Ellen B. Gwynn

D0284656

THE NEW
OXFORD COMPANION
TO LITERATURE IN
FRENCH

THE NEW
OXFORD COMPANION
TO LITERATURE IN
FRENCH

EDITED BY

PETER FRANCE

CLARENDON PRESS · OXFORD

1995

Oxford University Press, Walton Street, Oxford OX2 6DP

Oxford New York

Athens Auckland Bangkok Bombay
Calcutta Cape Town Dar es Salaam Delhi
Florence Hong Kong Istanbul Karachi
Kuala Lumpur Madras Madrid Melbourne
Mexico City Nairobi Paris Singapore
Taipei Tokyo Toronto

and associated companies in
Berlin Ibadan

Oxford is a trade mark of Oxford University Press

Published in the United States
by Oxford University Press Inc., New York

Introduction © Peter France 1995
Text © Oxford University Press 1995

All rights reserved. No part of this publication may be reproduced,
stored in a retrieval system, or transmitted, in any form or by any means,
without the prior permission in writing of Oxford University Press.
Within the UK, exceptions are allowed in respect of any fair dealing for the
purpose of research or private study, or criticism or review, as permitted
under the Copyright, Designs and Patents Act, 1988, or in the case of
reprographic reproduction in accordance with the terms of the licences
issued by the Copyright Licensing Agency. Enquiries concerning
reproduction outside these terms and in other countries should be
sent to the Rights Department, Oxford University Press,
at the address above

British Library Cataloguing in Publication Data

Data available

Library of Congress Cataloging in Publication Data

Data available

ISBN 0–19–866125–8

Set by Hope Services (Abingdon) Ltd.
Printed in Great Britain
on acid-free paper by
The Bath Press, Bath

CONTENTS

INTRODUCTION

La fureur des dictionnaires est devenue si grande parmi nous qu'on vient
d'imprimer un *Dictionnaire des dictionnaires*.

(Melchior Grimm, 1759)

We have come a long way since Grimm wrote this, and one wonders what he would
have said about our present situation. Our libraries are full of reference guides to all
kinds of topic, including literature written in French. When the idea of a new Oxford
Companion on the subject was put to me, I wondered therefore about the need to
add one more large volume to the list. Like most students of French literature, I have
long been used to referring to the *Oxford Companion to French Literature* (*OCFL*) of Sir
Paul Harvey and Janet E. Heseltine, first published in 1959, and the updated and
abridged version of it, the *Concise Oxford Dictionary of French Literature* (1976), edited by
Joyce M. H. Reid. These guides have served generations of readers well; specialists
and non-specialists alike have gone to them for information, but also to share the
authors' evident pleasure in their subject, its highways and some of its curious
byways. So why another *Oxford Companion*?

If in the end I took on the task of editing this volume, it was not just for the obvious reason that a great deal of new writing in French has appeared in the half-century
since most of the work on the *OCFL* was done. This is indeed the case, and particularly in the many other countries of the world where French is the main literary language (less than half of the world's French-speakers live in France). But if a sizeable
proportion of the headwords in the present volume do not figure in its predecessor,
this is also because, inevitably, the subject we label 'French Literature' or 'Literature
in French' is modified over time, reconstructed by new generations of readers, writers, critics, and scholars—indeed, the very shift from 'French literature' to 'literature
in French' reflects the way in which the assumptions of metropolitan culture have
increasingly been challenged (see below, pp. xii–xiv). New discoveries are made, the
emphasis shifts, interpretations and evaluations are revised. The task of a reference
work such as the present one is to record such transformations and (in modest measure) to contribute to them, offering what is meant as a *Companion* for readers of the
1990s and the beginning of the next millenium.

The history of literary knowledge and appreciation is not one of gradual and cumu-
lative progress. It entails a series of lesser or greater shifts, discontinuities, or even revolutions. It seemed essential, therefore, rather than simply seeking to update the
OCFL, to make a fresh start and produce an entirely new volume. This should not be
allowed to disguise our great debt to our predecessor. The reader will find a few
explicit references to it; these are only the tip of the iceberg. The *OCFL*, together with
other reference works such as those cited in the second part of the article ENCYCLOPE-
DIAS, have often served as points of comparison for editor and contributors, suggesting omissions, challenging priorities and judgements, or simply sending us back to
check our facts.

What then are the specific characteristics and aims of the *New Oxford Companion to Literature in French*? Perhaps the best way to answer this is to reflect a little on four of the principal words in the title.

Oxford. This is an Oxford book, but only in the sense that it is published by Oxford University Press. Some of its contributors are based in Oxford, but it has been edited in Edinburgh and written by a modern equivalent of what the *Encyclopédie* called a 'société de gens de lettres', a collection of some 130 contributors from many different places. Most are from Britain, but there are also colleagues from France, Ireland, the USA, Canada, the West Indies, Australia, and Africa.

Contributors from France are few in number. This is partly to obviate the need for massive translation. It would, perhaps, have been possible to translate into English one of the existing French literary encyclopedias, and this would have given readers an insider's view of the subject—how literature in French appears to the French themselves (obviously, the notion of insider/outsider is far more complicated than this French/non-French dichotomy suggests, particularly when one takes into account the many French speakers outwith France). Our aim, however, was different: to give the contextual information and illumination that are needed for foreign readers. In addition, it may be hoped that the outsider's view has its own value. English-speaking readers are often surprised at the way the French have exalted certain non-French writers [see, for instance, POE]; this surprise should be a productive one. In the same way, some of the priorities of this volume may seem idiosyncratic to francophone readers, but the distortions seen in a mirror placed across the Channel may also suggest that the internal view is not the only one.

So this *Oxford Companion* is a collective work, if not exactly a collegiate one. There were two main reasons for calling on so many different hands: speed and expert knowledge. If the aim was to produce a reference book for our time, it was essential to proceed rapidly—even so, since we cover living authors and recent events, some entries will already have dated by the time the book appears. As for expert knowledge, the *Companion* spans over a thousand years and covers places from Quebec to Madagascar; no one or two people could have hoped to deal adequately with all of this.

Those are the practical reasons for a multiplicity of authors. I hope too that readers will find value and pleasure in the resulting polyphony. All the contributors worked to the same broad guide-lines and all entries were edited by the same hand, but different voices mingle and contrast here, different styles of writing, different aesthetic, moral, or political perspectives. The impersonality of encyclopedias and dictionaries seems to me one of the myths of our age, and I have not attempted to iron out differences between contributors in the name of some impersonal, purely objective view of the subject. Except for the briefest entries (many of them by the editor), all entries are therefore attributed by initials, a key to which is on pp. xxiii–xxv.

A Companion. Boswell once wrote that if Addison seemed like a 'wise and accomplished companion', Johnson wrote like a teacher. Over against the pedagogue, in typical eighteenth-century fashion, stands the person of good company, the agreeable talker—though Addison too, with his 'Saturday sermons', was conscious of his role as teacher or preacher. The line between the two is not always clear, and the present volume aims, in Utopian fashion, to be both a source of information and a pleasant stimulus to reflection.

It is not, of course, a full-scale encyclopedia of writing in French. This would only fit into the present format if the choice of authors, texts, or subjects was deliberately limited to an unjustifiably small canonic body. Thus, while the more important works of an author are listed, there is no attempt at a complete listing. Nor do we offer a blow-by-blow account of writers' lives; the amount of biographical information given varies according to judgements as to its importance for a better understanding of the work. Similarly, while the burgeoning of scholarship would make it perfectly possible to produce lengthy bibliographies even for the least important topics and authors, we have suggested a small number of titles for further reading only in relation to most of the more substantial entries.

Nevertheless, as these hints for further reading suggest, together with entries such as HISTORIES OF FRENCH LITERATURE or BIBLIOGRAPHIES, this is a book meant not only for the general reader but for students and teachers. If anything, it is more university-orientated—but I hope not less companionable—than its predecessor. This no doubt reflects the way in which the universities have, for better or worse, strengthened their hold over literary culture.

Within and outwith the universities gloomy voices are often heard bemoaning the decline of first-hand acquaintance with foreign literature in the original. In spite of this, we have assumed, not too idealistically I hope, that it is not necessary to translate all French quotations into English, or to give English versions of the titles of books. In the bibliographical suggestions, works in French occupy as much space as works in English.

One particular feature, already visible to a certain extent in the *OCFL*, but extended here, is the presence of many longish articles on general topics. These reflect recent thinking and research, not only on the major literary genres from LYRIC POETRY to SERMON, TRAGEDY to AUTOBIOGRAPHY, but on many topics from literary, cultural, and political history, such as VERSIFICATION, FIN'AMOR, LIBRARIES, or OCCUPATION AND RESIS-TANCE (the entry on QUOTATIONS, however, offers relaxation from these more strenuous concerns).

As the example of OCCUPATION AND RESISTANCE makes clear, the entries are by no means confined to authors, texts, or strictly literary topics. Partly this reflects the move in French studies away from a concentration on language and literature to a more inclusive notion of cultural studies. But for those whose primary interest is in literature in the narrower traditional sense, it is still important for a Companion (as opposed to a dictionary) to offer the kind of broad context which would not be necessary for French readers. This extends from basic information on CURRENCY, WEIGHTS AND MEASURES, etc., through a vast range of historical references (note in particular the series of entries on aspects of *ancien régime* society, CLERGY, NOBILITY, TAXATION, and so on), to entries on science and philosophy, on language, and on other arts, including the more recent ones of CINEMA and TELEVISION. (Given the existence of such articles and the constraints of space, the number of individual entries on actors, painters, directors, and so on had to be quite strictly limited—and the selection is bound to seem arbitrary at times.) A list of the more important general articles is on pp. xix–xxi.

A Companion to Literature. 'Qu'est-ce que la littérature?'—'What is literature?', wrote an unjesting Sartre in 1947, and gave his own answer. The question has taken on a new urgency in recent decades, as the accepted literary 'canon', and sometimes the very notion of a canon, has been challenged on all sides.

The approach adopted here is a deliberately open and inclusive one. Literature is not a given and fixed entity, but a cultural construct. What has been called 'literariness' (that which distinguishes literature from non-literature) changes over time and depends in large part on communities of readers. Writing mainly of English cultural history, Raymond Williams showed in his *Keywords* (1976) how the modern restrictive meaning of 'literature' emerged in the early nineteenth century. From a different angle, the theorist Gérard Genette has written persuasively in *Introduction à l'archi-texte* (1979) of the highly dubious nineteenth-century reduction of literature to the so-called three great genres, lyric, epic, and dramatic. Modern library cataloguers often still struggle with this in their classifications, not knowing where to place Joubert's *Carnets* or Gibbons's *Decline and Fall*.

The story of the shifting boundaries of 'literature' (and of such cognate terms as *res litteraria, litterae humaniores*, letters, polite letters, belles-lettres) would take a long time to tell. Broadly, in older times the twin disciplines of rhetoric and poetics dealt with all kinds of writing which did not belong to such specialized fields as theology, law, medicine, or philosophy. Such a broad field includes not only what is sometimes called 'imaginative literature', but also various forms of oratory—particularly when they have a written form—history, satire and other didactic writing, letters, memoirs and journals, and eventually journalism. This is the wide and varied field which the present *Companion*, like its predecessor, sets out to prospect. Even so, there are grey areas on the margins, particularly for philosophy and science. Writers such as Descartes or Lévi-Strauss figure here as writers rather than as part of the intellectual context of a more narrowly defined literature.

One major recent development is an increased willingness to regard as 'literature' what previously went by names such as 'popular literature' or 'para-literature'. The Structuralist movement is often credited with having made it possible to discuss James Bond stories (in *Communications*, 8, 1970) alongside the novels of Flaubert and Stendhal. In fact, a glance at *OCFL* shows that such an enlargement of the canon beyond 'high literature' is no novelty. For the medieval period, indeed, the 'vulgar' genres (farces, *fabliaux*, and the like) have long been seen as worth studying alongside such nobler genres as epic or history. It is a constant of literary history that extra-canonic kinds of writing may become canonic, but only with time. The present volume makes room, not only for the time-hallowed popular song, folk-tale, or chapbook literature of the Bibliothèque Bleue, but for newer developments such as music-hall, detective fiction, science fiction, the *photo-roman*, and the literary form which has achieved such surprising academic respectability in France, the 'ninth art' of the *bande dessinée*.

Is everything, then, equally valuable, equally worthy of love and attention? Certainly, a strong case can be made for seeing the 'popular' (a very slippery term to define) as just as important an element in the life of a community as so-called high culture. Evaluation is arguably another matter. Here too, however, Pierre Bourdieu and many other sociological investigators have shown the extent to which taste is a function of social pressures. It would be naïve to ignore such determinations, and probably futile to attempt rational demonstrations of what we might personally think of as literary excellence. Debates about taste and aesthetic value are battlefields on which weapons of all kinds are deployed, not the least effective being the argument from authority. This is nicely captured in the story of a custodian at the Louvre whose lofty reply to an unimpressed visitor was: 'It is not the pictures that are on trial, sir.'

In practice, in any society or group of societies, over a longer or shorter period of time, a loose and fragile consensus emerges within what Stanley Fish has termed 'interpretive communities'—those who hold for the time being the power of interpreting and evaluating literary texts. Such groups, often competing, determine what goes into syllabuses, and what figures in works such as this *Companion*. It is not, perhaps, a satisfactory situation for those who aspire to more absolute values, but it is one we must live with. A work such as this cannot deny the existence of a canon (or canons) of literature in French; it can, however, hope to extend it and to do some justice to its shifting and conflictual nature.

In the first place, values change over time. It will be easy for readers, tracing inclusions and exclusions and comparing the amount of space allowed to a given subject, to see how our canon differs from the equally catholic one to be found in the *OCFL*. One striking example of a promotion is the much greater attention paid today to the writings of the marquis de Sade, and there are many more, especially for the late nineteenth and early twentieth centuries.

Such shifts do not occur without conflict. For example, at the time of writing one of the principal battles concerns the gender balance within the canon. It has been convincingly argued since the 1970s that there has been a conscious or unconscious exclusion from the syllabuses and histories of literature of women writers whose work calls for as much attention as that of their better-known male counterparts. A noteworthy case is Marceline Desbordes-Valmore, for a long time neglected by the canon-makers, now seen, as Baudelaire saw her, as one of the great poets of her time (Verlaine put the case in a double-edged way, proclaiming her 'la seule femme de génie et de talent de ce siècle'). The problems facing women writers and their treatment by the French literary establishment are discussed here in the entry on WOMEN WRITERS. Awareness of this kind of exclusion is a salutary guide to editors; it is, of course, no guarantee that their decisions will please all readers.

A simple way to assess the importance accorded to any particular writer or work is to measure the length of the entry. It is a crude form of assessment, and a misleading one. Other factors apart from a judgement of importance determine the length of entries. In some cases, with long-lived and prolific writers, there is simply a lot more to be said. Hugo receives more words than Rimbaud, Beauvoir than Weil, but no value judgement is implied. An additional factor is the need to give more information on hitherto-neglected subjects. In particular, for many writers from outside France, relatively long entries were needed since English-speaking readers are not, for the most part, very well informed about them.

Finally, in discussing the 'ins' and 'outs' of this volume, it goes without saying that the choice of immediately contemporary writers (some born since 1960) is something of a lottery. At one time it was not thought proper to study authors until they were dead, best of all if they were as dead as the classics of Greece and Rome. I believe it is better to take some risks here, knowing full well that a new *Companion* in thirty years time will see that 'we have done those things that we ought not to have done' and 'left undone those things that we ought to have done'. But I don't think one can conclude, with the Book of Common Prayer, that 'there is no health in us'. It is right that this should be a publication marked by time; it will give today's readers some pointers to current writing and will offer the interested readers of the future an idea of how some observers viewed the contemporary scene in the 1990s.

Literature in French. This part of the title reflects the single most important feature of the present *Companion* as compared with the *OCFL*: the place given to literature produced in French outside France. Some of the countries involved are France's neighbours: Belgium, Switzerland, and indeed medieval Britain. Writers from all of these places were often assimilated to the French tradition; in some cases they welcomed this, in others (e.g. Ramuz in Switzerland) they fought to maintain a national identity while avoiding the often limiting implications that this can easily entail. Such questions are discussed in BELGIAN LITERATURE IN FRENCH, SWISS LITERATURE IN FRENCH, and ANGLO-NORMAN LITERATURE.

Arguably more important than any of these, however, is the massive literary production in French, particularly over the last half-century or so, in countries which were (and in the case of Martinique, Guadeloupe, French Guiana and Reunion still are) French possessions overseas [see COLONIZATION; DECOLONIZATION]. There are more than 200 entries here devoted to individual writers from these countries, but also survey articles for the principal areas: AFRICA (SOUTH OF THE SAHARA), MAURITIUS AND REUNION, MADAGASCAR, ALGERIA, MOROCCO, TUNISIA, MIDDLE EAST, WEST INDIES, HAITI, LOUISIANA, QUEBEC, ACADIA. It is to these general entries that readers should look for the development of a particular genre in any given area, since generic articles such as NOVEL are primarily concerned with writing inside France, and it is only recently that this has been significantly influenced by models from other francophone countries. Some of the forms specific to other countries are identified in entries such as AFRICA (SOUTH OF THE SAHARA) and WEST INDIES.

I hope there is no need to argue the case for a full coverage of this large body of material, however difficult it is to do it justice within a limited space. The importance of what is usually called francophone writing is recognized not only in France, but increasingly in university French syllabuses in other countries. With the exception of some of the *Québécois*, however, I suspect that the francophone writers (unlike francophone film-makers) are still little known to the English-speaking public. No doubt more translations are needed; I hope that this *Companion* will help to spread the word.

The inclusion of both French and francophone writing in one volume is not unproblematic. Indeed, the very idea of 'francophone culture' has been a controversial one [see FRANCOPHONIE]. Is it not a new form of colonialist assimilation? Similar problems affect the English-speaking world; those concerned with Scottish writing, for instance, argue over whether it is preferable to develop the idea of a 'British literature' or 'literature in English' in which English literature will lose its central position, or to insist on the specificity of Scottish literature as a separate domain. In the same way, it might be argued that it is better to speak of Algerian literature rather than the Algerian contribution to francophone literature—all the more so because writing in French is only one part of Algerian literary production and needs to be seen in relation to Algerian writing in Arabic or Berber as much as to writing in French in other countries.

On the other hand, it is a matter of fact that many of the non-French writers included in this volume—whether it be Henri Michaux from Belgium, Jean-Jacques Rousseau from Geneva, Anne Hébert from Canada, or Tahar Ben Jelloun from Morocco—have established themselves in France. Their books have been published there, and they have played a vital part in French culture as well as in that of their native land. At the time of writing the latest winner of the French Prix Goncourt is the novel *Le Rocher de Tanios* by the Lebanese Amin Maalouf.

The expression 'literature in French' is not, then, as innocent as it might seem. Its use on the cover of this volume should not be taken to imply that 'French and francophone writing' is the right angle of vision from which to consider the writers included here. Many other angles are possible, and have found or will find their expression in other reference books, histories of literature and the like. The present gathering of French-speaking writers from many countries springs simply from the pragmatic perception of a gap in awareness that ought to be filled, a need that deserves to be satisfied.

From another angle, 'literature in French' is something of a misnomer, though no more so, perhaps, than 'French literature' would be. If it is essential to include writing in French from outside France, there is also writing in other languages within France. The typical Third-Republic history of France projected back into the past the French 'hexagon' which had been established by 1870 (when its boundaries were to be drastically, though temporarily, altered again). In fact, the idea of a French nation of its present-day dimensions is an anachronism for much of the past millennium. In the same way, the history of the French language defines itself by its finishing-point; it is the history of the gradual constitution of the modern French language. As lately as 1794, however, to judge by the results of abbé Grégoire's inquiry [see LITERACY], only a relatively small minority of the 'French' population were truly francophone; the majority spoke regional languages, often disparagingly called *patois* (indeed, the point of Grégoire's inquiry was to pave the way for the elimination of the *patois*, which was more or less completed over the following two centuries). Today, moreover, the hegemony of 'correct French' is open to many challenges. Writers such as Kourouma rework the French language to express the forms of Malinké; others in Quebec or the West Indies assert the value of local popular speech [see JOUAL; CREOLES]. In Europe, similarly, many writers have felt the appeal of what Queneau called 'le néo-français' [see ARGOT].

So French ('correct' French, French of the Île-de-France) has not been the language of the most of the inhabitants even of what is now France since the swearing of the Strasbourg Oaths in AD 842, the traditional foundation date for a written 'French' language. It may be objected that French was the language of the ruling and educated classes, the language of writing. This is broadly true for the modern period, but it leaves out of account two vitally important phenomena. The first is the rich Occitan literature of the early Middle Ages; previously called Provençal, this has often been subsumed under French literature, but it is important to stress its specificity [see OCCITAN LANGUAGE AND LITERATURE]. The second is the Latinity which prevailed in learned circles, in writing at least, until well into the seventeenth century. The poets of the Pléiade were bilingual in a literary sense, and Descartes, like Newton, wrote much of his philosophical work in Latin. One of the more significant developments in recent literary history has been the recovery of neo-Latin writing as an essential element of literary culture in early modern France [see LATINITY].

In addition to these two prestigious bodies of literature, one must remember the continuing existence, with its ups and downs, of post-medieval Occitan writing and of writing in the many *patois* and dialects of France. These are the subject of survey articles. And finally, a special place has been given to Brittany, where writing in Breton coexists with writing in French (by many of France's leading writers), and before that with writing in Latin. Without attempting an exhaustive coverage of non-French literature in France, I hope we have done some justice to these often neglected areas.

Such, briefly, are the aims of this *Companion* (more detailed points are dealt with in the Reader's Guide on pp. xv–xvi). It remains for me to thank the many people who have played an essential part in producing this book.

First, of course, all my contributors, from those who sent just one or two pieces to those who not only took on the large tasks offered them, but went beyond the call of duty to suggest further entries and were willing, in many cases, to add to their burden topics that had been overlooked or were hard to place. I had rather dreaded the job of editing work by so many different hands; in the event it turned out to be—usually—a pleasure.

Secondly, and more especially, the colleagues from various universities who acted as my advisers: for post-medieval France, in chronological order, Terence Cave, John Renwick, Ceri Crossley, Malcolm Bowie, and Elizabeth Fallaize. Such advice was most crucial for the francophone areas, and here I am much indebted to Richard Burton (Carribbean), Peter Hawkins (sub-Saharan Africa), Alex Hargreaves (Maghreb), and Ian Lockerbie (Canada) for the enthusiasm and care they gave to the task.

My greatest debt of gratitude, however, is owed to Sarah Kay, who agreed to be, in effect, co-editor for the important medieval component of the *Companion*, writing many entries herself and reading over all the other material relating to the Middle Ages. Her guidance both on the subjects to be treated and the right people to treat them was invaluable.

It was Kim Scott Walwyn of OUP who first persuaded me to take on the *Companion*; I greatly valued discussions with her and subsequently with Catherine Clarke. But it is above all with Frances Whistler of the Press that I have talked over the various problems that have arisen over the last three years; she has been a constant source of good advice and cheerful support. My thanks to them all, as also to Jason Freeman, to Jeff New, a vigilant copy-editor, and to all the highly professional OUP staff who helped with the publication of the *Companion*. I am very grateful too to those academic colleagues who gallantly took on the laborious task of proof-reading: Richard Burton, Alec Hargreaves, Peter Hawkins, Ann Jefferson, John Renwick, and Graham Runnalls.

Finally, and this is none the less true for being so often repeated over the years, I owe more than I can say to the contributor who figures as SR. For most of five years she has put up with this rival companion, and found time in a busy life to give the best of advice, criticism, and encouragement.

READER'S GUIDE

1. All entries are arranged in strict alphabetical order. When the heading consists of more than one word, the whole sequence of letters is used to determine the place of entries; thus SAINTE-BEUVE precedes SAINT-EXUPÉRY and DOMINIQUE precedes DOM JUAN. *Le, la, les, un,* and *une* are placed after the main names of titles, institutions, etc. Book titles beginning with *De* are treated in according with normal usage, e.g. DE L'AMOUR, but ESPRIT DES LOIS, DE L'.

2. Many medieval writers are classified, according with normal practice, under their first name (e.g. JEAN DE MEUN, COLIN MUSET); for some doubtful cases a cross-reference is given (e.g. BEAUMANOIR, Philippe de, see PHILIPPE DE BEAUMANOIR).

3. For proper names beginning with Du and Des (e.g. DU BELLAY, DES PERIERS) the Du or Des is treated as an integral part of the name. On the other hand, names beginning with De la (e.g. Jean de la Fontaine) will be found under La (LA FONTAINE), and names preceded by de or d' are placed under the initial of the principal name (e.g. VIGNY, HOLBACH). In a number of cases, such as de Gaulle, where the person is always referred to by the full name, there is a cross-reference (DE GAULLE, see GAULLE).

4. For names of persons the normal modern spelling is given—sometimes with a common alternative (e.g. BOULAINVILLER or BOULAINVILLIERS). Many medieval figures are commonly referred to by both English and French names (e.g. Alan of Lille, Alain de Lille); the most frequent usage has been adopted, with cross-references if necesary.

5. In book titles and quotations, spelling has been modernized wherever this can be conveniently done, for works from the 16th c. onwards. For the medieval period, the original spelling has generally been preserved, though for some titles which originate in more recent times, a modern spelling is used.

6. A short list of abbreviations used in the text will be found on p. xvii.

7. Dates are given as accurately as possible, although of course many remain uncertain or approximate; the indication '1450/5' means 'at some date between 1450 and 1455'. For books, unless otherwise indicated, the date is that of first *publication*; for plays and operas, unless otherwise indicated, the date is that of first *performance*.

8. An asterisk (*) placed before a word in the text refers to an entry under that word. Such indications are not given on every occasion when a word appears, but where helpful and relevant information will be found in the entry in question.

9. There are numerous entries devoted to individual works. Many works, however, are described in the entry devoted to their author; if this description is at all substantial, a cross-reference under the book's title directs the reader to it.

10. The suggestions for further reading given at the end of longer entries can be supplemented by reference to a group of articles which list useful resources for more detailed study. The most important of these are: BIBLIOGRAPHIES, DICTIONARIES, ENCYCLOPEDIAS, HISTORIES OF FRENCH LITERATURE, PERIODICALS.

11. Maps of France at different periods, maps of former French territories overseas, and a map of central Paris will be found on pp. xxvi–xxxv. A necessarily summary chronology is printed on pp. xxxvii–li.

12. Entries devoted to individual writers should be seen also in the context of more general entries—on genres, movements, historical events, etc.—which are listed on pp. xix–xxi.

13. The cut-off date for most entries is 1990; events and publications between 1990 and 1994 are covered less systematically.

ABBREVIATIONS

The following abbreviations will be found in the text of the *Companion*:

AOF	Afrique Occidentale Française
BN	Bibliothèque Nationale
CNRS	Centre National de la Recherche Scientifique
ENA	École Nationale d'Administration
ENS	École Normale Supérieure
FLN	Front de Libération Nationale (in Algeria)
MLF	Mouvement de Libération des Femmes
NRF	*Nouvelle Revue Française*
OAS	Organisation Armée Secrète (in Algeria)
PCF	Parti Communiste Français
PS	Parti Socialiste
SFIO	Section Française de l'Internationale Ouvrière
TNP	Théâtre National Populaire

LIST OF GENERAL ENTRIES

Listed below are the more important general entries; note that the entries devoted to genres are concerned principally with writing in France; French writing in other parts of the world is discussed under the appropriate country or area.

Political and Social History

ALGERIAN WAR
ANCIEN RÉGIME
ARMY, NAVY, MILITARY SERVICE
BONAPARTISM
COLONIZATION
COMMUNE DE PARIS (1871)
COURTS
CURRENCY
CRUSADES
DECOLONIZATION
FEUDALISM

FRONDE
HUNDRED YEARS WAR
HUNTING
MARRIAGE
MONARCHY
NATIONAL ASSEMBLIES
OCCUPATION AND RESISTANCE
    DURING WORLD WAR II
PEASANTS
POLICE
POPULAR FRONT

PRESIDENTS OF THE REPUBLIC
REGIONS AND DÉPARTEMENTS
REPUBLICS
RESTORATION
REVOLUTION
SLAVERY
TAXATION
WARS OF RELIGION
WEIGHTS AND MEASURES
WORLD WAR I

Intellectual and Cultural Movements

ABSURD, THEATRE OF THE
BAROQUE
CLASSICISM
COURTOISIE
CUBISM
DADA
DECADENCE
ENLIGHTENMENT
ENGAGEMENT
EXISTENTIALISM
FASCISM
FEMINISM
FIN'AMOR
HONNÊTETÉ
IDÉOLOGUES
IMPRESSIONISM

ILLUMINISM
LIBERTINS
MARXISM
MIDDLE AGES
NATIONALISM
NATURALISM
NÉGRITUDE
NEOCLASSICISM
NEOPLATONISM
NEOSTOICISM
NOUVEAU ROMAN
PARNASSE, LE
PERSONALISM
PETRARCHISM
PHENOMENOLOGY
PHYSIOCRATS

POSTMODERNISM
POST-STRUCTURALISM
PRECIOSITY
QUERELLE DES ANCIENS ET DES
    MODERNES
QUERELLE DES FEMMES
REALISM
RENAISSANCE
REPUBLICANISM
RHÉTORIQUEURS
ROMANTICISM
SENSIBILITÉ
STRUCTURALISM
SURREALISM
SYMBOLISM
UTOPIA

Religious History

ANTICLERICALISM
ANTISEMITISM
BIBLE
CATHOLICISM IN 20TH-CENTURY
  FRANCE
CLERGY

CONCORDAT
COUNTER-REFORMATION
DEISM
GALLICANISM
HERESIES
JANSENISM

JESUITS
JUDAISM AND JEWS IN FRANCE
ORATORIANS
PROTESTANTISM
QUIETISM
REFORMATION

Music, Art, Media

ACADÉMIE ROYALE DE PEIN-
    TURE ET DE SCULPTURE
CHANSON FRANÇAISE
CINEMA
FÊTES RÉVOLUTIONNAIRES

FONTAINEBLEAU
NOUVELLE VAGUE
OPERA
OPÉRA-COMIQUE
POPULAR SONG

RADIO
TELEVISION
WORDS AND MUSIC

Language and Science

ANTHROPOLOGY
ARGOT
DICTIONARIES
GRAMMARS

HISTORY OF THE FRENCH
    LANGUAGE
LINGUISTICS
PSYCHOLOGY

PSYCHOANALYSIS
SOCIOLOGY
VERSIFICATION

CONTRIBUTORS

HA-J   Hédi Abdel-Jaouad, Skidmore College, New York

RDA   Robert Anderson, University of Edinburgh

KRA   Keith Aspley, University of Edinburgh

GA-B   Gertrud Aub-Buscher, University of Hull

WA-B   Wendy Ayres-Bennett, Queens' College, Cambridge

DB   David Baguley, University of Durham

PJB   Peter Bayley, Gonville and Caius College, Cambridge

HEB   Helen Beale, University of Stirling

DMB   David Bellos, University of Manchester

PEB   Philip Bennett, University of Edinburgh

GPB   Geoffrey Bennington, University of Sussex

CJB   Christopher Betts, University of Warwick

JB   Jennifer Birkett, University of Birmingham

DSB   Dorothy Blair, formerly University of the Witwatersrand

AHB   Alistair Blyth, University of Stirling

HB   Hédi Bouraoui, York University, Toronto

MB   Malcolm Bowie, All Souls' College, Oxford

FPB   Frank Paul Bowman, University of Pennsylvania

CB   Celia Britton, University of Aberdeen

CHB   Charlotte H. Brunner, formerly Iowa State University

UPB   Peter Burke, Emmanuel College, Cambridge

RDEB   Richard Burton, University of Sussex

AB   Ardis Butterfield, University College, London

MMC   Margaret Callander, University of Birmingham

KCC   Keith Cameron, University of Exeter

JPC   Patsy Campbell, University of Edinburgh

PRC   Peter Campbell, University of Sussex

RC   Roger Cardinal, University of Kent at Canterbury

TCC   Terence Cave, St John's College, Oxford

AMC   Angela Chambers, University of Limerick

FNC   Firinne Ni Chréacháin, Centre of West African Studies, University of Birmingham

RJC   Rita Christian, College of North-East London

AC   Antoine Compagnon, University of Columbia; Université de Paris IV

MPC   Patrick Corcoran, Roehampton Institute

VC   Virginia Coulon, Université de Bordeaux I

GC   George Craig, University of Sussex

CC   Ceri Crossley, University of Birmingham

CMC   Christine Crow, University of St Andrews

JC   John Cruickshank, formerly University of Sussex

JMD   Michael Dash, University of the West Indies

PVD   Peter Davies, University of Glasgow

JDeJ   Joan DeJean, University of Pennsylvania

CD   Claire Duchen, University of Sussex

JHD   Jean Dunbabin, St Anne's College, Oxford

JD   John Dunkley, University of Aberdeen

CHE   Colin Evans, University of Cardiff

EAF   Elizabeth Fallaize, St John's College, Oxford

AMF   Alison Finch, Jesus College, Oxford

PJF	Philip Ford, Clare College, Cambridge	SK	Sarah Kay, Girton College, Cambridge
PF	Peter France, University of Edinburgh	JKa	Jackie Kaye, University of Essex
MG	Mary Gallagher, University College Dublin	JK	James Kearns, University of Exeter
SG	Simon Gaunt, St Catharine's College, Cambridge	HRK	Roderick Kedward, University of Sussex
RBG	Ralph Gibson, Lancaster University	MHK	Michael Kelly, University of Southampton
REG	Rhiannon Goldthorpe, St Anne's College, Oxford	WK	William Kidd, University of Stirling
LG	Lionel Gossman, Princeton University	DK	Diana Knight, University of Nottingham
RMG	Richard Griffiths, King's College, London	AK	Ambroise Kom, Université de Yaoundé, Cameroon
AGH	Alec Hargreaves, Loughborough University	RLK	Roberta Krueger, Hamilton College, New York
PGH	Peter Hawkins, University of Bristol	AL	Annette Lavers, University College, London
SH	Susan Hayward, University of Birmingham	FL	Françoise Little, University of Westminster
MJH	Michael Heath, King's College, London	SIL	Ian Lockerbie, University of Stirling
NH	Nicholas Hewitt, University of Nottingham	ML	Martyn Lyons, University of New South Wales
NHi	Nicki Hitchcott, University of Leeds	IM	Ian Maclean, The Queen's College, Oxford
CMH	Christina Howells, Wadham College, Oxford	GJM	Jonathan Mallinson, Trinity College, Oxford
HLlH	Humphrey Lloyd Humphreys, St David's University College, Lampeter	NM	Nicholas Mann, Warburg Institute, London
SJH	Sylvia Huot, Northern Illinois University	JAMM	John Marenbon, Trinity College, Cambridge
BEJ	Belinda Jack, Christ Church, Oxford	GDM	Graham Dunstan Martin, University of Edinburgh
CMSJ	Christine Scollen-Jimack, University of Glasgow	DM-S	Danielle Marx-Scouras, Ohio State University
SBJ	S. Beynon John, formerly University of Sussex	SMM	Sheila Mason, University of Birmingham
DJ	Douglas Johnson, formerly University College, London	CRPM	Cedric May, formerly University of Birmingham
GJ	Gillian Jondorf, Girton College, Cambridge	NM	Nicole Medjigbodo, formerly University of Ibadan
BJ	Bridget Jones, Roehampton Institute	AM	Ann Moss, University of Durham
MJ	Michael Jones, University of Nottingham	KM	Kerry Murphy, University of Melbourne
RMJ	Rosemarie Jones, formerly University of Sussex	VGM	Vivienne Mylne, formerly University of Kent at Canterbury
MKa	Mohamadou Kane, Université Cheikh Anta Diop, Dakar	SN	Suzanne Nash, Princeton University
MK	Maguèye Kassé, Université Cheikh Anta Diop, Dakar	SFN	Stephen Noreiko, University of Hull
		BNO	Beverley Ormerod, University of Western Australia

MP	Michael Palmer, Université de Paris III	IS	Ian Short, Birkbeck College, London
MDQ	Malcolm Quainton, Lancaster University	DAS	David Steel, Lancaster University
KR	Keith Reader, Kingston University	AJS	Alan Steele, formerly University of Edinburgh
WDR	Walter Redfern, University of Reading	JJS	James Supple, University of St Andrews
JR	John Renwick, University of Edinburgh	BCS	Bernard Swift, University of Stirling
IWR	Ian Revie, University of Edinburgh	JHMT	Jane Taylor, St Hilda's College, Oxford
SR	Siân Reynolds, University of Stirling	SSBT	Sam Taylor, University of St Andrews
AMR	Ann Ridehalgh, University of Southampton	DRDT	Dominic Thomas, University College, London
BR	Brian Rigby, University of Hull	ET	Ethel Tolansky, University of Westminster
CFR	Christopher Robinson, Christ Church, Oxford	DAT	David A. Trotter, University of Exeter
GVR	Vaughan Rogers, University of Edinburgh	DHW	David Walker, University of Sheffield
GAR	Graham Runnalls, University of Edinburgh	DRW	David Watson, University of Dundee
CS	Clive Scott, University of East Anglia	DWW	David Whitton, Lancaster University
ES	Eric Sellin, Tulane University, New Orleans	NW	Nelly Wilson, formerly University of Bristol
PS	Peter Sharratt, University of Edinburgh	DW	Dennis Wood, University of Birmingham
MHTS	Michael Sheringham, University of Kent at Canterbury	HZ	Hans Zell, Hans Zell Associates
JS	James Shields, University of Warwick	AZ	Abdelhamid Zoubir, University of Blida, Algeria

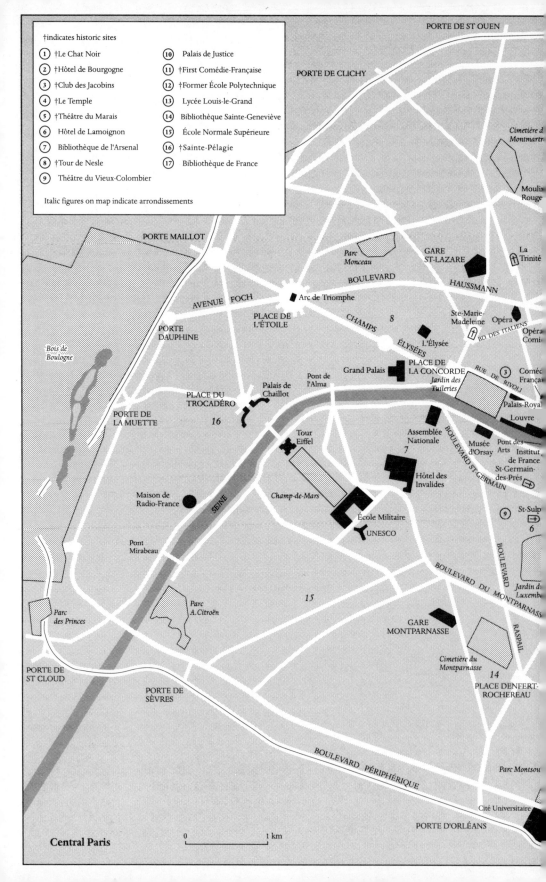

†indicates historic sites

1. †Le Chat Noir
2. †Hôtel de Bourgogne
3. †Club des Jacobins
4. †Le Temple
5. †Théâtre du Marais
6. Hôtel de Lamoignon
7. Bibliothèque de l'Arsenal
8. †Tour de Nesle
9. Théâtre du Vieux-Colombier
10. Palais de Justice
11. †First Comédie-Française
12. †Former École Polytechnique
13. Lycée Louis-le-Grand
14. Bibliothèque Sainte-Geneviève
15. École Normale Supérieure
16. †Sainte-Pélagie
17. Bibliothèque de France

Italic figures on map indicate arrondissements

PORTE DE ST OUEN

PORTE DE CLICHY

Cimetière de Montmartre

Moulin Rouge

PORTE MAILLOT

Parc Monceau

GARE ST-LAZARE

La Trinité

BOULEVARD HAUSSMANN

AVENUE FOCH

Arc de Triomphe

Ste-Marie-Madeleine

Opéra

PLACE DE L'ÉTOILE

CHAMPS

8

Opéra Comique

PORTE DAUPHINE

BD. DES ITALIENS

ÉLYSÉES

L'Élysée

Bois de Boulogne

Grand Palais

PLACE DE LA CONCORDE

RUE DE RIVOLI

3 Comédie Française

Pont de l'Alma

Jardin des Tuileries

Palais de Chaillot

Palais-Royal

PLACE DU TROCADÉRO

16

Louvre

PORTE DE LA MUETTE

Assemblée Nationale

Musée d'Orsay

Pont des Arts

Institut de France

Tour Eiffel

7

BOULEVARD ST-GERMAIN

St-Germain-des-Prés

Hôtel des Invalides

Maison de Radio-France

Champ-de-Mars

9 St-Sulpice

6

École Militaire

UNESCO

Pont Mirabeau

SEINE

BOULEVARD DU MONTPARNASSE

Jardin du Luxembourg

Parc A.Citroën

15

GARE MONTPARNASSE

RASPAIL

Parc des Princes

PORTE DE ST CLOUD

Cimetière du Montparnasse

14

PORTE DE SÈVRES

PLACE DENFERT-ROCHEREAU

Parc Montsouris

BOULEVARD PÉRIPHÉRIQUE

Cité Universitaire

PORTE D'ORLÉANS

Central Paris

0   1 km

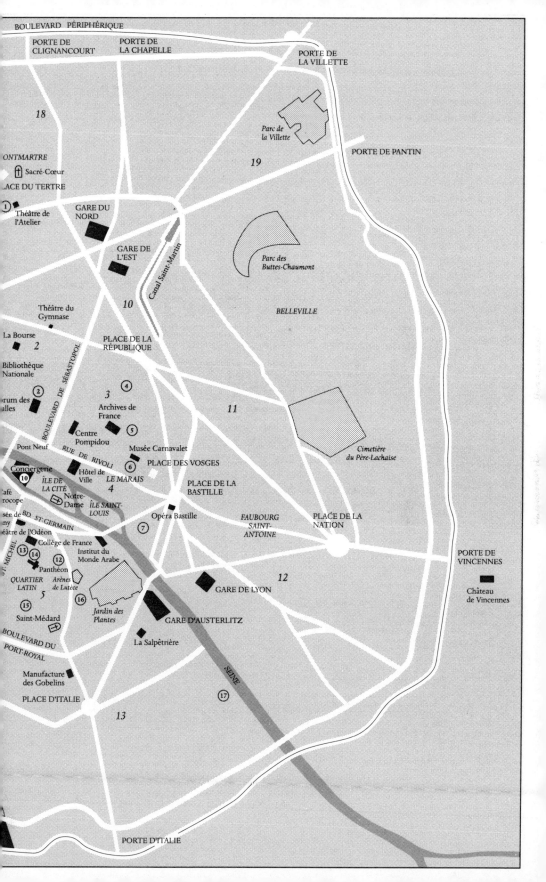

BOULEVARD PÉRIPHÉRIQUE

PORTE DE
CLIGNANCOURT

PORTE DE
LA CHAPELLE

PORTE DE
LA VILLETTE

PORTE DE PANTIN

18

Parc de
la Villette

ONTMARTRE

Sacré-Cœur

ACE DU TERTRE

19

Théâtre de
l'Atelier

GARE DU
NORD

GARE DE
L'EST

Parc des
Buttes-Chaumont

Canal Saint-Martin

10

BELLEVILLE

Théâtre du
Gymnase

La Bourse

2

PLACE DE LA
RÉPUBLIQUE

Bibliothèque
Nationale

④

3

11

rum des
alles

②

BOULEVARD DE SEBASTOPOL

Archives de
France

⑤

Centre
Pompidou

Cimetière
du Père-Lachaise

Pont Neuf

RUE DE RIVOLI

Musée Carnavalet

⑥

PLACE DES VOSGES

Conciergerie

⑩

Hôtel de
Ville

ÎLE DE
LA CITÉ

LE MARAIS

PLACE DE LA
BASTILLE

4

afé
rocope

Notre-
Dame

ÎLE SAINT-
LOUIS

Opéra Bastille

PLACE DE LA
NATION

sée de
ny
éâtre de l'Odéon

BD ST-GERMAIN

⑦

FAUBOURG
SAINT-
ANTOINE

Collège de France

Institut du
Monde Arabe

PORTE DE
VINCENNES

ST. MICHEL

⑬ ⑭

⑫

Panthéon

12

Château
de Vincennes

QUARTIER
LATIN

Arènes
de Lutèce

GARE DE LYON

⑯

5

⑮

Jardin des
Plantes

GARE D'AUSTERLITZ

Saint-Médard

BOULEVARD DU

PORT-ROYAL

La Salpêtrière

Manufacture
des Gobelins

SEINE

PLACE D'ITALIE

⑰

13

PORTE D'ITALIE

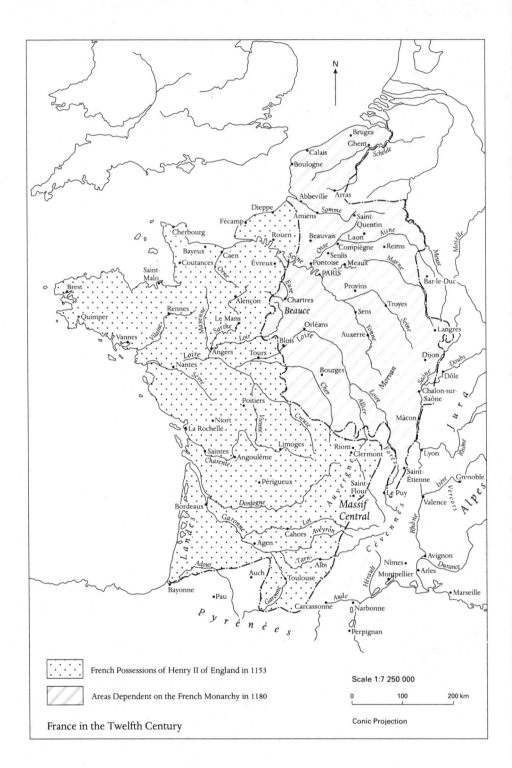

N

Bruges
Ghent
Calais
Boulogne
Schelde

Abbeville Arras
Dieppe *Somme*
Fécamp Amiens Saint-Quentin
Cherbourg Rouen Beauvais Laon *Aisne* Reims
Bayeux Caen *Oise* Compiègne *Marne*
Coutances Évreux Senlis *Meuse*
Saint-Malo *Orne* Pontoise Meaux Bar-le-Duc
Brest *Eure* PARIS
Seine

Quimper Alençon Chartres Provins
Rennes *Beauce* Sens Troyes *Seine*
Le Mans *Mayenne* Orléans Auxerre Langres
Vannes *Sarthe* Blois *Loire* *Yonne* Dijon *Doubs*
Vilaine Angers Loir Tours *Morvan* Dôle
Loire Bourges Chalon-sur-Saône
Nantes *Cher* *Loire* *Saône*
Sèvre Mâcon *Jura*

Poitiers *Allier*
Niort *Vienne* *Creuse* *Rhône*
La Rochelle Limoges Riom Lyon
Saintes Angoulême Clermont *Forez* Saint-Étienne
Charente *Isère* Grenoble
Périgueux Saint-Flour Le Puy Valence *Vercors*
Auvergne *Alpes*
Bordeaux *Dordogne* **Massif Central**
Landes *Garonne* *Lot* *Cévennes* *Rhône*
Cahors *Avéyron* Avignon *Durance*
Agen *Tarn* Albi Nîmes
Auch Toulouse Montpellier Arles
Bayonne *Adour* *Garonne* *Hérault* Marseille
Pau Carcassonne Narbonne
P y r é n é e s *Aude*
Perpignan

French Possessions of Henry II of England in 1153

Areas Dependent on the French Monarchy in 1180

Scale 1:7 250 000

0   100   200 km

France in the Twelfth Century

Conic Projection

N

ARTOIS
Arras ⊕ Douai
FLANDRE

PICARDIE

Rouen ⊕
ÎLE-DE-FRANCE

NORMANDIE
Paris
Bar-le-Duc ⊕
TROIS-
ÉVÊCHÉS ⊕ Metz
⊕ Nancy
LORRAINE
ALSACE
Colmar ⊕

CHAMPAGNE

Rennes ⊕
MAINE
BRETAGNE

ORLÉANAIS

ANJOU
Nantes ·
TOURAINE
SAUMUROIS

Dijon ⊕
Besançon ⊕
FRANCHE-
COMTÉ

BERRY
NIVERNAIS

BOURGOGNE

POITOU
BOURBONNAIS

AUNIS

MARCHE

SAINTONGE
LIMOUSIN
Clermont- ⊕
Ferrand
LYONNAIS

AUVERGNE
Grenoble ⊕

Bordeaux ⊕
DAUPHINÉ

GUYENNE ET GASCOGNE

Montauban
⊕
COMTAT VENAISSIN
(Papal State)
PROVENCE

Toulouse ⊕
Montpellier ⊕
Aix ⊕

Pau ⊕
LANGUEDOC

BÉARN

FOIX
Perpignan ⊕
ROUSSILLON

Boundaries

—·—·— France

— — — Gouvernements (military)

⊕   Seats of Parlements and other Sovereign Courts

Scale 1:8 000 000

0   100   200 km

Provinces of France in 1789

Conic Projection

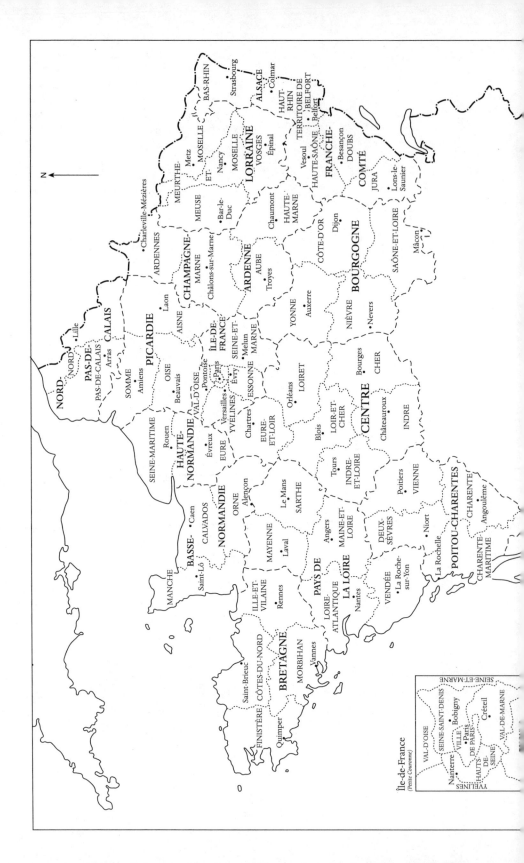

N ←

NORD- • Lille
NORD-

PAS-DE-
CALAIS
PAS-DE-CALAIS • Arras

PICARDIE
SOMME • Amiens
OISE • Beauvais
AISNE • Laon

ARDENNES • Charleville-Mézières

CHAMPAGNE-
MARNE • Châlons-sur-Marne
ARDENNE
AUBE • Troyes
HAUTE-MARNE • Chaumont

MEUSE • Bar-le-Duc

MEURTHE-ET- • Metz
MOSELLE • Nancy
MOSELLE

LORRAINE
VOSGES • Épinal

ALSACE
BAS-RHIN • Strasbourg
HAUT-RHIN • Colmar

TERRITOIRE DE BELFORT • Belfort

HAUTE-SAÔNE • Vesoul

FRANCHE-COMTÉ
DOUBS • Besançon
JURA • Lons-le-Saunier

CÔTE-D'OR • Dijon

BOURGOGNE
YONNE • Auxerre
NIÈVRE • Nevers
SAÔNE-ET-LOIRE • Mâcon

ÎLE-DE-FRANCE
VAL-D'OISE • Pontoise
Paris
SEINE-ET-MARNE • Melun
YVELINES • Versailles
ESSONNE • Évry
EURE-ET-LOIR • Chartres

HAUTE-NORMANDIE
SEINE-MARITIME • Rouen
EURE • Évreux

BASSE-NORMANDIE
MANCHE • Saint-Lô
CALVADOS • Caen
ORNE • Alençon

BRETAGNE
FINISTÈRE • Quimper
CÔTES-DU-NORD • Saint-Brieuc
MORBIHAN • Vannes
ILLE-ET-VILAINE • Rennes

PAYS DE LA LOIRE
MAYENNE • Laval
SARTHE • Le Mans
MAINE-ET-LOIRE • Angers
LOIRE-ATLANTIQUE • Nantes
VENDÉE • La Roche-sur-Yon

CENTRE
LOIRET • Orléans
LOIR-ET-CHER • Blois
INDRE-ET-LOIRE • Tours
CHER • Bourges
INDRE • Châteauroux

POITOU-CHARENTES
DEUX-SÈVRES • Niort
VIENNE • Poitiers
CHARENTE-MARITIME • La Rochelle
CHARENTE • Angoulême

Île-de-France
(Petite Couronne)
VAL-D'OISE
SEINE-SAINT-DENIS • Bobigny
YVELINES
VILLE DE PARIS • Paris
NANTERRE
HAUTS-DE-SEINE
VAL-DE-MARNE • Créteil
SEINE-ET-MARNE

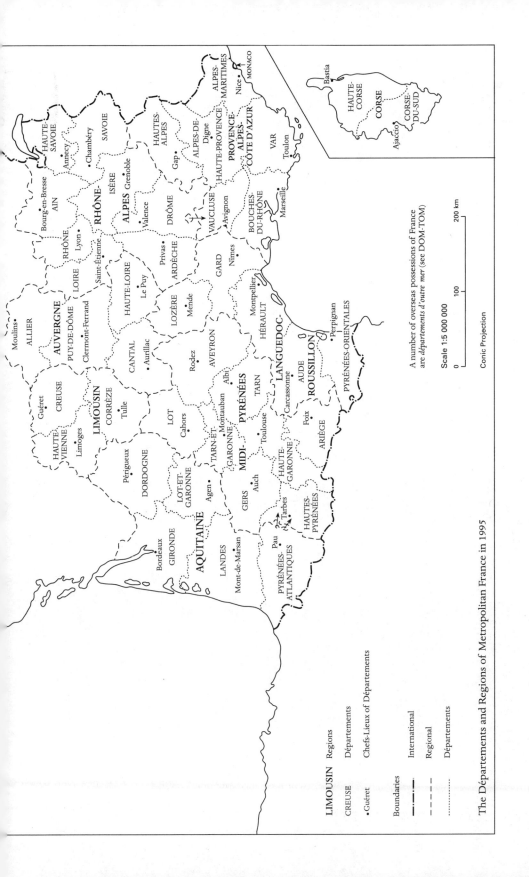

The Départements and Regions of Metropolitan France in 1995

A number of overseas possessions of France are *départements d'outre mer* (see DOM-TOM).

Scale 1:5 000 000

0	100	200 km

Conic Projection

LIMOUSIN Regions

CREUSE Départements

•Guéret Chefs-Lieux of Départements

Boundaries

——— International

– – – Regional

······· Départements

Newfoundland

Nouvelle
France

Saint Pierre &
Miquelon

Acadia
(Nova Scotia)

Louisiana

Saint-
Domingue
(Haiti)

Guadeloupe
Martinique
St Lucia

Saint Louis
Gorée

French
Guiana

French Colonial Expansion before 1763

Surat

Chandernagore

Yanaon

Mahé
Pondicherry
Karikal

Seychelles

Île de France (Mauritius)
Île Bourbon (Reunion)

Fort-
Dauphin

Principal territories colonized or controlled by France before 1763

Modern names are given in parentheses. For the chronology
of French expansion, see COLONIZATION

Scale 1:88 000 000

Modified Gall Projection

Saint Pierre &
Miquelon

Guadeloupe
Martinique

• Clipperton I.

FRENCH
GUIANA

MOROCCO

TUNISIA

ALGERIA

FRENCH WEST AFRICA

CAMEROON

TOGO

FRENCH EQUATORIAL AFRICA

The Division of French West Africa and French Equatorial Africa

Mauritania

F R E N C H   W E S T   A F R I C A

FRENCH

Sudan (Mali)

Niger

Chad

Senegal

Guinea

Upper Volta
(Burkina Faso)

EQUATORIAL

Ivory
Coast

Dahomey
(Benin)

Oubangui
(Central African Republic)

Togo

Cameroon

AFRICA

Gabon

Congo

- - - - Upper Volta boundary, 1947

Togo and Cameroon were mandated territories, 1939

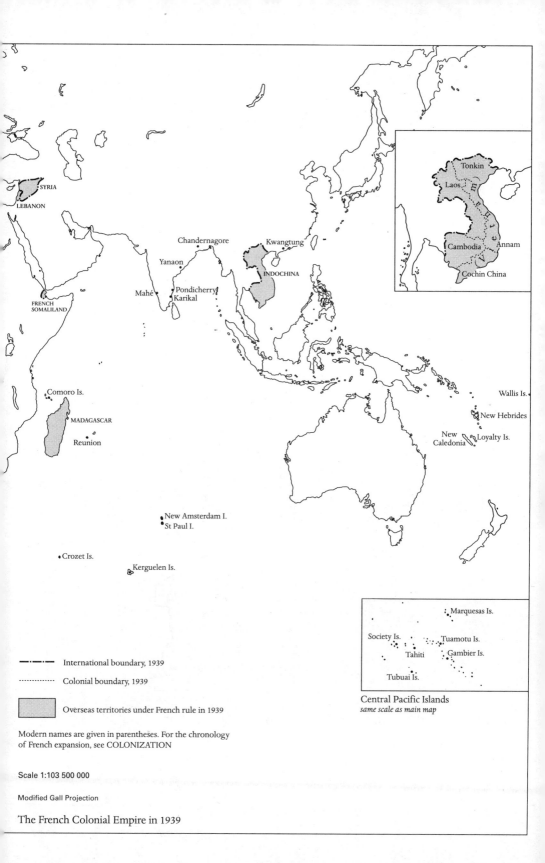

SYRIA

LEBANON

FRENCH
SOMALILAND

Chandernagore

Yanaon

Mahé
Pondicherry
Karikal

Kwangtung

INDOCHINA

Tonkin

Laos

Cambodia

Annam

Cochin China

Comoro Is.

MADAGASCAR

Reunion

Wallis Is.

New Hebrides

New
Caledonia

Loyalty Is.

New Amsterdam I.
St Paul I.

Crozet Is.

Kerguelen Is.

Marquesas Is.

Society Is.

Tahiti

Tuamotu Is.

Gambier Is.

Tubuai Is.

Central Pacific Islands
same scale as main map

—·—·— International boundary, 1939

············ Colonial boundary, 1939

Overseas territories under French rule in 1939

Modern names are given in parentheses. For the chronology
of French expansion, see COLONIZATION

Scale 1:103 500 000

Modified Gall Projection

The French Colonial Empire in 1939

CHRONOLOGY

THIS chronology lists some of the more important dates in French history and in the history of other French-speaking countries. Column 1 lists French monarchs (dates are those of reigns) and political regimes in France. Column 2 concerns political, economic, and social history, and Column 3 literary or cultural history—a small number of significant books, plays, etc. are given here under the date of their first production or publication. Column 4 places major authors not already mentioned in Column 3 at a point corresponding as nearly as possible to the time when they were most active (for dates, see the relevant entries above).

CHRONOLOGY

Reigning Monarch, or Regime (in France)	Political History	Cultural History	Authors
Merovingian Dynasty (481–751)			
481–511 Clovis		496 Baptism of Clovis	Boethius
511–61 Sons of Clovis (Thierry, Clodomir, Childebert, Clotaire I)		543 Foundation of Saint-Germain-des-Prés	
561–613 Sons of Clotaire I		**Early 7th c.** Benedictine rule comes to Gaul	
613–20 Clotaire II			
629–39 Dagobert	639 Power passes to Maires du Palais		
639–751 'Rois fainéants'	732 Victory of Charles Martel over Arabs at Poitiers		
Carolingian Dynasty (751–987)			
751–68 Pépin le Bref	778 Battle of Rencesvals (Roncevaux)		Alcuin
768–814 Charles I (Charlemagne)	**c.780** Monetary reforms	c.780 Carolingian script introduced	
	800 Charlemagne crowned emperor	c.790 Académie Palatine at court of Charlemagne	
814–40 Louis I	843 Division of Carolingian Empire	819 Einhard, *Vita Karoli Magni*	
840–77 Charles II		842 Strasbourg Oaths	
877–9 Louis II		858 Foundation of monastery of Vézelay	
879–82 Louis III and Carloman			
882–4 Carloman		880–2 *Séquences de sainte Eulalie*	
884–7 Charles le Gros			
887–98 Eudes			
893–923 Charles III (contested 893–8 and 922–3)	911 Beginning of Viking Duchy of Normandy	909 Foundation of abbey of Cluny	
922–3 Robert I			
923–36 Raoul of Burgundy			
936–54 Louis IV			
954–86 Lothaire			
986–7 Louis V			

Rulers	Historical events	Literary/cultural events	Authors
987–96 Hugues Capet		**End of 10th c.** *Vie de saint Léger*	
996–1031 Robert II	**11th–12th c.** Economic and demographic growth; development of towns	**c.1050** *Vie de saint Alexis*	
1C31–60 Henri I		**c.1080** *Chanson de Roland*	
		c.1098 *Chanson d'Antioche*	
1060–1108 Philippe I	**1066** Norman conquest of England	Paris pre-eminent as centre of learning from c.1100	Guilhem IX
	1095 Proclamation of First Crusade	**c.1100–1250** Troubadours and *trobairitz* active	Abélard
		1115 Saint Bernard founds abbey of Clairvaux	
1108–37 Louis VI		**1137** Suger begins construction of abbey of Saint-Denis	
1137–80 Louis VII	**1152** Eleanor of Aquitaine married to the future king of England	**12th c.** Beginnings of Vaudois heresy	Wace
		12th–13th c. *Chansons de geste*	Chrétien de Troyes
		12th–14th c. Arras a major cultural centre	Marie de France
		Mid-12th c. *Romans d'antiquité*; beginnings of *trouvère* poetry	
	1152–81 Rise of fairs in Champagne	**1163** Work begins on Notre-Dame de Paris	
	c.1180 Greatest extent of English Angevin Empire in France [see Map 1]	**Late 12th c.** Poems of Tristan (Béroul and Thomas); *Roman de Renart; Cycle de Guillaume*	
1180–1223 Philippe II (Philippe Auguste)	**1182–1215** Municipal 'communes' confirmed by Philippe-Auguste	**Late 12th c. onwards** Prose romances	Bodel
		Late 12th–14th c. *Fabliaux*	
	c.1200 Beginning of Capetians' attempts to impose royal currency	**1200** Charter of University of Paris	
	1204 Crusaders capture Constantinople	**Early 13th c.** *Aucassin et Nicolette*	Villehardouin
	1209–19 Albigensian Crusade against Cathars in Languedoc	**1216** Foundation of Dominican order	Jean Renart
	1214 Victory of French over English at Bouvines; Children's Crusade		
1223–6 Louis VIII		**c.1225** Beginning of *Le Roman de la Rose*	Thibaut de Champagne
1226–70 Louis IX (Saint Louis)		**1229** Foundation of University of Toulouse	
	1233 Papal inquisition established in Languedoc		
	1248 Saint Louis captured on Crusade	**Mid-13th c.** Brunetto Latini, *Li Livres dou tresor*	Rutebeuf
	1259 Treaty of Paris between France and England		
1270–85 Philippe III	**1270** Saint Louis's death marks end of Crusades		Adam de la Halle
1285–1314 Philippe IV	**1291** First Swiss confederation		
	1294 Outbreak of war between England and France		Joinville

Reign	Political events	Cultural / literary events	Authors
1498–1515 Louis XII	**16th c.** Rise of banking in France	**c.1500** Josquin des Prés	
	1503 French lose Naples		
	1504–7 First French expeditions to North America		Lemaire de Belges
	1513 French expelled from Italy		
	1516 Concordat between France and papacy	**1517** Luther's theses	Erasmus
1515–47 François Ier	**1520** Field of the Cloth of Gold		Lefèvre d'Etaples
	1521–59 Wars with Emperor Charles V	**1521–6** Evangelicals in Meaux	
	1525 French defeat at Pavia		Budé
		1528 Château of Fontainebleau remodelled	
		1530 Foundation of Collège des Lecteurs Royaux (future Collège de France)	
		1532–4 Rabelais, *Pantagruel* and *Gargantua*	Des Périers
	1534 Affaire des Placards	**1535** Olivétan's French Bible	Marot
	1534–43 Jacques Cartier in Canada	**1539** Edict of Villers-Cotterêts	
		1540 French translation of *Amadis de Gaule*	
		1541 Calvin, *Institution*	Dolet
	1541–64 Calvin in authority in Geneva	**1542** First Jesuit house in France	Scève
	1545 Massacre of Vaudois at Mérindol	**1545–63** Council of Trent	
1547–59 Henri II		**1549** Du Bellay, *Défense et illustration*	
		1550–1 Ronsard, *Odes*	Labé
		1552 Jodelle, *Cléopâtre captive*	Ramus
			Bèze
	c.1555 Financial collapse		
	1555–8 Villegagnon in Brazil		
	1558 Calais captured from English	**1558–9** Marguerite de Navarre, *Heptaméron*	La Boétie
1559–60 François II	**1559** Treaty of Cateau-Cambrésis	**1559** Amyot's Plutarch	
1560–74 Charles IX	**1560** Conjuration d'Amboise		
	1560–3 Regency of Catherine de Médicis		
	1561 Colloque de Poissy; Marie Stuart returns to Scotland		Grévin
	1562–94 Wars of Religion; inflation and economic collapse	**1562** Foundation of Jesuit Collège de Clermont	
		1563/4 Beginning of year fixed on 1 January	
		1564 Work starts on Tuileries palace	Belleau
		1570 Bibliothèque Royale transferred to the Louvre; foundation of Baïf's Académie de Poésie et de Musique	Henri Estienne
	1572 Saint Bartholomew's Day Massacre		Desportes
	1573 Future Henri III elected king of Poland		

Reigning Monarch, or Regime (in France)	Political History	Cultural History	Authors
1574–89 Henri III		**1574** Académie du Palais founded	Garnier
	1576 First Catholic Ligue	**1578** Ronsard, *Sonnets pour Hélène*	Bodin
		1580 First edition of Montaigne's *Essais*	Du Bartas
	1584 Major Catholic Ligue		
	1589 Henri III assassinated by Jacques Clément		
Bourbon Dynasty (1589–1792)			
1589–1610 Henri IV	**1594** Henri IV enters Paris	**1594** *Satire Ménippée*	Sponde
	1594–7 War with Spain		Du Vair
	1598 Edict of Nantes	**1599** Creation of theatrical company at Hôtel de Bourgogne	Béroalde de Verville
	1599–1611 Ministry of Sully	**1603** Carmelites introduced to France	Régnier
		1605 Building of Pont-Neuf	
		c.1606 Malherbe's commentary on Desportes	Malherbe
	1608 Champlain founds Quebec	**1607–27** D'Urfé, *L'Astrée*	
		1609 Reform of Port-Royal	
	1610 Henri IV assassinated by Ravaillac	**1610** François de Sales founds Visitandines	
1610–43 Louis XIII	**1610–17** Regency of Marie de Médicis	**1611** Bérulle sets up Oratorian Congregation in France	
	1614 Meeting of États Généraux	**1616** D'Aubigné, *Les Tragiques* (composed 1577)	
	1614–17 Nobles in revolt		
	1618 Beginning of Thirty Years War	**1618** Foundation of Maurist Congregation	Hardy
	1620–8 Huguenot risings	**c.1620–50** Hôtel de Rambouillet active	Théophile de Viau
	1624–42 Richelieu's ministry	**1625** Foundation of Lazarists by Vincent de Paul	Mlle de Gournay
			Racan
	1626 French expedition to West Indies	**1626** Edict forbidding duelling	Voiture
	1628 Defeat of Huguenots at La Rochelle		Mairet
		1631 Renaudot, *Gazette*	Gassendi
	1632 Insurrection of Gaston d'Orléans		
	1633 Beginning of slave-trade in Senegal	**1634** First meeting of Académie Française	
	1635 War declared with Spain	**1637** Corneille, *Le Cid*; Descartes, *Discours de la méthode*; Petites Écoles set up at Port-Royal	Sorel
	1639 Rising of *Va-nu-pieds* in Normandy		
	1642 Death of Richelieu; Mazarin first		Guez de Balzac

1643–1715 Louis XIV	**1643** Molière's Illustre Théâtre opened	Rotrou
1643 Condé's victory at Rocroi; French established in Madagascar		Tristan l'Hermite
1643–51 Regency of Anne d'Autriche	**1645** Italian opera introduced	La Calprenède
1648–53 Civil wars of La Fronde	**1647** Vaugelas, *Remarques*	Scarron
1648 Treaty of Westphalia concludes Thirty Years War	**1648** Founding of Académie Royale de Peinture et de Sculpture	Desmarets
1653 Papal condemnation of Jansenism	**1649–53** Scudéry, *Artamène ou le Grand Cyrus*	Cyrano de Bergerac
1659 Treaty of the Pyrenees ends war with Spain; France gains Roussillon, etc.	**1656–7** Pascal, *Provinciales*	Chapelain
	1656–9 Building of Vaux-le-Vicomte	
1660 Marriage of Louis XIV and Marie-Thérèse	**1658** Molière returns to Paris	Arnauld
1661 Death of Mazarin; arrest of Fouquet; 'personal reign' of Louis XIV begins		
1661–83 Colbert in office	**1663** Foundation of Académie des Inscriptions	Quinault
	1664 La Rochefoucauld, *Maximes*; first *fêtes* at Versailles	
1665 French in Saint-Domingue	**1664–9** *Tartuffe* affair	Saint-Évremond
	1666 Foundation of Académie des Sciences	
	1667 Racine, *Andromaque*	
1668 Paix de l'Église	**1668** La Fontaine, *Fables* (Book 1)	Villedieu
	1669 Académie Royale de Musique established by Lully	
	1670 Pascal, *Pensées* (posthumous)	Méré
		Thomas Corneille
1672–8 War with Holland	**1674** Boileau, *Art poétique*	Bourdaloue
		Bossuet
1675 Revolt of 'Bonnets Rouges' in Brittany		
1676 Affaire des Poisons	**1678** Lafayette, *La Princesse de Clèves*	
1678 Alsace and Franche-Comté come under French rule	**1680** Creation of Comédie-Française	Sévigné
1680 Dragonnades against Protestants	**1682** Court moves to Versailles	Bouhours
1682 Foundation of Louisiana		Deshoulières
1683 Louis XIV marries Mme de Maintenon	**1685** Fontenelle, *Entretiens sur la pluralité des mondes*	Malebranche
1684–93 Recurrent famines		
1685 Revocation of Edict of Nantes; Code Noir codifies slavery in colonies	**1687–8** Main phase of Querelle des Anciens et des Modernes	
1688–97 War of the League of Augsburg		

Reigning Monarch, or Regime (in France)	Political History	Cultural History	Authors
		1688 La Bruyère, *Les Caractères*	
		1690 Furetière, *Dictionnaire*	
		1691 Racine, *Athalie*	Dancourt
		1694 *Dictionnaire de l'Académie Française*	D'Aulnoy
		1697 Perrault, *Contes*; Bayle, *Dictionnaire*; expulsion of Italian actors	Regnard
		1699 Fénelon, *Télémaque*	Chaulieu
	1701–13 War of Spanish Succession	1704 Galland, *Les Mille et une Nuits*	Crébillon *père*
	1702–5 Camisard risings in the Cévennes		
	1709 Expulsion of nuns from Port-Royal		
	1713 Peace of Utrecht; Bull *Unigenitus*		Saint-Pierre
1715–74 Louis XV	1715–23 Regency of Philippe, duc d'Orléans	1715 Lesage, *Gil Blas*	Massillon
	1716–20 John Law's 'system', ending in financial collapse	1716 Return of Italian actors	Du Bos
	1726–46 Cardinal Fleury chief minister	1721 Montesquieu, *Lettres persanes*	La Motte
	1727–33 Jansenist 'convulsionnaires' at Saint-Médard	1726–9 Voltaire in England	Gresset
	1730–70 Growing prosperity in France	1731 Prévost, *Manon Lescaut*; Fleury closes Club de l'Entresol	Maupertuis
	1733–8 War of Polish Succession	1731–41 Marivaux, *Vie de Marianne*	Crébillon *fils*
	1741–8 War of Austrian Succession	1737 Beginning of regular salons of Académie de Peinture et de Sculpture	La Chaussée
	1745 Battle of Fontenoy		Saint-Simon
	1745–64 Mme de Pompadour in favour		
	1746 French conquer Madras	1746 Diderot, *Pensées philosophiques*	Duclos
	1748 Treaty of Aix-la-Chapelle	1748 Montesquieu, *Esprit des lois*	Vauvenargues
	1755 Lisbon earthquake	1749–89 Buffon, *Histoire naturelle*	La Mettrie
		1750 Rousseau, *Discours sur les sciences et les arts*	Condillac
		1751 First volumes of the *Encyclopédie*	
		1752–4 Guerre des Bouffons	D'Alembert
	1756–63 Seven Years War		
	1757 Damiens's attempt to kill Louis XV	1758 Helvétius, *De l'esprit*; attempts to suppress the *Encyclopédie*	Riccoboni
	1758–70 Choiseul ministry	1759 Voltaire, *Candide*	
	1759 French loss of Quebec	1761 Rousseau, *La Nouvelle Héloïse*	
	1762 Execution of Calas	1762 Rousseau, *Émile* and *Du contrat social*	Mably
	1763 Treaty of Paris; French loss of Canada and Louisiana		

1766–9 Bougainville's voyage around the globe		Marmontel
1768 France acquires Corsica		
1768–82 'Civil war' in Geneva		Saint-Lambert
1770–1 Maupeou affair	1770–80 Raynal, *Histoire des deux Indes*	
	1770 Holbach, *Système de la nature*	
	1774 Success of Gluck's *Orphée*	
1774–6 Turgot ministry	1777 First daily newspaper, *Le Journal de Paris*	Le Tourneur
1774–92 Louis XVI		
1776–81 Necker ministry	1782 Rousseau, *Confessions*; Laclos, *Les Liaisons dangereuses*	Rivarol
1778–82 French involvement in American War of Independence		
1783–7 Calonne ministry	1784 Beaumarchais, *Le Mariage de Figaro*	Parny
1787–8 Bad harvests in France	1787 Bernardin de Saint-Pierre, *Paul et Virginie*	Delille
		Chamfort
		Genlis
1788 États du Dauphiné in Vizille		Mercier
1789–99 Revolution [for details, see REVOLUTION, 1]	1789 *Déclaration des droits de l'homme*	André Chénier
1789 Assembly of États Généraux; fall of the Bastille; Assemblée Constituante; march on Versailles	1789–94 Revolutionary eloquence (Mirabeau, Danton, Robespierre, etc.)	
1790 Fête de la Fédération		
1791 Louis's flight to Varennes; Assemblée Législative; death of Mirabeau	1791 Sade, *Justine*	Volney
		Marat
1792 War declared on Austria		Hébert
First Republic (1792–1804)		
1792 Fall of the monarchy; September massacres; Battle of Valmy; Convention Nationale; declaration of the Republic		
1793 Execution of Louis XVI; war with England; defeat of the Girondins	1793 Académie Française dissolved	Mme Roland
1793–4 The Terror		
1793–6 War in Vendée		
1794 Execution of Dantonists and other 'factions'; downfall of Robespierre at Thermidor	1794 Fête de l'Être Suprême organized by David; foundation of École Normale Supérieure and École Polytechnique	Restif de la Bretonne
1795–9 Directoire	1795 Condorcet, *Esquisse*; foundation of Institut de France and Écoles Centrales	M.-J. Chénier
1796 Conspiration des Égaux, led by Babeuf		
1796–7 Napoleon's victories in Italy		
1798 Egyptian expedition; battle of Aboukir (the Nile); *coup d'état* of 18 Brumaire brings Napoleon to power		Sénac de Meilhan

Reigning Monarch, or Regime (in France)	Political History	Cultural History	Authors
	1799–1804 Consulate: Napoleon First Consul	1800 De Staël, *De la littérature*	
	1801 Concordat with Pius VII	1802 Chateaubriand, *Le Génie du christianisme*	Cabanis
	1802 Peace of Amiens		
First Empire (1804–14)	1803–14 Napoleonic campaigns		
	1804 Execution of duc d'Enghien; Napoleon crowned emperor; independence of Haiti	1804 Code Napoléon; first (German) edition of Diderot's *Neveu de Rameau* (begun c.1760)	Senancour
			Maine de Biran
	1806 Continental Blockade begins	1806–11 Creation of Imperial University	Joubert
	1812–13 Retreat from Moscow		Lamarck
Bourbon Restoration (1814–30) 1814–24 Louis XVIII	1814 Napoleon abdicates, retires to Elba; proclamation of the Charte	1814 Return of Jesuits to France	
	1815 The Hundred Days; Waterloo; Napoleon exiled to St Helena; White Terror; Holy Alliance		
		1816 Constant, *Adolphe*	De Maistre
		1819 Publication of Chénier's poems	Delavigne
	1820 Assassination of duc de Berry	1820 Lamartine, *Méditations*	Courier
	1821 Death of Napoleon		Fourier
	1821–7 Villèle ministry	1822 Hugo, *Odes*	Saint-Simon
1824–30 Charles X	1829–30 Polignac ministry	1822, **1827** English actors in Paris	Nodier
		1827 Hugo, *Préface de Cromwell*	
Orléans Monarchy (1830–48) 1830–48 Louis-Philippe	1830 July Revolution ('Les Trois Glorieuses'); Charles X abdicates; invasion of Algeria; kingdom of Belgium founded	1830 Battle of *Hernani* (Hugo); Berlioz, *Symphonie fantastique*; Stendhal, *Le Rouge et le noir*; Delacroix, *La Liberté guidant le peuple*	Béranger
			Desbordes-Valmore
			Scribe
	1831–4 Rebellion of Canuts in Lyon	1833–43 Michelet, *Le Moyen Âge*	
	1833 Conspiracy of duchesse de Berry		
		1834 Musset, *Lorenzaccio*	Lamennais
	1835 First French locomotive	1835 Vigny, *Chatterton*; *Servitude et grandeur*	Guizot
	1837–40 Insurrections in Quebec, followed by Act of Union	1840 Stendhal, *La Chartreuse de Parme*	Tocqueville
	1840 Napoleon's ashes returned to France	1840–59 Sainte-Beuve, *Port-Royal*	Tristan
			Comte

Political / Historical	Cultural / Literary	Authors
	1841 Balzac adopts title *La Comédie humaine*	Gautier
	1842 Dumas, *Les Trois Mousquetaires*	Sand
	1844 Viollet-le-Duc, first restorations	Sue
		Proudhon
c.1845 Railway boom in France		
1847–8 Guizot ministry	**1847–57** Michelet, *La Révolution*	
1848 Revolutions of February and June; abolition of slavery; Louis-Napoléon Bonaparte elected president		
Second Republic (1848–52)	**1849** Chateaubriand, *Mémoires*	Quinet
	1850 Courbet, *Un enterrement à Ornans*	
1851 *Coup d'état* of Louis-Napoléon	**1851–70** Hugo in exile	Leconte de Lisle
1852 Louis-Napoléon proclaimed emperor (Napoleon III)		
1853 Beginning of Haussman's reconstruction of Paris		
1854–6 Crimean war		
Second Empire (1852–70)	**1857** Flaubert, *Madame Bovary*; Baudelaire, *Les Fleurs du mal*	
	1861 Wagner's *Tannhäuser* at Paris Opera	Goncourt brothers
1859–93 French establish control of Indo-China	**1862** Hugo, *Les Misérables*	Veuillot
1860 French gain Savoie and Nice	**1863** *Le Petit Journal*; Renan, *Vie de Jésus*; Littré, *Dictionnaire*	Fromentin
1861–7 Mexican 'adventure' of Napoleon III	**1865** Bernard, *Introduction à l'étude de la médecine expérimentale*	Ségur
	1866 *Le Parnasse contemporain*	
	1866–76 Larousse, *Grand dictionnaire universel du XIXe siècle*	Banville
1867–9 Liberal reforms	**1869** Lautréamont, *Chants de Maldoror*; Flaubert, *L'Éducation sentimentale*	Mistral
1869 Opening of Suez Canal		
1870 Franco-Prussian War; defeat of Sedan; fall of Napoleon III		
Third Republic (1870–1940) [for list of presidents, see PRESIDENTS OF THE REPUBLIC]		
1870–1 Siege of Paris	**1871–93** Zola, *Les Rougon-Macquart*	Barbey d'Aurevilly
1871 Commune and repression ('La Semaine sanglante'); loss of Alsace-Lorraine	**1874** First Impressionist exhibition	Corbière
	1875–93 Taine, *Origines de la France contemporaine*	Verne
1875 Republican constitution established	**1876** Mallarmé, *L'Après-midi d'un faune*	Daudet
1876–98 Creation of French West Africa	**1880** *Les Soirées de Médan*	Vallès

Reigning Monarch, or Regime (in France)	Political History	Cultural History	Authors
			Becque
	1880 Amnesty for communards		
	1881–2 Lois Ferry on primary education		
		1884 Huysmans, *A rebours*	Maupassant
			Laforgue
			Villiers de l'Isle-Adam
	1886–9 Boulanger Affair		
	1889–3 Panama Scandal	1889 Eiffel Tower constructed; Universal Exhibition in Paris	Loti
			Dujardin
		1890 Claudel, *Tête d'or*	Darien
			Renard
		1894 Lanson, *Histoire de la littérature française*	Verhaeren
	1894–1906 Dreyfus Affair		Gourmont
	1895 Creation of Confédération Générale du Travail	1895 Louis Lumière's cinematograph	Brunetière
			Nelligan
	1896 Annexation of Madagascar	1896 Jarry, *Ubu roi*	France
		1897 Mallarmé, *Un coup de dés*; Gide, *Les Nourritures terrestres*	
	1898 Fashoda incident		
	1899 Founding of Action Française		
	1901 Founding of Radical Party	1901 First Salon de l'Automobile	Barrès
		1902 Debussy, *Pelléas et Mélisande*	Maeterlinck
	1903 Entente Cordiale with Britain	1903 First Tour de France	
	1904 Law against education by congrégations		
	1905 Creation of Socialist Party (SFIO); separation of Church and State	1905 Brunot, *Histoire de la langue française*	Jammes
		1906 Bergson, *L'Évolution créatrice*; Marie Curie first woman professor at the Sorbonne	
		1907 Picasso, *Les Demoiselles d'Avignon*	
	1909 Blériot flies across the Channel	1909 Ballets Russes in Paris; founding of *La Nouvelle Revue Française*	Péguy
			Segalen
	1911 Agadir crisis	1911 Colette, *La Vagabonde*	Alain-Fournier
	1912 French protectorate of Morocco		Larbaud
		1913 Apollinaire, *Alcools*	
	1914 Assassination of Jaurès	1913–22 Proust, *A la recherche du temps perdu*	
	1914–18 World War I	1913–24 Copeau at Le Vieux Colombier	
	1915–34 US occupation of Haiti	1916 Hémon, *Maria Chapdelaine*; Saussure, *Cours de linguistique générale*; Barbusse, *Le Feu*	
	1916 Battles of Verdun and the Somme		
	1919 Treaty of Versailles; Alsace-Lorraine becomes French again; victory of Bloc National in French elections		

1920 French mandate in Syria and Lebanon; Socialist congress at Tours; foundation of the French Communist Party	**1920** Dada in Paris	Ramuz
	1922 Valéry, *Charmes*	Jacob
1923–5 French occupation of Rhineland	**1922–40** Martin du Gard, *Les Thibault*	Duhamel
1924 Electoral victory of Cartel des Gauches	**1924** Breton, *Manifeste du surréalisme*	Alain
		Cendrars
		Roussel
1926 Poincaré government of 'Union Nationale'	**1925** Gide, *Les Faux-Monnayeurs*	
		Desnos
1927 Foundation of Croix-de-feu	**1927** Benda, *La Trahison des clercs*; theatrical cartel formed	Cocteau
1927–30 Period of Franco-German reconciliation	**1929** First talking pictures; Claudel, *Le Soulier de Satin* (written 1919–24)	Vitrac
		Éluard
		Pagnol
		Supervielle
1933 Hitler comes to power in Germany	**1932** Céline, *Voyage au bout de la nuit*	Reverdy
1933–4 Stavisky affair	**1932–46** Rolland, *Les Hommes de bonne volonté*	Mauriac
1934 Right-wing demonstrations in Paris (6 February), followed by anti-fascist general strike	**1933** Malraux, *La Condition humaine*	Jouve
		Michaux
		Nizan
1936 Victory of Popular Front in France; Blum opts for non-intervention in Spain	**1935** Guilloux, *Le Sang noir*	Giraudoux
1936–59 Union Nationale government of Duplessis in Quebec	**1936** Aragon, *Les Beaux Quartiers*	Bernanos
1937 Blum loses power	**1937** Picasso, *Guernica*	Saint-Exupéry
1938 Munich agreements		Montherlant
1939–40 'Drôle de guerre'	**1938** Sartre, *La Nausée*; Artaud, *Le Théâtre et son double*	Giono
		Simenon
Vichy Regime (1940–4) [for details, see OCCUPATION AND RESISTANCE]	**1939** Renoir, *La Règle du jeu*; Leiris, *L'Âge d'homme*	Drieu la Rochelle
1940 Fall of France; German occupation of northern France; Pétain comes to power; de Gaulle's broadcast of 18 June		Paulhan
		Weil
		Ponge
	1941 Aragon, *Le Crève-cœur*; Messiaen, *Quatuor pour la fin des temps*	Aymé
1942 Round-up of Jews in Paris; German occupation of southern France	**1942** Camus, *L'Étranger*; Vercors, *Le Silence de la mer*; creation of Éditions de Minuit	
1943 Forced labour in Germany (STO); formation of Conseil National de la Résistance	**1943** Sartre, *L'Être et le néant*	Bachelard
1944 Liberation of France; purges of collaborators		

Reigning Monarch, or Regime (in France)	Political History	Cultural History	Authors
Provisional government of de Gaulle (1945–6)	1945 Women vote for first time in French elections		
Fourth Republic (1946–58)	1946 Martinique, Guadeloupe, French Guiana, and Reunion become French *départements*	1946 Hébert, *Le Torrent*	Char
			Anouilh
			Vian
	1946 Indo-Chinese war of liberation		Diop, B.
	1947 Insurrection in Madagascar	1947 First *livres de poche*; first Avignon Festival; Le Corbusier begins 'la cité radieuse'; founding of *Présence africaine*; Césaire, *Cahier d'un retour au pays natal* (written 1938–9)	
		1947–8 Vogue of Saint-Germain-des-Prés	
		1948 Senghor, *Anthologie de la nouvelle poésie nègre et malgache*; Borduas, *Refus global*; Sarraute, *Portrait d'un inconnu*	
	1949 France a member of the Council of Europe and NATO	1949 Beauvoir, *Le Deuxième Sexe*; Braudel, *La Méditerranée*	Bataille, G.
			Bazin, H.
		1950 Ionesco, *La Cantatrice chauve*	Adamov
		1951 Founding of *Cahiers du cinéma*; polemic between Camus and Sartre	
	1953 Beginning of Poujadist movement	1953 Barthes, *Le Degré zéro de l'écriture*	Camara Laye
	1954–5 Mendès-France ministry	1954 Chraïbi, *Le Passé simple*	Sagan
	1954–62 Algerian War	1955 Aron, *L'Opium des intellectuels*	Bonnefoy
			Blanchot
			Dadié
	1956 Tunisia and Morocco gain independence; *loi-cadre* for autonomy of African colonies	1956 Butor, *L'Emploi du temps*; Beti, *Le Pauvre Christ de Bomba*; Kateb Yacine, *Nedjma*; Duras, *Moderato cantabile*	Audiberti
			Feraoun
	1957 French ratification of the Treaty of Rome	1957 Robbe-Grillet, *La Jalousie*; Camus, Nobel Prize speech	
	1957–86 Duvalier regime in Haiti	1958 Lévi-Strauss, *Anthropologie structurale*	Tardieu
			Alexis, J.-S.
			Memmi
Fifth Republic (1958–)	1958 Insurrection in Algeria; de Gaulle assumes power in France		
	1959 De Gaulle elected president	1959 Queneau, *Zazie dans le métro*	

1

A

ABBADIE, Jacques (1654–1727). French Protestant minister who lived in exile in Germany, England, and Ireland. He wrote a *Traité de la vérité de la religion chrétienne* (1684).

Abbaye, L'. Prison in Paris, founded in 1522, attached to the abbey of St Germain-des-Prés. Used originally for young and disorderly noblemen, it was the scene of some of the September Massacres of 1792 [see REVOLUTION, 1b].

Abbaye, Groupe de l'. A group of young French writers, artists, and theatrical people, sharing a disenchantment with the new capitalist, industrial, and anonymous society of the time, who decided to live and work together in a self-supporting community at Créteil between 1906 and 1908. The driving force and initiator of the enterprise was Charles *Vildrac. He was joined by Georges *Duhamel (who published his first volume of poetry there in 1907), René Arcos, Jules *Romains, and the painters Albert Gleize and Berthold Mahn. It was through art and literature, rid of all artifice, that a more humanitarian and socially just society, based on moral values, would be achieved. The group's association with Romains—it published his *Vie unanime*—and its emphasis on universal fraternity, led to the venture being linked to *Unanimism. They were in fact quite separate, but with shared ideals.

The material survival of L'Abbaye depended on the success of the hand-press printing venture, on paintings, and on visits and donations from like-minded people who wanted to participate in the simple, active, creative community life, in which each artist preserved his own individuality. The ideal lasted 14 months and came to an end through lack of an assured material future. The group's experience is the subject of Duhamel's book *Le Désert de Bièvres* (1937). [ET]

Abbé. The word can mean an abbot, but often implied no more than a minimal connection with the Church. The worldly *abbé* featured prominently on the fashionable literary scene in 17th- and 18th-c. France.

Abbesse de Castro, L'. One of Stendhal's *Chroniques italiennes.

ABÉGA, Séverin (b. 1955) Cameroonian writer. Educated at the University of Yaoundé, Abéga has worked as a research anthropologist and has pub- lished articles on 'myths'. His literary work often centres on peasant life and includes two collections of children's stories and a bitingly satirical novel, *La Latrine* (1989). [MPC]

ABEL, Antoine (b. 1934). One of the few writers from the Seychelles publishing in French, Abel has written three collections of fabulous tales in the form of prose poems: *Coco sec* (1969), *Une tortue se rappelle* (1977), *Contes et poèmes des Seychelles* (1977). He has also published a collection of poems, *Paille en queue* (1969). [BEJ]

ABÉLARD, Pierre (Peter) (1079–1142/4), quickly established himself as the leading logician of his day. Widely famed, he became the tutor and then the lover of Héloïse, an intelligent and highly educated girl. She wished to remain his mistress but, at Abélard's insistence, they were secretly married. When Héloïse's uncle and guardian, Fulbert, thought that Abélard had reneged on the marriage and sent Héloïse to a nunnery, he arranged for thugs to surprise him in his sleep and castrate him. Abélard then became a monk (c.1117), but he was back in Paris teaching logic and theology in the 1130s.

Abélard's main surviving works on logic—commentaries on Aristotelian logical texts and an independent treatise, the *Dialectica*—were probably written c.1114–22. In them, he urged a sharp distinction between real things and the non-things (such as states of affairs) which must be posited in order to understand the world. Abélard's later works include a much-revised theological treatise (*Theologia summi boni*, c.1120; *Theologia christiana*, 1120s; *Theologia scholarium*, c.1133–40) and two works mainly on moral philosophy (*Dialogue between a Christian, a Philosopher, and a Jew*, c.1125–6?; *Ethics*, 1138–9). There also survives an exchange of letters (almost certainly authentic, despite the doubts of some scholars) between Abélard and Héloïse, dating from the 1130s, when Héloïse was an abbess but still yearned after her former husband. *Jean de Meun was the first of many poets (who would include Petrarch and Pope) to respond sympathetically to the story told in these letters and in Abélard's autobiographical *Historia calamitatum* (*The Story of my Adversities*).

Despite the ecclesiastical condemnations of his writings at Soissons (1121) and, on St *Bernard's instigation, at Sens (1140), Abélard was not a heterodox thinker. He believed that the tools of logic can give only a partial understanding of mysteries such

1

as God's triunity; and he founded his ethical theory on love of God and obedience to his will. He died reconciled with St Bernard and the Church. [See SCHOLASTICISM.] [JAMM]

ABLANCOURT, PERROT D', see PERROT D'ABLAN-COURT.

Abraham sacrifiant. Innovatory Calvinist drama by Théodore de *Bèze, based on Genesis 22. First performed by Lausanne schoolboys in 1550, this 'tragédie française' (which none the less owes much to the medieval *mystery play) marries didacticism and drama. Like Abraham, Bèze suffered exile for his faith, and preaches through his characters the necessity of obedience to God and trust in His promises; dressing Satan as a monk, he satirizes Catholic worldliness and pride. The freshness and simplicity of the verse, the affectionate portrayal of the old couple, and the striking pathos of the scene of the sacrifice, raise the piece above mere sermonizing. [MJH]

Absurd, Theatre of the. Name given to a group of playwrights, and a type of drama, which constituted the French theatrical avant-garde of the 1950s. Critically imprecise, but ubiquitous and probably indispensable, the term was coined by Martin Esslin in his study of contemporary playwrights, *The Theatre of the Absurd* (1962). It refers to a group of writers, mainly though not exclusively in France, of whom *Beckett, *Ionesco, *Adamov, and (tenuously) *Genet are the main figures. Minor or occasional avatars of absurdist theatre are said to include *Arrabal, *Pinget, *Tardieu, *Vauthier, and *Vian, the Swiss Max Frisch and German Günter Grass, and the English-language playwrights Albee, Pinter, and N. F. Simpson. Among later playwrights, *Dubillard, *Obaldia, *Weingarten, and Tom Stoppard show absurdist influences. These writers cannot be said to constitute a school or movement, and it is important not to allow a label to obscure the huge differences between them. However, they have all on occasions drawn on a range of anti-naturalist techniques to express man's predicament in an irrational universe. It is this double alliance of content and dramatic style that is referred to by the expression 'Theatre of the Absurd'.

'Absurd' is taken loosely in the sense which it has in *Existentialist philosophy. It emphasizes (and generally does not go beyond) the purely negative side of *Sartre's Existentialism. More specifically, it is taken in the sense which *Camus gave to the word in Le Mythe de Sisyphe (1943), namely, 'out of harmony' with the universe. Camus identified the metaphysical anguish stemming from man's presence in a universe which denies any philosophical justification for his being. From this arises an awareness of the futility of human activity.

A sense of the absurd was a prominent feature of French literature immediately before and after World War II, though principally in philosophical writing, including Le Mythe de Sisyphe and L'*Être et le néant (1943), and novels such as La *Nausée (1938), L'*Étranger (1942), and La *Peste (1947). Camus's plays Le Malentendu (1944) and Caligula (1945), in so far as they express a view of existence as contingent and the world as being devoid of necessary meaning, might be said to anticipate an absurdist theatre. However, these plays, conventional in form, belong more to a traditional theatre of ideas because of their reliance on naturalistic situations and rational discourse. The Theatre of the Absurd, in contrast, does not discuss the human condition but represents it in absurd stage metaphors. For this reason, Jarry's *Ubu roi (performed in 1886), *Apollinaire's Les Mamelles de Tirésias, a proto-*Surrealist play written between 1903 and 1916, and indeed Surrealist theatre generally are often considered precursors: not in the philosophical sense, but for their use of anti-naturalist techniques such as narrative and psychological inconsistency, neologisms and nonsense language, and concrete stage imagery.

The archetypal plays of the Theatre of the Absurd are those which marked its emergence: Ionesco's La Cantatrice chauve (written 1948, produced 1950), Beckett's En attendant Godot (written 1947–9, produced 1953), and Adamov's La Parodie (his third play, produced 1952). These plays express significantly different world-views. Beckett emphasizes the meaninglessness of existence. Ionesco highlights non-communication and the uncomfortable contingency of the material world. Adamov communicates a tormented sense of mutilation and separation. Collectively, however, they exhibit the characteristic features of a type of theatre modelled on the absurd as a structural principle. The settings and characters are ahistorical, reflecting the metaphysical rather than social preoccupations of this type of drama. The mainstays of the conventional Aristotelian model of drama—plot, characters, and dialogue—are either discarded or subverted. The absence of plot emphasizes the futility and monotony of human existence. Characters lack motivation, and are seen to spend their time either waiting for something to happen (a motif common to all three playwrights) or engaged in meaningless exchanges of words. Cause and effect are dissociated, making events appear arbitrary and unpredictable. Material objects and stage properties appear incongruous. Time is elastic and non-linear. It is not by coincidence that the structure of such plays is typically circular (e.g. La Cantatrice chauve) or cyclical (En attendant Godot, La Parodie). The characteristic mood of these plays is tragicomic, inevitably so, because they express a nihilistic view of human existence whilst simultaneously denying man the dignity necessary to achieve genuine tragic stature.

The Theatre of the Absurd, which made Paris the dramatic capital of the world, was the major theatrical phenomenon of the 1950s. It was played out against the backdrop of the Cold War and under the shadow of Hiroshima, a period whose climate is best captured by Beckett in *Godot* and *Fin de partie*. By the early 1960s Beckett and Ionesco were established modern classics. Their success encouraged a spate of lesser absurdists, offering not so much a compelling global vision of life as minor variations of a mainly verbal and poetic kind. Beckett, meanwhile, continued to refine and condense his vision, in plays which became increasingly elliptical, culminating with the 30-second drama *Breath* in 1969. Ionesco's plays, reiterating ever more insistently his personal obsession with death, became increasingly allegorical. Adamov, repudiating his absurdist dramas as early as 1955, had adopted a Brechtian mode of committed theatre.

Absurdism helped to liberate playwrights from outmoded conventions, and gave rise to some powerful theatrical metaphors. Beckett's image of two tramps waiting beside a tree in a barren landscape became a universal icon of futile existence. But its nihilism represented a philosophical impasse. Moreover, it was the last theatrical avant-garde led by writers. After 1960 original dramatic writing fell into decline and directors took the initiative [see DRAMA IN FRANCE SINCE 1789]. [DWW]

See M. Esslin, *The Theatre of the Absurd* (1962); G. Serreau, *Histoire du 'nouveau théâtre'* (1966).

Acacia, L', see SIMON, C.

Académie is a word with several different meanings in French cultural history. In the world of *education it has designated since the time of Napoleon the 16 regional divisions (each with its *recteur*) of the Université de France. Between 1559 and 1685, however, there were *académies protestantes*, which were university-level establishments, and during the *ancien régime*, *académie* was the name given to schools in which noblemen learned the military and aristocratic arts.

In direct relation to literature, the term was used of groups of writers and scholars who met regularly not to teach, but to discuss matters of common concern, and in some cases to give prizes for literary works. Bodies of this kind existed under other names in the Middle Ages [see PUY, JEUX FLORAUX DE TOULOUSE], but the word *académie* came into general use in the 16th c. There were many such institutions in Renaissance Italy and the Italian example was widely followed over the next two centuries in France.

Jean-Antoine de *Baïf set up an *Académie de Poésie et de Musique in 1570 with royal patronage; this was supplanted by the Académie du Palais, which, unlike many of its successors, included female members. Among the most important private 17th-c. academies were those of *François de Sales, the *Dupuy brothers, d'*Aubignac, and *Lamoignon—and it was from an unofficial grouping of this type that the *Académie Française was

born. This was the first of several academies set up by *Richelieu, *Mazarin, and *Colbert as part of a policy of harnessing the arts and sciences to the greater prestige of throne and nation. Apart from the Académie Française, the most important were the *Académie des Sciences, the *Académie des Inscriptions et Belles-Lettres, and the *Académie Royale de Peinture et Sculpture, all of which were regrouped under the *Institut de France after the Revolution. Subsequently, Belgium acquired an Académie Royale de Langue et de Littérature Françaises de Belgique in 1920 and French Canada an Académie Canadienne-Française in 1944.

From the 1640s onwards academies were also set up in many provincial centres in France. These tended to be modelled on the Paris academies, and brought together local *notables* in an arena of intellectual equality comparable to the *salons. Their heyday was the 18th c., during which they came to interest themselves increasingly in scientific, economic, and political questions and propagated *Enlightenment values. Their importance may be gauged from the fact that *Rousseau wrote his two *discours* for the Académie de Dijon. [PF]

See F. A. Yates, *The French Academies of the Sixteenth Century* (1947); D. Roche, *Le Siècle des lumières en province* (1973).

Académie de Poésie et de Musique. Academy founded in 1570 by Jean-Antoine de *Baïf and the musician Joachim Thibault de Courville in order to create a closer union between poetry and music. Although Baïf's experiments with classically measured poetry and phonetic orthography were central to the origins of the Académie, there was also a comprehensive programme of other cultural and physical activities designed, after the *Neoplatonist manner of the Florentine academies, to harmonize body and mind, to moderate the passions, and to initiate the participants into higher intellectual and moral states. The Académie, the first French academy to be officially instituted by royal decree, attracted the best musicians and poets of the day and was active in Baïf's house in the rue des Fossés-Saint-Victor from 1571 to the death of *Charles IX (1574). Under *Henri III it continued to function, but was ultimately supplanted by the Académie du Palais, which met in the *Louvre and centred its activities more on philosophical and moral debate and oratory. Meetings of the Académie du Palais—a distant forerunner of the *Académie Française— were finally suspended in about 1584 as a result of civil war and lack of finance. [MDQ]

Académie des Inscriptions et Belles-Lettres. Academy set up by *Colbert in 1663 to compose inscriptions for royal medals and monuments. Consisting at first of only four members (including *Perrault), it was called the Petite Académie, then the Académie des Inscriptions et Médailles, before receiving its permanent name in 1716. During the

18th c. its activities expanded dramatically. It fostered research, published papers on such subjects as history and archaeology, and can be seen as the cradle of anthropology. Suppressed in 1793, it was incorporated in the *Institut de France under its original name in 1816.

[PF]

Académie des Sciences. Learned body set up by *Colbert in 1666 on the basis of previously existing informal meetings of scientists in circles such as those of *Mersenne and the *Dupuy brothers. It originally contained six classes, and was designed to encourage experiment and the communication of information and to apply science to the prestige and prosperity of the nation. Given the weakness of the universities [see EDUCATION], the Académie became a major centre of intellectual life in the 18th c., boasting members such as d'*Alembert, *Buffon, and *Lavoisier. *Fontenelle, who was Secrétaire Perpétuel from 1699 for over half a century, was responsible for the regular publication of reports, which brought scientific novelties to the attention of a broader public; he also composed *éloges of deceased academicians which constitute an embryonic history of science. Like the other royal academies, the Académie des Sciences was closed in 1793, but quickly re-emerged as a part of the new *Institut de France, and regained its original name in 1816.

[PF]

Académie du Palais, see ACADÉMIE DE POÉSIE ET DE MUSIQUE.

Académie Française. This hallowed institution began as a circle of writers grouped round *Conrart in c.1629. Getting wind of this initiative, *Richelieu decided to take it over as an instrument of national and personal prestige. In spite of the reluctance of some members, it began to meet in 1634, and its letters patent were ratified by the hostile Parlement de Paris in 1637.

Its form has changed little since the 17th c. The number of Academicians is limited to 40 ('les Immortels'), who are elected by their peers after a process of canvassing and visiting. They include not only writers, but important public figures (politicians, soldiers, lawyers, churchmen, etc.). Only in 1980 was the first woman academician, Marguerite *Yourcenar, elected.

The Académie's function is to establish and maintain linguistic and literary standards for the nation as a whole. At first this involved examining recent publications; one of its first operations was the notorious Sentiments de l'Académie sur Le *Cid, drafted by *Chapelain. Its principal task, however, was to be the preparation of a French dictionary, grammar, rhetoric, and poetics. The last two never materialized, and there was no official grammar until 1932 [see GRAMMARS], but the dictionary remains a regular part of the Académie's work. The first edition

appeared in 1964; since then there have been seven more, and the ninth is currently appearing in fascicles [see DICTIONARIES]. The Académie also awards literary *prizes, originally for poetry and eloquence, but currently numbering over 300, including the Grand Prix du Roman and the Grand Prix de la Francophonie. It is a rich institution, possessing several handsome properties, and its public activities are conducted with old-fashioned solemnity. From 1672 to 1806 it met in the *Louvre, since then under the 'coupole' in the former Collège des Quatre Nations across the river from the Louvre. Academicians still wear the bottle-green uniform established by Napoleon in 1801.

The early years of the Académie's history are described in *Pellisson's Histoire de l'Académie française (1653), continued by d'Olivet up to 1700. At first it was subject to pressure from above; Richelieu, the first 'protector', was succeeded by Chancellor *Séguier, but from 1676 onwards the king fulfilled this role. Under *Louis XIV, the Académie was expected to play its part in exalting the monarchy, and the monarch influenced the choice of new members. *La Fontaine's election, for instance, was delayed because he was out of favour. Similar pressures operated in the 18th c.—*Saint-Pierre was expelled for his political writings—but from the middle of the century the institution was infiltrated by the *philosophes; d'*Alembert as Secrétaire Perpétuel used it as an instrument of *Enlightenment. Even so, it was suppressed in 1793 as a part of the old aristocratic order. *Morellet saved its archives, and its surviving members formed the nucleus of the literary section of the *Institut de France, of which it became the first 'classe' under its original name in 1816. Since then, it has remained a central element of the cultural establishment.

From the beginning the Académie was criticized by those outside it (e.g. *Saint-Évremond)—and occasionally by those within. The slow pace of work on the dictionary (only marginally improved by *Colbert's creation of jetons or attendance tokens) attracted mockery, as did its claims to literary authority. One of its characteristics has always been its *salon-like mingling of writers with members of the social élite. Whereas the majority of past Academicians are now forgotten, many of France's greatest writers, particularly in the last two centuries, have not been members. Few Academicians are elected before reaching a respectable age, and the Immortals are a conservative rather than a creative force in French literary life. Nevertheless, the institution retains considerable prestige as part of France's cultural patrimony, its activities and elections are reported in the quality press, and its views on such matters as spelling—a French national obsession—continue to exert an influence. [PF]

See J.-L. Caput, L'Académie française (1986); M. Fumaroli, 'La Coupole', in P. Nora (ed.), Les Lieux de mémoire, II, La Nation, vol. 3 (1986).

Académie Goncourt. Founded in 1902 under the will of Edmond de *Goncourt, this society of ten writers meets annually over lunch to award the most prestigious of France's literary *prizes to what is judged the best imaginative prose work of the year. Their verdict has not always been ratified by posterity, but the prize guarantees unusually good sales.

Académie Palatine. Centre of learning and literary activity at the court of *Charlemagne. The English scholar Alcuin was one of its chief luminaries.

Académie Royale de Musique, see OPÉRA, THÉÂTRE DE L'.

Académie Royale de Peinture et de Sculpture. This academy was founded in 1648, in response to pressure from painters, who demanded official recognition that they belonged to a learned profession requiring intellectual abilities and an academic training, rather than to a trade. Previously art and crafts had been rigorously controlled by the guilds. Charles *Lebrun, Testelin, and Monsieur de Charmois persuaded the young Louis XIV to develop the Academy along the lines of those in Italy, to provide a system of instruction based on reason, rules, and study of the best masters. In 1665 the institution was given royal approval and funding. Rules, a code of practice, lectures, prize-givings, exhibitions, and a monopoly of life-classes were agreed and the Academy was given rooms in the *Louvre. *Colbert was appointed as vice-protector, and set about a programme of centralizing French art production and training which was to establish court and government control of patronage of the arts for over a century.

The social and political aims of the Academy were important, but the primary aim was educational. Students learned the practical aspects of painting or sculpture in the studios of their masters and only came to the Academy for instruction in drawing from Old Master drawings, then from casts, and finally from the life model. Painting was assumed to be an intellectual discipline requiring specialist education to be practised or understood. Mathematics, perspective, and geometry were taught, but the principal vehicle of indoctrination was the lecture or discourse.

Rules for young artists emerged from the analysis of pictures through a system of sequential categories. Fréart de Chambray identified the five most important visual categories as invention, proportion, colour, expression, and composition. Didactic qualities, expression, decorum, and appropriateness all figured in discussions about artistic scales of value. Attitudes to proportion and the intellectual pre-eminence of line were based on an understanding of the sacrosanct values of antiquity.

Competition was crucial to the idea of the Academy. Students were continuously assessed and graded. Those who attained the Grand Prix were given three years of subsidized advanced instruction in oil-painting. The Prix de Rome entitled the winner to four years of free study at the Académie de France in Rome—free, except that he must produce copies of the best (accredited) sculptures and paintings from Rome. The set subjects for this competition were, of course, drawn from classical writers.

In the early 18th c. the discourse system caused some Academic ideas to be discredited. The *Querelle des Anciens et des Modernes between the Rubenistes (de *Piles) and Poussinistes (Lebrun), which began in 1671, disputed the relative value of line and colour. The naturalism, realism, and truth attributed to colour triumphed over the abstract rigour of line. This refreshed official French taste and opened the doors of the Academy to a range of Venetian and Dutch-influenced artists such as *Watteau, *Fragonard, and *Chardin.

The first three decades of the 18th c. were a disrupted period. Exhibitions known as Salons were irregularly held [see ART CRITICISM], the established hierarchy of subject-matter was overturned, and still life—or subject-free art—attained the same importance as history painting, while variety, sprightliness, and grace became recognized as qualities to be admired.

Throughout Europe the central importance of individuality and intuition in all the creative arts came to dominate thinking. In Revolutionary France *David rebelled against the idea that genius could be taught or bounded by academies. The École des Beaux Arts replaced the Royal Academy in name, but the French system of academic art training continued to be very centralized and controlled, while painters continued to obtain their practical grounding in the studios of individual masters like David or Gros.

[JPC]

Acadia. Acadia is not a place. It is a certain way of being Canadian, the name given to the French-language culture of New Brunswick, Nova Scotia, and Prince Edward Island. The French first settled in Canada in the Bay of Fundy in 1603 and this settlement developed in isolation from the colony in the St Lawrence Valley [see QUEBEC]. Antonine *Maillet has shown that the oral culture of Acadia is preclassical, retaining much of the myth and popular wisdom found in *Rabelais. The British, masters in Acadia from 1713, judged this French population a threat to their success in the Seven Years War and scattered them heartlessly through eastern North America. Some settled in the Mississippi delta [see LOUISIANA] and others made their way back to the forests of New Brunswick, where they lived in hiding until timidly asserting themselves in the 1880s.

Antonine Maillet in her novels and plays, demythologizing Longfellow, has chronicled this exciting history of pilgrims, fishermen, and bootleggers, forging her own oral style to give a voice and identity to a silent, forgotten people. As in Quebec, CBC/Radio Canada has provided a training and a livelihood for young writers—Laurier Melanson and Herménégilde Chiasson are good examples; Chiasson is a modest, versatile, and talented graphic artist, broadcaster, theatrical producer, dramatist, and poet. The 1960s and 1970s produced a brief flowering of poetry of vituperation and lament (Chiasson, *Mourir à Scoudouc*, 1974, Raymond LeBlanc, *Cri de Terre*, 1973). Pierre *Perrault's film *L'Acadie, l'Acadie* documents uncannily the suppressed anger and faltering protest of this generation.

Acadia does not have a sufficiently large reading public to support even a daily paper—*L'Évangéline* closed in 1977. The Éditions d'Acadie have given a splendid service thanks to subsidies and valiant voluntary effort. Antonine Maillet and the brilliant novelist Jacques Savoie (*Raconte-moi Massabielle*, *Les Portes tournantes*) publish in Quebec. Édith Butler has made an international reputation as a singer-poet, but Acadia is kept alive not only by its stars but by the dedication of teachers, broadcasters, writers, genealogists, entrepreneurs, and volunteers in local-history and cultural associations.   [CRPM]

ACARIE, Madame, see DEVOTIONAL WRITING, 2.

ACHARD, Maurice (pseud. of Marcel-Augustin Ferréol) (1899–1974). Highly successful author of superior *Boulevard comedies over a period of 50 years. Full of quick repartee and a certain poetic fantasy, his plays all turn on affairs of the heart. *Voulez-vous jouer avec moa?* (1924) was produced by *Dullin; thereafter, with *Jean de la lune* (1929), *Le Corsaire* (1938), and other plays, he had a mutually fruitful partnership with *Jouvet.   [PF]

Acte additionnel aux constitutions de l'Empire, see NAPOLEON, 2.

Acte gratuit. Term used by *Gide to designate utterly unmotivated behaviour that defies routine, custom, and normal explanations. The hero of *Les *Caves du Vatican* exemplifies it when for no reason he pushes an old man to his death from a moving train. The notion attracted controversy and won devotees, especially among the *Surrealists. [DHW]

Action Française. Right-wing political movement founded in 1899, at the height of the *Dreyfus Affair, by Vaugeois and Pujo. *Maurras swiftly took control, making it royalist and (though he was an agnostic) supportive of the Church as a force for order and stability. In 1908 the daily *L'Action française* was founded, under the enthusiastic editorship of Léon *Daudet. The movement was strongly nationalistic, and implacably opposed to the Third Republic and to 'the enemy within' (Jews, *freemasons, *Protestants, 'métèques'). In Church matters, it strongly opposed all forms of modernism. During

World War I, attacks on the Republic were suspended in the national interest, and Action Française rode on a wave of popular approval. In the inter-war period, however, the movement gradually declined as an active force (Papal condemnation in 1926 and repudiation by the royalist pretender in 1937 did not help; nor did the rise of more energetic extra-parliamentary movements on the Fascist model). It retained influence in traditionalist circles, however, and there was a strong Action Française tinge to the Vichy government of 1940–4 [see OCCUPATION AND RESISTANCE]. Many French authors, critics, and historians were supporters, at one time or other, of Action Française, the most prominent being *Bernanos and *Maritain. [See NATIONALISM.]   [RMG]

ADAM, Juliette, née Lamber (1836–1936). French novelist and polemicist. Today she is remembered more for the seven volumes of her *Mémoires* (1902–10) than her literary output. She played a significant role in the intellectual life of the Third Republic, founding *La Nouvelle Revue* in 1879 and organizing a celebrated salon which met until the turn of the century.

ADAM, Paul (1862–1920), began his literary career during the 1880s with novels related to both *Naturalist and *Symbolist approaches to writing, in, for example, *Chair molle* (1885) and *Soi* (1886). He collaborated with Jean *Moréas, whose *Manifeste littéraire* (1886) applied the word 'Symbolism' to the literary movement, in the novel *Le Thé chez Miranda* (1886); and, under the pseudonym Jacques Plowert, he composed a *Petit glossaire pour servir à l'intelligence des auteurs décadents et symbolistes* (1888). He subsequently wrote novels of social and political commentary, and novels depicting military and family life in the early 19th c.   [BCS]

ADAM DE LA HALLE (or Adam le Bossu). Professional *jongleur and *trouvère active in *Arras from the 1260s to the 1280s. Autobiographical references in his works tell us that he spent most of his life in Arras, but went to Paris when young as a student (he was a *clerc*: Maistre Adam) and travelled with the count of Artois to Naples, where he probably died between 1285 and 1289. He married in the early 1270s, but experienced financial difficulties when the Pope withdrew certain fiscal privileges granted to married clergy; he may have returned to Paris at this point. Like Jehan *Bodel, his fame rested on his prolific and varied output, but unlike Bodel he was not only a poet but a musician. He was the author of 36 chansons, 16 *jeux partis, five motets, a *congé, an incomplete *chanson de geste (*Le Roi de Sicile*), and two plays, the *Jeu de la Feuillée* and the *Jeu de Robin et Marion*. He was a professional craftsman, and most of his works followed the conventions of the chosen genres; this is especially the case with the texts and music of the lyric poetry, though he was one of the few *trouvères* to have written music for three voices in his motets.

His three most substantial works, the *congé* and the two plays, though similar in some respects to Bodel's output, reject the latter's faith and sincerity in favour of irony and satire. In the *congé*, for example, Adam, as he takes leave of his friends, is not faced with imminent death; he is merely leaving to continue his studies interrupted by his marriage. His farewell to Arras includes a bitter attack on the dishonesty, coldness, and money-centredness of its inhabitants; and even his thanks to some friends and relations could be read as irony.

Adam's two plays could hardly be more different from each other (were they anonymous, no one would attribute them to the same author), but they have in common the fact that they are both dramatizations of lyric genres. The *Jeu de la Feuillée* (1100 lines, c.1276) is in effect a dramatized *congé*, in which Adam starts by declaring his intention to return to Paris to complete his education; he is fed up with life in Arras and disenchanted with marriage and his wife, whose youthful bloom has faded. This speech provokes an animated debate among his friends, his father Henri, and several successive passers-by. Their discussions touch on a number of Arras issues: greed, illness, sex, taxation, the morality of the higher clergy; Adam's problem is somewhat lost sight of. The passers-by include a doctor, a monk, a madman and his father, and a strange old witch, Dame Douche. The conversation is interrupted by nightfall and the arrival of three fairies, who discuss the prince du *Puy and other Arrageois, including Adam. They depart and the other characters reassemble in the tavern before making their separate ways home. The play is unusual in several ways. It is the first completely secular play in French; it is a play in which the author and his friends are not only actors but also characters, who mingle with other stereotypical or supernatural characters; it is full of local references, most of which critics have been able to understand; it has no apparent plot. Its enigmatic and elusive nature has inspired many contradictory interpretations, from Freudian to folkloristic.

The *Jeu de Robin et Marion* (760 lines, c.1283) was composed in Naples to entertain the army of the count of Artois. It is a staging of the plots of two traditional lyric genres, the *pastourelle and the pastoral *bergerie*. A knight Aubert meets the shepherdess Marion in a wood; he tries to seduce her, but she resists and Aubert leaves. Robin, her peasant lover, arrives bringing food and drink and then goes off to fetch his friends. Aubert returns and tries again to carry off Marion; Robin and his friends are too cowardly to intervene, but Marion manages to get rid of Aubert. Robin chases off a wolf, and the play ends with a series of rustic games and dances. The play begins and ends with songs, and there are several other sung passages, which explains why this play is sometimes called the first musical. A certain ambivalence hangs over this apparently simple play: who is laughing at whom? The knight (and the noble audience) at the peasants, or vice versa; or the author at them all? [GAR]

See H. Guy, *Adan de la Hale* (1898); D. H. Nelson, *The Lyrics and Melodies of Adam de la Halle* (1985); J. Dufournet, *Adam de la Halle: Le Jeu de Robin et de Marion* (1989); J. Dufournet, *Adam de la Halle: Le Jeu de la Feuillée* (1989).

Adam International Review. An Anglo-French quarterly devoted to literature and the arts, published in Bucharest and, since 1941, London. It features original writing by Aragon, Butor, Claudel, Cocteau, Duhamel, Éluard, Gide, Mauriac, Maurois, Simenon, and Sartre amongst other French contributors and a wealth of *inédits*. It has been doughtily edited from start to finish by Miron Grindea (b. 1909) who could justifiably have replied to any female enquirer after his thesaurus of modern literature with the Joycean palindrome 'Madam I'm *Adam*'. King's College, London, houses the *Adam* archive. [DAS]

ADAMOV, Arthur (1908–70). Russian-born playwright whose family moved to Paris in 1924. He was associated with the *Surrealists, developed an interest in Freudian analysis, and published a psychoanalytical autobiography, *L'Aveu* (1946), before turning to the theatre as a means of exorcizing his neuroses. His dramatic career covered two distinct phases. His early works (*L'Invasion, La Parodie, Le Sens de la marche, Tous contre tous*, and *Le Professeur Taranne*) were influenced by Strindberg and have affinities with the expressionist plays of Kaiser and Toller. With anonymous characters and locations, they project the inner world of a central author-character by means of anguished dream-like images of loneliness, persecution, and mutilation. Written between 1947 and 1953, and performed during the 1950s, they are often considered to be the most uncompromisingly bleak manifestations of the Theatre of the *Absurd.

In 1954–5, influenced by the discovery of Brecht and his association with *Planchon, he repudiated his earlier plays for their nihilism and lack of historical perspective. The theatre, he said, had to deal with both the incurable and the curable aspects of life. The incurable aspect was the fear of death, which had been the well-spring of his writing to then. The curable aspect was the social one, ignored by the absurdists. *Ping-Pong* (1955), depicting two young men whose lives are consumed by a pinball machine, marked a movement away from abstractionism and towards social reality. *Paolo Paoli* (1957), where the central consumer symbols are feathers and exotic butterflies, explores the laws of commerce and capitalism in *belle époque* society. It is a theatrically complex play, using documentary methods and drawing on Brechtian distanciation techniques. Its première, directed by Planchon, was hailed as the first throughgoing Brechtian production in France. Later committed plays dealt with the *Commune (*Le Printemps 71*, 1961), the judicial system (*La Politique des restes*, 1962), complacent moderation (*M. le modéré*, 1968), and the American Dream (*Off-limits*, 1969).

Although he had few successes in the theatre, Adamov was highly regarded by leading directors such as *Vilar, who admired the austerity of his early plays, and Planchon, to whom the Brechtian tendencies of his later plays appealed. He was the first French playwright to share Planchon's conviction of the political importance of *mise en scène*. The best production of his works was probably Planchon's posthumous tribute to him, A. A. *Théâtres d'Adamov*, performed at the TNP in 1975.

[DWW]

See R. Gaudy, *Arthur Adamov* (1971).

ADENET LE ROI (d. *c.*1300). Minstrel working at the courts of Henri III, duke of Brabant, 1261, and then Gui de Dampierre, count of Flanders. He was author of three *chansons de geste: Berte aus grans piés*, the story of Charlemagne's mother, based on the persecuted-wife motif; *Beuvon de Commarchis*, a reworking of *Le Siège de Barbastre* from the Cycle de *Guillaume; and *Les Enfances Ogier*, a courtly adaptation of the first episodes of *La Chevalerie Ogier de Danemark* [SEE OGIER LE DANOIS]. He also composed a long exotic romance, *Cleomadés*, in which the hero, son of the king of Spain, wins his bride, daughter of the duke of Tuscany, with the aid of a mechanical flying horse.

[PEB]

ADIAFFI, Jean-Marie (b. 1941). Regarded as one of the leading writers not only in Ivory Coast but also among the new generation of Black African writers. The cinema was his first vocation, but he became disillusioned while it and turned to philosophy and writing. As a novelist, playwright, and poet he has always claimed to write for the people, and throughout his writing there is a strong sense of innovation along with a concern for the aesthetic nature of his work. In his first novel, *La Carte d'identité* (1980), the colonial dimension serves as a framework for reflections on art, language, and cultural and personal identity; these issues are still topical today, and for this reason Adiaffi believes that there has been no fundamental change since so-called independence. For him, Africa must take root in its culture in order to develop. In *D'éclairs et de foudres* (1980) there is a strong desire to renew poetic discourse. The work is of a prophetic nature with real oneiric qualities, and contains a powerful denunciation of all forms of deception. In 1981 Adiaffi was awarded the Grand Prix Littéraire d'Afrique Noire.

[DRDT]

Adolescence clémentine, L', see MAROT, C.

Adolphe. Novel by Benjamin *Constant, probably begun in 1806 and published in London and Paris in 1816. The plot seems to echo many of Constant's own experiences: his time spent at German courts, his liaisons with a number of women, notably Anna Lindsay and Germaine de *Staël, and his difficult relationship with his father. Though generally considered to be in the tradition of the novel of psychological analysis initiated by *La *Princesse de Clèves*, *Adolphe* is also related to the *roman libertin* or novel of seduction, of which *Les *Liaisons dangereuses* was the most distinguished example. The story concerns the love affair between a young man, Adolphe, and the older Ellénore, mistress of the comte de P***; its originality lies in focusing more especially on their ensuing unhappy relationship, one from which Adolphe is unable to extricate himself because of a sense of loyalty, feelings of pity, and a fear of causing pain to Ellénore. Modern critics have seen in *Adolphe* variously a subtle study of the problematic relationship between language and feeling, a portrayal of the insidious power of the social group over the individual, and a projection of Constant's own complicated feelings towards women, the result of the early loss of his mother.

[DW]

Adonis, see LA FONTAINE.

ADOTEVI, Stanislas, see NÉGRITUDE.

Advertising. The language of 'la publicité' with its reflection and creation of the tastes of the times, its verbal economy, its striking images, its word-play, and its incessant search for novelty of expression, has of late become a subject of study. Whilst some '*pub*' language is memorable, and is devised to be so in the short term, it is patently not literature. Yet its linguistic features seem to overlap curiously with those of poetry. Just as they are features of verse, so alliteration, assonance, repetition, rhyme, simile, metaphor, textual compactness, telling imagery, and many other more specialized rhetorical devices are part too of the armoury of what Joyce called the 'gentle art of advertisement'. But for all their common denominators and despite poets' occasional turning to slogan-writing—*Cocteau coined 'Sans Kayser vos jambes ne seraient plus qu'un moyen de transport'—the advert, ephemeral as it may be, is not a lyrical construct and 'Dubo, Dubon, Dubonnet' no poem.

There has, none the less, been mutually fruitful interplay between advertising and literature. Indeed, the modern advert may have roots in the emblematic tradition of the Renaissance. Novelists have toyed with advertising material. *Balzac has Birotteau invent his 'Eau Carminative' and his 'Double Pâte des Sultanes' in his search for commercial success: 'il déploya le premier entre les parfumeurs ce luxe d'affiches, d'annonces et de moyens de publication que l'on nomme peut-être injustement charlatanisme.' *Zola wrote of the new fascination of *affiches* and *vitrines* in *Au Bonheur des Dames*, as did, more subtly, *Proust of the haunting 'cris de Paris' in *La Prisonnière*. Poets turned to the advert as textual model at the same time as, with the coming of colour lithography, painters like Toulouse-Lautrec began to design posters. The bizarrerie of at least one of *Lautréamont's disjointed similes purportedly stems from a contemporary newspaper 'réclame'. According to *Valéry, the typographical layout of adverts played a part in *Mallarmé's conception of the formal structure of *Un coup de dés* (1897). Thus it was that the musical model of *Symbolist poetry began to slip towards an iconographical one where, as in the advert, image and text worked together in close semantic support, a trend that reached its apogee in *Apollinaire's ideogrammatic *Calligrammes* (1918). Like Apollinaire, the *Dadaists were fascinated by street art, posters, and letterpress adverts in particular. Arcades and their *vitrine* displays were an important vector in the *Surrealists' understanding of mental transparency and the collapsing of perceptual barriers between reality and dream. *Breton's early concept of the image owed as much to 'réclame' as to *Reverdy. Indeed, a cynic might see the twin super-egos of Surrealism as Freud, the father of automatic associationism, and Bébé Cadum, the son of soap, respectively the private and public exponents of the expulsion of the Unclean and the satisfaction of Desire. It was not the Surrealists, however, but *Cendrars who promulgated a poetic genre he styled 'Publicité = Poésie'.

The 1920s, when unregulated advertising ran riot in the streets of Paris, and when literature itself first began to be 'marketed', by *Grasset, as a commodity, were undoubtedly the heyday of ad-lit intercourse, though novels such as *Perec's, and *Beauvoir's *Les Belles Images*, indicate that the affair is far from over.

[DAS]

Africa (South of the Sahara)

1. Oral Literature

The 'Dark Continent', the *terra incognita* of 18th- and 19th-c. European explorers, invaders, and colonizers, was believed to have no indigenous culture. Inhabited at best by the *bons sauvages* of the *philosophes*, at worst by the barbaric savages of the Positivists, Africa could have no 'literature'. When abbé *Grégoire published his *De la littérature des nègres* (1808), he could illustrate it only with verses written by freed slaves in America. In fact, despite the lack of written languages (in French West Africa, Arabic was reserved for Koranic studies), there was, throughout what we conveniently call 'Black Africa', a rich reservoir of oral literature

transmitted by professional chroniclers, praise-singers, and story-tellers known as *diéli* (*diali*) or *griots*. This collective lore is now sometimes known as 'orature'. The borderline between different genres is often blurred, but we can roughly distinguish the following:

a. Sacred texts. Prayers, invocations, religious songs, initiatory texts, which form part of the social, political, religious organization of peoples and regions, reflecting caste systems, nomadic or sedentary habits, presence of a king, growth of an empire or development of territorial groups under a local chief (e.g. songs for the enthronement or death of priests, chiefs, and kings). Invocations associated with agrarian rites, fishing, hunting, and annual renewal; stages in individual and social life: birth, baptism, circumcision or excision, marriage, death, epidemics, migrations, war or peace; those for practice of traditional crafts: weaving, forging, wood-carving, leatherwork; spells and magic incantations to make oneself invisible, overcome enemies or wild beasts, seduce women or conjure demons. (See G. Dieterlen, *Textes sacrés d'Afrique Noire*, 1965.)

b. Praise songs, associated with social and personal ceremonies, addressed, usually by the court or household *griot*, to a king, chief, warrior, or any individual who could pay for the service, recounting his exploits and ancestry.

c. Chronicles of the great empires (e.g. Ghana, Mali), their civilizations and warrior princes, from medieval to more recent times (e.g. El Hadj Omar, Lat Dior, Sundiata, Almamy Albouri). The mixture of heroic legend and historical fact makes these the *chansons de geste* of Black Africa.

d. Fable and folk-tale, popular 'science', didactic, supernatural, humorous, ribald, and romantic tales. While chronicles and praise-poems are specific to certain regions, most of the fables and folk-tales, with variants, are common to all parts of Black Africa, the animal protagonists varying according to geographic locality. Spider tales emanate from forest regions, the Hare is the hero in the savannah, the Tortoise and Antelope along the coast. (See M. Kane, *Essai sur les contes de Birago Diop*; F. V. Equilbecq, *Contes indigènes de l'Ouest africain*—NB the term 'Black literature' is used for the first time by Equilbecq to refer to the authentic oral heritage, which he transcribed and translated into French.) Many of the myths, fables, and legends have their counterparts elsewhere; the sacrifice of Iphigenia or Isaac can be compared with the legend of the Baoulé, in which Queen Abra-Pokou is called upon to sacrifice her only son to save the Baoulé tribe, whereupon the baobabs form a bridge over the River Comoé. We also find tropical equivalents of the Andromeda legend, in which a monster, usually a many-headed serpent, exacts the annual sacrifice of a virgin.

e. Myth and legend (e.g. cosmogonic, ethnic, heroic).

Africa

f. Popular wisdom: axioms, maxims, proverbs, riddles. These are mostly anonymous, but we may note the name of Kotje (or Cothe) Barma, the 18th-c. Senegalese sage, author of *dits faits*, mentioned by abbé *Boilat in his *Esquisses sénégalaises*. Birago *Diop contributed 'Kotje Barma ou les Toupets apophthègmes' to *L'*Étudiant noir*.

2. Written, Published Literature

a. The Colonial Era, 1850–1960. The first tentative efforts at literary composition by indigenous authors, during the period of French *colonization, were for the benefit of the colonial powers: accounts of travels, missionary or military expeditions, and descriptions of tribal life and customs by mulattos. The most important of these are *Panet and Boilat. Early Black writers of original works of fiction were often influenced by the cultural and administrative domination of France, directly or indirectly extolling the benefits colonization brought to the indigenous peoples and expressing respect for Christian and Western values. Ahmadou Mapaté Diagne's *Les Trois Volontés de Malic* (1920), an African version of the 'Three Wishes' theme, is an uplifting reader for use in primary schools in Senegal. Bakary *Diallo's more ambitious *Force Bonté* (1926) exalts the 'cardinal virtues' of France.

By the inter-war years, the revival of interest in African folklore taking place in Europe, combined with the growth of racial and cultural consciousness among Black intellectuals in Paris, eventually baptized as the *négritude* movement, resulted in the birth of an authentic Negro-African literature. One of the earliest calls was for the preservation in writing of traditional material transmitted by the old chroniclers and story-tellers. From 1935 to 1960 we find versions of folk-tales, myths, legends, and chronicles, from every region of West and Equatorial Africa, transcribed, translated, and retold with varying degrees of originality, the most important being Birago Diop's *Contes d'Amadou Koumba*. There followed full-length works of fiction based on chronicles transmitted by the local *griots*. Paul *Hazoumé's *Doguicimi* (1935) was the first African historical novel, a monument to Dahomey tradition. Twenty-five years later, the historian D. T. *Niane published his epic novel, *Soundiata*, the life of the legendary 13th-c. Mandingo warrior. Historical and legendary subjects, the repertoire of the *griots*, also formed the material, and provided heroes and heroines (e.g. Lat Dior, Shaka, Queen Pokou), for much dramatic literature during the colonial period (see particularly dramas by *Dadié, Cheik Aliou *Ndao, and *Senghor's dramatic poem *Chaka*).

Apart from works inspired by oral tradition, regional novels began to appear, depicting the existence, customs, and passions of rural, mainly animist, communities. Of these, Félix *Couchoro's first novel *L'Esclave* (1929), appearing when African literature was still embryonic, must be considered a pioneering work in theme, inspiration, and treatment. In the 1950s the outstanding regional novel was *Camara Laye's *L'Enfant noir* (1953). Émile Cissé's *Faraloko, roman d'un petit village africain* (1958) and *Ananou's *Le Fils du fétiche* (1955) also depict the customs of rural societies, the former, like *L'Enfant noir*, with nostalgia for the lost innocence of the author's childhood in Guinea, the latter casting the reformer's condemnatory eye on 'primitive', animist beliefs in rural Togo.

Novels with urban protagonists, pioneered by Ousmane *Socé's *Karim* (1935), begin to portray the dilemmas and vicissitudes of young people, influenced by contact with the West and caught at the crossroads of two cultures. Although depicting the clash of cultures resulting from colonization, sometimes with the heroes' unhappy experiences as student or worker in France, social-realist novels by *Sadji and *Naigiziki, like Socé's, are implicitly rather than explicitly anti-colonial. But in the immediate post-war decade, novelists, under the influence of *Fanon's *Les Damnés de la terre* and *Césaire's *Discours sur le colonialisme*, felt committed to using their literacy in the fight against colonialism, racism, and missionary subversion of African culture. They expressed their *engagement* in satirical, polemical novels. The bitterest, most powerful expression of militant *négritude* is found in *Dadié's autobiographical *Climbié* and the fiction of Mongo *Beti, Ferdinand *Oyono, and Ousmane *Sembène, as well as of lesser writers such as *Matip, *Malonga, *Badian, and J. Ikelle-Matiba.

Poetry, too, was committed to act as a war-cry. The traditional *Romantic, *Symbolist, and *Parnassian models adopted for early verse in the Caribbean were unacceptable in Africa, were taboo. Descriptions of nature, individual melancholy, personal experience, art for art's sake, were to be eschewed in the face of the need to proclaim the dignity of Black peoples, awaken them to an awareness of their alienation, extol the culture and traditions of Africa, and guide them in the search for their own identity. Verses dedicated to 'la femme noire' are less personal love poems than eulogies of 'Mother Africa'. Militant poets, following the example of Césaire, *Damas, Dadié, and David *Diop, sing of past and present oppression—the indignities, violence, and brutalities of slavery and colonial rule. Formally, the impact of the *négritude* movement, combined with the fact that this coincided with the *Surrealist school of poetry in France, caused a liberation of verse from classical rules of prosody. Under the influence of Senghor and Césaire, there is a widespread use of free or liberated verse patterns, and imagery, deliberately African in source, begins to reflect a telluric spirit and all aspects of the African landscape, while often exhibiting a sensuality and obsessive sexuality—not the eroticism of the West, but rather a preoccupation with the sources of life. Rhythms often echo the cadences of the

African dance or the beat of the tom-tom (Senghor actually prescribing the indigenous musical instruments which should accompany his verses).

b. *Post-Independence*. The date when the French colonies in West and Equatorial Africa gained independence [see DECOLONIZATION] is not only a political watershed but also a convenient point from which to assess new developments in creative writing from these regions. Changes, naturally, did not occur overnight. For one thing, many works published in the 1960s had been written in the previous decade. So, for some years poetry and social-realist novels still reflect a preoccupation with aspects of colonialism, although the edge of anti-colonial acerbity is generally blunted.

In poetry, Senghor's voice continues to dominate for another two decades, with his *Lettres d'hivernage* (1973) and *Élégies majeures* (1979). These still pay lip-service to *négritude*, which he redefines to include the expression of his personal mission to his homeland: 'Ma négritude est truelle à la main, est lance au poing | Récade . . . | Ma tâche est d'éveiller mon peuple au futurs flamboyants | Ma joie de créer des images pour le nourrir, ô lumières rythmées de la Parole!' Certain committed poets continue to militate in the name of suffering Africa and the search for Black identity (e.g. *Diakhate, *Joachim), or devote their talents to expressing national reconstruction or denouncing misery and oppression elsewhere in the world. Some make common cause with their 'brothers' in Chile, Angola, Vietnam, South Africa. But many of the new generation of poets, notably *Tchicaya U Tam'si, Malick *Fall, *Tati-Loutard, and Kine Kirama *Fall, are liberated from the commitments of *négritude* and take up universal themes of personal experience: solitude, exile, nostalgia, jealousy, pity, existential anguish, love and death. Bernard *Nanga ironically sums up his emancipation from commitment to an outdated loyalty: 'Qu'on ne me dise pas que je n'ai pas chanté | Ma vieille négritude. | Je la vis, | Il suffit. | Je hais les habitudes. | Nègre d'un temps nouveau, d'autres rêves hantés, | Je veux en homme libre | M'épanouir et vivre' (*Poèmes sans frontières*, 1987).

An important trend in the fiction of the first post-colonial decade is satirical, cynical, and lewdly picaresque social comedy (e.g. Oyono's *Chemin d'Europe*). Other novelists use their gifts to analyse the social and psychological problems of adapting to a changing world (*Ake Loba's *Kocoumbo*, 1960; *Kane's *L'Aventure ambiguë*, 1961). *Bhêly-Quénum's *Un piège sans fin* (1960) and Camara Laye's *Le Regard du roi* are both in different ways existential treatments of a search for identity in a hostile world. Another striking example is Malick Fall's allegorical *La Plaie* (1967). Some didactic fiction offers a blueprint for the future, illustrating how dignity, prosperity, and independence can be attained through a people's corporate efforts—physical toil hand in hand with education (e.g. *Nokan's *Le Soleil noir point*, 1962).

By the 1970s two new trends in prose writing reflect post-colonial social and political changes. One is the emergence of women writers. The other is the replacement of the evils of colonialism, as the satirists' target, by attacks on bureaucratic, corrupt, or dictatorial regimes in African republics. It did not take long to realize that independence did not bring the promised utopia, and the resultant disillusionment forms the theme for much satirical fiction, sometimes sombre, sometimes relieved by irony and savage humour. Such is *Kourouma's first novel, *Les Soleils des indépendances* (1968), denouncing the injustices, corruption, and inhumanity of the 'New Order'. Ousmane Sembène now uses the cinema, as well as the printed word (e.g. *Xala*, 1973), to illustrate the nepotism, exploitation, unscrupulous *arrivisme* of the new masters, the ever-increasing moral and economic gulf between the have-nots and the newly privileged black bourgeoisie. Aminata *Sow Fall (*La Grève des Bàttu*, 1979) and Ibrahima *Sall (*Les Routiers de chimères*, 1982) both use fiction to indict contemporary city life.

A reflection of the change in target from the colonial masters to indigenous tyrants is the fact that some writers have been imprisoned and many forced into exile by the uncompromising nature of their works and their implicit or explicit political stance. The repressive regime of President Sekou Touré in Guinea is the overt subject of a disillusioned Camara Laye's *Dramouss* (1966), and is thinly disguised in Fantouré's fictional, pessimistic *Cercle des tropiques* (1972). Sekou Touré is again the model for Tierno *Monénembo's sinister, cruel tyrant ruler in *Les Crapauds-Brousse* and Williams *Sassine's *Le Jeune Homme de sable* (both 1979). Mongo Beti broke a 16-year silence with novels virulently attacking President Ahidjo's oppressive rule in his native Cameroon: *Remember Reuben*, *Perpétue ou l'Habitude du malheur* (both 1974), and *La Ruine presque cocasse d'un polichinelle* (1979). The litany of violence and suffering in prison and concentration camps, accounts of plots and *coups d'état* which punctuate contemporary African politics, is taken up in *Dongala's short stories in *Jazz et vin de palme* (1982). But by the 1980s African writers were beginning to transcend the limitations of social-realism, using scatology, Rabelaisian farce, Ubuesque mock-heroics, and surreal fantasy in novels and plays to express their exasperation with neo-colonialism, totalitarianism and corrupt dictatorships. Tchicaya U Tam'si, the Congolese poet from an older generation, turns his hand to farce in his play *Le Destin glorieux du maréchal Nnikon Nniku*, while *Sony Labou Tansi heads the new generation of satirists with a series of savage surreal novels of contestation.

Finally, in the 1960s women writers begin to find their voice, mainly in prose. The tone and themes of their poetry are lyrical, both personal and universal, rather than militant. Annette *M'Baye, the pioneer of African women poets, expresses a frank sensuality in her love poems and a strong feminist note in all her verses, reminding us that there is suffering, revolt, and love that is specifically feminine as well as specifically African. Much of the verse of the new generation of women poets is undistinguished, but the young Senegalese Kine Kirama *Fall brings a freshness, economy, and spirituality to the expression of human loves and torments, her religious faith, and her love for the natural scenes of her birthplace. Véronique *Tadjo and *Werewere Liking both break new ground: Tadjo with prose poems original in theme and imagery drawn from her femininity, and arcane in their discreet personal references; Werewere Liking in hybrid creations, combining poetry, novel, and drama, as daring, violent, and provocatively feminist in theme and expression as they are innovative in form. Apart from Werewere Liking, who directs and writes for a theatre workshop, and Joséphine Kama-Bongo's play *Obali* (1974) about tribal customs in Gabon, there is little evidence of women's interest in dramatic writing.

The earliest prose works by women tend to be autobiographical, either histories from a variety of regions and backgrounds (e.g. *Pélandrova*, 1975, the eponymous author's story of her life as a Malagasy sorcerer, and Nafissatou *Diallo's account of a Muslim girl growing up in Dakar, *De Tilène au plateau*, 1976) or thinly disguised as fiction (e.g. the Cameroonian Thérèse Kuoh-Moukouri's *Rencontres essentielles*, 1969, and the Ivoirian Simone Kaya's *Danseuses d'Impé-éya: jeunes filles à Abijan*, 1975), two accounts from a woman's viewpoint of the clash of cultures resulting from a Western education in a traditional society. Ken *Bugul's *Le Baobab fou* (1982), a strikingly honest autobiographical novel, tells of a lonely, traumatized childhood and adolescence in rural Senegal, followed by the author's encounter with the permissive society and subculture of urban Europe.

The works of Aminata Sow Fall, the most prolific and versatile of French-African women writers, are not specifically feminist, but rather ironical, sociopolitical comments on false values in contemporary Senegalese society, perpetuated from tradition or resulting from Western influences. Mariama *Ba led the way in novels treating moral, psychological, and emotional dilemmas specifically affecting women, particularly problems of polygamy, social and religious constraints, and mixed marriages. Powerful works by the young novelists Calixthe *Beyala and Ananda *Devi, depicting the lives of women trapped in the bleak purgatory of Africa's urban slums, indicate that the future of African literature in French is safe in the hands of African women as well as men.

The post-colonial era has also seen moves towards 'linguistic decolonization' by fiction, poetry, newspapers, and films in indigenous languages. Wolof, spoken by the majority of Senegalese, with a grammar and orthography early drawn up at the University of Dakar, has proved the most widely adopted. Boubacar Boris *Diop and Cheikh Aliou Ndao have been at the forefront of this movement, the latter having written his first novel, *Buur Tileen*, in Wolof in 1963, before translating it for publication in French. B. B. Diop has written a play, as yet unpublished, and launched a newspaper in Wolof. Guinean poets are also beginning to publish locally in the vernacular. The practical and financial problems of publishing in a minority language do not apply to films, which can break out of a linguistic ghetto by the use of subtitles for international distribution. Ousmane Sembène, the pioneer African film-maker, first made both Wolof and French versions of his novel *Le Mandat*, and then original films such as *Ceddo* and *Camp Thiaroye*. In 1987 appeared *Kaddu Beykat/Lettre paysanne/Letter from my Village* by Safi Faye, the only African woman film-director to date. Souleymane Cissé (Mali) made the acclaimed *Yeelen* in the Bambara language, while Idrissa Ouedraogo, from Burkina Faso, the second poorest African country, which so far has produced no published literature in French, has three record-breaking features to his credit, filmed with local people and using the minimum of dialogue: *Yam daabo/The Choice*, *Yaaba*, and *Tilai/The Law*. [DSB]

See R. Finnegan, *Oral Literature in Africa* (1970); L. Kesteloot, *Les Ecrivains noirs de langue française: naissance d'une littérature* (1975); D. S. Blair, *African Literature in French* (1975); C. Wauthier, *L'Afrique des Africains* (1977); J.-P. Makoùta-Mboukou, *Spiritualité et cultures dans la prose romanesque et la poésie négro-africaine (de l'oralité à l'écriture)* (1983); A. Rouch and G. Clavreuil, *Littératures nationales d'écriture française* (1987).

African Literary Reviews. African literary and cultural magazines tend to have a somewhat precarious existence, the most important and most influential literary reviews having come from English-speaking rather than francophone Africa. In francophone Africa the greatest number of literary magazines has in fact come from a country that is bilingual, Cameroon. Arguably its most important literary and cultural review was *Abbia*. *Revue Culturelle Camerounaise/Cameroun Cultural Review*, which was started in 1963. It was dormant for many years, followed by brief flickers of life in the late 1970s, but it appears to be irrevocably moribund today. An important scholarly journal which commenced publication more recently, and which promotes research in the traditions of African theatre and thought, is *African Theatre Review* (1985–).

A fine journal published by Nouvelles Éditions Africaines in Ivory Coast, providing critical analysis of Black African Literature and its place in society, is the *Revue de littérature et d'esthétique négro-africaines* (1983–). The most significant cultural review published in Senegal, and which continues to be published fairly regularly, is *Éthiopiques. Revue socialiste de culture négro-africaine* (1974–), which aims to provide a platform for a dialogue for committed socialism, as well as analysis of African arts and cultures. *L'Afrique littéraire et artistique*, an attractively produced quarterly, was published from Senegal for several years (1968–?), and covered literature, drama, art, music, and the cinema. Finally, *ICA Information*, published by the Institut Culturel Africain (1975–), is a bilingual quarterly which provides regular information on cultural activities in member states of the ICA.

Muntu. Revue scientifique et culturelle du CICIBA (1984–) is a lavishly produced biannual journal from the Centre International des Civilisations Bantu; it provides multidisciplinary and comparative studies for research on all aspects of the cultural heritage of Bantu civilizations. Other little magazines of some note, published elsewhere in Africa (though showing little sign of life at the present time), include *Les Cahiers du Cercle Littéraire de Brazzaville* (1979–?) and *Ambario. Revue d'Animation Culturelle et Scientifique* (1978–?), which aims to promote cultural development in *Madagascar and to project an image of Madagascar's culture and literature to an overseas audience. [HMZ]

African Publishing Houses. Book-publishing is in crisis in most African countries. The deepening economic recession and chronic balance-of-payments problems have taken a severe toll on publishing and book development, and the resulting dearth of publishing outlets has meant that African writers are finding it increasingly difficult to place their work.

Until recently, it appeared that publishers in francophone Africa were better off than their colleagues in anglophone Africa, largely because they had access to a convertible currency, the CFA. However, recent developments (in 1990) indicate that they, too, have not escaped the recession, and government funding for textbooks or library development has dramatically declined, with the inevitable consequences for the book industries. A major publishing initiative taken in the early 1970s, the establishment of Les Nouvelles Éditions Africaines (NEA), would appear to be in danger of collapse.

Publishing activities in francophone Africa have always been heavily concentrated in two or three countries in West Africa: Senegal, Ivory Coast, and, to a lesser extent, Cameroon. The first full-scale indigenous publishing house was Éditions CLE in Yaoundé, Cameroon, founded in 1963 with the help of the Dutch and German Protestant churches. The number of new books from Éditions CLE has dropped sharply over the last decade or so, but its early list included names such as *Bebey, *Dadié, *Oyono-Mbia, and *Lopes. Other, smaller Cameroonian imprints have included *Philombe's Éditions Semences Africaines, which had a strong list focusing on poetry and drama, Buma Kor Publishing House, and Timothée Ndzaagap's Éditions Le Flambeau.

The launching in 1972 of the Nouvelles Éditions Africaines consortium was a significant publishing development. The main aims of NEA, a joint undertaking of the governments of Senegal, Ivory Coast, and Togo together with French publishing interests, were to foster African authorship, to promote the reading habit, and to produce school-books adapted to African, rather than European, realities and experience. NEA quickly became a major force in all areas of publishing, with a massive and impressive list which included most of the top names from the academic and literary world, among them Birago *Diop, Cheikh Anta *Diop, Amadou Hampaté *Ba, *Maunick, *Diakhaté, *Menga, *Nanga, *Sow Fall, *Sall, *Tati-Loutard, Mariama *Ba, and of course *Senghor. NEA also produced a wide range of attractive children's books, including some splendid comic-strip-type books.

Although the NEA experience has set an example of more enlightened government attitudes towards supporting indigenous African publishing, it could be argued that their dominance has stifled the growth of small independent publishers. The only other publisher of note in francophone West Africa is the Centre d'Édition et de Diffusion Africaines (CEDA) in Abidjan. Although the CEDA output has dropped substantially in recent years, they still maintain a strong literary list of novels, drama, poetry, and popular fiction, including a series co-published with Hatier in Paris. Dadié, *Adiaffi, *Diabaté, *Pliya, and *Sony Labou Tansi are among the internationally known CEDA authors. In Togo there have been a number of initiatives to set up small privately owned publishing-houses, including Éditions Akpagnon, owned by the writer and political activist Yves-Emmanuel *Dogbé, whose list has included fiction, poetry, and short-story collections, and Éditions HaHo ['for all'], launched in 1984 and publishing both in French and in African languages.

Publishing activities in other parts of French-speaking Africa, e.g. in Zaïre or the former Belgian colonies, are insubstantial. There is a fairly lively publishing industry in the Maghreb (especially *Algeria and *Morocco), but much of the literary publishing is of course in Arabic. In Africa south of the Sahara French publishers continue to dominate the markets, although the Canadians are beginning to make some inroads. Small autonomous publishing houses are unable to compete with the multinationals and the French publishing giants; and a viable publishing industry, which can produce books on a scale that matches local needs, is still a dream in most parts of the continent. [HMZ]

Afrique fantôme, L', see LEIRIS.

AGATHON, pseudonym used by Henri *Massis for co-authored works.

Âge d'homme, L', see LEIRIS.

Agence France-Press, see HAVAS.

Agésilas. Tragedy by P. *Corneille, set in ancient Ephesus, unusual in being written in *vers libres classiques.*

Agincourt, see HUNDRED YEARS WAR.

AGOULT, Marie de Flavigny, comtesse d' (1805–76), published under the pseudonym Daniel Stern, espousing the intellectual movements of her time with energy and enthusiasm. In the 1830s she had a celebrated affair with Liszt; their daughter, Cosima, later became the wife of Wagner. She is best known for a novel, *Nélida* (1845), but she also wrote interesting works of history and philosophy. [CC]

Agrégation. The *agrégation* originated in 1766, but took its modern form under Napoleon as a competitive examination for teaching posts. In law and medicine it remained a qualification for faculty teaching. In arts and science it was required for a full chair in a *lycée* [see EDUCATION]; *agrégés* were the élite among secondary schoolteachers, and many later moved into higher education. After the creation of girls' *lycées* in 1880, there were for many years separate *agrégations* for women. [RDA]

AGUESSEAU, Henri-François d' (1668–1751). Magistrate, orator, and Chancellor of France, author of a number of works on moral, political, and legal topics.

Aides, see TAXATION.

AIDS as a subject in modern writing, see GAY AND LESBIAN WRITING.

AIMARD, Gustave (1818–83), see ROMAN D'AVENTURE(S), 2.

Aimeri de Narbonne. *Chanson de geste* of the Cycle de *Guillaume. The surviving version by *Bertrand de Bar-sur-Aube dates from the end of the 12th c. Showing the influence of *romance, it tells of Aimeri's capture of Narbonne following Charlemagne's return from Rencesvals, and his struggles to hold the town. It provides the basis of *Aymerillot* in *Hugo's *Légende des siècles.* [PEB]

Aiol. *Chanson de geste* which forms part of the so-called 'Cycle de Saint-Gilles', being composed as a sequel to *Élie de Saint-Gilles.* It recounts the career of Élie's son Aiol who leaves Provence with his father's rusty armour and fine old horse Marchegai, and meets with derision from the better-accoutred though obviously less meritorious people whom he encounters on his way to Charlemagne's court. There, despite the machinations of the traitor Macaire and misadventures with Saracens, he finally establishes himself, marries, and has the traitor tried and executed.

Aiol is nearly 11,000 lines long and was composed in the late 12th–early 13th c. A lively and amusing work, it falls metrically into two parts, the first in decasyllables, the second in alexandrines. The decasyllabic lines are unusual in that they have a caesura after the sixth rather than the fourth syllable, a trait found in *Girart de Roussillon,* but otherwise virtually unknown in the *chansons de geste.* [SK]

AÏSSÉ, Mademoiselle (d. 1733). Circassian slave brought up in Paris, where she frequented salon society. She is remembered for her engaging letters. Her story provided a model for *Prévost's *Histoire d'une Grecque moderne.*

AJAR, Émile, see GARY.

AKE LOBA (b. 1927). Ivoirian novelist. Son of a traditional chief, Loba had a short and unimpressive school career before being sent to France by his father, where he obtained a baccalaureate by correspondence while an agricultural worker. Lacking funds to continue his education, he returned to Ivory Coast in 1959. His first novel, *Kocoumbo, l'etudiant noir* (1960), won the newly created Grand Prix Littéraire d'Afrique Noire. It describes the difficulties encountered by African students in France. Loba is basically an apologist for European bourgeois values. Generally indulgent towards his French characters (apart from the committed left-wing trade-unionists, whom he treats harshly), he tends to equate Westernization with progress. His second novel, *Les Fils de Kouretcha,* in which apologists of 'modernization' confront traditionalists, won the Houphouet Boigny Prize for Literature in 1970. He has published two other novels, *Les Dépossédés* (1973) and *Le Sas des parvenus* (1990). [FNC]

ALACOQUE, Marguerite-Marie, see DEVOTIONAL WRITING, 2.

ALADJI, Victor (b. 1941). Togolese novelist, short-story writer, and journalist; teacher at the Université du Bénin in Lomé. *Akossiwa, mon amour* (1971) and *L'Équilibriste* (1972) continue to be widely read in Togo. His novel *La Voix de l'ombre* (1985) met with less success than his earlier tales. [MPC]

ALAIN (pseud. of Émile-Auguste Chartier) (1868–1951). French philosopher, essayist, critic, teacher, and mentor of the *Radical party. The brief chapters of Alain's philosophical essays, the 5,000 lapidary *Propos* devoted to politics, literature, aesthetics, science, ethics, economics, education, and religion, and his admiration for thinkers as diverse as Plato, Spinoza, Descartes, Hegel, and Comte, might suggest an eclectic and unsystematic approach. None the less, Alain's work was unified by his insistence on the virtues of vigilant doubt, by his lasting concern with the interdependence of perception, judgement, and action, and by his faith in the will to freedom (*Quatre-vingt-un chapitres sur l'esprit et les passions*, 1921; *Histoire de mes pensées*, 1936). His belief that literature was a particularly rich source of 'real ideas' was borne out by his commentaries on *Valéry's *Charmes* and *La Jeune Parque* (1929 and 1936), and by his readings of *Balzac and *Stendhal: he extolled the vitality and material density of Balzac's world and the autonomy, integrity, and will-power of Stendhal's heroes (*Avec Balzac*, 1937; *Stendhal*, 1935).

Alain was a brilliant and unconventional *lycée* teacher (he refused an appointment at the Sorbonne) whose influence was acknowledged by generations of distinguished disciples, among them Simone *Weil, Georges Canguilhem, and Jean *Prévost. A man of independent mind, he belonged to no philosophical school. However, his emphasis on the inseparability of consciousness of self and consciousness of the world, and his interest in perception and imagination, anticipated the insights of French existential *phenomenology.   [REG]

ALAIN-FOURNIER (pseud. of Henri Alban Fournier) (1886–1914). French novelist. The child of two schoolteachers, Alain-Fournier failed to qualify for the profession. This was partly because of the time he spent writing poetry and frequenting Parisian literary circles with his schoolfriend Jacques *Rivière. It also resulted from his falling deeply in love with Yvonne de Quiévrecourt, whom he met briefly in 1905 and only saw again when she was a wife and mother. She appears as Yvonne de Galais in *Le *Grand Meaulnes* (1913), the novel by which he is mainly remembered. He was killed in the early weeks of World War I.

[JC]

ALAN OF LILLE (also Alain de Lille or Alanus ab Insulis) (d. 1203) wrote many works of practical and speculative theology, as well as the *De planctu naturae*, written in a combination of prose and verse, and the verse epic *Anticlaudianus*, which were enormously popular in the Middle Ages. In *De planctu*, a personification of Nature comes down to the world in order to bewail the prevalence of homosexuality. The *Anticlaudianus* recounts the creation of a perfect man, the celestial journey to receive his soul from God, and his victorious encounter with the vices. Both works provide ample opportunity for encyclopaedic digression and the display of a Latin style rich in grammatical metaphors and word-play.

[JAMM]

A la recherche du temps perdu. Novel by *Proust in seven volumes, published 1913–27 (the last three posthumously). It is the most important 20th-c. French novel, and is generally considered one of the masterpieces of European literature. Its plot is an odyssey of kinds: the narrator tells the story of his own life, recounting his errors and successes, and ends by explaining why he decided to write about this life (in, presumably, the novel we have just been reading).

A la recherche had an interesting publishing history. At first it was rejected by all the publishers Proust approached, and he had to pay to have the first volume published. Even after it was taken on by Gallimard, there were further difficulties. Some arose simply from Proust's own ceaseless reworking of his proofs, and his casual attitude to compositors' errors. But there were other complicating factors: he did not have time to revise the last three volumes properly before he died; and he was apparently making hasty decisions about the structure of the novel even while dying. The first Gallimard edition was thus full of errors and arbitrary editorial decisions.

In 1954 a new scholarly edition (the Pléiade) resolved most of these problems by sifting through the successive stages of Proust's proofs, as well as his typescripts and many of the notebooks in which he had drafted the novel (his famous 'Cahiers'). This edition became the standard one for the next 35 years. However, from the early 1970s on, scholars were exploring these 'Cahiers', typescripts and proofs, and studying new documents to which the Pléiade editors had not had access. It became clear that another edition was needed—one which would respect the last state of the text as overseen by Proust, but which could, in extensive notes, describe fully both Proust's reworkings and the problems posed by the posthumous volumes. (The sixth volume, *Albertine disparue*, has been a particular subject of debate.) A new Pléiade edition was therefore brought out in 1987–9. Since *A la recherche* came out of copyright in 1987 many competing editions have appeared; some over-dramatize their 'discoveries', and none is as satisfactory as the new Pléiade.

The first volume of the novel, *Du côté de chez Swann* (1913), describes a childhood in which the narrator grows up longing to be a writer, and filled with attractive but illusory images of travel, the aristocracy, and love. It opens with a painful scene which, says the narrator, is all he could remember as an adult, until one day, for the first time since childhood, he tastes some *madeleine* cake soaked in tea. This taste brings feelings of ecstasy and unexpectedly revives all the associated sensations—especially the pleasures—of significant periods of his childhood. The narrator now describes newly remembered landscapes, and early episodes concerning a number of characters who are to play a part in his adult life: for example, the family servant Françoise, the local snob Legrandin, the prestigious duchesse de Guermantes, his own friend Bloch, and particularly the family friend Swann. Swann shares many traits with the narrator, so much so that most of the second half of this volume is devoted to *Un amour de Swann*, the tale of Swann's most important love affair (which had taken place before the

A la recherche du temps perdu

narrator's birth): that with Odette, the woman he is eventually to marry. This affair is first helped, then hindered, by the Verdurins, an aspiring bourgeois couple who are to achieve startling social prominence in the course of the novel. After this, the volume returns to the narrator; he plays with Gilberte, the daughter of Swann and Odette, and begins with her what is to be his first unhappy relationship.

In the second part, *A l'ombre des jeunes filles en fleurs* (1919), the narrator, now an adolescent, frequents Odette's salon, where he meets the writer Bergotte. He visits the seaside town Balbec, and there goes to the studio of the painter Elstir; this painter, and the composer Vinteuil, influence his view of art. In Balbec he also makes friends with the nephew of the duchesse de Guermantes, Saint-Loup; he has curious encounters with the brother of the duc de Guermantes, the baron de Charlus; and he meets Albertine, who is to be the main object of his love. In the third part, *Le Côté de Guermantes* (1920–1), the narrator makes his way in society, and is eventually invited to dinner by the Guermantes. Meanwhile time is passing: the narrator's grandmother dies; Swann himself is dying; and the narrator is still not working at his writing. The fourth part, *Sodome et Gomorrhe* (1921–2), opens with the narrator's discovery of Charlus's (and others') homosexuality: Charlus's earlier inexplicable behaviour now becomes clear. Later in this volume Charlus falls in love with Morel, a young violinist; their relationship is to echo that of the narrator and Albertine. The narrator attends another important social occasion, a soirée given by the princesse de Guermantes. During a second stay in Balbec he visits the Verdurins, who are making their way in society, and renews intimacies with Albertine. He starts to suspect Albertine of lesbianism, suspicions apparently confirmed when she claims a close relationship with a couple known to be lesbian. Devastated, he brings her back to his flat in Paris, determined to marry her.

The fifth and sixth parts, *La Prisonnière* (1923) and *Albertine disparue* (1925), describe further social encounters with the Guermantes and the Verdurins, but focus mainly on the narrator's quasi-imprisonment of Albertine; the ebb and flow of his suspicions; her eventual flight and accidental death; his mourning; and the gradual waning of a jealousy that is at first unassuaged. At the end of *Albertine disparue* the narrator at last goes to Venice (a long-held desire). This visit in various ways helps him realize he no longer loves Albertine. On the way back he learns that Saint-Loup is to marry Gilberte, thus uniting the Guermantes and Swann sides of his life.

The last part, *Le Temps retrouvé* (1927), describes Paris during World War I; the war comes as a climax to a number of earlier scenes of callousness, cruelty, lying, rumour-mongering, and dissolution. The narrator has by now reached a nadir of discouragement. He has fulfilled his worldly ambitions, going to places he had wanted to visit (Balbec and

Venice); achieving social successes with the aristocracy; and forming relationships with three of the women he has desired (Gilberte, Madame de Guermantes, Albertine). But he has found that none of these experiences has brought him the hoped-for excitements, and that love can be agonizing. Furthermore, though his appreciation of art has matured and has brought him a certain wisdom, he cannot himself create. Nature no longer moves him; he cannot even believe in art as something unique. He retreats to a sanatorium, emerging eventually to go to a matinée given by the princesse de Guermantes (formerly Madame Verdurin). On his arrival a succession of physical sensations brings back to him a flood of involuntary memories. Previous involuntary memories (notably those brought by the *madeleine*) have seemed intensely pleasurable and significant. But, almost miraculously, it is these final ones which make him recognize the richness of his own life. They also confirm to him the continuity of his personality, which he has hitherto mainly experienced as disparate and contradictory. From these insights he gains the confidence to create at last his work of art: a book about his life. The knowledge that he and those around him are approaching death makes him all the more determined to write; he retreats from the world with a new sense of truth and a better understanding of both joy and mortality.

Within this relatively simple framework, Proust plays dazzling variations on certain conceptions of time, character, perception, and art—some his own; some clearly in a 19th-c. lineage; some coinciding startlingly with the ideas of other major contemporary thinkers whom he could not have read, like Freud. The best-known tenet of *A la recherche* is that promoting the power of involuntary memory, which Proust depicts as able to break down habit (the great blunter of perception) and as able to restore sensory and emotional impressions of years ago. He also illustrates over hundreds of pages his own assertion that we do not fall in love with the beauty, kindness, or intelligence of the beloved. Rather, we fall in love because we attribute to this beloved qualities and faults which issue merely from our own imaginations; or, more urgently, because we believe that she or he represents a world into which we wish to penetrate but from which we feel excluded. Proust uses bisexuality and homosexuality to stress both this subjectivity of love and its potential to exclude. His commentary on love also reinforces and informs his more general discussion of aesthetic ambiguity and of the subjectivity of perception.

A la recherche is remarkable not only for its powerful plot and its courageous ideas, but also for the beauty of its style. Proust usually writes long sentences which seem to recreate the multilayered quality of bodily sensations and inner associations. He achieves this illusion partly through his control of the most complex syntax to be found in French prose; partly through his play with phonetic patterns, metre, and other devices more often seen in verse than in prose; and partly through an extensive use of similes and metaphors that are paradoxically both apt and extraordinary. (Even Proust's generalizations tend at some point to move into a boldly physical vocabulary which integrates them into the wider network of sensory imagery.) These similes and metaphors are often marked by a quiet irony which allows one to enjoy their richness while reminding one that they are structures created by the mind.

A la recherche is not only tragic and ironic; it is also very funny, again in a way which both celebrates and deflates the objects of humour. Characters' pretences are stripped away to show pride, greed, tyranny, obstinacy, and prejudice for what they are, yet often the sheer preposterousness of these characters gives them a comic sublimity (for example, Madame Verdurin or the diplomat Norpois). In fact, all Proust's characters are amusing either occasionally or frequently: in particular, the gay baron de Charlus, by turns pathetic, outrageous, and perceptive, is one of the great comic creations of 20th-c. European literature. But Proust's humour lies perhaps chiefly in the particular linguistic talents he brings to the absurd. Among his favourite forms of wit are deliberately bathetic combinations of phrases; complex embroidery on an already-established joke after an interval of pages or even chapters; and comic metaphors which draw on comparisons taken from botany, mythology, painting, and many other spheres.

A la recherche is, finally, a political novel: it suggests that upper and lower classes view each other through rigid and mutually fascinating stereotypes; it makes detailed and penetrating analyses of social mobility; and it treats racism, poverty, homophobia, and war not just as symbols in an artistic structure, but also as historical realities.

The influence of A la recherche has been considerable. The development of the novel both inside and outside France has been deeply marked by its unprecedentedly bold use of a subjective first-person narrator; its stress on the relativism of perception; its manipulation of narrative chronology; and its ostentatious patterning by image, association, and coincidence. Thus, Gide's Les *Faux-monnayeurs probably derives most of its innovations from Proust. Even those rather later writers who can seem distinct from Proust—in, say, their more urgent exploration of political or social decisions—still often echo his psychological insights or adopt his methods of creating fluid or abruptly changeable character (for example, *Malraux, *Sartre, and *Camus). And, from the 1950s on, the *Nouveau Roman and similar works take up the aesthetic lessons of A la recherche to weave them into entertaining and complicated games. No subsequent French novel has, however, achieved so successful a blend of social and psychological insight, intellectual

and stylistic sophistication, tragedy and comedy. The range and moral dignity of A la recherche mark it off from those successors which, like it, relate or reflect the story of their own writing. Indeed, Proust—and his contemporary *Valéry—were already, in the early part of the century, offering the most mature and aesthetically finest expression of central modern preoccupations (preoccupations with, for example, the interpretation of chaotic material or with the structuring power of language).
[AMF]

See S. Beckett, Proust (1931); L. Bersani, Marcel Proust: The Fictions of Life and of Art (1965); J.-Y. Tadié, Proust et le roman (1971); J. Cocking, Proust (1982).

Alaric, ou Rome vaincue, see SCUDÉRY, G. DE.

Alba. Examples of this medieval lyric genre usually exhibit a popularizing tone, with relatively unsophisticated versification and the use of a refrain containing the word alba (dawn). They combine affective and narrative elements: there may be a narrator and one or more speakers, and the passage of time is crucial since the song is a response to dawn, when lovers must separate. The earliest known example is a *macaronic text from Fleury-sur-Loire. The *Occitan corpus is difficult to define; 18 examples are collected by Martin de Riquer (1944), but only nine plus a further four possible ones in B. Woledge's contribution to Eos: An Inquiry into the Theme of Lovers' Meetings and Partings at Dawn in Poetry (ed. A. T. Hatto, 1965), Woledge's criteria being more stringent and his collection correspondingly more homogeneous. Even so, the character of the alba varies widely: though many are anonymous, others are attributed to well-known *troubadours; and though most are resolutely secular, there are several whose main tonality is religious, the most famous being that by *Giraut de Bornelh. As a result, the origins of the genre are surrounded by controversy: is it clerical, and closely related to dawn hymns, or popular, and connected with other quasi-narrative lyric genres? The alba was clearly most successful in Occitania. There are five Old French examples in Woledge, and the form was also exploited in other languages. [SK]

ALBANY, Jean (1917–84). Poet from Reunion. Zamal (1951), Albany's first collection, is rightly regarded as breaking with a long-standing tradition of exoticism and out-moded *Parnassianism in the literature of Reunion [see MAURITIUS AND REUNION]. He was an early exponent of créolie (a neologism of Albany's), a localized form of *négritude, which sought to articulate an authentic réunionnais consciousness and to break with French models. He wrote a number of collections of poetry in both French and *Creole in addition to a P'tit Glossaire Piment de mots créoles (1974) and a Supplément (1983), beautifully illustrated dictionaries of a personal and literary kind. For non-Creole speakers these provide not only a particularly intimate access to Albany's Creole poems but to much of the island's poetry in that language.

[BEJ]

ALBERT-BIROT, Pierre (1876–1967). French poet and dramatist involved in the *Cubist and Futurist movements. His poetry, from *Trente et un poèmes de poche* (1917) to *Graines* (1965), constantly strives for new forms and imaginative combinations. His theatre (*Larountala*, 1919; *Le Bondieu*, 1922) draws on circus and pantomime to create fantastic effects. [EAF]

Albertine. Character in Proust's *A la recherche du temps perdu*.

Albertine disparue (1925). The sixth part of *A la recherche du temps perdu*, originally entitled *La Fugitive*.

ALBIACH, Anne-Marie (b. 1937). French poet, whose second volume, *État* (1971), attracted much critical attention. *Mezza voce* (1984) contains subsequent poems. Her demanding texts make original use of page layout and fragment normal discourse in a poetry of tense exploration. [PF]

Albigensian Crusade, see CATHARS.

Album des vers anciens, see VALÉRY.

Alceste. Principal character in Molière's *Le *Misanthrope*, an emblematic figure of awkward sincerity.

Alcionée, see DU RYER.

Alcools, see APOLLINAIRE.

ALCUIN (735–804), see LATINITY, 1; CHARLEMAGNE.

ALEMBERT, Jean le Rond d' (1717–83). French mathematician, scientist, and man of letters. The illegitimate son of Madame de *Tencin, he was left at birth outside the church of Saint-Jean-le-Rond, Paris—whence his second name. He was brought up by a glazier's wife, Madame Rousseau, remaining close to her as long as she lived. He never married. Contemporary accounts and his letters show him as an entertaining, irreverent companion, but little of this can be seen in his published works.

His precocious genius for mathematics led to his early admission to the *Académie des Sciences, and in 1743 he published the *Traité de dynamique*, which incorporates the principle for which his name is remembered in the history of mechanics. Further scientific works followed on a number of topics in physics, including the movement of fluids and the cause of winds. It was as an eminent scientist that he was invited to co-edit the *Encyclopédie* with *Diderot. In 1758, when the work ran into difficulties, he withdrew, but his contribution was an important one. In addition to overseeing the scientific and mathematical section, he wrote entries on general topics, including an attack on current secondary schooling ('Collège') and an appeal for the creation of a theatre in Geneva ('Genève'), which provoked *Rousseau's *Lettre à d'Alembert*. Above all, he composed the 'Discours préliminaire', a central text of the French *Enlightenment; it combines an analytic account of the acquisition of knowledge with a triumphalist picture of the development of enlightened thinking over the preceding two centuries.

In 1754 he became Secrétaire Perpétuel of the Académie Française. He used this position to promote the *philosophe cause and sought to enhance the Academy's dignity with his *Histoire des membres de l'Académie Française* (1785–7), which contains numerous *éloges of deceased Academicians, including *Fontenelle and *Montesquieu. In the 1750s and 1760s he also composed essays on many general topics, including style and language—see his *Mélanges de philosophie, d'histoire et de littérature*. His important *Essai sur la société des gens de lettres avec les grands* (1753) shows his desire to defend the autonomy of writers against the demands of polite society. Apparently a free-thinker, he was an ally of *Voltaire in his anti-clerical campaigns, and was active in stirring up opinion against the anti-*philosophe* Jean-Jacques Rousseau. [PF]

See R. Grimsley, *Jean d'Alembert* (1963).

ALEXANDER NEQUAM (d. 1217). A student of theology, medicine, and law at the University of Paris, he became an Augustinian canon at Cirencester (1197–1217). His *De naturis rerum*, a summation of contemporary knowledge on natural science, and his *De nominibus utensilium*, a treatise on technical instruments and their use, are only part of a prolific and versatile output. [IS]

Alexander Romances. Alexander the Great figures as the hero of several medieval romances from the 12th c. onwards. He is generally admired as a model of generosity and secular knighthood, though the enthusiasm of some poets is tempered by the fact that he was a pagan. The romances featuring him resemble the *romans d'antiquité* in their adaptation of classical legendary material, and in their combination of 'epic' themes such as warfare and dynasty with loving descriptions of objects of wonder. Alexander's career is particularly rich in occasions for introducing exotica: magical devices, monsters, enchanted places, oriental marvels, elaborately engineered artefacts from antiquity.

Even by medieval standards, the Alexander material assumes a striking variety of forms. Large numbers of Latin texts circulated, mostly deriving from a 2nd-c. Greek prose romance of Alexander now referred to as the work of Pseudo-Callisthenes. The earliest surviving vernacular poem, in Franco-Provençal, must have been written before 1155, when it was translated into German. The translator attributes his model to Alberic of Pisançon (= Besançon?); only the opening 105 lines of it have survived, composed in octosyllabic monorhymed strophes of varying length. The next French redaction is by a Poitevin poet, who recast the material used in Alberic's version to tell the story of Alexander's youthful exploits (or *enfances*) in 785 ten-syllable lines. From the late 12th to the early 13th c. the romance mushrooms, a whole series of further episodes being added, with preference now going to the 12-syllable line. One, attributed to a certain Eustache, tells of Alexander's raids in an episode known as the 'Fuerre de Gadres'. Another, composed by Lambert le Tort, continues Alexander's career with an account of his victory against Darius, king of Persia, and the plot to poison him. A final section attributed to Alexandre de Bernay, also known as Alexandre de Paris, tells of Alexander's death and the partition of his empire. It is thought that this last poet also reworked earlier sections of the romance and is to a large degree responsible for transmitting it to us in its present form. It was sufficiently popular for the name of the romance (or the *remanieur*) to become identified with its metre, hence the designating of 12-syllable lines as *alexandrines.

The verse text was recast as the *Alexandre en prose* sometime between 1206 and 1290. It also attracted a large number of verse continuations: two versions of the *Venjance Alexandre* in the 13th c. and the *Vœux du paon* by Jacques de Longuyon (c.1312). This in turn was continued by *Brisebarre (*Le Restor du paon*, 1338) and by Jean de la Mote (*Le Parfait du paon*, 1340). Another important redaction of the Alexander material in France is the Latin poem *Alexandreis* composed between 1178 and 1182 by Gautier de Châtillon [see LATINITY]. This work is more historical and less interested in embroidering on wondrous events than its vernacular counterparts. [SK]

Alexandre le Grand, see RACINE, J.

Alexandrine. The 12-syllable *vers alexandrin* takes its name from the 12th-c. *Roman d'Alexandre* [see ALEXANDER ROMANCES], though it was used earlier. From the 16th to the 19th c. it was the dominant metre in French poetry, being used for *tragedy, *satire, and many kinds of lyric and didactic verse. It was subject to strict formal constraints, which were modified and relaxed in the practice of 19th-c. poets [see VERSIFICATION].

ALEXIS, Jacques-Stephen (1922–61). One of the most admired of *Haiti's novelists, deeply influenced by the work of his predecessor Jacques *Roumain. He was one of the generation that challenged the ideas of *négritude by refusing to locate Haiti's identity exclusively in the African past and emphasizing the creolized nature of Haitian culture.

The son of a writer, born during the American Occupation of Haiti (1915–34), Alexis was shaped by the Marxism of Roumain as well as Breton's *Surrealism and the Surrealist-derived ideas of Alejo Carpentier. He rose to prominence as a leader of the student group La *Ruche, which helped overthrow President Lescot in 1946. After studying neurology in Paris, he returned to Haiti, where he wrote his major works. In 1956 he presented his famous essay on the *réalisme merveilleux of Haiti, to the first Congress of Black Writers in 1956. His left-wing Parti d'Entente Populaire challenged Duvalier in the early years of his presidency. Alexis was later killed by Duvalier's militia in an attempt to land clandestinely in Haiti.

Lyrical and dense, Alexis's novels focus on Haiti's urban poor. His first novel, *Compère Général Soleil* (1955), begins in the teeming slums of Port-au-Prince and contains extravagantly lyrical descriptions of the natural world that were to become a hallmark of Alexis's style. The plot turns on the massacre of Haitian cane-cutters in the Dominican Republic in 1937 by Trujillo's troops. Despite the sombre events depicted, Alexis concentrates on Hilarius Hilarion's capacity to survive both ideologically and emotionally. The same human potential appears in Alexis's second novel, *Les Arbres musiciens* (1957), which was inspired by the anti-superstition campaign in the early 1940s. Within the context of the Catholic Church's drive to eradicate voodoo, Alexis traces the fortunes of the Osmin family. This sprawling novel is as much about the emergence of a black middle class in a corrupt Haiti as it is about the changes taking place through an impoverished community's struggle to survive.

Alexis's later novels take even greater liberties with the novel form. *L'Espace d'un cillement* (1959) is a symbolic novel in which a prostitute, La Niña Estrellita, and a mechanic, El Caucho, represent a microcosm of the Caribbean's experiences. Again it is the protagonists' capacity to survive the humiliating world of the brothel that is highlighted. Alexis's last work, his *Romancéro aux étoiles* (1960), most fully illustrates his concept of the marvellous world of the popular imagination. These stories are not a gratuitous display of Haiti's rich folk culture but a demonstration of an inner recreative response to the horror of conquest, colonization, and repressive government. As in his novels, the poor are not seen simply as victims but as a part of a dynamic counterculture that ensures their survival. [JMD]

See M. Dash, *Jacques-Stephen Alexis* (1975).

ALEXIS, Paul (1847–1901). French novelist, short-story writer, dramatist, and journalist. He is mainly known as the faithful friend and first biographer of *Zola, as a staunch defender of *Naturalism, and the author of a legendary telegram, sent in response to Huret's literary survey (1891), stating: 'Naturalisme pas mort. Lettre suit.' He achieved little success in his own right with his novels,

Alexis, La Vie de saint

Madame Meuriot (1890) and *Vallobra* (1901), his collections of stories, notably *La Fin de Lucie Pellegrin* (1880), or his plays and stage adaptations. He contributed, however, to Les **Soirées de Médan*, and his work is of interest in typifying Naturalist themes and techniques.   [DB]

Alexis, La Vie de saint, see VIE DE SAINT ALEXIS.

Alexis, ou le Traité du vain combat, see YOURCENAR.

Algeria. Until the French conquest, which began in 1830 [see COLONIZATION], Algeria scarcely figured as a recognizable entity in French literature. The region was perceived primarily as part of the Barbary coast, notorious for its pirates. The experiences of French captives held for ransom were described in works such as *Regnard's La Provençale (1731)*. France's military conquest of Algeria, which was largely complete by the middle of the 19th c., created relatively safe travelling conditions for writers and artists. Their travelogues include Ernest *Feydeau's *Alger* (1862) and *Souna* (1876), *Fromentin's *Un été dans le Sahara* (1857) and *Une année dans le Sahel* (1859) and *Maupassant's *Au soleil* (1884). Algeria also served as a location for fictional works such as Alphonse Daudet's *Tartarin de Tarascon* (1872) and Gide's *L'*Immoraliste* (1902). Other works inspired by Gide's experiences in Algeria include *Les Nourritures terrestres* (1897) and *Amyntas* (1905). In most of these works Algeria is seen primarily as an exotic décor. The writings of Isabelle *Eberhardt, who embraced Islam, are more attentive to cultural traditions.

Algeria was unusual among French colonies in having a large settler population, though this was always heavily outnumbered by the indigenous Muslims. The settlers, who towards the end of the colonial period became popularly known as *pieds-noirs*, came not only from France but also from Spain, Italy, and other Mediterranean countries. By the end of the 19th c. a body of imaginative works was emerging from among the settler community. Writing under the pseudonym Musette, Auguste Robinet produced a series of tales featuring Cagayous, a plebian character who purveys the settlers' rough-hewn folk wisdom. The stories are liberally dosed with *pataouète*, a form of slang derived from the medley of languages which had been brought into contact with each other as a result of colonization.

The rude virtues of colonization were celebrated in a more heroic mould in the novels of Louis *Bertrand. With the creation of the Association des Écrivains Algériens in 1921, writers in the colony began to organize themselves around the banner of *algérianisme*. This term, originally coined by Robert *Randau in 1911, denoted a growing sense of cultural distinctiveness *vis-à-vis* France. While proud of their European roots and convinced of the inferiority of the Muslim population, the *algérianistes* emphasized the idea of a new people and culture being in the making in Algeria. Besides Randau, other prominent *algérianistes* included Jean Pomier, Louis Lecoq, and Charles Hagel. With the growth of Algerian nationalism among members of the Muslim élite, writers of European descent cultivated a less aggressive tone in a new movement known as the École d'Alger. Launched during the 1930s by Gabriel Audisio, this propounded a hedonistic 'Mediterranean' life-style seemingly insulated from the political pressures of the period. Typical of the École are the early narratives of Albert *Camus; other practitioners include *Roblès and Claude de Fréminville.

During the colonial period only a minority of Algerian Muslims learned to read and write. Most were educated in French rather than Arabic; the Berber language, spoken in relatively isolated regions such as Kabylia, was scarcely written at all. The earliest imaginative works in French by Algerians of non-European origin began to appear around the turn of the century. While most were highly derivative, they later diverged considerably from the models offered by metropolitan France and the settler community. Among the first to publish works of prose fiction was Abdelkader Hadj Hamou, who was closely associated with the *algérianistes*. Jean *Amrouche, who came from a Kabyle family converted to Christianity, struck a more original note in poems published from the 1930s onwards. As the Arabic and Berber languages offered easier access to theatre audiences, drama was to remain a marginal genre among francophone Algerian authors.

The pace of publication among non-European authors quickened after World War II. Mouloud *Feraoun's *Le Fils du pauvre* (1950) is often regarded as the earliest Algerian novel of real literary merit, though its critical reputation has since been eclipsed by that of Kateb Yacine's **Nedjma* (1956). Other important authors who began to publish during this period include Mohammed *Dib and Mouloud *Mammeri. Most of their early novels are inspired by both a semi-autobiographical urge and a determination to offer a more authentic representation of Algerian society than had been produced by writers of European origin. Cast mainly in a realist mode (*Nedjma* was an important exception), they were often described as works of 'ethnographic' fiction. They were sometimes criticized by Algerian nationalists for failing to identify unequivocally with the cause of independence. The protagonists, like the authors of these novels, feel distanced from traditional Algerian society by their internalization of French culture, yet at the same time are anxious to speak on behalf of their fellow countrymen against the injustices of the colonial system.

These tensions were accentuated during the Algerian War of Independence, which was launched by the nationalist Front de Libération Nationale (FLN) in 1954 [see next entry]. The main characters in the novels of Malek *Haddad are exiled in France while the armed struggle for national liberation rages in Algeria. In the political climate prevailing at the time, Kateb found it impossible to stage his anti-colonial play, *Le Cadavre encerclé*, in France; completed in 1954, it was first performed in Tunisia and Belgium in 1958. The conflict brought an outpouring of fiercely nationalist poetry by writers such as Djamal Amrani, Henry *Kréa, and Anna *Greki, and came to occupy a central role in many works of fiction, such as Dib's *Qui se souvient de la mer* (1962), Assia *Djebar's *Les Enfants du nouveau monde* (1962), and Mammeri's *L'Opium et le bâton* (1965). The war was to remain a major source of inspiration in all genres for many years after Independence, which came with the peace settlement reached at Évian in 1962.

Independence brought the mass exodus of the *pieds-noirs*. Only a small minority, including writers such as Jean *Sénac, who had sided with the FLN during the war, remained in the country. Most resettled in France, where they became known as *rapatriés*. Those who continued or began writing after 1962, such as Marie *Cardinal, contributed to a kind of exile literature.

The new Algerian state, controlled by the FLN, was firmly committed to a policy of Arabization, whereby the French language, regarded as a relic of colonial dependence, would be systematically replaced by Arabic in every sphere of life. Haddad stopped writing altogether, convinced that French—the only language in which he was literate—was inseparable from cultural alienation. He was among those who supported government-backed campaigns equating the national culture of Algeria with the exclusive use of the Arabic language. A major victory for this policy seemed to be scored when, in 1971, Kateb switched his main creative energies to theatre productions using Arabic dialect. Far from declining, however, Algerian writing in French has grown steadily since Independence, and still far outstrips in quantity that appearing in Arabic. Within Algeria, although it is easier to publish in Arabic, a steady flow of material continues to appear in French. In addition, many Algerian authors use publishers in France, where a significant number have taken up residence. The ideological inflexibility of the FLN, which held a near-monopoly of power until the end of the 1980s, tended to deter the most creative writers from seeking to publish in Algeria.

Dib was among those who chose to live in France, where he produced an acclaimed body of increasingly diverse and sophisticated works. Nabile *Farès explored the experience of exile in a mixture of poetry and prose, with mythical and lyrical modes increasingly supplanting conventional realism. In *Le Muezzin* (1968), Mourad *Bourboune created a powerful image of the alienation of many Algerian intellectuals from Islam, which is constitutionally enshrined as the country's official religion.

After a long period of residence in France, the poet and playwright Noureddine Aba returned in 1977 to Algeria, where he argued for mutual respect between the country's different linguistic and cultural traditions.

While publishing in France, novelists such as Djebar and Rachid *Boudjedra lived partly or primarily in Algeria, where they wrote about the problems of the post-Independence period with considerable candour. Influenced partly by the French *Nouveau Roman, Boudjedra experimented with complex narrative forms in trenchant explorations of social, political, and sexual injustices. Djebar was one of a growing number of Algerian women writers publishing in French. Others included Yamina *Mechakra, Myriam Ben, and Aïcha *Lemsine. Relations between the sexes within the changing contours of Algerian society before and after independence came under critical scrutiny in many of Djebar's novels, as also in Lemsine's *La Chrysalide* (1976), Mechakra's *La Grotte éclatée* (1979), and Ben's *Sabrina ils t'ont volé ta vie* (1986).

While Boudjedra chose to write in Arabic from 1982 onwards, the continued vitality of francophone writing in Algeria was attested by the emergence during the 1980s of new authors such as Rachid *Mimouni, Tahar *Djaout, Rabah Belamri, and Habib Tengour, who owed little or nothing to the colonial period. In novels such as *Le Fleuve détourné* (1982) and *Tombéza* (1984), Mimouni evoked the frustrations of life in a bureaucratic one-party state. Corruption and other abuses of power were dissected by Djaout in *Le Chercheur d'os* (1984), and by Belamri in *Regard blessé* (1987). Blending the poetic and the prosaic, historical displacements and contemporary references, Tengour confronted similar issues in works such as *Le Vieux et la montagne* (1983) and *Sultan Galiev ou la Rupture des stocks* (1985).

Meanwhile a fresh literary impulse came from the so-called *Beur generation, young men and women brought up in France by North African immigrant parents. Their works in some ways replicate the autobiographical and ethnographic features associated with the early development of the Algerian novel, but are often more humorous in tone and focus primarily on experiences in France, rather than Algeria. Whether they should properly be classed as part of Algerian or French literature is an open question. Although not herself a Beur, Leïla *Sebbar has also written extensively about the immigrant community.

Following the cancellation of general elections which the FIS, a militant Islamic party, had looked certain to win in 1992, Algeria entered a period of acute political crisis and terrorist violence. Francophone intellectuals such as Djaout were among the victims of terrorist murder squads. Others sought refuge abroad, particularly in France.

[AGH]

See C. Bonn, *La Littérature algérienne de langue française et ses lectures* (1974); J. Déjeux, *La*

Algerian War

Littérature algérienne contemporaine, 2nd edn. (1979); C. Achour, *Anthologie de la littérature algérienne de langue française* (1990).

Algerian War. Armed struggle against French rule launched by Algerian nationalists in 1954. By far the bloodiest and most traumatic episode in French *decolonization, the war ended with the independence of Algeria in 1962. Within France, the political strains provoked by the war brought the collapse of the Fourth Republic and the return to power of Charles de *Gaulle. The scale and brutality of the fighting, which included the widespread use of torture by French forces, resulted in heavy Algerian casualties and caused deep divisions of opinion among French intellectuals and the public at large.

The ferocity of the conflict arose from a combination of factors: the presence in Algeria of an unusually large and uncompromising settler population, a growing sense of exasperation among the indigenous, mainly Muslim, majority over the lack of reforms, a determination on the part of the French army to avoid another defeat of the kind which it had recently suffered in *Indo-China, and the conviction among leading French politicians that Algeria was an integral part of France. The myth of *Algérie française* had been nurtured not only by the large number of settlers, popularly known as *pieds-noirs*, but also by the geographical proximity of Algeria (compared with other colonies), its relatively early conquest from 1830 onwards, which marked the beginning of France's second colonial empire [see COLONIZATION], and a series of legal and administrative fictions woven by successive governments in Paris. Unlike other overseas territories, which were administered either by the Ministry of Colonies or by the Ministry of Foreign Affairs, Algeria came under the Ministry of the Interior. Its northern part, where most of the population was concentrated, was divided into *départements*, supposedly modelled on those in metropolitan France. In reality, the Muslims who made up the majority of the population were given an entirely different legal status, with none of the political rights enjoyed by the settlers.

Only a small number of Muslims passed through the French educational system. At first, most supported the colonial concept of *assimilation*, which promised the general diffusion of French culture and the extension of equal rights to the whole of the population. Disillusioned by French reluctance to honour these promises which, if implemented, would have undermined the privileged position of the settlers, Muslim leaders looked increasingly towards independence as a solution to their grievances. Nationalist sentiments hardened when, in 1945, pro-independence demonstrations in Sétif and other parts of north-eastern Algeria were brutally repressed. French promises of political reform in the shape of a new statute granted to Algeria in 1947 were effectively nullified by systematic ballot-rigging. Convinced that independence could be achieved only through military action, the nationalist Front de Libération Nationale (FLN) launched a guerrilla war on 1 November 1954.

In France there was all-party support for a policy of military repression. In 1956 parliament gave the government special powers to pursue the war by any means it saw fit, and the number of French troops in Algeria rose to over 400,000, many of them conscripts. The systematic use of torture to extract information from prisoners enabled French paratroopers, commanded by General Jacques Massu, to dismantle the FLN bombing network in the capital, Algiers, but fighting continued across much of the country. With the resolve of some politicians weakening and public opinion in France increasingly ill at ease over the war, on 13 May 1958 a coalition of settlers and army officers set up a Comité de Salut Public in Algiers in open defiance of the government in Paris. The committee called on de Gaulle, then in retirement, to take up the reins of power. Fearing political collapse, the French parliament voted to invest extensive powers in de Gaulle, who became the first president of the Fifth Republic. He maintained the confidence of most of the army by pursuing a vigorous military campaign in Algeria, while at the same time exploring the options for a peaceful settlement. When it became clear that he was prepared to grant independence to Algeria, dissident army officers staged an unsuccessful *putsch* in April 1961 and joined with hard-line settlers in the Organisation Armée Secrète (OAS), a terrorist organization dedicated to the cause of *Algérie française*. Under a peace agreement reached between France and the FLN at Évian in March 1962, Algeria became independent in July of that year. A scorched-earth policy by the OAS created panic among the settlers, almost all of whom fled to France, where they became known as *rapatriés*.

Its fundamental role in the constitution of an independent Algerian state gave the war a privileged position among Algerian authors [see preceding entry]. French writers and intellectuals found the war a more difficult issue to handle. Inhibited by his roots in the settler community, the normally outspoken *Camus retreated into silence on the Algerian conflict. *Sartre, whose play *Les *Séquestrés d'Altona* (1959) used German atrocities in World War II as an indirect way of exploring the use of torture in contemporary Algeria, became the target of OAS attacks because of his support for the FLN. Sartre's outright commitment to an organization seeking to defeat France militarily was comparatively rare. In the early stages of the war some of the main opposition inside France came from Catholic intellectuals grouped around the review *Esprit. Their denunciation of French military tactics, as in Pierre-Henri Simon's essay *Contre la torture* (1957), did not necessarily imply support for the independence movement in Algeria. The most active support for the FLN came from a clandestine network of Catholics, Communists, and others organized by Francis Jeanson, a friend of Sartre. When members of the network were prosecuted in 1960, their right to oppose the war was supported by the *Manifeste des 121*, whose 121 signatories—among them *Blanchot, Sartre, *Breton, *Sarraute, and *Vercors—reflected a broad spectrum of French cultural life. A counter-manifesto was signed by 300 supporters of the war, including *Dorgelès, *Nimier, and *Romains. [AGH]

See A. Horne, *A Savage War of Peace: Algeria 1954–1962* (1977); B. Droz and E. Lever, *Histoire de la guerre d'Algérie* (1982); J.-P. Rioux (ed.), *La Guerre d'Algérie et les Français* (1990).

ALIBRAY, Charles Vion, sieur d' (*c.*1600–*c.*1652). French poet and translator. His poetry ranges from *libertin* to devotional verse. His translations include Tasso's *Aminta* (1632), prefaced by an authoritative defence of the text's organic unity, and Bonarelli's *Soliman* (1637), but also works of renowned free-thinkers, such as Cremonini and Huarte. He was a friend of Grotius and *Pascal.

Aline et Valcour, see SADE.

Aliscans. *Chanson de geste* of the Cycle de *Guillaume. Composed in the 1170s it exploits material also known from the second part of the *Chanson de Guillaume. The hero, Rainoart, is the gigantic brother of Guillaume's wife, Orable-Guibourc. Guillaume finds him working as a slave in Louis's kitchen at Laon, whither he went to raise a new army following his failed attempt to avenge Vivien in the battle fought at Aliscans, a site associated with the Gallo-Roman cemetery at Arles. Rainoart fights with a *tinel* (a massive wooden yoke for carrying water-buckets). The poem's 8,000 lines mix epic cliché and inventive, often comic, verve. *Aliscans* exerted considerable influence on the later *romans de chevalerie*, as parodied by *Rabelais. [PEB]

ALLAIS, Alphonse (1854–1905). French humorist. Several collections of his tales, selected from his weekly contributions to *Le Chat noir, Le Journal,* and *Le Sourire* were published in his lifetime. Among the best-known, re-edited in recent years, are *A se tordre* (1891), *On n'est pas des bœufs* (1896), and *Le Captain Cap* (1902).

Expert in the logic of illogicality, in the practicality of the impractical, Allais was a master of the pun and a skilful exponent of many styles (notably the mock-literary and mock-academic). The often surreal quality of his humour was acknowledged by inclusion in *Breton's *Anthologie de l'humour noir*. At times as gently whimsical as Thurber, at others as black and sardonic as Ambrose Bierce, Allais recalls the fantasy and invention of the Cyrano de Bergerac of *L'*Autre Monde* and prefigures the word-play and absurdist vision of the *Vian of *L'Écume des jours* and *L'Automne à Pékin*. [AHB]

Alliance Française, L', see FRANCOPHONIE.

Almanac. Particularly during the *ancien régime*, the almanac was the stock-in-trade of *littérature de *colportage*, reading-matter for the barely literate. In its simplest form a calendar with pictures, costing from three to six *sous*, it was sold in massive quantities, above all to peasants. Typically (as in the *Grand Calendrier compost des bergers*) it also contained texts of various kinds, from astrological prophecies to news stories, religious or political discourses, songs, and poems. *Michelet dreamed of harnessing its popular appeal to the educational needs of modern democracy. [PF]

Almaviva, comte d'. Character in Beaumarchais's *Le *Barbier de Séville* and *Le *Mariage de Figaro*.

A l'ombre des jeunes filles en fleurs (1919). The second part of Proust's *A la recherche du temps perdu*.

Alouette, L' (1953). Play by *Anouilh, devoted to the story of *Jeanne d'Arc.

Alternance des rimes, see VERSIFICATION, 3.

ALTHUSSER, Louis (1918–90). Marxist philosopher. Born in Algeria, he joined the French Communist Party in 1948, and taught philosophy at the *École Normale Supérieure, eventually becoming its secretary. His best-known books, *Pour Marx* (1965) and *Lire le Capital* (1965), offered a strikingly original view of *Marxism, arguing that Marx had inaugurated the science of history in an 'epistemological break' with previous ideological notions put forward especially by Hegel. Attacking humanist interpretations, he proposed a theory of social formations, composed of four main 'practices', economic, political, ideological, and theoretical, in a structural relation to each other. Under criticism for 'theoreticism', he subsequently redefined Marxist philosophy as a revolutionary weapon rather than as the theory of theoretical practice. In a highly influential essay of 1970, 'Idéologie et appareils idéologiques d'État', he developed the notion that political power is primarily exercised through Ideological State Apparatuses, including religion and education. He defined ideology as a representation of the imaginary relationship of individuals to their real conditions of existence, functioning by calling upon individuals to recognize themselves as subjects, and therefore as subjected.

Althusser became internationally influential during the 1970s, though he was increasingly at odds with the PCF. In 1980, during a bout of depression, to which he was prone, he strangled his wife and spent his remaining years under psychiatric care. His posthumously published autobiography *L'Avenir dure longtemps* (1992) sparked renewed interest in him. [MHK]

Alzire

Alzire, ou les Américains (1736). Tragedy by *Voltaire, set in Peru under the conquistadors.

Amadas et Idoine. *Roman d'aventure* of c.1200–20 recounting the love of Amadas, son of the Seneschal of Burgundy, for Idoine, the duke's daughter. It exploits the false-death motif, the lover's madness, and the preservation of an unwilling bride's virginity by sorcery. The style is lively and scene-painting vivid in this patchwork adaptation of Arthurian and Byzantine romance motifs to a contemporary French setting. [PEB]

Amadis de Gaule. The most successful chivalric *romance in Renaissance France. Its origins are unknown for certain, but the first French version by Herberay des Essarts (1540) is based on Rodríguez de Montalvo's expansion of a fragmentary 15th-c. Spanish manuscript. It is a text of heroic and sensuous adventure centred on Amadis, the ideal knight, who encounters an array of giants, monsters, and enchanters in his loyal service of the princess Oriana. Its popularity in France (as in Spain) was extensive: by 1591 the four books of Des Essarts's original text had grown to 21 and had spawned countless imitations. In spite of a growing reaction, the work and the genre survived well into the 17th c. A further three books were added in 1615, and in the next decade interest was still evident, ranging from *Du Verdier's massive seven-volume compendium of chivalric commonplaces, the *Roman des romans* (1626–9), to Marcassus's abridged (and bowdlerized) *Amadis de Gaule* (1629) of just 368 pages. By the 1640s, though, the vogue had all but disappeared, and *La Calprenède, who was to develop a new, enormously popular style of quasi-historical fiction, could dismiss the genre as having 'ni verité, ni vraisemblance, ni clarté, ni chronologie'. [GJM]

Amadou Koumba, Contes d', see DIOP, B.

Amant, L' (1984). Autobiographical text by Marguerite *Duras narrating the author's passionate liaison as a schoolgirl in Indo-China with a young Chinese business man. The lovers accept that their separation is inevitable; 'la jeune fille', as the text names the heroine, leaves for France, and the unnamed lover marries the girl of his family's choice. Portraits of Duras's mother, of her younger, slightly retarded brother, and of her violent older brother, present in earlier texts, reappear. The text strongly evokes moments of the past, especially smells and sounds, but the author confesses simultaneously her conviction that 'l'histoire de ma vie n'existe pas'. [EAF]

Amboise, Conjuration d' (1560). A failed Protestant attempt to wrest the youthful François II from the domination of the *Guise family. Such direct action, even if justified on the grounds that it was directed at the king's 'evil advisors' rather than at the king

himself, was regarded with absolute horror. It helped provoke the *Wars of Religion.

American Influences, see BRITISH, IRISH, AND AMERICAN INFLUENCES.

Ami des hommes, L', see MIRABEAU, MARQUIS DE.

Ami des lois, L', see LAYA.

Ami du peuple, L', see MARAT.

Ami du Roi, L'. There were two journals of this name between 1790 and 1792, one of which became the official organ of the *émigrés* and the clergy.

AMIEL, Henri-Frédéric (1821–81). Professor of aesthetics and subsequently of philosophy at Geneva, Amiel was a poet and perceptive literary critic, but his reputation rests on his incomparable *Journal intime*, a monument of Romantic introspection. The act of writing helped to preserve the sense of personal identity in the face of the relentless onrush of time. Extracts from this vast undertaking first appeared in print in 1883. A complete critical edition of the text is currently being published (eight volumes, covering the period 1839–72, each of over 1,000 pages, had appeared by 1991). Amiel offers a detailed and probing form of self-analysis. He questions the stability of the self and the nature of its relation to the world, exploring the Romantic themes of loss and failure, flux and permanence, contemplation and action. In these pages we witness a hypersensitive mind turning inward and engaging in a dialogue with itself, investigating the processes of thought and their relation to the body. In addition to the insights drawn from self-analysis, the *Journal* is also valuable for its discussion of literature, history, philosophy, and religion. [CC]

Ami et Amile. Short (3,500-line) *chanson de geste* from the turn of the 12th and 13th c., telling a story which also appears as a saint's life [see HAGIOGRAPHY], a *romance, and a *miracle play, and whose main theme is male friendship.

Physically identical, Ami and Amile are spiritual twins, conceived and born on the same day; their meeting is preordained, and together they go to serve *Charlemagne. The allegorically named Ami substitutes without anyone's knowledge for Amile in a judicial duel, which Amile cannot fight himself because he knows that he is guilty, as accused, of having slept with the emperor's daughter. Ami swears his innocence and wins. Charlemagne, believing it is Amile who is innocent, proceeds to betroth the daughter to him; Ami, who cannot now reveal his true identity, accepts her. As he is already married, God punishes his prospective bigamy by afflicting him with leprosy. His wife drives him away from home. After years of illness, he meets Amile again, who learns from an angel that he can

24

cure Ami only by bathing him in the blood of his own children. With some misgivings Amile cuts his young sons' throats, Ami is healed, and a miracle restores the children to life. The friendship of the two heroes surpasses all other social relationships in the text to such an extent that in the end all other ties are abandoned and the friends leave France together. Relations with women are presented in a particularly negative light. The self-consciously confusing plot offers interesting insights into the roles of sexuality and the body, as well as of religion and the supernatural, in personal identity.   [SK]

AMILA, John, later Jean. French novelist Jean Meckert (b. 1910) signed this pseudonym to a score of *Série Noire novels, starting with the pseudo-American *Y'a pas de bon Dieu* (1950). From *Motus!* (1953) onwards, the settings are French. Populist and ecological, author of science fiction (*Le 9 de pique*, 1956) and also of film scripts, Amila writes about the poor and humble crushed by the power of money, war, or politics, and, against this background, the conflict of the sexes, most notably in *La Lune d'Omaha* (1964) and *Au balcon d'Hiroshima* (1985). *Terminus Iéna* (1973) questions history, truth, identity, and the novel.   [SFN]

Amour courtois, see FIN'AMOR.

Amour de Swann, Un. Part of *Du côté de chez Swann*, the first section of Proust's *A la recherche du temps perdu*. It is devoted to *Swann's love for Odette de Crécy.

Amour, la fantasia, L', see DJEBAR.

Amour la poésie, L', see ÉLUARD.

Amour médecin, L'. Comédie-ballet by *Molière, performed 1665, in which a lover dresses as a doctor to win a bride from her jealous father Sganarelle.

Amours, Les, see RONSARD.

Amours de Psyché et de Cupidon, Les, see LA FONTAINE.

Amours du chevalier de Faublas, Les, see LOUVET DE COUVRAY.

Amours jaunes, Les, see CORBIÈRE.

AMPÈRE, André-Marie (1775–1836). French physicist, founder of the science now known as electromagnetism. Ampère, a child prodigy in mathematics and later an inspired experimentalist, was the first to demonstrate, and to express mathematically, the relationship between electricity and magnetism. He initiated a standard system of measurement for electric currents. His works include an *Essai sur la philosophie des sciences* (1834–44) and the

posthumously published *Journal et correspondance*.
          [MB]

Amphitryon. Three-act comedy in free verse by *Molière, first performed 1668. It is an adaptation of a plot used also by Plautus and *Rotrou. The Greek general Amphitryon is married to Alcmène; his servant Sosie is married to Cléanthis. Jupiter desires Alcmène and adopts the physical guise of Amphitryon to obtain her favours, while Mercury adopts that of Sosie. The play exploits the confusions of identity which arise; it ends with the exposure of the double substitution. Amphitryon is comforted by the maxim that 'un partage avec Jupiter n'a rien du tout qui déshonore'. The play is often said to allude to the affair of *Louis XIV with Madame de *Montespan.

The same subject is treated, supposedly for the thirty-eighth time, in *Giraudoux's *Amphitryon 38*.
          [IM]

AMROUCHE, Fadhma Aïth Mansour (c.1882–1967). Algerian writer; she and her daughter Taos [see below] were the first Berber women writers. At 16, while working at a mission hospital near Michelet, she was baptized and married to Belkacem-ou-Amrouche, a young teacher attached to the mission, bearing him one daughter and seven sons. She spent most of her life in Tunis. In 1946 her son Jean [see next entry] persuaded her to write down her memories in French. These, with an epilogue written after her husband's death in 1959 and that of Jean in 1962, were published by Taos in 1968 as *Histoire de ma vie*. This unique work is a detailed account of a woman's personal history and a sociological document throwing light on existence in the remote villages of Kabylia at the turn of the century. Fadhma Amrouche was a singer, preserving traditional Kabyle songs learned originally from her own mother, and to these she added original poems, which Taos translated into French and included in her mother's autobiography.   [DSB]

AMROUCHE, Jean (1906–62). Algerian poet, son of the above. He benefited from a French education in Tunisia and Paris, and became a teacher. He is considered the founder of Algerian poetry written in French; his reputation spread through lectures, articles, and radio programmes. On his return to Algeria he worked with the Ministry of Information, and founded the review *L'Arche* in 1943. He had various posts in Algerian radio, but was sacked for political reasons in 1958. In the *Algerian War, he espoused the Algerian cause (see his poem 'Le Combat algérien'), but fought for peace and was one of the mediators between de Gaulle and Ferhat Abbas. He did not live to see Algerian independence.

Amrouche was primarily a poet, though he published very little. It was through poetry that he could express the anguish of his own and his people's situation. *Cendres* (1934) is the cry of the colonized against the colonizers who have brought death, destruction, indignity, and dispossession (*cendres*). The poet, perceived as a prophet, will be able to recapture the innocence of childhood, to search for his roots, his ancestors: 'Je veux trouver ma Famille.' In 1937 he published *Étoile secrète*, a metaphysical journey in search of God and Man couched in biblical language; in order to counteract despair, one had to believe in a merciful God and have faith in Man.

Amrouche returned to his roots and ancestral culture with his translations of *Chants berbères de Kabylie* (1939). His introduction to the poems, together with articles on indigenous poetry (e.g. 'Pour une poésie africaine', 1943), shows his interest in national identity and purpose. He developed this at greater length in his important essay *L'Éternel Jugurtha, proposition sur le génie africain* (1946), a description of the colonizers and the colonized, with Jugurtha rising up against his enemies and throwing off his shackles. Jugurtha represents the North African who, like Amrouche, feels the tension of two cultures: 'La France est l'esprit de mon âme, l'Algérie est l'âme de mon esprit.' [ET]

See R. Toulgoat-le-Baut, *Jean Amrouche: Itinéraire d'un colonisé* (1992).

AMROUCHE, Marie-Louise-Taos (1913–67). Daughter of Fadhma [see above]. Her autobiographical novel *Rue des Tambourins* (1960), published under the name Marguerite Taos, complements her mother's *Histoire de ma vie*, recounting from the adolescent's point of view the life of the Amrouche family in Tunis in the inter-war years. *Jacinthe noire*, written in 1935 but not published till 1947, the first novel in French by a Berber woman, is based on the author's arrival in France to study and the disturbing impact of her exotic origins on the inmates of the claustrophobic Catholic hostel where she is lodged. The narrator is a French girl who falls under the spell of this 'Black Hyacinth'. Taos's third semi-autobiographical novel, *L'Amant imaginaire*, appeared in 1975. With her brother Jean, she was passionately dedicated to preserving the Kabyle cultural heritage. Inheriting her mother's gift of song, she became a celebrated *chanteuse*, presenting traditional Kabyle songs throughout Europe, and translating Berber tales, songs, poems, and proverbs into French (published as *Le Grain magique*, 1960). [DSB]

AMYOT, Jacques (1513–93). French translator. A career as a tutor (notably for the future *Charles IX and *Henri III) and in the Church (abbé de Bellozane, 1548; Grand Aumônier de France, 1560; bishop of Auxerre, 1570) gave him the security he needed to devote himself to the work for which he is now most famous: translating Heliodorus, *Histoire éthiopique* (1547); Diodorus Siculus, *Les Sept Livres* (1554); Longus, *Les Amours pastorales de Daphnis et de Chloé* (1559); and, most importantly of all, two works by Plutarch—*Les Vies des hommes illustres grecs ou romains* (1559) and *Les Œuvres morales et mêlées* (1572). The two latter texts were particularly well received (notably by *Montaigne) since they corresponded to his countrymen's insatiable interest in ethics, history, mythology, and not least, in the psychology and motivation of great men. Amyot was regarded as a great stylist. His work considerably reinforced the efforts of the Renaissance translators (e.g. *Dolet) to reinforce the range and flexibility of the French language. [JJS]

An 2440, L', see MERCIER.

Ana. Name given to collections of *obiter dicta* and anecdotes of literary figures, particularly in the 17th c., when they give an image of the conversation in literary *salons. Among the best-known are the *Ménagiana*, the *Huetiana*, and the *Segraisiana*.

Anabase, see SAINT-JOHN PERSE.

ANANOU, David (b. 1917). Writer from Togo, where he worked as an *instituteur* from 1938. Despite health problems he completed his only major work, *Le Fils du fétiche*, in the early 1950s. Rather didactic and moralizing in tone, the novel contains much ethnographical information. [MPC]

ANCELOT, Jacques-Arsène (1794–1854) and Marguerite-Louise Virginie, née Chardon (1792–1875). Jacques Ancelot was a French playwright of the Restoration and July Monarchy. He was elected to the Académie Française in 1841. His wife was also a playwright and a novelist but is remembered as the hostess of an important literary salon. [CC]

Ancien régime. Name given to the regime which was abolished by the French *Revolution. Strictly speaking, it means 'former regime' rather than 'old regime', and as such was 'invented' by the revolutionaries to refer to what they hoped to abolish: it was therefore first conceptualized in 1789 and 1790. Many scholars have used the term to refer only to the decades immediately preceding the Revolution; for *Tocqueville it was the whole century before 1789. In fact, it was a system that integrated economic, social, ideological, juridical, and political aspects into a coherent structure, albeit one whose coherence is difficult to discern today. What disappeared in the crisis of 1789 was indeed its coherence, although many of its features, especially the economic and social structures, continued somewhat transformed until at least the mid-19th c.

The roots of the regime are to be found in the Middle Ages, when *monarchy and society took definitive shape. Three notions were particularly important in moulding it: hierarchy, corporatism, and privilege. The regime was full of inconsistencies, for it had evolved in an *ad hoc* fashion over many generations. Institutions such as the monarchy itself, the *parlements*, the privileged orders like the *nobility and *clergy, tended to base their claims to rights and authority on custom and precedence, and the conception of their corporate rights was intensely legalistic; quarrels over jurisdiction were frequent. Except in times of crisis, as during the civil wars, there was felt to be little need to explore the inherent contradictions of theory and practice. Only in the 18th c. did political conflict and the *Enlightenment lead to a demystification and desacralization of the monarchy, undermining the very basis of the regime. The extent to which the end of the old order in the crisis of 1787–9 should be viewed as a collapse resulting from the growing pressures of modernity and fiscal crisis, or as a revolutionary movement of Enlightenment ideology, is still very much a matter for debate [see REVOLUTION, 3].

The *ancien régime* has always been evaluated quite differently by the Right and Left. For those on the Right, in the tradition of *Taine, it was a stable, ordered society with much to admire in its hierarchy of values; while on the Left, where the influence of *socialism and of the Revolutionaries themselves has remained strong, it has been condemned for its inequality, privilege, and injustice, for its lack of personal liberty and excess of despotism. In a society still moulded by the Revolution, objective evaluation has been difficult.   [PRC]

    See A. de Tocqueville, *L'Ancien Régime et la révolution* (1856); D. Richet, *La France moderne: l'esprit des institutions* (1973); P. R. Campbell, *The Ancien Régime in France* (1988).

Ancien Régime et la Révolution, L', see TOCQUEVILLE.

Anciens, Les, see QUERELLE DES ANCIENS ET DES MODERNES.

ANDRÉ, Yves-Marie, père (1675–1764). Jesuit teacher, remembered for his *Essai sur le beau* (1741), a methodical treatise on aesthetics defending the idea of an unchanging 'beau essentiel' and stressing the links between beauty and morality.

ANDREAS CAPELLANUS (André le Chapelain) (*fl.* late 12th c.) was connected with the royal court at Paris and very probably that of Marie de Champagne at Troyes. His one known work, *De amore*, probably written *c*.1185, contains three books. The first discusses what love is and how it can be won; it includes imaginary dialogues between lovers of different ranks and describes a type of 'courtly love', a passion inspired by the beauty of the loved one, usually involving adultery. After a second book, which discusses how to preserve love, Andreas concludes with a third book attacking carnal love in traditional Christian (and anti-feminist) terms.

Scholars earlier this century took the work as a textbook of courtly love as it existed in reality [see FIN'AMOR]. More recently it has been argued that Books 1 and 2 are a sustained piece of irony. Certainly Andreas's contemporaries would have noticed how he apes theological discussions of Christian love in his analysis of romantic passion. But his treatise appears to be more of a *jeu d'esprit* than an attempt either to codify a real social phenomenon or to compose a moralistic satire. [JAMM]

ANDREVON, Jean-Pierre (b. 1937). A French writer of polemical science fiction, of left-wing persuasion, Andrevon uses the future to pursue a critique of present-day social and ecological issues. He entered print in 1968 when, according to him, French science fiction had its unpoliticized head in the clouds. His novels thus belong to 'l'anticipation à moyen terme', and particularly to the 'tradition catastrophiste' (e.g. *Le Désert du monde*, 1977; *Visiteurs d'apocalypse*, 1990), although he has also investigated time-travel (*Le Temps cyclothymique*, 1974) and the vagaries of inner space (e.g. *Sous le regard des étoiles*, 1989). This last preoccupation is the source of *Cauchemars de sang* (1986), one of his two contributions to the Collection Gore (Fleuve Noir Horreur).   [CS]

Andromaque. One of *Racine's most successful tragedies, first performed 1667. Set in Epirus after the Trojan War, it concerns four people locked in an impossible chain of unrequited passions. Andromaque, Hector's faithful widow, is the captive of Pyrrhus; he loves her and disdains the Greek princess Hermione, whom he is engaged to marry. Hermione loves Pyrrhus and is vainly loved by Oreste, who has been sent by the Greeks to claim Andromaque's infant son from Pyrrhus. A series of volte-faces and vacillations leads to the murder by Oreste of Pyrrhus, who is about to marry Andromaque. Hermione, having ordered the killing, disowns it and kills herself. Oreste succumbs to despair and madness. Andromaque is left in command; Troy has been avenged on Greece.   [PF]

Andromède, see CORNEILLE, P.

ANEAU, Barthélemy (*c*.1505–61). Principal of the Collège de la Trinité at Lyon and supposed author of the *Quintil Horatien* (1550), a satirical attack on Du Bellay's *Défense et illustration*. He translated into French the *emblems of Alciati (1549); his own *Picta poesis* (1552), commentaries on a series of printer's illustrations, appeared in both Latin and French. His translation of the third book of Ovid's *Metamorphoses* (1556) has an interesting theoretical preface. He also wrote plays and an extravagant prose fiction entitled *Alector* (1560).   [TC]

ANGÉLIQUE DE SAINTE-MADELEINE, mère (1591–1661). The name in religion of Jacqueline-

Angélique de Saint-Jean

Marie-Angélique Arnauld, sister of Antoine *Arnauld, who as abbess was responsible for the reform of the convent of *Port-Royal.

ANGÉLIQUE DE SAINT-JEAN, sœur, then mère (1624–84). Name in religion of Angélique Arnauld d'Andilly, niece of the above and daughter of *Arnauld d'Andilly. As mistress of the novices she led the resistance of *Port-Royal to official persecution. She is the central figure in Montherlant's *Port-Royal.

Angelo. Hero of a series of works (1949–58) by *Giono.

ANGENNES, Julie d'. Daughter of the marquise de *Rambouillet, recipient of the *Guirlande de Julie.

Anglomania, see BRITISH, IRISH, AND AMERICAN INFLUENCES.

Anglo-Norman Literature

1. Language

Anglo-Norman is the name given to the dialect of Medieval French imported into Britain in the wake of the Norman Conquest and used there, predominantly by royalty, the nobility, clerics and, increasingly, the higher bourgeoisie, as part of a complex bilingual culture. Anglo-Norman French was always a minority language, and there is no evidence that it ever penetrated significantly into the indigenous population. Its use grew progressively more anachronistic, especially from the second half of the 14th c., and by the middle of the 15th c. it had all but died out. It has, however, left an indelible trace on Modern English.

Anglo-Norman comprised at least four different registers: the first a spoken vernacular, the second an administrative language of record, the third an alternative language of instruction and adjunct to Latin, the fourth a literary language, which could range from the significantly dialectal to a form barely distinguishable from its Continental counterpart. Anglo-Norman must rapidly have ceased to function as a true spoken vernacular, becoming, through the natural processes of diglossia and bilingualism, a second, acquired language probably by the 1160s at the latest. By this date, the descendants of the Norman incomers would have been well able to understand and speak English. It was not, however, until the time of Chaucer that English was to regain its status as the dominant literary language, for Anglo-Norman continued throughout the 13th and 14th c. to be a living language of communication and of record as well as of literature. But, compared with English, which was accessible to both monolingual English speakers and bilingual French speakers, it remained more or less class-exclusive.

Anglo-Norman French had its own recognizable set of orthographic conventions: e.g. spellings such as *kaunt* (Continental *quant*), *lur* (*lour*), *cel* (*ciel*), *fei* (*foi*), *fere* (*faire*), *seignur* (*seigneur*), *joefne* (*jeune*); and certain distinctive dialect characteristics: e.g. rhymes of the type *tout / fut, mur / fleur, parler / chevalier*, and the syllabic instability of *e*. Other phonetic features included *castel* (for Continental *chastel*), *gardin* (*jardin*), *William* (*Guillaume*), *glorie* (*gloire*), *cherise* (*cerise*), and a range of aphetic forms such as *cater* (for *ac(h)eter*), *stoper* (*estoper*), and the antecedents of *chess* (*eschecs*), *spite* (*despit*), and *vanish* (*esvanir*). Occasionally doublets survive which preserve Insular and Continental reflexes of the same word: *cattle/chattel*, *warden/guardian*. The borrowing of English words, especially technical terms, is also encountered.

Anglo-Norman exerted a radical influence on the vocabulary of English, which absorbed many thousands of its lexical items, sometimes retaining early forms more or less intact: *faith, beast, fierce (fiers), voice*; sometimes preserving dialectal variants: *affray, spouse, meddle, fee, plank, finish, chive*; usually modifying both the pronunciation and the spelling of adopted forms—*beef, tower, jaw (joue), usher (uissier), nephew, purse*—occasionally to the point of obscuring their Anglo-Norman origins: *fashion (façon), mushroom (mousseron), jeopardy (jeu parti), puny (puis né), curfew (cuevre-feu),* and *wicket (guichet)*. The legal vocabulary of Modern English is almost exclusively Anglo-Norman in derivation. As a literary language, Anglo-Norman was, despite the fluidity of its spelling systems, not only perfectly grammatical but capable also of being highly expressive and inventive. Except occasionally in its later, more idiosyncratic phase, it was far from the bastardized jargon so often denigrated by Continental contemporaries. Its verse, however, frequently shows a less than rigorous adherence to regular syllabic models.

2. General Characteristics of the Literature

As far as Anglo-Norman literature is concerned, the very term is problematic. How valid a category is it? To what extent is its existence predicated on other than linguistic (dialectal) difference? In what relationship do its constituent elements stand to those of its Continental counterpart? How far does an exclusive delineation need to be made between, on the one hand, indigenous production of literary works and, on the other, Insular patronage, reception, and conservation of literary texts in Continental French? Seen as the whole corpus of writings produced in French in the British Isles from the time of the Norman Conquest until the close of the Middle Ages, Anglo-Norman literature can be said to occupy a significant place in the evolution of both Medieval French and Middle English literatures.

Among its most salient features are its quantity, its diversity, and its longevity. It clearly benefited from enlightened patronage, both clerical and secular, and the multicultural, polyglot environment in which it developed enabled it both to innovate and to thrive. Viewed historically, Anglo-Norman literature shows a quite remarkable precocity in its first century of production, the 12th, which sees the earliest appearance in French literature of the rhymed chronicle, Celtic and Arthurian narratives, eyewitness historiography, scientific, administrative, scholastic, and biblical texts. While certain of the traditional genres of medieval literature, such as devotional works and hagiography, are particularly well exemplified in Anglo-Norman, others, for instance the epic and the secular lyric, are noticeably under-represented. It is in the historiographical domain that Insular French makes its most durable literary impact through the transmission of the Arthurian *matière de Bretagne*. The romance flourished in Britain during the 12th and 13th c., though Anglo-Norman representatives of the genre show a marked preference for its non-courtly mode, privileging the adventure-narrative dimension, often within a dynastic framework. The shorter *lai* and the *fabliau* are also represented, and some Anglo-Norman drama has survived.

3. Narrative Forms

a. Romance. Only 3,000 lines survive from what must have originally been a 13,000-line romance of *Tristan* by Thomas. Incomplete though it is, this poem (*c.*1160–90) represents for many the finest achievement of Anglo-Norman literature. A pervading sense of human imperfection and necessary suffering is counterbalanced by a wealth of incisive psychological observation and analysis of the effects of fatal adulterous passion. Thomas's treatment of human love, with its unremitting vocabulary of affliction, stands in ambiguous contrast to much contemporary courtly writing on *fin'amor*. *Amadas et Idoine*, from the late 12th c., is a story of 'fine loial amour' which shadows the Tristan and Iseut legend to propose a model of ideal, socially integrated love.

Love occupies a less prominent role in the Anglo-Norman romance of *Horn* by Mestre Thomas (*c.*1170; later reworked into Middle English as *King Horn*), despite its being structured narratively round the hero's wooing of, and eventual marriage to, the princess Rigmel. This is not, however, a courtly romance, and its real theme is feudal vassalage and Horn's heroic pursuit of his birthright and dynastic justice. Set in a remote, archaic past reminiscent of the Danish invasions, but portraying a plethora of contemporary social detail, the narrative is skilfully patterned by parallelism and repetition. Its rhyming alexandrine *laisses* have clear epic resonances. The *Lai d'Haveloc* (*c.*1200), deriving from an episode interpolated into Gaimar's *Estoire des Engleis*, offers close thematic parallels with *Horn*. Influence of epic discourse is very much in evidence in Thomas of Kent's *Roman de toute chevalerie* (*c.*1175), an independent version of the *Alexander legend. The 13th c. *Amys e Amillyoun* belongs to the romance rather than to the epic tradition of this widespread and popular legend of brotherhood. [see AMI ET AMILE].

The tradition of the so-called Byzantine romance is represented in Anglo-Norman by two long narrative poems by Hue de Rotelande. A self-conscious writer with a sharp wit and a well-developed sense of literary irony, he uses parodic inversion to good effect. But his subtlety can easily be swamped by his narrative. However prolix and repetitive to the modern eye, runaway plots evidently appealed to contemporary audiences. *Ipomedon* (*c.*1180) treats the theme of love and chivalry within the courtly tradition, telling in a gently cynical way of the adventures that befall the King of Apulia's son in his amorous pursuit and ultimate conquest of La Fiere, duchess of Calabria. Ipomedon's son is the protagonist of Hue's second romance, *Protheselaus* (*c.*1190), which exploits, at considerable length and without much inspiration, what was destined to become the staple thematic diet of Anglo-Norman adventure-romance: unjust disinheritance/exile/return/reinstatement.

This narrative structure, already discernible in *Horn*, characterizes also the inordinately long *Roman de Waldef*, *Gui de Warewic*, and *Boeve de Haumtone*, all three dating from the first half of the 13th c. Satisfying an insatiable appetite for action and fast-moving unilinear plots that accumulate stock literary motifs, these breathless narratives follow the superhuman exploits of dispossessed baronial heroes across the length and breadth of Europe, sometimes even into Africa and the Middle East, until, covered in personal and dynastic glory, they return home to claim their rightful inheritance. *Fouke le fitz Waryn*, an early 14th-c. prose reworking of a lost poem from the later 13th c., celebrates with verve and humour the fictionalized exploits of the fitz Waryn family, highlighting particularly Fulk III's disinheritance by King John, his defiance and subsequent outlawry, and his eventual pardon and reinstatement. There is no firm evidence to substantiate the claim that *Waldef*, *Gui*, *Boeve*, and *Fouke* were initially patronized by specific Anglo-Norman families as dynastic propaganda, and their categorization as 'ancestral romances' is misleading. The British setting for the narratives of *Guillaume d'Angleterre*, a 12th-c. adventure romance sometimes attributed to *Chrétien de Troyes, and of *Fergus*, a 13th-c. Arthurian romance by Guillaume le Clerc, may possibly point to some sort of Insular patronage, but both are Continental French and not Anglo-Norman poems.

b. Lais. Among the shorter narrative forms in Anglo-Norman, pride of place must go to the curiously named Breton (meaning, of course, Celto-British) *lais, particularly those of *Marie de France. A skilful and learned Continental poet at the court of Henry II, she wrote a series of short lyrical narratives, for which she claims oral Celtic sources. Though her French is not distinctively Anglo-Norman, Insular culture inspires and pervades her work. Also attributed to Marie is a collection of fables (the *Ysopet*) and a version of *St Patrick's*

Anglo-Norman Literature

Purgatory. Le Lai del Desiré, a fairy-mistress story set at the court of the King of Scotland, has affinities with Marie's *Lanval* as well as with Chrétien's *Yvain*. *La Folie Tristan d'Oxford* (late 12th c.?) presents a résumé of the legend reminiscent of Thomas's version, blending analysis and realism within a moral perspective. *Le Donnei des amanz* (c.1180) is a debate between a lady and her lover in which each compares the other to Tristan and Iseut as models for emulation. Robert Biket's hexasyllabic *Lai du Cor* (c.1200?), a variation on the chastity-testing theme, is Arthurian and in the courtly mode, but parodically so. A handful of Anglo-Norman *fabliaux* survive which show no significant departures from the literary pattern established on the Continent. The 13th-c. *De la bounté des femmes*, perhaps from the pen of Nicole Bozon, deserves mention as a rare pro-feminist poem.

c. Epic. The closest we come to an indigenous Anglo-Norman epic is an 800-line Insular continuation, dating from the middle of the 13th c., of *La Destructioun de Rome*. Anglo-Norman copies of Continental epics are, however, plentiful, and epic influence is discernible in several Insular narratives. The survival, moreover, in Anglo-Norman manuscripts of the oldest extant text of the *Chanson de *Roland*, and of the unique copies of *Le *Voyage de Charlemagne*, *La *Chanson de Guillaume*, and **Gormont et Isembart* is adequate proof that the epic genre was known and appreciated in 12th- and early 13th-c. Britain. A fluent translation of the Latin prose *Pseudo-*Turpin Chronicle*, a clerical reworking of the *Chanson de Roland* tradition, was written (1214–16) by William de Briane.

4. Historiography

Anglo-Norman literature is perhaps most widely known for its early and innovative achievements in historiography, and these are no doubt to be explained in part by the multiculturism and multilingualism that characterized Insular society. Master Geffrei Gaimar used Latin, French, and English written sources to compile his long and ambitious rhymed chronicle charting the history of Britain from Jason and Brutus down to the death of Rufus (1100). Only the second part of this, *L'Estoire des Engleis* (c.1136–8), has survived. Much of it is a close translation of the *Anglo-Saxon Chronicle*, but in the post-Conquest section Gaimar is able to present a lively and lucid account of events. The first part of his chronicle was no doubt eclipsed by the appearance, in 1155, of *Wace's *Roman de Brut*, a highly influential text in the development of the *matière de Bretagne*.

The earliest example in French literature of contemporary historical writing in the vernacular is Jordan Fantosme's largely eyewitness account of the rebellion of the Young King in 1173–4. This curious, mixed-prosody poem, which offers an orthodox providential view of history, makes considerable use of epic language and maintains a good narrative

pace. Historians find some of Fantosme's material useful. The poet responsible for the *Song of Dermot and the Earl* (end of 12th c.?), a rhymed history of the Conquest of Ireland between 1152 and 1175, also looked to the epic for inspiration, but in vain.

L'Histoire de Guillaume le Maréchal (c.1225) was written under Insular patronage by a Continental poet who trod the broad common ground between the truth of events and the truth of literature. Over little short of 20,000 octosyllables he reconstructs a life of William Marshal which, though far from unrealistic, owes much to literary convention. His verses often lack, however, the refinement of romance discourse. Some historians grant the poem the status of biography. The rhymed *Des grantz geanz* (13th c.) proposes an alternative, female-oriented founding narrative to explain the name Albion: Albine and her Greek sisters arrived in Britain 260 years before Brutus. Peter of Langtoft, a canon of Bridlington, seems to have started his *Chronicle*, towards 1294, as an account of the reign of Edward I, but in subsequent redactions its scope was extended backwards as far as Brutus and forwards up to 1307. Historical writing continued unabated throughout the 14th c. with, amongst many others, Nicholas Trevet's *Chronicle* (1328–35), Sir Thomas Gray of Heton's *Scalacronica* (1355–60), the *Anonimalle Chronicle*, *Le Brut d'Engleterre*, and a life of the Black Prince (c.1385) by Chandos Herald.

5. Drama and Lyric

Though authoritative voices have claimed otherwise, evidence is slim for including the earliest surviving drama wholly in the French vernacular, the *Jeu* (or *Mystère*) *d'Adam* (c.1150–60?), within the Anglo-Norman canon. The first indisputably Anglo-Norman drama is *La Seinte Resurreccion* (c.1200, modern title *La Résurrection du Sauveur*), whose fragmentary narrative is that of the Descent and Entombment with the addition of the legend of Longinus. The prologue provides a particularly detailed description of the play's staging. The dialogue, in octosyllabic couplets and interspersed with narrative sections, is firmly structured and has a natural fluency, while its dramatic tempo is well maintained. It has been suggested that a series of mystery plays lies embedded in Herman de Valenciennes's *Li Romanz de Dieu et de sa mere*, though the Anglo-Norman provenance of this rhymed paraphrase of the Bible (c.1190) is far from clear.

*Macaronic verse, both religious and secular, is a characteristic of Anglo-Norman literature. 'En may . . .', for example, is an unusual Anglo-Norman/Latin *pastorela, 'Mayden moder milde' a song-prayer in alternating half-lines of English and French, while 'Dum ludis floribus' and 'De amico ad amicam' contrive to fuse French, English, and Latin into the traditional format of the love-song. A series of bilingual political songs, in French and English, from the reign of Edward I are incorporated by Peter of Langtoft into his *Chronicle*. Much

Anglo-Norman lyric poetry seems to have been designed for use in para-liturgical and homiletic contexts (there are numerous hymns to the Virgin), though poems such as 'Bele mere, ke fray?', a spirited example of the courtly *débat amoureux*, the *reverdie* 'Ferroy chaunsoun', the technically sophisticated 'El tens d'iver', and Bozon's anti-feminist 'Les femmes a la pie' serve to show that secular tastes were not only indulged but cultivated on occasion with skill and inventiveness. Gower's *Cinkante Balades* (1399–1400) are for the most part polished and highly proficient variations on conventional themes, written in a French which is more Continental than Insular.

6. Religious Writing

a. Hagiography. Anglo-Norman was used not only within the cloister as an alternative to Latin, but also among the wider religious community as a medium of moral instruction for the laity, and a particularly extensive corpus of doctrinal literature has come down to us. The field of vernacular *hagiography* was intensely cultivated in Anglo-Norman. Though preserved in its oldest form within the *St Albans' Psalter* (1120–30), the **Vie de saint Alexis*, in assonating decasyllabic stanzas of rare poetic beauty, is in all likelihood of earlier, Norman origin. To the nun Clemence of Barking, who composed *La Vie de sainte Catherine* in the last quarter of the 12th c., goes the credit of being French literature's earliest named woman author. Her octosyllabic poem is distinguished by the elaborate integration of the vocabulary of *fin'amor* into its pious narrative. Clemence may have been the same person as the anonymous nun of Barking who, in her *Vie d'Edouard le Confesseur* (1163–9?), defensively but quite unnecessarily apologizes for her 'faus franceis d'Angletere'. The murder of Thomas Becket in 1170 gave rise to vernacular *Lives* by the Continental Guernes de Pont-Sainte-Maxence (1170–4), and by Beneit, monk of St Albans (c.1184), who wrote in six-line tail-rhyme stanzas. Other monks composed saints' lives in French: Denis Pyramus, a Benedictine of Bury (St Edmund), and, also from Bury, Simon of Walsingham (St Faith). By the end of the 12th c., the ranks of Anglo-Norman hagiography had been further swollen by lives of St Nicholas and St Margaret (both by Wace), *La Passiun de seint Edmund*, *Saint Modwenna*, *La Vie de saint Laurent*, *La Vie de saint Gilles* by Guillaume de Berneville, *La Passion de saint George* by Simund de Freine, *La Vie de saint Josaphaz* by Chardri. Among the more interesting texts is *La Vie de saint Auban* (1235–57) by the St Albans monk and chronicler Matthew Paris, preserved in the author's illustrated holograph. It is archaic in form and tone, and the verse has a robust, epic quality. Matthew also translated the lives of Edward, Edmund of Abingdon, and Thomas Becket into Anglo-Norman, illustrating the texts himself and even circulating them among aristocratic ladies of his acquaintance. The other saints celebrated in

Anglo-Norman are too numerous to mention. Often classified as a saint's life, but wrongly so, is Benedeit's *Voyage de saint Brendan* (c.1106), a voyage narrative of Celtic origin, vividly written, tightly structured, and resolutely monastic in perspective. It inaugurated the use of the octosyllabic rhyming couplet.

b. Biblical Translation [see BIBLE]. When the monks of Christ Church, Canterbury compiled the lavish *Eadwine Psalter* (1155–60), they incorporated pre-existing Anglo-Norman translations between the lines of the Hebraicum. Several other Anglo-Norman Psalters survive from the 12th c. The translation of the Books of Samuel and Kings known as *Li Quatre Livre des Reis* (late 12th c.) deserves particular interest for the quality of its rhythmical, poetic prose. The Book of Judges was also translated into Anglo-Norman for the Templars during the 12th c. A prose translation of the Apocalypse appeared towards 1250, and William Giffard's rhymed version dates from the end of the 13th c. The Holkham Bible Picture Book (1320–30) has a full range of captions in Anglo-Norman octosyllables.

c. Religious Verse. Latin learning became more accessible through vernacular poetry. French literature owes its earliest scholastic text to one Sanson de Nantuil, whose *Proverbes de Salemon* (c.1150) translates the Book of Proverbs and its gloss into over 11,000 rhyming octosyllables. This was followed, around 1200, by Simund de Freine's *Roman de philosophie*, a verse vulgarization of **Boethius*, and by *La Petite Philosophie* (c.1230), a rhyming scientific treatise on the nature of the world. Among the Anglo-Norman religious verse written for secular instruction was St Edmund of Abingdon's much used manual of meditation, *Mirour de Seinte Eglyse*, the *Manuel des péchés* (c.1260), an encyclopaedic aid to confession of over 11,000 lines (translated by Robert Mannyng as *Handlyng Synne*), the even longer *Lumere as lais* (1267) by Pierre d'Abernon of Fetcham (sometimes Peckham), and Robert of Greatham's *Corset* and *Evangiles des domnees* (c.1260?). The *Château d'Amour* (c.1250), attributed to Robert Grosseteste, Bishop of Lincoln, makes more use of allegory, and this tradition is continued by Henry of Lancaster in his *Seyntz Medicines* (1354) and by Gower in his *Mirour de l'omme* (c.1380). Religious allegorical verse was but one of the accomplishments of the Franciscan Nicole Bozon (c.1280–1330); probably the most prolific and versatile of Anglo-Norman poets, his output ranged from poems on the Virgin, saints' lives, sermons and **exemplum* tales, to satires and proverbs.

7. Didactic Texts

Literary texts in Anglo-Norman could also serve more immediately practical functions. In 1113 Philippe de Thaon provided the chaplain to the king's steward with a translation into rhyming hexasyllabic couplets of the *Computus*, a treatise to calculate the Church calendar. Hardly less unexpected is the translation into Anglo-Norman verse of the Hospitallers' Rule (1181–5). The early use of Anglo-Norman in administrative life is shown in two vernacular charters of *c.*1140 and 1170, and a translation of the Laws of William the Conqueror (*c.*1150). Professional treatises on estate-management appeared during the 13th c. with Robert Grosseteste's *Reules*, Walter of Henly's *Dité de hosbonderie*, and the anonymous *Seneschaucie*. Administrative Anglo-Norman is particularly rich from the 14th c. onwards: municipal records, pleas, court proceedings, legal treatises, the parliamentary rolls, and the statutes of the realm.

Several literary texts take inspiration from the multilingualism that characterized the Insular nobility. Walter of Bibbesworth, whose rhymed *Tretiz pur aprise de langage* (second half of 13th c.) was based largely on distinguishing between homophones, wrote from within the learned tradition of glossaries and vocabularies. His aim was to provide his patron's presumably anglophone son with sufficient knowledge of French words to enable him to manage his estate. Walter's text was incorporated, together with a rhymed treatise on courtesy called *Urbain le courtois*, into a linguistic manual in verse known under the title of *Nova femina* (14th c.), in recognition of women's role as natural language teachers. The teaching of the written rather than the spoken language is the aim of the prose treatise *Orthographia gallica* (14th c.), which may well have been intended to meet the needs of the legal profession. Business and secretarial training in Anglo-Norman was catered for by manuals by Thomas Sampson and, in the early 15th c., William Kingsmill. Three versions of the *Maniere de langage* (1396–1415) teach Anglo-Norman by the conversational method, while John Barton's *Donnait françois* (1409) imparts grammatical knowledge in the more austere tradition of the schools.

8. Anglo-Norman Literature and the Continent

While some didactic works are obviously responses to needs peculiar to English society, it is much less easy to discern any significant Insular specificity within the broader totality of the Anglo-Norman literary texts produced in Britain between the 12th and the 15th c. French, it must be remembered, was an international language, and all literature in French belonged to a wide cultural hegemony. It is, therefore, as an integral part of French literature as a whole, rather than as an essentially national subculture, that Anglo-Norman literary production can be most profitably understood and evaluated. Far from coming to an end with the English loss of Normandy in 1204, cross-Channel relations continued to flourish throughout the Middle Ages. The works of Chaucer and Gower show close familiarity with Continental culture, and it is safe to assume that a large measure of literary interchange in both directions must always have been a feature of Anglo-French relations. Not even the *Hundred

Years War succeeded in compromising this shared culture: Richard II was an appreciative recipient and reader of *Froissart's verse, and *Charles d'Orléans whiled away his captivity after Agincourt composing poetry in English.

Much maligned, in the early part of this century, by French medievalists who condescendingly and proscriptively dubbed it 'le mauvais français d'Angleterre', and who considered its literature as belonging to an Insular backwater out of the Continental mainstream, Anglo-Norman is today able to claim its rightful place and status, that of an innovative and uniquely productive medium of oral and written communication which made a rich and varied contribution to both French and British cultures.   [IS]

See M. D. Legge, *Anglo-Norman Literature and its Background* (1963).

Angot, Madame. Character in the comic opera *Madame Angot, ou la Poissarde parvenue* (1797) by Maillot (or Demaillot). She is the *parvenue* who has not lost her **poissard* speech. Her popularity led to further comic operas devoted to her daughter and granddaughter.

ANGOT DE L'ÉPERONNIÈRE, Robert (*c.*1581–after 1640). Normandy satirist; his *Exercices de ce temps* (1622–31) contain some remarkably lively scenes from the everyday life of street and market-place.

Annales d'histoire économique et sociale. Journal (normally called simply *Annales*) founded in 1929 by *Febvre and *Bloch, and which radically reoriented French historiography. The 'Annales school' challenged the dominance of political and diplomatic history, with its emphasis on the narrative of events, and promoted an interdisciplinary and comparative approach involving geography, demography, and the social and economic sciences. They focused upon problems rather than periods ('absolutism' rather than 'the reign of Louis XIV'), sought to define the characteristics of collective mentalities, and analysed long-term processes and structures within a total material and cultural context.   [REG]

Annales galantes, see VILLEDIEU.

Annales politiques, civiles et littéraires, see LINGUET.

ANNE D'AUTRICHE (Anne of Austria) (1602–66). Daughter of Philip III of Spain, queen of Louis XIII, and regent during the minority of her son *Louis XIV. She (with Mazarin) was the object of much popular abuse during the *Fronde; as queen mother, she was a powerful member of the devout faction in the early years of her son's personal reign.

Année littéraire, L', see FRÉRON.

Annonce faite à Marie, L'. Written 1910–11, performed 1912, this play by *Claudel is a reworking of
La Jeune Fille Violaine (written 1892 and 1898–1900),
in which Violaine for her sister's sake renounces the
man she loves, and voluntarily suffers vilification,
exile, and death. The changes are significant:
influenced by his reading of *Huysmans, Claudel
moves the action to the Middle Ages, introducing
the theme of vicarious suffering, whereby Violaine's
trials have a universal significance; this is further
underlined by Violaine's leprosy (induced by an act
of charity, a kiss) and by powerful liturgical symbolism. [RMG]

Anonymity. In French as in other literatures,
'anon.' is a prolific and impressive author. The
Dictionnaire des ouvrages anonymes occupies four
large volumes of J.-M. Quérard's *Les Supercheries littéraires dévoilées* (2nd edn., augmented by G. Brunet
and P. Jannet, 7 vols., 1889). The association of
anonymity with 'supercherie' suggests that it is a
tactic of concealment, and this is indeed often the
case.
Anonymity may simply mean that the author is not
identifiable. This applies in particular to older texts
and those which were originally transmitted orally,
from *chansons de geste to *popular songs. The modern notion of *authorship, implying the individual
creation and ownership of a body of work, only
developed gradually in the Middle Ages. As late as
the 17th or 18th c., as with *La *Princesse de Clèves*,
anonymous publication might reflect the fact that a
work emanated from a group or salon. It might also
indicate that for social reasons the author of the text
(e.g. an aristocrat or a woman) did not wish to
figure as a writer. Alternatively—and here we are
coming nearer to the *hoax—anonymity might be
an attempt to suggest that a given work (e.g. the
Lettres portugaises) is not an author's creation but a
real-life document.
Very often, however, and particularly during the
ancien régime, anonymity is the result of prudence,
like the use of *pseudonyms (the line between the
two is unclear when the title-page reads 'Par M. de
***'). Vast quantities of scurrilous *pamphlets and
*libertin writings (e.g. *Diderot's *Bijoux indiscrets*)
appeared anonymously, as did some major works of
the *Enlightenment, from the *Lettres persanes to
*Helvétius's *De l'esprit*. In these two cases, the
author's identity was no secret, but *Morelly's
anonymous *Code de la nature*, for instance, was
attributed to Diderot throughout the 18th c. Since
the Revolution, while much journalism is still
unsigned, few important literary works have been
published anonymously. *Mérimée's *Chronique du
règne de Charles IX* is an exception. Perhaps because
of an increased sense of literary property, the pseudonym is more normal. [PF]

ANOUILH, Jean (1910–87) Playwright whose
prolific output, craftsmanship, versatility, and sus-

tained commercial success over fifty years made
him a phenomenon of the 20th-c. French stage.
After a period writing advertising copy and additional dialogue for films, he entered the theatre as
secretary to *Jouvet. Of his earliest plays, *Jézabel*
(1932) was unperformed and *L'Hermine* (1932),
Mandarine (1933), and *Y avait un prisonnier* (1935) were
unsuccessful. Thereafter, influenced by *Molière,
Shaw, Pirandello, and *Giraudoux, he produced a
stream of plays which won him an international
public.
Though Anouilh is never uninteresting, his plays
are uneven: he can be facile and meretricious as
well as moving, imaginative, and inventive. His is
pre-eminently a theatre of illusion. He creates an
artificial, self-consistent, and autonomous stage-
world in which pretence and make-believe of a
showy kind are central. He then artfully draws
attention to what is false in this world, inviting his
audience to be accomplices in a shared game. He
does this in several ways. He introduces many characters who are professional actors, like Madame
Alexandra in *Colombe* (1951); or else openly exploits
stock characters: sweet innocents, eccentric aristocrats, cuckolds, fire-eating generals. He scatters his
work with echoes, or sly pastiche, of major dramatists: Molière in *Ornifle* (1955), Chekhov in *Cher
Antoine* (1969). He revels in the device of the play
within a play, especially in *La Répétition* (1950),
where his own play is about the rehearsal of a play
by *Marivaux. He seizes on threadbare dramatic
conventions: gross melodrama in *L'Hermine*, bedroom farce in *La Valse des toréadors* (1952). In fact, he
pushes to its limit Shakespeare's 'all the world's a
stage', using this basic figure to articulate a great
variety of dramatic modes, themes, and moods.
The categories Anouilh applies to his plays do at
least indicate the range: *pièces noires, roses, brillantes,
costumées, baroques, secrètes*. The gamut runs from
anguish, wounded idealism, and misanthropic pessimism to sentimental charm and gaily exuberant
fantasy. What animates many of his plays is the
clash between exacting heroes and heroines
obsessed with their personal integrity ('pureté'),
with being true to themselves, and their all-too-
human antagonists who are ready to come to terms
with life. The idealists go down to a kind of ritual
defeat, often causing havoc in the process. Such are:
Frantz of *L'Hermine*, who commits murder to keep
his love for Monime 'immaculate'; Thérèse of *La
Sauvage* (1938), who sacrifices happiness with Florent
out of solidarity with her appalling parents; the
eponymous heroine of *Antigone* (1944), who dies
rather than be false to her own ideals; the spinster
aunt who commits suicide with her hunchback
lover in *Ardèle* (1948); *Jeanne d'Arc, who goes to
the stake in *L'Alouette* (1953) so as to remain true to
her vision; the archbishop, who spurns the king's
friendship and accepts martyrdom in *Becket* (1959)
rather than change his beliefs.
In Anouilh's earlier theatre, the only release from

the pressures of this stubborn integrity lies in pure escapism. The amnesic Gaston's exit in *Le Voyageur sans bagage* (1937) is a scene of tender fantasy at variance with the pain of his dilemma; Lucien's escape to a new life in Africa in *Roméo et Jeannette* (1946) hangs on the casual device of an unexpected letter; the prince's return to happiness in *Léocadia* (1940) occurs in a sort of romantic never-never land, as does that of the melancholy twin among the opulence of *L'Invitation au château* (1947). In the plays of the 1960s and 1970s, tragic intensity and buoyant escapist charm, so present in the earlier theatre, tend to be replaced by persistent, and sometimes sour, pessimism expressed in black farces like *Pauvre Bitos* (1956), his harsh cartoon of revolutionary fanaticism, and *Le Boulanger, la boulangère et le petit mitron* (1968), or melancholy comedies like *Cher Antoine*. Interesting in these later plays is the rehabilitation of compromise, as signalled in the figure of Louis XVIII in *La Foire d'empoigne* (1962). [SBJ]

See J. Harvey, *Anouilh: A Study in Theatrics* (1964); H. G. McIntyre, *The Theatre of Anouilh* (1981).

ANQUETIL-DUPERRON, Abraham-Hyacinthe (1731–1805). French orientalist who, after adventurous travels in the East, gave to the Bibliothèque du Roi a priceless collection of manuscripts, many of which he edited and translated.

Anthologie de l'humour noir. First published by *Breton in 1940, forbidden by the Vichy regime, and republished in an augmented edition in 1966, this inventively titled collection brings together many of the Surrealists' favourite authors, from Swift to *Jarry, Carroll to *Cravan.

Anthologies. Many medieval literary manuscripts, particularly of poetry, are in effect anthologies, containing work by several hands; only in the 14th c. do we find the rise of the single-author codex [see AUTHORSHIP]. Similarly, from the 16th to the 18th c. much poetry was first published in *recueils collectifs*, which occupied the position of literary journals in later times [see PERIODICALS]. These extremely numerous *recueils* have been catalogued for the period 1500–1700 by F. Lachèvre (*Bibliographie des recueils collectifs de poésies du XVIe siècle*, 1922; *Bibliographie des recueils collectifs de poésie de 1597 à 1700*, 4 vols., 1901–5); one should also mention the collections of *satires published in the early 17th c., for instance the *Cabinet satyrique* (1618–20).

These anthologies were put together by bookseller-publishers such as *Barbin; they were meant for the general public, not for schools, since French literature occupied a small place in the education of the day. There were, of course, school anthologies of the Greek and Latin classics, and when in the 19th c. French literature gained a bigger place in the syllabus, similar anthologies of French literature began to be published for school use. They have continued to this day; some, such as the classic series *Textes et littérature*, edited by A. Lagarde and L. Michard, offer secondary-school students a basic literary-historical introduction with selected texts; others, such as those published in the Garnier-Flammarion collection, are for more advanced use. At the same time, anthologies for the general public continue to appear in large numbers. They are not, as in the *ancien régime*, publications of new works, but are selections, often personal, of the best work in a given period or genre. Two imprints stand out for the range of their anthologies, the Bibliothèque de la *Pléiade, which includes collections of fiction, drama, history, oratory, and other forms as well as poetry, and the more recent series Bouquins, which offers adventurous selections from many genres, including *moralistes, *detective fiction, and *travel writing.

The following are among the most interesting poetry anthologies of recent decades, most of them concentrating on particular periods or types of poetry; those marked with an asterisk are bilingual editions:

A. M. Boase, *The Poetry of France* (4 vols., 1964–73).
B. Delvaille, *Mille et cent ans de poésie française* (1991).
C. Roy, *Trésor de la poésie populaire* (1967).
A. Pauphilet, *Poètes et romanciers du moyen âge* (revised R. Pernaud and A.-M. Schmidt, 1967).
A.-M. Schmidt, *Poètes du XVIe siècle* (2nd edn., 1964).
J. Rousset, *Anthologie de la poésie baroque française* (2 vols., 1961).
A. J. Steele, *Three Centuries of French Verse* (1961).
J. Roudaut, *Poètes et grammairiens du XVIIIe siècle* (1971).
B. Leuilliot, *Anthologie de la poésie française du XIXe siècle, de Chateaubriand à Baudelaire* (1984).
M. Décaudin, *Anthologie de la poésie française du XIXe siècle, de Baudelaire à Saint-Pol Roux* (1992).
*W. Rees, *French Poetry, 1820–1950* (1990).
C. A. Hackett, *Anthology of Modern French Poetry from Baudelaire to the Present Day* (1964).
M. Décaudin, *Anthologie de la poésie française du XXe siècle* (1983).
*M. Sorrell, *Modern French Poetry* (1992).
*G. D. Martin, *Anthology of Contemporary French Poetry* (1972).
C. A. Hackett, *New French Poetry* (1973).
L. S. Senghor, *Anthologie de la nouvelle poésie nègre et malgache de langue française* (1948).
C. Wake, *An Anthology of African and Malagasy Poetry in French* (1965).
L. Mailhot and P. Nepveu, *La Poésie québécoise, des origines à nos jours* (1980).
L.-F. Prudent, *Anthologie de la nouvelle poésie créole* (1984). [PF]

Anthropology. While the term is often used in its general sense of a philosophical conception of human nature or the human condition, it now more commonly refers to two groups of academic disciplines, both closely linked with archaeology.

Physical anthropology, which studies variations in characteristics of the human body, is closely related to the medical and biological sciences and has been controversially invoked in theories of race, by writers like *Gobineau. Social or cultural anthropology, also known as ethnology, is the better-known branch, in which French contributions have been internationally influential.

In this sense, anthropology is the study of human societies, and therefore closely related to *sociology. It has mainly focused on pre-literate or pre-technological societies which are often regarded as primitive, though many anthropologists have emphasized the extent of their similarity to modern industrial societies. The two broad directions of anthropological enquiry are the description and collection of data, often termed ethnography, and the theoretical reflection on it. In France, the two activities have tended to be separated. Many major writers have contributed significantly to ethnography, among them *Zola, *Gide, and *Leiris, while theoretical anthropology has been particularly important in intellectual debate.

In the 18th c., *philosophes like *Rousseau and *Diderot used the accounts of travellers to inform their work, though the specialist discipline of anthropology really emerged in the late 19th c. from the work of Émile *Durkheim, who stressed the distinctive role of social structures in forming individual behaviour, and Lucien *Lévy-Bruhl, who explored the relations between morality and customs, and proposed a theory of the evolution of human mind. These sociological and philosophical strands were brought together by Marcel *Mauss, the first major French anthropologist, whose Essai sur le don (1925) analysed the practices and rituals of gift-giving.

Undoubtedly the dominant figure in post-war anthropology is Claude *Lévi-Strauss, who blended ideas from *linguistics, *psychoanalysis, and *Marxism to produce a structuralist analysis which aimed to detect underlying patterns in kinship relations, myths and stories, religious practices, and art. His Anthropologie structurale (1958 and 1973) and Mythologiques (1964–71) outline his theory in detail, while his autobiographical Tristes tropiques (1955) has became a popular classic. André Leroi-Gourhan (1911–86) extended the scope of anthropology to analyse prehistoric mentality in both existing pre-literate societies and in societies accessible solely through archaeological remains. His conclusions are presented in Le Geste et la parole (1964–5).

Lévi-Strauss and Leroi-Gourhan established approaches to anthropology which have been widely followed nationally and internationally. Their distinctive contribution, springing from the French tradition they inherited, has been to valorize theoretical analysis over the description of data, and to assert that the ultimate goal of enquiry is to elucidate the nature and structure of the human mind. Both points remain matters of contention within anthropology and in wider intellectual debate.

[MHK]

Anticlericalism. The term is properly reserved for hostility to the activities of the clergy. In the French case this has nearly always meant the Catholic clergy. It should be distinguished from hostility to the Catholic faith—though the two have often coincided. Many anticlericals proclaimed themselves *deists of one form or another.

Anticlericalism in France is probably as old as Catholicism [see HERESIES], but it acquired a new importance during the *Enlightenment. Writers such as *Voltaire, *Diderot, and *Condorcet sharply attacked the Catholic clergy. They were hostile to what they perceived as the wealth and corruption of the upper clergy, and to the intolerance of the Catholic Church as an institution (as shown in the *Calas affair). They particularly attacked the religious orders, which they condemned as useless to society; the parish clergy, provided they showed themselves to be tolerant and rendered useful services such as the teaching of morality, were partially excepted from Enlightenment anticlericalism. The 18th c. also saw the development, in the artisanal working class of Paris, of a less intellectual but equally virulent anticlericalism, the reasons for which are still obscure.

Both strands of anticlericalism surfaced during the Revolution. Educated leaders (particularly the *Girondins) were much influenced by Enlightenment hostility to the Church. Popular anticlericalism was often expressed by the Parisian *sans-culottes. The two strands came together in the so-called 'de-christianization' campaign of 1793–4, when nearly all churches in France were closed and most of the remaining clergy compelled to abdicate. Anticlericalism during the Revolution was greatly exacerbated by the fact that many of the clergy sided with the king (unsurprisingly, in view of the close links between throne and altar under the ancien régime). Siding with the king came to mean siding with the foreign powers who were invading France; priests thus came to be perceived as traitors. This was one reason for the great bitterness of Revolutionary anticlericalism, which resulted in between two and three thousand priests losing their lives by violent means in the 1790s.

Anticlericalism became an important issue in French life again in the 1820s, when an attempt was made to re-establish the old alliance of throne and altar. Stendhal's Le *Rouge et le noir is a classic statement of the anticlerical mentality of the time—with particular focus on what the author perceived as the hypocrisy of the clergy. The 1830 Revolution reduced the political influence of the clergy, but anticlericalism remained a powerful force in French life. *Flaubert was one of the few non-Catholics to satirize it, in the character of *Homais, whose discourse includes all the commonplaces of 19th-c. anticlericalism—much of it inherited from the Enlightenment.

Antidote, L'

*Napoleon III's support for Catholic causes in the 1850s gave renewed impetus to anticlericalism among his republican opponents, as did the Catholic domination of the first parliament of the Third Republic [see REPUBLICANISM].

The anticlericalism of the Third Republic was thus in many ways a product of the clergy's support for earlier anti-republican regimes. There were also other causes. There is evidence (e.g. in the writings of *Michelet) that as Catholicism became more and more feminized in the course of the 19th c., republican men deeply resented the power that the clergy exercised over women. More generally, men seem to have resented the hierarchical structures of the Church, which demanded unquestioning acceptance by laymen of clerical authority.

For these and other reasons the Third Republic was dominated, between 1877 and 1914, by politicians who were strongly anticlerical. Their influence was particularly felt in *freemasonic lodges, which served as a kind of counter-church. The 1880s saw a flood of anticlerical legislation, notably with the secularization of public education and the reintroduction of divorce (1884). Clerical involvement against *Dreyfus gave renewed impetus to anticlericalism, resulting in the banning from teaching of any member of a religious order (thus almost destroying the Chruch's system of private schools), and in the separation of Church and State in 1905. More generally, Third Republic intellectual life was dominated by anticlericalism—as one can see notably in *Zola, though in La *Faute de l'abbé Mouret it takes a rather unusual form.

Joint support for the war effort in 1914 by both anticlericals and Catholics led to a lessening of hostility, and the 20th c. has been less marked by anticlericalism than the 19th. The old traditions of republican anticlericalism remain, however, deeply embedded in French life: the 1984 Socialist proposal to weaken the system of private Catholic secondary education was clearly a manifestation of it. The defeat of this proposal may not quite mark the end of traditional anticlericalism in France.   [RBG]

Antidote, L', see RABEMANAJARA.

Antigone, ou la Piété. Tragedy by *Garnier, published 1580. His longest play (2,741 lines), it draws on Seneca's Theban tragedy the *Phœnissae*, Statius' epic poem the *Thebais*, and Sophocles' tragedy *Antigone*. The theme of the Theban prince Polynice quarrelling with his brother and attacking the city which he wishes to rule allows for moralizing about civil war. Créon's treatment of Antigone (sentenced to death for disobeying his order not to bury the body of her brother Polynice) is judged by a chorus to be well-intentioned but mistaken. Multiple choruses are used to support various characters or represent segments of the population.

Antigone has been the subject of other French plays, including those by *Rotrou and *Anouilh.
        [GJ]

Antillanité, see GLISSANT.

Anti-Machiavel, L', see GENTILLET.

Antiquités de Rome, Les, see DU BELLAY.

Antisemitism [see also JUDAISM]. The spectacular success of *Drumont's La France juive (1886) marks the beginning of antisemitism as a modern mass movement in France. Much of its success is due to the rationalization of deeply embedded religious prejudices. Thus, Drumont's obsession with Jewry's fiendish power to destroy Christian/Aryan civilization by corrupting it belongs to a long anti-Judaic tradition which La France juive modernizes, presenting the Jewish peril, or judaization, in socio-economic and political terms.

Briefly summed up, the argument runs as follows: since Jewry's entry into French society, following the Emancipation Act of 1791, France has declined into Jewish materialism. Money is king and the king is Rothschild. Unlike his predecessors (*Fourier and Toussenel as well as Marx), Drumont did not regard judaization merely as a matter of socio-economic forces favouring a mercantile ethos, but of religious vocation: the chosen race was pursuing its God-given mission of world conquest. The whole of post-Revolutionary French history, from 'la Révolution juive' (1789), itself possibly a Jewish (or Judeo-Masonic) plot, to 'la République juive' (the Third Republic), was seen as stages in that triumphant conquest to which corresponded France's degeneration. The widespread feeling of decadence was thus given a simple cause, a 'Jewish explanation', as was done in medieval times for plagues and other disasters.

Drumont's originality lay in stating unequivocally that the Jewish Question posed a racial problem requiring a racial solution. Conversion, acculturation, socialization were dismissed as dangerous fantasies of equality. The *Dreyfus Affair (1894–9) provided an excellent opportunity for translating into politics theories of racial determinism, helped by a fanaticized public opinion. For this to succeed it was imperative not to allow the racial logic of Judas–Dreyfus–Jewry to be broken by rational discussion. The tactic, zealously pursued by the antisemitic press and eloquently supported by *Barrès and *Maurras (*Action Française was born in 1898), came close to succeeding: both government and the liberal press were terrified into silence by smear campaigns and by an anti-Jewish mass hysteria unprecedented in modern Western European history. In the event, Captain Dreyfus was eventually rehabilitated (1906) and the Republic emerged stronger from the ordeal, rehabilitations not easily forgiven.

It was not until the 1930s that large-scale antisemitism reappeared, with a vengeance, fuelled by a variety of factors, above all by a flood of refugees and by Léon *Blum's accession to the premiership in June 1936. It speaks well for the health of republican democracy that a Jew could head the French state at that time. Equally admirable is the sanity of the majority in the face of the demented propaganda unleashed against Blum and Jews.

And yet that same majority accepted without much protest the Vichy regime's *statuts des Juifs* (1940–1), which excluded French Jews, 'racially' defined in terms of number of Jewish grandparents, from all public office, imposed a quota system for the liberal professions and education, and aryanized property. The latest research suggests that Vichy's Jewish policy, including the handing-over of interned foreign Jews for 'resettlement' in the East, a measure to which there was growing public opposition, was not dictated by the occupying powers [see OCCUPATION AND RESISTANCE]. To what extent the French government actually knew of the deportees' fate is less certain. However that may be, extermination had no part in the tortuous state antisemitism defended by Vallat, who as commissioner-general for Jewish Affairs envisaged his role as surgeon not butcher. The story was different in occupied Paris, which had its ethnologists teaching people how to recognize the Jewish type, its exhibition of 'Le Juif et la France', its notorious round-ups carried out by the French police, and its collaborationist writers (among them *Brasillach, *Châteaubriant, *Céline, *Drieu La Rochelle, *Rebatet), looking forward to a new Franco-German Europe without Jews.

The following figures, very approximate, will help to put this dark chapter into perspective: over 75,000 French Jews perished in German camps; an estimated 250,000 survived the Occupation and Vichy, many thanks to the efforts of ordinary French people. How deep did racialism go in France? Deeper perhaps than good republicans, especially French Jewry, cared to admit. Nor were these ardent assimilationists aware of their own unwitting contribution by affirming that the Jewish Question did not exist, for in Republican France, One and Indivisible, there were no Jews.

The late 20th c. saw both a clearer acknowledgement of French responsibility for the fate of Jews in World War II, and the emergence of new tensions, now more related to the politics of the Middle East. [NW]

See M. Winock, *Édouard Drumont et Cie. Antisémitisme et fascisme en France* (1982); M. R. Marrus and R. O. Paxton, *Vichy France and the Jews* (1982); P. Birnbaum, *Anti-Semitism in France: A Political History from Léon Blum to the Present* (tr. M. Kochan, 1992).

ANTOINE, André (1858–1943). French actor, theatre director, and critic, founder of the Théâtre Libre set up in Paris (1887–94) on the basis of membership subscriptions as a means of evading censorship and providing an alternative to the stagnating commercial theatre. He staged new young dramatists, experimenting with the techniques of *Naturalism,

and established a pattern for studio theatres which sprang up throughout Europe and precipitated a theatrical revolution. He introduced Ibsen, Hauptmann, and Strindberg in France, pioneering acting and production styles appropriate to drama as a 'slice of life'. From 1906 to 1914 he was director at the *Odéon, where he continued his commitment to revitalizing the theatre. [DHW]

Antoine Bloyé, see NIZAN.

ANTOINE DE LA SALE, see LA SALE

Antsa, see RABEMANAJARA.

APOLLINAIRE, Guillaume (pseud. of Wilhelm de Kostrowitsky) (1880–1918). Born in Rome, the illegitimate child of a Vatican nobleman, who never recognized him, and a Finnish-born mother of Polish origin but Russian nationality, Apollinaire's early years were veiled in an often deliberate obscurity, and until he joined the French army in 1915 his identity papers described him as an 'Italo-Russe'. After a childhood spent in Monaco and Cannes, his subsequent wanderings from one casino town to another with a younger brother, mother, and a succession of 'uncles' inspired aspects of *Gide's Lafcadio and provided the future poet with a rich fund of dialect and folklore. When tutor to an aristocratic German family in the Rhineland, he met the English woman Annie Playden who was to mark so much of his early poetry, as was the painter Marie Laurencin with whom he had a stormy relationship in his early years in Paris. By 1911 his unorthodox background and avant-garde activities were such that, on the flimsiest of pretexts, he was briefly imprisoned for the theft of the Mona Lisa. An early champion of all that was new in poetry and painting, he was an unlikely recruit to the army, serving first in the artillery and subsequently, as a lieutenant, in the infantry. Invalided out, he married Jacqueline Kolb ('la jolie rousse') shortly before his death.

Although in recent years much more substantial attention has been paid to his other achievements, Apollinaire's reputation still rests principally on the two main collections of lyric poetry published in his lifetime—*Alcools* (1913) and *Calligrammes* (1918). But, perhaps fittingly for one who was an active colleague of the artistic avant-garde in the years before World War I, his first published collection of poems was a series of short and often humorous verses, illustrated by Raoul *Dufy's woodcuts: *Le Bestiaire, ou Cortège d'Orphée* (1911). He was a friend of the *Cubists, and although his contribution to the early debate surrounding their art—*Les Peintres cubistes* (1913)—was later dismissed by several among them, notably *Picasso, it remains what its originally intended title *(Méditations esthétiques)* proclaimed it to be: a collection of essays which attempts the evocation of the spirit of painting through words.

His early death from a combination of Asian

influenza and the aftermath of a head wound sustained in the trenches seemed to leave his posthumous standing as a leader of the avant-garde at the mercy of those who wished to take on this mantle themselves; he was accused of lacking sufficient audacity, of having failed to break free from the dead conventions of literature, by *Breton, *Aragon, and others. In an ironic parallel, more conservative opinion, while dismissing the experimental in his writing, valued the octosyllabic verses and shorter lyrics which undoubtedly make him one of the great French poets. Others, such as *Cendrars, were to allow his role as innovator to be undermined by charges of plagiarism.

Apart from personal factors, such controversy stems mainly from the multiplicity of readings which his poetry invites, not only through its variety of form and texture (*Calligrammes* has many poems written in the shape of objects), but also through its much more profoundly enigmatic nature. From the earliest poems of *Alcools*, which present a drama of the psyche in a mythical landscape imbued with Arthurian legend, to the last long poems of *Calligrammes*, there is a constant exploding of that unity of self which is normally found in lyrics of personal sensibility. At the same time the external universe seems to offer an immanent, if hermetic, meaning which is striven for from 'Merlin et la vieille femme' to the final verses of 'Les Collines'. While much scholarship has stressed the diversity of influences and heteroclite nature of his verse, it is impossible not to be aware of the strand of continuity in this poetry of exploration of self-in-the-world which Apollinaire produced at all stages of his life. It reveals the self as fractured subject whether in the lines of 'La Chanson du mal aimé', his earliest masterpiece, or the war poems such as 'Fête'.

An equally constant and paradoxically unifying strand in his poetry is his desire to make the language of his verse reflect the diversity of his experience and the often arcane nature of his erudition. Together with his friend Fernand Fleuret he produced the first catalogue of the *Enfer* of the *Bibliothèque Nationale, and an intimate knowledge of writers such as Aretino and *Sade is visible, though often in oblique fashion, in his work. Yet it was not only from the library shelf that he drew; his personal experience of Italian, particularly Roman, life and folklore, as well as the dialects and legends of Wallonia, the traditions and tales of the Rhineland, the rest of Germany, Czechoslovakia, provincial France, Monaco, and so forth made his poetry a dazzling and sometimes bewildering assemblage of fragments, which led to *Duhamel's dismissal of *Alcools* at the time of its publication as a 'boutique de brocanteur'. The jibe would have been better aimed at the residues of symbolism from which Apollinaire was trying to set free a new lyricism, and it is this liberation which remains the major achievement of *Alcools*.

Calligrammes, subtitled 'Poèmes de la paix et de la guerre', while containing much that is inspired from the same sources as the poems of *Alcools*—love affairs, encounters with the modern world and modern art—deserves also to be recognized as the finest poetic achievement of *World War I. Although a certain poetic record of the experience of the war remains in French, there is no equivalent of the group of poets (Owen, Sassoon, etc.) who define a moment in the history of English verse. Apollinaire is the only substantial poet in French whose work tries to engage with the business of being at war. His war poems have their moments of 'poetry in the pity', as is the case with 'Exercice', for example, and they have their moments of what may seem a crude jingoism and, worse, a personal revelling in military life, yet even at their most rebarbative for the pacifist, these poems not only record 'l'histoire de Guillaume Apollinaire | Qui fut à la guerre et sut être partout', they allow the reader to experience all aspects of the soldier's life and to place them in both a modern and a mythical context. They are never as naïve in their glorification of the warrior as some of Apollinaire's own letters (particularly the *Lettres à Lou*) might have led certain readers to suppose, and in their language they follow his constant habit of opening the poetic to the everyday and the modern in a way that is absolutely consistent with his pre-war aesthetic.

As a prose writer Apollinaire was inventive and highly unorthodox. He began as an anonymous pornographer but went on to put his name to the picturesque and inventive stories of *L'Hérésiarque et Cie* (1910), the whimsical and partly autobiographical *Le Poète assassiné* (1916), as well as *La Femme assise* (1920), which has been claimed as an early precursor of the *Nouveau Roman. His verse drama *Les Mamelles de Tirésias* (1918) might have been the beginning of a theatrical career in keeping with the invention and iconoclasm of the period. But it is his lasting achievement to have invented—perhaps with Cendrars—the first poetry, the first poetic language, of 20th-c. France.   [IWR]

See F. Steegmuller, *Apollinaire: Poet Among the Painters* (1963); M.-L. Lentengre, *Apollinaire et le nouveau lyrisme* (1984); T. Mathews, *Reading Apollinaire* (1987).

Apologie pour Hérodote, see ÉTIENNE, H.

Apostrophes. Highly influential television programme hosted by Bernard Pivot and broadcast on Friday evenings by Antenne 2 between 1975 and 1990. Lasting 75 minutes, the format consisted of a studio discussion among six authors, each of whom in turn answered Pivot's questions before being submitted to the comments and questions of the others. The studio atmosphere has been described as a cross between a literary salon and a boxing match. Although the programme offered an opportunity for writers of serious fiction to reach a mass audience, it became controversial as its influence over book-sales figures became evident. Bookshops began to have an 'Apostrophes' table for the books featuring in the week's programme, and Pivot was accused in 1979 by Régis *Debray of exercising a dictatorship over the market as he developed two spin-off programmes (*Apos* and *Strophes*) in addition to a monthly magazine entitled *Lire*. Michel Tournier, Philippe Sollers, and Bernard-Henri Lévy were amongst the most frequently invited authors. A few broadcasts were devoted to a long interview with a single author: amongst these figured Raymond Aron, Marguerite Duras, Julien Green, Claude Lévi-Strauss, and Marguerite Yourcenar. [EAF]

Appel à l'impartiale postérité, see ROLAND, MADAME.

Appel de la race, L', see GROULX.

Appel des arènes, see SOW FALL.

Approximations, see DU BOS, C.

'Après-midi d'un faune, L' ' (1876). Eclogue by *Mallarmé, most famous because of the prelude it inspired from *Debussy.

AQUIN, Hubert (1929–72). Canadian novelist, essayist, film-maker, and political activist. Born in Montreal and educated there and at the Institut d'Études Politiques in Paris, Aquin worked for Radio Canada between 1955 and 1959 and at the Office National du Film between 1959 and 1963, establishing himself as a virulent commentator on *québécois* affairs with an article published in *Liberté* in 1962 entitled 'La Fatigue culturelle du Canada français'. As vice-president of the Montreal section of the separatist Rassemblement pour l'Indépendance Nationale (RIN), Aquin was arrested for possession of firearms in July 1964; while he was interned awaiting trial, he wrote his first novel *Prochain épisode*, published shortly before his acquittal in December 1965. In 1966 his request for a Swiss residence permit was rejected on the grounds of his alleged terrorist connections, whereafter, returning to Canada, he was appointed national director of the RIN. His second novel, *Trou de mémoire* (1968), was awarded the Prix du Gouverneur Général du Canada, which Aquin refused to accept. A third novel, *L'Antiphonaire*, was published in 1969, followed by a collection of essays and other writings, *Point de fuite*, in 1971. In the 1970s Aquin pursued an often stormy career in journalism, film-making, and publishing. A fourth novel, *Neige noire*, appeared in 1974, but following his dismissal as literary director of Éditions La Presse in 1976, and apparently despairing of prospects for an independent Quebec, Aquin took his own life on 15 March 1977. He left behind him four novels of searing intensity, written in a language remarkable for its baroque extravagance, intricacy, and beauty and presenting the

quest for political and sexual liberation as inseparable aspects of an impossible quest for totality. Aquin's principal articles are collected in *Blocs erratiques* (1982). [RDEB]

See G. de Lafontaine, *Hubert Aquin et le Québec* (1978); R. Chambers, *Room for Maneuver* (1991).

AQUINAS, Thomas (*c*.1225–1274). Philosopher and theologian. For his thought see SCHOLASTICISM. For modern Thomism, based on his thinking, see MARITAIN.

ARAGO, François (1786–1853). French scientist, professor, and republican politician. Best known as an astronomer, Arago was elected in 1809 to the Académie des Sciences, for which he composed *éloges. He became a member of parliament during the July Monarchy. After the Revolution of February 1848 he entered the government as minister for the Navy. His political career ended when he was defeated in the 1852 elections. [CC]

ARAGON, Louis (1897–1982). A founding member of the *Surrealist movement and France's most distinguished Communist writer, Aragon excelled as a poet, novelist, and journalist. He was born in Paris, the illegitimate son of Marguerite Toucas and Louis Andrieux, a *député* and former préfet de police and ambassador to Spain, who gave him the name of Aragon. The quest for legitimacy and identity was to become one of the major themes of his work. After a brilliant school career, at the École Saint-Pierre in Neuilly and the Lycée Carnot, during which he showed a precocious literary talent, he enrolled as a medical student in 1916 and met André *Breton while attending courses at the Val de Grâce in 1917. He had a distinguished war career, in which he was awarded the Croix de Guerre, and saw service in occupied Germany until he was demobilized in 1919.

The first major period of his literary career began the same year, with the establishment, with Breton and *Soupault, of the review *Littérature*, which became the flagship of the French avant-garde. Initially closely allied to *Dada, Breton and Aragon broke with *Tzara in 1921 and moved on to found Surrealism in 1924. Aragon's writing of the 1920s constitutes some of the most accomplished and innovative production of the avant-garde. Novels such as *Anicet ou le Panorama* (1921) and *Les Aventures de Télémaque* (1922) owe much of their fantastic character to pastiche, whilst collections of poems, *Feu de joie* (1921) and *Le Mouvement perpétuel* (1926), make use of what was to become a constant feature of his work, collage. In particular, *Le Paysan de Paris* (1926), which proposes a new fantastic vision of the city, became a classic text of Surrealism. Aragon's Surrealist writing was theoretically underpinned by the violently polemical essay *Traité du style* (1928).

Aramis

In 1927 Aragon joined the French Communist Party (PCF), still believing that it was possible to make of Surrealism a genuinely revolutionary movement, but his meeting in 1928 with the Russian Elsa *Triolet, who was to be his companion until her death in 1970, led to closer contact with the Soviet Union and brought him to a more orthodox stance. On his return from the Revolutionary Writers' Congress in Kharkov in 1930, Aragon saw Surrealism and Communism as no longer compatible, a decision which led to his final break with Breton in 1932. Throughout the 1930s Aragon operated as an increasingly important figure in the French Communist apparatus, as a journalist, organizer, and writer. He had written for newspapers since the early 1920s, but in 1933 he became a regular journalist for L'*Humanité as well as editorial assistant for Commune. In 1937 he became director of the Communist daily evening paper Ce soir, a post he held until the paper was banned in 1939. At the same time, he became a central figure in the setting up and management of *Popular Front organizations, such as the Association des Écrivains et Artistes Révolutionnaires (AEAR) and the 1936 Congrès International pour la Défense de la Culture contre le Fascisme, as well as making frequent visits to the USSR. His writing during the 1930s veered from Surrealism to Socialist Realism, though he was careful to situate it clearly in a national cultural context which allowed him to continue some of the innovative techniques of the 1920s. Thus, whilst the poems of Hourra l'Oural (1934) show a marked return to traditional poetic form, the novels which make up the Monde réel cycle—Les *Cloches de Bâle (1934), Les *Beaux Quartiers (1936), and Les *Voyageurs de l'Impériale (1942)—continue the techniques of pastiche and collage which characterized the writing of the 1920s.

In 1940 a third major phase of Aragon's career began with his role in the Resistance [see OCCUPATION AND RESISTANCE]. He fought heroically in the Battle of France and, on the defeat of France, took a major part in the constitution of the intellectual resistance, both with the PCF and with Pierre *Seghers, with whom he and Elsa founded the Poésie series. From this period stems some of his finest poetry, Cantique à Elsa (1942), Les Yeux d'Elsa (1942), En français dans le texte (1943), and La Diane française (1945), in which mastery of lyrical form enables Aragon to equate love of woman with love of country and to celebrate the struggle against the Germans. After the war he emerged as the uncontested major Communist writer, though this did not prevent Party disapproval of works such as the novel Aurélien (1944), in spite its apparently orthodox character. Nevertheless, he continued to occupy key journalistic posts within the Party: he was made director of Ce soir in 1947, and director of Les Lettres françaises from 1953 to its closure in 1972. In fiction, he resumed his own brand of Socialist Realism with the cycle Les Communistes (1949–51),

though the abrupt ending of the project betrays growing doubts regarding Stalinism. He continued to publish poetry in the 1950s and 1960s, Elsa (1959) and Le Fou d'Elsa (1963), and novels: what is arguably his finest work, La *Semaine sainte (1958), La Mise à mort (1965), Blanche ou l'Oubli (1967), and a final collection of short stories, Mentir-vrai (1980). Although he remained a key figure in the PCF until his death and was given an official Party funeral, he became, particularly after May 1968 and the death of Elsa in 1970, increasingly distanced from orthodox Communism.

Aragon's reputation rests upon his importance within the Surrealist group, particularly through his Surrealist poetry and Le Paysan de Paris, and upon the poetry and fiction which resulted from his long relationship with Communism. The wartime Elsa poems in particular confirm him both as a major 20th-c. love-poet and as one of the most important poets of the Resistance. His fiction is important, not merely as the most successful illustration of Socialist Realism in France, but because of the way in which it transcends it to produce genuine textual complexity.   [NH]

See R. Garaudy, L'Itinéraire d'Aragon (1961); Y. Gindine, Aragon prosateur surréaliste (1966); J. Sur, Aragon, le réalisme de l'amour (1966); P. Daix, Aragon, une vie à changer (1975).

Aramis. One of the heroes of Dumas's Les *Trois Mousquetaires.

Arbres musiciens, Les, see ALEXIS, J.-S.

Archives. France has a very well-organized system of public archives. These include the Archives Nationales, created in 1794, the departmental archives in which local collections were centralized by a decree of 1796, and the archives held in every commune. The rich collection of the Archives Nationales has since 1808 been housed in the Hôtel de Soubise in the Marais district of Paris, where it acquired a fine new building in the 1980s. Much literary archival material is also located in major libraries, particularly the *Bibliothèque Nationale and the *Bibliothèque de l'Arsenal.   [PF]

A rebours (1884). Novel by *Huysmans, characterized by Arthur Symons as 'the breviary of the *decadence'. The wealthy neurotic Des Esseintes, incapable of sustaining the pressures of a society turning to democracy and mass consumption, retreats into his domestic interior to piece together in a sequence of fragmentary chapters a bewildering variety of alternative imaginative worlds.

In this ironic, consciously overwritten tale of self-indulgence, Des Esseintes is the would-be exclusive private consumer, recreating artificially pleasures he cannot enjoy in their commonplace form. Nature is the enemy. Ordinary food and drink can only be taken in novel artistic combinations or contexts, or joined to perverse sexual associations. Landscapes must be dark and derelict; flowers, dying, or exotic hybrids, symbolize and evoke perverse erotic pleasures. The terrors and humiliations of nightmare are more acceptable than the banalities of everyday living. As his imaginative and sexual potency dwindles, Des Esseintes depends on recapitulating the fragments of others' invention: the morbid erotic paintings of Gustave *Moreau or Odilon *Redon's embryonic grotesques; or, in literature, the gamey prose of the Latin decadence, the sadistic tales of *Barbey d'Aurevilly and *Poe, and the minor poetry of the modern decadence. In the end, however, what Des Esseintes considers the malignant forces of nature and history win out: for his own survival he is forced to return to the conventional world.

Huysmans's novel provided the stimulus for *Mallarmé's 'Prose pour des Esseintes'. [JB]

ARÈNE, Paul-Auguste (1843–96). Provençal playwright, novelist, journalist, and poet; friend of *Aubanel, *Mistral, and Roumanille; collaborator of Alphonse *Daudet. Following the success in Paris of his one-act comedy Pierrot héritier (1865), Arène left university and became an ever-struggling, full-time writer, known for agreeable tales and short stories set in Provence and displaying ironic wit and realistic detail, e.g. Jean des Figues (1868), La Gueuse parfumée (1876), Contes de Paris et de Provence (1887), La Chèvre d'or (1889). Other works include a dozen plays and charming French and Provençal verse, some published posthumously in the anthology Li Souleiado (1904). [PVD]

ARGENS, Jean-Baptiste le Boyer, marquis d' (1704–71). Voltairean free-thinker, author of capacious works modelled on Montesquieu's *Lettres persanes and displaying curiosity, scepticism, and a cosmopolitan spirit: Lettres juives (1736); Lettres cabalistiques (1737); Lettres chinoises (1739–40). He also wrote an unsystematic treatise, La Philosophie du bon sens (1737), memoirs, and libertine novels. [PF]

ARGENSON, René-Louis de Voyer, marquis d' (1694–1757). French political theorist and author of a valuable Journal. The son and brother of ministers, Minister of Foreign Affairs himself in 1744–7, and a friend of *Voltaire, he wrote before 1739 his Considérations sur l'ancien et présent gouvernement de la France, known only in manuscript until published in 1764. Monarchist in outlook, it proposed to move monarchy nearer to republicanism by extending the system of *États Généraux throughout the kingdom, the people thus having elected representatives at provincial level. D'Argenson was influenced by observing France's poverty when compared with neighbouring republics. [CJB]

His brother Marc-Pierre (1696–1764) was Directeur de la Librairie, War Minister, and founder of the École Militaire. The *Encyclopédie was dedicated to him. The story is told that when

*Desfontaines defended a pamphlet with the words: 'Monseigneur, il faut bien que je vive', he replied: 'Je n'en vois pas la nécessité.' [PF]

Argent, L'. Novel by *Zola, the 18th of the *Rougon-Macquart series, published in 1891. It takes up the story of Aristide Saccard, the ruthless speculator of La *Curée, who founds a bank and engages upon a titanic struggle on the stock-market with a Jewish banker, Gundermann, which ends in a disastrous defeat for Saccard. [DB]

ARGENTRÉ, Bertrand d' (1519–90), achieved prominence in two fields: he was the outstanding Breton jurist of his day, renowned for his Commentaires de la Coutume de Bretagne (1568) and for the revision of this Custom (1580). Secondly, he had a lifelong interest in Breton history, which culminated in his authoritative and officially commissioned Histoire de Bretagne (1582, revised 1588, and again in 1618 by his son, Claude). [MJ]

Argot. In the sense of thieves' slang, 'argot' has a presence in French literature that famously reaches back to the poems of *Villon, and it is still to be found in contemporary writing, although there is no unbroken strand of continuity. However, it is necessary, in order to understand the phenomenon properly, to extend the sense of the term to cover not only the language of the criminal classes but also that of the working class and all forms of popular French. These strands need to be treated together since they have become a rich source of invention and change in the politer forms of spoken language and one of the most powerful modifying factors in the evolution of written or literary French, particularly during the last hundred years. Just as in the 18th c. writers like *Restif de la Bretonne became aware of the inadequacy of the 'style noble' faced with the evocation of the daily— or nightly—life of the streets of the capital, so a strand of what was often only Romantic local colour has become an increasingly important presence in modern written French, as many writers have perceived the impossibility of confronting the modern (particularly urban) world through the medium of a literary language essentially fixed since the 17th or 18th c.

The 20th c. has seen an expansion of the uses of forms deriving from the oral language, from their provision of colour or realism in dialogues of Balzac to the assumption of their adequacy to any task which the novel, in particular, might undertake. In the works of *Céline the violence done to every aspect of classical French prose is both an aspect of the narrator's denunciation of the cultures, states, and societies which created World War I, the colonial empires, and the dehumanized world of 1920s capitalism, and a vehicle for his own feverish, nightmare vision of existence without hope. The hallucinatory quality of these novels begins with the

Arguments

destruction of formal syntax; this is interwoven with a strand of realism in so far as the text is a record of contemporary Parisian usage. In both vocabulary and syntax, it is the language of the capital and of specific sectors of its population which is the source of this new language, which, going far beyond realistic notation of spoken French, is at the heart of Céline's artistic project.

At the same time as Céline published *Voyage au bout de la nuit, *Queneau, afraid that the French language was on the brink of a schism as radical as that which separated Greek into its purely literary and demotic forms, was attempting to make spoken French—in his terms 'le troisième ou le néo-français'—into a literary instrument capable of anything. He claimed that an attempt to translate *Descartes's *Discours de la méthode* into the demotic was the origin of his first novel *Le *Chiendent*, which made apparent the rich comic possibilities opened up by the attempt to transcribe the spoken tongue (this vein was most notably exploited in his *Zazie dans le métro*). However, from the beginning, his works also embraced the most learned and literary forms of French and none is entirely composed in 'néo-français'. Queneau also made the popular language of Paris the vehicle for his verse and songs, carrying on a tradition which *Prévert had kept alive after the poems of Jehan *Rictus and the *chansonniers* of the post-Commune period. The contribution of Jacques Prévert—and that of his brother Pierre—extends beyond his poetry, which did much to spread the influence of ordinary speech in poetic language; he had an even greater impact through his work as a script-writer. The influence of the great French films of the 1930s, for instance those of *Renoir, *Duvivier, and *Carné, is contemporary with and perhaps equal to that of Queneau and Céline in this area.

While these ambitious attempts to change the nature of written French were going on, *detective fiction, which in France can be seen to reach back through Balzac to join with many of the phenomena mentioned above, continued to be written and read in vast quantity, and the use of argot as the sign of authenticity of observation of the criminal milieu continued to develop in its own right as well as to feed the vocabulary of everyday French. Moreover, the extent to which the informal registers have become more or less dominant in many forms of written French, up to and including essays such as *Au coin de la rue, l'aventure* by Pascal Bruckner and Alain Finkielkraut, is in part due to the emergence of generations which were able to read a language other than that taught in school.

While the 'polar' (thriller) is now the meeting-ground for the language of all who feel themselves to be in any way marginalized by conventional society, the autobiographical writers (e.g. *Boudard) from the poor working classes or the world of crime are able to use their linguistic inheritance to enrich a French prose which would otherwise be inadequate to their experience. Here, and in the works of *Cavanna, the humour endemic in popular language is a dominant characteristic. In this respect, it would be unthinkable not to mention the influence of *Dard, whose San-Antonio crime novels are, at their best, an irrepressible fountain of humour and verbal invention.

On a more discursive level the works of Claude *Duneton deal with what is a major post-war problem for many writers—which French to use, given that the language of the bourgeoisie is an alienating factor. Others, such as Jacques Cellier in his journalism and more extensive studies, have ensured that popular language is as well recorded and disseminated among the intelligentsia now as at any time in French history. The extensive imagery and poetry of popular speech in the hands of various writers has far outstripped the merely naturalistic usage that a criminal argot finds in many crime novels; and the existence of other genres, often grouped as 'paralittérature', such as *bande dessinée, together with the work of novelists such as Jean-Luc Bénoziglio, shows the enormous range of endeavour for which an 'unofficial' French is the medium.

[IWR]

See A. le Breton, *L'Argot chez les vrais de vrai* (1975); C. Duneton and J.-P. Pagliano, *Anti-manuel de français* (1978).

Arguments, see MARXISM.

Ariane, see CORNEILLE, T.

ARLAND, Marcel (1899–1986). French novelist and journalist. Having flirted with *Dadaism, Arland joined the *Nouvelle Revue Française*, which he co-directed from 1952. A witty and urbane critic and essayist, he wrote a score of short novels, typically analysing relations in small rural communities. He was elected to the Académie Française in 1968.

[MHK]

Arlequin, or Harlequin, is one of the most popular and ubiquitous stage figures from the 16th to the 19th c. Originating in Italian popular comedy (*commedia dell'arte*), he became acclimatized in France in the 17th c. and figured in innumerable comedies over the next century. There were many famous interpreters of the role, particularly *Molière's contemporary Domenico Biancolelli. His main home was the *Comédie-Italienne, where *Marivaux wrote for him, but he was also a favourite at the *théâtres de la *foire* [see PIRON]. Throughout his long life, Arlequin wore the familiar multicoloured costume and generally carried a wooden *latte*; at the beginning he wore a hirsute half-mask as a figure of animality, and was altogether less refined than in later incarnations. *Marmontel sums up his appeal in these words: 'The true model of his performance is the suppleness, agility, grace of a kitten, with a rough exterior which adds to the delight of his action; his role is that of a patient servant, loyal, credulous, greedy, always amorous, always getting his master or himself into a scrape, who weeps and dries his tears, with the ease of a child, whose grief is as amusing as his joy.' [PF]

Arlequin poli par l'amour, see MARIVAUX.

ARLETTY (1898–1992). The seductively world-weary queen of French screen acting, notably for *Carné in *Le Jour se lève* (1939) and *Les Enfants du paradis* (1945). Her richly sardonic voice was admirably suited to *Prévert's dialogues. Her career was badly affected by her affairs with German soldiers under the Occupation. [KAR]

ARLINCOURT, Charles Victor-Prévost, vicomte d' (1789–1856). Highly popular novelist of the Restoration and July Monarchy. His greatest success was *Le Solitaire* (1821).

Armagnacs and Burgundians. Parties which fought for power during the reign of Charles VI. The Armagnacs supported the king's younger brother, the duke of Orléans; the Burgundians favoured his cousin, Jean sans Peur, duke of Burgundy, and allied themselves with the English forces of Henry V [see HUNDRED YEARS WAR].

Armance (1827). *Stendhal's first novel. The noble Octave de Malivert is in love with his cousin Armance de Zohiloff. The strange and beautifully written story plots the psychological vicissitudes of their love, set against a satirically observed background of aristocratic society. The two lovers are typically Stendhalian superior beings, but the secret of Octave's eccentric melancholy, never disclosed to Armance or to the reader, but evident from the author's correspondence, is that he is impotent. After a brief 'mariage blanc', he takes poison and dies; Armance retires to a convent. [PF]

Army, Navy, Military Service. Until the middle years of the 17th c. the French army retained the characteristics of the *feudal system. Its recruitment was essentially feudal and seigneurial, with large bodies of mercenaries after 1445 to supplement these levies. The nobility responded more or less unwillingly to a call to arms—the *ban* and *arrière-ban*—and noble captains enrolled their servants as serving men at arms. Such a force was unreliable for the king, as it owed allegiance to other great lords whose interests might differ, and the troops were undisciplined. Pay was infrequent and they were expected to live off the land, taking from friend and foe alike and terrorizing town and countryside. The same could be said of mercenaries, except that they could be hired by the king who had more money than any single other lord. Active French involvement in the Thirty Years War led to a rapid expan-

sion in the numbers of men-at-arms, from 20,000 to about 150,000, and attempts at reform.

During the reign of *Louis XIV the secretary of state for war, Le Tellier, and his son *Louvois made great efforts to ensure promotion by seniority—which was difficult when officers bought their charge and often ended up out of pocket during campaigns. They did transform an almost privatized army into an army of the state and they strengthened discipline, by trying to pay officers more fairly, by building barracks for frontier garrisons, setting up supply depots, and promoting brutal punishments for infractions. Proper regiments were formed, company size was reduced to 40 men, with battalions of 15 companies, and specialized corps of grenadiers, fusiliers, and artillery were organized. The huge armies of the later wars of Louis XIV, 300,000–400,000 men, were made possible by conscription in the form of the *milice*, and even the peacetime army of the 18th c. numbered around 200,000, now predominantly infantry. Desertion remained frequent as conditions, though improved, were still harsh, and it was always the north-east and the eastern frontier provinces that provided the bulk of the recruits—those areas which suffered from invasion. The officer corps was increasingly aristocratic as military schools closed their doors to commoners and the Ségur ordinance of 1781 required four quarters of nobility (i.e. unmixed noble origins) for officers in certain regiments.

The navy suffered in comparison with the army, for although sporadic attempts were made before the 18th c. to organize one, its permanent establishment remained small. In the 16th c. it was no more than an hierarchy of officers and a small galley fleet. Ships of the line were run down in peacetime, and when war came private vessels were commissioned and the merchant marine put under colours. *Colbert and his later successors built up a naval force that numbered during the American War 79 ships of the line and 86 frigates.

If the *Revolution brought implementation of *ancien régime* reforms it also generated a transformation in the spirit of the armed forces. The officer corps emigrated in large numbers, conscription in the form of the *levée en masse* was instituted in 1793, and the army became a citizen army of patriots.

[PRC]

The ideal of the citizen army survived until the mid-20th c. For much of the 19th c. conscription into the army continued to be by lot, and it was still possible for richer young men to 'buy a man' in order to escape lengthy military service. Under the Third Republic compulsory male military service, although the subject of fierce political argument, was generally seen as an essential element in *republican culture, turning 'peasants into Frenchmen' (to use the title of a 1979 book by Eugen Weber). The wars of the 20th c. have been fought by armies consisting of regular soldiers, mercenaries (in the *Légion Etrangère), and conscripts. The use of conscripts in the *Algerian War, however, provoked considerable resistance to military service, since little provision was made for conscientious objection.

The regular army, on the other hand, has generally been on the right of the political spectrum. Since *Napoleon Bonaparte, France has seen a number of authoritarian military figures (*Napoleon III, *Boulanger, *Pétain, de *Gaulle) emerge as political leaders at moments of crisis; some historians have referred to this phenomenon as 'Caesarism'. The *Dreyfus Affair in particular showed the army establishment aligning itself with the monarchists and *Bonapartists against the republican forces of the Left.   [PF]

ARNAUD, Baculard d', see BACULARD D'ARNAUD.

ARNAUD, Georges (pseud. of Henri Girard) (b. 1918). French novelist, dramatist, and documentary reporter. His most famous work is the novel *Le Salaire de la peur* (1949), based on his experiences in South America (1947–9). An active critic of social injustices, Arnaud created a Hemingwayesque style marked by cinematic and journalistic influences.
                                                      [AHB]

ARNAULD, Antoine (1612–94). The youngest brother of Robert *Arnauld d'Andilly, he was a brilliant scholar who switched from law to theology under *Saint-Cyran's influence, becoming a doctor of the *Sorbonne in 1641. His career as the leading *Jansenist theologian and controversialist earned him the title 'le grand Arnauld'. In *De la fréquente communion* (1643) he defended Saint-Cyran's ideas, advocated a return to the purity and simplicity of early Christianity, and emphasized the need for true contrition before the sacrament of the Eucharist. Meanwhile, the controversy concerning Jansenius's *Augustinus* continued. In two works entitled *Apologie de M. Jansénius* (1643 and 1644), Arnauld supported Jansenius's arguments against sufficient grace and his teaching on reprobation (and, by implication, predestination). He also defended Jansenius in *Apologie pour les saints Pères de l'Église, défenseurs de la grâce de Jésus-Christ* (1651).

In 1653 five propositions allegedly taken from the *Augustinus* were condemned by Pope Innocent X. In reply, the Jansenists sought to distinguish between *droit* (were the propositions heretical?) and *fait* (were they part of the teaching of Jansenius?). This was the distinction made by Arnauld in the pamphlet *Lettre d'un docteur de Sorbonne à une personne de condition* (1655) and in a quarto volume, *Seconde Lettre à un duc et pair* (1656). The Sorbonne censured two of Arnauld's propositions and, despite the intervention of *Pascal, dismissed him. For the next 12 years he remained largely in hiding, but wrote tirelessly in defence of a strict Augustinianism. He also collaborated with *Lancelot and *Nicole, respectively, in publishing two very influential works, a *Grammaire*

générale et raisonnée (1660) and *La Logique, ou l'Art de penser* (1662). After the election of Pope Clement IX, the Jansenists experienced a period of respite between 1668 and 1679, during which Arnauld and Nicole wrote the anti-Protestant *Perpétuité de la foi de l'Église touchant l'Eucharistie* (1669–74).

In 1679 Louis XIV resumed his persecution of the *Port-Royalists, with the result that Arnauld spent his last 15 years in exile in the Spanish Low Countries and Holland. He continued to publish largely anonymous writings in defence of the Mons New Testament, in favour of a vernacular *Bible, against William of Orange, *Malebranche, and various Protestant writers. Above all, he pursued his campaign against the Jesuits in six volumes (1690–3 and 1695) which continued Pontchâteau's *Morale pratique des Jésuites représentée en plusieurs histoires arrivées dans toutes les parties du monde*.

Arnauld's sisters (Mère *Angélique de Sainte-Madeleine and Mère Agnès de Saint-Paul) and his niece (Mère *Angélique de Saint-Jean) were all abbesses of Port-Royal.   [JC]

ARNAULD D'ANDILLY, Robert (1588–1674). The eldest member of the Arnauld family to be closely identified with *Port-Royal. He married in 1613. Five of his daughters became nuns at Port-Royal and one son was a *solitaire* there. He held a series of court appointments but in 1645, eight years after his wife's death, he himself retired permanently to Port-Royal. He defended Port-Royal and the cause of *Jansenism, not least in direct and indirect correspondence with *Mazarin. He contributed to the evolution of French prose style in the 17th c. and produced much-admired translations of Augustine, Josephus, Teresa of Avila, etc.   [JC]

ARNAUT DANIEL (*fl. c*.1180–95). *Troubadour and impoverished minor nobleman from the Périgord. His 18 or 19 surviving songs are among the most virtuoso of the whole troubadour tradition; they were praised for their 'rare rhymes' in his *vida*, for their craftsmanship by Dante. Composing exclusively on the theme of love, Arnaut specialized in interweaving different registers of language—religious, technical, erotic, even comic—to produce a rich and initially somewhat impenetrable text whose artfulness was further enhanced by outrageously ambitious metrical schemes.   [SK]

Arnolphe. The comic protagonist of Molière's *L'École des femmes*.

ARNOTHY, Christine (b. 1930). French novelist whose first book, *J'ai quinze ans et je ne veux pas mourir* (1954), is an autobiographical account of the siege of Budapest in 1945. Later novels focusing on social and psychological analysis include *Toutes les chances plus une* (1980), dealing with the milieu of politics, and *Vent africain* (1989), set in California and Kenya.   [EAF]

ARON, Raymond (1905–83). French liberal sociologist and journalist. Aron studied philosophy at the *École Normale Supérieure and, in 1930–3, in Germany, introducing his close friend *Sartre to Husserl's *phenomenology. He also introduced Weberian ideas into French sociology. After spending the war in London as editor of *France libre*, he wrote for *Combat*, and in 1947 moved to *Le *Figaro*, where for 30 years he wrote a regular column arguing liberal and utilitarian centre-right positions. He combined prolific journalism with an academic career, and in 1955 became professor of sociology at the Sorbonne. He wrote extensively on the philosophy of history and the history of sociological thought, and his *Dix-huit leçons sur la société industrielle* (1963) popularized non-Marxist notions of the industrial society, economic growth, and structural change. He is particularly known for his polemics with Sartre and other left-wing intellectuals: his *L'Opium des intellectuels* (1955) and *Marxismes imaginaires* (1970) attacked as pure myth-making their attachment to Marxism, the Left, revolution, and the proletariat. They were, he argued, more interested in denouncing the world than in changing it. Hostile to the student movement in *May 1968 and to *Mitterrand's presidential candidacy in 1981, Aron none the less professed more affinity with those he criticized than with the intellectuals of the *Nouvelle Droite who took up his ideas.   [MHK]

AROUET, original name of *Voltaire.

ARRABAL, Fernando (b. 1932). Spanish-born playwright, film-maker, and novelist, resident in France since 1955. Profoundly influenced by a traumatic childhood in Spain during the Civil War, his work has a marked autobiographical basis. It has been likened to a gallery of private fantasies in which sado-masochistic images, neurotic obsessions (notably the image of a castratory mother-figure), and scatological fantasies are recurrent themes.

Before achieving notoriety in the 1960s he emerged in the late 1950s as the author of short *'absurdist' plays, of which the best known are *Pique-nique en campagne* (performed 1959), *Le Tricycle* (1963), and *Fando et Lis* (1964). With their stark situations and simple language, they are unpretentious plays expressing the loneliness of the individual in the face of a complex and hostile world. These tendencies are shown to best effect in *Le Cimetière des voitures* (written 1955, produced 1966), his first full-length play and the one most frequently performed.

In the 1960s his work acquired a more spectacular, baroque character. He developed an idea of theatre as a festive ceremony expressing the cruelty and confusion of life, but underpinned by a precise mathematical construction. He called these 'Panique' plays, after the movement he founded with Jodorowsky, Topor, and Sternberg. Of his many 'Panique' plays of the 1960s, including *La Grande Cérémonie*, *Le Jardin des délices*, and

L'Architecte et l'empereur d'Assyrie, the most successful is the last, a Freudian black comedy which dramatizes the fantasies and obsessions of two men marooned together on a desert island.

His experiences in prison in Spain, where he was arrested for blasphemy while on a visit in 1967, and the events of *May 1968, gave his subsequent work a political orientation. Plays such as *Et ils passèrent des menottes aux fleurs* (1967) and *L'Aurore rouge et noire* (May 1968) employ free imagistic techniques to depict provocative tableaux of repression and intolerance.

Of his large output (17 volumes of theatre up to 1987), a small number of plays have emerged as modern classics of their genre. While some of his plays fail to rise above exhibitionism, the best attain a powerful mythic dimension. Significantly, the most influential productions of his plays have been by the Latin-American directors *Garcia, *Lavelli, and *Savary, each of whom, in differing ways, has created bold stage images to express the ritualistic nightmare qualities of his plays. His first film, *Viva la muerte* (1971), depicting his childhood during the Civil War, is a masterpiece of surrealist cinema.
[DWW]

See A. Schifres, *Entretiens arec Arrabal* (1969); A. Berenguer, *L'Exil et la cérémonie* (1977); P. Podol, *Fernando Arrabal* (1978).

Arras, in north-eastern France, was especially important in the 12th and 13th c., when, thanks to the growth of the drapery trade and subsequently banking, it was one of the first French cities to have a strong bourgeoisie willing to patronize the arts, and particularly poetry, music, and drama. The output of its poets and musicians, e.g. *Adam de la Halle and Jehan *Bodel, and its industrial strength made Arras (and its dialect, Picard) a serious rival to Paris, until internal dissensions weakened it. The large number of professional entertainers in Arras led to the formation of the influential *Confréric des Jongleurs et Bourgeois d'Arras.   [GAR]

ARS, Le Curé d', see SERMON, 3.

Arsenal, L', see BIBLIOTHÈQUE DE L'ARSENAL.

Arsène Guillot, see MÉRIMÉE.

Arsène Lupin. Hero of popular detective novels by Maurice Leblanc.

Artagnan, Mémoires de M. d', see TROIS MOUSQUETAIRES, LES.

Artamène, ou le Grand Cyrus. Immense (15,000-page) novel by Madeleine de *Scudéry published in 10 instalments between 1649 and 1653. *Artamène* realizes the potential of the *roman héroïque*, the dominant form in the first half of the 17th c., when Scudéry was its leading practitioner. This version of the life of Cyrus the Great is both carefully documented—Scudéry's sources, notably Xenophon's *Cyropaedia*, are evident—and heavily novelistic: virtually all the great hero's actions are motivated by love for his beloved Mandane.

Before it closes on Cyrus's coronation and union with Mandane, the novel features endless twists—Cyrus is long disguised as Artamène; Mandane is repeatedly carried off—to keep the lovers apart. The plot is most frequently interrupted when one character tells another's story. Most of the final volume is devoted to 'The Story of Sappho', an episode which is simultaneously Sappho's first modern biography and a recreation of the life of Scudéry, often called 'Sapho'.

This simultaneity was the essence of *Artamène's* vast initial success. Contemporary readers found the historical setting exotic and pedagogical. They also read Cyrus's adventures as a thinly veiled recreation of the *Fronde, the contemporary civil war that blended military and amorous exploits in proportions similar to *Artamène's*. [JDeJ]

ARTAUD, Antonin (1896–1948). French poet, playwright, and theoretician of the theatre. Plagued by ill health and mental instability from an early age, he began writing poetry at school and joined *Lugné-Poë's Théâtre de l'Œuvre as an actor in 1920. He subsequently established himself as a man of the theatre with the companies of *Dullin and *Pitoëff, though his extravagance sometimes caused conflict. He was also to do a great deal of acting for the cinema, notably as Marat in *Gance's *Napoléon*. In 1924 he joined the *Surrealist movement and in 1926 founded the short-lived but controversial Théâtre Alfred Jarry with Roger *Vitrac.

A turning-point occurred for Artaud in 1931, when he witnessed Balinese dancers at the Colonial Exhibition in Paris. He published an article on the performance, which seemed to him to offer an alternative to decadent Western theatre. This was the first of a series of essays published in 1938 as *Le Théâtre et son double*. In 'Le Théâtre et la peste' and 'Le Théâtre de la cruauté' he expressed ideas which were to have a profound and lasting influence on the development of modern drama, arguing against the lifeless psychological, analytical content of the Western tradition and proclaiming the need for forms of theatre which inflicted an emotional, physiological contagion on the audience. He sought to establish that the essence of theatre was a type of delirium calling up the dark forces in humanity and nature. It is thus a challenge to civilization and ethics, relating to primitive levels of experience and operating on the stage through gesture, movement, lighting, colour, and music rather than through words.

In the mid-1930s Artaud struggled for money to establish a theatre where he could put his ideas into practice, and wrote a book on Heliogabalus, the mad Roman emperor, as well as outlines of plays to illustrate his method. In 1935 he managed to stage *Les Cenci*, based on the tragedy by Shelley, and full of blood, rape, incest, and murder; it was greeted with widespread incomprehension. None the less, his programme for a new type of theatre, revolutionizing everything from the architecture to the training of the actors, was to shape the work of a range of directors including *Brook and *Barrault. His life was dogged by mental illness and drug addiction; the anguish he sought to express through poetry and other writings made of him a modern visionary and a martyr to his art. [DHW]

See P. Virmaux, *Antonin Artaud et le théâtre* (1970); M. Esslin, *Antonin Artaud* (1976).

Art Criticism. In France, from the mid-18th to the late 19th c., art criticism was indissociably linked to the Salons. These were government-sponsored exhibitions, first held in 1667 on *Colbert's initiative and thereafter at irregular intervals until 1737, from when they were held either annually or biennially. From 1699 they had taken place in the Salon Carré of the Louvre, hence the name which remained in use even after the exhibition had been forced to change venues (in the mid-19th c.) as the need for greater exhibition space grew: by then the Salon had become the most important exhibition of contemporary art in Europe.

Initially reserved for the painters of the *Académie Royale de Peinture et de Sculpture, the Salon was opened to all artists in 1791. Seven years later it was placed under the control of a selection committee chosen by the government. Since the members of this committee were also the professors of the Academy, the Salon became the showcase for what was in effect a state-controlled monopoly of the production and evaluation of art. The expansion of the art market, the growing diversity of public tastes in art, the increased numbers of painters (and, therefore, of works rejected by the jury) eventually made this monopoly untenable, and in 1880 the state handed over control of the Salon to the Société des Artistes Français.

Deprived of official patronage, undermined by *Impressionism's challenge to its authority, and exposed to competition from exhibitions organized by dealers, private galleries, and artists themselves, the official Salon was unable to sustain its privileged position. The literary genre of Salon criticism in turn gave way to the increasingly professionalized literature of art necessitated by the proliferation and diversification of the avant-garde in painting from the beginning of the 20th c.

The literary genre of art criticism emerged in the mid-18th c. in response to the increased interest generated from 1737 by the regularity of the Salon exhibitions. In the 150 years which followed, the development of the press together with that of the art market transformed the demand for Salon reviews. For two main reasons the history of this Salon literature has still to be written. The first is that until quite recently art history considered it to be an irrelevant by-product of an academic system of painting discredited by the emergence of the modernist tradition from Impressionism onwards. The second is that, from an early stage in the 19th c., Salon literature had begun to establish its own canon, with the result that its histories have tended to focus on a small number of major figures: *Diderot, known throughout the 19th c. as 'le père de la critique d'art', whose Salons (written between 1759 and 1781 for the *Correspondance littéraire) were published in 1818, and his successors *Baudelaire, the *Goncourts, and *Zola.

In art criticism the central question is that of the nature of the transfer of image to words. For Diderot the obligation to recreate the painting, in the imagination of readers unable to see it demanded 'une variété de style qui répondît à la variété des pinceaux' (Salon de 1763), the assimilation of the principles of representation which governed the painting, and the creation of a verbal analogue by means of which the reader might realize the transfer in the opposite direction. Within the academic tradition this system was based on principles of composition established in terms of a hierarchy of subjects whose summit was occupied by those derived from Greek and Roman mythology. In these cases the transfer from image to word was facilitated by the existence of a classical source which the painting illustrated and to which the critic could refer to evaluate the pictorial performance of the text. At the other end of the scale was still life; devoid of any ennobling text, this confronted the critic with the problem of verbalizing that for which no system of discourse existed. Diderot was defeated by the problem in the Salon of 1763 when faced with the work of *Chardin—'On n'entend rien à cette magie'—only for this defeat to become a posthumous triumph when, 100 years later, changes in the artistic field gave a new status to still life and to a discourse which stressed the self-referential function of the material signs of art at the expense of their narrative function.

The critic's role as intermediary between painter and public became a rich source of friction between critic and painter, each dependent on the other for recognition of his or her activity but each vying with the other for jurisdiction over the artistic field. From *Delacroix onwards, the challenge to the authority of the academic system focused on the ambition to free the expressive potential of the medium from the subordinate role in the creation of narratives to which the academic system restricted it. A new role and significance was acquired in this process by colour, which confronted the critic with the limitations of discourse at the very time when literary *Romanticism was creating a poetic art criticism which threatened to channel the artist's exploration of form into new types of subordination to language. Baudelaire's achievement in his art criticism is to have integrated his understanding of the formal systems at work in the art of Delacroix and *Guys within a series of theoretical concepts which gave their formal research the weight needed to enter the modernist mainstream. Quite different but no less historically significant is the criticism of his great contemporary *Gautier, whose engagement with the visual arts throughout the crucial period from the July Monarchy to the Second Empire constitutes an anthology of the methodological and rhetorical strategies available to the 19th-c. salonnier.

With the demise of the official Salon and of the literary genre of art criticism derived from it, 20th-c. writers were able to explore their interest in the visual arts within a broader framework. As a result, their writing has taken many different forms. The most notable examples include *Valéry (on *Degas), *Claudel (Oriental art), *Saint-John Perse (*Braque), *Ponge (Braque, Chardin), *Malraux (in Les Voix du silence), *Barthes (L'Empire des signes), *Butor (Les Mots dans la peinture), while among 20th-c. writers, *Michaux represents to an unusual degree the practice of interrelating literature and the visual arts.

[JK]

Art de parler, De l', see LAMY.

Art d'être grand-père, L' (1877). Poetic collection by Victor *Hugo. *Sartre described his own Hugolian grandfather (in Les Mots) as 'la victime de deux techniques récemment inventées: l'art du photographe et l'art d'être grand-père'.

Arthénice. The name (an anagram of Catherine) by which Madame de *Rambouillet was known in her circle.

Arthur. Unlike his supposed historical prototype, the 6th-c. warrior chieftain of the Britons, the King Arthur of literature is above all the paragon of chivalric courtesy. His figure looms large over the *matière de Bretagne and French courtly romance. He and his court, the knights of the Round Table, are the touchstones of an ethos of refined chivalry, combining amorous and military service, set in a Golden Age. On to this, the medieval aristocracy projected its idealized self-image. The change in Arthur's role away from heroic combatant to justice-loving monarch presiding over a leisured society is embryonic in *Geoffrey of Monmouth, further emphasized by the time of *Wace's Brut, and more or less complete by the time of *Chrétien de Troyes, in whose romances he is an often somewhat passive, background figure representative of an older order. Although he continues to provide military leadership in later romances, his status is inevitably compromised by his wife Guenièvre's adulterous relationship with *Lancelot, which in La *Mort le roi Artu (c.1230) is one of the factors that contribute to the collapse of the Arthurian world. [IS]

ARTOIS, comte d', see CHARLES X.

Art poétique, L'

Art poétique, L'. Title used by *Boileau, *Peletier du Mans, *Vauquelin de la Fresnaye, and *Verlaine, among others.

Art pour l'art, L'. The theoretical origins of 'art for art's sake' lie in late 18th-c. German aesthetics and idealist philosophy. In France, anti-mimetic theories of the 'beau idéal' were relayed by *Quatremère de Quincy, *Cousin, and *Jouffroy. But the expression 'l'art pour l'art' is most strongly associated with the aggressive aestheticism that emerged in France after the 1830 Revolution, in opposition not only to the utilitarianism and philistinism of the new bourgeois regime, but also to the growing insistence from utopian socialists and humanitarians that literature and art should serve the interests of the repressed and immiserated majority and work for the progress of humanity. Gautier's preface to *Mademoiselle de Maupin* (1835) is the key text, but its militant aestheticism was to underpin avant-garde culture through the *fin de siècle* and into modernism. The notorious separation of form from content was also destined to become an obsessive preoccupation in 20th-c. literary criticism.   [BR]

Aspremont. Late 12th-c. *chanson de geste* celebrating the youthful exploits of *Roland prior to Rencesvals. The large number of surviving *Anglo-Norman manuscripts suggests that it was particularly popular in England. The poem ends with warnings of the rebellion against Charlemagne by Gurart de Fraite, a figure related to (and perhaps identical with) *Girart de Vienne and *Girart de Roussillon.   [SK]

Assemblée Constituante, Assemblée Législative, see REVOLUTION, I; NATIONAL ASSEMBLIES.

Assignats. Treasury bills first issued by the Revolutionary government in 1790, originally guaranteed by nationalized property, particularly that of the Church. They soon became simply paper money and depreciated dramatically.

Assimilation, see COLONIZATION.

Assommoir, L'. Novel by *Zola, published in 1877 and considered one of his finest literary achievements. Set in a working-class district in the north of Paris, it is the seventh of the *Rougon-Macquart series and tells of the misfortunes of Gervaise, a laundress, the daughter of Antoine Macquart and the mother of other significant characters in the novel cycle: Nana (in *Nana), Étienne Lantier (in *Germinal), Claude Lantier (in Le *Ventre de Paris and L'*Œuvre), and Jacques Lantier (in La *Bête humaine). Abandoned by Lantier at the beginning of the novel, the virtuous and hard-working Gervaise marries a slater, Coupeau, and their household prospers for a while. A daughter, Anna, is born. But Coupeau has a dramatic fall and, disgruntled at his fate, turns

to drink. Though her finances are depleted, Gervaise takes on a laundry of her own with the help of an admirer, Goujet. But, when Lantier returns and worms his way into the household, with Coupeau ever the worse for drink, the burdens of this *ménage à trois*, her own indulgences, and the growing hostility of her neighbours bring about Gervaise's ruin and her terrible physical and moral degradation. She also turns to drink; Coupeau dies in the throes of *delirium tremens* in a hospital; Anna (Nana) takes to prostitution; and Gervaise, reduced to a life of utmost squalor, dies of starvation. The novel is noteworthy for its scenes of popular life, its poignant and intense dramatic effects, its rigorous design, its symbolic and mythic configurations, and its innovative narrative techniques.   [DB]

ASSOUCY, Charles Coypeau d' (1605–77). Associate of *Cyrano de Bergerac and author of songs and *burlesque writings, including the *Aventures du sieur d'Assoucy* (1677), an account of his wanderings and misadventures.

Astérix. A comic strip created for the first number of *Pilote* (20 October 1959) by the writer René Goscinny and the artist Albert Uderzo. By the time Goscinny died in 1977, 24 albums had been published; Uderzo continued to produce the series on his own (e.g. *Le Fils d'Astérix*, 1983; *Astérix chez Rahâzade*, 1987). The first album, *Astérix le Gaulois* (1961), sets the pattern: successful Gallic resistance to the Roman occupation reverses history and allows revenge, and this resistance is led by unlikely anti-heroes in a burlesque epic which promotes, albeit ironically and self-parodically, chauvinistic and stereotyped attitudes. The text is rich in puns and learned allusion, as are the graphics. Astérix is an impudent answer to the immediately post-war influx of American supermen, the humble asterisk to their inflated stardom.   [CS]

Astragale, L', see SARRAZIN.

Astrate, see QUINAULT.

Astrée L'. Novel by Honoré d'*Urfé, published 1607–27 and widely seen as the culmination of the *pastoral tradition in France. It is set in 5th-c. Gaul and traces Céladon's troubled courtship of Astrée who, at the start of the novel, banishes him from her sight in the mistaken belief that he is unfaithful. Céladon attempts to kill himself in despair, builds a temple in the forest dedicated to his beloved, and is finally persuaded to return to her in the disguise of a girl. Around this classic plot of love, fidelity, and misunderstanding, d'Urfé constructs a network of other tales. Attitudes as varied as obsession and indifference, pride and insecurity, jealousy and timidity are explored in numerous different relationships, taking further the meditations on the nature of love so frequent in earlier pastoral fiction.

D'Urfé's analysis, both in the tales themselves and in the more extensive conversations and debates often inspired by them, is remarkable for its range and subtlety. He gives voice to a moral idealism which sees in love a means of spiritual transformation based on knowledge, respect, and aspiration, but he is clearly conscious too of all that is uncontrollably instinctive, selfish, and sensual in it. The scheming Polémas, the haughtily insecure Galathée, and the trenchantly epicurean Hylas all contrast with and complement the idealizing attitudes of the druid Adamas or the platonizing Silvandre; in the depiction of Céladon's relationship with Astrée we see how chaste admiration may coexist with self-doubt, misjudgement, and barely suppressed physical longing.

An early draft of the text is known to date from the 1590s, but the first volume was not published until 1607; this was followed by two further volumes in 1610 and 1619. Perhaps inevitably, the novel, which explores all that is shifting in human feelings and relationships, was left unfinished. After d'Urfé's death, his secretary *Baro completed and published the incomplete fourth part in 1627, and produced in the following year a fifth volume, derived purportedly from the author's notes. Few pastoral novels were written in the wake of this text—by the 1630s a taste for the quasi-historical *roman héroïque* was already taking hold—but it had a profound influence on the art and sensibility of the age. It continued to be read long into the 18th c.   [GJM]

See J. Ehrmann, *Un paradis désespéré* (1963); M. Gaume, *Les Inspirations et les sources d'Honoré d'Urfé* (1977); M. Bertaud, *L'Astrée et Polexandre* (1986).

Atala (1801). A tale by *Chateaubriand, which he originally intended to be part of *Les Natchez*, then integrated into his *Génie du christianisme*, but first published separately. Its instant success can be explained by its combination of lush North American exoticism, fatal passion, and religious sentiment, though the plot itself is not too edifying. Chactas, a Natchez who has been to France and was raised by the Christian Lopez, is captured by an enemy tribe who plan to kill him, but is saved by the young Atala, half-Spanish (Lopez is her father) and Christian, who has fallen in love with him. They flee, and after long wanderings are found in a storm by père Aubry, a French missionary who has founded a utopian Christian Indian enclave. Atala, alas, cannot marry Chactas for she has taken a vow of chastity, so she commits suicide by poison. The burial scene is particularly pathetic. The story is embedded in a series of frameworks; it is told by the blind, elderly Chactas to *René, and then transmitted across the years to the author-narrator, so that we learn also of the tragic end of Aubry, massacred by the Indians.   [FPB]

Ateliers nationaux. Workshops created to provide work for the unemployed after the Revolution of 1848 [see REPUBLICS, 2]; their speedy abolition was one of the factors provoking the June Days.

Athalie. *Racine's last tragedy (1691), composed like *Esther* for performance at *Saint-Cyr. It is a five-act play, magnificently written, with choruses between the acts. Based on accounts in the books of Kings and Chronicles, it tells of the overthrow of the usurper Athaliah by forces loyal to the house of David and the boy king Joas (a rare stage appearance by a child in 17th-c. theatre). The rising is managed by the inflexible high priest Joad, but the influence of Jehovah is felt throughout the play. It can be read either as the tragedy of the queen, the latest stage in the unending feud of two warring camps, or as a triumphal hymn to the true God, whose purposes are fulfilled by the crowning of Joas, the precursor of Christ. The play has also been interpreted as referring to contemporary events, in particular the English Revolution of 1688. It was greatly admired in the 18th and 19th c., even by those who, like *Voltaire, did not approve of its religious message.   [PF]

Athénée, L', see LYCÉE, LE.

Athos. One of the heroes of Dumas's *Les *Trois Mousquetaires*.

Atipa, roman guyanais, see WEST INDIES, 3.

Attila. Tragedy by Pierre *Corneille, first performed 1667. It is a play of love and ambition, culminating in the death of the hero from a bleeding nose.

AUBANEL, Théodore (1829–86). Foremost lyric poet of the *Félibrige; also dramatist, friend of *Mallarmé, admired by *Valéry. The rich head of a family printing business in Catholic Avignon, Aubanel began writing Provençal poetry after meeting Roumanille at a religious gathering. His love for working-class Jenny Manivet was thwarted by shyness and difference in status. Jenny entered a convent in 1854. Aubanel finally purged his five-year grief for 'Zani' in *La Mióugrano entreduberto* (1860), 49 sensitive, passionate poems in three sections, each ending with a Christian statement to comfort his bleeding heart (symbolized by the half-open pomegranate) from the memory of Zani in her red dress.

Acclaimed in Paris, the collection so enraged Avignon that Aubanel published nothing new until his play *Lou Pan dóu pecat* (1882, written 1863). Though his happy marriage, reflected in 'La Venus d'Arle' (written 1862), brought creative stability and recognition in the 1870s, Aubanel was fascinated by violence and the flesh. Some poems of *Li Fiho d'Avignoun* (1885, written 1866–7) express carnal desire; *Lou Pastre* (written 1866, staged 1960) and *Lou Raubatòri* (written 1872) concern rape and kidnapping. Misunderstood by the Félibrige and Avignon society, he died of apoplexy, leaving *inter alia* a posthumous collection, *Lou Rèire-Soulèu* (1899).

[PVD]

Aube, see ALBA.

AUBER, Daniel-François-Esprit (1782–1871). Composer, see OPERA; SCRIBE.

Auberon, see HUON DE BORDEAUX.

AUBERT, Jean-Louis, abbé (1731–1814). French journalist and critic, teacher at the *Collège de France, admired in his day as an author of fables.

AUBERT DE GASPÉ, Philippe (1786–1871). A colourful historical figure who collaborated with his son in writing the first French-Canadian novel, *L'Influence d'un livre* (1837), before producing, late in life, his own novel, *Les Anciens Canadiens* (1863), and a book of reminiscences, *Mémoires* (1866). The novel, clearly influenced by Sir Walter Scott, has a naïve charm and is as much a source of entertaining anecdotes about early French-Canadian society as the memoirs themselves. [SIL]

AUBIGNAC, François Hédelin, abbé d' (1604–76). French critic and dramatic theorist. A protégé of *Richelieu, he wrote poems, plays, and novels; from 1663 to 1671 he directed a semi-official Académie des Belles-Lettres. He was the author of essays on eloquence, and of *Conjectures académiques* (published 1715), in which he cast doubt on the existence of Homer. His most important work is *La Pratique du théâtre* (published 1657, written much earlier), the best summary of the *classical theory of tragedy; it contains detailed advice on ways of affecting an audience, stressing verisimilitude, the unities, and the rhetoric of the passions. [PF]

AUBIGNÉ, (Théodore) Agrippa d' (1552–1630). French poet, historian, satirist, and polemicist of the Protestant *Reformation, and also a long-serving soldier. He was educated in Paris and Geneva in both humanism and reformed doctrine. In 1560, after the Conjuration d'*Amboise, his father made him swear vengeance on the heads of those executed; he fought at Jarnac and in other battles and became a companion of Henri de Navarre (later *Henri IV). His love for Diane Salviati, niece of *Ronsard's Cassandre, was thwarted by her family and inspired his *Printemps* (*Hécatombe à Diane, Stances,* and *Odes*), written 1571–3, later repudiated as 'un printemps de péchés' and not published until 1874. In spite of some *Petrarchan preciosity, the evident sincerity of these poems and their basis in lived experience, together with the contrast between the serenity of love and the despair of rejection, conveyed by images of violence and war, continue to attract readers.

At the time of the *St Bartholomew's Day Massacre d'Aubigné was absent from Paris by chance, but this tragic event was of great psychological importance to him. During 1573–6 he joined Henri de Navarre in Paris and lived as a courtier, a life he later regretted. After being wounded at Castel-Jaloux in 1577, he broke with Henri and began to write *Les *Tragiques*, most of which was completed by 1579 and circulated in manuscript. He continued to fight for the cause until the conversion of Henri in 1593, which he had done his best to prevent. He then devoted his energies to Protestant assemblies. He continued to add to *Les Tragiques* after 1600, and published the book in 1616, and again, after condemnation by the Châtelet in 1620, with further additions in 1623.

D'Aubigné wrote another work, parallel to *Les Tragiques,* entitled *L'Histoire universelle*; he started it in 1601 and published it progressively from 1618 to 1620. This chronological prose version of some of the same events owes something to the historian de *Thou. D'Aubigné intended it to be more complete and impartial than *Les Tragiques,* but it is still passionately committed. In a lighter vein is the satirical prose work *Aventures du baron de Faeneste* (published 1617–30 and then not again until 1855), a picaresque novel which contrasts d'Aubigné himself, in the character of Enay (from the Greek *einai,* to be), with Faeneste (from *phainesthai,* to appear). The *Confession catholique du sieur de Sancy,* mostly written 1598–1600 but not published until 1660, is a court satire attacking Protestants who abjure their faith, directed primarily at Sancy, but also at cardinal *du Perron, who helped to convert him to Catholicism (this book has similarities with 'Princes' in *Les Tragiques*).

In 1620 d'Aubigné fled to Geneva after being involved in a conspiracy, and there he was entrusted with various military responsibilities. In 1628 he was present at the siege of La Rochelle. In the following year he composed his autobiography, *Sa vie à ses enfants,* and in 1630 (the year in which he died) he published his *Méditations sur les Psaumes* and *Petites Œuvres mêlées,* containing *Poésies religieuses* and *Psaumes en vers mesurés.* [PS]

See J. Bailbé, *Agrippa d'Aubigné. Poète des Tragiques* (1968); M. Soulié, *L'Inspiration biblique dans la poésie religieuse d'Agrippa d'Aubigné* (1977).

Au Bonheur des Dames. Novel by *Zola, published in 1883 and 11th in the *Rougon-Macquart series. This work depicts the Darwinian struggle, nominally during the *Second Empire, between small retail businesses and the new phenomenon of the department store. The enterprising Octave Mouret, the eldest son of François and Marthe Mouret and also the leading character in the previous novel of the series, *Pot-Bouille, transforms his wife's modest clothing business into a bustling and booming department store, putting to use his insights into the psychology of women's tastes and ruthlessly ruining his competitors in the business. He employs all the strategies of modern commerce to ensure the success of his enterprise. Though the novel is mainly of documentary interest as a story of modern commercialism and commodity fetishism, it contains a love story. A virtuous and energetic shop-girl, Denise Baudu, resisting Pamela-like the advances of the widowed and normally irresistible seducer Octave, is rewarded with reforms for her fellow workers and marriage to the boss. Zola called his novel 'le poème de l'activité moderne' and saw it as a vehicle for communicating a more positive view of life.   [DB]

AUBRY, Gilbert (b. 1942). Poet, and bishop of Reunion, whose collection *Rivages d'alizé* (1971) has been reprinted a number of times. His poetry is a vigourous yet conciliatory promotion of 'la Créolie' [see ALBANY]: 'Ici nous vivons de Créolie comme ailleurs de Négritude ou d'Occitanie.'   [BEJ]

Aucassin et Nicolette. One of the most delightful works of medieval fiction, this brief anonymous early 13th-c. tale is the unique instance of a *chantefable*, in which prose and assonanced verse are intermingled; it has been preserved in a single manuscript. Ostensibly a variation of the 'roman idyllique' such as **Floire et Blanchefleur*, the story recounts the forbidden love of Aucassin, son of a Christian count, for Nicolette, Saracen captive, and describes the perilous adventures the lovers undertake until their reunion and marriage. But the anonymous author's playful transformations of literary conventions are as remarkable as his style. We are treated to the sight of Aucassin refusing to fight until his father promises that he may hold Nicolette; to a scene where Nicolette bravely escapes from prison; to the courtly lovers' comic attempts to converse with shepherds; to the couple's fantastic adventures in the upside-down world of Torelore, and so on. The romance's clever mix of styles, generic registers, gender roles, and social classes exemplifies even as it gently derides the sophistication of courtly fiction.   [RLK]

Aude. Heroine of certain versions of *La Chanson de *Roland*, though her appearance in the most familiar version is only fleeting.

Au-dessus de la mêlée, see ROLLAND.

AUDIBERTI, Jacques (1899–1965). French poet, journalist, critic, novelist, and playwright. A fringe **Surrealist in the 1930s, recipient of the Prix Mallarmé for poetry in 1937, and author of some 30 novels, he was highly regarded by French critics for his erudition and his anti-war philosophy. Most of his monumental output has been eclipsed, whilst his standing as a playwright has grown steadily since his death. His work expresses a Manichean philosophy, which he called 'Abhumanism', an essentially dramatic vision of man and the universe, though in his plays it is often obscured by their verbal profusion.

His better plays, such as *Le Mal court* (winner of the Prix des Jeunes Compagnies in 1947), have an exuberant baroque texture suggesting a Surrealist **Claudel. Most of his plays have been staged by Georges Vital, whose acclaimed 1968 production of *Quoat Quoat* (first performed 1946) helped to rehabilitate Audiberti as a playwright. Other major plays include *La Fête noire* (1948), *Le Cavalier seul* (1955), *La Hobereaute* (1956), *L'Effet Glapion* (1959), *La Fourmi dans le corps* (1961).   [DWW]

AUDOUX, Marguerite (1863–1937). French novelist. During her deprived childhood in the Bourbonnais she worked as a shepherdess. Later she was a seamstress in Paris, where she knew Charles-Louis **Philippe and *Mirbeau. In 1910 she published the first and best of her novels, *Marie-Claire*, a deceptively naïve, linear account of the largely bitter experiences of an orphaned country-girl. Its subdued realism does fair justice to its subdued subject, although the writer hesitates to go below surfaces and organizes some of the sentimental situations into clichés.   [DAS]

AUDRY, Colette (1906–93). French writer and left-wing political activist; friend and colleague of Simone de *Beauvoir. She was a regular contributor of film criticism to *Les *Temps modernes*, author of critical essays on Blum (1955) and Sartre (1966), and won the Prix Médicis in 1962 for her first novel, *Derrière la barrière*.   [EAF]

AUGIER, Émile (1820–89). Successful French dramatist of the Second Empire who represents the 'école du bon sens', a reaction against the extravagances of Romantic drama and the superficiality of *Scribe. Beginning with a run of insipid plays in verse—*La Ciguë* (1844), *L'Aventurière* (1848), *Gabrielle* (1849)—he made his name with a succession of dramas about social problems. The lightest of these was *Le Gendre de Monsieur Poirier* (1854), a satire on the conflict between profligate nobility and thrifty bourgeoisie which echoes Scribe's sentimentality, facile patriotism, and love of happy endings. His later plays, well observed and skilfully constructed, are more searching studies of the social and economic conflicts of his day, though they accept too trustingly the conventional morality of his own class. *Le Mariage d'Olympe* (1855) is a critical study of the shadowy world of the *demi-monde*, while *Les Lionnes pauvres* (1858) tackles the problem of adultery. More forceful than these are his satirical attack on the press baron Vernouillet in *Les Effrontés* (1861) and his powerful exposure of the politics of clericalism in *Le Fils de Giboyer* (1862). Technically, he learned from Scribe's plotting but applied those skills to more serious ends.   [SBJ]

AUGIÉRAS, François (1925–71). French writer and painter. His striking autobiographical works, including *Le Vieillard et l'enfant* (1949, pseud. Abdallah

Chaamba), *Le Voyage des morts* (1959), and *Une adoles-cence au temps du Maréchal* (1968), are imbued with an atmosphere of often exotic homosexuality.   [DAS]

Augustinus, see JANSENISM.

AULNOY, Marie-Catherine Le Jumel de Barneville, comtesse d' (*c.*1650–1705). Writer of fiction and history, the latter being difficult to distinguish from the former. She had a turbulent married life, being suspected of trying to engineer the execution of her husband, 30 years her senior. Her writings on Spain (*Mémoires de la cour d'Espagne*, 1690; *Relation du voyage en Espagne*, 1690), ostensibly based on personal experience, are mainly plagiarized. Of her historical fiction, *Hypolite, Comte de Duglas* (1691) was immensely popular. Set in the England of Henry VIII, it is a swollen *nouvelle*, full of extravagant adventure, anticipating *Prévost in the sufferings of its star-crossed lovers (who are, however, united in a happy ending). Mme d'Aulnoy is remembered now for her fairy-tales. *Les Contes des fées* (1697) and *Les Contes nouveaux* (1698) contain some 30 stories in all, several of which have remained classics (*L'Oiseau bleu*, *La Chatte blanche*). Capitalizing on a current fashion (*Finette-Cendron* is an amalgam of *Perrault's *Le Petit Poucet* and *Cendrillon*), d'Aulnoy is more elaborately literary than Perrault, making plentiful use of fantastic metamorphoses and loading her stories with gold, jewels, and all kinds of exotic and extravagant accessories.   [PF]

Aurélia. *Nerval's autobiographical description of his Orphic descent into hell, his insanity, and his dreams, published in 1855, partly before his suicide, partly shortly thereafter. Unique in form and genre, the book is written in a poetic and yet disjunctive style, but many of the themes of both his dreams and his peregrinations in madness are echoes of his earlier writings and of the literary tradition. Marked by a sense of culpability towards the saving woman Aurélia, by conflict with his double and others, by doubts about religion, by a fear of the apocalyptic, the hero-protagonist finds reconciliation through fraternity with a double figure, and in a prose-poem section entitled 'Mémorables' he is pardoned, experiencing an epiphany of universal reconciliation and harmony. Much appreciated by the *Surrealists, the book is at the frontier of Romantic explorations of dreams and the irrational.   [FPB]

AURIER, Albert (1865–93). In his short life Aurier established himself as the leading authority on the visual arts within the French *Symbolist movement. A Neoplatonist and admirer of *Mallarmé, he promoted *Gauguin and *Van Gogh as the leaders of a Symbolist reaction to *Impressionism. His art criticism contains one of the first major definitions of the subjective, anti-realist trends which characterize much 20th-c. art.   [JK]

AUSONIUS, Decimus Magnus (*c.*310–90), see LATIN-ITY, 1.

Auteurs, Politique des, see CAHIERS DU CINÉMA.

Authorship (in the Middle Ages). The notion of vernacular authorship evolved with the growing importance of French as a written language during the later Middle Ages. Medieval views of authorship can be approached from various perspectives: the vocabulary used to refer to authors and authorial activity; the ways that authors represented the literary process; and the evidence of manuscript organization and illustration.

The numerous terms used by Old French writers to describe their authorial activity reflect the range of attitudes towards literary composition in the vernacular. The word *escrire* is not applied to the author of a text, being reserved for the activity of scribes. Often the author's activity is expressed in the word *faire*, implying the author as one who creates a text rather than one who duplicates written copies of it. Other terms also stress the identity of the author as one who finds or conceives an idea and works it out: *traire*, *imaginer*, and *trouver* and its nominal form *trouvère*. During the 12th and 13th c., the role of the author often blended with that of the performer. There is little distinction, for example, between *chanter* and *faire une chanson*. In the course of the later Middle Ages, however, a variety of terms came to express aspects of the technical craft of literary creation as distinct from performance, most of which stress a process of arranging and shaping the textual elements: *compiler*, *ordenner*, *former*. It is to be noted that such terms do not imply that the author has created the text *ex nihilo*; rather, the author is one who possesses the skills necessary to imagine a conceptual framework within which literary material can be artfully arranged. Lyric composition in the *formes fixes*, in particular, was portrayed less as a process of singing than as one of assembling words according to elaborate formal patterns. *Froissart even used the word *maçonner* for lyric composition: for him, the lyric poet was a verbal sculptor.

The importance of ordering, framing, and compiling in the literary process suggests that by the 14th c. the concept of vernacular authorship was moving away from that of performer and merging with that of writer. The terms *compiler* and *ordenner*, in particular, can refer to the act of literary creation, to the preparation of compendia and florilegia, and to the arrangement of anthology *manuscripts, ordinarily the domain of the scribe. That the medieval French poet should be thought of as the author of written texts, even of books, is an extremely important development in the history of French literature. This new status of the French author is reflected in the innovative application of the word *poète*—hitherto reserved for Latin authors—to Guillaume de *Machaut, in

*Deschamps's ballade commemorating Machaut's death (1377). The term was subsequently applied to *Jean de Meun, author of the second part of the *Roman de la Rose*. This shift in terminology is an important index of the growing status of French poetry as 'serious' literature, comparable to Latin letters, and of the concomitant rise in the status of the French versifier from story-teller or singer to authoritative poet and writer.

Medieval authors posit a variety of sources for their works; while these claims are sometimes fictional, they do serve to illustrate perspectives on the creative process. A medieval author may identify the origin of his or her writing in a pre-existing literary tradition, either written or oral; in the imagination or personal experience of an aristocratic patron; or in the author's own imagination or experience. Classical sources are common, both real—as in Jean de Meun's citations of Ovid, Lucan, *Boethius, and others—and fictional, such as the mysterious Latin book that supposedly provided the source for the prose *Tristan* and portions of the *Lancelot–Graal prose cycle. Acting (or posing) as translator, mediating between Latin letters and the French-speaking public, was a common stance for the medieval French author [see TRANSLATION]. In other instances, French verse might be used to preserve an oral Breton tradition, as in the *lais* of *Marie de France. In either case French literature was heir to previous traditions which it appropriated and adapted. The author was seen less as a creator or innovator than as one capable of making this material accessible to the French public, thereby participating in an unbroken tradition that bridged ancient and medieval cultures.

The medieval notion of authorship included not only the translation and adaptation of works in other languages, but also the revision or narrative continuation of works in French. Indeed, romance continuations are sometimes much longer than the text to which they are attached, and many are signed by name. In at least one case, that of the *Roman de la Rose*, the continuator, Jean de Meun, became far more famous than *Guillaume de Lorris, author of the original poem. It was fundamental to the medieval understanding of vernacular textuality that the literary text was never completely closed; it could always be reopened for continuation, interpolation, or other revision. As a result, the line between author, scribe, and *remanieur* can be extremely difficult to determine. It is not until the later Middle Ages, as French poets increasingly assumed responsibility for the written diffusion of their works, that we find a more stabilized textual tradition and a growing sense of the authority of the original text.

The role of the aristocratic patron is crucial to the representation of literary creation [see PATRONAGE]. The authors of both prose and verse romances often claimed to have received the source book, or the central idea, from their patron. In the narrative *dit*, especially popular in the late 13th and 14th c., the patron's own experiences may provide the subject-matter, with the author posing as witness and recorder. Both Machaut, in the *Fonteinne amoureuse* (*c*.1361), and Froissart in the *Prison amoureuse* (1372–3) and *Meliador* (1388), even claim to have incorporated lyric poetry written by a patron, a claim generally accepted only for the *Meliador*. An important aspect of the medieval concept of authorship is the author as collaborator with the patron, one who realizes the patron's ideas and who casts the patron's life in literary terms.

The author's own experiences, finally, are increasingly posited as literary material in the later Middle Ages, in works written in the tradition of the *Roman de la Rose*. When Guillaume de Lorris claimed his own dream as the subject of his romance, he was taking an unusual step, but subsequently dream-visions became a standard format, as did accounts of the narrator's adventures or misadventures in love. Allowing the narrator—closely identified with the author—to assume a central narrative role was an important step in late medieval French literature. It is part of the development towards a greater focus on the author as originator and crafter of the text, as one whose personal vision is expressed therein. The narrator/protagonist is often portrayed in the very act of writing and arranging the text or the anthology manuscript, a motif reflecting the growing emphasis on the author as writer and figure of authority.

These varying notions of the author are given visual shape in the author portraits that appear in manuscripts. As one might expect, *trouvères* and *troubadours are frequently portrayed as performers, sometimes with musical instruments; narrative poets are commonly represented holding or writing in a book. Lyric poets renowned for their learning, such as *Giraut de Borneil and *Adam de la Halle, were also sometimes portrayed with books. Both musical instrument and book are iconographic motifs rather than realistic details: *trouvères* did not necessarily play musical instruments, any more than a narrative poet would have composed texts by writing in a bound volume of blank parchment. What these pictures show is that the concept of the vernacular author included both the learned model of the scholarly writer and the performative model of the singer, reciter, or instrumentalist.

The organization of anthology manuscripts reflects changing attitudes towards the author. During the 12th and 13th c., manuscripts that were not simply miscellanies tended to be compiled according to generic classifications. Narrative texts—both *romance and *chanson de geste—were often arranged in an order corresponding to the internal chronology of the texts, resulting in the formation of narrative cycles. Authorship was rarely a factor in the compilation of such anthologies. In *lyric anthologies, on the other hand, no doubt due to the importance of the first person in lyric

Autobiography and Memoirs

discourse, songs were most commonly arranged by author. Author portraits are common in both French and Occitan *chansonniers*; many of the latter additionally contain the prose *vidas and *razos* that supply information concerning the identity of the poet and the genesis of his or her songs. While the *vidas* and *razos* must be regarded as largely fictional, and the portraits as stylized and conventional, such elements none the less serve to construct an authorial figure endowed with identifying features and located in a particular time and place. Still, non-lyric works by the same author were not included in the *chansonniers*; generic distinction outweighed the importance of authorship.

The earliest known example of a generically diverse collection of texts by a single author, arranged and presented as such, is the compilation of the complete works of Adam de la Halle—songs, motets, plays, and stanzaic verse—in the anthology manuscript Bibliothèque Nationale, fr. 25566, dating from the late 13th c. The earliest manuscripts containing the collected poems of *Rutebeuf date from the same period. The rise of the single-author codex, however, really takes place in the 14th c., beginning with the *dit* collections of such early 14th-c. poets as *Watriquet de Couvin and *Baudouin and Jean de Condé. The phenomenon is most fully represented by the great anthology manuscripts of Guillaume de Machaut, Jean Froissart, and *Christine de Pizan, carefully arranged and in some cases illuminated under the supervision of the author. The use of authorship as a basis for the compilation of anthology manuscripts reflects a strong sense of the text as primarily identified through its origins with a particular author, whose persona is strong enough to unite a diverse corpus and whose personal vision—informed by both learning and experience—is expressed therein. [For the post-medieval period see also ANONYMITY, PSEUDONYMS.]   [SJH]

See A. Minnis, *Medieval Theory of Authorship*, 2nd edn. (1988); S. Huot, *From Song to Book* (1987).

Autobiography and Memoirs. The word *autobiographie* was imported from Britain to France in the early 19th c. to designate a type of writing felt to be different from the traditional *mémoires*. The distinction between the two is not a hard-and-fast one; it has in fact been the object of some controversy in France since Philippe Lejeune proposed a precise and perhaps too exclusive definition of his subject in *L'Autobiographie en France* (1971). According to this, the writer of memoirs, usually a high-ranking or famous person, offers posterity a chronicle of his or her actions and an eyewitness account of contemporary people and events. Autobiography, on the other hand, implies the retrospective attempt to make sense of an inner destiny, the formation of a personality—and therefore almost always includes the story of the author's childhood (*récit d'enfance*).

Most narratives of the self written in France

before about 1750 fall into the former category, although such memoir-writers as Madame de *Staal and the duc de *Saint-Simon give a strong impression of their own personalities while recounting their memories, differing in this from the self-effacing medieval memorialists. *Montaigne is an exceptional case, but his prolonged introspection is not given narrative shape. Most memoirs, particularly those by men, are concerned with political or military life, but they may also depict high society and literary and artistic circles. These texts have been much used by historians: the 19th c. saw the massive publication of such generally unpublished memoirs in the *Collection des mémoires relatifs à l'histoire de France* of Petitot and Monmerqué (1819–29) and the *Nouvelle collection des mémoires pour servir à l'histoire de France* of Michaud and Poujolat (1836–8).

Among the most interesting of the innumerable memoirs of the *ancien régime* one may cite those of d'*Argenson, *Bassompierre, *Bernis, *Brantôme, *Commynes, *Hénault, *La Fare, *La Rochefoucauld, *Monluc, *Montpensier, *Motteville, *Nemours, *Retz, *Saint-Simon, *Staal, *Sully. The memoir tradition has continued in the 19th and 20th c. with the writings of such different figures as Raymond *Aron, *Beauvoir, *Berlioz, *Dumas *père*, *Genlis, *Guizot, *Herriot, André and Clara *Malraux, *Napoleon, Madame de *Rémusat, *Tocqueville, and Louise Weiss (*Mémoires d'une européenne*, 1968–76). The most remarkable modern memorialist is Charles de *Gaulle, whose skilfully crafted account of his destiny remains an essential (if suspect) source for historians.

A particular type of memoir, which may come closer to autobiography by its concentration on the inner life, is the account of a spiritual itinerary. The great models here are St Augustine and St Teresa of Avila. In French one can cite certain writers connected with *Port-Royal, such as Jean Hamon (*Relation de certaines circonstances de la vie de M. Hamon faite par lui-même*, 1702), the *Vie* of Antoinette Bourignon (1683), and in particular the autobiography of Madame *Guyon.

In 18th-c. France, one of the dominant forms of fiction was the *memoir-novel, in which a hero or heroine, sometimes of humble birth, describes his or her path through the difficulties of life. It seems likely that the popularity of this genre contributed to the development of modern autobiography. The founding text, Rousseau's *Confessions*, although its title proclaims a filiation with St Augustine, is in fact more similar to the narrations of *Lesage, *Marivaux, *Duclos, and *Prévost. What distinguishes Rousseau, apart from the quality of his writing, is his insistence on the inner life (*intus et in cute* is his epigraph), his willingness to reveal intimate secrets, and his stress on childhood. Something similar is found in the autobiographical texts of his younger contemporary *Restif de la Bretonne [see MONSIEUR NICOLAS] and his disciple Madame *Roland.

The *Confessions* tell the life of a commoner, albeit one who rose in the world through writing (*Jamerey-Duval and *Marmontel are comparable cases). From the late 18th c. there is a growing number of narratives of the lives of ordinary people who were not at all professional writers, from the glazier *Ménétra to Agricol Perdiguier (*Mémoires d'un compagnon*, 1853) to Émile *Guillaumin, Fadhma *Amrouche, or J.-B. Dumay (*Mémoires d'un militant ouvrier du Creusot, 1841–1905*, 1976). In a similar vein, the Breton writer *Hélias uses his memoirs to record the half-vanished rural culture of his native country. Recent historians have placed great value on the reports of such witnesses, often recorded orally. On the other hand, the literary genre of autobiography is dominated by the lives of writers. Important 19th-c. examples include *Quinet, *Sand, and *Renan; these are overshadowed by the *Vie de Henry Brulard* of Stendhal and the *Mémoires d'outre-tombe* of Chateaubriand. Both of these follow Rousseau's example in mingling the present and the past, thus blurring the distinction between autobiography and the *journal intime* which came to prominence at the same time [see DIARIES]. Chateaubriand's great work is at once memoirs and autobiography; it also contains a strong element of *travel writing, which in the *Romantic period began to take on an increasingly autobiographical character.

La Vie de Henry Brulard, as well as showing the way for much modern autobiography in its constant questioning of memory and self-knowledge, also anticipates later developments in presenting itself formally as a novel. In the 20th c. in particular, along with the growing favour for novels (often written in the first person) with a strong autobiographical element (*Proust, *Céline, *Sartre, *Duras, etc.), there has been a tendency to give the label *roman* to works which are really autobiographies (e.g. *Ernaux's *La Place* or *Camara Laye's *L'Enfant noir*). *Doubrovsky proposed the term 'autofiction' for his 'roman' *Fils* (1977), and the same term might be applied to his striking *Le Livre brisé*. The line between the two genres has become increasingly hard to draw.

Nevertheless, many writers of the 20th c. have written interesting texts which are indisputably autobiographies, among them Adamov, Althusser, Beauvoir (the first volume of her trilogy), Cavanna, Emmanuel, Gary, Gide, Green, Leclerc, Leduc, Pagnol, Sartre, Schlumberger, Simenon [see individual entries]. *Queneau characteristically broke the mould in writing a verse autobiography, *Chêne et chien* (1937), though he too calls it a 'roman', and his example was followed by Georges *Perros (*Une vie ordinaire*). The most remarkable autobiographical work of the century is, however, that of *Leiris, whose four-volume *La Règle du jeu* revolutionizes the whole concept of the genre, throwing overboard the normal chronological approach, scrutinizing particular events repeatedly and in great detail

and remaining constantly suspicious of his own motives and methods. This is at the opposite pole from the apparently unproblematic reminiscences of Pagnol or the polished self-presentation in Sartre's *Les Mots*.

Leiris's awareness of the pitfalls of the genre is echoed in the innovative autobiographies produced by writers associated with the *Nouveau Roman: *Sarraute (*Enfances*), *Robbe-Grillet (*Le Miroir qui revient; Angélique; Les Derniers Jours de Corinthe*), and *Simon (*L'Acacia*). Particularly striking examples of new directions in autobiographical writing are Claude *Mauriac's *Le Temps immobile*, *Laporte's 'biographies', several texts by *Perec, including *W, ou le Souvenir d'enfance*, and the inimitable, half-parodic *Roland *Barthes par Roland Barthes*, which carries as a kind of epigraph the words which best characterize a certain type of modern autobiography: 'Tout ceci doit être considéré comme dit par un personnage de roman.' [PF]

See P. Lejeune, *L'Autobiographie en France* (1971); *Revue d'histoire littéraire de la France*, special number on autobiography and memoirs (1975, no. 6); P. Lejeune, *Le Pacte autobiographique* (1975); M. Sheringham, *French Autobiography: Devices and Desires* (1993).

Automatic writing, see ÉCRITURE AUTOMATIQUE.

Automne à Pékin, L', see VIAN.

Autre Monde, L', ou les États et empires de la lune. A masterpiece of 17th-c. prose fiction. *Cyrano de Bergerac began it in the 1640s, but it appeared only posthumously, in a heavily expurgated version entitled *Histoire comique* (1657). Between 1908 and 1921 the complete text was finally published. It is clear that *L'Autre Monde* could not have appeared in Cyrano's lifetime.

The work recounts a young scholar's earthly and extraterrestial travels. It is a strange hybrid—part philosophical dialogue, part fantastic voyage, part Utopia, part *histoire comique* of the type produced by Cyrano's contemporaries *Théophile and *Tristan. The dialogue features Cyrano's narrator debating audacious topics from philosophical relativism and Epicureanism to the existence of God. The fantastic voyage blends eulogies of alchemy and defences of the new science (for example, the theories of Copernicus and the recently condemned Galileo). With its brilliant inventions, notably the narrator's various means of space travel, *L'Autre Monde* also prefigures modern *science fiction. The lunar *utopia displays biting social satire. The comic novel features risky topics such as the *Jesuits' machinations in Canada, and even flirts with blasphemy in literal readings of the Bible.

As provocative as it is unpredictable, *L'Autre Monde* has not lost the ability to astonish. [JDeJ]

AUVRAY (early 17th c.). Dramatist. In a brief career he wrote two free adaptations of plots taken from L'*Astrée, Madonte* (1628), and *Dorinde* (1630), both typical products of the prevailing fashion for involved and irregular tragicomedy. His letters, published in 1630, contain important insights into the literary life of the late 1620s. [GJM]

AUVRAY, Jean (*c.*1590–*c.*1633). A Normandy doctor and the author of poems in various genres, in particular the strongly worded satires contained in his *Le Banquet des muses* (1623).

Avalée des avalés, L', see DUCHARME.

Avare, L'. Five-act comedy in prose by *Molière, first performed 1668. Set in contemporary Paris, the play portrays the miserly widower Harpagon, who is a rival of his son Cléante for the hand of Mariane, a poor girl of unknown lineage. Harpagon's avarice dominates his household. His steward Valère, also of unknown lineage, courts Harpagon's daughter Élise; when a money-box goes missing, removed by Cléante's servant to be used as a bargaining counter, Valère is accused of the theft; but the arrival of Valère's and Mariane's long-lost father restores order to the household, makes possible the marriages of Harpagon's children, and reunites Harpagon with his money-box. [IM]

AVELINE, Claude (pseud. of Eugène Avtsine) (1901–92). French writer whose career as publisher, president of the Société Anatole France, Resistance writer ('Minervois', *Le Temps mort*, 1944), radio author (Prix Italia, 1955), novelist (*La Vie de Philippe Denis*, trilogy, 1930–55; *Le Poids du feu*, 1958), is eclipsed by his *Suite policière: L'Abonné de la ligne U* (1947), *Voiture 7, place 15* (1937), *Le Jet d'eau* (1947), *L'Œil-de-chat* (1970), *La Double Mort de Frédéric Belot* (1932). These stories turn on mystifications and impersonations, and are linked by the detective Belot, though he is a minor character in the second and third, and dead in the last. [SFN]

Avenir de la science, L', see RENAN.

Aventure ambiguë, L', see KANE.

Aventures du baron de Faeneste, Les, see AUBIGNÉ D'.

Avignon as a Publishing Centre, see BOOK TRADE, 2.

Avignon, Festival of. Theatre festival initiated by Jean *Vilar in 1947. A major theatrical event held each July, it was originally conceived by Vilar as a way of bringing high-quality theatre to the culturally deprived provinces and to large working-class audiences. His productions of the classics, on a wide stage in the courtyard of the Palais des Papes, played to audiences of several thousands. After 1951, when Vilar took over the TNP, the festival shared that theatre's repertoire and company, including Gérard *Philipe. Since the 1970s it has acquired a more fragmented character, with a vast array of fringe events alongside the official programme. [DWW]

Avignon Papacy. This is the period between 1309 and the early 15th c. when the popes lived at Avignon, an enclave in the Comtat Venaissin ceded to the papacy in 1229 after the Albigensian Crusades [see CATHARS]. Before the outbreak of the Great Schism in 1378 it was at Avignon that the medieval papacy's efforts to centralize the government of the Church reached their apogee. To house the papal household and administration (dominated by successive French popes and a majority of French cardinals) the enormous surviving palace was built in opulent style. But growing bureaucracy, constant financial demands, and papal secular concerns aroused violent contemporary criticism, from Petrarch among others. It was justifiably alleged that papal interests were frequently subordinated to those of France, even though the Avignonese popes, all men of real ability, strove valiantly to pursue independent policies. But use of the universal prerogative powers of their office was met by growing resistance from secular rulers anxious to protect 'national' churches from papal interference. Protestant and non-French Catholic historians have thus often depicted the ensuing struggle as marking a distinct decline, a 'Babylonish captivity', as the papacy slipped further into corruption and worldliness and failed to instigate effective reform, without a full recognition of the intractable problems the Avignonese popes faced. [MJ]

AVOST, Hierosme d' (*c.*1558–1592). A lawyer from Laval, d'Avost was in the service of *Marguerite de Valois and spent some time in Italy. He translated works from Italian and Spanish but also wrote his own poetry. A good example of provincial literary activity, his *Essais* (1584) show how translations of *Petrarch were moulded to contemporary taste. [KCC]

Axël, see VILLIERS DE L'ISLE-ADAM.

Aye d'Avignon. Short (4000-line) *chanson de geste which is remarkable for having a female protagonist. Aye is *Charlemagne's niece, and all the events of the text—machinations of traitors, assaults by Saracens, territorial interests—revolve around her. Although initially married by Charlemagne to a French baron, following her husband's death Aye marries a Saracen prince. The poem, composed in the late 12th c., is the oldest one in a group known as the 'Cycle de Nanteuil', another member of which—*Parise la Duchesse*—also has a female protagonist, a calumniated wife similar to the one in *Doon de la Roche*. The character of Aye was a popular one, frequently referred to in medieval works. [SK]

AYMÉ, Marcel (1902–67). Novelist. Brought up in the Jura, he was fond of a rural setting for his many novels, which practise an ironic humour and often treat the tensions between *anticlericals and Catholics (see also *Clérambard*, one of many plays written after 1942). Bawdiness (*La Jument verte*, 1933) and the fantastic (*La Vouivre*, 1943, and the short stories of *Le Passe-muraille*, 1943, and *En arrière*, 1950) are both essential elements of his work, giving edge to his ironic view of human beings and of the universe. Fantasy gives his work depth. Sometimes accused of lacking the philosophical dimension which would make him 'truly great', he was hated by the intellectual Left for his attack on them as bourgeois hypocrites in *Le Confort intellectuel* (1949). Despite his defending *Brasillach and *Céline, there is no question of his being a collaborator. He was a nonconformist opposed to both fascism and socialism, considered artists (unlike politicians) as the conscience of their era, and caused great offence to the legal establishment by his play *La Tête des autres* (1952). A more sympathetic reassessment of his work is overdue. It deals in (often conventional) types rather than individuals, but for that reason has been described as a 20th-c. human comedy. He is noted too for his comedies and children's stories (*Contes du chat perché*, 1934–58). [GDM]

AZEGGAGH, Ahmed (b. 1942). Algerian writer. Educated in France, he returned to Algeria in 1962, worked as a journalist, and finally settled in France. He is known primarily for his poetry, *Chacun son métier* (1966), *Les Récifs du silence* (1974), searching for national identity and political freedom in the post-liberation period. He is a committed writer, denouncing the corruption of power and the claustrophobic effect of the Algerian system, and is also a dramatist: *République des ombres* (1976). [ET]

AZÉMA, Jean-Henri (b. 1913). Poet from Reunion. After leaving his native island, Azéma settled first in Europe and then in Argentina. His *Olographe* (1978) represents a poetic return to the island. [BEJ]

AZIZA, Mohamed (pseud. of Chems Nadir) (b. 1940). Tunisian poet and essayist who seeks in his critical and poetic works to re-examine and update his Arab, Berber, and Islamic cultural heritage. His essays on the genesis and problematics of drama in the Arab world, *Le Théâtre et l'Islam* (1970) and *Regards sur le théâtre arabe* (1970), and on Maghrebian and African artistic forms of expression, *La Calligraphie arabe* (1971) and *Le Chant profond des arts de l'Afrique* (1972), contain the main ingredients of his poetic inspiration.

In his poetry—*L'Astrolabe de la mer* (1979), *Silence des sémaphores* (1978), *Le Livre des célébrations* (1983), and *Les Portiques de la mer* (1990)—Aziza taps oral literature and classical texts such as *Les *Mille et une Nuits* as well as pre-Islamic and Sufi poetry, for new sources of creative material. In the context of intellectual *decolonization, Aziza has resurrected the archetypal figure of Sinbad as a foil for Ulysses, and as an emblem of the modern Arab poet who constantly navigates between the past and the present, reality and fantasy. [HA-J]

B

BA, Amadou Hampaté (1901–92). Pioneering Malian historian, ethnographer, essayist, storyteller, and occasionally, novelist. His best-known literary work is based on the fruits of his academic research into folk-tales, *L'Étrange Destin de Wangrin* (1973), which was awarded the Grand Prix Littéraire d'Afrique Noire in 1974. He is the author of the proverbial phrase well-known throughout Francophone Africa: 'Quand un vieillard meurt, c'est une bibliothèque qui brûle.' His major historical work is a monumental collective reconstitution from oral tradition of the 19th-c. Fulani empire of Macina, *L'Empire peul du Macina* (2 vols, 1955–62). He has published many translations into French of Fulani poetry and folk-tales, as well as essays on religious subjects, in particular studies of the teachings of his spiritual mentor, *Tierno Bokar, le sage de Bandiagara* (1957). In 1971 he retired to Marcory, a suburb of Abidjan in Ivory Coast, and he is sometimes called 'the sage of Marcory'. [PGH]

BA, Mariama (1929–81). Senegalese novelist. *Une si longue lettre* (1980) takes the form of a series of letters from Ramatoulaye, a recent widow, to her friend Aïssatou, now divorced and living in New York. The letters recall both friends' marriages and chronicle Ramatoulaye's progress to independence—achieved against considerable obstacles—as a single woman and head of her family. The work embraces many aspects of Senegalese society, particularly the experiences of women from different social levels and generations.

Un chant écarlate (1981) depicts an intercultural marriage. Against the background of both families' disapproval, the upper-class French wife and Senegalese husband from a poor family find themselves unable to overcome their cultural differences. Ba analyses this mutual incomprehension with great sensitivity, detailing particularly the suffering of the wife. The relationship eventually breaks down, the husband takes a second, Senegalese wife, and the novel ends tragically.

Ba's work marks a milestone in the portrayal of women in the African novel. She shows the strength of women, but she could be reproached with pessimism: those who go against tradition suffer for it, and she tends to portray women's capacity to endure rather than suggesting any possibility of revolt or of change in society. [AMR]

BA, Thierno (b. c.1926). With his first play, *Lat Dior ou le Chemin de l'honneur* (1971), Ba joined the ranks of Senegalese post-1960 epic playwrights seeking to rehabilitate national history. He has also written a children's story, *Lat Dior* (1976), on the exploits of the national hero, and a second historical play, *Bilbassy* (1980). [FNC]

Babar. Elephant hero of cartoon books by *Brunhoff.

BABEUF, François-Noël, known as Gracchus (1760–97). Militant French Revolutionary, claimed by Communism as one of its first martyrs. Initially Babeuf was active in the rural revolution in Picardy (1789–91), winning the approval of *Marat. Next, in Paris, he played a useful, if subordinate, role on the far Left of the urban revolution working for Chaumette and the Paris *Commune. Abhorring State Terror, he then travelled some way with Thermidor and produced, in *Le Système de dépopulation* (1794), a (doubtless officially encouraged) denunciation of Carrier's excesses in the *Vendée. But detecting Thermidorian betrayal of that *Revolution for which, since 1790, he had suffered privation and imprisonment, Babeuf adopted the symbolically combative name Gracchus (5 October 1794) and re-entitled his periodical *Le Tribun du peuple*. It was then that, fully exploiting his talents as a publicist, he occupied the ground that had been deserted since the liquidation of the *Enragés. Transforming what had hitherto been his egalitarian Messianism into a visionary political programme (see his *Manifeste des plébéiens*, November 1795), he slowly realized his ambition to exercise a tribunate over public opinion and became the galvanizer of that new type of faction which was to be baptized the 'Conspiration des Égaux'. After the failure of the conspiracy (was it manipulated by the authorities?), Babeuf was put on trial and condemned to death. [JR]

Babouc, see MONDE COMME IL VA, LE.

BACHAUMONT, François de (1624–1702), author with *Chapelle of a *Voyage en Provence*.

BACHAUMONT, Louis Petit de (1690–1771). A knowledgeable French critic of painting, sculpture, and architecture. His name is now synonymous, however, with the *Mémoires secrets* (1777—89, 36 vols.), a valuable record of daily cultural and political life (1762–87) made by the élite *habitués* of the salon of Madame Doublet, in which Bachaumont was 'master of ceremonies'. He certainly edited the record for the period 1762–71 (vols. 1–6), but the method used for gathering the news (a 'registration' and 'verification' technique reminiscent of the *parlements*) has prompted certain critics to see Durey de Meinières (1705–85), a president of the Parlement de Paris, as the prime mover behind the initiative.

[JR]

BACHELARD, Gaston (1884–1962). French philosopher of science and literary critic. Bachelard argued that progress in science had been achieved through a series of radical discontinuities or 'epistemological breaks', exemplified notably by the emergence of relativity theory and quantum mechanics (*Le Nouvel Esprit scientifique*, 1934). Progress also implied the overcoming of tenacious 'epistemological obstacles'. He therefore proposed a non-reductive 'psychoanalysis' (and, later, a **'phenomenology'*) of irrational or mythical beliefs concerning the material world (*La Formation de l'esprit scientifique*, 1938), only to become fascinated by such 'rêveries matérielles' as a form of poetic truth which reveals our archetypal affinity with the four elements (*La Psychanalyse du feu*, 1938; *L'Eau et les rêves*, 1942; *L'Air et les songes*, 1943; *La Terre et les rêveries de la volonté*, *La Terre et les rêveries du repos*, 1948). As a scientist Bachelard conceived of matter as energy and vibration; as a reader he responded to images of its dynamism, rhythm, or metamorphosis, and to the sensuous and affective force of fluidity, viscosity, dissolution, or reflection, of flight or repose. Bachelard was less concerned with the structure of literary works than with the vectors of the writer's imagination and their prolongation in the reader; he thus influenced the 'thematic' approach of such critics as Georges *Poulet and Jean-Pierre *Richard. The postulate of discontinuity derived from microphysics informed Bachelard's anti-*Bergsonian rehabilitation of the instant in consciousness and time, while his notion of the 'epistemological break' was further elaborated by his pupil Michel *Foucault.

[REG]

Bachelier, Le, see VALLÈS.

BACULARD D'ARNAUD, François-Thomas-Marie de (1718–1805). Prolific French author of plays and fiction. *Les Amants malheureux* (1764, performed 1790) is a verse **drame* set in a catacomb; its atmosphere is described by Baculard as 'le sombre'. His greatest success was a collection of 24 novellas, *Les Épreuves du sentiment* (1772–80). His work was much derided by *Voltaire and others, but *Rousseau said: 'Monsieur Arnaud écrit avec son cœur'. His blend of romantic melancholy, Gothic horror, and improving sentiment was very popular in the years preceding the Revolution.

[PF]

BADIAN Kouyaté, Seydou (b. 1928). Malian novelist and playwright, best known for his first novel, *Sous l'orage* (1957), the story of an arranged marriage, told from the point of view of the reluctant bride, which becomes the symbol of the conflict between the older, traditionalist generation and the younger, westernized one. This work is widely studied in African schools, along with his politically committed epic drama about the Zulu warrior hero, *La Mort de Chaka* (1961). His later novels, *Le Sang des masques* (1976) and *Noces sacrées* (1977), remain overshadowed by his earlier works, despite their qualities and their similar theme of the conflict between tradition and modernity.

[PGH]

BADIANE, Cheikh (b. 1940). Senegalese novelist. The theme of mental illness, common in African literature, is given a slightly new slant in Badiane's first novel, *Aida Mbène ou les Fantasmes de Mor Diop* (1982), winner of the Senegalese Ministry of Culture prize. Unlike his better-known compatriot, Malick *Fall, Badiane explores the theme in a *petit-bourgeois* context. Badiane's second novel, *Les Longs Soupirs de la nuit*, was also published in 1982.

[FNC]

BADINTER, Elizabeth. French author of *L'Amour en plus* (1980), which argues that maternal love is not instinctive but the product, where it exists, of family and social history. Her later books demonstrate the dangers for women of an undue emphasis on sexual difference—see *L'Un est l'autre* (1985) and *Qu'est-ce qu'une femme?* (1989).

Bague de l'oubli, La, see ROTROU.

BAÏF, Jean-Antoine de (1532–89). French poet, the natural son of Lazare de *Baïf and a member of the *Pléiade. His work reveals an inventiveness and an erudition not always matched by poetic sensitivity and craftsmanship. His love poetry to the fictitious Méline (1552) and to Francine (1555) combines sonnets and 'chansons', *Petrarchism and sensual 'mignardise', whilst his 'Alexandrianism' and his predilection for mythological narrative poems, his considerable theatrical ability, and the Pléiade's attraction to scientific poetry find early expression in *Le Ravissement d'Europe* (1552), *Le Brave* (1567; an adaptation of Plautus's *Miles gloriosus*), and *Le Premier des météores* (1567) respectively.

From 1567 to 1573 Baïf devoted himself to the foundation of the *Académie de Poésie et de Musique and the related composition of classically measured verse and to the preparation of the *Œuvres en rime* (1572–3), his collective works which cover the creative period 1549–72 and contain four sections: *Poèmes, Amours, Jeux* (eclogues and theatrical productions), and *Passetemps* (mainly lighthearted epigrams). Baïf's most rewarding collection is the *Mimes, enseignements et proverbes* (1576, 1581, 1597). The earliest 'mimes' were predominantly gnomic and sententious but, in response to the continuing civil wars, Baïf developed the genre by an increasing emphasis on moral, satirical, political, and religious material. The same religious lyricism inspired his several psalters (1567–87).   [MDQ]

BAÏF, Lazare de (c.1496–1547). Father of the above. Lazare was an important diplomat in the service of *François Ier and a humanist scholar, whose publications included archeological works on ancient clothes (*De re vestiaria*, 1526) and naval matters (*De re navali*, 1536) and an alexandrine verse translation of Sophocles' *Electra* (1537).   [MDQ]

Baillage, bailli, see PARLEMENTS.

BAILLET, Adrien (1649–1706). French Jansenist priest and librarian to *Lamoignon. A devoted and ascetic scholar and compiler, he left a *Vie de Descartes* (1691) and a nine-volume work of bio-bibliography, *Jugements des savants sur les principaux ouvrages des auteurs* (1685–6).

Bajazet. Tragedy by *Racine, first performed 1672. Unusually for 17th-c. tragedy, the setting is modern Turkey. Bajazet, younger brother of the sultan Amurat, is held prisoner in the seraglio, where his fate depends on Amurat's favourite, Roxane. She loves Bajazet and wants him to marry her and wrest control of the country from the absent sultan; he, however, loves and is loved by Atalide, an Ottoman princess. Encouraged by the vizir Acomat, he attempts to play a double game; infuriated by jealousy, Roxane orders his death, which is rapidly followed by her own (at the hands of the sultan's emissary) and by Atalide's suicide. Only Acomat escapes the blood-bath which concludes this grim and claustrophobic play.   [PF]

BAKER, Josephine (1906–75). Singer and dancer. Leaving her native Saint Louis (Missouri) for Broadway, she joined the Revue Nègre, which brought her on tour to Paris in 1925. Scandal at her uninhibited jazz dancing launched her French career, which from 1927 included songs like 'J'ai deux amours' (1931) expressing her shared love affair with Parisian audiences.   [PGH]

Balcon, Le, see GENET.

Ballade. Provençal in origin (*ballada*, from *ballar*, to dance), the ballade assumed its classical fixity of form with its move northwards, and found a generic niche between the stately solemnity of the *chant royal and the engaging directness of the *rondeau. The commonest form of ballade is composed of three eight-line stanzas rhyming ababbcbC and a four-line *envoi* rhyming bcbC; as the capital letter indicates, the last line of the first stanza serves as a refrain, repeated at the last line of each stanza and of the *envoi* (which is the equivalent of the last half of one of the main stanzas). But there are several variations in length of stanza (particularly 10 or 12 lines) and thus of *envoi*, and the *envoi* may be variously

addressed to the 'Prince' (a nobleman, and particularly the presiding judge at a medieval literary tournament), or to some other noble or lady ('Sire', 'Reine', 'Dame') as homage or formula of leave-taking. The lines are usually octosyllabic or decasyllabic, depending on the stanza length (eight lines or ten); the so-called 'strophe carrée' was proposed as a principle by Jean *Molinet, who was also responsible for regularizing the *envoi*.

The ballade was standardized in the 14th c. by *Machaut, *Froissart, and *Deschamps, whose *Art de dictier et fere ballades et chants royaux* (1392) laid down the rules of the form exemplified in his own thousand-odd ballades. In the following century it was further developed by *Chartier, *Charles d'Orléans, *Christine de Pizan, and *Villon, who, perhaps best of all, exploited the two rhymes for their haunted melancholy or ironic insistence, and the refrain for its mixture of regret and worldly cynicism. The ballade continued to be practised up to the time of *Marot in the early 16th c., but was condemned by the *Pléiade, along with other medieval fixed forms, as one of the 'épiceries qui corrompent notre langue' (*Défense et illustration), as well as by classical successors in the 17th c. (with the exception of *La Fontaine), who regarded it as a barbaric survival; both *Molière and *Boileau make contemptuous allusions to it. Only with the *Parnassians, and particularly with *Banville's *Trente-six ballades joyeuses à la manière de Villon*, was the ballade revived and put into service by *Coppée, *Verlaine, *Richepin, and Maurice Rollinat (1846–1903). From 1896, Paul *Fort published innumerable 'ballades' in prose. The Romantic 'ballad' of *Hugo's *Odes et ballades* falls into the Anglo-Germanic tradition of the popular narrative ballad, as does *Musset's sly, parodic 'Ballade à la lune'. [See VERSIFICATION.]   [CS]

'Ballade des pendus, La', see VILLON.

'Ballade des dames du temps jadis', see VILLON.

BALLANCHE, Pierre-Simon (1776–1847). Catholic thinker whose philosophy of history was a formative influence on French *Romanticism. He sought to reconcile his Christian faith with a progressive interpretation of history grounded in the ideas of initiation and expiation, an interpretation which integrated the Revolution and did not regard it as aberrant. He is best known for *Du sentiment considéré dans ses rapports avec la littérature et les beaux arts* (1801) and his *Essai sur les institutions sociales* (1818). He was an epic poet as well as a social thinker; in 1829 he published *Orphée* and in 1831 *La Vision d'Hébal*, his most remarkable work. His platonic devotion to Madame *Récamier became legendary.   [CC]

Ballet de cour. An entertainment, extremely popular from the late 16th to the late 17th c., which exploited the different skills of poet, musician, choreographer, painter, and *machiniste* in a series of tableaux unified by a common theme. Of Italian inspiration, it became established after the spectacular *Ballet comique de la reine* of 1581. Free of constricting rules and traditions, it underwent multiple transformations in which, at different times, satire, melodrama, allegory, and the burlesque were given prominence; its thematic inspiration was similarly varied, drawing on ancient history or myth, chivalric romance or contemporary fiction. In some of *Molière's court entertainments, the role of librettist, often subordinated to that of musician and choreographer, became more pronounced; from these would develop the sophisticated art of *comédie-ballet. For all its diversity, it was characterized by its taste for spectacle, providing a refuge for the imagination as the *classical aesthetic took hold [see also MACHINE PLAYS]. But it also served social or political functions. In the early years, it reflected the aspirations of courtly society, with its representations of celestial harmony or the dawn of a new Golden Age; under *Louis XIV it often served a more specific purpose, helping to create and sustain the myth of the Sun King. [GJM]

Ballets Russes, Les. Formed in Paris in 1908–9 under the direction of Sergei P. Diaghilev, the Ballets Russes caught the attention of French composers, artists, and writers. *Cocteau collaborated with the Ballets, as did artists Léon Bakst and *Picasso, who contributed work on stage design, costumes, and posters. Diaghilev felt that the music must be an organic part of the conception of the ballet and commissioned the composition of works such as *Debussy's *Jeux* (1913), *Ravel's *Daphnis et Chloé* (1912), *Satie's *Parade* (1917), Stravinsky's *L'Oiseau de feu* (1910) and *Le Sacre du printemps* (1913), and works from members of Les *Six. The Ballets Russes disbanded with Diaghilev's death in 1929.

[KM]

BALZAC, Honoré [de] (1799–1850). French novelist, author of *La *Comédie humaine*. Son of a middle-ranking provincial civil servant, Balzac was educated at the Collège des Oratoriens at Vendôme and then apprenticed to a lawyer in Paris. He obtained permission to spend two years learning to write on his own, living in a garret, composed a tragedy in verse, *Cromwell*, and was then advised by family friends to abandon all literary ambition. In the 1820s he worked as a journalist and hack, penning several *genre* novels under the pseudonyms of Horace de Saint-Aubin and Lord R'Hoone (an anagram of Honoré); he then became a publisher, and, for a short while, a printer and type-founder. The collapse of these business ventures left him with large debts, principally to his mother. Balzac's slow development contrasts with the precocious genius of Victor *Hugo, almost his exact contemporary.

In 1828 he published a historical novel, *Le Dernier Chouan ou la Bretagne en 1800* (later renamed *Les *Chouans*), under his own name. *La Physiologie du mariage*, an anonymous compilation of anecdotes in the style of contemporary guides to practical subjects, caused a minor scandal in 1829 [see PHYSIOLOGIES]. Balzac first achieved public success in 1830 with *La *Peau de chagrin*, a 'philosophical tale' in a brilliant, irreverent, and wittily *Romantic style. After the July Revolution of 1830, and partly out of his disappointment with the new regime of the citizen king Louis-Philippe, Balzac adopted the style 'de Balzac' together with provocatively reactionary political attitudes. In that year he also published a set of sober short stories about marriage in the contemporary world, called *Scènes de la vie privée*, and it was to that vein that he returned in 1833 with the eight-volume series of *Études de mœurs au XIXe siècle*, which included *Eugénie Grandet*. From then on he worked at a tremendous rate, fuelling his imagination with coffee made from unroasted beans, sitting at his desk throughout most of the night wearing a monk's robe over his increasingly corpulent body. His ambition was to describe a whole society. The device of reappearing characters, first used in *Le *Père Goriot* (1834), links the plots of novels and stories set in widely differing social situations and has the effect also of creating gaps between the characters' reappearances, gaps which Balzac tried to fill with yet more stories. In 1841 he organized all that he had written into a single work to which he gave the title *La Comédie humaine*, and the first of the planned 16 volumes appeared in 1842. A 17th volume was added in 1847.

Balzac's father died in 1829, the last-but-one survivor of a tontine. (Had he lived a few weeks more, he would have solved his son's financial problems.) Balzac remained close to his mother, towards whom he felt considerable resentment and who outlived him. His warmest relationship was with his sister, Laure Surville. He had several amorous liaisons, notably with a much older woman, Laure de Berny, with the duchesse de Castries, with Caroline Marbouty, and with the Contessa Guidoboni-Visconti, by whom he may have had a child. In 1832 he received a mysterious message from a Russian countess, Evelyne de Hanska, and began a correspondence with her. It became the great affair of his life. Balzac's voluminous letters to Madame Hanska constitute an unusual record of a writer's life over a period of nearly 16 years, and are published separately from his other correspondence.

Balzac was also a society figure in the 1830s and, despite his debts, equipped himself with his own coach and horses. He could not keep such expensive trappings for very long. He was less in public view in the 1840s and became somewhat embittered at the success of the *roman-feuilleton, which overshadowed the publication of his complete works. He made attempts to write for the theatre, but his most substantial play, *Mercadet ou le Faiseur*, a brilliant comedy of manners and of money, was not performed until after his death. Somewhat adrift in revolutionary Paris in 1848, Balzac went to live with Madame Hanska on her estate at Wierzchownia, in the Ukraine; he finally married her at Berdichev in March 1850. (Chekhov's line, 'Balzac was married at Berdichev' has become a Russian proverb, meaning something like: fact is stranger than fiction.) Balzac fell ill on the return journey to Paris, took to his bed on arrival, and died. *Hugo wrote a moving account of him on his death-bed, and gave the funeral oration, in which he claimed that, 'whether he knew it or not, whether he wished it or not', the novelist had been a revolutionary writer.

Balzac's best-known novels—Le Père Goriot, Eugénie Grandet, La *Cousine Bette—contain many long and detailed descriptions of places, interiors, and people. He was fascinated by the relationship between outward appearance and inner reality, and subscribed, for example, to the bogus theory of phrenology, which attributed meaning to the shape of the skull. He strove to interpret the pictures which he painted in words, but he left much that is simply 'there': according to *Barthes, the residue of uninterpreted detail is what creates the 'reality effect' in Balzac's descriptions. His visual style of description was what first earned him the label of *Realist in the critical writing of *Champfleury and *Duranty. His novels also contain accurate information about the economic realities of Restoration France, and it is largely for this reason that he was considered a realist by Marx and by subsequent Marxist critics, in spite of the reactionary tone of much of the political sermonizing inserted into the later novels. For Georg Lukács, Balzac's 'critical realism' lies in the relationship which he establishes in his greatest novels between the course of history and the courses of individual lives.

Balzac has been criticized for the weakness of the endings of his novels. However, since each is but a chapter of the potentially infinite Comédie humaine, the relative lack of dramatic unity (much exaggerated by 19th-c. critics) is effectively determined by the overall design. Balzac was also attacked (notably by *Flaubert, in his correspondence) for the clumsiness of his style. It is true that his prose has little to do with academic notions of fine writing. He himself looked back to *Rabelais, whose 16th-c. spelling and vocabulary he pastiched in Les Contes drôlatiques. Balzac has a sense of verbal comedy as acute as Dickens's and is a masterful creator of dialogue. His special achievements are to have created a fictional world which closely resembles the real world of his own day and which also simulates the fragmentariness of ordinary life through the device of the reappearing characters; to have widened the permitted social range of literary heroes; to have created a gallery of 'typical' characters—the miser (Grandet), the erotomaniac (Hulot), the philistine (Crevel), the arch-crook (*Vautrin), the shady dealer (Gobseck), the abandoned lover (Madame de Beauséant), the arriviste

(*Rastignac), the jolly commercial traveller (Gaudissart), the femme fatale (Valérie Marneffe), the 'woman of thirty', the genius-inventor (David Séchard), and the philanthropist (Benassis)—who combine symbolic value with historical and human plausibility, and thereby to have contributed significantly to making the novel the dominant form of literary expression in the 19th c. [DMB]

See M. Bardèche, Une lecture de Balzac (1964); A. Maurois, Prometheus: The Life of Balzac (tr. N. Denny), 1965).

BALZAC, Jean-Louis Guez de (1594–1654). French prose writer and critic whose influence on his contemporaries was more considerable than the lasting impact of his published writings, but who contributed greatly to the creation of the paradoxically formal colloquial style which still holds sway in French literary and academic circles.

As a young man he spent some time in Rome as the agent of cardinal de Valette, and the experience marked him, not only with a taste for the virtues and style of classical antiquity, but with a conviction that France was the modern heir of Rome. There is a parallel with the career of *Du Bellay 70 years earlier; but whereas the poet had sought to enrich the French language by introducing the vocabulary of foreign models, Balzac wished above all to impose order, regularity, and gravity in prose, ignoring the risk of impoverishing the lexicon. The closer parallel is thus with *Malherbe.

At 30 he retired to a country estate in the southwest. Thereafter a stream of advice and censure issued from the Angoumois to the Parisian *classicists such as *Chapelain, *Conrart, or *Perrot d'Ablancourt. Balzac admired the *latinity of *Scaliger and Barclay; if he is to be considered a Ciceronian, it is because he imitates the elegant urbanity of Cicero's letters to Atticus in his own Epistolæ. And it is a transposition of that style into French which marks his formal Lettres, collections of which he published regularly from 1624. His Entretiens, which he envisaged as a modern version of *Montaigne's essay form and which were published posthumously (1657), maintain a similarly formal urbanity. His major prose works, though doubtless primarily written as exercices de style, attempt to build a bridge between antiquity and modernity in dealing with the burning issues of government (Le Prince, 1631) and religion (Socrate chrétien, 1652). The former may also have been composed in the hope of attracting royal patronage, but roused *Richelieu's suspicions and had to be reissued in an amended version. The latter attempts to temper Augustinianism with gentlemanly reasonableness. Aristippe (1658) applies the same deliberate reasonableness to questions of public administration. He began the work in the 1630s and returned to it repeatedly until his death. [PJB]

See R. Zuber, Les 'Belles Infidèles' et la formation du goût classique: Perrot d'Ablancourt et Guez de Balzac

(1968); J. Jehasse, *Guez de Balzac et le génie romain* (1977).

BAMBOTÉ, Pierre Makombo (b. 1932). The first writer from Centrafrique (Central African Republic) to be published: *La Poésie est dans l'histoire* (1962). He pursued a prolific career as poet, novelist, and short-story writer, culminating in a major novel, *Princesse Mandapu* (1972), a mysterious and inconclusive narrative about a petty local tyrant, set in a small Centrafrican town.   [PGH]

Bande dessinée (BD). Although the Swiss school-teacher Rodolphe Toepffer is perhaps the inventor of the strip cartoon (*Histoire de M. Vieux-Bois*, 1827, pub. 1837), the French BD had its origin in *La Famille Fenouillard* (1889) of Christophe (Georges Colomb). The following years saw the appearance of other legendary figures—Pinchon and Caumery's *Bécassine* (1905), Louis Forton's *La Bande des Pieds Nickelés* (1908)—but these were still narratives with illustration, the text running below the vignette; it was only in the relatively fallow 1920s that the integrated *bulle* (balloon) made its appearance, in Alain Saint-Ogan's *Zig et Puce* (1925) which, together with Hergé's *Tintin* (1929), gave a new impetus to the medium. But the Franco-Belgian BD still had two obstacles to overcome: its restriction to a child readership [see CHILDRENS' LITERATURE], and American imports—the 1930s were the decade of superheroes, from Mickey Mouse to Flash Gordon. These challenges were partly met by Pello's *Futuropolis* (1937-8), an adult *science-fiction series. After the war, and the censorship law of 16 July 1949 designed to stem American indoctrination, the gap was filled not so much by the French BD as by the Belgian: the success of the weekly *Tintin* stimulated the talents of E. P. Jacobs (*Blake et Mortimer*, 1946-72) and J. Martin (*Alix l'intrépide*, 1948), while *Spirou* drew on J. Gillain (Jigé) (*Jerry Spring*, 1954), A. Franquin (*Gaston Lagaffe*, 1957), Peyo (*Les Schtroumpfs*, 1958), and Morris (*Lucky Luke*, 1949). On the French side, the left-wing journal *Vaillant* owed its success to P. Gillon (*Fils de Chine*, 1950), Gire (*Pension Radicelle*, 1947), Coelho (*Ragnar*, 1954). The shift towards ideological and stylistic pluralism, and an adult readership, continued in René Goscinny's *Pilote* (1959) and *Astérix (1959); Gotlib, *Rubrique-à-Brac* (1968); Mandryka, *Le Concombre masqué* (1965); Gir, *Blueberry* (1963, with Charlier); Greg, *Achille Talon* (1963)—and in *Hara-Kiri* (1960, then *Hara-Kiri Hebdo*, 1969, and *Charlie-Hebdo*, 1970), founded by Georges Bernier and *Cavanna. Ironically the BD became a social fad, just when its function was fifth column, and drugs, counter-cultures, civil rights, and sexual liberation its preoccupations. The appearance of *Charlie mensuel* (1969), *L'Écho des savanes* (1972), *Métal hurlant* (1975), *Fluide glacial* (1975), and *Circus* (1975) confirmed the underground value of the BD. But with the popularity of the *album* (publication in volume form), and the corresponding decline of the serial, the journals have equally declined; merchandizing, take-overs by large publishers, and BD in paperback (1986) have put an end to subversion; the superhero has returned, and with him other species of the *roman d'aventures*: science fiction and thriller. Noteworthy among recent albums are: historical adventure—François Bourgeon's *Les Passagers du vent* (1978-84) and *Les Compagnons du crépuscule* (1982-90), and André Juillard's *Les Sept Vies de l'épervier* (with P. Cothias) (1982-9); political fantasy—Enki Belal's *Partie de chasse* (with P. Christin) (1982-3); *detective stories—Jacques Tardi's *Brouillard au pont de Tolbiac* (1981) and *120 rue de la gare* (1987-8); science fiction—Luc Schuiten's *Cités obscures* (with B. Peeters) (1982-); fantasy—François Boucq's *La Femme du magicien* (with J. Charyn) (1984-6).   [CS]

See P. Fresnault-Deruelle, *La Bande dessinée: Essai d'analyse sémiotique* (1972); P. Masson, *Lire la bande dessinée* (1985); S. Tisseron, *Psychanalyse de la bande dessinée* (1987).

Ban et l'arrière-ban, Le, see ARMY.

BANGUI, Antoine (b. 1933). Chadian novelist and author of *Prisonnier de Tombalbaye* (1980), an account of life as the political prisoner of his former leader, the first president of independent Chad, and an autobiographical novel, *Les Ombres de Koh* (1983), evoking his childhood in a divided and hunger-stricken Chad.   [PGH]

BANNY DE LIESSE, LE, see HABERT.

BANVILLE, Théodore de (1823-91). French poet and man of letters. He was at the centre of art for art's sake [see ART POUR L'ART] and *Parnassian developments in poetry and was highly esteemed both by contemporaries and later generations of poets, including *Mallarmé and *Rimbaud.

He was precociously gifted and soon discovered his distinctive poetic domain. His first collection, *Les Cariatides* (1842), already displayed his Hellenic inspiration, which was further evident in *Les Stalactites* (1846), although his rich deployment of *Ronsardian effects was also demonstrated here. Banville's poetic career and ambitions were closely linked with those of *Gautier and *Baudelaire. He shared their distaste for the prevailing ugliness, philistinism, and materialism of bourgeois and commercial culture. Like them, he wanted poetry to achieve the purity and perfection attained by other art forms. His *Petit traité de poésie française* (1872) is perhaps the single most impressive exposition of the forms and techniques of French poetry. *Mes souvenirs* (1882) is a valuable memoir of 19th-c. literary life. There is much of Banville yet to be discovered and appreciated. His *Odes funambulesques* (1857), with their interest in the theatre, the circus, and the everyday, go well beyond his reputation for the coldly marmoreal.   [BR]

BARANTE, Guillaume-Prosper Brugière, baron de (1782–1866). Best remembered for his *Histoire des ducs de Bourgogne* (1824–6), Barante occupies an important position among the French historians of the Restoration. In 1808 he published a *Tableau de la littérature française au XVIIIe siècle*, while as late as 1851–3 he brought out a history of the Revolutionary Convention. His political writings are of interest to students of Restoration liberal thought.   [CC]

BARBARA (pseud. of Monique Serf) (b. 1930). French singer-songwriter with a distinctively feminine, theatrical style and obsessively poetic refrains. Her career moved from the Left-Bank Parisian night-clubs of the 1950s (L'Écluse) to popular success in the music-halls of the 1960s (Bobino) and triumph in the concert venues of the 1980s (Le Zénith). Her delicate and sometimes playful songs celebrate recurrent fantasies and dreams—'L'Aigle noir' (1968), 'Marienbad' (1973)—memories of parents and childhood—'Nantes' (1963), 'Une petite cantate' (1964)—frustrated love—'Dis, quand reviendras-tu?' (1962)—and existential anguish—'Le Mal de vivre' (1964).   [PGH]

BARBEAU, Jean (b. 1945). Canadian dramatist, prominent among those in the 1970s who wanted to create a truly popular theatre in Quebec. Deliberately loose in construction and rudimentary in characterization, plays like *Le Chemin de Lacroix* (1970), *Ben-Ur* (1970), *Manon Lastcall* (1972), and others good-humouredly satirize official culture, high art, 'posh' French, institutionalized religion, and other embodiments of social pretension which exclude the working class. The **joual* which the characters speak is presented not derisively but with wry affection as the only form of speech in which working-class people can be authentically themselves (*Joualez-moi d'amour*, 1970). As in the case of other anti-establishment writers, Barbeau's inspiration dried up after the election of the Parti Québécois in 1976, but his theatre remains an engaging example of a Brechtian type of cultural project which was typical of Quebec in the 1970s.   [SIL]

'Barbe bleue, La'. One of Perrault's **Histoires ou contes du temps passé*, the story of Blue-Beard, perhaps connected with the historical *Gilles de Rais.

BARBEY D'AUREVILLY, Jules (1808–89). An important precursor of the late 19th-c. French Catholic Revival, converted in 1846–7, Barbey carried forward into the post-*Commune generation the dark Romantic inheritance of *Baudelaire and his anti-democratic dandy pose. *Huysmans, *Péladan, and *Bloy were all influenced by his extreme right-wing journalism and criticism (published in, for example, *Le Pays*, *L'Éclair*, *Le Constitutionnel*) and especially by his prose fiction. His major novels, exercises in sadistic melodrama tricked out, post-conversion, with the thrills of blas-phemous transgression, include *L'Amour impossible* (1841), *Une vieille maîtresse* (1851), *L'Ensorcelée* (1854), and *Un prêtre marié* (1865). The short-story collection *Les Diaboliques*, prosecuted by the police on first publication in 1874, enjoyed a *succès de scandale* when reissued with nine plates by the engraver Félicien *Rops in 1886.   [JB]

BARBIER, Auguste (1805–82). Barbier's reputation rests on one volume of satirical poetry, *Iambes* (1831), which brought together the angry verse he had published in the periodical press in the wake of the 1830 Revolution. His most successful long poem was *La Curée*, in which he denounced those who had jettisoned their republican convictions and had taken advantage of the *July Monarchy to further their own ambitions. Barbier was not the rival of *Chénier that he took himself to be, but his verse is at times powerfully effective. He also published poems which celebrated the oppressed genius of Italy, *Il pianto* (1833), and an unjustly neglected sequence, *Lazare* (1837), which includes a fine example of the French critique of the excesses of English industrialism.   [CC]

BARBIER, Edmond-Jean-François (1689–1771). Parisian lawyer who from 1718 to 1763 kept a *Journal* full of anecdotes and prejudice; it was published (with cuts) in 1847, and gives a vivid impression of the way events were experienced by an ordinary citizen.

BARBIER D'AUCOUR, Jean (1641–94). French Jansenist writer remembered for his polemics against the Jesuits, in particular *Bouhours (*Sentiments de Cléante sur les 'Entretiens d'Ariste et d'Eugène'*, 1671).

Barbier de Séville, Le (1775). Prose comedy in four acts by *Beaumarchais. Set in Seville, it reworks the themes and characters of Molière's *L'*École des femmes* and *Le Sicilien*: Doctor Bartholo, intent on marrying Rosine, his ward, keeps her jealously locked away from the world. The young Count Almaviva, having however caught sight of Rosine on her balcony, has fallen under her spell. The whole play revolves around the intrigues successfully woven by the supremely resourceful Figaro (formerly Almaviva's valet and now the eponymous barber) to ensure the young couple's marriage.   [JR]

BARBIN, Claude (1629–1700). Parisian bookseller-publisher who published the great classics of his day, as well as many lighter works, notably the *Recueil des plus belles pièces des poètes français* (1692, the *Recueil Barbin*).

Barbizon. Village near the forest of Fontainebleau, much frequented by artists (the École de Barbizon, including Corot, *Millet, Daubigny, and Théodore Rousseau) in the mid-19th c.

BARBUSSE, Henri (1873–1935). French novelist, poet, journalist, and left-wing activist. Barbusse made little impression on the public with his poetry or such naturalistic novels as *L'Enfer* (1908). However, with *Le Feu* (1916) he won the Prix Goncourt and wrote the most famous novel of protest published in France during *World War I. It contains horrifying scenes of trench warfare, of which Barbusse himself had direct experience. *Clarté* (1919) was also a war novel. After 1918 Barbusse organized the revolutionary *Clarté* movement. His radical journalism ended somewhat ingloriously with hagiographic biographies of Lenin (1934) and Stalin (1935). [JC]

BARCLAY, John, see LATINITY, 2.

BARCOS, Martin de (1600–78). *Jansenist religious thinker, who was influenced by the teaching of Jansenius in Louvain before becoming secretary to his uncle *Saint-Cyran, in 1631. Between 1643 and 1650 he lived at *Port-Royal, making a considerable impact on the community there and its leader Mère Angélique. Believing that the Church would not survive a further schism, he advised the nuns of Port-Royal to sign the formulary condemning five propositions by Jansenius. He was one of those Jansenists who preached total indifference to the world, believing in the spiritual value of humility and suffering in silence. [JC]

Bardamu, Ferdinand. The hero-narrator of Céline's *Voyage au bout de la nuit*.

BARÈRE DE VIEUZAC, Bertrand de (1755–1841). French lawyer and *Revolutionary politician, a *Montagnard member of the Comité de Salut Public until Thermidor, which he survived. His *Mémoires* were published in 1842–4.

Barlaam et Josaphat. A popular medieval hagiographic story, adapted to a Christian framework from the story of Buddha, recounting the conversion of an Indian prince Josaphat by Barlaam, a monk. Josaphat converts his father; then, on inheriting the kingdom, he leaves the secular world and dies a holy man. As well as numerous Latin versions of the story from the 12th c. onwards, there are three (plus a fragment) in Old French from the 13th c. and one in Occitan from the 14th c. [SK]

Barnabooth, A. O., a character in the writings of *Larbaud.

BARNAVE, Antoine-Pierre-Joseph-Marie (1761–93). Revolutionary politician. A Protestant from Grenoble, he was a dominant member of the popular party in the Assemblée Constituante, where his eloquence was second only to that of *Mirabeau. His active support for the monarchy led to his arrest (August 1792) and execution (November 1793) on a charge of treason. [PH]

BARNEY, Natalie, see GAY AND LESBIAN WRITING.

BARO, Balthasar (c.1600–1650). Secretary to d'*Urfé, he published in 1627 the fourth part of *L'*Astrée*, and a fifth, concluding volume, composed ostensibly from the author's notes. His theatrical output was varied, and includes the innovative *Célinde* (1628), which makes imaginative use of the play-within-the-play, and *Clorise* (1630), a pastoral which helped establish the trend towards regularity. [GJM]

BARON (pseud. of Michel Boyron) (1652–1729). French actor and playwright. *Molière's pupil and successor, he was the leading male actor of his generation. He retired in 1691, but made a come-back in 1720. Of his 10 plays, the best known is *L'Homme à bonnes fortunes* (1686), a satirical comedy of intrigue.

Baroque. A term long used disparagingly, but given positive value by Wölfflin to define non-classical form in post-Renaissance painting. Extended later to the other arts, its application to literature, though controversial, has led to the revaluation of much that was previously dismissed as of little worth. Baroque art is seen as forceful, restless, unitary in its impact, breaking out beyond its formal limits—in contrast with the stability and ideal clarity of classical art. It invites emotional response rather than intellectual contemplation. Primarily the term refers to the period between Renaissance classicism, founded on immanent reason and proportion, and the neoclassical revival, the high point of the baroque thus understood being the Rome of Bernini and Borromini. But this scheme is too simple: it does not allow for the complex relationship between the baroque and 16th-c. *mannerism, 18th-c. *rococo, or indeed 17th-c. French *classicism (many 'classical' authors display features usually associated with the baroque).

The term has acquired a thematic content rich enough to encompass the ethos and the pathos of an age. In the climate of near anarchy and religious war of late 16th-c. France, *Pléiade humanism and courtly mannerism could no longer suffice. There is blood and thunder in the dramas of *Hardy, unrestrained vituperation in satire, the love poetry of d'*Aubigné is violently expressionistic, religious poets like *Sponde and *Chassignet are obsessed with sin and death. But in France, as elsewhere, the deeper cultural crisis is ontological. The sense of universal mutability, the loss of bearings amidst 'ce tintamarre de tant de cervelles philosophiques' (*Montaigne), the social as well as the epistemological difficulty of discerning *l'être* from *le paraître*— such misgivings find appropriate means of expression involving enigma and illusion.

Theatrical values pervade the baroque. It sees the world as a stage, on which identities change, are called in question, confused, masked, and double-masked: a striking instance is Rotrou's *Le *Véritable saint Genest*, where the hero-actor suffers the martyrdom of the character he represents—in a play within the play. But the theatre is also a decor, in which art, with increasingly sophisticated techniques, challenges the authority of nature, both in the playhouse and in festive forms of make-believe like the *ballet de cour. Concurrently, the great outburst of visual imagery in Renaissance poetry is followed now by an extraordinarily free use of metaphor and conceit—stylistic means of metamorphosis. These may be played with for sheer pleasure or mannerist bravura, as by Marino and his French imitators; but for poets of the Catholic revival, like *Du Bois Hus or Martial de Brives, they serve also to display the glory of the Creator, whose artistry has conjured up so dazzling and kaleidoscopic a world, and one so fruitful in similitude and symbol. (The theory of metaphoric wit and the *pointe is fully elaborated by *Jesuit rhetoricians—Sarbiewski in Poland, Gracián in Spain, Tesauro in Italy.)

In itself, however, this world is insubstantial, illusory: it is a theatre for the existential drama of man. For God is the Lord not only of nature, but also of history, and of the grim and glorious epic of the Redemption. So, in *La Ceppède's intense spiritual exercises on the Passion, for instance, the symbolism is vividly realistic. Later, in a more self-assured Church, the tension eases. In Les *Tragiques, the Protestant d'Aubigné had set a blood-drenched stretch of lived-through history in its context of eternity; the mid-century Catholic national epics (owing much to Tasso), such as the Saint Louis of *Le Moyne, do the same for a history that is already legendary [see EPIC POETRY]. Always, though, whether intense or expansive, militant or triumphalist, in literature as in the visual arts, the baroque seeks to impress, persuade, convert: it urges towards the transcendent.

This is a climate for heroes, saints, and martyrs. It appeals to the spirit of chivalry and gloire still alive in the aristocracy, and also to the Christianized *Neostoicism, with its Roman resonance, spread in France by *Du Vair. Much of all this is reflected in Pierre *Corneille's theatre. And since the king himself is the Lord's anointed, the poetry of the Throne is as securely based as that of the Altar, drawing, with *Malherbe and many others, both on the Bible and on heroic mythology.

After the *Fronde, with the taming of the nobility and the elevation of the bourgeoisie, with the abating of religious fervour and the spread of *Jansenist severity, with the growth of critical thought and of the natural sciences, the climate changes. In the work of the grands classiques, the baroque still provides much of the internal dynamics, but the transcendental urge gives way to a searching scrutiny of human behaviour and motivation [see CLASSICISM].

[AJS]

See J. Rousset, La Littérature de l'âge baroque en France (1953); P. Butler, Classicisme et baroque dans l'œuvre de Racine (1959); P. N. Skrine, The Baroque (1978).

BARRAS, Jean-Nicolas-Paul-François, vicomte de (1755–1829). French soldier, then prominent *Revolutionary politician; he helped engineer *Robespierre's fall, then was one of the five members of the Directoire, but was forced out of politics by *Napoleon.

BARRAULT, Jean-Louis (1910–94). French actor, manager, and director. A disciple of *Dullin, *Artaud, and Decroux, he emerged in the 1930s as an actor of outstanding expressive power. His productions are noted for their physical inventiveness. Stylistically eclectic, he enriched the vocabulary of the stage with mime and oriental techniques, developed a form of 'total theatre' best illustrated by his productions of *Claudel, and did much to promote the emerging 'New Theatre' of writers such as *Ionesco, *Duras, and *Vauthier in the 1950s. With his partner Madeleine *Renaud, considered by many the leading actress of her time, he was a towering presence in French theatre for half a century.

[DWW]

BARRÈS, Maurice (1862–1923). French novelist, journalist, and politician of the Right. Barrès presented a distinctive voice which strongly influenced the young in the pre-war period, and a wide variety of authors of the next generation, from *Montherlant to *Mauriac. Born in Charmes-sur-Moselle, he was educated at the lycée of Nancy, studying philosophy under Burdeau. In 1883 he moved to Paris and was soon writing regularly for a number of prominent journals. In 1888 he published Sous l'œil des barbares, the first novel in his trilogy Le Culte du moi, in which he emerged as a fashionable exponent of the cult of individualism; the other two novels were Un homme libre (1889) and Le Jardin de Bérénice (1891).

Meanwhile, he was already showing a strong interest in politics. Having founded, in Nancy, a political journal, Le Courrier de l'Est, he stood successfully as a Boulangist [see BOULANGER] in the 1889 elections. His complex political attitudes at this stage combined authoritarian *republicanism, *nationalism, and an anti-capitalist desire for social reform.

In 1893 he lost his seat, and from then till 1906 he was to try repeatedly but unsuccessfully to return to the Chamber. He played a major part (1897–9) in the battles of the *Dreyfus Affair as an anti-Dreyfusard, his attitudes containing a strong element of *anti-semitism. His major political writings on the Affair were later gathered into Scènes et doctrines du nationalisme (1902). Under the influence of the physiologist Jules Soury, Barrès had become convinced of the importance of human intuition, seeing it as being not individual, but based on 'de très anciennes dispositions physiologiques'. In that we are the continuation of our parents, we must look for truth not in abstract theories but in instinctive urges.

In *Les *Déracinés* (1897), the first of a new trilogy of novels, Barrès developed his philosophy of 'la terre et les morts'; a group of young Lorrainers are uprooted from their province, and from the values of their forefathers, with disastrous results. The sequels, *L'Appel au soldat* (1900; on the Boulanger Affair) and *Leurs figures* (1902; on the *Panama Affair), provide a highly partisan account of the politics of their era. The last, in particular, is a masterpiece of literary polemic.

From 1904 onwards Barrès campaigned for the restitution of the lost provinces of Alsace-Lorraine, both in the press and in his novels *Au service de l'Allemagne* (1905) and *Colette Baudoche* (1908). In 1906 he was returned to the Chamber, where he was to remain until his death. His main themes were Alsace-Lorraine, the defence of the Church against *anticlerical policies, and the preservation of France's neglected churches.

Barrès's attitude to religion was complex; a fascination for the mystical, particularly in its least orthodox manifestations, was coupled with an appreciation of the Church as a continuity within the French tradition and as a force for order within society; and yet he remained an agnostic. These often conflicting attitudes were reflected in his novel *La Colline inspirée* (1913), a study of the brothers Baillard, the Vintrasian heretics who had set up their cult on the hill of Sion-Vaudémont in Lorraine.

Throughout World War I Barrès wrote a daily article for *L'*Écho de Paris* and was a leading patriotic contributor to France's war propaganda. In 1922 his novel *Un jardin sur l'Oronte*, an oriental love-tale, aroused a furore. The public had been accustomed to a political writer; the Church had begun to regard him as an apologist. Barrès, whose aim was here purely literary, became aware, under attack, that a 'committed' writer is condemned to being perpetually judged on 'committed' criteria.

In December 1923 Barrès died suddenly of a heart attack. The posthumous publication of his *Cahiers*, from 1929 onwards, revealed a far more complex and sensitive figure than had appeared from the published works of his heyday. Barrès was a man of contradictions: a *fin-de-siècle* aesthete thrust into the political arena; a simplistic political apologist whose bases for belief were highly complex; a proponent of discipline who was fascinated by the unorthodox. This heady mixture made of him the exciting and influential figure that he remains. [See DADA.]   [RMG]

See Z. Sternhell, *Maurice Barrès et le nationalisme français* (1972); P. Ouston, *The Imagination of Maurice Barrès* (1974).

BARTET, Julia (1854–1941). Distinguished French actress who began her career at the Vaudeville (1872–9) before entering the Comédie-Française in 1880, where she remained until her retirement (1919). She was especially admired for her elegance, finely modulated voice, and the restraint and dignity she brought to classical roles, notably in Racine's **Bérénice*.   [SBJ]

BARTHÉLEMY, Jean-Jacques, abbé (1716–95). A classical scholar of great erudition, he entered the *Académie des Inscriptions in 1747 and was named Garde des Médailles du Roi in 1753. He published learned works on coins, language, etc., but achieved popular success with *Le Voyage du jeune Anacharsis en Grèce* (1788). This voluminous work presents a young Scythian travelling through Greece in the age of Plato. There are many meetings with the famous, and descriptions of cities, buildings, institutions, and manners, all scrupulously annotated. A compendium of classics without tears, it was immensely popular in the 19th c.   [PF]

BARTHES, Roland (1915–80). As a writer, Barthes evades classification. He is famous as a semiologist and literary theorist, a high priest of *Structuralism, but in fact his output is very varied. Many of his most important writings are essays, in which the personal investment of the writer becomes increasingly evident. To use his own distinction, he is less an *écrivant* (one who uses language instrumentally) than an *écrivain* (one who works on and with words).

Even in his 'autobiographical' *Roland Barthes par Roland Barthes* (1975), he remains discreet about his personal life. He was born into the Bayonne bourgeoisie; his father, a naval officer, died the year after his birth, but he remained very close to his mother until her death shortly before his own. In 1934 he suffered an attack of tuberculosis, an illness which dogged him until 1947; he passed the war years in a sanatorium. He read classics and subsequently taught overseas for a time, but did not have a conventional academic career: it was only in 1960, after many years of research, writing, and journalism, that he became a director of studies at the *École Pratique des Hautes Études. Here he conducted a famous seminar, which led to many of his most important books. In 1976 he was elected to a chair of literary semiology at the *Collège de France.

The guiding thread running through Barthes's writings is a passionate concern with language, signs, and literature. His work does not develop in a straight line, but by a series of twists and turns; he compared it to a spiral in which the same element reappears, but transformed. A chronological account of his writings is therefore likely to give a false impression of coherence. As he wrote, he acted as a sounding-board, assimilating and reworking a series of favourite writers: *Gide, Brecht, *Saussure, *Lacan, *Proust, Nietzsche, etc.—the list of acknowledged masters is a long one, and it is by no means sure that he named the most important figures.

His first book, and one of his most famous, is *Le Degré zéro de l'écriture* (1953), an essay on modern literature much influenced by *Sartre; here he attempts a socio-historical description of the linguistic choices made by French writers, stressing the tragic lack of a common language in 'notre modernité'. At about the same time, however, his *Michelet* (1954), offers an *Bachelardian description of the inner world revealed in *Michelet's writings. His own commitment at this period to left-wing values is evident in the influential *Mythologies* (1957), a brilliantly witty and perceptive critique of the ideological codes at work in all kinds of cultural product, from all-in wrestling to song and cinema.

Mythologies ends with a theoretical attempt to define 'le mythe aujourd'hui', and this marks the beginning of Barthes's Structuralist period, what he later called his 'petit délire scientifique'. His aim was to develop the insights of Saussure and modern linguistics and create a new science of signs, semiology, which would describe the signifying systems that structure the world around us. *Éléments de sémiologie* (1965) was followed by *Système de la mode* (1967), a dry Structuralist description of the codes of fashion writing. However, much of Barthes's best writing in the 1960s (and thereafter) took the form of essays and articles, both critical and theoretical, one of the most important being the 'Introduction à l'analyse structurale du récit' (1966). The *Essais critiques* of 1964 were later completed by *Nouveaux essais critiques* (1972), and the posthumous *L'Obvie et l'obtus* (1982), *Le Bruissement de la langue* (1984), and *L'Aventure sémiologique* (1985).

The 1960s also saw a famous polemic, provoked by the Sorbonne professor Raymond Picard's attack on Barthes's idiosyncratic *Sur Racine* (1963). In *Nouvelle critique ou nouvelle imposture* (1965), Picard took Barthes to task for irresponsible neglect of basic standards of scholarship [see LITERARY HISTORY, 2]. Barthes riposted vigorously in *Critique et vérité* (1966), distinguishing criticism from science. This quarrel fixed him in the public eye as a leader of such new (and, for some, worrying) tendencies in criticism as the proclamation of the 'death of the author' and the consequent promotion of the critic.

The end of the 1960s saw Barthes, much influenced by *Lacan, *Derrida, and *Kristeva, moving away from a would-be scientific Structuralism and stressing the disruptive, plural values associated with 'le texte'. This is evident in *S/Z* (1970), a remarkable study of *Balzac's *Sarrazine*, where the Structuralist search for intelligibility (the codes of reading) is allied to a stress on difference and openness and a highly personal, symbolic reading. At about the same time he published a study of Japan, *L'Empire des signes* (1970), a happy counterweight to *Mythologies*, and an essay on the textual quality of three apparently very different writers, *Sade, Fourier, Loyola* (1971). The latter work prefigures the aphoristic *Le Plaisir du texte* (1973), which offers a psychoanalytically inspired defence of the modern, subversive text, and links reading, writing, and 'text' to the body, pleasure, and 'jouissance'.

Barthes's final years are marked by three major books in which he comes ever closer to writing about himself, and indeed, to the scandal of some devotees, to writing a novel. *Roland Barthes par Roland Barthes* (1975) plays with the forms of autobiography and textbook, setting before the reader an elusive, fragmentary, contradictory portrait of the writing self. *Fragments d'un discours amoureux* (1977), the record of a seminar, uses a similarly fractured form, full of allusions to Goethe's *Werther*, to speak indirectly of his own experience of (homosexual) love. And finally, *La Chambre claire* (1980), modestly subtitled 'Note sur la photographie', comes the closest of all his works to a Romantic self-expression worthy of one of the great loves of his final years, *Chateaubriand. His death in a street accident outside the Collège de France robbed France of a writer at the height of his powers.   [PF]

See A. Lavers, *Roland Barthes: Structuralism and After* (1982); J. Culler, *Barthes* (1983); P. Roger, *Roland Barthes, roman* (1986).

BARTLEBOOTH, Percival, a character in Perec's *La *Vie mode d'emploi*.

BARY, René (*fl.* 1640–80). The 'rhéteur des précieuses' [see PRECIOSITY], author of a *Rhétorique française* (1653), of works on philosophy for the ladies, and of model conversations and speeches. He was a mediocre writer, but his work helped to establish the polite culture of his day.

BASCH, Victor (1863–1944). French philosopher and human-rights activist. Professor of aesthetics at the Sorbonne and a specialist in German philosophy, he was an early *Dreyfusard and a leading figure in the Ligue des Droits de l'Homme. Basch and his wife were murdered by the Milice for their Resistance activities.   [MHK]

BASHKIRTSEFF, Marie (1860–84), was a Russian aristocrat and painter who lived half of her short life in Nice and Paris. She left a voluminous diary in French, begun in 1873 and continuing until a few days before she died of consumption. Intended for publication, and published posthumously (1887), the *Journal* was greatly admired for its frank and unflattering record of her inner life.   [PF]

BASNAGE DE BEAUVAL, Jacques (1656–1710). French Protestant scholar who lived in Holland after the Revocation of the *Edict of Nantes. He published a continuation of *Bayle's *Nouvelles*, the periodical *Histoire des ouvrages des savants* (1687–1709), and an augmented edition of *Furetière's *Dictionnaire*.

Basoche. An association of law clerks attached to the Parlement de Paris and other high courts of justice in the 15th c. Officially established by Philippe IV in 1305, they were set up to resolve disputes between the clerks. Their internal structure was modelled on that of the state, with a king, a chancellor, a *procureur*, an *avocat général*, etc. This serious purpose was later replaced by burlesque trials and carnavalesque ceremonies. It is estimated that by the end of the 15th c. there were 10,000 Basochiens in Paris alone; similar societies grew up in all provincial towns with a Parlement. The Basochiens were instrumental in the composition and performance of much late medieval drama, especially the **soties*; and their legal background and preoccupations are reflected in many *soties* and a few **farces*. Towards the end of the 15th c. the Basoches merged, or had members in common with, the **Enfants Sans Souci.* [GAR]

BASSOMPIERRE, François de (1579–1646). Half-German, half-*Lorrain*, Bassompierre (also known as the marquis de Chantérac) was one of the ageing **Henri IV's favourite companions. He acted as ambassador in Spain, Switzerland, and England, and was appointed marshal in 1622. Imprisoned in the Bastille by **Richelieu, he devoted much of his time to writing his memoirs (*Le Journal de ma vie*), which provide a particularly good insight into the last years of Henri IV. [JJS]

Bastille, La. Fortress built c.1380 at the Porte Saint-Antoine in Paris. In the 17th and 18th c. it was the most famous state prison, housing briefly, or not so briefly, many writers (e.g. **Voltaire, **Marmontel) who had fallen foul of the regime. When it was sacked in 1789 [see REVOLUTION, 1], it contained only a handful of prisoners, but its symbolic importance was immense; 14 July, the day of the 'prise de la Bastille', was celebrated in the **fêtes révolutionnaires* and since 1880 has been the main national holiday. [PF]

BATAILLE, Georges (1897–1962). Bataille's diverse writings emerge less from an intellectual system than from a turbulent confluence of obsessions, centred on the intensity of human impulse: 'J'appelle expérience un voyage au bout du possible de l'homme.' One might hint at the nature of his singular temperament by citing certain crucial experiences: watching a bullfighter being gored to death in the arena; reading an account of a potlatch when a Kwakiutl chieftain hurled piles of valuable copper plaques into the ocean; scrutinizing the faces of Chinese torture victims in an unspeakable photograph; or peering across the smoking lip of the Etna crater. Such are the touchstones of a sensibility which, in *La Part maudite* (1949), celebrates the human capacity to attain release through the spectacular discharge of surplus energy.

By profession a respectable librarian (at the Bibliothèque Nationale), Bataille regularly wrote obscene texts under various pseudonyms: works like *Histoire de l'œil* (1928), with its far-fetched perversities, or *Madame Edwarda* (1941), the tale of a street-walker transported by sacred orgasms, are symptomatic of a passion for uniting extremes, the ecstatic and the disgusting, the sublime and the scatological. Such excesses can have their comical side, though Bataille's ideas on laughter point more to black humour than facile joviality. Among his darkest books are *L'Érotisme* (1957) and *Les Larmes d'Éros* (1961), where harrowing illustrations punctuate an austere discourse (often reminiscent of **Sade) on the links between human sexuality, transgression, and death. The incandescent psychic states invoked in *L'Expérience intérieure* (1943) spring from processes of self-denying meditation coupled with sheer naked anguish, the dispossessed ego being finally credited with a kind of Stirnerian or Nietzschean sovereignty; the book was dismissed by **Sartre as an apologia for the worship of the abyss.

Bataille periodically sought to mobilize group activity, whether as editor of reviews like *Documents* in the late 1930s or *Critique* in the 1940s, as member of the **Collège de Sociologie, or as leader of short-lived secret societies. Typically, his alignment with **Surrealism never led to true participation—**Breton for one was chary of his apparent collusion with violence during the period of rising fascism—and Bataille thus remained a maverick in Parisian intellectual life, part devout mystic, part irrational sociologist, part latter-day **Dadaist, an unclassifiable, even opaque figure. His posthumous reputation as a bold theorist who exposed the taboos of Western culture has risen markedly, not least thanks to the cult-like attentions of the **Tel Quel* group in the 1970s. His *Œuvres complètes* encompass twelve volumes (1970–88). [RC]

See D. Hollier, *La Prise de la Concorde* (1974); A. Arnaud and G. Excoffon-Lafarge, *Bataille* (1978).

BATAILLE, Henry (1872–1922). French dramatist of the **Boulevard; influenced by the Romantics, his plays celebrate the natural and the instinctive over the rationality and morality of the bourgeoisie. From *Maman Colibri* (1904) to *Le Phalène* (1913), his lyrical portrayal of exceptional passions was greatly enjoyed by a generation of theatre-goers; today he is often viewed as didactic. [EAF]

Bataille de Pharsale, La, see SIMON, C.

Bâtarde, La, see LEDUC.

'Bateau ivre, Le', see RIMBAUD

Batouala, see MARAN.

BATTEUX, Charles, abbé (1713–80). A teacher of rhetoric, and professor of Greek and Latin at the **Collège de France, Batteux composed many theoretical and pedagogical works. *Les Beaux-Arts réduits à un même principe* (1746) bases a general theory of the arts on the imitation of 'la belle nature'; *De la construction oratoire* (1763) discusses the topical question of 'natural' word order; the *Cours de belles-lettres* (1747–50), later published with other works in *Principes de littérature* (1753), gave currency to the

notion of 'belles-lettres' and outlined a normative training in reading French and classical literature.
[PF]

BATY, Gaston (1885–1952). French theatre director, a prominent figure in the *Cartel and leading proponent of the director's role in production. Resistant to the influence of *Copeau and rejecting the tyranny of the text, he sought out works which left scope for directorial creativity, and never hesitated to cut or rewrite scripts. His purpose was to create a mood or atmosphere by exploiting decor, lighting, costumes, and music. Typical achievements were his staging of J.-J. *Bernard's *Martine* (1922), a play constructed around suggestive silences, and his adaptations of novels: *Crime et châtiment* (1933) and *Madame Bovary* (1936).   [DHW]

BAUDE, Henri (c.1430–c.1496). Although apparently resident in Paris, Baude was appointed royal tax-collector in the Limousin. In 1468 he was convicted of corrupt practices and thereafter had constant difficulties with the authorities, including the House of Burgundy. He was the author of a *morality play (now lost) which earned him another brief imprisonment, and of shorter poems, mostly satirical and referring under the veil of allegory to contemporary events. His *Dictz et moraulx pour faire tapisserie* prescribe an iconographic programme for a series of tapestries to illustrate short poems on proverbial and aphoristic themes.   [JHMT]

BAUDE FASTOUL (*fl.* 13th c.). Picard *trouvère. Seventy years after *Bodel, probably in 1272, Baude Fastoul likewise wrote a *congé shortly before death in an Arras leper colony. At 696 lines in 48 *strophes d'*Hélinand*, Fastoul's poem slightly exceeds Bodel's, whose horrific realism and expressions of friendship and faith it shares and develops with intermittent grotesque humour.   [PVD]

BAUDELAIRE, Charles (Pierre) (1821–67). French poet, art and literary critic, translator, and essayist. Following his father's death in 1827 and his mother's remarriage to Commandant (later General) Jacques Aupick in 1828, Baudelaire was educated at the Collège Royal de Lyon (1832–6) and the Collège Louis-le-Grand, from which he was expelled for indiscipline in 1839. He spent the next two years living what he later called a 'vie libre' in Paris, dissipating a good part of his paternal inheritance and making his first contacts in the literary-artistic milieu. An enforced voyage to Mauritius and Reunion (June 1841–February 1842) having failed to mend his ways, Baudelaire's access to what remained of his inheritance was restricted by the imposition of a *conseil judiciaire* in September 1844. By this time it seems likely that Baudelaire had written a substantial proportion of the poems that would later make up Les *Fleurs du mal*, most notably those inspired by Jeanne Duval, the mulatto

(*quarteronne*) whom he seems to have met shortly after his return from the Indian Ocean.

It was not, however, as a poet that Baudelaire first attracted the attention of his contemporaries, but as the author of the *novella La Fanfarlo* (1847), whose central character, Samuel Cramer, is in large part a self-portrait, and of critical reviews of the Salons of 1845 and 1846. These, particularly in their enthusiastic defence of the work of *Delacroix, placed Baudelaire in the forefront of mid-19th-c. critical thinking. During the Revolution of 1848 Baudelaire fought on the barricades in both the *journées de février* and the *journées de juin* [see REPUBLICS, 2]. In December 1851 he also took part in resistance to the military coup of Louis-Napoléon Bonaparte, and there seems little doubt that, at this stage of his career, Baudelaire was a dedicated left-wing republican.

Declaring himself to have been 'physiquement dépolitiqué' by the Bonapartist putsch, Baudelaire devoted much of the first half of the 1850s to translating the works of *Poe, which he had first encountered in 1847. Published at regular intervals in reviews, the translations were collected in *Histoires extraordinaires* (1856) and *Nouvelles Histoires extraordinaires* (1857), each preceded by an important critical study by Baudelaire himself; further translations from Poe were published as *Les Aventures d'Arthur Gordon Pym* (1858), *Eurêka* (1863), and *Histoires grotesques et sérieuses* (1865). In June 1855 Baudelaire published a sequence of 18 poems under the title *Les Fleurs du mal* in the *Revue des deux mondes; some of the poems are inspired by Marie Daubrun, with whom Baudelaire had a liaison in 1854–5 (and again in 1859), and by Aglaé-Apollonie Sabatier, to whom he addressed a series of anonymous poems between 1852 and 1854, and with whom he had a brief, and apparently catastrophic, sexual relationship in 1857, shortly after the trial and condemnation of *Les Fleurs du mal* when it appeared in book form.

The publication, in August 1857, of six prose poems offered a foretaste of what would, in the 1860s, become Baudelaire's preferred literary form. In 1858–9 he returned to the subject of drug addiction that he had already treated in *Du vin et du hachisch* (1851), translating substantial parts of De Quincey's *Confessions of an English Opium-Eater* which, accompanied by a major essay (*Le Poème du hachisch*) and supporting commentary by Baudelaire, was published as *Les Paradis artificiels* in 1860.

The year 1859, most of the first half of which Baudelaire spent living with his recently widowed mother at Honfleur, was the most productive of the writer's later life, witnessing the composition, in rapid succession, of 'Le Voyage', 'La Chevelure', 'Les Sept Vieillards', 'Les Petites Vieilles', and, at the year's end, 'Le Cygne', as well as of the important study on *Gautier, the *Salon de 1859*, and the first draft of the seminal essay on modern painting, *Le Peintre de la vie moderne*, published in 1863. The autobiographical notes collected under the titles *Fusées* and *Mon cœur mis à nu* also date from the late 1850s and early 1860s, as do the critical notices on contemporary poets which would be collected after his death in *L'Art romantique* (1869) under the title 'Réflexions sur quelques-uns de mes contemporains'. The same volume also contains the important essays 'Richard Wagner et "Tannhäuser" à Paris' (1861) and 'L'Œuvre et la vie d'Eugène Delacroix' (1863).

After the publication of the second edition of *Les Fleurs du mal* in February 1861 Baudelaire wrote comparatively little verse poetry, and directed his efforts increasingly towards the writing of short prose texts—to call them 'prose poems' is, in many instances, misleading—which, after appearing in reviews during his lifetime, were published posthumously in book form under the title *Petits poèmes en prose* in 1869: Baudelaire's own title, *Le Spleen de Paris*, is greatly to be preferred. By the early 1860s Baudelaire's mental and physical health was in a critical state. A *crise cérébrale* in January 1860 was followed by a recrudescence in 1861 of the venereal infection from which he had suffered in the 1840s, and in January 1862 he felt what he chillingly called 'le vent de l'aile de l'imbécillité' pass over him. Having failed to gain election to the Académie Française in 1862 and beset, as ever, by financial problems, Baudelaire left Paris for Belgium in April 1864 to give a series of public readings from his work; apart from one brief visit to Paris and Honfleur he remained in Belgium for the next two years in search of material for his never-completed denunciation of the country and its people, *Pauvre Belgique!* In March 1866 he suffered a serious fall in the Église Saint-Loup at Namur, after which he was unable to speak or write. Brought back to Paris in July 1866, he spent the last year of his life in a Parisian nursing home.

Baudelaire occupies a pivotal position in the development of modern French writing, not just as the poet of *Les Fleurs du mal*, but as the proponent, in his critical writings, of a modern, and specifically urban, aesthetic based on what he called the 'innombrables rapports' and encounters of city life; *Le Spleen de Paris* may be seen as an actualization in words of the programme for painting elaborated in *Le Peintre de la vie moderne*. Baudelaire, wrote *Laforgue, was the first poet to write of Paris 'en damné quotidien de la capitale'; more than any other French poet of his time, he marks the transition from the romantic to a proto-modernist poetic style and stance, and his influence on subsequent poets, both French (notably *Verlaine, *Rimbaud, *Mallarmé, and *Valéry) and foreign (Swinburne, Eliot, Rilke, and George amongst countless others), has been immense. [RDEB]

See J.-P. Sartre, *Baudelaire* (1947); W. Benjamin, *Charles Baudelaire: A Lyric Poet in the Era of High Capitalism* (tr. H. Zohn, 1973); C. Pichois and J. Ziegler, *Baudelaire* (1987).

BAUDOUIN DE CONDÉ (*fl.* 1240–80), and **JEAN DE CONDÉ** (*fl. c.*1300–50). Baudouin is author of 24 surviving *dits on different themes: moral (like *Le Dit des trois morts et des trois vifs*), amorous (*Li Contes de la rose*), or chivalric (*Li Contes du baceler*). His son left 75 poems, generally allegorical or moralistic, but including short *romans d'aventure* and the last five known *fabliaux. [JHMT]

BAUDRILLARD, Jean (b. 1929). French sociologist and cultural critic. He became known as a translator and critic of left-wing literature, which he combined with a career as a sociologist, culminating with a chair at Nanterre. He joined the *Tel Quel group, which was reformulating Marxism from a New Left perspective, and extended his criticism of the prevailing capitalist ideologies to encompass Marxist ideologies. Disillusioned by the failure of the Left after *May 1968, he argued that the proliferation of communications media in modern society has drowned out meaning and severed links between signs and their referents, whose reality must therefore be regarded as problematic (*La Société de consommation*, 1964). Often associated with *Postmodernism, he both castigates and celebrates the social and intellectual disintegration he describes. An English translation of his *Selected Writings* was published in 1988. [MHK]

Bavard, Le, see DES FORÊTS.

BAYART (Bayard), Pierre du Terrail, chevalier de (*c.*1473–1524). French knight known as the 'chevalier sans peur et sans reproche' [see CHIVALRY; CHAMPIER].

BAYLE, Pierre (1647–1706). Huguenot moralist and pre-*Enlightenment thinker, unsurpassed as a spokesman for religious toleration. He was the son of a Protestant minister in the remote south of France, but a brief conversion to Catholicism, then a return to Calvinism, made him a lapsed Catholic; at a time of growing official intolerance of the Huguenots, it was safer for him to leave his home region. Having tutored in Switzerland and Paris, he taught at a leading Huguenot academy, in Sedan, where he was befriended by *Jurieu. When the academy was officially shut down in 1681 both men emigrated, like the thousands of other refugees who formed the Huguenot diaspora [see REFUGE], and obtained posts at a French college in Rotterdam, where Bayle remained, never marrying, for the rest of his life.

In Holland, publishing flourished in comparative freedom from censorship. Bayle made his name as a writer with the *Pensées diverses sur la comète* (1682–3), a rational attack on the superstition that comets portend disaster, full of digressions and provocative arguments, many of which are covertly anti-Catholic. Bayle asked, for instance, whether atheism was better than superstition—a word inextricably associated, for Protestant readers, with the Catholic religion. A history of Calvinism by *Maimbourg, an ex-Jesuit, had portrayed it as subversive zealotry; Bayle published a *Critique générale* of Maimbourg in 1682. In Paris the *Critique*, urbane and effective, was officially banned and burned, but its success led to the arrest of Bayle's brother Jacob in 1685, just when the campaign against the Huguenots reached its height with the Revocation of the *Edict of Nantes. Jacob died in prison. Bayle's distress can be sensed in his angry descriptions of a France freed from 'heresy' in *Ce que c'est que la France toute catholique sous le règne de Louis le Grand* (1686), followed (still in 1686) by the first volumes of a cooler, more cogently argued attack on intolerance, *Commentaire philosophique sur ces paroles de Jésus-Christ, 'Contrains-les d'entrer'*. The words in question were the scriptural basis, according to St Augustine, for enforced conversion.

In 1687 a nervous breakdown made Bayle abandon the important journal he had begun for a Dutch publisher in 1684, *Nouvelles de la république des lettres*, which did much to foster the conception of a non-sectarian, international community of scholars and intellectuals. In the second period of his life his targets were more abstract: immoral behaviour in the name of religion and over-confidence in the religious powers of reason. He also quarrelled with Jurieu, first over tolerance, which Jurieu could not accept, then over the politics of the Huguenot diaspora. A pamphlet, *Avis aux réfugiés*, in which Bayle counselled loyalty to *Louis XIV, brought the final rift.

Jurieu's enmity eventually lost Bayle his teaching post, thus allowing him to devote himself to the preparation and publication of his greatest work, the *Dictionnaire historique et critique* (2 vols., 1697; 4 vols., 1702), an easily used and readable guide, on biographical lines, to figures and ideas of religious and philosophical importance since antiquity. The neutral main text is dwarfed by the enormous columns of notes, often outspoken. Bayle had to publish defensive *Éclaircissements*, notably for the article 'David', which emphasized the bad side of the Israelite king's conduct. Elsewhere he seems to delight in proving the incompatibility of faith and reason, always concluding that reason can prove nothing; only faith brings certainty. The most far-reaching arguments come in the relentlessly pessimistic exposition (especially in 'Manichéens', 'Pauliciens', and 'Marcionites') of the problem of evil; God's behaviour has to be accepted on faith, being rationally incomprehensible. Bayle's position, which prompted the composition of *Leibniz's *Théodicée*, remains controversial; it was within a certain Calvinist tradition, but has often seemed unconvincing from a writer so critical of dogmatism in general. In his last works he indefatigably elaborated previous arguments, for instance, against the rationalist Jean *Le Clerc in the *Réponse aux questions d'un provincial* (1703). During the Enlightenment his influence was enormous but one-sided, the Calvinist inspiration being neglected, while his scepticism and moral concern were used as weapons against religion and his arguments for tolerance served to foster indifference rather than the rights of conscience.   [CJB]

See E. Labrousse, *Bayle* (1983).

BAZIN, André (1918–58). France's leading cinema critic and theoretician, co-founder in 1951 of *Cahiers du cinéma*. A Catholic influenced by the *Personalism of *Mounier, Bazin laid great stress on the cinema's ontologically privileged status as window onto the real. His critical essays, published as *Qu'est-ce que le cinéma?* (1958–62), thus extol the 'realist' fluidity of directors such as Rossellini, Welles, and *Renoir rather than the stylization of an Eisenstein, and for this reason he fell into disfavour with the 'new' *Cahiers critics of the 1960s. Yet his conception of cinematic ontology is still influential, and essays such as those on *Carné's *Le Jour se lève* and *Bresson's *Journal d'un curé de campagne* remain unsurpassed.   [KAR]

BAZIN, Hervé (Jean-Pierre Hervé-Bazin) (b. 1911). Vigorous and witty French novelist, member of the *Académie Goncourt. His novels focus on problems of parental responsibility, collapsing marriages, and unstable values. His fathers can be overbearing or weak (*Au nom du fils*, 1960), but the mothers and wives are often impossibly capricious and egotistic (*Le Matrimoine*, 1967); for them love is a weapon in some unrelenting feud. However, the extraordinary Folcoche (*Vipère au poing*, 1948; *La Mort du petit cheval*, 1950) reaches near-mythic status with the concentrated energy of her stimulating virulence. Women can be admired for their toughness: Constance fights her paralysis to the end (*Lève-toi et marche*, 1952); Isa organizes a gyneceum in her family home, excluding the father of her child (*Qui j'ose aimer*, 1956). The semi-documentary *L'Île de la désolation* (1970) uses the Tristan da Cunha islanders in their British exile to attack consumerism; the 'wild man' of the woods in *L'Église verte* (1981) allows Bazin to question definitions of the 'natural'. His values are in fact conservative, if sceptical. But these novels are energized by the striking verve and irony of his style. Language is used eccentrically and inventively through his mainly first-person narrators as they articulate their hidden, pent-up passions. Brand-names, puns, neologisms, fantasies: this linguistic exuberance has been little analysed, and Bazin's work as a whole is undervalued.

[MMC]

BÉART, Guy (b. 1930). French singer-songwriter, also a cartoonist and television personality. He came to prominence in the late 1950s with songs modelled on the folk tradition, with clever lyrics containing ironic and detached commentaries on contemporary life and a singing style akin to that of *Brassens.   [PGH]

BEAUCHEMIN, Yves (b. 1941). Canadian novelist whose first work, *L'Enfirouapé* (1974), evokes the political kidnappings of October 1970 in Quebec in a lively blend of realism and fantasy. He is best known for *Le Matou* (1981), a fast-paced chronicle of life in Montreal with overtones of a mystery novel which is Balzacian in its narrative complexities and social sweep. Although without explicit political reference, it has been read as an expression of ethnocentric nationalism, construing the foreigner (the villainous Ratablavsky) as sinister. *Juliette Pomerleau* (1989) is another social chronicle, but with fewer fantastic elements. He has also published a personal journal, *Du sommet d'un arbre* (1986), and two novels for children. [SIL]

Beaudous, see ROBERT DE BLOIS.

BEAUHARNAIS, Marie-Françoise (known as Fanny) Mouchard, comtesse de (1738–1813). The daughter of a financier, she was the hostess of a Parisian literary salon frequented by *Dorat, *Cubières, *Mercier, and *Restif among others, and herself wrote plays, poems, and novels. Her younger cousin by marriage, *Joséphine de Beauharnais, married Napoléon Bonaparte in 1796.

BEAULIEU, Victor-Lévy (b. 1945). Canadian writer. He soon abandoned formal education and went from journalism to a wildly controversial career as writer and publisher. Since 1968 his prodigious mythopoeic imagination has spawned over 30 works. In addition to plays and television serials, his work combines fiction, (auto)biography, literary theory, and polemics, often within the same work. He has written tributes to his heroes, Hugo, Melville, Kerouac, and *Ferron, whose extravagant creative imaginations have captured images capable of fictionalizing a national culture; this has increasingly been his own ambition. His characters are forms of self-projection, living out sexual and other fantasies in a nightmare made even less coherent by excessive desires and heavy drinking: in *Jos Connaissant* (1970) the hero struggles touchingly with ignorance and ineptitude; *Don Quichotte de la démanche* (1974) shows Quebec's cultural aspirations hampered by rickets and madness; *Blanche forcée* (1976) is a poignant tale of psychological impotence.

Beaulieu's style has become less quirky, shedding the puns, neologisms, and shock-effects of the early writing. His *Manuel de la petite littérature du Québec* (1974) rescues temperance tracts and works of naïve spirituality, indicating sources of Quebec culture suppressed by the literary establishment. The subtext of his work is a passionate statement about the precariousness of the Quebec psyche and the awkward relations between artists and power which he experienced firsthand. [CRPM]

BEAUMANOIR, Philippe de, see PHILIPPE DE BEAU-MANOIR.

BEAUMARCHAIS, Pierre-Augustin Caron de (1732–99). French playwright. It is rarely appreciated that the creator of Figaro was not a professional man of letters, as the 18th c. had already begun to understand that term, but an entrepreneur with a chequered career. Initially he embraced his father's profession as a watchmaker but, when his novel escapement mechanism brought him notoriety (1753), the desire to succeed on a broader stage consumed him. Ten years later he had acquired the name de Beaumarchais, three royal offices, and the protection of Louis XV's daughters, and, not least, he had reached intimate, if mysterious, business understandings with the financier Pâris-Duverney.

'Capitalistic' enterprises (some more honest than others) were to dominate his whole life, gaining him considerable wealth but also a reputation as an unscrupulous adventurer and a succession of enemies who caused him serious discomfort. In 1770 he became embroiled with the ill-intentioned heir of Pâris-Duverney in a resounding lawsuit which was disastrously prolonged when Beaumarchais accused the equally ill-intentioned presiding judge, Goëzman, of corruption. Though he lost both cases, it was his four *Mémoires à consulter*, written against Goëzman, which exonerated him with the public and which epitomize Beaumarchais's essential traits: his combative nature, his ebullience, his refusal to be intimidated by notions of birth or authority.

If Beaumarchais constantly had the temerity to dare ('qui dit auteur dit oseur'), it was not for himself alone, though one must add that he often did dissimulate self-interest behind high principle. It was he who, having been sentenced to (pardonable) civic degradation, saved both Louis XV and Louis XVI from scurrilous pens (1774–5); he who helped persuade the government in 1776 to enter the American War of Independence on the side of 'suffering liberty' and who then equipped his own fleet of vessels to supply the insurgents; it was he, the dramatist, who founded in 1777 the Société des Auteurs Dramatiques in order to ensure fair remuneration for intellectual endeavours; he who created in 1780 the Société Littéraire et Typographique in order to mastermind, and to sell, the famous Kehl edition of *Voltaire's works. Many other (ad)ventures later, it was he who, as a patriotic though opportunistic Revolutionary, sought to purchase 60,000 guns in Holland so that France could face the Coalition in 1792.

His final years were equally turbulent: suspect and imprisoned (he narrowly escaped the September Massacres), suspect again and indicted, branded as an *émigré* (though on government business at the time), then reduced to poverty in Hamburg, it was only in July 1796 that Beaumarchais could return to Paris, to find both house and fortune devastated. After a display of typically combative tenacity, he died with his finances almost restored to their former glory.

In a life so geared to material success, there was always time for literature. For literature was another path to prominence and esteem. It was his farce-like *parades* (1757–63), written for appreciative society audiences, which encouraged him to produce *Eugénie*, a **drame larmoyant* (1767) which—even rehandled—prompted *Grimm to make one of his less accurate forecasts: 'Cet homme ne fera jamais rien, même médiocre.' Three years later, though now more confident of his talent, he attempted once more, but again without success, to reproduce current social and political reality with *Les Deux Amis, ou le Négociant de Lyon*. Real success came, however, with the *Mémoires à consulter* which are remarkable for brilliant inventiveness and sheer incandescent insolence. Here we find a polemicist, a moralist, an orator, and a satirist whose command of language and style is so assured that he was likened variously to Demosthenes, *Fénelon, Juvenal, and Horace, and whose sense of drama is so acute that Voltaire was moved to exclaim: 'Il n'y a point de comédie plus plaisante, point de tragédie plus attendrissante.' That success could only be enhanced by *Le *Barbier de Séville*—which lifted the comic theatre to heights unknown since *Molière—and then consecrated by *Le *Mariage de Figaro*. Unfortunately, Beaumarchais's inability to attain such heights again served only to underline the much lesser achievement of *La Mère coupable* (1792) with which he completed the Figaro trilogy and in which personal hatreds were the guiding muse. But this, and the even less successful opera *Tarare* (1787), are minor blemishes on such a singular career; few people so consistently electrified the social, political, and literary life of 18th-c. France as did Beaumarchais. [JR]

See G. de la Brenellerie, *Histoire de Beaumarchais* (1888); R. Pomeau, *Beaumarchais, l'homme et l'œuvre* (1967).

BEAUMONT, Christophe de (1703–81). Archbishop of Paris, author of a condemnation of Rousseau's **Émile*, to which Rousseau replied with a famous letter.

Beau ténébreux, Un, see GRACQ.

BEAUVOIR, Simone de (1908–86). French writer, philosopher, autobiographer, feminist, and political activist. Simone de Beauvoir is likely to be considered one of the major intellectual figures of the 20th c.; she has been hailed as the mother of post-1968 *feminism, but her actual production was much wider than this title suggests.

Born in Montparnasse into a conservative bourgeois milieu, she received the narrow secondary education thought appropriate for a 'jeune fille rangée'. Fortunately, a deterioration in the family fortunes led her parents to allow her to train for a teaching career, first at the Institut Catholique and the Institut Sainte-Marie, and then at the Sorbonne. Preparing here for the *agrégation* in philosophy, Beauvoir encountered Jean-Paul *Sartre, who remained a capital figure in

the rest of her existence. The couple they formed, in which each regarded the other as an 'essential' love whilst remaining free to experience other 'contingent' loves, has provoked a great deal of curiosity. They refused the idea of marriage and children, and never set up home together, preferring throughout the 1930s and 1940s to live separately in cheap hotels. Beauvoir always considered Sartre as the philosopher of the two, and in her early essays took Sartre's *L'*Être et le néant* (1943) as her chief reference point. In *Pyrrhus et Cinéas* (1944) and *Pour une morale de l'ambigüité* (1947) she explores Sartre's existentialism for its moral potential and develops the ways in which relationships between people could go beyond the conflictual.

Her real ambition, however, was to write fiction, and after a number of early attempts and the refusal of her volume of short stories *Quand prime le spirituel* (published only in 1979), her first novel, *L'Invitée*, appeared in 1943. Both an illustration of the Hegelian dictum: 'Chaque conscience poursuit la mort de l'autre', and a fictionalized account of the trio which she and Sartre formed with an ex-pupil, Olga Kosakievicz, the text plays out a highly charged set of psycho-sexual conflicts.

L'Invitée pays only scant attention to historical and social pressures, but the events of the late 1930s revolutionized Beauvoir's attitudes : 'l'histoire m'a saisie pour ne plus me lâcher', she later wrote of this period in *La Force de l'âge*. Her second novel, *Le Sang des autres* (1945), though still highly existentialist in its vocabulary and preoccupations, focuses on the moral dilemmas of a Resistance leader and argues a case close to the position of the French Communist Party at that time. Before the war Beauvoir had supported herself by teaching philosophy, first at a *lycée* in Marseille, then in Rouen and, from 1936, in Paris. After the war she devoted herself to writing, producing a third novel entitled *Tous les hommes sont mortels* (1946), which explores the potential of individual action for historical significance, and her only play, *Les Bouches inutiles* (1944).

In 1947 she spent five months in the United States on a lecture tour. On her return she published her impressions in *L'Amérique au jour le jour* (1948), an account which voices her criticisms of America but omits the fact that she had fallen in love. Her liaison with the American writer Nelson Algren, which lasted until 1951, created a major crisis in her life and provided some of the material for *Les *Mandarins* (1954), the novel for which she was awarded the Prix Goncourt (making her the third woman ever to receive it). From 1946 onwards, however, she had been working on *Le *Deuxième Sexe* (1949), a book which began as a short essay and which developed into two volumes of detailed analysis of women's oppression. Beauvoir herself was astonished by the situation which she uncovered; the book scandalized many of its French readers, and it was not until the early 1970s that Beauvoir was to find herself acclaimed as a feminist heroine.

Although a Communist sympathizer during the 1940s, she had not been a political activist. In the early 1950s she moved much closer to *Marxism, partly as a result of her debates with Claude *Lanzmann, who was 17 years younger than herself and shared with her for several years the flat behind the Montparnasse cemetery which she bought with the proceeds of the Goncourt Prize. During the 1950s she visited China and the Soviet Union with Sartre, and published *La Longue Marche* (1957) an enthusiastic essay on Communist China. She rejoiced at the defeat of the French in Vietnam and involved herself heavily in the campaign against French atrocities in the *Algerian War. In 1963 she wrote in *La Force des choses* that 'la guerre d'Algérie a porté au rouge l'horreur que m'inspire ma classe'.

She produced the first volume of her autobiography, *Mémoires d'une jeune fille rangée* in 1958; this was later followed by *La Force de l'âge* (1960), *La Force des choses* (1963), and *Tout compte fait* (1972). In 1964 she published *Une mort très douce*, an account of her mother's death. Twelve years after *Les Mandarins* she returned to fiction with *Les Belles Images* (1966), a sophisticated deconstruction of the language in which the bourgeoisie justifies its own existence, and *La Femme rompue* (1968), three short stories examining the ways in which women weave themselves into their own self-destruction. *La Vieillesse* (1970) analyses the problems of old age and denounces the conditions of the elderly in Western society.

*May 1968 found Beauvoir siding with the Maoist students and selling banned revolutionary papers on the streets. In the aftermath of 1968 the Mouvement de Libération des Femmes contacted her, and she began campaigning on abortion and other feminist issues. A strong influence on Anglo-American feminism, she had no sympathy with the new French feminism of sexual difference. She always remained implacably opposed to the family structure, which she considered basic to women's oppression. After Sartre's death she published *La Cérémonie des Adieux suivie d'Entretiens avec Jean-Paul Sartre* (1981); the publication of their correspondence and (posthumously) of Beauvoir's war diaries proved highly controversial, demonstrating that even a feminist heroine may have feet of clay. She died on 14 April 1986 and was buried with Sartre in the Montparnasse cemetery opposite her home. [EAF]

See E. Fallaize, *The Novels of Simone de Beauvoir* (1988); D. Bair, *Simone de Beauvoir: A Biography* (1990); T. Moi, *Simone de Beauvoir: The Making of an Intellectual Woman* (1994).

Beaux Quartiers, Les. Novel by *Aragon, published 1936, the second volume in the *Monde réel* trilogy. Whereas the first volume concentrates exclusively on Paris, the second volume opens in the fictional town of Sérianne-le-Vieux in the Midi and focuses on the family of Doctor Barbentane, the town's mayor, with ambitions to become a *député*. The first part of the novel dissects the corruption of the provincial bourgeoisie. It then follows the careers of the doctor's two sons: Edmond, who goes to Paris as a medical student, and Armand, who, initially destined for the priesthood, loses his faith, turns to socialism, rebels against his family, and runs away to join his brother in Paris. In the Parisian background, however, are the same sinister figures who dominate *Les *Cloches de Bâle*: the industrialist Wisner, the shady intermediary Joris de Houten, and the head of the taxi-owners Joseph Quesnel. Whereas Edmond is sucked into this world, abandoning his studies and making his fortune as the gigolo of Quesnel's mistress Carlotta, Armand, driven briefly by poverty to strike-break in Wisner's factory at Levallois-Perret, rejoins the unions' strike committee at the end of the novel. In spite of its powerful evocation of France on the brink of war, the novel lacks some of the formal virtuosity of its predecessor. [NH]

BEAUZÉE, Nicolas (1717–89). French grammarian and *philosophe, Beauzée is best known for contributing the grammatical articles to vols. 8–17 of the *Encyclopédie* (briefly with Douchet), after *Du Marsais's death (1756), and for his *Grammaire générale, ou Exposition raisonnée des éléments nécessaires du langage, pour servir de fondement à l'étude de toutes les langues* (1767). In this he expounds a rational and universal theory of language, aimed also at facilitating the learning of particular languages through the application of a subset of the rules of universal grammar. Beauzée's other works include moral and exegetic treatises, translations of Sallust and Quintus Curtius, and editions of *Girard's and Timothée de Livoy's synonym dictionaries and Newton's *Optics*.

[WA-B]

BEBEY, Francis (b. 1929). Cameroonian writer. In addition to the considerable reputation he has earned through his activities as a short-story writer and novelist, Bebey is also well-known as a composer, musician, musicologist, and broadcaster. He has written widely on all of these subjects.

The youngest of a family comprising nine children, he was orphaned at an early age and was brought up by his elder brother and sisters. Successful studies at the Lycée Technique de Douala earned him a scholarship allowing him to continue as a student at the *lycée* in La Rochelle and later at the Sorbonne. Between 1956 and 1961 he worked at Radio Française in Paris, Cameroon, and Ghana, and then for UNESCO between 1961 and 1974. During these periods he simultaneously pursued literary and musical careers. He regularly gave guitar recitals, and published his first novel, *Le Fils d'Agatha Moudio*, in 1967. It won the Grand Prix Littéraire d'Afrique Noire that year. His literary work (*Le Roi Albert d'Effidi*, and especially *La Poupée Ashanti*) lacks pretension and draws on themes close to the everyday lives of the people of West Africa. In recent years, he has devoted himself to music and has produced a number of his own albums. [MPC]

Bécassine. Popular **bande dessinée* heroine. The adventures of this simple but not defenceless Breton maid entertained readers of all ages from 1905 to World War II; from 1913 onwards they were written by Caumery and illustrated by Pinchon.

BECKET, Thomas, see HAGIOGRAPHY.

BECKETT, Samuel (1906–89). Irish-born playwright and novelist, winner of the Nobel Prize in 1969. Asked why he had chosen to write in French, Beckett replied that it made it easier to write without *style*. The style he sought to evade was principally his own: that of a hyper-literate Irishman, deeply imbued with French and Italian literature, whose literary ambitions had been nourished by personal acquaintance with James Joyce (whose secretary he was). Having, as an exceptionally bright middle-class Protestant youth, followed the customary path to Trinity College, Dublin, he excelled at French and, after a spell at the **École Normale Supérieure in Paris, returned to Trinity as a lecturer. Within two years he had abandoned academia, leaving an extraordinary monograph on **Proust (1931)—already brimming with Beckettian themes—as the main relic of this period.

Back in Paris, where, after a sojourn in London, he was eventually to settle, Beckett joined Joyce's circle, earned money through translations, and wrote poetry (*Echo's Bones*, 1935) and fiction: *More Pricks than Kicks* (1934) and *Murphy* (1938), the tale of a 'seedy solipsist'. Even more marginal and autistic than Murphy, the 'hero' of *Watt* (1953) is beset by linguistic maladies and finds it increasingly difficult to match words and things. Beckett wrote *Watt*, his last prose work in English for many years, during the **Occupation, while living incognito in Provence after the Resistance network of which he was a member had been broken up by the Germans (he was decorated for his Resistance work after the war).

The period following his return to Paris after the war was the most productive in Beckett's career, and it was at this point that he chose to write predominantly in French. Joycean exuberance, the free-wheeling virtuosity displayed in his English novels, no longer seemed appropriate. Instead of mastery, Beckett wanted his writing to enact feelings of impotence and ignorance, including the travails of expression admirably defined in his dialogues with Georges Duthuit (1948). To write in an alien tongue was to deny himself easy victories of style; it was to start from a sense of dispossession. Yet the break with English was also liberating; after warming up with some short stories and two novellas (including *Mercier et Camier*), in an extraordinary burst of creativity Beckett wrote *Molloy* (1951), two further novels, and his first theatrical masterpiece, *En attendant Godot* (1952).

The trilogy inaugurated by *Molloy* is the heartland of Beckett's mature work, where all his major themes and motifs are first realized or adumbrated: language and identity, vagrancy and purposelessness, physical dilapidation and mental ingenuity. The activity of narration, the business of trying to tell their stories, becomes the principal focus of attention as Molloy and Moran attempt to recount their failed encounters with one another, as Malone (*Malone meurt*, 1953) seeks, by telling stories, to cure himself of futile self-scrutiny, as the narrator of *L'Innommable* (1953) tries to fend off all those namable identities which claim to be 'him', asserting the conviction that as long as words keep coming, as long as there is language, he will be condemned to a radical anonymity and dispersion: 'Je suis en mots, je suis fait de mots . . . tous ces étrangers, cette poussière de verbe . . .'

The predominance of monologue in Beckett's fiction, further demonstrated in *Textes pour rien* (1955) and in *Comment c'est* (1961), helps explain the move to theatrical expression. With *En attendant Godot* he again pares his medium down to its essentials: an all-but bare stage; two men, then two more; two acts, the second in large measure a replay of the first. It is Beckett's distinction to have been a leading figure in two of the most important developments of French writing in the period after World War II: the **Nouveau Roman and the Nouveau Théâtre [see ABSURD]. In common with those of **Ionesco or **Genet, his plays explore the medium itself, using every aspect of theatre—repeated performances, the ambiguous dividing-line between stage and audience, conventions such as asides, exits, and entrances, stage 'business'—as a vehicle for his own vision. Linear plot is replaced by shape—both *Godot* and *Fin de partie* (1957) end as they begin—or by the sense that events are simply unfolding according to some unfathomable logic: 'quelque chose suit son cours', as Clov puts it in *Fin de partie*.

If the impact of Beckett's theatre has probably been greater and more lasting than that of his fellow dramatists, it is partly because his plays have greater resonance than theirs. A wealth of echoes and allusions links them not only to the rest of Beckett's work but also to important strands in European thought: from Zeno to Augustine and Dante, from **Descartes and **Pascal to **Baudelaire and Proust. But this should not tempt us to view Beckett too narrowly as a hermetic writer whose works require detailed exegesis. Commentators have sometimes been all too ready to turn him into a glum philosopher, with an exceptionally dark and austere world-view. Yet the responses of audiences often suggest otherwise, as they laugh or groan at the many jokes, puns, and witty exchanges; as they marvel at the extraordinary craftsmanship which (as Beckett's stage directions reveal) makes each of his plays a miracle of timing, marked by precisely modulated shifts of tempo and timbre; or as they register the surprisingly wide range of human emotions and aspirations with which Beckett deals.

Simple situations—waiting for a promise to be fulfilled, or for an anticipated end—become the prisms through which solitude and dependency, dominion and aggression, nostalgia and disgust, stoicism and despair, are refracted in exceedingly subtle and psychologically revealing ways. In later plays, unforgettable stage images—Winnie prattling cheerfully, half-buried in sand (*Oh les beaux jours*, 1963); Krapp scoffing at the pretensions of his erstwhile self preserved on tape (*La Dernière Bande*, 1959); the eternal triangle encased in urns (*Comédie*, 1963)—are the focal points of acutely detailed dissections of individual consciousness.

Beckett always shunned the literary limelight but worked closely with actors and directors he admired (e.g. *Blin, Madeleine *Renaud, Joe McGowan, Billie Whitelaw), participating very actively in some productions of his plays. His later work in both fiction and drama is that of a minimalist who compresses and refines his art, a tendency encouraged by the labour of translating his own works into English, or into French when he began writing in English again (the radio plays *All that Fall*, 1957, and *Embers*, 1959). There is great power and beauty in such brief prose pieces as *Bing* or *Assez* (both 1966), and in such plays as *Cette fois* and *Pas* (both 1978). *Compagnie* (1980) and *Worstward Ho* (1984) have a mellow autumnal grace. [MHTS]

See H. Kenner, *Samuel Beckett* (1966); R. Cohn, *Just Play: Beckett's Theatre* (1980); S. Connor, *Samuel Beckett: Repetition, Theory and Text* (1988).

BECQUE, Henry (1837–99). Though a solitary figure who eschewed allegiance to any particular school of writing, Becque was the one significant French playwright to emerge from the *Realist and *Naturalist movements of the 19th c. At the start of his career he hesitated between following the recipes for routine box-office success and writing more innovative plays. In his two best works, *Les *Corbeaux* (1882) and *La Parisienne* (1885), he demonstrates a gift for ironic observation of character and an ability to generate dramatic atmosphere without recourse to mechanical plot manipulation. His juxtaposition of comedy and tragedy, the unsettling objectivity of his dramatic technique, and his rejection of conventional plot devices meant that he had great difficulty in having his plays staged. His dialogue called for more natural acting styles than were current in his day, so that productions often met with uncomprehending reviews. His battles with theatrical managers and critics embittered and ultimately demoralized him (*Querelles littéraires*, 1890; *Souvenirs d'un auteur dramatique*, 1895), with the result that he failed to realize his considerable potential and left unfinished an ambitious play, *Les Polichinelles*. He was greatly admired as a pioneer by *Antoine and the generation of playwrights who succeeded him. [DI IW]

BÉDA, Noël (d. 1536). A syndic at the *Sorbonne and one of the foremost critics of humanists like *Erasmus (whom he accused of exceeding his competence when applying humanist learning to the scriptures) and of the Meaux group [see EVANGELI-CALS]. Having questioned the orthodoxy of *Marguerite de Navarre he was banished by *François Ier. He was also ridiculed by *Rabelais in the Bibliothèque de Saint-Victor (*Pantagruel*). [JJS]

BÉDIER, Joseph (1864–1938). Medieval scholar who broke with the post-Romantic tendency to view medieval texts from a historical distance, choosing rather to read them like other literary works. He developed an innovatory approach to editing established texts, not by attempted reconstruction of an archetype, but by following what the editor judges the best manuscript, which is emended only when necessary. [SK]

BEGAG, Azouz (b. 1957). Novelist of Algerian origin born and brought up in Lyon, where his father was an immigrant worker. Begag's autobiographical novels, *Le Gone du Chaâba* (1986) and *Béni ou le Paradis privé* (1989), retrace his childhood and adolescence in some of the poorest districts of Lyon. [AGH]

BÉGUIN, Albert (1901–57). Swiss-born Protestant, academic, translator, publisher, critic, and director of *Esprit after the death of *Mounier in 1950. He first gained prominence with his notable study of German Romanticism, *L'Âme romantique et le rêve* (1937). Yet, although drawn to the mysticism and the dream world of German poetry, he also wrote polemical articles and essays denouncing the Hitler regime of the 1930s while teaching in Germany. Returning to Switzerland, he was converted to Catholicism in 1940, taught at the University of Basle, and helped in 1941 to found and run *Les Cahiers du Rhône* with contributions from Resistance writers in France and prisoners of war. After the Liberation he settled in Paris, and his last years were spent in great literary activity, resulting in *Gérard de Nerval* (1945), *Balzac visionnaire* (1946), and *Léon Bloy, mystique de la douleur* (1948), among others. While director of *Esprit* he continued the *Personalist tradition of Mounier, trying to reconcile the differences of approach of the sociological and literary contributors, while stressing their individual contribution to the debates of the day. [ET]

BÉJART, Madeleine and Armande, see MOLIÈRE.

Bel-Ami. Novel by *Maupassant, published 1885. Georges Duroy, the 'Bel-Ami' of the title, is a dashing, ambitious, and unscrupulous journalist who exploits the women whom he seduces to further his career. From humble beginnings he becomes a successful reporter and political journalist with the help of his friend's wife, Madeleine Forestier, whom he later marries after her husband's death. He makes further gains through the wife of the owner of *La Vie française*, Madame Walter. After obtaining a fortune in some shady dealings, he divorces Madeleine, marries Madame Walter's daughter, Suzanne, and rises to the position of editor-in-chief. The novel presents a cynical picture of the world of journalism and a pessimistic view of the human condition.

[DB]

BELGHOUL, Farida (b. 1958). Novelist of Algerian descent born and brought up in Paris by immigrant parents. After making a number of short films and dabbling in *Beur politics, she wrote her first novel, *Georgette!* (1986). The text takes the form of an interior monologue narrated by a 7-year-old girl torn between the injunctions of her French schoolteacher and those of her illiterate Algerian father.

[AGH]

Belgian Literature in French. Aside from a tiny German-speaking area in the east, Belgium is essentially a bilingual country made up of Flemish-speaking Flanders in the north and French-speaking Wallonia (*la Wallonie*) in the south. The northern provinces were the home of four Flemish dialects, now close to standardization as modern Dutch, while the southern ones spoke the Walloon dialect, which has merged into modern French. Originally, in 1830, the Flemings and the Walloons joined forces to throw off Dutch rule and establish the modern Belgian state; yet intermittent separatist upsurges on either side have threatened national stability ever since, whether sparked off by quarrels over education, government power, and an uneven economy, or by the instinct of local patriotism. Any qualities deemed specific to Belgian francophone literature need to be mapped in relation to two opposed claims which challenge that specificity: on the one hand there is the position (defended in 1937 in a famous manifesto signed by prominent Belgian writers like Charles Plisnier, Marie Gevers, and Franz *Hellens) that Belgian literature forms an integral part of French literature at large; while on the other there is the view that it is the expression of an uncertain enclave whose suspect identity can only be maintained by artificially warding off the cultural impact both of France and the Netherlands.

Within Belgium at large, French has traditionally been the tongue of the educated and the politically powerful, as witness the dominance of French use among the cultured bourgeoisie in Flemish cities like Ghent and the fact that, though situated within Flemish Brabant, the country's capital, Brussels, is largely francophone. This has meant that the prestige of French as a medium of modern culture is interestingly tinged with self-conciousness and even an anxiety concerning the social and political dimensions of its use. Ought a francophone Belgian to opt for a modest horizon and address a provincial audience? Or ought that writer to set his or her sights on

Paris, settling for a local reputation only by default? It is true that Parisian literary models are as readily available as any others: but is the writer inside Belgium in a position blithely to ignore his or her cultural inheritance, with its unmistakable strain of 'Flemishness'? The paradox is that the majority of Belgium's best francophone writers come from the northern provinces rather than from Wallonia itself.

A rigid definition of what is typically 'Belgian' about Belgian literature in French would be merely caricatural, though as little is to be gained by stirring it indistinguishably into the French mainstream as by reducing it to a sluggish backwater of Dutch culture, marked by Flemish stolidity and an archaic ruralism. What *can* be isolated are some obvious references to geography and local custom; a less obvious cast of thought and temperament, where pragmatism coincides strangely with a certain mysticism; and an implicit awareness of linguistic difference and the cross-play of cultural codes even in daily life. To speak of cultural dualism may sound too pat: perhaps it is more a question of a sense of contrary options suspended in fertile tension—the cosmopolitan and the regional, the urban and the rural, the sophisticated and the popular, the visionary and the earthbound. Inadequate to the subtler task of characterizing individuals, such general notions at least offer points of orientation in the present overview, which will attempt simply to scan the considerable variety of Belgian francophone writing, naming prominent individuals while sketching general trends within the genres of poetry, fiction, and drama.

The first true wave of Belgian writing in French occurred in the 1880s, at a time of great social unrest. Writers largely belonged to the bourgeois class, yet were sympathetic to left-wing aspirations and often half-consciously associated their own anti-philistinism with contemporary anarchist ideals. The literary struggle was waged through a series of journals promoting neglected Belgian writers like Charles De Coster (1827–79), author of the overtly patriotic *Thyl Ulenspiegel* (1867), and emerging ones like Camille *Lemonnier or Émile *Verhaeren. In 1882 the young Max Waller (1860–89) took over the review *La Jeune Belgique* (1881–97) and made of it the lively, even noisy, forum of a Belgian literary renaissance whose first works, it is true, benefited from the Parisian styles of *Naturalism and *Parnassianism. Soon came a review called *La Wallonie* (1886–92), an epoch-making formulation which crystallized the very concept of a francophone homeland. Its editor, the Liège-based poet Albert *Mockel, at first advocated regionalism. Later, though, he turned the magazine into one of the foremost international platforms of *Symbolism, publishing work by Parisian 'stars' like *Ghil, de *Régnier, and *Mallarmé (who made a celebrated lecture tour through Belgium in 1890); the American Symbolist Stuart *Merrill; and a team of Belgian poets of the highest calibre—*Maeterlinck,

Verhaeren, *Rodenbach, *Van Lerberghe, and *Elskamp. The remarkable fact is that each of these last was brought up in Flemish-speaking Ghent; so that this first generation of major francophone writers strike a distinctively 'Belgian' note—with Verhaeren's muscular turbulence complemented by Maeterlinck's metaphysical quietism—while also holding their own alongside their foreign counterparts.

Much the same strategy of sustaining fruitful contact with Paris while nurturing local identity was pursued by Belgian *Surrealism during the inter-war years. The activities of Clément Pansaers (1885–1922), editor of the Dada magazine *Résurrection* (1918), prefigured those of Paul *Nougé, Marcel *Lecomte, Camille Goëmans (1900–60), and Louis Scutenaire (1905–87), who, along with the painter *Magritte and the musician André Souris, worked out a Brussels version of Surrealism which diverged from *Breton's Parisian blueprint in cultivating irony and enigma, as well as an occasional acerbic aggressiveness. A more idiosyncratic Surrealism was exemplified by the poet Achille *Chavée, a left-wing activist who fought in the Spanish Civil War; while a further non-aligned Surrealist was the poet Robert Guiette (1895–1976).

Among the poets of Brussels belonging to no particular group may be cited the varied examples of Jean de *Boschère, visionary mystic and friend of James Joyce; the short-lived Odilon-Jean Périer (1901–28), a graceful neoclassicist; and Géo *Norge, whose overtly regional, even earthy, themes place his work firmly at one extreme of Flemish francophone typology. The compulsive experimentalism of the painter-poet Henri *Michaux may be ascribed in part to his medical background, in part to his Surrealist affinities and his interest in exotic cultures. Michaux left his native Namur as a young man to travel in South America and Asia, and settled in Paris in 1937; even so, an argument might be made for seeing his anxious metaphysics as a throwback to Belgian Symbolism, while his tireless grapplings with collapsing verbal forms could be linked with the linguistic tensions mentioned earlier.

The poetry of Marcel *Thiry reflects a kinship with French post-Symbolist writers, and his colourful travels in Asia and America make of him in many ways another cosmopolitan. Despite this, Thiry does sound an appreciably Belgian note in his fantastic fiction. A capacity to tie the impossible and the outrageous to ordinary experience is indeed one of the distinguishing traits of Belgian writing of the *Fantastic, and may be found in varying measure in the work of Franz Hellens, Jean *Ray, and Jacques Sternberg (b. 1923). Their taste for things spectral or magical may be seen as a function of Belgian popular tradition, though there are equally plausible antecedents in Belgian Symbolism, with such proto-fantastic works as Rodenbach's novel *Bruges-la-morte* (1892), an uncanny suffusion of the macabre within a named locale. Certainly it can be said that a prag-

matic grip on real places is often a characteristic way for the Belgian literary imagination to launch its flights of fancy (though admittedly this general remark might prove to be applicable to Flanders and beyond, as well as to Wallonia).

The notion of a mingling of the poetic with the down-to-earth may also be traced back to certain writers of the 1880s who were not Symbolists. A certain lyrical realism informed the work of the popular novelist Camille Lemonnier, author of *Un mâle* (1881) and exponent of a *Naturalism somewhat cautiously responsive to *Zola's example, as well as that of the francophone Fleming Georges Eekhoud (1854–1927), who specialized in studies of provincial life in the Antwerp lowlands, as in *Kermesses* (1884). Some commentators have pointed out the tradition of earthy, folkloric regionalism in the work of Dutch-language novelists such as Félix Timmermans (1886–1947) and Ernest Claes (1885–1968); and, developing an enticing analogy with the peasant-life scenes of Pieter Bruegel, identify the Belgian francophone sensibility with the rural-archaic model. Certainly, an unrestrained devotion to the *genius loci* of her native Campine district by the River Scheldt is typical of the ruralist novelist Marie Gevers (1884–1975). More sophisticated shades of realism characterize Constant Burniaux (1892–1975), whose novels reflect his experiences as a schoolteacher; or Charles Plisnier (1896–1952), a one-time Communist whose chronicles of family life in provincial Belgium earned him, in 1937, the distinction of being the first foreigner to win the Prix Goncourt. An eye for telling detail informs the fiction of Georges *Simenon, whose notoriety as an expatriate crime-writer should not distract attention from his abilities as a serious novelist and what might be seen as his 'Belgian' concern with the atmospherics of concrete situations. Again, it is harder to find signs of national temperament in expatriates such as the Paris-based novelist Félicien *Marceau, author of the metropolitan extravaganza *Creezy* (1969), though Françoise *Mallet-Joris, daughter of the francophone Flemish author Suzanne *Lilar but now a French citizen, has written novels explicitly based on her Flanders upbringing.

In the domain of the theatre, Belgian writers seem always to have chosen to look to Paris, yet, apart from Maeterlinck, not to have become expatriates. Staged at the Théâtre de l'Œuvre by *Lugné-Poë, Maeterlinck's early Symbolist dramas were mystifying and exotic imports for Paris audiences accustomed to a French Realist diet. Lugné-Poë went on to stage the highly successful *Le Cocu magnifique* (1920) by Fernand *Crommelynck, the equal of *Giraudoux in the interwar Golden Age of Paris theatre, yet very much the Fleming in his Bruegel-like ebullience. Yet another Flemish francophone, Michel de Ghelderode, conquered that same stage in 1947 with his *Hop signor!*. This happened, however, only after a long apprenticeship with the

Vlaamse Volkstoneel, the Flemish People's Theatre, and Ghelderode remained loyal to Flemish popular culture throughout his prolific career, exploiting a vein of demonic and hallucinatory spectacle harking back not so much to Bruegel as to the weird fantasmagorias of Hieronymus Bosch. The religious drama *Barabbas* (1928) was seen in Paris and Brussels, but has become a regional classic by virtue of the Flemish version in which it has been performed each Easter since 1928. Indeed, the irreducibility of Ghelderode's regional attachment typecasts him as the paradigmatic Belgian francophone, always tempted by Paris yet never neglectful of his homeland, its folklore, its uneven cultural and linguistic fabric.   [RC]

See A. J. Mathews, *La Wallonie, 1886–1892: The Symbolist Movement in Belgium* (1947); V. Mallinson, *Modern Belgian Literature 1830–1960* (1966); R. Burniaux and R. Frickx, *La Littérature belge d'expression française* (1973).

Bel Immonde, Le, see MUDIMBE.

Bel Inconnu, Le. Late 12th- or early 13th-c. Arthurian verse romance (over 6,000 lines), written by one Renaut de Beaujeu, about whom nothing is known. The romance recounts the marvellous adventures of a knight who is dubbed 'the handsome unknown' because he knows neither his name nor his father. The young man overcomes awesome enemies and enchantments before learning his identity as *Gauvain's son and his name, Guinglain. He also experiences a powerful conflict between social obligation and private desire, which is presented within two interlacing love stories. Guinglain sets off boldly from Arthur's court to rescue the daughter of King Gringas, Blonde Esmerée, queen of Wales, whom he eventually saves by receiving a fearsome kiss from the serpent into which she had been transformed; she offers her kingdom and her hand in marriage. But *en route* to Esmerée's deliverance, Guinglain has met the enchanting Fée aux Blanches Mains, from whom he learns the joys and pains of desire. After twice deserting his beloved fairy, Guinglain agrees to a politically expedient marriage with the queen. In an intriguing epilogue, the narrator promises to let Guinglain lie again with the fairy mistress if only his beloved reader, whom he had addressed at several points during the story, will show him favour.   [RLK]

Bélisaire, see MARMONTEL.

BELLEAU, Rémy (*c*.1528–1577). French poet. A member of the *Pléiade, he was born in Nogent-le-Rotrou and educated under *Muret at the Collège de Boncourt. In 1556 his translation of the *Odes d'Anacréon* appeared together with a collection—the *Petites Inventions*—which revealed an early predilection for the descriptive realism of the *blason. Back in France after participating briefly in an Italian campaign in the cavalry of the marquis d'Elbeuf

(1556–7), Belleau wrote a commentary for *Ronsard's *Second Livre des Amours* (1560) and became tutor to the marquis's son, Charles de Lorraine, at the family estate at Joinville (1563–6), a setting idealized in Belleau's major work, the *Bergerie* (1565; revised and augmented, 1572).

Belleau's descriptive qualities are in evidence again in *Les Amours et nouveaux échanges des pierres precieuses*, a lapidary collection published in 1576 with verse adaptations of Ecclesiastes and the Song of Songs. A posthumous collective edition of his works (1578) contained for the first time an interesting verse comedy, *La Reconnue* (composed about 1563).

Although Belleau's work lacks lyrical intensity and sustained imaginative vision, his sensitive evocations of the physical and natural world (including art objects) reveal the delicate precision and the pictorial realism of a visual artist.   [MDQ]

'Belle au bois dormant, La'. One of Perrault's *Histoires ou contes du temps passé*, the story of 'Sleeping Beauty', with a final section in which the heroine's children are rescued from their mother-in-law, an ogress.

Belle Dame sans mercy, La, see CHARTIER.

Belle du seigneur, see COHEN, A.

Belle et la bête, La, see LE PRINCE DE BEAUMONT.

BELLEFOREST, François de (1530–83). Orphaned at an early age, Belleforest was raised by *Marguerite de Navarre. After studying law at Bordeaux and Toulouse, he moved to Paris, where he became Historiographe du Roi. He published over 50 titles: histories such as *Histoire des neuf rois Charles de France* (1568); *Les Grandes Annales . . . de France . . .* (1579), which stressed the Gaulish origins of the Franks; *L'Innocence de . . . Madame Marie, reine d'Écosse* (1572), a defence of the queen against Protestant criticism. He wrote poetry (see *La Pastorale amoureuse*, 1569), but is best remembered for his translations (Latin, Spanish, Italian), especially his adaptation of Bandello's *Histoires tragiques* (1560–80) [see BOAISTUAU].   [KCC]

BELLEGARDE, Jean-Baptiste Morvan de (1648–1734). French author of numerous works on ethics, religion, education, and particularly of influential books on polite behaviour and conversation. His *Réflexions sur le ridicule* (1696) and *Réflexions sur la politesse des mœurs* (1698) give a good idea of current ideas on the subject; together with cognate works, including a book of model conversations, they were several times reprinted and translated into English.   [PF]

Belles-sœurs, Les, see TREMBLAY.

BELLETTO, René (b. 1945), French novelist, scriptwriter, guitar-teacher, poet. His novels (*Le Revenant*, 1981; *Sur la terre comme au ciel*, 1982;

L'Enfer, 1986, Prix Fémina) combine the suspense of the detective story with humour (word-play, irony, and exaggeration) and sensitive characterization. *La Machine* (1990), in which two of the characters exchange personalities through technological manipulation, is more sombre, more disturbing, less satisfying. [PS]

BELLOY, Dormont de (pseud. of Pierre-Laurent Buirette) (1727–75). French dramatist. Orphaned in Paris at the age of 5, de Belloy was brought up by a lawyer uncle, who intended him for the bar. He wanted to act and, when his uncle opposed this, fled to Russia. His first tragedy, *Titus*, was first performed in St Petersburg in 1757, and two years later failed at the Comédie-Française. His 'national tragedy', *Le *Siège de Calais* (1765), was heavily promoted by Louis XV's government and won transient success. He is also remembered for *Zelmire* (1762), *Gaston et Bayard* (1771), *Pierre le cruel* (1772), and *Gabrielle de Vergy* (1777). He idealized the dynamism of the Middle Ages and early Renaissance, in contrast to the effeteness of his own time. [JD]

BELMONDO, Jean-Paul (b. 1932). French actor. His role in *Godard's *A bout de souffle* (1959) brought him fame as the leading male star of the *Nouvelle Vague. Latterly he has appeared mostly in popular films, where his cynicism allied to sensitivity is not so well used as in his greatest performance, again for Godard—*Pierrot le fou* (1965). [KAR]

BELON DU MANS, Pierre (c.1517–1564). French scientist and diplomat whose adventurous and disputatious life ended in assassination, probably by a Huguenot. Apart from detailed empirical studies of fish, birds, and trees, he published a lively account of his travels around the Mediterranean, *Les Observations de plusieurs singularités et choses mémorables* (1553). [MJH]

BEMBA, Sylvain (b. 1934). Congolese novelist, playwright, and essayist. He has worked in various capacities as a cultural adviser, has collaborated on the review *Liaison*, and is one of the most active members of Brazzaville intellectual circles. Bemba is a very prolific writer, particularly if one considers the list of his unpublished works (mainly plays). He has stated his affiliation to 'magic realism', a feature of all his writing, and is a strong social and historical critic of colonialism and modern societies, whether they be Western or African.

Rêves portatifs (1979) is a highly original novel. The 'rêves' are those which brought about 'independence', and they are dreams precisely because reality is so very different. The 'portatifs' corresponds to the increased role played by radio and television in everyday life and the way governments have used them to set up what Bemba calls 'radiotelevision dictatorships'. *Le Dernier des Cargonautes* (1984) is a satire of society; in its conversations and

discussions Bemba confronts many issues and warns against the evils which lie ahead. *Léopolis* (1984) explores the myth surrounding the assassinated leader Patrice Lumumba. Bemba was awarded the Grand Prix des Lettres by the Congolese president in 1977. [DRDT]

BEN ALI, Larbi (b. 1949). Tunisian poet living in Paris. Mostly self-taught, anti-intellectual, he has written two major volumes of poetry: *Prophéties insoumises* (1973) and *Le Porteur d'eau* (1976). His poetry, self-deprecating at times with touches of ironic humour and moving nostalgia, is a search for roots, identity, and meaning in a world that is itself in a constant state of flux. [ET]

BENDA, Julien (1867–1956). French essayist and critic. An acerbic and passionate advocate of disinterested contemplation and analysis, Benda promoted a universalistic morality based on fixed abstract principles, and an idealist, anti-pragmatic, anti-subjective rationalism. He denounced *Bergson's emphasis on intuition and his vitalist theories of dynamism, flux, and mobility; he castigated contemporary *intellectuals for abandoning the pure life of the mind and adopting worldly, practical, bourgeois, nationalistic, or crusading ends (*La Trahison des clercs*, 1927); and he indiscriminately attacked modern writers (*Gide, *Valéry, the *Surrealists) for their alleged formalism, anti-intellectualism, and obscurity (*La France byzantine*, 1945). [REG]

Benedictines. The Benedictine order follows the rule of St Benedict of Nursia (died c.550), a complete guide to cenobitical life structured around the eight offices of the day. This became by the 10th c. the standard rule in Western Europe. Benedictine monasteries were usually richly endowed, their inmates aristocratic. Primarily devoted to prayer, the monks also wrote chronicles, illuminated manuscripts, produced stained glass and other associated crafts, and dispensed hospitality and charity. After about 1050 their ascendancy was challenged by new orders, but they continued to play a major role in ecclesiastical affairs throughout the Middle Ages and beyond, and became particularly celebrated for their historical erudition [see MAURISTS]. Among the most famous French houses were Saint-Denis in Paris, *Cluny, Fleury (Saint-Benoît-sur-Loire), Saint-Martin in Tours, and Marmoutier. [JHD]

BENJAMIN, René, see WORLD WAR I.

BEN JELLOUN, Tahar (b. 1944). Moroccan novelist. Born in Fez, he moved at 18 with his family to Tangier where he attended the French *lycée*. Both towns were to play significant roles in his poetry and fiction. He then studied in Rabat, during which time he collaborated on the journal *Souffles and published his first poems, *Hommes sous linceul de silence* (1971), and a first novel, *Harrouda* (1973). He obtained a doctorate in psychiatric social work in France, his thesis being based on case histories of North African immigrant workers whom Ben Jelloun had counselled, mostly with regard to the sexual dysfunction they tended to suffer while in France. His second novel, *La Réclusion solitaire* (1976), fictionalized some of these case histories and his dissertation was subsequently published as *La plus haute des solitudes* (1977).

On the surface, Ben Jelloun's works are readily accessible tales, and yet one cannot have a full appreciation of his work without some idea of how Arabic language, Koranic imagery, and other aspects of traditional Moroccan culture—including the literary traits of errancy, delirium, fantasy, the quest voyage, and narrative framing found in the *Mille et une Nuits* and other classics of Eastern literature—have entered into French discourse.

Ben Jelloun's earlier novels include: *Harrouda* (1973), a haunting 'psycho-spatial' tale of the quite different urban experiences of Fez and Tangier; *Moha le fou, Moha le sage* (1978), the confused and tortured ravings of a man who yet speaks eloquently on behalf of the downtrodden and disenfranchised 'wretched of the Earth'; *La Prière de l'absent* (1981), which describes, against the backdrop of Moroccan politics and the legendary lives of the resistance patriots Krim and Ma-al-Aynayn, a quest to the south of Morocco by two mentally troubled men, Boby and Sindibad, an old woman, and an infant of destiny who has come under their care; and *L'Écrivain public* (1983), a remarkable but lesser-known novel whose story of the travails of a physical and psychological invalid is cleverly disclosed in letters, diaries, reminiscences, and dreams.

His most successful books to date have been *L'Enfant de sable* (1985) and its sequel *La Nuit sacrée* (1987, Prix Goncourt). The two books describe the psychological misshaping of a girl who is raised as a boy by her father and her subsequent rediscovery and affirmation of her female identity which she retrieves through a series of violent and erotic experiences. There followed *Jour de silence à Tanger* (1990), which is the interior monologue of an old man whose waning days are articulated primarily in listless introspection as he relives ancient, often erotic, memories; and *Les Yeux baissés* (1991), in which a girl, in an itinerary similar to that taken by Ben Jelloun and other francophone writers, moves from rural Morocco to France, becomes competent in French, and yearns to become a writer.

Ben Jelloun's poetry, ranging from brief enigmatic texts to surrealistic prose poems, is rich in imagery and highly lyrical. Representative poems may be found in *Les Amandiers sont morts de leurs blessures, suivi de A l'insu du souvenir* (1983), which includes such earlier collections as *Cicatrices du soleil* (1972) and *Le Discours du chameau* (1974).   [ES]

See A. Tenkoul, *Littérature marocaine d'écriture française* (1985); L. Mouzouni, *Le Roman marocain de langue française* (1987).

BENOIST, Alain de (pseud. of Fabrice Laroche) (b. 1943). French journalist, essayist, and lecturer who has been described as 'l'intellectuel numéro un de la *Nouvelle Droite'. He has published numerous polemical works, the most famous of which, *Vu de droite*, was awarded the Prix de l'Essai de l'Académie Française in 1978. This swingeing attack upon egalitarian values brought him to public prominence in 1979, when the media discovered the New Right. His extreme-Right activism began, however, in the early 1960s, with the pro-*Algérie française* Fédération d'Étudiants Nationalistes, leading to links with the proto-fascist Jeune Nation. He has played a major editorial role in the production of journals such as *Nouvelle École* and *Éléments* and written the media column in *Figaro Magazine*. His potential lasting influence was suggested by René Rémond's question: 'Alain de Benoist, serait-il le Charles *Maurras de sa génération?'   [GVR]

BENOÎT, Pierre (1886–1962). French author of a series of best-selling adventure novels set in wealthy and elegant social contexts. Moving between the world of Maxim's and the North African desert, the heroes of *Koenigsmark* (1918) and *L'Atlantide* (1919) become involved in complicated and exotic adventures before inevitably winning the day and the heroine. He was greatly appreciated in the inter-war period.   [EAF]

BENOÎT DE SAINTE-MAURE (*fl.* 12th c.). Author of *Le Roman de Troie* (*c.*1160), an adaptation into over 30,000 rhyming octosyllables of the supposedly eye-witness account of the Trojan War by Dares and Dictys [see ROMANS D'ANTIQUITÉ]. The role attributed to love is considerably amplified and foreshadows the courtly romance modes of later decades. Benoît's descriptive embroideries lend colour and variety to his sources. He also worked in England at the court of Henry II, where he succeeded *Wace as vernacular historiographer. He left his vast Norman history, the *Chronique des ducs de Normandie* (*c.*1175), incomplete, though it was already over 44,000 lines long.   [IS]

BÉNOZIGLIO, Jean-Luc, see ARGOT.

BENSERADE or **BENSSERADE,** Isaac de (1613–91). French poet and dramatist. In a long literary career he wrote witty verse, at least five plays, and a number of often satirical libretti for court ballets, composed in association with *Lully in the 1660s. Elected to the Académie Française in 1674, he became an outspoken *moderne* in the *Querelle.
        [GJM]

BENVENISTE, Emile (1902–76). French linguist. After pioneering work in comparative Indo-European grammar, he moved to pure linguistics, following a *Saussurean conception of general linguistics. He accepted that language was a system of signs, but challenged Saussure's account of the dualism of the sign, arguing that the relation between *signifiant* and *signifié* in verbal signs was not purely arbitrary and conventional. His analyses of temporality, person, and voice were taken up by *Barthes and others in theories of writing and literature. As professor at the *Collège de France, Benveniste vigorously promoted the extension of linguistic analysis to a wider range of communications, in the form of semiotics. See his *Problèmes de linguistique générale* (1966). [MHK]

BÉRANGER, Pierre-Jean de (1780–1857). Poet and songwriter. The son of a fairly humble Parisian family, he worked as a printer before obtaining a pension from Lucien Bonaparte and a clerical post in the University. He lost his post and was twice imprisoned under the *Restoration on account of his songs. His first publication was *Chansons morales et autres* (1815), containing the anti-Napeolonic 'Le Roi d'Yvetot'; this was followed by several more collections, the last being *Chansons nouvelles et dernières* (1833), with an important preface.

Béranger, who was much admired by *Stendhal and Goethe, was honoured at his death as a national poet. His witty, good-humoured poems and songs crystallized myths of the French rural past, of French popular mentality, and of *Bonapartism and spoke to the needs and aspirations of a wide range of readers at specific moments in history. His *anticlericalism and anti-royalism placed him in the central tradition of liberal *republicanism and made of him an exemplary opponent of the Restoration, his imprisonment further serving to enhance his legendary status.

It is generally accepted that his songs played a significant part in the 1830 Revolution [see JULY MONARCHY], and they continued to have a stirring effect on working-class republicans throughout the century. However, in the eyes of avant-garde writers such as *Baudelaire or *Flaubert—those committed to the quest for formal perfection and the exposure of hypocrisies and pieties of all factions—Béranger was worthy only of contempt. Baudelaire poured scorn on the easy sentimentality and hearty bawdiness of his songs. The same view has generally prevailed in literary circles; *Thibaudet even found Béranger indistinguishable from Flaubert's *Homais. Robert Louis Stevenson has a good and much more sympathetic piece about him in the *Encyclopedia Britannica* (11th edn.) [BR]

BÉRAUD, Henri (1888–1958). Right-wing French writer. As a journalist in Lyon and then in Paris, he gravitated towards extremist publications, notably *Gringoire*. Author of a novel and many political pamphlets, Béraud was a notorious wartime collaborator, for which he later spent 10 years in prison.

BERDIAEFF (English transliteration: Berdyaev), Nicolaï Aleksandrovitch (1874–1948). Christian existentialist philosopher. Born in Kiev, he first espoused Marxist ideas, then a mystical religion of

humanity, and finally a spiritually renewed Christianity. Forced into exile after the Bolshevik Revolution, he settled in Paris from 1925. His thought emphasized the free individual as the source of creativity and spiritual renewal. He developed an account of Communism which accepted its critique of capitalism, but rejected its subordination of individual spiritual aspirations to practical social struggles. He was particularly influential in the 1930s among the younger generation of Catholic intellectuals, whom he sought to innoculate against the temptation of Marxism. See his *Essai d'autobiographie spirituelle* (1948). [MHK]

Bérenger. Hero, or anti-hero, of several plays by *Ionesco.

Bérénice. Tragedy by *Racine, first performed in 1670 in competition with Pierre Corneille's *Tite et Bérénice*. Its plot can be summed up in a sentence from Suetonius: 'Titus, who was even said to have promised marriage to Queen Berenice, immediately sent her away from Rome against both their wishes.' Racine complicates this only by introducing Antiochus (who loves Bérénice) as an intermediary between the lovers. The preface states that 'invention consists in making something of nothing'; lacking in outward action, this moving play is made up of the conflicting and changing emotions of the characters as they confront their unbearable situation. As Roman emperor, Titus cannot marry a queen, nor can Bérénice return Antiochus's love. All the protagonists threaten suicide, but the play culminates in the grief-stricken acceptance of separation. Contemporaries saw in it an allusion to *Louis XIV's separation from Marie Mancini, Mazarin's niece. [PF]

BERGERAC, Cyrano de, see CYRANO DE BERGERAC.

Berger extravagant, Le, see SOREL, C.

Bergotte. Character in Proust's *A la recherche du temps perdu*, a novelist of genius.

BERGSON, Henri (1859–1941). One of the most influential French philosophers of his age. In 1900 he was appointed to a chair at the *Collège de France, where his lectures became a fashionable Parisian cult. He was awarded the Nobel Prize for Literature in 1927. His thought encompassed metaphysics, science, psychology, aesthetics, ethics, and religion, and he developed a philosophical method which reacted markedly against the scientific and analytic approach of contemporary positivism [see COMTE].

Bergson took as his starting-point our experience of time and change. In his *Essai sur les données immédiates de la conscience* (1889) he distinguished between time as we experience it, or duration as a fluid, continuous flow, and mechanical, spatial representations of time as divisible and measurable. He contended that the spontaneity, freedom, and creativity of consciousness had been obscured by the misapplication in psychology of determinist and mechanist laws more appropriate to the study of matter: the new task of philosophy was to investigate our living, qualitative apprehension of 'la durée réelle', unmediated by habit, social life, or linguistic convention. He addressed the relation between mind and body and between memory and perception in *Matière et mémoire* (1896), distinguishing between the 'pure' memory which preserves past images and events in their totality and uniqueness, and a utilitarian memory associated with repetition and bodily habit. The brain, argued, provides the mechanism whereby our pure image-memories are suppressed in the interests of practical action; they may reappear vividly and spontaneously if such constraints are relaxed. In *L'Évolution créatrice* (1907) the dynamic 'devenir' of our inner life is transposed to the level of the cosmos: the process of evolution itself is energized by an 'élan vital' which, in overcoming the resistance of matter, generates ever more diverse and complex forms, to become fully self-conscious in man. The assimilation of this lifeforce to a divine creative principle is adumbrated in Bergson's last major work, *Les Deux Sources de la morale et de la religion* (1932).

In the belief that conceptual language and analysis immobilize the object of knowledge, Bergson emphasized the role of intuition, allied to reflection, in grasping and revealing 'la durée réelle'. His own vivid metaphorical style exemplified this approach, as did his acknowledgement of the non-utilitarian vision and expressive power of art. Bergson's association of beauty with supple vitality and grace is illustrated by largely negative implication in *Le Rire* (1900). There he contended that a sense of the comic is provoked when natural spontaneity is reduced to a set of mechanical bodily responses; this automatism, perceived by society as a threat, releases the defensive reaction of laughter.

Bergson's influence was acknowledged by many writers and critics of his own and younger generations (e.g. *Péguy, *Thibaudet, *Deleuze), while comparisons between his insights and those of *Proust became a critical commonplace. His work anticipated a number of the themes of existential *phenomenology. [REG]

See I. W. Alexander, *Bergson* (1957); L. Kolakowski, *Bergson* (1985).

BERL, Emmanuel (1892–1976). French journalist and essayist. After military service in World War I, he joined the left-wing and pacifist movements of *Barbusse and *Rolland. His essay *Mort de la pensée bourgeoise* (1929) was one of several in which he diagnosed a moral and intellectual crisis, and called for revolutionary social transformations. After World War II he became a frequent broadcaster and wrote particularly on the exploitative intent behind European relations with Africa and Asia; see his

Nasser tel qu'on le loue (1968) and *Europe et Asie* (1969). [MHK]

BERLIOZ, Hector (1803–69). French composer and critic, who symbolizes for many the archetypal Romantic—the wild genius unappreciated in his time, whose life was inseparable from his art. Certainly it is difficult to try to separate them; all his orchestral music, for instance, has extra-musical associations relating both to literary inspirations and life experiences.

Berlioz was widely read and, although his two literary idols were Virgil and Shakespeare, he was familiar with French, German, and English contemporary literature. As a writer he is best known for his extraordinarily evocative *Mémoires* (1865). He also wrote some of his own opera libretti (*Les Troyens, Béatrice et Bénédict*) and was a highly respected music critic for much of his life (1834–62). His motivation in becoming a critic was both financial (for many years it was his chief source of income) and the need for a public venue in which to defend his ideals. No other French music critic of the time wrote as well or as much as Berlioz, and selections of his best criticism and short stories were published in his lifetime. [KM]

BERNABÉ, Joby (b. 1945). *Creole poet and virtuoso performer, often to music, of compositions which renew the oral traditions of Martinique (*Konmbo*, 1978). His well-received recitals blend humour, topical satire, and lyric fervour. He is also an actor and active in experimental theatre (see *Kimafoutiésa*, 1975, a collective creation attacking sponsored migration to France). [BJ]

BERNADETTE, Sainte, see LOURDES.

BERNANOS, Georges (1888–1948). With *Mauriac, Bernanos is the major Catholic novelist in France in the 20th c. and an equally important polemicist. Born in Paris, he joined *Action Française while a student at the Sorbonne and became one of the movement's journalists, editing *L'Avant-Garde de la Normandie* from Rouen before World War I. After a distinguished war career, during which he was seriously wounded, he became an inspector for an insurance company, covering the region of Northern France and Picardy, which was to be the location for his fiction. In the context of this financially insecure and semi-nomadic existence he became a novelist.

He published his first novel, *Sous le soleil de Satan*, in 1926. Based upon the career of the curé de Lumbres, the novel recounts the literal battle between a young country priest and the devil for the soul of a small country village, and sets the tone for the rest of Bernanos's fiction. His work is concerned with the concrete presence of evil, in apathy and corruption and violence, and with the search for privileged figures to combat it. In his next two novels, *La Joie* (1929) and *L'Imposture* (1931), the antidote to corruption is found in the innocence of the child, a theme he also explores in his later work. At the same time he turned to polemic, in the pamphleteering tradition of *Drumont and *Bloy, with La Grande Peur des bien-pensants (1931), in which he castigates his perennial enemy, the complacent, conventionally religious bourgeoisie.

In 1936 his struggle against poverty in France became too much, and he moved with his family to the cheaper life of Majorca. Not only was this period the most richly productive of his career, but it marked a major political turning-point. It was in Majorca that he produced his best-known novel, *Journal d'un curé de campagne (1936), which elevates the childlike innocence and heroism of a young country priest in his battle against evil to the level of sainthood, and Nouvelle histoire de Mouchette (1937), which depicts the emotional martyrdom of a young girl in a barren village. It was also in Majorca that he witnessed the brutality of the Spanish fascists; he denounced this in Les Grands Cimetières sous la lune (1937) and became an ardent Republican. Unable to settle again in France, he moved to South America; here he emerged as a major Gaullist propagandist during World War II and wrote his last novel Monsieur Ouine (1945), perhaps his most complex analysis of evil in the community; it was not published in its definitive form until 1955. His last years after the war were spent in North Africa.

Bernanos's Catholicism must be seen in the context of the Catholic Revival of the 1900s [see CATHOLICISM IN TWENTIETH-CENTURY FRANCE], as a vigorous reaction against materialist scientism and the hegemony of the bourgeoisie, and as a plea for mysticism and faith. Politically, this takes the form of a particularly anachronistic form of royalism: a return to the strength and cohesion of the Middle Ages. In his novels, it leads to an exploration of those figures who can transcend the finite limits of unbelief: the child, the saint, and the hero. In his cultivation of heroism as an antidote to the modern world, Bernanos enters the mainstream of French fiction of the 1930s; hence his close affinities with *Malraux and his adoption by the post-war right-wing *Hussards.   [NH]

See A. Béguin, Bernanos par lui-même (1954); M. Estève, Le Sens de l'amour dans les romans de Bernanos (1959); C. Nettelbeck, Les Personnages de Bernanos romancier (1970).

BERNARD, Catherine (c.1662–1712). A relative of the *Corneille brothers and a convert to Catholicism (1685), she published tragedies, notably Brutus (1691), and historical fiction (Le Comte d'Amboise, 1689; Inès de Cordoue, 1696). Her psychological novel Les Malheurs de l'amour (1687) was highly praised by *Fontenelle. The Académie Française awarded her poetry numerous prizes; the Ricovrati Academy of Padua elected her a member.   [JDeJ]

BERNARD, Claude (1813–78). French physiologist and professor at the *Collège de France, a leading figure in the development of experimental science as a system of hypothesis, proof, and refutation. In his Introduction à la médecine expérimentale (1865), he defined systematic medical experiment, distinguishing it from the randomness of empirical observation, and asserted the principle of scientific determinism, which, he held, was not to be confused with philosophical fatalism. Naturalist novelists, and particularly *Zola in Le Roman expérimental, published two years after Bernard's La Science expérimentale (1878), claimed mistakenly that Bernard's scientific method, which they did not understand clearly, could be applied in the novel.   [BCS]

BERNARD, Jean-Jacques (1888–1972). French playwright and novelist. He was the son of Tristan *Bernard and, though he later wrote novels, is remembered for the intimiste plays of his théâtre de l'inexprimé: Le Feu qui reprend mal (1921), Martine (1922, dir. Baty; 1985, National Theatre, dir. Hall, trans. Fowles), Le Printemps des autres (1924), L'Invitation au voyage (1924, dir. Baty), where allusion, suggestion, and the unspoken soberly articulate conflicts of heart and mind.   [DAS]

BERNARD, Jean-Marc (1881–1915). French poet and literary critic. He wrote both in Virgilian tones (Sub tegmine fagi, 1913) and in more piquant manner, founding the satirical review Les Guêpes in 1909 and associating with the *Fantaisistes *Carco and Dérème. Bernard's Villon-inspired 'De Profundis' is an anthology piece from the Golgotha of the trenches where he was killed.   [DAS]

BERNARD, Pierre-Joseph (1710–75). French poet. Known as Gentil-Bernard (a name given him by *Voltaire), he charmed the salons with his coolly elegant love poems, but was far from 'gentil' according to some contemporaries. He wrote an Art d'aimer (1775) and the libretto for *Rameau's opera Castor et Pollux (1737).   [PF]

BERNARD, Tristan (1866–1947). French humorist, journalist, playwright, and typical Parisian entertainer of the belle époque. His zestful and good-natured farces, light comedies, and satirical sketches of French middle-class life reflect an unerring talent to amuse, a quick-witted and ingenious handling of the mechanics of plot, a sharp eye for the ridiculous, and a relish in deflating his pompous characters. Plays favoured by his contemporaries include: L'Anglais tel qu'on le parle (1899); Triplepatte (1905); Monsieur Codomat (1907); Le Petit Café (1911). Also admired was his novel, Les Mémoires d'un jeune homme rangé (1899).   [SBJ]

BERNARD DE CLAIRVAUX, Saint (1091–1153), born of a noble family, renounced riches and worldly pleasures and founded the first *Cistercian monastery, at Clairvaux—his 'school of Christ', where the Rule of St Benedict was to be scrupulously followed. He emphasized the importance of monastic obedience and humility, by contrast with the arrogance of secular masters, in achieving true wisdom and happiness. Most notably in his *Sermons on the Song of Songs*, Bernard sought to express an understanding of God which was mystical rather than analytic. The eloquence of imagery and expression he brought to the task owed much to his reading, not merely of Christian authors, but of Cicero, an author who also, through his *De amicitia*, helped to shape Bernard's thoughts about loving God. Despite his classical learning, Bernard was deeply suspicious of the application of logical analysis to Christian doctrine. He was instrumental in bringing two of the leading masters of his day before ecclesiastical councils: *Abélard at Sens in 1140, Gilbert of Poitiers at Reims in 1148. He managed to secure the papal condemnation of Abélard, but despite his intrigues was outmanoeuvred by Gilbert, who in large measure succeeded in showing that Bernard had attacked what he was unable to understand. [JAMM]

BERNARDIN DE SAINT-PIERRE, Jacques-Henri (1737–1814). Novelist and naturalist. Born in Le Havre, he took a delight even as a child in romantic day-dreaming, and after reading *Robinson Crusoe* set sail for Martinique at the age of 12. On his return he studied under the Jesuits, became a military engineer, took part in the Seven Years War in Germany, and was punished by the army for indiscipline. Subsequent years were nomadic, filled with failed projects and disappointment: he became a geographer in Malta, a journalist in Holland, an engineer in Russia; in Warsaw and Vienna he lived by his wits; in Mauritius he appears to have lived as something of an opportunist. On his return to Paris, he became the friend of J.-J. *Rousseau, whose personality and philosophy were to have a profound influence on him. His *Voyage à l'Île de France* (1773) was not the success he had hoped; in great financial difficulty, he continued to write and at length published the *Études de la nature* (1784), which were enormously popular, especially with women, and which freed him at last from debt. His novel *Paul et Virginie* first appeared in volume 4 of the third edition of the *Études de la nature* (1788), and in the following year was published in a separate edition; this *pastorale* ensured his lasting fame and was followed in 1791 by *La Chaumière indienne*. He was eventually made Intendant of the *Jardin des Plantes and Cabinet d'Histoire Naturelle in 1792, Professeur de Morale at the *École Normale Supérieure in 1794, and a member of the *Institut in 1798. His support for Napoleon gained him an imperial pension.

Bernardin de Saint-Pierre's work has often suffered from his reputation as a man—quarrelsome, misanthropic, vain, greedy for money and honours. Though he could be confused in his thinking, excessively didactic and verbose, he nevertheless had an exceptional gift for poetic as well as accurate

description of exotic settings which makes him an important precursor of *Chateaubriand. A disciple of *Fénelon and Rousseau, he was filled with humanitarian zeal and a wish to reveal God through the wonders of nature. He looked not only back to a lost golden age of human happiness, which he had sought on his travels to distant lands, but also forward to a society purged of corruption, an ideal republic of justice and equality. *Paul et Virginie*, for which he is now primarily remembered, derives some of its lasting appeal from each of these aspects of his thought. [DW]

See *Études sur Paul et Virginie et l'œuvre de Bernardin de Saint-Pierre* (ed. J.-M. Racault, 1986).

BERNARD-LAZARE (pseud. of Lazare Bernard) (1865–1903) began as a *Symbolist writer, but before long threw himself into three overlapping battles. Against social injustice, he appealed to anarchism because it promised both bread and liberty. The battle against *antisemitism was less straightforward and the controversial *L'Antisémitisme, son histoire et ses causes* (1894) reflects the antisemitic and philo-Semitic stages of his thought. Thirdly, *Une erreur judiciaire: la vérité sur l'Affaire *Dreyfus* (1896) is the first history of the case and a precursor of 'J'accuse' [see ZOLA], alleging that the Affair was not a simple miscarriage of justice but an antisemitic creation. He died before Dreyfus's innocence was publicly recognized. [NW]

BERNART DE VENTADORN (*fl. c*.1147–70). *Troubadour. Described by his *vida* and by *Peire d'Alvernhe's satire as the son of a man-at-arms, Bernart was possibly a relative of the vice-comital house of Ventadorn in the Limousin where he started his poetic career; it would later take him to the courts of Henry II and *Eleanor of Aquitaine, and the count of Toulouse. His *c*.40 surviving songs are models of medieval lyric composition, their eloquent and impassioned appeals appearing effortless despite their formal exquisiteness. A principal architect of *fin'amor*, Bernart sensualized the remote love of *Jaufre Rudel and combated the stringent moralism of *Marcabru. His influence on later troubadours is exceeded only by his virtual domination of the work of the early northern French *trouvères. [SK]

BERNHARDT, Sarah (1845–1923). Arguably the greatest of all French actresses, she dominated the Paris stage from about 1872 to 1914. Noted for her beauty, grace of movement, superb voice, and technical versatility, she was especially memorable in Hugo's *Ruy Blas*, Racine's *Phèdre*, and *La Dame aux camélias* by *Dumas *fils*. [SBJ]

BERNIER, François (1620–88). French physician and traveller. Author of an *Abrégé de la philosophie de Gassendi*, he frequented *libertin circles and the salon of Madame de *la Sablière. A prolonged stay in

India, where he was physician to Aureng Zebe, produced several travel books (*Voyages*, 1699), combining recent history with interesting descriptions of cities, customs, commerce, and religion; though generally open-minded, Bernier is contemptuous of Hindu 'superstition'. [PF]

BERNIS, François-Joachim de Pierres de (1715–94). Thanks to female protectors such as Madame de *Pompadour, this elegant young French poet (nicknamed 'Babet la bouquetière') became a member of the Académie Française in his twenties, and subsequently minister of foreign affairs (1757–8), cardinal, and (from 1769) ambassador to Rome. His poetry, mainly written in his youth, is more interesting than its lightweight reputation suggests; it includes a philosophical poem in 10 cantos, *La Religion vengée*, and a descriptive poem in sprightly octosyllables on a then fashionable theme, *Les Quatre Saisons*. His memoirs are a useful source of information on 18th-c. literary life. [PF]

BERNSTEIN, Henry (1876–1953). French dramatist who dominated the Parisian stage between 1900 and 1917 and continued to enjoy success until his death with his portraits of a grasping, materialist society. His heroes are treacherous (*La Griffe*, 1906) and his heroines equally immoral (*Le Voleur*, 1906). A *Dreyfus supporter and himself a Jew, he treated the problem of Jewishness in *Israël* (1908) and *Judith* (1922). [EAF]

BÉROALDE DE VERVILLE, François (1556–c.1629). Son of the Calvinist Mathieu Béroald (erstwhile tutor to Agrippa d'*Aubigné), François became an inhabitant of Geneva in 1574 and developed an interest in the sciences. After the death of his father he became a teacher in Basle. Eventually he returned to France where he espoused Catholicism, becoming in 1593 a canon of Saint-Gatien in Tours. His publications were varied and revealed his many interests: alchemy (*Les Appréhensions spirituelles*, 1583); love (*Les Soupirs amoureux*, 1583); science (*Les Connaissances nécessaires*, 1583); personal and private morality (*L'Idée de la République*, 1584); metaphysics (*La Muse céleste*, 1593); theology (*Les Ténèbres*, 1599), etc. He also wrote an interminable novel, *Les Aventures de Floride* (1594–1601), but is best remembered for a satirical dialogue, *Le Moyen de parvenir* (1610), which adopts the scenario of Plato's *Symposium* and was for some time only attributed to Béroalde. Written in a Rabelaisian style, the dialogue satirizes contemporary views and mannerisms. Often coarse in its humour and criticized in its day for its obscenity, it is an interesting introduction to satirical form and to the *baroque mentality at the end of the 16th c. [KCC]

BÉROUL. Author of a late 12th-c. poem about *Tristan.

BERQUIN, Arnaud (1741–91). One of France's first writers of children's literature. He was known as 'L'Ami des enfants', this being the title of his popular serial publication (1782–3). The collection consists of little tales and dialogues, giving lessons in virtue, family affection, and manners; edifying and sentimental, with a personal touch and occasional moments of humour, it sold in great numbers throughout the 19th c. Berquin published other works in the same vein; when the Revolution came he turned to the peasants, preaching hard work and well-ordered family life in the periodical *Bibliothèque des villages* (1790). [PF]

BERQUIN, Louis de (d. 1529). Member of François Ier's Council, and thus the most prominent French victim of religious repression in the 1520s. Translator and apologist of *Luther and *Erasmus, Berquin was twice convicted of heresy but released by royal intervention. His hasty trial and execution on 17 April 1529 [see REFORMATION] caused consternation among the humanists, reflected in a moving letter by Erasmus.
[MJH]

BERRY, Charles, duc de (1778–1820). Second son of Charles X. His assassination seemed like the end of the *Bourbon dynasty, but he was survived by a posthumous son, the comte de Chambord, who was the Legitimist claimant to the throne ('Henri V') from 1836 until his death in 1883. In 1832 the duchesse de Berry, with support from *Chateaubriand among others, mounted an unsuccessful plot to restore the Bourbons.

BERSIANIK, Louky (pseud. of Lucille Durand) (b. 1930). Canadian feminist writer and poet. Her two main explorations of feminist themes (*L'Euguélionne*, 1976; *Le Pique-nique sur l'Acropole*, 1979) are impressive displays of wit and erudition, being parodies of the Bible and Plato's *Symposium* respectively.
[SIL]

BERTAUT, Jean (1552–1611), succeeded *Desportes as court poet to *Henri III, and retained the favour of *Henri IV, becoming bishop of Sées in 1606. His love poetry, mostly in *stances*, is abstract, rhetorical, and prolix, though mellifluous. He is fond of antithesis, often merely to create a *pointe, but sometimes to good oratorical effect. His official court or 'heroic' poetry owes much to *Ronsard, but, when set in the lyric mode, clearly anticipates *Malherbe in theme, manner, and tone, though without developing the same power. *Timandre*, a short story in verse, shows considerable psychological subtlety. [AJS]

Berte aus grans piés, see ADENET LE ROI.

BERTHELOT, Marcellin (1827–1907). French scientist, professor of organic chemistry at the *Collège de France, author of books on general philosophical topics [see ENCYCLOPEDIAS].

BERTIN, Antoine de (1752–90). Poet from the Île Bourbon (Reunion) who moved to France at the age of 9 and had a military career. He wrote sensual and elegiac love poetry (*Les Amours*, 1780) in the same vein as his friend *Parny.

BERTRAND, Adrien, see WORLD WAR I.

BERTRAND, Aloysius (Louis) (1807–41). Poet. Born in Piedmont, he grew up in Burgundy, and his early work was published at Dijon in the late 1820s. He subsequently moved to Paris, where he lived in difficult circumstances and suffered from ill health. Despite links with Romantic literary circles, he was unable to find a publisher for his major work, *Gaspard de la nuit: fantaisies à la manière de Rembrandt et de Callot*, published posthumously in 1842. This work reflects the Romantic taste for the medieval, the mysterious, and the bizarre, but its significance for literary history lies primarily in the contribution which it made to the development of the *prose poem in France.   [CC]

BERTRAND, Louis (1866–1941). French novelist best known for works such as *Le Sang des races* (1899), *La Cina* (1901), and *Pépète le bien-aimé* (1901), extolling the virtues of European colonists, particularly in French *Algeria. An influential figure in French colonial literature, he championed the idea of a Mediterranean civilization based on the legacy of imperial Rome.   [AGH]

BERTRAND DE BAR-SUR-AUBE. *Trouvère of the late 12th c. and known author of two *chansons de geste*: *Aimeri de Narbonne* and *Girard de Vienne*. In the latter he gives a famous definition of the three cycles of French epic poetry, le *Roi, *Doon de Mayence ('Revolt'), and Garin de Monglane or *Guillaume. In fact his work tends to blend features of all three.   [PEB]

BERTRAN DE BORN (late 12th c.). Aristocratic *troubadour from the Périgord who led a turbulent life, before becoming a monk (c.1196). Bertran's lyrics fuse *fin'amor with a brutal taste for violence to produce a startling, but powerful poetic symbiosis. Dante placed him in the Inferno because of his bellicose tendencies, but clearly admired his poetry, as did Ezra Pound, who translated several poems into English. There are frequent echoes in his *cansos and *sirventes of the conflicts in which he participated, particularly the war of 1180–4 between the sons of Henry II and *Eleanor of Aquitaine. The best edition of his poems is that of W. D. Paden (1986).   [SG]

BÉRULLE, Pierre de (1575–1629), was responsible for promoting many of the religious ideas of the *Counter-Reformation in France, and is a figure of much greater influence than his hastily compiled and inelegant literary remains suggest. As a reformer of religious orders, he collaborated with Madame Acarie to introduce the reformed Carmelites of St Teresa into France (1604), and in 1611 founded the French branch of the Congregation of the Oratory [see ORATORIANS], destined to propagate educational institutions rivalling the *Jesuit colleges in importance. Later he was involved in high politics, negotiating the Peace of Angoulême (1619), the arrangements with the Vatican for the marriage of Charles I to Henrietta Maria, and the Peace of Monçon with Spain. He was created cardinal in 1627, but fell from *Richelieu's favour in 1629. Through his extensive contacts, he touched intellectual and religious as well as political life at many points. In his mystical teaching he placed greater emphasis on the person of Christ than on dogma as a subject for meditation (*Discours des grandeurs de Jésus*, 1623), laying the ground for such modern devotions as the cult of the Sacred Heart and thus making a lasting mark on the temper of popular religious sensibility [see DEVOTIONAL WRITING, 2].
                                          [PJB]

BESSETTE, Gérard (b. 1920). Canadian novelist and critic, one of the first writers to gain prominence in the Révolution Tranquille period [see QUEBEC, 5]. His main contribution to Quebec literature has been as a formal innovator. While his first novels, *La Bagarre* (1958), *Les Pédagogues*, and *La Commensale* (1961 and 1975, respectively, but written earlier), adopt a traditional form of critical realism, they also hint at the more radical narrative experiments that were to follow in *Le Libraire* (1960), *L'Incubation* (1965), *Le Cycle* (1971), *Les Anthropoïdes* (1977), and *Le Semestre* (1979). Here Bessette borrowed creatively from such predecessors as *Camus, *Sartre, the French *Nouveau Roman, and Faulkner to achieve more powerful expressions of his themes of social and personal alienation. The overall impression left by his experiments is of a pioneering enrichment of Quebec literature, although ironically his most enduring creation may well be *Le Libraire*, the simplest and shortest of his works.

His Freudian approach as a literary critic has also been productive, yielding authoritative and illuminating readings of such classic Quebec authors as *Beaulieu, *Langevin, and Gabrielle *Roy.   [SIL]

Bestiaries. Translated around the 4th c. from a Greek original, the Latin *Physiologus* was a compilation of short, didactic animal stories designed to be read as Christian allegories. This early bestiary tradition was augmented during the 7th c. with material from Isidore's *Etymologiae*. The animal lore transmitted by the various different bestiary versions that developed subsequently comprises both real and fabulous creatures whose physical and symbolic attributes became part of the common fund of medieval perceptions of the natural world. Thus, the salamander has the power to extinguish fire; the lion resuscitates its stillborn cubs by breathing on them; the weasel conceives by the mouth and gives birth by the ear. The allegorical interpretations show considerably less imagination: the hedgehog is the devil and its spikes traps for the unwary; the phoenix rising from its own ashes represents Christ's resurrection; elephants who mate without lust by eating of the mandrake tree are the figural representations of Adam and Eve before the Fall.

The large number of surviving bestiary manuscripts and the text's wide influence on medieval art are sure indications of its popularity. The bestiary has been transmitted with a particularly rich tradition of illustration. One might conjecture that it could have served as a reading primer for aristocratic children. It was translated into French on several occasions. In the 13th c., Guillaume le Clerc's *Bestiaire divin* elaborates on the moral and exemplary dimensions of the text, while Richard de *Fournival's Bestiaire d'amour* draws courtly love into the bestiary tradition, transforming it, with humour, elegance, and irony, into a narrative of amorous conquest. In *Brunetto Latini's Livres dou tresor*, the bestiary is amplified into a discursive, encyclopaedic treatise which frequently attempts to rationalize inherited material.

In modern times *Apollinaire wrote a playfully poetic *Bestiaire*. [IS]

Bête humaine, La. Novel by *Zola, published in 1890, the 17th in the *Rougon-Macquart* series. One of Zola's most violent texts, this novel has as its principal character a homicidal maniac, Jacques Lantier, a third son of Gervaise Macquart who, unlike his brothers Claude and Étienne, does not appear in *L'*Assommoir*. Jacques, a mechanic on the Paris–Le Havre railway line, is witness to a murder on a train, meets Séverine and her husband Roubaud, who are responsable for the crime, and becomes her lover. In a fit of murderous desire, he kills Séverine. The novel ends with a fight to the death between Jacques and his stoker, Pecqueux, over the latter's wife, as the train that they are driving, carrying troops to the war with Prussia, runs on out of control. With elements of the detective story and echoes of both Dostoevsky and Jack the Ripper, *La Bête humaine*, much of which is set in dark, enclosed places, deals with the unconscious, atavistic urges that lie beneath the signs of modern progress and with instinctual associations between the sexual drive and the desire to kill. [DB]

BETI, Mongo (pseud. of Alexandre Biyidi) (b. 1932). Cameroonian writer. After secondary education in Yaoundé, he studied in France from 1951. Apart from two brief home visits, he has remained in self-exile in France as a teacher of literature, finding it impossible to accept the society produced by colonialism and neo-colonialism in his country. Two periods may be distinguished in his work: 1952–8 and post-1970.

'Sans haine et sans amour', a story published under the name Eza Boto in *Présence africaine* (1952), tells of a young Mau-Mau guerilla fighter, his hatred of whites and his disgust for their black friends. Although set in Kenya rather than Cameroon, it is the forerunner of the subsequent novels which denounce the devastating effects of colonial occupation, while rejecting the idyllic image of pre-colonial societies presented by, for example, *Camara Laye. Beti shows how the internal structural contradictions of feudal and clan society facilitated the colonial conquest, which in turn, while accelerating the breakup of traditional structures, also preserved and exploited their most oppressive features.

The four novels of the 1954–8 period depict a society which has lost its bearings, a prey to the colonial system, while in revolt against the constraints of patriarchal family and village life. Beti's conclusion is pessimistic: only a handful of very young characters put up a show of resistance, and this is individual and anarchic. He hardly refers to the collective struggle of the Union des Populations du Cameroun (UPC). Of these novels the first, *Ville cruelle* (1954), appeared under the pen-name Eza Boto; the others bore the name Mongo Beti. His second novel, *Le Pauvre Christ de Bomba* (1956), was banned in Cameroon because of pressure from the Catholic authorities, angry that Beti had exposed the links between missionary activity and the colonial conquest. *Mission terminée* (1957) and *Le Roi miraculé* (1958) develop themes from *Ville cruelle*: the resistance of young people to the patriarchal system, and the social destabilization caused by colonial rule.

Beti's 'Lettre de Yaoundé: Cameroun 1958' (*Preuves*, December 1958) expresses the author's difficulty, during a brief trip home, in identifying fully with his people's struggle. Despite his anger, he does not go beyond individual, psychological rebellion to an appeal for revolutionary action.

His second period was heralded by the publication of a pamphlet, *Main basse sur le Cameroun* (1972), denouncing the despotic rule of Ahidjo, a straw man set in place by the French to defend neo-colonial interests. It was banned in France. In two fictional works of this period, *Remember Ruben* (1974) and *La Ruine presque cocasse d'un polichinelle* (1979), Beti pays tribute to the founder of the UPC, Ruben Um Nyobé, assassinated by the French in 1958 as a member of the Cameroonian underground. *Perpétue* (1974) tells of the defection of a UPC activist and the plight of a woman, symbol of a conquered Africa, and a victim of neo-colonialism.

In 1978–9 Beti founded a journal, *Peuples noirs Peuples africains*, as a forum for criticizing the nature of Franco-African relations and *négritude. He also set up a publishing house, Éditions des Peuples Noirs, to issue works unacceptable to establishment publishers, including his own *Lettre ouverte aux Camerounais ou la Deuxième Mort de Ruben um Niobé* (1986), an attack on the neo-colonialist policies of Ahidjo's successor Paul Biya. In his two most recent novels, *Les Deux Mères de Guillaume Ismael*

Beur

Dzewatama, futur camionneur (1980) and *La Revanche de Guillaume Ismael Dzewatama* (1982), the main character is a young Frenchwoman married to a Cameroonian; she is a witness to the oppressive conditions and the absence of freedom of thought and expression in Cameroon. The works have structural weaknesses, and they suggest that the only effective way to contribute to radical change is as an individual living abroad. They are, in fact, similar to Beti's early works; there is a break between 1958 and the 1970s, but no real change in the author's perspective.   [NM]

See C. L. Dehon, *Le Roman camerounais d'expression française* (1989).

Beur. Popular term denoting a young person brought up in France by North African immigrant parents. A modified inversion of *Arabe*, the word was first adopted by youths of immigrant origin in working-class areas of Paris. It gained general currency in France during the 1980s, when large numbers of children born to North African immigrants, particularly Algerians, began reaching adulthood. A growing number of creative writers have emerged from among their ranks. These include Mehdi *Charef, Azouz *Begag, Ahmed *Kalouaz, Farida *Belghoul, and Arriz *Tamza. In Belgium, authors of North African descent such as Leïla *Houari may also be classed as Beurs, for their experiences closely parallel those of the immigrant community in France.

The writings produced by Beur writers resemble in some ways those of francophone writers in *Algeria, *Morocco, and *Tunisia. Most share a preoccupation with questions of personal and cultural identity, conditioned by the tensions between Arab-Islamic traditions on the one hand and secular French influences on the other. Even during colonial times, however, Europeans never constituted more than a minority of the population in the Maghreb, where Arabs and Berbers remained in the majority, albeit alongside powerful francophone influences. By contrast, the formative experiences of the Beurs have been those of a post-colonial ethnic minority situated in the margins of French society.

Beur poets and theatre groups became active during the mid-1970s, but it was not until the early 1980s that the first commercially published works by Beur authors appeared in print. The great majority of those published to date are works of narrative prose. Typically, they are heavily autobiographical. The material deprivations suffered by the immigrant community are often glossed over in a humorous way, and a colloquial tone in the mode of narration frequently serves to emphasize the familiarity of these authors with French society and culture at a grass-roots level, thereby undermining stereotyped ideas of ethnic minorities as fundamentally alien to the majority of the population.   [AGH]

BEUVE-MÉRY, Hubert (1902–89). French journalist and publisher. After studying law, he spent ten years in Prague, where he became correspondent for *Le *Temps*. Active in the Resistance, he then founded the daily newspaper *Le *Monde*, which he directed from 1944 to 1969.

Beuvon de Commarchis, see ADENET LE ROI.

Beverlei, see SAURIN.

BEYALA, Calixthe (b. 1960). Novelist, born in Cameroon and now living in Paris, whose writing has been the focus of much controversy because of both its feminist content and its innovative style: a fusion of oneiric lyricism and vulgar realism.

In her first novel, *C'est le soleil qui m'a brûlée* (1987), the political awareness of the heroine develops as a parallel to the evolution of her sexuality. Through a network of sexual relationships, Beyala deconstructs traditional myths about women and men, and presents a vision of woman as a 'New Eve', a potential source of knowledge and truth. *Tu t'appelleras Tanga* (1988) interweaves the life-story of an African child-prostitute with that of the young Jewish woman who shares her prison cell. Through the communion of these two women, the text promotes female solidarity as a possible escape from the figurative prison of patriarchal traditions. Beyala's most recent novel is *Seul le diable le savait* (1990), a supernatural tale which recounts the initiation of its heroine into the reality of Africa. This text, like the others, exposes the absurdity and madness which lie behind the social order, and suggests that what is real exists only 'au-delà des yeux'.

[NHi]

BEYE, Alioune Badara (b. 1945). A civil servant and director of the Senegalese publishing house Éditions Maguilen, he has published three historical plays. *Le Sacre du Ceddo* (1982) deals, like *Sembène's film *Ceddo*, with the struggle between animism and Islam in pre-colonial Senegal. This is also a theme of his latest play, *Nder en flammes* (1990), which focuses on the martyrdom of a group of noblewomen. His second play, *Dialawali, terre de feu* (1984), was adapted for Senegalese television.   [FNC]

BEYLE, Henri, original name of *Stendhal.

BEYS, Charles (c.1610–1659). French poet and dramatist. He published a collection of verse in 1652, and five plays. His most original and popular play was *L'Hôpital des fous* (performed 1634), a tragicomedy set in a lunatic asylum, which anticipates *Desmarets's *Les Visionnaires* in its ironic presentation of social types. It was rewritten as a comedy, *Les Illustres Fous*, performed in 1651.   [GJM]

BÈZE, Théodore de (1519–1605). Calvinist theologian and pastor often known by his Latin name, Beza. Born in Vézelay, he received a humanist edu-

cation and published secular poetry in Latin before fleeing to Switzerland in 1548 [see REFORMATION]; after teaching Greek in Lausanne and theology in Geneva, he succeeded Calvin as pastor in Geneva in 1564. He conducted abortive negotiations with the Catholics at Poissy (1561) and with the Lutherans at Montbéliard (1586). His voluminous writings in French and Latin include apologetics (Vie de Calvin, 1564; Du droit des magistrats, 1574), devotional works (Chrétiennes méditations, 1581), the influential Psaumes de David, 1553 (continuing Clément *Marot's version), and the innovatory drama *Abraham sacrifiant.
[MJH]

BHÊLY-QUÉNUM, Olympe (Codjo Eustache Marc Olympio) (b. 1928). Novelist and journalist from Dahomey, now Benin, descendant of the princely family of Gbhêly-Houénou and nephew of the writer Maximilien Quénum. The sense of the supernatural and the presence of mysterious powers in Bhêly-Quénum's fiction can be attributed to the influence of his mother, a Voodoo priestess, and his father, a freemason versed in the 'obscure forces of the Benin Gulf'. He left Africa in 1948 to complete his education in France. While teaching in the Paris region he published his first novel, Un piège sans fin (1960), acclaimed by Paulin Joachim as the first authentically African novel. There are, however, echoes of the Orpheus and Orestes myths, Crime and Punishment, *Sartre's Huis clos, Camus's L'*Étranger, and *Beckett's Fin de partie, while the narrative technique recalls the composition of *Manon Lescaut. Set in the colonial era, this is not a political work, but is intended to illustrate a philosophical and moral theme. The endless snares to which the hero, Ahouna, is exposed are supernatural powers that inspire him with an uncontrollable impulse to kill. In Le Chant du lac (1965), the supernatural is again present, with the author making a plea for the abolition of superstition, the demythification of the lake to exorcize the spell of the gods.

In 1963 Bhêly-Quénum took over the editorship of a short-lived magazine, La Vie africaine, then launched a bilingual (French–English) magazine, L'Afrique actuelle. A collection of short stories, Liaison d'un été (1968), contains some of his favourite themes: the presence of the supernatural, love affairs of mixed couples. The school reader, Un enfant d'Afrique (1970), recounts the life of Ayao Kilanko from the age of 6 until he becomes a primary-school teacher, and gives an authentic, lively account of life in the African bush. Bhêly-Quénum's third full-length novel, L'Initié (1979), is the most autobiographical of his works. The hero Kofi Marc Tingo is 'initiated' into esoteric lore, has a close association with freemasonry, marries a Frenchwoman, founds a literary magazine. But he studies medicine and sets up in practice in Cotonou, where his Western teaching and his knowledge as an 'initiate' give him the advantage over his rivals. Bhêly-Quénum has also published a number of short

stories. His numerous as-yet unpublished works include Les Appels du Vaudou, devoted to the life and death of his mother, and As-tu vu Kokolie? (on which he has been working for 25 years). [DSB]

See R. Mercier and M. and S. Battestini, Olympe Bhêly-Quénum, écrivain dahoméen (1964).

BIBAUD, Michel, see QUEBEC, 2.

Bible. Although there have been far fewer translations of the Bible into French than into English, and although there has never been one with the compelling power of the Authorized Version, the Bible has pervaded French writing from its beginnings to the present day. Biblical language appears in the 9th-c. Séquence de *Sainte Eulalie, in 10th- and 11th-c. *hagiography, in the Chanson de *Roland, and in 12th-c. *bestiaries and theatrical writing. The Bible was well known both through the Historia scholastica of Comestor (1170), a mixture of Bible-history, legend, and other material, and also, to clerics at least, in the Latin Vulgate. Priests, monks, and nuns approached it through the daily readings in the Latin breviary, and lay people listened to biblical readings in the liturgy, especially the Psalms and the Gospels, as well as in sermons. The illustrated Biblia pauperum and church art (carvings, glass, frescos) made it even more accessible.

French versions began to appear around 1100, with the first Psautier français and other isolated books in verse or prose translation [see BIBLES, MEDIEVAL]. By the mid-13th c. there was an edition of the whole Bible, translated by different hands (Bible de St Louis, c.1250, 'Bible du XIIIe siècle' (B.XIII), c.1280); noteworthy also is the Bible historiale of Guyart des Moulins (late 13th c.), an expanded adaptation of Comestor, and later revisions by Raoul de Presles (c.1380) and especially by Jean de Rély (1487), the latter often reprinted.

It is significant that the Bible was the first book to be printed, by Gutenberg, around 1450. The invention of *printing both facilitated the diffusion of editions in the original languages, in texts established according to humanist critical principles, and encouraged the faithful translation of these texts into the vernacular, for more popular use. As discrepancies between the new editions, such as *Erasmus's, and St Jerome's Vulgate became evident, religious controversy increased, and censorship followed [see REFORMATION]. New editions and translations were soon associated with the movement for reform. The *Evangelical writer *Lefèvre d'Étaples edited a Greek Testament (1518) and translated the Bible (NT, 1523; OT, 1528) from the Vulgate, basing himself on Rély's version and with some reference to the Greek. His translation was put on the Index in 1546.

The first Protestant translation was the work of Pierre *Olivétan (1535), relying on Lefèvre for the NT; it was revised by *Calvin and Robert *Estienne, and *Bèze's later revision became the official

Genevan translation. The Psalms particularly appealed to the imagination of the reformers: Clément *Marot produced verse translations of 49 psalms (1533–43) and Bèze completed the Psalter between 1551 and 1562. Other poets composed metrical paraphrases in French or Latin (e.g. *Buchanan). The Marot–Bèze version was the most popular, becoming the anthem, rallying cry, or song of the Protestant martyrs. Estienne concentrated his energies on editions of the Bible in the original languages, taking some account of Parisian manuscripts. His work was put on the Index in 1546. (It was Estienne who introduced the division into verses, from 1551.) There was one other original Protestant translation, by Sébastien *Châteillon (Basle, 1555) but it was not acceptable to Geneva. The Lyon printer Jean de Tournes found a compromise by which he saved himself from condemnation, publishing the Genevan text, but with Catholic prefatory matter. An approved Catholic Bible in French (Louvain, 1550) owes much to Lefèvre and perhaps even to Olivétan. The only Catholic Bible published in France during these years was by Pierre Benoist of the Paris faculty of theology (1566); it was heavily influenced by the Genevan version and was condemned in 1567.

In the 17th c. there were several new French translations: Samuel des Marets (Amsterdam, 1669, Protestant); abbé de *Marolles (1644 onwards, Catholic, though the project was stopped by Chancellor Séguier in 1671). Isaac *Le Maître de Sacy of Port-Royal completed the translation of the NT from the Vulgate in 1657 and began work on the OT in the Bastille ten years later. The NT was published in 1667 (called the 'Mons' NT but, in reality, Amsterdam, Elzevir), and the OT between 1672 and 1696. This harmonious, classical Port-Royal version, revised by *Arnauld and *Nicole, proved popular. A more scholarly version of the NT (Trévoux, 1702) was that by Richard *Simon, the founder of modern biblical criticism.

In the 18th c. there were two revisions of the Geneva Bible, by David Martin and J. F. Ostervald; they were followed in 1880 by Louis Segond's revision, the most commonly used Protestant Bible until quite recently. The standard Catholic Bible during the first half of the 20th c. was that by Pierre Crampon (Tournai, 1894–1904) based on the original Hebrew and Greek texts. The *Bible de Jérusalem* (1947–55), also translated from the originals, is a collective work directed by the Dominicans at the École Biblique in Jerusalem; it has proved generally acceptable to Catholic and Protestant alike and has itself been translated into other languages. Less well-known is *La Bible: traduction œcuménique*, published by the Société Biblique Française (NT, 1972; OT, 1975; one volume, 1985); this work looks forward to an even more ecumenical venture which would also be acceptable to Jewish readers. Although this aim has not yet been achieved, the translation by André Chouraqui (1947–9) captures the quality of the Hebrew and Greek poetry, and

the flavour of the Semitic world (though with much contrivance); different editions correspond to the Jewish, Catholic, and Protestant canons. Finally, it should be said that, in spite of this wealth of translations which reflect the style and the preoccupations of different ages, the version which has most influenced French literature until the present day is still St Jerome's Latin Vulgate. [PS]

See *The Cambridge History of the Bible*: vol. II, ed. G. W. H. Lampe (1969); vol. III, ed. S. L. Greenslade (1963) (two articles by R. A. Sayce); *La Bible de tous les temps*, ed. C. Mondesert, 8 vols. (1984); *Les Bibles en français*, ed. P.-M. Bogaert (1991).

Bible de l'humanité, La, see MICHELET.

Bible des poètes, La, see CLASSICAL INFLUENCES, I.

Bibles (Medieval). The term 'Bible' encompasses a wide variety of texts in medieval French, ranging from accurate prose translations of the Vulgate to verse adaptations of biblical texts, often in the form of *chansons de geste* or romances and frequently more akin to independent works of imaginative literature than to translations. In most cases the biblical text is accompanied by glosses and commentaries drawn from contemporary Latin sources; the texts, perhaps destined for a lay (and certainly non-Latinate) public, seem to have had a didactic function. Much biblical material remains in manuscript and has yet to be properly classified and edited. [DAT]

Bibliographies. The ancestors of modern literary bibliography in France are such works as *Sorel's *Bibliothèque française*, *Baillet's *Jugements des savants*, and *Goujet's *Bibliothèque française*, as well as the scholarly work of the *Maurists. The 19th and 20th c. have seen a vast and rather intimidating increase in such publications, devoted not only to French literature as a whole, but to genres, periods, and authors. The present entry aims simply to list some of the most helpful general works currently in use.

Two useful brief guides to the field are the *Manuel bibliographique des études littéraires* (1982) of B. Beugnot and J.-M. Moureaux and *French Language and Literature: An Annotated Bibliography* (1989), by F. Bassan, D. C. Spinelli, and H. A. Sullivan. For a full-length critical bibliography (now rather outdated in places), see the excellent *A Critical Bibliography of French Literature* (1947–) under the general editorship of D. C. Cabeen, J. Brody, and R. A. Brooks. Simple listings of titles of both primary and secondary material are given in G. *Lanson's *Manuel bibliographique de la littérature française moderne* (1909–14), a companion volume to his history of French literature, and this work is continued for the 16th to 18th c. in J. Giraud's *Manuel de bibliographie littéraire* (1921–55).

Much fuller listings, alphabetically arranged and

covering critical writing up to 1950–60, are contained in the series of bibliographies by A. Cioranescu, *Bibliographie de littérature française du 16e siècle* (1959), *Bibliographie de littérature française du 17e siècle* (1965–7), and *Bibliographie de littérature française du 18e siècle* (1969–70). For the Middle Ages, see R. Bossuat, *Manuel bibliographique de la littérature française du moyen âge* (1951, with supplements). The *Bibliographie des auteurs modernes de langue française* of H. Talvart and J. Place, dealing with the 19th and 20th c., began publication in 1928 and many volumes later had reached the letter M by the end of the 1980s. For a bibliography of hoaxes and anonymous writings, see J.-M. Quérard, *Les Supercheries littéraires dévoilées* (2nd edn., augmented by G. Brunet and P. Jannet, 1889).

For other francophone countries, some titles will be found in the entries for the different areas. See also J.-J. Luthi, A. Viatte, and G. Zananiri, *Dictionnaire général de la francophonie* (1986); A. Rouch and G. Clavreuil, *Littératures nationales d'écriture française* (1987); A. Berchtold, *La Suisse Romande au cap du XXe siècle. Matériaux pour une bibliographie* (1986); *Bibliographie des écrivains français de Belgique, 1881–1960* (Palais des Académies, Brussels, 1958–72); J. Déjeux, *Maghreb: littératures de langue française* (1993); C. Achour, *Dictionnaire des œuvres algériennes en langue française* (1990); J. Chévrier, *Littérature africaine* (1990); P. Hawkins and A. Lavers (eds.) *Protée noir* (1992); M. Lemir *et al.*, *Dictionnaire des œuvres littéraires du Québec* (1978–87); R. Lawless, *Haiti: A Research Handbook* (1990); *Notre librairie*, No. 106, '2,000 titres de littérature des Caraïbes' (July–September 1991).

All such works go out of date and need to be supplemented by annual bibliographies. The four main ones are: R. Rancœur, *Bibliographie de la littérature française*, published since 1951 in the *Revue d'histoire littéraire de la France*; the *Bibliographie der französischer Literaturwissenschaft*, founded by O. Klapp in 1956; and the relevant sections of *The Year's Work in Modern Language Studies*, a selective and critical bibliography published in Britain by the Modern Humanities Research Association, and of the Modern Language Association's *International Bibliography of Books and Articles on the Modern Languages and Literatures*. For specific periods, see in particular the annual *Bibliographie internationale de l'humanisme et de la Renaissance* and *French XX* (formerly *French VII*), a bibliography of 20th-c. French literature.

An important development of the 1980s and 1990s is the computerized bibliographical database. The essential one is the CD-ROM version of the *MLA International Bibliography*, covering the period since 1981 and regularly updated. See also, for example, the database on Maghrebian writing *LIMAG 2*, produced in Paris by the Coordination Internationale des Chercheurs sur les Littératures Maghrébines.

[PF]

Bibliothèque Bleue, La. The ancestor of the **livre de poche*. Early in the 17th c. publishers began to produce small books wrapped in blue sugar paper which were sold throughout France by pedlars (**colporteurs*). The trade was centred on Troyes, where the Oudot family occupied a dominating position, but other bookseller-publishers followed suit in Paris, Rouen, and elsewhere. The booklets were very cheap (as little as 1 *sou*), and they sold in massive numbers (about 1 million annually in the early 18th c.). Like **almanacs* and other related material, they were aimed at the non-book-buying classes of town and country. In some cases they were read aloud to the partly illiterate public at village *veillées*—evening gatherings where craft-work was combined with story-telling and similar entertainment.

Although some of the books are reprints of works by classic authors such as **Corneille, the majority were composed by literary journeymen, who drew on a varied and for the most part highly traditional repertoire. Religious writings, in particular lives of saints, works of popular devotion, and *cantiques*, were in great demand. The new thought of the **Enlightenment was slow to make an impact, but there were many handbooks of astrology, folk-medicine, letter-writing, and elementary civility. As far as 'belles-lettres' is concerned, two dominant elements are tall stories and burlesque comedy. There are many editions of popular old tales, including recyclings of the **Charlemagne legends, the adventures of **Robert le Diable and **Geneviève de Brabant, and the stories of **Gargantua which **Rabelais had promoted to the ranks of high literature. The story *Le *Bonhomme Misère* is probably the most famous item in the collection, which includes upwards of 4,000 titles, including reprints.

Under the *ancien régime*, the Bibliothèque Bleue was predominantly conformist in tone—indeed, it has been seen as a mechanism of social control. The Revolution saw spasmodic attempts to harness it to popular instruction, but it was in the 19th c. that it acquired a real political role, and came to be considered subversive and morally suspect. As part of the resulting attempt to control it under the Second Empire, **Nisard produced the first study of the phenomenon, his *Histoire des livres populaires ou de la littérature de colportage* (1864). His work is a mine of information, but his view of the blue books is patronizing and severe.

In recent years they have been more sympathetically studied, and sometimes this has led to a romantic image of them as a product of 'popular culture'. In fact, the relations between popular and learned culture are far from ones of simple opposition. The frontier between *littérature de colportage* and more prestigious productions was uncertain, and there was movement in both directions. The blue books reused the stories and ideas of learned literature (with a time-lag of a century or more), while fashionable readers and writers were interested in the pedlars' wares. *Perrault is a case in point: his verse tale *Griselidis* is indebted to the Bibliothèque Bleue, but his own *Contes* appeared before long between blue covers.   [PF]

See G. Bollème, *La Bibliothèque bleue: la littérature populaire en France du XVIIe au XIXe siècles* (1971); L. Andries, *La Bibliothèque bleue au dix-huitième siècle, Studies on Voltaire and the Eighteenth Century*, 270 (1989).

Bibliothèque de l'Arsenal. France's second great public library, situated in Paris on the site of the former arsenal. It began in the 18th c., was greatly developed by Revolutionary confiscations, and is particularly rich in manuscripts and medieval and dramatic literature. In the years following 1824 it was the scene of an important Romantic salon grouped round its curator, Charles *Nodier.

Bibliothèque française, La, see SOREL, C.

Bibliothèque Mazarine. Major Paris library, housed in the buildings of the *Institut de France, to which it now belongs. It originated in a legacy to the nation from Cardinal *Mazarin, and is rich in 17th-c. works.

Bibliothèque Nationale. France's principal public *library, one of the richest collections in the world. It originated in the private libraries of kings, particularly that of *François Ier at *Fontainebleau. In 1537 the system of *dépôt légal* was instituted, whereby a copy of all books published in France was deposited with the library. The Bibliothèque du Roi, as it came to be known, was greatly developed in the 17th and 18th c. on the initiative of *Mazarin, *Colbert, and others, and gradually became more accessible to scholars and the general reading public. From the second half of the 17th c. it occupied its present site in the Rue de Richelieu, although the main reading rooms date from the late 19th c. The Revolution brought the change to the present name (1792) and a great increase in holdings from the confiscated possessions of religious and other private libraries.

The library is now divided into four main departments (printed books, manuscripts, prints, medals) under the overall supervision of a *conservateur*. (There is a special section for obscene and blasphemous works known as the *Enfer*, which *Apollinaire explored and exploited at the beginning of the 20th c.) In 1926 it was for a time grouped with the *Bibliothèque de l'Arsenal, the *Bibliothèque Mazarine (now administered by the *Institut de France), and the *Bibliothèque Sainte-Geneviève (now a university library) in the Réunion des Bibliothèques Nationales de Paris. In the late 1980s plans were made for the move in 1995 to a monumental, purpose-built 'Bibliothèque de France' on the Left Bank of the Seine.   [PF]

Bibliothèque Sainte-Geneviève. Paris library dating from the early 17th c., originally the library of the Abbaye de Sainte-Geneviève, subsequently a national library, and now belonging to the University of Paris. It is housed in a particularly fine building opposite the *Panthéon.

Bibliothèque universelle des romans (1775–89). A periodical publication, with sixteen numbers each year. It provided résumés of, and occasionally extracts from, works of fiction from a wide range of periods and languages, together with background information and critical comment. The founders were Jean-François Bastide and the marquis de Paulmy d'Argenson. When the latter withdrew in 1778, Bastide continued as editor until 1788. In the early days the series had some scholarly pretensions, but these declined, possibly because of readers' reactions, and the number of contributions on ancient works became less frequent. In some cases, such as the *nouvelles* of Madame *Riccoboni, the *Bibliothèque* even published new works; it also admitted a few historical works, plays, poems, and tales from contemporary journals. Entries were classed under eight headings, as novels 'traduits du latin et du grec', 'de chevalerie', 'd'amour', 'de spiritualité', etc. In all, the collection provided about 1,000 articles, of which nearly one-third dealt with foreign works. While not directly reflecting the tastes of the reading public, the *Bibliothèque* does demonstrate increasing recognition of the novel as a reputable literary genre, and its commentaries illustrate the then current critical standards. It has been studied by A. Martin in *La Bibliothèque universelle des romans* (1985).   [VGM]

Bicêtre. Site of a hospital in outer Paris for disabled soldiers, which became in 1675 a notorious place of confinement, part prison, part asylum. It was the scene of massacres during the Revolutionary Terror.

BICHELBERGER, Roger (b. 1938), Novelist, poet, and literary critic. His work is deeply marked by his Catholic upbringing, his modest family background, and his experiences in the frontier region of Lorraine where he was born just before the outbreak of war. His novels—such as *Comme un éveilleur d'aurore* (1982), *Un exode ordinaire* (1983), and *Le Vagabond de Dieu* (1989)—avoiding provincialism and religious sectarianism, combine loyalty to his origins and an often rebellious independent spirit, dwelling on a quest for belief in a sometimes hostile or agnostic environment. He was awarded the Prix Henri Mondor of the Académie Française (1990) for his second collection of poems, *La Ténèbre des noces*.   [BCS]

Bienséance, see TRAGEDY, 2.

Biffures, see LEIRIS.

Bijoux indiscrets, Les (1748). An episodic novel by

*Diderot, set in an imaginary Africa; it is *libertin* in its freedom of thought and its *risqué* subject-matter.

BILLETDOUX, François (b. 1927). French novelist and dramatist. His three novels include *Royal Garden Blues* (1957), a satire of artistic and journalistic milieux, but he is better known as a dramatist whose popularity was at its height in the 1950s and 1960s. *Le Comportement des époux Bredburry* (1960) and, more particularly, *Va donc chez Torpe* (1961) were amongst his biggest successes, exemplifying the whimsical mode which he adopted, combining sardonic social comment with humorous situations, often focusing on the difficulties of communication, yet never falling into the camp of the Theatre of the *Absurd. He has also been interested in the cinema and has played an important role in French radio.

[EAF]

BINET, Étienne (1569–1639). French Jesuit priest and author of biographies and spiritual works popularizing the notion of the devout life among lay-folk in the spirit of his friend *François de Sales. His *Essai des merveilles de nature et des plus nobles artifices* (1621) is a moralized encyclopedia initially intended to provide preachers with a basis for comparisons and conceits. It is a treasure-house of curious, even bizarre information, mostly drawn from the Ancients, which went through a dozen editions up to 1660 and was a widely exploited source of poetic imagery. *Pascal writes disobligingly of Binet in the 9th *Provinciale*.

[PJB]

Biography. Biographies are probably as numerous in France as elsewhere, but the genre has never acquired the prestige there that it possesses in Britain, and can boast few if any great classics.

Early biographies are usually brief and laudatory and were composed according to rhetorical models, as in the medieval lives of saints [see HAGIOGRAPHY] or kings [see JOINVILLE], or the academic *éloges* which flourished in the 18th c. Beginning in the late 16th c., there are compilations of lives of artists or writers by Scévole de *Sainte-Marthe, *Perrault, *Goujet, and others, and this sub-genre is illustrated at greater length in *Baillet's *Vie de Descartes* (1691) or *Grimarest's *Vie de Molière* (1705), but without great distinction.

The 19th c. saw a considerable growth of interest in the life-stories of individuals. In 1811–28 the bookseller Louis-Gabriel Michaud produced the first edition of his *Biographie universelle*, of which the second edition (45 vols., 1843–61) remains the basic French biographical dictionary for the period up to about 1850 (for more recent years there is a *Dictionnaire de biographie française*, begun in 1933 under the direction of J. Balteau, M. Barroux, and M. Prévost—it had reached the letter H by 1989). Nevertheless, even in the 19th c. great biographies are few in number; they might include *Chateaubriand's very personal *Vie de Rancé* and—in a different vein—

*Renan's *Vie de Jésus*, or the monumental group biography in the *Port-Royal* of *Sainte-Beuve, who established biography as an essential part of *literary criticism.

In the 20th c. popular biographies have been written, for instance, by *Maurois, *Troyat, and *Rolland, and Jean Lacouture has produced important lives of *Malraux and *de Gaulle, but the most remarkable biographies remain *Sartre's imaginative lives of authors (*Baudelaire, *Genet, *Flaubert), which replace the 'l'homme et l'œuvre' approach of the classic French doctoral thesis by an attempt to understand the central 'project' of the writer. Having been out of fashion during the heyday of *Structuralism and the 'death of the author', literary biography enjoyed a renewal of favour in the 1980s, but many lives of French writers continued to be translated from the English (notably George Painter's accounts of *Proust and *Chateaubriand).

[PF]

BIZET, Georges (1838–75). French composer most famous for his operas, specially his *opéra-comique* *Carmen* (1875), based on the novella by *Mérimée. The term 'realist' (adapted from literature and visual arts) has been applied to *Carmen* for its subject-matter, social milieu, the use of on-stage music and local colour, and most importantly Bizet's detachment from his characters. The tragedy of *Carmen* is reinforced by Bizet's use of the traditional *opéra-comique* framework. In the 20th c. *Carmen* has inspired numerous adaptations in film, ballet, and theatre. Bizet also composed incidental music for Alphonse *Daudet's play *L'Arlésienne* (1872), and many songs to texts by the Romantic poets, in particular *Hugo.

[KM]

BLAIS, Marie-Claire (b. 1939). Canadian novelist, who has also written poetry and plays. A sequence of powerful imaginative novels has made her a leading figure in Quebec literature. From the traditional closed structure of the family in her early works to the looser random patterns of involvement in the novels of the 1980s, it is the interaction of social, religious, and moral pressures and tempestuous individual imperatives that creates the artistic texture of her writing. In *La Belle Bête* (1959) humiliation and frustration drive the main character to sadism, murder, and self-immolation: no other escape from the ritualized codes of the family seems possible. Later novels show educated women in their chosen professions, but they are often devastated by the callousness of those near to them and by the extent of the social deprivation they encounter: *Manuscrits de Pauline Archange* (1968) and its sequels *Vivre! vivre!* (1969), *Les Apparences* (1970), and *Visions d'Anna* (1982). Blais showed from early on a preoccupation with delinquency and deviance: *Tête blanche* (1961): *David Sterne* (1967). Male homosexuality is explored in *Le Loup* (1972), lesbianism in *Les Nuits de l'Underground* (1978).

Blanc

Some critics have considered all of Blais's work as a transposition into familial and personal terms of a social and political vision of Quebec. But she has specifically set out to probe and reflect the fabric, identity, and voice of Quebec society in a number of texts: *Un Joualonais sa joualonie* (1973), *Le Sourd dans la ville* (1979), *Pierre ou la Guerre du printemps* (1991). It would, however, be misleading to see any of these as realist novels. The strength and originality of Blais's writing lies in its blend of satire, fantasy, energy, and lyricism. Characters can take on mythical status, scenes become dream-like, language is transported. This extraordinary linguistic power is vested in the figure of Jean Le Maigre, the frail young genius of *Une saison dans la vie d'Emmanuel* (1965), Blais's most fêted novel. More than her other artist figures he testifies to a gritty resilience in the human spirit, as this startling imagination blossoms from the unlikely base of grinding rural poverty and a huge family, just the conditions that might be expected to stifle all individuality. But Blais's work is characterized by such paradoxes and insights, and the harshness of her vision is offset by respect and compassion. [MMC]

See P. G. Lewis (ed.), *Traditionalism, Nationalism and Feminism: Women Writers of Quebec* (1985).

BLANC, Louis (1811–82). Socialist historian, journalist, and political activist, who sums up the blend of socialism and nationalism which characterized many on the Left in 19th-c. France. He is best known today for his *L'Organisation du travail* (1839), which advocated a large role for the state in reorganizing industry and providing work. He played an active political role after the Revolution of 1848 [see REPUBLICS, 2] and his ideas inspired a number of attempted reforms. In the wake of the June Days he went into exile in England. His activism has tended to obscure his other achievements. He wrote a classic example of committed contemporary history, *Histoire de dix ans, 1830–1840* (1841–4), which went through numerous editions and translations, fuelling public antipathy to the *July Monarchy. In his *Histoire de la Révolution* (1847–62), Blanc opposed *Michelet's critique of Jacobinism and remained steadfast in his admiration for *Robespierre and his defence of the Convention. [CC]

Blancandin et l'Orgueilleuse d'amour. *Roman d'aventure* of the early 13th c. It tells, without any attempt to penetrate psychology or motivation, the adventures of the son of the King of Frise. Although the general frame owes much to the *Perceval* of *Chrétien de Troyes, the setting is oriental and the combats with Saracens are inspired by late *chansons de geste.* [PEB]

BLANCHOT, Maurice (b. 1907). French critic and novelist. After graduating, he worked as a journalist until 1940; from that time on he devoted himself exclusively to literary work, both on his own

account and for various publishing concerns, particularly Gallimard and the *NRF.*

Long known only to a small number of readers, he is now widely regarded as one of the greatest critics of the century; although it is not entirely clear why this change has come about. What is clear is that Blanchot himself has not abated one whit of his fierce, passionate, and wide-ranging commitment to the practice of literature. Over a period in which commitment itself has most commonly, as in what was called *littérature engagée*, been taken to imply the conviction that writing served causes or principles outside itself [see ENGAGEMENT], Blanchot has devoted his life to showing that it is in writing, not beyond it, that the central human choices are made. This revaluing of literature he has pursued both directly, in his more general essays, and by way of his readings of a number of writers, two of whom have perhaps paramount importance: *Mallarmé and Kafka. Blanchot's contention is that the stakes of literature are dauntingly high; the writer writing must come to terms, in one direction, with the tenuousness and narrowness of his or her hold on language, and, in the other, with the comparably overwhelming realities of silence and death. And so his exemplary figures are those who, like Mallarmé and Kafka, both remain wholly aware of these stakes and yet venture into the space of writing. One of Blanchot's best and most representative books of essays is called *L'Espace littéraire* (1955), and his explorations in that space and of those who, recognizing it, have made the venture into it form the core of his work.

Setting the highest standards, Blanchot treats his chosen writers with a respect that borders on veneration. At a time when Roland *Barthes was inveighing against the *doxa* of automatic respect for famous writers, so many statues that we piously dusted off, Blanchot, moving in an apparently opposite direction, was in fact showing how Barthes's polemical exaggeration was to be distinguished from mere iconoclasm. The notion of space implies that of boundaries, and much of Blanchot's critical writing is taken up with writers for whom, in their very different ways, boundaries are an urgent and constant preoccupation: Mallarmé and Kafka, but also, among others, *Sade, *Lautréamont, Rilke, *Beckett, *Duras. One essay opens with the words: 'Qui parle dans les romans de Samuel Beckett?' (*Le Livre à venir*, 1959), a question that succinctly anticipates much narratological theorizing. And the fact is that Blanchot himself stands at the convergence of many boundary-lines. The long speculation on language, death, and the creative process, and a disposition for philosophy that takes him from Plato through Hegel to Heidegger and *Levinas: these push him too to argument of a more general, though not more abstract kind. Thus, *L'Écriture du désastre* (1980) explores, in aphorisms, fragments, and longer pieces, the relation of language to catastrophe, whether it is the bereavement of individuals or the horror of Auschwitz. But even here he never forsakes the radically idiosyncratic *démarche* that is the mark of the writer, rather than that of the thinker or theorist: there can be no joining of a group or institution. His arguing is dense, demanding, urgent, and always and everywhere serious.

Blanchot's concerns find expression too in *récits* or novels, such as *Thomas l'obscur* (1941) or *Arrêt de mort* (1948), and in free-ranging reflective works such as *Le Pas au-delà* (1973). These, lacking perhaps the steadiness of focus that reference to other writers imposes, sometimes drift towards the portentous—always a risk in Blanchot. Interestingly counterposed to this tendency is *L'Entretien infini* (1969): again casting its reflective net freely and widely, but, connected always to particular readings, far surer in its movement. But, whether in book reviews, longer essays, or rhapsodic explorations, this fiercely private man celebrates as an intimate the essential strangeness of literature, of writing. [GC]

See R. Laporte and B. Noël, *Deux lectures de Maurice Blanchot* (1973); F. Collin, *Maurice Blanchot et la question de l'écriture*, 2nd edn. (1986).

BLANQUI, Auguste (1805–81). Revolutionary socialist and insurrectionary, prominently involved in the political upheavals of 1830, 1848, and 1870–1. His unwavering belief in armed rebellion as an instrument of political change led to long periods of imprisonment, during one of which he was elected president of the Paris *Commune of 1871. His writings were collected posthumously as *Critique sociale* (1885). [MB]

Blason. A genre of descriptive poetry, closely connected with the *emblem. It has its origins in 15th-c. poetry and heraldry, was practised principally in the 16th c., but lasted well into the next. *Sebillet defines it rather restrictively as 'a continual praising or blaming of the subject on which one has chosen to write'. Its clearest manifestation is to be found in the 'Blasons anatomiques' or 'Blasons du corps féminin', a kind of love-poem in vogue in the 1530s and 1540s. The first of these Renaissance *blasons*, the 'Blason du beau tétin', was written by Clément *Marot in Ferrara in 1535, and he was soon followed by *Scève (five poems) and other poets who gave detailed poetic praise to different parts of the body, and later to various objects and abstract qualities. The common nature of the poems was soon perceived and the first collected edition dates from 1543. The *blason* was sometimes paired with a *contreblason* (see Marot's 'Blason du laid tétin' or *Peletier's poems on the heart). A further development was the 'Hymne-blason' of the *Pléiade. The scope was later extended to include religious and satirical poems. The visual, even painterly, element is paramount, at least in the earlier *blasons*. [PS]

BLIN, Roger (1907–84). French director and actor. He directed the first production of *En attendant Godot* (1953) and the French premières of numerous subsequent plays by *Beckett. Although his name is primarily associated with that of Beckett, who regarded him as his preferred director, other important and influential productions included *Genet's *Les Nègres* (1959) and *Les Paravents* (1966). [DWW]

BLOCH, Jean-Richard (1884–1947). French novelist and essayist. After a short university career, he contributed to cultural reviews of the Left, notably *Europe*, which he co-founded in 1923 with Romain *Rolland and Jean *Guéhenno. A sympathizer of the PCF, his Resistance activities and his Jewish background obliged him to leave France, and he became a regular wartime broadcaster in French on Radio Moscow. Bloch wrote novels including . . . *et Cie* (1917), many short stories in the Balzacian realist tradition, several texts for the theatre, and a large body of cultural criticism and travel reportage. Among the committed intellectuals of his day he was a humanist and moralist rather than a political theorist. [MHK]

BLOCH, Marc (1886–1944). French historian, co-founder of *Annales. A champion of comparative and 'structural' history who owed much to the theories of *Durkheim, Bloch examined the relationship between collective beliefs, political and social institutions, and ideas of kingship in *Les Rois thaumaturges* (1924). He traced long-term developments and extended the scope of historical evidence in *Les Caractères originaux de l'histoire rurale française* (1931), drawing upon artefacts, ancient maps, place-names, aerial surveys, and folklore; and in *La Société féodale* (1939–40) he analysed the mental attitudes and ways of life underlying feudal organization. [REG]

BLONDEAU, Dominique (b. 1937). French-Canadian novelist. In her novels the characters pursue elusive, impossible goals and are forced to reckon with their own isolation. Sequences are dream-like, and there is no clear linear structure. In *Que mon désir soit ta demeure* (1975) the narrative voices are particularly complex. Her novels include *Les Visages de l'enfance* (1970); *Demain c'est l'orient* (1972); *L'Agonie d'une salamandre* (1979); *Un homme foudroyé* (1985); *Les Feux de l'exil* (1991). [MMC]

BLONDEL DE NESLE. *Trouvère from Picardy, active late 12th and early 13th c., sometimes identified as Jehan II, lord of Nesle-lès-Péronne (1202–32). He composed some 22 extant *chansons courtoises*, whose style is sometimes simple, sometimes precious and prosodically complex. He was probably an associate of *Gace Brulé and *Conon de Béthune, but not of Richard Cœur-de-Lion as legend claims. [PVD]

BLONDIN, Antoine (b. 1922). French novelist. A member of the right-wing *Hussards group, he began his career as an extreme right-wing polemicist for the semi-clandestine *La Dernière Lanterne* and continued as a major writer for *Rivarol* in the 1950s. His first novel, *L'Europe buissonnière* (1949), draws upon his experience with the Service du Travail Obligatoire in Germany and presents a picaresque view of World War II, in which events and characters are governed by chance. This anti-historicist, anti-*Existentialist stance is continued in his later fiction, such as *Les Enfants du Bon Dieu* (1952) and *Un singe en hiver* (1959, Prix Interallié), with a poignant sense of humour and a wry evocation of the emptiness of post-war life. [NH]

BLOY, Léon (1846–1917). French writer of prose fiction, journalist, and diarist. A precursor of the late 19th-c. Catholic Revival [see CATHOLICISM IN TWENTIETH-CENTURY FRANCE], Bloy was the first to combine with any degree of success the dual functions of the Catholic writer as creative artist and defender of an absolute faith. For some, his ironic and satirical journalism is the best part of his production. Bloy himself preferred his autobiographical novels *Le Désespéré* (1887) and *La Femme pauvre* (1897), his multi-volume *Journal*, transpositions of the frustrations of his own poverty and passions into the redeeming language of Crucifixion and Apocalypse, and his prophetic tomes on reparatory suffering and the imminent advent of the Holy Spirit (*Le Salut par les Juifs*, 1892; *Celle qui pleure*, 1908, on the penitential cult of La Salette). [JB]

BLUM, Léon (1872–1950). French socialist leader, prime minister during the *Popular Front. Trained as a lawyer, in his youth he was literary critic for the *Revue blanche*. Lucien *Herr converted him to socialism, and Blum was thereafter deeply influenced by *Jaurès. At the Congress of Tours (1920), when the bulk of the French Socialist Party (SFIO) rallied to Lenin's Third International to form the French Communist Party, Blum led the minority loyal to 'la vieille maison'. In the inter-war period he rebuilt the SFIO, and when the Popular Front won the 1936 election, Blum became premier, presiding over the historic social legislation of the period. His reluctant non-intervention in the Spanish Civil War helped widen splits in the Left alliance, and after defeat in the senate over the economy, he resigned in June 1937, occupying office only briefly thereafter. During the war he was arrested by the Vichy authorities, but his defence testimony was so eloquent that his trial was halted. *A l'échelle humaine* (1945), written in prison, is a testament of faith in humanist socialism. After his release from Buchenwald in 1945, he was briefly caretaker premier in December 1946, and remained an elder statesman of the Fourth Republic till his death.

Blum inspired both affection and hate, the latter often antisemitic in inspiration. He endured both verbal and physical attacks during the 1930s, mostly from the extreme Right: *Maurras wrote of him: 'Voilà un homme à fusiller, mais dans le dos.' He was not always popular with the Left either, for in an age of extremes, his socialism was moderate and reformist, inspired by moral concern and respect for legality. Retrospectively, however, Blum has become a venerated figure on the Left, associated with the achievements of the Popular Front, of which he wrote: 'I felt . . . I had brought a little sunshine, a moment of happiness into difficult lives.' His many and varied writings were collected in the *Œuvres complètes* (1954–66). [SR]

BOAISTUAU, Pierre (1517–66). Famous in his day as the author of works of compilation, in particular *Le Théâtre du monde* (1558), an encyclopedic account of 'les misères du monde', he is remembered mainly as the first editor of the *Heptaméron* and the translator of six of Bandello's *Novelle*, the very popular *Histoires tragiques* (1559), later continued by *Belleforest. He was interested in monsters and prodigies (*Histoires prodigieuses*, 1560). [PF]

BOCAGE, Pierre-François (1797–1863). Handsome *Boulevard actor whose impassioned and expressive style of acting owed much to the English actor *Kean, and who excelled in melodrama and Romantic drama. His performances in *Dumas père's *Antony* (1831) and *La Tour de Nesle* (1832) made him the darling of the younger generation. [SBJ]

BOCCACCIO, see ITALIAN INFLUENCES.

BODEL, Jehan (d. 1210). Professional *jongleur and *trouvère, active at the very end of the 12th c. in *Arras, of whose *Confrérie des Jongleurs et Bourgeois he was a member. Its records show that he died in 1210, but already by 1202 he had withdrawn from society owing to leprosy. He probably took part in the Fourth Crusade from 1199 to 1201. He was one of the first of a line of distinguished writers who benefited from the particularly favourable circumstances in Arras. Bodel worked in a variety of genres, producing *fabliaux, *pastourelles, a *chanson de geste, a *congé, and a play; in the first three cases, he followed established models, in the last two he created something new.

His nine *fabliaux* are typical examples of the genre and include the usual stories of greed, stupidity, and lechery. In *Le Vilain de Bailleul*, a wife who is caught *in flagrante* by her peasant husband convinces him that he is not only ill, but dead, and thus can do nothing to prevent her making love to the priest. The five *pastourelles* are also typical, though the genre was still very new in northern France. In 'L'autre jor, les un boschel', the courtly narrator tells how he came across a shepherdess weeping, because she had lost a lamb and her peasant lover had abandoned her. The knight finds it only too easy to console the shepherdess and to seduce her.

Like most *chansons de geste*, the *Chanson des Saisnes* results from multiple authorship, and only the first 3,300 lines can confidently be attributed to Jehan Bodel; even they probably result from the reworking of an earlier text. The main subject is *Charlemagne's war against the Saxon Guitaclin, and the poem, in its longest (*c*.8,000-line) versions, ends with the conversion of Saxony. But its interest, like that of other epics of its day, lies in the confrontation between an older, feudal model of social organization, and the rising current of *chivalry and individualism. This latter element is manifested by Charlemagne's nephew Baudouin, and his love affair with the Saxon queen Sebile. While the feudal army stagnates on the banks of the Rune (the Rhine?), Baudouin swims back and forth having *galant* adventures. Glamour aside, his early death suggests a certain reluctance on the part of the poet to embrace social change. The song is remarkably well-written, its alexandrine lines maintaining real power and resonance.

The *Jeu de Saint Nicolas* (1,540 lines) is undoubtedly Bodel's masterpiece and most original work, even if traces of his earlier writings appear in it; it is in effect the earliest surviving example of a French *miracle play, though no later miracle is like Bodel's. Using Latin and vernacular sources, he creates a play out of the legend of St Nicolas of Myra, in which the saint proves his ability to guard treasure left in his protection; but Bodel sets the action in an unusual and ambiguous context. After a battle between Christians and Saracens, in which all the Christian soldiers are killed, the Saracens find a 'preudom' (a simple Christian) praying to a wooden statue of Nicolas. They reprieve him when he says the statue will protect any treasure entrusted to it and decide to test the 'preudom''s claim. Whilst all are asleep, three Arras thieves, who have heard about the situation, steal the treasure. When this is revealed, the 'preudom', his life now threatened, prays again to Nicolas, who visits the terrified thieves and forces them to put the treasure back. Next day the Saracens find it not only safe but multiplied, and they are converted to Christianity. Into this fundamentally religious drama, Bodel introduces not only epic and crusading elements (topoi, vocabulary, versification) but also the humour of the *fabliaux* (drinking, cheating, swearing), as well as many local references to Arras. This mixing of the genres, which baffled earlier critics, is now seen as the play's most original feature. According to a possibly inauthentic prologue, it was performed before an Arras *confrérie* on a 5 December in the early 1200s.

The *congé*, probably Bodel's last work, can also lay claim to originality, as it is the oldest surviving example of a genre in which the poet, faced with his real or imaginary death or departure, looks back over his life. *Congés* were written by *Baude Fastoul and *Adam de la Halle; *Villon's *Testament* is also a form of *congé*. In Bodel's poem (540 lines, 45 stan-

zas), the poet takes leave of his friends, wishes them well in the future, and prays to our Lady for his own salvation as he departs for the leper-house.   [GAR]

See C. Foulon, *L'Œuvre de Jehan Bodel* (1958); A. Henri, *Le Jeu de Saint Nicolas* (1965); A. Brasseur, *La Chanson des Saisnes* (1989).

BODIN, Jean (1529/30–96). Political and religious thinker. Born in Angers, he studied law in Toulouse, where he hoped to be instrumental in setting up a new humanist college. He became a member of the Parlement de Paris in 1561, and was obliged to sign an oath of Catholic alliegance. His Protestant sympathies, however, led him to oppose the policies of oppression recommended at the États Généraux at Blois in 1576. He is, in consequence, regarded as one of the more influential members of the moderate *Politique movement. His later decision to ally himself with the Catholic *Ligue was probably taken under duress.

He is most famous for his *Six livres de la République* (1576, republished in Latin in 1586), in which he was the first to provide an autonomous definition of the principle of sovereignty. His analysis of the various kinds of sovereignty, and in particular of the various factors which influence its nature and development, looks forward to Montesquieu's *Esprit des lois*; but he is evidently preoccupied with contemporary Protestant justification of tyrannicide: hence his overwhelming desire to create a strong—and just—monarchy. Certain checks and balances are allowed for, but sovereignty is seen as being vested solely in the monarch. In this way, Bodin's work prepares the way for 17th-c. theories of the divine right of kings [see MONARCHY].

His *Réponse aux paradoxes de M. de Malestroit* (1568) provides the first rigorous analysis of the mechanisms which fuel inflation. As such, it too is 'modern' in outlook, as is the *Methodus ad facilem historiarum cognitionem* (1566), which insists on the need for rigorous method in the field of 'universal' (i.e. comparative) history.

The *Colloquium Heptaplomeres* (which remained in manuscript until the middle of the 19th c.) also shows Bodin to be a man who is not afraid to open up radically new perspectives. It is a discussion between a Catholic, a Lutheran, a Jew, a Moslem, and a Deist. Different speakers are occasionally allowed to score points over each other; but, in the end, no single view is allowed to prevail. Bodin would seem, therefore, to be recommending a basic tolerance. The modern reader will be all the more surprised, therefore, by his *Démonomanie* (1580), in which he vigorously defends the witch trials which *Montaigne so earnestly deplored.   [JJS]

See J. H. Franklin, *Jean Bodin and the Rise of Absolutist Theory* (1973).

BOETHIUS, Anicius Manlius Severinus (Boèce) (*c*.480 524/6), an aristocratic Roman, served Theodoric, the Ostrogothic ruler of Italy, until he was imprisoned on trumped-up charges of disloyalty and finally executed. His Latin translations of most of Aristotle's logical works became standard, and through his commentaries and textbooks he transmitted to medieval readers the late antique Greek logical tradition. His five short theological treatises provided medieval scholars with an example of how Aristotelian logic could be applied to Christian doctrine. Even more influential was his *De consolatione Philosophiae*, written in prison. In an imaginary dialogue, with verse interludes, a personification of Philosophy reasons the character Boethius out of initial despair at his unjust condemnation: honour, fame, riches, power, and pleasure are all transitory goods of fortune; only the Highest Good, on which all these depend, is stable; and it is identified with God. *De consolatione* was commented on frequently, from the 9th c. to the 14th. It influenced both Latin authors (for instance, Bernardus Silvestris and *Alan of Lille), and vernacular writers, such as *Jean de Meun (who translated the work into French) and, outside France, Dante, Petrarch, and Chaucer.   [JAMM]

Boeve de Haumtone, see ANGLO-NORMAN LITERATURE, 3a.

Bohème, La. The penniless, provocatively unconventional, and mostly unsuccessful circles of artists and writers attempting to establish themselves in Paris in the 1830s and 1840s, and, by extension, any eccentric artistic group, so named after *Nodier's fantastical *Histoire du Roi de Bohême et de ses sept châteaux* (1830) (itself a play on the established meaning of *bohémien* as 'a person of irregular and disreputable habits'). The original 'Bohemians', such as Petrus *Borel, Philothée *O'Neddy, and Théophile *Gautier, lived communally, on occasions, in the derelict Hôtel Pimodan, in the Impasse du Doyenné, and in Montmartre, experimented with drugs, and took the battle of *Romanticism to extravagant limits [see BOUSINGOTS; JEUNES-FRANCE]. The 'Bohème' of the July Monarchy probably constitutes the first self-defined 'counter-culture' in France, from which the long tradition of the artistic and social avant-garde springs. [See MURGER.]
                                                    [DMB]

BOÏELDIEU, François-Adrien (1775–1834). Composer, see OPÉRA-COMIQUE.

BOILAT, David, abbé (1814–1901). Senegalese writer. Born of a French father and half-caste mother, he was educated in a French seminary, and returned to Senegal in 1842 as missionary and educator. Appointed director of education by Baron Roger, he founded the first secondary school in the colony. He wrote an important ethnological study, *Esquisses sénégalaises* (Physionomie du pays—peuplades—commerce—religions—passé et avenir—récits et légendes) (1853), with 24 illustrations by the author of types and costumes of different native

peoples. His Wolof Grammar (1856) was awarded a prize (founded by *Volney) for linguistics.   [DSB]

BOILEAU, Gilles (1631–69). Older brother and occasionally rival of *Boileau-Despréaux, whose poetic gift he failed to emulate.

BOILEAU-DESPRÉAUX, Nicolas, known to contemporaries as 'Despréaux', now always known as 'Boileau' (1636–1711). Poet, satirist, and critic. The label 'régent [or 'législateur'] du Parnasse', which Boileau humorously applied to himself, has stuck; he was by turns venerated (in the 18th c.) and reviled (in the 19th) as the schoolteacher or lawgiver of French *classicism. The reality is more interesting.

He came from the legal bourgeoisie and lived all his life in or near Paris. A childhood operation left him impotent, and he never married. After studying law (which he hardly ever practised), he threw himself into literary life. An outspoken and often bitter man—reputedly the model for Alceste in Molière's *Le *Misanthrope*—he made many enemies, including *précieux* circles and the writers pensioned by *Colbert. His aggressive temperament is evident in his *Satires*, of which the first nine were written between 1660 and 1667, followed by three more between 1692 and 1708. The tenth satire concerns women and the twelfth is an attack on *Jesuit casuistry; in the early ones the targets are sometimes socio-political (tax-farmers, corrupt officials, etc.), but usually literary. The same vein is exploited in his mischievous *Dialogue des héros de roman* (composed c.1666), an attack on the *roman héroïque*.

Boileau began in a bohemian way; some of his early friends (including *Molière and *Chapelle) were close to the world of the *libertins. Soon, however, he was taken in hand by respectable backers, notably the *Lamoignon group, who channelled his energies away from satire to moral epistles and a more serious interest in poetics. He wrote 12 *Épîtres* between 1668 and 1696, and in 1674 published his Art poétique, together with an influential translation of the *Traité du sublime* of pseudo-Longinus. The Art poétique (in four cantos) combines the personal mockery of the *Satires* with an exposition of what we now call 'classicism'; Boileau stresses the truthful imitation of nature, the value of 'reason', the need for both inspiration and control, and discusses more technical questions of versification and the poetic genres. The translation of Longinus sets him among those who preferred the high ambitions of classical literature to modern politeness. A critic engaged in the debates of the day, he nailed his colours to the mast in his defence of *Racine and Molière.

He had cultivated the royal favour in dedications and epistles, and in 1677, together with Racine, a close friend of his later years, he was appointed 'historiographe du roi'. The two poets accompanied the king on his campaigns, and produced a *Précis his-*

torique des campagnes de Louis XIV, but little else. The awkward Boileau, who did not hide his sympathy for the *Jansenists, was not a successful courtier, though he did exploit this apparent lack of savoir-faire adroitly in a number of court poems. After 1688, having been elected to the Académie Française in 1684, he was the chief of the ancien camp in the *Querelle des Anciens et des Modernes, attacking *Perrault vigorously in his 12 Réflexions critiques sur quelques passages du rhéteur Longin (1694–1713).

Boileau is important for his influence on literary taste in France and elsewhere in the 18th c.—and equally for the way he was later taken as an emblem of classicism at its most limited. But he was also a poet. His poetic work is almost all in alexandrine couplets, which he uses with considerable mastery, combining often exuberant wit with such memorable, if blunt, formulations as: 'Ce que l'on conçoit bien s'énonce clairement.' The Satires, Épîtres, and Art poétique are in their different ways all verse discourses which vary between the playful and the solemn, the idiosyncratic and the commonplace. Boileau's favourite self-image was that of 'l'ami du vrai', the fearless truth-teller and enemy of humbug, inflation, and equivocation. He believed in the role of the satirist as the scourge of bad writing. But he was also wary of the role of teacher or preacher, and his work is notable for its tone of ironic self-deprecation. This no doubt prevented him from writing the elevated poetry that he so admired in the ancients. Instead, he composed a mock-heroic epic in six cantos, Le Lutrin (1674–83), which tells a ridiculous story of petty clerical squabbles in a parody of high tragic verse. It can be seen as a model for Pope's Rape of the Lock, just as the Art poétique prefigures his Essay on Criticism. [PF]

See Boileau, Œuvres complètes, ed. C.-H. Boudhors, 7 vols. (1934–43); J. Brody, Boileau and Longinus (1958); G. Pocock, Boileau and the Nature of Neo-classicism (1980).

BOILEAU–NARCEJAC. Pierre Boileau (b. 1906) and Thomas Narcejac (pseud. of Pierre Ayraud) (b. 1908) wrote crime fiction separately before corresponding, meeting, and collaborating on L'Ombre et la proie, serialized in 1951, followed by Celle qui n'était plus (1952; filmed as Les Diaboliques, 1954) and 40 years of crime novels, stories, films, and plays for radio and television. Theorizers, occasionally pasticheurs, of crime fiction, they sought a vein different from English puzzle and American violence in an implacable irony of situations where victims, often would-be killers, are more important than detectives, and blows awaited strike from, sometimes even in, unexpected quarters. [SFN]

BOINDIN, Nicolas (1676–1751). French scholar and man of letters, elected in 1706 to the *Académie des Inscriptions. A sceptical *philosophe, he frequented café society, supported the modernes [see QUERELLE], and professed atheism. He wrote several light comedies and academic dissertations on such topics as phonetics and the ancient theatre. [PF]

BOISGUILBERT or BOISGUILLEBERT, Pierre le Pesant de (1646–1714). French economist, who made a considerable fortune and opposed *Colbert's system (see his Détail de la France, 1695).

BOISROBERT, François Le Métel, sieur de (1589–1662). French poet, novelist, and dramatist. A man of easy literary talent, he wrote witty love poetry, devotional verse, a novel, four free adaptations of Spanish novelas, and 18 plays. His Pyrandre et Lisimène (performed 1631–2) was one of the first regular tragicomedies, and his numerous comedies of the 1650s exploited the popularity of Spanish comedia. [GJM]

BOISSARD, Maurice. Pseudonym used by *Léautaud.

BOISTE, Pierre-Claude-Victoire, see DICTIONARIES, 4.

Bollandistes. A group of scholars, named after the Fleming Jean Bolland (1596–1665); mainly Jesuits, they were responsible for publishing lives of the saints [see HAGIOGRAPHY] in over 50 volumes of Acta sanctorum between 1643 and 1794. They were reconstituted in Belgium in 1837 and have continued their work, in an increasingly scholarly spirit.

Bomston, Milord Edouard. English character in Rousseau's La *Nouvelle Héloïse. His love story was eventually omitted from the novel.

BONALD, Louis, vicomte de (1754–1840). French Catholic philosopher and politician, adversary of the democratic spirit in all its forms. He regarded 18th-c. rationalism as an abomination, accusing it of eroding the social organism and leading directly to the dislocation of 1789. For him society was not the construction of the rational will of individuals; individuals were formed by society and only existed in and through social relationships. The principles of social life were embedded in tradition and in language which transmitted God's will. Bonald exerted considerable influence during the Restoration. However, he quite lacked the literary gifts of Joseph de *Maistre. His major works are Théorie du pouvoir politique et religieux (1796) and La Législation primitive (1802). [CC]

Bonaparte, see NAPOLEON.

Bonapartism has always been associated with the cult of the Bonaparte family, and Corsica has invariably been the stronghold of any movement connected with it. In political terms Bonapartism has usually been classified as right-wing, but a number of reservations have to be made.

*Napoleon I ended the Revolution, but he attempted to bring about the reconciliation of the French. He established authoritarian government, but sought to preserve the work of the Revolution. He established the rule of *notables*, gave guarantees to property-owners, distributed hereditary titles, and increased centralization, but maintained the abolition of privileged casts and corporations and declared that careers were open to talent. *Napoleon III was accused of establishing a police state and suppressing public opinion, but at the same time he was concerned with economic growth and with the plight of the poor. The notion that Bonapartism is impossible to define seems to be confirmed when one remembers that Napoleon I was famous for his military victories, while Napoleon III's defeats have never been forgotten.

The essence of Bonapartism is that it seeks to be a unifying force in a divided country and tries to achieve this by concentrating on the talents and reputation of an individual. Both emperors drew support from many varied sectors of the population. After 1870 Bonapartism did not die out; it was in the Bonapartist tradition that *notables* were elected to the National Assembly, and that striking miners shouted 'Vive Napoléon IV!' The movement led by General *Boulanger to capture power between 1886 and 1892 had many of the characteristics of Bonapartism. The same has often been said of *Gaullism. [DJ]

Boncourt, Collège de, see PLÉIADE.

Bonheur d'occasion, see ROY, G.

Bonhomme Misère, Le. Anonymous tale, one of the most popular in the *Bibliothèque Bleue: it was acclaimed by *Champfleury as the epic of the poor. A peasant, Misère, has as his only wealth a pear-tree; two unknown travellers (Peter and Paul), to whom he gives lodging, grant him the favour that anyone who climbs into his tree will remain stuck there. He uses this to catch a thief, and then, when La Mort comes for him, he traps her too in his tree; as a result, Misère (i.e. Poverty) will remain among men as long as there is life on earth. [PF]

BONI, Nazi (1912–69). Novelist, politician, and *député* in the French National Assembly. Born in Upper Volta (now Burkina Faso), he was author of a widely admired historical novel tracing 300 years of life in an African village, *Crépuscule des temps anciens* (1962). [PGH]

BONIVARD, François, see SWISS LITERATURE IN FRENCH, 1.

BONNARD, Pierre (1867–1947). In the artistic and literary circles of the French *Symbolist milieu, Bonnard was known chiefly as a decorative artist (posters, drawings, and lithographs for the *Revue blanche,* 1894; lithographs and wood engravings for *Verlaine's Parallèlement,* 1900). In his early paintings of landscapes and domestic scenes, he sought to integrate the *Impressionist colour surface and Japanese composition, but following his discovery

in 1909 of the light of southern France, he devoted himself to the expression of vibrant and subtle harmonies of colour. [JK]

BONNECORSE, Balthasar de (1631–1706). Poet from Marseille, a friend of the *Scudérys, *La Fontaine, and *Pellisson. Although he wrote some pleasing poems, he is remembered only because of being gratuitously mocked by *Boileau in *Le Lutrin,* to which he responded with a satire in 10 cantos, *Le Lutrigot* (1686).

BONNEFOY, Yves (b. 1923). Since publication of his first major collection in 1953, Bonnefoy has often been hailed as the leading French poet of the postwar generation. The dense, hieratic poems of *Du mouvement et de l'immobilité de Douve,* while not without echoes of *Scève or *Mallarmé, introduced a wholly original poetic voice marrying authentic philosophical questioning with lyrical intensity. The mysterious central figure of Douve, fleetingly a woman of flesh and blood, a dying body, a mythical emanation of the natural world, a disembodied voice, a *genius loci,* an absent interlocutor, pointed to central questions: where is the *place* of poetry, what kind of knowledge, if any, can poetry foster, and what is the relationship between the poet's medium and the world he seeks to encounter? In meditative essays written at about the same time as *Douve* (and collected in *L'Improbable,* 1959), Bonnefoy defined poetry as an act directed at what he called 'la présence', an engagement with the here and now of lived experience in the real world. Purely conceptual knowledge denies *présence* by affirming universality; the virtues of poetry—that 'parole jetée matérielle contre l'origine et la nuit'—stem from its links with subjective utterance, with the materiality of language, and with the wellsprings of myth.

Bonnefoy's great achievement is to have pursued with great persistence a searching interrogation into the ends and ethics of poetry, not only through the medium of poetry itself—as in *Hier régnant désert* (1958) and *Pierre écrite* (1965)—but also through essays, criticism, translation, and teaching. His extensive translations of Shakespeare and Yeats prompted insights into the language of poetry. Prose fables such as *L'Arrière-pays* (1972) and the narratives collected in *Récits en rêve* (1987) situate the poetic quest in a wider context of experiences. Bonnefoy has written widely on other poets, and his assessments of *Baudelaire, Mallarmé, *Rimbaud, *Breton, or *Jouve are uniquely penetrating and authoritative. Equally important, however, are his writings on the visual arts, which include monographs on French Romanesque art and on the baroque period in Rome, and numerous essays on contemporary artists such as Miró, Balthus, Hopper, and Garache. The vast book on the sculptor *Giacometti (1991), like the earlier *Rimbaud par lui-même* (1959), indicates a central preoccupation, shared by Geneva critics such as *Poulet and

*Starobinski, with the links between works of art and the existential project or personal destiny of the artist.

Time and again, in the essays collected in such volumes as *Le Nuage rouge* (1977) and *La Vérité de parole* (1988), Bonnefoy seeks to establish the point at which the poem becomes no more than a linguistic object, or the painting an empty triumph of form over fact. In *La Présence et l'image*, the lecture delivered on his accession to a chair at the *Collège de France in 1981, Bonnefoy suggests that poetry should involve a 'guerre contre l'image': a place where the lure of imaginary, Utopian perfection in both life and art is given its due but also sedulously resisted in furtherance of an open-ended commitment to genuine communication and to authentic love for the given world—'ce qui est'. This is also the great theme of later collections, from *Dans le leurre du seuil* (1977) to *Ce qui fut sans lumière* (1987) and *Début et fin de la neige* (1991), often more straightforward than the early poems, but no less charged with a fervent belief in the vital role of poetry in human existence. [MHTS]

See G. Gasarian, *Bonnefoy: la poésie, la présence* (1966); J. Naughton, *The Poetics of Yves Bonnefoy* (1984).

Bonnes, Les. Play by *Genet, written at the request of *Jouvet, who first produced it in 1947. Awakening echoes of the notorious case of the Papin sisters who murdered their mistress and her daughter in 1933, two maids indulge in rituals of role-play as a means of coping with the resentment and self-hate their lowly functions provoke in them. Initially performed naturalistically, the work has since become a classic of avant-garde theatricality. [DHW]

Bonnet rouge, Le. The red cap was adopted as a sign of revolutionary allegiance by many French men and women from 1789 and became an official emblem of the Revolution in August 1792. It has its origin in the *bonnet phrygien*, a Roman symbol of liberty, but also in the red caps worn by convicts. In Brittany, 'les Bonnets rouges' was the name taken by the participants in the great peasant rising of 1675.

BONSTETTEN, Charles-Victor de (1745–1832). Swiss critic and philosopher. He epitomized the cosmopolitan spirit of the intellectuals who surrounded Madame de *Staël at *Coppet. His most important publications are *L'Homme du midi et l'homme du nord* (1824) and *Études sur l'homme* (1821).

Book Trade [see also LIBRARIES; LITERACY; MANUSCRIPTS; PRINTING IN FRANCE UNTIL 1600]

1. An Unchanging Regime

The organization of the French book industry changed little between the age of Gutenberg and the early 19th c. Until the changes wrought by the Revolution and its aftermath, books were manufactured by artisans, traditionally grouped in small workshops in the capital, around the university, the law courts, and Notre-Dame. When the Imprimerie Royale was set up in 1640, with seven presses under one roof, it was an exceptionally large establishment for its time. Printers carried out several different functions at once, acting as booksellers and publishers. Before 1750 the French book industry produced fewer than 500 titles annually. This did not mean that nothing at all had changed in book production since the 16th c.: the proportion of books produced in Latin, for example, was already a minority by the mid-16th c., and it fell to less than 20 per cent of total production from the 1660s onwards. Nevertheless, the description of provincial printing offered by Balzac in *Illusions perdues* would probably have looked familiar to a printer of the 16th or 17th c.

The Revolution dealt a decisive blow to the guild system and to monarchical control, and by the 1830s the introduction of mechanization and of capitalist methods began to transform the typographical *ancien régime*. Overall, however, the book trade was still characterized by centralized government control (see Section 2 below), and the domination of Paris.

2. Organization and Control before 1789 [see also CENSORSHIP]

Printing and publishing in *ancien régime* France was governed from the beginning of the 16th c. by the grant of a royal *privilège*. A *privilège* conferred fiscal rights, for books were tax-free, and in principle guaranteed a protected home market. A *privilège* was thus an authority to publish a given book, which conferred a virtual monopoly on the successful publisher. It might be limited to 20, 10, or just a few years: enough to allow the publisher to produce not just one edition, but the repeated editions which alone could make a book profitable. Until 1777, a *privilège* was renewable.

Printers before the Revolution thus worked within a protected system of temporary monopolies, and the book trade was at the mercy of the royal pleasure. Royal favour played an important additional role in the disbursement of *patronage. A wide range of pensions and sinecures was available to support writers and artists. In these different ways, the *ancien régime* monarchy policed, supervised, and repressed the book trade. The mechanisms of control were installed as the bureaucracy of royal absolutism expanded in the late 17th c.; the abbé Bignon's term as Directeur de la Librairie (1699–1714) is usually identified as a crucial period in this process.

In practice, the *privilège* system was very centralized. Parisian publishers, in close contact with both authors and bureaucrats, seized the lion's share of lucrative *privilèges*. Provincial publishers complained bitterly that they were left only the crumbs discarded by their larger Parisian colleagues. These complaints were partly justified. In Lyon, for example, far less was printed in the 18th than in the 17th c. The city had 30 printers in 1701, but only 12 were active there by 1777. The domination of Parisian publishing drove the Lyon book trade to rely on resale and distribution, buying in Holland and Germany and reselling in Spain. Similar stagnation set in in Languedoc, except perhaps in Toulouse, where the *parlement*, clergy, and university kept local printers in work for at least two-thirds of the year. Provincial publishers were often forced to wait for Parisian *privilèges* to expire, and the works concerned to become public property, but they were frustrated by the frequent renewal of *privilèges*. As a result, provincial centres like Rouen were driven into a close reliance on illegal and contraband works.

Illicit literature was smuggled into France from abroad, chiefly from Holland and Switzerland, through various underground networks in the 18th c. Illegal books might be hidden among other goods, their passage facilitated by bribing customs officials, or carriers might exchange their freight clandestinely, before it arrived 'under seal' at the nearest *chambre syndicale* (see Section 4 below) to the French border. Rouen was an important distribution point for contraband from Holland; and Avignon, as a superbly situated Papal enclave, and a tax haven, was a paradise for publishers of books banned in France. Avignon publishers could produce best-sellers with no *privilèges* to infringe, and without paying authors a fee. They could undercut their French competitors by between 25 and 50 per cent.

It required a vast network of corruption to organize regular shipments and distribution of prohibited books. It could also be very expensive. Contraband passed through so many hands on its devious route from Switzerland to such places as Versailles, that its price was thereby increased by at least 25 per cent. There was nevertheless a considerable market for pornography, satires on religion and the court, and a few extremist works of *Enlightenment philosophy.

The domination by Paris of the book trade in the Midi was part of a more general European pattern in which, by the 18th c., the north of Europe supplied the south and east. In the decade of the 1780s, three-quarters of all books published in Paris but reissued in the provinces were produced north of a line between Avranches and Besançon. Outside the area north of this imaginary line, only Toulouse and Lyon showed any vitality as book publishers.

The Avranches–Besançon (or Saint-Malo–Geneva) line coincides with the division often made between the literate north-east of France and the relatively illiterate west, centre, and Midi. It is also echoed in the distribution of printing-shops. In 1777 the network of printing-shops was densest in the north-east, with the usual exceptions of Toulouse and Bordeaux. In the centre of France there was only one printing-shop for a quarter of a million inhabitants. Between 1701 and 1777 the number of provincial printers declined by almost 30 per cent. There were very few booksellers anywhere in the vicinity of the capital, which drew all such activity like a magnet to the Quartier Latin. There were hardly any in port cities, but many around provincial *parlements*. Studies of book-purchasing habits conducted in the 1940s suggest that this north-east/centre-west division has remained a permanent feature of French cultural space.

3. Authors and Publishers

Until the position of the author became fully professionalized in the 19th c., writers under the *ancien régime* enjoyed little legal protection, since their property rights were not fully recognized. Authors sold their manuscript once and for all to a publisher, and were not entitled to the benefits of anything resembling a royalty system. *Rousseau received no payment for the hundreds of articles on music he contributed to the *Encyclopédie*, and the Amsterdam publisher Rey paid him only 1,000 *livres* for the *Contrat social*. Writing for the theatre could be more lucrative, because fees rose in proportion to box-office receipts, as long as the latter covered the theatre's expenses. Only a few writers were able to earn large sums by their pen in the *ancien régime*: *Buffon was one, and *Restif de la Bretonne another. It was more common for authors to be treated like amateurs, and to be satisfied with an offer of several luxury-bound copies of their own work in payment.

The Revolution, however, redefined the nature of private property in literary works as in everything else. On 19 July 1793 the Convention gave authors, painters, and composers the right to dispose of their own works during their own lifetime, and the same right was to be enjoyed by their heirs up to ten years after the author's death. The Revolution ended the system of royal *privilèges*, and invented a primitive form of copyright.

4. The Printing Trade

The Revolution also suppressed the corporate organization of the entire printing industry. Under the *ancien régime*, a mass of detailed legislation controlled entry into the book trade, the recruitment of workers, and access to the coveted *maîtrise*. Apprentices had to be of the Catholic faith, and were required to have a knowledge of Greek and Latin. The number of apprentices was limited, to protect existing practitioners from too much competition. The government tried to reduce the number of printers to make policing easier, and the monarchy found ready accomplices within the trade itself.

The printers' community had an exclusive membership, its own autonomous structure and social life, electing its own officials on the feast of St John the Evangelist, the patron saint of printers. The guild also had its own local *chambre syndicale*, where corporation officials checked imported books to eliminate contraband and illegal competition. Opening the trade to unrestricted competition would, it was argued, lead to serious deterioration of the typographer's art. Not only did the corporation stand in the way of free competition and the progress of book production along capitalist lines, but the guild was also a willing instrument of the monarchy's police apparatus. Its exclusive policies helped to isolate a number of aspiring authors and publishers, who formed a growing intellectual proletariat in Paris in the dying years of the *ancien régime*.

For the apprentices and journeymen who produced the literary masterpieces of the *ancien régime*, the working environment was noisy, the hours long, but the pay probably good. The labour market was very insecure; printers joined other *compagnons* on their *Tour de France in search of work, experience, and the occasional bout of drunken fighting in defence of their lodge, or 'Devoir'. They lived from job to job, travelling wherever work was offered. Inside the printing-shops workers were paid by the task, or by the thousand impressions. Work rhythms varied erratically, with periods of intense activity alternating with periods of total rest or redundancy. In Neuchâtel, for instance, workers took holidays exactly as they wished, and worked at their own pace. They were craft-workers whose working life was not subject to the regularity and discipline which industrial capitalism was later to demand.

Before the technical innovations of the 19th c., printing used technology inherited from the 16th c. Ink was sold by the pint, in a container made of boiled leather. It was usually made from a mixture of walnut, turpentine, and resin, and just one barrel might cost as much as a second-hand printing press. Until rubber was introduced as an eraser in the reign of Louis XVI, bread was a normal correcting medium. Paper itself was manufactured from cloth, supplied by a host of rag-pickers all over the country. The material had to be soaked in unpolluted water, left to ferment, and then pounded into pulp. The pulp was then spread out in thin layers, squeezed, hung up to dry, smoothed, and polished with stone.

The cost of paper was normally the largest item on the budget of an 18th-c. publisher. In a production budget for a work in octavo or in duodecimo, on ordinary paper, with a normal print-run of 1,200 or 1,500, the publisher expected paper to absorb between 60 and 75 per cent of expenses. In this era of the hand-made book, buyers paid great attention to the thickness and smoothness of the paper, and the care observed by the printer. Subscribers might threaten to cancel their subscription if a book appeared with too many misprints or an excess of fingermarks in the margin.

The technology of printing on the eve of the French Revolution therefore bore a striking resemblance to the state of the art in the age of Gutenberg. Books were printed by hand-operated wooden presses, operated by a pre-industrial workforce. Only in the first half of the 19th c. did mechanization, industrial concentration, and professional specialization change the industry. Until then, the total annual production of books in France only exceeded 1,000 titles per year in the 1780s, while the average print-run remained at well under 2,000 copies per title.

5. The Nineteenth Century

In the early 19th c. a series of inventions began to transform the printing industry. After the Napoleonic wars, Ambroise-Firmin Didot bought one of the new Stanhope presses in London, and French manufacturers started to copy it. The Stanhope was the first all-metal press, with a platen large enough to print a complete folio at one pull. In 1811 Koenig invented a cylindrical press, driven by steam, capable of producing 1,000 copies per hour.

At first only large-circulation newspapers found the investment in such machines worthwhile [see PRESS]. In 1833 there were only 67 mechanically operated presses in Paris: only 7 per cent of the total. In 1830, however, the year of Revolution, printing-workers smashed the mechanical presses in the Imprimerie Royale—one indication of an industry in the throes of an important growth period. By the 1840s about one Parisian press in six was mechanically operated, although small printing workshops with a small number of employees were still the norm.

In the 19th c. the book became an object of everyday consumption. The publisher emerged as a specialist profession for the first time, and a few became household names. When the French first began to order books by the names of their publishers, rather than by their titles or authors, it was a *Hachette or a *Larousse they were demanding. Charpentier produced the single-volume, small-format novel (in octodecimo) which led eventually to the production of cheap, mass-produced fiction. Books were sold in new ways: not by subscription, but through new retail outlets, like the station book-stalls which made a fortune for Hachette in the 1850s and 1860s. Authors, too, eventually benefited from the rapid commercialization of book production. A royalty system developed, and in 1838 they organized themselves into the Société des Gens de Lettres to defend their interests. Legislation of 1854 confirmed the author's copyright, and that of his or her heirs, and reciprocal international copyright agreements were put into place.

The trade was still regulated by Napoleonic legislation, enacted between 1811 and 1814. A printer or bookseller needed a *brevet*. To obtain the *brevet*, it was necessary to swear an oath of allegiance and submit trade references and a certificate of good morality. All printers were strictly policed, and a decree of 1811 fixed the maximum number allowed to operate in Paris at 80. In 1870 the printer's *brevet* was at last abolished.

Bordeaux

Large-scale publishing enterprises demanded large injections of capital, which were usually beyond the resources of individual publishers. The arrival of the modern capitalist publisher is clearly demonstrated in the career of Michel and Calmann Lévy. By the Second Empire, the Lévy brothers had established a successful business on the basis of their theatrical publishing. In 1856 Lévy launched a new collection of novels and poetry, the Collection Michel Lévy, in the octodecimo format (the old 'format Charpentier'), at the price of only 1 franc per volume. This series, and its rock-bottom price, were the foundation of the Lévy empire. Their diverse investments included interests in French and Italian railways, the Marseille Gas Company, Algeria, and Bordeaux vineyards. The profits they made from Renan's *Vie de Jésus* alone paid for their new building in the rue Auber—publishing was moving away from the Quartier Latin and the *Palais-Royal to the brash world of the boulevards.

In the early years of the 19th c. novels were rarely produced in print-runs of more than 1,000 or 1,500 copies. By the 1840s editions of 5,000 copies were more common, while in the 1870s the cheapest editions of Jules *Verne appeared in editions of 30,000. New categories of reader had joined the reading public: *children, for instance, with the expansion of literacy and primary *education (which became free, compulsory, and secular in the 1880s). Schools, as Hachette realized, were an increasingly important part of the market. The new readers of the 19th c. also included the lower middle classes, especially the white-collar workers and clerks who devoured cheap magazines and *romans-feuilletons. The reading public had also undergone a process of feminization in the 19th c., and many publishers and writers identified women as the true and natural novel-reading audience of their time.

6. The Twentieth Century

In the 20th c. print culture has continued to thrive, in spite of competition from the electronic media and from new commercialized leisure pursuits. Book production, stagnant earlier in the century, has expanded since 1945, and a survey by the Syndicat National de l'Édition of 1966-7 showed that television owners bought more books than non-owners. The screen and the book are not necessarily incompatible.

The paperback revolution has transformed the book and the nature of reading. In 1970 61 per cent of all books produced in France were paperbacks. Nevertheless, according to a SOFRES poll for Le Figaro in 1972, only one Frenchman in four reads more than one book per month. In 1990 the French still spent more on cigarettes than they did on books, and perhaps 40 per cent of the population are not generally buyers or readers of books. The *livre de poche has not opened up new markets, but has better served the readership which already existed.

Methods of distribution have changed: only one-

third of French readers buy their books in bookshops. Other outlets are increasingly important for the trade, such as newsagents, book clubs, and large stores.

Industrial concentration has accelerated in the 20th c. In 1970 17 publishing houses were responsible for about one-half of the turnover of books in France. Today, however, the field is dominated by just three giant corporations—Hachette, Les Presses de la Cité, and Larousse-Nathan. These firms control 80 per cent of turnover, and are themselves controlled by international companies, for whom French books are a secondary financial activity.

The internationalization of the French book trade is perhaps inevitable. Less than 5 per cent of the world's reading public is French-speaking, and although this is not a measure of the language's international importance, the growing power of English in the world is undeniable. Since 1970 France's book imports have been more significant than her book exports, which have been sold in France's traditional, but limited, export market of *Belgium, Canada [see QUEBEC], and *Switzerland. For French publishers, it is increasingly important to handle *translations, both into and out of English, and to invest in publishing concerns in the English-speaking world.   [ML]

See J. Cain et al., Le Livre français: hier, aujourd'hui, demain (1972); R. Darnton, The Business of Enlightenment: A Publishing History of the Encyclopédie, 1775-1800 (1979); J.-Y. Mollier, Michel et Calmann-Lévy ou la Naissance de l'édition moderne, 1836-1891 (1984); H.-J. Martin and R. Chartier (eds.), Histoire de l'édition française, 4 vols. (1983-6); M. Lyons, Le Triomphe du livre: histoire sociologique de la lecture dans la France du 19e siècle (1987).

BORDEAUX, Henry (1870-1963). French novelist and essayist, author of solid detailed narratives supporting an ethic of family loyalty, self-sacrifice, and traditional moral and religious values. Professional milieux (legal, medical) are carefully evoked, also urban and provincial settings (Savoie). His best work dates from the early 1900s: La Peur de vivre (1902), Les Rocquevillard (1906), La Croisée des chemins (1909), La Robe de laine (1910).   [MMC]

BORDEU, Théophile de (1722-76). French doctor whose modern theories (Recherches sur le pouls, 1756) won him considerable celebrity. He contributed to the *Encyclopédie and *Diderot used him as a mouthpiece in Le *Rêve de d'Alembert.

BORDUAS, Paul-Émile (1905-60). Canadian essayist and painter, born in Saint-Hilaire, south-east of Montreal. He left school at 15 and was apprenticed to the 'sage de Correlieu', Ozias Leduc, church-decorator in his native village. Leduc sent him to the Montreal art school and then to France, where he worked on church restoration with Maurice Denis. He saw work by *Matisse and *Picasso, but felt uneasy in France and returned to teach at

Montreal's École du Meuble. He describes movingly in *Projections libérantes* (1949) his patient, disturbingly silent teaching methods and his brushes with authority. His gaucheness, unorthodoxy, and hatred of academicism contributed to his success. He attracted a group of disciples, writers, painters, sculptors, and dancers—Riopelle, the *Gauvreau brothers, Masson, Guilbault—whose originality he fostered and who had a subversive effect on Quebec's cultural progress from the 1940s. Borduas saw the need to free Quebec from the dead hand of clericalism. His group, Les Automatistes, exhibited in Montreal in 1942, in a variety of styles from Cubism to Fauvism. A collective manifesto in 1948, *Refus global*, cost Borduas his job. He left for Cape Cod and New York in 1951 and then for France in 1955, where he died a pauper and recluse.

When *Breton invited the Automatistes to join the *Surrealists, Borduas declined. Breton's dreams were not his. A prolific painter, he was a man of few words. His essays are a terse, angry, but eloquent testimony to one man's courage in challenging the clerical hold on thought and taste in post-war Quebec. *Refus global* paints the history of Quebec in the grip of fear and nausea. 'Au diable le goupillon', spits Borduas. It is beyond Christianity that we discover the ideal of human brotherhood. He denounces the twin hegemonies of capitalism and Marxism and makes an impassioned plea for freedom: 'Place à la magie! Place à l'amour!' Pierre *Vadeboncœur salutes in Borduas the one *Québécois* courageous enough to assume the risks of art and go to the limits of his own artistic vision.   [CRPM]

BOREL, Pétrus (pseud. of Joseph-Pierre Borel d'Hauterive) (1809–59). Nicknamed 'the Lycanthrope', he was perhaps the most outrageous exponent of the 'genre *frénétique' practised by the members of the *Petit Cénacle. He claimed to draw on the republicanism of 1830 in his rebellious and shocking prose and poems (*Rhapsodies*, 1831; *Champavert, contes immoraux*, 1833; *Madame Putiphar*, 1839), but the anarchy of sentiment and the deliberate playing with literary conventions have more in common with *Surrealism (which acknowledged its debt) than with early 19th-c. political literature. In the late 1840s he was for a while a colonial administrator in Algeria.   [BR]

BORY, Jean-Louis (1919–79). French author of a cycle of 20 novels entitled *Par temps et marées* covering a wide variety of periods and themes, often experimental in narrative structure. He was an active campaigner in defence of homosexuals. His first novel, *Mon village à l'heure allemande* (1945), drawing on his experience in the Resistance, won the Prix Goncourt.   [EAF]

BOSCHÈRE, Jean de (1878–1957). Belgian poet, novelist, and artist. A tortured figure who rarely received the recognition he sought (despite the support of *Artaud, *Suarès, and others), Boschère achieved notoriety in British literary circles thanks to Harold Munro, who introduced him to Pound, F. S. Flint (who translated his poems), and the Imagist circle. Leaving London in 1922, he lived briefly in Italy and then in France, first in Paris and then at La Châtre. Sombre and mystical in their tonality, but also intensely sensual and marked by a consistent search for spiritual illumination, Boschère's works, accompanied by his illustrations, include verse and prose poetry (*Dressé, actif, j'attends*, 1936; *L'Obscur à Paris*, 1937), novels (*Satan l'obscur*, 1933), and the posthumous *Journal d'un rebelle solitaire* (1981).   [MHTS]

BOSCO, Henri (1888–1976). Novelist and poet. Bosco's native Provence is the atmospheric constant of texts that weave rural mysteries in a moody, hybrid language of paganism and Christianity, where description dominates narrative. He reached a wide readership with *L'Âne Culotte* (1938), *Hyacinthe* (1940), *Le Mas Théotime* (1945, Prix Renaudot), *Le Jardin d'Hyacinthe* (1945), and *Malicroix* (1948). *L'Enfant et la rivière* (1945) and *Barboche* (1957), both sometimes considered *ouvrages pour la jeunesse*, are lighter introductions to his work. He also wrote poetry.   [DAS]

BOSQUET, Alain (b. 1919). Poet and novelist. The son of Ukrainian refugees, brought up in Belgium, he worked for the American army during World War II. He was associated with *Breton in New York. Most of his poetry, which is remarkable for its wit and brilliant imagery, is collected in *Le Livre du doute et de la grâce* (1977—a sceptic's view of God), in *Poèmes, un* (1979) and *Poèmes, deux* (1981), and in *Sonnets pour une fin de siècle* (1980), a painfully savage portrait of the contemporary world. He has also written fine, ironic novels (e.g. *Les Bonnes Intentions*, 1975) and the autobiographical *Une mère russe* (1978) and *L'Enfant que tu étais* (1982).   [GDM]

BOSSUET, Jacques-Bénigne (1627–1704). As an orator, churchman, educationalist, political thinker, and historian, Bossuet was one of the leading intellectuals at the court of Louis XIV. He came from a *parlementaire* family in Dijon, where he was educated at the Jesuit college. When his father moved to Metz, he became a youthful canon of the cathedral there, eventually rising to the post of archdeacon. Meanwhile he pursued a brilliant career of study at the Collège de Navarre in Paris, gaining a reputation as a preacher. This solid humanist education, deployed with exceptional aptness and judgement, swiftly led him to be entrusted with other duties. In the 1660s he was invited to preach four Lenten and two Advent courses of sermons before the court, and was consecrated bishop of Condom in 1669. In 1670 he was appointed tutor to the dauphin, and was elected to the Académie Française a year later. Realizing that residence in his see would be impossible, he resigned it in 1671; but after the dauphin's marriage ended tutorial duties,

Bossuet became in 1681 bishop of Meaux, close to the court, where until his death he remained a central figure in political and theological affairs.

For his royal pupil he developed a theory of history which highlights the intervention of Providence in human affairs. The *Discours sur l'histoire universelle* (1681) contains only the first part of a planned history of the world: its chronological first section—much of it a paraphrase of the Old Testament—ends with Charlemagne. The second section discusses Judaism and Christianity, and the third considers the rise and fall of ancient empires in terms which emphasize the ultimate sovereignty of God. Many of these ideas naturally recur in his preaching, especially his funeral orations. But there they are allied to an intense preoccupation with the salvation of the individual soul characteristic of the later *Counter-Reformation.

The links between religion and public affairs dominate much of his writing, and in his final years Bossuet largely abandoned the pulpit for ecclesiastical politics and theological controversy. He was a stout defender of *Gallican independence and royal influence in the Church against the claims both of Rome and of *Port-Royal. He strongly supported the revocation of the *Edict of Nantes and the persecution of the Huguenots. His *Histoire des variations des églises protestantes* (1688) is a classic account of the fissiparous tendencies of Christian bodies which break away from the unity of Rome; and he corresponded with *Leibniz over the possibilities of Christian reunion. His last years were devoted to remorselessly bullying *Fénelon in the quarrel over *Quietism, not least by bringing his long-standing influence to bear at Versailles. Although doubtless sincerely motivated by what he saw as the dangerous moral passivity and lack of common sense inherent in Madame *Guyon's doctrine of the disinterested love of God, he unscrupulously published and distorted her private conversations and cast suspicion on her morals (*Relation sur le quiétisme*, 1698), and thus ended his career by condemning Fénelon, his most brilliant disciple, to permanent exile from the court and blighting the development of mysticism in the French Church for at least a century.

At his death a considerable proportion of his writings—including all but one of his sermons, all his panegyrics on the saints, and the *Élévations sur les mystères*—remained unpublished, and his nephew the abbé Bossuet prepared (and in several cases modified) them for the press. He also completed the book for which Bossuet is best known among historians of political thought, the *Politique tirée des propres paroles de l'Écriture sainte* (1709). This treatise in ten books is the fullest French statement of the theory of absolute *monarchy and the divine right of kings. The first six books were written for the dauphin; after 1679 Bossuet set the work aside and took it up again only in 1700. Basing himself largely on the Old Testament, he argues for the necessity of political and legal institutions in

human society after the Fall, affirming that God has providentially ordained hereditary monarchy in the image of his own sovereignty. The later books extend these principles to such practical matters as the rights of the Church, just wars, and fair taxation, ending with a timely reminder that God punishes rulers who forget they are but his ministers. The distinction between absolutism and arbitrariness is thus grounded in the monarch's obedience to divine law.

But if such theories are now of purely historical interest, it is as a literary artist that he has survived; *Valéry devoted a famous essay to the power of his style and *Lanson called him the greatest lyric poet of the 17th c. Some of his sermons, notably *Sur l'éminente dignité des pauvres dans l'Église* (1659), *Sur la mort* (1662), and on the Carmelite profession of the king's former mistress Louise de *La Vallière (1675), together with the funeral orations for Queen Henrietta Maria of England (1669), her daughter the duchesse d'Orléans (1670), and *Condé (1687), have remained a cultural reference-point and source of literary allusion akin to the Authorized Version of the Bible in the English-speaking world. Their effect depends upon the way an abstract Christian doctrine, be it the mysterious workings of Providence, the immortality of the soul, or the vanity of human wishes, is powerfully allied to vivid instances and memorably concrete images. Bossuet tends to impose a fundamentally antithetical structure on his subject-matter, which thus emerges shot through with drama: worldliness wars with austerity, sin with righteousness, death with life. In the breadth, precision, and syntactic control of his rhetoric Bossuet owes much to the oratorical school of Cicero; but in his love of stirring contrasts and emotive colouring he stands in the tradition of the Old Testament prophets and the early Fathers of the Church. With *Pascal, he represents the high point of religious writing in France.   [PJB]

See J. Truchet, *La Prédication de Bossuet* (1960); T. Goyet, *L'Humanisme de Bossuet* (1965); J. Le Brun, *La Spiritualité de Bossuet* (1972).

BOUCHART, Alain (*fl.* 1471–1514). Author of the *Grandes Croniques de Bretaigne*, the first published history of medieval Brittany. He was a lawyer by training, ducal secretary in 1484, and *maître des requêtes* for both Duke François II and King Charles VIII, in whose service he moved to Paris. He retained a lifelong attachment to his native province and its privileges, a major theme of his history.   [MJ]

BOUCHER, François (1703–70). French painter. Early in his career (1737–9 and 1744–8) Boucher designed stage scenery at the *Opéra, for example for *Les Indes galantes* in 1743 and the ballet *Les Fêtes chinoises* of 1753. He came to the attention of Madame de *Pompadour, and from 1746 enjoyed her patronage in a series of enviable royal commissions. His portraits of her as an educated and accomplished director of public taste rank amongst his most entrancing paintings. He was immensely influential. In addition to holding all the high positions possible for a French artist, Boucher became one of the most prolific French book illustrators. Prints of his independent drawings were issued by Gilles Demarteau (1722–76) and achieved wide circulation. *Diderot denounced Boucher's work, but he could not entirely dismiss the magic of his pictorial effects. [JPC]

BOUCHET, Guillaume (c.1514–1594). Poet and printer of Poitiers; his prose work in the 'table-talk' tradition, *Les Serées* (three instalments, 1584–98), purports to record 36 conversations, consisting of short stories, jokes, and *exempla*, which paint an interesting picture of bourgeois tastes and preoccupations of the period. [MJH]

BOUCHET, Jean (1476–1557). Barrister of Poitiers and prolific poet associated with the *Rhétoriqueurs. A stern moralist (*Les Renards traversants*, 1503) and painstaking chronicler (*Les Annales d'Aquitaine*, 1524), he was one of the earliest French writers to attack *Luther in the vernacular (*Les Triomphes de la noble et amoureuse dame*, 1531). [MJH]

Boucicaut, Le Livre des fais du bon messire Jehan le Meingre, dit (1409). This anonymous biography of Boucicaut, marshal of France from 1401 to 1409, mixes documentary and selective panegyric. The chivalric adventures of the knightly paragon—his occasional brutalities left obscure—is offered for the emulation of posterity. [JHMT]

BOUDARD, Alphonse (b. 1925). The native *argot of Boudard's sardonic autobiographies brings to life characters met in the Resistance: *Bleubite* (1966), *Les Combattants du petit bonheur* (1977), *Le Corbillard de Jules* (1979); as criminal and convict: *La Métamorphose des Cloportes* (1962), *La Cerise* (1963); as consumptive: *L'Hôpital* (1972); or screen-writer: *Cinoche* (1974). His education, sentimental and otherwise, is depicted in *Le Café du pauvre* (1983), *L'Education d'Alphonse* (1987); and other scenes of contemporary life in *Le Banquet des léopards* (1980), *Les Enfants de chœur* (1982), *La Fermeture* (1986). *La Méthode à Mimile* (with Luc Étienne, 1970) is an argotic primer. [SFN]

BOUDJEDRA, Rachid (b. 1941). Algerian writer. He studied in Tunis from 1951 to 1958, joined the Liberation Army in 1959, and acted as an FLN representative in Madrid from 1960 to 1962. After graduating in philosophy at the Sorbonne in 1965, he wrote a master's thesis on *Céline. After a short stay in France, where he married, he moved to Morocco and taught in a *lycée* at Rabat.

The publication of his first novel, *La Répudiation* (1969), established him as one of the most subversive writers of post-colonial Algeria. His *Topographie idéale pour une agression caractérisée* (1975), however, diminished the impact of his first

novel as well as modifying the favourable comment provoked by *L'Insolation* (1970); critics pointed out his tendency to exaggeratedly narcissistic language. *Topographie*, like *Le Vainqueur de coupe* (1981), fabricates a strange world of neurotic characters, whose obsession with female sexual troubles appears arbitrary. *Discours sur les femmes dans l'œuvre de Rachid Boudjedra* (1982) suggests something of his personal obsession with women, which could in a sense explain the narrowness of his themes. His other preoccupation is his conversion from writing in French to Arabic. *Le Démantèlement* (1982), which he has declared to be a translation of *Ettafakouk*, the Arabic version, is in fact in the line of his French works, and the reader may wonder whether it was not written in French first, and suspect that Boudjedra is trying to profit from the national debate in Algeria on language and religion. [AZ]

BOUELLES, Charles de, also known by his Latin name, Bovillus (c.1480–1533). A Janus-figure, looking both back towards the Middle Ages (he was influenced by Nicolas of Cusa and Raymond Lull) and towards the High Renaissance: his *De sapiente* (On the Wise Man, 1510) develops ideas on human dignity which we normally associate with Pico della Mirandola. He regarded the instability of the vernacular as making it inferior to Latin, but his call for a flexible grammar helped promote the cause of the French language (*De . . . gallici sermone varietate*, 1533). He published his *Geometrie pratique* in 1510, but his French poetry (which sometimes indicates an unworldly, Christian view) was not published until the 19th c. [JJS]

BOUFFLERS, Stanislas-Jean, chevalier de (1730–1815). Poet, author of pleasant light verse with a personal touch. His mother (not to be confused with *Rousseau's patron, the duchesse de Boufflers, later maréchale de *Luxembourg) was a leading beauty at the court of Lorraine at Lunéville. The chevalier (later marquis) was a governor of Senegal, and lived in exile from 1792 to 1802. [PF]

BOUGAINVILLE, Louis-Antoine, comte de (1729–1811). French explorer. Also a lawyer and mathematician, he fought in Canada, attempted to colonize the Falkland Islands, and circumnavigated the globe (1766–9). His *Voyage autour du monde* (1771) is a well-told tale, full of geographical and ethnographic interest; it contains lyrical pictures of the newly discovered Tahiti, which inspired Diderot's *Supplément au Voyage de Bougainville*. [PF]

BOUHOURS, Dominique, père (1628–1702). Critic and grammarian. Born into the Paris bourgeoisie, he joined the *Jesuits as a novice in 1644 and taught in their colleges before taking orders in 1662. Settling in Paris, he frequented literary gatherings, including the Académie *Lamoignon and the salon of Madeleine de *Scudéry, making a name as an expert on matters of style and language—*Racine sent him *Phèdre* for vetting. He also engaged in theological and literary polemic with the *Jansenists.

His *Doutes sur la langue française* (1674) and similar works show him to be a dogmatic codifier of polite usage in the manner of *Vaugelas. Classical taste is tempered with a love of fashionable wit, the limits of which he explores in *La Manière de penser dans les ouvrages d'esprit* (1687) and the related anthology *Pensées ingénieuses des anciens et des modernes* (1689). His most enduring work is *Les Entretiens d'Ariste et d'Eugène*, a subtle set of six conversations in which two men of the world discuss the sea, the French language, secrecy, wit, the *je ne sais quoi*, and the art of *emblems. [PF]

BOUILHET, Louis (1822–69). French poet and dramatist, and close friend of *Flaubert from 1846 until his death. The two men relied on each other for frank criticism of their writing, and Bouilhet was regularly consulted over *Madame Bovary, Salammbô*, and *L'Éducation sentimentale*. Flaubert had a high opinion of Bouilhet's work, and organized the posthumous staging of his last play, *Mademoiselle Aïssé*. Flaubert also published a collection of poems at his own expense (*Les Dernières Chansons*, 1872), prefaced with an enthusiastic 'Hommage à Louis Bouilhet'. Other works include *Melaenis, conte romain* (1851), *Festons et astragales* (1859), *Madame de Montarcy* (1856), and *Le Château d'Amboise* (1866).

[DK]

BOUKMAN, Daniel (pseud. of Daniel Blérald) (b. 1936). Dramatist, teacher, and journalist from Martinique. Influenced by *Fanon, he worked from 1962 in Algeria. Boukman, a critic of *négritude from a Marxist standpoint, is best known for a lively polemical play on migration, *Les Négriers* (1971), later filmed as *West Indies* by Med Hondo. He has composed several other agitprop pieces and some *Creole verses. [BJ]

BOULAINVILLER or **BOULAINVILLIERS**, Henri de (1658–1722). French polymath, free-thinker, and political theorist. Personally unfortunate, of ancient lineage, he devoted himself to scholarly writing, mainly historical and religious, which is original to the point of eccentricity. He was a friend of *Saint-Simon, who reports on his astrological pursuits, and *Fréret, who wrote a memoir on his life. His political works— for instance, the *Essais sur la noblesse de France* (1732)—were well-known and influential but unpublishable until after his death because of their hostility to royal policy. They express an extreme version of the 'thèse nobiliaire', the argument for giving political power to the aristocracy: the nobles of the Germanic tribes which conquered Roman Gaul ruled by right of conquest and were equal in authority to the king; their prerogatives, gradually eroded by the increase in power of the king and the bourgeoisie, should be restored to their descendants, superior to commoners by blood. Feudalism was 'le chef d'œuvre de l'esprit humain'.

Boulainviller probably remained true to Catholicism, but was attracted by *Spinoza, and wrote a deistic *Vie de Mahomet* and series of essays on the religious beliefs of the ancients [see CLANDESTINE MANUSCRIPTS]. [CJB]

BOULANGER, Georges (1837–91). French general and politician. He acquired great popularity as war minister in 1886–8, was elected a *député* in 1889, and seemed poised to come to power in a right-wing coup to provide strong executive government. The Boulangist movement failed, however, and its leader fled the country and committed suicide after being discredited as having conspired with the monarchists against the Republic.

BOULANGER, Nicolas-Antoine (1722–59). French civil engineer whose geological observations led him to develop theories about the early history of mankind. Studying ancient texts in many languages, he traced religious customs and theocratic government back to fear caused by the Flood and other natural catastrophes. These ideas are outlined in *Encyclopédie* articles such as 'Déluge' and spelt out at length in works published posthumously by the *Holbach circle, notably *Recherches sur l'origine du despotisme oriental* (1761) and *L'Antiquité dévoilée* (1766). Although he condemns follies and injustices, his approach is dispassionately scientific. But his books were used in Holbach's anti-Christian campaigns and the baron published his own *Le Christianisme dévoilé* under Boulanger's name. [PF]

Boule-de-suif (1800). Story by Maupassant, included in the *Soirées de Médan*. Set in the *Franco-Prussian War, it tells of the humiliation of a generous-spirited prostitute.

Boulevard, Théâtre de. A term originating in the theatres lining the Boulevard du Temple in early 19th-c. Paris and providing raw popular entertainment from *pantomime, puppets [see GUIGNOL], and *vaudeville to the *melodramas of *Pixerécourt. Since the 1890s it has been applied pejoratively to the commercial stage and its diet of easy entertainment for a bourgeois public. It has been variously used of *Feydeau's farces, Sacha *Guitry's comedies of adultery, *Bernstein's hectic dramas of passion, the plays of *Anouilh, and even of some plays with serious pretensions (e.g. *Salacrou). Specifically, the Boulevard is distinguished from the avant-garde (e.g. *Vitrac, *Beckett). [SBJ]

BOULEZ, Pierre (b. 1925). French composer, conductor, teacher, and writer, one of the most important figures in contemporary music. Since 1976 he has been director of IRCAM (Institut de Recherche et Coordination Acoustique/Musique) and has for many years been a member of the *Collège de France. Many of his compositions have literary inspirations. *Le Marteau sans maître* (1952–4, revised 1957), for instance, is based on the work of *Char. He has written two musical portraits of poets,

*Mallarmé in *Pli selon pli* (1957–62) and E. E. Cummings in *e. e. cummings ist der dichter* (1970). Boulez has written extensively about his own and other people's music, musical institutions, and aesthetic issues. Much of his writing is extremely polemical. [KM]

BOULLÉE, Étienne-Louis (1728–99). Influential through his well-known pupils (such as *Ledoux and J.-N.-D. Durand), Boullée wrote a famous treatise on architecture which remained unpublished. His *Diderotian writing and drawings commend the combination of terse, abstract, mathematically based designs with a passionate, romantic conception to produce sublime, transcendental effects. His best-known design is the spherical monument to Newton. [JPC]

BOUNIN, Gabriel (1535–c.1586). Barrister and bureaucrat of Châteauroux, author of *La Soltane* (1561), the first tragedy in French on a modern subject. Bounin's Senecan account of the assassination of Soliman the Magnificent's heir is marred by prosodic ineptitude. He later published circumstantial poetry, political pamphlets, and a morality play on the religious wars, *La Piaffe et la picquorée* (1579). [MJH]

BOURAOUI, Hédi (b. 1932). One of the best-known *émigré* Tunisian writers and academics, and professor of contemporary French literature at York University, Canada, after studying in France and the United States. He is a prolific writer with a number of published volumes of poetry (e.g. *Musoktail*, 1966), essays (*Créaculture I, II*, 1971), and critical works. His aim as a poet is to extend the frontiers of language—'Je m'élastique dans les mots'—assimilating other cultures, playing and experimenting with words: *Éclate module* (1972), *Vesuvia* (1976), *Haïtu-vois* ('aïe, tu vois') (1980). His poetry is hermetic, and access is deliberately difficult, to encourage the reader to break away from his 'module' and escape from the chaotic, unjust, and self-destructive world of modern technology. He attacks nationalisms, defending 'la conjoncture métisse'. As editor of the francophone review *Dérives*, he favours the development of multi-culturalism in Canada. *Poésies*, with introductory articles by Tunisian critics, was published in 1991. [ET]

BOURBON-BUSSET, Jacques de (b. 1912), a pupil of *Alain, abandoned a distinguished public career to devote himself to writing, in the seclusion of Salernes (Var), with his wife Laurence, known as 'le Lion'. Member of the Académie Française, novelist, author of an extensive *Journal*, he elaborated the notion of an 'amour fou durable'. [BCS]

Bourbons. Royal house descended from Robert de Clermont, sixth son of Louis IX. Its fortunes were eclipsed following the treachery of Charles de Bourbon under *François Ier, but restored when *Henri IV succeeded *Henri III, the last of the *Valois. Henri IV restabilized the monarchy, which had been weakened by the *Wars of Religion. There were subsequent crises during the minority of his son, Louis XIII, and his grandson, *Louis XIV [see FRONDE]. The experience of civil war and the absence of any other viable political structures led, however, to the increasing absolutism of the Bourbons. The monarchy proved unable to cope with the financial and political crisis of the late 18th c. and was toppled during the *Revolution. The dynasty returned to power briefly after the fall of *Napoleon [see RESTORATION] and continued to command support after its final downfall in 1830 [see BERRY]. [JJS]

BOURBOUNE, Mourad (b. 1938). Algerian novelist. Born in Jijel in Kabylia, Bourboune was a militant in the Fédération de France of the FLN and from 1963 to 1964 the president of the cultural commission set up by the political bureau of the FLN. Bourboune's first novel, *Le Mont des genêts* (1962), is of little interest now, but *Le Muezzin* (1968) is an extraordinary work which guarantees its author a place amongst the most talented of the 1962 generation of Algerian writers.

Bourboune is interested in the pagan elements of Berber culture which have been overlaid by Christianity and Islam. His novel is a fierce satire on the 'Arab' created by French colonialism for its own purposes and amalgamating cultural variety into a composite portrait of 'simili-humains' and 'hommes troncs'. The onslaught, however, is not confined to colonialism: the novel's tone of shame and disillusion extends to the post-Independence period and to those who have conspired to thwart the revolution and to make of Algeria a 'swindle'. The novel's ironically named hero, 'le muezzin', plans to blow up the mosque, the symbol of all corruption, but finally desists as even this gesture of nihilism would be too meaningful in a culture of 'nécrophages'. His desire to recreate again from nothing leads him to disappear into the deserts of the south. The novel uses a great variety of forms and a mingling of poetry, dialogue, and chorus to create a theatrical effect, to reproduce the plurilingual polyphony of Algerian culture, and to expose the hypocrisy of discourses of power. *Le Muezzin* must rank as one of the most strikingly bitter and disillusioned works of 20th-c. African literature. [JKa]

BOURDALOUE, Louis (1623–1704). French Jesuit priest whose sermons were the most assiduously followed of all the fashionable Parisian preachers of his day, largely perhaps because he took social and personal morality for his subject-matter at a time when secular writers had generated a taste for the *moraliste portrayal of types and characters. He was much sought after as a confessor. He shows a striking capacity for combining methodical examination with a perceptive, though dispassionate, language of psychological analysis. The rigorous divisions and

Bourdet

subdivisions of his sermons made his points easy for his congregation to retain: he was sometimes described as 'the blind preacher' because of a habit of speaking with his eyes shut, the better to recall the order of his argument. The written versions of his addresses that have survived are somewhat unvaried in tone, though their objective and rational vocabulary may be said to have contributed to the development of character study as a suitable literary subject: he was widely commended as a model in the 18th c. Comparing and contrasting his sermons with those of *Bossuet became a scholastic exercise akin to the more famous parallel between *Corneille and *Racine. [PJB]

BOURDET, Édouard (1887–1945). Inter-war French playwright and reforming administrator of the *Comédie-Française (1936–40). His psychological studies of lesbianism (La Prisonnière, 1926), male homosexuality (La Fleur des pois, 1932), and incest (Margot, 1935) alternated with sharp satire of French social and commercial life: Vient de paraître (1927), Le Sexe faible (1929), Les Temps difficiles (1934). [SBJ]

BOURDIEU, Pierre (b. 1930). French sociologist of culture and education. Bourdieu's research is designed to test empirically the proposition that the power of dominant social groups and classes is reinforced by the inheritance and investment of 'cultural capital' in the fields of knowledge, language, social skills, style, values, and taste, and perpetuated by the 'symbolic violence', tacitly accepted as legitimate, which is imposed upon dominated groups through social institutions such as the educational system (La Reproduction, 1970; La Distinction, 1979). More recently Bourdieu has investigated the structures of power and prestige which sustain and are promoted by professional groups within the University and the Grandes Écoles (Homo academicus, 1984; La Noblesse d'état, 1989). [REG]

Bourgeois de Paris, Journal d'un. A conventional but misleading name: the anonymous writer was probably a cleric rather than a bourgeois, and probably wrote retrospectively, at the end of a given year. The Journal (published in part in 1653, in full in 1729) runs from 1405 to 1449 and is a remarkable social and economic document, especially valuable for episodes revealing mentalities in Paris, but much less accurate on larger-scale, distant events, where his Burgundian sympathies dominate. [JHMT]

Bourgeois gentilhomme, Le. Three-act comedy-ballet by *Molière, first performed 1670. The play is a sharp satire on the social pretensions of Parisian nouveaux-riches. Monsieur Jourdain wishes to acquire the social skills commensurate with his wealth; he employs a number of tutors for this purpose. In his efforts to obtain the favour of a marquise he enlists the help of Dorante, an unscrupulous aristocratic parasite. Monsieur Jourdain refuses snobbishly to allow his daughter Lucile to marry Cléonte because

he is not a nobleman, until a charade is organized by Cléonte's servant Covielle in which Cléonte, disguised as the son of the 'Grand Turc', marries Lucile, and Monsieur Jourdain is created a 'mamamouchi', or Turkish nobleman, in a humiliating ceremony. The play was very popular in Molière's day. [IM]

BOURGES, Élémir (1852–1925). French novelist, remembered for his grandiose, rather Stendhalian novel of contemporary manners, Le Crépuscule des dieux (1884), his pessimistic decadent novel Les Oiseaux s'envolent et les fleurs tombent (1893), and an epic prose poem, La Nef (1904 and 1922). He was a learned bibliophile who found inspiration especially in the classical and Shakespearian theatre, and cultivated an exclusive ideal of literary perfection. He was highly respected by his contemporaries, but his vast and somewhat heavy tragic frescos are now thought to show that his inspiration and literary ambition outstripped his execution. [BCS]

BOURGET, Paul (1852–1935). French novelist and essayist who studied philosophy and medicine before turning to literature. Following early poetic works, his Essais (1883) and Nouveaux essais de psychologie contemporaine (1886) examined intellectual and moral attitudes through the study of contemporary writers, and during the 1880s he developed these sharp insights in fictional form. Probably his best-known novel, Le Disciple (1889), was an indictment of positivist determinism which marked a turning-point in his career. Thereafter, his novels and critical essays became increasingly a defence of conservative, Catholic, and monarchist values, and are often regarded as tendentious. [BCS]

Bourgogne, Hôtel de, see HÔTEL DE BOURGOGNE.

BOURIGNON, Antoinette, see DEVOTIONAL WRITING, 2.

BOURSAULT, Edme (1638–1701). French playwright. Having thrown himself incautiously into polemics with *Molière (Le Portrait du peintre, 1662, an attack on L'École des femmes) and *Boileau (Satire des Satires, 1669), he achieved success with his comedies: Le Mercure galant (1683, a gallery of satirical portraits renamed La Comédie sans titre to placate *Donneau de Visé); Les Fables d'Ésope (1690); Ésope à la cour (1701). [PF]

Bousingots, Les. Group of writers on the margins of respectable society who in the early 1830s advocated artistic freedom in ways which challenged the values of the bourgeois monarchy. Whereas the *Jeunes-France were an essentially literary avant-garde, the Bousingots were more willing to link their ideas about art with *republicanism in politics.

BOUSQUET, Joë (1897–1950). Permanently invalided after a 1918 war-wound, Bousquet filled notebook upon notebook with suggestive aesthetic, poetic, mystical, and erotic meditations, and published them in such compilations as *La Tisane de sarments* (1936) and *Traduit du silence* (1941), and, posthumously, *Mystique* (1973) and *Papillon de neige* (1980). His novels, gathered in *Œuvre romanesque complète* (4 vols., 1979–84), lend shape to a world of metaphysical premonition. The Carcassonne bedroom where he lay behind closed shutters became a place of pilgrimage, with Bousquet playing the role of spiritual mentor to visitors as diverse as Louis *Aragon and Simone *Weil. Letters to contemporaries like *Gide, *Breton, and Hans Bellmer make up his *Correspondance* (1969), while tender letters to a young woman appear as *Lettres à Poisson d'Or* (1967). Bousquet's reputation is still growing, and the posthumous publication of his journals and jottings proceeds steadily. That of *Le Cahier noir* (1989) disclosed an unsuspected physical explicitness to Bousquet's erotic fantasy-life, though even here the quasi-pornographic detail manifests an ethereal translucency.   [RC]

BOUSSENARD, Louis (1847–1910), see ROMAN D'AVENTURE(S), 2.

Bouts de bois de Dieu, Les, see SEMBÈNE.

Bouts-rimés. A poem composed to rhymes set in advance. It was popular as a game in 17th-c. *salons.

Bouvard et Pécuchet. Unfinished novel by *Flaubert, published posthumously in 1881, his most extraordinary and manic undertaking, both for the basic conception and for the infinite consultation of written sources logically required to carry it through. He was aiming at 'une encyclopédie critique en farce', which readers would not know whether or not to take seriously. He developed a simple source story whereby two copy clerks retire to the country, get mortally bored, and return to a life of voluntary copying at each other's dictation. Flaubert explodes the proportions, taking his two autodidacts through a massive survey of every branch of human knowledge (agriculture, archaeology, historiography, science, metaphysics, aesthetics, etc.) with a repeated pattern of events. Bouvard and Pécuchet consult a pile of books, apply their knowledge to the world with disastrous effects, relook at the sources, realize they all contradict each other, become disillusioned, and move on to a new topic. Flaubert had planned that they should be arrested for demoralizing the local population whilst delivering an adult-education lecture. Released as harmless fools, they would return to copying. Their *copie* was to form a second volume of the novel, the status of which is not clear in Flaubert's notes and statements of intent, but which was probably to be made up of quotations from their original sources as well as from the *Dictionnaire des idées reçues* which Flaubert had first

conceived in the 1850s. *Bouvard et Pécuchet* is the quintessential Flaubert text for those who like his modern and 'undecidable' side.   [DK]

BOUVET (erroneously Bonet), Honoré (*c*.1340/5 –*c*.1410), prior of Selonnet, studied law at Avignon and played a minor role as a French diplomat. His considerable literary output included satirical poetry and polemical tracts, but his lasting importance rests on *L'Arbre des batailles* (*c*.1386–90), the most widely read late-medieval French commentary on the laws of war.   [MJ]

BOUVIER, Nicolas, see TRAVEL WRITING.

BOYER, Claude (1618–98). Prolific French dramatist, described by *Chapelain as second only to Pierre *Corneille. Throughout his long career he wrote tragedies which followed prevailing theatrical tastes, and several plays which sought to incorporate music, dance, and machines. The particular success of his spectacular *Ulysse dans l'île de Circé* (performed 1648) saved the Marais theatre from bankruptcy.   [GJM]

BOZON, Nicole, see ANGLO-NORMAN LITERATURE, 6c.

Bradamante. Tragicomedy by *Garnier, published 1582. The subject is taken from Ariosto's chivalrous epic poem *Orlando furioso*. The plot concerns the mutual love of the converted Saracen knight Roger and the French warrior-maiden Bradamante. She will marry only a man who can defeat her in single combat; Roger achieves this, but fighting under the name of his high-born rival Leon. A happy outcome is assured by Leon's magnanimity and Roger's elevation to a throne. Praise of France and moralizing about political matters are incorporated into the play, whose varied tone embraces the homely discussions of Bradamante's parents, the dignified seriousness of Charlemagne, and the outpourings of unhappy lovers.   [GJ]

BRANTÔME, Pierre de Bourdeilles, seigneur de (*c*.1540–1614). French memorialist. The third son of an ancient family, he was appointed *abbé commandataire* of Brantôme by Henri II in recognition of services rendered by his brother. He had been a student in both Paris and Poitiers, and was rather proud of his learning. A traditional noble at heart, however, he was infatuated by the military life, serving in Italy, in the *Wars of Religion, and even fighting against the Turks. He was, in consequence, crippled by a riding accident and sought compensation in writing. Far from writing only memoirs, however, he provides, in a series of posthumously published *Vies* (*des dames galantes, des hommes illustres*, etc.), a vast portrait of Renaissance society, describing not only fellow soldiers but also—and it was for this that he used to be most famous—a description of the ladies of the Valois court. His work tends to be of anecdotal rather than of historical value, but he had a sharp eye for detail and his judgements reveal the value system of an above-average though not (in moral or intellectual terms) outstanding member of the military aristocracy. Madame de *Lafayette used his work in order to paint the 16th-c. background for *La *Princesse de Clèves*.　　　　　　　　　　[JJS]

BRAQUE, Georges (1882–1963). French painter. An essential figure in 20th-c. painting and one of the most important exponents of still life in Western art, Braque had assimilated the lessons of *Impressionism and *Fauvism when, in 1907, his discovery of *Cézanne's work and of *Picasso's revolutionary *Les Demoiselles d'Avignon* led him to initiate, along with Picasso, the *Cubist revolution in painting. In addition to *Apollinaire, who acclaimed his Cubist phase in *Les Peintres cubistes* (1913), his work has engaged some of the major poets of the century. These include *Char, in *Recherche de la base et du sommet* (1955), *Ponge, in a series of articles written between 1946 and 1971, and *Saint-John Perse, for whose 'poetic meditation', *L'Ordre des oiseaux* (1962), Braque produced 12 coloured lithographs.　　[JK]

BRASILLACH, Robert (1909–45). French novelist, political journalist, and literary critic. His career took off with his appointment to *L'*Action française* in 1931, and his strong belief in international *fascism was promulgated in his journalism, as editor of *Je suis partout* from 1937 onwards, and in his most successful novel, *Les Sept Couleurs* (1939). In *Notre avant-guerre* (1941) he traced the emotional and intellectual climate in which his generation had developed towards fascism. A prisoner of war in 1940–1, after his release he resumed his journalistic activities in *Je suis partout* as a wholehearted supporter of collaboration [see OCCUPATION AND RESISTANCE]. In 1945 he was executed for treason.　　　　　　　[RMG]

BRASSENS, Georges (1921–81). French singer-songwriter, also poet, novelist. This gruff, shy stage performer, hiding behind a thick southern accent and an even thicker moustache, shocked his early audiences with his explicitly sexual subject-matter and his use of 'bad language'. He allowed his provocatively comic style ('La Mauvaise Réputation', 1952) to mask a craftsman of archaically regular verse, steeped in poetic tradition and capable of making popular songs out of poems by *Villon, *Aragon, or *Hugo. His 'monotonous' musical style, using only two acoustic guitars and double bass, mixes traditional French folk-song with influences of jazz and swing from the 1930s and 40s. His early lyrics often evoke a pastoral village community ('Brave Margot', 1953); his later songs are usually less idyllic and more philosophical ('Mourir pour des idées', 1972). He celebrates friendship ('Les Copains d'abord', 1964) and generosity of spirit ('Chanson pour l'Auvergnat', 1954). He prefers the traditional submissive virtues of women to their sexual demands or their middle-class pretensions, and refuses to be tied down by conventional values ('La Non-demande en mariage', 1966). His early *suc-*

cès de scandale developed into a durable popularity, of which he was mockingly sceptical. He will be remembered for re-infusing into French popular song a sense of its literary heritage, both classical and *Rabelaisian; as the best example of the *troubadour in the age of the electronic mass media.　　[PGH]

BRAUDEL, Fernand (1902–85). French historian. Braudel epitomized the interests and methods of the *Annales* school. He distinguished between three historical time-scales: *la longue durée*, or the slow development of underlying structures (climatic, demographic, agrarian); *la conjoncture*, or medium-term social, economic, and institutional trends; and *l'événement*, or the superficial succession of political and military events. All three were explored in his masterpiece *La Méditerranée et le monde méditerranéen à l'époque de Philippe II* (1949), which ranged far beyond the ostensible limits of its subject in both space and time. His last work, *L'Identité de la France* (1986), confirmed his interest in the material determinants of culture.　　　　　　　　[REG]

BRAULT, Jacques (b. 1933). Canadian poet. He studied philosophy in Montreal, Paris, and Poitiers and then taught literature in Montreal. His popular origins and work as a docker while a student gave him his rugged common sense and earthy realism. But this unpretentiousness combines with sophisticated thought to make him one of the best commentators on the work of *Nelligan, *Grandbois, *Saint-Denys Garneau (whose Œuvres (1970) he edited with Benoît Lacroix), and the writer he called '*Miron le magnifique'. His training as a philosopher helped him to handle with enviable ease the themes of time, love, despair, and death in *Alain Grandbois* (1968). His early poems were collected as *Mémoire* (1968), celebrating his love for his father and for his brother Gilles, killed in Sicily in 1943. *La Poésie ce matin* (1971), its title from *Apollinaire's 'Zone', with whom he could say: 'J'écoute les bruits de la ville', contains a moving, unsentimental tribute to his 'petite mère'. Through *L'En-dessous l'admirable* (1975), *Trois fois passera* (1981), and *Moments fragiles* (1984), he remains one of the outstanding lyric poets of his age, his lyricism becoming steadily more spare, mixed with anger and a calm determination not to 'crever dans la stupeur'.　　　　　　　　　　[CRPM]

BRÉBEUF, Georges de (1618–61). Poet and man of letters, the friend of *Conrart, *Ménage, and Pierre *Corneille, with whom he shared a Normandy background. In the manner of *Scarron he burlesqued the epics of antiquity (*L'Énéide de Virgile en vers burlesques*, 1650; *Lucain travesti en vers enjoués*, 1656). Brébeuf is now best known on account of the numerous unkind references *Boileau makes in the *Art poétique* to his translation of Lucan's *Pharsalia*, and the scarcely more charitable couplet: 'Malgré son fatras obscur | Souvent Brébeuf étincelle.'

　　　　　　　　　　　　　　　　[PJB]

BREL, Jacques (1929–78). Singer-songwriter, also actor, film director. Fleeing the bourgeois conformity of the family cardboard factory in Brussels, in the early 1950s Brel brought his guitar and his songs of naïve Catholic idealism to the Montmartre cabaret Les Trois Baudets. His early love-songs ('Quand on n'a que l'amour', 1956) became more bitter ('Ne me quitte pas', 1959) and soon gave way to songs of existential despair and revolt ('Le Moribond', 1960) as well as caustic satire ('Les Flamandes', 1959). In the early 1960s Brel's records present a gallery of portraits, often caricatured but also compassionate ('Amsterdam', 1964). At the same time his performing style developed to a high pitch of dramatic intensity as he conquered the audiences of the Parisian music-halls (Bobino, 1959; Olympia, 1961). With François Rauber, his arranger, and Gérard Jouannest, his pianist, he created an original, hybrid musical style which combines classical music, brass band, and the accordion in a way sometimes reminiscent of Kurt Weill. At the height of his fame in 1967 Brel abandoned his music-hall career for the cinema, first as an actor, then as a director. His last years of failing health were spent sailing around the world, eventually settling in the Marquesas Islands in the South Pacific. He returned to Paris in 1977 to record one last album of songs which sum up in exacerbated form the themes of his writing.   [PGH]

BREMOND, Henri, abbé (1865–1933). French literary critic and historian. His scholarly 11-vol. *Histoire littéraire du sentiment religieux en France* (1916–1933) investigated links between poetry and mysticism, romanticism and religion, and celebrated Sainte-Beuve. Between the wars his notion of **poésie pure* (see the essay with that title, published 1926) temporarily inflected critical attitudes. His first-hand knowledge of English Catholicism led to his writing several books on the subject.   [DAS]

BRESSON, Robert (b. 1901). The greatest of French Catholic film-makers began his career with *Les Anges du péché* (1943), though his distinctive cinematic style does not appear fully until the *Bernanos adaptation, *Journal d'un curé de campagne* (1951). This is characterized by elliptical narration, the eschewal of anything that might resemble psychologial 'explanation', and above all the refusal of 'actors' in favour of 'models' whose apparent emotional neutrality acts like a window onto the soul. These ideas are aphoristically set out in *Notes sur le cinématographe* (1975), and reach perhaps their highest development in *Pickpocket* (1959), a homage to Dostoevsky, and *Au hasard Balthazar* (1966).   [KAR]

Brethren of the Common Life. An influential pre-*Reformation lay movement, founded in the Low Countries by the disciples of the mystic Gerard Groote (1340–84). Their way of life is encapsulated in the *Imitation of Christ* attributed to Thomas à Kempis; dwelling in quasi-monastic communities (without taking vows), they placed personal piety, humility, and right conduct above ceremonies, sacraments, and 'vain and worldly learning'; their emphasis on meditation and simple vernacular preaching seemed an implicit reproach to the established Church. Their help was sought in reforming monasteries and education in Paris in the 1490s; their teaching influenced *Luther, *Erasmus, and *Lefèvre d'Étaples.   [MJH]

BRETON, André (1896–1966). French poet, who was not just a founder-member and the chief theoretician of the *Surrealist movement but also its heart and soul. He abandoned his medical studies in favour of poetry, went during his honeymoon to see Freud, was briefly a member of the Communist Party (1927), met Trotsky in Mexico (1938), and spent most of World War II in the USA. Although he could command unswerving loyalty, his detractors saw him as authoritarian—some even labelled him the 'pope' of Surrealism.

At first influenced by *Mallarmé and the *Symbolists, he subsequently discovered *Jarry, *Rimbaud, and *Lautréamont and established contact with *Valéry, *Apollinaire, and *Reverdy. Some of these influences are discernible in the poems of *Mont de piété* (1919), but his discovery in that year of automatic writing [see ÉCRITURE AUTOMATIQUE] led to a radical change of style. This can be seen in his contributions to *Les Champs magnétiques* (1920), written in collaboration with Philippe *Soupault, and especially in the 'historiettes' of *Poisson soluble* published in 1924 in the same volume as the *Manifeste du surréalisme*. He periodically brought out new collections of poetry, full of surprising and evanescent imagery: *Clair de terre* (1923, but revised and enlarged in 1966), *Le Revolver à cheveux blancs* (1932), *L'Air de l'eau* (1934), *Poèmes* (1948), and the posthumous *Signe ascendant* (1968), in addition to significant individual poems, e.g. 'L'Union libre' (published anonymously in 1931), 'Violette Nozières' (1933), 'Pleine marge' (1940), 'Fata Morgana' (1941), 'Les États généraux' (1944), and *Ode à Charles Fourier* (1947).

Breton's questioning of the novel genre was seen not only in the *Manifeste* (1924) but also in *Nadja* (1928), a quasi-autobiographical work written in a variety of modes despite Breton's avowed quest for a clinical style: here he investigated in turn the nature of his own identity, the special gifts of the eponymous 'heroine', and her value as a herald of the new love that enters the text at the end. *Nadja* may be viewed as the first of a sequence of works (the 'prose quartet'), continued by *Les Vases communicants* (1932), essentially an examination of the relationship between dream and reality, *L'Amour fou* (1937), a presentation of objective chance and the chance encounter as well as a study of love (like the rest of this quartet, based on his own experience), and *Arcane 17* (1944), a lyrical prophecy of a veritable emancipation of Woman, an affirmation of Breton's belief in youth and a championing of the three great causes of poetry, love, and liberty.

His lifelong interest in art was demonstrated by the successive editions of *Le Surréalisme et la peinture* (1928, 1945, 1965), by *L'Art magique* (1957), written with Gérard Legrand, and the little prose-poems of *Constellations* (1959), inspired by Miró's wartime set of gouaches. Apart from the 1924 *Manifeste*, his theoretical or critical works include the *Second Manifeste du surréalisme* (1930), *Qu'est-ce que le surréalisme?* (1934), and the collections of essays and articles, published either in his lifetime—*Les Pas perdus* (1924), *Point du jour* (1934), *La Clé des champs* (1953)—or posthumously (*Perspective cavalière*, 1970). *Entretiens* (1952), primarily the texts of a series of radio interviews, may be seen as his memoirs.

Breton and his colleagues constantly adopted a revolutionary political stance, but in the widest sense of the term. As early as 1922 he had stressed the importance of a poet's way of life: in his case this is exemplified by his peregrinations around Paris in the cause of Surrealism, by his 'organization' of the group's activities, from regular meetings and discussions in cafés to the collective drafting of pamphlets, and by his persistent refusal to compromise his principles.   [KRA]

See M. Bonnet, *André Breton: naissance de l'aventure surréaliste* (1975); H. Béhar, *André Breton: le grand indésirable* (1990).

Breviari d'amor. Widely distributed part-spiritual, part-secular Occitan encyclopædia of 34,597 lines composed between spring 1288 and *c*.1292 by Matfre Ermengaud of Béziers. Somewhat convoluted and inconsequential, it enlivens stock philosophical, moralizing, and scientific material with local colour. The world is seen as manifesting love in various forms.   [PVD]

BRIAND, Aristide (1862–1932). French politician. He was prime minister several times, and was active after World War I in promoting reconciliation with Germany and the establishment of a durable European order. He won the Nobel Peace Prize in 1926.

BRIÇONNET, Guillaume (1472–1534), was successively bishop of Lodève (1489) and Meaux (1516) and leading spirit among the *Evangelicals. His correspondence (1521–4) with *Marguerite d'Alençon [de Navarre], full of mystical piety, and his innovations in worship and preaching in his diocese, are attractive and influential features of the early *Reformation in France.   [MJH]

BRIERRE, Jean (1909–92), Poet, dramatist, and Haiti's ambassador to Argentina. He emerged in the 1930s as a poet and militant in the backlash against the American Occupation (1915–34). His thundering epic verse celebrated the heroes of Haitian independence and the black race. His *Black Soul* (1947) and *La Source* (1956) are well-known Haitian examples of the poetry of *négritude.   [JMD]

BRIEUX, Eugène (1858–1932). French dramatist remembered for plays attacking current social evils: *Blanchette* (1892), with its country girl drifting into prostitution; *Les Trois Filles de M. Dupont* (1897), an indictment of arranged marriages; *La Robe rouge* (1900), an assault on judicial corruption; *Les Avariés* (1901), a grim study of syphilis.   [SBJ]

Brigade, La, see PLÉIADE.

BRILLAT-SAVARIN, Anthelme (1755–1826). French writer on gastronomy with deep intellectual roots in 18th-c. philosophy, whose work has become increasingly celebrated, in recent times by Roland *Barthes. His *Physiologie du goût* (1825) is notable for its vitality, originality of style, and abundance of pithily expressed aphorisms, many of which have entered into common currency.   [BR]

BRION, Maurice (1895–1984). French author of many biographical studies of writers and artists, particularly of the Italian Renaissance and German Romanticism (*L'Allemagne romantique*, 1963–78). He also wrote *L'Art fantastique* (1961) and novels which are fantastic tales of the discovery of vanished or imaginary worlds (*La Folie Céladon*, 1935; *La Ville de sable*, 1959).   [PF]

BRISEBARRE, Jean le Court, known as (*fl.* 1312–38). Author of pious works and more particularly of the *Restor du Paon* (before 1338), a pseudo-epic poem claiming to fill lacunae in the *Vœux du paon* [see ALEXANDER ROMANCES].

BRISSET, Jean-Pierre (1837–1923). An erudite yet eccentric philologist whose biography remains obscure, Brisset came to light in the 1980s when French linguistics began to address various marginal cases. Brisset's grand aim was to reveal the origins not only of language but of Creation itself. Words, he contends, originate in God-the-Logos; they are always linked to things; hence all aspects of language open onto cosmology. Publications such as *La Grammaire logique* (1883) and *La Science de Dieu* (1900), which he financed himself, are replete with delirious puns and sound-permutations, yet have an unremitting seriousness. One of his more provocative ideas is that Man is descended from the frog, a claim based on phonetic evidence and confirmed, Brisset triumphantly notes, in the empirical fact that human sperm resembles tadpoles.   [RC]

BRISSOT, Jean-Pierre, known as Brissot de Warville (1754–93). French Revolutionary leader. After a chequered literary and political career, he was elected a *député* in 1789 and became leader of the 'Brissotin' party, subsequently the *Girondins, promoting it in his newspaper *Le Patriote français*. He fell with his party and met his death on the scaffold [see REVOLUTION, 1C].

Britannicus. Tragedy by *Racine, first performed 1669. Racine draws on Tacitus in depicting the struggle between Nero, as 'monstre naissant', and his mother Agrippina. Having ordered the abduction of Junie, the beloved of his half-brother Britannicus, whom he has ousted from the throne, Néron falls in love with her, but woos her in vain. Agrippine attempts to regain her ascendancy over her son by taking the part of Britannicus and Junie. Finally, swayed by his evil counsellor Narcisse, Néron disregards the advice of the upright Burrhus and has Britannicus murdered, thus deliberately signalling his mother's downfall. Junie flees to the Vestal Virgins, and the stage is set for Néron's career of crime. *Britannicus* is perhaps Racine's most striking representation of the psychology of power.

[PF]

British, Irish, and American Influences

1. Before 1700

The English crown held sway over much of what is now France for long periods in the Middle Ages. After the Norman Conquest, however, French was the dominant literary language in England for three centuries; even at the end of the 14th c., Gower was writing as much in French as in English and Latin. *Anglo-Norman literature was continuous with its continental French counterpart, and specifically English literature had little influence in France for most of the Middle Ages. On the other hand, the Celtic *matière de Bretagne* penetrated into France in the 12th c. and was massively exploited by writers of *romances. In addition, numerous natives of Britain played an important part in French intellectual life through the medium of Latin [see SCHOLASTICISM]. The Scot George *Buchanan, teaching at Bordeaux, was to make a significant contribution to French Renaissance humanism, although it does not appear that, even at the time of the Auld Alliance, the rich Scottish literary tradition was much known in France.

Throughout the great flowering of English literature in the 16th and 17th c., the attention of French writers and readers was turned more to Italy and Spain than to their northern neighbours. There was some two-way movement between France and Britain, certain themes from British history appear in French tragedies and novels, and there are occasional examples of specific literary contacts (e.g. Cyrano's use of a text by Godwin in *L'*Autre Monde*), but no large-scale influence. *Saint-Évremond lived in London for some 40 years, but was able to move in a French world there.

2. 18th Century

This was the time when Britain became fashionable. The peak of 'Anglomania' was reached in the last three decades of the *ancien régime*, though this does not mean that French writers abandoned their national traditions so as to write like their neighbours. Much English and Scottish literature was translated in the 18th c. and became an essential point of reference for educated people. The key figure was *Voltaire, who, after living in England for two years, sang the praises of English life, philosophy, and literature in his *Lettres philosophiques*. Other important early commentators were the Swiss Béat Louis de Muralt (*Lettres sur les Anglais et les Français*, 1725), abbé Jean-Bernard Le Blanc (*Lettres d'un Français*, 1745), *Prévost, who translated extensively and wrote about England in his novels and journalism, and Montesquieu, who drew on his stay in England in *De l'*esprit des lois*.

Perhaps the most significant area was philosophy. D'*Alembert's 'Discours préliminaire' to the *Encyclopédie* indicates the immense prestige enjoyed by Bacon and by many British scientists, but above all by Newton and Locke. Newton was only gradually acclimatized, principally by *Maupertuis and Voltaire, in the face of strong resistance from the followers of *Descartes. Locke not only provided a model for the epistemology of *Condillac, *Helvétius, and others; his writings on politics and education were highly influential, not least on Jean-Jacques *Rousseau. Other widely known philosophers included Hobbes, Mandeville, Shaftesbury (a major influence on *Diderot), Hume (though more as a historian), and the 'common sense' Scottish philosophers, who enjoyed a great reputation among the *Idéologues and their successors.

It was in the 18th c. that *Shakespeare began to be known and admired (though with reservations). His plays were translated in P.-A. de la Place's *Théâtre anglais* (8 vols., 1745-9); this also included work by Jonson, Dryden, Otway, and others. In the second half of the century the 'domestic tragedy' of Lillo and Moore struck a chord in the partisans of the *drame. Milton, whose *Paradise Lost* was translated several times in both prose and verse (first by Dupré de Saint-Maur, 1729), became established as an example of 'sublime' writing. Thomson's *Seasons* provided a model (alongside Virgil's *Georgics*) for the descriptive poems of *Delille, *Saint-Lambert, and *Roucher, and the 'graveyard' poems of Gray and Young (translated by *Le Tourneur) found echoes in the developing current of *sensibilité. But the most important poets for the French were Pope and 'Ossian'. Pope, much translated, was at first seen largely as a verse philosopher, his *Essay on Man* causing considerable controversy; later in the century *Colardeau's version of *Eloisa to Abelard* launched a vogue for the emotional 'héroïde'. James Macpherson's 'translations' of *Fingal* and other poems attributed to the 5th-c. Caledonian bard Ossian found a ready audience among those interested in primitive art; translated by Le Tourneur, the poems of Ossian won the allegiance of *Napoleon, *Chateaubriand, and many other admirers in France and beyond.

Of the prose writers, Swift and particularly Addison were among the first to make an impact. *Gulliver's Travels*, translated by *Desfontaines (1727), seems to have inspired *Marivaux and Voltaire before becoming a children's classic; Addison's *Spectator*, imitated by Marivaux and others, set a standard for polite journalism. Defoe's *Robinson Crusoe* was an exceptional case; it became a European classic and was presented in Rousseau's **Émile* as the one book needful to a boy, 'le plus heureux traité d'éducation naturelle'. In general, though, Richardson was the English novelist most admired in 18th-c. France (in the inadequate translations of Prévost); the influence of *Clarissa* on Rousseau's **Julie* has been exaggerated, but Richardson found an enthusiastic champion in Diderot (*Éloge de Richardson*). Goldsmith and Sterne were also appreciated (*Tristram Shandy* gave Diderot the starting-point for **Jacques le fataliste*), as was Fielding, though the latter was most influential on *Stendhal some decades later. Late in the century, the English 'Gothic' novel appealed to the readers of *Baculard d'Arnaud or *Mercier and to the spectators of the budding *melodrama.

3. 19th and 20th Centuries

English and Scottish writing benefited from the Romantic celebration of Nordic literature, launched principally by Madame de *Staël. Chateaubriand, who spent several years in England, admired and translated *Paradise Lost* and inserted several pages on English literature in his **Mémoires d'outre-tombe*. He gives pride of place to Byron, who was the only British Romantic poet to make much of a stir in France (though *Pichot drew attention to the Lake poets, later important for *Sainte-Beuve, and Stendhal was an admirer of Shelley). But the dominant British writer in France at this time (along with Shakespeare) was Walter Scott, who not only followed 'Ossian' in creating a Romantic image of Scotland, but provided a model for the historical novel which was followed by *Vigny, *Mérimée, and *Hugo, and applied to the recent past by Stendhal and *Balzac. None of the other great 19th-c. British novelists was to have a comparable impact, though Dickens, Thackeray, and Eliot received considerable critical praise. De Quincey's *Confessions of an English Opium-Eater* was given new currency by *Baudelaire.

North America had long been the subject of travel writing, and Chateaubriand, for instance, who travelled there in 1791–2, set his main fictional works in America. In the early 19th c. French opinion began gradually to take note of American writers, including Fenimore Cooper and Washington Irving. Then, in the 1850s, Baudelaire translated many of the writings of *Poe, thus launching him on an extraordinary French career.

American literature, particularly the novel, has naturally occupied an ever-greater place on the French literary horizon. Particularly important was the French discovery of the modern American novel in the 1930s; Faulkner, Steinbeck, Hemingway, Dos Passos, Dashiel Hammett, and others offered a mode of fiction very different from the traditional

French psychological novel: fragmentation, simultaneous action, objective narration, 'hard-boiled' style, a 'behaviourist' view of human actions. Such techniques were praised and imitated by writers such as Malraux (*L'*Espoir*), *Sartre (*Le Sursis*), and Camus (*L'*Étranger*). Faulkner in particular was very popular, and his influence can be seen in writers as diverse as Anne *Hébert, *Kateb Yacine, and Claude *Simon. But perhaps the greatest single American contribution has been in the field of *detective fiction. The *Série Noire was from the outset dominated by translations from the American, just as the Hollywood thriller has been an inescapable model for the post-war cinema.

The impact of British and Irish writing has been more diffuse and difficult to pinpoint. At the end of the 19th c. writers such as Wilde and Swinburne found a following among the *Symbolists and *Decadents, and *Proust translated Ruskin. Some 19th-c. writers were 'rediscovered' and acclaimed in the 20th c. because they offered something different from mainstream culture: Gide praised Hogg's *Confessions of a Justified Sinner*; the maximalism of *Wuthering Heights* appealed to Georges *Bataille and others; Hopkins won a following in the brilliant translations of Pierre Leyris; Lewis Carroll captivated the *Surrealists; story-tellers and travel writers found inspiration in the work of Robert Louis Stevenson. Certain 20th-c. critics and translators made a speciality of the British, notably *Maurois, with his biographies of Byron, Shelley, and others, and *Larbaud, who translated Joyce's *Ulysses*. This, with *Finnegans Wake*, has perhaps been the strongest single influence on experimental French writing, from the Surrealists to *Perec, and the impact of Irish literature is reinforced by the work of *Beckett, straddling two cultures. Most major British and Irish writers have had translators and admirers; it seems likely, for instance, that *Sarraute found support for her explorations in the example of Virginia Woolf. There have also been writers, often resident in France, whose reputation has been greater there than in Britain, e.g. Graham Greene, Charles Morgan, Lawrence Durrell, and the Scottish poet Kenneth White. And, finally, British writing has been much used in areas where there were gaps in the native tradition: *children's literature, for instance, or popular romance.

Certain major writers are conspicuous by their virtual absence from the French literary scene, for instance Burns and Austen. As for those who are present at the end of the 20th c., it is interesting to scan the list of those accorded the classic status of the Bibliothèque de la *Pléiade: Carroll, Conrad, Defoe, Dickens, Faulkner, Fielding, Hemingway, Joyce, Kipling, Poe, Shakespeare, Swift.   [PF]

See F. C. Green, *Minuet: A Critical Survey of French and English Literary Ideas in the Eighteenth Century* (1935); P. van Tieghem, *Les Influences étrangères sur la littérature française* (1967).

Brittany. The distinctiveness of Brittany is due to large-scale immigration from south-western Britain in the Dark Ages. The Brittonic or insular Gaulish language thus introduced is thought to have fused with surviving Armorican Gaulish and ensured that peninsular Brittany would remain massively Celtic-speaking until the beginning of the 20th c. In 850 the Bretons extended their hegemony deep into Romance-speaking territory, annexing definitively the large cities of Rennes and Nantes, which became the centre of gravity of a bi-ethnic duchy. The frontiers of Brittany remained stable until 1789, although its autonomy, already variable in medieval times, was further limited by a treaty of union with France in 1532.

1. Writing in Breton

Old Breton (800–1100), quite abundantly, if fragmentarily, attested in glosses and proper-names, is very similar to Old Cornish and Old Welsh. Technical terms indicate its use in learning and government, though one can only speculate as to its literary traditions on the basis of evidence found sparingly in Middle Breton texts (1450–1659) and more abundantly—but more problematically—in the *matière de Bretagne* and in Modern Breton oral literature.

Middle Breton, when after three barely documented centuries it appears in writing, is heavily Gallicized in spelling and vocabulary. There is no evidence of any official use of the language, and beyond two dramatized lives of British saints and one Arthurian fragment, the literature, dominated by religious verse and drama, shows little thematic originality. Evidence for a tradition of cultivation by trained practitioners is to be found, however, perhaps in the relative uniformity of the language and certainly in the versification. This makes systematic use of elaborate schemes of internal rhyme, a feature found in the more complex and more consonant-based *cynghanedd* of Welsh.

Early Modern Breton printed texts are almost exclusively devotional and practically all translations. There is, however a substantial body of manuscript plays which, although rarely original, cover a wider spectrum of themes. Their performance by humble amateurs for mass audiences was repeatedly proscribed under the *ancien régime*, yet the tradition survived down to the mid-19th c. The 19th c., through a Romantic nationalism sharpened by counter-revolution, reawakened the interest of intellectuals, bringing the first wave of puristic standardization in the work of Le Gonidec. Oral literature was first presented to a general public in Hersart de La Villemarqué's *Barzaz-Breiz* (1839), a collection of ballads with translations. Their basic authenticity has only recently been finally demonstrated, but the texts were very heavily edited and accompanied by generally spurious historical explanations. With increasing literacy popular publications became numerous, with secular material increasing; these were mainly didactic and traditionalist in character.

Literacy in Breton had never been a majority phenomenon and, after nearly 40 years of compulsory schooling exclusively through the medium of French and the upheavals of World War I, the 1920s saw the traditional readership of Breton begin to melt away quite rapidly. This is when Roparz Hemon (1900–78) launched as a supplement to the nationalist *Breiz Atao* the bimonthly *Gwalarn*, whose declared policy was to develop a Breton-language literature aimed at a modern educated middle class. Despite deep-seated tensions and contradictions, these ambitions have to some extent been realized in the last 30 years. More is being published in Breton than ever before, with 60 or more books appearing every year. There are 50 or more writers of sustained and regular productivity, but given the small size of their public, they cannot live by their pens and are generally confined to the shorter genres. It is remarkable to find so much variety and reassuring to find some real creative skill, but not surprising to find that the works with most depth to them are autobiographical [see HÉLIAS]. This is all happening against the depressing backdrop of the rapid collapse of Breton as a community language, with speakers representing less than a third—an ageing third—of the peak figure of 1,500,000 estimated for 1914.

There have in recent times been attempts to develop the Romance vernaculars of Upper Brittany, traditionally referred to as *le(s) patois gallo(s)*, as a written medium, often in this case called *la langue gallèse*. In substance, they are very close to the vernaculars of rural Maine and Anjou, but being more peripheral to the Île-de-France have rather more archaisms. One important figure from the *Pays gallo* is Paul Sébillot (1843–1918), whose *Revue des traditions populaires* and collection *Littératures populaires de toutes les nations* were milestones in the study of oral literature in France.

Before passing on to French texts, which after all represent the great bulk of literature emanating from both halves of Brittany, it should be noted that the Breton language has considerable symbolic power. Some writers ignore or reject it, while at the other end of the spectrum others claim it to be the sole defining characteristic of Bretonness. A strange, though not uncommon, phenomenon can be found in critics' claims that the Breton language is viscerally present in French works in which the Breton-speaker would never discover any such thing. Paradoxically, in written Breton literature French influences are all-pervasive: very few texts in any period are the work of monoglots.

2. Writing in French

Throughout the Middle Ages, Latin was cultivated as elsewhere in Europe. *Hagiography was the most interesting genre of the period, with the first complete text dating from the 9th c. The most notable medieval French texts produced in Brittany are: *La Chanson d'Aiquin*, a verse epic located in north-eastern Brittany, a 12th-c. composition preserved in a 15th-c. manuscript; the 12th-c. satirical *Livre des manières* by Étienne de Fougères, also a productive Latinist; and *Meschinot's allegorical *Lunettes des princes* (1491). An interesting feature is a late-medieval school of historiographers best represented by Pierre *Le Baud and Alain *Bouchart, continued by Bertrand d'*Argentré; this provided the basis for further development by Dom Lobineau (1667–1727).

16th-c. production extends from mystery plays (a *Vie de sainte Catherine* being published as late as 1576) to typical Renaissance verse best exemplified by Charles d'Espinay (1531–91); the outstanding author is Noël *du Fail. The 17th and 18th c. show greater integration with French norms, with what is specifically Breton tending to be confined to works of erudition, of which the Celtomania of père Paul-Yves Pezron's *Antiquité de la nation et de la langue des Celtes* (1703) is fortunately not typical, although it turned out to be quite influential. In a general climate of conformism, the *Enlightenment was far from absent, especially in parliamentary circles—the *Encyclopédie* sold 400 copies in Rennes. The novelist *Lesage, the critic *Fréron, the essayist *Trublet, and the philosopher *Maupertuis made their careers on the Parisian scene, as have many Breton writers.

Of the three best-known names of the 19th c., *Chateaubriand and *Lamennais show no specific Bretonness, whereas *Renan, despite his travels and erudition, never lost contact with the Breton-speaking milieu of his childhood. For most outside observers such as *Balzac and *Mérimée, Brittany was a convenient reserve in which to imbibe the local colour of savages both noble and otherwise from a perspective of authoritative ignorance; *Flaubert and *Loti are the honorable exceptions. Poetry is abundant throughout the century, with Auguste Brizeux (1803–58) the best-remembered of the Romantics and Tristan *Corbière the most striking in his cultivation of the barbaric—his father Édouard, a Morlaix slave-trader, wrote seafaring novels. Paul *Féval was the most prolific of the novelists, a popular and successful writer of cloak-and-dagger fiction, some of it specifically set in Upper Brittany. The interpretation of Lower Brittany and its inhabitants to a French-speaking public is a genre which developed and expanded; the precursor was Émile Souvestre (1806–54), and the most important name Anatole Le Braz (1859–1926).

The 20th-c. writers who have established themselves firmly in the general French literary scene have almost all been primarily novelists. The first generation is represented by *Segalen and Max *Jacob, both innovative, the former in his quest for the exotic, the latter in his *Surrealism. Next come *Guéhenno, *Queffélec, and *Guilloux, and the much younger Le Quintrec, Mohrt, and *Hallier, all of them classic in the sense that they associate reflection with careful naturalistic observation. *Robbe-Grillet, the best-known of them, stands out

as a pioneer of the *Nouveau Roman. The less public literature of poetry is also widely practised, the foremost names being *Guillevic, Angèle Vannier (b. 1917), Le Gouic (b. 1936), Le Men (b. 1943), and Keineg (b. 1944). Themes range from the cosmic to the political, often associated with the sudden changes in both society and landscape which economic change has brought since World War II. The question of identity is ever-present and some of its aspects can be profitably followed up in Morvan Lebesque's influential pamphlet *Comment peut-on être breton?* (1965). [HLlH]

See J. Balcou and Y. Le Gallo, *Histoire littéraire et culturelle de la Bretagne* (1987).

BRIZEUX, Auguste, see BRITTANY, 2.

BROGLIE. French noble family, many of whom have played important parts in the nation's history. Victor, duc de Broglie (1785–1870), left important *Souvenirs* (1886) devoted to his early years. Two of his grandsons, Maurice and Louis, were distinguished physicists.

BROOK, Peter (Stephen Paul) (b. 1925). English director and founder of the International Centre of Theatre Research in Paris. He won international acclaim for his sensational productions with the Royal Shakespeare Company, including Peter Weiss's *Marat/Sade* (1964), influenced by *Artaud's Theatre of Cruelty. In 1970, with the help of Jean-Louis *Barrault, he created the ICTR in the Bouffes du Nord, an abandoned music-hall near the Gare du Nord. With performers of many nationalities, the company explores diverse production styles and modes of theatre aimed at transcending cultural and national barriers. Their most celebrated production was of the entire Indian epic cycle of the *Mahabharata*, first performed in a quarry outside Avignon in 1985. [DWW]

BROSSARD, Nicole (b. 1943). Canadian poet and novelist, a leading figure in the Quebec avant-garde. Her poetic work, collected in *Le Centre blanc* (1978), and her first novels, *Sold out* (1973) and *French Kiss* (1974), undertook the subversion of traditional literary forms. In the 1980s a commitment to feminism and lesbianism added a political dimension to the deconstructive project. *Amantes* and *Le Sens apparent* (both 1980) assimilate the process of writing to the release of women's sexual desires. *Le Désert mauve* (1987) makes the same statements but with a greater degree of narrative coherence than hitherto. [SIL]

BROSSES, Charles de (1709–77). President of the Parlement de Dijon, friend of the *philosophes*, and in *Diderot's words 'une petite tête gaie, ironique et satirique'. His learned publications include important work on the origins of language (*Traité de la formation mécanique des langues*, 1765) and on 'primitive' religion (*Du culte des dieux fétiches*, 1760). His *Lettres familières écrites d'Italie en 1739 et 1740*, published posthumously in 1799 and much loved by *Stendhal, offer a model of personal travel writing, in which detailed accounts of art works and monuments, not always complimentary, or a careful description of Vesuvius, addressed to *Buffon, are interspersed with sprightly, enthusiastic accounts of the peculiarities and the aesthetic and sensual pleasures of life in Italy. [PF]

BROUARD, Carl (1902–65), poet and 'enfant terrible' of Haitian *indigénisme*, helped found *La Revue indigène* (1927–8) and later became director of *Les *Griots* (1938–40). Restless, bohemian, and mystical, he left his wealthy background to live in the slums of Port-au-Prince. His poetry was marked by voodoo mysticism and he became a strident apologist for *noirisme*. Catholic mysticism dominates his final poetic ramblings. [JMD]

BRUANT, Aristide (1851–1925). Singer-songwriter, also popular novelist and dramatist. Despite his reputation as the singer of Parisian low-life in the *belle époque*, immortalized in the *Toulouse-Lautrec posters, he was in fact born and bred among the provincial bourgeoisie of Courtenay (Loire), and only settled in Paris when he was 17. Early in his career he was associated with the famous Montmartre cabaret, Le *Chat Noir. His best-known songs celebrate the romantically glamorized underworld of the popular quarters of Paris: 'A Montmartre', 'A la Bastille', 'A Saint Lazare', 'Rue Saint Vincent', etc. The refrains of his songs are simple; but his voice, one of the first to be recorded, is as distinctive as his image. [PGH]

BRUÈS, Guy de, see PYRRHONISM.

Brumaire, Coup d'état du 18, see NAPOLEON, I.

BRUNEAU, Alfred (1857–1934). French composer of operas and pupil of *Massenet, Bruneau was a close personal friend of *Zola. All his libretti are either adapted from Zola novels, for instance, *Le Rêve* (1891), *L'Attaque du moulin* (1893), or as in the case of *Messidor* (1897) and *L'Ouragan* (1901) written specially for the composer. His operas have been termed 'realist' works. [KM]

BRUNETIÈRE, Ferdinand (1849–1906). French critic, teacher at the *École Normale Supérieure, director of the *Revue des deux mondes* from 1893, and author of *Études critiques sur l'histoire de la littérature française* (1880–1925). A dogmatist, he stressed the moral responsibility of literature, and fought the impressionism of *France or *Lemaître. Following *Sainte-Beuve and *Taine, influenced by Darwinism, he introduced genre and its evolution as a factor in the explanation of literature, along with biographical and social conditions (*L'Évolution de la poésie lyrique en France au XIXe siècle*, 1894). Committed to *classicism, he censured contemporary literature, notably Baudelaire and (in *Le Roman naturaliste*, 1882) *Zola. Despite his militancy against *Dreyfus and late con-

version to the Catholic faith, his *Manuel d'histoire de la littérature française* (1897) was a major influence on the literary canon of the Third Republic. [AC]

BRUNETTO LATINI (c.1220–c.1294). Florentine scholar and statesman, author of *Li Livres dou tresor*, an important early French prose encyclopaedia in three books: the first treats philosophical, doctrinal, historical, and scientific topics, the second ethics, and the third rhetoric and politics. A vast undertaking, this work combines the 'new' science and philosophy derived from Greek sources from the mid-12th c. onwards with a more conservative, *Neoplatonic tradition of thought. Dante stages a meeting between himself and Brunetto Latini in the *Inferno*. [SK]

BRUNHOFF, Laurent de (b. 1926). Author of best-selling books for children based on the character of an elephant named Babar, created by his father Jean de Brunhoff in *Histoire de Babar, le petit éléphant* in 1931. The imaginative illustrations and the gentle nature of the elephant account in large part for the charm of the stories. [EAF]

BRUNO, G., see TOUR DE LA FRANCE PAR DEUX ENFANTS, LE.

BRUNOT, Ferdinand (1860–1938), is known to all French philologists for his monumental *Histoire de la langue française* (1905–53), covering the internal and external history of French; vols. 12 and 13 were completed after his death by Charles Bruneau. Brunot's synchronic study, *La Pensée et la langue* (1922), conceives grammar as constituted on a psychological rather than a formal basis, and examines the relationship between thought and language with particular reference to French. Brunot's other works include a fierce criticism of the Académie Française *grammar (1932), a study of *Malherbe's linguistic thought (1891), and proposals for spelling reforms (1905, 1922). [WA-B]

BRUNSCHVICG, Léon (1869–1944). French philosopher. A proponent of idealism and humanism, Brunschvicg argued that our mental processes, through synthesizing acts of judgement, constitute a world which is the world for us (*Les Modalités du jugement*, 1897). He believed that the goal of philosophy was to reveal intellectual activity moving, throughout the historical development of mathematics, science, and ethics, towards ever greater self-awareness and unity (*Le Progrès de la conscience dans la philosophie occidentale*, 1927), and he stressed the freedom and inventiveness of the intellect in creating not only new categories of thought but new spiritual values. [REG]

BRUSCAMBILLE (or Deslauriers). Early 17th-c. comic actor, 33 of whose popular *Prologues*, spoken at the *Hôtel de Bourgogne and close in tone to contemporary satire, were published in 1610.

Brut, Le Roman de

Brut, Le Roman de, see WACE.

Brutus. Tragedy by *Voltaire, performed 1730. The play revolves around the conflict experienced by Titus, who is torn between his love for Tullie (daughter of the tyrant Tarquin, recently expelled from Rome by his own father, Lucius Junius Brutus) and his commitment to the liberty of the young Republic. Finally ensnared by love, he joins the supporters of Tarquin conspiring for his return, but his treachery is discovered. The Senate leaves his fate to Brutus, who has him executed. The tragedy was published with an important preliminary discourse (dedicated to Bolingbroke) which helps to pinpoint Voltaire's feelings on tragedy after two years' intimate contact with English models.   [JR]

BUABUA WA KAYEMBE MUBADIATE (b. 1950). Zaïrean poet-playwright. Of his plays, *Les Flammes de Soweto* (1979) treats of the death of Steve Biko, while *Le Délégué général* (1982) and *Mais les pièges étaient de la fête* (1988) discuss corruption and the pressures of society on individuals. His poems combine lyricism with social commitment.   [AMR]

BUCHANAN, George (1506–82), *humanist, textual critic, poet, playwright, historian, and political theorist, was a Scotsman who taught for many years in Paris, Bordeaux, and Coimbra. A friend of the *Pléiade, especially *Du Bellay, he wrote in Latin, not French, yet his poems and plays helped to shape vernacular writing. From the 1530s onwards he wrote witty, elegant satires and erotic and scientific poems, but did not publish them until he was 60. His plays were performed in Bordeaux in the 1540s, with his pupil *Montaigne among the actors: translations of Euripides' *Medea* (1544) and *Alcestis* (1556), and two original works, *Jephthes* (1554) and *Baptistes* (1577). Buchanan was the first to write classical tragedy in France, adapting Euripides and Seneca to biblical subjects, and following Aristotle's principles. After condemnation and imprisonment by the Portuguese Inquisition for his Protestant sympathies, during which time he worked on his metrical paraphrases of the Psalms, he returned to Paris, and then Scotland (1561), where he became tutor to the young James VI (later James I of England). He wrote there *De iure regni apud Scotos* (1579), discussing royal authority and tyrannicide and attacking Mary Queen of Scots, and his subjective and controversial *Rerum scoticarum historia* (1582).   [PS]

BUDÉ, Guillaume (1467–1540). Humanist. Born in Paris, he studied law at Orléans, and learned and later taught Greek; from 1522 he was secretary and librarian to François Ier. A scholar of vast erudition, he was the most eminent French humanist of his generation, and was responsible in 1530 for persuading the king to appoint the 'royal readers' in Hebrew, Greek, and Latin who formed the nucleus of the future *Collège de France. Among his principal works are a commentary on the Pandects (1508) and a treatise on ancient coinage (*De asse*, 1514), both of which reveal the breadth of his learning, his pioneering skills as archaeologist and philologist, and his insistence on returning to the original texts and documents. His *Commentarii linguae graecae* (1529) and his translations of Plutarch firmly placed Hellenism on the agenda of Renaissance scholarship. He attempted in his writings to reconcile ancient Greek and Christian thought, while keeping a firm distinction between them: in *De transitu hellenismi ad christianismum* (1535) he shows how pagan learning can educate the mind, while Christian learning forms the soul. The stress here, as in his *De l'institution du prince*, is moral rather than theological; Budé thus exemplifies the most important features of Renaissance *humanism.   [NM]

BUFFIER, Claude (1661–1737). French Jesuit who contributed to the *Mémoires de *Trévoux* and published many pedagogical works, including a *Grammaire française* (1709), a *Traité de la poésie* (1728), and a *Cours des sciences* (1732). Some of his work was used without acknowledgement in the *Encyclopédie*.

BUFFON, Georges-Louis Leclerc, comte de (1707–88). Often remembered today for his inaugural address to the Académie Française, the *Discours sur le style* (1753), Buffon was the most prestigious scientist of his day and one of the enduring influences emanating from the French *Enlightenment. In the field of scientific erudition he was an entrepreneur of genius, impressive not merely in his practical achievements as superintendant of the Jardin du Roi (now the *Jardin des Plantes) from 1739 until his death, but also in the scope and authority of his literary projects. The *Histoire naturelle générale et particulière* (1749–1804) eventually comprised 36 volumes. Produced with a series of collaborators, notably *Daubenton, it aimed at a comprehensive account of the cosmological beginnings of the earth, and also of the composition and evolution of organic life. By methodically consolidating knowledge of the natural world the *Histoire* complemented the *Encyclopédie*, whose status in publishing history it rivals.

Buffon was born in Montbard into a family of the new nobility. Following legal, medical, and botanical studies, his education was completed in the company of an English nobleman on the Grand Tour (1729–32). Thus his first projects were translations of Evelyn's *Sylva* and Hales's *Vegetable Staticks* (1735). Such learned forays were typically reinforced by Buffon's proprietorial interest in forestry. Throughout his career the practical, the profitable, and the scientific were interlinked, subsequent ventures in iron-founding and coal-mining having their cosmological and geological resonance in the theories of the *Histoire naturelle* and *Les Époques de la nature* (1778).

The *Histoire naturelle*, with volumes on cosmology, geomorphology, mineralogy, zoology, and botany, displays an exhaustive conception of natural history. While respecting the tenets of observation and experiment, Buffon's genius lay in synthesizing the findings of others in order to isolate salient principles, and in articulating these with great clarity and precision. He claimed only to assemble facts methodically, and indeed long tracts of the work, notably on ornithology, hardly rise above the mundanely descriptive. Yet while he may be criticized today for the timid anthropocentricity and moralism of his treatment of organic life, he successfully implanted such pregnant hypotheses as marine sedimentation and the evolution of species from primitive prototypes under environmental pressure. In *Les Époques de la nature* he revised his theories, establishing the classic division of rocks into igneous, metamorphic, and sedimentary. He also massively expanded the time-scale of terrestrial evolution from its minute biblical span.

Thus, he successfully focused his generation's imagination on the awesome fecundity and interconnection of all natural phenomena. While avoiding direct conflict with the Church, his conception of human nature and origins was unrepentantly heretical. This audacious vision transcends the observational neutrality practised by contemporaries like *Réaumur and Bonnet, who criticized him. Modern historians of science applaud him for daring to rescue systematic understanding from their myopic particularism, and above all for endorsing the Cartesian creed of faith in the human mind and in its scientific vocation.   [SMM]

See J. Roger, *Buffon: un philosophe au jardin du roi* (1989).

BUGUL, Ken (b. 1948). The only work of this Senegalese woman writer, an autobiographical novel, *Le Baobab fou* (1982), warmly received by Western critics, is a frank account of the author's experience of the world of drugs and sexual degeneracy in Europe. Bugul's work differs from other examples of the alienation theme (e.g. *Socé and *Kane) in identifying the roots of alienation in a personal experience (she was abandoned by her mother, and Ken Bugul is in fact a pen-name meaning 'unwanted child') rather than in the French colonial policy of *assimilation*.   [FNC]

Burgraves, Les. Epic verse drama of concealed identity by Victor *Hugo. Set in 13th-c. Germany, it concerns the fratricidal struggle for power between the emperor, Frederick Barbarossa, and a house of princes led by Frederick's older brother Job. Performed at the Comédie-Française in 1843, the play, with its long speeches and absence of any love story or comic relief, was a dismal failure, inspiring many parodies, and ended Hugo's 20-year career as France's most successful dramatist.   [SN]

Burgundian Court Literature. It is customary to date 'Burgundian court literature' from the creation

of the Valois dukedom for his fourth son, Philippe le Hardi, by Jean le Bon of France in 1363, to the death of the last great duke, Charles le Téméraire, in 1477. The dukedom comprised two distinct geographical entities, united by marriage: Burgundy proper, centring on Dijon, and from 1384 the northern provinces of Flanders. As marriage and conquest expanded the latter territories, Brussels came to displace Dijon as the capital.

The Valois dukes (Philippe le Hardi, duke from 1363 to 1404; Jean sans Peur, 1404–19; Philippe le Bon, 1419–67; Charles le Téméraire, 1467–77) were among the wealthiest magnates of the age, and their court was royal in all but name, universally admired as a centre of refined opulence: the dukes retained an astonishing array of architects, artists, musicians, *tapissiers*, and jewellers. They entertained lavishly, with great feasts, tournaments, and court pageantry. In this artistic hothouse, literature played a major part. The dukes—and their family and entourage—assembled one of medieval Europe's outstanding libraries, catalogued in a series of inventories from 1404 to 1504 and consisting ultimately of over 1,000 volumes, the product of a veritable stable of the finest copyists, calligraphers, miniaturists, and bookbinders. The dukes themselves had pronounced literary leanings; Philippe le Bon in particular had *anciennes histoires* read before him every day; he collected so effectively that he was said to be 'le prince le mieux garni de autenticque et riche librairie'. The dukes' tastes differed. Philippe le Hardi's interest in hunting is reflected in his commissioning of *Gace de la Buigne's *Deduit des chiens*, and he was also the dedicatee of *Gaston Phébus's *Livre de la chasse*, whilst Charles le Téméraire's classical interests were reflected in his commissioning of translations, for example, of Julius Caesar, Xenophon, and Cicero.

Certain procedures are characteristic of the ducal libraries. The dukes' interest in history was extensive, fed by the acquisition and copying of Latin histories, and by commissions to re-compile and translate them, often in luxurious and lavishly illuminated manuscripts; thus in 1448 *Wauquelin compiled a great history of Alexander the Great, and in 1454 Jean *Mansel anthologized Livy and Sallust among others to produce *Les Histoires romaines*. They had a particular predilection for history with local relevance; Philippe le Bon commissioned a series of *chroniques*, of France, Flanders, Holland, characterized by genealogical preoccupations designed to ground the history of the dukedom in the remotest antiquity. Similar preoccupations also underlie commissions such as David Aubert's huge four-volume compilation, *Histoire de Charles Martel et de ses successeurs* (1448), and his three-volume *Conquestes de Charlemagne* (1458), a compilation of *chansons de geste* modernized into prose, and bibliographically one of the jewels of the Burgundian library.

This last procedure—*dérimage*—is a permanent preoccupation of Burgundian literary industry. The

Buridan

princes admired the chivalrous deeds described in epic and romance, but preferred prose to the strait-jacket of verse, 'pour le langaige quy est plus entier et n'est mie constraint'. The dukes' library contained *mises en prose* of epics and romances: the **Chastelain de Coucy*, **Cleomades*, *Gilles de Chin*, and many more. The *mises en prose* of **Chrétien's Cligés* and *Erec et Enide* are typical, but typically disappointing: we lose not only the rhythm and tension of the rhymed couplets, but also much lively description and subtle monologue, since the compilers aimed, says Wauquelin ominously, to 'retranchier et sincoper prolongacions et mots inutiles'. At the same time, however, the Arthurian prose romances were acquired and copied: the later inventories note multiple copies of the prose **Tristan* and the Vulgate cycle [see ROMANCE, 2]. The dukes' tastes were conservative; the fiction they commissioned built on existing popularity and they encouraged the production, or at least the propagation, of more recent Arthurian romances: all the manuscripts of the **Perceforest* emanate from Burgundian circles.

The two fields where the Burgundian contribution was most original are historiography and lyric poetry. Unsurprisingly, the dukes' interest in history was carried forward into a concern for the proper presentation to posterity of their own achievements. On the one hand, they encouraged the frankly partisan: the *Geste des ducs Philippe et Jehan de Bourgogne*, for instance, running from 1384 to 1412. More interestingly, however, they also retained as *indiciaires*, or official historians of their courts, **Chastellain ('perle et estoile de tous les historiographes') until his death in 1474, followed by **Molinet until 1506, retained for 120 *livres* in 1485 as 'bon et leal historiographe et chronicqueur'. Both historians pride themselves on impartiality, but are sincerely convinced of Burgundian superiority; their works are, of course, panegyrics, couched in sonorous prose, theatricalizing contemporary events. They and their fellow Burgundian Olivier de **La Marche accord central importance to the Burgundian court as the locus of *haute noble chevalerie*, and pay particular attention to the festivities whose etiquette and choreography La Marche in particular documents. Like virtually all their contemporaries, the writers view history anachronistically, through the prism of **chivalry, with a didactic note inviting readers to draw moral lessons from contemporary events.

Chastellain and Molinet are also court poets, as indeed was La Marche—and it is in this capacity that they illustrate the second strand of Burgundian originality, a type of lyric verse commonly attached to the so-called **Rhétoriqueurs. This poetry is didactic and politically involved; over half of Molinet's *Faits et dits* is devoted to court matters. It sets store by the writer's technical skill, his erudition, his linguistic ingenuity, even the physical disposition of the words on the page.

Brilliant propagandists, the dukes made the most of their patronage; what is typical of Burgundian court literature, finally, is the imbrication of politics and literature: the **Vœux du paon* inspire the theatrical crusading vows at the Vœux du Faisan ceremony (1454), and **Jacques de Lalaing's essentially histrionic *pas d'armes*, La Fontaine aux Pleurs (1449–50), inspires **La Sale's *Saintré*.   [JHMT]

See G. Doutrepont, *La Littérature française à la cour des ducs de Bourgogne* (repr., 1970).

BURIDAN, John (*c.*1295/1300–after 1358), became a master of arts at the University of Paris in *c.*1320 and spent the rest of his life teaching there in the Faculty of Arts. He was rector of the university in 1328 and again in 1340. According to **Villon, the queen of France ordered him to be tied in a sack and thrown into the Seine (no other source recounts this incident).

Among Buridan's works are logical treatises (*Tractatus de consequentiis*, *Sophismata*, *Summulae de dialectica/Compendium logicae*) which offered sophisticated treatment of the *logica modernorum*, the branches of logic newly devised by medieval logicians; and *quaestio*-commentaries on a very wide range of Aristotle's writing, including the *Nicomachean Ethics*, the *Metaphysics*, *Politics*, and many of the texts on natural science. Like his English near-contemporary, William of Ockham, Buridan was a **nominalist: he denied that anything exists which is not individual. He did not, however, follow Ockham in his rejection of Aristotelian epistemology, nor does his moral thought show the strong emphasis—characteristic of Ockham and many 14th-c. nominalists—on the distinction between God's absolute power (what in theory God can do) and his ordained power. As an arts master, Buridan was content to develop Aristotle's ethics in Aristotle's own terms, as a practical science.

The sophism known as Buridan's Ass, which presents a donkey dying of hunger because unable to choose between two equal bundles of hay, appears to have been falsely attributed to him.   [JAMM]

Burlesque. Although used more broadly of many kinds of playful, parodic writing [see PARODY AND PASTICHE], in French literary history, the term refers to a genre briefly fashionable in the years following 1643, before being vigorously condemned by critics [see CLASSICISM]. It is associated with **Scarron, who introduced it from Italy with his *Recueil de quelques vers burlesques* and illustrated it in his *Typhon* and the seven books of his unfinished *Virgile travesti*. It was also practised by such poets as **Saint-Amant, **Sarasin, **Perrault, and d'**Assoucy.

This burlesque genre is the playful presentation of a noble subject (e.g. the *Aeneid*) in a 'low' setting and 'low' language—usually deliberately trivial octosyllabic verse. It could easily become vulgar and obscene, and as such lent itself to popular satire, as in the **mazarinades*. It also found a place in the

*Bibliothèque Bleue. It was not so much an anti-establishment genre, however, as a literary play on stylistic levels, comparable to its elevated counter-part, mock-heroic, which *Boileau described in the preface to *Le Lutrin* as a 'burlesque nouveau'.   [PF]

BUSSIÈRES, Jean de (1607–78). French Jesuit poet whose *Descriptions poétiques* (1648) offer, in Alan Steele's words, 'an orgy of the lesser baroque'.

BUSSY-RABUTIN, Roger de Rabutin, called comte de (1618–93). French military man, known as much for his amorous conquests as for his martial exploits. He was imprisoned for the first time, and his regiment abolished, after he was judged responsible for the financial misdealings undertaken by the men serving under him while he was courting a prominent noblewoman. Widowed in 1646, he was convicted in 1648 for the attempted kidnapping of a rich young widow. His literary career was similarly controversial. He co-authored the *Carte de la Braquerie* (from 'bragues', related to codpiece), a 1654 parody of the *carte de Tendre* and *preciosity. His obscene portraits of prominent court women were leaked by a mistress. Despite the ensuing outcry, he was admitted to the Académie Française, just days before the *Histoire amoureuse des Gaules* (1665), his scandalous court chronicle, appeared without his authorization. During the imprisonment and exile that followed, he maintained a prolific correspondence, notably with his cousin *Sévigné, and composed his memoirs.   [JDeJ]

BUTOR, Michel (b. 1926). French writer. His novels *L'*Emploi du temps* and *La *Modification* gave him a prominent position in the Parisian literary avant-garde of the 1950s and 1960s, and are still his best-known works. But the novels—these two plus *Passage de Milan* (1954) and *Degrés* (1960)—constitute only a small fraction of his output. From *Mobile* in 1962 onwards, this extremely well-read, much-travelled and prolific writer has produced a series of texts which are not conventional fiction or conventional criticism or conventional travel writing but contain elements of all three.

Throughout the 1960s he was part of the politically committed Parisian intelligentsia, protesting against the *Algerian War and participating in the events of *May 1968. Since 1970 he has combined writing with university teaching, first at Nice, later at Geneva. He is one of the most intellectually sophisticated writers of the post-war period; his background in philosophy, especially the work of Hegel and *Sartre, sets him apart from the other writers of the *Nouveau Roman with whom he was initially associated. Like them, he saw the novel as a domain of structural experiment; unlike them, he insisted that its purpose was to enlarge the reader's understanding of social and historical reality.

Répertoire I (1960) contains the articles which first formulate his theory of the novel as a narrative which articulates our everyday reality, not via any authorial message but through its overall structure, which he sees as 'a way of forcing the real to reveal itself'. It therefore has to be very carefully worked out in advance—but will inevitably be modified once the actual writing is under way. These same concerns are carried through to his later work, albeit in an increasingly fluid, fragmented, collage-like form; all Butor's texts are characterized by the methodical precision and subtlety of their construction, and the preliminary 'schemas' he describes are often intimidatingly complicated.

The structure of the text reflects, amplifies, and hence elucidates the largely unconscious cultural structures in which our existence is grounded. A central emphasis here is the relation between individual self-consciousness and collective historical situation: we cannot spontaneously discard our ideological matrix, but can liberate ourselves through a slow, painful process of *conscious* reappraisal of our historical and cultural determinants. Butor sees history as a series of collective representations of reality; the individual writer, therefore, is working not on raw objective reality, but on (and in) a pre-existing complex of representations which he or she partially transforms through the 'illumination' of blind spots that had hitherto been repressed. Each new text situates itself inter-textually, modifying an existing literary corpus and leaving itself open to future modification. Cultural monuments, too, are represented not as fixed absolutes but as enmeshed in a historical and spatial 'polyphony'— the *Description de San Marco* (1963) or the 'liquid monument' of Niagara Falls in *6,810,000 litres d'eau par seconde* (1965).

He has an acute sense of cultural difference. For Butor, a product of European Catholic society, encounters with America, Egypt, Australia, and the Far East are a fascinating revelation of otherness. His evocations of foreign places, many of which appear in the four volumes of *Le Génie du lieu* (1958, 1971, 1978, 1988), challenge European notions of colonial dominance and embody in their own 'stereophonic' form the decentred heterogeneity of cultural reality. This, however, is just one of the series of volumes which Butor has produced. The five volumes of *Répertoire* are devoted to critical writings, as is a newer series based on his classes at Geneva: *Improvisations sur *Flaubert* (1984), *Improvisations sur Henri *Michaux* (1985), *Improvisations sur *Rimbaud* (1989). In addition, he has written separately on *Montaigne (*Essais sur les Essais*, 1968), *Baudelaire (*Histoire extraordinaire*, 1969), and *Fourier (*La Rose des vents*, 1970), among others. *Illustrations* (I, 1964; II, 1969; III, 1973; IV, 1976) form another sequence written in response to paintings, etchings, photographs, etc.

But perhaps the most productive and original series from the mid-1970s onwards is that of the five volumes of *Matière de rêves* (1975, 1976, 1977, 1981, 1985); these 'dream narratives' are not records of actual dreams, but texts which develop according to a non-realist, dream-like logic characterized by loss of identity, metamorphoses, polymorphous sexuality, and the fragmentary incorporation of paintings, music, and literature. Butor's later texts—too numerous to list exhuastively—are not widely read, but they confirm his position as one of the most rigorous and original writers of his period.

[CB]

See J. Roudaut, *Michel Butor ou le Livre futur* (1964); A. Helbo, *Michel Butor: vers une littérature du signe* (1975).

C

Cabale des Dévots, La, see SAINT-SACREMENT, COMPAGNIE DU.

CABANIS, Pierre-Jean-Georges (1757–1808). French physician and prominent *Idéologue. As a professor of clinical medicine and member of the *Institut, Cabanis championed improvements in public health; as a member of the Conseil des Cinq-Cents and senator, he supported the *coup d'état* of 18 Brumaire, but opposed Napoleon's subsequent drift to dictatorship.

His principal work, *Rapports du physique et du moral de l'homme* (1802), elaborates a rigorous psychophysiological materialism. Going beyond the abstractive epistemology of *Condillac and the exclusive environmentalism of *Helvétius, Cabanis argued that all mental processes were derived from sensation and contingent upon a complex interplay of physical determinants. Though influential for later Positivism [see COMTE], Cabanis's medical philosophy and the secular ethic which it proclaimed were stymied by Napoleon's political aims and by the revival of religion and metaphysical idealism in the early 19th c.   [JS]

Cabaret is often employed in the sense of 'tavern'; such *cabarets* were favourite meeting-places of male writers, at least until the appearance of *cafés. For the more recent sense of the word see CHANSON FRANÇAISE.

CABET, Étienne (1788–1856). Born in Dijon, Cabet became a lawyer active in leftist causes and was elected deputy in 1831, but his extreme opinions led to his being sentenced to five years' exile in England. He there wrote his *Histoire populaire de la révolution française* and *Voyage en Icarie*, both published in 1840 after his return to Paris. A *Utopian novel, *Voyage* describes Cabet's programme for a Communist society with common ownership of everything and the motto: 'from each according to his capacities, to each according to his needs.' The rather weak love plot derived from La *Nouvelle Héloïse* is followed by an anthology of citations from past writers supporting Cabet's views. In *Le Vrai Christianisme* (1846) he demonstrated that Jesus was a Communist. He had many followers, some of whom in 1848 moved to the United States to found Icaria; Cabet joined them, but their efforts were marked by disputes and schisms and he left the colony for St Louis, Missouri, where he died; the last colony dissolved in 1894.   [FPB]

Cabinet des fées, Le. Collection of 17th and 18th-c. fairy-tales published in 41 vols. in 1785–6 by Charles-Joseph de Mayer. It includes oriental tales as well as stories belonging to the tradition of *Perrault [see SHORT FICTION].

Cabinets de lecture. Commercial lending-libraries, which began in the 18th c. as newspaper reading-rooms (see Stendhal's *Lucien Leuwen*), and mushroomed in the 1820s as providers of educational and leisure reading to the fast-rising number of readers who could not afford to buy books. By 1835 there were 500 *cabinets de lecture* in Paris alone, ranging from handsome libraries of contemporary fiction to dingy backrooms, charging 1 *sou* for reading a volume on the premises, and 2 *sous* for reading at home. The *cabinets de lecture* allowed the literature of the Romantic period to reach a mass public despite low print-runs and high prices. Pirated Belgian printings, then cheaper newspapers, and finally mass reprints brought the price of reading-matter down sharply between 1840 and 1860, and the *cabinets de lecture* faded away. [See LIBRARIES, PUBLIC.]   [DMB]

CABON, Marcel (1912–72). An important Mauritian literary figure, whose poetry is dispersed in often obscure journals. His novel *Namasté* (1965) is about Indo-Mauritian peasant life. It is a novel of *enracinement* and of nostalgia for the ancestral past.   [BEJ]

Cacouacs. Mocking name given to the *philosophes in a pamphlet published anonymously in 1757 by J.-N. Moreau (1717–1803), who later became librarian to Marie-Antoinette.

CADOU, René-Guy (1920–51). French poet. Following in the footsteps of his parents and grand-parents, Cadou became a teacher in his native Brittany. By the time of his early death he had written a considerable body of poetry, finally collected in 1977. This lyrical and mellifluous writing seeks to blend into one harmonious vision the power of his feelings for the natural world, love of his wife (celebrated in *Hélène ou le Monde végétal* 1947), and fraternal solidarity with friends and fellow poets. Still widely admired for its freshness and urgency, Cadou's poetry is characteristic of the École de *Rochefort, of which he was a leading member.
[MHTS]

Caesura, see VERSIFICATION, 2.

Café-concert, see MUSIC-HALL.

Cafés and Restaurants

Cafés and Restaurants. Coffee-drinking reached France from the Middle East in the 17th c. Cafés were set up in Marseille and then in Paris, and soon became a prominent feature of cultural life, partly replacing the *cabarets* (taverns) where male writers had previously met. There were over 300 of them in Paris by 1720 and (according to *Mercier) some 700 in 1785. One of the first and most famous was the Procope, close to the *Comédie-Française on the Left Bank; others included the Régence (described in Diderot's *Neveu de Rameau), the Laurent, and the Café de Foy.

As against the *salons, the cafés, following the example of the English coffee-house, were mainly masculine preserves, where conversation was freer and less refined. They played a vital role in the development of *Enlightenment thought, being places where new or subversive ideas could be fairly openly discussed (though police spies haunted them). In addition, news was circulated and journalists gathered here (see *Voltaire's L'Écossaise ou le Café, 1760), new books and plays were judged, reputations were made.

During the *Revolution, the Parisian cafés took second place to clubs as hotbeds of ideas and intrigue, but they emerged into new prominence in the 19th c., when they tended increasingly to specialize in particular types of clientele (fashionable, poetic, political, artistic, etc.). Old cafés such as the Procope survived and were joined by new establishments as favourite meeting-places for writers connected with various cliques, movements, and journals, particularly at the end of the century. These included at various times the Momus, the Vachette, the Tortoni, the Café de Paris, and the Closerie des Lilas.

The second half of the 19th c. saw the development of the *café-concert* [see MUSIC-HALL], where professional entertainment gave a new spice to normal sociability. Such places, alongside the *cabarets artistiques* such as the *Chat Noir or the Lapin Agile, were characteristic of *Montmartre when it was a fashionable artistic centre around the turn of the century. Between the wars, the cafés and *brasseries* of *Montparnasse played a similar role. With the *Occupation, however, cafés became a vitally essential living-space for some writers; these included the group around *Beauvoir and *Sartre, whose favourite cafés at *Saint-Germain-des-Prés, the Flore and the Deux Magots, became the headquarters of popular *Existentialism after World War II.

Alongside cafés, restaurants have had an important part to play in French literary life. The most famous was the Restaurant Magny (in the Latin Quarter), where writers and artists met for the fortnightly *dîners Magny* between 1862 and 1875, among them *Flaubert, Turgenev, *Gautier, *Renan, *Sainte-Beuve, *Taine, and the *Goncourt brothers. And it is in a restaurant that the *Académie Goncourt meets every month over lunch and annually chooses the winner of the Prix Goncourt. [PF]

Cahier d'un retour au pays natal, see CÉSAIRE, A.

Cahiers, Les, see VALÉRY.

Cahiers d'André Walter, Les, see GIDE.

Cahiers de doléances. Lists of grievances (drawn up by parishes, corporations, municipalities, etc.), digests of which were then prepared by electoral assemblies for examination by the États Généraux in May 1789 [see REVOLUTION, 1a].

Cahiers de la quinzaine, Les, see PÉGUY.

Cahiers du cinéma. This journal, co-founded by André *Bazin in 1951, has exercised an influence in the world of French cinema equalled only by Les *Temps modernes or *Tel Quel in their fields. In its earlier days, when many subsequent *Nouvelle Vague directors wrote for it, it promoted the 'politique des auteurs', which caused Hollywood cinema to be taken seriously by ascribing to its leading directors the status of authorship. Its second major period of influence came in the late 1960s under the editorship of Jean-Louis Comolli, when it was marked by a structuralist/Marxist/psychoanalytic vocabulary similar to that of Tel Quel. [KAR]

Cahiers vaudois, see SWISS LITERATURE IN FRENCH, 4.

CAILLAVET, Gaston Arman de, see FLERS.

CAILLOIS, Roger (1913–78). A sociology student in Paris in the 1930s, Caillois briefly participated in *Surrealism, and was later a co-founder of the *Collège de Sociologie. Caught up by events while visiting South America in 1939, he was exiled there till 1945, becoming a keen publicist for writers like Neruda and Borges. Caillois's early work includes sociological studies such as Le Mythe et l'homme (1938) and L'Homme et le sacré (1939), but his post-war writing became increasingly hard to pigeon-hole. Once he realized his true specialism to be 'les sciences diagonales', he flung himself into the pursuit of illuminating analogies across all sorts of subject boundaries. It was in such an interdisciplinary spirit that he founded the review Diogène in 1952. With a neo-Romantic's eye for the telling convergence of natural and cultural signs, Caillois elaborates on such favourite topics as dreams and myths, butterflies and carnivorous flowers, the poetry of *Saint-John Perse, masks, and magical places (he travelled world-wide after 1948 as an emissary for UNESCO). Le Mimétisme animal (1963) treats of animal mimicry and camouflage, complementing Au cœur du fantastique (1965), a salute to the tradition of the *Fantastic in painting. The superb L'Écriture des pierres (1970) explores the art-like aspects of his personal mineral collection. Caillois's work is informed both by a strong aesthetic sense and an appetite for all things oblique, ambiguous, and irregular. [RC]

'Ça ira'. One of the most popular songs of the French Revolution, first sung to a country-dance tune in 1790. The title/refrain expresses confidence in the future. Its most famous lines are: 'Ah! ça ira, ça ira, ça ira! | Les aristocrates à la lanterne!'

CALAS, Jean (1698–1762). Protestant merchant of Toulouse, brutally executed on the false charge of killing his son for wanting to become a Catholic. *Voltaire, in his campaign against 'l'infâme', made of this a *cause célèbre* and by tireless campaigning had Calas rehabilitated in 1765.

Calendars. During the Middle Ages there were in France, as elsewhere in Europe, different ways of fixing the beginning of the year, the main dates being 25 December, 1 January, 25 March, and Easter. An edict of Charles IX of 1 January 1563/4 prescribed 1 January as the standard date. A few years later, in 1582, the Gregorian calendar was adopted in place of the Julian, with the consequent loss of 10 days.

1792 saw the introduction of a quite new calendar to mark the inauguration of the Republic on 22 September (1 Vendémiaire, An I). At first, the Republican era was deemed to have begun on 1 January 1792, so that documents from 1 January 1793 to 21 September 1793 were dated An II, but it was decreed in October 1793 that An I had begun with the declaration of the Republic on 22 September 1792. The Revolutionary calendar came into general use in December 1793 and was abolished by Napoleon in 1805, France returning to the Gregorian calendar on 1 January 1806 (12 Nivôse, An XIV).

Under the Revolutionary calendar, the year was divided into twelve months of 30 days, each of them divided into 3 *décades*, in which the days bore arithmetical names (*primidi, duodi*). The extra five or six days a year were observed as festivals known as *sans-culottides*. The months were given poetic new seasonal names devised by *Fabre d'Églantine: Vendémiaire, Brumaire, Frimaire, Nivôse, Pluviôse, Ventôse, Germinal, Floréal, Prairial, Messidor, Thermidor, Fructidor. [PF]

CALET, Henri (1904–56). French author of populist novels and short stories written between 1935 and 1956 which met with considerable success on being republished in the 1980s. Largely based on his own experiences and knowledge of Paris, novels such as *La Belle Lurette* (1935) and *Les Grandes Largeurs* (1954) recount the everyday tragedies of ordinary people in a spare, often melancholic tone. [EAF]

Caliste, see CHARRIÈRE.

Calligrammes, see APOLLINAIRE.

Calmann-Lévy, publishing firm, see BOOK TRADE, 5.

CALVIN, Jean (1509–64). Religious Reformer whose doctrine still exerts a powerful influence, especially in northern Europe and North America. The son of an ecclesiastical lawyer from Noyon, Calvin received theological and legal training at Paris, Orléans, and Bourges; though destined originally for the Church,

and already the possessor of two benefices, he also pursued humanist studies, publishing a learned commentary on Seneca's *De clementia* in 1532. Attracted by *Evangelical circles in Paris, he fled the city in 1533 when his Erasmian friend Nicolas Cop delivered an imprudent rectorial oration, partly written by Calvin. After a period of wandering, during which he visited *Marguerite de Navarre at Nérac and wrote a preface for his cousin *Olivétan's French Bible (Neuchâtel, 1535), Calvin settled at Basle where the first version of his master-work, *Christianae religionis institutio*, was published in 1536.

In July of that year Guillaume *Farel persuaded Calvin to settle in Geneva and assist in establishing a Reformed church; Calvin became a pastor, but an ill-judged attempt to impose a Confession of Faith on the citizens resulted in another flight. Between 1538 and 1541 Calvin was pastor of the French Reformed Church at Strasburg, whence he was recalled to Geneva by the Council, who recognized belatedly his unique powers of leadership and organization. Once there he published a French version of the *Institutio* (*Institution de la religion chrétienne*) to be followed by four revisions, in both Latin and French, culminating in the definitive text of 1559–60. The book's principles were the basis of Calvin's ordering of the Genevan community: his first tasks were the drafting of new civil and penal codes of law for the city, and the establishment of an oligarchical hierarchy of Orders. During the next 23 years he presided over a theocratic government, based on a devoted and rigidly supervised pastorate which strove to impose a rigorous moral code and strict religious conformism: all this authorized by direct reference to the revealed word of God. Energetic proselytism soon began, since Calvin's experiences had convinced him that the pietistic Lutheran 'church of the converted' must become a 'church of conversion'. It was particularly successful in south-western and western France. The French Calvinists, who held their first general synod in Paris in 1559, were increasingly perceived as a threat to monarchical and ecclesiastical authority, and such suspicions contributed much to the outbreak of the *Wars of Religion.

Calvin's authority in Geneva was tested, and eventually strengthened, by the notorious affair of the aggressive Spanish anti-trinitarian Michael Servetus, who had attacked Calvin's *Institutio* in his *Christianismi restitutio*. In 1553 Servetus was sent to the stake for heresy by the Genevan Council, relying largely on Calvin's evidence. This apparently inquisitorial behaviour provoked protests, especially from Calvin's erstwhile colleague Sébastien *Châteillon, but Calvin's opponents in Geneva, having sided with Servetus, were irretrievably damaged by the Spaniard's conviction. Calvin resumed his pastoral and educational tasks. The Genevan Academy, with *Bèze as rector, was established in 1559, a model for the later seminaries which helped carry Calvin's reformation into the world.

Camara Laye

The springs of Calvin's doctrine were, as with Luther and other Reformers: his impatience with the perceived worldliness and decadence of the Roman Church (see his *Traité des reliques*, 1543), his concern at the spread of impiety and spiritual laxity (*Traité des scandales*, 1550), and his desire, accentuated by his humanist and patristic studies, to return to the lost purity of the gospel teaching and of the primitive Church. Although Calvinism is frequently identified with the single doctrine of the predestination of the elect, it is of course more complex. Though in broad agreement with Luther on justification by faith, the bondage of the will, and mankind's total depravity, Calvin differed fundamentally over the central doctrine of the Eucharist: he did not accept that the sacrament of Communion was necessary to salvation (which is through faith in the Word alone), and rejected Lutheran consubstantiation in favour of the view that the bread and wine are the 'spiritual substance' of Christ's body, accessible only to the faithful (*Traité de la cène*, 1541). His controversial views on the necessity of discipline in the Church (the 'communion of saints'), on the Church's guiding role in the life of the State, and on the impracticability of compromise with Rome, were expounded in a flood of treatises in Latin and French. Calvin's French is distinguished by a dignity, simplicity, and clarity which make him a precursor of the classical style, but also by flexibility of register, humour, and sarcasm, as the need arose to persuade a less-cultivated audience.   [MJH]

See Calvin, *Three French Treatises* (ed. F. M. Higman, 1970); T. H. L. Parker, *John Calvin* (1975); R. S. Wallace, *Calvin, Geneva, and the Reformation* (1988).

CAMARA LAYE, (1924–80). Guinean prose writer. Born at Kouroussa in Upper Guinea, the son of the town's leading goldsmith and blacksmith, Camara Laye underwent schooling in French before moving on to studies in the capital, Conakry, and then Paris. His early life is thus in many ways typical of the experience of many young African intellectuals in that he was drawn increasingly away from the culture and traditions of his own family and people into the alien world of European culture and values. For Camara Laye, the conflicts of culture and identity which this experience seems to have engendered were apparently lived with particular poignancy, as his first novel, *L'Enfant noir*, indicates. Written while he was working in the Simca car factory near Paris and published in 1953, it is a largely autobiographical account of childhood experiences. The passage from childhood to adolescence and manhood is a journey which is paralleled in the novel by the journey from a traditional African world to a modern, Europeanized world in which old customs and practices can no longer have any real meaning. Hence, it is not only the boy who is developing into a man, it is also the society in which

he lives which is radically changing. By the time the protagonist leaves for Europe at the end of the novel, he has lost the sense of magic and mystery with which he viewed events in his early childhood. The plane which takes him to Paris is separating him from two equally fragile, equally mystical, and equally irrecuperable worlds: the emotional universe of his own childhood and the gentle, traditional world of pre-colonial Africa.

On publication, the novel was attacked by many, Mongo *Beti in particular, who refused to understand how a novel describing events taking place under colonial rule could avoid referring to the exploitation, the cruelty, and the daily injustices suffered by blacks under that system. Such criticism by politically committed writers indicates a failure to appreciate or accept the underlying motivation for all Camara Laye's work. For him the emphasis on the often mystical African experience of African cultural realities is essentially a question of sensibility. His project is to explore such experiences and not to use literature as a platform for socio-political purposes. Thus, the other-worldly quality which is present in his first novel heralds the symbolic and mythical tone of the second, *Le Regard du roi* (1954). The protagonist, Clarence, is a white man rejected by his own kind, whose quest is to enter the service of the king. The journey he undertakes has the qualities of a dream, peopled with mysterious characters and beset with strange adventures. It is also, for Clarence, a voyage of self-discovery.

Camara Laye returned to Guinea at its independence in 1958 but quickly grew disillusioned with the brutality of the regime. His third novel, *Dramouss* (1966), recounts some of the background to his subsequent departure into exile in Senegal, but it remains a disappointing work in comparison with the earlier novels.

In the latter years of his life, despite illness and exile from his native country, Camara Laye continued to work at collecting Malinké versions of great epics, interviewing and recording the accounts of *griots* throughout the region. Some of this work was published in 1978 as *Le Maître de la parole*. [MPC]

See A. King, *The Writings of Camara Laye* (1980).

Cambronne, le Mot de. The word euphemistically thus referred to, 'Merde!', is said to have been spoken by the Napeolonic general Cambronne, when called on by the English at Waterloo to surrender against overwhelming odds. The nobler version of his response is: 'La garde meurt et ne se rend pas.'

Camisards (word derived from the old Provençal *camisa*, a shirt). Protestant inhabitants of the Cévennes, who rebelled against the Revocation of the *Edict of Nantes. Attempts to suppress the eschatological Calvinism nurtured by male and female prophets led to the Guerre des Camisards (1702–4), sparked off by the assassination of abbé du Chayla at Pont-de-Montvert. There were probably never more than 1,500 Camisards under arms at any one time, but they mounted a highly effective guerrilla campaign, which took 25,000 royal troops to put down. Even by 1715 there was an irreducible heartland round Saint Hippolyte-du-Fort. There is little evidence that this was a conscious class war, but most of the combatants were peasants, artisans, or small tradesmen, and they had little upper-class leadership. Their memory is still celebrated locally, their writings and songs have been preserved, and their saga has become a symbol of resistance to persecution. [RBG]

CAMPISTRON, Jean-Galbert de (1656–1723). French playwright, would-be successor to *Racine, backed by the Vendôme circles of the *Temple. His tragedies, including *Alcibiade* (1685) and *Tiridate* (1691), are simple in construction, derivative in style and subject. 'Sur le Racine mort, le Campistron pullule', wrote *Hugo. [PF]

CAMUS, Albert (1913–60). Novelist, playwright, essayist. Camus was born and raised in a working-class European milieu in Algeria. His early intellectual promise was spotted by Jean *Grenier and he went on to pursue studies in philosophy that might have made of him a distinguished academic. However, the onset of tuberculosis at the age of 17 ruled out an academic career, and the disease was to dog him for the rest of his life. His first published writings were lyrical essays inspired by a passion for existence and an intense capacity for communion with nature, coupled with a sharp perception of life's fragility and bleakness. The title of the 1937 collection, *L'Envers et l'endroit*, highlights this dualistic conception of the human predicament which was to remain a constant throughout his work (see *L'Exil et le royaume*, 1957).

In the late 1930s he took a succession of menial jobs while developing various interests: political, involving brief membership of the Communist Party; theatrical, through the foundation of two companies for which he adapted, wrote, directed, and acted; journalistic, as a campaigning reporter on the radical newspapers *Alger républicain* and *Soir républicain*. He also completed his first novel, *La Mort heureuse* (published posthumously), and began work on his play *Caligula*, as well as the novel *L'*Étranger* and the philosophical essay *Le Mythe de Sisyphe*. When published in 1942, the latter two works established his reputation as the spokesman for a philosophy of the absurd. The essay begins by asking whether suicide is not a legitimate reaction to life's futility and analyses the components of the human condition, concluding that the absurd results from the incompatibility between, on the one hand, the indifferent natural universe and the incomprehensible circumstances of existence, and, on the other hand, man's desire for order and sense. Thus, an authentic response to the human lot requires that the individual maintain the tension between his or her needs and aspirations and the world's refusal to satisfy them. We are like Sisyphus condemned perpetually to push a boulder up a mountain, whence it will inevitably roll back down again: in the endless and ever-defeated effort to surmount this fate, we must, argues Camus, imagine Sisyphus happy and emulate his resilience. Meursault, the anti-hero of *L'Étranger*, leads a life which can be seen as a manifestation of this vision, and through his terse narrative became an icon for his alienated era.

As these works appeared, Camus had actually moved beyond what to him was only an initial premiss for the individual, and was more concerned with collective attitudes. Trapped in occupied France where he had gone for medical treatment in 1942 just before the Allied landings in North Africa, he worked for the Resistance newspaper *Combat while writing La *Peste*, his allegorical depiction of life under oppression. This novel demonstrates how the tension characterizing the absurd develops into resistance and revolt against a common lot in a movement of solidarity which has implications on the political as well as the metaphysical plane. The clandestine publication of the first of the *Lettres à un ami allemand* (1943) expressed something of the practical relevance of this theory of revolt which was the next stage in Camus's thought.

At the Liberation of France, Camus, as editor-in-chief of *Combat*, now a national newspaper, was a major figure in French intellectual life. Through his editorials he informed public opinion on the crucial issues of the day: the post-war purges of collaborators, the establishment of a new constitution and a new political regime in France, the beginnings of the Cold War (see *Ni victimes ni bourreaux*, 1946). He was linked with *Sartre as a leader of radical opinion, but took pains to distance himself from the latter's Existentialism, as his own notion of revolt presupposed moral values Sartre was bound to deny. The publication of *La Peste* in 1947 was a prelude to a cooling in their hitherto close relations; when *L'Homme révolté* (1951) was analysed in Sartre's review *Les *Temps modernes* it precipitated a bitter controversy which severed links definitively. In this essay tracing the origins and development of revolt, Camus had been concerned to show that Hegelian historical determinism constituted a perversion of the rebel's true aim and had inevitably opened the way to totalitarianism, both fascist and Marxist.

Moving towards a third stage in his philosophical evolution, Camus was beginning to direct his efforts towards defining an ideal of balance or measure: but in practice this brought him further wounding isolation and estrangement, as he was driven equally to denounce the abuses of Communism and to protest against Western hypocrisy, both in the workings of capitalism and in the failure to support the freedom being snuffed out in Eastern Europe. The mid- and late 1950s were particularly soured for Camus by the *Algerian War. Throughout his career he had castigated the injustice inherent in Algeria's political status within France; but his position exposed him to criticism from all sides as, unable to contemplate the transformation of his homeland into a country which was not French, he determined to refrain from public comment for fear of inflaming partisan passions. In 1958 a volume of his journalism, *Actuelles III* (following previous collections of 1950 and 1953), presented over 20 years' writings on the subject: it was met with virtual silence. His demoralization was exacerbated by personal difficulties and by doubts about his creative powers; but his artistic gifts were triumphantly vindicated in *La *Chute* (1956), which converted his own perceived shortcomings into a mirror sardonically turned on his contemporaries. Though his output as a playwright—*Le Malentendu* (1944), *Caligula* (1945), *L'État de siège* (1948), *Les Justes* (1949)—failed to match the impact of his other works, in the 1950s he was a much-respected theatre director and produced successful adaptations of other authors. Following the publication in 1957 of his short stories *L'Exil et le royaume*, he was awarded the Nobel Prize for Literature. He was working on a substantial new novel, *Le Premier Homme* (published 1994), when killed in a car accident.   [DHW]

See J. Cruickshank, *Albert Camus and the Literature of Revolt* (1960); H. Lottman, *Albert Camus* (1978); R. Grenier, *Albert Camus: soleil et ombre* (1987).

CAMUS, Jean-Pierre (c.1584–1652). A prolific spiritual writer and one of the first French bishops to espouse the ideals of the Council of Trent. Born in Paris, he became bishop of Belley in 1609. He owed this youthful preferment to his father's reputation as a loyalist supporter of *Henri IV: parts of the diocese had been transferred to the French crown from Savoy as recently as 1601. His close episcopal neighbour was *François de Sales, whose ardent disciple he became: the *Esprit du B. François de Sales* (1639–41) remains his best-known work. Under that influence, Camus resided in his diocese and preached tirelessly, publishing a dozen volumes of sermons. Their profusion of images and quotations, couched sometimes in note form, made them particularly apt as sources for other preachers, and they were constantly reprinted until his death. In 1621 he initiated with *Agathonphile* a series of over 30 spiritual romances. Earlier, between 1609 and 1618, he had published 37 books of *Diversités*, an immense, rambling compilation of essays after the manner of *Montaigne which display an impressive and bizarre range of reading. In 1640 he resigned his see and devoted his retirement to the work of the Hôtel des Incurables in Paris.   [PJB]

CAMUS, Renaud (b. 1946). French novelist and essayist. He is an outspoken supporter of gay rights; in his reflections on homosexuality, particularly *Notes achriennes* (1982), he evokes the relativity and subjectivity of sexual identity. His 'novels' began with experiments in polyphonic writing and collage

(e.g. *Passage*, 1975; *Été*, 1982), but moved towards more traditional narrative with the pseudo-historical novels *Roman roi* (1983) and *Roman furieux* (1986). His works do not, however, observe conventional generic boundaries, moving freely between autobiography, critical essay, and fiction.   [CFR]

Canada, French, see ACADIA; QUEBEC.

Canard, see PRESS, 1.

Canard enchaîné, Le. French satirical weekly founded in 1915; it is the greatest success this century in a long tradition of newspapers that mock authority and expose its failings. The *Canard* of 1915–16 was adapted from an anti-militarist tract of the troops in the trenches by Maurice Maréchal, who directed the paper until 1940. Independence personified—it carries no advertising—the *Canard* is a power in the land: it relates rumours, stories, and news, secreted in government, political, financial, and journalistic circles. Its record of exposing scandal and investigative journalism perhaps explains why the authorities, in the 1970s, placed hidden microphones in the *Canard's* new offices. Henri Jeanson, Morvan Lebesque, and André Ribaud, whose long-running pastiche 'La Cour' portrayed de *Gaulle as Louis XIV, *à la* *Saint-Simon, have graced its pages, as have many caricaturists.   [MP]

Candide, ou l'Optimisme (1759). Philosophical tale by *Voltaire. It bitterly satirizes the Optimism of *Leibniz and others because, placed in the hands of trusting adepts, this easily becomes a form of fatalism, schooling men to accept the human condition, whereas Voltaire's own experience suggested that man was better employed in reacting against his condition, however puny the end-result might be. With its controlled anger and its deliberate ironic distancing, his *conte* makes for painful, if amusing and instructive, reading.

Candide, a trusting young man, has been taught by his tutor Pangloss to believe that 'all is for the best in the best of all possible worlds'. Brutally expelled, at the end of Chapter 1, from the household at Thunder-ten-Tronckh, an 'earthly paradise' of calm and unquestioning Optimism, Candide wanders from Europe to the Americas and back again, now re-finding, now again losing sight of, the other members of the household, who are also discovering the real world which constantly and cruelly contradicts the Optimism of Pangloss.

Having for 30 chapters experienced every evil known to man, the little family (with several new members, including the bitter Manichean Martin) comes full cycle and is reunited, outside Constantinople, on a smallholding which proves, like Thunder-ten-Tronckh, to be another 'earthly paradise'. Now, however, it is one of calm and sceptical realism: Candide has learned that life in all its evil does not necessarily have to be accepted. He now knows that the ultimate wisdom requires like-minded people to pool their meagre resources in determined opposition to the hostility of the world. The book ends with his dismissal of Pangloss's unrepentant philosophizing: '"Cela est bien dit", répondit Candide, "mais il faut cultiver notre jardin."'

[JR]

Canon. The notion of a more-or-less official canon of French literature is a recent development. In earlier centuries the demands of the education system produced a relatively stable list of the essential Latin and Greek classics. Only in the 18th c., however, did French literature come to be seriously studied in schools and colleges, and one finds in the work of *Rollin, *Batteux, and other pedagogues of the time the beginnings of a national canon. Outside the schools, the *Academies, the *salons, the *press, and critics from *Boileau to *La Harpe contributed to establishing a hierarchy of French literature, but this remained flexible as long as it was not dominated by the education system.

It was in the 19th c., with the development of national programmes of education, that the literary canon began to take a more fixed shape. Throughout the 19th c. it was dominated by the *classical writers of the 'grand siècle' (the age of Louis XIV); only under the Third Republic did that other 'grand siècle' (the age of Enlightenment) come to occupy an equivalent position. Medieval literature was gradually introduced, at first from a philological standpoint [see MIDDLE AGES, 3], and space was found for the newly revalued writing of the Renaissance, even including the once-despised *Rabelais. In the early 19th c. the Romantics had been in revolt against the official hegemony of classicism; they too were fairly quickly taken up into the canon. In the 20th c. certain écrivains maudits (e.g. *Baudelaire, *Zola) were only grudgingly given the place they now occupy.

No doubt one can exaggerate the importance of school programmes for people's actual reading habits, but they represent a form of authority which seems to call for challenge and modification. Recent decades have seen many changes, including the following: the 'histoire des mentalités' suggested by the *Annales historians has given strength to the anti-élitist movement to extend the canon beyond the realms of high culture; much work has been done to revive the fortunes of neglected or ostracized movements and writers, from the *Rhétoriqueurs to the *précieuses, from the 17th-c. *libertins to *Sade; the forgotten work of female authors has begun to be properly explored [see WOMEN WRITERS]; the importance of writing in French outside France has been belatedly recognized. Issues such as these—and indeed the very existence of a canon—continue to be hotly debated both inside and outwith France (notably in the USA); further discussion of their relation to the present Companion will be found in the Introduction.

[PF]

Canso. Medieval Occitàn lyric genre (the word means 'chanson'). Early troubadours like *Guilhem IX and *Marcabru refer to their compositions indiscriminately as vers, but from about 1150 *troubadours distinguish between cansos, *sirventes, and other genres. Approximately half of the extant corpus of troubadour lyrics are cansos. Originally set to music, cansos are devoted exclusively to singing about *fin'amor. They are generally composed of between four and eight stanzas (coblas) of the same length and form and one or more shorter stanzas which replicate a part of the form of the other stanzas (envois or tornadas). Though some cansos have relatively straightforward rhyme-schemes, some are metrically extremely complex. A common metaphor in cansos equates the quality of a troubadour's love with the quality of his poetry, and troubadours like *Arnaut Daniel took pride in inventing demanding metrical forms which show off their technical skills. Cansos are often densely metaphorical and highly conventional, giving them an abstract flavour to the modern reader; they rarely reveal the identity of the lady to whom they are ostensibly addressed. The canso was clearly a very popular form throughout Europe; the Occitan genre certainly had a profound influence on the love poetry of the Northern French trouvères, on the German Minnesingers, and on Italian poets like Dante and Petrarch.

[SG]

Canso de la crotzada. This Occitan song recounting the Albigensian Crusade (1209–29), waged ostensibly against *Catharism, is an incomplete epic poem of 9,582 lines, the work of two authors. The first third, covering the period 1204–July 1213, is by a Navarrese priest residing in Montauban, Guilhem de Tudela, who condemns heresy but also brutality on either side. The remainder, an anonymous continuation to June 1219 begun the previous year, while upholding orthodoxy, expresses attachment to the southern cause and the future Count Raymond VII of Toulouse. Though factually accurate, the account shows selective bias.

[PVD]

Cantatrice chauve, La, see IONESCO.

Canuts. Name given to the Lyon silk-workers, who rose against their masters in 1831 and 1834 and were harshly put down. They are the subject of one of the great French popular songs, 'C'est nous les Canuts'.

Capetians. The Capetian dynasty ruled France from 987 to 1328, with remarkably few succession disputes and inter-family rivalries throughout the period. From unimpressive beginnings it slowly built up the royal demesne and consolidated royal power, especially in the legal and ideological spheres, until the French crown became pre-eminent in Europe. The most famous rulers of the line were Philippe II (*Philippe-Auguste) (1180–1223), who annexed much of the Angevin empire, Louis

IX (1226–70), whose justice aroused such admiration that he was subsequently canonized as Saint Louis, and Philippe IV (1285–1314), who imposed his will upon Pope Boniface VIII. Although the direct line ended in 1328, the *Valois and *Bourbons were branches of the dynasty, and *Louis XVI was tried for his life under the name of 'Louis Capet'. [JHD]

Capitaine Fracasse, Le, see GAUTIER.

Capitale de la douleur, see ÉLUARD.

Caprices de Marianne, Les. Bitter comedy by *Musset, published 1833, first performed 1851. It is set in Naples. The ingenuous Celio is caught up in an intrigue between the cynical Octave and Marianne, the wife of Claudio. Loving Marianne himself, he goes in Octave's place to a rendezvous with her and is killed on the orders of her husband. *Renoir's film *La Règle du jeu* is based on Musset's play. [PF]

Caquets de l'accouchée, Les. Eight short satirical 16th-c. *recueils*, not published as a single volume until 1623. The fiction of pregnant women gossiping provides an amusing account of everyday life, 'où se voient les mœurs, actions et façons de faire de ce siècle'. [JJS]

Caractères, Les, see LA BRUYÈRE.

CARCO, Francis (pseud. of François Carcopino-Tusoli) (1886–1958). Born in New Caledonia , Carco was a *Fantaisiste poet, dramatist, art critic, and biographer, but is remembered particularly as a novelist. Bohemian *Montmartre on the eve of World War I furnished the stimulus for his career, and the underworld of Pigalle the subject of a sequence of novels, which Carco prolonged into the inter-war period in spite of the increasingly nostalgic and historical interest of his subject. *Jésus-la-Caille* (1914), *L'Homme traqué* (1922), and *Brumes* (1935) represent well Carco's fascination with the criminal mind and the exotic appeal of the language, character, and haunts of those who peopled the Parisian underworld. [AHB]

CARDINAL, Marie (b. 1929). Born in Algeria, Cardinal is the author of over a dozen best-selling texts, many of autobiographical inspiration, in which the problems of the couple, of motherhood, and of writing dominate. She is best known for *Les Mots pour le dire* (1975), a novel fictionalizing her long, painful, but ultimately successful psychoanalysis. *Autrement dit* (1977) follows up some of the issues raised by her experience, and situates it more firmly in a feminist perspective. *Au pays de mes racines* (1980) explores her feelings about her native Algeria; *Les Grands Désordres* (1987) deals with the problems of heroin addiction within the framework of a mother–daughter relationship. [EAF]

CARÊME, Marie-Antoine (known as Antonin) (1784–1833). Celebrated cook who worked for *Napoleon, *Talleyrand, and various European monarchs. He wrote several classic works on cooking, including *Le Cuisinier français* (1833).

Caribbean, see WEST INDIES.

'Carmagnole, La'. Famous Revolutionary dancing song, apparently composed in 1792; it exists in many versions. The *carmagnole* was a coat or costume worn by the *fédérés*.

Carmelites. Monastic order founded on Mount Carmel in the 12th c. It became an important mendicant order in medieval Europe. The reforms of St Teresa, introducing greater austerity, led to the formation of a separate order, the Discalced Carmelites (Carmes Déchaussés), who wore sandals rather than shoes and stockings. This reformed order was introduced to France in 1604 by *Bérulle and Madame Acarie. The Carmelites occupied a significant place in *ancien régime* society. [PF]

Carmen. (1847). The most famous tale by *Mérimée, in part because of *Bizet's somewhat sweetened opera version (libretto by *Meilhac and Halévy). The narrator, an archaeologist similar to Mérimée but criticized by the text for his incomprehension, encounters and befriends Don José, a soldier turned bandit who is under sentence of death. José recounts his passion for the gypsy Carmen who led him into a life of crime, robbery, and murder, all the while betraying him with other men, at times for venal reasons, finally out of love for the picador Lucas. José murders her, motivated by despair rather than rage. In an economic but intense style, Mérimée explores the relationship between passion, crime, and death. Primitive passions in crude form are presented as both admirable and disastrous in their results. The emotional impact is controlled by the narrator's erudite if impersonal observations, including a final chapter on the history, customs, and language of the gypsies. [FPB]

CARMONTELLE (pseud. of Louis Carrogis) (1717–1806). French portraitist, architect, and playwright, he published two collections of comedies, the *Théâtre du prince Clenerzow* (1771) and the *Théâtre de campagne* (1775), as well as works on painting. He is chiefly remembered for his *proverbes dramatiques*, of which he published over a hundred between 1768 and 1781. The accurate observation of the speech and manners of the wide range of ordinary people who figure in the proverbs has given them a recognized documentary value. [JD]

CARNÉ, Marcel (b. 1909). The French director with whom 'poetic realism' in the cinema is always associated. His collaboration with *Prévert is famous for the mordant fatalism of *Quai des brumes* (1938) and *Le Jour se lève* (1939), both starring Jean *Gabin and often seen as mirroring the disillusionment of the post-*Popular Front years. *Les Enfants du paradis* (1945), a theatre drama of the 1830s starring *Arletty and *Barrault, was for generations of British cinema-goers the definitive 'Continental film'. Carné's post-war work, without the collaboration of Prévert, does not stand comparison with the earlier films: to quote the Larousse *Dictionnaire du cinéma*: 'finis le manichéisme, l'amour fou, le destin.' [KAR]

Carolingians. Dynasty founded in 751 when Pépin le Bref, *Maire du Palais of Austrasia, obtained papal approval for his coronation at the expense of the last *Merovingian ruler. Members of Pépin's family ruled in East Francia until 911, and (with inter-ruptions) in West Francia until 987. After the brilliance of Pépin's and *Charlemagne's reigns, their successors had to face division of their empire, declining resources, internal strife between broth-ers, and invasions from Vikings, Saracens, and Magyars. But despite their weakening political grip, the Carolingians patronized learning, reformed the Church, and continued to evoke loyalty from their people. [JHD]

CARON, Louis (b. 1942). Canadian novelist whose major concern is with the theme of French-Canadian identity as it has been transmitted through history. In *L'Emmitouflé* (1977), the story of a draft-dodger in Quebec in 1917 is connected to the conscientious objection of his Franco-American nephew to the Vietnam War, 50 years later. The three-volume saga of *Les Fils de la liberté* (1981–90) follows the fortunes of the Bellerose family from the Patriote rebellion of 1837 to the October crisis of 1970. While the intertwining of individual and col-lective destiny is more powerfully achieved in the first two volumes than in the contemporary third part, Caron remains the finest exponent of the typi-cal Quebec genre of the family saga. He has also written a charming novel of childhood, *Le Bonhomme sept-heures* (1978). [SIL]

CARRÈRE, Emmanuel (b. 1957). French novelist. In *La Moustache* (1986) the hero, having shaved off his moustache, discovers that, according to his wife and friends, he had never had one. Reality begins to col-lapse around him. Both the realist interpretation (that he goes mad, killing himself at the end for Freudian reasons) and the modernist reading (that this is a debunking of fictional realism) are too banal. In fact, the novel treats the interplay between subjectivity, the beliefs of others, and reality, and toys with the notion of alternative universes (see his essay *Le Détroit de Behring*, 1986). [GDM]

CARRIER, Roch (b. 1937). Canadian novelist. A native of rural Quebec, he studied in Montreal and Paris and taught literature before becoming a full-time writer. As well as novels, he has published col-lections of short stories including *Joli deuils* (1964) and *Les Enfants du bonhomme dans la lune* (1979), and plays, including *La Céleste Bicyclette* (1980). A natural story-teller, writing with an attractive verve and simplicity, he has been one of the most widely read *québécois* writers in English Canada.

He is best known for his early 'trilogie de l'âge sombre', in particular *La Guerre, yes sir!* (1968). This shows the impact of the 'English' World War II on a Brueghelian rural Quebec; the realities of oppres-sion are there, but presented in a grotesque light. *Floralie, où es-tu?* (1969) is the dream-like transposi-tion of a troubled wedding night, while the final part of the trilogy, *Il est par là, le soleil* (1970), is the nightmarish depiction of a country boy's degrada-tion in Montreal.

Carrier's subsequent six novels continue to offer a fantastic refraction of Quebec life. One of the most interesting is *Il n'y a pas de pays sans grand-père* (1979), made up of the thoughts of an old man who asserts the continuity of Quebec culture in solidarity with his grandson, in prison for anti-monarchist protests. *La Dame qui avait des chaînes aux chevilles* (1981), another interior monologue, is the dramatic story of a 19th-c. heroine who attempts to poison her hus-band for abandoning their child in the snow. Carrier's most ambitious work to date is *De l'amour dans la ferraille* (1984), a leisurely satirical panorama of village life and politics. Since then he has pub-lished two books combining story-telling and travel writing, about Australia (*L'Ours et le kangourou*, 1986) and Jordan (*Chameau en Jordanie*, 1988). [PF]

Carte de Tendre, La, see TENDRE.

Carte d'identite, La, see ADIAFFI.

Cartel, Le. Name of a loose association formed in 1927 of four Paris theatres run by *Jouvet, *Baty, *Dullin, and the *Pitoëffs. They published a mani-festo expressing a common policy of resisting crude commercialism and improving the quality of theatre production. Their influence was dominant through-out the 1930s [see THEATRES AND AUDIENCES, 2.] [DHW]

Cartesian, Cartesianism, see DESCARTES.

CARTIER, Jacques (1491–1557), see COLONIZATION; QUEBEC, I.

CARTOUCHE, Louis-Dominique (1693–1721). Like *Mandrin, a hero of French popular legend, whose exploits are recounted in plays, songs, and stories. The leader of a spectacularly daring band of rob-bers, reputed to have had dealings with the Regent, he was broken on the wheel, and met his death with a courage that was much admired. [PF]

CASANOVA de Seingalt, Giacomo (1725–98). Italian memorialist. Though not the polymath he claimed to be, Casanova was gifted and well-informed. He travelled widely, often moving on because he was expelled for some shady transaction. Many of his works, including a translation of the *Iliad* (1775–8), were in Italian. His major writings in French are a Utopian novel, *Icosameron* (1788), and the celebrated *Mémoires* first published in German in 1822, then in a bowdlerized French edition in 1826, but only available in complete form since 1960–2. This lively picture of 18th-c. mores, once thought to be more fiction than fact, is now held to rely on exaggeration rather than sheer invention. Casanova's reputation as an indefatigable womanizer has given him a quasi-mythical status comparable to Don Juan.   [VGM]

Cassandre, see LA CALPRENÈDE.

CASSOU, Jean (1897–1986). Eminent art historian and director of the Musée de l'Art Moderne, Paris. A native of the Spanish Basque Country, he also translated many texts from the Spanish, and is a novelist whose elusive fictions (e.g. *Les Inconnus dans la cave*, 1933) are marked by a discreet Romanticism and a protest against modern alienation. A non-Stalinist Communist, he took a heroic part in the Resistance and when imprisoned in 1941–2 wrote his beautiful *Trente-trois sonnets composés au secret*, published under the pseudonym Jean Noir in 1944.   [PF]

Castelain de Couci, Le Roman du, see CHASTELAIN DE COUCI.

CASTELLOZA (*fl.* first half of 13th c.). *Trobairitz*, author of four surviving love songs, all expressive of bitter misery and powerlessness.

CASTIGLIONE, Baldassare (1478–1529), see COURTOISIE.

CASTORIADIS, Cornélius (b. 1922). Political philosopher. Born in Greece, he came to Paris in 1945 and pursued first a career as an economist with the OECD, publishing his political analyses under various pseudonyms. With Claude Lefort, he founded the influential review *Socialisme et barbarie* (1948–65), which offered critiques of Soviet *Marxism, especially of the bureaucracy it engendered. Turning away from Marxist and Hegelian thought towards *psychoanalysis, he developed a prophetic conception of revolution based on the mobilization of radical imagination.   [MHK]

Cateau-Cambrésis, Treaty of (1559). This treaty signalled the acceptance by *Henri II that, following the disastrous defeat of Saint-Quentin (1558), France was no longer in a position to challenge Spain for the domination of the Italian peninsula. Henri gained Metz, Toul, and Verdun, but had to cede Savoy and Piedmont. Anxious to counter the spread of Protestantism at home and to cement a new alliance with the Habsburgs, Henri arranged the marriage of his sister, Elizabeth, with Philip II of Spain. Franco-Spanish rivalry was, however, to remain as intense as ever.   [JJS]

Cathars. The Cathars—or Albigensians, as their southern French adherents were called—were dual-

ists, believing that the world is dominated by the opposing principles of Good and Evil. They owed their theology to the Bogomils of the Byzantine empire, who had long preserved Manichean traditions and whose disciples spread the word in the second half of the 12th c. in Flanders, the Rhineland, France, and Lombardy, wherever anticlericalism had created fertile soil. Two schools of theologians, the mitigated and the absolute dualists, contended for supremacy among believers.

But the appeal of Catharism in southern France lay less in its theology than in the ethical values it taught, and in the way of life of the *perfecti*, the élite of the sect. These men abandoned family and home, embraced the life of apostolic poverty, foreswore sexual relations and meat-eating, rejected oath-taking (that necessary element in medieval social life), and concentrated on ministering in the vernacular to their adherents and on developing a ritual for their Church. They exercised so strong a hold on their followers' imaginations that Catholics were forced into imitating them; the *Dominican order of friars was designed to promote a similar life-style combined with rigid orthodoxy. The *credentes*, those who accepted the authority of the *perfecti* but did not aspire to their standards, undertook to accept the *consolamentum*, the sacrament of heretication, on their deathbeds. Otherwise few rules were imposed upon them. Many castellans and lesser aristocrats of southern Languedoc in the 12th and early 13th c. united resentment of the Catholic clergy's moral claims with affection for a heretical ministry that required no tithes for its maintenance. Their female relations were attracted by the Cathar nunneries, and perhaps also by the less blatantly sexist character of the heretics' ecclesiology.

Pope Innocent III saw in these supporters the primary danger to Christianity. In 1208 he launched the Albigensian Crusade [see CANSO DE LA CROTZADA] against them, which embittered all southerners, whether heretic or not, against the predominantly northern crusaders. Though Catharism survived the crusade, it then suffered from the Inquisition, instituted by Pope Gregory IX in 1231. The usual penalty for support of the *perfecti*, forfeiture of land, slowly forced the southern aristocracy back into the clutches of the Catholic Church, and Catharism became an underground movement, increasingly found only in the Pyrenean villages beyond the Inquisitors' reach. After Jacques Fournier's inquest (1318–25) into the heretics of Montaillou [see LE ROY LADURIE] and its surroundings, no more was heard of it.   [JHD]

See C. Thousellier, *Catharisme et valdéisme en Languedoc*, 2nd edn. (1969); R. Lafont *et al.*, *Les Cathares en Occitanie* (1982).

Cathédrale, La, see HUYSMANS.

CATHERINE II, Empress of Russia, see DIDEROT; RUSSIA AND FRANCE.

CATHERINE DE MÉDICIS (1519–89). Daughter of Lorenzo II de' Medici, duke of Urbino, and cousin to Pope Clement II. She was chosen as bride for the future *Henri II as part of *François Ier's Italian policy. She allowed the *Guise brothers to dominate François II, but came into her own when named regent on the accession of *Charles IX, only losing her ascendancy towards the end of the reign of *Henri III. She was much hated by the Protestants because of her responsibility in the *St Bartholomew's Day Massacre, but did much to ensure the survival of the French monarchy during a period when it was so nearly eclipsed by the rival factions in the *Wars of Religion.   [JJS]

Catholicism in 20th-Century France. [The earlier history of the Catholic Church in France is covered in a number of entries, in particular CONCORDAT, CLERGY, DEVOTIONAL WRITING, GALLICANISM, HERESIES, JANSENISM, ULTRAMONTISM, and entries on the principal religious writers.]

In the aftermath of the *Dreyfus Affair, relations between Church and State turned on the bitter conflict between the idea of the French Republic [see REPUBLICANISM] and the public (i.e. clerical) authority of the Church. The radical *anticlerical Émile Combes broke the grip of the Church on education, and the law separating Church and State, unilaterally rejecting the *Concordat, was approved in 1905. Intended and perceived as a defeat for the Church, the Separation was almost certainly beneficial: while leaving the Church materially weakened, it removed state interference and effectively encouraged concentration on spiritual and moral matters. The disadvantages of Church association with the state were illustrated briefly under the Vichy regime [see OCCUPATION AND RESISTANCE], by which time, however, the patriotism and indeed republicanism of individual Catholics, manifest already during World War I and recognized implicitly in the canonization of *Jeanne d'Arc, were scarcely in doubt; and during the century, while anticlericalism—not confined to opponents of the Church—remained deep-seated, conflict between Church and Republic ceased generally to arouse great passion, being largely superseded by conflict within the Church, sometimes with political overtones.

Although the association of Catholicism with monarchism and political authoritarianism, as seen in Maurras's *Action Française, dies hard, the Church also witnessed efforts to foster democratic republican and socialist policies, including Sangnier's *Sillon movement, condemned by Pius X in 1910, which attracted the interest of François *Mauriac and prefigured the establishment of the Mouvement Républicain Populaire (MRP) after World War II, the development of Catholic youth movements and Catholic action groups, and the 'worker-priest' experiments initiated in the 1950s. In response to dechristianization, the liberalizing policies of the Second Vatican Council (1962–5), empha-

sizing collegiality, social conscience, and religious tolerance, appeared to reinforce the spiritual intentions of such developments. However, in the confusion following the Council, conflict between traditional authoritarianism and the claims of individual conscience caused renewed tensions within the Church, both in liturgical reform and, for example, in relation to priestly celibacy and moral questions of birth control and contraception. A traditionalist counter-reaction, often known as *intégriste* and sustained notably by Marcel Lefebvre, the ardent anti-Communist archbishop of Dakar and bishop of Tulle, confronted the Vatican and the French hierarchy. In 1972 he established a rebel traditionalist seminary at Écône in Switzerland; he was suspended from official functions in 1976, and his differences with the Vatican remained unresolved, risking schism. At the same time, to the dismay of liberal Catholic intellectuals, the Church tended in the 1970s and 1980s to encourage clerical obedience and traditional moral theology by the appointment of conservative bishops.

Before and after the Separation, a Catholic revival, with associated triumphalism, had seen a series of spectacular conversions, including those of *Claudel, *Péguy, *Maritain, and *Rivière. The 'revival' itself, following the authoritarian reaffirmations of the First Vatican Council (1869–70), had contributed to the decline of *Gallicanism: in response to the scepticism generated by scientific and scholarly rationalism and to virulent political anti-Catholicism, it was in many ways a reversion to intransigent *Ultramontane traditionalism, and found expression in a Catholic literary revival, as seen for instance in writers such as *Bourget and *Huysmans. However, in the most prominent Catholic novelists of the 20th c., *Bernanos and Mauriac, spiritual conviction was accompanied by deep scepticism concerning the Church's exercise of temporal power and by a degree of anticlericalism. Frequently regarded as 'Catholic novelists', they distanced themselves from the misleading idea of the 'Catholic novel'. In the late 20th c., with the waning of triumphalism and the challenges of pluralism, anti-ideological writers such as Jean *Sulivan, who take Catholic themes and attitudes as their subject-matter, tend to regard themselves not as 'Catholic writers' but as writers 'who are also Catholics'.

[BCS]

See A. Latreille and R. Rémond (eds.), *Histoire du Catholicisme en France* (1962); J. Duquesne, *Les Catholiques français sous l'Occupation* (1966); R. Griffiths, *The Reactionary Revolution: The Catholic Revival in France (1870–1914)* (1966); R. Etchegaray and F. Marty (eds.), *France, que fais-tu de ton baptême?* (1980).

CAU, Jean (1925–93). French novelist, journalist, and essayist who was *Sartre's secretary from 1947 to 1956. His essays on the political and moral decline of the century are typified by *Réflexions dures pour une* *époque molle* (1981); his memoirs include *Croquis de mémoire*, evoking Sartre. Among his novels, *Pitié de Dieu* (1961) won the Prix Goncourt.   [EAF]

CAUMONT DE LA FORCE, see LA FORCE.

Causeries du lundi, see SAINTE-BEUVE.

CAUSSADE, Jean-Pierre de, see DEVOTIONAL WRITING, 3.

CAUSSIN, Nicolas, père (1583–1651). French Jesuit father and royal confessor, author of an important Latin treatise on rhetoric (adapted for the lay public as *La Cour sainte*, 1624) and of Latin tragedies.

CAVANNA, François (b. 1923). Humorist and polemicist (*Coups de sang*, 1991). Cavanna recounts his childhood among Italian immigrants in *Les Ritals* (1978), wartime forced labour in *Les Russkoffs* (1979), beginnings as a cartoonist and journalist in *Bête et méchant* (1981), disenchantment in *Les Yeux plus grands que le ventre* (1983). In his novels, *Les Fosses carolines* (1986), *La Couronne d'Irène* (1988), as in his other work, he uses the direct style pioneered in the journals *Hara-Kiri* and **Charlie-Hebdo*, copying the cadences and vocabulary of spoken French, and feigning dialogue with the reader. A prototypical autodidact, he is a defender of the French language: *Mignonne, allons voir si la rose . . .* (1989).   [SFN]

Caveau, Le. Literary club or cabaret founded in 1729 by *Piron, *Crébillon *père*, and others; it continued to flourish, with interruptions and changes of name, well into the 19th c., when *Béranger's songs were sung there.

Caves du Vatican, Les. Novel by *Gide, published 1914; Gide called it a **sotie*. Its central idea derives from real events: in the 1890s a band of confidence tricksters exploited the rumour that the Pope had been kidnapped and replaced by an impostor as a means of extracting money from gullible believers. The resulting crusade to rescue the pontiff draws in a cast of characters of various satirico-comic dimensions: the unworldly Amédée Fleurissoire, ineffectual hero and victim; the scientist and free-thinker Anthime Armand-Dubois, subject of a mock-miraculous conversion; the arch-respectable novelist Julius de Baraglioul, toying feverishly with the notion of the gratuitous act (**acte gratuit*) as the subject of his next work. Most notorious of all is Lafcadio Wluiki, a free spirit in search of adventure, who pours scorn on convention and commits a gratuitous act by pushing Fleurissoire to his death from a moving train. Labelled a *sotie* by the author to signal that he did not consider it a true novel, the work's multiple ironies set up complex debates around the notions of freedom and determinism, reality and belief, chance and intention. With its intrusive narrator, its novelist-within-the-novel, and its challenges to narrative convention, the text is a prime example of self-conscious fiction.   [DHW]

CAYLUS, Claude-Philippe de Tubières, comte de (1692–1765). An aristocratic French archaeologist, draughtsman, and collector, Caylus wrote his *Recueil d'antiquités égyptiennes, étrusques, grecques, romaines et gauloises* (1752–67) on his return to Paris from a study tour of Italy and Greece. As an Academician he helped to re-establish the standards of classical art, in particular the central role of drawing, in the training of an artist. He read his *Vie de Watteau* to the Academy in 1748. Our knowledge of 18th-c. Parisian life owes a great deal to his lively accounts, such as the *Vies d'artistes du XVIIIe siècle* (ed. A. Fontaine, 1910). He also wrote a variety of playful and **libertin* literary texts (*Œuvres badines complètes*, 1787).   [JPC]

CAYROL, Jean (b. 1911). Writer from Bordeaux whose early poetic talent was seen in two books published in *Les Cahiers du Sud*: *Le Hollandais volant* (1936) and *Les Phénomènes célestes* (1939). His long poems of mythical and biblical figures, upheavals of the cosmos, loneliness, revolt, destruction, and resurgence, culminate in the prophetic *Le Dernier Homme (Adam)* (1940).

Cayrol's participation in the Resistance, his capture, and time spent in the Mauthausen concentration camp under the severe *Nacht und Nebel (nuit et brouillard)* regime changed his career and literary output. His poems, *Miroir de la rédemption* (1943), were smuggled out of prison and published by *Béguin. Emerging from the descent into hell, he produced *Poèmes de la nuit et du brouillard* (1945). The 40 or so books he has written since the war—novels (*Je vivrai l'amour des autres*, 1947, Prix Renaudot), essays, poetry, films (*Nuit et brouillard*, 1956, produced with *Resnais and probably the best film about the camps, and *Muriel*, 1963, also with Resnais)—are all variations on the themes of disintegration, reintegration into society, personal relationships, sincerity with the self, and the portrayal of man at 'l'état zéro'. The two essays in *Lazare parmi nous* (1950) discuss the possibility of a literature born of the concentration camp in a world that is still 'un univers concentrationnaire'. For Cayrol, using language is life, a proof of existence: *Les Mots sont aussi des demeures* (1959). He received the Grand Prix de Poésie in 1984 and has recently published a cycle of poems: *A voix haute* (1990), *De vive voix* (1991), *A pleine voix* (1992).   [ET]

CAZALIS, Henri (1840–1909). Now remembered almost solely as one of *Mallarmé's closest friends and his most important correspondent during the 1860s, Cazalis was a *Parnassian poet of some stature during the final third of the 19th c. (*Vita Tristis*, 1865; *Melancholia*, 1868; *L'Illusion*, 1875). In addition to medical articles (he was a doctor by profession), he published widely on European and oriental literatures. In his poetry and criticism, his literary, philosophical, and scientific interests combine to create a pessimistic but stoic humanitarianism characteristic of the Parnassian generation to which he belonged. [JK]

CAZOTTE, Jacques (1719–92). French writer, most of whose varied literary output involves the *merveilleux* and/or the occult. He is chiefly remembered for *Le Diable amoureux* (1772), the first significant example of the *conte fantastique* [see FANTASTIC]. In this case, unlike his previous fiction, the supernatural elements are not rationally explicable. Having fallen in love with Biondetta, the female form assumed by the Devil, the hero eventually manages to resist 'her' temptations. The story illustrates Cazotte's anti-rationalist beliefs (he was later a follower, briefly, of *Saint-Martin's Illuminist movement). He also opposed the Revolution, seeing it as a manifestation of Evil, an attitude which led to his execution. [VGM]

CÉARD, Henry (1851–1924). French novelist, short-story writer, journalist, and critic. He is most closely associated with *Naturalism and was the author of *Une belle journée* (1881), usually considered to be a model Naturalist novel, a work of considerable technical achievement in the manner of the banal anti-novel that owes more to *Flaubert and his ideal of the 'book about nothing' than it does to *Zola. His other works include his contribution to *Les *Soirées de Médan*, a second novel, *Terrains à vendre au bord de la mer* (1906), a number of short stories, some fine critical articles, and his unsuccessful theatrical ventures. He was known for his keen intelligence and profound pessimism. [DB]

Célibataires, Les. This *Montherlant novel (1934) depicts the inexorable decline of two ruined members of the provincial nobility, Élie de Coëtquidan and Léon de Coantré, and the many problems they have in coping with the modern world. On the one hand, it is a critique of the contemporary society to which Montherlant had returned after the war; on the other, it is a sympathetic depiction of two individuals who fail to adapt to circumstances, and of a class which, despite its many virtues, seems doomed to failure and neglect. From their refusal to bow to change, the heroes may seem to prefigure the heroes of Montherlant's later drama; but their obstinacy is in no way heroic, and their solitude arouses pity rather than admiration in the reader. The last words of Léon de Coantré, begging his cook Mélanie not to leave him, as he does not wish to die alone, sum up the pessimistic mood of the novel. While not as adventurous technically as *Les *Jeunes Filles*, which immediately succeeded it, *Les Célibataires* is nevertheless a very powerful novel, which revealed to the public the presence of a brilliant new novelist. [RMG]

Célimène. Principal female character in Molière's *Le *Misanthrope*, the flighty object of Alceste's love.

CÉLINE, Louis-Ferdinand (pseud. of Louis Ferdinand Destouches) (1894–1961). For the last part of his life and in the early years following his death, Céline's reputation was overshadowed by the public's perception of him as a collaborator, a fascist, and an antisemite. Similarly, as a novelist, because of his exploitation of spoken French and his establishment of a narrator bearing considerable similarities to the author, he was long regarded both as an extreme example of the survival of *Naturalism in fiction and, at best, as an inspired primitive using his novels to convey a bleak moral message. Gradually it has become possible, however, to see the style and the narrative persona as careful contrivances and to see both Céline's fiction and non-fiction as complex and ambiguous, consciously operating within the framework of French modernism.

He was born in Courbevoie, that Parisian industrial suburban heartland which remains at the centre of his work, the son of an insurance clerk and a shopkeeper specializing in lace and antiques. Shortly after, the family moved to the Passage Choiseul in the 2nd *arrondissement* of Paris, the traditional centre of the Parisian *petite bourgeoisie* beginning to decline with the dawn of the new technological century. After attempts at various artisanal trades, with no conspicuous success, Céline joined the cavalry in 1913 and saw service in the first months of World War I, being wounded and decorated for gallantry. After travelling in England and French West Africa, he belatedly began medical studies in Rennes and finally qualified as a doctor in 1924, with a thesis on *La Vie et l'œuvre de Philippe-Ignace Semmelweis*, a work which announces much of his later fiction and non-fiction. After a period in Geneva as a medical official for the League of Nations, during which he briefly visited the Ford factory at Detroit, he settled as a doctor in Paris in 1928, first in private practice and then in the municipal clinic in the industrial suburb of Clichy. At this time he wrote two plays, to be published later, *L'Église* (1933) and *Progrès* (1978), a number of medical polemics on the subject of hygiene and social medicine, and began his first novel, *Voyage au bout de la nuit*.

The publication of this novel in 1932 and the award of the Prix Renaudot established Céline as a major author instantly. Its depiction of a picaresque journey through World War I, the colonies, America, and the industrial suburbs, conveyed a philosophical and social pessimism which attracted Left and Right alike. The publication of his second novel, *Mort à crédit*, in 1936, alienated much of this support, on account of the bleakness of its depiction of the family, its stylistic lack of compromise, and its calculated obscenity. This alienation was compounded, in so far as the Left was concerned, by his denunciation of Soviet Russia, following a journey there, in *Mea culpa* (1936), and by the publication of a violent antisemitic pamphlet, *Bagatelles pour un massacre* (1937). This was followed by two further pamphlets, *L'École des cadavres* (1938) and *Les Beaux Draps* (1941). Whilst their antisemitic content undoubtedly situated Céline on the extreme Right, the ambiguity

Cénacle

and complexity of the pamphlets were barely perceived. In fact, they manipulate consciously an entire tradition of polemic, from Swift and Defoe to *Bloy and *Bernanos, and contrive to parody conventional antisemitic polemic whilst conveying a more insidious form of antisemitism. It is likely that their stylistic virtuosity provided a release from the block in which Céline found himself with his third novel, *Casse-pipe* (1949).

During the *Occupation, he frequented collaborationist circles without becoming heavily implicated, and concentrated on a two-novel evocation of London during World War I, *Guignol's Band I* (1944) and *Guignol's Band II* (1964), in which the stylistic experimentation of *Mort à crédit* and the pamphlets is continued to create a consciously Shakespearian atmosphere. In 1944 he left France with the Vichy government for Sigmaringen and from there fled to Denmark, where he was interned pending extradition by the Liberation authorities. In spite of French attempts, he was not returned to France and remained under house arrest in considerable hardship until he was finally allowed back in 1951, settling in his last house in the suburb of Meudon.

The last ten years of Céline's life were his most productive. A further two-novel cycle, *Féerie pour une autre fois I* (1952) and *Féerie pour une autre fois II: Normance* (1954), weaves a complex operatic fantasy around Montmartre Bohemia and the bombing of the Butte in 1944. The *Entretiens avec le professeur Y* (1955) constitute his major *art poétique*, emphasizing the necessity of 'la petite musique' to his style, the directness of which he defines as a 'metro émotif'. Finally, the trilogy evoking his experiences in Germany at the end of the war, *D'un château l'autre* (1957), *Nord* (1960), and *Rigodon* (1969), is a culmination of his fictional experimentation.

Early critics of Céline identified his originality in the bleakness of his moral vision. In fact, it lies both in the precision and complexity of that vision itself and in the stylistic and textual sophistication with which the vision is conveyed. Céline's general despair at humanity is forged from a precise awareness of social and economic processes which have cut him and his class off from their past. The psychological tension generated by such a loss is the basis both for Céline's pessimism and for the linguistic form in which it is couched. His language, which consciously, like that of *Queneau, attempts to reinvigorate literature with the vibrancy of spoken French, is a careful compound of popular French and varying layers of *argot, given a jazz-like musicality through the use of exclamations separated by three dots. Similarly, the Célinian text is not the direct reflection of a moral or social reality which it was once thought to be, but the product of layer upon layer of cultural and literary references, of which *Proust is one of the most important. In this perspective, Céline stands as one of the foremost French modernist novelists. [NH]

See F. Vitoux, *Céline* (1978); H. Godard, *Poétique de Céline* (1985); I. Noble, *Language and Narration in Céline's Novels* (1986); N. Hewitt, *The Golden Age of Louis-Ferdinand Céline* (1987).

Cénacle. Name given to groups of *Romantic poets and writers; the most famous of these met during the Restoration in *Nodier's salon at the Arsenal and at *Hugo's house in the rue Notre-Dame-des-Champs. In the early 1830s a group of Hugo's younger admirers formed the *Petit Cénacle. See Balzac's *Illusions perdues* for the picture of a *cénacle*.

CENDRARS, Blaise (pseud. of Frédéric Sauser) (1887–1961). Born in Switzerland to a father of French anabaptist origins and a Scottish mother, Cendrars led a life of wandering and adventure which was the basis of much of his writing in verse and prose. His *Vol à voiles* (1932) was long taken as a source for information about his early life, but Cendrars himself spoke of it as a 'divertissement', and like most things that he wrote or said about himself (and others) it is better viewed as a playful fictional construct loosely related to reality. He worked in St Petersburg from 1904 to 1907 and returned there in 1911 prior to going to New York in December of that year, where his stay lasted until June 1912. These experiences contributed to two of his most famous poems—'Les Pâques à New York' (1912) and 'La Prose du Transsibérien' (1913)—which alone place him among the foremost poets of the avant-garde in the Paris of 1912–14. The latter is in itself a poem-object, or in Cendrars's own terms 'un livre simultané', being published on one long unfoldable sheet which carried the accompanying paintings of Sonia *Delaunay, thus taking its place in the history of painting also. The former may have, to some extent, influenced *Apollinaire's 'Zone'. Cendrars certainly allowed it to be said that it had, after Apollinaire's death.

In August 1914 he enrolled in the Foreign Legion and lost an arm in the battle for the Marne in September 1915. Something of his experiences can be found in his *La Main coupée* (1914), although, bizarrely, the title does not allude to his own loss.

In the field of poetry, his *Du monde entier* (1919), *Dix-neuf poèmes élastiques* (1919), *Documentaires* (1924)—originally entitled *Kodak*, but changed for legal reasons—and *Feuilles de route* (1927–8) are the best of his contribution to the modernism of the period. The omnipresent themes of wandering and the world as poem, together with a narrative strand, are the characteristic marks of this author, whose impact on French poetry is over by the 1930s. His *L'Anthologie nègre* (1921) also contributed to the contemporary cult of the primitive and the exotic in avant-garde art.

His prose works, of which the best-known are *L'Or* (1925), *Moravagine* (1926), *Le Plan de l'aiguille* and *Les Confessions de Dan Yack* (both 1929), *Rhum* (1930), *L'Homme foudroyé* (1945), and *Bourlinguer* (1948), also mix truth and fiction (whatever their nominal genre) in a way that owes much to their author's gifts as a 'raconteur' and his notions of 'divertissement'. As one critic has put it: 'the most famous imaginary hero created by the Swiss writer could well be Blaise Cendrars.'

See J. C. Fluckiger, *Au cœur du texte* (1977); J. Bernard (ed.), *Cendrars, l'aventurier du texte* (1992).

Cendres, see AMROUCHE, J.

'Cendrillon'. One of Perrault's *Histoires ou contes du temps passé*, the familiar 'Cinderella', without the more brutal elements found in the Grimm version.

Censorship in France. 'A rigid rule, a lax practice' was how de *Tocqueville characterized the administration of the *ancien régime*, though a more accurate description might be that the regime wavered alternately between authoritarianism and paternalism. In the same way, one could say that the repressive nature of *ancien régime* censorship was mitigated by its inefficiency. The *Revolution briefly inaugurated one of the most liberal press regimes ever known; but Imperial and Bourbon authorities reimposed strict controls over the printed word.

1. Reformation to Revolution

The history of censorship in France begins essentially with the introduction of *printing. In the 16th c. the monarchy, anxious to combat the progress of the Reformation, gave considerable powers of censorship to the Paris theology faculty. Decrees of 1547 and 1551 prohibited the sale or printing of any book concerning holy scripture without the prior sanction of the *Sorbonne. This legislation was intended to restrict the importation of Reformation texts and Bibles from Germany and Geneva. The printer Robert *Estienne left for the freer air of Geneva, but the humanist printer *Dolet was executed in 1546.

In the 17th c. the state assumed control of censorship. In the reign of Louis XIV the monarchy first established close supervision of all printed materials, and was prepared to prosecute 'immoral' publications. The machinery of state censorship was operating effectively by the end of the 17th c., to enforce ideological conformity and to protect French publishing from foreign competition.

The apparatus of royal repression expanded rapidly during the 18th c. Before 1660 there had been fewer than 10 censors; in the early 1730s there were 41 royal censors, appointed by the Garde des Sceaux. By the eve of the Revolution their number had increased to 178, based for the most part in Paris. The censors were unpaid officials, although long service was often rewarded by a royal pension. They were lawyers, *savants*, librarians, editors of journals, and they were in close touch with the authors they were censoring. Some writers, like *Fontenelle and *Condillac, were themselves employed as censors, and it was common for

authors to discuss their work with the censor, to ensure that it defended religion, monarchy, and *les bonnes mœurs* to official satisfaction. Censorship was a meeting-place where the royal administration worked out a compromise with the *Enlightenment intellectuals.

There were ways of evading or subverting the apparatus of ideological coercion, but the repressive capacity of the *ancien régime* should not be underestimated. In 1753 the Rouen printer Machuel lost his *maîtrise*, and his printing-shop was closed. The censor demanded 23 alterations to La *Nouvelle Héloïse*, some of them substantial. *Marmontel and *Voltaire were briefly imprisoned in the Bastille, and *Diderot served a sentence in Vincennes. The Lieutenant de Police maintained a network of *inspecteurs de la librairie* to enforce royal prohibitions. Almost 1,000 offenders went to the Bastille between 1660 and 1789 for publishing-related violations (usually poor book-pedlars), about 17 per cent of all those imprisoned there. The crowd that stormed the Bastille in 1789 found only half-a-dozen unfortunate inmates to release; but the prison also contained thousands of books, by *Mercier, *Linguet, *Raynal, and others, which had been incarcerated as threatening and subversive.

The monarchy was not the only censoring authority: the Parlement de Paris as well as the Sorbonne also claimed the power to censor literary productions. In the age of enlightened absolutism the monarchy tried to eliminate the medieval pretensions of these rivals, but their influence could never be completely neglected. In 1758 the Parlement mounted a celebrated and successful challenge to the publication of *Helvétius's *De l'esprit*, after it had been approved by the censor Tercier. On this occasion, the Parlement not only secured the revocation of the royal *privilège*, but also managed to remove the unfortunate Tercier himself. The Parlement de Paris ordered the arrest of Rousseau, after the appearance of *Émile* in 1762. In 1781 Raynal was in turn wanted by the Parlement, after the publication of his *Histoire des deux Indes*. In the 1750s the *Encyclopédie* was a victim of these multiple pressures, from Parlement, the Sorbonne, and the clergy.

A distinguished author like Voltaire might shake off these problems, and exploit a short and not-uncomfortable spell in prison for publicity purposes. For a publisher or a printer, however, it was not so easy. He stood to lose money in fines or in impounded books, and his livelihood was at stake if he took too many risks with illegal publications. In 1745 the Toulouse publisher Delrieu was condemned by the local *parlement* to hard labour for life in the prison hulks, for publications contrary to the Roman Catholic religion. This was an exceptionally severe sentence, and the victim had sensibly fled before it could be carried out.

The first blow to this system came from within the government itself. The first relaxation can be

Cent ballades

linked with the tenure of office of *Malesherbes as Directeur de la Librairie (1750–63). Malesherbes did not object to royal censorship out of any liberal idealism. He was a pragmatist, whose main complaint was that the system of censorship did not, and could not, work. He wished to loosen royal control, because it was powerless to prevent an outpouring of pirated and illegally imported works. He also realized that the enforcement of censorship put the French book industry at a severe disadvantage with foreign competitors.

Malesherbes encouraged new techniques of circumventing regulations. He granted publishers authorizations to print, which did not amount to the grant of an official *privilège*. Malesherbes allowed this system of *permissions tacites* and simple *tolérances* to flourish. They did not give publishers a guaranteed monopoly, but they constituted a promise that the government would not prosecute. *Permissions* were thus given to many new works, by authors like *Beaumarchais, *Mably, and *Condillac. In Languedoc they were used for a specific purpose: to allow the circulation of Protestant books. By the 1780s almost as many works were being produced with a *permission tacite* as with a *privilège*. By this time royal censors had acquired a highly developed sense of their own futility.

2. Since 1789

The first years of the Revolution saw the abolition of censorship and an astonishing explosion of print. Between 1789 and 1799 over 2,000 new newspapers appeared in Paris alone (many did not survive more than a few editions). In the provinces there were over 1,000 new journals in the Revolutionary decade. Subsequent regimes, both Revolutionary and Napoleonic, drastically modified this brief period of liberalism: the Act of 1819, for instance, prohibited books which contained offence to public decency, religion, and good morality.

Under the July Monarchy infringements of the censorship laws were tried by jury: but the courts heard only about four cases annually, concerning non-periodical publications, between 1835 and 1847. The 1848 Revolution introduced another very liberal interlude, until the oppressive administration of *Napoleon III again silenced republicans and deprived offenders of the right to trial by jury.

The most famous attempt to suppress undesirable writing under the Second Empire concerned *Madame Bovary*. In 1857 Flaubert, together with the owner and printer of the *Revue de Paris*, appeared before the Tribunal Correctionnel on charges of offending public morality and religion. The deathbed scene offended Catholics, and the erotic nature of Emma Bovary's religious devotion was shocking. They were acquitted since, according to the magistrates, the work had not been written with the sole aim of encouraging sexual licence or insulting public decency, and because the book's blameworthy passages were few and short, considering its overall length. Les *Fleurs du mal* was prosecuted in the same year, and the prosecution was led by the same lawyer, Pinard, who argued that Baudelaire's realism was obscene and blasphemous. The magistrates ordered the removal of a few erotic poems from the collection, and fined Baudelaire 300 francs.

In 1881 the Third Republic promulgated its 'law on the freedom of the press', which annulled the legal restrictions introduced since 1819, and reintroduced trial by jury for publishing offences. Since then, with brief exceptions, notably World War I and the Vichy period [see OCCUPATION AND RESISTANCE], there has been no advance censorship of works published in France. In various francophone countries (e.g. *Haiti), however, authoritarian regimes have at various times had recourse to harsh controls. [For press censorship, see also PRESS; for state control of the theatre, see THEATRES AND AUDIENCES.]   [ML]

Cent ballades, Le Livre des (1388/9). A collaborative work composed according to the *Livre des faits de *Boucicaut* by Boucicaut and three other aristocrats during a crusading expedition in 1388/9. A legal fiction, it dramatizes a debate on the relative values in love of Loyauté and Fauseté (the first preached by the venerable knight Hutin, the second by the more frivolous Guignarde ('coquette')), in a series of elegant ballades with different and sophisticated rhyme-schemes. According to the frame fiction, the debate was submitted for judgement later to other notables such as the duc de Berry and Guy de la Trémoïlle.   [JHMT]

Cent nouvelles nouvelles (1456–61). This collection of prose tales was composed for Philippe le Bon of Burgundy by an anonymous writer (sometimes identified with Antoine de *La Sale). Like his model, Boccaccio, he attributes his tales to different speakers, members of the Burgundian court, including the duke himself; he does not, however, develop a frame narrative as does Boccaccio. The writer prides himself on having given a 'novel slant' to his collection, for while much of the narrative material is appropriated from the *Decameron* itself and from *fabliaux*, he insists that the events represented are recent, underpinning this claim with a pretence of historical accuracy—names, dates, places—and a wealth of concrete detail. The cast-list is familiar from the *fabliaux*—deceived husbands, wily clerics, naïve or exploitative wives—but prose allows for the fleshing-out of character and the elaborating of dialogue. While the majority of the tales are comic—principally featuring seduction stratagems, but also drunkenness, military anecdotes, unscrupulous clergy—some are serious, even tragic: a woman commits suicide to escape rape (98); another dies having unwittingly married bigamously (69). The tales thus allow, interestingly, for a blurring of genres, a shifting moral perspective.   [JHMT]

Centre National de la Recherche Scientifique (CNRS). The principal public body for funding scientific research in France. Created by laws of 1941 and 1948 which amalgamated previous bodies, it has expanded greatly and offers lavish support for work in the human sciences, including literary research.

Cent Vingt Journées de Sodome, Les, see SADE.

CERCAMON (second quarter of the 12th c.). Early *troubadour who worked at the court of Guilhem X of Poitiers (d. 1137), possibly at the same time as *Marcabru. Cercamon's small surviving corpus includes one of the earliest *tensos and some of the first conventional *cansos. Cercamon is a pseudonym meaning 'he travels the world'. His poems have been edited by V. Tortoreto (Modena, 1981).
[SG]

Cercle des tropiques, Le, see FANTOURÉ.

CERF, Muriel (b. 1951). French writer whose first texts, *L'Antivoyage* (1974) and *Le Diable vert* (1975), describe her exotic travels. A dozen novels, written in an elaborate and poetic style, often focus on portraits of women. Antonella Piattio, a characteristic heroine, appears in three novels, beginning with *Marie Tiefenthaler* (1982). *Julia M. ou le Premier Regard* (1991) returns to an autobiographical vein.   [EAF]

Cerisy-la-Salle. International cultural centre situated in the Cotentin district of Normandy, scene of regular colloquia on literary and cultural topics, including celebrated debates on literary criticism, the *Nouveau Roman, etc.

CERTEAU, Michel de (1925–86). French cultural historian. Originally a Jesuit theologian, with a training in history, literature, and anthropology, de Certeau spanned several disciplines with enormous erudition. His membership of *Lacan's École Freudienne (1964–80) informed his many books on the religious and cultural history of the 16th, 17th, and 18th c. Close in some respects to *Foucault, he was particularly concerned to identify the strategies by which dominated groups sought to resist the constraints imposed on the meanings and activities available to them. See his *L'Invention du quotidien* (1974) and *L'Écriture de l'histoire* (1975).   [MHK]

CERVANTES, Miguel de, see SPANISH INFLUENCES.

CÉSAIRE, Aimé (b. 1913). Martinican poet, dramatist, historian, politician, and, with Léon *Damas and Léopold Sedar *Senghor, the founder of the *négritude* movement of West Indian and African writers in French.

Césaire grew up in a black lower-middle class family (his father was a tax inspector, his mother a dressmaker) in which French rather than *Creole was the normal language of communication. From the Lycée Schoelcher in Fort-de-France (where Damas was a fellow pupil), Césaire proceeded, in 1931, to the Lycée Louis-le-Grand in Paris (where he met Senghor) and thence, in 1935, to the *École Normale Supérieure. Elected president of the federation of Martinican students in Paris, Césaire collaborated with Senghor and a number of fellow French West Indian students on the sole number of the journal *L'*Étudiant noir* (1935). In it he published an article, 'Nègreries. Jeunesse noire et assimilation', which contains in embryo all the themes that he was to elaborate in his later writings, most notably a rejection of the assimilationist assumptions of French colonialism and the need for colonized Africans and West Indians to assert their separate cultural, psychological, spiritual, and racial identities.

Césaire began to write his first and most influential work, *Cahier d'un retour au pays natal,* in 1935, while on holiday in Yugoslavia. He claims to have been inspired by the sight of the Adriatic island of Martinska to embark upon a passionate *défense et illustration* in poetry of Martinique and its people from the period of slavery up to the present. In 1936 he visited Martinique for the first time in five years and completed the poem in 1937. Alternating violently between phases of despair and resignation and phases of hope and revolt, the shift from one to the other being mirrored in the text's frequent shifts from prose to verse, the *Cahier* describes the journey of a colonized black West Indian from a condition of physical, cultural, and existential exile back to the 'native land' of his authentic self; in it the language and imagery of Surrealism are placed at the service of the emerging concept of *négritude.*

After rejection by French publishers in 1937–8, the first version of the *Cahier* was finally published by the review *Volontés* in August 1939, at the very moment when Césaire, with war about to erupt in Europe, returned along with his wife, the Martinican poet Suzanne Roussy, to his *pays natal.* He remained there till 1944, teaching at the Lycée Schoelcher and influencing a whole generation of young Martinicans, including *Fanon and *Glissant. In 1941 Césaire, his wife, and a number of other Martinican writers founded the review *Tropiques* which, in the face of continuous threats of censorship by the local version of the Vichy regime, developed the project of racial, cultural, and psychological self-assertion initiated by the *Cahier.* The *Tropiques* group's advocacy of *Surrealism as a means of combating the multiple alienations of colonialism was encouraged by the brief visit of André *Breton to Martinique in 1941. It was Breton's essay, 'Un grand poète noir', which, serving as the preface to an enlarged and revised version of the *Cahier* published (with a translation into English) in New York in 1947, brought Césaire and his work to the attention of a wider public in France, its colonial empire, and elsewhere.

After an extended visit to *Haiti in 1944, Césaire was approached by Martinican Communists to stand as the party's candidate as mayor of Fort-de-France and *député* for the central constituency of

Martinique at elections for the Assemblée Nationale Constituante convened in Paris following the Liberation. Despite having had no previous contacts with the Communist Party in either its local or metropolitan version, Césaire accepted; in 1945 he was duly elected to both positions, which he held without interruption for over four decades until standing down as *député* in 1993. In 1946 he was parliamentary *rapporteur* for the law which transformed Martinique, along with Guadeloupe, Guyane, and Reunion, into a *département* of France. The same year saw the publication by Gallimard of poems that had appeared in *Tropiques* during the war, under the title of *Les Armes miraculeuses*; the volume also contained a striking drama entitled *Et les chiens se taisaient* on the subject of slavery, colonialism, and racism. A further volume of poems entitled *Soleil cou coupé* was published in 1948, followed by *Corps perdu*, illustrated with 32 engravings by Picasso, in 1950.

In 1947 Césaire was active, along with Senghor, Damas, Alioune *Diop, and others, in founding the review *Présence africaine*, and in 1949 attended Communist-sponsored peace-conferences in Poland and Romania. In 1950 his *Discours sur le colonialisme* gained him a world-wide reputation as an enemy of colonialism and advocate of the distinctive destiny of colonized peoples. By 1953 he was increasingly troubled by the growing contradiction between his essentially race- and culture-based assertion of the distinctive identity of Black people in his literary and polemical works and the class-based universalist assumptions of the political party to which he belonged. After delivering a communication entitled 'Culture et colonisation' at the first Congrès International des Écrivains et Artistes Noirs held in Paris in September 1956, Césaire the following month announced his resignation from the Communist Party in his celebrated *Lettre à Maurice Thorez*. In 1958 he formed his own Parti Progressiste Martiniquais, with autonomy (i.e. local self-government within the context of a continued relationship with France) as its preferred solution to the political, economic, and cultural problems of Martinique; it should be noted that at no point has Césaire advocated out-and-out independence for his *pays natal*.

In 1960 a new book of poems, *Ferrements*, was published. Its title indicates the two poles—'ferments' and 'ferrements' (i.e. irons)—that had dominated Césaire's experience in the 1950s and would continue to do so in the years that followed. In 1960, too, Césaire published a major historical study of Toussaint *Louverture, and in 1961 *Soleil cou coupé* (1948) and *Corps perdu* (1950) were republished in much-revised and abridged form under the joint title of *Cadastre*. Increasingly, though, it was the theatre rather than poetry that became the centre of Césaire's literary activities. In 1963 he published the first of a trilogy of 'drames de la décolonisation', *La Tragédie du Roi Christophe*, which, focusing on post-independence Haiti, was first staged at Salzburg in

1964 and, amid much controversy, at the Théâtre de l'Odéon in Paris in 1965. Recent events in Africa formed the theme of *Une saison au Congo* which, published in book form in 1966, was performed in Venice and Paris the following year. The trilogy was completed by an adventurous rewriting of Shakespeare's *Tempest*, *Une tempête*, which, following productions in Tunisia and Paris in 1969, was performed in Martinique in 1972 on the occasion of the first Festival Culturel de Fort-de-France, the first time that one of Césaire's plays had been seen by a Martinican audience.

After the early 1970s Césaire's career as a writer showed a definite falling-off, with only two collections of poems, *Noria* (included in the three-volume *Œuvres complètes* published in Fort-de-France in 1976) and *Moi, laminaire . . .* (1982). In the course of two decades he seemed increasingly dominated by day-to-day politics in Martinique and the French Assembly. Politically, he became more and more of an establishment figure, voting with the French Socialist Party in the Assembly and, in 1982, becoming the first president of the newly constituted Conseil Régional de la Martinique which, in the view of a younger generation of Martinican nationalists, is merely one further mechanism of French neo-colonialism in the island. His belief in the fundamental 'African-ness' of West Indian cultures has come under attack from the proponents of *créolité [see CONFIANT]. There was always a tension between the radicalism of Césaire's poetic and dramatic works and the moderation and frequent uncertainty of his political praxis, but, on the strength, above all, of *Cahier d'un retour au pays natal*, his place as the 'grand poète noir' hailed by Breton remains secure. [RDEB]

See R. L. Scharfman, '*Engagement'and the Language of the Subject in the Poetry of Aimé Césaire* (1980); A. J. Arnold, *Modernism and Negritude: The Poetry and Poetics of Aimé Césaire* (1981); R. Toumson and S. Henry-Valmore, *Aimé Césaire Le Négre inconsolé* (1993).

CÉSAIRE, Ina (b. 1942). Daughter of the above, ethnologist specializing in oral tradition (two collections of *Creole folk-tales and numerous commentaries). Using family lore and personal narratives, her play *Mémoires d'Isles* (1985) recreates the lives of two Martinican grandmothers. She has also adapted 'Ti-Jean' tales for the stage (*L'Enfant des passages*, 1987) and has documented Caribbean culture on film. [BJ]

César, see GRÉVIN.

César Birotteau. Novel by *Balzac (1837); its full title is *Histoire de la grandeur et de la décadence de César Birotteau, maître-parfumeur.* Perhaps the first business epic of French literature, Balzac's novel is both a comic narrative of narrow philistinism and an encomium to the values of self-help and single-minded hard work. Birotteau's rise is due to skilful marketing of a cure for baldness; his downfall due to the dishonesty of his accountant and the machinations of financiers. Through the exemplary story of a single shopkeeper, Balzac allows the reader to glimpse the complex machinery of the circulation of money in Restoration France and the workings of an entire social system, the subject of La *Comédie humaine* of which *César Birotteau* is a constituent part. [DMB]

CESBRON, Gilbert (1913–79). French writer and broadcaster. A lawyer by training, he held various media positions and was administrator of Radio Luxembourg for a period after 1945. From 1972 he was heavily involved in charitable works. Throughout the post-war period he wrote many plays, novels, and essays, usually focusing on the morality of a particular social issue, dramatized with his characteristic Catholic sentimentality. His best-known works are *Les Saints vont en enfer* (1952), a novel based on the experience of the worker-priest movement, and *Il est minuit, docteur Schweitzer* (1952), a play eulogizing the work of medical missionaries. [MHK]

C'est le soleil qui m'a brulée, see BEYALA.

CÉZANNE, Paul (1839–1906). One of the decisive sources of 20th-c. painting, Cézanne grew up in Aix with *Zola. In 1886 the friendship ended with the publication of L'*Œuvre*, Zola's novel of the Impressionist movement, when Cézanne decided that Zola had based the failed Impressionist, Claude Lantier, on him. Cézanne's achievement was to integrate the formal innovations of *Impressionism with the abstract patterns he admired in the classical masters. Representing sunlight through colour harmonies and assimilating nature within basic geometrical forms (cylinder, sphere, and cone), his paintings both reproduced external reality (landscapes, still life, portraits) and created autonomous pictorial structures. In doing so, they opened the way to the revolution of *Cubism. [JK]

CHABROL, Claude (b. 1930). Popular film-maker associated with the *Nouvelle Vague, of which he was one of the leading figures.

CHABROL, Jean-Pierre (b. 1925). Radio and television story-teller, and novelist, Chabrol sets in his native Cévennes novels of religious dissent (*Les Fous de Dieu,* 1961), Popular Front (*Les Rebelles,* 1965–8), and Resistance (*Un homme de trop,* 1958). He portrays the same revolt and solidarity elsewhere in *Le Canon Fraternité* (1970) and *Le Bout-Galeux* (1955). [SFN]

Chagrin et la pitié, Le, see OCCUPATION AND RESISTANCE, 7.

CHALLE or **CHASLES,** Robert (1659–1720). French writer, who was also a soldier, lawyer, and merchant. Two of his works were published posthumously: the *Journal d'un voyage aux Indes orientales*

(1721), a highly personal and lively record; and the *Mémoires,* written in 1716 but not published until 1931. Another work sometimes attributed to him, *Difficultés sur la religion,* came out in 1767 as *Le *Militaire philosophe*. Challe thus saw in print only his two works of fiction: a volume which continued Filleau de Saint-Martin's sequel to *Don Quixote,* and *Les Illustres Françaises* (1713).

The latter was at first highly successful, going into some 20 re-editions by 1780. Subsequently it fell into oblivion, though *Champfleury did draw attention to Challe as a precursor of the *Realist novel. Modern critical interest in Challe was aroused by Frédéric Deloffre's new edition of the work in 1959. *Les Illustres Françaises* consists of seven interlinked *nouvelles* set in a frame narrative. All the heroines, faced with obstacles to their love, show fidelity and strength of character, though in two cases with tragic consequences. The milieu, a group of aristocrats and prosperous bourgeois, is vividly portrayed, with a good deal of practical detail. Challe's style sometimes lacks elegance, but he creates characters of interesting complexity and has a notable gift for story-telling. [VGM]

Chambre ardente. Court set up in the 16th c. in the Parlement de Paris to try heretics [see REFORMATION]. The *chambre,* which was draped in black and lit by torches, also dealt with cases of poisoning.

Chambre bleue, La, see RAMBOUILLET, HÔTEL DE.

Chambre claire, La, see BARTHES.

Chambre des Députés, La, see NATIONAL ASSEMBLIES.

Chambre syndicale, see BOOK TRADE, 4.

CHAMFORT, Sébastien-Roch Nicolas, known as (1740–94). Dramatist and essayist who neglected none of the proven recipes for literary and social success: he won five prizes at various academies, wrote two comedies (*La Jeune Indienne,* 1764; *Le Marchand de Smyrne,* 1770) and a tragedy (*Mustapha et Zéangir,* 1776), cultivated influential members of the literary establishment, was patronized by the powerful, pensioned by the monarchy, and was finally elected to the Académie Française (1781). In the process, he gained painful knowledge of himself and *ancien régime* society in which everything was for sale: bodies and consciences, allegiances and pens. In the ten years preceding 1789, surveying a system which, with its topsy-turvy values, consecrated every conceivable injustice, he gathered ammunition for a radical demolition of France's imperfections to be entitled *Produits de la civilisation perfectionnée.*

The material, published posthumously by *Ginguené, appeared as *Maximes, pensées, caractères et anecdotes* (1795). In this collection, much admired by Schlegel, Schopenhauer, Nietzsche, and *Camus, Chamfort espouses *Rousseau's position: man *was* born free and yet *is* in chains because life in society (made necessary perhaps by man's nature) has corrupted then enslaved him, leaving him with a fearful dilemma: *not to live or to live corrupted*. Chamfort's pessimism has its limits however. Perhaps man *is* condemned to decline. But, indifferent to metaphysical speculation and its consolations, Chamfort proposes that man himself holds the remedy. True, he may not be all goodness, yet neither is he radically bad. True, nature is both a negative and a positive principle, bringer of order and disorder, but élite souls can attempt to fathom the opposites and the contrasts. Chamfort fully experienced the pain of such contrasts and contradictions. With his ardent desire for transparency and independence, he is the energetic individualist, free from illusion and false hope. And yet his ideal seemed now to galvanize, now to paralyse him. Motivated, however, by so much hatred and so much hope, faced with a world which he wished at once to save and to destroy, he greeted the Revolution—that consecration of his own revolt—as a sure means of moral regeneration, now not just of élite souls, but as a new beginning for humanity.

By mid-1793 the Revolution seemed, however, intent on denying its very *raison d'être*. Chamfort the moralist spoke out again. Immediately suspect, he was for months thereafter cruelly harassed. Learning that he was to be imprisoned again (14 November 1793), he reaffirmed his inner liberty with a courageous (but horribly clumsy) attempt at suicide and died five months later, as surely a victim of the Terror as André *Chénier.   [JR]

See. J. Renwick, *Chamfort devant la postérité* (1986); C. Arnaud, *Chamfort* (1988).

Chaminadour, see JOUHANDEAU.

CHAMOISEAU, Patrick (b.1953). Martinican novelist, playwright, and theoretician, whose particular interests are the sociopolitical and literary status of French *Creole, and the affirmation of Martinican cultural identity. These issues, earlier raised by *Glissant, are debated in *Éloge de la créolité* (1989), jointly authored by Chamoiseau, R. *Confiant, and Jean Bernabé, and in *Lettres créoles* (1991) co-authored with Confiant. They are also variously illustrated in Chamoiseau's autobiographical *Antan d'enfance* (1990) and his novels *Chronique des sept misères* (1986), *Solibo magnifique* (1988), and *Texaco* (1992, Prix Goncourt). He employs many features associated with the Creole folk-tale—wit, zest, irony, audience participation, and a sometimes brutal realism—in order to convey his humane and subtly subversive view of Caribbean social history.   [BNO]

CHAMPAGNE or **CHAMPAIGNE,** Philippe de (1602–74). French painter who combined in his portraits and religious paintings the rich colour of Rubens, the authoritative classical composition of *Poussin, and the interest in texture and individual-

ity of the Flemish school. He worked for Louis XIII, although his best known portrait is of *Richelieu, full-length, in cardinal's robes and Van Dyckian pose. He contributed to philosophical debates at the *Académie Royale de Peinture et de Sculpture. From 1643 all his work for the convent of *Port-Royal was powerfully affected by *Jansenism. His numerous portraits of officials, dignitaries, ecclesiastics, bourgeois, and personal friends convince through their original severity and acute psychological perception.   [JPC]

Champ-de-Mars, Le. Open space on the left bank of the Seine in Paris, now the site of the *Eiffel Tower. Originally the parade ground of the École Militaire, it was the scene of *fêtes révolutionnaires* and subsequent great open-air occasions.

CHAMPFLEURY or **FLEURY** (pseud. of Jules Husson) (1821–89). French novelist, art historian, and critic, whose novels include *Chien-Caillou* (1847), the story of an engraver, *Les Aventures de Mademoiselle Mariette* (1853), a bohemian tale based on his own life and acquaintance, and *Les Bourgeois de Molinchart* (1855), the plot of which is based on provincial adultery. He wrote an important *Histoire de la caricature* (1865–90), but is best remembered for his support for the painter *Courbet, and for his polemic on behalf of *Realism in art and writing. *Le Réalisme*, a collection of articles, was published in 1857.   [DK]

CHAMPIER, Symphorien (*c*.1472–*c*.1540). A doctor practising mainly in Lyon, and physician to Antoine, duc de Lorraine, with whom he travelled in Italy, he was appointed for a while in 1515 to the prestigious University of Pavia. As a magistrate (*échevin*) he saw his house ransacked during the Rebeine (Great Revolt) of 1529. A cousin through marriage of *Bayart, he wrote *Les Gestes, ensemble la vie du preux chevalier Bayart* (1525), whose success outshone its merit. A staunch supporter of the noble order, he published in 1535 *Le Fondement et origine des titres de noblesse*. We owe him numerous treatises (in Latin) on medical subjects and works on local history. He is above all memorable as one of the introducers into France of *Neoplatonism (*La Nef des dames vertueuses*, 1503).   [KCC]

CHAMPLAIN, Samuel de (1567–1635), see COLONIZATION; QUEBEC, I.

CHAMPMESLÉ, Marie Desmares (1642–98). Actress famous for her creation of many tragic roles by *Racine, whose mistress she was.

CHAMPOLLION, Jean-François (1790–1832). Linguist, decipherer of hieroglyphics, and founder of the modern discipline of Egyptology, for which he supplied a manifesto in the form of his *Lettre à M. Dacier relative à l'alphabet des hiéroglyphes phonétiques* (1823). Building upon the work of the physicist

Thomas Young on the Rosetta Stone, Champollion produced a complete decipherment, which was followed by a grammar and a dictionary of the ancient Egyptian language. His essential insight was that the symbols were of three kinds: alphabetic, syllabic, and 'determinative' (i.e. making reference to earlier portions of text). Most of his later writings were published posthumously by his brother Jacques (1778–1867). [MB]

Champs magnétiques, Les, see SURREALISM, I.

CHAMSON, André (1900–83). French historian, art critic, and novelist, who was also an important civil servant and an active participant in the Resistance [see OCCUPATION AND RESISTANCE]. His literary output ranged from novels (*Roux le bandit,* 1925; *Les Hommes de la route,* 1927), to historical essays (*Clio,* 1929), to writings on art (*La Peinture française au musée du Louvre,* 1948), to works of broader brush (*Le Puits des miracles,* 1945). His Cévenol Protestant origins, the Mont Aigoual, and its surrounding region loom large in his early fictional imagination which is sturdily realistic. [DAS]

CHANDERNAGOR, Françoise (b. 1945). Author of a best-selling imaginary autobiography by Madame de *Maintenon entitled *L'Allée du roi* (1981). The fictional trilogy of Christine Valbray, begun in *La Sans Pareille* (1988), pursued in *L'Archange de Vienne* (1989) and *L'Enfant aux loups* (1990), creates the life of a contemporary woman, interspersed with the commentaries of her 'autobiographer'. [EAF]

Change (1968–85). French cultural journal and 'collective', founded by Jean-Pierre *Faye. Other important editorial members included Philippe Boyer, Jean-Claude Montel, Jean Paris, Léon Robel, Mitsou Ronat, and Jacques *Roubaud. The 'collective' was international and interdisciplinary in scope. It brought together writers, linguists, philosophers, mathematicians, and biologists. Influenced by linguistic and poetic theory (from the Russian Formalists to Noam Chomsky and Morris Halle) and by Marx, *Change*'s objective was to show the impact of the 'change of forms' on material social change. Viewed as a real presence and not an abstract entity, language had to be transformed if society was to be transformed. Thus, the important formal and political notion of 'transformationism' for *Change*: 'the thought that thinks through language and history'. Profoundly influenced by the events of *May 1968 and their aftermath, the journal devoted numerous essays and special issues to linguistic minorities throughout the world, and to political oppression in North and South America, Europe, and South-East Asia. [DM-S]

Channel Islands, see PATOIS AND DIALECT WRITING.

Chanson, see CANSO; GRAND CHANT COURTOIS

Chanson d'Antioche, La, see CRUSADE CYCLE.

Chanson de geste. Major medieval French narrative genre, with a distinctive verse form and broadly historical content: *geste* means 'history' as well as 'deed'; it can also mean 'lineage'. *Chansons de geste* are often also referred to as '*epic poems', because they are substantial works running to many thousands of lines whose major subject-matter is heroic action; the term 'epic' also serves to underline the opposition between them and medieval '*romance', the other major narrative genre of the period. The best-known examples of *chansons de geste* are those celebrating the heroic careers of *Roland and William of Orange [see GUILLAUME, CYCLE DE], both of whom appear to have been real historical figures from Carolingian times. *Chanson de geste* texts are difficult to date, but the genre flourished from at least the late 11th until the early 14th c., and longer if one includes the recasting in prose (or *mise en prose*) [see BURGUNDIAN COURT LITERATURE] of earlier verse texts throughout the 14th and 15th c.; these *mises en prose* continued to be printed in the 16th c. There are over 100 surviving *chansons de geste*, not all of which have yet been edited. Nearly all are anonymous. The earliest named author is *Bertrand de Bar-sur-Aube (late 12th c.).

Unlike romances, which share the same metre as many other medieval French genres, *chansons de geste* are immediately recognizable because their metrical form is virtually unique to them. (It is also found in some saints' lives.) They are composed in strophes of varying length called *laisses*; all the lines of each *laisse* share the same assonance or rhyme. *Laisses* may be as short as three or four lines, or as long as several hundreds. In some early poems there is a close correspondence between narrative shape and *laisse* division; the story develops in a manner similar to the English ballad, with an episode being recounted in each strophe. Another ballad-like feature of these early poems is their use of repetition. Similarities of phrasing from one *laisse* to another impart a lyrical quality to the poems, and by the same token diminish their narrative impetus. It is sometimes unclear whether the same events are being re-narrated from different points of view, or whether different events are being described with a disconcerting similarity. The lyricism of the *chansons de geste* was probably also manifested in performance, since it appears that they were sung or intoned, and not, as were romances, simply read aloud.

Chansons de geste are usually monometric, i.e. all the lines are of uniform length, the decasyllabic line predominating but coming under increasing competition from the *alexandrine from the late 12th c. onwards. A very few texts—including the early *Gormont et Isembart*—are in octosyllables. Whatever its length, the line is divided into two by a regularly placed caesura, which cuts the decasyllable 4–6 (exceptionally 6–4), and the alexandrine 6–6. Just as the *laisse* tends to correspond to a unit of narrative, so these 4- or 6-syllable hemistichs are often

Chanson de geste

syntactically self-contained; and as there is repetition between *laisses*, so there is a tendency for hemistichs to recur, both within a given poem, and from poem to poem. This feature has led to the *chansons de geste* being described as 'formulaic', the repeated hemistichs being termed 'formulae'.

This terminology derives from Homer studies, and reflects a concern to compare the *chansons de geste* with other epic literatures. The degree of 'formulaicness' of *chansons de geste* and other epic texts has been diversely calculated, and the results used to defend the view that the *chansons de geste* were originally an oral genre. 'Formulae', it is suggested, were a stock of ready-made poetic building-bricks enabling a singer to put together in performance the details of a narrative whose overall framework he would reproduce from memory (and which, moreover, would be already known to his audience). The manuscript versions which we have are merely the fossilized remains of poetic material which in the Middle Ages lived through constant recreation and retelling. Writing preserves individual texts, but it also distorts the fluidity and plurality of the medieval works.

The respective roles of *orality and writing in the production of the *chansons de geste* are, however, a matter of controversy. Even though the poems were performed orally, they may not have been performed entirely from memory, or with a high degree of improvization. In cases where the same *chanson de geste* survives in several manuscript copies, variations between the copies may result from rival oral versions, but they may equally arise from editorial decisions or from the vagaries of medieval scribal practice. 'Formula' might be a romantic term for 'cliché', and certainly there could be reasons other than oral improvization for cultivating patterns of repetition. Given the disagreement on these issues, it is difficult to give a straightforward account of the form of the *chansons de geste*.

There are analogous problems when we address their content. Here the major puzzle is that most *chansons de geste* have some kind of anchorage in historical fact, usually from the *Carolingian era. How did 8th- and 9th-c. material find its way into 12th-c. poems? Were they composed in the manner of historical novels, using chronicle sources for information? The main weakness of this solution is the poems' wild inaccuracies: they seem as eager to misrepresent historical incidents as to dramatize them. Alternatively, was there a continuous tradition of oral narrative, stretching back to contemporary celebrations of historical events, but eventually distorting them through its constant retelling and embroidering upon them? The major problem with this hypothesis is that such evidence as survives for this alleged 300-year period of activity is insufficient to prove that there was a continuous *literary* tradition, as opposed to a tradition of family or local legends with no fixed form. The question of sources

and origins is complex and, it would appear, irresolvable. There is no doubt, however, that the *chanson de geste* texts we now have show traces of reworking, or *remaniement*; how far back in time such *remaniements* extend, and whether they were predominantly oral or written, remains unknown.

An interesting testimony to the character of the *chansons de geste* is that of Jehan *Bodel. In the prologue to his *chanson de geste*, *Les Saisnes*, he characterizes them as 'true' in contrast with Arthurian romances ('empty and entertaining') and adaptations of the classics ('learned'). The 'truth' of the *chansons de geste* may not be informed by learning, and certainly not by the accuracy sought by modern historians, but they do capture perceptions about historical reality. These poems are concerned with lived experience, which they construct as a curious amalgam of present moral and political preoccupations and past circumstances. France's heroic age—the Carolingian empire—becomes a fictional setting for heroic figures onto whom contemporary dilemmas can be displaced and through whom they can be investigated.

In the prologue to his *Girart de Vienne, Bertrand de Bar-sur-Aube classifies *chansons de geste* into three *gestes*: those of the emperor Charlemagne; those dealing with William of Orange and his family; and those that deal with rebels or traitors. This analysis is far from satisfactory for categorizing texts (*Girart de Vienne* itself could be said to belong to all three), but it does suggest three ways of envisaging the roles of king and aristocracy in the *chansons de geste*, and thus of categorizing their political content. In the *geste du roi*, barons collaborate with the king, usually in a context of holy war or *crusade; in the William poems a weak king Louis, son of Charlemagne, is only kept in power by the selfless service of his vassals; and in the poems featuring rebel barons, the social fabric is represented in various stages of disintegration as powerful factions within France war with each other, and the king is either under attack himself (as in *Renaut de Montauban) or powerless to end the fighting (as in *Raoul de Cambrai). The historical struggles represented in the *chansons de geste* are a powerful lens through which to view broader political and moral issues: the value and cohesion of social bonds such as *feudalism, friendship, lineage, or the emergent concept of 'the nation'; the validity of different means of settling disputes or enforcing authority, such as violence, coercion, litigation, or negotiation; the acceptability of social difference created by factors such as race, religion, legitimacy, gender; the threat to political stability posed by ambition, duplicity, or illicit sexuality.

It is impossible to judge the audience of the *chansons de geste*. They may have been heard by all social groups. The 12th-c. chronicler William of Malmesbury alleges that a *jongleur* performed the *Chanson de Roland* to encourage the invading force at the Battle of Hastings, but modern scholars take this account with a pinch of salt. From the late 12th c. onwards, with the rise in importance of the poems dealing with rebel barons, *chansons de geste* become less favourable to the aristocracy and more akin to social satire, and this change may have brought with it a widening of audience.

Poems from all three of the *gestes* enumerated by Bertrand are reworked in prose. *Jean d'Outremeuse (14th c.) and David Aubert (15th c.) both made massive prose compilations of earlier epic poems, and many other *mises en prose* survive that are anonymous. Although the date, status, and origins of our *chanson de geste* texts are all uncertain, it is clear that they were an enormously succesful and influential genre throughout the French Middle Ages.   [SK]

See François Suard, *Guillaume d'Orange. Étude du roman en prose* (1979); D. J. A. Ross, 'The Old French *chansons de geste*', in A. T. Hatto (ed.), *Traditions of Heroic and Epic Poetry* (1980).

Chanson de Guillaume, La. *Chanson de geste* related to the Cycle de *Guillaume. The earliest portions, relating the death of Vivien at L'Archamp, date from about 1100. In a first interpolation (*c*.1150) Guillaume 'al curb nés' ('Hooknose') is aided by his nephew Gui, whose *enfances* are narrated. At line 1980 Guillaume has successfully avenged Vivien; at line 1981 he is viewing the wreck of another defeat. The revised ending, dating from the 1170s, exploits material related to *Aliscans. The real hero is now the giant Renewart. The poem is remarkable for its mixture of stark grandeur, especially in portraying the desolation of war, and burlesque humour.
     [PEB]

Chanson de Jérusalem, La, see CRUSADE CYCLE.

Chanson de Roland, La, see ROLAND.

Chanson de sainte Foy, La. Sancta Fides, or St Foy, was a historical figure. She was martyred in 303 and her remains were taken first to Agen, then transferred to the abbey of Conques (in Aquitaine) some time before 883. The 593-line Occitan narrative poem commemorating these events was written in rhyming octosyllabic *laisses* [see CHANSON DE GESTE] *c*.1170, probably in the extreme south of Occitania (Cerdagne). Its early date qualifies it as what philologists call a 'monument', but its interest is far from solely linguistic: its portrayal of the Occitan protagonist as a lover of Christ despite the seductions and butchery of the Romans forms an extraordinary preface to the productions of the *troubadours which were shortly to follow.   [SK]

Chanson d'Ève, La, see VAN LERBERGHE.

Chanson française. The term 'chanson' covers a variety of different forms of expression, both literary and musical: from epics to short lyric poems; from anonymous folk-songs with simple, traditional refrains [see POPULAR SONG] to settings of Symbolist poems by late 19th-c. composers [see WORDS AND

MUSIC, 2]. The adjective 'française' in recent times has served to distinguish from these other forms the modern French popular song that emerged at the end of the 19th c., as exemplified by such figures as *Bruant, *Piaf, or *Brassens. It can be linked to the growth of a mass popular culture and the development of the electronic media, which distinguish it from the folk-song and cabaret tradition out of which it evolved.

Several features mark this transition: the creation of 'star' performers, with their own style and audience, in the context of the *music-hall and *café-concert*. Some of these also composed their own songs, reinforcing the 'star' persona: Bruant is an early example of this. During the 19th c. writers of popular lyrics, such as *Béranger and *Pottier, escaped from their earlier anonymity, but were not usually known as performers.

The songs thus created differ from the art-song or *lied* not only in the relative simplicity of their musical form, but also in the fact that the lyrics take precedence over the music. Whereas the lyric of the art-song, however literary its origins, is used as the pretext for a musical composition, in the popular song the music serves rather as a support for the lyric. Indeed, in the *chansonnier* tradition the music was often not an original composition, but a well-known folk-tune: in this way, the term *chansonnier* has come to mean 'comedian' or 'satirist', rather than singer or songwriter.

The French popular song has always played an important role as a vehicle for social comment, and as a rallying point for political causes. It also has much closer links with literature than its English-language counterpart, and quite apart from the art-song it has been fairly common for poems to be turned into popular refrains or for literary figures to turn their hand to lyric-writing: the repertoires of *Guilbert or *Greco bear witness to this. In broad terms, one can distinguish two general currents of *chanson française*: one a vehicle for free-wheeling social commentary, political satire, or protest; the other a personal expression of feeling of a poetic kind, including the perennial love-song.

At the end of the 19th c., with the development of the modern popular *chanson*, some further distinctions can be made. On the one hand, there is the cabaret song, as practised in the 1890s by Bruant, Jules Jouy, or Mac Nab in places such as the *Chat Noir in Montmartre: satirical, individualistic, with some literary and intellectual pretentions. This style underwent a revival in the cellars of *Saint-Germain-des-Prés in the 1940s and 1950s, with the emergence of such figures as Greco, *Ferré, *Vian, Brassens, and *Brel. On the other hand, there are the songs of the music-hall, *café-concert*, or revue, popular in the commercial sense, less controversial: the repertoires of Mistinguett, *Chevalier, Josephine *Baker, or Piaf. A similar distinction, but not a symmetrical one, can be drawn between singer-songwriters who create their own repertoire, such

Chansonnier

as Bruant, *Trenet, or *Barbara; and the many teams of professional songwriters producing songs for others: André Willemetz and Henri Christiné, for instance, who were responsible for Chevalier's 'Valentine', Mistinguett's 'En douce', and musical comedies such as Phi-phi (1918).

In the 1920s, 1930s, and 1940s the phonograph gradually replaced sheet music as the principal form of song publishing. This process was speeded up by the growth of radio broadcasting, which tended to identify songs with particular singers. In the 1950s and 1960s the arrival of television further increased the emphasis on charismatic performers such as Piaf or Brel, and the development of the long-playing record allowed modern troubadours such as Brassens to create albums of songs analogous to collections of poems. The 1970s saw the eclipse of the cabaret and the music-hall as venues for the live performance of chanson: only the Olympia in Paris survives. Their place has been taken by giant concert halls such as the Zénith at La Villette or the Palais des Sports at Bercy, with a corresponding decline in the dramatic subtlety available to performers. At the same time new media resources have opened up, in the form of video. Live performances can be recorded and distributed, providing a permanent record of an ephemeral occasion, and the video-clip, despite the production costs, provides a new dimension in the dramatic presentation of a song, and can be used to good effect by television programmes. It is too early to say what effect these new media will have on the chanson tradition, but it is clear at the end of the 1980s that the indigenous style is in danger of being swamped by the international marketing of British and American products, whose influence had hitherto been assimilated in a creative way by singers like *Souchon, *Gainsbourg, or *Renaud.

The chanson française none the less represents a distinctively French phenomenon, and has developed through the electronic media into a kind of parallel literary tradition. It is commonplace, with the blessing of the Académie Française, to treat Brassens or Brel as major poets: they have taken their place in the pantheon of cultural monuments.
[PGH]

See C. Brunschwig, L.-J. Calvet, J.-C. Klein, Cent ans de chanson française (1981); L. Rioux, 50 ans de chanson française (1993).

Chansonnier, see MANUSCRIPTS; CHANSON FRANÇAISE.

Chansons de mal-mariée. Songs expressing the grievances of an unhappy wife, traditional in northern and southern France and Italy, reflect the social reality of customary male dominance. The genre seems native to both regions of France despite the imbalance of surviving early examples (Old French outnumbering Old Occitan). These are mostly anonymous and probably late 12th- or early 13th-c. pseudo-popular adaptations of lost, orally transmit-ted folk-songs originating in May festivals—hence perhaps the high proportion of dance-song forms employed.

Typically, a young, occasionally coquettish wife complains that against her will she has married an old, impotent, yet cruel and jealous boor but desires a real or imaginary young lover. Variations include the reluctant fiancée (15th c. onwards); the nun reluctantly wedded to the Church but yearning for a male liberator (13th and 14th c. onwards); the drudge in penury, losing her youthful charms, married to a boozing womanizer and nostalgically recalling an old flame (more realistic variant, 15th c. onwards); the dwarf's wife (comically grotesque variant, attested 1724, probably much earlier); the predatory husband-seeker. All probably pre-date their earliest written attestation. Further variations are the complaint of a henpecked husband, comic (*Colin Muset) or wryly ironic (Le Mariage *Rutebeuf), and objective condemnation of the jealous husband or the youngster-marrying hag (13th c. onwards). Pierre Bec surveys the genre and edits 12 examples in La Lyrique française au moyen âge (XIIe–XIIIe siècles) (1977–8).
[PVD]

Chansons de toile or **Chansons d'histoire.** Names given in early- and mid-13th-c. romances by *Jean Renart and Gerbert de Montreuil to third-person narrative *trouvère lyrics, short love stories allegedly sung by ladies at their needlework or linen-weaving. Only 15 complete examples and 6 fragments, all pre-14th c., survive in langue d'oïl [see LANGUE D'OC]. They are conveniently edited by Michel Zink in his study Les Chansons de toile (1978). Motets and rondets de carole draw on other lost specimens. On average the complete lyrics have 61 lines in nine to ten stanzas with a short refrain. Five are ascribed to Audefroi le Bastart (fl. 1200), the rest being anonymous. Their simplicity of style (contrasting with their melodic ornamentation), occasional lapses into assonance, frequent use of Germanic names, and freedom from the conventions of *fin'amor may reflect an archaic northern French tradition (only one Occitan fragment survives). But the archaism may be false and the genre contemporary with other, similarly uninhibited chansons de femme.

These love stories usually end happily with triumph over an obstacle: parental opposition, a forced betrothal, a husband's cruelty, gossip, a third person's presence, geographical distance, a lover's unwarranted suspicion. Or at least fulfilment is promised. But generally any gratification rewards the suffering of the main protagonist, a young, nobly born beauty whose complaint or predicament engages audience sympathy through subjective lyricism or dramatic tension. One chanson d'histoire unexpectedly switches to the first person to contrast the happy couple with the lonesome narrator. Another ends unhappily with the death of one partner, the other becoming a nun.
[PVD]

CHANTAL, Jeanne-Françoise de (Madame Chantal), see FRANÇOIS DE SALES.

'Chant des ouvriers, Le', see DUPONT.

'Chant du départ, Le'. Revolutionary song with words by M.-J. *Chénier and music by Étienne-Nicolas Méhul; probably first sung on 14 July 1794, it became an official national song, sharing the patriotic, militaristic character of 'La Marseillaise'.

Chant du monde, Le, see GIONO.

Chant écarlate, Un, see BA, M.

Chantefable, see AUCASSIN ET NICOLETTE.

CHANTELOUVE, François de (dates unknown). This obscure Gascon from near Libourne was a poetic mediocrity. His play, or rather dramatized pamphlet, *La Tragédie de feu Gaspard de Colligny* (1575), is a curious document defending the murder of the admiral [see COLIGNY]. He also published a tragedy, *Pharaon,* and other poetic works (1577). [KCC]

Chant royal. Relatively fixed verse form standardized by *puys, employed from the early 14th to the 16th c., occasionally revived in the 19th. It developed the form of the *chanson courtoise,* which by *Adam de la Halle's time generally comprised five stanzas plus optional *envoi* keeping the same rhyme endings throughout. The *chant royal* added a one-line concluding refrain to each stanza and any *envoi.* It was thus an extended *ballade,* one stanza shorter than the *double ballade,* similarly allowing for variation in number and length of lines and number of rhymes per stanza. The form was reserved for serious treatment of love, religion, etc. Exponents included *Machaut, *Deschamps, *Crétin, *Marot, and Parmentier. [PVD]

Chants berbères de Kabylie, see AMROUCHE, J.

Chants de Maldoror, Les, see LAUTRÉAMONT.

Chaos et la nuit, Le, see MONTHERLANT.

CHAPELAIN, Jean (1595–1674). French critic and theorist. His ponderous epic *La Pucelle* (1656) was savaged by *Boileau, who was much indebted to his theoretical writings. Chapelain occupied a key position in literary France for many years, being a founder member of the *Académie Française, principal author of the Academy's critique of Le *Cid, and subsequently *Colbert's main literary agent. A series of writings such as his 'Lettres sur la règle des vingt-quatre heures' (1630) lay down the principal doctrines of *classicism, but he also left an interesting correspondence (e.g. with Guez de *Balzac) and a 'Dialogue de la lecture des vieux romans' which shows a fascinatingly ambivalent attitude to medieval *romance. [PF]

Chapelain décoiffé, Le, see PARODY AND PASTICHE.

CHAPELLE, Claude-Emmanuel Lhuillier, known as (1626–86). French poet and *libertin, friend of *Gassendi, *Boileau, and *Molière. His most notable work is the *Voyage en Provence* (1663), written with Bachaumont, a series of lively anecdotes in prose and verse. Renowned for his scathing wit, he was credited with some of the most powerful satires of the day, including the *Chapelain décoiffé.* [GJM]

CHAPSAL, Madeleine (b. 1925). French writer. She began as a journalist on L'*Express, where she published a series of interviews with writers including *Beauvoir and *Lacan later republished as *Les Écrivains en personne* (1960). Subsequently she wrote best-selling novels, such as *La Maison de jade* (1986), describing an older woman's devastation when her young male lover leaves her. She is a member of the Prix Fémina jury. [EAF]

CHAR, René (1907–88). French poet. Dense and often hermetic, but also intensely lyrical and impassioned, Char's work reflects the rugged beauty and radiant light of his native Provençal landscape. Born at L'Isle sur la Sorgue (Vaucluse) he retained traces of *l'accent du midi* and remained resolutely unmetropolitan despite long periods of residence in Paris. The names of cherished sites: Thouzon, Le Thor, Buoux, Richerenches, Les Névons (a family domain sold against Char's wishes after his mother died in 1954), recur frequently in his work, where a sense of the world's threatened beauty is omnipresent (Char campaigned against nuclear installations in the 1960s). Yet it would be wrong to see him as a regional or nature poet. Char's concern with place, which was to be echoed by many poets of the post-war generation, is ultimately ethical in character and relates to the question of how we should 'dwell' (in the German philosopher Heidegger's phrase) on earth. A correspondence with Heidegger, who shared Char's interest in the pre-Socratic philosophers and their affirmation that all phenomena were in permanent flux, led to seminars held at Le Thor in the 1960s. Yet, if the Char–Heidegger encounter represents a vital convergence of poetry and philosophy, Char's poems are not potted treatises and require no specialized knowledge.

He is none the less a difficult poet, for a number of reasons. First, the forms Char favoured—the *prose poem and the aphorism—are not the most easily accessible. Secondly, his poems are often elliptical, seemingly alluding to events in his life without supplying specific detail. Thirdly, readers sometimes feel a discrepancy between the power and urgency of Char's rhetoric and its lack of clear purport. His discourse appears to remain close to its initial inspiration and thus to make a certain necessary obscurity part of its message: 'j'aime qui éblouit puis accentue l'obscur à l'intérieur de moi.'

Between 1930 and 1935 Char participated in the *Surrealist movement (*Le Marteau sans maître,* 1934), his early poems having attracted the attention of *Éluard. Although he mistrusted automatic writing and found it hard to toe a party line, Surrealism suited his natural combativeness and disdain for authority, and the promotion of poetry to the centre of human existence made a lasting impression. The *Occupation marked a turning-point for Char. He played a leading role in the Resistance, becoming, under the pseudonym Capitaine Alexandre, 'chef départemental (Basses-Alpes) des Forces françaises combattantes', and leading many dangerous missions. He chose not to publish during the war but never stopped writing, and the works which emerged after the Liberation are among his most widely admired (*Fureur et mystère*, 1948).

Seuls demeurent (1945) initiated a lasting friendship with *Camus, who in 1946 published Char's *Feuillets d'Hypnos*—notes and reflections written in the *maquis*—in his collection L'Espoir for *Gallimard. In different ways both works show how for Char the urgent interrogation of the nature of poetry, and in particular the role and credentials of the poet, was the pathway towards unveiling more general truths. Indeed, poetry, in his writing, becomes the embodiment of the irreducibly enigmatic nature of human experience as disclosed in such diverse fields as love, eroticism, political aspiration, art, and philosophy. Many of his most resonant aphorisms—'L'Éclair me dure', or 'Le poème est l'amour réalisé du désir demeuré désir'—stress the provisional, fragile nature of poetic truth, placing the emphasis on possibility rather than actuality. Poetry is a disruptive force, a form of violence which questions the *status quo*: 'la réalité sans l'énergie disloquante du poème, qu'est-elle?' The poet's role is to keep open the door to a transformed future: 'A chaque effondrement des preuves le poète répond par une salve d'avenir.'

In Char's hands the prose poem, poised between abstract discourse and narrative, harks back to *Rimbaud's *Illuminations*, and his mastery of the form, in *Les Matinaux* (1950) or *Le Nu perdu* (1971), is consummate. One should not neglect, however, his many poems in free verse where, as in his haunting plays (*Trois coups sous les arbres*, 1967), a certain musicality relieves the fragmentary abruptness of his manner. The visual arts were of paramount importance to Char and he counted many painters among what he called his 'alliés substantiels': from Georges de *la Tour, *Poussin, and *Braque to Nicolas de Staël and Viera da Silva. In *La Nuit talismanique* (1972) he reveals his own talent for visual creation.

[MHTS]

See M. A. Caws, *L'Œuvre filante de René Char* (1981); J.-C. Mathieu, *La Poésie de René Char ou le Sel de la splendeur*, 2 vols. (1984–5); E. Marty, *René Char* (1990).

CHARCOT, Jean-Martin (1825–93). The founder of modern neurology, Charcot established the classic descriptions of numerous nervous diseases, and pioneered new diagnostic techniques. He was particularly noted for his studies of hysteria, which he refused to categorize as an exclusively female disorder, and for the use of hypnosis in its investigation. While emphasizing organic factors and thereby underestimating the role of suggestion in the development of hysteria, he acknowledged the relevance of psychological traumas, dissociated from the patient's consciousness, in determining the nature of its symptoms. Freud was indebted to Charcot, having attended his celebrated clinical examinations in 1885 and 1886 [see PSYCHOANALYSIS]. [REG]

CHARDIN, Jean (1643–1713). Probably the most important French author of travels in the Orient. A Protestant jewel merchant, he spent 13 years in Persia; after the Revocation of the *Edict of Nantes he took refuge in England and Holland. His *Journal du voyage du chevalier Chardin en Perse* (1686) was much praised and translated; his complete *Voyages* in 10 vols. appeared in 1711. He gives a detailed and objective account of Persian society, based on serious research and a knowledge of the language and its literature. His writings, with *Tavernier's, are a major source of Montesquieu's *Lettres persanes*.

[PF]

CHARDIN, Jean-Baptiste Siméon (1699–1779). French painter. In 1737 he exhibited *La Fontaine* and *La Blanchisseuse* at the Salon, and the art collector Mariette recorded in 1759 that engravers competed for the right to reproduce them—often with a moralizing sub-text. Chardin exhibited until 1773 in the Salon, where *Diderot admired his deceptively direct, morally elevating genre scenes. He reserved his most unstinting praise, however, for the paint handling and naturalism of Chardin's still-life subjects. Royalty, members of the aristocracy, and many major artists collected his paintings. The king allotted him rooms in the Louvre (1757), and he held high office in the Academy. After a period of eclipse his reputation was restored around 1846. *Proust wrote an essay on Chardin, included in *Contre Sainte-Beuve*. [JPC]

CHAREF, Mehdi (b. 1952). Algerian-born novelist and film-maker, the first *Beur writer to arouse significant public interest. Since the age of 11 he has lived in Paris, where his father was an immigrant worker. *Le Thé au harem d'Archi Ahmed* (1983), which Charef later turned into his first feature film, is a slightly fictionalized account of his adolescence in a working-class Paris suburb. *Le Harki de Meriem* (1989) interweaves scenes from the *Algerian War with racist incidents in France a quarter of a century later. [AGH]

Charivari, Le. Satirical paper founded by Charles Philipon in 1832, famous for its subversive treatment of life in the July Monarchy and the Second Empire. Though less political than its stable-mate *La Caricature*, it published material which ruthlessly

exposed social and political corruption, as in
*Daumier's Robert Macaire series (1836–8).   [BR]

CHARLEMAGNE (Charles I) (742–814). The son of
Pippin (Pépin le Bref), first Arnulfing king of
Francia, Charles succeeded to the throne in 768.
Initially his reputation rested on the successes of his
Frankish armies in Aquitaine, in Italy, against the
Avars, and against the Saxons, his only military dis-
aster being the destruction of his rearguard at
Rencesvals (Roncesvalles)—the subject of the
*Chanson de *Roland—in 778. Victory guaranteed him
a degree of authority over all the dukes and counts
of his disparate realms.

Charles inaugurated a thoroughgoing reform of
the Frankish Church. He called scholars—Alcuin the
Englishman, Theodulf the Goth, Paul the Deacon, a
Lombard—to his court, where they revived the
study of classical Latin so that patristic literature and
early codes of canon law should again be fully comprehensible [see LATINITY]. Charles participated in
their discussions, promoted them to positions of
trust, commanded others to imitate them, encouraged the copying of manuscripts, and patronized a
concomitant revival of late antique art forms. In 800
he was summoned by Pope Leo III to Rome, where
on Christmas Day he was crowned emperor. The
revival of the ancient title (extinct in the West since
476) consolidated Charles's authority and after his
death in 814 perpetuated his fame as a Christian hero.
In succeeding centuries he was remembered as the
ideal French king, and portrayed in *chansons de geste
as a warrior against the infidel.   [JHD]

Charles. For French kings of this name, apart from
Charles IX and Charles X, see the Chronology.

CHARLES IX (1550–74) inherited the throne on the
premature death of his brother, François II, in 1560.
His mother, *Catherine de Médicis, initially acted as
regent and attempted to maintain a powerful influence over him. He followed Catherine's decision to
conciliate the Protestants, but was persuaded to
sanction the *St Bartholomew's Day Massacre,
which finally alienated the Protestants and led them
to develop new theories of popular sovereignty and
the right of resistance. Despite his weaknesses,
Charles was much loved by *Ronsard.   [JJS]

CHARLES X (1757–1836). Grandson of Louis XV,
younger brother of Louis XVI and Louis XVIII, the
last *Bourbon king of France. As comte d'Artois he
was a bitter enemy of the *Revolution, going into
emigration in 1789. He led the *ultras after the
*Restoration. Succeeding to the throne in 1824, he
precipitated his downfall in July 1830 by his reactionary policies. The faithful Chateaubriand gives a
haunting description of his exile in Prague in the
*Mémoires d'outre-tombe.   [PF]

CHARLES D'ORLÉANS (1394–1465). Poet. Nephew
to Charles VI, Charles was brought up in a cultured,
cosmopolitan court. In 1407, however, his father,
the duke of Orléans, was assassinated at the order of
his cousin, the duke of Burgundy, and Charles, pursuing retribution, was thrust into the political tur-
moils of the late *Hundred Years War. Captured at
Agincourt in 1415, he spent the next 25 years as a
prisoner in England. His imprisonment, while courteous, was solitary and conducive to poetry. Charles
had already composed a few lyrics and a short,
rather unfocused allegory, *La Retenue d'Amours*; in
England he found his forte, the shorter fixed forms
such as *chanson* and *ballade. Freed in 1440, he first
attempted to pick up the threads of his inheritance
and political ambitions; soon disillusioned, he settled from about 1450 until his death in 1465 almost
exclusively in Blois, where he cultivated poets and
artists. His personal manuscript for these later years
survives; it preserves not only his own *œuvre* (in
these years the *rondeau predominates) but also
works composed by his entourage, including
*Villon.

Charles's rank means that we have an unusual
wealth of biographical information; this and his
romantic life-history tempt critics to read the poems
of exile autobiographically, insisting on images of
imprisonment or attempting to identify Charles's
unnamed 'dame'. But although the ballades are
attributed to an insistent poetic *je*, this persona
remains shifting and fragmented. A recurring dialectic is established between the poetic *je* and its counterpart, 'mon cuer', in which the former is the
detached analyst, the latter the victim of conflicting
personifications. Thus emotional conflicts are the-
atricalized, and out of the conventional metaphors
of *fin'amor (whose traditional character should
warn us against reading the lyrics too confession-
ally) Charles creates a coherent poetic landscape ('le
logis de mon cuer', 'la nef de Bonne Nouvelle',
'l'ermitage de Pensee', 'la forest d'Ennuyeuse
Tristesse', the 'moustier amoureux'). Within this
frame, dramatically represented, abstractions and
poetic persona interact: the poetic *je* plays chess
with Dangier, takes council with Confort, and—typically self-reflexive—reads the 'rommant de Plaisant
Penser'.

From 1440, particularly in the rondeaux, this elaborate allegorical world achieves even greater sophistication. A new conflict becomes a *leitmotiv*: the
poetic *je* is increasingly torn between Melancolie
and Nonchaloir, an elegant, faintly amused detachment, even indifference. Reading and writing are
visualized not simply as acts, but as objective states
which in turn objectify the poet's sentiments
('Dedens mon Livre de Pensee | J'ay trouvé escrip-
vant mon cueur | La vraye histoire de douleur, |
De larmes toute enluminee'). And the range of allegorical settings is increased: war and conflict are
conventional enough, but more original are the
hunt or the law-courts, the tournament or the *fête
champêtre* ('Les fourriers d'Esté sont venus | Pour
appareillier son logis, | Et ont fait tendre ses tappis,
| De fleurs et verdure tissus').

This revitalization of metaphor is matched by formal and linguistic flexibility. Charles's vocabulary is not wide, but his shifts of register, his conversational syntax, his use of proverbs or technical terminologies give an impression of ease and intimacy. His handling of the fixed forms which he favoured is masterly: the essential musicality of ballade and rondeau, the discipline of the refrains, and the metric constraints provide a spatial framework in which he flourishes. His most lasting contribution is his centring of the poetic enterprise on self-exploration; like Villon's or *Machaut's, Charles's poetic *je* is one of the pioneers of the landscape of the self. [JHMT]

See D. Poirion, *Le Poète et le prince* (1965); J. Fox, *The Lyric Poetry of Charles d'Orléans* (1969); D. A. Fein, *Charles d'Orléans* (1983); D. H. Nelson, *Charles d'Orléans: An Analytical Bibliography* (1990).

CHARLES LE TÉMÉRAIRE (1433–77). The last great duke of Burgundy, he was killed in battle against the French [see BURGUNDIAN COURT LITERATURE].

CHARLEVOIX, Pierre-François-Xavier, père de (1682–1761). French Jesuit missionary in Canada, subsequently a contributor to the *Mémoires de *Trévoux*. He published historical accounts of Japan, Paraguay, and San Domingo. His most famous work is the monumental *Histoire et description de la Nouvelle France* (1744), which brings together previous work on the settlement of North America with a journal of his own travels. [PF]

Charlie-Hebdo. Founded in 1960 by *Cavanna, with Cabu, Choron, Gébé, Reiser, Willem, and Wolinski, the monthly *Hara-Kiri*, 'journal bête et méchant', set out to shock and provoke. Setting a new tone, it established complicity with readers, but often fell foul of press laws. *Hara-Kiri Hebdo*, launched in 1969, aiming at greater topicality, fared even worse. The derisive headline on de *Gaulle's death, 'Bal tragique à Colombey: un mort', alluding to a dance-hall fire, incurred a complete ban, and *Charlie-Hebdo*, named after the group's other monthly, specializing in *bandes dessinées*, took its place from 1970 until publication ceased in January 1982. It was relaunched in 1992. [SFN]

Charlus, Palamède de Guermantes, baron de. Memorable and comic character in Proust's *A la recherche du temps perdu*; from *Sodome et Gomorrhe* on his homosexuality becomes one of the main themes of the work.

Charmes, see VALÉRY.

CHARON, Jean-Émile-Octave (b. 1920). French physicist, on the Commissariat à l'Énergie Atomique 1955–61, and author of the theory of Complex Relativity, an attempt to reconcile Einstein with quantum theory. The universe is two-sided, having an outer, entropic, and an inner, negentropic, space, the former being the physical, the latter the mental, world. Mental space is located within electrons, which are indestructible particles. Books such as *L'Homme à sa découverte* (1963) and *L'Esprit et la relativité complexe* (1983), therefore, propose that mind is a necessary and immortal denizen of the universe. [GDM]

CHARPENTIER, François (1620–1702). French man of letters, academician, author of works on painting, and defender of the cause of the *modernes* [see QUERELLE] in his *Défense de la langue française* (1676) and *L'Excellence de la langue française* (1683).

CHARPENTIER, Marc-Antoine (c.1645–1704), French composer, principally of sacred music, but also of *pastorales*, chamber operas, and two *tragédies lyriques*, one, *Médée* (1693), to a libretto by Thomas *Corneille. He replaced *Lully as *Molière's musical collaborator in 1672–3, and after Molière's death still worked with his company until 1686, writing *intermèdes*, prologues, and general incidental music for plays. [KM]

CHARRIÈRE, Isabelle de (1740–1805). Born into a Dutch aristocratic family, Belle de Zuylen, now more usually known as Isabelle de Charrière, is important principally as a novelist and letter-writer, and as the friend of James Boswell and later of Benjamin *Constant.

Brought up at Slot Zuilen, near Utrecht, she early showed an independent and unconventional turn of mind. Before her marriage in 1771 to Charles-Emmanuel de Charrière, a member of the Swiss gentry, she had engaged in a clandestine correspondence with a married man, Constant d'Hermenches, uncle of Benjamin Constant, and published a *conte* satirizing aristocratic pride of ancestry, *Le Noble* (1762). After 1771 she lived at Colombier, near Neuchâtel, where she wrote novels, political and literary pamphlets, plays, and poetry, some of which remained in manuscript until the publication of her *Œuvres complètes*, ed. J.-D. Candaux and others (1979–84).

Her fiction brings a keen and probing intelligence to bear on moral questions, particularly where relations between the sexes are concerned. *Lettres neuchâteloises* (1784) and *Lettres écrites de Lausanne* (1785) scrutinize the workings of class and gender in provincial communities, while *Lettres de Mistriss Henley* (1784), a microscopic *Madame Bovary*, portrays with a degree of dark wit the plight of a *mal mariée*. Her best-known novel, *Caliste* (1787), written as a sequel to *Lettres écrites de Lausanne*, anticipates *Corinne and *Adolphe. It is the study of a heroine whose conduct in the past has transgressed society's norms for sexual behaviour, and whose hesitant and indecisive admirer, William, is held back from making a firm commitment to her by his father's disapproval. [DW]

Charroi de Nîmes, Le. *Chanson de geste* of the Cycle de *Guillaume, probably composed in the 1150s or

1160s to provide a bridge between *Le *Couronnement de Louis* and *La *Prise d'Orange*. The first 600 lines present a confrontation between Guillaume and the emperor Louis, provoked by the latter's failure to grant his most faithful vassal a fief. Lines 783–1485 relate the expedition to Nîmes as a swashbuckling adventure, borrowing its central motif (the hero disguised as merchant with an army hidden in barrels) from a folk-tale akin to Ali Baba. With his clumsy power, mighty punch, and hearty laugh, Guillaume is also assimilated to folk-tale giants. [PEB]

CHARRON, Pierre (1541–1603). Moral philosopher. Born in Paris, he began a career in the law, then became a priest and was renowned for his preaching. He shifted allegiance in 1589 from the *Ligue to the *Politiques; at about the same time *Montaigne befriended him. In 1593 he published *Les Trois Vérités*, in which he argued that religion is necessary and that God exists; that Christianity is revealed truth; and that Roman Catholicism is the only authentic version of Christianity. His targets in this work were atheists, infidels, and Protestants. In his more famous work *De la sagesse* (1601), he shifts his attention away from strictly theological issues to man himself. Borrowing heavily from Seneca, Plutarch, *Du Vair, Justus Lipsius, Huarte, and especially Montaigne, he sets out a sceptical and *Neostoic philosophy which is founded on the close interrelationship of practical wisdom with knowledge and personal integrity. His reliance on Montaigne is so great that some chapters of his work are no more than transcriptions of passages from the *Essais*. *De la sagesse* appeared no less than 49 times between 1601 and 1672, and is almost as important as the *Essais* themselves as a source of information about Montaigne's ideas. Although he was attacked in the 17th c. as a *libertin because of his positive attitude towards scepticism, there is little reason to doubt Charron's personal orthodoxy. [IM]

Charte, La, see RESTORATION.

CHARTIER, Alain (1380/90–c.1430). Chartier entered the service of Charles VII—then dauphin—shortly before 1417, and remained there as royal notary and secretary until after 1428. A trusted emissary, he acted on several occasions as ambassador to various European courts. Nearly 200 manuscripts of his work are extant, a measure of his prestige.

His literary production was considerable, in Latin and in French; the former mainly consists of official discourses interesting for the light they throw on Chartier's own Latinity. His French writings, prose and verse, accounted for his reputation in his own time. His earliest poems are courtly and conventional, but his first notable work, *Le Livre des quatre dames* (c.1416), holds a typically delicate balance between poet as lover and poet as commentator. The poet as character meets four ladies lamenting their distress in the wake of what is clearly the battle

of Agincourt; all four castigate those who fled. The poem is a debate: which of them has suffered the most, the first who is widowed, the second whose husband is imprisoned, and so on.

Certain formal features—the poet as observer, the debate form—recur in his best-known and most popular poem, *La Belle Dame sans mercy* (1424), whose tone is an interesting mixture of the courtly and the mildly satirical. The poet overhears a conversation between a mournful, languishing Amant and a briskly sceptical, rational Belle Dame proof against all the Lover's emotional appeals. Elsewhere in his writings debate goes hand in hand with despair at the plight of France. The *Debat du herault, du vassault et du villain* (after 1415) externalizes this despair with a debate between a despondent knight, a herald looking for a return to the old values, and a brusque peasant. The poem anticipates his best-known prose work, the *Quadrilogue invectif* (1422). This stages another debate, this time between France herself and representatives of the different estates: a nobility cowardly and idle, a clergy intent on worldly pleasure, a people demanding and discontented. The debate, conducted with a sophisticated dialectic, is couched in an eloquent, rhetorical, Latinate prose, its austere and measured periods balancing the sense of distance created by allegory and a genuine indignation inspired by contemporary disasters. His last major work, the unfinished *Lai d'esperance* (1428–9), betrays a growing sense of disillusionment: in this allegory, Defiance, Indignation, and Deseperance invite him to suicide; he is rescued from his despair only by the three theological virtues. [JHMT]

See F. Rouy, *L'Esthétique du traité moral d'après les œuvres d'Alain Chartier* (1980).

CHARTIER, Émile-Auguste, see ALAIN.

Chartreuse de Parme, La. *Stendhal's second great novel, dictated in less than two months, published in 1839. The publisher forced cuts on Stendhal, and the later sections are more abrupt than intended.

Though based on a 17th-c. chronicle of a Renaissance story, it is set in modern Italy—an Italy shaped by its author's desires. It opens with the burst of life brought to Milan by the armies of Napoleon. The hero, Fabrice del Dongo, apparently the natural son of the marquise del Dongo and a French officer, is brought up on Lake Como by his mother and his aunt, Gina Pietranera, who after her husband's death becomes the duchesse de Sanseverina in an arranged marriage. Fabrice, who is at odds with his official father and elder brother (humourless devotees of the Austrian authorities who succeed Napoleon), goes as a naïve young man to fight for his hero at Waterloo—the famous unheroic description of the battle inspired Tolstoy's *War and Peace*. On his return he pursues—without conviction—a successful ecclesiastical career in the petty tyranny of Parma, where his aunt is living with her lover, the worldly-wise yet passionate Count Mosca, chief minister to the prince. Made uneasy by Gina's undeclared love for him, Fabrice avoids her, has an affair with an actress, whose lover he kills in a fight, and is eventually imprisoned in the lofty citadel of Parma. Here he finds his true love, Clélia Conti, the young daughter of the commandant. Against his will, he agrees to escape from prison, but soon returns, and is only narrowly saved from poisoning by Gina's agreement to sleep with the young prince (successor to the tyrant whom she has had murdered in revenge for his treatment of Fabrice). In the final chapters Fabrice finds his way back to the heart of Clélia, who has married and made a vow never to *see* him again. They are reunited in darkness, and know three years' happiness, before Fabrice's desire to see his and Clélia's son results in the death of child and mother. He retires to the Carthusian monastery of the title and dies a year later, soon followed by Gina.

Stendhal dedicated La Chartreuse to the 'Happy Few', and it was not very successful at first. Like Le *Rouge et le noir, it combines brilliant political satire (much admired by *Balzac) with a romantic love story. The four main characters are finely matched: Fabrice is superstitious and weak-willed, Clélia naïve, but both are beautiful figures of romance, set against the more experienced and richly characterized Gina and Mosca. The novel is a great poem of Italy, playful and passionate, full of Stendhal's own presence, an equivalent in words to the operas of Mozart he so loved. [PF]

CHASLE, Raymond (b. 1930). A Mauritian diplomat, Chasle is also a poet. His collections include *Vigiles irradiées* (1973) and *L'Alternance des solstices* (1975). He is fascinated by the *calligramme*, and his poetry is often described as 'ascensionnel'. [BEJ]

CHASLES, Philarète (1798–1873). The son of a member of the Convention, this influential and prolific literary critic and professor was a pioneer of the comparative spirit. He wrote widely on French, classical, and English literature and was appointed to the *Collège de France in 1841. His *Mémoires* (1876-7) form a valuable source for our knowledge of the literary life of the Romantic period.

CHASLES, Robert, see CHALLE.

Chasse spirituelle, La, see HOAXES.

CHASSIGNET, Jean-Baptiste (c.1570–c.1635). Lawyer and poet from Besançon; like *La Ceppède, *Favre, and other contemporary provincial poets, he played a significant role in local government. He published a substantial collection of Christian poems on death (Le Mépris de la vie et consolation contre la mort, 1594) and paraphrases of sacred texts. The preface of Le Mépris claims that it was inspired by the *Wars of Religion. Borrowings from *Ronsard's Derniers vers, *Montaigne's Essais, and other prose writers are detectable in this collection: the latter supply a number of *Neostoic motifs. Chassignet's evocations of the ephemeral nature of life and the horror of death are often regarded as characteristically *baroque.
[TC]

CHASTELAIN DE COUCI, LE. Celebrated *trouvère now generally identified as Gui, the powerful castellan of Coucy-le-Château (Aisne), attested in charters from 1186 to 1201. Oddly, no document gives Gui his dynastic surname 'de Torote', which prompts speculation that he may be identical with *Gace Brulé's friend Gui de Ponceaux. *Villehardouin reports that, on the Fourth Crusade, Gui joined a faction of temporarily dissident crusaders shortly before his death and burial at sea (May 1203). Of 34 lyrics ascribed to the Chastelain in manuscripts, seven are unquestionably authentic and six possibly genuine. All 13 *chansons* are elevated in style, 11 expressing *fin'amor and 2 being a crusader's complaint at having to leave his lady. While observing the conventions and conceits of the *grand chant courtois, they suggest a degree of physical attraction, even eroticism, unusual in the noble register and successfully convey a hint of natural sincerity.

The Chastelain's fame as poet and ill-starred crusader inspired Jakemes's late 13th-c. *Roman du castelain de Couci et de la dame de Fayel*, a 8,266-line extravaganza which, like a *razo* [see VIDA] to a lyric by *Guilhem de Cabestaing, reworks the well-known folk-tale about the lady who inadvertently eats her dead lover's heart. [PVD]

Chastelaine de Vergi, La. This brief, anonymous 13th-c. verse romance recounts the violent end of a tragic love affair with remarkable elegance and precision. The châtelaine of Vergy grants her love to a knight on the condition that he never speak of their affair to anyone. But their courtly liaison is destroyed by the jealous duchess of Burgundy, who loves the knight in vain. Like Potiphar's wife, she complains to her husband that the knight has tried to seduce her. In order to avoid the accusation of treason when confronted by the angry duke, the knight reveals that he loves the châtelaine. The news travels from duke to duchess and finally to the châtelaine, who dies of sorrow when she realizes that her lover has broken his vow. The knight kills himself at his lady's side, and the duke delivers a fatal blow of the sword to his wife. The tale's poetic artistry contrasts with the sordid plot of deception and death; it was frequently copied and cited, and was adapted in the 15th and 16th c. in verse and prose, notably by Marguerite de Navarre in the *Heptaméron. [RLK]

CHASTELLAIN or **CHASTELAIN,** Georges (c. 1415–1475), nicknamed 'le grand Georges'. Chronicler and poet, often seen as 'father' of the *Rhétoriqueurs. He was born in Flanders and held various posts at the court of *Burgundy under Philippe le Bon and then Charles le Téméraire. Although he was an official historian, his unfinished prose *Chroniques* often attempt to take a relatively objective view and are not always hostile to France. His verse includes lengthy political or moralizing pieces such as *Les Princes* (sometimes interpreted, though unconvincingly, as a satire against Louis XI), *Le Trône azuré* (rejoicing in France's defeat of the English), the *Dit de Vérité* (bitter reproaches against the French), and *Le Miroir de Mort*, as well as ballades and rondeaux on various topics.   [CMSJ]

CHASTELLUX, François-Jean, marquis de (1734–88). A French aristocrat and a soldier, he charmed the *salons and sympathized with the *philosophes. His *De la félicité publique* (1772) is a rebuttal of *Mably's pessimism. Influenced by Vico, Hume, and *Voltaire, he tries to demonstrate historically that happiness depends on good government and enlightenment, and that we should not despair of progress. Chastellux later fought for American independence; his *Voyages dans l'Amérique septentrionale* (1786) are a straightforward account of everyday life, the natural world, cities and battlefields, written in diary form.   [PF]

Chastiements. 13th-c. moralizing and didactic tracts in verse on various topics, comparable to the Occitan *ensenhamens. Old French *chastiement* means both 'punishment, rebuke, correction' and 'instruction, advice'. Critical and corrective intent inspires two anonymous diatribes, *Le Chastiement des clers* (60 anti-goliardic alexandrines in rhyming couplets) and the sermon *Por chatoier les orgueilloz* (216 octosyllabics in sixains; composed 1250–75), which predictably condemns all prevalent sins, notably pride and acquisitiveness, from an eschatological viewpoint. Criticism passes for instruction in the anonymous anti-feminist satire *Le Chastie-musart* (two versions), whose author claims to be poor and therefore free to denounce the folly of love which dupes simpletons (*musars*). Traditional coarse humour and jibes at female unreliablity, illogicality, venality, vanity, etc. are hardly tempered by occasional admissions that exceptional women are virtuous and poor ones pardonable. Violence to punish female misbehaviour is advocated.

Purely instructive, however, is *Robert de Blois's *Chastoiement des dames* (757 octosyllabics in couplets; composed *c*.1233–66), a ladies' guide to etiquette. Modesty of dress and behaviour are advised, but extra-marital affairs condoned if of long standing. The anonymous *Chastoiement d'un père à son fils* (two versions), moralizing tales with some linking narrative, adapts the 12th-c. *Disciplina clericalis* by the Hispano-Jewish author Petrus Alfunsi.   [PVD]

'Chat botté, Le'. One of Perrault's *Histoires ou contes*, the story of Puss in Boots.

CHATEAUBRIAND, François-René, vicomte de (1768–1848). Born in Saint-Malo of an old Breton noble family whose declining fortunes his father somewhat restored, Chateaubriand spent his youth there or with his grandmother, or particularly at Combourg, a medieval château acquired by his father which provided rich material for his Romantic imagination. Destined for the army, he was presented at court in 1787 but also frequented literary circles with *Fontanes, *La Harpe, *Ginguené, and particularly *Malesherbes. Partly at the latter's prompting, after witnessing the beginnings of the Revolution, Chateaubriand set forth for North America (June 1791–January 1792), visiting Philadelphia, New York, Niagara Falls, and venturing west as far as Ohio. Recent scholarship has established that the itinerary he claimed, often considered fantastic, was quite accurately described. Chateaubriand was to put his American sojourn to considerable literary profit, writing a prose epic, *Les Natchez* (published 1826), of the amorous and other adventures of the Frenchman René among the Indians and in the French and Indian wars.

After his return to France he joined the army of the émigré princes, was wounded at the Battle of Thionville, and made his way from there to Jersey and then England, only returning to France in 1800. In England, his life was difficult, but he wrote extensively and in 1797 published his *Essai historique, politique et moral sur les révolutions anciennes et modernes dans leurs rapports avec la révolution française*, a deeply pessimistic book equating all revolutions, announcing the end of Christianity, combining political theory and personal outpourings. Back in France, he achieved fame with the publication of *Atala (1801), originally a part of *Les Natchez*, and then of *Le Génie du christianisme* (1802), which happily coincided with *Napoleon's efforts to restore Catholicism. The chapter on the prototypical Romantic hero *René was much appreciated. According to *Le Génie*, man's desire for the absolute is infinite, and only religion can satisfy that desire. Christianity satisfies the imagination and the emotions, inspires beautiful works of art, contributes to civilization and progress. The aesthetic, positivistic aspect of his apologetics—Christianity is true because it is good and beautiful—was to have widespread influence.

An appreciative Napoleon sent him to Rome, but he there tangled with Cardinal Fesch. In 1804, indignant at the assassination of the duc d'*Enghien, he resigned and became increasingly hostile towards the Napoleonic regime. He moved to La Vallée aux Loups, a country house to the south of Paris where he redesigned both house and garden. In 1806 he embarked on a lengthy trip to the Orient (Constantinople, Jerusalem, Egypt, Carthage, finally Spain) which led to his *Itinéraire de Paris à Jérusalem* (1811). Like much travel literature of the period, the book is something of a compendium and a rewriting, but many of the descriptive passages are rich. He also produced *Les Martyrs ou le Triomphe de la religion chrétienne* (1809), another prose epic about the triumph of Christianity over paganism. The Christian hero loves a pagan maid, she becomes converted, they are separated, then reunited, then martyred.

He also regularly wrote political journalism for the *Mercure de France*, and had a series of amorous engagements with often notable women (his marriage, made hastily in 1792, was not a happy one) including Delphine de Sabran, contesse de Custine and mother of Astolphe de *Custine, Claire de Kersaint, duchesse de *Duras, and, especially from 1817 until his death, Juliette *Récamier.

He was elected to the Académie Française in 1811, but not allowed to read his anti-Napoleon *discours de réception*. In 1814 he published *De Buonaparte et des Bourbons*, a virulent attack against Napoleon then in exile on Elba (Chateaubriand had written it before his fall from power); Louis XVIII said the volume 'was worth an army'. He accompanied Louis XVIII to Ghent during the Hundred Days. Under the second Bourbon *Restoration he had a highly chequered political career, largely because he sought to combine loyalty to legitimacy with the defence of political liberties, especially the liberty of the press; also, his political ambitions were not always accompanied by the necessary competence and skills. His *De la monarchie selon la Charte* (1816), a defence of Louis XVIII's policies but with a conclusion sharply critical of some governmental actions, led to his fall from favour and one of many serious financial crises, forcing him to sell La Vallée aux Loups. He soon returned to partial favour, served as ambassador to Berlin and to London, was present at the Congress of Verona, and was minister of foreign affairs at the time of the 1823 intervention in Spain. His relations with *Charles X were quite strained, but he was appointed ambassador to Rome in 1828.

After the July Revolution, Chateaubriand, who in many ways had prepared its advent, chose to resign from the Chambre des Pairs out of loyalty to the elder branch of the Bourbons, and began writing his *Histoire de France* (1831). In 1832 his support of the duchesse de *Berry in her effort to foment a civil war and restore the Bourbons led to two weeks' imprisonment, but he was acquitted. His voyages and efforts to reconcile Charles X with his quixotic daughter-in-law were quite unsuccessful. In 1838 he and his wife moved from their home in the rue d'Enfer (next to an infirmary she had directed and supported by the sale of chocolate) to the Hôtel de Clermont-Tonnerre, in the rue du Bac and near L'Abbaye-aux-Bois where Madame Récamier lived and where Chateaubriand went daily; it was one of the most prestigious literary salons of the time. At the behest of his spiritual director, he wrote a *Vie de *Rancé* (1849); the work is also a meditation by Chateaubriand on his own life. In 1847 he finished his *Mémoires d'outre-tombe*, perhaps his most appreciated work today. He was buried, as he had carefully planned, in the Romantic island setting of the Grand Bé, in the Atlantic near Saint-Malo.

Considered by the Romantics and many since as their founding father, with his melancholy vision and his interest in the exotic, the passions, the imagination, Chateaubriand was also a perceptive observer of and important participant in the political scene of his days, and possessed real merit as an apologist of the Christian faith and as an historian and essayist. His combination of acuity, at times bordering on cynicism, revery, and sensibility produced writings which have been greatly appreciated by writers as different as *Hugo, de *Gaulle and *Barthes.   [FPB]

See J.-P. Richard, *Paysage de Chateaubriand* (1967); P. Clarac, *A la recherche de Chateaubriand* (1975); G. Painter, *Chateaubriand* (1979).

CHÂTEAUBRIANT, Alphonse de (1877–1950). French novelist and polemicist. His initial fame came as a Catholic novelist, his *Monsieur des Lourdines* (1911), a nostalgic depiction of the values of a country gentleman, winning the Prix Goncourt, and *La Brière* (1923) the Grand Prix du Roman. He later expressed strong enthusiasm for Nazi Germany in *La Gerbe des forces* (1937), and during World War II edited *La Gerbe*, a leading collaborationist journal. He was condemned to death in 1945, but died in exile.   [RMG]

CHÂTEILLON (Castalio), Sébastien (1515–63). Scholar and Genevan Reformer who collaborated but subsequently quarrelled with *Calvin; celebrated for his eloquent advocacy of religious toleration in *De haereticis* (1554, on the Servetus affair) and *Conseil à la France désolée* (1562, after the massacre of Wassy [see WARS OF RELIGION]). His French translation of the Bible appeared in 1555.   [MJH]

Châtelaine de Vergy, La, see CHASTELAINE DE VERGI.

CHÂTELET, Madame du, see DU CHÂTELET.

Châtiments, Les. A collection of satirical poems by Victor *Hugo attacking *Napoleon III after the *coup d'état* of 1851. Written during the poet-statesman's first year of political exile and published in Brussels in 1853, the work had an important underground success in France. It was re-edited in 1870 after the fall of the Second Empire. Juvenalian satire, rich in historical reference, alternates with prophecy in this work, structured according to the Christian scheme of Fall, Expiation, and Redemption.   [SN]

Chat noir, Le. Café-cabaret in *Montmartre, frequented by writers and artists from 1881 to 1897. A sign over the door said: 'Passant, sois moderne.'

CHATRIAN, Alexandre, see ERCKMANN-CHATRIAN.

Chatterton (1835). Prose drama by *Vigny, who uses the 18th-c. English poet Thomas Chatterton as a symbol of the suffering poet, spurned by a materialist society. The poor hero lodges in London with John Bell, the rather crudely drawn epitome of the philistine, industrial spirit. He is attracted to Bell's wife Kitty, a tender creature devoted to her children, and the two recognize each other as kindred spirits. He writes to the lord mayor requesting assistance, but the latter mocks him, treating him like a servant. In despair, Chatterton poisons himself. Kitty, who has not revealed her true feelings, dies broken-hearted. [CC]

CHAULIEU, Guillaume Amfrye, abbé de (1639–1720). French poet. Although an ecclesiastic, he spent his time in worldly, free-thinking circles, particularly at the *Temple and Sceaux [see MAINE, DUCHESSE DU]. His verse, like that of his bosom friend *La Fare, is presented as that of a worldly amateur; it is harmonious and subtle, and includes many poems addressed to friends and patrons, verse epistles, and letters mixing prose and verse. He named *Chapelle as his poetic master, but his 'muse libertine' also harks back to the *badinage* of *Marot and his successors. His epicurean enjoyment of the privileged pleasures of love, the table, and the countryside is tempered by a melancholy resignation to decline and death. [PF]

CHAUMEIX, Abraham-Joseph de (c.1730–1790). Author of *Préjugés légitimes contre l'Encyclopédie* (1758–9), a voluminous attack on the *Encyclopédie* and *Helvétius's *De l'esprit*.

Chaumière indienne, La, see BERNARDIN DE SAINT-PIERRE.

CHAVÉE, Achille (1906–69). Chavée could simply be presented as one of the leading members of the Belgian *Surrealist group, but that would not do full justice to this self-styled prophet in his own country (see his 1957 poem beginning 'Minuit le temps d'une seconde'). In the 1930s he founded the 'Rupture' group in La Louvière before going to Spain to fight in the International Brigades. He was a believer in the Absolute, his poems tend to be cryptic, and his imagination oscillates between the childlike and the adult. His numerous collections of poems include *Une foi pour toutes* (1938), *D'ombre et de sang* (1946), and *De vie et mort naturelles* (1965). [KRA]

CHAWAF, Chantal (b. 1948). First published by Éditions des Femmes in 1974 with *Retable: la rêverie*, Chawaf has produced more than a dozen texts. Her highly elaborated 'écriture du corps' brings into language areas of pre-verbal experience which have been cut off from language in the Cartesian separation of mind and body. *Blé de semences* (1976) draws on myth and fairy-tale to explore in archetypal terms the drama of the adolescent girl's ambiguous attachment to the mother. *Elwina, le roman-fée* (1986) satirizes an unscrupulous male publisher's attempt to exploit a young woman whose writing is literally a search for the mother. [EAF]

CHAZAL, Malcolm de (1902–81). Mauritian writer. André *Breton declared, with reference to him: 'On n'avait rien entendu de si fort depuis *Lautréamont.' Chazal's enigmatic, fragmentary texts were originally published as *Pensées* (seven

vols.; vol. 7 is entitled *Sens plastique*) on *Mauritius between 1940 and 1945. Gallimard reissued a selection which was published under the title *Sens plastique* (1948).

Chazal's work displays the influence of *Swedenborg, theosophy, and certain cabalistic practices, and his often violent, aphoristic, anthropomorphic texts establish correspondences and syntheses between the human body and the physical, intimately known environment—animal, vegetable, and mineral—of Mauritius. The essential poetic project involves a quest for an original secret harmony accessible through language.

La Vie filtrée was published in 1949; *Petrusmok* (1951) and *Sens magique* (1956) belong to Chazal's 'mythico-biblical' period. Poet, visionary, and mystic, his *L'Homme et la connaissance* and *Sens unique* (both 1974) provide an important insight into the theory which he developed alongside the production of a large corpus of texts. [BEJ]

CHEDID, Andrée (b. 1920). Poet, novelist, and playwright. Born in Egypt but of Lebanese Maronite extraction, Chedid settled in Paris in 1946. The landscape and history (both ancient and modern) of Egypt and Lebanon are constantly present in her work, discreetly in her poetry, more explicitly in her novels, short stories, and plays. A poet first and foremost, Chedid has published many *recueils* which have been collected in two volumes: *Textes pour un poème (1949–1970)* in 1987 and *Poèmes pour un texte (1970–1991)* in 1991. Delicate and often brief, sinuously rhythmical and urgently phrased, her best poems blend metaphysical preoccupations (mortality, the search for unity) with personal, corporeal experience (the human face is a key motif in her work). Chedid has written nearly a dozen novels, several of which are set in Egypt, including *Le Sommeil délivré* (1952), *Le Sixième Jour* (1960), *L'Autre* (1969), *La Maison sans racines* (1985), and many short stories (*Derrière les visages*, 1983). Her plays, of which the best-known is *Bérénice d'Égypte* (1981), have been widely performed. In both her novels and plays Chedid shows a particular concern for women's experience and often combines social realism with more universal or mythic elements. [MHTS]

Chef d'œuvre inconnu, Le. A hunting novella about a failed artist, one of the *Études philosophiques* in Balzac's *Comédie humaine*.

Chemin des ordalies, Le, see LAÂBI.

Chemins de la liberté, Les. Unfinished trilogy of novels, composed and published by *Sartre in the 1940s. Its setting is France at the onset of World War II. *Les Chemins* is a more technically ambitious work than *La *Nausée*; it interweaves a variety of different viewpoints in a form of subjective third-person narrative, similar in some ways to *Flaubert's *style indirect libre*. In the first volume, *L'Âge de raison* (1945), the perspective changes from chapter to chapter throughout the account of a 48-hour period; in volume 2, *Le Sursis* (1945), the time-span is a week, but the viewpoint shifts more rapidly, moving sometimes within a single phrase from one character's perspective to another's. This narrative technique, used here to stress the simultaneity of different reactions to the early years of the war and the phoney peace of 1940, was probably influenced by the American novelist John Dos Passos. The lack of punctuation, the juxtaposition of perspectives, and the intensity created by the single focus of a multiplicity of characters work together to convey the common humanity and intersubjective experience of the French on the verge of war. Necessarily lived as unique, the events are common to all. Volume 3, *La Mort dans l'âme* (1949), reverts to a slower pace of perspectival change.

L'Âge de raison is less experimental than *Le Sursis* but thematically richer. It shows the quest of Mathieu, a university teacher, for the money to pay for his lover Marcelle's illegal abortion. Mathieu is an exemplary failure as an *Existentialist, obsessed with freedom to the extent that he will never commit himself to anything [see ENGAGEMENT]. The two days of his search bring him into contact with a variety of characters: the weak Marcelle, whose opinion on her accidental pregnancy he never seeks; the homosexual Daniel, trapped in his own essentialist vision of his nature; his brother Jacques, a contemptible bourgeois in Mathieu's eyes, who none the less has an uncannily clear insight into the reasons underlying Mathieu's reluctance to commit himself; his student Ivich, with whom he is infatuated, and whose gratuitous, adolescent freedom he covets; his old friend Brunet, a Communist, who is Mathieu's counterpart in that he has accepted the sacrifice of his freedom for the sake of full political commitment. *Les Chemins* shows a wide spectrum of existential positions, none of them fully authentic, all of them familiar options, in the vivid setting of wartime Paris. [CMH]

Chemins qui montent, Les, see FERAOUN.

CHÊNEDOLLÉ, Charles-Julien Lioult de (1769–1833). French writer of didactic and nature poetry (*Le Génie de l'homme*, 1807; *Études poétiques*, 1820). An important figure for early French Romantic poets, he has had a merely antiquarian significance for later readers. He was an associate of *Constant, Madame de *Staël, and *Chateaubriand, an acolyte of *Rivarol, and lover of Lucile de Chateaubriand. [BR]

CHÉNIER, André (1762–94). The most gifted French poet of the 18th c. When he died a victim of the *Revolution, his poems were unknown; they were published for the first time in 1819. Thereafter, for reasons both poetic and political, Chénier was adopted by the *Romantics as a heroic precursor, and a noble legend formed about his name.

He was born in Constantinople of a French father and Greek mother, and always considered himself partly Greek, though he lived in France from the age of 2. After attending the Collège de Navarre, he led a life of study and pleasure, and was secretary of the French ambassador in London. An atheist and fierce critic of the abuses of the *ancien régime*, he welcomed the Revolution, but quickly decided it had got out of hand and threw in his lot with the moderate *Feuillants. He was an impressive orator and journalist, attacking the *Jacobins in virulent articles in the *Journal de Paris*. His stance here, as in his poetry, is an aristocratic one, that of the free spirit, belonging to no party, scorning the crowd, and speaking his mind fearlessly. During the Terror he lay low outside Paris, but was arrested, held in Saint-Lazare prison, and executed two days before *Robespierre's downfall.

Chénier's surviving work is like a great sculpture yard, full of unfinished sketches. These include prose works, notably an 'Essai sur les causes et les effets de la perfection et de la décadence des lettres et des arts', and the beginnings of two philosophical epics, *Hermès* and *L'Amérique*, devoted to the physical history of the globe and human progress from darkness towards the light. Like his friend *Lebrun, he had a high idea of the poetic calling, expressed in a remarkable *ars poetica*, 'L'Invention'. His scorn for modern decadence and triviality was fuelled by an admiration for ancient simplicity and grandeur; he knew Greek literature exceptionally well.

His small body of finished poetry includes the beautifully orchestrated *Bucoliques*, apparently impersonal treatments of ancient themes (the most famous being a lament, 'La Jeune Tarentine'), the more personal *Élégies* (mainly on love), epistles, epigrams, and odes. In his verse, he often recaptures both the music and the eloquence of *Racine. His poetic language combines sonorous classical allusion with the naïveté which he saw as the essential poetic gift. Anticipating *Hugo, he reshapes the rhythms of the alexandrine to give it a new expressive power, using *enjambement* in an unprecedented way. These qualities are perhaps most evident in his satirical and political poems. The *Iambes*, written in alternating alexandrines and octosyllables just before or during his imprisonment, leave an unforgettable picture of the Terror seen by its most eloquent victim. [PF]

See P. Dimoff, *La Vie et l'œuvre d'André Chénier jusqu'à la Révolution française* (1936); F. Scarfe, *André Chénier: His Life and Work* (1965).

CHÉNIER, Marie-Joseph (1764–1811), brother of André [see previous entry], was essentially a dramatist who was intent, like *Voltaire, on making the stage a place for *philosophie*. He had enormous success with his controversial *Charles IX* (November 1789) which, depicting a French king who was the murderous enemy of his subjects, was readily understood as an indictment of Louis XVI. With similar political intentions, he then wrote between

1791 and 1794 *Henri VIII, Calas, Fénelon,* and *Timoléon* (which Robespierre—shades of *Charles IX!*—disliked as intensely as another of Chénier's tragedies, *Caïus Gracchus*). Given his parallel output of patriotic, republican songs and hymns (e.g. 'Le Chant du départ'), Versailles sent Chénier to the Convention. There he was prominent in the reorganization of state education and the founding of the Conservatoire de Musique, the *Institut, and the *École Polytechnique. He emerged from hiding after 27 July 1794 as a right-wing Thermidorian, sat in the Conseil des Cinq Cents, supported Napoleon at Brumaire (even wrote *Cyrus* for his coronation) but, realizing his mistake, redeemed his republicanism with the *Épître à Voltaire,* the *Promenade à Saint-Cloud,* and *Tibère* (staged only in 1844). He spent his declining years composing armchair political tragedies, verse translations from Sophocles, and a useful *Tableau de la littérature française depuis 1789 jusqu'à 1808,* which attacks Romanticism and defends the Enlightenment and the ideals of l'An II.

[JR]

CHÉREAU, Patrice (b. 1944). French theatre director. Co-director (1972–82) of the TNP with *Planchon, and director of the Théâtre des Amandiers, Nanterre, since 1982. Sharing Planchon's Marxist tendencies, he aims to re-situate texts historically in their social and political context. His controversial but influential productions of Wagner's *Ring* cycle at Bayreuth (1976–80) applied similar principles to opera. [DWW]

Chéri. Novel by *Colette, published in 1920, and one of her most popular works. It narrates the relationship between the young Chéri and the older Léa, and explores the tenderness and poignancy of such a liaison, culminating in the positive acceptance by Léa of her final solitude.

Cheval de troie, Le, see NIZAN.

Cheval d'orgueil, Le, see HÉLIAS.

Chevalerie Vivien, La. *Chanson de geste* composed to provide a prologue to *Aliscans in the Cycle de *Guillaume, replacing the first part of the non-cyclic *Chanson de Guillaume. In this version Vivien provokes his own death by vowing, when knighted, never to retreat one pace, then slaughtering a boatload of Saracen prisoners to incite a retaliatory expedition. [PEB]

Chevalier au cygne, Le, see CRUSADE CYCLE.

Chevalier au lion, Le, see CHRÉTIEN DE TROYES.

Chevalier de la charrette, Le, see CHRÉTIEN DE TROYES.

CHEVALIER, Jacques (1882–1962). French Catholic philosopher. Professor of philosophy at Grenoble, his Catholic *Bergsonism influenced *Mounier,

*Lacroix, and others. Briefly minister of education, and of the family, under Vichy, Chevalier is best known for his compendious *Histoire de la pensée* (1955–61).

CHEVALIER, Maurice (1888–1972). Singer, occasionally lyric-writer—the archetype of the popular singer from the French *music-hall, with his dinner-jacket, boater, and thick Parisian accent. His early poverty-stricken years in Belleville led to a youthful debut in the local music-hall and durable success as the partner of Mistinguett at the Folies Bergère in 1912. The peak of his career came between the wars at the Casino de Paris and the Bouffes Parisiens, when around 1924 he first adopted his immortal stage costume and sang 'Valentine'. His stay in Hollywood from 1928 to 1935 did nothing to diminish his popularity in France, but his very public personality created problems during the *Occupation, when he was accused of collaboration and his reputation was seriously compromised; but he managed to retain his role as the singing ambassador of French frivolity until his farewell 80th birthday concert in 1968. [PGH]

Chevallerie Ogier, La, see OGIER.

CHEVREAU, Urbain (1613–1701). French dramatist, translator, and critic. His varied literary output includes poetry, tragedies and tragicomedies, a satirical comedy, two heroic novels, and a translation of Joseph Hall's *Characters*. His most significant work is his literary criticism, which reveals a talent for comparative analysis and a rigorous, at times rigid, conception of classical aesthetic principles. [GJM]

CHEVREUSE, Marie de Rohan, duchesse de (1600–79). An energetic noblewoman, active in unsuccessful intrigues against *Richelieu and *Mazarin, including the *Fronde. She was a possible model for Émilie in *Cinna.

CHEYNET, Anne (b. 1938). Writer from *Reunion, best known for her militant novel *Les Muselés* (1977). Subtitled 'roman réunionnais', the novel focuses on the lives of the island's poor. Cheynet is also a poet. [BEJ]

CHIASSON, Herménegilde, see ACADIA.

Chiendent, Le (1933). *Queneau's first novel, which he claimed was the result of an attempt to translate into modern demotic French *Descartes's *Discours de la méthode*. It does indeed owe much to philosophical enquiry into the nature of being, establishing the existential novel in French well before *Sartre. However, he later revealed that it was Dunne's *An Experiment with Time* which he intended to translate, although his reading of Descartes did play a major role in his conception of the work, particularly in imparting 'le doute méthodique à l'égard de son art'. The novel otherwise obeys a strict set of formal rules such as might govern the construction of a poem—the numerous characters appear and disappear in patterns according with Queneau's notion that 'on peut faire rimer des situations ou des personnages'—and each section of the novel observes the rules of the three unities. There are 91 such sections, 91 being the product of 7 and 13, Queneau's favourite numbers—7 because both his names have 7 letters and 13 for its unlucky and fatal connotations. The sum of the digits of 91 being 1, Queneau thus marked his novel with the numerical symbols of the beginning and the end (since for him 13 was associated with death). [IWR]

Children's Literature. History has not heeded *Rousseau, who thought the reading of books the 'scourge of childhood', although it has canonized the single text he allowed his *Émile, *Robinson Crusoe*. Today it is acknowledged that 'la littérature pour la jeunesse' is a significant marginal area of French writing—for some readers, indeed, it may be the only fictional material approached during a lifetime. There persists, however, a debate about the frontiers of the genre.

From pop-ups to Le *Petit Prince, the concept of children's literature extends from quasi-toys to classics. Do texts addressing a reader of 6 belong with those of interest to a 12-year-old? Are teenage books children's books? Some recognized masterpieces of children's literature are of equal, if not greater, charm for adults. Does, then, the place in the adult canon of La Fontaine's *Fables exclude them from the genre? Have accompanying pictures or a happy ending anything to do with the defining criteria? Should the term encompass the strip-cartoon, itself a Swiss-French invention?

And then there is the question of orality. It was only with the advent of compulsory, free, state primary *education in 1882—nearly two centuries after the appearance of *Perrault's fairy tales—that the majority of French children were taught to read [see LITERACY]. Yet before then a great many had absorbed 'literature', if only in the shape of *formulettes, *comptines*, or lullabies, preserved for posterity by largely female transmitters of an oral culture. These must be included in any definition of children's literature, which will be taken here to mean literature designed primarily to be read or listened to by children up to the age of adolescence.

It may be true that the great British children's classics (much translated into French) by Defoe, Stevenson, Carroll, Kipling, Barrie, Tolkien, Dahl, and others have few counterparts in French, and that the endearing and profound nonsense tradition of Carroll, Lear, or Belloc is largely absent across the Channel, despite some Surrealist output by *Aragon (who translated *The Hunting of the Snark*), Desnos, and others. In France as in Britain, however, a specifically children's literature gradually came into existence from the 17th c. onwards, one of the products of what Philippe Ariès in his controversial *L'Enfant et la vie familiale en France sous*

l'ancien régime (1960) termed the modern 'invention of childhood'.

Animals play a large role in children's books in France as elsewhere, be it the indispensable Milou (Snowy) in Hergé's *Tintin, the green-trousered elephant of Jean de *Brunhoff's *Babar* series, or the denizens of Marcel *Aymé's *Contes du chat perché*. This tradition goes back a long way, as far as the Brer Fox of the 13th-c. *Roman de Renart*, which flowed into post-Renaissance popular culture. With La Fontaine's *Fables* (1668–78), animal characters acquired a place in Versailles court culture, and French children's literature a classic in every sense, not least that of still being taught today in the classroom. Perrault's equally classic stories followed (1691 onwards), inscribing popular oral culture on the page with a mixture of inventiveness and simplicity, magic and realism, which has continued to captivate French children. His Griselidis, le Petit Poucet, and their companions appeared in print virtually contemporaneously with the creation of Racine's tragedies for young ladies, *Esther and *Athalie—the latter of which presented perhaps the first convincing child character in French literature, Joas. Nor should Fénelon's best-selling Odyssey sequel *Télémaque be forgotten.

The *grand siècle*, in short, was also great in terms of children's literature; to the trio of *Corneille, *Racine, and *Molière corresponds that of La Fontaine, Perrault, and Fénelon. A pity that most French children of the 17th c., like most adults, were illiterate. Most talk and writing about fairies, for which there was a contemporary vogue [see SHORT FICTION], took place in the salons of ladies such as Madame d'*Aulnoy, Marie-Jeanne *L'Héritier, Madame Castelnau-Murat, or Anne *Bernard. Only in the mid-18th c. did their tales filter down into the chapbooks that fuelled the imagination of the humble [see BIBLIOTHÈQUE BLEUE].

The taste for the fairy-fantastic was later to be resurrected, for adults, by Romantics such as *Nodier. In between came the moralizing Arnaud *Berquin, creator of *L'Ami des enfants* (1782–3), the first periodical for children, and the prolific Madame de *Genlis. Then, in the mid-19th c., at a time when the expanding *book trade and the progress of education were widening the reading public, appeared the delightful *contestataire* writer and publisher Pierre-Jules *Hetzel (P.-J. Stahl), who produced first the 20 volumes of his *Nouveau magasin des enfants* (1843–7), prettily bound and beautifully illustrated, and then, from 1864, the *Magasin d'éducation et de récréation*, eventually pooled with the famed Bibliothèque Rose (founded 1855) of *Hachette. Among Hetzel's illustrators were *Grandville and *Doré.

It was Hetzel who had the vision to publish the work of possibly the greatest French writer for young readers, Jules *Verne. *Cinq semaines en ballon* (1863) was the first of more than 60 illustrated *Voyages extraordinaires*, the first editions now collectors' items, which took the reader to the heights, depths, and lengths of the planet, often by means of futuristic inventions under the command of doughty leaders such as Captain Nemo of *Vingt mille lieues sous les mers* (1870). Captains, from Nemo to Hook, Haddock to Corcoran, are the stuff of the child's imagination—the text is the vessel, the author at the wheel, the child reader on board like a cabin-boy in the apple-barrel.

It was in 1863, the year of Verne's balloon book, that the 64-year-old comtesse de *Ségur, already the author of nine volumes for children, published *François le bossu*, with *Les Malheurs de Sophie* (1864) and more than half her output still to come. Although variously accused at different times of prejudice and immorality, her books still appeal, thanks to her talent for stories strongly rooted in the reality of her times. Other best-selling 19th-c. children's writers whose works are still in print include Zénaïde Fleuriot, Alfred Assollant (*Le Capitaine Corcoran*, 1867), G. Bruno (*Le *Tour de la France par deux enfants*, 1877), and the much-underrated Hector *Malot, author of the foundling novel *Sans famille*. Malot—like Alphonse *Daudet, whose *Le Petit Chose* was adapted for children by Hetzel (1868)—wrote very much in a post-Dickensian manner.

With advances in printing and especially colour-printing techniques, the pictorial element was to play an ever-increasing part in 20th-c. children's books and periodicals, this process being complicated by the advent of *cinema and *television. Albert Lamorisse's film *Crin blanc* itself became a book in 1953—and his film for children, *Le Ballon rouge* (film 1955, published 1956), remains unequalled. As for television, few British viewers realized that *The Magic Roundabout* was originally Serge Danot's *Le Manège enchanté*.

Where *bande dessinée* is concerned, the relation of word and image is more complex still. Most 20th-c. children's classics in France seem to have been strip-cartoons rather than texts proper. After *La Famille Fenouillard*, *Bécassine, Les Pieds nickelés*, and *Zig et Puce* came Hergé in 1930 with Tintin (de *Gaulle's only acknowledged international rival), and later, in 1959, Goscinny and Uderzo's *Astérix.

Sometimes publishing series themselves have become the classics, Hachette's Bibliothèque Verte (from 1924), Flammarion's Albums du Père Castor (from 1931), Folio Junior (from 1977). There have also been numerous periodicals such as *Spirou* (from 1938) or *Okapi* (from 1971). Nevertheless, memorable children's books have continued to be published: *Pergaud's *La Guerre des boutons* (1912), *Maurois's *Patapoufs et filifers* (1930), Saint-Exupéry's *Le Petit Prince* (1943), Boyer's *Bébert et l'omnibus* (1952), Berna's *Le Cheval sans tête* (1955), perhaps Queneau's *Zazie dans le métro* (1959), if this can be called a children's book. And there is a recent return to orality with Henri Gougaud (*Contes de la Huchette*, 1987), Pierre *Gripari and many others . . . 'et ils vécurent heureux et eurent beaucoup d'enfants'.   [DAS]

See M.-T. Latzarus, *La Littérature enfantine en France dans la seconde moitié du 19e siècle* (1924); P. Hazard, *Les Livres, les enfants et les hommes* (1932); F. Caradec, *Histoire de la littérature enfantine en France* (1977); J. Glénisson, 'Le Livre pour la jeunesse', in H.-J. Martin and R. Chartier (eds.), *Histoire de l'édition française*, vol. III (1985).

Chimène. Heroine of Corneille's *Le Cid.

Chimères, Les, see NERVAL.

Chivalry. The abstract noun 'chivalry' (*chevalerie*) is derived from the contemporary term used for a medieval mounted warrior or knight, *chevalier*. Its precise meaning remains elusive: chivalry, as it evolved from the 11th c., meant different things at different times in different places. Ideal forms of chivalry are described in a rich vernacular literature, of which the *Chanson de *Roland is the earliest exemplar. This particularly emphasized military values like courage, honour, and loyalty to a master as befitting a knight's conduct. These characteristics were both reinforced and modified in *romances written from the mid-12th c. by *Chrétien de Troyes and his successors, including the German minnesingers Wolfram von Eschenbach and Gottfried von Strasbourg. Together with those brought up in the Occitan *troubadour tradition, they attributed a larger place to women in their poems, encouraging respect for and service to noble ladies as worthy knightly attributes. They elaborated sophisticated ideas of courtly love [see FIN'AMOR]. At the same time churchmen, once extremely hostile to the undisciplined martial activities of the early medieval nobility, began to channel this aggressiveness into crusading, urged restraint in aristocratic dealings with the weak, poor, and defenceless, equated the highest ideals of knighthood with piety and service to Christ, and provided liturgies for blessing arms and newly dubbed knights. By these means the nobility's continuing hold on political and economic power was justified in a society that was viewed conventionally as comprised of three Orders (those who prayed, fought, or laboured).

Later medieval centuries not only added further influential literary models for chivalric imitation (the *Arthurian and *Alexander romance-cycles rivalled that of *Charlemagne and his paladins in popularity), but also provided exemplars from life. The *Histoire de Guillaume le Maréchal* (c.1225–30), accounts of other famous soldiers like Bertrand du Guesclin (d. 1380) or Maréchal *Boucicaut (d. 1421), or the panorama of western European knighthood in the 14th c. furnished by *Froissart's *Chroniques* and other chivalric historians were widely circulated. In the 15th c. the court of the dukes of *Burgundy was especially influential in promoting all forms of chivalric endeavour, with knights engaging in quests, *pas d'armes*, and *tournaments, when not employed in real warfare, but their enthusiasm was still widely shared by most of the nobility

Chivalry

of Europe. After 1325 most states of any importance in the West saw the creation of exclusive secular Orders of Chivalry like the Band of Castile (1330), the Garter in England (1347–8), or the Golden Fleece of Burgundy (1430) under the close control of their sovereigns, and where the inspiration of the Arthurian Round Table is sometimes directly obvious.

Medieval authors also continuously drew on biblical or classical sources of inspiration to provide exemplars worthy of imitation. From an early stage in chivalric writing the topos of a lost Golden Age and criticism of modern knights for failure to live up to standards set by their ancestors became common; it occurs already in Étienne de Fougères's *Livre des manières* (*c*.1170). Many of these themes came happily together at the beginning of the 14th c. in Jacques de Longuyon's *Vœux du paon* [see ALEXANDER ROMANCES], in which the cult of the Nine Worthies, archetypal warrior-figures chosen from classical antiquity, the Bible, and medieval history, makes its first literary appearance. Hector, Alexander, and Julius Caesar represented antiquity; Joshua, David, and Judas Maccabeus were the biblical heroes; and Arthur, Charlemagne, and Godfrey de Bouillon exemplified the recent past. The deeds of Du Guesclin led Eustache *Deschamps to dub him the tenth *preux*, whilst in Scotland Robert Bruce was deemed worthy of that honour. An equivalent list of nine *preuses*, chosen from antiquity, was latterly augmented by the addition of *Jeanne d'Arc.

There was also an important technical literature of chivalry with treatises and instructional manuals on knightly behaviour, training, and the art of war. These combined lessons derived from Vegetius' *De re militari* (translated by *Jean de Meun as *L'Art de chevalerie*) and other Roman authorities like Frontinus, with those taught by recent experience of warfare and contemporary legal theory (itself largely based on the Justinianic Civil Code or, in the case of the concept of the Just War, on St Augustine and Canon lawyers). An anonymous *Ordene de chevalerie* (*c*.1250) and Ramon Lull's *Libre del ordre de cavalyeria* (also quickly translated into French) provide two early examples, whilst Honoré *Bouvet's *L'Arbre des batailles* and *Christine de Pizan's *Livre des fais d'armes et de chevalerie* were two widely circulated late-medieval examples of books explaining the moral dimensions of war and exhorting knights to observe accepted conventions of the 'laws of war' which now governed actual fighting. New editions, translations, or adaptations of these key texts on the theory and practice of chivalry had been produced in all major European languages by the 15th c. The vogue was further enhanced by the invention of printing, when chivalric works were amongst the earliest and most popular printed books. Lull's *Libre*, for example, was Englished by Caxton and three further French editions appeared in the early 16th c. That the images of knighthood they portrayed remained influential is made plain by the career of *Bayart, a late example of a *chevalier sans reproche*.

It is thus against the varied patterns of behaviour attributed to fictitious as well as real figures that the diversity of actions contemporaries recognized as chivalric during the Middle Ages must be measured. Initially the product of a very specific set of historical and social circumstances, a working definition is that chivalry ('what the horse soldiers did') was an ethical code in which 'martial, aristocratic and Christian elements were fused together' (Keen). Although some features which went into its composition are universal military virtues—bravery, loyalty, and generosity towards companions in arms—the area in which chivalry came to birth and quickly achieved its most durable characteristics is widely agreed to be France. It was particularly in northern France in the 11th and 12th c. that a society dominated by great princes and aristocrats, ably seconded by lesser military figures, a *feudal society, was formed. But many other parts of the medieval West also contributed to the shaping or expression of chivalric ideals, whilst the remarkable military successes of western knights from around 1100 in Muslim Spain, Byzantium, the eastern Mediterranean, the Middle East, and the Baltic entailed a wide dissemination of these ideals, which became normative for the European aristocracy for the rest of the Middle Ages and beyond.

The main military development encouraging the rise of chivalry was the use by cavalry troops of the lance as a thrusting weapon rather than as a missile like a spear or javelin. The Normans were pioneers in these tactics; the Bayeux Tapestry (*c*.1080) catches the changes they entailed at a critical moment. But by the early 12th c. cavalry in most parts of the West had adopted the new weapons and tactics, their spread probably encouraged by the simultaneous development of the tournament, a form of mock-warfare in which knights practised their newly won skills. Success in tournaments, as the career of William the Marshal (Guillaume le Maréchal) admirably showed, might lead to wealth and political power for a landless knight. In the 13th c. several of these international events, like those at Hem in 1278 ('a marvellous piece of Arthurian theatre'—Keen) or at Chauvency in October 1285 were commemorated in verse, whilst the jousts at Saint-Inglevert (1390) between Anglo-French knights during a lull in the *Hundred Years War were celebrated by Froissart.

It was in this context that heraldry also developed: a system of rules governing the adoption of personal and family devices borne by the knighthood as an aid to recognition. Heraldry was an essential adjunct to medieval chivalry, allowing observers to record outstanding or infamous deeds in the lists or on the battlefield. The first known hereditary insignia or coats of arms came into use in England, France, and Spain *c*.1130–40. Heralds, who are first found at late 12th-c. tournaments, slowly assumed the leading role in their increasingly ritualized organization and as guardians of the complex science of blazon, whose traditional language is still based today on Old French as it was in the late Middle Ages. By then most of Europe was divided into Heraldic Marches, each with its own hierarchy of kings of arms, heralds, and poursuivants. Recognized internationally as enjoying personal immunity, heralds were also frequently employed as messengers for diplomatic missions, besides officiating at every kind of ceremonial or court occasion.

The combination of a social system dominated by a nobility with its own distinctive moral and ethical values based on the code of chivalry proved to be remarkably durable and influential. Other medieval social groups (leading townsmen in the Low Countries, Germany, and Renaissance Italy, for instance) held these values in high esteem. Aspects of chivalry came to affect the content of education beyond the princely courts and noble households where it found its fullest expression. Among chivalry's legacies to the post-medieval world is the concept of the 'gentleman', the man of honour, breeding, and social distinction [see COURTOISIE; HONNÊTETÉ], whilst the 'laws of war', to which chivalric warfare gave rise, helped prepare the way for the formulation of international law in more recent centuries.   [MJ]

See G. Duby, *The Chivalrous Society*, tr. Cynthia Postan (1977); M. Keen, *Chivalry* (1984); P. Contamine, *War in the Middle Ages* (1984).

CHODERLOS DE LACLOS, see LACLOS.

CHOISY, François-Timoléon, abbé de (1644–1724). Perhaps the 17th c.'s most curious figure. In his ecclesiastical career, he served the cardinals of Bouillon and *Retz as a diplomat, followed *Louis XIV in his campaigns of the 1670s, and participated in the 1684 embassy to Siam. He won election to the Académie Française for his *Journal du voyage de Siam* (1687). From 1668 on, Choisy often lived publicly as a woman, calling himself first Madame de Sancy, then the comtesse des Barres. He left curious accounts of this other life, *Histoire de Madame la comtesse des Barres* (published 1735) and fragments (published 1862), and a story, *Histoire de la marquise-marquis de Banneville* (1695–6).   [JDeJ]

CHOLODENKO, Marc (b. 1950). French poet and novelist whose first publications were collections of poetry (*Parcs*, 1971; *Cent chants à l'adresse de son frère*, 1975). His novels, of increasingly complex narrative structure, combine psychological analysis with a penchant for the erotic. He was awarded the Prix Médicis for *Les États du désert* (1976). *Métamorphoses: autobiographie d'un autre* (1992) is again a work of uncertain narrative status.   [EAF]

CHOQUETTE, Robert-Henri, see QUEBEC, 3.

Choses, Les, see PEREC.

Chouannerie. Name given to extensive counter-revolutionary peasant movements active in many parts of France, particularly Brittany and Normandy, from early in the *Revolution until 1815. The Chouans, whose name (meaning 'owl') derives from the nickname of their first leader, the smuggler Jean Cottereau, joined forces with the insurrectionary armies in the *Vendée in 1793.

Chouans, Les. Historical novel by *Balzac, first published 1828 as *Le Dernier Chouan ou la Bretagne en 1800* and announced as the first chapter of 'une histoire pittoresque de la France' in imitation of Walter Scott's *Waverley* novels.

CHRAÏBI, Driss (b. 1926). Leading Moroccan writer of the 'Generation of '52'. His first novel, *Le Passé simple* (1954), was a literary bombshell. Published at the height of the French–Moroccan conflict, Chraïbi's invective text spared neither French colonial rule nor Moroccan, patriarchal society. His compatriots accused him of betraying his country at a time when it was seeking independence from France. French critics and journalists, on the other hand, used the book to justify the preservation of the French protectorate in Morocco. Disturbed by the controversy, Chraïbi publicly disowned his novel in 1957, only to regret this gesture years later.

Born in El Jadida, Morocco, Chraïbi was one of a token few native Moroccans to pursue secondary studies in a French *lycée*. In 1945 he left for Paris, where he studied chemical engineering and neuropsychiatry. Disillusioned with science, he abandoned his formal studies and travelled throughout Europe and Israel. He has held various jobs in France, where he now lives.

Chraïbi is the author of 12 novels and a collection of short stories, all published in Paris. In *Les Boucs* (1955), *L'Âne* (1956), *De tous les horizons* (1958), *La Foule* (1961), *Un ami viendra vous voir* (1967), and *Mort au Canada* (1975), he explores a variety of themes in diverse geographical settings. They include the plight of immigrant workers in France, racism, political corruption in the Third World, women's liberation, and interpersonal relationships in the West. Despite his attempts not to be labelled a regional writer, Chraïbi's most successful works are those dedicated to the Maghreb and its people: *Le Passé simple*, *Les Boucs*, *Succession ouverte* (1962), *La Civilisation, ma mère!* . . . (1972), *Une enquête au pays* (1981), *La Mère du printemps (L'Oum-er-Bia)* (1982), *Naissance à l'aube* (1986), and *L'Inspecteur Ali* (1991).

Although *Le Passé simple* was hailed as a classic tale of revolt against the father, Chraïbi contended in 1983 that it was really about love for the mother, who also symbolizes the homeland. Yet it is only in *Succession ouverte*, which depicts the return to the native land, that Chraïbi displays real empathy towards the mother and her land. In *La Civilisation, ma mère!* . . . the emancipation of the narrator and the future of the Maghreb is viewed in relation to the social evolution of women. The angry and violent tone of Chraïbi's early novels makes way for a tender and lyrical style in his later works.

If there is one underlying theme that unites all of Chraïbi's works, it is the indictment of civilization. In a century characterized by ethnocide and in a world full of dispossessed, it is only fitting that this Moroccan Berber and exiled writer should choose to write for and about those who have endured centuries of foreign conquest and domination. He writes on behalf of those peoples who have had to relinquish their land, their historic past, their voice, and their identity: all the minorities who comprise, Chraïbi reminds us, the great majority of this world.

Many years have passed since the angry young man of Le Passé simple decided to break with his past and turn to the West. In the mystical and life-celebrating prose of Naissance à l'aube, a 60-year-old exile finds the way back to his native land and to the historic past of his people. [DM-S]

See H. Kadra-Hadjadji, Contestation et révolte dans l'œuvre de Driss Chraïbi (1986); Revue CELFAN Review, 5, 2 (1986), devoted to Chraïbi; D. Marx-Scouras, 'A Literature of Departure: The Cross-Cultural Writing of Driss Chraïbi', Research in African Literatures, 23, 2 (1992).

CHRÉTIEN DE TROYES (fl. 1160–85). Author of five Arthurian verse narratives, Chrétien de Troyes set the course for the emerging genre of *romance in France and other European countries.

The author who signed his name 'Crestiens' left no historical trace other than the names of his patrons, Marie de Champagne and Philip of Alsace. He was evidently a well-educated cleric, for he claims to have translated Ovid's Art of Love and tales from the Metamorphoses; he was also versed in the *romans d'antiquité, in the early *matière de Bretagne, as well as in folklore and popular proverbs. His authorship of two lyric poems in the style of the *troubadours and his association with Marie, daughter of *Eleanor of Aquitaine, suggest that he knew the poetry and precepts of *fin'amor. The precise dates of his romances remain uncertain.

Chrétien composed elegant octosyllabic couplets that were intended to be read aloud before women and men at court. His poems are voiced by a narrator who comments upon his material and his craft. Deft description and characterization, clever dialogue, rhetorical play, and a gently comic perspective on courtly conventions mark his narrative art, which, while it generally supports *chivalric values, is never overbearingly didactic. The master romancer showed particular talent for juxtaposing complementary or contrasting episodes in such a way that their literal events would suggest a deeper significance. His use of ambiguous symbolism and of marvellous events and objects enhanced the mystery and charm of his creations without ever destroying their human scale. The romances' irony and ambiguity must have inspired medieval readers to ponder moral and social questions. Modern critics continue to debate the many possible interpretations of his works.

In Erec et Enide, which is the first surviving full-length Arthurian romance, Chrétien announces his intention to surpass popular story-tellers by making a 'molt bele conjointure'—a harmonious narrative structure—out of an adventure story. As the romance dramatizes the conflict between love and chivalry, it also examines dominance within marriage. After winning Enide's hand through prowess, Erec abandons chivalry for the amorous delights of his new wife. When he overhears her lament over what others have said about him, the knight sets off to regain his reputation; he commands his wife to accompany him and to remain silent. Enide repeatedly defies his orders and alerts Erec to danger, thereby allowing him to defeat his enemies. The romance ends joyously and with great ceremony, but Chrétien will continue to explore the complex web of psychological and sexual tensions first spun in Erec.

Literary sophistication combines with striking irony in Cligés, a bipartite tale that recasts the *Tristan story in a Byzantine frame. Chrétien illustrates the motif of translatio studii, the transference of learning from Greece to Rome and then to England and France, by sending Alexander, son of the emperor of Greece and Constantinople, off to King Arthur's court. The knight experiences Ovidian lovesickness for Soredamours, whom he eventually marries. Their son Cligés, wrongly deprived of the throne by his uncle Alis, falls in love with his usurper's wife, Fenice. By means of magic potions and with the help of her maidservant, Fenice makes her husband believe that he enjoys physical possession of her in marriage, although it is only a dream; later, she feigns death and escapes to a marvellous hideaway, where she lives with Cligés. In contrast to Tristan and Iseut, the lovers manage to live their love exclusively, if not painlessly, until they marry after Alis's death. Throughout Cligés, the narrator's ingenious literary transformations rival his characters' clever ruses.

Chrétien heightens the ambiguity of his hero in Le Chevalier de la Charrette (Lancelot), a romance that portrays the adulterous love of *Lancelot and Guenièvre, Arthur's wife. Because Chrétien states in his Prologue that he has derived his matière and sens from Marie, countess of Champagne, and because the romance is completed in the voice of one Godefroy de Leigni, some critics have assumed that Marie ordered Chrétien to write a story about courtly love that he found distasteful and subsequently abandoned. But the romance's alternately mysterious and gently parodic treatment of the hero, who rides ignominiously on a cart in pursuit of his lady, suggests that Chrétien may have sought to leave his readers puzzled and amused. The unresolved issues of this romance inspired in part the 13th-c. prose Lancelot.

For many readers, Le Chevalier au Lion (Yvain) is Chrétien's most accomplished work. Since the romance contains allusions and intertextual references to *Lancelot*, critics have speculated that the two romances were written simultaneously or in alternation. *Yvain* further explores the conflict between marital and chivalric duties broached in *Erec*. It recounts first how Yvain, with the help of a clever intermediary, Lunete, convinces the reluctant widow of a knight he has defeated to marry her husband's conqueror and then how he neglects his new wife, Laudine, by overstaying the leave she has accorded him. Her refusal to pardon and receive him plunges Yvain into madness. In the course of the expiatory adventures he undertakes to regain his reason and her love, he rescues a lion, who becomes his faithful companion and symbolizes, perhaps, his emergent humanity. Yvain happily wins back Laudine, although he does so by means of a verbal ruse set by Lunete; the romance forestalls easy conclusions about the hero's moral progress.

Chrétien's final and longest romance, *Le Conte du Graal* (*Perceval*), dedicated to Philip of Alsace, count of Flanders, was never completed; it remains his most enigmatic work. Although the narrator claims to have derived the *Grail story from a book supplied by his patron, we know neither what the source was nor what Chrétien himself may have invented. Like Erec and Yvain, Perceval makes an initial mistake for which he must atone: when he sets off to Arthur's court to become a knight, he rides away without tending to his mother, who has fallen in a sorrowful faint. Perceval seeks to apply literally the courtly precepts his mother and mentor have imparted to him, but he lacks the deeper moral sense that would allow him to empathize with others. Perceval's comic *naïveté* has tragic consequences. When the hero fails to enquire about the purpose of the bleeding lance and the Grail, he misses his chance to heal the wounded Fisher King. The romance breaks off in the midst of a section devoted to *Gauvain's more worldly adventures; four verse continuations by others provided two distinct endings. Critics speculate that Chrétien wished to contrast profane and spiritual knighthood in the Gauvain–Perceval opposition, but the author never wrote his final word on the subject.

Some critics have attributed to Chrétien *Guillaume d'Angleterre*, an edifying non-Arthurian tale of a king's tribulations, as well as the account of the rape of Procne's sister by her husband, the *Philomena*, which survives in the early 14th-c. *Ovide moralisé*. But it was for his Arthurian romances that Chrétien was most influential throughout the European Middle Ages; his work directly or indirectly inspired continuators, imitators, adapters, and innovators. After the decline of chivalric romance in the early modern period, Chrétien's brilliance remained obscured until the 19th- and 20th-c. revival of medieval studies. By now the romancer has fully regained his prominence as a master of irony and ambiguity and as one of the most important forebears of European fiction.   [RLK]

See J. Frappier, *Chrétien de Troyes* (1957); D. Kelly (ed.), *Chrétien de Troyes* (1985); T. Hunt, *Chrétien de Troyes: 'Yvain'* (1986).

CHRISTINE DE PIZAN (sometimes Pisan) (*c*.1364–*c*.1431). Poet and scholar. The rapidly proliferating bibliography devoted to Christine, after some centuries of disparagement, is an index of her fascination as a personal and a feminine, indeed a feminist, voice. After a prosperous childhood at the court of the French king Charles V with her father, the court astrologer, and after a happy marriage, she was left a widow in 1390 with her financial affairs embarrassed and with no resource other than her pen. These masculine responsibilities turned her—a revealing metaphor—into a 'vray homme', and she became one of the earliest professional *femmes de lettres*.

Her earliest works consist of lyric poetry—*ballades, *rondeaux, a *virelai—some plainly commissioned, others where one can read a confessional sincerity ('Seulete suy, et seulete vueil estre | Seulete m'a mon doulz ami laissiee'). The autobiographical should not be exaggerated, however: formally and thematically, the poems use the discourse of desire and loss of the medieval courtly lyric.

Much less conventional is Christine's entry on equal terms into the arena of intellectual debate. Her *Epistre au Dieu d'Amours* (1399) takes issue with *Jean de Meun's misogyny [see ROMAN DE LA ROSE]; the epistle—her first resort to a device she would often use as a persuasive strategy—instituted a poetic debate, the *Querelle des Femmes, in which Christine found powerful allies. The defence of women underlies much of her early work. In *Le Livre de la cité des dames* (1404–5) she imposes her own thematic and polemical construct, setting *exempla drawn largely from Boccaccio in a dream allegory: Raison, Justice, and Droiture enlist her aid in constructing an ideal city as a refuge for unprotected women; the city is peopled by the great women of history and legend who have made positive contributions to civilization. On a more contemporary note, *Le Livre des trois vertus* or *Trésor des dames* (1405) is a mirror for women of every class: the same allegorical voices are borrowed to explain women's duties. Christine's insistence on women's dignity and right to a role other than the subservient underpins what are essentially apologias for her sex.

Christine was now ready to move into a less woman-centred sphere. Already in *c*.1400 she had produced the *Epistre d'Othea*, a *miroir des princes idiosyncratically employing a fictional correspondence: written in verse and prose, it purports to give the goddess Othea's model advice to the ideal knight Hector of Troy (aged 15), each piece of advice being assigned a moral gloss in Christine's own voice. *Le Livre du corps de policie* (1404/7), perhaps a pendant to the *Livre des trois vertus*, is addressed to men, and puts forward moral precepts based on *exempla* mainly from antiquity. More unusually, *Le Livre des fais d'armes et de chevalerie* (1410), based primarily on a French translation of Vegetius, instructs the ideal prince in his military duties and strategies.

Christine's growing reputation led to a commission in 1404 to write *Le Livre des fais et bonnes meurs du sage roy Charles V*, a panegyric partly based on the **Grandes Chroniques de France* but also incorporating personal details furnished by *gens notables* at court. By this date her preoccupations seem generally more historical than personal. True, her *Livre de la mutacion de fortune* (1400–3) hints at an allegorical autobiography, but personal and practical experience serves mainly to apprehend political and social realities, and the work is rather a seven-part universal history. *Le Livre du chemin de long estude* (1402) is similarly couched in the first person, but narrates an allegorical journey into a world where the Virtues debate the choice of a prince able to save the world from destruction.

Much of Christine's later work, however, focuses directly on the lamentable state of France. Her *Lavision Christine* (1405) is a complex dream vision interweaving several allegorical threads. Set in a universal history, it diagnoses the moral decay of France. Her *Lettre a la reine Isabeau de Baviere* (after 1405) appeals to the queen to intercede in the cause of peace. Similar laments preoccupy her *Lamentation sur les maux de la guerre civile* (1410) and her *Epistre de la prison de vie humaine* (1416/8); only her *Livre de la paix* (1412–14) offers the glimmer of a solution: dedicated to Louis de Guyenne, it deplores the weakness of contemporary rulers but hopes to appeal to his sense of responsibility. Fortunately, Christine's last surviving work, the *Ditié de Jehanne d'Arc* (1429), takes a more hopeful view: God, in the person of the Maid [see JEANNE D'ARC], has brought the sun back to Christine's life, triumphantly vindicating the woman warrior: 'Hee! quel honneur au femenin sexe!'

Christine's *œuvre*, then, is remarkably varied. Almost more than her preoccupation with the cause of women, her engagement with contemporary politics is a constant. Her voice is a scholar's, with a striking skill in deploying learned quotation. Her lyric writing has fluency and pathos; her prose is experimental, with a supple if sometimes convoluted Latinate syntax which puts her at the forefront of contemporary stylists. [JHMT]

See C. C. Willard, *Christine de Pizan* (1984); A. J. Kennedy, *Christine de Pizan: A Bibliographical Guide* (1984).

Chronique du règne de Charles IX, see MÉRIMÉE.

Chroniques des ducs de Normandie, see BENOÎT DE SAINTE-MAURE.

Chroniques italiennes. Collection of stories by *Stendhal, written 1829–36, published anonymously in journals and as a collection posthumously in 1855. Based on manuscripts from Italian archives, they range from a short novel (*L'Abbesse de Castro*) to brief tales. Stendhal presents them, not quite accurately, as raw, truthful accounts of incidents 'qui jettent un jour singulier sur les profondeurs du cœur humain'; they show the 'Italian' energy which he liked to set against the pettiness of life in France. He did not simply translate his sources, but transformed them into typically Stendhalian texts, admirably bare and fast-moving. The characters are passionate seekers after love, honour, or power, with little respect for law or conventional morality: *Les Cenci* (a subject also treated by Shelley and *Artaud) is a story of oppression, revenge, and terrible punishment, while in *L'Abbesse de Castro* a frustrated lover-turned-bandit attempts to storm the convent where his beloved is confined. The stories are distanced from the unromantic present. One, *Vanina Vanini*, is set in recent times, two (including *Suora scolastica*) in the 18th c., and the rest in a somewhat legendary 16th c., which prefigures that painted by Burkhardt or Nietzsche. [PF]

Chrysolite, La, see MARESCHAL.

Chute d'un ange, La, see LAMARTINE.

Chute, La. Novel by Albert *Camus, published 1956, taking the form of a monologue delivered by Jean-Baptiste Clamence. Formerly a successful lawyer, he has become a prey to remembered events which have destroyed his earlier certainties about his character and motives. Pursued by guilt from his past, he has retired to a bar in Amsterdam where he now waylays customers, consoling himself by demoralizing others, through his own sardonic confession eliciting from them an acknowledgment of their sins. Camus satirizes his own high-mindedness as well as the moral blackmail he had seen exercised by ideological dogmatists. [DHW]

Cid, Le. Tragicomedy by Pierre *Corneille, first performed 1637. Set in medieval Spain, it centres on the noble young lovers Rodrigue and Chimène. To avenge an insult to his father, Rodrigue kills Chimène's father in a duel. Chimène is then honour bound, in spite of their mutual passion, to seek revenge. Rodrigue leads an army which defeats the Moorish invaders, and on his return disarms Chimène's champion, whereupon the king, having given him the grandiose title of Cid (Lord), presses Chimène to relent and marry him. The play ends in uncertainty as to the final outcome.

With its vibrant poetry of love and heroism, the play was an immense success ('tout Paris pour Chimène a les yeux de Rodrigue', wrote *Boileau). It also gave rise to vigorous disputes. Georges de *Scudéry attacked it, and the *Académie Française, encouraged by Richelieu, published the *Sentiments de l'Académie sur le Cid* (written by *Chapelain), in which the play's improprieties and irregularities were noted. It was considerably modified in later editions, and from 1648 was labelled a tragedy. [PF]

Cinema

'Cimetière marin, Le'. *Valéry's most famous poem, included in *Charmes*.

Cinema. The connections between cinematic and literary culture have always been particularly close in France, from the *Surrealists' fascination with the silent director Louis Feuillade, via the involvement of *Cocteau or *Pagnol, to the more recent directorial ventures of novelists such as *Duras, *Robbe-Grillet, and Jean-Philippe *Toussaint. If there is a world capital of film culture, it has to be Paris, where the first public film screening took place in 1895 and where the concentration of cinemas remains unrivalled in the Western world.

The films shown at that first screening were short 'home-movie' documentaries, directed by Louis Lumière, who ran a photographic factory near Lyon and saw moving pictures as a piquant adjunct to his main business. The other name associated with the 'prehistory' of cinema in France is that of Georges Méliès, a professional magician whose films (such as *Le Voyage dans la lune*, 1902) rely upon illusion and special effects. From the outset, the dichotomy—in many respects a false one, but none the less firmly entrenched—between film as documentary record of the 'real' and film as dream-factory was established.

Serials (such as Feuillade's *Les Vampires*, 1915–16) and literary adaptations formed, along with the comedies of such as Max Linder, the bulk of the early silent output. Visual experimentation flourished as resources increased in the 1920s; Surrealist-influenced short films (Germaine Dulac's *La Souriante Madame Beudet*, 1923; Buñuel and Dali's *Un chien andalou*, 1928) and the epic extravagance of Abel *Gance indicate the range the silent film could cover.

The arrival of sound (1929) had an initially disastrous effect upon the French industry, outstripped as it was by its American and German competitors. 'Safe' adaptations of *Boulevard plays and literary classics were the norm, though the names of *Guitry and *Pagnol show that such cinema was not necessarily so hidebound as has often been thought. A still more important literary contributor was Jacques *Prévert, whose mordant scripts for *Carné, Grémillon, and *Renoir are arguably his finest work. Studio filming was the rule until about the mid-1930s, reflecting not only industrial conservatism but the superb quality of set design (often by Lazare Meerson or Alexandre *Trauner) and the number of actresses and actors (e.g. Jules Berry, Louis *Jouvet, Madeleine *Renaud) who had come from the theatre.

Renoir's work more than that of any other director promoted location shooting and suggested that the sound cinema could produce artistic masterpieces [see also CARNÉ; DUVIVIER; VIGO]. The war obviously had a disruptive effect; the major French directors who went to Hollywood, René Clair and Renoir, were far less successful there than their German counterparts such as Fritz Lang and Douglas Sirk, and, while the Occupation yielded a masterpiece such as Carné's *Les Enfants du paradis* (1945), it also badly affected the careers of actresses and actors who collaborated (*Arletty, Pierre Fresnay, Robert le Vigan). Post-war reconstruction was hindered by these divisions within the industry and by the flood of American films onto the French market. The 15 years after the Liberation were to be stigmatized by the *Nouvelle Vague critics as those of the 'cinéma de qualité' (also known as the 'cinéma de papa'), though recent revaluations of its leading directors (Claude Autant-Lara, René Clément, Henri-Georges Clouzot) have been rather kinder to their work. Gangster movies, made by such directors as Yves Allégret, Jacques Becker, and Jean-Pierre Melville, were an important counterweight to the more overt production values of the 'cinéma de papa', and also fed into the Nouvelle Vague's output.

The Nouvelle Vague, the most important movement in post-war French cinema, is the subject of a separate entry. Although the term was originally a journalistic invention and never covered a coherent body of theory and practice, the films, together with the polemic declarations of faith, of directors such as *Godard, *Resnais, and *Truffaut, had a powerful collective impact, whether negative or positive, both in France and abroad. It is partly as a result of the 'politique des auteurs' championed by the principal organ of the Nouvelle Vague, *Cahiers du cinéma*, that Godard came to be an *auteur* as much studied as *Butor in French courses in the English-speaking countries.

The Nouvelle Vague remained dominant in serious French cinema probably until 1968–9, beginning a period which unsurprisingly inaugurated a major return to the historical via critical documentaries (Marcel Ophuls's *Le Chagrin et la pitié*, 1971) and reconstructions (Louis Malle's *Lacombe Lucien*, 1974). These remained, however, less popular with the general public than big-screen films starring such names as Alain Delon, Brigitte Bardot, Yves *Montand, or Simone *Signoret. Major new directors to appear in the 1970s included Bertrand Blier, Maurice Pialat, and Bertrand Tavernier; woman directors, in France as elsewhere, have generally been few and far between (Agnès *Varda is by far the best-known).

The dominant trends in French cinema by 1990 were at the opposite pole to the values of the Nouvelle Vague. Gaudy studio filming eschewing any suspicion of realism, with minimal or inconsequential narrative, characterizes the 'video-clip' world of such directors as Jean-Jacques Beineix and Luc Besson, while big-screen costume drama—'cinéma de qualité' with a vengeance—reestablished itself with Claude Berri's Pagnol adaptations *Jean de Florette* and *Manon des sources* (both 1986), the most successful foreign-language films ever in Britain, and Bruno Nuytten's *Camille Claudel* (1989), starring Isabelle Adjani. Yet many younger directors, such as

169

Léos Carax and Eric Rochant, were making films clearly influenced by the Nouvelle Vague, and French cinema culture remained remarkable in its openness and diversity. [KAR]

See J.-P. Jeancolas, *Le Cinéma des Français* (1979) and *Quinze ans d'années trente* (1983); J.-L. Passek (ed.), *Dictionnaire du cinéma français* (1987); S. Hayward and G. Vincendeau (eds.), *French Film: Texts and Contexts* (1990).

Cinémathèque, La. The Cinémathèque de Paris will always be associated with the name of Henri Langlois, who co-founded it with the director Georges Franju in 1936 and was synonymous with it until his death in 1977. Langlois, with a team including Mary Meerson, Lotte Eisner, and Marie Epstein, devoted boundless energy to buying up and stocking copies of films that would otherwise have been lost, and the Cinémathèque has since the war offered an unrivalled range of repertory screenings. Langlois's allegedly amateurish management led to *Malraux's attempt to dismiss him in February 1968, which successfully mobilized the cinematic world against the government and can be seen as a precursor of *May 1968. [KAR]

CINGRIA, Charles-Albert, see SWISS LITERATURE IN FRENCH.

Cinna. Tragedy by Pierre *Corneille, first performed 1641. Inspired by his love for Émilie, whose father has been killed by the Roman emperor Augustus (Auguste), Cinna leads a plot against Auguste's life, and persists in it even when he and his fellow conspirator Maxime have been consulted by the blood-weary emperor, who wants to abdicate. The conspiracy is betrayed by Maxime, who is vainly in love with Émilie. Helped by the advice of his wife, Livie, Auguste conquers the impulse to have the conspirators executed. His clemency wins the hearts of Cinna, Maxime, and even the irreducible Émilie, and the play ends on a note of moral and political apotheosis. [PF]

Cinq Auteurs, Les, see RICHELIEU.

Cinq grandes odes, see CLAUDEL.

Cinq Grosses Fermes, Les, see TAXATION.

Cinq-Mars (1826). Historical novel by *Vigny which takes as its subject the failed plot by Cinq-Mars and the nobility against *Richelieu. Vigny admires Cinq-Mars's loyalty to his king and shares his aversion for Richelieu and his unscrupulous henchman, le père Joseph. At the same time, influenced by Walter Scott, he sets out to recreate a broad picture of 17th-c. society. The novel was an immediate success. However, Vigny's treatment of historical fact raised important questions and to justify his willingness to transform his data he included in the fourth edition (1829) an important preface, 'Réflexions sur la vérité dans l'art'. [CC]

CIORAN, Émile-Marcel (b. 1911). Romanian essayist and aphorist, resident in France since 1937. He studied philosophy in Bucharest, writing a thesis on *Bergson, and in 1933 published his first literary work there, *Pecumile disperării* (On the Peaks of Despair). In a sequence of essays in French—*Précis de décomposition* (1949), *Syllogismes de l'amertume* (1952), *La Tentation d'exister* (1956), *De l'inconvénient d'être né* (1973), *Aveux et anathèmes* (1987)—he displays an acute demythologizing intelligence and a sombre verbal wit. Cioran is a philosophical minimalist, endlessly seeking an imagined point of emptiness from which an unillusioned quest for being might be launched. [MB]

Cistercians. The Cistercian order began in 1098 when a group of reforming monks founded the abbey of Cîteaux in Burgundy. The order's distinctive features came to be its literal observance of the Rule of St Benedict, its cultivation of internal piety, its requirement of manual labour, its rejection of tithes and manorial dues, and its preference for sites hitherto unexploited, including frontier lands in Spain, Scandinavia, and Germany. Under the influence of *Bernard de Clairvaux the order spread rapidly across Europe; by 1153 there were 344 houses. But its initial enthusiasm and high standards proved hard to sustain. [JHD]

Cité antique, La, see FUSTEL DE COULANGES.

Cités du termite, Les, see FANTOURÉ.

Civilité, see HONNÊTETÉ.

CIXOUS, Hélène (b. 1937). French writer, theorist, critic, and teacher, Cixous is best known in Britain and America for her theorization of sexual difference. However, she cannot be characterized as simply or even principally a theoretician; all the texts within her wide creative range carry an immensely poetic charge. She was born into a Jewish family in Algeria, of a German mother and French father, and questions of difference and alienation have always been prominent in her work. Her doctoral thesis on James Joyce, subsequently published, was entitled *L'Exil de Joyce* (1969). Throughout the 1970s her work focused on an exploration of feminine subjectivity and its otherness in a series of texts which had an enormous impact on thinking about difference and sexual identity; in 'Le Rire de la Méduse' (1975), *La Jeune Née* (1975), and 'La Venue à l'écriture' (1977) she called on women to write through their bodies and began to theorize the practice of an *écriture féminine*, a writing which would emerge from the multiple nature of the feminine libidinal economy.

Her own prolific output of fictional prose texts from *Dedans* (1969) onwards, through *La* (1976), *Angst* (1977), *Limonade tout était si infini* (1982), and many others, explores femininity, otherness, and the transformation of subjectivity within complex narrative structures designed to retain as much openness to the reader as possible. *Le Livre de*

Promothéa (1983), focusing on problems of writing and on the powers of love, throws into question the whole issue of authorial identity. In 1977 she founded the Centre d'Études Féminines, where pioneering work on sexual difference and its relation to the literary text has been carried out. She herself has written essays on Joyce, Kleist, Hoffmann, Poe, and on the Brazilian novelist Clarice Lispector, whom she much admires.

Much of her work in the 1980s was written for the theatre in a shift from what she has called 'the scene of the unconscious to the scene of history'; questions of otherness and of the struggle for freedom and for identity continue to be addressed, but the focus on feminine subjectivity becomes part of a broader concern with the ethical dimensions of contemporary history. *L'Histoire terrible mais inachevée de Norodom Sihanouk, roi du Cambodge* (1985) dramatizes the sufferings of the Cambodians after the withdrawal of the French as a colonial power; *L'Indiade ou l'Inde de leurs rêves* (1987) deals with the Indian struggle for independence from British rule. She also continues to write fictional prose: *Jours de l'an* (1990) and *L'Ange au secret* (1991) continue the exploration of subjectivity and of writing which, for Cixous, itself has transformative powers.   [EAF]

See M. Shiach, *Hélène Cixous: A Politics of Writing* (1991).

CLAIRAUT, Alexis-Claude (1713–65). Eminent French astronomer and mathematician, sent with *Maupertuis to Lapland by the *Académie des Sciences to measure the meridian. A Newtonian, he wrote important works on the shape of the earth, the movements of the moon, and Halley's comet (on the last of which he quarrelled with d'*Alembert).

CLAIRON, Mademoiselle (pseud. of Claire-Josèphe Léris de la Tude) (1723–1803). Leading tragic actress who performed in many of *Voltaire's plays at the Comédie-Française and collaborated with *Lekain in reforming acting styles of the time. See her *Mémoires et réflexions sur l'art dramatique* (1779).

CLANCIER, Georges-Emmanuel (b. 1914). Poet, novelist, and author of important essays on poetry. He paints a loving picture of his native Limousin in the family saga *Le Pain noir* (4 vols., 1956–61). Much of his best poetry (e.g. *Terres de mémoire*, 1965) ressuscitates the past and celebrates the present in short texts of mysterious simplicity which recall *Éluard.   [PF]

Clandestine Manuscripts. Publication during the *ancien régime* was not free; *censorship was constant, though often ineffective, and the penalties serious. In consequence a thriving trade in all sorts of clandestine literature grew up; pornography was banned, but so were *Pascal's *Lettres provinciales*. Most of the established canon of *Enlightenment works (except for *Rousseau's) was published

anonymously and in some degree of secrecy, either outside France or without the permission to publish that was legally required.

Among works that long remained in manuscript form are, in philosophy, *Voltaire's *Traité de métaphysique*, of about 1735, and in political thought d'*Argenson's *Considérations*, not to mention some of *Diderot's most important writings. The term 'clandestine manuscripts' has come to refer particularly, however, to works that were subversive or critical of established religion. Among them are some that now seem genuinely Christian, such as Pierre Cuppé's *Le Ciel ouvert à tous les hommes* (1712), which argues that none need go to Hell, but the majority are critical of religion or even violently hostile, such as the *Traité des trois imposteurs*, which accuses Moses, Jesus, and Mohammed of founding their religions on falsehood and fraud. Equally extreme and much more elaborate critiques of Catholic Christianity, one atheist, the other deistic, were made by *Meslier and the '*Militaire philosophe'. Madame *du Châtelet left similar works in manuscript.

Perhaps the most typical example of these manuscripts is the widely disseminated *Examen de la religion*, dating from *c*.1705, another anonymous *deist work that criticizes the Catholic apologists' arguments. Known in three versions, with varying titles, sometimes attributed to *Saint-Évremond, it is virtually a collective work of early 18th-c. free thought: copying by hand gave opportunities for revision and addition as manuscripts circulated. Others too were ascribed to reputed free-thinkers, such as *Boulainviller and *Fréret, some of whose writings were certainly clandestine. After *c*.1760 many of the manuscripts were published (Meslier's by Voltaire and the Militaire philosophe's by *Holbach), still clandestinely and with little regard for fidelity to the originals. Their presence is perceptible in the background of *philosophe* literature, such as Rousseau's *Profession de foi du vicaire savoyard*. One of the most interesting manuscripts, *Le Philosophe*, found its way into the *Encyclopédie* (article 'Philosophe'). The manuscripts' significance remains debatable, but they do at least bear witness to widespread intellectual opposition to imposed religious orthodoxy at a date prior to the writings of the greatest *philosophes*.   [CJB]

See I. O. Wade, *The Clandestine Organization and Diffusion of Philosophic Ideas in France from 1700 to 1750* (1938).

Clarens. Estate by Lake Geneva which is the idyllic setting for the later books of Rousseau's *La *Nouvelle Héloïse*.

CLARI, Robert de (*fl.* *c*.1204–1220). Picard knight who accompanied his lord Pierre d'Amiens on the Fourth *Crusade, participated in the famous siege and sack of Constantinople in 1204, returned home in 1205 bearing relics for his local church, and subsequently (apparently after 1216) dictated his memoirs to a scribe. His account of the crusade (which is now known as *La Conquête de Constantinople*) is valuable both in historical and in literary terms. Excluded from the debates of the commanders, he expressed the opinions of the less privileged, their discontent with the inadequate share of booty granted them, and their pride in the achievements of simple knights. He provided a vivid picture of the crusaders' dilemmas before their arrival at Constantinople, in which can be detected an absence of enthusiasm for the leader, Boniface of Montferrat, and for the Venetians. He also related the negotiations between the victorious Latins and their new neighbours after the fall of the city. His descriptive powers were considerable, as was his natural curiosity, which led him investigate some aspects of Byzantine history. As one of the first writers of French prose, he employed a strictly limited vocabulary, yet harnessed it to an effective narrative form in which traces of epic conventions are evident. [JHD]

Clarté. Political and literary journal established in 1919 by *Barbusse, who was its first editor. Its initial position of humanist internationalism evolved towards greater sympathy with the Communist Party, and with Trotskyism, and it did much to introduce the new Soviet literature to France [see also SURREALISM].

Classical influences

1. Medieval

Knowledge, assimilation, and exploitation of classical literary texts, identified since the 9th c. as the characteristic property of the educated élite of western Europe and functioning as a currency common to linguistically diverse vernacular literatures, constitute one of the most sensitive indicators of fluctuations in literary theory and practice. Like Boccaccio in 14th-c. Italy, French writers towards the end of the Middle Ages invariably defined 'poetrie' as fiction, and, more specifically, fictions derived from ancient authors. Vernacular versions of classical fictions were usually the latest in a series of reformulations of the original source. Most commonly, ancient fictions were transmitted through the medium of compilations, in the form of brief synopses arranged in lists, to be abbreviated further and redeployed in new catalogues by a *Villon, a *Champier, and, later still, a Jean *Bouchet. Alternatively, they came by way of paraphrases (sometimes, as in the case of Homer's *Iliad*, through Latin intermediaries). These were couched in a narrative style where dialogue predominated at the expense of visual effects, as in the 14th-c. *Ovide moralisé* and its late 15th-c. derivative, the *Bible des poètes*, which continued the manner well into the 16th c.

Another major factor which distanced late-medieval versions of classical fiction from their originals was the interposition of allegorical interpretations. Characters, objects, and events were transformed into the components of substitute narrations which plotted historical, scientific, moral, and religious 'truths' onto the fiction. The *Bible des poètes*, in editions printed up to 1531, transmitted just such an allegorical reading of the *Metamorphoses*, combining previous French and Latin retellings of Ovid. *Lemaire de Belges, in his *Concorde des deux langages* (1511) and his *Illustrations de Gaule et singularités de Troie* (1510–13), set late-medieval French modes of reading classical fictions against an explicitly Italian response to the pagan poets. Lemaire's 'Italian' manner is characterized by sheer aesthetic delight in visual mimesis, uninhibited by allegorical displacements and neither diffused by interpolated dialogue nor diminished in reductive summaries.

2. Sixteenth Century

In the first 50 years of the 16th c. French verse *translations of Ovid, from the *Heroïdes* of Octovien de *Saint-Gelais at the turn of the century to Clément *Marot's two books of the *Metamorphoses* (1534 and 1543), were symptomatic of a new closeness to the language and the vision of classical texts. But, in the shift in the reception of classical literature which was to be so profoundly influential, translation was of less importance than pedagogical techniques promoted by *humanist schoolmasters. By the late 1540s most young French writers had received an education focused exclusively on Latin and, to a lesser extent, Greek texts embracing literature, *rhetoric, moral philosophy, and history. They heard these texts read with an explanatory commentary which drew attention to linguistic expressions, rhetorical niceties, and historical context, with cross-references to parallel material: they extrapolated their texts into systematically ordered commonplace books; they wrote Latin prose and verse composition in which they reproduced the ideas and the stylistic mannerisms of their prescribed authors [see LATINITY]. This training in the analysis and production of persuasive discourse evolved a canon of model authors and established criteria for evaluating styles of writing.

The standards inculcated in the class-room were applied directly to the vernacular by practitioners and also by theorists, especially *Du Bellay and *Peletier du Mans. Writers of French set themselves to imitate and emulate classical texts which they had read in their original languages, in their original form, and accompanied by commentaries which explained the historical and literary culture which had produced them. Systematic allegorical interpretation, with its tendency to anachronism now unacceptable to historically minded humanists, was only sporadically imposed; but classical fictions were invariably read as exemplifications of moral truths and, more often than not, as representations of the behaviour of natural phenomena, as well as models of rhetorical artifice and repositories of reusable quotations.

The long-term effects on French literature of the humanist method of teaching classical authors were to downgrade the pre-existing vernacular tradition in favour of contemporary exercises in literary imitation (Du Bellay); to create a literature fully accessible only to an educated élite able to recognize the allusions in which much of its meaning was coded (fully exemplified in the commentary *Muret appended to *Ronsard's poems in 1553); and to naturalize the concept of a literary culture which spoke a language quite different from that of the prevailing Christian ideology and which could claim its own autonomy (see Ronsard's answers to his Protestant critics in the 1560s). In the short term the most obvious effect was to force a restyling of literary production in order to replicate the genres practised in antiquity. The contrast between the treatises of *Sebillet (1548) and Du Bellay (1549) measures the change envisaged.

In practice, experiments in producing epics in the ancient mould foundered (Ronsard's *Franciade). However, short narrative mythological poetry in the Ovidian manner was thoroughly acclimatized in French (Ronsard, *Baïf, *Belleau), as were odes, Pindaric and Horatian (Ronsard, *Malherbe), and hymns in the manner of ancient, pagan Greece, mediated by the Latin Marullus (Ronsard). In the absence of a commercial theatre in the second half of the 16th c., drama was largely a literary, even a school, exercise, subject to the procedures of literary imitation, which ensured that it acquired the characteristics of ancient dramatic writing, particularly that of Seneca (*Jodelle, *Garnier). The rhetorical phraseology of French poetry after 1550, its repertory of figures, and its frame of reference were determined by classical influence, which even prompted attempts to write quantitative metre in French (Baïf's 'vers mesurés à l'antique').

Classical influence also in large measure decided that poetry should be the privileged mode in French literature between 1550 and 1600. Antiquity had left few examples of prose fiction to imitate, and certainly no theories of prose fiction to counterbalance Horace, whose precepts for writing poetry (along with those of contemporary Italians) set the agenda for French theoretical writing in the 16th c., or Aristotle, whose influence is discernible, but relatively weak, in French texts before the 17th c. Theoretical discussion of prose writing took the form of rhetorical prescription, closely based on Cicero (Fouquelin, 1555 [see RAMUS]; Courcelles, 1557). *Montaigne was part of an anti-Ciceronian reaction, but he too was the product of his humanist education, with its moralizing preoccupations and its method of excerpting passages to juxtapose them and then generate discourse by playing them off against each other.

Montaigne had a profound familiarity with Latin literature, but a limited first hand knowledge of Greek, as was true of most pupils of humanist schools (apart from professional Greek scholars and

the writers inspired by *Dorat's teaching, notably Ronsard). It was for this reason that, whereas the translation of Latin literature into French was an occupation held in low esteem in the second half of the 16th c. and generally practised by minor figures (*Habert for Ovid and Horace, *Des Masures for Virgil), translation from Greek had a much higher status. The numerous French translations of Platonic and *Neoplatonic texts, Belleau's translation of 'Anacreon' (1556), the *Iliad* begun by Salel and completed by *Jamyn (1545–80), and *Amyot's Plutarch (1559 and 1572) enriched French literature and gave it new directions.

3. Seventeenth Century

By contrast, in the 1650s and 1660s publishers were making quite an industry out of the translation of Latin literary texts, in response to the much larger market which by then existed for vernacular versions of the best-known Latin authors. By that stage knowledge of classical literature had permeated well beyond the class-room and had become a culture common to the whole of literate and even non-literate society, Latinate or not. But the study of classical texts in their original languages had ceased to be the main agent of transmission, displaced by vernacular literature itself, now predominantly classical in idiom [see CLASSICISM], and by works of reference. In addition, translations and commentaries in French, adjusted to the taste of gentlemen (and lady) amateurs (e.g. the much-reprinted *Metamorphoses* of Nicolas Renouard, 1606), reached a much wider readership than contemporary Latin scholarship, which was beginning to specialize exclusively in textual and historical criticism. Another primary source of dissemination was through art, in the form of mythological picture-books, painting, sculpture, and decorative motifs.

The appropriation of classical culture by a nonspecialist public finds expression in the familiar and even superior tone which 17th-c. authors adopt towards their classical material, from the liberties taken by a *Théophile de Viau to *burlesque versions of Ovid and Virgil in the 1640s and ironical retellings of mythological fictions. The latter is best exemplified by *La Fontaine's *Les Amours de Psyché*. This slightly sceptical distancing, which only adds charm to the classical make-believe, takes its cue from a momentous change in attitude towards the cultural legacy of humanism. The conviction that ancient literature, and in particular its mythological apparatus, was the vehicle of more-or-less arcane truths was customary in French and Latin commentaries up until the mid-century, and persisted even later in mythological handbooks. But in his criticism of Renaissance schooling (*Discours de la méthode*), *Descartes denied that the classical literature at the core of its curriculum was true in any sense. Under the influence of the Scientific Revolution the language of truth became mathematics. The 'scientific' textual and historical criticism of contemporary classical scholars (beginning with Casaubon and Joseph Scaliger) had also tended to divest their texts of their aura of vatic authority. *Boileau's *Art poétique* (1674), still overridingly Horatian, despite his translation of Longinus, affirms the essentially classical stylization of contemporary French literature, but the necessary paraphernalia of mythological reference are no more than 'ornements reçus'. The one literary genre where this polite scepticism was suspended was *tragedy. There Aristotle's *Poetics* and works derived from it set the grounds for critical discussion and increasingly exercised prescriptive force. Even so, it was perhaps ancient history more often than ancient fiction that provided the plots for French 'classical' tragedies.

4. Eighteenth to Twentieth Centuries

The sense of history and historical anachronism, originally fostered by the humanists' investigation of the ancient world, was to be more influential on literary developments than the authority of classically derived theory. In the last 30 years or so of the 17th c. opposition to the cultural hegemony of defunct classical languages and literatures became assertively articulate in the *Querelle des Anciens et des Modernes. In the 18th c. modern vernacular literature, portraying modern society in modern genres (notably prose fiction) apparently relegated ancient authors to the schoolroom, or at least marginalized ancient culture in its own narrow specialisms and the peripheral areas of occasional verse and decorative embellishment. But in the schoolroom classical teaching kept alive the possibility of a non-Christian ethic of citizenship; among historians the classical example legitimized speculation about alternative systems of government; and the iconography of the Revolution and the Napoleonic era was *Neoclassical.

Elsewhere the study of classical art and literature took an even more revolutionary turn in the late 18th and early 19th c., but in spite of the isolated and inspiring example of André *Chenier, it registered only weakly in France's rather etiolated version of *Romanticism. It was not until later in the 19th c. that French authors seized vigorously on the prototypes which classical literature provided for figures of genius, visionaries, and poets (*Hugo's 'satyre', *Mallarmé's faun, the early *Rimbaud, *Valéry in *Charmes). Activated by *Symbolism, this recovery of ancient mythology invented a metonymical reading of classical fiction which renewed the potency of its figures, making them signify in areas out of reach of cultural and rational discourse: the primitive and the subconscious. But this use of classical prototypes presupposed a classically educated readership, as did the peculiarly French fashion of the inter-war years and just after, when *Gide, *Cocteau, *Giraudoux, *Sartre, and *Anouilh played on the ironies involved in their modern restylings of Greek fictions to create initial shock and deliver topical messages.

The decline of classical education in the post-war period threatens to impoverish literary communication, but classical literature remains a potent resource. In 1964–5 *Barthes had good cause to entitle his seminar on classical rhetoric an 'aide-mémoire', yet since then the most seminal development in literary theory has been the recovery and reassessment of ancient and Renaissance *rhetoric. Classical influences are still present in French literature, but they are harder to uncover. The favourite textual metaphors of modern writers (*Foucault, *Pinget, *Butor) are excavation, commentary, palimpsest.   [AM]

See J. Seznec, *La Survivance des dieux antiques* (1940, 2nd edn. 1981); R. R. Bolgar, *The Classical Heritage and its Beneficiaries: From the Carolingian Age to the End of the Renaissance* (1954); T. M. Greene, *The Light in Troy: Imitation and Discovery in Renaissance Poetry* (1982).

Classicism

1. Legend and Counter-Legend

The words *classicisme* and *classique* are applied to many periods, from antiquity to the early 20th c. of *Gide and *Valéry, thus implying the existence of an eternal classicism, opposed to an eternal *romanticism or *baroque. The terms are most used, however, of the literature of the second half of the 17th c., though the *âge classique*, may be seen as extending well into the 18th c. *'Neoclassicism', often used as a synonym by English-speaking writers, is best kept for the quite different artistic movement of the late 18th c.

17th-c. classicism is largely a construction of later generations, who used it for their own ideological purposes. The so-called classical writers did not see themselves as such. The word had originally meant the best (usually ancient) writers, and those who were suitable for class-room study. In the mid-18th c., as French literature was more studied in the schools, a set of writers came to be seen as the modern equivalent of the classics of antiquity. This phalanx, with *Racine as its central figure, was seen as transcending the disorder, confusion, and licence of earlier generations. *Voltaire in his *Siècle de Louis XIV* enshrined the notion of a cultural high point, comparable to the centuries of Pericles or Augustus. *La Harpe, in his influential *Lycée*, reiterated the classical poetics worked out over the previous 150 years and offered the French classical writers as unequalled literary models. They were to retain their position in the national *patrimoine* and the school curriculum during the 19th and much of the 20th c.

Because classicism was seen as associated with power, both the royal power of the 17th c. and the power of teachers and academies in the 19th, it became the object of fierce attacks. Romantics such as *Hugo or *Stendhal saw classical rules as hostile to freedom, imagination, and creativity. *Foucault's description of oppressive classical culture in his

Histoire de la folie is a modern variation on this theme. Against the idea of a serene order of clarity, harmony, and good taste, modern literary history has therefore tended to stress the variety of 17th-c. writing, paying more attention to the first half of the century and the *irréguliers* or *libertins* (e.g. *Théophile, *Cyrano de Bergerac) who had been overshadowed by the generation of 1660. The baroque and *preciosity have come to be viewed more positively, and the importance of women's writing in this period has been more fully recognized.

A different strategy, beginning with the *Histoire de la littérature classique* (1940) of Daniel Mornet, has been to stretch the idea of classicism to include many qualities previously excluded. This is already visible in Gide's definition of it as 'un romantisme dompté', and may be likened to the Nietzschean notion of Greek tragedy as a marriage of Apollo and Dionysus. On this view, classicism does not suppress energy, wit, and passion, but holds them in a productive and satisfying equilibrium. It is characterized less by rules than by its interest in taste, pleasure, and the inexplicable *je ne sais quoi*.

2. Theories

At one time it was customary to speak of a 'doctrine classique'. In so far as this implies a shared body of theory which governed writing it is, like the idea of classicism, a *post facto* construction. Theorists argued with one another, and writers did not necessarily take much notice of them. Even so, the classical period is marked by the new importance given to poetics and *criticism, which had an official headquarters in the newly created *Académie Française. The discussions among writers, theorists, and amateurs concerned above all *tragedy, but also *epic poetry, prose *eloquence and *lyric poetry, and to a lesser extent *comedy, *history, and even the *novel. The most prominent 17th-c. theorists included d'*Aubignac, *Balzac, *Boileau, *Bouhours, *La Ménardière, *Le Bossu, and *Rapin, followed in the 18th c. by *Batteux, *Marmontel, and others. Boileau, in the *Art poétique* (1674), the most important single critical work of the time, signalled the role of *Malherbe ('Enfin Malherbe vint') in establishing a verse language worthy of literature, and language and *versification remain central theoretical preoccupations. Other notions which commanded fairly general respect are:

a. *Imitation of antiquity*. The theorists of classicism, like those of the *Renaissance, saw modern literature as working in a tradition which went back to the great writers of antiquity [see CLASSICAL INFLUENCES]. Although certain theorists were deferential to Aristotle (as interpreted by 16th-c. scholars) and to the rules which he had supposedly extrapolated from ancient practice, the notion of imitation meant re-creation rather than copying. Nevertheless, respect for antiquity was shaken during the 17th c., particularly in the *Querelle des Anciens et des Modernes.

b. *Truth to nature*. This very elastic concept has served many different literary movements. In the 17th c. it had negative and positive functions. Negatively, it condemns the extravagance attributed to previous generations (what we now call the *baroque); positively, it means finding the best possible way of writing about *human* nature, seen not so much in its local manifestations as in its unchanging essence. A key concept is that of *vraisemblance* (verisimilitude), which is preferred to attested historical truth; it is *vraisemblance* which underlies the rule of the three unities [see TRAGEDY].

c. *Reason*. Closely associated with truth to nature, 'la raison' does not mean rationalism, nor does it rule out imagination and creativity. It does, however, imply a taste for order, measure, and harmony. In its social manifestation it enjoins the writer to observe the decorum designated by the term *bienséance* [see TRAGEDY]. This sets the classical culture of the *honnêtes gens apart from the world of peasants, children, or savages.

d. *Instruction*. Poetry was no longer invested with the grandiose philosophical or religious mission assigned it by a *Ronsard, but almost all critics spoke of its didactic function. Aesthetic pleasure was not an end in itself. In its extreme form, in the writing of *Le Bossu, this meant the assimilation of the *Iliad* to the Aesopic fable.

e. *Pleasure*. While writers had a duty to instruct, they were no less obliged to give pleasure—'plaire et toucher'; indeed, pleasure makes instruction possible. Critics and theorists, although not always preaching subservience to the taste of the audience, insisted on the need to avoid idiosyncratic independence and pedantic scholarship. Classical culture was far from monolithic, but compared with later generations it shows a remarkable harmony between writer and polite public.

3. Writers

The writers thought of as classical are sometimes grouped under the label 'l'école de 1660'. In fact, although some of them were linked by friendship, the writers who came to prominence in the 1660s are far from forming a school. For the period 1660-90, the major figures often described as classical are: Pierre *Corneille, *Pascal, *La Fontaine, Boileau, *Molière, Racine, *Bossuet, *La Fayette, *La Rochefoucauld, *Sévigné, *La Bruyère, and perhaps *Fénelon, with a second rank including *Bourdaloue, *Fléchier, *Quinault, Thomas *Corneille, and *Saint-Évremond. Some important writers of the period are generally excluded from the list as representing tendencies which are inimical to classicism, e.g. Madeleine de *Scudéry, *Perrault, *Fontenelle, *Villedieu, *Bayle.

When one considers this list, it does not look like a coherent group whose writing embodies the theories outlined above. At one extreme, it has been suggested that Racine is the only truly classical writer—particularly if one accepts the view of him as the incarnation of taste and equilibrium, ignoring the extravagance and violence of his theatre. P. Corneille, belonging to an earlier generation, was at odds with the rule-makers and many of their principles. Molière can only be made classical by forgetting a large part of his work, from the farces to the *comédies-ballets*. La Fontaine was a free spirit. Boileau was the champion of classical poetics, but his own satiric poetry hardly conforms to it. Sévigné and La Fayette wrote in genres that were barely recognized by critics, and the *moralistes*, like Pascal, favoured fragmentary, discontinuous forms. Bossuet's eloquence is Christian before it is classical, though the two are not necessarily at odds.

Nevertheless, in at least two respects these writers belong together. First, all are preoccupied with understanding human nature and finding the best way of expressing this understanding. Psychological and moral curiosity dominates the age, and this is addressed above all to the social behaviour of human beings. Secondly, all show a powerful *rhetorical awareness of their audience. They may not flatter it, sometimes they shock its expectations (La Bruyère, Pascal), but they belong in the society for which they write. One sign of this is the marked stress on *orality in their works.

Of course these characteristics were not unique to the writers of the late 17th c.; they continued to define most French writing of the 18th c. What is more specific is that these writers belonged to a court-dominated, absolutist society, and this affected what they wrote. Not that one can equate classicism with authoritarianism; although many of the writers mentioned above enjoyed official patronage, and some took part in the academies that mediated royal power in the arts, none were simply pillars of the establishment. Most had a strongly critical streak; in the absence of any perspective of social or political change, this often found expression in a vision that was ironic, world-denying, or tragic. [PF]

See H. Peyre, *Le Classicisme français* (1942); E. B. O. Borgerhoff, *The Freedom of French Classicism* (1950); J. Brody (ed.), *French Classicism: A Critical Miscellany* (1966); *Continuum* I, 'Rethinking Classicism' (1990).

CLAUDEL, Paul (1868–1955). French Catholic dramatist and poet who revived poetic drama in the modern period. Claudel is something of a paradox: reactionary in his religious and political ideas, he was nevertheless a constant innovator in his writings, building on contemporary trends in the theatre for a series of new and original departures. Too often dismissed as a religious bigot or a political backwoodsman, Claudel is best considered in literary terms, as a great dramatist and dramatic poet (his lyric poetry being at its best when sharing the rhetorical characteristics of his writing for the theatre, as in the Cinq grandes odes, published in 1910). His strange version of Catholic belief, often verging

on the heretical, was particularly effective in producing dramatic situations of great power. One does not need to share his beliefs in order to appreciate the dilemmas involved.

He was born at Villeneuve-sur-Fère in 1868, of a middle-class family which moved to Paris in 1881, where Paul studied at the Lycée Louis-le-Grand. A Catholic by birth and upbringing, he nevertheless became strongly influenced by the contemporary pessimism based on Schopenhauer. A reading of *Rimbaud in 1886 convinced him, however, of the existence of something beyond external reality. Influenced by what many have seen as a misreading of Rimbaud, he underwent a profound religious experience which was succeeded by four years of doubt and uncertainty, before his 'conversion définitive' in 1890.

Claudel's first poetry and drama were essentially *Symbolist. To the vagueness and lack of definition of much of the Symbolist theatre, however, Claudel added two new elements: cores of symbolism (particularly Christian symbolism) around which a coherent meaning could establish itself; and a powerful voice based on the *verset claudélien*, free verse written for declamation and based on the breath group, as well as on biblical and liturgical techniques of repetition.

His first two plays, *Tête d'or (written 1889, published 1890) and La Ville (written 1890, published 1893), already display this power. They are, however, large-scale, complicated plays in which the symbolism is still often rather confused. Much of this may have been caused by uncertainty of message. In Tête d'or, a Nietzschean desire for freedom and self-fulfilment stands alongside the Christian message; in La Ville, the symbolism of anarchism (destruction, purification) fits rather better with a Christian statement of the need for renewal. La Jeune Fille Violaine (written 1892, but not published until 1926) was a new departure, in that the main lines of the action are much simpler. The theme of this play, based on suffering and renunciation, is centrally Christian.

Claudel's diplomatic career (1893–1935) was often to influence his plays and poetry, which took much from the cultures that surrounded him. Vice-consul in New York and Boston (1893–4), he was posted as consul to China in 1895, where, apart from visits to France (1900–1 and 1905–6), he was to remain until 1909. Consul in Prague (1910–11) and Frankfurt (1911–13), consul-general in Hamburg (1913–14), he returned to France at the outbreak of war and performed missions in Rome (1915–16) and Rio de Janeiro (1917–19). After service in Denmark on the Schleswig Commission (1920–1), he became ambassador to Japan (1921–7), to the United States (1927–33), and to Belgium (1933–5).

His first posting in the United States produced *L'Échange* (written 1893, published 1900), in which American capitalism is a major theme. Restricted to four characters, it continued the new move to simplicity, which was reinforced when, between 1895 and 1898, he rewrote *La Ville* (this version being published in 1901), reducing the number of characters from 29 to 8. This, and the new version of *La Jeune Fille Violaine* (written between 1898 and 1900, published 1901), also show a move towards a more real primary action (as in *L'Échange*), with the symbolic meaning of events residing within a realistic *cadre*.

*Partage de Midi (written 1905, published privately—150 copies—in 1906, and not properly published until 1948) is the climax of this trend. In it two lovers, conversing within the formulae of contemporary social discourse, become nevertheless aware of their mystical union on another plane. Transitions from one mode of existence to another are effected by mysterious incantatory phrases. What on one plane would appear a banal story of adultery becomes a cosmic drama.

The power of the emotions in this play is something new. Where, in the second *La Ville* for example, the heroine Lâla had moved from man to man because of symbolic necessity rather than human desire, in this play human desire is uppermost, and the symbolism is designed to explain it. The new immediacy appears to have been a result of Claudel's own experience. In 1900 he had returned to France from China to present himself for a monastic vocation, and had been refused. In disarray, on the boat back to China he started a passionate affair with a married woman, details from which were to colour most of his plays from now on. *Partage* is an expression of the conflict between Christian morality and the Romantic view of a predestined passion. Here the conflict is not resolved; within a few years, however, thanks to Claudel's reading of *Huysmans, the doctrine of vicarious suffering, in an extreme form, was to become central to his work, and was to explain how the separation of suffering lovers could be efficacious in saving the world, with their love being part of God's plan. This explains the central role of such suffering in the Trilogy (*L'*Otage*, *Le Pain dur*, and *Le Père humilié*), in the extensive reworking of *La Jeune Fille Violaine* entitled *L'*Annonce faite à Marie* (written 1910-11, published 1912) and, above all, in *Le *Soulier de Satin* (written 1919-24, published 1929).

This last play was a dramatic new departure. Influenced by all the new trends in European drama, and also drawing on the techniques of the Noh theatre observed during his period in Japan, Claudel turned his back on the conventions of realism in the theatre and produced a wide-ranging, disconcerting, humorous, tragic, universal drama which is like nothing else before or since. He was already making extensive use of music, and of modern media such as the cinema screen, to enhance his drama. *Le Livre de Christophe Colomb* (written 1927, published 1935) continued this trend, which culminated in the opera *Jeanne au bûcher* (written 1935, published 1939, music by Honegger).

A new career was to start with his collaboration with the actor-producer Jean-Louis *Barrault. In 1943 they produced, on the Paris stage, a new version of the previously unperformed *Soulier de Satin*. Barrault's productions of *Partage de Midi* (1948), *L'Échange* (1951), *Christophe Colomb* (1953), and *Tête d'or* (1958) created a new realization of the theatrical power of Claudel's drama, and opened the way to a new generation of producers (*Vitez, *Lavelli, *Bourdet) who have used Claudel as an incomparable resource.   [RMG]

See A. Vachon, *Le Temps et l'espace dans l'œuvre de Paul Claudel*·(1965); F. Varillon, *Claudel* (1967); M. Lioure, *L'Esthétique dramatique de Paul Claudel* (1971); M. Malicet, *Lecture psychanalytique de l'œuvre de Claudel*, 3 vols. (1978-9).

CLAUDE LE LORRAIN, Claude Gellée, known as (1600-82). French painter. Claude was so popular and well established in Rome by 1637, with commissions from the Pope, cardinals, and the king of Spain, that he had to keep meticulous visual records of his work to defeat forgers. His evocative classical and biblical landscapes, often with the same titles as those of his scholarly friend *Poussin, are very different in interpretation. In subjects derived from Ovid's *Metamorphoses* or the *Aeneid* and *Georgics* of Virgil, his landscape settings reflect the appropriate human sentiments in their weather conditions, times of day, poetic light effects, and lyrical moods. His work and that of his contemporary Gaspar Dughet (1615-75) were particularly influential on the development of landscape gardening and the *Picturesque movement in 18th-c. England.   [JPC]

Claudine. Heroine of several books by *Colette.

CLAVEL, Bernard (b. 1923). French novelist; the son of a baker and once apprenticed to a *pâtissier*. His best-selling novels evoke a traditional France in epic terms and have frequently been adapted for the screen. *Les Fruits de l'hiver* (1968) was awarded the Prix Goncourt but, elected to the prize jury in 1971, Clavel resigned in protest at the jury's machinations.   [EAF]

CLAVEL, Maurice (b. 1920). French novelist, dramatist, and television critic. His plays and novels such as *Une fille pour l'été* (1957) and *Le Tiers des étoiles* (1972) combine social and political realism with metaphysical preoccupations. His essays—*Ce que je crois* (1975), *Dieu est Dieu, nom de Dieu!* (1976)—denounce Marxism in favour of Christianity.

                                                  [EAF]

CLAVERET, Jean (*c*.1600-1666). Dramatist. He was one of the first to write comedies with modern settings, of which *L'Esprit fort*, first performed in 1630, is the only one to survive. He quarrelled with Pierre *Corneille, whose own comedies were following a similar course, and became the unfortunate victim of scathing attacks in the Querelle du *Cid.   [GJM]

Clélie, histoire romaine

Clélie, histoire romaine. Vast (13,000-page) novel by Madeleine de *Scudéry published in ten instalments between 1654 and 1660. The work, now called a *roman héroïque*, often resembles romance more than novel. *Clélie* begins *in medias res*, just before the marriage between Clélie and Aronce. Suddenly, an earthquake separates the lovers. After many fantastic adventures (Clélie is repeatedly kidnapped by Aronce's rivals, for example), they are eventually reunited. However, that happy end is delayed by a variety of intercalated narratives: one character tells another's life story; groups embark on lengthy discussions of themes ranging from the qualities of successful *letter-writing to the value of *inclination* or sudden passion. Despite its setting in classical Rome, *Clélie* was very much a novel for its times.

The best-seller of the century, *Clélie* was the favourite reading of the *précieuses* [see PRECIOSITY]. Much intercalated material was borrowed from their actual discussions—the *carte de *Tendre*, for instance, was invented in Scudéry's salon. And the issues *Clélie* raises, in particular its critique of marriage as legal 'slavery' for women, were hotly debated in the *salons. Contemporary readers praised Scudéry's intimate knowledge of the human heart. In fact, *Clélie* inaugurates the French novel's close association with psychological realism. [JDeJ]

CLEMENCEAU, Georges (1841–1929), nicknamed 'Le Tigre'. He qualified as a doctor, but suffered prison and exile for his opposition to the *Second Empire. Under the Third Republic he edited the Radical newspaper *La Justice* and had a turbulent career as politician and journalist, but his finest hour came as war leader (prime minister 1917–20). Among other writings he left a political testament, *Au soir de la pensée* (1927).

CLÉMENCE DE BARKING, see ANGLO-NORMAN LITERATURE, 6a.

CLÉMENT, Catherine (b. 1939). Feminist thinker who adopts a psychoanalytic and Marxist viewpoint. *La Jeune Née* (1975, with *Cixous) analyses Western representations of women, focusing on the roles of the witch and the hysteric. *Vies et légendes de Jacques *Lacan* (1981) defends Lacanian theory and argues its usefulness for *feminism. [EAF]

CLÉMENT, Jean-Baptiste (1836–1903). Journalist and political song-writer. A miller's son and manual worker, he took part in the *Commune of 1871, went into exile, and on his return continued his militant career in *Guesde's party. His songs include 'Le Temps des cerises' and 'La Semaine sanglante'.

Cléomadès, see ADENET LE ROI.

Cléopâtre, see LA CALPRENÈDE. A quite different Cléopâtre (queen of Syria) is the evil heroine of Corneille's *Rodogune*.

Cléopâtre captive. Lyrical verse tragedy by *Jodelle, first performed in 1552/3 with *Belleau and *La Péruse in principal roles. Loosely modelled on Plutarch's life of Antony, *Cléopâtre* was enthusiastically received in *humanist circles and marked the beginnings of French neoclassical *tragedy and of Jodelle's association with the *Pléiade. Of limited dramatic and psychological interest by modern standards, the tragedy centres on Octavien's unsuccessful attempt to dissuade Cléopâtre from committing suicide. It introduced many standard features of later French classical tragedy—five acts, historical subject, noble characters, confidants, a chorus, unities of time and action, moral and philosophical *sententiae*, the supernatural (dreams, prophecies), stichomythia, a declamatory and rhetorical tone. [MDQ]

Clergy. During the Middle Ages and the *ancien régime*, the Catholic clergy formed the First Estate in the French society of orders. Its members and institutions were privileged, exempt from military service and from most taxes, such as the *taille, octrois, aides*, on the grounds that the Church's true function was to pray to God. In processions the clergy usually came first. Clerical justice existed alongside royal justice, and although the *Gallican Church was inextricably bound up with the monarchy, it was also a fully distinct institution with representation. From the 1580s a Grande Assemblée du Clergé met every ten years with a *petite assemblée* taking place five years later, and a number of special assemblies were called; all of these might discuss questions of finance and theology.

The order was divided into secular clergy—archbishops, bishops, *abbés, canons, curés, vicaires*, deacons—and the regular clergy of the religious orders. A further distinction was made between the upper clergy of bishops and abbots, and the lower clergy of monks, *curés*, and canons (but note that the term *abbé* was commonly used to mean any priest having taken orders, not just wealthy abbots). This clerical divide was both social and economic: the upper clergy was recruited overwhelmingly (about 85 per cent from 1600 to 1789) from the nobility, with an increasing tendency towards the older and sword nobility; the lower clergy came from the bourgeoisie, the artisanal class, and the richer peasantry, with a decided decline in social origins taking place from the mid-18th c. The regular clergy of *Benedictines, *Cistercians, *Carmelites, *Dominicans, *Franciscans, and Augustines had been founded chiefly from the 10th to the 13th centuries, the Minims in 1440. As the nature of piety altered so too did the nature of vocations, and the foundations of the 17th c. were rarely for mendicants but rather for more active orders. The two decades before the Revolution saw a rapid decline in the number of regulars, by about one-third.

The Catholic Church was immensely wealthy; its many separate institutions owned together about 10–20 per cent of France, with consequent seigneurial dues and rents. Half of its revenue came from the clerical tithe, the *dîme*, paid by Catholics and representing about 7 per cent (an average from wide local variations) of the crop, levied usually in kind. However, although the clergy avoided taxation by paying a 'free gift' (*don gratuit*) to the king, the crown siphoned off some wealth in the form of loans secured upon the Church which were never in fact repaid. The lower clergy was poor. Incomes were very low, a *portion congrue* for a *curé* being 200–300 *livres* in the 17th c., rising to 500 *livres* after 1768, while *vicaires* received sometimes less than 100 *livres*. Differences of wealth and the evident misuse of the riches of the Church fuelled the hostility of the lower clergy to the episcopal establishment. The revenues of the upper clergy were large—episcopal incomes averaged 30,000–40,000 *livres* in the 18th c., with many sees bringing in twice that amount or more—and this wealth enabled younger sons of the nobility to live in a truly noble style. The Concordat of Bologna (1519) had seen the papacy recognize clerical sees as an important element in the royal system of appointments and therefore of patronage, with a portion of revenues often being diverted to non-clerical candidates through the 'commendatory' benefice. Benefices were conferred on suitable candidates by the king's confessor and some influential councillors; under *Louis XIV the *feuille des bénéfices* was held by the Jesuit Pères *La Chaise and Le Tellier successively.

In the Middle Ages neither the secular clergy nor the laity was always 'Christian' according to the definition inculcated after the 16th-c. Catholic reformation associated with the Council of Trent [see COUNTER-REFORMATION]. Before this, clerics were frequently uneducated, absent from their sees, of dissolute habits, and unable to fulfil their pastoral duties, while Catholicism was a mixture of animism, popular religion, 'pagan' rituals, and often ill-understood received theology. A reform was long overdue [see also REFORMATION]. The great age of religious renewal was the 17th c., 'the century of saints', the first half of which witnessed the wider establishment of the *Jesuits in France and the foundation of numerous new orders by devoted Christians such as *Bérulle (the *Oratorians), St *François de Sales (the Visitandines), St *Vincent de Paul (the Lazarists, the Sisters of Charity), and Angélique Arnauld, who reformed the convent of *Port-Royal. Around the mid-century seminaries were founded to train priests, and by the end of Louis XIV's reign almost every diocese had one. *Congrégations* specialized in charitable care, teaching, and missionary work, with the numerous female orders offering opportunities for active participation by daughters of the bourgeoisie and nobility. The result was a better-trained, active, and missionary clergy able to persuade and pressurize the population to adopt the more interior and hierarchical vision of the Church.

With education of the priesthood, theological differences developed wider constituencies—for example, on the question of grace debated between

*Jansenists and Jesuits—and the lower clergy began to assert its rights *vis-à-vis* the episcopate according to the arguments of Edmond *Richer. In the 18th c. the clergy was divided by Jansenism and under assault from the *Enlightenment. Although many *curés* welcomed the *Revolution at first, it was to bring turmoil to the clergy, nationalizing Church property, abolishing the religious orders, and requiring a divisive oath to the *Constitution Civile in 1791; poverty, strife, and persecution was the lot of bishops and priests as *anticlericalism took root, together with a renewal of popular and superstitious religious practices in many areas.

The 19th c. brought recovery and renewal for the clergy, whose numbers had drastically fallen. From 1796 to 1880 nearly 400 new *congrégations* were founded, and the number of nuns increased tenfold to 130,000. A feminization of piety occurred as women in a male-dominated society responded to the opportunity for self-fulfilment as sisters, and the Marian cult flourished. The parish priesthood expanded rapidly under the Second Empire to 56,000 priests in 1869 for 42,000 parishes; they were now better educated but, under the anticlerical Third Republic, poor and beleaguered village notables of the Right, often subservient to the local élite. Recruitment was mainly from rural areas in what have, since the Revolution, remained traditionally Catholic and conservative regions: the west, Brittany, the Massif Central, and Lorraine.

The 1880s marked a high point for vocations, followed by stabilization and, since World War II, drastic decline. Society was becoming increasingly secular, with only nominal Catholicism for rites of passage being practised by more than 50 per cent in 1986. Diocesan priests fell in number from 46,000 in 1960 to 28,695 in 1985, of whom only 10 per cent were under 40, and ordinations have fallen back to the low level of the era of the Revolution, only 100 a year. The Church responded to the crisis of declining numbers and increasing age of the clergy by ending its hostile relationship to the State and muting the harsher approach of the lay Action Catholique movement with its emphasis on authority, in the face of more 'popular' religious opinions among the laity. [For more recent developments, see CATHOLICISM IN 20TH-CENTURY FRANCE.]

[PRC]

See J. Delumeau, *Le Catholicisme entre Luther et Voltaire* (1971); F. Lebrun (ed.), *Histoire des catholiques en France* (1980).

Cleveland (*Le Philosophe anglais, ou Histoire de monsieur Cleveland*), see PRÉVOST, A.-F.

Cligès, see CHRÉTIEN DE TROYES.

Climbié, see DADIÉ.

CLITANDRE, Pierre (b. 1954). Haitian writer, painter, and journalist, who in 1978 became editor of the cultural weekly *Le Petit Samedi-Soir*. A victim of Duvalierist repression, after 1980 he lived in exile in New York, director of the newspaper *Union*. His novel *Cathédrale du mois d'août* (1982) is written in the vein of **réalisme merveilleux*. Although graphically portraying the struggles of the poor in the slums of Port-au-Prince in the face of brutal political oppression, Clitandre also delights in the imaginative richness of Haitian culture: Voodoo symbolism, oneiric figures from folklore, echoes of a heroic past.   [BJ]

Cloches de Bâle, Les. Novel by *Aragon, published 1934, and the first volume of the *Monde réel* trilogy. The novel is set in 1912, as Europe moves towards war, and as Paris is terrified by the anarchist Bande à Bonnot and paralysed by an extended taxi-strike. The novel is in three parts, the first of which focuses upon the bourgeoisie, represented by the entourage of Diane de Nettencourt: the world of generals, shady financiers, and bought politicians, determined to crush attempts at working-class organization. The third part of the novel concentrates upon an example of such organization; its hero, Victor, is one of the leaders of the strike of Paris taxis, which is eventually starved into submission. The link between the two worlds is Catherine Simonidzé, the daughter of a Georgian oil-well owner, who lives in relative poverty with her mother and sister in Paris. Although by caste and through financial links close to the world of Diane de Nettencourt, she instinctively rejects the conventions and interests of the bourgeoisie and sides with the working class, although she is attracted more by anarchism than Socialism. The novel ends with an epilogue describing the Socialist Basle Congress and its affirmation of its resistance to war. Significantly, for a novel which shows history through its women characters, it ends with an evocation of the German Socialist Clara Zetkin as an image of the future. Considered an example of French Socialist Realism, the novel is a complex and ambitious piece of writing, with Aragon's characteristic use of pastiche and authorial intervention.   [NH]

CLOOTS, Anarcharsis (pseud.of Jean-Baptiste du Val de Grâce, baron de Cloots) (1755–94). Prussian in origin, he espoused the **philosophe* cause, was made a French citizen by the Revolutionary Convention Nationale, and expounded a doctrine of cosmopolitanism and the cult of reason in writings such as *L'Orateur du genre humain* (1791) and *La République universelle* (1792). He was executed with the **Hébertistes*.

CLOUET. The name of two portrait painters, father and son, both nicknamed Janet. Jean (*c.*1485–1541) came from the Low Countries, and worked for François Ier from 1516; he painted **Budé* (New York), *Man with a Petrarch* (Windsor), *Madame de Canaples* (Edinburgh), and probably *François Ier* (Louvre), as well as producing many drawings (Chantilly). François (*c.*1510–1572) succeeded him as royal

painter; his work includes *Pierre Quthe* (Louvre), a full-length portrait of Charles IX (Vienna), *Femme au bain* (Washington), and numerous drawings (Chantilly). **Ronsard's Élégie à Janet*, addressed to François, compares the poet's and the painter's ideals of feminine beauty.   [PS]

CLOVIS, first Christian king of France, see MEROVINGIANS; see also DESMARETS DE SAINT-SORLIN.

Clubs, see CORDELIERS; ENTRESOL; JACOBINS.

Cluny. Abbey founded in 909 by William the Pious, duke of Aquitaine, during the revival of Benedictine monasticism that marked the post-Viking period. Its foundation charter, which placed it under the protection of the Apostolic See, guaranteed it independence of secular and episcopal control. Under a series of outstanding abbots, monks from Cluny reformed many other monasteries and federated them to the mother house. Cluniacs devoted themselves to intercessory prayer, advocated penitential pilgrimages (the Cluniac pope Urban II launched the First Crusade), and were staunch supporters of the reforming papacy. Cluny's fortunes declined in the later 12th c.   [JHD]

COCTEAU, Jean (1889–1963). A leading figure in the avant-garde in Paris in the first decades of the century. Born in Maisons-Laffitte, he entered at an early age the world of the 'tout-Paris', including the salon of Anna de *Noailles. He constantly sought to respond to Diaghilev's celebrated command, 'Etonne-moi'. Although he was involved in all forms of artistic and cultural activity, he preferred to regard himself as a poet, so much so that he referred to his novels as 'Poésie de Roman' and his plays, ballets, and libretti as 'Poésie de Théâtre'.

Paradoxically, it is not for his poetry proper that he is now best known. He published his earliest volume of verse, *La Lampe d'Aladin*, in 1909, but his more important collections include: the Futurist (or Cubist, or Dadaist) long poem *Le Cap de Bonne Espérance* (1919), dedicated to the aviator Roland Garros; the more traditional poem (or poems) of desire, doubtless inspired by *Radiguet, *Plain-Chant* (1923); the staccato, modernist, word-play-ridden pieces addressed to *L'Ange Heurtebise* (1925): the opium-inspired *Opéra* (1927) that Cocteau himself considered to be his quintessential expression; the shapely, richly textured poems of *La Crucifixion* (1946); and his poetic testament, perhaps his poetic masterpiece, *Le Requiem* (1962), in which he pays tribute to a wide range of precursors, from Homer to Góngora, from Dante to *Mallarmé.

His 'Poésie de Roman' began with the almost unclassifiable verbal-cum-artistic fantasia *Le Potomak* (1919), dedicated to Stravinsky, continued with the 1923 novellas *Le Grand Écart* and *Thomas l'Imposteur*, and reached its climax with *Les Enfants terribles* (1929), a tale of rebellious youth centred on a brother and sister, Paul and Élisabeth. These works of the 1920s are characteristically controlled concoctions of personal experience and vivid imagination, dream and reality, truth and falsehood, all larded with provocative aphorisms.

It is Cocteau's 'Poésie de Théâtre' that is the most obvious interface with the other arts. For the ballet *Parade* (first performed 1917) he collaborated with *Satie, *Picasso, and Massine; for *Les Biches* (1924) he worked with *Milhaud and *Poulenc; for *Phèdre* (1950) Georges Auric composed the music and Serge Lifar was the choreographer. In the preface which he wrote in 1922 to *Les Mariés de la Tour Eiffel* he contemplated a new 'genre théâtral' to be produced by 'un groupe amical' rather than an individual dramatist; that play involved collaboration with five of Les *Six. His adaptation, or contraction, of Sophocles' *Antigone*, first staged in 1922, became the libretto for Honegger's 'tragédie lyrique' six years later. The Latin translation of the text of his adaptation of *Oedipus Rex* similarly served as the basis of Stravinsky's opera-oratorio. More importantly, it was the stimulus to the reworking of the Oedipus story in *La Machine infernale* (1934), where Cocteau was able to incorporate allusions to Freud. The Greek myth with which he felt the most personal affinity, however, was that of Orpheus, for which he found a dramatic structure first in the play *Orphée* (1927) and subsequently in the film version (1950). The cinema was possibly his ideal medium; he made his debut with *Le Sang d'un poète* (1930), and his best films include *L'Éternel Retour* (1943) and *La Belle et la bête* (1945), as well as *Orphée*, but not the embarrassingly egocentric *Le Testament d'Orphée* (1960). [KRA]

See J.-J. Kihm, E. Sprigge, H.-C. Béhar, *Jean Cocteau: l'homme et les miroirs* (1968); F. Steegmuller, *Cocteau* (1970).

Cocu magnifique, Le, see CROMMELYNCK.

Code Civil, Le (also known as the Code Napoléon). Although there were earlier proposals for a codification of French law, it was the Revolution which put forward serious plans for an official code. These were brought to fruition during the Consulate and Empire. *Napoleon himself was involved in the preparation of the code, though much of the drafting was done by Jean-Étienne-Marie Pontalis (1746–1807). Five different codes, concerning civil law, civil procedure, commercial, criminal, and penal law, were drawn up; the first and most important, the Code Civil, was promulgated in 1804. It was temporarily imposed on countries subject to the Empire, and was subsequently taken as a model in various European and Latin American countries. In France, although progressively revised, it has remained in force until the present day.

Divided into three sections (the law of persons, the law of things, and the law of the acquisition of rights), the Code is partly based on the customs of Paris and Orléans, but takes other material from

Roman law and elsewhere. Above all, it is a rational legal code, embodying the liberal individualism of the Revolution, but also reinforcing the authority of fathers and husbands. Its clarity of expression has been much admired; *Stendhal told *Balzac that while writing the *Chartreuse de Parme* he read a page or two of the Code every day as a stylistic discipline. [PF]

Code de la nature, Le, see MORELLY.

COËFFETEAU, Nicolas (1574–1632). Preacher to *Henri IV, bishop, and noted controversialist. His *Essai des questions théologiques* (1607) was not the first theological treatise to be written in French (see *Calvin and *Du Plessis-Mornay), but his work contributed substantially to the development of French prose. His works were frequently cited in the *Dictionnaire de l'Académie Française*. His classicizing tendencies are evident in his *Histoire romaine* (1621). [IJS]

Cœlina, ou l'Enfant du mystère, see PIXERÉCOURT.

Cœur simple, Un, one of Flaubert's *Trois contes*.

Coffee Houses, see CAFÉS AND RESTAURANTS.

COHEN, Albert (1895–1981). Swiss novelist, essayist, and autobiographer. His individualistic major work of fiction, *Solal et les Solal*, appeared in three volumes, *Solal* (1930), *Mangeclous* (1938), and (most famously) *Belle du Seigneur* (1968). The life of a Cephalonian Jew, told in richly original style, becomes the ground for a complex and often satirical fresco of love and cosmopolitan politics, which, in its later stages, attains a Proustian pitch of insight and emotional intensity. A cloying note mars some of his autobiographical work (*Le Livre de ma mère*, 1954). [DAS]

COIGNARD, Gabrielle de (c.1540–1594). Poet, whose father and husband were presidents of the Parlement de Toulouse. After her husband's death she found consolation in composing her *Œuvres chrétiennes*, which were published posthumously in 1594 by her two daughters. They consist of *stances*, odes, and around 150 sonnets, exploring mainly religious themes, in language which is often highly erotic; her poetry has been described as 'pétrarquisme spirituel'. Its form owes much to the *Pléiade and possibly Louise *Labé, but her spirituality may derive from Spanish devotional literature. She shows some feeling for external nature, a rarity in women writers in the 16th c. [CMSJ]

COIGNET, Jean-Roche (1776–1865). His two-volume *Cahiers du capitaine Coignet* (1851–3) recounting his runaway rural childhood, service as a barely literate grenadier in Napoleon's Garde, and eventual retirement in his native Yonne, give a robust, vernacular account of the real life of a foot-soldier and faithful *grognard* from the Italian campaign to Waterloo. [DAS]

COLARDEAU, Charles-Pierre (1732–76). French poet and playwright. He translated Tasso, as well as Young and other English poets; his imitation of Pope's *Eloisa to Abelard* under the label 'héroïde' (1758) launched a vogue for such verse epistles attributed to famous figures.

COLBERT, Jean-Baptiste (1619–83). Chief minister of *Louis XIV from 1661. The son of a merchant, he came to power by engineering *Fouquet's downfall, and was responsible for a vigorous and often unpopular programme of economic and administrative reform, protecting French commerce and rebuilding the navy. Seeing the importance of the arts for national prestige, he fostered *academies and libraries and elicited royal propaganda by giving pensions to writers selected by *Chapelain.   [PF]

COLET, Louise, née Revoil (1808–76). Prolific French writer whose importance in her day is difficult to assess due to the misogyny of so-called friends and critics. Mainly remembered as *Flaubert's clinging mistress and recipient of important parts of his correspondence, she is an interesting phenomenon in her own right. Born in Aix-en-Provence, she married a poor musician without the blessing of her family, followed him to Paris (they eventually separated), and struggled to establish herself as a writer. She supported herself through fluctuating state pensions, literary prizes for her poetry, earnings from published books and articles, and with money from Victor *Cousin, who believed himself the father of her daughter. Cousin, Flaubert, *Musset, and *Vigny were her best-known lovers, her salon in the rue de Sèvres was frequented by many writers, and she exchanged letters with *Hugo and *Quinet. Works featuring fictional versions of Flaubert are *Une histoire de soldat* (1856) and *Lui, roman contemporain* (1860), the latter just one of the epidemic of novels portraying George *Sand's relationship with Musset. She was a feminist and socialist who joined Flora *Tristan's Union Ouvrière and supported the Paris *Commune in 1871.   [DK]

COLETTE, Sidonie-Gabrielle (1873–1954). Colette, who published her early work under the names of Willy and ˚Colette Willy, was long regarded as a writer limited historically to the *belle époque* and the Third Republic and thematically to minor genres of psychological and nature writing. Her reputation has increased significantly, however, particularly through feminist criticism, so that she is now regarded, not only as a major 20th-c. woman writer, but also as a major literary figure of the first half of the century.

She was born in the Burgundian village of Saint-Sauveur-en-Puisaye. Her father was a retired army captain; invalided out of the army when his leg was amputated, he had become the local tax-inspector. Her mother, Sidonie, who is celebrated in much of her later work, such as *La Maison de Claudine* (1922)

and *Sido* (1929), was a major influence upon her, both through the establishment of a loving maternal relationship and through her introduction of her daughter to the world of nature, which became such an important part of Colette's later work. This idyllic childhood was overshadowed by constant financial difficulties, which led in part to her early marriage in 1893 to Henri Gauthier-Villars who, under the name of Willy, was making a reputation for himself as a journalist and popular novelist. This reputation was based in large part on his extensive exploitation of *nègres*, poor writers who produced work to Willy's prescription which was published under his name. Colette was immediately enrolled into this group and, using material from her own adolescence, with titillating detail added at Willy's instruction, produced the four phenomenally successful Claudine novels, *Claudine à l'école* (1900), *Claudine à Paris* (1901), *Claudine en ménage* (1902), and *Claudine s'en va* (1903), and the two Minne novels, *Minne* (1904) and *Les Égarements de Minne* (1905).

This literary slavery, compounded by Willy's constant infidelities, caused the marriage to break up definitively in 1906, and Colette embarked upon a period of what was considered scandalous independence, appearing until 1913 as a music-hall artiste, often in sketches and plays adapted from her own novels, such as *Claudine à Paris*, and forming, until 1910, a liaison with the marquise de Morny, known as 'Missy'. At the same time she began to assert her literary independence. Two novels, *La Retraite sentimentale* (1907) and *L'Ingénue libertine* (1909), were still very much under the shadow of Willy's popular style, but *La *Vagabonde* (1910), with its evocation of the world of the music-hall and its exploration of the assertion of independence of its heroine, breaks new ground and establishes a very real originality.

Colette's period of bohemianism ended in 1912 with her marriage to Baron Henry de Jouvenel, with whom she had one daughter, 'Bel-Gazou', born in 1913. It was during the 12-year marriage to de Jouvenel that Colette established herself firmly as a writer, particularly through *Chéri* (1920), probably her best-known novel, *Le Blé en herbe* (1923), and the beginning of a whole series of personal reminiscences with *La Maison de Claudine* (1922).

Her second marriage ended in 1924, and in 1925 she met Maurice de Goudeket, whom she was to marry in 1935 and who remained with her until her death. Until the war her writing consisted of novels, such as *La Fin de Chéri* (1926), *La Seconde* (1929), *La Chatte* (1933), and *Duo* (1934), and an increasingly successful body of autobiographical and semi-fictional work, such as *La Naissance du jour* (1928), *Sido* (1929), *Le Pur et l'impur* (originally *Ces plaisirs*, 1932), and *Mes apprentissages (Ce que Claudine n'a pas dit)* (1936). She spent the war years in Paris, concerned for the safety of her Jewish husband, and produced two volumes of memoirs about the period, *Journal à rebours* (1941) and *De ma fenêtre* (1942), as well as two novels,

Julie de Carneilhan (1941) and *Gigi* (1944), and two collections of short stories, *Chambre d'hôtel* (1940) and *Le Képi* (1943), which mark a return to the *belle époque* and the subject-matter of the earlier fiction. From the Liberation to her death, she was one of the major figures of the French literary establishment.

Colette's work has too often been considered to be limited by its historical time-scale and by its subject-matter (the role of woman). This is because her work, whether fiction or non-fiction, is essentially autobiographical. Yet it uses autobiography to establish a general vision which is comprehensive and challenging. Her works are concerned with the progress towards authenticity: against the corruption and hypocrisy of *belle époque* society and the prevailing and continuing male-dominated way of seeing, she explores sexual and emotional relationships, the process of ageing, and the acceptance of a wholeness of existence in the world of nature. The key to her work is in the vision itself: not merely in the extraordinarily acute powers of observation for which she was so justly praised, but in the rectification of that male-dominated way of seeing. This required the construction of a new perception and a new style in which to embody it.   [NH]

See Y. Resch, *Corps féminin, corps textuel* (1973); N. Ward Jouve, *Colette* (1987); D. Holmes, *Colette* (1991).

COLIGNY, Gaspard de, amiral (1519–72) replaced *Condé as military and political leader of the French Protestants until his assassination in the *St Bartholomew's Day Massacre. He owed his importance to the fact that the more eminent members of the Bourbon faction were minors and to his own prestige as an experienced soldier and as an austere Calvinist.

COLIN MUSET (*fl.* 1230–70). A professional *trouvère-jongleur* employed at courts in Lorraine and Champagne. He is credited with 18 lyrics: nine attributed to him in manuscripts, three more naming him, one implausibly attributed to another person, and five *anonyma*. His seven *chansons jongleuresques* and three *serventois* express his preferences and aversions, predictably condemning lordly avarice and naïvely celebrating the good life which satisfies all appetites. Ironic self-mockery offsets the moralizing. Although in a *tenso* Muset answers Jacques d'Amiens with cynicism, his whimsical good humour (conveyed partly by diminutives) relieves the clichés of *fin'amor* in his remaining lyrics, which include two *descorts* and a *lai*. [PVD]

Collaboration during World War II, see OCCUPATION AND RESISTANCE.

COLLÉ, Charles (1709–83). Versatile French author, who wrote *parades* [see FARCE] for the financier Meulan, and subsequently for the duc d'Orléans, as well as *opéras-comiques*, vaudevilles, and comedies. He is remembered for a successful *drame, Dupuis et*

Des Ronais (1763), and more especially for *La Partie de chasse de Henri IV*, written in 1763 but banned until 1774. His *Journal historique et littéraire* (1748–72) is generally severe on contemporary life and letters.
[JD]

Collège. Many colleges were founded by charitable endowment in the University of Paris in the Middle Ages [see SCHOLASTICISM]; these were originally residences for students (for the most part teenagers), but acquired a teaching role. Among the most famous were those of Boncourt, Coqueret, Montaigu, and Navarre, and above all the *Sorbonne. Many subsisted until the Revolution; in the 16th c. some played an important part in the *humanist revival, especially Boncourt (where Jodelle's *Cléopâtre* was performed), and Coqueret, where *Dorat taught *Ronsard, *Du Bellay, and others. A later arrival was the Collège des Quatre Nations, founded under *Mazarin's will for young men from four provinces newly acquired by France; its buildings became the home of the *Institut in 1806.

The word also applies to the secondary schools of the pre-Revolutionary teaching orders (the most prestigious were the Collège de Clermont—later Collège Louis-le-Grand—of the *Jesuits in Paris and the Collège de Juilly of the *Oratorians). Many were shut at the Revolution and their place taken by state-run *écoles centrales* and lycées. Today *collège* usually means a state school offering the first stage of secondary education [see EDUCATION].   [PF]

Collège de France (formerly Collège Royal). In 1530 Guillaume *Budé persuaded *François Ier to found a *humanist centre of learning in Paris, a 'collège des trois langues', first projected in 1517, which would be able to stand side by side with the conservative *Sorbonne and challenge its intellectual leadership. In spite of subsequent objections the king stood firm. The guiding principles were freedom of research and teaching and free access to all. At the first foundation there were two professors of Greek (Toussaint and Danès), two of Hebrew (*Vatable and Guidacerio), one of Latin (Latomus), and one of mathematics (Fine), soon followed by *Postel (oriental languages). Vicomercato (Greek and Latin), and Vidius and Dubois (medicine). The initial programme is reflected in *Rabelais's letter of Gargantua to Pantagruel (1532), which features the same forward-looking spirit of enquiry and encyclopedic aim in its 'abîme de science'. The second generation of teachers under *Henri II included *Ramus, *Turnèbe, *Dorat, and other close associates of the *Pléiade. In 1566 *lettres patentes* of *Charles IX formally established the statutes.

Under various names the Collège Royal (Collège de France since the Restoration) has successfully traversed 460 years; it was respected by the Revolution and survived unchanged. Among its many prominent members we find in the 17th c. especially philosophers, mathematicians, and orientalists, and in the 18th, scientists. In the following century science, history, Egyptology, and medicine were notable areas of research, and in the 20th c. it has continued to be progressive, above all in new disciplines and in crossing intellectual boundaries. Today it is under the control of the Ministère de l'Éducation Nationale and there are just over 50 professors.

For centuries the college existed only in name and in the person of its teachers, lacking premises and financial security. At first lectures took place either in university colleges or even in the open air, in the rue du Fouarre, and for decades payment was either delayed or non-existent. A sumptuous building was planned on the site of the *Institut de France but never built; in 1610 building began on the present site, next to the Sorbonne, but the work was not completed until 1774, and there has been much alteration since then.   [PS]

Collège de Sociologie, Le. This somewhat abstruse organization took shape in Paris in 1937 as a circle of researchers led by *Caillois, *Bataille, and *Leiris. Its avowed aim was to advance the study of *la sociologie sacrée*: that is, to identify and analyse those aspects of modern Western culture—rituals, cultic objects, irrational crazes—which bear comparison with the tribal phenomena which are the normal stuff of anthropology. Most participants had relevant qualifications—for example, Caillois had studied with the sociologist *Mauss, as had Leiris, veteran of the 1931 Dakar–Djibouti expedition—but there was no agreement on a firm scientific agenda, and the enterprise foundered in 1939 amid quarrels largely provoked, it is said, by Bataille's unmanageable demands.   [RC]

COLLETET, Guillaume (1598–1659). Poet and critic, who sought in his own work to synthesize the conflicting poetic traditions of the 1620s. One of the first members of the Académie Française, he wrote poetic treatises on the epigram and sonnet and other verse genres (*Art poétique*, 1658), and prepared a substantial history of French literature, never published, which was largely destroyed in 1870.   [GJM]

Colline inspirée, La, see BARRÈS.

COLLOT D'HERBOIS, Jean-Marie (c.1750–1796). Actor, playwright, and theatre manager who attained fame as a *Jacobin politician during the *Revolution. He wrote the popular *Almanach du père Gérard* (1791), became a member of the Comité de Salut Public, then helped engineer *Robespierre's downfall, after which, falling victim to the Thermidorean reaction, he was deported to French Guiana, where he died.   [PF]

Colomba. Novella by *Mérimée, published in 1840, set in Corsica. The hero, Orso Antonio, a military officer who saw action at Waterloo, on returning from France is urged by his sister, Colomba, to partake in a vendetta to punish the murderers of his father, but Orso also falls in love with an English tourist, Lydia Nevil, who at first opposes such uncivilized customs. Colomba, by various strategies, maintains the need for revenge, and finally Orso, ambushed, kills the two sons of the murderer. He hides in the *maquis*, Colomba leads Lydia to visit him there, and they declare their love. He is cleared of charges, in large part thanks to the testimony and influence of Lydia and her father. Lydia and Orso marry, but Colomba remains merciless when faced with the senile and grieving murderer. It is one of Mérimée's most probing studies of the conflict between civilized and primitive value codes, written with deft irony, in a style which is both concrete and distancing, based in part on his own, by then thorough, acquaintance with Corsica.   [FPB]

Colonel Chabert, Le (1832). Short novel by *Balzac about a soldier presumed dead who returns to find his place taken. It is one of the *Scènes de la vie privée* in *La *Comédie humaine*.

Colonization. France has won and lost two colonial empires during the last 500 years. The first was acquired mainly in the Americas, beginning in the 16th c., as well as in the Indian Ocean and the Indian subcontinent during the 17th and 18th c. By the beginning of the 19th c. the bulk of these territories had been ceded to Great Britain as a consequence of French military defeats in Europe or overseas. France built up a second colonial empire during the 19th and early 20th c. in Africa, Indo-China, and Oceania; most of these colonies were to gain their independence after World War II. [See maps on pp. xxxii–xxxv]

France's earliest efforts at overseas expansion were concentrated in North America. Dispatched by François Iᵉʳ in 1534, Jacques Cartier discovered the St Lawrence River and advanced up it as far as Hochelaga (Montreal). It was not until the beginning of the following century that a serious attempt was made at settling La Nouvelle France, as Canada was called at that time [see QUEBEC]. Samuel de Champlain founded Quebec in 1608, explored the Hudson River to the south, and pushed as far west as Lake Huron. The Mississippi basin was claimed for France in 1682 by Robert Cavelier de La Salle, who named it *Louisiana in honour of Louis XIV. Effective colonization was slow, however: the number of settlers living in French North America is thought never to have totalled more than 80,000.

There were almost as many settlers in the much smaller but more productive territories held by France in the Caribbean. Guadeloupe, Martinique, and the western part of Saint-Domingue (*Haiti) were among the most important *West Indian islands to pass under French control from 1625 onwards. A colony was also created on the South American mainland, in French Guiana. Sugar and other commodities produced in the Caribbean accounted for most of the trade generated by the French empire. The labour needs of the Caribbean islands were dependent on African slaves, who out-numbered white settlers by more than ten to one [see SLAVERY]. The slave-trade was supported by trading posts such as Saint-Louis and Gorée on the coast of Senegal, in West Africa.

Island colonies acquired by France in the Indian Ocean during the 17th and 18th c. included Île Bourbon (Reunion), Île de France (*Mauritius), the Seychelles and, for a brief period, small parts of *Madagascar. Among the trading posts established on the Indian coast from the 1660s onwards were Pondichery, Chandernagor, and Mahé. French expansion into the interior was carried furthest by Joseph François Dupleix, who by 1754 had established a French protectorate over a large part of the Indian subcontinent.

This marked the high-water mark of France's first overseas empire, which at that stage covered an area of approximately 10 million square kilometres with an estimated population of 30 million. Most of this, including eastern Louisiana, was lost to Britain as a consequence of the *Seven Years War (1756–63). The remainder of Louisiana was sold to the United States in 1803. There were further losses during the Napoleonic Wars (1803–15), at the end of which France retained only a few Caribbean possessions together with a handful of territories situated for the most part around the rim of the Indian and North Atlantic oceans.

The beginning of France's second colonial empire was marked by the conquest of *Algeria, which was initiated in 1830 and largely completed by the middle of the 19th c. under the command of Marshal Thomas Bugeaud. From their bases on the coast of Senegal, French forces led by General Louis Faidherbe began pushing into the West African interior. Cochin-China (southern Vietnam) was annexed in 1859, and Cambodia was made a French protectorate in 1863. In the Pacific Ocean, where explorers such as *Bougainville had made initial contacts the previous century, France established a protectorate over Tahiti in 1842 and annexed New Caledonia in 1853.

The major phase of expansion came under the Third Republic. Under the premiership of Jules *Ferry, France gained protectorates over *Tunisia as well as over Annam and Tonkin (central and north-ern Vietnam). French *Indo-China became complete with the creation of a protectorate over Laos in 1893. Madagascar was annexed in 1896 and French control in North Africa was extended through a protectorate over *Morocco in 1912. The biggest territorial gains came in sub-Saharan *Africa. By the beginning of the 20th c. France held sway over most of West and Central Africa, where her territories were grouped together respectively as Afrique Occidentale Française (AOF) and Afrique Équatoriale Française (AEF). France's final acquisitions came after World War I with the defeat of Germany and the Ottoman Empire, whose colonies were redistributed among the victorious powers under the aegis of the League of Nations; in this way, France gained mandates over Syria and Lebanon in the Middle East and over the West African territories of Togo and Cameroon.

At its height, between the World Wars, this new French empire was second only to that of Great Britain. It covered more than 12 million square kilometres and contained a population of nearly 70 million, almost twice that of metropolitan France. Indo-China accounted for more than one-third of all the inhabitants. Sub-Saharan Africa contained similar numbers, but they were more thinly spread across a much larger area. There were in all one-and-a-half million settlers. The great majority of these were in the North African territories, particularly Algeria, which constituted the only *colonies de peuplement* among the newly acquired empire. The remainder served as *colonies d'exploitation*, where economic development was directed by relatively small European élites.

The long-term goal often claimed by colonial propagandists was *assimilation*, i.e. the wholesale re-creation of the overseas territories and their inhabitants in the image of French civilization. In practice, the empire was designed to support, rather then duplicate, the economy of France; native peoples were denied political rights, and educational facilities (an essential prerequisite for cultural assimilation) touched only a minority of the population. By the early 20th c. French colonial practice had been rationalized into a new doctine known as *association*, according to which colonizers and colonized would each retain their separate cultural identities while collaborating for the mutual benefit of all concerned. Ironically, the small native élites who passed through the French educational system were to play a leading role in pressing for *decolonization.

Three categories of writers may be distinguished in the literary mediation of the colonial experience. Some wrote about the overseas territories without ever visiting them, a tradition which goes as far back as *Rabelais in *Pantagruel* and *Montaigne in the essay 'Des cannibales'. Others, such as *Fromentin or *Loti, visited the colonies and, in describing their experiences, contributed to French *travel writing. A third body of literature was produced by the permanent inhabitants of colonies, particularly where there were substantial numbers of settlers, as in Algeria. While writers of French descent were initially to the fore among those based overseas, members of the French-educated indigenous élites became increasingly prominent during and after decolonization.

The literatures of the French territories overseas are discussed in entries for specific regions or countries.   [AGH]

See X. Yacono, *Histoire de la colonisation française* (1969); M. A. Loutfi, *Littérature et colonialisme: l'expansion coloniale vue dans la littérature romanesque française, 1871–1914* (1971); J. Meyer, et al., *Histoire de la France coloniale*, 2 vols. (1991).

Colportage

Colportage, Littérature de. Term used to describe the varied literary wares hawked around town and country by pedlars (*colporteurs*) during the *ancien régime* and into the 19th c. *Colporteurs* were poor for the most part, and were subject to police control and sometimes to persecution for distributing subversive material. They nevertheless played a vital part in distributing the printed word to unprivileged members of society, in particular to the peasants. Their stock was made up largely of the booklets of the *Bibliothèque Bleue, but also of *almanacs, broadsheets, and popular prints, of which the *images d' *Épinal* are the best-known example.   [PF]

Combat. Daily paper published in Paris 1944–74, originally a clandestine news-sheet for the Resistance network of the same name. With Albert *Camus as editor, it became a model of high journalistic standards, extending the ethos of the Resistance into post-war political life. In 1947 Camus resigned in the face of financial difficulties threatening the paper's editorial independence.   [DHW]

COMBAZ, Christian (b. 1954). Novelist, brought up in the Bordelais. His *Oncle Octave* (1983) offers the intriguing picture of an innocent mistreated by fate and by those around him, to whom he is an unbearable reminder of the terrors of eccentricity and failure. Combaz is a subtle moral observer of human behaviour. See also *La Compagnie des ombres* (1985), *Le Cercle militaire* (1987), *Chez Cyprien* (1990).
                                                    [GDM]

COMBES, Émile (1835–1921), jokingly called 'le petit Père Combes'. Leader of the *Radical Party at the time of the separation of Church and State [see ANTICLERICALISM].

Combray. Remembered setting of important scenes from the narrator's childhood in Proust's *A la recherche du temps perdu*. It is usually identified with Illiers, near Chartres.

Comédie-ballet. Theatrical genre invented by *Molière for court performance. It combines comedy or farce with interludes of song, dance, and music derived from the *ballet de cour*. The first such piece was *Les Fâcheux*, performed at *Vaux-le-Vicomte for *Fouquet in 1661. *Comédies-ballets* make up a large part of Molière's work, including such well-known plays (now often performed with the ballet element scaled down) as *George Dandin*, *Le *Bourgeois gentilhomme*, and *Le *Malade imaginaire*, for which *Lully wrote the music.   [PF]

Comédie-Française (sometimes Théâtre Français). In conformity with his policy of centralization and prestige, Louis XIV officially founded the Comédie-Française in 1680. It was constituted by the fusion of the *Hôtel de Bourgogne and the Théâtre de Guénégaud [see THEATRES AND AUDIENCES]. Under royal protection, the new company, of 27 members,

received the exclusive rights to perform plays in French in and around Paris and, from 1682, an annual grant of 12,000 *livres*. In reaction to long-standing ecclesiastical and social disapproval, the actors signed their first act of association (*acte de société*) in January 1681, thus forming a co-operative responsible for raising money, mainly for building work, and the payment of common debts. They lived on the profits from the sale of theatre places, according to an agreed division into shares (*parts*). Twice Louis XV agreed to defray their debts, in 1757 and 1766. Over time, the price of government aid has always been increased managerial intervention by the authorities.

The Revolution abolished the company's monopoly in 1791, and political dissension divided the members in 1793, with (most notably) *Talma and Dugazon leaving to form the Théâtre de la République at the Palais-Royal, while the remainder stayed at Saint-Germain as the Théâtre de la Nation (closed the same year). In 1799 the company was reunited and moved into the Salle Richelieu. The Comédie still occupies this location, which has several times been extensively modified [for previous locations, see THEATRES AND AUDIENCES]. Modern technology has enhanced the quality of the theatre; the number of places has, however, gradually been reduced from 1,900 to 892.

Under Napoleon, the state grant, suppressed in 1790, was restored (1802), and a new *acte de société* signed in 1804. The company's monopoly was partially restored in 1806. Though the successive political systems of the 19th c. modified the precise terms of the relationship between the company and the state, their basis was laid in the *décret de Moscou* of 1812. The most significant subsequent ruling was made in 1850, when the provision was introduced for the overall administrator, a post dating from 1847, to be appointed by the appropriate Ministry (then the Ministry of the Interior, now that of Culture). The 19th-c. statutes essentially formed the basis of those introduced in 1946 and modified in 1975.

Today the administrator appoints *pensionnaires* on an annual contract renewable for up to 10 years. A *pensionnaire* can be proposed for election as a *sociétaire* by the general assembly of *sociétaires*, subject to ministerial ratification. Nearly all the present *sociétaires* have passed through the Conservatoire, the prestigious actors' training-school, though in practice the choice of actors, like that of plays, is in some measure in the hands of the producers.

Two-thirds of the *Comédie's* income derives from a state grant, but its artisitic independence is still preserved. It has been described as 'une troupe au service d'un répertoire'. This formula emphasizes the unique function it has acquired from the mid-18th c. onwards of defining and preserving the nation's dramatic heritage, in terms first of the works performed, and secondly of the style of presentation. The history of the Comédie-Française has been closely identifiable with that of French dramatic literature. The Salle Richelieu hosts more than 400 performances a year. Of the 2,500 plays performed in the first 300 years of its existence, some 2,000 were *créations* (i.e. first performances in France, in French), representing the work of over 875 authors. The most frequently staged play was *Tartuffe*. [JD]

Comédie humaine, La. Title given by Honoré de *Balzac to his collected stories and novels, casting his copious fictions as a single, secular reply to Dante's *Divine Comedy*. La Comédie humaine was published in 16 vols. by Furne, Paulin, Dubochet, and *Hetzel between 1842 and 1846; a 17th supplementary volume, containing Les Parents Pauvres (La *Cousine Bette and Le *Cousin Pons), appeared in 1847. Modern editions of Balzac's works are based on the author's corrected copy of the Furne edition, known as the *Furne corrigé* or 'FC'. In the Furne edition, La Comédie humaine contains 89 separately titled works [for a list, see below], but, given Balzac's plans to add numerous further 'scenes' and sections and the uncertain status of the Contes drolatiques, the number is somewhat arbitrary.

La Comédie humaine was the last in a series of attempts by the author to expand the limits of fiction whilst continuing to write relatively unitary novels and stories. The title, adopted in 1841, was a means of regrouping works already written, many of which were already linked together by reappearing characters; it also served to prompt plans for further writing. In the last prospectus Balzac wrote (in 1845) for his still-incomplete encyclopedia of social life, La Comédie humaine was to have the monumental form of a pyramid, standing on a broad base of fictions describing contemporary society (the Études de mœurs), supporting a tier of texts considering the causes of social phenomena (the Études philosophiques), and topped by a small set of Études analytiques, offering an analysis of the abstract principles of social life itself. Only La Physiologie du mariage and a few other fragments were written for the Études analytiques. La *Peau de chagrin, *Louis Lambert, and *Séraphîta are the principal elements in the Études philosophiques, which interested Balzac mainly in the period 1830–5. The bulk of La Comédie humaine thus consists of Études de mœurs, and it is on these formally diverse and wide-ranging social fictions that Balzac's influence and value rest. They are themselves subdivided into six sets of 'scenes': Scènes de la vie privée, Scènes de la vie parisienne, Scènes de la vie de province, Scènes de la vie de campagne, Scènes de la vie politique, Scènes de la vie militaire. The 'countryside', 'political' and 'military' scenes are less copious by far than the first three categories, in which the majority of Balzac's greatest and most widely read novels fall. The Contes drolatiques, 'droll stories' written in a pastiche of 16th-c. French, decorate the base of Balzac's asymmetric pyramid like a fresco or bas-relief.

The 'Avant-propos' of La Comédie humaine was written in 1842, long after many of its major pieces had been published and, in several cases, already rewritten, and it can be read as a retrospective rationalization of Balzac's Promethean creativity as well as a self-prescriptive plan for his ensuing work. It presents the whole of La Comédie humaine as a gallery of 'types' or 'species' of humanity analogous to the species of the natural world described by *Geoffroy Saint-Hilaire, to whom the whole work is dedicated. Balzac also declares that he writes 'in the light of two eternal truths, monarchy and catholicism', whilst remaining 'only the secretary' of French society, the lowly transcriber of the history which it made for itself.

La Comédie humaine is not a series of novels in the manner of Scott's Waverley Novels, or Zola's later *Rougon-Macquart; nor is it a unitary compendium like Proust's *A la recherche du temps perdu which, for all its complexity, has a single reading order. It is a unique construction, less like the monument to which Balzac aspired than it is like a permanent building site, or a labyrinthine and still-living city with uncountable points of entry and infinitely many ways through it. La Comédie humaine contains over 2,000 named characters; of these, about 500 appear in more than one novel; about 50 characters constitute the core of Balzac's fictional universe, and are dealt with at length in several different stories. The sheer scale of Balzac's creation (done without card-indexes or any of the tools of the historian or of the secretary which Balzac claimed to be) is dizzying; the consistency of the physical, social, and emotional world seen from dozens of different fictional perspectives gives Balzac's Paris, Balzac's aristocracy, Balzac's bourgeoisie, Balzac's publishers, critics, writers, artists, misers, traders, widows, wives, daughters, and concierges a kind of lifelikeness which real life rarely possesses. Balzac was reputed to have become entirely wrapped up in his own creation and to have called, on his deathbed, not for a real doctor, but for Horace Bianchon, the medical student in Le *Père Goriot who rose in the course of La Comédie humaine to being the most respected doctor in Balzac's Paris.

La Comédie humaine, despite its intoxicating grandeur, is irrelevant to the reader of Balzac's individual novels, many of which function independently as 'human comedies' on a smaller (but by no means trivial) scale. Le Père Goriot, La Cousine Bette, *Illusions perdues, *Splendeurs et misères des courtisanes, La *Rabouilleuse all present several different social settings, have several separate and related intrigues, and have casts of characters ranging from servants to duchesses, from traders to crooks Each of Balzac's major works implies the Promethean and encyclopædic ambition of La Comédie humaine, which itself adds little rational structure to sort out the teeming multiplicity of the world he created again and again. Balzac's achievement lies in his novels, as novels. His driving ambition to exhaust the social world he created in the image of the real one generated both the structure of *La Comédie humaine* and the masterpieces within it; but it is the latter, not the former, which constitute the major literary monument of the 19th c. [DMB]

See H. J. Hunt, *Balzac's Comédie Humaine* (1959); P.-G. Castex, 'L'Univers de la Comédie humaine', in vol. 1 of *La Comédie humaine*, ed. P.-G. Castex (1976).

The works which make up *La Comédie humaine* are as follows:

ÉTUDES DE MŒURS:

SCÈNES DE LA VIE PRIVÉE: *La Maison du chat qui pelote* (1830); *Le Bal de Sceaux* (1830); *Mémoires de deux jeunes mariées* (1841–2); *La Bourse* (1832); *Modeste Mignon* (1844); *Un début dans la vie* (1842); *Albert Savarus* (1842); *La Vendetta* (1830); *Une double famille* (1830); *La Paix du ménage* (1830); *Madame Firmiani* (1832); *Étude de femme* (1830); *La Fausse Maîtresse* (1841); *Une fille d'Ève* (1838–9); *Le Message* (1832); *La Grenadière* (1832); *La Femme abandonnée* (1832); *Honorine* (1843); *Béatrix* (1839); *Gobseck* (1830); *La Femme de trente ans* (1831–4); *Le Père Goriot* (1834–5); *Le *Colonel Chabert* (1832); *La Messe de l'athée* (1836); *L'Interdiction* (1836); *Le Contrat de mariage* (1835); *Autre étude de femme* (1842).

SCÈNES DE LA VIE DE PROVINCE: *Ursule Mirouët* (1841); *Eugénie Grandet* (1833); *Les Célibataires*— (i) *Pierrette*, (ii) *Le *Curé de Tours*, (iii) *La Rabouilleuse* (1840, 1832, 1841–2); *Les Parisiens en province*— (i) *L'Illustre Gaudissart*, (ii) *La Muse du département* (1833, 1843); *Les Rivalités*—(i) *La Vieille Fille*, (ii) *Le Cabinet des antiques* (1836, 1836–8, 1839); *Illusions perdues*—(i) *Les Deux Poètes*, (ii) *Un grand homme de province à Paris*, (iii) *Les Souffrances de l'inventeur* (1837, 1839, 1843).

SCÈNES DE LA VIE PARISIENNE: *Histoire des Treize*— (i) *Ferragus*, (ii) *La *Duchesse de Langeais*, (iii) *La Fille aux yeux d'or* (1833, 1833–4, 1834–5); *Histoire de la grandeur et de la décadence de *César Birotteau* (1837); *La Maison Nucingen* (1838); *Splendeurs et misères des courtisanes* — (i) *Comment aiment les filles*, (ii) *A combien l'amour revient aux vieillards*, (iii) *Où mènent les mauvais chemins*, (iv) *La Dernière Incarnation de Vautrin* (1838–47); *Les Secrets de la Princesse de Cadignan* (1839); *Facino Cane* (1836); *Sarrasine* (1830); *Pierre Grassou* (1840); *Les Parents pauvres*—(i) *La Cousine Bette*, (ii) *Le Cousin Pons* (1846, 1847); *Un homme d'affaires* (1845); *Un prince de la Bohème* (1840); *Gaudissart II* (1844); *Les Employés* (1837); *Les Comédiens sans le savoir* (1846); *Les Petits Bourgeois* (posth.); *L'Envers de l'histoire contemporaine*—(i) *Madame de la Chanterie*, (ii) *L'Initié* (1842, 1848).

SCÈNES DE LA VIE POLITIQUE: *Un épisode sous la Terreur* (1830); *Une ténébreuse affaire* (1841); *Le Député d'Arcis* (1847, finished in 1854 by Ch. Rabou); *Z. Marcas* (1840).

SCÈNES DE LA VIE MILITAIRE: *Les *Chouans* (1829); *Une passion dans le désert* (1830).

SCÈNES DE LA VIE DE CAMPAGNE: *Les *Paysans* (1844);

*Le *Médecin de campagne* (1833); *Le *Curé de village* (1839); *Le *Lys dans la vallée* (1835).

ÉTUDES PHILOSOPHIQUES:

La Peau de chagrin (1830–1); *Jésus-Christ en Flandre* (1831); *Melmoth réconcilié* (1835); *Massimilla Doni* (1839); *Le *Chef-d'œuvre inconnu* (1831); *Gambara* (1837); *La *Recherche de l'absolu* (1834); *L'Enfant maudit* (1831–6); *Adieu* (1830); *Les Marana* (1832–3); *Le Réquisitionnaire* (1831); *El Verdugo* (1830); *Un drame au bord de la mer* (1835); *Maître Cornélius* (1831); *L'Auberge rouge* (1831); *Sur Catherine de Médicis* (1841); *L'Élixir de longue vie* (1830); *Les Proscrits* (1831); *Louis Lambert* (1832); *Séraphîta* (1834–5).

ÉTUDES ANALYTIQUES:

Physiologie du mariage (1829); *Petites misères de la vie conjugale* (1830, 1840, 1845).

Vol. 12 of the Pléiade edition of *La Comédie humaine* (ed. P.-G. Castex, 1981) contains indexes of the fictional and real characters in Balzac's work.

Comédie-Italienne. Since 1570 French kings had obtained visits by *commedia dell'arte* groups by arrangement with the dukes of Milan and Mantua. But it was only in 1653 that an Italian theatre was located permanently in Paris. Though the Italian theatre (subsequently known as the Comédie-Italienne or Théâtre Italien) was initially a colony of the *commedia dell'arte* (directed by Fiorilli–*Scaramouche), its location and circumstances entailed a separate and unique development. From its repertoire of stock characters, some specifically Italian ones were dropped, and the *Arlequin character assumed increasing prominence. The company obtained permission to use French in 1684. Entertaining rather than instructive, they performed topical and satirical plays and parodies, but their chief dramatic resources were spectacle, songs, and action. Among the dramatists who wrote for this 'Ancienne Troupe' were *Regnard, *Dufresny, Delosme de Monchesnay, Palaprat, Fatouville, and Gherardi. Though the *Italiens* were initially supported by the king, the licentiousness of their performances increasingly displeased the authorities, and a series of performances of *La Fausse Prude*, in which allusions to Madame de *Maintenon were detected, brought their expulsion from Paris in 1697.

The Regent brought the 'Nouvelle Troupe Italienne' back to the *Hôtel de Bourgogne under Luigi Riccoboni (Lelio) in 1716. A fruitful period of collaboration with *Marivaux followed from 1720 to 1743. Along with Thomassin, who transformed the role of Arlequin, the actresses were the company's strongest performers, and Marivaux's *innamorate* were conceived specially with Flaminia and Silvia in mind. Other important writers for this company were Autreau, *Gueullette, *Sedaine, Coypel, and Delisle. As improvisation declined from the 1730s, the inclusion of music and songs increased, French actors came to outnumber Italian ones, and the Italian language was rarely used. In 1762 the Italian company merged with the *Opéra-Comique. Its Italian repertoire was suppressed in 1779, and its official title changed to 'Opéra-Comique' in 1793.   [JD]

Comédie larmoyante. An untheorized genre dating mainly from the 1740s, which prefigures the *drame, though it almost always uses verse, is not specifically bourgeois, and has no social mission. Its greatest exponents were Madame de *Graffigny (whose Cénie, a prose work, was performed in 1750) and Nivelle de *La Chaussée. *Voltaire, in Nanine (1749), and *Marivaux, in La Mère confidente (1735), also flirted with the genre. The plays present serious and highly artificial domestic situations, conceived for their sentimental appeal. Secret marriages, false identities, and (artifically delayed) recognition scenes are the hallmarks of the genre, along with psychological oversimplification. Though now neglected, these plays were none the less immensely popular with contemporary audiences.
[JD]

Comedy

1. Before 1700

The word comédie can be misleading in French. In the 17th c. it was used of all kinds of play; 'aller à la comédie' meant to go to the theatre, and comédien still means simply an actor in the 20th c. Even when used more technically, comédie did not necessarily imply laughter or amusement; Pierre *Corneille gave to some of his serious plays with happy endings the label 'comédie héroïque'.

If one were to judge by the use of the word, comedy did not exist in France before the 16th c., when its arrival was heralded in Du Bellay's *Défense et illustration, with its call for the re-creation of comedy alongside other ancient forms such as ode or tragedy. But of course much drama in the Middle Ages (not to speak of other genres) is essentially comic [see MEDIEVAL THEATRE]. Comic elements existed within the liturgical plays, the liturgy was shadowed by the parodic 'fête des fous', and the *jongleurs maintained a tradition of open-air popular entertainment. As for the comic theatre proper, we still have the 13th-c. 'jeux' of *Bodel and *Adam de la Halle in Arras, and the numerous didactic or satirical *soties, *morality plays, or *farces performed in the 15th and 16th c. by such groups as the *Enfants sans Souci or the *Basoche. *Patelin is the best-known example of this entertaining popular theatre.

The mid-16th c. saw the humanists attempting to create a more literary type of comedy. Rejecting native farce, they looked for models to the Latin New Comedy (Plautus, Terence) and more directly to the Italians. Classical French comedy is above all Italian in origin. The theories adumbrated by *Peletier du Mans, *Larivey, and others anticipated 17th-c. doctrine, and plays such as *Jodelle's Eugène (still close to the medieval farce in some respects), *Grévin's Les Ébahis and La Trésorière, and the skilfully written comedies of Larivey suggested future

directions for the comic theatre. They failed, however, to find a real theatrical public [see THEATRES AND AUDIENCES].

Throughout the ancien régime farce and other forms of popular theatre continued to attract crowds. The trio of farceurs at the *Hôtel de Bourgogne [see FARCE], *Tabarin on the Pont-Neuf, *Bruscambille, and the white-faced *Jodelet all performed amusing short pieces. Companies from Italy played commedia dell'arte, at first in their own language, but eventually in French, with an ample element of slapstick [see COMÉDIE-ITALIENNE]. And from the late 17th c. the théâtres de la *foire attracted mixed audiences to varied entertainments in which farce mingled with music and spectacular effects. Some of these currents flowed together in the 18th c. to create the genre of *opéra-comique.

Meanwhile a more literary form of comedy established itself on the Parisian stage during the first third of the 17th c. The Italian *pastoral plays, imitated by *Hardy, *Racan, and *Mairet, were a formative influence. *Du Ryer, *Rotrou, and *Desmarets among others made significant contributions, but the essential figure was Pierre *Corneille, whose early comedies transfer the pastoral love intrigue to a nicely observed contemporary urban reality. His *Illusion comique is an exceptional tour de force.

The years between 1640 and 1660 saw the consolidation of 'la grande comédie', literary comedy of manners and intrigue in five acts and in verse. Although less discussed by theorists than tragedy, it was shaped according to similar precepts to those governing its more serious elder sister. From about 1640 *Spanish theatre exerted a powerful influence, seen notably in Pierre Corneille's Le *Menteur and the plays of Rotrou, *Scarron, and Thomas *Corneille.

Many new comedies were written in the years after 1660 by authors including *Quinault, *Donneau de Visé, *Racine (Les Plaideurs), and Hauteroche, but the comic stage at this time was dominated by *Molière. Supported by the king, the 'premier farceur de France' combined elements from popular and learned theatre, together with court spectaculars (*comédies-ballets) in an unparalleled creation which appealed equally to la cour and la ville, to the honnêtes gens and the ordinary people. Molière became the standard model proposed to subsequent comic playwrights. Unfortunately, however, critics from *Boileau on tended to concentrate on a small number of Molière's more 'serious' comedies (Le *Misanthrope, Le *Tartuffe, Les *Femmes savantes, etc.), neglecting the more lively elements in the name of literary decorum, and making of him the champion of 'la comédie de caractère'.

2. After 1700

The century following Molière's death was a golden age for comedy, which occupied a central position in the French literary culture of the time. Before and after 1700 *Regnard, *Dancourt, *Dufresny, *Lesage, and others produced witty, cynical comedies of intrigue and social observation. Of these, *Turcaret* is the finest example. *Marivaux, working mainly for the Comédie-Italienne, developed a brilliantly original type of comedy, founded on the elegant and subtle exploration of amorous feeling. Some of his later plays show a tendency to a more moralizing or sentimental strain, which can be seen equally in the work of *Voltaire (*L'Enfant prodigue* and *Nanine*), *Gresset (*Le Méchant*), *Piron (*La Métromanie*), and above all *Destouches, whose plays (notably *Le *Glorieux*) combine fashionable sensibility and comic verve. This line was further developed in the *comédie larmoyante* of *La Chaussée and the *drame* of *Diderot or *Sedaine; here comedy takes second place to emotion and instruction.

A more light-hearted comedy persisted, not only in the popular theatre but in the 'théâtres de société', private theatricals which enjoyed a great vogue in the 18th c. Here the *proverbes dramatiques* of *Carmontelle or the plays of *Collé were performed, together with *parades*, of which *Gueullette made a speciality [see FARCE, 2]. *Beaumarchais too wrote *parades*, as well as *drames*, and elements of both combine with comedy of intrigue and socio-political satire in Le *Barbier de Séville* and Le *Mariage de Figaro*. These two plays were the great events of French comic theatre in the last quarter of the 18th c.

Comedy continued to be performed in France during the Revolutionary, Napoleonic, and Restoration years. It was largely based on existing models (*Fabre d'Églantine, *Pigault-Lebrun, L.-B. Picard (1769–1828), *Delavigne, etc.). This period also saw the remarkable rise of the quintessentially French *vaudeville, the most popular form of theatre throughout the 19th c. After 1820 the comic theatre was dominated by two figures, *Scribe and *Musset. The tightly crafted if shallow *comédies-vaudevilles* of the former provided a model of the well-made play for successors such as *Sardou (and Ibsen). Musset's far more interesting plays, on the other hand, are full of charm, variety, and poetic fantasy; some execute variations on the *proverbe dramatique*, others, such as Les *Caprices de Marianne* or *On ne badine pas avec l'amour*, come close to the world of tragedy or *drame*.

There is indeed a growing tendency, from the early 19th c. onwards, for the once-separate theatrical genres to merge. Tragedy no longer exists in a recognizable form; comedy, the more flexible form, combines with tragedy and *drame* in many different ways, from the *comédie sérieuse* of *Dumas *fils*, *Augier, and *Becque to the 20th-c. *comédie poétique* of *Giraudoux, *Anouilh, or *Schéhadé [see DRAMA IN FRANCE SINCE 1789].

On the other hand, a relatively pure comic tradition does persist, notably in the farces or vaudevilles of *Labiche, *Feydeau, *Courteline, or *Romains

(*Knock*, 1923), the comic operettas of *Meilhac and Halévy, the sharp social observation of *Porto-Riche and Jules *Renard, and the 20th-c. *Boulevard comedies of writers such as *Aymé, *Achard, *Pagnol, Sacha *Guitry, and André Roussin (b. 1911, the great supplier of the post-World War II Boulevard).

In a quite different vein, following Jarry's *Ubu roi*, the avant-garde theatre contains a strong element of grotesque comedy or farce; this is evident in the work of *Cocteau, *Apollinaire, *Vitrac, and the Belgians *Crommelynck and *Ghelderode. It culminates in the far from light-hearted comedy of *Ionesco and other writers associated with the Theatre of the *Absurd.

[PF]

See P. Voltz, *La Comédie* (1964).

Comité de Salut Public, Comité de Sûreté Générale, see REVOLUTION, IC.

Commedia dell'arte. Italian popular theatre, first brought to France in the 16th c. It was originally a theatre of improvisation, relying on the reappearance of stock types, or masks, such as the servants Arlecchino [see ARLEQUIN], Scaramuccia [see SCARAMOUCHE], *Scapino, and Pedrolino (Pierrot), the old man Pantalone, and a pair of young lovers, whose desires form the basis of the plot. Acrobatics and physical business (*lazzi*) played a large part in this theatre, as did verbal wit and innuendo. The *commedia* was the origin of the *Comédie-Italienne in France, and exerted a great influence on *Molière. A full treatment of the subject will be found in the *Oxford Companion to the Theatre*. [PF]

Commentaires, see MONLUC.

Comment j'ai écrit certains de mes livres, see ROUSSEL.

Commune de Paris. Assembly formed by Parisian electors on 15 July 1789, following the storming of the *Bastille. It appointed a mayor, created the *Garde Nationale, and was responsible for municipal administration. On 10 August 1792 it was replaced by a left-wing 'Commune insurrectionnelle' [see REVOLUTION, 1b]; this wielded considerable power in the ensuing period, bringing popular pressure to bear on the Convention. Its members suffered wholesale repression on the downfall of *Robespierre. [PF]

Commune de Paris (1871). Insurrection against the government of Adolphe *Thiers, following the siege of Paris during the *Franco-Prussian War. During the siege, male citizens were armed and formed battalions of the *Garde Nationale. The French capitulation on 28 January was seen by many as humiliating and unnecessary, and the decisions of the monarchist assembly, elected in February and meeting in Versailles instead of Paris, infuriated sections of the city's population already exasperated by hardship. The Thiers government negotiated with the Prussians, repealed the rent freeze, and ordered the return of cannon paid for by public subscription. Regular troops attempting to seize the cannon on 18 March were met by popular resistance during which two generals were shot. The government fled Paris for Versailles, leaving a power vacuum, filled first by the central committee of the Garde Nationale, then by the Commune, effectively the municipal council of Paris, elected by male citizens on 26 March. The name deliberately echoed that of the Revolutionary Commune de Paris [see above]. Many wealthy Parisians had left the city and the radical and proletarian composition of the Commune mainly reflected the politics of the working-class districts.

Negotiations with Versailles collapsed, and the Commune became a kind of insurrectionary counter-government, with collective leadership rather than any single leader. Some of its actions were practical, aimed at alleviating hardship: rent extensions, free redemption from pawnshops. Others were potentially further-reaching and ideologically inspired: free, compulsory, secular schooling, bans on night work, co-operative take-over of abandoned businesses—but stopped short of raiding the vaults of the Banque de France. There was an explosion of free speech, which had been severely limited under the Second Empire: meetings were held nightly in newly opened clubs, including several for women. But the Commune barely had time to exist before it was crushed. Similar uprisings in provincial cities (notably Marseille) had collapsed. The Prussian army stood by while Thiers regrouped French troops for an assault. Pro-Versailles forces entered Paris on 21 May, the beginning of the 'semaine sanglante', as the Communards put up desperate but uncoordinated resistance behind barricades, after burning public buildings and executing their clerical hostages, including the archbishop of Paris. The Versaillais repression was severe: possibly 30,000 Parisians were killed and thousands more were sentenced to deportation or exile.

The Commune came to have symbolic importance for the Left, both inside and outside France. It has been described both as 'a festival of the oppressed' and as a 'glorious harbinger of new events'. But although Lenin is said to have rejoiced when the Bolshevik revolution had lasted longer than the Commune's 54 days, the socialist nature of the uprising is not self-evident. Patriotic republicanism among the pre-industrial working class may have been equally important. The Commune also drew on the *Revolution's heritage and imagery. It was chronicled by *Vallès in L'Insurgé, and *Rimbaud's early writings are associated with it. J.-B. *Clément's song 'Le Temps des cerises', although written earlier, came to be a lament for the Commune, while *Pottier's 'L'Internationale' was inspired by it. Its historical significance has to some extent been buried

under its tragic end and the long shadow it cast over the French labour movement, which took many years to rise from the ashes. [SR]

See S. Edwardes, *The Paris Commune* (1971); J. Rougerie, *Paris Libre* (1971); E. W. Schulkind, *The Paris Commune: The View from the Left* (1972).

COMMYNES, Philippe de (1447–1511). Born at Renescure in Flanders, the future statesman and memorialist began his career in the household of Charles, count of Charolais, during the War of the Public Weal (1465) between Louis XI and his nobles. At Péronne in 1468 he mediated between Charles, now duke of Burgundy, and *Louis XI. Growing admiration for the king led Commynes to desert ducal for royal service. Between 1472 and 1477 he enjoyed considerable influence in executing French foreign policy, especially towards Burgundy. After Charles's death (January 1477), he was temporarily estranged from the king and despatched on missions to Italy, though he was present at Louis's deathbed (August 1483). During Charles VIII's minority he became increasingly disillusioned, joining the duke of Orléans, leader of the anti-royal party in the Guerre Folle. Arrested and imprisoned (1487–9), he was later confined to his estates. The French invasion of Italy in 1494 provided a chance to rebuild his diplomatic career. He was sent as ambassador to Venice and fought at Fornovo (July 1495), before returning to Venice, but his mission finally ended in failure. Back in France, he remained on the fringe of the court. The accession of Orléans (Louis XII) in 1498 brought few rewards and his last years were troubled by acrimonious litigation.

Commynes's reputation as a writer rests on his *Mémoires*, of which there is no autograph manuscript nor any surviving copies dating from his lifetime. According to the prologue they were begun after a request from Angelo Cato, archbishop of Vienne, for materials to use in a history of Louis XI. It is obvious, however, that they were intended to stand on their own and to be read by a wider audience. The first six books, composed between 1489 and 1493, cover the period from 1464 to 1483, and were first published in 1524. Two final books, dealing with Charles VIII's Italian expedition and completed by 1498, were published in 1528. A full edition first appeared in 1552; a century later they had already been translated into at least 10 languages and have remained to the present a major source for western European history in the late 15th c.

Written in a generally direct, often conversational, style, the *Mémoires* provide analysis and informed reflection on contemporary events and leading personalities not unlike the best contemporary Italian humanist historical writing. They explain affairs rationally and with psychological insight. For centuries readers have accepted that Commynes was an honest, impartial, and well-informed observer, as *Saint-Beuve suggested in his *Causeries du lundi*. But in recent years two converging lines of investigation—into the accuracy of the historical material they contain and the form and intention of the *Mémoires*—have overturned received opinion. As a result, their reputation as the dispassionate, objective reminiscences of an elder statesman has been replaced by the view that they are an extremely clever, deliberately artificial, mendacious, and highly selective treatment of events by an embittered man seeking posthumous revenge on personal enemies whom he blamed for his own ultimate lack of success. Whilst this hypercritical assessment in its most developed form has yet to gain full acceptance, it has undoubtedly revealed Commynes as a complex, subtle, and intelligent writer, whose *Mémoires* must no longer be taken at face value but require the most careful handling.   [MJ]

See Philippe de Commynes, *Mémoires*, ed. J. Calmette and G. Durville, 3 vols. (1924–5, repr. 1965); *Memoirs: The Reign of Louis XI*, trans. M. Jones (1972).

Compagnie du Saint-Sacrement, La, see SAINT-SACREMENT.

Compagnons, compagnonnage, see TOUR DE FRANCE. *Le Compagnon du Tour de France* is the title of a novel by *Sand.

Compère Général Soleil, see ALEXIS, J.-S.

Complainte, see POPULAR SONG.

Comptine. Children's counting rhyme, but the term is often applied to all kinds of children's rhymes. Like other forms of popular song, these began to be seriously collected in the 19th c., though a rich anthology, *La Fricassée crotestylonnée*, was published in 1602. Many 20th-c. poets, in particular the *Surrealists, have found pleasure and inspiration in these rhymes; Philippe *Soupault used the radio to collect them from France, Belgium, Switzerland, and Canada. An accessible modern collection is *Les Comptines de langue française*, ed. J. Baucomont (1961). [See also POPULAR SONG.]   [PF]

COMTE, Auguste (1798–1857). French thinker; the leading proponent of Positivism, often also regarded as the founder of *sociology. Originally a disciple of the comte de *Saint-Simon, he elaborated a systematic philosophy of science, expressed in his influential *Cours de philosophie positive* (1830–42). Comte argued that human understanding of the world was initially religious, supposing supernatural forces; that it advanced to a metaphysical stage, postulating abstract principles; and that it finally acceded to a stage of positive or scientific knowledge, based on an empirical grasp of the relations between observable phenomena. The physical sciences had followed this *loi des trois états*, and it was now time for the study of society to advance to the third, scientific stage in a 'social physics', for which he coined the term 'sociology'. He elaborated a historical

method and a system of general laws constituting the statics and dynamics of society, from which proposals for action could be derived. Following an intense relationship with Clotilde de Vaux, Comte felt that moral and emotional life should also be brought within the positivist framework. As a vehicle for this work, he developed a 'religion of humanity', complete with a calendar, liturgy, and institutions, which had some success in Europe and North and South America. Comte's ideas were popularized later in the century by *Littré and supported by *Taine and *Renan, among others.

Positivism may be understood as simply a synonym for Comte's own work, including its more flamboyant social and religious manifestations. However, it has acquired the more enduring meaning of a theory of knowledge, which has informed a large body of work in philosophy, history, and the social sciences. Put simply, it is the view that knowledge depends solely on what can be observed, and on what can legitimately be deduced from observed facts. As against those who argue the importance of prior theoretical constructions, positivism rejects any proposition which cannot be positively verified by experience, or which cannot be proved false by some conceivable empirical event. In this sense, Comte's thought is not wholly consistent with positivism.   [MHK]

See D. G. Charlton, *Positivist Thought in France* (1959); L. Kolakowski, *Positivist Philosophy* (1972).

Comte d'Anjou, Le Roman du. Written by Jehan Maillart, this early 14th-c. romance concerns the daughter of a count of Anjou, who is tempted to incest by her outstanding beauty. Fleeing to Orléans, she earns her living by embroidery, but attracts the love of the comte de Bourges. Calumnies persuade the latter that their child is not his; he condemns her to death, but his servants disobey and she returns to Orléans with the child. He husband's suspicions are finally laid to rest and all is made right. The work celebrates charity, especially the charity of the poor; it offers a pleasingly realistic picture of bourgeois life.   [JHMT]

Comte de Monte-Cristo, Le. Novel by Alexandre *Dumas *père*. Serialized in *Le *Journal des débats* (August 1844–January 1846), *Le Comte de Monte-Cristo* had an immense success and marked a high point of the fashion for the *roman-feuilleton*. As with many of his other novels, it was written in collaboration with Auguste *Maquet, who provided Dumas with chapter plans and historical and factual material. It offers a thrilling and sensational narrative of escape, social triumph, and revenge, which has retained a profound and lasting appeal in modern mass culture. Dumas drew on his own previous revenge novel *Georges* (1843) and on the *cause célèbre* of François Picaud, who, wrongfully imprisoned under the Empire, returned after 1814 to exact violent retribution on his accusers. In *Le Comte de Monte-Cristo* the imprisoned Bonapartist conspirator Edmond Dantès escapes, discovers the treasure of Monte-Cristo, and returns to Paris to settle scores with Restoration society. His campaign of revenge becomes an epic conflict between good and evil, as Dantès, the agent of Providence, destroys high-society schemers and crooks. But the text is not underpinned by the social humanitarianism of an Eugène *Sue. Dantès is a Byronic hero and sweet revenge is complicated by a gnawing sense of guilt.

[BR]

Comte d'Essex, Le, see CORNEILLE, T.

COMTESSA DE DIA (end of 12th or beginning of 13th c.). *Trobairitz, whose four songs, varied in tone and metre, reflect on and probably ultimately reject the role of courtly *domna* created by the male *troubadours. [SK]

Comtesse de Rudolstadt, La, see CONSUELO.

Comtesse de Tende, La, see LAFAYETTE, COMTESSE DE.

Conciergerie, La. Ancient prison in central Paris, which housed many famous prisoners, particularly during the *Revolution. For a description see Balzac's *Splendeurs et misères des courtisanes.*

Concordat. Term used for a treaty between the papacy and a civil state. There have been two significant concordats in French history, in 1516 and 1801.

The Concordat of 1516 was essentially a measure whereby François Ier imposed his power on the French Church. It conferred on the king the effective power to nominate to senior positions in the Church, including bishoprics. Together with other regalian rights, this gave the crown a decisive role in Church affairs until the Revolution.

The Concordat of 1801 was a compromise which guaranteed freedom of worship for Catholics after the persecutions of the 1790s, in return for certain forms of state control over the Church. Catholicism was recognized as 'the religion of the great majority of French citizens'. Church buildings that had not been sold during the Revolution were placed at the disposition of bishops. Clerical salaries were to be paid by the state. Bishops were to be nominated by the government (though there was effectively a papal veto). The appointment of parish priests was subject to government approval. The Church agreed not to trouble the consciences of those who had acquired ecclesiastical property during the Revolution. The concordat of 1801 remained the basis of Church–State relations in France until the Separation of Church and State in 1905 [see ANTI-CLERICALISM]. [RBG]

Concorde des deux langages, La, see LEMAIRE DE BELGES.

CONDÉ, Louis Ier, prince de (1539–69) was the uncle of the future *Henri IV. Although only a second

son, he was, as a prince of the blood, one of the more important Huguenot leaders in the *Wars of Religion. The extent of his involvement in the Conspiration d'*Amboise is unclear, but he would almost certainly have been executed if it had not been for the premature death of François II. He was killed in cold blood following his defeat at Jarnac.

[JJS]

CONDÉ, Louis II de Bourbon, prince de ('le grand Condé', known after his father's death in 1646 as 'Monsieur le Prince') (1621–86). He attained heroic status (echoed in *Corneille's tragedies) as the victor of the Battle of Rocroi against the Spaniards (1643), but came into conflict with the royal party during the *Fronde. In his retirement at Chantilly, he was a major patron of artists and writers (*Boileau, *Racine, *La Bruyère). A noted free-thinker for much of his life, he was the subject of a magnificent funeral oration by *Bossuet. [PF]

CONDÉ, Maryse (b. 1937). A highly prolific writer in a variety of genres, whose historical saga centred on the Bambara kingdom, *Ségou* (1984–5), was the first best-seller by a Caribbean author. Born in Guadeloupe, she has taught in West Africa, Europe, and the United States, and draws on her knowledge of the black diaspora to explore kinship networks and inter-racial intimacies: *Heremakhonon/En attendant le bonheur* (1976); *Moi, Tituba sorcière* (1986); *Traversée de la mangrove* (1989). Work in drama, criticism (*La Civilisation du bossale*, 1978), and translation amplifies the concern of her fiction to make accessible through individual portraits a lucidly commonsensical view of ethnic issues. [BJ]

CONDILLAC, Étienne Bonnot, abbé de (1714–80). The most purely philosophical of the 18th-c. *philosophes, Condillac devoted his life to thought and teaching. Born into a noble family in Grenoble, the younger brother of *Mably, he studied with the Jesuits, attended a seminary in Paris, and took orders in 1740. Though known as abbé de Condillac, he is said to have celebrated mass once only. Between 1740 and 1758 he frequented Paris society, including Madame de *Tencin's salon, and was on friendly terms with men of letters such as *Diderot and *Rousseau. In 1758, after the success of his philosophical writings, he was appointed tutor to the young prince of Parma, Louis XV's grandson; he stayed in Parma for nine years, writing for his pupil a *Cours d'études*, which was published in 16 vols. from 1776 to 1789. He was a member of the Academy of Berlin (1749) and the Académie Française (1768).

His principal writings, which make up a coherent body of theory, were published over a period of ten years: *Essai sur l'origine des connaissances humaines* (1746); *Traité des systèmes* (1749); *Traité des sensations* (1754); *Traité des animaux* (1755). All of them concern the philosophy of mind, the way in which human beings acquire their ideas, and the role of language

Condition humaine, La

in the process; Condillac is interested both in describing how we think, and in helping us to think, talk, and write better. Against the great 17th-c. system-builders such as *Descartes and *Leibniz, he adopts Locke's premiss that ideas come from experience, in the first instance from sensations. Using the fiction of a statue which is successively exposed to the impressions of the various senses, he describes the way in which simple ideas are linked by association, forming the basis of all thought.

In this process, language is crucial. False reasoning comes from a faulty use of language, and Condillac's aim is to reform language so that it will properly reflect true ideas. He sees a desirable progress from the poetic, imaginative language of earlier times to the greater accuracy (and perhaps dryness) of modern languages such as French, which facilitate the essential philosophical activity, analysis. Since the faulty use of language is acquired in childhood, a reform of education is called for. The *Cours d'études*, alongside many volumes on history, contains a *Grammaire*, an *Art d'écrire*, an *Art de raisonner*, and an *Art de penser*, all of which are really one single art, which can be applied to social, political, and economic problems. These admirable manuals, though they had little success with the untalented prince of Parma, were very influential in France, where the *Idéologues proclaimed themselves Condillac's disciples.   [PF]

See R. Lefèvre, *Condillac* (1966); I. F. Knight, *The Geometric Spirit: The Abbé de Condillac and the French Enlightenment* (1968).

Condition humaine, La (1933). Novel by *Malraux, awarded the Prix Goncourt. Set in China, the novel opens in March 1927 with the Kuomintang (nationalist) army led by Chiang Kai-shek at the gates of Shanghai. Their Communist allies inside the city organized an insurrection in preparation for the army's take-over, but Chiang Kai-shek instead concluded a deal with foreign capitalists and swooped on the Communists on 12 April. The majority of the novel's heroes are massacred in this coup. The novel marks a turning-point in Malraux's fiction in that the heroes are no longer adventurers but politically committed revolutionaries. Nevertheless, as the novel's title indicates, metaphysical anguish in the face of the human condition remains paramount. 'Il faut toujours s'intoxiquer', declares the novel's sage figure, Gisors. Gisors uses opium; Ferral, the foreign capitalist, drugs himself with the exercise of power; Tchen the anarchist is obsessed with murder; May lives for love; Clappique escapes into mythomania. Yet it is the faith and fraternity of the Communist leaders, Kyo and Katow, which carry the greatest lyrical weight. Kyo dies convinced that 'il mourait pour avoir donné un sens à sa vie. Qu'eût valu une vie pour laquelle il n'eût pas accepté de mourir?'   [EAF]

Condition ouvrière, La, see WEIL.

Condition postmoderne, La, see LYOTARD.

CONDORCET, Jean-Antoine-Nicolas, marquis de (1749–94). 'The last of the *philosophes*', as *Michelet called him, was a mathematician and scientist who involved himself in Revolutionary politics and perished by it, leaving an exemplary statement of *Enlightenment beliefs. This level-headed rationalist has acquired a tragic aura from the fact that his most famous work was written in the shadow of imminent death.

He came of a noble Picardy family, studied with the Jesuits, and soon showed remarkable mathematical gifts. This brought him to the attention of d'*Alembert, who introduced him to the salons and the world of the *philosophes*, notably *Turgot. In 1769 he entered the *Académie des Sciences, and in 1773 published his *Éloges des académiciens morts depuis l'an 1666 jusqu'en 1699*, a sequel to the work of *Fontenelle and a pioneering text in the history of science. He was made Secrétaire Perpétuel of the Academy in 1776, and composed further *éloges*.

In 1774 he was appointed to a post in the ministry of finance by Turgot, whose economic reforms he defended in a series of pamphlets. On his patron's fall he returned to mathematical work, concentrating on probability theory, which he wanted to see applied to social science and politics. In 1782 he was elected to the Académie Française, and began to devote himself increasingly to political activity, notably on behalf of women and blacks. In 1786 he married Sophie de *Grouchy, who was 20 years his junior.

Condorcet had supported the American Revolution; in 1789 he welcomed the Revolutionary movement in France. He joined the *Jacobin club, and was elected to the Assemblée Législative and the Convention, where his position was close to that of *Brissot and the *Girondins. In 1792 he presented an important project for the reform of public education, and thereafter worked on a revised constitution, which was never implemented. After the Girondins' fall, his arrest was ordered; he went into hiding for eight months and was found dead in his cell, probably by suicide, on the day following his arrest.

During his last months Condorcet wrote the work for which he is now remembered, the *Esquisse d'un tableau historique des progrès de l'esprit humain*, the outline of a projected *magnum opus*. Setting out a vision of humanity's progress in ten *époques*, it is at the same time 'philosophical history', history of science, and a political profession of faith. Against religious obscurantism and political oppression, human progress is traced equally in science and in morality; for Concorcet better science meant a better society. The ninth *époque*, a tableau of Enlightenment from *Descartes to the Revolution, is followed by a tenth which paints a golden future; man's perfectibility, aided by the new mathematical science, will allow progress to continue indefinitely. The *Esquisse* is the best 18th-c. exposition of the new doctrine of progress, and a poignant testament of the 'age of reason'. [PF]

See K. M. Baker, *Condorcet: From Natural Philosophy to Social Mathematics* (1975); E. and R. Badinter, *Condorcet, un intellectuel en politique* (1988).

Confession d'un enfant du siècle, La (1836). Novel by *Musset which draws on his relationship with George *Sand. The hero, Octave, is a rich, happy, and idle young man whose universe collapses when he discovers that his mistress is having an affair with his best friend. The act of betrayal destroys the harmony between Octave and the world; henceforward he doubts everything and distrusts everyone—especially women. The former idealist becomes a materialist, the naïve lover becomes a libertine who no longer believes in the possibility of love. However, in the countryside he encounters Brigitte Pierson, the embodiment of the natural and the good as opposed to the urban and the artificial. Unfortunately the happy relationship between Octave and Brigitte disintegrates because Octave cannot escape the libertine he once was. He persecutes the loyal and tender Brigitte, coming close to murdering her. Finally, and rather ambiguously, Octave achieves a degree of inner peace by renouncing his love for Brigitte and smiling on her departure with another man, Smith. The novel also contains as its second chapter a classic statement of the *mal du siècle, the spiritual sickness suffered by a disillusioned generation born too late to fight in Napoleon's armies and unable to discover a stable meaning in life. [CC]

Confessions du comte de ***, Les, see DUCLOS.

Confessions, Les. Jean-Jacques *Rousseau's account of his life, the founding text of literary *autobiography. It was written in exile from France, between 1764 and 1770, and published posthumously. Part I (Books 1–6), tells of his childhood, his adventures as a young man, and his relationship with Madame de Warens; it was written at leisure, in Switzerland and England, and the tone is relaxed and often humorous, with memorable evocations of youthful happiness. Part II (Books 7–12) deals with the years 1742–66, Rousseau's career as a writer, his quarrels with the *philosophes, and his first years of exile. It was written more rapidly and feverishly, in the growing conviction of a universal conspiracy against him, and is often painful reading.

Rousseau's account is inaccurate in detail, and in places distorted by the desire for self-justification. But it is a remarkable attempt to tell the inner truth of his life as he saw it. The stress on childhood, the frank explorations of sexuality, and the importance attached to the feelings and thoughts of a commoner make of it, as he puts it in his provocative prologue, 'an unprecedented enterprise'. It met with a mixed reception at first, many admirers being taken aback by what they saw as trivial or sordid revelations, but has increasingly been regarded as his masterpiece. [PF]

CONFIANT, Raphaël (b. 1951). Martinican novelist, journalist, and proponent of the idea of *créolité. He has published three novels written entirely in *Creole (*Bitako-a*, 1985; *Kòd Yanm*, 1986; *Marisosé*, 1987), and two novels (*Le Nègre et l'Amiral*, 1988; *Eau de café*, 1991, Prix Novembre) which employ a highly distinctive blend of standard French and Creole to impart a vision of Martinique that emphasizes above all the heterogeneity of the island's culture, language, and people; *Le Nègre et l'Amiral* is especially noteworthy for its vivid recreation of Martinique under the Vichy régime. He also published *nouvelles* and poems in Creole. Confiant is joint author (with Jean Bernabé and *Chamoiseau) of the manifesto *Éloge de la créolité* (1989) and (with Chamoiseau) of *Lettres créoles* (1991). A bitter opponent of *négritude, he has often attacked *Césaire (*Aimé Césaire: une traversée paradoxale du siècle*, 1993). He has contributed frequently to nationalist publications in Martinique, notably *Antilla* and *Karibèl*, of which he was one of the founders, and is active in the Martinican ecology movement and the international Creole movement, Banzil Kreyol. [RDEB]

Confréries. Religious associations of lay people devoted to the cult of a saint or the Virgin Mary or a special feast day. Some were independent; others were attached to trade guilds (*corporations*), in which case the saint was usually the patron of the trade, e.g. St Éloi for the goldsmiths of Paris, St Crespin and St Crespinien for the shoemakers of Rouen. Their activities consisted principally of religious services, processions, mutual help, and charity. Their literary significance is that in the Middle Ages many *confréries*, especially those in Paris and the north-east of France, organized poetry competitions held at their regular meetings (*puys), and occasionally performed plays, often based on the life of their patron, e.g. the *Miracles de Nostre Dame par personnages. The *confréries* flourished from the 13th c. A few unusual *confréries* made major contributions to medieval literature. The Confrérie des *Jongleurs d'Arras included many of the most famous *Arras poets, such as Jehan *Bodel. The Confrérie de la Passion performed many large-scale *mystery plays in Paris in the 15th and 16th c. [see HÔTEL DE BOURGOGNE]. [GAR]

Congé. *Medieval lyric poem of farewell. Two distinct types exist: 1) the *congé d'amour* (troubadour *comjat*) expressing farewell to love in general or to an unforthcoming lady in particular without going so far as the *chanson de change*, which indicates preference for a new mistress; 2) the *congés d'Arras*, three 13th-c. stanzaic poems without music written by *Bodel, *Baude Fastoul, and *Adam de la Halle to take leave of friends when entering a leper colony or going elsewhere to study. This localized genre has few surviving antecedents, scarcely resembling the leper *Gautier de Châtillon's lament 'Versa est in luctum' (composed c.1184) or *Hélinand's Vers de la mort, whose rhyme-scheme it nevertheless adopts. [PVD]

Congrégation, La. An organization of Catholic ultra-royalist sympathizers particularly active in the 1820s. The old aristocracy was strongly represented, particularly at leadership levels. For ordinary members, it was simply an organization for the practice of Christian charity and the propagation of monarchical ideas. At the top, however, was a small nucleus of the Chevaliers de la Foi, dedicated to secret political work in defence of an ultra-royalist system. This gave some basis to the Liberal belief in a conspiratorial secret society, which they called simply 'the Congregation'. The 'secret note' episode in Stendhal's Le *Rouge et le noir is based on this belief. [For congrégations in general, see CLERGY.] [RBG]

CONON DE BÉTHUNE. Outstanding *trouvère, warrior, and statesman. The fifth son of a lord of Béthune (Picardy) related to the house of Flanders, Conon led forces in the Lombard war (1176–83), joined the Third Crusade (1189–93), and, according to *Villehardouin, featured prominently in the Fourth (1202–4). A seneschal by 1217, he became regent of the Empire in 1219, but died in that or the following year. To Conon are ascribed: a pungent and witty fictive *tenson; a bilingual *jeu parti with the troubadour Raimbaut de Vaqueiras; a serventois against linguistic prejudice; two crusading songs; and six chansons courtoises, one of them heavily moralizing, another switching unexpectedly from praise to abuse of the beloved. [PVD]

Conquérants, Les (1928). Novel by *Malraux set in Hong Kong at the time of the strike of 1925. Essentially it is a portrait of the hero, Garine, who works with the Communists against the English, but who is indifferent to political systems since he believes all forms of social organization to be stigmatized by the absurd. Perfectly lucid, he immerses himself in action for action's sake. His death inevitably signals his failure, since it interrupts action. In the novel he is contrasted with the professional revolutionary Borodine and the moral idealist Tcheng-Dai. Trotsky wrote a famous objection to the novel. [EAF]

Conquête de Constantinople, La, see CLARI; VILLEHARDOUIN.

Conquête de Plassans, La. Novel by *Zola, the fourth in the *Rougon-Macquart series, published in 1874. In this anticlerical work, abbé Faujas, a Bonapartist agent, uses his spiritual authority to consolidate the power of the imperial regime in the fictitious Provençal town of Plassans. His influence

drives Marthe Mouret to religious hysteria and her husband, François, to madness. [DB]

CONRART, Valentin (1603–75). Although Conrart published relatively little himself, he is important for his role in the founding of the *Académie Française and in helping to shape classical taste. From the weekly gatherings of men of letters at Conrart's home to discuss matters of language and style, *Richelieu constituted the Academy in 1634, and Conrart became its first Secrétaire Perpétuel. Considered an authority on grammar and style, he examined meticulously numerous manuscripts he was asked to read, including that of *Vaugelas's Remarques. Of particular interest are his letters and especially his Mémoires, which provide valuable information about the political, religious, and literary history of his age, and notably of the *Fronde. [WA-B]

Conseil d'État, for the ancien régime see MONARCHY; since 1799 the Conseil d'État has been the supreme judicial body in France.

Considérations sur la France, see MAISTRE, J. DE.

Considérations sur les causes de la grandeur des Romains et de leur décadence. This is *Montesquieu's 'rise and fall of the Roman Empire', an essay published in 1734. Originally intended as part of De l'*esprit des lois, it sets natural causality against the providential schemes of *Bossuet's Discours sur l'histoire universelle, arguing that the growth of the empire was due to such factors as the size and economy of the early Roman state, which pushed its people towards wars of conquest, and its decline to the corruption brought on by excessive expansion. It is written in an impressively sober, laconic style. [PF]

Considérations sur les mœurs de ce siècle, see DUCLOS.

Consolation de Philosophie, La, see BOETHIUS.

Conspiration, La, see NIZAN.

Conspiration des Égaux, La, see BABEUF.

CONSTANT, Alphonse-Louis (1810–75). Educated for the priesthood, he first wrote religious poetry strongly marked by Marian devotion, then became politically involved with the socialist movement and combined religious themes with social protest, notably pro-feminist. La Mère de Dieu (1844), a prose epic, best represents this period of his career. After 1851 he published, under the name of Eliphas Lévi, widely read expositions of the occultist 'metaphysical' tradition and his own meditations on aspects thereof. His Dogme et rituel de la haute magie (1856) was much appreciated by many authors, including *Villiers de l'Isle-Adam and Catulle *Mendès. [FPB]

CONSTANT, Benjamin (Henri-Benjamin de Constant de Rebecque) (1767–1830). Noted in his own lifetime as a theoretician of liberalism, as an exceptionally eloquent *député* in the French parliament, and as an author of works on the history of religion, Constant is now best known as a novelist (*Adolphe, 1816; and *Cécile*, published only in 1951) and writer of autobiographical works (*Le Cahier rouge*, more properly known as *Ma vie*, first published 1907, and the *Journaux intimes*). There was nevertheless in the 1980s a revival of interest in him as one of the founding fathers of modern liberalism.

Constant's background was Swiss, Protestant, and aristocratic. He was born in Lausanne and his mother died shortly after giving birth to him. Educated privately, Constant was intellectually precocious. He mastered German and English as well as Latin and Greek and, after study at the universities of Erlangen and Edinburgh, spent a number of years as a court official in the service of the duke of Brunswick, where he made an unhappy and short-lived marriage to Wilhelmina von Cramm, whom he divorced. He became a close friend of Isabelle de *Charrière, whom he had met in Paris in 1787 and with whom he corresponded until her death. His political career began in France in 1794 after the beginning of his celebrated and stormy liaison with Germaine de *Staël. With her he worked for the moderate republican cause, and like her he came into conflict with *Napoleon during the period of the Tribunate, of which he was a member and from which he was expelled in 1802 for his attacks on the increasing authoritarianism of the First Consul. From the late 1790s Constant's relationship with de Staël had become an increasingly unhappy one. Yet despite a passionate relationship with the Irish *demi-mondaine* Anna Lindsay, begun in 1800, and an affair in 1806 with Charlotte von Hardenberg, who became his second wife in 1808, he was unable to break de Staël's hold over him until 1811. Years of scholarly work on the history of religion were followed by an unhappy passion for Juliette *Récamier and a disastrous return to political activity; during Napoleon's Hundred Days, Constant supported the ex-emperor, believing him to be converted to respect for the law and the rights of the individual. During semi-exile in London in 1816 he published the first edition of *Adolphe*. In 1819 he was elected *député* for the Sarthe, and thereafter had a successful parliamentary career in the liberal opposition, championing such causes as the freedom of the press, the abolition of the slave-trade, and Greek independence. He also distinguished himself as a journalist and polemicist. He was given a state funeral.

Central to Constant's writings is a concern for the freedom of the individual. His strong criticism of Rousseau's *Du *contrat social* stems from his desire that the individual should be protected from the potential tyranny of the group. His autobiographical works, journals, and correspondence reflect not only his restless emotional life but also a fierce personal desire for independence: in *Adolphe* this desire in the central male protagonist comes into tragic conflict with the demands of another individual, Ellénore, and of society and its representatives. Among Constant's writings on religion, *De la religion* (1824–31) shows both an Enlightenment belief in human perfectibility and an acknowledgement of the importance of religious feeling and the capacity for self-sacrifice: the outward forms of religion may develop and change, but, in Constant's eyes, religious feeling remains an important and permanent feature of human beings. [DW]

See W. W. Holdheim, *Benjamin Constant* (1961); E. Hofmann, *Les 'Principes de politique' de Benjamin Constant* (1980).

Constituante, La, the Assemblée Constituante, see NATIONAL ASSEMBLIES.

Constitution Civile. The Civil Constitution of the Clergy was voted by the Revolutionary Assemblée Constituante on 12 July 1790. It contained various measures to end abuses in the upper clergy and to weaken their authority over parish priests. Clerics were to be paid a stipend (instead of the former complex system based on the tithe). Bishops and parish priests were to be elected by 'active' citizens—i.e. the clergy was to be subject to lay control. The Pope was to have no say in episcopal appointments, or indeed in the general running of the Church in France. When the Assembly then decreed that all clergy paid by the State must swear an oath of loyalty to the Civil Constitution, about half the parish clergy refused (the 'réfractaires'), leading to a bitter split in the French Church. [RBG]

Constitutionnel, Le. After three changes of title in six months (1815), this newspaper was a flag-bearer of Liberalism during the Restoration and the July Monarchy, but championed *Napoleon III during the Second Republic and Second Empire. In the 1830s it supported the governments of *Thiers, who was long one of its leading journalists and, indeed, a shareholder. Dr Véron relaunched the daily in 1844: the serial novel, *Le Juif errant*, by *Sue, helped boost circulation. *Sainte-Beuve published his literary criticism in *Le Constitutionnel* before moving to *Le *Moniteur*. It declined rapidly in the 1870s. [MP]

Consuelo (1842). This lengthy novel by George *Sand, together with its sequel *La Comtesse de Rudolstadt* (1843), is a blending of a novel of initiation, a love story, the expression of hopes for a Utopian society of fraternity and justice, and meditations on the meaning of religion, philosophy, and the arts, especially music, which is given important symbolic status. The heroine, a student of Porpora, becomes a music tutor to the Rudolstadt family, whose scion Albert embodies ancient revolutionary traditions. She marries him out of pity, achieves fame as a singer, is inducted into the radical fraternity of the Invisibles, is reunited with Albert, whom she now deeply loves and whom she thought dead, and they roam through Eastern Europe preaching the socialist gospel of universal charity.   [FPB]

Consulat, Le, see NAPOLEON, I.

Conte, see FOLK-TALE; SHORT FICTION.

Conte du graal, see CHRÉTIEN DE TROYES.

Contemplations, Les. Considered by many to be *Hugo's most accomplished collection of lyric poetry, published during his exile in 1856. Conceived as a kind of spiritual autobiography and allegory of human destiny, the work is divided into two parts: 'Autrefois (1830–1843)' and 'Aujourd'hui (1843–1855)'. The year 1843, when the poet's daughter, Léopoldine, drowned in the Seine, marks the symbolic turning-point whereby a personal lyricism, focusing on love and nature, is transformed into the visionary poetry of a disembodied 19th-c. prophet. A masterful handling of rhythm, syntax, and extended metaphor produces deeply moving and hallucinatory effects in both intimate and visionary texts.
[SN]

Contents, Les. Prose comedy by Odet de *Turnèbe, probably written about 1580, published 1584 after its author's early death. In form and technique it is a typical learned comedy, in five acts, with unity of place and time, and conventional characters. The language, however, is earthy and often obscene, with much bawdy humour. The young lovers Basile and Geneviève are thwarted by her mother's preference for another suitor. Basile disguises himself as the favoured suitor in order to enter the house and make love to Geneviève so that her mother will be obliged to let the couple marry. This is achieved after many complications.   [GJ]

Conte philosophique, see SHORT FICTION.

Contes cruels, see VILLIERS DE L'ISLE-ADAM.

Contes d'Amadou Koumba, see DIOP, B.

Contes de la rue Broca, see GRIPARI.

Contes de ma mère l'Oye. Title usually given to Perrault's *Histoires ou contes du temps passé.*

Contes d'Espagne et d'Italie, see MUSSET.

Contes drolatiques. Light-hearted stories by *Balzac, imitating the manner of *Rabelais and 16th-c. storytellers; first published separately, they were included in La *Comédie humaine.*

Contes et nouvelles, see LA FONTAINE.

Contes moraux, see MARMONTEL.

CONTI, Armand, prince de (1629–68). Member of a collateral branch of the *Bourbon family, brother of

'le grand *Condé'. He took part in the *Fronde and was a protector of *Molière, but on becoming devout turned against the theatre (see his *Traité de la comédie,* 1666).

Contrat social, Du. Treatise on political right, published by Jean-Jacques *Rousseau in 1762. It is one of the most discussed texts of European political theory, and has been presented both as a cornerstone of democracy and as a breviary for totalitarianism. It is best understood in the context of its author's theories of human nature and his own experience; the model of political organization it proposes is like an idealized version of Genevan government. It was not meant to be put into practice directly, but to serve as a yardstick by which to judge existing governments.

Rousseau's starting point is man's original freedom, memorably expressed in the opening words: 'L'homme est né libre, et partout il est dans les fers.' Rejecting theories of the natural or god-given rights of rulers, he sees the basis of political obligation in a pact, which is tacitly made between all the citizens of a state (as distinct from a pact between ruler and subjects). The citizens together form the 'sovereign' and make the laws, whose execution is entrusted to a government (which may be a single person or a group). Freedom (as opposed to natural independence) is defined as obedience to laws which are the expression of the 'general will' (a peculiarly difficult concept, not necessarily the same thing as majority rule). The essential purpose of the work is the protection of individual rights, or, in Rousseau's terms, to 'find a form of association which can defend and protect with all the power of the community the person and possessions of each associate, and by which each person unites himself with all, but only obeys himself and thereby remains as free as before'.

The work was immediately condemned by the authorities in France and Geneva. It had a considerable influence on thinking in France during the *Revolution, and more generally played an essential role in establishing the doctrine of popular sovereignty.   [PF]

Contre Sainte-Beuve, see PROUST.

Contr'un, see LA BOÉTIE.

Convention Nationale, La, see REVOLUTION, I; NATIONAL ASSEMBLIES.

Convulsionnaires, Les, see PÂRIS.

Cookery Books, see HOUSEHOLD MANAGEMENT TREATISES.

COPEAU, Jacques (1879–1949). French actor, director, and theoretician of the theatre. Co-founder of the *Nouvelle Revue Française* with André *Gide in 1909, Copeau set up the Théâtre du Vieux-

Colombier in 1913 and the École du Vieux-Colombier in 1920 to put into practice his programme for a renewal of the French stage. He dismissed extravagant trappings and commercialism, seeking a return to essentials through an austere, simple, and disciplined approach to both staging and acting. Hostile to compromise, Copeau had a difficult career, but as collaborator or teacher formed most of the generations which dominated French theatre through to the 1950s.   [DHW]

COPPÉE, François (1842–1908). Now chiefly remembered as one of the *Parnassian jury which in 1875 excluded work by *Mallarmé, *Verlaine, and *Cros from the third volume of the *Parnasse contemporain* (1876), Coppée was one of the best-known poets and dramatists of the 1870s and 1880s. His play *Le Passant* enjoyed enormous success in 1869, due in part to its revelation of Sarah *Bernhardt. In successive volumes of poetry, notably *Intimités* (1868), *Poèmes modernes* (1869), and *Les Humbles* (1872), he drew upon the descriptive realism he admired in Parnassian poetry to create a picturesque, idealized representation of working-class Paris life which helped to establish a tradition of popular poetry.   [JK]

Coppet. A château on the shores of Lake Geneva between Geneva and Lausanne bought in 1784 by Jacques *Necker, father of Germaine de *Staël. It is most usually remembered for the 'Groupe de Coppet', the brilliant group of writers that gathered there around the exiled Madame de Staël during the first decade of the 19th c. and formed a centre of opposition to Napoleon's repressive policies and to the values of his empire. The year 1808 is generally reckoned to have been a peak in the Coppet group's intellectual activities. Cosmopolitan in origin and liberal in outlook, the group had in common an interest in philosophy, notably Kant, and in what might now be called comparative literature and the comparative history of different cultures. Though others spent periods at Coppet, the nucleus of the group were Madame de Staël, Benjamin *Constant, Prosper de *Barante, Charles Victor de *Bonstetten, the Bernese historian and philosopher, the historian *Sismondi, and August Wilhelm von Schlegel, the German critic and translator. Coppet was noted for the high level of its philosophical and literary discussions, and for the wit displayed by Constant and de Staël when in conversation together. *Stendhal was to call Coppet 'les états généraux de la pensée européenne'.   [DW]

Coq-à-l'âne. Writing or dialogue in which normal logical links are suspended, creating a nonsense effect. Practised by Clément *Marot, verse of this kind was fashionable for a time in the 16th c.

COQUELIN, Benoît-Constant (1841–1909), known as Coquelin aîné. The finest comic actor of his day, he excelled in the great roles of classical comedy, espe-

cially *Molière, though he gave memorable performances in new plays by *Augier, *Dumas *fils*, and *Sardou. He had a sensational success in *Rostand's *Cyrano de Bergerac* (1897).   [SBJ]

Coqueret, Collège de, see PLÉIADE.

Coquillards. A celebrated band of brigands and discharged soldiery, perhaps numbering as many as 1,000 men, which took its name from the pilgrim's badge of a shell (*coquille*), and was active in Burgundy in the 1450s. Their secret language (*jargon*), customs, and organization under a 'king' are revealed by confessions and the *ballades en jargon* of *Villon.   [MJ]

COQUILLART, Guillaume (c.1452–1510). Highly regarded by Clément *Marot and his generation, this playwright came from a prosperous family in Reims and studied law. His early work, associated with the *Basoche, was written primarily for an audience of law-students, hence the mock-legal frameworks. Later, as well as shorter poems, he produced a range of comic satiric performance pieces (monologues, dialogues, some of doubtful attribution), including notably a parodic *Débat des dames et des armes*.   [JHMT]

Corbeaux, Les. Play in four acts by *Becque, written around 1874, staged at the Comédie-Française in 1882. The sudden death of Mousieur Vigneron leaves his wife and three daughters a prey to his business associates who display the rapacity and lack of scruple that characterized much 19th-c. commerce. The drama of the women's expropriation is handled with unnerving objectivity and a grim comedy that spares neither the foibles of the victims nor the duplicity of the predators. The subtle realism of the play's dialogue and structure broke with theatrical convention and anticipated techniques used by Ibsen and Chekhov.   [DHW]

CORBIÈRE, Tristan (Édouard-Joachim) (1845–75). One of the great original poets of the 19th c. His father Édouard was a fine seaman and a novelist. Tristan, born at Coat-Congar in Brittany, settled for a time in Roscoff, where he sailed his boat and shocked the inhabitants by his grotesque dressing-up. He was sickly, deformed by arthritis, and many of his poems express disgust at his own ugliness. He seems to have been spiritually 'adopted' (1871) by Count Rodolphe de Battin and his mistress, 'Marcelle', whom he worshipped. *Les Amours jaunes* (1873) were totally ignored by the public. In December 1874, transported to hospital by his friends, he writes to his mother: 'Je suis à Dubois, dont on fait les cercueils.' Recognition began only later when Verlaine wrote about him in *Les Poètes maudits* (1884).

The rhythms of popular speech are crammed into regular verse, giving it new life. Corbière senses the power and onward flow of the traditional French alexandrine strongly (e.g. 'Bambine'), and in his hands its energy is so intense that it becomes disrupted, rather as magnifying the energy of waves causes them to break. This is one of the secrets of his brilliant sea poetry.

A self-ironist like *Laforgue, Corbière's masks are intended to reveal rather than conceal. Unlike Laforgue, what is revealed is not facetious, but tragic and tormented. Sincerity is achieved through irony, subverting the conventional categories of emotion. The registers of popular speech are introduced, along with many different voices. The latter are often those of sailors—for the ordinary man's experience of life is more immediate, hence more poetic. 'La Fin', one of his greatest poems, is an outburst against the landsman's romantic clichés to be found in *Hugo's 'Oceano Nox'. What does Hugo know of the sailor's duel with death? Poetry, Corbière implies, needs above all reality.   [GDM]

See A. Sonnenfeld, L'Œuvre poétique de Corbière (1960); F. F. Burch, Corbière (1970); R. L. Mitchell, Corbière (1979).

CORDAY, Marie-Anne-Charlotte de (1768–93). An educated woman from Normandy and supporter of the *Girondin cause, she attained fame by stabbing *Marat to death in his bath, and was guillotined, becoming a heroine for anti-*Jacobins.

Cordeliers, Club des (Société des Amis des Droits de l'Homme et du Citoyen). This Revolutionary club was constantly a radical, republican body spearheading popular distrust of the government. Until 1792 it shared influence and policies with the *Jacobins, but being, unlike the latter, open to all (including women), and being less compartmentalized and hierarchical, it showed more individual initiative. Under the growing influence of the Commune and the Hébertistes, it became increasingly resistant to the policies of the two great Committees, and its leaders, falling victim to a general proscription against conspirators, were executed (24 March 1794). The Club then purged itself of those remaining members who displeased the victors in the Convention and thereby condemned itself to complete impotence.   [JR]

CORDIER, Mathurin (1479–1564). Humanist and educator. After lecturing in Paris, where *Calvin was his pupil, Cordier embraced the Reform in 1534 and taught in Geneva, Neuchâtel, and Lausanne, establishing elementary schools there (see his much-imitated Civilité puérile, 1560). His many schoolbooks include editions of Cicero's Letters and a classic treatise on spoken Latin.   [MJH]

Corinne, ou l'Italie. Novel by Germaine de *Staël, begun 1805, published 1807. It recounts the doomed love between Corinne, a poetess living in Italy who is creative, inspired, and passionate, and a Scottish aristocrat, Lord Oswald Nelvil, melancholy and reserved. The plot is built upon the antithesis between the supposed characteristics of northern and southern Europeans, described in de Staël's De l'Allemagne and De la littérature, but, as its subtitle implies, the book also contains much informed comment on the art and architecture of Italy. Corinne is a free spirit, fiercely independent of popular prejudices: Oswald is disturbed by her positive and outward-going personality, and, feeling himself under an obligation to his late father's wishes, finally marries Lucile, who embodies the quiet domestic virtues he feels must characterize a wife. Not the least interesting aspect of the novel is its richness of symbolic and atmospheric detail: in particular, images of fire, water, and light abound in it. The central theme of Corinne has much in common not only with *Adolphe but also with Isabelle de *Charrière's Caliste (1787): the male protagonist's weakness and hesitancy in the face of his father's wishes and of (often hypocritical) public opinion, both of which are hostile to his relationship with the woman protagonist, lead to a final betrayal of her by him. As in Adolphe, an oblique criticism of the values of society under Napoleon seems to have been intended.   [DW]

CORM, Charles, Lebanese writer, see MIDDLE EAST.

CORNEILLE, Pierre (1606–84). One of France's greatest dramatists, author of 32 plays. His reputation has waxed and waned, often in relation to his rival *Racine; in recent decades Racine has been the more performed and appreciated, even though Jean *Vilar, for instance, regarded Corneille as the more genuinely popular playwright. Only a small part of his work is now familiar to the broad public, and generalizations about 'Cornelian tragedy' or 'the Cornelian hero' are often based on a handful of plays.

He was born into a middle-class family in Rouen, where he lived for most of his life. His father was a magistrate who acquired noble status, which Corneille inherited. He married a local woman and was the father of seven children. His studies at the local Jesuit college left him with an excellent knowledge of Latin and a lasting attachment to the eloquence and humanist values of his masters. He worked for many years as a lawyer and administrator in Rouen, but lost his post as an indirect result of the *Fronde. A loyal subject, he had troubled relations with *Richelieu and *Mazarin; Richelieu at first 'protected' him, but Corneille was an independent spirit, and the minister encouraged his newly founded Académie Française to censure Le *Cid. The playwright became a member of the Academy only in 1647. Generally he was adept at securing patronage; in 1658 he acquired the favour of *Fouquet, and in the 1660s he received a royal pension and wrote court poetry.

He was a master of verse, and throughout his career wrote in various genres, from love poetry and salon pieces to works of devotion. Between 1651 and 1656 he made a complete verse translation of the *Imitation of Christ* (first published in 1656); subsequent religious translations included *L'Office de la Vierge* (1669). But it was the theatre which made him. Or rather, like one of his heroes, he created his own identity by bringing a new glory to the French stage.

The date of his early plays—and indeed of many later ones—is uncertain. They were performed in Paris by the young company of Mondory, later known as the Théatre du Marais—to which he remained attached, though for his later plays he preferred the *Hôtel de Bourgogne [see THEATRES AND AUDIENCES]. With the exception of the swashbuckling tragicomedy *Clitandre* (1630), they are all comedies: *Mélite* (1629/30), *La Veuve* (1631?), *La *Galerie du Palais* (1632?), *La *Suivante* (1632/3), and *La *Place Royale* (1633/4). Eschewing the easy laughs and stock types of farce, Corneille models himself rather on the *pastoral. His comedies take place, however, in a stylized modern urban setting. They are concerned with love and marriage (the realities of money not being forgotten), and the action usually revolves around two young couples. In this world of deception and matrimonial negotiation, feelings are uncertain, and identity is created by the playing of parts. In this respect, the comedies prefigure the later tragedies, the most interesting character being the heroically ridiculous Alidor of *La Place Royale*.

Corneille's first tragedy was his reworking of a grim classical subject, *Médée* (1635). This was immediately followed by the play-within-a-play, *L'*Illusion comique* (1635), which is like a self-reflexive prelude to the four great tragedies, *Le Cid* (1637), *Horace* (1640), *Cinna* (1640/1) and *Polyeucte* (1641/2). These plays established Corneille as the outstanding tragedian of the day, and they have been the four pillars of his fame ever since. All of them, while evoking distant times and places, had a topical political relevance which did not escape contemporaries.

There followed two further comedies, *Le *Menteur* (1644) and *La Suite du Menteur* (1644), and four Roman tragedies, *La *Mort de Pompée* (1644), *Rodogune* (1645), *Théodore* (1646), and *Héraclius* (1647). The last three of these show an increasing preference for a bewildering complexity of plot and for shocking subjects taken from little-known corners of ancient history. *Théodore*, with its story involving martyrdom and prostitution, was Corneille's first theatrical failure.

In 1648, on Mazarin's request, he wrote the text (in 'vers libres') for the *machine play *Andromède*; it was performed, with grandiose sets by Torelli, in 1650. The next three plays, *Nicomède* (1651), *Pertharite* (1651), and *Don Sanche d'Aragon* (1650), all reflect the current political situation, in particular the troubles of the Fronde. *Don Sanche* was given the new label of 'comédie héroïque' to denote a serious play that ends well.

After the failure of *Pertharite*, Corneille retired

from the theatre for several years, only returning in 1659 with *Œdipe*, written at the request of Fouquet. The following year he published a complete edition of his plays (1660), for which he revised the earlier plays extensively, writing a critical 'examen' for each of them, as well as three important theoretical pieces, the *Discours du poème dramatique*, the *Discours de la tragédie*, and the *Discours des trois unités*.

In 1662 he moved to Paris with his brother Thomas [see next entry], and continued to write for the theatre until 1674. His production includes a collaboration with *Molière on the court spectacular *Psyché* (he had earlier written the text for a similarly grandiose piece, *La Toison d'or*, produced in 1661). But the bulk of his work is made up of tragedies or 'comédies héroïques': *Sertorius* (1662), *Sophonisbe* (1663), *Othon* (1664), *Agésilas* (1666), *Attila* (1667), *Tite et Bérénice* (1670), *Pulchérie* (1672), and *Suréna* (1674). These years were embittered by a growing feeling of neglect and failure, and by the success of his aggressive young rival, Racine. His later plays do not have the surging confidence and eloquence of his greatest period, but they make up a fascinating and varied body of work, and do not deserve the neglect which they have suffered.

In his attitude to the theatre, Corneille was proudly independent. He did not accept the authority of Aristotle and his interpreters on all points. For instance, improbable but true subjects might override the dictates of *vraisemblance* [see TRAGEDY], and the emotion aroused by tragedy could be admiration as well as pity or terror. His prefaces and 'examens' show his desire to dazzle the audience. His plays are full of exceptional characters (from the saintly Polyeucte to the monstrous Cléopâtre in *Rodogune*), terrible dilemmas, and surprising turns of events—the complexity of plays such as *Othon* or *Héraclius* is enough to baffle the inattentive spectator. Above all, his plays are remarkable for their eloquence. His heroes and heroines are living examples of the humanist ideal of the orator, as it was inculcated in the Jesuit colleges.

The Jesuits may also have instilled in him an optimistic faith in human nature. In his theatre exceptional individuals, members of a heroic élite, create their own identities, based on an ethic of *gloire* (reputation) and *générosité* (magnanimity) which is not generally felt to be at odds either with the national interest or with Christian values. Love plays a crucial part in this ideal; although it is often opposed to the demands of honour or duty, it remains an essential part of the heroic life, and the creation of the couple is a central element in Corneille's tragedies and comedies alike.

This optimism does not go unchallenged, however. *L'Illusion comique* shows in a comic light his awareness of the theatrical fraud. The spectator is always conscious of the pain associated with heroism, and of the vulnerability of the ideal. In the later plays in particular, love and heroism are often seen as at odds with selfish calculation and with the Machiavellian politics known as 'raison d'état'; his swan-song, *Suréna*, is exemplary in this respect.

Moral and political issues are debated with passionate seriousness in Corneille's tragedies; he was clearly fascinated by such questions and their topical applications, and he often seems to give his approval to particular positions. In recent years critics have shown (often in contradictory ways) how his plays appear to echo contemporary ethical discourse. But it would be wrong to see him as essentially an ideologist. He was a first and foremost a playwright.   [PF]

See P. Bénichou, *Morales du grand siècle* (1948); B. Dort, *Corneille dramaturge* (1957); G. Pocock, *Corneille and Racine: Problems of Tragic Form* (1973); M. Fumaroli, *Héros et orateurs: rhétorique et dramaturgie cornéliennes* (1990).

CORNEILLE, Thomas (1625–1709). Dramatist and lexicographer, eclipsed for posterity by his older brother Pierre. He married his brother's wife's sister, and the two families lived in close harmony. Pierre protected and helped Thomas, who in turn championed Pierre's reputation and encouraged the début of their nephew *Fontenelle, giving him access to the *Mercure galant*, which Thomas directed with Donneau de Visé. On his brother's death Thomas was elected in his place to the Académie Française, for which he prepared a new edition of *Vaugelas's *Remarques* and composed an important two-volume *Dictionnaire des arts et des sciences* (1694).

He was the author of over 30 plays or operas. More flexible than his brother, he had no distinctive manner or style; many of his works are modelled on existing plays. Several early comedies, performed between 1647 and 1656, are adapted from the Spanish. *Le Festin de pierre* (1677) is a flat verse adaptation of Molière's *Dom Juan*, which it supplanted until the mid-19th c. Several of his tragedies (e.g. *Stilicon*, 1660; *Camma*, 1661) are vigorous tales of love and power in the manner of his brother. *Timocrate* (1656) was a huge success; it is an improbable love story whose hero, king of Crete, appears under a false name in Argos, which he defends against his own armies. *Ariane* (1672), his best play, tells the story of Ariadne's betrayal by Theseus with a simplicity that owes much to *Bérénice. His other most successful tragedy, *Le Comte d'Essex* (1678), combines the appeal of unrequited love and political intrigue.   [PF]

Cornet à dés, Le, see JACOB.

CORNU, Auguste (1888–1981). Historian of *Marxism. His doctoral thesis of 1934 was the first French academic work on Marx. After World War II he moved to East Berlin, and his scholarly volumes on Marx's and Engels's early years sparked vigorous debates in France during the 1960s.

COROT, Jean-Baptiste-Camille (1796–1875). French painter, whose delicate and luminous landscapes make him a forerunner of *Impressionism.

Correspondance littéraire, philosophique et critique. A manuscript journal, of which some 15 copies were regularly distributed to wealthy and titled subscribers throughout Europe, including Catherine the Great and Frederick II of Prussia. It began as a continuation, perhaps a rival, of the *Nouvelles littéraires*, compiled irregularly by *Raynal between 1747 and 1755. Its chief editor from 1753 to 1773 was Melchior *Grimm, who was increasingly helped by Madame d'*Épinay, *Diderot, and J.-K. Meister. Meister took over the editorship from 1773 to 1793, and attempted with little success to revive the journal after 1794.

The *Correspondance littéraire* (as it is usually known) was dispatched at first at monthly, but soon at fortnightly intervals; this rhythm was maintained with some variations until the 1770s, when it reverted to monthly distribution. Each number was a sizeable production. The most famous of a number of similar journals [see BACHAUMONT; MÉTRA], it offers a rich account of cultural life in Paris, reporting at length on new publications, plays, and art exhibitions, but also including original works, most notably by Diderot, who used it as an outlet for many of his most important writings which could not be openly published. It was for the *Correspondance* that he composed his *Salons.

The journal generally reflects the views of the *philosophe* circle, responding rapidly to the intellectual issues of the day. Grimm's personal contribution is remarkable for its acute, if biased, judgements and its consistently readable style, which is sometimes serious, occasionally fulsome, but often mischievously ironic or downright rude.

The *Correspondance* was edited by M. Tourneux in 16 vols. (1877–82).   [PF]

'Correspondances'. Sonnet by *Baudelaire, drawing on the teachings of *Illuminism and very important for *Symbolism.

Corvée, see FEUDAL DUES.

Cosroès. Tragedy by *Rotrou, performed c.1648, published 1649. It is set in 7th-c. Persia, where the succession to the old king Cosroès is contested between his elder son Syroès and Mardesane, the son of his scheming and ambitious second wife Syra. Syroès enjoys popular support but is less ruthless and unprincipled than his opponents, and his scruples make him irresolute and ineffectual. Finally Mardesane, Syra, and Cosroès commit suicide, leaving Syroès victorious but dismayed. Although Syroès is the central character, Syra is the most forcefully portrayed. The play is exciting, and gives a sinister picture of the lust for power.   [GJ]

COSTAR, Pierre (1603–60). Learned man of letters, friend of Guez de *Balzac and *Ménage, enemy of

*Chapelain; he left a number of works in defence of *Voiture's poetry and a correspondence of some interest.

COSTER, Charles de, see BELGIAN LITERATURE.

Côté de Guermantes, Le. The third part of Proust's *A la recherche du temps perdu.*

COTGRAVE, Randle (*c*.1570–1634). English lexico-grapher whose monumental *Dictionary of the French and English Tongues* (1611) is an indispensable guide to the language of 16th-c. France. Drawing on popular as well as on literary and scientific sources, it is a gold-mine of proverbial and familiar expressions; *Rabelais's translator *Urquhart was indebted to it. [MJH]

COTIN, Charles, abbé (1604–82). Court preacher, academician, and poet, remembered now because of *Boileau's unrelenting and intemperate attacks on him (motivated in part by Cotin's own denigra-tion of the *Satires*). He was the model for the grotesque Trissotin in Molière's Les *Femmes savantes.* [PF]

COTON, Pierre, père (1564–1626). French *Jesuit preacher who attracted *Henri IV's attention by his vigour in controversy with the Huguenots. He worked for the Edict of Rouen (1603), which relaxed the ban imposed on the Jesuits in 1595, and was appointed royal confessor in 1608. But in 1610 the king's assassin Ravaillac was widely rumoured to have been influenced by Jesuit political theory epit-omized in Mariana's defence of tyrannicide. Coton wrote an open letter to Henri's widow, Marie de Médicis, rebutting these reports. Widely translated, it attracted a flood of international reaction known as the 'Anti-Coton'. He continued as Louis XIII's confessor until falling from favour in 1617. [PJB]

COTTIN, Sophie, née Marie Ristaud (1770–1807). Hugely popular sentimental novelist of the early 1800s. Her best-known work was *Élisabeth ou les Exilés de Sibérie* (1806).

COUCHORO, Félix (1900–68). Novelist and journal-ist, a native of Dahomey (Benin). After publishing *L'Esclave* in 1929, he produced little until the 1950s, when for six years he lived in political exile in Ghana. His prodigious output of novels in the 1960s were published in serial form in *Togo-Presse*. [MPC]

Couleur locale. A characteristic feature of *Romanticism. Authors appealed to the imagination of their readers by including visual and picturesque details. A concrete sense of time and place was con-sidered essential. Descriptive techniques evolved which tried to emulate the painter's eye for detail. However, the vogue for local colour implied more than using description and the selection of detail in order to evoke a particular setting or period. This approach reflected the repudiation of *classicism with its veneration for the timeless and the univer-sal in favour of Romanticism's sense of nationhood, diversity, and the value of cultural difference. Local colour was part of the Romantic writer's attempt to capture a new truth, to render social reality in its complexity, to locate his subject within a broader context. At the same time it allowed the writer to express dissatisfaction with present reality and depict an alternative to conventional morality. Romantic writers were drawn to foreign cultures (Spain, Italy, the Middle East, and North Africa) and to earlier periods (the Middle Ages and the Renaissance). Exoticism often carried an erotic charge, and local colour helped open up a literary space in which violent passions could be displayed. [CC]

Counter-Reformation. The term, which dates from the 19th c., would seem to imply that the phenome-non concerned was the product of a Catholic reac-tion against the Protestant *Reformation. According to this interpretation, it is seen as beginning in 1517 (the same date as *Luther's 95 theses) and as culmi-nating in a series of anti-Protestant measures: the appointment of militant popes (e.g. Pius IV in 1555); the convocation of the Council of Trent (which was held, with substantial interruptions, between 1545 and 1563); the foundation of the *Jesuits (the 'shock troops' of the Counter-Reformation); the creation of a new, more effective Inquisition (1542); and the establishment of the Index of Prohibited Books (1559).

It is true that the Council of Trent marked a deliberate rejection of any attempt at finding ritual and doctrinal compromises. Whereas many of the monarchs of Europe wished to use the Council as a means of removing abuses in the Church (thereby making compromise easier to achieve), the papacy made sure that it concerned itself above all with doctrinal issues. The decisions made in this domain deliberately precluded any possibility of reaching an understanding with the more moderate Protestants: Luther's view of justification by faith alone was rejected; the importance of good works was stressed, as was the role of the priest as intermedi-ary between God and the sinner; the Lord's Supper was interpreted in a rigorously traditional way and was, furthermore, to be celebrated only in Latin.

There is no doubt that the Counter-Reformation would have been very different if there had not been a Protestant Reformation against which to react. Modern historians prefer, however, to avoid such a tendentious title and to refer to the 'Catholic Reformation', which they then seek to interpret in the context of a desire for religious reform extend-ing well back into the Middle Ages. Seen in this per-spective, the Counter-Reformation appears as only another (though extremely important) manifesta-tion of the desire for a purer spirituality which inspired the *Brethren of the Common Life, the German medieval mystics, and the 15th-c. conciliar movement (as exemplified by *Gerson).

The other most recent change in attitudes towards the Counter-Reformation concerns its duration. It used to be argued that the movement was over by 1650, or even by 1600. Modern historians tend to emphasize the progressive nature of the reform, which took several centuries to complete. This viewpoint is particularly appropriate in the case of France, where the progress of the Counter-Reformation was seriously impeded by the *Wars of Religion. The creation by *Henri II of the *chambre ardente and his acceptance of the Peace of *Cateau-Cambrésis demonstrated his intention to eradicate heresy from his lands. His sons, however, ruled over a country torn by factional and religious strife. On the one hand, the monarchy was often forced to offer concessions to the Protestants in the hope of obtaining peace. On the other, it often had to resist the pressures applied by the extremists of the Catholic *Ligue. The strong *Gallican traditions of the French Church often led the French king (and the Parlement) to oppose measures (like the publication of the decrees of the Council of Trent) which they felt would reinforce the position of the Spanish/Ultramontane party. For these reasons, the full flowering of the French Counter-Reformation was delayed until the 17th c. Even then, progress was often patchy, but the appointment of more and more reforming bishops, the increasing influence of Jesuit schools (with such famous pupils as *Corneille, *Descartes, and *Mersenne), and the guidance of ecclesiastics like *Bérulle and *François de Sales slowly but steadily enabled the spirit of the French Counter-Reformation to penetrate the hearts and minds of more and more of their contemporaries. [JJS]

See J. Delumeau, Catholicism between Luther and Voltaire (1977); M. Mullet, The Counter-Reformation (1984).

Coup de dés, Un, see MALLARMÉ.

Coup de grâce, Le, see YOURCENAR.

Coup d'état. The two most celebrated coups in French history are those of 18 Brumaire 1799 [see NAPOLEON, I] and of 2 December 1851 [see NAPOLEON III]. The latter was mockingly compared by Marx to the former.

Coupe enjambante, coupe lyrique, see VERSIFICATION, I.

COURBET, Gustave (1819–77). The leading representative of the *Realist movement in French painting, Courbet succeeded in fusing a powerful naturalist style with a socialist vision of society and art derived from *Proudhon. In Parisian artistic and literary circles in the late 1840s, his friends included *Baudelaire (whose portrait he painted c.1847) and *Champfleury. Following the Revolution of 1848 his representation of contemporary social reality, his land- and seascapes, and his female nudes freed

from conventional idealism embodied his rejection of the academic tradition. During the Universal Exhibition held in Paris in 1855 he staged a rival exhibition of his own work, which marked an important stage in the collapse of state control of painting, a process accelerated by the *Impressionists. [JK]

Cour d'amour. Late 13th-c. allegorical poem by Mahieu le Poirier (4,430 lines: start missing). In Love's castle a narrator attends an eight-day hearing of 32 amatory grievances. The God of Love's bailiff and 12 peers (e.g. Biau Parler) pass judgement despite partly successful attempts by Dame Envie to disrupt proceedings. There is also an Occitan version. [PVD]

Cour des Aides. Under the ancien régime, a law court dealing principally with cases involving taxation.

Cour des Miracles, La. Headquarters of beggars in medieval Paris, described by *Hugo in Notre-Dame de Paris.

COURIER, Paul-Louis (1772–1825). Professional soldier who served in the Revolutionary and Napoleonic armies, but whose distaste for military campaigns and whose obstreperous temperament put him firmly in the disgruntled 'grognard' type. Under the *Restoration, and from his vantage-point as a new landowner in the Touraine, he jealously protected his own situation and robustly defended the interests of the little man against Church and State in a series of caustic pamphlets (Pétition pour les villageois qu'on empêche de danser, 1821; Pamphlet des pamphlets, 1824). An accomplished Greek scholar, he translated Xenophon and Les Amours pastorales de Daphnis et Chloé by Longus. [BR]

Couronnement de Louis, Le. *Chanson de geste of the Cycle de *Guillaume, probably composed in the late 1130s in the legitimist atmosphere of the abbey of Saint-Denis. Apparently loosely episodic, its five sections, in which Guillaume d'Orange defends the *Carolingian succession to the French crown and Holy Roman Empire, are tightly structured to give a uniform ideological message. Louis, Charlemagne's heir, is presented as childishly weak, while Guillaume's loyalty, though severely tested, remains unshaken. In the second episode (a duel with the demonic giant Corsolt), Guillaume receives the wound which furnishes his nickname 'au court nez' (Shortnose) in the cyclic poems. The Carolingian fiction covers references to the reigns of Louis VI and Louis VII (the latter perhaps providing the model for the epic Louis), and conflicts between the Capetian kings and their vassals, especially the dukes of Normandy. The poem, which is not lacking in robust humour, contrasts the loyalty of knights, common people, and reformed regular clergy with the traitorous ambitions of the great feudatories and secular clergy. Although it is composed in the 'oral style' common to epics, the prologue and first episode (the coronation) show that the poet was literate and had access to chronicles for the Carolingian period. [PEB].

Courrier de l'Est, see BARRÈS.

Courrier Sud, see SAINT-EXUPÉRY.

Cours de linguistique générale, see SAUSSURE.

Cours d'études, see CONDILLAC.

COURT DE GÉBELIN, Antoine (1725–84). A Protestant and a freemason, he was the author of the *Lettres toulousaines* (1763), a defence of *Calas, and of a monumental but unfinished nine-volume work, *Le Monde primitif* (1773–82). This shows all languages to derive from a common tongue, which corresponds to the true nature of things. Not only language but all sorts of relics of antiquity can be read allegorically: 'le monde entier n'est qu'une allégorie, un miroir fait pour nous conduire à la connaissance d'un monde supérieur.' His mystical thought was admired by *Saint-Martin. [PF]

COURTELINE, Georges (pseud. of Georges-Victor-Marcel Moinaux) (1858–1929). While still a French civil servant he wrote humorous columns for popular newspapers before embarking on fiction that hilariously subverted hallowed institutions: the army in *Les Gaîtés de l'escadron* (1886), the civil service in *Messieurs les ronds-de-cuir* (1893). Turning to the stage, he wrote hard and racy farces, mostly in one act and in rapid, short scenes. In these he combines acute social observation with extravagantly comic situations, excelling at showing how individuals are deformed by rigid adherence to rules and conventions, whether in military life (*Lidoire*, 1891), the law (*L'Article 330*, 1900), or marriage (*La Paix chez soi*, 1903). [SBJ]

COURTILZ DE SANDRAS, Gatien de (1644–1712). French novelist. Courtilz spent some 15 years in military service, first as a musketeer then as a cavalry captain, before beginning his literary career. His first book was published in 1678, and in all he produced 36 works. Only one of these, *Les Aventures de la comtesse de Strasbourg* (1716), is a novel with purely imaginary characters. The remaining works draw heavily on his knowledge of public personages and military campaigns. They show a general progression from *chroniques scandaleuses* and romanced biographies to the pseudo-memoirs for which he is chiefly remembered [see MEMOIR-NOVELS]. His best-known work is the *Mémoires de M. d'Artagnan* (1700). [VGM]

COURTIN, Antoine de (1662–85). French diplomat and civil servant, known for his *Nouveau traité de la civilité* (1671), one of the most popular manuals of politeness for the upwardly mobile. As well as basic table manners, he preaches modesty and a proper respect for rank.

COURTIN, Nicolas, see EPIC POETRY.

Courtly Love, see FIN'AMOR.

Courtois d'Arras. A 650-line dramatization of the parable of the prodigal son. Composed in Arras in the early 13th c., it sets the action firmly in contemporary Artois and expands the scenes in which the country-bumpkin son, ironically named Courtois, is robbed by two prostitutes in a tavern. Each of the surviving manuscripts contains a small number of narrative lines, which suggests that *Courtois* is one of several texts (e.g. *La Seinte Resureccion, La Passion d'Autun*) whose dramatic status was uncertain; belonging to the repertoire of the *jongleurs, it could have been either a true play or a lively narrative. [GAR]

Courtoisie. French courtly traditions go well back into the Middle Ages [see FIN'AMOR; CHIVALRY]. For the Renaissance period the most important contemporary influence was Castiglione's *Il Cortegiano* (1528), which was first translated into French by Jacques Colin in 1537. Castiglione comments specifically on the philistinism of many members of the French aristocracy, thereby reinforcing a tradition which was to continue well into the 17th c. There is evidence that many of the criticisms were exaggerated; the nobles in question were often merely complying with the accepted view of what a nobleman should be like: essentially a soldier and a huntsman. But with the increased importance of the royal *court and of the role of women within it (both developments were particularly noticeable under *François Ier), requirements changed. Thus, Castiglione demands that the perfect courtier should be able to sing and dance, play musical instruments, write prose and verse, and have a good knowledge of the humanities; and, above all, that he should be able to show off these attributes with an effortless grace.

Castiglione's ideal, which also has an ethical dimension (the courtier should be his prince's political and moral advisor), bears the imprint of Italian *Neoplatonism. As such, it was unlikely to be successfully transferred to France—where, indeed, there was something of a backlash, as witnessed by the anti-courtier trend evident in much contemporary literature. The advent of the *Wars of Religion had an ambiguous influence. On the one hand, it disrupted social life in a way which often made courtly developments hard to sustain. On the other, the brutalizing effects it had on the *nobility made many of its members (*La Primaudaye and *La Noue, for instance) aware of the pressing need to re-educate the *noblesse d'épée*. Their approach to education was, however, very different and often more utilitarian than Castiglione's. The real link between *Il Cortegiano* and 17th-c. *honnêteté is provided by the *Essais* of *Montaigne: in particular, 'Du pédantisme', 'De l'institution des enfants', and 'De l'art de conférer'. Montaigne's view of the ideal conversation is probably rather more challenging than *Faret's or *Méré's; but his views on the educational needs of the gentleman and especially his hatred of pedantic display had an enormous influence on subsequent concepts of *honnêteté*. [JJS]

Courts, Royal [see also MONARCHY]. The ambiguities in the concept of 'court' are conveniently summarized in the *Dictionnaire* of *Furetière, who defines this term first as a place inhabited by a king, then as the king and his council, and finally as the king's suite. The reason for these ambiguities was the fact that most of the private life of kings was lived in public. The court included not only the king's servants in his capacity as ruler, but his household, with all its cooks, valets, secretaries, laundresses, falconers, buffoons, guards, and so on. Like other lords, the king was also surrounded by a clientele of lesser men, the courtiers, who shared his hours of leisure. The most successful courtiers became 'favourites' (*mignons*, as they were often called in the 16th c.). The competition for favours disgusted some observers, and attacks on the court (such as Alain *Chartier's *Curial*) became a popular literary genre. There were also temporary visitors, suitors who 'courted' the king in the hope of favours.

The court was, therefore, comparable to a small town, its population fluctuating between 2,000 and 15,000. It was generally itinerant from the Middle Ages to the end of the 17th c. Up to the reign of *Louis XIV most kings circulated between a few favourite residences, including Blois, *Fontainebleau, Chambord, Vincennes, and St-Germain-en-Laye, spending relatively little time in Paris despite the various rebuildings of the *Louvre. Even Louis was itinerant, despite his love for *Versailles. On his death in 1715 the court moved to Vincennes and then to the Tuileries, but returned to Versailles in 1722. *Napoleon followed the example of his predecessors: he moved into the Tuileries in 1800, when he was still First Consul, and made it his base for the next 14 years.

Besides its domestic and political functions, the court was an educational institution, 'the school of all that is honourable' as one 15th-c. writer put it. Noble boys were sent to court to serve as pages and squires, and girls to wait on the queen. Participation in the court's rituals was a school of deportment, while court gossip was a form of political education. The court style of dress, conversation, and so on was followed with increasing attention by provincial élites (one of the main functions of the *Mercure galant* was to tell ladies in the provinces about the latest court fashions). [UPB]

See J.-F. Solnon, *La Cour de France* (1987).

COUSIN, Victor (1792–1867). French philosopher who rose from humble origins to become a professor at the *Sorbonne in 1815. His name is linked with the Eclectic school which, rather than advocating a radically new doctrine, held that the systems of the past should be sifted and reassessed. His best-known work is *Du vrai, du beau et du bien* (1836), based on lectures delivered in 1818. Before 1830 he was a rallying-point for the intellectual opposition to the Restoration (the government suspended his lectures between 1820 and 1827). In the longer term, however, Cousin offered a spiritualist alternative to those of a more conservative disposition who feared Catholicism's allegiance to reactionary royalism. He held a number of key administrative posts during the *July Monarchy. [CC]

Cousine Bette, La. Novel by *Balzac, published 1847 as the first part of *Les Parents pauvres*. It tells the story of the fall of the house of Hulot, precipitated by Lisbeth Fischer, the 'cousin Bette' of the title, a poor spinster and hanger-on. Hector Hulot is a military administrator whose career had flourished in the Napoleonic era, to which he remains attached in the more commercially minded 1830s, when the novel's plot begins. In middle age Hulot has become an obsessive womanizer, and Bette's plot of revenge on the household which has treated her with condescension for decades turns on the manipulation of Hulot's sexual desire. Valérie Marneffe, a physically irresistible middle-class whore, acting in collusion with her husband and with Bette, strips Hulot of every penny he has, and of all that he has borrowed and hopes to pay back from a racket set up with his brother-in-law in the recently acquired colony of Algeria. The Algerian racket is uncovered, Hulot is caught *in flagrante delicto* with Valérie and forced to resign his post at the Ministry of War, and he disappears into squalid working-class quarters of Paris to live under anagrammatic pseudonyms with a string of child-mistresses. Adeline, Hulot's wife, an exemplary figure of Christian goodness, first attempts to save the family fortunes by offering herself to Hulot's rival and comrade-in-skirts, the wealthy buffoon Crevel, and finally accepts Hulot back into her now impoverished home. She dies when she hears the unrepentant 'prodigal father' offering to make the scullery maid the second Baroness Hulot; Crevel and Valérie die from poison administered by a jealous Brazilian lover; Bette dies of disappointment and sickness; but Hulot lives on at the end of this sombre and powerful novel, no longer a man but a mere wreck symbolizing the force of desire itself. [DMB]

Cousin Pons, Le. The last of *Balzac's major novels, published 1847 as the second part of *Les Parents pauvres*, telling the tragic story of the musician Sylvain Pons, the 'poor relation' of a tribe of wealthy middle-class families. Pons is phenomenally ugly, lives with his bosom companion, a German pianist called Schmucke, who is perhaps even uglier, and has a passion for good food which makes him a parasitical caller on the Camusots, the Cardots, and the

Popinots, to whom he is related. He is also a passionate and learned collector of antiques, in the manner of Du Sommerard, Balzac's contemporary, whose collection now forms the basis of the Musée de Cluny. When Pons is banished from the wealthy tables at which he has picked and falls ill with a disease of the liver, his former protectors begin to grasp the value of the bric-à-brac amassed in his flat, and become parasites in their turn. Madame Camusot, 'one of the most venomous and intriguing women of the *Comédie humaine' (H. J. Hunt), uses middlemen to exploit the gullible Schmucke, and the dying Pons sees the finest of his pictures appropriated by the philistine family which had condescended to feed him. Pons dies; Schmucke tries but fails to save his inheritance, cedes it for a risibly small sum, and follows his old friend to the grave. *Le Cousin Pons* is remarkable for its portrayal of sexuality 'sublimated' in eating and collecting, and of a tender friendship between two bachelors. Like *La *Cousine Bette, Pons* is a sombre work, held together by a complex web of metaphors and mythical allusions, offering little hope for kindness and sensitivity in a world ruled by greed and corruption.   [DMB]

COUTHON, Georges-Auguste (1775–94). Lawyer, then *Revolutionary politician. Though confined to a wheelchair, he was a vigorous member of the Comité de Salut Public. A close ally of *Robespierre and *Saint-Just, he died with them.

CRAVAN, Arthur (pseud. of Fabian Lloyd) (1887–?1920). Anticipating *Dada, Cravan rejected art and preferred the poetry of scandalous living. He was a boxer and a traveller; in 1914 he disappeared from Paris to North America and Mexico. His review *Maintenant* (5 numbers, 1912–15) contains almost all his writing, since republished as *J'étais cigare* (1971): adventurous poems reminiscent of *Rimbaud, prose pieces including a celebration of Wilde and a mocking account of the bourgeois *Gide, and a scurrilous review of the Exposition des Indépendants.   [PF]

CRÉBILLON, Claude-Prosper Jolyot de (1707–77). French novelist. Son of Prosper Jolyot de Crébillon [see below], 'Crébillon *fils*' wrote a number of novels and tales, using a wide variety of forms. His first published work, *Le Sylphe* (1730), is a short *conte*. Later he produced two much longer tales, *L'Écumoire* (1734) and *Ah! quel conte* (1754). These are satirical in tone, using fairies and magical effects in pseudo-oriental settings. *L'Écumoire*, however, touched on religious and political issues (the 'skimmer' symbolizes the Bull *Unigenitus*), and earned Crébillon a brief spell in the Bastille. For *Le Sopha* (1742) he was exiled from Paris for three months. In this work Amanzéi relates various scandalous encounters he witnessed when, in a previous incarnation, his soul inhabited a sofa. Crébillon had already published a more conventional *memoir-novel, Les *Égarements du cœur et de l'esprit (1736–8).

He wrote three *epistolary novels: *Lettres de la marquise de M**** (1732) and his two final works, *Lettres de la duchesse de **** (1768) and *Lettres athéniennes* (1771). The marchioness and the duchess have serious love-stories to tell. In the 'Athens' (= Paris) of the last novel there are several correspondants, chief of whom is Alcibiades, a cynical libertine. The second half of *Les Heureux Orphelins* (1754) also consists of letters. Crébillon was probably helped in this work by his English wife, as the first part is translated from Elisa Haywood's *The Fortunate Foundlings*. Finally he wrote two accomplished and entertaining *contes dialogués*, *La Nuit et le moment* (1755) and *Le Hasard du coin du feu* (1763). In 1759, somewhat paradoxically in view of his literary reputation, he became one of the royal censors [see CENSORSHIP].

Crébillon *fils* used to be dismissed as a minor licentious author. Due to the current interest in narratology and the interpretation of ambiguous texts, as well as changes in moral standards, he now attracts more appreciative critical attention. His style, always chaste as to vocabulary, is complex and relies on implications and *sous-entendus*. The works themselves are often morally ambivalent: while he ridicules promiscuous women and rakes, the scenes of libertinage are written with an engaging zest. Moreover, his preferred forms—letters, memoir-narratives, dialogues—preclude any qualifying comments from an external narrator. Just as many of his characters mask their true intentions, so Crébillon himself leaves us to deduce his own values.   [VGM]

See B. Fort, *Le Langage de l'ambiguïté dans l'œuvre de Crébillon fils* (1978).

CRÉBILLON, Prosper Jolyot de ('Crébillon *père*') (1674–1762). Playwright who wrote nine extant tragedies based on mythology and ancient politics in a career which spanned the years 1705 to 1754. He was elected to the Académie Française in 1731, and was appointed royal censor in 1733 and police censor in 1736. His plays preserved the classical tragic form of five acts in verse. His one significant innovation was the exploitation of the horror which his mythological sources authorized, as in *Atrée et Thyeste* (1707), in which Atrée almost tricks Thyeste into drinking the blood of his murdered children. Crébillon's best works were *Atrée et Thyeste, Électre* (1708), and *Rhadamiste et Zénobie* (1711). In his later years he was promoted by the court as a tragic rival to *Voltaire, who reworked five of Crébillon's subjects in consequence of the mutual animosity generated by Crébillon's uncharacteristically persistent censorship of *Mahomet* (1742). Aesthetic conservatism marks both his plays and his activities as a censor, and he was hostile to the adaptation of English dramatic material for the French stage. Louis XV financed the production of a luxury edition of his works in 1750. A requiem mass for him, organized by the Comédiens Français, provoked an ecclesiastical incident.   [JD]

Crémazie

CRÉMAZIE, Octave (1827–79). Usually considered to be the first major French-Canadian poet. His great popularity in the 19th c. rested on his patriotic verse in which French Canada, despite its military defeat and subjection to the British Empire, is depicted as remaining nobly true to the religion and language it inherited from pre-Revolutionary France. Following a visit to France in 1856 and his discovery of the French Romantic poets, he turned to more private themes of sadness, exile, and death. Strangely, permanent residence in France, following a business failure in Canada, led him to give up poetry completely, but he engaged in an exchange of letters with the abbé Casgrain and other correspondents in Canada which throw an interesting light on his literary and social ideas. His works were not collected until after his death (1882) and the definitive *Œuvres complètes* (2 vols.) were published only in 1972–6. [SIL]

CRENNE, Hélisenne de (pseud. of Marguerite Briet) (c.1500–?1555). Author of the first autobiographical novel in French. *Les Angoisses douloureuses qui procèdent d'amours* (1538, some ten editions by 1560) is the story of an unhappy adulterous love affair, intended as a cautionary tale for women readers. The *Épîtres familières et invectives* (1539) and the long allegorical piece *Le Songe* (1540) reveal her as a champion of women's interests. Even her prose translation of the first four books of Virgil's *Aeneid* (1541) has 'feminist' leanings, for she enlarges considerably on the tragic fate of Dido. Her florid, Latinate prose, which, though often clumsy, suggests a degree of humanist learning, gave rise to the legend initiated by *Pasquier (but long since discredited) that she was the model for *Rabelais's *écolier limousin*. [CMSJ]

Creoles. The French term *créole* is used to designate either a person (in the *West Indies specifically a white person of French origin) born in the former colonies, or forms of language (in some islands also known as *patois*) spoken in Martinique, Guadeloupe with its dependencies, Guyane, *Haiti, parts of Louisiana, the Commonwealth countries of Dominica, St Lucia, Grenada, and Trinidad, as well as the Indian Ocean islands of Reunion, *Mauritius, Rodrigues, and the Seychelles. It is this latter sense which will be treated here, with special reference to the Caribbean.

French (or 'French-based') creoles are contact languages born, in the case of the *West Indies, as a result of the meeting of French colonizers and slaves brought from West Africa in the 17th and 18th c. [see COLONIZATION]. Today they are the native language of the majority of the population in the French West Indian *départements* and in Haiti, and to a lesser extent in Dominica and St Lucia, but survive only marginally in Grenada and Trinidad.

Most of their vocabulary derives from French or Gallo-Romance dialects. Differences between the lexis of modern standard French and the Gallo-

Romance lexical items in Creole are explained by the date of the initial contact (e.g. *balier*, 'balai'; *bwèt*, 'boîte'; *espérer*, 'attendre'); by the regional origin (mainly north-western or western France) of the first settlers (e.g. *palaviré*, 'slap given with the back of the hand'; *marrer*, with a general sense of 'to tie'; *vèt*, 'vert', with a sounded final consonant); by semantic developments which took place once the Creole was established (e.g. *driver*, 'to loiter'); and, for their form, by the phonetic structure of Creole, which leads, for instance, to the replacement of the front-rounded vowels (e.g. *mi*, 'mûr'; *pé*, 'peut'; *pè*, 'peur') and the loss of *r* at the end of a word or before a consonant (e.g. *mi*, 'mûr'; *macher*, 'marcher'). Typical of all French creoles is the agglutination of an element probably derived from the French article, e.g. *lapot*, 'porte' ('the door' would be *lapot la*); *zé*, 'œuf' and 'œufs'; *diri*, 'riz'. Non-French items have come mainly from the African languages spoken by the slaves (e.g. terms relating to food, customs, religious beliefs, and the description of people such as *béké*, a white person born in the West Indies); from the Amerindian languages of the original inhabitants, particularly names of plants and animals; and from other European languages, especially Spanish and English, spoken in the Caribbean.

Creole grammar is very different from that of written French, though less so when compared with the spoken language. The origins of this difference are disputed; it has, for example, been attributed to the influence of the native languages of the African slaves who came into contact with French, to a Portuguese trading pidgin, to the fact that the French input was entirely spoken, and to a bioprogramme which lies at the basis of universal features of language learning. Whereas the morphology is simpler than that of French (there is no grammatical gender; nouns, adjectives, and verbs are not inflected), complex syntactic relationships are expressed by a system of markers, such as the particles placed before the verb to mark tense and aspect. The basic grammatical structure is shared by all the French creoles, though there are major differences between the Caribbean creoles and those of the Indian Ocean, and differences of detail between island and mainland creoles, between the speech of the eastern Caribbean and that of Haiti, and even between the dialects of different eastern Caribbean islands or parts of Haiti.

As a mainly spoken language, Creole does not enjoy the prestige of the standard national languages with which it coexists, but it is essential for intimate conversations, jokes, teasing and swearing, and for many speakers replaces the less formal registers of the standard language. It is the only language in which most Haitians can function with confidence. Literacy classes in Creole and experiments with using it as the language of instruction in schools have a history of several decades in Haiti, and in 1983 it was decided that Creole could be used as a medium for teaching in the French overseas *départements* in the Caribbean. Various orthographies have been proposed, but there is as yet no universally agreed system.

Creole is the vehicle of a rich oral literature of tales (notably animal stories featuring as their hero Compère Lapin in the Caribbean and Compère Lièvre in the Indian Ocean), songs, proverbs, and riddles. Many of these find close parallels in the oral literature of West Africa, and remain alive even in the countries (Grenada, Trinidad) where French Creole is dying out.

Examples of writing in Creole go back as far as the mid-18th c., when the language was at a very early stage of development, e.g. Duvivier de la Mahautière's *Lisette quitté la pleine* (Haiti, 1757), and the translation of *La Fontaine's fables into Creole was a favourite pastime in the 19th c. in both the Caribbean and the Indian Ocean. The use of Creole in written literature has developed most consistently in poetry, e.g. Oswald Durand, *Choucoune* (1884), Sonny Rupaire, *ti cou-baton* (1973). In the novel, after Parépou's early attempt to write in Creole (*Atipa*, 1885), the language appeared mainly in the form of isolated terms or phrases (see Jacques *Roumain's *Gouverneurs de la rosée* and Patrick *Chamoiseau's *Chronique des sept misères* for particularly successful examples), but in recent decades there have also been whole prose works in Creole, starting with Frank *Étienne *Dézafi* (1975). A movement to create serious theatre in Creole began in Haiti in the 1950s with the adaptation of classical Greek plays by Félix Morisseau-Leroy and Frank Fouché; original plays entirely in Creole have followed in both Haiti and the French islands. The interplay of Creole and French for dramatic and stylistic effects is exemplified in the plays of Ina *Césaire and in films such as Euzhan Palcy's screen version of *Zobel's *La Rue Cases-Nègres*. Even when not overtly used, Creole and its sonority, rhythms, and imagery underlie much of Caribbean literature in French, since it is the native language of nearly all those writing in French in the region.

[GA-B]

See A. Valdman, *Le Créole: structure, statut et origine* (1978); R. Chaudenson, *Les Créoles français* (1979); J. Bernabé, *Fondal-natal: grammaire dialectale approchée des créoles guadeloupéen et martiniquais* (1983).

Créolité. A theory of French *West Indian literature, culture, and identity, most fully formulated in *Éloge de la créolité* (1989) by Jean Bernabé, *Chamoiseau, and *Confiant and in the last two writers' *Lettres créoles* (1991). Unlike the rival theory of *négritude, créolité emphasizes not the survival of 'African' cultural forms in the Caribbean, but the creation, out of a multiplicity of constituent elements (African, European, Amerindian, Asian), of a composite creole culture distinctive to the Caribbean. It commends the use of *Creole as a literary medium for French West Indian writers and

uses the language as a paradigm for the formulation of a racially inclusive (rather than, in the manner of *négritude*, racially exclusive) theory of Caribbean identity, insisting on the necessary complexity and heterogeneity of Caribbean cultures. [For *créolie* see ALBANY.] [RDEB]

CRÉTIN, Guillaume (*c.*1465–1525). Born in Paris, one of the *Rhétoriqueurs, Crétin had a distinguished ecclesiastical career. His works include a number of patriotic, moralizing pieces for Louis XII and François Ier. He wrote many *épîtres*, ballades, rondeaux, and *chants-royaux* and an unfinished *Chronique française*. His interests were also musical, and one of his longer poems was on the death of the musician Okeghem, the *Déploration sur le trépas de feu Okergan*. Despite the mediocrity of his poetry, his contemporary fame was considerable. Crétin was probably the model for Raminagrobis in Chapter 21 of *Rabelais's *Tiers Livre*, and the rondeau quoted there is by him. [CMSJ]

CREVEL, René (1900–35). French Surrealist who initiated experiments with hypnotic sleep. His greatest contribution to the movement, however, was to demonstrate that *Surrealism and the novel could be reconciled. Whether texts such as *Détours* (1924), *La Mort difficile* (1926), *Babylone* (1927), *Êtes-vous fous?* (1929), and *Les Pieds dans le plat* (1933) are called 'romans' or 'fictions', the role of language itself in their elaboration is arguably the key element. *Mon corps et moi* (1925) is a confessional monologue and *L'Esprit contre la raison* (1927) is his Surrealist manifesto. For him, suicide, an obsessive theme in a number of his works, was the ultimate solution.
[KRA]

CRÉVIER, Jean-Baptiste Louis (1693–1765). Historian and teacher at the Collège de Beauvais in Paris. He completed *Rollin's *Histoire romaine*, wrote an ill-judged critique of Montesquieu's *De l'*esprit des lois*, and achieved honourable success with his very traditional *Rhétorique française* (1765).

Crispin rival de son maître, see LESAGE.

Critical Theory, see LITERARY THEORY.

Criticism. The term can mean, and has meant in France, many different ways of writing or talking about literature. It is not so much a literary genre as a set of practices, often at odds with each other. French literary history shows striking changes in the dominant functions assumed by criticism, the institutions where it is produced, and the value placed upon it, from the Romantic scorn for the critic as uncreative parasite to the extraordinary respect shown to certain *maîtres à penser* of the late 20th c.

1. Medieval and Renaissance

The words 'la critique' (criticism) and 'le critique' (critic) did not have their modern meaning until the

Criticism

late 16th and 17th c. Medieval France, however, was familiar with several kinds of criticism, practised mainly in the universities in relation to Latin texts, both biblical and classical. There were biographies of writers, some in the vernacular [see VIDA], but above all there was a highly developed art of commentary. This paid attention to the intention and genre of works, their moral value, their usefulness as a source of expressions and rhetorical devices, and to their often hidden meaning, interpreted according to sophisticated allegorical schemes. The latter continued into the *Renaissance period and beyond; they are mocked in the prologue to *Rabelais's *Gargantua.*

The Renaissance saw a great flourishing of philology, as practised by such *humanist scholars as *Dolet or *Dorat. This was applied first and foremost to ancient texts [see CLASSICAL INFLUENCES], but also to difficult writings in French, as in *Muret's commentary on *Ronsard. At the same time, there was criticism of a more polemic nature in various prefaces, and particularly in the arguments about the value of the new programme of the *Pléiade, which was carried on in *Sébillet's *Art poétique français* and *Du Bellay's *Défense et illustration.* This overlapped with the development of formal criticism or poetics. Late medieval rhetoricians (e.g. Jean *Bouchet) had produced manuals of poetic devices, but the 16th c. saw the recovery of Aristotle's *Poetics* and Horace's *Ars poetica* and the publication of commentaries and treatises on poetics in Latin (Castelvetro, *Scaliger) and increasingly in French (Ronsard, *Peletier du Mans).

2. 17th and 18th Centuries

Such theoretical works, sometimes polemic in nature, are a major feature of 17th-c. literary history [see CLASSICISM]. They include the works of *Chapelain, *La Ménardière, *Colletet, *Rapin, *Le Bossu, and *Boileau. Boileau, however, is much less the dogmatic lawgiver of legend than the committed and often prejudiced critic, passionately concerned with evaluating and promoting the literature of the present. A related mode of criticism in this period is the fault-finding commentary, concentrating on questions of language and decorum. *Malherbe's commentary on *Desportes is the classic example, together with Chapelain's *Sentiments de l'Académie sur le *Cid.*

More entertaining than pedantic discussions of this kind were the relatively informal discussions of French and foreign literature in fashionable society and the writings read there. *Montaigne may be seen as a precursor; his *Essais* abound in agreeably personal discussions of his reading. In the 17th c. the *salons provided a new venue for literary conversations (the *Académie Française itself was originally a kind of salon). The *honnêtes gens* of the salons were the public for the numerous essays, letters, dialogues, reflections, and the like which contain the best of 17th-c. criticism—one may cite the writings of *Balzac, *Sarasin, *Méré, *Bouhours, *La Bruyère, and *Saint-Évremond, together with the novels of Madeleine de *Scudéry and the prefaces of writers such as *Corneille, *Racine, and Boileau. This 'amateur' critical tradition, whose aim is to create, consolidate, or revise the literary norms of polite society, continues throughout the 18th c. in innumerable writings, including those of *La Motte, *Bayle, *Fénelon, *Marivaux, *Diderot, *Voltaire (who also practised the more pedantic mode in his commentaries on Corneille), and *Chamfort. Of the more theoretical works produced in the 18th c., the most important are probably those of *Dubos and *Marmontel.

In the *ancien régime,* as in more recent times, literature was often a place of controversy. In the 17th c. there were violent onslaughts by *Bossuet, *Nicole, and others on the immoral tendencies of imaginative writing, and the use of religious subjects in profane literature was defended by *Desmarets in the face of Boileau's attacks. The turn of the century saw the *Querelle des Anciens et des Modernes, in which first Boileau and *Perrault, and then Madame *Dacier and *La Motte took leading parts. In the 18th c. literary quarrels came to have an increasingly political nature (for or against the *Enlightenment). An important new development was the appearance of book-reviewing periodicals such as the *Journal des Savants,* the *Mémoires de Trévoux,* *Fréron's *Année littéraire,* *Linguet's journals, and *Grimm's less public *Correspondance littéraire.* This was the birth of the professional journalist-critic, who was to flourish in the following century.

3. 19th and 20th Centuries

During the 18th c. French literature had begun to be systematically studied in the *rhetoric classes of secondary schools. This normative teaching is enshrined in *Batteux's *Cours de belles-lettres;* from now on the criticism of modern literature and pedagogy were to become ever more closely entwined. *La Harpe continued in the same vein for the adult audiences of the *Lycée. His *Cours de littérature* is a culmination of the old tradition of dogmatic evaluation, but at the same time it is a history of European literature. Literary history in its modern sense, however, makes its appearance in the works of de *Staël and *Chateaubriand. And it was the historical approach which was to dominate the criticism and eventually the teaching of literature in the following century or more with the voluminous writings of *Villemain, *Sainte-Beuve, *Taine, *Brunetière, *Lanson, and many others. [For this development, and the subsequent conflict between literary history and 'la nouvelle critique', see LITERARY HISTORY.]

Meanwhile, evaluative, essayistic criticism remained vigorous and often combative, as in the work of *Stendhal, *Nodier, *Nisard, or *Saint-Marc Girardin or the prefaces of most of the major writers of the 19th c. Sainte-Beuve, for all his 'scientific' biographical ambitions, was above all an opinion-forming journalist, and periodicals such as the *Revue de Paris* and the *Revue des deux mondes* provided a forum for critical debate. In the later 19th c., in reaction to positivistic literary history, there was a flourishing of 'impressionistic' criticism, exemplified by the work of Jules *Lemaître. After 1909 the *Nouvelle Revue Française* in particular provided a home for creative criticism by writers such as *Du Bos, *Thibaudet, *Rivière, and *Paulhan. In modern times, moreover, some of the best personal criticism has been written by those who are better known as poets or novelists: for instance, *Baudelaire, *Proust, *Gide, *Valéry, *Blanchot, *Butor, and *Bonnefoy. *Sartre is a special case, pursuing the same type of investigation into human motives and actions in his fiction and drama and in his writings about literature.

4. 'La Nouvelle Critique'

The second half of the 20th c. is marked by the emergence of a varied set of tendencies sometimes grouped together as 'la nouvelle critique'. These are united principally by their opposition to traditional university criticism ('l'homme et l'œuvre') on the one hand, and to essayistic impressionism on the other. Most refer explicitly to some theoretical foundation and subvert 'common-sense' readings of texts based on philological and historical information or authorial intention. The first group to be given this label were the critics sometimes known (rather inaccurately) as the *Geneva School (*Raymond, *Poulet, *Richard, etc.), who used a thematic analysis largely inspired by *Bachelard to illuminate the 'moi profond' of the writer. A second group were the revisionist Marxist critics such as *Goldmann, who attempted to go beyond the simple reflection model of classic *Marxism. A later development of Marxist criticism is that of the *Althusser school, notably *Macherey, who made use of some of the ideas of *Structuralism to stress the contradictory positions that go into the 'production' of literary works. Around 1968 the group associated with *Sollers, *Kristeva, and *Tel Quel also attempted to bring together Marxism and late Structuralism.

It is no doubt Structuralism that has had the greatest impact on the study of literature. This is described in a separate entry, but it should be stressed here that Structuralist theory and criticism were intimately bound up with new movements in creative writing such as the *Nouveau Roman. Such a commitment to the new is seen at its best in the work of *Barthes, probably the most constantly rewarding critic of recent decades. He, like many of his colleagues, made the move from Structuralism to *Post-Structuralism around 1968, abandoning hopes for a 'science of literature' in favour of approaches stressing the openness and contradictions of the text, which thus becomes the ground for the creative activity of the reader. Two dominant features of criticism between 1970 and 1990

were the impact of *feminism, particularly in the 1970s, and the massive influence on literary interpretation of *psychoanalysis. This was a period in which the intellectual leaders of French modernity (Barthes, *Lacan, *Derrida, *Foucault, Kristeva, *Irigaray, *Lyotard) exerted a powerful influence well beyond the frontiers of France.

It should not be thought that these developments have meant the end of more traditional modes of criticism in France. Much journalistic criticism is relatively unaffected by such ideas, although journals such as *Critique*, *Littérature*, and *Tel Quel* have been among the centres of new critical activity. And the universities, while their attitude to various types of 'nouvelle critique' is warmer than in the 1960s, have continued to produce much-needed philological and historical work. Indeed, one of the most hopeful signs of the early 1990s is the development outlined at the end of the entry LITERARY HISTORY. [PF]

See R. Fayolle, *La Critique littéraire* (1964); G. Poulet (ed.), *Les Chemins actuels de la critique* (1968); J. Sturrock (ed.), *Structuralism and Since* (1979); A. J. Minnis and A. B. Scott, *Medieval Literary Theory and Criticism* (1988).

Critique. Influential journal founded by Georges *Bataille in 1946, devoted mainly to in-depth discussions of new books on literature or social science.

Critique de la raison dialectique, SEE SARTRE.

Critique de l'École de femmes, La, SEE MOLIÈRE.

Croisset. Location of the house outside Rouen where *Flaubert, the 'hermit of Croisset', lived and wrote for more than half his life.

Croix, La. Launched as a popular, combative daily in 1883 by the Assumptionist order, *La Croix* was backed by La Bonne Presse, one of the major print media groups of the past century. After a chequered spiritual, political, and commercial history, the newspaper—renamed *La Croix l'événement* in 1956— has survived to be France's sole Catholic daily. [MP]

Croix-de-feu, La. Nationalist and militarist association with fascist leanings, led from 1931 by Colonel François de la Roque. Its supporters took to the streets of Paris on 6 February 1934 on the pretext of the *Stavisky affair; the rise of the *Popular Front was in part a reaction to this demonstration.

CROMMELYNCK, Fernand (1886–1970). Dramatist with roots in Belgium, where he became known for plays such as *Nous n'irons plus au bois* (1906) and *Le Sculpteur de masques* (1908). In 1920 *Le Cocu magnifique* was staged at the Théâtre de l'Œuvre in Paris with the director, *Lugné-Poë, in the principal role. This variation on the theme of the deceived husband gives the old tale an outrageous twist by having the man himself incite others to cuckold him, at first intoxicated by his delight in possessing so desirable a

211

wife and then driven to pre-empt the attentions of a feared seducer. So intense a passion generates a bold farce that is not without a certain poignancy. This production was a pronounced success, but subsequent works were greeted with less enthusiasm: *Les Amants puérils* (1921) and *Carine ou la Jeune Fille folle de son âme* (1929) failed to achieve the same balance of the comic and the touching, and disconcerted Parisian audiences with their brusque switches from poetry to vulgarity. *Tripes d'or*, played in Brussels in 1930, was more warmly received there. His last play, *Une femme qu'a le cœur trop petit* (1934), confirmed the playwright's vigorous invention by showing how a woman's austere personality drives all in her household to debauchery. [DHW]

Cromwell, Préface de. Appended to Victor *Hugo's unperformed play about English regicide in 1827, this anti-classical manifesto connects poetic form to stages in human history: primitive times and natural man to the lyric; antiquity and the awakening of nationhood to the epic; modern times and a self divided between material and spiritual to the drama. The critical consciousness born of this division can no longer repress the ugly from the beautiful ideal. Hugo calls for the dynamic grafting of *sublime and grotesque and the abolition of the unities of time and place, but maintains verse for the more concentrated rendering of ideas. [SN]

CROS, Charles (1842–88). A talented amateur scientist from the Midi, Cros is credited with the invention of an automatic telegraph, a recipe for colour photography, and the 'paléophone' of 1877, a device narrowly pre-dating Thomas Edison's better-known phonograph. A friend of *Verlaine and *Manet and later the humourist Alphonse *Allais, Cros frequented such mock-serious literary groups as the Paris of the 1870s as the Hydropathes and the Zutistes. As a writer, he had higher pretentions than to be known exclusively as the author of the scatty nursery-rhyme 'Le Hareng saur', but was refused entry into the solemn circle of Le *Parnasse contemporain under *Leconte de Lisle, which judged him a mere joker. In fact the author of Le *Coffret de santal* (1873) was as earnest and fastidious a technician as any Parnassian, and a poem such as 'Hiéroglyphe' offers a remarkable mosaic of verbal sonorities. Many poems reflect his love for the salon-hostess Nina de Villard and express erotic yearnings tinged with metaphysical disquiet; Cros's blend of desperateness and mordant self-irony prefigures *Laforgue and led to his consecration by *Breton as a master of black humour. However, it was not until 1954 that his *Œuvres complètes* finally saw print. [RC]

Crusade Cycle. Collective title for medieval poems about the *Crusades. It is usually subdivided into the First and Second Cycles. The First Cycle comprises a sequence of epic poems preserved in several cyclical manuscripts; it purportedly describes the events of the First Crusade (1096–9) and the estab-

lishment of the Latin Kingdom of Jerusalem, and was composed between the end of the 11th c. and the late 13th c. In practice, only the earliest poems of the First Cycle (*Chanson d'Antioche*, dealing with the siege of Antioch; *Chanson de Jérusalem*, describing the capture of Jerusalem) have any claim to historical accuracy; subsequent accretions are increasingly fictional in nature and increasingly concerned with the implausible adventures (amorous and military) of a range of thoroughly romanticized Christian and Saracen heroes. In this respect, the First Crusade Cycle is typical of the later *chansons de geste.

The composition of the First Cycle also conforms to the practice found in, for instance, the *Guillaume Cycle: the poems or 'branches' composed first (the most historical) constitute the central sections of the corpus, with both the prehistory of these episodes and their subsequent development being added later. Thus, the ancestry of one of the heroes of the First Crusade, Godefroy de Bouillon, is provided by the branches preceding the historical nucleus: the poems known as the *Enfances Godefroi* and *Le Chevalier au Cygne* (legendary material accommodated to the framework of the Crusade Cycle by means of a spurious genealogy), then a branch devoted to the *enfances of the Swan Knight himself, are added in the 13th c. Promotion and glorification of Godefroy, both by exaggerating his role in the First Crusade and by endowing him with famous ancestors, seems to be one of the aims of the First Cycle. A transitional branch between the *Chanson d'Antioche* and the *Chanson de Jérusalem*, a semi-fictional account of the adventures of a number of Christian Knights captured *en route* to Jerusalem (*Les Chétifs*), had been added earlier.

The *Continuations*, describing events after the capture of Jerusalem in 1099, constitute the last branch to be appended to the First Cycle. In form and style the First Crusade Cycle is a *chanson de geste* cycle; retrospective modification of historical events abounds. Where it differs from the other epic texts is in its subject-matter, nearer to current events than is the norm. It must not be forgotten that none of the cyclical manuscripts is contemporary with the First Crusade: all date from at least a century later, and the more developed manuscripts (those with most branches) are later still. It may be that the dates at which the manuscripts were copied (the time of the Third Crusade, the period of Louis IX's expeditions) correspond to moments when interest in the (by then) legendary First Crusade had grown. Divergences between different manuscripts point to an important part being played in the composition of the First Cycle by the scribes-cum-*remanieurs*. A collective edition is in progress under the aegis of the University of Alabama.

The Second Cycle consists of three 14th-c. poems, the *Chevalier au Cygne et Godefroid de Bouillon* (a reworking of the Swan Knight theme), *Baudouin de Sebourc*, and the *Bâtard de Bouillon*. To these may be added *Saladin*, a *mise en prose* of a lost epic concerning this archetypical Saracen hero. The Cycle endeavours to update and continue the First Cycle, by adding accounts of later expeditions; and it continues the process of romanticization of the crusades begun in the First Cycle, thus moving further still from historical reality. The introduction of *romance themes and motifs is very evident throughout the works of the Second Cycle.

The Crusade Cycle provides evidence of the vitality of epic form, used in this case to celebrate relatively recent historical events which (perhaps partly because of the chosen form) are none the less imbued with legendary and mythological qualities. It also illustrates the interplay between history and fiction (and the extent to which no such distinction was made in the Middle Ages) which is characteristic of medieval writing.   [DAT]

See R. F. Cook and L. S. Crist, *Le Deuxième Cycle de la Croisade* (1972); K.-H. Bender (ed.), *Les Épopées de la croisade. Colloque de Trèves, 1984* (1987); D. A. Trotter, *Medieval French Literature and the Crusades* (1988).

Crusades. Sometimes described as Western Europe's first colonial venture, the Crusades were inaugurated by Pope Urban II at the Council of Clermont in 1095. Spurred by a request for military aid from the Byzantine emperor Alexius Comnenus, Urban proclaimed an armed pilgrimage to free Jerusalem and the Eastern churches from the menace of the Seljuk Turks. The pope's call to battle appealed to French aristocrats and their knightly entourages, some of whom had already experienced war against the infidel in Spain. They were attracted not only by the prospect of plunder and adventure but also by ecclesiastical protection for their property during their absence, alleviation of the burden of sin, and, if they died on the journey, the promise of immediate entry to heaven.

Though the pope's message was directed to soldiers, the preachers who spread it caught the imagination of a wider audience. In response, Peter the Hermit set off in 1096 with a large force drawn principally from the towns of Flanders and the Rhineland. It proved hard to control—similar groups slaughtered Jews in northern France and Lorraine—and because it had made inadequate financial provision for the expedition it aroused antagonism by pillaging as it marched. Yet the fate of Peter the Hermit's army—it was decimated by the Turks in Asia Minor—did not deter other noncombatants from participating in later expeditions. And Peter was celebrated in the chronicles and songs that emerged over the next few years.

The main armies of the First Crusade, drawn from Languedoc, the Île-de-France, Flanders, Normandy, Lorraine, and Norman Italy, met in Constantinople in 1097. Thence they set off on the dangerous route across Asia Minor to Antioch, which they captured in 1098, an adventure described in detail in the *Chanson d'Antioche* [see CRUSADE

CYCLE]. In June 1099 the Latins reached Jerusalem, which they besieged for four weeks before it fell. The event was greeted ecstatically in Europe, where the returning crusaders were fêted as Christian heroes. Their exploits were amply recorded, particularly by the anonymous South Italian knight who participated in the expedition and wrote the *Gesta Francorum* as he went along. His text apparently provided the foundation for a number of subsequent chronicles. 12th-c. readers habitually identified 'Franci' as 'French', and this encouraged a somewhat exaggerated view of the French contribution to crusading, and thus contributed to the growth of French national consciousness.

While most of the soldiers returned from the East in 1100, a small group of warriors remained to settle what became known as Outremer. The relative ease with which the First Crusade had captured Jerusalem made the task of securing the Latin states in the East appear too easy. So long as the various Seljukid emirs in Syria squabbled among themselves, things went well. But gradually, under Zengi's and Nur ad Din's leadership, greater unity emerged. And by 1174, when Saladin had united the Turkish armies with the navy and financial resources of Egypt, Outremer's days seemed numbered.

In 1144 Zengi captured Edessa, an event that horrified the West. Two large armies, led by Conrad III of Germany and Louis VII of France, set out to reverse the defeat, but succeeded only in embittering Franco-Byzantine relations (as the account of Odo of Deuil makes clear) and in drawing the Turks together. The total failure of the Second Crusade provoked disillusionment. As a consequence, the defence of the Latin states came to rest increasingly on the military orders, the Knights Templar and Hospitaller, whose special role it was seen to be.

But apathy disappeared when the news reached Europe of Saladin's capture of Jerusalem in 1187. In response to papal command, and drawing on revenues raised by new forms of taxation, the emperor Frederick Barbarossa, Philippe II of France, and Richard the Lionheart set off for Outremer in 1189. The Third Crusade (described from Richard's point of view in Ambroise d'Evreux's *Estoire de la guerre sainte*) succeeded in restoring a Latin kingdom based on the coastal strip between Acre and Jaffa, though not including Jerusalem itself. For the next century the efforts of western Christendom were directed to maintaining this strip in the face of Ayyubid, Mongol, and Mameluke forays, and to attempting to secure Jerusalem. To these ends conventional strategy dictated a preliminary attack on Egypt, seen as the vulnerable supply centre of enemy armies.

This was the initial plan of the Fourth Crusade, the Flemish, French, and Venetian expedition described by *Villehardouin and *Clari, which gathered in Venice in 1202. Exactly how that expedition was diverted to the capture of Constantinople in

Cubières

1204 has long been the subject of historical dispute. But the results of that diversion are clear: undying Byzantine hatred for the Latins, and the creation of an unstable empire controlled by western lords which provided an alternative focus for crusading activity until 1261 and established more durable French interests in Greece.

The 13th c. saw another distraction from war in Outremer when Innocent III extended crusading privileges to those prepared to fight heretics in Europe. In 1208 he launched the Albigensian Crusade against the supporters of the *Cathar *perfecti* in southern France, a brutal campaign that was swiftly caught up in the mesh of Languedocian politics. As a consequence of the bitterness aroused by the papal army under Simon de Montfort, soldiers from the Midi, who had made substantial contributions to the armies of the first three crusades, played a negligible role in later efforts to hold on to Outremer.

Among northern Frenchmen, Thibaut IV de Champagne nursed ambitions in Outremer deriving from his grandfather's rule there between 1192 and 1197. But after the failure of his crusade in 1240, French interest lagged. It took the piety and commitment of Louis IX to rekindle enthusiasm. However, the royal crusade of 1248–52, described by *Joinville, resulted in total defeat in Egypt, followed by a profitless stay in Outremer. Louis's second crusade was a disaster, ending in his death in Tunisia in 1270. The only positive result of his endeavours was to create an obligation on future French kings to interest themselves in the fate of Outremer. Therefore, long after the fall of Acre in 1291 which marked the end of the Latin kingdom, Louis's successors planned expeditions to the East and raised taxation for that purpose. But none actually set sail.

[JHD]

See S. Runciman, *The Crusades* (1951–4); H. E. Mayer, *The Crusades*, 2nd edn., trans. J. Gillingham (1988).

CUBIÈRES, Michel de, known as Cubières-Palmézeaux, Dorat-Cubières, etc. (1752–1820). Author of innumerable forgotten works (light poetry, satires, odes, *drames*, etc.). A friend of *Dorat, he was close to Fanny de *Beauharnais and later wrote admiringly of *Mercier and *Restif, members of the same circle. He distinguished himself by his hostility to *Boileau. After 1789 he proclaimed himself 'le poète de la Révolution' and wrote patriotic verse, including *Le Calendrier républicain* (An IV); later he praised Napoleon and the Restoration monarchy. [PF]

Cubism. Artistic Cubism developed from *Picasso's fusion in *Les Demoiselles d'Avignon* (1907) of the lessons of *Cézanne and the forms of Negro and Iberian sculpture. Working first separately, then together, Picasso and *Braque sought to represent the complete structure of the object and its relationship of volume and space by juxtaposing different views of it in interlocking planes. As Cubism evolved, this analysis of the object's volumes and spatial extension became subordinate to the construction of an internal unity of planes, colours, and shapes in which the object was the means rather than the end.

The label 'Cubist' covers a multitude of pictorial practices which create difficulties of taxonomy when it is extended beyond painting. Even as these practices evolved during the period 1908–14, such were the contacts in Paris between avant-garde painters and poets that this extension was inevitable. *Apollinaire, in *Les Peintres cubistes* (1913), related Cubist painting to Nietzsche and non-Euclidian geometry. The same year, *Cendrars published 'the first simultaneous book', the *Prose du Transsibérien*, illustrated by Sonia *Delaunay. *Jacob considered his own poetry in *Le Cornet à dés* (1917) and that of *Reverdy to be the most Cubist. In the first issue of *Nord–Sud* (1917), Reverdy's important essay 'Sur le cubisme' established a theoretical framework for the analogies between Cubist painting and literature (notably in his aesthetic of the image), and his various projects in collaboration with Juan Gris offer important examples.

Though the diversity and range of Cubist painting make precise analogies between poems and paintings difficult to establish, it is clear that Cubism gave an important impetus to avant-garde poetics during the period 1908–14. It reinforced the idea that poetry was an autonomous intellectual structure, freed from the obligation to represent external reality, an interplay of fragmented, discontinuous verbal segments, simultaneously rather than hierarchically presented (with all that this implied for syntax, punctuation, linguistic register). This in turn led poets to define a literary lineage for these developments in the work of *Mallarmé and *Rimbaud, sometimes even to see Cubist painting as an offshoot of it. The poetry of Apollinaire, Jacob, Reverdy, *Salmon, *Cocteau, and *Albert-Birot continued actively to engage these issues. [JK]

Culte du moi, Le, see BARRÈS.

Cunégonde. Heroine of Voltaire's *Candide.

Curé de Tours, Le (1832). A scene from clerical life by Balzac, included in the *Scènes de la vie de province* in *La *Comédie humaine*.

Curé de village, Le. Novel by Balzac, first published 1838–9. A thriller set in central France, it was included in the *Scènes de la vie de campagne* of *La *Comédie humaine*.

Curée, La. Novel by *Zola, published in 1871, the second of the *Rougon-Macquart* series. It is a picture of unscrupulous financial speculation and moral corruption in Paris during the *Second Empire. Aristide, son of Pierre Rougon and brother of the hero of *Son Excellence Eugène Rougon* (1876), is a man of ruthless ambition, who has followed his brother to Paris to make his fortune. Soon after the death of his wife, he seizes the opportunity offered by a marriage of convenience to Renée Béraud du Châtel, who is pregnant by a married man and whose respectable family wishes to preserve their reputation. Taking on the name Saccard, Aristide amasses a huge fortune in shady property dealings, made possible by the *haussmannisation of Paris. His wife, avid for extravagant pleasures and new sensual experiences, embarks upon an affair with her effeminate stepson, Maxime, which Saccard tolerates out of financial interest. Abandoned by Maxime, who marries for money and status, and ruined by her husband, Renée dies soon after withdrawing from the society whose corruption she finally comes to recognize. Her husband will reappear as a financier in L'*Argent (1891). La Curée is remarkable for its evocations of Paris as a new Sodom, its highly charged imagery, its satire and parody, its descriptions of the transformation of Paris and decadent life under Napoleon III, and its reworking of the Phaedra theme. [DB]

CURIE, Marie, née Sklodowska (1867–1934). Physicist. Born in Poland, she was one of the first scientists to investigate the phenomenon which she named radio-activity. She and her fellow physicist, Pierre Curie (1859–1906), whom she married, discovered the elements polonium and radium (1898), and gave their name to a measure of radioactivity. She became the first woman professor at the *Sorbonne, against considerable odds, and a champion and role model for higher education opportunities for women. Her pioneering work gained her Nobel Prizes for physics (1903) and chemistry (1911). Her daughter and son-in-law, Irène and Frédéric Joliot-Curie, were also Nobel Prize-winning nuclear physicists. [MHK]

Currency. From the time of *Charlemagne until the *Revolution, the basic money of account used in France was the livre (originally one pound of silver), divided into 20 sous (or sols), which were in turn divided into 12 deniers (cf. English £.s.d.). After the break up of the Carolingian empire different livres were in use in different regions of France, the two principal ones being the livre tournois (used in the south) and the livre parisis (used in the *Capetian domains, valued one-fourth higher than the livre tournois). The livre parisis gradually went out of use and was abolished in 1667.

Over the centuries the metallic equivalent of the livre declined steadily as a result of royal decrees, so that by the 18th c. it was worth about 100 times less than the original quantity of silver. Coins began to be replaced by banknotes in the 17th and 18th c., although *Law's system undermined confidence in paper money. Coinage did not correspond to the money of account; among the many different coins used at various times during the ancien régime, some of the most frequently encountered are:

Écu:	in the Middle Ages a gold coin usually worth one livre; from the 17th c. a silver coin worth three livres. In more recent times the term is used to mean five francs.
Franc:	from the time of *Henri III a silver coin worth one livre.
Denier:	a coin of silver or base metal.
Liard:	a small coin worth three deniers.
Louis:	or louis d'or, gold coin first issued under Louis XIII, worth between 10 and 24 livres. During the First Empire it bore *Napoleon's effigy and was called the napoléon.
Pistole:	a gold coin of Spanish origin, equivalent of the louis; from the 18th c. the term was sometimes used to mean 10 livres or francs.

Under the Revolution the livre was officially replaced by the franc, divided into 10 décimes (this term was rarely used) or 100 centimes. The word sou continued in popular use for such expressions as 'cent sous' (5 francs). Gold and silver coins continued in official use in the 19th c., but in the early 20th c. were taken out of circulation in favour of paper money and coins of base metal.

In 1960 President de *Gaulle revalued the franc (called at first the 'nouveau franc') to 100 times its previous value. Members of the older generations continued to speak in terms of the old franc, especially for larger denominations ('un million', in slang 'une brique', for 10,000 new francs).

It is virtually impossible to give present-day equivalents for money of earlier periods. By way of illustration, in the mid-18th c. a loaf of bread might cost three sous in a good year, but several times as much in times of shortage. In the same period, the first edition of the *Encyclopédie cost nearly 1,000 livres, the first edition of *Émile 15 livres, and an annual income of 6,000 livres a year was considered 'respectable' in Paris. In the 18th c. the pound sterling was worth about 24 livres, in 1930 about 124 francs, in 1958 about 1,150 old francs, and at the end of 1992 about 8 new francs. [PF]

CURTIS, Jean-Louis (pseud. of Louis Laffitte) (b. 1917). Novelist and essayist who received the Prix Goncourt and became famous overnight for his novel Les Forêts de la nuit (1947), a portrait of Resistance and Collaboration set in a small town near the demarcation line in Occupied France during World War II. He has continued throughout his writing career to produce novels and short stories with a strong sense of social and historical background, including the aftermath of the Liberation, the consumer society of the 1960s, *May 1968, and beyond. He was elected to the Académie Française in 1987. [EAF]

CURVAL, Philippe (b. 1929). After an unsettled early career, Curval was, from 1953, one of the champions of *science fiction in France, publishing nouvelles, criticism, and collages in Fiction and Satellite. He went on to publish his first novels, *Les Fleurs de Vénus* (1960) and *Le Ressac de l'espace* (1962, Prix Jules Verne), with the collection Le Rayon Fantastique. In the course of the 1960s his work moved increasingly towards 'fiction spéculative' (e.g. *La Forteresse de coton*, 1969). With the publication in 1975 of *L'Homme à rebours* and of *Cette chère humanité* in 1976, Curval's projections of a human future were more clearly marked by *Surrealism (the oneiric and erotic) and the *roman noir*, tendencies memorably married in *Tous vers l'extase* (1981), whose heroine, Sadie mac Key, is a sexually free-wheeling feminine version of a Chandlerian private eye. Black humour, political satire, and the heroism of the Romantic rebel are the recurrent features of his recent writing.

[CS]

CUSTINE, Astolphe de (1790–1857). Scion of a noble family—his father and grandfather were both guillotined, and his mother, née Delphine de Sabran, was *Chateaubriand's mistress—Custine wrote a somewhat autobiographical novel, *Aloys* (1829), which reveals some of the tensions resulting from his homosexuality (he was involved in a public scandal in 1824 which rather served to liberate him). His most widely read book was his perspicacious *La Russie en 1839* (1843), which created a considerable polemic. His correspondence is also of exceptional interest.

[FPB]

CUVIER, Georges (1769–1832). A commanding figure in the history of biology, whose empirical discoveries, classificatory schemes, and powerful opinions placed him in the forefront of scientific debate during the first three decades of the new century. Educated in Stuttgart (1784–8), and greatly influenced by the new *Naturphilosophie*, Cuvier developed an encompassing view of animal life, present and past. As a comparative anatomist, he put forward the principle of 'correlation of parts', by which the structure and function of individual bodily parts could be related to those of the body as a whole, and in his study of fossils he used this principle in the hypothetical reconstruction of whole animals from their fragmentary remains. His firm belief in the immutability of species brought him into conflict with *Lamarck and *Geoffroy Saint-Hilaire, although much of the evidence he assembled prepared the ground for the evolutionary biology of Darwin.

[MB]

Cymbalum mundi, see DES PÉRIERS.

CYRANO DE BERGERAC, Savinien de Cyrano, known as (1619–55). One of his century's most colourful and controversial figures and most talented and original French writers. He was initially a soldier, known for his bravery. Fact and fantasy are hopelessly entangled in his subsequent biography. Already in 1640, while he was a student of the philosopher *Gassendi, contemporaries began to circulate larger-than-life legends about him, notably the story of his single-handed rout of 100 men. This triumphal image is one early example of Cyrano's gradual transformation into a fictional character, a process that culminated in *Rostand's (largely fictive) *Cyrano de Bergerac*. Cyrano's complicity in his own fictionalization is undeniable: the various signatures he began to use in the 1630s include Hercule de Bergerac and Alexandre de Cyrano Bergerac.

The young mythomaniac frequented writers, especially the *libertin* circle in which *Tristan L'Hermite and *Scarron moved. By 1645 he was known as the author of a comedy, *Le Pédant joué* (published 1654), a satire of educators and educational methods from which his friend *Molière later borrowed choice bits. Early in the *Fronde he published a number of virulent *mazarinades, notably *Le Ministre d'état flambé* (1649). He subsequently switched sides and defended Mazarin, for example in *Lettre contre les frondeurs* (1651). During this period he broke off relations with all his former literary friends. Cyrano achieved his greatest prominence after the war with the staging of his tragedy, *La *Mort d'Agrippine* (1653), especially during the ensuing scandal, when he was often accused of atheism.

As early as 1650 Cyrano was reported to have written a work called *L'*Autre Monde. However, he did not include it in his *Œuvres diverses* (1654). He undoubtedly realized that the novel was so irreverent regarding matters religious and philosophical that the censors would never have allowed it to be made public. In 1654 he was struck on the head by a falling beam, an incident for which, even in the absence of evidence, his enemies have been blamed. He died the following year from complications due to the accident. *L'Autre Monde* was finally published in 1657, under the title *Histoire comique*, in an edition heavily expurgated by the author's friend Lebret. A second posthumous edition, *Nouvelles œuvres* (1662), made public the novel's unfinished sequel, *États et empires du soleil*. His second imaginary voyage, while it contains dazzling flights of imagination, cannot compare with the sustained brilliance of *L'Autre Monde*.

Cyrano virtually disappeared from the French collective imagination throughout the 18th c. He later became a cult figure for writers such as *Nodier and *Gautier, whose rehabilitation prepared the way for Rostand's fiction and also for the editions that, in the early 20th c., finally made the unexpurgated *L'Autre Monde* available, revealing its startling originality. [See also POINTE.]

[JDeJ]

See J. DeJean, *Libertine Strategies* (1981).

Cyrano de Bergerac (1897). Swashbuckling and fanciful verse drama on the above by *Rostand, a great popular success, and in 1990 the basis of a best-selling film starring *Depardieu.

Cyrus (or *Le Grand Cyrus*), see ARTAMÈNE.

D

DABIT, Eugène (1898–1936). French novelist, diarist, painter, and art critic. His *Hôtel du Nord* (1929), the basis for *Carné's film, won the first Prix du Roman Populiste in 1931. He was a Parisian locksmith by trade, then a talented painter before turning to literature. A socialist and an authentic reporter of contemporary working-class life, he wrote mainly of the *petites gens* of the capital in soberly realistic novels—*Petit Louis* (1930), *Un mort tout neuf* (1934)—or stories (*Faubourgs de Paris*, 1933; *Train de vies*, 1936). His fine *Journal intime* (1936) records his melancholic sensitivity and self-questioning. He died suddenly on a visit with *Gide to Soviet Russia. [DAS]

DACIER, André (1651–1722). Student of the noted classicist Tanneguy Le Fèvre, he married his childhood friend and fellow classical scholar Anne Lefebvre *Dacier. He edited and/or translated, among others, Aristotle, Plato, Sophocles, and Plutarch. He was a member of the Académie Française and defended the ancients in the *Querelle des Anciens et des Modernes. [JDeJ]

DACIER, Anne, née Lefebvre, (c.1651–1720). The greatest French woman Hellenist, the most celebrated Hellenist of her day, and a world-class philologist whose editions remained authoritative for decades. She was the daughter and student of the noted humanist and classicist Tanneguy Le Fèvre. She married another of his students, André *Dacier. She was among the directors of the famous *ad usum Delphini* collection of classical texts [see DAUPHIN]. She edited and/or translated, among others, Homer, Sappho, Aristophanes, Anacreon, and Plautus. Her *Des causes de la corruption du goût* (1714) was a major defence of the ancients in the *Querelle des Anciens et des Modernes. [JDeJ]

Dada. Launching an out-and-out attack on received values in the arts and in culture at large, the Dada movement erupted almost simultaneously in different cities amid the turmoil of World War I: there were Dada groups in Zurich, Berlin, Cologne, Hanover, even New York and Barcelona, as well as in Paris. It received its name (meaning 'gee-gee', but reputedly chosen at random from a dictionary) at a gathering in Zurich in the spring of 1916, where the Dadaists sabotaged all preconceptions by their wild multi-media antics at the Cabaret Voltaire. From Zurich, the Dada virus was transported to France in the person of Tristan *Tzara; his eagerly awaited arrival in January 1920 catalysed a Paris group led by *Breton and *Aragon, whose journal *Littérature* had already veered alarmingly away from the cultural orientation of its title. There ensued a brief yet impassioned season of provocations and scandals, largely orchestrated by Tzara and culminating in a 'Festival Dada' held at the respectable Salle Gaveau in May 1921, when an exasperated audience threw vegetables at the Dadaists on stage as they made weird music, or declaimed nonsense poems and outrageous manifestos of destruction. A crisis in the group surfaced at the mock-trial *in absentia* of Maurice *Barrès, targeted as the incarnation of establishment rectitude: it emerged that Tzara wanted only to engage in negative clowning, while Breton and others were intent on drawing up an indictment of the cultural system as a prelude to organized reconstruction. The ensuing quarrels and scissions in the group led to Dada's demise and a period of gradual and difficult reorientation that saw the stirrings of nascent *Surrealism.

A short-lived but exemplary gesture, Dada represented the least inhibited challenge one could imagine to the ideology underlying bourgeois culture and art: it was anti-patriotic, anti-aesthetic, and anti-conventional in the extreme. It was also, in principle, against permanence, yet, paradoxically, it left a legacy of enduring works, from the baffling though often funny pictures of *Picabia and the young Max Ernst to the free-wheeling poems of Tzara and *Péret, and the astringent prose of Jacques *Rigaut and the early Aragon. Among its most satisfying products are dual-media collaborations such as *Éluard's *Les Malheurs des immortels* (1922), with collages by Ernst, and Tzara's *Cinéma calendrier du cœur abstrait* (1920), with woodcuts by Hans Arp. [RC]

See M. Sanouillet, *Dada à Paris* (1965).

DADIÉ, Bernard Binlin (b. 1916). Poet, playwright, and 'chronicler' from Ivory Coast. His autobiographical novel *Climbié* (1956) tells of his schooling, work in the fields, followed by the École *William Ponty and work in the education department of the AOF in Dakar. Experiences of the hardships of rural life under the colonial regime and discovery of the works of Marcus Garvey turned him into a political activist; Charles Béart's enthusiasm for theatrical activities at William Ponty inspired him to become a playwright; discussions with Alioune *Diop attached him to the *négritude movement and confirmed him as a committed poet. He founded the periodical *Dakar Jeunes*, in which he published traditional folk-tales, retold in French, and in addition issued two slim volumes of poetry, before returning to Ivory Coast, where his political activities led to his imprisonment in 1949. One of the most prolific and gifted of this early generation of African writers, Dadié's literary works (apart from his political journalism) fall into the following categories:

(i) *Poetry*. After the juvenilia mentioned above came *Afrique debout!* (1950), a clarion call to arms to his people and a litany of protest against colonial domination. In *La Ronde des jours* (1954), less truculent, the defiance is tempered with Christian humility. This volume contains one of the most moving and dignified protest poems of the *négritude* movement, 'Je vous remercie mon Dieu, de m'avoir créé Noir'. *Hommes de tous les continents* (1967) shows a maturing of Dadié's philosophy, his humanism, and his command of subtler poetic effects.

(ii) *Folklore*. Work at the Institut Français d'Afrique Noire inspired him to collect material from the oral heritage of Ivory Coast for *Légendes africaines* (1953) and *Le Pagne noir* (1955), which include historical legends, cosmogonic myths, moral fables, and spider stories. *Les Belles Histoires de Kakou Ananze, l'Araignée* (1979) are spider stories presented as a school reader.

(iii) *Drama*. First produced in 1936, *Assémien Déhylé, chronique agni* was presented by the William Ponty pupils in Paris for the Exposition Internationale in 1937 and published as *Assémien Déhylé, roi du Sanwi* (1965), a series of tableaux interspersed with aphorisms and local wisdom. *Papassidi, maître escroc* (1975) is a Moliéresque farce about a charlatan, while *Monsieur Thôgô-Gnini* (1970) offers the comic portrait of a profiteer and seducer, illustrating the evils accompanying the arrival of the white man in Africa. *Béatrice du Congo* (1970), a pageant of symbolic events covering the history of the colonization of West Africa by the Portuguese, is an anti-colonial diatribe in tragic mode. *Les Voix dans le vent* (1970), an allegorical tragedy, studies the corrupting influence of power, and *Îles de tempête* (1973) traces the history of the colonization of *Haiti. In *Mhoi Ceul* (1979) Dadié returns to social satire.

(iv) *Fiction. Climbié*, published as a novel, is autobiography. In 1980 two volumes of short stories, *Commandant Taureault et ses nègres* and *Les Jambes du fils de Dieu*, set in the colonial era, are inspired by the author's early memories.

(v) *Other prose works*. Dadié's travels in Europe and America furnish him with material for ironic chronicles. *Un nègre à Paris* (1959), based on his first journey to France, adopts the artifice of a supposed long epistle to an African correspondent. *Patron de New York* (1964) and *La Ville où nul ne meurt* (Rome) (1968) continue his meditations on the influences moulding different societies. These chronicles, like Dadié's dramatic works, demonstrate his virtuosity in handling the resources of the French language, juggling with idiom, puns, and adding new dimensions to worn-out clichés. *Opinions d'un nègre* (1979) is a collection of aphorisms, summing up his mature philosophy. [DSB]

See C. Quillateau, *Bernard Binlin Dadié* (1967).

DAGUERRE, Louis-Jacques-Mandé (1787–1851). Inventor of a 'diorama', a popular attraction creating illusions of nature, and (with Nicéphore Niépce) of the daguerreotype, one of the earliest photographic processes, whose existence was officially announced in 1839.

DAIVE, Jean (b. 1941). French poet, founder in 1970 of the journal *Fragment*. He has published several interrelated volumes, including a sequence with the general title *Narration d'équilibre* (1982–90). His tense, elliptical poems explore the difficulties of existence in an enigmatic world. [PF]

DAKEYO, Paul (b. 1948). Cameroonian poet, anthologist, and publisher. In 1980 he founded Silex Éditions in Paris where he now lives. A committed poet, Dakeyo has published several volumes, including *Les Barbelés du matin* (1973), *Chant d'accusation* (1976), *Soweto! Soleils fusillés* (1977), and *La Femme où j'ai mal* (1989). He has edited, in collaboration with others, three anthologies of African poetry, and notably *Aube d'un jour nouveau* (1981), devoted to South African poets in French translation. [VC]

D'ALEMBERT, see ALEMBERT.

DAMAS, Léon-Gontran (1912–78). Poet of *négritude, associated with *Senghor and Aimé *Césaire in the literary expression of a specifically black consciousness. Born in Cayenne, French Guiana, a fragile asthmatic child, Damas studied at the Lycée Schoelcher, Martinique, and then in Paris, mixing with black students, artists, and workers from Africa and the Americas, who were active in the margins of small magazines (*Légitime défense, L'*Étudiant noir*). Studies in ethnology resulted in a 1934 mission to the maroon 'Noirs réfugiés' of French Guiana. He briefly played a more active political role, succeeding René Jadfard as Socialist *député* in 1948–51. Involved in publishing and radio work, he travelled widely, collecting material for anthologies of black poetry, giving lectures and readings, epitomizing the evangelical post-war solidarity of *Présence africaine*. From 1970 to his death he was based at Howard University, Washington, DC.

The early poetic collection *Pigments* (1937) was a landmark in the expression of major *négritude* themes, outlining the traumatic history of the New World slave ('La Complainte du nègre'), reclaiming lost Africa ('Limbé'), and dwelling on the alienation of the black man in European society ('Solde', 'Un clochard m'a demandé dix sous', 'Pareille à ma légende'). Most memorably, Damas created in 'Hoquet' a sarcastic monologue which dramatizes the voice of a mother scolding a little mulatto boy who resists being socialized into French respectability: table manners and catechism, history homework and piano lessons, and of course 'le français de France'—a rueful, witty view of *assimilation* at its most painful and intimate. Much offence was given by poems mocking the loyalty to France of black troops, and Damas was outspoken against European racism. In form his best poems are strongly rhythmical, with the colloquial verve of oral tradition in their repetitions and word-play, and a particular skill in melodic 'blues' ('Il est des nuits'). Other, more lyrical collections (*Névralgies*, 1966) have not attracted the same interest, though the extended confessional poem in four movements, *Black-Label* (1956), has been successfully dramatized with musical accompaniment.

Damas's pre-war return home inspired two prose works: *Retour de Guyane* (1938), a bitter survey deploring the state of a still-wretchedly underdeveloped penal colony, and *Veillées noires* (1943), a volume of *Creole folktales, adapted into French and seasoned with the author's characteristic sardonic wit. Damas was relatively little read in French Guiana until his death inspired the creation of a literary magazine, *La Torche*. [BJ]

See D. Racine *Léon-Gontran Damas: l'homme et l'œuvre* (1983); K. Q. Warner (ed.) *Critical Perspectives on Léon-Gontran Damas* (1988).

Dame aux camélias, La, see DUMAS FILS.

Dame de chez Maxim, La, see FEYDEAU, G.

DAMIENS, Robert-François (1714–57). Author in 1757 of an attempt on the life of Louis XV which alarmed the authorities about the possible subversive effects of *Enlightenment ideas. Condemned to a horrible death, he is said to have remarked: 'La journée sera rude', to the huge admiration of *Diderot.

Damnés de la terre, Les, see FANON.

D'Amour, P.Q., see GODBOUT.

DANCOURT, Florent Carton (1661–1725). French playwright. Having trained as a lawyer, he married an actress in 1680 and entered the theatre. After a brief provincial career, he and his wife joined the Comédie-Française in 1685 and worked with it until his retirement in 1718. His talents were appreciated by royalty, and he acted as orator for the company; he also gave his name to *dancourades*, one-act plays written to support the main performance. Many of his shorter plays (e.g. *Les Vendanges de Suresnes*, 1695) retained their popularity until the 19th c., while of his five-act comedies the most notable are *Le Chevalier à la mode* (1687) and *Les Bourgeoises à la mode* (1692). He was particularly gifted in writing lively satirical sketches with a topical flavour. His general view, like that of *Regnard and *Lesage, is one of amusing and morally uncommitted cynicism which, though inherently critical, remained within the prevailing limits of acceptability. [JD]

Dandy, dandysme. 'Le dandysme est un soleil couchant', wrote *Baudelaire in *Le Peintre de la vie moderne* (1863), an aristocratic mode of being which was doomed to extinction by the inexorable rise of republicanism in 19th c. France. It was in the 1820s and 1830s that the largely British phenomenon of the dandy, exemplified in different ways by Byron and Brummel, found a French home among the Anglophile aristocratic exquisites who cultivated in their art of dress and manners an aesthetic unity with which to express their superiority over the utilitarian values of the rising bourgeoisie. *Musset in 'Mardoche' (*Contes d'Espagne et d'Italie*, 1830), *Gautier in *Fortunio* (1838), and *Balzac, in numerous essays and novels, gave the dandy a central place in their critique of contemporary culture. With *Barbey d'Aurévilly's 1844 essay on Brummel, the literary representation of the dandy gives way to a philosophy of *dandysme* in which artificiality, detachment, self-control, and the cult of surprise become active spiritual exercises through which the dandy maintains a stoic, existential revolt. Baudelaire espoused these views except for the detachment, and saw *Guys as the modern artist most representative of a less blasé dandyism. *Mallarmé extended in *La Dernière Mode* (1874) dandyism's poetics of fashion, but le *dandysme* returned to marginality through association with the *decadent spirit embodied in Des Esseintes's pursuit of refined, artificial sensation (Huysmans, *A Rebours*). The changes consequent on World War I consigned it to history, one which *Camus analysed in *L'Homme révolté* (1951) as that of the destructive, nihilist side of the *Romantic revolt. [JK]

DANGEAU, Philippe de Courcillon, marquis de (1638–1720). Soldier, diplomat, and consummate courtier, he kept a *Journal* from 1684 onwards in which he recorded impassively events both great and small. Though curiously flat, it is a valuable primary source for the reign of *Louis XIV and was much used by *Saint-Simon, who found it infuriatingly boring. [PF]

DANIEL, Gabriel, père, see HISTORIOGRAPHY, 8.

DANIEL-ROPS, Henri (pseud. of Henri Petiot) (1901–65). French writer and Church historian. He wrote many novels and essays on edifying themes, and a major *Histoire de l'Église*. A Catholic humanist, Daniel-Rops was a staunch European federalist; he was elected to the Académie Française in 1955.

Danse macabré. Jean *Lefèvre uses the expression in 1376—so spelt consistently until the 16th c.—and may possibly have written a poem so named, but the first documented manifestation of the theme in France are the frescos painted at the Cimetière des Innocents in Paris in 1424–5. They consisted iconographically of a series of couples, a mummified *Mort* with a living victim, arranged hierarchically, lay and cleric, from pope and emperor to hermit and babe-in arms, and framed by images of an *Acteur* (author). Underneath were verses, each dancer being allocated one eight-line octosyllabic stanza: the message combines a *memento mori* with satisfaction at Death's levelling of the estates. The frescos were destroyed, but the verses were copied and printed in 1485 by the Parisian printer Guyot Marchant, with fine engravings possibly drawn from the Innocents. A *Danse macabré des femmes* followed in 1486, possibly devised by *Martial d'Auvergne.

Several uncertainties subsist: the word *macabré* is unknown before 1376 and its precise meaning is obscure (it has been traced to Hebrew and Arabic roots; the motif may have German origins; the idea of a dance may have roots in folklore; the message may be related to mendicant sermons. Its popularity, however, was remarkable: images and verses were copied in churches all over France, and in manuscripts and incunabula. The motif remained popular beyond the 16th c. and figures in 18th-c. chapbooks [see BIBLIOTHÈQUE BLEUE]. [JHMT]

Dans le labyrinthe, see ROBBE-GRILLET.

DANTON, Georges-Jacques (1759–94). French Revolutionary leader and orator of great stature. His influence over both *Commune and people helped prepare the fall of the monarchy. Originally indefatigable in defence of the popular revolution as minister of justice (August 1792) and as a Conventionnel (in 1792–3 he galvanized resistance to invasion and helped found the revolutionary armies, then in March 1793 initiated the Revolutionary Tribunal and, the following month, became a founding member of the Comité de Salut Public), he veered gradually towards moderation. Though he was for a time a supporter of *Robespierre in the attack on dechristianizers and *Hébertistes, his espousal of *indulgence* ultimately gave his opponents the opportunity to dispose of him as an 'enemy of the Republic'. He was guillotined on 5 April 1794 after a farcical trial.

As a vigorous orator, who often spoke extempore, Danton had few rivals. Some of his statements have become proverbial. His speech on 2 September 1792 to the Assemblée Législative after the Battle of Longwy contained the stirringly immortal: 'Le tocsin qui va sonner n'est point un signal d'alarme, c'est la charge sur les ennemis de la patrie. Pour les vaincre, Messieurs, il faut *de l'audace, encore de l'audace, toujours de l'audace* et la France est sauvée.' [JR]

DARD, Frédéric (b. 1921). Prolific French author of parodic detective fiction, much of it under the penname of San-Antonio, the sexually irresistible and apparently immortal narrator-hero of over 150 linguistically inventive novellas. Dard's Rabelaisian style, combining vulgarity with punning neologisms, is occasionally as brilliant as the *néo-français* of Queneau's *Zazie dans le métro*, which it resembles. His self-designatedly 'big' novels, notably *La Vieille Dame qui marchait dans la mer* (1988), give a vision of life as sombre as those of *Simenon, whose

La Neige était sale Dard also adapted for the stage. Dard's ribald plots are often weak, his reappearing characters are shallow; but his vast output, motivated by Christian moral convictions, can be read as an irreverent answer in a 'low culture' genre to the 'high theory' of the *Nouveau Roman. [DMB]

DARIEN, Georges (pseud. of Georges Adrien) (1862–1921). French novelist, polemicist, founder of the review *L'Escarmouche* (1893–4). Little is known of his life. Of Protestant descent, Darien attended the Lycée Charlemagne in Paris. In 1881 he enlisted and served five years in North Africa, of which almost a whole year was spent in a military prison-camp. Between 1893 and 1905 he lived frequently in London; his financial situation remains a mystery. After his first novel, *Bas les cœurs!* (1889), a corrosive satire of the panicky Versailles bourgeoisie in 1870–1, Darien inflates in *Biribi* (1890) his experiences in a North African disciplinary battalion into a savage indictment of official brutality. Less focused, *Les Pharisiens* (1891) is a highly ambivalent attack on profiteering antisemitism. In 1897 came his best novel, *Le *Voleur*.

Darien's major essay, *La Belle France* (1900), excoriates the forces ranged against individualism from the viewpoint of an alienated patriot. It is by turns exhilarating and infuriating. A comparable mixture of intimate acquaintance and extraterritorial perspective energizes *L'Épaulette* (1905). This novel concerns itself with military castes rather than outcasts, as in *Biribi*. The army is second nature to the trimmer father and the narrating, brain-warped son. Though weak-willed, the son manages to unveil familial, social, and military scandals. The device of a semi-assimilated but open-eyed narrator gives *L'Épaulette* genuine bite and density. Darien also wrote, in English, *Gottlieb Krumm, Made in England* (1904), a fascinating study of an immigrant con-man. Darien's general proneness to melodrama and to speechifying spokespeople works against, but does not finally outweigh, his penetrating gaze, pointed wit, and capacity for sustained indignation. He escapes pigeonholing on Right or Left. [WDR]

DAUBENTON, Louis-Jean-Maire (1716–99). French naturalist. He collaborated with *Buffon on the volumes of the *Histoire naturelle* concerning animals. A member of the Académie des Sciences, he worked in the Jardin du Roi (later *Jardin des Plantes), organized the Muséum, lectured, published many scientific papers, and was a pioneer of French sheep-breeding. [PF]

DAUDET, Alphonse (1840–97). French novelist and story-teller. He was born in Nîmes and died in Paris after a long illness. He began his writing career in 1858 with a collection of poems, *Les Amoureuses*, followed by a short story in verse, *La Double Conversion* (1861), and theatrical sketches, but he finally established himself as a writer of prose fiction and succeeded in becoming a popular author who also appealed to more discriminating readers.

His most lasting works are *Le Petit Chose* (1868), a partly autobiographical novel of which the first section is quite closely related to his own boyhood, his *Lettres de mon moulin* (1869), evoking scenes of life in Provence, and the *Contes du lundi* (1873) and *Contes et récits* (1873), primarily patriotic tales related to his experiences during the *Franco-Prussian War. He is remembered particularly for his larger-than-life, ambitious, and cowardly *provençal* character *Tartarin, in *Tartarin de Tarascon* (1872) and subsequent novels, and for *Numa Roumestan* (1881), dwelling on the contrast between *méridional* and Parisian life. His later novels of Parisian manners are less known. Although he is commonly associated with *Naturalist realism, his most memorable works are delicate transpositions and subtle evocations of human suffering. [BCS]

DAUDET, Léon (1867–1942). French novelist, essayist, journalist, and polemicist. Eschewing the delicate impressionism of his father Alphonse [see above], Léon abandoned a medical career to attain fame with his novel *Les Morticoles* (1894) before embracing reactionary monarchism and becoming the thunderous editor and daily leader-writer of *L'*Action française*, where he rampaged as an extremist bully in the French politico-literary china shop. Abhorred and beloved for his virulent prejudices, purple diatribes, and scandal-ridden private life, he was a prolific author and a more important writer and social commentator than he has generally hitherto been judged—see *Le Voyage de Shakespeare* (1896), *Fantômes et vivants* (1914), *L'Hérédo* (1916), *Le Rêve éveillé* (1926), *Écrivains et artistes* (8 vols., 1927–9), *Paris vécu* (2 vols., 1929–30). [DAS]

DAUMAL, René (1908–44). The major theoretician of the group Le *Grand Jeu. After he had met Alexandre de Salzmann and then Gurdjieff, his quest for authentic spiritual experience led him to the East, to Hinduism, and to the sacred Sanscrit texts, some of which he translated. In his lifetime he published the gnomic, or ironic, or colloquial poems of *Le Contre-Ciel* (1936) and the *'pataphysical *récit*, *La Grande Beuverie* (1938). His posthumous publications include *Le Mont Analogue* (1952), an allegorical account of a journey to another world, the essays and notes of *Chaque fois que l'arbre paraît* (1953), *Poésie noire, poésie blanche* (1954), the metaphysical treatise *Tu t'es toujours trompé* (1970), and *Mugle* (1978), a series of prose cantos vaguely reminiscent of *Lautréamont's *Les Chants de Maldoror*. His writings stress the importance of negation as a positive act, together with an eternal quest for poetry, self-knowledge, and the Absolute. [KRA]

DAUMIER, Honoré (1808–79). French lithographer and cartoonist, whose memorable satirical images

of life during the July Monarchy and the Second Empire attracted many readers to papers such as *La Caricature*, *Le *Figaro*, and *Le *Charivari*. It was in *Le Charivari* that he published his legendary Robert Macaire series, devoted to the fraudulent dealings of a character first invented in a melodrama of 1823 (*L'Auberge des Adrets*) and played by Frédérick *Lemaître. [PF]

DAUNOU, Pierre-Claude-François (1761–1840). *Idéologue politician and historian who played an important role in formulating the education policy of the Directoire [see REVOLUTION, 1d]. In addition to politics he pursued an administrative and academic career and was *Michelet's superior at the Archives Nationales. He wrote a study of the papacy. The lectures he delivered at the *Collège de France were published posthumously as *Cours d'études historiques* (1842–5). [CC]

Dauphin. Originally the title of the rulers of Dauphiné (who had a dolphin on their coat of arms), this became the title of the eldest son of the king of France after Dauphiné was ceded to France in 1349. The classics 'ad usum Delphini' were texts by Greek and Roman authors edited for the son of *Louis XIV ('le Grand Dauphin') under the direction of *Huet and *Bossuet.

Daurel et Beton. 12th-c. Occitan *chanson de geste* on the theme of male friendship. Two companions enter a pact that one will inherit the assets, including the wife, of the other. The poorer of the two murders his friend in a faked hunting accident, assumes his estates, and forcibly marries the reluctant widow. The surviving son, Beton, is rescued from the murderer by a *jongleur, Daurel, who is so loyal to his old lord that he sacrifices his own baby to save his lord's child. They flee together, and when Beton grows up he defeats the treacherous companion and regains his land. After some 2,000 lines the sole manuscript breaks off at the point when Beton prepares to attack *Charlemagne, who had sanctioned the traitor's transactions. [SK]

DAVID, Jacques-Louis (1748–1825). French painter. A brilliant *Neoclassicist, David responded in his paintings to contemporary philosophical, political, and literary developments during France's most dynamic period of change. Much of his work during the Revolution was ephemeral, in the form of pageants and huge propaganda processions [see FÊTES RÉVOLUTIONNAIRES]. He was dictator of the arts after the execution of Louis XVI. His subjects, originally drawn from classical mythology, moved to the Stoic writers propounding national as opposed to domestic virtues. His most famous works, *The Oath of the Horatii* and *Brutus*, were executed in the 1780s. The theme of the suffering hero, sacrificing personal, family loyalties to state duties (e.g. *The Death of Marat*, 1793) was replaced by the idea of conciliation (*Sabine Women*, 1799) and then

Débâcle, La

by the hero triumphant (*Napoleon crossing the Alps*) during the Empire. David drew inspiration from the Antique but also from his great 17th-c. compatriot *Poussin. His character was complex, and much of his portraiture of condemned aristocrats has a strong element of Romantic handling and interpretation.   [JPC]

Débâcle, La. Novel by *Zola, published 1892, the 19th in the *Rougon-Macquart* series. The setting is the *Franco-Prussian War, France's disastrous defeat at Sedan, and the *Commune of 1871. The novel follows the fortunes and friendship of two French soldiers, Jean Macquart, who was the protagonist in La *Terre*, and Maurice Levasseur. These characters are supposed to represent two opposing sides of France: Jean, the reasonable, wise, and healthy pragmatist; Maurice, the wild Romantic dreamer, seeking glory and justice. After suffering together the painful preliminaries of war and the horrors of the Battle of Sedan, which occupy most of the novel, the two men find themselves on opposing sides in the civil strife. Symbolically, Jean, now in the Versailles army, inflicts a lethal wound on his 'brother', now a *communard*, when they meet by coincidence fighting on a barricade. Despite the fearful bloodshed, the novel ends on an optimistic note of renewal.   [DB]

DEBARS, Riel. Poet from Reunion. *Sirène de fin d'alerte* (1979) is protest poetry which denies the realities of the exotic tradition and focuses on the poverty of Debars's native island.   [BEJ]

DEBORD, Guy, see SITUATIONISM.

DEBRAY, Régis (b. 1941). French intellectual and novelist. After studying at the *École Normale Supérieure under *Althusser, he travelled widely in Latin America, studying revolutionary strategies and eventually accepting a philosophy chair in Havana. He joined Che Guevara's guerillas in Bolivia, was arrested in 1967, and spent three years in prison. Debray has written prolifically, reformulating Marxist political theory, and in *Le Pouvoir intellectuel en France* (1979) and *Le Scribe* (1980) analysing the relation between intellectuals, the media, and the state. He was appointed political adviser to President *Mitterrand in 1981. His novels, including *La Neige brûle* (1977), draw on his Latin American experiences and explore the connection between personal relations and political commitment.   [MHK]

DEBUSSY, Claude (1862–1918). Possibly the French composer most influenced by literature, Debussy was involved in literary circles, was friendly with the important literary men of his time, and reportedly drew more inspiration from literature than from music. In his musical *œuvre*, works with text predominate, the most numerous of which are his 87 solo songs. The writers who were most important to his music were the *Parnassians and

*Symbolists: *Banville, *Baudelaire, *Verlaine, *Mallarmé, *Louÿs, and *Maeterlinck. His greatest number of songs have words by Verlaine, and in general he appears to have been most inspired musically by poetry of merit. Debussy wrote his own poems for the song cycle *Proses lyriques* and some libretti based on *Poe short stories. He was also a music critic from 1901 to 1914.

In his setting of texts Debussy was always sensitive to the rhythms and natural inflections of the French language. This is particularly evident in his opera *Pelléas et Mélisande* (1902), but also apparent in his songs. Apart from these, many other works were inspired by literary texts (including a large number of unfinished stage works). See, for instance, his incidental music for *Le Martyre de Saint Sébastien* (1911) to a text by Gabriele d'Annunzio, and his orchestral work based on Mallarmé, *Prélude à l'après-midi d'un faune* (composed 1892–4).   [KM]

Decadence. The late 19th-c. Decadence is a European phenomenon with its focal point in the Paris of the 1880s and 1890s: *Haussmann's metropolis, reconstructed to answer the needs of mass society, expanding capital, and the nascent mass market. The themes and motifs of Les *Fleurs du mal* (1867), Baudelaire's complicit satire of bourgeois corruption, Richard Wagner's hymns to the decay of culture and aristocracy and the apotheosis of love and death, together with the new feminine icons and fantastic landscapes of the English Pre-Raphaelite poets and painters, all contribute to the representation of a specific political moment and mood, out of whose complexities was to emerge much of 20th-c. European modernism.

In France itself, the Decadent moment spans the period between the *Commune of 1871 and *World War I. At first ambivalent, it sometimes appears as a regenerative revolt against the mediocrity of bourgeois consensus in, for example, the novels of the socialist Jean Lombard (*L'Agonie*, 1888; *Byzance*, 1890) or the anarchist Octave *Mirbeau. But the weight of the movement is conservative, clinging to traditional concepts of authority, hierarchy, and power in opposition to the challenges of contemporary socialism and feminism. With the help of new techniques of large-scale printing, reproduction, and distribution, the writers and painters of the Decadence peddled an élitist ideology to the pre-political masses of a new consumer society.

The (mis-)representations of decadent dream are simple stereotypes drawn from old prejudice. Life is portrayed as a conflict between the virtuous male spirit and evil feminine nature. Woman is the scapegoat, vampire (Helen, Salome, Medusa), or victim (Ophelia, Galatea). Man is the Artist or Magus, creator of all things, frustrated by Woman and the mob. His art enshrines his neurotic impotence and the perversion of his frustrated desire: an adolescent eroticism, marked by fetishism, violence, incest, torture, homophobia (often, a repressed homophilia), murder, and madness (see the short stories and novels of *Rachilde, Jean *Lorrain, *Huysmans, *Louÿs). In the 1880s revived interest in the marquis de *Sade went hand-in-hand with the vogue for Leopold von Sacher-Masoch. The ghoulish terror of the mask, evoked by Jean Lorrain, is a key symbol. Elsewhere, rage at the refusal of the natural world to be confined by the frame of individual will finds a different expression in mystical evasions. A variety of occult systems provide new languages for artistic discourse: *Rosicrucianism, Theosophy, Satanism (see e.g. the epic novel cycle *La Décadence latine*, 1884–1907, by Joséphin *Péladan, founder of the Salons de la Rose+Croix).

Decadent style oscillates between often-parodied cliché and significant linguistic experiment. Huysmans's and de *Gourmont's rediscovery of the gamey style of the Latin Decadence, their interest in rare, specialist, technical vocabulary, or in the manipulation of language (after Baudelaire) to collapse the positivist boundaries between sense-experience, represent influential efforts to engineer the decay of language and generate new forms. [JB]

See J. Birkett, *The Sins of the Fathers: Decadence in France 1870–1914* (1986); B. Dijkstra, *Idols of Perversity: Fantasies of Feminine Evil in Fin-de-Siècle Culture* (1986); M. Teich and R. Porter (eds.), *Fin de Siècle and its Legacy* (1990).

Décade philosophique, littéraire et politique, La. The *Décade*, founded by *Ginguené in 1794, appeared every ten days, in accordance with the *Revolutionary calendar. Favoured by the Directoire, it had many important contributors and was a vehicle for the *Idéologues. Against the spiritualism of *Chateaubriand's *Génie du christianisme* it defended *Enlightenment values, and became an organ for the liberal opposition under *Napoleon, who obliged it to fuse with the *Mercure de France* in 1807. [PF]

Décentralisation théâtrale, La. State-sponsored programme launched in 1947 to remedy the lack of theatrical provision in the provinces. It had long been recognized that the capital's cultural hegemony, encapsulated in the catch-phrase 'Paris et le désert', effectively meant that the majority of French people were theatrically disenfranchized. Whereas earlier attempts to remedy this situation— e.g. *Gémier's Théâtre National Ambulant (1911–12)—had been abortive, the post-war programme under the direction of Jeanne Laurent created seven Centres Dramatiques Nationaux: Le Grenier de Toulouse, the Centres Dramatiques de l'Est (Strasbourg), de l'Ouest (Rennes), du Sud-Est (Aix-en Provence), and du Nord (Tourcoing), La Comédie de Saint-Étienne, and Le Théâtre de la Cité (Villeurbanne). A second tier was created by the provision of subsidies for a number of existing semi-permanent provincial companies, some of which were designated Troupes Permanentes.

Further impetus derived from a parallel programme launched in 1959 to create provincial *Maisons de la Culture (often endowed with excellent up-to-date theatre facilities). Of the numerous festivals which have also sprung up since the war, the most flourishing are those of *Avignon and Nancy. Although often marked by local disagreements over objectives and specific programmes, *décentralisation* has been a major achievement of French cultural politics and has led to some of the most innovative and creative theatrical work being conducted in the provinces [see THEATRES AND AUDIENCES, 2]. [DWW]

Déclaration des droits de l'homme et du citoyen. This canonic text, consisting of 17 articles and a preamble, was adopted by the Assemblée Nationale on 26 August 1789 [see REVOLUTION, 1b]. It was the work of a committee, and draws on the American Declaration of Independence as well as the ideas of *Rousseau, *Montesquieu, *Mably, and the *Physiocrats. Few changes have been introduced over the last 200 years. The declaration does not have force of law, but is a founding text of the French *republican tradition. The basic rights enshrined in it are freedom, property, security, and resistance to oppression. It makes no mention of women [see GOUGES]. [PF]

Decolonization. Most of the overseas territories colonized by France during the 19th and 20th c. [see COLONIZATION] gained their independence between 1945 and 1962. A similar process of decolonization occurred at about the same time in the overseas empires of the other European powers. It resulted from a combination of developments both within the colonies and in the wider international environment. During the early decades of the 20th c. Western-educated native élites became increasingly articulate in their political demands. World War II weakened the colonial powers, and persuaded many that it was time to divest themselves of their overseas possessions.

While decolonization was in this sense part of a general historical trend, it proved in many ways a more difficult experience for France than for other colonial powers such as Great Britain. Because of the humiliation suffered by France during the German *Occupation of 1940–4, leading politicians generally resisted decolonization, seeing in the overseas empire a means of reasserting the country's status as a great power. Writers and intellectuals were also slow to embrace the trend towards decolonization. While many, such as the liberal and leftist Christians grouped around the review *Esprit*, criticized the excesses of colonialism, few wished to see the end of empire as such. Contributors to Sartre's *Les *Temps modernes* were relatively isolated in calling for the outright independence of colonial territories. Although independence was eventually granted to most sub-Saharan colonies with

223

Decolonization

relatively little bloodshed, the French relinquished *Indo-China and *Algeria only after long and bitter wars.

The conferring of independence was not in the logic of French colonial traditions. The instincts of most policy-makers were heavily conditioned by the concept of *assimilation*, which, far from preparing for separation, envisaged an ever-closer affiliation between France and her overseas possessions. Assimilation, which promised the wholesale diffusion of French civilization, was initially accepted as an ideal by many among the French-educated élites which gradually emerged from among the native peoples overseas. There was impatience, however, over the flagrant inequalities which persisted between colonizers and colonized, and this would later turn to distrust over the sincerity of French promises. The denigration of native cultures implicit in the idea of assimilation was also challenged by increasing numbers of non-Europeans, giving rise to the *négritude* movement among black African and Caribbean intellectuals during the 1930s. The anti-colonial aspects of Marxist ideology influenced those who, like the Vietnamese nationalist Nguyen Ai Quoc (later known as Ho Chi-Minh), visited the Soviet Union between the wars.

The success of the Bolshevik Revolution in 1917 had established for the first time a significant power prepared to back anti-colonial struggles. Though initially weak and compelled to moderate its stance when threatened by the rise of fascism, the Soviet Union helped to render the international climate less conducive to colonialism, as did the anti-colonial rhetoric voiced by leading American politicians. World War II greatly accelerated the forces leading towards decolonization. Defeated and occupied by Nazi Germany, France was shown to be far more vulnerable than many in the colonies had previously thought. The dwarfing of the European powers by the victorious American and Soviet allies placed further international constraints on the colonial system.

In 1936 Syria and Lebanon, over which France had gained control in 1920 under a League of Nations mandate already conditioned by American misgivings over colonialism, were promised independence within three years. Although this was delayed, initially by internal disturbances and later by the course of the war, in 1945 the two countries became the first to gain their independence from France. Yet de *Gaulle, who, after rallying resistance to the Nazi occupation, headed France's first post-war government, was determined to hold on to the rest of the empire. During the war he had used the colonies as a base from which to work for the liberation of France. The Brazzaville Conference, organized at his initiative in 1944 to lay down a blueprint for the empire after the war, specifically ruled out independence or even autonomy.

During the war French authority in Indo-China, which had remained loyal to the collaborationist Vichy government, had been weakened by Japanese expansionism. In 1945 the nationalist Viet-Minh, led by Ho Chi-Minh, seized control of Vietnam and declared the country independent. De Gaulle refused to recognize these claims. When he left office the following year the seeds were sown for the Indo-China War (1946–54), during which France unsuccessfully attempted to reimpose her authority by military means.

Conscious of the growing criticisms aroused by the colonial system, in 1946 the constitution-makers of the Fourth Republic renamed the empire the Union Française. Three main groups of territories were distinguished. Long-established colonies such as Martinique and Reunion, together with Algeria, were declared to be *départements d'outre-mer* (DOM). In sub-Saharan *Africa and *Madagascar, the colonies were officially termed *territoires d'outre-mer* (TOM). Protectorates such as those in Indo-China, *Morocco, and *Tunisia were called *états associés*. These changes did little to stem the tide of pro-independence movements. In 1946 black Africans campaigning for independence set up the Rassemblement Démocratique Africain under the leadership of Félix Houphouët-Boigny. An insurrection in Madagascar was crushed in 1947, but in Indo-China, despite a huge military effort, the French were forced to concede independence after being defeated at Dien Bien Phu in May 1954.

The eight-year-long *Algerian War, which began in November 1954, brought France to the brink of political collapse and finally persuaded a significant part of the intelligentsia that the colonial system could no longer be justified. By weakening France, the conflict in Algeria also hastened the pace of decolonization elsewhere. Morocco and Tunisia became independent in 1956, and under a *loi-cadre* introduced the same year a measure of autonomy was granted to sub-Saharan Africa, where Houphouët-Boigny and other black African leaders such as *Senghor had adopted a relatively moderate stance. Under the new constitution established by de Gaulle on his return to power in 1958, the Union Française was replaced by La Communauté, a much looser form of association under which most of the remaining overseas territories were given the right to independence at a later stage. Guinea alone voted to reject this arrangement, preferring instead to become independent immediately. Only two years later all the other sub-Saharan territories, together with Madagascar, opted for complete independence. From the former federations of French West Africa and French Equatorial Africa, 11 new states were thus created in 1960: Senegal, Mauritania, Mali, Upper Volta (subsequently Burkina Faso), Niger, Ivory Coast, Dahomey (subsequently Benin), Gabon, Congo, Central African Republic, and Chad. Cameroon and Togo, sub-Saharan territories mandated to France by the League of Nations after World War I, also became independent at this time. With Algerian independence in 1962 French decolonization was virtually complete, except for a few small territories scattered around the globe [see DOM-TOM].

Under a policy known as *coopération*, France instituted economic and cultural aid programmes with most of the ex-colonial territories. She also concluded defence agreements with the majority of newly independent states in sub-Saharan Africa. *Tiers-mondistes*, i.e. supporters of Third World countries, have criticized these arrangements on the grounds that they smack of neo-colonialism. Culturally, the most significant legacy of colonization and its aftermath is la **francophonie*. The continuing use of the French language by political and cultural élites in ex-colonial territories has been the seedbed from which a rapidly expanding body of literature in French has emerged outside France during the second half of the 20th c. [see entries for different regions and countries].   [AGH]

See X. Yacono, *Les Étapes de la décolonisation française* (1971); P. C. Sorum, *Intellectuals and Decolonization in France* (1977); A. Ruscio, *La Décolonisation tragique: une histoire de la décolonisation française, 1945–1962* (1987).

Décor simultané, see MEDIEVAL THEATRE.

Dedications, see PATRONAGE.

Défense et illustration de la langue française, La. Composed in response to **Sebillet's Art poétique* (1548) and indebted to an Italian treatise by Speroni, the *Défense* was published in **Du Bellay's* name (1549) as the manifesto of the future **Pléiade*. Inspired by the nationalistic desire to emulate the example of Italy, it advocates the renewal of French as a poetic language by means of a programme of linguistic, stylistic, and metrical enrichment and a process of imitation of Greco-Roman and Italian genres and sources (imitation involved a dynamic method of *innutrition*, the spontaneous and personalized expression of assimilated and fully digested reading).   [MDQ]

DEFFAND, Madame du, see DU DEFFAND.

DEGAS, Edgar (1834–1917). One of the most important painters of the **Impressionist* movement, Degas devoted himself to the representation of modern life to which he brought innovative pictorial strategies (such as cropped borders and unusual angles of vision) and unrelenting experimentation with materials and techniques. Unlike **Monet* he was not interested in the *plein-air* study of nature, preferring the urban subjects (girls training for ballet, laundresses, cabaret and circus performers, prostitutes) also prominent in the novels of **Zola*, **Huysmans*, and the **Goncourts*, and in whom is enacted the complex relationship between representation and sexuality in Third-Republic France. Despite **Valéry's* belief that Degas could have been a major poet, his sonnets are more remembered for having provoked **Mallarmé's* famous advice to

him: 'My dear Degas, it is not with ideas that one writes poetry. It is with words.'   [JK]

DE GAULLE, see GAULLE.

Degré zéro de l'écriture, Le, see BARTHES.

DEGUY, Michel (b. 1930). French poet, whose ability to find ever-renewed ways of fusing poetry and poetic theory accounts for his emergence in the 1970s as a major figure on the French intellectual scene, as well as a prominent poet. A trained philosopher, Deguy was well placed to mediate between the contemporary poetic tradition and the radical shake-up of ideas engendered by **Structuralism* and **Post-Structuralism*, a project which informs the influential review *Po&sie* he has edited since 1972.

His early collections—*Fragments du cadastre* (1960), *Poèmes de la presqu'île* (1962), *Biefs* (1964)—centred on the poet's vigilant 'auscultation de l'espace', constantly anticipating those rare coincidences of moment and place which stake out the periphery of Being. But the emphasis placed on the cardinal role of metaphor paved the way for the new orientation perceptible in *Actes* and *Ouï-dire* (both 1966), where language takes centre stage: 'la poésie comme l'amour risque tout sur les signes.' *Actes* and its successors, which include *Figurations* (1969) and *Tombeau de Du Bellay* (1973), are remarkable fusions of poem and precept composed in an exceptionally lively style, bristling with neologisms, rare words, and coinages arrived at by hyphenation ('la ruse du trait d'union'). Widening the angle again, subsequent collections, including *Jumelages suivi de Made in USA* (1978) and the admirable *Gisants* (1985), show us the poet at large—as traveller, lover, editor, consumer of mass media, intellectual—bringing the exigencies of poetry to bear on the signs and discourses of the modern world.   [MHTS]

DEIMIER, Pierre de (1570–1618). French poet and poetic theorist. A native of Avignon, he belonged to an important group of poets in Provence [see also LA CEPPÈDE; MALHERBE]; later (c.1603), he joined the court circle of **Marguerite de Valois* in Paris. His *Académie de l'art poétique* (1610) has much in common with the reforms of Malherbe, emphasizing the importance of reason in poetic composition and deploring obscurity; however, earlier poets (**Ronsard*, **Desportes*, **Du Bartas*) are also referred to approvingly. Other works include translations of Latin and Italian poetry, imitations of Spanish poetry and romance, and biblical paraphrase.   [TC]

Deism. An 18th-c. movement in religious belief for the educated laity, especially the **philosophes*; not confined to France. The word originated in the 16th c. as a pejorative term for antitrinitarian and similar ideas among sects such as the Socinians, and was taken over to denote analogous views in secular writings: the deist is essentially one who, on the positive or constructive side, limits his religion to the belief in God, and on the negative or critical side remains independent of Christianity, and often hostile. 'Natural religion', often taken as synonymous, is in principle compatible with Christianity, or can even be its basis.

As a form of free thought, critical deism in the *Enlightenment is the historical successor to *libertinage. Its positive aspect seems to have stemmed chiefly from 17th-c. French rationalism; *Descartes and *Malebranche were the inspiration of several of the first French deists, such as *Gilbert and the *Militaire philosophe. Fully developed by about 1730, notably in the *clandestine manuscripts, deism was already popularized (for instance in the huge epistolary works of d'*Argens) well before the movement reached its apogee in the 1760s. It is clearly perceptible in the *Encyclopédie (even the articles by clerics are strongly influenced by deistic rationalism) and given perhaps its fullest expression in Voltaire's *Dictionnaire philosophique and *Rousseau's Profession de foi du vicaire savoyard. They contrast strongly: Voltaire prefers implication, reduces the positive side to a minimum, and is mockingly aggressive towards Catholicism; Rousseau argues directly and in detail, in treatise fashion, is influenced by the moralizing tendency of Calvinism, and is more conciliatory. Of the other major philosophes, *Montesquieu is comparatively mild on the critical side; utilitarian and indifferentist, he argues that religion should serve the secular needs of society (he attacks monasticism, for instance). *Diderot, typically for a later generation, moves to atheism after a problematical deist phase. By the 1770s atheism was already outflanking deism as a radical form of religious thought; enemies said that deism was merely a step on the way. With its 'Supreme Being' but lacking a church, deism can appear somewhat unreal and literary, despite the patent sincerity of many adherents. It is often found in *Utopias and as the belief of fictional foreign visitors or inhabitants of exotic surroundings. In a cosmopolitan but still religious age, its appeal was partly that under its remote, rational deity the danger of religious conflict seemed to recede. It was never an organized movement, unlike some of its 19th-c. successors, secular religions such as *Comte's, though during the Revolution the Supreme Being was briefly the object of official worship [see also THÉOPHILANTHROPIE].   [CJB]

DÉJAZET, Virginie (1798–1875). One of the most popular French actresses of her time, she had a string of brilliant successes in *vaudeville and light comedy at the Palais-Royal, the Variétés, and the Gaîté, specializing in travesti parts—soldiers, students—as well as in pretty country girls and grand ladies.   [SBJ]

DELACROIX, Eugène (1798–1863). The leading representative of *Romanticism in French painting, Delacroix applied his powerful imagination and audacious composition and use of colour to a huge range of subjects. He mastered one series of pictorial motifs and ideas after another: Italian and Flemish artists studied in the Louvre, British colourism and Romantic literature discovered through Bonington, North African subjects drawn from his visit there in 1832. From the 1830s onwards his mastery of traditional subject-matter and monumental form won him a series of major state commissions. Idolized by *Baudelaire, who hailed him as 'the true painter of the nineteenth century' (Salon de 1846), Delacroix was the link between the Old Master tradition and the most contemporary problems of art theory and practice, of which his three-volume Journal is an essential text.   [JK]

De la littérature considérée dans ses rapports avec les institutions sociales, see STAËL.

De l'Allemagne, see STAËL.

De l'amour. Essay by *Stendhal, published anonymously in 1822. Rather chaotically constructed, it purports to be a scientific account of the phases and varieties of love, proposing the famous theory of 'crystallization' (whereby love is born of frustration and imagination), distinguishing between 'amour-passion', 'amour de tête', 'amour de vanité', and 'amour physique', and discussing national differences in amorous behaviour. In reality it is a deeply personal work, full of coded references to his recent love for Mathilde Dembowski (Métilde): 'Je tremble de n'avoir écrit qu'un soupir, quand je crois avoir noté une vérité.'   [PF]

DELARUE, Paul, see FOLK-TALE.

DELAUNAY, Marguerite-Jeanne Cordier, see STAAL.

DELAUNAY, Robert (1885–1941). French painter who pursued la peinture pure in his paintings, theoretical writings, and lectures. The heavy paint layer of early works, a pulsating mosaic of touches, ceded to his invention of *Orphism (brighter palette, a kaleidoscope of shifting planes, zones of warm and cool colour, lyricism channelling kinetic energy). He executed series paintings (the city, windows, the Eiffel Tower); he combined time and movement, tradition and invention, in La Ville de Paris (1910–12); and his 'simultaneous' compositions, with light and colour creating form, embrace movement and modernity. *Apollinaire, who lived with the Delaunays briefly, and whose tastes corresponded, coined the term 'Orphism', matching it poetically in 'Les Fenêtres'.   [HEB]

DELAUNAY, Sonia, née Terk (1885–1979). Russian-born designer and painter resident in France from 1905. For some time after marrying Robert *Delaunay in 1910 she worked predominantly in the decorative and applied arts, but without relinquishing painting, where her collaboration in research with Robert was crucial. They shared theories of colour and movement, and a preference for simple, geometric shapes and near-abstraction. Her designs, initially for her home, became recognized internationally by the avant-garde: textiles, fluid dresses and theatre costumes, 'simultaneous' scarves, book-bindings, poster designs. A friend of Blaise *Cendrars, she illustrated *La Prose du Transsibérien et de la petite Jehanne de France* (1913). [HEB]

DELAVIGNE, Casimir (1793–1843). French poet and dramatist, famous in his day. His sequence of poems *Les Messéniennes* (1816–18) combines a hymn to national glories, praise of liberty, a lament on the allied occupation of France, and a fervent appeal to national unity. It was triumphantly received, as were his tragedies, notably *Les Vêpres siciliennes* (1819), a chauvinistic treatment of the French occupation of Sicily, *Le Paria* (1821), and *Marino Faliero* (1829), a defence of liberalism among the corruptions of Venice. These succeeded through combining political liberalism with cautious experiment on the language and forms of traditional tragedy. [SBJ]

DELAY, Florence (b. 1944). French actress, theatre critic, dramatist, and novelist; her stylish and imaginative work often crosses boundaries. Thus, *Graal-Théâtre* (1979) adapts medieval narratives for the stage, whilst her novel *Le Aie aie de la corne de brume* (1975) recreates the conventions of courtly love in a modern context. *Etxemendi* (1990) dramatizes another problem of boundaries—the Basques. [EAF]

DELÉCLUZE, Étienne-Jean (1781–1863). French artist and critic, pupil of *David. He is best remembered for his *Souvenirs* (1862) and his *Journal* (1948), which provide many insights into Parisian literary life.

De l'esprit des lois, see ESPRIT DES LOIS.

DELEUZE, Gilles (b. 1925). One of France's most versatile contemporary philosophers; his interests are particularly wide-ranging. His early work (1953–67) is concerned primarily with original studies of a number of major philosophers, including Nietzsche, Kant, *Bergson, and Spinoza. The middle period (1967–80) is the most controversial, as Deleuze turned his attention to literature (*Proust, Kafka, *Tournier, and *Zola, amongst others) and *psychoanalysis, allying himself with the radical anti-Freudian analyst Félix Guattari in a two-volume study of capitalism and schizophrenia, *L'Anti-Œdipe* (1972) and *Mille plateaux* (1980). Since 1980 his major publications have been concerned with the aesthetics of contemporary painting and cinema, with a notable study of the work of *Francis Bacon* (1984).

Like *Derrida, Deleuze is a philosopher of difference. He describes himself as an empiricist and a philosopher of multiplicity. He aims to view reality positively, in terms of what it is, rather than what it is not, that is, as differentiated and multiple, marked by specificity and individuality, rather than

according to the abstractions generated by philosophies (such as Hegel's or *Sartre's) which give priority to human consciousness and see the world in terms of negation, contradiction, opposition, and lack. In his contributions to psychoanalysis and literary theory the underlying common preoccupation is a critique of *interpretation*. Deleuze is resolutely anti-hermeneutic. Interpretation presupposes what it claims to uncover: in psychoanalysis, the fantasm, the unconscious, the Oedipus complex; in literature, a totalized, unified meaning. His study of Proust (1964, revised 1970), for example, rejects the traditional view of his work as organic, totalizing, and Platonizing, and argues that it is fragmented, heteroclite, and violent. Deleuze's 'schizoanalysis' repudiates Freudianism as reductive and repressive; it believes individual 'complexes' to originate in specific social structures, not in universal, triangular family relations; it does not envisage desire as arising from lack but considers it a positive means of breaking away from social and political restrictions. For Deleuze, art is never neurotic; in his terms, it is psychotic and revolutionary: 'schizoanalysis' aims to uncover the revolutionary power of the text, its explosive potential energy. Malcolm Lowry, Deleuze claims, comes closest to his own conception of the literary text as a 'sort of machine'. His concern is with what it can *do*, not with what it may *mean*. He does not interpret a text but rather asks what its uses may be, and argues that these are as varied and multiple as the domains of human desire. Deleuze's own texts are difficult, eccentric, and stimulating. [CMH]

See R. Bogue, *Deleuze and Guattari* (1989).

Délie, objet de la plus haute vertu, see SCÈVE.

DELILLE, Jacques (1738–1813). French poet whose verse translation of the *Georgics* (1769) won for him the chair of Latin poetry at the *Collège de France and election to the Académie Française (1774). He had revolutionary intentions for poetry, wishing to free it from classical aesthetic prejudices, to give it novel subject-matter and new, more musical verse forms, whether in his early descriptive, or 'agronomic', poetry (*Les Jardins*, 1782) or his late 'philosophical' works (*L'Imagination*, 1806; *Les Trois Règnes*, 1808). The theory contained in his prefaces, which is not without modern resonances, is certainly fascinating, though his practice is another matter. His status as the 'greatest contemporary poet' was reflected in his 'funérailles d'apothéose'. [JR]

Déliquescences d'Adoré Floupette, see HOAXES.

DELLY, pseudonym of Marie (1875–1947) and Frédéric (1876–1949) Petitjean de la Rosière, joint authors of some 100 romantic novels, which still enjoy considerable popularity. Of slight literary merit, the novels rest on recurrent elements of popular sentimental escapism. For R. Quilliot (*La

Mer et les prisons, 176), they are the source of the extravagant sentence attributed to the perfectionist author Grand in *La *Peste* ('Par une belle matinée de mai, une svelte amazone . . . '). [AHB]

DELORME, Marion (*c*.1611–1650). Courtesan known to *Richelieu, *Saint-Évremond, and others; the subject of a verse drama by *Hugo, *Marion de Lorme* (1831).

DELORME, Philibert (*c*.1510–*c*.1570). Son of a master mason, Delorme studied in Italy before becoming *surintendant des bâtiments* for Henri II. Among his most lasting work (much of it now destroyed) are the Château de Saint-Maur, the Château d'Anet (for *Diane de Poitiers), and François Ier's tomb in Saint-Denis. He designed the Tuileries for *Catherine de Médicis, but his plans were carried out only in part. His role in adapting classical and Italian architecture to French tastes was further enhanced by the publication of his *Nouvelles inventions pour bien bâtir* (1561) and his *Architecture* (1567). [JJS]

Delphine. Novel by Germaine de *Staël, published 1802, which has for its epigraph: 'A man must know how to brave public opinion, a woman how to submit to it.' Delphine d'Abbémar, a young widow, falls in love with her cousin's fiancé, Léonce de Mondoville, but the couple are kept apart by misunderstandings and social obstacles. As in *Corinne*, there is something of a role reversal between the central male and female protagonists, Delphine being recklessly courageous, having 'modern' ideas about love and being willing to defy social taboos, while Léonce is indecisive. Society's conventions and beliefs finally prove too strong for her: the couple are kept apart by spiritual barriers, Léonce is shot during the *Vendée campaign, and Delphine commits suicide. The novel seems to have grown out of de Staël's own experience of the unhappiness caused by the powerful taboos of society barring the way to individual fulfilment, a theme later taken up in *Corinne*. The institution of marriage, religious vows, and conventional disapproval of suicide are all challenged in the novel, and the importance of individual freedom is asserted. [DW]

DELPHY, Christine (b. 1941). Feminist theorist. Described by Simone de *Beauvoir as 'France's most exciting theorist', co-founder of the review *Nouvelles questions féministes* in 1977, she is the author of many articles, some of which are translated in *Close to Home* (1984). Her work is rooted in a materialist analysis of relations between men and women, stressing the economic oppression of women within the household, but rejecting both a Marxist analysis as inadequate on patriarchy, and the radical *feminism of Psych et Po as insufficiently aware of economics. [SR]

DELTEIL, Joseph (1894–1978). French writer. His first novel, *Sur le fleuve Amour* (1923), was a racy

adventure-story in whose title it is difficult to see just the name of the Asian river. He was one of the early *Surrealists but was expelled from the group after winning the Prix Fémina for *Jeanne d'Arc* (1925). His abandonment of literature in 1930–1 has been attributed both to ill health and to *l'amour fou*. He resumed his literary career after World War II with such works as *Jésus II* (1947), *François d'Assise* (1960), the intriguingly titled *La Cuisine paléolithique* (1965), which relies on the imagination of a primitive universe, and *La Deltheillerie* (1968). [KRA]

Démocratie en Amérique, De la. Study by *Tocqueville, published in two vols. (1835, 1840) after a year's visit to America. Tocqueville describes the constitutional form of the state, the major political institutions (parties, press, etc.), the legal system, and the way that democratic rule operates. He emphasizes the customs and culture which in his view underpin American political and economic success, and in particular the combination of robust individualism with a tradition of cohesive and effective organization. He points out the defects of American society, especially its corruption, conformism, and racism, but argues that its liberal virtues of freedom, equality, and democracy hold lessons for France. The work was enormously successful both in France and in the United States. [MHK]

DENISOT, Nicolas (1515–59), wrote under the pseudonym of 'le comte d'Alsinois'. He organized the *tombeau* for *Marguerite de Navarre (1550). His *Cantique du premier avènement de Jésus-Christ* (1553) is noteworthy for the way in which it attempts to adapt the aims of the *Pléiade to Christian ends. He may also be the author of the so-called Théodose Valentinian's *L'Amant ressuscité de la mort d'Amour* (1558), which explores, through the medium of the novel, the relationship between human and divine love. [JJS]

DENON, Dominique-Vivant (1747–1825). Baron Denon's career in the French diplomatic service survived several changes of regime from the reign of Louis XV to the Restoration. A skilled engraver, he produced an album illustrating Bonaparte's Egyptian expedition and was later appointed first director of the Louvre. His literary reputation rests on one brief masterpiece in the *libertin* mode, *Point de lendemain* (1777), a tale of adulterous love told with impeccable discretion. *Balzac liked it so much that he cited it in full in his *Physiologie du mariage* (1829), warning off husbands while recommending it to bachelors as 'une délicieuse peinture des mœurs du siècle dernier'. [RC]

DÉON, Michel (b. 1919). One of the *Hussards of the post-war period identified with the creation of a new literature of the Right in opposition to left-wing writers. A large fictional production, often set in countries embodying for him a purer past, includes *Le Balcon de Spetsai*, 1961 (Greece), *Un taxi mauve*, 1973 (Ireland). He was elected to the Académie Française in 1978. [EAF]

DEPARDIEU, Gérard (b. 1948). In 1990 French cinema's leading male actor. His early roughneck qualities (Blier's *Les Valseuses*, 1974), have been enriched by a capacity to communicate anguish and distress (*Resnais's *Mon oncle d'Amérique*, 1980) and social marginality (Berri's *Jean de Florette*, 1986). In Rappeneau's *Cyrano de Bergerac* (1990) he shows that he has the makings of a major 'literary' stage actor. [KAR]

Départements, see REGIONS AND DÉPARTEMENTS.

DEPESTRE, René (b. 1926). Haitian poet and novelist. Influenced by the nationalism of post-Occupation *Haiti as well as Marxism, *Surrealism, and the Resistance poetry of *Éluard and *Aragon, he was a founder of the student magazine *La *Ruche* which helped overthrow President Lescot in 1946. Like his contemporary *Alexis, he was to challenge the ideas of *négritude* in his essays *Pour la révolution, pour la poésie* (1969) and *Bonjour et adieu à la négritude* (1980). Since 1946 he has spent most of his time in exile and lived for 15 years in Cuba. Disillusioned, he left Cuba in 1979 to work with UNESCO in Paris.

Depestre's first poems, in *Étincelles* (1945) and *Gerbe de sang* (1946), are exuberant celebrations of revolution. While some of those written in the early 1950s are little more than Marxist tracts, his later *Minerai noir* (1956), *Journal d'un animal marin* (1964), and *Un arc-en-ciel pour l'occident chrétien* (1967) reveal a fuller range from lyrical love poetry to wry evocations of exile. The prose works *Alléluia pour une femme jardin* (1973) and *Le Mât de cocagne* (1979) extend the themes of erotic love and political commitment. His most recent novel, *Hadriana dans tous mes rêves* (1988), written in the tradition of *réalisme merveilleux*, was awarded the Prix Renaudot. [JMD]

Dépit amoureux, Le. Early comedy of intrigue by *Molière.

Déracinés, Les. Novel by *Barrès, published in 1897, the first in his trilogy *Le Roman de l'energie nationale*. It depicts the moral and physical uprooting of seven young Lorrainers. In Lorraine their schoolteacher Bouteiller (based on the philosopher and politician Burdeau), by his version of Kantianism, detaches them from the firm basis of traditional morality. Thereafter they are physically uprooted from their province, moving to Paris, filled with a desire to fulfil themselves to their utmost. Their fates are disparate: two, Racadot and Mouchefrin, of peasant origin, have little natural defence against what Barrès sees as intellectual anarchy, and end up as assassins; Renaudin becomes an unscrupulous political journalist, Suret-Lefort a successful Third-Republic lawyer-politician. Three turn out, in Barrès's terms, reasonably well: Sturel, an impassioned Boulangist [see BOULANGER, G.]; Roemer-

spacher, a *Tainian historian; and Saint-Phlin, a traditional aristocrat who remains solidly linked to Lorraine land and tradition. This *roman à thèse* is well-constructed, its themes skilfully interwoven. Above all, it gives a full (if partisan) picture of the political life of the period. It was of great influence, giving the word 'déraciné' to the political vocabulary and spelling out the influential doctrine of 'la terre et les morts'. [RMG]

DERÈME, Tristan, see FANTAISISTES.

Dernier de l'empire, Le, see SEMBÈNE.

Dernier des justes, Le, see SCHWARZ-BART, A.

Dernier Jour d'un condamné à mort, Le, see HUGO.

DEROULÈDE, Paul (1846–1914). Writer and politician. After military service in the *Franco-Prussian War, Deroulède wrote a series of controversial plays of a sharply nationalistic tone, and joined the extreme right-wing movement of General *Boulanger. Elected to the Assemblée Nationale, he became a vociferous opponent of the Third Republic and participated in the abortive military coup of February 1899. Exiled to Spain, he continued to write aggressively chauvinistic essays. [MHK]

DERRIDA, Jacques (b. 1930). Widely recognized today as the most important contemporary French philosopher, Derrida, whose work has been indissociably associated (especially outside France) with the term 'deconstruction', has since the late 1960s been the object of considerable, and often polemical, interest. He was born into a Jewish family in Algeria, and moved to Paris to prepare for entry to the *École Normale Supérieure in 1949, subsequently passing the *agrégation* in 1956 and returning to the École to teach from 1964 to 1984, since when he has held a post at the École des Hautes Études en Sciences Sociales and several visiting professorships in the USA.

After a prize-winning introduction to a translation of Husserl's *Origin of Geometry* (1962), it was with *La Voix et le phénomène*, *De la grammatologie*, and *L'Écriture et la différence* (all 1967), and subsequently *Marges de la philosophie*, *La Dissémination*, and *Positions* (all 1972), that Derrida made a spectacular publishing entry into a French intellectual scene in transition from *Structuralism into a more fragmented future. With immense scholarly and argumentative authority, Derrida argued, on the basis of texts ranging from Plato to Heidegger and from *Rousseau to *Artaud and *Jabès, that the tradition of western philosophy ('Western metaphysics') had systematically attempted to organize its thinking in terms of binary oppositions, that this organization was violent and dogmatic, and that careful reading of the texts concerned showed how more powerful forces worked to unravel that binary organization. Binary oppositions are never the neutral descriptive operators they pretend to be, says Derrida, but always operate according to an evaluative hierarchy whereby one term of the opposition is presented as original, primary, or preferable, and the other as derived, secondary, and to be avoided if possible.

Improbably enough, Derrida first and most famously attempts to show this by investigating the opposition of speech and writing, showing how, from Plato to *Saussure via Rousseau and Husserl, western thought has systematically presented writing as a dangerous, derivative form of language, and speech as its natural home. Against this, Derrida argues as follows: writing is traditionally described as being (merely) the sign of a sign, or even the (graphic) signifier of a (naturally phonic) signifier; but in fact all language can be described in such terms, in the wake of Saussure's dictum about language being a system of differences without positive terms, so the traditionally devalued term (writing) would in fact provide the more accurate description of language as a whole. All language is writing in this sense, although this sense can no longer quite be the sense given to writing by the tradition. This 'deconstruction' of the opposition first inverts the traditional evaluation of the terms, placing writing on top, as it were, but then attempts to displace the whole opposition by arguing that writing is no longer one term, but the description of the whole field previously divided into two. Keeping the term 'writing' or 'text' for the whole field appears to be a gesture inviting misunderstanding, as in the notorious dictum 'there is nothing outside the text', but Derrida argues that only by thus maintaining and displacing old terms can metaphysics be effectively contested.

On the basis of this deconstruction, Derrida argues that *all* the values associated with speech and writing, and motivating their traditionally oppositional description, are similarly displaced: thus (especially, and following Heidegger in this) presence and absence, but also life and death, proximity and distance, literal and figural meaning, meaning and lack of meaning, sanity and madness, inside and outside, masculine and feminine. This opens a vast perspective of deconstructive work to be done throughout a philosophical tradition redescribed as 'logocentric', and the simplest (and only slightly over-simple) way of reading Derrida's own prolific subsequent writing, and that of his followers, is as the pursuit of this programme, with polemical digressions on contemporary thinkers (*Foucault, Habermas, *Lacan, *Lévi-Strauss, Searle). Since 1972 Derrida has published a further 20 or so books, most notably perhaps *Glas* (1974, juxtaposing readings of Hegel and *Genet), *La Carte postale* (1980, on Freud and Lacan), two large collections of essays—*Psyché: inventions de l'autre* (1987) and *Du droit à la philosophie* (1990, on questions of philosophy as an institution, in part surrounding Derrida's own involvement with the Collège International de Philosophie, of which he was the founding president)—and two

works involved more or less directly in the 'affairs' surrounding Heidegger and De Man (*De l'esprit*, 1987; *Mémoires pour Paul de Man*, 1986–8).

Some critics have assumed that questioning binary distinctions commits Derrida to making everything the same, but his point is to avoid the quick domestication of difference implied by binary thinking, in the interests of a field of indefinitely plural differences and singularities, which would also have ethical and political implications. Once one has avoided the error of assuming that Derrida is straightforwardly and predictably promoting the previously secondary term over the previously valorized term (the matrix of many misreadings of Derrida's work, which forget or ignore the moment of displacement), then this becomes a powerful set of readings of texts whose familiar interpretations are quite dramatically destabilized.

Derrida works extensively with literary texts (he has published important readings of *Baudelaire, Genet, *Mallarmé, *Ponge, among others), and he works with philosophical texts in a way that most readily recalls the type of close reading associated with literary criticism. Few would deny the brilliance and perspicuity of his readings, even if they would resist some of his conclusions. This may go some way towards explaining the attraction his work has held for many literary scholars, although it has been anathema to devotees of more traditional approaches, and the object of much ill-informed criticism, due perhaps to its philosophical difficulty. Literature, even in quite a traditional conception, seems clearly to illustrate some of Derrida's main contentions about language in general: literary theory has long recognized that texts function independently of authorial intention, that they give rise to many, often incompatible, interpretations, that the tradition of reading texts is in principle endless, and that texts often generate their most powerful effects by courting the charge of meaninglessness. Derrida's effort has been to show how these features, when more rigorously formulated, are in fact features of language in general, which constantly escapes philosophical (and literary-critical) attempts to master it, irrepressibly generating new possibilities in a way which will always outplay the equally irrepressible desire for determinate and reliable meanings. [GPB]

See R. Gasché, *The Tain of the Mirror* (1986); G. Bennington and J. Derrida, *Jacques Derrida* (1991); D. Wood (ed.), *Jacques Derrida: A Critical Reader* (1992).

DES AUTELS, Guillaume (1529–81). Friend of *Ronsard, who dedicated an *Élégie* (1560) to him in reply to his verse and prose commentaries on contemporary events such as the Conjuration d'*Amboise. He also wrote a comic narrative in the manner of *Rabelais (1574), a treatise on French orthography (1548) attacking the reforms of *Meigret, and some lyric poetry. [TC]

DES BARREAUX, Jacques Vallée, sieur (1599–1673). One of the most notorious of the *libertins*, a close friend of *Théophile. Probably an atheist, he had a reputation for debauchery. Although interested in philosophy, he was not primarily a writer, but has been credited with a body of anonymous verse, including some vigorously anti-religious and pessimistic sonnets. [PF]

DESBORDES-VALMORE, Marceline (1786–1859). French author of numerous volumes of poetry: *Élégies, Marie et romances* (1819), *Élégies et poésies nouvelles* (1825), *Poésies* (1830), *Les Pleurs* (1833), *Pauvres fleurs* (1839), *Bouquets et prières* (1843). She also published a number of collections of short stories and tales, some of them particularly for children. There is an early novel, *L'Atelier d'un peintre* (published in 1833), which is interesting both as an autobiographical text and as a depiction of the milieu of painters in the early 19th c.

Although some of her poetic qualities were recognized in her day by writers such as *Baudelaire, and later by *Verlaine and the *Symbolists, she had in general carried a reputation as a lightweight lyrical poet. Only in relatively recent times has serious critical attention been turned to her works and their true value been acknowledged. The undervaluation of Desbordes-Valmore has certainly been in large part due to critical blind-spots, misconceptions, and prejudices concerning women's writing. She has long been thought of as having written passively and sentimentally about her tragic and often solitary personal life (unfulfilled love affair with the writer Henri de Latouche, death of her children and closest friends). What now strikes the modern reader is precisely her ability to deal with tragic experience directly and unflinchingly, never evading the pain of memory, loss, and remorse. Seen in the context of other contemporary French Romantic poets, her powers of precise observation and her ability to catch the detail of nature and everyday life are rare indeed. One is, therefore, not surprised that a modern poet such as Yves *Bonnefoy, in his selected edition of her poetry (1983), has called for a complete revaluation of 19th-c. French poetic history which would accord her a central place, and which would also force a reassessment of all those supposedly more eminent (male) Romantic poets who, in their grandiose mystical and visionary projects, had so signally failed to incarnate the real world in their poems.

Few poets of any period have, in fact, succeeded like Desbordes-Valmore in finding such concrete ways of writing about the presence of the absent and the absence of the present—losing the body but still seeing the reflection, losing the voice but still hearing the echo. It is perhaps her treatment of family relationships and family affections which now seems the most important and most moving feature of her work, in those poems which nostalgically and painfully confront the fragility and unre-coverability of original patterns of loving, feeling, and belonging. [BR]

DES CARS, Guy (1911–93). One of the most popular and widely read novelists of the post-World War II period. His prolific output of best-selling novels largely depends on strong plot and a formulaic treatment of human passions. The titles of novels such as *L'Impure* (1949), *Le Boulevard des Illusions* (1953), or *L'Insolence de sa beauté* (1972) indicate in themselves his characteristic themes. [EAF]

DESCARTES, René (1596–1650). One of the principal creators of modern philosophy and science, an emblematic figure of the power of independent thinking.

He was born in Touraine and educated at the Jesuit college of La Flèche. From 1618 to 1620 he served in the army; in November 1619, while garrisoned in Germany in a 'poêle' (a small house heated by a central stove), he experienced a spell of 'enthusiasm' in which he discovered 'les fondements d'une science admirable'. Between 1620 and 1629 he travelled, but was based in Paris, frequenting scholarly circles. In 1629, having decided to devote himself to philosophy, he settled in Holland, where he lived for the rest of his life. His voluntary exile gave him freedom and solitude, though he entertained many visitors and kept up a voluminous and fascinating correspondence.

In his early years in Holland he was much occupied by scientific research, but metaphysics became his dominant concern in the late 1630s. Having refrained from publishing for many years, he grew increasingly concerned to win over readers to his philosophy, and to oust *scholasticism from the schools. In 1649 he accepted an invitation from a royal admirer, Queen Christine of Sweden, but fell ill and died in Stockholm.

Descartes's youthful writings are only preserved in fragmentary form. His first major work, the *Regulae ad directionem ingenii* (*Règles pour la direction de l'esprit*), written in Latin before 1629, was published posthumously. It contains 21 'rules' designed to establish a method for achieving, within the field open to human understanding, a scientific certainty as firm as that of mathematics. Using this method, which combines intuition, observation, experiment, and deduction, he then worked on a treatise, *Le Monde, ou le Traité de l'homme*, in which he offered a mechanistic account of the universe (a heliocentric system) and of human beings, their bodily motions, and sensations. The work was completed by 1633, but Descartes abandoned publication on hearing of Galileo's condemnation.

His first published book, and his most famous, was the *Discours de la méthode*, published in French in 1637 together with essays on optics, meteorology, and geometry. It is a complex work, whose six parts are given unity as the story of the author's search for truth. In Part 1, starting from the premiss that 'le bon sens est la chose du monde la mieux partagée', Descartes offers his intellectual autobiography as a possible model for the proper conduct of the mind. He tells of his book-centred Jesuit education, which failed to satisfy his desire for certain knowledge, and of his decision to make a clean break and think for himself. Part 2 recounts, with superb confidence, the discovery of the true method; as in the *Regulae*, this consists in taking nothing for granted, accepting only ideas which are entirely self-evident, and proceeding from them by orderly 'chains' of reasoning. In Part 3 he sets out the prudently conformist 'provisional ethics' which he adopted until he had arrived at a rationally based morality.

Part 4, the centre of the book, sets out Descartes's first metaphysical discoveries. Having submitted all ideas to methodical doubt, he is left with the unshakeable principle: 'Je pense, donc je suis' (*Cogito, ergo sum*, often referred to as 'the cogito'). He proceeds from this to a radical distinction between the thinking substance (mind, spirit, or soul) and the material world; this is the famous Cartesian 'dualism'. The final basic principle in Part 4 is the existence of a perfect being, God, which is deduced from the very fact that we possess an idea of perfection. God in turn guarantees the value of sense experience, and thus of experimental science. Part 5 contains a summary of the doctrine of *Le Monde*, emphasizing the distinction between human beings, with their immaterial souls, and animals, which are seen as 'machines'—an aspect of Descartes's philosophy that caused much controversy. Part 6 is a fascinating discussion of his publishing strategy and the way he sees his public responsibility as a scientist.

His later works develop the ideas of the *Discours*. The *Méditations* (published in Latin in 1641, in French in 1647) is his most important work of pure philosophy. Using the first-person form again, it attempts to establish more firmly the metaphysics of the *Discours*, in particular the existence of God and the mind–matter distinction. Methodical doubt is given added force here by the fiction of a 'mauvais génie' dedicated to deceiving us. The work is followed by a number of lengthy replies to objections from readers such as *Gassendi, Hobbes, and *Arnauld.

The *Principes*, published in Latin in 1644 and in French in 1647, is Descartes's fullest account of his philosophy. Book 1 is devoted to metaphysics, Books 2–4 to physical science, including cosmology. The work is designed to replace existing school manuals, and is divided into easily assimilated short chapters; declaring that all normal people are capable of philosophy, Descartes in a preface of 1647 urges readers to read it in the first instance 'like a novel'. An unfinished dialogue, *La Recherche de la vérité*, shows a similar concern for popularization.

His last major work, *Les Passions de l'âme* (1650), written at the request of Princess Elizabeth of Bohemia, explains the passions in accordance with his dualistic principles. The pineal gland in the brain is declared to be the place of interaction between body and mind. If the body affects the mind, the converse is also true; writing in *Neostoical vein, and expressing values also embodied in the heroes of Pierre *Corneille, Descartes exalts the free will of the 'généreux'.

His ideas, powerful in their own right, are given added force by his rhetorical skill. His tone and style—even his choice between Latin and French—correspond to his projected readers, whose reactions are provoked, anticipated, and answered. The man is very present in the writing. At times he is disarmingly modest, at times fiercely ironic. His plain style is often lifted to a higher plane by the striding rhythm of his sentences and his striking images.

Descartes's philosophy, Cartesianism, exercised a great influence, even when it was rejected. His cosmology, with its 'horror of the vacuum' and its planets whirled around in vortices (*tourbillons*) of ether, succumbed to Newtonian physics, though not before supplanting Aristotle in the colleges. His doctrine of 'innate ideas' was ousted, or at least modified, by Locke's sensationalism. His body–soul dualism, with its need to explain the reciprocal action of the two substances, continued to tease philosophers, notably *Malebranche and *Leibniz. But his greatest legacy was his method, together with his confidence in the possibility of explaining and conquering nature. For better or worse, he was one of the fathers of the Scientific Revolution; his methodical doubt and his independence of mind continued to inspire *Enlightenment thinkers, even if they discarded many of his scientific theories as fantasies. [PF]

See A. J. P. Kenny, *Descartes: A Study of his Philosophy* (1968); G. Rodis-Lewis, *L'Œuvre de Descartes* (1971); B. Williams, *Descartes* (1978).

DESCAVES, Lucien (1861–1949). French novelist. A disciple of *Huysmans and of the *Goncourt brothers and a practitioner of *écriture artiste*, he was an exponent of *Naturalism, whose tendencies he took to extremes in novels such as *Le Calvaire d'Héloïse Pajadou* (1883) and *Une vieille rate* (1883), yet he was one of the signatories of the 'Manifesto of the Five' against Zola's *La *Terre*. The scandal provoked by his anti-military novel, *Sous-Offs* (1889), made him famous. Though acquitted of charges of offending the army and public morality, he was stripped of his military rank. [DB]

DESCHAMPS, Eustache (*c.*1340–1404). French poet. Also known as Eustache Morel, he was born in Vertus, near Épernay. His early education was provided by the poet-musician Guillaume de *Machaut, perhaps his uncle. He probably studied law at Orléans. He held minor posts at the French court in the reigns of Charles V and VI, and in 1389 was nominated *bailli* (judge) at Senlis. For most of his life he enjoyed royal favour, and was a more-or-less official court poet, writing pieces for royal occasions or simply to amuse his patrons. Like *Froissart, Deschamps provides an invaluable (often first-hand) account of many of the major historical events of the last third of the 14th c. (e.g. personal experience of the *Hundred Years War, the burning of his own home town and house by the English).

Deschamps left an impressive body of works, including the first *art poétique* in French, *L'Art de dictier* (1392), some dramatic pieces (e.g. *La Farce de Mestre Trubert et d'Antrongnart*, the *Dit des quatre Offices de l'Ostel du Roy*), and long moralizing poems like *Le Miroir de mariage* (an unfinished misogynist marathon of some 12,000 lines). However, the most accessible to the modern reader are probably the vast number of ballades, *chants-royaux*, rondeaux, and *virelais*—more than 1,300—nearly all of which show considerable mastery of the intricacies of the *formes fixes*. In these poems Deschamps is often tediously moralizing, as he grumbles away at the state of the world, but many are fresh and quirkily original, particularly in their evocation of the trivia of everyday life. The breadth of Deschamps's experiences as courtier, diplomat, soldier (and consequently great traveller) is reflected in his poetry. He is particularly good at conveying physical experiences, cold, hunger, seasickness, toothache. His traveller's tales of fleas in beds and disgusting foreign food are particularly entertaining. Indeed, a great many of his poems are about food and drink, giving a vivid impression of the culinary habits of 14th-c. Europe.

Deschamps wrote touching poems about his own home, comic verses about the problems of bringing up children, and eulogistic poems on 'Paris sans per'. His satirical pieces are probably his best: he is a sharp-tongued critic of mores at court. His experiences as a judge give rise to a number of amusing, if savage, pieces about criminals and marginals—Deschamps was a great hanger and flogger (one of his refrains reads 'Prenez, pandez, et ce sera bien fet'). Many of his satirical poems are misogynistic, though his works also include a fair measure of conventional love poetry. He also wrote about a dozen Aesopian fables, with particularly vivid evocations of animals, the best-known of which is probably *Le Chat et les souris*, with its catchy refrain 'Qui pendra la sonnette au chat'. His anti-English poems, referring to the old legend that Englishmen have tails and using scraps of English, are highly entertaining, and he also addressed a eulogistic poem to Chaucer.

In many ways Deschamps anticipates *Villon, by whom he was eclipsed. He comes at a decisive moment in the evolution of poetry—the decline of the courtly tradition as the dominant mode. The *Art de dictier* represents a radical break from Deschamps's master Machaut, and marks the definitive divorce of poetry and music [see WORDS AND MUSIC, 1]. Although Deschamps was not the inventor of the *formes fixes*, he was responsible for their consolidation, and vastly extended their thematic

range. His influence is difficult to assess, for although his poetry is a positive compendium of the themes and forms of the late Middle Ages, encapsulating much that is typical of the often sombre mood of the 14th c. and containing many elements that lead on to the poetry of the *Rhétoriqueurs, his complete works survive in only one massive manuscript, and his name is little mentioned by subsequent generations. [CMSJ]

See E. Hoepffner, *Eustache Deschamps Leben und Werke* (1904, repr. 1974); D. Poirion, *Le Poète et le prince: l'évolution du lyrisme courtois de Guillaume de Machaut à Charles d'Orléans* (1965).

DESCHAMPS, Léger-Marie, dom (1716–74). Benedictine monk, author of an audacious Utopian system. He criticized contemporary *philosophes such as *Holbach, but in the name of his own brand of atheism, based on an elaborate metaphysics and reminiscent of *Spinoza. Against the existing 'état de lois', he advocated an 'état de mœurs' free from private property, oppression, and exploitation. He published only two short books, seeking rather to make influential converts by personal contact. *Diderot incorporated his ideas in the *Supplément au Voyage de Bougainville*. Deschamps's manuscript, entitled 'La Vérité, ou le Vrai Système', has not been published in full (for a selection, see *Dixhuitième siècle*, Nos. 4 and 5). [PF]

DESCHAMPS (DESCHAMPS DE SAINT-AMAND), Antoine (called Antony or Antoni) (1800–69). French poet. Younger brother of Émile Deschamps and a disciple of *Hugo and *Vigny, he translated Dante's *Divine Comedy* in 1829 and published lyric poetry of quite distinct and intense quality. He lost his mental health in 1834, and was treated, like *Nerval, by Dr Blanche; some of his poems describe the sufferings of his insanity. [FPB]

DESCHAMPS (DESCHAMPS DE SAINT-AMAND), Émile (1791–1871). Brother of Antoni Deschamps, active in the Romantic movement and known for his translations and adaptations of Spanish, German (Goethe, Schiller), and especially English texts, including Shakespeare. His *Études françaises et étrangères* (1828) included a preface defending Romantic doctrine. He wrote the librettos for Rossini's *Ivanhoe* and *Berlioz's *Roméo et Juliette*. Deschamps also composed fantastic tales, poems (including one in defence of *Baudelaire), and journalism. [FPB]

Désert de l'amour, Le. Novel by *Mauriac, published in 1925, and one of his bleakest. It opens in a fashionable Parisian bar, with the hero, Raymond Courrèges, recognizing Maria Cross, who scandalized Bordeaux when he was an adolescent there 17 years earlier. Through a long flashback, characteristic of much of Mauriac's fiction, the novel describes the respectable bourgeois world of Bordeaux and the passion which both Raymond and his doctor

Désert, Le

father develop for the *demi-mondaine*, a passion which remains unexpressed and unfulfilled and which engenders in Raymond a lingering desire for revenge. The chance encounter in the bar leads to a meeting with Dr Courrèges, in Paris for a conference, which underscores the tragedy: the passion which has so dominated the lives of Raymond and his father has been unrecognized by Maria Cross herself. Maria, the challenge to bourgeois hypocrisy, is both the meeting-point between father and son and the permanent instrument of their torture, with no salvation in sight. [NH]

Désert, Le, see PROTESTANTISM, 1.

Désert, Le, see MEMMI.

DES ESCUTEAUX, Antoine (*fl.* 1600–20). Novelist, often coupled with *Nervèze as an author of absurd and extravagantly written romances.

Des Esseintes. The hero of Huysman's **A rebours.* *Mallarmé's 'Prose pour des Esseintes' is inspired by him.

Des Femmes. Feminist publishing house set up in 1974 as a collective by the Psychanalyse et Politique group [see FEMINISM]. It published many hitherto unknown women writers in the 1970s and launched a series of recordings of women's texts. It was reorganized in the 1980s along more traditionally commercial lines, with the name of the group's key figure, Antoinette Fouque, now on the cover. [EAF]

DESFONTAINES, Pierre-François Guyot, abbé (1685–1745). French critic and translator, who ran successively several periodicals, notably *Observations sur les écrits modernes* (1735–43). He was a traditionalist, hostile to the neologisms and affectations of the *modernes,* but sufficiently interested in English literature to translate *Gulliver's Travels.* A pugnacious character, he clashed with *Voltaire (*La Voltairomanie,* 1738). [PF]

DES FORÊTS, Louis-René (b. 1918). French poet and novelist, whose high reputation rests on a few books which have never achieved popularity. He is the author of a group of *récits, La Chambre des enfants* (1960), a poem in alexandrines, *Les Mégères de la mer* (1967), and two novels, *Les Mendiants* (1943) and *Le Bavard* (1946). The latter is an extraordinary monologue, like a parody of Rousseau's *Confessions* filtered through Dostoevsky, in which a narrator exhibits his humiliation in a convoluted prose which is constantly undermining itself. Since 1967 Des Forêts has published little, apart from fragments of an autobiography in progress and the *Poèmes de Samuel Wood* (1988). [PF]

Des Grieux, chevalier. The protagonist-narrator of Prévost's *Manon Lescaut.*

DES HOULIÈRES, Antoinette du Ligier de La Garde (1638–94). It was logical that Des Houlières

should have been the recipient of the first prize for poetry ever awarded by the Académie Française (in 1671). She was the most highly regarded contemporary lyric poet. She composed in many genres, from songs to tragedies, but was best known for her pastoral poetry. Her most moving poems are frank, personal evocations of the ageing process. She frequented the *salons and first published in the *Mercure galant.* Her tone often evokes *La Rochefoucauld's philosophy of detachment; like him, she never forgot the ideals of the *Fronde. [JDeJ]

DÉSIRÉ, Artus (c.1510–1579). Normandy priest, poet, and polemicist, whose numerous writings against the Reformers are marked by vituperative satire and parody, and illustrate the intensity and intolerance of contemporary propaganda; his *Contrepoison des 52 chansons de Cl. Marot* (1560) parodies and debunks *Marot's influential psalm paraphrases. [MJH]

DESMARETS DE SAINT-SORLIN, Jean (c.1600–1676). Polymath, who entered the French literary scene through his active participation, as performer as well as creator, in *ballets de cour.* He gained fame by serving *Richelieu's interests. He was, for example, principal author of several plays on which Richelieu may have collaborated, of which the comedy *Les Visionnaires* (1638) is the best-known. He was among the founder-members of the Académie Française and among the authors of the *Sentiments de l'Académie sur le *Cid* (1637). In 1654 he underwent a conversion and began to write devotional prose, becoming violently antagonistic to those (like the *Jansenists) whose doctrines he opposed. From this period date his epic poem, *Clovis, ou la France chrétienne* (1657, extensively rewritten for the 1673 edition) and his biblical poems. He ended his career with numerous contributions to the *Querelle des Anciens et Modernes, all of them defences of modern literature. [JDeJ]

DES MARQUETS, Anne (d. 1588). A Dominican nun best known for her *Sonnets, prières et devises en forme de Pasquins* (1562), which were inspired by the Colloque de Poissy, and for her translations of the *Carmina sacra* of Marcantio Flaminio, which are followed by sonnets developing *Counter-Reformation themes (sin, salvation, etc.). Much of her work was not published until the 17th c. [IJS]

DES MASURES, Louis (c.1515–1574). Soldier, poet, courtier, friend of the *Pléiade, he left the French court at the accession of Henri II and spent much of the rest of his life outside France. His best-known work is a trilogy of plays about David (*David combattant, David triomphant, David fugitif,* 1566) with a strong Protestant message about perseverance and faith in the face of persecution, and in form combining elements of classical tragedy as imitated by other French humanists at the time (*Jodelle, *Garnier) and of the traditional French *mystère. He

234

also wrote *Bergerie spirituelle*, a *morality play, and translations of Virgil and of the Psalms.   [GJ]

DESMOULINS, Camille (1760–94). A lawyer and early *Cordelier, he was already visible on 12 July 1789 exhorting the people to rise against Louis XVI and was at the storming of the Bastille. His essential role was not, however, as demagogue or man of action, but as a polemicist, pamphleteer, and journalist (*Révolutions de Paris et de Brabant*) who was dangerous for all who opposed the popular revolution: his *Histoire des Brissotins* (1793) was, for example, to help bring down the *Girondins.

His name now conjures up *Le Vieux Cordelier* (5 December 1793–24 January 1794), which was less a journal than a series of (only seven) fulgent pamphlets directed by an *old* Cordelier against the newer versions (e.g. the *Hébertistes) who, overtaking the Revolution on the far Left, were betraying the original Cordelier values of generosity and commitment to a programme of justice and equality. After long following *Robespierre, Desmoulins allied increasingly in the Convention with *Danton and the Indulgents: Number 4 of the *Vieux Cordelier* called for a reversal of the Terror and the creation of a 'Comité de clémence'. Number 6 (his political *credo*), then Number 7 (an audacious attack on the Comité de Salut Public) were judged to be even more dangerous and marked him out for inevitable retribution. He accompanied Danton to the guillotine (5 April). [See also REVOLUTION, I.]   [JR]

DESNOS, Robert (1900–45). French poet. A very inventive *Surrealist, he made contact with *Breton in 1922. In the experiments with hypnotic sleep, he turned out to be the best subject, capable of writing in a trance. Even if the aphorisms of *Rrose Sélavy* (1922–3) were not the result of transatlantic telepathic communication with Marcel *Duchamp, the latter provided the model. Desnos's first published book, *Deuil pour deuil* (1924), an almost unclassifiable prose text, paved the way for the erotic fantasy *La Liberté ou l'amour* (1927). In his lifetime he brought out two major volumes of poetry: *Corps et biens* (1930), covering the decade from 1919 until his exclusion from the Surrealist group, includes the linguistic experiments of 'L'Aumonyme' and 'Langage cuit' (1923), the lyrical apostrophe 'A la Mystérieuse' (1926) and 'Les Ténèbres' (1927); *Fortunes* (1942) shows how he continued to explore the whole gamut of poetry, despite his radio and newspaper work. He also wrote two cantatas with *Milhaud, *Pour l'inauguration du Musée de l'homme* (1937) and *Les Quatre Eléments* (1938), a novel, *Le Vin est tiré* (1943), a 'play', *Le Place de l'Étoile* (1945), and essays, e.g. *Félix Labisse* (1945). A Resistance poet, he died in a concentration camp. His posthumous publications include *Choix de poèmes* (1946), *Domaine public* (1953), *Cinéma* (1966).   [KRA]

Désordres de l'amour, Les (1675). Collection of four historical novellas by *Villedieu set in 16th-c. France

during the *Wars of Religion. Villedieu borrowed her story-line from the historian *Mézeray. To his blend of political and amorous intrigue she added psychological depth and affective motivation. The work helped launch a new genre, the *nouvelle historique* or *nouvelle galante*, which dominated late 17th-c. prose fiction. All historical novellas illustrate a common philosophy, that the major events of history can be explained by the influence of love on those in power: in this case, all public misfortunes, even war, are portrayed as 'love's disorder'.   [JDeJ]

DES PÉRIERS, Bonaventure (c.1510–c.1544). French prose writer. Born in Burgundy, he was raised by the abbot of Saint-Martin in Autun. We first hear of him collaborating on *Olivétan's French Bible (1535). Introduced into the service of *Marguerite de Navarre, he became one of her secretaries. Mixing with the literati of Lyon, he sympathized with the *Evangelicals, translated works from Latin and Greek, took *Marot's defence in *Pour Marot absent . . . contre Sagon* (1537), and worked with *Dolet on the *Commentarii linguae latinae* (1536–8). The latter and the works of Origen are said to have helped cultivate the healthy religious scepticism to be seen in his best-known work, *Cymbalum mundi* (1539), published under the pseudonym of Thomas du Clevier (an anagram of Thomas l'incrédule?). In four short Lucianic dialogues, he examines the dangers of reason and eloquence; the work's enigmatic or hermetic nature has prompted differing interpretations. Attacked by Protestants and Catholics alike, the book was condemned by the Parlement but Marguerite interceded in Des Périers's favour. He also left a collection of short stories, the *Nouvelles récréations et joyeux devis* (c.1538, published 1558), which bear the stamp of Boccacio and *Rabelais, yet which reveal a certain originality of style and psychological observation. After he left Marguerite's service in 1541 little is known about him: Henri *Estienne claimed he committed suicide.   [KCC]

DESPORTES, Philippe (1546–1606). French poet. He was born in Chartres, the son of a well-to-do mercer. By 1566 he was in Paris, working as a member of the royal secretariat. When the duc d'Anjou was elected king of Poland, Desportes went with him to Cracow, but was glad to return on his master's accession to the French throne as Henri III. His continuing services to the crown were rewarded with four abbacies *in commendam* (he took only minor orders). Now very wealthy, and his peace made with Henri IV after some involvement in the *Ligue, he built up an impressive library and was a generous patron to scholars and writers, including his nephew Mathurin *Régnier.

Most of Desportes's poetry had been written by 1573, for the Italianate high society of Charles IX's reign, particularly the salon of the maréchale de Retz. For such a public, poetry was no longer a cultural adventure, as it had been with the *Pléiade, but current coin for social, and especially amorous, exchanges. His sonnets and *stances* draw on the hackneyed material of the neo-*Petrarchan manner, and on a fund of recurring images, conceits, and allusions, the whole forming as it were a data-bank and a programme for unlimited variations within very narrow limits overall. The thematic analysis of his *univers poétique* remains unconvincing because of this restricted range and the derivative nature of the texts (many of his poems are closely modelled on Italian originals), but even more because very many were written with the purely practical aim of furthering the amorous pursuits of other people. Such is the degree of socially imposed abstraction, however, that it is often hard to discern which poems were written to whom and in whose name—the poet himself included: the arrangement into sequences is to a considerable extent artificial. At its best, this sophisticated yet undemanding poetry, with its langorous music, conveys a mood of entranced adoration; elsewhere, paradox and metaphor lose their virtue through excessive elaboration. In some of his elegies, however, freed from the conventions of his chosen *milieu*, he strikes sharper and livelier notes. He also wrote some devotional poems, and his translation of the Psalter proved popular throughout the Catholic revival, thanks to the approval of *François de Sales.

From about 1570 Desportes's prestige grew until eventually it eclipsed that of *Ronsard; but a major revolution in taste is foreshadowed by the highly critical marginal notes made by *Malherbe in his copy of the 1600 edition of the *Œuvres*. [AJS]

See J. Lavaud, *Philippe Desportes* (1936); G. Mathieu-Castellani, *Les Thèmes amoureux dans la poésie française, 1570–1600* (1975).

DES ROCHES, Madeleine (c.1520–1587) and Catherine (c.1542–1587). Mother and daughter were humanists whose literary salon in Poitiers was famous. Catherine is best known through *Pasquier's *La Puce de Madame des Roches* (1583). On a visit to the salon he is said to have spied a flea on her bosom: the assembled company, including Catherine, then composed verses on the flea in French, Spanish, Italian, Latin, and even Greek. More significantly, the two women also produced an important body of work, mainly poetry, published in the *Œuvres* (1578) and the *Secondes œuvres* (1583). Madeleine, whose verses are anecdotal and personal, treats themes like women's education, widowhood, the death of a friend, in a variety of forms (epistles, sonnets, odes). Catherine's poetry, more formally accomplished, includes a sonnet cycle on the loves of Sincero and Charite. [CMSJ]

DESROSIERS, Léo-Paul (1896–1967). Canadian novelist, best known for *Les Engagés du grand portage* (1939), an epic account of the struggles, hardships, and commerical rivalry of the early days of the fur trade in the Canadian north. *Nord–Sud* (1931), which recounts the migration of French-Canadian farmers and lumberjacks to take part in the Californian gold rush, although less vivid, has similar qualities. Later works, like *L'Ampoule d'or* (1951), which attempt greater literary sophistication are less successful. [SIL]

Destinées, Les, see VIGNY.

DESTOUCHES (pseud. of Philippe Néricault) (1680–1754). Comic playwright. After a diplomatic career during the Regency, Destouches retired in 1727 to devote himself to writing plays. He wrote 19 for the Comédie-Française, and success came with the first, *Le Curieux impertinent* (1710). His most successful plays thereafter were: *L'Ingrat* (1712), *L'Irrésolu* (1713), *Le Médisant* (1715), *Le Triple Mariage* (1716), *Le Philosophe marié* (1727), *Le *Glorieux* (1732), and *Le Dissipateur* (published 1736, performed 1753). Though not without their lighter side, his plays are intended to be serious and to edify the spectators by appealing to their sensibility. They illustrate the trials of virtue and the aberrations of fundamentally good characters, and reflect a systematically optimistic vision. [JD]

DESTUTT DE TRACY, Antoine-Louis-Claude, comte (1754–1836). French philosopher and acknowledged leader of the *Idéologues. Despite his noble rank and army commissions under the king, he supported the Revolutionary cause, though not the Revolution in all its excesses; he was imprisoned for a year during the Terror.

Influenced by *Condillac and Locke, Tracy elaborated a 'science of ideas' which reduced all mental processes to sense-impressions: thought is a function of our physical organization: 'penser, c'est sentir'. The four-volume *Éléments d'idéologie* (1801–15), which forms the main corpus of his philosophical writings, seeks to provide a methodology for explaining the development of thought from its sensory origin.

Tracy had a powerful effect on the young *Stendhal among others, but found his influence curtailed when *Napoleon suppressed the Class of Moral and Political Sciences within the *Institut in 1803. [JS]

DES VIGNES ROUGES, Jean, see WORLD WAR I.

Detective Fiction. Although *Sue, *Ponson du Terrail, or *Vidocq can be cited as precursors, with *Poe an obvious influence, detective fiction in French begins with *Gaboriau. It presupposes the existence of scientific method and a regular police force (though from the start amateur detectives rival professionals) for its subject-matter, and a public for its consumption.

Some 300 titles a year are now published in France, generally in collections of which Le *Masque and *Série Noire are the best known (others have come and gone). Writing to a formula, authors are frequently prolific, their names trademarks: 'Peter Randa' (André Duquesne), reportedly in the 1960s and 1970s the criminals' favourite author, wrote some 300 Fleuve Noir titles. Challenge is intrinsic to detective fiction: Maurice *Leblanc's Arsène Lupin, 'gentleman-cambrioleur' and, like Gaboriau's Lecoq, a master of disguise and solver of riddles, defies established order in a series of novels from 1905 to 1939, and is even pitted against 'Herlock Sholmès' (1908); the reporter Rouletabille, in Gaston Leroux's *Le Mystère de la chambre jaune* (1907), outwits the police in an archetypal closed-room enigma. To the anarchic heroes of this first period succeed more law-abiding investigators.

Because of its artificially strained invention, detective fiction was classed as a minor genre, the term *roman policier* being decried even in 1908 by Leroux in *Le Parfum de la dame en noir*, but the sterility of translation and imitation was avoided by, for example, S.-A. Steeman (*Six hommes morts* 1931), *Aveline, Pierre Véry (*L'Assassinat du Père Noël*, 1934), Pierre Nord (*Double crime sur la ligne Maginot*, 1936), and, outside the main current, *Simenon. The American hard-boiled school and Série Noire set a new fashion, from which *Malet escaped and against which *Boileau–Narcejac reacted. More recently, as the term *polar* replaces *roman policier*, the genre becomes more self-assured, conscious of its traditions: all tendencies coexist, with Boileau–Narcejac producing new Arsène Lupin titles in the 1970s and *Manchette producing political crime thrillers. Literature for mass-consumption, detective fiction also implies a duel between author and reader: *Exbrayat's archness of tone, the *argot of Simonin or Auguste Le Breton, San-Antonio's truculence [see DARD], stem from this. There is cross-fertilization between film and fiction: Série Noire titles inspire many films; authors such as 'Sébastien Japrisot' (pseud. of Jean-Baptiste Rossi) and Jean *Vautrin also make films, while film is a motif in for example René *Belletto's *Sur la terre comme au ciel* (1982), itself filmed as *Péril en la demeure* (1985). [See ROMAN NOIR.]
[SFN]

Deuxième Sexe, Le (1949). Simone de *Beauvoir's famous and important *feminist text which studies multiple aspects of women's situation to demonstrate that 'on ne naît pas femme, on le devient'. The introduction stresses the *Existentialist approach of the study but it becomes more materialist as it proceeds. Taking in turn biology, psychoanalysis, Marxism, history, literature, education, socialization within the family, marriage, maternity, and other social roles for women, Beauvoir shows how femininity is socially constructed and how women are cut off from freedom and cast in the role of 'other'. This is found to be partly a result of male myth-making and partly of women's connivance; Beauvoir accepts no biological or other predetermining absolutes, and encourages women

to wrest what she considers universal values from the male preserve. The roles of wife and mother are viewed with particular opprobrium (even distaste) and love is described as a danger to women, since, while the power balance remains unequal, it encourages women to live their lives vicariously through men. Independent work and socialism are proposed as the way forward, though after 1970 Beauvoir herself declared this to be an inadequate solution and argued that the feminist struggle had to be conducted independently. [EAF]

DEVI, Ananda (pseud. of A. D. Nirsimloo-Anenden) (b. 1957). Mauritian writer. In 1973 she won Radio France Internationale's short-story prize. Her stories, *Solstices* (1977), show astonishing maturity and originality of vision, imagination, and expression for so young a writer. *Le Poids des êtres* (1987) was singled out for honorable mention by the jury for the *Noma Award. Her novels, *Rue La Poudrière* (1989), *Le Rêve carnassier*, *L'Arbre-fouet* (both 1991), analyse in dense, poetic prose the violence, passions, dreams, and nightmares of life in the slums of Port-Louis, demythifying the Romantic vision of *Mauritius. She is also the author of socio-anthropological studies in English and French, including 'Identité ethnique du groupe telegu de l'île Maurice' (1990). [DSB]

DEVILLE, Patrick (b. 1957). French novelist. *Cordon bleu* (1987) is a story of detection with a shadowy central character and a minimal plot grudgingly revealed; even the mystery is elusive and irony prevails. *Longue vue* (1988) highlights an ornithologist looking back in dreams, memory, and imagination to his past and a woman he loved, and rediscovering them in a long-lost daughter: a novel of recognition rather than of suspense. *Le Feu d'artifice* (1992) describes a series of exhilarating, hallucinatory journeys across Europe, presenting the brittle emotions of three characters in a world of high tech, fast luxury cars, and consumerism. Deville's writing is spare, yet not jejune, at times clinically exact, but leaving room for wit. [PS]

Devin du village, Le (1752). Successful and innovative pastoral opera by Jean-Jacques *Rousseau.

Devoir de violence, Le, see OUOLOGUEM.

Devotional writing. The literature which describes the techniques and experience of prayer and religious meditation is in French primarily in the Roman Catholic tradition, though heterodox, Protestant, and non-Christian traditions are present. Devotional literature may take many forms: autobiographical texts, journals, texts teaching how to meditate, verbal prayers, poems, etc. [see also SERMON].

1. Middle Ages and Renaissance

The most widespread text is surely the *Imitation of Christ* (c.1418) by Thomas à Kempis; many versions and translations of it exist in France from the 1460s

Devotional writing

on, often entitled *L'Éternelle Consolation*. The origins of devotional literature were, however, in the Bible and the early Church Fathers. Before the Renaissance it was mostly written in Latin, and even with the Renaissance the major authors influential in France—Ruysbroek, Ignatius Loyola, Teresa of Avila, John of the Cross—were foreigners. It is difficult to speak of a specifically 'French' school of spirituality except in the 17th c.

Spiritual writing in France can be traced back as far as the 2nd c. It develops considerably during the medieval period, when individual, personal piety, including private prayer, increasingly supplements the collective, communal worship of the early Church. The great monastic foundations were the prime source of much of this spirituality. *De diligendo deo* of *Bernard de Clairvaux is perhaps the first major treatise on mysticism written in France; in proclaiming that God must be loved purely and solely because he is God, he initiated the tradition of 'pure love' which was to be so strong in France. Richard of St Victor (d. 1173), is representative of another tradition: that the contemplation of the order and beauty of creation can lead to a consciousness of the divine.

While manuals of devotion for the laity exist from the 9th c. on, *hagiography and liturgically inspired iconography or drama [see MEDIEVAL THEATRE] probably played a more important role until the 13th and 14th c., when the need to combat *heresy led to the forming of the Dominicans, the *Franciscans, the *Carmelites, and a renewal of spirituality among regular clergy, secular clergy, and laity, with an appropriate literature. The spiritual ladder, the beatific vision, the adoration of the Child Jesus and of the Sacred Heart, of the Compassion of Mary and her seven sorrows, became widespread, but the distinctions between prayer, meditation, and reading are still not clear-cut.

15th-c. France had one major spiritual author, *Gerson. His *La Montagne de contemplation* (1400), *Dialogus de perfectione cordis* (1417), and *Tractatus super Cantica Canticorum* (1429) reject *nominalism's excessive rationalism in favour of a return to the tradition of mysticism stretching from the 5th-c. Pseudo-Dionysius to Ruysbroek in the 14th c. By the end of the century printed books had become widespread, including *livres d'heures* and devotional manuals, generally quite Christocentric.

The 16th-c. humanistic concern with the study of the Bible and the Church Fathers [see EVANGELICALS] led to an increased familiarity with the traditions of mysticism. And the *Counter-Reformation also produced a spiritual renewal. The founder of the Minims, Francis of Paola, and others of the Franciscan tradition emphasized devotion to the humble Jesus, silence, humility; *Béda's *Internelle Consolation* (1542) is perhaps the most representative text of this internal piety. In 1529 the *Jesuits arrived in Paris bringing Ignatian meditation, where the movement of the imagination is intellectually guided towards a sympathetic identification with the major scenes of the Bible, leading to a reshaping of the individual soul.

2. Seventeenth Century

The struggle against the Protestant reform led to a real 'interior crusade', marked not only by renewed catechetical zeal but also by the publication of a mass of devotional tracts, selections of prayers, etc., including the chapbooks of the *Bibliothèque Bleue. This ferment of activity, together with the translation of such major authors as Luis of Grenada, Catherine of Sienna, John of the Cross, and Teresa of Avila, explain in part the rich French flowering of the 17th c. The Englishman William Fitch (in religion, the Capuchin Benedict Canfield, 1502–1611), who spent his religious career in France, prepared the way by propounding the necessity of dying to the self and of total abandonment to God, as did *Richelieu's 'éminence grise', Joseph Tremblay, with his adaptation of Loyola in the *Introduction à la vie spirituelle par une facile méthode d'oraison* (1616).

France was to become for a period the centre of mystical activity and literature. A major instigating role was played by Madame Acarie (1566–1618) who, deeply moved by the translation of the autobiography of Teresa of Avila (1601), founded the reformed Carmelites in France and, after the death of her husband, entered the order in 1613, taking the name of Marie de l'Incarnation; before that, her salon exercised a seminal influence, especially on *Bérulle, the founder of the French Oratory. Bérulle reflects the Augustinian influence and the Christocentric orientation which characterizes the great French spiritual writers of the age.

Of these, the greatest was surely *François de Sales, whose *Introduction à la vie dévote* and *Traité de l'amour de Dieu* remain classics. The former, written for the laity who intend to remain in the world, underlined that the spiritual life is available to all, and is manifested primarily by the love of God and neighbour; it proposes a daily schedule of spiritual exercises centred on the practice of mental prayer.

Bérulle and François de Sales were followed by a noted generation of mystics: Charles de Condren (1588–1641), strongly marked by Augustine, emphasized complete abandonment and self-annihilation. Jean-Jacques Olier (1608–57), the founder of the Saint-Sulpice seminary, believed that we must annihilate our humanity as Christ does his sacred humanity in the sacrifice of the mass. Jean Eudes (1601–80), the founder of the Eudists, together with Marguerite-Marie Alacoque (1647–90), popularized devotions to the Sacred Hearts of Jesus and Mary. Alacoque wrote a remarkable spiritual autobiography and Eudes *Le Cœur admirable de la mère de Dieu* (1670) and *La Vie et le royaume de Jésus* (1637). Mention should also be made of Marie Guyard (Marie de l'Incarnation), first superior of the Ursulines in Quebec, whose *Retraites* (1682) and *L'École sainte* (1684) are the primary works of

French-Canadian spirituality, and of Nicolas Herman (Frère Laurent de la Résurrection) (c.1605–1691), who spent his life working in the kitchen of his monastery; his posthumously published *Maximes spirituelles* (1692) and *Maximes et entretiens* (1694) are among the best manifestations of the passive tendency of French spirituality (he was much cited by *Fénelon). Finally, the remarkable Jesuit Jean-Joseph Surin (1600–65), an exorcist at Loudun whose spiritual autobiography recounts his own 'possession' or madness and his eventual restoration to grace and sanity; his *Fondements de la vie spirituelle* (1667) and *Dialogues spirituels* (1704–9) are exemplary of the quest to lose oneself in the presence of God.

Much of the later 17th-c. spiritual writing is marked by the quarrels over *Jansenism and *Quietism. *Pascal expresses the Jansenist concern with man's tragic situation between *grandeur* and *misère*, which can only be ameliorated by faith centred on the person of Christ. Both the enemy of Quietism, *Bossuet, and its defender, Fénelon, wrote spiritual as well as didactic, polemic, or historical literature; Bossuet's *Élévations sur les mystères* and *Méditations sur les Évangiles* are masterpieces of spiritual prose, as is Fénelon's *Explication des maximes des saints*, with its careful delineation of the differences between true and false mysticism.

Such delineation was necessary by that date because of the writings of two profuse, if not always gifted or orthodox authors, Madame *Guyon and Antoinette Bourignon (1610–80). Guyon, best known for her *Moyen court et très facile de faire oraison*, wrote an autobiography and some 30 other volumes. Bourignon, born at Liège, also wrote extensively (including two autobiographies), and shifted from Quietism to Pietism; she broke with the Church in 1661, proclaiming herself 'the woman clothed with the sun' of the Apocalypse.

3. After 1700

As a result of these excesses and quarrels, the mystical tradition in France fell somewhat into disrepute during the first half of the 18th c. Two notable exceptions were Louis-Marie Grignion de Montfort (1673–1716), whose *Traité de la vraie dévotion à la Sainte Vierge* was only published in 1842, and particularly Jean-Pierre de Caussade (1675–1751), a Jesuit whose *Instructions spirituelles en forme de dialogue sur les divers états d'oraison* (1741) and *L'Abandon à la divine providence* (published 1867) provided an orthodox, acceptable statement of what was best in the Quietist tradition, often quoting Bossuet to that end. Late in the century the heterodox, *Illuminist tradition found its most gifted French exponent in *Saint-Martin.

Late 18th- and 19th-c. French spirituality has been less studied. Much scarred by the Revolution, the Church did produce, particularly among the exiled clergy, some devotional writers of quality, but whose emphasis on the value and meaning of suffering, whose intense and graphic style, may seem somewhat extreme. Devotions to the Sacred Heart, the Sacred Wounds, Our Lady of the Seven Sorrows, mark the period. Exemplary are Jean-Nicolas Grou (1731–1803), author of *L'Intérieur de Jésus et de Marie* (1815), and Jean-Baptiste Lasausse (1740–1826), author of *Le Chrétien brûlant d'amour pour Jésus-Christ crucifié* (1825), whose title is revelatory of content and emphasis. Translations and republications of the classics, including Thomas à Kempis and Teresa of Avila, are numerous, but even the movement centred on *Lamennais produced little in the way of properly spiritual literature, the notable exception being Philippe Gerbet (1798–1864), whose Eucharist-centred *Considérations sur le dogme générateur de la piété chrétienne* (1829) was much appreciated by George *Sand. Ulrich *Guttinguer provided a Christianized version of Saint-Martin, and Eugénie de *Guérin wrote a deeply spiritual *Journal*. There was, above all, a transfer of the techniques and vocabulary of mysticism into poetic practice, often marginal in its relation to Catholicism: the paganism of Maurice de *Guérin, or the various meditations, elevations, contemplations of *Lamartine, *Hugo, even *Baudelaire. The turn of the century did see two great mystical writers: Thérèse de Lisieux (1873–97) continued the Carmelite tradition with her *Histoire d'une âme* (1898), an autobiography recounting no extraordinary grace, but a pure oblation to merciful love as it can be known by a simple soul; and Charles de Foucauld (1858–1916), who left the Trappist order to lead a hermit's life in Algeria, where he met martyrdom after bearing witness to his faith by a life of ecumenical charity (see his posthumous *Écrits spirituels*, 1923). He was influential on Louis Massignon, who pioneered the task of introducing Muslim mysticism to France.

Authors such as Simone *Weil, Lanza del Vasto, and *Teilhard de Chardin have followed the spiritual way in a deeply Christian sense, but showing a limited debt to the traditional techniques of meditation. Indeed, the emphasis of contemporary *Catholicism on common, especially liturgical, participatory worship is not always propitious to the introspective pursuit of the mind's road to God. The masterpieces of devotional literature are often published and appreciated only posthumously, however, and the French mystical tradition remains the subject of scholarly and critical work by such scholars as Jean Orcibal and Michel de *Certeau. [FPB]

See H. Bremond, *Histoire littéraire du sentiment religieux en France*, 12 vols. (1916–36; repr. 1967); J. Orcibal, M. de Certeau, A. Rayez, *et al.*, *Histoire spirituelle de la France* (1964); J. Aumann, *Christian Spirituality in the Catholic Tradition* (1985).

DHÔTEL, André (1900–91). French novelist. Although he wrote extensively on Rimbaud (*L'Œuvre logique de Rimbaud*, 1933; *Rimbaud et la révolte moderne*, 1952; *La Vie de Rimbaud*, 1965),

Dia

Dhôtel is best known for his numerous novels, the most successful of which, *Le Pays où l'on n'arrive jamais* (1955) won the Prix Fémina and typifies his fiction—*Campements* (1930), *Les Chemins du long voyage* (1949), *Un jour viendra* (1970)—where reality is haloed with a sense of magic and where constituent elements are nature, nomadism, young love, and the quest for a tantalizingly elusive *ailleurs*.   [DAS]

DIA, Amadou Cissé (b. *c*.1915). The first play of this Senegalese writer, *La Mort du Damel* was performed in the late 1930s by the École *William Ponty. In the Ponty tradition, it portrays Lat Dior, king of Cayor, who resisted the French invasion, as a local, feudal tyrant rather than the national resistance figure he was to become in post-Independence literature. Dia's second play, *Les Derniers Jours de Lat Dior* (1947), while still betraying vestiges of colonial ideology, can also be seen as a forerunner of the nationalist theatre of the 1960s.   [FNC]

DIA, Malick (b. 1934). Like many post-Independence Senegalese writers, Dia is preoccupied with the moral vacuum resulting from the loss of traditional values. His first novel, *L'Impossible Compromis* (1979) deals with a black–white love relationship. In *Le Balcon de l'honneur* (1984), a somewhat melodramatic novel with less-than-convincing characters, a young wife, in obedience to tradition, commits suicide when her marital fidelity is compromised.   [FNC]

DIABATÉ, Massa Makan (1938–90). Malian writer. He published short stories and plays but is best known for the novels which make up the 'Kouta trilogy': *Le Coiffeur de Kouta* (1980), *Le Boucher de Kouta* (1982), *Le Lieutenant de Kouta* (1979). Here, following in the line of *Kourouma and *Niane, Diabate gives to the adventures of his characters a truly Malinké flavour, both in form and in content.

He was also a translator and poet, continuing the family *griot tradition in *L'Aigle et l'épervier ou la Geste de Sunjata* (1975) and *Janjon et autres chants populaires du Mali* (1970); the latter work belongs to the epic cycle of his bardic race. His initiatory *Comme une piqûre de guêpe* (1980) embodies song, dance, and pantomime like the Kotèba or Malian popular theatre.

At once a traditionalist and a modernist, Diabaté brings to life the great figures of Malinké memory: Sunjata, Samory, Ba-Bemba, Sikasso. He celebrates the beliefs and practices of the people of Kouta, their friendship, *joie de vivre*, solidarity, courage, respect for elders and for promises. His stories are a manifesto of the aesthetics of the word among the Malinké, in that he aims for a faithful rendering of Malinké dialogue, making use of artful comparisons and the infinite resources of the proverb.   [AK]

Diable amoureux, Le, see CAZOTTE.

Diable au corps, Le, see RADIGUET.

Diable boiteux, Le. Novel by *Lesage, published 1707, inspired by Guevara's *Diablo cojuelo* (1641). The 'lame devil' of the title, the spirit Asmodée, is released from a bottle by the student Cleofas; in return, he lifts the roofs of the houses of Madrid for Cleofas to see what is really going on. The result is a series of satirical sketches of Parisian society, loosely linked by an amorous intrigue. With its combination of modern rationalism, lightness of tone, and playful use of the supernatural, the work has been seen by Roger Laufer (in *Lesage ou le Métier de romancier*, 1971) as characteristic of the *Rococo aesthetic.   [PF]

Diable et le bon dieu, Le. Play by *Sartre, first performed 1951. Like *Les *Mains sales*, it contests the bourgeois values of idealist heroism and absolute ethics by revealing them as theatrical posturing. A medieval pageant in 11 tableaux, centred on the German Peasant's war, it shows the leader Goetz espousing first Evil and then Good, and wreaking havoc in both the personal and social spheres, until his final conversion to 'une morale historique et humaine'. The play stresses socio-historical conditioning, situational ethics, and the individual's inability to transcend his or her circumstances if they are sufficiently constricting: the priest, Heinrich, seems doomed to betray either his Church or the people he loves. But the play is not unequivocally pessimistic, and there is a tension between Goetz's final embrace of a war destined to defeat, and, on the other hand, his apparently radical free choice of his course of action.   [CMH]

Diaboliques, Les, see BARBEY D'AUREVILLY.

DIAKHATÉ, Lamine (1928–87). Senegalese poet, novelist, critic, a product of French *assimilation* policy and disciple of *Senghor and the *négritude movement. Of his poetry, 'La Joie d'un continent' (1954), a seven-stanza ode, was later incorporated into *Primordiale du sixième jour* (1960), which celebrates the Creation, with new poems on Senegal's independence and the agony of the then Belgian Congo. Like Senghor his tone is scholarly, reflective, and moderate in expression. *Temps de mémoire* (1968), a rhetorical chronicle and praise poem, expresses the poet's nostalgia for his 'terre millénaire' and 'la sérénité des premiers âges'. *Nigérianes* (1974), 19 short odes resulting from Diakhaté's stay in Nigeria as Senegalese ambassador, are in part a discreet private dialogue (an unmistakable echo of Senghor's *Chants pour Naëtt* and 'Lettre à une Princesse'), and in part the expression of a profound personal experience.

His first fictional work is *Prisonnier du regard* (1975), two stories with a factual basis. *Chalys d'Harlem* (1978), like the stories, is based on actual persons and historical events; it is a well-documented, lively study of a unique personality and black society, ranging from Senegal's legendary past to present-day Harlem. His critical works include *Contribution de l'Afrique Noire et de Madagascar à la littérature contemporaine* (1965); *Lecture libre de 'Lettres d'hivernage' et de 'Hosties noires' de L. S. Senghor* (1976).   [DSB]

Dialectique, La, see RAMUS.

Dialect Literature, see PATOIS AND DIALECT WRITING.

Dialects of Medieval French, see HISTORY OF THE FRENCH LANGUAGE.

DIALLO, Bakary (1892–1978). The only literary work of this Senegalese ex-serviceman, *Force-Bonté* (1926), is an account of his experiences in World War I. A herdsman before joining the colonial army, Diallo, who was self-educated, wrote his account with the aid of French friends. Although the victim of a number of injustices, Diallo is an ardent apologist for colonialism. *Force-Bonté*, republished in 1985, is seen by some literary historians as the forerunner of the francophone African novel.   [FNC]

DIALLO, Nafissatou (1941–82). Senegalese novelist. The three works she published in her lifetime are an autobiographical novel, *De Tilène au plateau* (1976), a historical novel, *Le Fort maudit* (1980), and a children's story, *Awa la petite marchande* (1981). A fourth novel, *La Princesse de Tiali*, came out posthumously in 1987.   [VC]

Dialogue. The dialogue or *entretien*, which sought to imitate urbane conversation [see ORALITY, 2], was a very important literary genre of the *ancien régime*. Although it has continued to be used in more recent times by writers such as *Renan, *Claudel (*Conversations dans le Loir-et-Cher*, 1935), or *Valéry (*Eupalinos ou l'Architecte*, 1923), it has lost its central place in the literary field. Speech is, of course, represented in fictional and dramatic writing of all periods, and certain medieval genres such as the dialogue of allegorical figures or the *jeu parti* or *tenso* embody the dialogic principle, but the prose imitation of urbane conversation really begins with the Renaissance. *Erasmus's *Colloquia*, which were partly aids to learning Latin, enjoyed great popularity in the 16th c. and beyond, but the main models were Plato, Cicero, and Lucian, as mediated by Italian culture. In addition, *Montaigne's *Essais*, although not formally dialogues, offered examples of the unpedantic, conversational discussion of ideas.

Sometimes the dialogue was meant simply to give an agreeable image of talk, but usually this attractive form was a vehicle for putting forward opinions, or at least for raising ideas for discussion. Guez de *Balzac's *Entretiens* (in reality a one-sided conversation), *Méré's *Conversations*, the framing conversation of *La Fontaine's *Les Amours de Psyché*, and the works of *Saint-Évremond and *Bouhours are among the best examples of the more urbane, less didactic type of dialogue in the 17th c.; they are

succeeded in the following century by the works of such writers as *Rémond de Saint-Mard. Often the form lends itself to the discussion of literature; this is the case notably in *Perrault's *Parallèle des anciens et des modernes* and *Fénelon's *Dialogues sur l'éloquence*, but *Desmarets, *Huet, and many others couched their criticism in dialogue form. *Molière's *Critique de l'École des femmes* transfers such imaginary conversations to the stage.

At other times, the dialogue is more overtly philosophical, sometimes quite strenuously so. In *Bodin's *Colloquium Heptaplomeres*, a challenging examination of religious questions, no dominant view emerges [see also TAHUREAU], but elsewhere dialogue often serves a cause, as in *La Mothe le Vayer's sceptical *Dialogues* or the unfinished *La Recherche de la vérité* in which *Descartes tried to embody his distinctly monologic philosophy. Similarly, *Malebranche was to express difficult ideas in accessible form in his *Entretiens sur la métaphysique*. It was probably *Fontenelle who achieved the greatest success with the form in the 17th c., first with his influential piece of scientific popularization, *Entretiens sur la pluralité des mondes*, where a male philosopher casts his thought into conversational form for a willing female learner, and then with his *Dialogues des morts*, where a Lucianesque genre is used for exercises in irreverent scepticism. Fénelon also made use of the dialogue of the dead to teach lessons to the young duc de Bourgogne, while *Montesquieu raised political questions in his *Dialogue de Sylla et d'Eucrate*. (A more elementary form of instructive dialogue is the catechism, which was adapted for political purposes during the Revolution.)

The high point of philosophical dialogue in France is reached with *Diderot, who draws not only on the classical tradition but also on English examples, notably Shaftesbury. His dialogues are sometimes expository in the style of Fontenelle (e.g. the anti-religious *Entretien avec la Maréchale*) but are more often exploratory, as in Le *Rêve de d'Alembert* or the *Supplément au Voyage de Bougainville*. In the exceptional case of Le *Neveu de Rameau*, philosophical dialogue comes close to fiction or drama. *Voltaire, on the other hand, while sometimes writing serious dialogues of ideas (*Dialogues d'Ephémère*, Le Dîner du comte de Boulainvilliers*), more often follows the example of Lucian or of *Boileau's *Dialogues des héros de roman*, creating ridiculous conversations for satirical purposes. Jean-Jacques Rousseau, finally, having used the dialogue form for a preface to La *Nouvelle Héloïse*, returned to it when writing the sequel to his *Confessions, Rousseau juge de Jean-Jacques*. Here dialogue no longer represents urbane conversation, but a divided self and a tragic destiny.   [PF]

See B. Beugnot, *L'Entretien au XVIIe siècle* (1971); D. J. Adams, *Bibliographie d'ouvrages français en forme de dialogue, 1700–1750* (1992).

Dialogue de Sylla et d'Eucrate

Dialogue de Sylla et d'Eucrate, see MONTESQUIEU.

Dialogue Novel. Stories conveyed wholly or largely through dialogue. Only isolated examples of this genre occurred before 1750. From then until about 1800 it enjoyed a minor vogue, with a resurgence from the 1880s onwards. Its subject-matter is extremely varied, ranging from the obscene—Barrin, *Les Délices du cloître* (1672)—to works such as Martin du Gard's **Jean Barois.* Among the best-known writers in the genre are *Crébillon *fils* and *Diderot. The most prolific practitioner was undoubtedly *Gyp, whose best works, like *Bijou* (1896), skilfully exploit the resources of the form. Dialogue novels still appear occasionally, e.g. *Pinget's *L'Inquisitoire* (1962) and Mariella Righini's *La Passion, Ginette* (1983), a 'telephonic' novel [see also SARRAUTE]. [VGM]

Dialogues des morts, see FÉNELON; FONTENELLE.

DIANE DE POITIERS (1499–1560). The middle-aged mistress of *Henri II, over whom she seems to have cast a spell. The story that she gave herself to *François Ier in order to save the life of her father is, despite *Hugo's *Le Roi s'amuse,* almost certainly apocryphal. Under Henri's rule, she was all-powerful; but we have few primary sources concerning their relationship. She is best remembered today as a possible model for *Diana the Huntress* (School of *Fontainebleau) and as the fortunate recipient of the Château d'Anet. [JJS]

Diaries. The literary genre of the *journal intime* appears in France in the 19th c. Previously, many diarists kept and left records of their daily doings and observations, which are of great interest to the historian; notable examples include the 15th-c. so-called *Journal d'un *bourgeois de Paris,* the court diary of *Dangeau, the 18th-c. journal of E.-J.-F. *Barbier, or the *livre de raison* of the 16th-c. Normandy squire Gouberville, which is presented by *Le Roy Ladurie in his *Le Territoire de l'historien* (1973). A particular variant is the *travel journal; these are very numerous, two of the best-known being *Montaigne's Italian journal and *Montesquieu's account of his European travels. There are also many more recent journals containing principally an individual's observation of his or her social world, e.g. *Hugo's *Choses vues,* the diaries of the *Goncourt brothers, or *Léautaud's formidable *Journal littéraire.*

As in the case of Léautaud, it is often difficult to distinguish between 'spectator' diaries and the true *journal intime.* The latter is above all a prolonged exercise in regular introspection—'un registre exact de toutes les pensées de son esprit', as *Diderot put it in a letter to Sophie Volland (14 July 1762). The *Romantic concern for individual subjectivity provided a fertile soil for this new genre, but the diary also had an educative function, particularly for girls. Most private diaries remained unpublished and were little known before the work of Michelle

*Perrot and of Philippe Lejeune (*Le Moi des demoiselles,* 1993). In some cases, however, the diary was immediately recognized as a work of literature. The most striking figure is *Amiel, who owes his fame entirely to his immense *Journal*; one may also cite the much admired diaries of Eugénie de *Guérin and Marie *Bashkirtseff.

Most celebrated *journaux intimes* are the work of figures who are well known as writers in other genres. Remarkable examples over the last two centuries include *Maine de Biran, *Joubert, *Stendhal, *Delacroix, Maurice de *Guérin, *Michelet, *Barrès, Jules *Renard, *Gide, *Pozzi, *Du Bos, *Mauriac, *Jouhandeau, *Green, and *Sartre (*Carnets de la drôle de guerre*). In some cases the journal is less a place of self-scrutiny than a record of mental exploration, the most remarkable case being undoubtedly the *Cahiers* of *Valéry.

Most diaries, even those of writers, have been published posthumously, not having been intended for the public eye. From the 1840s, however, with the publication of the journals of Maine de Biran, Joubert, and Eugénie and Maurice de Guérin, the *journal intime* attained the status of a literary genre, and from this time on, if not before, diarists have usually been conscious of writing not for themselves alone, but for future readers. In some cases, such as those of Gide, Mauriac, and Green, they began to publish their journals in their own lifetime. [PF]

See B. Didier, *Le Journal intime* (1976).

DIARRA, Mandé-Alpha (b. 1954). Malian novelist. Educated at Alfort, Paris, and Montpelier, Diarra alternated writing with veterinary and economics studies and development work at home. His novel, *Sahel! Sanglante sécheresse* (1981), depicts the harsh realities of starvation, necrophagy, and drought in a Mali village victimized by a corrupt bureaucracy. [CHB]

DIAWARA, Gaoussan. Malian playwright, winner of Radio France Internationale theatre prize for *L'Aube des béliers* (1976). He has also published poetry—*Afrique ma boussole* (1980)—and short stories: *La Grande Panique* (1980) and *Les Nouvelles maliennes* (1982). [PGH]

DIB, Mohammed (b. 1920). Algerian poet and novelist. Born in Tlemcen, Dib held various jobs as a teacher, accountant, weaver and rug designer, interpreter, and journalist before turning to full-time writing. In 1959 he moved to France, where he has continued to reside, although he returns regularly to Algeria.

With the death of *Kateb Yacine in 1989, Dib became the undisputed *doyen* of Algerian literature. He was not only one of the first Maghrebian francophone authors of the post-World War II renaissance, publishing poems as early as 1947, but also continued to be both prolific and innovative. Unlike some of his contemporaries, Dib has constantly sought to renew and revitalize his writing. Besides being Algeria's foremost living novelist, he is a major poet.

Dib was, with *Feraoun, *Mammeri, and Kateb, a member of the 'Generation of 52', so dubbed because of the appearance in 1952 of important first novels by Dib (*La Grande Maison*) and Mammeri (*La Colline oubliée*) and sometimes renamed the 'Generation of 54' to refer to the major political event of modern Algerian history, the outbreak of the war of independence.

La Grande Maison, the first volume of a loosely knit trilogy (*L'Algérie*), is a naturalistic description of life in the streets and housing projects where the poor live. In this work the main characters are, in Zolaesque fashion, subordinate to the looming allegorical presence of Hunger. The remaining volumes (*L'Incendie*, 1954; *Le Métier à tisser*, 1957) continue to reflect Dib's left-wing social and political commitments during the 1940s and 1950s. His early novels have been widely read in Algeria and have been introduced into the school and university curricula.

Dib's work took a dramatic turn in the early 1960s when he forsook the naturalistic, 'ethnographic' novel for a more interiorized and oneiric discourse. His best known novel, *Qui se souvient de la mer* (1962), ostensibly deals with the *Algerian War, but is particularly remarkable for its many-layered, surreal, and futuristic imagery. In a liminary note, Dib acknowledges the importance to his creative vision of *Picasso's *Guernica* and science fiction, but we also find evidence of the influence of Freud and Jung in the subterranean and oceanic worlds where the action unfolds as well as in the mythic portrayal of the woman and the mother.

Dib also published, at this time, the first of a series of brilliant collections of poetry. *Ombre gardienne* (1961), although highly rarefied, provides an early link to the novels, for several of the texts in the collection first appeared as songs inserted into the trilogy. If the prose has evolved over the years, the poetry has, on the contrary, remained fairly consistent in style, perhaps because, as Dib once remarked, he is unable to practise spontaneous automatic writing in writing his novels—even when the result seems oneiric—whereas he often uses such procedures in composing the poems.

Dib's many novels may be divided roughly into four groups: the early naturalistic trilogy; the interiorized psychological, oneiric novels, usually set in Algeria (*Qui se souvient de la mer*; *Cours sur la rive sauvage*, 1964; *La Danse du roi*, 1968; *Habel*, 1977); the two novels of an unfinished trilogy about Algeria during the years of crisis in the early 1970s (*Dieu en Barbarie*, 1970; *Le Maître de chasse*, 1973); and the 'nordic novels' set in Algeria, Finland, and France (*Les Terrasses d'Orsol*, 1985; *Le Sommeil d'Ève*, 1989; *Neiges de marbre*, 1990). Some works defy easy classification, however, being transitional, such as some of the early short stories in *Au café* (1955) and *Le Talisman* (1966) and the at-once realistic and psycho-

logical *Un été africain* (1959), in which the identity quest of a young girl unfolds before the muted sounds and imagery of the Algerian War.

Dib's poems in *Formulaires* (1970), *Omneros* (1975), *Feu beau feu* (1979), and *Ô vive* (1987) are hermetic and derive much of their power from their linguistic virtuosity—including neologisms, plays on names and words, and deliberate ambiguities—and half-revealed urgencies, such as erotic innuendoes, which allow the reader's imagination to play freely around these exquisitely understated texts.   [ES]

See J. Déjeux, *Mohammed Dib, écrivain algérien* (1977); *Revue CELFAN Review* ('Mohammed Dib'), 2: 2 (1983); C. Bonn, *Lecture présente de Mohammed Dib* (1988).

Dictionaries [See also ENCYCLOPEDIAS]

1. Medieval and Renaissance

The origins of French lexicography lie in bilingual French–Latin glossaries of the medieval period, themselves inspired by Latin monolingual glossaries and notably Joannes Balbus's *Catholicon* (composed c.1286, first published 1460). Bilingual French–Latin glossaries of the 13th and 14th c. deriving from such works include the oldest surviving example, known as the *Abavus* (c.1285) and the *Aalma* (second half of the 14th c.), essentially an adaptation of the *Catholicon*. With Firmin Le Ver's bilingual *Dictionarius* (1420–40) the number of entries increases to some 45,000 words. There are only two known examples of exclusively French glossaries in the medieval period, both primarily intended to explain the texts they accompany: 'Li Ars d'amour' (c. late 13th/early 14th c.) and a late 15th-c. rhetorical treatise.

The 16th c. is dominated by the typically Renaissance polyglot dictionaries and, from 1552 on, bilingual dictionaries featuring French and another modern language (e.g. Flemish, 1552; Spanish, 1562; English, 1570). The best-known polyglot dictionary is that termed *Le Calepin* in France. Ambrosius Calepinus's Latin *Dictionarium* (1502) was constantly augmented during the century until it featured 11 languages, with French included for the first time in 1545.

The most significant publication for the history of lexicography in the 16th c. was Robert *Estienne's *Dictionnaire français–latin* (1539). For all its defects, not least that it is primarily the inverse dictionary of his earlier Latin–French dictionary (*Dictionarium Latino–Gallicum*, 1538), itself preceded by a *Latinae linguae thesaurus* (1531), the French–Latin version is notable as a precursor of French monolingual dictionaries, for where no Latin equivalent of a French term is available, a French explanation is offered.

2. Seventeenth Century

The most important of subsequent reworkings of Estienne's material was Jean Nicot's *Trésor de la langue française* (1606), comprising some 18,000 entries. Nicot still provides Latin equivalents for the

Dictionaries

French words, but has more sophisticated monolingual entries offering explanations of the meaning of words and details of their orthography, gender, etymology, and usage. From 1606 to 1680 no major original monolingual French dictionary appeared; the majority of works published before 1680 are thus bilingual, and notably Latin–French dictionaries (e.g. Philibert Monet, *Inventaire des deux langues française et latine*, 1635), although there are also important modern-language bilingual dictionaries (e.g. *Cotgrave's French–English dictionary of 1611). Note too *Ménage's *Origines de la langue française* (1650, 2nd edn. 1694), an early French etymological dictionary.

It was therefore not until 1680, some 70 years later than for Italian and Spanish, that the first entirely monolingual dictionary of French appeared, César-Pierre Richelet's *Dictionnaire français*. Although conceived as a dictionary of good usage, this lexicon of some 25,500 entries includes a whole range of words shunned by purists, and notably technical terms. Variationist labels indicate the usage and currency of the words and the entries are supported by literary quotations. Richelet's work continued to appear right up to 1811. If Richelet is the ancestor of descriptive dictionaries, *Furetière's *Dictionnaire universel* (1690), embracing some 40,000 words, with technical and medical terms especially well represented, presages the vast general and encyclopedic dictionaries of the following century. The *Dictionnaire de l'*Academie française*, first promised in the Academy's statutes of 1635, finally appeared in two vols. in 1694. *Chapelain's original plan was for the dictionary to feature examples of literary usage on the model of the Italian Crusca dictionary, but this was subsequently revised as work progressed painfully slowly, notably after *Vaugelas's death in 1650. The Academy reflects the prescriptive mentality of the age, banishing from its dictionary of some 15,000 words those terms considered too old, too new, technical, of low register, 'd'emportement ou qui blessent la pudeur'; in practice, however, it was somewhat more tolerant. The most striking feature is the presentation of the material by roots, so that derivations and compounds are treated under their primes. The exclusion of old and technical terms from the dictionary was compensated for by the Academy's *Dictionnaire des arts et des sciences*, edited by Thomas *Corneille (1694).

3. Eighteenth Century

The different methods of Furetière, Richelet, and the Academy each had their successors in the following century. Following Furetière, the 18th c. particularly favoured universal dictionaries and encyclopedias, the proportions of which increased considerably during the century. We may also note the inventories of specialist and technical terms, such as Augustin-Charles d'Aviler's *Dictionnaire d'architecture civile et hydraulique* (1755) and the first synonym dictionaries by Gabriel *Girard (1718, 1736).

In 1701 Furetière's dictionary had been revised by *Basnage de Beauval. The *Jesuits of Trévoux then decided to expand the work further by including Latin equivalents, historical information, and additional scientific and technical terms. The resulting *Dictionnaire universel français et latin* (3 vols., 1704), commonly known as the *Dictionnaire de Trévoux*, continued to expand until by 1771 it comprised eight folio volumes, only declining in importance in the face of the *Encyclopédie*.

The Academy published four new editions of its dictionary during the century. The second (1718) continued the Academy's selective policy, but adopted an alphabetical presentation; whilst the third (1740) introduced some spelling reforms. By the fourth (1762) and fifth (1798), some new scientific, technical, and Revolutionary terms were included.

With the general increase in volume of dictionaries came the need for abridged or original pocket dictionaries, especially during the economic crisis of 1780–1820. Initially these covered specialized domains (e.g. Prévost's dictionary of rare and specialized words, the *Manuel lexique* of 1751), but subsequently more general works appeared. Occasionally, with the new vogue for expansion in the 19th c., abridged dictionaries were re-expanded. Perhaps the most interesting work and best source of information about late 18th-c. usage is Jean-François Féraud's *Dictionnaire critique de la langue française* (1787–8), with its moderately purist approach and use of literary examples.

4. Nineteenth Century

The 19th c. extended 18th-c. practice in providing large and usually learned dictionaries, although occasionally quality is sacrificed to quantity. These sometimes comprise more than 150,000 words, include ever more documentation, and become increasingly open to neologisms. Pierre-Claude Victoire Boiste's *Dictionnaire universel de la langue française* of 1800 (14th edn., 1857), subsequently renamed *Pan-lexique*, sets the trend in containing an abundant, if somewhat excessive, word list. This was followed by Bescherelle's *Dictionnaire national ou Grand dictionnaire critique de la langue* (1843). The 19th c. is also typified by the increased use of diachronic material and the citation of classical authors; the best-known example is *Littré's *Dictionnaire de la langue française* (1863–72, supplement 1877). Another major publication was Pierre *Larousse's *Grand dictionnaire universel du XIXe siècle* (1865–90), part dictionary, part encyclopedia, containing a vast but not excessive number of terms and making extensive use of citations from 19th-c. authors. As well as abridged and specialized versions of Larousse's dictionary, we may note the appearance of the *Nouveau Larousse illustré* (1898–1907). The end of the century saw the publication of the *Dictionnaire général de la langue française*, edited by Adolphe Hatzfeld, Arsène Darmesteter, and André Antoine Thomas (1898–1900), in which considerable emphasis is placed on the historical material, the etymologies and datings by now becoming more accurate.

Two new editions of the Academy's dictionary appeared in the 19th c. (1835, 1878), and abridged versions and complements of additional terms were also popular (e.g. by Légoarant, 1841). The growing historical preoccupations of the 19th c. are reflected in Frédéric Godefroy's 10 vol. *Dictionnaire de l'ancienne langue française* (1880–1902). Specialized works continued to appear, such as the synonym dictionaries of Guizot (1809) and Lafaye (1857).

5. Twentieth Century

The 20th c. has witnessed the re-edition of the great 19th-c. dictionaries and the appearance of new large-scale encyclopedic dictionaries. For instance, Larousse's publications include the *Larousse du XXe siècle* (1928–33), *Grand Dictionnaire encyclopédique Larousse* (1982), and *Grand Larousse de la langue française* (1971–8). Special mention must be made of Paul Robert's *Dictionnaire alphabétique et analogique de la langue française* (1953–64, 1970; 2nd edn., 1985), which includes numerous literary citations from the 16th to the 20th c. and features words associated with the headword through synonymy, antonymy, etc. In 1932–5 the eighth edition of the Academy's dictionary appeared and the ninth is currently being issued in fascicles (1986–).

Alongside the vast lexicons, there has been notable growth in two areas: concise dictionaires aimed at the general public and specialized works. Larousse, for instance, publishes a whole range of dictionaries, such as the *Larousse des débutants* (1957), aimed at children and foreigners, or the *Larousse de base, dictionnaire d'apprentissage du français* (1977). Particularly popular and known for its openness to neologisms is the *Petit Larousse*, which appears annually. Also worthy of note is Jean Dubois's *Dictionnaire du français contemporain* (1966), which adopts a structuralist approach. Robert has produced the popular *Petit Robert* (1967) and the *Micro-Robert* (1971) containing *c*.30,000 'mots primordiaux'.

The vast range of specialist works is too extensive to detail. There has been a growth of dictionaries covering earlier periods of the language's history, both large-scale (e.g. Tobler-Lomatzsch's dictionary of Old French, 1925–) and of more modest proportions. Virtually every aspect of language has been represented in a specialized work, including dictionaries of difficulties, pronunciation, synonymy, neologisms, and *argot. Walther von Wartburg's *Französisches Etymologisches Wörterbuch* (1922–) dominates etymological dictionaries, but the Robert *Dictionnaire historique de la langue française* (1992) is worthy of note; there are also valuable more concise dictionaries, notably Bloch and Wartburg's *Dictionnaire étymologique de la langue française* (1932, 5th edn. 1968).

Two new developments must be mentioned finally. First, the growth of the study of lexicography as an academic discipline, both in its theoretical and historical aspects; and secondly, from 1960 on, the use of mechanized and electronic techniques for the gathering of data and compilation of dictionaries. Most major publishing-houses specializing in dictionaries now plan computerized dictionaries. Use of on-line technology has been of importance in a major 20th-c. project to produce a *Trésor de la langue française* (TLF), which will cover the history of French in four or five broad periods. Publication has begun for the period 1789–1960 (*TLF, XIXe–XXe s.*, 1971–). As well as using the *Inventaire général de la langue française*, the project has collected its own computer database of some 90 million examples. Words not selected for the dictionary (to comprise *c*.85,000 words) will be published in specialized inventories. [WA-B]

See G. Matoré, *Histoire des dictionnaires français* (1968); B. Quemada, *Les Dictionnaires du français moderne 1539–1863* (1968); *Wörterbucher, Dictionaries, Dictionnaires*, ed. F. J. Hausmann and others, vol. 2 (1990).

Dictionnaire critique et historique, see BAYLE.

Dictionnaire des idées reçues. Humorous collection of banal remarks (e.g. 'Actrices. La perte des fils de famille') compiled over many years by *Flaubert, who put similar statements into the mouths of his bourgeois characters. It was published posthumously.

Dictionnaire philosophique portatif, Le. *Voltaire's compact, personal response to the cumbersome *Encyclopédie* of which he said: 'Twenty folio volumes will never make a revolution. It is the little portable volumes costing thirty *sous* that are to be feared. Had the Gospel cost twelve hundred sesterces the Christian religion would never have been established.' Voltaire was working on his *Dictionnaire* in that spirit as early as September 1752, and restarted work on it in 1760 following the ban on the *Encyclopédie*. When it appeared (July 1764), incorporating 73 articles of vastly differing lengths, its kaleidoscopic variety of styles and stances (ranging from the serious or the ironic to the mock-naïve, the comic, or the grotesque) did not even momentarily obscure the fact that this work exemplified the radical, utilitarian spirit of the *Enlightenment. It was equally evident (particularly to the authorities who repeatedly banned it) that the *Dictionnaire*, with its pitiless examination of morals and the religion of the arrogant established Church (which he presents as the source of countless ills), also had an underlying unity of purpose. For it presented a coherent counter-image of Voltaire's ideal society: a laicized place of free thought which is quintessentially tolerant, for tolerance is the key to stability, prosperity, and happiness. Such was the success of the work that, by 1769, it had already had 16 editions (sometimes appearing under the title *La Raison par* *alphabet*), and had been expanded to include an extra 45 articles. In 1770 Voltaire started producing an overlapping companion (the *Questions sur l'Encyclopédie*), which itself went through a dozen editions before his death. [JR]

DIDEROT, Denis (1713–84). Regarded today as one of the three greatest French writers of the 18th c., Diderot is a striking example of a writer whose reputation has grown with time. Many of his best works were unknown to his contemporaries, for whom he was principally the editor of the *Encyclopédie*. For the 19th c. he was above all a freethinking *philosophe* and was claimed as an ancestor by left-wing and anticlerical thinkers. More recently, as the full range of his work has become better known, readers have been most impressed by the adventurous and subtle qualities of his immensely varied writings.

He was born in Langres, the son of a cutler whose virtuous image haunts many of his works. His mother died when he was young. Of his two sisters, one died mad in a convent, while his younger brother became a priest. He attended the local Jesuit college, then moved to Paris, where he graduated as Master of Arts at the age of 18. Rejecting a legal career, he launched into a bohemian life of expedients, including translation from the English. In 1742 he married the penniless Antoinette Champion; of their several children only one, Angélique, reached adult years.

His first significant publication was a relatively free translation from the English moralist Shaftesbury, the *Essai sur le mérite et la vertu* (1745); this book announces the views that permeate much of his later writing. At the same time he embarked on a major undertaking, the editing of the *Encyclopédie*, which occupied many years of his life and enabled him to make a living from literary earnings. Apart from his editorial work (which entailed writing a vast number of filler articles), his main contributions were in the fields of philosophy, science, art, and technology.

In the late 1740s he wrote some fiction, notably the episodic *Les Bijoux indiscrets* (1748), which combines an exotic and licentious plot with some adventurous philosophical explorations. In the same period a series of essays on religion and philosophy, the *Pensées philosophiques* (1746), *La Promenade du sceptique* (1747), and the *Lettre sur les aveugles* (1749), show him working his way from a form of *deism tinged with scepticism to a position of materialist atheism; to this, with some hesitations, he adhered for the rest of his life. The *Lettre* deals largely with the problems of perception posed by Locke's philosophy, and illustrates Diderot's typical mixing of empirical evidence and imagination in dealing with philosophical problems; it is most remarkable for the eloquent cosmic vision attributed to the blind mathematician Saunderson, in which Diderot for the first time envisages the great flux of nature

which knows no Newtonian order. For this work he was imprisoned in the Château de Vincennes, and was only released on promising to publish no further subversive books—a promise which had a considerable effect on his subsequent writing, forcing him to adopt indirect methods, or to write for posterity. Two philosophical works followed. The *Lettre sur les sourds et muets* (1752) is mainly concerned with questions of art and language; in places it anticipates Romantic notions of poetry. The *Pensées sur l'interprétation de la nature* (1753) is a series of richly suggestive reflections on scientific method and owes a good deal to the writings of Francis Bacon. In these early works one can already see Diderot's characteristic modes of writing; using dialogue to test out views one against another, and allowing himself the digressive freedom of loose forms such as the letter, he enjoys pushing ideas to the limit, challenging the reader with bold, paradoxical insights.

By 1750 he was a leading figure in Paris literary circles and in the *philosophe* movement. Among his close friends were *Grimm, *Condillac, d'*Alembert, *Holbach, and above all Jean-Jacques *Rousseau, with whom he was to quarrel bitterly and irreconcilably in 1758. In 1755 he fell in love with an unmarried woman, Sophie Volland, to whom he addressed over the next twenty years an unparalleled sequence of letters, his nearest approach to an autobiography.

The theatre was one of his main interests in the 1750s. Two theoretical works, *Entretiens sur le Fils naturel* (1757) and *Discours sur la poésie dramatique* (1758), spell out his proposals for a new kind of theatre, the *drame or serious play of contemporary middle-class life, written in prose and making considerable use of gesture and tableau effects. His two plays which illustrate these theories, *Le Fils naturel* (1757) and *Le Père de famille* (1758), seem declamatory and sentimental to modern taste, but Diderot's innovatory approach was very influential all over Europe in the next 150 years.

Prose fiction also occupied him a great deal. In the *Éloge de Richardson* (1762) he praised the realism and emotional power of the English novelist, and in 1760 he wrote his own novel of female suffering, *La *Religieuse*. At about the same time, smarting from the persecution of the *Encyclopédie*, he began one of his masterpieces, *Le *Neveu de Rameau*. He also became increasingly involved with the visual arts, and in 1759 produced the first of his many accounts of the biennial exhibitions of the *Académie Royale de Peinture et de Sculpture, the *Salons*; in connection with these he wrote in 1766 his theoretical *Essais sur la peinture*.

Diderot was keenly interested in mathematics and the natural sciences, attending chemistry lectures and following recent developments in medicine and biology. The latter are the subject of his *Eléments de physiologie* (1773) and of the remarkable group of dialogues entitled *Le *Rêve de d'Alembert*

(1769), in which he proposes an eloquent materialist account of human and animal life.

In order to provide a dowry for his daughter (who married in 1772), he accepted patronage from Catherine the Great of Russia, who was anxious to present herself as an enlightened monarch. In 1773, therefore, he travelled to St Petersburg, staying there for several months and having frequent and lengthy meetings with the empress, whom he tried to win over to his own views on government and society. His disillusionment with her reforms is reflected in the political writings which assume an increased importance in his later years. In works such as *Mémoires pour Catherine II* (1773) and *Observations sur le Nakaz* (1774), he adopts a democratic and often radical standpoint. This is even more true of his voluminous and anonymous contributions to Raynal's *Histoire des deux Indes.

But he was more a moralist than a political thinker. He was fascinated by the moral dilemmas faced by would-be free individuals in 'civilized' society, and this preoccupation is evident in a number of remarkable tales and dialogues of the 1770s, *Entretien d'un père avec ses enfants, Les Deux Amis de Bourbonne, Ceci n'est pas un conte, Madame de la Carlière*, and the *Supplément au Voyage de Bougainville*. Related questions are discussed at about the same time in a critical commentary on *Helvétius's De l'homme* and in a much-discussed work of dramatic theory, *Le Paradoxe sur le comédien* (1773), where he defends the view that great acting requires detachment rather than involvement. The most important work of his later years, however, was the novel *Jacques le fataliste*. He continued writing up to the year before his death, the last significant titles being the comedy *Est-il bon? Est-il méchant?* (1781) and the *Essai sur les règnes de Claude et de Néron* (1782). The former is his most successful dramatic work, and shows him attempting to come to terms with his own moral contradictions; the *Essai*, in the form of an extended commentary on the life and writings of Seneca, is in fact an *apologia pro vita sua*, partly provoked by the imminent publication of Rousseau's *Confessions.

During his lifetime many of Diderot's greatest writings were not published, and circulated only in manuscript, notably in his friend Grimm's *Correspondance littéraire*. They have only gradually become known over the ensuing 200 years. Together they make up an astonishing body of work. In almost every field he touched on—art criticism, metaphysics, biology, moral philosophy, political thought, theatre, fiction—he made innovative contributions. The central theme of his thought is probably to be found in the elaboration of a materialist view of the world, and the consequential search for an appropriate morality, aesthetics, and politics. But it would be wrong to reduce him to a single philosophy. He thrives on contradiction. Characteristically weaving together reflection and story-telling, he is always testing theory against experience. As a writer, he is notable for his Protean energy, his humour, irony, and openness. Adopting, transforming, and combating the ideas of others, he brings opposing voices and views into contact and conflict, and involves his reader in an adventure of the mind. [PF]

See A. Wilson, *Diderot* (1972); J. Chouillet, *Diderot* (1977); P. France, *Diderot* (1982).

Didon se sacrifiant, see JODELLE.

Dien Bien Phu. The dramatic French defeat here in 1954 marked the end of the French colonial presence in *Indo-China.

DIERX, Léon (1838–1912). Poet. In 1898 Dierx, who had left his native Reunion to become a civil servant in Paris, succeeded *Mallarmé as 'prince des poètes'. Like his *Parnassian associates, Dierx no longer holds a significant position within the French canon but, like *Leconte de Lisle and *Parny, belongs to a remarkable group of writers born on Reunion who constitute for most literary historians the origins of the island's francophone literature. Dierx's Œuvres complètes were published in 1872 (an augmented edition appeared in 1888). His best-known poems, which are descriptive of biblical scenes, are closer to linguistic equivalents of paintings than rewritings of scripture. [BEJ]

Dieu, by Victor Hugo, see LÉGENDE DES SIÈCLES.

Dieux ont soif, Les, see FRANCE.

Dîme royale, La, see VAUBAN.

Diogène, see CAILLOIS.

DIOP, Alioune (1910–80), see PRÉSENCE AFRICAINE.

DIOP, Birago Ismaël (1906–89). Senegalese poet and fabulist, one of the pioneers of Negro-African writing in French. Though encouraged by his brother Massyla in his early flair for writing, he followed the example of another brother in studying veterinary medicine at Toulouse. After qualifying he rejoined his compatriots and contemporaries, *Senghor and Ousmane *Socé Diop, in Paris, and contributed to the newly founded L'*Étudiant noir translations of the *dits faits* (aphorisms) of the Senegalese sage, Kotje Barma, and tales told in his childhood by his grandmother and the family *griot. Appointed veterinary surgeon to western Sudan, he began consciously to collect folk-tales and legends of French West Africa.

Caught up in France from 1942 to 1946 by the German occupation, he contributed with Senghor, *Damas, and Alioune Diop (no relation) to the literary and political aspects of the *négritude movement, publishing poems, original stories, and traditional folk-tales in various magazines, including the first number of *Présence africaine. His *Contes d'Amadou Koumba* (1947) shared the Grand Prix

Diop

Littéraire d'Afrique Occidentale Française with Socé Diop's *Karim*. From 1950 to 1960 he worked as chief of veterinary services in Ivory Coast, Upper Volta, and Mauretania, while putting the finishing touches to the *Nouveaux contes d'Amadou Koumba* (1958). The last volume of the trilogy, *Contes et lavanes* [riddles in the form of short songs] (1963) won the Grand Prix Littéraire d'Afrique Noire. Selections from the three volumes have been published in English as *Tales of Amadou Koumba*. His collected poems, with the punning title *Leurres et lueurs* (1960), like his tales, express the spirit of non-militant *négritude*, but his real poetic talent is manifested in his tales. While modestly claiming to be merely the scribe and translator of his household *griot*, he is in fact a totally original writer, a master of sophisticated narrative, passing from reality to fantasy, with a very personal gift for urbane, economical irony, alternately comic, poetic, and dramatic. Some of his tales have been successfuly dramatized and two made into films.

From 1960 to 1966 he represented the newly independent Republic of Senegal as ambassador to Tunis, then returned to Dakar to open a veterinary clinic. After a decade of silence, protesting that he had broken his pen, Birago produced the first volume of his memoirs, *La Plume raboutée* (1978), followed in 1982 by the second, *A rebrousse-temps*. These offer an insight into the educational system of colonial Senegal, the social life of young people in Dakar, and the activities of black intellectuals in France in the inter-war years. They also demonstrate the literary qualities that form the charm of his *Contes*: humour, urbanity, observation of people's mannerisms, and the ability to weave drama and tension into the fabric of real episodes.

[DSB]

See M. Kane, *Essai sur les Contes d'Amadou Coumba: du conte traditionnel au conte moderne d'expression française* (1981).

DIOP, Boubacar Boris (b. 1946). Senegalese writer. Among the most artistically and philosophically serious writers of his generation, Diop, journalist and co-founder of the Senegalese weekly *Sud-hebdo*, has published two novels and a play. *Le Temps de Tamango* (1981) is a re-creation of the historical events of 1968 in Senegal, viewed from a 21st-c. perspective in which the neo-colonial state has been replaced by communism. Diop is preoccupied not only with the incompetence of the present leadership but with the nature of revolutionary movements and the role of intellectuals in revolutionary activity. *Tamango*, though spiked with healthy scepticism and leaving no room for facile illusions, is written in a style which bubbles with energy and dry humour. At the formal level, the novel breaks with all the conventions of traditional Western narrative. Diop's second novel, *Les Tambours de la mémoire* (1987), less formally innovative, is also more sombre: the intellectual, no longer able to identify with urban radical movements, tries to join up with a peasant resistance organization in the forest, led by a legendary female figure. Both Diop's works have won prizes: *Les Tambours* was the first winner of the Abdou Diouf Literary Award in 1990. His play, *Thiaroye terre rouge* (1981), is a powerful forerunner of *Sembene's film, *Camp de Thiaroye*. Diop is also actively involved in the national languages movement.

[FNC]

DIOP, Cheikh Anta (1923–86). Philosopher, linguist, Egyptologist, mathematician, and scientist, one of the most profoundly revolutionary thinkers francophone Africa has produced in the 20th c. In 1946 he left his native Senegal for further studies in France. His first doctoral thesis, rejected by the Sorbonne, was published in 1954 under the title *Nations nègres et culture*. Two later theses finally resulted in Diop being awarded a *doctorat d'état*.

On his return to Senegal at Independence, Diop worked as a researcher at the Institut Fondamental d'Afrique Noire (IFAN). Several more works were published, including *Antériorité des civilisations nègres: mythe ou vérité historique?* (1967), *Les Fondements économiques et culturels d'un état fédéral d'Afrique noire* (1974), and *Parenté génétique de l'égyptien pharaonique et des langues négro-africaines* (1977), but, despite his growing international reputation, he was never permitted to lecture at the University of Dakar. He set up three successive political parties, all of which were banned, and was arrested and imprisoned several times. He died in 1986 and received posthumously the national recognition he had been denied throughout his life: the university in which he had been banned from lecturing was named after him.

Diop's fate at the hands of the French and of *Senghor can be explained in terms of his ideas and the political implementation he sought to give them. In his radio-carbon laboratory at IFAN he developed techniques which enabled him to prove that, contrary to the claims of European Egyptologists, many of the ruling class of the ancient Egypt whose achievements Europeans have revered had been black Africans. Diop thus undermined the Western theory of African cultural inferiority, an ideologicial corner-stone of colonial exploitation. Secondly, using linguistic and other forms of cultural evidence, Diop demonstrated the underlying unity beneath the surface diversity of African cultures, thus calling into question the Balkanization of Africa by the colonial powers. Politically Diop was a pan-Africanist and federalist, the francophone counterpart of Nkrumah and, like the latter, an obvious threat to Western interests in Africa.

Efforts by the colonial and neo-colonial establishments to marginalize Diop have proved unsuccessful in the long term. His theory of the black African contribution to ancient Egyptian civilization is now generally accepted, and has become increasingly popular as a weapon in the struggle of black minorities against racism.

[FNC]

DIOP, David (1927–60). Poet of Cameroonian-Senegalese parentage, who spent his early childhood in Senegal and his adolescence in France. In his teens he was already writing militant anti-colonial poetry and took part in the setting-up of *Présence africaine* in Paris in 1947. On his return to Senegal, Diop taught in a secondary school in Dakar. In 1956 his only collection of poems, *Coups de pilon*, was published. In 1960 he was killed in a plane crash. A member of the Parti Africain de l'Indépendance, in his politics and in his poetry Diop opposed *Senghor. Although the latter included Diop in his 1948 anthology, he regretted Diop's 'lack of romanticism' and hoped he would 'grow more human with age'. Other critics have appreciated the deep humanism of Diop's revolutionary poetry. Because he adopts the point of view of the unprivileged majority, his picture of Africa foregrounds the pain and humiliation of colonialism. His work throbs with an infectious hatred of injustice and a confidence in the ability of Africans and all oppressed peoples to rise up and overcome it. His revolutionary commitment has been seen as inimical to the interests of poetry, but his poems, though brimming over with a seemingly spontaneous energy and intensity, are carefully crafted and have stood the test of time.   [FNC]

DIOP, Massyla (1885–1932). Older half-brother of Birago, editor of the short-lived *Revue africaine littéraire et artistique*, in which he published poems and a realist novel in serial form of Senegalese town life, *Le Réprouvé, le roman d'une Sénégalaise* (1925), which profoundly influenced Ousmane *Socé Diop and Abdoulaye *Sadji, as well being his brother's 'bush of fire'. He anticipated the tenets of *négritude by advocating a return to the values of Africa's past.
                                              [DSB]

Directoire, Le (the Directory), see REVOLUTION, 1d.

Disciple, Le, see BOURGET.

'Discours à Madame de la Sablière', see LA FONTAINE.

Discours antillais, Le, see GLISSANT.

Discours de la méthode, see DESCARTES.

Discours de la servitude volontaire, see LA BOÉTIE.

Discours des misères de ce temps, see RONSARD.

Discours des passions de l'amour, see PASCAL.

Discours sur les sciences et les arts (1750). The academic discourse which brought fame to J.-J. *Rousseau, and in which he first sketched out his vision of human history.

Discours sur l'histoire universelle, see BOSSUET.

Discours sur l'inégalité (often known as the 'Second Discourse'), see ROUSSEAU, J.-J.

Discours sur l'universalité de la langue française (1784). *Rivarol's prize-winning essay for the Academy of Berlin. He argued that French had been destined to grow, over the years, into a matchless vehicle for civilized exchange. It deserved this pre-eminence, since its inherent qualities made it the language of logic and clarity: 'Ce qui n'est pas clair n'est pas français.' Although all languages are mortal, they gain a type of immortality thanks to the masterpieces written in them. French will thus become a dead language only when it ceases to have great writers.   [JR]

Disparition, La (1969). Full-length novel by *Perec from which the letter *e* is entirely absent.

Dispute, La. Late one-act comedy by *Marivaux, first performed 1742. Long neglected, it has attracted directors in recent decades. In order to settle an argument as to whether love is a natural emotion, the protagonists of a frame play watch unseen the behaviour of two couples brought up in the 'state of nature'. Both sexes show the characteristics of civilized humanity: 'vices et vertus, tout est égal entre eux.'   [PF]

Dit. A type of poem that began to appear in the late 13th c. and remained popular into the 15th. It was not a strictly defined genre. Poems identified as *dits* were often written in octosyllabic couplets, but other verse forms were possible. The *dit* could range from around one hundred to several thousand lines. It could be either narrative or expository; and, although it was never set to music, it could include lyric insertions with musical settings. The *dit* could address a variety of topics, including love, social and political satire, moral and spiritual matters, and eulogy.

In spite of such variety, certain traits can be associated with the *dit*. It is always constructed on first-person discourse. Thus the narrative *dits*, in which a narrator identified with the author recounts events that he or she experienced or observed, can be distinguished from the *lai*, narrated in the third person and often set in the distant past. Because of the importance of this first-person voice, *dits* are frequently transmitted along with other works by the same author, and can be associated with the rise of the single-author codex at the beginning of the 14th c. [see AUTHORSHIP]. Early examples of poets whose *dits* were compiled and transmitted as authorial collections are *Rutebeuf, *Baudouin de Condé and his son Jean, and *Watriquet de Couvin. Subsequently, the narrative *dits* of *Machaut, *Froissart, and *Christine de Pizan were transmitted in anthology codices containing the collected works, both lyric and narrative, of those poets.   [SJH]

Divorce, see MARRIAGE.

Dix années d'exil, see STAËL.

Djamal, see KRÉA.

DJAOUT, Tahar (1954–93). Algerian novelist. In *L'Exproprié* (1984), *Les Chercheurs d'os* (1984), *L'Invention du désert* (1987), and *Les Vigiles* (1991) he describes the difficulties of daily life in post-Independence Algeria, warning against bureaucracy, despotism, and religious fanaticism. Assassinated by an unknown assailant, he was the first in a series of Algerian intellectuals murdered in terrorist attacks attributed variously to Islamist insurgents and state-backed death squads. [AGH]

DJEBAR, Assia (pseud. of Fatima-Zohra Imalayène) (b. 1936). Algerian novelist, historian, and filmmaker. Born in Cherchell, she studied in Algiers, Paris, and Tunis, and was the first Algerian woman to enter the École Normale Supérieure de Sèvres. She taught history at the University of Rabat and, after the War of Independence, at the University of Algiers, where she was also involved in literary criticism, journalism, and broadcasting; in the early 1970s she collaborated in theatre-centred activities in Paris. She currently lives mainly in France.

Djebar's novels foreground women's exploration and definition of their personal, sexual, and social identity, in relation to the family, the male, and the community of women, in a world ordered by tradition but invaded by history. The young heroines of the first two novels, *La Soif* (1957) and *Les Impatients* (1958), rebel against the norms of family and society but with unforeseen, calamitous results. *Les Enfants du nouveau monde* (1962) and *Les Alouettes naïves* (1967) are set against the wider perspective of the *Algerian War and follow the trajectories of a number of women whose development and destinies are bound up with the national struggle.

After a 10-year silence Djebar returned to fiction with the collection of short stories *Femmes d'Alger dans leur appartement* (1980); the war and its aftermath form the background, but a strong note of female solidarity is introduced, prelude to a more overtly feminist stance. *L'Amour, la fantasia* (1985) is the first volume of a planned tetralogy. Scenes from the public history of the French conquest, into which Djebar introduces a female presence, are juxtaposed with incidents from the life of a girl growing up in the mid-20th c.; she moves in the enclosed world of women with its muted voices, rich texture of relationships, and store of memories and tradition, but at the same time takes the first steps towards independence through education. The second volume, *Ombre sultane* (1987), is the story of Isma, the sophisticated first wife of a man who has since married the more traditional Hajila, and of the latter's revolt against the constraints imposed upon her. Djebar has also directed the films *Nouba des femmes du mont Chenoua* (1978) and *La Zerda et les chants de l'oubli* (1982), and has published a volume of poetry and co-authored a play. [RMJ]

See J. Déjeux, *Assia Djebar: romancière algérienne, cinéaste arabe* (1984).

DJIAN, Philippe (b. 1949). French novelist. After a collection of short stories, *50 contre 1* (1981), a lyrical thriller, *Bleu comme l'enfer* (1982, filmed by Yves Boisset in 1986), and an ostensibly autobiographical novel, *Zone érogène* (1984), Djian caught the public imagination with *37°2 le matin* (1985, filmed by Jean-Jacques Beineix in 1986); it tells of Betty, whose passionate quest for fulfilment, her own or vicariously the writer's, plunges her into madness under the narrator's lucid but powerless gaze. *Maudit manège* (1986) presents itself as a sequel, continuing this autobiographical vein, and *Échine* (1988), though the narrator is more obviously fictional, still pursues the theme of conflict between commitment to writing and the demands of lovers, friends, and family. Djian, an admirer of American writers such as Miller, Kerouac, and Brautigan, writes of drop-outs and drifters in an unidentified setting which could be his native south-west France; his books are ironically narcissistic, dealing with his personal and sexual intimacy, but tempering the apparent revelations with the reserve of a carefully crafted prose style and wry humour. Djian returned to the short story with *Crocodiles* (1989), and widened his scope with *Lent dehors* (1991) and *Sotos* (1993). [SFN]

Djinn, see ROBBE-GRILLET.

Docteur Pascal, Le. Novel by *Zola, published 1893, the final volume of the *Rougon-Macquart* series. The action is set in Plassans in Provence, where the series began. The doctor and genealogist Pascal Rougon, who keeps files on the hereditary history of the family, lives with his mother Félicité, his niece Clotilde, the daughter of Aristide (Saccard), and their servant Martine. The plot centres on the struggle between, on the one hand, Pascal's scientific faith and, on the other, the religious prejudices and mysticism of the other characters, who seek to destroy the doctor's files. Clotilde is converted to Pascal's faith and the 'biblical' couple enjoy an idyllic love, until Pascal dies, leaving Félicité and Martine free to destroy his manuscripts. But Clotilde saves the genealogical tree and bears her uncle's child, in whom hope for the future is lyrically invested. *Le Docteur Pascal* summarizes the *Rougon-Macquart* series and, with dramatic scenes in which several of the diseased offspring of the family are shown dying out, rounds it off on an optimistic note. The novel is also a response to the religious revival in France at the end of the century. [DB]

Doctrinaires, Les, see GUIZOT.

DOGBÉ, Yves-Emmanuel (b. 1939). Writer from Togo. Born in Lomé, Dogbé worked as a teacher in Togo and Benin before continuing his studies in philosophy and sociology in Paris. He is probably the most prolific of living Togolese writers, and the breadth of his interests is as impressive as the quantity of his published works. He has written novels, stories, fables, poetry, and essays, and it is difficult to associate him too narrowly with any one of these genres at the expense of the others.

His essays illustrate a commitment to developmental models which respect, as far as possible, African values. He has written on famine, education, literacy, and the need for popular participation in politics, always driven by a desire to increase awareness of important social issues in his own country and Africa at large. His doctoral thesis, published in 1973 as *Négritude, culture et civilisation*, is an analysis of the importance of ideology in the African context. It is Dogbé's conviction of the need for change, coupled with his firm belief in the power of the written word, which led him to found his own publishing house, Éditions Akpagnon, in 1979. Although his novels *La Victime* and *L'Incarcéré* have had little success outside Togo, his poetry is more widely read. One collection, *Le Divin Amour*, won the Charles-Vildrac Prize in 1979. Dogbé now lives and works in Paris. [MPC]

DOGBEH, Richard. Poet from Dahomey (now Republic of Benin), author of several collections of poems: *Les Eaux du Mono* (1963), *Rives mortelles* (1964), *Voyage au pays de Lénine* (1967), *Cap Liberté* (1969). [PGH]

Doguicimi, see HAZOUMÉ.

DOLET, Étienne (1509–46). Printer and humanist scholar who, after studying in Paris, Padua, and Toulouse, began his career as *correcteur* for the printer Sebastian Gryphius at Lyon in 1534. Having established his own press there four years later, he produced more than 80 volumes, including works by several classical authors, *Marot, *Rabelais, *Calvin, and himself. Twice condemned to death (in 1536 and 1542), he twice received a royal pardon, but was finally burned at the stake for heresy in Paris in 1546.

He contributed significantly to the growth of *humanism through his encouragement of neo-Latin poets in Lyon, his printing and editing of classical works, and his own writings. These include the virulently anti-Erasmian *Dialogus de imitatione ciceroniana* (1535), his monumental *Commentarii linguae latinae* (1536–8), and his *Cato christianus* (1542), suspected of heterodoxy. He was also active as a translator, publishing *La Manière de bien traduire* in 1540 as a prelude to a series of translations: Cicero's *Epistolae ad familiares* (1542) and *Tusculan Disputations* (1543), and the pseudo-Platonic dialogues *Axiochus* and *Hipparchus* (1544). Dolet was a vain, irascible, and difficult man, but a passionate and evangelically minded scholar; his scepticism, regarded as heretical, reflected his constant concern to promulgate the ideas of classical authors. [NM]

Dolopathos. A rhymed translation from Latin (*c.*1220–5) by the *trouvère* Herbert of an adaptation of the 'Seven Sages of Rome'. Exploiting the 'Potiphar's wife' motif and the technique of delay by cyclic story-telling, it tells how Lucinien, son of Dolopathos, king of Sicily, is saved by his tutor, Virgil, from his stepmother's accusation of rape. [PEB]

DOLTO, Françoise, née Marette (1908–88). French childhood analyst whose *Psychanalyse et pédiatrie* (1939), *Le Cas Dominique* (1971), and the celebrated *Lorsque l'enfant paraît* (1977) influenced a generation of practitioners and parents. A sometime member of the Société Psychanalytique de Paris and *Lacan's École Freudienne, she also wrote on psychoanalysis and religion, female sexuality, and a remarkable *Autoportrait* (1988). [EAF]

DOMENACH, Jean-Marie (b. 1922). French Catholic philosopher and journalist. Active in the Resistance in Lyon, he joined the staff of Mounier's review *Esprit at the Liberation, becoming editor and later director. Domenach has written many essays on cultural and political themes, including *Le Retour du tragique* (1967), on the consciousness of tragedy in contemporary culture. [MHK]

DOMERGUE, Urbain, see GRAMMARS, 2.

Dom Garcie de Navarre. *Molière's only *comédie héroïque*; it features a hero tormented by jealousy. A failure when it was produced in 1661, it provided its author with some passages for *Le *Misanthrope*.

Dominicans. Order of Preaching Friars founded by St Dominic in 1215 to combat the *Cathar heresy in southern France. It combined an austere way of life with the high standard of education that was judged necessary for missionary work and the refutation of unorthodox opinion. Among its greatest scholars were Albertus Magnus and Thomas Aquinas, whose writings became classics of *scholastic philosophy and theology. The order played a major role in the evolution of the Inquisition, and its friars were renowned as preachers and confessors. Its annual general chapters excited admiration as models for representative institutions. [JHD]

Dominique. Novel by *Fromentin, first published 1862. Dominique falls in love with Madeleine at the moment when she marries Monsieur de Nièvres. He continues to nourish an unconsummated passion for her. Eventually, during a stay at her husband's château, the question of their mutual love becomes unavoidable. After scenes of increasing tension and 'danger', she dismisses him for ever. Dominique retires to the country to marry, beget children, and forget his ambitions for romantic passion. Critics have often seen the message of the book as commonsensical: one must turn one's back on passion, accept reason and reality. The book, however, embodies the classic Romantic conflict between love and morality—a conflict whose purpose is to inflame the sensibilities. Dominique feels alive only when inflamed. Once he renounces Madeleine, he relapses into autumnal melancholy.

Augustin, his puritanical mentor, is a bloodless figure; Olivier, though a roué, provides the voice of reason; but the author punishes him for it by disfigurement. The novel thus fails to reconcile emotion and reason, and reads as a typically Romantic act of worship to the goddess of frustration.   [GDM]

Dom Juan. Five-act comedy in prose by *Molière on a popular subject, first performed 1665. Before the play begins, Dom Juan, a dissolute Spanish nobleman and a *libertin*, has murdered the father of one girl he has dishonoured in a duel, and is being pursued by the family of another, Done Elvire, whom he enticed away from a convent and married. Unrepentantly, he continues his life of unrestrained pleasure-seeking in the company of Sganarelle, his superstitious valet. His seductive charms are exercised on peasant girls, creditors, Done Elvire, and his father, whom he eventually fools with a display of feigned devoutness. Having visited the grave of the man he murdered and flippantly invited him to dinner, Dom Juan is confronted with the statue from the tomb, who drags him off to hell after he has refused to repent. The play uses a number of theatrical effects—a nodding statue, the mouth of hell, a ghostly apparition—which were especially popular at the time.   [IM]

DOM-TOM. Acronym for *départements et territoires d'outre-mer*, overseas territories (mainly islands) administered by France. They are the last surviving remnants of France's former colonial empires. The four *départements d'outre-mer*, Guadeloupe, Martinique, French Guiana (Guyane), and La Réunion, date back to the earliest stages of French *colonization, and are treated in many, though not all, respects as ordinary *départements* within metropolitan France. The *territoires d'outre-mer* are more diverse in their administrative structures. They include another of France's earliest colonial acquisitions, Saint-Pierre et Miquelon, off the coast of Newfoundland, mineral-rich New Caledonia (the scene of violent conflicts between French settlers and other ethnic groups during the 1980s), and Polynesia, where France has her atomic-weapons test sites.   [AGH]

DONAT(US), see GRAMMARS, I.

DONGALA, Emmanuel Boundzeki (b. 1941). Congolese novelist and short-story writer. He studied in the Congo, the USA, and France before becoming lecturer in chemistry at the University of Brazzaville. The central character of *Un fusil dans la main, un poème dans la poche* (1973) is an ex-student who joins the southern African freedom fighters, then becomes leader of his country. It is both a satire on ultra-leftism and a meditation on power in the post-colonial era. The themes of *Jazz et vin de palme* (short stories, 1982) range from the persistence of belief in the supernatural, through political corruption, to black life in New York. *Le Feu des orig-*

ines (1987) follows one (reputedly immortal) character from the pre-colonial to the post-independence period. Both novels show innovative structure and handling of time. Dongala's works also demonstrate a concern with psychology and with the search for a fusion of traditional wisdom and modern science. While opening up debate on political problems, Dongala does not propose solutions. He consistently attacks the self-seeking of the new political élite; at the same time, he mercilessly punctures Romanticism, refusing to show the pre-colonial period as a golden age.   [AMR]

Don Japhet d'Arménie, see SCARRON.

DONNEAU DE VISÉ, Jean (1638–1710). Author of topical *nouvelles* and of a number of plays, including some successful comedies of manners (*La Mère coquette*, 1665; *La Devineresse*, with Thomas *Corneille, 1679). His most important literary role was that of founder and editor of the *Mercure galant*.

Don Sanche d'Aragon. Comédie héroïque by Pierre *Corneille, first performed 1650. This romantic story of the rise to royal power of an apparently humbly born hero was thought to allude to the favour enjoyed in France by *Mazarin.

Doon de la Roche. Late 12th-c. *chanson de geste of 4,600 lines, in which social breakdown results from Doon's mistakenly repudiating his wife for adultery and rejecting his son for being a bastard. The son and wife together eventually re-establish justice and order. An unusual *chanson de geste* for its concentration on the delinquence of the father/husband, its story is recast in the Spanish romance *Istoria de Enrique, fi de Oliva*.   [SK]

Doon de Mayence. *Chanson de geste surviving only in an undistinguished 13th-c. redaction, but of which an earlier version probably existed in the 12th c.; its protagonist is cited by *Bertrand de Bar-sur-Aube in the prologue to his *Girart de Vienne* as the progenitor of the lineage of traitors. The term 'Cycle of Doon de Mayence' is used to refer, rather improperly, to *chansons de geste* on the theme of barons in revolt.   [SK]

DORAT, Claude-Joseph (1734–80). Prolific author of plays and poems in several genres. He was most successful in light verse, where we find an epicurean attitude to life and love and the wit or *persiflage* which he defends in *Mes fantaisies* (1768).

DORAT, Jean (Auratus) (1508–88). Teacher of Greek and Latin literature at the Collège de Coqueret from 1547 (where *Ronsard, *Du Bellay, and *Baïf were his pupils), and at the Collège Royal (1556), royal poet and translator. He published an annotated Greek edition of Aeschylus' *Prometheus Bound* (1548), a small collection of French verse, and many Latin poems in various genres (*Poematia*, 1586). Unlike his academic colleagues Lambin and *Turnèbe, Dorat did not publish his commentaries and conjectures; his legendary, inspired classical learning survives only in student notes and the work of people like Henri *Estienne. Ronsard said of him: 'il m'apprit la poésie'; this he did by explaining the Greek dramatists, especially Aeschylus, and the poets Homer, Pindar, and Callimachus, by providing both an allegorical and a moral interpretation, and by confirming the poet in his role as prophet. In 1571 he collaborated with Ronsard, the sculptor Germain Pilon, and the painter Nicolò dell'Abate on the *royal entry of *Charles IX and Élisabeth d'Autriche. Dorat's religious attitude has been seen as pagan rather than Christian and his justification of the *St Bartholomew's Day Massacre as political as much as religious polemic. [PS]

DORÉ, Gustave (1832–83). A precocious, versatile, and productive artist, Doré now owes his reputation mainly to the illustrations he produced for more than 200 books. Entirely self-taught, he was already well known for his caricatures when, in the early 1850s, he discovered in literary texts a richer terrain for his unconstrained imagination. His illustrations of *Rabelais (1854) enjoyed enormous success and were followed by those of *Balzac, *Perrault, Cervantes, *Chateaubriand, Milton, *Hugo, Tennyson, Dante, *La Fontaine, the Bible, and numerous lesser-known works. His detailed, energetic images illustrate the fantastic and obsessional in *Romanticism's analysis of the anguish, cruelty, and mystery of the human condition, and encompass the range of complex relationships between word and image in the 19th c. [JK]

DORGELÈS, Roland (pseud. of Roland Lecavelé) (1886–1973). Author of novels, short stories, travel literature, and memoirs of bohemian life. He is best known for *Les Croix de bois* (1919), a novel published on the very day of his demobilization. It recalls *Barbusse's *Le Feu*, though it is less political in its reaction to war. Other war books include *La Machine à finir la guerre* (1917, with Régis Gignoux), *Le Cabaret de la belle femme* (1919, collected short stories), *Le Réveil des morts* (1923), *Souvenirs sur les Croix de bois* (1929), *Bleu horizon* (1949). Reminiscences of bohemia include *Quand j'étais Montmartrois* (1936). [JC]

DORIOT, Jacques (1898–1945). A leading member of the French Communist Party, Doriot left the Party in 1934 after a bitter controversy with *Thorez. In 1936 he became the charismatic leader of the Parti Populaire Français, France's nearest approach to a *fascist party, with *Drieu la Rochelle as one of his leading apologists. He was a prominent collaborationist in 1940–4. [RMG]

DORVAL, Marie (1798–1849). A gifted and moving actress who, like *Bocage, was influenced by the style of acting of an English company visiting Paris in 1827–8. She had a succession of triumphs in Romantic plays: *Dumas *père's* *Antony* (1831), *Hugo's *Marion de Lorme* (1831), and Vigny's *Chatterton* (1834). [SBJ]

Double Inconstance, La. Comedy in three acts by *Marivaux, first performed at the *Comédie-Italienne in 1723. The naïve and rustic love of Arlequin and Sylvia is troubled when the prince falls in love with Sylvia and has the lovers brought to court. Flaminia, playing on Sylvia's vanity, brings her to abandon her childhood love in favour of the superior qualities of the prince, who remains incognito until the end of the play. Arlequin is consoled by marriage to Flaminia, but not before he has mocked the vanities of court life and criticized the prince's injustice. A light-hearted comedy with sinister overtones of manipulation. [PF]

DOUBROVSKY, Serge (b. 1928). French critic and novelist. Author of studies of *Corneille and *Proust, Doubrovsky intervened in the debate over new methods of literary *criticism with his *Pourquoi la nouvelle critique?* (1966), showing the diversity of approaches which lay beneath this label. Of his five novels the most remarked upon is *Le Livre brisé* (1989), an autobiographically based text which begins as a diary, turns, at his Austrian wife's insistence, into a frank account of the depths to which their once-idyllic relationship has sunk, and then brutally becomes an anguished post-mortem as his wife dies suddenly. It was awarded the Prix Médicis. [EAF]

DOUDAN, Ximénès (1800–72). Literary journalist of the July Monarchy. He is remembered for his entertaining *Mélanges et lettres* (1876–7) and his *Des révolutions du goût* (1881).

DOUMBI-FAKOLY (b. 1944). Born in Mali of Senegalo-Malian origin, Doumbi-Fakoly has spent his life between Senegal, Mali, and France, where he has worked in banking since 1980. His first novel, *Morts pour la France* (1983), deals with French colonial treatment of African ex-servicemen and includes a version of the Thiaroye Massacre. The second novel, *La Retraite anticipée du guide suprême* (1984), is an indictment of African leaders' thirst for power. [FNC]

Doyen de Killerine, Le, see PRÉVOST, A.-F.

Dragonnades. These were a form of persecution of Protestants, in the lead-up to the Revocation of the *Edict of Nantes. From May 1685 troops were billeted on Protestants who refused to convert, and given a licence to do what they liked. This was an old tactic, previously used against peasant rebellion or to get taxes in, and had been used episodically against Protestants since 1659. A *dragon* was a cavalry soldier armed with gun and sabre; other troops were also used. The soldiers committed numerous atrocities, including pillage and rape. The method was often very effective in persuading Protestants to go through the motions of conversion to Catholicism; it was even more effective in fanning the hatred of such *nouveaux convertis* for the Catholic Church (even though such persecution was largely a state decision, about which the clergy were not always happy). [RBG]

Drama in France since 1789 [see also THEATRES AND AUDIENCES]

1. Revolution and Romanticism

The frontier between *tragedy and *comedy had been considerably blurred in the 18th-c. French theatre by the arrival of intermediate genres such as the *comédie larmoyante* and the *drame*. The events of 1789–94, displacing the *ancien régime* connoisseurs, accelerated this breakup of the old dramatic system. While comedies and tragedies continued to be written in the 19th c.—indeed comedy, *farce, and *vaudeville have pursued a triumphant career on the *Boulevard and elsewhere—the 'serious' or mixed theatre of the 19th and 20th c. is best described under the heading 'drama'.

The theatre of the Revolutionary period [see REVOLUTION, 2] was often partisan or didactic. The events of those years also developed a public taste for sensational spectacle; the moralizing and the sensational come together in the *melodrama of *Pixérécourt and others. It is melodrama that provides the link between the 18th-c. *drame* and the very different *drame romantique* which was the major new development of the first half of the 19th c.

Romantic drama has roots also in German theatre, notably Schiller (*Constant published an adaptation of *Wallenstein* in 1809), and above all in *Shakespeare. English companies acted Shakespeare in Paris in 1822 and 1827 [see KEAN]: Stendhal, in *Racine et Shakespeare*, defended Shakespearian-style historical drama against the partisans of *classicism: and *Vigny's verse translation of *Othello* created a furore at the *Comédie-Française in 1829 with its mention of the indecorous 'mouchoir'.

Historical drama in prose was an important strand of the Romantic theatre. It began with *Mérimée's *Théâtre de Clara Gazul* (1825), reached the stage with *Dumas père's *Henri III et sa cour* (1829), and produced such major works as Vigny's *Chatterton* (1835), which resembles an 18th-c. *drame*, and Musset's outstanding *Lorenzaccio* (1834). Musset also wrote plays which mix the tragic and the comic in an original way, in particular *On ne badine pas avec l'amour* and Les *Caprices de Marianne*.

But it was *Hugo above all who stamped his mark on the *drame romantique*. His Preface to *Cromwell sets out the theory of an art form suitable for the modern world, mixing the *sublime and the grotesque, and his *Hernani* was the great public battle between the old and new theatre. His historical dramas in verse, written with great panache, offered the kind of strong emotional effects and

moral lessons to which the audiences of melodrama were accustomed. After the failure of Les *Burgraves* in 1843, however, this type of theatre went into decline; Dumas continued to produce historical melodramas, but Hugo's poetic drama found no real followers, except perhaps the *Rostand of *Cyrano de Bergerac* half a century later.

2. Realism, Symbolism, and Poetic Theatre

Paris theatrical life continued to flourish after the decline of the *drame romantique* [see COMEDY], but no major serious drama emerged until the end of the century. *Scribe taught writers of comedy and drama the virtues of the well-made play, and under the *Second Empire the 'école du bon sens' used this style of drama to depict contemporary life and social problems, though often in a relatively comic mode. The two most important playwrights in this tradition during the *Second Empire were *Dumas *fils* and *Augier. During the 1880s something close to *Naturalism found a place on the French stage, with the adaptation of novels by *Zola or the *Goncourt brothers, and particularly the pioneering plays of Becque (Les *Corbeaux*, 1882). *Antoine's Théâtre Libre provided a home for these, for the plays of writers who were active in their time such as Georges Ancey (*Monsieur Lamblin*, 1888) or François du Curel (*L'Envers d'une sainte*, 1892), and for translations of Ibsen, Strindberg, and Hauptmann. The tradition of realistic stage investigations of contemporary society and psychology continued in the first half of the 20th c. in the works of Henry *Bataille, *Bernstein, *Bourdet, *Vildrac, *Porto-Riche, Jules *Renard, François *Mauriac, and many others.

The crucial development of the late 19th c. is, however, the emergence of the anti-realistic theatre of *Symbolism, which sought to use the stage, with its music, lighting, and decor, as a means for exploring metaphysical concerns. This movement centred on the Théâtre de l'Art of Paul *Fort and the Théâtre de l'Œuvre of *Lugné-Poë and *Mauclair. Many influences were at work here, including the work of *Mallarmé and his circle and the revelation of Wagner. The plays themselves ranged from the iconoclastic *Ubu roi* of Jarry to the ethereally suggestive poetic dramas of *Maeterlinck. Playwrights associated with this movement also included *Villiers de l'Isle-Adam (whose *Axël* was never actually staged), *Rachilde, *Dujardin, *Péladan, and even the young *Gide and *Duhamel. But the dominating figure was that of *Claudel. His first plays were so grandiosely poetic as to be virtually unstageable, but he later recast them and began to write increasingly with stage performance in mind. From 1912 his work was produced by Lugné-Poë, *Copeau, and others, and his much later collaboration with *Barrault meant that he remained a living force in the theatre.

Although Symbolist theatre in its pure form is confined to two decades around the turn of the century, its hostility to realism, experimental approach to staging, and taste for allegory exerted a definite influence on the poetic or literary theatre which flourished in France in the decades following World War I. Copeau at the Théâtre du Vieux Colombier and subsequently the producers of the *Cartel, *Vilar, Barrault, and others encouraged writing which is situated somewhere between the true avant-garde and the Boulevard. Playwrights of this kind include J.-J. *Bernard, *Lenormand, *Salacrou, *Obey, *Cocteau, and above all *Giraudoux, whose collaboration with *Jouvet resulted in a series of scintillating plays in which the word reigns supreme.

Giraudoux also illustrates an important development characteristic of the theatre in the middle years of the 20th c.: the use of subjects taken from history, legend, or myth to discuss moral and political issues. Already at the beginning of the century Romain *Rolland had produced his *Théâtre de la Révolution*, which was successfully revived in the effervescent climate of 1936. Beginning in 1942, *Montherlant produced a series of intellectually ambitious costume dramas, and *Camus (e.g. *Les Justes*) and *Sartre (e.g. *Le *Diable et le bon dieu*) used a similar technique to argue out the political dilemmas of *Existentialism. A fashionable genre for many years was the play of ideas in which a classical myth is reworked, often with deliberate anachronism; characteristic examples are Cocteau's *La Machine infernale*, Giraudoux's *La Guerre de Troie n'aura pas lieu*, Sartre's *Les Mouches*, Camus's *Caligula*, and *Anouilh's *Antigone*. The versatile Anouilh is a particularly good example of a playwright who combines serious concerns, theatrical inventiveness, and commercial success.

3. The Theatre of the Absurd, and After

A different line is that of the genuinely avant-garde theatre, often a theatre of derision and absurdity. This may be seen as deriving from Jarry's perennially subversive *Ubu roi*; it continues in the work of *Apollinaire and the *Surrealists, particularly in the fierce comedies of *Vitrac, and finds its prophet in *Artaud and his Theatre of Cruelty. Its culmination is the post-war Theatre of the *Absurd, illustrated above all by *Beckett, *Ionesco, *Adamov, and perhaps *Genet.

Paradoxically, this anti-literary theatre was also perhaps the last movement in France to produce a body of texts which have become literary classics (Ionesco became a member of the *Académie Française in 1970). The 1950s had seen the French discovery of Brecht, mediated in particular by *Vilar and the *Théâtre National Populaire. This led, in Paris and particularly in the provinces [see DÉCENTRALISATION THÉÂTRALE] to a more political, open-textured theatre, such as that of *Gatti, which is often less easily converted into texts for reading than the plays of Beckett (however theatrical these may be). Important political plays were also written

about this time by *Césaire, *Kateb Yacine, and Adamov.

At the same time the theatrical director gained in importance at the expense of the author. In the 1970s and 1980s the most important theatrical productions, in Paris and elsewhere, tended to be revivals and adaptations of classic texts by directors such as *Brook, *Vitez, *Planchon, and *Chereau. Alternatively, in the wake of *May 1968 they might be street theatre, café theatre, or multi-media collective creations such as those produced at *Savary's Grand Magic Circus. The most striking example was *Mnouchkine's Théâtre du Soleil, where the text was often not the essential element (any more than it was in the 'théâtre lyrique' of operetta and the like which long remained the most popular form of theatre in France). Mime and 'performance theatre' of various kinds all contributed to separate theatre ever further from literature.

Nevertheless, 'author theatre' has continued to be written, produced, and published in France. Apart from the writers already mentioned, some of the most important playwrights to have emerged since World War II are: *Audiberti, *Arrabal, *Billetdoux, *Dubillard, *Grumberg, *Koltès, *Marceau, *Novarina, *Obaldia, *Sarraute, *Schéhadé, *Tardieu, *Vinaver, and *Weingarten. Most of these write plays which are in some way creative in their use of language; some, such as Arrabal and Tardieu, are followers in the line of the Theatre of the Absurd. In addition, the French theatre has been much enriched by plays from francophone countries outside France [see AFRICA (SOUTH OF THE SAHARA) and other national entries].   [PF]

See M. Descotes, *Le Drame romantique et ses grands créateurs* (1955); M. Lioure, *Le Drame* (1963); D. Knowles, *French Drama of the Inter-War Years* (1967); D. Bradby, *Modern French Drama, 1940–1980* (1984).

Drame. The theatre of 17th- and 18th-c. France was divided into the realms of *tragedy and *comedy. Unlike the heroic verse *tragicomedy of the 17th c., the *drame* (or *drame bourgeois*) which emerged in the mid-18th c. sought to break down this barrier by offering serious representations, in prose, of the lives of ordinary contemporaries.

The first important theorist of the genre was *Diderot, though *Beaumarchais (*Essai sur le genre dramatique sérieux*, 1767) and *Mercier (*Nouvel essai sur l'art dramatique*, 1773) also made significant contributions. Inspired by English playwrights (Lillo, Moore), and following the example of the *comédie larmoyante*, Diderot put forward in his *Entretiens sur le Fils naturel* (1757) and *Discours sur la poésie dramatique* (1758) proposals for intermediate genres avoiding the remoteness of tragedy and the frivolity of comedy: 'tragédie bourgeoise', 'drame philosophique', and 'comédie sérieuse'. The distinctions between them are not very significant, the important thing being a convincing portrayal of contemporary social life, with appropriate sets, costume, diction, and physical action, which would involve the audience's sympathy, appealing to the fashionable *sensibilité* of the day. The resulting emotion should be edifying; the *philosophes* saw the *drame* as part of the struggle for social and moral progress.

Diderot's own *drames* (*Le Fils naturel*, 1757; *Le Père de famille*, 1758) suffer from melodramatic didacticism, as do those of Beaumarchais (e.g. *Eugénie*), *Baculard d'Arnaud, and Mercier (the most assiduous toiler in this vineyard). The best example of the genre is Sedaine's *Le *Philosophe sans le savoir*. The 18th-c. *drame* had to endure contemporary ridicule and hostility, and produced no masterpieces, but its long-term effects were considerable. The clear separation of tragedy and comedy proved unsustainable in France and elsewhere. Diderot's arguments won a hearing in Germany by way of Lessing, and much serious European drama of the 19th and 20th c. is arguably a descendant of the movement of the 1750s. [For this, and for the *drame romantique*, see DRAMA IN FRANCE SINCE 1789.] [PF]

Dreyfus Affair (*L'Affaire Dreyfus*). One must distinguish between the judicial Dreyfus Case and the Affair which grew out of it. The Case was very simple: in December 1894 Captain Alfred Dreyfus, a Jewish officer serving with French Military Intelligence, was found guilty of spying for the Germans and sentenced to life imprisonment on Devil's Island. In the next few years the discovery of new evidence led a number of people to the realization that a serious miscarriage of justice had taken place.

Colonel Picquart's discovery in 1896 of evidence pointing to another figure, Commandant Esterhazy, was a turning-point; but it was the public revelation of these suspicions in late 1897 which led to the crisis of the Affair. The controversy which raged thereafter divided France into two violently opposed camps. Dreyfus himself, and the initial miscarriage of justice, tended to be lost from view. Though, for a significant number of Dreyfusards, the case remained one purely and simply of justice, the Affair became a battleground for an already deeply divided France, in which fear of the other side, and the necessity for its defeat, became paramount for both parties. Generalizations are dangerous, and many figures crossed the expected lines; but on the whole military men, Catholics, *antisemites, monarchists, *Bonapartists, and ex-Boulangists [see BOULANGER, G.] tended to be anti-Dreyfusards, and *anticlericals and anti-militarists to be Dreyfusards. One side attacked Jews, freemasons, Protestants, and republicans; the other, the army and the Church. The Affair was a symptom rather than a cause; but it exacerbated these hatreds still further.

For two years, 1897–9, the fortunes of both sides waxed and waned, with animosities at fever-pitch. Finally Dreyfus was brought back in August 1899 for retrial; but he was found guilty once more. By now the choice was between Dreyfus and the army's honour. Dreyfus received a pardon, but was finally exonerated only in 1906. Many of the political forces that had jumped on the Dreyfusard bandwagon extracted advantage from the outcome of the Affair, as some of the purer Dreyfusards noted with concern.

The Affair was a catalyst that produced some remarkable polemics and saw the emergence of the *intellectuals who were so prominent in 20th-c. French history. *Zola's article 'J'accuse' (13 January 1898) was a turning-point, and leading parts on the Dreyfusard side were played by *Bernard-Lazare, *Jaurès, *Clemenceau, *Péguy, and *Mirbeau, together with extreme anti-militarists and anticlericals like Urbain Gohier and Laurent *Tailhade. Prominent anti-Dreyfusard polemicists included *Barrès, *Rochefort, *Maurras, *Drumont, and the cartoonists Forain and Caran d'Ache. Among sympathizers, Dreyfusards included *Proust and Anatole *France, anti-Dreyfusards *Claudel, *Léautaud, and *Valéry.

The Affair also figures in various ways in literary works of the succeeding period, e.g. Martin du Gard's *Jean Barois, France's M. *Bergeret à Paris* and *L'Île des pingouins*, Proust's *A la recherche du temps perdu*, and Zola's *Vérité*. Outstanding among later commentaries on the Affair is Péguy's *Notre jeunesse* (1910), where the author's concern at the political use that had been made of the Affair in its aftermath is translated into a brilliant polemical attack on those who had thus sullied the ideal 'mystique' of Dreyfusism. [See NATIONALISM.] [RMG]

DRIEU LA ROCHELLE, Pierre (1893–1945). A French novelist and essayist of the inter-war period, Drieu la Rochelle was imbued with a sense of the decadence of contemporary society, which led him into a variety of forms of escape, including a political commitment to *fascism. His collaborationist policies during World War II led to an initial neglect of his work in the post-war period; but he is now recognized as one of the more remarkable novelists of his time.

World War I was a major influence upon him. But even before the war certain tendencies in his thought were already established. Above all, there was the influence of Nietzsche and of *Barrès, and a personal tendency to depression and despair, leading to thoughts of suicide. The war brought him action and a sense of liberation from the mediocrity and futility of human existence. His war poems, published in the collection *Interrogation* in 1917, express the need for 'la force du soldat', and for struggle, suffering, and danger.

Back in post-war civilian life, Drieu felt 'dépaysé'. The world around him appeared to have learned none of the lessons of the war. He plunged into a despairing quest for pleasure amid the distractions of post-war Paris, including varied sexual adventures. He moved in fashionable literary circles, and through *Aragon became involved with the *Surrealist movement. His writings, up to 1934, reflect his continuing disillusion. On the one hand, the novels (e.g. *L'Homme couvert de femmes*, 1925; *Blèche*, 1928; *Une femme à sa fenêtre*, 1930; *Drôle de voyage*, 1933) and the short stories express the futility of sexual encounters and a desire for escape from tedium and mediocrity. On the other, a series of essays seriously examines the political and social situation (*Mesure de la France*, 1922; *Le Jeune Européen*, 1927; *Genève ou Moscou*, 1928; *L'Europe contre les patries*, 1931); he invites France to accept her diminished position in the post-war world, and to see herself as part of a greater federal Europe which, rejecting both old-style nationalism and the outmoded distinction between capitalism and communism, could counteract the power of Russia and America. In 1931 he wrote a masterpiece which stands out from his contemporary output, *Le Feu follet*, the stark depiction of the last days in the life of a drug-addict before he commits suicide.

The year 1934 produced an enormous change in Drieu's ideas. The riots of 6 February [see CROIX-DE-FEU] convinced him of the healthy renewal for France that could be achieved through fascism. Later that year his *Socialisme fasciste* declared the need for one party on the fascist model. By 1936 he had joined *Doriot's Parti Populaire Français, whose theorist he became in regular contributions to the party newspaper, *L'Émancipation nationale*, many of which were gathered into the volume *Avec Doriot* (1937). Typically, however, he was soon disillusioned with the party, at one stage considering suicide because of his sense of universal futility. In January 1939 he broke with Doriot.

It was the disillusionment of 1938–9 which was to produce his greatest novel, *Gilles* (1939), whose hero Gilles Gambier goes through a political and social development similar to Drieu's own. The theme of purification through war recurs in the final section, where the hero participates in the Spanish Civil War.

After the French defeat in 1940, Drieu, despite his contempt for the Vichy regime [see OCCUPATION AND RESISTANCE] and his continuing disillusionment with fascism in practice, strongly advocated collaboration with the Germans. He accepted the editorship of the *Nouvelle Revue Française*. In 1943 he produced a final novel, *L'Homme à cheval*, one of his best works. After the Liberation he committed suicide on 15 March 1945, to evade arrest.

In the last year of his life Drieu produced three remarkable documents, which were eventually published in 1961 under the title *Récit secret*. These were: a treatise in which, prior to producing a philosophy of suicide, Drieu describes his various suicide attempts from childhood onwards, culminating in a full description of his feelings the day before his last attempt in August 1944; a 'Journal' from 11 October 1944 to 13 March 1945 (touching on the political situation, his own pressing concerns, his attraction towards suicide, his readings, and his progress on the novel he was writing); and finally the outline of his own defence (for the trial he expected), in which he described his political evolution from 1918 to 1945.

Drieu, by his cult of action and his despair at the decadence and aimlessness of modern life, parallels a number of other writers of the inter-war period, including *Malraux, whom he described as his 'frère en Nietzsche et en Dostoievski', and the German author Ernst Jünger. Like them, he found a temporary outlet in political commitment; but his individualism always prevented him from espousing for long any precise cause. The tensions thus aroused, and his complex and neurotic personality, combined, however, to produce a handful of remarkable works of art. [RMG]

See F. Grover, *Drieu la Rochelle* (1962); R. Soucy, *Fascist Intellectual: Drieu la Rochelle* (1979).

Drôle de guerre, La. Name given to the waiting period between the declaration of war between France and Germany on 3 September 1939 and the German offensive of May 1940 (cf. the English term 'Phoney War').

DROUET, Juliette, see HUGO.

DROUET, Minou (Marie-Noëlle) (b. 1947). A child-poet prodigy, allegedly, the authenticity of whose *Arbre, mon ami* (1956) became a contemporary *cause célèbre*. See A. Parinaud, *L'Affaire Minou Drouet* (1956), and *Barthes, *Mythologies*. [DAS]

DRUMONT, Édouard (1844–1917). France's foremost antisemite of the period 1880–1900, Drumont had his first great success with *La France juive* (1886), a turgid diatribe attacking Jewish power in contemporary society, which became the driving force behind contemporary political *antisemitism; other similar works followed, such as *Le Testament d'un antisémite* (1891). In 1892 he founded the highly successful newspaper *La Libre Parole*, which played a prominent part in the *Panama Scandal and in the *Dreyfus Affair. He was a *député* for Algiers 1898–1902. Thereafter his fortunes were in decline. He died in obscurity and penury in 1917. [RMG]

DRUON, Maurice (b. 1918). French novelist. His first books, inspired by wartime experiences, were followed by chronicles of the inter-war years (*Les Grandes Familles*, 1948) and a vast fresco of the French Middle Ages, *Les Rois maudits* (1955–77), which enjoyed great success when adapted for television.

DU BARTAS, Guillaume de Salluste (1544–90). French soldier and diplomat, and a religious epic poet of considerable influence. He studied law at Toulouse, in 1566 inherited the title of nobility conferred a year earlier on his father, and in 1567 became Doctor of Law. Having retired to his estate, he wrote a theoretical work advocating poetry of a Christian nature (*La Muse chrétienne*, 1574), which he published together with several didactic poems of Calvinist or cosmic inspiration composed between 1567 and 1572 (*Judith, Uranie, Le Triomphe de la foi*).

Less intransigent than his co-religionist d'*Aubigné, Du Bartas nevertheless fought in the *Wars of Religion as an officer attached to the court of Navarre. The same partisan commitment and religious zeal are present in his two major biblical and scientific epics, the *Première Semaine ou Création du Monde* (1578), and the unfinished *Seconde Semaine ou Enfance du Monde* (1584). Gentilhomme Ordinaire to Henri de Navarre (later *Henri IV) from 1585, Du Bartas undertook diplomatic missions to Scotland and Denmark. Shortly after celebrating the Battle of Ivry in a poem, he died fighting against the *Ligue.

Du Bartas's fame, which threatened even to rival the poetic supremacy of *Ronsard, was established by the *Première Semaine*, a work which was translated into several languages, which ran into some 25 editions in as many years (several accompanied by learned commentaries by Simon *Goulart), and which either inspired or was admired by d'Aubigné, Tasso, Milton and, later, Goethe. Based on patristic commentaries on Genesis (St Basil, *Hexaemeron*), the structure of the French text is dictated by its hexameric theme. It attempts an encyclopaedic inventory of human knowledge within a tradition of scientific poetry which includes *Scève, *Baïf, and *Peletier, and within a didactic and religious framework which traces the variety and harmony of creation to the unique glory of God. Past critics emphasized Du Bartas's lapses of taste, his excesses of style, his infelicities of language, his absence of selection, and his proselytizing manner, but more recently scholars have reappraised his poetry within the perspective of *'baroque' aesthetics and have demonstrated how, by a complex networking of symbolic correspondences and analogies, by detailed and evocative descriptions, by sustained use of metaphor, and by linguistic, rhetorical, and phonic inventiveness, he creates a universal language which stylistically imitates diversity within unity by associating microcosm and macrocosm, words and things.   [MDQ]

See J. Dauphiné, *Guillaume Salluste du Bartas, poète scientifique* (1983); J. Miernowski, *Dialectique et connaissance dans 'La Sepmaine' de Du Bartas* (1992).

DUBÉ, Marcel (b. 1930). With *Gélinas, Dubé is the most significant Quebec dramatist before *Tremblay. In his prolific production for the theatre, radio, and television, it is his early working-class tragedies which remain his most powerful pieces. *Zone* (1953), *Un simple soldat* (1957), and *Florence* (1957) express the social alienation of their characters with a realism of language and setting that has poetic force. In contrast to the strong popular feel of these works, his later plays, *Bilan* (1960), *Au retour des oies blanches* (1966), and *Les Beaux*

Dimanches (1965), among others, are concerned with the hypocrisy and moral failures of a bourgeois élite. This shift in social focus seems to have been partly motivated by the debate in the 1960s over the state of Quebec French. Whereas Tremblay and other Quebec dramatists opted for proletarian *joual, Dubé argued that the theatre should set an example of the articulate use of language and thus be worthy of a new emerging nation. But if his later plays gain much from their seriousness of purpose and from his command of technique, the search for a more elevated theatrical style only led to the creation of rather stereotyped middle-class characters who lack the vitality and social significance of the characters of the earlier plays.   [SIL]

DU BELLAY, Joachim (*c*.1522–1560). The most important poet of the *Pléiade after *Ronsard, Du Bellay was born near Liré (Anjou) into a noble family already renowned for its diplomats, church dignitaries, and soldiers. Fragile in health and orphaned at an early age, he was brought up by an elder brother who neglected his education. Encouraged in his early poetic activities by *Peletier, he abandoned his legal studies (begun in Poitiers in 1545) and joined Ronsard and *Baïf at the Collège de Coqueret, where from 1547 to 1549 he received a *humanist education under *Dorat.

April 1549 saw the publication in Du Bellay's name of the *Défense et illustration de la langue française*, a theoretical programme faithfully illustrated in his collections of 1549–50: the first sonnet cycle in French poetry of essentially *Petrarchist love poems (*L'Olive*), two collections of Horatian odes (*Vers lyriques, Recueil de poésie*), and an allegorized battle between the muses of poetry and ignorance (*La Musagnœomachie*). Prematurely aged and partially deaf after a lengthy serious illness (1550–2), Du Bellay discovered in poetry consolatory and therapeutic values. Certain poems published in collections of 1552–3 are more personal and less humanist in nature and distantly look forward to *Les Regrets*. The elegaic tone of *La Complainte du désespéré* (1552) and the satire of Petrarchism in *A une dame* (1553) anticipate, for example, the two major inspirations of *Les Regrets*, whilst the Christian content of the *Hymne chrétien* and *La Lyre chrétienne* (1552) prefigure Du Bellay's religious concerns as a *Gallican Catholic found in *Les Regrets*.

April 1553 marked his departure for Rome in the retinue of his cousin Cardinal Jean du Bellay. Enthusiastic to undertake the humanist pilgrimage to Italy and perhaps ambitious for advancement in a diplomatic career, Du Bellay was to be disappointed in his expectations. Although too much credence must not be placed on the personal witness of *Les Regrets*—allowance should be made for hyperbole and literary convention—he describes his Roman stay as an exile and as a series of disappointments. He returned to Paris in 1557 to further disappointments (family and legal disputes, continuing poor health, dissatisfaction with the French court), but with the consolation of publishing in 1558 four very different collections of poetry: the *Poemata* (four books of Latin verse), the *Divers jeux rustiques* (a composite collection of recreational pieces, largely facetious, satirical, and rustic in inspiration), and two sonnet sequences, the *Antiquités de Rome* and *Les Regrets*, which finally liberated the sonnet cycle from its associations with love poetry and Petrarchism.

A dense and suggestive mosaic of assimilated humanist themes and images, the 32 alternating decasyllabic and alexandrine sonnets of the *Antiquités* and the 15 allegorical sonnets of the *Songe* which follows (translated by Edmund Spenser as *The Visions of Bellay*) contrast the past glory of Rome with her present decay, reflect on the causes of her downfall within a cyclical view of history (*translatio imperii*), and draw general philosophical and political lessons from the Roman experience concerning the vanity of human endeavour and the vulnerability of France on the eve of civil war.

Distancing himself from the more elevated principles of the *Défense* and from the erudite concerns of Ronsard, Du Bellay defines the 191 alexandrine sonnets of *Les Regrets* as a natural and simple record of personal thoughts and feelings. The two principal inspirations—elegiac and satirical—lament the areas of dissatisfaction of the poet's 'exile', pass under mordant review the moral decadence and the spiritual barrenness of the papacy and the Vatican, and, in sonnets written on Du Bellay's return to France (which anticipate *Le Poète courtisan* of 1559), satirize the philistinism and hypocrisy of the French court. Although some critics emphasize the 'modern' and 'sincere' aspects of *Les Regrets*, the roles of poetic convention and literary reminiscence must not be underestimated, for not only have Ovid (*Tristia*) and Horace (*Satires*) shaped the conception of the collection and the persona Du Bellay presents, but familiarity with contemporary Italian burlesque poetry has influenced the scope and nature of the French poet's satire.

Whilst Du Bellay lacks the vitality, the breadth of vision, and the sublime eloquence of Ronsard, his reputation is assured by the evocative power and suggestivity of his language, the visual impact and the picturesque precision of his imagery, the delicate resonance of his sensibility, his command of the sonnet form, and his sureness in matters of rhythm, musicality, and rhetoric.   [MDQ]

See R. Griffin, *Coronation of the Poet: Joachim Du Bellay's Debt to the Trivium* (1969); G. Gadoffre, *Du Bellay et le sacré* (1978); G. H. Tucker, *The Poet's Odyssey: Joachim Du Bellay and the 'Antiquitez de Rome'* (1990).

DUBILLARD, Roland (b. 1923). French playwright. With *Obaldia, *Weingarten, and *Vauthier, he belonged to the second wave of *Absurdist writers who sought to renew the language of theatre by verbal experiments. His plays bear the influence of his earlier career as an actor performing cabaret sketches and as radio producer. Their plots are minimal, and often amount to a kind of amiable chit-chat exposing the solitude of the characters. His most admired play is *Naïves hirondelles* (1961). Other plays are: *Si Camille me voyait* (1953), *La Maison d'os* (1964), *Où boivent les vaches* (1972), *Diablogues* (1975), *L'Eau en poudre* (1978). He has also published poems and fiction.   [DWW]

DU BOIS HUS, Gabriel (1599–1652 or later). French poet who carries to an extreme the baroque panegyric of throne and altar in his poems *La Nuit des nuits* and *Le Jour des jours*—i.e. the nativities of the *Dauphin du Ciel* and the *Dauphin de la Terre*—published in tandem in 1641. Excessive hyperbole mars his rhetoric, but skilful handling of a tricky stanza-form helps to control his proliferating concetti. His description of expectant Nature at the Nativity is a masterpiece of baroque word-painting, often compared with Milton's poem on the same theme.   [AJS]

DU BOS, Charles (1882–1939). Born into a rich cosmopolitan family, with a knowledge of languages and a European education, Charles du Bos was the archetype of the leisurely man of letters with immense cultural knowledge and broad interests. Among his wide circle of literary friends were *Gide, *Schlumberger, *Ghéon, *Valéry, *Maurois, and *Rivière. He contributed to many reviews, including the *Gazette des beaux-arts* and the *Nouvelle Revue Française*; his articles are collected in *Approximations* (1922–37). As a critic he moved easily through different art forms (literature, painting, and music) and through different cultures, producing works on Goethe, Byron, the Brownings, *Mérimée, and Benjamin *Constant. He kept up an extensive correspondence with the German scholar Curtius, Gide, and Valery *Larbaud, among others.

His journal, begun in 1908, revealed behind the urbane, cultured conversationalist the drama of Du Bos's inner life; the search for an impossible happiness, the problem of reconciling individualism and self-fulfilment with the possibility of loving someone other than oneself, the attainment of spiritual values in art while rejecting God, a desire for total sincerity. The battle between intelligence and God was resolved by his conversion in 1927, and in 1932 appeared *François Mauriac et le problème du romancier catholique*. In 1937 he left France for the University of Notre Dame, Indiana, where he wrote *What Is Literature?* (1940).   [ET]

DU BOS, Jean-Baptiste, abbé (1670–1742). An influential figure in the development of aesthetics, Du Bos acted as a French diplomat before devoting himself to history (*Histoire critique de l'établissement de la monarchie française dans les Gaules*, 1734) and to discussions of the arts. His major work, the *Réflexions critiques sur la poésie et la peinture* (1719), locates the enjoyment of art in feeling rather than reason, explaining the appeal of tragedy by the pleasure of experiencing strong emotion in safety. The power of poetry resides not in its ability to instruct, but in the way poetic language affects the senses, the imagination, and the passions. Painting, with its direct representation of objects, is even more affecting. And since pleasure is the criterion of judgement, public taste is a more reliable guide than the experts. However, Du Bos accepts the classical canon of greatness, and attempts to show how the appearance of artists of genius, in ancient Greece for instance, may be explained by historical and climatic conditions. [PF]

DU BOUCHET, André (b. 1924). French poet. Instantly identifiable by its distinctive fragmentation and *mise en page* (reminiscent of *Mallarmé's Un coup de dés*), a poem by Du Bouchet challenges the reader to repeat a trajectory which, as it leaps across gaps between words and phrases, seeks to stick as closely as possible to a concrete experience occuring concurrently in the spheres of language and of sensory reality. The publication of pages from the *Carnets 1952–1956* (1989), on the basis of which the early collections *Le Moteur blanc* and *Dans la chaleur vacante* (1961) were written, illuminates Du Bouchet's desire to capture, in bursts of verbal energy, mental and bodily sensations experienced when out walking in arid and elemental mountain country. In a series of volumes—*Où le soleil* (1968), *Laisses* (1975), *L'Incohérence* (1979), *Rapides* (1980), *L'Avril* (1983), *Ici, en deux* (1986)—Du Bouchet has experimented with different kinds of syntax and typography. At the same time he has progressively explored his conception of poetry and creation through meditations on other poets: Hölderlin, *Reverdy, *Baudelaire, Celan; or painters: *Giacometti (*Qui n'est pas tourné vers nous*, 1972), Tal Coat (*Cendre tirant sur le bleu*, 1965). [MHTS]

DUBUFFET, Jean (1901–85). French painter and writer. As original with the pen as with the brush, Dubuffet used both instruments to state his belief in the demolition of orthodoxy, and in art as *révolution permanente* and *fête amusante*. He celebrated his own notion of *l'art brut* ('raw art', including the work of psychotics and children), and donated a large collection of naïve painting to the city of Lausanne. His robustly inventive tracts, essays, articles, and poems, many collected in *Prospectus et tous écrits suivants* (1967), decry the asphyxiation exercised on originality by bourgeois culture. [DAS]

DUBY, Georges (b. 1919). Influential French medieval historian of the *Annales* school. Duby's major contribution to medieval social history is his monumental study *La Société aux XIe et XIIe siècles dans la région mâconnaise* (1971); he has also published on many aspects of French social and economic history from the 11th to the 13th c. His work on the social behaviour of young aristocratic males, and on

medieval marriage, has greatly influenced understanding of the themes of knighthood, *chivalry, and *fin'amor in literary texts of the 12th c. Duby's influence extends outside the academy. He has overseen publications intended to bring knowledge of medieval France to a wider public, directs the series *Histoire de la vie privée*, and is president of the Conseil de Surveillance de la Société d'Édition de Programmes de Télévision. [SK]

DU CAMP, Maxime (1822–94). French journalist, writer, and early photographer, for around 10 years close friend of *Flaubert. In 1847 the two men produced alternate chapters of *Par les champs et par les grèves*: they travelled together in the Middle East from 1849 to 1851. Du Camp's photographic record, *Égypte, Nubie, Palestine et Syrie*, was published in 1852. He was an editor of *La *Revue de Paris* (in which *Madame Bovary* first appeared in serial form) and of *La *Revue des deux mondes*. He produced a novel (*Forces perdues*, 1867), political memoirs (*Souvenirs de l'année 1848*, 1876; *Les Convulsions de Paris*, 1878–9), and the better-known *Souvenirs littéraires* (1881–2). [DK]

DU CANGE, Charles du Fresne, seigneur (1610–88). Eminent French scholar, author of two indispensable dictionaries of medieval Latin and Greek [see MIDDLE AGES, 2], and of pioneering studies of Byzantine history (*Histoire de Constantinople sous les empereurs français*, 1657).

DUCASSE, Isidore, see LAUTRÉAMONT.

DUCHAMP, Marcel (1887–1968). French artist who originated the *objet trouvé* and was associated with successive avant-garde movements. *Apollinaire included him in *Les Peintres cubistes*; his painting *Nu descendant un escalier*, influenced by chronophotography, imitates progressive movement. Duchamp's humour, irreverence, and inventiveness prompted his ready-mades, such as the urinal *Fontaine*; his move from paintings to objects was important to *Dadaism, whose herald, *New York Dada*, was the creation of Duchamp, *Picabia, and Man Ray. *Éluard owned his construction on glass, *La Mariée mise à nu par ses célibataires même*; Duchamp's accompanying commentary appeared in a Surrealist journal, with an introduction by *Breton. [HEB]

DUCHARME, Réjean (b. 1942). Canadian novelist and playwright. Since the sensation caused by his first published novel, he has remained a mysterious figure, revealing little of his private life except that he was born between Montreal and Quebec and 'did various jobs and travelled'. It is impossible to tell how directly his novels, mainly first-person narratives, correspond to his lived experience. They are remarkable texts, full of the poetry of refusal, escape, and despair; their contradictions and complexities tease the reader, and they are written in an exhilaratingly original language, reminiscent of *Céline, in which literary allusions, word-play, and ordinary speech are combined to create a new poetry.

L'Avalée des avalés (1966), first published in Paris (like most of Ducharme's work), is the monologue of Béatrice Einberg, a child who refuses adult compromises in a violent itinerary leading from Quebec to war in Israel. *Le Nez qui voque*, written earlier but published in 1967, is another novel of the despair of growing up, narrated by a boy who reneges on a suicide pact with his girl-friend. *L'Océantume* (1968), also written before *L'Avalée des avalés*, recounts the epic escape of a young heroine, Iode Ssouvie, in search of the sea. In all these novels the young protagonists seek refuge from the crazy civilized world in a poetic pantheon where *Nelligan and *Rimbaud are powerful divinities. The later novels, following the deliberately ridiculous verse epic, *La Fille de Christophe Colomb* (1969), are told by disillusioned if nostalgic adult narrators, and the reference is now not so much to poetry as to modern mass culture. André and Nicole Ferron, the heroes of *L'Hiver de force* (1973), set themselves to watch television exhaustively in a refusal of all meaningful existence (involving some sharp satire on the nationalist intelligentsia), but their refusal is the counterpart of an intense desire for love. A similar sense of paradise lost pervades *Les Enfantômes* (1976), the middle-aged Vincent Falardeau's chaotic memoirs.

In the late 1970s and the 1980s Ducharme wrote for the theatre (e.g. *HA ha!*, 1982) and for the cinema (notably the screenplay for Manckiewicz's *Les Bons Débarras* of 1979, another story of an untamed child at odds with the world). He returned to the novel only in 1990 with *Dévadé*, in which the Célinian poetry of marginality remains strong. [PF]

See R. Leduc-Park, *Réjean Ducharme: Nietzsche et Dionysos* (1982).

DU CHÂTELET, Émilie Le Tonnelier de Breteuil, marquise (1706–49). Physicist and mathematician; a pupil of *Maupertuis. Although a devotee of Newton, whose *Principia* she translated, she defended *Leibniz's metaphysics in her *Institutions de physique* (1740). From 1733 she lived with *Voltaire at her château of Cirey; as well as being lovers, they worked together on scientific and philosophical questions; when he left her she began an affair with *Saint-Lambert, and died in pregnancy. An independent and original character, she left a *Discours sur le bonheur*, which places equal value on love and intellectual endeavour. [PF]

Duchesse de Langeais, La. Short novel by *Balzac, first published as *Ne touchez pas à la hache* in a section of *Études de mœurs au XIXe siècle* entitled *Histoire des Treize*. Ostensibly a cloak-and-dagger drama of the 'Thirteen' daring men sworn to support each other, *La Duchesse de Langeais* is the vehicle for Balzac's firmest portrait of the heartless woman incapable of real affection. Antoinette de Langeais is a society coquette whose frivolous disre-

gard for the feelings of the men she entrances provokes an old soldier, Armand de Montriveau, to plan violent revenge. Balzac's theme is a personal one (recurring notably in *La *Peau de chagrin* and in *Le *Père Goriot*), but also part of a general denunciation of the aristocracy of his day. [DMB]

DUCIS, Jean-François (1733–1816). French author of two tragedies, *Œdipe chez Admète* (1778) and *Abufar* (1795), but best known for his verse adaptations of existing prose translations of *Hamlet* (1769), *Romeo and Juliet* (1772), *King Lear* (1783), *Macbeth* (1784), and *Othello* (1792), in which Shakespeare is made to comply with the norms of French tragedy. He refused Napoleon's favours, and in his later years wrote some personal lyrics of considerable charm. [PF]

DUCLOS, Charles Pinot (1704–72). Novelist and moralist. Born in Dinan (Brittany), he completed his education in Paris, where he lived most of his life, while remaining involved in Breton affairs. He quickly made a reputation as a wit in café and salon circles and subsequently at court. In 1755 he was elected Secretaire Perpétuel of the Académie Française. Louis XV once remarked: 'Pour Duclos, il a son franc parler', and he was indeed known for his frankness; this and his democratic inclinations brought him close to *Rousseau, his friend for many years. Having fallen foul of authority over the *La Chalotais affair, he toured Italy in 1767, writing a sharply observant *Voyage en Italie*, whose originality was highly praised by *Stendhal.

Duclos wrote some history: his *Histoire de Louis XI* (1745) won him the post of official historiographer, and his *Mémoires secrets sur le règne de Louis XIV, la Régence et le règne de Louis XV* (published 1791) drew on *Saint-Simon's manuscripts. He was also the author of essays on such subjects as the Celtic languages, duelling, and the theatre, but is remembered now for his fiction and his accounts of contemporary society. His *Histoire de Mme de Luz* (1740), a historical novel of unhappy virtue in the manner of *La *Princesse de Clèves*, was followed in 1741 by *Les Confessions du comte de ***. This *memoir-novel tells the story of a reformed rake; the aristocratic narrator gives a brisk, somewhat superficial, account of his many seductions, enlivened by sharp social observations, but at the end he is turned to virtue by the love of a good woman.

The moralist comes into his own in Duclos's best-known work, the *Considérations sur les mœurs de ce siècle* (1750). His declared aims are scientific (observation, leading by induction to general truths) and he spends a good deal of time on terminology (distinguishing, for instance, between *probité*, *honneur*, and *vertu*), but the book consists essentially of critical reflections on the manners and values of upper-class society. It is less lively than *La Bruyère's *Caractères*, but is distinguished by a robustly independent stance. Duclos writes as a citizen, stressing usefulness and honesty, attacking frivolity and

Du contrat social

privilege. His values are close to Rousseau's at times, but unlike his friend he attributes great importance to men of letters, whose influence he welcomes as an important new feature of 18th-c. French society. [PF]

See J. Brengues, *Duclos, ou l'Obsession de la vertu* (1978).

Du contrat social, see CONTRAT SOCIAL

Du côté de chez Swann. The first part of Proust's **A la recherche du temps perdu* (it contains *Combray, Un amour de Swann,* and *Noms de pays: le nom*).

DUCRAY-DUMINIL, François-Guillaume (1761–1819). French popular novelist in vogue around 1800. He is best-known for *Victor ou l'Enfant de la forêt* (1796).

DU DEFFAND, Marie de Vichy, marquise (1697–1780). She distanced herself from her bad marriage and participation in the **Regency's promiscuity when she became a pillar of *salon society. The assembly she founded about 1730 shaped French intellectual life for half a century. Du Deffand's celebrated literary discernment was honed by voracious reading. Her salon was more aristocratic than that of her rival *Geoffrin. It was less open to **philosophes* but more accessible to women, including her protégée *Lespinasse, with whom she parted company when Lespinasse set up her own salon. Her correspondence is celebrated, especially the letters she exchanged for 15 years with Horace Walpole. [JDeJ]

DU FAIL, Noël (*c.*1520–1591). Lawyer and storyteller. Born near Rennes, Du Fail studied in Paris and was at the Battle of Cérisoles (1544). He completed his studies on the long way back from Italy to Brittany, where he settled as a barrister in Rennes and later was a member of the Parlement de Bretagne. Accused at one time of Calvinist sympathies, he sided with the king against the *Ligue. Like many 16th-c. lawyers, he turned to literature for recreation. His short stories are characterized by their Breton flavour, their unusual **coq-à-l'âne* structure, their underlying parody of the law and social customs, and their *Rabelaisian use of dialogue. The stories create a contrast between times past and present, with a certain regret for the age that is gone, and extol the pleasures of country life. They offer a picture of Breton peasant existence which appears convincing, yet is highly stylized. They span the whole of his legal career, with the *Propos rustiques* (1547), *Les Baliverneries* (1548), and finally the *Contes et discours d'Eutrapel* (1585). He signed his first two publications Léon Ladulphy, and the last, 'le feu seigneur de la Herissaye'. He also left an important work on Breton customary law, the *Mémoires . . . des plus notables et solennels arrêts du Parlement de Bretagne* (1579). [KCC]

DU FRESNOY, Charles-Alphonse, see PILES.

DUFRESNY, Charles Rivière (1648–1724). Despite general acknowledgement of Dufresny's talents in several areas—music, landscape-gardening, the plastic arts, and literature—his work has been overshadowed by that of more-easily classifiable contemporaries, such as *Regnard, with whom he collaborated in the 1690s, and *Lesage. His best-known plays were written for the Comédie-Française: *L'Esprit de contradiction* (1700), *Le Double Veuvage* (1702), *La Coquette de village* (1715), *Le Mariage fait et rompu* (1721). He wrote initially, however, for the Comédie-Italienne, and his compositions, fusing music, dance, and text, had a strong influence over its subsequent development. Without adopting the moralizing tone of some later comedies, he highlights social and personal corruption, through characters who exemplify the general malaise of an age of changing values. His work is generally marked by a taste for the unusual and the irregular. He is also remembered for his prose narrative *Les Amusements sérieux et comiques* (1699)—one source of inspiration for Montesquieu's **Lettres persanes*—and for his innovative and personalized editorship of *Le *Mercure galant* (1710–13). [JD]

DUFY, Raoul (1877–1953). French painter. With his painting, mural decorations, theatre and fabric designs, ceramics, and posters, Dufy was a major source of the modern visual sensibility. The woodcuts and lithographs which he produced to illustrate works by *Apollinaire, *Mallarmé, *Daudet, *Gide, and *Colette, among others, constitute some of the most important modern examples of the creative collaboration between word and image. [JK]

DU GUILLET, Pernette (*c.*1518–1545). Poet from Lyon, author of a single volume of *Rymes*, published posthumously in 1545 by Jean de Tournes at her husband's request. Du Guillet's association with *Scève is well known and their poems contain reciprocal allusions, though she owes more to *Marot and the *Rhétoriqueurs than to him. Her small collection embraces several different metres and genres: 60 epigrams (*dizains* and *huitains*), 10 *chansons*, five elegies, and two *épîtres*. Her love is seen as predestined, a mixture of chaste Platonic idealism and desire frankly expressed; although sometimes prosaic and unimaginative, she shows sensitivity and an independent spirit. [PS]

DUHAMEL, Georges (1884–1966). A doctor turned writer and member of the Groupe de l'*Abbaye, Duhamel, now a largely forgotten figure, achieved fame before World War II, being elected to the Académie Française in 1935. He is remembered for two cycles of novels: *Vie et aventures de Salavin* (1920–32), whose hero is a precursor of the antiheroes of *Sartre and *Camus, and the popular *Chronique des Pasquier* (1933–45). Writing with warmth and humour, he used the saga of the

Pasquier family to attack materialism and defend the rights of the individual against the collective forces of society. He wrote passionately against war and its atrocities (which he had experienced at first hand) in *La Vie des martyrs* (1917), and against the rise of Hitlerism in *Défense des lettres* (1937). [ET]

DUJARDIN, Édouard (1861–1949). French dramatist, novelist, poet, critic of literature, painting, and music, and founder and co-editor of literary reviews (*La Revue wagnérienne*, *La Revue indépendante*), Dujardin played a pivotal role in the *Symbolist movement. He and *Wyzewa promoted in the *Revue wagnérienne* the idea of 'art intégral' (a loose fusion of Wagnerian Total Art and *Baudelairean *correspondances*) central to the Symbolist aesthetic. He persuaded *Mallarmé to attend the 1885 Lamoureux Wagner concert, to publish in the review his 'Richard Wagner, rêverie d'un poète français' and his sonnet in homage to the musician, and in 1886–7 to become drama critic of the *Revue indépendante*, which published Mallarmé's 'Notes sur le théâtre'. His efforts to apply to literature the procedures of Wagnerian music had two important consequences. The first was his contribution to the theory and practice of the *vers libre*, which he adopted for his own dramatic work, *La Légende d'Antonia*, a trilogy based on *Parsifal* and whose oratorios, incantations, and symbolic characters make it a period piece of Symbolist theatre. The second was his creation, in *Les Lauriers sont coupés* (1888), of the interior monologue technique, based on an analogy with Wagner's use of musical motifs. Joyce later asserted that this was one of the sources of *Ulysses*. [JK]

DULAC, Germaine (1882–1942). Feminist filmmaker and theorist of the silent period; she directed the sensational *La Coquille et le clergyman* (1927), scripted by *Artaud [see CINEMA; SURREALISM].

DULAURENS, Henri-Joseph Laurens, known as (1719–93). Unfrocked monk, author of satires, parodies, and risqué 'philosophical' tales, notably *Irmice* (1765) and *Le Compère Matthieu* (1766).

DULLIN, Charles (1885–1949). French actor and theatre director who collaborated with *Copeau before achieving prominence with his own company, L'Atelier, throughout the 1920s and 1930s. Scrupulous in his attention to detail, attaching great importance to the text of a play, he shared Copeau's ideal of the actor's vocation. He was a co-founder of the *Cartel. [DHW]

DU LORENS, Jacques (1580–1655). Poet from Normandy, author of pamphlets and numerous *Satires* (1624, 1633, 1646), which voice a vigorous, if repetitive, distaste for contemporary vices and hypocrisies.

DU MARSAIS, César Chesneau, sieur (1676–1756). He wrote on religious and philosophical topics, but

is remembered as a grammarian, author of many articles on language in the *Encyclopédie* and of the posthumous *Logique et principes de grammaire* (1769). His philosophical, somewhat eclectic, theory of language stresses the universal validity of 'natural' word order. In opposition to this, figurative and poetic language is seen as expressive, emotive, or decorative. The recent revival of *rhetoric has focused attention on his *Traité des tropes* (1730), which offers a theory of the origin and proper (i.e. discreet) use of tropes, of which he lists 19 species. His work was continued by *Fontanier. [PF]

DUMAS, Alexandre ('Dumas père') (1802–70). Dramatist, novelist, travel writer. On a world scale Dumas is perhaps the best known of all French novelists. His massive fictional output brought him an enormous readership in his day, and his key novels have continued to attract a large popular audience, being repeatedly adapted for popular serialization, cinema, and television.

His father was a legendary general in Napoleon's army who had distinguished himself by a famous victory over the Piedmontese in the Alps, and whose exploits were recounted by Dumas himself in *Mes mémoires* (1852–5). His grandfather was a minor aristocrat who had settled in San-Domingo, and his grandmother, Marie-Cessette Dumas, was a black slave-girl.

Dumas's literary career started in the early 1820s when, together with literary collaborators, he began to write *melodramas and *vaudeville sketches, the earliest example of which was produced at the Ambigu-Comique in 1825. A volume of tales, *Nouvelles contemporaines*, appeared in 1826. Dumas's first theatrical triumph came with the performance of *Henri III et sa cour* at the Comédie-Française in 1829, a glamorously produced historical drama, rich in melodramatic incident, which made him a leader of the Romantic revolution in the theatre. Henceforth, Dumas was a celebrated figure in Parisian literary circles. He strongly supported the republican cause in 1830. In the early 1830s he rapidly confirmed his notoriety with the sensational success of the play *Antony* (1831), which at the time seemed to epitomize all the supposed danger and subversiveness of the new Romantic literature. He maintained his power to enthral and shock with the tragedy *La Tour de Nesle* (1832), which played a central part in the contemporary obsession with all things medieval. His other outstanding theatrical success was *Kean ou Désordre et génie* (1836), in which the actor Frédérick *Lemaître played the virtuoso role.

Dumas's truly colossal literary and social celebrity, however, came with his career as a writer of *romans-feuilletons*. In very close collaboration with Auguste *Maquet, he contributed serial novels to the press throughout the late 1830s and early 1840s. From 1844 (when he published both *Le *Comte de Monte-Cristo* and *Les *Trois Mousquetaires*) until

1848, he dominated the field of the *roman-feuilleton* with such titles as *Vingt ans après* (1845), *La Reine Margot* (1845), *Joseph Balsamo* (1846–8), and *Le Vicomte de Bragelonne* (1848–50). With *Les Mohicans de Paris* (1854–7) he demonstrated his continuing inventiveness in the field of popular fiction. [BR]

See F. W. J. Hemmings, *The King of Romance* (1979).

DUMAS, Alexandre ('Dumas *fils*') (1824–95). Playwright, often bracketed with *Augier as the most influential dramatist of the Second Empire. Natural son of Alexandre Dumas *père*, the circumstances of his birth and upbringing induced in him a lifelong concern with the problems of adultery, illegitimacy, and prostitution. *La Dame aux camélias* (1852), his play about the doomed passion of a courtesan and the scion of an honourable family, has achieved legendary status and was turned into an opera, *La Traviata*, by Verdi. Unlike Augier, who was drawn to broader subjects like the ethics of commerce, the power of the press, and the influence of the Church, Dumas *fils* concentrates narrowly on sexual morality, arguing a case for or against certain values and attitudes. His dialogue is brilliant and showy, involving carefully orchestrated rhetorical exchanges, and he handles surprise and suspense skilfully. He tends to sensationalize his subject-matter, as one can see from *Le Demi-monde* (1855), his play about an unscrupulous woman of easy virtue; *Le Fils naturel* (1858), a curious study of his own predicament; *Les Idées de Madame Aubray* (1867), where a 'fallen woman' is redeemed; and the lurid *La Femme de Claude* (1873), which exposes the adulteress undermining society. [SBJ]

Du mouvement et de l'immobilité de Douve, see BONNEFOY.

DUNETON, Claude (b. 1935). French writer, novelist, and linguistic commentator, notable for his popularizing work on the history of the French language, e.g. *La Puce à l'oreille* (1985) and the encyclopaedic *Le Bouquet des expressions imagées* (1990). Iconoclastic in approach, as in *Anti-manuel de français* (1978), which rejects the traditional academic 'explication de texte' in favour of a wide-ranging semiotics-based discourse analysis, his concern for the contemporary language is best represented in *Parler croquant* (1973), in which he pillories the colonializing impact of 'standardized French' on regional languages, in particular Occitan, and on the 'language of the people' in general. [AHB]

DU NOYER, Anne-Marguerite, née Petit, (*c.*1663–1720). Protestant who spent years, before and after her marriage to Guillaume du Noyer, outside France fleeing religious persecution. She edited a periodical, *La Quintessence des nouvelles* (1711). Her *Lettres historiques et galantes* (1713) prefigure the *Lettres persanes.* Her pseudo-memoirs (1720) are a rich source for the history of private life. [JDeJ]

DUNOYER DE SEGONZAC, Pierre, see URIAGE.

DUPARC, Henri-Eugène-Marie, see WORDS AND MUSIC, 2.

DU PERRON, Jacques Davy, cardinal (1556–1618). French poet. The son of a Huguenot minister, but converted to Rome, he was *lecteur* to *Henri III, becoming bishop of Évreux, archbishop of Sens, and cardinal. A man of encyclopaedic learning, formidable intellect, and persuasive speech, he was instrumental in the conversion of *Henri IV. His poetry shows some parallels with that of his friend *Bertaut, and works by the one have sometimes been attributed to the other, but in the best of his relatively small output he displays a brilliance and energy not to be found in Bertaut. Like the latter, in his poems for throne and altar he clearly anticipates *Malherbe (whom he drew to the king's notice in 1600). The posthumous *Perroniana* (1669) contain some succinct remarks on poetic style with which Malherbe would have agreed—perfection is reached when not one word in the poem can be bettered for propriety, significance, or euphony; metaphor should be unobtrusive, and it should operate on the level of general terms, so as to ensure sustained nobility of tone. [AJS]

DUPLESSIS-MORNAY, Philippe (1549–1623). Surnamed 'le pape des Huguenots', Duplessis-Mornay was a leading Calvinist propagandist, and stalwart supporter of Henri de Navarre (later *Henri IV) during his struggle for the crown. His posthumous *Mémoires* are a rich source for the history of the *Wars of Religion. He is often identified with the anonymous author of the *Vindiciae contra tyrannos* (1579) which, written in the aftermath of the *St Bartholomew's Day Massacre, developed the theory of popular sovereignty and the right to revolt. [JJS]

DUPONT, Pierre (1821–70). Famous French *ouvrier-poète* who attracted the admiration and patronage of important writers (including *Sand and *Baudelaire) and whose celebrity reached its peak during the Revolution of 1848. Baudelaire famously paid tribute to the poignant realism of 'Le Chant des ouvriers' (1846), a poem which became a rallying-cry of the dispossessed. [BR]

DUPONT DE NEMOURS, Pierre-Samuel (1739–1819). French economist, an active member of the *Physiocrat group, whose ideas he propagated in his journals, the *Journal de l'agriculture* and the *Éphémérides du citoyen.* He also published *Quesnay's *Physiocratie* (1768) with an important introduction. He survived the Revolution in spite of his moderate views, emigrated for a time to America, and refused official protection under Napoleon. [PF]

DUPREY, Jean-Pierre (1930–59). French sculptor and poet. For the *Surrealist gesture of urinating on the

flame of the Unknown Soldier, he was imprisoned, then transferred to a psychiatric ward. Shortly after release he committed suicide, another Surrealist gesture. *La Fin et la manière* (1965) celebrates annihilation with frightening verbal brilliance. See also *Derrière son double* (1965), *La Forêt sacrilège* (1970).
[GDM]

DUPUY, Jacques (1591–1656) and Pierre (1582–1651). Archivists and librarians who organized meetings of scholars at the Parisian house of the président de *Thou, which came to be known as the Académie Putéane. Jacques was de Thou's librarian; Pierre was a historian in his own right, and was in royal service from 1624. Their considerable collection of books and manuscripts was left to the king and incorporated into his library in 1657.
[IM]

DURAND, Étienne (1585/90–1618), *poète ordinaire* to *Marie de Médicis, was much involved in the production of *ballets de cour*, notably the *Ballet de Madame* (1615) and the *Ballet de la Délivrance de Renaud* (1617). He was executed in 1618 for intriguing against the king in the queen mother's interest. Durand has a sure rhythmical eloquence, and his love poetry often rings true psychologically. In his most impressive poem, the 'Stances à l'inconstance', mutability, a favourite topos of the time, takes on a quasi-religious tonality.
[AJS]

DURAND, Gilbert (b. 1921). Cultural anthropologist and literary critic. Inspired by *Bachelard and Jung, Durand created a typology of images and symbols, drawing upon the elemental categories developed by the former and the archetypal patterns established by the latter (*Les Structures anthropologiques de l'imaginaire*, 1960). He became increasingly critical of *Lévi-Strauss's 'formal' *Structuralism and developed a 'figurative' approach which emphasized the integrative and generative power of mythical and symbolic motifs both in the structure of individual literary works and in the cultural dynamics of specific historical moments (*Le Décor mythique de la Chartreuse de Parme*, 1961; *Figures mythiques et visages de l'œuvre*, 1979).
[REG]

DURAND, Marguerite (1864–1936). *Grande dame* of early 20th-c. *feminism. Well educated and of bourgeois family, she was by turns an actress at the Comédie-Française, hostess to the Boulangists [see BOULANGER, G.], and journalist on Le *Figaro, before being converted to feminism in 1896. She founded (and funded) a newspaper, *La Fronde*, written and produced by an all-woman team. It appeared daily from 1897 to 1903 and intermittently thereafter, and was taken seriously enough to be described as '*Le Temps* en jupons'. Marguerite Durand remained an ardent campaigner for women's rights and bequeathed her collection of books on women to the feminist library in Paris which bears her name.
[SR]

DURAND, Oswald, see HAITI, 1.

DURANTY, Edmond (1833–80). Co-editor of the review *Réalisme* (1856–7) and militant spokesman for Realist doctrines. His novels—especially *Le Malheur d'Henriette Gérard* (1860) and *La Cause du beau Guillaume* (1862)—are interesting and individual works which go beyond the programmatic theory of *Realism he propounded.
[BR]

DURAS, Claire Lechat de Kersaint, duchesse de (1778–1828), maintained an important literary salon and also wrote three remarkable novels about impossible love. Classically simple in style and plot, they treat what were then somewhat scandalous subjects in a moving way. *Ourika* (1824) is the pathetic tale of the hopeless love of a young black for a noble Frenchman; she enters a convent and dies. In *Édouard* (1825) the son of a worker adopted by a nobleman falls in love with his adopted sister and, aware of the impossibility of the misalliance, seeks death as a soldier. *Olivier* (posthumously published, 1971) deals with physical impotence as an obstacle to love, and inspired *Stendhal's *Armance*.
[FPB]

DURAS, Marguerite (pseud. of Marguerite Donnadieu) (b. 1914). France's most celebrated woman writer of the late 20th c., Duras has produced over 50 novels, plays, and films. Moving constantly beyond the various schools and movements with which critics have associated her, creating texts which increasingly abolish the boundaries between novel, film, and play, her work pushes formal constraints to their limits and defies any easy classification.

She was born and brought up in Indo-China, where her parents were both teachers. Her father died when she was 4, and she led the marginalized life of the child of a poor white family as her mother struggled to bring up three children. Disaster struck the family when her mother decided to buy and farm a small plot of land; the first year the whole rice crop was lost when the land was flooded. Despite her mother's heroic efforts to construct dams, the tragedy was repeated the following year and financial ruin ensued. Indo-China figures largely in Duras's work, as does, increasingly, the episode of the flood and the tensions between the neurotic mother, the slightly retarded younger brother whom Duras adored, and the violent older one.

Duras left Indo-China in 1932 to study in Paris; here she met her first husband Robert Antelme, whom she married in 1939, and her second, Dionys Mascolo, with whom she had a son in 1942. The same year she published her first novel, *Les Impudents*, followed by *La Vie tranquille* (1944); both are family sagas set in the French provinces, which were compared to the novels of *Mauriac. She signed them Duras, the name of a French village near which her father had owned a property.

During the war she was active in the Resistance (a period recounted in the stories of *La Douleur*, 1985) and was a member of the Communist Party, with which she remained involved until her expulsion in the early 1950s.

In 1950 she published *Un barrage contre le Pacifique*, an autobiographical novel strongly evoking Indo-China and drawing on the flood disaster of her childhood. Although it remains a family saga, dominated by the portrait of the mother, it has echoes of contemporary American writing and a clear political thrust in its denunciation of the colonial system. It was subsequently filmed by René Clément.

Her next three novels (*Le Marin de Gibraltar*, 1952; *Les Petits Chevaux de Tarquinia*, 1953; and *Le Square*, 1955) chart a steady progress in her gradual paring-down of the traditional narrative framework. *Le Square*, for example, presents the dialogue of an older man and a young nursemaid who meet by chance on a park bench; the action lasts an hour or two at most, and the significance of the meeting remains uncertain. *Moderato cantabile* (1958), which firmly established her literary reputation, accelerated this process; a recognizably Durassian voice, with its ambivalencies, silences, and disruptive desires had emerged.

In the same period Duras was approached to write a film scenario; *Hiroshima mon amour* (1959, directed by *Resnais) was a great success and was to open up new directions in her work. Her first play, *Les Viaducs de la Seine-et-Oise* (1960), followed the same year, dealing with the psychological enigma of a macabre crime (a favourite theme). The same crime was later to be taken up in a novel, *L'Amante anglaise* (1967)—an example of the way in which Duras increasingly reworks material in different narrative forms.

Considered as being on the fringes of the *Nouveau Roman, Duras continued throughout the 1960s to produce novels and plays in which formal elements are reduced to a minimum, characters remain elusive, and plot is replaced by the orchestration of a number of details. Silences, hesitations, the weight of what is not said become the hallmark of her work. *Le Ravissement de Lol V. Stein* (1964), another work which can be considered a turning-point, presents, in a skeletal script, the case of Lol, whose mental balance is disturbed when her fiancé leaves her for Anne-Marie Stretter. It opens up an enigmatic cycle of linked works, including *Le Vice-Consul* (1966), in which both Anne-Marie Stretter and an apparently unrelated beggar-woman figure; *India Song* (1973, both a text and a celebrated innovatory film), which takes up the same narrative with a different ending; *L'Amour* (1971), one of Duras's most hermetic texts; and *La Femme du Gange* (1973), a film and script based on *L'Amour*, in which Anne-Marie Stretter and Lol reappear. In 1965 Duras had no less than three plays produced and published: her adaptation of *Le Square* (the revision of a version produced in 1957), *Les Eaux et forêts*, a comic absur-

dist piece, and *La Musica*, a dialogue between a divorced couple reviewing their life together. The three were published together as *Théâtre I*; a second volume of plays, including *Suzanna Andler*, was published as *Théâtre II* (1968).

The mood of *May 1968 matched Duras's own hopes for a social revolution, and it found a ready echo in her imagination. *Détruire, dit-elle* (1969, text and film) pits the subversive force of desire against conventional attitudes to sexuality; *Nathalie Granger* (1972, text and film) links the violence of the young to their frustrations, and has a strong feminist element. Attempts have been made to claim Duras's writing as an 'écriture féminine' (see Marini below); *Les Parleuses* (1974), a dialogue between Duras and Xavière Gauthier, is Duras's most overtly feminist text.

Throughout the late 1970s and the 1980s Duras continued to produce a wide range of films and texts, often replaying and reworking each other. *L'Éden cinéma* (1977) adapts for the stage her novel of 1950, *Un barrage contre le Pacifique*; in *Les Lieux de Marguerite Duras* (1977) the author reviews her past life in a dialogue with Michelle Porte. *Le Navire Night*, the account of a passion lived entirely over the telephone, is both film (1978) and text (1979). Since 1980 much of her work has been marked by the presence of Yann Andréa in her life. In *L'Été 80* (1980) he watches a child on the beach with Duras; *Yann Andréa Steiner* (1992) self-evidently revolves around him. His own book *M.D.* (1983), recounting Duras's brush with death during a detoxification treatment, is said by Duras to have inspired her to write *L'Amant* (1984), an autobiographical narrative returning to the Indo-China period which won the Prix Goncourt and brought, in its relative accessibility, a mass audience to Duras. *L'Amant de la Chine du Nord* (1991) approaches the same narrative again from a different direction. In the preface Duras writes: 'Je suis redevenue un écrivain de romans.'

[EAF]

See M. Marini, *Territoires du féminin* (1977); C. Blot-Labarrère, *Marguerite Duras* (1992); L. Hill, *Marguerite Duras: Apocalyptic Desires* (1993).

DURKHEIM, Émile (1858–1917). A founding father of modern sociology, Durkheim believed that the social cannot be reduced to the psychological, that man becomes distinctively human only within society, and that society is the source of morality, exercising constraint upon individual behaviour through a collective system of beliefs and values. He referred to social factors as 'things' which, being unavailable to introspection, should be studied scientifically. His concern with establishing objective indices of social solidarity or disequilibrium led to his pioneering statistical analysis of suicide rates (*Le Suicide*, 1897) and to his study of religion as a source of social cohesion (*Les Formes élémentaires de la vie religieuse*, 1912).

[REG]

DURTAIN, Luc (pseud. of André Nepveu) (1881–1959). A doctor by profession, close to the Groupe de l'*Abbaye and *Unanimism, he published several volumes of poetry, including *Quatre continents* (1935), travel books, and novels, some of them under a general title, *Conquêtes du monde*, which sums up the humanist ambitions of his writing.

DU RYER, Pierre (*c*.1600–1658). French dramatist. After serving in the royal household as a young man, and then as secretary to the duc de Vendôme (illegitimate son of *Henri IV), Du Ryer seems to have been able to support himself by writing (mostly working as a translator from Latin and Greek) from about 1640. His 18 plays include pastoral, comedy, tragedy, and tragicomedy. His comedy *Les Vendanges de Suresnes* (performed 1633 or 1634, published 1635 or 1636) is interesting for its emphasis on the setting amid the vineyards round Suresnes and for its comic characters (notably the vine-grower Guillaume, originally played by the famous 'farceur' Gros-Guillaume). Other plays include a biblical tragedy, *Saül* (performed *c*.1639, published 1642), a Roman tragedy *Scévole* (performed 1642–3, published 1647, and much reprinted in the 17th c.), and *Alcionée*, a tragedy dealing with political problems, freely adapted from Ariosto (performed 1637, published 1640). This play was much admired by, among others, *Richelieu and Queen Christina of Sweden, who were no doubt gratified by its tendency to support absolute monarchy. Du Ryer was elected to the Académie Française in 1646, in preference to Pierre *Corneille. [GJ]

DUTACQ, Armand, see SIÈCLE, LE.

DUTOURD, Jean (b. 1920). French novelist and journalist who became famous with *Au bon beurre* (1952), a humorous and ironically deflating account of life under the German *Occupation. His prolific production includes *Un ami qui vous veut du bien* (1981), replying to the many anonymous letters which his work provokes; *Mémoires de Mary Watson* (1980) imagines the life of the wife of Sherlock Holmes's assistant. He was elected to the Académie Française in 1978. [EAF]

DU VAIR, Guillaume (1556–1621). French magistrate, politician, diplomat, and *Neostoic moralist, bishop of Lisieux from 1617 to his death. He became involved in the political struggles of the *Wars of Religion, first on the side of the *Ligue, then on that of the *Politiques. His defence of Salic law made him popular with *Henri IV and led to his appointment as senior magistrate in Provence (1597) and, later, Garde des Sceaux (1615). He wrote on political and linguistic issues, and published his *Méditations sur les psaumes* in 1580; but he is best known for his promotion of Stoic philosophy. His translation of Epictetus' *Enchiridion* appeared in 1591 and was frequently reprinted. This was followed by the publica-

tion of a number of influential tracts which he had composed earlier: *De la constance et consolation ès calamités publiques* (1597); *La Philosophie morale des stoïques* (1598); *La Sainte Philosophie* (1600). He aspired to reconcile ancient Stoicism with Christianity; like *Montaigne and Justus Lipsius, he stressed the importance of controlling the will and developing a personal philosophy as an antidote to the vicissitudes of fortune, the evils of the times, and the uncertainty of happiness. His works, which also include the treatise *De l'éloquence française* (1594), were very influential in the first half of the 17th c., and enjoyed frequent republication. [IM]

DUVALIER, François, see HAITI, 3.

DU VERDIER, Gilbert Saulnier, sieur (1598–1686). French novelist. His prolific and heavily derivative output reflected popular tastes, and includes a pastoral novel, *La Diane française* (1624), the massive *Roman des romans* (1626–9), a compilation of commonplaces from the chivalric romance, and the satirical *Chevalier hypocondriaque* (1632). Some substantial historiographical work followed in the 1650s. [GJM]

DU VERGIER DE HAURANNE, see SAINT-CYRAN.

DUVERT, Tony (b. 1946). French novelist and essayist. His major fiction, notably *Le Voyageur* (1970), *Paysage de fantaisie* (1973), and *Journal d'un innocent* (1976), exploits the formal achievements of the *Nouveau Roman in pursuit of the subversion of conventional values. In particular, he sets out to disturb his readers by focusing on adolescent male sexuality and pederasty, using a pornographic lyricism reminiscent of *Genet. His essays, *Le Bon Sexe illustré* (1974), and *L'Amour au masculin* and *Abécédaire malveillant* (1989), are virulent attacks on current concepts of morality as a subordination of human values to the requirements of capitalism. [CFR]

DUVIGNAUD, Jean (b. 1921). French sociologist. Active in left-wing politics in the post-war period, Duvignaud was a member of the PCF until 1951, and went on to co-found the journal *Arguments* with *Morin and *Lefebvre. He was particularly concerned with the relationship between culture and society, which he approached from a humanistic Marxist perspective. He established the sociology of art as an academic discipline, and his work on the sociology of theatre has been particularly influential. See his *Sociologie de l'art* (1967) and *Spectacle et société* (1970). [MHK]

DUVIVIER, Julien (1896–1967). The great journeyman director of pre-*Nouvelle Vague cinema. His prolific career spanned nearly 50 years and ran the gamut from literary adaptations—the two versions of *Renard's *Poil de carotte*: silent (1925) and sound

Duvivier

(1932)—through exotic melodramas, to the Franco-Italian 'Don Camillo' films of the early 1950s. *La Belle Équipe* (1936), a major *Popular Front film, and the Algiers gangster drama *Pépé le Moko* (1937) gave Jean *Gabin two of his greatest roles, and *La Fin du jour* (1939), set in a home for retired actors, is a moving homage to Michel *Simon and Louis *Jouvet.

[KAR]

E

Ébahis, Les, see GRÉVIN.

EBERHARDT, Isabelle (1877–1904). Novelist and travel writer shaped by an unusual medley of cultural traditions, inspired mainly by colonial North Africa, where she travelled extensively between 1897 and 1904. Born in Switzerland of Russian parents, she scandalized the colonial establishment in North Africa by embracing Islamic beliefs, criticizing French rule, and masquerading as a man. Virtually all her works, such as *Dans l'ombre chaude de l'Islam* (1906), *Notes de route: Maroc, Algérie, Tunisie* (1908), *Pages d'Islam* (1919), and *Trimardeur* (1922), were published posthumously, initially by the journalist Victor Barrucand, whose editorial role has been the subject of considerable controversy; later editions are more reliable. [AGH]

EBONY, Noël X. (1944–86). Ivoirian poet, civil servant, and journalist, Ebony was editor-in-chief of *Africa International* until his accidental death. The book of verse, *D. E. J. A. V. U. suivi de Chutes* (1983), singled Ebony out as a sophisticated poet, a promising member of a new generation of post-*négritude* writers. He left several unpublished manuscripts, including poetry and a novel. [VC]

Écailles du ciel, Les, see MONENEMBO.

Échange, L', see CLAUDEL.

ECHENOZ, Jean (b. 1947). French author of six novels published by *Minuit: three stories of espionnage and detection, *Le Méridien de Greenwich* (1979), *Cherokee* (1983, Prix Médicis), *Lac* (1989), and two of adventure, *L'Équipée malaise* (1986) and *Nous trois* (1992), which combines an earthquake in Marseille and a journey in space. *L'Occupation des sols* (1985) is a work apart, a 15-page vignette about a father and son and the only remaining image of their dead wife and mother, a psychologically and socially sensitive piece. The plots of the other five are ingenious and intricate, with many characters obliquely introduced, minimally delineated, and brought together by a convergence of chances. These works are never far from pastiche (see the farcical botched denouement of *Lac*). The writing is taut, economic, and precisely descriptive, and at the same time inventive and alive with neologisms (nouns converted into strong verbs) and syntactic tricks. Humour, and especially irony, abounds. [PS]

Écho de Paris, L'. This daily, launched in 1884 as a lightweight *Boulevard title, underwent many changes. In 1900 it was the mouthpiece of the anti-*Dreyfusard Ligue de la Patrie Française and became perhaps the best-written of conservative newspapers of the early 20th c. It published *Barrès's *Chronique de la grande guerre,* an exercise in maintaining morale in war-time adversity. Between the wars *L'Écho's* readership declined; the paper remained the preferred reading of the military and the right-thinking bourgeoisie. Contributors included the young François *Mauriac. [MP]

École des femmes, L'. Five-act comedy by *Molière, first performed 1662. Arnolphe, a pretentious Parisian known also as 'M. de la Souche', thinks that he has successfully brought up Agnès to be a perfect wife—passive, submissive, and ignorant. Horace, the son of one of his friends, courts her, however, and not knowing of Arnolphe's double identity, tells him of all his schemes to further the relationship. In spite of this forewarning, Arnolphe is unable to thwart Horace's plans; in the end, Agnès's long-lost father appears and reveals that she is in any case betrothed to Horace. The play gave rise to a protracted debate about theatrical decorum and the value of comedy throughout 1663 to which Molière contributed two one-act plays that discuss the literary, social, and theatrical issues raised by the play: *La Critique de l'École des femmes* and *L'Impromptu de Versailles.* [IM]

École des maris, L', see MOLIÈRE.

École Nationale d'Administration (ENA). Training school for higher civil servants and diplomats, created 1945. Entry is by competitive examination at postgraduate level, and the 'énarques' enjoy considerable prestige.

École Nationale des Chartes. The state institution training archivists and librarians in France. It was founded in 1821.

École normale, see EDUCATION, 2C.

École Normale Supérieure. This *grande école* in the rue d'Ulm, Paris, traces its origins to 1794, though its early history was not continuous. Its main purpose was always to train teachers for higher and secondary education, but its prestige within the competitive educational system meant that it attracted an intellectual élite which later made its mark in politics, literature, and philosophy as well as in academic life. It also drew its pupils from less privileged social classes than most *grandes écoles.*

Being residential, the ENS had an intense internal life which strongly marked its graduates, and the *esprit normalien* was seen as the quintessence of the critical independence and literary discrimination which were thought characteristic of French intellectual habits; the scientific side of the school was also important, but has attracted less attention. Although the ENS has produced some distinguished conservative thinkers, it has generally been identified with the Left—liberal in the 19th c., often socialist in the 20th—and *normaliens* were prominent in controversial episodes such as the Revolution of 1848, the *Dreyfus Affair, and the ideological struggle between fascism and Communism. In 1903 the ENS was brought into closer association with the University of Paris, but retained its autonomy and special character. An equivalent school for women was founded at Sèvres in 1881, and the two schools were amalgamated in the 1980s. [RDA]

École Polytechnique. Founded in 1794 to train engineers for the army and state service, Polytechnique rapidly established a prestige which it has never lost. It was a centre around 1830 of the *Saint-Simonian cult of industrial progress, and produced some notable civil engineers. Later its influence extended into the civil service and private business, and its rigorously competitive entrance examination, the lucrative positions to which it leads, and the social influence of its 'old boy' network have both maintained its position at the head of the *grandes écoles* and tended to give it a socially privileged clientele. [RDA]

École Pratique des Hautes Études. Graduate school created in 1868, associated with the University of Paris. Like the *Collège de France, it does not deliver degrees. Its research seminars, conducted by figures such as *Barthes or *Bourdieu, are at the forefront of intellectual life in Paris.

Écoles centrales. These secondary schools, founded in 1795, were one of the few concrete educational achievements of the *Revolution, and embodied a radical ideal of education derived from the *Enlightenment. They broke with existing classical traditions by emphasizing science and other modern subjects, and giving their pupils a free choice instead of a fixed curriculum. They also excluded religion, which deterred many conservative-minded parents, and in 1802 Napoleon replaced them with the *lycées*, which returned to the traditional model [see EDUCATION]. But though short-lived, the *écoles centrales* were an experiment which inspired many later attempts at modernization. [RDA]

École William Ponty, see WILLIAM PONTY.

Économistes, Les, see PHYSIOCRATS.

Écossaise, L' (1760). Comedy by *Voltaire, mainly remarkable for its satirical portrait of his enemy *Fréron. See also REINE D'ÉCOSSE, LA.

Écriture artiste. Name given by Edmond de *Goncourt (in the preface to his novel *Les Frères Zemganno*, 1879) to the highly mannered and impressionistic prose style practised by the Goncourt brothers and their imitators. This manner attempts to employ original expressions and turns of phrase, vying with Impressionist painters, to render immediate sensations in prose. As Edmond de Goncourt wrote in the *Journal* (22 March 1882): 'Je voudrais trouver des touches de phrases, semblables à des touches de peintre dans une esquisse: des effleurements et des caresses, et, pour ainsi dire, des glacis de la chose écrite, qui échapperaient à la lourde, massive, bêtasse syntaxe des corrects grammairiens.' This form of writing is characterized by nominal syntax, weak verbal forms, the inversion of subject and verb, abstraction, an accumulation of participles and adjectives, and an abundance of metaphors. [DB]

Écriture automatique. An age-old technique, rediscovered by *Breton in 1919. It became one of the methods employed by the *Surrealists to gain access to subconscious thought and to explore the nature of lyricism and inspiration. They distinguished it from the automatic writing practised by spiritualist mediums, but it has connections with Freud's 'free association' (*la pensée parlée*). The basic idea was to write down quickly, without having a preconceived subject, whatever came into one's head. Breton was the 'author' of the most famous texts produced in this manner: *Les Champs magnétiques* (1920), in collaboration with *Soupault, and *Poisson soluble* (1924). [KRA]

Écriture du désastre, L', see BLANCHOT.

Écriture et la différence, L', see DERRIDA.

Écriture féminine. Name given to a particular approach to the question of women's writing, exemplified by Hélène *Cixous and her 'études féminines' seminar. Central to this approach is the belief that sexual difference is inscribed in language in ways that can be detected. The two theoretical texts which expound Cixous's thinking on this question are 'Le Rire de la Méduse' and 'La Jeune Née', both produced in the mid-1970s.

Femininity as it exists in patriarchy is held to be a male-defined concept, and women need to discover and uncover a non-phallic form of femininity. Writing is an important part of this process of discovery. 'Écriture féminine' describes what is referred to as the 'effet-femme' in language and texts, and reflects 'feminine libidinal economy' whose organizing principles are linked to notions such as a particular relation to spending and giving, starting and ending, linearity and circularity, accepting risk and uncertainty, not seeking origins or authority, asserting a different notion of self and other, of property and ownership.

Masculine and feminine are not the same thing as

male and female: male and female writers have both masculine and feminine within them to a greater or lesser extent. Cixous sees the feminine in male writers such as Kleist, Joyce, and *Genet. Female writers whose work can be described as feminine include Virginia Woolf, Cixous herself, Marguerite *Duras, and the Brazilian writer Clarice Lispector. According to proponents of 'écriture féminine', the feminine is disruptive of phallologocentric practices: while language and language-use may be oppressive to women in that women may experience things in ways that have no form of expression, 'écriture féminine' at least disturbs the tranquil surface of discourse, both by writing in other ways and writing about other things. [CD]

Écume des jours, L', see VIAN.

Edict of Nantes. In April 1598 *Henry IV (himself an ex-Protestant who had converted to Catholicism to ensure his control of the whole country) issued the Edict of Nantes [see WARS OF RELIGION]. This complex edict guaranteed the existence in France of the Calvinist religion as an independent force. It was not motivated by a belief in toleration for its own sake (a principle in which neither Catholics nor Protestants at that time believed), but by a recognition that some settlement would have to be reached with the Calvinists (or Huguenots) if further civil war was to be avoided. The Edict guaranteed the freedom of Protestant worship, under certain strict limitations, particularly concerning where churches might be set up. Most importantly, it nominated about 150 *lieux de refuge*, of which 66 were *places de sûreté*, garrisoned by Protestant troops paid out of royal funds. La Rochelle and Montauban were the most famous. This meant in fact that Protestantism constituted a sort of state within a state.

As French absolutism intensified in the 17th c. this situation was unlikely to last. There was sporadic fighting from 1615 onwards (accompanied by far from sporadic atrocities on both sides), culminating in *Richelieu's siege and subjugation of La Rochelle, followed by the Peace of Alès in 1629, which put an end to the *places de sûreté* and to the military independence of the Calvinists—though without much effect on their numbers. In the 1680s repression was stepped up, culminating in 1685 in the *dragonnades*. On 17 October 1685 Louis XIV issued the Edict of Fontainebleau, formally revoking the Edict of Nantes, and making even the practice of the Protestant religion in private homes illegal. At least 200,000 Huguenots fled the country [see REFUGE]; most others conformed outwardly, but maintained the Protestant tradition underground [see CAMISARDS; PROTESTANTISM]. [RBG]

Education. [For education in the Middle Ages see SCHOLASTICISM.] The history of French education since the Renaissance falls into three phases. Under the *ancien régime*, it belonged to a cultural domain largely controlled by the Catholic church. Between the 1789 Revolution and the early 20th c. the expansion of schooling as part of the social apparatus of an industrializing nation was accompanied by intense conflict between the Church and the secular, centralizing State. Since World War I attention has concentrated on breaking down the barriers of class and gender, to substitute a unified system for one in which élite and mass education formed separate spheres. Throughout these phases, the use of education to impose a common set of values may be seen as a characteristically French emphasis.

1. The Ancien Régime

The early history of popular education is difficult to separate from that of *literacy, which spread slowly and patchily, especially among the rural population. *Petites écoles* giving a rudimentary education were left to local initiative, and came under religious superintendence. The *Reformation and *Counter-Reformation gave them a marked stimulus. While Protestants laid special stress on reading the Bible, Catholics relied on education to evangelize the countryside, combat heresy, and instil new devotional disciplines. Occasional support was forthcoming from the State, but the real work was done by the local clergy, by charitable individuals, and by religious orders like the Frères des Écoles Chrétiennes founded by Jean-Baptiste de *la Salle. As with literacy, there were striking regional variations within France, and by 1789 high levels of school attendance existed north and east of the 'line from Saint-Malo to Geneva'. But even within literate areas, large numbers escaped schooling altogether; schools were most highly developed in towns, and more likely to be attended by boys than girls.

At the popular level, institutional schooling was slow to replace informal means of socializing children. For the social élite, however, a standard pattern of humanist secondary education in *collèges* and universities was established in the late 16th c. The *Jesuits had the leading role, but religious orders like the *Oratorians were also active, and there were Protestant colleges in the early years [see also PORT-ROYAL]. Latin was at the heart of this education, which sought to train pupils in the written and oral skills of *rhetoric, and to immerse them in a timeless world where the standards of beauty, truth, and conduct taught by the classical authors were fused with the Christian faith. This model also prevailed in the residential *colleges which were attached to universities and prepared younger students for their degrees in arts, colleges which were especially numerous and powerful in Paris. The university system inherited from the Middle Ages expanded in the 16th and 17th c. as the lay professional faculties of law and medicine came to enjoy equal prestige with theology. But by the 18th c., although the universities' social role remained important (recent research has done something to rehabilitate their intellectual reputation), their

Education

academic life had become stagnant, with ossified teaching and examining procedures. They failed to contribute creatively to *Enlightenment thought, remaining dominated by religious orthodoxy when the French élite was rejecting the direction of the Church.

The colleges and universities had a special appeal for those urban social groups—*noblesse de robe* and bourgeoisie—whose aspirations centred on legal training and access to public offices and professions, though they also attracted pupils from more modest backgrounds aiming at the clergy. The older nobility still favoured an education stressing gentlemanly and military accomplishments, combining the college with private education through tutors. A domestic ideal was also preferred in girls' education, which was largely in the hands of religious orders; convent schools cultivated a family atmosphere, and did not copy the intellectual rigour of the boys' colleges.

2. 1750–1914

a. Reform and Revolution. In the mid-18th c. new ideas about childhood and the formation of the personality, as expressed notably in Rousseau's **Émile*, brought a reaction against the stereotyped forms of élite training. Like other leading figures of the Enlightenment, Rousseau was ambivalent towards the education of the masses. But the Enlightenment belief in rational social reform stimulated thinking about national systems of education directed by the State. The closing of the Jesuit Colleges in 1762 brought upheaval, and the 1789 Revolution made the crisis more general, as the revenues of the Church were confiscated, religious orders dissolved, and priests expelled. The 24 universities then existing were abolished in 1793, and schools survived with difficulty. The 1790s saw several far-reaching reform plans, notably that of *Condorcet, but political instability and lack of money meant that little was achieved. The *écoles centrales* (1795), secondary schools on a radical new model, were the most interesting innovation. It was only after Napoleon seized power and restored the Church that the fortunes of education revived, though he was content to leave influence over the masses to the clergy, and concentrated on the training of officers and bureaucrats. The new bourgeois élite was to have a secular ethos, and ecclesiastical influence was excluded from the 'university' created in 1808—the centralized corporation of administrators and teachers. Napoleon's administrative structure, including the grouping of departments into regional *académies* headed by *recteurs*, was to prove long-lasting.

b. Élite Education. Lycées replaced the *écoles centrales* in 1802. Supplemented by municipal colleges in smaller towns, they followed a standard curriculum leading to the new *baccalauréat*, returning to the humanist traditions of the colleges whose buildings they often occupied. Latin now shared the honours with Greek, French literature, mathematics,

and philosophy (taught in the final year); élite culture remained deeply marked by an emphasis on analytical clarity and verbal expression. This *culture générale* became a badge of bourgeois status, but one angled towards the professions and the bureaucracy rather than industry and commerce. There were periodic attempts to introduce science and other modern subjects, but only in 1902 were alternative paths to the *baccalauréat* given equal status.

Since the *lycées* gave a complete liberal education, the demand for higher education was limited. Instead of restoring the universities, Napoleon created separate faculties; the vocational law and medical schools flourished, but letters and science attracted few students. The ambitious preferred the *grandes écoles*, specialized schools which recruited through competitive examinations. In the 19th c. their numbers were limited, the *École Polytechnique and the *École Normale Supérieure being the most distinguished. Later, *grandes écoles* multiplied, particularly in commerce and engineering. Their entrance examinations required intensive preparation, especially in mathematics, and the Paris *lycées* specialized in this task—part of the progressive concentration of educational and scientific institutions in the capital. Alongside the *grandes écoles*, the faculties underwent significant reform and expansion under the Third Republic. Germany's victory in 1870–1 was attributed to her intellectual and scientific superiority, and the German universities became the model for the reform policy directed by Louis Liard. The provincial faculties were developed with an eye to local industrial needs, the *Sorbonne was rebuilt, laboratories and research institutions were founded, and the faculties of letters and science acquired a new clientele of full-time students, now including women. Reform culminated in 1896 with the constitution of 15 universities, and the system thus established changed little before the 1960s.

Another achievement of the Third Republic was the creation of *lycées* for girls (1880), though the curricula for boys and girls remained different until the 1920s (and it was not until the 1960s that mixed secondary education became general). The girls' *lycées* were a challenge to the Church, which previously dominated the field, and were accompanied by attacks on Catholic secondary schools for boys, which had revived in the 19th c. despite Napoleon's legal restrictions. Republicans saw Catholic institutions for the élite (which included Catholic faculties from 1875) as dangerously divisive and anti-modern, and it was true that Catholic colleges had a social cachet which appealed to the nobility and the more conservative bourgeoisie.

c. Popular Education. *Anticlericalism was fundamental to *republican policy on popular education. The *lois *Ferry, which made education free (1881) and compulsory (1882), have usually been seen as a turning-point, but they really marked the consolidation of a long development. Every government after

1815 encouraged the provision and improvement of schools, in co-operation with the Church and local authorities. The *loi* *Guizot of 1833 required every commune to provide a public school, and created departmental *écoles normales* for training teachers. Guizot himself was typical in combining religious and humanitarian motives with the idea of social control, looking to the schools to moralize the masses and provide social stability. The *loi Falloux* of 1850 reinforced the influence of the Church, and *Napoleon III made only limited legislative changes despite the modernizing character of his regime. Yet throughout these years schooling was steadily extending, as its social and economic value became more evident. Regional disparities were evened out, the education of girls was no longer neglected, and school attendance became part of the accepted pattern of childhood among both peasants and urban workers. Ferry's reforms filled the gaps, and created a well-financed national system.

They also reflected the passionate republican belief, already evident in 1848, that education was the instrument of democracy, social progress, and popular emancipation. The positivist creed of science provided an ideology for *anticlericalism, and Ferry enforced the principle of state neutrality in religion (*laïcité*): religious instruction was replaced by 'civic' teaching, and only lay persons could teach in state schools. The reforms of the Third Republic were also inspired by *nationalism, using the school to break down regional loyalties and form French citizens; this entailed the imposition of standard French, and a war against *patois and non-French languages. The village school was one of the most characteristic institutions of the Third Republic, which had no more zealous servants than the elementary teachers (*instituteurs* and *institutrices*). On the other side of the Church–State battle, Catholics denounced the 'atheist' state schools, and devoted much energy to building up their own, especially in devout areas like the west. In the heated political atmosphere after the *Dreyfus Affair, the republicans attempted to eliminate even Catholic private schools by banning religious orders; tensions were reduced after World War I, but only in the 1950s was a compromise reached by admitting Catholic schools to state subsidy.

3. Since World War I

Élite and popular education developed as separate, self-contained systems, reflecting the rigid class structure. Universities and *lycées* were strongholds of liberal values, symbolizing the principles of merit and talent asserted in 1789 against birth and privilege, but they had no direct connection with elementary schools, and although there were many individual success stories, the channels of social mobility were narrow. The advent of the Third Republic brought no substantial change, and before 1914 only about 3 per cent of the age-group received secondary education, 1 per cent reaching the *bac-*calauréat. But after World War I a new impulse towards democratization created the ideal of the *école unique*. Instead of being divided between free elementary and fee-paying secondary sectors, each serving a wide age-range, schools would be organized in successive stages, allocating pupils to different types of secondary education according to ability. This programme was accomplished in stages between the 1920s and 1960s, but gradual reform was then overtaken by an educational 'explosion', driven partly by a rising birth-rate, partly by a growing demand for qualifications. More pupils staying on at school meant a surge in demand for higher education, and the consequent overcrowding helped provoke the student disturbances of *May 1968. The short-term response to these was to subdivide large universities and found new ones (producing more than 60 separate institutions), and to allow more autonomy from the state; in the long term, governments accepted the need to move from élite to mass higher education. For similar reasons, the barriers within secondary education were dismantled, and schools were reorganized into two stages, the *collèges* common to all, and the *lycées* for advanced pupils, giving various forms of technical and vocational as well as academic education. The *baccalauréat* expanded accordingly. But the system remained highly competitive, with the *grandes écoles* retaining their place at its apex. As sociologists like *Bourdieu pointed out, bourgeois privilege could survive within formal meritocracy, and the power of education to mould the social structure was less than idealists over the centuries had supposed.

[RDA]

See L.-H. Parias (ed.), *Histoire générale de l'enseignement et de l'éducation en France*, new edn. (1983); R. Chartier, M.-M. Compère, and D. Julia, *L' Éducation en France du XVIe au XVIIIe siècle* (1976); A. Prost, *Histoire de l'enseignement en France, 1800–1967*, 6th edn. (1986).

Éducation sentimentale, L'. Novel by *Flaubert, published in 1869 (an earlier novel by Flaubert bearing the same title was written in 1843–5). It develops the theme of the provincial student making his way in Paris against the recent historical period of 1840 to 1851. Flaubert wanted to record the 'histoire morale' of his own generation and chose his hero and his group of Parisian friends to represent a range of social and political positions. He undertook massive research for the novel over the five years he spent writing it. Climactic moments in Frédéric Moreau's love-life are dramatically juxtaposed with the outbreak of the February Revolution of 1848 and the 1851 *coup d'état* (all political positions, from revolutionary to reactionary, are derided with Flaubert's familiar cynicism). Flaubert worried that the historical background was swamping the foreground of the hero's amorous adventures. In fact Frédéric is a mere spectator of the history making itself under his nose, and, despite the parallel themes of disillusionment, the novel lacks the causal links between private and historical spheres of, say, a novel by *Balzac.

Indeed, an early allusion to Le *Père Goriot implies that Frédéric has been deliberately conceived as an anti-*Rastignac, passive and not really ambitious, throwing away lucky breaks (an inheritance, useful social connections), which could have acted as a springboard for a career in business or politics. There are elements of the Romantic artist figure in Frédéric, but even here the theme is half-hearted and degraded. He dabbles in the commercialized art world of Jacques Arnoux, who runs an art magazine and sells paintings before becoming a ceramics manufacturer. At the same time Frédéric is obsessively in love with the virtuous and rather ordinary Madame Arnoux, but, unable to act, he instead takes over Arnoux's mistress, the prostitute Rosanette. Possible marriages with Louise Roque, an unsophisticated provincial neighbour, and with Madame Dambreuse, widow of a wealthy banker, complicate Frédéric's life but come to nothing. Flaubert's detailed descriptions of the contrasting interior settings of Madame Arnoux, Rosanette, and Madame Dambreuse form the basis of the moral and aesthetic atmosphere of the novel, while the streets of Paris form a poetic as much as a political backcloth. In a famous epilogue to the novel Frédéric is visited by Madame Arnoux after a gap of 15 years. The dividing-line between sentiment and narrative irony as they discuss their great but unconsummated love is narrow indeed, and this scene more than any has led to critical debate over the intended value of this relationship. Indeed, critics remain intrigued by their own inability to get to the bottom of the ideological, moral, and aesthetic ambivalence of this ambitious but wilfully insipid novel. [DK]

Égarements du cœur et de l'esprit, Les. Novel by *Crébillon *fils*, published in three parts (1736–8). Though unfinished, it is generally considered to be one of his best works. Cast in the form of a *memoir-novel, it shows the young Meilcour's initiation into the world of *galanterie*. His heart is won by the virtuous young Hortense de Théville, but Crébillon's story stops just as Meilcour has been seduced by an older woman, Madame de Lursay. The hero's cynical mentor, Versac, expresses a philosophy akin to that of Valmont in Les *Liaisons dangereuses*. Crébillon's style is complex and subtle, often relying on ambiguity to achieve its effects. [VGM]

Egypt, see MIDDLE EAST.

EIFFEL, Gustave (1832–1923). Engineer, designer of numerous major projects, in particular the 300-metre metal tower on the Champ-de-Mars which bears his name and was constructed for the Exhibition of 1889 (to commemorate the Revolution). The *Oxford Companion to French Literature* describes it as 'intrinsically hideous' but possessing 'a beauty of familiarity which defies aesthetic standards'; it has seemed to many writers and artists of the 20th c. the very symbol of modernity (see the paintings of Robert *Delaunay or the opening of *Apollinaire's 'Zone'). [PF]

EINHARD. Soldier and counsellor to *Charlemagne and Louis Iᵉʳ, author of a *Life of Charles the Great* (*Vita Karoli Magni*) between 819 and 831. Modelled on Suetonius' *Lives of the Caesars*, drawing on official documents, and enlivened by first-hand impressions, it portrayed Charles as a warrior, judge, and father of his people. [JHD]

ELEANOR OF AQUITAINE (1122–1204). Granddaughter of William IX, duke of Aquitaine (*Guilhem IX, the troubadour), Eleanor was the child of Aenor of Chatellerault and Duke William X. When her father went on a pilgrimage in 1137 to Compostella (where he died), he left her in the guardianship of the ailing king Louis VI, who married her to his son and heir Louis. As queen of France and duchess of Aquitaine from 1137, Eleanor bore her husband two daughters, but not the son for which he yearned. Although she accompanied Louis on the Second *Crusade, the marriage was by then under serious strain, and in 1152 they were divorced on (spurious) grounds of consanguinity. Immediately she married Henry, duke of Normandy and count of Anjou, soon to be crowned Henry II, king of England. After the birth of four sons and two daughters, Henry in 1168 sent Eleanor back to Aquitaine to govern the province and induct their second son Richard Lionheart into the ways of the duchy. But in 1174 she was imprisoned for supporting her sons in rebellion against their father, and thereafter ceased to exercise authority apart from two brief periods, the first during Richard's absence on crusade, the second in the early years of John's reign.

High claims have been made for Eleanor as the chief transmitter to northern France of southern *troubadour culture, as an avid patron of poetry and music, as the proponent of passionate love and the poetic exaltation of adultery, and also as the promoter of *tournaments. Richard the Poitevin praised the atmosphere in her entourage; *Bernart de Ventadorn mentioned her in four songs; *Wace dedicated his *Roman de Brut* to her and to Henry; and *Andreas Capellanus had her preside over the court of love he described in his *De amore* (which at least suggests he knew she would enjoy the work). She may have encouraged *Marie de France; she probably influenced her daughter Marie, countess of Champagne (who, with her husband Henry the Liberal, patronized learning and piety), and also her son Richard, who wrote competent poems in the troubadour style. But because her role was backstage, her precise contribution to the sudden emergence of the courtly culture that bloomed in later 12th-c. France remains uncertain. [JHD]

See W. W. Kibler (ed.), *Eleanor of Aquitaine: Patron and Politician* (1976); D. D. R. Owen, *Eleanor of Aquitaine: Queen and Legend* (1993).

ELEBE Lisembe, (Philippe) (b. 1937). Zaïrois poet and playwright. African authenticity is a major theme of Elebe's ten volumes of verse, which include *Mélodie africaine* (1970), *Orphée rebelle* (1972), *La Joconde d'ébène* (1977), and *Les Cailloux de l'espoir* (1987). Anti-colonialism dominates his plays: *Simon Kimbangu ou le Messie* (1972); *Le Sang des Noirs pour un sou* (1972); *Chant de la terre/Chant de l'eau* (1973).   [VC]

Électre, see GIRAUDOUX.

Éléments de la philosophie de Newton, see VOLTAIRE, 2.

Éléments de littérature, see MARMONTEL.

EL GOULLI, Sophie (b. 1932). Tunisian writer. Born in Sousse, Tunisia, educated in Tunis and Paris, she has worked as an art critic and lectures on history of art in Tunis. She has published collections of poems: *Signes* (1973), *Nos rêves* (1980), and *Vertige solaire* (1981); a study of a Tunisian painter, *Ammar Fehrat et son œuvre* (1979); and a collection of short stories for children, *Contes: le Joueur d'échecs, le Roi qui s'ennuyait, le Soleil et la pluie* (1983).   [FL]

EL HOUSSI, Majid (b. 1942). Tunisian poet and academician. El Houssi practises in his four volumes of poetry, *Je voudrais ésotériquement te conter* (1972), *Imagivresse* (1973), *Ahméta-O* (1980), and *Iris Ifriqiya* (1981), a poetics of lyrical violence: his verse is full of audacious, sacrilegious, and *Surrealist imagery couched in the traditional but renovated form of oratory, *dhikr,* or incantation. Childhood in a colonial situation and the subsequent cultural and linguistic alienation of the colonized are major themes in his poetry. Like the majority of Tunisian poets in French, El Houssi attempts to reactualize motifs, modes of expression and art-forms from the past in a continuous effort to explain and update reality.
          [HA-J]

Élise, ou la Vraie Vie, see ETCHERELLI.

Elision, see VERSIFICATION, I.

Elle. Up-market women's magazine, founded in 1945, which achieved an avant-garde reputation in the 1950s and 1960s for its handling of sexual issues and its publication of Simone de *Beauvoir. Overtaken by second-wave *feminism in the early 1970s, it had reorganized by 1980 as the thinking woman's fashion magazine.   [EAF]

Elle sera de jaspe et de corail, see WEREWERE LIKING.

Éloge. With the rise of the various French *academies, this ancient branch of oratory established itself as a literary genre. It can be seen as the lay equivalent of the funeral oration as practised by *Bossuet or *Fléchier. Normally an *éloge* was read out after the death of an academician, and published shortly afterwards as an obituary. In some cases *éloges* were composed for those long dead (Cicero, *Henri IV, etc.) in competitions for academic prizes. There were also discourses in favour of professions, virtues, etc.—and these gave rise to mock encomia, ranging from *Erasmus's *Praise of Folly* (echoed by *Rabelais) to the trivial *Éloge du pet* (1799) of Mercier de Compiègne.

In the 18th c. the acknowledged master of the genre was A.-L *Thomas, who left an *Essai sur les éloges* (1773). More important are the series of *éloges* composed for the *Académie des Sciences by *Fontenelle and *Condorcet, and for the *Académie Française by d'*Alembert. For all their solemnity, these pieces (and those of the 19th c. which follow in the same tradition) offer not only biographical information, but also an embryonic history of science and literature, enhancing the corporate (male) self-image by the praise of great predecessors.   [PF]

Éloges, see SAINT-JOHN PERSE.

Eloquence. 'Prends l'éloquence et tords-lui son cou', wrote *Verlaine. One striking feature of modern French literary history is the disappearance of eloquence or oratory. Of course, eloquent writing persists in the theatre and in written genres such as the novel, essay, pamphlet, newspaper article, or even occasionally poetry, but one would look in vain for chapters on eloquence in most accounts of modern literature.

In the *ancien régime* and even the 19th c. it was different. *Rhetoric taught poetry and eloquence as the two parts of what came to be known as literature. The *Académie Française offered prizes in both fields. The two were customarily distinguished ('Poets are born, orators are made'), but the dividing-line was unclear, and critics, theorists, and teachers such as *Rapin, *Perrault, or *Batteux moved to and fro between them.

Eloquence, like theatre, is a performance art; indeed, the classical theatre was a major forum for eloquence, and one of the few in which the female voice could be heard. Like drama, oratory too survives in written texts. These might be composed in advance, or written down during or after the speech, but they were often published, sometimes in anthologies (e.g. *Vaumorière's *Harangues sur toutes sortes de sujets,* 1687), and as such became the object of study, appreciation, and imitation. The field was usually divided into four areas:

a. The eloquence of the pulpit. For many centuries this was the dominant kind of oratory: it is the only one which has left a significant mark in histories of literature [see SERMON].

b. Academic eloquence. All the *academies, both Parisian and provincial, encouraged oratory. Jean-Jacques *Rousseau came to fame with a discourse composed for the Dijon academy. The main kind of oratory practised in these assemblies was demonstrative, that of praise or blame [see ÉLOGE].

c. *Forensic eloquence*. This existed wherever there were law courts, but attained a new prestige with the Ciceronian revival of the *Renaissance. Much pleading in the 16th and 17th c. was remarkable for its rich literary erudition, its use of quotations and elaborate metaphors–this was criticized in Claude *Fleury's *Dialogues sur l'éloquence judiciaire* (composed 1664) and mocked in *Racine's *Les Plaideurs*. In the late 17th c. a simpler style came into fashion. Most speeches continued to be read from written texts until the 19th c., when legal oratory became less literary, more improvised. Few barristers have gained a place in literary history; they include Antoine *Lemaître, *Patru, and d'*Aguesseau in the 17th c., and in the 18th *Linguet, Henri Cochin (1687–1747), and two lawyers who defended *Calas, Elie de Beaumont and Loyseau de Mauléon. *Mirabeau *fils* and *Beaumarchais also produced remarkable speeches when pleading their own cases.

d. *Political eloquence*. This came into its own during the *Wars of Religion, when in university assemblies or at the *États Généraux orators such as *Pasquier, *L'Hôpital, or *Du Vair defended their causes. For most of the 17th and 18th c. there were no representative assemblies, and political oratory could only find a home in the law-courts (*parlements*). This was notably the case in the Parlement de Paris during the *Fronde, and again at the time of the expulsion of the *Jesuits (*c.*1761) and the *Maupeou affair (1770). But generally, 18th-c. commentators looked with some envy to Britain as a place where political eloquence could flourish.

The *Revolution rapidly changed all that. The National Assemblies, but also the clubs and public meetings, provided the forum for a great explosion of political eloquence, which now seemed capable of changing the fate of the nation. This eloquence has been much debated, usually in partisan terms. Some have seen it as the cradle both of modern political speaking and of a new kind of language prefiguring *Romanticism; for others, it is sinister, grotesquely inflated, full of 'noble Roman' posturing. The speeches of the great orators, notably Mirabeau, *Barnave, *Danton, *Vergniaud, *Robespierre, *Saint-Just, have mostly been published, even though we cannot be sure whether what we read is what was said. But to gain a truer impression of the reality of political debate, one needs to go back to the contemporary records printed in journals such as the *Moniteur*.

*Napoleon's regime suppressed most political eloquence except his own, which was remarkable for its vigour, clarity, and concision. Thereafter, as parliamentary government established itself in France, political oratory became a normal part of the nation's life. Among politicians who acquired particular fame in the 19th and 20th c., one should mention *Constant, Pierre-Antoine Berryer, *Lamartine,

*Thiers, *Guizot, and *Jaurès. Charles de *Gaulle above all, mastering the new possibilities of television and radio, used his quite traditional eloquence very effectively to sway public opinion and action; his speeches are as much a part of 'literature' as the great sermons of the 17th c.   [PF]

See J. Starobinski, 'La Chaire, la tribune, le barreau', in P. Nora (ed.), *Les Lieux de mémoire*, II, *La Nation*, vol. 3 (1986).

ELSKAMP, Max (1862–1931). Belgian *Symbolist poet, who lived all his life in Antwerp and evoked its people and traditions in naïve-seeming, yet subtle verse, combining musicality and syntactic innovation (*Enluminures*, 1898; *La Louange de la vie*, 1898). After a silence of 23 years he published several slim volumes, including the nostalgic *Chanson de la rue Saint-Paul* (1922), in which a darker note is heard, perhaps heralding the mental illness to which he succumbed.   [PF]

Elstir. Character in Proust's *À la recherche du temps perdu*, the representative of modern (Impressionist) painting.

ÉLUARD, Paul (pseud. of Eugène Grindel) (1895–1952). 'De l'horizon d'un homme à l'horizon de tous'—this famous line gives a clue to the wide appeal which makes Éluard a truly European poet, alongside Rilke, Montale, or Lorca, and one of France's best-known 20th-c. writers. For him the poet was above all a mediator: 'J'établis des rapports . . . entre ma solitude et toi.' Poetry could confine itself at times to mediating between the ecstasies or vicissitudes of the lover and the world of everyday communication, or even to becoming simply the extension of love at its most intensely sensual: 'D'une grande écriture charnelle j'aime.' But for much of his career Éluard saw his writing as mediating between the personal and the political—*La Vie immédiate* and *La Rose publique*, to borrow the titles of two of his collections, from 1932 and 1934 respectively.

*Surrealism played a decisive part in Éluard's poetic orientation. The son of prosperous lower-middle-class parents from the Paris suburb of Saint-Denis, he turned to poetry when ill health, which dogged him all his life, led to long spells in Swiss sanatoria (1912–13). The meeting with Gala (*Lettres à Gala*, 1984), a fiery Russian who was to be his first wife and muse, and the experience of working as a nurse during World War I provided inspiration for his early work, but it was the encounter with *Paulhan, *Breton, and *Aragon in 1919, and participation in *Dada, then Surrealist, activities in the 1920s, which gave Éluard's work the tonality it was to retain until his early death in 1952. Wholeheartedly committed to the Surrealist programme— liberation of the unconscious, celebration of desire, appeal to the marvellous in everyday life—Éluard usually refrained from ideological pronouncements and never entirely espoused Surrealist methods.

The poems of *Capitale de la douleur* (1926) and *L'Amour la poésie* (1929) are Surrealist in their linguistic freedom, their lack of immediate referential anchorage, the radicalism of their lyric charge, but they are also classical by dint of economy, purity of diction, and syntactical control. Rather than flamboyant imagery, Éluard's Surrealist poetry derives its energy from an incomparable virtuosity in repetition and variation, juxtaposition and ellipsis, phrasal modulation and rhythmic fluidity. Very much an individualist, he participated fully none the less in the collective side of Surrealism, often collaborating with others: *Ralentir travaux* (1930), poems written *à trois* with Breton and *Char; *L'Immaculée Conception* (1930), where he and Breton attempted to replicate the verbal symptoms of various mental disorders. *Les Malheurs des immortels* (1922), with Max Ernst, was the first of many collaborations with painters (*Picasso, Man Ray), to whom he also devoted many poems and some interesting essays (*Donner à voir*, 1939).

Éluard subscribed fully to the Surrealist view that moral or religious constraints should not interfere with sexual freedom, and his biographers report numerous liaisons in addition to the relationships explicitly celebrated in his poems: with Gala (who deserted him for Salvador Dali), then Nusch (whose sudden death in 1946 left him devastated), Jaqueline (*Corps mémorable*, 1947), and finally Dominique—*Le Phénix* (1951). Strongly linked to the cult of woman and the feminine, another Surrealist trait, love permeates Éluard's poetic universe, and the 'Je–Tu' relationship is the linchpin of poem after poem. Transmuted into poetry, Éluardian love becomes an infinite set of variations involving the same basic ingredients—the four elements, eyes, reflections, parts of the (female) body. Far from providing stability, however, love is presented as a dynamic process, a generative dialectic involving dark moments as well as epiphanies.

The expansive movement whereby love opens vistas beyond the purview of the solitary individual provides, in poetic terms at least, the bridge between love and politics. The injustice of economic deprivation (that of the French worker in the 1930s) or political dispossession (that of the Spanish republicans from 1936, whose struggle Éluard actively supported) could be represented as severing men and women from the replenishing power of love. In the course of the 1930s the increasing ascendancy of socio-political consciousness in Éluard's poetry does not greatly alter its rhetorical or thematic nature. Along with other Surrealists he had joined the Communist Party in 1927, and been expelled in 1933. His *rapprochement* with the Party in 1938 led to a definitive break with Breton, but paved the way for the important role Éluard was to play during the *Occupation as organizer for the Comité National des Écrivains, anthologist of clandestine poetry, and poet actively committed to the resistance effort (his poem 'Liberté', widely distributed

as a tract, is one of the most famous of the period). Somewhat more controversially Éluard travelled widely on behalf of international Communism after the war, and his *Poèmes politiques* blemish his work in certain eyes. Some of his finest love poems, however, also date from this time.   [MHTS]

See M. Jean, *Paul Éluard* (1965); J.-C Gateau, *Paul Éluard et la peinture surréaliste* (1982); N. Boulestreau, *Paul Éluard* (1985).

Élysée, Palais de l'. Since 1873 the official residence of the president of the French Republic. It is situated in the 8th *arrondissement* of Paris, between the rue du Faubourg Saint-Honoré and the rue de l'Élysée.

Émaux et camées. The best-known collection of short poems by *Gautier, first published 1852, with subsequent, enlarged editions.

Emblem. A literary mode, highly popular throughout Europe from the 16th to the 18th c., characterized by its formal tripartite structure (motto, woodcut illustration, epigrammatic interpretation in prose or verse) and its moralistic intention. It may be distinguished from the *devise*, which is enigmatic and personal, whereas the emblem is symbolic and universal. Emblems usually appear in collections, one to a page. The first emblem-book, by the lawyer Alciati, was published in Latin in Augsburg in 1531 (also Paris, 1534, French translation 1536). The first French example was Guillaume de la Perrière's *Théâtre des bons engins* (1540). Others were composed by Gilles Corrozet, Guillaume Guéroult, and Pierre Cousteau; one of the most distinguished was *Aneau's *Picta poesis*, which appeared in French as *Imagination poétique* (1552). See also Georgette de Montenay's *Emblèmes, ou Devises chrétiennes* (1571) and *Bèze's *Quarante-quatre emblèmes chrétiens* (1581). The main source is to be found in medieval and Neoplatonic allegory and symbolism and in hieroglyphics. Their chief interest does not lie in their literary or artistic value, but in the way text and picture combine to convey a moral, and point to the intellectual and ethical concerns of a fascinated public.   [PS]

Émigré, L', see SÉNAC DE MEILHAN.

Émile, ou De l'éducation. Jean-Jacques *Rousseau described this work, published 1762, as his treatise on human nature. His fullest and most mature account of the positive philosophy he elaborated as an answer to the catastrophic situation diagnosed in his first writings, it takes the form of a pedagogical novel in five books, telling of the education of a solitary boy by a wise tutor. The fifth book is devoted to Émile's partner, Sophie, who is brought up to play a traditional wifely role.

Rousseau's programme, partly inspired by Locke, is centred on the notion that the child is a human being in its own right. Émile is not educated to fit into existing society, but to develop his individual potential to the full. This involves a 'negative' education, preserving him from harmful social influences and respecting a gradual 'natural' development, where the training of the senses precedes book-learning and moral and religious education (the latter being extensively treated in Book 4 in the 'Profession de foi du vicaire savoyard'). In the last two books the 'savage' is reintegrated into society, and learns the lessons of Du *contrat social. An unfinished sequel, Émile et Sophie, ou les Solitaires, shows him coming to grief in contemporary France and falling back on his qualities of self-reliance.

Émile was condemned by the Sorbonne and the Parlement de Paris for its unorthodox religious doctrine. In the following two centuries it exerted an incalculable influence on innovatory theory and practice in education. [PF]

Éminence grise, L'. Name given to the Capuchin friar Joseph le Clerc du Tremblay (1577–1638), *Richelieu's agent and adviser, and subsequently to individuals exercising hidden influence on public affairs [see DEVOTIONAL WRITING, 2].

EMMANUEL, Pierre (pseud. of Noël Matthieu) (b. 1916). Born at Caën, educated in a religious school at Lyon, his poetic work and theory were initially inspired by *Jouve. His pen-name betrays his vision of the poet—both priest and prophet—and he is a leading Catholic poet in the *Hugolian, *Claudelian tradition of eloquence. His poetic journey is described in Autobiographies (1970), where he explains that poetry is akin to contemplation, often written in a trance-like state, and that poetic language is a reality, not a symbolic system. Psychic and spiritual reality 'fill' each poetic word as water fills a goblet. 'Speech seems to me like a fifth element, as natural as the four others—the spiritual element which makes them concrete. . . . The words that [poetry] employs are indivisible from the things they name.' It seems a dangerous doctrine to assume that human words can express the logos, and despite his genuine poetic gift (e.g. the poems of 'Nef', Sophia, 1973), the eloquence of Emmanuel is too often empty, his grandiose rhythms too often turgid. His output is large, including Tombeau d'Orphée (1941), Sodome (1944), Babel (1951), Visage nuage (1956), Jacob (1970). [GDM]

Empire, see NAPOLEON; SECOND EMPIRE.

Emploi du temps, L'. Novel by *Butor, published 1956. Presented as the diary of Jacques Revel, a young Frenchman spending a year in 'Bleston', an industrial city in the north of England inspired by Manchester, where the young Butor had spent two years, the novel charts his struggle to survive in an alienating environment. Realizing that the blind rage Bleston provokes in him is merely self-destructive, he turns instead to writing as a means of exploring, articulating, and hence mastering the city's malign powers. An increasingly complex contrapuntal system of time sequences develops as he goes over different sections of the past year, juxtaposing them in different patterns, while the present simultanously evolves as he writes. Understanding the past means sacrificing the present: he becomes so absorbed in the diary that he loses two potential fiancées. His representation of Bleston incorporates the city's own cultural signs, notably a cathedral window depicting Cain, a series of medieval tapestries illustrating Greek myths, and a detective story set in the town. He identifies with the Old Testament fratricide, Theseus confronting the Minotaur, and the detective seeking the truth. But he discovers the necessity of going beyond pre-existing representations which, though helpful, are inevitably distorted and incomplete: making sense of reality is an open-ended, constantly unfinished process, and his diary, too, will be unable to fill in all the gaps.

[CB]

Ems Dispatch, see FRANCO-PRUSSIAN WAR.

En attendant Godot, see BECKETT.

Encyclopedias have been composed in France from the High Middle Ages on. The earliest examples were in Latin, in particular the Speculum majus of *Vincent of Beauvais, which enjoyed great success even beyond the invention of printing, the last edition being produced in 1624. Early French encyclopedic writings include the poems of Philippe de Thaon [see ANGLO-NORMAN LITERATURE], the versified Ymage du monde (1247) of Gautier de Metz, and in particular the prose Li Livres dou trésor of *Brunetto Latini. Brunetto, like his counterparts who write in Latin, arranges his material by subject-matter, but sometimes uses alphabetical order within sections.

There is something of a lull in French encyclopedic production at the time of the Renaissance, although one can point to such compilations as those of *Belon du Mans and *Binet. The latter's Essai des merveilles shows the way an encyclopedia can be used as a source-book by writers and orators. *Rabelais was the first French writer to use the term 'encyclopédie', though his attitude to encyclopedic learning is not without an element of mockery.

In the 17th c. the modern encyclopedia begins to emerge in France (following the lead given by Bacon in England and Comenius in Holland). *Moreri's Grand dictionnaire historique (1674) long remained a much-used work of reference for history, geography, and biography; it was criticized and corrected in that influential monument of encyclopedism, *Bayle's Dictionnaire. At about the same time, *Furetière in his dictionary often goes beyond the mere definition of words—the 'dictionnaire de mots' was at first not clearly distinguished from the 'dictionnaire de choses', and even in more recent times the line between the two is far from sharp [see DICTIONARIES].

In 1694 appeared Thomas *Corneille's Dictionnaire des arts et des sciences, the scientific pendant to the dictionary of the *Académie Française. The interest in technology was carried further, not without some plagiarism, in the greatest French encyclopedia, the *Encyclopédie* (1750–72) of *Diderot and d'*Alembert, which aimed both to provide an account of the current state of knowledge (excluding the kind of historical material covered by Moreri) and to 'change the general way of thinking'. The alphabetically ordered material of the *Encyclopédie* was subsequently rearranged and augmented (but without the excitement of the original) in the immense *Encyclopédie méthodique* masterminded by *Panckoucke.

The second great French encyclopedia, *Larousse's *Grand dictionnaire universel* (1865–90), sets itself deliberately in the tradition of Diderot and d'Alembert. It is a splendidly combative, often idiosyncratic compendium of progressive views of the time and a work of massive proportions which combines the historical information of Moreri with the scientific and philosophical interests of the *Encyclopédie*. It is also the first of the great family of Larousse dictionaries and encyclopedias which occupy a central place in modern French culture, though none of them has the originality of their ancestor. They are mainly exhaustive encyclopedias with many short entries (the latest in the line being the *Grand Larousse universel* of 1985, 2nd edn. 1992); Larousse's *La Grande Encyclopédie* (1971–6), on the other hand, is composed of more substantial articles. A particular place is occupied by the *Petit Larousse illustré*, an endlessly republished and revised dictionary-encyclopedia with a section for proper names and the famous 'pages roses' of quotations, a refuge for France's Latin culture.

Of the many other general encyclopedias of the 20th c., four deserve special mention. The 31-vol. alphabetical *Grande Encyclopédie* (1885–1901), directed by Marcellin Berthelot, is something like a French equivalent of contemporary versions of the *Encyclopedia Britannica*. The 21-vol. *Encyclopédie française*, directed by Lucien *Febvre, began publication in 1934 and was finished in 1966; it is arranged non-alphabetically, the material being ordered according to an original conception of the map of knowledge. The *Encyclopédie de la Pléiade* (1956–), whose first general editor was Raymond *Queneau, is an open-ended collection, with separate volumes for particular subjects; it conforms more closely to traditional academic disciplines and contains material of a very high standard. And finally the *Encyclopedia Universalis* (1st edn., 1968–75) is the major encyclopedic venture of the last third of the 20th c.; it combines a 4-vol. 'Thesaurus-Index' of short entries with a 23-vol. 'Corpus' which contains many original, often controversial, essays by important authors, but it is not so complete as the Larousse volumes.

Innumerable encyclopedias are devoted to particular branches of knowledge. In the literary field, technical terms are interestingly treated in H. Morier's *Dictionnaire de poétique et de rhétorique* (1961;

2nd edn., 1989) and B. Dupriez's *Gradus: les procédés littéraires* (1984). The *Dictionnaire des lettres françaises* (7 vols., 1951–72), under the general direction of Cardinal G. Grente, contains a vast amount of information about writers from the Middle Ages to the end of the 19th c. (the medieval volume was reissued in a completely revised form in 1992). It has, however, been partly superseded by the *Dictionnaire des littératures de langue française* (3 vols., 1984; 2nd edn., 4 vols., 1987), edited by J.-P. Beaumarchais, D. Couty, and A. Rey. This covers francophone and regional literatures well; many articles are very substantial, and as a result the number of authors treated is more limited than in the Grente volumes. In English, apart from the present volume and its Oxford predecessor, the second volume of the *Guide to French Literature* of A. Levi (1992) offers detailed accounts of the lives and works of approximately 200 major authors since 1789; a similar volume for the pre-1789 period appeared in 1994. [See also BIBLIOGRAPHIES.] [PF]

See A. Rey, *Dictionnaires et encyclopédies* (1982); H. Meschonnic, *Des mots et des mondes: dictionnaires, encyclopédies, grammaires, nomenclatures* (1991).

Encyclopédie, L'. One of the most important publishing ventures of the 18th c., often regarded as the best embodiment of the ideas and values of the French *Enlightenment. The *Encyclopédie, ou Dictionnaire raisonné des sciences, des arts et des métiers* was published in 17 large volumes, augmented by 11 splendid volumes of plates, between 1751 and 1772. It had originally been conceived by a consortium of booksellers as a translation of Ephraim Chambers's *Cyclopedia*; under the general editorship of *Diderot and d'*Alembert it quickly grew into something much more ambitious: an extensive account of the arts, sciences, and technology of modern Europe written from the critical and reforming standpoint of the *philosophes* (indeed, *encyclopédiste* became a synonym for *philosophe*).

The publishing of the work was fraught with difficulties. It met with fierce hostility from the *Jesuits (expressed principally in the *Memoires de *Trévoux*), and after the scandal caused by the publication in 1758 of *De l'esprit* by *Helvétius, further publication was forbidden by the Parlement de Paris. At this stage d'Alembert retired from the enterprise, and Diderot considered continuing publication abroad. Nevertheless, thanks to the protection of the Directeur de la Librairie, *Malesherbes, the final 10 volumes of text (which had been surreptitiously censored by the publisher Le Breton) were issued in France in 1765 under a *permission tacite*.

The *Encyclopédie* was advertised as the work of a 'société de gens de lettres', and its numerous (generally unpaid) contributors included priests, doctors, noblemen, civil servants, scientists, artists, business men, and skilled craftsmen. Most of them were new authors—including the as-yet relatively obscure

Enfance

*Quesnay, *Turgot, and *Rousseau (who wrote on music and political economy)—but there were some famous names, in particular *Voltaire and *Montesquieu, both of whom wrote on literary topics. It was Diderot who effectively co-ordinated the whole undertaking and personally wrote a vast number of articles, both large and small. He was greatly ·aided by the unassuming chevalier de *Jaucourt, who relieved him of much of the routine work of compilation.

There is a striking 'Discours préliminaire' by d'Alembert, which paints a triumphant picture of the progress of enlightenment in modern Europe, paying tribute to such precursors as Bacon, Locke, and *Descartes. It also sets out a scheme of the totality of human knowledge based on the operations of the mind. In theory, this permits a rational ordering of all the material; in reality, despite many cross-references, the alphabetical order adopted means that the work is often disconcertingly disparate. In addition, the scope, tone, and quality of the entries vary greatly.

In the scientific domain, the best and most up-to-date articles are probably those on the higher mathematics (by d'Alembert) and on medicine and natural history (see 'Animal' by Diderot). History, law, and politics occupy an important place; the contributors, who include several of the *Physiocrats, put forward a reforming line on such matters as administration and taxation. Particularly significant is the attention devoted to useful manual arts; Diderot expounds the approach adopted in 'Art', and the various crafts and trades are fully described and beautifully illustrated.

What distinguishes the work, however, is its 'philosophical' standpoint; this can be largely attributed to its principal editor, whose aim was to 'change the general way of thinking'. It finds expression in Diderot's audacious series of articles on the history of philosophy, in the primacy accorded to this-worldly concerns over theology and metaphysics, and, in the subversive tone of such articles as 'Agnus Scythicus', an attack on credulity, particularly in matters of religion. Cross-references serve the same purpose; in one famous instance a 'pompous eulogy' of the Franciscan order is undermined by a reference to a comic entry on a trivial debate about the shape of the friars' hoods.

Whether because it was useful or because it was entertaining, the *Encyclopédie* was a huge success. A complete set of the first edition cost close on 1,000 *livres*, and there were over 4,000 subscribers. It made a fortune for its publishers, and was quickly pirated and reprinted in cheaper editions. Subsequently the publisher *Panckoucke issued supplements, before transforming and revising the whole work in the *Encyclopédie méthodique*, which ran to over 200 vols. A similar methodical arrangement was adopted in the *Encyclopedia Britannica*, first published in Edinburgh in 1771. [See also DICTIONNAIRE PHILOSOPHIQUE.] [PF]

See J. Proust, *L'Encyclopédie* (1965); R. Darnton, *The Business of Enlightenment* (1979).

Enfance, see SARRAUTE.

Enfance d'un chef, L'. Novella by *Sartre, included in *Le Mur*. It paints a mocking portrait of the psychological roots of right-wing authoritarianism.

Enfances. In medieval texts the word refers to the first deeds of arms of an aspirant knight. Many *chansons de geste* deal with this period of precocious heroic activity, in which characteristic events of the hero's maturity are prefigured. There are many autonomous poems on this theme, including *Les Enfances Vivien*, *Les Enfances Guillaume*, and *Les *Narbonnais* from the Cycle de *Guillaume, *Mainet* (the 'Enfances Charlemagne'), and *Les Enfances Ogier* by *Adenet le Roi. Frequently *enfances* sections are found in longer poems. Two versions of the 'Enfances Roland' exist in *Aspremont* and *Girart de Vienne*. *Enfance* poems were frequently the last to be composed in a cyclic sequence. [PEB]

Enfant, L', see VALLÈS.

Enfant de la haute mer, L', see SUPERVIELLE.

ENFANTIN, Barthélémy-Prosper (1796–1864), see SAINT-SIMON, COMTE DE.

Enfantines, see LARBAUD.

Enfant noir, L', see CAMARA LAYE.

Enfants Sans Souci, Les. One of the names taken by the many societies of laymen in late medieval France devoted to the composition and performance of comic plays; the Gallants Sans Souci was another such name. They are linked in particular with the *soties; the Enfants Sans Souci were often the *sots* in these plays. Their relationship with the societies of law clerks called the *Basoches is complex. The Enfants Sans Souci were *compagnies joyeuses* of young men from good families; they called their leader the *prince des sots*. They flourished especially in the north-east of France, and initially had no specific connection with the legal profession. But many Basochiens were also members of the Enfants Sans Souci, and the co-operation between the two types of association encouraged the rapid growth of comic drama in the late 15th and early 16th c.; in particular, the Enfants were able to avoid the censorship which began to be imposed on the Basochiens inside the lawcourts [see MEDIEVAL THEATRE]. [GAR]

Enfants terribles, Les, see COCTEAU.

Enfer, L', see BIBLIOTHÈQUE NATIONALE.

Engagement. French word for commitment, possessing both a general and a historically specific sense. That life, art, or literature should be committed to a cause is arguable and comprehensible in all epochs. But the term was used with particular political intent in France in the 1940s and 1950s and associated primarily with left-wing and radical *Existentialist commitment. When applied to literature, the term generated much controversy. Its 'manifesto' could be said to be *Qu'est-ce que la littérature?* (1948), in which *Sartre argued that art, literature and particularly novels were *necessarily* committed. Sartre's argument is that all literature implicitly presents a certain world-view, and that the novelist cannot escape the political and ethical consequences of the kind of world she or he presents to readers. For this reason, writers should also be committed in a fully conscious sense, recognizing the influence of their works and using this in a positive way to work for a better, fairer, and freer world. Writers then both *are* committed, and have a duty to commit themselves. Since Sartre does not believe anyone should prescribe a particular mode of action for this, because we are all responsible for making our own free choices, he does not attempt to lay down any universally applicable criteria for the form that *engagement* should take. But, in accordance with Existentialist thinking on ethics, he argues that literature should contribute to making a world which respects freedom, works for the liberation of the oppressed, and creates an environment of social justice and equality. This has implications for literary aesthetics as well as for subject-matter: omniscient narrators, predetermined characters, destiny, are all rejected in favour of a more fluid, relative, subjective narrative, which respects the *phenomenological experience of temporality and recognizes its readers' freedom to (re-)create the novel they are reading. [CMH]

ENGHIEN, Louis-Antoine-Henri de Bourbon, duc d' (1772–1804). A member of the house of *Condé, he emigrated under the Revolution, but was kidnapped in March 1804, brought back to France, and executed on the trumped-up charge of plotting to overthrow Napoleon (who saw in him a possible rival for power). His killing provoked great indignation, expressed notably in Chateaubriand's *Mémoires d'outre-tombe*. [PF]

English Influences, see BRITISH, IRISH, AND AMERICAN INFLUENCES.

Enjambement. [See VERSIFICATION.] The term used to describe the run-on of a syntactical unit from one line to the next, or from one half-line (hemistich) to the next. In other words, the juncture at the end of the line, or at the caesura, does not coincide with a natural syntactical break but, rather, interrupts the syntactical unit and compels it to straddle the line-ending or caesura:

Et, pour sa voix, lointaine, et calme, et grave, elle a
L'inflexion des voix chères qui se sont tues.

These lines from *Verlaine's 'Mon rêve familier' have both an end-of-line enjambement, and an end-of-hemistich enjambement:

L'inflexion des voix | | chères qui se sont tues. (4 + 2 + 1 + 5)

Lines with enjambement at the caesura are often more comfortably read as *trimètres*:

L'inflexion | des voix chè: | res qui se sont tues. (4 + 3 + 5) [CS]

Enlightenment

1. General Characteristics

The Enlightenment was an international movement of ideas, well described by Norman Hampson as 'less a body of doctrine than a number of shared premisses'. Beginning in the late 17th c. and generally reaching a peak in the mid-18th, it took different forms in different countries. Somewhat misleadingly, most historical accounts have focused on France, as in the famous secondary definition in the former edition of the *Shorter Oxford Dictionary*, which reflects 19th-c. anti-Enlightenment thinking: 'shallow and pretentious intellectualism, unreasonable contempt for authority and tradition, etc., applied *esp.* to the spirit and aims of the French philosophers of the 18th c.'

In France, the 'Siècle des Lumières' (there is no exact equivalent to 'enlightenment') is an essential part of the national heritage, alongside and in some ways opposed to *classicism. It has often been associated with the *Revolution and the values espoused by *republicans and the Left. There is indeed a myth of the Enlightenment, already present in d'*Alembert's account of the move from darkness to light in the 'Discours préliminaire' to the bible of Enlightenment, the *Encyclopédie. The myth has provoked many counterblasts, anticipated in the tirade of Beaumarchais's Bartholo (in Le *Barbier de Séville): 'Sottises de toutes espèces: la liberté de penser, l'attraction, l'électricité, le tolérantisme, l'inoculation, le quinquina, l'encyclopédie et les drames.'

The main thrust of the movement can be summed up in Kant's 'Dare to know!', implying both critical and constructive thinking. The former had its limits; it can be argued that the *philosophes (committed enlighteners) showed a faith in reason, nature, or progress which they denied to existing practices or beliefs. Generally, however, Enlightenment thinking was inspired by *Descartes's methodical doubt: customs, religions, laws, governments were subjected to scrutiny and rejected if found wanting. Typically, the *philosophes* only criticized in order to create or reveal an order more in harmony with human nature and desires and therefore more conducive to general happiness. Their preferred values were tolerance, sociability, and freedom. Laws, government, and education were to be remade on rational lines. Above all, science, freed from the constrictions of religious dogma, would lead to fuller knowledge of the natural world (which included the human) and to the technical and material progress on which greater happiness depended.

Enlightenment

Most of these characteristics were common to Enlightenment thinking across Europe. The French Enlightenment, however, differs from that in Germany, Switzerland, or Scotland by its more radical tone. Where an Adam Smith was well integrated into his society, a *Diderot or a d'Alembert, while they had friends in high places, were embattled against a political and religious establishment which used its power to suppress their ideas by *censorship, imprisonment, and other penalties. Their position was consequently often more extreme or seditious, particularly in relation to the Church: witness *Voltaire's 'Écrasez l'infâme'. Until the last quarter of the century the *philosophes* were fairly remote from the actual conduct of affairs, and were thus more inclined to speculate freely and follow ideas to their uncomfortable conclusions.

Enlightenment France was by no means uniformly enlightened. Not only were many members of the privileged classes hostile to the *philosophes*, but the latter's ideas reached only a minority of the population. Many 'enlightened' writers expressed disdain for the dark masses, who continued to live in a customary world of popular culture and 'superstition'.

2. Historical Development

a. The period between about 1680 and 1715 was described by Paul Hazard as the 'crisis of European consciousness'. In France it was the time of the *Querelle des Anciens et des Modernes, which among other things reflected a growing confidence in the new science and philosophy. *Fontenelle in his *Entretiens sur la pluralité des mondes* and *Histoire des oracles*, *Bayle in his *Pensées diverses sur la comète* and *Dictionnaire*, and Richard *Simon in his biblical criticism gave examples of the rational examination of established beliefs. Fontenelle also anticipated the High Enlightenment by popularizing the new science in an attractive, witty manner. In the wake of the *libertins* of the 17th c. and the early *Utopian thinkers, the new Parisian coffee-houses [see CAFÉS] and circles such as the *Temple and the group round *Boulainviller were centres for free-thinking on religion and politics; this found expression in the *clandestine manuscripts of *Fréret and others (the most radical manuscript, however, comes from a different segment of society—the 'Testament' of the country priest *Meslier). In their different spheres, the *Académie des Sciences and the *Académie des Inscriptions were also beginning to be forces for intellectual change.

b. The years between 1715 and c.1745 are those of the early (or first-generation) Enlightenment. They see the acceleration of scientific enquiry and philosophical speculation, the growing attraction of *deism, the radical discussions of the Club de l'*Entresol, and above all the emergence of two major figures, *Montesquieu and *Voltaire. The *Lettres persanes* of the former anticipates many essential Enlightenment themes and attitudes, while his *De l'*esprit des lois* is one of the great texts of the movement. Voltaire, while at first more poet than *philosophe*, emerged in 1734 with the *Lettres philosophiques* as the militant leader of Enlightenment thought that he was to remain until his death 44 years later. It is significant that this work was inspired by Voltaire's stay in England, where he had admired political liberty, religious tolerance, and the work of Newton and Locke. At this time English influence was dominant; it can be seen also in the work of *Marivaux, who shared many Enlightenment values; his journalism is directly modelled on the *Spectator* [see BRITISH, IRISH, AND AMERICAN INFLUENCES].

One of the most important developments of this period is indeed the rise of the periodical *press, with the appearance of many journals in which Enlightenment ideas were expressed and criticized. Equally important is the creation of provincial *academies; these provided a socially mixed forum in which philosophy and science could be advanced on a broad front. In addition, the major Parisian *salons were increasingly permeated by *philosophe* ideas as the century progressed.

c. The years from about 1745 to 1770 are those of the High Enlightenment, in which the *philosophes* form a party around the *Encyclopédie*; this great production, for all its faults, is the summation of Enlightenment thinking, and its chequered history reflects the battle between the *philosophes* and their many enemies (the most prominent of these, the *Jesuits, were expelled from France in 1764). This is the most militant period, marked by the materialistic theses of *Helvétius, the anti-religious propaganda of *Holbach and his associates, and Voltaire's campaign against the *infâme*.

The generation of *philosophes* born between 1705 and 1725 includes some very different figures, ranging from discreet scholars to coat-trailing propagandists; some of the most important are d'Alembert, *Boulanger, *Du Châtelet, *Condillac, *Duclos, *Grimm, Helvétius, Holbach, *La Mettrie, *Mably, *Marmontel, *Raynal, the slightly younger *Morellet and *Turgot, and the *Physiocrats. Three figures stand out: Diderot, whose position as editor of the *Encyclopédie* made him the leader of the *philosophes*, although his most important writing was not generally known until after his death; *Buffon, who kept his distance from the party, and whose scientific work had great philosophical implications; and *Rousseau, who from being a contributor to the *Encyclopédie* emerged as a paradoxical *frère ennemi*, denouncing the progressive ideals of his former colleagues, yet offering a more radical critique of the *status quo* and a visionary ideal.

d. From c.1770 Enlightenment thinking acquired power and respectability. The *Encyclopédie* was a great success; the *Académie Française was infiltrated by d'Alembert; the Physiocrats, in the person of Turgot, were given the official opportunity to try out their theories in the real world. R. Darnton, in

The Literary Underground of the Old Regime (1982), argues that in the pre-Revolutionary years there was a split between the official Enlightenment, in which figures such as Marmontel, *Thomas, *Suard, *La Harpe, *Morellet, *Rivarol, and even *Chamfort could pursue comfortable careers with pensions and sinecures, and a swarming 'Grub Street' of pamphleteers, pornographers, and the like, out of which emerge such major figures as *Restif or *Mercier, as well as many Revolutionary leaders, *Brissot, *Marat, *Hébert, etc.

This thesis remains controversial, but it is certain that the 'late Enlightenment' sees an explosion of radical political thought (much influenced by Rousseau), often messianic or Utopian in tone. Enlightenment values become entangled with more mystical currents, which prefigure some aspects of *Romanticism, from the theories of Dom *Deschamps and *Court de Gébelin to *freemasonry, *Illuminism, and *Mesmerism. Nevertheless, the old Voltairean rational influences continue to work, and are superbly incarnated in the work of his editor, *Beaumarchais. A different strand of Enlightenment thinking, the materialism of Holbach and Diderot, is pushed to unexpected extremes in the novels and pamphlets of the marquis de *Sade. But it is perhaps *Condorcet who, in the shadow of the guillotine, produced the best resumé of classic Enlightenment thinking.

3. Significance and Influence

This remains the subject of vigorous debate. The traditional Marxist view was that the Enlightenment represented the values of the rising bourgeoisie, which seized power in 1789; it was thus one of the causes of the *Revolution (the same view was expressed by enemies of the Revolution—'c'est la faute à Voltaire, c'est la faute à Rousseau'). Against this, modern historians have argued that the Enlightenment was a movement *within* an élite, which included both nobles and bourgeois. It is certainly true that the 'société des Lumières', as seen, for instance, in the contributors and subscribers to the *Encyclopédie*, is drawn from different social groups, including aristocrats, bourgeois, and artisans. On the other hand, it is clear that the values propagated by the Enlightenment—values which later generations take too much for granted—were essentially inimical to the old politico-religious regime.

One might hesitate today before naming the Enlightenment among the principal causes of the Revolution. Nevertheless, while many of the earlier *philosophes* (Voltaire, Montesquieu, Buffon) were far from revolutionary in their political thought, and while many of their successors (Marmontel, Condorcet, Morellet) fell foul of the Revolution, the Revolutionary leaders themselves were impregnated with various kinds of Enlightenment thinking. Rousseau in particular was the *maître à penser* of *Robespierre and his colleagues. In subsequent years, the *Idéologues and the *écoles centrales helped to maintain the Enlightenment tradition. Although much attacked by both reactionaries and Romantics, this was to survive and triumph, often in caricatural form, in the progressive, *anticlerical *republicanism of the later 19th c.   [PF]

See J.-M. Goulemot and M. Launay, *Le Siècle des Lumières* (1968); P. Gay, *The Enlightenment: An Interpretation*, 2 vols. (1967–70); R. Porter and M. Teich (eds.), *The Enlightenment in National Context* (1981).

Enragés, Les. A loose political grouping during the *Revolution led by Jacques Roux (1752–94), ex-priest and member of the Commune de Paris. Like the *Hébertistes, they supported the Terror, emphasizing its social and economic aspects, but were repressed as extremists by *Robespierre in late 1793.

Enseignements, see ENSENHAMENS.

Ensenhamens. 12th- and 13th-c. didactic poems in Occitan. An *ensenhamen* is usually written in octosyllabic rhyming couplets and ostensibly addressed to a social group: e.g. courtly ladies, damsels, knights, or *jongleurs*. The behaviour prescribed for courtly men and women in the *ensenhamens* is suspiciously similar to that required of their counterparts in the courtly *canso*; the *ensenhamens* probably tell us more about literary ideals than life at the courts where they circulated. The repeated insistence, in the *ensenhamens*, on generosity to poets and *jongleurs* probably indicates wishful thinking on the part of their authors; in the 13th c. their popularity appears to be due primarily to nostalgia for a golden age of courtly poetry. The related Old French *enseignements*, written by poets like *Robert de Blois, are possibly more realistic than the *ensenhamens*, but even these are highly stylized, clearly conflating literary paradigms with historical reality. The early *ensenhamen Cabra juglar*, by Guiraut de Cabrera, a contemporary of *Marcabru's, purports to instruct a *jongleur* on the texts he should have in his repertoire; it is one of our best sources of information on literary culture in Occitania in the first half of the 12th c. The *ensenhamens* have been published in *Testi didattico-cortesi di Provenza*, ed. G. E. Sansoni (Bari, 1977).   [SG]

Entre les eaux, see MUDIMBE.

Entresol, Club de l'. Following the English model, this club met at the Parisian house of President *Hénault for free discussion of political and economic questions from 1724 to 1731. D'*Argenson, abbé de *Saint-Pierre, and *Montesquieu attended regularly, as did the Englishmen Walpole and Bolingbroke. Cardinal *Fleury, having considered making it into an academy, ordered its closure because it was too critical of his administration.   [PF]

Entretien avec Monsieur de Sacy, see PASCAL.

Entretiens d'Ariste et d'Eugène, Les

Entretiens d'Ariste et d'Eugène, Les, see BOUHOURS.

Entretiens sur la pluralité des mondes, see FONTENELLE.

Entretiens sur les sciences, see LAMY.

Envers et l'endroit, L', see CAMUS, A.

Épaulette, L', see DARIEN.

Epic Poetry. Epic poetry, while broadly covering long heroic poems which recount legendary or historical narratives of national importance, has in fact meant very different things over the centuries in France. Central to literary production in the high Middle Ages, it continued to enjoy great critical prestige in later centuries, even though the numerous epic efforts of French writers since the Renaissance have for the most part failed to win a place in the canon. Only in the 20th c., dominated by the novel, has the epic ceased to attract poets.

The earliest mention of epic poetry in France comes in *Einhard's Vita Karoli* (9th c.), in which we learn that *Charlemagne ordered ancestral songs of the Franks to be collected. These were presumably oral compositions in Frankish, and provided one stream leading to the great flowering of *chansons de geste* in the 12th and 13th c. By the end of the Middle Ages these poems had undergone considerable influence from the *romance, whose themes and narrative techniques were adopted and grafted onto subjects drawn from the traditional stock relating to Carolingian or Merovingian times, to the Crusades, or to ancient Greece and Rome through the influence of the *romans d'antiquité.* The surface form of the *chansons de geste* was preserved, although rhyme had replaced assonance in the *laisse* and the standard line was now the alexandrine rather than the decasyllable.

Originally a communal literature, epic had become the province of individual poets like *Bertrand de Bar-sur-Aube and *Bodel as early as the 12th c., and, under the increasing influence of humanistic thought in the 15th and 16th c., it came to be seen as the pinnacle of achievement to be aimed at by poets. The models adopted were Virgil, Statius, and to a lesser extent Homer. In his *Franciade* Ronsard elaborated a legend first propounded in Fredegarius's history of the Franks (7th c.) in providing a Trojan ancestry for the kings of France. Despite some moments of poetic grandeur the academic sterility of the thematic conception led to the poem's failure as an epic model. *Les Tragiques* by Agrippa d'*Aubigné could not provide a model for future generations either, but its firm rooting in the personal experience, and prejudices, of its Protestant author during the *Wars of Religion give the poem an immediacy and power lacking in Ronsard's erudite imitation of antiquity. *Du Bartas's *Semaines,* while not epic poems in the traditional sense of the word, were perhaps the most influential long French poems of the period; they

had a powerful impact on English poets from Spenser to Milton.

While the 17th c. did not abandon Greco-Roman models and themes, the inspiration of Tasso and the resurgence of a sense of national identity and cultural self-confidence, especially in the second half of the century, led to the reawakening of interest in great figures of the French Middle Ages. This produced poems on Clovis (by *Desmarets, *Clovis ou la France chrétienne,* 1657), St Louis (by *Le Moyne, *Saint Louis ou la Sainte Couronne reconquise,* 1653), and Charlemagne (by Le Laboureur, *Charlemagne,* 1664, and by Nicolas Courtin, *Charlemagne ou le Rétablissement de l'empire romain,* 1666, and *Charlemagne pénitent,* 1687). These tend to be of chronicle inspiration, with unwieldy rambling plots; Desmarets seeks essentially to provide a model of Christian kingship for the young Louis XIV, while Le Laboureur and Courtin, in his first poem, present the career of the first Holy Roman Emperor in the colours of a national hero and popular saint. Courtin's second poem, which may reflect changing attitudes at Louis XIV's court, if not intended as a 'mirror of the prince', makes Charlemagne's soul the battleground between mere imperial glory (represented by the devil) and self-domination (represented by St James of Compostela). Le Moyne's poem, although marred like its contemporaries by a weight of digressions, achieves a certain breadth of inspiration by drawing not only on national historiography, but also on Tasso's vision of the crusade and on native epic and romance traditions. The 17th c. also saw a plethora of moralistic poems combining Old Testament subjects (Susanna and the Elders, Judith and Holofernes, Saul and David, the Creation) with classical models.

The 18th c. produced only one epic of note, Voltaire's *La Henriade,* a belated treatment to add to the many contemporary eulogies of the king of Navarre, which presents Henri IV as an enlightened enemy of *l'infâme.* The 19th c. took its premisses for writing epic poetry from a different source than that in vogue from the 16th to 18th c. The rise of Romanticism in Germany in the late 18th c. had renewed interest in *Volksepos* as an expression of national identity, and the work of Herder and Diez was soon communicated to France. The great epics of antiquity, and the freshly rediscovered epics of the Middle Ages, were considered to be the result of compilation and polishing by learned poets of short songs produced more or less spontaneously by participants in the events recounted. This provided Romantic poets with a new method of structuring epics by thematic groupings of shorter, more intense poems, enabling them to recapture the lyric aspect of epic lost since the mid-12th c. Along with the rediscovery of the Middle Ages proper came a renewed appreciation of Renaissance and early Baroque literature, which was often confused with the medieval.

A blend of mysticism and humanism (drawn

from Dante, Petrarch, and Shakespeare) and the politico-philosophic legacy of *Rousseau mark all attempts at epic in the Romantic period. *Lamartine conceived a monumental epic of humanity, Visions, in 1821. The project was never completed, but elements of it were absorbed into other works, like the 12,000 line 'fragment' La Chute d'un ange (1838–40) and the 'episode' Jocelyn (1836). The former deals with the conflict between humanity and barbarism and the role of civilization in human development, ending rather pessimistically with the Flood; the latter, much more optimistic, mixes an idyll of human love with the ascetic renunciation required by divine love, both of which are superseded in an appeal to transcendent humanism. Jocelyn is notable for its explicit mix of narrative and lyric forms. *Vigny's Poèmes antiques et modernes (1826) and Les Destinées (1864) are thematic constellations of poems dealing with the relationship of man to nature, the conflict of humanity and barbarism, and the common heroism of all sentient creatures faced with the inimical fate imposed by a jealous God. *Hugo's La *Légende des siècles, produced in three series (1859, 1877, 1883) with its two posthumous companion poems, La Fin de Satan (1886) and Dieu (1891), treats similar themes on a broader canvas, taking in universal history, but concentrating on medieval and Revolutionary France. In all of these poems the sense of individual or communal heroic struggle against physical odds typical of early epic is lost in the purely transcendental conflict of Good and Evil. It is perhaps in the novels of the period, particularly in those of *Balzac and *Hugo, that this essential aspect of epic is best captured. [PEB]

See R. A. Sayce, The French Biblical Epic in the Seventeenth Century (1955); D. Maskell, The Historical Epic in France, 1500–1700 (1973); W. Calin, A Muse for Heroes (1983).

Épinal, Images d'. Popular prints, often sold by itinerant pedlars [see COLPORTAGE]. They were, in fact, produced in many centres, but the town of Épinal in north-eastern France came to specialize in them in the 19th c. Originally woodcuts and subsequently lithographs, the prints are brightly coloured (predominantly red and blue) and naïve in style. They often combine words and images (e.g. stories of *Geneviève de Brabant), and are close to the broadsheet or canard [see PRESS, 1]. Many are religious in theme, sometimes connected with *confréries; others convey popular wisdom and humour. Topical political subjects are also common, particularly in relation to the *Revolution and the exploits of *Napoleon; *Napoleon III used the Épinal industry to propagate Bonapartism. From the 17th c. they attracted amateurs (such as *Marolles), and were very popular with collectors in the 18th c. There are notable collections in the Bibliothèque Nationale, the museum of Épinal, and the Musée des Arts et Traditions Populaires in Paris. [PF]

ÉPINAY, Louise-Florence d'Esclavelles, Madame d' (1726–83). Wife of a tax-farmer, she was at the centre of a circle including *Diderot, her lover *Grimm, to whose *Correspondance littéraire she contributed anonymously, and *Galiani, with whom she corresponded after 1769. She patronized and then quarrelled with Jean-Jacques *Rousseau; her version of the affair is given in the Histoire de Madame de Monbrillant (or Pseudo-Mémoires), published in 1818, and very popular in the 19th c. A woman of intelligence and sensibility, she resented the limits placed on her sex; her Conversations d'Émilie (1775), while stressing motherhood, propose anti-Rousseauist views on women's education. [PF]

Epistolary Art, see LETTER-WRITING.

Epistolary Novel. Some early French novels contained letters, but the type of novel consisting wholly of letters took off slowly, with only a handful of instances before 1700. The *Lettres portugaises (1669) proved very popular. It contains little in the way of plot, and the same holds true for the next landmark of the genre, Montesquieu's *Lettres persanes (1721), which was followed by a number of similar works, largely vehicles for the discussion of ideas. Well-known instances include the work of d'*Argens and Madame de *Graffigny's Lettres d'une Péruvienne (1747). The first major work of *Crébillon fils was a love-story in letters, but even more popular in terms of re-editions was the now-forgotten Lettres de Ninon de Lenclos (1750) by Damours.

The most prolific period for the genre was from 1750 to c.1820, peaking in the 1780s: some 450 letter-novels appeared in French, of which nearly one-third were translations of English works. The most notable of these was the 1751 version, by *Prévost, of Richardson's Clarissa. *Rousseau too combined a love-story with serious moral issues, in La *Nouvelle Héloïse (1761). Other popular authors such as Madame *Riccoboni kept the genre alive, and it gained further impetus from Les *Liaisons dangereuses (1782), a technical masterpiece. In the 19th-c. *Balzac's rather weak efforts in this form, like George *Sand's, show the genre in decline. 20th-c. letter-novels in French, such as Nicole's Les Lions sont lâchés (1955), are rare.

Many epistolary novels are presented by an 'editor', who relates how he came by the letters and/or adds explanatory footnotes to the text. While the most frequent subject of the plot is love, letters also lend themselves to debates on any and every topic. The 'epistolary' heading covers several narrative forms. With a single letter-writer the missives may be simply instalments of an autobiography; or an account, sent to a confidant, of what the writer is living through; or the more active relationship of a woman writing to her lover. Most 'duologue' letter-novels consist of exchanges between lovers, but alternatively the duologue may cover a situation where a confidant merely comments on the protagonist's missives. With three or more corre-spondants we have the 'polyphonic' novel, provid-ing opportunities for a greater variety of situations, characters, individual styles, and differing points of view.   [VGM]

See J. Herman, *Le Mensonge romanesque: paramètres pour l'étude du roman épistolaire en France* (1989).

Épreuve, L'. One-act comedy by *Marivaux, one of his most popular, first performed 1740. Lucidor puts his beloved Angélique to a somewhat cruel test, proposing to marry her to a rich suitor (his valet in disguise), before finally declaring his own love.

Équivoque. A play on words of identical sound and different meaning. At its simplest, it is the ordinary pun; at its most complex (beloved of the *Rhétoriqueurs) it may cover two whole lines of verse (*distique holorime*), e.g. *Hugo's

Gall, amant de la reine, alla, tour magnanime,
Galamment de l'Arène à la Tour Magne à Nimes.

Eracle, see GAUTIER D'ARRAS.

ERASMUS, Desiderius (*c*.1469–1536). The great Dutch scholar, theologian, and satirist had many connections with France, indeed, France 'gave him his freedom' in 1495 when he enrolled in the University of Paris, after several stultifying years in the monastery of Steyn. Despite the rigours of life as a student of theology at the Collège de Montaigu, Erasmus cultivated Parisian men of letters, includ-ing the humanist Gaguin and the royal poet Fausto Andrelini. In Paris he published his first book, a col-lection of Latin poems, and in 1500 the *Collectanea*, originally a short handbook on Latin style for his private pupils, which was to expand into the cele-brated *Adagia*, one of the corner-stones of *Renaissance humanism. There the proverbial wis-dom of the ancient world was married to modern experience in Erasmus's moralizing commentaries; the work was thus a forerunner, not only of erudite compilations and dictionaries, but also of *Montaigne's *Essais*, whose author joked (III. 2) that he would have taken Erasmus's most trivial utter-ances for adages and apophthegms. In 1511 Erasmus published in Paris his most enduringly famous book, the *Moriae encomium* (Praise of Folly), whose complex irony delighted French satirists, especially *Rabelais in his *Tiers Livre*.

After 1501 Erasmus lived only occasionally in France—despite pressing invitations from *François Ier—but he corresponded with *Budé and *Marguerite de Navarre, amongst many others, and his scholarly and theological writings left their imprint on a generation of French intellectuals. In particular, his revision of the Greek New Testament (1516) and his commentaries on St Paul inspired the *Evangelicals gathered round *Lefèvre d'Étaples and *Briçonnet. On the other hand, the theologians of the *Sorbonne suspected him of complicity with *Luther, and campaigned strenuously against him;

his translator *Berquin was burned at the stake in 1529.

Erasmus's style too had its influence: his use of Lucianic dialogue, for example, in the *Colloquia* and the *Julius exclusus*, to mock superstition and reli-gious imposture is echoed most notably in *Des Périers's *Cymbalum mundi* and by Rabelais, who also embraced Erasmus's Christian humanism in such fields as education and statecraft.

After his death the hardening of religious atti-tudes brought Erasmus's relative moderation into disrepute; not until the advent of the *philosophes did he return to the forefront of intellectual life, with a dubious reputation as the champion of ratio-nalism which clung to him for two centuries. Modern readers appreciate rather his moderation, common sense, and wit.   [MJH]

See R. H. Bainton, *Erasmus of Christendom* (1969); M. M. Phillips, *Erasmus and the Northern Renaissance* (rev. edn., 1981).

ERCKMANN-CHATRIAN (Émile Erckmann, 1822–99; Alexandre Chatrian, 1826–90). In the mid-1850s Erckmann and Chatrian began their lifelong collaboration by supplying Parisian journals with tales based on the Alsace-Lorraine region, which remained their constant source of literary inspira-tion. Their considerable popular success came with *Histoire d'un conscrit de 1813* (1864), the series of 'romans nationaux', and *Histoire d'un paysan* (1868–70), all of which related the history of France from the point of view of the ordinary Frenchman. Their stirring and patriotic works, with their deep sense of place, were not only commercially success-ful, but were much in favour with the Ministry of Education in the Third Republic.   [BR]

Erec et Enide, see CHRÉTIEN DE TROYES.

Ère du soupçon, L', see SARRAUTE.

Ériphile. Female character invented by Racine to provide a relatively happy ending to *Iphigénie*.

Ermitage, L'. The country house on Madame d'*Épinay's estate near Montmorency where J.-J. Rousseau lived in 1756–7 and about which he wrote in the *Confessions*.

ERNAUX, Annie (b. 1940). French novelist. Ernaux's writing is strongly marked by her childhood and working-class origins in Normandy. Her early nov-els have strong feminist themes: *Les Armoires vides* (1974) is narrated by a student from a working-class background undergoing an abortion; *Ce qu'ils disent ou rien* (1977) has a younger female narrator who finds herself confronted one summer by hitherto unsuspected gender roles and sexual codes; *La Femme gelée* (1981) is the narrative of an intellectual married woman, again of humble social origins, whose ambitions and desires have been smothered by marriage and motherhood. 'Je cherche ma ligne de fille et de femme', writes the narrator, echoing Ernaux's project in examining the social and cultural meaning that her gender holds. With *La Place* (1981) and *Une femme* (1988) she takes a new direction, producing narratives which combine an autobiographical, historical, and social dimension. *La Place* focuses on her father, exploring her relationship with him and the abyss which her middle-class culture acquired through education has created between them. The text lovingly recreates her father's habits, tastes, and language. *Une femme*, written immediately after her mother's death, similarly evokes her mother's life, this time accompanied by the particular ambivalences of daughter–mother love and identification. [EAF]

Eroticism and Pornography. Erotic literature concerns itself with representations of the sexual appetite designed to elicit a sensual response. Georges *Bataille's definition, due allowance made for its distinctive mystique of transgression, goes straight to the point: 'De l'érotisme, il est possible de dire qu'il est l'approbation de la vie jusqu'à la mort. . . . S'il s'agissait de définition précise, il faudrait certainement parler de l'activité sexuelle de reproduction dont l'érotisme est une forme particulière' ('One can say of eroticism that it is the acceptance of life, even to the point of death. . . . If a precise definition was needed, one would certainly have to speak of the sexual activity of reproduction, of which eroticism is one particular form') (*L'Érotisme*, 1957).

On the sliding-scale of intellectualized lust, the distinction between literary kinds (the love story, the erotic tale, the pornographic narrative) depends on the relation set up between narrator, text, and reader, which in its turn depends on a delicate and historically variable interplay of literary, linguistic, and forensic conventions. The history of the variation of the terms, which late 20th-c. criticism has been writing and debating (see e.g. Susan Sontag, 'The Pornographic Imagination', in *Styles of Radical Will*, 1969; Walter Kendrick, *The Secret Museum: Pornography in Modern Culture*, 1987), is not a simple question of styles of writing. 'Erotic' writing, deemed aesthetically better, more often than not simply speaks a more discreet and exclusive code than the 'pornographic' text, in its description of physical parts, its degrees of fetishization, and its evocation of the aggressive and oppressive interplay of sexual relations. Post-Freud and, even more so, post-*Foucault, the question appears much more one of social history, and has to do most of all with the politics of freedom and repression—themselves highly problematic terms, as may be seen in Bataille's discussions of the 'liberating' effect of the work of *Sade.

It is worth noting that the Enlightenment, which laid the foundations for the bourgeois state, saw the origins of the present categories. *Bayle, adding to the 2nd edn. (1702) of his *Dictionnaire* an 'Éclaircisse-ment sur les obscénités', argued for the right to pleasure, and to the pleasure of the text. In the convention that 'obscenities' be confined to Latin, Bayle saw an unacceptable political as well as intellectual élitism. The *Grand Robert* (2nd edn., 1985), crediting the first printed use of the term 'érotisme' to *Restif de la Bretonne in 1794, unwittingly highlights the socio-political connotations of the category. The exhibitionistically frank author of *Monsieur Nicolas* claimed on behalf of his whole class the right to speak with the same frankness as society's darling, Jean-Jacques *Rousseau, and arrogated to himself the right to police the sexuality of his contemporaries at the same time as he sought to set up his own preferences as the norm.

The *Oxford Companion to French Literature* had no entry under this heading. Nevertheless, France has long been seen abroad as a country where adventurous or scurrilous writing flourishes. It was in Paris, for instance, that in the first half of the 20th c. journals and presses such as the Olympia Press or the Obelisk Press published works by English-language authors (including Henry Miller and James Joyce) which were forbidden in Britain or America. And in French literature itself there is a well-known erotic tradition, with several different strands. The best-known is perhaps the eroto-comic line that runs from *gauloiserie* (bawdry) to Gallic wit. Beginning with the medieval *fabliaux*, the *blason and contre-blason*, and the anal eroticism of the *Rabelaisian carnival, this goes underground in the 17th c. to re-emerge in the libertine gaieties of the 18th, in the writings of *Mirabeau *père*, the racy tales of the *philosophes*, and the light narratives of *Crébillon *fils*, *Nerciat, *Fougeret de Monbron, *Denon, and *Louvet de Couvray, whose slight-minded but entertaining hero Faublas, a spoiled *fils de famille*, sets the fashion for generations. The next change of style is in the 20th c., with the black absurdist humour of *Apollinaire and his *Surrealist successors, who remained undeterred by Bataille's censure of the hypocrisy signalled by laughter at sex: 'L'extrême licence liée à la plaisanterie s'accompagne d'un refus de prendre au sérieux—j'entends *au tragique*—la vérité de l'érotisme' (Preface to *Madame Edwarda*, 1937).

Equally long in its antecedents is the lyrical line that runs from *Jean de Meun's continuation of the *Roman de la Rose*, through the Petrarchan sonnets of the *Pléiade, and into the paler symbols of the 19th c. At the end of the latter period, the pallid decency of, as it were, the official erotic is interestingly offset by a crude underground: the 'humanist' Pierre *Louÿs's unacknowledged narratives, or *Verlaine's homosexual poetry.

The 18th c.'s fascination with the politics and the philosophy of the body generates another kind of erotic writing. On one level, the philosophical and revolutionary pamphleteers use sexual smear and caricature in their attack on established authority (or, as the century wears on, on one another). A collection of essays edited by Lynn Hunt (*Eroticism and the Body Politic*, 1991) has brought to this theme the fresh perspective of feminist criticism. Equally well-known is the double preoccupation of serious novelists of the period with the invention of a new language for the representation of erotic pleasure and with exploring the significance of authoritarian pretensions to circumscribe individual sexual experience. The reader receives a double invitation to share philosophical or political insights, and to join in the voyeuristic peep through the keyhole. The first half of Rousseau's *La *Nouvelle Héloïse* argues its defence of individual desire from within substantial passages of linguistic exhibitionism, in overheated precious periphrases. Diderot's *La *Religieuse*, with its famous sadistic and lesbian sequences, investigates with physiological precision the violence done to individual sexuality by institutionalized repression. *Thérèse philosophe* (1748), attributed to a number of authors, including the marquis d'*Argens, is one of many less high-minded versions of the same anticlerical theme (see also *Le Portier des Chartreux*, 1741). The thrill of sexual power games evoked in Laclos's *Les *Liaisons dangereuses* is embedded in a bitingly ironic reconstruction of the other games aristocratic society plays with and against its unruly members. In the Gothic fictions of the marquis de *Sade, narrating in crude, precise detail the sexual violences practised on the weak by the strong, philosophy and politics are both subordinated in the economy of the narrative to the procurement of strong sensations. Lengthy discourses on nature, instinct, and reason serve variously as interludes or preludes to the orgiastic spectacle. What Sade reveals of the sexual politics of his period has, of course, its own interest: his highlighting, for example, of the centrality of incest for the contemporary erotic imagination—the Oedipal taboo. The same motif resurfaces at the end of the next century, in the *Decadent fictions of such writers as *Barbey d'Aurevilly, *Huysmans, and *Mirbeau, at another moment of radical challenge to concepts of authority.

In so far as erotic pleasure thrives (*pace* Sade) on difference, or novelty, the reinvigoration of erotic writing in recent years has come from writers exploring hitherto ignored perspectives. Homosexual texts by men, such as the prose and drama of *Genet, display alternative power relations and make different play with the inherited images. As regards the feminine erotic, here too an alternative tradition is being created. In the 18th c. the few women writing erotic texts did so for a predominantly male readership, for example, Barbe-Suzanne-Aimable Giroux de Morency, author of *Illyrine, ou l'Écueil de l'inexpérience* (c.1799), the first erotic novel in French to be signed by a woman. *Rachilde's writing is still tied to the male gaze, despite its self-proclaimed rejection of the patriarchal prescription for pleasure. *Colette offers more original representations of the heterosexual relationship from the female perspective, which tip into bisexual or lesbian experience. In the course of the 20th c. the latter has become an important focus of literary interest. Liane de *Pougy's poetry (*Idylle saphique*, 1901) is slight, but significant, in its effort to reclaim a sensuality until then the property of *Brantôme and *Baudelaire. The prose of Violette *Leduc sets new benchmarks for frankness. A world apart is the work of Monique *Wittig, in which the battle for sexual freedom, in every sense, is a battle for the language of representation (*Les Guérillères*, 1969). Wittig's *Le Corps lesbien* (1973) takes over the most disabling codes of heterosexual discourse to write a representation of lesbian passion. The traditional grammar of eroticism embodied in Baudelaire—the sado-masochistic mode, the fetishizing *blason* of female parts, the symbol that stereotypes woman as divinity or animal, predator or victim—is turned into a new syntax of homosexual relations embodied in the new model of Sappho. [See GAY AND LESBIAN WRITING.]   [JB]

ESCARPIT, Robert (b. 1918). French novelist and critic noted for his work on the sociology of literature. *La Révolution du livre* (1960) and *Le Littéraire et le social* (1970) analyse the conditions of production of the book and of mass literature. His later work, including *L'Écrit et la communication* (1972), extends into a theory of literary communication.   [EAF]

Esclarmonde. Sequel to *Huon de Bordeaux*.

Escoufle, L', see JEAN RENART.

Esméralda. Gypsy heroine of Hugo's *Notre-Dame de Paris*.

Espace littéraire, L', see BLANCHOT.

Espion turc, L', see MARANA.

Espoir, L' (1937). *Malraux's novel about the Spanish Civil War, written and published while the war was still in progress, partly in order to raise funds for the Republican side. Opening in July 1936 with the routing of the right-wing coup in Madrid and Barcelona, the novel ends on the Republican victory of Guadalajara in March 1937. Since the Republicans eventually lost the war (in 1939) the novel is to some extent given the lie by history. A sophisticated text which avoids propaganda, it nevertheless argues firmly that the Republican cause is a just one, and that victory can only be achieved through the agency of the Communist Party. This is for technocratic rather than ideological reasons—the major characters are well aware of the drawbacks of the Party. The novel brings into play a vast number of characters, representing numerous views of the war, and is episodic in structure. As it progresses an inexorable logic develops: 'faire' (action and results) must dominate over 'être' (idealism and individualism); efficacy must come before morality. 'L'action est l'action et non la justice', declares

Magnin, a revolutionary socialist working with the Communists. Nevertheless, he is painfully aware of the costs of this bleak lesson.   [EAF]

Esprit. Monthly review founded by Emmanuel *Mounier, Georges Izard, and Denis de *Rougemont in October 1932. Mounier developed in its columns his doctrine of *Personalism. The review's circulation probably never exceeded 4,000 copies, but its religious and intellectual influence has been considerable. Mounier ran *Esprit* as a forum for debate between believers and non-believers. Considerable friction arose with other titles of the Catholic press—*L'Aube*, for instance—which also sought a dialogue with non-believers.   [MP]

ESPRIT, Jacques (1611–78). Having been a novice with the *Oratorians, he acquired the reputation of a witty conversationalist in the salons and became a close associate of *La Rochefoucauld. He had a part in the latter's *Maximes*, which are close in spirit to his own *Jansenist-inspired condemnation of pagan virtue, *De la fausseté des vertus humaines* (1677–8).   [PF]

Esprit, De l', see HELVÉTIUS.

Esprit des lois, De l'. Treatise by *Montesquieu, published 1748, the culmination of over 20 years of work. It is divided into 31 books, each containing up to 45 chapters. The reader's first impression, ultimately misleading, may be of the disorderly accumulation of fascinating material drawn from a great variety of sources, both books and observation. Noting the author's fondness for sharp turns of phrase, Madame *du Deffand famously (and inappropriately) called his book 'de l'esprit sur les lois'.

Faced with the multiplicity of laws in societies past and present, Montesquieu's stance is that of the scientist—indeed, he has been called the father of social science. Rather than saying what should be, he tries to account for what is, to show the laws governing the making of laws. The work may be divided into two parts. The first part (Books 1–13) is concerned with political organization; it describes the working of the three types of society, republic (including democracy and aristocracy), monarchy, and despotism. These are distinguished not only by their constitutional arrangements, but more importantly by what Montesquieu calls their 'principle', the human qualities on which their operation depends. These are virtue (i.e. public spirit) for republics, honour for monarchy, fear for despotism.

The second part (Books 14–31) deals with the many other factors, moral and physical, which influence laws and social behaviour. One of these is climate, to which Montesquieu attributes a powerful influence, but other important chapters are devoted to the size and population of states, and to commerce and to religion. All of these go to make up the 'general spirit' of a nation; this differs greatly from country to country, producing very different legal systems. The final four books are devoted to medieval *feudalism, which was important from the point of view of a champion of the nobility.

Montesquieu was not content simply to describe and explain, accepting the *status quo*, however repugnant it might be. He presents despotism as a horrible state to be avoided, and his analyses show how a nation may be freer and happier by virtue of good government and legislation. Although the early books paint an alluring picture of the republics of antiquity, Montesquieu's real preference goes to more stable, 'moderate' regimes, in particular constitutional monarchies, where the ruler's power is held in check by 'intermediate bodies' such as the nobility and the lawcourts. Book 11 contains high praise for the English Constitution, with its separation of powers and its system of checks and balances.

An equally important element in his liberal programme is the critique of laws which are arbitrary or unduly severe, or infringe unnecessarily on private freedom. He is hostile to religious and moral intolerance, and speaks out against torture and slavery. All of this contributed to the work's prestige with contemporaries and with posterity. Although its message seemed unduly conservative to *Helvétius and to many subsequent radicals, it exerted a great influence on the framing of the American Constitution, and has been one of the key texts for the liberal tradition in Europe.   [PF]

Esprits, Les, see LARIVEY.

Espurgatoire Seint Patric, see MARIE DE FRANCE.

ESQUIROS, Henri-Alphonse (1812–76). French poet, journalist, and political writer. Esquiros began as a Romantic religious poet and author of fantastic tales; then, in the 1830s, he became involved with the mystical socialist movement, publishing his *Évangile du peuple* (1840), whose revolutionary and pro-violence interpretation of the Gospels led to his imprisonment, and his *Histoire des Montagnards* (1847), a justification of the Terror, especially of *Marat, as corresponding to Christian ideals. He spent the Second Empire in exile in England and wrote a number of volumes about English life, religion, and culture. Returning to France in 1869, he was elected to the Assemblée Nationale, later to the Senate. Interested in occultism, Utopian socialism, and feminism, Esquiros also showed real talent as an observer of contemporary society.   [FPB]

Esquisse d'une philosophie, see LAMENNAIS.

Esquisse d'une théorie des émotions, see SARTRE.

Esquisse d'un tableau historique des progrès de l'esprit humain, see CONDORCET.

Essais, Les, see MONTAIGNE.

Essais de morale

Essais de morale, see NICOLE.

Essais sur la noblesse en France, see BOULAINVILLER.

Essais sur la peinture, by *Diderot, see SALONS, LES.

Essai sur les données immédiates de la conscience, see BERGSON.

Essai sur les mœurs et l'esprit des nations (1756). Voltaire's most ambitious historical work, pirated originally as the *Abrégé de l'histoire universelle* (1753). Constantly sceptical of the evidence available to the historian, increasingly aware of the interplay between commerce, economics, politics, culture, customs, and manners, this was Voltaire's revolutionary approach to the story of mankind and the *Enlightenment's surer guide to the 'meaning of life' than *Bossuet's equally vast but providentialist explanation. Isolating the causes and symptoms of a prosperous, civilized society, Voltaire proposes that—despite much cruelty and obscurantism, and despite the baneful influence of Christianity—mankind does make progress and is, on the whole, responsible for its own destiny. Between 1753 and 1778 this work went through 27 editions.   [JR]

Essai sur les règnes de Claude et de Néron, see DIDEROT.

Essai sur l'indifférence en matière de religion, see LAMENNAIS.

Essai sur l'inégalité des races humaines, see GOBINEAU.

Estates General, see ÉTATS GÉNÉRAUX.

ESTEBAN, Claude (b. 1935). French poet, a pithy, icily minimal stylist whose poems evoke empty spaces and anxieties, 'à mi-chemin de l'être | et de l'oubli'. From *Terres, travaux du cœur* (1979) to *Le Nom et la demeure* (1985) he inches, as if reluctantly, towards the fervency which floods his essays in favourite poets in *Critique de la raison poétique* (1987). A sensitive translator from the Spanish, he has also written a monograph on the sculptor Chillida (1972).   [RC]

Esther. Play in three acts with choruses by *Racine. It tells the biblical story of the captive Esther who saves the Jews from persecution by the Persian king Assuérus. This edifying piece was written in 1689 at the request of Madame de *Maintenon to be performed by the girls at the school of *Saint-Cyr. The performances, with music by Moreau, were glamorous ceremonies to which *Louis XIV invited courtiers and favoured guests.   [PF]

ESTIENNE, Henri II (1531–98). Most distinguished member of the dynasty of printer-scholars founded by Henri I Estienne (c.1470–1520). Like his father Robert (see below), Henri II found that his interest in humanism led naturally to Calvinism. He spent most of his life in Geneva. His independent mind

and more particularly his passion for salacious stories, however, caused problems with the Genevan authorities, whose censorship was in many ways more rigorous than that of the *Sorbonne. His contribution to Greek scholarship is evident in his *Thesaurus linguae graecae* (1572). In the literary field, he is renowned for his edition of the Pseudo-Anacreon (1554), which helped inspire the *Pléiade, and for a chaotic but none the less important work, the *Apologie pour Hérodote* (1566), which has similarities with the prose fiction of Bandello, Boccaccio, *Des Périers, and *Marguerite de Navarre (whom he sometimes uses as sources).

The *Apologie* ostensibly makes a comparison of ancient and modern customs with the intention of demonstrating that the Greek historian's stories are no more incredible than customs to be found in modern Europe. In this sense it can be regarded as a forerunner of the *Querelle des Anciens et des Modernes. Estienne intends, however, to apply his satirical gifts even more directly to contemporary affairs and to provide a biting attack on the Catholic Church, targeting priests, monks, and the concept of transubstantiation (which is seen as being even more horrendous than ancient cannibalism). His satire of this 'théophagie' might seem to align him with *Rabelais's criticism of the 'Papimanes'; but, like *Calvin, he is deeply suspicious of his predecessor, whom he regards as a dangerous free-thinker.

Another target of attack is provided by the 'Philausones': the Italophile scholars and courtiers who are the butt of his satire in the *Épître de Monsieur Celtophile aux Ausoniens* (1578). His hatred of Italian claims to cultural hegemony combines with his love of Greek in his *Deux dialogues du nouveau français italianisé* (1578) and in *De la précellence du langage français* (1579). Here he argues, as previously in the *Traité de la conformité du langage français avec le grec* (1566), that Greek is superior to all other languages (including Latin) and that, of all modern languages, French is most like Greek. In this way Estienne can be seen to contribute, like *Du Bellay and *Pasquier, to the growing cultural nationalism of the French Renaissance.   [IJS]

See C. Lenient, *La Satire en France ou la Littérature militante au XVIe siècle* (1877).

ESTIENNE, Robert (1503–59). Scholar, printer, publisher, and bookseller, father of Henri II Estienne (see above). Royal printer of Latin and Hebrew (from 1539) and Greek (1544–51), he published many editions of the classics (Terence, Plautus) and neo-Latin writers (*Budé, Macrin); also grammar and lexicography: *Thesaurus linguae latinae* (1531), *Dictionarium latinogallicum* (1538), *Dictionnaire français–latin* (1539), valuable records of bilingual interaction; finally editions of the Bible in Hebrew, Greek, and Latin, based on early manuscripts in Paris. Because of *Sorbonne opposition to these Bibles, Estienne moved to Geneva in 1551 and there published *Calvin, *Bèze, and new editions of the Bible.   [PS]

Est-il bon? Est-il méchant?, see DIDEROT.

Estoire du Saint Graal, see GRAIL ROMANCES.

États Généraux. The assembly of the representatives of the three orders, or estates, of the realm: namely, the *clergy, the *nobility, and the *Tiers-Etat. It was convoked by the king in times of royal weakness and national emergency, usually when he needed to seek consent to fiscal subsidies. Both the system of election and the number of deputies varied, and voting was by estate. Meetings usually lasted several weeks and the king would promise redress of grievances presented in *cahiers de doléances* drawn up by *bailliage* and then by estate. Assemblies were held in 1302, 1347, 1355–7, 1380, 1413, annually from 1423 to 1439, 1468, 1484, 1506, 1560, 1561, 1576, 1588, 1593 (convoked by the Catholic *Ligue), 1614, and 1789 [see REVOLUTION, 1a]. [PRC]

ETCHART, Salvat (1932–c.1980). Novelist. The whole direction of Etchart's life and work was set by his decision to leave France and settle in Martinique. There, the work shows, his imagination was taken over by his experience of colonial reality. His political sympathies are clear—the title and epigraph of his best novel, *Le Monde tel qu'il est* (1967, Prix Renaudot) are taken from Engels—but the focus is human and social: the web of relations and differences in which are caught whites and blacks and all the colours between. Appalled and fascinated by distinctions that are now fine, now crass, he invents a writing that combines passionate lyricism with sharp analysis, subtleties with simplifications. The grim pun which sustains *Le Monde tel qu'il est*—the narrative setting is a 'day at the races'—allows the play of all of these. But not just as spectacle, for the very awareness that informs them dramatizes the question of Etchart's own location.

Etchart's other novels include *Les Nègres servent d'exemple* (1964) and *L'Homme empêché* (1977). [GC]

ETCHERELLI, Claire (b. 1934), won the Prix Fémina for *Élise ou la Vraie Vie* (1967), describing the experiences of a young woman working on a factory shop-floor and her secret love affair with an Algerian political activist during the *Algerian War. In *A propos de Clémence* (1971), the humble Clémence tries to cope with the violence and fears of a self-publicizing Spanish political refugee. *Un arbre voyageur* (1978) has a more optimistic ending; Milie and Anna somehow survive the daily struggle for existence for themselves and their children and find themselves instinctively in tune with the events of *May 1968 on which the novel closes. [EAF]

Été, L', see WEINGARTEN.

Ethnology, see ANTHROPOLOGY.

ÉTIEMBLE, René (b. 1909). The son of peasants, a polyglot, and an expert in Chinese philosophy, he worked in the USA during World War II, then at the University of Alexandria, before returning to a brilliant French academic career. He wrote the three-volume *Le Mythe de Rimbaud* (1952–70); also several novels, including the scandalous *Enfant de chœur* (1937) and the erotic *Blason d'un corps* (1961). He will remain famous for putting a new word into the language through his forceful and humorous polemic denouncing the invasion of French by English words (*Le Franglais*, 1964). [GDM]

ÉTIENNE, Franck (b. 1936). Poet, novelist, and dramatist, a teacher of mathematics and Haiti's foremost writer in *Creole (his works appear under the creolized name Frankétienne). He established his reputation in the 1960s with his poems *Au fil du temps* (1964), *Mon côté gauche* (1965), and *Chevaux de l'avant-jour* (1967). He founded the movement known as 'Spiralisme', which advocated a freer narrative form, as seen in his novels *Mûr à crever* (1968), *Ultravocal* (1972), and *Dézafi* (1975). The latter, written in Creole, was the start of a new phase of writing in Creole for the theatre. His most successful play, *Pèlin-tèt* (Head Traps), was forced to close in 1978 by the Duvalier regime. [JMD]

Étourdi, L'. Early comedy of intrigue by *Molière, first acted in Lyon in 1653/5, remarkable for the role of the inventive valet Mascarille.

Étrange Destin de Wangrin, L', see BA, A.

Étranger, L'. Novel by Albert *Camus, published 1942. It is a stylistic *tour de force* which conveys the authentic flavour of the universe of the absurd and was important to such subsequent writers and critics as *Barthes, *Robbe-Grillet, and *Sarraute. The narrator is Meursault, an Algerian of instinctive but undemonstrative temperament who in Part 1 recounts the everyday random events of his life between his mother's funeral and his own murder of an Arab on a beach. In Part 2 minor details are turned into damning evidence at his trial. The arbitrary mechanisms of the judicial system and capital punishment provoke Meursault to assert the value of life in the face of mortality. [DHW]

Être et le néant, L'. *Sartre's best-known philosophical work, published 1943. Subtitled 'Essai d'ontologie phénoménologique', it embodies the main preoccupations of his 'classical', *Existentialist period. Despite its balanced title, the work's primary concern is not with *being*, the fixed, self-identical *être-en-soi* of physical objects and entities, which earns about six of the text's 660 pages, but rather with *le néant*, the 'nothingness' of human consciousness as it constructs a world out of the brute 'being' which confronts it. In epistemological and ontological terms, Sartre is trying to steer a course between (objective) realism and (subjective) idealism. But it is the psychological aspect of the text which is of more general interest.

Être Suprême

For Sartre, consciousness is radically free: free, through its capacity to imagine, to construct a meaningful human world, free also to construct a life, a self, a project of being-in-the-world. But the consequences of radical freedom are total responsibility and an inability ever to achieve peaceful self-identity. One reaction is *angoisse*. Furthermore, consciousness does not simply have the physical world to contend with, it also has other consciousnesses with *their* projects, plans, and imagined future lives. Human relations are presented in terms of conflict, of attempts at mastery of the other, be it through evidently power-based intentions such as sadism and oppression, or, more disturbingly, through apparently desirable attitudes such as love or tolerance. All these, in Sartre's description, are riddled with inauthenticity and alienation; relations with others are never free from the desire to dominate or be dominated. This grim picture is what we try to mask from ourselves in *mauvaise foi* (bad faith), a form of self-deception which is the commonest kind of inauthenticity. All this, says Sartre in a famous footnote, does not exclude the possibility of an ethics of deliverance and salvation. But *L'Être et le néant* is not the place to find it. [CMH]

Être Suprême, Fête de l'. Festival stage-managed by *David and held at *Robespierre's instigation at the Tuileries on 20 Prairial (8 June) 1794. It was meant to inaugurate a deistic cult complete with an 'Hymne à l'Être Suprême', but caused considerable mockery and disaffection.

Étude et le rouet, L', see LE DŒUFF.

Études de mœurs au XIXe siècle. Group title of an eight-volume series of novels and stories by *Balzac published 1833–5, including notably *Histoire des Treize* and *Eugénie Grandet*.

Étudiant noir, L'. Pioneering black student review of which only one number (March 1935) is known for certain to have appeared. In it, a group of Martinican students, notably Aimé *Césaire, Gilbert Gratiant, and Léopold Sainville, were for the first time joined by an African student, Léopold Sédar *Senghor, in protesting against the assimilationist theory and practice of French colonialism. The review is commonly, if with some exaggeration, regarded as marking the beginning of the *négritude movement in French African and French West Indian thought and writing. [RDEB]

EUDES, Jean, see DEVOTIONAL WRITING, 2.

Eugène, see JODELLE.

EUGÉNIE DE MONTIJO (1826–1920), a Spanish aristocrat, became empress of France on her marriage to *Napoleon III in 1853. She was the centre of a brilliant court, which included her devoted friend *Mérimée.

Eugénie Grandet. Novel by *Balzac, written and published in 1833 in the first series of *Études de mœurs au XIXe siècle and subsequently placed in the *Comédie humaine amongst the Scènes de la vie de province, of which it is both the model and the masterpiece. It is a meticulous study of the constricted life of a girl brought up in a miser's household in Saumur—a life so pinched and mean that it almost defies modern imagination. As in many of Balzac's provincial scenes, the gulf between Paris and the provinces provides the novel's narrative impulse. Cousin Charles arrives from the capital; with his city clothes and sophisticated trinkets, he seems to Eugénie to have come from another planet, and she falls in love. Charles's father has been ruined in business; news of his suicide reaches Saumur a few hours later. Eugénie gives Charles the gold coins she possesses to help him start a new life in the Indies, and civil war breaks out in the household between Grandet and his daughter. The old man is a grasping miser of extraordinary cunning ('financially speaking, something between a tiger and a boa constrictor') who has amassed a huge fortune in gold coins, to which he devotes an exclusive and almost sensual passion. Upon his death Eugénie makes a sensible marriage, and devotes the rest of her life to good works. Around this minimal plot, Balzac creates a memorable portrait of a household, of a whole way of life, and of two unusually powerful characters. [DMB]

Eulalia, see SAINTE EULALIE, SÉQUENCE DE.

Europe. Literary periodical created in 1923 by a group round Romain *Rolland. Its editors have included *Guéhenno and *Cassou.

Evangelicals. Although the term has wide connotations, in French intellectual history it is usually associated with a group of early Reformers, inspired particularly by the *Brethren of the Common Life and *Erasmus; whilst acknowledging the necessity of religious reform by recourse to the original sources of the Church's inspiration, the *Évangéliques* laboured to reform the Church from within and resisted the extreme positions which eventually led to schism. By the opening of the Council of Trent (1545), most members of the group had been reabsorbed into the Roman Church, though some joined Lutheran or Calvinist sects [see REFORMATION].

Most easily identifiable is the Groupe de Meaux: in 1521 Guillaume *Briçonnet brought together in his diocese a number of humanist theologians and preachers, including his mentor *Lefèvre d'Étaples, Guillaume *Farel, the Hebraist François *Vatable, and Gérard Roussel, protégé of *Marguerite d'Alençon (de Navarre), who took a profound interest in their work and corresponded with Briçonnet on spiritual and mystical questions. Despite the *Sorbonne's opposition, the group proclaimed, in print and from the pulpit, their programme for checking the worldliness and laxity of the clergy, for simplifying the forms of worship, and for bringing the people into closer communion with the revealed word of God by preaching and translation. Lefèvre's *Commentarii* on the Gospels (1522) summarize the group's aims. But within four years, amid the turmoil caused by defeat at Pavia and by repression of *Luther's 'heresy' in France, the group had dispersed, with Farel preaching radicalism at Basle, and even Lefèvre and Roussel briefly in exile at Strasburg.

Despite the failure of the Meaux experiment and the hostility of the Sorbonne, Evangelical ideas persisted into the 1530s; some commentators argue that *Marot embraced them, and *Rabelais clearly supported their synergist attitude to justification. Roussel, appointed Marguerite's chaplain, introduced many of the planned reforms in Navarre, and preached a famous series of Lenten sermons to the court at the Louvre in 1533. The latitudinarianism of the Evangelical movement may be illustrated by the fact that in 1536 Farel was *Calvin's colleague in Geneva, whilst Roussel became bishop of Oloron.

[MJH]

See G. Bedouelle, *Lefèvre d'Étaples* (1972); J. K. Farge, *Orthodoxy and Reform in Early Reformation France* (1985).

Évangiles. Term used variously in the Middle Ages to refer to (*a*) verse and prose adaptations of the Gospels, including homiletic commentary, based on readings from the Gospels prescribed for Sundays in the liturgy (e.g. by Jean de Vignay, Robert of Gretham); (*b*) accounts of Christ's early years (infancy gospels) deriving from apocryphal gospel material (e.g. the Old French and Anglo-Norman *Évangile de l'Enfance*, based on the Latin Gospel of Pseudo-Matthew); (*c*) translations of the apocryphal Gospel of Nicodemus. The first category provides evidence of the use of French in a liturgical context; the others are typical of medieval adaptations of the *Bible and related texts. [DAT]

Ève future, L', see VILLIERS DE L'ISLE-ADAM.

Évolution créatrice, L', see BERGSON.

EXBRAYAT, Charles (1906–89). Though famous for detective fiction, Exbrayat wrote first for the theatre. His first novel, *Jules Matrat* (1942), was a *roman du terroir*, as were later *Un matin elle s'en alla* (1969) and *Les Bonheurs courts* (1981–2). He wrote film scripts before being invited to contribute to Le *Masque. *Elle avait trop de mémoire* (1957) and *Vous souvenez-vous de Paco?* (1958) began a long series of crime and spy novels: settings range from caricatural Britain (*Ne vous fâchez pas, Imogène*, 1959) or Spain (*Olé! Torero!*, 1963) to French provinces (*Les Dames du Creusot*, 1966), but with a constant humorous vein. [SFN]

Exemplum (plural *exempla*). A story (true or fictional) which provides concrete illustration of an abstract ethical point. Mentioned as a device in the *Rhetorica ad Herennium* (1st c. BC), the *exemplum* had an important role in medieval textbooks of poetics. In his *Poetria nova* Geoffrey of Vinsauf discusses the use of *exempla* both to begin and to end a narrative. Manuals of preaching placed even greater stress on the use of these illustrative stories, and a number of collections of *exempla* were made for the use of homilists. Many vernacular genres acknowledge their kinship with *exempla*, with apparent seriousness in *historiography, with varying degrees of good faith in *romances, and seemingly parodically in the *fabliaux*. [JAMM]

Exil, see SAINT-JOHN PERSE.

Exil et le royaume, L' (1957). Collection of five stories by Albert *Camus, three of which are set in Algeria; written for the most part in a classical style, all explore existential problems.

Existentialism. A philosophy which gives priority to human existence, that is to say, subjective experience of the world, rather than to abstract or 'objective' structures or essences. It views human existence as radically different in nature from the existence of the physical world, in so far as men and women are free to make of themselves the kind of people they want to be and, to some extent, to make for themselves the kind of world they want to live in. This freedom entails concomitant responsibilities; it is not freedom in a void, for each person's freedom comes into contact and possible conflict with that of everyone else. Our 'being-in-the-world' is bound up with our 'being-with-others', and in this sense Existentialism has an overriding moral dimension, even if it eschews any notion of moral rules or absolutes. In fact, Existentialists usually espouse a situational ethics, in which the consequences of a particular act in particular social and historical circumstances take priority over absolute ethical norms. This is quite contrary to any view of a 'moral law' (e.g. Kant's), but not necessarily radically incompatible with a certain kind of liberal Christianity. Indeed, the first Existentialist is generally considered to be the 19th-c. Danish theologian, Søren Kierkegaard, who set out to defend subjective experience against the totalization and objectivization of the Hegelian system. 20th-c Existentialists are generally more keen to explore all the implications of a thoroughgoing atheism, though there have been several notable Catholic Existentialists, such as Gabriel *Marcel in France.

Heidegger's *Sein und Zeit* (Being and Time, 1927) and Sartre's *L'Être et le néant* (1943) are probably the best-known Existentialist works of this century [Sartre's thought is more fully treated in the entries devoted to him and to *L'Être et le néant*]. Neither discusses individual human existence in the usual sense: Heidegger's work centres on *Dasein* (being-there, existence) which is not individuated, and, although Sartre's adoption of Corbin's translation of

Existentialisme est un humanisme, L'

Dasein as 'la réalité humaine' has been criticized for its humanism, it does avoid the individuation inherent in the notion of a 'human being'. Sartre's own examination of the *pour-soi* of human consciousness is also distinct from any notion of person or individual ego. Existentialists prefer to explore 'consciousness' or perhaps the 'subject', rather than the 'self', for the former terms do not imply that identity or essence which is called in question by Existentialism.

Existentialism is popularly associated with the notoriety it enjoyed in Paris in the 1940s, when its opposition to the dominant encoded forms of power and ideology was discussed and perhaps lived out in the hothouse atmosphere of Saint-Germandes-Prés cafés and night-clubs. The identification of a philosophical movement with the life-style of its major proponents (here, principally, Sartre and Simone de *Beauvoir) is, however, necessarily short-lived, and existential philosophy has wider implications than the youthful revolt encapsulated in the Left-Bank protest movement. It is possible that post-war France needed the sugar-coating of a cult movement to help it swallow Existentialism's high moral seriousness. [CMH]

Existentialisme est un humanisme, L', see SARTRE.

Expérience intérieure, L', see BATAILLE, G.

Explication des Maximes des saints, see FÉNELON.

Express, L'. Founded in May 1953 by Jean-Jacques Servan-Schreiber, who had already made his mark on *Le *Monde*, *L'Express* was initially a committed journal, opposed to the prosecution of the *Algerian War, close to *Mendès-France, but open to a diversity of views—including the Gaullist solution for Algeria espoused by Jean Daniel, and the regular columns ('blocs-notes') where *Mauriac rallied to de *Gaulle. Relaunched as a news magazine in 1964, with a technocratic centrist stance, *L'Express* aimed at the 'engineer from Grenoble'. It suffered from the political or ideological toings-and-froings of its chief proprietor (be it Servan-Schreiber or James Goldsmith), but it succeeded in becoming France's premier news magazine. Former staff members founded other weeklies: Jean Daniel *Le *Nouvel Observateur*, Claude Imbert *Le Point*. [MP]

F

Fables. Collection by *La Fontaine, first published in 1668 as *Fables choisies, mises en vers*. This contained six books, with about 20 fables in each. A second edition, containing 11 books, appeared in 1678–9, and a 12th book in 1694. In the first edition La Fontaine draws on familiar fables of Aesop and Phaedrus such as 'The Wolf and the Lamb'. Rejecting the purist advice of *Patru, who saw brevity as the rule of the genre, he endows his fables with 'novelty and gaiety', creating vivid dramas, with evocative rural settings and characters whose animal and human traits are cunningly intermingled. Irregular verse is used with supple mastery; the story-teller plays ironically across all the registers of language, delighting in setting heroic rhetoric against down-to-earth speech. In the second edition he writes with greater freedom, drawing his stories from many sources and developing them at greater length. The pretence that the fables are meant for children is abandoned here. The figure of the poet assumes increasing importance, as he offers personal confidences or meditates on the philosophical implications of his material. In particular, he challenges human arrogance; the 'Discours à Madame de la Sablière' in Book 9 is a critique of *Descartes's notion of the animal as machine.

The fable is meant to teach a lesson, and La Fontaine accepted this view. Even though his main concern was the creation of beautiful little comedies, his fables are indeed instructive, but do not usually yield a simple lesson. Often no explicit moral is given; if it is, it may well seem to contradict the story. 'La raison du plus fort est toujours la meilleure'—the moral of 'Le Loup et l'agneau'—is like an echo of *Pascal's cynical politics, suggesting at most that the weak do well to keep their heads down. What the *Fables* convey—with great poetic richness and inimitable lightness of touch—is a vision of the world in which the simple desire for happiness is corroded and thwarted by the cruelty of life.

Other French authors have written fables [see MARIE DE FRANCE; LA MOTTE; AUBERT; FLORIAN], but La Fontaine remains the unequalled model.   [PF]

See O. de Mourgues, *La Fontaine: Fables* (1960).

Fabliaux. Short comic narratives, composed between the late 12th and the 14th c. The number of *fabliaux* varies according to the criteria used to define them, but there are roughly 140, about 60 of which are designated as *fablel* or *flabel* by their authors. This term, which is simply the diminutive of *fable*, is not particularly illuminating as a description, since although a minority of *fabliaux* are related to existing fables with an all-human cast, tales with anthropomorphized animals as protagonists are not generally regarded as *fabliaux*. A few authors of *fabliaux* are known by a name and no more (Guérin, Durand), and there are several poets who composed *fabliaux* as well as works in other genres (*Bodel, *Rutebeuf, Watriquet de Couvin, Jacques de Baisieux, Jean de Condé [see BAUDOUIN DE CONDÉ]) but the majority of texts are anonymous. Most *fabliaux* are written in octosyllabic rhyming couplets, and are well under 1,000 lines long.

Earlier this century *fabliaux* were regarded as a marginal genre, and were certainly not considered suitable for students; an early student anthology (ed. Johnston and Owen, 1957) complains that 'half of the total violate modern susceptibilities to a serious extent', and confines itself to exemplars that are 'reasonably acceptable' (p. ix). Many *fabliaux* are indeed very explicit about sexual behaviour, and especially sexual fantasy. Whereas fables anthropomorphize animals, in *fabliaux* it is often genitals that are endowed with independent agency, and assimilated to animals (*L'Escuiriel*; *La Sorisete aus estopes*; the various versions of *La Damoisele qui ne pooit oïr parler de fotre*; etc.). Some of the *fabliaux* are also pornographic, in the sense that their narratives revolve quite blatantly around the size and suitability of sexual organs, and the quantity or frequency of sexual performance. Others are scatological. In general, they focus attention on the lower body (including the stomach—eating and drinking are also prominent themes) and are dismissive of any attempt to valorize 'higher' concerns. In their irreverence towards idealism the *fabliaux* recall the *Roman de Renart*: theirs is a world where belief in abstract ideals is generally misplaced, if not a downright handicap.

This earthiness of the *fabliaux*, combined with their liking for non-noble characters, led to their initially being categorized as 'bourgeois literature'. They have also been seen as 'popular' in their ethical attitudes, and in their perpetuation of classic 'jokes'. A major turning-point in *fabliaux* scholarship came with the realization that many of them are burlesques of courtly texts, and that their obsession with what goes on below the belt results not from lower-class philistinism, but from carefully targeted parody (Nykrog, 1957). *Fabliaux* and *romances might, it became apparent, be enjoyed by the same audiences; they might even be composed for them by the same authors.

Fabre

This critical move reclaimed the *fabliaux* for literary attention. Since then, the wit and linguistic sophistication of these texts have been increasingly demonstrated. Although no longer seen as exclusively burlesquing courtly texts, they are now accepted as a highly 'literary' genre, and even as epitomizing 'literariness'. For the *fabliaux* represent a world in which the ingenious triumph over the unimaginative. Those who trust in the fact that they possess power, or money, or a wife, can be guaranteed humiliation, loss, or cuckolding, for most *fabliau* heroes are tricksters, capable of turning their very lack of such possessions to their own advantage.

A theme which is found in several *fabliaux* involves the trickster punishing a wealthy household which has refused him hospitality. In *Le Bouchier d'Abevile* a butcher, refused admission by a priest, offers to pay for accommodation with a sheep he has stolen from the priest's herd; he also buys sexual favours from the priest's mistress and maidservant by promising them the sheepskin. Only when he has left do the members of the household discover how they have all been tricked. Sometimes the unimaginative try their hand at trickery, only to have their own trick rebound against them. One recurring *fabliau* plot (e.g. *La Borgoise d'Orliens*—it is also found in the one surviving *Occitan fabliau*) is that of the 'mari cocu, battu et content'. A rich husband suspects his wife of infidelity and determines to catch her out. He pretends to leave, then comes back disguised as the suspected adulterer. His wife sees through the disguise, but plays along with it: pretending to be furious at the intrusion of a would-be seducer, she has him soundly beaten. The husband is locked up overnight, congratulating himself on his wife's virtue, while she entertains the real lover. Such *fabliaux* can be seen as 'literary' in their play with rival representations.

In many cases the successful representations, like literature, are linguistic: the dupe is deceived by a form of words, whether it is a husband believing his wife's account of being 'healed' by a long thin flask from which came drops of unguent (*La Saineresse*) or St Peter letting a **jongleur* into heaven (*Saint Pierre et le jongleur*). Many of these linguistic deceptions show an uncanny familiarity with clerical skills such as biblical commentary; some tricksters are clearly intellectuals in mufti. If the *Roman de Renart* reflects, albeit distantly, scholastic debates of the period, so do the *fabliaux*; their major point of contact with **scholasticism* is their common interest in language and epistemology. Chaucer adapted several *fabliaux* in the *Canterbury Tales*, and there are also analogues in Middle High German, but the wit and naughtiness of the *fabliaux* remain predominantly French phenomena.   [SK]

See P. Nykrog, *Les Fabliaux* (1957); W. Noomen and N. van den Boogaard (eds.), *Nouveau recueil complet de fabliaux* (1983–); M. J. S. Schenk, *The Fabliaux, Tales of Wit and Deception* (1987).

FABRE, Jean-Henri (1823–1915). French entomologist. The son of a peasant, he became a teacher and scientist, publishing numerous textbooks. He is remembered for his *Souvenirs entomologiques* (10 vols., 1879–1907), of which a best-selling selection was published in 1910 as *La Vie des insectes*. Based on his observations and experiments in Provence, it describes in great detail the behaviour of insect species, showing the infinite variety of life in a few acres of land. The flowery style and anthropomorphic presentation may raise a smile today, but the work is a treasure-house of precise observation.
[PF]

FABRE, Joan-Batista, see OCCITAN LITERATURE (POST-MEDIEVAL).

FABRE D'ÉGLANTINE, Philippe-François-Nazaire (1755–94). Modestly successful French playwright who was especially known for *Le Philinte de Molière* (1790), but who became much better known, then and now, as an enthusiastic Revolutionary: founder member of the **Cordeliers, member of the Paris Commune, the Convention, and the original Comité de Salut Public, and author of the Revolutionary **calendar. A faithful friend of **Danton and supporter of *indulgence*, he perished along with the other Dantonistes. Fabre is the author of the much-loved 'Il pleut, il pleut bergère'. He called himself Fabre d'Églantine because he had won a gold *églantine* (a well-known poetry prize) at the **Jeux Floraux de Toulouse.   [JR]

FABRE D'OLIVET, Antoine (1768–1825), a playwright whom success stubbornly eluded, diversified late into the study of the languages and cosmogonies of the ancient world. His unquestionable erudition was, however, undermined by his visionary temperament, exalted imagination, and his taste for the occult, which led him to propound fantastical hypotheses. Fabre deserves recognition, however (though in a smaller way than **La Curne de Sainte-Palaye, **Raynouard, and **Fauriel), as a distant precursor of the **Félibrige, for *Le Troubadour, poésies occitaniques du XIIIe siècle* (1804), a collection of verse (some of it authentic) couched in various dialècts with Fabre's translations.   [JR]

FABRI, Pierre (c.1450–c.1535). Author of the *Grand et Vrai Art de pleine rhétorique* (1521), in which, in traditional medieval fashion, he regards poetry as a special kind of rhetoric. He also provides a survey of the medieval genres (ballade, rondeau, etc.) which the **Pléiade, reacting against its medieval heritage and against **Rhétoriqueur poetry, will ostentatiously spurn.   [JJS]

Fabrice del Dongo. Romantic hero of Stendhal's *La *Chartreuse de Parme*.

Fâcheux, Les, see MOLIÈRE.

FAGUET, Émile (1847–1916). French literary critic. A disciple of **Sainte-Beuve and **Taine, he was a successful lecturer and published innumerable critical books, mainly essays grouped by centuries under the title *Études littéraires*, but also monographs. A defender of tradition, he concentrates on the intellectual and moral stance of writers. His work has a tone of reassuring authority which has not worn well. [PF]

FALBAIRE DE QUINGEY, Charles-Georges Fenouillot de (1727–1800). Inspecteur Général of a salt-works and contributor to the *Encyclopédie*. He wrote *drames*, the most famous being *L'Honnête Criminel* (1767), a protest against the position of Protestants in France.

FALCONET, Étienne-Maurice (1716–91). French sculptor, creator of the famous statue of Peter the Great (the 'bronze horseman') in St Petersburg. He exchanged a series of letters with *Diderot between 1765 and 1767, in which he attacked the *philosophe's* view that artists are driven by the desire for immortality.

Falconry, see HUNTING.

FALL, Aminata Sow, see SOW FALL.

FALL, Kiné Kirama (b. 1934) is Senegalese. In his preface to her first collection of poems, *Chants de la rivière fraîche* (1976), *Senghor commented on her typically African combination of spirituality and sensuality. The poem in *Les Élans de grâce* (1979) have the stark simplicity of old Irish love songs and the sensual-spiritual ambiguity characteristic of the *troubadours. They have also been compared with medieval Arab mystic poetry. [FNC]

FALL, Malick (1920–78). Malick Fall combined an interest in literature with work as a bureaucrat in Senegal's Department of Information; he later went on to pursue a career as a diplomat. In spite of the fact that he published very little, Fall's novel, *La Plaie* (1967), has justly earned him the reputation as one of Senegal's more important novelists of the post-Independence period.

Fall's first published work was a collection of poems, *Reliefs* (1964), which were composed over a long period spanning an eventful era in Senegalese history. Many of the poems reflect the preoccupations of the colonial period, while others offer a much more personal perspective on the conflicting hopes and fears of the independence process. In these poems, Fall rejects the stereotypical exoticism associated with *négritude. *La Plaie* can be read as a satire on urban life and the various forms of disruptive influence which Western society has imposed upon traditional African ways. The protagonist, Magamou Seck, is drawn to the city to seek work but, injured in a lorry crash, he is reduced to a life of begging. Magamou's wound marks him as a social outcast. But it also has a symbolic significance which relates to the other possible reading of the

novel as a quest for freedom, meaning, and a sense of identity. [MPC]

Family Life, see MARRIAGE.

FANCHETTE, Jean (b. 1932). A Mauritian writer, Fanchette co-founded with Anaïs Nin the bilingual journal *Two Cities* (1959–64). He has also written an essay on psychodrama and some poetry. His novel *Alpha du centaure* (1975) oscillates between the contrasting realities of Mauritius and Paris. [BEJ]

Fanfarlo, Le, see BAUDELAIRE.

Fanny, see FEYDEAU, E.

FANON, Frantz (1925–61). Martinican-born psychoanalyst, theorist of anti-imperialist revolution. Born into a lower-middle-class family of mixed racial origin, Fanon was educated at the Lycée Schoelcher in Fort-de-France (where one of his teachers was Aimé *Césaire), and came to political consciousness in an island colony controlled in the name of the Vichy regime by the French navy. In 1943 he escaped, at the third attempt, from Martinique to the neighbouring island of Dominica, whence he joined the Forces Françaises Libres. He subsequently fought with them in Morocco, Algeria, and France, gaining the Croix de Guerre in 1945. Between 1947 and 1951 he studied medicine, specializing in psychiatry, at the University of Lyon, and in 1952 published his seminal work on the psychology of racism and 'race relations', *Peau noire masques blancs*. Heavily influenced by Freud, Jung, Hegel, and *Sartre, the work begins as a humanistic or rationalist investigation, but reaches authentically revolutionary conclusions.

Fanon married a Frenchwoman, José Dublé, in 1952 and, after a short period as psychiatric intern at Pontorson in Normandy, was appointed psychiatric consultant at the Hôpital Blida-Joinville in Algeria in 1953. A sympathizer with the FLN from the outbreak of the *Algerian War in 1954, Fanon resigned from his psychiatric post in 1956 in order to devote himself entirely to the insurgent cause. Expelled from Algeria by the French in January 1957, he went to Tunisia where he worked as a psychiatrist and also contributed regular artricles to the FLN newspaper *El Moudjahid*, which are reprinted, along with other writings, in the posthumous *Pour la révolution africaine* (1964). In 1959 a searching analysis of the sociology and psychology of the war in Algeria, *L'An Cinq de la révolution algérienne*, was banned by the French government, and in the same year an attempt was made on Fanon's life in Rome, where he had gone for medical treatment following injury in a land-mine explosion on the Tunisian–Algerian border.

In 1960 Fanon was chosen to represent the Gouvernement Provisoire Algérien in Ghana, but fell ill and, in December 1960, was diagnosed as suffering from incurable leukaemia. Following treatment in Moscow, he returned to Tunisia and there, in the space of ten weeks, wrote his last and most influential work, *Les Damnés de la terre* (1961), in which he argues not only that colonialism cannot be overthrown without violence but also, and still more controversially, that *only* violent struggle can truly liberate colonized humanity from the multiple psychological alienations from which it suffers. It was published shortly after his death with a preface by *Sartre. Translated into English as *The Wretched of the Earth*, the work had a massive influence on anti-colonial and anti-racist struggles throughout the world, not least in the United States where it was an inspirational text of the Black Power Movement in the 1960s and early 1970s. Though its conclusions concerning violence seem increasingly questionable, its analysis of the social psychology of colonialism remains unsurpassed.   [RDEB]

> See D. Caute, *Fanon* (1970); J. McCullough, *Black Soul White Artifact: Fanon's Clinical Psychology and Social Theory* (1983); H. A. Bulhan, *Frantz Fanon and the Psychology of Oppression* (1985).

Fantaisistes, Les. Group of poets who came together *c.*1911. Their immediate inspiration was *Toulet, and they aimed for a light, tender, sometimes mocking poetry which would 'fleurir la route où est passée une humaine douleur' (M. Rat). They included *Carco, Jean-Marc *Bernard, *Klingsor, Tristan Dérème (pseud. of Philippe Huc, 1889–1941), and Jean Pellerin (1885–1921).

Fantasio. Bitter and witty comedy by *Musset, published 1834 in *Un spectacle dans un fauteuil*, first performed 1866. The hero, a gentleman disguised as the king of Bavaria's jester, is a transposition of the Romantic poet.

Fantastic, The. Fantasy, taken broadly to mean a more-or-less light-hearted play with the impossible and the imaginary, is of course a permanent element in French literature. It can be traced, for instance, in the supernatural aspects of *folk-tale, *pastoral, and *opera, in the imaginary voyages of *Rabelais, *Cyrano de Bergerac, or Voltaire (e.g. *Micromégas*), and in modern *science fiction. The present entry, however, is confined to the fantastic in its more recent and narrower definition as a literature of mystery and horror.

In spite of the charge that 'les Français n'ont pas la tête fantastique' (Louis Vax), a characteristic strain of fantastic writing can be traced in French literature from the giddy devilries of *Cazotte's *Le Diable amoureux* (1772), through the supernatural tales of *Romanticism, and on to the erotic phantasmagoria of *Surrealism, and even, it may be argued, the suave enigmas of a *nouveau romancier* like *Robbe-Grillet. According to the Structuralist criteria of Tzvetan *Todorov, the effect of the literary Fantastic is to implicate the reader in the hesitation experienced within the narrative by characters unable to decide if certain events are real or unreal. A tale such as *Mérimée's *La Vénus d'Ille* (1837) perfectly fits this model in so far as its narrator, for all

his scholarly self-importance, cannot finally resolve whether or not he has witnessed the murder of a young man by a statue come to life. A story like *Maupassant's *Le Horlà* (1886–7), with its diary format, offers a complementary demonstration in inviting the reader to enter the mind of a man in the grip of hallucinations.

French practitioners of this international genre tend to owe less to the horror-inducing strategies of English Gothic than to the milder thrills of *Les *Mille et une Nuits* or the uncanny fantasies of E. T. A. Hoffmann; so that Romantics like *Gautier, with his yarn about a glamorous vampire, 'La Morte amoureuse' (1836), or Surrealists like *Mandiargues, with his story on a similar theme, 'Le Passage Pommeraye' (1946), might be thought to offer rather more wit and baroque decoration than is compatible with the wholehearted escalation of disquiet and panic. Even so, the persuasive insights into the psychotic sensibility of Nerval's semi-autobiographical *Aurélia* (1855), the macabre imaginings of *Villiers de l'Isle-Adam's *Contes cruels* (1883), and the unfettered and morbid frenzies of *Lautréamont's *Chants de Maldoror* (1868–9) are evidence that the French can hold their own against foreign 'shockers' like *Poe or Gustav Meyrink. The history of the genre of the Fantastic is one of evolving self-consciousness and narrative subtlety, and, while in the 1940s francophones like Marcel *Brion and Jean *Ray could still exploit classic formulae, supremacy was to shift to South America and the urbane ironies of Jorge Luis Borges, whose masterly fictions, translated by Roger *Caillois, were a major revelation of the 1950s.   [RC]

> See P.-G. Castex, *Le Conte fantastique en France: de Nodier à Maupassant* (1951); R. Caillois, *Anthologie du fantastique*, 2 vols. (1966); T. Todorov, *Introduction à la littérature fantastique* (1970).

Fantômas. The Fantômas adventures, originally dictated in alternate monthly instalments for serial publication by Pierre Souvestre (1874–1914) and Marcel Allain (1885–1969)—their contributions supposedly marked by 'néanmoins' and 'toutefois' respectively—and by Allain alone from 1919, recount in 32 volumes of a hasty style, from 1911 to 1962, the Manichaean struggles of this protean criminal hero, loved by Lady Beltham, against Inspector Juve and the forces of authority. Neither side ever triumphs, and Fantômas forever returns as surprises follow reversals. Fantômas, 'le Génie du crime', 'l'Insaississable', caught the imagination of readers of all categories, including *Apollinaire, *Aragon, *Breton, and the *Surrealists, and the adventures gave rise to a number of films.   [SFN]

FANTOURÉ, Alioum (pseud. of Mohamed Touré) (b. 1938). Guinean economist, working for the United Nations Industrial Development Organization in Vienna. His first novel, *Le Cercle des tropiques* (1972), attacking the dictatorial regime of

President Sékou Touré (a distant relative), was awarded the Grand Prix Littéraire d'Afrique Noire in 1973. This original, well-constructed, powerful work, opens the way for a long line of post-independence political satires [see AFRICA (SOUTH OF THE SAHARA)]. Fantouré describes with insight and irony the political machinations and election-rigging leading up to independence in a fictional former African colony, 'Les Marigots du Sud', under the ruthless despot-dictator, the Messie-koï Baré-Koulé. Multinational monopolies and international organizations condone his repressive rule in the interest of neo-colonial hegemony. After the inevitable military coup and death of the tyrant, a brief, cynical epilogue reminds us that there is no hope, that tyranny is a hydra-headed monster.

The structure of Fantouré's next, equally pessimistic novel, Le Récit du cirque . . . de la vallée des morts (1975, under the name Mohamed-Alioum Fantouré), is totally innovatory, mingling poetry and prose, owing something to the *Nouveau Roman, with borrowings from folk-tales, cinematic techniques, and theatrical improvizations. The 'action' takes place in a theatre of sorts, which becomes a prison, with echoes of Dante's Inferno, where the fate of the protagonists (interpreted by actors) is manipulated by a 'metteur en scène', Saïbel-Ti. The spectators can intervene by operating remote-control switches. The final disillusioned message to the blasé international audience, desensitized to the fate of the Third World, is: 'Retournez à votre indifférence.'

Fantouré again demonstrates his versatility with his next ambitious venture, a historical trilogy, Les Cités du termite. Volume 1, L'Homme du troupeau du Sahel (1979), tells of the early vicissitudes of the ambiguous hero, Mainguai, entrusted with the mission of leading the Unité Tsé-tsé to trace an invisible flock and bring it to Conakry, where a factory-ship intends to embark a supply of mutton for Europe. Here fiction, farce, satire, and historical fact are interwoven in an epic drama of modern colonial Africa. Volumes 2 and 3 are Le Voile ténébreux (1985) and Le Gouverneur du territoire (1989). [DSB]

Faramond, see LA CALPRENÈDE.

Farce

1. Medieval

The farce in the Middle Ages was a short comic play without moralizing or satirical intentions (as opposed to the *morality and the *sotie). It derived its humour from amusing situations, tricks, verbal dexterity, and sudden reversals of the action; a classic plot is one in which a would-be deceiver is finally himself deceived. About 150 farces have survived, mostly in four main collections dating from the late 15th and 16th c.; the period of the farce's popularity extends from the end of the Middle Ages well into the Renaissance, and its influence is still apparent in *Molière. The word farce is usually interpreted as meaning 'stuffing', thus implying that farces were originally comic interpolations in serious *mystery plays; but only one example of this has survived, in the 15th-c. Vie de saint Fiacre. Separate farces were sometimes performed after a mystery play to amuse or retain the audience. Another interpretation links farce to fart, meaning deceit, a notion which is present in nearly all the plays.

The origins of the farce are uncertain; there appears to be a gap in the surviving comic drama between the 13th-c. *Arras plays and the farces. Some critics suggest that the *fabliaux of the 13th and 14th c. fill this gap, in that they are the narrative reflections of a lost dramatic tradition. Undoubtedly the themes, settings, and structure of the fabliaux are similar to those of the farces.

Farce performances were of two main types: those organized by the *Basoches, usually farces in a legal setting; and those performed by semi-professional troupes of four or five actors (men played women's roles), who would set up their stage in an open space or a market-place or a large hall. Stages were small and simple: planks supported by barrels or trestles at head-height, divided in two by a curtain behind which the actors changed. These physical limitations restrict the dimensions of most farces, which are rarely over 500 lines long and require only two, three, or four actors. Although aimed primarily at the general public, farces were much appreciated by the upper classes; nobles and kings (e.g. *René d'Anjou) employed farceurs on a permanent or occasional basis.

The characters in the farces were not abstractions, as in the *soties and *moralities; they were apparently real people, with names, jobs, and problems. The most frequent settings for farce plots are the home or the market square, and the recurrent themes are petty dishonesty, illicit love, stupidity, and stubbornness; but these human failings are a source of laughter, not satire. A typical farce will show (a) a ménage à trois in which the lover, often the local priest, attempts to seduce the willing wife of a jealous but foolish husband (L'Amoureux, Martin de Cambrai); or (b) a simple dispute and exchange of insults between husband and wife (L'Obstination des femmes); or (c) a series of attempts at dishonesty (Le Pasté et la tarte). Though the action is set in the real world, the characters are not realistic. The main characters are stereotypes—jealous husband, lecherous priest, unfaithful wife, dishonest merchant, adoring father, semi-educated teacher, etc. They do not develop in the course of the action, which springs from the conflict between several of these stereotypes in a particular situation. The outcome of a farce is usually a predictable surprise. The stereotypical woman of the farces—she is deceitful, stubborn, crafty, foul-mouthed, and over-sexed beyond her husband's capacity—has caused some critics to claim the genre is anti-feminist; but the stereotypical men are no more admirable, and are often stupider.

Farel

The sources of humour in the farce are not only the characters and the situations, but also the language. The best farces, e.g. *Pathelin, Martin de Cambrai*, use language not merely as a supplementary means of provoking laughter (verbal jokes, puns, insults), but as central to the misunderstandings and arguments. The importance of language, together with the restrictions of versification (octosyllabic couplets with mnemonic rhymes, and frequent *rondeaux-triolets*) and the need to create a tightly structured denouement, meant that, even if the public of the farces was ill-educated and illiterate, this was certainly not true of the authors.

[GAR]

See B. Bowen, *Les Caractéristiques essentielles de la farce* (1964); J.-C. Aubailly, *Le Théâtre médiéval profane et comique* (1975); A. Tissier (ed.), *Recueil de farces*, 6 vols. (1986–90).

2. 1550 to the Present

There are many affinities and common elements linking the medieval farces which flourished *c*.1450–1550 with the *Comédie-Italienne of the 17th c., the noisy pantomime at the Théâtre des Funambules in the 1830s, the topical verve of the *vaudevilles popular around 1815–45, and the more literary farces of *Labiche and *Feydeau. Although the use of verse is now the exception rather than the rule, all these dramatic forms draw on stock characters and are, in varying degrees, irreverent, boisterous, and subversive of authority. With the exception of the mimes, they all revel in word-play, some of it, especially in the 17th and 18th c., indecent or scatological. They also share a fondness for practical jokes and elaborate comic business.

The native French farce of the early 17th-c. *Hôtel de Bourgogne was associated with former mountebanks like *Tabarin, Turlupin, *Gaultier-Garguille, and fat Gros-Guillaume. It originated in the fairground booths where travelling quacks used *parades*, crude dramatic sketches, to attract customers. During the 17th c. this broad native farce, elements of which find their way into *Molière's *Les Fourberies de Scapin* (1671), was rivalled, though not displaced, by the greater virtuosity of the Comédie-Italienne, itself a naturalized version of the Italian *commedia dell'arte* with its stock characters, masks, colourful costumes, acrobatic skills, and improvised ensemble playing based on an outline sketch (*scenario*). Borrowing some of the characters of the Comédie-Italienne, the native *parade* evolved in the course of the 18th c. into a racy entertainment with topical allusions and scatological word-play. Its appeal went beyond popular audiences and it was taken up *c*.1730 by the gentry in a vogue which lasted until the Revolution of 1789.

The ideological pressures of the Revolution and the censorship and cultural pretensions of the Napoleonic regime militated against the gross levity of traditional farce, but the reforms of 1806–7 eventually made it possible for licensed theatres like the Variétés and the Vaudeville to continue the disrespectful and scabrous traditions of old farce without the coarseness and horseplay of the original. Advances in public education and aspirations to gentility among the rising commercial and manufacturing classes in the mid-19th c. diminished the appeal of broad and indecent farce, but the power of farce to shock and challenge conventional society is confirmed in the second half of the century by the fast, witty, and inventive plays of Labiche and Feydeau, which dispense with scatology and crude knockabout routines, and by Jarry's violent and aggressive parody, *Ubu roi, which does not. A revolutionary development of farce in the 20th c. is *Beckett's *En attendant Godot*, where the routines and patter of the music-hall are used to metaphysical ends.

[SBJ]

FAREL, Guillaume (1489–1565). A disciple of *Lefèvre d'Étaples and member of the *Evangelical Groupe de Meaux. He settled in Geneva, where he persuaded *Calvin to establish himself in 1536. Having been expelled from Geneva with Calvin, he worked principally from Neuchâtel as an active organizer of the *Reformation. He was a vehement preacher and left many doctrinal works in Latin and French.

[PF]

FARÈS, Nabile (b. 1940). Algerian writer from Collo in Petite Kabylie. As a *lycée* student he participated in strikes against French rule in Algeria. He studied philosophy and wrote a thesis in anthropology, and settled to live and teach in France.

Farès's fictional writings are concerned with the roots of Kabylian culture and the experience of exile. His major work is *Un passager de l'Occident* (1971). The experimental form of this work calls into question the nature of fictional structures, though the use of an epistolatory style seems rather old-fashioned. Farès's concern is with cultural decolonization and he problematizes the language of literary creativity in what he calls 'la reconnaisance d'une dialectique interne'. He suggests that the themes of Algeria's colonial past should be abandoned in favour of the crystallization of national consciousness and that the authentic personality of the nation lies in the pagan heritage: 'Après la décolonisation française de l'Algérie viendra la décolonisation islamique.' This fairly simple proposition is, however, made highly complex by being articulated in an elaborate discourse borrowed from *Derrida, which ranges far beyond the powers of comprehension of Algeria's illiterate majority. Like *Yahia, pas de chance* (1970), *Un passager* is basically an autobiography which calls into question the post-1962 political choices facing Algeria with respect to Islam and Arabic culture. Farès's options are aesthetic rather than political, but the novel is far less naïve politically than the many works devised in response to the one-party system's stranglehold on the definition of Algerian identity during the 1970s.

Other works include *Le Champ des oliviers* (1972), *Mémoire de l'absent* (1974), *L'Exil et le désarroi* (1976), *La Mort de Salah Baye ou la Vie obscure d'un Maghrébin* (1980). [AZ]

FARET, Nicolas (1596–1646). One of the first members of the Académie Française, he published a volume of letters and a work inspired by Castiglione, *L'Honnête homme ou l'Art de plaire à la cour* (1630), which was one of the founding texts of the 17th-c. doctrine of *honnêteté*.

FARGUE, Léon-Paul (1876–1947). French poet. Born in Les Halles in the very heart of Paris, and proud of it, Fargue epitomizes the type of the early 20th-c. urban poet in the lineage of *Baudelaire's flâneur*. Nourished on nocturnal wanderings, prose fabulations such as *Le Piéton de Paris* (1939) inventorize the streets, parks, markets, and cafés which make up what Fargue called 'ma géographie secrète', a cityscape of ragged vistas and spectral silhouettes. The post-*Symbolist musicality of his early verse (*Pour la musique*, 1912) evolved into a breathless poetic prose whose rhythms propel the apocalyptic dream-fugue of *Vulturne* (1928). [RC]

FARRÈRE, Claude (pseud. of Frédéric Bargone) (1876–1957). Novelist best known for adventure stories set in exotic locations. As a young man, he was an admirer of *Loti, under whom he served briefly during his career as a naval officer. Farrère's works are, however, less lyrical and more theatrical than those of Loti. His early successes include *Les Civilisés* (1905), *L'Homme qui assassina* (1907), and *La Bataille* (1911), set respectively in Indo-China, Turkey, and Japan. A political reactionary, his adulation of strong men is reflected in the frenetic pace of his fictional works, where outlandish incidents increasingly outweigh literary craftsmanship. [AGH]

Fascism. Analysis of fascism has produced an immense literature, for which the definition of the term is a major problem. This is especially acute in the French context. The most restrictive definition, limiting it to the Italian original and foreign imitators who adopted the name 'fascist' or a direct translation of it, can provide only a few unimportant examples. The problem is made worse by indiscriminate use of the word as a term of political abuse. Between these two extremes, however, there is a consensus in academic discourse that fascism is an 'ideal type' derived from an amalgam of Mussolini's Italy and Hitler's Germany.

The essence of the concept is that fascism seeks, by electoral means, by violence, or by both together, to overturn the institutions of parliamentary liberal democracy, replacing them with a single party led by a dictator. This brings about not only a political, but a social and economic revolution, creating a new type of totalitarian society and defending the nation against internal and/or external threats, notably that posed by Marxist communism.

*Antisemitism, a vital element in Nazism, is absent from Italian fascism before 1938. In that it often invokes left-wing ideas, if only to pervert them, fascism differs from the conservative or the outright reactionary position, both of which have been prominent in France.

Given this broader use of the concept, several French movements can be seen as fascist, and others are important as pre-1914 precursors. Some authorities include even Napoleon I among the precursors; more widely, the *Bonapartism of the Second Empire, Boulangism [see BOULANGER, G.], and the antisemitic and *nationalist movements of 1885–1914 have been depicted as proto-fascist, notably by Zeev Sternhell. This interpretation has been strongly challenged by French historians, especially René Rémond, who posits a Bonapartist tradition distinct from fascism.

All participants in the controversy accept that fascism never succeeded in France; there is nothing comparable to what happened in Italy and Germany. French fascism, even widely defined, never won power or really widespread support. Fascism is a phenomenon of the period between the two World Wars, whose pre-1914 origins and post-1945 penumbra can be analysed, as long as it is remembered that they are not identical with it. Bonapartism and Boulangism were successful, but were at best forerunners, whose relationship with fascism is remote and problematic. France since 1945 has seen many tiny groups of the fascist type, but their support has been minimal. There is an inverse relationship between their closeness to the fascist model and their success. The populist movement led by Pierre Poujade in 1956–8 and the more recent Front National gained more support, but are close to fascism only in certain elements of their programmes.

During the inter-war period there is the same inverse relationship between proximity to the fascist model and political success. Some movements have been wrongly categorized as fascist, while those which were genuinely fascist were tiny, ephemeral, and fissiparous. The latter, and their leaders, include the Faisceau (G. Valois, 1925–7), Solidarité Française (F. Coty, 1933–4), the Socialistes Nationaux (G. Hervé, 1932–4), Francisme (M. Bucard, 1933–6). Slightly more long-lived was Jeunesses Patriotes (P. Taittinger, 1924–38), linked to the pre-1914 Ligue des Patriotes [see NATIONALISM] and the remnants of the Bonapartist parties, and thus not specifically fascist. The only truly fascist party that had broad support was the Parti Populaire Français (PPF), founded by *Doriot in June 1936. Until 1938 it was prominent on the political scene, exaggeratedly claiming a membership of 300,000 and attracting the support of intellectuals such as *Drieu la Rochelle. Like the smaller parties, it was weakened by internal dissension; in rapid decline at the outbreak of war, it was later resurrected as a German instrument.

The movement led by Colonel de la Roque was

even more successful [see CROIX-DE-FEU]. In spite of its superficial characteristics, however, it was not really fascist in character, and after 1936, as the Parti Social Français, it became a mainstream parliamentary conservative party. It was set to become a major political force, but like the PPF never had its strength tested by national elections. La Roque did not become a collaborator.

*Action Française, born out of the anti-*Dreyfusard campaign, survived, but its significance was intellectual rather than directly political. Moreover, although included in some surveys of fascism, *Maurras's ideology was quite different; a traditional counter-revolutionary theory, it lacked nearly all the specifically fascist elements. One should look here rather than to fascist ideology for the inspiration of the 'Révolution nationale' of Vichy [see OCCUPATION AND RESISTANCE].

An aspect of French fascism worth mentioning is the admiration for fascism displayed by writers and intellectuals, the most notable being *Drieu la Rochelle, *Brasillach, *Céline, *Chateaubriant, and *Rebatet. Some, but not all, of them had been influenced by Maurras. France was more important for the development of fascist ideology than for direct fascist political activity. Much of Mussolini's system can be traced to Georges *Sorel, while antisemitism, notoriously central to Nazism, was outlined in 19th-c. France more strongly than elsewhere. Inoculated with the fascist virus before 1914, France, with its liberal republican tradition, reacted vigorously. In the inter-war period fascism was foreign, even if some of its roots were French. This alien character enhanced its appeal to some, especially after the defeat of 1940, but ensured that it was rejected by the great majority.

[DRW]

See Z. Sternhell, *La Droite révolutionnaire, 1885–1914* (1978) and *Ni droite, ni gauche, l'idéologie fasciste en France* (1983); P. Milza, *Fascisme français, passé et présent* (1987); A. Chebel d'Apollonia, *L'Extrême-Droite en France, de Maurras à Le Pen* (1988).

Fatrasies. Short nonsense poems fashionable in Picardy and Artois in the 13th c. They are found in two collections. The 54 anonymous *Fatrasies d'Arras* and 11 *fatrasies* by Philippe de Rémi [see PHILIPPE DE BEAUMANOIR] observe a strict formal pattern yet anarchically accumulate *non sequiturs* and semantic contradictions (e.g. flying castles, singing onions), controlled only by exigencies of rhyme. Satire may underlie the facetious word-play. Yet, despite recurrent vocabulary, grammatical structures, and motifs (religion, death, animals, geographical localization, violence, weather), unlike most medieval lyric genres, *fatrasies* defy thematic analysis. Differently constructed, but derivative, is the 14th- and 15th-c. *fatras*. [PVD]

Faubourg Saint-Germain. A district of Paris, on the Left Bank, which became a centre of aristocratic

society in the 17th and 18th c. and particularly after the *Restoration. As such, sometimes without a precise geographical location, it figures prominently in novels by *Stendhal, *Balzac, and *Proust.

FAUCHET, Claude (1530–1602). A friend of *Pasquier, with whom he shared a keen interest in French history and institutions—witness his *Recueil des antiquités gauloises* (1579, 1599) and his *Recueil de l'origine de la langue et poésie françaises* (1581). His work is noteworthy for its critical interest in medieval philology and for his use of manuscript sources. [JJS]

FAUJAS DE SAINT-FOND, Barthélémy (1741–1819). French geologist who travelled to the Scottish Highlands in 1784 and wrote an interesting *Voyage en Angleterre, en Écosse, et aux Îles Hébrides* (1797).

FAURE, Élie (1873–1937). Self-taught French art historian; humanitarian socialist. A disciple of *Lamarck, Faure believed that mind and matter, God and Nature, formed an organic and ceaselessly developing unity. In his five-volume *Histoire de l'art* (1909–27) he lyrically evoked the energy of art as the expression of man's physical and spiritual needs and desires, and as a creative impulse evolving in harmony with the rise, decadence, and renewal of civilizations. He pioneered the study of primitive art and recognized the aesthetic potential of the machine age, seeing the cinema, with its collective appeal and its technical resources, as the art of the future. [REG]

FAURÉ, Gabriel (1845–1924). French composer, performer, and teacher. From 1907 to 1920 he was head of the Paris Conservatoire, where he initiated numerous innovations. Although he composed music for almost all genres, Fauré represents for many the quintessence of French song-writing. Most of his songs, or *mélodies*, were set to poems by *Hugo, *Gautier, *Leconte de Lisle, *Baudelaire, *Verlaine, and the lesser-known Armand Silvestre. Verlaine arguably inspired his best songs. Although not rigid in its adherence to texts (he would omit or split stanzas), his musical response to the subtleties of the poetry results in an extraordinarily sensitive moulding of poetry to music. [KM]

FAURIEL, Claude (1772–1844). Professor, administrator, and historian. A French Philhellene and a man of liberal convictions, he contributed significantly to the growing interest in foreign literatures, translating tragedies by Manzoni (1823), bringing out a collection of Greek popular poetry (1824–5), and doing pioneering work on Provençal poetry. See his *Histoire de la Gaule méridionale sous la domination des conquérants germains* (1836) and *Histoire de la poésie provençale* (1846). [CC]

Fausses Confidences, Les. Comedy in three acts by *Marivaux, performed by the *Comédie-Italienne in

1737. Dorante, a poor, well-bred, and good-looking young man, falls in love with the rich widow Araminte. He has himself taken on as her steward, and with the aid of some complex and not entirely scrupulous intrigues, masterminded by his former valet Dubois, he little by little brings Araminte to love him and confess her love, to the scandal of her mother, the snobbish Madame Argante, who wanted her to marry a count. To redeem his tarnished reputation, Dorante owns up to his trickery, and the play ends with the prospect of marriage.

[PF]

Faustroll, Dr, see JARRY; 'PATAPHYSIQUE.

Faute de l'abbé Mouret, La. Novel by *Zola, fifth in the *Rougon-Macquart series, published 1875. It takes the form of a religious allegory or philosophical tale, depicting the struggle between the Church and Nature for the 'soul' of Serge Mouret, the son of François Mouret and Marthe Rougon. Serge, the parish priest in a small Provençal hamlet, is intensely devoted to the cult of the Virgin Mary and falls ill as a result of his excessive devotions, losing his memory. His uncle, the hero of the later novel Le *Docteur Pascal, takes him to the wild garden, le Paradou, where, in a patent transposition of the myth of Adam and Eve, a young girl, Albine, tempts him back to new life, with the active complicity of surrounding nature. The formidable frère Archangias, however, invades the Paradou to reclaim Serge for the Church. The young priest, repentant, denies the call of nature and the pregnant Albine, who dies as a result of his rejection. The novel is in the form of a triptych and has been admired for its lyrical qualities, its lush descriptions, and its representation of peasant life before La *Terre.

[DB]

Fauvism. Derived from the French word fauve, 'wild beast', with which the critic Louis Vauxcelles described *Matisse, *Vlaminck, Derain, *Rouault, and Marquet when he saw the flat patterns and strong colours of their works exhibited in 1905 in the Salon d'Automne in Paris, Fauvism briefly brought together these painters who were seeking, in the wake of *Gauguin, *Van Gogh, and *Cézanne, to explore the expressive potential of colour. In its emphasis on the material, sensuous element of painting, it has been related to the emergence in literature of the poetic movement known as 'le naturisme', which in the closing years of the 19th c. played a major role in the reaction against *Symbolism.

[JK]

Faux-Monnayeurs, Les. The only work of his which *Gide was prepared to call a novel, published 1926. It depicts aspects of Parisian life in the early decades of the 20th c. in such a way as to suggest that each generation, having criticized the preceding one, goes on to replicate its behaviour. From a complex tapestry emerges a view of humanity as being essentially subject to self-delusion, incapable of distinguishing between the real and the imagined. The victims of this state of affairs, it is suggested, are the young, manipulated by unscrupulous or inept elders to the detriment of their potential authenticity. Illustrating what to Gide was a key feature of the genre, the novel deploys a multiplicity of narrative points of view as the story is shaped through what the characters themselves have to say in conversations, letters, or diaries. The narrator, who also features in the text, frequently confesses his ignorance of certain matters; his voice, together with the presence of a novelist (Édouard) working on a novel called Les Faux-Monnayeurs, highlights the relativity of perception and anticipates the formal self-consciousness of the *Nouveau Roman. Le Journal des Faux-Monnayeurs (1926) gives insights into the elaboration of the work.

[DHW]

FAVART, Charles-Simon (1710–92). French dramatist. The son of a pastry-cook, he became a very successful author of *opéras-comiques, many written in partnership with his wife, a brilliant actress. In 1758 he became director of the Opéra-Comique (the new theatre built for the company in 1783 is still called the Salle Favart). Bastien et Bastienne (1753), for which Mozart later composed music, is a parody of *Rousseau's Le Devin du village. Haydn wrote tunes for his masterpiece, Les Trois Sultanes (1761), a patriotic light comedy in vers libres in which a Frenchwoman outwits the emperor Soliman. Patriotism is even more evident in the one play Favart wrote for the *Comédie-Française, L'Anglais à Bordeaux (1763).

[PF]

FAVRE, Antoine (1557–1624). Jurist, magistrat, and poet. A close friend of *François de Sales and d'*Urfé, Favre was one of a distinguished group of literary figures in Savoy in the early 17th c. In addition to his legal writings, he composed several collections of devotional poetry comparable with *La Ceppède's, and a series of moral quatrains regularly printed with those of *Pibrac.

[TC]

FAYE, Jean-Pierre (b. 1925). French writer; member of the *Tel Quel group from 1963 to 1967 and co-founder of the *Change 'Collective' in 1968. Faye's prolific work encompasses all genres: poetry, narrative prose, theatre, literary criticism, political philosophy, and sociology. He is noted particularly for his analyses of literary and political language: Théorie du récit (1972), Langages totalitaires (1972), La Critique du langage et son économie (1973), Dictionnaire politique portatif en cinq mots (1982), La Raison narrative (1990); and for his narrative work 'Hexagramme', comprising Entre les rues (1958), La Cassure (1961), Battement (1962), Analogues (1964), L'Écluse (1964, Prix Renaudot), Les Troyens (1970), followed by Inferno—versions (1975), L'Ovale—détail (1975), Les Portes des villes du monde (1979), Yumi. Visage caméra (1983). Exploring the world and demystifying language go hand in hand for Faye.

The key to concrete language lies in the critique of language rather than in ideologies. The writer's task is to uncover the formal and ideological mechanisms underlying representation; to dismantle the powers of language that hold us captive. For Faye, literature is 'being able to say by what signs our reality comes to us'. [DM-S]

February Revolution (of 1848), see REPUBLICS, 2.

FEBVRE, Lucien (1878–1956). French historian; co-founder of *Annales*. Febvre's originality lay in his integration of other disciplines, such as geography and psychology, into the study of social and intellectual history, and in his investigation of the limits imposed upon the cultural constructs of a given period by the linguistic and conceptual tools available to it. While recognizing the importance of material factors, he stressed the freedom of man in interaction with his environment, and, as in his most influential work, *Le Problème de l'incroyance au XVIe siècle: la religion de Rabelais* (1942), he combined the analysis of collective mentalities with an emphasis upon the ideas of exemplary individuals. [REG]

Fédérés, Les. Delegates, often members of the Garde Nationale, sent from the provinces to Paris for the Fête de la Fédération on 14 July 1790 and again in 1792, when many were involved in the deposition of Louis XVI [see REVOLUTION, 1b].

Fée aux miettes, La, see NODIER.

'Fées, Les'. One of Perrault's *Histoires ou contes du temps passé*. A girl who is kind and well-spoken to a fairy in disguise sees all her words transformed into precious stones; her rude sister's words become serpents.

Félibrige, Le. Influential Provençal literary movement launched in Avignon in 1854 by seven writers, including Joseph Roumanille (1818–91), his former pupil *Mistral, and acquaintance *Aubanel. They aimed to raise awareness of Provençal traditions, history, and language, to codify Provençal grammar and spelling, and to demand that Provençal be taught in schools. Despite its Catholic conservatism, the movement was intellectually modern and cultivated contacts with Parisian writers. It attracted many Occitan authors, including Félix Gras (also from Avignon), under whose leadership (1891–1901) it declined. Yet, past schisms, polemics, and rivalries notwithstanding, it still survives. [See OCCITAN LITERATURE (POST-MEDIEVAL).] [PVD]

Feminism in France has shared many features familiar to the anglophone world through the feminist movements in the United Kingdom and the USA: on the one hand, the desire and the struggle to attain equal rights for women; on the other, involvement with political movements that contested the republican state and believed that

women's oppression would only end with the end of patriarchy.

The specificity of French feminism derives from the intellectual as well as the political climate in which it has developed. Most particularly, in the late 20th c. the dominance of *Marxism, *psychoanalysis, and *Post-Structuralism in intellectual discourse has shaped contemporary French feminist theory as it is generally understood outside France. The aspects of French feminism which parallel those with which anglophone readers are familiar in their own countries—its political struggles, its work in sociology, political science, and history—tend to be ignored (and untranslated) while the aspects which are exciting in their unfamiliarity are stressed (see below, Section 4). The resultant paradox is that, while feminist theory is marginalized (if not ignored completely) in French intellectual life today, its impact on academic life outside France is highly significant.

1. Origins

The first manifestations of feminism in France were as part of an intellectual debate. Beginning with the *Querelle des Femmes in the 13th c., the debate was originally theological, concerning the nature of 'Woman': women's inferiority was held to be proved through arguments based in theology, medicine, and law. This proof was challenged, and debates followed concerning the relative virtues and vices of the sexes, with women defended most notably by *Christine de Pizan, sometimes called the first feminist. These debates continued for four centuries.

In the 16th–18th c. individual women (and some men) spoke out in favour of women's emancipation or women's excellence (Louise *Labé, Mademoiselle de *Gournay), but their words had few literary or political echoes. It has been argued that the women associated with *preciosity could be thought of as feminists. Ridiculed or despised for their excessive attention to the niceties of language, they represented a threat to patriarchy precisely because their challenge to the current use of language symbolized an attack on male values. The 17th-c. philosopher *Poulain de la Barre questioned the inequality between men and women and concluded that, as women had the same potential for rational thought as men, their inferior status was created socially and was not justifiable; women should be given the same opportunities for advancement and fulfilment as men. His argument remained without concrete effect.

The most influential *Enlightenment philosophers did not espouse feminism, but *Helvétius and *Condorcet did advance the notion of the equality of the sexes and suggest that no rational argument could justify the continued subordination of women. (Some historians of French feminism consider that Poulain de la Barre and Condorcet between them provided the theoretical framework to which women were to refer throughout the 19th c.) Furthermore, in spite of the fact that the Enlightenment was not especially enlightened as far as women were concerned, it did bring some changes, in that the 18th-c. emphasis on (male) individualism gave women a model and a language for their own struggle.

2. Revolution to World War II

It was during the *Revolution that women came to political action in France. They demonstrated alongside men and also separately; they filled the *cahiers de doléances* with demands; they formed women's political clubs (women not being permitted to join or speak in most of the men's clubs). After 1793 the women's clubs were closed down, and women were literally sent back to the home. In 1792 Olympe de *Gouges published the celebrated *Déclaration des droits de la femme et de la citoyenne*, and other women equally made their mark as activists (Etta Palme d'Aelders, Pauline Léon, Claire Lacombe). The male revolutionaries were not favourable to these separate actions and ideas; nor was Napoleon, and his *Code Civil of 1804 reinforced women's subordination to the father or husband.

In spite of this, the early 19th c. saw the beginning of sustained political activity by and on behalf of women. They formed a fundamental part of the *Saint-Simonian and *Fourierist socialist movements (Claire Démar, Suzanne *Voilquin) in the 1830s, with their desire to found new societies with different relationships between the sexes. Even within these movements, however, some of these politically active women were marginalized by their 'unfeminine' behaviour and/or by their unacceptably radical ideas (Flora *Tristan, Pauline Roland). Saint-Simonian women also set up their own newspapers and spoke about the specific oppression of women, as a distinct form of oppression, as well as linking it with that of the working class. When, in 1848, universal male suffrage was introduced [see REPUBLICS, 2], women's subordination was felt even more strongly. As in previous periods of revolution, women's clubs and newspapers had been started after the February Days, only to be suppressed in June. Jeanne Deroin, a working-class feminist inspired by Utopian socialism, did not give up, but presented herself as a candidate in the 1849 legislative elections in the name of republican integrity— liberty, equality, and fraternity for all. Her candidacy was not admitted because she was a woman.

In the Second Empire, particularly in its later, more liberal, period, women sought to improve their rights within the context of the existing French state. The distinction between two types of feminism (one contesting the bourgeois republic, the other working to improve women's lives and extend women's rights within it) was, possibly artificially, asserted by women involved in the nascent *socialist movement. The type of feminism thought of as liberal humanist feminism had its focus on legislative reform: demands such as improved educational opportunities for women, the right to divorce, and other reforms of the Code Civil— protection for women workers, concern for the moral welfare of working-class women—as well as the first calls for female suffrage, continued into the Republican decades of the 1870s and 1880s (Maria Desraismes, André Léo, Marguerite *Durand). It is possible to trace the achievements of this liberal humanist feminism via a chronology of legislation and of pioneering actions. Some women identified themselves, at least briefly, as both socialist and feminist (Hubertine Auclert, Madeleine *Pelletier), while for others, class politics always came first (Louise *Michel, Louise Saumoneau). The relationship between the two areas of struggle has never been simple.

In the 20th c. suffrage became far more central to feminist concerns (Jane Misme, Cécile Brunschvicg), as did the question of peace (Hélène Brion) and, influenced by the neo-Malthusians and following the 1920 laws on contraception and abortion, the issue of birth control (Nelly Roussel, Madeline Pelletier).

The influence of feminism on socialism, or the effect of socialist feminism on women's lives and status, is harder to gauge as it cannot be judged by concrete achievement. The struggle of socialist women meant that they engaged with the Republic, which oppressed them as workers and as women, with the theory of Marx, which ignores gender, and with the misogyny of their socialist brothers. This multiple struggle continues within all the parties of the Left on the level of theory and in daily practice.

3. Since World War II

Post-war 'women's rights' feminism in France grew partly out of the pre-war campaigns, although with the granting of female suffrage (1944) different issues came to the fore. Frenchwomen voted for the first time in April 1945, and the principle of equal pay for men and women was asserted in the 1946 Décret Croizat. The 1950s seemed to be dormant as far as feminism was concerned, but in fact the ground for later achievements was being prepared. However, there was no self-defined feminist movement to lead any campaigns or to build on the foundations provided for feminist analysis by Simone de Beauvoir's Le *Deuxième Sexe* (1949).

The 1960s brought a rise in women's participation in the labour market, increased levels of schooling for girls, and a significant number of reforms brought about primarily through women's pressure-groups. Reform of the marriage laws (1965) and the liberalization of the laws on contraception (1967) were the most far-reaching of these. The presidency of Valéry Giscard d'Estaing (1974–81) is often characterized as a period during which society became more open and tolerant, and during which women's rights made progress. In 1974 a secretary for the condition of women (Françoise *Giroud) was appointed, made a frustrated attempt to improve women's situation, and resigned after two years; but also in 1974 the law legalizing abortion subject to certain conditions was brought to parliament by minister of health Simone Veil, and became law in 1975. Divorce by mutual consent also became possible (1974).

After the Socialist victory of 1981, Yvette Roudy became the first minister for women's rights in France and continued a tradition of issue-based feminism within the broader challenge of changing 'les mentalités'. The Ministry also developed new sets of priorities, some of which caused havoc and provoked outraged opposition: the law on professional equality (1983); commissions to reform language practices and to change images of women in schoolbooks; the attempt to enact an anti-sexist law. Other issues, still relatively taboo—such as sexual harassment and domestic violence—were raised publicly for the first time.

This 'women's rights' feminism made great progress in the 1980s, but still faced problems: equality may have been achieved in law, but it remained mainly theoretical, and the implementation and monitoring of legislation was not always possible. Women still formed a tiny part of the political, intellectual, and business élites in France, while providing the majority of the low-paid, unskilled workers and of the unemployed. Abolished during the 1986-8 period of political 'cohabitation', the Ministry for Women's Rights was not replaced at such a high level after the return to power of a Socialist government in 1988. Under prime minister Michel Rocard there was a junior minister responsible for women's rights (Michèle André); being without the status, the prestige, the budget of a full minister, she remained fairly low key. The appointment in 1991 of Édith Cresson as France's first woman prime minister was accompanied, however, by an increase in the number of women in high-level political positions.

4. The MLF

After *May 1968 a different form of feminism was born, known as the Mouvement de Libération des Femmes (MLF). Sharing in the upheaval of ideas of the May movement, while experiencing marginalization within the movement itself, MLF feminists decided to form women-only consciousness-raising groups, in order to understand women's oppression, identify the oppressors, and seek collective solutions. These feminisms (for they were many) broke from a 'women's rights' focus, condemning participation in politics as 'reformist', whereas the new—or second-wave—feminisms were considered to be 'revolutionary'. Some of the MLF feminisms gave priority to the relation between women's oppression and class oppression (*tendance lutte des classes*); others suggested a complete separatism and

development of a woman-centred existence (Psych et Po, short for Psychanalyse et Politique [see DES FEMMES]). Seeking acceptance into a male-dominated and male-defined world was no longer the goal; it was replaced by a direct challenge to so-called male values, a revaluing of feminine specificity, a challenge to the foundations of knowledge as well as to the corner-stones of society (the family, heterosexuality).

MLF feminists engaged in political action mainly as pressure-groups, preferring to remain outside party politics. The most successful mobilizing campaign of the earliest post-'68 years was for the legalization of abortion, but a whole range of initiatives began, from a number of feminist journals to communes and courses. Feminism claimed that the personal was political and that this had to be demonstrated in women's lives.

Contemporary feminist thinking is reflected in—and indeed gave rise to—a rich textual production. Women write about their own lives and about women's lives in general (*Ernaux, *Rochefort, *Letessier, *Cardinal, *Leclerc); there has been important and innovative theoretical work concerned with gender and class, psychoanalysis and language, epistemology, history (Guillaumin, *Delphy, *Irigaray, *Cixous, *Le Dœuff, *Kristeva, Fraisse, Fauré, *Perrot); there has been experimentation within fiction (*Duras, *Chawaf, Cixous) and theatre; Beauvoir has been read and reread, admired and criticized, while remaining present as activist as well as figurehead until her death in 1986. Feminism is concerned with the production of woman-centred theory, and feminist scholars took issue with the male masters dominant in the 1970s—Freud, *Lacan, *Structuralists and *Post-Structuralists. The intellectual exploration associated specifically with French feminism in recent years has concerned the Lacanian positing of woman as unknowable, indefinable 'other', a view challenged by those who seek to discover a non-patriarchal feminine identity and a post-patriarchal existence for women in the late 20th c.

While Lacan posited 'woman' as unknowable, as inevitably 'other' and excluded from the symbolic, feminist theoreticians have suggested ways of undermining the phallocentric and logocentric symbolic order which positions woman in this way. Key concepts connected with 'the feminine' for Luce Irigaray and Hélène Cixous, for instance, are multiplicity (which operates at both the sexual and the discursive level) and alterity, which suggests a femininity that is something else, different—but different on its own terms. Challenging the supremacy of the Phallus and the Logos might be achieved through the multiplicity and the alterity inherent in female sexuality, through language, and through writing [see ÉCRITURE FÉMININE]. The subversion of notions surrounding the subject, identity, and meaning—notions introduced by male philosophers—has been used by feminists (although the theoreticians named here and usually identified as 'French feminists' would not necessarily accept the label) to imagine a post-phallocentric, post-logocentric world of alterity which does not always consider the feminine in relation to the (superior) masculine and does not keep women subordinate to men. [CD]

See M. Albistur and D. Armogathe, *Histoire du féminisme français* (1977); H. Bouchardeau, *Pas d'histoire, les femmes* (1977); E. Marks and I. de Courtivron (eds.), *New French Feminisms* (1980); M. Perrot, 'Naissance du féminisme', in *Le Féminisme et ses enjeux: 27 femmes parlent* (1988); C. Duchen, *Feminism in France* (1986); G. Duby and M. Perrot (eds.), *Histoire des femmes*, Vols. 4 and 5 (1991, 1992).

Femmes, see SOLLERS.

Femmes illustres, Les, see SCUDÉRY, M. DE.

Femmes savantes, Les. Five-act comedy by *Molière, first performed 1672. Three members of a middle-class household—Philaminte, Chrysale's wife, her sister Bélise, and her daughter Armande—are obsessed with the life of the spirit to the exclusion of that of the flesh and devote their time to philosophy and literature. Philaminte wishes her other daughter Henriette to marry Trissotin, a *précieux* author [see PRECIOSITY]; but Henriette loves Clitandre, who has the support of Chrysale and his brother Ariste. By spreading a false rumour that the family's fortunes have been lost, Ariste exposes Trissotin as interested only in Henriette's money; Clitandre remains loyal to her, and is rewarded with her hand. Trissotin is a thinly disguised portrait of *Cotin; his companion in the play, the pedant Vadius, was said to represent *Ménage. [IM]

FÉNELON, François de Salignac de la Mothe- (1651–1715). French churchman and mystic whose extensive writings also display a versatile talent as educationalist, story-teller, and constitutional theorist, and whom banishment from the court of *Louis XIV transformed into an epitome of dignified political exile.

The scion of a noble but impoverished family of the Périgord, he was educated for the Church, first at Cahors, then at Paris, where he shone as a preacher—his *Dialogues sur l'éloquence*, posthumously published in 1718, date from this time—and as an energetic rural missionary to Protestants. He was taken up by the devout circle around Madame de *Maintenon, became superior of the Nouvelles Catholiques (an institute for newly converted Huguenot girls) from 1679, and wrote the *Traité de l'éducation des filles* (1687). In 1689 he was appointed tutor to the duc de Bourgogne, grandson of the king. His most enduringly popular works were written for his difficult royal pupil, though published later. In the enchanting *Dialogues des morts composés pour l'éducation d'un prince*, based on the young prince's own exercises in composition, leading figures of antiquity and modern times converse with hindsight on power, corruption, destiny, and the vanity of human ambition. Classical and natural themes were inculcated by prose fables and short stories. *Télémaque*, the famous pedagogical romance, is based on the same fusion of classical narrative with moral, indeed constitutional, lessons.

He seemed destined for great worldly success: his pupil adored him; he basked in the approval of *Bossuet, tutor to the earlier royal generation; he was elected to the Académie Française in 1693, and appointed archbishop of Cambrai in 1695. But while at court he had developed an interest in Christian mysticism, and he fell under the spell of Madame *Guyon at the very moment when Madame de Maintenon had grown suspicious of her promoting the principles of *Quietism among the young. Though it was at Fénelon's suggestion that Bossuet was called in to advise, he was shocked at his mentor's treatment of the issue and appealed to wider opinion, first by an approach to Rome and eventually in his *Explication des maximes des saints* (1697), a point-by-point attempt to justify the disputed doctrines. Opinion at court turned against him. In the year of the *Explication* he was ordered to reside in his diocese, and early in 1699 he was formally discharged from his duties as tutor. Two months later came a papal condemnation of his book engineered by Bossuet with the support of Louis XIV. The latter's suspicions were doubtless confirmed when, weeks after, an unauthorized edition of *Télémaque* began to circulate, for it was easy to interpret its author's message to his pupil as a serious critique of the regime. The disgrace was total.

Fénelon never saw Versailles again. In a celebrated gesture of submission he proclaimed from the pulpit of his own cathedral the brief of Innocent XII forbidding the faithful to read the *Explication*. His episcopal administration, zeal against *Jansenism, and charitable hospitality towards armies fighting in Flanders became legendary. *Saint-Simon's *Mémoires* draw an unforgettable portrait of this phase of his life. His well-bred manners and almost feline subtlety of mind emerge, too, from the vast correspondence he maintained in exile, much of it unpublished until recently, though his letters of spiritual direction came out in 1718; and his *Lettre à l'Académie française* of 1714 is an influential contribution to aesthetics in the aftermath of the *Querelle des Anciens et des Modernes. But his political views remained unchanged. Already, from the *Lettre à Louis XIV*, probably written early in 1694 and never sent, more distinctly from *Télémaque*, and unambiguously from the *Tables de Chaunes*, composed with the duc de Beauvilliers in 1711 as an explicit manifesto, one can deduce a programme of reforms based on a theory of the ancient constitution which absolutism is deemed to have perverted. The independence of the Church and the nobility are to be restored, the good of the people to be preferred to the self-aggrandizement of the monarch. There was a real chance of translating such policies into reality when, on the death of the grand dauphin in 1711, the duc de Bourgogne became the heir-apparent to his elderly grandfather. It was widely assumed that Fénelon would be the leading personality of the new reign. All hopes were dashed when the new dauphin himself died, aged only 20, in 1712. By a final irony, Fénelon's own death (from complications arising from a road accident) in January 1715 preceded his still-implacable enemy Louis XIV's by a mere eight months.   [PJB]

See J.-L. Goré, *L'Itinéraire de Fénelon* (1957); V. Kapp, *Télémaque de Fénelon* (1982).

FÉNÉON, Félix (1861–1944). The most important French art critic of the late 19th c., Fénéon defined the theoretical and formal basis of Neo-*Impressionism in his 1886 brochure, *Les Impressionnistes en 1886*. As an editor of avant-garde literary journals he played an important part in the *Symbolist movement and was one of the group of 30 tried in 1894 for anarchist sympathies.   [JK]

FERAOUN, Mouloud (1913–62). Algerian novelist, one of the first of Muslim descent to publish significant works in French. Born in Kabylia, a Berber-speaking region to the east of Algiers, he was educated and in turn taught in French colonial schools. A friend of *Roblès and later of *Camus, he was influenced by these and other authors of *pied-noir* (settler) origin, but was one of the earliest voices to articulate in French the experiences of Algeria's indigenous population. During the *Algerian War he was torn between respect for French humanist values and the desire to see an end to colonial oppression. He was assassinated by the OAS, a terrorist organization run by colonial die-hards, a few days before the conclusion of the Évian peace agreements which brought independence to Algeria.

Feraoun's first novel, *Le Fils du pauvre* (1950), is highly autobiographical. Its opening pages, in which the narrator-protagonist, Menrad Fouroulou, contrasts his insider's view of Kabyle society with that of casual tourists, typifies the way in which early Algerian novelists continued to address an essentially French audience even while distancing themselves from the colonial standpoint. The remainder of the novel focuses on Menrad's experiences as a schoolboy of peasant origin in French Algeria.

In his second novel, *La Terre et le sang* (1953), as in the series of tableaux collected in *Jours de Kabylie* (1954), Feraoun's picture of life in Kabylia is again tailored to a French audience. The pretext for these descriptions in *La Terre et le sang* is the return to his native village of the protagonist, Amer, after having spent 15 years as an immigrant worker in France. Algeria's indigenous traditions are explained to Amer's French wife, Marie, as she attempts to integrate into village life. The sequel, *Les Chemins qui*

montent (1957), features their son, also called Amer, who is better educated and more critical of the colonial system than was the older man. At the same time, the unsympathetic portrayal of Mokrane, a fanatical Muslim, suggests that little would be gained from a return to Algeria's pre-colonial culture. The younger Amer's suicide appears emblematic of the impasse into which many of Algeria's French-educated élite felt themselves to have been led by the political and cultural contradictions endemic in the colonial system.

In *Les Poèmes de Si-Mohand* (1960) Feraoun presented and translated an important collection of Kabyle poetry. The posthumously-published *Journal* (1962) kept by him during the war of independence is one of his most powerful pieces of writing. It is a candid and stoical account of his attempt to maintain a sense of personal integrity while being pressurized from all sides to commit himself unequivocally to one or other of the warring camps. Miscellaneous essays and unpublished writings were collected in *Lettres à ses amis* (1969) and *L'Anniversaire* (1972).   [AGH]

See C. Achour, *Mouloud Feraoun: une voix en contrepoint* (1986).

Fergus, see ANGLO-NORMAN LITERATURE, 3a.

Fermiers généraux, see TAXATION.

Fermina Marquez, see LARBAUD.

FERNANDEZ, Dominique (b. 1929). Distinguished Italianist, son of Ramon *Fernandez. His prolific output (some 30 books since *Le Roman italien et la crise de la conscience moderne*, 1958) includes *Les Événements de Palerme* (1966), psycho-biographies of Pavese (1967) and Eisenstein (1975), writings on choral music, opera, and travel, a novel of the 'castrati', *Porporino ou les Mystères de Naples* (1974, Prix Médicis), and *Dans la main de l'ange* (1982, Prix Goncourt), an 'imaginary' biography of Pasolini. Though his neo-Freudianism has become less prominent since *L'Arbre jusqu'aux racines* (1972) and *L'Étoile rose* (1978), in which the narrator's homosexuality, courageously assumed, reflects the author's, psycho-affective as well as cultural influences are powerfully acknowledged in *L'École du sud* (1991) and *Porfirio et Constance* (1992), which mediate the lives of the writer's parents through the traditional theme of conflict between north and south.   [WK]

FERNANDEZ, Ramon (1894–1944). Emblematic committed intellectual of the inter-war years, who established his literary and philosophical credentials in works such as *Messages* (1926), *De la personnalité* (1928), and a *Vie de Molière* (1929). Mexican by birth but French-educated, a contributor to the *Nouvelle Revue Française* from 1923 until 1943 and a member of the *Gallimard Comité de Lecture, Fernandez also published two novels (*Le Pari*, 1932, Prix Fémina; *Les Violents*, 1935) and an ideological treatise, *L'Homme est-il humain?* (1936). A militant anti-fascist in 1934–5, he joined *Doriot's Parti Populaire Français in 1937; wartime studies of *Proust and *Barrès partly redeemed the dogmatic excesses of his collaborationism, without recapturing the promise of his early years.   [WK]

Ferney. The estate just across the border from Geneva where Voltaire settled in 1758 [see VOLTAIRE, 4].

Ferraille, see REVERDY.

FERRAND, Anne de Bellinzani, présidente (1657–1740). French writer known for her novels of women unhappily married, especially the *Histoire nouvelle des amours de la jeune Bélise et de Cléante* (1689). Her *Lettres galantes* (1691) is a one-sided epistolary novel indebted to the *Lettres portugaises.* Ferrand's own unhappy marriage to a prominent magistrate was fabled; it ended in legal separation in 1686.   [JDeJ]

FERRÉ, Léo (1916–93). Singer-songwriter, composer, conductor, also poet, novelist. He is one of the masters of the genre of *chanson française.* His unfulfilled ambitions as a classical composer and his love of French poetry combined to produce some of the most memorable of modern popular songs ('Jolie Môme', 1960; 'Avec le temps', 1972), including settings of poems by *Rutebeuf, *Baudelaire, *Verlaine, *Rimbaud, *Apollinaire, and *Aragon. His career began in the night-clubs of Saint-Germain-des-Prés in 1947, and he developed slowly from Left-Bank cult figure to nationally known music-hall star by 1960. Transformed by the combination of a domestic crisis and the events of *May 1968, his long-held anarchist sympathies led him to express the revolt of a younger generation in violent texts, declaimed rather than sung against the accompaniment of a rock band ('Le Chien', 1969) or a symphony orchestra ('Il n'y a plus rien', 1973). He moved to Italy in the early 1970s, and his subsequent self-produced recordings celebrated his love of classical music and his identification with the Romantic figure of the artist as prophet and outcast ('Les Artistes', 1977).   [PGH]

Ferrements, see CÉSAIRE, A.

FERRON, Jacques (1921–85). Canadian writer. He was born in Louiseville and attended the Collège Brébeuf with Pierre Trudeau. He was saved from the worst effects of this élitist education by appointments as a doctor at the Valcartier military base and on the Gaspé peninsula, and practised for most of his career in the working-class Ville Jacques-Cartier (Montreal). He deplored the consequences of mass urbanization. One of the most original and independent writers in Quebec, he revelled in polemics, and elevated letters to the press into a literary genre. Over 200 of these have been collected by Pierre Cantin in *Les Lettres aux journaux* (1985); here, with wit and cruel sarcasm, Ferron denounces medical neglect and the shocking state of mental-health provision, defends young extremists in the 1960s against the near police-state conditions resulting from terrorism, debunks Quebec stereotypes, demolishes writers and critics. This pugnacious and playful spirit pervades most of his work as a novelist, short-story writer, playwright, and essayist. Confessing his lack of inventiveness as a story-teller, he reworks universal myths—Orpheus in *Le Ciel de Québec* (1969), where he pillories *Saint-Denys Garneau and his friends; the Annunciation in *Papa Boss* (1966); Alice in Wonderland in *L'Amélanchier* (1970). *Le Salut de l'Irlande* (1970) tilts at the notion of the racial purity of the *Québécois.* The Parti Rhinocéros which he founded aimed at a similar ironic treatment of Canadian federal politics.   [CRPM]

FERRY, Jules (1832–93). Third-Republic politician, twice prime minister, who is remembered (and commemorated in the name of many *lycées*) as the architect of the *lois Ferry* (1881–2) which brought in free compulsory primary *education for all. He was assassinated by a madman.

Fête des Fous, La, see SOTIE.

Fêtes révolutionnaires. Revolutionary France publicly celebrated such a multiplicity of things, in such differing ways, that it is perhaps more accurate to talk, not about *fêtes révolutionnaires,* but *fêtes de la Révolution française.* Similarly, though it is unwise to generalize about these complex phenomena, it is probably helpful to distinguish between early and later *fêtes.* The early *fêtes* (1789–91) tended to reflect local habits and to be a happy mixture of old (religious) and new (civic) elements: the former (Mass; *Te Deum*; sermons) betokened continuity, a keeping of faith with an avowable past, while the latter expressed gratitude and support for political regeneration. They were uniformly fervent affairs. With their classical décor, pealing bells, patriotic songs, stirring speeches, fraternal embraces, and solemn oath-taking, their military formations, flags, drums, bugles, clarion calls, and cannonades, they constantly appealed to the senses and the emotions.

These early *fêtes* (given the preponderance of the military elements) seemed to gravitate increasingly around, even be initiated by, the *Garde Nationale. Its presence seems to have been organizationally decisive: all the later *fêtes* (1792–4)—almost always decided on by, and decreed from, Paris—adopted the same symmetrical, tightly controlled, highly organized approach. The Revolutionaries were passionately interested in the civic education of the citizen and sought to entrust this undertaking to the theatre, to the popular societies and, not least, to the *fêtes.* The festivals devised by the technocrats and the doctrinaire Revolutionaries were, therefore, not an end in themselves, but an enabling mechanism towards the ultimate implementation of great political designs: the Republic started to commemorate

Feudal Dues

dates of Revolutionary history or to celebrate new divinities, new martyrs, new guiding principles. Such new *fêtes* (their rationale is conveniently summarized by Robespierre in his *Rapport sur les rapports . . .*) imposed in turn new dogmas (**Déclaration des droits de l'homme*, the Constitution, etc.), new ceremonial or ritual practices, and created a symbolism surrounded by mystical veneration (e.g. the Tricolor, the Tree of Liberty). The intention, irrespective of *fête*, was to engineer an exhilarating, sacralizing contact with political rightness, to foster selfless devotion to the *res publica*, and therewith to create a rampart against the possible decadence and decay of the Revolution itself.

These attempts to create and to perpetuate a sacred sense of communal purpose should have been successful. All the lessons of antiquity, the insights of *Rousseau and the **philosophes* theoretically favoured the Republican innovators. Their highly stylized, austere, regimented *fêtes* served gradually, however, to alienate all save the fanatically committed. The break with time-honoured local preferences was too great and too rapid. Though still part of Republican ritual down to 1799, the *fête révolutionnaire* was in reality moribund by mid-1794.   [JR]

See M. Ozouf, *La Fête révolutionnaire* (1976); *Les Fêtes de la Révolution*, Colloque de Clermont-Ferrand, 1974 (1977).

Feudal Dues. Honorific or useful rights attached to the medieval and early modern *seigneurie*, known loosely throughout the *ancien régime* as *droits féodaux*, and abolished during the *Revolution. Honorific seigneurial rights included the privilege of a pew in church, keeping pigeons, hunting, and fishing. Useful, profitable rights were in the form of quitrents; labour services (*corvées*); the *champart*, a levy in kind of a small proportion of the crop; the *cens*, originally a money equivalent to labour but which soon became a nominal sum because of inflation; and *banalités*, the monopoly of the mill, oven, and press for flour, bread, and grapes in the fief.

The incidence of these dues varied considerably from region to region and is now impossible to calculate precisely. In the south, where the principle was 'nul seigneur sans titre', the system weighed very lightly, if at all. In the north, the customary assumption was 'nulle terre sans seigneur' and the burden was much heavier. Even so, it has sometimes been exaggerated, for it rarely amounted to as much as one-twelfth of the peasant's income. However, in provinces like Brittany and Burgundy heavy payments were often exacted by the lords. *Beaumarchais's *droit du seigneur* was, of course, an amusing invention, but many historians have contended, arguably, that in the last decades of the *ancien régime* dues were exacted more systematically and with a keener sense of profit. It is certain that dues were increasingly resented by the peasantry in the pre-Revolutionary decades.   [PRC]

Feudalism was not a term used in the medieval period; but the adjective 'feodalis' was found in the 12th c., and the noun 'feudum' went back to Carolingian times. Recent research on the vocabulary and institutions regarded as feudal has revealed so wide a range of often-conflicting ideas, both among medieval people and among historians, as to lead to a call for the abandonment of the category in historical research. But there can be no justification for abandoning the study of words actually used in the medieval period. And as for 'feudalism', it seems better to define it clearly and continue to use it, rather than to let a term that has played so rich a part in historiographical tradition become incomprehensible to future generations.

To economic historians, feudalism is the exploitation of dependent peasants' labour by an aristocratic landowning class. To lawyers and constitutional historians, it implies the enforcement of law and exaction of taxes, not by the state, but by landowners. And to social historians, it is a system of social relations dependent on vassalage and fiefs. Because these conceptions differ so markedly, it is scarcely surprising that there has long been disagreement as to when, if ever, feudalism existed. On the other hand, though not confined to the medieval world, all three types of feudalism were found at different times and to different degrees in medieval societies. And the conceptions continue to be useful in highlighting distinctive aspects of medieval life, even if historians no longer regard any of them as either adequate or precise descriptions. Though the two great authoritative studies of the subject, Marc *Bloch's *La Société féodale* and F. L. Ganshof's *Qu'est ce que la féodalité?*, now seem over-schematic, they still contain material of great value. It would be unfortunate if the search for ideal categories led to the destruction of the traditional ones before better had been established.

For those interested in medieval literature, feudalism usually refers to the networks of relationships between lords and their men that flourished in the High Middle Ages, and were extensively described in the **chansons de geste*. In **Raoul de Cambrai*, for example, Raoul's acceptance of Bernier into his household and his gift of arms to the youth creates an obligation on Bernier which transcends his duty to his mother. The poem investigates the point at which the lord's ill-treatment of his man justifies the man's disloyalty, and whether the slaying of a lord by his man should be regarded as treason, even after a formal renunciation of fealty. The connection between this theme and the historical realities either of the late 12th c., when the poem was composed, or of the 10th c., when the historical Raoul de Cambrai lived, has been much debated.

Historians are hampered by a relative absence of sources in their attempts to aid literary experts on so contentious a question. Lord–man relationships, which had their roots in both the Roman and the Germanic worlds, were commonplace in the

*Carolingian empire. Yet they apparently acquired new vigour and definition in the later 9th and the 10th c., which saw the development of a more militarized society, of castles, and of bands of professional soldiers employed to defend great churches and comital palaces, and tied to their employers' service by bonds of vassalage. Most historians would therefore agree with Marc Bloch in seeing this as the 'first feudal age'. But because the social ties under investigation bound laymen, they were discussed in the vernacular and not recorded. The Latin texts that survive for the period before 1200 cast only a partial and sometimes distorting light on the issue. Nevertheless, because they are all we have apart from the vernacular poems, they have to be exploited. Most of these sources fall into two categories: didactic writings by the clergy, and charters or other legal documents.

There is a famous description of the obligations of a man towards his lord in the letter written in 1020 by Bishop Fulbert of Chartres to the duke of Aquitaine (see F. Behrends (ed.), *The Letters and Poems of Fulbert of Chartres* (1976), no. 51). Fulbert declared that a man must not injure his lord, must keep his secrets and his castles secure, must maintain his judicial rights and and all his possessions, and must not hinder him in the fulfilment of any of his plans. The bishop concluded that these somewhat negative commands should be complemented by helpful counsel and support on all occasions. And in return the lord should similarly aid his man. What he described was a bond of mutual insurance between unequals. The letter was deliberately constructed in mnemonic form, proof that its writer regarded it as of immediate relevance.

Legal records offer a rather different picture. To take one example, Norman charters show aristocrats holding castles of the duke of Normandy in return for services that, by the beginning of the 12th c., were normally restricted to castle guard, campaigning, and suit of court, but in emergencies could be far more exacting; these castellans then enfeoffed knights on much the same terms to help them fulfil their duties. This relationship has often been regarded as classically feudal—binding members of the military aristocracy, defining military obligations, involving the bestowal of a fief held contractually, and taking for granted the existence of a court for thrashing out disputes between lords and their men. But in the *Anglo-Norman realm this was combined with two other features that do not fit well into the classical picture: an army that was largely composed of soldiers paid for their services (i.e. not fighting in return for fiefs); and a ruler who not only maintained tight control over his tenants-in-chief but also intervened in the affairs of their tenants. In other words, feudalism here, far from conferring state rights on landowners, offered the state an alternative means of controlling its lesser subjects.

Fulbert's letter and the Norman charters mark the two poles of feudal discourse: the one concerned essentially with personal relations based on loyalty, very loosely and rather negatively defined; the other regulated by contract and law. It used to be thought that the first was expressed by a promise of fealty, suitable for free men, while the second demanded homage and an oath of vassalage, which in origin were exacted only from the unfree, though by the High Middle Ages they had largely lost their servile connotations. The difference was, therefore, not just a matter of perception, but of legal fact. But more intensive research on the lord–man relationship in various parts of France suggests that this is something of an oversimplification. Historians have tended to regard the south as less feudalized in the 11th and 12th c. than the north. But the content of lordship depended less on the form of oath demanded (which was determined by geography and custom), than on the ability of the lord to command obedience. And the contract was not usually irrevocable: an aggrieved man normally claimed the right publicly to renounce his loyalty to his lord, provided he also gave up any benefit he had received in return.

In the later 12th and the 13th c. French feudalism became more coherent, yet less relevant to spheres of life other than politics and law. The French kings tightened vassalic discipline, not only within the royal demesne, but also over their great princes, whom they constrained to submit to the decisions of the royal court [see MONARCHY]. The princes likewise attracted to their courts local lords who had hitherto preferred independence. But at the same time the fiefs of knights and lesser lords became hereditary, thus depriving great men of an element of their dominion. And local courts increasingly came under the control of local communities. With greatly improved communications, the rapid intensification of the money economy, the development of a land market, increasing reliance on mercenaries for warfare, and the declining military significance of local defences, by 1300 the conditions in which feudalism had flourished were fast disappearing. [See also FEUDAL DUES.]

[JHD]

See M. Bloch, *La Société féodale* (1939–40); F. L. Ganshof, *Qu'est-ce que la féodalité?* (1944): E. A. K. Brown, 'The Tyranny of a Construct: Feudalism and Historians of Medieval Europe', *American Historical Review*, 89 (1974), 1063–88.

Feu, Le, see BARBUSSE.

Feuillants, Club des. Club of right-wing, generally royalist Revolutionaries, formed in July 1791 by secession from the *Jacobins. Led by *Barnave, it was very influential for a brief period, but was eliminated from the political scene by the events of 1792 [see REVOLUTION, 1b].

FEUILLET, Octave (1821–90). Highly popular French novelist and dramatist. His blend of gentility and sentimentality secured for him a large public under the Second Empire, when social mobility and uncertain standards made his idealized images of the gentry congenial to the expanding class of novel-readers who looked to fiction for guidance on their 'betters'. They found it in *Roman d'un jeune homme pauvre* (1858), the tale of an apparently penniless young man and a rich heiress. The same vein is tapped in *Julia de Trécœur* (1872) and in plays like *Le Pour et le contre* (1853) and *La Belle au bois dormant* (1867). [SBJ]

FEUILLADE, Louis, see CINEMA.

Feuille villageoise, La, Revolutionary newspaper, see LITERACY.

FÉVAL, Paul (1817–87). Leading exponent of the **roman-feuilleton* who, with *Les Mystères de Londres* (1844), offered an early challenge to *Dumas's supremacy. It was, however, during the Second Empire that Féval came to dominate the market in serialized fiction. His most popular and effective novel was *Le Bossu*, which appeared in *Le *Siècle* in 1857. [BR]

FEYDEAU, Ernest (1821–73). Realist novelist and friend of *Flaubert. His most famous novel was the scandalous story of adultery and jealousy, *Fanny* (1858), published a year after **Madame Bovary* and compared by *Sainte-Beuve to Constant's **Adolphe*. He also wrote travel notes [see ALGERIA], a learned study of ancient funeral rites, essays, and plays. [PF]

FEYDEAU, Georges (1862–1921). Son of Ernest *Feydeau, he was the master *farceur* of the 1890s in France. While English farce of the Victorian period is cosy and genial, Feydeau's treatment of marital deceit and discord is sharply subversive of family life. His farce suggests a well-oiled machine designed to destroy order, rationality, and established pieties. *Labiche's world, though fantasticated, is rooted in ordinary life; Feydeau's is cruel, claustrophobic, and smacks of mania. The obsessive precision of his stage directions is matched by fiendishly complicated plots and a breathless tempo which whirls his characters along from one crisis to the next. Plot and props (electric bells, etc.) are primary, character is reduced to a cog in the machine. Failures of communication are endemic (mislaid notes, foreigners with poor French) and physical disabilities are played for laughs—Mathieu's stammer in *L'Hôtel du libre échange* (1894), Fontanet's bad breath in *Un fil à la patte* (1899). Ritual humiliation is common, as when 'la môme Crevette' is covered with a rug and used as a seat in *La Dame de chez Maxim* (1899). Feydeau represents the acme of farce as the disguised fulfilment of repressed desires. [SBJ]

Fierabras. A **chanson de geste* of the last quarter of the 12th c. explicitly linked with the *Chanson de *Roland*, not only by the roles allotted to Roland, Oliver, and Ganelon, but by a specific prediction of Rencesvals in the last *laisse*. The theme of the poem is the conversion of the giant Fierabras and the rescue and bringing to France from Rome of the relics of the Crucifixion, but in the depiction of battles, the exploitation of supernatural devices (including a healing balm associated with the Entombment), giants, and love-struck Saracen princesses, the epic is transformed into a **roman d'aventure*. 'Fierabras' later became a generic name for boastful warriors. [PEB]

Figaro. Barber, valet, man of wit and resourcefulness, a character in Beaumarchais's *Le *Barbier de Séville*, *Le *Mariage de Figaro*, and *La Mère coupable*.

Figaro, Le. In 1854 the press magnate Hippolyte de Villemessant resurrected a title previously used in 1826. Initially a weekly, *Le Figaro* became a political daily towards the end of the Second Empire (1866–7). The most lastingly successful of various *Boulevard newspapers, it revived the journalism of epigrams and society gossip exemplified by *Le *Mercure galant*. 'Parisian wit' flourished in columns adorned, from *Baudelaire onwards, by many stars of the French literary firmament. *Le Figaro* was not published between November 1942 and August 1944. Liberal-conservative in politics, the paper enjoyed renewed prestige under Pierre Brisson's stewardship (1944–64). In 1975 it became part of the group controlled by Robert Hersant. [MP]

Filles du feu, Les, see NERVAL.

Fils de la liberté, Les, see CARON.

Fils du pauvre, Le, see FERRAOUN.

Fils naturel, Le (1757). Sentimental domestic drama by Diderot, an illustration of the theories expounded in the three *Entretiens sur le Fils naturel* which were published with it; the composite volume makes up a curiously contradictory narrative.

Fin'amor. In the 18th and 19th c., when French scholars first began to interest themselves in medieval texts, they called the kind of love they found there *amour chevaleresque*. Later in the 19th c. Gaston *Paris pioneered the use of the term *amour courtois* or 'courtly love', which is still used widely today. The term most usually found in medieval texts of the 12th c., however, is *amour fine*, equivalent to the Occitan *fin'amor*, which means something more like 'true love' or 'pure love'. (In Medieval French and Occitan *amour|amor* is feminine; hence the adjectival agreement *fine*, or *fin'*, for *fina*.)

This variety in terminology highlights the problem of characterizing an emotion which is experienced at the level of the individual, but also helps to give shape and direction to a wider community that we might call 'courtly culture'. The term *amour chevaleresque* centres emotion on the male lover-hero, a lover who is also a knight. *Lancelot would be an obvious example: engaged in a constant series of chivalric encounters, he fights, at least in part, because inspired by love, and is loved, at least in part, because of his successes as a knight. Individual emotion, on this account, expresses itself primarily in action, which, although placed at the service of the lady, also serves the interests of community since the hero's opponents merit their defeat.

The term *amour courtois* highlights instead the requirements of decorum and discretion in love. It helps direct our attention to the ways in which love is regulated by principles of exchange in the same way as other feudal and courtly institutions. The lover, indeed, is involved in a complex way with his community, since the court helps to define his status and identity, and he in turn contributes to its welfare by his heroic actions. Individual emotion, on this account, is framed by social pressure and communal interest.

The term *amour fine*, finally, places the emphasis much more firmly on the individual sensibility of the lover, on his or her quality of interiority and personal inspiration. The metaphor is from metal refining; the term *esmeré*, 'refined (metal)', is often used as well, both by *troubadours and northern French writers. An extended example of this image occurs in the epilogue of *Li Roman du castelain de Couci* [see CHASTELAIN DE COUCI]: true lovers, purified in the fire, are cleansed of their weaknesses and enabled to endure their sufferings. These differences of nomenclature suggest a major shift in values, whereby what for medieval poets seemed 'personal' and 'inner', for later readers seemed 'communal' and directed outwards, into the sphere of action. In the 12th c., 'true' love seems to have offered a new experience of interiority, even though now it can appear as one more variant of the concern with sociality so evident throughout medieval literature.

A prominent role in the development of ideas of love in the Middle Ages was played by the *Tristan legend. Its importance is attested not only by the actual Tristan texts, but by the proliferation of allusions to the legend in troubadour and *trouvère lyrics from the early 12th c. onwards, and by the large number of narrative works (several of the romances of *Chrétien de Troyes, most notably his *Cligés*) which can be seen as recasting scenes or themes from it. The potion in the Tristan story was brewed in order that the married couple, Iseut and Mark, should fall in love with each other. It was intended, that is, to promote the existence of a single order: one where personal desire would merge with political advantage, and private sentiment be effortlessly integrated to the public institution of marriage. But although Iseut married Mark, it is she and Tristan who drink the potion by mistake, and consequently fall in love: their love is adulterous, if only by default, and the worlds of inner sentiment

and public institutions are driven irrevocably apart. An unbridgeable divide is created between two quite separate orders of reality. The domain of *fin'amor*, inhabited by the lovers and their confidants, lies sometimes alongside the public world of the king and his feudal barons (especially in what survives of Beroul's version of the Tristan), and sometimes outside it (as when one or both of the lovers are exiled from Mark's court; this is particularly characteristic of the ending of the Thomas version). But wherever love is located, it cannot be properly understood by people from the other world, an incomprehension responsible for many of the most famous scenes in the Tristan story, such as Iseut's ambiguous oath (which means one thing to her and Tristan, but something quite different to everyone else), or Mark's discovery of the lovers sleeping with the sword between them (which he interprets, wrongly, as proof of their innocence).

The separation between different worlds of value which in the Tristan legend is engendered by the potion is simply assumed in a large number of other texts that deal with *fin'amor*. It produces a wealth of irony. A frequent scenario of both *lyrics and *romances, for example, is the punishment of someone who opposes the lovers. This scenario is inherently paradoxical, in that the lovers' opponent is 'wrong' precisely because he is 'right': in terms of the public order, his suspicions are well founded, but the lovers, mysteriously entitled to protection, can ironically reverse the values of right and wrong. Irony is also exploited as a stylistic resource, to guarantee the discourse of the lovers against comprehension by others. Courtly rhetoric constantly appeals to a play of inclusion and exclusion. Elaborate metaphors, for instance, or other forms of indirectness such as allusion or euphemism, are offered to the discerning audience with the gratifying assurance that they alone will understand them; the vulgar and undeserving will have no share in their understanding.

Fin'amor remains the emotion of an élite even when, as is often the case, the emotion in question is not transgressive. In Old French narrative, love which leads to an uncontroversial wedding is more common than an adulterous affair conducted in the teeth of an existing marriage. (It is worth noting that it is always the wife who is the adulterous partner; she is the best placed to expose the irony, and indeed the anxiety, arising when an object acquired in a public contract turns out to be a subject with private desires of her own.) And in the poetry of the troubadours and *trouvères*, despite constant appeals for secrecy and discretion, there are virtually no explicit indications that the lady for whom the poet sings is married. The interiority of individual emotion always seems to be under threat, even if there is no apparent reason why the public order would condemn it. It can only survive in the noblest and best; and it can only be shared with other like-minded individuals—the constituents of what I earlier termed 'courtly culture'. *Fin'amor* is thus both individualistic and social in its orientation: it turns away from the existing social order to found a new (and perhaps imaginary) community of its own.

There are many theories about what historical circumstances led to the success of *fin'amor* as a literary theme. One line of thought, which has been in disfavour for some time and is probably due for revival, discerns analogies between it and developments in Christian spirituality in the 12th c. Current explanations look to changes in *feudal society, and especially in marriage practices. It could be, for instance, that *fin'amor*, with its emphasis on individual choice, was an appropriate ideology for an emergent monarchical state, in which relationships were perceived as being mediated via the abstract notion of the state rather than by the old, personal bonds of homage, and in which personal responsibility and private conscience were beginning to supersede earlier notions of honour and shame. This view is associated with the writings of R. H. Bloch. Or it could be that the gradual encroachment of the Church into marital law and practice focused fresh attention on love and emotional choice, and particularly on the status that being loved by a socially well-placed woman could confer on a man. Furthermore, the difficulties encountered by many young noblemen in finding a bride, when their families were reluctant to settle property on any of their children except the eldest son, may have made them a ready audience for the literature of *fin'amor*, offering them as it did fantasies of enhanced value and erotic success which were the reverse of their lived experience. This view is promoted by Georges *Duby.

Whatever the historical reasons for it, *fin'amor* marked a turning-point in European culture. It put gender at the top of the ideological agenda and gave to the feminine (though probably not to real historical women) a literary prominence never before enjoyed. Although diverse in its manifestations even in the 12th c., *fin'amor* was sufficiently vital to inspire poets throughout the Middle Ages and beyond. [SK]

See R. Boase, *The Origin and Meaning of Courtly Love* (1977).

Fin de partie, see BECKETT.

Fin de Satan, La, by Victor *Hugo, see LÉGENDE DES SIÈCLES, LA.

Fin de siècle, see DECADENCE.

Fiscal System, see TAXATION.

Flamboyants, Les, see GRAINVILLE.

Flamenca. This Occitan romance, sometimes also referred to as *Las Novas de Guilhem de Nevers*, was probably composed after 1263. Just over 8,000 lines of it survive in a single manuscript whose beginning

and end are lost. A dedicatory passage suggests the author's name was Bernardet, writing in the service of a lord of Alga in the Rouergue. Although composed in the extreme south of Occitania, the romance is set in northern France. The Flemish heroine, Flamenca, is married to a count of Bourbon who jealously locks her up, allowing her out only to church and to the spa baths. She is eventually seduced by another northerner, Guilhem de Nevers, who ingeniously poses as cleric. He whispers two syllables to her each time she comes to church, and arranges to meet her at the baths, where she 'heals' his lovesickness and vice versa. At the end of the surviving text Flamenca has persuaded her husband to trust her, and she and Guilhem carry on their affair under his nose without his realizing it. Guilhem's two-syllable messages combine with Flamenca's two-syllable replies to construct five lines of octosyllables strongly reminiscent of those lyrics of *Peire Rogier that represent an inner dialogue. Indeed, at every turn the behaviour of the lovers recalls the poetry of 12th-c. *troubadours. Multiply ironic, a work of extraordinary wit and poise, the romance seems to be offering a wry look at Occitan culture from the perspective of those who felt cut off from its heyday by the victory of the northern French in the Albigensian Crusade [see CATHARS]. [SK]

FLAMMARION, Ernest (1846–1936). French bookseller and publisher. He successfully launched his still-flourishing family publishing venture in 1867 with the *Astronomie populaire* of his brother, the astronomer Camille Flammarion. The firm published *Drumont (*La France juive*, 1885), Hector *Malot, *Colette, and a wide list of medical, scientific, geographical, and historical works, including the Père Castor children's series. [DAS]

FLAUBERT, Gustave (1821–80). French novelist, a major figure of world literature. Henry James called him the 'writer's writer' in recognition of his obsession with literary form, and Flaubert has been admired by many creative writers. He has also intrigued literary critics of every persuasion.

He grew up in accommodation attached to a hospital in Rouen, where his father was a well-known surgeon. He enjoyed his schoolwork, especially history, and developed a precocious literary talent from around the age of 14. His very early works repay study for their insight into Flaubert's psychology, and for their close thematic links with the mature works. Short stories such as 'Un parfum à sentir', 'La Peste à Florence', and 'Bibliomanie' (1838), or 'Quidquid volueris' and 'Passion et vertu' (1837), were followed by a romantic first-person confession, *Mémoires d'un fou* (1838), and a philosophical drama, *Smarh* (1839). Expelled from his *lycée* in 1839, he passed his *baccalauréat* by private study, and enrolled reluctantly as a law student in Paris. There he completed *Novembre* (1842), a pessimistic confession which was more sophisticated than *Mémoires d'un fou*, switching (*Werther*-like) from first to third person, and including an intercalated episode with Marie, a prostitute who initiates him sexually before recounting her own mirror-image story.

The writing of the first *L'Éducation sentimentale* (which shares only its title with the 1869 novel) was interrupted by the event that was to shape the rest of Flaubert's life. In January 1844 he suffered a major epileptic fit and entered a long period of recurrent illness. In his large-scale study of Flaubert, *L'Idiot de la famille*, *Sartre suggests that his epilepsy was hysterical, representing a radical option for failure and passivity, allowing him to escape the demands of the adult world and to accede, via the condition of *rentier*, to the status of an artist. Certainly the plot of *L'Éducation*, finished in 1845, reveals a shift of interest from the worldly Henry to Jules, an introspective would-be artist whose life to date has been a failure. And certainly it was agreed that Flaubert should give up the legal studies which he hated (he had failed his second-year examination in 1843). He adapted readily enough to life at Croisset, the house outside Rouen which his father purchased for the benefit of his son's health, and which was to be his home and writing-base for the rest of his life. The household was an unusual one, for Flaubert's father and sister both died early in 1846, leaving just Flaubert, his mother, and his baby niece Caroline, who was brought up by his mother.

In July 1846 Flaubert met Louise *Colet in Paris; the first phase of their intense but famously difficult relationship lasted nearly two years. Flaubert was unwilling to spend much time with her, despite the passion expressed in their almost non-stop correspondence. In 1847 he found time to spend three months on a walking holiday in Brittany with Maxime *du Camp. The two friends collaborated on a set of literary travel notes, *Par les champs et par les grèves*, writing alternate chapters. The year 1848 was marked less by the Revolution and its aftermath than by the death of a close boyhood friend, Alfred Le Poittevin, whose speculative, metaphysical bent no doubt influenced Flaubert's *La *Tentation de saint Antoine*. On its completion in 1849 Flaubert accompanied Du Camp on an 18-month expedition to Egypt and the Middle East, of which he produced a rich account in his letters and travel notes, and during which he seems to have clarified his aesthetic principles.

Flaubert's mature period can be seen to start here. He returned with a new sense of purpose, and a willingness to embark upon his first novel for publication. This was to be *Madame Bovary*, on which he worked for five years. Its early period of composition is admirably recorded in his correspondence with Louise Colet, with whom he renewed relations (albeit excessively spaced out), until finally breaking with her in 1854. Flaubert was acquitted in 1857 of the criminal charge of publishing a morally offensive book; the trial ensured the success of *Madame*

Bovary, and Flaubert, for the first time, became a well-known writer. From this time on he seems to have accommodated himself happily to Second Empire society. He had a close friend and literary advisor in Louis *Bouilhet, he corresponded and occasionally socialized with many of the literary and artistic figures of the day (*Sainte-Beuve, the *Goncourt brothers, *Gautier, and *Renan), and after the successful publication of *Salammbô* in 1862 he formed a friendship with the Princesse *Mathilde, cousin of the emperor. He was also close to George *Sand, despite their differing views on literature.

His life went less well from 1869. He was disappointed by the reception of *L'*Éducation sentimentale*, devastated by the death of Bouilhet, and experienced the collapse of the Empire in 1870 as the end of the world in which he felt at home. He despised both Prussians and *communards*. The early 1870s were marked by other bereavements: close friends, and above all his mother in 1872. Financial problems followed from the sale of property in 1875 (to rescue his niece's husband from bankruptcy), and by 1879 he was obliged to accept a small pension organized for him by his friends. However, he was befriended by a younger generation of writers in the late 1870s, published *Trois contes* in 1877, and had almost completed the first volume of *Bouvard et Pécuchet* when he died suddenly in May 1880.

Flaubert was less of a hermit than legend has it. Recent scholarship has interestingly revealed the existence of a long-standing relationship with Juliette Herbert, his niece's English governess, and over the years he clearly had many good friends. He pretended to hate everybody, and especially the French bourgeoisie, but he seems to have hated the working classes far more. His misanthropy (real or insincere), his obsession with *la bêtise* and with the *idées reçues* of the bourgeois world-view, the noisy humour that seems to have marked his social persona, are doubtless signs of an uneasy assumption of his own class position as a provincial *rentier*. For despite his pretence of disassociating his literature from ideological positions, the content of Flaubert's mature works, as much as their over-wrought language, is marked by an extraordinary tension. This finds its concrete form in an ironic tone and narrative attitude which are notoriously difficult to place.

[DK]

See J.-P. Sartre, *L'Idiot de la famille*, 3 vols. (1971–2); J. Culler, *Flaubert: The Uses of Uncertainty* (1974); D. Knight, *Flaubert's Characters: The Language of Illusion* (1985).

FLÉCHIER, Esprit (1632–1710). French orator and churchman, bishop of Lavaur (1685) and Nîmes (1687). Active as a young man in the literary salons of Paris (see his playful *Mémoires sur les Grands-Jours d'Auvergne*, 1665, published 1844), he was appointed *lecteur* to the dauphin in 1671 and received into the Académie Française in 1673 on the same day as

*Racine. A distinctly *précieux* elegance and wit [see PRECIOSITY] mark his preaching, especially the funeral orations for the great (*Turenne, Le Tellier, Maria-Teresa of Austria, Julie d'Angennes), which contemporaries loved to contrast with those of *Bossuet and on which his fame largely rests. They were first collected for publication in 1680.   [PJB]

FLERS, Robert de (1872–1927), and **CAILLAVET,** Gaston Arman de (1869–1915). French playwrights who, in collaboration before World War I, were fashionable purveyors of brittle and sophisticated plays about high society. They were not *farceurs*, like their near contemporaries *Courteline and *Feydeau, but versatile makers of light comedies of manners. Their style varies from the smart and cynical, in *Les Sentiers de la vertu* (1903), to the sentimental *L'Amour veille* (1907). When they resort to satire, their tone is waspish and their targets rather grand: the Assemblée Nationale in *Le Bois sacré* (1911); the Académie Française in *L'Habit vert* (1913).   [SBJ]

Fleurs de Tarbes, Les, see PAULHAN.

Fleurs du mal, Les. The title of *Baudelaire's great collection of lyric poems appears to have been suggested by the critic Hippolyte Babou (1824–78), and was first used by Baudelaire when he published a sequence of 18 poems under that title in 1855. A substantial proportion of the poems included in the first edition of *Les Fleurs du mal* had been completed by the mid-1840s, and at intervals during the 1840s and early 1850s Baudelaire announced their forthcoming publication, first under the title of *Les Lesbiennes* (1845–7) and then of *Les Limbes* (1848–51), under which title a sequence of 11 sonnets did indeed appear in 1851. When *Les Fleurs du mal* was published in book form in late June 1857 its often scabrous and sacrilegious content immediately attracted the attention of the authorities, and on 20 August 1857 Baudelaire was fined 300 francs by the Sixième Chambre Correctionnelle for 'outrage à la morale publique'; in addition, six poems in the collection were ordered to be suppressed. A second edition appeared in February 1861, 'rajeuni, accru et fortifié', in Baudelaire's words, by a large number of new poems composed in 1859–60, notably 'La Chevelure', 'Les Sept Vieillards', 'Les Petites Vieilles', 'Le Cygne', and the new collection's culminating piece, 'Le Voyage'.

In February 1866 Poulet-Malassis published the six banned poems, along with 17 other poems, in a Belgian edition entitled *Les Épaves*; the condemnation of 1857 was finally quashed in May 1949. A third edition of *Les Fleurs du mal* containing 25 extra poems, some of them juvenilia or discarded works, others (notably 'L'Imprévu' and 'Recueillement') post-1861 compositions, was prepared by *Banville and published after Baudelaire's death.

Baudelaire was adamant that his 'livre atroce' was not 'un pur album' and that the individual poems yielded their full significance only when read within the 'cadre singulier' in which he had set them. Introduced by the celebrated dedicatory piece 'Au lecteur', the 100 poems of the 1857 edition were divided into five sequences or 'chapters' ('Spleen et Idéal', 'Fleurs du mal', 'Révolte', 'Le Vin', and 'La Mort'), while a new section, 'Tableaux parisiens', was inserted into the revised structure used for the 126 poems of the 1861 edition. *Les Fleurs du mal* records, in poetry in which lyricism and irony are fused, the quest of divided modern man for an 'ideal'—variously sought in art, eroticism, travel, drugs, and political, social, and metaphysical revolt—that forever eludes him, plunging him back into the agony of isolation and despair that Baudelaire called 'spleen'. Oscillating from one extreme to another, the quest is open-ended, ever to be renewed, and takes the seeker beyond the realms of life and death 'au fond de l'Inconnu pour trouver du *nouveau*' ('Le Voyage').   [RDEB]

See J. Prévost, *Baudelaire: essai sur la création et l'inspiration poétiques* (1953); A. Fairlie, *Baudelaire: 'Les Fleurs du Mal'* (1960); F. W. Leakey, *Baudelaire and Nature* (1969).

FLEURY, André-Hercule, cardinal de (1653–1743). Having been Louis XV's tutor, he was minister of state from 1726 until his death. An adroit politician, jealous of his own power, he managed France's affairs cautiously and economically.

FLEURY, Claude, abbé (1640–1723). Historian and teacher. Educated by the Jesuits, he qualified as a lawyer, took orders in 1669, and was tutor to the children of 'le grand *Condé' and the grandchildren of *Louis XIV. A peaceful, studious man, he left a voluminous body of writings. His weightiest work is the *Histoire ecclésiastique* (1691 onwards, 36 vols., of which 20 by Fleury), in which narrative history alternates with summaries of patristic thought. It was placed on the Index because of its *Gallican tendencies. Other didactic writings include the *Catéchisme historique* (1679), *Les Mœurs des Israélites* (1681), and *Les Mœurs des chrétiens* (1682). Fleury's important *Traité du choix et de la méthode des études* (1683) lays stress on the value of sound, unprofessional reasoning, and offers a radical reclassification of studies: the useful (including economics and politics), the agreeable (including languages), and the useless (including scholastic philosophy). A similar originality is visible in his *Discours sur Platon*, written for the *Lamoignon academy in 1670, and in his advocacy of the grand sublimity of ancient Greek and, above all, Hebrew poetry (*Discours sur la poésie des Hébreux*). He is one of the most impressive of the *anciens* [see QUERELLE DES ANCIENS ET DES MODERNES].   [PF]

Fleuve caché, Le, see TARDIEU.

Fleuve détourné, Le, see MIMOUNI.

FLINS DES OLIVIERS, Louis Carbon de (1757–1806). Magistrate, poet, and during the

Revolution author of comedies, including a satire on monasticism, *Le Mari directeur* (1791).

Floire et Blanchefleur. Anonymous tale from the mid-12th c. in rhymed octosyllabic couplets. This brief 'roman idyllique' recounts the childhood love of Floire, a pagan prince, for Blanchefleur, daughter of a Christian captive. Born on the same day, the children grow up and are educated together; they fall in love as they read ancient love literature. But Floire's parents contrive to separate the lovers as they reach adulthood. Floire undertakes fantastic adventures to rescue Blanchefleur, who has been bought and held captive by the cruel, misogynistic emir of Babylon. After penetrating into the emir's domain by hiding in a flower-basket, Floire eventually tells the story of his voyage and moves the captor's court to mercy. Floire and Blanchefleur are joyously reunited; Floire inherits his parents' kingdom and converts to Christianity. An early version of the tale, sometimes dubbed 'aristocratique', incorporates allusions to Ovid and to the Troy legend; its author delights in describing luxurious and marvellous objects, such as Blanchefleur's false tomb or a golden cup decorated with the story of Troy. A later version abridges refinements and expands the chivalric content. [RLK]

Floovent. Short (2,500-line) *chanson de geste* of the early 13th c., the hero of which is thrown out of court for pulling a nobleman's beard, but returns triumphant after romantic adventures. The story has attracted interest because it may contain historical material from the reign of Clovis [see MEROVINGIANS]. [SK]

FLORIAN, Jean-Pierre-Claris de (1755–94). Born into a noble family in the Cévennes, he served in the army, and then devoted himself to letters in Paris, becoming a member of the Académie Française (1788). His health was broken by the prisons of the Revolution. His works include *romans héroïques*, pastoral idylls, and plays. These are generally sentimental and edifying, like his collection of *nouvelles* set in various countries, but the *nouvelles* are brief, simple, and well told. 'Le doux Florian' is remembered for his *Fables* (1792), the most successful attempts to imitate *La Fontaine, but lacking the liveliness and toughness of the original. [PF]

FLORIO, John (c.1553–1625). Translator. Born in London the son of an Italian Protestant, he taught languages and composed textbooks and a dictionary before publishing in 1603 his great translation of *Montaigne's *Essais*, a free yet faithful version which left its mark on innumerable English speakers, including Shakespeare. [PF]

Florus et Lyriopé, SEE ROBERT DE BLOIS.

FOIGNY, Gabriel (c.1630–1692). French writer. His *La Terre australe connue* (1676), always paired as a

*Utopia with that of *Veiras, tells of a virtuous, anarchic, and hermaphrodite society which is perfect as regards social organization and technological advance, but not entirely happy. The book is important for its *deism, or natural religion. [CJB]

Foire, Théâtres de la. Term used to cover a variety of popular entertainments which from the late 16th c. were presented at the two main Parisian fairs, the Foire Saint-Germain in winter and the Foire Saint-Martin in summer. The *forains* included jugglers, rope-dancers, and so on, but they also produced plays, above all *farces; by the late 17th c. these were rivalling the appeal of the official theatres, the *Comédie-Française and the *Opéra, whose monopoly of sung and spoken theatre they infringed, and who repeatedly had them outlawed. To get around legal bans the *forains* had recourse to such expedients as puppet plays, monologues, and in particular the *pièce à écriteaux*, in which a dumb-show was accompanied by placards of *vaudevilles for the audience to sing.

Their repertoire was essentially comic (with *Arlequin playing a central role); often their productions mocked and parodied the serious theatre of the time. Many of the shows were spectacular, enchantment being an important element; and, above all, music and words were closely interwoven. From 1715 the term *opéra-comique begins to be used for the fairground shows; the genre was subsequently developed by *Favart, whose Opéra-Comique fused with the *Comédie-Italienne in 1762. The *théâtres de *boulevard were the direct descendents of the *théâtres de la foire*.

Among the authors who wrote for the Foire were *Piron (see his remarkable monologue, *Arlequin-Deucalion*, 1772) and *Lesage, who wrote or colloborated on approximately 100 scripts between 1712 and 1735, and wrote the preface to the 10-vol. *Le Théâtre de la foire ou l'Opéra-comique* (1721–37). [PF]

Folie du sage, La, SEE TRISTAN L'HERMITE.

Folie Tristan, La, SEE TRISTAN.

Folk-tale. The French *conte populaire* belongs to the vast European treasure of folk-tales which has been extensively explored over the last two centuries. While unique versions of particular tales have been recorded in France, all are related to stories told throughout Europe and beyond. Nevertheless, researchers have usually recognized some specificity in the French tale, seeing it as less fantastic, more down-to-earth, than its Germanic or Slavonic counterparts.

The *conte populaire* is an oral genre, part of a popular culture which also includes song, dance, ritual, and custom. The stories, passed down from teller to teller by word of mouth, were more or less ritually recounted in a variety of settings, from long sea voyages to the village *veillée*, an evening gathering in which work combined with the pleasures of story and song. Story-telling was a skilled business, each *conteur* both re-enacting and renewing the traditional stock. The stories themselves have been grouped (though not without controversy) into a number of classes: the *conte merveilleux* (fairy-tale), the *conte d'avertissement* (warning tale), the animal story, the *légende* (recounting stories connected with local beliefs), and so on. It is essential to remember that these stories were not originally addressed to children, although many of them have become part of children's lore in recent times.

Except in certain limited milieux, the old practice of story-telling was virtually killed by the modernization of society. It hardly exists in present-day France—though it has held its own better in other francophone countries [see AFRICA (SOUTH OF THE SAHARA)]. Attempts have recently been made to rekindle the old embers, and story-telling has enjoyed a certain vogue, with festivals such as that of Saint-Rémy de Provence. For the most part, however, the *conte populaire* survives only in written records.

Folk-tales have been an important source for writers over the centuries; they have left their mark on texts as different as the medieval *fabliaux* and romances, the work of 16th-c. *conteurs* such as *Rabelais or *Du Fail, and the stories of modern writers from *Nerval to *Tournier. None of these gives direct access to the actual folk-tale. The first significant attempt to transcribe oral tales was *Perrault's *Histoires ou contes, which certainly draw on the spoken tradition to some extent (exactly how much remains a matter for dispute). However, Perrault adapted his material to the polite taste of his day, as did all the other *conteurs* who catered for the surprising vogue for fairy-tales at the end of the 17th c. [see SHORT FICTION].

Perrault's beautiful stories have had an unfortunate effect, in that for many readers they have obscured the real folk-tales from which they were drawn. What is more, their success and reuse in the chapbooks of the *Bibliothèque Bleue had a knockback effect on the original stories; by the time collectors began to record these more scientifically from peasant story-tellers, they often bore the marks of Perrault.

The serious recording of folk-tales came rather later in France than in many parts of Europe. The golden age was the period between about 1870 and 1920, which saw the foundation of journals such as the *Revue des traditions populaires* (1888–1919) and the publication of many collections of tales from different regions (e.g. Emmanuel Cosquin's *Les Contes populaires de Lorraine*, 1887). A second phase in the collection of folk-tales began after World War II, with modern methods of mechanical recording. In 1953, with the support of the CNRS, the Société d'Ethnographie Française began publication of the journal *Arts et traditions populaires*. Major research projects were undertaken (just before it was too late) in various parts of France and in French Canada,

where old French tales continued to be told. Brittany has been a particularly fruitful source of stories; *Hélias's *Les Autres et les miens* (2 vols., 1977) is both a re-creation in French of Breton stories from the Pays Bigouden and a celebration of the storyteller and traditional peasant culture. In similar fashion, *Pourrat produced his own version of stories of the Auvergne in *Le Trésor des contes* (1948–62).

The years 1953–6 saw the publication of seven volumes of *Contes merveilleux des provinces de France*, under the direction of Paul Delarue; since then, many other texts and recordings have been made available, notably the series of *Récits et contes populaires* launched by Gallimard in 1978. The essential scholarly work for the whole of France is, however, *Le Conte populaire français* (1957–) of Paul Delarue and Marie-Louise Ténèze, a complete catalogue with examples of all the principal story-types recorded. [PF]

See M. Simonsen, *Le Conte populaire français* (1981); G. Massignon, *De bouche à oreilles* (1983).

FOLLAIN, Jean (1903–71). French poet. Dedicated to simplicity of style and intimacy of focus, Follain's tenuous verse and scarcely weightier prose poems assiduously prospect a narrow vein of nostalgia, reconstructing glimpses of the country town of his childhood (*Canisy*, 1942). He insists on isolating trivial objects and gestures which, once poetically framed, emerge as poignant microcosms whose resonances transcend the minimalism of their overt content—as witness the poem 'Métaphysique' (from *Exister*, 1947), where the fragile bowl with the floral design which a countrywoman lifts up before her breasts becomes a cipher for human mortality and the sanctity of bodily existence.   [RC]

Folle Journée, La. The subtitle of Beaumarchais's *Mariage de Figaro.

FOMBEURE, Maurice (1906–81). French poet. Fombeure's first collection, *Silences sur le toit* (1930), reflected his desire to steer poetry away from lofty abstraction and linguistic excess towards a renewal of its popular roots and a natural simplicity—'la poésie des gouttes d'eau'. This orientation brought him into the orbit of *Cadou and the poets of the École de *Rochefort, with whom he collaborated. In the best poems of subsequent volumes, such as *A dos d'oiseau* (1942), *Sortilèges vus de près* (1947), *Le Vin de La Haumuche* (1952), Rabelaisian gusto blends successfully, or alternates effectively, with a more elegiac inspiration. Although his poetry is primarily rural, inspired by his native Touraine, Fombeure, a teacher by profession, was an habitué of the Brasserie Lipp in Paris and an enthusiastic celebrant of the literary life who impressed contemporaries with his ability to inject everyday living with humour and poetry.   [MHTS]

Fontainebleau. Château in the Île-de-France where in 1528 the mason-architect Gilles Le Breton remodelled a fortified hunting-lodge into a palace for *François Ier, housing his library (forerunner of the *Bibliothèque Nationale) and art collections.

The building, now much altered, is one of the best examples of French Renaissance architecture, Italianate but reaching out towards a distinctive French classical style (among its early architects were Serlio and *Delorme). Its decoration is equally important. Two artists dominate, the Florentine Giovanni Battista Rosso ('Le Roux') and Francesco Primaticcio from Bologna. The Galerie François Ier (1530s) was mainly decorated by Rosso in an Italian Mannerist style, with paintings and stucco (masks, swags, fruit, strap-work); the iconography show the king as Renaissance prince, Roman emperor, and classical god. Primaticcio decorated the Galerie Henri II (ballroom) and the Galerie d'Ulysse (1540s onwards); the latter was destroyed in the 18th c., but is known through engravings and tapestries and Primaticcio's Ulysses and Penelope, based on one of the panels.

The castle was the setting for royal ballets and other festivities (*Ronsard's Bergerie, 1563-4), and became known as a centre for artists and a style of art. The 'École de Fontainebleau' included Niccolò dell'Abbate, who assisted Primaticcio from 1552, and other artists working elsewhere, such as the sculptor Jean Goujon. To them must be added the engravers, notably Luca Penni, Léonard Thiry, and Jean Mignon: it was through engraving that the art of Fontainebleau became internationally known. The style of Fontainebleau is essentially decorative, characterized by its tall human figures, with long necks and small heads, moving with sensual grace through leafy landscapes studded with classical ruins. Later in the century there was a second school of Fontainebleau, of which the principal artists were Ambroise Dubois, Toussaint Dubreuil, and Martin Frémiet. At Fontainebleau French writers were able to look at Italian Renaissance art naturalized in a French setting and enjoy a visual representation of classical mythology and ancient history, the purpose of which was partly aesthetic pleasure and partly royal and national propaganda. The poets of the *Pléiade reflected this dual intention.   [PS]

See D. and E. Panofsky, 'The Iconography of the Galerie François Ier at Fontainebleau', in Gazette des Beaux-Arts, 2 (1958); L'École de Fontainebleau, exhibition catalogue, Grand Palais (1972); J.-J. Lévêque, L'École de Fontainebleau (1984).

FONTANES, Louis de (1757–1821). Important figure who typifies the Neoclassical moment in French literature in the Revolutionary and Empire periods. He had a significant influence on *Chateaubriand, who addressed his Lettres à Fontanes sur la campagne romaine (1804) to him. His own preferred genre was didactic poetry, but none of his works has found favour with modern readers. Although originally a free-thinker who sympathized with the early Revolution and went into exile, he later adopted a conservative stance and was supported by Bonaparte. He was editor of the *Mercure de France and grand-maître of the Napoleonic University. [BR]

FONTANIER, Pierre (1768–1844). Obscure French author of two works, Manuel classique pour l'étude des tropes (1821) and Les Figures autres que tropes (1827), both republished by *Genette as Les Figures du discours in 1968 during the *Structuralist revival of *rhetoric. Following *Du Marsais, they give a full account of the traditional classifications.   [PF]

FONTENELLE, Bernard Le Bovier de (1657–1757). French polymath whose career stretched from the middle of the reign of Louis XIV to the middle of the publication of the *Encyclopédie. In his long life (he died just short of 100), he wrote many works in many genres, from pastoral poetry to scientific treatise. Perhaps none of them is an undoubted classic, but together they make of him a figure of great importance, the first *philosophe, an example of critical modernity.

He was born in Rouen, a nephew of the *Corneille brothers—he championed Pierre against *Racine and was much helped by Thomas, whose scientific work he continued. With a Jesuit education and a degree in law behind him, he settled in Paris and was quickly involved in literary life in circles round the *Mercure galant. He was elected to the Académie Française in 1691, and in 1699 was appointed Secrétaire Perpétuel of the *Académie des Sciences, a post he occupied for over half a century. He frequented the *salons, in particular that of Madame de *Lambert, and received patronage from the Regent (a pension and a lodging in the Palais-Royal). He never married.

For him poetry was a frivolous activity associated with the childhood of humanity. But he wrote many poems, tragedies, comedies, and pastorals. These have sunk without trace; his tragedy Aspar (1680) was such a flop that its performance was maliciously described as the origin of the whistle of derision in the French theatre. His writings on literature are those of a rationalist, for whom the agreeable effects of poetry can be explained and codified. The Histoire du théâtre français (published 1742) shows an unexpected curiosity about medieval poetry, while the Digression sur les Anciens et les Modernes (1688), coming down on the side of the modernes, shows little respect for Homer and the primitive Greeks [see QUERELLE].

Fontenelle's important work was done in prose genres marginal to mainstream literature. The Nouveaux dialogues des morts (1683) modernize Lucian to express through paradox a sceptical and mocking assessment of humanity. The Entretiens sur la pluralité des mondes (1686) was a highly influential piece of scientific popularization; it expounds the Copernican world system and the mechanistic physics of *Descartes in elegant dialogues between a philosopher and a lady, speculating about the inhabitants of other planets and relativizing the importance of our own. The *Histoire des oracles* (1687) is a lesson in critical method; its demolition of unfounded notions about pagan oracles extends by implication to all irrational beliefs, including Christianity. The interest in the history of human error is taken further in the caustic *De l'origine des fables* (published 1724), where the follies of mythology are explained historically, and the anti-Christian line is pursued in the notorious brief allegory, *Relation de l'île de Bornéo* (1686).

In the second half of his life Fontenelle's main work was scientific. He published work of his own, but his principal contribution was his *Histoire de l'Académie des Sciences*, an annual summary of the work of the Academy, with prefaces, the first of which, in 1702, concerns 'l'utilité des mathématiques et de la physique'. He also published (in 1733) a volume devoted to the earlier history of the Academy, and virtually invented a new genre in writing over 60 *éloges* of deceased academicians, including a striking account of Peter the Great. (His own *éloge* was written by d'*Alembert.) All of this contributed greatly to making science more generally accessible, and even fashionable.

Fontenelle was a man of great gifts and equable temperament. Portraits, including that by Madame de Lambert, tend to show him as a cold fish, not given to enthusiasm or devotion. A famous anecdote recounts him saying that if he had a hand full of truths, he would not open it. He was indeed a prudent writer at a time when intellectual daring was dangerous, but he worked long and hard to discredit false authority and promote rational thinking; 'penser juste' was humanity's great triumph. Cynicism about science and humanity in his youthful *Dialogues* gave way to a measured belief in progress; in his wary way, he was a committed modernist. As such he was revered by the *philosophes*, even though they had doubts about his caution, mocked his flowery wit, and regretted his obstinate refusal to accept Newtonian physics. [PF]

See R. Shackleton (ed.), *Entretiens sur la pluralité des mondes* (1955); A. Niderst, *Fontenelle à la recherche de lui-même* (1971) and (ed.), *Fontenelle. Actes du colloque de Rouen, 1987* (1989).

Fontenoy. Village in Belgium, scene in 1745 of an important battle of the War of Austrian Succession, in which the French under the maréchal de Saxe defeated the Anglo-Allied troops under the duke of Cumberland. Here the French commander d'Anterroche reputedly issued the invitation to Lord Hay: 'Messieurs les Anglais, tirez les premiers!'

Force-Bonté, see DIALLO, B.

Force de l'âge, La, and *La Force des choses.* Second and third volumes of the memoirs of Simone de *Beauvoir.

Formes fixes. Term used to refer to the numerous set forms of verse which dominated medieval *lyric poetry, and have continued to be used in more modern times, often playfully, with the aim of obtaining an archaic flavour. The most important are the *ballade, *vireli (virelai), *rondel (rondeau), and *chant royal. More recent *formes fixes* include the *villanelle and above all the *sonnet. A full list, with examples, can be found in H. Morier, *Dictionnaire de poétique et de rhétorique* (2nd edn., 1989).

FORMEY, Jean-Henri-Samuel (1711–97). Protestant minister and teacher who lived in Germany and became secretary of the Academy of Berlin. The author of philosophical and pedagogical works, he attacked *Rousseau in his *Anti-Émile* (1763).

FORNERET, Xavier (1809–84). French poet, playwright, and critic. He is remembered for some bursts of visionary writing. His name was rescued from obscurity by *Breton, who saw in him a precursor of *Surrealism.

FORT, Paul (1872–1960). French poet, editor, and theatre director, Fort created the short-lived Théâtre d'Art (1890–2) as a forum for *Symbolist theatre and the journal *Vers et prose* (its title a homage to *Mallarmé), which he directed between 1905 and the outbreak of World War I and which brought together the literary and artistic avant-garde of *Montparnasse. As a poet his name is associated with the 'ballade'; he published his first collection in 1896 and remained faithful to the form for the rest of his life (*Ballades françaises*, 17 vols., 1922–58). Written in prose but with the sound-structures and rhythms of poetry, they celebrate love, nature, and death in a tone of spontaneity which provides a link between the French lyrical tradition and *popular song. [JK]

Fortune des Rougon, La. Novel by *Zola, the first in the *Rougon-Macquart* series, published in 1871. It recounts the prehistory of the Rougon-Macquart family, establishing the basis for the whole series, and presents a satirical picture of the brutal and opportunistic seizure of power by the Bonapartists, in the wake of Louis-Napoléon's *coup d'état*, in Plassans, a fictional provincial town in Provence, where a republican uprising is violently repressed. [DB]

FOUCAUD, Charles de, see DEVOTIONAL WRITING, 3.

FOUCAULT, Michel (1926–84). French philosopher, literary critic, and historian, one of the most charismatic figures in the galaxy of thinkers who, in the 1960s and 1970s, became associated in the public mind with the *Structuralist movement. His radical questioning of the categories which permit us to think means, however, that no element in the present entry might go unchallenged by him or by some readers.

The Structuralist label suits the title—professor of the History of Systems of Thought—which he chose in 1970 for his chair at the *Collège de France, where he was appointed after a meteoric career as teacher and administrator in French universities and institutes, in Sweden, Poland, Germany, Clermont-Ferrand, and the experimental university of Paris-Vincennes. This title shows an awkwardness which can only be attributed to Foucault's keen desire to describe the double thrust, historical and structural, of his method, an awkwardness exceptional in a writer whose arresting, if sometimes rhetorical, brilliance was regularly commented on by sometimes puzzled critics more used to the sober style of contemporary history, sociology, or art criticism.

This literary dimension is conspicuous in the book which made him famous, *Folie et déraison: histoire de la folie à l'âge classique* (1961), which raised the concerns of his first work, *Maladie mentale et personnalité* (1954, revised 1966), to something altogether different and utterly original. In the *Histoire de la folie*, which blends historical sociology, epistemology, considerations on architecture, and literary analysis, the modern cult of Reason is shown to rest on the inexorable exclusion of areas which had a place and a role in earlier epochs. This exclusion took a tangible form in the middle of the 17th c. with the 'grand renfermement', the building of 'general hospitals' which would house all the heterogeneous categories which could be construed as social deviants, and thereby guarantee the social norm. This institution is the prototype of others, like the prison, which Foucault either studied himself in *Surveiller et punir: naissance de la prison* (1975) or evoked with disciples exploring penal archives; these yielded the 19th-c. text *Moi, Pierre Rivière, ayant égorgé ma mère, ma sœur et mon frère . . .*, edited by Foucault in 1973. Epistemological concerns are prominent in *Les Mots et les choses: une archéologie des sciences humaines* (1966), *L'Archéologie du savoir* (1969), and in his inaugural lecture, *L'Ordre du discours* (1971). A prison of another kind is introduced in the paradoxical thesis of *La Volonté de savoir* (1976), where Foucault attacks contemporary liberationist discourses as the prelude to a full *History of Sexuality*. He only had time to publish two other volumes, however, *L'Usage des plaisirs* and *Le Souci de soi* (both 1984). Here an analysis of sexual morality in ancient Greece and Rome shows a move from the exploration of objectifying processes to that of the processes whereby a human subject constitutes itself through experiences and codes, which lead to an art and aesthetics of existence.

Foucault described himself as a historian, and, in tracing the genealogy which relates concepts and practices (madness, clinical medicine, punishment, sexuality) to the institutions of various social power structures, he made use of a mass of historical data yielded by innumerable and often totally forgotten texts, asserting that one must 'read everything'. But the points he was making were bold, controversial, and far-reaching in a way which can only be called philosophical.

His writing is solidly anchored in historical material, yet—like that of his mentors of the *Annales* school reconstructing 'mentalities'—it concentrates on synchrony, identifying intellectual configurations in which disciplines that are contemporaneous derive their coherence more from their relations with each other than from a one-to-one correspondence with disciplines which might seem to be their predecessors or successors. Thus, *Les Mots et les choses* purports to show that the triad found in the discourse of the 'classical age'—'natural history', which deals with living beings, 'the analysis of wealth', which deals with economic exchange, and 'general grammar', which deals with language—cannot be unproblematically related to the triad found in 19th-c. discourse, that of 'biology', 'political economy', and 'philology'. Despite his critical attitude towards all master-thinkers, the three areas chosen by Foucault to illustrate his point were something of a commonplace in a period already dominated by Marx, Freud, and the great figures of modern linguistics, a period inclined to treat linguistics as a 'pilot-science'.

As for the ideology of periodization and the stress on epistemology, they are typical Structuralist concerns, and generated one of his most original concepts, that of *episteme*. This is the tacit experience of order which stands between the fundamental codes of a culture (its language, perceptions, modes of exchange, techniques, values, and practices) and the scientific and philosophical interpretations it produces. This notion has been much criticized, as were elements in Foucault's work such as: the emphasis on historical ruptures (comparable to Kuhn's 'paradigm changes'); the denunciations of the spurious continuity produced by traditional history of ideas; the apparent ignoring of any need to account for the 'mutations' between synchronic states; and what struck some readers as nihilistic glee when he described Man as a recent invention produced by the structure of 19th-c. knowledge, an invention whose imminent demise, perceptible in contemporary letters and sciences, possibly heralded a totally new *episteme*. Much of this criticism is epitomized in *Sartre's claim that what Foucault produced is not an archaeology but a geology of knowledge.

In doing so, however, he has attracted equally intense admiration and gratitude. His discrediting of facile humanistic certainties which use an allegedly ahistorical Reason as a guarantor of progress left him free to concentrate on the detail which makes visible the 'microphysics of power', the strategies of its social dissemination and its paradoxically productive effects. This theoretical work which renovated our vision of 'carceral' institutions—asylums, prisons, schools, hospitals, barracks, factories—reinforced the general 1960s trend towards self-help groups among people united by the same situation, whether of gender, race, language, sexual orientation, geographical origin, or physical predicament.

It resulted likewise in activism for Foucault, who had consistently stressed the need to restore their right of speech to groups silenced by their place in the structure. The identification one senses with his subject-matter gives an extra dimension to his enterprise (for his private life, see Miller's 1993 biography): it raises him to a kinship with all the literary and artistic 'madmen'—*Sade, *Roussel, *Artaud, or *Van Gogh—whose experience of 'unreason' he had early on identified as the core, and not the margin, of human experience. Whatever part provocation played in his denunciation of the modern discourse of liberation, there is an unquestionably liberating effect in the work of Foucault, which comes from the fact that he was, in the words of one of his idols, *Blanchot, 'a man at risk, a man on the move'; in so being, he accomplished what he hoped: to make the ground stir under our feet.

[AL]

See A. Sheridan, *Michel Foucault: The Will to Truth* (1980); H. Dreyfus and P. Rabinow, *Michel Foucault: Beyond Structuralism and Hermeneutics* (1982); M. Cousins and A. Hussain, *Michel Foucault* (1984); D. Eribon, *Michel Foucault, 1926–1984* (1989); J. Miller, *The Passion of Michel Foucault* (1993); D. Macey, *The Lives of Michel Foucault* (1993).

FOUCHÉ, Joseph (1763–1820). Revolutionary politician, who distinguished himself by his de-Christianizing policy and repressive activities. Having helped engineer *Robespierre's downfall, he became a protégé of *Barras and then *Napoleon's unscrupulous minister of police. He was largely responsible for the strict censorship imposed under the Empire.

FOUCHET, Max-Pol (1913–81). French poet, editor of *Fontaine*, a Resistance review in World War II. He was a humanist and friend of *Camus and *Mounier. His poetry, collected in *Demeure le secret* (1961), expresses a lyrical belief in the future of mankind. His interest in peoples and their civilizations led him to write on Portugal, Carthage, India, and Africa.

FOUGERET DE MONBRON, Louis-Charles (1706–61). Writer from Picardy, who drew on his bohemian travels throughout Europe for *Le Cosmopolite ou le Citoyen du monde* (1750), showing a cynicism akin to that of *Diderot's Rameau. He also wrote satirical accounts of Paris and England, parodies, a translation of *Fanny Hill*, and a scurrilous story of prostitution, *Margot la ravaudeuse* (1750). [PF]

Fouke le fitz Waryn, see ANGLO-NORMAN LITERATURE, 3a.

FOUQUELIN, Antoine, see RAMUS.

FOUQUET or **FOUCQUET,** Nicolas (1615–80). Surintendant des Finances under *Louis XIV until

1661, when he was disgraced, tried, and imprisoned for supposed malversation (in reality because of his power, ambition, and wealth). He had assembled a luxurious court at *Vaux-le-Vicomte, and was a lavish patron of writers, including *Molière, *Corneille, *Pellisson, and *La Fontaine, many of whom continued to support him in his disgrace. [PF]

Fourberies de Scapin, Les (1671), comedy by *Molière, see SCAPIN.

FOURIER, Charles (1772–1837). Born in Lyon of a rich family which lost its wealth during the Revolution, Fourier was an eccentric Utopian socialist whose peculiar style, sharp criticisms of the horrors of civilization, and exultation of desire and complexity, continue to excite interest. Applying Newton to the social world, he proposed that in a harmoniously organized society attractions would be proportionate to destinies and the 13 passions would all be satisfied—those of the five senses, of honour, friendship, love and parenthood, of concordance, of intrigue, and the 'butterfly' passion for variety (in work or sex), plus unityism (the opposite of egotism). Such harmony could only be realized by organizing society into phalansteries of around 1,620 members each, where equality would not be practised but where a complex system of shifting hierarchies, occupations, and relations would be created, all of which Fourier described in great detail. Providing a synthesis of *Rousseau and *Sade, he offered many telling illustrations (Nero would have made an excellent butcher) and many wild fantasies (the ocean would become as lemonade). His wry humour is sometimes hard to evaluate. He worked out his proposal in great detail, including minute descriptions of the architecture and the daily rhythm of life in the new world of harmony.

His pioneering attention to the problems of motivation in education and work, to what was to become vocational testing, astound, as do his pre-Freudian insights into the mechanisms of the passions (the limits placed on their expression by 'civilization' produce perversions); he was a profoundly original thinker. The full sexual amplifications of his theories were only revealed with the publication of his *Nouveau Monde amoureux* (1967). *La Théorie des quatre mouvements* (1808) is the first exposition of his system, which hardly varied thereafter. *Le Nouveau Monde industriel* (1829) is his most clear and concise work but leaves out his cosmogony (the planets copulate). Categorizing endlessly, ceaselessly indulging in neologisms, Fourier's tone is also quite idiosyncratic, with unexpected shifts from the serious to a comic which is at times wry, at times hilarious. He had many followers, in France, England, and elsewhere. In the United States, at Brook Farm, Arthur Brisbane tried to put his principles into practice. Other attempts to found phalansteries were equally abortive, except for the much-modified 'familistère' at Guise which survived into the 20th c. He was much appreciated by the *Surrealists and again during *May 1968; *Barthes wrote about him in Sade, Fourier, Loyola (1971). [FPB]

See M. Spencer, Charles Fourier (1981); J. Beecher, Charles Fourier, the Visionary and his World (1986).

FOURNIVAL, Richard de (b. 1201). Canon and chancellor of Amiens and canon of Rouen, author of both Latin and vernacular texts. In 1246 he was granted the right to practise as a surgeon. Highly educated, he assembled a remarkable library—described in his Biblionomia—which passed eventually to the library of the *Sorbonne.

Fournival's vernacular works include a corpus of songs in the trouvère style and the prose Bestiaire d'amours (mid-13th c.), in which the traditional *bestiary material is adapted to become an allegory of erotic love. The material, a blend of conventional didacticism and lyrical subjectivity, is handled with both humour and erudition; the text, richly illustrated, survives in numerous manuscripts. Three other prose treatises on love, the Consaus d'amours, Commens d'amours, and Poissanche d'amours, are of doubtful attribution. Two independent verse redactions of the Bestiaire are known, one of which—surviving only in fragmentary from—may be the work of Fournival himself. The Bestiaire also inspired a continuation in which the lover wins his lady's affections, and an anonymous prose response in the voice of the woman to whom it is addressed, the Response au bestiaire. [SJH]

FOURQUEVAUX, Raymond de Beccarie de Pavie, sieur de (1508–74). French soldier and diplomat, whose correspondence and memoirs illuminate French relations with Spain and Scotland at crucial periods. He is the presumed author of an influential treatise on warfare, inspired by Vegetius and Machiavelli, Instructions sur le fait de la guerre (1548, falsely attributed to Guillaume du Bellay). [MJH]

FOURRÉ, Maurice (1876–1959). French novelist. Although he published a novella 'Patte-de-bois', in 1907, Fourré was 'discovered' late in life by the *Surrealists: *Breton wrote the preface for his first novel, La Nuit du Rose-Hôtel (1950), describing it as an 'œuvre toute de ferveur et d'effusion'. This was followed by La Marraine du sel (1955). Arguably his most intriguing work, however, was the surreal whodunnit Tête-de-Nègre (1960), with its unusual mode of authorial intervention and echoes of the *Grail legend and even of *Lautréamont. The other posthumous publication was Le Caméléon mystique (1981), a whimsical love-story that is much more than a love-story. In Fourré's brand of magic realism, the lyrical prose is often interspersed with little poems. [KRA]

Fous de Bassan, Les, see HÉBERT, A.

Fragments d'un discours amoureux, see BARTHES.

FRAGONARD, Jean-Honoré (1732–1806). French painter, whose long career reflects the movement of taste between *Rococo and *Romanticism, though he is best known as the author of elegantly erotic scenes. His most enthusiastic patrons were drawn from the worlds of finance, music, and theatre. In 1771 Fragonard's glamorous series of decorative paintings The Progress of Love for Madame du Barry at Louveciennes were rejected in favour of works in the newly fashionable Neoclassical style by Vien. [JPC]

Français peints par eux-mêmes, Les (1839–42). Multi-instalment publication in which Léon Curmer harnessed the talents of many writers and illustrators. It is a vital source for the social and cultural history of the *July Monarchy, not least for its treatment of lower-class types and street life. Walter Benjamin called it an example of 'dioramic literature'. [BR]

FRANCE, Anatole (pseud. of Jacques-Anatole-François Thibault) (1844–1924). Novelist and critic, Nobel laureate (1921), son of a royalist Parisian bookseller. His early work (1862–77) as a reviewer and publisher's editor produced a sympathetic study of *Vigny (1868) and a variety of slight but suggestive essays on authors ranging from Apuleius to *Zola, some reprinted in Le Génie latin (1913). Criticism written for Le *Temps (1887–93) during the years of his fame as a writer, and reprinted in four volumes of La Vie littéraire (1888–92), reveal a subtle and elegant mind but no great originality or force. Whether judging *Balzac, *Baudelaire, or *Dumas fils, he is lucid, appreciative, but lacks rigour and penetration. He embarked on poetry but soon abandoned it. Poèmes dorés (1873) and a poetic drama, Les Noces corinthiennes (1876), reflect *Parnassian sympathies but, while displaying flashes of sensuous life, lack a personal voice.

Though his erudite reflections on a variety of subjects, from war to morals, won him admirers for Le Jardin d'Épicure (1894) and Sur la pierre blanche (1905), France's fame rests on the witty, mocking, and urbane scepticism pervading his impressive body of short stories and novels. Of these, the barely fictionalized 'novels' evoking his childhood—Le Livre de mon ami (1885), Pierre Nozière (1899), Le Petit Pierre (1919), La Vie en fleur (1922)—have a simple directness and charm which contrast with the arch pastiche of 18th-c. life to be found in La Rôtisserie de la reine Pédauque (1893) and Les Opinions de M. Jérôme Coignard (1893). More impressive are the fine short stories in Balthasar (1889), L'Étui de nacre (1892), Le Puits de Sainte-Claire (1895), etc. Thaïs (1890), an exotic tale of courtesan turned saint, and Le Lys rouge (1894), a study of sexual jealousy in Florence, represent France's most ambitious attempts to write about human passion, but they cannot rival his later novels. First among these must be Les Dieux ont soif (1912), his vivid and masterly study of Revolutionary fanaticism and corruption. Next come the four volumes of his *Histoire contemporaine*: *L'Orme du mail* (1897), *Le Mannequin d'osier* (1897), *L'Anneau d'améthyste* (1899), *Monsieur Bergeret à Paris* (1901), offering their scathing mockery of French politics. Finally, *L'Île des pingouins* (1908), his disenchanted allegory of human progress, and *La Révolte des anges* (1914), his playful but subversive account of Christianity, reveal a true satirist.   [SBJ]

See R. Virtanen, *Anatole France* (1968).

Franciade, La. *Ronsard's unfinished national *epic—only 4 of the planned 24 volumes were published (1572). It was conceived in 1550 and was designed to trace the origins of France's royal dynasty to the legendary Trojan hero Francus, son of Hector. The *Défense et illustration* had devoted an entire chapter to the epic and its classical models (Homer, Virgil), but in spite of inspired fragments the *Franciade* is disappointing: the decasyllabic line (imposed by *Charles IX) lacks vigour and amplitude, the narrative structure is slack and repetitious, and fidelity to classical sources (notably Virgil) is constraining. It nevertheless exercised considerable influence on the theory and practice of 16th- and 17th-c. historical epic.   [MDQ]

Francion, La Vraie Histoire comique de (1623), by Charles *Sorel, is one of the most original novels of the 17th c. and one of its outstanding literary successes. It traces the adventure-filled life of Francion and his dealings with a wide range of characters from pedants to go-betweens, fashionable ladies to second-rate poets. Its narrative complexity allows different levels of reading. In the tradition of *conte* and *fabliau*, it provides scenes of *gaulois* incident designed to provoke laughter. As a satire, it unleashes a series of powerful attacks on the vulgarity of peasants, the corruption of lawyers, or the ignorance and scheming of nobles. And, in certain richly imaginative and elusive scenes, such as the hero's dream which combines erotic fantasy with metaphysical allegory, or his evocative vision of a *libertin* Utopia, it suggests a radical questioning of social, moral, and religious convention. In recent years its embodiment of different narrative languages and traditions has aroused particular critical attention. The novel went through three separate forms, from the bold and outspoken first edition of 1623, to an enlarged but expurgated version published three years later, to the final text of 1633, where a more orthodox moralizing voice was introduced.   [GJM]

Franciscans. When St Francis gathered his first followers, he envisaged an order of laymen practising apostolic poverty, living by labouring and begging, and sharing in his spirituality of obedience and freedom. But before he died in 1226 he had himself accepted some modifications to this plan. Subsequently the Franciscans acquired convents, accepted bequests, took holy orders, and were attracted to university education, especially at Paris. These changes caused serious internal rifts, with the dissidents, known as Spiritual Franciscans, finding support in the Midi in the later 13th and early 14th c. Nevertheless the Franciscans flourished, counting among their members notable scholars, missionaries, inquisitors, mystics, and preachers.   [JHD]

FRANCK, César (1822–90). Composer, teacher, and organist of Belgian origin. He was a deeply religious man, and his combination of classicism and intense emotionalism inspired many young composers. Franck based some of his songs and symphonic poems on Romantic texts (e.g. by *Leconte de Lisle and *Hugo), and his music was greatly appreciated in many artistic and literary circles. The Belgian avant-garde movement 'Les Vingt' performed Franck's chamber music, including the première of his violin sonata, and on his death a memorial concert of his works. *Proust was a great admirer of Franck's chamber music; his violin sonata is possibly one of the sources for the Vinteuil sonata in *A la recherche du temps perdu*.   [KM]

Franco-Gallia, see HOTMAN.

FRANÇOIS Ier (1494–1547) became king of France on the death of Louis XII (1515). He was immensely popular with his nobility because of his energetic participation in the Italian wars. Early successes like that of Marignano (1515) gave way, however, to the defeat of Pavia (1525), which led to the king's imprisonment in Madrid and to the establishment of Spanish hegemony in Italy. François's pursuit of dynastic aims in Italy shows that he was still, in many ways, a medieval monarch; but his dogged compaigns against the encircling power of the emperor Charles V showed him to be very much aware of the importance of power politics. He shocked Europe by signing an alliance with the Turks and infuriated Catholic opinion at home by supporting the German Protestants.

Although a sincere Catholic, he tolerated moderate reform in France until the Affaire des *Placards, which convinced him that Lutheranism was fundamentally seditious [see REFORMATION]. His earlier, more tolerant attitude was born of a desire to establish France's reputation as a centre for the New Learning, which often went hand-in-hand with *Evangelical leanings of the kind associated with his sister, *Marguerite de Navarre. It bore more permanent fruit in the Collège Royal (later *Collège de France) and in his handsome library, which was to become the basis of the *Bibliothèque Nationale. François was also aware of the prestige to be obtained as a patron of the visual arts. He succeeded in luring the ageing Leonardo da Vinci to France and, for a time, the more ebullient Cellini. His name is more particularly associated, however, with the rebuilt Palace of *Fontainebleau, which he had decorated in the Mannerist style by Il Rosso and Primaticcio. His achievements will outlast the image of the philanderer-king presented by *Hugo's *Le Roi s'amuse*. [JJS]

FRANÇOIS DE SALES, Saint (1567–1622). A man of great holiness whose piety was uncompromising yet engagingly humane. Many regarded him as a saint during his lifetime and he was canonized in 1665.

Born in the Duchy of Savoy, he received a humanist education in Paris and Padua. He had a deep sense of religious vocation, however, and was ordained in 1593. In the same year he began a dangerous, but ultimately successful, four-year mission to the Chablais area converting Calvinists to Catholicism. From 1602 until his death he was bishop of Geneva. He proved an inspiring preacher, a successful spiritual director, a voluminous letter-writer, and a conscientious administrator of 450 parishes. His long association with St Jeanne-Françoise de Chantal began in 1604. Six years later they founded the Congregation of the Visitation (the Visitandines), which achieved the status of a full religious order in 1618. François de Sales is known above all as the author of *Introduction à la vie dévote* (1609, definitive edn. 1619)—one of the most continuously successful manuals of the devout life ever written [see DEVOTIONAL WRITING, 2]. His more difficult *Traité de l'amour de Dieu* (1616) was addressed to 'souls that are advanced in devotion'.

[JC]

Françoise. The faithful family servant in Proust's *A la recherche du temps perdu*, a treasure-house of traditional modes of thought and speech.

François le Champi. Novel by George *Sand, published in periodical form in 1847–8, as a book in 1850. The hero is a foundling raised first by a good but illiterate poor woman, then by Madeleine Blanchet despite the opposition of her mother-in-law and her husband, a miller who falls into the clutches of drink and an evil woman. François is forced tearfully to depart and seek work elsewhere, where he succeeds, then returns to restore the health and fortunes of the widowed Madeleine, thanks in part to a large gift from his unknown mother. Eventually he and Madeleine marry, though she is somewhat his elder, but filial affection becomes transformed into marital bliss. Somewhat melodramatic in that the characters are either very good or very bad, the novel presents a skilful literary use of *patois* for scenes of provincial daily life. It is preceded by an interesting discussion of the problems and virtues of writing in that mode. [FPB]

Francophonie, La. Literally, the ability to speak French; more commonly denotes the global community of French-speakers. Usage of the term often connotes a commitment to strengthening that community. Estimates as to the overall number of francophones vary widely, depending on the level of proficiency and the purposes for which French is used. The most reliable estimates put the total at over 120 million. Less than half of these are in France. Most of the others live in France's former colonial territories [see COLONIZATION]; smaller numbers are found in the *DOM-TOM (overseas departments and territories still administered by France) as well as in European states bordering on France. Sub-Saharan *Africa and the *Maghreb contain by far the largest concentrations of francophones outside France. The next largest groups are in North America (especially *Quebec) and the *West Indies, as well as Europe (particularly *Belgium and *Switzerland). Most of the remainder are in the *Middle East and *Indo-China, together with parts of Oceania.

The term *francophonie* was originally coined by Onésime *Reclus in his book *France, Algérie et colonies* (1880), but was little used until the 1960s when, in the immediate aftermath of *decolonization, it was taken up by those committed to strengthening the position of French as a world language. Political leaders in a few French-speaking areas, such as *Algeria, refused to associate themselves with this movement on the grounds that it amounted to a form of neo-colonialism. Most newly independent francophone states joined the movement, however, with presidents *Senghor of Senegal and Bourguiba of *Tunisia particularly to the fore. The position of Quebec, where most of the population speak French, was made difficult by its status as a province within the predominantly anglophone state of Canada, whose leaders were wary of international links which might help to foster a separatist movement. These fears were fuelled by a visit in 1967 during which the French president Charles de *Gaulle shocked the Canadian government by crying 'Vive le Québec libre!'

In most so-called francophone countries outside France, French is spoken by only a minority of the population. However, this minority usually encompasses the most educated social groups, for French remains the language of instruction in the schools of many former colonies, and in sub-Saharan states in particular it still serves as the language of government. Spearheaded by French-educated élites in the years leading up to decolonization, francophone writing outside France has become a major feature of the post-colonial period [see separate entries on individual regions and countries]. In addition, the continuing prominence of French-speakers in the upper echelons of ex-colonial states means that *la francophonie* is significant not only culturally but also economically and politically.

Numerous organizations have been set up to develop links among the francophone community. Some, such as the Alliance Française, founded as a private organization in 1883 to improve France's international standing by providing French-language tuition for foreigners, were set up before decolonization, but most were created more recently. The Association des Universités Partiellement ou Entièrement de Langue Française (AUPELF) was founded in 1961 to foster co-operation between academics. The Association des Écrivains de Langue Française (ADELF) is the post-colonial successor to the Société des Écrivains Coloniaux, which was set up in Paris in 1926, while the rival Fédération Internationale des Écrivains de Langue Française (FIDELF) was established in Montreal in 1982. An international panel of experts appointed to the Haut Conseil de la Francophonie, created at the initiative of President François *Mitterrand in 1984, functions as a kind of think-tank generating new ideas for the promotion of the French language.

Since 1970 the Agence de Coopération Culturelle et Technique (ACCT) has encouraged cultural and technical co-operation between more than 30 French-speaking states. The delicacy of Quebec's constitutional position blocked proposals for a full-scale summit of francophone heads of state until an agreement with the Canadian prime minister Brian Mulroney cleared the way for the first such meeting, which took place in Paris in 1986. Here, Canada distinguished herself as the only serious challenger to France's dominance within the francophone community, the bulk of which consists of Third World countries unable to match the economic and political might of the industrialized world. Significantly, the second francophone summit was held in Quebec in 1987. Despite their numerical weight, black Africans had to wait until 1989 before hosting the third summit, held in Dakar. [AGH]

See J.-J. Luthi, A. Viatte, and G. Zananiri, *Dictionnaire général de la francophonie* (1986); M. Tétu, *La Francophonie: histoire, problématique et perspectives* (1987).

Franco-Prussian War and **Siege of Paris** (1870–1). Under *Napoleon III, France unwisely embarked on war with Prussia in the summer of 1870. Against a background of smouldering confrontation, the official *casus belli* was a dispute over the candidate for the Spanish throne; less officially, a diplomatic snub, leaked in the famous Ems dispatch, provoked an outbreak of bellicosity in Paris. The outcome was a humiliating defeat for France. Superior manpower and deployment led to a series of Prussian victories in August, and the French emperor was captured at Sedan on 2 September. A republic was proclaimed in Paris on 4 September, and a government of national defence hastily assembled as the capital was besieged by the Prussian army. The siege lasted until January 1871, its later stages bringing severe hardship to the Parisians.

The French capitulation of 28 January 1871 was followed by nation-wide elections in February, and the resulting government, led by Adolphe *Thiers, negotiated with Prussia; by the Treaty of Frankfurt (10 May 1871), France paid a heavy indemnity and ceded the two captured provinces, Alsace and Lorraine, thus inspiring over 40 years of revanchism. Meanwhile, the circumstances of the siege combined with political and social tensions in Paris to produce the uprising known as the *Commune (March–May 1871). The long-term result of France's crushing military defeat was deep-seated anxiety about German technological and demographic superiority, later reinforced by the events of the 20th c. [SR]

Franglais, Le, see ÉTIEMBLE.

FRÉCHETTE, Louis (1839–1908). Canadian poet, dramatist, and prose writer whose varied and eventful career and literary output made him a highly popular public figure. He was equally at home in lyric, satirical, and epic verse. His most ambitious work is *La Légende d'un peuple* (1887), a large-scale evocation in poetic tableaux of the history of French Canada, inspired equally by *Garneau's *Histoire du Canada* and Victor *Hugo. He had already taken Hugo as a model for *La Voix d'un exilé* (1886), a polemical attack in prose and verse on the Canadian Confederation Act of 1867, which he wrote while living in Chicago. His work for the stage included a highly Romantic melodrama and two spectacular patriotic plays, now largely forgotten. As a prose writer, he is best known for his ironic caricatures of French-Canadian social types, *Originaux et detraqués* (1892). [SIL]

FREDERICK THE GREAT (Friedrich II, king of Prussia) (1712–86). Succeeding his notoriously anti-intellectual father Friedrich-Wilhelm in 1740, he was a partisan of French culture and the *philosophes. He spoke French habitually, wrote both verse and prose in the language, and made it the language of the Academy of Berlin, of which *Maupertuis became director. He was the friend, correspondent, and protector of many French men of letters, including d'*Alembert and *Voltaire; the latter lived at Potsdam from 1750 to 1753 before quarrelling with Maupertuis and the king. [PF]

Freemasonry. Compared with its British counterpart, the French masonic movement has always been reforming and *anticlerical, though it was also linked in the 18th and 19th c. with various mystical or *Illuminist currents. It was supposed by many to have been one of the influences preparing the way for the *Revolution, and in the 19th c. it became strongly associated with *republicanism. As a result, reactionaries have often denounced freemasons, along with Jews, Protestants, and other supposedly alien elements, as enemies of true French nationhood. Under the *Occupation of 1940–4 masons were subjected to severe harassment.

There are three masonic organizations in France, the Grand Orient, the Grande Loge de France, and the Grande Loge Nationale Française; the last of these, founded in 1913, is recognized by masons of Britain and other countries. [PF]

FRÉNAUD, André (1907–93). Poet, native of Burgundy. For most his life he held an office job with French Railways. His two-year imprisonment in Germany after the collapse of France in 1940 is a main source of his first collection, *Les Rois Mages* (1943).

He has a great range of manners and tones: at times highly concrete and down-to-earth, as warm, humorous, and bluff as his own personality (see, in addition to the collection just mentioned, *La Sainte Face*, 1968, 1985)—at other times appealing to archetypal symbols, particularly in the long poems which he was unusual in continuing to write (e. g. *La Sorcière de Rome*, 1973). The key experience in Frénaud is 'visitation', in which a surge of energy (carrying with it a sense of unity) constructs a miraculous 'château' of words. In his trance, the poet has felt himself 'another', but is sadly restored to his everyday self at the end of the experience, and inspects his poem with mingled wonder and disappointment. Despite its great energy, Frénaud's poetry has a pedal-note of melancholy. His output is large: see also *Il n'y a pas de paradis* (1962) and *Haeres* (1982), and consult the interviews of *Notre inhabileté fatale* (1979). [GDM]

French-Canadian Writing, see QUEBEC; ACADIA.

French Language, see HISTORY OF THE FRENCH LANGUAGE.

French Revolution, see REVOLUTION.

Frénétique, Littérature. In the years immediately following 1830 there emerged groups of writers who asserted their marginality and opposition to bourgeois respectability. They valued artistic freedom and their work displayed a self-conscious alienation joined with a spirit of negation. 'Frenetic' writing often dealt with the themes of excess, violent death, and suicide. *Gautier and *Nerval wrote texts in the 'frenetic' manner. Other writers of note were Petrus *Borel, Philothée *O'Neddy, and Charles Lassailly. In this context we should also include the *Mémoires* written in prison by Pierre-François Lacenaire before his execution for murder in 1836. [CC]

Frère Jean des Entommeures. Combative monk and companion of *Rabelais's giants [see PANTAGRUEL AND GARGANTUA].

FRÉRET, Nicolas (1688–1749). Classical and Chinese scholar and chronologist. Famous for his free-thinking, incarcerated in the Bastille in 1714 (probably for anti-Jesuit writings), he was almost certainly the author of the *Lettre de Thrasybule à Leucippe* (1722), the most ambitious of the *clandestine manuscripts, not published until 1766. It is a full-length treatise, supposedly written in the 2nd c. AD, mainly attacking revealed religion from an atheist and materialist standpoint; it contains a very clear statement of the pleasure–pain principle. Other manuscript works attributed to Fréret include a scholarly and forceful *Examen critique du Nouveau Testament.* [CJB]

FRÉRON, Élie-Catherine (1718–76). Journalist. Heaving completed his 'apprenticeship' under *Desfontaines, he produced his own publication: *Lettres de la Comtesse* (1745–6), followed—after a hiatus occasioned by official displeasure—by his *Lettres sur quelques écrits de ce temps* (1749), which became in 1754 the famous *Année littéraire*. Actively engaged as both Catholic and monarchist in all the polemics of his effervescent times, he was a constant irritant for the *philosophes*. It is regrettable that *Voltaire's scurrilous and repeated denigration of him should so balefully have obscured the value and the unity of his compendious criticism. [JR]

FROISSART, Jean (b. 1337; d. after 1404). Though best known in the modern period for his chronicles, Froissart is also the author of a significant poetic corpus, including lyric compositions in the *formes fixes*, *pastourelles*, narrative *dits*, and a chivalric romance of more than 30,000 lines, the *Meliador*. Aside from the latter, Froissart's poetry participates in the tradition inspired by the *Roman de la Rose*; he was particularly influenced by his older contemporary, Guillaume de *Machaut. Like Machaut, Froissart prepared anthology manuscripts of his poetic works (excluding *Meliador*), with *dits* arranged in chronological order and lyric compositions arranged by verse form.

Little is known of Froissart's life beyond his literary contributions. He was a native of Valenciennes. As a writer he enjoyed the patronage of the high aristocracy, including, among others, Philippa of Hainaut, queen of England, with whom he was associated from 1361 until her death in 1369; Wenceslas of Brabant, whose own compositions appear as lyric insertions in *Meliador*; Gui, comte de Blois, who appointed Froissart court chaplain; and *Gaston Phébus, comte de Foix and vicomte de Béarn, whom Froissart entertained during the winter of 1388–9 with an oral reading of *Meliador*. By 1373, he had taken holy orders and been granted a benefice at Estinnes-au-Mont, which he held for the next ten years. It was also at about this time that he turned from the composition of lyric poetry and *dits* in order to devote himself to *Meliador* and to his chronicles. In the 1380s, due to his growing ties with Gui de Blois, Froissart received canonries in Chimay and Lille.

Froissart frequently hints at a love affair with a lady named Marguerite. This name is encoded into the *Espinette amoureuse*, and in several other pieces Froissart declares his love for the daisy (*marguerite*), even inventing a myth to explain its origins. It has not been possible, however, to identify a historical woman of that name who might have played an important role in Froissart's life, and the motif may be a purely literary one. It is none the less an important thread running through Froissart's poetic corpus, with allusions to the daisy or to the name 'Marguerite' appearing, in various forms, in many of his works.

Froissart composed in the standard lyric *formes fixes* of the 14th c. No music has survived for his compositions, although it is possible that they were sometimes set to the melodies of other songs. His work is typical of late medieval lyric in the tradition of Machaut: love poetry, often incorporating mythological figures and allusions to allegorical personifications. Like Machaut, Froissart included lyric insertions in his narrative *dits*.

His three major *dits* are the *Espinette amoureuse* (c. 1369), *Prison amoureuse* (1372–3), and *Joli Buisson de Jonece* (1373); he also composed numerous shorter pieces. Like those of Machaut, Froissart's *dits* feature a first-person amorous protagonist, closely identified with the author, who is portrayed as inept in love but successful in the composition of lyric and narrative poetry, both in the service of the lady and for aristocratic patrons. The most distinctive feature of Froissart's *dits* is his incorporation of pseudo-Ovidian myths, adapted to fit the context in which they are placed. These may be either an alteration of known myths or entirely new stories, involving characters with pseudo-Greek names.

The verse romance *Meliador* (1388) features a five-year quest competition, jointly proclaimed by King Arthur and the king of Scotland, whose purpose is to select a husband for the Scottish princess. The resulting text, in which the adventures of several knights are interlaced, provides the occasion for a thorough review of chivalric values, both amorous and military. In the *Meliador*, as in the chronicles, Froissart expresses his belief in these values as the underpinnings of an aristocratic society.

Froissart worked on his *magnum opus*, the *Chroniques*, from approximately 1360 to 1400. He began with an adaptation of the chronicle of *Jean le Bel, which covered the period 1326–56, and then continued with an account of contemporary events, focusing on the political intrigue and military exploits of the *Hundred Years War. Froissart's sympathies lay entirely with the nobility; he had little patience with the claims of the bourgeoisie. His *Chroniques* provide invaluable evidence for social mores and political attitudes of the time; he is particularly noted for his vivid descriptions of pageantry and ceremony, and for his lively vignettes of court life. [SJH]

See P. Dembowski, *Jean Froissart and his Meliador* (1983).

FROMENTIN, Eugène(-Samuel-Auguste) (1820–76). French writer. Though professionally a painter, he is famous for his one novel, *Dominique, which has strongly autobiographical elements. In his youth he had a (probably reciprocated) passion for Jenny Chessé, a married woman three and a half years older than himself, who died of cancer in 1844. After her death Fromentin wrote fascinating journals on his travels in the African deserts, and devoted himself with great official success to painting in the orientalist style, but still regarded himself as a writer *manqué*. 15 years later the editor of *La Revue des deux mondes* 'ordered' a novel from him. The result was *Dominique*, first published in the review in 1862. In paying homage to his love-affair, Fromentin transforms it into a classic of romantic frustration. He died too early to witness the great popular success of his novel, republished three months after his death.

Fromentin is also remembered for his illuminating essays on Dutch and Flemish painting, published in 1876 as *Les Maîtres d'autrefois*. [GDM]

Fronde, La. A period of civil insurrection (1648–53) during the minority of *Louis XIV, named after the *fronde*, or sling, used in children's games. It saw the union of two uneasy allies with different reasons for revolting against *Mazarin's policies: the *parlements*, who wished to limit the fiscal powers of the royal government, and the turbulent high nobility, whose power had been eroded under the administration of *Richelieu and who grasped the opportunity to reassert their traditional independence. During four years of desultory skirmishing throughout France, Paris swung first one way then another; at one point the court and Mazarin were forced to flee, as a series of concessions followed by retractions heightened the atmosphere of instability. *Condé, the uncle of the king and the highly successful commander of the French army during the 1640s, was arrested in 1651, unleashing a second period of revolt; but his involvement with Spain, still technically at war with France, cost him the support of the *parlements*, and *Retz, who had been responsible for rallying the Parisian mob against Mazarin, was won over to the royal side by the promise of a cardinal's hat. Louis XIV was able to enter Paris in triumph in 1652; Bordeaux and other provincial cities continued to resist royal authority until 1653, but peace was restored by October of that year.

The Fronde witnessed several deeds of daring, not least by noblewomen such as the duchesse de *Montpensier and the duchesse de *Longueville. It figures prominently in the memoirs written about this period by Retz, *La Rochefoucauld, Madame de la Guette, and others, and it saw the prolific outpouring of pamphlet literature known as *mazarinades*, which express in virulent and often pungent terms factional opposition to the hated first minister of the crown. It is often taken to be the watershed of the century, dividing the swashbuckling, optimistic mood of the 1630s and 1640s from the more sombre outlook of the generation of *Pascal and *Racine. [IM]

Front National, see FASCISM.

Front Populaire, see POPULAR FRONT.

Fruits d'or, Les, see SARRAUTE.

Fugitive, La. Original title of *Albertine disparue*, the sixth part of Proust's *A la recherche du temps perdu*.

FULBERT, see LATINITY, I.

FUMET, Stanislas (1896–1983). Writer and critic. Founder and director of the liberal Catholic review *Temps présent*, he was a prolific critic of art and literature. After World War II Fumet became director of the Catholic publishing house Desclée de Brouwer. See his *Claudel* (1958) and *Le Néant contesté* (1972).

[MHK]

Funeral Oration, see SERMON.

FURETIÈRE, Antoine (1619–88). Satirist and lexicographer. A member of the Parisian legal bourgeoisie, he lived all his life in the capital, acquiring a sinecure as an abbot in 1662. In 1648 he published a *burlesque parody of Book 4 of the *Aeneid*, and in 1655 a volume of *Poésies diverses*; this includes five realistic 'satires' of bourgeois life, notably the picturesque 'Jeu de boules des procureurs'. His *Nouvelle allégorique* (1658) is a rather ponderous literary satire; it praises the *Académie Française, to which Furetière was elected in 1662. At this time he collaborated with *Boileau and *Chapelle in the parody of Le *Cid, *Chapelain décoiffé, and in 1666 published, with little success, his *Roman bourgeois. His most important work is the *Dictionnaire universel*, which he produced single-handed, in competition with the dictionary of the Academy [see DICTIONARIES]. The Academy had Furetière's work banned, accused him of plagiarism and disloyalty, and expelled him in 1685. He defended himself in three truculent *Factums* (1685–8), showing that his dictionary was quite different from (and superior to) the Academy's. Posterity has endorsed his arguments, appreciating the richness of his work, which was finally published in Holland in 1690, after his death.

[PF]

FUSTEL DE COULANGES, Numa-Denis (1830–89). Professor of history at Strasbourg until 1870, thereafter at the Sorbonne, Fustel is best known now as the author of *La Cité antique* (1864), one of the earliest histories without dates, events, or names of individual personalities. At the same time that Marx and his associates were emphasizing class conflict and arguing that material relations of production were the foundation of all social relations and of culture, Fustel emphasized the organic unity of society and the fundamental importance of religion. Society was held together by beliefs, not economic relations (the institution of property, for instance, arose out of the cult of the dead and of ancestors), and divisions emerged as common beliefs were weakened and replaced by material interests. Fustel's influence is clearly felt in the work of his most brilliant student, *Durkheim, but his ideas are equally compatible with the themes developed in the novels of *Barrès. The latter undoubtedly appreciated both Fustel's claim, in a famous polemic with the German scholar Mommsen after the German annexation of Alsace, that shared political myths rather than language are the basis of national identity, and his request, despite his religious agnosticism, that he be buried according to the rites of the religion of his native France. Fustel's elegantly austere and impersonal style (in reaction against the overblown Romantic rhetoric of the revolutionaries of 1848) helped to mask the political significance of his work. The 75th anniversary of his birth in 1905 was thus the occasion of a violent dispute over his legacy between those of his students who supported the Republic (notably Durkheim, a Jew, and Gabriel Monod, a Protestant) and the right-wing nationalists of *Action Française.

[LG]

G

Gabelle, La, see TAXATION.

GABIN, Jean (1904–76). For André *Bazin, 'Œdipe en casquette', the French cinema's proletarian tragic hero *par excellence*. Rumour had it that he insisted on dying violently at the end of each film, as in *Renoir's *La Bête humaine* (1938) and *Carné's *Quai des brumes* (1938) and *Le Jour se lève* (1939), the last perhaps French cinema's greatest tragic acting performance. His pre-war career at its peak—from *Duvivier's *La Belle Équipe* (1936)—is intimately associated with the triumph and downfall of the *Popular Front. Only Humphrey Bogart has given the cinema such a troubled incarnation of a masculinity at once violent and tender. [KAR]

GABORIAU, Émile (1832–73). Secretary to the novelist Paul *Féval, and journalist, Gaboriau began *detective fiction in French by creating the first detectives; his admiration for *Poe was an obvious influence. *L'Affaire Lerouge* (1866, but serialized in 1863) presents le père Tabaret, significantly nicknamed 'Tire-au-clair', and Inspecteur Lecoq, in a mystery to be solved logically and scientifically. Gaboriau also wrote *Le Crime d'Orcival* (1867), *Le Dossier 113* (1867), *Les Esclaves de Paris* (1869), *Monsieur Lecoq* (1869), *La Vie infernale* (1870), *La Clique dorée* (1871), *La Dégringolade* (1873), *La Corde au cou* (1873). The later novels feature Lecoq, master of disguise and deduction alike. The crimes are presented as problems to be solved by observation and analysis, but Gaboriau's villains use misleading clues and false trails, so that solving the crime becomes a duel between villain and detective, and also between the author and the reader, whom he deliberately sets out to baffle and amaze. Detective fiction was not, however, sufficently established and recognized as a genre for the detective's enquiries to constitute the sole interest, and Gaboriau's novels still retain, alongside the astute deductions, the melodramatic devices of the *roman-feuilleton*. [SFN]

GACE BRULÉ. Knight and outstanding early *trouvère, whose life remains obscure. His surname apparently refers to a heraldic device on his shield (*brulé* = *bur(e)lé*, 'barred', 'barry'). Gace's lyrics link him with Champagne and Brie, whose countess he ostentatiously obeys in one lyric, but also with Brittany, to which he perhaps travelled with Count Geoffroi (d. 1186), mentioned in three *chansons* and possibly Gace's partner in a *jeu parti*. This western connection suggests that 'Gatho Bruslé/Bruslez' attested near Dreux (Eure-et-Loire) and Mantes

(Yvelines) in 1212–13 may be the poet. Gace's friends included *Blondel de Nesle and *Gautier de Dargies. His lyrics were widely quoted, imitated, and explicitly admired by later writers. The manuscripts ascribe 104 to him—more than to any other *trouvère*—though editors doubt almost half these attributions in varying degrees. All lyrics indisputably by Gace are delicately nuanced *chansons courtoises*, expressing doomed *fin'amor* which threatens death. The poet-persona appears compulsively yearning, frustrated, suffering, melancholic, introverted, reflective, apprehensive, sensitive to others' rivalry and malice, paralysed by inhibition sometimes formally conveyed through prosodic complexity. Only artistic creativity, self-expression through song, seems to sustain him. Art may be his true passion, the lady being a shadowy, abstract pretext. [PVD]

GACE DE LA BUIGNE. King's chaplain and author of the long and unclassifiable *Roman des deduis* (1359–c.1377), lauding *deduis* (diversions) as instilling aristocratic elegance. It opens with a battle of virtues and vices but quickly shades into a debate on the value of falconry as against *hunting. Set in a legal framework, it is notable for its hunting details. [JHMT]

GAGNON, Madeleine (b. 1938). Canadian poet and writer whose work combines a vision of Quebec, its roots and its specificity, with a strong political and feminist commitment. Her first collection of poetry, *Pour les femmes et tous les autres* (1974) demonstrates strong Marxist-feminist sympathies: committed to the women's struggle and to a rejection of high literature, these poems have a markedly oral and popular flavour, drawing on the everyday speech of women of Quebec. The typographical arrangement of the text on the page, often vertical as well as horizontal, emphasizes the desire of the poet to disrupt literary and social norms. The title of her second collection, *Poélitique* (1975), itself announces that the poetic is to coincide with the political; taking as its theme a history of syndicalism in Quebec, the volume underlines the need for a poetic revolution to accompany a social transformation. The strongly lyrical voice which emerges in these collections, and which prevents them from being merely ideological, is affirmed in *Retailles* (1977), written jointly with Denise Boucher, in which the expression of the subjective and of the body in an uncensored textual flow becomes dominant. In the same year she collaborated with Hélène *Cixous and Annie *Leclerc on *La Venue à l'écriture*, a collection of essays theorizing '*écriture féminine'. *Antre* (1978) pushes the logic of subjectivity into a search for the maternal and an opening up to the unconscious through metaphor, especially through metaphors of the body. *Lueur* (1979), an 'archaeological novel', presents metaphor as a path to knowledge. Yet both these texts also suggest the impossibility of writing, an impossibility expressed in extreme terms in *Au cœur de la lettre* (1981), a fragmented text accompanied by the author's own illustrations. *La Lettre infinie* (1984) continues to explore writing and the self, seen through the prism of relationships between mother, son, and absent father. Two volumes of poetry published in 1986, the prize-winning *Les Fleurs du catalpa* and *L'Infante immémoriale*, express a reflective, intimate meditation on a series of interwoven themes, including North America, women, and history. The forms employed are fluid, sometimes merging into poetic prose, but also convey an air of discreet restraint. In 1989 she published a volume subtitled 'Autographie 2', collecting together critical commentaries and texts reflecting on writing. She emphasizes here that this kind of writing can only artificially be separated from her creative work. The title of the volume, *Toute écriture est amour*, characterizes perfectly her attitude to writing.   [EAF]

See L. Dupré, *Stratégies du vertige* (1989).

GAIMAR, Geffrei, see ANGLO-NORMAN LITERATURE, 4.

GAINSBOURG, Serge (pseud. of Lucien Ginzburg) (1928–92). Singer-songwriter, also film director, painter. At his debut in the 1950s in the night-clubs of the Parisian Right Bank, his awkward stage presence and icily ironic delivery inhibited his popular success, which came when his songs were interpreted by others such as *Greco and France Gall. The sexual innuendoes of these, the explicit heavy breathing of 'Je t'aime moi non plus' (1968), and his reggae version of 'La *Marseillaise', 'Aux armes et caetera' (1979), gave him an image of professional *provocateur*. The witty word-play of his lyrics and his ostentatious cynicism have made him an anti-hero of French popular culture.   [PGH]

Gai Saber, the 'gay science' of Occitan poetry, see JEUX FLORAUX DE TOULOUSE.

Galaad (Galahad). Pure-hearted hero of the later *Grail Romances, where he replaces the unworthy *Gauvain, *Lancelot and Perceval.

Galerie du Palais, La. Comedy by Pierre *Corneille, first performed *c*.1632, remarkable for its realistic presentation of contemporary Paris.

GALIANI, Ferdinand, abbé (1728–87). Secretary at the Neapolitan embassy in Paris from 1759 to 1769. He was a member of *philosophe* circles, who appreciated his wit—in *Diderot's words, 'le plus joli petit Arlequin qu'ait produit l'Italie, mais sur les épaules de cet Arlequin était la tête de Machiavel'. Sceptical of his friends' optimism, he attacked *Physiocrat doctrines in his *Dialogues sur les blés* (1770).   [PF]

GALL, Franz Joseph (1758–1828), originated a theory of phrenology which explained the characteristics of the human mind in relation to the configuration of the cranium. German by birth, he lectured in Paris in 1807 where his message was well received. He took French nationality in 1819. His psychophysiological theories appealed to the generation of *Balzac.   [CC]

GALLAND, Antoine (1646–1715). Orientalist and translator. He studied in Paris, was a secretary at the French embassy in Constantinople, and spent many years in the east for the Compagnie des Indes Orientales. Returning to Paris in 1688 he worked as a scholar, publishing d'*Herbelot's *Bibliothèque orientale* and becoming a professor at the *Collège de France in 1709. He translated the Koran, but is known above all for his version of *Les *Mille et une Nuits*. This was first-hand work, done largely from manuscripts and oral sources over a period of about 40 years. He also left a *Journal* of his travels.   [PF]

Gallicanism was a nexus of ideas (usually in opposition to *Ultramontanism) which tended to restrain the pope's authority in the French Church in favour of that of the bishops or of the temporal ruler. It is useful to distinguish between 'royal Gallicanism' (often vigorously supported by the *parlements), which defended the French state against any interference in its affairs by Rome, and 'episcopal Gallicanism', which defended the French Church against control by the papacy.

Such doctrines go a long way back in French history. They are already very apparent in the Pragmatic Sanction of Bourges (1438), which gave the French Church authority to control its own senior appointments and its own temporal administration independent of the pope. The *Concordat of 1516 conferred power to control senior Church appointments on the king; this was the beginning of royal Gallicanism. The Declaration of 1682, which became the key text of Gallicanism, reasserted both strands. It denied that temporal rulers could be deposed by ecclesiastical authority, or that their subjects could be dispensed by the Church from the obedience they owed; it declared that the rules, customs, and constitutions of the Gallican Church were inviolable, and that in matters of faith the decisions of the pope were subject to appeal to a council of the Church. This was the basis of French Gallicanism, dominant in the 18th c. It is often argued that much of Gallican doctrine was enshrined in the *Constitution Civile of 1790. After the Revolution, and particularly after the fall of the last Bourbon in 1830, royal Gallicanism became rather irrelevant. Ecclesiastical Gallicanism, however, continued to oppose the upsurge of Ultramontanism until the First Vatican Council (1870), which declared the pope infallible when making *ex cathedra* statements on matters of faith and morals, dealt it a final and fatal blow.   [RBG]

Gallimard. Publishing house founded in 1911 by *Gide, *Schlumberger, and Gaston Gallimard to publish the works of the contributors to the *Nouvelle Revue Française*, notably Gide, *Claudel, *Martin du Gard, *Péguy, and *Valéry. It was run from 1919 onwards by Gaston Gallimard, and then by his son Claude. Its first Goncourt-prize-winning author was *Proust in 1919, for the second volume of *A la recherche du temps perdu*; Gallimard had refused the first volume but bought the rights back from *Grasset in 1917. It became a major force in French literary life, publishing modern authors, both French and foreign, such as *Breton, *Sartre, *Beauvoir, Hemingway, Dos Passos, and Faulkner. Its Bibliothèque de la *Pléiade is probably the most prestigious collection of any French publishing house.   [EAF]

GALLO, Max (b. 1932). Historian and socialist politician, Gallo complements a score of historical works with nearly as many novels on contemporary historical themes, in particular *Le Cortège des vainqueurs* (1972) and his Nice trilogy: *La Baie des Anges* (1975), *Le Palais des Fêtes* (1976), *La Promenade des Anglais* (1976).   [SFN]

GAMALEYA, Boris (b. 1930). Poet from Reunion. *Vali pour une reine morte* (1972) is a long dramatic poem which introduces the archetypal figures of the poet's native island: 'l'île-reine', 'l'esclave révolté', 'le chasseur de nègres marrons'. The violence of his texts stems from the juxtaposition of dislocated images of different cultural referents and languages: French, *Creole, Malagasy, and African and Indian languages.

His other work includes *Les Contes populaires créoles* (1974), the poetry of *La Mer et la mémoire* (1978), and the dramatic poem *Le Volcan à l'envers ou Madame Desbassyns, le diable et le bon Dieu* (1983).   [BEJ]

GAMBETTA, Léon (1838–82). Republican politician, opponent of the regime of *Napoleon III, famous as an orator. He made a memorable balloon escape from besieged Paris in the *Franco-Prussian War, was hostile to the *Commune, and played a prominent role in the beginnings of the Third Republic.

Ganelon. The traitor in *La Chanson de *Roland*.

GANCE, Abel (1889–1981). Probably the most imaginative, certainly the most grandiose French film director of the silent era. The eight-hour, three-screen *Napoléon* (1926) is filmed history (and the *Napoleonic myth) at its most lyrically spectacular. The advent of sound and his *Pétainist sympathies

caused a decline of interest in his work, and for a long time *Napoléon* was available only in shortened versions until Kevin Brownlow succeeded in reconstructing a complete version in 1981. This, with live orchestral accompaniment, has been triumphantly screened to large audiences round the world.
[KAR]

GARASSE, François (1585–1631). A Jesuit who was in the forefront of the *Counter-Reformation reaction to sceptics, occult writers, and *libertins*. His *Doctrine curieuse des beaux-esprits de ce temps* (1623) and his *Somme théologique* (1625) contain violent attacks on such authors as *Vanini, *Charron, and *Théophile de Viau.   [IM]

GARAT, Dominique-Joseph (1749–1833). Journalist and teacher at the *Lycée, author of several *éloges* (e.g. of Fontenelle). He was a minister under the Convention, and a senator under Napoleon. As 'professeur d'analyse de l'entendement humain' at the *École Normale Supérieure, he was close to the *Idéologues.

GARAUDY, Roger (b. 1913). Marxist philosopher. A Protestant by background, Garaudy joined the Communist Party in 1933, becoming in 1945 a member of its leadership and official guardian of Stalinist orthodoxy. His prolific writings on intellectual, literary, and artistic issues included polemics with leading *Existentialists. After 1956 he espoused an eclectic humanist *Marxism which sought dialogue with other currents of thought, especially Catholicism, and sharply opposed the theoretical Marxism of *Althusser. Expelled from the PCF in 1970 for criticizing its position on the student movement and Czechoslovakia, he called for an alternative revolutionary strategy based on a metaphysics of hope. Subsequent religious conversions led him to Catholicism and later to Islam.   [MHK]

GARCIA, Victor (1934–82). Stage director. He created audacious baroque spectacles based on an overall environmental setting and employing strong visual and auditory effects. Like Artaud, he believed the director was the master-creator in theatre, yet his most powerful productions were those based on existing texts, notably *Genet's *Les Bonnes*, *Arrabal's *L'Architecte et l'Empereur d'Assyrie*, and Lorca's *Yerma*.   [DWW]

Garde Nationale. Originally a volunteer citizen's militia created in 1789, then a compulsory armed force (1793). Becoming a volunteer body again, its fortunes varied during the 19th c., but it was an increasingly conservative force for keeping bourgeois order. However, many of its sections supported the *Commune, and it was disbanded in 1871.

Gargantua. The giant hero of a series of popular burlesque romances featuring well-known characters from the Arthurian legends, usually referred to collectively as *Les Chroniques gargantuines* and later included in the *Bibliothèque Bleue. The version printed in 1532 seems to have prompted *Rabelais to invent Pantagruel, son of Gargantua, then to tell his own version of the story of Gargantua [see PANTA-GRUEL AND GARGANTUA]. He at first uses some of the traditional motifs, but soon outstrips the scope of his model even at the narrative level; he also adds multiple layers of other materials (e.g. from classical antiquity and the Bible), and turns the work into a vehicle for contemporary satire. [TC]

Garin de Loheren, see LOHEREN CYCLE.

Garin de Monglane. *Chanson de geste* of the 13th c. dealing with the ancestor of Guillaume d'Orange. Although one of the last of the Cycle de *Guillaume to be written, it tells of the origins of the *Narbonnais clan, following the established romance-influenced pattern of the conquest of a lady and a fief. [PEB]

GARNEAU, François-Xavier (1809–66). Canadian historian and author of the most influential work of the 19th c. in French Canada: *Histoire du Canada depuis sa découverte jusqu'à nos jours* (3 vols., 1845–8). Conceived as a response to the threat of assimilation of French Canada into English Canada posed by the Act of Union (1841), it is written from an enthusiastically nationalist point of view and sought as much to fire its readers with a faith in the future of French Canada as to record history. Few French-Canadian writers and poets for the rest of the century failed to pay tribute to Garneau and to acknowledge his influence. [SIL]

GARNEAU, Saint-Denys, see SAINT-DENYS GARNEAU.

GARNIER, Pierre (b. 1928). Poet who, after publishing some quite traditional verse, came to prominence in the 1960s as the main French representative of concrete poetry; see *Perpetuum mobile* (1968), the programmatic *Spatialisme et poésie concrète* (1968), and *Spatialisme/Anthologie, 1960–1990* (1990).

GARNIER, Robert (1545–90). The most prolific of the humanist playwrights in the ambit of the *Pléiade, Garnier studied law at Toulouse (where in 1564 and 1566 he won prizes for poetry) and, after spending some time in Paris, became a provincial magistrate. Of his seven tragedies, three (*Hippolyte*, 1573; *La Troade*, 1579; *Antigone*, 1580) are on subjects from Greek epic or tragedy, three (*Porcie*, 1568; *Cornélie*, 1574; *Marc-Antoine*, 1578) from Roman history, and one (*Les *Juives*, 1583) from the Bible. He also wrote a tragicomedy, *Bradamante* (1582), derived from Ariosto, and some non-dramatic verse, notably *Hymne de la monarchie* (1567).

Although he had some acquaintance with Greek dramatists, his main dramatic model was Seneca. All plays are in five acts, the *alexandrine is used for dialogue, the unities are respected, and the tragedies have a chorus or choruses. Speeches are often very long, the first act sometimes consisting of a single speech followed by a choric ode. Action is reported, often giving rise to lamentation. Variety is provided by a rich range of rhetorical effects, by contrasts between strongly stylized speakers, and by the use of a diversity of lyric metres in the choric poems.

Garnier's prefaces make clear that several of his subjects are chosen for the parallels they offer to the contemporary *Wars of Religion. Through the violence and pathos of his battle-scenes, through his depiction of the sufferings of civilian populations in war, and through his references to kings and kingship he conveys a strong desire for peace and an attitude of not-uncritical loyalty to the crown. He was a Catholic, and towards the end of his life was briefly a member of the *Ligue, but may have joined under duress. Garnier seems to have been admired by his contemporaries, but his tragedies inevitably fell out of favour in the following century, although *Bradamante* is in the repertory of the travelling theatre company in Scarron's *Roman comique*. When interest in Garnier's theatre revived, it was at first mainly as a precursor of French 17th-c. classical theatre that he was valued; then a growing interest in *rhetoric led to a more sympathetic appreciation of his plays. *Antigone* and *Hippolyte* have been revived (with some abridgement) in the professional theatre in Paris in the 20th c. [GJ]

See J. Holyoake, *A Critical Study of the Tragedies of Robert Garnier (1545–90)* (1987).

GARROS, Pey de, see OCCITAN LITERATURE (POST-MEDIEVAL).

GARY, Romain (pseud. of Romain Kacew) (1914–80). Novelist. Of Russian-Jewish origin, spending his childhood and early adolescence in Vilnius and Warsaw, he obtained French nationality in 1935. The influence of his early cultural, social, and ethnic background marks many of his works, particularly his first novel, *Éducation européenne* (1945), his last, *Les Cerfs-volants* (1980), and the most autobiographical, *La Promesse de l'aube* (1960).

Awarded the Prix Goncourt in 1956 for *Les Racines du ciel*, Gary was to achieve the unusual distinction of winning this prize a second time, under the pseudonym of Émile Ajar. For six years and in four novels Gary successfully mystified the French literary establishment, duplicating and indeed revitalizing his literary career. The most significant of the Ajar novels is *La Vie devant soi* (1975, Prix Goncourt). A moving, humorous, ardent defence of wounded human dignity, it is a remarkable exemplification of the strong humanitarian message which pervades Ajar/Gary's work.

The final novel, *Les Cerfs-volants*, is in many ways a summing-up of Gary's strengths. His blending of fantasy and realism of characterization, of East

European and French cultures, of rational pessimism and idealistic optimism, constitutes, in essence, a literary match for the paintings of that other French-Russian Jew, Chagall.   [AHB]

GASCAR, Pierre (pseud. of Pierre Fournier) (b. 1916). French writer. His short stories (*Les Bêtes*, 1953) and many of his novels (*Le Temps des morts*, 1953; *Le Fugitif*, 1961) deal with the theme of captivity (he was imprisoned in World War II). His travels to China led him to write a series of essays, including *La Chine ouverte* (1955) and *Voyage chez les vivants* (1958).   [EAF]

Gaspard de la Montagne, see POURRAT.

Gaspard de la nuit, see BERTRAND, A.

GASSENDI, Pierre (1592–1655). Priest, philosopher, and astronomer, considered in his own day *Descartes's most formidable French opponent. A native of Provence, he completed his university education in the south, and became known through the publication of the first volume of his anti-Aristotelian *Exercitationes* in 1624. Soon after he made contact with *Mersenne, *Descartes, *Peiresc, and others. The final 30 years of his life were divided almost equally between Provence and Paris. He published a number of works on astronomical observations, and biographies of such astronomers as Tycho Brahe and Copernicus, but he is best known today for his exposition of the philosophy of Epicurus and his defence of scepticism. These aspects of his work, together with his commitment to the new science, have led some historians to associate him with the *libertins, but it seems much more appropriate to see in him a member of that group of progressive thinkers and participants in the nascent European republic of science and letters for whom an attachment to traditional Catholicism was compatible with the pursuit of mechanistic science, empiricism, anti-Aristotelianism, and an opposition to metaphysics in all its forms. It was this last feature of Gassendi's thought which led him into conflict with Descartes, on whose works he wrote a number of penetrating critiques.

His own scientific endeavours, whether theoretical or practical, are not particularly innovative; nor did he grasp the importance of the mathematical and quantitative approach to science which informed the work of his contemporaries and friends. But he represents the new spirit of free rational enquiry liberated from scholastic physics and cosmology. His work on Epicurus was directed at removing the taint of hedonism from Epicurean philosophy, and rehabilitating materialism, which, he argued, was not incompatible with Catholic theology. A collected edition of his works appeared posthumously in Latin in 1658; *Bernier produced a French account of his philosophy in 1675. He was one of the 'tétrade' of friends, with *Naudé, *La Mothe le Vayer, and later *Patin, who were active in the philosophical and literary life of Paris in the middle years of the century.   [IM]

See H. Berr (ed.), *Pierre Gassendi* (1955).

GASTON PHÉBUS (1331–91). Gaston III, comte de Foix, known as Phébus because of his golden good looks, was a passionate hunter, and is principally known as author of the outstandingly popular *Livre de la chasse* (1387–91). Mainly based on personal experience and observation, this five-part treatise deals with the habits of game-animals, hunting-dogs and their ailments, the training of hounds, the tracking, killing, and butchering of stags and other game, and finally—but with a touch of aristocratic distaste—with the use of traps and nets. Many copies have informative, detailed miniatures; one (BN, f. fr. 616) is among the finest manuscripts in the world.
                    [JHMT]

GATTI, Armand (b. 1924). French playwright, filmmaker, journalist, and poet. A committed artist of anarchist tendencies, he embraced theatre and other performance media as a means of testifying to the struggles of the modern world. His plays are challenging in both content and form. They seek not to unite audiences, nor to communicate a reassuring revolutionary faith, but to force spectators to confront uncomfortable questions concerning contemporary reality. In an attempt to reveal the multiple aspects of a situation, Gatti employs a complex dramaturgy, which he calls 'théâtre éclaté', with actions and characters situated on several planes and in different time-scales.

In the 1960s much of his writing was autobiographical. *La Vie imaginaire de l'éboueur Auguste Geai* (1962) presents his father, an Italian immigrant worker, at five formative stages of his life. In *La Deuxième Existence du camp de Tatenberg* (1962) Gatti, himself an escapee from a Nazi concentration camp, explores the long-term effects of the experience on former inmates. Among other plays from this period, *Un homme seul* deals with the Chinese Civil War, *La Naissance* with the Guatemalan independence movement, *La Cigogne* with the survivors of Nagasaki, *Chant public devant deux chaises électriques* with the execution of Sacco and Vanzetti.

Frustration with the restrictions of established theatre, especially after the government's intervention in 1968 to ban the TNP production of *La Passion du Général Franco*, led him to explore more open and participatory structures permitting fuller contact with audiences. He also became a peripatetic artist, documenting his plays by drawing on lived experience in a specific community: in Northern Ireland, for example, where he produced a film, *Nous étions tous des noms d'arbres* (1982), and a play, *Le Labyrinthe* (1982). An uncompromising poet who seeks to express complex truths through a combination of reportage and telling images, he stands as the foremost committed dramatist of post-war years.
                    [DWW]

GAUCELM FAIDIT (*fl. c.*1172–1203). *Troubadour. His large output (65 songs of certain attribution) is very varied in style and genre; his most famous pieces are a crusade song and a lament (*planh*) for the death of Richard Lionheart, but he also wrote love songs in which *fin'amor* and misogyny compete interestingly for dominance. [SK]

GAUGUIN, Paul (1848–1903). Considered today one of the founders of 20th-c. painting, Gauguin initially exhibited with the *Impressionists before developing his own technique in which rich colour, heavy outline, and the flattening of the picture-surface were used to represent the artist's subjective, emotional response to external reality. The result was hailed by *Aurier in 1891 as the pictorial equivalent of literary *Symbolism. Gauguin also collaborated with the poet and critic *Morice on Noa Noa, an account of his life and work during his first journey to Tahiti (1891–3). His formal experimentation and interest in all types of primitive art were of great importance, notably for *Matisse and *Picasso. [JK]

GAULLE, Charles de (1890–1970). Soldier and statesman. He was born in Lille; his family was of the lesser nobility, Catholic, and intensely patriotic. Educated at Catholic establishments, he began his military career when he entered *Saint-Cyr in 1909. Serving as a junior officer in World War I, he used his time as a prisoner-of-war to study military and German history. His analysis of German military leadership, La Discorde chez l'ennemi (1924), stressed the importance of maintaining harmony between civilian and military leadership.

Throughout the inter-war period de Gaulle distinguished himself by his writing and lectures. Le Fil de l'épée (1931) examined the qualities needed for leadership. Vers l'armée de métier (1934) put forward the need for a small, highly trained professional army. La France et son armée (1938) begins with the words: 'La France fut faite à coups d'épée', and fits in well with his 1924 remark: 'l'histoire est ma passion.' But these books did not endear him to his colleagues, especially when he challenged the prevailing military orthodoxy. His career languished, and it was with difficulty that he was promoted to the rank of colonel.

However, when on 10 May 1940 the Germans launched their offensive, de Gaulle found himself at the centre of battles around Laon and Abbeville. On 6 June he was made under-secretary at the Ministry of Defence. In the turmoil of defeat, when *Pétain came to power, de Gaulle left for London and on 18 June, supported by Churchill, he made his famous broadcast proclaiming the existence of La France Libre. Although a little-known general without an army, he established himself as the leader of the French Resistance, both inside and outside France [see OCCUPATION AND RESISTANCE]. He entered Paris in triumph in August 1944 and directed the provisional government.

In January 1946 he resigned in protest against the way the new constitution was evolving. There began a long period of unsuccessful political activity and isolation, from which he only emerged when the *Algerian War created a crisis in 1958. Acting with superb tactical skill, he imposed himself on a country fearful of civil war and created the Fifth Republic, with its strong presidential powers. From 1958 to 1969 the history of de Gaulle is the history of that Republic. He assumed a prestigious place in world affairs, but his position in France was severely shaken by the events of *May 1968. The following year he promoted a complicated referendum on constitutional reform which was defeated. He resigned and withdrew from public life, dying the following year.

During his first retirement he wrote his Mémoires de guerre (3 vols., 1954–9), and after 1969 he worked on his unfinished Mémoires d'espoir (2 vols., 1970–1). Since 1946 many volumes have been published of his Discours et messages and since 1970 Lettres, notes et carnets. His writings and speeches have been much praised for their style. He was influenced by such classical authors as *Montesquieu, by Romantic writers including *Michelet and *Chateaubriand, and by more recent figures: *Barrès, *Péguy, *Bergson. Some of his words are frequently quoted, above all the opening of the Mémoires: 'Toute ma vie, je me suis fait une certaine idée de la France.' His friend and colleague André *Malraux claimed that he was 'le dernier grand homme qu'ait hanté la France'. [DJ]

See B. Ledwidge, De Gaulle (1982); J. Lacouture, De Gaulle, 3 vols. (1984–6).

Gaullism. Political movement characterized by its fidelity to the ideas of Charles de *Gaulle, in particular the defence of French national identity and sovereignty. It has gone under different names, currently (1990) the Rassemblement pour la République (RPR), led by Jacques Chirac.

Gauloiserie, SEE EROTICISM AND PORNOGRAPHY.

GAULTIER-GARGUILLE (pseud. of Hugues Guéru) (d. 1633). Member of a famous trio of *farceurs* who played at the *Hôtel de Bourgogne in the early 17th c. The other members were Gros-Guillaume (Robert Guérin, d. 1634) and Turlupin (Henri Legrand, d. 1637). They also performed in tragedies.

GAUTIER, Théophile (1811–72). Poet, novelist, and critic. He spent his whole life in Paris and was a central figure in the world of literature and art for nearly half a century, moving from the brash young Turk of the *Petit Cénacle to the established member of Second Empire high society.

More than most other important writers, Gautier has suffered from being made to exemplify a series of positions and postures beloved of traditional literary history: youthful Romanticism at the time of Hugo's *Hernani (chronicled in Gautier's own

Gautier d'Arras

Histoire du romantisme, 1872); dandyish aestheticism in his *Préface de *Mademoiselle de Maupin*; cold and formalistic Parnassianism in *Émaux et camées* (1852). Not that any of the traditional characterizations are exactly false; rather, they tell only a very small part of the story. Gautier's work is, in fact, rich and varied. His critical writings on literature, fine art, theatre, pantomime, ballet, and dance, for the most part originally published in the periodical press, fill many volumes, including *Les Grotesques* (1844— essays on writers such as *Villon or *Théophile), *L'Art moderne* (1855), *Histoire de l'art dramatique depuis vingt-cinq ans* (6 vols., 1858–9). The value and interest of this work has yet to be fully acknowledged, as has that of his large body of travel writing (including *Voyage en Espagne*, 1845).

His reputation for impersonal formalism or rococo sensuality has for too long perpetuated an image of Gautier as superficial, frivolous, and even heartless. In fact, even in his early self-dramatizing and provocatively *risqué* works, one can detect a writer who, while amply given to play and paradox, none the less shows himself to be engaged with a set of deep obsessions concerning sexuality and death which would continue to preoccupy him in all his later works. He displayed enormous virtuosity and self-assurance in his early works, and his assault on the utilitarianism and philistinism of bourgeois society in the *Préface de Mademoiselle de Maupin* remains a remarkably lively and pertinent piece of writing. It was here that Gautier put forward the aggressive version of l'*art pour l'art* with which he has most commonly been identified.

He was a successful exponent of many fashionable forms, from the two long narrative poems playing on fantastic or Byronic themes, *Albertus* (1832) and *La Comédie de la mort* (1838), to the Hoffmannesque *fantastic tales such as 'La Morte amoureuse'. But his success was not merely a fashionable one, and his importance was handsomely acknowledged by *Baudelaire when he dedicated *Les *Fleurs du mal* 'au poète impeccable', 'au parfait magicien ès lettres françaises'. In Gautier a lifelong belief in the superior values of art and artifice went together with a readiness to work with the most difficult verse forms (particularly the octosyllabic quatrain). His aestheticism was at one with the themes of literary decadence, and he was to have a great influence upon English *fin-de-siècle* culture. He has also remained popular with the general public for his historical adventure novel, *Le Capitaine Fracasse* (1853). [BR]

See P. E. Tennant, *Théophile Gautier* (1975).

GAUTIER D'ARRAS (*fl.* 1160–85). Author of the octosyllabic verse romances *Ille et Galeron* and *Eracle*, he enjoyed the patronage of Marie de Champagne, Thibaut V of Blois, husband of her sister Aélis, and of Baudouin—probably Baudouin V—of Hainaut. *Ille et Galeron* relates the story, also treated by *Marie de France, of a man between two women.

Ille, having lost an eye in battle and fearing that his wife Galeron will no longer love him, departs for Rome. His military exploits are appreciated by the emperor, whose daughter Ganor falls in love with him. Galeron meanwhile has searched Europe for her husband and finds him just before he can be married to Ganor. Ille and Galeron live happily in Brittany for some years until Galeron retires to a convent; Ille subsequently marries Ganor. The eponymous hero of the rather less coherent *Eracle* has the marvellous ability to distinguish the true worth of gemstones, horses, and women. His gifts impress the emperor of Rome, whose wife he chooses. The situation of *Ille et Galeron* is inverted when the empress, poorly treated by her husband, takes a lover; the emperor magnanimously releases his wife to marry Paridès. The scene then shifts to Constantinople, where Eracle is elected co-emperor; in conclusion he restores the True Cross to Jerusalem. [RMJ]

GAUTIER DE CHÂTILLON (b. 1135). One of the most illustrious Latin poets of the 12th c., author of the epic *Alexandreis* about Alexander the Great (written in hexameters, probably between 1178 and 1182) and of much lyric poetry. He is credited with inventing the Goliardic metre *cum auctoritate* (i.e. rhythmical stanzas ending in a hexameter or pentameter). [PJF]

GAUTIER DE COINCI (1177–1236). Born of noble stock, Gautier became a Benedictine novice at Saint-Médard de Soissons in 1193 and prior at Vic-sur-Aisne in 1214, returning to Saint-Médard to be grand prior (1233) until his death. His single work, preserved in nearly 80 manuscripts, is the massive *Miracles de Nostre Dame*, written at Vic (1214–27) and occupying some 30,000 lines in two books. Besides prologues, epilogue, and two sermons on chastity and fear of death, it contains 22 lyrics celebrating the Virgin (*contrafacta* of Latin para-liturgical songs or of vernacular courtly lyrics) and 76 Marian legends which freely adapt Latin sources. [PVD]

GAUTIER DE DARGIES. *Trouvère* from Dargies, near Grandvilliers (Oise), historically attested in 1195, 1201, 1206 (as a *vavasour*), and 1236 (as a knight); he probably joined the Third Crusade. He composed some 24 extant lyrics—one motet, one *tenson* advising a young Richard (de *Fournival), and 19 *chansons* plus three *descorts* treating *fin'amor*. He was an associate of *Gace Brulé. [PVD]

Gauvain. Renowned hero of medieval French romance, son of King Lot, nephew of King *Arthur, and one of the pre-eminent knights of the Round Table. Although less known today than his peers *Lancelot or Perceval, Gauvain (or Gawain) was one of the most popular and most frequently treated figures in the *matière de Bretagne. Oral stories about this stock character doubtless preceded and spread alongside Gauvain's literary characterization, which develops in the hands of different authors throughout the evolution of *romance. The knight's status as a paragon of prowess and courtesy is established in his first vernacular appearance in *Wace's Brut. In *Chrétien de Troyes's Yvain he is the 'sun of chivalry', the standard against which other knights are measured. But, as early as Yvain and Lancelot, and more strikingly in the Conte du Graal, Gauvain finds himself in situations that compromise his status as the perfect knight: he backs the wrong side in a judicial case; he fails to protect women to whom he owes allegiance; his amorous dalliances lack commitment; compared with Lancelot or Perceval, his adventures have no emotional or moral purpose. In the verse continuations of the Conte du Graal, the authors play up the contrast between Perceval's seriousness and Gauvain's superficiality, sometimes portraying Gauvain with humour, sometimes presenting a darker picture.

Gauvain's failure to live up to his perfect reputation made him a favourite figure of romancers who sought to burlesque or critique courtly conventions; he is featured in a number of 13th-c. verse romances that demystify the courtly ideal (i.e. *Raoul de Houdenc's La Vengeance Raguidel). By the time of the monumental Vulgate cycle [see LANCELOT; GRAIL ROMANCES], Gauvain's character as a ladies' man was well established. As a result of his superficial attraction to female beauty he is clearly unqualified to complete the Grail quest. Although he remains a model of courtesy and Arthur's closest advisor, he recedes in the hierarchy behind Lancelot, Perceval, and Galahad. In the Queste del Saint Graal and La *Mort le roi Artu, Gauvain displays a violent streak that culminates in his final, tragic vengeance against Lancelot. His wrath brings about his own death and contributes to the eventual destruction of the Arthurian kingdom. Gauvain's complex, often ironic, presentation in Old French romance inspired one of the masterpieces of English medieval literature, Sir Gawain and the Green Knight.   [RLK]

See K. Busby, Gauvain in Old French Literature (1980).

GAUVIN, Axel, see MAURITIUS AND REUNION.

GAUVREAU, Claude (1925–71). Canadian poet and dramatist who practised the *Dadaist and *Surrealist techniques associated with the Automatiste (automatic writing) movement in Quebec. He was a signatory of the famous Refus global manifesto of *Borduas. In his lifetime neither his poetry, which includes Dadaist experiments in howls and screams, nor his plays had much success. Consecration has come through highly successful posthumous productions of two of his reputedly 'unstageable' plays, La Charge de l'orignal épormyable (1956) and Les Oranges sont vertes (1970). Both deal with the figure of the persecuted artist, which Gauvreau made part of his personal legend. The first, which draws on his own experience of psychiatric treatment, departs

less from conventional dramatic form than the second, which has a hallucinatory extravagance of speech and action.   [SIL]

GAVARNI, Paul (pseud. of Sulpice-Guillaume Chevalier) (1804–66). Artist, engraver; a central figure in the lively world of illustration in the July Monarchy and beyond. He tended to stay clear of serious political subjects and specialized in elegant and witty treatments of fashionable topics. He particularly favoured the cheeky, erotic portrayal of the lorette type of woman.   [BR]

Gavroche. Heroic street urchin in Hugo's Les *Misérables.

Gay and Lesbian Writing. There has been as yet no substantial investigation of the role of homosexuality in French literature before the 20th c. This is in part because gay writers tended to work outside the mainstream, as in the cases of *Théophile de Viau and *Cyrano de Bergerac, in part because writers did not perceive themselves as having a gay identity or as being part of a separate homosexual culture—the very term 'homosexuality' is a late 19th-c. invention.

From the 1870s the growth of a medico-pychiatric discourse tending to identify homosexuality as an involuntary condition rather than a series of voluntary acts, and as a sickness rather than a sin, coincided with the emergence of a succession of writers, nurtured on the Romantic image of the writer as pariah and on the *Baudelairean rejection of nature, who drew on their own sexual orientation to develop these themes. At the same time there was a growing awareness of contemporary English and German defences of an idealized Greek pederasty which provided the only model for a positive literary account of any aspect of homosexuality. The foundations for 20th-c. French gay male writing lie in the generation born between 1840 and 1880, in the works of writers such as *Verlaine, *Rimbaud, the Belgian novelist and critic Georges Eekhoud (1854–1927), Pierre *Louÿs, Jean *Lorrain, *Gide, and *Proust. Unsurprisingly, given the context of its formation, the immediate legacy of this generation was twofold: a literature of pederastic apologia and a gay male literature of guilt.

The situation for lesbian writers was slightly different. Lesbianism, although it made a more serious appearance in *Balzac's La Fille aux yeux d'or and *Sand's Lélia, had been a permitted theme of mildly erotic literature, most of it written by and intended for the titillation of male heterosexual readers, throughout the 19th c.. One such work, Loti's Les *Chansons de Bilitis (1894), paradoxically became the inspiration for the group of lesbian writers surrounding the poet and essayist Natalie Barney (1876–1972) and the poet Renée Vivien (1877–1909) who 'launched' French lesbian writing at the start of the 20th c. on a tone often much more positive than that of their male counterparts.

Gay and Lesbian Writing

The first phase of modern gay writing runs from Proust to *Genet, via *Cocteau. These writers, lacking any model for a positive account of adult male homosexuality, project a negative self-image. All three were fascinated by male homosexual desire as a pursuit of *otherness*. In the case of Proust this 'otherness' was most often found in class difference, and offered a direct parallel with the 'otherness' imposed by Jewishness. Proust also subscribed to the view propounded by contemporary German sexology, that homosexuals were spiritual hermaphrodites, possessing the soul of one sex in the body of the other, and thereby condemned to love 'real' (i.e. heterosexual) men, who by definition would be unable to return that love. Proust's account of homosexuality is depressing, first because all the images he uses for it suggest an inescapable negative condition, and secondly because he depicts it as creating structures within society which, by cutting across normal social boundaries, undermine it, making of it a phenomenon which inevitably invites repression.

Cocteau projects a comparable negative self-image. His *Le Livre blanc*, published anonymously in 1928, while it poses as a plea for social acceptance, projects a series of impossible, doomed homosexual passions which offer a mirror-image of the doomed heterosexual passions in his plays. The motif of love-as-death also occurs in the idea that beauty deals the artist a fatal wound, an image recurrent in his poems and in *Les Enfants terribles*. Homosexuality for Cocteau, as for Proust, is congenital, inescapable, and a factor which dissolves social structures, but, whereas for Proust salvation through art is thematically separated from homosexuality, for Cocteau his sexual orientation, triggered by the 'wound of beauty', is a prerequisite for artistic creation.

Far from breaking away from the tradition of the homosexual as a doomed outlaw whose existence is only justified if it gives birth to art, Genet carried it one step further. In his novels homosexuality is a state characterized by isolation and guilt. He uses it, together with murder, as the ultimate manifestation of evil. While his lyrical treatment of homosexual acts marked a breakthrough in gay writing, the heavy sexual stereotyping and the insistent coupling of homosexuality with criminality made his work go rapidly out of fashion in the socially more tolerant climate of the 1970s.

In the period 1900–50 *positive* images of male homosexuality were largely confined to pederastic literature. The growth of a 'literature of adolescence' before World War I and its extension into a cult of youth by right-wing writers in the inter-war period coincides with Gide's expounding of the Greek mentor–pupil model of male love. Gide's defence of pederasty as physically normal and morally healthy in *Corydon*, his exemplification of such a relationship in *Les *Faux-monnayeurs*, and his confession of his own sexual experiences in North Africa in *Si le grain ne meurt* paved the way for a considerable literature in the period 1940–70 exploring adolescent sexuality in a pederastic context, by writers as diverse as Julien *Green, *Montherlant, and Roger *Peyrefitte, a tradition degenerating into coy salaciousness and even downright pornography. Over the same period (1900–50) lesbian literature, while often projecting a positive self-image, tended, after the initially isolationist approach of Barney's circle, to explore the issue of female identity, particularly female sexuality, within a bisexual context. This approach, cultivated especially by *Colette and continued into the next generation in the works of Christiane *Rochefort, is coherent with the way in which lesbian writing in France has become increasingly more a facet of women's writing and less closely tied to gay writing than is true in the English-speaking world. The tortured texts of Violette *Leduc, which form a bridge with progressive lesbian writing of the 1960s and after, were retrogressive in so far as they are based on self-hatred, but achieved a frank expression of female sensuality comparable in importance to that of Genet in gay writing [see also EROTICISM AND PORNOGRAPHY].

In the 1950s and early 1960s there were signs of a gradual relaxation in gay attitudes. In 1954, for instance, with the support of Cocteau and Peyrefitte, André Baudry founded an association, Arcadie, and a serious monthly review of the same name, dedicated to discreet defence and exploration of what the Arcadians preferred to term 'homophilie'. On the other hand, in the same year *Jouhandeau still felt it necessary to publish his eulogy of sodomy, *Tirésias*, anonymously. But the end of the 1960s, partly under the spur of the events of *May 1968, partly in response to developments in the USA after the Stonewall Riot in 1969, saw a dramatic change in the status and nature of homosexual literary expression in France in all three aspects—gay, pederastic, and lesbian. Negative self-images continue to appear in the works of Michel *Tournier and Yves *Navarre, for example, but there also appeared works in which, for the first time, homosexuality is not so much an issue as a simple fact, the focus of the work being elsewhere, as in *Bory's *La Peau des zèbres*.

Gay issues became politicized, notably through the FHAR (Front Homosexuel d'Action Révolutionnaire) formed in 1971 by a group including Guy *Hocquenghem, and its successor GLH (Groupes de Libération Homosexuelles) formed in 1974, and the founding of the periodical *Gai pied* provided a mouthpiece for a more polemical generation of writers, including Hocquenghem and Renaud *Camus. This politicization is reflected in particular in Tony *Duvert's powerful and disturbing essays and novels promoting pederasty, and in the radical lesbian texts of Monique *Wittig; both writers argue that capitalism promotes heterosexuality as a tool of social control. Meanwhile in Canada Michel *Tremblay began to explore cultural, political, and sexual marginalization as interrelated phenomena.

The advent of AIDS ('le SIDA') in the 1980s

caused a further significant shift in gay writing. Because AIDS principally affects gay adult males, it has temporarily eclipsed pederastic literature and has hastened the alignment of lesbian writing with the broader current of *feminist literature. It has also caused an unexpected convergence of previously divergent streams of gay writing. Once again outlawed by society, gay males have been faced with the choice of accepting pariah status passively, even willingly (e.g. Jean-Noël Pancrazi, *Les Quartiers d'hiver*, 1991, Prix Goncourt; Alain-Emmanuel Dreuilhe, *Corps à corps: journal du Sida*, 1987), welcoming the status while rejecting its negative implications (Dominique *Fernandez), or contesting it (Navarre, Hervé *Guibert). Through the expression of the physical and psychological experience of AIDS and the attempt to constitute a 'living' memorial to the dead, AIDS writing is reassessing the relationship between life and art and the value of both.

Perhaps the most notable uniting factor in gay and lesbian writing in the 20th c. is its reluctance to conform to prevailing aesthetic orthodoxies. Although conceptually rooted in previous tradition, Proust and Gide broke new ground aesthetically; Genet, Colette, and Violette Leduc ignored conventional generic distinctions; *Yourcenar, Hocquenghem, and Fernandez sought new uses for historical fiction; Wittig and Duvert re-harnessed the techniques of the Nouveau Roman to broadly 'political' ends. In particular, Michel Tremblay has developed a complex system of intertextual reference, within his own work and outwards to metropolitan French literature, to link personal, social, and cultural issues. Above all, AIDS writing, notably in the texts of Guibert, has activated all these approaches, together with techniques of documentary fiction, in its attempt to find both a fulfilment and a justification in art for lives tragically cut short.

[CFR]

See G. Stamboulian and E. Marks (eds.), *Homosexualities and French Literature* (1979); C. Robinson, *Homosexuality and Twentieth-Century French Literature* (1994).

GAY, Sophie (1776–1852). French novelist. In her work, pre-Romantic sensibility is combined with classical economy and analytical precision; *Léonie de Montbreuse* (1813) and *Anatole* (1815) are perhaps the best of her novels. Her *Souvenirs d'une vieille fille* (1834) provide at times amusing insights into the Romantic movement and contemporary celebrities. She was the mother of Delphine Gay de *Girardin.

[FPB]

Gazette, La, see PRESS, I; RENAUDOT.

GELÉE, Claude, see CLAUDE LE LORRAIN.

GÉLINAS, Gratien (b. 1908). Canadian actor and playwright who was the first important dramatist in modern Quebec theatre. Before *Dubé he put the québécois working class on the stage, using a vernac-

ular that was authentic and colourful. The source of his inspiration is to be found in the pre-war *Fridolinades*, a series of variety-hall satirical sketches, whose hero Fridolin (played by himself) is a diminutive street urchin, wise beyond his years, occasionally wistful as well as cheeky. The anti-hero of *Tit-Coq* (1948) is an older, wryer Fridolin, whose status as a bastard and resultant exclusion from family happiness poignantly express the contemporary québécois feeling of cultural and social disinheritance. In *Bousille et les justes* (1954) the tone darkens further, the little man-cum-orphan hero being abused and driven to suicide by a society now seen as problematic and hypocritical. Only *Hier les enfants dansaient* (1968), on the topical political debate over separatism, does not have its roots in working-class humour and pathos, and is less convincing as a result. Although not without flaws of form and substance, Gélinas's work as a whole remains a vivid and touching chronicle of the evolution of québécois sensibility.

[SIL]

GÉMIER, Firmin (1869–1933). French actor and director. A pupil of *Antoine and the creator of the role of Père *Ubu, he became interested in popular theatre, directing Romain *Rolland's *Le 14 juillet* in 1902, creating the short-lived Théâtre Ambulant (1911–12), which toured France by rail, and becoming the director of the first *Théâtre National Populaire in 1920.

Gendarmerie, see POLICE.

Gendre de Monsieur Poirier, Le, see AUGIER.

GENET, Jean (1910–86). French playwright and novelist. Courting scandal throughout his life, Genet first achieved notoriety as a criminal who, on paper stolen from the prison workshops, secretly wrote texts that combined aesthetic aspirations with largely pornographic content. Discovered by *Cocteau, who on the strength of Genet's first poem proclaimed him a literary genius and secured a presidential pardon for him, his reputation was established by his first novels: *Notre-Dame-des-fleurs* (1944), a prison-cell fantasy woven around celebrated murderers and figures of Parisian low-life, and *Miracle de la Rose* (1946), evoking the mystical adoration directed by youthful delinquents in Mettray Reformatory towards the murderer awaiting execution in Fontevrault Prison. Another early admirer and friend was *Sartre, who wrote the monumental *Saint Genet, comédien et martyr* (1951) which established Genet as an *Existentialist hero and helped enshrine the legend of the artist emerging spontaneously from the outcast. Although it is true that Genet was a foundling, never knew his mother nor the identity of his father, and spent his youth in state institutions or wandering Europe in more or less abject poverty, there is plenty of evidence to indicate that his literary bent pre-dated his prison career. That he provocatively cultivated his criminal image is evident in *Journal du voleur* (1948); in his other novels, *Querelle de Brest* and *Pompes funèbres* (1947), the narratorial voice delights in challenging the bemused reader to distinguish between reactions of scandal and complicity.

Being canonized and comprehensively explained by Sartre proved a deeply unsettling experience, and for a while Genet was haunted by the prospect of literary sterility. None the less, he re-emerged in the mid-1950s as a powerful and innovative dramatist. He had written *Haute surveillance* and *Les *Bonnes* in the late 1940s, but the relatively conventional productions these had received tended to restrict their impact to that of their author's notoriety. *Le Balcon* (1956) depicts a brothel whose clients, accustomed to fantasizing in roles such as Judge, General, and Bishop, are called upon to stand in for these figures of authority when a revolution threatens to overturn the ruling regime outside. The script inevitably provoked new scandal, with the result that it was two years before a production in French could be mounted. The theatrical ambition was far-reaching, amounting to an assault on stage conventions of a kind envisaged by *Artaud. Genet himself expressed outrage at the inadequacy of the first production, in English, which this play received.

Of the plays that followed, *Les *Nègres* (1958) articulated the psychology of racial hatred in uncompromising terms. Roger *Blin staged a French production in 1959 which won the author's wholehearted approval, and *The Blacks* ran for three years in the United States in a 1961 production which coincided with and contributed significantly to the rise of the Civil Rights movement. *Les Paravents* (1961), set in Algeria and not staged in France until four years after the end of the *Algerian War, succeeded even at this remove in causing outrage through its vigorous enactment of colonial conflict. While his depiction of power relations has a visceral, emotional impact, the dramatic method Genet explores involves a high degree of theatrical self-consciousness, in which magnificent ritualized spectacle plays tantalizingly with the distinction between illusion and reality. These texts draw on the richest theatrical traditions to produce effects which are profoundly original and challenging.

Apart from essays on Rembrandt and Giacometti and other fragments, Genet virtually ceased literary publication after 1961, devoting himself instead to the support of political and social groups with which he could identify. It seems likely that he sought in this way to re-establish with society the relationship of hostility and exclusion to which he had become accustomed, and which he feared losing on becoming a successful artist. He witnessed the student uprising of *May 1968 in Paris, and went on to seek more convincing militancy in the American Civil Rights movement and among the Black Panthers. Subsequently he wrote a preface to the prison letters of Black activist George Jackson,

and created a furore in 1977 with an article supporting the Baader-Meinhof terrorists. He also developed a long-standing allegiance to the Palestinian Liberation Organization, his relations with which figure prominently in *Un captif amoureux* (1986), a prose work he completed shortly before his death.

[DHW]

See R. Coe, *The Vision of Jean Genet* (1968); J.-B. Moraly, *Jean Genet, la vie écrite* (1988); E. White, *Genet* (1993).

GENETTE, Gérard (b. 1930). French critic and theorist. His *Structuralist approach seeks to map the formal possibilities of literary art rather than to offer interpretations of works. A series of essays, *Figures* (3 vols., 1966, 1969, 1972) culminates in a theory of narratology, illustrated from Proust's **A la recherche*. Subsequent volumes have been concerned with ideas of a language corresponding to reality (*Mimologiques*, 1976), literary genres (*Introduction à l'architexte*, 1979), the relationship of texts with preceding texts (*Palimpsestes*, 1982), and the beginnings of works (*Seuils*, 1987). [PF]

Geneva School of Criticism. Name somewhat misleadingly given to a loose grouping of critics most of whom were Swiss and/or taught at Geneva. The leading figures are *Béguin, *Raymond, *Poulet, *Rousset, *Starobinski, and *Richard. Inspired by the critics of the *NRF, by *Bachelard, and by German philosophy, they used thematic analysis to approach the 'monde imaginaire' or 'moi profond' of the writer, seeking identification between critic and author. Their intuitive approach was very influential until about 1970, when it was challenged by the development of a more hard-headed formalist or *Structuralist criticism. [PF]

Geneviève de Brabant. Legendary heroine, victim of the machinations of her husband's seneschal Golo, whose advances she had rebuffed. Her life figures in the **Légende dorée*; it was popular in the *Bibliothèque Bleue, has been the subject of songs, plays, and stories, and is depicted on the lantern slides recalled with nostalgia by the narrator of **A la recherche du temps perdu*.

GENEVOIX, Maurice (1890–1980). French novelist. He wrote carefully documented, vivid studies of soldiering in *World War I, reissued as *Ceux de Verdun* (1950), and then a long sequence of solidly crafted novels with a strong regional core, centring on the Val de Loire: *Rémi des Rauches* (1922), *Roboliot* (1925, Prix Goncourt) on poaching in the Sologne, *Marcheloup* (1934). Closeness to nature, like childhood (*La Loire, Agnès et les garcons*, 1962), is seen as conferring unique insights, and animals too are valued. A specialized vocabulary is used for every rural activity, from barrel-making to stag-hunting. Some of his works reflect visits to Canada (1940s) and Africa (1950s). [MMC]

Génie du christianisme, Le, see CHATEAUBRIAND; ROMANTICISM, 2.

Génie du lieu, Le, see BUTOR.

Génitrix. Novel by *Mauriac, published 1923. One of his most powerful evocations of domestic and provincial claustrophobia, it explores the obsessive possessiveness of Félicité Cazenave towards her son Fernand, resulting in her virtual murder of his wife Mathilde. This has the effect of turning Fernand against his mother, and she dies in her turn, leaving Fernand alone. A ray of hope is introduced at the end of the novel with the return of the family servant, Marie. [NH]

GENLIS, Stéphanie-Félicité du Crest, Madame de (1746–1830). French educationalist, novelist, and memoir-writer. She was briefly the mistress of the duc de Chartres and thereafter governess to his children, but her constitutionalist politics lost her the favour of the European courts, which she had won by her works on education (*Adèle et Théodore ou Lettres sur l'éducation,* 1782) and her stories and plays for children (*Les Veillées du château,* 1784; *Théâtre à l'usage des jeunes personnes,* 1779–80). In exile she turned to rewriting history in the form of memoirs and popular historical novels, and continued with both after her return to France in 1800 (e.g. *Mademoiselle de la Fayette,* 1813; *Les Parvenus,* 1824; *Mémoires inédits sur le XVIIIe siècle et la révolution française,* 1825–8.) [JB]

GENTIL-BERNARD, see BERNARD, P.-J.

GENTILLET, Innocent (d. *c.*1595). Protestant magistrate from Grenoble who fled to Geneva in 1572. He is now remembered for his *Discours d'état . . . contre Machiavel* (1576), which reflects Protestant fury at the *St Bartholomew's Day Massacre. Gentillet's work is important in so far as it enabled the Protestants to present their resistance to the French monarchy as legitimate self-defence. It also did more than perhaps any other contemporary text to spread the view of the 'murderous Machiavelli' in France. His attacks were directed in particular at *Catherine de Médicis, the granddaughter of the man to whom *Il Principe* had been dedicated. Catherine was certainly involved in the plot against *Coligny; but she was far from being the cynical disciple of Machiavelli (whose views are in any case distorted) presented by Gentillet. The *Anti-Machiavel* (as it is often known) is typical, however, of the growing anti-Italian feeling of this period. [IJS]

GEOFFREY OF MONMOUTH (d. 1155). An Anglo-Welsh Augustinian canon resident at Oxford, Geoffrey rapidly became the most popular historian of the 12th c. following his *Historia Regum Britanniae* (1135–8), an account of the early history of Britain from its foundation by the Trojan Brutus until the establishment of the Saxon hegemony in the late 7th c. Supposedly exploiting a 'very ancient book in the British [i.e. Welsh] tongue', it recreated the Celtic past, complementing laconic Insular historiography by free and imaginative use of alternative, no doubt oral, sources. It gave particular prominence to King *Arthur, whose literary vogue it initiated by way of *Wace and the *matière de Bretagne. Geoffrey also wrote the *Prophetiae Merlini* as well as a *Vita Merlini* in hexameters. He died in 1155 as bishop of St Asaph in North Wales. The survival of well over 200 manuscripts of his *Historia* is a measure of his literary success. [IS]

GEOFFRIN, Marie-Thérèse, née Rodet (1699–1777). At the time of her marriage in 1713 to a wealthy older man, nothing indicated that Geoffrin would become the most powerful woman in the Republic of Letters. In 1730 she met the reigning *salonnière,* *Tencin, who formed Geoffrin as her successor. In her house in the rue Saint-Honoré she opened a *salon frequented by prominent writers such as *Fontenelle and d'*Alembert, and the most important contemporary artists and musicians—Mozart first played for Parisian society there. Friend to the *philosophes, she entertained many foreigners, from Walpole to Hume, attracted by the period's intellectual ferment. She corresponded regularly with numerous foreign courts and visited Poland at the invitation of King Stanislas Poniatowski, whose mentor she was for decades. From what was known as her 'royaume de la rue Saint-Honoré', this bourgeoise exercised influence over crowned heads. *Saint-Beuve called her salon 'l'une des premières institutions de l'Europe'. [JDeJ]

GEOFFROY SAINT-HILAIRE, Étienne (1772–1844). Eminent natural scientist. He was active during the Revolution and in 1793 became professor at the Muséum d'Histoire Naturelle. In 1798 he participated in the expedition to Egypt. His scientific work can be viewed as extending that of *Lamarck. His name is linked with the theory of transformism, with an understanding of the role of development in the natural universe. In 1830 he was involved in a famous debate with his erstwhile friend and colleague *Cuvier, who accepted the role of final causes, supported fixism, emphasized functionality and morphology, and viewed science in terms of the establishment of taxonomies. Geoffroy argued in favour of what he called the unity of plan and of composition, an approach which looked for affinities and homologies between species and which viewed life as a process of transformation. Whereas Cuvier was a conservative in politics as well as in science, Geoffroy defended ideas which appealed to the progressive ideology of liberals and republicans. He also had a metaphysical, pantheistic understanding of nature which his many literary friends found attractive. Balzac's *Comédie humaine* is dedicated to him. [CC]

George Dandin

George Dandin, ou le Mari confondu. *Comédie-ballet* by Molière, first performed at court in 1668. Shorn of its ballet surroundings, the comedy is a three-act farce based on a traditional plot. Dandin, a rich peasant, has married above himself; his wife, Angélique, deceives him with the aristocratic Clitandre, and every time he calls his parents-in-law, the grotesque Sottenvilles, to witness his humiliation he is forced by her trickery to eat his words—his bitter refrain is: 'Vous l'avez voulu, George Dandin.' [PF]

Géorgiques, Les. Novel by Claude *Simon, published 1981. This monumental novel consists of three intertwined narratives, centred on 'L.S.M.', a general in Napoleon's army, a cavalry trooper in 1940, and 'O', an English volunteer in the Spanish Civil War. Juxtaposed to the destruction of war is the theme of the land alluded to in the Virgilian title: the seasonal time-scale of nature and agriculture which, ironically, is not contrasted with but echoed by a similarly cyclical historical time in which wars merely repeat themselves. A network of analogies links the three soldiers. For instance, they all write: L.S.M.'s life is reconstructed through his letters and records (based on a real collection of papers found in Simon's family home); the cavalryman has written a novel which appears to be *La *Route des Flandres* (whose hero is *Georges*); and O is *George* Orwell, whose *Homage to Catalonia* is 're-written' by Simon. Probing the truth of these texts, the novel problematizes the diverse relationships between writing, knowledge, and history. But it is ultimately dominated by the stoic figure of L.S.M., the 'ancestor', returning after a lifetime's campaigning to die on his beloved estate. [CB]

GERBET, Philippe, see DEVOTIONAL WRITING, 3.

GÉRICAULT, Théodore (1791–1824). French painter, major precursor of Romanticism, who created in *Le Radeau de la Méduse* one of France's most widely recognized paintings, still invoked by political cartoonists. Extensive preparatory work for it includes studies of severed heads and amputated limbs. *Balzac, fascinated like many contemporaries by physiognomy and character-types, admired Géricault, whose series of portraits of the insane (the various *Monomanes*) is, moreover, remarkable for his empathy with their distress. Black models are not unusual in his work (*Le Radeau*, *Le Nègre Joseph*). He painted officers not only leading charges but retiring from the fray, prompting *Michelet to praise his symbolic evocation of the sad fortunes of France during 1812–15. [HEB]

Germanic Influences. The history of the French literary response to genres, themes, and styles originating in the germanophone cultures dates back at least to the 1760s, when translations of the prose *Idylls* of the Swiss pastoral poet Salomon Gessner extended the vogue for delicate emotionalism launched by Rousseau's *La *Nouvelle Héloïse* (1761). Though digests of German-language works had seen print in the 1770s in the *Bibliothèque universelle des romans*, it was Madame de *Staël's 1810 conspectus *De l'Allemagne* which most empatically drew French attention to such major figures as Goethe and Schiller and established an enduring paradigm of Germanic creativity. Goethe's best-known works were that epitome of extravagant feeling, *Werther*, which influenced Chateaubriand's *René*, Sénancour's *Oberman*, and Constant's *Adolphe*; and *Faust*, a dramatic text whose reverberations were international, complex, and profound. By the 1820s Schiller's noble tragedies and the doom-laden plays of Zacharias Werner had combined with the example of *Shakespeare to set a standard for Romantic theatre, one which French playwrights, and Victor *Hugo in particular, never really met.

Among the host of Romantic novelists and poets whose work betrays Germanic influences—*Nodier, *Balzac, *Vigny, Hugo, even *Stendhal—Gérard de *Nerval stands out as the best-read and most widely travelled. His translations of both parts of *Faust* were motivated by a private affinity with its story of the doomed aspirant to universal knowledge, while his anthology *Poésies allemandes* (1830) introduced work by Heine and Gottfried Bürger, whose spook-ballad 'Lenore' was the most imitated poem of the age. The renown of that maestro of the *Fantastic E. T. A. Hoffmann has obscured the less-obvious impact of Romantic theorists like Friedrich Schlegel and Novalis, as well as that of Fichte and Schelling, the philosophers of Idealism. The advent of *Symbolism in France saw Richard Wagner enshrined as a cultural saint, with *La Revue wagnérienne* drawing a characteristic equation between music and poetry; while the tenets of German Idealism underpin the writings of *Mallarmé and *Villiers de l'Isle-Adam (not to mention the introspective essays of the Belgian Symbolist *Maeterlinck, who translated Novalis). Poets like *Laforgue and *Apollinaire spent time in Germany and furthered the literary stereotype of the Germanic soul-scape, wistful and bitter-sweet.

By the turn of the century the French had perfected the myth of the Germanic writer as a creature of intuition rather than of logic, an earnest visionary in the mould of Jean-Paul Richter, whose literary dreams had been first circulated by Madame de Staël. The gradual diffusion of Kantian and Hegelian philosophy tended only to confirm an alluring image of Germanic thought as obscure and profound, the ordained complement to the surface clarity and logicality of its Gallic counterpart. Even such a quintessentially 'French' apologist of lucidity as *Valéry devoted years to reflecting upon the shadow-side of mental life, and finally paid homage to Goethean conceptions in the unfinished play *Mon Faust* (1946). André *Breton, theorist of *Surrealism, with his contempt for facile realism and his championship of the irrational, worked up an even more extreme version of the myth, equating the Germanic mind with fertility and the Gallic with sterility; he had no qualms about annexing a foreign Romantic like Achim von Arnim to the Surrealist cause, nor about situating the scientific work of Freud in the self-same imaginative tradition. Elsewhere, themes of irrationality and heroism gleaned from the writings of Nietzsche were to leave an imprint upon the young *Gide, *Malraux, *Camus, *Saint-Exupéry, and *Bataille. Dozens more such literary and philosophical influences could be cited—that of Hofmannsthal upon *Du Bos; of Husserl upon *Sartre; of Kafka upon *Camus, *Beckett, and *Blanchot; of Brecht upon *Gatti; of Heidegger on *Char and on much recent *literary theory. Perhaps the best-informed Germanophile in the 20th c. was *Giraudoux, who studied in Munich and wrote novels and plays unashamedly indebted to Kleist, Novalis, Chamisso, and Fouqué, and defending the value of intuitive, non-cultural knowledge.

Whereas successive military invasions in 1870, 1914, and 1940 have understandably qualified the image of Germany in the French national consciousness at large, there persists within the literary sensibility a strain of nostalgia for Germanic culture, as may be evidenced in a succession of novels including Rolland's *Jean-Christophe (1904–12), Giraudoux's Siegfried et le Limousin (1922), and *Vercors's admittedly guarded wartime assessment Le Silence de la mer (1942). (The unequivocal homage embodied in 1937 in L'Âme romantique et le rêve by the Swiss critic Albert *Béguin springs from a less-troubled context of cultural transmission.) More recent symptoms of this same nostalgia occur in the work of *Gracq, an admirer of Kleist and Ernst Jünger, of *Tournier, who studied German philosophy for four years in Tübingen, and whose Le *Roi des aulnes (1970) is based on Goethe's ballad 'Der Erlkönig'; and of *Jaccottet, who has translated Hölderlin, Rilke, and Musil. The lasting prestige in France of the germanophone poet Paul Celan (who in 1970, like Heine before him, died in Paris) suggests a persistent French attraction to introspective writings of intense metaphysical hue. It might be added that Celan shares with the German Romantics a love of the fragmentary, and with the Idealist philosophers an idiom that is dense and cryptic. The evidence is that, while it may veer towards the caricatural, the association of the Germanic imagination with qualities of density, intuitiveness, and a bold, archetypal energy continues to colour the receptivity of French intellectuals to publications from across the Rhine.

[RC]

See L. Reynaud, L'Influence allemande en France aux XVIIIe et XIXe siècles (1922); L. Le Sage, Jean Giraudoux, Surrealism, and the German Romantic Ideal (1952); P. Van Tieghem, Les Influences étrangères sur la littérature française (1550–1880) (1967).

Germinal. Novel by *Zola, published 1885, the 13th work in the *Rougon-Macquart series, and often considered to be his masterpiece. It is the story of a strike in a mining community in the north of France under the Second Empire. The hero, Étienne Lantier, son of Gervaise Macquart and her lover Lantier from L'*Assommoir, finds work in a mine in Montsou and, horrified by the inhuman working and living conditions of the miners, organizes a strike against the mining company and the capitalist system. A love intrigue is provided by the struggle between Étienne and a brutal mineworker, Chaval, for the affection of Catherine Maheu, the daughter of a typical working-class family in the community. The strike turns violent and the army fires on the workers. A Russian nihilist, Souvarine, sabotages and destroys the Voreux mine. Trapped for days in the flooded mine with Catherine and Chaval, Étienne kills his rival and makes love to Catherine, but she dies in his arms. Rescued after his long ordeal, Étienne leaves Montsou for Paris to go to fight for the emancipation of the workers.

The novel is at once an impressive realistic evocation of the living conditions and the attitudes of the working class and the bourgeoisie in this industrial context, a depiction of the class struggle and of conflicting ideological positions at the time, and a powerful work of poetical and mythical representations. Its ambiguous message, evoking both revolutionary action and natural evolution, is contained in the novel's symbolic title (Germinal is the seventh month—March/April—in the Revolutionary *calendar).

[DB]

Germinie Lacerteux. Novel by the *Goncourt brothers, published 1864. The most influential of their works, particularly as a model of literary *Naturalism, it tells the story of a country girl in service in Paris who, after early experiences of rape and pregnancy, becomes the servant of the elderly Mademoiselle de Varandeuil. Germinie lives a double life of devotion to her mistress and wild dissipation with her lovers Jupillon, the son of a creamery proprietor, and Gautruche, a vicious, drunken signpainter. Exploited and abused by her lovers, she sinks ever deeper into fits of hysteria and promiscuity, drunkenness and theft, until she dies in a state of utter wretchedness. In a high-sounding, *Hugolian preface, the authors claimed that their novel was original in depicting the miseries of life in the lower classes and in creating a new form of tragedy. The story is based on the life of Rose Malingre, the servant of the Goncourt brothers; like Mademoiselle de Varandeuil, they knew nothing of her excesses until after her death.

[DB]

Géronte. Name often given to foolish old men in traditional comedies, for instance the gullible victim of *Scapin in Molière's Les Fourberies de Scapin.

GERSON, Jean Charlier de (1363–1429). Notable humanist scholar, theologian, and statesman who studied at the Collège de Navarre in Paris, taught in the Faculty of Theology there for 23 years, and became chancellor of the University in 1396, playing an active role at the Council of Constance (1415–18). His works include numerous treatises on theological and spiritual matters [see DEVOTIONAL WRITING, 1], and over 500 sermons and speeches. Many of these are in French, and reveal his mastery of vernacular prose, as also a considerable classical culture. In the *Querelle des Femmes, he took the side of *Christine de Pizan against Jean de Meun's *Roman de la Rose. [NM]

Geste, Chanson de, see CHANSON DE GESTE.

Geste d'Ève, Le, see TROYAT.

GHELDERODE, Michel de (1898–1962). Belgian dramatist whose plays first began to be known in France in 1947 and had a great impact in the 1950s, though he had been performed in Belgium from 1925, both in Flemish and in French. His most characteristic works were written between 1925 and 1940: *Barabbas* (1928), *Fastes d'enfer* (1929), *Mademoiselle Jaïre* (1934), *Sire Halewyn* (1938).

Gheld14 draws on expressionism and combines elements of popular tradition with medieval Flemish legend and folklore; his range encompasses earthy farce and flamboyant lyricism. Avoiding intellectualism, his plays are markedly visceral in intention and impact; characters such as Faust, Lazarus, and Jairus's daughter and events such as the Crucifixion are presented in down-to-earth contexts, even if the treatment is farcical, macabre, or grotesque. The flesh and physical decay are typical motifs; the lyricism of the dialogue constantly calls on images of matter and appeals to the senses, though the ultimate and overriding obsession with death draws higher mysteries into play. The primitive appetites of the body are thus linked to a tragic horror at life's uncertainty; the sacred and the sacrilegious go hand in hand. The playwright's sumptuous, baroque style is used to clothe characters who are virtual marionettes acting out a derisory masquerade. [DHW]

GHÉON, Henri (pseud. of Henri-Léon Vangéon) (1875–1944). Critic and poet (*Chansons d'aube*, 1897), whose love of the theatre was encouraged by his friendship with *Copeau. A meeting with *Gide in 1897 proved decisive and, with *Schlumberger and Copeau, he became a founder-member of the *Nouvelle Revue Française in 1909, and a regular contributor. While on military service in 1916 he returned to Catholicism, and henceforth his activities were to be the 'témoignage d'un converti'. He wrote lives of saints, religious and mystery plays— 'le théâtre pour le peuple fidèle'; *Les Trois Miracles de Sainte Cécile* (1919) and *Job* (1932) were performed in parish halls by his itinerant troupe, Les Compagnons de Notre Dame. However, his rushed and over-diversified output (over 50 plays) precluded success. [ET]

GHIL, René (1862–1925). Initially a disciple of *Mallarmé, whose preface to Ghil's *Traité du verbe* of 1886 placed the young poet at the forefront of the *Symbolist movement, Ghil broke with him in 1888 to develop his own 'verbal instrumentism'; in this he adapted elements from Wagner, *Baudelaire, and *Rimbaud into a theory of poetic expression which claimed to provide a scientific basis for the aesthetic equivalence of musical sound, colour, and phoneme. This synthesis of artistic forms would in turn express the hidden laws of humanity's history and development which form the subject of Ghil's verse, more important for its ambition than its achievement. [JK]

GIACOMETTI, Alberto (1901–66). Swiss-born sculptor who rethought the sculpted human figure (as skeletal transparency, not mass). Expelled from the *Surrealist group in 1935 when he returned to working from nature, he battled by various routes (minute observation, memory, copying the art of the past) to reproduce reality and to capture movement. In his sculptures, paintings, and drawings (including portraits of writers) Giacometti was absorbed by the relation of the figure to the surrounding space, or *le vide*. *Sartre introduced him to *Genet: both wrote illuminatingly about what Giacometti's work signified in post-war French experience. Sartre divined how the figures are seen—even close to—in distant perspective. *Éluard dedicated 'Marines' (1941) to him; *Ponge and *Bonnefoy also empathized with his work. [HEB]

GIDE, André(-Paul-Guillaume) (1869–1951). French novelist. When he was awarded the Nobel Prize for Literature in 1947, André Gide had been a leading light on the French intellectual scene for 40 years.

His vocation as a writer was conceived at a very early age, according to his autobiography *Si le grain ne meurt* (1926). An only child, he was the product of a strict Protestant upbringing and an almost exclusively female environment following the death of his father when Gide was 11. His mother's insecurity drove her to be excessively protective of her son, who had an unsettled childhood with little regular schooling. At the age of 13 he conceived a pious and spiritual love for his cousin Madeleine Rondeaux, which soon came into conflict with his sexual impulses. Intense religious fervour alternated with erotic obsessions throughout his adolescence: the conflict led him to write his first novel, *Les Cahiers d'André Walter* (1891), and offer it to Madeleine as a proposal of marriage, in the hope that his devouter aspirations, finding an ally in her, would ultimately triumph. On the advice of their families she refused, and Gide was left to resolve his dilemma alone.

He examined his predicament in the *Journal* he had been keeping from his early teens, and which over a lifetime would come to constitute a major landmark of French literature in its own right. He perceived himself to be a victim of the contradiction, particularly acute within Protestantism, between freedom of conscience and orthodox morality: determining on sincerity at all costs he set out on a series of trips to North Africa during the mid-1890s, in the course of which he realized his homosexuality, conceived Les *Nourritures terrestres, and fought the last of his battles with maternal authority. On the sudden death of his mother in 1895, however, he felt compelled to marry Madeleine, attaching himself thereby to an anchor which would serve to check and balance his wilder inclinations.

The achievement of balance without sacrificing any of the contradictory elements in his nature became the guiding principle in Gide's life and works. The writing bears a special relationship to the biography: in his fiction Gide explores aspects of his personality to which he could not give unfettered expression in his life. Thus, although characters such as André Walter, or the Michel of L'*Immoraliste (1902), are recognizably derived from Gide's own experience, and while their narratives, like that of La *Porte étroite (1909), reproduce the circumstances of Gide's life, they go well beyond positions Gide was prepared to endorse. In writing such works, Gide rid himself of troublesome temptations that threatened to monopolize his energies and left himself free to envisage alternatives—often diametrically opposed ones, as in the exemplary contrast between L'Immoraliste and La Porte étroite: the former explores gratification of the instincts, while the latter examines self-denial. Ultimately, Gide was happy to remain a man divided, having, by the time of *Thésée (1946), learned to nourish his contradictions and demonstrated that indecision and inner dialogue could be a source of creativity, and by extension become the mark of an authentic human being.

Gide's literary début coincided with the heyday of *Symbolism, when the realist novel was widely disparaged for ignoring the subtler intuitions which it was considered the true artist's task to enshrine in his work. Aspiring none the less to be a novelist, Gide was intent on demonstrating that the novel can be a work of art with a harmonious structure and the capacity to shape and stylize reality rather than produce a slavish copy. His texts are intensely patterned, with complex formal symmetries. On the other hand, Gide casts doubt on the novel's capacity to record reality as such, suggesting, for instance, that the subject of Les *Faux-Monnayeurs (1926) is the conflict between the real world and the representations of it which humans attempt. He experimented with forms of lyricism, allegory, parody, and satire before fixing on a form of ironic first-person narrative which he termed récit and which he was to make his own in works such as L'Immoraliste, La Porte étroite, La *Symphonie pastorale (1919), and L'École des femmes (1929). Here a character tells his (sometimes her) own story, though the account is coloured or distorted by an emotional involvement with events. Hence, the reader is obliged to adopt a critical stance, reading between the lines to re-establish the facts as far as possible, often at the expense of the credibility or moral stature of the narrator-protagonist.

These narrowly focused works failed to satisfy Gide himself, and he pursued his experiments with the novel form in search of a panoramic construction which would encompass something of the social dimension. In Les *Caves du Vatican (1914) he mingled the influence of Dostoevsky with the novel of adventure, but his critical sense and propensity to irony got the better of his avowed intent, turning the work into a comic pastiche for which ex post facto he borrowed the label sotie from medieval farce. Only in Les Faux-Monnayeurs was he willing to see a genuine novel, though here too the life of the characters and the development of plot share the stage with reflections upon the novel form and with highly self-conscious devices such as the novel-within-the-novel.

Gide's literary stature also derived from his prominent role in the creation of the *Nouvelle Revue Française, from his plays (Saül, 1896; Œdipe, 1930), and from his work as a distinguished essayist, critic, and translator. He further shaped the cultural climate of his time through the example of individual integrity he sought to illustrate in his life and writings. He attracted controversy by his defence of pederasty (Corydon, 1924) and his denunciations of colonialism (Voyage au Congo, 1927; Retour du Tchad, 1928). He emerged as the model of the committed intellectual in his study of the workings of the judicial system (Souvenirs de la Cour d'Assises, 1914) and his brief flirtation with Soviet Communism (Retour de l'URSS, 1937; Retouches à mon Retour de l'URSS, 1938). [DHW]

See G. Brée, André Gide (1963); C. Martin, André Gide par lui-même (1963); D. Walker, André Gide (1990).

GIGUÈRE, Roland (b. 1929). Canadian poet and graphic artist who publishes his own poetry and that of others in handsome art editions. The work collected in L'Âge de la parole (1965), La Main au feu (1973) and Forêt vierge folle (1978) is some of the finest in modern Quebec poetry. He has strong affinities with French *Surrealism, writing in a dense metaphoric style within which he can range from alliterative musicality to a simple sobriety of expression. A black despair at the inhumanity of the world, particularly present in his earlier work written under la grande noirceur of the Duplessis regime, is increasingly relieved by an intense belief in the regenerative powers of the imagination, human solidarity, and love. [SIL]

GILBERT, Claude (1652–1720). A Dijon lawyer whose *Utopia, Histoire de Calejava (1700), printed but unpublished, is set in northern Lithuania. It is largely a description of a rational, deistic natural religion, much influenced by *Malebranche but critical of aspects of Catholicism, Gilbert presumably having had Huguenot connections.   [CJB]

GILBERT, Gabriel (*c*.1620–*c*.1680). French poet and dramatist. His large output includes eclogues, pastorals, tragedies, and a sparkling comedy of intrigue (*Les Intrigues amoureuses*, 1663). His first play, *Marguerite de France* (performed 1640), earned the praise of *Chapelain, and his rewriting of the Phèdre myth, *Hypolite* (performed 1645), in which the heroine is engaged, but not married, to Thésée, was certainly known to *Racine.   [GJM]

GILBERT, Nicolas-Joseph-Laurent (1751–80). Poet from Lorraine who failed to achieve success in Paris and expressed his bitterness in *Le Dix-huitième Siècle* (1775), a satire against the *philosophes* dedicated to *Fréron. Just before dying he composed a memorable 'Ode imitée de plusieurs psaumes'. *Vigny gave currency to a legend that, like *Malfilâtre, he died in poverty.   [PF]

Gil Blas. Novel by *Lesage. The first six books of the *Histoire de Gil Blas de Santillane* were published in 1715, Books 7–9 in 1724, and Books 10–12 in 1735. A vital influence in the development of the *memoir-novel, it is the fictional autobiography of a man of humble birth who rises, after a long series of adventures, to become the favourite of the Spanish prime minister. As the book progresses the hero grows older, and so does the narrator. The early books display the verve of youth, the middle ones are marked by vigour and irony, while the final volume, narrated from the perspective of country retirement, tends more to sentimental moralizing. The hero's life is frequently interrupted by the narratives of other characters.

Gil Blas is not distinguished by any heroic qualities, nor does his account of his life show much psychological curiosity. He is an Everyman, whose entertaining escapades are recounted with an innocent amorality. His Spain is not particularly Spanish; it is the modern world, not unlike the world of *La Bruyère, in which money is the supreme value. The appeal of the novel lies above all in the vigour, speed, and humour of the narration. It enjoyed immediate and lasting success, and was praised to the skies by Walter Scott, but has lost critical favour in the last century or so.

The title *Gil Blas* was also used by a popular daily newspaper, founded in 1879, which lasted until the outbreak of World War I.   [PF]

Gilles. Long, semi-autobiographical novel by *Drieu la Rochelle, published 1939. The hero, Gilles Gambier, searches in vain for a role in a futile world. In the first of the four parts, wounded and on leave in Paris, he develops a taste for debauchery and luxury; but, disgusted at this life, he volunteers for the front again, aiming to find heroism and death. In Part 2, after the war, he continues his aim-

less life, dabbling in the shallow world of the literary avant-garde and of cynical Third-Republic politics. The loss of the one woman he loves, and the suicide of a young man destroyed by his associates, finally make him break with this society. In Part 3 the love of a new woman restores his desire to live; he becomes a political journalist, and marries her. Disgusted by the inadequacy of contemporary politics and politicians, and inspired by the riots of 6 February 1934 [see STAVISKY], he turns to fascism. But this too is found wanting; France falls back into sterility. His wife dies of cancer. Gilles despairs. In the epilogue a character called Walther (whom we perceive to be Gilles) fights for Franco and finds satisfaction in the re-found virility of war, and in death.   [RMG]

GILLES DE RAIS (sometimes Retz) (*c*.1404–1440). Frequently identified as a prototype for *Perrault's Bluebeard, Gilles was in reality a paedophile, who murdered many of his victims. Inheritor of vast estates in the Loire valley, he accompanied *Jeanne d'Arc to the relief of Orléans in 1429 and was promoted to be a marshal of France. But his increasingly dissolute lifestyle (the first murders were committed *c*.1426) caused mounting financial difficulties. These were cynically exploited by Duke Jean V of Brittany and his servants, until Gilles had irretrievably mortgaged his substance. Then, as public disquiet over his crimes grew, Gilles was handed over for trial on charges of heresy and sorcery to a church court which condemned him to public execution on the gibbet at Nantes.   [MJ]

GILSON, Étienne (1884–1978). Philosopher, professor at the *Sorbonne and the *Collège de France. He wrote major works on medieval philosophy and on the influence of Thomas Aquinas and *scholasticism on modern civilization and philosophy, particularly that of *Descartes.

GINGUENÉ, Pierre-Louis (1748–1815). French poet and critic who came into his own during the Revolution. He worked on *La Feuille villageoise*, produced in 1795 the first edition of *Chamfort's *Œuvres complètes*, and then edited the *Correspondance* of *Mirabeau and Chamfort (1797). In parallel, he—chief among other *Idéologues—founded and edited the *Décade philosophique*. At the same time he pursued a varied administrative, political, or diplomatic career until marginalized by Napoleon. His energy then went into his courses at the Athénée which were to become the much-appreciated *Histoire littéraire d'Italie* (9 vols., 1811–19), a forerunner of the discipline of comparative literature.   [JR]

GIONO, Jean (1895–1970). Novelist, born in Manosque (Basses-Alpes) in 1895, the son of a shoemaker of Italian descent. He enjoyed a happy childhood and attended the local school, which he left at 16 to work in the town bank. He served in the infantry in World War I, married in 1920, and returned to the bank until the success of his first books enabled him to become a full-time writer.

Rooted but not regionalist, a born fabulator, Giono created, like Faulkner, an imaginary South. Even his autobiographical *Jean le bleu* (1932) is luxuriantly fictionalized. Throughout his work he invents landscapes with figures: individuals shaped by and collaborating or struggling with a physical locale. This is amply shown in his 'Pan-trilogy': *Colline* (1929), *Un de Baumugnes* (1929), *Regain* (1930). Against the traditionally hostile depiction of peasant life, Giono sets natural aristocrats, peasant thoroughbreds. Meshed with the theme of natural living is that of the human capacity for gainsaying reality and fabricating an alternative. This theme propels *Naissance de l'Odyssée* (1930), an inverted epic where Ulysses becomes semi-accidentally the subject of a legend, which proliferates by oral transmission around his seedy person. The lie—panicky, self-defensive, or self-assertive—is central to Giono's imaginative strategy.

Though he had a native tendency to exalt and to denounce, his equally inborn anarchism prevented his preaching virtuous lessons. The sensual frankness of relationships between his individuals is not corseted by social conventions, established religion, or organized government, national or local. A recurrent figure is the 'guérisseur', or mid-husband, who rescues others in difficulties, but remains ultimately solitary.

Unabashed hyperbole is the commonest mode. Giono's war-novel, *Le Grand Troupeau* (1931), is his dystopia, in which the modern age bursts murderously into a previously atemporal realm. Even here, however, the life-force, memorably pictured in the rodents' fastidious feeding off the dead, counteracts the unnatural, man-made massacre. The constant shuttle between the country home and the front saves this novel from the claustrophobia of trench-confined war-fiction. *Le Chant du monde* (1934) brings battle on to a more human scale. Telling of a feud between families, conducted like a European Western, it is one of Giono's finest fictions, in which he succeeds in giving an insistent voice and life to natural phenomena alongside his human protagonists. The most poetical of French novelists, Giono expends cornucopian imagery to celebrate the joys of instinctual living. He once described his aim as being to batter the sensibilities of his readers. His people are all of a piece, and not mutilated by the demands of life in mass-society.

In 1935–9 Giono veered into rabidly pacifist pamphlets, urging the unlistening peasantry towards civil disobedience. The novel *Que ma joie demeure* (1935) coincided with an experiment in organized anarchy on the Contadour plateau. It depicts a, finally failed, attempt to install a small-scale working Utopia which also makes time for luxury pastimes. The idyll is wrecked by the ravages of selfish love, but even more by Giono's unreadiness to conceive of successful groups, however well-intentioned. The apocalyptic *Batailles dans la montagne* (1937) shows upland people coping heroically with a flood. Despite resisting annexation by Left or Right, Giono was imprisoned in 1939 for encouraging defeatism, and again in 1944 for collaboration; he was guilty on neither score. From 1940 onwards his fictional world grew darker, more violent, more beset by *ennui*, although his heroes continued to be select souls engaged in various artifices of self-preservation. The new mentors, replacing Homer and Virgil, were Machiavelli and *Stendhal. *Noé* (1947) yields some clues and much mystification about his methods of composition. Subsequent 'chroniques' (*Un roi sans divertissement*, 1947; *Les Âmes fortes*, 1949; *Les Grands Chemins*, 1951; *Le Moulin de Pologne*, 1952) exploit fragmented viewpoints and a minimum of synthesis or explanation of motive. His adopted cynicism seems as hyperbolic as his earlier, more open-hearted pursuit and defence of happiness.

A different series (*Mort d'un personnage*, 1949; *Le Hussard sur le toit*, 1951; *Le Bonheur fou*, 1957; *Angelo*, 1958) relates the exhilarating adventures of Angelo Pardi, a 19th-c. individualist of great charm, generosity, and idealism, amid a cholera epidemic, in revolution, and in love. *Deux cavaliers de l'orage* (1965) and *Ennemonde* (1968) are family sagas, exalting physical prowess and passionate relationships. In all of these texts, and especially his last novel, *L'Iris de Suse* (1970), Giono writes with the apparently negligent ease of Picasso painting. He presents a baroque mixture of the ancient Greek (numinous landscapes, grandiose dramas), the Western (poker faces, sibylline dialogue), and the Gothic (horrors recounted deadpan). The post-war fictions of this great animator substitute skeleton and muscle for the earlier tendency to flabby opulence. Giono's ambiguous genius ensured that he could write principally only of strength. As a narrator of tales mostly beyond orthodox values of good and evil, he has very few equals. [WDR]

See W. D. Redfern, *The Private World of Jean Giono* (1967); P. Citron, *Giono* (1990).

GIRARD, Gabriel, abbé (1677–1748). French grammarian, remembered for his influential dictionary, *Synonymes français* (1736, originally published 1718 as *La Justesse de la langue française*), which was much used by *Diderot and his colleagues for the *Encyclopédie*.

GIRARD, René (b. 1923). French philosopher. Born in Avignon, Girard has spent most of his adult life teaching French in American universities. His approach is characterized by a close reading of literary, religious, and mythological texts. His *Mensonge romantique, vérité romanesque* (1961) is an important study of the novel. In his major work, *La Violence et le sacré* (1972), he argues that the mimetic nature of desire is at the origin of all human conflicts, which can only be resolved by sacrificial rituals of expulsion. In *Des choses cachées depuis la fondation du monde* (1978) he proposes the solution in a non-sacrificial reading of the New Testament. [MHK]

GIRARDIN, Delphine Gay de (1804–55). The daughter of Sophie *Gay and wife of Émile de *Girardin, she wrote verse, some of which appeared in *La Muse française* [see ROMANTICISM, 2]. Under the pseudonym Charles de Launay she published what is perhaps the first gossip column, with the title *Lettres parisiennes* (1836–9, as a book 1843). She also published a number of comedies, novels, and short stories, which are often witty satires of contemporaries such as *Balzac, of *Fourierism, etc. She maintained an important salon, and her talent and beauty were much appreciated by the Romantics. [FPB]

GIRARDIN, Émile de (1806–81). Dynamic press entrepreneur who in 1836 inaugurated the publication of the *roman-feuilleton* in *La Presse* [see PRESS, 2]. He had already made his fortune in the late 1820s and early 1830s by launching a series of magazines which, each in its way, caught the mood of the moment—from the dandyish *La Mode* to the *Journal des connaissances utiles* and the *Musée des familles*, the latter two of which both spoke directly to the utilitarian and domestic concerns of the rising bourgeoisie. Always a key figure in politics and literature, it was he who handed Louis-Philippe the terms of abdication in February 1848. [BR]

GIRARDIN, René-Louis, marquis de (1735–1808). Author of an admired work on landscape gardening, *De la composition des paysages, ou Des moyens d'embellir la nature*. *Rousseau spent his last days as his guest at Ermenonville with its beautiful English garden. The romantic tomb Girardin created for Rousseau on the Île des Peupliers became a place of pilgrimage. [PF]

Girart de Roussillon. Occitan *chanson de geste* of the second half of the 12th c., closely related to the Northern French **Girart de Vienne*. Its 10,000 lines result from several stages of composition, but the poem we have is the work of a superb poet who paints a sombre view of political and moral disintegration in the prolonged warfare between Charles Martel and his vassal Girart. Initially motivated by sexual jealousy and territorial rivalry, their struggle raises the question of how far it is possible for human social and legal institutions ever to conform to God's will. The text is remarkable for its many long council scenes in which action, the 'proper' content of a *chanson de geste*, gives way to debate and commentary of a very high order. The final solution also comes from outside the epic domain of masculine action and politics: Girart abandons warfare under the guidance of his wife, Berte, and collaborates with her in the foundation of the church at Vézelay. [SK]

Girart de Vienne. *Chanson de geste* related to the Occitan **Girart de Roussillon*, and likewise charting a war between vassal (Girart de Vienne) and sovereign (Charlemagne). Like the Occitan poem, *Girart de Vienne* combines sexual and territorial themes: the king marries the bride he had originally destined for Girart, provoking her animosity as well as his, and Girart is accused of failing in his feudal obligations. The 7,000-line text appears to result from the recasting, c.1180, of an earlier poem which is now lost; it is attributed to the first author of *chansons de geste* to be known to us by name, *Bertrand de Bar-sur-Aube, to whom we also owe **Aimeri de Narbonne*. Bertrand is an informed commentator on previous *chansons de geste*; the prologue to *Girart de Vienne* classifies them into three principal groups, or *gestes*, on the basis of their protagonists. He is also a subtle writer. One immediate cause of the war between Girart and Charles is Girart's outrage at discovering, when he meant to kiss Charlemagne's toe as a gesture of submission, that the queen has tricked him into kissing hers instead. As well as black humour, this scene manifests the political duplicity characteristic of court life in *Girart de Vienne*. Bertrand also paints spirited portraits of the youthful *Roland and Oliver, and gives a vivid account of the origins of their companionship. [SK]

GIRAUDOUX, Jean (1882–1944). Diplomat, novelist, playwright, and critic. Son of a minor civil servant, he was brought up in a series of small country towns and after a number of academic successes entered the French diplomatic service in 1910. After World War I, when he was wounded and decorated for bravery, he returned to diplomacy, filled several important posts, and finally, at the outbreak of World War II, was appointed commissioner for information. Here he was not a success and retired from the service (1940). His war memoirs of 1914–18 are contained in *Lectures pour une ombre* (1917), *Amica America* (1919), and *Adorable Clio* (1920), while his later political reflections are found in *Pleins pouvoirs* (1930), *Armistice à Bordeaux* (1945), and *Sans pouvoirs* (1946).

He began as a writer of fiction. *Provinciales* (1909), a loose collection of three stories of childhood, a tale of love gone wrong and a couple of sketches of country life, establishes his manner and prefigures all his later fiction. Stylistically it is in strong reaction against *Naturalism. Giraudoux's preference is for the greater richness and complexity of 16th-c. French—he loved *Ronsard—and for the fanciful and mysterious excursions of German Romantics like E. T. A. Hoffmann. He sings the praises of country life, relishing its charms, slow rhythms, and eccentricities, but he defamiliarizes the real world, rescuing it from its banality through verbal alchemy. His prose is highly imaged, full of fanciful similes, ingenious analogies, odd juxtapositions, ironies, paradoxes, and hyperbole. Fancy embellishes the world, revealing the intricacy and wonder of nature and the kinship between human and animal. There is no strong narrative line and characterization is impressionistic, dealing in types rather than individuals. Much is made of the freshness and mystery of young girls and of the natural code of living they embody. Subsequent novellas and short stories recreate this imaginary world, *L'École des indifférents* (1911) and *La France sentimentale* (1932) being the most successful. The novels take up the search for harmony and the poetic possibilities of ordinary life: *Suzanne et le Pacifique* (1921), where the virginal heroine abandons Paradise of her own free will; *Siegfried et le Limousin* (1922), a rather fey treatment of the differences between France and Germany, which greatly preoccupied him and which surface again in his first play, *Siegfried* (1928); *Bella* (1926), with its witty satire of political notables woven into a version of Romeo and Juliet; *Choix des élues* (1939), where the loves of Jacques and Maléna are played out in an American setting.

Giraudoux's meeting with *Jouvet in 1928 was crucial in helping him to discipline the poetic fancy of his prose fiction to the needs of the stage. The ensuing partnership produced a series of memorable plays, still highly verbal and stylized, but strikingly effective in performance. They range from the witty duel between the human and the divine in *Amphitryon 38* (1929), and the clever and moving debate over peace and war in *La Guerre de Troie n'aura pas lieu* (1935), to the clash of sacred and profane love in *Judith* (1931) and the ingenious recasting of Greek myth in *Électre* (1937), where a sinister beggar is the voice of inexorable fate. This is a highly rhetorical theatre which reinstates traditional dramatic devices like monologue and *tirade* so as to give shape, order, and coherence to fragmented experience. Within the plays women emerge as the key to Giraudoux's persistent quest for harmony, and the exalted status he gives to love is inextricably linked with their qualities of delicacy, naturalness, candour, and fidelity. The plays in which harmony is attained have buoyancy and charm: *Supplément au voyage de Cook* (1935), with its triumph of 'natural' morality in the South Seas; *Intermezzo* (1933), where the unspoilt Isabelle rejects a proffered immortality; *Amphitryon 38*, in which married love is vindicated. Later plays are more pessimistic about the prospects of harmony: *Ondine* (1939), where knight and seamaiden prove incompatible; *Sodome et Gomorrhe* (1943); *Pour Lucrèce* (posth., 1953), where innocence is defeated; even *La Folle de Chaillot* (posth., 1945), where only madwomen believe in love and honour. Giraudoux also wrote criticism—*Les Cinq Tentations de La Fontaine* (1938); *Littérature* (1941)—and scripts for two films. An unfinished novel, *La Menteuse* (c.1936), and play, *Les Gracques* (c.1941), were published in 1958. [SBJ]

See L. Le Sage, *Jean Giraudoux, His Life and Works* (1959); D. J. Inskip, *Jean Giraudoux, the Making of a Dramatist* (1958).

GIRAUT DE BORNELH (Borneil) (*fl. c.*1162–c.1199). One of the most popular *troubadours of his day, Giraut's reputation endured throughout the 13th c., when he was known as the Master of the Troubadours. Dante placed him in Paradise as a *poeta rectitudinis*, but implied that he thought *Arnaut Daniel a better poet. Though rebarbative to modern taste when they adopt the high moral tone that recommended them to Dante, Giraut's songs are not devoid of lyricism or humour. He was formally inventive and composed in a variety of genres: *cansos, *sirventes, *pastorelas, and *tensos. His best-known piece is an *alba. Giraut was a key figure in the controversy over the *trobar clus, which some of his poems either illustrate or attack. His poems have been edited by R. V. Sharman (1989). [SG]

Girondins. Revolutionary grouping led at first by *Brissot, and known to contemporaries as the Brissotins. The principal figures included *Vergniaud, *Condorcet, and *Roland. It was not a formal party or club, but a loose grouping which met in a number of salons (e.g. Madame Roland's), so that it is difficult to say who exactly was a Girondin (their enemy *Marat produced a list of 102, but the criteria he used are unclear). A number of them came from the rich south-west (the *département* of the Gironde), and they tended to represent a relatively moderate, anti-Parisian position. Many were originally associated with the *Jacobins, and after the deposition of Louis XVI in August 1792 they emerged as the controlling faction, taking France into war on several fronts. Suspected by the people of wanting to 'stop the Revolution', they engaged in a fierce struggle with the more radical *Montagnards, led by *Robespierre and actively supported by the Paris crowd [see REVOLUTION, IC]. After their defeat on 2 June 1793 many were imprisoned and executed, but subsequently acquired a romantic and heroic aura, exemplified in *Lamartine's *Histoire des Girondins*. [PF]

GIROUD, Françoise (b. 1916) worked in the film industry and journalism before becoming minister of state for women (1974–6) and then for cultural affairs (1976–7). Her very varied output includes collections of articles, a novel, a statement of her credo (*Ce que je crois*, 1978), and biographies of Marie *Curie (1981), Alma Mahler (1987), and Jenny Marx (1992). [EAF]

GIROUX, Suzanne, see EROTICISM AND PORNOGRAPHY.

GLISSANT, Édouard (b. 1928). Martinican novelist, poet, playwright, and essayist; the most distinguished and influential French Caribbean writer of the second half of the 20th c. His major preoccupation is with Caribbean cultural identity, a concept central to his important theoretical work, *Le Discours antillais* (1981). An advocate of independence for

Martinique, he deplores what he terms the cultural dispossession associated with the island's quasi-colonial status as a DOM [see DOM-TOM]. In his view, France's economic and socio-cultural predominance in her Caribbean territories is a barrier to the development of a sense of West Indian nationhood, since the embracing of metropolitan French values negates the racial and cultural bonds formed throughout history between the many Caribbean islands. Here, as in his earlier essay *L'Intention poétique* (1969), Glissant emphasizes the significance of history in the quest for national identity. Martinican indifference to Caribbean folk traditions (African in origin), and the inferior status accorded to *Creole, are seen as symptomatic of a profound rejection of self-knowledge and self-acceptance. Glissant's theory of *antillanité* suggests that the Caribbean region has a cultural unity that overrides racial and linguistic differences. A literary corollary of this theory is the identification of affinities between French Caribbean and other writing in the Americas, particularly the fiction of Latin America and the southern United States. These ideas are further developed in *Poétique de la relation* (1990).

Glissant's principal collections of poetry (*Poèmes*, 1963; *Boises*, 1979; *Pays rêvé, pays réel*, 1985, *Fastes*, 1992), like the two versions of his play *Monsieur Toussaint* (1961, and 1978, with Creole additions to the text), are rooted in Caribbean history, densely allusive, and sound a characteristic note of ironic restraint. The ancestral loss of Africa and the bitter suffering of generations of anonymous slaves in the West Indies are linked with the poet's current distress over the destruction of the natural landscape in Martinique, and the difficulty of re-establishing an ill-recorded folk history.

Glissant's fiction is consistent with his belief in the need to rediscover the past in order to understand and reshape the present. His five loosely connected, unconventional novels move between real and imagined moments in the social history of Martinique. In *La Lézarde* (1958), the poetic, almost abstract account of a murder on the eve of the 1946 elections becomes a critique of the structures of colonial society. *Le Quatrième Siècle* (1964) traces the evolution of two archetypal groups during the era of slavery: the fugitive maroons, and the captives who learned endurance and survival in the unsparing world of the plantation. *Malemort* (1975), perhaps the most influential of Glissant's works, is a bleak allegory of French hegemony that presents modern Martinique as a cultural and ecological disaster-zone, devoid of any creative impulse. *La Case du commandeur* (1981) shows the individual members of a peasant family, over many decades, vainly seeking to retrace their origins and define themselves. *Mahagony* (1987), in keeping with the harsh pun of its title, juxtaposes the tenacious struggle for freedom and the relentless quelling of insurrection throughout Caribbean history. A further related novel, *Tout-monde*, appeared in 1993. [BNO]

See D. Radford, *Édouard Glissant* (1982).

Globe, Le. Daily paper founded in 1824 by Pierre *Leroux and P.-F. Dubois. It was the organ of liberal *Romanticism, with collaborators including *Sainte-Beuve and Charles de *Rémusat. After 1830 it became briefly the journal of the *Saint-Simonians, closed in 1832, and was twice relaunched later in the 19th c.

Glorieux, Le. Five-act verse comedy by *Destouches, performed 1732. Tufière is a poor Gascon noble, purportedly good at heart, save for his amply illustrated, obsessive rank-consciousness. This fault is cured when his poorly dressed father, Lycandre (impoverished by a legal miscarriage, finally righted) forces his son to recognize him in front of his mistress, Isabelle, and her rich bourgeois family. The play includes recognition scenes, parallel and interconnected love affairs, an example of the *cri du sang*, and some well-known moral aphorisms. Pasquin, Tufière's imitative but readily self-critical valet, Philinte, his absurdly self-deprecating rival, and Lisimon, his over-familiar prospective father-in-law, all generate mild amusement. The play (of which the preface is an important indicator of the direction which comic drama was taking) is acknowledged as one of Destouches's finest works. [JD]

Glossaire, j'y serre mes gloses, see LEIRIS.

GLUCK, Christoph Willibald von (1714–87). German composer who in the 1760s 'reformed' the Italian *opera seria* by placing the emphasis on the text rather than the music. Several of his innovations were derived from French sources and his 'Reform *operas', particularly *Iphigénie en Aulide* (1774), can be seen as a continuation of the French operatic tradition. He made repeated visits to Paris in the 1770s and even rewrote *Orfeo* and *Alceste* for French audiences. His operas became the centre of a Parisian literary polemic in the 1770s, Gluckists versus Piccinistes (partisans of the Italian Nicola Piccini). [KM]

GLUCKSMANN, André (b. 1937). French philosopher, writer, and human-rights advocate. *La Cuisinière et le mangeur d'hommes* (1975) and *Les Maîtres penseurs* (1977) placed Glucksmann at the forefront of the *Nouveaux Philosophes movement. Other works include: *Le Discours de la guerre* (1967, published with a new essay, 'Europe 2004' in 1979); *Stratégie et révolution en France* (1968); *Cynisme et passion* (1981); *La Force du vertige* (1983); *La Bêtise* (1985); *Silence, on tue*, with Thierry Wolton (1986); *Descartes c'est la France* (1987); *Quelques mots sur la parole*, with Václav Havel (1989); and *Le XIe Commandement* (1991). All of Glucksmann's works denounce the various forms of oppression inscribed in philosophical and political thought, and their manifestations in contemporary times (totalitarianism, concentration camps, nuclear war). [DM-S]

Gobelins, Manufacture des. Tapestry-works in Paris, dating from the 15th c. It became state property under Louis XIV, and played an important part in royal propaganda.

GOBINEAU, Joseph-Arthur de (1816–82). French diplomat, poet, novelist, historian, and ethnographer. He was largely ignored during his lifetime, but his reputation has grown steadily in the 20th c. His long verse romances are deservedly forgotten, but a few of his historical novels continue to appeal: *Ternove* (1847), *L'Abbaye de Typhaines* (1849). Nowadays his fame rests on his later fiction. First are the striking short stories, rich in colour and incident and marked by irony, elegance, and psychological penetration. Best are: *Mademoiselle Irnois* (1847) and *Adélaïde* (1869), fine studies of female passion and frustration; and intriguing exotic tales collected in *Nouvelles asiatiques* (1876). Of considerable distinction is *Les Pléiades* (1874), a novel of friendship expressing Gobineau's cult of a natural élite. His gallery of Renaissance portraits, *La Renaissance* (1877), is vivid, as is the reportage of *Trois ans en Asie* (1859). His oriental scholarship is now suspect, as are the racial theories of *Essai sur l'inégalité des races humaines* (1853–55), a work exploited by the Nazis. In this, the decay of civilization is attributed not, as traditionally, to luxury, corruption of manners, irreligion, or systems of government, but to racial inequality and miscegenation. *Tocqueville challenged his historical pessimism. [SBJ]

Gobseck. Avaricious money-lender who figures in the story of the same name (1830) by Balzac, and in other volumes of his *Comédie humaine*.

GODARD, Jean-Luc (b. 1930). A Swiss by birth, the most controversial of French-language film-makers. His first feature, *A bout de souffle* (1959), made a great impact through its parody of *film noir* conventions and the studiedly amoral cool of *Belmondo and Jean Seberg. The role of improvisation, the dislocation of sound and image, the incorporation into the cinematic text of other texts (literature, music, paintings, references to films, posters, etc.) are constants in an *œuvre* of Protean diversity. *Pierrot le fou* (1965) is a moving love story in Technicolour which also presages the political concerns that were for a while to dominate his work. *La Chinoise* (1967) is the masterpiece of his 'Maoist' period and an extraordinary prefiguration of *May 1968.

His political commitment, a motorcycle accident, and an interest in experimenting with video successively kept him away from the 'conventional' cinema for more than a decade. His subsequent films (*Sauve qui peut/la vie*, 1979; *Prénom Carmen*, 1983) have revealed a continuing obsession with the sound/image relation and (some would say) with the bodies of young women. [KAR]

GODBOUT, Jacques (b. 1933). Canadian novelist, journalist, and film-maker, one of the best-known of the writers who came to prominence during the Révolution Tranquille [see QUEBEC, 4]. Born in Montreal, he attended a Jesuit college and the Université de Montréal. He wrote a thesis on *Rimbaud, and spent three years as a university teacher in Ethiopia, returning to Canada in 1957. Founder president of the Union des Écrivains Québécois and one of the founders of the journal *Liberté, he was actively involved in the nationalist movement.

His first books were volumes of poetry, and he has published a collection of essays (*Le Réformiste*, 1975), but his reputation rests essentially on his fiction. His first two novels, *L'Aquarium* (1962) and *Le Couteau sur la table* (1965), are experimental in form and pose political problems in an allegorical way. His most popular book, however, and the one in which the personal and political themes of his work are most effectively interwoven, is *Salut Galarneau!* (1967). It is an engaging story of alienation and discovery, set in Montreal, where the hero, disaffected from *québécois* society, keeps a stall called 'Au Roi du Hot Dog'. He writes his own life story in a racy inventive style, in which *joual and high culture mingle; when his girlfriend deserts him, he has himself walled into his house, but overcomes his despair and proclaims his ambition to mix life and writing ('vécrire').

D'Amour, P.Q. (1972) is another richly inventive text; it dramatizes the conflicts between classes and cultures in the love-affair of a writer and his typist, suggesting again a possible liberation through writing from the tensions of modern society. Godbout's subsequent novels include *L'Île du dragon* (1976), *Les Têtes à Papineau* (1981), a funny yet despairing image of the situation facing 'celui qui parle français en Amérique', and *Une histoire américaine* (1986), a satirical political thriller set in California. In 1994 he returned to his earlier hero, a quarter-century on, in *Le Temps des Galarneau*. [PF]

GODEAU, Antoine (1605–72), a favourite of the salons, and one of the first members of the Académie Française, became bishop of Grasse in 1636 (later of Vence). While keeping in touch with Parisian circles, he proved an admirable pastor and reforming bishop, showing some sympathy with the *Jansenists. He was very prolific in both prose and verse, and, though wary of the theatre, thought it right that religion should benefit from the graces of poetry. His own poetry on devotional subjects (eclogues, odes, descriptive and narrative poems, paraphrases, etc.) is felicitously cadenced, expansive, and decorative. [AJS]

GODEFROI DE BOUILLON, see HAGIOGRAPHY.

GODET, Philippe, see SWISS LITERATURE IN FRENCH, 3.

GODIN, Gérald (b. 1938). Canadian poet and politician who was one of the founders of the literary journal *Parti pris. He vigorously practises the use of *joual in his own poetry, especially Les Cantouques (1967), as advocated by the review, but in his case without any pejorative intention or effect. He has a natural delight in popular speech of all kinds, and has developed his own inventive mixture of joual and other registers of Quebec French to produce a rich, accessible poetry of frequently infectious musicality. His work expresses social anger and compassion, but also love and tenderness. Poems up to 1986 are collected in Ils ne demandaient qu'à brûler (1987). He was elected to the Quebec National Assembly in 1976 as a member of the nationalist Parti Québécois and occupied several ministerial posts in successive Quebec governments. [SIL]

GODOLIN, Pèire, see OCCITAN LITERATURE (POST-MEDIEVAL).

Goguette, see POPULAR SONG.

GOLDMANN, Lucien (1913–70). Leading exponent of sociological and structural approaches to literature and philosophy. After studies in his native Bucharest, and in Vienna, Paris, and Geneva (with *Piaget), he taught in Paris, and later Brussels. His celebrated and contentious study of *Pascal and *Racine, Le Dieu caché (1955), correlates their tragic vision with contradictions in contemporary social structures. His Pour une sociologie du roman (1964) suggests homologies between the structures of 20th-c. novels, especially *Malraux's, and those of modern capitalism. Drawing on the early Lukács, he proposed to reconcile *Marxism and *Structuralism in a 'genetic structuralism' which was influential, especially in the sociology of literature and culture, during the 1960s. [MHK]

GOMBAULD, Jean Ogier de (c.1570–1666). Of French Huguenot origin, he was a minor favourite of Queen Marie de Médicis, who gave him a pension. As a friend of *Conrart he belonged to the founding nucleus of the *Académie Française, and helped to compile its statutes. He was also a friend of *Malherbe, whose mantle as literary and linguistic censor he to some extent inherited. His poetry, first collected and published in 1646, is appropriately meticulous, but the result is frigid; *Boileau singles out his sonnets for criticism. His allegorical novel (Endimion, 1624), pastoral drama (L'Amaranthe, 1631), and a tragedy (Les Danaïdes) were all considered failures. [PJB]

GOMBERVILLE, Marin Le Roy, sieur de (1600–74). French poet and novelist. A fertile poetic imagination characterizes his earliest verses and novels, including Carithée (1621), which combines historical romance with pastoral idyll, and his continuation of d'*Urfé's unfinished L'*Astrée (1626). His most famous work, Polexandre (1619–37), is a complex and sophisticated adventure novel which blends the exotic and the real, psychological insight and visionary power, as it traces the hero's courtship of

Alcidiane, queen of the 'île inaccessible'. Cythérée (1639–40), a mixture of myth and spiritual fantasy, marks the start of a more pious phase in his career which culminates in the allegorical La Jeune Alcidiane (1651), of *Jansenist inspiration. [GJM]

Gommes, Les, see ROBBE-GRILLET.

GONCOURT, Edmond (1822–96) and Jules (1830–70). Novelists, historians, men of letters, and authors of the famous Journal, which provides a fascinating, frank, personal (and often biased) view of their age and an invaluable source of anecdotes and portraits of contemporary figures for the period 1851–1896. Edmond was born in Nancy, Jules in Paris. Supreme aesthetes, highly neurotic, utterly misogynist, with refined tastes and a mania for collecting objets d'art, the Goncourt brothers devoted their whole lives to art and literature. They developed together a distinctive, impressionistic style, called *écriture artiste, achieving a remarkable symbiosis in their collaboration, writing as one until the death of Jules. The survivor, Edmond, always sought to keep alive his brother's spirit. They frequented the salon of Princess *Mathilde during the Second Empire and featured in the famous 'dîners Magny', the fortnightly gatherings that brought together leading men of letters and science and George *Sand) at a Paris restaurant in the 1860s. After 1885 Edmond presided over a literary salon, the Sunday meetings at the 'Grenier', and in his will left money to found the *Académie Goncourt which began to meet in 1903, when the Prix Goncourt was also founded [see PRIZES, LITERARY].

Their career as novelists began inauspiciously with En 18.. (1851), which ran foul of the imperial censors. Their first novel of note was Les Hommes de lettres (1860), later called Charles Demailly (1868), the story of a young writer and journalist driven mad by his shrewish wife and his enemies in the press. Sœur Philomène (1861) is a simple love story, a 'clinical analysis' set in a hospital, whilst Renée Mauperin (1864), a novel of bourgeois manners, has a more complex plot and seeks to represent the 'modern young woman'. The brothers published three more novels before the death of Jules: *Germinie Lacerteux (1864), their most significant work; Manette Salomon (1867), which returns to the theme of the artist destroyed by woman; and Madame Gervaisais (1869), which is set in Rome and deals with the religious hysteria of the main character, who dies in the presence of the pope. Seeing a direct equivalence between writing history and novels ('L'histoire est un roman qui a été, le roman est l'histoire qui aurait pu être', Journal, 24 November 1861), with their passion for anecdotal detail, tableaux, and revealing documents, they wrote a series of monographs on 18th-c. history and art, notably on famous women such as *Marie-Antoinette and the mistresses of Louis XV. Their play Henriette Maréchal had a hostile reception at the Comédie-Française in 1865, but fared better when revived in 1885.

After 1870, along with his studies of Japanese art, Edmond published *La Fille Élisa* (1877), a novel on prostitution and prison life; *Les Frères Zemganno* (1879), about two brothers who are circus performers; *La Faustin* (1882), the story of an actress; and *Chérie* (1884), another 'psychological and physiological study' of a young woman.   [DB]

See R. Ricatte, *La Création romanesque chez les Goncourt (1850–1870)* (1953); R. Baldick, *The Goncourts* (1960).

Gormont et Isembart. A fragmentary *chanson de geste*, dating from the end of the 11th c. The surviving 661 octosyllabic lines relate, in parallel *laisses* punctuated by refrain-like quatrains generating an incantatory rhythm, the attempts of vassals of Louis to kill the pagan king, Gormont. Victory is achieved by the emperor himself at the cost of his own life, and interest then passes to the fate of the renegade Isembart, who repents when fatally wounded. This extremely archaic poem evokes the Viking invasions (Gormont, 'king of Cirencester', fights on foot) and exploits such folk motifs as the magical dwarf and the father–son duel. The 13th-c. *Chronique rimée* of Philippe Mousket assimilates the poem to the Revolt Cycle [see DOON DE MAYENCE].   [PEB]

GORZ, André (b. 1924). Essayist and political philosopher. Born in Austria, Gorz adopted an independent Marxist perspective under the influence of *Sartre, whom he joined as co-director of *Les *Temps modernes* in 1961. Starting from an economic analysis, he developed a sharp critique of the communist and socialist parties' preoccupation with state power, and in *Adieux au prolétariat* (1980) prophetically proclaimed that free time rather than employment should be the goal of progressive political movements.   [MHK]

GOT, Edmond (1822–1901). Prominent actor and *doyen* of the Comédie-Française, where he spent his entire career, earning praise for his technique; he enjoyed success in classical comedy, especially *Molière, and in a wide range of modern plays, e.g. *L'Étrangère* by *Dumas *fils*. His *Journal* (1910) is an interesting account of plays and players at the Comédie-Française.   [SBJ]

GOUDAR, Ange (c.1720–1791). Nomadic writer, author of works in many genres, including *philosophe* pamphlets and treatises of political economy, as well as a *Testament politique de *Mandrin* (1755) in praise of the famous contrabandist.

GOUGENOT (early 17th c.). French dramatist and novelist. His *Roman de l'infidèle Lucrine* (1634) blends romanesque incident with analysis of character, but his most notable achievement was *La Comédie des comédiens* (1631), one of the first French plays to explore and promote the value of the acting profes-

sion. It inspired *Scudéry's play of identical title, and anticipates Corneille's L'*Illusion comique.   [GJM]

GOUGES, Olympe de (pseud. of Marie Gouze) (1748–93). Early champion of women's rights. Born in Montauban, she had little education and dictated to a secretary the plays and pamphlets she published after arriving in Paris. Of nonconformist views and ambiguous social status, she attracted mixed publicity. One play, *Zamore et Mirza* (performed 1789), attacked slavery, but she is now best known for her pioneering pamphlet, *Déclaration des droits de la femme et de la citoyenne* (September 1791). Little noticed at the time, it systematically applied the 1789 *Déclaration* to women's rights, arguing that those who might go to the scaffold for their views should at least have the right to voice them. Her own outspokenness against the *Jacobins led to her execution during the Terror.   [SR]

GOUJET, Claude-Pierre, abbé (1697–1767). Literary historian. A *Jansenist, fiercely hostile to the Jesuits, he wrote the continuation of *Fleury's *Histoire ecclésiastique*. He is known for his *Bibliothèque française* (1740–56), a useful if unexciting compilation in 18 vols., containing separate histories of major genres, with summaries of many works.

GOULART or **GOULARD,** Simon (1543–1628). Calvinist scholar and apologist who succeeded *Bèze as president of the Genevan synod in 1605. His diverse output includes important collections of documents relating to the *Wars of Religion (*Mémoires de l'état de France*, 1576; *Histoire ecclésiastique*, 1580) and a popular compilation of *Histoires admirables et mémorables* (1600).   [MJH]

GOUNOD, Charles (1818–52). French composer; his opera *Faust* (1859) won lasting popularity.

GOURMONT, Rémy de (1858–1915). Described by T. S. Eliot as 'the critical conscience of his generation', this French poet, novelist, essayist, and co-founder of *Symbolist reviews (*Mercure de France*, 1890; *L'Ymagier*, 1894) was one of the most wide-ranging representatives of late 19th-c. intellectual trends. He was the foremost spokesman within the Symbolist movement for Schopenhaurian Idealism, with its emphasis on individual subjectivity. His novels (notably *Sixtine*, 1890, and *Lilith*, 1892) explore this theme within *Decadent variations on the relationship between sexuality and artistic creativity. Of more lasting impact, however, was his critical writing (notably *Livres des masques*, 1896–8; *Esthétique de la langue française*, 1899; and *Le Problème du style*, 1902), in which his concept of the subjectivity of writer and critic resulted in a theory of creative or poetic criticism which became an essential strand in Anglo-American New Criticism.   [JK]

GOURNAY, Marie le Jars, demoiselle de (c.1566–1645). Independent writer and the 'fille d'alliance' (adopted daughter) of *Montaigne, she was born into the minor nobility, taught herself Latin, and was so uplifted by her reading of the *Essais* that she made contact with their author and arranged that he should visit her. After his death she was entrusted, together with the poet Pierre de Brach, with the edition of the final version of the *Essais*. In 1596 she moved to Paris, and remained there until her death, living in reduced circumstances on the margins of the fashionable literary world. She was the butt of a number of malicious practical jokes and was subjected to satire both for her defence of the Jesuits and for her spirited advocacy of the language of *Ronsard and Montaigne. She published at her own expense a feminist tract, occasional verse, moral essays, and some translation, which she collected together in her *Ombre* (1626), later revised and renamed *Les Avis et presents* (1634, 1641). She is remembered today for her *Égalité des hommes et des femmes* (1622), her derivative short story, *Le Promenoir de M. de Montaigne* (1594), and her views on style.   [IM]

Gouverneurs de la rosée, see ROUMAIN.

GOYÉMIDÉ, Étienne (b. 1942). Novelist, playwright, and poet from the Central African Republic. His first novel, *Le Silence de la forêt* (1984), examines the world of the pygmies, which provides the framework to the story of the protagonist, who suddenly decides to give up everything and reconsider his values in search of the true meaning of existence. The originality of his second novel, *Le Dernier Survivant de la caravane* (1985), lies in the fact that it does not deal with the conflict between the indigenous and colonial populations, but concentrates on the violent clashes with the slave-traders who came from the north in the 19th c.   [DRDT]

GOZLAN, Léon (1803–66). Journalist, minor novelist, and dramatist. He knew *Balzac, about whom he published a volume of reminiscences, *Balzac en pantoufles* (1856).

Graal, see GRAIL ROMANCES.

GRACQ, Julien (pseud. of Louis Poirier) (b. 1910). French novelist and essayist, in ordinary life a teacher of history and geography in a Paris *lycée*. After meeting André *Breton in 1939, Gracq discreetly situated his own ideas and work within the orbit of *Surrealism, though abstaining from direct involvement in the Paris group. His work comprises novels, *récits*, and prose poetry, two plays (of which one is an adaptation of Kleist's *Penthesilea*), literary essays, and leisurely books devoted to elective places such as the Nantes he knew as a schoolboy in the 1920s (*La Forme d'une ville*, 1985) or the Rome he first visited at the age of 66 (*Autour des sept collines*, 1989). An adept of a prose of great acuity and gracefulness which advances with an almost somnambulistic equipoise, Gracq constantly slows down the

action in his fictions with poetic descriptions of a world steeped in psychic resonances and hermetic symbolism. The hypnotic atmosphere of the novels sustains a curious tension amid torpor, the sensation of being on the brink of either catastrophe or sublime fulfilment: the protagonists spend long hours confined alone or in small groups, as in *Un beau ténébreux* (1945), where people linger out of season in a seaside hotel in Brittany, in the grip of foreboding and expectancy. Psychologically implausible, Gracq's characters are invariably exceptional beings, brooding loners and devotees of impassioned gestures, like the hero of *Le Rivage des Syrtes* (1951), who launches a naval attack on an unseen enemy and sparks off a war. Themes of exile, fatality, transgression, and sombre yearning are indebted to Romantic antecedents, as well as to the *Grail cycle, the Parsifal legend, and the Gothic tradition (see *Au château d'Argol*, 1938).

An impressive occasional writer, Gracq draws up notes on his readings as well as sketches of personal and historical reminiscence, publishing them from time to time in collections such as *Lettrines* (2 vols., 1967 and 1974), *En lisant, en écrivant* (1980), or *Carnets du grand chemin* (1992). His essay *André Breton* (1948) foregrounds Breton's prose style and comes across as a literary portrait of singular empathy, perhaps even an oblique self-portrait. Gracq once dubbed his criticism 'une critique de l'émoi', and it is true that he is content with a small shelf of favourites like *Poe, Novalis, *Chateaubriand, *Stendhal, and Ernst Jünger, on whom he can make comments, now playful, now solemn and penetrating. A resolute dissenter from the rituals of Parisian literary life, which he pilloried in the pamphlet *La Littérature à l'estomac* (1950), Gracq adamantly refused the Prix Goncourt for which he was nominated in 1951. [RC]

See *Julien Gracq. Actes du colloque international d'Angers* (1982); M.Murat, *Julien Gracq* (1991).

GRAFFIGNY or **GRAFIGNY,** Françoise d'Issembourg d'Happoncourt, Madame de (1695–1758). Originally a resident of Lunéville, where she was under the protection of the ducal court of Lorraine, she moved to Paris at the age of 44, frequented literary circles, and eventually became a writer. Her *epistolary novel *Lettres d'une Péruvienne* (1747) was among the century's best-sellers; the tale of a kidnapped Inca princess, it blends romance, feminist protest, and social satire. Her sentimental play *Cénie* (1750) was also a major success. Graffigny wrote short plays and fables for the children of the imperial court at Vienna, and left an extensive and interesting correspondence.   [JDeJ]

Grail Romances. The Grail and the quest to discover its whereabouts or the secret of its mysteries provided one of the most popular themes of later medieval literature and art, and has continued to inspire artists as diverse as the Pre-Raphaelites, Wagner, and Julien *Gracq in modern times. Its popularity probably stemmed from the open-endedness of the theme, combined with an appeal to the highest ideals of *chivalry and religion, which, while essentially orthodox, allowed a whole range of esoteric interpretations.

The first mention of the Grail, or rather of a grail (a broad serving dish capable of holding a whole salmon), comes in Le Conte du graal written by *Chrétien de Troyes between c.1180 and 1192. This unfinished romance claims as its source a book shown to the author by his patron, Philip of Flanders. Chrétien's romance was highly problem-atic as it was unfinished and also contained two par-allel sets of stories: that of the uncouth Perceval, who should have asked the question: 'Whom does the grail serve?', which would put an end to the dev-astation of the land of the Fisher King; and that of *Gauvain, who rambles from chivalric adventure to chivalric adventure, nominally questing the bleed-ing lance which accompanies the grail, until caught in the womb-like web of the castle of his own mother and grandmother. Some critics believe that the Perceval and Gauvain material belong to sepa-rate romances amalgamated after Chrétien's death. While there may be some literary evidence for this within the text, the manuscript tradition lends no support to the view. Perceval's failure to ask the restorative question opens a perspective of death and destruction of apocalyptic proportions which, with the essentially chivalric aspects of Chrétien's work, are elaborated in the first two verse Continuations by anonymous authors c.1195–1210.

The First Continuation takes Gauvain as its hero; although he visits the Grail Castle and asks appro-priate questions, the devastation is not ended as he falls asleep from exhaustion before hearing the answers. This continuation is purely an adventure romance and interpolates another entire story based on Welsh folk-tales, that of Caradoc Briebras. The Second Continuation reverts to Perceval as hero, but again has little interest in the moral or spiritual dimensions of Chrétien's work. Perceval also rides from adventure to adventure, hunting the white stag, retrieving a magic hunting dog, doing battle in enchanted lands. The author is so little concerned with piety and chastity that not only does Perceval spend a night with Blancheflor, his love from Chrétien's poem, but he also sleeps with the lady on whose behalf he hunted the white stag. The contin-uation breaks off at the point where Perceval was about to ask the spell-breaking questions. Two fur-ther verse continuations, by Manessier and Gerbert de Montreuil, dating from the late 1220s or 1230s, finally bring the story to a close, but only after sev-eral more peripeteia, which are chivalric in nature and not obviously linked to the quest. However, both these writers have experienced the influence of the ascetic Queste del Saint Graal (c.1225–30, see below); they accentuate the Eucharistic features of the story and emphasize Perceval's chastity.

Despite some allusions towards the end of Chrétien's account, the first systematic treatment of Eucharistic symbolism in the Grail stories is due to *Robert de Boron. His Estoire du Saint Graal (or Joseph d'Arimathie) exploits Genesis and Exodus, *Geoffrey of Monmouth's Historia Regum Britanniae, and *Wace's Roman de Brut, as well as the Gospels and apocrypha, to make the Grail both the dish from which Christ ate the Paschal lamb and the ves-sel in which His blood was collected at the Crucifixion, and to have it transported with its guardian priesthood to Britain, while the lance becomes the Lance of Longinus, the Roman centu-rion who pierced Christ's side. The Merlin uses the figure of the Celtic wizard-prophet, sired by an incubus on a virgin, who was instrumental in the birth and education of Arthur, to make the Arthurian realm central to a universal scheme of sal-vation. Perceval, the last part of Robert's trilogy, introduces the Grail-winner to the Round Table, where he is identified by the splitting of the 'stone of destiny' when he sits in the Siege Perilous. He visits the Grail Castle twice under the close tutelage of Merlin before asking the required questions and inheriting the duties of priest-king, guardian of the Grail. The 'speaking stone' is made whole and the adventures of Arthur's realm come to an end.

At about the same time as the prose adaptations of Robert de Boron's works were being made (c.1200–12), the monks of Glastonbury produced their own version of the Grail story, Le Haut Livre du Graal or Perlesvaus. This text has demonstrably pious intentions (several sections begin with invocations of the Trinity), but it was also intended to promote the abbey's Arthurian relics, and so puts much emphasis on chivalric adventure. There are three principal questers (Perceval, Lancelot, and Gauvain), none of whom is debarred by sin from participating, although Perceval remains the hero. Unlike in any other version, the Fisher King dies and the Grail and Lance are removed from Britain to a spiritual home before Perceval completes the quest, which thus centres on the winning of 'Grail substitutes', notably a gold circlet. The quest com-pleted, Perceval travels over the western seas to a blessed land, amid reminiscences of Celtic myth and folk-tale and of the Voyage de saint Brendan [see ANGLO-NORMAN LITERATURE, 6a].

Like all the other texts considered so far, the Perlesvaus remains firmly committed to the courtly ethos, but the Queste del Saint Graal, composed as part of the *Lancelot cycle, takes a firmly ascetic, uncourtly stance at the hands of a Cistercian writer. Gauvain fails because he is an habitual homicide and womanizer; Lancelot carries the stigma of his adultery with Guenièvre, and is seared by the Grail. He is given the role of penitent. Perceval is demoted to a subsidiary role, dying at the completion of the quest. The new hero is the virgin Galaad, predes-tined to his role in a purely religious and non-heroic sense. The enemies to be overcome are devils and sins personified, and the allegorical meaning of every adventure is expounded by White Monks. The narrative scheme embraces the whole divine plan of salvation from Eden to the New Jerusalem, represented by Sarras, the city where Galaad officiates as priest-king on the model of Melchisedech, and where he contemplates the final mystery of the Grail, which centres on the nature of the Trinity and transubstantiation. After the ultimate mystical experience Galaad is translated to Heaven, leaving his other companion Bohort to return to Arthur's court to recount what he knows. The marvels of Britain are at an end, as is the purpose of the Round Table, which will be destroyed in the bloody, internecine strife of *La *Mort le Roi Artu.*   [PEB]

See J. Marx, *La Légende arthurienne et le graal* (1952); J. Markale, *Le Graal* (1982); C. Méla, *La Reine et le Graal* (1984).

GRAINVILLE, Patrick (b. 1947). French novelist who draws on a baroque and fantastical imagination. *La Toison* (1972), *La Lisière* (1973), and *L'Abîme* (1974) form a 'mythical autobiography' reaching from the erotic fantasies of a student to his crisis of old age. *Les Flamboyants* (1976) won the Prix Goncourt; set in black Africa, it focuses on the figure of King Tokor, whose indulgence in both pleasure and violence fascinates and disturbs a young white European. *La Diane rousse* (1978) creates the mystical and erotic vision of a blind man; *Les Forteresses noires* (1982) is a futuristic fantasy, whilst *L'Orgie, la neige* (1990) presents an adolescent initiation into death and sexuality amidst the snow.
[EAF]

Grammaire générale et raisonnée. The 'Grammaire de Port-Royal', composed by *Arnauld and *Lancelot [see GRAMMARS, 2].

Grammars

1. Medieval and Renaissance

France was slow in producing its own vernacular grammars. The earliest works on the French language, typically intended for the English, are essentially practical in orientation. These include orthographic treatises and works treating basic noun and verb morphology (e.g. *Traité de la conjugaison française, c.*1250; *Orthographia gallica, c.*1300), dialogues, model conversations or letters, texts for beginners such as Walter de Bibbesworth's *Tretiz . . . pour aprise de langage (c.*1250? 1290?) or the late-14th-c. *Manières de langage,* and early grammars written in England which depend heavily on the Latin grammarian Donatus, as represented by the earliest extant example, the *Donat françois (c.*1400), composed by 'plusieurs bons clercs' from Paris for Johan Barton.

Grammars for and by the English continued to appear, one of the most original examples being John Palsgrave's *L'Éclaircissement de la langue française* (1530), written in English, which unfortunately had virtually no influence in France. 16th-c.

practical grammars for foreigners (e.g. G. du Wes, 1532; J. Pillot, 1550, for Germans; C. de Sainliens or Holyband, 1566, 1573) were written sometimes in Latin, sometimes in the vernacular.

It was thus not until 1531 that the first grammar written by a Frenchman was published in France, Jacques Dubois (or Sylvius)'s *In linguam gallicam isagwge.* The advent of *printing and increased use of the vernacular had led to calls for the language to be codified and fixed so as to lend it prestige and inhibit change (e.g. Geoffroy *Tory's eloquent plea in *Champ fleury,* 1529). Dubois's grammar, still in Latin, illustrates the difficulties experienced by early French grammarians who tried to force French into Latin models even where the languages differed fundamentally, as in noun morphology or use of articles. Typical also is its descriptive approach and format comprising a treatment of letters or sounds and a basic morphology; little space is devoted to syntax before Charles Maupas's *Grammaire française* (1607). Only gradually, as the century progressed, were grammarians such as Louis *Meigret, whose *Tretté de la grammere françoeze* (1550) was the first written in French, able to see French at least to some extent on its own terms. This engendered debate as to which usage should constitute the norm, whether that of the educated, the royal court, the people, the lawcourts, or the chancellery. Robert *Estienne's *Traité de la grammaire française* (1554) is essentially a synthesis of Dubois and Meigret, whilst his son Henri's *Hypomneses de gall. lingua* (1582) contains some new insights helped by his knowledge of Greek, but still attributes to French a declension system and neuter gender. Other works by Henri *Estienne (e.g. *Deux dialogues,* 1578) attack Italian lexical borrowings. Pierre de la Ramée (Petrus *Ramus)'s *Grammaire* (1562, 1572) is of interest for its formal approach.

Meigret and Ramus, along with others such as Jacques *Peletier du Mans, also took up the cause of reforming French orthography to bring it closer to pronunciation, albeit to no avail (for an example of Meigret's spelling see his *Tretté* cited above). The most radical proposal was by Honorat Rambaud (1578) for a completely new alphabet.

2. Seventeenth and Eighteenth Centuries

The 17th c. continued to produce practical grammars retaining the traditional format and often intended for foreigners, but increasingly grounded on a firmer theoretical basis and including general insights (e.g. C. Maupas, *Grammaire française,* 1607; A. Oudin, *Grammaire française,* 1632; C. Irson, *Nouvelle méthode,* 1656; L. Chiflet, *Essai d'une parfaite grammaire de la langue française,* 1659). Two new and influential currents emerged. First, *Vaugelas's *Remarques* (1647), born from the Academy and salon milieu, is a collection of observations on good French usage, defined as that of the soundest part of the court and contemporary authors. Despite its avowed emphasis on usage, the work gave rise to normative works codifying French to the last detail and often espousing a rigorous, not to say inhibitive, purism, as typified in the work of *Bouhours. Vaugelas's format was also influential, producing a whole series of observations; even *Ménage adopted it for his erudite *Observations sur la langue française* (1672, 1676). Secondly, the 'Port-Royal grammar', *Arnauld and *Lancelot's *Grammaire générale et raisonnée* (1660), combining the tradition of medieval speculative grammar with Cartesianism, inaugurated philosophical rational grammar in France. The fundamental premiss that language reflects thought helps shape not only a novel analysis of the parts of speech but even the work's format. 'Method' becomes a keyword in later 17th-c. grammars (e.g. Denis Vairasse d'Allais's *Grammaire méthodique*, 1681).

The beginning of the 18th c. witnesses the continuation of purism, notably in commentaries on classical authors and in works which look to usage or often have a practical or didactic aim, but which nevertheless prepare the way for the great general grammars (e.g. *Régnier-Desmarais, *Traité de la grammaire française*, 1705; *Buffier, *Grammaire française*, 1709; P. Restaut, *Principes généraux et raisonnés de la grammaire française*, 1730). The 18th c., especially from 1740, is, however, the age of philosophical and rational grammars and the apogee for theoretical works on French; we might note, for instance, the two principal grammarians of the *Encyclopédie*, *Du Marsais, whose *Traité des tropes* (1730) marks a move towards increased abstraction, and *Beauzée, author of a *Grammaire générale* (1767) in which 'la grammaire particulière' is subordinated to the rules of general grammar. Rather than observing usage themselves, there was a tendency for the *philosophes* to include a certain category in universal grammar and then 'discover' it in French. Moreover, features observed by previous usage grammarians became the subject of necessary and absolute rules. Also worthy of note are Gabriel *Girard's *Les Vrais Principes de la langue française* (1747) and *Condillac's *Essai sur l'origine des connaissances humaines* (1746) and *Grammaire* in Volume I of his *Cours d'études* (1775). Condillac and the *Idéologues dominated the linguistic thought of the end of the century, eclipsing, for instance, Jean-François Féraud's *Dictionnaire critique de la langue française* (1787–8). The end of the century witnessed a decline in works with theoretical orientation, with the most original contributions coming from Urbain Domergue (1745–1810), author of a *Grammaire générale analytique* (1785) who also founded a 'Société des Amateurs de la Langue Française' and a *Journal de la langue française* (1784–9, 1791–2), and Antoine-Isaac Sylvestre de Sacy, who in 1799 published his *Principes de grammaire générale*. Dieudonné Thiébault's *Grammaire philosophique* (1802) and *Destutt de Tracy's *Éléments d'idéologie* (1801–15) signal the demise of general grammar in the early 19th c.

3. Nineteenth and Twentieth Centuries

From a position of pre-eminence in the study of language, French linguistic thought declined markedly in quality in the 19th c. The work of the Idéologues was superseded by a proliferation of school grammars intended for primary and secondary use. Providing above all rules for the written language, they were essentially designed for teaching French orthography, and notably past-participle agreement. Charles-François Lhomond's *Éléments de la grammaire française*, first published in 1780, ran to numerous editions, as did the most successful work of the 19th c., Joseph-Michel Noël and Charles-Pierre Chapsal's *Nouvelle grammaire française* (1823). Compilations were also popular, notably Charles Girault-Duvivier's *Grammaire des grammaires* (1811), containing all the decisions of past usage grammarians. Ideals of purism and correctness were kept alive in such works as Desgrouais's *Gasconismes corrigés*, constantly re-edited from 1766 on.

Whilst historical comparative grammar and the study of Indo-European were important elsewhere in Europe, historical grammar only really penetrated into France from about 1880 with the work of Michel Bréal and Arsène Darmesteter; a particular interest was shown in semantics and semantic change (M. Bréal, *Essai de sémantique*, 1897; A. Darmesteter, *La Vie des mots*, 1887). Later, the study of comparative grammar and Indo-European were taken up in France, notably by Antoine Meillet.

School grammars have continued to appear in the 20th c., largely unaffected by changing theoretical perspectives. Many grammars of the early part of the century remained traditional (e.g. A. Dauzat, *Grammaire raisonnée*, 1947), but there was an important number of psychologically based grammars, such as Jacques Damourette and Édouard Pichon's *Des mots à la pensée* (1928–40) or Ferdinand *Brunot's *La Pensée et la langue* (1922). Major publishing houses produce their own grammars (e.g. *Grammaire Larousse du français contemporain*, 1964). The long-awaited *Grammaire de l'Académie Française* of 1932, first promised in 1635, proved a disappointment; the standard reference work today for most educated Frenchmen is the Belgian Maurice Grevisse's *Le Bon Usage*, first published in 1936. While adopting a traditional grammatical format, the work also focuses on problematic questions.

On the whole, the findings of general and theoretical linguistics, especially *Structuralism, have only slowly been assimilated into French grammars (e.g. G. Gougenheim, *Système grammatical de la langue française*, 1939). However, since the late 1950s a variety of different theories have left their mark on the description and analysis of French, including dependency grammar (L. Tesnière, *Éléments de syntaxe structurale*, 1959), Structuralism (T. Cristea, *Grammaire structurale du français contemporain*, 1974), and generativism (J. Dubois and M. Gross, *Grammaire transformationnelle du français*, 1965–77).
[See also LINGUISTICS.]   [WA-B]

See: F. Brunot, *Histoire de la langue française des origines à 1900*, 13 vols. (1905–53); L. Kukenheim, *Esquisse historique de la linguistique française et ses rapports avec la linguistique générale*, 2nd edn. (1966); J.-C. Chevalier, *Histoire de la syntaxe: naissance de la notion de complément dans la grammaire française (1530–1750)* (1968); G. A. Padley, *Grammatical Theory in Western Europe 1500–1700*, 3 vols. (1976–88).

Grammatologie, De la, see DERRIDA.

Gramont, Mémoires du comte de, see HAMILTON.

GRANDBOIS, Alain (1900–75). Canadian poet, born in Saint-Casimir, west of Quebec. The name comes from forests owned by his ancestors. After a very free childhood, he took a leisurely law degree in Charlottetown and then at Laval. At 21 a legacy permitted him to roam the world between the wars. His short stories, *Avant le chaos* (1945, 1964, 1991), set in China, Djibouti, London, and the south of France, recall the long sea voyages, the chance encounters with expatriates, the storms and doldrums of elegant despair, overshadowed by the chaos of war. His first work was a biography of his forebear the explorer Louis Jolliet (1645–1700), *Né à Québec* (1933), followed by a magical rewriting of the *Voyages de Marco Polo* (1941). Impoverished after World War II, he relived his experiences in a long series of radio broadcasts, later published as *Visages du monde* (1971, 1991). He was a gifted story-teller, combining narrative and human interest, reverie and dialogue.

Grandbois's first six poems (1934) were published by a French adventurer in Hankow, China, and reappear in *Les Îles de la nuit* (1944). *L'Étoile pourpre* (1948) and *Rivages de l'homme* (1957) complete his collected *Poésies*, published by the Éditions de l'Hexagone in 1963. The critical edition of his work currently being published by Bibliothèque du Nouveau Monde (Montreal) includes much unpublished writing. A number of *Poèmes inédits* were provisionally published in 1985. A stoic and elegiac poet, influenced by *Vigny and the Bible, his free but disciplined verse protests at the inexorability of time, the ephemeral nature of beauty and passion, the unassuageable thirst of man for light and meaning, his restless and fruitless quest for peace in the bosom of the Other:

Je suis le veuf de la nuit [. . .]
Je suis le veuf d'une invisible terre
La nuit m'a enseigné la cloison de ton visage.

Passionate love-letters to the Quebec poet Simone Routier throw light on the strong but discreet erotic strain in his poetry. Grandbois, torn between immanence and transcendence, clearly belongs to the age of *Malraux, *Supervielle, and *Saint-John Perse. He has had no imitators, but the Hexagone group [see QUEBEC, 5] and poets as different as Jacques *Brault and Raoul Duguay have acknowledged their indebt-

edness. Pierre *Emmanuel recognized in Grandbois one of the great poets in the French language.
[CRPM]

Grand chant courtois. Somewhat ambivalent term of medieval scholarship adapted from the rubric *grant chant* in a *trouvère songbook (Oxford, Bodleian, Douce 308), which classifies lyrics by genre. The rubric heads 91 lyrics, all *chansons courtoises* (*cansos) apart from seven *chansons pieuses* and a *serventois*, a *chanson satirique*, and a *tenson fictive. Some scholars, therefore, equate *grands chants courtois* with *chansons courtoises*. Others extend the sense to cover *serventois* (*sirventes) pronouncing on topical social or political issues, *troubadour *planhs* mourning dead persons, *tensons and *jeux partis (envisaged as two interlocking *sirventes), and those *chansons courtoises* and *serventois* which introduce a crusading theme.
[PVD]

Grand Cyrus, Le, novel by Madeleine de *Scudéry, see ARTAMÈNE.

Grande Mademoiselle, La. Name by which the 17th-c. duchesse de *Montpensier was known.

Grande Maison, La, see DIB.

Grande Peur, La, see REVOLUTION, 1b.

Grandes Chroniques de France, Les. An unwieldy compilational history of France composed over some 200 years (1250–1450) by a number of different hands, some sections being translated from Latin, some composed in French. It covers France from Troy to 1450. Historically it is unreliable, but its glorification of France and the monarchy is a valuable index of changing attitudes among historians and public.
[JHMT]

Grandes Écoles, Les, see EDUCATION, 2b.

Grand Guignol, see GUIGNOL.

Grand Jeu, Le. A 'para-*Surrealist group' led by René *Daumal, Roger Gilbert-Lecomte, Roger *Vailland, and the painter Joseph Sima, it saw itself as 'une communauté en quelque sorte initiatique'. Born out of the Simpliste group founded by the youthful Daumal, it was active between *c.*1928 and 1933. The review *Le Grand Jeu* ran to three numbers between 1928 and 1930.
[KRA]

Grand Meaulnes, Le. This novel, published by *Alain-Fournier in 1913, delicately handles the themes of love, memory, adventure, and childhood. It is partly a fictionalized account of the author's own adolescent love for Yvonne de Quiévrecourt. Alain-Fournier creates a poetic, dream-like atmosphere as the narrator, François Seurel, tells how his schoolfellow Augustin Meaulnes chanced upon a mysterious country estate, watched festivities celebrating the engagement of Frantz de Galais, fell in love with Frantz's sister Yvonne, but could never discover the way back there. François eventually found it, Meaulnes married Yvonne, left to help Frantz find his fiancée, and eventually returned home where Yvonne had died in childbirth. [JC]

Grand Prix Littéraire d'Afrique Noire, Le. Prize created in 1960 to replace various colonial awards. Organized by the Association des Écrivains de Langue Française (ADELF), the judges' panel is composed as follows: three ambassadors of francophone African countries serving in Paris, drawn by lots each year; three academics from institutions such as the Académie Française; a representative from the Ministère de la Coopération; and three ADELF committee members. The first winner was *Ake Loba's *Kocoumbo, l'étudiant noir* in 1961. While several winners have become classics (e.g. *Kane's *L'Aventure ambiguë*), other widely acclaimed works, like *Sembène's *Les Bouts de bois de Dieu* and *Kourouma's *Les Soleils des indépendances*, have not been similarly honoured. [FNC]

Grand Siècle, Le. Name often given to the 17th century in France, in particular to the reign of *Louis XIV [see CLASSICISM, I].

GRANDSON, Oton de (c.1340–1397), was greatly admired by contemporaries for his elegant poetry and his chivalry, in spite of his death in a judicial duel. His verse emulates *Machaut's notably in the long verse *Livre messire Odo*, an amorous 'autobiography' inset with ballades and *chansons*. [JHMT]

Grand Troupeau, Le, see GIONO.

GRANDVILLE (pseud. of Jean-Ignace-Isidore Gérard) (1803–47). French artist, a contributor to Le *Charivari*, admired by *Baudelaire among others for his fantastic imagery, including portrayals of contemporaries as animals. He illustrated many classic texts, including *Don Quixote*, *Gulliver's Travels*, La Fontaine's *Fables*, and works of *La Bruyère and *Béranger.

Grasset. Publishing-house founded in 1905 by Bernard Grasset (1881–1955), which built a reputation for publishing contemporary authors. It played an important part in French literary life of the 1920s with its collection 'Cahiers Verts' and the publication of works by *Mauriac, *Morand, *Montherlant, *Drieu la Rochelle, *Mauriac, and *Giraudoux. Bernard Grasset himself published a book about publishing entitled *Remarques sur l'édition* in 1928. [EAF]

GRATIANT, Gilbert (1895–1985), Martinican writer, see WEST INDIES, 4, 6.

Great War, The, see WORLD WAR I.

GRÉBAN, Arnoul (c.1425–c.1495). Author of the most influential of medieval *Passion plays. Born probably in Le Mans, Gréban studied theology and music in Paris; he was the organist at Notre-Dame, when he composed his Passion in about 1450. He later worked for Charles duc du Maine until 1473, when he went to Italy as a musician.

His four-day, 30,000-line Passion play is generally recognized to be the masterpiece of the genre; exceptionally, several identical complete manuscripts of the play have survived. It was borrowed and reworked, directly or indirectly, by many later *fatistes* (mystery-play compilers). Jehan Michel expanded the second and third days, and versions of the complete play were performed in Troyes in the 1490s and in Mons in 1501; large sections of it appear in the two *Passions de Valenciennes* of 1547 and 1549. Gréban followed the model of the *Passion d'Arras*, using the *Procès de Paradis* as the framework for four days dramatizing respectively the childhood of Christ, his public life, the Passion proper, and the Resurrection; but he preceded this with a *Création abrégée*. Gréban's writing is more supple than his predecessors'; his success is attributable not only to his rapidity of movement and his skilful versification, but also to his incorporation of numerous learned sources, including Nicolas de Lire, pseudo-Bonaventure, and a narrative Passion composed for Isabeau de Bavière, the result of which is to emphasize the role of the Virgin Mary. [GAR]

GRÉCO, Juliette (b. 1927). French singer and actress. Famous in her teens as 'la muse de *Saint-Germain-des-Prés', she made a career as a subtle and theatrical cabaret performer, interpreting songs with lyrics by literary figures such as *Sartre, *Prévert, *Desnos, and *Queneau, as well as by fellow singers like *Ferré, *Brel, and *Béart. [PGH]

GRÉCOURT, Jean-Baptiste Joseph Willart, abbé de (1683–1743). French poet. Although a priest, he frequented *libertin circles and composed a great deal of light verse: burlesque, fables, epigrams, madrigals, epicurean love poetry.

Greek Influences on French Literature, see CLASSICAL INFLUENCES.

GREEN, Julien (b. 1900). Catholic novelist, dramatist, and memorialist, born of American parents from the Southern states, which serve as a location for some of his fiction, but brought up in Paris and of French nationality. His early novels, such as *Mont-Cinère* (1926), *Adrienne Mesurat* (1927), and *Léviathan* (1928), evoke a claustrophobic world in which the characters' attempts to escape turn to passion, violence, and madness; they reflect Green's difficulties in reconciling sexuality, particularly homosexuality, with Catholicism. His work in the 1930s explores the possibility of escape from this bleak world through fantasy, and his later fiction, including *Moïra* (1950), *Chaque homme dans sa nuit* (1960), and *L'Autre* (1971), moves towards a more optimistic vision in which salvation is finally

Grégoire

possible. In the 1950s he turned to drama, with three plays, *Sud* (1953), *L'Ennemi* (1954), and *L'Ombre* (1956), which show considerable dramatic talent and reflect the concerns of the novels. His spiritual and aesthetic evolution is recounted and explored in a third major area, his work as an autobiographer and, especially, diarist, whose *Journal*, begun in 1926, constitutes, with those of *Gide and *Mauriac, one of the major 20th-c. examples of the genre.   [NH]

GRÉGOIRE, Henri, abbé (1750–1831). Revolutionary reformer. He was born in Lorraine and began his career as a country priest. In his *Essai sur la régénération physique, morale et politique des Juifs* (1788) he blamed the state of the Jews on the antisemitic legislation governing them and demanded its abrogation [see JUDAISM]. Elected deputy of the clergy to the *États Généraux, he was among the first to join the deputies of the Third Estate, and played a major legislative role throughout the Revolution, speaking and writing extensively in favour of the rights of Jews, blacks, and those of mixed blood (especially in *Haiti). He proposed projects for education reform, for the elimination of *patois and the universalization of the use of French (which he considered essential to effective democracy), for the enrichment and development of the Bibliothèque Nationale, and was extremely active in attempting to preserve historical monuments from revolutionary vandalism. Grégoire is pre-eminently representative of the Revolutionary effort to realize the hopes of the Enlightenment.

Named bishop of Blois in the Constitutional Church, he was a major force in organizing and maintaining that institution whilst showing charity towards the non-juror priests [see CONSTITUTION CIVILE]. Of great personal courage, he refused to renounce his episcopal functions during the Terror, bravely pleading for religious tolerance, and after the *Concordat refused to deny the validity of his episcopate or of the experiment of the Constitutional Church. He encountered Napoleon's wrath because he refused as senator to approve of the divorce with Josephine; he roundly condemned the emperor also for his reinstitution of slavery.

Grégoire suffered much persecution under the Restoration; elected *député* in 1819, he was accused of having been a regicide and not seated. His *Histoire des sectes religieuses* (1814, 2nd edn. 1828–45) reflects his *Gallican and Jansenist convictions, but also his concern with ecumenicity. *De la littérature des noirs ou Recherches sur leurs facultés intellectuelles* (1808) proposed that, as with the Jews, the state of the blacks stemmed from social and cultural conditions (especially slavery) and that they had made and could make great contributions in science, letters, music, religion, and politics.   [FPB]

GREGORY OF TOURS, see LATINITY, 1.

GREIMAS, Algirdas Julien (1917–92). Linguist. Born in Lithuania, he took a doctorate in literature at the Sorbonne in 1947 and was for many years director of studies in general semantics at the *École Pratique des Hautes Études. His *Sémantique structurale* (1966) was a founding text of semiotics, analysing lexical units, 'lexemes', into minimal semantic units, 'semes', and contextual semantic units, 'sememes'. His structural analysis of discourse was highly influential in the *Structuralist approach to literary and mythological texts. See also his *Du sens: essais sémiotiques* (1970).   [MHK]

GREKI, Anna (pseud. of Colette Anna Melki, née Grégoire) (1931–66). Algerian poet. She was born in Batna and educated in Collo and Philippeville, then worked as a primary-school teacher in Annaba and Algiers and joined the Parti Communiste Algérien. Arrested in 1957, she was imprisoned and tortured in Barberousse, transferred to Beni-Messous, and expelled from Algeria in 1958. She lived in Tunis and only resumed her teaching career in Algeria in 1965. She left two collections of poems (the second published after her sudden death in 1966) in which, in a lyrical manner, she combines love for her country with an ardent hope and support for its imminent liberation: *Algérie, capitale Alger* (1963), *Temps forts* (1966).   [FL]

GRENIER, Jean (1898–1971). French philosopher and essayist. Raised in Saint-Brieuc, where he met Louis *Guilloux, from 1930 to 1938 he taught philosophy at the Grand Lycée d'Alger: among his pupils was Albert *Camus, who was profoundly influenced by *Les Îles* (1933) and *Essai sur l'esprit d'orthodoxie* (1938); their *Correspondance 1932–1960* (1981) reveals a mutual respect and friendship. Upholding a philosophy of existence rooted in concrete experience and informed by a love of Greek civilization, Grenier also won renown for his studies of oriental philosophy, especially Taoism, as well as for his literary criticism and his writings on art (*L'Esprit de la peinture contemporaine*, 1951).   [DHW]

GRENIER, Roger (b. 1919). French novelist and critic. Active in the Resistance during the *Occupation, he joined *Camus as a reporter on the newspaper *Combat* in 1944 and later worked for *France-Soir*. An essay on crime reporting, *Le Rôle d'accusé*, appeared in 1948, and his first novel, *Les Monstres* (1953), drew on his experience as a journalist, also reflected in *La Salle de rédaction* (1977). As well as *Ciné-roman* (1972, Prix Fémina) and a dozen other novels up to *Partita* (1991), his output includes volumes of short stories (*Le Silence*, 1961; *Miroir des eaux*, 1975) and critical essays, notably on Camus (*Soleil et ombre*, 1987).   [DHW]

GRESSET, Jean-Baptiste-Louis (1709–77). Poet and dramatist. A native of Amiens, he was a pupil of the Jesuits and taught for a time in their colleges. Elected to the Académie Française in 1748, he devoted much of his later life to the Academy of Amiens, where he was loved and admired. He wrote a number of odes and eclogues, but is at his best in easy-going narrative or satirical verse, such as 'La Chartreuse' or 'Les Ombres'; these poems, like his epistles, are lively and unpompous, making good use of shorter verse lines. He won fame at the age of 24 with *Ver-Vert* (1733), a mock-epic about a parrot who is the pride and joy of a convent, but shocks his hearers by learning bad language. *Édouard III* (1740) is a tragedy in the Racinian manner, loosely based on British history; Gresset also wrote two comedies: *Sidnei* (1745), a sentimental English piece about averted suicide, and the better-known *Le Méchant* (1747), a fairly traditional matrimonial comedy containing some sharp social satire.

[PF]

GREUZE, Jean-Baptiste (1725–1805). French painter. Greuze developed Charles *Lebrun's theories of distinguishable human expressions in immensely popular paintings composed like theatrical tableaux. Instead of Greek heroes he portrayed ordinary families fulfilling simple duties of moral or social significance such as *Le Père de famille expliquant la Bible* (1755). *Diderot perceived a link with *Rousseau and devoted much favourable comment to Greuze in his *Salons*. He approved of the realism of portraits like Babuti, the *sensibilité* in his *La Jeune Fille qui pleure son oiseau mort* (1765), and the human emotions in his monumental set pieces of *La Malédiction paternelle* (1777) and *Le Mauvais Fils puni* (1778).

[JPC]

Grève des Bàttu, La, see SOW FALL.

Grève, Place de la. On the site of the present place de l'Hôtel-de-Ville in Paris, this was a centre of river traffic and the water trade, but best known as a place of public execution until the early 19th c. Discontented workers gathered there, whence the expression 'se mettre en grève', to go on strike.

GRÉVIN, Jacques (1538–70). French dramatist, translator, and poet. Grévin studied in Paris at the Collège de Boncourt, where the teachers included *Buchanan and *Muret, and where Jodelle's *Cléopâtre captive* was performed, probably while Grévin was a student there. His first publications, in 1558 and 1559, were occasional poems. Meanwhile he was studying medicine and received his doctorate in 1562. In 1560 his *Olimpe* (odes, a pastoral, satirical sonnets, and love sonnets) appeared, graced with poems by *Ronsard, *Du Bellay, and *Belleau. Grévin's surviving dramatic output consists of a tragedy and two comedies, published in 1561. *César* somewhat resembles an earlier Latin play, Muret's *Julius Caesar* (1552), but with notable differences (the introduction of Mark Antony, the representation of Caesar as hesitant and uneasy, the fact that the chorus consists of soldiers who have fought under Caesar). The comedies are among the best of their period. In *La Trésorière* two men compete for the love of a married woman. Amorous and financial concerns are ingeniously interwoven. In *Les Ébahis*, Madelon's rival lovers are an old man (who turns out to be already married), a boastful Italian soldier (mocked for his nationality, his serenading, and his cowardice), and a young lawyer (who is successful).

[GJ]

GREVISSE, Maurice, see GRAMMARS, 3.

GRIGNAN, comtesse de, see SÉVIGNÉ.

GRIGNON, Claude-Henri (1894–1978). Canadian journalist and novelist who achieved fame through his portrayal of Séraphin Poudrier, a hard-bitten country miser, in *Un homme et son péché* (1933). Twice made into a feature film, the novel achieved still greater popularity as a long-running serial on radio (1936–65) and on television (1956–70). If Grignon's character achieved an even greater hold on the popular imagination than *Lemelin's Plouffe family, it is no doubt because he was set in an earlier historical period and in more remote rural locations. The combination effectively captured that powerful nostalgia for its agrarian past which is a major feature in the culture of modern urban Quebec. [SIL]

GRIMAREST, Jean-Léonor Le Gallois, sieur de (1659–1713). Author of a *Vie de M. de Molière* (1705), containing sharp criticism of contemporary acting. He followed this up by giving interesting rhetorical advice to actors in the *Traité du récitatif* (1707).

GRIMM, Frédéric-Melchior, baron de (1723–1807). German man of letters who made his career in France. He was a close friend of *Diderot, and the lover of Madame d'*Épinay, whose part he took in her quarrel with her former friend Jean-Jacques Rousseau; Rousseau paints a black picture of him in the *Confessions*. In the *Guerre des Bouffons, he defended the Italian cause in a pamphlet, *Le Petit Prophète de Bœhmischbroda* (1753). He then cultivated patrons throughout Europe; it was for them that he composed the journal for which he is best remembered, the *Correspondance littéraire*. At the Revolution he went into exile. [PF]

GRIMOD DE LA REYNIÈRE, Alexandre-Balthazar-Laurent (1758–1838). Author of the pioneering and much-imitated *Almanach des gourmands servant de guide dans les moyens de faire grande chère* (1803–12), in which he drew on his own considerable experience to provide readers with lively information on all aspects of cooking and eating out, and helped to establish a new genre of modern gastronomic writing. [BR]

GRINGORE, Pierre (c.1475–1538). Born in Normandy, a *Rhétoriqueur, he was one of a group of writers used by Louis XII to produce propaganda. But he was best known for his association with a *confrérie*, the *Enfants Sans Souci, as actor, producer, and writer, providing them with *soties and moralités, like the *Jeu du prince des sots* (1512). His

Griot

stage-name, 'mère sotte', is often used for his publications. He also wrote a lengthy mystery play, *La Vie de monseigneur sainct Loys*. Two of his most famous works, satirical, moralizing pieces, were the verse *Folles Entreprises* (1505, inspired by Brant's *Narrenschiff*) and *Les Fantaisies de Mère Sotte* (1516), which mixed verse and prose. The character Gringoire in Hugo's *Notre-Dame de Paris* is based on Gringore. [CMSJ]

Griot is the generic name given to the members of a particular 'caste' of men, who have performed a wide variety of functions within traditional West African society. At one and the same time official story-teller, historian, musician, poet, and praise-singer, the *griot* continues to play an important ceremonial role at all the significant events in the life of the community: births, marriages, funerals, and so on. In pre-literate societies the importance of the oral tradition cannot be overestimated, and the essential function of the *griots* was to ensure the passage from generation to generation of a poeticized account of the people's history, its myths, and the genealogies of its celebrated individuals and families. The *griots* have thus come to be known as 'the guardians of the word' (see *Camara Laye's *Le Maître de la parole*). Their performances, generally accompanied by music, rely on highly developed mnemonic techniques and often make use of a stylized and poetic linguistic register. In traditional societies the *griots* were highly respected members of the community, but colonization and the social upheavals which have followed in its wake have dramatically altered their status. As West Africa has become literate, the *griots* have lost much of their *raison d'être*. [MPC]

Griots, Les (1938–40). Quarterly journal and organ of *noirisme* in *Haiti. Formed in 1932 by Louis Diaquoi, Lorimer Denis, and François Duvalier, the group included the poets Carl Brouard and Magloire Saint Aude. Inspired by *Price-Mars, they saw Haitians as genetically Africans, praised voodoo, and demanded a return to cultural authenticity. [JMD]

GRIPARI, Pierre (1925–90). A fantasy writer, whose best-selling book is *Contes de la rue Broca* (1967) (for children). The predictable moral expectations of *Perrault's 'Les Fées' are reversed in 'La Fée du robinet': the naughty child is rewarded, the good child punished, for fairies do not understand the modern world. Gripari is the spokesman of a more ironic view of life, in which the old moral certainties have shifted. See his autobiography, *Pierrot la lune* (1963), and 'P.G. vu par P.G.', in P. Gripari, *Critique et autocritique* (1981). [GDM]

'Griselidis'. Story of the patient Griselda, told in verse by *Perrault. The original is in Boccaccio and is retold by Chaucer in the Clerk's Tale, as well as figuring in the *Bibliothèque Bleue.

GROS-GUILLAUME, see GAULTIER-GARGUILLE.

GROSJEAN, Jean (b. 1912). French poet. For a time a priest, he left the Church and married. His work is intensely concerned with spiritual questions. Several books of poems, beginning with *Terre du temps* (1946), culminate in *La Gloire* (1969), a meditation on 'le dieu' and poetry. These books are mainly in a form akin to *Claudel's *versets*; his most recent collection of simpler, valedictory poems, *La Lueur des jours* (1991), is in near-traditional verse. He has also written several *récits* and translated the Bible, the Koran, and Greek tragedy. [PF]

GROUCHY, Marie-Louise-Sophie, marquise de Condorcet (1764–1822). Having been converted to the new philosophy, she married *Condorcet in 1786, shared his political commitments, and supported him in the difficult Revolutionary years. Her salon was a meeting-place for advanced thinkers and writers, from *Beaumarchais to *Chamfort, Beccaria to Tom Paine, and for many of the future *Idéologues. After Condorcet's death she edited his works and translated Adam Smith's *Theory of Moral Sentiments*. [PF]

GROULT, Benoîte (b. 1920). Novelist, journalist, and feminist. In 1963 she published a book written jointly with her sister Flora, *Journal à quatre mains*, based on their diaries of the German Occupation. *Ainsi soit-elle* (1975), an essay on women, marks a turning-point in her feminist consciousness. Later novels include *Les Vaisseaux du cœur* (1988). [EAF]

GROULX, Lionel-Adolphe (1878–1967). Canadian priest, historian, and novelist who was the major intellectual force behind French-Canadian nationalism from the 1920s to the 1960s. He exercised his influence through the politically militant Action Française movement (not to be confused with *Action Française of Maurras) and its journal *Action française* (founded 1921, later *Action nationale*), but also through his prolific and highly readable historical works, which have had a much wider audience.

His objectives as a historian were to defend and celebrate the crusading role of the Church in the construction of French Canada, and to draw inspiration from the past for the nationalist cause (*Notre maître le passé*, 3 vols., 1924–44). He lived to see many of his aspirations fulfilled by the Révolution Tranquille of the 1960s (which adopted one of his rallying cries, 'maîtres chez nous', as its slogan), but the neo-nationalism of this period was significantly less conservative than his own [see QUEBEC, 5]. He carried over his political commitment into his literary work, especially the controversial *L'Appel de la race* (1922). Portraying the two founding peoples of Canada as irreconcilably divided 'races', and suggesting that intermarriage between them was doomed to failure, this work has led critics (especially in English Canada) to denounce his ethnic determinism and to seek other evidence of racist beliefs—notably antisemitism—in his writings. In comparison, his other literary productions were uncontroversial. *Rapaillages* (1916) is a set of idyllic sketches of the traditional rural life of French Canada, while *Au Cap Blomidon* (1932) is a didactic tale of a young French *Acadian who, by hard work, recovers his family's ancestral farmlands in Nova Scotia. [SIL]

GRUMBERG, Jean-Claude (b. 1939). French playwright. His work reflects his experiences as the son of Jewish immigrant workers, whose father was deported and disappeared during the German *Occupation. His early experimental plays, written in the 1960s and 1970s, include *Demain une fenêtre sur rue*, *Amorphe d'Ottenburg*, *Dreyfus*, and *En r'venant de l'Expo*. His biggest success to date was with *L'Atelier* (1979), a more conventional naturalist-style drama. Set in a small clothing workshop in the immediate post-war period, it gives an understated and moving picture, seasoned with Yiddish humour, of the life of survivors of the Holocaust. [DWW]

Guadeloupe, see WEST INDIES.

GUATTARI, Félix, see DELEUZE.

GUÉHENNO, Jean (1890–1978). French critic and essayist. In the 1930s he edited the left-wing reviews *Europe* and *Vendredi*, and published sharp criticisms of French culture and class attitudes. Moving to *Le *Figaro* in 1945, Guéhenno wrote prolifically; he was elected to the Académie Française in 1962.

GUÉNEAU, Agnès, see MAURITIUS AND REUNION.

Guénégaud, Hôtel de, see THEATRES AND AUDIENCES, I.

Guêpes, Les, see KARR.

Guérillères, Les, see WITTIG.

GUÉRIN, Eugénie de (1805–48). The sister of Maurice de *Guérin, she brought him up, consecrated her life to him and, after his death, to his fame and the publication of his works. She kept a *Journal intime* from 1834 to 1842 (published posthumously, 1862) remarkable for its analytical and spiritual depth, description of nature, and prose style. She spent almost all her life at the Château du Cayla near Albi. [FPB]

GUÉRIN, Maurice de (1810–39), was born and died at the Château du Cayla (Tarn). After his mother's death he was brought up in an atmosphere of religious austerity by his sister Eugénie de *Guérin. He was intended for the Church, and in 1832 he joined *Lamennais's Christian Community at La Chesnaie. After the dissolution of the Community in 1833 he attempted to earn his living by writing and teaching, but his health was weakened and he eventually died of tuberculosis.

His was a fragile and troubled nature, and his attitudes and ideas combine the mystic and the pagan. His verse is generally considered to be mediocre; his strength and literary reputation lay in his prose poems, *Le Centaure* (1840) and *La Bacchante* (1862), and in his *Journal* and letters. The poems bring together a Dionysiac sensuousness and a sense of pervading anxiety. His reputation was established initially by George *Sand, *Barbey d'Aurevilly, and *Sainte-Beuve, and since the early 20th c. his works have been regularly in print. [BCS]

GUÉRIN DE BOUSCAL, Guyon (1613–57). French dramatist. He wrote a novel and 11 plays, including *Oroondate* (performed 1643), which parodies the widespread literary models of heroic courtship, and a trilogy based on *Don Quixote* (performed 1638–9), notable for its accomplished use of the burlesque. It is thought to have been adapted and played by *Molière's troupe in 1660. [GJM]

Guermantes. Name of the noble family with whom the narrator is obsessed in Proust's *À la recherche du temps perdu*.

Guerre des Bouffons, La. A battle of words waged in Paris in 1752–4 over the respective merits and demerits of Italian and French music, particularly *opera. Although not a new issue, it was ignited in August 1752 with the performance of Pergolesi's comic intermezzo *La serva padrona* by a visiting Italian *opera buffa* troupe. The debate intensified in January 1753 with the performance of Mondonville's heroic pastorale *Titon et l'aurore*, and over 30 pamphlets and letters were written in a period of nine months. The *philosophes* were heavily involved, with *Grimm, *Holbach, *Diderot, and *Rousseau all contributing personally. The articles on music in the *Encyclopédie* provided much of the ground material, and the two most important pamphlets were Grimm's *Le Petit Prophète de Bœhmischbroda* (January 1753, unsigned) and Rousseau's *Lettre sur la musique française* (November 1753). The quarrel was artificially inflamed by the enthusiasm of many of the contributors for a debate of any sort. It ended in 1754 with the successful revival of *Rameau's *Castor et Pollux* and *Platée*, and the consequent departure of the Italians. While the debate did not result in the adoption of Italian opera by the nationalistic French, the Guerre probably hastened the rapid changes that took place in French music shortly afterwards. [KM]

Guerre des boutons, La, see PERGAUD.

Guerre de Troie n'aura pas lieu, La, see GIRAUDOUX.

Guerre, yes sir!, La, see CARRIER.

GUESDE, Jules (pseud. of Jules Bazile) (1845–1922). Socialist leader and popularizer of *Marxism in France. Converted to Marxist socialism in the 1870s, he collaborated with Marx, Engels, and Lafargue to write the nascent French Socialist Party's Le Havre Manifesto of 1880. In an age of schisms, Guesde led his own 'collectivist' Parti Ouvrier Français until Socialist unity in 1905. A spellbinding orator, he conveyed his simplified version of Marxism to many French workers, especially in the industrial north. Although Marx was thinking of the Guesdists when he said he was 'not a Marxist', much of Guesdism survived in the French Communist Party.　　　　[SR]

GUEULLETTE, Thomas-Simon (1683–1766). A cultured Parisian lawyer, Gueullette was a prolific and successful writer, widely translated, and especially appreciated in England. He wrote several collections of exotic tales, a novel, *Mémoires de Mademoiselle Bontemps* (1738), and some 70 plays (mainly *farces or parades) for private theatres, for the *théâtres de la *foire, and for the *Comédie-Italienne. He collaborated with the Parfaict brothers on the *Dictionnaire des théâtres de Paris* (1756), and published important editions of *Montaigne (1725), *Rabelais (1732), and of *La Sale's *Le Petit Jehan de Saintré* (1724).　　　　[JD]

GUÈVREMONT, Germaine (1873–1968). Canadian writer whose handling of the 'roman du terroir' (regional novel based on the land) makes her work both the summation of a tradition in Quebec writing and the point of rupture with it. *En pleine terre* (1942), a collection of short stories, precedes the saga of the Beauchemin family recounted in her two novels *Le Survenant* (1945) and *Marie-Didace* (1947). As is traditional in the genre, the family is closely anchored to the land and to the family house, symbol of the family's continuation through the generations. However, in both novels the arrival of a stranger is the signal for the disruption and eventual destruction of the family lineage.　　　　[EAF]

GUIBERT, Hervé (1955–91). French writer, whose work shifts easily across generic boundaries—novel, short story, documentary essay, intimate journal, *photo-roman—but maintains a clearly autobiographical orientation. The first of his 19 books—*La Mort propagande*—was published in 1977 and immediately established his idiom: succinct, uncompromisingly lucid, surgical in its examination of illusion, amoral but sternly principled. It also introduced an abiding preoccupation with the mechanisms of the human body. This culminated in an almost clinical study of the progression of AIDS in his own body (*A l'ami qui ne m'a pas sauvé la vie*, 1990), followed by another text with AIDS as its subject, but taking renewed pleasure in the adventures of mind, *Le Protocole compassionnel* (1991). Characteristically, his last story *Mon valet et moi* (1991), in which 'moi' is a wealthy 80-year-old, is subtitled 'roman cocasse'. His work was also nourished by his enthusiasm for photography, most directly in the image-less *L'Image fantôme* (1981), the text-less *Le Seul Visage* (1984), and a collection of earlier writing, *Vice* (1991). He was the photography correspondent for Le *Monde* up to 1985.　　　　[CS]

GUIBERT DE NOGENT (1053–1124). Benedictine abbot, author of an autobiography, *De vita sua* (c.1114), notable for its local colour, and of a history of the first crusade, *Gesta Dei per francos*, written c.1110 in Latin prose interspersed with poetry. He also wrote biblical commentaries, proposing four modes of reading the Bible: *historia, allegoria, tropologia, anagogia.*　　　　[PJF]

Gui de Warewic. Surviving in 15 manuscripts and twice translated into Middle English, *Gui de Warewic* (first half of 13th c.) was by far the most popular of the *Anglo-Norman adventure romances, and is the best example of the genre. It is set in Anglo-Saxon England at the time of King Athelstan. Its success may be due in large measure to its double focus as love romance and epic saint's life. After a purely secular first part tracing the fulfilment of Gui's desire for worldly glory under the inspiration of love, a second, didactic part shows the realization of a new mission as God's champion against the pagans: having conquered the world as a chivalric hero of love, Gui recovers it as an epic hero for God.　　　　[IS]

Guignol. Name given to a French puppet believed to have originated in Lyon in the late 18th c., and possibly invented by the puppet-master Laurent Mourguet. Guignol represented the · droll, open-hearted Lyonnais silk-weaver given to drink, and a local variant of Polichinelle or Punch, themselves puppet figures derived from the Pulcinella of the *commedia dell'arte*. Though more genial than the aggressive, humpbacked Punch, Guignol still moves in the familiar world of brawls, boisterous fun, and low comedy and, like Punch, invites his audience to join in the spirit of misrule. Traditional Guignol performances continue to be direct and unsophisticated. They are not to be confused with the refined puppet shows of Henri Signoret's Petit Théâtre des Marionnettes (1888), which presented adaptations of Aristophanes, Cervantes, and Shakespeare. The elements of violence and sadism in Guignol shows help to explain 'Grand Guignol', a term applied to cheap thrillers, often from the pen of André de Lorde, which were staged in the little theatres of Montmartre during the closing years of the 19th c. These were gory exercises in suspense and horror designed to assault the nerves of the audience. The tradition continues in modern horror films.　　　　[SBJ]

Guignol's Band, see CÉLINE.

GUILBERT, Yvette (1867–1944). French singer and songwriter. An improbable music-hall star of the 1890s, like the heroine of her famous song, 'Madame Arthur', she had a considerable *je ne sais quoi*. Her stage presence and dramatic skills were developed through her long apprenticeship, from actress to cabaret singer, when she finally adopted the stage costume of green satin with black gloves celebrated in the posters of *Toulouse-Lautrec. Her style was comically tragic, full of erotic innuendoes or worldly-wise irony. Her lyrics were usually written by others—Paul de *Kock, Mac Nab, Xanrof—but she often set them to her own music.   [PGH]

GUILHEM IX (1071–1126). The earliest *troubadour whose work has survived, as duke of Aquitaine Guilhem was one of the most powerful men in Europe as well as a gifted poet. Twice married, he had a long-term adulterous affair for which he was excommunicated (1114), invaded Toulouse twice (1097 and 1113), embarked on a disastrous expedition to Palestine (1101–2), and more successfully fought the Moors in Spain (1120). Chroniclers portray him as an impulsive yet shrewd statesman with a taste for high living and a marked irreverence for the Church.

His small corpus of extant poems seems to reflect this personality: there are obscene but witty boasting poems, a humourous, though similarly ribald, narrative poem, a *congé, and love lyrics which appear to herald the conventions of *fin'amor. His songs affirm his poetic and sexual superiority, metaphorically linking his prowess with power in a manner which was to become typical of the courtly lyric. Because of his apparent position as the 'first' troubadour, Guilhem has fascinated modern critics, despite being somewhat marginal in the manuscript tradition. He seems, however, to have been an influential figure for subsequent early troubadours like *Marcabru and *Jaufre Rudel, perhaps because he made the Poitevin court such an important cultural centre. His poems have been edited by N. Pasero (1973).   [SG]

GUILHEM DE CABESTANH (*fl.* c.1212). *Troubadour. He is less remembered now for his seven love songs than for his *vida, a version of the 'cœur mangé' story also found in the Roman du Castelain de Couci [see CHASTELAIN DE COUCI]. According to this grisly literalization of courtly metaphor, a husband, discovering his wife's adultery, has her lover killed and his heart served to her to eat. She learns what she has eaten and dies; he relents, and has them buried together.   [SK]

GUILLAUME, Gustave, see LINGUISTICS.

Guillaume, Cycle de. Name properly applied to six *chansons de geste (Les *Enfances Guillaume, Le *Couronnement de Louis, Le *Charroi de Nîmes, La *Prise d'Orange, La *Chanson de Guillaume, Le *Moniage Guillaume) dealing with Guillaume d'Orange, his turbulent relationship with the emperor Louis, son of *Charlemagne, and his incessant struggle against the 'pagan' Saracens in the south of France, and to five other poems (Les Enfances Vivien, La *Chevalerie Vivien, *Aliscans, La Bataille Loquifer, Le Moniage Rainouart) dealing principally with Guillaume's nephew Vivien and his brother-in-law Rainouart. The title is usually given, however, to the complete set of some 24 poems about the deeds of the Narbonnais clan and their ancestor *Garin de Monglane (after whom the cycle was originally named by *Bertrand de Bar-sur-Aube).

Of the three different cycles named by Bertrand, only the Garin de Monglane, or Guillaume, cycle was seriously elaborated by manuscript compilers, whose copy-shops produced three major redactions or 'editions' of the texts. These are known to modern editors as AB (six MSS in Paris, London, and Milan), CE (three MSS in Paris, Boulogne-sur-mer, and Berne), and D (one MS in Paris). It is notable that no manuscript contains the complete sequence, and that the bulk concentrate on the biography of Guillaume himself, although the two commonly grouped as B contain the 'grand cycle' of most of the 24 poems. There are also related manuscripts devoted to *Aimeri de Narbonne and *Girart de Vienne, Guillaume's father and grandfather, and to Vivien and Rainouart. The garbled state of the text of some poems, notably Le Charroi de Nîmes and La Prise d'Orange in D (Bibliothèque Nationale, fonds français 1448), has fuelled the debate between neo-traditionalists (who consider the manuscript a transcription of a *jongleur's performance) and individualists (for whom it is a copy made from memory).

The kernel of the cycle is provided not by the Chanson de Guillaume, which never actually figures as a text in cyclic manuscripts, but by the combination of Vivien–Rainouart material found in Aliscans and La Prise d'Orange. Although the earliest manuscripts date from the 13th c., the elaboration of the cycle occurred in the second half of the 12th c. Le Charroi de Nîmes, composed to provide a prologue to La Prise d'Orange (c.1125) in a 'proto-cyclic' compilation, probably dates from the 1150s or 1160s, to judge from the treatment of 'la Dame de Saint-Gilles' in an episode justifying Guillaume's 'crusade' in the south of France. Attempts to create a consistent cycle are sporadic, however: La Prise d'Orange, for instance, which was given its final cyclic form in the 1190s, never takes into account the data of Les Enfances Guillaume (c.1190–1200).

With the exception of the early Le Couronnement de Louis, all the poems of the cycle reveal strong romance influence and a tendency to robust comedy in the person of Guillaume, the development of whose character seems to have been considerably influenced by that of the comic folk-tale giant Rainouart, and of his perpetually young but pertly precocious nephew Gui. The biography of St Guillaume de Gellone, Charlemagne's cousin, count of Toulouse and commander of the army that captured Barcelona for the Franks in 803 AD, provides an essential frame for the core of the cycle, accounting for a particular atmosphere of dedication and martyrdom (in La Chevalerie Vivien and Aliscans), an almost mythographic contact with powers of evil (in Le Couronnement de Louis, Le Moniage Guillaume, and the non-cyclic Chanson de Guillaume), and a sense of real regret for homicide, even when the victims are Saracens (in *Le Charroi de Nîmes*). Most of the poems, however, elaborate the traditional motif of the young hero's quest for a bride and a fief. These include the story of the founder of the clan, *Garin de Monglane*; that of Guillaume's father, *Aimeri de Narbonne*; *Les *Narbonnais* (one of the *enfances* poems at the heart of the cycle, which recounts in boisterous and often comic vein the establishment of six of Aimeri's sons, first at Charlemagne's court, then in fiefs they have to conquer); *La Prise d'Orange*; and later poems like *Guibert d'Andrenas* and *La Prise de Cordres et de Sebille*.

Many of the poems establish links with the Cycle du *Roi, including *Girart de Vienne* (which makes Roland's companion Oliver a collateral member of the Narbonnais clan) and *Les Enfances Vivien* (in which Vivien is sent as hostage to Spain to secure the release of his father Garin, captured at Rencesvals). Several texts exploit the episode of the siege of the hero's city (frequently defended by a loyal spouse during his absence) and the mythological motif of the apocalyptic battle, given initial poetic form in the *Chanson de Guillaume* and finding cyclic expression in *Aliscans*. The cycle's unity is assured by the tireless energy of Guillaume, the mutual loyalty of the clan, and the stubborn support of legitimism by the Narbonnais in the face of perpetual imperial ingratitude. It is notable that the women of the cycle, especially Guillaume's wife Guibourc (the baptized name of Orable, the Saracen queen of Orange) and Aimeri's wife Hermengart, show a force of character and independence of action that makes them stand out in a period in which the woman's role in literature, whether epic or courtly, was severely circumscribed. [PEB]

See J. Frappier, *Les Chansons de geste du cycle de Guillaume d'Orange* (1955 and 1964); M. Tyssens, *La Geste de Guillaume d'Orange dans les manuscrits cycliques* (1967); *Les Chansons de geste du cycle de Guillaume d'Orange—hommage à Jean Frappier* (1983).

Guillaume d'Angleterre. A late 12th-c. *romance written in a language and style highly reminiscent of *Chrétien de Troyes, and indeed claiming as its author one 'Crestiiens' who worked on material provided by 'Roger the Clever'. Set in Britain, it tells of a bewildering series of accidents that befall its God-fearing royal protagonist and his wife Graciene as, exiled and separated, they each suffer humiliation and social degradation before eventually being reunited and reinstated. Its narrative is a particularly rich hotchpotch of commonplaces (shipwreck, pirates, fortuitous encounters), and it is close in both spirit and structure to the adventure romance so popular in *Anglo-Norman literature. [IS]

GUILLAUME D'AQUITAINE, see GUILHEM IX.

GUILLAUME DE DIGULLEVILLE (1295–after 1380). A monk in the Cistercian abbey of Chaalis, Digulleville composed three long allegorical poems

in octosyllabic couplets: *Le Pelerinage de vie humaine* (c.1330–1), which survives in two redactions and describes the moral life of the soul; *Le Pelerinage de l'ame* (c.1355–8), describing the soul's experiences in the afterlife; and *Le Pelerinage de Jhesucrist* (c.1358), recounting the life of Christ. His works were widely read and were translated into Dutch, German, English, and Spanish. [SJH]

GUILLAUME DE LORRIS (first half of the 13th c.). The author of the first part of the *Roman de la Rose* (c.1225–40), whose name is known only through *Jean de Meun's citation in his continuation of that poem. His name is derived from the town of Lorris, located between Orleans and Montargis. Nothing is known of his life. [SJH]

GUILLAUME DE MACHAUT, see MACHAUT.

Guillaume de Palerne. A loosely composed, episodic *roman d'aventure* of the early 13th c., set in southern Italy. It combines elements of the werewolf legend and idyllic love romance to recount in a mode reminiscent of oral epic techniques the adventures of Guillaume, heir to the throne of Sicily. [PEB]

GUILLAUME LE MARÉCHAL (William Marshall), see ANGLO-NORMAN LITERATURE, 4.

GUILLAUMIN, Émile (1873–1951). Writer of peasant stock who spent his life in Ygrande (Allier), devoting it to farming and, through novels, essays, and articles, to *la cause paysanne* in general. In 1904 he published his accomplished early example of 'green' literature, *La Vie d'un simple*, an account of the experiences of a *métayer* farmer, the hardness of whose life is mellowed by a deeply perceived sense of communion with nature. [DAS]

GUILLERAGUES, Gabriel-Joseph de Lavergne, vicomte de (1628–85). He began as a lawyer in Bordeaux, later moved to Paris, where he frequented literary circles and was known for his wit and occasional writings. He found royal favour, culminating in an ambassadorship to Constantinople (1669). The *Lettres portugaises* are now usually attributed to him. [JDeJ]

GUILLEVIC, Eugène (b. 1907). Poet. He was born at Carnac in Brittany, but never learnt the Breton language. He joined the Communists during World War II; the resulting *Gagner* (1949) suffers from political *engagement*, *31 sonnets* (1954) from bathos. He later returned to his earlier manner, in which he communicates the authentic poetic thrill.

The purpose of poetry (he says) is to arouse the sense of Being: it is to help others to live everyday life in a state of 'presence' to oneself and to things (*Vivre en poésie*, 1980). A Guillevic poem tends towards the brevity of a haiku, offering a moment of intense, almost mystical, concentration, akin to contemplation. It is surrounded by white paper and silence, and stands vertically on the page 'like a dam across time', as if, when reading it, time stops. Words obtain their 'real meaning' only within poems. Religions are poetry which has succeeded too well and become sclerotic.

Some of Guillevic's major collections are *Terraqué* (1945), *Exécutoire* (1947), *Carnac* (1961), *Sphère* (1963), *Euclidiennes* (1967), *Ville* (1969). See also a further collection of interviews, *Choses parlées* (1982). [GDM]

GUILLOUX, Louis (1899–1980). Novelist. Born in Saint-Brieuc in Brittany, Guilloux attended the local *lycée*. In the 1920s and 1930s he worked in journalism. Though he never joined a political party, he devoted much energy to anti-fascist activities (e.g. congresses) and to the relief of the unemployed and refugees. After World War II he collaborated in the establishment of several provincial *Maisons de la Culture. He is a much-undervalued writer.

Guilloux's autobiographical novel, *La Maison du Peuple* (1927), evokes a close-knit family whose shoe-maker father organizes a *Proudhonist group with other artisans. Despite setbacks, they build a 'Maison du Peuple', combining educational, cultural, and trade-union facilities. The outbreak of war suspends the enterprise. It is a persuasively understated novel which eschews sentimentality. After other, more intimist, fictions—*Dossier confidentiel* (1930), *Compagnons* (1931), *Hyménée* (1932), and *Angélina* (1934)—Guilloux achieved his masterpiece in *Le *Sang noir* (1935). *Le Pain des rêves* (1942) celebrates family love and household deities (a complex grandfather, an exotic aunt). The people here are sleepwalkers attempting to combat miseries by imaginative flights. His most ambitious experiment was *Le Jeu de patience* (1949), an intricate text demanding patient reconstitution by the reader. Micro- and macro-history collide: the horrors of war, and anarchist and *Popular Front politics or right-wing coups, impinge violently on private dramas. It is a haunted kaleidoscope, often hallucinatory. The writer is a remembrancer, saving others from oblivion—an obsessive theme in his memoirs, *L'Herbe d'oubli* (1984). *Les Batailles perdues* (1960), another large-scale work, is less successful in its effort to track the loss, maintenance, or reinvigoration of the revolutionary spirit. *La Confrontation* (1967) is a psychological detective story, a quest for a missing person and for the self. It is a disappointing finale for a fine story-teller. [WDR]

GUIOT DE PROVINS (*fl.* late 12th and early 13th c.). Lyric *trouvère and encyclopedist, author of the didactic and satirical *Bible Guiot* [see BIBLES].

GUIRAUD, Alexandre, baron (1788–1847). Poet and dramatist, with the blend of royalist and Catholic views which typified the *Romanticism of the Restoration. A founder of the *La Muse française* (1823–4), he was elected to the Académie Française in 1826. In 1839 he published an interestingly eccentric Catholic philosophy of history. [CC]

GUIRAUT RIQUIER (*c.*1230–*c.*1292). One of the last important *troubadours, Guiraut worked at the courts of Castile (*c.*1270–9) and Rodez (*c.*1280–5). He composed *cansos, *sirventes, devotional poetry, *pastorelas, and longer discursive poems. His *cansos* particularly impart a strong sense of nostalgia for a golden age of courtly poetry and *fin'amor. [SG]

Guirlande de Julie, La. Collection of short poems written by the *habitués* of the Hôtel de *Rambouillet in honour of the marquise's daughter, Julie d'Angennes, to whom the elegantly calligraphed book was presented on New Year's Day, 1634. It is often taken as a symbol of literary *preciosity.

Guise. Princely family which wielded great power in 16th-c. France. Contemporaries argued whether the family (which hailed from Lorraine) was truly French; but *Henri II heaped honours upon them, thus putting the French monarchy in an impossible position when (following his premature death) he was replaced by ineffectual rulers. François II's domination by François de Guise and his brother, the cardinal de *Lorraine, led to the failed Protestant coup, the Conjuration d'*Amboise. François de Guise set the *Wars of Religion in motion when his men massacred worshipping Protestants at Wassy (1562). His assassination (1563) helped prompt the much later assassination attempt on *Coligny and thus the *St Bartholomew's Day Massacre.

François's son, Henri de Guise (1550–88), profited from *Catherine de Médicis' fear at the growing influence of Coligny to avenge the assassination of his father. His victory over the German (i.e. Protestant) army at Auneau and Vimory (1588) confirmed his status as a hero in the eyes of the Catholic *Ligue. Unable to counter his influence in any other way, *Henri III had him assassinated at the États Généraux of Blois.

*Marie Stuart was the cousin of François de Guise. [JJS]

GUITRY, Lucien (1860–1925). Actor and father of Sacha *Guitry, he was an admired leading man of the Paris stage in the 1890s, often playing opposite *Bernhardt and *Réjane. His personal magnetism, intelligence, and naturalness brought him many successes, e.g. in *Mirbeau's *Les Mauvais Bergers* (1897) and *Rostand's *L'Aiglon* (1900). [SBJ]

GUITRY, Sacha (1885–1957). Actor-playwright, son of Lucien *Guitry. An accomplished, if showy, actor, he appealed to fashionable theatre-goers between the wars, usually when performing in his own plays at the Théâtre de la Madeleine. He was the prolific author of frothy light comedies and costume plays (130 between 1902 and 1949), many intended as star vehicles for himself and his second wife, Yvonne Printemps. Most of the comedies—*Quand jouons-nous la comédie?* (1935), *N'écoutez pas, Mesdames* (1942)—are about adultery. The costume plays—*Pasteur* (1919), *Mozart* (1925)—deal lightly with large subjects. He was also an important film director. [SBJ]

GUIZOT, François-Pierre-Guillaume (1787–1874). French statesman, historian, educationalist, writer on religious affairs; his long career was distinguished in all its many fields.

Born of a Protestant family at Nîmes, educated partly at Geneva, he began as a journalist and with his first wife Paulin founded the review *Annales de l'éducation*. In 1812 he began teaching history at the Sorbonne; his lectures of 1822–4 and 1828–30, and their publication, made him famous. The *Histoire générale de la civilisation en Europe* (1828) and the *Histoire de la civilisation en France* (1829) were outstanding. His first two volumes studying the English revolution of the 17th c., *Histoire de la Révolution d'Angleterre* (1826–7) were widely read and discussed.

He was also active in politics, within the administration from 1814 to 1820, as a pamphleteer (some of his works were collected in *Mélanges politiques et historiques*, 1869) and as a *député*, and was associated with *Royer-Collard in the Doctrinaire group defending the constitutional monarchy against the *ultras. After the July Revolution he was minister for public instruction from 1832 to 1836 and minister for foreign affairs from 1840 to 1847, when he was virtually the head of government (which he actually became in 1847).

After 1848 he continued to write on English history, wrote a series of *Méditations chrétiennes*, and was active in the Académie Française, to which he had been elected in 1836. His *Mémoires pour servir à l'histoire de mon temps* (8 vols., 1858–67) begin with the telling words: 'Je suis de ceux que l'élan de 1789 a élevés et qui ne consentiront point à descendre'; they provide many documents, especially concerning education, relative to the history of France up to 1848. [DJ]

See D. Johnson, *Guizot: Aspects of French History (1787–1874)* (1963); P. Rosanvallon, *Le Moment Guizot* (1985).

GUTTINGUER, Ulrich (1785–1866). French novelist, best known for *Arthur* (1836), an autobiographical novel begun in collaboration with *Sainte-Beuve. Converted in 1829, Guttinguer revised his project, describing his unhappy love-life, a beneficent woman's influence, and his conversion. Sainte-Beuve's *Volupté* resulted from this collaboration, and Balzac imitated both in *Le *Lys dans la vallée*. Guttinguer also published poetry and devotional works. [FPB]

Guyane (French Guiana), see WEST INDIES.

GUYARD, Marie, see DEVOTIONAL WRITING, 2.

GUYON, Jeanne-Marie Bouvier de la Motte- (1648–1717). Spiritual writer, a rare instance of a laywoman mystic, and the central figure in the controversy over *Quietism. After a disturbed provincial childhood and an unhappy arranged marriage, Madame Guyon was left a widow of considerable means, which she devoted to promoting her doctrines of spiritual self-abnegation, passive contemplation, and the disinterested love of God. Her *Moyen court et très facile de faire oraison* (1685) brought her in turn popularity in devout court circles, friendship with *Fénelon and Madame de *Maintenon, violent accusations of heterodoxy, hysteria, and immorality, police interrogation, imprisonment at Vincennes, and exile to Blois. Most of her writings, including an autobiography and *Les Torrents spirituels*, were published posthumously by devoted disciples. [PJB]

GUYOTAT, Pierre (b. 1940). One of the most avant-garde and subversive French novelists of the later 20th c. Guyotat's works examine the violence of language, sexuality, politics, racism, and war. His first two works, *Sur un cheval* (1961) and *Ashby* (1964), received little critical attention. It was his third novel, *Tombeau pour 500,000 morts* (1967), in which he recounts in oneiric fashion his experiences as a French soldier in Algeria, that established his reputation as a controversial writer. His fourth novel, *Éden, Éden, Éden* (1970), was declared obscene and censored. A defence was launched on his behalf by *Foucault, *Barthes, *Leiris, *Sollers, and other intellectuals (*Littérature interdite*, 1972). Subsequent works include *Prostitution* (1976), *Le Livre* (1984), and *Vivre* (1984). [DM-S]

GUYS, Constantin (1805–92). The name of Guys is now indissociably linked to that of *Baudelaire, who described him as 'le peintre de la vie moderne' in his famous essay of that name written in 1859. In his watercolours, engravings, and drawings of café life, military scenes, and fashionable Parisian society of the Second Empire, Guys's summary handling and mastery of light seemed to the poet to exemplify his ideal of the modern artist's relationship with his subjects: the ability to depict the combination of the ephemeral and the eternal essential to modern forms of beauty and to see the world with a child-like freshness of vision. [JK]

GYP (1849–1932) (pseud. of Sybille-Gabrielle Marie-Antoinette de Riquetti de Mirabeau, comtesse de Martel de Janville). French novelist. She began publishing in 1882, chiefly to earn money. She produced sketches for magazines, notably *La Vie parisienne*; plays, of which more than 20 were staged; numerous political articles, taking the anti-*Dreyfus line; three autobiographical books; some art-criticism; and over 100 works of fiction. These were extremely poplar and frequently reprinted. Much of Gyp's fiction consists of *dialogue novels, including both satirical and serious works. Some are mere pot-boilers but others, such as *Bijou* (1896), are well-constructed, carefully written, and worth critical attention. She was admired by readers as diverse as Nietzsche, Anatole *France, and Henry James. [VGM]

H

H, see SOLLERS.

HABERT, François (*c*.1508–*c*.1561), under the pseudonym 'le Banny de Liesse' (banished from joy), was a prolific but mediocre poet and translator. He enjoyed royal favour under François Iᵉʳ, and Henri II conferred on him the title 'poète du roi'. His works include encomiastic verse for Henri II, edifying poems in a style reminiscent of the *Rhétoriqueurs (e.g. *Le Temple de Vertu*, 1542), and *recueils* influenced by *Marot (*La Jeunesse du Banny de Liesse*, 1541). He translated Ovid's *Metamorphoses* and Horace's *Satires* and *Epistles*. [CMSJ]

HACHETTE, Louis-Christophe (1800–64). French bookseller and publisher. He bought the Librairie Brédif in 1826, renamed it Hachette, and published educational books and, later, dictionaries, encyclopedias, and famous series, including *Les Grands Écrivains de la France*, *Littré's dictionary, and that of the *Académie Française. Hachette's children's list, which took over *Hetzel's, included the wide-selling Bibliothèque Rose. In 1852 the firm won exclusive rights to railway station news-stand book-sales, and in 1898 created the Messageries Hachette, a monopoly national distribution service which lasted until 1944. Still under family leadership, Hachette is a leading player in book and newspaper publishing and distribution in France, including *Livre de Poche publications. [DAS]

HADDAD, Malek (1927–78). Algerian poet and novelist. Haddad developed the idea that the ethnolinguistic extraction of Algerian francophone writers is bound to lead them to merely instrumental uses of the French language, while they retain a nostalgia for their mother tongue, Arabic or Berber, which the coercive French educational system vainly attempted to eradicate after the military occupation of Algeria in 1830.

He was involved in political and cultural issues as a result of his personal experience of French schools in his native Constantine and in the university of Aix-en-Provence, which he left on the eve of the *Algerian War. His first publications were newspaper articles in *Alger républicain*, the dominant organ of the Parti Communiste Algérien, between 1948 and 1950. *La Dernière Impression* (1958), *Je t'offrirai une gazelle* (1959), and *Écoute et je t'appelle* (1961) are his most acclaimed novels, but his reputation rests mainly on his poetry, collected in *Le Malheur en danger* (1956), and an essay, 'Les Zéros tournent en rond' (1961), which embody the paradoxes of his mastery of the French language: 'Nous écrivons le français, nous n'écrivons pas en français.' The relation between the Algerian writer and the French language is felt by him as a historical absurdity.

From 1961 to the independence of Algeria Haddad travelled as an FLN spokesman to the Soviet Union, Egypt, and India, where he advocated the case for the war against the French. After 1962 he organized the cultural supplement of the newspaper *An-Nasr* and contributed several articles in French until 1968. In spite of his active participation in the Premier Colloque Culturel National in June 1968, in the First Panafrican Festival in July 1969, and more generally in the creation of a new literary tradition, when he objected to the continued use of French and when he acted as a general secretary for the Union des Écrivains Algériens in 1974, Haddad was never able to come to terms with a guilty feeling of bi-cultural ambiguity: 'En vérité, je crois n'avoir jamais été à ma place. Je me suis trompé d'époque . . . l'histoire a voulu que j'aie toujours été à cheval sur deux époques, sur deux civilisations.' [AZ]

Hagiography (Medieval). The writing of biographies of holy men and women is common to all great religions, and the aims of the biographers vary with time, place, and religion. In Christian France of the Middle Ages the purpose of vernacular hagiography was essentially the instruction and edification of a non-Latin-speaking laity. Unlike other literary genres, hagiography is definable only by its content, and to some extent by the structure of that content, not by its form. In the 11th and early 12th c. it is clearly related to *chansons de geste (very early texts of the 10th c. may be so related, but evidence is lacking); from the later 12th c. onwards hagiographic texts share formal features with *romance and chronicle literature, being composed first in octosyllabic couplets, then in prose, although verse no more died out in hagiography than it did in romance. From the 13th to the 16th c. saints' lives, particularly martyrs' lives, are represented in the drama.

Vernacular hagiography in medieval France is also distinct from other types of texts in being essentially a secondary literature; that is, virtually all surviving examples are translated from, or at least dependent on, Latin originals. These originals could have two purposes: to provide evidence for a canonization process or to provide readings (replacing the Epistle at Matins or during mealtimes) on the saint's feast day. In the former case rules of presentation were steadily elaborated by the Curia and became relatively fixed by the 13th c. The saint's birth and childhood were considered at least briefly as prefigurations of an adult life of sanctity; consequently contemporary literary prejudices tended to encourage borrowing from epic or romance *enfances models, while social prejudices led to the hierarchical promotion of the subject, stressing the future saint's aptitude for success in the world, were his or her sights not firmly fixed on the next. A precocious aptitude for learning is common, as are other marks of piety and divine favour, extending occasionally to the performance of miracles. A spiritual crisis or conversion experience (even in the case of children born into Christian families) is frequently depicted during the subject's late teens or early twenties or at a significant ceremony (marriage or knighting), and opposition or obstacles to the career of sanctity have to be overcome. Finally, whether as martyr or confessor, the saint must imitate Christ in his death, which frequently provokes further conversions. Such imitation may be limited to the day (Friday) or hour ('nones'—three in the afternoon) inscribed as the time of death. Although there may be some reference to miracles in biographies, these were generally, and increasingly in the 13th and 14th c., reserved for separate works (Miracula) devoted to the thaumaturgic aspects of sanctity.

As may be expected in an essentially patriarchal society one distinctinction observed between male and female saints concerns chastity. While the observance of chastity is a mark of most male saints, it does not figure as a major theme of sanctity, many male saints enjoying a normal married life, and some, including St Augustine, having illegitimate children before their conversion. Virginity and its preservation in the face of extremely aggressive persecution by male oppressors is, by contrast, a defining feature of the majority of female saints' lives. It is notable that the version of La Vie de sainte Catherine by Clemence of Barking, the only known female hagiographer of the 12th c., does not differ from other versions in this respect, but in the courtly treatment of psychology evident in the depiction of the persecuting emperor.

The earliest literary texts in French are all related to hagiography: both the Séquence de *sainte Eulalie (late 9th c.) and La *Vie de saint Léger (10th c.), being martyrs' lives, concentrate on the ultimate crisis; Jonas (10th c.) recasts the Old Testament story in hagiographic mould; La *Vie de saint Alexis and the Occitan *Chanson de sainte Foy d'Agen (both 11th c.), while having close formal links to epic, reveal already the classic disposition of the 'chronicle' biography. The same epico-hagiographic model was applied to the Occitan Boecis, a biography of *Boethius, adapted from the De consolatione Philosophiae. Even works having a long existence in Latin prior to translation show the influence of folktale and non-Christian myth. The Oedipus myth structures both La Vie de saint Gregoire and La Vie de

saint Julien l'Hospitalier, while the latter, like St Hubert, also encounters a marvellous stag which determines his 'fate' as a saint. Such beasts may, like their romance counterparts, be drawn from Celtic folklore. An extreme case of this tendency is Le Voyage de saint Brendan, which applies to the 6th-c. abbot of Clonfert ancient Irish 'odyssey' tales (immrama), notably exploiting the legend of Bran and his call beyond the sea to the Land of the Blessed by Mannanan. Such 'artificial' restructuring may not be absent even from the biographies of canonized personalities from the comparatively recent past of the hagiographer. Thus, Matthew Paris's Vie de seint Ædward le rei, like its Latin sources (lives by Osbert of Clare and Aelred of Riveaulx), creates for Edward the Confessor a character and career deliberately constructed to conform to hagiographic models, with Earl Godwin cast as a Judas figure. The new biography, whose bias is created from an inextricable mixture of political and ecclesiastical motivations, is quite at variance with what is known from other sources.

Where a biblical personality like John the Baptist is involved, hagiographers were generally more scrupulous in following the Gospels, or at least the apocrypha. Even so, the 12th-c. fragment of John's Life in alexandrine couplets adheres to established patterns by having him learn his letters before the age of 5, at which point, fleeing the temptations presented by his playmates, he adopts the eremitical life described in the Bible. For its part the 14th-c. Vie de saint Jean-Baptiste pads out the few received details with didactic digressions and replaces the enfances section with a lengthy account of the invention of the saint's relics. Even in the case of a recently dead figure like St Thomas Becket, where the author of the vernacular Life, Guernes de Pont Sainte-Maxence, consulted eyewitnesses and used chancery documents, the exploitation of Latin Vitae, which imposed received models, applies. Thus Becket's early piety and scholastic aptitude are stressed, and it becomes impossible to tell whether his widely reported crisis of conscience and conversion to extreme asceticism on being appointed archbishop of Canterbury is a reality, a conventional motif, or a case of life imitating art. At one extreme of hagiography lies *Joinville's La Vie de saint Louis, which centres on his recollections of Louis IX's crusading expedition to Damietta, on which the author was a close companion of the king. The framework of traditional hagiography is broken in this personal memoir. At the other extreme are found accounts of fictitious or legendary (*Guillaume d'Angleterre, *Ami et Amile, Berthe au Grand Pied) or fictionalized (Godefroi de Bouillon, first crusader king of Jerusalem) heroes and heroines borrowed from other genres, whose biographies were adapted to hagiographic norms, without the original epic or romance features being suppressed. [See also ANGLO-NORMAN LITERATURE, 6a; BOLLANDISTES.]   [PEB]

See H. Delehaye, *The Legends of the Saints*, trans. D. Attwater (1962). P. Johnson and B. Cazelles, *Le Vain Siècle guerpir* (1979); B. Cazelles, *Le Corps de sainteté* (1982).

Hain teny. A genre belonging to the oral tradition of *Madagascar, *hain teny* translated literally means 'linguistic science' or 'science of words'. Different from, but related to, *ohabolana* (proverb), *kabany* (public oratory), and *angano* (folk-tale), the distinctive features of the *hain teny* relate to its original function as a means of resolving lawsuits. The two opponents in the dispute improvised a dialogue based on proverbial, aphoristic statements. Often under the metaphorical disguise of a love quarrel, it is dialogic and develops by means of antitheses, parallelisms, oppositions, and reversals.

It was principally Jean *Paulhan's interest in the genre which assured its continuing importance as an influence within the francophone Malagasy written tradition. In 1913 he published *Les Hain-teny merinas, poésies populaires malgaches*, which was composed of texts transcribed from oral sources and translated. Divorced from the context of their performance, fixed in a written form, and translated into a European language, Paulhan's *hain teny* are more gnomic and cryptic than their 'source', and have passed through a series of contextual and linguistic transitions which bring them close to a form such as the *chant alterné*. They are texts which greatly interested *Apollinaire, *Jacob, and *Éluard. A number of young Malagasy poets (in particular *Rabearivelo and *Ranaivo) were encouraged and inspired by Paulhan's enterprise.

The important discovery and publication of mid-19th-c. manuscripts compiled under King Ranavalona I provided further material for the study of the *hain teny*.   [BEJ]

See B. D. Ramiaramanaan, *Du ohabolana au hain teny: langue, littérature et politique à Madagascar* (1983).

Haiti

1. The Nineteenth Century

Haiti, formerly the French colony of Saint-Domingue, became independent in 1804 as a result of a slave rebellion led by Toussaint *Louverture. The declaration of independence meant the beginning of French Caribbean literature and arguably Caribbean literature as a whole [see WEST INDIES]. The first decades of independence produced a range and sophistication in literary activity unlooked-for in an ex-colony. French colonialism in Haiti, as elsewhere in the Caribbean, was characterized by the plantation system and justified in terms of black inferiority. Such societies with their brutal beginnings were not expected to produce a literary or intellectual culture.

Haitian writing in the 19th c. was invariably motivated by political events. Pride in their defeat of Napoleon's army, the need to inspire ideals of nationhood and solidarity, and the celebration of Haiti's redemptive mission in a world where slavery still existed, dominated the 'littérature de circonstance' of these early years. Despite the instability of the first two decades of civil war, there was intense literary activity among the urban élite. Evidence of this can be seen in such literary journals as Jules-Solime Milscent's *L'Abeille haytienne* (1817) and Hérard Dumesle's *L'Observateur* (1819).

The fierce nationalism of these early years was reinforced by the influence of French *Romanticism. The themes of the quest for identity, the importance of the imagination, and the influence of environment over sensibility have a shaping impact over this formative period. During the 23 years of relative calm under President Boyer, an early form of *indigénisme* was advocated in the newspaper *Le Républicain* (1837), founded by Ignace and Émile Nau along with the Ardouin brothers. These writers insisted on the value of literature in earning the respect of the outside world. They also criticized imitativeness and argued that Haitian artists should strive for a freshness and originality in their work.

This belief in the need to articulate a peculiarly Haitian world-view prepared the way for the achievement of Oswald Durand, whose *Rires et pleurs* (1896) was an ambitious attempt to describe Haitian flora and fauna as well as present-day culture. He is best known for his *Choucoune*, the first significant attempt to write poetry in *Creole. Durand's contemporary Massillon Coicou had similar concerns, and his collection *Poésies nationales* (1892) was dedicated to celebrating the grandeur of Haitian independence.

At least as important as the creative writers of the 19th c. were Haiti's early pamphleteers. The first of these was the secretary of the short-lived king Henry Christophe, Le Baron de Vestey, whose *Le Système colonial dévoilé* (1814) is the first Caribbean critique of European colonialism and defence of national sovereignty. This tradition continued into the late 19th c., despite political uncertainties. Haiti's essayists defended their country against racist theorizing current at the time. For instance, in response to *Gobineau's *Essai sur l'inégalité des races humaines*, which argued that the black race was incapable of civilization, Haiti produced a number of sophisticated responses. The titles of some of these polemical works speak for themselves: Louis-Joseph Janvier's *L'Égalité des races* (1884), Anténor Firmin's *De l'égalité des races humaines* (1885), and Hannibal Price's *De la réhabilitation de la race noire* (1900). Their concern with how to maintain independence after winning it anticipates the discussion of the issue of neo-colonialism which would emerge much later in the rest of the Caribbean.

2. 1900–1940

By the turn of the century, Haiti was a country in crisis. The internal divisions between rural peasantry and urban élite were acute. Equally apparent

Haiti

was the collapse of political authority and the persistent threat of outside intervention. Despite the gloom of these years, Haiti's literary production was remarkable. It is at this time that the prose narrative emerged in Haiti. These novels were either political satires or depictions of peasant life. In their application of the tenets of French *Realism to their writing, Haiti's novelists produced political satire such as Frédéric Marcelin's *Themistocle Epaminondas Labasterre* (1901), social commentary in Justin Lhérisson's *La Famille des Pitite Caille* (1905), and a peasant novel in Antoine Innocent's *Mimola* (1906).

Poetic activity at the turn of the century was centred on the journal *La Ronde* (1898–1902), which represented a rejection of too parochial an approach to literature and advocated a new eclecticism. It was founded by Pétion Gerome and published the poetry of Etzer Vilaire, Edmond Laforest, and Georges Sylvain among others. In contrast to the novels, which are regionalist, the poetry of the generation of *La Ronde* was marked by French *Symbolism with its insistence on an impersonal aesthetic. The delicate and allusive world of their poetry is strikingly different from the nationalistic verse of their predecessors. Vilaire was awarded a prize by the Académie Française for his poetry and a French edition of his work appeared in 1910. The glory of *La Ronde* was, however, short-lived, as chronic instability was making Haiti more vulnerable to outside intervention.

Haiti had seven presidents between 1910 and 1915, the last of whom was killed by a mob after ordering the execution of political prisoners. The following day the United States occupied Haiti. The Occupation lasted from 1915 to 1934 and had a profound effect on Haitian culture in the 20th c. Haitians, divided by colour and class when left to themselves, become united in the name of race and nation when there is a threat from outside. Consequently, the neo-colonial American presence in Haiti provoked a new wave of nationalism which manifested itself in different ways. There was a short-lived peasant revolt, the 'caco' rebellion, led by Charlemagne Peralte. The poet Georges Sylvain founded L'Union Patriotique in 1920 to protest against atrocities committed by the Americans. Opposition to the Occupation came to a head in 1929 with a series of strikes initiated by the students at the School of Agriculture. A younger and more radical generation of Haitians would now dominate intellectual life.

It is this generation which launched the movement of *indigénisme* in Haiti, and the movement was marked by their iconoclastic and anti-intellectual posture. Their restlessness was fed by the antiestablishment attitudes of Paris in the 1920s, and soon became apparent in the pages of such journals as *La Nouvelle Ronde* (1925), *La Trouée* (1927), and *La Revue indigène* (1927–8). The major poets of this movement—Émile Roumer, Jacques *Roumain, Carl *Brouard, and Philippe *Thoby-Marcelin—

wanted to go beyond the fashionably bohemian posturing of the time. They wished to end Haiti's intellectual isolation and introduce the writing of the Harlem Renaissance and of Latin America. They also felt that poetry might allow access to Haiti's soul. They were influenced by the ideas of *Maurras in this quest for 'l'âme haitienne'.

Their indebtedness to Maurras led them to embrace the ideas of one of Haiti's most influential thinkers, Jean *Price-Mars. His *Ainsi parla l'oncle* (1928), which advocated that Haitian peasant culture was the key to understanding 'l'âme haïtienne', pushed *indigénisme* in the direction of *noirisme, with its belief in the essential Africanness of Haitian culture. This interest in race and ethnology appealed equally to a sense of solidarity with a homogenous Pan-American diaspora. Literature in the 1930s was pervaded by concern with Haiti's Afro-Latin heritage. Perhaps the best-known poem on this theme is Léon Laleau's 'Trahison' (1931), which describes the Haitian soul as torn between 'des mots de France' and 'le cœur . . . de Sénégal'.

The ideology of *noirisme* was formulated at this time by the Griot movement begun by Louis Diaquoi, François Duvalier, and Lorimer Denis. *Indigénisme* was too bland for the *noiristes, and the pages of their journal *Les *Griots* (1938–40) are filled with the advocacy of black nationalism and the verse of Carl Brouard inspired by voodoo mysticism. They did not challenge the political establishment in the 1930s, however, and their movement provoked little more than ridicule from members of the francophile mulatto élite such as Dantès Bellegarde.

The nonconformist 1930s also embraced Marxism, which did challenge the existing order. The Communist Party was founded by Jacques Roumain in 1934. Roumain's ideas were characterized by a view of culture as ever-changing and dynamic, which distinguished him from the reductionist notions of culture shared by both *noiriste* intellectuals and the francophile élite. His major works, inspired by a visionary Marxism, were the poems of *Bois d'ébène* (1945) and the novel *Gouverneurs de la rosée* (1944). These works, and Roumain's brand of Marxism, were to leave an indelible mark on generations of writers to come.

3. Since 1940

The 1940s in Haiti were a period of intellectual effervescence. This atmosphere was created by the influence of World War II and the radicalism of the post-Occupation period, and was intensified by the visits of writers such as Alejo Carpentier, Nicolas Guillen, Aimé *Césaire, and André *Breton. *Surrealism, which had previously been criticized by Roumain and was evident only in the hermetic verse of Magloire Saint-Aude, received a tremendous boost from Breton's visit. It combined explosively with current radicalism and led to the overthrow of the conservative, pro-American regime of Elie Lescot by the student activists of the newspaper La *Ruche in 1946.

The group was led by René *Depestre and Jacques-Stephen *Alexis. However, if the 1940s meant the intellectual ascendancy of Marxism and Surrealism, it also signified the political success of *noirisme*. The latter took centre stage in the regime of President Estimé, and the firebrands of La Ruche were shrewdly provided with scholarships to study abroad. Alexis became one of the first to challenge the ideas of *négritude* with his essay on *réalisme merveilleux* read at the First Congress of Black Writers held in Paris in 1956. Depestre would, in a response to criticism from Césaire, stress the need for cultural autonomy in Haiti in his 'Introduction à un art poétique haïtien' (1955). Both writers ran foul of *noirisme* as practised by the Duvalier regime, which came to power in 1957. Depestre spent most of his life in exile and Alexis was killed by Duvalier's militia in 1961.

The Duvalier regime lasted for 29 years in Haiti. After 'president for life' François Duvalier died in 1971, he was succeeded by his son Jean-Claude, who was overthrown in 1986. Duvalierism contained the elements of xenophobia, racial mystification, and authoritarianism that characterized Griot ideology. The Duvalier regime in Haiti by the 1960s had stifled not only all dissent but also almost all intellectual activity. François Duvalier's collected works were tellingly entitled Œuvres essentielles (1966) to indicate that they were the ultimate authority on all subjects. As a result, writing dwindled within Haiti and was taken over by Haitians in exile in Montreal, Paris, New York, and Dakar.

Within Haiti, the only movement with any impact was *spiralisme*, founded by Franck *Étienne in the late 1960s. Never openly political, *spiralisme* advocated a literary experimentation which was totally opposed to the closed discourse of authoritarian politics. It was only during the somewhat more relaxed regime of Jean-Claude Duvalier that *spiralisme* began to confront the Haitian state in Étienne's theatre, written exclusively in Creole. Outside Haiti, however, writing was characterized by a strident anti-Duvalierism. Novels by Depestre, Gérard Étienne, and Anthony Phelps were some of the most successful in the genre but never attained the high quality of the Latin American novels about dictatorship. Indeed, some of the most successful writing outside Haiti was not single-mindedly anti-Duvalierist, but began to question some of the received ideas of Haitian writing—cultural authenticity, national identity, and belief in the written word. The work of Anthony Phelps and Jean-Claude Charles rather provocatively addresses these issues and makes a plea for a reassessment of exile.

Since 1986 Haiti has entered a period of political uncertainty and intense self-questioning. It is no coincidence that the anti-Duvalier movement has no intellectual leadership and that its language is *Creole. Now the burning issues are no longer literary. [JMD]

See A. Viatte, *Histoire littéraire de l'Amérique française* (1954); N. Garret, *The Renaissance of Haitian Poetry* (1963); M. Dash, *Literature and Ideology in Haiti, 1915–1961* (1981).

HALÉVY, Élie (1870–1937). French historian, son of the librettist Ludovic Halévy. A philosopher by training, he rejected materialist interpretations of history, preferring to emphasize the central ideas and systems of value and belief which informed political movements and specific public policies. He thus analysed the development and internal contradictions of English utilitarianism and its role in the growth of liberalism (*La Formation du radicalisme philosophique en Angleterre*, 1901) and, in the seminal first volume of *Histoire du peuple anglais au XIXe siècle* (1912–32), he explained the stability of English society in 1815 in terms of the moral and social effects of evangelical religion. [REG]

HALÉVY, Ludovic, see MEILHAC.

HALLIER, Jean-Edern (b. 1936). French novelist and polemicist. He co-founded the review *Tel Quel*, and was a prominent activist in *May 1968, explaining his evolution from wealthy origins to left-wing convictions in *La Cause des peuples* (1972). Editor of the radical newspaper *L'Idiot international* and author of truculent political pamphlets, a succession of flamboyant, provocative postures earned him notoriety (*Chaque matin qui se lève est une leçon de courage*, 1978; *Carnets impudiques*, 1988). His novels are highly coloured outgrowths of his own biography (*L'Évangile du fou*, 1986), often situated in the exotic locations he has visited as a reporter (*Chagrin d'amour*, 1974; *Fin de siècle*, 1980). [DHW]

HAMILTON, Anthony (c.1646–1720). Because his parents followed Charles II into exile, Hamilton was educated in France; he spent the last 30 years of his life at Saint-Germain. His published works, written in French, include light verse, letters, and some stories which parody fairy-tales and oriental tales. Hamilton's chief claim to fame rests on the *Mémoires du comte de Gramont* (1713), a romanced biography of his brother-in-law. Starting in about 1640, this offers anecdotes concerning the army and court life in France, leading up to a *chronique scandaleuse* of Charles II's court. Though over-praised by some critics, the work is witty and quite entertaining. [VGM]

HANSKA, Évelyne, comtesse, see BALZAC.

Hara-Kiri, see CHARLIE-HEBDO.

HARDY, Alexandre (c.1572–1632). French dramatist. Little is known of his life, save that he was an actor as well as a writer, and was for many years employed as playwright to various companies, including the company based, when in Paris, at the *Hôtel de Bourgogne. Thus he could be considered the first professional French playwright, and he dominates our picture of the French theatre in the first two decades of the 17th c. His output must have been very large; he claimed to have written over 600 plays, but only 34 have survived (tragedies, tragicomedies, and pastorals); these, which he published in the last decade of his life, are presumably the ones he thought his best.

Compared both with 16th-c. humanist tragedy and with 17th-c. classical *tragedy, Hardy's plays are crude but eventful. They ignore the unities and violate *bienséance*, not least by their portrayal of violence on stage, including rape (in *Scédase*). They were presumably composed to be acted with a *décor simultané*, which accommodated changes of scene. The time-span often covers many years. Their subjects include classical literature (*Théagène et Chariclée*, *Didon*), history (*Panthée*, *Coriolan*), and myth (*La Gigantomachie*, *Ariadne ravie*); Jewish history (*Mariamne*); and plots taken from Spanish or Italian authors (Cervantes: *Cornélie*, *La Force du sang*, *La Belle Égyptienne*; Lope de Vega: *Lucrèce*; Boccaccio: *Gésippe*). Hardy's vocabulary and style are somewhat old-fashioned for his period and his phrasing often convoluted and elliptical; his abundant use of classical and mythological allusion sometimes seems out of place, as in *Lucrèce*, a rather seamy 'modern' subject of double adultery where the characters use incongruously high-flown imagery. Hardy seems clumsy and unpolished compared with later 17th-c. dramatists, but his plays must have been exciting to watch and, although physical action on stage was to disappear in succeeding decades, many features of later tragic drama are already present in Hardy's plays. These are analysed by G. Brereton in *French Tragic Drama in the Sixteenth and Seventeenth Centuries* (1973); this critic also points out some textual echoes of Hardy in *Corneille. There has been no complete re-edition of Hardy's theatre since the edition by E. Stengel (1884, repr. 1967), but several plays have now appeared in modern critical editions.   [GJ]

See J. Scherer (ed.), *Théâtre du XVIIe siècle*, vol. 1 (1975).

Harlequin, see Arlequin.

Harpagon. Molière's classic portrayal of the miser, in *L'*Avare*.

HART, Robert-Edward (1891–1954), One of the most important francophone Mauritian literary figures of the first half of the century. Initially his work was influenced by *Parnassianism, and then by a Gidean carnality and sensuality. Later his texts became musical, mystical, and spiritual, and the presence of *Mauritius's varied cultural elements became important: e.g. Indian philosophy in *Poèmes védiques* (1941). In addition to numerous collections of poetry he wrote a cycle of novels, *Pierre Flandre* (1928–36), focused on a quest for origins. *Plénitudes* (1948) is his most famous collection of poetry; it dis-

plays a wide range of characteristic themes and obsessions.

Although Hart's work has often been described as reactionary in its form, and although as representative of modern Mauritian literature his work was quickly superseded by the work of younger Mauritian writers, his writing is very much the foundation of much that was written later, particularly because of his introduction of varied Mauritian cultural references—Buddhist, Islamic, Chinese, African. He is resolute in his admiration of French poetry and the French poetic tradition, but his imagery is drawn from a properly Mauritian (rather than an abstractly 'exotic') landscape.   [BEJ]

HARVEY, Jean-Charles (1891–1967). Canadian journalist and writer, best known for *Les Demi-Civilisés* (1934), a novel which gained notoriety from being condemned by the Church as dangerously freethinking. But the novel is too stereotyped in expression to carry conviction as a clarion call for freedom of thought and speech. Moreover, its thesis that modern Quebec has fallen from the natural simplicity of its agrarian past into the decadence of a semi-educated society is strangely conservative and substantially undercuts its ostensible radicalism.   [SIL]

Haussmannisation. Name commonly given to the transformation of Paris undertaken, under the aegis of *Napoleon III, by Baron Georges Haussmann (1809–91), prefect of Paris from 1853 to 1869. Under Haussmann's direction, the overcrowded central *quartiers* of the city were demolished, and a system of rectilinear boulevards—notably the boulevards de Strasbourg, de Sébastopol, Saint-Michel, and Saint-Germain—was constructed, which for the first time bound the city together as a single structural entity. Other structural innovations included the radiating circles of the place de l'Étoile (place Charles-de-Gaulle), place du Château d'Eau (place de la République), and place d'Italie; the construction of new bridges over the Seine (notably the ponts de l'Alma, des Invalides, and de Solférino); the transformation, by the landscape-gardener Alphand, of the Bois de Boulogne and the construction of new parks (Parc Monceau, Parc des Buttes-Chaumont); and the creation, by the engineer Belgrand, of a modern sewage and water system. New wings, designed by Visconti, were added to the *Louvre, the Halles Centrales were completely reconstructed using cast-iron and glass by Baltard, and work was begun on Garnier's new Théâtre de l'*Opéra. *Haussmannisation* divided Paris into a preponderantly middle-and upper-class west and an overwhelmingly working-class east (Belleville, Ménilmontant, La Chapelle, La Villette), and this redistribution of population is generally thought to have contributed to the *Commune of 1871. Its effects are evoked in Zola's *La *Curée* (1872), *Le *Ventre de Paris* (1873), and *Au Bonheur des Dames*

(1883) and, most movingly, in *Baudelaire's poem 'Le Cygne'. [RDEB]

HAUTEROCHE, Noël le Breton, sieur de (1617–1707). Comic actor and playwright at the *Hôtel de Bourgogne; his plays include *Crispin médecin* [see POISSON].

Hauteville House. The house on Guernsey where Victor *Hugo lived in exile from 1856 to 1870.

Havas, Agence. Founded—first as a modest translation bureau—by Charles Havas (1783–1858), the agency quickly achieved during the 1830s a dominant position. Either directly, or through subsidiary companies, Havas also became France's leading *advertising agency. It supplied provincial newspapers with feature material—*variétés*, *romans-feuilletons*, etc.—as well as news and advertising copy. Between the two world wars it was increasingly attacked, by left-wing politicians such as Léon *Blum, as one of the oligopolistic and capitalist forces responsible for the corruption of the press. In 1940 Pierre Laval 'nationalized' Havas-news, and created the official news agency, l'Office Français d'Information. In 1944 l'Agence France-Presse (AFP) began operations as part of the general reform of the press. Remaining separate from Havas, which continued as one of France's leading communications groups (being privatized in 1987), AFP became one of the world's three leading international news agencies. [MP]

Haveloc, Le Lai d', see ANGLO-NORMAN LITERATURE, 3a.

HAZOUMÉ, Paul (1890–1980). Novelist from Dahomey (now Benin). He came to prominence for his unique historical novel *Doguicimi* (1935), the fruit of 25 years of research into the history and customs of his people, drawing heavily on oral chronicles collected from local *griots. It is the first full-length prose work of fiction—if we except *Maran's *Batouala*—written by an African and inspired totally by an African subject. Set in pre-colonial Dahomey during the reign of King Ghêzo, 'Master of the World', it tells of events during the expedition undertaken by the kings of Abomey against the neighbouring Mahi tribe. The eponymous heroine is portrayed as the model of a national heroine, endowed with beauty and superhuman courage, inspired by exalted ideals of stoicism, fierce national pride, and conjugal fidelity to endure imprisonment, torture, and death. Care for historical accuracy and local colour (minute descriptions of life at the court and long passages detailing the lay and religious rituals of betrothals, burials, and military preparations) make *Doguicimi* an African *Salammbô.

Hazoumé is also the author of the ethnological study *Le Pacte du sang au Dahomey* (1937), *La France contre le racisme allemand* (1940), and *Cinquante ans d'apostolat au Dahomey de Mgr. Steinmetz* (1950). [DSB]

HÉBERT, Anne (b. 1916). Canadian poet and novelist. Born in the village of Sainte-Catherine de Fossambault, she grew up in family homes there and in Quebec. It was a happy environment, in which she was encouraged to write by her father, a civil servant and a writer, and strongly influenced by her cousin, the poet *Saint-Denys Garneau, whose accidental death in 1943 precipitated a powerful movement of revolt in her writing. Her early work was published in Canada, but since the 1950s she has been mainly published in Paris, and has made her home there, with frequent visits to her native land.

Hébert first became known as a poet. *Les Songes en équilibre* (1942) explores in a free verse of great purity the experience of being in the world, and particularly the natural world of Quebec. In *Le Tombeau des rois* (1953) the link between the poet and the world is broken; under the influence of her cousin's death, the poet confronts destruction and negation, embodying her quest in powerful symbols, notably that of the ancient tomb suggested in the title poem, which begins memorably: 'J'ai mon cœur au poing | Comme un faucon aveugle.' *Mystère de la parole* (1960) suggests a partial victory of light over darkness and a reconciliation of the poet and the world through the power of the word.

The symbolic force so evident in Hébert's poetry is also constantly present in the prose fiction for which she is now best known (she has also written a number of plays). The novella *Le Torrent* (written 1945, published 1950) announces many of the themes of her novels. The hero-narrator of this monologue is literally struck deaf by his fierce mother, who destined him for the Church to expiate the sins of her youth, but this deafness draws him towards the turbulent forces of life and death, the 'torrent' of the title. This terrible parable has been described as 'l'expression la plus juste qui nous ait été donnée du drame spirituel du Canada français' (G. Marcotte). Similar conflicts of instinct and repression, nature and culture, are explored in a series of impressive novels, all set in Quebec province and figuring passionate and violent protagonists, particularly women. *Kamouraska* (1970, Prix des Libraires) is based on a real-life murder case in 19th-c. Quebec; *Les Enfants du sabbat* (1975), set in the 1940s, is a story of witchcraft in a convent; *Les Fous de Bassan* (1982, Prix Fémina) is an extraordinary Faulknerian evocation of the violent natural world of the Gaspé peninsula and an investigation by six different narrators of a crime of rape and murder. More recently, *Le Premier Jardin* (1988) is less haunted by violence; it shows the return to Quebec city of an ageing actress who uncovers and accepts her half-forgotten youth. All of these novels are distinguished not only by their dramatic power, but by narrative inventiveness and a use of words which is that of the poet. [PF]

See R. Lacôte, *Anne Hébert* (1969).

HÉBERT, Jacques-René (1757–94). Radical Revolutionary, member of the *Cordeliers, of the Commune Insurrectionnelle (9–10 August 1792), and deputy *procureur syndic* of the Paris *Commune (December 1792). A vigorous, highly popular spokesman for the people with his periodical *Le Père Duchesne*, he almost naturally replaced the assassinated *Marat as the chief of the popular party. He was an implacable enemy of the *Girondins and a radical proponent, along with Chaumette and *Cloots, of de-Christianization. Denounced by *Saint-Just as a dangerous factionalist and 'enemy of the Revolution', he was inevitably guillotined (22 March).

The Père Duchesne was a legendary Parisian character, well known long before 1789, whose name was synonymous with crude, down-to-earth statements. It was the *Feuillant Lemaire, deliberately attempting with his *Lettres bougrement patriotiques du Père Duchesne* to subvert the people by using one of its favourite characters, who prompted Hébert to create his own, deliberately coarse anti-journal (*Les Grandes Joies et les grandes peines du Père Duchesne*) in order to counterbalance the vituperation of Lemaire's and other royalist periodicals. Founded in September 1790, *Le Père Duchesne* appeared almost without interruption until Hébert's execution. Its name was massively copied in other Revolutionary periodicals, tracts, or brochures because of its popularity and extraordinary effectiveness. [JR]

HEGEL, Georg Wilhelm Friedrich, see HIPPOLYTE; KOJÈVE.

HÉLIAS, Pierre-Jakez (b. 1914). A Breton teacher of French and classics of humble peasant origin, he became known to the public when he was given responsibility for the weekly half-hour of Breton-language broadcasting established in 1946. He systematized and deepened his researches into traditional society and its language as a source of materials. His writing was largely in Breton, though many texts were accompanied by a translation. This is the origin of his very successful auto- (or perhaps rather ethno-) biographical work *Le Cheval d'orgueil* (1975)—originally appearing in weekly bilingual instalments in *Ouest-France*. A second volume, *Le Quêteur de mémoire* (1990), is subtitled 'quarante ans de recherche sur les mythes et la civilisation bretonne'. In *Les Autres et les miens* (1977) he presents and illustrates the story-telling tradition of his native Pays Bigouden. He has also published plays and novels in French. [HLlH]

HÉLINAND DE FROIDMONT (c.1160–c.1230). Cistercian author chiefly remembered for his *Vers de la mort* (1194–7), a didactic poem concerning death and how to prepare for it. The formal influence of the so-called 'Hélinand strophe', a 12-line stanza of octosyllables, has been detected in later writers; Hélinand's poem was emulated by Robert le Clerc in the 13th c. [DAT]

HELLENS, Franz (1881–1972). Belgian novelist. Educated at a francophone school in Flemish-speaking Flanders, Hellens exploited his cultural dualism in fictions which mesh the chimerical and the down-to-earth; one collection bears the programmatic title *Réalités fantastiques* (1923). From 1922 to 1925 he edited the avant-garde review *Le Disque vert*, where *Michaux first published. Hellens's abundant *œuvre* ranges from the surrealistic visions of the early novel *Mélusine* (1920) to the matter-of-fact account of a young woman's hideous disfigurement in *La Mort dans l'âme* (1935), finally veering towards psychological realism in the novel *Moreldieu* (1946), with its treacherous and vicious hero. [RC]

Héloïse, see ABÉLARD.

HELVÉTIUS, Claude-Adrien (1715–71). A rich tax-farmer who attained fame as a philosopher, though he also wrote poetry. Early influenced by *Voltaire, he allied himself with the *philosophes; his principal work, *De l'esprit* (1758), was condemned by the Parlement de Paris along with the *Encyclopédie. This made him cautious; his second book, *De l'homme*, was published posthumously in 1772. He and his wife were sociable, hospitable people, and he kept up an important correspondence.

Helvétius's ambition was to be the Newton of the moral world, to provide a scientific account of human behaviour. His system, derived in part from Locke, presents vices and virtues as the result of physical sensation, of the human desire to maximize pleasure and minimize pain. Human beings are impelled by self-interest; the task of the legislator and the educator is, therefore, to create harmony between the individual interest and the general good. Individuals are all born with similar potential, so that genius, for instance, can be created by proper conditioning. These arguments were criticized by *Diderot (who was broadly in sympathy with Helvétius's position) because of the dogmatic crudity with which they are expressed. Nevertheless, they influenced the *Idéologues considerably, and *Stendhal saw in Helvétius 'the greatest of the French philosophers'. [PF]

HÉMON, Louis (1880–1913). Novelist, born in Brittany. He spent some years in England, wrote short stories and the sporting novel *Battling Malone* (1925), then emigrated to Canada, where he used his experience to write the novel for which he remains famous, *Maria Chapdelaine*.

HÉNAULT, Charles-Jean-François (1685–1770). Son of a tax-farmer, and a magistrate at the Parlement de Paris, 'le président Hénault' was an Academician, and a frequenter of literary circles, notably that of the duchesse du *Maine. He wrote poetry and plays, but his most solid achievement was the *Nouvel abrégé chronologique de l'histoire de France* (1744, frequently revised and reissued), a manual concentrating on political and military history from the beginnings to 1715. His *Mémoires* were published in 1855. [PF]

HÉNAULT, Gilles (b. 1920). Canadian journalist and poet, who has been both a trade-union organizer and director of the Museum of Contemporary Art in Montreal. While he is not a political poet, his work is inspired by themes of social justice, freedom, and concern for the future, expressed in a dense but clear poetic language, shot through with humour and irony. In *Totems* (1953) he pays homage to the original Amerindian peoples of Canada, while the titles of *Sémaphore* (1962) and *Signaux pour les voyants* (1972) show his humanitarian concern to make connections and to communicate. [SIL]

HENEIN, Georges (1914–73). Egyptian poet, editor, and journalist. For over a decade (1937–48) Henein led an active *Surrealist group in Cairo, keeping up its contacts with the main movement and writing many poems, tracts, manifestos, and short stories (*Déraisons d'être*, 1938; *Pour une conscience sacrilège*, 1945). After a rift with *Breton, Henein created a more informal and eclectic grouping, centred on the journal *La Part du sable*, where Egyptians figured alongside French writers such as *Bonnefoy, Henri *Thomas, and Jean *Grenier. When, like his Jewish friend *Jabès, Henein (a Copt) bowed to Arab nationalist pressures and left Egypt in the late 1950s, he turned to political journalism. Although from 1956 he eschewed publication, he never stopped writing creatively, and the works published since his death, including *Pour un pays inutile* (1977), *La Force de saluer* (1978), and *L'Esprit frappeur* (1983), have attracted increasing attention as they reveal an unusual alliance of intellectual brilliance, polemical drive, and poetic fancy. [MHTS]

HENNEQUIN, Émile (1859–88). In *La Critique scientifique* (1888) Hennequin sought to build on the theories of *Taine to create a scientific theory of artistic production in which the work's internal organization could be subjected to three levels of analysis, aesthetic, psychological, and sociological. This 'esthopsychology' or 'science of the work of art as sign' enjoyed renewed interest in the 1960s, when it was seen as a precursor of 'la nouvelle critique'. [JK]

HENNIQUE, Léon (1851–1935). Novelist, short-story writer, and dramatist, he published a number of works that are typical of the themes and techniques of *Naturalism, notably *La Dévouée* (1878), *L'Accident de Monsieur Hébert* (1883), and *Les Funérailles de Francine Cloarec* (1887). Though he contributed to *Les *Soirées de Médan*, he came to be associated more with the *Daudets and Edmond *Goncourt than with *Zola. He wrote for *Antoine's Théâtre-Libre, and his varied theatrical works range from naturalist plays to pantomime. [DB]

HENRI II (1529–59) inherited the throne from his father, *François Ier, in 1547. He continued the latter's attempts at increasing the power of the monarchy, but made the mistake of promoting the *Guise family, which was to cause his sons so much difficulty in the *Wars of Religion. Henri inherited his father's anti-Habsburg policies, allying himself with the German Protestants and with the Turks. Increasing financial difficulties, as well as the disastrous defeat of Saint-Quentin, led him, however, to make peace with Philip II (Treaty of *Cateau-Cambrésis). His death in a jousting accident left the monarchy painfully weak at a time when it was facing internal religious and political challenges. [JJS]

HENRI III (1551–89). Third son of *Henri II. Having been elected king of Poland in 1573, this intelligent but unstable man succeeded *Charles IX on the throne of France in 1574. Popular with contemporaries for his early military prowess, he earned their increasing disdain—and subsequently the fierce attacks of d'*Aubigné—because of his adoration of his favourites and his excessive indulgence in religious devotions. He eventually decided to free himself from the dominance of the Catholic *Ligue by having its leaders assassinated, and paid the price when he himself fell victim to the assassin's knife. He was a generous patron of the arts [see ACADÉMIE DE POÉSIE ET DE MUSIQUE]. [JJS]

Henri III et sa cour, see DUMAS, PERE.

HENRI IV (1553–1610). Henri de Bourbon, roi de Navarre, acceded to the French throne after the assassination of *Henri III in 1589. The latter's decision to assasinate the duc de *Guise had already removed the greatest obstacle to Henri's accession; but he had to win back his kingdom piecemeal, convert to Catholicism, and find a compromise which he could impose on his former co-religionists (the *Edict of Nantes). He was aided in the task of rebuilding his kingdom by his own personal qualities and by the dedication of his aides: Jeannin and Laffemas, who concentrated on industry and commerce, and *Sully, who emphasized the importance of agriculture. He was, however, mistrusted both by the Protestants, who felt that he had abandoned them, and by the Catholics, who felt that his abjuration was probably the result of a political calculation rather than a sincere conversion. Hence the large number of assassination attempts, culminating in his death at the hands of Ravaillac. The war which he was planning against Spain—which France could ill afford and might well have lost—would certainly have made him unpopular, but his untimely end led to the creation of the legend of 'Henri le Grand', saviour of the monarchy and father of his people. For the *précieuses*, he became 'le Grand Alcandre' [see PRECIOSITY]. For the *parlementaires* suffering under *Louis XIV's more absolutist rule, he was the liberal king. As a champion of tolerance, he is the hero of Voltaire's *La *Henriade*. For the *Physiocrats, he became the great protector of the peasantry, anxious that each family should have

Henriade, La

'une poule au pot'. The popular imagination of today remembers him above all as a brave soldier, as an astute military commander, and as 'le vert galant'. [JJS]

Henriade, La (1728). Epic poem in ten cantos by *Voltaire, first published (as *La Ligue*) in 1723. It was Voltaire's attempt, after aiming to be the French theatre's Sophocles, to give his country an epic poem worthy of the name, and was enormously popular with his contemporaries, who considered it his masterpiece (more than 60 editions in his lifetime). The subject is ostensibly the siege of Paris undertaken by Henri III, assisted by Henri de Navarre, in 1589. But in reality the *Henriade* proposes a philosophical panorama of religious fanaticism and a sustained meditation on civil discord, both anathema to Voltaire. [JR]

HENRI D'ANDELI (*fl.* 13th c.). Clerical author of the *Lai d'Aristote*, an unusually long, 'courtly', and highly polished *fabliau*. He also composed a *Bataille des vins blancs* and a *Bataille des sept arts*.

HENRI DE FERRIÈRES (14th c.). Author of the curiously disparate, bipartite *Livres du Roy Modus et de la Reine Ratio* (dated 1354–76), in prose with occasional verses. In the first part, *Le Livre de la chasse*, an invaluably comprehensive treatise, Roi Modus explains in dialogue and with moralizations the different hunting methods and habits of game animals; he adds a verse debate on the value of falconry as against hunting [see GACE DE LA BUIGNE]. The following *Songe de pestilence* stages Modus and Ratio complaining before God that Charity, Truth, and Humility are supplanted by the World, the Flesh, and the Devil—hence the disasters of the 14th c. [JHMT]

HENRIETTE D'ANGLETERRE (1644–70). Daughter of Charles I of England and Henrietta Maria, unhappily married to Philippe, duc d'Orléans, the brother of *Louis XIV. Her death was the subject of a famous funeral oration by *Bossuet, of which posterity has remembered the words: 'Madame se meurt, Madame est morte!' Her life was written by her friend Madame de *Lafayette.

HENRIOT, Philippe (1889–1944). Extreme rightwing politician and publicist. Born in Reims, he became active in Catholic political movements in the 1920s, was a *député* for Bordeaux from 1932, and wrote extensively in the extreme right-wing press. After the fall of France he enthusiastically supported *Pétain's policy of collaboration, which he promoted tirelessly in articles and speeches. His propaganda broadcasts on Radio Vichy during the last year of the *Occupation were particularly effective in demoralizing opponents in country areas with little access to printed media. An early member of the hated Milice, he became propaganda minister in January 1944, and was assassinated by the Resistance the following June. [MHK]

HENRY, Charles (1859–1926). As a scientist at the *École des Hautes Études in Paris, Henry carried out research in experimental psychology which played an important part in aesthetic debates in the 1880s, notably in *Seurat's theories of colour and in literary *Symbolism's efforts to establish a scientific basis for their theories of the relationship between the arts. [JK]

Heptaméron, L'. A collection of 72 stories (originally intended as 100, but unfinished) by *Marguerite de Navarre, not published in her lifetime. The first edition by *Boaistuau was entitled *Histoire des amants fortunés* (1558); the name *Heptaméron* was first used by Claude Gruget in a new edition the following year. The cycle is clearly inspired by Boccaccio's *Decameron*, of which a French translation, commissioned by Marguerite, had appeared in 1545. Five noblemen and five ladies, cut off by floods in the Pyrenees, gather in a monastery and tell stories while waiting for a bridge to be constructed. Each tale is followed by a discussion of its moral implications, inevitably bringing out the divergence of opinion between the sexes. A number of the storytellers have been identified, e.g. Parlamente as Marguerite herself and Hircan as her husband Henri.

As in Boccaccio's cycle, the tales vary widely in length and manner, from the brief and excremental (stories 11 and 52), through the equally bawdy sexually explicit (several), to the high-minded with an unhappy ending (e.g. 19, where two lovers unable to marry end up in holy orders). There are also some 20 tales about lubricious clerics, especially the *Franciscans. But unlike the comic anticlericalism of the *Decameron*, Marguerite's, characteristic of the Reformation, involves unequivocal denunciation of corrupt clergy.

The unity of the cycle is thematic, virtually all the tales being about relationships between the sexes—love, marriage, adultery, rape. In contrast with the *Decameron* and the misogynistic *Cent nouvelles nouvelles*, the *Heptaméron*, particularly in the discussions, presents a vigorous defence of woman and a highly sympathetic portrayal of her problems in a society where a courtly veneer conceals brutal sexual mores. But Marguerite sees as almost impossible the reconciliation of male needs for endless conquest with female ideals of chastity and conjugal fidelity. While there is a case for seeing Marguerite as an early feminist, she seems largely to accept the traditional male view of woman: she portrays more unfaithful wives than husbands, and her libertine women are unambiguously condemned by all the speakers. Although we are invited to attach considerable importance to Parlamente's *Neoplatonic definition of human love as leading to divine love (19), more earthly points of view which see the sexual side of love as legitimate are not rejected.

Though neither as skilful nor as witty as the

Decameron, the *Heptaméron* represents both a considerable literary achievement and an invaluable evocation of life in Renaissance France.   [CMSJ]

See L. Febvre, *Amour sacré, amour profane: autour de l'Heptaméron* (1944); M. Tetel, *Marguerite de Navarre's 'Heptaméron': Themes, Language and Structure* (1973); N. Cazauran, *L'Heptaméron de Marguerite de Navarre* (1976).

Heptaplomeres, see BODIN.

Héraclius. Tragedy by Pierre *Corneille, first performed 1647. Set in Constantinople, it is remarkable for the complexity of the plot, which turns on false and uncertain identities.

Heraldry, see CHIVALRY.

HÉRAULT DE SÉCHELLES, Marie-Jean (1759–94). French magistrate and Revolutionary politician, executed with *Danton. He wrote a *Voyage à Montbard* (1785) about *Buffon, and fascinating notes on many subjects, including eloquence, in his *Codicille politique et pratique d'un jeune habitant d'Epone* (written before 1789).

Herbe, L', see SIMON, C.

HERBELOT DE MOLAINVILLE, Barthélémy d' (1625–95). French orientalist, professor at the *Collège de France, author of the *Bibliothèque orientale* (1697), a work of encyclopedic erudition on things oriental, completed and published by *Galland.

HERBERAY DES ESSARTS, Nicolas d' (d. *c*.1552), see AMADIS DE GAULE.

HEREDIA, José-Maria de (1842–1905). French poet, born in Cuba of Spanish–French parentage. Among the second generation of poets who recognized in *Leconte de Lisle the source and model of their poetic practice, it was Heredia who most systematically applied in his verse the *Parnassian principles of impersonality, historical reconstruction, and formal perfection. From the early 1860s his chosen form was the *sonnet, whose concision and formal symmetries offered the most effective framework for the creation of images of visual beauty in historical or natural settings to which Heredia aspired. His collection *Les Trophées*, published to great acclaim in 1893, forms an anthology of 'transpositions d'art' and summarizes the achievements and limitations of the Parnassian effort in French poetry.   [JK]

Heresies. Derived from the Greek word for choice, heresy came to be defined by the medieval Church as 'an opinion chosen by human perception, founded on the scriptures, contrary to the teaching of the Church, publicly avowed and obstinately defended'. Since disputes as to what was unorthodox were a prime means of stimulating the Church to clarify its teaching, efforts were made to distinguish heretics from proponents of views later declared to be heretical, a distinction that tended to shield academic theologians from opprobrium. But once a teaching had been accepted as part of the Church's tradition, those who continued to oppose it could legitimately be required to abandon their opinion. Detection and persecution of heresy was, therefore, common in periods of intellectual ferment. And since in practice schism or refusal to accept ecclesiastical discipline was also often punished as heretical, the offence was found at most times. But the Church in the early Medieval West was in general too preoccupied with diocesan organization and missionary work to notice deviant opinions.

The early 11th-c. intellectual awakening in western Europe was accompanied by sporadic outbreaks of heresy in French towns, which sent ecclesiastics scurrying back to patristic sources both to identify and to deal with the new problem. By the end of the century popular heresy threatened to become endemic in Flanders, the Rhineland, and parts of northern France, where it was often associated with weavers. To some extent heterodoxy grew from a sceptical reaction against the Church's sharper definition of the sacraments, particularly the mass, but also baptism and marriage. At the same time it developed rapidly under the impact of the general call for ecclesiastical reform and for the suppression of simony and clerical marriage, which encouraged charismatic leaders to lambast the clergy and attracted crowds to their cause.

The tough response of northern bishops and counts to the tumultuous mobs collected by anti-clerical preachers such as Tanchelm of Antwerp or Henry of Lausanne led their sympathizers to drift southwards to areas of weaker political control in the first half of the 12th c. Their numbers were swelled by critics of the now wealthy and aristocratic Church, who called for its rejection in favour of sects practising apostolic poverty, among which the Waldensians or *Vaudois were outstanding. Admiration for apostolic poverty intensified under the impact of dualist ideas imported from the Eastern empire around 1140, after which *Catharism became a major force in southern France and Lombardy. The swelling tide of anticlericalism merging into heresy caused lay rulers to introduce the death penalty for adherents of sects, and forced ecclesiastics to concentrate on their extirpation. In 1208 Innocent III proclaimed the Albigensian Crusade; in 1231 Pope Gregory IX instituted the Inquisition, which, though it aimed to induce penitence, was prepared to invoke state aid and capital punishment when necessary.

Unsurprisingly, repression, while not unsuccessful, could induce obstinacy, especially when dissidents like the Fraticelli were fortified by prophecies of the imminent destruction of the Roman Church. And the papal authority that authorized repression was automatically called into question—both

Boniface VIII and John XXII were accused of heresy. Furthermore, the widespread exploitation of repressive processes for political ends (e.g. in the crushing of the French Templars) encouraged cynicism, which the Great Schism did nothing to still. The Conciliar Movement's attempt to define the means whereby the Church's traditions could be authoritatively stated came to grief on the rock of national interests. Meanwhile, as literacy and private devotion grew, Lollardy in England, Hussitism in Bohemia, and the Brethren of the Free Spirit in the Low Countries testified to the importance of vernacular writings, local conditions, and sometimes incipient nationalism in framing doctrinal views. Uniformity began to seem Utopian.

The *Reformation altered the scale of the problem without changing its nature—each religious community now had its own dogmas to defend by repression. In most of Europe the 16th and 17th c. saw the continued involvement of state power in the maintenance of doctrinal purity. The toleration briefly extended to the French Huguenots by *Henri IV in 1598 was withdrawn by the Revocation of the *Edict of Nantes in 1685. Only gradually did state power recede, leaving the individual Churches to deal with their own dissidents as they thought best. Thereafter excommunication became, and remains, the standard punishment for heresy.

[JHD]

See C. Thouzellier, *Catharisme et valdéisme en Languedoc* (2nd edn., 1969); R. I. Moore, *The Origins of European Dissent* (1977); B. Hamilton, *The Medieval Inquisition* (1981).

HERGÉ, see TINTIN.

HERLIN, Louise (b. 1925). Cairo-born poet, who has also lived in England and America. Her harmonious, restrained verse expresses an intense vision of place. Her principal collections are *Le Versant contraire* (1967), *Commune mesure* (1971), *Crayons, le béton la plage* (1981), *L'Amour exact* (1990). [PF]

HERMAN, Nicolas, see DEVOTIONAL WRITING, 2.

Hernani. Verse drama by Victor *Hugo set in 16th-c. Spain. The plot hinges on the conflict between honour and passion that emerges from the rivalry for the noble Doña Sol between an outlawed noble (Hernani), the king of Spain, and a grandee representing the values of old Spain. Written to reflect the anti-classical principles of the Preface to *Cromwell, the play became a *cause célèbre* that established Hugo as the leading Romantic dramatist when it was presented at the Comédie-Française on 25 February 1830. In his *Histoire du romantisme* *Gautier describes the fighting that broke out at the opening line between Hugo's followers and defenders of classicism. [SN]

Hérodias. The third of Flaubert's *Trois contes.

HÉROËT, Antoine (1492–1568). Poet, courtier of *Marguerite de Navarre, and bishop of Digne from 1552. He is the author of a '*blason de l'œil' (1535). *L'Androgyne* (1535, published 1542) is a decasyllabic poetic adaptation of part of Plato's *Symposium*, following Ficino's translation and commentary. *La Parfaite Amie* (1542) is a personal meditation on love, yet within the Platonist tradition, influenced by Castiglione and Italian treatises: love is divinely inspired, mutual, and leads to self-knowledge and virtue, but perfect union is achieved only after death. Praised by both *Sebillet and the *Pléiade, Héroët is a sensitive and urbane poet. [PS]

Héroïde. For this type of poetry, fashionable in the 18th c., see COLARDEAU.

HERR, Lucien (1864–1926). Philosopher and socialist intellectual. Born in Altkirch, Alsace, he studied in Paris, entering the *École Normale Supérieure to take the philosophy *agrégation*. Travelling in Russia and Germany, he encountered Hegelian philosophy and socialism, which he later did much to propagate in France. He became librarian at the École Normale, which occupied the rest of his life and made him an influential figure for generations of *normaliens*. He joined the Possibiliste branch of the French *socialist movement, and directed many of his students towards it, including Jean *Jaurès. Always something of an *éminence grise*, he is often regarded as the major socialist intellectual of his time. [MHK]

HERRIOT, Édouard (1872–1955). President of the *Radical Party 1919–35, repeatedly minister and prime minister, and mayor of Lyon for 50 years. He was popular for his tolerant humanism and his eloquence, remained hostile to Vichy, and published books on various subjects, including memoirs (*Jadis*, 1948–52).

HERTEL, François (pseud. of Rodolphe Dubé) (1905–85). Canadian poet, novelist, and essayist who left the Jesuit order for voluntary exile in France in 1949 as a protest against the spiritual and cultural stagnation of French Canada. His philosophical meditations and ardent nationalism, expressed in a prolific stream of publications, were influential in the 1950s. His most enduring work is likely to be the bitter poetry of self-doubt in *Mes naufrages* (1951). [SIL]

HERVÉ, Pierre (b. 1913). French polemicist and political philosopher. Active in the Communist Youth and later the Resistance, Hervé became leader-writer for L'*Humanité and editor of *Action*. Expelled from the PCF for his pamphlet *La Révolution et les fétiches* (1956), he subsequently joined the Parti Socialiste.

HETZEL, Jules (1814–86). Bookseller, publisher, and writer. In 1862 he opened a Paris bookshop specializing in children's books, founding the hugely successful *Magasin d'éducation et de récréation* in which he published the work of Jules *Verne amongst many others. Under the pseudonym P.-J. Stahl, he wrote entertaining works including *Scènes de la vie publique et privée des animaux* (1851) and *Histoire d'un homme enrhumé* (1859). In 1886 his titles were bought by *Hachette. [DAS]

Hexagone, L', see MIRON; QUEBEC, 5.

Histoire. Novel by Claude *Simon, published 1967, awarded the Prix Médicis. The events of a day in the narrator's life are interspersed with memories of his childhood, his mother's death, etc., and with his attempts to imagine his parents' courtship and honeymoon (the novel ends with a description of him in his mother's womb): a hypothetical reconstruction sparked off by her collection of postcards. These and other pictorial elements play a major role in generating the text. The title is doubly ironic, implying the impossibility of presenting one's life either as *story*—a linear ordered composition—or in an intelligible relation to *history*; his memories of participating in the Spanish Civil War expose the irreducible gap between the abstraction we call 'History' and the meaningless confusion of the individual's experience of events like war. The fragility of identity, adrift in a chaotic flow of perceptions, is further expressed in intermittent identifications with his uncle Charles: both men's wives, apparently, committed suicide, and this sense of sexual loss haunts the novel. Hence also the absences and lacunae underlying the text: the father whom he never knew, the breakdown of his marriage which is never fully told. Consequently the language of the text does not so much represent a coherent fictional 'reality' as pursue a desperate, often bitter, yet richly sensuous trail of associations. [CB]

Histoire amoureuse des Gaules, see BUSSY-RABUTIN.

Histoire critique du Vieux Testament, see SIMON, R.

Histoire de Charles XII, see VOLTAIRE.

Histoire de la folie à l'âge classique, see FOUCAULT.

Histoire de ma vie, see AMROUCHE, F.-A.-M.; SAND.

Histoire des deux Indes (full title *Histoire philosophique et politique des établissements et du commerce des Européens dans les deux Indes*). Multi-volume history of European colonization, masterminded by *Raynal, first published in 1770, with augmented editions in 1774 and 1780. Much of the work was written by other *philosophes*, including *Holbach, Deleyre, Pechméja, and above all *Diderot, who wrote up to one-third of the total. It is Diderot's contributions, unattributed in the text, which have most interested 20th-c. scholars, and they are often published separately. In its time, however, the *Histoire* made its impact in its own right.

It describes in turn the colonial establishments of the European powers in the East Indies, South America, the West Indies, and North America (Raynal planned another work on Africa), and concludes with a highly 'philosophical' account of modern Europe, its recent progress, and the enlightened way ahead. There are many useful, though not always accurate, accounts of the geography, fauna and flora, society, and commerce of the colonies, with picturesque descriptions of coffee, hummingbirds, etc. But Raynal's success with contemporaries was largely due to discussions of such questions as slavery, commerce, savage life, or religion. These express *Enlightenment views, often with great eloquence, particularly the pieces written by Diderot. *Voltaire, described the *Histoire* as 'du réchauffé avec de la déclamation', and the modern reader is struck by its many contrasts and contradictions. Nevertheless, it had a huge success, going into numerous editions and being translated into several languages. It was also condemned to be burned by the public executioner in France, and Raynal was forced into honourable exile. [PF]

Histoire des oracles, see FONTENELLE.

Histoire des Treize. Group title of three novels by *Balzac: *Ferragus*, La *Duchesse de Langeais*, and La *Fille aux yeux d'or*, included in *Études de mœurs au XIXe siècle*.

Histoire d'O., see MANDIARGUES.

Histoire d'une Grecque moderne, see SEE PRÉVOST, A.-F.

Histoire d'un paysan, see ERCKMANN-CHATRIAN.

Histoire ecclésiastique, see FLEURY, C.

Histoire naturelle, see BUFFON.

Histoires de déserteurs, see MAJOR.

Histoires naturelles, see RENARD, J.

Histoire socialiste, see JAURES.

Histoires ou contes du temps passé. Collection of stories by *Perrault, usually known as the *Contes* or *Contes de ma mère l'Oye* (Mother Goose Tales). There are eight stories in prose, 'La Belle au bois dormant', 'Le Petit Chaperon rouge', 'La Barbe bleue', 'Le Chat botté', 'Les Fées', 'Cendrillon', 'Riquet à la houppe', and 'Le Petit Poucet'. These were published in 1697 along with three previously published verse tales, 'Griselidis' (based on the story in Boccaccio), 'Peau d'âne', and 'Les Souhaits ridicules'. It is the prose tales which have been remembered; they were first issued under the name of Perrault's son Pierre, who did indeed have some part in their composition.

Most of the stories come from popular sources [see FOLK-TALE], and may have been inspired by genuine story tellers, but they are also much indebted to literary precedents and are written in an artistically naïve way so as to appeal to fashionable audiences as much as to children. Each story is followed by one or two morals in verse (often omitted in modern editions for children). In his interesting prefaces, Perrault associates them with his campaign on behalf of the *modernes* [see QUERELLE], presenting them as a more moral equivalent to the fables of antiquity.

These beautifully told stories were an immediate success, and helped create a vogue for fairy-tales [see SHORT FICTION]. They quickly became a children's classic, and through popular editions influenced the oral tradition from which they had come (Grimm's fairy tales show signs of this). Some readers such as André *Chénier or Bruno Bettelheim (see his *The Uses of Enchantment*) have despised or criticized them, and they have tended to be omitted from discussions of French classical literature, but they have continued to shape the minds of children and adults in France and abroad. [PF]

Histoire universelle, see AUBIGNÉ.

Histories of French Literature. The rise of modern French 'histoire littéraire' is charted in a separate entry [see LITERARY HISTORY]. The present entry lists some of the main histories of French literature currently available. These are numerous and cater for all levels of interest. [For other Francophone countries see bibliographies for the relevant entries.]

Of the classic early 20th-c. histories, the most impressive in some ways is the single-author, single-volume *Histoire de la littérature française* (1895, frequently revised) of the principal founder of the discipline, *Lanson. At the same time L. Petit de Julleville edited a much longer *Histoire de la langue et de la littérature françaises* (8 vols., 1896–9), for which *Brunot treated the history of the language. In 1923 came the 2-volume *Littérature française* of J. *Bédier and P. Hazard, which retained its classic status for a quarter-century (in 1948 P. Martino produced a new edition).

There have been several multi-volume histories in French since 1950. The *Histoire de la littérature française* (new edn., 1955–64), directed by J. Calvet, contains 10 volumes, each written entirely by one author, as is the case in the 16-volume *Littérature française* (1970–9), directed by C. Pichois. The five volumes published by the Presses Universitaires de France under the heading *Précis de littérature française* (1985–91, one volume per century from the 16th to the 20th) are collective works, each under a separate editor. The first volumes of another collection launched in 1992 by the same publishers under the heading 'Collection Premier Cycle' follow a similar pattern of multiple authorship, with the exception of M. Zink, *Littérature française du moyen âge* (1992).

Two general histories stand out. Volume 3 of the *Histoire des littératures* in the Encyclopédie de la Pléiade is entitled *Littératures françaises, connexes et*

marginales (1978); as well as excellent chapters on periods, genres, and authors, it contains sections on *francophone, regional, and *patois writing. The *Histoire littéraire de la France* (1974–80), under the general direction of P. Abraham and R. Desné, contains 12 multi-author volumes which, from a generally left-wing perspective, provide a good account of the historical development of French literature in relation to social, political, and economic movements. In addition, the brief *Histoire de la littérature française* (1991) by R. Balibar, published in the 'Que sais-je?' series, radically scrutinizes all three terms, 'histoire', 'littérature', 'français', and suggests a different way of telling the story.

There are many histories of individual genres or particular periods. Some of the former are mentioned here under the relevant entries; of the latter the most impressive is the rich *Histoire de la littérature française du XVIIe siècle* (5 vols., 1948–56) of A. Adam. One might also mention the personal but well-documented account of recent writing by P. de Boisdeffre, *Histoire de la littérature de langue française des années 1930 aux années 1980* (1985).

In English there have been a number of one-volume surveys, such as G. Saintsbury's *A Short History of French Literature* (1882), L. Strachey's *Landmarks in French Literature* (1912), and G. Brereton's *A Short History of French Literature* (1954), all of which naturally bear the marks of their author and his time. Of collective publications, the six volumes of *French Literature and its Background* (1968–70), edited by J. Cruickshank, each contain some 15 essays by various hands on authors and historical topics. In *A Literary History of France* (6 vols., 1967–74), edited by J. Charvet, each period, for the most part a century, is treated by a single author. A totally different approach is to be found in *A New History of French Literature* (1989), edited by D. Hollier, which submits the traditional narrative to an idiosyncratic fragmentation into some 200 short essays, some unexciting, some brilliant. [PF]

Historiettes, see TALLEMANT DES RÉAUX.

Historiography. As in other parts of Europe, French historical writing has gone through a number of more or less distinct phases since the Middle Ages, of which it may be useful to distinguish seven. The labels are ones of convenience, and the phases should be viewed as overlapping, with periods of transition in which rival styles of historiography appealed to different readers and writers.

1. Chronicles

The chronicle was essentially a narrative of events, political, military, or ecclesiastical. Earlier medieval chronicles were usually written in Latin by monks (notably Raoul Glaber, *c*.985–*c*.1046), and concentrated either on local or on 'universal' history (i.e. the history of the world from Adam onwards). Later chronicles were more often written in a vivid and colloquial vernacular by secular priests or laymen (including the nobles *Joinville and *Villehardouin), and emphasized the history of France. The most famous examples of the latter type are *Froissart's Chroniques, which told the story of the main feats of arms in France, England, and Spain from 1325 to c.1400, and the Mémoires of *Commynes, on the period 1464–95. However, the first book printed in French, in 1477, was the *Grandes Chroniques de France, a collective work by the Benedictine monks of Saint-Denis, the custodians of the memory of the deeds of the French kings.

2. Humanist History

The dominant form of history written in the 16th c. was the work of the *humanists, and it followed classical models much more closely than the chroniclers had done, gaining in clarity and losing in immediacy in the process. Narratives such as the Gesta Francorum (c.1520) by the Italian humanist Paulus Aemilius were combined with literary portraits of the protagonists and put speeches into their mouths in order to explain their motives, in the manner of Livy. Even memoirs, like the Commentaires (1592) of the soldier Blaise de *Monluc, owed something to the classical tradition (in this case, to Caesar). Another important form of humanist history was the study of the history of institutions, well exemplified by the Recherches de la France (1560) by the lawyer Étienne *Pasquier, and the reflections on the development of the various forms of government in *Bodin's Methodus (1566), a treatise concerned with 'the easy comprehension of history'.

3. Pragmatic History

In reaction against what he considered the rhetorical excesses of some of the humanists, notably the invention of speeches, the magistrate Jacques-Auguste *de Thou (1533–1617) wrote a Latin history of his own time, the age of the *Wars of Religion, in a plain style and an impartial tone. An equally detached treatment of a controversial problem was the methodological treatise De re diplomatica (1681) by the Benedictine scholar *Mabillon, a study in the antiquarian tradition of the humanists, which laid down the principles on which genuine documents (medieval charters, for the most part) could be distinguished from forgeries. Historical reference books began to appear, notably *Moreri's Grand Dictionnaire historique (1674). Pragmatic in a more political sense of the term were the works funded by the government, such as the Histoire de France (1643–51) by François *Mézeray, and *Maimbourg's hostile Histoire du calvinisme (1682), which was part of the campaign leading to the Revocation of the *Edict of Nantes.

4. Philosophical History

The famous Dictionnaire historique et critique (1697) by *Bayle was intended to give the impression of an impartial scholarly work as well as to demolish Moreri, but it was as much the expression, indeed the vehicle, of a world-view as the historical works of *Bossuet, the Discours sur l'histoire universelle (1681) and the Histoire des variations des églises protestantes (1688). Philosophical history, in the sense of history informed by general ideas and attempting to persuade the reader of their validity, was the dominant genre in the 18th c. It was wide-ranging, taking the world as its province and concerned with economic, social, and cultural developments over the long term as well as with the narrative of events or the growth of political, legal, and ecclesiastical institutions. It was also a reaction against what the philosophical historians considered as the myopia of the antiquarians, their preoccupation with petty details. Meanwhile the Benedictines of St Maur (*Maurists) in particular were carrying on the antiquarian tradition, publishing collections of sources like the Recueil des historiens des Gaules et de la France (1738–52) and reference books such as L'Art de vérifier les dates (1750). The four outstanding examples of French philosophical history are the *Considérations sur les causes de la grandeur des Romains et de leur décadence (1734) by Montesquieu, the *Essai sur les mœurs (1756) by Voltaire, the *Histoire des deux Indes (1770–80) by Raynal, and the Esquisse d'un tableau historique des progrès de l'esprit humain (1795) by *Condorcet.

5. Romantic History

Romantic history was written in conscious reaction against the philosophical history of the Enlightenment, which was increasingly considered too cosmopolitan and too bloodless. There was a revival of narrative, under the influence of novels such as Scott's Quentin Durward (1823) and Hugo's *Notre-Dame de Paris (1831). The focus shifted from society to the nation or even the 'race'. There was a growing interest in medieval history, formerly dismissed by 'enlightened' scholars as an age of darkness. Prosper de *Barante's Histoire des ducs de Bourgogne (1824–6) was concerned to tell a story, and above all to paint a picture of the late Middle Ages, full of 'local colour', rather than to explain or to judge. The Histoire de la conquête de l'Angleterre par les Normands (1825) of *Thierry interpreted medieval English history as a story of conflict between two races, Normans and Saxons. The 11-volume Histoire de France (1833–67) of *Michelet was a story told in a highly dramatic fashion, the hero of the drama being 'France' rather than any individual person. His seven-volume La Révolution française (1847–53) had a similar focus on 'the People'. Closer to the tradition of philosophical history were the Histoire de la civilisation en France (1829–32) by *Guizot, better known as a statesman; Thierry's Essai sur l'histoire de la formation et des progrès du Tiers État (1853); and *Tocqueville's still more famous L'Ancien Régime et la révolution (1856).

6. Positivist History

A reaction against Romantic history was not long in coming. According to some critics, the concentration on events and picturesque details took the ideas out of history. They wanted a grand narrative of the type offered by the philosophical historians and by the sociologist Auguste *Comte, charting the progress of humanity from religion to 'positive philosophy' and revealing the operation of the laws of history. According to others, what was wrong with Romantic historians was their reliance on narrative sources ('chronicles') rather than official documents ('records'). They wanted historiography to become 'positivist' in the sense of adopting a more scientific method. The struggle between these two tendencies dominates the later 19th c. In the centre we may situate *Fustel de Coulanges, whose masterpiece *La Cité antique* (1864) discussed the function of pagan religion in ensuring the cohesion of the family and the state. The philosophical wing of positivist history is exemplified by *Taine, whose *Origines de la France contemporaine* (1875–93) viewed French history as the field of interaction between three forces: 'race', 'milieu', and 'moment'. The empiricist wing included Gabriel Monod, who founded the *Revue historique* (1876) to promote a more scientific and a more professional approach to history in the manner of Leopold von Ranke and his followers, and Ernest *Lavisse, best known as the editor of a multi-volume history of France (1900–11). The positivist approach, documentary and evolutionist, can also be seen in the history of science practised by Pierre Duhem, the history of French literature by Ferdinand *Brunetière, and the history of the French language by Ferdinand *Brunot. The achievements and limitations of positivist history are revealed most clearly by the methodological textbook of Charles-Victor Langlois and Charles Seignobos, *Introduction aux études historiques* (1898).

7. Annales *History*

Seignobos in particular came to symbolize traditional historiography in the eyes of Lucien *Febvre and Marc *Bloch when they launched their campaign for its renewal at the University of Strasbourg following World War I, a campaign which culminated in the foundation of the journal *Annales d'histoire économique et sociale* in 1929. Bloch and Febvre opposed the dominance of the history of political events and they preached and practised the history of economic and social structures and also of what they called 'historical psychology' or 'the history of collective mentalities'. This 'new history', drawing on the ideas of economists and sociologists, was a minority movement in their day, but it became the dominant tendency after World War II, under the leadership of Fernand *Braudel, whose wide-ranging study *La Méditerranée et le monde méditerranéen à l'époque de Philippe II* was published in 1949, and of Ernest *Labrousse, whose work on economic cycles in the 18th c. inspired generations of research students. The so-called 'Annales school' still exercises intellectual hegemony over French historical writing today, and includes scholars of the distinction of Georges *Duby, Jacques *Le Goff, and Emmanuel *Le Roy Ladurie. However, it has diversified to the point of fragmentation in the process of incorporating new ideas (notably those of *Lévi-Strauss and *Foucault) and of finding new objects such as the history of women, the history of reading, and the history of the body.

8. Authors and Readers

The history of historical writing requires a social dimension, a concern not only with writers but also with publishers and readers, indeed with the 'historical culture' of the French, the changing place of history in their everyday life. Looking back over the centuries, changes in the role and functions of French historians are clearly visible. In the first place, secularization. The history of the French was largely written by the clergy not only in the Middle Ages but also in the early modern period (to the Benedictines mentioned above one might add the Jesuit Gabriel Daniel, whose *Histoire de France* of 1713 remained authoritative till the later 18th c., when it was replaced by that of another Jesuit, Paul-François Velly). Only after the Revolution was historical writing dominated by the laity. The second major change was the professionalization of history in the 19th c., with the foundation of the *École des Chartes (1821) to train students in the study of the sources, and with the foundation of chairs of history in the universities. Today, professional historians are among the leading intellectuals of a country where the role of intellectual is still taken very seriously.

Despite the appeal of chronicles to medieval nobles, it is likely that the readership of historical works was mainly clerical until about 1600. As for the laity, library inventories suggest that lawyers (including the magistrates of the *parlements*) were the main consumers of history during the old regime. In the 18th c., the rise of social history coincided with the rise of women readers and the possibility of making a profit from publishing. Voltaire's *Essai* went through 15 editions between 1756 and 1784, while Velly was paid 1,500 francs a volume for his history of France. The vogue of historical painting in the 18th and 19th c. made the past more vivid to thousands of spectators. In the later 19th c. the textbook-reading public became important for the first time, as the government encouraged the study of the history of the nation in order to legitimate the Third Republic and transform 'peasants into Frenchmen'. In the course of the recent shift from the book to the screen, history has retained an important place, and the faces of Duby and Le Goff, for example, are familiar on French television.

[UPB]

See P. Gay, *The Enlightenment*, vol. 2 (1969); D. Kelley, *Foundations of Modern Historical Scholarship* (1970); P. Archambault, *Seven French Chroniclers* (1974); C.-O. Carbonell, *Histoire et historiens 1865–85* (1976); S. Bann, *The Clothing of Clio* (1984); P. Burke, *The French Historical Revolution* (1990).

History of the French Language

1. Latin to Old French

The colonization of Gaul by the Romans in the first two centuries BC led to the introduction of Latin into Gaul and the gradual Romanization of Gaul's education and administration. The term 'Latin' covers a whole range of different varieties including the 'Classical' Latin of Cicero and Caesar and what is often misleadingly referred to as 'Vulgar Latin', embracing the spoken language of the legionaries, and popular and late written forms which in their differences from classical norms are thought to be closest to speech and the common ancestor of the modern Romance languages. Diachronic developments attested in Latin, such as the simplification of the nominal declension system, increased use of prepositions and determiners, and the formation of new compound tenses, point the way to the new Romance vernaculars.

Pre-5th-c. texts suggest a relatively homogeneous language over the Empire, and the influence of the Celtic substrate in Gaul is most obviously lexical, notably in the fields of daily and country life (*mouton*, *sapin*, *chemise*). In the 5th c., however, Germanic tribes invaded Gaul, with the Visigoths settling south of the Loire, the Burgundians in the Rhône and Saône vallies, and the Franks in the north. On this occasion, in the face of the prestige of Roman language, law, and education, and with the conversion of the Frankish king Clovis to Christianity, the conquerors did not impose their language but gradually adopted Latin. In the south of Gaul, where Germanic influence was weakest, the language remained closer to Latin but, in the north, Germanic influence caused important changes. For instance, the strong expiratory accent of the Germanic speakers may well be responsible for phonological changes (such as the diphthongization of tonic free vowels) which differentiate northern Gaul (the *langue d'oïl* area and the ancestor of Modern French) from the south (*langue d'oc*) and from a third, wedge-shaped area in central eastern France (*franco-provençal*). Germanic vocabulary was assimilated into the lexicon, including outdoor, military, and affective terms (e.g. *haie*, *guerre*, *honte*, *orgueil*).

There is much dispute as to when it is appropriate to speak of a French vernacular distinct from Latin, but the *Strasbourg Oaths (842 AD) are generally identified as the earliest extant text in the vernacular of Gaul. For convenience, the history of French is usually divided into broad periods, if possible using a combination of external or historical factors and key internal or linguistic changes. The period of Early Old French may be said to cover broadly the mid-9th c. until the end of the 11th c. Although termed 'Early Old French' it was not a single, undifferentiated language which emerged in Gaul. As well as the major division into *langue d'oïl*, *langue d'oc*, and *franco-provençal*, there was within each area a network of dialects which sometimes gradually shaded into each other, sometimes changed abruptly on either side of a geographical barrier.

The 'heyday' of Old French in the 12th and 13th c. witnessed a number of important developments. First came the gradual acceptance of *francien*, the language of the Île-de-France, and notably that of Paris, as the desirable spoken norm. Paris became the political, legal, and educational focus, and nearby Saint-Denis provided a spiritual centre. In occupying a fairly central position in the *langue d'oïl* area, *francien* was, moreover, linguistically less differentiated from the other dialects than those on the periphery. The prestige of *francien* is evident from the much-quoted 12th-c. comment by Garnier de Pont-Saint-Maxence: 'Mes langages est buens, car en France fui nez' ('My language is good because I was born in France [i.e. Île-de-France]'). It is significant that there appears to be no text written in 'pure' dialect, for even the earliest texts show incompatible 'Parisian' forms alongside regional features to a degree which cannot be explained in terms of regional differences between author and scribe. By the end of the 12th c. *francien* had made considerable progress as the written norm, even before Paris became an important literary centre in the following century. In the 13th c. the strongest regional colouring was *picard*; *champenois* too appeared for a time as a possible competitor to *francien*, especially during the time of *Chrétien de Troyes, but towards the end of the 13th c. its influence began to wane. *Anglo-Norman was used by the ruling classes in England throughout the Old French period, and had a rich and abundant literature.

Throughout its history, the 'standard' language has had to compete not only with other dialects, but also with Latin [see LATINITY]. During the 13th c. French was introduced to some extent in local documents in Picardy and from 1254 it was permitted alongside Latin in the royal chancellery. In the *langue d'oc* area, the role of Occitan as a literary language [see OCCITAN LANGUAGE AND LITERATURE] was diminished by the Albigensian Crusade (1208–13) [see CATHARS], which led to the demise of the Toulousain dynasty and the eventual submission of the south to the Crown; it nevertheless continued to be used for everyday purposes.

What are the principal characteristics of Old French? Phonologically, Old French possessed a whole range of vowel sounds including diphthongs and triphthongs. Broadly speaking, its spelling, used to transcribe an essentially oral literature, espoused the phonological principle, albeit imperfectly since the Roman alphabet was inadequate for representing all the new Romance sounds. Morphologically, Old French is characterized by a two-case nominal declension system which, although not always formally distinct, allowed to some extent the differentiation of subject and non-subject functions. The word order of Old French was fairly fluid, but favoured structures with the verb in the second position. Alongside the Germanic vocabulary, Old French exploited its own processes of word-formation, possessing great variety in the number and use of its suffixes.

2. 'Middle French'

Of all the period labels, 'Middle French' is probably the most controversial. Usually a date in the first half of the 14th c. is taken as the *terminus a quo*, but there is less agreement as to its end-point, notably as to whether the 16th c. should be considered a separate period of 'Renaissance French'. Whatever the case, it is a period of significant change and restructuring of the language system, and of a growing national consciousness which had important linguistic repercussions.

The literature of the late Middle Ages is composed in French, which in the 14th c. means *francien* with a light *picard* colouring. Most of the early printed texts appeared in Latin, but gradually the use of French spread to official records and legal texts. In the south, Occitan continued to be the usual spoken language, but either French or Latin was used for written purposes and French gained ground in official documents. Outside France, however, French lost its influential position, for instance in southern Italy, Sicily, and Cyprus.

Some of the principal changes in the language may be summarized briefly. Phonologically, the period is marked by the levelling of Old French diphthongs and triphthongs, the lowering of nasal vowels, and the loss of final consonants. The spelling of Middle French came under the control of the *practiciens*, or legal clerks, who favoured an etymological spelling, essentially for the eye rather than the ear. As French pronunciation continued to evolve, this led to an ever-widening gap between sounds and letters. By the beginning of the Middle French period, the disintegration of the two-case nominal system was virtually complete. With this came increased use of determiners. Irregularities or variation of either verb stems or endings introduced by the 'blind' operation of sound change were removed by analogical reworking. Syntactically, there is an increase in Suject-Verb-Complement constructions, but Middle French sentences are typically loosely structured, showing, for instance, the separation of relatives and antecedents and unattached participle clauses. The vocabulary was enriched as required, especially with Latinisms, which sometimes form doublets with their 'popular' counterparts (e.g. *esmer/estimer*); borrowings from Italian also begin to feature, a fashion which reached its peak in the 16th c.

3. The Sixteenth Century

The 16th c. witnesses the spread of French to further domains such as theology, science, mathematics, and dialectic, and early attempts to analyse and describe the language with the first *grammars of French published in France. Despite the unrest caused by wars with Italy and the Holy Roman

Empire and outbreaks of civil war, the political unification of France proceeded. In the south, French slowly gained ground with the literate minority, although the number of speakers remained very small. In the north, French increasingly rivalled Latin in official documents. A series of royal edicts from 1490 promoted the use of French in legal proceedings, the most famous of which, the Ordonnances de Villers-Cotterêts of 1539, prescribed that all deeds and court proceedings were to be recorded henceforth 'en langage maternel françois et non aultrement'. Abroad, French continued to be employed by the aristocracy and for trade and diplomacy.

Early discussions of French focused on the need to give it stability and rules to lend it the dignity of Latin. It was believed that one way to 'improve' French was through lexical innovation, with the doctrine of *richesse* typifying attitudes to language; there was, therefore, an openness to neologisms, archaisms, dialect terms, calques, and borrowings. Early in the century there was also a positive attitude to Italianisms, but in the second half of the century the change of attitude is symbolized by Henri *Estienne's polemic against these borrowings.

During the century the relationship of French and Latin permeated much linguistic thought, and early grammarians found it difficult to free themselves from Latin descriptive models [see GRAMMARS]. The question of the degree to which French should depend on its ancestor also surfaced in the debate on spelling reforms. Despite the attempts of reformers (such as Louis *Meigret) to introduce a phonologically based spelling system for French, the traditional etymological spelling showing family relations, morphological function, and differentiating homonyms dominated, as represented in Robert *Estienne's French–Latin dictionary of 1539/40 [see DICTIONARIES, 1]. Nevertheless, some simplification of orthography was achieved, and the cedilla, acute accent on final close *e*, and apostrophe became established.

The use of French by writers in the 16th c., especially the first half, is equally typified by Latin influence, encouraged at least in part through the work of translators of Latin into French [see TRANSLATION, 1]. Not only is the lexicon full of learned material, there was also direct imitation of Latin constructions. This, however, abated as the century progressed, so that even before *Malherbe's arrival at court at the beginning of the 17th c., the use of French was tending towards greater independence from Latin and clarity of expression.

4. Seventeenth and Eighteenth Centuries

The 17th and 18th c. are the period of classical and neoclassical French. The rise of absolutism, culminating in the reign of *Louis XIV, is paralleled by increased regimentation and codification of the language in the 17th c. In the 18th c., with the decline of the influence of the court and the rise of the bourgeoisie during a period of wars and financial crises under Louis XV, there came some relaxation of linguistic control, especially as regards the lexicon, but on the whole the entire period is characterized by the establishment of the written norms of standard French, essentially unchanged to the present day. The influence of Latin continued to wane, and dialect speakers were increasingly stigmatized. In the north of France the upper classes normally spoke French, whilst the lower classes either used French with a regional colouring or were bilingual in French and dialect. In the south the use of French continued to spread, especially in towns. From 1714 French was adopted in international treaties. Its prestige abroad is reflected in the essay subject set for a prize offered by the Berlin Academy in 1782: 'Qu'est-ce qui a rendu la langue française universelle?' The 17th c. was also the first period of French *colonization, with settlement in Canada, Louisiana, the West Indies, Africa, and on the Indian continent.

The tone of much of the linguistic writing of the century is set by *Malherbe's annotations on the poetry of *Desportes. The ideal of quantity of terms characteristic of the 16th c. is replaced by one of quality of usage, so that the vocabulary is purified by the banishment of neologisms, archaisms, technical terms, and regionalisms, and syntax made more explicit and regular. The same desire to fix and purify the language is evident in the aims of the *Académie Française, founded in 1635. It is in the context of a climate of linguistic awareness, with discussion of language being common in the *salons and *cabinets* of the age, that we must view the *Remarques* of *Vaugelas, who established an élitist norm for good usage and laid the basis for much subsequent usage. Throughout the period every aspect of the language was codified, with very high demands made in terms of clarity and choice of the *mot juste*. While the essentials of modern French usage date from this period, the spoken language has continued to evolve, with the gap between the two media widening.

In classical and neoclassical French, spelling remained essentially etymological, but some reforms did gradually permeate usage. Sound changes included the dropping of h from pronunciation, the restoration of some final consonants, and the debate between the *ouïstes* and *non-ouïstes* as to the correct pronunciation of words like *chose* (versus *chouse*). Use of the past historic and imperfect subjunctive declined in speech. Above all, the syntax was dominated by concern for clarity and explicitness and the Subject-Verb-Complement word order was adopted as the norm. In some cases elaborate, not to say complex, rules were established.

5. Since the Revolution

The period from the Revolution to 1945 is marked by increased standardization and the loss of many dialects [see, however, PATOIS AND DIALECT WRITING].

Contemporary French dates from the end of World War II, a period when the French have felt the need to protect their language from Anglicisms and casual usage, and assert its role as a world language by promoting la *francophonie.

The Revolutionaries considered that a unified language would help achieve the political ideals of the *Revolution. Abbé *Grégoire was charged with establishing the extent of the knowledge of the language in France. Of an estimated population of 25 million, at least 6 million, mainly in the south, knew no French at all, and only 3 million were able to speak it correctly [see LITERACY]. The title of his report of 1794 is significant: *Sur la nécessité et les moyens d'anéantir les patois et d'universaliser l'usage de la langue française*. Since then, linguistic unification has been dramatic [see EDUCATION, 2c]. At the turn of the 20th c. Gilliéron and Edmont, aware of the rapid decline of the dialects, recorded them in the *Atlas linguistique de la France* (1902–10); since then further loss has occurred. With this has come the rise of regional varieties of French, French which differs little syntactically from the standard language, but has local terms and regional pronunciation. We should also not forget the minority languages spoken in France: Occitan, Breton [see BRITTANY], Flemish, Catalan, Corsican, and Basque. In 1951 the *Loi Deixonne* went some way towards protecting the study of Basque, Breton, Occitan, and Catalan by allowing them as optional subjects for the *baccalauréat*; in 1974 Corsican was added.

The period 1830–1918 was a second major period of French colonialism, with the establishment of a considerable empire in Africa, the Far East, and Oceania. French, as the language of the conqueror and the élite, became widely established. In the 20th c. much of this empire has been lost, but this has not necessarily entailed the demise of French [see FRANCOPHONIE]. Today, French is one of few languages spoken in all five continents, although there are few speakers left in Asia. Realistically, we may think of some 90–100 million native speakers of French world-wide, with some 200 million more using it as a second language. Its status ranges from that of official language used only by an élite, as in the 22 countries of Black *Africa south of the Sahara, through being widely used but not the official language, as in *Algeria, *Tunisia, and *Morocco, to being the native language as in *Quebec and parts of *Belgium and *Switzerland.

Whilst the speed of evolution has been slowed somewhat by normative grammar, the French language has changed since the Revolution. If the essential syntactic rules of correct written French have remained fairly constant, stylistic variants such as the use of *reprise* (i.e. the 'picking-up' of a substantive by a pronoun allowing greater freedom of word order) or the narrative imperfect have become more prevalent. Moreover, the spoken language shows marked differences, such as the reduction of negative *ne . . . pas* to simple *pas* or the avoidance of inversion, especially for interrogation, and in more informal registers the differences are even more pronounced. The vocabulary of Modern French has had to expand to meet new political, cultural, and technical needs. By far the most common sources of new words are derivations and compounds, which frequently make use of Latin and Greek elements. More controversial has been the influx of Anglo-American borrowings, which have engendered a series of adverse reactions from the purists—ranging from the satire of *Étiemble to legislation (the so-called *Loi Bas-Lauriol* (1975) proscribing the use of anglicisms in the description of products and political bodies). There have also been proposals throughout the 20th c. to reform and simplify French spelling, but if the past is anything to judge by, reformers will have a tough battle against French purism and conservatism.   [WA-B]

See M. K. Pope, *From Latin to Modern French* (1934); G. Price, *The French Language: Present and Past* (1971); P. Rickard, *A History of the French Language*, 2nd edn. (1989).

Hiver de force, L', see DUCHARME.

Hoaxes. J.-M. Quérard's *Les Supercheries littéraires dévoilées* (2nd edn., 1889) contains seven large volumes listing all manner of literary frauds. In a sense all the innumerable *memoir-novels, *epistolary novels, and similar works of the 18th c. could be regarded as hoaxes, which attempt to pass off fiction as truth. Sometimes, as in the case of the *Lettres portugaises* (if these are indeed the work of *Guilleragues), the trick was very effective, and one might speak of forgery. In the same way, while the use of *pseudonyms for tactical or other purposes did not take in the readers of *Candide* (attributed to 'le docteur Ralph') or *L'*Ingénu* (attributed to *Quesnel), the claim that *Holbach's *Le Christianisme dévoilé* was the work of *Boulanger was plausible enough.

The hoax proper, however, implies the desire to mock readers and critics by fooling them into taking a forgery as genuine. There have been a number of famous cases where this succeeded—together with others where the jury is still out. *Mérimée's *Théâtre de Clara Gazul* and *La Guzla* both took in competent judges (including Pushkin for the latter). In 1885 an improbably titled satirical spoof by Henri Beauclair and Gabriel Vicaire, *Déliquescences, poèmes décadents d'Adoré Floupette*, was taken seriously by some readers, as was Pierre *Louÿs's 'translation', *Les Chansons de Bilitis* (1894). *La Chasse spirituelle* (1949), published as a long-lost prose poem by *Rimbaud, was in reality a *pastiche by two actors, Madame Akakia-Viala (Marie-Antoinette Allévy) and Nicolas Bataille; apparently unintentionally, they hoodwinked a number of connoisseurs. More recently, Romain *Gary tricked the French literary public by winning the Prix Goncourt for a second time under the name of the mysterious Émile Ajar; arguably

this was a case of pseudonymy rather than a hoax [see also VIAN; NUGUET].   [PF]

HOCQUENGHEM, Guy (1946–88). French novelist and essayist. At the forefront of *gay activism in the 1970s, he helped found the Front Homosexuel d'Action Révolutionnaire in 1971 and published polemical essays, including *Le Désir homosexuel* (1972) and *La Dérive homosexuelle* (1977). His beliefs on sexual liberation were tied to radical politics. In his five novels he explored the condition of the outsider, experimenting with the historical novel in *La Colère de l'agneau* (1985) and *Les Voyages et aventures extraordinaires du frère Angélo* (1988). His masterpiece, *Ève* (1987), written when he was dying from an AIDS-related disease, uses the biblical myth to reflect on the status and achievement of the gay artist.   [CFR]

HOLBACH, Paul-Henri Thiry, baron d' (1723–89). Atheist and materialist philosopher. Born in Germany, he was brought up in France by an uncle whose title and fortune he inherited. He had an excellent education, culminating in a stay in Leiden, a centre of new scientific thought. Settling in Paris in 1749, he became the 'maître d'hôtel de la philosophie', generously entertaining visitors from all over Europe in his town house in the rue Royale and his country house at Le Grandval. He was very close to *Diderot and made an important contribution to the *Encyclopédie*, mainly in the fields of chemistry and metallurgy. In Paris he was, with *Naigeon, the centre of a workshop for the production of anti-Christian propaganda, editing *clandestine manuscripts (*Fréret, *Boulainviller, *Du Marsais, *Boulanger, etc.), translating the works of English free-thinkers, and composing original pamphlets and treatises. 'Il pleut des bombes dans la maison du Seigneur', Diderot wrote of this activity in 1768.

Almost all Holbach's own writings were published anonymously or under other names (e.g. that of Boulanger). Before 1770 he wrote or collaborated on several critiques of Christianity and other religions, notably *Le Christianisme dévoilé* (1766) and *La Contagion sacrée* (1768); these continue the free-thinking tradition of the *libertins, pushing it towards an intransigent, scientific atheism. A second group of works, beginning with the famous *Système de la nature* (1770; summarized in *Le Bon Sens*, 1770) and including *Le Système social* (1773) and *La Morale universelle* (1776), expose a global, materialist philosophy of nature. All phenomena are explained in terms of matter and movement, free will and the immortality of the soul are declared to be illusory, and politics and ethics are placed on a new, natural foundation. Holbach is not an elegant or subtle writer. Diderot mocked his friend's ponderousness, and Goethe wondered that his 'grey', 'deathlike' writing could have attracted devotees, but for all its literary failings, his great body of work played a vital role in the movement of ideas of the late 18th c.

[PF]

Homais, Monsieur. Comic yet sinister chemist in Flaubert's *Madame Bovary*; a memorable caricature of the liberal Voltairean bourgeoisie of the 19th c.

HOMER, see CLASSICAL INFLUENCES; QUERELLE DES ANCIENS ET DES MODERNES.

Homme approximatif, L', see TZARA.

Homme aux quarante écus, L' (1768). Satirical narrative by *Voltaire, mainly attacking *Physiocrat proposals for a single land tax, but incidentally scattering barbs in all directions.

Homme de la pampa, L', see SUPERVIELLE.

Homme-machine, L', see LA METTRIE.

Homme qui rit, L' (1869). Novel by Victor *Hugo, set in late 17th-c. England. Full of Hugolian archetypes, this grotesque romance seems to reflect the promise and the failure of revolutionary ideals that shaped 19th-c. French political history. The hero, Gwynplaine, mutilated by order of the king, has had a smile carved into his face so that he will not be recognized as the heir to a nobleman who refused to accept a Restoration monarchy after the fall of Cromwell's republic. When he discovers his identity, Gwynplaine gives a moving speech to the House of Lords, pleading the cause of the people. The grimace causes the audience to dissolve into hilarity, and the novel ends with the suggestion of Gwynplaine's suicide. The mixture of satire and romance, comedy and tragedy, grotesque and sublime recalls the aesthetic programme of Hugo's preface to *Cromwell. [SN]

Homme rapaillé, L', see MIRON.

Homme révolté, L', see CAMUS, A.

Hommes de bonne volonté, Les. The largest of the *romans-fleuves*, consisting of 27 volumes published by Jules *Romains between 1932 and 1946. Six of these volumes (19–24) first appeared in the USA between 1941 and 1944. However, it differs from other serial novels in character as well as scale. For example, Romains does not use the laws of heredity, as in Zola's *Rougon-Macquart* cycle, or the personality and career of a single hero, as in Romain Rolland's *Jean-Christophe*, but introduces the concept of *Unanimism. This is the idea that social life and individual life are dominated by human groups or crowds: the city, the army, the congregation, the mob, etc. So Romains concentrates more on social groupings than on an individual hero. This also means, as he makes clear in his preface, that the structure of his vast fictional creation is not linear, characters and events are not necessarily linked, and episodes may sometimes lead nowhere. The broad range of characters and incidents is designed to give the reader a greater sense of the collective life of society, and Romains claimed that a clear, straight-forward style would encourage a very wide readership.

Les Hommes de bonne volonté covers a precise quarter-century from 6 October 1908 to 7 October 1933. The collective life of Paris presides over all, with particularly memorable descriptions of the city in 1908, 1918, 1922, 1928, 1933. The pace of the work, though leisurely throughout, inevitably varies. For example, the opening volume only covers a single day in Paris and its environs, whereas the first nine months of 1933 are covered by the last three volumes. In the intervening pages there is a picture of the different social classes, from aristocrats, through industrialists, speculators, etc., to manual workers. Political and artistic life are both portrayed in considerable detail. As regards the history of the period, there is much about pre-war disquiet, post-war cynicism, *Marxism, *fascism, and the political and ideological conflicts of the 1930s. *World War I itself is very much the centre-piece of the work. Volumes 15 and 16, *Prélude à Verdun* and *Verdun*, remain the best-known section of Romains's novel, although he had no direct experience of warfare. His Unanimist theories lent themselves particularly well to the portrayal of war, even though he was now linking characters and episodes more conventionally than had been his original intention. [JC]

Homosexual Writing, see GAY AND LESBIAN WRITING.

Honnêteté. The French tradition of courtly behaviour was renewed in the Renaissance period under the influence of Castiglione and Italian politeness [see COURTOISIE]. By the 17th c. the word *courtoisie* was old-fashioned, but the values it implied continued to mould not only upper-class social behaviour, but also writing. Literature became increasingly detached from humanist learning (heavy, erudite volumes in Latin), and aligned itself more with the habits and expectations of polite society. Writers were under pressure (which they sometimes resisted) to be people of good company, clear, entertaining, and witty.

The values associated with *courtoisie* might be expressed in the 17th and 18th c. by several different words. *Civilité* did not generally enjoy any great prestige; it signified the fairly elementary polite behaviour which was essential for social intercourse, but could be learnt by anyone; in a tradition going back to *Erasmus, it was inculcated in popular manuals such as those of *Courtin and *La Salle. *Urbanité*, a more exalted concept, was felt to be a Latin borrowing, and never established itself as 'urbanity' did in Britain. The two essential words were *honnêteté* and *politesse*, both of which designated an ideal of élite behaviour. Between them, they generated a sizeable literature.

It was in the mid-17th c. that the theory of *honnêteté* and the image of the *honnête homme* were elaborated. The most successful work, *Faret's *L'Honnête Homme* (1630), was much indebted to

Hopil

Castiglione; however, its subtitle ('l'art de plaire à la cour') indicates that its author, of bourgeois origins, is concerned with social advancement as much as with polite behaviour. A less pragmatic approach is found in the works which relate to the *salons, which until about 1660 were a more important centre of politeness than the court. Of particular importance are the long novels of the period, from *L'*Astrée* to *Clélie*; these were seen by contemporaries as a reflection of the behaviour and conversation of polite circles. Later in the century *Méré, in his *Conversations* and *Discours*, gave a clear account of what his society meant by *honnêteté*: it is both moral and aesthetic, involving apparent modesty, naturalness, taste, and wit. For Méré, as for *La Rochefoucauld, true *honnêteté* is a rare achievement, for which noble birth is a necessary but not sufficient condition. Similarly, while the courtier was often seen as the model to be imitated, life at court did not always match up to the high standards of a Méré.

Honnêteté did not, therefore, have a great deal to do with honesty; it was an aristocratic ideal of social performance. Nevertheless, there were those who continued to believe that the *honnête homme* ought to be an 'homme d'honneur', that morality was more important than distinction. This is a central theme of Molière's Le *Misanthrope*, where the Alceste–Philinte couple provided a term of reference for a debate that continued over the following century or more, generally in relation to the term *politesse*. Politeness, which could refer not only to individual behaviour but to a broader notion of civilization, was widely thought of as a French speciality. As such it was often mocked abroad, and in France itself was the subject of endless debate. There were treatises and essays from writers such as *Bellegarde, *Vaumorière, *Trublet, or Madame de *Lambert, but the subject also figures prominently in many other works. *La Bruyère, for all his pessimism, offered a positive view of politeness as a form of altruistic behaviour, a conquest over our savage nature. *Marivaux, in his essays, plays, and novels, notably La *Vie de Marianne*, depicts a politeness which is essentially moral and has little to do with rank. Going further in the same line, *Duclos and even Jean-Jacques *Rousseau try to imagine a politeness worthy of a less hierarchical and artificial society. But *politesse* was too much associated with refinement for this attempt to succeed. The following century saw the term reduced to its current, more limited meaning; literature, meanwhile, ceased to be so closely tied to élite society and to the notion of politeness. [PF]

See M. Magendie, *La Politesse mondaine et les théories de l'honnêteté en France, au XVIIe siècle, de 1600 à 1660* (1926); P. France, *Politeness and its Discontents* (1992).

HOPIL, Claude (*c.*1585–after 1633). Poet about whom little is known, but whose unusually intense mystical canticles (*Les Divins Élancements d'amour*, 1629; *Les Doux Vols de l'âme amoureuse de Jésus*, 1629) have attracted considerable attention in recent years. In striking negative images he attempts to express the inexpressible, and his 'Cantique sur l'indifférence' seems to prefigure the *Quietism of the end of the century. [PF]

Horace. Tragedy by Pierre *Corneille, first performed 1640, published 1641 with a dedication to *Richelieu. Rome, at the beginning of its expansion, is at war with the neighbouring city of Alba. To resolve the conflict, the champions of Rome, Horace and his two brothers, fight the champions of Alba, Curiace and his two brothers, even though Horace is married to Curiace's sister, Sabine, and Curiace betrothed to Horace's sister, Camille. Horace brings Rome victory by killing all three Curiaces, but is then provoked by the taunts of the grief-stricken Camille into killing her. The final act is a trial in which Horace is defended by his father and pardoned by the Roman king, Tulle, because of his supreme usefulness to the state. Even so, his honour is irreparably tarnished. *Horace* is one of Corneille's most tragic plays. [PF]

'Horla, Le' (1886–7). A story of horror and madness by *Maupassant, one of his principal contributions to the literature of the *Fantastic.

Horn, see ANGLO-NORMAN LITERATURE, 3a.

Hôtel de Bourgogne, L'. The principal *theatre of Paris in the 17th c. Situated on the right bank, it was built in 19548 for the *Confrérie de la Passion, who performed *mystery plays there during the 16th c., and then let it out to various companies, above all the Comédiens du Roi. Here, in far from convenient surroundings, *Racine's tragedies were performed. Subsequently it passed to the *Comédie-Italienne.

HOTMAN, François de (1524–90). This Protestant jurist and polemicist was the author of one of the most effective pamphlets written during the *Wars of Religion, the *Epître envoyée au tigre de France*, which was directed against the cardinal de *Lorraine. Hotman is much more famous, however, for the *Franco-Gallia*, which is one of the most significant Protestant contributions to political theory. It was probably composed at least in part before the *St Bartholomew's Day Massacre of 1572, but its publication in 1573 was particularly opportune since it enabled the Huguenots to challenge the power of the now discredited monarchy. [JJS]

HOUARI, Leïla (b. 1958). Moroccan-born novelist brought up from the age of 7 in Belgium. In *Zeida de nulle part* (1985) she depicts the identity crisis of an adolescent girl torn between her desire for personal freedom and loyalty to her immigrant parents. Similar cross-cultural themes are explored in a collection of short stories, *Quand tu verras la mer. . .* (1988). [AGH]

HOUDAR(T) DE LA MOTTE, see LA MOTTE.

HOUDETOT, Élisabeth-Sophie, comtesse de (1730–1813). Sister-in-law of Madame d'*Épinay, remembered as the object of J.-J. Rousseau's unavailing passion which he poured into *La *Nouvelle Héloïse*. Her *amant en titre* was *Saint-Lambert.

HOUDON, Jean-Antoine (1741–1828). Sculptor who made a series of terracotta busts of *grands hommes*, including *Diderot and *Napoleon. His best known are those of *Voltaire, made from a few sittings after Voltaire had admired Houdon's bust of *Molière at the Comédie-Française. Stark naturalism and compelling concern with anatomical accuracy are evident in his *Écorché* (1767).   [JPC]

Hours, Books of, see LIVRES D'HEURES.

Household Management Treatises. Works on all aspects of domestic economy, including cookery, have enjoyed continuing popularity down the centuries; books such as those of *Brillat-Savarin have achieved literary celebrity. Their interest for linguistic and cultural history has given them particular importance for the medieval period. The largest category is culinary. The earliest in French is found in an Anglo-Norman manuscript (late 13th c.), entitled *Coment l'en deit fere viande e claree*. Much more considerable are Taillevent's *Viandier* (1326–95), a handbook for the professional cook written by Charles V's master cook, and Chiquart's *Fait de cuisine* (1420), written as a record of lavish feasts provided by the master cook of Amadeus VIII, duke of Savoy. Intended for masters of the craft, not mere householders, these are *aide-mémoires*: quantities and cooking-methods are left undefined. The Ménagier de Paris (c.1393), on the other hand, includes recipes as just one of a range of household skills—everything from veterinary hints to gardening—essential to his inexperienced young bride; his recipes, many of them copied from the *Viandier*, are revised to make them more informative.   [JHMT]

HOUSSAYE, Arsène (1815–96). An outstanding example of the literary entrepreneur created by the rapid expansion of the *press in the 19th c., Houssaye practised every literary genre, but it was in art history and criticism that he made his most significant contribution. A member during the 1830s of the literary and artistic Bohemia of *Romanticism, Houssaye founded *L'Artiste*, which quickly became a focus for 'l'*art pour l'art'. Appointed in 1849 director of the Comédie-Française, the Romantic bohemian became a Second Empire dandy, but maintained his commitment to the Romantic dramatists of his youth, in particular the exiled *Hugo, whose works he staged despite official disapproval. He was the dedicatee of *Baudelaire's *Le Spleen de Paris*.   [JK]

HUE DE ROTELANDE, 12th-c. romance writer, see ANGLO-NORMAN LITERATURE, 3a.

HUET, Pierre-Daniel (1630–1721). Huet has frequently been referred to as the most learned man of his age. The clearest 17th-c. precursor of the following century's encyclopedic intellectual mode, he worked in fields as diverse as theology and astronomy, and was the outstanding contemporary Hellenist and Hebraist. As a young man he frequented the *salons. He later chose an ecclesiastical career and was named bishop of Avranches in 1692. Huet often used his vast erudition and knowledge of antiquity for the defence of modern literature, notably in his celebration of the novel, *De l'origine des romans* (1670), published as a preface to Lafayette's *Zayde*.   [JDeJ]

HUGO, Victor-Marie (1802–85). Leader of the *Romantic school between 1830 and 1850, he dominated 19th-c. French literature with the prodigious flow and bold originality of his work until his death. During his 20 years of voluntary exile in the Channel Islands under the *Second Empire, he symbolized the promise of spiritual regeneration and the humanitarian ideals of *republicanism, and was greeted upon his return to France as a revered national patriarch. *Flaubert called him the 'immense vieux'. Translated into many languages before his death and read by a popular as well as an intellectual public, Victor Hugo's work has had a wide-ranging influence.

    Born in Besançon, he had a tumultuous childhood. His father, Joseph-Léopold-Sigisbert Hugo, an officer in the Republican army, met his mother, Sophie Trébuchet, a strong-minded young Breton woman, after being sent to help quell an uprising in the Vendée in 1793. Married in 1797, they had three sons: Abel, 1798; Eugène, 1799; and Victor, 1802; but the marriage was fraught with tension. Sophie resented uprooting her family to follow her husband, whose status in Napoleon's army eventually rose to that of general and count as he moved from France to Corsica, and, with the protection of Joseph Bonaparte, to Italy and Spain. Both parents developed other attachments. Twice Sophie took the children by coach through war-ravaged landscapes to join her husband: once to Italy in 1807 and once, more memorably for the precocious child, to Spain in 1811 with a royal escort; but despite Joseph Bonaparte's efforts to reconcile the couple, Sophie returned to Paris in 1812, where she took charge of the education of her children, preparing them for careers as men of letters.

    By the age of 13 Victor had already begun writing stories and classical tragedies; at 16 he received first prize from the Académie des *Jeux Floraux at Toulouse for an ode entitled 'Le Rétablissement de la statue de Henri IV' and had written a draft of his first novel, *Bug-Jargal*. In 1819 he and his brothers founded a royalist literary journal, *Le Conservateur* *littéraire*, which appeared regularly from December 1819 until March 1821. Victor, whose learning and energy were already extraordinary, was the major contributor with literary criticism, the drama review, and numerous works of his own. In 1822 he published a volume of *Odes*, for which he was awarded a royal pension, enabling him to marry Adèle Foucher. Their first child, Léopold, died after a few months. They had four others: Léopoldine, 1824; Charles, 1826; François-Victor (the translator of *Shakespeare), 1828; and Adèle, 1830. During these years as Hugo acquired a critical mastery of classical French verse forms, he read the German and English Romantics, discovered Shakespeare, and became closely associated with the conservative *Cénacle of *La Muse française* headed by *Nodier. In 1825 Hugo's stature was such that he was invited to the coronation of Charles X at Reims; but he had already begun to connect modernist practice in the arts with revolutionary politics. The prefaces to the five editions of the *Odes*, which became the *Odes et ballades* in 1826 and 1828, reflect the shift towards republicanism that occurred after the death of his mother and reconciliation with his Bonapartist father.

By 1826 the Hugo salon had replaced Nodier's as a vital centre for Romantic artists and writers. The period 1826–30 was one of intense creativity. *Sainte-Beuve praised the *Odes et ballades* in the liberal newspaper, *Le *Globe*, and became a regular of the Hugo entourage. In 1827 Hugo read the preface to *Cromwell* to his friends. This anti-classical text, demanding the inclusion of the grotesque and the ugly for a genuinely contemporary notion of the beautiful, became a founding document for French Romantic theory. In 1829 he published *Les Orientales*, a virtuoso collection of poems demonstrating the originality of his control over a wide range of verse forms, and one month later a deeply moving novel against capital punishment, *Le Dernier Jour d'un condamné à mort*, written from the point of view of the condemned man. The culmination of Hugo's meteoric rise to fame came in October 1830 with the performance of *Hernani* at the Comédie-Française. Fighting broke out on the opening night between the defenders of classicism and Hugo's friends, strategically planted in the audience. The event heralded the ascension of the Romantic avant-garde to aesthetic dominance.

The year 1830 marks a turning-point both in French political history and in Hugo's personal life. After the birth of her fifth child Adèle Hugo withdrew from her husband and began cultivating an intimate relationship with Sainte-Beuve that lasted, off and on, for many years. In 1833 Hugo himself began a liaison that would become a lifetime commitment with Juliette Drouet, a minor actress in his play *Lucrèce Borgia*. Hugo and his wife remained friends throughout their marriage, but they were no longer the ideal family of the 1820s painted by Louis Boulanger. The lyric collections, *Les Feuilles d'automne* (1831) and *Les Chants du crépuscule* (1835), contain poems commemorating Hugo's attachment to his family and to Juliette; those published later in the decade, *Les Voix intérieures* (1837) and *Les Rayons et les ombres* (1840), focus more on the metaphysical nature of poetic consciousness than on the personal love lyric.

With the performance of *Hernani*, Hugo became a leading dramatist under the *July Monarchy. Despite the censorship of *Le Roi s'amuse* in 1832 for its cruel depiction of François Ier, the royal family offered Hugo his own playhouse, the Théâtre de la Renaissance. It opened in 1838 with *Ruy Blas*, his most successful play. In 1831 he published *Notre-Dame de Paris—1482*) a dark, multi-layered novel set in 15th-c. Paris. The descriptions of the cathedral revolutionized contemporary attitudes toward medieval architecture and caused the creation of a Commission of Historic Monuments to save France's buildings from further destruction. Re-editions of his early novels, *Le Dernier Jour d'un condamné à mort*, *Han d'Islande*, and *Bug-Jargal*, followed the publication of *Notre-Dame de Paris*, and a new novel against capital punishment based on a real event, *Claude Gueux*, appeared in 1834. Hugo was nominated to the Légion d'Honneur in 1837 and elected to the Académie Française in 1841.

In the 1840s Hugo's political ambitions caused a lessening of his poetic output. In 1845 he was named peer of France. But several events prepared the way for a major change in his life. In 1843 his drama *Les *Burgraves* was booed off the stage after five performances. Later in the same year his adored daughter, Léopoldine, drowned in a sailing accident. In 1845 the recently elected peer caused a national scandal when caught *in flagrante* with Léonie d'Aunet. After the fall of the July Monarchy in June 1848, Hugo was elected *député* from Paris to the Assemblée Constituante and began publication of a newspaper, *L'Événement*, in which he supported the candidature of Louis-Napoléon Bonaparte for the presidency of the new Republic. In May 1849 he was re-elected, but to a conservative Assembly, where, isolated from both the Left and the Right, he made impassioned but ineffectual speeches on poverty, universal suffrage, freedom of the press, lay education, and capital punishment. By February 1851 he openly opposed the government of the future *Napoleon III, fleeing to Belgium to avoid arrest after the *coup d'état* of 2 December. After publishing a virulent pamphlet, *Napoléon le petit*, denouncing the usurper, he moved his family to the Channel Islands, first Jersey and then Guernsey in 1855, where he remained until the emperor's abdication in 1870.

During the exile years Hugo wrote his greatest poetry: the powerful satirical verse of *Les *Châtiments* (1853), the personal and metaphysical poems of *Les *Contemplations* (1856), *La Fin de Satan* and *Dieu*, the epic poems of *La *Légende des siècles* (1859), and the erotic and pastoral lyrics of *Les Chansons des rues et des bois* (1865). He also finished the great social novel Les *Misérables (1862) begun in 1845, wrote his essay on the nature of genius, *William Shakespeare* (1864), and two other visionary social novels, Les *Travailleurs de la mer* (1866) and *L'*Homme qui rit* (1869). His popularity in France was unparalleled, even after other literary movements had displaced Romanticism.

When Hugo returned to France in 1870 he was elected to the new conservative Assembly in 1871, but resigned after a few months. Although opposed to the *Commune, he sheltered fleeing *communards* in his house in Belgium. *L'Année terrible* (1872) captures the complexity of his feelings surrounding these events. He returned to Hauteville House in Guernsey to write his last great novel, *Quatrevingt-Treize* (1874), describing the civil war in the *Vendée. When Hugo was elected senator in 1876, he asked for amnesty for the supporters of the Commune. A second series of *La Légende des siècles* and *L'Art d'être grand-père* appeared in 1877. After a stroke in 1878 Hugo virtually stopped writing, but previously finished works continued to appear: *La Pitié suprême* (1879), *L'Âne* and *Religion des religions* (1880), *Les Quatre Vents de l'esprit* (1881), *Torquemada* (1882), and a final series of *La Légende des siècles* (1883). Hugo died in 1885 and was entombed in the Pantheon after a state funeral attended by 2 million people and delegates from every country in Europe. Posthumous publications include: *La Fin de Satan* (1886), *Le Théâtre en liberté* (1888), *Dieu* (1891), *Les Années funestes* (1898), *Dernière Gerbe* (1902), *Océan* and *Tas de pierres* (1942).

From his earliest writings Hugo insisted on the social responsibility of the writer, and after 1850 conceived of himself as a spiritual guide, whose vocation it was to reveal the providential order underlying personal and historical events. He interpreted his own life as exemplary of the fate of a collective, historical self, and was not adverse to substituting dates of symbolic significance on his manuscripts to make the links in the mythopoetic story clear. Many of Hugo's prefaces as well as the allegorical structuring of his works point to the way the past inhabits and animates the present. *Littérature et philosophie mêlées* (1834) was one of his first efforts to combine writings from the early royalist period of 1819 with those of 1830 to show the invisible connections linking them.

Like other Romantic historians, Hugo saw the Revolution as a major turning-point in his progressivist concept of history; but he never became reconciled to the excesses of the Terror and the violence of mass uprisings. The startling discontinuities in his own work seem to underscore the arbitrariness of his idealizing claims. As history repeatedly wipes away the redemptive design, every century must find a prophet to reconstruct the providential story in a language appropriate to its time. The birth of democracy is reflected in the hybrid forms that typify Hugo's work—the grotesque hero with the sublime soul, the stylistic blending of familiar and lofty diction, history as an amalgam of folklore and erudition. His formal innovations in all genres—the broken rhythms of the alexandrine, the vast new lexicon of common and proper names, and the visionary treatment of metaphor; the symbolic complexity of theatrical set and costume design; or the treatment of the novel as a total work blending drama, philosophy, epic, and history—are meant to reflect the confusion and potential freedom of the post-Revolutionary era.

If Hugo's Utopian view of history has met with derision, his modernist heirs recognize the enormous importance of his contribution to the revitalization of poetic forms. As *Valéry put it 50 years after his death, Hugo's greatness can be judged by the controversy his work continues to inspire.   [SN]

See J. Massin's 18-vol. edition of the *Œuvres complètes* (1967–70) for a wealth of informed commentary on all of Hugo's works; J. Gaudon, *Le Temps de la contemplation* (1969); A. Ubersfeld, *Le Roi et le bouffon* (1974); S. Nash, 'Les Contemplations' of Victor Hugo: An Allegory of the Creative Process (1976); V. Brombert, *Victor Hugo and the Visionary Novel* (1984).

HUGUENIN, Jean-René (1936–62). French novelist. Fame came with his first and last novel *La Côte sauvage* (1960), a subtly contained but atmospheric treatment of a compelling brother–sister attraction in a Breton setting. His telling *Journal* (1964) expresses the aspirations of his new Romanticism and bears on his founding of *Tel Quel with *Sollers and *Hallier. Most of his journalistic articles are brought together in *Une autre jeunesse* (1965).   [DAS]

Huguenot. Name given to Calvinists and to *Protestants in general. It apparently derives from the German *Eidgenossen* (confederates), which relates to a medieval Swiss federation for mutual defence.

Huis clos, see SARTRE.

Humanism. This term, first coined in the 18th c., is used, broadly speaking, in two different senses which it is important not to confuse. In *Renaissance studies it refers to a scholarly movement devoted to the thoroughgoing revival of the writings of classical antiquity and embodied in a pedagogical programme designed to supersede the logic-based *scholasticism of the later Middle Ages [see CLASSICAL INFLUENCES]. The term *humanista* was coined in the late 15th c. from the classical Latin phrase *studia humanitatis* to designate students and scholars who chose this kind of study. As the name implies, a central aim of such 'humanists' was to promote a more human-based approach to learning, including a cultivation of eloquence for practical purposes and a study of disciplines such as history and moral philosophy. But this did not entail an abandonment of Christian belief: indeed, most humanists—especially in northern Europe—were deeply concerned to demonstrate the compatibility of ancient culture with Christian faith and values. In modern times 'humanism' has been used, by contrast, to refer to a philosophical outlook in which man is assigned value in his own right, and hence normally implies an atheistic or at least an agnostic frame of reference: thus, for example, *Sartre's claim that 'l'existentialisme est un humanisme'.

[TC]

Humanité, L'. Founded by *Jaurès in 1904, France's leading left-wing daily newspaper has had a distinguished but controversial history. In 1905 it became the mouthpiece of the SFIO (Socialist Party) and published articles from a wide range of left-wing politicians and intellectuals (*Guesde, Paul Lafargue, Edouard Vaillant, etc.) In 1920, following the separation of the *Socialists from the Communists, L'Humanité became the national daily of the PCF. Banned on 26 August 1939, it became an underground publication in 1944. In the euphoria of the Liberation its circulation rose to over 400,000. Its decline—mirroring in part that of the PCF—has been persistent: with circulation down to 65,000, L'Humanité feared imminent closure in 1993.   [MP]

HUMBERT, Marie-Thérèse (b. 1940). Mauritian-born novelist, resident in France since 1968. Her first novel, A l'autre bout de moi (1979), was a succès de librairie and was awarded the Prix Littéraire des Lectrices d'Elle. Although it was to have been situated in France originally, this novel's strength is its vivid, if at times over-written, evocation of the landscape and ethnic mix of Mauritius. It portrays in particular the unhappy social position of Franco-Mauritians of mixed race, dramatized in the story of twin girls from this stricken background. Narrated in the first person (by one of the twins), this tale of ambivalent self-rejection seems to elucidate complex and oppressive ethnic divisions. Le Volkameria (1982) and its sequel, Une robe d'écume et de vent (1989), also have a confined island setting. However, as the territoire d'outre-mer in question is entirely fictional, these novels are not anchored in the reality of a particular place and time and thus seem strangely dream-like. They retain the strongly atmospheric writing of the first novel, but claustrophobic family drama has entirely displaced the sociopolitical dimension of Humbert's earlier writing.

[MG]

Hundred Days, The, see NAPOLEON, 2.

Hundred Years War, The. A phrase popularized in the mid-19th-c. to describe a series of Anglo-French wars between 1337 and 1453, now seen as a distinct phase of a longer rivalry as the modern nations of France and England grew out of the feudal, family 'empires' that preceded them. In this perspective the war's origins lie in the Norman Conquest of 1066 and the Angevin inheritance that made medieval English kings also vassals of the Capetians.

It was the definition and exercise of their rights that principally led to war in 1337.

In return for territorial concessions, Henry III of England in the Treaty of Paris (1259) acknowledged holding his lands in France by liege homage. But as lawyers in the late 13th c., under the influence of Roman law, formulated a clearer doctrine of sovereignty, the relationship changed. In practice, the development of the Parlement of Paris as an appellate court and close supervision in the field severely circumscribed the English king's freedom of action as duc de Guyenne and caused endless disputes with Crown officials.

These developments provoked two initial conflicts (1294–1303 and 1324–7), during which Guyenne was twice confiscated and overrun by French forces. Anglo-French ill feeling was also engendered by a French alliance with Scotland, rivalry in the Netherlands, piracy, and naval warfare. The extinction of the *Capetian dynasty (1328) allowed Edward III to claim the French throne, though he afterwards temporarily recognized the election of Philippe de Valois. In 1337, after more frustrated diplomacy and mutual recrimination, Guyenne was confiscated again. Edward III retaliated by assuming the title 'king of France' and exercising 'sovereign' rights in Guyenne.

The conflict which followed can be divided into several phases. Initially it went badly for Edward III, but between 1340 and 1360 English arms enjoyed spectacular success (Sluys, 1340; Crécy, 1346; Poitiers, 1356), whilst warfare in provinces like Brittany attracted soldiers eager for personal enrichment. The capture of the French king Jean II at Poitiers represented a nadir in French fortunes. Widespread social unrest and financial hardship followed as the country struggled to find the king's ransom and humiliating territorial concessions were agreed. The Treaty of Brétigny (1360), however, marked the beginning of a slow revival. Its momentum increased under Charles V (1364–80), though the effort to eject the English completely proved impossible. The war was punctuated by truces as exhaustion set in on both sides.

Domestic divisions under Charles VI (1380–1422) allowed the English to renew their offensive in 1415 [see ARMAGNACS AND BURGUNDIANS]. At Agincourt, French forces suffered another catastrophic defeat. Henry V overran Normandy and formed a powerful alliance with Burgundy. By the Treaty of Troyes (1420) a double monarchy was established: the dauphin was disinherited; his sister, Catherine, married the English king; and succession to both kingdoms was entailed on their issue. But after Henry's premature death (1422) the dauphin as 'king of Bourges', Charles VII, slowly recovered the initiative, thanks to the intervention of *Jeanne d'Arc. In 1435 the Burgundians were reconciled and in 1436 Paris was recaptured. Although the English fought tenaciously in Normandy, adequate resources were lacking, whilst French military and financial reorganization allowed Charles VII to mount a decisive campaign in 1449–50. In 1453 Guyenne was finally conquered, effectively ending the war.

From an early point the conflict stimulated a wide range of literary expression. Military campaigns and individual feats of valour were celebrated in chivalric works, reaching their apogee in *Froissart's Chroniques. The lives of famous captains were also commemorated in a last flourishing of the *chanson de geste tradition. The darker side of war and its impact on ordinary people find sympathetic treatment in the poetry of Eustache *Deschamps, the Quadrilogue invectif of Alain *Chartier, and the realism of chroniclers like Jean de Venette or the *Bourgeois de Paris. Bitter laments came from loyal servants of the French crown, like Jean Jouvénal des Ursins, who savaged the royal administration for its shortcomings. Propaganda pieces and pamphlets also proliferated, as did treatises on the art of war (Honoré *Bouvet, *Christine de Pizan). 'Official historiography' enjoyed a particular vogue as the Valois kings continued the Capetian tradition of encouraging the monks of Saint-Denis to write the *Grandes Chroniques de France, until the last decades of the war.   [MJ]

> See C. Allmand, The Hundred Years War (1988); C. Sumption, The Hundred Years War, vol. I, Trial by Battle (1990).

Hunting. As a popular pastime of the nobility, it is hardly surprising that hunting in its various forms should play an important part in medieval fiction. Like tournaments, hunting scenes, whether involving falcons, hounds, or simply the bow and arrow, are extensively used in imaginative writing. Often, such episodes are purely decorative, without any real narrative function. Frequently, though, the hunt is both a social occasion and an opportunity for the demonstration of bravery and agility; and the locus of the hunt itself, the forest, offering the possibility of becoming separated from one's companions or entourage, provides an appropriate setting within which adventures (natural and supernatural) can readily arise. In some cases the pursuit of mythical or magical creatures may be traced back to folk-motifs common to many cultures. The value attached to falcons and hawks is amply demonstrated by the readiness with which they are presented (and received) as gifts; their symbolic importance is exemplified by their role in prophetic dreams and, on a less exalted level, in the use (notably in the *chansons de geste) of images concerning their rapidity, with which that of knights or their horses is habitually compared. In some contexts the hunt is also the occasion for bloodshed and murder, and can serve as an image for destructive sensuality.

As well as appearing in fictional texts, hunting gave rise to another form of literature. A number of, often highly technical, treatises on the subject survive; some, like the 14th-c. Livres du Roy Modus et de la Reine Ratio of *Henri de Ferrières (written for an aristocratic patron) and the very popular Livre de la chasse (1387–91) by Gaston III, comte de Foix (*Gaston Phébus), were originally composed in French and are elaborate expositions of the theory and practice of the chase; others, translations of Latin works such as Frederick II's De arte venandi cum avibus, or of the treatises on falconry by Alexander Medicus and King Dancus, provide further evidence that there was a demand for practical and instructive works on the subject written in French. Some of this material was also translated into other Romance languages. Treatises of this sort complement and confirm the detailed descriptions of hunting given in fiction, and they underline the growing use of the vernacular for didactic and scientific purposes in the later Middle Ages.   [DAT]

> See G. Tilander (ed.), Les Livres du Roy Modus et de la Royne Ratio (1932); G. Tillander (ed.), Gaston Phébus, Livre de la chasse (1971); La Chasse au moyen âge: actes du colloque de Nice, 1979 (1980).

Huon de Bordeaux. *Chanson de geste of the early 13th c., combining the theme of barons in revolt (Huon spends most of the 10,000-line text in exile) with marvels and faerie: his chief companion is Auberon, later to become the Shakespearean Oberon. The poem was extremely successful and soon became the core of an epic cycle, its immediate neighbours being Auberon (which serves as its prologue) and Esclarmonde (its sequel).   [SK]

Huron. Name given by the French to the tribes of Iroquois Indians living in parts of North America. In 18th-c. France 'le Huron' was the typical noble savage [see INGÉNU, L'].

Hussards, Les. Name given to a group of young right-wing French writers of the 1940s and 1950s, particularly Roger *Nimier, from whose novel Le Hussard bleu (1950) the group's name is derived, Antoine *Blondin, and Jacques *Laurent. The group, which also included Michel *Déon, Kléber Haedens, and Stephen Hecquet, was characterized by its rejection of the spirit of the Resistance and of the Fourth Republic and its antagonism to *Existentialism.   [NH]

HUYGHE, René (b. 1906). French art historian; professor of the psychology of art at the *Collège de France. His many monographs include studies of *Delacroix and *Van Gogh. Dissatisfied with the limitations of verbal language, Huyghe analysed the means of communication available to art and emphasized its power to create new expressive forms within its social context (Dialogue avec le visible, 1955). He interpreted the image as a dynamic projection of the unconscious (L'Art et l'âme, 1960), established correspondences between natural structures (the crystal, the spiral) and the archetypal forms of art, and believed that its development was informed by biological, psychic, and spiritual energies evolving towards an obscure and infinite goal (*Formes et forces*, 1971). [REG]

HUYSMANS, Joris-Karl (1848–1907). Though he first became known as a writer of *Naturalist fiction (*Marthe, histoire d'une fille*, 1876; *Les Sœurs Vatard*, 1879; 'Sac au dos', in *Les *Soirées de Medan*, 1880; *En ménage* 1881), Huysmans's first publication, *Le Drageoir à épices* (1874), was an experiment in non-Naturalist form which points forward to the *Decadent exercises of *À rebours* (1884), *En rade* (1887), and *Là-bas* (1891). His art criticism (collected in *L'Art moderne*, 1883, and *Certains*, 1889) shows the same sensitivity to the movement of contemporary culture, taste, and the market. Open initially to art and architecture which celebrates technological advance and the life of the modern city, it moves rapidly towards the masters of escape, dream and nightmare, mysticism and magic (Gustave *Moreau, Odilon *Redon, and Félicien *Rops).

Neurotic antagonism to contemporary society encouraged Huysmans's movement in the early 1890s towards the Catholic Church (*En route*, 1895): not the embryonic modernist movement, engaging sympathetically with the secular masses, but the traditionalist version reinstated by Vatican I (1870), rooted in the nostalgic and élitist cult of authority, superstitious and obscurantist. The misogyny at the centre of his earlier writing, expressed in a cruel and perverse eroticism, is transformed into the cult of female martyrs and saints committed to reparatory suffering, taking on death and disease in imitation of Christ to redeem the world (*Sainte Lydwine de Schiedam*, 1901). Only the Virgin Mary, the focus of Huysmans's devotion and the centre of the worship at Chartres which he exhaustively evokes in *La Cathédrale* (1898), escapes the humiliation of the feminine without which he appears unable to form any image of himself.

Huysmans's transition from Naturalism to *Symbolism and Catholicism can be variously viewed. It represents the political refusal of the desk-bound civil servant that Huysmans remained all his life to engage with the challenges of industrialization and democratization. It is an evasion into idealism that is linked with right-wing and regressive political factions. But it is also the fruitful recognition of the exhaustion of certain aesthetic options, particularly the rationalist and positivist strait-jacket of Naturalism, and it raises the possibility of new ways of writing and thinking. What most critics, however, agree on is Huysmans's tenacity in carrying over into his later writing his original Naturalist vision. This is both a weakness and a strength. It enables him to bring a vivid intensity of expression into the realms of the abstract and the ideal, but it also confines those realms within simple, restrictive, and conservative limits. [JB]

See R. Baldick, *The Life of J.-K. Huysmans* (1955).

Hymnes, see RONSARD.

Hymns (Medieval). The best preserved sub-genre of the medieval religious lyric, hymns became an integral part of the sung liturgy and were subsequently introduced into the Mass, first in the form of tropes and then of the sequence. The formal variations of the *versus* and the *conductus* were later developments. Among the most celebrated and enduring examples of the genre are Venantius Fortunatus's 'Vexilla regis prodeunt' from the end of the 6th c. and Hrabanus Maurus's 'Veni creator spiritus' of the early 9th c. *Abélard was a particularly prolific and original author of hymns, while the sequences of Hildegard of Bingen (c.1150) exploit a rich gamut of visionary imagery. Both metrical ('quantitative') and accentual verse forms are used, and alongside orthodox imagery and themes, classical and contemporary allusions are sometimes incorporated. The influence of Latin hymnody on secular poetic forms is best illustrated in the *Carmina Burana*. Apart from the early Old French *Séquence de *sainte Eulalie* (882) and the *Occitan 'Mei amic e mei fiel', whose melody is based on a Latin Christmas hymn, vernacular continuations of the Latin tradition are largely confined to hymns to the Virgin, of which a substantial corpus survives in Medieval French and particularly in Medieval Spanish (Alfonso X, el Sabio). [IS]

HYPPOLITE, Jean-Gaston (1907–68). Philosopher prominent in the neo-Hegelian revival. Attracted by Hegel's early spiritual writings, Hyppolite undertook a major study of his *Phenomenology of Mind*, which traces the forms and development of human consciousness. He produced the first, and the authoritative, French translation of it (1939–41) and a doctoral thesis which carefully analyses its genesis and structure (1946) and endeavours to elucidate Hegel's text in its own terms, at the risk of being thought intellectually timid. After the war Hyppolite sought to bring together the concerns of *Existentialism, socialism, and Christian spirituality. He proposed Hegelian philosophy as the basis for an understanding of human development, capable of discerning a meaning and purpose in history. His interpretation of Hegel was refined in the light of Marx's early criticisms, which centred on the need to consider alienation in social, rather than just spiritual, terms. Later, challenged by Heidegger's critique of humanism, he turned to Hegel's *Logic* and developed a less socially optimistic philosophy of being and language. From his important posts in the *Sorbonne, the *Collège de France, and the *jury de l'agrégation*, Hyppolite was highly influential in French academic philosophy during the 1950s and 1960s, counting among his pupils *Foucault, *Deleuze, *Althusser, and *Derrida. [MHK]

HYVRARD, Jeanne (b. 1945). French author of a series of poetic texts exploring the themes of identity, madness, women, and language in a highly personal style and vocabulary. Strongly marked by a period spent in the French Caribbean, she wrote on returning *Les Prunes de Cythère* (1975), followed by *Mère la mort* (1976), and *La Meurtritude* (1977). Her essays argue her belief in fusional and transnational thinking (see *Canal de la Toussaint*, 1986, and *La Pensée corps*, 1989). A short-story collection, *Auditions musicales certains soirs d'été* (1984), and *La Jeune Morte en robe de dentelle* (1990), a striking text addressed to her mother, employ a more traditional form.

[EAF]

I

Iambes. Title used for collections of satires by A. *Chénier and A. *Barbier.

Ibrahim ou l'Illustre Bassa (1641). A *roman héroïque* set in Constantinople, the joint work of Georges and Madeleine de *Scudéry, with an important preface by Georges.

Idéologues. A loose-knit group of philosophers, scientists, *littérateurs*, and political reformists under the intellectual leadership of *Destutt de Tracy and *Cabanis. Much influenced by the epistemology of *Condillac and the ethical utilitarianism of *Helvétius, they developed 18th-c. sensationalism into the early years of the 19th c. After the fall of Robespierre in 1794, Ideology became the quasi-official philosophy of the Republic, institutionalized in the Class of Moral and Political Sciences of the *Institut and propagated in the pages of La *Décade philosophique. The Idéologues proved particularly influential for a time in educational reform, pioneering the experiment of the *écoles centrales (1795–1802) and exerting a powerful influence upon one of their most celebrated pupils, *Stendhal.

Meaning literally the 'science of ideas', Ideology sought to provide a methodology for the study of all mental operations, classified by Tracy as sensation, memory, judgement, and will. Since ideas were, as Condillac had argued, compounds of sensation, they were held by the Idéologues to be resolvable, through analysis, into the sense-data from which they arose. For them, the analysis of ideas was the primary philosophical discipline. If ideas could be verified at each stage of their development, from the simplest apprehension to the most complex intellectual concept, errors of cognition and reasoning would be eradicated and knowledge would be founded on a sure empirical basis, free of all religious and metaphysical speculation.

Though disciples of Condillac, the Idéologues went beyond his abstractive epistemology, placing their 'science of ideas' within the ambit of 'zoology'. Since all thought derives from experience as mediated through the senses, there can be no meaningful distinction between the 'physical' and the 'moral' realms. Physiology, the analysis of ideas, and moral philosophy were, as Cabanis asserted, 'les trois branches d'une seule et même science, qui peut s'appeler, à juste titre, la science de l'homme'.

As a philosophical programme aimed at practical reform, Ideology was encyclopaedic in its range. With its insistence on the need for a tightly defined language as the vital instrument of analysis, it boasted a methodology applicable not only to scientific enquiry but to ethics, politics, history, legislation, and even the arts. The writings of the Idéologues are suffused with a belief in the perfectibility of humankind through education. When their humanitarian and liberal-republican sympathies came into conflict with *Napoleon's imperial ambitions, their role as institutional reformers was abruptly curtailed. Though their influence was felt among later Positivists [see COMTE], their philosophy was denounced as atheistic and eclipsed by the revival of religion and metaphysical idealism in the early 19th c.   [JS]

See G. Gusdorf, *La Conscience révolutionnaire: les Idéologues* (1978); E. Kennedy, *A 'Philosophe' in the Age of Revolution: Destutt de Tracy and the Origins of 'Ideology'* (1978).

Idiot de la famille, L'. Study of Flaubert by *Sartre, an extensive illustration of late Existentialist biographical method.

IKOR, Roger (1912–86). Journalist and novelist, best known for his novel cycles. *Les Fils d'Avrom* (including *Les Eaux mêlées*, 1955, Prix Goncourt) recounts the gradual acclimatization of a Jewish family in France over three generations. After the suicide of his son, painfully described in *Je porte plainte* (1981), he campaigned against the influence of quasi-religious sects over young people.   [EAF]

Île Bourbon, L'. Former name for Reunion; see MAURITIUS AND REUNION.

Île de France, L'. Former name for *Mauritius. Within France, the Île-de-France is the region surrounding Paris.

Île de la raison, L'. Philosophical three-act comedy by *Marivaux, loosely based on *Gulliver's Travels*.

Île des esclaves, L'. Philosophical comedy by *Marivaux, in which masters and servants are made to change places when washed up on an island governed by former slaves. The masters mend their ways and regain their position.

Île des pingouins, L' (1908). A satirical account of human progress by Anatole *France, with an ironic picture of the *Dreyfus Affair.

Île mystérieuse, L'. Serialized in *Le Magasin d'éducation et de récréation* (1874–5), this most Vernian of *Verne's novels links *Les Enfants du capitaine Grant*

(1867) to *Vingt mille lieues sous les mers* (1869); it combines a balloon, struggle against oppression, contrasting Robinsons, science (especially electricity), and taming the wilderness, with the revelation of Nemo's identity and his entombment under the volcanic island which then erupts. During the American Civil War a hurricane drives engineer Cyrus Smith, Nab his servant, Top the dog, reporter Gédéon Spillett, Pencroff the sailor, and young orphan Harbert Brown, captive Northerners escaping by balloon from besieged Richmond, to an island. Destitute, with only their clothes and what their pockets contain, they survive and even establish themselves comfortably, thanks to their talents and Smith's scientific culture, producing bricks, steel, and explosives before finding a chest of tools. They build a boat, rescue and re-educate Ayrton, the solitary castaway of *Grant*; they construct an electric telegraph, which mysteriously summons them: dying Nemo, the hidden benefactor who had been watching over them, is revealed as Prince Dakkar, the Indian independence fighter. After Lincoln Island's destruction, Nemo's treasure enables the castaways, rescued by Captain Grant's expedition, to re-create their colony on the mainland. [SFN]

Ille et Galeron, see GAUTIER D'ARRAS.

Illuminations, Les, see RIMBAUD.

Illuminism. A current of philosophical and religious thought which, indebted to the gnostic tradition, *Neoplatonism, *Swedenborgianism, and more recently discovered Eastern religions, enjoyed considerable popularity in the late 18th c. and the *Romantic age. The major writers associated with it include *Saint-Martin, *Fabre d'Olivet, and *Dupont de Nemours. Illuminism was influential on such varied writers as Joseph de *Maistre, *Ballanche, *Nerval, *Sand, *Baudelaire, *Hugo, and also such later figures as *Teilhard de Chardin.

The doctrine varies from author to author, but generally conceives of creation as an emanation from God through the Sophia (Wisdom), then the Word, with matter resulting from the Fall because of disobedience; but the divine Word remains present in all creation. Man alone, at the centre of the great chain of being, is free and is charged with the redemption of matter and the restoration of the lost harmony and unity of the universe. For many, this restoration involves a form of metempsychosis where, by continued reincarnation and expiatory suffering, souls move gradually toward the reintegration of the divine. All created being is symbolic of the divine, whence a series of 'correspondences' or harmonies among the various levels of the chain of being. Knowledge of the truth is acquired by introspection and by a process of initiation which includes a descent into hell, dying to be born again.

Many Illuminists were religious syncretists, proposing that all religious systems express, in varying symbolic modes, the same truth; they vary in their attitude towards Christianity, for some a perversion, for others (if properly understood) the best expression of the truth. Nor was Illuminism without its interplay with certain aspects of scientific thought, be it magnetism (*Mesmer, Puységur), physiognomony (Lavater), or theories of evolution (*Geoffroy Saint-Hilaire). The tradition continues to this day, and later in the 19th c. was popularized by such authors as Eliphas Lévi (A.-L. *Constant) and Joséphin *Péladan. [FPB]

Illusion comique, L'. Comedy by Pierre *Corneille, first performed 1635/6, subsequently entitled *L'Illusion*. This 'étrange monstre', as he called it, has attracted attention in recent years thanks to the revival in the fortunes of *baroque literature. The magician Alcandre conjures up for Pridamant the adventures of his erring son Clindor who, after serving a braggart captain (Matamore) and being in danger of execution for killing a man, finds his vocation as an actor. As well as playing with different levels of illusion, the comedy celebrates the new value accorded to theatre by contemporary society. [PF]

Illusions perdues. Novel, or more properly a huge novel-cycle, by *Balzac, first published 1837 (Part 1, 'Les Deux Poètes'), 1839 (Part 2, 'Un grand homme de province à Paris'), and 1843 (Part 3, 'Les Souffrances de l'inventeur'), which both invents and exhausts the 'novel of disillusionment'. *Illusions perdues* follows the career of Lucien Chardon, who adopts his mother's nobler name to become Lucien de Rubempré, from his youth in the provincial town of Angoulême (in Part 1) to Paris, where he achieves brief celebrity as a poet before sinking into the lower reaches of journalism and hack-writing (in Part 2). In Part 3 he returns to Angoulême, defeated and ridiculed, to complicate the dramatic business adventures of his old friend David Séchard. He is saved from suicide at the very end by a mysterious traveller, who whisks him back to Paris (and to the further adventures of *Splendeurs et misères des courtisanes*).

Lucien is a 'weak vessel', a young man of talent, charm, and ambition, lacking that dogged consistency which alone, for Balzac, leads to greatness. David Séchard is his complementary opposite, a 'genius' in Balzac's own unconventional terms, whose fictional invention of vegetable-based paper (made in historical fact some years after Balzac's death) is only defeated by the perfidy of local money-lenders and rivals. In Angoulême, Lucien rises from the 'low town' of L'Houmeau to the one literary salon of the 'high town', where he is lionized by Madame de Bargeton, his elder by 15 years. The description of the complex social structure of the town is a masterpiece of sociography, enlivened by satirical portraits of provincial types.

Part 1 ends with the elopement to Paris of the provincial muse and her poet-protégé. In the capital the scales fall from Lucien's eyes, and he quickly abandons Madame de Bargeton, who now seems to him to be an ungainly, dry old stick. He comes up against the miserliness of publishers and book-sellers, and finds he can earn his living only from journalism, not from his slim set of poems entitled *Les Marguerites* (the extracts given were written by *Gautier). He becomes a member of a literary circle or *cénacle* around Daniel d'Arthez—who prefers the obscurity of a life devoted to his art—whilst also mixing in the dangerous circles of the theatre, hack journalism, and the fringes of politics; and he is soon caught out and sinks into debt. Balzac gives the first and fundamental analysis of a star system, in which a few writers earn large fees and an inexhaustible supply of hangers-on are manipulated by venal editors and publishers; the second part of *Illusions perdues* remains the standard Romantic demonstration of the plight of the (real or would-be) artist in an age of commercial culture. The scene where Lucien writes drinking-songs by candle-light to earn a few francs as his lover Coralie dies of consumption in their freezing attic is, for all its period pathos, absolutely convincing.

The business saga of Part 3 is no less a critical analysis of the injustices of early capitalism than the spectacular myths of the poet in Paris; Balzac's explanations of paper-making technology, of patents, bills of exchange, and legal skulduggery are as exciting as the adventures of Dumas's Les *Trois Mousquetaires*. Despite its three-part structure, its vast range of topics, locations, and characters, *Illusions perdues* has a fundamental unity provided less by the vacillating character of Lucien de Rubempré than by the consistent, impassioned, and critical vision of the realities of French life in the period. [DMB]

Illustres Françaises, Les, see CHALLE.

Illustres Bergers, Les, see PASTORAL.

Illustre Théâtre, L', see MOLIÈRE.

Il ne faut jurer de rien. *Proverbe dramatique* by *Musset, first published 1836, performed 1848. The unsuccessful wager in question is that women are faithless.

Il n'y a pas de pays sans grand-père, see CARRIER.

Image d'Épinal, see ÉPINAL.

Imitation de Jésus-Christ, see DEVOTIONAL WRITING, I; CORNEILLE, P.

Immoraliste, L'. Novel by André *Gide, published 1902 and termed by him a *récit*, being narrated in the first person by the main protagonist. After a near-fatal illness while on honeymoon in North Africa, Michel is obsessed with his vision of an authentic inner self previously stifled by culture, custom, and morality. He destroys his wife Marceline in his pursuit of a higher set of values which are redolent of the Nietzschean superman but which in reality are a pretext for egoism and a latent homosexuality. Telling his story after her death becomes an attempt at self-justification. [DHW]

Immortels, Les. Name given to the *quarante* of the *Académie Française.

Imposteur, L'. Subtitle of Molière's *Tartuffe*.

Impressionism derived its name from a derogatory remark made by a journalist about *Monet's painting *Impression, soleil levant*, exhibited in 1874 in the first exhibition organized by the Société Anonyme des Peintres, Sculpteurs, Graveurs, which included works by *Cézanne, *Degas, Monet, *Morisot, Pissarro, *Renoir, and Sisley. Between this first Impressionist exhibition and the eighth and last in 1886, this diverse and fractious group secured a victory in their struggle with the official institutions of French painting which opened the way to the modernist tradition of 20th-c. art.

Impressionism was a rejection of the principles and practices taught by the professors of the Academy, who also formed the jury for the annual Salon exhibition [see ART CRITICISM]. In the École des Beaux-Arts the student learned to represent an intellectual idea of a subject through techniques based on drawing and chiaroscuro. From early in the 19th c. alternative practices developed from which the Impressionists would learn, notably *Delacroix's brush-stroke and use of colour, the landscapes of Corot and the *Barbizon group, *Courbet's realism, and Manet's treatment of modern subjects. Building on these and on new scientific accounts of colour perception, they used more brilliant colour, wider tonal range, and broken brushwork to represent more faithfully the play of natural light on objects. The effect of this new role of light and colour as organic elements of picture-making was to discredit academic theories of composition, drawing, and the hierarchy of subjects. More recently, however, the modernist emphasis on Impressionism's experimentation with autonomous formal means has been challenged by studies of the relationship between Impressionist technique and subject-matter (notably the forms of bourgeois leisure in Paris, its suburbs, and the surrounding countryside).

From the outset the work of Manet and the Impressionists engaged writers. In the 1860s *Zola praised Manet's *Naturalism, and in the mid-1870s *Mallarmé wrote an essential article on his open-air painting. *Huysmans championed Impressionism (notably in Degas), while *Laforgue related it to developments in poetry, music, and philosophy. Such exchanges gave rise to the idea of an Impressionist literature, of stylistic developments in prose and poetry analogous with Impressionist painting. *Hugo called Mallarmé his 'cher poète impressionniste', Zola claimed to have applied Impressionist technique in certain of his descriptions, and the term has frequently been used with reference to the novels of the *Goncourts and the poetry of *Verlaine. Since there was no single technique common to the Impressionist painters, the term is necessarily a loose one; it usually refers to attempts to represent through syntactic variation the fragmentary and discontinuous nature of the sensations of modern, particularly urban, civilization. [JK]

See A. Callen, *Techniques of the Impressionists* (1982); R. L. Herbert, *Impressionism: Art, Leisure and Parisian Society* (1988).

Imprimerie Nationale. Establishment originating in the appointment of an 'imprimeur du roi' by *François Ier. Under names that have changed with the regimes, it has continued to print official papers, but also prestige editions of French classics.

Impromptu de Versailles, L' (1663). One-act prose comedy by *Molière, representing his company at rehearsal, and defending his L'*École des femmes.

Indiana (1831). First novel written by *Sand without a collaborator, a romantic story set partly on the Île Bourbon (Reunion).

Indigénisme. A radical movement in *Haiti signalling a literary renaissance, provoked by the nationalist reaction against the American Occupation (1915–34). Iconoclastic in spirit, it demanded a rejection of European values and a celebration of Haiti's indigenous culture, or 'l'âme haïtienne'. Its organ was *La Revue indigène* (1927–8), edited by *Brouard and *Thoby-Marcelin among others. Similar in thrust to the Harlem Renaissance and Afro-Cuban movements, its ideals are best represented by Émile Roumer's *Poèmes d'Haiti et de France* (1925). Ideologically it gave way to *noirisme and *Marxism in the 1930s. [JMD]

Indo-China. The French occupation of Indo-China was relatively brief, finishing in a bitter war and the defeat of Dien Bien Phu [see COLONIZATION, DECOLONIZATION]. Both the colonial period and the withdrawal left their mark on France in a number of ways; the war did much to worsen relations between the army and the government, and prepared the way for some of the conflicts connected with the *Algerian War.

A number of important French literary works reflect aspects of the Indo-Chinese experience, notably Malraux's *La *Voie royale* and Duras's *L'*Amant* (Duras was born in Indo-China and spent her childhood there; her work might therefore be seen as belonging to 'Indo-Chinese literature in French'). The colonial authorities sought to encourage the teaching and use of French in Indo-China as in the rest of the empire. Indo-Chinese intellectuals spent time in France before, during, and after World War II; the revolutionary leader Ho Chi Minh, for instance, lived there for several years and wrote political tracts in French. Raphaël Barquissau's *L'Asie française et ses écrivains* (1949), an anthology

published a few years before the final French withdrawal in 1954, shows a certain development of French-language writing, both by colonists and by indigenous authors. There was indeed a modest flourishing of Vietnamese fiction in French, one of the leading figures being Pham Van Ky (b. 1916), who settled in France in 1938 and published many novels with Indo-Chinese or oriental subjects, including *Perdre la demeure* (1961, Grand Prix du Roman de l'Académie Française). In general, however, the French presence in Indo-China was too short-lived and the native cultural traditions too strong to allow the growth of a significant national literature in French. [PF]

Inès de Castro. Heroine of plays by *La Motte and *Montherlant [see REINE MORTE, LA].

Inès de las Sierras, see NODIER.

Infâme, L', see VOLTAIRE.

Infini, L'. Journal directed by *Sollers, taking the place of *Tel Quel* in 1983.

Ingénu, L' (1767). Philosophical tale by *Voltaire. A guileless young Frenchman, raised among the Hurons, returns in 1689 to a corrupt France where his innate good sense and acute awareness of natural justice are tested in situations which progress from the comical to the cruel. He is imprisoned in the Bastille for having shown compassion towards the suffering Huguenots. Mademoiselle de Saint-Yves, whom he loves, obtains his freedom, but only by sacrificing her honour to Saint-Pouange, a powerful 'sous-ministre'. The struggle between love and conscience causes her death. The story, in two unequal halves, moves from amusingly wicked attacks on the usual politico-religious absurdities towards the sentimental (Saint-Yves's sacrifice and death). The resultant uneasy tension has given critics trouble. [JR]

Ingénue Saxancour, see RESTIF DE LA BRETONNE.

INGRES, Jean-Dominique (1780–1867). French painter, as dominant in early 19th-c. French painting for draughtsmanship and classicizing traits as *Delacroix was for colour. The two are often contrasted too baldly as exponents of Classicism and Romanticism. In the representation of the female form and certain compositional details, Ingres was indebted to Raphael. He shows mastery of line, sometimes with elongation for stylistic effect (e.g. the odalisque's back in *La Grande Odalisque*, 1814). Attentive to contemporary fashion and skilful in handling drapery, Ingres excelled as a portraitist, with an interesting motif of reflections in mirrors. For *Baudelaire, while he honours the antique ideal, he falls short of genius because he lacks passion and imagination, and over-systematizes his drawing. [HEB]

Initié, L'

Initié, L', see BHÊLY-QHÉNUM.

Innommable, L', see BECKETT.

Inquisition, see HERESIES.

Inquisitoire, L', see PINGET.

Insolences du Frère Untel, Les, see JOUAL.

Institut de France (until 1806, Institut National). Learned body founded in 1795, incorporating many members of the former royal *academies, grouped in three 'classes' (Mathematical and Physical Sciences, Moral and Political Sciences, Literature and Fine Art). In 1816 it was reorganized: the *Académie Française, *Académie des Sciences, *Académie des Inscriptions, and *Académie Royale de Peinture et de Sculpture (now Académie des Beaux-Arts) resumed their separate identities under the umbrella of the Institut; in 1832 a fifth class was added, the Académie des Sciences Morales et Politiques. Meetings were at first in the *Louvre; in 1806 the Institut moved to its present home, the former Collège des Quatre Nations on the Left Bank.
[PF]

Instituteurs, institutrices, see EDUCATION, 2C.

Institutions de la religion chrétienne, see CALVIN.

Insurgé, L', see VALLÈS.

Intellectuals. The French term *intellectuels* first came into common usage during the *Dreyfus affair, when it was applied by *Clemenceau to those 'men of ideas, scholarship and creativity', such as Seignobos and Anatole *France, who signed a manifesto in support of *Zola's article 'J'accuse'. Then as now, the term could be two-edged, attracting the scorn of *Barrès among others. Although the concept might be applied retrospectively, without too great distortion, to such groups as the philosophers of the *Enlightenment or to renowned academics like *Michelet, it is most often used of 20th-c. groups or individuals and usually implies a high level of formal education. French intellectuals have often taken full advantage of the privileged position of philosophy within the school curriculum. But the term also bears the mark of its origins: it tends to imply both a certain collective identity, often created by membership of institutions such as the universities or the *École Normale Supérieure, and a willingness, sometimes interpreted as a duty, publicly to express opinions on issues of the time [see ENGAGEMENT]. *Benda, in *La Trahison des clercs*, argued by contrast that it was not the role of this educated 'clerisy' to descend into the forum, but his advice was mostly honoured in the breach: *Barthes later described the intellectual as 'à mi-chemin entre le militant et l'écrivain'. Examples of self-conscious collective action by intellectuals, apart from the petitions signed for and against Dreyfus, are the anti-fascist committee in the 1930s and the petitions against the *Algerian War. Although historically more associated with the Left than with the Right, French intellectuals have ranged across the political spectrum [see EXISTENTIALISM; MARXISM; OCCUPATION AND RESISTANCE; NOUVEAUX PHILOSOPHES]. The growth of the broadcast media and the expansion of higher education have lately blurred the edges of what was once an identifiable (and largely male) élite.
[SR]

Intendants were *maîtres des requêtes* (royal jurists) provided with royal letters of commission, sent out into the provinces to oversee the collection of taxes and military affairs, and to help keep order. Such commissioners are to be found infrequently in the late 16th c., but after 1635, when France was actively participating in the Thirty Years War, most provinces had an *intendant*. They were accorded increasingly wide powers of interference, which made them vastly unpopular with the venal office-holders in the localities. The *Fronde Parlementaire insisted on their abolition, but they made a reappearance as *commissaires départis* in the 1650s, and were soon resident in each *généralité* (administrative region). Numbering about 30 in 1700, they were destined to become the most powerful royal agents in the 18th c. They then established permanent bureaux with clerks and sub-delegates. A long-standing historical view has seen them as all-powerful agents of centralization and the final step in the development of a modern state. In truth, they were far from being entirely modern administrators, enmeshed as they were in webs of clientage, almost all intermarried within their corps, and anxious to return to Paris. They were so overburdened with tasks by the government that their role as effective centralizers is to be seriously questioned, and many defended their localities against unsuitable royal policies. In the late *ancien régime* several intendants were notably enlightened, such as *Sénac de Meilhan and *Turgot.
[PRC]

'Internationale, L' ', see POTTIER.

Introduction à la connaissance de l'esprit humain, see VAUVENARGUES.

Introduction à la médecine expérimentale, see BERNARD, C.

Introduction à la méthode de Léonard de Vinci, see VALÉRY.

Introduction à la vie dévote, see FRANÇOIS DE SALES.

Invalides, Hôtel des. This Parisian monument, begun in 1670, was and still is a hospital for injured war veterans. Its domed chapel, designed by *Mansart, was chosen in 1840 as the resting place for the sarcophagus containing *Napoleon's remains.

Invitée, L', see BEAUVOIR.

IONESCO, Eugène (1912–94). Playwright and leading exponent of the Theatre of the *Absurd. His original dramatic techniques redefined the boundaries of drama in the 1950s and had a profound influence on theatre world-wide.

The son of a Romanian father and a French mother, his early years were divided between La Chapelle-Anthenaise and Bucharest, where he lived between the ages of 13 and 26 before settling in Paris in 1938. The recurrent themes of his plays—nostalgia for a luminous childhood, an interest in the phenomenon of language and the relativity of received ideas, an aversion to ideology—seem to have been shaped by these experiences. Like *Beckett, he came to the theatre late, and his first writing for the stage met with indifference or hostility. His early works played to thin audiences in small Left-Bank theatres, but by 1953 they were attracting the attention of figures such as *Queneau and *Anouilh. In Britain, his work gave rise to a celebrated polemic involving Orson Welles, Lindsay Anderson, George Devine, and Philip Toynbee. Conducted in the *Observer* in 1958, it was led by Kenneth Tynan, who attacked Ionesco for his lack of social or political purpose. His reply—that a playwright simply writes plays—helped to define him as a writer concerned only to communicate his personal anguish rather than to engage in ideological debate. In the 1960s his plays were taken up by *Barrault and Orson Welles. His entry to the repertoire of the Comédie-Française in 1966, and election to the Académie Française in 1970, completed his canonization as a modern classic.

His earliest and most innovative works were one-act nonsense plays: *La Cantatrice chauve* (produced 1950), *La Leçon* (1951), *Les Chaises* (1952), and *Jacques ou la Soumission* (1955). These absurdist sketches, to which he applies epithets such as 'anti-pièce', 'pseudo-drame', and 'farce tragique', express the modern sense of non-communication and alienation, but with a surreal comic force. As well as castigating bourgeois conformism, they parody conventional theatrical forms. Disregarding psychology and coherent dialogue, they depict a dehumanized world with mechanical, puppet-like characters mouthing platitudes and *non sequiturs*. The plays have no story-line, but deploy a simple and effective dramatic structure based on an accelerating rhythm. Language becomes increasingly reified, words and material objects acquire a life of their own, the stage is steadily invaded by objects and cacophony, overwhelming the characters and creating a growing sense of menace.

With his second full-length play, *Tueur sans gages* (1959; the first was *Amédée, ou Comment s'en débarrasser*, 1954), he began to explore more sustained dramatic situations. This play also marks the appearance of more humanized characters, notably a central character called Bérenger. A comically naïve individual who engages the spectator's sympathy, Bérenger is an autobiographical figure who projects the author's sense of wonderment and anguish in the face of the strangeness of reality. In *Tueur sans gages*, while visiting the Utopian 'Cité radieuse', Bérenger encounters the ineluctable face of death in the figure of a serial killer. In *Rhinocéros* (1960) he sees his friends transformed one by one into pachyderms, until he stands alone against the conformist tide. Inspired by the rise of the fascist Iron Guard in Romania in the 1930s, *Rhinocéros* expresses most forcibly the author's horror of ideological conformism, seen as a contagious mental mutation. *Le Roi se meurt* (1962) shows le roi Bérenger Ier, an allegorical Everyman, struggling to come to terms with the inevitability of his own death. These hallucinatory plays are outstanding for the memorable theatrical metaphors—a motiveless killer, a disintegrating kingdom, weightlessness—with which ontological states are expressed.

Le Piéton de l'air (1963) marked the end of the Bérenger series. His later work, which has generally received less attention, includes *La Soif et la faim* (1966, premiered at the Comédie-Française); *Jeux de massacre* (1971), inspired by Defoe's *Journal of the Plague Year*; *Macbett* (1972), a free adaptation of Shakespeare; and *Ce formidable bordel* (1973).

Apart from an unproduced libretto for an opera, he did not write for the stage after *Voyage chez les morts* in 1981. But the legendary production of *La Cantatrice chauve*, which transferred to the 80-seater Théâtre de la Huchette in 1952, was still playing there in 1993.   [DWW]

See G. Tarrab, *Ionesco à cœur ouvert* (1970); R. Coe, *Ionesco: A Study of his Plays* (rev. edn., 1971).

Iphigénie. Tragedy by *Racine, first performed at Versailles in 1674. Inspired by Euripides' *Iphigenia in Aulis*, it was presented by Racine in his preface as a witness to the supremacy of the Ancients [see QUERELLE]. It centres on Agamemnon, who is ordered by an oracle to sacrifice his daughter Iphigénie so as to obtain favourable winds to sail to Troy. He lures her and her mother Clytemnestre to the camp on the pretext of her marriage to Achille. When the secret comes out, Achille and Clytemnestre defy Agamemnon, but urged on by the army he proceeds with the sacrifice. To avoid the unacceptably miraculous denouement of the Greek play, Racine invents a captive princess, Ériphile, Iphigénie's unhappy rival in love; her real name is finally revealed to be Iphigénie, and her death by suicide satisfies the oracle (if not the spectators), and opens the seas to the Greek army.   [PF]

Ipomedon, see ANGLO-NORMAN LITERATURE, 3a.

IRIGARAY, Luce. Radical French *feminist thinker and practising psychoanalyst whose work has given rise to very diverse interpretations. *Speculum de l'autre femme* (1974), her first major contribution to feminist theory, argues that Western thought is grounded in a destructive male *imaginaire* [see

LACAN], estranged from the maternal and the feminine. In order to find a way forward, Irigaray undertakes a psychoanalysis of western philosophers and thinkers, especially Freud and Plato, seeking the 'repressed' of western culture. *Ce sexe qui n'en est pas un* (1977) attacks the Freudian model of feminine sexuality and sets up one based on women's irreducible multiplicity and fluidity [see FEMINISM; ÉCRITURE FÉMININE]. The issue of language and gender, already addressed in *Parler n'est jamais neutre* (1985), is taken up in *Langages* (1987) and *Sexes et genres à travers les langues* (1991), which analyse empirical work on language and sexual difference. *Éthique de la différence sexuelle* (1984) addresses the symbolic division which imprisons the feminine in the corporeal and the material while closing the masculine off in the spiritual and the intelligible. Irigaray is working towards an as-yet unrealized symbolization of the feminine which would allow an 'amorous exchange' between the masculine and the feminine and point the way towards her (perhaps necessarily) Utopian vision of the future. [EAF]

Irish Influences, see BRITISH, IRISH, AND AMERICAN INFLUENCES.

Isengrin. The wolf in the *Roman de Renart*.

Iseut, see TRISTAN.

Islam in France. The French encounter with Islam goes back at least as far as Charles Martel's victory over Arab invaders at Poitiers in 732. During the 19th and 20th c. *colonization brought French domination in many Muslim countries, notably in the *Maghreb and the Middle East. Since World War II, large numbers of Muslim immigrants from former colonies have settled in France, which now has the largest Muslim population in any western European country. Estimates as to the exact number vary, but there are generally thought to be around 3 million Muslims in France, which in size makes them second only to Roman Catholics among the country's religious communities. Most are Sunni Muslims, but they are divided by numerous ethnic and ideological cleavages which have so far prevented them from speaking with a single voice in their dealings with the state, which has in any case been reluctant to grant any formal recognition to the Islamic community.

Early literary references to Islam feature in medieval works inspired by the *Crusades. During the colonial period, travel writers such as *Loti emphasized the exotic dimension of Islam, while *Psichari was sufficiently fearful of its strength among the colonial masses to convert to Catholicism, which he saw as an essential mark of French authority. More recently, a handful of intellectuals such as the dissident Communist Roger *Garaudy and the publisher Michel Chodkiewicz (director of the Éditions du Seuil) have converted to Islam. The majority of Muslims in France are of Maghrebian immigrant origin. They include the so-called *Beur generation, whose writings are marked by a weakening in the influence of Islam, when compared with its importance among first-generation immigrants. [AGH]

Isolé Soleil, L', see MAXIMIN.

Isopet, see YSOPET.

ISSA, Ibrahima (b. 1922). Native of Niger and author of a pseudo-historical, would-be philosophical novel, *Les Grandes Eaux noires* (1954), aiming to reclaim the glory of an ancient Saharan civilization. He has also published a collection of poems, *La Vie et ses facéties: poèmes* (1979). [DSB]

ISTRATI, Panaït (1884–1935). Novelist. 'Un autodidacte qui trouve la Sorbonne où il peut', the Greco-Romanian-born Istrati spent his early life, like his picaresque protagonist Adrien Zograffi, 'on the road' throughout the Near East, informing the talents which, under the tutelage of Romain *Rolland and in expressive, self-taught French, he later displayed in his vibrant, colourful stories, part lyrical, part realistic: *Kyra Kyralina* (1924), *Oncle Anghel* (1925). In *Vers l'autre flamme* (1927) he castigated the Soviet regime. [DAS]

Italian Influences. A balance-sheet of literary exchange over some seven centuries would doubtless show that Italy's debt to France began earlier, and was the greater, but between the 14th and the end of the 17th c. there are significant instances of Italian influence upon the development of French literature. The earliest occur as a direct result of the intense contact between the two cultures during the period of the *Avignon Papacy (1309–77). From the start, however, Italian literature (and strictures against France by Petrarch in particular) provoked a nationalistic response: Jean de Hesdin and Nicolas de Clamanges began in the late 14th c. a debate that was to be continued well into the 16th by Jean *Lemaire de Belges (*Concorde des deux langages*, 1511), Symphorien *Champier (*Duellum epistolare*, 1519), Henri *Estienne (*Deux dialogues*, 1578), and Thomas *Sébillet (see below).

Of the three dominant figures of Italian medieval literature, Dante was the least influential in France, remaining neglected, even after his translation in 1596–7, until his rediscovery in the early 19th c. The Latin writings of Petrarch (especially *De remediis utriusque fortune*, translated in 1378 and 1503) and of Boccaccio, on the other hand, were to have considerable impact, and were frequently cited as sources of sound moral doctrine and historical information by such early writers as *Christine de Pizan; their presence is often a sign of nascent humanism. Petrarch's Latin translation of Boccaccio's story of Griselda was to enjoy considerable popularity in France from 1385 onwards and, as an extreme example of feminine virtue, contributed to the *Querelle des Femmes which was to last well into the 17th c.

Petrarch was also admired for his Latin style and classical scholarship, areas in which his humanist successors remained predominant, as is revealed by the presence among the first books printed in Paris in 1470 of works by Barzizza and Valla.

Petrarch's *Trionfi*, already known in France in the late 15th c., were translated in 1514 by Georges de la Forge and *c*.1530 by Simon Bourgouyn. Above all, however, his *Canzoniere* (not fully translated—by Vasquin Philieul—until 1548–55) inspired in the 16th c., in France as everywhere else in Europe, that poetic phenomenon known as *Petrarchism: use of the sonnet form (probably first imitated in French by Clément *Marot *c*.1530), of a complex structure to hold together a sequence of love-poems, and of a vast vocabulary of poetic conceits. *Scève's identification of the tomb of Petrarch's beloved Laura in Avignon, and his *Délie* (1544), reflect the interest that the *Canzoniere* held for him and other Lyonnais poets such as Louise *Labé; in 1549 *Du Bellay published the first French Petrarchan sonnet-sequence (*L'Olive*), and from then onwards the *Pléiade and poets such as *Magny and *Desportes continued to draw on Petrarch and his Italian imitators (in particular Cariteo, Tebaldeo, Serafino, Bembo, Ariosto, and Sannazaro). Du Bellay himself obligingly provides the theoretical underpinning for, and an example of, imitation in his *Défense et illustration de la langue française*, heavily dependent upon a dialogue by Sperone Speroni; similarly, in his *Art poétique français* *Sebillet urges his compatriots to absorb all that they can of what Italy and classical antiquity have to offer. In the 17th c. *Saint-Amant, *Scudéry, and *Tristan l'Hermite were still to find inspiration in Italian sources such as the love-poetry of *Marino or the satirical verse of Berni [see SATIRE], while Tasso was to have a considerable influence upon the development of the French historical *epic.

Boccaccio's *Decameron* (translated in 1400 and 1485) left its mark on French prose fiction. It was already known to the author of the *Cent nouvelles nouvelles; a new translation was made in 1545 for *Marguerite de Navarre, in whose *Heptaméron its traces are visible, as in the anonymous *Comptes du monde aventureux* of 1555. Boccaccio's *Filocolo* and *Fiammetta*, both translated early in the 1530s, were, like other short stories by Poggio Bracciolini and Aeneas Sylvius Piccolomini, to provide French writers with further versatile Italian narrative models.

But the content of the narrative, as the *Heptaméron* shows, is increasingly influenced by *Neoplatonism. Petrarchist love-poetry, such as that of Louise Labé or the Pléiade, also frequently echoed ideas deriving from Ficino and Pico della Mirandola; the demand for Italian dialogues and treatises of a broadly Neoplatonic slant led to the translation of Bembo's *Asolani*, Leon Ebreo's *Dialoghi d'amore*, Cariteo's *Peregino*, Sannazaro's *Arcadia*, and others. The impact of Castiglione's *Cortegiano* (first translated in 1537) on *Héroët's *Parfaite Amie* is clear, and it remained popular well into the latter half of the century [see COURTOISIE]. Meanwhile other ideas of partly Italian origin were also gaining currency in France: the rationalist and sceptical views of Pomponazzi and the Paduan Averroists, the political thought of Machiavelli and Guicciardini, the latter not appreciated for his anti-French sentiments.

One more major area in which Italian influence may be discerned is the theatre. Troupes of Italian actors were already active in France in the 16th c., importing the stock figures of the *commedia dell'arte*; from the middle of the century onwards Italian comedies were increasingly imitated and translated, notably by *Larivey. Traces of the same comic tradition are evident in the plays of *Molière and *Marivaux, and in the activities of the Italian actors [see COMÉDIE-ITALIENNE], who were expelled from Paris in 1697 but later returned, merging in 1762 with players of the *théâtres de la *foire to form the nucleus of what was in 1780 to become the Opéra-Comique. Finally, the *pastoral, deriving especially from Tasso and Guarini, left a profound stamp both on the prose narrative of d'Urfé's *Astrée and on the plays of *Hardy, *Racan, and *Beaumarchais.

Except in the domains of the theatre and opera, there is little more Italian literary influence in France before the 19th c. The rediscovery of Italy which took place then was partly a physical one, the result of increased travel; in literary terms it is marked more by the adoption of historical themes than by the influence of texts, and by a long-overdue interest in Dante, hero of a romantic myth of the Middle Ages which lasted at least until *Baudelaire. But Madame de Staël's novel *Corinne (1807) started a fashion which was underpinned by histories of Italian literature by *Ginguené (1811–19) and *Sismondi (1812), and above all by the writings of *Stendhal. Venetian themes were explored by *Gautier and *Balzac, and Florentine ones by *Dumas *père* and *Musset; by the middle of the 19th c. Italy was firmly established as a setting for adventure and romance. [NM]

See F. Simone, *Il rinascimento francese* (1961); L. Sozzi (ed.), *Mélanges à la mémoire de Franco Simone*, vol. 3 (1984); J. Serroy (ed.), *La France et l'Italie au temps de Mazarin* (1986); F. Braudel, *Le Modèle italien* (1989).

Itinéraire de Paris à Jérusalem, see CHATEAUBRIAND.

J

JABÈS, Edmond (b. 1912). Poet, born in Cairo, from where he moved to Paris in 1957. *Je bâtis ma demeure* (1959) contains most of his early work—folk-song-like poetry, often concerned with the Holocaust. The multi-volumed *Livre des questions* (1963–73) and *Livre des ressemblances* (1976–80) sometimes read like pages of the Talmud. Rabbis interrogate rabbis on the meaning of word and world. He is often called a disciple of *Blanchot, and of modern theories of linguistic self-reference, but more profoundly he is a mystic: words misrepresent the nature of ultimate, or even ordinary, reality. Only paradox and aphorism can point the way. He speaks about poetry in *Du désert au livre: entretiens* (1980).   [GDM]

JACCOTTET, Philippe (b. 1925). Poet. Swiss by birth, Jaccottet settled in a French village in the Drôme, a region of wooded hills and mountainous prospects from which he derives a landscape poetry of non-specific and universal resonance. The early verse collections *L'Effraie* (1953) and *L'Ignorant* (1958) address notions of place, moment, and obliviousness to self, ascribing poetic virtue to the ephemeral nuance of non-human life. Trees and birds, rain and snow, moon and stars are the archetypal features of a world dense with intimations of harmony and transfiguration. Inspired by Hölderlin, Rilke, and Ungaretti, each of whom he has translated, Jaccottet celebrates those rare moments of participatory insight when contingent phenomena, lyrically voiced, accede to the status of metaphor or metaphysical symbol. The haiku-like poems of *Airs* (1967) epitomize a 'crystalline' aesthetic of laconic poise; while the more ruminative verse of *Pensées sous les nuages* (1983), the meandering prose of *Paysages avec figures absentes* (1970), and the scattered notations serially issued under the title *La Semaison* (1963, 1971, 1984) reflect a never-assuaged Romantic yearning to elicit higher meaning from the scrutiny of natural signs.   [RC]

'J'accuse'. *Zola's famous contribution to the *Dreyfus Affair, published in *L'Aurore* on 13 January 1898.

Jacinthe noire, see AMROUCHE, M.-L.-T.

JACOB, François (b. 1920). French biologist and historian of the biological sciences (*La Logique du vivant*, 1970), awarded the Nobel Prize in 1965, jointly with André Lwoff and Jacques Monod. In his genetic researches at the Institut Pasteur he studied, *inter alia*, the relationship between 'regulator' and 'structural' genes within the cell.   [MB]

JACOB, Max (1876–1944). Mystic and *farceur*, poet and parodist, Breton and Jew, night-owl and hermit, Jacob brought pathos, humour, and linguistic *brio* to the exercise of his Protean talents. In a remarkable trajectory, his life led him from Quimper (whose *menu peuple* figure repeatedly in his work) to the Montmartre of *Apollinaire, *Picasso, and *Salmon, where he painted gouaches and had two visions of Christ, to Saint-Benoît-sur-Loire where, after his conversion to Christianity, he spent long periods of monastic solitude, and finally to the transit camp at Drancy where, after his arrest as a Jew, he died of pneumonia. With their dazzling word-play and parodic verve, the prose poems of *Le Cornet à dés* (1916) rank with the writings of Apollinaire as cardinal expressions of the spirit which, after the eclipse of the *Symbolists, was to infuse the modernist movement in France. Ever willing to give the initiative to language, and to whatever might emerge from a memory nourished by eclectic reading—popular fiction, folk legends, devotional texts, and the Cabbala—Jacob turned his hand to verse poems (*Le Laboratoire central*, 1921), bizarre novels (*Le Cabinet noir*, 1922), religious texts (*La Défense de Tartuffe*, 1924). Bringing a touch of fantasy to everything he did, Jacob also composed Breton 'chants' under the pseudonym Morven le Gaélique, wrote interesting meditations on poetry, and maintained a vast correspondence through which he gave much valued advice and support to younger writers, who included *Leiris and *Jabès.   [MHTS]

Jacobins, Les. In May 1789 a group of Breton deputies to the *États Généraux founded the Club Breton, which soon became a place for debate for other patriotic deputies. That October the club, following the Assembly to Paris, quartered in the library of the Dominicans, or Jacobins, in the rue Saint-Honoré, where the Société des Amis de la Constitution (rebaptized Société des Jacobins after the fall of the monarchy) continued to be an amorphous body of deputies linked solely by their 'constitutionalism'. However, in 1790, impelled by fear of real (and imaginary) counter-revolution, the club—aided by a succession of schisms and departures—started to move leftwards. By late 1792, thanks to judicious recruitment, increasing democratization, tighter discipline, and periodic purges, the Left—though divided—controlled the club. Internal division did not, however, impair the influence it wielded outside. In its heyday (1791–4) the club, as two Assemblies discovered, was a significant force. For it was not merely a Parisian pressure-group. It genuinely represented a national movement: from 1790 onwards it coordinated and inspired (manipulated even) the efforts of all its affiliated branches throughout France. The result was a 'climate of opinion' which was most significant during l'An II (1793–4), when the Jacobins counted some 2,000 provincial branches and provided most of the personnel for the *comités de surveillance* and the *armées révolutionnaires*. Yet it was at that height of influence that there came a series of fratricidal disputes between *Montagnards and *Girondins, then between *Robespierristes, *Maratistes, *Hébertistes, and *Dantonistes, which badly compromised the vitality of the club. Harassed by the Thermidorians, and finally suppressed by law (23 August 1795), the Jacobins thereafter slowly declined into obscurity, though some did join *Babeuf in 1796.

In 1791–4 the importance of the Jacobins was such that their name became universally synonymous with 'radical Revolutionary' (though they were much less radical, much more prudent, than the *Cordeliers). Later, 'Jacobin' became a term of abuse. Marx and traditional Marxists, though influenced in their conception of the socialist revolution by the Jacobinism of 1792–4, found the movement wanting; for them Jacobinism has symbolized the romantic belief that human will rather than economic realities can shape history. Most people now understand Jacobinism to mean contempt for democratic processes and majority opinion. In modern parliamentary terms, 'Jacobin' designates an intransigent democrat who is hostile to any weakening of the central, centralizing authority of the state. [JR]

JACQUEMONT, Victor (1801–32). French botanist and geologist. This liberal intellectual was a friend and correspondent of *Stendhal and *Mérimée, and frequented the literary salons of the *Restoration. In 1828 he embarked upon a scientific expedition to India on behalf of the Muséum d'Histoire Naturelle. His *Voyage dans l'Inde* appeared posthumously in 1841–4. [CC]

Jacquerie, a peasant rising, see PEASANTS.

Jacques de Lalaing, Le Livre des faits de (later 15th c.). Charolais, the author of this biography often attributed to *Chastellain, was a herald and close companion of the hero. He concentrates on the latter's exploits in the lists and in elaborately devised deeds of arms. [JHMT]

JACQUES DU CLERCQ (1420–1501). Author of lively *Mémoires* (1448–67) where admiration for the Burgundian court is tinged with some realism, and which are marked by a strongly anticlerical streak and a predilection for everyday life in *Arras. [JHMT]

Jacques le fataliste. Novel by *Diderot, begun c.1771, published posthumously. Impossible to clas-

sify, this comic novel or anti-novel can be set in a tradition including *Don Quixote*, the work of *Rabelais, and Sterne's *Tristram Shandy*. It consists essentially of a series of dialogues. In the framing dialogue, between 'author' and 'reader', Diderot teases us with paradoxes of realism and illusion. Then there is the running dialogue between Jacques, formerly a peasant, now a valet, and his master; together they ride through France, staying at inns and talking endlessly, telling one another, inconclusively, the stories of their love affairs. Their conversations are interrupted by encounters and further conversations, which bring new stories, ranging from comic anecdotes to the fully developed novella of the failed vengeance of Madame de la Pommeraye on her fickle lover. These stories and discussions allow Diderot to pose moral questions, to explore individual idiosyncrasy, and to play with the teasing problems of free will and fatalism. The novel proclaims, but also mocks, the fatalism professed by Jacques (and elsewhere by Diderot himself), testing it against the realities of life. It also calls into question the conventions of novel writing, and as such has been seen as an ancestor of modernist fiction. Goethe, more vigorously, called it a 'feast worthy of Baal'. [PF]

Jacques Vingtras. Hero of the trilogy of novels by *Vallès.

Jadis et naguère. Poetic collection by *Verlaine, published 1885; it contains his 'Art poétique'.

Jalousie, La. Novel by *Robbe-Grillet, published 1957. An apparently impersonal text reveals itself as emanating from someone whose presence is detectable only from the movements of his gaze and traces left on his surroundings—an extra table setting, etc. Various scenes are described, mainly featuring a woman, 'A.', and a neighbour, Franck; we guess that A. is the narrator's wife and he suspects her of sleeping with Franck—hence the title. But this is never stated: the word *jalousie* occurs only in its other meaning of 'Venetian blind'. The novel provokes conflicting interpretations. Some critics see it as a representation of the mind as a screen traversed by images—perceived, remembered, or imagined: the text, in the present tense throughout, does not differentiate. Subjectivity is thus essentially perception, but perception limited and distorted by emotion. Alternatively, the descriptions, which follow no realistic chronological sequence, have been seen as elements of an abstract textual composition based on a play of repetition and variation. [CB]

JALOUX, Edmond (1878–1949). French novelist and critic, a native of Marseille. The delicacy of his art belies the robustness of his output (his works of fiction run to some 300, whilst his critical pieces are to be counted by the thousand). His novels, which delineate the pleasures and pains of love, often portray idealized figures in a dream-like landscape— *Le Démon de la vie* (1908), *Le Reste est silence* (1909), *La Fin d'un beau jour* (1920), *O toi que j'eusse aimée!* (1926). His critical output, including *L'Esprit des livres* (1923) and *D'Eschyle à Giraudoux* (1946), ventures well beyond the bounds of French literature— *Figures étrangeres* (1925)—and is elegant, intelligent, and perceptive. His memoirs, *Les Saisons littéraires* (1942–50), make charming and rewarding reading.

[DAS]

JAMEREY-DUVAL, Valentin (1695–1775). Peasant from the Yonne who rose to become librarian at the court of Lorraine. His *Mémoires*, written *c*.1733–47, but published in full only in the 20th c., pre-date Rousseau's **Confessions* as the personal autobiography of an upwardly mobile man of letters and give a striking picture of a difficult, nomadic adolescence.

[PF]

JAMMES, Francis (1868–1938). The poet of the south-west of France, where he spent his life, Jammes celebrated the beauty and authenticity of the experience of nature. His first volume, *De l'Angélus de l'aube à l'Angélus du soir* (1898), made him the most admired poet of the 'naturist' anti-*Symbolist movement and a major representative of the tradition of provincial literature established during the 19th c. The apparent spontaneity of his poetic language, which included the full resources of the *vers libre*, does not disguise the mastery with which he created a naïve, lyrical, occasionally melancholic vision of the countryside. Encouraged by *Claudel, he returned to Catholicism. His subsequent work, notably *L'Église habillée de feuilles* (1906) and *Géorgiques chrétiennes* (1911–12), celebrate this rediscovered faith.

[JK]

JAMYN, Amadis (1540–93), French poet. Having studied under the leading humanists *Dorat and *Turnèbe, Jamyn became *Ronsard's secretary and companion. In the 1570s he participated in the *Académie du Palais and belonged to a group of court poets which also included *Desportes. He translated parts of the *Iliad* and the *Odyssey*, and wrote amorous and religious verse.

[TC]

JANET, Pierre, see PSYCHOANALYSIS.

JANIN, Jules (1804–74). French critic who first made his mark around 1830 with novels that exemplified the young generation's taste for horror mixed with humour, cynicism, and some despair (*L'Âne mort et la femme guillotinée*, 1829). He occupied a key position in the Parisian literary world of the mid-century as a very regular contributor to the press. Only now is the interest of his literary and theatrical criticism and his sizeable correspondence being fully apprehended. *La Fin d'un monde et du *Neveu de Rameau* (1861) has a significant place in the history of Diderot's text.

[BR]

JANKÉLÉVITCH, Vladimir (1903–85). Philosopher. Born in Bourges, Jankélévitch headed the philosophy *agrégation* list in 1926. He brought a wide range of classical cultural references to his highly personal style of writing, and wrote extensively on music. He developed a non-substantialist philosophy of time and the instant, strongly influenced by *Bergson. His books focused on moral and psychological themes, such as death, evil, lying, irony, boredom, purity, and forgiveness, which he analysed in their existential dimensions. He became professor of philosophy at the Sorbonne in 1952.

[MHK]

Jansenism. This religious movement took its name from the theologian Jansenius (Cornelius Jansen, 1585–1638). He taught a strict Augustinianism, insisting that human beings cannot achieve goodness without the intervention of God's grace and that a minority of individuals has been predestined by God for salvation. The anti-Jansenist and pro-Jansenist factions were prolonging a late-16th-c. conflict between the worldly and other-worldly teachings of *Jesuits and Augustinians respectively. In *Mars gallicus* (1635) Jansenius attacked *Richelieu's foreign policy and, with his close friend and ally *Saint-Cyran, rejected the *raison d'état* doctrine of Richelieu which identified the interests of religion with those of the state. Saint-Cyran, who was consequently imprisoned from 1638 to 1643, had become spiritual adviser of the abbey of *Port-Royal in late 1635. He fulfilled this role for seven years and helped make the abbey a vital centre of Jansenist theory and practice.

Meanwhile, Jansenius's major work, his *Augustinus*, had been posthumously published in 1640. It was condemned by the Inquisition in 1641 and by Pope Urban VIII in 1643. Five propositions allegedly taken from it, and said to represent Jansenist theology, were proclaimed heretical by Pope Innocent X in 1653 and Pope Alexander VII in 1656. The reply of many Jansenists, including Antoine *Arnauld and *Nicole, was to make the famous distinction between *le droit* and *le fait*, accepting that some propositions were heretical, but denying that they were to be found in the *Augustinus*. Two of the strongest defences of the claims of individual conscience and of Jansenist teaching generally appeared when the duc de Liancourt, because of his clear Jansenist leanings, was refused absolution by his confessor. Arnauld replied with a brochure, *Lettre d'un docteur de Sorbonne à une personne de condition* (1655), and a quarto volume, *Seconde lettre à un duc et pair* (1656). This defence of Jansenism led to his dismissal from the Sorbonne, despite *Pascal's mauling of his Jesuit adversaries in the witty and caustic *Lettres provinciales* (1656–7).

In 1655 the Church authorities demanded that all clergy should sign a formulary condemning the five propositions. New formularies were drawn up in 1657 and 1661, when monks and nuns were also required to sign. Between 1661 and 1668 pressure was especially renewed against Port-Royal. Pascal was one of those who supported the nuns, the great majority of whom did not sign despite personal visits from the Archbishop of Paris and the presence of royal troops. In the end a compromise was worked out, and peace between the Jansenists and the Holy See, the so-called 'Paix de l'Église', lasted from late 1668 to early 1679.

By 1679 various influential protectors of Port-Royal, including the duchesse de Longueville, had died, and Louis XIV resumed his attacks on Jansenism, which he suspected of encouraging republican attitudes. In 1709 the nuns of Port-Royal des Champs were finally and forcibly dispersed, and two years later the abbey was razed to the ground on the king's orders.

This severe blow was followed by the papal bull *Unigenitus* (1713) which condemned *Quesnel's *Réflexions morales* (1692). But Quesnel's leadership and organizational powers did much, despite persecution, to maintain the influence of Jansenist doctrine throughout the 18th c.; this was reinforced by the weekly *Nouvelles ecclésiastiques* (1728–1803). A number of French Jansenists found relative freedom in the Netherlands during this time. In France, after Napoleon's *Concordat of 1801 with Pope Pius VII, Jansenism was restricted to a very small number of individuals.

Jansenism influenced some of the outstanding literary figures of the 17th c., including *Racine, Pascal, *Boileau, *La Rochefoucauld, and *La Fayette. It produced an important vernacular *Bible, and between 1637 and 1660 offered the boy pupils of its 'Petites Écoles' an original education including science and Greek. No doubt the movement displayed the self-righteousness typical of small minority groups, but it attracted widespread admiration for its rejection of moral compromise, its questioning of absolute government, and its contribution to a growing sense that individual conscience and private conviction had a right to be heard and expressed.   [JC]

See L. Cognet, *Le Jansénisme* (1961); A. Adam, *Du mysticisme à la révolte* (1968); A. Sedgwick, *Jansenism in Seventeenth-Century France* (1977); C. Maire (ed.) *Jansénisme et révolution: chroniques de Port-Royal* (1990).

Jardin des Plantes, Le. Botanical garden on the left bank of the Seine in Paris, inaugurated in 1635 and known from 1640 as the Jardin du Roi. Lectures in botany, chemistry, and related subjects were given there, and it was greatly developed in the 18th c., when *Buffon was for 49 years the director. A menagerie was set up in 1792 at the instigation of *Bernardin de Saint-Pierre. Under the Revolution the Jardin acquired its modern name, and 1793 saw the creation there of the Muséum d'Histoire Naturelle, whose first 12 professors included two of the *Jussieu brothers, *Geoffroy Saint-Hilaire, *Lamarck, and *Cuvier.   [PF]

Jardin des supplices, Le, see MIRBEAU.

Jardin sur l'Oronte, Un, see BARRÈS.

JARRY, Alfred (1873–1907). French writer and eccentric, whose life and work anticipated and inspired *Dadaism, *Surrealism, and much of the modern avant-garde.

As a precocious schoolboy in Rennes he contributed to the classroom lore prompted by an inept physics teacher; this laid the basis of his life's work, giving rise to the character of Ubu, the coarse, vicious, and vulgar tyrant to whom much of Jarry's writing is devoted. In the Paris of the 1890s he frequented the *Symbolists, publishing poems and other texts collected in *Les Minutes de sable mémorial* (1894) and earning notoriety for his arcane practical jokes and odd life-style. At the same time he worked on the plays of the Ubu cycle, which he first presented as puppet shows to his friends, as he had since his schooldays. This material began to be published from the mid-1890s; *Ubu Roi* appeared in 1896, at which point Jarry installed himself as factotum for *Lugné-Poë at the Théâtre de l'Œuvre and devoted himself to persuading Lugné to stage the play, which received two performances, the public dress rehearsal and the first (and last) night, on 9 and 10 December 1896.

The ensuing controversy established Ubu as a force to be reckoned with; and in accompanying articles and commentaries Jarry articulated the principles of a far-reaching revolution in techniques of staging and attitudes to the theatre. His production was a challenge to conventional taste and realistic presentation, featuring a bizarre composite backdrop of palm trees, a mantelpiece, fields of snow, etc., in front of which an elderly man tiptoed between scenes to hang up placards indicating changes of location. Jarry had intended that the actors be concealed behind masks and restrict their movements to puppet-like gestures. In fact, he saw no other stagings in his lifetime apart from marionette presentations.

Jarry went on to complete further pieces of the cycle: *Ubu cocu* (1897), *Ubu enchaîné* (1900), *Ubu sur la Butte* (1901), while himself increasingly adopted the persona, speech, and mannerisms of Ubu, both as a rejection of the world and as a challenge to its stupidity. He also wrote novels, including *Messaline* (1901), *Le Surmâle* (1902), and *Gestes et opinions du Docteur Faustroll, 'pataphysicien*, published posthumously in 1911. These adumbrate a mock-solemn vision informed by the contingency of the real world, asserting the equivalence of opposites, cultivating paradox and other deliberate challenges to sense which underlie his notion of *'pataphysics.
                    [DHW]

See N. Arnaud, *Alfred Jarry* (1974); K. Beaumont, *Alfred Jarry* (1984).

Jasmin

JASMIN (Jacme Boèr), see OCCITAN LITERATURE (POST-MEDIEVAL).

JASMIN, Claude (b. 1930). Canadian novelist whose early novels caught the feverish mood of social and political change in the Quebec of the early 1960s. In *La Corde au cou* (1961) and *Ethel et le terroriste* (1964), among others, the revolt of his proletarian protagonists against the established order leads them to frustrated acts of murder or to political terrorism. Typically there is a flight from justice which is also a quest for self, and the first-person narratives mix violence and eroticism with a despairing lyricism. From the 1970s his work has been more eclectic, combining autobiographical writing, polemical journalism, and novels of diverse inspiration. Of note are *La Petite Patrie* (1972), memoirs of his working-class Montreal childhood, and *La Sablière* (1979), a touching novel about a retarded child.   [SIL]

JAUCOURT, Louis, chevalier de (1704–80). A Protestant doctor, author of a life of *Leibniz, and *Diderot's principal work-horse on the *Encyclopédie*, for which he wrote innumerable derivative articles on all kinds of subject, working for many hours a day with selfless dedication.

Jaufre. An Arthurian romance in Occitan of about 11,000 lines, interweaving two quests, one to avenge an insult to *Arthur, the other to win a rich and beautiful heiress. Each produces moments of irony and comic excess, offset against the more serious themes of the religious value and social function of knighthood. Whether the resulting text is burlesque or committed is hard to judge. Its date is likewise controversial, a dedication to a king of Aragon producing three candidates, of whom the most likely is Peter II (1196–1213). *Jaufre* would then have been composed in the wake of the romances of *Chrétien de Troyes; it is particularly reminiscent of his *Perceval*.   [SK]

Jaufre Rudel. This early *troubadour is the shadowy Jaufre Rudel II, lord of Blaye (Gironde), who appears in two charters between 1120 and 1143 and was dead by 1164. A *sirventes* by *Marcabru addressed 'A·N Jaufre Rudel outra mar' shows that Rudel joined the Second Crusade, as his otherwise fictitious *vida* relates. Rudel's six extant authentic lyrics are proto-*cansos* expressing an enigmatic *fin'amor* at once quasi-mystical yet erotic, thwarted by geographical (and perhaps psychological) distance, sometimes supplemented by the prohibition or curse of a relative (husband, brother, godfather). The complex meaning is conveyed with an artlessly simple style and haunting imagery.   [PVD]

JAURÈS, Jean (1859–1914). Socialist leader, journalist, orator, and historian. Born in Castres (Tarn), Jaurès was an *agrégé* who forsook teaching for politics. He sat in the Assembly for most of the years from 1885 to his death, first as an independent social-

ist, later as a leading figure in the *Socialist Party he had tirelessly worked to unify in 1905. An ardent *Dreyfusard, he was celebrated for his humanitarian and democratic vision of socialism and for his legendary powers of oratory. Founder of *L'*Humanité* in 1904, he wrote much journalism, but his *magnum opus* was the *Histoire socialiste (1789–1900)*, of which he was general editor and author of the volumes on the French Revolution. His assassination by a right-wing activist on the eve of World War I came as he strove to organize resistance to the rush to war. His memory is venerated on the French Left; *Blum wrote of him that he bore 'the stamp of genius'.   [SR]

Javert. The police inspector in Hugo's *Les *Misérables*.

JEAN, Raymond (b. 1925). University teacher, novelist, literary critic, and journalist. His novels include: *Le Village* (1966) set in Vietnam; *Les Deux Printemps* (1971); *Photo-Souvenir* (1980) set in South America; *L.* (1982); *La Lectrice* (1986). Among his essays are *Pratique de la littérature* (1978), *La Singularité d'être communiste* (1979), and the autobiographical *Belle clarté Chère raison* (1985). Jean's writing is classically lucid and harmonious, imaginative, yet passionately anchored in lived experience, either personal (see *L.*) or political. Although he rejects the label 'communist writer', this commitment dominates.   [PS]

Jean Barois. Novel by *Martin du Gard, published 1913. Through the life of the hero, it portrays *fin-de-siècle* France, the clash of scientism and Catholicism, the *Dreyfus Affair, and *Zola's 'J'accuse' and his subsequent trial; it is today significant above all as a major technical experiment. His love of theatre led Martin du Gard, in his earliest works, to adopt a new manner of writing, namely, a transposition to the novel of scenes in dialogue form accompanied by 'stage directions'. It was in *Jean Barois* that he was to develop this manner to its fullest.

Predominantly in dialogue, the novel goes beyond this basic format to include the text of telegrams, letters, and speeches, all of which sit naturally, in their spontaneity, with the immediacy of the dialogue scenes, giving the reader that 'optique de spectateur' which Martin du Gard sought to achieve.

Having initially considered the application of this manner to the writing *Les *Thibault*, he was forced to concede that, in spite of the life which the 'roman dialogué' could communicate, the drawbacks (a lesser density of content, a diminished range of narrative devices) were too significant for a work of the dimensions in which *Les Thibault* was conceived.   [AHB]

Jean-Christophe. Ten-volume *roman-fleuve* first published by Romain *Rolland in *Péguy's *Cahiers de la quinzaine* between 1904 and 1912. Its idealism is indicated by Rolland's own description: 'une œuvre de foi' in 'une époque de décomposition morale et sociale'. The eponymous hero is a musical prodigy, and the first three volumes describe his upbringing and early compositions in a small Rhineland town. Left-wing politics and a violent fracas cause Jean-Christophe Krafft to leave for Paris, and Volume 5 (*La Foire sur la place*) is a memorably severe indictment of Parisian intellectual, artistic, and social life during the first decade of this century. Jean-Christophe eventually meets Olivier Jeannin, a young French intellectual, who shows him some better aspects of French life and with whom he becomes involved in left-wing activities. In the course of a riot Olivier is fatally wounded and Jean-Christophe, having shot a policeman, is spirited away by friends to Switzerland. By the last volume he is again in Paris as a highly successful composer, but eventually dies of pneumonia. It was immensely popular in its day, but some of the idealistic enthusiasms and socialist simplicities of *Jean-Christophe* now appear very dated. [JC]

JEAN DE CONDÉ, see BAUDOIN DE CONDÉ.

JEAN DE MEUN (Jean Chopinel or Clopinel of Meung-sur-Loire) (d. 1305). Best known as continuator of the *Roman de la Rose* (c.1270–8), Jean de Meun was also an important translator. Still surviving are his renditions of the *De re militari* of Vegetius, the epistles of *Abélard and Héloïse, and *Boethius' *De consolatione Philosophiae*, dedicated to Philippe IV le Bel. In the prologue to the latter, Jean additionally claims to have translated Aelred of Riveaulx's *De spirituali amicitia* and Gerald of Wales's *De mirabilibus Hiberniae*. Scholars are divided as to his authorship of three texts attributed to him in the manuscript tradition, the *Testament*, *Codicille*, and *Sept articles de la foy*. [SJH]

JEAN D'OUTREMEUSE (1338–1400), clerk of the Official of Liège, certainly composed at least two *chansons de geste*, a chronicle, and a lapidary, one of the few works attributed to him that has survived complete. In *Ly Myreur des histors*, an ambitious universal history, giving particular prominence to his native city, he inextricably mixed legendary and historical material. [MJ]

JEAN LE BEL (c.1290–1370), canon of Saint-Lambert de Liège, but attracted more to the life of princely courts and camps, chronicled the earliest phases of the *Hundred Years War. He placed particular emphasis on military affairs, pioneering the chivalric form of reportage which *Froissart, who began by plagiarizing his work, later made so popular. [MJ]

JEANNE, Max (b. 1945). Writer and teacher from Guadeloupe, contributor to the cultural magazine *CARE*, with a particular interest in theatre. Jeanne is not one to suffer fools of any complexion; his writings include the 'ciné-poème' *Western* (1978), a hectic, sarcastic 'spectacle sang et lumière' of his island's history, and *La Chasse au racoon* (1980), a novel set in the margins of the May 1967 uprising in Pointe-à-Pitre. [BJ]

JEANNE D'ARC (c.1412–1431). An illiterate girl from a prosperous peasant family of Domrémy in the Barrois, Jeanne played a brief but decisive role in restoring the fortunes of the *Valois monarchy when at their lowest ebb in the *Hundred Years War. Contemporary mystery, posthumous legend, and Romantic imagination have transformed her into the unrivalled heroine and saint of French national history, celebrated in art, cinema, and an enormous literature, recently augmented by gender studies.

In her own day Jeanne was seen by some churchmen as threatening traditional values in two main respects: by her assumption of the archetypal male profession of soldier (including, for obvious practical reasons, its dress) and because she made 'prophetic' claims. Moved by 'voices' she identified as those of Saints Michael, Catherine, and Margaret, Jeanne crossed enemy territory to reach the royal court at Chinon in February 1429 on a 'divine' mission to save France. There she galvanized the uncrowned dauphin (Charles VII) into sending an army to the relief of Orléans, besieged by the English, and then urged him to go to Reims for coronation (17 July), her most signal service. She was already a pawn in the factional intrigues about the king, and there followed several unsuccessful military ventures in which the Maid participated until taken prisoner at Compiègne in May 1430 by Burgundian forces. Deserted by Charles VII, Jeanne was handed over to the English in Normandy, who arranged a trial for sorcery before an augmented Church court. At Rouen on 30 May 1431 she was burned as a relapsed heretic after a harsh imprisonment bravely endured.

Several 'false Joans' appeared immediately after her death and a legal process, begun in 1450, 'rehabilitated' her. In the 17th c. she was the subject of *Chapelain's ill-fated national epic *La Pucelle* (as also, later, of a scurrilous mock-epic of the same name by *Voltaire), but it was not until the 19th c. that the image of La Pucelle as a 'national saviour' was principally created. She was canonized in 1920. Popular interest in her career appears insatiable, whilst some recent scholarly appraisals have usefully employed insights gained from modern feminist studies. [MJ]

See Marina Warner, *Joan of Arc: The Image of Female Heroism* (1981).

Jeannot et Colin (1764). Short moral tale by *Voltaire, a story of metropolitan corruption and sterling provincial goodness.

JEAN RENART (*fl.* first third of 13th c.). Author, probably from Picardy, to whom three verse romances have been generally attributed: *L'Escoufle*, *Le Lai de l'ombre*, and *Le Roman de la rose ou de Guillaume de Dole*; less certain is his authorship of *Galeran de Bretagne*.

Critics consider Jean Renart as a major creator of

the 'roman réaliste', an important step in the evolution of Old French *romance. His work departed from Arthurian romance by omitting marvellous events and by including contemporary personages and geographical sites. He excels in detailed, realistic descriptions of social events that must have appealed to his courtly audiences. He is also a master of astute characterization through dialogue. *L'Escoufle*, probably his earliest work, expands the model of the 'roman idyllique' found in **Floire et Blanchefleur*; it describes at some length the adventures of two young noble lovers, Guillaume, son of the count of Normandy, and Aelis, princess of Rome, who were born on the same day and were childhood companions. The lovers become separated during their escape from disapproving parents when Guillaume chases after an *escoufle* (a bird of prey) which stole the alms-purse given by Aelis as a love-token. In the seven years that elapse before their fortuitous reunion, Aelis behaves as a resourceful heroine who supports herself by embroidering.

A briefer and more lyrical narrative, the *Le Lai de l'ombre*, which alludes to *L'Escoufle*, is notable for its ambiguous presentation of love in a flirtatious debate between a lady and a knight. The *Lai* is the only work claimed directly in a manuscript by 'Jean Renart'. The author's most brilliant work is his last, *Le Roman de la rose ou de Guillaume de Dole*; it combines the realistic attention to social detail of *L'Escoufle* with the psychological finesse and courtly refinement of *Le Lai de l'ombre*. The poet incorporates 46 fragments of lyric poetry into a narrative where songs and story are mutually enhancing. In a variation upon the wager motif wherein two knights place a bet upon the chastity of the wife or friend of one of them, the romance recounts how Lienor, Guillaume de Dole's sister, defends her honour against the treacherous seneschal by means of clever verbal manipulation. She earns the admiration and hand in marriage of Emperor Conrad, who had previously loved her only as a distant object of desire. The narrator's skilful embroidery of lyric and narrative effects a subtle critique of love and honour as presented in courtly literature.   [RLK]

See R. Lejeune, *L'Œuvre de Jean Renart* (1968); M. Zink, *Roman rose et rose rouge* (1979).

JEAN SANS PEUR (1371–1419). Duke of Burgundy from 1404 to his death, at the height of Franco-Burgundian rivalry [see BURGUNDIAN COURT LITERATURE].

Jean Santeuil. Unfinished novel by *Proust, written in the third person, adumbrating many of the themes of **A la recherche du temps perdu*.

JEHAN BRETEL. *Trouvère* and Arras cloth merchant (attested 1256, d. 1272), head ('prince') of the local *puy for a time. His extant work comprises seven courtly lyrics and **jeux partis* with 19 fellow *trouvères*, including *Adam de la Halle. These debates often treat preposterous topics in humorous, familiar, or ironically pedantic style.   [PVD]

Jehan de Paris, Le Roman de (1490–1500). This last medieval romance centres patriotically on the king of France's amorous rivalry with the king of England for the hand of the Infanta of Castille. Jehan's splendid progress to Spain disguised as a rich merchant, his chivalric triumph, is set against a caricature of the luckless English monarch.   [JHMT]

Jehan et Blonde, see PHILIPPE DE BEAUMANOIR.

Je ne sais quoi, Le. An expression which became popular in polite circles in the 17th c. to refer to elements in human affairs or art which are difficult to explain in terms of classical rationalism. It is discussed in the fifth of the *Entretiens d'Ariste et d'Eugène* by *Bouhours, who sees in it a mysterious touchstone of refined taste.   [PF]

Jesuits. The Society of Jesus, founded by the Spaniard Ignatius Loyola in 1534, soon established itself in France, and played a vital role in French history over the following centuries. While acquiring considerable influence at times, the Society encountered great hostility; it has often been presented caricaturally as the *bête noire* of French *anticlericalism. 'Mangeons du Jésuite' is the cry of the 'Oreillons' in Voltaire's *Candide.

The Society is a religious order whose purpose is to combat for the Catholic faith in the world (as opposed to the convent). Its role was for a long time a militant one, seeking converts, winning the ear of the powerful, and educating the young. The Jesuits' *Ultramontane loyalty to Rome was often seen as being in conflict with France's national interest. Their sympathies with the *Ligue caused them to be popularly associated with the assassinations of *Henri III and *Henri IV, and they were expelled from the country for a brief period beginning in 1594.

In the 17th c. the Jesuits established themselves increasingly firmly in France, allying themselves closely with the monarchy of *Louis XIV, two of whose influential confessors, the pères *La Chaise and Le Tellier, belonged to the order. They conducted a running feud with the *Jansenists, whose theology had been condemned by the Pope. *Port-Royal responded with *Pascal's *Provinciales*, which fixed the image of the Jesuit as worldly casuist in the French imagination. In the 18th c. they found themselves equally opposed to the new philosophy, and attacked the *Encyclopédie* in their periodical *Mémoires de *Trévoux. In 1762, however, disaster struck: following their expulsion from Portugal and a financial scandal in Martinique, their schools were closed by the Parlement de Paris, and two years later they were expelled from France; this time they were not allowed back until 1814. Thereafter, they regained power and influence, and were involved in politics on the side of the clerical ultra-royalists.

They were again expelled in 1880 and in 1901, and their subsequent influence on French society appears to be much diminished.

The Jesuits were very active as a missionary order outside Europe, notably in India, Japan, and China, in North America, and in Brazil and Paraguay. In the last of these they set up a remarkable colony which drew the fire of Voltaire (in **Candide*) and Diderot (in the **Supplément au Voyage de Bougainville*). As missionaries, they produced numerous reports (*relations*) on the countries they lived in, including a series on Canada published in Paris between 1632 and 1671; the perspicacity of these texts make them important forerunners of ethnography.

The Society produced untold quantities of literary texts, both published and unpublished. It numbered among its French members theologians such as **Petau, preachers such as **Coton, literary critics such as **Bouhours and **Rapin. The Jesuits' contribution to French literature resides less in their own writings, however, than in their role as teachers. Until 1762 they were the dominant teaching order of the *ancien régime* [see EDUCATION]. Their network of secondary schools (*collèges*) covered France, the most important being the Collège de Clermont (subsequently Collège Louis-le-Grand) in Paris. Many of France's leading men (for these were all-male colleges) were taught by them, including numerous writers, from **Corneille to Diderot. Their education was Latin-centred, giving a central place to **rhetoric as a practical, performing skill, extending to the composition and acting of innumerable Latin plays—a genre whose cultural importance has been insufficiently recognized. There were innovators and brilliant teachers among the Jesuits, but their teaching, regulated by the *Ratio studiorum* first laid down in 1599, remained essentially traditional. Their philosophy and science lagged many years behind new developments, to which they were often bitterly opposed. Nevertheless, they remained a dominant educational power in France after the Restoration and under the Second Empire.   [PF]

See F. de Dainville, *L'Education des Jésuites* (1978); M. Fumaroli, *L'Âge de l'éloquence* (1980); J. Lacouture, *Les Jésuites* (1990–).

Jeu d'Adam, Le (*Ordo Representacionis Adae*), is a unique Norman, or **Anglo-Norman, play dating from the mid-12th c. Its basic framework is (*a*) the Latin responses of the Septuagesima mass, which recount the Creation, Temptation, and Fall of Adam and Eve, and the story of Cain and Abel, and (*b*) the Latin Procession of Prophets. In performance, each of these Latin elements, having been sung by the choir, is 'translated' in dramatized form into the vernacular; but this dramatization is particularly free in section (*a*), where the psychology of Adam and Eve is illustrated with great intelligence. The text includes numerous Latin stage directions, and is preceded by detailed instructions concerning

the style of acting and the appearance of the set representing the Earthly Paradise. Though the *Jeu d'Adam* has close links with the liturgy, no similar Latin liturgical drama has survived; it is thus sometimes called a semi-liturgical drama. In spite of the traditional view that it was performed outside the west front of a church, an indoor performance, which would underline its liturgical connections, is more probable. In the only surviving manuscript the text is followed almost immediately by a sermon on the Fifteen Signs of Judgement, which some critics consider to be an integral part of the play.   [GAR]

Jeu de la feuillée, Le, see ADAM DE LA HALLE.

Jeu de l'amour et du hasard, Le. Comedy in three acts by **Marivaux, performed at the **Comédie-Italienne in 1730. Sylvia and Dorante are destined by their families to marry but have never met; they independently decide to exchange roles with their servants, Lisette and Arlequin, so as to size one another up before agreeing to marriage. They fall in love, each taking the other for a servant. Dorante declares his identity at the end of Act II, but Sylvia leads him to agree to a misalliance before revealing who she is, whereupon the play ends joyfully with the prospect of a double marriage of masters and servants.   [PF]

Jeu de patience, Le, see GUILLOUX.

Jeu de Paume, Le Serment du, see REVOLUTION, 1b.

Jeu de Robin et de Marion, Le, see ADAM DE LA HALLE.

Jeu de saint Nicolas, Le, see BODEL.

Jeune Belgique, La, see BELGIAN LITERATURE IN FRENCH.

Jeune Fille Violaine, La. Title of the first version of Claudel's *L'*Annonce faite à Marie.*

'Jeune Parque, La', see VALÉRY.

Jeunes Filles, Les. A sequence of four novels by **Montherlant: *Les Jeunes Filles* (1936), *Pitié pour les femmes* (1936), *Le Démon du bien* (1937), *Les Lépreuses* (1939). The hero, a famous writer called Pierre Costals, cynical and *libertin*, is depicted in a series of relationships with women who are in love with him: Thérèse Pantevin, a religious fanatic who writes from afar; Andrée Hacquebaut, who is obsessed by him but in whom he finds no attraction; Solange Dandillot, a simple young girl to whom he himself is strongly attracted. The novels are experimental in technique, mingling letters, extracts from diaries, third-person narration, documents, and 'essays' on general topics in which we cannot be sure who is speaking. Footnotes create a 'Montherlant' who is yet another character. From it all we glimpse a Costals made up of opposites, in whom pity and cruelty, play-acting and simulated discourse, create unpredictable effects and make it difficult for him, for other characters, and for the reader to assess where the truth lies. Underlying it all is a profound misogyny, expressed in a series of generalizations about the disparate natures of men and women.   [RMG]

Jeunes-France, Les. Name given *c*.1830 to a group of *Romantic writers and artists, including *Nerval, *Borel, and *Gautier, whose extreme views or unusual behaviour shocked public opinion, e.g. in the battle of *Hernani.

Jeu parti. Old French name for a lyric genre which in Occitan is called the *partimen*. In dialogue form, it resembles the *tenso*, or *tenson*, but developed at a slightly later date and involves more formal control: whereas in the *tenso* the topic seems to arise spontaneously, in the *jeu parti* one speaker proposes a dilemma in the opening stanza and asks the second participant which of two sides he will take. That choice being made, the first speaker defends the option remaining. The sides in the argument are thus formally distributed, or *parti*. The speakers then defend their position in alternate stanzas. Exceptionally, a judgement is recorded in favour of one or the other, but usually, after three or so stanzas each, the discussion simply breaks off. There are a number of obscene *jeux partis*, but the majority deal with love in its courtly aspect, and great pleasure seems to be taken in the (?mock-)serious discussion of theoretical niceties. A good example is the Occitan *partimen* between the *troubadour Gui d'Ussel and *trobairitz Maria de Ventadorn on the question: Are two people who love each other equal, or should the man be subordinate to the woman? Gui, defending equality, in fact implies that women should do what men want them to. The *tenso* never became established in northern France, but some of the most famous *trouvères* (*Gace Brulé and *Thibaut de Champagne) wrote *jeux partis*. The majority, however, are associated with the *trouvères* of *Arras. A. Langfors's edition of the French *jeux partis* (1926) contains 182 examples.   [SK]

Jeux Floraux de Toulouse. Poetry festivals held, probably annually, in Toulouse from 1324 onwards and organized by a *puy founded the previous year called the Sobregaia Companhia dels Sèt Trobadors de Tolosa or the Consistòri del Gai Saber. At each festival prize-winning poets received a golden violet, eglantine, or marigold. The festivals became a battle-ground for the acceptance of *Occitan in the 16th and 17th c., French prevailing in 1694. Despite *Du Bellay's strictures (*Défense et illustration de la langue française*, II. iv) and frequent restructuring, the institution flourished, honouring *Du Bartas, *Mistral, and *Hugo among others.   [PVD]

JOACHIM, Paulin (b. 1931) Poet. Born in Benin, Joachim left for France, where he attended secondary school. While still a student he became

*Soupault's secretary. Moving in the direction of journalism he published articles in both *Présence africaine* and the Catholic students' *Tam Tam*, before embarking on a course for journalists. He first worked for *France Soir* and in 1960 moved to *Bingo* as chief editor. In 1971 he founded *Décennie*. 17 years without major publications separate his collection of poems *Anti-grâce* (1967) from *Oraison pour une renaissance* (1984). In 1964 he had published the poems of *Un nègre raconte*. The early collections are densely surrealistic, while *Oraison* is more immediately coherent and directed, concerned with establishing links with a mystical and mysterious ancestral past.   [BEJ]

Joad, the inflexible High Priest, a dominant character in Racine's *Athalie*.

JOAN OF ARC, see JEANNE D'ARC.

Jocelyn, see LAMARTINE.

'Joconde'. The first of *La Fontaine's *Contes*, written in *vers libres classiques* and based on a story of marital infidelity in Ariosto. *Boileau defended it in his sprightly *Dissertation sur la Joconde* (1665).

JODELET (pseud. of Julien Bedeau) (*c*.1595–1660). French actor, famous for his floured face and nasal manner of speaking. He enlivened and refined traditions of *farce, creating Cliton in Corneille's *Le *Menteur* and inspiring comedies by *Scarron and d'*Ouville which gave prominence to the valet's role. He joined *Molière's troupe in 1659, and acted in Les *Précieuses ridicules*.   [GJM]

JODELLE, Étienne (1532–73). Dramatist, poet, and member of the *Pléiade, Jodelle was born in Paris of modest origins, educated at the Collège de Boncourt, and is remembered essentially for having written the first classical French tragedy (*Cléopâtre captive*, 1552/3). A second lyrical tragedy, *Didon se sacrifiant* (written in 1555), appeared in Jodelle's collective works (1574), and his *Eugène* (composed 1552) marked an important stage in the restoration of classical comedy advocated in the *Défense et illustration*. Disgraced at court because of a disastrous entertainment he organized in honour of *Henri II and François de Lorraine (February 1558), Jodelle spent the 1560s attempting to regain favour by composing anti-Protestant and official court poetry. Although admitted to the salon of the maréchale de Retz, he died in July 1573 in poverty and abject misery.

Besides his dramatic work, the *Œuvres et mélanges poétiques* (1574) contain poetry covering a lengthy creative period and a diversity of inspirations (including love sonnets addressed to the maréchale de Retz, a bitter collection of *Contr'Amours*, and violent poems directed against the Protestants and approving of the *St Bartholomew's Day Massacre). Jodelle's verse is characterized by an emotional intensity, a verbal virulence, a disturbing vision, and a rhythmical energy admired by d'*Aubigné and judged *'mannerist' or 'pre-baroque' by certain critics. [MDQ]

Joie de vivre, La. Novel by *Zola, the 12th of the *Rougon-Macquart series, published 1884. Set in a fishing port in Normandy, ironically named Bonneville, this edifying text is the story of Pauline Quenu, an orphan taken in by relatives, the Chanteau family. Despite all the sufferings and misfortunes that surround her and the sacrifice of her inheritance and her love for the pessimistic Lazare Chanteau, she affirms her belief in life. [DB]

JOINVILLE, Jean, sire de (b. 1225). Chronicler. His father's family, that of the hereditary seneschals of Champagne, had a long and distinguished tradition as crusaders. Like other Champagne noblemen, in youth Jean was much drawn to the royal court in Paris, where he grew close to King Louis IX. Hence he naturally accompanied his king on the famous *crusade of 1248, during which he was captured and ransomed in Egypt, went to Acre (where he produced a credo to console the dying), and returned to France in 1252. In the later part of Louis's reign he was only rarely at court. But in 1282, when canonization of the king was first mooted, Joinville was called to give evidence before a royal commission. Many years later he acceded to the request of Queen Jeanne of Navarre, and produced his great work Le Livre des saintes paroles et des bons faiz de notre roy Saint Looys in 1305–6, adding a dedicatory letter to Prince Louis, heir of Philippe IV, in 1309. After this little is known about him, and the date of his death is disputed.

In producing his famous Life, Joinville drew extensively on Guillaume de Nangis's writings for the later years of the reign, and on the Enseignements and the Établissements de St Louis. His description of the king's deathbed came from Louis's son Pierre d'Alençon. Otherwise most of his testimony was firsthand. The Life is divided into two parts, a short introduction identifying the king's outstanding characteristics and owing much to standard hagiographical writing, and a far longer piece in more chronological form, devoted principally to the crusade. Joinville swung between portraying Louis as the ideal king obedient to the commands of Christ, and offering the occasional personal glimpse of a man who dressed unsuitably for his office, who enjoyed banter, and who did not love his wife. Joinville chose to counterpose his picture of Louis as the humble saint with one of himself as the embodiment of the military man's point of view, a contrast which creates memorable incidents. The detailed account of the crusade in Egypt was probably intended to ensure that Philippe IV and Prince Louis, who were engaged in planning an expedition to the East at the time he was writing, were well informed about the problems they might face. [JHD]

See N. L. Corbett, La Vie de Saint Louis: le témoignage de Jean, seigneur de Joinville (1977); M. Slattery, Myth, Man and Sovereign Saint: King Louis IX in Jean de Joinville's Sources (1985).

Jongleurs. Medieval professional entertainers. In the earlier part of the Middle Ages their activities were extremely varied, and included juggling, acrobatics, and dancing, as well as music and storytelling. Later they tended to specialize more; the musicians and story-tellers rose in public esteem, whereas the others fell. The jongleurs were especially important in the 13th c., when their repertoire bridged the already narrow gap between the oral presentation of narrative material and true theatre. They memorized and performed in front of live audiences—at a seigneurial court, in a market-place, or along a pilgrimage route—not only narrative *chansons de geste and *fabliaux, which they may have composed themselves, but also dramatic monologues and *dits. Some jongleurs were attached to seigneurial courts and were called menestrels. In the 13th and 14th c., as the feudal structures which produced many of their patrons declined, jongleurs congregated more in the cities and formed *confréries to defend their interests, e.g. in *Arras. *Rutebeuf, *Bodel, and *Adam de la Halle are examples of the most famous creative jongleurs. [GAR]

JORDAN FANTOSME, see ANGLO-NORMAN LITERATURE, 4.

JORIF, Richard (b. 1930). Novelist of Martinican origin. His first novel was Le Navire Argo (1987), whose hero, when discovered in a cellar at the age of 18, speaks the French of *Rabelais. He returns to the contemporary world on a raft of words, piloted by the reading of *Littré's dictionary, which he sees as a great fund of living experience. Language often actuates reality in the modern French novel—but rarely with such irony. [GDM]

Joseph Delorme, Vie, poésies et pensées de, see SAINTE-BEUVE.

JOSÉPHINE, Empress (Joséphine de Beauharnais) (1763–1814). A relation by marriage of Fanny de *Beauharnais, she married Napoleon in 1796 (her first husband having been guillotined), was crowned empress by him in 1804, but was divorced in 1809 because she bore him no children.

Joseph Prudhomme. The typical self-satisfied bourgeois of the 19th c., as caricatured by Henri *Monnier.

Joual. Name given to a form of popular French spoken in Quebec province and particularly in Montreal. The word is a transliteration of the dialect pronunciation of the noun cheval. Joual has been mocked and attacked, notably by Jean-Claude

Desbiens in *Les Insolences du Frère Untel* (1960), as a degraded form of the language, ungrammatical, phonetically corrupt, and full of Anglicisms. From the mid-1960s, however, many *québécois* writers used it to give their work the authentic ring of common speech and to promote the real language of the majority to the dignity of literary language. A good example of literary *joual* is *Tremblay's *Les Belles-Sœurs*.

JOUBERT, Joseph (1754–1824). Author of *pensées*, maxims, and some remarkable letters. He was early in contact with *Diderot, and later a friend of *Chateaubriand, *Bonald, *Fontanes, *Chênedollé, and other major figures of the age. Suffering from poor health, he led a retired life, except for serving under Napoleon in the education ministry.

Much admired for the concise, accurate, at times witty quality of his writing, he refused to compose any work of length, preferring the private 'carnet', in which he combines a classical quest for concision with an introspective, analytical bent. He writes in the *La Rochefoucauld tradition, but with a more tolerant, even Epicurean view of mankind; his critical judgements on writers are often remarkable for their acuity. A collection of his *Pensées* was published by Chateaubriand in 1838, followed by the fuller *Pensées, maximes, essais et correspondance*, published by P. de Raynal in 1842. [FPB]

Joueur, Le. Comedy in five acts and in verse by *Regnard, first performed at the Comédie-Française in 1696. The play's theme is topical, but its structure is a fantastic medley of comic clichés. Valère, a *petit-maître* whose main vice is (incompetent) gambling, has a mistress, Angélique, in whom his interest is always in inverse proportion to his success at gambling. When she finally dismisses him, he resolves to console himself with further gambling. Its *lazzi* [see COMMEDIA DELL'ARTE] and some of its characters give *Le Joueur* affinities with the Italian comedy. Its cast includes Valère's sharp servant Hector, an ageing coquette, a patient and wronged mistress with a domineering maidservant, a gullible and irascible father, an *entremetteuse*, a dissipated marquis, and a crooked gambling teacher. The movement of the play is rapid, and its exploitation of the resources of dramatic language, masterly. [JD]

JOUFFROY, Simon-Théodore (1796–1842). Philosopher who taught at the Sorbonne and the *École Normale Supérieure. With *Cousin and *Royer-Collard, Jouffroy was part of the spiritualist reaction to 18th-c. thought. He translated Dugald Stewart and spread the ideas of the Scottish philosophy of common sense in France. During the Restoration he wrote articles for *Le *Globe*, the intellectual organ of the liberal opposition. He is probably best remembered today for his famous essay *Comment les dogmes finissent*, in which he gave eloquent expression to the Romantic sense of the loss of faith and meaning. His articles and lectures were collected and pub-

lished as *Mélanges philosophiques* (1833), *Cours de droit naturel* (1834–5), and *Cours d'esthétique* (1843). [CC]

Joufroi de Poitiers. A *roman d'aventure* of the mid-13th c., woven loosely around the *vida* of *Guilhem IX and exploiting names relating to the houses of Anjou and Poitiers in the 12th c. It recounts, without recourse to the marvellous, and using motifs known to the *fabliaux*, the cynical career of the count of Poitiers and his equally cynical squire, Robert, interlaced with personal reflections on love by the narrator. [PEB]

JOUHANDEAU, Marcel (1888–1979). Unorthodox mystic Catholic novelist and memorialist, closely allied to the *Nouvelle Revue Française* group of *Gide, *Martin du Gard, and *Paulhan. He uses an evocation of his native town of Guéret, in the Creuse, under the fictional name of *Chaminadour* (1934), to paint an acerbic portrait of small-town life which transcends mere social depiction to become a mystic allegory of the struggle between man and God. In his writing, his tempestuous and disastrous marriage and his homosexuality, recorded in *Chroniques maritales* (1938) and the 27 vols. of *Journaliers* (1961–81), are integrated into his tortured religious vision. [NH]

Journal de Paris, Le, see PRESS, 1.

Journal des débats, Le. Founded in 1789 to report the National Assembly, *Les Débats* became noted for fine writing (*Chateaubriand, *Royer-Collard, Julien-Louis Geoffroy, etc.). Napoleon rebaptized the paper *Journal de l'empire* and sequestered its property. From 1814, and for the next half-century, *Les Débats* championed liberalism and opposed ultra-royalism and Bonapartism; under the stewardship of the Bertin family it favoured a constitutional monarchy. A *journal des notables*, with an élite readership, *Les Débats* continued to nurture fine writing—the mordant *Saint-Marc Girardin and the irony of *Prévost-Paradol, for instance. It remained a distinguished journal of comment after 1870, but its influence declined as that of *Le *Temps* rose. [MP]

Journal des demoiselles, Le, see MIDDLE AGES, 3.

Journal des savants, Le. In a century when authors were beginning to produce scientific works in their native languages, but when the notion of independent criticism had yet to gain acceptance *Louis XIV—encouraged by *Colbert—authorized the publication of a journal monitoring developments in the sciences and the arts. Launched in January 1665 by Denis de Sallo, the *Journal des savants* reviewed French and European books. Its directors included abbé Gallois, secretary of the Académie des Sciences, and abbé Bignon, a friend of *Fontenelle. Much respected and imitated, this ancestor of scientific and literary journalism was published at irregular intervals. In the later 18th c. it gradually lost its former prestige. [MP]

Journal de Trévoux, Le, see TRÉVOUX.

Journal d'un curé de campagne. Novel by *Bernanos, written in Majorca and published 1936. It depicts the struggle of the unnamed priest against the evil, corruption, and apathy of the Picard village of Ambricourt. Helped by the neighbouring curé de Torcy and by the cynical yet courageous Dr Delbende, who commits suicide in the course of the novel, the *curé*, armed only with extraordinary resilience and a childlike innocence, resists the engulfing apathy and animality of the village and saves the local countess from the sin of despair. His death from cancer at the end of the novel elevates him from the level of innocence and heroism to that of sainthood, as he takes upon himself the sins of the village. Bernanos's most accomplished novel, it owes its power both to the pathos of the *curé* and the darkness of the village, and develops into a heroic struggle between the unprepossessing figure of the young priest and the evil around him. As such, it is not merely a major Catholic novel but an important contribution to the literature of heroism of the inter-war years. [NH]

Journal d'une femme de chambre, see MIRBEAU.

Journaliers, see JOUHANDEAU.

Journal intime, see DIARIES.

Journalism, see PRESS.

Journal, Le. In 1892 Fernand Xau launched a popular daily, offering the cream of French writing for 5 centimes. *Barrès, Léon *Daudet, Jules *Renard, *Mirbeau, and *Zola contributed to Le Journal, and *Allais, Tristan *Bernard, and *Courteline provided humourous pieces. Elsewhere, however, Daudet and Mirbeau depicted the *parvenu* manners and politicking of the Belgian businessmen called Letellier who owned the paper. Engaged in a newspaper war with Le *Matin, Le Journal became a leading mass-circulation daily. But it never recovered from suspicions that its director, Charles Humbert, had used the paper for arms-trafficking purposes during World War I. [MP]

Journal littéraire, see LÉAUTAUD.

Journal officiel, see MONITEUR.

Journals, see PERIODICALS.

Journées de février, Journées de juin. The two main episodes in the Revolution of 1848 [see REPUBLICS, 2].

JOUVANCY or **JOUVENCY,** Joseph, père de (1643–1719). Jesuit educator and scholar, for *Hugo the symbol of 18th-c. pedantry. His *Appendix de diis et heroïbus poëticis* (1705), a student's guide to mythology, was a schoolroom best-seller; like his pedagogical treatise *De ratione discendi et docendi*, it was much reprinted in Latin and in French. [PF]

JOUVE, Pierre-Jean (1887–1976). French poet, novelist, and critic. 'Inconscient, spiritualité, catastrophe'—the title of Jouve's important preface to *Sueur de sang* (1935) provides a key to his poetry and fiction, where the links between eroticism and spirituality, sexuality and death, the unconscious and the apocalyptic, poetry and the absolute, are paramount. Up to *c.*1920 Jouve had been a different kind of writer, influenced first by the Neo-*Symbolists, then by the *Unanimism of *Romains and then, during World War I, by the altruistic humanitarianism of Romain *Rolland. A personal crisis, brought on partly by the war and accompanied by a discovery of the mystics and of *psychoanalysis (Jouve married the analyst Blanche Reverchon), led him to repudiate his earlier work. In a series of strange and haunting narratives, from *Paulina 1880* (1925) to *Vagadu* (1931)—probably the first French novel to be based on a psychoanalytical case-history—Jouve rehearsed his obsessions. Conjointly, in the resonant poems of *Noces* (1931) he elaborated a network of symbols—the eye, the mouth, the stag—and the characteristic rhetoric, at once carefully crafted and elliptical, which were to be maintained and extended in the magnificent poems of *Matière céleste* (1937), dominated by the mythical figure of 'Hélène' and the theme of *Nada* (the void) derived from the Spanish mystics. At Dieulefit and then Geneva, Jouve composed the poems of *La Vierge de Paris* (1946), which gave expression to a spirit of resistance nourished by mythic images of revolutionary and medieval France. An admirer of *Nerval, *Rimbaud, *Mallarmé, and above all *Baudelaire (*Tombeau de Baudelaire*, 1958), Jouve—a fine critic—also often expressed his intense admiration for Monteverdi, Mozart, and Alban Berg. [MHTS]

JOUVET, Louis (1887–1951), actor and director, contributed to the theatrical revival after World War I and gave prominence to the director's function. He began his acting career at the Vieux-Colombier with *Copeau in 1913, and went on to score many successes with parts on stage (often in his own productions) and in the cinema. A member of the *Cartel, he stressed the importance of the text in drama, though noted for the elegant theatricalism of his sets. Eclectic and keen to entertain, his most notable productions included *Knock* by Jules *Romains (1923) and involved a sustained partnership with *Giraudoux (*Siegfried*, 1928; *La Guerre de Troie n'aura pas lieu*, 1937). [DHW]

Judaism and Jews in France. The history of Jews and Judaism in France falls into two broad sections: before and after the emancipation act of 1791, which accorded full citizenship to the Jewish 'nations'. The early pre-Revolutionary history could be summarized as a brief golden age, up to the First *Crusade (1096), followed by the long, dark Middle Ages of

417

persecution, increasing segregation, and a series of expulsions and readmissions, depending on the state of the royal coffers.

On the eve of the Revolution, though the 1394 expulsion edict remained in force, a Jewish community of some 40,000 was unevenly concentrated in two main areas: a relatively wealthy, privileged, and well-established minority of Sephardis (Jews of Spanish origin) in the Bordeaux and Bayonne areas, and the majority (78 per cent) of poor and unassimilated Ashkenazis (east-European Jews) living under severe residential and professional restrictions in Metz, Alsace, and Lorraine. Not surprisingly, the first protests against the chaotic and degrading system of privileges, really a denial of rights, came from the north-eastern community leaders (Cerf Berr, Isaie Beer Bing, and Berr-Isaac-Berr. They proved to be remarkable fighters as the discussion on how to improve Jewry's lot developed into the much wider emancipation debate.

The conclusion to that debate in 1791 constitutes a momentous event in modern Jewish history and had a profound influence on shaping French-Jewish mentality. Yesterday they had still been slaves, the Lorraine leader told his community on Day One of the New Era; today they were not only men and citizens but Frenchmen. Much of what came to be known as Franco-Judaism is already present in the 'before and after' view of things expressed here. With the implicit rejection of what went before, a great deal of French as well as Jewish history was repressed. Acceptable French history began with the Revolution which, in its turn, closed Jewish history. It was inappropriate, Théodore Reinach observed in 1884, to speak of French Jews after 1791. Even the term 'Jewish' caused embarrassment because of its alleged association with Judaea and Jerusalem. The most striking expression of Franco-Judaism is found in the rabbinical sermons delivered on the occasion of the centenary of the Revolution (*La Révolution française et le rabbinat français*). Not only was 1789 celebrated as the modern Passover, the second Sinai Law, the coming of the Messianic age; but values and aspirations which had once formed the patrimony of Israel were transferred to France, as if the former's role had been absorbed, fulfilled by the latter. Exit Israel in a blaze of glory, having given birth to 1789. The rabbinate and the Consistoire, the main official bodies and both centralized Napoleonic institutions, proved ideal for spreading Franco-Judaism, a creation after the emperor's own heart. He had gone to dramatic length, in convening the Grand Sanhedrin (1807), to ensure that Jewish law should be compatible with state law. At critical *antisemitic moments the poetry of *civis gallicus sum* dictated a political strategy of silence, of waiting for non-Jewish personalities to take up the fight.

The *Dreyfus Affair was one such moment. With some notable exceptions (e.g. *Bernard-Lazare, Joseph Reinach) the community remained silent, hoping that the storm would pass. Assimilation had broken down one essential survival mechanism: solidarity. *Blum deplored this silence in the 1930s, and was in turn regarded with suspicion by the Jewish Establishment both for his politics—not in tune with its rather conservative republicanism—and for his undiplomatic open Jewishness and support of immigrants. It became increasingly difficult to live up to the image of total assimilation; the Vichy years further complicated matters [see OCCUPATION AND RESISTANCE], though even then we have some moving testimonies of how Marc *Bloch, for example, was sustained by the poetry of being French (*L'Étrange Défaite*, 1946).

Alongside mainstream Franco-Judaism, we find variants, opposition, even French Zionists (Bernard-Lazare, André Spire). There were French-Jewish writers such as Edmond Fleg, who came to understand his Frenchness better after he had discovered his Jewishness. Generally, it would seem as if artists had fewer complexes about having 'plusieurs patries' than the Establishment. At least this used to be the case. The Jewish community today, the biggest and most active in Europe, much revitalized by a considerable contingent of North African Jews, appears to thrive on its internal diversity as well as on an uninhibited affirmation of ethnicity within the larger context of French society.   [NW]

See Rabi, *Anatomie du judaïsme français* (1962); B. Philippe, *Être juif dans la société française* (1979).

Jugement dernier des rois, Le, see MARÉCHAL.

Juif errant, Le. The story of the Wandering Jew, who failed to help Jesus carry the Cross and has walked the earth ever since, is a very ancient one. It was a favourite of the *Bibliothèque Bleue and popular prints, and was given a new lease of life by *Sue in a political *roman-feuilleton*.

Juives, Les. Tragedy by *Garnier, published 1583. It shows the persecution by Nabuchodonosor (Nebuchadnezzar) of the captive Jewish royal family. Nabuchodonosor is a ferocious tyrant who, rejecting all pleas and arguments for mercy, has the Jewish royal children murdered and the king, Sédécie (Zedekiah), blinded, unaware that he is being used by God to punish the Jews and will be punished in his turn. The Jewish women who form the chorus are led by the queen-mother, Amital, an impressive embodiment of grief. Sédécie is an ideal 'Christian' monarch, concerned for his people. The choric poems, especially those modelled on the Psalms, show Garnier's lyric skill.   [GJ]

Julie, see NOUVELLE HÉLOÏSE, LA.

Juliette, L'Histoire de, see SADE.

July Monarchy is the name given to the reign of the Orléanist king Louis-Philippe. He came to power in 1830 after the Parisian insurrection of the July Days—the *trois glorieuses*, 27, 28, and 29 July—

had driven Charles X from power into exile [see RESTORATION]. In some respects the July Monarchy was a continuation of the previous regime, with a monarch, two chambers, and a small, wealthy electorate (though this continued to grow significantly throughout the reign). On the other hand, the style of the regime was less reactionary; there was greater press freedom and an extension of popular *education. It was a period of industrial growth, in which the power of the rich bourgeoisie was consolidated (and became a favourite target of satirical writers and artists, from *Stendhal to *Daumier). Henri *Monnier's Joseph Prudhomme symbolizes the middle-class smugness associated with the regime.

There were pro-Bourbon movements under the July Monarchy [see BERRY], but it also saw the growth of working-class movements. The regime fell in February 1848 [see REPUBLICS, 2], partly as a result of economic difficulties, though the immediate trigger was the government's refusal to allow a patriotic banquet. Louis-Philippe abdicated on 24 February and took refuge in England. [PF]

JUMINER, Bertène (b. 1927). Guyanese doctor and writer who has combined a distinguished academic career in medicine with literature. His fiction deals especially, after *Fanon, with the psychological complexities of *decolonization, drawing on extensive personal experience in the Caribbean, and West and North Africa. Les Bâtards (1961) denounced neglect, mismanagement, and racial discrimination

through the perspective of newly qualified doctors returning to French Guiana. Both Au seuil d'un nouveau cri (1963) and La Fraction de seconde (1990), set in Guadeloupe, explore modern Caribbean characters within narrative frames of the traumas of slavery. La Revanche de Bozambo (1968), also a radio play, humorously lampoons whites colonized by blacks.

[BJ]

JURIEU, Pierre (1637–1713). Calvinist minister and tireless controversialist. In 1681, having taught in a Protestant academy at Sedan, he took refuge with *Bayle in Rotterdam, whence he directed a stream of polemic against *Bossuet, *Arnauld, and many other opponents. After the Revocation of the *Edict of Nantes he published Lettres pastorales adressées aux fidèles qui gémissent sous la captivité de Babylone (1686-9), which combine theological argument, history of the early Church, and modern martyrology.

[PF]

JUSSIEU, Antoine de (1686–1758), Bernard de (1699–1777), Joseph de (1704–79). These brothers were all botanists, famous for their plant-gathering expeditions and their contributions to the Jardin du Roi (later *Jardin des Plantes). Bernard was a teacher of genius, who had a decisive influence on botanical history. His nephew, Antoine-Laurent (1748–1836), wrote a crucially important treatise (Genera plantarum, 1789) on the 'natural' system of plant classification. [PF]

Justine, ou les Malheurs de la vertu, see SADE.

K

KA, Abdou Anta (b. 1931). One of the most original and gifted of Senegalese post-Independence writers, Ka is self-educated. His collection of plays, *Quatre pièces* (1972), includes what he calls 'a poor man's Shaka', recognized by Dorothy Blair as the best of the francophone adaptations of Mofolo's novel about this semi-legendary Zulu king. *Quatre pièces* also contains a study of mental illness, *Pinthioum-Fann*, set in the Dakar mental hospital where Ka was treated for alcoholism. His plays, and his collection of short stories, *Mal* (1975), are full of irony and humour. His lightness of touch in no way diminishes the force of his indictment of neo-colonial exploitation and the spiritual bankruptcy of the Senegalese bourgeoisie. Although *Pinthioum-Fann* won the American Arts d'Afrique award in 1969, the work of this confirmed non-conformist has not received the type of international recognition it deserves. [FNC]

KAHN, Gustave (1859–1936). French poet, editor, and critic who played a major role in the *Symbolist movement between 1886 and 1895. As co-editor of *La Vogue* in 1886, he published poems by *Rimbaud and *Laforgue which contributed to the development of *vers libre*, whose cause he also advanced in his 1887 volume of poetry, *Les Palais nomades*, and in the preface to his collected *Premiers poèmes* of 1897 [see VERSIFICATION]. One of the most important art critics of the late 19th c., he helped to establish Symbolism's discourse on painting, in which the *Impressionism of *Degas and the *Neo-Impressionism of *Seurat were reconciled with the most recent expressions of the idealist tradition in the work of *Moreau and *Puvis de Chavannes.

[JK]

KALOUAZ, Ahmed (b. 1952). Algerian-born poet, novelist, and dramatist brought up from an early age in France. The son of an immigrant worker, he explored the condition of Algerian women in his first novel, *L'Encre d'un fait divers* (1984), and produced a powerful narrative on French racism in *Point kilométrique 190* (1986). The poems collected in *A mes oiseaux piaillant debout...* (1987) mix personal and political themes. Through the circus folk depicted in the play *Double soleil* (1989), Kalouaz explores the theme of marginalization. [AGH]

Kamouraska, see HÉBERT, A.

KANE, Cheikh Hamidou (b. 1928). Senegalese novelist. The son of a chief, he was educated first in the Koranic school, speaking only Fulbe (the language of the Fulani) until the age of 10, followed by the local French primary school, secondary school in Dakar, and university in Paris (1952–9). He returned to Senegal bringing with him his one novel, *L'Aventure ambiguë*. It was published in 1961, obtaining the Grand Prix Littéraire d'Afrique Noire in 1962.

Although on one level autobiographical, with the wider implications of the quest or initiation novel, the primary theme of *L'Aventure ambiguë* is the crisis of a traditional society in transition, presented through the impact of Western secular culture, education, and philosophy on a deeply devout Muslim youth. This theme of acculturation is widespread in West African fiction, but nowhere is it developed with such art and profundity.

The hero, Samba Diallo, like the author a member of a noble Fulani clan, spends his early years under the absolute guidance of the ascetic master of the Koranic school, who recognizes the child's purity and picks him to succeed him as the spiritual guide of the Diallobé country. But political expedience demands that Samba leave his tutelage to attend French lay schools and subsequently the Sorbonne, where he is steeped in the philosophies of *Descartes, *Pascal, and Nietzsche. The ambiguities of his existence, suggested by the title, are the consequences of snatching the youth from traditional influences and replacing these with Europe's materialistic dialectics. And, because the rootlessness postulated here is more intellectual and spiritual than social, Kane offers no facile solutions. Rather than compromise, his hero finds release from his dilemma in an ambiguous death, which is a sort of suicide.

The substance of Kane's novel is not in its incident, but in its argument, presented by way of parable, metaphor, and symbol. It is structured as a series of confrontations and dialogues, each presenting a stage in the quest for the Absolute, a facet of a complex spiritual dilemma, or, at the lowest level, a search for a strategy to halt the destruction of the basic values of Islam by the inroads of westernization. The novel's symmetrical structure, economical framework, and elegant simplicity of language give it its classic proportions and make it a work of sombre poetic beauty, in keeping with the austere beauty of the landscape and the gravity of its quintessential problems. [DSB]

Karim, see SOCÉ DIOP.

KARONE, Yodi (pseud. of Alain Ndongo Ndiye) (b. 1954). Cameroonian writer, living in Paris. He is the author of two plays, but is best known for his novels, *Le Bal des caïmans* (1980), *Nègre de paille* (1982), *Les Beaux Gosses* (1988), and *A la recherche de cannibale amour* (1988). The first of these takes place in a concentration-camp world, the others represent a challenge to the neo-colonial world and a quest for freedom, with picaresque heroes roaming through Africa, Europe, and America. [AK]

KARR, Alphonse (1808–90). French journalist known for his caustic commentaries on the events and personalities of the Parisian literary scene during the July Monarchy in his satirical paper *Les Guêpes*. He was also the author of minor sentimental and humorous novels (*Sous les tilleuls*, 1832) and, later, of texts in the domestic genre (*Voyage autour de mon jardin*, 1845). [BR]

KATEB Yacine (1929–89). Algerian writer. Kateb is the most important and influential *Maghrebian author and his novel *Nedjma the best-known work by a Maghrebian.

After early instruction at Koranic school, he entered the French colonial school system where he excelled in French language studies. He was arrested during the 8 May 1945 nationalist demonstration in Sétif. Kateb would later say that this episode was crucial in his intellectual and political development, for it was in prison that he discovered the two most important things in his life: revolution and poetry.

His first book of poems, *Soliloques* (1946), consists of apprentice pieces reminiscent of poems by French *Symbolist and *Decadent poets of the 19th c. He also demonstrated his precocity as well as his commitment to national liberation in a lecture on the 19th-c. Algerian patriot Abdel-Qader, which he delivered at the Salle des Sociétés Savantes in Paris when he was not yet 18.

Kateb claimed that his writings constitute 'a single work written in one long breath'. Indeed, the first clear expression of this open-ended work was a poem entitled 'Nedjma ou le poème ou le couteau' (1948), in which we encounter many of the icons, symbols, and mythic figures which abound in his other works: ancestors, the stars, palm trees, blood, sun, steeds, camels, the infinite desert and, above all, Nedjma. The quest for the evanescent character of Nedjma, based on a real-life cousin who represented a haunting but impossible love object for Kateb, weaves a common thread through his principal novels and plays.

In 1956, at the height of the *Algerian War, the Éditions du Seuil issued his masterpiece, *Nedjma*. Its publication was a literary event, partly because of the political impact of an Algerian work of *Nedjma*'s stature appearing in Paris during those volatile times, but especially because the novel's manifest brilliance and highly fragmented nature had no precedent in Maghrebian literature.

Many of the characters in *Nedjma* are found in Kateb's other works written in the 1950s and 1960s. He had the habit of rewriting and republishing extracts of his texts, and there is often no clear line of demarcation among genres. For example, 'Le Fondateur', a poetic text published in a journal and reprinted in an anthology, ended up assimilated into the prose of Kateb's second novel, *Le Polygone étoilé* (1966), which was developed from the many cuttings resulting from the radical abridgement of *Nedjma* that the publisher had required.

Kateb also used drama to explore the same themes. *Le Cercle des représailles*, published in 1959, includes a dramatic version of the Nedjma theme (*Le Cadavre encerclé*), a farce (*La Poudre d'intelligence*), a drama (*Les Ancêtres redoublent de férocité*), and a dramatic poem, 'Le Vautour'. After the publication of a play about the Vietnam War and colonialism, *L'Homme aux sandales de caoutchouc* (1970), Kateb turned away from French and produced plays in colloquial Arabic, undertaking another major French-language work only in his last years, a play in commemoration of the bicentenary of the French Revolution. Kateb's early dramatic style is Brechtian and the later plays in French and Arabic continue and exaggerate this trend, even bordering on political caricature of the sort found in so-called 'guerilla theatre'.

In 1987 Kateb was awarded the French Grand Prix des Lettres for his contribution to literature. His work has been a fundamental point of reference for other postmodern Maghrebian writers, such as the Moroccan Abdelkebir *Khatibi and Algerian novelists Rachid *Boudjedra, Rachid *Mimouni, Tahar *Djaout, and Mohamed Magani. [ES]

See J. Arnaud, *Recherches sur la littérature maghrébine de langue française: le cas de Kateb Yacine* (1982).

KAYO, Patrice (b. 1942). Cameroonian writer, formerly director of *Le Cameroun littéraire* and author of numerous works in various genres—poems, fables, stories, essays—the most important being probably *Tout le long des saisons* (1983), *Déchirements* (1983), and *Les Sauterelles* (1986). A partisan of *négritude, he seeks for a harmony between African and European civilization. Above all, he is a spokesman for the ordinary people, whom he seeks to wake from their lethargy to an awareness of their oppressed condition. His socio-political commitment does not, however, prevent his poetry from expressing love, friendship, and fraternity. [AK]

KEAN, Edmund (1787–1833). Great English actor whose dynamic style of playing excited the literary and artistic élite of Paris and inspired a number of rising young French actors (*Bocage, *Dorval, *Lemaître) during the visit of an English theatre company (September 1827–July 1828), when 33 performances of plays by *Shakespeare were given. Kean's own performances as Othello and Richard

III, like those of the other leading players (Charles Kemble, Macready, Harriet Smithson), revealed Shakespeare in a wholly new light and profoundly influenced the future character of French Romantic *drama and the actors associated with it. He was the subject of plays by *Dumas *père* (1836) and *Sartre (1953). [SBJ]

KÉBÉ, Mbaye Gana (b. 1936). A prolific writer, Kébé, who has worked for the Senegalese Ministry of Culture and as a school inspector, has produced poetry, short stories, plays for radio and TV, novels, and children's books, several of which have won prizes. His collection of poetry, *Ébéniques* (1975), whose title echoes *Senghor's *Éthiopiques*, clearly shows the latter's influence. His early work often echoes the conciliatory tone which characterizes Senghor's approach to the French. On the other hand, his first novel, *Le Blanc du nègre* (1979), looks at the role of French *coopérants* with a satirical eye, and the second, *Le Décret* (1984), is an even more bitingly satirical comment on contemporary Senegalese politics. The television adaptation of *Le Décret* proved immensely popular in Senegal. [FNC]

Keepsake, see SHORT FICTION.

KEITA, Aoua (b. *c*.1915). As the title of by far her most important work suggests, *Femme d'Afrique: la Vie d'Aoua Keita racontée par elle-même* (1975), Keita's text is autobiographical and historical, describing her involvement as a militant during the 1960s in Mali. Among the first generation of African women writers, Keita is one of many women to have written a text which falls outside the purely literary. [BEJ]

KESSEL, Joseph (1898–1979). French journalist and novelist whose active life is the basis for much of his fiction. His adventurer-heroes fight in air-battles (*L'Équipage*, 1923), participate in the Resistance struggle (*L'Armée des ombres*, 1946), and travel to exotic countries. *Belle de jour* (1928), later filmed by Buñuel, creates a woman whose desires conflict with her social role. [EAF]

KHAÏR-EDDINE, Mohammed (b. 1941). Berber writer from the south of *Morocco whose early work *Agadir* (1967), taking its inspiration from the earthquake which destroyed that town, gained much notoriety because of its modernistic techniques and its iconoclasm. Its apparent attack on the monarchy led to a long period of living abroad for its author. Khaïr-Eddine's later work has been more autobiographical in tone and is extensively concerned with his Berber roots. *Une vie, un rêve, un peuple, toujours errants* (1978) is based on the traditional story-telling and legends of the Sousse. In *Légende et vie d'Agoun'chich* (1984) Khaïr-Eddine relates the story of an outlaw figure of this area whose demise coincided with the arrival of the French. This novel is one of the very few francophone works in Morocco to deal directly with French colonialism. Khaïr-Eddine returned to Morocco in 1980. [JKa]

KHATIBI, Abdelkebir (b. 1938). One of the most influential contemporary Maghrebian writers. He was born in El Jadida, Morocco, and from 1949 to 1957 attended the Collège Sidi-Mohammed in Marrakesh. While a student there, he became interested in French literature and culture as well as creative writing. He then studied sociology at the Sorbonne and in 1965 defended a thesis on *Le Roman maghrébin* (1968). He directed the Institut de Sociologie in Rabat from 1966 until 1970 and currently holds a position of university research professor at the Institute of Scientific Research at the Université Mohammed V.

As an adolescent, Khatibi wrote under a pseudonym poems in Arabic and in French which were published and read on the radio in Rabat, as well as plays which were produced. His first novel, *La Mémoire tatouée* (1971), signalled a new approach to writing in Morocco. The discontinuity of the discourse is quite different from that of earlier works by Maghrebian writers such as *Chraïbi, *Feraoun, *Dib, *Mammeri, and *Memmi.

In his novels and such major socio-critical works as *La Blessure du nom propre* (1974), *Amour bilingue* (1983), and *Maghreb pluriel* (1983), Khatibi pays special attention to the impact of the Maghrebian writer's mother tongue upon the acquired French in which he or she writes, coining a 'third code' or discourse based on an 'interior calligraphy' and reflecting an aesthetics of the 'palimpsest', or what Khatibi has termed a *bi-langue*, prominent in francophone and other bilingual literatures. Khatibi's aesthetic preoccupations with bilingualism, biculturalism, and inter-semiotic activity (including what he has called *bi-pictura*) surface frequently in his works and constitute the focal point of such books as his *L'Art calligraphique arabe* (1976; in collaboration with M. Sijelmassi), *Le Livre du sang* (1979), and *Ombres japonaises* (1988). He is also deeply concerned with social relations on a number of levels, from male–female courtship to international understanding. In recent years he has been formulating a concept of human emotional interaction, or *aimance*, that relies on the individual's heightened ability to *capter*, or tune into, the feelings of others. On a broader scale, Khatibi's interest in other cultures—particularly their urban spaces—and in the transcendence of cultural differences is explored in such works as *Figures de l'étranger dans la littérature française* (1987), *Le Même Livre* (1985, in collaboration with J. Hassoun), and his most recent novel, *Un été à Stockholm* (1991). [ES]

See C. Buci-Glucksmann *et al.*, *Imaginaires de l'autre: Khatibi et la mémoire littéraire* (1987).

Kingship, see MONARCHY.

Kings of France, see the Chronology at the end of the volume.

KLINGSOR, Tristan (pseud. of Léon Leclère) (1874–1966). The work of this French poet, painter, musician, and art critic is distinguished by his love of legends and by his experimentation with metre and with traditional popular verse forms. Whether the legends were those of the *Symbolist movement's medieval and Wagnerian themes (*Filles-Fleurs*, 1895) or those of oriental literature (*Schéhérazade*, 1903), his mastery of French verse forms and rhythms (including those of the *vers libre*) resulted in the very personal, flexible, light, and humorous poetry which made Klingsor one of the inspirations of the *Fantaisistes in the period immediately preceding World War I.   [JK]

KLOSSOWSKI, Pierre (b. 1905). Novelist and essayist, born in Paris of Polish parents, and brother of the painter Balthus. Klossowski was much influenced by Georges *Bataille, and shared his admiration for *Sade (*Sade mon prochain*, 1947). His main fictional work, the trilogy *Les Lois de l'hospitalité* (1954–60), brings a self-consciously classicizing diction to bear upon a sequence of transgressive erotic scenarios.   [MB]

Knock, ou le Triomphe de la médecine (1923). Comedy by Jules *Romains, performed with great success by *Jouvet. Doctor Knock succeeds in building up a thriving country practice from nothing by terrorizing the healthy local people into hypochondria.

KOCK, (Charles-) Paul de (1793–1871). Hugely popular novelist and author of comedies and *vaudevilles. This good-natured and humorous observer of *le petit peuple* wrote rollicking stories full of life, movement, and gaiety, sometimes coarse and scabrous, often grossly sentimental, occasionally with a moral lesson tacked on. Known as the master of the *roman gai*, he contributes significantly to our picture of French social life, especially during the Restoration and the July Monarchy. Marx read him avidly for both entertainment and instruction. Typical of his manner are: *Gustave ou le Mauvais Sujet* (1821), *Le Cocu* (1831), *La Jolie Fille du faubourg* (1840).   [SBJ]

KOFFI, Raphaël (b. 1942). Ivoirian writer. Following an early novel, *Les Dernières Paroles de Koimé* (1961), Koffi turned his attentions to theatre. His play *Le Trône d'or* was commended by the jury of the Concours Théatral Interafricain in 1968.   [MPC]

KOFMAN, Sarah (b.1934). French philosopher. Her work draws on the thought of Freud and Nietzsche, both of whom she has subjected to 'symptomatic' readings, uncovering the discursive strategies they employ. In criticizing Freud's analysis of women she argues that he devised hasty pseudo-solutions to mask his profound uneasiness on this matter.
                [MHK]

KOJÈVE, Alexandre (1902–68). Neo-Hegelian philosopher. Kojève (originally Kozhevnikov) left his native Russia in 1920, and studied philosophy in Germany before settling in Paris in 1927. His early work in the philosophy of religion drew on Soloviev, Heidegger, and Marx. From 1933 to 1939 he conducted a now-legendary seminar at the *École Pratique des Hautes Études on Hegel's *Phenomenology of Mind*, with a small but distinguished audience including *Bataille, *Queneau, *Lacan, *Merleau-Ponty, *Aron, and *Breton. Substantively published as *Introduction à la lecture de Hegel* (1947), it strongly influenced the Hegel revival and popularized Kojève's interpretation of Hegel's analysis of the Master–Slave relationship. In a conflict, he argued, the Master desires recognition more than he fears death, and conquers the Slave who prefers life even at the price of submission. However, recognition by a Slave cannot satisfy the Master, who also becomes dependent on the Slave's work, while the Slave in his fear and subjection learns self-awareness, self-mastery, and control over the material world. This dialectical account of human consciousness was adopted by *Existentialists and applied to many social and political contexts. Kojève's post-war philosophical activity was limited by his career as a senior civil servant, but his posthumous and unpublished works continued his attempt to reformulate Hegel's philosophical system.   [MHK]

KOLTÈS, Bernard-Marie (1948–89). French playwright. Author of ten plays, he emerged as the most distinctive and important dramatic voice of the 1980s with productions of *La Nuit juste avant les forêts* (1977), *Combat de nègre et de chiens* (1983), *Quai Ouest* (1986), *Dans la solitude des champs de coton* (1987). His plays examine the transactional nature of human relationships, exploring the interaction of psychological motivation and ideological context in a situation which Koltès calls a 'deal', but which is not always overtly commercial. With highly charged dramatic situations and language, and the cultural and racial mix of their settings, they offer striking images of life in the late 20th-c. 'global village'.
                [DWW]

KONÉ, Amadou (b. 1953). Ivoirian writer, born in Burkina Faso. A professor of African literature, he has written novels, plays, and essays. His theatre is didactic in nature, the most recent play being *Les Canaris sont vides* (1984). His novels, *Les Frasques d'Ebinto* (1975), *Jusqu'au seuil de l'irréel* (1976), *Sous le pouvoir des Blakoros* (1980–2), and *Liens* (1982) resemble the work of traditional story-tellers in both form and content. See his essay, *Du récit oral au roman* (1985).   [AK]

KOUROUMA, Ahmadou (b. 1927). Novelist and playwright from Ivory Coast. His personal history encompasses student radicalism, four years spent in Indo-China as a punishment for 'subversive' behaviour during his military service, qualification as an actuary, and appointment as director of the Institut National des Assurances in Yaoundé.

Koyré

Perhaps the most strikingly original francophone African novel to date, Kourouma's *Les Soleils des indépendances* (1968) was hailed by some as the first truly African novel in French, and condemned by others for its unapologetic disregard for standard French syntax. The story of a Malinké prince reduced to the status of a beggar in the Independence era, *Les Soleils* is set in two West African republics whose fictive names hardly conceal their real identities (Ivory Coast and Guinea). The novel is a brilliantly humourous satire of the regimes of both Houphouët Boigny and Sékou Touré, and of the one-party state in general, though Kourouma does betray marginally more sympathy for the socialist option.

The novel's originality lies more in its style than in its content. It is the first real attempt to subordinate the French language to the artistic demands of African reality. Malinké idioms are translated literally not only in the dialogue but in the body of the text. Kourouma is a highly sophisticated artist, master of both modern Western and African literary cultures, and he exploits the differences between the two traditions to marvellous comic effect. Though he sometimes gives the impression of merely revelling in neo-colonial Africa's multiple ironies for their own sake, *Les Soleils*, in bringing the pre-colonial prince and the neo-colonial masters face to face, is, in fact, a serious attempt to grasp the basic mechanisms of African history.

After a virtual silence of 22 years (apart from the brief appearance of a play, *Tougnantigui, diseur de vérité*, performed in Abidjan, banned in mid-run, and never published), Kourouma's second novel, *Monnè, outrages et défis* appeared in 1990. Like *Dongala and *Fantouré, having dissected neo-colonialism Kourouma now returns to the final days of the pre-colonial era, to the French invasion and conquest, to re-examine the roots of Africa's present crisis. *Monnè* was awarded the annual prize of the French Association des Nouveaux Droits de l'Homme.

[FNC]

KOYRÉ, Alexandre (1892–1964). French historian of science and philosophy. A student of Husserl, *Bergson, and *Brunschwicg, he was convinced of the fundamental unity of intellectual activity: he believed that the development of science was inseparable from the history of philosophy and religion, and demonstrated in his studies of 16th- and 17th-c. science that metaphysical and scientific revolutions are closely connected (*Études galiléennes*, 1939; *La Révolution astronomique*, 1961). His own approach involved setting aside modern priorities in order to reconstruct the presuppositions, intentions, and methods of scientific innovators, together with the apparent errors and failures which revealed the mind at work in the process of discovery. [REG]

KRÉA, Henri (b. 1933). Algerian writer whose dual inheritance, from his French father and his Algerian mother, has profoundly influenced his work. Unlike other Algerian writers of his generation, who have sought for evidence of national identity in pre-colonial history and culture, Kréa believes that nationality is a question of choice and commitment. He claimed, therefore, to write in 'Algerian'; the cover of his first novel *Djamal* (1961) asserted that 'le langage est l'algérien, langue en formation, aussi différente du français que l'américain est de l'anglais'. However, the language of the work is Algerian-French, not Francarabe, colloquial Arabic, or Berber. The book's hero, Mourad, claims: 'Moi, je suis Arabe et je parle français!' He is an Algerian because he chooses to be. Kréa's use of local French words like *coulo, frangaoui, makrout, zalabia*, etc., show the change undergone by French in Algeria. (The subsequent disappearance of many of these neologisms shows the extent to which they were the product of settler French.) *Djamal*'s fragmented syntax and experiments with mimetic dialogue are attempts to authenticate the French of Algeria as a separate language. His works also include *La Révolution et la poésie sont une seule et même chose* (1957) and *Tombeau de Jugurtha* (1968). [JKa]

KRISTEVA, Julia (b. 1941). French-Bulgarian theorist, writer, psychoanalyst, and professor of linguistics; former member of the *Tel Quel editorial board (1970–82). Kristeva came to Paris in 1965 to study at the *École Pratique des Hautes Études, where she became a protégée of *Goldmann and *Barthes. In less that two years she managed to conquer the Parisian intelligentsia with such publications as 'Bakhtine, le mot, le dialogue et le roman' and 'Pour une sémiologie des paragrammes', which appeared in *Critique and *Tel Quel. Her first collection of articles, *Séméiotiké: recherches pour une sémanalyse*, came out in 1969. That same year Kristeva published *Le Langage, cet inconnu* under the name of Joyaux (the family name of her husband, Philippe *Sollers). Her doctoral theses, *Le Texte du roman* and *La Révolution du langage poétique*, appeared in 1970 and 1974. The latter represents the culmination of her work in semiotics and literary theory from the late 1960s to mid-1970s. Drawing on linguistics, philosophy, psychoanalysis, and avant-garde literature, she here elaborated a theoretical discourse centred on the question of subjectivity in language and history.

After a trip to China in 1974 Kristeva published *Des Chinoises*, which explores the evolution of Chinese women in relation to the Chinese Cultural Revolution. In 1975 she co-edited *La Traversée des signes*, a series of articles on linguistic theory and poetic practice in non-Western cultures. *Polylogue* (1977) contains essays on linguistic theory and avant-garde writing, as well as on the place of femininity and motherhood in Western thought and culture. *Folle vérité* (1979) is a collective work stemming from a seminar on psychotic discourse and truth. In *Pouvoirs de l'horreur* (1980), *Histoires d'amour* (1983), *Au commencement était l'amour* (1985), and *Soleil noir:*

dépression et mélancolie (1987), she examines the representations of abjection, love, and melancholy in Western culture from a psychoanalytical perspective.

Kristeva has also published a novel on the Parisian intelligentsia entitled *Les Samouraïs* (1990). Her second novel *Le Vieil Homme et les loups* came out a year later. With *Étrangers à nous-mêmes* (1988) and *Lettre ouverte à Harlem Désir* (1990), she engages with the political issues of the 1980s—immigration and racism—and more generally with the question of exile, which has been one of her fundamental preoccupations as a foreigner in France.

Kristeva's position as a linguist, analyst, and writer enables her to conceptualize Western thought and culture essentially from the perspective of the human subject and its relation to language, sexuality, and politics. Like *Benveniste and Barthes, she has made subjectivity a fundamental concern of semiotic theory. Her notion of the 'subject-in-process' goes hand in hand with a theory of signification that concentrates on the crisis or subversion of meaning—hence the importance she accords both to clinical practice and to the texts of modernity (e.g. *Mallarmé, Joyce, *Artaud, *Céline). Kristeva's socialist background and her status as an *émigrée* in France have been fundamental in determining her theoretical and ethical concerns. Highly suspicious of totalizing systems and global models, she has opted for an ethics of singularity and a theory of exceptions in art and literature.

[DM-S]

See T. Moi, *The Kristeva Reader* (1986); J. Lechte, *Julia Kristeva* (1990).

KRÜDENER, Barbara Juliane de Vietinghoff, baronne de (1764–1824). Novelist and mystic of Russian origin. She was deeply interested in *Illuminism and for a time exerted an influence over Tsar Alexander I. Her literary reputation rests essentially on her novel *Valérie* (1803).

L

LAÂBI, Abdellatif (b. 1942). The major Moroccan francophone writer of the post-Independence period and one of the major 20th-c. literary figures in the Maghreb. Editor of *Souffes*, politically active in the Parti de la Libération et du Socialisme, he was arrested, tortured, and imprisoned in 1972 for 'délits d'opinion'. Adopted as an Amnesty International prisoner of conscience, he was awarded the Prix de la Liberté, PEN Club, and the Prix International de Poésie by the Fondation des Arts, Rotterdam, while still in jail. He was released in 1980 and now lives in France.

Laâbi's imprisonment is not coincidental to his work but fundamental, as it arose from his insistence on the intensely political nature of writing. His use of French, rather than Arabic, is a deliberate choice in his attempt to find a language which can detraditionalize as well as decolonize the Moroccan consciousness. Laâbi's writing constantly refers back to the orality of Morocco. He moves amongst genres in a style which he himself terms 'itinéraire', as he constantly seeks to elude conventional modes and responses. His constant terror is of being submerged by the aphasia which is colonialism's lasting legacy and which tyranny in Morocco has perpetuated. His achievement is the creation of a new literary language which is constantly preoccupied with the nature of writing; his failure is inevitable given the paradox of a committed revolutionary writer in a society of illiterates.

It was during his imprisonment that Laâbi's creativity developed to full maturity, leaving only a trace of the rather false surrealism of his early *L'Œil et la nuit* (1969). In *Le Règne de barbarie* (1976), *Sous le baillon* (1981), and *L'Écorché vif* (1986), called *prosoèmes*, he strives for a language which is refined, lucid, and angry and which is free from the pseudo-mimetic function of prose, while not being afraid to incorporate authentic material such as letters to Mario de Andrade and to his son in *L'Écorché vif*. In *Le Chemin des ordalies* (1982), Laâbi transformed his prison letters, later published as *Chroniques de la citadelle d'exil* (1983), into a lucid prose poem which is one of the most memorable accounts of imprisonment ever written.

In interviews, such as that with Jacques Alessandra published as *La Brûlure des interrogations* (1985), Laâbi explores honestly and with great historical insight the dilemma of the relationship between the intellectual and the state, a dilemma which faces all writers from impoverished and despotic societies and which is often evaded or marginalized. By consistently problematizing the role of the writer, Laâbi's work has held out the possibility of the emergence of an uncompromised literary voice in the Maghreb; in this his role is second only to that of *Kateb Yacine in Algeria.

Laâbi has also been responsible for several translations from Arabic into French, including the writings of the Iraqi poet Abdelwahab Al Bayati, *Autobiographie du voleur de feu* (1987). Other works include a theatrical piece, *Le Baptême chacaliste* (1987), and the poetry sequences *Discours sur la colline arabe* (1985) and *Histoire de sept crucifiés de l'espoir* (1980). In 1980 a collection of essays by distinguished authors and scholars was published as *Pour Laâbi*.   [JKa]

LA BARRE, Jean-François Lefèvre, chevalier de (1747–66). A young man who was beheaded and burnt on a charge of blasphemy and of mutilating a crucifix. *Voltaire fought in vain for his rehabilitation, which was decreed by the Convention in 1793.

Là-bas (1891). *Huysman's second major novel, like *A rebours an attempt to reconstruct contemporary reality through imagination and art. *Là-bas* is constructed on two intersecting planes. The historical novel which the hero, Durtal, is writing plunges back into a representation of a vigorous, violent, and intensely spiritual Middle Ages. Durtal narrates with censorious relish the crimes, condemnation, and penitential suffering of the 'enigmatic' *Gilles de Rais, the Bluebeard of tradition, sadist, pervert, and Satanist. This purportedly historical reconstruction runs alongside Durtal's investigations of the equally horrendous, though less visible, war of black and white magic in contemporary Paris. The techniques and tone of the contemporary plane of the text (vivid circumstantial detail, conventional realistic settings, dialogue and psychological analysis, and Durtal's sceptical stance), set against the clearly imaginative status of the medieval narrative, blur the boundaries between fiction and reality. For the credulous reader in 1890s Paris, swept by occult fevers (Rosicrucianism, Theosophy, Luciferism, Vintrasism, Satanism), the novel acquired authoritative, documentary status. Huysmans was in fact acquainted with the circles he described, though whether their activities had quite the power and extent which he attributed to them is another matter.   [JB]

LABAT, Jean-Baptiste (1663–1738). French Dominican missionary in the *West Indies, whose voluminous *Nouveau voyage aux îles d'Amérique* (1722, augmented edn. 1742) is an encyclopedic account of fauna, flora, local customs, commerce, etc., written in a lively, attractive style.

LABÉ, Louise (*c*.1520–1566), lived in Lyon and published a single volume of poetry there in 1555, containing 24 sonnets, one of which was in Italian, three elegies, a prose 'Débat de Folie et d'Amour', and 24 poems by others in her honour. Her lasting reputation depends on the sonnets, often republished and translated. The first two or three poems of the sequence consciously place her in the *Petrarchan tradition, employing techniques such as antithesis to convey alternating states of hope and fear, or the frustrations of love which is unreturned or has gone cold, and using hyperbole for intensity of feeling, such as the joyful memory of past love. Labé's structures and conceits are traditional, and she speaks the ordinary language of love, but her own poetic voice comes through distinctly. Her achievement lies in the expression of emotion and desire, creating at least an impression of spontaneity and sincerity. Her writing is usually sensual and pagan (she compares herself to the recently discovered Sappho). Linguistically less inventive than *Scève or *Ronsard, she also rejects their mythological and imaginative complexity.

The elegies, less distinguished than the sonnets and rather stilted, owe much to Ovid, Tibullus, and Propertius, and they too treat of the absent lover and the ravaging effects of desertion. The 'Débat' is a witty dialogue reminiscent of *Erasmus, with classical and medieval resonances. The feminist dedicatory epistle to the whole volume, often quoted today, urges women to leave aside their spinning, jewelry, and fine clothes in favour of literature and other cultural pursuits, and so to rival men. As a woman poet she herself successfully challenged prevailing attitudes; yet to talk of her 'écriture en direct' as specifically feminine writing is to diminish her intellectual and artistic stature. [PS]

LABERGE, Albert (1877–1960). Canadian journalist and novelist who was a self-proclaimed disciple of the French *Naturalist school of *Zola and *Maupassant. The bleak pessimism of his rural novel *La Scouine* (1918) partly derives from his French models, but was also a reaction against what he saw as the stultifying complacency of the agrarian myth propagated in French Canada by the Church. Inevitably censored and ostracized by official organs of culture, he published little during his long public career as a sports journalist but devoted his years of retirement to the production of numerous volumes of short stories which have the same qualities of harshness and uncompromising realism as his early novel. It was these qualities which led to the rehabilitation of his work in the 1960s, when he was hailed as a courageous pioneer in the demystification of traditional rural values. [SIL]

LABERGE, Marie (b. 1950). Canadian dramatist whose first plays, *Ils étaient venus pour . . .* (1976), *C'était avant la guerre à l'anse à Gilles* (1980), are striking dramatizations of socio-historical subjects. Increasingly, however, she has turned to themes of tangled personal relationships, especially within traumatized families. Often built round emotional confrontations and painful confessions of frustration, as in *Jocelyne Trudelle, trouvée morte dans ses larmes* (1980) and *L'Homme gris* (1982), her plays can also be tender and elegiac, as in *Aurélie, ma sœur* (1988). She has also published two novels, *Jalousie* (1989) and *Quelques adieux* (1992). [SIL]

LABICHE, Eugène (1815–88). Master of farce under the Second Empire. Of about 173 plays written with collaborators between 1837 and 1877, the earliest reflect the loose, improvisatory techniques of the popular *vaudeville. Later plays pay more attention to individual characterization and the comedy of manners, mocking bourgeois attitudes to money, property, and marriage. In the free-wheeling invention evident in farces like *Un chapeau de paille d'Italie* (1851), *Le Voyage de Monsieur Perrichon* (1860), and *La Station Champbaudet* (1862), scheming lovers, pompous fathers, and purblind husbands are propelled at dizzying speed through the hoops of deceit, dowry-hunting, and marital infidelity. [SBJ]

LA BODERIE, Le Fèvre de, see LE FÈVRE DE LA BODERIE.

LA BOÉTIE, Étienne de (1530–63) studied law at Orléans before becoming a magistrate in the Parlement de Bordeaux, where *Montaigne became his colleague in 1557. Their friendship was immortalized by the latter in 'De l'amitié' (*Essais*, I. 28). Following La Boétie's untimely death, Montaigne published much of his work, but thought better of including the *Discours de la servitude volontaire* (sometimes known as the *Contr'un*) because it had been published by the Protestants. Montaigne complained bitterly that a sincere but fundamentally academic diatribe against tyranny had been hijacked by the Huguenots, who (following the *St Bartholomew's Day Massacre) turned it into an attack on the monarchy. La Boétie's fundamental conservatism is evident in his *Mémoire sur la pacification des troubles* (formerly known as the *Mémoire touchant l'édit de janvier*), where he presents a cogent case for permitting only one religion (Catholicism) and for punishing those guilty of disturbances. He exhibits in so doing a shrewd mixture of respect for the individual and awareness of the political dangers of making doctrinal concessions. [JJS]

LA BORDERIE, Bertrand de (*c*.1507–after 1547). One of *Marot's disciples, though also influenced by the *Rhétoriqueurs, he is best known for his *Amie de cour* (1541), in which, reacting against *Petrarchan and *Neoplatonist values, he has a female mouthpiece argue that it is wrong to place woman on a pedestal [see HÉROËT; QUERELLE DES FEMMES]. [JJS]

LABROUSSE, Ernest (1895–1988). French historian, influenced by *Marxism and associated with the *Annales* school. He directed research at the *École Pratique des Hautes Études, did pioneering work on the economic history of the *ancien régime*, and edited with *Braudel a four-volume *Histoire économique et sociale de la France* (1970–9).

LA BRUYÈRE, Jean de (1645–96). *Moraliste*, the last great figure of French *classicism, and in some ways a precursor of the *philosophes*. He was born into a well-to-do middle-class family in Paris, where he lived until his death. Not a great deal is known about his life. He studied law, and in 1673 bought a sinecure as *trésorier général*. In 1684 he was appointed tutor to Duke Louis de Bourbon, grandson of *Condé, to whose household he remained attached. The experience was not a satisfying one. In 1693 he was elected to the Académie Française, and in his combative reception speech sided with the *anciens* in the *Querelle des Anciens et des Modernes; a sharp polemic ensued. He never married, and died poor.

La Bruyère is the man of one book, *Les Caractères*. The first edition of 1688 presented itself as a translation of the *Characters* of the Greek author Theophrastus together with 'les Caractères ou les mœurs de ce siècle'. In fact, La Bruyère had begun work on his own *caractères* several years earlier and Theophrastus was an ancient pretext for his own modern writing. In a series of eight editions between 1688 and 1694 La Bruyère more than doubled the size of his work, changing its nature considerably.

In its final form the work consists of 1,120 sections, from one line to several pages in length. They are of three types: general maxims and aphorisms similar in form to those of *La Rochefoucauld; somewhat longer reflections, generally devoted to aspects of contemporary society; portraits of individuals. The last category is the one which most readers associate with La Bruyère; numerically it is less important than the previous two, although it is more prominent in later editions. Some of the portraits are developed at length, the longest being that of Ménalque, the absent-minded man. La Bruyère insisted that his portraits, with their Greek names, did not represent particular individuals, but contemporaries had no hesitation in giving 'keys' for many of them.

These three categories, which overlap considerably, are grouped into 16 chapters; most of these are devoted to particular subjects (e.g. literature, conversation) or to social groups (e.g. the court, women), but others range very broadly, particularly the central section, 'De l'homme'. La Bruyère claimed that there was an overall plan to the work, leading (like *Pascal's *Pensées*) from a satirical view of the world to a religious conclusion in the final section: 'Des esprits forts'. This seems to be no more than a posteriori special pleading; the work's unity does not come from a plan, but from an over-all vision.

La Bruyère's chosen stance is that of the philosopher—not the creator of a system of thought, but the detached, clear-sighted observer of the follies of human nature; his writing has much in common with *Boileau's satires and *Molière's comedies. He ridicules all sorts of human weakness, and at times writes vehemently against what he terms the 'ferocity' of man to man. Many of his observations concern contemporary society, in particular the glamorous but vicious court, the abuses of power, the new wealth of the financiers, the corruption of the Church. A famous, though untypical, observation presents the wretched state of the peasants ('certains animaux farouches'). The standpoint from which he makes his criticisms is a Christian one, and many of his remarks show a strong desire for a better, more charitable social order, but he is no revolutionary; for all his attacks on the rich and powerful, and his identification with the victims, his political stance is that of a conservative monarchist with a somewhat golden view of former days.

It is not these traditional values that make *Les Caractères* memorable, but the extraordinary style in which La Bruyère represents his men and women. He has many interesting things to say about writing, and is very conscious of himself as an artisan of the word. His style conveys an original vision of the world. Piling up short sentences and repetitive details, he tends to dehumanize his characters, transforming them into automata. His vision of a spiritually empty society gives a new twist to the old image of the world as stage; he presents his readers with a grotesque comedy of masks or puppet show. The result is a bitter, yet attractive text. Its appeal to 18th-c. readers is witnessed in David Hume's words: 'La Bruyère passes the seas, and still maintains his reputation.' [PF]

See O. de Mourgues, *Two French Moralists* (1978); J. Brody, *Du style à la pensée* (1981).

'Lac, Le'. Lamartine's most famous poem, published in his *Méditations poétiques* (1820).

LA CALPRENÈDE, Gauthier de Coste, sieur de (*c.*1610–1663). French playwright and novelist. His literary career divides into two phases. From 1635 to 1642 he wrote six tragedies and three tragicomedies, some exploiting contemporary successes by *Tristan and *Mairet (e.g. *La Mort des enfants d'Hérode*, 1638), others exploring the less familiar ground of English history (e.g. *Le Comte d'Essex*, 1637). From 1642 he published a series of long, quasi-historical romances: *Cassandre* (1642–5), *Cléopâtre* (1646–57), and the unfinished *Faramond* (1661–3). Although confused in construction and unashamedly anachronistic, these novels were enormously popular for their heroic mythification of contemporary courtly ideals. They inspired the plots of many plays, most notably Thomas *Corneille's *Timocrate* (1656). [GJM]

LACAN, Jacques (1901–81). Psychiatrist, psychoanalyst, founder of a distinctively French Freudian tradition, and author of *Écrits* (1966), one of the talismanic texts of *Post-Structuralism.

Lacan was educated at the Collège Stanislas and the Paris Medical Faculty and came to *psychoanalysis by way of an orthodox psychiatric training. His doctoral dissertation, *De la psychose paranoïaque dans ses rapports avec la personnalité* (1932), was both a case-study of an individual patient ('Aimée') and a vigorous polemic against the dominant clinical attitudes and diagnostic procedures of the day. For Lacan, the psychotic patient was not an empty site in which a predetermined mental process played itself out, but a *person* endowed with an emotional history, a vision of the future, intellectual aptitudes, and the power of speech. A stress on speech as the mainspring of clinical understanding was again present in the long article on the family that Lacan contributed to the *Encyclopédie française* (1938; repr. as *Les Complexes familiaux dans la formation de l'individu*, 1984), and was to become central to his theory of subjectivity in such later papers as 'Fonction et champ de la parole et du langage en psychanalyse' (1953), 'L'Instance de la lettre dans l'inconscient ou la Raison depuis Freud' (1957), and 'Subversion du sujet et dialectique du désir dans l'inconscient freudien' (1960).

'L'inconscient est structuré comme un langage': this is the most quoted of Lacan's many gnomic pronouncements, and still usefully encapsulates a major dimension of his theory. The human infant, as he/she acquires speech, is inserting him/herself into a pre-existing symbolic order, and subjecting his/her passion to the controlling pressures of the verbal domain. Unconscious desire, for Lacan, is unstoppable and insatiable; its goals are perpetually in flight. The symbolic order of language through which this desire passes is one in which the human subject is endlessly divided, displaced, and reconstituted. The principal aim of Lacan's psychoanalysis is to allow the subject fully to inhabit the symbolic order, to heed the language of his/her desire, and to remain in process, uncompleted, unillusioned, and directed desiringly towards a future.

These views are at variance with one of the traditional aims of psychoanalysis: that of protecting the ego against other, disruptive, mental agencies. Analysts who set out to fortify the ego as the seat of personal identity are under constant attack from Lacan: they are trying to make a public monument from a will-o'-the-wisp. The source of this error, for Lacan, is the realm that he calls the 'imaginary' in contradistinction to the symbolic order. The imaginary comes into being at the 'mirror phase', as postulated in 'Le Stade du miroir comme fondateur de la fonction du JE' (1949). Between the ages of 6

months and 18 months the human individual is first able to envisage him/herself as a coherent entity, sees him/herself in a mirror, identifies with the image, and delights in the power to control its movements. An ideal notion of personal completeness is born at this phase and, with it, a tendency in the individual to seek identity in dealings with others and with the world of objects. It is at this phase that the ego is first glimpsed. The terms 'subject' (*sujet*) and 'ego' (*moi*) are antonyms for Lacan. Where the ego is the illusory product of successive imaginary identifications, or mirrorings, the subject proper is born of otherness, lack, and discord.

The dialectic between the Symbolic and the Imaginary orders is called on to perform much of the theoretical work that Freud had assigned to competing mental agencies: the unconscious and the conscious in his first main model and the id, ego, and superego in his second. The virtue of Lacan's approach is that his 'orders' necessarily connect the inner workings of the mind to the outer workings of society. The danger, of which he was aware, was that such an approach might become merely dualistic—yet another instance of 'imaginary' identification. To combat this tendency, he introduced the concept of the 'Real'. The Real is that which constantly exceeds the imaginary and symbolic constructions of the individual and often comes close, in Lacan's usage, to meaning 'the impossible' or 'the ineffable'.

Throughout Lacan's career as a theorist, two distinct tendencies are visible. On the one hand, he is a simplifier and a systematist: *Saussure's *signifiant* and *signifié* are called on to introduce a new principle of economy into the Freudian lexicon, and the triad comprising Symbolic, Imaginary, and Real is manipulated as a grand key to the mysteries of mind and society. On the other hand, he is restless and acquisitive: his concept of the 'Other' is derived from *Kojève's reading of Hegel, his temporality from Heidegger, and many of his incidental modelling devices from mathematics and symbolic logic. This eclecticism goes hand in hand with a famously 'difficult' literary manner, a cult of ambiguity, and an insistent ironic playfulness. Lacan is the author, therefore, both of a system and of a style, and 'Lacanians', correspondingly, are of two broad kinds: those who single-mindedly apply his theory to cultural products and those who imitate his literary manner.

Lacan's achievement lay not simply in re-dramatizing Freud's doctrine but in making it mappable onto a wide variety of other social discourses. His unremitting stress on lack and self-division in the lives of speaking creatures has given Lacan an exemplary status for observers in neighbouring intellectual disciplines: he is a theorist for whom 'theory' is an impossible calling. [For the feminist critique of Lacan, see FEMINISM, 4.] [MB]

See M. Marini, *Jacques Lacan* (1986); S. Felman, *Jacques Lacan and the Adventure of Insight* (1987).

LACARRIÈRE, Jacques (b. 1925). French travel writer, author of many books on Greece, literature, theatre, religion, and mythology. He has written personal and engaging narratives of wandering, including *L'Été grec* (1976) and a fascinating account of a 1,000-kilometre walk across France, *Chemin faisant* (1977). [PF]

LACENAIRE, Pierre-François (1800–36). Famous criminal whose cynical freedom of demeanour appealed to his Romantic contemporaries [see FRÉNÉTIQUE].

LA CEPPÈDE, Jean de (c.1548–1623). Magistrate and religious poet. As a *conseiller* in the Parlement of Aix-en-Provence, then president of the Chambre des Comptes, La Ceppède—like *Chassignet, *Sponde, and *Vauquelin de la Fresnaye—played a major role in provincial administration. He published para-phrases of the penitential psalms (1594) and of other sacred verse, but his major work was *Les Théorèmes* (1613–21), a cycle of sonnets accompanied by prose commentaries and forming an extended semi-narrative meditation on the Passion and its sequel up to Pentecost. His flamboyant, emotive, yet also erudite devotional style is characteristic of *Counter-Reformation taste. [TC]

LA CHAISE, François d'Aix, père de (1624–1709). *Louis XIV's Jesuit confessor from 1675 and an active enemy of the *Jansenists. An estate where he sometimes lived became in the 19th c. the famous Père-Lachaise cemetery where many writers and artists are buried, and the site of the Mur des Fédérés, where the Left gathers to celebrate the memory of those shot there during the *Commune of 1871. [PF]

LA CHALOTAIS, Louis-René de Caradeuc de (1701–85). Breton magistrate who played an active part in the expulsion of the *Jesuits, and published plans for a new education system, *Essai d'éducation nationale* (1763). He was later exiled for his defence of the rights of the Parlement de Rennes; this famous case led to the *Maupeou affair. [PF]

LA CHAMBRE, Martin Cureau de (c.1595–1669). Physician and founder member of the Académie Française. He wrote scientific works in French, including a treatise on psycho-physiology, *Les Caractères des passions* (1640?).

LA CHAUSSÉE, (Pierre-Claude) Nivelle de (1692–1754). Author of plays in several genres, chiefly remembered as the inventor of the *comédie larmoyante* and as the author of *La Fausse Antipathie* (1733), *Le Préjugé à la mode* (1735), *Mélanide* (1741), *L'École des mères* (1744), and *La Gouvernante* (1747). His plays exploit, in verse, the tear-jerking potential of a dramatic formula whereby virtuous or near-virtuous middle-class private individuals are involved in serious and deplorable situations (of social inequalities and abuses, for example), with an artificially delayed outcome, in order to generate pathos and hence move audiences to admire and imitate virtuous behaviour. Contemporary audi-ences were enthusiastic, but modern critics, while recognizing La Chaussée's place in the history of drama, have been generally severe on the dramatic value of his works. [JD]

LACLOS, (Pierre-Antoine-François) Choderlos de (1741–1803). The literary reputation of Laclos rests on a single work, his *epistolary novel *Les *Liaisons dangereuses* (1782). He was by profession an army engineer. Before 1782 he had published some light verse and written the libretto, based on Madame *Riccoboni's *Ernestine*, of an *opéra-comique*. He wrote, but did not publish, three essays on the edu-cation of women (the first two in 1783 and the third after 1795). His critique of *Vauban's theory of siege fortifications (1786) attracted disapproval from his superiors, and in 1788 he left the army to become Philippe d'*Orléans's secretary. Later he joined the Société des Amis de la Constitution and for a brief period edited their *Journal*. He was twice impris-oned, facing execution in 1794. However, he was subsequently allowed to resume his military career; as a brigadier-general he saw action with the Rhine army. He was on his way to a posting in Naples when he died of dysentery and malaria at Tarento.

Because of *Les Liaisons dangereuses*, some of his contemporaries suspected Laclos of being another Valmont: cynically immoral, self-serving, and given to conspiracy. Among critics this view of him per-sisted well into the 20th c. Such an interpretation of his character is now generally rejected, particularly in the light of his affection for his wife and family, as seen in his letters. His political sympathies—first royalist, then republican, then an admirer of Bonaparte as a great general—still raise queries, but in more general terms he can be seen as a man of conventional morality, and in many respects a disciple of *Rousseau. [VGM]

Lacombe Lucien, see MODIANO.

LA CONDAMINE, Charles-Marie de (1701–74). French mathematician and scientist. A member of the Académie des Sciences, he was sent by that body in 1736 to South America, to make astronomi-cal observations [see MAUPERTUIS]. Having stayed there for ten years, he wrote fine accounts of his travels, notably the *Journal d'un voyage fait par ordre du roi à l'équateur* (1751). [PF]

LACORDAIRE, Jean-Baptiste-Henri (1802–61). Converted to Catholicism in 1824, Lacordaire was a fervent disciple of *Lamennais until the latter's break with Rome in 1834. He entered the Dominican order and achieved fame as a preacher with his *Conférences* (1835 ff.), renewing the form and content of the *sermon, reintroducing Thomist theology, and proposing that faith was compatible with reason, whilst also emphasizing the mystical aspects of Christianity. Politically active, he was a member of the Assemblée Constituante in 1848. [FPB]

LACOUE-LABARTHE, Philippe (b. 1940). French philosopher. A student of *Derrida, he has written extensively on Nietzsche and Heidegger, particularly analysing the relationship between literature and philosophy, and the problem of the subject: who speaks and in whose name? He has written an intricate study of the relation between Heidegger's Nazi politics and his radical philosophy. He works closely with Jean-Luc *Nancy. [MHK]

LACRETELLE, Jacques de (1888–1985). French novelist, best known for *Silbermann* (1922), which followed the introspective, melancholy *La Vie inquiète de Jean Hamelin* (1920). The strong, economical narrative of *Silbermann* charts the appearance of a gifted, compelling Jewish boy in the life of the insecure, lonely Protestant narrator, and the enthusiasms and betrayals of their alliance. A sequel, *Le Retour de Silbermann* (1929), is harsher, more Gidean. Lacretelle wrote family chronicles—*Les Hauts Ponts* (1932–35)—and treated public themes (civilian resistance to German occupation: *La Bonifas*, 1925) but in his work the focus is always not so much political as psychological. He translated Mary Webb and Emily Brontë. [MMC]

LACROIX, Jean (1900–86). French Catholic philosopher and essayist. A student of *Chevalier, he taught philosophy in lycées in Dijon and Lyon. A founder member and regular contributor of the review *Esprit, he was active in several centre-left movements of Catholic intellectuals. He wrote innumerable popularizations of philosophy and was weekly philosophy columnist of Le *Monde (1945–80). [MHK]

LACROSIL, Michèle. Guadeloupean novelist whose fiction is concerned with racial and class antagonisms in the Caribbean. These unresolved conflicts, presented as the root of individual obsession in *Sapotille et le serin d'argile* (1960) and *Cajou* (1961), are examined in the broader context of plantation society in *Demain Jab-Herma* (1967). [BNO]

LA CURNE DE SAINTE-PALAYE, Jean-Baptiste de (1697–1781). Medievalist. Born in Burgundy, he studied at the Oratorian Collège de Juilly, and was briefly a diplomat. As a member of the *Académie des Inscriptions (1724) he produced many papers on medieval subjects. His principal works were the influential *Mémoires sur l'ancienne chevalerie* (2 vols., 1759), a *Histoire littéraire des troubadours* (3 vols., 1744), and a *Glossaire de l'ancienne langue française*, published fully only in 1875–82. His evocation of a more 'primitive' society appealed to both conservative and radical readers, and his scholarship was highly regarded until well into the 19th c. [PF]

LA FARE, Charles-Auguste, marquis de (1644–1712). French poet. After a military career he became a close friend of *Chaulieu and an habitué of the *Temple. His (perhaps underrated) poetry includes playful amorous verse as well as reflective pieces on such themes as modern corruption and rural retreat. He also translated Latin poetry and left valuable *Mémoires sur les principaux événements du règne de Louis XIV* (published posthumously). [PF]

LAFAYETTE, Marie-Joseph, marquis de (1757–1834). Soldier and politician. An aristocrat who believed in liberty and the rights of man, he fought in the American War of Independence and was a major figure in the first years of the French Revolution. He was the commander of the *Garde Nationale, but his loyalty to the royal family caused him to become a refugee. In 1830 he was one of those most responsible for bringing Louis-Philippe to the throne, saying that this was the best of republics [see JULY MONARCHY]. *Sainte-Beuve considered him 'le plus précoce, le plus intrépide et le plus honnête' of those who attacked the *ancien régime*, and he has remained the 'chevalier' of revolution. [DJ]

LAFAYETTE or **LA FAYETTE,** Marie-Madeleine Pioche de La Vergne, comtesse de (1634–93). No author influenced early prose fiction more decisively than this woman who entered the literary scene as a young *précieuse* during the golden age of the salons [see PRECIOSITY]. Her first published work was a verbal portrait of her lifelong closest friend, *Sévigné. She went on to write a series of historical novels that permanently altered the novel's shape (*La Princesse de Montpensier*, 1662; *Zayde*, 1670; *La *Princesse de Clèves*, 1678; *La Comtesse de Tende*, published 1724). Her contributions to the history of her age, *Histoire de Madame Henriette d'Angleterre* and *Mémoires de la Cour de France pour les années 1688 et 1689*, were published posthumously (1720, 1731).

For a brief period after her marriage (1655), Lafayette resided on her husband's estate in Auvergne. She gave birth to her two sons at this time. The rest of her life she lived as a Parisian, at the centre of French intellectual life. The most notable literary figures of the day frequented her salon. Many of them collaborated in the production of her novels, common practice at a time when, in the salons, aristocrats and bourgeois regulary crossed class lines to make literature together. Thus, at Lafayette's request, *Huet and *Segrais helped revise her romance *Zayde*, to make its style less reminiscent of that of her favourite author, Madeleine de *Scudéry; her long-time companion *La Rochefoucauld was so intimately involved with the creation of *La Princesse de Clèves* that he has often been referred to as the novel's author.

Lafayette was at home in political circles. She managed her family's considerable estate, influenced political appointments, and carried on diplomatic negotiations with the house of Savoie. Louis XIV

Lafcadio

gave the first private tour of the newly completed *Versailles to this woman of wide-ranging influence.

The type of novel Lafayette invented both reflected this range of influence and expanded prose fiction's horizon. Like many of her precursors she wrote historical fiction, but she documented it to a previously unheard-of degree, so thoroughly that the line between history and fiction is often blurred. She used historical fact as a vehicle for political commentary—for example, on the corrupting influence of court life. The shape Lafayette gave her narrative was perhaps her greatest innovation. Instead of the extended fictions of earlier novelists, she created works of striking concision. Her collaborators testify to her desire to reduce plot to the bare essentials, especially by eliminating almost entirely the intercalated tales and digressions that constitute the bulk of earlier fiction. Her narrative tautness demanded greater attentiveness from readers. More than any other writer, she can be said to have revolutionized the very process of reading prose fiction.

Lafayette also invented the psychological novel: she replaced the action-oriented model of earlier prose fiction with a microcosm centred on issues of interiority. In plots carefully reconstructed from 16th-c. French history, she introduced fictive situations that 17th-c. readers saw as related to emotional issues important in their own private lives. For months after the publication of La Princesse de Clèves, the *Mercure galant printed letters from its readers interpreting the princess's behaviour as if she were an actual, contemporary woman. Was she right to tell her husband of her attraction to another man? Were her expectations of marriage reasonable? What would be the consequences if women today imitated her behaviour? Indeed, Lafayette's characters often seem to be encouraging this type of reading. The prince de Clèves, for example, discusses how husbands should treat their wives in a precise situation. In addition—in a progression from the princesse de Montpensier to Zayde and to the princesse de Clèves—her protagonists engage in a quest for interior, private space in which they can dissect their emotional response to situations in which they find themselves. Whenever the princesse de Clèves is able to find privacy in the midst of the invasiveness and public displays of court life, she comes to terms with her actions in increasingly extended interior monologues.

In salon society participants frequently tried to define what they sensed were the changing conditions for male–female relations. Lafayette gave their debates literary form. Contemporary readers saw this as the sign of her innovativeness. 20th-c. readers recognize in this new interiority the mark of her modernity. [JDeJ]

See R. Duchêne, Madame de Lafayette (1988); J. DeJean, Tender Geographies (1991).

Lafcadio. The hero of Gide's Les *Caves du Vatican, perpetrator of the original *acte gratuit.

LAFITAU, Joseph-François, père (1681–1740). French Jesuit missionary to Canada, author of Mœurs des sauvages américains comparées aux mœurs des premiers temps (1724). This pioneering work of anthropology and comparative religion presents a favourable picture of the American 'savages', drawing parallels between their religions, customs, and government and those of classical antiquity in such a way as to stress the idea of a common humanity. [PF]

LA FONTAINE, Jean de (1621–95). Poet, known above all for his *Fables, which have been read, learned, and recited by French children and adults for three centuries. He wrote much else besides, in a variety of genres. Often seen as one of the principal authors of French *classicism, he appears rather as an idiosyncratic individualist. His tastes ranged from Plato to *Rabelais, from the *romances of chivalry to *Malherbe, and his writings show a love of experiment as well as a sensitivity to contemporary taste.

The son of a government official, he was born in Château-Thierry, to the east of Paris, and maintained his connection with his provincial home throughout his life. After an education at the local Jesuit college and a brief and apparently unenthusiastic period as a novice with the *Oratorians, he obtained a legal qualification in Paris. He was married to Marie Héricart in 1647 and in 1652 bought a post as maître des eaux et des forêts. On his father's death he inherited two more such posts, but these official functions had to be surrendered in 1671. Even before this his finances were precarious, and all his life he depended a good deal on *patronage. His first patron was *Fouquet, to whom he remained loyal after the surintendant's disgrace. From 1664 to 1672 he had a sinecure as a gentilhomme servant at the Palais du Luxembourg; thereafter he was given lodging in Paris by Madame de la *Sablière and by Monsieur d'Hervart. His relation with royal power was an uneasy one, even though he addressed many official poems to the royal family; when he was elected to the Académie Française in 1683, his admission was blocked for a year by the king.

As a writer, he did not belong to any camp. Throughout his life he remained a close friend of *Maucroix, and was on good terms with the other poets he met in Paris in the 1640s, including *Pellisson and Charles *Perrault. The old idea of the 'quatre amis de Psyché' (*Molière, *Racine, *Boileau, and La Fontaine) is something of a myth, though La Fontaine admired Molière and was on good terms with Racine. In the *Querelle des Anciens et des Modernes he took the ancien side, but in an undogmatic, diplomatic way.

His writings are often personal in tone; they helped create an image of the poet in which legend and reality are hard to disentangle. He figures as an easygoing, independent, pleasure-loving person, a lover of women but also of solitude, savouring natural beauties and the melancholy sweetness of passing time. On his own admission, he was an 'âme inquiète' and inconstant—he devoted little care to his wife and son. At the same time, though, he was ambitious, and his fables show a tough-minded cynicism which contrasts with the relaxed hedonism of his self-image. At the end of his life he was converted, and publicly condemned the immorality of his *Contes*.

He began publishing relatively late, in 1654, but once launched he devoted himself to his art. His output is very varied. There are many pieces of occasional verse, ranging from flattering odes to witty epistles and epigrams. Among his most appealing poems are the elegies and *discours*, in particular the 'Élégie pour Fouquet', written shortly after his patron's downfall, the four amorous 'Élégies', the 'Épître à *Huet' of 1687, which offers a subtle profession of poetic faith, and the 'Discours à Madame de la Sablière' (written c.1683), a rueful self-portrait which echoes many passages in the *Fables*.

He also wrote some longer poems: *Adonis* (1658), much admired by *Valéry, is a poetic exercise on a classical theme, showing remarkable mastery of the alexandrine; *Clymène*, written at about the same time, is even more clearly a piece of poetic display, grouping a series of pastiches around an amorous theme; *La Captivité de Saint Malc* and *Le Quinquina* can best be regarded as responses to the challenge of unpromising subjects (the triumph of virginity and quinine respectively). There are also a number of dramatic efforts, ranging from an adaptation of Terence, *L'Eunuque* (1654), to the unfinished tragedy *Achille*. La Fontaine had no great gift for the theatre, but was fascinated by its possibilities, in particular the beautiful illusion, magic, and metamorphosis of the opera. His libretto *Daphné* was rejected by *Lully (this provoked some sharp polemic verse, notably the 'Épître à M. Niert'), and his *Astrée* (1691), based on the ever-popular novel of d'*Urfé, was a failure.

One of his favourite forms was the medley of prose and verse. He uses this in letters, notably an agreeable series addressed to his wife in 1663 when he travelled to the Limousin, in *Le Songe de Vaux*, a decorative portrayal of Fouquet's château, and in what is perhaps his most ambitious work, *Les Amours de Psyché et de Cupidon* (1669). This leisurely retelling of the old story from Apuleius is enhanced by being framed in an entertaining conversation between four friends who walk through the still-unfinished gardens of *Versailles, praising the monarch and discussing such literary questions as the respective difficulties and merits of tragedy and comedy.

If the *Fables* are La Fontaine's true claim to fame, his first success came from his *Contes et nouvelles*, which were much imitated and provided the subject for many comedies. They are poetic versions of old stories from many sources (medieval and Renaissance France, Boccaccio, Rabelais, Ariosto).

In the first edition (1664) the reader is offered the choice between two styles, the supple irregular verse of *La Joconde* (praised by Boileau) or short lines in rhyming couplets and archaic language reminiscent of *Marot and old French *farce. Encouraged by success, La Fontaine kept enlarging his book, in which the two styles continue to mingle. The stories belong to the tedious 'gaulois' repertoire of cuckolds, lecherous priests, and wanton young women; they become more scurrilous in later editions, though verbal decency is maintained. The fourth edition (1674) was banned, and after his conversion the author disowned his book. Earlier, he presented the *Contes* as harmless fun; what mattered was the manner of telling, not the subject. And indeed they do derive their appeal from the ease with which the narrator handles the verse and storyline, digressing freely and engaging his reader in conversation about the work.

La Fontaine is one of France's great poets and a dedicated artist, in spite of his pose of nonchalance. His works show great verbal mastery and a constant taste for experiment and novelty. They also stand out in their time by their personal charm, their evocation of natural beauty and of the pleasures of dream and illusion. He creates his masterpiece in the *Fables*, where this charm engages with the harsh world of power, cruelty, and failure.   [PF]

See M. Guitton, *La Fontaine: Poet and Counterpoet* (1961); M. Gutwirth, *Un merveilleux sans éclat: La Fontaine, ou la Poésie exilée* (1987); M. O. Sweetser, *La Fontaine* (1987).

LA FORCE, Charlotte-Rose de Caumont de (c.1646–1724). French Protestant writer who helped launch the passion for fairy-tales (*Les Contes des contes*, 1698). She composed numerous historical novels (*Histoire secrète de Bourgogne*, 1694; *Histoire secrète de Henri IV*, 1695). *Les Jeux d'esprit, ou la Promenade de la princesse de Conti à Eu* (1701) is her most original work.   [JDeJ]

LAFORGUE, Jules (1860–87). A great and original French poet, one of the creators of modernism, always detested by the French for his facetiousness. The question is: can one be a great poet if one continually sends up the most solemn things, including language itself? Influenced by Walt Whitman, he was in turn a major influence on T. S. Eliot. Born in Montevideo, the son of a French teacher, he was educated in Tarbes in the Pyrenees and in 1876 came to Paris, where he led a poor and solitary life. He took a post of reader at the court of Empress Augusta of Germany (1880). A stormy affair occurred with an unidentified 'R'. In 1886 he married an English girl, Leah Lee, who died of tuberculosis in 1888, as he had the previous year. His *Derniers vers* were published in 1890; earlier volumes include *Les Complaintes* (1885) and *L'Imitation de Notre Dame de la lune* (1886). Had Laforgue foreseen his life, it would not have surprised him, for his mentors were Schopenhauer and E. von Hartmann, and he took the universe to be an irony practised against its inhabitants.

After some early verse of *Hugolian portentousness, he adopts a playfully provocative stance, daring the reader to glimpse the true Laforgue through a series of violently shifting masks, attitudes, tones of voice, and registers. One attitude is no sooner struck than it is debunked by the next one. These procedures are embarrassed and defensive, and Woman seems to be in league with the jeering universe. But it is also true that he declares his true self to be unknown to its owner. His persona is the pierrot, a mournful, absurd, yet pitiable clown. He expands the techniques of poetry almost explosively, for every register of French is used, from the highest to the lowest, every emotional attitude is touched upon, the attitude of the poet flickers like a turning crystal, the brilliance of his imagery knows no limits either of propriety or of reason, and the verbal inventiveness is breathtaking. Scrupulous attention is paid to the emergence of shifting moods from the unconscious (Hartmann's pre-Freudian collective unconscious). The prose pieces of *Moralités légendaires* (1887) spread these procedures much more thinly and, though funny, are so in a dishearteningly facetious way. His masterpiece, *Derniers vers*, combines these techniques with a moving seriousness, in which pity and despair render life more meaningful and acceptable.   [GDM]

See W. Ramsey, *Laforgue* (1953); D. Arkell, *Looking for Laforgue* (1979).

LA GRANGE, Charles Varlet, sieur de (1639–92). Male lead in *Molière's company from 1659, and administrator of the company after Molière's death. He kept a detailed register of productions, takings, etc., which is an essential source of information for the history of the theatre.   [PF]

LAGRANGE, Joseph-Louis (1736–1813). Important French mathematician and astronomer, for a time director of the Academy of Berlin, author of a *Mécanique analytique* (1788).

LA GRANGE-CHANCEL (François-Joseph de Chancel, sieur de La Grange) (1677–1758). A youthful prodigy, he won court favour and wrote a number of mediocre tragedies, beginning with *Adharbal* (1694). He achieved fame and disgrace with *Les Philippiques*, five odes composed c.1717–18, containing fierce and libellous attacks on the duc d' Orléans and the corruption of the *Regency.   [PF]

LA HARPE, Jean-François de (1739–1803). French poet, playwright, and critic. As a young man he associated with the *philosophes* and modelled himself on *Voltaire. Fame came with the tragedy *Le Comte de Warwick* (performed 1763), set in medieval England. His plays, poems, and discourses were successful in their day—in particular his controversial *drame, *Mélanie* (published 1770, performed 1791)—

but he is now remembered for his influential *Le Lycée ou Cours de littérature* (1799–1805). Based on lectures given at the *Lycée, this aimed to be first complete literary history of Europe. Ignoring the Middle Ages, misrepresenting the Greeks, and giving pride of place to French classical tragedy, it offers a strongly traditionalist, not to say reactionary, view of the subject. La Harpe, having welcomed the Revolution, turned virulently against it when he was imprisoned, and published a striking diatribe, *Du fanatisme dans la langue révolutionnaire* (1797). The *Lycée* contains vitriolic attacks on *Diderot, *Rousseau, and the philosophic spirit in general.

[PF]

LAHBABI, Mohammed Aziz (1932–93). Moroccan writer, professor of philosophy in Rabat and Algiers, and one of the leading academics in Morocco. A central figure in the cultural life of his country, he was awarded many honours at home and abroad. As a student of philosophy in France he came under the influence of *Bergson. At the intersection of European philosophy and Islamic thought, Lahbabi evolved a Muslim humanism and *Personalism: see his doctoral thesis *De l'être à la personne* (1954), followed by *Le Personnalisme musulman* (1964).

Apart from a novel, *Espoir vagabond* (1972), written first in Arabic, Lahbabi's main literary interest was poetry. In *Les Chants d'espérance* (1952) and *Misères et lumières* (1958), he endeavours to define his own role as a poet aesthetically and spiritually: 'le poète fait vibrer les couleurs du Verbe'. He explores this idea in *Ma voix à la recherche de sa voie* (1968). His poetry is characterized by a strong metaphysical concern for the situation, role, and future of man, the questioning ending in hope, faith, and fraternity (*Ivre d'innocence* 1980).

Lahbabi wrote a number of works in Arabic and felt the tension between the two cultures, and the desire to return to one's roots: *Florilège poétique arabe et berbère* (1964). His essay *Du clos à l'ouvert: vingt propos sur les cultures nationales et la civilisation humaine* (1961) advocates abandoning the rigidity and narrowness of nationalism and monoculturalism, for tolerance and dialogue between cultures.   [ET]

LA HONTAN, Louis-Armand, baron de (1666–after 1715). French military officer and adventurer who spent some years in Canada while it was still being explored and colonized, and published in Holland in 1703 interesting *Nouveaux voyages* and *Mémoires* on the subject, including conversations with a prominent Iroquois chieftain. In the *Dialogues de Lahontan* (also 1703), partly ghosted by a former monk, Nicolas Gueudeville, the chieftain, 'Adario', becomes a 'noble savage' with revolutionary ideas and a spokesman for *deism, the natural religion of Native Americans being coupled with some criticisms of Catholic Christianity. Adario may have influenced Voltaire's Huron hero in *L'*Ingénu*.

[CJB]

Lai. 1. A lyric form of the *troubadours, also called *descort*.

2. A complex lyric form of the 14th and 15th c. having 24 stanzas paired by rhyme and an overall circular structure.

3. A short narrative form of the late 12th and 13th c. Earlier examples deal with Arthurian material, and many, including the major collection by *Marie de France, allude to the origins of the form in Celtic *clarsach* (harp) melodies. While Marie's *lais* tend to emphasize the psychological and social problems of love, stressing personal integrity, others exploit folktales of the fairy-mistress type to produce exotic adventure stories. The chastity-test motif is used in two, Robert Biket's *Lai du cor* and *Le Lai du mantel*. The former treats Arthur's court with comic disrespect, the latter introduces bitter anti-feminist satire. In the 13th c. the *lai* becomes a witty narrative, often with a contemporary setting, as in *Le Lai de l'ombre* [see JEAN RENART]. [PEB]

Laïcité. Term used to indicate the neutrality of the state in matters of religion. It has been invoked above all on the question of *education; the *lois Ferry* of 1881 enforced the principle of secular education, which was a central tenet of Third-Republic *republicanism. Although often thought to be a thing of the past, the reflex of *laïcité* has surfaced from time to time since World War II over the question of state subsidies for religious schools. [See also ANTICLERICALISM.]

LAINÉ, Pascal (b. 1942). French philosopher and novelist, educated at the École Normale Supérieure de Saint-Cloud. His teaching experiences in Paris and the provinces (Saint-Quentin) informed early works such as *B comme Barabbas* (1967) and *L'Irrévolution* (1971, Prix Médicis), a disabused, neo-*Sartrian account of *May 1968. Lainé remains best-known for *La Dentellière* (1974, Prix Goncourt), a study of emotional mismatch and socio-intellectual alienation whose underlying themes—absent or inadequate parental figures, lack of communication, the quest for identity, the problem of stereotyping—are those of his *œuvre* as a whole, which, from *Si on partait* (1978) to *Dialogues du désir* (1992), reveals a *Queneau-like fascination with different fictional genres, humorous, erotic, historical. [WK]

Lais, Le, see VILLON.

Laisse. Verse form characteristic of the *chanson de geste*.

LAKANAL, Joseph (1762–1845). A member of the Convention Nationale, he was responsible for many Revolutionary projects for educational reform, and for the organization of the Muséum d'Histoire Naturelle in the *Jardin des Plantes.

LALONDE, Michèle (b. 1937). Canadian poet who was prominent among the many Quebec writers in

the 1960s who committed themselves publicly to the nationalist cause through public performances, poster poems, marches, and manifestos. Her famous poem 'Speak White' (1968), popularizing the analogy between Quebec and a colonized country that was already current in nationalist writings, is a moving and angry protest at anglophone hegemony in Canada. *Défense et illustration de la langue québécoise* (1979) collects most of her 'interventionist' poems and prose, including her contributions to the debate on the status of Quebec French. [SIL]

LA MARCHE, Olivier de (c.1426–1502). Poet and chronicler. His literary production was a logical extension of his 60 years' service to the *Burgundian court: treatises on etiquette and tournament technique, and above all his *Mémoires* covering the years 1435–88, often inaccurate in historical detail, but a minute record of court life and its festivals. [JHMT]

LAMARCK, Jean-Baptiste de (1744–1829). French biologist, originator of the evolutionary theory of *transformisme*, according to which organisms continually improve and develop by adapting to the environment. He taught at the Muséum d'Histoire Naturelle, but died blind and poor. His work combines observation and taxonomy with the desire to understand the processes of life as a whole, in which human beings are considered a part of nature; these ideas are impressively formulated in his *Philosophie zoologique* (1809). His most famous theory, the inheritance of acquired characteristics, has been superseded by Darwin's natural selection, but he has continued to inspire thinkers and writers. [PF]

LAMARTINE, Alphonse de (1790–1869). French poet, politician, historian, writer of travel books and popular literature. Son of an aristocratic and military father and a noble and religious mother, Lamartine grew up on the relatively modest estate of Milly near Mâcon. In turn melancholic and dissipated, he spent his youth and early manhood pursuing a sequence of romantic and casual liaisons. His love for the consumptive Julie Charles provided the inspiration for his most famous poem 'Le Lac'. Immediate poetic success led to distinguished diplomatic postings in Italy and, later, to eminence in national politics. Lamartine's political fame rests on the leading role he took in the provisional government during the 1848 Revolution (and no less, perhaps, on the spectacular failure of his presidential candidacy at the end of that year).

Lamartine's importance as a poet is still seen primarily in terms of the reputation he acquired on the publication of his earliest work, *Méditations poétiques* (1820). This collection is enshrined in traditional literary history as the first poetic text of the 'Romantic revolution' in France, and in 'Le Lac' it contains the poem commonly considered to offer the quintessential example of Romantic lyrical poetry, with its treatment of lost love and lost time. His many other collections of lyrical and meditative poetry have been little read in modern times (*Nouvelles médita-tions poétiques*, 1823; *Harmonies poétiques et religieuses*, 1830; *Recueillements poétiques*, 1839). His completed 'fragments' of a vast Christian epic (*Jocelyn*, 1836; *La Chute d'un ange*, 1838) are indispensable for an under-standing of 19th-c. religious ideas and testify to cru-cial 19th-c. poetic ambitions, but these poems have remained alien to modern poetic sensibilities [see EPIC POETRY].

Although *Méditations poétiques* conferred on Lamartine the status of a Romantic poet, literary historians have stressed that the poems were, in fact, firmly rooted in the late-18th-c. neoclassical and elegiac tradition. Critics have repeatedly pointed to the dominance of unreconstructed neoclassical practice in Lamartine's verse (stale, conventional poetic diction; over-dependence on classical and bib-lical sources). Those who have spoken positively of the qualities of his poetry have tended to invoke such vague criteria as 'musicality', fluidity', and 'dreamy luminosity'. English-speaking readers and critics, with their taste for original metaphor and eye-on-the-object recreations of the natural world, have found Lamartine's conventional and abstract verse particularly hard to admire. His portentous metaphysics has been equally difficult to swallow.

Initially considered as a French Byron, Lamartine could not see beyond the adolescent and mystifica-tory posturing of Byron's early verse. Byronic irony and self-mockery were understood in France only in terms of a rebellious Satanism. In trying to under-stand the impact of Lamartine's early verse, one has to acknowledge that readers responded to the ago-nized self-questioning, and saw in it a profounder form of French poetry than what had gone before. The central paradox of Lamartine's poetic success was that, while he exploited conventional poetic devices, he nevertheless injected into his works a new existential urgency. His poems of love and loss, time and death, faith and doubt, despair and conso-lation, are some of the most characteristic works of French *Romanticism*, which is most centrally defined by its intense preoccupation with religious and metaphysical questions, at a time of post-revolutionary upheaval and fundamental challenge to established orthodoxies.

Apart from the *Histoire des Girondins* (1847), which is said to have been influential in 1848 and which remains a significant text on the French Revolution, his historical output is not highly regarded. It was largely the product of the literary drudgery of his later years and was intended to clear his heavy financial debts. More deserving of attention, and still almost completely undiscovered, are his popu-lar educational works (especially the vast *Cours fami-lier de littérature*, 1852–69). Lamartine had long been interested in 'the People' and the social question. His liberal humanitarianism was imbued with the idealistic spirit of early socialism. He believed litera-ture should be used as a prime instrument in the progress of humanity (*Des destinées de la poésie*, 1834),

and he devoted numerous literary and journalistic projects to the cause of popular education. He also wrote sentimental and idealized tales about working people (*Geneviève, histoire d'une servante*, 1850; *Le Tailleur de pierres de Saint-Point*, 1851).   [BR]

See M. E. Birkett, *Lamartine and the Poetics of Landscape* (1982); W. Fortescue, *Alphonse de Lamartine* (1983).

Lamba, see RABEMANANJARA.

LAMBERT, Anne-Thérèse de Marguenat de Courcelles, marquise de (1647–1733). Her learning and literary discernment were celebrated, but Lambert began to frequent the *salons only upon her widowhood in 1686. After prolonged litigation to settle her husband's estate, in 1710 she opened the salon that established her as *Rambouillet's heir and inaugurated the Enlightenment's salon tradition. Her assembly proved so influential that half the elections to the Académie Française were allegedly sealed in its discussions. She wrote extensively and is best known for *Avis d'une mère à sa fille* and *Avis d'une mère à son fils* (1726–8), composed for her chil-dren, and for *Réflexions sur les femmes* (1728).   [JDeJ]

LA MÉNARDIÈRE or **LA MESNARDIÈRE,** Hippolyte-Jules Pilet de (1610–63). A doctor and a rather laboured salon poet (*Les Poésies*, 1656), who is now remembered, if at all, for his *Poétique* (1639), only Volume 1 was published); this attempt to set out Aristotelian rules for tragedy contains some interesting remarks on language.   [PF]

LAMENNAIS or **LA MENNAIS,** Félicité de (1782–1854). A Breton, ordained when he was 34, Lamennais achieved fame with his *Essai sur l'indif-férence en matière de religion* (1817, 1821, 1823), a demonstration of the social virtues of Christianity which offered also as proof of Christianity that it was the faith of the *sens commun*, believed every-where, always, by all, in however corrupted a form. His *Ultramontanism led him to battle for the end of government interference in religious matters, whence a move to political opposition culminating in his highly popular *Paroles d'un croyant* (1834), a protest against political oppression, war, the misery of the lower classes, written in a poetic, prophetic, neo-biblical style. He counted among his disciples many of the intellectuals of the Church, including *Lacordaire, Ozanam, and *Montalembert. His writings provoked papal condemnation, and he broke with the Church to pursue a career as an active republican pamphleteer (*Le Livre du peuple*, 1837). His *Esquisse d'une philosophie* (1840–6) was an ambitious synthesis of *Romantic aesthetics, German transcendental philosophy, Christianity, and dreams of a new faith yet to come. He retired to private life after Louis-Napoléon's *coup d'état* of December 1851, was never reconciled with the Church, and, as he had requested, was given a pau-per's burial.   [FPB]

LA METTRIE, Julien Offray de (1709–51). Doctor and materialist philosopher. Born in Saint-Malo, the son of a rich merchant, he studied with the Dutch physician Boerhaave, several of whose works he translated. In Paris he frequented the society of aristocratic free-thinkers, but after the publication of highly unorthodox books, and of a series of satirical pamphlets directed against his fellow doctors, he had to take refuge in Leiden. Here too his works raised a storm; in 1748 he accepted an invitation from Frederick II of Prussia to settle in Berlin, where he died of food-poisoning, to the satisfaction of those who detested his views.

In his *Histoire naturelle de l'âme* (1745), *L'Homme-machine* (1748), and *L'Homme-plante* (1748), La Mettrie sets out in a brisk and uncompromising way arguments, based on his medical experience, to the effect that human actions, thoughts, and feelings are all part of the material world. He was not embarrassed by the moral implications of this view, proclaiming the supreme value of happiness and pleasure, rejoicing in free-thinking, and seeing no incompatibility between atheism and virtue. His vigorous, crude, and often entertaining writing made him few friends, and even those, such as *Diderot, whose ideas were close to his, spoke disparagingly of him. [PF]

Lamiel. Unfinished novel by *Stendhal, begun in 1839. Lamiel is a Normandy girl, adopted by a bourgeois family, protected by a duchess, and devoured by the desire to discover all about life and love. Encouraged in her amoral individualism by the cynical Sansfin, a hunchbacked doctor, she elopes to Rouen with the duchess's son, then makes her way to Paris and the world of fashionable kept women. She shares with many of Stendhal's heroes a sharp mind, a strong will, a lack of affectation, and a hatred of the boredom and hypocrisy of contemporary French society, which is portrayed with the satirical verve of *Lucien Leuwen*. [PF]

LAMOIGNON, Guillaume I de (1617–77). Member of a powerful legal family, Premier Président of the Parlement de Paris from 1658. He presided impartially over the early sessions of *Fouquet's trial, and as a member of the Compagnie du *Saint-Sacrement blocked the performance of Molière's *Tartuffe*. A highly educated man, he gathered around him an impressive 'academy', whose members included *Patin, *Rapin, *Pellisson, Claude *Fleury, and *Boileau (whom he guided in his career). The group, which was hostile to *Colbert's ministry, devoted itself to serious discussion of philosophy and literature; it was here that some of the ideas of the *anciens* were expressed in their purest form [see QUERELLE DES ANCIENS ET DES MODERNES].

Lamoignon's son, Chrétien-François, was Avocat-Général at the Parlement, a much-admired legal orator, and a friend of *Racine, Boileau, and many other men of letters. A notable member of the family in the 18th c. was *Malesherbes. [PF]

LA MOTHE LE VAYER, François de (1588–1672). Parisian magistrate and member of the 'tétrade' of friends which included *Gassendi, *Naudé, and *Patin. His long career falls into three phases. Between 1630 and his association with *Richelieu and the Académie Française in 1639 he was active as a proponent of scepticism, and published under the pseudonym Orasius Tubero nine *Dialogues faits à l'imitation des anciens* (1630–1) which show the influence of *Montaigne in their blend of suspension of judgement with discreet conformism. While under the patronage of Richelieu, and later as tutor of *Louis XIV from 1652 to 1660, his scepticism disappeared from view, but it reasserted itself in the final phase of his career, during which he wrote *Du peu de certitude qu'il y a dans l'histoire* (1668) and the *Hexaméron rustique* (1670). In his middle period he wrote on linguistic issues and was the author of a treatise *De la vertu des payens* (1642), written against the *Jansenists. [IM]

LA MOTTE, Antoine Houdar(t) de (1672–1731). French playwright and poet. Educated by the Jesuits, he qualified as a lawyer but devoted himself to literature. His work includes fables, odes, opera, pastorals, and tragedies. The odes were overshadowed by those of J.-B. *Rousseau, and his plays the only one to achieve success was *Inès de Castro* (1723), an edifying tragedy on a medieval subject [see REINE MORTE, LA]. A friend of *Fontenelle, he championed the cause of the moderns in the *Querelle des Anciens et des Modernes, prefacing his 'improved' version of the *Iliad* (1714) with a discourse criticizing the Greek poet from the point of view of modern rational politeness. He argued against Madame *Dacier's criticism and attacked uncritical admiration of antiquity in his urbane and unrepentant *Réflexions sur la critique* (1715). A prolific poet, for whom the main merit of verse lay in 'la difficulté vaincue', he later argued for the superiority of prose, producing prose versions of Sophocles' *Oedipus* and Racine's *Mithridate*. [PF]

LAMY, Bernard, père (1640–1715). French *Oratorian teacher and priest who fell foul of his order for his espousal of *Descartes's philosophy and his *Jansenist sympathies. He is best known for two books. The innovative rhetorical treatise *De l'art de parler* (1675, much augmented in 1688 and later editions, when its title becomes *La Rhétorique ou l'Art de parler*) is sometimes called the 'Rhétorique de Port-Royal': i.e. an equivalent to the *Logique* of *Arnauld and *Nicole and the *Grammaire* of Arnauld and *Lancelot; it contains discussions of phonetics and other linguistic topics, as well as a theory of persuasion based on the dynamic psychological function of the rhetorical figures. His *Entretiens sur les sciences* (1683) is a book of advice on reading for future Oratorian teachers; it had a

Lancelot

considerable influence on the self-education of Jean-Jacques *Rousseau.   [PF]

LANCELOT, Claude (1616–95). Teacher in *Port-Royal's 'Petites Écoles' counting *Racine among his pupils. His various grammars—Greek, Latin, Spanish, Italian—explained the rules in French rhymes which children could memorize. He taught Greek and Latin through French rather than Latin. With Antoine *Arnauld he produced the influential *Grammaire générale et raisonnée* (1660) [see GRAMMARS, 2]. His *Mémoires* appeared posthumously (1738).   [JC]

Lancelot Romances. The story of Lancelot of the Lake and his love for *Arthur's queen, Guinevere (Guenièvre), with its mixture of highly idealized chivalric prowess and equally idealized love, has furnished western culture with one of its most enduringly popular legends.

The earliest extant French romance of Lancelot is *Le Chevalier de la charrette* by *Chrétien de Troyes, which links the rescue of Guenièvre from Gorre ('The Land from which None Returns'), following her abduction by the diabolical Meleagant, to an exposition of *fin'amor* as found in *Occitan lyric poetry and adapted to its new narrative context. The abduction story is an avatar of the Persephone myth, incorporating a general redemption of Arthurian chivalry by a knight given distinct Christological features in his role as saviour.

That Lancelot is not without legendary antecedents is shown by the appearance of his name in two lists of knights in Chrétien's earlier romances, *Erec et Enide* and *Cligés*, and by a biographical romance, really the product of the stitching-together of a series of similar tales of the *Bel Inconnu* type, in which Lancelot perpetually assumes the central role. Thus he acquires a number of wives, won as the culmination of each adventure. In this text he is already associated with the 'Lady of the Lake' but is not the rescuer of Guenièvre, nor does she number among his loves. That innovation appears due to Chrétien de Troyes, or perhaps to Marie, countess of Champagne, who provided the material on which he worked, and is very probably the result of borrowing from the legend of *Tristan and his love for Iseut, his uncle's consort. The French original of the romance is lost, but the text is preserved in the German *Lanzelet*, translated from French by the Swiss poet Ulrich von Zatzikhoven *c*.1200.

The principal romance of Lancelot, however, is the 13th-c. prose romance also known as the *Lancelot-Graal*. This vast compilation actually contains three romances: *Lancelot*, *La Queste del Saint Graal* [see GRAIL ROMANCES], and *La *Mort le Roi Artu*. The cycle, fictitiously attributed to Walter Map in the manuscripts, was completed by the addition of three further elements: *L'Estoire du Graal* and *La Suite du Merlin* (elaborating elements from the

works of *Robert de Boron) and *Le Livre d'Artus* (dealing with Arthur's origins and early adventures). The 'Lancelot proper' can further be divided into three sections: 'Galehaut' (dealing with Lancelot's origins as orphaned son of King Ban de Benoyc, his upbringing in the care of the lake fairy, his early adventures and meeting with Guenièvre, his friendship with the ill-fated giant Galehaut); 'Charrette' (a reworking of Chrétien's romance, including a prologue explaining Meleagant's role as one of jealous rivalry, sexual and chivalric, with Lancelot, and sequels in quests and adventures provoked by events in Gorre); 'Agravain' (the story of the origins of the Grail quest, with the conception of the new Grail-winner, Galaad, and of the clan rivalry and jealousy which will ultimately break out into civil war destroying Arthur's kingdom in *La Mort le Roi Artu*).

The exact date of the prose romance is a matter of controversy, as is the question of whether it was conceived in cyclic terms, with *La Queste del Saint Graal* and *La Mort le Roi Artu* as integral parts of the structure, or was first conceived as a non-cyclic work dealing essentially with the 'Enfances Lancelot', approximately corresponding to the extant 'Galehaut' episode. The main argument in favour of the latter view is that in this first section of the romance a number of manuscripts refer to the Grail-winner as Perceval or Perlesvaus. The author's outlook also seems much less ascetic here than in the *Queste*, and much less doom-laden than in the *Mort Artu*, attitudes which develop predominantly in the 'Agravain' section. This would suggest that an initial non-cyclic romance (probably dating from *c*.1215–20) elaborating material from Chrétien de Troyes, Robert de Boron, and the early Grail continuations was reworked (*c*.1225–35) as a cyclic text designed to incorporate the *Queste* and the *Mort Artu*.

The main structural innovation of the prose *Lancelot* is the consistent use of *entrelacement* to create a broad canvas. By this means a number of quests and adventures are carried on simultaneously, and the reader follows one 'thread' until it intersects with that of another knight's story, which is then taken up. Many such 'threads' can be followed before the original one is rejoined. Since many adventures are formulaically repetitive (conquest of an enchanted castle or graveyard; abduction, imprisonment, and madness through love of a knight or lady; substitutions and impersonations; vows to avenge wounded or murdered knights) the impression is created of a whole world on the move.

As the romance progresses, it becomes clear that any attempt to bring order out of this chaos, and to impose a golden age at the point of the sword of even the best knight in the world, is doomed to failure because of the inherent flaws in society, which crystallize symbolically around the antagonism between Lancelot's clan and *Gauvain's, the increasingly condemned adulterous love of Lancelot and Guenièvre, and the almost abstract malignant antagonism of Arthur's sister, Morgain. These forces will lead to the removal of Grace from Arthur's kingdom, in *La Queste del Saint Graal*, and to its final disintegration in *La Mort le Roi Artu*, romances in which Lancelot and his lifelong obsession still play a key role, although Lancelot can no longer be said to be the hero of either. None the less, his reputation was so enduring that in the funeral oration that Malory has Sir Ector de Maris speak over him at the end of *La Morte d'Arthur* he can still be remembered as 'the courteoust knight that ever bare shield . . . the meekest man and the gentlest that ever ate in hall among ladies . . . the sternest knight . . . that ever put spear in rest'.

[PEB]

See F. Lot, *Étude sur le Lancelot en prose* (1918, repr. 1954, with additional material); E. Kennedy, *Lancelot and the Grail* (1986); A. Micha, *Essais sur le cycle du Lancelot-Graal* (1987).

LANG, Jack, see SOCIALISM AND COMMUNISM.

LANGEVIN, André (b. 1927). Canadian novelist whose work is typical of the mood of depression and confinement often present in *Quebec literature before the Révolution Tranquille of the 1960s. Among his early works *Poussière sur la ville* (1953) is a moving depiction of the stoic despair of sensitive individuals in stagnant small-town communities. His later work remains faithful to this initial vision, reflecting little of the social advances made in Quebec since 1960. *L'Élan d'Amérique* (1972) and *Une chaîne dans le parc* (1974) are powerfully written, but present characters for whom the future is barren and without hope. [SIL]

Langue d'oc, langue d'oïl. These terms refer respectively to the southern (or *Occitan) and northern dialects of France. They are based on the words for 'yes', the southern *oc* deriving from Latin *hoc* and the northern *oïl* from Latin *hoc ille*. Both terms date from the 13th c., but reflect an earlier distinction [see HISTORY OF THE FRENCH LANGUAGE].

LA NOUE, François de (1531–91). Protestant nobleman and professional soldier who became one of the foremost advisors to Henri de Navarre (the future *Henri IV). He was one of the few participants in the *Wars of Religion to benefit from an almost universal reputation for virtuous conduct. He was once regarded as the probable author of a letter advising Henri de Navarre to abjure Protestantism; but his commitment to his religion (which he died trying to protect) was such that he is unlikely to have recommended this course of action. This did not prevent him, on the other hand, from making an eloquent plea for Protestants and Catholics to remember that they were all Christians and for a non-violent solution to be found. See his *Discours politiques et militaires* (1587), which is the

work of a moralist with broad humanitarian sympathies. [JJS]

LANOUX, Armand (1913–83). French novelist, historian of the Paris *Commune (*La Polka des canons*, 1971, and *Le Coq rouge*, 1972); also an essayist-biographer. The three strands of his work are evident in *Adieu la vie, adieu l'amour* (1977), a 'novel' based on wartime (1914–18) correspondence of Roland *Dorgelès. Similarly, in *Bonjour, Monsieur Zola* (1954) *Zola is the 'hero' of a solidly documented fictionalization of the author's life and times. Lanoux's own war experiences formed the historical basis for the trilogy *Margot l'enragée*: *Le Commandant Watrin* (1956, Prix Interallié), *Le Rendezvous de Bruges* (1958), and *Quand la mer se retire* (1963, Prix Goncourt). [AHB]

LANSON, Gustave (1857–1934). Critic and historian of French literature. A professor of rhetoric and belles-lettres by training and a disciple of *Brunetière, he became the promoter of *literary history in France, later known as 'Lansonism'.

His influence was at its peak between the *Dreyfus Affair and the separation of Church and State in 1905. He stood for the democratization and laicization of the *lycée*, through the substitution of history for rhetoric, and allied himself with historians and sociologists, thus giving new scientific legitimacy to literary studies. He applied classical philology to modern literature, and at the same time called for a vast social history of literary life. After conventional essays (e.g. *Bossuet*, 1891), his *Histoire de la littérature française* (1895, many times reprinted) became the standard textbook of the Third Republic; with his *Voltaire* (1906), he shifted the balance from the 17th to the 18th c. in the training of citizens. His critical editions, of Voltaire's *Lettres philosophiques* (1909) and *Lamartine's *Méditations* (1915), and his *Manuel bibliographique de la littérature française moderne* (1909–14) long set the standards for academic scholarship. His method, formalized by his followers (for instance Gustave Rudler, for many years a professor in Oxford, in *Techniques de la critique et de l'histoire littéraire*, 1923) and reduced to a positivistic study of sources and influences, had the effect of cutting off literary studies from literary life until the attacks of 'la nouvelle critique' in the 1960s [see CRITICISM, 4]. [AC]

Lantier. Name of a family whose members figure prominently in many volumes of Zola's *Rougon-Macquart* series.

LANZMANN, Claude (b. 1925). Colleague of *Sartre and *Beauvoir on *Les Temps modernes* from 1952 onwards; editor since 1986. He is the author of a cinematic work in two parts entitled *Shoah* (1985), of which the text appeared the same year. The films, which took 11 years to make, reconstitute the genocide of the Jews carried out between 1941 and 1944. [EAF]

Lapalissade. A statement of the obvious, as in the old popular song about the maréchal de la Palisse (or la Palice), who died at the battle of Pavia in 1525: 'Un quart d'heure avant sa mort | Il était encore en vie.'

LA PÉRUSE, Jean Bastien de (1529–54). Member of the humanist group which studied under *Buchanan and *Muret at the Collège de Boncourt. He imitated Seneca (and to some extent Euripides) in his *Médée* (1556), which was one of the first neo-classical plays to be produced in the entourage of the *Pléiade mouvement.

LA PLACE, Pierre-Antoine de (1707–93). French translator who published an influential *Théâtre anglais* in 8 vols. (1745–9) [see BRITISH, IRISH, AND AMERICAN INFLUENCES, 2].

LAPLACE, Pierre-Simon, marquis de (1749–1827). French astronomer, physicist, and mathematician, who also had a political career under *Napoleon. His main contributions concern probability (*Théorie analytique des probabilités*, 1812) and above all the solar system (*Exposition du système du monde*, 1796).

LAPLANCHE, Jean (b. 1924). French psychoanalyst, co-editor with J.-B. Pontalis of a complete (and controversial) translation of Freud into French [see PSYCHOANALYSIS].

LAPOINTE, Gatien (1931–83). Canadian poet who, in *Le Temps premier* (1962) and especially *L'Ode au St Laurent* (1963), a Whitmanesque celebration of the land of Quebec, set the tone for a whole generation of Quebec poets who, in the 1960s, proclaimed the reappropriation of their culture and country. The *poésie du pays* is still present in *Le Premier Mot* (1967), but juxtaposed with a more sombre preoccupation with death. After a 12-year silence, there is a change of direction in his last publications *Arbre-radar* (1980) and *Corps et graphie* (1981), which are more tersely private in theme and more fragmented in form.   [SIL]

LAPOINTE, Paul-Marie (b. 1929). Canadian poet who is one of the leading exponents of a new poetics in Quebec. He was initially inspired by *Rimbaud and *Surrealism in *Le Vierge incendié* (1948); his later work marries a strong lyrical impulse with a passion for the materiality of language. His monumental poem 'Arbres' in *Le Réel absolu* (1971) is comparable in inspiration to the *Ode au St Laurent* of his namesake Gatien *Lapointe, but totally different in expression since here the celebration of country and heritage is expressed simply through a long enumeration of the botanical names of native trees. *Écritures* (1979) carries further his disruption of syntax and use of words as autonomous signifiers.   [SIL]

La Pommeraye, Madame de. Heroine of a celebrated story of amorous revenge inserted in Diderot's *Jacques le fataliste*.

LAPORTE, Roger (b. 1925). A philosopher by training, Laporte is primarily known as the author of a series of unusual works (including *La Veille*, 1963; *Fugue*, 1970; *Moriendo*, 1983) where attention focuses on the activity of writing itself, to the virtual exclusion of other subject-matter. Assembled in one volume (*Une vie*, 1986), the nine separate texts are experiments in a new genre, labelled 'biographie' (see *Carnets*, 1979; *Lettre à personne*, 1988), where the writer's self is apprehended in its primordial relationship to language and utterance. Austere but rigorous and elevating, Laporte's work often invokes kindred spirits such as *Mallarmé, *Artaud, and *Blanchot, on whom he has written with penetration (*Quinze variations sur un thème biographique*, 1975).   [MHTS]

LA PRIMAUDAYE, Pierre de (1546–1619). An eminent representative of the enthusiasm for moral philosophy which characterized the late 16th c. in France. His best-known work is *L'Académie française*, published in successive volumes between 1577 and 1596. As the title suggests, he provides an example of the many projects involving the creation of an *academy. It is not clear whether the academy really existed (in which case it would be an early example of a Protestant academy) or whether the speakers merely provided a convenient fiction for La Primaudaye's dialogues.   [JJS]

LAPRADE, Victor Richard de (1812–87). French poet, critic, and professor of French literature at Lyon. A Catholic poet with a strong sense of the power of external nature, Laprade combined a Romantic sensibility with classical influences to produce one major poem, *Psyché* (1841), and a considerable quantity of verse of a rather mediocre quality. As a young man he was an enthusiast for the ideas of *Ballanche and *Quinet. After 1848 his conservatism increased. He concluded that the crisis of the present sprang from three main causes: the egalitarianism of the Revolution, the spread of industrialism, and the rehabilitation of the flesh proclaimed by the Utopian socialists.   [CC]

LA RAMÉE, Pierre de, see RAMUS.

LARBAUD, Valery (1881–1957). Novelist, poet, essayist, and translator. He was an *angliciste* by training. His immense Vichy-St-Yorre wealth and taste for travel coloured the cosmopolitanism of his fictional Barnabooth, whose *Poèmes par un riche amateur* (1908) comfortably pre-date the internationalist currents in *Apollinaire or *Cendrars and are a neglected marker in modernism. A 1913 re-edition added to them a short story and a *journal intime*, under the title *A. O. Barnabooth: ses œuvres complètes*, revealing in the diary a Barnabooth (Perec's Bartlebooth in *La *Vie mode d'emploi* is an obvious avatar) of more humanist bent. From 1910 his literary erudition and appetite for translation made him a mainstay of the *NRF*, where he also published novellas, essays, and poems. He translated Italian, Spanish, and much British writing, including that of James Joyce. Inspired by Joyce and *Dujardin, he experimented with interior monologue in the novella 'Amants, heureux amants' (*NRF*, 1921).

His *Beauté, mon beau souci* (1920) is more sharply worked than his better-known study in adolescence, *Fermina Marquez* (1911), though it too resorts to the curious, self-effacing narrative displacement in mid-text that makes so many of his protagonists seem ineffectual. Larbaud is to the novella what Balthus is to painting—witness his *Enfantines* (1918)—for much of his writing is a delicate meditation on the mysterious graces and favours—invariably ungranted—of young girls, known or dreamt-of. Yet for all its genteel fantasies and cossetted comforts, his fictional world, where libertinage and emotion play awkwardly together, appears pervaded by solitude. A subtle psychologist and a travel writer of charm (*Jaune bleu blanc*, 1927; *Aux couleurs de Rome*, 1938), he was a pivotal figure in the Anglo-French literary landscape of his day.   [DAS]

LARIVEY, Pierre de (*c*.1540–1612). French dramatist and translator, possibly of Italian descent. His plays are nine prose comedies, six published in 1579 and a further three in 1611. They are adapted from Italian models and through them are derived ultimately from Latin comedy. The best known is *Les Esprits* (1579), one of whose central characters is a miser, perhaps a model for Molière's Harpagon in *L'*Avare*. The title of the play refers to the ghosts or demons alleged to haunt the miser's house (a ruse devised to keep him out of it).   [GJ]

LA RIVIÈRE, Mercier de (*c*.1720–93). Member of the *Physiocrat group, author of the influential *L'Ordre naturel et essentiel des sociétés politiques* (1767). *Voltaire mocked this work in his *L'Homme aux quarante écus*, but it won La Rivière an invitation to Russia from Catherine the Great.

LA ROCHEFOUCAULD, François, duc de (1613–80). Together with *La Bruyère, La Rochefoucauld is the best-known of the French *moralistes*, famous for his exploration of the role of 'amour propre' in human behaviour. Heir to a prestigious title, he was known until his father's death as the prince de Marcillac. After an aristocratic education he was married in 1628, entered military service the following year, and embarked on a career of court intrigue, where pride and chivalry engaged him on the side of the queen-mother (Marie de Médicis) and the queen (Anne d'Autriche) against *Richelieu. He was not a born man of action; later he played a prominent but ineffectual part in the *Fronde as an ally of *Condé against *Mazarin. Seriously wounded and disgraced, he retired from active life. He then frequented *salons, particularly that of Madame de *Sablé, and from 1665 was a close friend of Madame de *Lafayette.

During his retirement he wrote *Mémoires* devoted to his adventures. A faulty Dutch edition of 1662 describes the Fronde episode, and subsequently he wrote about his earlier years; the complete text only appeared in the 19th c. The story is told in a curiously dry way; little attempt is made to analyse motives and emotions, and in the later books the author refers to himself in the third person. He does, however, give a striking image of the confusion of the Fronde and the folly and vanity of its noble protagonists.

The disillusionment of the *Mémoires* is given more memorable expression in La Rochefoucauld's essential work, the *Réflexions ou Sentences et maximes morales* (usually called the *Maximes*). The immediate stimulus for these came from conversations in the Sablé circle, where the composition of pithy moral maxims was a kind of game. La Rochefoucauld's correspondence with Sablé and with Jacques *Esprit, author of *De la fausseté des vertus humaines*, show him working on what he calls his *sentences*. The manuscripts and the successive editions demonstrate the care he gave to revising them, polishing the style and aiming for greater concision. The first authorized edition dates from 1665; many maxims were subsequently deleted from this. The definitive edition, containing 504 maxims, came out in 1678, but over 50 more were published posthumously.

The *Maximes* are not all very short; the first edition opened with a remarkable 2-page analysis of the workings of 'amour-propre' and closed with a similarly full account of the 'scorn of death'. Nevertheless, the dominant type consists of only a few lines of generalized moral comment. Many of these seem too easy at first, and not a few are indeed flippant, but at their best (e.g. 'Nous avons tous assez de force pour supporter les maux d'autrui') they provoke the reader to fill out from personal experience the brief statements in which the author has condensed his own experience; it has been said that a maxim is like an extremely concentrated novel.

Needless to say, the *Maximes*, for all their apparent objectivity, give a subjective view of life, the view of a disillusioned male aristocrat. They show considerable openness and uncertainty before the complexities of human psychology, but the prevalent tone is cynical, as the author shows the sordid motives, generally described in terms of 'interest' and 'amour-propre', behind apparently virtuous behaviour. It seems certain that his stance is partly religious in origin, echoing the *Jansenists' denunciation of the falsity of pagan virtue; however, he is at pains to phrase his thought in a secular manner. It is possible to read his maxims as a dispassionate description rather than a denunciation. What is more, not all is negative; the use of expressions such as 'le plus souvent' allows one to glimpse a positive ideal of genuine nobility, love, etc. which can be set against the false virtues that have usurped their place. Among other things, La Rochefoucauld contributes to the elaboration of a theory of *honnêteté.

Although he owes his celebrity to the steely concision of the *Maximes*, La Rochefoucauld composed in his last years a set of *Réflexions diverses* on traditional moral topics, in which he gives himself more space for a subtle and less cynical exploration of human behaviour and motives. [PF]

See W. G. Moore, *La Rochefoucauld* (1969).

LA ROCHE-GUILEM or **LA ROCHE-GUILHEM,** Anne de (*c*.1644–*c*.1707). Protestant who fled France after the Revocation of the *Edict of Nantes. She wrote most of her many novels in England. She was known for her *nouvelles historiques* and *galantes* in the mode of *Villedieu, notably *Almanzaïde* (1674), *Le Grand Scanderberg* (1688), and *Histoire des favorites* (1697). [JDeJ]

LAROMIGUIÈRE, Pierre (1756–1837). French philosopher, professor at the Sorbonne. He was a transitional figure who modified the sensationalism of the *Idéologues in a way which gave an increased role to consciousness. He is usually seen as a bridge between *Condillac and *Maine de Biran. His lectures were published as *Leçons de philosophie sur les principes de l'intelligence* (1815). [CC]

LAROQUE, Gilbert (1943–84). Canadian novelist. His most important works are *Après la boue* (1972), *Serge d'entre les morts* (1976), and *Les Masques* (1980), all of which use a stream-of-consciousness technique to express the obsessive and sometimes morbid state of mind of characters wrestling with traumatic family memories. [SIL]

LAROUSSE, Pierre (1817–75). Lexicographer and publisher. His *Grand dictionnaire universel du XIXe siècle* (15 vols., 1865–76; supplements 1878, 1890) is one of the best French *encyclopedias, a treasure-house of information and a reflection of moderate progressive thought of the time. Over the past century the house of Larousse has been the major French publisher of *dictionaries and encyclopedias, together with grammars, textbooks, and the popular cheap 'Classiques Larousse'. [PF]

LA SABLIÈRE, Marguerite Hessein de (*c*.1636–1693). After she had obtained a legal separation from her inconstant husband, this well-educated daughter of a wealthy Protestant family created a famous *salon. There, philosophical and especially scientific debate shared the stage with literary matters. La Sablière received instruction in science and mathematics from members of the Académie des Sciences; *Bernier translated and abridged *Gassendi's philosophical works at her request. She was the patroness of *La Fontaine, who dedicated his reception speech for the Académie Française to her. She was the author of *Maximes chrétiennes*, long included in editions of *La Rochefoucauld's maxims. [JDeJ]

LA SALE, Antoine de (*c*.1385–*c*.1460). Prose writer. La Sale spent his life in the service of princely houses: page at 14 to Louis d'Anjou, tutor from 1434 to the son of *René d'Anjou, and then from 1448 to the sons of Louis de Luxembourg. His early works reflect the pedagogue: *La Salade* (1441) and *La Sale* (1451) are miscellaneous compilations of *exempla, reminiscence, episodes from ancient history, and improving tales which even their editor calls *indigestes manuels*. The first is distinguished, however, in incorporating an account of Antoine's visit to the *Paradis de la reine Sibylle*, in Italy.

Next in his heterogeneous œuvre comes *Le Réconfort de Madame du Fresne* (1447/8), a consolatory epistle for a mother whose first child had died, interesting for its inclusion of two *exempla* from real life, including the tragic history (somewhat fictionalized) of Madame du Chastel, forced to choose between her husband's honour and her little son's life, and choosing the former. His final treatise, *Des anciens tournois et faicts d'armes* (1459), uses memories of the great *tournaments of his youth at the court of Anjou to prescribe correct chivalric practices.

Of all his works, however, *Le Petit Jehan de Saintré* (1456) is the most successful. The heroine, a young widow known only as Madame des Belles Cousines, picks out a young page, Jehan, as a future knightly champion. She offers him an oddly intercut torrent of good advice and hard cash and ensures his courtly and chivalric success, while exacting his obedience. Saintré, hero of a fictional crusade, finally asserts his independence merely by inventing his own deed of arms; piqued, the lady retires to her estates where she falls in love with a *bon vivant* Damp Abbé. Saintré's return disturbs a sensual idyll: taunted by Madame, he is first thrown in wrestling by Damp Abbé, then in turn defeats his enemy and wounds him shamefully, taking revenge on Madame by disclosing her infidelity at court. The work is an intriguing mixture of courtly romance and *fabliau: the domineering heroine, finely drawn, understands the rituals but not the essence of *fin'amor, and the *Bildungsroman* charts Saintré's transformation from shy page to champion of the masculine world of war and tournament. Critics persistently see it as evidence of chivalric decline, but in fact La Sale ironizes everything *except* chivalry, whose values ultimately predominate. [JHMT]

LA SALLE, Jean-Baptiste, abbé de (1651–1719). Founder in 1679 of the Frères des Écoles Chrétiennes, who were providing free primary *education in over 100 French schools by 1789. His textbooks, *Les Devoirs du chrétien* and *Les Règles de la bienséance et de la civilité chrétienne*, were massively reprinted until well into the 19th c. He was canonized in 1900. [PF]

LAS CASES, Emmanuel, comte de (1766–1842). French historian. Loyal to *Napoleon, he accompanied him in exile to St Helena until he was expelled by the British authorities in 1816. His *Mémorial de Sainte-Hélène* (1822–3) records his master's life in exile and his recollections of past events. It is personal as well as historical (describing, for instance, the speed with which Napoleon dictated, so that Las Cases had to invent a form of shorthand to keep up). The book was an important contribution to the Napoleonic legend; it is Julien Sorel's bible in Stendhal's *Le *Rouge et le noir*. [DJ]

LA SERRE, Jean Puget de (1600–65). Librarian of Gaston d'*Orléans and prolific author of novels and histories, much mocked by *Boileau's generation for his mediocrity and his *pointes. He composed a manual of *letter-writing, *Le Secrétaire à la mode* (1625).

LASNIER, Rina (b. 1915). Canadian poet. Lasnier's first publication, *Féerie indienne* (1939), testifies to her deep attachment to her land and its history, through a poetic evocation of an Iroquois heroine, Catherine Tekakwitha. The natural world that she has always been so close to offers her not only a series of themes or images, but a living texture through which can be perceived the spiritual and the transcendent; the tree, for instance, is a vigorous vertical symbol of this, yet it can be cut down or consumed by fire in a few minutes, and so become 'other', and it is also the cross, a different link between heaven and earth. Humans are viewed in a similar way, as there is continuity between all life in Lasnier's world. This is the paradox of the 'présence de l'absence' that is omnipresent in her work, and is signalled in so many of her titles: *Le Chant de la montée* (1947), *Escales* (1950), *Présence de l'absence* (1956), *Mémoire sans jours* (1960), *L'Arbre blanc* (1966), *L'Invisible* (1969), *La Part du feu* (1970), *L'Échelle des anges* (1975), *Les Signes* (1976), *Matin d'oiseaux; palier de paroles* (1978), *Chant perdu* (1983). Her vision is inward and intense, but hers is also an ambitious project, encompassing a new cosmogony, in which creation emerges from 'la malemer' (*Mémoire sans jours*), Eve's fall is reinterpreted, and the earth is seen through the gaze of the angels, those 'souffleurs' of God's word to humans (*L'Échelle des anges*), while the stone eyes of funerary sculptures, Etruscan couples, and Christian 'gisants' challenge and penetrate the mystery of death (*Les Gisants*, 1963).

Lasnier distances herself from poetic theory and what she sees as linguistic games. She cites an unusual range of poets as important in her development: Francis Thompson and G. M. Hopkins (from her period at school in England), the Persian poets, *Segalen, Rilke, *Claudel. Her poetry often appears in compact regular lyric forms, but she also uses a long Claudelian and biblical *verset* for reflective or celebratory expression. All is distilled and concentrated, linked by an assonanced harmony. The questioning is constantly renewed but never arid;

Lasnier has too strong a belief in the power of love and transformation, too immediate a sense of dynamism for her poetry not to be, in the end, affirmatory. [MMC]

See P. G. Lewis (ed.), *Traditionalism, Nationalism and Feminism: Women Writers of Quebec* (1985).

LASSAY, Armand-Léon, marquis de (1652–1738). French author of a conservative *Utopia, *Le Royaume des Féliciens*, included in his *Recueil de différentes choses* (1727). This happy realm has a constitutional monarchy, a nobility, and freedom of trade; dress denotes social position; the religion is deistic and tolerant. [CJB]

LA SUZE, Henriette de Coligny, comtesse de (1618–73). French poet. Renowned for her conversion to Catholicism, divorce from a brutal husband, and several lengthy and ruinous court cases, she was much admired for her elegies, characterized by their passionate but rigorously unsentimental expression of love. Her salon was widely frequented, and she corresponded with Christina of Sweden and *Saint-Évremond. [GJM]

LA TAILLE, Jean de (*c*.1533–1608). French humanist playwright and author of an essay, *De l'art de la tragédie* (published 1572 as a preface to his biblical tragedy *Saül le furieux*), which sets out the conventions of tragedy as then perceived (lamentable subject-matter; unity of time and place; violent action reported, not represented; five acts, progressing towards the catastrophe; a moderately virtuous hero). His own two tragedies combine biblical subjects with formal and stylistic imitation of Seneca (*La Famine, ou les Gabaonites*, 1573). His other writings include two prose comedies (1573), *Le Negromant* (translated from Ariosto) and *Les Corrivaux* (adapted from Boccaccio). [GJ]

Latin Influences on French Literature, see CLASSICAL INFLUENCES.

Latinity. The various educational systems in France up until the time of the Revolution, both ecclesiastical and secular, ensured that a sound knowledge of Latin and a good acquaintance with Latin authors were acquired by those who attended school. Latin was the language of the classroom (and even the playground) until the second half of the 18th c., and, as a result, pupils learnt to compose verse and prose in Latin before they did in French. Many continued to write in Latin after leaving school, and this resulted in a vast corpus of literature which remained vital and innovative until at least the mid-17th c., and which enjoyed a richly symbiotic relationship with the vernacular.

1. Medieval

Until the 11th c. Latin was virtually unrivalled as the literary language of France. The poetry of the late classical writer Ausonius (*c*.310–*c*.395), written in a wide range of quantitative metres, contains works which movingly express his affection for his native Bordeaux and for his relatives and friends, as well as the famous 'Idyll' on the Moselle, notable for its appreciation of the natural world. His *Epistles* contain poems to and from his pupil Paulinus of Nola (353–431); these touchingly bear witness to their friendship, and also to Paulinus's Christianity, which in later years inspired him to write a new kind of poetry: classical in form and style but Christian in sentiment. Following this example, the 5th c. saw a surge of Christian Latin poets, of whom the Lyon-born Sidonius Apollinaris (*c.*430–479) is the most significant as the author of a collection of 24 extant poems, including 8 panegyrics, and of 9 books of prose epistles. In the 6th c. it is the Italian Venantius Fortunatus (*c.*540–*c.*600), author of the beautiful Passion hymn 'Pange, lingua', who is the main writer of both religious and secular poetry in France and who marks, in his hymns, a break with quantitative metres and a move to rhythmical and rhyming verse. The *Historia Francorum* of Gregory of Tours (*c.*538–*c.*594) provides us with a rare historical work from this early period.

Subsequently, it was not until the 8th c. and the Carolingian Empire that Latin literature again flourished in France, with scholars from all over Europe being attracted to the court of *Charlemagne: the Englishman Alcuin (*c.*735–804), who helped to systematize the teaching of the *trivium* (*grammar, *rhetoric, dialectic); the Spaniard Theodulf (*c.*760–821), bishop of Orléans, whose literary inspiration came largely from the classical tradition; the Italian Paulinus of Aquileia (d. 802), who did much to establish rhythmical metres, modelled on popular Latin verse. After the death of Charlemagne in 814 literary writing declined somewhat, though the monastic schools maintained a strong interest in classical literature, and verse composition formed part of the regular curriculum. This tradition was continued in the cathedral schools of the 10th and 11th c., for example at Reims, and at Chartres under the direction of Fulbert (*c.*960–1028), himself the author of both quantitative and rhythmical poetry. Of the many writers of this period, it is worth mentioning Hildebert de Lavardin (1056–1133), Bérenger de Tours (999–1088), Baudri de Bourgueil (1046–1130), and Marbode de Rennes (*c.*1035–1123), the author of a rhetorical work *De ornamentis verborum* and the *Liber lapidum* on the properties of precious stones, as well as of lighter verse. Quantitative metres (particularly the elegiac couplet) continued to coexist with rhythmical and rhyming metres.

Although the final years of the 11th c. saw the beginning of a rich vernacular literature in France in the form of the *chanson de geste*, Latin literature, with its international audience of scholars and churchmen, went from strength to strength in the fertile intellectual climate of 12th-c. France. Paris became firmly established as the intellectual capital of Europe, where the great debates between rival philosophical schools were acted out [see SCHOLASTICISM]. Autobiographical writings reveal something of the personalities of such men as *Abélard (in the *Historia calamitatum*) and *Guibert de Nogent, famous too for his history of the Crusades, while Abbot Suger (1081–1151) composed a biography of Louis VI. Later we have the eloquent prose writing of Pierre de Blois (*c.*1140–1212) as an example of the epistolary genre, and the influential *De amore* of *Andreas Capellanus, which codified the rules of courtly love [see FIN'AMOR]. Religious poetry continued to be important. The imposing abbey of *Cluny housed a number of religious poets, including Pierre le Vénérable (*c.*1092–1156) and Bernard de Morlaas (b. early 12th c.); and both Abélard and the mystic *Bernard de Clairvaux contributed impressive works to the genre. Later, the sequence, a verse form originally used to embellish the *Alleluia* of the Mass and now regularized in rhythm and rhyme, became the dominant verse form, particularly in the hands of Adam de Saint Victor (d. *c.*1177). Secular poetry reflects the concerns and interests of the age. Philosophical works were composed by Abélard (*Astrolabius*), Bernard Silvestris de Tours (*fl.* 1145–53), author of the Platonizing *De mundi universitate*, and *Alan of Lille, famous for his *Anticlaudianus*, one of the earliest medieval works to make systematic use of allegory. His satire, the *De planctu naturae*, also exploits allegory. As a satirist, Bernard de Cluny is far more outspoken in his condemnation of worldly vices, including those of the Church.

Epic poetry, in some cases inspired by the vernacular *chansons de geste*, flourishes in the 12th c., with the *Alexandreis* of *Gautier de Châtillon representing the best example. Of considerable importance too is the 12th-c. Latin lyric, with its highly personal content and style, which has maintained an abiding appeal, especially with regard to the so-called Goliardic poets, authors of secular, often scurrilous verses. Hugues Primat d'Orléans (*c.*1093–*c.*1160), in his famous 'Dives eram et dilectus', clearly demonstrates his poetic gifts in a vigorous rhythmical and rhyming verse-form in which he gives free rein to his often violent feelings. Gautier de Châtillon could be no less acerbic in his satires, though his poetry is often in a gentler vein, on the changing seasons or love, and his works inspired many other writers. Later we have the more moralizing poetry of Philippe le Chancelier (d. 1236). An important genre in the early Middle Ages was didactic writing, typified by the *Ars versificatoria* of Mathieu de Vendôme (b. *c.*1130) and the highly influential *Doctrinale* of Alexandre de Villedieu, which was still being used to teach Latin in the early 16th c.

Latin drama during the Middle Ages was largely centred upon the Church, with the development, from the 9th to the 13th c., of liturgical drama based originally upon tropes introduced into services celebrating the important feasts of the Christian year, in particular Easter [see MEDIEVAL THEATRE].

Subsequently Latin *miracle plays made their appearance. Other 'dramatic' forms developed in the 12th c., notably the *comœdia*, inspired by Plautus and Terence, and itself inspiring the vernacular *fabliau*. Examples are the *Amphitryo* and the *Aulularia*, attributed to one Vitalis who was writing in the latter part of the century, along with the *Milo* of Mathieu de Vendôme.

2. Renaissance and Modern

After the literary heights of the 12th c. Latin literature had to wait until the Renaissance before a vigorous new tradition offered any sort of rivalry with the vernacular. The study of Latin continued in the schools and universities, and there are indeed a few authors who have survived from the 14th c., e.g. Jean *Gerson and Nicolas de Clamenges (*c.*1360–1440). But as early as the 15th c. there was a growing awareness that Latin was known imperfectly, and the reforms of the University of Paris by Cardinal d'Estouteville in 1452 were partly designed to correct this decline. Scholars such as Guillaume Fichet (1433–*c.*1480) and Robert Gaguin (*c.*1423–1501) further helped to prepare the ground for the neo-Latin writers of the 16th c. The invention of the *printing press opened up the world of classical literature to a much wider audience than hitherto, and later *François Ier provided a climate in which learning could flourish. In humanist colleges Alexandre de Villedieu's *Doctrinale* was finally replaced after 1511 by the grammar of Johannes Despauterius, which went into considerable detail on all aspects of Latin grammar and versification, and proved so successful that it continued to be used throughout the 17th c. However, its apparent emphasis on exceptions and its synchronic treatment of classical Latin led to what some purists felt to be a hybrid language, and indeed the century is marked by a protracted debate on Ciceronianism.

Imitation of the ancients, of course, lay at the heart of the new literary movement in France, and, during the first half of the century it was neo-Latin authors, at least in the realms of poetry and drama, who led the way. Verse composition was a central exercise for pupils in the *humanist colleges which now formed the main educational establishments in France, and, of those who continued to compose in Latin in later years, it is worth mentioning Jean Salmon Macrin (1490–1557), who was one of the first writers to use the Horatian lyric metres in France in his *Odes*; Nicolas Bourbon (*c.*1503–*c.*1550), many of whose epigrams are sharply satirical; the Ciceronian Étienne *Dolet; Marc-Antoine *Muret, whose commentary on Catullus helped popularize the *style mignard*; Jean *Dorat, whose poetry is less impressive than his influence as a teacher; Théodore de *Bèze, a highly competent epigrammatist in his pre-Geneva days; the Scotsman George *Buchanan, who during his time in France composed fine works in the full range of classical genres; Joachim *du Bellay, whose Latin poetry during his period in Rome was

so successful, despite his own strictures on neo-Latin composition in the *Défense et illustration*; and Michel de *l'Hôpital. Between them, they would help to establish the status of poetry as a serious exercise, capable of enhancing national prestige and of influencing public opinion, especially on religious issues.

French humanist drama also has its origins in neo-Latin writers. Whilst the medieval tradition is continued by Nicolas Barthélemy de Loches (b. 1478) in his Passion play *Christus xylonicus* of 1529, Buchanan and Muret during their time at the Collège de Guyenne in the 1540s wrote original plays for performance by the pupils (including *Montaigne), and, when subsequently they taught at the Collège de Boncourt in Paris, they clearly inspired a whole generation of vernacular playwrights (*Belleau, *La Péruse, *Jodelle, Jean de *la Taille, *Grévin).

The works of Renaissance Latin prose-writers are essentially scholarly (e.g. *Budé) or religious (e.g. *Calvin) in nature, though *Erasmus's *Moriae Encomium* was to have a strong influence on the development of satire, and J.-C. *Scaliger's *Poetices libri septem* of 1561 was responsible for popularizing Aristotelian literary ideas in France. It is really at the beginning of the 17th c. that imaginative neo-Latin prose reaches its peak with John Barclay (1592–1621) in his *Euphormionis Lusini Satyricon* of 1607 inspiring a tradition of satirical *romans à clé*. Also of note are the philosophical works of *Descartes and of *Gassendi.

Towards the end of the 16th c. *Jesuit education began to take over from the humanist colleges in Catholic Europe, and with it Jesuit drama also became firmly established. Some of the best-known French exponents of the genre are Denis *Petau, Louis Cellot (1588–1658), and Nicolas *Caussin. It is the Jesuits too who provide much of the neo-Latin poetry of the 17th c., with a proliferation of *epic verse (typified by Pierre Mambrun's *Constantinus* of 1658), agricultural works (inspired by Virgil's *Georgics*) written by René *Rapin and Jacques Vanière (1664–1739), while a non-Jesuit, Claude Quillet (1602–61), is the author of one of the more refreshing works of the period, the *Callipaedia* of 1655. The Jesuit emphasis on purity of expression and content, coupled with an increasing unease at the inevitable mixture of the sacred and the profane in Latin composition, completed the decline of humanist Latin literature in the 17th c. Although the study of the classics continued to play an important part in education, Latin compositions outside the classroom are few and far between from the 18th to the 20th c. There is, however, the long Christian apologia in verse, the *Anti-Lucretius* of Melchior de Polignac, published in 1742. For the 19th c. it is worth mentioning the Latin poems of *Baudelaire, and the libretto of Stravinsky's opera *Oedipus Rex* (translated from *Cocteau's version by Jean Daniélou) offers a rare 20th-c. Latin work of art.
[See also CLASSICAL INFLUENCES.]   [PJF]

See E. R. Curtius, *European Literature and the Late Middle Ages* (1953); K. Strecker, *Introduction to Medieval Latin* (1957); J. IJsewijn, *Companion to Neo-Latin Studies* (1990).

LATOUCHE, Henri de (pseud. of Hyacinthe Thabaud de Latouche) (1785–1851). French poet, playwright, and novelist. His novel *Fragoletta* (1829) continues to command critical attention. In 1819 he brought out a highly influential edition of the works of André *Chénier.

LA TOUR, Georges de (1593–1652). French painter. Very few works can be attributed to him, although records show him to have been rich and popular with the French administration at Nancy. His dramatic lighting effects clearly show the influence of Caravaggio. His early work is minutely descriptive of surface textures and is divided between genre and biblical subjects. A series of theatrically posed candle-lit scenes gradually developed into an intense, still, contemplative type of religious subject using very simplified forms, in tune with French classical taste. [JPC]

LA TOUR, Maurice Quentin de (1704–88). An eccentric, La Tour revolutionized French portaiture with his enormous sequence of vivacious, informal portraits in pastel. His studio at the Louvre was visited by all the notables and literati of the day, including *Diderot, who commented on his intense concentration. He exhibited his interpretations of the royal family, leading philosophers, singers, actors, and dancers at the Salons. Our knowledge of the appearance of French society depends heavily on his images. In his important life-size pastel portrait of Madame de *Pompadour (1755), the setting, with its prominent art portfolio and volumes of Guarini's *Il Pastor fido*, *La *Henriade*, *De l'*esprit des lois*, and the *Encyclopédie* was used to glorify her intellectual freedom and patronage. [JPC]

LA TOUR DU PIN, Patrice de (1911–75). French poet. *La Quête de joie* (1933), published while he was still a student in Paris, brought La Tour du Pin to the attention of such writers as *Supervielle and *Gide, who were impressed by his ability to combine spiritual fervour with classical precision and an atmosphere of legend. Descended from Irish kings on his mother's side, he was brought up on the family estate in Sologne where he was to spend much of his life. After a long imprisonment in Germany (1940–3) La Tour du Pin drew up the plan for an epic work in three parts, or 'Jeux', the first concerned with man's relationship to himself, the second with his relation to the world of others, and the third with the relationship to God. The first part of *Une somme de poésie*, dating from 1946, consists of nine 'books', which feature a variety of legendary protagonists who represent different aspects of the poet's spiritual itinerary. The second part, subtitled 'La Contemplation errante' (1959), is more austere

and philosophical, while the third, comprising such collections as *Petit théâtre crépusculaire* (1963) and *Une lutte pour la vie* (1970), is dominated by the poet's attempt to reconcile poetic writing and religious faith, and to combine them in a *théopoésie* where poetry becomes a form of prayer. *Une somme de poésie* is a rich and rewarding work in its scope and structure (revised more than once before the poet's death), and in the way the best poems combine traditional rhythm and metre with a modern use of diction and imagery often drawn from the natural world. [MHTS]

LA TOUR LANDRY, Le chevalier de (c.1330–1405). Author of a *Livre pour l'enseignement de ses filles* (1371/2), designed to instruct his daughters in the art of finding and keeping husbands. His rambling treatise is a cross between memoir and homily, with biblical *exempla*, snippets from saints' lives, and anecdotes that are sometimes surprisingly risqué. There were two English translations, including one by Caxton, and the German translation was still being reprinted in the 17th c. [JHMT]

LAUNAY, Rose de (Marguerite Cordier), Madame de Staal, see STAAL.

LAURE (1903–38). Colette Peignot, known as Laure, was the cherished companion of Georges *Bataille until her untimely death in her mid-thirties. Her literary remains appeared in 1971 and 1977 as *Écrits de Laure*. They comprise *Histoire d'une petite fille*, an account of her childhood rebellion against religion; poetic texts grouped under the heading *Le Sacré* and heightened by the urge for lucid communication before the menace of death; and letters to friends like Simone *Weil, with whom she shared a self-sacrificing political idealism and a distaste for the chicaneries of French cultural life. [RC]

LAURENDEAU, André, see QUEBEC, 3 and 5.

LAURENT, Jacques (b. 1919). A member of the right-wing *Hussards group and, like all its members, both a novelist and a polemicist. He was the founding editor of *La Parisienne* in 1953 and from 1954 to 1959 was editor of *Arts*. His polemic of the 1940s and 1950s was consistently anti-Gaullist and anti-*Existentialist: in *Paul et Jean-Paul* (1953) he castigates both *Bourget and *Sartre for reducing literature to didacticism. His own fiction, especially *Les Corps tranquilles* (1949), *Le Petit Canard* (1954), and *Les Bêtises* (1971, Prix Goncourt) combines a serious view of the war and Liberation with considerable formal innovation. Under the pseudonym of Cécil Saint-Laurent, he was the author of the best-selling *Caroline chérie* (1958). [NH]

Laure persécutée, see ROTROU.

LAUTRÉAMONT, comte de (pseud. of Isidore Ducasse) (1846–70). Prose poet. Haloed in eldritch glamour, the Montevideo-born Ducasse is one of the *maudits* of French literature, his premature death a sign, however, that he was beloved at least by gods of the savage sort. So little indeed is known about his brief life that his writing appears almost as the work of some unknown midnight *taggeur*, whose moving finger wrote and having writ moved on.

Printed in 1868–9 (but published in full only in 1874), his six *Chants de Maldoror*, written in prose, celebrate the unbridled predatory misdeeds of a prowler monster whose shape is as indefinite as his age. 'Peindre les délices de la cruauté' is the avowed intention, and the reader is engulfed in a flux of nightmarish scenarios that unfurls with a strangely rhythmic insistence. Gothic paraphernalia and a grotesque menagerie of animal metamorphoses underpin a vision of man once innocent but now transmogrified into a wild beast. Male adolescents are the preferred prey, charmed, abducted, and destroyed in an atmosphere of psychopathic mayhem that smacks of the homosexual, but equally subverts any such inference. Meanwhile Lautréamont's eccentric vision unleashes images of uninhibited novelty with dislocatory pre-*Surrealist similes that still astonish.

However, behind this apparently spontaneous pageant of the subconscious at play is a writer in full control of the effects he wishes to create. The *Chants* is a discreetly self-conscious text which busies itself periodically with the problems of its own organization, recognizes the weirdness of its manner, and is alive to varieties of reader response. From time to time the writer teasingly collapses the terrors he creates. Some of his artifices, borrowed from the *roman-feuilleton*, from medical treatises, or popular scientific magazines, he deliberately makes apparent, and a parodic understanding often infiltrates our reading.

This vein of parody governs his *Poésies* (1870), which appeared in the year of his death in Paris. They are in two parts, are not poetry, and represent a curious and possibly suspect volte-face in relation to the *Chants*. The first section is a brief *ars poetica* in prose rejecting Romanticism and all its rites and writers. The second is largely an unattributed collection of maxims, sayings, and texts by classical authors, rewritten in such a way as to divert or destabilize their original meaning. The technique is an interesting early form of deconstruction but makes disjointed reading. It is for the wild, worrying beauty of the *Chants de Maldoror*, a reservoir for many of the resources of later modern writing, that the darkly fulgurant Ducasse is remembered. [DAS]

See M. Blanchot, *Lautréamont et Sade* (1949); G. Bachelard, *Lautréamont* (1956); M. Philip, *Lectures de Lautréamont* (1971); A. de Jonge, *Nightmare Culture* (1973).

LA VALLIÈRE, Louise de la Baume le Blanc, duchesse de (1644–1700). *Louis XIV's mistress from 1661 until she was supplanted by the more aggressive *Montespan. She retired to a Carmelite convent in 1674; *Bossuet preached a famous sermon when she took her vows the following year.

LA VARENDE, Jean-Balthazar-Marie Mallard, comte de (1887–1959). Aristocratic author of many nostalgic novels and stories of his native Normandy (e.g. *Pays d'Ouche*, 1936; *Nez-de-cuir*, 1937). Written in a lightly archaic style, these evoke a vanished social order and a class of brave, life-loving leaders with an ideal of sacrifice and service. [PF]

LAVELLI, Jorge (b. 1932). Argentinian-born theatre director who came to prominence in the 1960s with baroque productions of plays by Gombrowitz, Copi, and *Arrabal. His ritual productions, influenced by *Artaud, are characterized by rhythm, musicality, and precise geometrical movements. His later experimental work in opera made him, together with *Chéreau, one of the leading renovators of the genre. [DWW]

LA VIGNE, André de (d. *c*.1515). Author of poems and plays, in particular a *mystery play about St Martin performed in 1496. He accompanied Charles VIII on his Italian campaign and wrote a verse account of it.

LAVISSE, Ernest (1842–1922). French historian, director of the *École Normale Supérieure (1904–19). He directed two massive collective works of national history, *Histoire de France* (9 vols., 1900–11) and *Histoire de la France contemporaine* (10 vols., 1921–2), which remained authoritative for many years, as well as primary-school manuals which helped mould the national consciousness of generations of French people. [PF]

LAVOISIER, Antoine-Laurent de (1743–94). One of the founders of modern chemistry. His most important discoveries concern oxygen and the composition of air and water (see his *Traité élémentaire de chimie*, 1789). His many scientific and practical interests included the manufacture of gunpowder and a scheme for gas lighting. He held a post of tax-farmer, as a result of which—in spite of his liberal views—he was guillotined under the Revolution. [PF]

LAW, John (1671–1729). Financier. Born in Edinburgh, he took refuge from justice on the Continent, becoming a successful gambler and proponent of a system of public credit. In 1716 the Regent called him in to restore France's finances. He set up a bank in the rue Quincampoix, soon to become a state bank, took over trading companies such as the Compagnie du Mississippi and the Compagnie des Indes, and issued vast amounts of paper money without any solid backing. Instead of encouraging commerce, this generated a wave of speculation, ending in a crash where many fortunes were lost. Law fled to Italy. His 'système' was often held responsible (e.g in the *Lettres persanes*) for the social instability and corruption associated with quick fortunes; it gave banks and public credit a bad name in France for several generations. [PF]

Law Courts, see PARLEMENTS.

LAYA, Jean-Louis (1761–1833). Poet and dramatist who enjoyed great success during the Revolution (e.g. *Les Dangers de l'opinion*, 1790; *Jean Calas*, 1793,). He is remembered especially for *L'Ami des lois* (2 January 1793), which attacked the Convention at a delicate moment (Louis XVI was on trial) and depicted *Marat in the guise of Duricrane, *Robespierre as Nomophage. Arrested soon afterwards, Laya remained in prison until 9 Thermidor. Thereafter his career was varied: dramatist once again, then journalist, literary critic, and teacher (it was he who, in 1813, succeeded *Delille in the chair of literary history and poetry in the Sorbonne).
[JR]

LAYE, Camara, see CAMARA LAYE.

Lazarists, see VINCENT DE PAUL.

LÉAUTAUD, Paul (1872–1956). Novelist, essayist, theatre critic, and diarist. Léautaud, an admirer of *Voltaire, *Diderot, *Chamfort, and *Stendhal, was a spirit of the French 18th c. stranded in the 20th. A bachelor of biting tongue and a writer of uninhibited mordant prose, he worked as secretary to the *Mercure de France* from 1908 to 1941, first coming to notice as the co-author, with van Bever, of the anthology *Poètes d'aujourd'hui 1880-1900* (1900), which he followed with a tender, slightly risqué autobiographical novel *Le Petit Ami* (1903), set in the *demi-monde* of his childhood. As 'Maurice Boissard' he was for many years the idiosyncratic drama critic of the *Mercure*, later of the *Nouvelle Revue Française* (*Le Théâtre de Maurice Boissard 1907–1923*, 1926). Quietly plying his quill pen at the hub of Parisian literary life, he remained largely unknown despite occasional volumes of aphorisms, reflections, and souvenirs (*Mélange*, 1928; *Passe-temps*, 1929) until, in old age, his sparkling and irreverent radio conversations of 1950 with Robert Mallet (*Entretiens avec Robert Mallet*, 1951) launched him into fame. His masterpiece remains the 19 volumes of his revealing and acerbic *Journal littéraire 1893–1956* (1956–66), largely written amongst cats, candlelight, and cobwebs in the ramshackle *pavillon* at Fontenay-aux-Roses which was his modest hermitage for the 46 years preceding his death. [DAS]

Lebanon, French Literature of, see MIDDLE EAST.

LE BAUD, Pierre (*fl.* 1480–1505), produced the most important medieval history of the Duchy of Brittany in 1480 (*Croniques et ystoires des Bretons*, BN, MS. fr. 8266; incomplete edn., 1907–22). He was encouraged to revise it by Queen Anne. A presentation copy was completed by September 1505 (British Library, Harleian MS. 4371; first edn., 1638; full modern edn., 1986). [MJ]

LEBESQUE, Morvan, see BRITTANY, 2.

LEBLANC, Maurice (1864–1941). French author of some 20 novels in the *Arsène Lupin* cycle (1907–39), featuring the romantic, dandyish, fiendishly clever, and physically resourceful detective Arsène Lupin. Published first in *Je sais tout* and then in the daily *Le *Journal*, Leblanc's novels were still palpably indebted to the great 19th-c. forebears of the *roman-feuilleton*. [BR]

LE BOSSU, René, père (1631–80). French author of a *Traité du poème épique* (1675) which was influential in its day, particularly in England. It argues implausibly that the essence of an epic is its 'fable', which, like Aesop's stories, should be seen as conveying a universal moral lesson.

LE BRIS, Michel, see TRAVEL WRITING.

LE BRUN, Annie (b. 1942). Active in Paris *Surrealism until its dissolution, Le Brun has published prose poetry (*Annuaire de lune*, 1977), an essay on the poetic sensibility (*Appel d'air*, 1988), and a reappraisal of *Sade (*Soudain un bloc d'abîme, Sade*, 1986). She is best known for her provocative critique of French feminism, *Lâchez tout* (1977). [RC]

LEBRUN, Charles (1619–90). Virtual dictator of the arts in France until the death of *Colbert in 1683. He established his reputation by a series of decorative schemes, and his own greatest compositions, which immortalize the achievements of the crown, are at *Versailles. He became a founder, rector, chancellor, and finally director of the *Académie Royale de Peinture et de Sculpture. He was also director of the *Gobelins factory and Premier Peintre (1664). His *Tent of Darius* (1661), for Louis XIV, is a model of legibility, with the explicit and varied gesture and expression of the figures deriving from ideas expressed by *Poussin. Lebrun's influential treatise, *Méthode pour apprendre à dessiner les passions* (1698), codified human emotions and provided a visual system by which a painting might be read like a written text. [JPC]

LEBRUN, Ponce-Denis Écouchard (1729–1807). Poet who won success both by his epigrams and by his lofty lyrical and philosophical poems. His contemporaries called him (in all seriousness) Lebrun-Pindare, and he professed a high poetic ideal, which he communicated to his young friend André *Chénier. In his lengthy odes, on subjects ranging from the Lisbon earthquake to the Revolution and the Empire, the forced sublimity often topples over into absurdity. His long philosophical poem, *La Nature*, begun in 1760, remained unfinished, but shows him nobly attempting to do poetic justice to the immensity of the universe revealed by modern science. [PF]

LECLERC, Annie. Author of *Parole de femme* (1974), an influential text of the French *feminist movement of the 1970s, celebrating the female body in lyrical terms. The text's assumption of female specificity and acceptance of traditionally female domestic tasks made it controversial, though Leclerc's main purpose was to revalue women's experience. Arguing that women have historically been closer to their bodies than men, she calls on women in 'La Lettre d'amour' (in *La Venue à l'écriture*, 1977) to write from their bodies. After *Épousailles* (1976) and *Au feu du jour* (1979), affirming women's special relationship to life forces, *Hommes et femmes* (1985) focuses on the common language of love between men and women; sexual difference is still strongly expressed but as a dialectic rather than as a biological given. A collection of short stories, *Le Mal de mère* (1986), was followed by *Origines* (1988), a text addressed directly to *Rousseau and relating her lifetime passion for his work (it also evokes her marriage to Nicos *Poulantzas). At the same time it is an account of her own relationship with writing. *Clés* (1989) is a short text exploring the power of words through the Bluebeard myth. All Leclerc's writing is highly poetic and is closely bound up with her own experience. [EAF]

LE CLERC, Jean (1657–1736). Scholar and journalist. Born in Geneva, he became a convert to Arminianism in Holland, where he wrote voluminously. His eminence in the 'république des lettres' came from editions of classical texts, translations of and commentaries on the Bible, and particularly the sober and knowledgeable review-articles in his journals: *Bibliothèque universelle et historique* (1686–93); *Bibliothèque choisie* (1703–14); *Bibliothèque ancienne et moderne* (1714–26). One of his specialities was English writing; another, science. He clashed with *Simon over biblical criticism (*Sentiments de quelques théologiens*, 1685); against *Bayle, in a resounding controversy (1704–6), he defended religious rationalism. [CJB]

LECLERCQ, Théodore, see PROVERBE DRAMATIQUE.

LE CLÉZIO, Jean-Marie (b. 1940). French novelist, born in Nice of a French mother and an English father whose family emigrated from Brittany to Mauritius in the 18th c. His first published novel, *Le Procès-verbal* (1963, Prix Renaudot), was hailed for its stylistic virtuosity and its bold departures from narrative convention; *Le Déluge* (1966), *La Guerre* (1970), and *Les Géants* (1973) developed its vision of the misfit, alienated by a mechanistic, urban, consumer civilization, often depicted in apocalyptic terms. Striking typographical experiments are a feature of the author's drive to catalogue the texture of everyday life in the material world, an impulse present in the meditations of *L'Extase matérielle* (1967). His subsequent experience of living in Mexico and among Indians in Panama produced several works on Latin American civilizations. Later novels evoke Third World encounters with the West, as in *Désert* (1980), whose heroine leaves her desert homeland for the infernal life of the French city. The narrative of *Le Chercheur d'or* (1985) moves from Mauritius to France and back again; Le Clézio's own childhood experience of travel in Africa also informs *Onitsha* (1991). These texts are increasingly marked by lyrical celebrations of primitive landscapes and life-styles. [DHW]

LECOMTE, Marcel (1900–66). Active in the group producing the avant-garde journal *Correspondance* in Brussels in 1924, Lecomte made his mark within Belgian *Surrealism with stories and prose poems celebrating the uncanny and the marvellous which haunt the underside of urban normality. Such collections as *L'Accent du secret* (1944) and *le Carnet et les instants* (1964) orchestrate tiny coincidences and quirks of human appearance or gesture, to disclose a distinctive, because infinitely discreet, surreality. His reflective essays on contemporary literature were issued as *Les Voies de la littérature* (1988). [RC]

LECONTE DE LISLE, Charles-Marie (1818–94). French poet, born on Reunion, whence he came to France in 1837 and became the leading figure in the *Parnassian movement in French poetry.

Leconte de Lisle's first volume of verse, *Poèmes antiques* (1852), signalled his break with *Romanticism. Ten years later the publication of the *Poèmes barbares* confirmed his status as the leader of the post-Romantic generation in poetry. Later collections are *Poèmes tragiques* (1884) and *Derniers poèmes* (1895). His reputation, eclipsed for much of this century by those of *Baudelaire and the major poets associated with *Symbolism, is now benefiting from the re-evaluation of the Parnassian movement's pivotal role in 19th-c. French verse.

Profoundly disappointed at the failure of the Revolution of 1848, Leconte de Lisle sought in poetry and the study of ancient Greek and Indian cultures an alternative form of engagement with the ideas of his time. In his verse and critical writings he rejected didactic and utilitarian art and Romantic poetry's expression of the self in favour of resurrecting past civilizations in which art and science were indissociable. He reconciled in his writing a cult of objective impersonality and deeply held intellectual commitments. This historian of antiquity and barbarism expressed a sense of the void at the centre of modern civilization and dismissed the consolations of religion. Instead, he proposed the beauty of the arrangement of word, sound, and image expressed in poetry's traditional forms, particularly the alexandrine, a lesson which *Mallarmé would extend. [JK]

LE CORBUSIER (pseud. of Charles-Édouard Jeanneret) (1887–1965) was born in Switzerland, settled in Paris in 1917, and besides being this century's best-known architect (Unité d'Habitation de Marseille, Chapelle de Ronchamp, Chandigarh), was also the author of several influential books. A Purist painter himself, he collaborated with Amédée Ozenfant on *Après le cubisme* (1918), and articles for *L'Esprit nouveau* (1921–4), which he had founded in 1919. His principal works are: *Vers une architecture* (1923), *La Ville radieuse* (1935), *Quand les cathédrales étaient blanches* (1937), *La Charte d'Athènes* (1943), *Manière de penser l'urbanisme* (1946), *Le Modulor* (1950). Le Corbusier's revolutionary theory and practice of architecture and town-planning were rationalist, functionalist, and brutalist, and he was often accused of inhumanity, yet, as *Le Modulor* proclaims, it is man who is (literally) the measure of everything, and he advocates a Utopian return to nature ('soleil, espace, verdure'). The writing parallels the architecture: it is lucid, dogmatic, provocative, and élitist, at times austerely mathematical, at others poetic and striving for 'la forme pure dans des rapports précis'. [PS]

LECOUVREUR, Adrienne (1692–1730). Notable French tragic actress. After her death in mysterious circumstances she was refused church burial because of her profession. Her friend Voltaire stigmatized this act of intolerance in his *Lettres philosophiques*.

LE DŒUFF, Michèle (b. 1948). French philosopher and translator (of Bacon and Shakespeare). Her most ambitious work to date, *L'Étude et le rouet* (1989), is a vigorous reflection on women's relation to philosophy, inspired by Hipparchia of Thrace, who devoted to study 'the time she should have wasted at her distaff'. It seeks to undermine the universalist claims of a philosophical tradition which has not contained thought by and about women, that is, to 'analyser le discours sot tenu sur les femmes par des gens qui en principe n'ont pas droit à la sottise'. Central to the book is a comparative criticism of the work of *Sartre and *Beauvoir, and it concludes with a call for full *mixité* within the French intellectual tradition. [SR]

LEDOUX, Charles-Nicolas (1736–1806). Brilliantly inventive French architect, whose total conception of the design, furnishing, and decoration of Madame du Barry's Pavillon de Louveciennes (1771) confirmed French *Neoclassical taste. The theatre at Besançon (1775–84) is his classical masterpiece, together with the Romantic salt works at Arc-et-Senans, where *Poussin's idea of the Greek modes is expressed by the fountains of salt water formed like primitive, natural rocks. [JPC]

LEDUC, Violette (1907–72). French writer. *La Bâtarde*, a key work of modern autobiography published in 1964 with a preface by Simone de *Beauvoir, brought Leduc the success which had previously eluded her. All her writing, as she acknowledged, is concerned with the attempt to lay the ghosts of her past. She initially wrote intense, and at best hauntingly obsessive, fiction: *L'Asphyxie*

(1946), *L'Affamée* (1948), *Ravages* (1955), and *Thérèse et Isabelle* (1966). *La Bâtarde*, autobiography proper as opposed to autobiographical fiction, gave Leduc greater scope to exercise her by-then highly developed gift for controlling and reappraising her experiences by means of stylistic manipulation. Less focused, her posthumous volumes of autobiography, *La Folie en tête* (1971) and *La Chasse à l'amour* (1973), are disappointing, although her qualities—unflinching lucidity and inexpugnable narcissism laced with wry humour—are still much in evidence. Leduc has found a new readership in the wake of literary *feminism and the concept of *écriture féminine*. [MHTS]

LEFEBVRE, Georges (1874–1959). Professor at the Sorbonne, historian of the Revolution, which he interpreted along republican and broadly Marxist lines in works of great erudition, including *La Grande Peur de 1789* (1932), *Quatre-vingt-neuf* (1939), and *La Révolution française* (1951).

LEFEBVRE, Henri (1901–91). The most prolific French *Marxist intellectual of the 20th-c. Attracted to Communism in the 1920s, he developed a humanistic Marxist philosophy, inspired by Hegel and early Marx, combining the dialectical method with a theory of alienation. His post-war books on *Rabelais, *Descartes, *Diderot, *Musset, aesthetics, and philosophy were innovative, and often critical of prevailing views in the French Communist Party, which he left in 1958. He turned to sociology, specializing in urban sociology and the sociology of everyday life, for which he is now best known. See his *Matérialisme dialectique* (1939), *La Somme et le reste* (1959), *La Vie quotidienne dans le monde moderne* (1968). [MHK]

LEFÈVRE, Jean (c.1320–c.1387). French lawyer and translator of (among other works) the virulently misogynistic *Lamentations* of Matheolus. His original works are the *Respit de la mort* (1376), written after a near-mortal illness and cast as a suit in due form for a stay of execution, and *Le Livre de Leesce* (1380/7), a meticulous rebuttal of the *Lamentations*. He may also have written the *Danse macabré*. [JHMT]

LE FÈVRE DE LA BODERIE, Guy (1541–98). Polymath, polyglot, and poet. His knowledge of ancient and oriental languages enabled him to contribute to the preparation of the Antwerp polyglot Bible; as a disciple of the visionary scholar Guillaume *Postel, he was also familiar with *Neoplatonist and hermetic thought. He wrote some religious verse and two long 'scientific' poems: the *Encyclie des secrets de l'éternité* (1571) traces a spiritual ascent from reason and formal theology to biblical and cabbalistic insight; the *Galliade ou la Révolution des arts* (1578–82) is an encyclopaedic work coloured by nationalistic and *Counter-Reformation beliefs. [TC]

LEFÈVRE D'ÉTAPLES, Jacques (c.1460–1536). French scholar, theologian, and father-figure to the *Evangelicals. Early visits to Italy inspired him to publish in France the new Latin versions of Aristotle made by Italian scholars, and to advocate a new critical approach to the original texts; contact with Florentine *Neoplatonism led to editions of Dionysius the Areopagite, Ramon Lull, and other mystical writers, as well as of certain Greek Fathers—in particular, the Platonizing Origen. Philology, mysticism, and patristics all prepared the way for his major work on the scriptures: in 1512 appeared his Latin translation and commentary on St Paul, followed in 1522 by his commentary on the Gospels, and by a French translation of the *Bible in 1523 (New Testament) and 1528–30 (Old Testament). Protected by *François Ier, and especially by *Marguerite de Navarre, he weathered the wrath of the *Sorbonne and, despite a brief period of exile in 1525–6, continued to inspire the now-scattered French Evangelicals. He died at Marguerite's court at Nérac. [MJH]

LEFRANC, Martin (c.1401–1461). Born in Normandy, he studied in Paris and travelled widely, spending much of his adult life in the service of the dukes of Savoy, notably under Amédée VIII, later antipope Felix V, to whom he was secretary. Of his three main works, two—Le Champion des dames (1442) and the Complainte du livre du champion des dames—were important (if prolix) pro-feminist contributions to the contemporary *Querelle des Femmes. The third, L'Estrif de Fortune et Vertu (1447–8), composed of alternating sections of verse and prose, raises interesting questions of determinism, and counts Pertrarch and classical writers among its sources. [NM]

LEFRANC DE POMPIGNAN, see POMPIGNAN.

Légataire universel, Le. Comedy by *Regnard, produced 1708, a witty, cynical play of trickery over a will.

Légende de saint Julien l'Hospitalier, La. The second of Flaubert's *Trois contes.

Légende des siècles, La. Collection of 'little epics' by Victor *Hugo composed between 1840 and 1877, published in three series in 1859, 1877, and 1883. Two other poems, La Fin de Satan, representing Evil annihilated by Liberty, and Dieu, representing God as Love, were to form a trilogy with these poems on Humanity, but they remained unfinished and were published posthumously.

The first series is the culmination of a decade of intense poetic creativity during which Hugo wrote his greatest verse, including Les *Châtiments and Les *Contemplations. The poems of La Légende combine legend and history in a depiction of Humanity's historical and spiritual development, from biblical times, through deepening experience of evil, to the new collective moral awareness of the post-Revolutionary present and beyond. Each century imposes its own mask on the face of Humanity. Part 1, 'D'Ève à Jésus', begins with a lush evocation of Eden ('Le Sacre de la Femme'), where humanness is equated with fecundity and sensuality. With the fall out of Paradise, Humanity's lineage is transferred to the sleeping patriarch of the Book of Ruth in 'Booz endormi' and ultimately, in what is perhaps the greatest poem of the series, 'Le Satyre', to a libidinous and prophetic Pan figure, more powerful than the gods because he is capable of capturing the terrible beauty of creation with his song. Passing rapidly over oriental, Greek, and Roman antiquity, Hugo devotes most space to medieval times, when French epic literature was born, with narrative poems (e.g. 'Le Mariage de Roland', 'Le Petit Roi de Galice', 'L'Aigle du casque') that stress the barbarism of the 'dark' ages. The poems on the 19th c. ('Les Pauvres Gens') and the 20th c. ('Pleine mer', 'Plein ciel', 'La Trompette du jugement') are apocalyptic in tone and style. The additions of the second and third series overseen by Paul Meurice tend to blur the original outlines of the epic plan. [SN]

Légende dorée, La (Legenda aurea). A compilation of digests of saints' lives [see HAGIOGRAPHY] made by the Italian Dominican Jacobus de Voragine (d. 1298). The stories stress uncomplicated piety and the miraculous to provide daily readings and objects of meditation for private devotion following the cycle of the liturgical year. The collection proved very popular and was twice translated into French in the 14th c., by Jean de Vignay and Jean Belay, whose version provided the basis for early printed editions. The folk-tale simplicity of the biographies guaranteed their popularity, and the openness of the structure of the collection enabled many hands to add to the stock of stories. [PEB]

LÉGER, Fernand (1881–1955). French painter who, after *Cubism and *Orphism, independently sought an art for the people in an age of machines. *Apollinaire in Les Peintres cubistes praised his genuineness and the 'simplicité' of his art. War service (1914–18, including Verdun) marked him professionally and personally: comrades took him for a house-painter, which he found meritorious. The drawings published with his war correspondence (1990) reveal the regular shorthand of echoing shapes (volumetric or cylindrical) which characterize his paintings. Metallic sheen, outline, and a bright palette enliven paintings of workers and machines. Communism was a bond between Léger and *Éluard, who responded with 'Les Constructeurs' to the painting of that name; Léger illustrated Éluard's 'Liberté'. [HEB]

Léger, Saint, see VIE DE SAINT LÉGER.

Légion d' Honneur. Order created by Bonaparte to unite civilians, soldiers, and clergy in the cult of the fatherland. Today it has a grand'maître (the president of the Republic) and five classes (*chevalier, officier, commandeur, grand officier*, and *grand-croix*). When official insignia are not worn, members are distinguished by the 'rosette' worn in the buttonhole.

Légion Étrangère. The French Foreign Legion was created in 1831 for foreign recruits serving in French armies overseas. It now has many French soldiers, and in 1962, at the end of the *Algerian War, its headquarters moved to metropolitan France. Numerous books and films have created a romantic (or sometimes anti-romantic) image of the Legion as a place of criminality, male comradeship, and adventure.

Légitime Défense. French *West Indian literary-political review, published in Paris, of which only one number (June 1932) appeared. In it a group of Martinican students, notably Etienne Léro (1910–39), René *Ménil, and Jules Monnerot *fils* (b. 1909), looked to a fusion of *Marxism, Freudianism, and *Surrealism as a means of revolutionizing the practice of French West Indian writing and the social, political, and racial structures it reflected.   [RDEB]

Legitimists. Name given to the supporters of the *Bourbon dynasty after its fall from power in 1830; they were opposed to the partisans of the *Orléans dynasty (Orléanists).

LE GOFF, Jacques (b. 1924). Important French social historian of the Middle Ages, and co-editor of *Annales*. Le Goff was receptive to the influence of anthropology and wrote pioneering studies of medieval urban life (*Marchands et banquiers du moyen âge*, 1956), scholarly milieux (*Les Intellectuels au moyen âge*, 1957), and what he calls the medieval 'imaginary' (*L'Imaginaire médiéval*, 1985)—the study of mentality and symbolism.   [SK]

LE GRAND D'AUSSY, Pierre Jean-Baptiste, see MIDDLE AGES, 3.

Legs, Le. Comedy in one act by *Marivaux, one of his most successful, first performed 1736. After some complex skirmishes, the marquis, offered a rich legacy if he will marry Hortense, sacrifices 200,000 *livres* in order to marry the comtesse, whom he loves.

LEIBNIZ, Gottfried Wilhelm (1646–1716). Philosopher, whose work covers most fields of human knowledge and thought. Born in Leipzig, he went to France in 1672 on an unsuccessful diplomatic mission; having made intellectual contacts in Paris, he used French for many of his principal writings (*Essais de théodicée*, 1710, an answer to *Bayle; *Principes de la nature et de la grâce*, 1714; *Principes de la philosophie* (*Monadologie*), 1714). *Fontenelle pronounced his funeral *éloge*, but his great metaphysical system had a limited impact in 18th-c. France and his disciples were caricatured in Voltaire's *Candide*.
[PF]

LEIRIS, Michel (1901–90). Leiris is a key figure in 20th-c. French culture whose work combines poetry, ethnography, linguistics, *psychoanalysis, and autobiography in strikingly innovative ways. Brought up in a well-heeled Paris suburb, a background which always made him uneasy, he was influenced early on by the examples of Raymond *Roussel (a family friend) and Max *Jacob, who encouraged him to write. The painter André Masson introduced him to the *Surrealists, and here his fascination with language found expression in the remarkable verbal experiments of *Glossaire j'y serre mes gloses* (1925), a fantastic lexicon based on potential analogies between the physical properties of words and their meanings, and *Aurora* (1946), where he constructs a dream-like narrative on the basis of extravagant linguistic permutations. *Haut mal* (enlarged edn., 1969) collects the bulk of Leiris's verse.

Various factors, including a turbulent personal life which led him to undergo psychoanalysis, and a collaboration with Georges *Bataille, at that time editor of the interdisciplinary review *Documents*, lie behind the sudden decision to become secretary to the Mission Dakar–Djibouti, an ethnological field-trip across Africa in 1931-3. Although Leiris's own record of the journey, the strongly subjective diary *L'Afrique fantôme* (1934), annoyed the professionals, the expedition led to a position at the Musée de l'Homme and a distinguished career marked by notable publications on Black Africa and the Caribbean (*Cinq études d'ethnologie*, 1969).

From the 1930s onwards Leiris adopted autobiography as his principal form of literary activity, and the radical approach he took to the genre was to prove immensely productive and influential. Through autobiography, with its dual commitment to literary form and documentary fact, Leiris sought to explore his conflicting desires for the transcendent intensities of poetic language, and for radical transformation in both the personal and the sociopolitical spheres. *L'Âge d'homme* (1939) jettisoned conventional chronological structure and featured a method combining Surrealist collage, psychoanalytical free association, and ethnographic description. Starting from feelings inspired by a painting, Cranach's diptych of Judith and Lucretia, Leiris excavates the 'mythology' of his erotic life, identifying deep-rooted fears and desires behind his liking for opera, bull-fighting, allegories, or classical myth. Yet, as he ruefully explained in 'De la littérature considérée comme une tauromachie', a brilliant preface added to the 1946 reissue, he had wanted the composition of *L'Âge d'homme* to liquidate rather than consolidate his fantasies and fears. His aim had been that writing autobiographically should involve a risk analogous to that of the bullfighter (*Miroir de la tauromachie*, 1938, is a remarkable philosophical meditation on the *corrida*). Conscious that this had not been the case, he embarked on a further experiment in autobiography, *La Règle du jeu*, the four-volume work widely regarded as a masterpiece to be compared with *Montaigne's *Essais* and Rousseau's *Confessions*, that was to occupy him for some three decades.

Biffures (1948) opens with a series of densely written essays focused initially on Leiris's subjective experiences in the field of language. Entitled '...reusement' (the child's erroneous construal of the word 'heureusement'), the first piece concerns his discovery of the irremediably social aspect of language; in 'Perséphone' Leiris constructs an elaborate network out of a wide range of memories concerning his imaginary relationship to natural phenomena. As in *L'Âge d'homme*, chronology is replaced by associative patterning, but here, rather than juxtaposition and classification, what predominates is an intricate weaving together of small data—things seen, heard, or imagined, and at some point recorded in a journal or card-index.

The method is basically the same in *Fourbis* (1955) and *Fibrilles* (1966), although in these works thematic analysis is applied increasingly to particular events or periods in the author's life whose 'mythic' character is elicited by minute scrutiny: a deathly sound heard as a child, a relationship with a prostitute during the *drôle de guerre*, a suicide attempt. Leiris constantly questions his motives and methods, interrupting his narration and evaluating his progress in a quintessentially modern way, but always in the light of long-term objectives, which are ultimately ethical in character, bearing on death, art, memory, writing, and revolution. In *Frêle bruit* (1976), the fragmentary coda to *La Règle du jeu*, and in such late works as *Le Ruban au cou d'Olympia* (1981), *Langage tangage ou Ce que les mots me disent* (1985), and *A cor et à cri* (1988), Leiris reaffirms his enduring conviction that poetic aspiration and political change, while necessarily at loggerheads, are vitally connected. His diaries began to be published posthumously in the 1990s.

The visual arts played an important part in Leiris's life (his wife Louise was a leading Parisian art dealer), and with customary lucidity he wrote illuminatingly on his friends *Picasso, *Giacometti, and Francis Bacon. [MHTS]

See P. Lejeune, *Lire Leiris* (1975); R. H. Simon, *Orphée médusé* (1984).

LEKAIN (pseud. of Henri-Louis Cain) (1729–78). The most famous male tragic actor of the 18th c. He acted many of *Voltaire's leading parts at the Comédie-Française. With *Clairon, he was responsible for important reforms, including the suppression of on-stage seats and the introduction of somewhat more authentic costume.

LE LABOUREUR, Louis, see EPIC POETRY; QUERELLE DES ANCIENS ET DES MODERNES.

Lélia, see SAND.

LE LIONNAIS, François, see OULIPO.

LEMAIRE DE BELGES, Jean (*c.*1475–before 1525). Born in Bavai (also called Belges), Hainault, he was one of the last, but one of the best, of the *Rhétoriqueurs, often seen as a precursor of the Renaissance. A godson of *Molinet, he was educated in Valenciennes and Paris. He had a good knowledge of Latin and Italian literature, and a lively interest in painting and sculpture. In his career as court poet and historiographer he was principally attached to Marguerite d'Autriche, later to Anne de Bretagne. His most significant works in verse include *La Couronne margaritique* (1504–5, on the death of Marguerite's second husband, Philibert de Savoie), *Les Chansons de Namur* (1507, in support of a popular revolt), *La Concorde des deux langages* (1511, i.e. French and Italian—a plea for cultural unity), *Les Épîtres de l'amant vert* (1505, burlesque epistles, supposedly written by Marguerite's parrot, which dies because of its love for her). His prose chronicle in three books, *Les Illustrations de Gaule et singularités de Troie* (1510–13), treats the Trojan origins of the French. In both poetry and prose his language is more supple and subtle than that of the earlier Rhétoriqueurs, and contains interesting descriptive elements, particularly in the evocation of the natural world. [CMSJ]

LE MAÎTRE, Antoine (1608–58). French barrister, who in 1637 gave up a brilliant career at the bar to become the first *Port-Royal *solitaire*. Noted for his austerity and humility, he was soon joined by *Lancelot, Singlin, and his younger brothers Simon Le Maître de Séricourt and Isaac *Le Maître de Sacy—all much influenced by *Saint-Cyran. His *Plaidoyers et harangues* were considered showy by classical theorists of eloquence. [JC]

LEMAÎTRE, Frédérick (1800–76). Virtuoso French actor of the *Romantic period, he was famed for the uninhibited power of his acting. At home in several genres, he earned a legendary reputation for magnetic performances in plays of strong emotions: *L'Auberge des Adrets* (1823), *Dumas *père's *Kean* (1836), Hugo's *Ruy Blas* (1838). [SBJ]

LEMAÎTRE, Jules (1853–1914). French critic and playwright, who gave up teaching to devote himself to writing. His journalistic essays, grouped in two collections, *Les Contemporains* (10 vols., 1885–1924) and *Impressions de théâtre* (11 vols., 1888–1920), are avowedly impressionistic and personal ('des impressions sincères, notées avec soin'), but open-minded and often witty and stimulating. In later years he adopted the right-wing positions of *Action Française. [PF]

LE MAÎTRE DE SACY or **SACI,** Louis-Isaac (1613–84). Confessor at *Port-Royal. Having completed the translation of the New Testament begun by his brother Antoine *Le Maître (the Mons New Testament, 1667); he published his annotated translation of the Old Testament between 1672 and 1696.

He also translated the *Imitation of Christ* (1662), and his name is associated with *Pascal's *Entretien avec M. de Saci*. [JC]

LEMELIN, Roger (1919–92). Canadian novelist and journalist, best known for two colourful and lively chronicles of French-Canadian working-class life: *Au pied de la pente douce* (1945) and *Les Plouffe* (1948). The initial impact of these works was magnified by subsequent television serials and film versions, which made the Plouffe family a cultural institution in Quebec. Set in 1936–40, both works show social change weakening the grip of the two great forces of traditional French-Canadian life: the Catholic Church and the family (the latter being symbolized by the redoubtable figure of *la mère Plouffe*). *Pierre le magnifique* (1952), loosely linked to the first two novels, and a belated sequel, *Le Crime d'Ovide Plouffe* (1982), were less successful. [SIL]

LEMERCIER, Népomucène (1771–1840). Extremely prolific French playwright and poet. He attacked Romantic drama, but made 'Shakespearean' experiments in tragedy (*Agamemnon*, 1797; *Christophe Colomb*, 1809) and invented a new genre, the *comédie historique* in prose (*Pinto*, 1800). His long poems are magnificently unreadable; see *L'Atlantiade* (1812), an epic of modern physics, with an extraordinary cast of new divinities. [PF]

LEMIERRE, Antoine-Marin (1733–93). Winner of several prizes from the Académie Française, author of two long didactic-descriptive poems, *La Peinture* (1769) and *Les Fastes* (1779), and of tragedies, including *Hypermnestre* (1758), *Guillaume Tell* (1766), and *La Veuve du Malabar* (1770), in which suspense and local colour serve a Voltairean ideology. [PF]

LEMONNIER, Camille (1844–1913). Belgian writer, author of a series of novels on the theme of rural and urban poverty (notably *Le Mâle*, 1881, and *Happe-Chair*, 1886), which reveal the influence of *Zola's *Naturalism. He edited and contributed to numerous French and Belgian literary reviews and his extensive art criticism includes important early studies of *Courbet and *Rops, among others. In works such as *Nos Flamands* (1869) and *La Belgique* (1888) he helped to create a *Belgian francophone literary identity, and for almost 50 years was a major link between French and Belgian literary circles. [JK]

LE MOYNE, Pierre (1602–71). French Jesuit moralist and poet. He was attacked, unfairly, by *Pascal in the *Lettres provinciales*. Heroic virtue is a favourite theme with him, for instance in *La Galerie des femmes fortes*, and in his *Saint Louis* (1653) he attempted to create a national Christian *epic. His poetry, though very uneven, is altogether exceptional in the range and power of its imagery, the poet's office being, in his view, to display the wisdom and power of the Creator by revealing the latent symbolism of the world. [AJS]

LEMSINE, Aïcha (b. 1942). Algerian novelist, born in the Némencha, married to a diplomat, Ahmed Laïdi. She has published two novels. *La Chrysalide* (1976) purports to follow the evolution of the family and the role of women in Algeria, but the result is ambiguous. *Ciel de porphyre* (1978) describes the *Algerian War through a diary written by an adolescent surrounded by stereotyped female characters living in an inauthentic world. Her essay *Ordalie des voix* (1983) was translated into Arabic as *Hukm al-aswat*. [FL]

LE NAIN, Antoine (*c*.1588–1648), Louis (*c*.1593–1648), and Mathieu (*c*.1607–1677). The Le Nain brothers were French painters of unusual avant-garde naturalistic scenes. Antoine produced small scenes of bourgeois or peasant families. Louis specialized in remarkable peasant scenes, calm and monumental in effect though small in scale. Mathieu painted candle-lit militia scenes. Their themes of cardplaying, music-making, and the much-discussed *Chambre de rhétorique* correspond more closely to French 18th-c. literary ideas. [JPC]

LENCLOS, Anne, called Ninon de (*c*.1620–1705). Among the most renowned intellects of her day, she was also her century's most celebrated courtesan—although she was technically not a kept woman, since she had independent means. She moved in literary and *salon circles, wrote poetry, and shared the feminism of the *précieuses* [see PRECIOSITY]—'Je me fais homme' is her alleged response to patriarchal privilege. Her open sexuality was as legendary as the free-thinking she had in common with her lifelong friend *Saint-Évremond. Nevertheless, she was considered the best representative of Parisian style and her company was sought by men and women, libertines and prudes alike. [JDeJ]

LENÉRU, Marie (1875–1918). Diarist, playwright, and critic, born in Brest into a distinguished naval family. Measles at 14 left her deaf, half-blind, and with speech difficulties. Her perceptive *Journal*, posthumously published in 1922 (as was her percussive essay *Saint-Just*), records in epigrammatic style her loss of faith and the acumen and zest which she summoned to surmount her handicaps and her condition as a woman. From 1910 her well-constructed plays *Les Affranchis*, *La Triomphatrice*, *Le Redoutable*, *La Paix*, *Le Bonheur des autres*, and *La Maison sur le roc* treated serious moral issues, though they seem dated now because of their settings. [DAS]

LENGLET-DUFRESNOY, Nicolas (1674–1755). French diplomat and historian, several times imprisoned, and author of books on many subjects, including hermetic philosophy. His *De l'usage des romans* (1734) defends novels as providing insights into life and love not offered by standard history; it includes a full bibliography going back to medieval romance. [PF]

LE NOBLE, Eustache (1643–1711). Author, during an adventurous life full of travel, banishment, and prison, of a vast number of mainly mercenary but often lively works, histories, pamphlets, stories, fables, translations, etc., culminating in *Uranie ou les Tableaux de la philosophie* (1694–7), which expounds and defends astrology. [PF]

LENORMAND, Henri-René (1882–1951). Best known as a dramatist and theorist of the avant-garde French theatre of the 1920s, when his pessimistic plays, often drawing on Freudian ideas, excited praise and controversy. He was associated with the director Georges *Pitoëff, whose productions of his plays brought out vividly their sense of doom and claustrophobia. The bias of his work is deterministic, whether in the baleful effects of climate and colonialism in *Le Simoun* (1920) and *A l'ombre du mal* (1924), or in the ravages of suppressed desires and emotions: incestuous passion in *Le Simoun*, childhood trauma in *Le Mangeur de rêves* (1922). [SBJ]

LE NÔTRE, André (1613–1700), garden designer, see VERSAILLES.

LÉONARD, Nicolas-Germain, see WEST INDIES, 1.

LE POITTEVIN, Alfred, see FLAUBERT.

LEPRINCE DE BEAUMONT, Marie, Madame (1711–80). French novelist and story-writer. The only work of hers which is still read is her version of *La Belle et la bête* (an abridgement of Madame de Villeneuve's original text). This and other fairy-tales are included in *Le Magasin des enfants, ou Dialogues d'une sage gouvernante et plusieurs de ses élèves* (1756), a work which went into dozens of editions, lasting well into the 19th c. She published three similar educational works, for 'des adolescentes', 'des jeunes dames', and 'des pauvres'. Although she also produced a number of novels and *contes moraux*, she is interesting chiefly for her efforts—manifested before Rousseau's *Émile*—to make education enjoyable. [VGM]

LEROI-GOURHAN, André, see ANTHROPOLOGY.

LEROUX, Gaston (1868–1927). French journalist, barrister, and author of popular novels [see DETECTIVE FICTION; ROMAN D'AVENTURES].

LEROUX, Pierre (1797–1871). French socialist philosopher and propagandist. His best-known work is *De l'humanité* (1840), in which he expounded a quintessentially Romantic creed grounded in a faith in mankind as a collective being progressing through history. His idealistic socialism and its accompanying aesthetics influenced George *Sand. Leroux's political thought foregrounded the notions of equality and, above all, solidarity. He was elected to the National Assembly during the Second Republic, spent the early years of the Empire in exile in England and in Jersey, but returned to France after the amnesty of 1859. In 1863 he published his last important work, *La Grève de Samarez*. [CC]

LE ROY, Louis (c.1510–1577). French humanist scholar, professor of Greek at the Collège Royal in 1572, who utilized his own translations of Plato and Aristotle in his voluminous political and historical writings; his masterwork is *De la vicissitude ou variété des choses en l'univers* (1576), a pioneering work on cyclical change in cultural history. [MJH]

LE ROY LADURIE, Emmanuel (b. 1929). French historian. In his doctoral thesis, *Les Paysans de Languedoc* (1966), which covered the period from 1450 to 1750, Le Roy Ladurie continued the *Annales tradition of studying both material determinants and collective mental attitudes in a long-term perspective. He combined an emphasis on quantitative methods with an interest in historical geography (*Histoire du climat*, 1967), and moved towards historical anthropology in the best-selling *Montaillou, village occitan, 1294–1324* (1975), a vivid reconstruction, based on an innovative interpretation of traditional source material, of the ecology, customs, beliefs, and kinship networks of a single community. [REG]

LÉRY, Jean de (1534–1613). Pugnacious Burgundian Calvinist, active as a pastor during the *Wars of Religion, who left eyewitness accounts of the sieges of Sancerre and La Charité. His principal work is the *Histoire d'un voyage fait en la terre du Brésil* (1578), an account of the ill-fated colonial expedition under *Villegagnon in 1555–8. Successive editions developed a polemic against André *Thevet, whose *Singularités*, purportedly a first-hand account of the expedition, blamed the Calvinist members for its failure. Léry's book probably provided material for *Montaigne's essay 'Des cannibales'. [MJH]

LESAGE, Alain-René (1668–1747). Novelist and playwright. A Breton by birth, he attended the Jesuit college at Vannes, studied law, and settled in Paris, where he married and had four children. He was a professional writer of a new type, depending partly on *patronage, but mainly on earnings from his writings. He used material from many literary sources (Turkish, Italian, above all Spanish), adapting it to the taste of his public. Translation, imitation, and original work are hard to tell apart in his voluminous output. Most of this is now forgotten; Lesage's continuing celebrity is due to two novels and two comedies.

As a novelist, he began with the *Lettres galantes d'Aristénète* (1695), adapted from the Greek, and *Les Nouvelles Aventures de l'admirable Don Quichotte de la Manche* (1704), a largely original work inspired by a sequel to Cervantes. *Le *Diable boiteux* (1707, enlarged edn. 1726) was an immense success and was much imitated. Lesage appears to have made a considerable contribution, as 'rewriter', to *Les Mille et un Jours* (1710–12), translated by Pétis de la Croix, a rival publication to Les *Mille et une Nuits. His masterpiece, the Histoire de *Gil Blas de Santillane, was published in three instalments between 1715 and 1735, and achieved immediate and lasting success. He used a similar formula, the series of adventures attributed to a single hero, with intercalated stories, in several more novels, but with less success. Among these, Les Aventures de Robert Chevalier, dit de Beauchêne (1732) is based on a true story set in Canada, whereas the Histoire de Guzman d'Alfarache (1732) and Le Bachelier de Salamanque (1736) continue to exploit the Spanish vein.

Lesage was also a prolific writer for the theatre. His first success was Crispin rival de son maître, performed at the Comédie-Française in 1707; this entertainingly cynical one-act comedy of errors and intrigue, in the traditional mode, shows the valet Crispin, under a false identity, coming close to supplanting his master in love. The valet actually supplants the master in the next comedy, the brilliant *Turcaret (1709); production of this play was delayed and its success compromised by reactions to its fierce satire. Thereafter Lesage broke with the Comédie-Française and worked for the théâtre de la *foire, composing or collaborating on dozens of scripts for entertainments, ranging from harlequinades in dumb-show to comic operas. With his colleague d'Orneval, he published ten volumes of Le Théâtre de la foire ou l'Opéra-comique (1721–37), with an interesting preface.

He was a writer for his time, an artisan of letters, and a supporter of the modernes in the *Querelle. He wrote for a broad public, and Gil Blas in particular was much appreciated by readers of many countries for two centuries. Critics have sometimes viewed him rather more patronizingly, condemning the diffuse nature of his narratives and the banality or superficiality of his morality and his psychology. Yet he is in many ways a fascinating witness of his period. His writing is sharp and up to date, he has a gift for the dramatic scene and a keen eye for the masks and pretences of a corrupt society. While reusing old literary material, he nevertheless gives a strong sense of life in a real, unidealized world.

[PF]

See R. Laufer, Lesage ou le Métier de romancier (1971).

Lesbian Writing, see GAY AND LESBIAN WRITING.

LESCONVEL, Pierre (c.1650–1722). Author of a *Utopian novel, the Voyage du prince de Montberaud dans l'Île de Naudely (1703), strongly influenced by Fénelon's *Télémaque. The island is France idealized, complete with absolute monarch, aristocracy, and Church; trade and agriculture prosper, but wealth and rank are not abused. [CJB]

LESPINASSE, Julie de (1732–76). Of noble but illegitimate birth, she entered the Parisian literary scene as *Du Deffand's companion. The latter repudiated her because Lespinasse had, under her protector's

roof, created a rival *salon. Her modest apartment became a force that shaped French public opinion: the evolution of the *Encyclopédie was debated there, as were elections to the Académie Française and even affairs of state (the ministers *Turgot and *Malesherbes were among her regulars). Her assembly was more open than others to illustrious foreigners, such as Hume (she was fluent in English, Spanish, and Italian). Immortalized in Diderot's *Rêve de d'Alembert, she was famous for her spontaneity, her devotion to d'*Alembert (who parted company with Du Deffand for her), and the fervour of her attachments to the Spanish marquis Gonsalvo de Mora and the comte de Guibert. Her passionate correspondence with Guibert illustrates *letter-writing's paradoxical double status in the French tradition. In the manner of Héloïse's letters, it is read simultaneously as personal outpouring and literary masterpiece. [JDeJ]

LE TELLIER, Michel (1603–85), see LOUVOIS.

LETESSIER, Dorothée (b. 1953). French novelist. 'Une OS en personne qui prend la plume' (B. Poirot-Delpech). Her freshly written and accessible novels are rooted in her experience as a factory-worker in Brittany. Voyage à Paimpol (1980) tells the story of the flight of a young mother from the prison of marriage, motherhood, and factory life, and Loïca (1983) that of a nonconformist who disrupts the male-friendly patterns of both family and work-place.

[SR]

LE TOURNEUR, Pierre (1736–88). French translator. Through his prose versions of Young, Hervey, and Gray, he was responsible for the vogue enjoyed on the Continent by the 'graveyard' school of English poetry. He also translated Ariosto, Goldsmith, Johnson, and Richardson, but is best remembered for his version of Ossian (Poésies galliques, 1777), which conveyed Macpherson's work to all corners of Europe, and for his prose Shakespeare (20 vols., 1776–82), which served as a basis for *Ducis's verse adaptations. In both cases Le Tourneur renders the original meaning reasonably faithfully, but dilutes the style to comply with polite French practice.

[PF]

Letter-Novels, see EPISTOLARY NOVELS.

Letter-Writing. In French literature letter-writing achieved a status more elevated and lasting than in any other national tradition. For over 200 years beginning in the late 16th c., letter-writing continued to diversify, until throughout the 18th c. it occupied a central position on the literary horizon.

Letter-writing is not a genre but a form with different manifestations—letter manuals, private correspondences collected for publication, *epistolary novels. First to appear in the 16th and 17th c. were volumes of familiar letters by individual writers and letter-manuals. The letters included in these collections had varying origins: writers collecting their own correspondence juxtaposed letters to different recipients; editors of manuals mixed letters by different authors and letters fictive and authentic. In both cases the personal was de-emphasized to give the letters a predominantly rhetorical status. Familiar letters, e.g. *Pasquier's (1586), were intended to inspire creative imitation, in particular to encourage others to write in French rather than Latin. By the early 17th c., however, imitation was defined less creatively in manuals such as *La Serre's *Le Secrétaire à la mode* (1625), which simply proposed model letters designed to fill various epistolary needs. Letter-writing at this time was a cog in the vast enterprise of sociability. The composition of letters—of compliment, gallantry, and so forth—was part of the fine art of worldly conduct being refined and practised in the early *salons [see HON-NÊTETÉ]. At the same time, the letter was recognized as an effective didactic or polemic genre, as in *Pascal's *Provinciales*.

The depersonalized use of the letter, which valorized correct form over individual expression, paradoxically helped generate more personal manifestations of the epistolary form, the great correspondences and novels which make up its golden age. Manuals first grouped together letters dealing with different subjects, then arranged them so that a plot was implied from their order, thereby paving the way for the epistolary novel.

The 18th-c. epistolary explosion was initiated in the second half of the 17th c. by writers who made letter-writing synonymous with personal intimacy. In addition, the major epistolary successes of this time, notably the *Lettres portugaises*, made letter-writing the expression of what Richardson, who knew his French precursors well, called 'writing to the moment', the exploration of the fullness of the present tense and narrative immediacy. Finally, these texts suggest that women have privileged access to epistolary communication and almost make letter-writing synonymous with women's writing. By the time the first major French correspondence, *Sévigné's, was edited in the early 18th c., the age of the epistolary novel was under way. However different their style and content, its masterpieces—notably *La Nouvelle Héloïse* (1761), Les *Liaisons dangereuses* (1782), and Richardson's novels, which were immensely influential in *Prévost's French translation—all present the letter as the privileged mode of immediate and full personal revelation and reinforce the association between women and letter-writing.

The importance of letter-writing in literary history can be seen as a function of the degree to which it questions the limits of literature. Sévigné's correspondence, for instance, has been admired both for its sophisticated literary technique and for the absence of such sophistication, for its instinctive impulse. Similarly, the *Lettres portugaises* has been praised alternately as a literary masterpiece and an outpouring of authentic sentiment. This endless conflict about the nature of the form can be traced to the absence of a clear distinction between public and private spheres of discourse.

It is, for instance, rarely certain that the vast majority of 16th- and 17th-c. epistolary texts were destined for publication. Moreover, their various contexts of publication often recast them in formats so radically dissimilar that the text's meaning was repeatedly transformed. Witness the example of Sévigné's letters, which were edited only in 1725, 30 years after her death. Over the next 30 years the first four editions of her correspondence appeared. In each of these, and in virtually all the numerous editions that appeared over the next century and a half, the correspondence appears in a new light—at times exclusively personal (a mother's letters to her daughter), at times exclusively political (a high-born woman's view of a powerful court). The first epistolary masterpiece in the French tradition, the letters exchanged by Héloïse and *Abélard in the 12th c., shared a similar fate when they became famous in French translation in the 17th c. Now celebrated as a powerful expression of personal passion, these letters were domesticated by being infused with the worst excesses of *preciosity.

Similar problems are associated with virtually all the vast early-modern epistolary production. To what extent can we consider a work edited for publication as the creation of the individual listed as its author? To what extent is our reading of a letter influenced by the certainty that it is an authentic record of its author's private thoughts and opinions, intended only for its original recipient? Such issues, today the foundation of any critical reading of letter-writing, were largely responsible for the form's immense success in the early-modern period, when the voyeuristic gaze onto another's private life was a new-found pleasure and when letter-writing was central to the project of opening literature to the personal.

The 18th c. also inaugurated the golden age of personal correspondence. Inspired by the epistolary novel's cult of narrative immediacy, individuals carried on intense, long-term epistolary involvements. Some of these, e.g. *Du Deffand's correspondence with Walpole, have become celebrated. The age's best-known writers (*Voltaire, *Rousseau, *Diderot) composed voluminous correspondences—and wrote increasingly with the sense that they would be edited for publication.

It may have been the letter's prominence in the second half of the 18th c., when the modern French pedagogical system was being created, that brought about the form's eclipse. Until the early 20th c. letter-writing was an integral part of the French curriculum. Famous letters were included in all pedagogical manuals—once again as models of sociability and eloquence. Thus domesticated and distanced from its partnership with immediacy and authenticity, letter-writing ceased to be a French passion. [JDeJ]

Lettre à d'Alembert

See 'La Lettre au dix-septième siècle', *Revue d'histoire littéraire de la France*, 78 (1978), 6; L. Versini, *Le Roman épistolaire* (1979); J. Altman, *Epistolarity* (1982).

Lettre à d'Alembert sur les spectacles (1758). A long public letter by J.-J. *Rousseau, attacking the contemporary theatre and defending the traditional, unsophisticated manners of Geneva, where d'*Alembert had proposed establishing a theatre.

Lettre à l'Académie française, see FÉNELON.

Lettre de Thrasybule à Leucippe, see FRÉRET.

Lettres de cachet. Under the *ancien régime* these letters were issued (and could be obtained by powerful people) to order the imprisonment or exile of individuals; they were used in particular for family affairs. The Assemblée Constituante abolished them in 1790.

Lettres de mon moulin. Much-loved sketches of Provence life by Alphonse *Daudet, first published in *Le Figaro* in 1866, then in book form in 1868.

Lettres d'une Péruvienne, see GRAFFIGNY.

Lettres écrites de la montagne, see ROUSSEAU, J.-J.

Lettres familières écrites d'Italie, see BROSSES, DE.

Lettres françaises, Les. A literary journal of the Resistance, launched 1942 [see OCCUPATION AND RESISTANCE, 6].

Lettres persanes. Novel in letter form by *Montesquieu, published anonymously in 1721. It was an immense success, and attracted official disapproval. There are 161 letters by many writers, the most important being two Persians, the serious-minded Usbek and the more light-hearted Rica, who go to France on an extended visit. The essence of the work is the contrast of cultures, embodied in the exclamation: 'Comment peut-on être Persan?' The Orient is seen as a place of traditional order and oppression, whereas France is free, changing, and frequently ridiculous. The outsider's gaze allows Montesquieu to satirize many aspects of his society—politics, religion, salon conversation—in the years before and after the death of *Louis XIV. At the same time, we see the Persians adopting many of his cherished values, and the letters contain serious discussions of such topics as natural justice, political economy, and demography. There is an ironic contrast between Usbek's progressive enlightenment and his unsuccessful attempt to maintain despotic control over his harem in Persia; throughout the novel we see tension mounting among his wives, slaves, and eunuchs, and it ends bloodily with the defiant suicide of his favourite wife, Roxane. [PF]

Lettres philosophiques, Les, were first published in London as *Letters concerning the English Nation* (1733; ed. N. Cronk, 1994) and had been written in large part by *Voltaire in English. They appeared in parallel in France as *Lettres sur les Anglais*. However, with the inclusion (1734) of the 25th (and final) letter on *Pascal—that force for darkness despite all his intellectual brilliance—Voltaire re-entitled his work, thereby deliberately underlining his militant drift. For the work had been meant to suggest, through its examination of English religious, political, and cultural life, how France's neighbours, promoted now to the role of idealized model, had liberated themselves from obscurantism by their own *philosophical* endeavours. [JR]

Lettres portugaises. This slim volume, published anonymously in 1669, was among the most influential works of its century. Today the letters are generally attributed to *Guilleragues, but 17th-c. readers never doubted that they were, as the original edition proclaimed, 'traduites en français'. These readers did not consider the possibility that this could be a work of literature and instinctively took the letters for the authentic account of the woman whose voice we hear in them. Early readers were not interested in the identity of this woman, who describes herself only as a Portuguese nun and calls herself simply Mariane, although they did try to determine that of the unfaithful French lover to whom the letters were addressed. The theory identifying the letters' author with an actual Portuguese nun, Mariana Alcoforado, dates from the 19th c. For her first public, Mariane was beyond identity, a primal voice of female passion. *Sévigné, for example, identified the archetypal woman's writing expressed in a burning love-letter simply as 'une portugaise'.

The five original 'portugaises' read like an extended cry from the heart. Mariane's obsession with her passion is so all-consuming that she sacrifices the external world to it. It is ultimately unclear, for instance, whether she exclaims 'my love' to the man who has betrayed her or to her passion personified. In an effusion that early readers saw as the authentic, unbridled female voice, but that recent critics praise as controlled disorder, Mariane pours out a tale of abandonment that becomes a victory over abandonment as she transfers her passion to writing.

Lettres portugaises is still usually published anonymously. Such indeterminacy is appropriate for a work that has most often been admired for its intense authenticity. The five 'portugaises' define the paradox of *letter-writing as a genre poised between the real and the fictional. [JDeJ]

Lettres provinciales, see PASCAL.

Lettres sur la liberté du commerce des grains, see TURGOT.

Lettre sur les aveugles, see DIDEROT.

Lettre sur les sourds et muets, see DIDEROT.

LE VAU, Louis (1612–70), architect, see VERSAILLES.

LÉVESQUE, René, see QUEBEC, 5.

LÉVI, Eliphas, pseudonym used by A.-L. *Constant.

LEVINAS, Emmanuel (b. 1906). Moral and religious philosopher, belatedly influential on *Post-Structuralism. Born in Lithuania of Jewish family, he studied in Strasbourg and Freiburg, where he was impressed by *Bergson, Blondel, Husserl, and Heidegger, completing a doctoral thesis on intuition in Husserl (1930). He took French nationality and met many leading French intellectuals. Mobilized in 1939, he was captured and spent the war in a prisoner-of-war camp. Returning to Paris, he taught in a Jewish teacher-training college and, after completing his state doctorate, *Totalité et infini* (1961), held philosophy chairs at Poitiers, Nanterre, and the Sorbonne. Steeped in the Talmudic tradition of textual analysis, Levinas published many essays of biblical exegesis, and essays on Judaism, notably *Difficile liberté* (1963). His philosophical framework was based on *phenomenology, though he considered that its account of human experience and intentionality gave excessive importance to self-consciousness. He argued that the prior relation of the self to the Other is inscribed in experience as *mauvaise conscience*, which implies that every person has a fundamental and infinite responsibility for the other person. He therefore asserted the primacy of ethics over ontology, and the priority of moral and religious experience over rationality and reflection.

[MHK]

LÉVI-STRAUSS, Claude (b. 1908). Structural anthropologist. Like the linguist *Saussure, to whom he owes much, his theories have been influential in many domains beyond academic anthropology and have helped to form the way of looking at the world associated with *Structuralism. Born in Brussels, educated in Paris, Lévi-Strauss took his first degree in law and the *agrégation* in philosophy. In 1934 he went to teach at the University of São Paulo, Brazil, where he developed an interest in social anthropology. After a brief stay in France in 1939 he returned to America, lecturing in New York (1940–5), and becoming Conseiller Culturel at the French Embassy in Washington at the end of the war. In 1948 he returned to Paris and was appointed director of studies at the *École Pratique des Hautes Études from 1950 to 1974, and professor of social anthropology at the *Collège de France from 1959. He is a member of the Académie Française.

Lévi-Strauss's career has not been conventional. His training as a philosopher rather than as an anthropologist meant that he was considered something of an amateur in ethnographic fieldwork by certain British and American anthropologists, particularly because of the brevity of his periods of observation and his inability to converse fluently in their own language with the peoples he studied. His

analyses of kinship theory (in *Les Structures élémentaires de la parenté*, 1949) have been subject to particularly strong criticism for their alleged superficiality and poor evidence. But Lévi-Strauss's Structuralist technique does not depend for its verification on a multiplicity of empirical evidence, for the data is not used cumulatively in the same way as in a more traditional pragmatic or positivistic enquiry.

His background in philosophy did not, however, ensure that he was taken seriously by philosophers either. As an anthropologist in the broad sense of the term, he crossed swords publicly with *Sartre in 1962 in *La Pensée sauvage*, protesting against what he saw as Sartre's misrepresentation of the complexity of the thought-processes of primitive peoples in the *Critique de la raison dialectique* (1960). Sartre retaliated by accusing Lévi-Strauss of having no comprehension of the nature of dialectical as opposed to analytic reason; though now 30 years old, the controversy has not been definitively settled. It is evidently unfair to hold the broad nature of Lévi-Strauss's formation against him, not least because he certainly *became* a specialized anthropologist. But he himself describes intellectual activity with positive approval as a kind of *bricolage*, the putting-together creatively of various previously unconnected odds-and-ends. In his remarkable autobiographical essay, *Tristes tropiques* (1955), he stresses the wide variety of factors at work in his own intellectual background, presenting himself as formed initially by the triple impact of *Marxism, *psychoanalysis, and geology, from which three disparate domains he claims to have learnt that 'understanding consists in the reduction of one type of reality to another, and that the true reality is never the most obvious'.

The idea that understanding is necessarily reductive is the foundation-stone of Lévi-Strauss's brand of Structuralism. The structures that may be discovered beneath the apparent diversity of reality are in a strong sense *common*, for they have their origin in the universal structures of the human mind. It is not individual human subjects that pattern the world for Lévi-Strauss; it is rather Mind that, as part of nature, plays out its determined destiny in its individual embodiments. Lévi-Strauss's massive four-volume study of the logic of myths, *Mythologiques* (1964–71), shows the practical implications of this view most clearly, for individual myths are studied not for their *intrinsic* meaning, but for their place in the wider network of myths from which their meaning is differentially derived. But its implications are further-reaching than this, affecting areas as diverse as psychoanalysis and aesthetics (Structuralism is broadly supportive of the notion of universal unconscious patterns in life and art) and history and ethics (it is anti-ethnocentric, anti-anthropocentric, and anti-historicist, for it displaces the human subject from its central position as creator of order) Ironically, however, its major influence has been in the domain of literary theory, in ways which

Lévi-Strauss himself views with considerable suspicion. Structures, he believes, are evident only through comparative study. A Structuralist analysis of a single text (such as *Barthes's *S/Z*) is a contradiction in terms. For Lévi-Strauss, literary Structuralism is founded on false premisses and leads only to a dead-end.   [CMH]

See D. Sperber, *Le Structuralisme en anthropologie* (1968); E. Leach, *Lévi-Strauss* (1970).

LÉVY, Bernard-Henri (b. 1948). One of the leading *Nouveaux Philosophes, Lévy became an international media celebrity with the publication of *La Barbarie à visage humain* in 1977. Subsequent works include *Le Testament de Dieu* (1979), *L'Idéologie française* (1981), *Questions de principe 1, 2, 3* (1983, 1986, 1990), and *Éloge des intellectuels* (1987). Lévy has also published two novels, *Le Diable en tête* (1984, Prix Médicis) and *Les Derniers Jours de Charles Baudelaire* (1988). In opposition to such notions as reason, progress, nationalism, and revolution, he advocates an ethics of resistance, whose bases are a philosophy of the subject and monotheism.   [DM-S]

LÉVY-BRUHL, Lucien (1857–1939). French anthropologist. In his early work Lévy-Bruhl postulated a fundamental difference between the mentalities of modern and primitive societies. He argued that the collective representations of the latter bear witness to a pre-logical mentality governed by the principle of 'participation', which does not differentiate between the material and the spiritual, the natural and the supernatural, the self and the non-self (*Les Fonctions mentales dans les sociétés inférieures*, 1910). Lévy-Bruhl later gave precedence to the affective and mystical aspects of pre-logical thought and, influenced by the criticisms of *Durkheim and *Mauss, sharply attenuated his distinction between the primitive and the logical mind.   [REG]

LEYRIS, Pierre, see TRANSLATION, 3.

Leys d'amors. Long Occitan treatise codifying rhetoric, prosody, and grammar, produced by Guilhem Molinier of Toulouse and collaborators for the Consistòri del Gai Saber [see JEUX FLORAUX DE TOULOUSE]. Its two extant prose versions (written 1328–c.1337 and 1355–6) diverge considerably, emphasizing linguistic and philosophical matters respectively. It was adapted into verse c.1337–43.   [PVD]

L'HÉRITIER DE VILLANDON, Marie-Jeanne (1664–1734). French woman of letters who published in a wide range of fields. Like her uncle Charles *Perrault, she wrote fairy-tales. She translated Ovid's *Heroides* (1732) and edited the duchesse de *Longueville's memoirs (1709). In *Le Triomphe de Madame *Deshoulières* (1694) and *L'Apothéose de Mademoiselle de *Scudéry* (1702) she paid tribute to her precursors.   [JDeJ]

L'HÔPITAL, Michel de (c.1505–1573). A French humanist author with a solid reputation and a supporter of the *Pléiade, he is now best known as the chancellor to whom *Catherine de Médicis turned when attempting to implement a policy of conciliation towards the beginning of the *Wars of Religion. He played a key role in the Colloque de Poissy, in which moderate Catholics and Protestants attempted to find a solution to their doctrinal differences. Certain of his administrative reforms bore fruit; but the failure of Catherine's conciliatory policies led to his resignation in 1568. His name remains associated with the *Politique movement, which contributed substantially to the accession of *Henri IV.   [IJS]

Liaisons dangereuses, Les. Published 1782, this work by *Laclos is probably the most skilfully crafted *epistolary novel ever written. It is a 'polyphonic' work, and Laclos has created an appropriate voice or style for each character. The protagonists, Valmont and Madame de Merteuil, are libertines by conviction. The novel shows the working-out of two projects: the seduction by Valmont (at Merteuil's suggestion) of Cécile de Volanges, a girl fresh from convent-school; and the seduction of Madame de Tourvel, a young woman whose virtue and religious faith Valmont sees as a challenge. Although Valmont and Merteuil were once lovers, they are now rivals in libertinage, and their latent hostility eventually becomes overt. Fatally wounded in a duel with Danceny (who is in love with Cécile), Valmont gives him Merteuil's letters. When these are circulated in Paris, her reputation is ruined; in addition she contracts smallpox, which mars her beauty; and she loses an important lawsuit. It therefore appears that the wicked characters have been duly punished. But the victims suffer too: Tourvel dies, heart-broken, and Cécile decides to become a nun. Moreover, the quantity and quality of the protagonists' letters, which display their superior intelligence and strength of will, mean that the reader may well feel some admiration for Valmont and Merteuil. The two conflicting prefaces to the novel (both by Laclos) do little to clarify its moral ambiguity.

Initially a *succès de scandale*, the work was frequently reprinted up to about 1800. For much of the 19th c., however, it was dismissed as immoral and indeed officially banned. Modern critics take a less censorious view of Laclos's ethical position.

Two other aspects of the book have provoked discussion. It had long been argued that Laclos's *exposé* of corrupt aristocratic society helped to bring about the Revolution. This view is now generally discredited. More recently, critics have suggested that Merteuil is a feminist *avant la lettre*. However, while rejecting male domination, she shows little sympathy for other women; her 'feminism' is therefore debatable. Most of the remaining discussions by modern critics concern the literary merits of the novel and Laclos's masterly exploitation of the epistolary form.   [VGM]

See J.-L. Seylaz, 'Les Liaisons dangereuses' et la création romanesque chez Laclos (1958); R. Pomeau,
Laclos (1975); S. Davies, Laclos: 'Les Liaisons dangereuses' (1987).

Libelle, see PAMPHLET LITERATURE; PRESS, 1.

Libération, daily newspaper, see PRESS, 2.

Liberté. Canadian literary journal. Its foundation in
1959 by a group including the novelist *Godbout
gave an outlet for the new cultural and intellectual
energies in *Quebec which marked the beginnings
of the Révolution Tranquille. Unlike the slightly
later *Parti pris, Liberté had no declared political
position, but in the general fervour for reform of
the times it shared many of the demands of its more
radical sister journal, especially the call for French
unilingualism in Quebec as the necessary condition
of cultural survival. Its eclecticism has enabled it to
outlive Parti pris. Although no longer as influential
as in the past, it is still a force on the Quebec literary
scene, being particularly noted for its special numbers.
    Liberté is also the title of the collected prose writ-
ings of *Senghor.   [SIL]

Libertins. Term used to describe a number of disparate literary, social, and philosophical groups
from the late 16th to the end of the 17th c. It was at
one time claimed that libertins were rationalistic
atheists who derived their philosophical doctrines
from the Averroists of the School of Padua, notably
Pomponazzi (1462–1525) and, later, Cremonini
(1550–1630). But this view has now been widely discredited both by those who argue that Paduan
Aristotelianism was not Averroist in nature and by
those who, like Lucien *Febvre, claim that the 16th
c. was 'un siècle qui veut croire' and that the notion
of God was indispensable to the operation of its systems of thought.
    The word libertin emerged in the late 16th c. as a
term of abuse directed at those who rejected traditional authority and were indifferent or irreverent in
matters of religion. By 1620 it was associated with a
broad group of 16th-c. radical thinkers, including
Pomponazzi, Cardano (1501–76), Bruno (1548–1600),
and Campanella (1568–1639), many of whom were
to be linked subsequently with the authorship of the
notorious Traité des trois imposteurs (i.e. Moses,
Jesus, and Mohammed). *Montaigne's brand of
*Pyrrhonian scepticism was also an important factor
influencing its development. In France, the association with scandalous religious opinion was extended
to include a debauched, hedonistic way of life which
was the outward expression of an indifference
towards, or denial of, the afterlife: this is the version
of libertinage against which *Garasse fulminated in
his Doctrine curieuse des beaux-esprits de ce temps (1623)
and which *Mersenne impugns in his Impiété des
déistes, athées et libertins de ce temps (1624). These
attacks were stimulated not only by the writings of

*Vanini, who was executed in Toulouse in 1619 for
spreading allegedly materialistic doctrines, but also
by the behaviour of a free-living group of noblemen
in Paris whose acknowledged leader was the
Protestant poet *Théophile de Viau.
    Various literary works are associated with this
group: the collection of anonymous bawdy poetry
extolling the pleasures of the flesh, implicitly produced for a dissolute male tavern audience, entitled
Le Parnasse satirique; Sorel's *Francion (1623), a novel
celebrating the immoral and feckless life-style and
the irresponsible 'nouvelle philosophie' of its eponymous hero, a poor French nobleman; and
Théophile's poetry, in which are found hints of
Lucretian atomism, a description of death as the end
of all things, a celebration of sensuality, and, aesthetically, a linking of freedom of thought with freedom of form. Théophile suffered imprisonment and
trial in 1623–5; his fate heralded a greater circum-
spection in libertin circles, which was accentuated
further by the stricter regime of *Richelieu
(1630–42).
    Another manifestation of libertinage flourished
even in that period: the so-called 'libertinage érudit'
of the group of philosophers, scholars, and writers
which included *Gassendi, Diodati, *Naudé,
*Mersenne, and *Patin. This developed out of the
learned meetings which were presided over by the
*Dupuy brothers in Paris. Many of the members of
this group shared a passionate commitment to the
free exchange of scientific and cultural information
at a time when outside France the effects of the
Roman Index of forbidden books and the
Inquisition were felt strongly. For this reason, and
also because a number of the group were themselves in religious orders, great discretion was
shown in their discussion of the new empirical theories of Bacon, Copernican and Galilean astronomy,
Epicurean materialism, mechanical philosophy, and
the ideas of 16th-c. radical Italian philosophers. It
may well be that certain members of this group
were free-thinkers; but it now seems implausible
that the group as a whole shared these convictions,
even if their discretion is taken to indicate that they
knew that their discussions were potentially subversive to traditional beliefs.
    A number of literary figures are associated with
this coterie: *La Mothe le Vayer, whose Dialogues
faits à l'imitation des anciens of 1630–1 express a sceptical view of theology; *Cyrano de Bergerac, whose
libertin writings are mainly associated with the second period of unconstrained publication in France,
from the beginning of the *Fronde (1648) to the
accession to power of *Louis XIV (1661); *Des
Barreaux, now remembered for his libertin poetry;
*Saint-Évremond, who was banished for having
written against *Mazarin's Spanish policy in 1661.
Most of the other publications associated with the
libertins érudits appeared in Latin: Naudé's editions
of works by Nifo and Cardano, Gassendi's life of
Epicurus and account of Epicurean philosophy,

Librairie

Mersenne's mathematical works. Between 1648 and 1655 the principal members of the group died, bringing to an end an early but important episode in the development of the *République des lettres*.

After 1661, and especially after the *Tartuffe* affair of 1664–9, discussion of libertinage becomes much more circumspect in the new, increasingly repressive atmosphere of absolutism; the Revocation of the *Edict of Nantes of 1685 had a yet more drastic effect, as did the persecution of other heterodox religious practices (such as *Jansenism and *Quietism). This did not bring to an end intellectual enquiry coloured by free-thought. The *clandestine manuscript *Theophrastus redivivus* of 1659, together with the early *deist writing of *Foigny, testifies to its continuance; but the expression of materialist beliefs takes on a more muted, melancholic, and urbane form, as in the works of *Deshoulières, Saint-Évremond, and *Chaulieu. By the end of the century the term *libertin* had become detached from the nexus of connotations which it possessed in 1620; atheism was no longer socially shocking, provided that discretion was shown in its expression; and to express belief in the new astronomy was no longer scandalous. It is therefore not surprising that the term lost much of its colour and slipped eventually, by the middle of the 18th c., to designating mere rakes and debauchees.   [IM]

See J. S. Spink, *French Free Thought from Gassendi to Voltaire* (1959); A. Adam, *Les Libertins au XVIIe siècle* (1964).

Librairie, see BOOK TRADE.

Libraries, Private. In the 16th and 17th c. Parisian book-owners, like the owners of manuscripts in the Middle Ages, belonged to clearly defined social groups. These included above all the legal profession and the educated clergy. Private libraries were the exclusive possessions of the wealthy and powerful, who stocked their shelves with *Counter-Reformation theology and works of classical antiquity. In 16th-c. Amiens, similarly, only 20 per cent of inventoried estates belonged to book-owners. Over 70 per cent of lawyers and nobles owned books in Amiens, but only one-twelfth of merchants and artisans. Their small private libraries were principally composed of books of hours (*livres d'heures).

In the 18th c., however, the presence of books was increasingly noticeable in the households of the *petite bourgeoisie*. This emerges from studies of *inventaires après décès* (post-mortem inventories), a limited source, since not everyone was fortunate enough to have an estate to bequeath and because notaries who compiled the inventories tended to discard any literary matter which had no material value. The possession of a library did not always indicate a keen reader. Some libraries were accumulated by collectors, others for decoration, others were inherited and virtually ignored. They did not even indicate literacy. One Breton nobleman, de Combles, who asked the Revolutionary authorities to return his confiscated library, was incapable of signing the letter of application.

The possession of books varied from place to place. In Châlons-sur-Marne, only one inventory in ten revealed the presence of books at the end of the 18th c., which is a warning not to overestimate the size of the book-buying public in the provinces. In Lyon, 20 per cent of artisans owned books, and three-quarters of members of the liberal professions did so, sometimes owning ten times as many as the artisans. In the capital, familiarity with literary culture was more widespread: 35 per cent of the post-mortem inventories of the Parisian lower classes contained books in 1780. Moreover, the number of books found in each individual library multiplied considerably during the 18th c. Works of piety and religion abounded on Paris bookshelves [see DEVOTIONAL WRITING], and the total number of books inventoried in 18th-c. Paris expanded fivefold.

The reading public was proportionately larger in Paris than in the provinces then, but it was still circumscribed within social limits. The clergy, for example, almost always had a well-stocked library, which tended to have very traditional contents. Monastic collections, like that of the Franciscan library at Sospel, contained biblical and patristic texts, works of theology, hagiography, and church history. Occasionally, religious libraries held a copy of the *Encyclopédie*, as did the Benedictines of Mont Saint-Michel in their well-stocked library of 4,630 volumes. The Carthusians were especially well-provided-for. At Solignac, the 13 monks each had 80 volumes of piety, theology, or religious history in their own cells.

The liberal professions, too, would own good libraries, and their books might include not only works necessary for professional consultation, but also classical literature and works of history, and their family might well include novel-readers. Artisans could be expected to own fewer books, and their literary tastes were mixed and elusive for historians. In early 19th-c. Paris, books were owned by 60 per cent of the liberal professions, 35 per cent of business men (*négociants*), but only 6 per cent of shopkeepers.

Books remained rare and precious items in peasant households. In the countryside of the Mâconnais in the 19th c. only 12 per cent of all post-mortem inventories revealed the presence of any books, and these were usually to be found in the country houses of urban business men. The peasant's 'library' might contain *almanacs, which, like other household objects, would hang from the ceiling on a nail. In the Rouergue the peasant's library would consist of a piece of wood suspended over the main table, on which would be stored the family's reading-matter: almanacs and perhaps a missal.

The last century has seen a great increase in book-buying. In 1981 a Ministry of Culture survey reported that 80 per cent of the French population were book-owners, and about one-half of them owned more than 100 books each. Levels of book-ownership are still determined by social and educational factors. The absence of books at home is particularly marked in rural households and among people over the age of 70. Novels make up the largest part of private libraries today, although two-thirds of French readers own dictionaries and encyclopedias, and half of them own works of history.

[ML]

Libraries, Public. The French public library system developed much more slowly than its equivalents in Britain or the USA. Whereas, at the beginning of the 20th c., the city of Leeds had a central library with 14 branches open all day, Lyon, a city of almost identical size, had only six popular libraries, open in the evening only. It was only in the late 1860s that the French library system had begun its process of democratization. This backwardness was a result of France's lower *literacy rate, its slower urbanization, and its centralized administration. In addition, French workers probably worked longer hours at the end of the 19th c. than their counterparts in western Europe, and therefore had less time for reading.

The French Revolution's attempts to establish public libraries in every administrative *district* had little effect. By 1848 fewer than 200 French towns had a public library. Only a few of them were open for more than a few hours per week, and even fewer went so far as to lend books to the public.

The problem was certainly not the quantity of stock: many municipal libraries inherited the libraries of dissolved convents, seminaries, and the sequestered estates of *émigrés*. Some boasted a very impressive stock. This was true of Parisian libraries like the Bibliothèque du Roi (*Bibliothèque Nationale), one of the largest in Europe, and the *Bibliothèques Sainte-Geneviève, Mazarine, and de l'Arsenal. Important stocks were also held in provincial centres like Montpellier, where there was a considerable library attached to the medical school. These stocks, however, consisted mainly of theological and judicial treatises, Latin and Greek classics, and works of antiquarian local history. They sorely lacked works of literature, reference, and general culture.

Municipal libraries catered for local savants, not for the general public. At Limoges in 1855 the library closed throughout September and October, and only opened between 10 a.m. and 4 p.m., which effectively excluded the working classes. There was little or no funding for new purchases, and there was usually no efficient catalogue or sorting system. Librarians were poorly paid, and had no career structure in the early 19th c., and so had no incentive to improve amenities. Their job was a sinecure, which provided a comfortable retirement for ex-servicemen. They inhabited *bibliothèques-musées*, and many librarians regarded the rare arrival of a reader as an unwelcome intrusion.

Readers went elsewhere, to *cabinets de lecture, where they could hire books or newspapers for a small fee. Most *cabinets de lecture* were conveniently situated on the Boulevards, and they stocked a high proportion of the novels which the public demanded.

Liberal reformers attempted to democratize libraries. They realized that the Catholic Church had been relatively successful in launching lending-libraries in the 1820s and 1830s. Fearing that dissemination of socialist and Bonapartist tracts in the countryside had produced the 'excesses' of the 1848 Revolution, and its anti-liberal liquidation at the hands of Louis-Napoléon, they detected a need to provide the new reading public with edifying and instructive literature, which would counteract undesirable political influences—popular libraries could also challenge the demoralizing influences of *colportage literature and the *cabaret. They admired the Mechanics' Institutes in Britain, and the quiescence of the Lancashire operatives during the cotton famine caused by the American Civil War led them to adopt British methods of social discipline and to encourage the idea of workers' 'self-improvement'. Popular lending-libraries could play a part in achieving all these aims.

The establishment of popular libraries was the work of two main philanthropic organizations: the Société Franklin and Jean Macé's Ligue de l'Enseignement. Macé's Ligue, founded in 1866, aimed to give intellectual sustenance to the blighted industrial region of eastern France. It remained, however, a local effort, well-supported by local Rhineland manufacturers, including several Protestants, looking to improve the effectiveness and education of their own work-force.

Macé was also involved in the foundation of the Société Franklin, set up in 1862 to establish libraries and supply them with books. By 1902 there were 3,000 bibliothèques populaires in France, although many had tiny budgets, small stocks, and short opening hours. The Society recommended cheap books and advised on library management. Many librarians still viewed their new clientèle with trepidation. In Toulouse, the bibliothèque populaire refused to lend at all, which defeated the object of the exercise. In Paris itself, the municipal bibliothèques populaires only dared to lend in 1879. The Bibliothèque Ferney in Paris was so suspicious of its readers that it opened in 1886 with two police agents patrolling the reading-room.

By the end of the 19th c. local administration had accepted some financial responsibility for the library network, and accordingly asserted bureaucratic control of what had once been private ventures. In 1883 Paris had 22 municipal libraries, including 17 bibliothèques populaires subsidized by the Hôtel de Ville. In the 1890s the movement probably reached a peak: by 1894 50 libraries operated in Paris, lending 1.75 million books per year.

This, however, did not mean that popular

lending-libraries had achieved their original purpose. Library reformers had set out to eliminate impiety, obscenity, socialism, and religious bigotry, as peddled by *colporteurs* and popular novelists. The manual worker was to be provided with intellectual sustenance, which would refresh and ennoble his spirit. He was to be offered works of sound morality and useful technical knowledge. To inculcate a true moral sense, however, the ancients and the classics of the 17th c. were recommended. The model catalogue of the Société Franklin included *Fénelon, *Pascal, *Bossuet, *Corneille, *Racine, *Molière, and *La Fontaine. A strong dose of Seneca was seen as the antidote to *almanacs, works of piety, ridiculous fairy-tales, and the sensational melodramas of Eugène *Sue. To encourage the reading of fiction would be to betray the aims of popular library reform.

Popular readers did not necessarily accept the edifying book-lists patronizingly offered by middle-class reformers. Moreover, the working class did not flock to use the libraries, whose clientele fell into four main social groups. First, the libraries appealed to a number of women, who were unemployed and/or *propriétaires*. They made up 20 per cent of Parisian borrowers. A second group of borrowers consisted of white-collar employees and clerks. A third group, often emphasized by provincial librarians, were schoolchildren. Finally, the borrowers did include a number of *ouvriers* and *ouvrières*, who represented between one-tenth and one-third of library readership. Non-working-class readers were, therefore, in a large majority amongst library borrowers.

The tastes of these readers never reflected the reformers' preference for moral and instructive literature. Instead, they had an insatiable appetite for novels. This exasperated the librarians, who could not stem the demand for Scott, Cooper, *Notre-Dame de Paris*, and *Le *Comte de Monte Cristo*. Generations after their initial publication, such books found a new audience in the lending-library. In spite of themselves, popular lending-libraries played an important role in spreading consumption of the popular novel during the Third Republic.

Today, however, only a small minority of readers are public-library borrowers. By the 1980s only one adult French inhabitant in ten used a library as often as once a month. Borrowers were especially to be found among the female, student, and professional population. Libraries, therefore, have not created new readers, but rather assisted those who are already keen book-purchasers.   [ML]

See M. Lyons, *Le Triomphe du livre: une histoire sociologique de la lecture dans la France du 19e siècle* (1987).

LIGNE, Charles-Joseph, prince de (1735–1815). Known during his lifetime as a field-marshal and military writer, as the friend of many members of European literary and court society, as a wit and a lover of women, the prince de Ligne is now remembered primarily as a letter-writer and author of aphorisms and memoirs, the latter containing portraits of famous contemporaries such as *Voltaire and *Rousseau. His written style was that of his speech—he was a noted raconteur. Late in his life Germaine de *Staël undertook, with his approval, the stylistic revision and publication of a volume of his selected writings (*Œuvres choisies*, 1809). His *Lettres et pensées* have been edited by R. Trousson (1989).   [DW]

Ligue, La. The Catholic League created in December 1584 had a crucial role to play in the closing years of the *Wars of Religion. It had many predecessors, notably the League of 1576, formed in Picardy under the leadership of the *Guise family in order to oppose the Peace of Monsieur, which had granted favourable terms to the Protestants. *Henri III was able to bring this movement to a swift end by declaring himself its head. The League of 1584, on the other hand, was created in very different circumstances and had much more catastrophic consequences. Its immediate cause was the death of the king's brother, which left the Protestant Henri de Navarre (the future *Henri IV) as heir presumptive. Extremist Catholics had no intention of tolerating the possibility of a heretic king or of allowing Henri III to persuade Henri de Navarre to convert. Their intention was to take power for themselves either by removing Henri III or by reducing him to a mere figurehead, and then to exterminate the Protestants.

Many historians have failed to take the Ligue seriously. This was partly because of its close connection with the king of Spain, which led 19th-c. French historians to regard it as unpatriotic, and partly because it was ill served by *Politique historians like *L'Estoile and de *Thou. More recent experience should make us aware of the power—and sincerity—of religious fanaticism. This said, it is true that, in many cases, religious motivation served as a mask to disguise personal ambition (notably in the case of Henri de Guise) or as a means of reclaiming lost independence. Ultimately, it was these factors which led to the movement's destruction. The demagogic, semi-republican nature of the movement in Paris alienated its aristocratic leaders, who were themselves suspect to many of their contemporaries because of the blatantly self-interested way in which they pursued their objectives. Once the future Henri IV had converted to Catholicism the Ligue's support was bound to ebb very quickly, especially when he began to buy off its more aristocratic supporters. The involvement of Spain made it particularly hateful in the eyes of Protestants, Politiques, and other moderate Catholics. The extent to which it had lost the hearts and minds of more moderate Frenchmen is amply demonstrated by the *Satire Ménippée. In the early 18th c. it was excoriated in Voltaire's *La *Henriade*.   [JJS]

See E. Barnavi, *Le Parti de Dieu* (1980); F. J. Baumgartner, *Radical Reactionaries: The Political Thought of the French Catholic League* (1976).

Ligues. The name has been adopted in more-recent times by various groups, usually of a right-wing persuasion, such as *Deroulède's Ligue des Patriotes. Such *ligues* played an active part in the disorders preceding the *Popular Front.

LIKING, Werewere, see WEREWERE LIKING.

LILAR, Suzanne (1901–88). Belgian novelist. Raised as a francophone in Flemish-speaking Ghent, Lilar established a Paris reputation with a play about Don Juan, *Le Burlador* (1945). In more intimate vein, her *Journal de l'analogiste* (1954) muses upon poetic perceptions which intensify daily life as well as art. Her erotic novel *La Confession anonyme*, printed anonymously in 1960 and filmed by André Delvaux as *Benvenuta* in 1983, portrays a woman surrendering to a love both mystical and carnal. *Le Couple* (1963) attacks the depreciation of amorous values in modern society, a position elaborated in an analysis of *Sartre, *A propos de Sartre et de l'amour* (1967). Lilar's late work turns to nostalgic reminiscence, as in *Une enfance gantoise* (1976), of which extracts appeared as *A la recherche d'une enfance* (1979) alongside family snapshots. The novelist Françoise *Mallet-Joris is her daughter. [RC]

LIMBOUR, Georges (1900–70). French poet, prose writer, and art critic. A friend of *Crevel and *Vitrac, he was a *Surrealist from the outset, only to be excluded for frivolity by the end of the 1920s. A university teacher and traveller, he is best known for his fantasy *récits* such as *Les Vanilliers* (1938), infused with surrealistic dream imagery. See *Soleils bas, suivi de poèmes, de contes et de récits* (1972). [DAS]

LINDON, Jérôme, since 1948, influential director of the Éditions de *Minuit, who was instrumental in publishing and promoting the *Nouveau Roman.

LINGENDES, Jean de (c.1580–1616). Poet, author of melodious if trivial verse in the pastoral mode (*Les Changements de la bergère Iris*, 1605).

LINGUET, Simon-Nicolas-Henri (1736–94). Though neglected by modern historians, Linguet must be judged one of the most intriguing and prolific French controversialists and political analysts of the later 18th c. Temperamental and arrogant, he was nevertheless capable of courageous and original work.

Born in Reims, he had three successive careers, as soldier, fashionable advocate, and journalist. The mastery of forensic rhetoric displayed notoriously in his *mémoire* for the comte de Morangiès may be contrasted with his defence of justice on behalf of the chevalier de *la Barre's co-defendants (1766), of the Brabant insurgents (1789–90), and finally of the political rights of Dominica (1791). During his editorship

the *Journal de politique et de littérature* (1744–8) was noteworthy for its coverage of English life. Sometime ally and opponent of *Voltaire, he drew on him for his own dramatic and satirical works (*Socrate*, 1764; *La Cacomonade*, 1766), and dedicated the best of his critical writing to him (*Examen des ouvrages de Voltaire*, 1788). His *Annales politiques, civiles et littéraires* (1779–90) are a notable source work for the period. Best known, the *Théorie des lois civiles* (1767), ostensibly refuting Montesquieu, offers some of the most subversive political analysis of the century. Behind a façade of reactionary pessimism, Linguet projects law and social institutions together as legitimations of brigandage rather than bastions of freedom. Thus, while he was guillotined for advocating despotism, we may more accurately judge him an ally of *Rousseau and a precursor of Marx. [SMM]

Linguistics. The arts and sciences of language have a long history in France [see RHETORIC; GRAMMARS], but linguistics as presently understood came of age in the 20th c., during which there has been a tremendous growth in the volume and diversity of linguistic studies, particularly since the 1950s. 19th-c. linguistics, centred in Germany, was principally concerned with the comparison of languages and their historical dimension; important representatives in France include Michel Bréal and Arsène Darmesteter, who were especially preoccupied with semantic change. The publication of *Saussure's *Cours de linguistique générale* (1916) marked a major shift of emphasis and a resurgence of synchronic studies; French linguistics has been greatly influenced by his structural treatment of language and his view of language as a social phenomenon. The same sociological interpretation of language, typical of the 'French school', is found in the work of another powerful influence on French linguistics, Antoine Meillet, comparativist and general linguistician, who was concerned, for instance, with the external causes of semantic change. Two works reflect French interest in the relationship between language and thought, *Brunot's *La Pensée et la langue* (1922) and J. Damourette and E. Pichon's *Des mots à la pensée: essai de grammaire de la langue française* (1927–40).

The influence of Saussurian *structuralism via Prague-school phonology is perhaps best represented in France by André Martinet (b. 1908)'s functionalism, with its emphasis on the needs of communication and the effect of speakers' choices. For many years Martinet's functional approach dominated both synchronic and diachronic phonology in France (see e.g. *Phonology as Functional Phonetics*, 1949; *Économie des changements phonétiques*, 1955), and is continued, for example, in the work of Henriette Walter. Functional syntactic studies have also been produced by Martinet, G. Gougenheim, and J. Gagnepain. French linguistics was, however, much slower to embrace American distributionalism; not

Lipogram

until the 1960s do we find Jean Dubois's *Grammaire structurale du français* (1965–9) or Maurice Gross's *Grammaire transformationnelle du français* (1968), which is greatly influenced by Zellig Harris's notion of transformation. Chomskyean generative grammar has also found its supporters in France, especially at the University of Paris-Vincennes: notable are the Belgian-born N. Ruwet, the American-born R. Kayne, and, as regards phonology, F. Dell. Recently newer models such as generalized phrase-structure grammar have also been applied to French.

Two important 'home-grown' theories are those of Lucien Tesnière (1893–1954) and Gustave Guillaume (1883–1960). Tesnière's posthumous *Éléments de syntaxe structurale* (1959) uses a dependency model to describe syntactic functions. Guillaume's 'psychosystematic' model, which is primarily concerned with the semantic content of grammatical categories, created an important school in France, but his work has had little impact abroad, perhaps because of the abstractness of his thought and the abstruseness of his terminology.

Semantic preoccupations are also evident in more recent developments in linguistic theory in France such as Bernard Pottier's structuralist approach to semantics, the logico-semantic theories of Robert Martin and J.-B. Grize, or G. Fauconnier's work on cognitive semantics. In the last two decades theories of enunciation (*énonciation*), and to a lesser extent pragmatics (see e.g. O. Ducrot's work on presupposition, *Dire et ne pas dire*, 1972), have dominated much of French linguistic thought. Émile *Benveniste's important *Problèmes de linguistique générale* (1966–74) defines enunciation as the 'mise en fonctionnement de la langue par un acte individuel d'utilisation', and it is thus especially concerned with deictic elements, such as the first- and second-person personal pronouns. Antoine Culioli's work on enunciation is equally a theory not of sentences but of utterances (relegated to performance by Chomsky); it aims to model the construction of utterances by speakers in enunciative situations.

Alongside this work on linguistic theory, a great range of linguistic studies have flourished in France in the fields of stylistics, phonetics, dialectology, lexicology and lexicography, statistical and applied linguistics, etc. Since the 1950s, linguistics, including that of the Russian Roman Jakobson, has exercised a powerful influence on French literary theory and literary production; for a discussion of this, see STRUCTURALISM. [WA-B]

See B. Pottier (ed.), *Les Sciences de langage en France au XXème siècle* (1980).

Lipogram. A literary curiosity of classical origin in which one or more letters of the alphabet are avoided. The device was 'rediscovered' by *Queneau and used by *Perec in *La Disparition* (1969), a novel in which the absence of the letter *e*, the commonest of the French alphabet, is not always noticed by readers. [DMB]

Lit de justice, see PARLEMENTS.

Literacy. The rise in literacy was one of the most significant developments of the Age of *Enlightenment. Literacy can be measured through the study of signatures, usually those of spouses or conscripts. The real value of the signature test, however, cannot be appreciated except in the broad context of contemporary pedagogic methods and of the ways students learned to read and write. Up to and including the 19th c., reading and writing were usually taught as quite separate, consecutive processes. French school inspectors of the 1830s complained of a great gap between learning to read, which came first, and learning to write, which came second. The signature was the first thing anybody learned to write; therefore, it was a sign that some reading ability had already been acquired, even though it reveals little about writing competence. This justifies the interpretation of the signature as an intermediate point in the student's cultural apprenticeship.

Signatures to marriage contracts tend to test the literacy of a certain age-group, ranging from about 20 to the early thirties, and there may also be a social selection here, for those who married at a later age may well have been from a higher social stratum, in which case they may be expected to be more literate.

In addition, there were those who could read, but not sign their name competently. This was largely a female group. The Church had tried as far as possible to encourage people to read their bibles and catechisms, but not to write. Perhaps for this reason, many women in *ancien régime* France could read but not sign. In some families there was a rigid sexual division of literary labour, in which the women would read to the family while the men would do the writing and account-keeping. The signature test of literacy must, therefore, be used with caution, and with the knowledge that it almost certainly underestimates the real reading ability of the signers, and particularly that of female signatories.

On the eve of the Revolution almost half of the male population of France was able to read, but male literacy appears from the signatures to have been almost double that of women. Literacy was generally higher in the north and east, France's most prosperous and urban-industrial areas. Literacy was higher in towns than in the countryside, and higher in large towns than in small towns. Even in the north, older administrative centres like Douai, with lawcourts, religious establishments, or universities, had higher literacy rates than newly industrialized areas like Roubaix. Rich *faubourgs* everywhere were more literate than poor ones, and the gap between male and female literacy was much narrower in urban centres than in the countryside.

Literacy varied everywhere according to social status. In the west of France only about 11 per cent of domestic servants could read and write, but by

1789 the literacy of urban artisans, the future *sans-culottes*, had risen to about 40 per cent. Great variations in literary ability existed even within the artisan classes. In Lyon, for example, on the eve of the Revolution, 75 per cent of *boulangers* were literate, as well as 76 per cent of *boulangères*. Amongst Lyon hatters, on the other hand, half of the men were literate and only one quarter of the women. This was the difference between *boutique* and *atelier*: literacy was higher among the trades which required regular contact with the public. Literacy varied, too, according to levels of skill. The rate for Lyonnais day-labourers was only 37 per cent for men and 29 per cent for women. In the Midi agricultural workers were rarely more than 10 per cent literate, and their wives never reached even 10 per cent literacy.

In the capital, however, the popular reading public was distinguished by a much higher rate of literacy. By 1789 90 per cent of Parisian men and 80 per cent of the women could sign their wills. Two Parisian wage-earners out of three could sign the inventories of their deceased spouses. Two-thirds of the inhabitants of the Faubourg Saint-Marcel could read and write in 1792. These statistics alone suggest a huge potential audience for Revolutionary printed propaganda amongst the popular urban classes.

Illiteracy here means illiteracy in French; it is a concept which does not recognize the widespread usage of non-French languages. According to the abbé *Grégoire, in l'An II (1794) at least 6 million Frenchmen were ignorant of the French language, and as many again could not sustain a conversation in it. They included almost a million Breton-speakers, France's German, Italian, Flemish, and Basque speakers, not to mention the exclusively *patois*-speaking populations of the centre, south, and south-west. Only a minority of French men and women were exclusively francophone at the end of the 18th c., and for millions of citizens the French Revolution, like the affairs of the *ancien régime* monarchy, was conducted in a foreign language. The historian Fernand *Braudel stressed the diversity of France, which he described as a country of 'micro-regions' and 'micro-dialects'. Linguistic uniformity and widespread literacy in French was an achievement of the late 19th and early 20th c.

The ability to use French in speech or writing was a trait which distinguished the bourgeois from the artisan or the labourer, in town or countryside. In the Aveyron, Grégoire was informed, the French-speakers were retired soldiers, doctors, clergymen, nobles, and *négociants*. In Bordeaux, aspiring artisans would use French as a sign of status, to distinguish themselves from the Gascon populace. The phenomenon of bourgeois bilingualism should not disguise the fact that it was the educated bourgeoisie and local *notables* who were the chief agents of the spread of the French language, and therefore of the nationalist ideology of the Revolution and of republicanism.

The transition from *patois* to French usage was a transition from a predominantly oral to a written language and culture. The illiterate, of necessity, recognized the increasing power of the written word over their lives. The burning of the *terriers* (feudal title deeds) by the peasantry in revolt in 1789 may be seen as the vengeance of rural illiterates against the power of written culture. The written word took some time to penetrate the oral universe of the French peasantry. In 1848 peasants in the Périgord were under the impression that *Lamartine (or 'La Martine') was the mistress of the politician Ledru-Rollin: a mistake they probably would not have made if they had been accustomed to reading Lamartine's name in print.

The statistics of illiteracy hide the wide possibilities of oral reading. It took only one reader to read aloud a poster to a crowd gathered in the street, only one orator to read *Marat's *L'Ami du peuple* in a political club, a café, or local wineshop. In the *ancien régime* official notices were usually publicly proclaimed before being posted, to the sound of the drum and trumpet. In 1790 Cerutti's *La Feuille villageoise* appealed directly to local *notables*, landowners, professional people, and clergy to read the paper aloud on Sunday after Mass, and the editor received several letters from subscribers who reported that they actually had read it publicly in this way.

Examples like that of *Jamerey-Duval, the Lorraine farm-boy and shepherd, demonstrate the role of the oral and visual in the act of learning to read. The illiterate Duval dated his literary apprenticeship from a chance encounter with Aesop's *Fables*, which he made other shepherds read aloud and explain to him. He repaid his friends and fellow workers later by reciting stories in public to his companions.

Jamerey-Duval learned through memory, recitation, and oral reading. His case is a reminder that the literacy figures are not the whole story. There was a vast 'reading public' which was a listening public, among the illiterate.   [ML]

See F. Furet and J. Ozouf, *Lire et écrire: l'alphabétisation des Français de Calvin à Jules Ferry*, 2 vols. (1977).

Literary History

1. The Establishment of the Discipline

Before the 19th c. and the modern definition of both history and literature, there existed chronicles of writers and books (including both *belles-lettres* and the sciences), e.g. the monumental 12 volumes of the *Histoire littéraire de la France* by Dom Rivet and Dom Clémencet (1733–63) [see MAURISTS]. But the awareness of literature as a social institution related to nations and historical periods hardly appeared in France before German *Romanticism inspired Germaine de *Staël's *De la littérature* (1800), which asserted the 'influence of religion, customs, and laws on literature', and *Chateaubriand's *Génie du* *christianisme* (1802), which explained aesthetic value by the religious quality of a civilization.

Whereas *La Harpe's *Lycée* (1799–1805) still dogmatically judges works of art against a rational, Aristotelian ideal of beauty, the basic assumption of literary history will henceforth be that the beautiful is not universal, but historically relative—this poses the difficult question of the possible survival into future ages of a historically conditioned beauty. *Villemain, in his *Tableau de la littérature française au XVIIIe siècle* (1828–9), and *Sainte-Beuve, in *Port-Royal* (1840), paved the way for the separation of literary history both from impressionist criticism and from mere history of literature understood as a collection of separate studies. Literary history increasingly contextualized literature in order to determine the meaning of texts. Sainte-Beuve explained individual works through the biography of their authors, giving portraits of the groups with which they were associated. *Taine, more positivistic in his determinism [see COMTE], appealed to the three necessary and sufficient elements of *la race, le milieu*, and *le moment*. *Brunetière added the evolution of genres, modelled on Darwin's evolution of species. It was *Lanson who finally established literary history as the alternative to *rhetoric and *belles-lettres* both in *lycées*, where it became an official part of the syllabus in 1880, and in the universities, which were reformed in 1902. Whereas rhetoric allegedly served to reproduce the élite of orators, literary history was to train all the citizens of a modern democracy.

Literary history thus became the academic discipline which defined how literature was taught and studied from the 1890s on. As a discipline, it grounded its scientific and social legitimacy in the positivist history of the late 19th c.—*Péguy mocked the 'well-organized gang' of historians who reorganized France's educational system after the defeat of 1870—but it also touches upon and borrows from sociology and criticism. As a historical genre obsessed with the method of establishing facts, it extends the application of the reliable tools of classical and medieval philology to modern literature. In this view, literary facts of the past are primarily texts. Literary history first proceeds to the collection and identification of documents, the rigorous establishment of texts, and the editing of unpublished material. It then compiles biographies and bibliographies, and compares individual works and group mentalities in order to specify originalities and to distinguish schools and movements.

Lanson never wanted to limit the new discipline to textual erudition. He consistently insisted that it should (as a part of sociology) aim also at global descriptions and explanations of all literary phenomena and institutions pertaining to the production and reception of books. After the series of monographs and authors was available, the next step would be to attempt what he called the 'portrait of the literary life of the nation, the history of culture and of the activity of the faceless crowd of readers

as well as of the famous élite of writers'. Literary history would relate literature to the social, political, moral, and intellectual life of the nation (Lanson's literary history explicitly aimed to serve the *patrie*) and, beyond the nation, to other European literatures and cultures (comparative literature was in France a by-product of literary history). Such a comprehensive programme appealed to *Marxists and was approved by Plekhanov in an article of 1897. Finally, as it related to criticism, literary history was not expected to reduce works of literature to archival documents, but also to generate a proper evaluative discourse and explain why certain works, which we call classics, still affect us and become, so to speak, immortal, while others do not survive their own times. For Lanson, the insistence on historical relativity did not preclude an enquiry into the permanence of emotion and taste. The object of literary history, he wrote, was not to dismiss impression and sympathy, but to reduce the 'element of personal sentiment in our knowledge to an indispensable and legitimate minimum, while still granting it all its value'.

As a result of this extremely ambitious and probably Utopian programme, literary history always remained a hybrid and ambiguous field of research. It soon became limited to and identified with the search for sources and the tracking of influences. Sources and influences superficially reconcile the concern for originality and the ideology of causality, as they apparently resolve individual facts into social sequences, but literary historians were often accused of being content with accumulating dates and facts around texts. Our analyses, Lanson said, are 'approaches to genius', thus conceiving genius as the irreducible residue of historical and generic determinism. The intellectualist notion of the human mind and of aesthetic creation that literary history perpetuated was in conformity with associationist psychology at the very time when *psychoanalysis called for a new type of understanding.

2. Attacks on Literary History

Initially ridiculed on political grounds by the reactionary circles of the *Action Française, who saw it as an imitation of German erudition and a rejection of the classical humanities, literary history was soon censured both by social historians and creative writers. The former, like Lucien *Febvre, argued that it was not acceptable cultural history, and that Lanson's admirable project of an 'histoire provinciale de la vie littéraire en France', forgotten by his disciples, remained a dream. The creators, like Péguy or Proust, reacted against the misconception of individuality and the reduction of the essentiel plurality of meaning in literature to the historical sense or the sense of the author. But the strongest attacks came in the 1960s from 'la nouvelle critique'.

This sought to ground literary studies on renewed paradigms borrowed from the social sciences—e.g. psychoanalysis, *linguistics, Marxism— that had replaced history and challenged the principle of the rational and historical intelligibility of literary meaning. After *Barthes published *Sur Racine* (1963), exposing the myth of the classical Racine by reference to psychoanalytic anthropology, Raymond Picard, author of *La Carrière de Jean Racine* (1956) and representative of the Lansonian Sorbonne, launched a vigorous counter-attack in *Nouvelle critique ou nouvelle imposture* (1965). Barthes claimed that literature was utterly foreign to history and that, if a vast social history of literary life was indeed desirable, according to the excellent programme set by Lanson and later revived by Febvre and the historians of *Annales*, it would be irrelevant to the *meaning* of literature. The 'nouvelle critique' of the 1960s and 1970s brought back into the foreground allegory, as a model of the hermeneutics of the hidden, and *rhetoric, as a paradigm of inquiry into forms and techniques, both of which were approaches that literary history had repudiated. Paradoxically, however, the critique of traditional literary history as a veiled ideology consolidated, in its return from the text as document to the text as monument, literary history's main ideological legacy, the canon of authorized great books. Meanwhile the German scholar Hans Robert Jauss set out to replace a history of literature written from the point of view of its production with an 'aesthetics of reception'; this implied a new attempt to combine history and literature through the study of public and private reading. But the history of reading, which is consistent with Lanson's programme, still remains a theoretical project more than a practical realization.

3. A Return to Literary History

After the initial popularity of 'la nouvelle critique' had declined, there was a return to literary history in the 1980s. This could be explained by saying that its hold on French education was so powerful that its institutional domination was never seriously threatened, and that, after an interlude, literary studies returned easily to the type of erudition that had served them between the 1890s and the 1960s. But the literary history of the end of the 20th c. is not exactly the old literary history of Lanson. It has taken up the challenge of 'la nouvelle critique' and registered the change of historical paradigm since positivism, in particular the dispute about the notion of fact—e.g. literary fact—as independent from the mentality of the historian. Today a history of literature cannot, for instance, take for granted the Romantic periodization of centuries conceived as living entities, or the canon of great works handed down by tradition. If the revision of the canon has never been radical—though it has rehabilitated *Baroque poetry, long dismissed under the evolutionist label of 'preclassicism', and 18th-c. novels, especially those by women—it has demonstrated a willingness to observe the larger literary production of any period, including popular and so-called marginal or para-literature. The long-awaited enterprise of a vast social history of literary life has also been seriously undertaken. Such collective works as Henri-Jean Martin and Roger Chartier's *Histoire de l'édition française* (1983–6) have introduced the quantitative tools of statistics into literary history, and more attention has been given to literary institutions by sociologists of literature. But such descriptions of literature as a social activity leave aside such questions as what constitutes a text as literary, and whether its 'literarity' can be constructed as a historical object.

Even textual criticism has been modified by modern hermeneutics, and 'literary genetics' has attempted to move critical editions and the inevitable source studies away from associationist psychology and the attempt to isolate the so-called residue of genius. The focus is now on the production of the text itself rather than on its raw materials. A critical edition, the epitome of literary history encompassing all that is necessary for the comprehension of a given text, now looks quite different— e.g. Proust's *A la recherche du temps perdu* in the new *Pléiade edition (1987–9). It includes drafts which stress the process rather than the product, at the risk of dissolving the notion of 'definitive' text just as that of canon can be lost in social history. Literary history has become more complex as a result of 'la nouvelle critique'. This does not mean that there exists such a discipline as a 'new literary history', but that the historical understanding of literary phenomena remains one of the indispensable paths to the study of the literature. [See CRITICISM.]   [AC]

See G. Lanson, *Essais de méthode, de critique et d'histoire littéraire* (1965); C. Cristin, *Aux origines de l'histoire littéraire* (1973); A. Compagnon, *La Troisième République des lettres* (1983); C. Moisan, *L'Histoire littéraire* (1990).

Literary Theory. Theoretical approaches to literature are as old as Aristotle; they include in France the poetics of *classicism and the lessons of *rhetoric. The term 'literary theory', however, came into favour in the 1970s and 1980s to refer to certain modern approaches to the study of literature, differing on the one hand from *literary history, and on the other from the less systematic kinds of literary *criticism. In many cases this involved applying to literature insights derived from philosophy or the human sciences (notably *linguistics and *psychoanalysis). French intellectuals played a prominent part in this explosion and found disciples in many other countries, particularly the USA.

Some of these approaches are discussed under CRITICISM, 4; see also BACHELARD; BARTHES; DERRIDA; FEMINISM; FOUCAULT; LACAN; LÉVI-STRAUSS; MARXISM IN FRANCE; PHENOMENOLOGY; POST-STRUCTURALISM; STRUCTURALISM; TEL QUEL.   [PF]

Littérature. Provocatively entitled journal launched by the *Surrealists in 1919. *Littérature* is also the title of a periodical devoted to literary theory (1971–).

LITTRÉ, Émile (1801–81). French historian of medicine, philosopher, linguist, philologist, and translator, best known for his *Dictionnaire de la langue française* (1863–72, Supplement 1877), a landmark in the history of French lexicography [see DICTIONARIES].

Littré studied first medicine, then Greek, Sanskrit, and Arabic. He became a disciple, but not a slavish follower, of Auguste *Comte. Independent of Comte in his political thinking, Littré remained a Positivist, helping to disseminate Comte's ideas in such works as *Auguste Comte et la philosophie positive* (1863) and *La Science au point de vue philosophique* (1873).

Littré's dictionary records contemporary usage, but conceived in the broadest sense as dating from *Malherbe on. The dictionary's greatest originality lies in the extensive use of citations, both in the definitions and in the entries' historical content. Typically, older authors, especially 17th-c. ones, are preferred and 19th-c. writers, notably those post-1830, are neglected. Littré equally adopts a relatively conservative stance, including many archaic, technical, and dialectal terms in his word lists, but being more selective in his inclusion of neologisms. This attitude relaxes somewhat in the Supplement.

Littré also published works on the history of the French language (1862) and semantic change (1888). His translations include versions of Hippocrates (1839–61) and of Strauss's *La Vie de Jésus* (1839–50), Dante's *Inferno* (1879), and Pliny's *Histoire naturelle* (1848–50).   [WA-B]

Livre de la chasse, Le, see GASTON PHÉBUS.

Livre de poche. A cheap paperback format launched in France in 1953 by Henri Filipacchi. Originally the name of a collection, it has come to mean a modestly priced format of relatively small size, cheaply produced and with high print-runs. Its ancestors include the *pamphlets and treatises of earlier centuries designed to reach a wide audience and, more recently, the English Penguin Books, launched in 1935. Filipacchi worked for *Hachette but conceived of the *livre de poche* as a universal collection at the disposal of all publishers, a 'populist *Pléiade' which would put the great works of literature at the disposal of the masses. The first three titles were launched on 9 February 1953 and cost 150 (old) francs. The monopoly set up by agreements between publishers assured the new collection of a superb catalogue: *Sartre, *Camus, *Aymé, Faulkner, and *Proust came from *Gallimard; *Colette and Daphne du Maurier from Albin Michel; *Mauriac, *Malraux, *Giraudoux, *Zola, *Daudet from Grasset-Fasquelle. Print-runs sold out in weeks in this golden age of the *livre de poche.* By 1962 the four monthly new titles had become twelve and publishers were queuing up to get their titles into the catalogue.

Competition inevitably resulted: Flammarion set up their 'J'ai Lu' series in 1958, followed by Presses de la Cité's 'Presses Pocket' in 1962 (a patent obliges other publishers to use the circumlocution 'format de poche'). The biggest blow, however, came in 1971–2 when Gallimard withdrew and launched its own 'Folio' collection: 500 titles disappeared from the Livre de Poche lists; the panic to draw in new titles and publicize them led to volumes being given away free with Elf petrol for a short period. However, despite the subsequent withdrawal of Plon (1975) and Seuil (1981), the market stabilized after 1975, with most of the publishers widening their catalogues.

By the 1980s more than one-third of all books published in France were in the *poche* format and more than two-thirds of literary texts. Other important collections include 10/18 (Union Générale d'Éditions), Points (*Seuil), and the cheap classics in the Garnier-Flammarion series. No longer merely the books of the impecunious, *poches* have made an inestimable contribution to the desacralization of the book in France and the extension of the reading public. *Le *Grand Meaulnes* has sold more than 3 million copies in *poche*; *Germinal, Daudet's *Lettres de mon moulin*, and *Vercors's *Le Silence de la mer* all over 2 million. Jean *Giono wrote to Filipacchi in 1958: 'J'estime qu'aujourd'hui le livre de poche est le plus puissant instrument de culture de la civilisation moderne.'   [EAF]

Livre des quatre dames, Le, see CHARTIER.

Livre des saintes paroles et des bons fais de notre roy Saint Looys, Le, see JOINVILLE.

Livres d'heures. Breviaries designed for the layman, and therefore attractively presented and easy to refer to. The typical *livre d'heures* has at its core the *Hours of the Virgin* (the prayers, hymns, and lessons prescribed for the canonical hours of Matins, Lauds, etc.), but generally includes, for instance, the Penitential Psalms or the Office of the Dead. Manuscripts exist from as early as the 11th c., but especially in the 15th c. *livres d'heures* are produced in an astonishingly rich variety, and by some of the most remarkable artists of the ducal courts of Burgundy and Berry.   [JHMT]

Livres dou tresor, Li, see BRUNETTO LATINI.

LOAISEL DE TRÉOGATE, Joseph-Marie (1752–1812). One of the many late-18th-c. practitioners of the sentimental novel. His works were much appreciated by the public during the Revolution. His main novel is *Dolbreuse ou l'Homme du siècle ramené à la vérité par le sentiment et la raison* (1777), whose hero bears a striking resemblance to Senancour's *Oberman and especially to Chateaubriand's *René. Other works include *Les Soirées de la mélancolie* (1777) and *La Comtesse d'Alibre* (1779).   [BR]

LOAKIRI, Mohamed, see MOROCCO.

LOBA, Ake, see AKE LOBA.

Logique, ou l'Art de penser, La, the 'Logique de Port-Royal', an innovative treatise by *Arnauld and *Nicole.

Loheren Cycle. A group of *chansons de geste* composed from the late 12th c. onwards, recounting the territorial rivalry and consequent enmity between two great families, those of Lorraine and of Bordeaux. The Loherens are the heroes, principally represented in the oldest poem of the cycle, *Garin le Loheren*, by the Garin of the title and his brother Begon, and in the next poem by the eponymous hero Gerbert de Mez. The Loheren barons' struggles against the treacherous Bordelais are wars of attrition, presented with a degree of realism rare in the *chansons de geste*. Through constantly renewed sieges, skirmishes, and the occasional pitched battle, small territorial gains and losses are chalked up. On each side members of the families are killed or die, grow older, and are supplemented by the arrival of new generations. In this way the cycle grew to include *Anseÿs de Mez, Hervis de Mez* and, later, *Yon ou la Vengeance Fromondin*. Although they seem to have no basis whatever in historical fact, the Loheren poems convey a remarkable sense of historicity. They are also striking metrically. Like other *chansons de geste* they are composed in monorhymed strophes called *laisses*, but here the *laisses* are unusually long and virtually all assonate or rhyme in -i, not an assonance commonly favoured by other epic poets. Such relentless repetition over thousands of lines (*Garin* alone is 15,000 lines long) accords well with the unrelieved grimness of events in this cycle.
[SK]

Loire, Châteaux de la, see RENAISSANCE, 2.

Lokis (1869). Fantastic tale by *Mérimée, set in Lithuania; the hero is half-bear, half-man.

LOMBARD, Jean, see DECADENCE.

LONGEPIERRE, Hilaire-Bernard de Roqueluyne, baron de (1659–1721). Courtier, tutor to princes of the blood, translator of Greek poetry, and champion of the ancients (*Discours sur les anciens,* 1687) [see QUERELLE]. He praised *Racine in his *Parallèle de Corneille et de Racine* (1686) and imitated him in his tragedies (*Médée,* 1694; *Électre,* performed 1702). [PF]

LONGUEVILLE, Anne-Geneviève de Bourbon-Condé, duchesse de (1619–79). Sister of *Condé and *Conti, wife of the third *Fronde leader (married 1642). She was called the 'soul' of the insurrection because of her leadership and legendary daring while these princes were imprisoned. After her conversion (1663), she divided her life between the *Carmelites and the *Jansenists. [JDeJ]

LOPÈS, Henri (b. 1937). Congolese novelist and short-story writer. From 1969 to 1973 he held various ministerial posts including prime minister (1973); later he was deputy-director of UNESCO. His work is characterized by commitment to ordinary people and a stress on the interrelation of the personal and the political. The short stories in *Tribaliques* (1971) deal largely with the difficulties (and the necessity) of remaining true to exacting ideals and resisting the temptations of the easy life. This theme is further developed in the novel *Sans tam-tam* (1977), in which a schoolteacher in the bush refuses promotion to an overseas posting. *La Nouvelle Romance* (1976) again deals with corruption and laziness, while demonstrating the importance of recognizing the potential of women. *Le Pleurer-Rire* (1982), a satirical study of an African dictator, is a scathing attack on neo-colonialism; technically innovative, it also demonstrates Lopès's acute ear for colloquial speech. *Le Chercheur d'Afriques* (1990) and *Sur l'autre rive* (1992) both deal with problems of individual and group identity: in the former, the protagonist is part-African, part-European; in the latter, a Congolese woman living under an assumed identity in Guadeloupe. The range, complexity, and symbolism of Lopès's recent work indicate how much he is continuing to develop both technically and thematically. [AMR]

Lorenzaccio (1834). Prose drama by *Musset originally published as part of *Un spectacle dans un fauteuil* and not intended for performance. The greatest French Romantic historical drama, it takes as its subject Lorenzo de' Medici's assassination of Alexander, duke of Florence. It describes a failed attempt to transform society by an act of murder, but it is also a profound analysis of the complex psychology and motivations of the main character. In order to be in a position to kill the duke, Lorenzo has been forced to don the mask of the corrupt libertine; however, he discovers that he has not simply been playing a role in order to gain the duke's confidence: he has become a real debauchee. He kills the duke, not out of any belief that his action will regenerate society, but because the act of murder is the only link which still binds him to his once-idealistic self. At the close of the play Lorenzo is in turn the victim of an assassin. The old order reasserts itself. The message of the play is pessimistic. It undermines the Romantic belief in the progressive movement of history and questions man's power to initiate purposeful change, reflecting the mood of French society in the years which followed the July Revolution of 1830. [CC]

LORET, Jean, see MUSE HISTORIQUE, LA.

LORRAIN, Claude le, see CLAUDE LE LORRAIN.

LORRAIN, Jean (pseud. of Paul Duval) (1855–1906). Successor to *Huysmans as the keeper of the *Decadent flame; his vast literary and journalistic production is an indispensable compendium of *fin-de-siècle* attitudes. In a series of novels (notably *M. de Bougrelon*, 1897, and *M. de Phocas*, 1901), he chronicled the erotic, sadistic, and criminal fantasies of the Decadent spirit, for which the articles he contributed to influential newspapers helped to find an audience in fashionable Parisian society.   [JK]

LORRAINE, Alain (b. 1946). Poet from Reunion. The title of his principal work, *Tienbo le rein suivi de Beaux visages cafrines sous la lampe* (1975), is a *Creole expression meaning both 'Stick together!' (in times of trouble) and 'Hold tight!' (in an amorous embrace). Lorraine's texts are militant and passionate. Both the form and thematics of *Tienbo le rein* are reminiscent of *Césaire's *Cahier d'un retour au pays natal*. Lorraine has also written a number of simple, direct, and accessible poems about the life of the poor on the island.   [BEJ]

LORRAINE, Charles de Guise, cardinal de (1524–74). Younger brother of one of the most important figures of the first *Wars of Religion (François de *Guise), he was an extremely influential figure in his own right. He played a key role in the Colloque de Poissy and in the last meeting of the Council of Trent. Although prepared at times to consider compromise, he was a resolute enemy of Protestantism and the subject of *Hotman's bitter attack *Au tigre de la France*.   [IJS]

LOTI, Pierre (pseud. of Julien Viaud) (1850–1923). Author of travel narratives and novels set mainly in exotic locations which he visited during his career as a naval officer. Most of his works are heavily autobiographical in inspiration, though this is lightly disguised in early novels such as *Aziyadé* (1879), *Le Mariage de Loti* (1880), and *Le Roman d'un spahi* (1881), set respectively in Turkey, Polynesia, and West Africa. *Pêcheur d'Islande* (1886), a tale of Breton fishermen, is perhaps his most finely crafted novel. Increasingly, however, Loti abandoned all pretence at fiction in favour of lyrical travel narratives such as *Au Maroc* (1890), *Jérusalem* (1895), *L'Inde (sans les Anglais)* (1903), *Vers Ispahan* (1904), and *Un pèlerin d'Angkor* (1912). In works such as *Turquie agonisante* (1913) and *La Mort de notre chère France en Orient* (1920), he engaged in a series of polemics on behalf of Turkey, whose faltering empire was dismembered in the wake of World War I. Two volumes of retrospective autobiography were published as *Le Roman d'un enfant* (1890) and *Prime jeunesse* (1919). Fragments from his journal appeared as *Un jeune officier pauvre* (1923), *Journal intime, 1878–1881* (1925), and *Journal intime, 1882–1885* (1929).   [AGH]

Louis. 18 kings of France bore this name, beginning with Louis le Débonnaire, son of *Charlemagne [see Chronology]. Apart from *Louis XIV (Louis le Grand), the most noteworthy are:

Louis IX (Saint Louis), leader of the Third *Crusade [see JOINVILLE];

Louis XI, who fought the *Burgundian duke Charles le Téméraire and was responsible for the extension and consolidation of French territory;

Louis XIII (le Juste), whose first minister was *Richelieu;

Louis XV (le Bien-Aimé), whose long reign saw growing economic prosperity and the rise of the *philosophes;

Louis XVI, who fell victim to the *Revolution, which he only half-heartedly accepted, and was guillotined as 'Louis *Capet';

Louis XVIII, grandson of Louis XV, who spent the Revolutionary and Napoleonic years in exile, returning in 1814 [see RESTORATION].

The so-called Louis XVII, son of Louis XVI and Queen *Marie-Antoinette, died in prison in 1795 and never reigned.

LOUIS XIV (1638–1715), son of Louis XIII and Anne of Austria, succeeded to the throne in 1643. His coronation, delayed by the troubles of the *Fronde, took place in 1654. He married Marie-Thérèse (daughter of Philip IV of Spain) in 1660, thus setting the seal on the peace between the two kingdoms signed the previous year. Louis was trained for the task of ruling by Cardinal *Mazarin, and on the latter's death in 1661 took the decision to rule without a first minister. There followed a decade in which French pre-eminence in Europe was asserted by every conceivable means, from diplomatic incidents in London and Rome to the invasion of the Spanish Netherlands in pursuit of territorial claims through the queen. The next decade was dominated by a war against the Dutch Republic in which the king again campaigned in person. The period 1679–89 was one of peace, but for the rest of his reign Louis was usually in armed conflict with the emperor, the Dutch, and the British, from the War of the League of Augsburg (1689–97) to the War of the *Spanish Succession (1701–13). The king's greatest successes, at a high price in men and money, were the acquisition of Franche-Comté and Strasbourg and the placing of his grandson Philippe of Anjou on the Spanish throne.

On the domestic front, Louis's reign is most often remembered for the economic policies of *Colbert; for the Revocation, in 1685, of the freedom of worship for French Protestants guaranteed by the *Edict of Nantes; and for the lavish royal *patronage of the arts, from the building of *Versailles to the pensions given to men of letters, who regularly compared the king to Alexander, Augustus, and Apollo. The young king was an enthusiast for hunting, music, plays, beautiful women (notably Mademoiselle de *La Vallière and Madame de *Montespan), and dancing (he made regular appearances in the *ballet de cour). As gout and the fistula forced him to adopt an increasingly sedentary life-style, the king showed more interest in the visual arts. Under the influence of Madame de *Maintenon (whom he married in secret soon after the death of Marie-Thérèse in

1683), Louis became increasingly devout. Throughout his reign he devoted from six to ten hours a day to the business of government.   [UPB]

See F. Bluche, *Louis XIV* (1988).

Louisiana. France had lost most of her American empire by the early 19th c. [see COLONIZATION]. However, French continued to be spoken not only in the *West Indies, *Quebec, and *Acadia, but in various parts of Canada and the USA, particularly New England and Louisiana. The latter figures quite prominently in French literature (e.g. *Manon Lescaut* and works by *Chateaubriand). Books in French had also been written there from the early 18th c., the earliest being histories and travel writing. The 19th c. saw a flourishing of literature, journalism, and theatre. Playwrights such as Auguste Lussan, Placide Canonge, and Victor Séjour, imitating French Romantic drama and melodrama, had their plays performed in New Orleans. Poets and song-writers included Tullius Saint-Céran, Adrien and Dominique Rouquette (disciples of Chateaubriand and champions of Louisiana literature), and the black poets included in the anthology *Les Cenelles* (1845). Many novels were published, by writers including Alexandre Barde and Charles Testut, both *émigrés* from France, and particularly Alfred Mercier (1816–94), who with his brother Armand founded the Athénée Louisianais for the defence of French-language culture. Mercier's most important work is *L'Habitation Saint-Ybars* (1881), a plantation novel based on childhood memories. The last significant Louisiana novelist was Sidonie de la Houssaye, parts of whose uncompleted *roman-fleuve, Les Quarteronnes de la Nouvelle Orléans*, were published in 1894–8.

Written French literature seemed dead in Louisiana at the beginning of the 20th c. However, an oral culture of songs, tales, etc. survived in rural regions settled by 18th-c. refugees from Acadia ('Cajuns'). In 1968 a Conseil pour le Développement du Français en Louisiane was set up, and there was the beginning of a revival of written literature, based on the oral tradition and often written in Cajun French—which was also given wide currency in France when Jean *Vautrin's novel, *Un grand pas vers le Bon Dieu*, set in Louisiana and drawing on Patrick Griolet's scholarly work on the language, won the Prix Goncourt in 1989.   [PF]

Louis Lambert. Novel by *Balzac, written in several versions between 1832 and 1835. *Louis Lambert* is in part the biography of a fellow scholar at the Collège des Oratoriens at Vendôme, where Balzac, like the narrator, was educated, and in part an exposition of Balzac's materialist metaphysics, dealt with in more summary manner and in a fantastical context in *La *Peau de chagrin*. The main argument is that will-power is a virtually physical substance (a 'fluide vital') which can achieve unlimited power by force of concentration. Balzac also posits a difference between the inner action of will and thought in the 'être actionnel' and its outer action in the real world (the 'être réactionnel'). Louis Lambert, the eponymous hero of this novel, develops his inner action to such a pitch that he becomes incapable of living in the outer world and goes mad. Balzac's reinvention of the Cartesian duality of mind and body is heavily marked by his interest in *Illuminism, taken to further extremes in *Séraphîta*, and by his belief that a total explanation of mental life would be provided one day by scientific means.   [DMB]

LOUIS-NAPOLÉON, see NAPOLEON III.

LOUIS-PHILIPPE, King (1773–1850). A member of the *Orléans dynasty. For his reign, see JULY MONARCHY.

Lourdes. In 1858 Bernadette Soubirous, a 14-year-old peasant girl, saw a series of visions of the Virgin Mary near the village of Lourdes. The apparitions were almost immediately followed by miraculous cures, initially mostly associated with the water of the nearby spring. Lourdes rapidly became a place of pilgrimage, especially after the establishment of a rail-link in 1869. By the early 20th c. more than half-a-million pilgrims (mostly French, and mostly women) went to Lourdes each year. In the 1960s 2 million pilgrims a year came from all over the world. Of about 5,000 cures reported by the end of 1959, 58 have been declared miraculous by the Church.

Lourdes is the title of the first of *Zola's *Les Trois Villes*.   [RBG]

LOUVERTURE, Toussaint (c.1743–1803). Born a slave and freed by his owner in 1776, François-Dominique-Toussaint Bréda, later known as Toussaint Louverture (sometimes L'Ouverture), led the slave uprising in Saint-Domingue (*Haiti) from 1794 to 1802, when he was captured by the French and taken to France. There he died, a prisoner in the Forteresse de Joux (Haut-Doubs), a year before his country achieved full independence. His life has inspired numerous literary works, notably plays by *Lamartine (*Toussaint Louverture*, 1850) and *Glissant (*Monsieur Toussaint*, 1961), and a major study by *Césaire (*Toussaint Louverture: la Révolution française et le problème colonial*, 1960).   [RDEB]

LOUVET DE COUVRAY, Jean-Baptiste (1760–97). French novelist, who from 1789 onwards was actively involved in politics and was a powerful orator. He joined the *Girondins, was prominent in attacking *Robespierre, and had to spend a year as a fugitive. His *Mémoires*, not published in full until 1889, are useful for the Revolutionary period. Most 18th-c. readers, however, knew him as the author of two novels: *Émilie de Varmont* (1791) deals with divorce and the marriage of priests; but it was his long *memoir-novel, *Les Amours du chevalier de Faublas* (1787–90), which made and has maintained his reputation. The light-hearted liaisons of the hero's youth lead to a sombre close, with several deaths and Faublas's temporary madness.   [VGM]

LOUVOIS, François-Michel le Tellier, marquis de (1641–91). Son of the powerful statesman and minister of Louis XIV, Michel le Tellier (1603–85), Louvois worked with his father in the royal service, above all as a ruthless war minister. He played an active part in the repression of the *Protestants at the Revocation of the *Edict of Nantes.

Louvre, Le. Changing its purpose over the centuries, this hybrid unfinished building by the Seine has seen service as fortress, prison, palace and symbol of the monarchy, centre for artists, museum, and now French cultural symbol. Started by Philippe-Auguste in about 1190, transformed into a royal residence and library by Charles V, rebuilt by François Ier, it was enlarged by succeeding kings but rarely inhabited. In 1546 Pierre Lescot built the Cour Carrée, later enlarged to its present form, and in 1564 Catherine de Médicis commissioned Philibert de l'Orme to build the Tuileries Palace to the west. Claude Perrault's colonnaded east front dates from 1667.

Already under Henri IV the Louvre was a place where artists could work, and under Louis XIV it also housed the *Academies. Plans to turn it into a museum were realized after 1792, and Napoleon's spoils enriched it. The Tuileries, joined to the Louvre in 1857, were burned down by the *Commune in 1871. Since 1983 the museum has been revitalized. The architect Ieoh Ming Pei has tried to give it unity by his grandiose new entrance, covered by a pyramid of glass, steel, and aluminium. In 1988 President Mitterrand opened Le Grand Louvre, designed as the greatest art museum in the world.   [PS]

LOUŸS, Pierre (originally Pierre Louis) (1870–1925), was celebrated by contemporaries as an erudite Hellenist who transposed into his own prose the pagan sensuality and aesthetic purity of the Greek ideal. His best-selling hoax 'translation', Les Chansons de Bilitis (1894), gave scholarly respectability to erotic fantasies in which morbid, misogynist violence is veiled in classical style. His novels include Aphrodite (1896), in which the courtesan Chrysis's love for the great sculptor Démétrios ends in her death and the production of his finest work; La Femme et le pantin (1898); and Les Aventures du roi Pausole (1901). The discreet eroticism of these works is in striking contrast to Louÿs's posthumously published pornographic novels (Trois filles de leur mère, 1926).   [JB]

LOZEAU, Albert, see QUEBEC, 3.

Lucien Leuwen. Novel by *Stendhal, written 1834–6, set in contemporary France. Lucien, having been expelled from the *École Polytechnique for radicalism, is posted as an unambitious junior officer to Nancy, where he is welcomed by provincial *ultra society and falls in love with a young widow, Madame de Chasteller. Tricked into thinking she has had an illegitimate child, he returns brokenhearted to Paris and civilian life and with the help of his father, a rich and cynical businessman, enters political life, an amoral game which he plays with brio. Stendhal never wrote the final section in which Lucien was to serve as a diplomat in Italy and be reunited with his love.

The first 18 chapters were published as Le Chasseur vert in 1855, but the novel as a whole has to be reconstructed from manuscripts; the best edition is that of H. Martineau (1952). Although unfinished, it is among Stendhal's finest works, remarkable for its leisurely depiction of a timid reciprocal love against a background of political intrigue, for the contrast between worldly-wise father and romantic son, and for its entertaining and acute view of Louis-Philippe's France, with a cast ranging from the king and his ministers to grotesque provincials of all parties.   [PF]

LUCINGE, René de (1554–c.1615). Savoyard diplomat, ambassador to the court of *Henri III, of which he left interesting memoirs. His major work, De la naissance, durée et chute des états (1588), is a Machiavellian account of political change, based on history and on observation of the Ottoman empire, whose downfall he optimistically predicts.   [MJH]

LUGNÉ-POË, Aurélien (1869–1940). Theatre director who worked for a time with *Antoine but broke away to develop anti-naturalistic techniques at his Théâtre de l'Œuvre from 1893 [see JARRY]. He exploited highly stylized methods to enhance the suggestiveness of a performance but, although audacious and innovatory, remained eclectic in his approach.   [DHW]

LULLY, Jean-Baptiste (Lulli, Giovanni Battista) (1632–87). Composer, performer, and dancer of Italian birth, Lully was initially known for his *ballets de cour and *comédies-ballets. From 1664 to 1670 he collaborated with *Molière on comédies-ballets—a genre in which dramatist and composer worked as equals. Lully is regarded as the founder of French *opera. Under the patronage of *Louis XIV he had autocratic control over all operatic performance in France. He called his operas tragédies en musique (renamed tragédies lyriques in the 18th c.), with the tragedy or libretto being of primary, not secondary, importance. Most were written with *Quinault, with others by *Corneille and *Fontenelle, on subjects drawn from mythology or legends of chivalry. Lully modelled his operas on the famous tragedies of the day and based his recitatives on the declamatory style used by the actors at the *Comédie-Française. He made little distinction between airs and recitatives; the time of the action more or less coincides with the music, whereas in contemporary Italian opera time was effectively suspended during the arias. Every *tragédie* consisted of a prologue glorifying the king, followed by five acts. Ballet was an essential ingredient, most notably in the *divertissements*. Lully's *tragédies* established a genre which remained active for over 100 years in France.   [KM]

LUMIÈRE, Louis (1864–1948), see CINEMA.

Lumières, Le Siècle des, see ENLIGHTENMENT.

Lundis and *Nouveaux lundis,* see SAINTE-BEUVE.

Lunettes des princes, Les, see MESCHINOT.

Lupin, Arsène. Hero of detective stories by M. *Leblanc.

LUTHER, Martin (1483–1546). The impact upon France of the great German Reformer's writings and campaigns was most marked in the three decades following his original protest at Wittenberg in 1517, when his teachings on justification by faith, the bondage of the will, consubstantiation, mankind's total depravity, and the iniquities of Rome, were fiercely debated. In later years the French *Reformation was dominated by the teachings of *Calvin.

As early as February 1519 Luther's 95 theses and his *Resolutiones* expounding them were being read and welcomed in *humanist circles in Paris; Lyon and Avignon were not far behind. In April 1521 the *Sorbonne followed Pope Leo X's excommunication of Luther by publishing its *Determinatio* (final judgement) on his works, which amounts to proscription; in August the Parlement de Paris ordered that all Lutheran books be surrendered. Philip Melanchthon's replies to these censures were similarly condemned by the Sorbonne in 1522, and thereafter study of Luther became clandestine and hazardous. In 1523, after a show trial, Louis de *Berquin formally abjured his 'Lutheran errors', but an Augustinian from Normandy, Jean Vallière, was the first 'Lutheran heretic' to go to the stake in France.

As the persecution intensified, French refugees in the great publishing centres of Basle, Antwerp, and Strasbourg helped to disseminate Luther's works in France, where controversy surrounded the association of *Marguerite de Navarre and *Marot with Lutheran ideas. Marguerite's support was never explicit, and the *Evangelical influence of *Lefèvre, *Briçonnet, and others was strong; but in a famous case the Sorbonne attempted to censor her *Miroir de l'âme pécheresse* (1531: issued by Simon Dubois, notorious as a publisher of Lutheran works). Marot was accused of Lutheranism as early as 1526 (see his *Épître à Monsieur Bouchard* and *Enfer*), and was proscribed after the second Affaire des *Placards in 1535. Thereafter Lutheran fortunes waxed and waned with *Francois Ier's political relations with the German Lutheran princes; the king encouraged several attempts to negotiate a doctrinal compromise,

particularly with the more pliant Melanchthon, but little was achieved.

An important literary feature of the Lutheran debate was the widespread dissemination of satires, such as the *Livre des marchands* (1533: on the worldliness of the Roman Church) and the *Alcoran des Cordeliers* (1560 in French), which exhibit the characteristic abrasiveness and broad humour of Luther's own satires.   [MJH]

See W. G. Moore, *La Réforme allemande et la littérature française* (1930); J. Wirth, *Luther* (1981).

Lutrin, Le, see BOILEAU.

LUXEMBOURG, Charles-François-Frédéric de Montmorency-Luxembourg, maréchal-duc de (1702–64). Distinguished soldier. He and the maréchale (the former duchesse de Boufflers), were J.-J. *Rousseau's protectors after his quarrel with Madame d' *Épinay.

Luxembourg, Palais du. Built in 1615–20, this was for a time owned by the *Orléans family; it now houses the Senate, and is adjoined by a park full of literary associations. For the Théâtre du Luxembourg, see ODÉON.

LY, Ibrahima (1936–89). Malian author of two novels, *Toiles d'araignées* (1982) and *Les Noctuelles vivent de larmes* (1988), and the short story 'Une main ouverte' (in *Paris-Dakar et autres nouvelles*, 1987). A Marxist and political activist, he was imprisoned by the military regime from 1974 to 1978; *Toiles d'araignées* reflects this experience.   [AMR]

Lycanthrope, Le. Name adopted by the *frénétique* poet Petrus *Borel.

Lycée, see EDUCATION.

Lycée, Le. Parisian institution offering public lectures in natural and social sciences, French, and foreign literature to fashionable audiences. Set up by the balloonist Pilâtre de Rosier in 1781, it became the Lycée in 1786 and continued to function successfully until 1849, latterly as L'Athénée. The roll-call of lecturers includes many famous names, from *La Harpe to *Constant, *Cuvier to *Comte.

Lycée, ou Cours de littérature, Le, see LA HARPE.

Lyon School. Term sometimes used of the group of poets writing in Lyon c.1540–50, notably *Scève, *Labé, and *Du Guillet.

LYOTARD, Jean-François (b. 1924). French philosopher. His work came to international prominence with *La Condition postmoderne* (1979), although he had a considerable following in the 1960s and 1970s in France as a 'philosopher of desire', associated with *Deleuze, and was known for his earlier political involvement with the Socialisme ou Barbarie group and in the *May 1968 movement.

Lyric Poetry

This philosophy is first developed in the monumental (and underrated) *Discours, figure* (1971), the essays collected in *Dérive à partir de Marx et Freud* and *Des dispositifs pulsionnels* (both 1973), and the scandalous *Économie libidinale* (1974), which marked Lyotard's break with *Marxism and is essentially an attempt at a neo-Nietzschean politics and aesthetics of intensity, developed from a non-*Lacanian reading of Freud. Around the late 1970s he abandons this for a quasi-Wittgensteinian philosophy of language dominated by a concern to formulate the possibility of judgement and justice (see especially *Au juste*, 1979), in the wake of the perceived collapse of traditional metaphysical absolutes and the dispersion of events and singularities briefly associated with *Postmodernism. It is this concern which dominates his next major work *Le Différend* (1983), and subsequent essays collected in *L'Inhumain* (1989). [GPB]

Lyric Poetry

1. Medieval

a. General Characteristics. The term 'lyric', although widely used today to refer to a particular tradition of French poetry in the Middle Ages, was not available to medieval poets; they deploy instead a range of more or less precise generic terms to designate a wide range of compositions which tend to be short, strophic, sung to music, and organized around a first-person voice, and which deal prominantly (though by no means exclusively) with the theme of love. Terms such as *vers* (in Occitan) or *chanson* in French have a relatively unspecific meaning. Some medieval terms (such as *sirventes) designate content primarily, since *sirventes* are often formal imitations (*contrafacta*) of existing love songs. Others (such as *jeu parti*) are mainly formal: a great variety of topics are debated in these texts, it is the debate form itself which defines the genre. Yet others (such as *alba*, the dawn song) highlight both narrative content (lovers' separation at dawn) and a characteristic formal feature (a refrain word, *alba*). The analysis of medieval lyric poetry cannot straightforwardly assume the priority of either substantive or formal characteristics.

A typological distinction which has proved useful is that between 'aristocratic' (*aristocratisant*) and 'popularizing' registers, elaborated by Pierre Bec. By 'register' here is meant a common store of potential constituents for a song of a particular type: characteristic motifs, phraseology, verse forms, and so on. The 'popularizing register' comprises lyric verse with a narrative cast like the *alba* or the *pastourelle; verses apparently conceived as dance-tunes, such as the *estampie* or the *rondeau; verses incorporating 'popular' refrains; first-person songs in a woman's voice (*chansons de femme*, *chansons de toile*, *chansons de mal-mariée*); comic or burlesque songs—any song, in short, which does not share the perspective of a courtly male speaker. 'Aristocratic' genres include love songs (*cansos in Occitan, the *grand chant courtois* in French); reflective, moral, religious, or politi-

cal songs using similar forms (e.g. *sirventes*, songs to the Virgin such as those by *Gautier de Coinci, and crusade songs); and the debate genres. The terms 'popularizing' and 'aristocratic' do not imply the expected social class of either composer or audience. Both 'aristocratic' and 'popularizing' songs can be ascribed to the same poet, such as *Thibaut de Champagne. And poets who emerge from the towns or from clerical milieux, rather than from the aristocracy, such as *Adam de la Halle, may compose 'aristocratic' songs.

This distinction becomes less helpful in the later Middle Ages, with the rise of a new kind of poetic voice: that of the clerk, in the sense the term had in the Middle Ages, when it designates not so much a cleric as a scholar and intellectual. With such figures as *Rutebeuf and *Machaut the writer's craft becomes an important component of the lyric. Formal skill, developed in the *formes fixes* (such as the *ballade or *virelai), becomes an index less of inherent refinement (as in earlier 'aristocratic' song) than of writerly achievement. Music remains an important element of lyric composition (notably in the case of Machaut, celebrated as a composer and musical innovator) [see WORDS AND MUSIC, 1]. But after Machaut lyric poetry tends to be increasingly divorced from music and inserted into other written texts, such as *dits. Thus *Villon, for example, inserted 19 lyric pieces of various genres into his *Grand Testament.* Musicality comes to be regarded as an inherent trait of poetry which no longer needs the addition of a musical accompaniment; thus *Deschamps's *Art de dictier* (1392) emphasizes the 'musique naturelle' of verse in opposition to the 'musique artificielle' of music, an idea repeated as late as *Molinet's *Art de rhétorique* (1492).

b. Before 1300. Despite the difficulties of classification, and hence of generalization, lyric poetry to the end of the 13th c. tends to be thought of as dominated by the love song (*canso* or *grand chant courtois*), even though this makes up less than half of the surviving texts, because so many other genres (especially the 'aristocratic' ones) are formal calques of it. In this period, text and music seem to have been closely associated. Poets (*troubadours in Occitan, *trouvères in northern French) were also composers, and their songs were composed in strophes, each of which, in any song, shared the same metrical structure and thus could be sung to the same tune. (One genre, the *descort*, is defined by the fact that it flouts this convention and gives each successive stanza a different metrical shape.) In the love song, both metre and tune were usually unique to their particular song. This gave an especial prominence to the opening stanza, which often contains the most striking imagery, or the most dramatic claims, of the whole song. In subsequent stanzas, form and tune are recapitulated and the content elaborated, but with the exception of a few poets (*Bernart de Ventadorn, *Thibaut de Champagne) the central part of the song is not made the occasion for rhetorical display. Instead, poetic energy is gathered for the end, often a direct request for love or action, which may be expressed in the final stanza and/or in a partial stanza, termed a *tornada* in Occitan, an *envoi* in French, soliciting the favour of the poem's addressee(s).

Composed to be sung, and presumably usually sung from memory without the support of a written text, the opening and, to a lesser extent closing stanzas are those whose position is most fixed. Intermediate stanzas appear in different manuscript copies with a considerable variety of orderings, and sometimes stanzas are omitted or interpolated. The close correspondence between melody and metre was probably a useful mnemonic. But the rhyme scheme of a lyric does not necessarily correspond with its musical form; and it far oustrips the requirements of a memory-aid. Rhyme schemes are sometimes so intricate and the rhyme words so unusual as to be a song's principal form of ornament. Rather than the rhymes conforming to the music, the music is made to serve and enhance the rhymes, protracting the rhyme syllable with elegant swirls of notes (*melismata*).

The content of love songs in this period rehearses the paradoxes of *fin'amor. The first-person singer represents his feelings as simultaneously worthy and transgressive. He loves a lady, but often assimilates her, by the use of feudal imagery, to a man. Other paradoxes abound. A singer professes to sing under the compulsion of personal feeling, but also in the hope of pleasing a lady or patron. A song is both new and traditional, conventional and sincere. The formal exquisiteness of the lyric is therefore made to house, and hold in balance, a set of tensions and contradictions which yield interesting reflections on conceptions of the self, the social, and the relation of sentiment to language.

Northern French *trouvères* who begin their songs with professions of sincerity and novelty are being particularly disingenuous, since so many of their songs follow the form and phraseology of Occitan models. Lyric poetry had become a prestige medium and the lyric subject is characterized in terms similar to a hero of *romance. The desire these texts express can be seen as the desire to be the subject of a lyric, rather than to succeed in whatever the ostensible theme of a song might be. When, from the end of the 13th c. onwards, new forms such as the ballade and the *virelai* rise to prominence, this sense of participating in a literary tradition increases rather than diminishes.

c. Later Middle Ages. The poets of the 14th and 15th c. take this process a stage further: the desire of Machaut, *Charles d'Orléans, or Villon could be said to be the subject not just of the lyric but of the *œuvre*. It is characteristic of these writers that, like Machaut, they should be concerned with the materiality of their production: its copying, its anthologization, the disposition of stanza and line on the page itself; that they should wish, like Deschamps or

Molinet, to analyse and codify the very essence of the lyric project; that they should show a predilection for the more weighty, flamboyantly difficult verse-forms such as the *lai or the *complainte*. Technical virtuosity foregrounds and solemnizes the poetic *je*, its conflicting impulses dramatized through allegorical figures in the wake of the *Roman de la Rose*, or through exteriorizations of a fragmented self such as Cœur, Penser, or Corps. The poet's analysis is directed inwards (*Christine de Pizan's widowhood; Machaut's mildly ironic old man's passion in the *Voir Dit*) or conscious of a political and social mission (Deschamps's vituperative counterpart to the vices of his time; Alain *Chartier's sonorous denunciations of the princes of France). The poet, in other words, is not a mere entertainer, but a person of substance whose self merits examination and whose opinions have weight.

This shift in perspective—from periphery of court life to centre of the moral universe—characterizes the *Rhétoriqueurs, officially constituted court poets *par excellence*, whose words are designed to be in themselves a memorial of those whom they serve, and demand, therefore, a maximum of poetic sophistication. To display learning, to manipulate an elegant allegory, to multiply linguistic and prosodic virtuosities, is to attach to poetry all the solemnity of their official verse. [SK and JHMT]

See D. Poirion, *L'Évolution du lyrisme courtois de Guillaume de Machaut à Charles d'Orléans* (1965); P. Bec, *La Lyrique française au Moyen Âge: contribution à une typologie des genres poétiques*, 2 vols. (1977-8).

2. Modern

a. Renaissance. The domination of 16th-c. French poetry by the *Pléiade should not be allowed to obscure the talents of its immediate predecessors. Clément *Marot still belongs to the medieval tradition, cultivating the stylistic complexity of the *Rhétoriqueurs, but his later verse epistles show an elegant *badinage* and his biblical paraphrases an unadorned lyric vigour which are humanist. *Neoplatonic and *Petrarchan influences are first felt in the work of the Lyon poets, particularly in *Scève's *Délie*. But Scève's restrained, hermetic art has little in common with the searing passion of Louise *Labé's sonnets. The object of Labé's unrequited love is assumed to be Olivier de *Magny, whose poems of spiritual exile in Rome, *Soupirs*, pre-date *Du Bellay's similar *Regrets* by a year. The link between the Lyon school and the Pléiade is provided by *Pontus de Tyard, who, with *Jodelle, *Peletier du Mans, *Baïf, *Belleau, Du Bellay, and *Ronsard, makes up the constellation. The 'programme' of these poets enjoins a thoroughgoing imitation of classical models (hence Baïf's attempts to introduce quantitative principles into French verse). The immediate successor of the Pléiade was the proto-*précieux *Desportes, whose detached urbanity sets him far apart from the rough-hewn, tumultuous commitment of contemporary Protestant poets, such as *Du Bartas, d'*Aubigné, and *Sponde.

b. *Seventeenth and Eighteenth Centuries.* *Malherbe presides over the poetry of the first decades of the 17th c. as its brusque lawgiver: precision of language, fixity of caesura, prohibition of hiatus, chevilles, and commonplace rhymes, semantic integrity of stanzas—in short, poetic intensity through formal rigour and linguistic spareness. Malherbe's theories are only available in his *Commentaires sur Desportes* and the account of his disciple *Racan, who with his master and *Mainard represented a tendency firmly resisted by *Régnier and *Théophile de Viau. These poets worked to reinstate the claims of spontaneous inspiration, decoration, and a syntax and diction freely conceived. With the development of the *salons and of *preciosity, poetry became the preserve of a social élite set on refining feelings and language to a paroxysm of exquisiteness. *Voiture was the 'court poet' of the Hôtel de *Rambouillet, and his entourage included *Benserade, *Gombauld, and *Malleville. Independent of the cult of preciosity, but not untouched by it, were the 'baroque' poets *Tristan l'Hermite and *Saint-Amant, who excelled in the *burlesque. A much sterner enemy of the précieux was *Boileau, who championed Malherbe's classical principles; but Boileau's reputation is also founded on his Juvenalian Satires, his mock-epic Le Lutrin, and his Horatian Épîtres. By Boileau's standards, the *vers libres classiques of La Fontaine's *Fables are excessively free; the attraction of these vers mêlés lies not only in their improvised and virtuosic quality, but also, and paradoxically, in their apparently unlaboured naturalness, a quality seen also in several poets of the late 17th c.: *Deshoulières, *Chaulieu, *La Fare.

The lyric suffered in the 18th c. from a surfeit of ossified diction, mythological allusion, and unwieldy rhetoric. Poets found it difficult to occupy the middle ground between ratiocinative gravity and social entertainment. To some (*La Motte, *Fontenelle) poetry seemed wilful mystification and a dangerous enthralment of judgement; *Voltaire had to admit that 'de toutes les nations polies, la nôtre est la moins poétique', rich in poetics, poor in poetry. J.-B. *Rousseau, a protégé of Boileau's, is best known for his odes, cantatas, and epigrams: his hetero-metric and hetero-stanzaic structures have a diversity of pace and metrical eventfulness which can please over larger spans. Le Franc de *Pompignan's 'Ode sur la mort de J.-B. Rousseau' has an adroit mixture of paradox and pathos, found also in his biblical verse. The ode is equally the forte of Écouchard *Lebrun. After the mid-century, the influence of English topographical and seasonal poetry was felt: Virgil and James Thomson combined to engender *Saint-Lambert's Les Saisons, *Roucher's Les Mois, and *Delille's Les Jardins. The

century's poetry culminated in the work of André *Chénier: elegies, odes, epistles, idylls, scientific and philosophical poems, and the bitterly satirical Iambes.

c. *Romantic Poetry.* Chénier's poems were finally published in 1819, shortly after the intense, confessional Élégies et romances of *Desbordes-Valmore, and a year before Romanticism's 'official' poetic inception with *Lamartine's Méditations ('Je suis le premier . . . qui ai donné à ce qu'on nommait la Muse, au lieu d'une lyre de sept cordes de convention, les fibres mêmes du cœur de l'homme . . .'). Very different from Lamartine's suave melancholy is *Vigny's blunt and clear-headed disillusionment, his stoical idealism, expressed in poems published between 1822 and 1864 (Les Destinées). Vigny has little of the verse and ironic fantaisie associated with *Musset's earlier verse, qualities which were transformed into the altogether darker hues of Les Nuits. Bestriding the century, both as figurehead and survivor of Romanticism, is *Hugo, whose work explores all dimensions of the movement: the picturesque and exotic (Les Orientales), the sentimentally familial (Les Feuilles d'automne), the politically committed (Les *Châtiments), spiritual autobiography (Les *Contemplations), and cultural history (La *Légende des siècles). Throughout Hugo's work one finds moments of intense visionary encounter, involving both memory and fantasy; similar encounters are recorded in *Nerval's Les Chimères, different, however, in their unaffected familiarity with myth, in their peculiarly confident hermeticism.

d. *Symbolism and Parnassianism.* The achievement of vision in and through language is a central concern of the *Symbolist poets, whether in *Baudelaire's 'surnaturalisme', in *Rimbaud's 'long, immense et raisonné dérèglement de tous les sens', or in *Mallarmé's image of the poet as 'une aptitude qu'a l'Univers spirituel à se voir et se développer'. These enterprises involve the suppression of the personal voice of the poet, as he yields the initiative to words or inhabits other consciousnesses (Baudelaire's 'sainte prostitution de l'âme', Rimbaud's 'Je est un autre'). Alongside the visionary runs the intimate, the tracing of feelings which do not have the unambiguous, self-justifying power of Romantic feeling, but are fleeting, mixed with sensation, multiple (*Verlaine, Henri de *Régnier, *Samain). A third current derives from the irony cultivated by Baudelaire in the figures of the dandy and the fallen angel: the poem becomes the site of psychological investigation, a probing of the layers of consciousness which exist between the poet and his self, poet and reader; the contract of complicity with the reader is broken, and meaning constantly shifts in the relationship of mutual distrust, while language flouts the poetic in the prosaic or whimsical (Verlaine, *Cros, *Corbière, *Laforgue).

From the 1850s, and particularly *Gautier's Émaux et camées, dates the other large trend of the latter half of the 19th c., *Parnassianism, whose coherence is difficult to establish other than negatively. That there was a reaction against the facility and self-exposure of the Romantics, their amateurism and glorification of the poetic gift, cannot be doubted. But this response is common to *Symbolism too. Gautier makes a virtue of difficulty, to the point of virtuosity, as does, in even more acrobatic vein, *Banville, with his revival of fixed forms. But this aesthetic prizing of the *dulce* over the *utile* does not square with *Leconte de Lisle's philosophical and positivistic historicism, with its appealing note of unappeasable yearning, nor with the domestic realism of François *Coppée, nor with the melancholy moralizing of *Sully-Prudhomme. And *Heredia's sonnet-cycle, *Les Trophées*, for all its epic historical scale, is full of Symbolism in its suggestive ellipses and compressions.

e. Twentieth Century. Symbolism's heritage in the 20th c. runs through the dynamic socialism of *Verhaeren and the rustic Catholicism of *Jammes, and culminates in *Valéry's subtle enquiry into creative consciousness and a purified poetic act, an enquiry reopened much later by *Deguy and the poet-mathematician *Roubaud. The Catholic tradition of the early century found its most powerful expression in the ample, magisterial versets of *Claudel's *Cinq grandes odes* and in the obsessive insistence of *Péguy's verse. The all-encompassing, rhapsodic, Whitmanian strain in Claudel is to be found in other poets, in the *Unanimists (Jules *Romains), in globe-trotting poets such as *Cendrars, *Larbaud, and *Saint-John Perse. Cendrars shared with *Apollinaire an enthusiasm for the contemporary arts, and particularly for the aesthetic of simultaneity; the latter's *Calligrammes* explore the 'idéogramme lyrique', while *Reverdy, in his turn, uses layout to project his linguistic *Cubism. Reverdy's definition of the image ('Plus les rapports de deux réalités rapprochées seront lointaines et justes, plus l'image sera forte') lies at the heart of *Surrealist poetics, itself inextricably linked with the visual arts [see BRETON; ÉLUARD; DESNOS; ARAGON]. On the fringes of Surrealism, *Supervielle pursued his intuited presences, while *Jouve fused Freud with Christianity in a prophetic mode; the voice of Christian vision is also to be heard in Jouve's disciple Pierre *Emmanuel and in Patrice de *La Tour du Pin.

Éluard, Aragon, Desnos, Emmanuel were poets of the Resistance, as was *Char, whose later collections are suffused by an elliptical elementalism. A vein of wit in modern French poetry is represented by *Prévert, *Queneau, and *Tardieu; these poets achieve their effects by adopting the unauthorized point of view, as indeed do the poets who adopt 'le parti pris des choses', *Ponge and *Guillevic. In many senses Ponge and Guillevic are in search of the same revelation of inalienable being as *Bonnefoy; the answer of Henri *Michaux to the blankness or hostility of available reality lies in the exorcizing power of language itself. *Jacottet and *Réda, on the other hand, aim to capture the epiphanies of past and passing sensation, the one in a poetry drastically pared down, the other in a fuller, elegiac mode. If the French language is a means of transformation and redemption for some, for others it is full of potential treacheries and misrepresentations: the founding poets of *négritude, *Senghor and *Césaire, had to colonize French to express the universals of blackness; and, in their footsteps, a francophone poetry of alternative ethnic identities and histories has proliferated in sub-Saharan *Africa, the *West Indies, the countries of the *Maghreb, and *Quebec. [See also ANTHOLOGIES; VERSIFICATION.]   [CS]

See G. Brereton, *An Introduction to the French Poets: Villon to the Present Day* (rev. edn., 1973); S. Brindeau, *La Poésie contemporaine de langue française depuis 1945* (1973); R. Sabatier, *Histoire de la poésie française*, 9 vols. (1975–88); K. Aspley and P. France (eds.), *Poetry in France* (1992).

Lys dans la vallee, Le. Sentimental novel by *Balzac, written in 1835–6, partly as a reply to *Sainte-Beuve's *Volupté*. Cast in the form of a letter to Nathalie de Manerville, Balzac's novel consists of a first-person account of Félix de Vandenesse's first love, for an older married woman, the virtuous Henriette de Mortsauf, the 'lily' of the novel's title, whose idyllic château of Clochegourde lies in the lush valley of the Indre, not far from Tours. Henriette allows the impetuous young man to become a house-guest and, in reminiscence of Rousseau's *La *Nouvelle Héloïse*, a sighingly romantic but always unconsummated passion develops through long disquisitions on morality and motherhood. Félix then has a brief political career in Paris, where he is swept off his feet by the man-eating Lady Arabella Dudley. Félix takes Arabella back to Clochegourde, where she confronts Henriette. The older woman dies, perhaps of a broken heart, suddenly regretting the life of virtue which she has led and which held the one man she might have loved at bay. Henriette's eleventh-hour reversion to a real and tragic awareness of her own suppressed feelings, and the reply from Nathalie de Manerville which closes the novel, are of great psychological and literary power, in stark contrast to the moralizing sentimentality of Félix's over-long account of his earlier feelings. The technical accomplishment of an *epistolary novel, containing a first-person confession in which several other narrative levels are nested, is not inconsiderable.   [DMB]

M

MAALOUF, Amin (b. 1949). Lebanese historian, journalist, and novelist, living in Paris since 1976. He is editor of *Jeune Afrique*, and his writing bridges the gap between Europe and the Arab world, for instance *Les Croisades vues par les Arabes* (1983), *Léon l'Africain* (1986), and *Les Jardins de lumière* (1991). In 1993 he won the Prix Goncourt for the novel *Le Rocher de Tanios*, a weave of history and fiction whose hero comes from a village in mid-19th-c. Lebanon.   [DSB]

MABILLE, Pierre (1904–52), was a veritable polymath: surgeon, sociologist, active *Surrealist from 1934; French cultural attaché in Haiti and first director of the French Institute there (1945); art critic, student of alchemy, astrology, and voodoo. He taught at the École d'Anthropologie and the Faculty of Medicine in Paris (1949–51). As a Surrealist, his most important book is *Le Miroir du merveilleux* (1940), a wide-ranging and critical anthology. As a thinker, his profession of faith is found in *La Construction de l'homme* (1936). His desire for a synthesis of different branches of knowledge is revealed in *Égrégores ou la Vie des civilisations* and *La Conscience lumineuse* (1938). He also published a psychoanalytical-cum-sociological study, *Thérèse de Lisieux* (1937).   [KRA]

MABILLON, Jean (1632–1707). French Benedictine monk of the reformed *Maurist congregation who has been called the Galileo of historical scholarship. His *De re diplomatica* (1681) lays down the principles which have ever since guided the critical study of historical documents. Professed at Reims (1654), Mabillon migrated in 1664 to the abbey of *Saint-Germain-des-Prés in Paris, already a celebrated centre for historical and textual research, where he edited the works of *Bernard de Clairvaux and St Augustine. In his *Traité des études monastiques* (1691) he defended these activities against the views of the austere Trappist *Rancé, for whom learning was an obstacle to monastic perfection.   [PJB]

MABLY, Gabriel Bonnot, abbé de (1709–85). Elder brother of *Condillac, he wrote on politics and ancient and modern history, devoting himself to study except for a few years' experience of political life in the foreign ministry. His numerous works include a history of diplomacy and international relations. The *Entretiens de Phocion* (1763) make a patriotic appeal for morality in political behaviour. *Des droits et devoirs du citoyen* (1789) brought posthumous fame; written many years earlier, it asks how far to take opposition to an unjust government, con-tains communistic views on property, and appeared prophetic in its plan to hold *États Généraux. In his refusal of modern corruption and admiration for Spartan virtue, Mably resembled J.-J. *Rousseau, but he lacked the Genevan's contagious eloquence.
                                             [CJB]

Macaire, Robert, see DAUMIER.

Macaronic Verse. Burlesque, often mock-epic, poetry tagging Latin endings on to vernacular words became fashionable in Italy from 1490. It was introduced to France by 'Arena', *alias* Antoine des Arens, whose *basses danses Ad suos compagnones* (1529) and satire *Meygra entrepriza catoliqui imperatoris* (1537) facetiously incorporate Gallicisms and Provençalisms. Subsequent practitioners include *Belleau (*De bello huguenotico*), *Molière (*Le Malade imaginaire*), and one Josselin, SJ, who shortly before 1700 described festivities in Autun. The tradition of bilingual or multilingual verse, sometimes loosely considered 'macaronic', began among Anglo-Norman, French, and Occitan poets in the late 12th c. and continues with *Prévert's 'Chant song' (*Spectacle*, 1949).   [PVD]

MACHAUT or **MACHAULT,** Guillaume de (*c.*1300–1377). A prolific writer of both lyric and narrative poetry, Machaut was also an important composer. His works were admired and imitated both inside and outside France. In his youth Machaut served as personal secretary to John of Luxembourg, king of Bohemia. In the course of his career he also enjoyed the patronage of Bonne, John's daughter and wife of the dauphin; Charles le Mauvais of Navarre; and Jean, duc de Berry. In 1337 he received a canonry at Reims, which he held until his death. Most of his poetry dates from after this time.

While Machaut's compositions were occasionally copied independently, they are for the most part transmitted in anthology manuscripts of his collected works. Most of these are richly illuminated. Machaut exercised a supervisory role in the preparation of manuscripts, the precise extent of which is not known; at the very least he was probably involved with codex organization and with the design of illustrative programmes. Machaut's role in book production is linked to his interest in establishing a poetic identity powerful enough to unify his entire literary and musical *œuvre*. His important position in the evolution of French literature is reflected in Eustache *Deschamps's ballade commemorating Machaut's death, in which Machaut is designated as 'poète': the first known application of this term to a vernacular author.

While Machaut did not invent the lyric *formes fixes*, his work helped to establish these forms as canonical. The hierarchy of forms is nowhere so clear as in the *Remède de Fortune* (c.1341), which contains an example of each with musical accompaniment. The pieces are arranged in descending order of poetic complexity—from *lai* to rondeau—and in ascending order of musical complexity, moving from monody to polyphony. In the anthology manuscripts of Machaut's collected works, lyric pieces are grouped according to verse form. A group of poems without musical accompaniment is transmitted under the title *La Louange des dames*.

Machaut's narrative *dits* are in the tradition of the *Roman de la Rose*. He employs first-person narrative; the subject is love, including both the representation of love experience and the didactic exposition of proper behaviour in love; and he frequently makes use of the dream-vision format and of allegorical personification. Machaut may present himself as lover, as in the *Dit du Vergier* (before 1340), the *Remède de Fortune*, and the *Dit de l'Alerion* (before 1349); or he may act as witness and recorder of another's love, as in the *Dit du Lyon* (1342) and the *Fonteinne amoureuse* (c.1361). In all of these poems Machaut presents an intellectualized vision of love, one largely separated from erotic desire. Love provides inspiration for literary and musical composition, and is the basis for a cheerful optimism sustained by contemplation of the lady's many virtues.

The *Jugement du roy de Behaingne* (c.1340), written for John of Luxembourg, presents a debate in love casuistry, in which it is determined that a man whose lady has betrayed him has suffered more than a lady whose lover has died. Its sequel, the *Jugement du roy de Navarre* (1349), written for Charles le Mauvais, reverses the judgement after a lengthy debate in which the narrator is accused of defaming women. An interesting forerunner of the 15th-c. *Querelle des Femmes*, this pair of *dits* provided an important model for *Christine de Pizan's debate poetry.

Machaut's most enigmatic and most self-reflexive work is the *Voir Dit* (True Tale), written near the end of his career. In it he portrays himself, an elderly and ailing poet, carrying on a love-affair with a teenage girl. The affair consists largely of poetry and prose epistles exchanged between the lovers and reproduced in the text. The *Voir Dit* is quite literally the story of its own day-by-day composition, and includes such details as the poet's complaint that he cannot reconstruct the proper order of the earlier love letters, which do appear in an illogical order. This state of affairs has led to debate concerning the veracity of the *Voir Dit*, which most scholars now regard as fictional.

Only two *dits* treat topics other than love. The *Confort d'ami* (1357) offers advice and consolation to Charles le Mauvais, and includes numerous mythological *exempla*. The *Prise d'Alexandrie* (after 1369), Machaut's last major composition, recounts the exploits of Pierre I de Lusignan, king of Cyprus.

Machaut's contributions to French literature include a complex blend of amorous and learned registers; a strengthening of the concept of vernacular poetic authority; and a humorous ironizing of the first-person narrator. His poetry is highly mannered, ornamental, and self-conscious. While building on the example of the *Roman de la Rose* and exploring the conventions of courtly poetry, Machaut proved himself a brilliant and original poet. [SJH]

See W. Calin, *A Poet at the Fountain* (1974); K. Brownlee, *Poetic Identity in Guillaume de Machaut* (1984); J. Cerquiglini, *'Un engin si soutil': Guillaume de Machaut et l'écriture au XIVe siècle* (1985).

MACHEREY, Pierre (b. 1938). French Marxist philosopher and literary theorist. Macherey developed *Althusser's philosophy, applying the results to literature. His influential *Pour une théorie de la production littéraire* (1966) attacked humanistic literary criticism, which sees literary works as the creation of an author whose meaning must be elucidated. Instead he proposed a theoretical approach which examines how a text has been produced and how it produces its effects. Since literary texts are coherent structures, he argued, they often display as formal problems the incoherences inherent in the ideological material from which they are produced. More recently he has advocated a Marxist philosophy based on Spinoza rather than Hegel. [MHK]

Machine infernale, La (1934). Play by *Cocteau, reworking and modernizing the Oedipus myth.

Machine Play (*pièce à machines*). Before the 17th c. spectacular stage effects had been popular in such para-theatrical entertainments as *royal entries and *ballets de cour*. From about 1640 the French theatre followed the Italian example in cultivating such effects. *Richelieu and *Mazarin brought Italian designers, notably Giacomo Torelli, to Paris, where they worked in the Palais Cardinal and the Salle du Petit Bourbon [see THEATRES AND AUDIENCES, I]. Machinery allowing for sunrises and sunsets, flights and descents from heaven, rocks that opened and fountains that played, became increasingly important, achieving its apotheosis in the *fêtes* of *Vaux-le-Vicomte and *Versailles and in the *operas of *Quinault and *Lully. The term 'machine play' is given to a variety of works (tragedy, pastoral, etc.) in which the spectacular element predominates, usually with a strong admixture of music and dance. The most famous examples of the genre are Pierre *Corneille's *Andromède* (1650) and *La Toison d'or* (1661) both performed at the Théâtre du Marais, which came to specialize in such shows. Although derided by defenders of the more literary type of tragedy, machine plays, like the opera, were very popular with contemporary audiences.   [PF]

MAC ORLAN, Pierre (pseud. of Pierre Dumarchey) (1882–1970). The most prominent of the Montmartre writers of the inter-war years, with *Carco and *Dorgelès. After a pre-war apprenticeship in Montmartre bohemia as a caricaturist and comic journalist, he became, with *Le Chant de l'équipage* (1918), an outstanding practitioner of the adventure novel, with a conscious debt to Conrad and Stevenson. Strongly marked by his experience of World War I and by his observation of post-war Germany, his novels, notably *Malice* (1923) and *Le Quai des brumes* (1927), constitute a powerful evocation of post-war 'inquiétude' in the context of what he termed 'le fantastique social'.   [NH]

MACRIN, Jean Salmon, see LATINITY, 2.

Madagascar. The sections devoted to Malagasy literature in French in *Senghor's influential *Anthologie de la nouvelle poésie nègre et malgache de langue française* (1948) and in *Damas's *Poètes d'expression française* (1947) are of a length comparable to the sections devoted to the whole of Africa. After the 1947 anti-colonial uprising on the island had been brutally suppressed, the poetry of the three best-known Malagasy poets, Jean-Jacques *Rabearivelo, Jacques *Rabemananjara (then in prison for alleged involvement in the planning of the uprising), and Flavien *Ranaivo, represented a commitment to Malagasy cultural and literary traditions, seen, for example, in attempts to transpose the *hain teny* into poetry in French. Rabemananjara's poetry became increasingly militant. For the editors of the anthologies mentioned above, Malagasy literature in French was a new departure.

Between the wars, however, two colonial writers, Pierre Camo and later Octave Mannoni, had already been giving support to Malagasy literature in French, particularly in their commitment to literary periodicals. Four journals were significant: *18° latitude sud*, *Capricorne*, *Du côté de chez Rakoto*, and the official *Revue de Madagascar*.

In addition to the three major poets mentioned above, a number of less well-known figures sustained the francophone Malagasy literary tradition in the 1940s: Élie Charles Abraham (*Les Saisons de mon cœur*, 1940), Randriamarozaka (*Illusoire ambience*, 1947), P. Nomyard (*Souffles du printemps*, 1947), Régis Rajemisa-Raolison (*Les Fleurs de l'île rouge*, 1947), and Paul Razafimahazo (*Une gerbe oubliée*, 1947), for whom the *hain teny* was an important formal influence. During the 1950s a number of varied works were published, mostly highly imitative of French models, by Louis Sumski, Michel-François Robinary, Jean-Louis Ranaïvoson, Fidelis-Justin Rabetsimandranto, and Paul Rakotonirina.

The political atmosphere after Independence in 1960 did not encourage literary activity. Both Rabemananjara and Ranaivo sought political exile in France. A number of uninteresting works appeared, a collection of poems by Paul Randrianarisoa (*Premiers visages*, 1961), and the first francophone fiction, Rabearison's moralizing *Les Voleurs de bœufs* (1965) and Aimée Andria's equally moralizing but less politically motivated stories in *Brouillard* (1967) and *Esquif* (1968). The period of intense 'malgachisation' which followed the change of regime in 1973 also tended to militate against writing in French, though a number of notable writers continued to contribute to the francophone tradition. Some younger writers have been nominated for important literary prizes, above all for short stories (Patrick Andriamangatiana, Tsilavina Ralaindimby, Marie-Danielle Rason, Zefaniasy Bemananjara). Two other important woman writers, Michèle *Rakotoson, who has written some exciting plays, and the poet Jocelyne Trime (*Moïka*, 1984), confirm the impression that the contribution of women to the francophone tradition on the island is likely to remain significant.   [BEJ]

Madame Bovary. Novel by *Flaubert, published in instalments in the *Revue de Paris* in 1856, and as a book in 1857. It is Flaubert's most famous and important work, begun on his return from the Middle East in 1851 and worked upon for many hours a day for nearly five years. Flaubert's long apprenticeship as a writer is evident in this work, which has intrigued critics as much by its tone and ideological ambivalence, as by its quest for stylistic perfection. Flaubert's correspondence from the period of composition, especially that with Louis *Colet, is a rich source of information on his aesthetic aims for a prose work deliberately conceived at the limits of possibility. The letters record his endless struggles with 'les affres du style', and explore such famous ideals as the 'book about nothing', an art that would 'faire rêver', and the impersonality implied by a complete lack of authorial comment. In the finished novel an undecidable narrative voice is in part achieved by Flaubert's innovative use of *style indirect libre* for the reporting of speech and thoughts.

Flaubert was prosecuted in 1856 for his supposedly obscene and blasphemous handling of a tale of provincial adultery ending in suicide. He was acquitted thanks to a defence lawyer who demonstrated that Emma Bovary was a moral warning rather than an object of admiration. In retrospect it seems that the nihilistic quality of the writing, more perhaps than the plot as such, lay behind the prosecution's focus on such phrases as 'les souillures du mariage et la désillusion de l'adultère'. The novel is a devastatingly negative account of both marriage and adultery. It is critical of Emma's selfish and sometimes silly aspirations, yet this romantic farmer's daughter is given a dull and inarticulate husband, the country doctor Charles Bovary, two selfish and mediocre lovers (Rodolphe and Léon), and a deadly set of village neighbours. While Lheureux the money-lender exploits her increasing depression and precipitates her ruin and suicide, a long-standing battle between the priest Bournisien and the chemist Homais, a progressive anti-clerical, moves towards a grotesque resolution. As they watch over Emma's dead body, Flaubert juxtaposes the priest sprinkling holy water with the chemist sprinkling disinfectant. The husband howls with grief somewhere in the background; the reader struggles to cope with sympathy, irony, and gruesome descriptions of the corpse, just as Flaubert lived through every detail and emotion of the novel.   [DK]

Madame, Mademoiselle, Monsieur. Used without further addition, these were titles given in the 17th and 18th c. to members of the royal family. 'Madame' was either the king's eldest sister or the wife of 'Monsieur', the king's eldest brother. Thus, until her death in 1670 'Madame' was the name given to *Henriette d'Angleterre, duchesse d'Orléans. 'Mademoiselle' designated the first princess of the blood while she remained unmarried, 'La Grande Mademoiselle' being the title given in the 17th c. to the duchesse de *Montpensier.

Madeleine, La Petite. At the beginning of Proust's *A la recherche du temps perdu* it is the taste of a small cake, a *madeleine*, which activates the narrator's involuntary memory of his childhood visits to Combray.

Mademoiselle, see MADAME.

Mademoiselle de Maupin (1835–6). Novel by Théophile *Gautier, whose 'Préface' is better known than the novel itself as a manifesto of l'*art pour l'art. The novel was, however, much admired by *Baudelaire and *Balzac, and by fin-de-siècle writers and artists, both in France and elsewhere, as a pure expression of dilettantish and dandyish aestheticism and eroticism. It is destined to attract new readers because of its surprising and complex play with narrative procedures and with gender roles and identities. Gautier's refusal to let anything be what it appears was obviously part of his *enfant-terrible* strategy to confuse and scandalize the flat-footed, moralizing bourgeois and humanitarian readers he stigmatized so wittily in his 'Préface'. In alternating epistolary and third-person forms, the novel shows the hero d'Albert as in turn melancholic and idealistic, cynical and libertine (but always narcissistic), and above all desperate to break out of solipsism and monotony and find true beauty embodied in corporeal form. Based on the strange adventures of the 17th-c. bisexual Madeleine de Maupin, who dressed and behaved like a swashbuckling swordsman and horseman, Gautier's novel, in conscious imitation of *As You Like It*, plays on the erotic attractions and misunderstandings of a young foursome.   [BR]

Madrigal. A short, light poem of no fixed form, very popular in 17th-c. France.

MAETERLINCK, Maurice (1862–1949). Belgian poet, dramatist, and essayist, Nobel laureate (1911), and a leading figure in the *Symbolist movement. He began as a poet (*Serres chaudes*, 1889; *Douze chansons*, 1896) before turning to the stage and creating a series of strange, innovatory 'dramas of inaction' in which symbolic figures move like sleep-walkers across a dimly lit stage. In a dream-like imaginary world, where death is always an implied presence, characters are depicted as the playthings of invisible and fateful powers. Influenced by the contemporary vogue for pantomime, puppets, and shadow-plays, he envisaged the characters of the three plays he published in 1894—*Alladine et Palomides*, *Intérieur*, and *La Mort de Tintagiles*—as being played by puppets. This epitomizes his desire to break away from the prevailing theatrical conventions of *Naturalism and from the virtuoso styles of performance employed by the acting stars of the 1890s, in order to create a poetic universe full of intimations of mystery and spirituality. Haunting examples of this early manner can be found in *L'Intruse* (1890), where a family is gripped by the expectation of death, and *Les Aveugles* (1890), in which a sightless man is more attuned to the realm of the spirit than the sighted. Subsequently he exploited other conventions in the theatre: legend in *Pelléas et Mélisande* (1893), with its doomed lovers in a medieval setting; fairy-tale in *L'Oiseau bleu* (1908), a charming entertainment for children; social realism in *Monna Vanna* (1902) and *Le Bourgmestre de Stilemonde* (1918), a drama about civilian heroism in World War I; sentimental religious fable in *Marie Magdeleine* (1910) and *Sœur Béatrice* (1910), where a nun is miraculously replaced by the Virgin Mary. Influential on contemporaries like *Claudel, Yeats, and D'Annunzio, Maeterlinck's static theatre anticipates *J.-J. Bernard's 'drama of the unspoken', and even *Beckett.   [SBJ]

Magasin pittoresque, Le. The first French popular illustrated magazine, founded by Édouard Charton in 1833 on the model of *The Penny Magazine*. It is an invaluable source, not only for its exceptional pictorial interest, but also for the evidence it provides of the concerted attempt in the July Monarchy to promote the 'morale de Franklin'.   [BR]

Maghreb. An Arabic term now widely used in French to denote the western half of North Africa, primarily the former colonial territories of *Algeria, *Morocco, and *Tunisia; in some contexts it also includes Mauritania and Libya. Together with its derivative *maghrébin*, the term became current after *decolonization, partly because it had fewer of the colonial, and sometimes pejorative, overtones associated with expressions such as *Afrique du Nord*, *Nord-Africain, Arabe.   [AGH]

483

Magny, Dîners, see CAFÉS AND RESTAURANTS.

MAGNY, Olivier de (1529–61). French poet. Having joined the circle of court poets in 1547, Magny produced collections of love-poetry in the manner of *Ronsard (*Amours,* 1553; *Gayetez,* 1554; *Soupirs,* 1557). In the mid-1550s he travelled to Rome, where he met Joachim *du Bellay; he is mentioned in a number of Du Bellay's *Regrets.* [TC]

MAGRITTE, René (1898–1967). Belgian *Surrealist painter who associated with *Breton, *Aragon, and *Éluard while living near Paris from 1927 to 1929. His theoretical writings include 'Les Mots et les images' (*La Révolution surréaliste,* 1929) and *La Pensée et les images* (1954). He made illustrations for Éluard, who dedicated two poems to him and owned several of his paintings. Magritte's works evoke the transforming imagination (interchanging shapes, textures) and sometimes incorporate the written word, notably *Ceci n'est pas une pipe.* His major themes include time and memory. The viewer is disturbed by veiled, sightless heads, stillness, expressions of alarm, or by the absence of human beings; incongruous juxtapositions are intensified by photographic verisimilitude of style. [HEB]

Mahomet (1742). *Voltaire himself provides the best synopsis of this tragedy, which depicts an unscrupulous religious charlatan's cynical attempt at domination over men's minds. 'It concerns a young man [Séide] born virtuous, who, seduced by fanaticism, murders an old man [Zopire] who loves him, a young man who, thinking to serve God, unknowingly becomes a parricide; it concerns an impostor [Mahomet] who orders his murder, and who promises the murderer [Séide] an incest for reward [Palmire is in reality the long-lost sister of Séide]' (letter to Frederick II, 30 December 1740). Voltaire clearly indicated his philosophical intention with the later title (1743): *Le Fanatisme ou Mahomet.* The play was dedicated to Pope Benedict XIV in 1745. [JR]

Maigret. The detective hero of numerous novels by *Simenon.

MAILLARD, Olivier (c.1430–1502). Franciscan preacher. A Breton by birth, he occupied a number of important posts in his order and was entrusted with several delicate diplomatic missions. Since almost all the extant texts of his sermon-courses for Lent, Advent, feast-days, and Sundays are in Latin, or in a curious mixture of Latin and French, they have sometimes given rise to a mistakenly derogatory view of 15th-c. preaching in general. In fact he usually preached in French, but made or dictated notes in the language of the Church as models for other preachers to use. [PJB]

MAILLET, Andrée (b. 1921). Montreal-born author of a significant and varied output. Her poetry (*Elémentaires,* 1964) has strong links with oral traditions; her short stories often have mythical and fantastic elements. *Profil de l'orignal* (1952), a prose work, satirizes the traditional Quebec consciousness, whilst *Les Montréalais* (1962) and *Les Remparts de Québec* (1965) participate in the upsurge of the Révolution Tranquille [see QUEBEC, 5]. [EAF]

MAILLET, Antonine (b. 1929). Canadian novelist, born in Bouctouche, New Brunswick. She is the chief representative of the *Acadians of the Maritime Provinces, a people with a development quite distinct from that of Quebec. Persecution, isolation, and lack of social opportunity have given the Acadians an oral culture of folk-tales, proverbs, racy language, and a life-style suited to survival through fishing and subsistence farming. Maillet maintains that Acadia escaped the dubious advantages of French *classicism ('Malherbe vint, mais pas chez nous'), and her thesis, *Rabelais et la culture populaire en Acadie,* traces the survival of French traditions in New Brunswick. It is this vigorous popular speech, folk-history, and humour which she has exploited with great skill in her monologues, *La Sagouine* (1971) and *Gapi* (1976), and in plays like *Les Crasseux* (1973), and carefully distilled in her novels through her own blend of orality and narrative.

Creating a modern fictional form for an unsophisticated oral culture has been an impressive innovation, and Maillet has achieved this while losing little of her verve. She plays off the bootlegger, rum-runner, village scold, against the establishment, priest, teacher, mayor, prude, entrepreneur, to great satirical effect. Her first novel, *On a mangé la dune* (1962), created a delightfully innocent portrait of childhood, poking fun at the smugness of adult society. Her latest work, *L'Oursiade* (1990), uses animals and children to paint an idyllic picture of primal harmony, contrasting good-naturedly with the prejudice, greed, and malice of those who 'own' the world. The tantalizing illusion of peace between man and animals becomes credible. Maillet's other Homeric task has been to redraft Acadian history from the expulsion by British troops in 1755, through the great trek back from the Carolinas (*Pélagie-la-Charrette,* 1979, Prix Goncourt), to the reconquest of legitimacy at the Congress of 1881 after *Cent ans dans les bois* (1981, published in France as *La Gribouille,* 1982). Antonine Maillet is a member of the Haut-Conseil de la Francophonie and a delightful spokeswoman for the diaspora. Her narrators are aged story-tellers, 'défricheteux de parenté', defenders of the disenfranchised and guardians of the collective memory. [CRPM]

MAIMBOURG, Louis, père (1610–86). French religious historian, author of numerous works. His Gallican sympathies led to his expulsion from the Jesuits in 1682. His history is eloquent and biased; the *Histoire du calvinisme* (1682) gave rise to vigorous polemic with Protestant champions such as *Bayle and *Jurieu. [PF]

MAINARD or **MAYNARD,** François (1582–1646), 'L'homme de France qui savait le mieux faire des vers' (according to *Malherbe, whose poetry seminars he attended) was secretary to *Marguerite de Valois (1605–7), president of the presidial court at Aurillac (1612–28), and one of the original members of the Académie Française, but he never acquired the wealth or status he thought were his due, and from 1633 spent most of his time on his estate at Saint-Céré, regretting the more generous patronage of the Valois princes. Stricter on some points than Malherbe himself, he argued for a division of the *sizain* at the third line and, against *Racan, for a break at the seventh as well as the fourth in the *dizain*; on the other hand he defended the 'irregular' sonnet, with variant rhymes in the quatrains. He tends to make each line as self-contained as possible and, though he wrote some heroic odes in the manner of Malherbe, is happier in shorter forms, considering himself to be 'l'épigrammatiste de France'. His elegant wit, caustic or playful, is balanced by his sense of the world's vanity and the end of all things, impressively conveyed in his ode 'Alcippe, reviens dans nos bois'.   [AJS]

MAINE, Louise de Bourbon, duchesse du (1676–1753). Granddaughter of *Condé, wife of Louis XIV's legitimated son. Her court at Sceaux was a brilliant centre of social and cultural life, frequented by *Voltaire and *Fontenelle among others; it is well described in the memoirs of *Staal-Delaunay.

MAINE DE BIRAN, Marie-François-Pierre Gont(h)ier de Biran, known as (1766–1824). Philosopher and statesman. A moderate royalist, he served in the king's guard before escaping the Terror to devote himself to philosophical study. Elected to the Conseil des Cinq-Cents and, later, the Chamber of Deputies, he held various public posts from the Directoire through to the *Restoration.

In 1802 Biran's *Influence de l'habitude sur la faculté de penser* won first prize in an essay competition sponsored by the *Institut. This marked the beginning of a philosophical career which saw him develop beyond the sensationalist epistemologies of *Condillac and the *Idéologues towards an original synthesis between passively felt sensation and actively generated perception. In the *Mémoire sur la décomposition de la pensée* (1805) and subsequent writings, Biran posits a distinction between the 'outward' experience of sense-impression and the 'inward' experience of self (*sens intime*), arguing that the latter, through willed endeavour (*effort voulu*) and its associated perceptions, constitutes a rich source of primary knowledge. His evolution towards an increasingly spiritual conception of human nature was marked by growing belief in the existence of a divine force, free will, and moral responsibility. His *Journal intime* is a fine example of French introspective writing.   [JS]

Mains sales, Les. Play by *Sartre, first performed 1948. It confronts a political pragmatist (Hoederer) with a moral idealist (Hugo) in a situation which ends in the death of both protagonists. The play focuses on the problems within the Communist Party in the imaginary state of Illyria towards the end of World War II. Hoederer's stance of compromise leads to his assassination by the young bourgeois party-neophyte Hugo, who is later put to death himself by the Party when Hoederer's murder becomes a source of political embarrassment. Sartre claimed his preference was for Hoederer's situational ethics, but public sympathy went to Hugo, and the play was interpreted as anti-Communist. In consequence, Sartre banned its production for several years.   [CMH]

MAINTENON, Françoise d'Aubigné, marquise de (1635–1719). Second wife of *Louis XIV. Granddaughter of Agrippa d'*Aubigné, she married the crippled *Scarron. After her husband's death she was protected by Madame de *Montespan, looking after her royal children, and eventually supplanted her in the king's favour. He married her secretly in 1683, and it was largely under her influence that his court became devout. She played some part in public affairs behind the scenes, but devoted most attention to the school she founded at *Saint-Cyr for poor girls of good family. It was for Saint-Cyr that she commissioned *Racine to write 'trois mille vers de piété', *Esther* and *Athalie*. She left an interesting correspondence, which has been much admired.   [PF]

Maires du Palais (Mayors of the Palace). Under the *Merovingian kings these were the heads of the royal household. They became increasingly powerful, virtually ruling the kingdom after the death of Dagobert I in 639. Charles Martel, the victor of the battle of Poitiers, was a mayor of the palace; his son, Pépin le Bref, founded the *Carolingian dynasty after a palace *coup* in 751.

MAIRET, Jean (1604–86). French dramatist. Born in Besançon, Mairet began his education there, and later studied in Paris. As a young man he became attached to the household of the duc de Montmorency, which led to friendship with *Théophile de Viau, also protected by Montmorency, while the Italian duchesse de Montmorency encouraged an interest in Italian drama. Mairet wrote 12 plays (including tragedy, tragicomedy, comedy, and *pastoral). All were composed quite early in his long life, his last play (*Sidonie*) being performed *c.*1637. His second play, the pastoral tragicomedy *La Sylvie* (performed probably 1626, published 1628), was one of the most successful in that mode, and in its setting and characters is typical of the genre, although with some distinctive features such as a magical element in the plot and, in the third scene, a celebrated 80-line dialogue in cross-rhymed couplets between the shepherdess heroine Sylvie and an unwanted suitor.

Maison de rendez-vous, La

Another pastoral tragicomedy, *La Silvanire* (performed 1630, published 1631) was in its published form accompanied by a preface in which Mairet recommends, on grounds of *vraisemblance* and contemporary taste, the adoption of the unities of action, time, and place. He writes with particular reference to comedy, although indicating at several points that the same 'conditions' apply to tragedy. Three years later his tragedy *Sophonisbe* (1634) reintroduced regular tragedy to France, respecting both the unities and *bienséance*. The subject had been treated by others and was later to be used by *Corneille and *Voltaire. In Mairet's version Syphax, the elderly husband of the Numidian queen Sophonisbe, is conveniently killed between Acts I and II, in battle against the Romans' Numidian ally, Massinissa. Sophonisbe immediately marries Massinissa, and both hope that he will be able to protect her from the Romans. Sophonisbe takes poison (the gift of Massinissa) to escape captivity, expressing noble defiance, and Massinissa commits suicide over her body. Mairet comments in the dedication of the play that audiences were moved to tears by the lovers' deaths.

Mairet was very active in the Querelle du *Cid*; indeed, he launched the Querelle by an offensive poem addressed to Corneille in the voice of the Spanish author of Corneille's source. Perhaps it was Corneille's growing reputation (particularly after *Horace*, performed 1640) that caused Mairet to abandon the theatre. He became a diplomat, representing the Franche-Comté at the French court, and eventually retired to Besançon. [GJ]

See G. Dotoli, 'Statut du héros de Jean Mairet', in M. de Rougemont *et al.* (eds.), *Dramaturgies, langages dramatiques: mélanges pour Jacques Scherer* (1986).

Maison de rendez-vous, La, see ROBBE-GRILLET.

Maison des jeux, La, see SOREL, C.

Maison de Sylvie, La, see THÉOPHILE DE VIAU.

Maison du peuple, La, see GUILLOUX.

Maisons de la Culture. The opening of Maisons de la Culture from the early 1960s onwards in certain key urban centres throughout France (and also in overseas territories) was the symbolic culmination of the post-war drive to democratize and decentralize French cultural life. When André *Malraux was put in ministerial control of cultural affairs in 1959 cultural development became part of the central planning process. Malraux saw the Maisons de la Culture as institutions which would make the important works of the world's cultural heritage available to the largest possible number of French people. The creation of the Maisons de la Culture was closely allied with, and indebted to, the movement of *décentralisation théâtrale*, which had exemplified the democratic cultural ideals of a whole post-war generation. In a broader sense, the idea of

Maisons de la Culture was part of the Utopian dream of cultural democracy promoted by the *Popular Front in 1936.

Although the Maisons de la Culture were given multi-purpose facilities, it was theatre that was at the heart of their work of cultural creation and diffusion, not least because theatre was considered to offer the aesthetic and spiritual communion that Malraux and the high-minded people of the theatre found so obviously lacking in the rapidly growing domain of the mass media. In this respect, it is important to remember that the Maisons de la Culture came into existence just when television was entering the homes of most French people. Malraux opened the first Maison de la Culture in Le Havre in 1961, and by 1973 there were 12 in total. After this date no more were built. They soon proved to be cumbersome and excessively expensive institutions. Serious financial problems led to constant crisis, and in some cases finally to closure. Long before this, however, they had been shown not to be fulfilling their aim of reaching uneducated people. In *May 1968 they came under special attack, as the democratic idealism that underpinned the creation and operation of the Maisons de la Culture was denounced as bourgeois oppression and mystification. In later years they rationalized and diversified their activities and became more responsive to local needs. In addition, a national network of more modest Centres d'Action Culturelle was formed. [BR]

'Maison Tellier, La'. Comic story of a brothel by *Maupassant; it gave its name to a collection of tales.

MAISTRE, Joseph de (1755–1821). The most influential theorist of the Counter-Revolution. Fleeing his native Savoy in 1792 when the armies of Revolutionary France invaded, he pursued a diplomatic career, spending many years in Russia. His thought was closely attuned to the spirit of his violent times. In his writing, the *Revolution became at once a satanic, destructive event and a collective act of expiation, a blood sacrifice, presaging national regeneration. Disdaining the idea of individual freedom and roundly condemning what he considered the unholy negations of the *Enlightenment, Maistre disinterred a chilling *Ultramontanism which he incorporated into a cosmic theodicy. A great stylist, he penned memorable pages on the necessity of suffering and war, and on the centrality of the public executioner, whom he viewed as the cornerstone of a stable hierarchical society. Maistre is at his best in his polemical *Considérations sur la France* (1797). His belief in papal infallibility is articulated in *Du pape* (1819). His extended reflections on language, history, and Providence constitute his highly influential *Les Soirées de Saint-Pétersbourg* (1821). Maistre's Catholic royalism, with its rejection of the notion of individual rights, was to haunt those who in 19th-c. France worked to achieve an accommodation between Christianity and modernity. His thought is an essential component of the authoritarian tradition of the French Right; it also exercised a considerable influence on *Baudelaire.

[CC]

MAISTRE, Xavier de (1763–1852). Novelist and brother of the above. He served in the forces of Sardinia and later in the Russian army. His literary reputation rests upon his prose fiction, especially *Voyage autour de ma chambre* (1794).

Maître de la parole, Le, see GRIOT; LAYE.

Maître de Santiago, Le (1947). In this *Montherlant historical drama on a Spanish theme, Don Alvaro Dabo, master of the Order of Santiago, judging that Spain is destroying her honour in pursuit of riches in the Americas, refuses to go there, even when it becomes clear that his daughter's marriage and happiness depend on it. In the end, he and his daughter dedicate themselves to religion, in a scene of mystical exaltation. This powerful play contrasts with the *Claudelian concept of the Catholic heroism of the *Counter-Reformation; its own form of heroism lies in nobility, Stoicism, and almost fanatical renunciation. [RMG]

Maîtres sonneurs, Les, see SAND.

MAJOR, André (b. 1942). Canadian novelist and poet who was originally associated with the *Parti pris* group. His early works, *Le Cabochon* (1964) and especially *La Chair de poule* (1965), exemplify the literary programme of the group by showing the blighted lives of working-class characters and using *joual and disjointed literary form to prod the bourgeois reader into political awareness. Shortly afterwards he broke with the group and in the rest of his work adopts a more distanced form of social criticism. The fictional trilogy entitled *Histoires de déserteurs* (1974–6) offers a bleak picture of the stagnation of Quebec bourgeois society, without drawing explicit conclusions. The emphasis is rather on the literary complexity and formal elaboration of the three novels, often described as Faulknerian both in their handling of time and in the sense of fatality which pervades them. Essentially the same approach is to be found in *La Folle d'Elvis* (1981) and *L'Hiver au cœur* (1987). [SIL]

MAKHELE, Caya (b. c.1945). Congolese writer. He is editor and a regular contributor to the review *Équateur*, and runs a series devoted to new writing at the Autrement publishing house. Active for a long time in Brazzaville literary circles, he co-wrote the play *Le Coup de vieux* in 1982 (with his close friend *Sony Labou Tansi) and published his first novel, *L'Homme au fardeau*, in 1988. [DRDT]

MAKOUTA-MBOUKOU, Jean-Pierre (b. 1929). Prolific Congolese writer since 1970 of novels, poetry, essays, and literary criticism. In an adventurous output of uneven quality, his best-known work is perhaps the violent tale of a quest for vengeance, *Les Dents du destin* (1984). [PGH]

Malade imaginaire, Le. Three-act *comédie-ballet by *Molière, first performed 1673. Argan, a hypochondriac whose failing is exploited by his rapacious second wife Béline, vetoes the marriage of his daughter Angélique to Cléante because he wants a doctor for a son-in-law. His choice falls on the pedantic Thomas Diafoirus. Argan's brother Béralde and his servant Toinette join forces to thwart both the marriage and the designs of Béline on her husband's money. By making Argan counterfeit death, they expose his wife's callousness and his daughter's real affection for him; Béralde then convinces Argan to become a doctor himself in order to satisfy his desire for constant medical attention. The play ends with a ballet representing a burlesque admission ceremony of a doctor into the Faculty of Paris. On the fourth performance of the play Molière collapsed on stage and later died. [IM]

MALAVAL, François (1627–1719). French poet and religious writer, blind from early childhood. He published devotional works close to *Quietism, and quasi-mystical *Poésies spirituelles* (1671).

Mal court, Le (1947). Comedy by *Audiberti.

Maldoror, see LAUTRÉAMONT.

Mal du siècle, Le. The spiritual sickness of *Romanticism. The Romantic self felt displaced, exiled; the *mal du siècle* was the manifestation of an alienated subjectivity seeking to unite with something greater than itself. It produced disillusionment, melancholy, and a weariness with life; but also feelings of violence and aggression. According to *Chateaubriand in *Le Génie du christianisme*, the malady arose on account of the discrepancy between the true object of human desire, which was the infinite, and the terrestrial goals which human beings could actually achieve. But it was also a condition which testified to the uncertainties of the new world ushered into being by the Revolution. In the case of Chateaubriand it sprang, at least in part, from the concerns of an aristocracy which had been displaced from its leading role. For the later generation of *Vigny, *Musset, and *Quinet, the experience was different and was related to the loss of hope represented by the collapse of the imperial dream. Dissatisfaction with the present involved not only melancholy but also impatience with the world as it was, with the obstacles which were placed against the fulfilment of desire. The *mal du siècle* was the most serious symptom of the general Romantic crisis in belief and reflected a broader quest for meaning and purpose in the universe. [CC]

MÂLE, Émile (1862–1954). French art historian. Rejecting the prevailing emphasis on formal analysis and purely descriptive iconography, Mâle explored the sources, subject-matter, and symbolism of art from the Middle Ages to the 17th c., and brought out the moral and spiritual motives underlying its modes of representation and changes in style. In his pioneering work *L'Art religieux du XIIIe siècle* (1898) he traced the connections between art, literature, religious practices, and secular history, stressing the encyclopedic nature of medieval art and, notably, of the great cathedrals, which ordered and made visible the knowledge and beliefs of the time. [REG]

MALEBRANCHE, Nicolas (1638–1715). Catholic philosopher, the most important French thinker of the later 17th c. In his work the opposition between faith and reason, often considered irreducible, is overcome. Much indebted to *Descartes (the rigour of the argumentation in *L'Homme*, which he picked up by chance in 1664, deeply impressed him), he was no less influenced by the Augustinian tradition of the *Oratorians, among whom he spent his life as a priest. Gentle but resolute in character, he developed his philosophy in a series of restatements and answers to objections.

The best general exposition is in the *Entretiens sur la métaphysique* (1688). His first and probably most widely read work, *De la recherche de la vérité* (1674–5), has a manifestly Cartesian title and plan, being in outline a guide to the avoidance of error and defining truth in mathematical fashion. It also puts forward his best-known philosophical theory, that of 'la vision en Dieu'. The *Traité de la nature et de la grâce* (1680), which brought Malebranche into conflict with *Jansenism, interprets the miraculous as the result of God's general laws of nature. *Arnauld attacked especially the argument that pleasure is a true form of happiness; the *Traité* was eventually banned by the Vatican. The *Traité de morale* (1684) is notable for its affirmation of a rational 'ordre immuable' in ethics, which in principle allows the exact calculation of degrees of value. In Malebranche's works of apologetics the reconciliation of faith and reason is particularly clear; hostile critics (among them *Bossuet) saw this as rendering faith unnecessary.

Both 'la vision en Dieu', which is a theory of perception, and Malebranche's theory of causality, that of 'causes occasionnelles', address problems arising from the rigid Cartesian division between mind and matter, or thought and extension. To the question of how the mind, which is immaterial spirit, can perceive material objects, Malebranche replies that it is through communication with the divine mind, which contains the ideas of all created things. The doctrine of occasionalism explains analogously how the immaterial mind, by willing, causes a material thing, the body, to move. According to Malebranche, matter can be moved directly only by God's infinite power. What happens when a human act of will is followed by a bodily movement is that the willing is the 'occasion on which' God causes the body to move.

Another example of Malebranche's theocentrism, or emphasis on God (which distinguishes him from Descartes), is his view of motivation. He held that we desire the good that is universal, namely God, in all our desires for limited and specific goods. Such views gave his rational Christianity an appeal verging at times on the mystical and resembling that of *Fénelon. His contemporary influence was very considerable; as regards the 18th c., it still awaits full assessment. One significant case is *Montesquieu's definitions of justice as a 'rapport de convenance' and laws as 'rapports nécessaires', phrases typical of Malebranche's ethical thought. [CJB]

See H. Gouhier, *La Philosophie de Malebranche* (1926); G. Rodis-Lewis, *Nicolas Malebranche* (1963).

MALESHERBES, Chrétien-Guillaume de Lamoignon de (1721–94). A member of the *Lamoignon dynasty, he was Directeur de la Librairie (i.e. the book trade) from 1750 to 1763. His even-handed and tolerant administration won him the praise of the *philosophes; he looked kindly on the *Encyclopédie and protected *Rousseau. Having defended Louis XVI before the Convention, he was guillotined. [PF]

MALET, Léo (b. 1909). French song-writer, anarchist, a *Surrealist in the 1920s and 1930s, Malet turned, on release from wartime captivity, to initially pseudonymous crime fiction ('Frank Harding') and to historical romance. *120, rue de la Gare* (1943) introduced Nestor Burma, the irreverent, irrepressible 'détective de choc', who featured notably in the unfinished *Nouveaux mystères de Paris* (1954–9), set in 15 of the 20 *arrondissements*: *Le Soleil naît derrière le Louvre* (1954), *Boulevard . . . ossements* (1957). His *Trilogie noire*: *La Vie est dégueulasse* (1948), *Le Soleil n'est pas pour nous* (1949), *Sueur aux tripes* (1969), brings together all aspects of his work. [SFN]

MALFILÂTRE, Jacques-Charles-Louis de Clinchamp de (1733–67). Poet from Normandy who, after a brief success with his ode 'Le Soleil fixe au milieu des planètes', failed to make his way in Paris; *Gilbert's line 'La faim mit au tombeau Malfilâtre ignoré' brought him his posthumous celebrity. His translations of Virgil and his long mythological poem *Narcisse ou l'île de Vénus* (1769) show an original gift for melodious verse. [PF]

MALHERBE, François de (1555–1628), reformer of French poetry, was born at Caen, and studied at Basle and Heidelberg. Converted to Catholicism, he went to Aix-en-Provence as secretary to the governor, Henri d'Angoulême; he spent the years 1577–86 and 1595–1605 in Provence, the intervening years in Caen. In 1587 he presented to Henri III 'Les Larmes de Saint Pierre', a florid, manneristic poem which he later excluded from the canon of his work. In

1600 he recited his 'Ode à la reine sur sa bienvenue en France' at the reception given to Marie de Médicis in Aix; on the strength of this poem, *Du Perron drew Henri IV's attention to Malherbe's talent in the courtly heroic vein. Not until 1605, however, was he attached to the court, and, although his position as official poet continued unchallenged during the regency and under Louis XIII, wealth never came his way.

Malherbe's 'doctrine'—imparted at seminars held in his lodgings— can be reconstituted, chiefly from his caustic annotations on the poetry of *Desportes. He demands at the outset coherence and clarity of thought, then a careful adequation of expression to substance, an evenness of tension such that the reader is neither puzzled by complication nor defrauded by superfluity of words. This rhetorical basis is to be complemented by observance of current polite usage. Nor is it enough to avoid cacophony: hiatus and *enjambement are proscribed, the caesura must be regular, rhyme must be exact, rich when possible, and facile matchings avoided. The same distrust of facility led Malherbe in his own work (understandably limited in quantity) to avoid long sequences of alexandrines in favour of stanzaic forms, in which he sought above all to adapt the sentence-structure rhythmically to the metre.

*Boileau later wrote in his Art poétique: 'Enfin Malherbe vint.' Malherbe's 'reform', with its insistence on craftsmanship, was in fact the culmination of a process begun long before him. None the less, by sheer impact of personality he gave form and force to what had been only a trend, and the new orthodoxy thus set up proved all the more enduring through its coincidence with a certain stabilization of the French language. Not until the 1620s, though, was his pre-eminence assured, particularly with the publication of the Recueil des plus beaux vers des poètes de ce temps (1627), containing mainly poems of his own or by his acknowledged disciples.

His emphasis on reason and usage made of Malherbe a 'modern', and he was brusquely dismissive of *Pléiade humanism. *Ronsard came to seem aberrant, with his creative freedom and his ambition to bridge the gap between his own world and that of the Greeks. The imprint of Rome, on the other hand, remained indelible on two traditions very influential in Malherbe's time: *rhetoric and *Neostoic philosophy. His conception of high poetry is essentially rhetorical, and his outlook on life basically Stoic (he translated several works of Seneca). The well-known 'Consolation à M. du Périer' argues from the impermanence of life and the demoralizing effect of sentimentality (as distinct from natural feeling) towards a rational assent to the divinely willed order of nature, and a resolution to turn necessity into virtue.

As court poet, Malherbe could not but lend his talent on occasion to furthering the amorous designs of Henri IV among others. But when the monarch is perceived not merely in baroque fashion as a demigod, but as the God-given saviour of a sorely troubled nation, a vein of genuinely patriotic poetry, pro bono publico, opens up. From this angle, Malherbe appears in retrospect as Ronsard's heir in spirit, and even to some extent in form (with his revival of the ten-line lyrical strophe). In the handful of poems he wrote in this vein, of which the 'Prière pour le roi allant en Limousin' (1605) is the most impressive, Malherbe reaches the height of his eloquence, drawing on classical, but especially on Old Testament, material to strike a resounding prophetic note.

In another late poem he memorably develops the opening verses of Psalm 145 into a disenchanted dismissal of the vanity of the world, royalty and all. At heart, despite his notorious gruffness and mordant wit, Malherbe was a vulnerable man, as his correspondence reveals, particularly his letter to his wife on the death of their daughter in 1591. [AJS]

See R. Fromilhague, Malherbe: technique et création poétique, and La Vie de Malherbe, 1555–1610 (1954).

MALLARMÉ, Stéphane (1842–98). French poet in verse and prose, patron saint of the *Symbolist movement, and essential reference-point for countless later writers, artists, and theorists. From *Valéry to *Sartre, *Blanchot, and *Bonnefoy, and from *Surrealism through *OULIPO to *Derridean deconstruction, Mallarmé's work has come to represent a nec plus ultra of the self-absorbed literary imagination. Academic critics have responded to the famous obscurity or 'difficulty' of his writing with a multitude of competing interpretations, and in the process have conferred upon his slender corpus of poems an atmosphere of strenuous cerebration. Yet if Mallarmé is read without undue regard for this daunting posthumous reputation he often seems strikingly direct in his address to the reader. He writes about sexual desire, parenthood, and friendship, about ceremonious social conduct and the anxieties of the isolated individual, about the ordinary life of the senses and the daily presence of pain and death in human affairs. The arresting diction in which he handles these fundamental experiences is at certain times plain and lucid, and has at others an air of ecstatic incantation.

Outwardly, Mallarmé's life was not crowded with incident. His father and maternal grandfather were civil servants, and he himself, upon completing his lycée education in Sens, embarked upon a series of modest appointments as an English teacher; these took him to Tournon, Besançon, Avignon, and eventually back to Paris, his birthplace. His domestic life with Maria Gerhard, to whom he was married in 1863, was tranquil, though occasionally disturbed by financial difficulties and periods of ill health. The story of Mallarmé's ruling passion for literature, however, is altogether more eventful. By the age of 12 his literary career was launched, and from his mid-teens he was a voracious reader of modern poetry. *Gautier, *Hugo, *Baudelaire, and

Mallet du Pan

*Poe all had a profound impact upon his developing craft, and throughout the period of his apprenticeship he had a circle of close friends who understood and nurtured his single-minded artistic enthusiasm. Bereavement had a special role in his literary career: his mother died when he was 5, and his second child, Anatole, at the age of 8 in 1879; as his poetic masters disappeared one by one, and were commemorated in a sequence of verse 'tombeaux', loss and mourning came to occupy a central place in his writing. His sonnet 'Quand l'ombre menaça de la fatale loi' (1883), perhaps the finest of his elegiac works, is at once a requiem for all dead artists and a heroic celebration of his own creative gift. For Mallarmé, poetry was an exemplary act of resistance in a dark and godless world.

Mallarmé was a writer's writer who embodied an entire spectrum of attitudes to the verbal medium. At one extreme, literature was, or was to become, the supreme mechanism for making the world intelligible. The epistemological claims of literature were akin to those of science and philosophy in so far as it sought knowledge of the true nature of things, but literature outstripped these kindred disciplines in that it alone recapitulated and re-enacted within itself—or in the supreme Book that it foreshadowed—the creativity of the cosmos. This exalted vision, together with the generous encouragement he gave to the younger writers who sought his advice and, from 1880, attended his mardis, made Mallarmé into an almost priestly figure. But at the same time he was a jobbing writer for whom the pen had many worldly and potentially lucrative uses. He compiled a fashion journal (La Dernière Mode, 1874) and a number of school textbooks (including Les Mots anglais, 1877, and Les Dieux antiques, 1880); he was a translator, a reporter, a reviewer, a loyal and energetic correspondent, the author of lectures, tributes, and addresses, the master-confectioner of messages in verse to accompany Easter eggs and glacé fruits.

There is no contradiction, for Mallarmé, between these different styles or intensities of verbal performance: the frivolous-seeming journalism that he wrote as 'Miss Satin' or 'Marguerite de Ponty' contains brilliant set-pieces in praise of the great couturier's structural audacity, and 'serious' philosophical works like 'Prose pour des Esseintes' (1884) or the picture-poem Un coup de dés jamais n'abolira le hasard (1897) are alive with word-play and ingenious conceits. The learned etymologies that he catalogued, and occasionally invented, for his school pupils reappear, charged with a new intensity of meaning, in the elaborate faceting of his verse.

A clear line of development may be traced from such early works as 'Les Fenêtres' (1863) or 'Brise marine' (1865), in which Baudelaire's presence is everywhere visible, through the middle-period poems in alexandrines (e.g. the eclogue 'L'Après-midi d'un faune', 1876; two sections of the dramatic poem, Hérodiade, 1876–87), in which Mallarmé

found his distinctive density of expression, to elliptical late works in octosyllables such as 'A la nue accablante tu' (1895). Mallarmé moves gradually from a semi-allegorical narrative manner towards a style that brings together a host of criss-crossing metrical, syntactic, and acoustic pathways. Yet these are differences of degree, not kind, for all Mallarmé's poems, early and late, hesitate between consecutive and simultaneous methods of textual organization—between the desire to go somewhere, in story or in argument, and the desire to explore the layered and interconnected elements that any one moment of perception comprises. The characteristic sensation that his verse, and to a lesser extent his prose (see Divagations, 1897), affords is that of stable structure being pursued in a semantic force-field which constantly threatens to overwhelm it. Images suggesting an underlying or an overarching principle of order in the universe—a constellation in Un coup de dés, a genus of ideal flowers in 'Prose pour des Esseintes', a bird's triumphant flight in 'Le Vierge, le Vivace et le Bel Aujourd'hui' (1885)— emerge from within busy verbal textures that speak of chance, contingency, and fragmentation. This tension between the possibility and the impossibility of poetry continues to make Mallarmé's work provocative and topical, more than a hundred years after its first appearance in print.   [MB]

See J.-P. Richard, L'Univers imaginaire de Mallarmé (1961); E. Noulet, Vingt poèmes de Stéphane Mallarmé (1965); G. Millan, The Throw of the Dice: The Life of Stéphane Mallarmé (1994).

MALLET DU PAN, Jacques (1749–1800). Born in Geneva and editor of the Genevan Journal historique et politique, this anti-republican writer began his career by attacking the *philosophes and ended it by conducting an anti-Revolutionary campaign from London, where he was editor of the Mercure britannique from 1798 to 1800. He had previously edited the *Mercure de France, in which he passionately defended constitutional monarchy as the spokesman of the *Feuillants. In exile he moved between Switzerland, Belgium, and England. His most notable single work was Considérations sur la nature et la durée de la Révolution en France (1793).
                                                                                      [BR]

MALLET-JORIS, Françoise (pseud. of Françoise Lilar) (b. 1930). Born in Antwerp, the daughter of Suzanne *Lilar, she is a member of the Académie Goncourt and the Prix Fémina jury. Her first novel, Le Rempart des béguines (1951), describes the sentimental education of its heroine, who, through a lesbian relationship with an older woman, learns to free herself from illusions. Male delusions are pursued in L'Empire céleste (1958) and Dickie-Roi (1980). Divine (1991) traces the revolution in a woman's life when she decides to lose weight. Two biographies of Marie Mancini (1964) and Jeanne Guyon (1978) reassess women historically misunderstood. Lettre à *moi-même* (1963) describes her quest for God, whilst *La Maison de papier* (1970) raises the problem of conflicting demands for the writer. [EAF]

MALLEVILLE, Claude de (1597–1647). French poet. A founder-member of the Académie Française and contributor to the *Guirlande de Julie*, he was a typical representative of the new *salon poetry, comparable to *Voiture in his sonnets and rondeaux.

Malone meurt (1951). Novel by *Beckett, the second in a trilogy beginning with *Molloy*.

MALONGA, Jean (1907–85). Congolese novelist. He was successively seminarist, bank clerk, and male nurse before being elected *député* to the French National Assembly in 1946. He was later head of Congo National Broadcasting. Both Malonga's novels appeared in 1954. *Cœur d'aryenne* deals with interracial love, and is an appeal for racial harmony. *La Légende de M'foumou Ma Masono* depicts an exotic Africa tailored to the taste of the European reader of the 1950s. *Cœur d'aryenne* was widely acclaimed when it appeared, its success stemming more from the nature of the subject-matter than from the work's literary qualities. [FNC]

MALOT, Hector (1830–1907). Writer of children's stories, whose novel *Sans famille* (1878) is one of the great popular classics of French culture. The moral and didactic adventure story of the boy Rémi, a foundling who goes in search of his own identity, has struck deep chords in generations of readers and is still much read. [BR]

MALRAUX, André (1901–76). French novelist, politician, and art critic. Malraux's life and work are closely tied to the history of his century. Born at its beginning, reaching adolescence with World War I, he gained a reputation as an adventurer when he embarked in 1923 on a dubious enterprise in Indo-China. From here, however, he witnessed the beginnings of the Chinese revolution as well as involving himself in the problems of colonial French Cambodia. During the 1930s he was a prominent anti-fascist, and in 1934 went with *Gide to Berlin to petition Goebbels. In 1936 he was again at the centre of events when he commanded an air squadron fighting on the Republican side in the Spanish Civil War. In World War II he served first in a tank unit and then, after his capture and escape, in the Resistance. After the war he shifted away from the Left, abandoning any sympathy with Communism and becoming a strong personal admirer of de *Gaulle. When de Gaulle gained power, he made Malraux minister for information (1945–6) and later the first minister for cultural affairs (1959–69). In this role Malraux created the *maisons de la culture and initiated the cleaning of many of Paris's most famous monuments. He supported de Gaulle at the time of the events of *May 1968 and followed him in his fall from power in 1969.

Malraux's personal life was marked by a series of tragic deaths and by the difficulties he experienced in maintaining close relationships over a sustained period. The themes of death and of the near impossibility of human relations mark his fiction deeply. His parents separated when he was 4, and he was brought up by his mother and aunt. His grandfather committed suicide in 1909; his father was to do the same in 1930 (both deaths are fictionalized in a number of Malraux's texts). In 1921 he married Clara Goldschmidt, who later described their life together in her memoirs. In 1936 he separated from Clara and set up home with Josette Clotis, with whom he had two sons. In 1944 Josette fell under a train and died; both Malraux's brothers had also died during the war. In 1948 he married his elder brother's widow, Madeleine, with whom he lived until 1965. His two sons by Josette were killed in a car accident in 1961. From 1966 he lived with the poet and writer Louise de *Vilmorin, until her death in 1969.

He began writing essays and short stories in the 1920s, heavily influenced by the contemporary movements of *Cubism, *Dadaism, and, to a lesser extent, *Surrealism. His short stories bore titles such as 'Lunes en papier' (1921) and 'Royaume farfelu' (1928); both these texts are strongly marked by the satirical and the grotesque, but also introduce the themes of death, destiny, and the futility of action which reappear throughout his work. Two essays of this period, *La Tentation de l'Occident* (1926) and *D'une jeunesse européenne* (1927), describe European civilization as in crisis: the death of belief in God has been followed by the death of belief in Man; the West's entire metaphysical system, which pays lip-service to the ideals of action and individualism, has consequently been cut off from its foundations and conceals a fundamental absurdity. The only possible attitude to this state of affairs is complete lucidity; this is the point from which the heroes of his first two novels, Les *Conquérants* (1928) and *La *Voie royale* (1930), start out. These texts, in which the adventurer heroes endeavour to stretch individualism to its limits in what they know to be an impossible attempt to defeat death itself, are sometimes seen as Malraux's period of Nietzschean temptation. In the following group of three novels, *La *Condition humaine* (1933), *Le Temps du mépris* (1935), and *L'*Espoir* (1937), the characters may recognize the absurdity of their own existence, but new values and solutions beyond the individual begin to emerge. All three novels combine the presentation of a contemporary political situation (the Chinese revolution in *La Condition humaine*, the rise of fascism in Hitler's Germany in *Le Temps du mépris*, the Spanish Civil War in *L'Espoir*) with a metaphysical analysis of 'the human condition'—the title of this novel could stand for all Malraux's work. Death, the passage of time, old age, physical incapacity, social constraints, the individual's own past, all combine in Malraux's novels to form the weight of a destiny which only fraternity, human dignity, and the sacrifice of individual interests to a greater cause can begin to alleviate. Yet Malraux once described his aim as being to 'donner aux hommes quelques images de la grandeur humaine', and it can be argued that the lyrical force of certain scenes in his texts ultimately does impose this vision. His last novel, *Les Noyers de l'Altenburg* (1943), poses the possibility of art as a force against destiny, a theme implicit in some of his early work.

Malraux's growing belief in the power and significance of art dominated his production from the late 1940s onwards. Between 1947 and 1949 he published the three volumes of reflections on painting entitled *Le Musée imaginaire*, *La Création artistique*, and *La Monnaie de l'absolu*. These make up *La Psychologie de l'art*, modified and retitled in 1951 as *Les Voix du silence*. Essays on sculpture (*La Musée imaginaire de la sculpture mondiale*, 1952–4), on Goya (*Saturne*, 1950), and on Picasso (*La Tête d'obsidienne*, 1974) followed. In 1967 he published a highly unconventional volume of autobiography, appropriately entitled *Antimémoires*, and an account of his last meeting with de Gaulle in *Les Chênes qu'on abat* (1971). *Lazare* (1975), his last publication in his lifetime, is part autobiography, part an essay on death. *L'Homme précaire et la littérature* (1977) discusses his literary preferences.

Malraux died in 1976, not, like his protagonists, in the thick of battle, but in a hospital bed. 'La mort transforme la vie en destin', he had written in 1930 in *La Voie royale*. It is surely his destiny to be considered as one of the most powerful and lucid writers of his century. [EAF]

See C. Jenkins, *André Malraux* (1972); J. Lacouture, *André Malraux* (1973); W. Langlois, *Via Malraux* (1986).

Mamelles de Tirésias, Les. Play by *Apollinaire, produced 1918; the prologue contains the first use of the word 'sur-réalisme'.

MAMMERI, Mouloud (1917–89). Algerian novelist, ethnologist, and essayist, a native of Kabylia. Mammeri's reputation in Algeria cannot be measured solely by his relatively small literary output, for he is revered by the Kabyles and Berbers across the Maghreb as a defender of their civil and political rights and as a custodian and promoter of their cultural values.

He was educated first at the local primary school and then in Rabat (Morocco), Algiers, and Paris. During World War II he fought for the French and the Allies in Algeria and in Europe. In 1957, at the height of the *Algerian War, he went to Morocco, returning to Algeria after independence was won in 1962. He taught at the University of Algiers and directed a research centre at the Bardo Museum, later founding and directing a research centre for the study of Berber culture in Paris.

Mammeri published only four novels, two anthologies of Berber poetry, a Berber grammar, and a handful of plays, stories, and essays on Berber culture, the latter having been collected posthumously in a volume entitled *Culture savante, culture vécue: études 1938–1989* (1991). His first two books are 'ethnographic novels' depicting local mores familiar to the author's countrymen but instructive, even exotic, to European readers. *La Colline oubliée* (1952) is a novel about growing up in a small Kabyle town and the first encounters with the colonial world, and *Le Sommeil du juste* (1955) recounts a young man's emancipation first from the narrow culture of his village and then from the impact of the colonial educational system. *L'Opium et le bâton* (1965) describes the questioning and the adventures of an Algerian doctor, against the backdrop of the Algerian War; the arena is vaster here than in the first two books, the style and vision more open. Finally, *La Traversée* (1982) is a poetic fable: a small group crosses the Sahara, a 'crossing' which assumes different symbolic functions, from a simple travel adventure to the historical evolution of Algeria and to the recapitulation of the protagonist Mourad's life, which comes full circle as he returns, ill and disillusioned, to die in the *djemaa*, or public square, of his native village. [ES]

See M. Mortimer, *Mouloud Mammeri, écrivain algérien* (1982).

MANCHETTE, Jean-Patrick (b. 1942). Author of several works of crime fiction (many of them filmed) in the new-style *polar* manner [see DETECTIVE FICTION], of which he is one of the principal exponents. His work blends the strands of American hard-boiled detective fiction with a post-*May 1968 vision of an entirely corrupt bourgeois world. Echoes of contemporary political events, such as the *affaire Ben Barka*, can be found in his books, of which *L'affaire N'Gustro* (1971), *Nada* (1972), *Morgue pleine* (1973, also published as *Polar*), *Fatale* (1977), and *La Position du tireur couché* (1981) are among the best known. He is also a critic, screen-writer, and author of *bandes dessinées*. [IWR]

Mandarins, Les. Novel by Simone de *Beauvoir which won the Prix Goncourt in 1954. It is a long, rich, and complex text intertwining two narratives, the first presented in the third person and focused through Henri, a writer and journalist, and the second a first-person narrative voiced by Anne, a psychotherapist. Both present the political and moral dilemmas of the French left-wing intelligentsia in the immediate post-war period in France (1944–8), struggling with their own attitudes to the Communist Party, with the shock of the news of Hiroshima and of the existence of the Soviet labour camps, with the problem of meting out justice to ex-collaborators, and with the issue of the relative priorities to be accorded to literature and politics. The central question of the nature of the relationship between political efficacy on the one hand and morality on the other is constantly returned to.

Paralleling these dilemmas is the problem of choice within the heterosexual couple. Both Anne and Henri make difficult personal choices, but whereas Henri emerges with renewed strength, Anne is left contemplating suicide. Beauvoir's first novel after *Le *Deuxième Sexe*, it exhibits an acute awareness of Anne's problems as wife and mother.   [EAF]

Mandat, Le, see SEMBÈNE.

MANDEVILLE, Jean de (*c*.1300–1372). Travel writer. Although writing in French, the author claims, probably fictionally, to be English and to have started his journeys in 1322; some evidence suggests he may have lived in Liège. Except perhaps for his description of the Middle East, his *Voyages* (*c*.1356) are highly derivative; rather than a record, this is a summary of the known world, real and imaginary. Geography, fauna, and especially people and customs are described with real intellectual curiosity and remarkable tolerance; his contention that the earth is round may well have influenced Columbus. His style is lively and very readable, perhaps explaining his immense popularity: more than 300 manuscripts, 90 editions, and translations into 10 languages.   [JHMT]

MANDIARGUES, André Pieyre de (1909–91). A tangential figure in post-war Paris *Surrealism, Mandiargues specialized in elegant fictions about disturbing erotic experiences, minutely tabulated and often involving scenes of sacrifice and exacting ritual reminiscent of *Sade or *Bataille. The early fantasias of *Le Musée noir* (1946) exploit a thematics of perverse encounters and bloody struggles in the dark. The less sombre *Le Lis de mer* (1956) celebrates the almost metaphysical aura of anonymous sex, as the heroine alluded to in the title arranges for her own deflowering on a nocturnal shore in Sardinia. The interaction of desire and external setting dominates Mandiargues's imaginings, as in the novel *La Marge* (1967), set in the feverish alleys of Barcelona's red-light district, or the story 'La Marée' (1971), whose hero times his climax to coincide precisely with high tide. A connoisseur of the *outré*, Mandiargues devoted essays (*Le Belvédère*, 1958; with further vols. in 1962 and 1971) to the Gothic novelist Charles Maturin and the Surrealist artist André Masson, as well as to such personal discoveries as the monstrous Baroque sculptures at Bomarzo in Italy or the modern graffiti he copied down in the park at Versailles. His salute to *Histoire d'O.* (1954), a pornographic classic signed by the pseudonymous Pauline de Réage, may be tongue-in-cheek, given that he is widely suspected of complicity in its composition.   [RC]

MANDRIN, Louis (1725–55). French brigand, whose combats with the hated tax-collectors made him a Robin Hood-like folk-hero, often coupled with *Cartouche. He was broken on the wheel; his edifying death is the subject of the popular 'Complainte de Mandrin' ('Nous étions vingt ou trente . . .').   [PF]

Manekine, La, see PHILIPPE DE BEAUMANOIR.

MANET, Édouard (1832–83). One of the most important painters of the 19th c., Manet combined a deep awareness of pictorial traditions and practices, a commitment to the representation of contemporary reality, and a willingness to experiment with every aspect of the painter's art. His modern subjects and technical innovations (summary brushwork, bold colour, informal composition) challenged the entire academic tradition and were of decisive importance for the *Impressionists. *Baudelaire encouraged his commitment to modernity and *Zola applauded his sincerity and defence of pictorial values against the literary subject-matter of academic painters, but it was *Mallarmé who most clearly recognized the extent to which his fundamental revision of the aims and means of painting opened the way to future developments.   [JK]

MANICOM, Jacqueline (1935–76). Born into a large rural family of East Indian origin in Guadeloupe, Jacqueline Manicom qualified in midwifery, and played an important role in family planning and the feminist *Choisir* movement. The semi-autobiographical *Mon examen de blanc* (1972) charts a black woman doctor's sexual and political liberation. *La Graine: journal d'une sage-femme* (1974), set in a large Parisian maternity hospital, amplifies the plea for women's rights through case-histories of poor, often immigrant, mothers and sketches of Caribbean junior staff.   [BJ]

Manifeste des 121, Le, see ALGERIAN WAR.

Manifeste des Cinq, Le, see TERRE, LA.

Manifeste du surréalisme, by *Breton, see SURREALISM.

Mannerism. A term used to indicate art understood less as the expression of a substantive content of thought or emotion than as a demonstration of the artist's inventiveness in creating variations on a received norm—which may themselves become clichés and so compose from individual 'manners' a period style. A mannerist art usually arises from the exploitation of suggestions already present in a preceding organic or 'classical' phase, and answers a social (usually courtly) need for decoration or entertainment. The term is applied primarily to the late-Renaissance shift from the equilibrium of a Bramante or a Raphael towards effects of surprise, multi-focal interest, movement, distortion, or stylized elegance—an aesthetic which spread into France mainly through *Fontainebleau. Its application to literature remains controversial, particularly when used to characterize a period. Beginning in the later 16th c., however, there are certainly features in French literature that can be related (not

493

always reduced) to a mannerist aesthetic—persistent refining on *Petrarchan paradoxes, play with figures such as antithesis, tours de force with conceits or with sound effects, intricacies of plot in tragicomedy, the pastoral, or the novel. *Preciosity may be seen as a late outcrop. [AJS]

Manon Lescaut. This short novel, whose full title is Histoire du chevalier des Grieux et de Manon Lescaut (1731), appeared as the final volume of *Prévost's Mémoires d'un homme de qualité. It is the story of the chevalier's love for Manon, who sets a life of pleasure above physical fidelity. Des Grieux resorts to progressively graver crimes to obtain money for her. When Manon is deported to America she does come to reciprocate his love, but this chance of happiness vanishes with her death. We see events only through the self-justifying narrative of Des Grieux. Manon herself has become an exemplar of faithless women who inspire an overwhelming passion.
[VGM]

MANSART, Francois (1598–1666). French architect. Mansart designed distinctively French buildings, many of them private houses in Paris. Innovative in design, unusual in form, but severe and classical in mood, always for intelligent bourgeois patrons, Mansart's work was admired by *Voltaire. Jules Hardouin-Mansart (1646–1708), his great-nephew, displayed more theatrical tendencies at *Versailles.
[JPC]

MANSEL, Jean (1400–c.1473). Burgundian author of the immense Fleur des Hystoires (1467), an ambitious compilational history of the world in four books running from the Creation to the reign of Charles VI. Sources are heterogeneous: the Bible, hagiography, Latin histories, and even an abridged *Girard de Roussillon. [JHMT]

MANSOUR, Joyce (1928–86). Poet. Born in England of Egyptian parents, she was a leading member of the post-war *Surrealist movement. There is a strongly sado-masochistic element in her work. Some of her poetry can be found in Rapaces (1960), which has a quite individual note of feline savagery.
[GDM]

Manuscripts.

1. Medieval

The manuscripts that transmit medieval French literature are extremely varied. They range from small, undecorated, inexpensive productions—possibly designed, in some cases, for use by itinerant performers—to large-format, lavishly illustrated books commissioned by members of the high aristocracy. Some contain but a single text, though many are anthologies; the latter range from extremely diverse miscellanies to carefully organized collections of a single author or literary genre. The earliest surviving example of Old French poetry is the Séquence de *sainte Eulalie, transcribed in a Latin manuscript of the late 9th c. Only a modest number of manuscripts written in French have survived, however, from before the 13th c., at which time vernacular manuscript production increased significantly. It was not replaced by the printing press until the 16th c.

One important category of Old French manuscripts is the chansonnier, which may be devoted to the songs of the *troubadours or *trouvères, to motets, or to compositions in the lyric *formes fixes. Only a small fraction of troubadour songs are preserved with music, but most chansonniers in the langue d'oïl [see LANGUE D'OC] include musical settings. Anthologies of the trouvères and troubadours are usually arranged by author, often with conventionalized author portraits. In addition, troubadour manuscripts commonly contain the prose *vidas (biographies of the poets) and razos (narrative explanations of the genesis of a given song). These texts provide commentary, albeit fictional, on the poems and create a vivid sense of the authorial persona. The incidence of variant readings among the various manuscripts of a given song is extremely high for both the troubadour and the trouvère corpora. This state of affairs can be attributed to the fact that the earliest surviving chansonniers post-date the earliest songs by over a century. The texts that have come down to us thus reflect the accumulated effects of variations introduced by performers and perhaps by scribes during a period of largely oral transmission. The phenomenon of textual variation is generally known by the term mouvance, made standard by Paul *Zumthor.

Narrative anthologies, though sometimes miscellaneous, are often governed by thematic or generic considerations, resulting in anthologies of saints' lives, of *fabliaux, and so on. Collections of texts on a given topic are sometimes arranged in such a way as to create a chronological progression throughout the manuscript. *Chansons de geste, for example, are typically compiled into large narrative cycles. Similarly, compilations of the *romans d'antiquité provide an extended romance coverage of ancient history, sometimes completed by examples of Arthurian *romance. As in the lyric tradition, narrative texts are subject to mouvance. Some variants no doubt derive from a practice of oral reading or recitation, reflecting a performer's efforts to adapt the text to his or her audience; others can be attributed to scribal error. In many cases, however, scribes themselves exercised editorial functions, choosing to expand, abridge, or otherwise modify the texts they copied. Copyists might even consult more than one manuscript of a text, preparing a composite version.

The path from manuscript to modern edition entails numerous problems that must be solved by the editor. Discussion of editorial practices is generally expressed in terms of a debate between two schools of textual criticism, identified with the great philologists Joseph *Bédier and Karl Lachmann respectively. The Bédieriste editor favours a conservative edition of the manuscript judged as best—or even parallel editions of every surviving manuscript—on the grounds that this method reproduces an authentic medieval text and not a hypothetical re-creation. The Lachmannian editor, on the other hand, aims for a reconstruction of the original text that would have given rise to the existing manuscript versions, arguing that the words of the author are to be preferred, whenever possible, over those of copyists. Many editors seek a middle path between these two extremes, balancing an effort to identify and correct errors and scribal alterations against a need to present a text that accurately reflects the surviving manuscripts. The characteristics of a given text—the number, date, and quality of its manuscripts and the extent of variation among them—are crucial in determining the procedures best suited to its edition.

Scribal editorial work was not limited to the compilation of anthologies and the transcription of a faithful or altered copy of the text. Scribes also had to decide where to introduce breaks in the text by means of enlarged ornamental initials, sometimes containing narrative illustrations. Some copyists employed a hierarchical system of initials of different sizes and degrees of ornamentation in order to indicate a range of divisions and subdivisions within the text. Scribes also devised programmes of rubrication, ranging from terse indications of the title or the main topic addressed in individual sections to lengthy explanations in verse or prose. Rubrics of the latter sort provide a running commentary that guides the reader through the text. With long texts, such as the *Roman de la Rose* or the *Perceforest*, rubrics might be recopied at the beginning of the manuscript to form a Table of Contents.

Scribes were also involved in the illustration of manuscripts, since it was up to them to leave spaces for miniatures; and the rubrics that served as captions for the illustrations may have served as a guide to the artist. The choice of whether or not to illustrate a given text, however, would be informed by a variety of factors, including not only the judgement of the scribe but also that of workshop artists, as well as the wishes of the patron, his or her financial resources, and the availability of models from which miniatures could be copied. Some texts, such as the *Roman de la Rose* and *Guillaume de Degulleville's Pelerinage de vie humaine*, quickly developed standard iconographic programmes, although individual manuscripts do show some variation and an individual artist could always choose to create new images. Many texts, however, never developed a standard iconography, and the choice of which passages to illustrate and how to represent a given scene may vary widely from one manuscript to another.

It is not until the 14th c. that one finds substantial evidence for the involvement of vernacular authors in manuscript production. Earlier examples do exist. *Gautier de Coinci clearly conceived his Miracles de Nostre Dame (1214–27) as an illustrated compendium; but as a monastic poet he would have had both the education and the resources to oversee manuscript production. Aristocratic poets similarly possessed the means of acting as both author and patron, exerting some control over the written production of their works; examples of this phenomenon are *Joinville's exposition on the *Credo* (1250–1), clearly conceived as an illustrated text, and the songs of *Thibaut de Champagne (1201–53), which, according to the *Grandes Chroniques*, were written down at his instigation. In the 14th c., however, there are manuscripts devoted to the works of a single non-noble author and evidently compiled with at least some degree of supervision by the author: e.g. the collected *dits* of *Watriquet de Couvin and the more diverse anthology codices of Guillaume de *Machaut, Jean *Froissart, and *Christine de Pizan.

Manuscripts are a source of information about the interests and reactions of medieval readers, recorded in marginal annotations. The most common annotation is 'Nota', which generally identifies proverbs or moral teachings; from this practice it is clear that medieval readers placed a high priority on a text's didactic content, and that they responded to the use of proverbs and formulaic discourse. The indication 'Nota' could, however, also be used to mark humorous passages that parody sententious discourse. More elaborate glosses, though not common in vernacular manuscripts, are occasionally used to identify historical figures; to cite Latin sources or analogues; to enter a proverb that serves to comment on the text; or simply to record a personal reaction such as agreement, surprise, or sorrow. From the number of Latin glosses it is clear that the audience for vernacular literature was by no means limited to the unlettered.

The evidence of library inventories, colophons, inscriptions, and wills confirms that manuscripts of Old and Middle French literature were owned by men and women of the aristocracy, the bourgeoisie, and the clergy, as well as by ecclesiastical and university libraries. Through a study of the many features of the manuscripts—organization, textual variants, illustrations, rubrication, annotations, and patterns of ownership—one can trace not only the history of the book in the pre-printing era, but also the reception and interpretation of French literature by generations of medieval readers.   [SJH]

See A. Foulet and M. B. Speer, *On Editing Old French Texts* (1979); S. Huot, *From Song to Book* (1987); J. Lemaire, *Introduction à la codicologie* (1989).

2. Post-Medieval

Even after the generalization of printing, manuscripts continued to be widely used in certain circumstances for the transmission of literary works. Manuscripts circulated in the *salons [see PRECIOSITY]. The great majority of Latin plays written and performed in *Jesuit colleges in the 17th and

18th centuries exist only in manuscript. Similarly a work such as père Houbigant's 'Traité des études' circulated in manuscript copies in the *Oratorian colleges. A particularly important development was the use of manuscripts for the circulation of subversive writing [see CLANDESTINE MANUSCRIPTS]. [PF]

Manuscrit trouvé à Saragosse, see POTOCKI.

MAQUET, Auguste (1813–88). French novelist. Principal collaborator of *Dumas *père*, Maquet wrote drafts and provided historical information for him to rework in his many *romans-feuilletons*, including the most celebrated. After their partnership came to an acrimonious end, Maquet wrote serialized fiction under his own name (*La Belle Gabrielle, Le Comte de Lavernie*, both 1854–5). [BR]

Maquis. Term originally referring to rough country in Corsica, used of the bands of Resistance fighters in rural areas during the German *Occupation of France in World War II.

MARAN, René (1887–1960). Poet and novelist, born of Guyanais stock in Martinique. His father was in the Colonial Service and moved to Gabon, whence the young child was sent at 7 years of age to be educated in Bordeaux. Life for the black schoolboy was not easy (see his novel *Le Cœur serré*, 1931), but he developed well and mixed with the young literati, publishing in 1909 his first volume of poetry, *La Maison du bonheur*, which reveals a debt to Henri de *Régnier. During his 13 years in Africa from 1910 he wrote *Batouala*, which won the Prix Goncourt in 1921. The book created a rumpus and roused strong criticism of Maran for his description of conditions in Ubangui Chari and his plea for African culture. Acclaimed as the father of *négritude*, he has been condemned by others for being more a 'Frenchman with a black mask' (his own conflict is reflected in *Un homme pareil aux autres*, 1947). A lifelong and unflinching worker for the African cause, he contributed to the bimonthly *Les Continents*, wrote documentaries on Africa (e.g. *Le Tchad*, 1931), animal novels with an African setting written in a highly poetic style (e.g. *Bacouya le Cynocéphale*, 1953), biographies (e.g. *Livingstone*, 1938), and a number of collections of poetry. During the 1920s and 1930s his Paris home became a meeting-place for Afro-Caribbean writers. Maran kept a low profile, but his influence was considerable. [KCC]

MARANA, Gian-Paolo (1642–c.1693). Genoese emigrant to France, now accepted as the author of a multi-volume series of letters published (1684–97) in French and English under various titles, and usually known in France as *L'Espion turc*. Often reprinted, it provided the framework and some ideas for the *Lettres persanes*. Mahmut is supposedly an agent of the Ottoman emperor who reports back from Paris, in the years 1637–82, on political and other events; he has correspondents elsewhere in Europe. His political opinions are very pro-French (Marana's patron was an ambassador for *Louis XIV), but eclectic and unorthodox on religion. [CJB]

MARAT, Jean-Paul (1744–93). A physician and indefatigable intellectual, born in Neuchâtel, whose pre-Revolutionary activity demonstrated both professional and broad philosophical interests and who, not unlike *Linguet, crossed swords with all and sundry with little concern for personal repose. Politically active early in 1789, Marat began to broadcast his radical democratic principles even more widely with his *Publiciste parisien* (12 September 1789), which became, five issues later, *L'Ami du peuple* and which lived vigorously, with two changes of title (*Journal*—then *Publiciste*—*de la République française*) until Marat's death. Always incendiary in defence of the popular revolution (though no more violent than many royalist adversaries), he was constantly one of the most powerful (for some, loathed and frightening) men of the whole period: though often notable for good sense and political astuteness, *L'Ami du peuple* became, above all, synonymous with accusation and denunciation, with the notion that pre-emptive strikes or purges of named individuals or groups 'hostile' to the Revolution made good political sense. Marat had a wide, devoted following among the ordinary people and the radical bourgeoisie (whom he also represented in the Convention), who looked upon him as their oracle and tribune. Assassinated by Charlotte *Corday (13 July 1793), he became a Republican martyr. [JR]

MARCABRU (*fl. c.*1130–*c.*1156). *Troubadour who worked in Spain as well as at the courts of Poitiers and Toulouse. He knew *Jaufre Rudel, and possibly *Cercamon, *Bernart de Ventadorn, and *Peire d'Alvernhe. Marcabru's identity is unknown, the name being a pseudonym, but his detailed knowledge of the Bible and the Church Fathers, together with a striking command of rhetoric, suggest he was a clerk. Intensely polemical, his work is savagely ironic, frequently obscene, and often slanderous. The majority of his songs are virulent satires or parodies, entertaining but obsessive attacks on the immorality of the aristocracy and other troubadours. He deplores the birth of illegitimate children and is unusually misogynistic, even by medieval standards. A key figure in the development of the conventions of *fin'amor*, Marcabru was also influential in the evolution of troubadour style [see TRO-BAR CLUS]. The combination of outspoken criticism of courtly society with exceptional poetic talent secured him notoriety well after his death; in later texts he is virtually the only early troubadour mentioned by name. Apart from numerous satires, Marcabru wrote one of the earliest *tensos*, the first *pastorela*, and the famous *Vers del Lavador* (1149), in which he advocates participation in the *reconquista* in Spain rather than the Crusade in the Holy Land. [SG]

MARCADÉ, Eustache. 15th-c. author of the *Passion d'Arras* [see PASSION PLAYS].

MARCEAU, Félicien (pseud. of Louis Carette) (b. 1913). Novelist, essayist, and dramatist of Belgian origin whose work, whether in the form of novels such as *Les Élans du cœur* (1955) and *Creezy* (1969, Prix Goncourt) or plays such as *L'Œuf* (1956), explores the conflict between the individual and social ritual. [EAF]

MARCEL, Gabriel (1889–1973). Christian philosopher, drama and music critic, and playwright. Marcel's independent thinking anticipated and influenced the development of existential *phenomenology in France. Concerned with the mysteries of incarnated being and of 'being-with-others', Marcel attempted to recover, through a higher-order reflection, the immediacy of concrete experiences such as those of existing, possessing, and belonging (*Être et avoir*, 1918–33), and of fidelity, hope, and anxiety (*Homo viator*, 1945). His earlier plays dramatized the psychological aspects of metaphysical and spiritual tensions (*Un homme de Dieu*, 1925); he later explored their more ideological implications (*Rome n'est plus dans Rome*, 1951). [REG]

MARDRUS, Dr Joseph-Charles-Victor (1868–1949). Author of the modern translation of the *Arabian Nights*, under the title *Mille nuits et une nuit* (1898–1904) [see MILLE ET UNE NUITS].

Mare au diable, La (1846). One of George *Sand's rustic novels. The widowed farmer Germain is urged to remarry an eligible widow of a neighbouring village; he heads there with his eldest son and Marie, a poor girl off to her first job. Becoming lost, they spend the night by a haunted pond; Germain falls in love with Marie. The widow turns out to be shallow and pretentious, and Marie's new employer tries to seduce her. She flees, returns to their village with Germain, but refuses for some time to admit that she reciprocates his love. Of particular interest is the Appendix which offers a detailed portrait of marriage customs in provincial France before the Industrial Revolution. [FPB]

MARÉCHAL, Sylvain (1750–1803). French dramatist and publicist whose early works—for which he suffered—hinted heavily at the atheism he would later preach openly. An early *Jacobin, he was ardent in the popular cause from 1789 to 1794; he wrote for various periodicals (e.g. *Les Révolutions de Paris*), though the main thrust of his production was still in the area of atheistic thought (*Dieu et les prêtres*, 1790, etc.). Predictably, he played an important if still badly understood role in the dechristianization movement. His best-known works—produced to promote the popular cause—date from 1793: his *Jugement dernier des rois* (now seen as the masterpiece of the *sans-culotte* theatre, foreshadowing *Adamov or Mayakovsky) is an exalted prophecy of

universal republican victory despite the then-dark days of foreign invasion, counter-revolution, and civil war, while his opera, *La Fête de la Raison* (music by Grétry), depicts the abjuration of a patriotic priest and makes a noteworthy attempt to fuse opera and the *fête révolutionnaire*.

After Thermidor he went through a period of disorientation until meeting *Babeuf, then played an important, if shadowy, part in the Conspiration des Égaux (1796), when he was a member of the Secret Directory, charged with drafting the *Manifeste des Égaux*. Inexplicably the authorities overlooked these treasonable activities and Maréchal ended his career obscurely, but as active as ever in producing atheistic literature (*Dictionnaire des athées*, 1800). [JR]

Maréchale d'Ancre, La, see VIGNY.

Maréchaussée, La, see POLICE.

MARESCHAL, André (*c*.1603–*c*.1650). French dramatist and novelist. His plays range from unselfconsciously irregular tragicomedies—his preface to *La Généreuse Allemande* (1630) is a powerful defence of aesthetic freedom—to comedies of considerable importance. His *Inconstance d'Hylas* (performed 1630) was the first French comedy to concentrate on character rather than plot, and *Le Railleur* (performed 1635) is an innovative modernization of the Italian comic tradition. His most original work is his novel, *La Chrysolite* (1627), which combines biting social satire with a study of emotional instability rarely matched in novels of the century, and whose important preface explores the aims of *vraisemblance* in fiction. [GJM]

MARGUERITE DE NAVARRE (also known as **MARGUERITE D'ANGOULÊME** or **D'ALENÇON**) (1492–1549). Born in Angoulême, daughter of Charles d'Angoulême and Louise de Savoie, she received the same humanist education as her younger brother, the future *François Ier. She was married in 1509 to Charles d'Alençon (d. 1525), then in 1527 to Henri d'Albret, king of Navarre. Her daughter, Jeanne d'Albret, was mother of the future Henri IV. Throughout her life she was intimately involved in the political life of France, particularly in the period following François Ier's captivity in Spain (1525–6). There were periods when she found it prudent to take refuge in her own kingdom of Navarre because of her religious views (e.g. after the Affaire des *Placards in 1534). She was strongly influenced by the archbishop of Meaux, Guillaume *Briçonnet, and the *Evangelical group around him. Passionately interested in the ideas of *Luther and *Calvin, she protected some of the leading Reformers—such as *Lefèvre d'Étaples—and was the patron of writers like *Marot, Bonaventure *des Périers, and *Rabelais.

She was a prolific writer, leaving a voluminous correspondence and numerous poetic and dramatic works, though her most lasting achievement is

Marguerite de Savoie

undoubtedly the cycle of 72 tales known as the *Heptaméron*. Her poetry is mostly religious and often mystical, comprising *rondeaux*, the *Chansons spirituelles*, and many long allegorical meditations. One of her earliest works of this type, *Le Miroir de l'âme pécheresse* (1531), was banned by the *Sorbonne in 1533. A large body of her poetry was published in the *Marguerites de la Marguerite des Princesses* and the *Suite des Marguerites* (1547), including *La Coche*, a dialogue on perfect love. Some important works remained in manuscript until the 19th c. (e.g. two long poems—*Les Prisons*, describing the progressive liberation of the human soul; *Le Navire*, a monologue evoking her distress at the death of François Iᵉʳ). Her plays include secular pieces with a strong moralistic content, such as the *Comédie jouée à Mont de Marsan* or the *Farce de Trop, Prou, Peu, Moins*, and the more specifically religious four-part *Comédie de la nativité de Jésus-Christ*.

Though Marguerite's writing reflects her involvement in *Renaissance humanism, *Neoplatonism, and Evangelism, her choice of genres and use of allegory look back to the Middle Ages. As much as for her literary achievements, she is noteworthy for her role as a political figure and as a protector of major Evangelical writers and thinkers. [CMSJ]

See P. Jourda, *Marguerite d'Angoulême, duchesse d'Alençon, reine de Navarre (1492–1549). Étude biographique et littéraire*, 2 vols. (1930, repr. 1978).

MARGUERITE DE SAVOIE (1523–74). Daughter of *François Iᵉʳ, queen of Philibert-Emmanuel de Savoie. She wrote poems and encouraged the poets of the *Pléiade.

MARGUERITE DE VALOIS (1553–1615), daughter of *Henri II and *Catherine de Medicis, married Henri de Navarre (later *Henri IV) in 1572. In 1583 they were separated, and the marriage was annulled in 1599. She then moved to Paris, and became an influential patroness of letters, as well as an author of poetry and memoirs in her own right. She was known affectionately as 'la reine Margot', and was the subject of several scurrilous pamphlets. [IM]

Maria Chapdelaine. Novel by *Hémon, evoking the hard yet beautiful pioneering life in northern Quebec. Maria, daughter of an indefatigable settler, is in love with the adventurous fur-trader François Paradis. After his death in the wild and the death of her mother, she rejects the chance to move to the comfortable south and marries her peasant neighbour Eutrope Gagnon, remaining true to the family vocation. The novel, simply written with some use of rural Canadian speech, appeared in France in serial form and then as a book in 1916. After some resistance, it became a mythical text of 'la survivance' for French Canadians [see SAVARD]; since the 1950s its message has been regarded with more suspicion. [PF]

Mariage de Figaro, ou la Folle Journée, Le. *Beaumarchais's dynamic, fast-moving sequel to *Le*

Barbier de Séville. Three years have passed. Almaviva is married to Rosine and, though jealous of her fidelity, freely indulges his own sensuality. The gracious comtesse still loves her husband, though—suffering cruel neglect—she is stirred by vague 'romantic' longings. Figaro, now the caretaker of the castle and the comte's *valet de chambre*, loves Suzanne, the comtesse's chambermaid. The comte has agreed to their marriage and has promised them a fine bedroom between his own and the comtesse's. Suzanne knows, however, that the generosity hides ulterior motives. The plot concerns, therefore, these rival claimants for the vivacious Suzanne: on the one hand, Figaro with his native wit and intelligence; on the other, the comte with all the advantages of birth and authority but who is—for our greater amusement—constantly thwarted; the young page Chérubin (fast becoming an embryonic Almaviva) is in love with the comtesse and further complicates the general situation by making the comte jealous. The denouement comes when the comtesse, masquerading as Suzanne, meets the comte after dark at the trysting-place her maid had arranged with him: the comte is exposed to the ultimate but emotionally useful indignity of courting his own wife. Unmasked, he can no longer hinder the marriage of Figaro.

The comedy, completed in 1781, was performed (with immense success) only in 1784, not because of Beaumarchais's incessant rewriting but because Louis XVI, shocked by the play's constant disrespect for authority, blocked its performance, thereby giving it exaggerated (retrospective) claims to revolutionary subversiveness, which it does not really have. Figaro the 'frondeur' is probably less interested in destroying the established order than in becoming part of it. [JR]

Mariamne, La. Tragedy by *Tristan L'Hermite, first performed 1636. The upstart king Hérode sees in a terrifying dream the shade of Aristobule whom he has had drowned, the brother of Mariamne his wife. This Maccabean princess, wed for political reasons, but for whom Hérode is now besotted with love, hates and despises her husband. Phérore and Salome resentfully persuade their brother Hérode that she is plotting to kill him, but moved by her noble grief for her children he is ready to spare her, when a false suspicion of adultery fires his jealousy and ensures her execution. The final act shows Hérode maddened by remorse.

*Hardy and *Voltaire also wrote plays on this subject. [AJS]

Marianne. Female symbol of the *Republic. The name originated in the *Revolution, and was at first used pejoratively (with possible connotations of prostitution) by enemies of the new order; since then Marianne has been represented in many guises, which are traced in M. Agulhon's *Marianne au combat* (1979).

MARIE-ANTOINETTE, Queen (1755–93). Daughter of the emperor of Austria, she married the future Louis XVI in 1770. Her love of pleasure and devotion to the interests of her native country made her widely unpopular, and she was the target of scurrilous pamphlets. Having encouraged her husband to resist reform and revolution, she was put on trial and guillotined nine months after him.

MARIE DE FRANCE (*fl.* second half of 12th c.) is commonly assumed to be a woman writer from the Île-de-France who lived in England and perhaps wrote at the court of Henry II Plantagenet. More precise identification of Marie with a historical person is disputed. The name 'Marie' appears in three works attributed to the same author, the *Lais*, the *Fables*, and (with less certainty) the *Espurgatoire seint Patriz*. Judging from these texts, Marie was an educated person of the nobility who knew Latin, English, and French, was well-versed in classical culture as well as popular traditions, was a sensitive observer of social and amorous problems, and a sophisticated, self-conscious artist. Many readers, medieval and modern, have assumed that the author was a woman; some have seen in the writings a woman's distinctive perspective upon love, social relationships, and courtly literature.

Marie's *Lais* (written between 1160 and 1178) rank among the best-loved works of medieval literature. Extant wholly or partly in five manuscripts, of which one alone contains all 12 stories, these brief tales in rhymed octosyllabic couplets are inspired by and named after the songs, or **lais*, sung by Bretons to commemorate an extraordinary or dramatic event, an *aventure*. In the Prologue, Marie states her desire for poetic originality: she chooses not to translate from Latin, because so many others have done so, but to remember the *lais* she has heard. With stylistic economy, thematic complexity, and symbolic richness, the *Lais* recount the sufferings of lovers who struggle, often unsuccessfully, against social constraints. The *Lais'* Breton setting mixes feudal reality with other-worldly fantasy. The *merveilleux* often intrudes in the form of fairies and magical animals, objects, or plants, but it never distorts the human dimension of the lovers' plight.

Incorporating diverse sources and multiple perspectives, Marie's tales are irreducible to a single moral or theme. *Guigemar*, whose unhappily married heroine is ultimately united with the eponymous hero, shows a debt to Ovid and the **romans d'antiquité*; *Equitan*, where the adulterous couple conspire to kill the husband and are ultimately punished, prefigures the materialism of the **fabliaux*. An unfaithful wife who schemes against her werewolf husband gets her due in *Bisclavret*, a variation of a beast fable. The Arthurian court is the backdrop for the knight's betrayal of his fairy mistress in *Lanval*; courtly conventions are parodied in *Chaitivel*. Symbolic objects or animals often emblematize the lovers' plight and provide poetic fulfilment in the place of real-life solutions: in *Deus Amanz* a flowering mountainside commemorates the magic potion spilled by a lover who dies as he carries his lady to the summit. In *Laüstic* the lady embroiders her story in a cloth to shroud the nightingale that her jealous husband has killed, and she then sends the relic to her lover. In *Yonec* the lover himself takes the form of a hawk who flies through the window to visit an unhappy wife until he is treacherously killed. In *Milun* the bird motif reappears in a swan who carries the lovers' messages, allowing the constant couple to be reunited with their son after the jealous husband has died. The briefest *lai*, *Chevrefoil*, recounts a poignant episode of the **Tristan legend; the longest, *Eliduc*, portrays the plight of a man betrothed to two women, who is saved through the altruism of the first wife. Sympathy between women is also remarkable in *Fresne*.

The *Fables* or *Ysopet* (the generic name for fable collections in the Middle Ages), which appear to have been written after the *Lais*, are 103 brief narrative poems, **exempla* for moral instruction that Marie claims to be translating from an English source. Some 40 fables correspond closely to a Latin adaptation of Aesop; the others have diverse origins. Protagonists include peasants, knights, and ladies, as well as beasts. A distinctive authorial style conveys sharp observations of social injustice. Their concise moral endings are often ironic or obliquely related to the tale. The *Espurgatoire seint Patriz*, based on a Latin text and possibly Marie's last work, casts the voyage of a knight, Owein, to the underworld as a chivalric adventure.

The recent revival of critical interest in Marie's work suggests that she fulfilled her intention, implied in the *Lais'* Prologue, to put wisdom and eloquence to good use in the creation of distinctive, subtle texts that encourage her readers to add the 'surplus' (or additional meaning) of their own interpretation.   [RLK]

See E. Mickel, *Marie de France* (1974); P. Ménard, *Les Lais* (1979); H. Spiegel, *The Fables* (1987).

MARIE DE MÉDICIS (1573–1642). Queen to *Henri IV after his divorce from *Marguerite de Valois in 1600 and regent from 1610 to 1617.

MARIE STUART (Mary Queen of Scots) (1542–87), daughter of James V of Scotland and Marie de Guise, became queen at six days old, was educated at the French court, and married the dauphin (the future François II) in 1558. After the death of *Henri II (1559) she was also queen of France until her husband's death 18 months later. In 1561 she returned to a turbulent Protestant Scotland where she married Darnley (1565), by whom she had a son, later James VI and I; soon after Darnley's murder (1567) she married Bothwell. Mary was imprisoned in England for 19 years by her cousin Queen Elizabeth and executed in 1587.

As a girl she had been idolized by the French

court; a poet herself, she was praised by *Ronsard, *Baïf, *Buchanan, and *L'Hôpital for her gentleness, wit, and beauty (evident in *Clouet's portraits) and celebrated by *Brantôme. At times she was the subject of sordid pamphleteering in France, England, and Scotland (notably by Buchanan). Her poems and essays in French, unpublished in her lifetime, include occasional elegiac verses, and religious and philosophical meditations on betrayal and the reversal of fortune; the writing is simple and direct, yet *topoi* and *exempla* abound. Her tragic life, with its real or imagined faults, has been the subject of plays (see *Montchrestien's *L'Écossaise*, 1601), operas, films, and romanced biographies. Mary remains controversial; it is still often difficult to separate historical reality from romantic legend.   [PS]

MARIMOUTOU, Carpanin (b. 1956). Literary critic, literary activist, and poet from Reunion. Marimoutou advocates the exclusive use of *Creole and regards the use of French as a sign of bad faith. *Arracher cinquante mille signes* is his most important collection.   [BEJ]

MARINI, Giovanni Battista (1569–1625). Italian poet who in 1615 took refuge in France, where he was known as 'le cavalier Marin'. His long poem *Adone* (Adonis), written in French, and published in 1623 with a preface by *Chapelain, was much admired. 'Le marinisme' was the name given to a style of poetry characterized by its display of verbal wit.   [PF]

Marion de Lorme (1831). Romantic drama by Victor *Hugo [see DELORME].

MARITAIN, Jacques (1882–1973). France's leading 20th-c. Catholic philosopher. Converted by *Bloy in 1906, he became the major figure in the pre-war Thomist revival. A strong supporter of *Action Française from 1911, Maritain broke with *Maurras after the papal condemnation of 1926. In *Primauté du spirituel* (1927) he attempted to redefine the relationship between politics and the Catholic faith. He thereafter played a major part in the liberal Catholic camp in the 1930s. Opposed to Vichy, he spent the war in America. His importance rests above all on his purely philosophical writings, particularly those which appeared in the 1930s.   [RMG]

MARIVAUX, Pierre Carlet de Chamblain de (1688–1763). Playwright, novelist, and essayist. The son of an administrator, he grew up in the provinces and subsequently lived in Paris. Little is known of his private life. He married in 1717; his wife died six years later, and his one daughter became a nun. Partly ruined by the collapse of *Law's system, he was never well off and died a poor man.

With the exception of one play, *Le Père prudent et équitable*, his early writings were for the most part burlesque parodies of the classics, such as *L'Iliade travestie* (1716) and *Le Télémaque travesti* (published in 1736). He knew little Latin and less Greek, and followed *Fontenelle and *La Motte in their hostility

to the *anciens* [see QUERELLE DES ANCIENS ET DES MODERNES]. He frequented Parisian *salons, notably those of Madame de *Lambert and Madame de *Tencin, both of whom are portrayed in his *La *Vie de Marianne*. Contemporary accounts speak of his witty conversation and his excessive sensitivity to praise and criticism. In 1743 he was elected to the *Académie Française, for which he composed 'Réflexions' on a variety of topics.

He achieved fame, and remains best known, as the author of over 30 comedies (his one tragedy, *Annibal*, was a failure). They were written in almost equal proportions for the *Comédie-Française and the *Comédie-Italienne; many of his most successful parts were written for the Italian players, in particular the leading lady Silvia and Thomassin, who played *Arlequin. One fascinating comedy, *Les Serments indiscrets* (1732) is in five acts, but most of the best-known are in three: they include *La *Surprise de l'amour* (1722), *La *Double Inconstance* (1723), *Le Prince travesti* (1724), *La Fausse Suivante* (1724), *La Seconde Surprise de l'amour* (1727), *Le *Jeu de l'amour et du hasard* (1730), *Le Triomphe de l'amour* (1732), *L'Heureux Stratagème* (1733), *Le Petit-Maître corrigé* (1734), *La Mère confidente* (1735), and *Les *Fausses Confidences* (1737). There are also many one-acters, including *Le *Legs* (1736), *Les Sincères* (1739), and *L'*Épreuve* (1740). A special group is formed by plays on 'philosophical' themes such as the relations between the sexes (*La Nouvelle Colonie*, 1729, and *La *Dispute*, 1744) or between social classes (*L'*Île des esclaves*, 1725); *L'Île de la raison* (1727) exploits in three acts the recent precedent of *Gulliver's Travels*.

The one-act *Arlequin poli par l'amour* (1720) sets the tone for the plays that follow. In a fairy-tale setting, the love of a shepherdess (Silvia) transforms the rustic Arlequin. This popular comic figure appears in many of Marivaux's subsequent plays, where he represents a force of nature—naïve, gluttonous, and attractive—but is increasingly downgraded to the role of foolish servant. In all these plays a constant theme is the discovery of love, in which men and women are brought by the machinations of others to recognize their desires, which have been evident to the spectators all along. The obstacle to love is no longer, as in *Molière, the tyrannical father; the difficulties lie in the hearts and minds of the lovers, which are explored with great subtlety. In spite of a disquieting stress on weakness and irrationality and the bitterness of some of the social observation, the action usually ends reassuringly with a wedding, often a double wedding involving both masters and servants. The subjects are superficially similar, but the tone varies greatly, from the stylized light-heartedness of *La Surprise de l'amour* to the overt cynicism of *La Fausse Suivante* or *Le Legs*, where money plays an important part. Later plays, in particular *Les Fausses Confidences*, show a growing interest in depicting contemporary society.

After early successes, the comedies met with an increasingly hostile reception on the grounds of their supposed obscurity or triviality, and Marivaux devoted more time to journalism, essays, and fiction. From 1717 he had written sketches of Paris life for the *Mercure. Between 1721 and 1724 he published the 25 numbers of Le Spectateur français, inspired by the success of the English Spectator. These are not so much essays as capricious combinations of narrative and moral reflection, often placed in the mouths of fictional narrators and adopting the standpoint of the detached observer. He continued in this vein in the seven numbers of L'Indigent philosophe (1727), where he takes on the persona of a modern Diogenes, and in Le Cabinet du philosophe (1734).

Marivaux's 'journalism' led naturally to the writing of novels. His first piece of fiction had been Les Effets surprenants de la sympathie (1713–14), which was followed by comic works such as Pharsamon (inspired by Don Quixote) and La Voiture embourbée. But his great achievement as a novelist is his two memoir-novels, both published in instalments and left unfinished, La *Vie de Marianne (1731–42) and Le *Paysan parvenu (1734–35). These free-wheeling, digressive texts display most fully their author's gift for combining psychological exploration and moral reflection.

In all his works, Marivaux shows a strong concern for moral and social questions. His views on such matters are personal, but rarely very original. Much of his writing turns on love between the sexes, and shows great sensitivity to the problems of women in contemporary society. He pleads the cause of kindness and fellow-feeling against social arrogance. But he stops short of the radical positions of the *philosophes, for whom he had little sympathy—and the feeling was mutual.

What is most striking is his language. This was constantly criticized by contemporaries as being affected and obscure. He defended his original style against the pressure to conform, claiming that it was more adequate to psychological reality and truer to authentic speech than the standard polite language. Even so, for generations the word 'marivaudage' came to mean, as *Voltaire put it, 'beaucoup de métaphysique, et peu de naturel', and his writings were seen as decorative, frivolous products of the Regency years. Only fairly recently, partly as a result of pioneering theatrical productions by *Vilar, *Planchon, and others, has his language been fully recognized as the medium for the creation of attractive, compelling, and often disturbing images of social and sexual behaviour. [PF]

See J. Rousset, Forme et signification (1962); E. J. H. Greene, Marivaux (1965); F. Deloffre, Une préciosité nouvelle: Marivaux et le marivaudage, 2nd edn. (1967); H. Coulet and M. Gilot, Marivaux; un humanisme expérimental (1973).

MARKALE, Jean (b. 1928) Author of over 30 books on the mythology and folk-tales of the Celtic countries. He has written on the *Grail, King *Arthur, Merlin, Mélusine, the Celtic woman, *Eleanor of Aquitaine, and Vercingetorix. A writer of vast learning and challenging ideas, he insists that the multiplicity of possible interpretations (Éliade, Jung, Freud, the social experience of the peasant, traces of prehistoric religion, etc.) is the measure of the folk tradition's richness. Myth and folklore strike down to deeper meanings than the university's élitist 'literature'. [GDM]

Marly. Country palace between *Versailles and Saint-Germain, built by *Mansart for Louis XIV as a place of retreat from the pressures of court life. 'Être de Marly' was a singular honour for his courtiers. The nearby 'Machine de Marly' was a pump to raise waters from the Seine for lakes, fountains, and cascades.

MARMIER, Xavier (1809–92). French critic, poet, novelist, and travel writer. He came to public attention with the publication of his Lettres sur l'Islande (1837). In 1839 he was appointed to teach foreign literature at Rennes but soon abandoned the university and followed a career as a librarian, notably at the *Bibliothèque Sainte-Geneviève. His case illustrates particularly well *Romanticism's interest in foreign countries and cultures. [CC]

MARMONTEL, Jean-François (1723–99). 'L'enfant gâté de l'Ancien Régime' (F. Aulard), Marmontel enjoyed a highly successful, sociologically interesting career: a poor tailor's son, called to Paris by *Voltaire in 1745, he was one of the first to make of literature a profession, ultimately becoming Historiographe de France (1772) and Secrétaire Perpétuel de l'Académie Française (1783). By his own admission, his lifelong passion was literary theory. His first articles, published in the *Encyclopédie, underwent successive rehandlings (e.g. Poétique française, 1763), and when finally they appeared as Éléments de littérature (1787) they confirmed Marmontel's contribution to the discipline as both distinguished and sometimes prophetic (the work contains developments that *Baudelaire and *Valéry could have called their own; others, without acknowledgement, quite shamelessly did).

Besides being a theorist, Marmontel also participated actively in the *Enlightenment. His internationally successful Contes moraux (1755–65) had made 'la philosophie' and the practice of virtue reassuringly attractive. But it was Bélisaire (1767)—a retelling of the story of the Roman general Belisarius, designed to persuade Louis XV to become the badly needed Philosopher-King—which proved to be his most useful contribution. Chapter 15, containing a plea for the civil toleration of *Protestants, caused a furore involving the *philosophes and the religious establishment which left the government pensive. Provoked by the same affaire de Bélisaire, Les Incas (1767–77), which was to enchant both *Chateaubriand and Mickiewicz with its prose poetry, was in turn another powerful plea for toleration. Though these works, engines of war in the service of suffering humanity, may not suit modern tastes, they helped the cause of Huguenot emancipation. For this reason 'they remain important works' (Jean Fabre).

Recent criticism has re-evaluated Marmontel's career and work, and has recognized the importance of both. Notwithstanding, it is still true that the public will spontaneously read only his *Mémoires* (1792–4), that charming and revealing historical record that he left of his own century which he knew so well: the world of the *salons, the attributes of the *honnête homme*, the numerous personalities of the literary and political establishment. More recently, however, critics have perceived that the *Mémoires* also have a profoundly human value and hence doubly deserve to be read, for they not only reproduce the complexity of the man and of his world, but also mirror the contrasts of the age and of the 'human condition'.   [JR]

See S. Lenel, *Marmontel* (1902); J. Renwick, *Marmontel, Voltaire and the 'Bélisaire' Affair*, (1974); M. Cardy, *The Literary Doctrines of Marmontel* (1982).

Marne, Battle of the. Conflict early in September 1914 at which the advancing Germans were turned back as they approached Paris. The 'taxis de la Marne' were Parisian taxis requisitioned to take troops to the Front.

MAROLLES, Michel de, abbé de Villeloin (1600–81). French translator of many Latin texts, including the New Testament. Of his generally unimpressive prose versions of Latin poetry, the best known were of Martial's epigrams. His *Mémoires* for the period up to 1655 are chatty, self-satisfied literary reminiscences. He was a notable collector, whose prints were the origin of the Cabinet des Estampes at the *Bibliothèque Nationale.   [PF]

MAROT, Clément (1496–1544). Protestant poet, born in Cahors, son of Jean *Marot. Clément moved to Paris when his father became secretary to Anne de Bretagne. He may have studied law, and it is known that he was page to Nicolas de Neufville some time between 1510 and 1519. In 1519 he became *valet de chambre* in the household of *Marguerite d'Alençon (later de Navarre), who was to protect him throughout his life, and in 1526, after the death of his father, he succeeded him as *valet de chambre* to *François Ier. He was imprisoned in the Châtelet in 1526 for breaking the Lenten fast, indicative of his Protestant sympathies. His earliest poems date from around 1515, and his first collection of poetry, *L'Adolescence clémentine*, was published in 1532, followed by the *Suite de l'Adolescence clémentine* in 1533. Forced to flee in the wave of persecution of Protestants following the Affaire des *Placards in 1534, he took refuge firstly with Marguerite in Navarre, and then in Italy, with another French princess of Protestant sympathies, Renée de Ferrare. In 1536, when François Ier declared a general

amnesty for exiled Protestants, he returned to France, solemnly abjuring his errors in Lyon. During a further period at the French court Marot enjoyed considerable literary success, his *Œuvres* being published in 1538. He had been working on his translations of the Psalms for many years, and it was probably the publication of the *Trente psaumes de David* in 1541, coinciding with a renewal of anti-Protestant measures, which led to a second period of exile from 1542 in Geneva, where he was welcomed by *Calvin. He died of the plague in Turin in 1544.

Marot's poetry is immensely varied, both in genre and in tone. Among his early works are a number of long allegorical pieces: e.g. the 'Temple de Cupido', a pure *Rhétoriqueur poem; 'L'Enfer', a curious hybrid of medieval allegory and Renaissance protest, which recounts his experiences in the Châtelet prison; the 'Déploration de Florimond Robertet', a medieval funeral *complainte* used as a vehicle for Protestant theology. They also contain examples of two of the medieval *formes fixes*, ballades and rondeaux. He was perhaps at his best in the *Épîtres*, which he wrote throughout his life. The majority are light pieces, many of them begging-letters to patrons or friends, e.g. 'Au roi pour avoir été dérobé' (a request for money) and 'A son ami Lyon' (a plea to his lifelong friend Lyon Jamet to secure his release from prison). Virtually all the *Épîtres* are in decasyllabic rhyming couplets, but the *coq-à-l'âne*, a sub-species of the *épître*, are ludic, anarchic, satirical poems written in octosyllables. Many of his *Épigrammes*, the best of them wittily satirical, show the influence of classical writers such as Martial. Among them, the two *blasons, 'Du beau tétin' and 'Du laid tétin', which sparked off a *Concours des Blasons*, are very revealing of contemporary attitudes to women. His long plaintive *Élégies* are love poems, though not particularly successful ones. In his own day his supreme lyrical achievement was probably seen as the *chansons* and the translations of the Psalms—songs of love, profane and sacred, their popularity in both cases being enhanced by their musical settings.

Marot was undoubtedly many-sided. On the one hand a frivolous court entertainer—summed up by *Boileau's 'Imitons de Marot l'élégant badinage'—on the other a committed Protestant polemicist. As a poet, he is a Janus-like figure who both looks back to the Middle Ages (his earliest works perpetuate late-medieval poetic traditions, and he edited *Villon and the *Roman de la Rose), and at the same time ushers in the first phase of the French *Renaissance (he translated Virgil, Ovid, and Petrarch, and he may well have been the first to write sonnets in French). He was a witty and sometimes biting satirist, often savagely anticlerical, but with a buoyant confidence in the New Age. Marot was rapidly eclipsed by the *Pléiade, but remained both popular and influential when the Pléiade fell into disfavour in the 17th and 18th c.   [CMSJ]

See C. A. Mayer, *Clément Marot* (1972); R. Griffin, *Clément Marot and the Inflections of Poetic Voice* (1974).

MAROT, Jean (*c*.1465–1526). A *Rhétoriqueur, secretary to Anne de Bretagne from 1506, and *valet de chambre* of François Ier from about 1514. His major works are his verse accounts of Louis XII's Italian expeditions, *Le Voyage de Gênes* (1507) and *Le Voyage de Venise* (1509). His mediocre poetry has survived largely because it was often published with the works of his son Clément [see previous entry].

[CMSJ]

Marriage. A civil contract and a religious sacrament, marriage in old France was intended to continue the lineage, to join together families and fortunes. For the lower orders at least, it was an economic necessity. It was much too important a matter to be left to the children. Affectivity or personal satisfaction had little to do with choice of partners by the parents; 'love' was a term reserved for God and 'tendre amitié' was a bonus in a relationship structured by patriarchal authority and female respect—the latter having definite overtones of fear.

The marriage ceremony would be followed by a feast and dancing, all characterized by a rich variety of local customs much recorded by folklorists. A dowry was normal for the bride, and although it was usually managed by the husband it remained legally the woman's property; a widow was entitled to the return of her dowry and a portion of the inheritance for her subsistence—so family strategies and struggles commonly developed in order to keep such monies in the family. The importance attached to the chastity of the bride and the close moral and physical control of her person show how crucial it was that the legitimacy of progeny be assured if inheritance strategies were to succeed. Clandestine marriages without parental consent could, after an edict in 1557, lead to disinheritance for men under 30 or women under 25 or to annulment for minors, while impediments such as consanguinity, civil and spiritual paternity (guardianship or godparenthood), ecclesiastical status, or impotence would all lead to annulment. Divorce was not possible until 1792, but was restricted by *Napoleon and then abolished under the *Restoration, to be brought back in 1884 only on grounds of adultery, cruelty, slander, and severe criminal sentence. Separation was possible, but for reasons of economic and moral constraint was practised almost solely by the richest and poorest couples; it could lead to divorce only after 1908.

Marriage, therefore, was the strategic union between two kinship networks for mutual economic and 'political' advantage. Consequently, most marriages took place between representatives of families on the same social level, with similar fortunes and often within the same corporate group. A master tailor married a tailor's heiress if possible, a magistrate married the daughter of a colleague, a courtier another courtier, and unequal marriages simply for the sake of money were rare enough to be adversely commented upon. Kinship connections were a favoured route to advancement in society, and marriage meant access to a wider and more useful network.

Most other defining characteristics of unions were dictated by social group, wealth, and cultural geography. The nobility, for instance, married young, at 23–5 years old for men and 18–20 for women, with very young unions quite frequent. Other classes were more constrained by the diminishing prospect of an inheritance large enough to set up and support a household. Therefore, as the population increased and land-hunger developed as rural France slowly changed from a lightly populated state of 16 million inhabitants after the Black Death and *Hundred Years War to the chronicly overpopulated territory of 28 million inhabitants in the late 18th and early 19th c., the average age of first marriage rose accordingly. In 1500 it was about 24 for men and 20 for women; by 1700 it had risen to 26½ and 24½ respectively, and in the late 18th c. reached about 28 for men and 24 for women (where it remained more or less steady until after World War II). Because mortality was so high and life-expectancy so short (38–40 for those who reached adulthood), remarriages were frequent in all classes of society, for one partner might die much earlier than the other. Men found it easier to remarry than older women, but step-parents, wicked or otherwise, were a normal fact of life for many children.

Under the *ancien régime* children tended to die young, a quarter before they reached the end of their first year and a quarter of those remaining before their fifth year—only half reached the age of 20. Mortality was particularly high for foundlings and those whom fashion or economic necessity dictated should be sent to wet-nurses. Each family would have on average five children, and with high mortality the population could increase only slowly. Prospects improved with the demographic revolution of the 19th c.; this consisted largely of a reduction of infant mortality and the control of some diseases. The population, however, rose only slowly to 39 million in the 1870s and stagnated thereafter, as late marriage and contraception (the 'sinful secret' of *coitus interruptus* was apparently discovered by the peasantry from the mid-18th c.) helped family limitation in the countryside. With greater mobility, the rise of cities, and the decline of the strict moral censure associated with small rural communities, there came an increase in cohabitation and illegitimacy.

In the household economy of the *ancien régime* (which continued in most cases throughout the 19th c.), spouses had hierarchically defined roles to play, the patriarch having responsibility for outdoor work, accounts, and discipline, while the wife's tasks were limited to less-valued, though essential ones such as cooking, cleaning, and child-rearing, but also including farm-work or serving in a shop in the case of a modest master craftsman's wife. The marriage was lived out in a household that usually included servants and often kin, such as an elderly parent or unmarried younger brothers or sisters. The nuclear family was the most frequent family structure, especially in towns, but the stem family was common at certain stages in the life-cycle in rural areas and predominated in some southern areas. Much depended on the inheritance customs in force in a region: they varied from primogeniture to equal partition, with many local variations, and all this affected marriage strategies. The main concern was to keep the family inheritance together, and if possible accrue more wealth. Romantic love developed late, along with individualism and a sense of the private sphere, and until the 20th c. existed far less in reality than in literature.

In the 20th c., and particularly since World War II, the picture of marriage has altered in several ways. After a brief flurry of postponed marriages had swollen the statistics up to 1950, the marriage rate was almost 95 per cent until the 1970s. French people married younger again, and the average age-difference between partners was reduced to only about two years. The massive rise in couples choosing each other stems from the decline of family strategies in a mobile society and the rise of romantic love—although for sociological reasons partners continue to be selected from similar social backgrounds. Divorce rose to 10 per cent in the 1950s, but marriages now lasted over 40 years as against 20 during the ancien régime. Within marriage, sentiment, and a whole ethic of intimacy and shared moments, have replaced the predominantly economic arrangement of earlier centuries. However, from the 1970s the trend changed: marriage in the last decades of this century is usually preceded by cohabitation, frequently supplanted by it, and one-third of the time ends in divorce (three-quarters of which are requested by the woman). [PRC]

See J.-L. Flandrin, Families in Former Times (1979); M. Segalen, Mari et femme dans la société paysanne (1980); Y. Lequin (ed.), Histoire des Français, vol. 1 (1984).

MARS, Mademoiselle (pseud. of Anne-Françoise-Hippolyte Boutet) (1779–1847). Talented and perennially fresh actress who triumphed on the stage of the *Comédie-Française for many years. She was particularly noted for her roles in the comedies of *Molière, *Marivaux, and *Scribe, but was also successful in dramas by *Dumas père and *Hugo. [SBJ]

'Marseillaise, La', see ROUGET DE LISLE.

MARTEAU, Robert (b. 1925). French poet who spent much time in Spain (as a lover of the bull-fight). His collections, including Royaumes (1962), Travaux sur la terre (1966) and Sibylles (1971), Fragments de la France (1990), and Liturgie (1992), give eloquent expression to a rich vision of elemental life. He has also published novels and other prose writings. [PF]

MARTIAL D'AUVERGNE (1430/5–1508). An influential lawyer with a varied œuvre. His best-known work, the gently comic Arrêts d'amour (c.1460), adopts an accurate legal framework, purporting to be the record of 51 cases heard before a Cour d'amour. Most rest on the courtly topos of a suit brought by a martyred lover against Belle Dame Sans Merci; they often shade into absurdity. His other major work, Les Vigiles de Charles VII (1471–83), is a long panegyric based mainly on chronicles and structured liturgically, with responses sung for instance by 'France' or 'Noblesse'. As well as another liturgical piece, the Matines de la Vierge, he probably wrote a *Danse macabré des femmes. [JHMT]

MARTIAL DE BRIVES, père (c.1600–before 1653). Capuchin monk and religious poet. His Parnasse séraphique (1660) contains richly baroque elaboration of devotional themes.

MARTIN DU GARD, Roger (1881–1958). French novelist, playwright, and diarist, winner of a Nobel Prize in 1937. Much of Martin du Gard's work is a monument to mimesis, for he aimed for absolute transparency of presentation. It is none the less arguable that his lifetime's labours to achieve that goal in his multi-volume Les *Thibault (1922–40) and the unfinished Lieutenant-Colonel de Maumort (1983) diminished the artful narrative talents evident in *Jean Barois (1913) and in shorter works such as Confidence africaine (1931), the delightfully bleak Vieille France (1933), or even his subtly robust peasant farce Le Testament du père Leleu (1914). Jean Barois, a vigorous quasi-cinematographic analysis of Third Republic mentalities, earned him entry to the NRF group. The novels of Tolstoy and Dickens are the models for his major work, Les Thibault, which presents the lives of two middle-class brothers from adolescence onwards and celebrates youthful revolt, secular integrity, medicine, socialism, and sexuality, with death as the axis of the human condition. A similar tragic humanism characterizes the posthumously published Maumort. Martin du Gard was a man of judgement and counsel; his Correspondance générale (7 vols. to date) is important, notably his exchange of letters with *Gide (2 vols., 1968). His Journal (vol. 1, 1992) erodes the intriguing discretion in which he veiled his personal life. [DAS]

MARTINET, André, see LINGUISTICS.

Martin Guerre. Hero of a famous episode in 16th-c. Gascony. A rich peasant returns to his family after a long absence, lives happily with his wife for four years, but is revealed as an impostor by the true Martin Guerre. The resulting law case, written up by the judge Jean de Coras, was sensationally popular; it has been the subject of novels, a play, and a film, and has been fascinatingly analysed by Natalie Zemon Davies (*The Return of Martin Guerre*, 1983).

[PF]

Martinique, see WEST INDIES.

MARTIN LE FRANC (1410–61). Didactic writer who undertook (in *Le Champion*) the defence of women [see QUERELLE DES FEMMES] and reflected (in *L'Estrif*) on fortune and virtue.

Martyrs, Les, see CHATEAUBRIAND.

Marxism in France. Marxism was developed as a theory of history and society by Karl Marx and Friedrich Engels during the mid-19th-c. It has usually been associated with radical movements, especially Communist, but exists also as an intellectual framework distinct from them.

Marx lived in Paris during the formative years 1843–5. He and Engels saw France as a model of modern political development and wrote influential analyses of French history, especially the periods 1848–51 and 1870–1. Their political theory drew on *Rousseau and 19th-c. French socialists, though in a famous polemic, *Misère de la philosophie* (1847), Marx criticized *Proudhon for underestimating the importance of economic issues and workers' organizations.

Marx's daughters, Laura and Jenny, and their French husbands, respectively Paul Lafargue and Charles Longuet, helped to spread his ideas in France, where they were little known before the 1880s. With Jules *Guesde, Benoît Malon, and others, they coined the term 'Marxism' and propagated a simple economic determinism, which prompted Marx's irritated comment that, in this sense, he was not himself a 'Marxist'. Other socialists, notably Jean *Jaurès, were attracted to Marx's dialectical method, adapted from Hegel. Georges *Sorel also aroused interest in Marx's philosophy. But with the unification of the French Socialist movement in 1905, theoretical discussions were largely abandoned as divisive. After *World War I the movement split into the Proudhonist Socialists under Léon *Blum, and the Communists, who affiliated to the Moscow-based Third International [see SOCIALISM AND COMMUNISM]. During the 1920s the Socialists promoted translations of Marx's philosophical writings, while the Communists promoted Lenin, Engels, and Marx's political works.

After a sporadic and often marginal existence in France, Marxism emerged in the 1930s as a dynamic movement which had a formative influence on almost all the major writers of the second half of the century. The prestige of the Soviet Union and the role of the French Communist Party (PCF) were contributing factors, but Marxism also appealed as a more attractive philosophy than the main alternatives. During the *Popular Front period many *intellectuals welcomed the combination of theory with practical action, confirming a notion of the committed *intellectual which went back to the *Dreyfus Affair. Henri *Lefebvre's dialectical humanism, Paul *Nizan's caustic materialism, Auguste *Cornu's careful Marxian scholarship, and Georges *Politzer's polemical rationalism were all strands of a flourishing pre-war Marxist intellectual culture.

Several Marxist intellectuals were killed during World War II. However, the role of the Soviet Union and the PCF ensured a ready audience for Marxist ideas at the Liberation. Among their proponents were established figures in literature (*Aragon, *Éluard), art (*Picasso, *Léger), science (Joliot-Curie, Langevin, Wallon), history (Georges *Lefebvre, Soboul), and other intellectual spheres. A flood of young intellectuals joined the PCF, eager to learn. Catholics and Existentialists incorporated Marxist insights into their own thinking, and initiated promising dialogues with young Marxist thinkers like Pierre Hervé, Roger *Garaudy, Henri Lefebvre, and Jean-Toussaint Desanti. However, with the hardening polarizations of the Cold War, the PCF retrenched behind a dogmatic Stalinism, imposed from Moscow by Andrey Zhdanov and from Paris by Laurent Casanova. There followed a flow of self-criticisms, and several departures among browbeaten intellectuals.

By the end of 1956 international and domestic crises had helped to divide French Marxism into many divergent currents. The PCF slowly abandoned attempts to impose an orthodox Marxism-Leninism on its members, and within the party conflicting new interpretations flourished. One grouping, led by Garaudy and Aragon, looked towards Italian conceptions and proposed a neo-Hegelian Marxism as a broadly inclusive humanist perspective, open to dialogue with other philosophical and religious doctrines and potentially converging with them. Another grouping, led by Louis *Althusser at the *École Normale Supérieure, looked towards Mao Tse-tung's China and argued for a radical break with Hegelian and humanist ideological illusions, to produce a rigorous scientific Marxist-Leninist theory. This aggressively original approach was influential with many young philosophers and social scientists, including Nicos *Poulantzas, Étienne Balibar, Pierre *Macherey, and Georges Labica. Not all Althusserians were Communists, and, of those who were, most either left or were excluded from the party during the 1970s, as was Garaudy. Between these hostile camps, Lucien *Sève led the attempt to construct a non-dogmatic dialectical Marxism, supported by Solange Mercier-Josa, who reappropriated Hegelian concepts, and André Tosel, who looked rather to Gramsci.

Outside the PCF many forms of Marxism sprang up from the 1950s onwards, often animated by ex-Communists or by the small but active Trotskyist groups. Many Marxists were grouped round reviews

Mascarille

like *Socialisme ou barbarie* (1949–65) and *Arguments* (1956–63), including Pierre *Naville, Edgar *Morin, Claude Lefort, Pierre Fougeyrollas, Cornélius *Castoriadis, Alain *Touraine, Serge Mallet, Kostas Axelos, and François Chatelet. They developed critiques of Stalinist Communism and, within a broadly humanist framework, explored the limits of notions such as history, philosophy, social class, and the state. They also examined the possibilities of combining Marxism with other disciplines, including *psychoanalysis, *linguistic theory, or structural *anthropology, and with such conceptions as the End of History and the End of Philosophy.

Jean-Paul *Sartre moved towards Marxism in the mid-1950s, declaring that it was the conceptual horizon of the age and attempting to reconcile his earlier *Existentialism with it in his *Critique de la raison dialectique* (1960). Joined by Simone de *Beauvoir, he gravitated towards the vociferous Maoist groups, though other Existentialists, like *Merleau-Ponty and *Gorz, found different accommodations with Marxism. Leading *Structuralists, including *Lévi-Strauss and *Barthes, absorbed elements of Marxism. Many of the *Post-Structuralists and *Postmodernists were marked by it, though they often chose subsequently to reject it. And it formed a major, if at times uncomfortable, part of *feminist and environmental theory.

In the decade after *May 1968 Marxism achieved something close to a hegemonic position in French intellectual life. However, in the late 1970s and 1980s the political and philosophical tide turned against it. The crisis of Soviet-style Communism and the critique of overarching world-views or Master Narratives have reversed the conditions which first projected Marxism to popularity in the 1930s and now pose the question of how far and in what forms it will survive. [MHK]

See M. Poster, *Existential Marxism* (1975); M. Kelly, *Modern French Marxism* (1982); T. Judt, *Marxism and the French Left* (1986).

Mascarille. The name, suggesting a small mask, is given to the tricky valet in several of *Molière's comedies, notably *L'Étourdi* and *Les *Précieuses ridicules*.

MASCARON, Jules (1634–1703). Court preacher under *Louis XIV and, like *Massillon, an *Oratorian. Between the mid-1660s and the mid-1690s he gave no fewer than six Advent and four Lent series of sermons before the king. He was also a popular funeral orator, best remembered for his orations for Anne d'Autriche (1666) and *Turenne (1676). Only the latter was published in his lifetime; and since a mere selection of his work was posthumously printed on the basis of notes, his reputation rests largely on the good opinion of his contemporaries, notably Madame de *Sévigné. He was appointed bishop of Tulle in 1671 and translated to Agen in 1680. [PJB]

MASPÉRO, François (b. 1932). French publisher and journal editor. One of the most influential phenomena of post-1968 French publishing, the Petite Collection Maspéro had the aim of constituting a series of well-produced but cheap volumes of classic left-wing texts and original essays by left-wing intellectuals. In the spirit of *May 1968, the series concentrated upon anti-Stalinist Communist theoreticians and upon writers from Third World revolutionary movements, such as Guevara, Kenyatta, and *Fanon. In the 1970s Maspéro's bookshop, La Joie de Lire, was a major focal point in Paris for alternative culture. He himself demonstrates considerable gifts as a writer with his autobiographical novel *Le Sourire du chat* (1984) and his investigation into the life of the Parisian suburbs in *Les Passagers du Roissy-Express* (1990). [NH]

Masque, Le. Founded in 1927 by Albert Pigasse, Le Masque is the oldest *detective fiction collection in France, remaining faithful to its unillustrated yellow cover with the mask-and-quill symbol, and also to the classic detective puzzle. Though publishing many translations, it has also attempted to nurture a French tradition. [SFN]

MASSENET, Jules (1842–1912) was in his time an extraordinarily successful and prolific French opera composer. His musical style has a melodic charm and grace, aptly described by d'Indy as a discreet and quasi-religious eroticism. His most famous operas are *Werther* (1892, based on Goethe's novel), *Manon* (1894, based on *Prévost's novel), and *Thaïs* (1894, based on a novel by Anatole *France). He also collaborated with Catulle *Mendès on two operas and based compositions on works by *Hugo, Alphonse *Daudet, *Flaubert, and many other contemporary authors. Professor of composition at the Paris Conservatoire from 1878 until his death, Massenet had an impact on a generation of French composers, some of whom reacted violently against what they saw as the facile charm of his music. [KM]

MASSILLON, Jean-Baptiste (1663–1742). French *Oratorian and preacher much appreciated at Versailles (he preached an Advent series in 1699 and Lent series in 1701 and 1704, along with important funeral orations including that of *Louis XIV himself). It was in 1718 that he preached, in the presence of Louis XV, the ten sermons entitled the *Petit Carême*, which became the most highly regarded model of pulpit eloquence of the century (and beyond). Though he was strongly marked by the Christian rationalism of the 17th c., he also exemplified that emergent current of religious sensibility which typifies the 18th c. As the 'Racine de la chaire', he disengaged from the austere pulpit erudition of a *Bourdaloue and from the stark appeals to dogma and theology of a *Bossuet and, meditating on the infinite sadness of suffering humanity, approached the same emotional regions as a century which was fast becoming secularized. His general concern for mankind, expressed with limpid classical purity, earned for him the admiration of the *philosophes (e.g.*Voltaire, d'*Alembert, and *Marmontel). In fact, he was doubly a priest after their own hearts: having become, despite his *Jansenist leanings, bishop of Clermont-Ferrand in 1717, he was for over 20 years a model divine, constantly devoted in all Christian charity to his flock and his episcopal duties. [JR]

MASSIS, Henri (1886–1970). Never a major writer, Massis was nevertheless central to right-wing French politics and literature in his period. His early tracts (co-authored under the pseudonym 'Agathon'), L'Esprit de la nouvelle Sorbonne (1911) and Les Jeunes Gens d'aujourd'hui (1913), were influential expressions of the new Right. A supporter of *Action Française, he became editor in 1920 of La Revue universelle, pursuing both political and literary disputes with great vigour. Vicious and often personalized, his polemics were nevertheless highly effective. He served under Vichy, and after the war continued to support right-wing causes, from Salazar's Portugal to French Algeria. [RMG]

MASSON, André (b. 1921). Born in Rose Hill, *Mauritius, Masson became a journalist having failed to be admitted to the priesthood. Less prolific than his brother, Loys [see below], and less tempted by exile, André is best known for his violent, hallucinatory realist novel, Un temps pour mourir (1962), in which tropical cyclones and equally unpredictable and uncontrollable passions tear through the text. Le Chemin de pierre ponce (1963) is a novel which focuses on totalitarianism. His third novel, Le Temps juste (1966), is a metaphysical work which explores Being and Time. [BEJ]

MASSON, Jean (also known as Papire) (1544–1611), studied Greek and Hebrew and shared the humanists' love of manuscripts. His interest in primary sources gives particular value to his history of Gaul (1577). The latter is written in Latin, but emphasizes his links with vernacular historians like *Pasquier. He was the friend of *Dorat and many of the *Pléiade writers. [JJS]

MASSON, Loys (1915–69). Poet, essayist, humorist, novelist, and dramatist, Masson is the author of some 40 works published in Paris. Born on *Mauritius, he left in 1939 and never returned. The island is nevertheless relevant to his work in a number of ways, most obviously in L'Étoile et la clef (1945), a novel which explores its social injustices. Certain recurrent images in his work are also related to Mauritius: the homosexual rape of a white child by a coloured man, the curse on the 'race de Caïn'. Children are the heroes of Masson's work: it is they who are prepared to transgress, to overstep social and racial boundaries.

His early poetry is reminiscent of *Malraux's. In the 1950s he published two symbolic sea novels: Les Mutins (1951) and Les Tortues (1956). Le Notaire des noirs (1961) is set on Mauritius, Les Noces de la vanille (1962) on Reunion. Le Lagon de la miséricorde (1964) and Les Anges noirs du trône (1967) are set in the Pacific. [BEJ]

Mateo Falcone. Corsican story by *Mérimée, in which a father personally sacrifices his own son to the family honour.

MATHILDE, Princesse (1820–1904). Niece of Napoleon I, cousin of Napoleon III. Her salon in Paris and at Saint-Gratien was visited by many leading writers, including *Flaubert, *Sainte-Beuve, and *Gautier, to the last of whom she gave a sinecure post as her librarian.

Matière céleste, see JOUVE.

Matière de Bretagne, La. The 'Matter of Britain' is the term used to describe the corpus of Celtic, more specifically Arthurian, legend that provided the narrative framework for so much medieval French *romance. How it reached the Continent from Britain is not known. Equally unclear is who *Arthur was, and how a chieftain of the Britons who apparently distinguished himself against the invading Saxons at the Battle of Mount Badon early in the 6th c. came to be rescued from historical oblivion in the second quarter of the 12th c. by the inventive genius of *Geoffrey of Monmouth. Whether or not Arthur lurks behind the name of Ambrosius Aurelianus celebrated by the 6th-c. historian Gildas, and however authentic or otherwise the appearance of his name may be in the Old Welsh Gododdin (c. 600), the Annales Cambriae (9th–10th c.), and the Pseudo-Nennius (9th c.), it seems certain that he must have lived on as a folk hero in the collective memory of the Celts for many centuries.

Transmogrified by Geoffrey's Historia regum britanniae (1135–8) into the glorious monarch of a resplendent Golden Age, fit to rival Alexander and Charlemagne, Arthur the king makes his debut in French literature in Le Roman de Brut (1155), a rhymed translation and adaptation of Geoffrey's Latin text by the Anglo-Norman poet *Wace. He considerably amplified that part of his Latin source devoted to Arthur, portraying the king as a paragon of *chivalry and dwelling in particular on the splendours of his coronation and the courtesy of his court. He also added (from where it is not known) the Round Table. A scholarly and critical writer, Wace, in the wake of William of Malmesbury, drew attention to the many fables relating to Arthur circulating amongst the Britons at the time, and to their belief in his eventual return from Avalon. Wace clearly gave these stories little credence and did not see fit to embroider any into his narrative, which remains by and large faithfully close to Geoffrey's.

*Chrétien de Troyes, the earliest and best exponent of French courtly *romance, certainly read Wace, but his works exploit a great deal of Celtic material which does not figure in either Wace or Geoffrey, and he clearly had access to sources other than these. *Marie de France, a Continental poet writing at the English court of Henry II, also had access to Celtic material. This, she tells us, she obtained from oral sources, from narrative songs (lais) that she heard from the lips of 'Bretuns'. Unlike 'Bretaigne' (Britain) that could be distinguished from 'Bretaigne menur' (Brittany), no linguistic differentiation was made in medieval French between Britons and Bretons, and we cannot therefore know whether Marie's sources were Cymric or Armoric—or both. But since in any case the Welsh and the Bretons shared a language which, though no longer common, may still presumably have been mutually intelligible in the 12th c., it is probably unnecessary to attempt to make any further distinction. When, however, Geoffrey of Monmouth used the term 'Britannici sermonis' to describe the language of 'the very ancient book' which he claimed as his source, he could only mean Welsh, as his contemporary Gaimar confirms.

The existence, at all events, of Celtic legend circulating orally in 12th-c. Britain provides an alternative source to that of written Latin and French texts to explain the availability of such material in Champagne and beyond. Indeed, the Matter of Britain had already reached Italy in the first two decades of the century, as the Arthurian-inspired archivolt of Modena Cathedral shows. Whatever the intermediary here, transmission to France in particular may very well have been made by itinerant, Celtic-speaking story-tellers such as Bleheris/Bledri, whose literary activity is referred to by 12th-c. contemporaries, or by bilingual Anglo-Norman versifiers plying their cross-Channel trade. Equally probable candidates for the role of intermediaries were the professional interpreters attached to the royal and baronial courts, who assured communication between the Celtic-speaking and francophone inhabitants of 12th-c. Britain. Some of these channels might have passed through Brittany, others need not have.

Another, and more direct, source of contact would, of course, have been Welsh literary texts, but these, preserved only in much later copies, are difficult to date. Apart from some brief and possibly early mentions of Arthur in, for example, the Black Book of Carmarthen (early 13th c.), the first significant texts are those of the Mabinogion. The oldest of these, and probably the only one to pre-date Chrétien de Troyes, is Culhwch and Olwen, a bridewinning tale featuring Arthur, Kay, Bedevere, Gawain, and Guenièvre. The Dream of Rhonabwy dates from the 13th c. As for Gereint Son of Erbin, it has very clear narrative affinities with Chrétien's Erec et Enide; the Lady of the Fountain stands in the same relation to Yvain, while Peredur has links, but less close, with Perceval. More French than Celtic, in fact, these 14th- and 15th-c. Welsh texts appear to have themselves undergone the influences of Chrétien's romances.

Even if the problems of defining what the Matter of Britain actually consisted of, and in what forms it could have been transmitted to France, remain unresolved, it is clear that the imaginative appeal of Celtic legend to French romance writers and their audiences was real and, in literary terms, highly productive. The matière de Bretagne was to persist into the great prose romances of the 13th and 14th c., ultimately to return to the land of its birth at the end of the Middle Ages with Malory. [IS]

See J. S. P. Tatlock, The Legendary History of Britain (1950); R. S. Loomis (ed.), Arthurian Literature in the Middle Ages (1959); C. Bullock Davies, Professional Interpreters and the Matter of Britain (1966).

Matière de Rome, La, see ROMANS D'ANTIQUITÉ.

Matière et mémoire, see BERGSON.

Matière des rêves, see BUTOR.

Matin, Le. Launched in 1884, this newspaper championed 'Anglo-Saxon' news-values; adorned by pictures of telegraph wires, and boasting correspondents world-wide, Le Matin initially had no *romans-feuilletons and was politically eclectic. Its owner, Alfred Edwards, sold out to fellow press tycoons Henry Poidatz and Maurice Bunau-Varilla. The latter, France's closest approximation to 'Citizen Kane', ran Le Matin until 1944, when it was closed down. He played the media mogul, megalomaniac, and bully-boy, boasting 'my empire is worth three thrones'. In 1899 Le Matin slashed its sale-price to 5 centimes and grew to six pages. After a bitter war with Le *Journal, its circulation was 1.6 million in 1916. Its aggressive nationalism took the paper ever further to the Right and to collaboration during the *Occupation. Before 1914 Gaston *Leroux was one of its star-reporters and novelists (Chéri-Bibi, etc.), as later was Joseph *Kessel. [MP]

MATISSE, Henri (1869–1954). French painter. With *Picasso and *Braque, Matisse was one of the major innovators in European painting in the early 20th c. His work gave colour a new autonomy and power of expression, which caused uproar in the Salon d'Automne of 1905 and was labelled *Fauvist, though his colour was usually characterized more by a peaceful sensuality than by violence. He brought the same sense of design to a range of media. In addition to his graphic work, he designed the scenery and costumes for the 1938 ballet of Le *Rouge et le noir, and became one of the most important book illustrators of the century (notably the poetry of *Mallarmé, 1932, *Ronsard, 1948, and *Charles d'Orléans, 1950). His work was the subject of *Aragon's major analysis of artistic creation, Henri Matisse, roman (1971). [JK]

Matter of Britain, The, see MATIÈRE DE BRETAGNE.

MATTHEW PARIS, see ANGLO-NORMAN LITERATURE, 6a.

MATTHIEU, Pierre (1563–1621). French royal historiographer under Henri IV and Louis XIII. Earlier, he wrote political tragedies, especially *La Guisiade* (1589), supporting the *Ligue and advocating tyrannicide. His *Tablettes de la vie et de la mort* (1613), quatrains on moral themes in the manner of *Pibrac and *Favre, enjoyed lasting popularity.

MAUCLAIR, Camille (pseud. of Camille Faust) (1872–1945). French poet, novelist, art critic, and travel writer. A champion of *Impressionism and *Symbolism and a prolific author of unusual critical flexibility, Mauclair abandoned poetry and the novel to produce books on writers, musicians, painters, and picturesque places. With *Lugné-Poë he founded the Théâtre de l'Œuvre. His novel, *Le Soleil des morts* (1898), with its reverential portrait of *Mallarmé as Calixte Armel, is still in print. [DAS]

MAUCLAIR, Jacques (b. 1919). French theatre director. Believing the director's role to be subordinate to that of the author, and dedicated to producing new plays, he made a significant contribution in providing a stage for emerging playwrights in the 1950s, particularly *Ionesco. A disciple of *Jouvet, he looked to the dialogue and dramatic rhythms to communicate the text. [DWW]

MAUCROIX, François (1619–1708). French poet and translator, chiefly remembered as the friend of *La Fontaine. A lawyer by training, he was obliged by poverty to take orders and accept a canonry at Reims. The fact that he wrote mildly indecent poetry did not prevent him from assiduously carrying out his cathedral duties: Christian sentiment exists side by side with the tradition of the 'esprit gaulois'. His epicurean stance, though entirely unsystematic and largely owed to Horace, leads him to praise a tranquil existence enlivened by good company and good cheer. His madrigals, epigrams, *chansons*, and odes appeared in collective *recueils*. [PJB]

MAUNICK, Édouard (b. 1931). Mauritian poet. He worked on Mauritius as a teacher and then librarian, and in 1954 published his first collection of poetry, *Ces oiseaux de sang* (1954). In 1960 he left for Paris and, while continuing to publish poetry, embarked on a career as a critic, commentator, and journalist principally concerned with francophone Africa, and working for both radio (for which he also wrote a number of plays) and the press. For a number of years he was editor of *Demain l'Afrique*. Later he became assistant director of UNESCO publications.

Maunick's poetic self is the half-caste: 'n'oubliez pas que métis est mon état civil'. This duality combines with numerous other antitheses: of blood and race, whiteness and blackness, sea and island, land and water, interior and exterior. His texts exist in relationship, in poetic archipelagos, sharing fundamental similarities in terms of concrete imagery but focused on different themes. In *Les Manèges de la mer* (1964), *Ensoleillé-vif* (1976), and *En mémoire du mémorable* (1979), the same presences appear: White Woman (also represented as snow and the Island-Mother), the sea (place and medium of transition), father (related to blood, time, and death), and *la parole* (once again associated with woman). Advocating cultural and racial plurality and multiplicity, Maunick always sees exile as temporary, a moment on a journey *from* and *to*. [BEJ]

MAUPASSANT, Guy de (1850–93). French short-story writer, novelist, and journalist. He is usually associated with *Naturalism and contributed to *Les *Soirées de Médan* the story *Boule de suif* which launched his career, but he always maintained an independent position in relation to the movement, with little respect for *Zola's theories, despite his admiration for his works.

He was born in Normandy of aristocratic stock and raised by his mother after her separation from his unfaithful father. Unsubstantiated rumour had it that he was the illegitimate child of *Flaubert, who took a paternal interest in his literary development and inspired in him a scrupulous concern for style. After taking part in the *Franco-Prussian War, which interrupted his law studies in Paris, Maupassant worked in the civil service until he was able, after 1880, to live by his writings. He achieved enormous success with his short stories and novels. For ten full years he was able to lead an extravagant life, travelling much, moving in high-society circles, and entertaining a prodigous number of mistresses. His biographers have emphasized the contrasting sides of his character: on the one hand a robust, sporty individual, with a passion for rowing and other outdoor sports, whose prowess saved the English poet Swinburne from drowning; on the other hand a nervous, morbid, anxious, suicidal individual, whose health was soon undermined by his hectic life-style, syphilis, and inherited maladies (his mother was depressive and his brother died insane). By 1890 his health had seriously declined, with fits of depression and the onset of paralysis. By 1891 he could no longer write and he attempted suicide the following year. Interned in an asylum, he died insane in considerable physical and mental distress.

In the early part of his career, Maupassant wrote a collection of poems, *Des vers* (1880), and some plays, then later a number of travel journals, but he made his mark as a master of the short story. His *contes* and *nouvelles* were usually published first in the press, where Maupassant perfected the art of the piquant *chronique*. Many were reworked before appearing in his collections of tales, such as *La Maison Tellier* (1881), *Mademoiselle Fifi* (1882), *Contes* *de la bécasse* (1883), *Miss Harriet* and *Les Sœurs Rondoli* (1884), *Toine* and *Contes du jour et de la nuit* (1886), *Le Horla* (1887), and *L'Inutile Beauté* (1890). The lucidity of his style and the conciseness of form of his stories derive more from Flaubert than from his naturalist contemporaries. These works deal with the meanness of peasant life, the mediocrity and hypocrisy of bourgeois manners, and the vanities of high society, and are remarkably varied in theme, tone, form, and genre: they include the tragic, the comic, the farcical, the satirical, the fantastic, always with a common concern to depict human foibles and obsessions and cynically to reveal the sordid, selfish underside of human actions. Maupassant is particularly skilled at presenting suggestive details and anecdotes that reveal with a few deft strokes a whole system of values and a philosophy of life. His works are marked by a profound pessimism, nourished by his reading of Schopenhauer. As his preface to *Pierre et Jean* shows, his realism deals as much with the illusions of the mind as with the realities of life. He made an important contribution, notably with 'Le Horla', to the genre of the *fantastic tale.

Maupassant published six novels. *Une vie* (1883), his first and most Naturalist novel, heavily influenced, however, by the manner and themes of Flaubert's Realist works, is the sad story of the disillusionment and suffering of a wife and mother. After this pessimistic picture of a woman's failings, *Bel-Ami* (1885) presents an equally cynical and much less sympathetic view of a man's success. *Mont-Oriol* (1887) is a story of dowry-hunting and adultery set in a spa in the Auvergne countryside. *Pierre et Jean* (1888) is usually considered to be Maupassant's best novel. *Fort comme la mort* (1889) is the story of an ageing painter who falls in love with the young daughter of his mistress, and *Notre cœur* (1890) the story of a young man's relationship with an attractive young widow whose salon attracts distinguished artists from the high society of Paris.   [DB]

See E. Sullivan, *Maupassant the Novelist* (1954 and 1972); A. Vial, *Guy de Maupassant et l'art du roman* (1954).

MAUPEOU, René-Nicolas-Charles-Augustin de (1714–92). Chancellor of France under Louis XV; his attempts to reform the *parlements*, followed by the exile of the recalcitrant lawyers in 1771, provoked fierce hostility and were overturned on the accession of Louis XVI in 1774.

MAUPERTUIS, Pierre-Louis Moreau de (1698–1759). Philosopher-scientist, remembered as the target of *Voltaire's malicious *Diatribe du docteur Akakia*, in fact an adventurous and original thinker. Born in Saint-Malo, he was briefly a soldier before devoting himself to science. In a *Discours sur les différentes figures des astres* (1732) he introduced Newtonianism to France. As a result, he was sent by the *Académie des Sciences to Lapland to make measurements designed to determine the shape of the globe [see LA CONDAMINE]; as well as scientific reports, he published a fascinating *Relation* (1749) of this daring expedition. In 1745, invited by *Frederick the Great to reorganize his Academy, he settled in Berlin; it was here that he became embroiled in acerbic disputes with Voltaire and others.

His scientific and philosophical works, written in an admirably clear style, cover many subjects, from the origin of language to cosmological proofs of the existence of God, which he based on the principle of the law of least effort. The originality of his thinking is best seen in his work on biology and genetics, notably the *Vénus physique* (1745), in which he attacks orthodox preformationism and anticipates the transformist thinking of *Diderot and *Buffon.
    [PF]

Mauprat, see SAND.

MAURIAC, Claude (b. 1914). Son of François *Mauriac, author of critical essays on his father, *Breton, *Proust, and others. His attachment to the *Nouveau Roman and to the importance of form is evident in *L'Alittérature contemporaine* (1958), and in his own novels. *Le Temps immobile* (10 vols., 1974–) constructs a set of non-chronological—and continuing—memoirs.   [EAF]

MAURIAC, François (1885–1970). With *Bernanos, the major French Catholic novelist of the 20th c. Mauriac concentrates upon the hypocrisy and materialism of his class, the provincial bourgeoisie, and observes the struggles of those who refuse to conform, often at the risk of their own souls. The reconciliation of this heroic intransigence with salvation is the continuing theme of his fictional work.

He was born in Bordeaux, into a rich Catholic bourgeois milieu, with interests in timber and wine and property in the Landes, and this milieu becomes the essential locus of much of his later fiction. After a Catholic education in Bordeaux, towards the end of which he was influenced by both *Barrès and *Jammes and became briefly attracted to Marc *Sangnier's *Sillon movement, he moved to Paris in 1907, to study for entrance to the *École des Chartes. In 1909, however, he left the École to devote himself to literature, initially through journalism and poetry, in the collections *Les Mains jointes* (1909) and *Adieu à l'adolescence* (1911), and experiments with fiction, in *L'Enfant chargé de chaînes* (1912) and *La Robe prétexte* (1914). In 1913, he married Jeanne Lafon, and his first son, Claude, was born in 1914 [see above]. Rejected from the army on medical grounds, he served briefly until 1917 as a medical auxiliary in Salonica with the Red Cross.

It was in the 1920s that Mauriac's literary reputation was established. A *mondain* writer, with close contacts with the group who frequented the nightclub Le Bœuf sur le Toit, such as *Cocteau, *Radiguet, and *Rigaut, he was also closely allied to the Right, under the influence and friendship of

Barrès, writing for the right-wing *Le Gaulois* and with intimate links with *Maurras and *Action Française. His first novel to obtain major recognition was *Le Baiser au lépreux* (1922), followed closely by *Le Fleuve du feu* (1923), *Génitrix* (1923), *Le *Désert de l'amour* (1925), and *Thérèse Desqueyroux* (1927), all of which, in the claustrophobic geography of the South-West, explore the constraints of the bourgeois family, the search for love and individuality, and spiritual barrenness.

From 1928 to 1931 he suffered a major religious and personal crisis, stemming from his inability to reconcile sexuality and Christianity; his subsequent work exhibits a more positive perspective on the issues raised in the fiction of the 1920s, beginning with the novel *Ce qui était perdu* (1930) and continuing with *Le *Nœud de vipères* (1932), *Le *Mystère Frontenac* (1933), and *La Fin de la nuit* (1935), a sequel to *Thérèse Desqueyroux*, in which the heroine moves closer to salvation. This novel was the subject of *Sartre's famous attack on Mauriac, in 'M. François Mauriac et la liberté', in which he accused the author's God-like narratorial stance of preventing the freedom of his characters: 'Dieu n'est pas romancier. Monsieur Mauriac non plus.' Mauriac had already pre-empted this criticism to a certain extent in essays such as *Le Roman* (1928) and *Le Romancier et ses personnages* (1933); he attempted to rectify it with the first-person narration of the implicitly anti-Vichy *La *Pharisienne* (1941).

Elected to the Académie Française in 1933, Mauriac was still firmly on the Right but, like Bernanos, was moved to adopt a left-wing stance by the Spanish Civil War. A courageous member of the literary Resistance during the *Occupation and a fervent Gaullist, he was a prominant left-wing intellectual during the Fourth Republic and was one of the founder members of the editorial board of *L'*Express*, adopting an uncompromising opposition to French use of torture during the *Algerian War. With the return to power of de *Gaulle in 1958 he became the chief literary apologist of the Fifth Republic, through his column *Bloc-notes* in the *Figaro littéraire*. His final years were marked by a return to the novel, with *L'Agneau* (1954), and particularly *Un adolescent d'autrefois* (1969) and its posthumous sequel, *Maltaverne* (1972).

A distinguished journalist and author of important diaries and memoirs, Mauriac is outstanding as a practitioner of a form of realist fiction which carries acute psychological analysis of the claustrophobia of provincial bourgeois society to metaphysical significance.   [NH]

> See J. E. Flower, *Intention and Achievement: The Novels of François Mauriac* (1969); J. Touzot, *Mauriac avant Mauriac 1913–1922* (1977); J. Lacouture, *François Mauriac* (1980).

Maurists. Members of the *Benedictine Congrégation de Saint-Maur, which was originally founded in 1618 to promote the reform of the order,

but became famous for the learning of its members. The Maurists produced monuments of erudition, editions, histories, collections of documents, mainly concerned with theology and church history, but including the *Histoire littéraire de la France*, which aims to describe all works produced in France until 1500. 12 volumes were produced in the 18th c. under the leadership of Dom Rivet and Dom Clémencet; the work was continued after the Revolution by the *Académie des Inscriptions.   [PF]

Mauritius and Reunion. Mauritius (formerly the Île de France) was a French colony from 1715 until it was ceded to Britain in 1810, and after this date French continued to be the language of culture. Reunion (formerly the Île Bourbon) has been a French possession almost uninterruptedly since 1649 and is now a DOM [see DOM-TOM]. The literary contribution of both islands was considered a part of the French tradition in the 18th and 19th c. In the late 18th c. the poems of *Parny and *Bertin (both of settler families) represented Reunion, while *Bernardin de Saint-Pierre, who spent three years on Mauritius, wrote descriptions of the island and made it the setting for his very popular *Paul et Virginie*.

In the 19th c. the work of the Mauritian poet Thomi Pitot de la Beaujardiève (1779–1857) was heavily influenced by *Béranger. However, François Chrestien (1767–1846), in *Le Bobre africain* (1882; *bobre*: guitar), introduced references to African culture and included a number of poems in *Creole. *Leconte de Lisle, leader of the *Parnassians, and Léon *Dierx, elected 'prince des poètes' after *Mallarmé's death, were the two great 19th-c. poets from the Île Bourbon.

During the first half of the 20th c. the literary production on both islands followed the general tendencies of *Romanticism and *Symbolism. On Mauritius, Léoville l'Homme (1857–1928) and, most notably, Robert Edward *Hart produced significant and at times more obviously Mauritian poetry. The influence of *Surrealism is visible in the later volumes of Loys *Masson. His work, most particularly his novel *Le Notaire des noirs* (1961), includes important contributions to a specifically Mauritian literature. The texts of Malcolm de *Chazal, for example, *Sens plastique*, though clearly in the tradition of André *Breton, are often rooted in a recognizably Mauritian landscape. André *Masson has produced a number of esoteric religious writings and Édouard-J. *Maunick, whose work includes an African dimension, is sometimes associated with the literature of *négritude. Africa is also important in the poetry of André Legallant. Marcel *Cabon, in a number of works, but most notably his novel, *Namasté* (1965), uses clear, uncomplicated language to depict ordinary Mauritian life. Some Creole phrases are incorporated into the French.

On Reunion, the 'francotropisme' (to use a neologism created by the Mauritian literary historian

Maurois

Jean-Georges *Prosper) of the 19th c. continued into the first half of this century. The publication in 1951 of Jean *Albany's collection *Zamal* represents the beginnings of a specifically *réunionnais* poetry, rooted in the history, landscape, and culture of a particular island, rather than an unspecified 'exotic' space, seen from the perspective of France. He has also written a *P'tit glossaire: le piment des mots créoles* (1974) and a *Supplément* (1983).

Boris *Gamaleya, in his long poem *Vali pour une reine morte* (1972), dramatically juxtaposes the major 'figures' of the island—'l'île reine', 'l'esclave révolté', 'le chasseur de nègres marrons'. It is a violent text which emphasizes the diversity of the island, manifest in the peoples, landscapes (and seascapes), flora, and fauna.

A more overtly militant text is the long poem by Alain *Lorraine, *Tienbo le rein* (1975), dedicated 'aux z'enfants de la misère de ce pays qui vient'. Other poets are Gilbert *Aubry (bishop of Reunion), Agnès Guéneau, Jean-Henri *Azéma, and Riel *Debars.

A *roman réunionnais* emerged later. The term is used by Anne *Cheynet as the subtitle to her work *Les Muselés* (1977). Axel Gauvin's *Quartier Trois-Lettres* (1980) and Agnès Guéneau's *La Terre Bardzour, Granmoune* (1981) also depict, in simple language, the poverty and deprivation experienced by many on the island. Gauvin's novel is also interesting in its language, which reads as an accessible Creole or obviously creolized French. He has answered those who accuse him of unacceptable compromise by translating the work into standard *réunionnais* Creole—*Kartyé trwa lèt* (1984). Daniel Honoré's *Louis Redona* (1980) is one of the few novels in Creole.

A number of important historical novels have also been written: Firmin Lacpatia's *Boadour* (1978) about Indian indentured labour in the 19th c., Jean-François *Sam Long's *Terre arrachée* (1982), and Daniel Vaxelaire's two novels about slavery in the 18th and 19th c.: *Chasseur d'esclaves* (1982) and *L'Affranchi* (1984).

[BEJ]

See J.-G. Prosper, *Histoire de la littérature mauricienne de langue française* (1978); D.-R. Roche, *Lire la poésie réunionnaise contemporaine* (1982).

MAUROIS, André (pseud. of Émile Herzog) (1885–1967). The foremost popular biographer in France in the 20th c., his subjects include Shelley (1923), Disraeli (1927), Byron (1930), Turgenev (1931), *Chateaubriand (1938), *Proust (1949), George *Sand (1952), Victor *Hugo (1954), Madame de *Lafayette (1961), and *Balzac (1965). The popularity of his biographies undoubtedly owes much to the semifictional techniques of character-analysis and narration on which they are based. A devoted anglophile, Maurois also produced an *Histoire d'Angleterre* (1937), as well as two amusing novels which draw upon his experience with British troops during World War I

and which established his literary reputation: *Les Silences du colonel Bramble* (1918) and its sequel, *Les Discours du docteur O'Grady* (1922).   [NH]

MAURON, Charles (1899–1966) trained as a scientist, but deteriorating sight and the patronage of Roger Fry led to a career in translation (of contemporary English authors, including E. M. Forster) and literary criticism. *Aesthetics and Psychology* (1935) foreshadowed *Des métaphores obsédantes au mythe personnel* (1962), which purported to go beyond previous psychopathological studies of the artist (Marie Bonaparte on *Poe, René Laforgue on *Baudelaire), by revealing the unconscious associations underlying textual creation. Sensitively applied, his psychocriticism yielded suggestive interpretations of *Mallarmé and *Racine, but his attempt to reconcile formalism and reception theory, briefly influential during the 'nouvelle critique' debate of the 1960s [see CRITICISM, 4], is currently neglected.   [WK]

MAURRAS, Charles (1868–1952). A leader of the French intellectual Right from the *Dreyfus Affair to the end of World War II, Maurras was a brilliant political journalist who influenced many major writers, from *Maritain to *Bernanos. He was also a literary critic, devoted to the cause of classicism. His political beliefs were authoritarian, anti-republican, antisemitic, xenophobic. A founder-member of *Action Française in 1899, he soon became its leader, and made of it a Royalist movement which was to dominate French right-wing politics for over 40 years. An agnostic, he strongly supported the Catholic Church as a force for order.   [RMG]

MAURY, Jean-Siffrein, abbé (1746–1817). Celebrated French preacher, author of an *Éloge de Fénelon* (1771) and an *Essai sur l'éloquence de la chaire* (1777). He played a prominent part as a deputy and orator in the early years of the Revolution, defending the nobility and clergy in debates with *Mirabeau. In 1792 he emigrated to Rome, where he was made a cardinal, returning to France under Napoleon. He is credited with inventing the term *sans-culotte*, referring jokingly to women.   [PF]

MAUSS, Marcel (1872–1950). French anthropologist; nephew and collaborator of *Durkheim. Mauss argued that the intellectual categories and symbolic systems of a given society (its concepts of time, space, number, and hierarchy; its linguistic and religious practices) are conditioned and interrelated by the specific features and material conditions of the corresponding social structure. His emphasis on the 'total social phenomenon' was exemplified in *Essai sur le don* (1925), in which the laws and mechanisms of gift-exchange are seen to be fundamental to the organization and cohesion of the societies in which it is practised. Mauss's methods were later applied and developed by *Lévi-Strauss.   [REG]

Mauvaise foi. For this central concept of *Sartre's Existentialism see ÊTRE ET LE NÉANT, L'.

MAX, Édouard de (1869–1924). Of Romanian origin and accent, he was a prominent leading man on the Paris stage of the 1890s, an exotic, talented, but uneven actor who created a following. He played opposite *Bernhardt in many plays, including *Sardou's *La Sorcière* (1903) and a revival of Racine's *Andromaque* (1903). [SBJ]

Maximes, Les (*Réflexions ou Sentences et maximes morales*), see LA ROCHEFOUCAULD.

Maximes, pensées, caractères et anecdotes, see CHAMFORT.

MAXIMIN, Daniel (b. 1947). Writer and teacher from Guadeloupe, closely associated for many years with the journal *Présence africaine*, a sensitive critic steeped in the developing traditions of black literature in French. *L'Isolé Soleil* (1981) is a densely allusive novel, setting up textual exchanges (notebooks and diaries, fragments of song and story) to mimic the historical interpenetration of 'nos quatre races, nos sept langues, nos douzaines de sangs' and to reflect on the meaning of Caribbean experience. *Soufrières* (1987) also creates both appealing characters and a text of poetic density, dominated by the symbolism of the erupting volcano. [BJ]

Maximum, Le. The Revolutionary Convention's attempt to control the economy by price-fixing. On 4 May 1793 sale of grain was thus regulated; on 29 September the so-called 'General Maximum' included all foodstuffs and commodities.

May 1968. The *événements de mai*, as they are widely known, continue at once to stimulate and to baffle analysis. 'Ce qu'il faut comprendre, c'est à la fois l'énormité et l'insignifiance de mai 68' (Edgar Morin)—or, in other words, how the most spectacular and unpredictable period of civil disorder experienced by a Western democracy since World War II culminated in the biggest majority in French electoral history for the incumbent regime. The cultural and (in an *Althusserian sense) ideological results of May have always been more apparent than its political ones; yet it could be argued that these latter include the fall of de *Gaulle, the rise of *Mitterrand and the Parti Socialiste (PS), and the terminal decline of the Parti Communiste Français (PCF).

Unrest in the student milieu had been manifest for several months before May, primarily in the form of protests against the Vietnam War and the restrictive conditions under which students lived. These converged on the new campus at Nanterre in the Paris suburbs, where male students were not allowed to visit women in their rooms, and the administration block was occupied on 22 March in protest against the arrest of a Nanterre student who had taken part in an attack on the American Express building in Paris. Libidinal emancipation (as evidenced by the slogan 'Jouissez sans entraves') and direct action—two of the major themes of May—

were articulated here. Robert *Merle's novel *Derrière la vitre* (1970) is set in Nanterre (where its author taught) on 22 March.

Discontent escalated and spread to the Quartier Latin, whose student traditions made of it the opposite pole to Nanterre. (It is interesting to note how the educational institutions most closely associated with May were the time-hallowed—the *Sorbonne, the *École Normale Supérieure— and the very new—the Paris universities of Nanterre and Censier.) It was the occupation of the Sorbonne by the police and the imprisonment of students that led to the 'May' familiar from countless photographic images. The night of 10–11 May—the 'nuit des barricades'—saw fierce street-fighting on the Left Bank and aroused the sympathy of many young workers for the students, despite the hostility of the Confédération Générale du Travail (CGT) and the PCF, for whom the students (and Daniel Cohn-Bendit in particular) were spoilt brats playing a dangerously diversionary game.

In the days that followed, strikes and occupations spread from the Paris university world to, on the one hand, the provinces, and on the other the factories. When on 17 May the Renault factory at Boulogne-Billancourt, heart of the CGT/PCF's industrial empire, was occupied, it was clear that the established Left had been outstripped by the movement's heterogeneous and contagious dynamism. Trotskyist, Maoist, and anarchist militants were joined by many thousands of others previously not politicized.

De Gaulle's attempts to master a crisis he himself described as 'insaisissable' appeared doomed to failure, as his address to the nation on 24 May was greeted with derision and the supposedly generous economic terms of the Accords de Grenelle were rejected at Billancourt on 27 May. It looked increasingly as if the work-force's dissatisfaction with its pay and conditions might combine with the vehement denunciations of capitalism and imperialism emerging from the occupied universities to bring about the downfall of the regime: workers and students alike were opposed to Gaullism's hierarchical gerontocracy.

The leaders of the established Left—*Mendès-France, Mitterrand, Waldeck Rochet—in different ways threw their hats into the ring, and when de Gaulle literally disappeared for the afternoon of 29 May (on a mission to General Massu, commander of the French forces in Germany, that not even his prime minister *Pompidou knew about), his days seemed numbered. With hindsight, and bearing in mind the all-pervasive theatricality of the events, it now seems unsurprising that within 24 hours the pendulum had swung in the opposite direction. In his radio speech on 30 May de Gaulle refused to resign, announced parliamentary elections, and delivered a cavernous warning of the dangers of totalitarian Communism. That evening a massive Gaullist counter-demonstration filled the

Champs-Élysées. Exactly a month later the second round of the elections yielded an unprecedented Gaullist landslide.

Less than a year later, however, de Gaulle was to resign—defeated in a referendum on regional reform that everybody knew to be a vote of confidence. It seems quite clear that his patriarchal domination had been irretrievably shattered by May. The PCF was the other major casualty; its loss of contact with youth and belated attempt to turn from condemnation of the events to annexation of them severely weakened its credibility, and it is arguable that the PS became the major Left party because (at least until it was in government) it was better able to identify with the concerns and the spirit of May [see SOCIALISM AND COMMUNISM].

What was this spirit? Its two main qualities can be summed up as a rejection of unaccountable hierarchies (which bore fruit in the democratization of universities and the recognition of work-place union branches) and a broadening of political terms of reference away from worker-ist economism to include such areas as *feminism, the Third World, the environment, and questions of (in the widest sense) culture. Nothing changed after May, yet everything was—remains—*different*.   [KAR]

See A. Delale and G. Ragache, *La France de 68* (1978); A. Schnapp and P. Vidal-Naquet, *Journal de la commune étudiante* (1969, new edn. 1988); L. Joffrin, *Mai 68* (1988).

MAYNARD, see MAINARD.

MAZARIN, Cardinal Jules (Giulio Mazarini or Mazzarino) (1602–61). After training in the law, some military service, and experience as a papal diplomat, Mazarin came to France in 1634, entered the service of *Richelieu, and was naturalized in 1639. He succeeded Richelieu as first minister in 1642 and remained in that post until his death. His early years were marked by military successes abroad, but his government was shaken by revolts during the *Fronde (1648–53), and his own popularity fell to a very low ebb [see next entry]. He was responsible for selecting and training the administrators who were to establish *Louis XIV's absolutist reign: *Fouquet, *Colbert, and Le Tellier. He was an avid patron of the opera and of letters, continuing to protect those who had been favoured by Richelieu: *Chapelain, *Desmarets, *Corneille, *Ménage. Above all, he was a book-collector, in which he was abetted by his librarian *Naudé. By 1651 his library numbered 57,000 volumes; he left it to the nation.
[IM]

Mazarinades. *Pamphlets in verse or prose produced during the *Fronde, mostly directed against *Mazarin, the Queen Mother Anne d'Autriche, or the financiers. Published in vast numbers (several thousand for the period 1649–53), they continued the tradition of pamphleteering from the *Wars of Religion. *La Mazarinade* (1651), generally attributed

to *Scarron, gave its name to the whole series, which quickly began to be collected by *amateurs*. Many of the pamphlets are anonymous, but well-known writers such as *Patru and *Sarasin were also involved; one of the major authors writing for *Retz was Jacques Carpentier, known as Marigny. Many *mazarinades* take the form of popular songs, set to existing melodies. Their tone is often highly scurrilous; in vocabulary and in verse forms (notably the octosyllable) they echo the contemporary vogue for the *burlesque.   [PF]

M'BAYE D'ERNEVILLE, Annette (b. 1926). Senegalese poet and journalist. Her *Poèmes africains* (1965) and *Kaddu* (1966) establish her as the pioneer of Senegalese women writers, and she has been a source of inspiration and encouragement to younger women. Kaddu means 'spoken words' in Wolof, and in her poems she speaks for all African women, living and dead, members of her family, and friends from her Paris days. She reminds us that there is suffering, revolt, love that is specific to women, and at the same time specifically African: e.g. 'Kassack' (a circumcision song) addressed to her son; 'Labane', a young girl's lament on being deflowered by the husband imposed on her against her will. Intensely personal, her verses speak of betrayal, shared passion, maternal love, love of humanity, nostalgia, bitterness, mourning, solitude, regrets, and despair, but we also glimpse some of the themes of *négritude: Mother Africa, slavery— from the viewpoint of the woman violated to breed a 'négresse marron'. Every poem is constructed on a striking visual image, with a musical tempo appropriate to the theme: the rhythm of the blues, the beat of the tom-tom, the syncopation of dance music in a Paris night-club, the sensual panting of metre adapted to explicit erotic effects. She has also published a book of verses for children, *Chansons pour Laïty* (1976).   [DSB]

MBENGUE, Mamadou Seyni (b. 1925). Senegalese dramatist. *Le Procès de Lat Dior*, Mbengue's contribution to Senegalese nationalist theatre, won the RFI Inter-African Theatre Competition in 1970. Plays by other writers about Lat Dior, the 19th-c. Senegalese national hero of resistance to the French, are written in epic style, but in Mbengue's version Lat Dior is tried by a modern jury. His sacrifice of the lives of his people is condemned, but he is ultimately acquitted. Mbengue, who has held a number of important posts in the Senegalese Ministry of Information, has also written a historical novel, *Le Royaume de sable* (1976), set in Cayor immediately after the colonial conquest.   [FNC]

Meaulnes. The poetic young hero of Alain-Fournier's *Le *Grand Meaulnes*.

Meaux. Town to the east of Paris, of which *Bossuet was bishop for many years, whence his nickname 'l'Aigle de Meaux'. For the 16th-c. Groupe de Meaux see EVANGELICALS.

MECHAKRA, Yamina (b. c.1954). Algerian writer and psychiatrist; author of one of the most remarkable literary texts on the *Algerian War. Devoid of revolutionary idealism and abstract heroism, *La Grotte éclatée* (1979) is as much a love poem as it is a novel about the impact of war. This prose poem is dedicated to the memory of a freedom fighter, tortured and killed by the French before Mechakra's very eyes, but who appears to have taught his daughter, Yamina, that human dignity and compassion transcend hatred and revenge.   [DM-S]

Méchant, Le (1745). A somewhat bitter comedy of manners by *Gresset.

MEDDEB, Abdelwahab (b. 1946). Tunisian novelist, poet, and essayist of the younger generation after Independence. His first novel, *Talismano* (1979), established him as an experimental writer who uses the art of displacement with great skill, establishing a complicity with the Arabic language and culture. In his second novel, *Phantasia* (1986), he raises the fundamental Maghrebian questions of selfhood and alterity, dealing with the voluntary exile of the artist. Thus, we witness a confrontation of occidental and Arabo-Islamic cultures. In his collection of poems, *Tombeau d'Ibn Arabi* (1987), his poetic prose captures the letter and the spirit of the most important medieval Arabic poet whose young Persian lover, Nidam, foreshadows Dante's Beatrice. Meddeb is also an essayist and a translator from Arabic to French (see his *Les Dits de Bûstami*, 1989).   [HB]

Médecin de campagne, Le. Novel by *Balzac, written in 1832–3, the first of the works to be included in the *Scènes de la vie de campagne* in *La *Comédie humaine*. It tells the story of Dr Benassis, the country doctor of the title, a Catholic Utopian who brings morality and relative prosperity to a peasant community in a fertile valley of the lower Alps. The novel is of some formal interest, combining an original use of the 'guided tour', a retrospective confession which alters the reader's perception of the main character and his motivations at the very end, and a celebrated insertion, 'La Vie de Napoléon racontée dans une grange', which is perhaps the first self-conscious transcription of oral history in French literature. It is said that Balzac borrowed the idea of this bravura passage from Henri *Monnier; whatever his sources, he succeeded in giving popular form to an important national myth in which ancient superstitions support a belief in the possibility of achievement and progress. *Le Médecin de campagne* as a whole is also one of the few novels of *La Comédie humaine* to be imbued with 19th-c. optimism, the sense that self-interest controlled by hierarchy and religion can bring progress, self-respect, and collective improvement.   [DMB]

Médecin malgré lui, Le. One of *Molière's best farces, performed 1666. Forced by a trick of his wife Martine to act the doctor, the woodcutter Sganarelle 'cures' Géronte's daughter Lucinde by introducing the young beau Léandre as his apothecary. When asked why he refers to the heart as being on the right side, Sganarelle explains: 'Oui, cela était autrefois ainsi, mais nous avons changé tout cela.'   [PF]

Médée. Tragedy by P. *Corneille, first performed 1635. Inspired by Euripides and Seneca, this vigorous play is notable for the self-assertion of its heroine, Medea.

Medieval Theatre. A theatrical performance in the Middle Ages was much more than just an example of a literary genre; it was often a social, religious, and commercial event affecting a whole community and involving not only the spoken word, but also spectacle, music, and even dance. Moreover, drama was arguably the most pervasive of all literary genres, since the illiteracy of the public was no barrier to a play's reception. Although much medieval literature had a dramatic or para-dramatic dimension—*lyric poetry was sung at seigneurial courts, *chansons de geste* were declaimed, *romances and *fabliaux* were narrated before live audiences—the theatre, especially by the end of the Middle Ages, was able to reach the widest possible public.

The popularity of drama in France in the Middle Ages is attested by the survival of some 600 texts and by archive records of thousands of performances from the late 11th to the mid-16th c. These texts reflect a wide range of types of dramatic literature: liturgical drama, *miracle plays, *mystery plays, *farces, *soties, *morality plays, etc. Traditional criticism divides medieval French drama into two types, religious and comic.

Religious drama in Europe is generally believed to have its origins in the liturgy of the medieval Catholic Church. Tropes (musical and verbal embellishments) introduced into first the Easter, then the Christmas, Mass grew into semi-independent units called an *Ordo* or a *ludus* dramatizing the story of the Resurrection or the Nativity. This Latin liturgical drama, sung by monks in abbeys and churches across Europe, developed in complexity betwèen the 9th and the 15th c., and drew on an increasingly wide range of material, including saints' lives [see HAGIOGRAPHY] and the Bible. Some of these dramas contained refrains or interpolated passages in the vernacular.

The earliest dramas in French, the 12th-c. *Jeu d'Adam* and the *Seinte Resurreccion*, are often held to owe much to the traditions of liturgical drama, although these plays were written at the same time as, if not before, some of the most complex liturgical dramas. The theatre of medieval France stands out from that of its European neighbours in that a number of important early (pre-14th-c.) texts have survived. In particular, a remarkable group of plays were composed in *Arras in the 13th c. The first two of these, *Courtois d'Arras and the *Jeu de Saint Nicolas, are partly comic adaptations of religious sources, respectively of the parable of the prodigal son and of a miracle performed by Saint Nicolas. At the end of the century *Adam de la Halle wrote two completely secular plays, the Jeu de la Feuillée and the Jeu de Robin et Marion, both dramatizations of lyric genres. Though the Arras plays seem to have had little influence on later drama, they introduced some of the technical aspects of composition found in all subsequent plays, in particular, the use of the octosyllabic couplet and the mnemonic rhyme, where the last line of each speech rhymes with the first line of the next. The Arras plays owe much to the social structure of the city where they were composed, and above all to the expansion of the *confréries and trade guilds.

It was the confréries, associations of lay people meeting to worship a particular saint or to celebrate a special feast, who were largely responsible for the development of the French miracle play, the genre which dominated the 14th c. These plays, usually between 1,000 and 3,000 lines long, dramatize some of the vast quantity of narrative literature based on miracles allegedly accomplished by the Virgin Mary or by the saints; though clearly religious in inspiration, the plots of miracle plays are set in the real world. They thus contribute to a secularizing tendency already seen in the Arras plays. About 50 French miracle plays survive, 40 in one major collection, the *Miracles de Nostre Dame par personnages, performed by a confrérie of the Parisian goldsmiths. Performances often took place indoors, in a guild-hall, with a system of staging, now called décor simultané, which was used in all religious drama from the 12th to the 16th c.: all the sets required by a play were placed in the playing area at the beginning of the performance; there was no curtain, no scene changes. This system greatly influenced not only the shape of medieval theatres (never permanent, but always constructed ad hoc), but also dramaturgical writing and other practices.

Mystery plays flourished in the 15th and early 16th c. Their subject-matter included not only that of the earlier miracle plays, especially saints' lives, but also biblical material; the life and crucifixion of Christ was the subject of a special type of mystère, the *Passion play. Their most striking features are an increasing length and a tendency to mix extremes of tone. The average mystery play is about 10,000 lines long, many are around 30,000, and a few almost 60,000. These enormous dimensions meant that a performance was an exceptional event, the organization of which was beyond a small confrérie. Normally the cooperation and financial subsidy of a town's administration were required; preparations were costly, involved hundreds of people, and extended over many months. They frequently made a financial loss, but attracted trade from the specta-

tors coming from afar. Stages were normally constructed in a town square or other similar large, open space, and audiences had to pay; but virtually all members of the community were able to attend. To attract such an audience for a long period of time, plays needed variety of tone; serious episodes were interspersed with comic scenes and characters, as well as violence and vulgarity.

Historically, one notes two parallel developments. As the stage used for medieval religious drama moves from the church to the guild-hall, and finally out into the town square, so the content and style of the plays change from the sobriety of the earliest texts to extreme variety. It is thus a mistake to see mystery plays merely as religious drama; indeed, they anticipate the mixing of genres later to be characteristic of the *Romantic period.

Of the so-called comic genres, the farce and the sotie clearly see laughter as their principal aim; this is less obvious in the morality play. These genres do not appear before the 15th c. and their origins are problematic. If the soties, with their apparently plotless, disordered conversations between sots, have a strong satirical undercurrent, the farces, usually dramatizations of *fabliau-like situations based on deceit or trickery set in a ménage à trois, have no moralizing purpose. These plays, rarely longer than 500 lines (though the Farce de Maistre Pierre *Pathelin is an outstanding exception), were normally performed by small groups of travelling professional players like the *Enfants Sans Souci or by societies of law students known as the *Basoche. Moralities, however, sit uneasily across the religious–comic divide, their function being the teaching of a moral lesson by means of a dramatic action involving abstractions or personified virtues and vices. It is their treatment of this subject-matter which makes them comic, and, of course, the fact that the conclusion is always a happy one. Evil characters provoke mockery and laughter, as do the devils in mystery plays.

Such problems of classification did not preoccupy the medieval public, who enjoyed all of these genres, as well as such para-dramatic works as *sermons, *sermons joyeux, *dits, and dramatic monologues. The theatre's popularity reflects the largely oral and visual culture of the Middle Ages, appealing to all social and intellectual groups. The large-scale medieval spectacles strengthened the sense of social cohesion. The intellectuals wrote the texts; the artists provided the sets; aristocrats and bourgeois commissioned, organized, and acted in the plays; the local artisans built the stages; and the whole community watched.   [GAR]

See G. Frank, The Medieval French Drama (1953); E. Konigson, L'Espace théâtral médiéval (1975).

Méditations métaphysiques, see DESCARTES.

Méditations poétiques, see LAMARTINE.

MEIGRET, Louis (c.1500–after 1558). Humanist and translator, notably of classical authors, Meigret produced the first French *grammar written in French (*Traité de la grammaire française*, 1550). He was a principal protagonist in the debate on spelling reform, favouring in his *Traité touchant le commun usage de l'écriture française* (1542) an orthography based on pronunciation—thus the title of his grammar was spelt *Tretté de la grammere françoeze*. [WA-B]

MEILHAC, Henri (1831–97), and **HALÉVY,** Ludovic (1834–1908). Legendary duo celebrated for their collaboration in charming drawing-room comedies (*Froufrou*, 1869; *La Petite Marquise*, 1874), but above all as the authors of irreverent and entertaining libretti for the operettas of Offenbach, mostly staged at the Théâtre des Bouffes-Parisiens, and distilling the hedonistic spirit of *Second Empire Paris: *La Belle Hélène* (1864), *La Vie parisienne* (1866), *La Grande Duchesse de Gérolstein* (1867), etc. Halévy was also the author of amusing, if sentimental, pictures of family life: *Abbé Constantin* (1882), *La Famille Cardinal* (1883). His interesting journal was published posthumously: *Carnets* (1935). [SBJ]

MEILLET, Antoine, see LINGUISTICS.

MEISTER, Jacques-Henri (1744–1826), see CORRESPONDANCE LITTÉRAIRE.

Mélanide. *Comédie larmoyante*, in five acts and in verse, by Nivelle de *la Chaussée. The best example of the genre, *Mélanide* was first performed at the Comédie-Française in 1741, and it remained fairly popular until 1815. It is adapted from *Gueullette's *Mémoires de Mademoiselle Bontemps* of 1738. Its complicated plot turns on the themes of separation, illegitimacy, concealed identity, recognition, and reunion. The intricacies of the plot were less important to the author and his audiences than the emotional experiences they afforded, such as empathy with the sufferings of virtue and the admiration of patience, forgiveness, and magnanimity. The roles are largely uninteresting, and the Parisian setting conventional. The title and tone of the play are broadly tragic, and the diction (unlike that of the later *drames) elevated and stylized. [JD]

Meliador, see FROISSART.

MÉLIÈS, Georges, see CINEMA.

Mélite, see CORNEILLE, P.

MELLAH, Fawzi (b. 1946). Tunisian novelist, essayist, and playwright. In his essays and creative work Mellah deals with post-colonial social problems that have their roots in the past as well as with myths and legends that have currency and relevance in today's Tunisia. His novels, *Le Conclave des pleureuses* (1987) and *Elissa la reine vagabonde* (1988), draw on reality and myth to explore the multiple layers of the Maghrebian psyche and imagination. [HΛJ]

Mélodie, see WORDS AND MUSIC, 2.

Melodrama. The French *mélodrame* is derived from the Greek word for 'music-drama', and was applied to a form of dramatic performance in which one or more actors recited to music. It became popular in France in the second half of the 18th c. and was used of J.-J. *Rousseau's *Pygmalion* (1775), a *scène lyrique* in which brief spoken passages alternate with expressive instrumental music. Its current meaning dates from about 1802, when *Pixerécourt applied it to big stage-plays with incidental music, spectacular scenic effects, and sensational plots, of which he was the acknowledged master and which were wildly popular. Many features of the melodrama—its stock characters, violent emotions, inflated language, and moral sententiousness, together with its passion for crime and punishment, remorse and retribution—are drawn from 18th-c. models, including the English Gothic novel, the *comédie larmoyante*, and the *drame bourgeois*. The novelty of Pixerécourt's melodrama lies in the degree to which it theatricalizes these features by exploiting all the resources of the stage (music, costume, scene-painting, machinery) in order to produce a fast-moving action, peopled with heroes and villains, that is fully integrated with the spectacular sets (designed by Ciceri and others) representing wild, picturesque, or sinister places. [See DRAMA IN FRANCE SINCE 1789.] [SBJ]

Mélusine, Le Roman de. Two versions exist, one in verse by Jean d'Arras (1392–3), one in prose by Coudrette (*c*.1402). The former claims to have adapted his version from a chronicle given him by his patron Jean de Berry, but it is more probably derived from local legend. It concerns Mélusine, daughter of a fairy, who marries Raimund on condition that he never follow her on Saturdays. Mélusine gives birth to ten sons, thus establishing the Lusignan dynasty, and they pursue chivalric success all over Europe and the East. Eventually Raimund transgresses, and finds that his wife is transformed into a serpent; she disappears, but since then, beneficent, she watches over her descendants. The legend continued in common currency for several centuries. [JHMT]

MEMMI, Albert (b. 1920). By far the most prestigious and prolific Tunisian francophone writer, Memmi is one of the founders of Maghrebian literature. His novels deal with the Jewish community in the *hara* of the Tunisian capital. They also attempt to trace ancestral origins in order to establish the fluctuating identity of the Jewish community in an Arabo-Islamic context. His first novel, *La Statue de sel* (1953), deals with enigmatic Jewish selfhood within the cultural matrix of colonialism; it centres on Alexandre Mordekhaï Benillouche's struggle in relation to family, tradition, and the outside world. In *Agar* (1955) Memmi deals with the problem of intermarriage between a European and a Maghrebian. *Le Scorpion* (1969) shows Memmi at his best in experimental narrative. He treats the oppression of tradition while recapturing a cultural identity constantly fluctuating between occidental and oriental in a series of interwoven narratives which shatter linearity. *Le Désert* (1977) is a masterpiece in which Memmi, a sociologist, becomes a kind of historian pushing his novelistic rock, like Sisyphus, through the history of the family, the tribe, and the itinerary of 'the life and adventures of Jubaïr Ouali El-Mammi'. Again, the imaginary taps all the sources of the Tunisian heritage, above all the founder of modern sociology, Ibn Khaldoun. In *Le Pharaon* (1988) Memmi shows again his talent as story-teller, telling us the tale of a professor of Egyptology within the struggle for Tunisian independence. Here he criss-crosses the destinies of known political figures, both French and Tunisian, with the love story of his main characters.

Memmi is also a great essayist, whose *Portrait du colonisé* (1957) had certainly the greatest impact for all the African and post-colonial nations, but also for Quebec. A fundamental essay dealing with the relationship—psychological, sociological, political—between the colonizer and the colonized, its importance cannot be overestimated. Other essays include *Portrait d'un Juif* (1962), *La Libération du Juif* (1966), *L'Homme dominé* (1968), *Juif et Arabe* (1974), *La Dépendance* (1979), and *Le Racisme* (1982). In the earlier books he dealt primarily with the problems arising between the Jewish and Arab communities: because he attempts to strike a balance, his works have been viewed as controversial by both. In his later works Memmi deals with more universal issues, always in relation to the dialectic of peoples: the couple, race, culture. He has also published interviews: *Entretiens* (1975), *La Terre intérieure* (1976), *Ce que je crois* (1984). Many of his books have been translated into several languages. [HB]

See R. Elbaz, *Le Discours maghrébin: dynamique textuelle chez Albert Memmi* (1988).

Memnon (1749). Short philosophic tale by Voltaire, mocking the desire to be perfectly wise; also the original title of **Zadig*.

Mémoires à consulter, see BEAUMARCHAIS.

Mémoires de la vie d'Henriette-Sylvie de Molière, see VILLEDIEU.

Mémoires d'Hadrien, see YOURCENAR.

Mémoires d'outre-tombe. *Chateaubriand's autobiography, published posthumously (1849–50). He conceived the project in 1803, began in 1809, finished in 1847. Much of the writing was done after 1830, but he integrated into the text fragments published earlier and elsewhere. An analysis of both his self and his age, the work is marked by a paradox of despair (both past and future are impossible) and hope, with an idealization of the real, a personification of his dreams, a desire for happiness combined with disappointments about life. It is divided into four sections (his early years, travels, military career, and exile; his literary career during the Consulate and the Empire; his political career under the *Restoration; and the years of his retirement); the large-scale text contains sharp portraits of *Napoleon, Charles X, and many others, and highly evocative, vivid scenes, some derived from his travels, some from his appreciation of nature. It is perhaps the most appreciated of Chateaubriand's works today and a benchmark in the French *autobiographical tradition. [FPB]

Mémoires d'une jeune fille rangée (1958). The first and most personal volume of Simone de *Beauvoir's memoirs.

Mémoires d'un touriste, see STENDHAL.

Mémoires et aventures d'un homme de qualité (1728–31). Long novel by abbé *Prévost which includes *Manon Lescaut.

Mémoire tatouée, La, see KHATIBI.

Memoir-Novel. This term could cover all novels in which a character tells his or her life-story, but in practice it is applied almost exclusively to works up to the early 19th c. This is doubtless because the 18th c. is held to be the 'golden age' of novels in this form. Sorel's **Françion* (1623) is the earliest major French novel in which autobiographical narrative is important; and *Le Page disgrâcié* (1642) by *Tristan l'Hermite is another landmark. As historical memoirs became more numerous, some novelists composed 'pseudo-memoirs' in which the lives of real people were narrated as though they had written the story themselves. A celebrated example is *Hamilton's *Mémoires du Comte de Gramont*, and *Courtilz de Sandras produced several such works, including the *Mémoires de M. d'Artagnan* (the basis for Dumas's *Les *Trois Mousquetaires*).

In a second type of memoir-novel the narrator is a fictional character, but historical personages and events are introduced as a kind of authentification. *Prévost frequently used this technique. Finally there are memoir-novels which, while they may claim to be 'true', do not rely on historical elements. The first major example is Madame de *Villedieu's *Mémoires de la vie d'Henriette-Sylvie de Molière* (1672). A variation in form makes some memoir-novels akin to *epistolary novels: thus, Marivaux presents the instalments of *La *Vie de Marianne* as letters sent by Marianne to a friend.

Memoir-novels include works in a wide range of styles and subject-matter, from the edifying to the obscene. Among the most successful examples are **Gil Blas* (1715–35), which illustrates the comic and picaresque vein; *Les *Égarements du cœur et de l'esprit* (1736–8); *La *Religieuse*, for many readers the most gripping 18th-c. work in this form; and *Les Amours de Faublas* (1787–90) by *Louvet de Couvray, which moves from initial frivolity to a sombre, quasi-Romantic ending.

The importance of memoir-novels, in terms of literary history, lies in the opportunities offered by this form for analysis and exploration of the narrator's personality. This subjective approach opened the way to more subtle and complex characterization than had appeared in most previous novels with external narrators. [VGM]

See R. Démoris, *Le Roman à la première personne* (1975).

Memoirs, see AUTOBIOGRAPHY.

'Mémorial, Le'. The document recording his second conversion that *Pascal carried sewn into his clothing.

Mémorial de Sainte-Hélène, see LAS CASES.

MÉNAGE, Gilles (1613–92). By training a lawyer but a constant presence in Parisian literary circles, he was a friend of *La Mothe le Vayer and *Méré, and the flirtatious 'professor' of Madame de *Lafayette and Madame de *Sévigné. He thus belonged to the group of self-appointed censors of language and taste who have been credited with the creation of French *classicism, and may be the original of *Molière's Vadius (*L'École des femmes*, III. 3). His *Origines de la langue française* (1650), though hardly satisfying modern philological standards, offers an insight into the linguistic preoccupations of the day. [PJB]

Ménagier de Paris, Le, see HOUSEHOLD MANAGEMENT TREATISES.

Menaud, maître-draveur, see SAVARD.

MENDÈS, Catulle (1841–1909). Versatile, prolific, and superficial, Mendès is now more remembered for his critical writing than for his poetry, novels, and plays. With the support of *Gautier (whose daughter, Julie, he later married), he founded *La Revue fantaisiste* in 1861 and five years later cofounded *Le Parnasse contemporain*, two reviews which figured prominently in the poetic movement linking the *Romantic and *Symbolist generations. He was a friend of *Mallarmé, who addressed to him some of his most significant statements on poetry, and was one of the first and most ardent French defenders of Wagner. His eyewitness account of the *Commune of 1871 is a revealing statement of the *Parnassian separation of art and politics, and his *Légende du Parnasse contemporain* (1884) and *Rapport sur le mouvement poétique français* (1902) remain important histories of the poetry of the period. [JK]

MENDÈS-FRANCE, Pierre (1907–82). The last important leader of the once powerful French *Radical Party. After participating in the Resistance, he became a *député* in 1946 and prime minister in 1954, when he succeeded in extricating France from the war in *Indo-China. His austere policies attracted much hostility, and he was defeated in 1955

and never returned to power, but his vision and commitment have remained a source of inspiration to many on the Left. [PF]

MÉNESTRIER, Claude-François (1631–1705). French Jesuit father who became a specialist in organizing *royal entries and *fêtes* and a theorist of heraldry, court ballet, and allegorical or spectacular art of many kinds. See his *L'Art du blason* (1661), *L'Art des emblèmes* (1662), *Traité des tournois, joutes, carrousels et autres spectacles publics* (1669).

MÉNÉTRA, Jacques-Louis (1738–after 1803). Glazier whose *Journal de ma vie* (ed. D. Roche, 1982) is a rare example of an 18th-c. working-man's autobiography. This spirited text gives a remarkable glimpse of ordinary Parisian life in the years preceding the Revolution.

MENGA, Guy (b. 1935). Congolese teacher turned journalist, Menga was head of National Broadcasting in Brazzaville but experienced political difficulties after the change of regime in 1968 and was dismissed from public service in 1971. He moved to France and became head of the African section of Radio France Internationale. A prolific writer, he has won numerous prizes for his plays, novels, and short stories. His works dominated Congo theatre in the late 1960s. His first play, *La Marmite de Koka Mbala*, a social satire in which the villagers ultimately free themselves from the oppressive clutches of the fetish priest, was performed at the Festival of Black Arts in Dakar in 1966. *L'Oracle*, another social satire on the traditional oppression of women and youth, won an Inter-African Theatre Competition prize in 1967. Menga's first novel, *La Palabre stérile*, awarded the Grand Prix Littéraire d'Afrique Noire in 1969, is a not wholly successful cocktail of well-known themes: gerontocracy, the problems of urban life, drugs, and the role of mysticism (Matswanism) in politics. Set in the colonial era, the novel lacks the verve of the comedies. He has written two other novels: *Kotawali* (1977), the story of a woman resistance fighter's attempt to raise the consciousness of a lorry-driver, and *La Case de Gaulle* (1984). [FNC]

MÉNIL, René (b. 1907). Martinican poet, essayist, and political thinker, contributor to *Légitime défense* and *Tropiques* and for many years a leading Communist intellectual in Martinique. His major writings are collected in *Tracées: identité, négritude, esthétique aux Antilles* (1981). [RDEB]

MENOT, Michel (d. 1518). Franciscan preacher. Very little is known of his early life, other than that he was a student at Orléans. He was appointed guardian of the Franciscan house in Chartres in 1514, and restored its buildings. He gave Lenten series of *sermons in Amiens (1496), Tours (1508), and Paris (1517 and 1518), dying there in the latter year at the height of his fame. His sermons were first published in 1519. They are remarkable for the vigour of their language and the range of anecdotes and fables they contain as *exempla.   [PJB]

Menteur, Le. Comedy by Pierre *Corneille, inspired by Lope de Vega, first performed in 1644. Dorante, a law student newly returned to Paris from the provinces, invents a glamorous life for himself to impress two young women, Lucrèce and Clarice. He courts Clarice, thinking her to be Lucrèce, fights a duel with her lover, becomes embroiled in an ever-growing web of lies which shock his simple valet Cliton and his honourable father Géronte, but in the end extricates himself by fast talking and marries the real Lucrèce. This entertaining play reads in places like an ironic reflexion on Corneille's tragedies. A sequel, *La Suite du Menteur* (1645), is less successful.   [PF]

Mépris de la vie, Le, see CHASSIGNET.

Meraugis de Portlesguez, see RAOUL DE HOUDENC.

MERCIER, Alfred, see LOUISIANA.

MERCIER, Louis-Sébastien (1740–1814). French polymath who was for long judged in accordance with the dismissive evaluation of his contemporaries; for he was a resolute nonconformist in all things who fell foul of censorship, of the Comédie-Française, of the literary establishment, of the monarchy, of *Robespierre, of *Napoleon . . . but who has found more favour with the Romantics and the late 20th c.

He was first known, throughout France and Europe, as the author of some 50 *drames bourgeois, which all suffered from the curse of the genre: a surfeit of didacticism and high moral purpose. Conversely, his prefaces to those plays and his manifestos are of capital importance because they contain visionary opinions and insights which were to resurface with the young Victor *Hugo. Indeed, Jules Janin was to characterize the *Nouvel essai sur l'art dramatique* (1773) as Mercier's *Préface de *Cromwell.* With exactly the same prescience, *Mon bonnet de nuit* (1784) contains a rich collection of thoughts concerning the future of French poetry (which any historian of *Romanticism must read), while, similarly, the basic contention of *Néologie* (1801)—in which Mercier once again bridges the rationalism of the 18th c. and the burgeoning literary imagination of the 19th—is that French poets will be mere versifiers until such time as a revolution has been accomplished in imagery and vocabulary. Prefiguring Hugo once more, it was really Mercier who put a 'bonnet rouge' on the dictionary.

The earliest of Mercier's works which is still read for genuine enjoyment and stimulation is *L'An 2440* (1770), a work of political radicalism which—springing from a novel conjunction of past experience, present observation, and prophetic extrapolation—is the only genuinely creative contribution to

*Utopian literature in the 18th c. Mercier's fame is, however, inseparable from his *Tableau de Paris* (1781–9) and *Le Nouveau Paris* (1793–8), 18 volumes of disorganized sketches of Parisian life seen through its people, its places, and its institutions, which appeared to his classical contemporaries as a peripatetic's artless, even chaotic, collection of 'choses vues', but which—with its vitality, its acuity of vision, its implicit classification of social types, and its underlying antithesis between *grandeur* and *misère*—possibly prefigures *Balzac. One can fairly say that Mercier's historical importance and literary qualities have only been properly assessed by modern criticism, which sees his *œuvre* as original, imaginative, and exciting.   [JR]

See H. Temple Patterson, *Poetic Genius: Sébastien Mercier into Victor Hugo* (1960).

MERCIER DE LA RIVIÈRE, see LA RIVIÈRE.

Mercure de France, Le. In 1724, following a government reorganization of publishing, this title was conferred on a publication whose previous names included *Le Mercure français* (1605), the forerunner of the periodical press in France, and *Le *Mercure galant.* France's leading literary review, *Le Mercure de France* was wide-ranging in subject-matter, but prudent in its politics: it was government-controlled. Directed between 1758 and 1760 by *Marmontel, the journal numbered *Voltaire and *La Harpe among its collaborators, and helped promote the *Encyclopédie. After 1778 it prospered under the management of *Panckoucke, covering politics as well as the arts. Generally published weekly, it declined during the Revolution, but was one of the few non-specialist reviews to continue publication under Napoleon.

In 1889 *Symbolist authors founded a literary review entitled *Le Mercure de France* that lasted until 1965 and gave birth to a publishing house in 1894. Rémy de *Gourmont, Jules *Renard, and *Jarry published in the review.   [MP]

Mercure galant, Le. Periodical founded by *Donneau de Visé in 1672. At first published at irregular intervals, it became a monthly in 1678.

Immediately upon the appearance of its inaugural issue in March 1672 it was evident that there was an eager readership for the new public paper. It featured readers' responses to the issues raised by its articles; debate was intense and often prolonged. A veritable flood of gazettes and news-sheets had been launched in the course of the preceding decade, and in the process a new breed of writer, the first true precursor of the modern journalist, came into existence. The first papers contained only political news, on the model of *Renaudot's government-sponsored *Gazette*, which provided the official version of contemporary events. The next papers reported on the world of high society, even its scandals.

Donneau de Visé put journalism at the service of special-interest groups. Well-connected in aristocratic milieux, he produced a public paper whose contents are structured like a *salon discussion. He even reproduces the view of public life painted in the historical fiction of his contemporaries, *Lafayette and *Villedieu. In Le Mercure galant's inaugural issue he explains that it will feature the circumstances—in particular, marriages and law-suits—always omitted from official accounts, that really explain the balance of French power. Le Mercure galant also helped launch new works, notably in 1678, when Donneau de Visé directed the first true publicity campaign, for the appearance of La *Princesse de Clèves. In this way and in many others, he promoted the values of literary 'moderns'.

In collaboration with a team of associates led by Thomas *Corneille, Donneau de Visé ran the paper until his death in 1710. A series of editors, notably *Raynal and *Marmontel, continued Le Mercure galant throughout the 18th c.—under such names as Le Mercure and Mercure de France [see previous entry]. Subsequent editors never re-created Donneau de Visé's formula, the blend of light fiction, occasional verse, and long, gossipy letters that makes the original Le Mercure galant an invaluable source of information on the tastes and the fascinations of the intellectuals who had come of age in salon society.					[JDeJ]

MÉRÉ, Antoine Gombaud, chevalier de (1607–84). A member of the old French nobility, he made his debut as a writer late in life. Drawing on a good education (he was a devotee of Greek literature) and a lifetime's experience of high society, he published six Conversations (1668), followed by three Discours (1677) concerning charm, wit, and conversation, and six further Discours, published posthumously. He is the principal theorist of *honnêteté, which he presents as a compendium of aesthetic and moral values (naturalness, good taste, politeness, charm). It is an ideal of individual excellence, but inseparable from aristocratic hegemony. Paradoxically, given that the honnête homme is the opposite of the pedant, he tends to adopt a pedagogical tone. He corresponded with *Pascal, but his influence on the latter has been exaggerated.   [PF]

Mère coquette, La (1665). Verse comedy by *Quinault.

Mère coupable, La (1792). Sentimental drama by *Beaumarchais, presenting the difficulties of Figaro's married life.

Mère Sotte, see SOTIE.

MÉRIMÉE, Prosper (1803–70). French author of short stories, novels, plays, and historical and archaeological studies, Mérimée was born of a good bourgeois family (his father taught fine arts), first studied the law, but soon opted for a literary career. Marked by Romantic themes and concerns, but often treating them playfully or with ironic distance,

Mérimée began his literary career with two hoaxes. Le Théâtre de Clara Gazul (1825, 1830) presents six mostly short plays set in Spain or South America and somewhat inspired by the liberties of Spanish Golden Age theatre. La Guzla (1827) is a collection of mostly spurious Illyrian folk-songs, etc. La Jacquerie (1828) is a historical drama, but full of violence and revolt, as is La Famille de Carvajal (1828), a dramatic reworking of the Cenci tale which initiates Mérimée's long-standing concern with the relations between eroticism and death. His historical novel, Chronique du règne de Charles IX (1829), is one of French Romanticism's better efforts at the genre; he was a more meticulous historian than either *Dumas or *Vigny, but hardly hides his anticlericalism in this recounting of the *St Bartholomew's Day Massacre.

The rest of his literary output is essentially short stories or novellas, always tersely written, usually exemplifying a ghastly tragic situation but with a distance created by framing devices, by the use of understatement and ambiguity, and by various forms of irony. The collection Mosaïque (1833) included Mateo Falcone, a Corsican tale of a youth who betrays his family honour for a silver watch and is killed by his father; Tamango, about a revolt on a slave ship and the tragic death or bitterly farcical end of all involved; and Le Vase étrusque, where unjustified suspicions of infidelity lead to the lover's death by duel, and the heroine's by heartbreak. In 1841 appeared perhaps his two best tales, *Colomba and La Vénus d'Ille, the latter a fantastic tale in which it is made to appear that a statue of Venus has killed the less-than-sympathetic hero and driven his fiancée to madness; here Mérimée's sceptical narrator is in many ways a self-portrait. *Carmen (1852) was accompanied by Arsène Guillot, a tale of triangular love where the working-class heroine is sacrificed, but with tragic effect, to the devout but adulterous lady of high society. Later in life Mérimée published fewer tales, but they remained remarkable, in particular Djoûmane (1873), which blends the oneiric, the exotic, and the sexual; Lokis (1869), again an archaeological tale set in Lithuania and dealing with miscegenation between bear and woman and the resultant vampire activities of their offspring; and La Chambre bleue (1871), a rather *Maupassant-style tale where an adulterous tryst is marked by blood and death, comfortingly revealed to be only wine and drunkenness.

Literature was a secondary activity for Mérimée, who earned his living as inspector of historical monuments and did much for the preservation of Vézelay, Avignon, etc.; despite his friendship with *Viollet-le-Duc, he generally favoured preservation over restoration. His tireless efforts to preserve the vestiges of France's historical and architectural past produced a number of highly readable volumes of travel literature. He also wrote several historical studies, some still of solid value, on Russian and Spanish history; the best is probably his Histoire de

Don Pèdre Ier, roi de Castille (1848). He had known
*Eugénie de Montijo, Napoleon III's empress, since
her childhood and was always devoted to her and
hence loyal to the regime of her husband; he lived
to see the defeat of France and the fall of the Second
Empire in 1870. He was a close friend of *Stendhal,
and also of Turgenev. Very familiar with English
and Russian literature (he learned Russian as an
adult), he did much to introduce Turgenev, Gogol,
and others to French literature. His correspondence
has been ably edited and provides rich, compre-
hending, and yet caustic judgements on the literature, politics, and personalities of his age. He
combined to a rare degree radical doubts about all
belief-systems—religious or political—with a love
for individual, heroic, even criminal behaviour, and
a sense of how aesthetic distance could maintain
both awareness and perspective.   [FPB]

See A. Raitt, *Prosper Mérimée* (1970); J. Autin,
Prosper Mérimée, archéologue, homme politique (1983).

MERLE, Robert (b. 1908). An academic English specialist in France, Merle has also written plays, history, and novels. His early novels, classic in
construction, are varied in theme: war and its side-
effects in *Week-end à Zuydcoote* (1949, Prix Goncourt)
and *La Mort est mon métier* (1952); the Bounty story
revisited in *L'Île* (1962); Nanterre (where he was professor) in *May 1968* in *Derrière la vitre* (1970). He
also edges into science fiction in *Un animal doué de
raison* (1967), *Malevil* (1972), and *Les Hommes protégés*
(1974), and oneiric suspense in *Madrapour* (1976). For
his saga of the *Wars of Religion, *Fortune de France*
(1977–85), Merle invents an Occitanized 16th-c.
French.   [SFN]

MERLEAU-PONTY, Maurice (1908–61). French
philosopher and essayist; noted for his distinctive
contribution to the development of *phenomenology. In his major work, *Phénoménologie de la perception* (1945), he took the situated body-subject, rather
than pure consciousness, to be the medium of our
insertion in the world; he explored the lived experience, prior to scientific explanation or reflective
analysis, in which self, world, and others are recip-
rocally implicated in non-determinate and ambiguous interrelations. His descriptions of the body–
world nexus of spatial experience, temporality and
history, sexuality and social relationships, and of
language as creative expression and as both innate
and sedimented structure, went far beyond the
nominal range of his title. His interest in the visual
arts owed much to his reflections on perception. A
painting is both expressive and 'autofigurative'; it
makes visible not a representation of an object but
the embodied essence of the act of seeing and of the
creative gesture; it makes manifest the latent meanings of the world through the 'coherent deforma-
tion' of style. As political editor of *Sartre's
influential review *Les *Temps modernes*, Merleau-
Ponty at first adopted a Marxist approach to con-

temporary problems; however, his disillusion with
Communism at the time of the Korean War led to a
bitter critique of the increasingly committed Sartre.
           [REG]

Mérope. Tragedy on a Greek subject by *Voltaire,
first performed 1743.

Merovingians. Frankish dynasty named after King
Merovech (d. 457), who fought for the Romans
against Attila the Hun and established his own rule
in the region of Tournai in what was later to
become Flanders. His son Chilperic confirmed
Frankish authority over this region and was succeeded by his son, Clovis (466–511), memories of
whom may survive in the *chanson de geste
*Floovant. Clovis extended the Frankish kingdom to
the whole of Gaul, which thereby became 'Frankia'
(later 'France'), with its capital at Paris. Through a
combination of warfare and alliances he won control over the Central and Southern Germans
(Thuringians and Alemanni); he also led successful
campaigns against the Visigoths in Aquitania and
Toulouse, thus laying the foundations of what
would later become the *Carolingian empire. He
was the first Germanic king to convert to
Christianity, embracing Roman Catholicism after
his defeat of the Alemanni and thereby consolidating his rule in Gaulish territory, since the Gallo-
Romans were Catholic also. Clovis's empire was
ruled by his successors until the 8th c. (the territory
being sometimes, as was customary, divided
between several sons at once) but, increasingly, real
power passed to the *Maires du Palais, who ousted
the Merovingians in a palace coup in 751 and
installed Pépin le Bref, father of *Charlemagne, on
the throne.   [SK]

MERRILL, Stuart (1863–1915). Poet. American-born
but French-educated and of socialist and pacifist
sympathies, Merrill settled in France, where he cultivated the art of friendship and penned poems of a
*Symbolist persuasion, sometimes exaggeratedly so,
though distinguished by their refinement and sense
of social concern (*Les Quatre Saisons*, 1900; *Une voix
dans la foule*, 1909). He was gently satirized as
Hubert in *Gide's *Paludes*.   [DAS]

MERSENNE, Marin (1588–1648). French mathematician and theologian who, like *Peiresc and
*Gassendi, combined an adherence to the new sci-
ence with firm commitment to Catholicism. He was
educated at the Jesuit Collège de la Flèche and
became a Minim in 1611. His first publications were
on theological issues; he opposed both atheism and
hermetic philosophy, and wrote a pamphlet in 1624
against the *libertins. His most important mathematical work was in the field of acoustics and optics. He
attacked the scepticism of *Montaigne and was an
ardent defender of Galileo. Like the latter, he
argued that essences were unknowable, but that
precision in observation and experiment could pro-

vide the basis for quantitative mathematical analysis. His scientific empiricism is close to that of Bacon, but in matters of language and communication his work bears the mark of rationalism. His house was an important meeting-place for philosophers and scientists: the young *Pascal met *Descartes there in 1647. Gassendi was one of his close friends. Mersenne is associated with the origins of mechanistic philosophy. Like Peiresc, he engaged indefatigably in international correspondence. [IM]

Merteuil, Madame de. Character in Laclos's Les *Liaisons dangereuses.

MÉRY, Joseph (1798–1867). French journalist, poet, novelist, and dramatist. He was celebrated for his wit, and his political verse satire La Villéliade (1826) was immensely successful, notwithstanding the platitude of its classical couplets.

MESCHINOT, Jean (c.1420–1491). A Breton *Rhétoriqueur (and soldier) attached to the dukes of Brittany. His works include love poetry in the form of rondeaux and ballades, and a sequence of 25 satirical ballads, Les Princes, modelled on *Chastellain's work of the same name. His most famous work, a mixture of prose and verse, was a long allegorical, moralizing piece on the four cardinal virtues, Les Lunettes des princes. Meschinot's fame was considerable, and in the early 16th c. there were more editions of his works than of any other poet except *Villon. [CMSJ]

MESCHONNIC, Henri (b. 1932). French poet and professor of linguistics. His poems (e.g. Dédicaces proverbes, 1972) and biblical translations are closely related to a theoretical enterprise beginning with Pour le poétique (1970–8), an ambitious attempt to overcome the dualities characteristic of modern thinking about literature and language. [PF]

MESLIER, Jean (1664–1729). Curé of a village near Reims and famous in the 18th c. and since for anti-Christian views concealed until his death. His enormous Mémoires (or 'Testament'), perhaps the leading *clandestine manuscript, contain a comprehensive attack on all aspects of Christianity couched in the strongest terms. His philosophy was atheist; it developed out of the materialist side of Cartesianism by way of a critique of *Fénelon. *Voltaire published part of the Mémoires with a deist conclusion. Meslier also violently attacked social injustice and, having sketched out a kind of rural *Utopian communism, has been much studied as a predecessor of socialism. [CJB]

Mesmerism. Doctrine of animal magnetism put forward by Friedrich Anton Mesmer, an Austrian doctor who came to France in 1778, lecturing and conducting healing sessions. Mesmerism was extremely fashionable in France in the years preceding the Revolution, but quickly fell into disrepute.

MESSIAEN, Olivier, see OPERA.

MÉTRA, François (c.1714–1786). One of the authors of an anonymous Correspondance littéraire secrète published in Holland from 1775, and containing much political and literary gossip of the day, some of it scandalous or subversive.

Metric System, see WEIGHTS AND MEASURES.

Métromanie, La (1738). Verse comedy by *Piron, a play of courtship and marriage in which the humour comes from the self-infatuation of poets.

METZ, Christian (b. 1927). France's leading cinema theoretician of the 1960s and 1970s. He followed a path characteristic of much literary theory in moving from an early concern with narrative taxonomy reminiscent of *Genette (Essais sur la signification au cinéma, 1968) to work influenced by *Lacan's psychoanalysis (Le Signifiant imaginaire, 1976). [KAR]

MEUN, Jean de, see JEAN DE MEUN.

Meunier d'Angibault, Le, see SAND.

Meursault. The 'outsider' hero of Camus's L'*Étranger, supposedly named after a favourite wine of the author.

MEYERBEER, Jacques (or Giacomo) (1791–1864), see OPERA.

MÉZERAY, François Eudes, sieur de (1610–83). Historian. Son of a Normandy surgeon, he studied at the University of Caen and served in the army before becoming a man of letters under the protection of *Richelieu, *Séguier, and *Colbert. He contributed to *Renaudot's Gazette and translated and revised histories of Byzantium and the Turks, as well as producing his famous illustrated Histoire de France from 'Faramond' to Henri IV in three large volumes (1643–51), best known in its abridgement, the Abrégé chronologique (1667). Mézeray's criticisms of French kings for over-taxing their subjects infuriated Colbert and led to the loss of the author's pension as Historiographe de France. [UPB]

MICHAUD, Louis-Gabriel, creator of the major French biographical dictionary, see BIOGRAPHY.

MICHAUX, Henri (1899–1984). A profoundly original and independent writer, Michaux was above all an explorer, by all possible means, of his own inner space, conceived not psychologically but in terms of movements, divisions, subsidences, deviations, encounters, 'Émergences-Résurgences' (the title of one of his collections).

Born in Belgium, educated in Flemish, he rebelled against his narrow background and in 1921 signed on as a seaman, making his way eventually to Brazil. He moved to Paris in 1924 (but did not take French nationality until 1955) and was inspired to write by the discovery of *Lautréamont and the encouragement of *Paulhan (*Gide, another admirer, wrote an important essay on Michaux in 1941). Between 1925 and 1939 he travelled extensively in South America, India, China, and Indonesia, reporting on his journeys in *Ecuador* (1929) and *Un barbare en Asie* (1933), and at the same time transforming them into an essentially inner quest. This quest is inaugurated in *Qui je fus* (1927), continued in *Mes propriétés* (1929), *Voyage en grande Garabagne* (1936), and *Un certain Plume* (1930), where the mishaps of the eponymous hero, a Chaplinesque *alter ego*, are handled with a humour which was to be an important dimension of Michaux's writing. The dominant note, however, is that of an intensely emotional engagement with the minute-by-minute ebb and flow of mental and bodily feeling conveyed in a restless, staccato style which concretizes—in such figures as the ghostly Meidosems—the pockets and currents of inner life.

Writing itself becomes a particular form of experience which may aim to exorcize (*Épreuves, exorcismes*, 1945) or to achieve a magical serenity. Influenced by Klee, Ernst, and Chirico, and by oriental calligraphy, Michaux also used graphic means to summon up and pin down his inner world, producing a remarkable body of work, regularly exhibited from the 1950s onwards, which was to lead other artists in the direction of what became known as 'tachisme'. Another important development was the experimentation with drugs, particularly mescalin, recorded in such works as *Misérable miracle* (1956), *L'Infini turbulent* (1957), *Connaissance par les gouffres* (1961), and *Les Grandes Épreuves de l'esprit* (1966), where drug-induced experiences are seen not as a means of escape but as extensions of a constant quest for knowledge. [MHTS]

See M. Bowie, *Henri Michaux* (1973); J.-M. Maulpois, *Michaux passager clandestin* (1985).

MICHEL, Jehan. Author of a four-day, 30,000-line *Passion play, performed in Angers in 1486. No manuscript has survived but several printed editions were published in Paris between 1490 and 1540. Michel based his play on the second and third days of Arnoul *Gréban's Passion play; 65 per cent of the lines are taken from Gréban. But the result is very different. Michel rejects all Old Testament material, the early part of Christ's life, and the Resurrection, in order to concentrate on his public life. The purpose of this original adaptation is to underline Christ's moral and exemplary role; two major techniques are used to achieve this end. First, Michel increases the number of sermons, which emphasize the individual's own responsibility for his salvation and his need to be ready for the coming of Christ. Secondly, he illustrates this lesson by expanding greatly the biographies of some secondary characters. Marie Madeleine is almost the heroine of the second day, where her life before her conversion is dramatized vividly; and Judas, who kills his father and marries his mother before encountering Jesus, becomes an Œdipus fig-

ure for the first time on the French stage, although the Judas incest legend was an old one.

Michel's play rapidly became famous throughout France, partly due to its having been printed. It was best known, however, in a compilation, when it was framed by Gréban's first and fourth day; this vast, 50,000-line text was performed in Mons in 1501 and in Paris in 1507. [GAR]

MICHEL, (Clémence-)Louise (1830–1905). French anarchist orator, active in the Paris *Commune. A schoolteacher and republican during the 1860s, she was both an active speaker and an armed combatant during the Commune, for which she was deported to New Caledonia. On her return in 1880 she became a touring heroine of the anti-authoritarian movement. A passionate and altruistic individual, she recorded her life in infuriatingly disorganized style in her *Mémoires* (1886). [SR]

MICHELET, Jules (1798–1874). The reputation of the greatest of French Romantic historians has been uneven. A supporter, then a critic, of the regime of Louis-Philippe, he was dismissed from his post as keeper of the National Archives and professor at the *Collège de France under Napoleon III (1851) and went into exile for a time. The Third Republic, in contrast, made him required reading in schools and turned him, as it turned *Hugo (whom he resembles in many ways), into a pillar of its own version of republican ideology. The appropriation of Michelet by the state, together with the ardent nationalism of his writings, his rejection of the central role of class conflict in history, and his insistence on the organic unity and identity of the nation (he was the first historian, he declared, to see France 'as a person'), led some historians, especially Marxists, to consider him irretrievably old-fashioned and *petit-bourgeois*. The historical professionalism that came in with the founding of the *Revue historique* (1876) was suspicious of his typically Romantic belief in universal symbolism, his poetic prose, and his passionate political commitments.

However, a reaction against positivist historiography in the 1920s and 1930s led historians like *Febvre and *Braudel to discover virtue in Michelet's approach to history and to applaud his Romantic rejection of specializations, his ideal of a 'total history', and his highly imaginative view of the range of historical enquiry. Finally, a growing awareness of the rhetorical and literary dimension of all writing, including writing in history, anthropology, and the other social sciences, together with a broadly based questioning of the radical distinction often drawn between the scientific and the non-scientific, has focused renewed attention on Michelet as writer. What the positivist historians condemned as idiosyncratic and irresponsible speculation can be seen instead as imaginative insight into unexplored areas of historical existence (*mentalités*, nutrition, sexual practices, etc.).

Michelet was one of a new class of young professionals who supported and benefited from the 1830 Revolution. The son of an impecunious printer, he carved out a successful career as tutor to the daughters of Louis-Philippe, professor at the *École Normale Supérieure, director of the National Archives, and professor at the Collège de France. His early works, notably his *Introduction à l'histoire universelle* (1831)—a glorification of progress and civilization, of Revolutionary and Republican France as the providentially appointed leader of the march of history in the modern age, and of the 1830 Revolution as the fulfilment of the Revolution begun in 1789—and the early volumes of his *Histoire de France* (vols. 1–6, 1833–44), in which he painted a glowingly sympathetic portrait of the popular culture of the Middle Ages, won him both a large readership and official approval. Soon, however, he became an outspoken critic of the timid and conciliatory foreign policy of Louis-Philippe and his ministers and of the regime's social and economic liberalism, both of which he saw as betraying the spirit of the Revolution. He interrupted his *Histoire de France* to collaborate with his friend *Quinet on *Les Jésuites* (1843), a pamphlet attacking the expanded role of the Church in education and reaffirming the principle that the education of the people is the right and responsibility of the nation alone. Shortly afterwards, in *Le Peuple* (1846), he warned that the liberal economic policies of the regime were creating deep social divisions that threatened the unity of the nation as the Revolutionary fathers had conceived it. Finally, he began work on the seven volumes of his *Histoire de la Révolution française* (1847–53), the express aim of which was to revive the original Revolutionary faith and to serve as the gospel of a new religion of France. When he returned to his *Histoire de France* in 1855 it was to celebrate the Renaissance and to retract his earlier enthusiasm for the *Middle Ages.

Deprived by the regime of Napoleon III of his regular salary as a government appointee, Michelet was forced to write for the new mass public created by universal education. In addition, the loss of easy access to the archives and the influence of his second wife, Athénaïs Mialaret—a young woman 28 years his junior, in whom he saw a new Jeanne d'Arc come to save him at the time of his deepest despair about himself and France in 1849—encouraged Michelet to try to bring off the *livre populaire* he always dreamed of writing in the more 'feminine' field of natural history (as opposed to the 'masculine' field of political history). Written in collaboration with Athénaïs, *L'Oiseau* (1856), *L'Insecte* (1858), *La Mer* (1861), and *La Montagne* (1868) were intended to appeal to women and the people, as well as to men. Athénaïs's contribution, however, carefully set off between quotations marks, was distinctly subordinate, in keeping with Michelet's typically 19th-c. views of the proper relation of man and woman, reason and feeling, form and generative

power, science and imagination, prose and poetry, etc.

Michelet's universal symbolism, learned from the German Romantics, made it inevitable that the history of nature would reveal the same patterns and carry the same progressivist and integrationist message as the history of political society. All his writing, from the *Histoire romaine* of 1831 to the brilliantly imaginative sketch of a history of woman, to which he gave the title *La Sorcière* in 1862, and the remarkable private *Journal*, published only recently, proposes a single master-design uniting natural history, the history of humanity, the history of continents and nations, and the history of the individual. The historian's personal history follows the same pattern as that of nature or mankind or France. That is what makes it possible to write history in the first place. 'De quoi l'histoire s'est-elle faite sinon de moi?', Michelet wrote in his *Journal*; 'De quoi l'histoire se referait-elle . . . sinon de moi?' History, for Michelet, is not an analytical activity, it is essentially hermeneutic, a writing from the inside. It does not set out to investigate a problem or answer a question. It is, in Michelet's own definition, 'résurrection de la vie intégrale'.

As the true historian of France is identical with his subject ('Je suis la France', Michelet proclaimed), the history he makes out of himself and offers to his fellow citizens is a kind of Eucharist, uniting them in a new communion, the fellowship of France. Michelet's historian is a Christ figure. He gives up his own life to redeem the living and the dead; he restores the unity of the nation by resurrecting or re-presenting his own buried past and the buried past of the nation: the otherness he had to repress in himself (his humble origins, his femininity), in order to develop and 'progress' as an autonomous individual and a man; and the otherness of everything that has been repressed in the official records of the national past—the 'silences de l'histoire' that mark the passage of those on whom the victorious present has been built.

The past presented itself to Michelet in the form of the female body—'la grande blessée'—whose blood and suffering are the condition of new life. While moving forward on the inevitable march of history, he argued repeatedly, the present must acknowledge and redeem the past from which it sprang. Thus, the industrious, intellectual, 'masculine' Occident overtakes the luxuriant, material, 'feminine' Orient, but at the same time spiritualizes it and saves it from the cyclical world of repetition for eternal life. The male, dependent in his infancy on the frightening, primitive female, at once nurse and Circe, source of life and harbinger of death, overtakes her and brings her to dependency on him, but at the same time raises her lovingly above her natural, material existence; the son becomes a protective husband and the mother a consoling daughter. History (spirit and freedom) overtakes geography (material necessity), not by denying it but by turning it to 'higher' ends. France emerges from her diverse provinces, taking their place and at the same time ensuring that they will live eternally in her. As nature's 'higher' creatures emerge from the more primitive without destroying the source of life from which they sprang, Man learns to measure and master the sea (*la mer*) or the primitive slime (*terra mater*), while at the same time respecting their inexhaustible restorative as well as destructive powers. The bourgeoisie emerges from the womb of the people and imposes its leadership, not to dominate and exploit it, but to educate it towards the future. Where domination is mere violence, Michelet insists, there is no genuine progress, only an unending alternation of repression and revolt (the return of the repressed). The history of England, as learned from *Thierry, exemplifies this pattern of repetition. The history of France, in contrast, offers humanity the model of a successful historical dialectic, in which revolution is a moment in evolution.   [LG]

> See G. Monod, *La Vie et la pensée de Jules Michelet* (1923); R. Barthes, *Michelet par lui-même* (1954); P. Viallaneix, *La Voie royale: essai sur l'idée du peuple dans l'œuvre de Michelet* (1959).

Microcosme, see SCÈVE.

Micromégas. Philosophical tale by *Voltaire, published 1752, probably begun 1739. In the manner of *Gulliver's Travels*, it reduces human pretensions to importance by bringing an eight-league-tall traveller from Sirius to inspect the earth. His reactions are divided between horror at the folly and cruelty of humanity and admiration for modern science. [PF]

Middle Ages, The

1. Origins of the Term

The notion of a Middle Age (*medium œvum*) separating the ancient world from modern times was first developed by *humanists in the 14th c., although the term itself was not used until the beginning of the 17th c. Petrarch and his contemporaries were aware that a 'dark age' separated 'modern' Italians from their Roman roots. Petrarch's own attitude was ambivalent, since, while deprecating the 'barbarities' of pre-Dante Italian and regarding his own Italian writings as unworthy trifles, he admired the *troubadours and, like Dante, used their example to develop his own poetics. It was the French humanists of the mid-16th c. who rejected out of hand an age identified with the *Sorbonne and scientific logic expressed in a Latin which had remained a living idiom, in favour of a 'renaissant' return to Ciceronian purity of style and rhetoric. *Rabelais, who also exploited both medieval epic and romance for subject-matter, and preaching manuals for narrative techniques, was most influential in inspiring scorn for the period, with his use of the pejorative words 'gothique' and 'languegoth' (which he coined on the model of *langue d'oc) to describe respectively a whole culture and a literary style.

2. Political and Ideological Exploitation of the Term

The 'Middle Ages' have been more subject to manipulation for political and ideological ends than any other of the artificially identified segments into which Western historiography has traditionally divided its culture. It did, however, require a certain distance in time to provide a perspective within which the notion could be deployed as a symbolic shorthand in discourse on contemporary problems. The 16th c., engaged in defining its own distinctiveness, largely eschewed this temptation (although Claude *Fauchet used his knowledge of medieval texts to bolster *Gallicanism, an attitude which earned him *lettres de noblesse* in 1586); it is not until the reign of Louis XIV that we find the first manifestations of the phenomenon. The background to the *Fronde was steeped in the idea, derived from a view of *feudalism, of the peers as equals not only of each other but of the king, whose personal domination they sought to resist. The attitude is satirized in section 20 of 'De la cour' in *La Bruyère's *Caractères*, in which a nobility marginalized by the king and his ministers seeks refuge in heraldic quarterings, crusader ancestors, and the 'gothic quaintness' of its non-modernized châteaux.

The use of the medieval past to resist the centralized rule of an absolutist monarchy supported by non-noble ministers became a commonplace at the end of the reign of Louis XIV and throughout the 18th c., finding expression in dictionaries, encyclopaedias, and treatises on nobility and chivalry. The *Glossarium ad scriptores mediæ et infimæ latinitatis* of *Du Cange was published in three volumes in 1678. While its prime purpose was purely erudite, to provide a dictionary of medieval Latin, a number of articles included explanatory quotations from literary texts and charters in Old French. This aspect of the work, spotlighting ancestral French custom and culture, was consistently expanded by revisers producing successive new editions of the dictionary throughout the 18th c. Like Du Cange, *La Curne de Sainte-Palaye was essentially a lexicographer, whose Old French dictionary received only partial publication in the author's lifetime. More influential in forming a view of the Middle Ages, and in fostering a sense of caste among the nobility, was his monumental *Mémoires sur l'ancienne chevalerie*. The image he presented from sources in both narrative romance and lyric texts was of a *libertin* age in which chivalry represented a nobility of rough-and-ready independence. *Boulainviller was perhaps the most seminal writer in forming the idea of a nobility independent of and equal to the king. While his *Histoire de l'ancien gouvernement de France* and *Essais sur la noblesse de France* were published posthumously, his opposition to monarchic rule is already seen in his *Mémoire pour la noblesse de France contre les ducs et pairs* (1717). Despite the efforts of these writers and of Montesquieu's careful analysis of the development of feudalism up to the period of

Hugues Capet, in Books 30 and 31 of De l'*esprit des lois, the Revolutionary period, perhaps because of the polemics of *Voltaire and the *philosophes, firmly identified feudalism and the Middle Ages with the abuses of the ancien régime. Thus, France from Directoire to First Empire preferred to turn to republican Rome for political models at just the time when other parts of Europe were rediscovering their 'medieval' past as a way of breaking the cultural hegemony of French *classicism.

It was only with the Restoration that royalist Romantics, led by Victor *Hugo, found in the Middle Ages a source of sound governance and national pride. The mood did not last, however, and the transformations can be plotted through the shifting attitudes expressed in successive redactions of *Michelet's Histoire de France, notably in those essays dealing with the Crusades and *Jeanne d'Arc. While the original versions are a paean to the vigour and independence of the French people under feudal monarchy, later redactions stress the ignorance, superstition, and oppression institutionalized by the alliance of Throne and Altar. The shift to a diabolic and barbaric Middle Ages represented in part an opposition to the espousal of medieval fashions by the regime of *Napoleon III. A reaction against that view of the period was provoked by the events of 1870 [see FRANCO-PRUSSIAN WAR]. During the 19th c. the scientific investigation of the Middle Ages had been led by German philology, thus enshrining the view of the period as Germanic. After the French defeat at Sédan the links of the nation's 12th-c. culture to classical Latin models became emphasized to distance France from the victor. This attitude hardened during the period from 1914 to 1945, when the national epic and 'resistance' heroes and heroines such as Jeanne d'Arc were used as rallying symbols. The same tendency to link the Middle Ages to a humanistic pan-European ideal also surfaced in Germany, where scholars like Erich Auerbach and Ernst Robert Curtius used it to focus their opposition to Nazism.

3. Scholarship and the Medieval Canon

In spite of the condemnation of the *Pléiade, the process of preserving a corpus of medieval literature began in the 16th c. Clément *Marot, in his translation of Le *Roman de la Rose and his edition of *Villon's Testament, was largely concerned with keeping alive a tradition of native culture still seen as vital. This was also the attitude of Fauchet, whose essentially philological researches into the origins and development of the French language incidentally preserved a large corpus of texts relating to French literature and to customary law. The 17th c. saw a hiatus in this activity, and interest in medieval texts was not seriously renewed until the 18th c., apart from the continued circulation of epic and romance texts as chapbook literature [see BIBLIOTHÈQUE BLEUE]. The first attempt to produce a comprehensive history of the literature of the period was the monumental Histoire littéraire de la France, inaugurated by the *Maurists in 1733; this is still proceeding under the auspices of the *Académie des Inscriptions et Belles-Lettres. The comte de *Tressan shows both his extensive knowledge of, and supercilious attitude to, medieval theatre in his article 'Parade' in the *Encyclopédie, an ambivalence which is also manifest in his translations and adaptations in the *Bibliothèque universelle des romans, which included not only texts that have remained in the canon, like *Huon de Bordeaux, but more marginal texts like the late prose romance Petit Artus de Bretagne. These were treated according to the tastes of the roman libertin. Rather more precious and moralistic in approach was Pierre Jean-Baptiste Le Grand d'Aussy, whose adapted editions of medieval contes and *fabliaux (1781) tended to edulcoration. In 1756 Étienne Barbazan produced an anthology of texts transcribed from manuscripts in the Bibliothèque Royale and published in the original Old French, ranging from obscene fabliaux like Le Sentier battu, through *Aucassin et Nicolette and the *congés of the Arras poets, to pious and didactic works such as the Miracles de Nostre Dame of *Gautier de Coinci and L'Ordene de chevalerie. The vogue for vulgarization did not die with the new century, and popular scholars like Achille Jubinal contributed regularly to periodicals, including women's magazines. Notable in this area was Le Journal des demoiselles which, in the 1830s and 1840s, specialized in 'medievalism', including adaptations of literary texts and biographies of great figures, among them several women, including *Christine de Pizan.

The main thrust of work in the 19th c. was, however, philological. The first-generation editors were concerned with unearthing monuments from the libraries of Europe (Francisque Michel's telegram from Oxford: 'J'ai trouvé la Chanson de Roland', remains famous). In this period textual editing was still an art rather than a science, with little sense of how to date either manuscripts or works; the texts produced, in such important series as 'Les Romans des Douze Pairs' and 'Les Anciens Poètes de France', were based on an impressionistic view of the best manuscript. It was in the second half of the century, as the lessons of the German philologist Lachmann's work on establishing stemmata codicon from a collocation of 'common errors' were absorbed, that editors started trying to recreate the 'archetype' or author's text by a meticulous comparison of all known manuscripts. This was also the period that saw the founding of the Société des Anciens Textes, whose mission remains to publish a definitive corpus of medieval French literature to the highest scientific standards.

The first half of the 20th c. saw both the apogee of scientific philology, in which critical editions were regarded primarily as material for linguistic study, and the first serious attack on that position by one of its great practitioners, Joseph *Bédier [see MANUSCRIPTS]. The abandonment of the Lachmann-style critical edition has been particularly notable in recent years in all areas except courtly romance, and even there editorial precedence is now given to the base manuscript. In epic studies theories of oral transmission have led to the preference for synoptic editions. The theory of the instability of medieval texts in manuscript transmission has produced similar solutions for lyric, *lais*, and *fabliaux*. Since World War II theories of oral composition have influenced attitudes to the poetics of the epic, which, like romance, has been analysed for mythographic content using techniques borrowed from anthropology, folklore, and religion. Since the 1960s Structuralist, semiotic, and deconstructionist approaches have been applied to medieval as to modern literature. The concept of *histoire des mentalités* of the **Annales* school has helped open the way for the use of reception theory, and for sociological and feminist approaches.

4. The Middle Ages in Art, Literature, and Film

It is not possible here to do more than mention one or two moments in the history of representation of the Middle Ages. The 15th c. was already exploiting nostalgically an image of the 'High Middle Ages', a monument to which is seen in *René d'Anjou's Livre du Cueur d'amors espris*, and in the 16th c. Marguerite de Navarre included a version of *La *Chastelaine de Vergi* in her *Heptaméron*. It was, however, the 19th c. which saw the flood of medievalism into art and literature, with the architectural Gothic recreations and 'restorations' of *Viollet-le-Duc, the *style troubadour* in decorative arts, and literary reconstitutions, such as Hugo's *Notre-Dame de Paris* and *Flaubert's *Saint Julien l'Hospitalier*. The diabolic and mystic interpretation emerged in Hugo's *Légende des siècles*, and in *Axël* by *Villiers de l'Isle-Adam. The 20th c.'s ambivalence to the period can be seen in *Tournier's exploitation of the *Gilles de Rais legend in *Le Roi des aulnes*, in *Cocteau's satirical *Les Chevaliers de la Table Ronde*, and in *Gracq's mysterious reworking of the Grail story in *Au château d'Argol*. In the theatre *Anouilh alternates between the pageant of *L'Alouette* and the whimsical satire of *Becket*, while in cinema *Bresson's dark and bloody *Lancelot du Lac* contrasts with *Rohmer's falsely naïve *Perceval*.

[PEB]

See R. Pernoud, *Pour en finir avec le moyen âge* (1977); J. Le Goff, *Pour un autre moyen âge* (1977); P. Zumthor, *Parler du moyen âge* (1980).

Middle East. A local French-language culture flourished in Egypt and Lebanon in the early 20th c., reaching its peak in the inter-war period.

Although short-lived, *Napoleon's Egyptian expedition (1798–1801) created a lasting sphere of influence. While French scientists, scholars, and engineers embarked on ambitious projects (including the remarkable *Description de l'Égypte*, 1820–30), numerous French schools were established by religious orders which forged links with a sizeable Christian community (the Copts being the largest single group) receptive to non-Islamic influences. Within a couple of generations an indigenous francophone community constituted one of the many strands of Egyptian society. It was to develop its own press and cultural institutions and to produce works in all the main literary genres.

Much French-Egyptian writing was inevitably derivative, but the best writers contrived to assimilate influences (including those of the many French writers who visited Egypt) and create works communicating a personal vision or perspective. In fiction, social issues were often predominant, as in *Le Livre de Goha le simple* by Albert Adès (1893–1921) and Albert Josipovici (1892–1932), with its mythical popular hero, or the many novels concerning the plight of Egyptian women, such as *Les Répudiées* by Niya Salima (1878–1908), the cycle of novels including *Zenouba* (1950) by Out-el-Koloub (b. 1908), or the more recent *L'Égyptienne* (1975) by Fawzia Assad (b. 1929). The bleak novels of Albert Cossery (b. 1913), such as *La Maison de la mort certaine* (1944) or *La Violence et la dérision* (1964), depict the predicament of the underprivileged.

The appeal of the French language and the poetic quality of Egypt's history and sites are conjoined in the verses of Raoul Parme (b. 1904) and others. The reaction against such conventionality marks some of Egypt's most challenging francophone writers, notably Georges *Henein, who established links with the French *Surrealists and, in the 1940s, created a circle which included Edmond *Jabès and, at a distance, Joyce *Mansour.

In Lebanon, where French contacts date back to the Crusades, and where the language has often served as a *lingua franca*, writers in French were especially active after 1920 (when the country came under French mandate). Chekri Ganem's play *Antar* (1910), with its Cyrano-like hero, was a great success at the Paris Odéon in 1910. In the 1920s and 1930s the *Revue phénicienne* of Charles Corm (1894–1963), and his novel *La Montagne inspirée* (1934), sought to rally support for a post-Ottoman, 'Phoenician', and effectively French Lebanon. In literary terms the most original and stimulating writers, who include Georges *Schéhadé and Andrée *Chedid, emerged primarily in the period after World War II. Despite the ravages of civil war (since the mid-1970s), interesting work has continued to appear from such poets as Fouad Gabriel Naffah (1925–83), Nadia Tueni (1935–83) and Vénus Khoury Ghata (b. 1937), the poet-diplomat Salah Stétié (b. 1925), the poet-novelist Nohad Salameh (b. 1945), and the historian and novelist Amin *Maalouf.

Like their predecessors Henein, Jabès, and Chedid, who all based themselves in Paris from the 1950s onwards, francophone writers (including the Syrian Fereydoun Hoveydah, b. 1936) tend now to be writers in exile. In view of the rise of Islamic movements, among other political and economic factors, the future of an indigenous French literature in the Middle East must be seen as precarious.

[MHTS]

See J. J. Luthi, *Introduction à la littérature d'expression française en Egypte (1798–1945)* (1974); S. Khalaf, *Littérature libanaise de langue française* (1974).

MIGNE, Jacques-Paul (1800–75). Editor of numerous theological writings [see SERMON].

MIGNET, François-Auguste (1796–1884). French historian, archivist, and collaborator with *Thiers on *Le National*. His works include *Histoire de la Révolution française* (1824), *Histoire de Marie Stuart* (1851), and *La Rivalité de François Ier et de Charles-Quint* (1875).

MILET, Jacques (1425–66). Much admired by the *Rhétoriqueurs, he was the author of the allegorical *Forest de tristesse* and of a vast theatrical *Istoire de la destruction de Troye la grant* (1450/2), designed to be performed on four successive days and setting the history of France's Trojan origins as a *mystery play.

[JHMT]

MILHAUD, Darius (1892–1974). Prolific composer of largely dramatic music for opera, theatre, ballet, and film, and an important member of the group known as 'Les *Six'. His music makes use of popular-music idioms—for instance, his ballet *La Création du monde* (1923) is strongly influenced by jazz. He was a close friend of *Claudel and based many works on Claudel texts, including innovative music for an entire 'Oresteia' trilogy (1913–22) and an allegorical opera, *Christophe Colomb* (1928). He also worked with *Cocteau, their most successful collaboration being the chamber opera *Le Pauvre Matelot* (1927). Milhaud wrote three books, one his autobiography.

[KM]

Militaire philosophe, Le. Appellation of both an anonymous author and his work, one of the most important *clandestine manuscripts, probably dating from 1705–10, entitled *Difficultés sur la religion proposées au père Malebranche*. The author, an officer with a technical training, knew *Malebranche's *Recherche de la vérité* well and turned its rationalism against Christian apologetics, attacking all the arguments devised by Malebranche and many others to prove the truth of Christianity. The work's final part (omitted in a truncated version published by *Holbach) expounds a complete system of *deism in which God is transcendent justice. [CJB]

Mille et une Nuits, Les. *Galland's version of the oriental tales known in English as the *Arabian Nights* launched the work on its vastly influential European career. Published in 12 volumes between 1704 and 1716, it was not the translation of an existing book, but the result of firsthand work on manuscripts and oral sources. Galland himself chose the stories and the order of their telling; his translation is, for its time, quite scrupulous, but he felt free to omit lengthy descriptions, vulgar elements, and the repetitions that characterize oral story-telling. His elegant, rapid style is that of his time, and some readers have thought that he dresses up his Orientals in fashionable French attire—but this no doubt contributed to its success.

Its popularity was phenomenal. Capitalizing on the taste for oriental material witnessed by such works as Racine's *Bajazet* or the travels of *Tavernier, and equally on the recent vogue for fairy-tales [see SHORT FICTION], Galland's work was much reprinted, imitated, and translated into many languages (the first English version done from Arabic originals only appeared in 1838). To his annoyance, *Les Mille et un Jours* (tr. Pétis de la Croix with help from *Lesage) appeared along with his own work in 1710, and there were many similar collections. A new, more accurate translation entitled *Mille nuits et une nuit* was published by J.-C.-V. Mardrus in 1898–1904.

Galland's work offered not only a more or less realistic image of a foreign culture (*Gobineau later praised its accuracy), but the vision of a world and a world-view that caught the Western imagination. The chance-dominated fatalism of his stories inspired *Voltaire, even though the introduction to *Zadig sets the seriousness of the *conte philosophique* against the meaninglessness of oriental tales. The *merveilleux* element in the *Nights* offered food to the Romantic dreamer (*Stendhal loved them), and their discreet but unembarrassed eroticism was endlessly imitated by novelists and *conteurs* in the following two centuries. [PF]

MILLET, Jean-François (1814–75). French painter, famous for his scenes of peasant life, in particular *L'Angélus*, an iconic image of rustic peace. He was himself a farmer's son from Normandy; for the last 30 years of his life he worked in *Barbizon.

MILLEVOYE, Charles-Hubert (1782–1816). French poet. Although he wrote in a diversity of poetic forms, Millevoye has been exclusively identified with the elegy (*Élégies*, 1812). He had a significant influence on *Lamartine, and *Sainte-Beuve was also attracted to his melancholy and fatalism. Two of his poems have been constantly picked out and anthologized: 'La Chute des feuilles' and 'Le Poète mourant'. [BR]

MILOSZ, Oscar Vladislas de Lubicz (1877–1939). A night of mystical illumination on 14 December 1914 divides the *Symbolist of *Le Poème des décadences* (1899) from the poet-philosopher of *Les Arcanes* (1926) and *L'Apocalypse de Saint-Jean déchiffré* (1933), works influenced by the *Illuminist tradition, by alchemy, and by the cabbala. Born in Belorussia of Lithuanian extraction, Milosz came to France at the age of 12 and wrote exclusively in French. The creation of the Lithuanian Republic in 1918 led to a diplomatic career and to works inspired by

Mimouni

Lithuanian folklore, but from 1925 Milosz lived largely as a recluse dedicated to arcane speculation conducted in dense, mysterious language. He is best known for his play *Miguel Mañara* (1912), centred on the figure of Don Juan, but his later poetry (*Adramondoni*, 1918) and the hermetic works in which he sought to elaborate a cosmology based on the notion of 'le rien' have commanded increasing respect among specialists.   [MHTS]

MIMOUNI, Rachid (b. 1945). Algerian writer; professor of economics in Algiers. Mimouni's short stories (*La Ceinture de l'ogresse*, 1990) and novels denounce the injustices and corruption of post-Independence Algeria. His first two novels, *Le Printemps ne sera que plus beau* (1978) and *Une paix à vivre* (1983), were published in Algeria. Although concerned with the unkept promises of post-revolutionary Algeria, they are mild in tone compared with his later works, all published in Paris.

Le Fleuve détourné (1982) established Mimouni's literary reputation. The novel is about a martyr of the revolution, who has been declared dead. He returns to his native village in search of the present. A victim of amnesia, he is unable to recover his identity in a corrupt and oppressive society that has diverted the ideals of the revolution. *Tombéza* (1984) centres on a monstrous protagonist who symbolizes, both as victim and executioner, the misery, horror, and violence of contemporary Algeria. Algerian society is paralysed not only by its past, but also by the absence of a viable political perspective. In *L'Honneur de la tribu* (1989) Mimouni argues that the memory of a people is only worth recovering if it is mindful of the future. *Une peine à vivre* (1991) is about love and power in a totalitarian state; *De la barbarie en général et de l'intégrisme en particulier* (1992) is a virulent pamphlet against fundamentalism in Algeria.   [DM-S]

Minotaure. A very glossy, eclectic, and lavishly illustrated review that came out between 1933 and 1939. Although Skira and Tériade were its editors, the *Surrealists played prominent roles. In a thought-provoking and innovative way, it covered art and literature in relation to ethnography, archaeology, music, and dance, setting the highest of standards.   [KRA]

Minuit, Éditions de. Publishing-house founded clandestinely by Pierre de Lescure and *Vercors during the *Occupation in 1942. Its first publication was Vercors's *Le Silence de la mer*, followed by 43 other texts by authors including *Aragon and Elsa *Triolet published clandestinely before the Liberation. In 1948 the direction was taken over by Jérôme Lindon. He gradually built up an outstanding reputation for avant-garde literature, publishing Samuel *Beckett from 1951 onwards and then the *Nouveaux Romanciers, whose names were so associated with their publisher that they were also known as 'l'école de Minuit'. The award of the

Nobel Prize to Claude *Simon and the standing of Marguerite *Duras have enhanced Minuit's reputation still further.   [EAF]

MIRABEAU, Honoré-Gabriel Riqueti, comte de (1749–91). Famous Revolutionary statesman and orator. His early career as profligate son of the marquis de *Mirabeau and wayward husband was scandalously nonconformist, earning him lengthy imprisonment. From 1780 to 1788 he led a second adventurous existence as pamphleteer, speculator, and secret agent. These were, however, years when Mirabeau, using professionally competent (and sometimes illustrious) ghost-writers, learned how to be a redoubtable polemicist (*Des lettres de cachet*, 1782; *Considérations sur l'ordre de Cincinnatus*, 1784; *La Monarchie prussienne sous Frédéric le Grand*, 1788; *Histoire secrète de la cour de Berlin*, 1789). Having played a significant role in the agitation leading up to the Revolution, he was elected to the États Généraux, then to the Assemblée Constituante where, with his commanding presence and extraordinary oratorical powers, he became almost the spokesman for the Third Estate. But, paradoxically, his political views—after the writings of the earlier years when he had slain dragons—proved to be surprisingly moderate. He was, in a memorable phrase, 'too much of a monarchist for the Revolution, too revolutionary for the monarchy'. Not surprisingly, and not without good reason (for, in addition, he was venal and versatile, even Machiavellian), he was—shortly before his death—discredited with both Royalists and *Jacobins.   [JR]

MIRABEAU, Victor de Riqueti, marquis de (1715–89). A disciple of *Quesnay, he devoted himself to improving his estate and composing works which set out in a confused way the doctrines of the *Physiocrats. See in particular *L'Ami des hommes* (1756—Mirabeau adopted for himself the title of this book) and *Théorie de l'impôt* (1760). He was a strange individual, a despotic liberal, lover of mankind, writer of erotic tales, protector of *Rousseau, and persecutor of his family, especially his more famous son, Honoré-Gabriel [see above]. Although a writer, he affected to despise 'la canaille philosophique'.
                    [PF]

Miracle Plays. Medieval dramatizations of stories relating the miraculous events occurring as a result of the intervention of the Virgin Mary or the saints, in response to the prayers of a true believer in need of help. A large number of narrative Marian miracles and saints' lives, in Latin and French, circulated widely in the Middle Ages [see HAGIOGRAPHY]; they were ideally suited to dramatization. Religious in inspiration yet set in the real world, the plots inevitably contained a striking theatrical climax. Miracle plays flourished especially in the 13th and 14th c. and were often performed by religious *confréries. The earliest miracle plays may have been influenced by Latin liturgical dramas of a similar nature. The best-known are *Bodel's *Jeu de Saint Nicolas*, *Rutebeuf's *Miracle de Théophile*, and the collection of *Miracles de Nostre Dame par personnages*. Most were relatively small-scale plays, rarely more than 2,500 lines long, performed by the *confréries* in their hall. Miracle plays contributed to the development of drama not only in their increasing secularization, but also in giving scope for the elaboration of complex technical devices, called *feintes*, needed to stage the miraculous climax. The term *miracle* is rarely used to describe religious plays after the 14th c., though many *mystery plays dramatize similar subject-matter, especially those based on saints' lives. [GAR]

Miracles de Nostre Dame par personnages. Collection of 40 *miracle plays performed annually between 1339 and 1382 at the meetings of the *Confrérie Saint-Éloi of the Parisian Goldsmiths' Guild. The Goldsmiths were one of the most prosperous of the Paris trade guilds and their wealth was reflected in increasingly lavish celebrations—masses, processions, banquets, poetry competitions—held on the only day in the year when they were permitted to assemble, on or near 6 December, the feast of their patron saint, Eloi. The two-volume, illustrated manuscript which preserves the 40 plays, as well as some of the winning poems, reveals that the performances took place indoors in the hall of the *puy des orfèvres*. The time available for the performances, as well as the restricted dimensions of the makeshift theatre, limited the plays' length (between 1,000 and 3,000 lines) and their staging complexity (usually six or seven sets and between ten and thirty actors).

The subjects of the plays are much more varied than the label 'miracle' might suggest. Although many are typical of the genre (e.g. *L'Enfant donné au diable*, *L'Abesse grosse*, *Le Pape qui vendi le basme*, *La Femme que Nostre Dame garda d'estre arse*) or are straightforward saints' lives (e.g. *Valentin*, *Silvestre*, *Panthaléon*, *Alexis*), others are adaptations of *romances and *chansons de geste (e.g. *La Femme du Roy de Portigal*, *La Marquise de la Gaudine*, *Ami et Amile*, *Clovis*). A few are based, not on written, literary sources, but on 'real' miracles, e.g. *L'Enfant ressuscité*. The non-miracle sources are always adapted in such a way as to include a miraculous intervention by Notre Dame.

This annual succession of performances developed its own internal traditions, as later authors drew on their predecessors' plays and included evidently popular items, such as descents of angels from Heaven to Earth singing *rondeaux, sermons incorporated into the action, and scenes of torture, imprisonment, and childbirth. Though undoubtedly religious in intent and spirit, they often reflect the preoccupations of the wealthy bourgeoisie from which they sprang: scenes involving trade and money are frequent. One notes however, two surprising absences—humour and the Devil. [GAR]

See G. A. Runnalls, *Le Miracle de l'enfant ressuscité* (1972).

Miracles de Nostre Dame, Les, see GAUTIER DE COINCI.

MIRBEAU, Octave (1848–1917). French journalist, art critic, and novelist. His trajectory from extreme Right to anarchist Left is a microcosm of the complex politics of the bourgeois intellectual in 1880s France. His autobiographical novels, *Le Calvaire* (1887), *L'Abbé Jules* (1888), and *Sébastien Roch* (1890), trace his disillusionment with authoritarian Catholic ideology and the state which it supports. *Le Jardin des supplices* (1899), a brilliant account of decadent sadism, is an ironic analysis of power relations in contemporary society, showing how individual imagination is drafted into the service of collective oppression. The racy sexuality of *Le Journal d'une femme de chambre* (1900) is also an exposé of the ideology of the *Dreyfus era and the violence below the surface of conservative order. [JB]

Mirèio, see MISTRAL.

Miroir de l'âme pécheresse, Le, see MARGUERITE DE NAVARRE.

Miroir qui revient, Le (1985). Autobiographical work by *Robbe-Grillet.

Miroirs des princes. These codifications of the art of good government have a long history in Latin; moralists and churchmen such as John of Salisbury (in his *Policraticus*), Giraldus Cambrensis, Ramon Lull, and *Gerson had for centuries designed programmes to promote true kingship. The later Middle Ages saw a number of similar works in the vernacular, among them *Robert de Blois's *Enseignement des princes* (mid-13th c.), *Watriquet de Couvin's *Mireoir as princes* (1327), or, less explicitly titled, *Christine de Pizan's *Livre du corps de policie* (1404/7). The writers share a faith in the malleability of the child: tyranny is to be avoided by careful teaching and learning (*clergie*), without which a king is like an ass with a crown. The writers propose programmes to inculcate proper religious, moral, and intellectual development: exemplars are sought among the great of antiquity and the Bible, and more especially among the prince's own ancestry. The topics covered vary from the proper administration of justice to military science; the writers hope to inculcate both a proper humility and a sense of dynasty and mission. Later treatises, such as *Erasmus's *Institutio principis christiani* (1516) or *Nicole's *Éducation d'un prince* (1670), follow in the same tradition. [JHMT]

MIRON, Gaston (b. 1928). Canadian poet who is one of the most prominent figures in contemporary Quebec literature. In 1953 he founded, with others, the publishing house L'Hexagone, which has had a major influence on the course of Quebec poetry. In his own poetry he became the voice of the 1960s generation of Quebec writers who made the reappropriation of their language and culture the main purpose of their writing. Loss of identity is expressed in his work in the drama of a fragmented self which can only achieve integration through the recovery of country and language. His reflections on the semantic perversion of Quebec French through subordination to English inspired the whole language debate in Quebec. He has published little since *L'Homme rapaillé* (1970), which collects most of his work, but even today that volume and Miron's personal dedication to the cause of a distinctive national literature remain indispensable points of reference for the understanding of contemporary Quebec.   [SIL]

Misanthrope, Le. Five-act comedy by *Molière, first performed in 1666, generally considered to be his masterpiece.

In her Parisian salon, the coquettish Célimène's favours are sought by a number of habitués, among them Oronte and Alceste, the misanthropist, who insists on saying what he thinks. His contrary nature sets him at odds with Oronte on a point of honour (the merits of Oronte's poetry), with the law, and with Célimène herself. His anti-fashionable behaviour contrasts with that of his friend, the moderate though less principled Philinte. Célimène is eventually confronted with evidence of her coquettishness; all her suitors abandon her except Alceste, but she is unable to accept his condition for marriage, that they withdraw from polite society. The play ends (unusually) not in reconciliation but in social dispersal. *Rousseau violently attacked Molière in his *Lettre à d'Alembert* for making Alceste's sincerity a subject of ridicule.   [IM]

Mise en abyme. Term from heraldry, meaning the reduced reproduction of an image within itself. It was popularized by *Gide to refer to a similar phenomenon in literature (play within play, novel within novel, etc.) and featured prominently in the *Nouveau Roman.

Misérables, Les. Victor *Hugo's most popular novel, published 1862, about the socially and spiritually damned. Begun in 1845 after extensive research on problems of poverty, penal reform, and capital punishment, the writing of the manuscript, originally called *Les Misères*, was interrupted by the Revolution of 1848 and picked up again in 1860.

The action begins on the eve of Waterloo in 1815 when an escaped convict, Jean Valjean, hardened by being imprisoned for stealing a loaf of bread to feed his sister's family, now steals from a kindly bishop who has given him shelter. We follow the hero, whose name implies 'Everyman', through the various stages of his moral regeneration, rendered perilous and exciting by the relentless pursuit of Javert, an intransigent agent of the law. Features of the plot recall the popular *feuilleton* literature of Sue's *Les

Mystères de Paris. The action moves abruptly from 1815 to 1817 when Jean Valjean, who now calls himself Monsieur Madeleine, has become a wealthy and respectable bourgeois. After a battle of conscience, he reveals his former identity and returns to prison to save the life of a derelict wrongly accused of being Jean Valjean. Freedom of choice is underlined when he escapes arrest temporarily to promise the dying prostitute, Fantine, that he will care for her child, Cosette. He develops a passionate paternal attachment to Cosette, with whom he lives in isolation from society, but possessiveness gives way to self-sacrifice when he saves the life of her fiancé, Marius, by carrying him through the sewers of Paris.

The novel abounds with memorable characters: Gavroche, the witty and heroic street urchin who dies on the barricades during the Revolution of 1830, the evil Thénardiers who abuses Cosette, and pre-*Haussmann Paris in all its mystery and diversity. The narrative is interrupted by long digressions of historical and sociological interest: a flashback to Waterloo, a critique of the pathology of convent life, a disquisition on slang, a visionary description of the Paris sewers. This incomparably rich story about the coming into being of a free individual ends with Jean Valjean's return to anonymity, as nature effaces his name from his tombstone. Thus, the social and political allegory takes on the familiar pattern of Hugo's metaphysical view of history as a force that continues its path beyond human memory.   [SN]

Mission terminée, see BETI.

MISTRAL (Joseph-Etienne-)Frédéric (1830–1914). Celebrated Provençal narrative poet, leader of the *Félibrige (1876–88) and the second Occitan renaissance, Nobel prize-winner (1904). Mistral's life in the Bouches-du-Rhône, first at his parents' *mas*, then in nearby Maillane, made him an incomparable regional ethnologist. An eclectic reader, at 10 he began writing Provençal poetry (*Li Meissoun*, 1927), a pursuit encouraged by Roumanille, his teacher at the *lycée* of Avignon. He began compiling a dictionary, which would become *Lou Tresor dóu Felibrige* (1878–86). From 1851 Mistral devoted his life to poetry, publishing with a French translation for the Paris market and abroad.

After publishing ten short poems in *Li Prouvençalo* (1852), Mistral spent seven years writing the 12 cantos first of *Mirèio* (1859), then of *Calendau* (1867). The former, a simple tale of young, blighted love, violence, and death in the Alpilles, Crau, and Camargue, combines elements of realism, folklore, animism, and Christian faith. The latter tells of heroic action in a world of seafarers (Cassis), brigands (Nice), fantasy and magic (Mont Gibal), with love triumphant. The same mix occurs in *Nerto* (1884), which transposes the Faust legend into 14th-c. Provence, also the setting for *La Rèino Jano* (1890), a five-act tragedy. In *Lou Pouèmo dóu Rose* (1897), however, Mistral recognizes that modern progress dooms his beloved traditional Provence. *Lis Isclo d'Or* (1875), a disparate collection of short narrative and other poems, was republished, much revised, in 1889. A mellow tone permeates *Moun espelido: memòri e raconte* (1906) and the unstructured poetry collection *Lis Oulivado* (1912), named after the last crop of the year in Provence. Posthumous works are *Proso d'Armana* (1926; sequels 1927, 1928), *Escourregudo pèr l'Itali* (1930).   [PVD]

Mithridate. Tragedy by *Racine, first performed at Versailles in 1674. It centres on the death of Mithridates, king of Pontus and inveterate enemy of Rome. On the point of launching an invasion of Rome, Mithridate is betrayed by his son Pharnace and reduced to heroic suicide. Before this he has also been at odds with his younger son Xipharès, his rival for the hand of the princess Monime. The young lovers are finally united and vow to carry on Mithridate's struggle. The king appears as a cruel yet pathetic figure, reduced from glory to military impotence and humiliating jealousy, but Racine allows him to go out in glory. The play was a favourite with *Louis XIV.   [PF]

MITTERRAND, François-Maurice (b. 1916). French politician, president of the Republic from 1981.

Educated in a Catholic school in Angoulême and the École Libre des Sciences Politiques in Paris, he was destined to be a lawyer. But the war made him a sergeant and a prisoner until he escaped in December 1940, after which he took a job with the Vichy government concerned with the welfare of prisoners-of-war. He was active in the Resistance, and after the Liberation entered politics as one of the leaders of a party which had emerged from the Resistance, the Union Démocratique Sociale et Républicaine. With only one brief interruption (1958–9), he was a *député* or senator for the Nièvre until 1981. Under the Fourth Republic he served as a minister in many governments. After 1958 he became a leader of the left-wing opposition, standing against de *Gaulle in the presidential election of 1965 and winning 45 per cent of the votes. In 1971 he became leader of the reconstituted Parti Socialiste [see SOCIALISM AND COMMUNISM] and, having been narrowly beaten in the presidential election of 1974, was victorious in those of 1981 and 1988, thereby becoming the first man in French history to be twice elected president of the Republic by universal suffrage. By 1981 he had published some 13 books, including the autobiographical *Ma part de vérité* (1969).   [DJ]

MNOUCHKINE, Ariane (b. 1934). French theatre and film director, founder of the Théâtre du Soleil. Although her film *Molière, une vie* (1979) is highly regarded for its interpretation of *Molière's theatrical career and its cinematic inventiveness, she is best known for her successful experiments in *création col-*

lective. In reaction to the arguably excessive power of theatre directors, she created the Théâtre du Soleil as a workers' collective, seeking to make the theatrical process a shared responsibility. Its work is underpinned by left-wing political convictions and a desire to make theatre accessible and relevant to ordinary people. The company has experimented with diverse performance styles, from circus and *commedia dell'arte* to Japanese *kabuki* and *bunraku*. Its aim is to fabricate a new theatrical language with which to interpret social and political themes. Its first major success was the celebrated *1789* (1970), an exuberant interpretation of the French Revolution in a popular fairground style. Two subsequent spectacles, *1793* (1972) and *L'Âge d'or* (1975), one historical, the other contemporary, were also created from documentary sources. Turning to Shakespeare in the 1980s, the company employed its unrivalled ensemble performance skills, to stunning visual effect, in oriental-style productions of *Richard II* (1981), *Twelfth Night* (1982), and *Henry IV, Part 1* (1984). Oriental techniques were also applied to the ambitious epics based on the lives of Prince Sihanouk of Cambodia (1985) and Mahatma Gandhi (*L'Indiade*, 1987), both scripted by Hélène *Cixous, and in *Les Atrides* (1990).   [DWW]

Mobile. Text by *Butor, published 1962. *Mobile* belongs to none of the normal generic categories. Subtitled 'Étude pour une représentation des États-Unis', it is an intertextual montage of very diverse American 'voices'. Quotations from Jefferson or Franklin are interwoven with mail-order catalogues, tourist brochures, the history of the American Indians, etc., together with fragments of fictional speech and an unobtrusive but eloquent authorial discourse. Out of all this a representation of America, seen by a foreigner, gradually emerges. The structure is complex and precise: a journey across the continent in which each section of the text represents one state and one hour of time, but the states are ordered alphabetically rather than geographically, and transitions between them are effected by a coincidence of place-names: we move from Concord in Alabama to Concord in North Carolina, for instance. This 'mobile' construction effectively reinstates the plurality of American culture, against the white racism which tries to obliterate black and Amerindian reality. It also sets up a counterpoint between the ideological voices of colonialism and consumerism and the repressed memories, fears, and desires which, if made conscious, could lead to the 'liberation' of a new America.   [CB]

MOCKEL, Albert (1866–1945). Belgian poet and critic, Mockel founded in 1886 *La Wallonie*, which, in the seven years of its existence, became one of the major journals of the *Symbolist movement. His *Propos de littérature* (1894) and *Stéphane *Mallarmé, un héros* (1899) are among the most important critical

Moderato cantabile

writing produced by the younger Symbolist generation, and his early support helped to establish the reputations of *Claudel and *Verhaeren.   [JK]

Moderato cantabile (1958). Short novel by Marguerite *Duras centring on the encounter between Anne Desbaresdes, wife of an industrialist, and Chauvin, the latter's employee. Not a love story in the conventional sense, the text presents a series of dialogues in which the couple construct a fantasized version of the circumstances surrounding a *crime passionnel* witnessed by Anne. At their final meeting they carry out what appears to be a symbolic re-enactment of the murder. It is a formally innovative text in which elliptic dialogue, significant detail, and structural patterning largely replace traditional characterization and plot. Duras collaborated with Peter *Brook in the film version made in 1960.   [EAF]

Modernes, Les, see QUERELLE DES ANCIENS ET DES MODERNES.

Modeste Mignon (1844). One of the *Scènes de la vie privée* in Balzac's *Comédie humaine*; the heroine, a provincial heiress, writes a fan letter to the poet Canalis, but finally marries his secretary Ernest, who has impersonated Canalis.

MODIANO, Patrick (b. 1945). A novelist associated initially with the post-Gaullist re-evaluation of the *Occupation and Resistance, Modiano has extended his field of exploration into the 1960s whilst retaining many of the same psychological preoccupations. His trilogy on the Occupation, *La Place de l'Étoile* (1968), *La Ronde de nuit* (1969), and *Les Boulevards de ceinture* (1972), shows a fascination with the world and psychology of collaboration and constitutes an important rectification of the traditional demarcation-lines between Resistance and collaboration. The same preoccupation underlies the film scenario he wrote with Louis Malle, *Lacombe Lucien* (1974); the depiction of a young country boy who joins the Gestapo almost by accident after having been rejected by the Resistance and the fascinated evocation of the *demi-monde* of collaboration were widely criticized as glamorizing the Right and helping to establish a 'mode rétro'. His later work, *Villa triste* (1975), *Livret de famille* (1977), *Rue des boutiques obscures* (1978), *Une jeunesse* (1981), *De si braves garçons* (1982), and *Quartier perdu* (1984), whilst retaining echoes from the Occupation period, establishes a new domain in its evocation of the 1960s as a period of social and moral sterility.   [NH]

Modification, La. Novel by *Butor, published 1957. Léon Delmont goes by train to visit Cécile in Rome, to tell her that he has decided to leave his wife and live with her. But by the time he arrives he has changed his mind. The text, written in the second person (*vous*), enacts a process of 'modification' whereby Léon's initial project is gradually seen to derive from a false sense of himself and his possibilities. He discovers that personal identity is inseparable from historical and cultural forces, and that individuals living in the dispersed, fissured society of the post-imperial world are condemned to psychological 'cracks' as well—ambivalence, compromise, and disunity. Léon's simplistic self-image breaks up under the pressure of previously repressed insights and memories, sparked off by elements of external reality presented to him by the train journey and expanding into dreams and the mythical archetypes of a collective cultural unconscious. This 'mental machine' takes him over—and the reader, too, is inexorably caught up in it. We are given no direct explanation of what is happening to Léon; rather an evolving structure of repetitions, parallels, contrasts, and transformations of images means that understanding slowly emerges from the structure of the text as a whole.   [CB]

Modulor, Le, see LE CORBUSIER.

Mœurs, Les, see TOUSSAINT, F.-V..

Mœurs des sauvages américains, see LAFITAU.

Mois, Les, see ROUCHER.

Moïse sauvé, see SAINT-AMANT.

MOLIÈRE (pseud. of Jean-Baptiste Poquelin) (1622–73). Widely considered to be one of the greatest comic playwrights of all time, Molière belonged to a brilliant generation of artists and writers who flourished under the patronage of *Louis XIV. He was born in Paris, the son of an upholsterer attached to the court, and after a solid education at the Jesuit Collège de Clermont seemed destined for a career in the law. But in 1643 he abandoned his studies and renounced his succession to his father's trade in order to found the 'Illustre Théâtre' with the Béjart family and others; it was at this time also that he adopted the name 'de Molière'. The Illustre Théâtre survived little more than a year in Paris, and was plagued by debt and other difficulties; in 1645 the company abandoned the attempt to establish itself in the capital and moved to the provinces. For 13 years Molière's troupe performed in provincial cities and noblemen's houses; its repertoire included plays by leading contemporary playwrights, and farces and comedies composed by Molière himself, notably *L'Étourdi* (1653/5) and *Le Dépit amoureux* (1656). Molière's success in the capital would be inexplicable but for the training as an actor and as a manager and theatre director which these years provided.

He attracted provincial patrons of increasing power and wealth; eventually he was promised the protection of Monsieur, brother of Louis XIV, and returned to Paris in 1658. There he shared the Salle du Petit-Bourbon with an Italian company; his troupe also acted in private houses and at court festivities. The first play he composed after his return to Paris, Les *Précieuses ridicules*, was performed in November 1659; it was an immediate success. A topical social satire, dealing with the affected prudishness inspired by the novels of Madeleine de *Scudéry, it inaugurated a series of comedies on current affairs which were to involve Molière in violent literary and theatrical feuding. He had already attracted the attention of the king, and it is likely that royal support enabled the company to move to its own theatre, the Salle du Palais-Royal, in 1660–1 [see THEATRES AND AUDIENCES, 1]. Louis's support did not stop there, however; a royal pension was granted to Molière in 1663 and his company was accorded the title 'Troupe du Roi' in 1665. A sign of the personal affection of the monarch for his favoured playwright is Louis's agreement to be godfather to Molière's son Louis, born in 1664. In 1662 Molière had married Armande Béjart, the sister of his rejected mistress Madeleine; contemporary gossip suggested that Armande was not Madeleine's sister but her daughter, and implied that the relationship was incestuous. The fact that the king stood sponsor for Molière's first child in these circumstances shows that he was willing to defend him publicly.

In his 15 years in Paris Molière showed a remarkable versatility in his output of plays, which range from one-act *farces to *comédie-ballet, and from *machine plays to high comedy. He began by composing farces, adding new elements to this traditional genre. Les Précieuses ridicules, for example, was, unusually for farce, topical; and the eponymous hero of *Sganarelle ou le Cocu imaginaire (1660) is not a stereotype, but a character who reflects comically on his own failings. In 1661, Molière experimented with a heroic comedy, *Dom Garcie de Navarre. This play was a flop, not only because the theme of jealousy was rather unsatisfactorily treated, but also because Molière's troupe, and especially Molière himself, considered to be the greatest comic actor of his day, were much more successful in performing comedy than serious drama. Also in 1661 Molière produced Les Fâcheux for an entertainment given by *Fouquet to Louis XIV at *Vaux-le-Vicomte; this was the first of a number of successful comédies-ballets, designed to appeal to the court.

Louis XIV had himself suggested to Molière one of the characters to be included in Les Fâcheux, in which a parade of court bores pass before the eyes of the spectators; Molière's next plays have been said to be further contributions to Louis's artistic and social policies. Apart from the brief Le Mariage forcé and the comédie-ballet La Princesse d'Élide (both 1664), they were all contentious. L'*École des femmes (1662) is a five-act verse comedy which supplanted the tragedy normally performed as the main element of a theatrical soirée; like L'École des maris of the previous year, it places on stage representatives of contemporary manners and attitudes (in this case, a potentially repressive husband) and advocates moderate permissiveness and social con-

formism. The play provoked a storm of protest on both literary and social grounds, to which Molière replied by producing two short conversation pieces set respectively in a salon and in a theatre: La Critique de l'École des femmes and L'Impromptu de Versailles. The latter play expressed his confidence in the king's support and carried on his feud with the rival troupe, the *Hôtel de Bourgogne, which specialized in the performance of tragedy.

The furore raised by L'École des femmes, however, was nothing in comparison to the reception which awaited his next play, Le *Tartuffe. Molière dared in this comedy to put on stage a religious hypocrite; this touched a very raw nerve in the entourage of the king and provoked the ecclesiastical and devout party at court to conspire in banning the play in spite of the fact that the king apparently approved of it. The play did not obtain a licence for public performance until 1669, five years after its first, partial performance at a court festivity; it then became financially the most successful of all of Molière's comedies. Like Les Précieuses ridicules and L'École des femmes, it was set in contemporary Paris and even made direct reference to the *Fronde and to the king, who is eulogized in the last act of the play.

Political and social issues are raised also in the plays written by Molière while waiting for *Tartuffe to be licensed for performance: *Dom Juan (1665) portrays a *libertin nobleman who is punished at the end of the play by being dragged off to hell, but not before he has commented darkly on the religious hypocrisy of the age; Le *Misanthrope (1666) shows the socially unacceptable behaviour of a number of aristocratic habitués of a salon; L'*Avare (1668) demonstrates the corrosive effect of the pursuit of money on human relations; *Amphitryon of the same year, which may well refer discreetly to Louis XIV's notorious affair with Madame de *Montespan, appears to advocate prudence and silence in an absolutist state. The plays of this period, which also include the lighter-hearted L'Amour médecin (1665), Le *Médecin malgré lui (1666), Mélicerte, Pastorale comique, and Le *Sicilien (all 1666–7), are famous for some of Molière's most memorable creations: Dom Juan, whose urbane manipulation of those about him is highly entertaining, and only becomes disturbing towards the end of the play; Alceste the misanthrope, whose tempestuous and contradictory pursuit of sincerity at all costs wreaks havoc in the circles in which he moves; Harpagon, whose obsessive avarice is as sinister as it is funny.

There is some evidence that Molière's finances were in crisis just before the release of Tartuffe in 1669, and this may in part account for the new direction his dramatic production took at around that date. In conjunction first with *Lully, and later with *Charpentier, Molière undertook to produce a number of comédies-ballets for the court: *George Dandin (1668), *Monsieur de Pourceaugnac (1669), Les Amants magnifiques (1670), and most notably Le *Bourgeois

Gentilhomme (1671). This last play combined a satire of the *nouveaux-riches* and their pretensions to social graces with the vogue for all things Turkish at court. The portrayal of contemporary vice and folly is as sharp as in the earlier plays, but the whimsicality of the pseudo-Turkish ceremonies of the end of the play relieves it of some of its sting. Similarly, the harsh portrayal of the cuckolded farmer George Dandin, who has foolishly married above his station, is attenuated by the pastoral ballet episode at the end of the play. Molière even experimented with a combination of tragedy and ballet, as happens in *Psyché* of 1671. At the same time he produced the farces, *La Comtesse d'Escarbagnas* and *Les Fourberies de *Scapin* (both 1671), and two more memorable comedies of manners: *Les *Femmes savantes* of 1672 and the three-act *comédie-ballet* Le *Malade imaginaire*, famous for its portrayal of the hypochondriac Argan. It was ironically in the course of the fourth performance of this play in 1673 that Molière collapsed on stage; he died later in the same evening.

Throughout his brilliant though tumultuous Parisian career, Molière set out to satisfy two audiences: on the one hand, the court and especially the king; and on the other, those who attended his theatre, many of whom belonged to the bourgeoisie. His satire is clearly designed to appeal to these very different clients; this conferred complexity on his plays, and may well have contributed to their enduring popularity and to the almost infinite range of interpretations to which they can be subjected.

He is often said to be a classical writer of comedies, which might seem to suggest that he represents timeless models of human vice and folly—the miser, the hypochondriac, the hypocrite, the misanthropist, and so on; but his plays have been successfully adapted to innumerable cultural settings from the 17th c. to the present day. This may be explained through Molière's sheer professionalism: he was an actor and a theatre director as well as a playwright, and had a virtuoso command of the techniques of all the theatrical genres of his day—*commedia dell'arte*, native French farce, high comedy, machine plays. Molière was as able to exploit the lowest tricks of farce—bawdy jokes, stageplay, stereotypical characters—as the most refined comedy of language which provokes not a guffaw but, as one of his contemporaries put it, a 'rire dans l'âme'. Above all, he seems to have an effortless command of the psychological trigger of laughter, as is demonstrated by the reaction to his plays of audiences of many different generations and cultures.

Molière has been presented under many different guises: a precursor of the *drame* of the 18th c.; a comic genius indifferent to social issues; a moralist who employed comedy to 'corriger les hommes en les divertissant'; a defender of bourgeois values; a toady of the aristocracy. All of these opinions may have something in them: but Molière's multifaceted plays transcend them all. [IM]

See R. Bray, *Molière, homme de théâtre* (1953); W. D. Howarth, *Molière* (1982); J. Grimm, *Molière* (1984).

MOLINET, Jean (1435–1507). Born in Desvres (near Boulogne), one of the *Rhétoriqueurs. After studies in Paris, he was attached to the duke of Burgundy (Charles le Téméraire) from 1464. A tireless purveyor of *Chroniques* and official poetry (e.g. *Le Trône d'honneur*, a long allegorical poem on the death of Charles), he also wrote ballades and rondeaux (some frivolous or obscene), and produced the *Roman de la Rose moralisé* (in prose) and an *Art de rhétorique*. Though often tedious and verbose, he was nevertheless inventive in his use of verse forms and metre. His popularity at the beginning of the 16th c. is attested by the frequent references to him and by the editions of his works, *Les Faictz et dictz*. [CMSJ]

Molinists. Name sometimes used loosely (usually pejoratively) in the 17th c. to refer to the *Jesuits, but meaning the followers of the Spaniard Luis Molina, who aimed to reconcile free will with grace and divine foreknowledge.

Molloy (1951). Novel by Beckett, the first in the trilogy also including *Malone meurt* and *L'Innommable*.

Monarchy. [For a listing of kings of France, see Chronology, pp. xxxvii.] The election of Hugues Capet in 987 as king of France saw the start of a long line of monarchs who ruled territories that were enlarged and gradually welded together to form the French state. The *Capetians were to survive in the direct line until 1328, when a *Valois became heir, and the Valois kings were in turn succeeded by the *Bourbons from 1589 to 10 August 1792. The *Revolution abolished the monarchy in 1792, but it was re-established in 1814 [see RESTORATION] and was to last until the Revolution of 1848 [see REPUBLICS, 2]. Although contenders for a throne had no chance of success under the Third Republic, the monarchical principle re-emerged as a strong intellectual force in French politics at the end of the 19th c. with the formation of *Action Française.

Throughout the *ancien régime* the precise limits of royal power were unclear. The close link maintained by the kings with the Church was an essential element in their authority. Kings were seen as God's lieutenants on earth and so had a sacred quality and a duty to defend the true (Catholic) religion. God was the supreme judge, and so too was the king in earthly matters. In popular tradition these qualities had been exhibited in exemplary fashion by St Louis (Louis IX) in the 13th c., and they were still emphasized, until the end of the regime, by the coronation ceremony, during which the new king was anointed with holy water. The popular definition of kingship hardly altered between the Middle Ages and the last decades of the regime: the king could do no wrong (although he might have evil advisers), was wise and blessed with the gift of 'the royal touch', curing scrofula by the laying on of hands. Learned juristic definitions wavered between an emphasis on the medieval seigneurial origins of royal power [see FEUDALISM], which was later buttressed by conciliarist notions applied to the secular sphere, and the revived Roman tradition, which attributed far wider powers to the king than the former, more contractual concepts.

From the late 14th c. onwards royal jurists tended to apply to internal affairs that maxim first exploited against papal pretentions: *rex in sui regno imperator est*, arguing that the powers of the king over his territories were akin to those of the Roman emperors. Although such claims were never incorporated into royal edicts, they gave rise to much learned debate, particularly during the *Wars of Religion. However, in his *Traité des seigneuries* (3rd edn., 1610) Loyseau could still put into words what many had believed for a long time, namely that there were five regalian rights: the king could make laws, create offices, decide upon peace and war, have the final decision in judicial matters, and mint coin. Beyond these rights, which hardly amounted to a constitution (though many historians have indeed claimed that France did have an 'unwritten, customary, constitution'), most other areas of the exercise of royal power were open to differing interpretations—according to political theory, local customs, or provincial and corporate privileges. For example, the right to tax people without their consent [see TAXATION] remained contentious because many continued to believe that the king should live off his own estates except in wartime. Additionally, and fundamentally, all agreed that, because God had instituted rulers for the benefit of mankind, kings had a duty to defend the commonwealth and protect the life and security of their subjects.

Strictly speaking, no king was bound by the decisions of his predecessors. However, monarchical states need continuity between rulers and their laws must not die with them, so a fiction had developed that the king never died: 'the king is dead, long live the king!' In this way the royal office passed without interruption through the male line, and thus jurists solved the problem of the continuity or lapse of royal legislative acts over succeeding generations. In addition to its theoretical attributes, French kingship was a dynastic affair in which the interests of the royal family clearly counted for as much as any regalian duties.

To protect their own interests and those of their subjects, and thereby fulfil their monarchical duties, the kings had evolved certain judicial, financial, and administrative structures. Most of these had made their first appearance during the 13th and 14th c., during the period of strengthening royal power before the *Hundred Years War. Often built upon pre-existing areas of administration, either feudal or religious, these institutions had created a stable, if complex, administrative geography by the 16th c.

During the 16th c. secretaries of state emerged and the royal council (*Conseil d'État* or *Conseil d'en haut*) developed. The extensive use of *intendants* from the 1630s reveals the need to control royal officials and coerce the population into paying heavier taxes. Many historians have seen the emergence of 'the modern state' in such administrative developments, and identify the notion of 'absolute monarchy' with these changes. However, the term 'absolute monarchy' was a description of the undivided nature of royal sovereignty—the ultimate power of decision lay with the king alone, and not, for example, with an aristocratic council or a representative assembly—and should not, strictly speaking, be applied to the institutional structures, while the word 'absolutism' is a neologism dating from the 1830s and best forgotten, so misleading is it.

There is an important distinction to be made between theoretical sovereignty in the *ancien régime* and the actual exercise of power; if royal sovereignty was in theory 'absolute', royal authority was in practice very restricted in comparison with the modern state; its exercise was subject to a host of traditional, customary (but legal) checks. Even writers who interpreted royal authority as being truly unlimited stated that the king would never want to act unjustly, which was to say, despotically. The kings were therefore 'absolute' monarchs constrained by the laws of the land, not despots, and were not by any means all-powerful. For this reason, persuasion, propaganda, bluff, negotiation, and compromise were as much a part of the normal techniques of monarchical rule as were bureaucratic or administrative practices.

During the 16th and 17th c. the royal *court greatly developed as an instrument of government, reaching its apogee under *Louis XIV at *Versailles. Far from being merely a place where the nobility was domesticated, the court was a crucially important central institution, the fount of *patronage, the centre-piece of the financial system—it was an arena in which administrators were expected to be courtiers and where aristocratic values dominated. Louis XIV was as much a prisoner of the court as his leading servants, a fact which should cause us to question the orthodox view that his reign saw the triumph of an 'administrative monarchy'. For the monarchy, in parallel with bureaucratic channels, patronage and clientage remained important instruments of government. Even so, royal power was so restricted by privileges that political crises of both a judicial and fiscal nature were frequent from the early 17th c. Political debate from the 1750s combined with religious scepticism to undermine the legitimacy of monarchical authority, so that it had few defenders by the late 1780s. The final crisis of the monarchy in 1787–9 revealed a monarchy unable to overrule privileged resistance to fiscal reform, in an age when the exercise of royal power was increasingly regarded as 'despotic'. Unable to surmount the crisis, the 'absolute' monarchy collapsed in 1789, to be replaced by a constitutional monarchy until 1792. [PRC]

See D. Richet, *La France moderne: l'esprit des institutions* (1973); P. R. Campbell, *The Ancien Régime in France* (1988).

MONCRIF, François-Augustin Paradis de (1687–1770). While holding various official positions (reader to the queen, censor, etc.), he wrote in a number of different genres: comedies, stories, songs, poems, and a famous work of mock erudition, *Histoire des chats* (1727).

Monde, Le. In 1944 de *Gaulle wanted France to have a newspaper commanding international respect, to replace *Le *Temps.* Under Hubert *Beuve-Méry's direction (1944–69), *Le Monde* became France's authoritative newspaper of record and comment; it defeated several attempts by politicians and financiers to suborn its independence. Four directors later—Jacques Fauvet, André Laurens, André Fontaine and, from 1991, Jacques Lesourne—*Le Monde* remains obligatory reading for intellectuals, business men, and politicians alike. Its investigative reporting during the *Rainbow Warrior* affair (1985) helped restore the tarnished fortunes of a paper politically left-of-centre, and with an average circulation of 450,000 copies. [MP]

Monde, ou le Traité de l'homme, Le, see DESCARTES.

Monde comme il va, Le. Philosophical tale by *Voltaire, subtitled 'Vision de Babouc'. Babouc is sent by an angel to see whether Persepolis (Paris) should be destroyed or reformed. Torn between admiration and horror, his report persuades the angel to leave things as they are: 'si tout n'est pas bien, tout est passable.'

Monde primitif, Le, see COURT DE GÉBELIN.

Monde tel qu'il est, Le, see ETCHART.

MONÉNEMBO, Tierno (b. 1947) Guinean novelist. Still a child when Sékou Touré came to power in 1958, Monénembo (a pseudonym) fled from Guinea in the late 1960s. After some time in Ivory Coast and Senegal, he completed his studies in France, where he obtained a post as a teacher of biochemistry.

He has written two novels, both of them indictments of Sékou Touré's régime. In *Les Crapauds-brousse* (1979) the young idealist intellectual returns to Guinea after completing his studies abroad, and is progressively disillusioned by the brutality, corruption, and incompetence of the regime. The second novel, *Les Écailles du ciel* (1986), is even more pessimistic. Broader in scope, it spans modern Guinean history from before the French conquest to the death of Sékou Touré and its immediate aftermath. The first section, which covers life in a pre-colonial village, seeks with considerable success to convey the Fulani world through the medium of French, much as *Kourouma had done with the Malinké.

While in no way idealizing this era, Monénembo paints it with an affectionate, positive touch completely lacking in the rest of the novel, which ends on a totally nihilistic note: there is no way forward for Guinea, nor any point in discussing the country's future further. [FNC]

MONET, Claude (1840–1926). One of the leading figures of the *Impressionist movement, Monet specialized in the representation of light's interaction with formless elements such as water, steam, and mist, or the variations of form created by changes of light, as in the series paintings executed on a single motif (grainstack, poplar, cathedral). His research culminated in the water-lilies executed for the Orangerie Museum, Paris, in which forms are dissolved into shimmering pools of intense, vibrant colour. Initially defended by *Zola (*Mon salon*, 1866, 1868) in the name of *Naturalism, Monet's work was seen by the *Symbolists as part of a wider, subjective, anti-Naturalist move to transcend logical, utilitarian representations of reality; his series paintings came to be considered as the pictorial realization of *Bergson's distinction between duration and spatial time. This link between pictorial technique and intellectual trends informs subsequent literary responses to Impressionist painting, such as the descriptions of Elstir's paintings in Proust's *A la recherche du temps perdu*, and theories of the material imagination, such as those of *Bachelard. [JK]

Money, see CURRENCY.

Mon Faust, see VALÉRY.

MONGE, Gaspard (1746–1818). Mathematician and physicist, one of the founders of the *École Polytechnique and one of the first teachers at the *École Normale Supérieure. He was much honoured by Napoleon.

Moniage Guillaume, Le. *Chanson de geste* of the Cycle de *Guillaume, loosely inspired by the historical Guillaume's retreats to Aniane and Gellone. The tone is predominantly comic, the hero failing to adapt to monastic life, although Guillaume's final rescue of Louis when Paris is under attack, his abduction by Saracens, and his fight with a demon near his hermit's cell add more serious epic touches. [PEB]

Moniage Rainouart, Le. *Chanson de geste* of the Cycle de *Guillaume dating from 1190–1200 imitating *Le *Moniage Guillaume* and repeating many incidents from that poem. It tells how Rainouart retires to a monastery following the death of his wife and the abduction of his son. The giant's inability to adapt to monastic life is recounted with much comic verve. [PEB]

Moniteur, Le (full title *La Gazette nationale, ou le Moniteur universel*). In 1789, once the king and the National Assembly had moved to Paris, Charles-

Joseph *Panckoucke, the publisher of the *Encyclopédie méthodique* and of newspapers such as the *Mercure de France*, founded a broadsheet daily to report Assembly debates rapidly and extensively, as well as foreign and domestic news. Recognized for the quality of its parliamentary coverage, *Le Moniteur* received government privileges and subsidies. *Napoleon made the daily the centre-piece of his propaganda machine. Occasionally contributing articles himself, he awarded Panckoucke's heirs the monopoly of the publication of government measures and of official news—a role it retained until 1869, when its place was taken by the *Journal officiel*.

[MP]

MONLUC, Blaise de (*c.*1502–1577). French memorialist. A member of the generation which fought in the Italian Wars before participating in the *Wars of Religion, he won great renown in the former as a result of his stout but unavailing defence of Sienna, and great notoriety in the latter as a result of his brutal methods. He was sceptical about the motives of the various leaders of the civil war, but sincerely believed that the only way to end it quickly was to act ruthlessly. His *Commentaires*, which were not published until 1592, were originally begun partly as a work of self-justification and partly in order to serve as a model for future captains, but they expanded into a lively panorama of the wars in which he participated. Monluc shared the view of most of his fellow nobles that the aristocrat's chief role should be military, but was aware of the fact that social and political changes would make it more and more necessary for the *noble d'épée* to receive a good education. Although more interested in 'le bien faire' than 'le bien dire', he became increasingly aware of the value of his memoirs.

[IJS]

MONNIER, Adrienne (1892–1955). Paris bookseller, writer, and editor. From 1915 her 'Maison des Amis des Livres' at 7, rue de l'Odéon (across from Sylvia Beach's 'Shakespeare and Company') became a writers' forum and 'le foyer d'idées le plus attractif de l'époque' (*Breton). See *Les Gazettes 1925–45* (1953) and her memoirs, *Rue de l'Odéon* (1960). [DAS]

MONNIER, Henri (1799–1877). French satirist, known for the creation in his 1830 *Scènes populaires* of the character of Joseph Prudhomme, the typical bourgeois—good-hearted but stupid and pretentious, naïve and limited but very verbose. His *Les Bourgeois de Paris* (1834) and *Mémoires de Joseph Prudhomme* (1857) combine wit and realism in their presentation of the foibles and pretentions of the middle class. He illustrated his own works. Actor as well as artist and writer, he contributed much to *vaudeville, puppet theatre, etc. [FPB]

MONOD, Gabriel, see HISTORIOGRAPHY, 6.

MONOD, Jacques (1910–76). French biochemist; awarded the Nobel Prize in 1965. In his most widely read work, *Le Hasard et la nécessité* (1970), Monod demonstrated that evolution has its source in chance disturbances and random combinations at the microscopic level; their effects are replicated and transmitted through the rigorous mechanisms of the genetic code, and filtered, in the process of natural selection, by the teleonomic or goal-directed behaviour of organisms. A number of philosophical implications were seen to follow. Monod argued that man's cognitive frames of reference are innate, and that man's cognitive functions are not immediately linked with speech. He attacked the pseudo-scientific claims of dialectical materialism, and sought to ground authentic action and discourse in an ethical commitment to the principle of objectivity in knowledge, on which a scientific and humanist socialism might be based. [REG]

Monsieur, see MADAME.

Monsieur de Pourceaugnac. *Comédie-ballet* by *Molière, first performed for the court at Chambord in 1669. It features a grotesque provincial from Limoges who is cruelly humiliated to prevent his marriage to Orgon's daughter Julie, who prefers the young Parisian Éraste.

Monsieur Nicolas ou le Cœur humain dévoilé. *Restif de la Bretonne's 16-vol. autobiography (1794–7), a frank account of the life, passions, and philosophy of the ordinary man ('je disséquerai l'homme ordinaire, comme J.-J. Rousseau a disséqué le grand homme'). Monsieur Nicolas sees himself as a mirror for his contemporaries: that middle section of society (well-to-do peasants and urban artisans) come to new status and self-consciousness in the pre-Revolutionary *Enlightenment. The text conveys the material reality of daily life in vividly observed detail, with anecdotes, tableaux, portraits, and lively dialogue anticipating the realist techniques of 19th-c. prose: the family farm at Saci, boarding-school, printing-shops in Auxerre and Paris, Paris streets and lodging-houses, the prostitute and libertine world, the life of the theatre. The driving force is the hero's exacerbated sensuality, generating prolix accounts of his sexual precocity, his frenzied cult of the ideal feminine, and, most of all, a plethora of passing sexual adventures. Sexuality and writing are indissolubly linked and jointly designated as the source of self-consciousness. Restif is acutely aware of the material reality and power of language. When he draws up his calendar of the women named in his text (bourgeoises, shopgirls, actresses, prostitutes), he explains that he is drawing them from obscurity into a new historical place: 'Parler de quelqu'un, c'est augmenter son existence. N'en rien dire, c'est aider la mort.' [JB]

Monsieur Ouine, see BERNANOS.

Monsieur Songe. Character who figures in several stories by *Pinget.

539

Monsieur Teste

Monsieur Teste. Imaginary intellectual figure in the 'Cycle Teste' by *Valéry, a series of pieces from different periods of his life, the first and best-known of which, written in 1894 shortly after his youthful mental crisis, is *La Soirée avec Monsieur Teste* (1896). Preferring potentiality or inner mental power to actual creation or the communication of his talents, Teste is in fact a monstrous high priest of the intellect (Mr 'Head', from an old form of *Tête*), whose aim is total self-mastery by knowing his limits as a physical organism ('Que peut un homme?'). Introduced by an already highly self-aware narrator ('I cannot abide stupidity' was the opening line of the first English translation), he is seen, for example, not only minimizing the outer circumstances of his life as much as possible, but examining the sensation of physical pain. (We also see him at the opera, characteristically observing himself observe the audience of which he himself forms part.)

Teste for Valéry was a literary experiment (one of his many comments in the Pléiade edition of his collected works) in extracting the most intense moments of a mind observing its own operations and composing from them a whole way of life. In other pieces we are given extracts from Teste's Log-Book or, in the often comical *Lettre de Madame Émilie Teste* (1924), a view of this 'mystique sans Dieu' as seen by his conveniently complementary wife. Representing a certain direction of Valéry's own mind taken to parodic extreme, Teste himself was partly modelled on *Poe's Dupin, as well as on *Degas and on *Descartes, with whom Valéry associated the autobiographical element absent from modern philosophy; Teste in turn is thus associated with the 'roman moderne'. This was Valéry's only venture into novelistic form. [CMC]

Montagnards. Name given to the radical deputies who sat in the most elevated section ('La Montagne') of the Convention Nationale during the *Revolution; the group included about one-third of the deputies by Spring 1793. They struggled victoriously against the *Girondins, but did not long survive the downfall of *Robespierre. The moderate *députés*, who gave unreliable support to the Montagnards, were known as 'La Plaine' or 'Le Marais'.

Montagne du lion, La, see TLILI.

MONTAIGNE, Michel de (1533–92). Moralist and author of the *Essais*, composed during the last 20 years of his life, which have left an indelible impression not only on French but on European culture. In the eyes of many of his contemporaries he was a striking example of a *Neostoic author; to the sceptics and *libertins* of the 17th c. he was their precursor and inspiration; in the following century, *Diderot admired him as a *philosophe avant la lettre*, and *Rousseau saw in him the first of the great confessional writers. More recently, Nietzsche praised him as a destructive relativist, and *Gide saw in him

a proponent of sexual honesty and liberation. One of the peculiar qualities of his *Essais* is to reflect the intimate preoccupations of their readers; it is thus hardly surprising that for his most modern critics his work is marked by the aesthetics of the fragmentary; that it exemplifies intertextuality (incorporating as it does 1,264 explicit quotations, as well as countless other allusions); and that Montaigne himself anticipated reader-response theories of interpretation. This protean quality assures the *Essais* their status as a classic.

Montaigne was born in Gascony of a recently ennobled well-to-do family, and given a solid humanist education at the Collège de Guyenne. He was destined for a career in the law, and after university studies at either Toulouse or Paris he became in 1557 a minor magistrate at the Parlement de Bordeaux, where *La Boétie was his colleague and friend. He sold his post in 1570 in order to 'retire into the bosom of the learned Virgins'. His father had died two years before, leaving him the estate of Montaigne, where he resolved to devote the remainder of his life to reading, contemplation, and writing in the tower of his château, which housed his extensive library and whose exposed beams were inscribed with his favourite quotations.

His retirement was, however, not entirely uneventful; he left it to travel extensively in France, Switzerland, Germany, and Italy in 1580–1, leaving an interesting *Journal de voyage* which was discovered and published in 1774. Subsequently he became mayor of nearby Bordeaux (1581–5). Between 1570 and 1588 he was intermittently involved in high-level diplomatic negotiations on behalf of *Henri III and Henri de Navarre, later *Henri IV, the heir presumptive to the throne, both of whom conferred honours on him. He died in 1592, of the painful hereditary disease (the kidney stone) of which his father also died. By that time he was a famous author whose works had run through several editions. He published the first two books of *Essais* at his own expense in Bordeaux in 1580, and had them reprinted in a revised version in 1582; in 1588 an enlarged edition, which included the third book, appeared in Paris; at the time of his death he was working on a much-expanded edition, which came out in 1595, edited by Marie de *Gournay, his 'fille d'alliance'.

This bare outline of his life does not reveal the intense and exciting intellectual journey on which he embarked when he retired in 1570, and which ended only at his death. He may have intended only to read and meditate; but he soon began to write, and scholars have been able to establish with some certainty the order in which he wrote the *Essais*. Why he began to write is not altogether clear, even though he offers various reasons. An important factor might well be the death of his closest friend, the moralist Étienne de la Boétie, in 1563; it has been plausibly suggested that the *Essais* are a one-sided continuation of their conversations together.

Another factor could be the existence of loosely organized books of gleanings from the ancients, which offered Montaigne a model for arranging by theme and subject the notes he himself made from his reading. In giving his work the novel title 'Essais', which suggests 'experiments' or 'trials', Montaigne may well be alluding to aspects of this work of compilation and reflection. It is the very reverse of a confident or assertive title. Nor did Montaigne claim to be writing for the benefit of anyone other than his intimates and immediate family; indeed, the prologue of 1580 tells the casual reader that he would do better not to bother with the book at all.

The subjects which most interest him initially are those closest to his own preoccupations and to those of his contemporaries. Montaigne belonged to the post-*Reformation generation for whom the schism in the Church was an irreversible fact and a burning personal issue: some of his own siblings had become Protestants, although he was to remain a staunch Catholic. The optimistic era of *humanist learning was past: but attention was still paid to the principal topics of humanist concern: education, war, moral philosophy, history, politics, and the higher disciplines of law and medicine. Montaigne's early interests revolve around human inconsistency, ambition, and above all pain and death in this broad context. His reading and writing are designed to console him and strengthen him against what he perceives as future threats: death from a painful disease, social disorder, religious uncertainty, personal perplexity. This is often said to be his Neostoic phase, characterized by his essays on philosophizing as learning to die (I, 20) and solitude (I, 40), in which the wise man is said to withdraw from public life and even social contact and to make himself master of his own happiness by steeling himself against misfortune. But even in this phase, Montaigne's penchant for paradox and issues of doubt is clear, and his awareness of the bewildering diversity of human character and experience is explicit (I, 23; I, 31).

A major development in his writings—sometimes called the 'sceptical crisis'—occurred in the middle years of the 1570s when Montaigne had a medal struck with the device 'Que sçay-je?' It is sometimes connected with the incident he records in the chapter on practice (II, 6), in which the experience of falling off a horse and apparently drifting towards death makes him realize that his policy of steeling himself against future misfortune is misplaced. But it may have much more to do with his defence of Raymond Sebond (Sabunde), which he was apparently commissioned to write by *Marguerite de Valois, the Catholic wife of Henri de Navarre. Montaigne had translated the 15th-c. Sebond's *Theologia naturalis* in 1569 at the behest of his father; it is a work which purports to prove God's existence by rational means, and which describes man's pre-eminence in God's creation. Montaigne's 'Apologie

de Raymond Sebond' (II, 12)—an apologia presumably against Protestant critiques—is a thoroughgoing though unsystematic exercise in *Pyrrhonism. It constitutes a withering sceptical attack on all forms of dogmatic philosophy and on all of man's intellectual pretensions. Man is shown to be no higher than the animals; his reason, weak and faulty; his senses, through which he acquires all knowledge, fallible and untrustworthy; and his moral convictions, lacking secure rational bases. Diversity and difference, not similarity and consensus, are shown to be ubiquitous; and the whole universe, in continual, incommensurable flux. Man, his faculty for judging and reasoning, and the objects of his perception are perpetually changing and unstable. Not only Sebond's adversaries, but arguably Sebond himself was demolished by this radical sceptical critique.

But it did not produce despair in Montaigne: instead, in his later *Essais*, he began cautiously to search for new bases for human enquiry. Ancient moral philosophies had failed to come up with a way of achieving happiness which was generally applicable; it was clear, therefore, that everyone had to search for their own answers by beginning their enquiries with that which they knew best: themselves. Personal anecdotes had been related by Montaigne from the very beginning of his writing; but they did not amount to fully fledged self-study. Self-study requires a method, however; Montaigne's was a unique form of non-self-indulgent introspection. This had to be honest, and unconstrained by convention; it had to be unselective; it had to take into account the fundamental mutability of man. As a practice, it led to self-portrayal: the recording of facts and opinion about the self in an infinitely extendable list. Because man changes constantly, the self-portrait cannot be revised, only augmented. In Book 3 of the *Essais*, and in the additions inserted in the first two books, the results of this method unfold. Montaigne records his most intimate sexual and gastronomic practices, as well as his most lofty thoughts; he leaves contradictions and inconsistencies in his text as a proof of its veracity; his arguments and discussions are rarely sustained for more than a paragraph or two (indeed, the titles of the *Essais* seldom indicate adequately their contents, and sometimes, playfully, have nothing to do with them whatsoever); he records his judgements on other people and other subjects as evidence about himself as much as about these people or subjects.

The conclusions of this enquiry are, if anything, yet more surprising for their day. Man is seen as a corporeal more than a rational being. He is an amalgam of vice and virtue, in which the two elements are inseparable. He is irreducibly individual, but every man 'porte la forme entière de l'humaine condition' (III, 2). All men share the same nature, but their social, political, and (implicitly) religious institutions are relative to specific societies, political systems, and religions. This relativistic attitude leads to a plea for toleration and the expression of horror at unjustifiable repression in the name of law, religion, or 'reason': the chapters which deal with the burning of witches and the Spanish treatment of Amerindians (I, 31; III, 6; III, 11) are especially eloquent condemnations of intolerance. But Montaigne himself derives political and religious conformism from his relativistic and sceptical stance.

The *Essais* accumulated additions (with few amendments) over the period of their composition; one can only imagine that, had Montaigne lived longer, they would have continued to do so, because he tells us that he has discovered an inexhaustible vein of rich material to exploit. As his confidence in his enterprise grows, so the *Essais* become more complex, more paradoxical, more playful, more idiosyncratic in expression. Indeed, one of their most remarkable features is their style.

By adding to his own essays Montaigne becomes an alien reader of his own writing, and offers many penetrating insights into the reading process itself. Towards the end of Book 3 the *Essais* become a celebration of reading and writing, of human conversation and friendship, of living life to the full, which contrasts with the stiffly Neostoic attitudes expressed in the first period. Experience, not Seneca or Cato, has taught him the best way of managing pain; he is able to rejoice in the legitimate pleasures of life, and the very last quotation in his *Essais* has a distinctly pagan, hedonistic ring to it. But to suggest that this is the conclusion of such a multifaceted and complex work would be wrong. Just as scepticism is present from the beginning, so also is a certain sort of Stoicism present at the end. Plausible it may be to see a development in the *Essais* from one philosophical stance to another: but it is more plausible to see them all as expressions of the complex personality of an author whose investigation into human nature marks a turning-point in man's enquiry into man.

[IM]

See R. A. Sayce, *The Essays of Montaigne* (1972); P. Burke, *Montaigne* (1981); I. Maclean and I. McFarlane, *Montaigne* (1982).

Montaillou, see LE ROY LADURIE.

MONTALEMBERT. Charles-Forbes-René, comte de (1810–70). Catholic writer and politician. He belonged to the group of liberal Catholic intellectuals which surrounded *Lamennais at the time of *L'Avenir* (1830–2). However, he broke with Lamennais after the papal condemnation of *Paroles d'un croyant*. Montalembert pursued an active political career during the July Monarchy and the Second Empire as a stout defender of Catholic interests. He also published a seven-vol. *Histoire des moines d'Occident* (1860–77). [CC]

MONTAND, Yves (pseud. of Ivo Livi) (1921–91). Italian-born film actor. He grew up in Marseille and became known as a popular singer, strongly committed at first to the Communist Party. His long acting career, for much of which he was married to Simone *Signoret, was crowned by his appearance as a Provençal peasant in *Jean de Florette* and *Manon des sources* [see CINEMA].

MONTCHRESTIEN, Antoine de (c.1575–1621). French dramatist, author, during his twenties, of six tragedies (*Sophonisbe*, published 1596; *L'Écossaise, Les Lacènes, David, Aman,* all published 1601, with a revised version of *Sophonisbe,* renamed *La Carthaginoise; Hector,* published 1604, along with revised versions of the other plays, *L'Écossaise* being renamed *La *Reine d'Écosse*). The subjects are taken from classical epic and history, the Bible, and modern history. There has been debate as to whether Montchrestien's revisions, particularly of *Sophonisbe,* were influenced by a meeting with *Malherbe in about 1600. The evidence is inconclusive. The plays (verse tragedies in five acts, with a chorus or choruses who conclude each act with a stanzaic poem) are similar in form and technique to those of earlier humanist playwrights such as *Garnier and *La Taille. Montchrestien's only known later work is a *Traité de l'économie politique* (1615), which argues that the state should protect French manufacturers and merchants against foreign competition. In 1621 Montchrestien joined a Huguenot revolt (it is not certain that he was a Protestant) and was killed in a skirmish; after his death he was tried for rebellion and a sentence of breaking and burning carried out on his body. [GJ]

MONTEILHET, Hubert (b. 1928). French historian and amateur theologian. Monteilhet uses suspense and changing perspectives, in crime fiction from *Les Mantes religieuses* (1960), *Les Pavés du diable* (1963), to *La Part des anges* (1990); pastiche (*Sophie,* 1970); fantasy (*Les Queues de Kallinaos,* 1981); and historical novels (*Neropolis,* 1984; *La Pucelle,* 1988). [SFN]

MONTÉPIN, Xavier de (1823–1902), see ROMAN D'AVENTURE(S), 2.

MONTESPAN, Françoise-Athénaïs de Rochechouart, marquise de (1640–1709), became *Louis XIV's mistress in 1667, ousting Louise de *la Vallière. She bore him seven children, later legitimized, before losing her position in the late 1670s. She was a patron of *Racine and *Boileau, but was also suspected of involvement in black magic and poisoning [see POISONS, AFFAIRE DES].

MONTESQUIEU, Charles de Secondat, baron de (1689–1755). Political philosopher, historian, and novelist, remembered above all for his *magnum opus, De l'*esprit des lois,* but also highly regarded as a master of French prose.

Montesquieu was a member of the military and legal nobility of the Bordeaux region. His rank was important to him; indeed, much of his political writing is devoted to a defence of the privileges and functions of his caste. Born at the Château de la

Brède, in a prosperous wine-growing region, he was educated at the *Oratorian college of Juilly and at the law faculties of Bordeaux and Paris. In 1715 he married Jeanne Lartigue, a rich Protestant, who subsequently looked after the estate and the family during her husband's frequent and prolonged absences. In 1716 he inherited a fortune, together with the office of *président à mortier* in the Parlement de Bordeaux—he exercised his legal functions until resigning in 1725 to devote himself to travel, study, and writing.

As a young lawyer in Bordeaux he was an assiduous member of the local *academy, writing numerous papers for it. Some are devoted to moral or political topics, but many are on scientific subjects, and it was in a scientific spirit that he later studied law, politics, and society. His first major publication was the *Lettres persanes* (1721), the success of which made him a fashionable figure in Paris. Between 1722 and 1728 he frequented various Paris *salons, and in particular the *Club de l'Entresol, where politics was high on the agenda; for admission, he wrote a *Dialogue de Sylla et d'Eucrate*, a critique of tyranny and heroic individualism, and one of a number of pieces in which a Roman subject allows him to discuss general political issues. At about the same time he composed essays on such topics as natural law and moral obligation. His involvement in fashionable society is reflected in some lightweight but sometimes subtle fictional writings: *Le Temple de Gnide* (1725) is a rather wearisome pseudo-Greek pastoral whose aim is to give 'une peinture poétique de la volupté'; the *Voyage de Paphos* (1727) is similar. In 1727, against the opposition of the prime minister *Fleury, Montesquieu was elected to the Académie Française.

The years 1728 to 1731 were devoted to European travel, taking in Austria, Hungary, Italy, Germany, Switzerland, and Holland, and culminating with a two-year stay in England, which greatly influenced his political views. He was a keen observer: his travel journals, particularly those written in Italy, show a powerful desire to document all aspects of the places he visited. These writings were an essential preparation for his master-work *De l'esprit des lois*, to which he devoted himself whole-heartedly on his return to France. He divided his time between La Brède and Paris, reading voraciously and taking copious notes (some of which were subsequently published under the titles *Geographica* and *Spicilège*).

The first fruit of his studies was the *Considérations sur les causes de la grandeur des Romains et de leur décadence* (1734). At about this time he also wrote further short works of fiction, the most interesting being the posthumously published *Histoire véritable*, a picaresque tale of metempsychosis, covering many lands and many centuries, in which he exploited the satirical vein of the *Lettres persanes*. In 1748, after years of assiduous work that more or less cost him his sight, he published *De*

l'esprit des lois. The work was controversial; it was attacked by Jesuits and Jansenists alike, and in 1750 Montesquieu published a *Défense de l'Esprit des lois*. In 1752 it was placed on the Index. In the last years of his life he was a revered figure among the younger *philosophes*. His last work, the *Essai sur le goût*, figures as the article 'Goût' in the *Encyclopédie*, and D'*Alembert's *Éloge de Montesquieu* was placed at the head of vol. 5 of that work. *Diderot is said to have been the only man of letters at his funeral.

Montesquieu seems to have been at home in the world, where he occupied a privileged place. Although many of his writings are bitterly critical of his society and the way it was developing, his writing is never tragic. In religious matters he avoided controversy, but was apparently a deist rather than a convinced Christian. The richly interesting collection of jottings known as *Mes pensées*, which contains the first draft of many thoughts that were developed in his published works, also offers a self-portrait, in which he speaks of his naturally happy disposition: 'Je m'éveille le matin avec une joie secrète; je vois la lumière avec une espèce de ravissement. Tout le jour je suis content.'

His influence on following generations was immense; he has been variously called the father of liberalism, the father of constitutions, and the founder of social science. His conservative attachment to the stability of the existing hierarchy was married to a desire for moderate reform. In many ways, he was the archetypal champion of *Enlightenment, his aspiration being towards unblinkered clarity of vision and understanding. This meant getting outside himself—the *Lettres persanes* is made of many voices, and stresses the relativity of cultural values. His stance as a writer is customarily one of detached curiosity; in *De l'esprit des lois* this all-accepting scrutiny of the way things are plays fascinatingly against his committed view as to how they should be.

His manner of writing conveys all of this wonderfully well. It is generally reasonable, and sometimes eloquent in a traditional way, but its hallmark is a cool brevity, often witty, and capable of delivering a sharp shock. Later writers such as *Flaubert, and particularly *Stendhal, greatly admired the 'style coupé' of passages such as this, from the *Considérations*: 'quelques soldats entrèrent dans le palais, pour piller: ils trouvèrent, dans un lieu obscur, un homme tremblant de peur; c'était Claude: ils le saluèrent empereur.' [PF]

See J. Starobinski, *Montesquieu par lui-même* (1951); R. Shackleton, *Montesquieu* (1961); J. Shklar, *Montesquieu* (1987).

MONTESQUIOU, Robert de (Montesquiou-Fezensac, comte de) (1855–1921). Poet, essayist, art critic, and aesthete. A rich homosexual dandy, Montesquiou bravely flaunted his eccentrically refined tastes for perfumes, fabrics, and luxury artefacts at high-society extravaganzas, often lavishly orchestrated and funded by himself. His several volumes of poetry, including *Les Chauves-souris* (1892) and *Les Hortensias bleus* (1896), are similarly affected and of less substance than his essays on artists and literary figures. *Les Pas effacés* (1923), his embittered memoirs, appeared posthumously. Purportedly the model for *Huysmans's Des Esseintes and *Proust's Charlus, Montesquiou probably owes survival more to their writing than to his own.   [DAS]

MONTFLEURY (pseud. of Antoine Jacob) (1639–85). French dramatist, son of a famous actor at the *Hôtel de Bourgogne. His plays include comedies of intrigue, *L'Impromptu de l'hôtel de Condé* (1663), a satirical response to Molière's mockery of his father's acting style, *Le Mari sans femme* (1664), which makes innovative use of musical interludes, and the imaginative *Comédien poète* (1674), in which actors appear both as themselves and in their theatrical roles.   [GJM]

MONTHERLANT, Henry de (1868–1971). Montherlant had two almost entirely separate careers, as a novelist (1922–39) and as a dramatist (1942–71). In both, he specialized in the close examination of the irrationality and unpredictability of human behaviour.

Born in Paris, into a family of the minor aristocracy, Montherlant attended a number of schools, ending with the Catholic Collège de Sainte-Croix in Neuilly, from which he was expelled in 1912 (in circumstances reflected in his *La Ville dont le prince est un enfant*). A rather aimless existence thereafter was transformed by the experience of the war, in which he served in the infantry and was severely wounded.

His early writing (1920–32) was heavily coloured by the experience of life in a Catholic college, of sporting activity, and of the exhilaration of war. The message tended to be one of male heroism, of the fraternity of war and action, and of the dangerous dilution of all this by sentimentality and the 'feminine' virtues. His first work, a collection of essays entitled *La Relève du matin* (1920), emphasized the ambiguous moral and spiritual effect of the college, and the moral impact of the trenches. In the novel *Le Songe* (1922), the hero Alban de Bricoule finds fulfilment in the 'ordre mâle' and the fraternity of war. *Les Olympiques* (1924) is a collection of essays, poems, and short stories in praise of sport and its physical effort, its sense of fraternity, its purity of spirit. The next novel, *Les Bestiaires* (1926), takes us back to the pre-war Alban, who finds heroism in the bullring. *Mors et vita* (1932) collects together various pieces, inspired by the war, that Montherlant had been writing since 1918.

It was when he turned to new themes and techniques, however, that Montherlant was to show his true capabilities. *Les *Célibataires* (1934) was a successful new departure, consolidated by the sequence of four novels *Les *Jeunes Filles* (1936–9), in which various experimental techniques help to underline that 'syncrétisme et alternance' in human psychology which Montherlant had defined in the essay of that name in *Aux fontaines du désir* (1927): the simultaneous, or alternating, presence of opposites within human motivation. These novels were to be praised by writers as diverse as *Aragon, *Bernanos, and *Malraux.

He continued as an essayist, too, with the collections *L'Équinoxe de septembre* (1938), which railed at the mediocrity of contemporary France, and *Le Solstice de juin* (1941) which, in the aftermath of defeat, expressed similar anxieties and called for a new spirit within the country.

Up to 1942, then, Montherlant was known almost exclusively as a novelist and essayist. Nobody could have foreseen that from 1942 onwards he was to write above all for the theatre. La *Reine morte* (1942) was the result of a commission to translate for the Comédie-Française a play by Guevara; in the event, Montherlant wrote a play entirely his own, which set the pattern for his mature drama. A historical play with elevated tone, it dealt with the complexity and inconsistency of human motivation and behaviour. It was the first of a series of historical dramas: *Malatesta* (1946), *Le *Maître de Santiago* (1947), *Port-Royal* (1954), *Don Juan* (1958), *Le Cardinal d'Espagne* (1960), *La Guerre civile* (1965). Alongside them were written a number of other plays in modern dress: *Fils de personne* (1943), *Demain il fera jour* (1949), *Celles qu'on prend dans ses bras* (1950), *La Ville dont le prince est un enfant* (1951), *Brocéliande* (1956). These two strands, which have often been contrasted, have much in common. Montherlant's originality does not lie in his stage techniques, which are surprisingly traditional amid the experimentation of the post-war theatre, but in the introduction of a novelist's ambiguities into the theatre, and a rejection of shape, coherence, or synthesis, particularly in the field of psychological motivation. He rejects the 'theatre of ideas', and presents us with human situations of infinite complexity, to which there are no certain conclusions, and certainly no 'authorial message' (hard as many critics have tried to ascribe one to him). Certain themes, admittedly, fascinate him: heroism, stoicism, the clash of ideals—and, above all, religion. As an agnostic, Montherlant is nevertheless convincingly able to depict, from his detached standpoint, Christian problems of grace and the appeal of Christian renunciation. His powerful dramatic work has aroused much controversy in France; one thing that is sure is that it cannot be ignored.

In the 1950s and 1960s Montherlant published a number of volumes of diary-based writings containing his ideas and reactions, over the years, to a wide variety of subjects; these included *Carnets (1930–1944)* and *Va jouer avec cette poussière (Carnets 1958–64)*, as well as similar volumes containing observations about his own plays. He also produced a remarkable last novel, *Le Chaos et la nuit* (1963), in which the theme of death and its effect on the human psyche is explored, with indifference finally being seen as the only defence against both the illusions of life and the certainty of death.

Montherlant died by his own hand on the day of the autumn equinox; his ashes were scattered on the Forum in Rome.   [RMG]

See H. Perruchot, *Montherlant* (1959); J. Cruickshank, *Montherlant* (1964).

Montmartre. Hill to the north of Paris, now in the 18th *arrondissement*. The 'Butte' saw fierce fighting during the 'Commune of 1871, after which the pompous basilica of the Sacré-Cœur was erected there as an act of expiation. It remained rustic in character until the end of the 19th c. and was a popular pleasure resort, with many bars, cabarets, and dance-halls (e.g. the Moulin Rouge), which were much frequented by artists and writers around the turn of the century.   [PF]

Montparnasse. District in the 14th *arrondissement* of Paris, south of the Boulevard Montparnasse, adjacent to the Montparnasse cemetery. Between about 1910 and 1940 its cafés, bars, and night-clubs were fashionable meeting-places; many writers and painters, both French and foreign, lived and worked there.

MONTPENSIER, Anne-Marie-Louise d'Orléans, duchesse de, known as Mademoiselle or la Grande Mademoiselle (1627–93). First cousin to Louis XIV and most important heiress of her century. Her exploits during the *Fronde were legendary. Because of them, her cousin exiled her to her château, Saint-Fargeau. There she began her memoirs, so controversial that their posthumous first edition was suppressed by royal decree. From her collaboration with *Segrais resulted the *Nouvelles françaises* published under his name (1656–7), two collective volumes that made verbal portraiture fashionable, and the novellas *Relation de l'île imaginaire* and *Histoire de la princesse de Paphlagonie* (all 1659). Her long-desired marriage to the adventurer Lauzun was ill-fated.   [JDeJ]

MONTREUX, Nicolas de (1561–1610). French historian (*Histoire universelle des guerres du Turc*, 1608) and dramatist (producing a comedy and three tragedies, including *Isabelle*, 1592, inspired by Ariosto), but best known as one of the continuators of the *Amadis* cycle. The latter helped prepare the way for L'*Astrée*, as did Montreux's pastoral novels (e.g. *Les Amours de Cléandre et de Domiphille*, 1597).   [JJS]

Moraliste. Word used to describe authors of reflections on human nature and society. While this characteristically French term can be applied to authors of large-scale works such as *Montaigne or *Rousseau, it tends to be used primarily of those writers of the 17th and 18th c. who specialized in the brief maxim, sketch, portrait, or thought. *Pascal's *Pensées* may be seen as the work of a *moraliste*,

though they were meant as materials for a different kind of book. The pungent maxims of *La Rochefoucauld proved a more typical model; to them should be added the *Caractères* of *La Bruyère, whose concern is as much with social observation as with so-called universal human traits. In both cases, what the reader derives from these short texts is less a moral truth than a stimulus to self-examination, observation, reflection, and discussion. Such maxims and portraits belong essentially in a *salon culture.

Of later *moralistes*, *Vauvenargues and *Chamfort are outstanding, though one might also mention the aphoristic writings of *Diderot (e.g. *Pensées philosophiques*), *Voltaire (e.g. *Le Philosophe ignorant*), or *Rivarol. *Montesquieu's *Mes pensées* and *Joubert's *Pensées* are examples of revealing private writings which acquired the status of *moraliste* texts when published posthumously.   [PF]

Morality Plays. Medieval plays teaching a moral lesson through a drama involving personified abstractions; they were a major genre of the 15th and 16th c. and reflect the contemporary taste for allegory. Some are short and light, and have much in common, in terms of style, versification, and stage requirements, with the *soties*; others are much longer and closer to *mystery plays, e.g. *L'Homme juste et l'homme mondain* (30,000 lines, 84 characters). Plots are based on a conflict between two opposing sets of virtues and vices, who may be fighting over the soul of Everyman, Le Monde, or Povre Peuple. These satirical plays are comic in two senses; virtue normally triumphs, and the actions and eventual discomfiture of the vices provoke laughter. Moralities can be classified according to their subjects. Some attack universal sins, like greed (in *La Condamnation de Banquet*, Gourmandise, Friandise, and Bonne Compagnie gorge themselves with Dîner, but soon meet Apoplexie and Paralysie; later, Banquet is executed by Sobriété and Diète), or more topical issues, like fashions in education (*Les Enfants de maintenant*), social injustice (*Povre Peuple*), ecclesiastical disputes (*Le Concile de Basle*), and politics (*La Paix de Péronne*). There are also some *moralités religieuses*, which are allegorizations of material more typical of mystery plays, e.g. *La Vendition de Joseph*. The performances of these plays, of which about 80 have survived, were organized by societies devoted to the purpose, like the *Enfants Sans Souci and the *Basoche.   [GAR]

MORAND, Paul (1888–1976). A sophisticated French diplomat and careful stylist, Morand is best known for his fiction of the 1920s, particularly the two collections of short stories *Ouvert la nuit* (1922) and *Fermé la nuit* (1923) and the novel *L'Europe galante* (1925), which depict the corruption of post-war European and particularly Parisian high society. As a travel writer he excelled in portraits of cities: *New York* (1929), *Londres* (1933), and *Bucarest* (1935), and in his novel *Bouddha vivant* (1927) he explored the same contrast between Eastern and Western civilization as that evoked in *Malraux's *La Tentation de l'Occident*. His reputation suffered considerably from his having served as Vichy ambassador in Romania and Switzerland during World War II.   [NH]

MORÉAS, Jean (pseud. of Iannis Papadiamanto-poulos) (1856–1910). A major figure in the *Symbolist movement, the Greek-born Moréas wrote its manifesto (*Le Figaro*, 18 September 1886), expounded its theories (*Les Premières Armes du symbolisme*, 1889), and took part in its experimentation with *vers libre*. In 1891 he defected to found an 'École Romane' which promoted a return to 16th-c. traditions. His poems (*Les Stances*, 1899–1920) reveal his search for a compromise between Symbolist and classical tendencies in poetry.   [JK]

Moreau, Frédéric. The weak-willed central character of Flaubert's *L'*Éducation sentimentale*.

MOREAU, Gustave (1826–98). Known to his contemporaries as the 'jeweller' for the rich, lacquered technique with which he painted biblical and mythological subjects, Moreau had a profound impact on the *Decadent and *Symbolist movements in French literature. This was largely due to Huysmans who, in *A rebours* (1884), presented Moreau's *Salomé dansant devant Hérode* and *L'Apparition* (both exhibited in the *Salon of 1876) through the tortured and misogynistic eroticism of the central character, Des Esseintes. As if to distance his work from such responses, Moreau produced in 1886 a series of delicate and innovative watercolours to illustrate the *Fables* of La Fontaine.   [JK]

MOREAU, Hégésippe (1810–38). French poet. He published in the year of his death a collection of tales and poems, *Les Myosotis*, many highly imitative of Romantic and pre-Romantic modes; some, evoking his childhood, his nostalgia for the pastoral, his intellectual and religious crises, are impressive for their lyric directness and profundity. Illegitimate, orphaned at an early age, poor, a misfit, Moreau is the image of the Romantic 'suffering poet'.   [FPB]

MOREAU, Jeanne (b. 1928). French actress who, having played opposite Gérard *Philipe in *Le Cid* at the TNP, made a brilliant film career. She has worked for many of the major directors of the period (e.g. *Truffaut, *Jules et Jim*; *Duras, *Nathalie Granger*).

MOREL, Jean de (1511–81). Centre of a salon frequented by Michel de *l'Hôpital, Nicolas de Bourbon, Jean *Dorat, Salmon Macrin, and the poets of the *Pléiade, including *Du Bellay. He was the editor of the first collected edition of Du Bellay's works (1568). The salon's appeal was progressively reduced by the Calvinist tendencies displayed by various members of the Morel family. Morel himself served as tutor to d'*Aubigné.   [JJS]

MORELLET, André, abbé (1727–1819). Publicist and economist. The son of a Lyon paper merchant, he studied theology at the Sorbonne with *Turgot before being admitted to *philosophe circles, in particular the *salons of Madame *Geoffrin, *Holbach, and *Helvétius. He was a vigorous polemicist (Voltaire wrote his name: *Mords-les*) and was imprisoned in the Bastille for two months in 1760. A partisan of free-trade, he attacked the Compagnie des Indes and wrote against *Necker and against *Galiani's *Dialogue sur les blés*; he also planned, but never completed, a large-scale dictionary of commerce and made an unpublished translation of Adam Smith's *Wealth of Nations*. Among his published translations, the most important was Beccaria's *Traité des délits et des peines* (1765). Elected to the *Académie Française in 1785, he saved its archives and the manuscript of the dictionary when it was closed down in 1793; on its reopening as part of the *Institut in 1803, he was one of its most faithful members. His *Mémoires* (1822) and his correspondence paint a nostalgic picture of the lost world of the salons, and contain fascinating, if subjective, portraits of *Rousseau, *Diderot, and other famous acquaintances.   [PF]

MORELLY (forename and dates unknown) published from 1743 to 1755 works on many subjects and became famous for attacking private property in his *Utopian *Code de la nature* (1755). Considered to be an early example of socialist thought, its inspiration is often drawn from religious ideas, and has much in common with *Rousseau's early works. Based on the principle that man is by nature not wicked but well disposed to his fellows, it argues for an egalitarian society with common ownership of property, and culminates in a detailed plan for the establishment of the perfect state. Morelly also wrote a Utopian prose epic, *Naufrage des îles flottantes ou la Basiliade* (1753).   [CJB]

MORERI, Louis (1643–80). French priest and author of *Le Grand Dictionnaire historique* (1674), a successful encyclopedia. Originally a single folio volume, it was greatly expanded and revised by subsequent editors, including Jean *Le Clerc (6th edn., 1691, 4 vols.). The last edition was the 20th (1759) in 10 folio volumes, generally reckoned the best.

MORGAN, Michèle (b. 1920). One of the best-loved pre-*Nouvelle Vague screen actresses, immortalized by *Gabin's 'T'as de beaux yeux, tu sais' in *Carné's *Quai des brumes* (1938). Grémillon's *Remorques* (1941) gave her a similar role as the innocent *femme fatale* in a misty French seaport.   [KAR]

MORICE, Charles (1861–1919). With the publication in 1889 of *La Littérature de tout à l'heure* in which he analysed the mystical sources and ambitions of the *Symbolist movement and their relationship to the language and technique of poetry, Morice became, albeit briefly, its leading spokesman. In the 1890s he collaborated with *Gauguin on *Noa Noa*, a romanticized account of the painter's experience in Tahiti.

[JK]

MORIN, Edgar (b. 1921). French writer and sociologist. Attracted to Communism in the Resistance, he worked as a writer and journalist for the Communist Party, but eventually rejected doctrinaire Stalinism and espoused an oppositional and humanistic *Marxism during the 1950s. His career is vividly described in his *Autocritique* (1959). He became director of the review *Arguments* (1957–63), which developed a non-Communist Marxism influenced by *Existentialism. Turning to an academic career in sociology, he pioneered the sociology of culture and communication. His study of the phenomenon of rumours was strikingly original, but he is best known for his work in the sociology of cinema.

[MHK]

MORISOT, Berthe (1841–95). French painter. While concentrating on a more limited range of subjects (notably domestic and garden scenes) than many of her male colleagues in the *Impressionist movement, Morisot made a discreet but decisive contribution through her influence on *Manet during the 1870s, her efforts on behalf of the Impressionist exhibitions between 1874 and 1886, and her own audacious adaptation of its formal innovations. *Mallarmé paid tribute to her achievement in his preface to the catalogue of the exhibition held in 1896 on the first anniversary of her death.

[JK]

Morocco. As is true of all overseas francophone areas, except perhaps *Quebec and *Haiti, the most significant era of French-language literary production in Morocco began shortly after World War II. The intellectuals of the French colonies and protectorates, having witnessed the humiliation of France in 1940 and having made many sacrifices fighting for the Allied forces, were reluctant to resume the subordinate socio-political status they knew before the war. In Morocco, *Algeria, and *Tunisia a literary flowering occurred in the late 1940s and early 1950s. Modern Moroccan literature in French offers a rich and varied corpus of writing, encompassing, as it does, the Arab, the Berber, and the Judaeo-Maghrebian experiences which, while sharing common traits, yet maintain their unique cultural essences.

The first Moroccan writer of the post-war period to attract critical attention was Ahmed *Sefrioui, author of a collection of stories *Le Chapelet d'ambre* (1949) and a novel *La Boîte à merveilles* (1954). Many of the Maghrebian stories and novels of the 1950s were, like these, 'ethnographic' narratives describing local customs and conflicts and published in France for the edification and pleasure of a French readership. The poet, novelist, and essayist Mohammed Aziz *Lahbabi also began publishing in the late 1940s, and many of his francophone works, including translations from the work of Arabic-language poets (e.g. *Douleurs rythmées*, 1974), have been published in the Arab world, where he is particularly admired.

Le Passé simple (1954) by Driss *Chraïbi conformed to the formula of the ethnographic novel, but also had great influence on developing Moroccan writers. It addresses many of the fundamental questions with which Moroccan and other Maghrebian writers are concerned, such as the bicultural dilemma of the young European-educated intellectual; the generation gap, aggravated by the cultural chasm between the traditionally authoritative father and the Europeanized son, and the special role women, especially mothers, play in the lives of young Moroccan males. Chraïbi, who later moved to France, altered his style and wrote a series of novels in which he analyses the history and civilization of Morocco.

In the mid-1960s there was a major renewal in Moroccan literature, paralleled by similar phenomena in Algeria and Tunisia, a revolt against earlier models, bolstered, no doubt, by the political upheaval in France in *May 1968. This renewal was signalled by the activism of the group of writers who founded and/or were affiliated with the journal *Souffles, launched in 1966 by Abdellatif *Laâbi. This poet's work, at first experimental (e.g. the poetic novel *L'Œil et la nuit*, 1969), soon became politically militant. He has written moving accounts in both prose and poetry of his and other activists' ordeals in prison.

Major novelists who emerged as part of the renewal include Mohammed *Khaïr-Eddine, Abdelkebir *Khatibi, and Tahar *Ben Jelloun. If Chraïbi is the doyen of Moroccan writers, these three might also compete for that title on the basis of the length of their careers or the reputations they have achieved. The writing of Khaïr-Eddine has been described as vituperation, vociferation, and spleen-venting. He established his reputation with his novel *Agadir* (1967), and went on to publish such vitriolic, surrealistic poems and prose works as *Soleil arachnide* (1969), *Moi l'aigre* (1970), *Le Déterreur* (1973), *Ce Maroc!* (1975), and *Une odeur de mantèque* (1976).

Khatibi's brilliant first novel, *La Mémoire tatouée* (1971), introduced Postmodern techniques to Moroccan literature; if Khaïr-Eddine embodied and renewed an age-old Arabic literary tradition of spontaneous dream, errancy, eroticism, and violence, Khatibi analyses the various strata of being and language as they interact in the bilingual writer. His novels and essays are almost indistinguishable, for he is generally preoccupied by the task of defining consciousness in a process reminiscent of that practised by Valéry's *Monsieur Teste. His other major works explore the interaction of the Maghrebian writer's native and acquired tongues, language in the broadest semiotic sense, and such codes as those of urban space and the human emotional intercourse which he labels *aimance*.

Tahar Ben Jelloun established his reputation with

a novel, *Harrouda* (1973), and powerful evocative poems like those of *Les Amandiers sont morts de leurs blessures* (1976). His graduate studies and case work as a social psychologist dealing with the trauma of impotence among Maghrebian immigrant workers in France had a great impact on his work. In recent years, half a dozen absorbing, brilliantly crafted novels, including *La Nuit sacrée* (1987, Prix Goncourt), have established Ben Jelloun as a major writer.

A new generation of novelists, led by Abdelhak *Serhane, has obvious roots in the Moroccan literary tradition. Serhane's principal works, *Messaouda* (1983) and *Les Enfants des rues étroites* (1986), based on his early years in Azrou, are brutally naturalistic even as they experiment with interwoven discourses and symbolism. Omar Berrada's *L'Encensoir* (1987) crams into fewer than 150 pages almost all of the clichés of the Moroccan novel, clichés which he manipulates with considerable humour. Another novelist who shows promise is Leïla *Houari.

Poetry and theatre are not the strongest genres in Moroccan literature. Critics have made the remark that, despite appearances, poetry has thrived in Moroccan literature, but *in the prose*. Indeed, much of the best poetry is by the well-known novelists (e.g. Khaïr-Eddine, Ben Jelloun) or is found in the novels themselves (e.g. these writers plus Khatibi and the later Chraïbi).

As for poets *per se*, we should mention—in addition to Khaïr-Eddine, Khatibi, Ben Jelloun, Lahbabi, and Laâbi—Mostafa Nissaboury (b. 1943) and Mohamed Loakira (b. 1945). Nissaboury, a cofounder of *Souffes*, has published little, but his booklength poem *La Mille et deuxième Nuit* (1975) was very influential, restating in the modern context the importance to Moroccan literature of *Les *Mille et une Nuits*. Loakira has based some of his complex poetic discourse on the street songs, children's chants, and proverbs of his native Marrakesh (*Marrakech*, 1975) and has sometimes shaped his poetic cadences to the rhythms of Afro-Arab Gnawi music (*Semblable à la soif*, 1986). Other poets worthy of mention include Mohamed Alaoui Belrhiti (b. 1951), Abdallah Bensmaïn (b. 1948), Abdallah Bounfour (b. 1946), Rachida Madani (b. 1951), and Zaghloul Morsy (b. 1953). [ES]

See J. Déjeux, *Litterature maghrébine d'expression française* (3rd edn., 1980); M. Gontard, *Violence du texte* (1981); *Revue CELFAN Review* ('Moroccan literature'), 2: 3 (1983); L. Mouzouni, *Le Roman marocain de langue française* (1987).

Mort à crédit. *Céline's second novel, published 1936, is in the tradition of the late-19th-c. French family novel, like *Vallès's *L'Enfant* or Jules *Renard's *Poil de carotte*. Exemplifying Céline's mature style, which exploits the properties of spoken French and *argot and makes use of a 'telegraphic' series of exclamations, Ferdinand, the narrator, recounts the increasingly disastrous progress of his childhood and adolescence. His parents, Auguste and Clémence, belong to the Parisian *petite bourgeoisie*; they impose on their son their exaggerated hopes for the future and their outrage when he inevitably fails to comply. After two jobs lost in Paris and a disastrous journey to England, Ferdinand is so incensed by his father's constant criticism that he attempts to kill him. The long final section of the novel recounts Ferdinand's experiences with the eccentric inventor Courtial des Pereires, who, after all his schemes have collapsed, commits suicide, leaving the narrator in complete nervous collapse.

The novel is arguably the most ambitious and accomplished of Céline's works, for it is based both upon an acute historical perception and a complex psychological structure. Socially and economically, the novel charts, through Ferdinand and his family, the decline of an entire social class, the Parisian artisanal *petite bourgeoisie*, at the turn of the century. For this reason, the Universal Exhibition of 1900 is given considerable prominence as the symbolic moment when the new technology and the new economy took over, an economy which leads to the death of the *petite bourgeoisie*, just as the 'crédit' of the title is linked to 'mort'. The psychological relations within the novel are linked, moreover, to this economic process: the neurosis of the father, Auguste, stems from it and inflicts a similar neurosis upon the son, both as child and as mature narrator. There is every evidence that Céline, who had a professional knowledge of Freud at the time, was exploring a deep-seated Oedipal relationship, which accounts for the constant frame of Proustian references. [NH]

Mort d'Agrippine, La. *Cyrano de Bergerac's only tragedy (published 1654). When it was staged (1653), a scandal erupted after 'Frappons, voilà l'Hostie' (the victim) was misread as blasphemy. The sombre plot, featuring the conspiracy against the emperor Tiberius fuelled by Agrippina's desire to avenge her dead husband, Germanicus, culminates in the assassination of all conspirators. [JDeJ]

Mort de César, La. Tragedies of this name were written by *Grévin and *Voltaire, among others.

Mort de Pompée, La. Tragedy by Pierre *Corneille, first performed 1644. It concerns the killing of Pompey in Egypt after his defeat at Pharsalia. In order to curry favour with César, the Egyptian king Ptolomée, egged on by evil counsellors, has Pompée put to death. But César, who is in love with Ptolomée's sister Cléopâtre, disowns the murder. Ptolomée then plots to kill César, but the plot is revealed by Pompée's widow, Cornélie, in spite of her desire for revenge, and the play ends with the death of the conspirators. *Pompée* is remarkable for the epic grandeur of its verse, its broad historical sweep, and its vivid depiction of Machiavellian politics set against the heroic 'générosité' of Cornélie.

[PF]

Mort de Sénèque, La (1644). Tragedy by *Tristan l'Hermite.

Mort le roi Artu, La. A prose romance composed *c.*1230, forming the final branch of the cyclic compilation *Le Lancelot-Graal.* Unlike the earlier branches, this one, recounting the dissolution of the Arthurian world, has no clear hero, although the story of *Lancelot and Guenièvre is still central, and their adultery the ultimate cause of the disintegration of *Arthur's kingdom. However, the specifically Cistercian ideology which marked *La Queste del Saint Graal* [see GRAIL ROMANCES] is replaced by a mixture of fatalism (symbolized by Arthur's dream of the Wheel of Fortune) and the explicitly human antagonisms which divide clans at court, in the meshes of which Arthur is helplessly caught. Moreover, the immediate cause of the disaster, Mordred's rebellion, itself provoked by a mixture of treasonous and adulterous motives, reflects a basic unsoundness at the heart of the chivalric world, since in the Vulgate Cycle Mordred is Arthur's son born of incest, not merely his nephew as in *Geoffrey of Monmouth and *Wace. Several themes are continued from the Vulgate *Lancelot*, including the quest for the missing knight, Lancelot's madness, and Guenièvre's doubts and jealousies, but all are recounted without recourse to marvels, in a world where tournaments, murders, and private intrigues have replaced magical adventures. The sense of immense human tragedy implicit in this vision so gripped the later Middle Ages that Malory made it the focus of his whole *summa* of the Arthurian world, calling it *Le Morte d'Arthur.* [PEB]

Mort propagande, La, see GUIBERT, H.

Mosca, comte de. Central political character in Stendhal's *La *Chartreuse de Parme.*

MOSTEGHANEMI, Ahlem (b. 1953). Algerian poet, born in Algiers, educated in Algiers and in Paris, where in 1980 she gained a doctorate for a thesis published as *Algérie, femme et écritures* (1985). She then worked at the Centre Arabe de Documentation et d'Information in Paris, broadcasting a daily programme on poetry on Algerian radio, and writing for the newspaper *Ech-Chaâb.* Her two collections of poems are *Au hâvre des jours* (1972) and *L'Écriture dans un moment de nudité* (1976). [FL]

MOTIN, Pierre (1566–*c.*1614). Little is known of this poet, but about 150 of his poems figure in satirical collections of the day. As well as obscene verve and inventiveness, his work sometimes reveals a light touch and a preoccupation with dream and inconstancy which set him apart from his contemporaries *Sigogne and *Régnier. [PF]

Mots, Les (1960). Autobiographical text by *Sartre, a disenchanted and beautifully written account of his childhood and his choice of writing as a career.

Mots et les choses, Les, see FOUCAULT.

MOTTEVILLE, Françoise Bertault, dame Langlois de (*c.*1615–1689). After a brief marriage to an elderly magistrate, she became Anne d'Autriche's confidant until the queen's death. She then retired from the court, composed her *Mémoires pour servir à l'histoire d'Anne d'Autriche* (1723), which features the events of the *Fronde, and exchanged memorable letters with *Montpensier. [JDeJ]

Mouches, Les. Play by *Sartre, an Existentialist reworking of the Electra story produced in occupied Paris in 1943.

MOUHY, Charles de Fieux, chevalier de (1701–84). French author of plays, writings on the theatre, and many novels, including *La Mouche* (1736), *Le Masque de fer* (1737), and *Lamedis* (1735–7). The last of these, described by Jacques Bosquet as 'le type même du chef d'œuvre inconnu', contains proto-Romantic metamorphoses, dream sequences, and voyages to subterranean worlds. [PF]

MOUNET-SULLY, Jean Sully Mounet, known as (1841–1916). French actor. Idol of the Comédie-Française in his generation, he dominated the great tragic roles of the classical repertory. His commanding presence, voice of remarkable range and beauty, and strong lyrical vein inspired memorable performances, e.g. in Sophocles' *King Oedipus*, Corneille's *Polyeucte*, and Hugo's *Ruy Blas.* [SBJ]

MOUNIER, Emmanuel (1905–50). French thinker; the leading progressive Catholic intellectual of the 1930s and 1940s. Weaned on *Bergson and *Péguy, he abandoned academic philosophy in 1932 to direct the monthly review *Esprit.* His *Personalism focused Catholic social doctrine on the human person as a whole, and facilitated Catholic participation in the Centre and Left of French politics. Under Vichy he published *Esprit* for a year and taught at *Uriage until banned. Imprisoned for several months, he was subsequently decorated for his Resistance activities. Influential with Socialists and Christian Democrats, Mounier was an important participant in the intellectual debates of the post-war period, notably pioneering Catholic dialogue with Communists. Many of his views became commonplaces of modern Catholicism, but his *Traité du caractère* (1946) is still widely read, and *Esprit* remains an influential Left-Catholic review. [MHK]

MOUSTAPHA, Baba (pseud. of Mahamet Moustapha) (1952–82). Chadian playwright, author of *Le Maître des Djinns* (1977), *Makarie aux épines* (1979), and *Le Commandant Chaka* (1983). His works are generally subversive and satirical, questioning the use of outworn traditions to manipulate people, the domination of the city, and neo-colonial regimes. [AMR]

Moyen de parvenir, Le, see BEROALDE DE VERVILLE.

MUBADIATE, see BUABUA WA KAYEMBE MUBADIATE.

MUDIMBE, V. Y. (Vumbi Yoka or Valentin Yves) (b. 1941). Zaïrean poet, philosopher, and one of the most challenging African novelists writing in French today. Mudimbe obtained a doctorate from Louvain, and taught in Zaïre before moving to Duke University in the USA.

Although his poetry (in several collections, including *Déchirures*, 1971, and *Les Fuseaux, parfois . . .*, 1974) is characterized by dream-like, hermetic imagery, Mudimbe insists that poetry is compatible with the exigencies of revolution. Of his several works in the field of philosophical anthropology, the best-known are *L'Autre Face du royaume* (1973) and *L'Odeur du père* (1982). What predominates in these, and in most of Mudimbe's writings, is a stringent epistemological critique of Western Africanist discourse. He believes that 'pour l'Afrique, échapper réellement à l'Occident suppose d'apprécier exactement ce qu'il en coûte de se détacher de lui'. He consistently develops this thesis, particularly in relation to the problems of conscience and consciousness raised by Christianity in Africa and in relation to the vicissitudes of politics in postindependence Zaïre.

Mudimbe's first novel, *Entre les eaux* (1973), about an African priest turned resistance fighter, was awarded, in 1975, the Grand Prix Catholique de Littérature. *Le Bel Immonde* (1976), a provocative reflection on the pathology of power, tells of an affair between a corrupt government minister and a prostitute. In another novel, *L'Écart* (1979), a clear link is suggested between the hero's mental breakdown and that cultural dis-ease which is the legacy of colonialism. Technically, this novel is Mudimbe's most ambitious: its form and style suggest very effectively a severely disturbed subjectivity. *Shaba deux* (1990) also probes the complex, painfully internalized trauma originating in relations between Africa and 'the West'. In the form of a diary kept by a young African nun in a Belgian order as she confronts her own feelings of confusion and guilt in a violent, revolution-torn Zaïre, this novel raises questions about law and order in Africa, and about the nature of that order. Like all of Mudimbe's work, his novels are enriched but never swamped by an impressive range and depth of philosophical, and indeed cross-cultural, thought, and particularly by the author's acute awareness of the paradoxes inherent in such cross-reference.   [MG]

See B. Mouralis, *V. Y. Mudimbe ou le Discours, l'écart et l'écriture* (1988).

Muezzin, Le, see BOURBOUNE.

MULLER, Charles, see REBOUX.

Mur, Le (1939). A collection of five very different stories by *Sartre ('Le Mur', 'La Chambre', 'Éros-trate', 'Intimité', 'L'Enfance d'un chef'), all exploring existential dilemmas and choices.

MURET (Muretus), Marc-Antoine (1526–85). French scholar and teacher who taught *Jodelle in Paris and *Montaigne in Bordeaux. He is the author of Latin poems (*Juvenilia*, 1552), including a play, *Julius Caesar*, one of the first plays written in France on a classical subject and a good example of formulary rhetoric, and he published annotations, mainly mythological and intertextual, to the second edition of *Ronsard's *Amours* (1553) and many editions of the classics. He left for Italy accused of sodomy and taught law and philosophy in Venice and then Rome. He was ordained a priest and published *Hymnorum sacrorum liber* (1576) and Ciceronian speeches on academic and political occasions.   [PS]

MURGER, Henry (1822–61). French Realist writer, serio-comic chronicler of Parisian literary and artistic low life. He was the popularizer (even creator) of enduring myths of how, due to the harshness of a materialistic and philistine society, idealistic Parisian young men repeatedly fail to fulfil their dreams of creating genuine masterpieces and of finding true love. Now known almost exclusively for *Scènes de la vie de bohème* (1851), source of Puccini's opera, he also wrote other characteristically sentimental, cynical, and fitfully amusing accounts of the Parisian world of arts and letters: *Le Pays latin* (1851), *Le Roman de toutes les femmes* (1854), *Les Buveurs d'eau* (1853–4).   [BR]

Musée imaginaire, Le, see MALRAUX.

Muse française, La. Literary review, published 1823–4 [see ROMANTICISM, 2].

Muse historique, La. A weekly gazette in doggerel verse by Jean Loret; it takes the form of gossipy epistles about social and artistic life between 1650 and Loret's death in 1665. This pioneering venture quickly found a competitor in the *Muse héroique* (1654–5) of Charles Robinet, to be followed by other similar news-sheets.

MUSET, Colin, see COLIN MUSET.

Muséum d'Histoire Naturelle, see JARDIN DES PLANTES.

Music-hall. A form of public entertainment, especially popular with the French urban working classes from the late 1860s to the 1950s. It originated in London as a concert of songs—ribald, sentimental, or patriotic—given in a hall built on to the Canterbury Arms (1848). Later, comedians, dancers, acrobats, conjurors, etc. were added. In France it had its roots in the *café-chantant* or *café-concert*, a modest diversion in the form of a local singer offered by some Paris cafés (e.g. Café du Midi, 1847) to their customers for the price of a drink. The innovation was soon copied by other cafés and open-air dance venues, like the Bal Mabille. Subsequently cafés set up makeshift stages with a small band and a *corbeille*, a half-circle of girls who joined in the choruses. With the rise in eating out and public entertainment which characterized the *Second Empire, the *cafés-concerts* multiplied, expanded, and grew more luxurious. An edict of 1867, granting them the right to mount more varied and costumed productions, virtually turned the *cafés-concerts* into music-halls. This led to the big variety-halls (Eldorado, Ba-Ta-Clan, Folies-Bergère); the singing stars (Mogador, Thérésa, Paulus); the hit songs ('La Femme à barbe', 'En revenant de la revue'). In the first half of the 20th c. these stage-shows became increasingly spectacular, bringing other halls and stars to prominence, e.g. Mistinguett and Maurice *Chevalier at the Casino de Paris. Eventually the music-hall fell victim to the popularity of *cinema and *television.   [SBJ]

MUSSET, Alfred de (1810–57). French poet, dramatist, and novelist. Musset grew up in Paris, the son of an important government official with literary interests. He sampled a number of careers, including medicine and banking, but found none satisfactory, feeling he had an overwhelming literary vocation. In 1828 he published a French version of De Quincey's *Confessions of an English Opium Eater*, and in 1830 made his name as a leading *Romantic author with a series of narrative poems, the *Contes d'Espagne et d'Italie*. However, Musset's independent spirit indicated that he could not be expected for long to remain identified with any particular literary movement. The poems abounded in verve, *couleur locale*, metrical inventiveness, and dramatic incident, but they also pointed to Musset's ironic temperament.

He next turned to the theatre. His first theatrical venture, *La Nuit vénitienne* (1830), was a failure, and after this setback he wrote drama intended to be read rather than performed, what he called *Un spectacle dans un fauteuil* (1833–4). The first series contained the dramatic poems *La Coupe et les lèvres*, *A quoi rêvent les jeunes filles*, and *Namouna*. There followed his major dramatic works, *On ne badine pas avec l'amour* and Les *Caprices de Marianne*. Here he explored the experience of love with a lightness of touch and a verbal dexterity unequalled among his contemporaries. In 1834 he published *Fantasio* and *Lorenzaccio*, the play which today ranks as the finest French Romantic historical drama.

In 1836 Musset brought out a novel, *La *Confession d'un enfant du siècle*, in which he drew on the experience of his tempestuous love affair with George *Sand in an attempt to provide a diagnosis of the ills of a generation suffering from the *mal du siècle*. Musset portrayed his contemporaries in a state of spiritual disarray: the religious and moral certitudes of the past had been destroyed, but nothing meaningful had come to replace them. The novel held out the ambiguous hope that the meaning of existence might be revealed through the experience of love. Much of Musset's work reflects the spiritual crisis of his times, sometimes directly, as in *L'Espoir en Dieu* (1838), more often by the suggestion that a gain in knowledge can lead to doubt, debauchery, and death in a world from which any transcendent meaning and purpose have been drained (see *Rolla*, 1833).

Musset took up the major themes of Romanticism but he lent them a distinct edge. In his work the stability of the self was undermined and the sense of a secure personal identity was threatened. He returned obsessively to a number of motifs: the irrevocable loss of childhood innocence, a masochistic enjoyment of suffering, an anguished awareness of the distance between appearance and reality, a fascination with the relationship between knowledge, sexual desire, and death. At the same time his work was suffused with irony, with a sense of distance. Not for him the humanitarianism of the Romantics who wanted art to serve the cause of social progress. He remained a subversive, independent, unpredictable spirit, for whom art was the only redemption possible. His most famous poetic achievement, *Les Nuits* (1835–7), is a sequence of four poems dramatizing the experience of personal crisis and suffering in the form of an exchange between the poet and his muse. The poet confesses the truth of his being in some of the best-known Romantic lyric verse, but he employs a rhetoric of dolorism which may strike the modern reader as self-indulgent.

Musset's really important work belongs to the 1830s, though some his later production deserves attention (*Histoire d'un merle blanc*, 1842; *Il faut qu'une porte soit ouverte ou fermée*, 1846). His physical condition declined after 1840 as a consequence of his life of excess. He was elected to the Académie Française in 1852.   [CC]

See Ph. van Tieghem, *Musset* (new edn., 1969); D. Sices, *Theater of Solitude: The Drama of Alfred de Musset* (1974).

Mystère de la Charité de Jeanne d'Arc, see PÉGUY.

Mystère Frontenac, Le. Novel by François *Mauriac, published 1933. Regarded as one of his most positive works, coming soon after the resolution of his religious and emotional crisis, it uses the family, often in the earlier novels a négative force of constraint, as a mystical reflection of divine love. Blanche Frontenac, after the death of her husband Michel, brings up her three sons and two daughters in the Catholic faith and in veneration of the family name and traditions, helped by Michel's brother Xavier, who has a religious devotion to his brother's family, abandoning to them his fortune and hiding from them his mistress Joséfa. Attention focuses on the three sons, Jean-Louis who inherits the family timber business, José who joins the colonial army and will die in the war, and the youngest, the poet

Yves. Even in crisis, at its most acute in the case of Yves, there is an instinctive mysterious link between the three brothers, the uncle, and the mother, their estates in the Landes, and the love of God, which transcends the pessimism of Mauriac's earlier writing. [NH]

Mystères de l'amour, Les, see VITRAC.

Mystères de Paris, Les. Novel by Eugène *Sue. Serialized in the *Journal des débats* from June 1842 to October 1843, *Les Mystères de Paris* is the most celebrated *roman-feuilleton* and the quintessential example of the genre. The novel has not retained its place in modern mass culture, as have *Dumas's novels, and the characters have long ceased to be household names. Nevertheless, *Les Mystères de Paris* had a profound effect on the development of the popular fiction of mystery, suspense, criminality, and low life. In the figure of Rodolphe it also introduced one of the first charismatic superheroes of popular culture who devote their lives to meting out justice and exacting retribution. The redemptive powers of Rodolphe are linked to Sue's socialist and humanitarian mission to help the poor and oppressed. The serialization of the novel constituted one of the first sensational media events of a nascent mass culture. It brought large and different sections of society together into a community of readers, all desperately awaiting the next number. Sue received a shoal of fan letters, many of which have been preserved. They are a precious and rare source, revealing how ordinary people actually responded to literature at this period. [BR]

Mystery Plays (*Mystères*). Large-scale religious plays performed throughout France in the 15th and early 16th c. Though the word *mystère* rarely appears before the 15th c., in fact many mystery plays dramatize the same subjects as the 14th-c. *miracle plays, e.g. saints' lives; many others, however, are based on biblical material—a few on the Old Testament, but most on the New Testament. Those plays dealing with the life of Christ constitute a special group, called *Passion plays.

Over 200 mystery plays have survived, the shortest being less than 1,000 lines (e.g. *Sainte Venice*) and the longest over 50,000 (e.g. *Les Actes des Apôtres*); the average is about 10,000 (e.g. *Saint Martin*). Some saints worshipped nation-wide were the subject of several different plays, e.g. Martin, Sébastien, Barbe; but many small communities performed plays on the life of their local saint (e.g. Didier in Langres). There are also a few mystery plays on non-religious subjects, e.g. the *Siège d'Orléans* and the *Destruction de Troye*. In contrast to the comic genres like the *farce, the *sotie, and the *morality, mystery plays were perceived as historical plays recreating real events of the past; they were not seen as fictional or imaginary.

Their length was such that most performances were commissioned, organized, and subsidized by a whole town, through its local government; but a few exceptional *confréries (e.g. the Confrérie de la Passion) were capable of such undertakings. A typical performance spread over three or four days (*journées*), though some lasted eight, twenty, twenty-five or more, and required hundreds of speaking roles. Preparations—composition of the text, copying out the various manuscripts for actors and producers, rehearsals—inevitably occupied several months. Most important of all, the theatre had to be built. There were no permanent theatres in the Middle Ages; every performance of a mystery play necessitated a purpose-built theatre. Normally, a large wooden structure was erected in a wide, open public space, e.g. the town square or a cemetery. Such buildings, which were taken down after the performance, usually contained two sorts of seating; wealthy spectators would buy a box (*loge*) for the whole play, whereas the general public would pay a daily fee, perhaps a few *deniers*, for admission to the *gradins*.

The shape of the stage or playing area is a subject of controversy; some critics hold that most mystery plays were performed in the round, others maintain that a variety of stages were used—in the round, linear, square, horseshoe, etc. It is undoubtedly the case that some plays were performed in the round: see Jehan Fouquet's miniature of the *Martyre de Sainte Apolline*. Medieval stages appear to have had two distinct types of sets, a station or *lieu*, where groups of actors waited, visible to the spectators, before entering the main playing area, and the *mansion* or *échafaud*, which represented a place (a town, a church, a house). All the sets required for a given *journée* were on stage throughout that *journée*; there were no curtains or scene changes. This arrangement meant that spectators could see action going on at two or three places on the stage at the same time—simultaneous action, an effect more frequently achieved today in the cinema than the theatre. The shape of the theatre and the possibility of simultaneous action affected the way plays were written; many mystery plays are made up of short episodes rapidly moving from one set to another, with mimed action at one set accompanying dialogue at another. The two most important sets were usually Paradise and Hell, placed opposite each other, Paradise to the east and Hell to the west, thus underlining the supernatural conflict at the heart of all mystery plays. The visual and aural aspects of a mystery play—stage machinery, *voleries*, *feintes*, trap-doors, pyrotechnic effects in Hell, music, noise—were arguably more important than the spoken text. Certainly, producers were paid more than poets.

The characters appearing in the plays were not only saints and martyrs, or pagans and devils; there were many ordinary people, tradesmen, soldiers, peasants, and their wives, even *sots*, who, by their words and deeds, introduced everyday life into the action; thus the serious and inspiring aspects are balanced by an earthy realism. Mystery plays were earnest religious plays; but they were also realistic, comic, and even scabrous. Such brusque contrasts often disturb modern critics, used to a clearer separation between tragedy and comedy. Mystery plays were genuine popular theatre; their end did not come about because of the disaffection of the public. They were, in effect, suppressed by the religious and political establishment, who reflected the changing spiritual and intellectual ethos of the mid-16th c. [GAR]

See L. Petit de Julleville, *Les Mystères* (1880); M. Accarie, *Le Théâtre sacré de la fin du moyen âge* (1979); C. Davidson, *The Saint Play in Medieval Europe* (1986).

Mythe de Sisyphe, Le, see CAMUS, A.

Mythologies, see BARTHES.

Mythologiques, see LÉVI-STRAUSS.

N

Nabis, Les. Formed in the autumn of 1888 and taking their name from the Hebrew word meaning 'seer', the Nabis were a group of young French painters (including *Bonnard, *Vuillard, Maurice Denis, and Paul Sérusier) who, influenced by *Gauguin and Japanese prints, rejected *Naturalism in favour of the flat decorative patterning of the picture surface. *Aurier defined their work as a pictorial equivalent of literary *Symbolism, but their illustration work, notably for the *Revue blanche, and their décors for *Lugné-Poë's Théâtre de l'Œuvre represent a more significant contribution to late-19th-c. literature.   [JK]

NADAR (pseud. of Félix Tournachon) (1820–1910). French photographer. He began as a writer of satirical sketches and a caricaturist. In 1853 he opened a photographic studio; here, influenced by contemporary research in physiognomy, he produced a remarkable series of portraits, including profound images of *Nerval, *Baudelaire, *Desbordes-Valmore, *Hugo, and many other literary figures. Subsequently he invented aerial photography, working from a balloon.   [PF]

Nadja, see BRETON.

NAIGEON, Jacques-André (1738–1810). Atheist *philosophe, forthright rather than subtle. He wrote for the *Encyclopédie and reworked subversive manuscripts for *Holbach's anti-religious campaign. Later he produced the first collected edition of *Diderot (1798) and an edition of *Montaigne's *Essais* (1802).   [PF]

NAIGIZIKI, J. Saverio (b. 1915). Pioneering literary figure of Rwanda, author of *Escapade ruandaise* (1949), a semi-autobiographical novel, *L'Optimiste* (1954), a controversial play, and a two-volume development of his earlier fiction, *Mes transes à trente ans* (1955).   [PGH]

NAÏNDOUBA, Maoundoué (b. 1948). Chadian playwright and short-story writer. *L'Étudiant de Soweto* (first performed 1978) centres on a student activist in the 1976 Soweto Uprising and combines crowd scenes with individual argument and poetry. Naïndouba has also written short stories for radio: *La Double Détresse* (1973) and *La Lèpre* (1979).   [AMR]

Naissance de l'Odyssée, see GIONO.

Namouna, see MUSSET.

Nana. Novel by *Zola, published 1880 and ninth in the *Rougon-Macquart series. As a sequel to *L'*Assommoir, this famous text narrates the brilliant life and horrific death of the courtesan Anna Coupeau. Rather than developing a plot, the work consists of a series of episodes, recounting Nana's extravagant escapades, her chequered fortunes, and the fortunes that she makes and destroys. Her seduction, exploitation, betrayal, and humiliation of the religiously inclined but sensual comte Muffat does, however, provide an element of continuity in the tale. Having escaped the miserable conditions of her parents' life in the slums, Nana makes her mark first in the theatre, then becomes one of the *lionnes* of the Second Empire, coming to symbolize the regime itself in all its dissipations, dying of smallpox on the very day that the *Franco-Prussian War breaks out. More a mythical creation than a character in a novel, she is pictured in larger-than-life dimensions, as a 'Golden Fly' issuing from the filth of the slums to avenge the people by corrupting the upper classes with her irresistible sexuality, as a 'femme fatale', a 'man-eater', an all-powerful Venus born of the gutters of Paris.   [DB]

NANCY, Jean-Luc (b. 1942). French philosopher. A student of *Derrida, he has written widely on the major figures in Western philosophy. His analyses of Hegel's concept of *Aufhebung* and Kant's categorical imperative have been influential. His strict reading of *Lacan, with Philippe *Lacoue-Labarthe, led him to focus on theories of meaning and its textual construction, exploring the boundaries of literature and philosophy. His work explores the limits of notions of meaning, identity, community, and freedom, acknowledging their fragility with an almost mystical sense of awe.   [MHK]

NANGA, Bernard (1934–85). Cameroonian poet and novelist. A professor at the University of Yaoundé, he entered and departed from Cameroonian literature like a meteor, and his death remains shrouded in mystery. The author of *Les Chauves-souris* (1981), awarded the Grand Prix Littéraire d'Afrique Noire, *La Trahison de Marianne* (1984), awarded the *Noma Award, and *Poèmes sans frontières* (1987), Nanga is the apostle of a new social and cultural order.

The first-person narrator of *La Trahison de Marianne,* deeply rooted in his native earth but attached to his wife 'Marianne', is torn between Africa and the West. To live out his *négritude for him does not mean looking back nostalgically, but working for the triumph of a new serenity. Africa must be freed from the 'chauves-souris' who oppress it and force it to mark time, when they are not actually barbarizing it. Fallen victim to Africans who are incompletely liberated from colonialism, wholly unaware of their responsibilities, and concerned only with satisfying their basic appetites, the continent is dying. For Nanga, Africa is in urgent need of liberation from the Africans.   [AK]

Nanine, ou le Préjugé vaincu (1749). Verse comedy by *Voltaire, a sentimental play in the manner of Nivelle de *la Chaussée.

Nantes, Édit de, see EDICT OF NANTES.

NAPOLEON (Napoléon Bonaparte, Emperor Napoléon I) (1769–1821)

1. The Rise to Power

Bonaparte was born in Ajaccio, Corsica; his family was of Italian descent. Educated in France at Autun, the military college of Brienne, and the École Militaire in Paris, he served in the École d'Artillerie d'Auxonne. Although he distinguished himself at the Siege of Toulon, he only became a national figure with his suppression of an insurrection in Paris on 13 Vendémiaire (5 October 1795), his marriage on 9 March 1796 to Josephine de Beauharnais, who had an influence in Parisian political circles, and his brilliant leadership of military campaigns in Italy in 1796–7. He sought to attack British power in the Mediterranean and India by his campaign in Egypt, but was foiled by Nelson's defeat of the French fleet at Aboukir Bay (August 1798).

When he returned to France, he found a number of squabbling politicians engaged in conspiracies, fearful of a neo-*Jacobin revival and fearful too of the royalists. Bonaparte was an obvious ally, and on 18–19 Brumaire (9–10 November 1799) he forced the legislature to establish a Consulate made up of *Siéyès, Ducos, and himself. But Bonaparte was different from the mediocre men who had led France in the years preceding 1799 [see REVOLUTION, 1d]. He was a man of energy, determination, and intelligence, whose abilities as a soldier and administrator were so outstanding that they have sometimes been regarded as unique. He emerged as first consul, then as consul for life (1802), and finally, in 1804, as emperor.

Napoleon (as he should now be called) wished to establish effective government. Important in this process was the codification of laws in a manner that maintained the social hierarchy and asserted the authority of the male, the father, and the state [see CODE CIVIL]. A centralized financial system with the Banque de France controlling the currency was introduced in 1800. Elected bodies were largely ignored, and the regime became more dependent on the administrative system, in which nobles of the *ancien régime* and a new nobility, derived from the bourgeoisie and the popular classes and attracted by

the *Légion d'Honneur, cooperated. Censorship was rigorously imposed, dissident groups were brutally suppressed, and the monarchist threat was disposed of by the execution of the duc d'*Enghien, an incident which provoked great indignation.

In 1800 Napoleon initiated negotiations with the papacy with a view to establishing religious peace at home (there was once again organized rebellion in parts of western France—see VENDÉE). The result was the *Concordat of 1801, which officially reconciled the Church with the Republic. But Napoleon continued to act high-handedly towards the Church. On 2 December 1804 the pope was present at Notre-Dame, supposedly to crown the emperor and thus sanction his elevated status. But at the crucial moment Napoleon crowned himself, and proceeded to crown Josephine. Years later he forced one of his archbishops to allow a divorce, so that he could marry Marie-Louise of Austria (1810). This was so that he could have a son and heir, who was born a year later (he was proclaimed 'roi de Rome' in his cradle, and was briefly recognized as Napoleon II in 1815, but never reigned and died in exile in 1832).

2. The Napoleonic Campaigns

The Revolution had shown that the destiny of France was bound up with the rest of Europe. It had been war that had transformed the Revolution in 1792, it was French victory that had helped bring down *Robespierre's type of government, and it was continuous warfare that destroyed the Directoire and brought Napoleon to power. Although the Consulate promised peace and succeeded in imposing peace on Austria at Lunéville (1801) and on Britain at Amiens (1802), these treaties accepted many French gains of territory and were unlikely to be lasting. Military operations and diplomacy were directed towards imposing not only a French political system on the remainder of Europe, but also, through the anti-British Continental System (*blocus continental*), an economic hegemony that would stimulate French enterprise.

In a continuous series of campaigns from 1805 to 1809 Napoleon won considerable victories (including Austerlitz, Jena, Eylau, Wagram), and established an empire which, through annexation and the establishment of vassal states, covered most of Europe, excluding Russia. He distributed thrones and territories to his relatives and favourites. But he could not always be absent from Paris. The campaigns were improvised; his armies were not properly supplied; the rate of desertion was high; the British were successful in organizing a series of coalitions against him. The Spanish campaign (1808–13), where Napoleon led his forces for a relatively short time, saw his first defeats. The Russian campaign (1812) was a disaster. A new coalition was formed against France, and at Leipzig (1813) he was forced to make his greatest retreat. Faced with the invasion of France, he won some remarkable victories but was unable to halt the allies, who

Napoleon II

entered Paris on 30 March 1814. Napoleon, at Fontainebleau, found himself isolated, and abdicated (6 April). He was given the kingdom of Elba, where he installed himself and his court.

He was to re-emerge. Bored with Elba, fearful that he was to be transferred to another, quite undesirable island, and calculating that there was much discontent within France, he escaped and landed in France, near Antibes, on 1 March 1815. Now began the Hundred Days, or *vol d'aigle* (using another metaphor, Marshal Ney, who had been sent to arrest him, later said: 'Je ne pouvais arrêter l'eau de la mer avec mes mains'). Napoleon entered Paris on 20 March. He introduced a form of liberalism with the 'Acte Additionnel aux Constitutions de l'Empire' (1 June), promising liberty of the press and a form of parliamentary government, but it aroused little enthusiasm in political circles. Once again his fate was sealed by a battle on a foreign field, *Waterloo. He abdicated again (22 June), and after seeking permission from the British government to go to America, he accepted exile on the Atlantic island of St Helena, where he lived under close supervision with a small group of followers, mainly occupied with the composition of his memoirs.

3. Significance and Legend

It is difficult to sum up Napoleon's significance. He was always a Corsican, viewing the Mediterranean as the vital centre of the world and underestimating the importance of the Atlantic and the Baltic. He was a soldier, seeking and finding military solutions to problems. Politically, it should be remembered that he had been a member of the *Jacobin club; there was always in his ideas the belief that strong government should be surrounded by popular approval. Finally, it must be said that he was an adventurer and a gambler, believing in his destiny, prepared to stake everything on one campaign or one battle. He acted as if he knew that he was only to be in power for a short time, and that his power was fragile. *Guizot, an experienced politician and perceptive historian, summed him up with these words: 'C'est beaucoup d'être à la fois une gloire nationale, une garantie révolutionnaire, et un principe d'autorité'.

The young Bonaparte had had literary ambitions; he wrote several pamphlets and *contes* and envisaged greater works, such as a history of Corsica. He was much influenced by *Rousseau. His best-known work was *Le Souper de Beaucaire* (1793), a series of conversations posing the question of the authority of the Republic over a dissident Marseille. He had studied many classical authors, and at the imperial court the librarian was regularly summoned to tell the emperor about recent publications; for all his interest in literature, however, he did not approve oppositional writers such as *Chateaubriand and Madame de *Staël. His own proclamations and orders of the day have been much admired for their laconic vigour.

From the time of the Consulate, Bonaparte had been preoccupied with his own history and with what became known as the Napoleonic legend. On St Helena he requested from the British government that he be sent several hundred volumes, mostly on French history. All his companions, including generals Bertrand, de Montholon, and Gourgaud, were expected to help him to write his history, and from this work many volumes emerged, sometimes containing several versions, notably the *Mémoires pour servir à l'histoire de France sous Napoléon* (6 vols., 1823–5) and the *Mémorial de Sainte-Hélène* of *Las Cases.

Meanwhile in France the legend was cultivated by *Béranger, *Hugo, and *Balzac. The government of Louis-Philippe contributed to it by having Napoleon's remains brought to Paris and installed in the *Invalides. Louis Bonaparte profited from the legend in his political career, and as *Napoleon III set up editorial committees (on some of which *Mérimée and *Sainte-Beuve served) to publish Napoleon's correspondence. 32 volumes appeared between 1858 and 1870, but they are very incomplete.

One understands why *Barrès, who continued the Napoleonic legend, hailed him as 'Napoléon, professeur d'énergie' and 'capable de servir de centre, de point de contact aux imaginations françaises, aux plus simples comme aux plus civilisés'. [See also BONAPARTISM.]   [DJ]

See P. Geyl, *Napoleon: For and Against* (1949); J. Tulard, *Napoléon ou le Mythe du sauveur* (1977); C. Emsley, *The Longman Companion to Napoleonic Europe* (1993).

NAPOLEON II, see NAPOLEON, 2.

NAPOLEON III (Louis-Napoléon Bonaparte) (1803–73). Son of Louis Bonaparte, the brother of the emperor Napoleon, and of Hortense de Beauharnais, daughter of the emperor's first wife. He became the recognized leader of the Bonapartes after his elder brother's death. In exile in England he wrote *Des idées napoléoniennes* (1839), a highly successful publication which sketched out a future *Bonapartist regime and put forward his belief that the state should play a decisive role in running the economy. When in prison in Ham after an unsuccessful attempt to seize power in France, he wrote *L'Extinction du paupérisme* (1844), which extended his ideas. He was also the author of an artillery manual.

Returning to France at the outbreak of the Revolution of 1848, he was elected a *député*, then prince-president of the Republic [see REPUBLICS, 2]. On 2 December 1851 his *coup d'état* made him president without any constitutional limitations. He proclaimed himself emperor in December 1852. He organized the transformation of Paris into a modern and beautiful city, through the work of Baron *Haussman [see SECOND EMPIRE].

The defeat of his armies in the *Franco-Prussian

War (he was captured in person at Sedan) led to the fall of the Second Empire. He settled in England with the Empress *Eugénie. His only son and heir, Prince Eugène, was killed fighting with British forces in Zululand. [DJ]

Narbonnais, Les. *Chanson de geste* of the Cycle de *Guillaume relating the *enfances* of the seven sons of Aimeri de Narbonne. In a distorted reflection of the move to primogeniture in 12th-c. France, Aimeri reserves Narbonne for his youngest son; the other six must either conquer fiefs for themselves or fill posts at *Charlemagne's court. The poem ends with the six successful elder brothers returning united to relieve Narbonne besieged by the Saracens. [PEB]

NARCEJAC, Thomas, see BOILEAU-NARCEJAC.

Natchez, Les. Prose epic by Chateaubriand, inspired by his American travels and begun c.1794, published 1826. Its plot expands on those of *René and *Atala.

National, Le. Newspaper founded in 1830 by *Thiers, *Mignet, and Armand Carrel. It helped to provoke the Revolution of 1830 [see JULY MONARCHY] and favoured English-style constitutional monarchy. It ceased publication in 1851.

National Assemblies (in France). Although the *États Généraux and the *parlements* were able to influence law-making and government to a certain extent under the *ancien régime*, parliamentary government only began with the Revolution. The name 'Assemblée Nationale' was taken by the *Tiers État on 17 June 1789; for the successive Revolutionary assemblies, the Assemblée Constituante (1789–91), the Assemblée Législative (1791–2), the Convention Nationale (1792–5), and the Directoire (1795–9) see REVOLUTION, I.

The Directoire first introduced a bicameral form of legislature, the two chambers being the Conseil des Cinq Cents and the Conseil des Anciens. Under the Consulate and the Empire [see NAPOLEON] there were various legislative bodies, the most important being the Sénat Conservateur, but they exercised little real power.

After the *Restoration, the constitutional 'Charte' provided for two chambers, the Chambre des Députés and the Chambre des Pairs. Since then, with the partial exception of the *Occupation period of 1940–4, when the assembly was adjourned but not formally dissolved, France has had an elected lower house (usually Chambre des Députés, but Corps Législatif under the Second Empire and Assemblée Nationale under the Fourth Republic) and an upper house, for the most part indirectly elected (usually Sénat, but Conseil de la République under the Fourth Republic). The relations of power between national assemblies and heads of state has varied considerably from regime to regime [see REPUBLICS]. [PF]

Nationalism is a concept that arose in the 19th c. among peoples who became aware of their national identity without having a national state; in these cases nationalism had first to be affirmed linguistically and culturally, then be given political embodiment. In France, the state came first, and over the centuries created the nation, so that the roots of national self-consciousness can be traced long before the concept or word existed. French nationalism was clearly one of the driving forces of the Revolutionary and Napoleonic periods, but the word *nationalisme* appeared in a dictionary only in 1874.

It is significant that this was after the French defeat of 1870–1 and the loss of Alsace and Lorraine. France now felt herself to be a multilated nation. It was at this time that, in order to refute German claims to the lost provinces, *Renan delivered his seminal lecture, 'Qu'est-ce qu'une nation?' (1882). *Barrès subsequently gave widespread currency to the word and the idea (*Scènes et doctrines du nationalisme*, 1902). Political groups developed: the Ligue des Patriotes (1882), Ligue de la Patrie Française (1899), and *Action Française (of which *Maurras soon became the leader). These are collectively referred to as the nationalist movement.

The impulse for *revanche* against Germany soon took second place, however, and the nationalist groups focused on domestic forces that were seen as sapping national strength. Thus, rather than uniting the nation against a foreign enemy, the nationalist movement became divisive, above all in its lost battle against the defenders of *Dreyfus, whose campaign was seen as a threat to the army. In the course of this conflict, nationalism, which from 1789 to 1885 had been associated with the Left, was adopted by the Right. It thus became intertwined with the main theme of Left–Right conflict, the battle between the Catholic Church and the Republic. Elements of the nationalist movement that had originally been *anticlerical became absorbed in this traditional conflict of the 'two Frances', and the specifically nationalist aspect of their programme was attenuated.

However, the 'union sacrée' of 1914–18 showed that when the foreign threat materialized in earnest, the disputes of nationalists against republicans were submerged in a united patriotic effort. This union was symbolized by the government of the ex-Dreyfusard *Clemenceau, who became 'Père-la-Victoire' and was panegyrized by Action Française. After 1918 the specific sense which nationalism had acquired fades out, although some extreme-Right movements of the inter-war period are referred to as nationalist Ligues. An echo of this terminology is the self-description of the Vichy regime as 'la Révolution nationale' [see OCCUPATION AND RESISTANCE]. [DRW]

See R. Girardet (ed.), *Le Nationalisme français, 1871 1914* (1966); R. Tombs (ed.), *Nationhood and Nationalism in France from Boulangism to the Great War, 1889–1918* (1991).

Naturalism

Naturalism has traditionally been considered a crude and exaggerated successor to *Realism, nourished by the pseudo-scientific theories of its chief exponent, *Zola. Amongst the major writers usually associated with the movement along with Zola—Alphonse *Daudet, *Huysmans, the *Goncourt brothers, *Maupassant, and lesser figures such as *Alexis, Paul Bonnetain, *Céard, *Descaves, Louis Desprez, *Hennique, and Gabriel Thyébaut—there was little agreement, interest, or consistency in theoretical matters.

Zola used the term *naturaliste* in the 1860s to denote a heritage of realist literature, inspired by the positivist tradition in philosophy, science, and the arts, that rejected the idealistic aspirations of the Romantic movement. *Balzac was the main literary model, *Taine the model critic and theoretician, *Comte and Claude *Bernard the intellectual mentors of the scientific age to which Zola linked the movement. The term 'Naturalism' conveniently evoked the natural sciences, in which Zola sought to ground Naturalist methods; materialist and positivist philosophy, which provided the broad philosophical framework of the movement; and contemporary art criticism and practices, to which the Naturalist writers frequently had recourse, not only for their themes and techniques, but also for their aesthetic principle of the exact imitation of nature. Zola's theorizing culminated in *Le *Roman expérimental* (1880), heavily influenced by Claude *Bernard's *Introduction à l'étude de la médecine expérimentale* (1865). Here he established a controversial analogy between the writer and the scientific experimenter. The comparison between the naturalist in literature and the scientist or doctor is also made by Céard, a more sober theorist, but only to insist that Naturalism was above all a method, relying upon the close observation of reality. In very general terms, the Naturalists shared a materialistic, mechanistic view which tended to subject mankind to deterministic factors, like the laws of heredity or influences from the environment.

The more solid links amongst the Naturalist writers were at the level of their literary practices rather than their theories. Despite the diversity of Naturalist texts, two fundamental types can be defined. A Goncourtian type depicts tragic dramas of degeneration caused by such determining factors as hereditary taints, neurotic dispositions, adverse social conditions, in which the victims, usually women, as in Zola's *L'*Assommoir*, submit to an inevitable socio-biological fate. A second, more Flaubertian type of work, less scientific and more philosophical than the first, inspired in many cases by Schopenhauer's pessimism, presents the disillusionment and frustrations of a (usually male) protagonist caught up in the dilemmas of daily existence. There is also much social satire in Naturalist texts, as well as a tendency to favour, as relief from the grim realities, decorous descriptions in the manner of contemporary painters.

Historically, the first Naturalist texts, which became models for later writers, date from the 1860s, notably the Goncourt novel *Germinie Lacerteux* (1864), Zola's *Thérèse Raquin* (1867), and Flaubert's *L'Éducation sentimentale* (1869). But it was only in the late 1870s, after the furore caused by the publication of *L'Assommoir* (1877), that a discernible group of writers with common interests formed. With the exception of Zola's novels and two texts by Huysmans, *Marthe, histoire d'une fille* (1876), and *Les Sœurs Vatard* (1879), few Naturalist works had in fact been published before the so-called 'Médan Group' issued their collection of stories, *Les *Soirées de Médan*, in 1880. The sense of solidarity in the group was fostered more by their common opposition to the hostility with which Naturalist texts were being received by the critics than by a common literary programme; there were dissensions in the group. However, in 1880s, a flood of Naturalist texts appeared, novels, collections of short stories, and theatrical productions. The 'Manifeste des Cinq' against *La *Terre* (1887) was considered to be a critical breach in the defences of the Naturalist school, though, in fact, the five young 'Naturalists', supposedly representatives of a new Naturalist generation, were never acknowledged by Zola as his disciples and, by then, most of the members of the 'Médan Group', had gone their own way. By the time Jules Huret published the results of his *Enquête sur l'évolution littéraire* (1891), which, notwithstanding the famous telegram from Alexis ('Naturalisme pas mort. Lettre suit.'), pronounced the movement dead, it was already enjoying considerable success abroad and exercising a lasting influence on writers in France.

Naturalism also had an undeniable influence on the theatre. Numerous works of fiction, mainly by the Goncourt brothers and Zola, were dramatized and the stage adaptation of *L'Assommoir* (1879), in particular, had a considerable impact. But, in general, the best and most successful works for the stage were produced by writers not associated directly with the Naturalist movement (Becque, *Les *Corbeaux*), or by professional men of the theatre who came later, like *Antoine and the Théâtre Libre, or by foreign playwrights like Ibsen and Strindberg. [DB]

See Y. Chevrel, *Le Naturalisme* (1982); A. Pagès, *Le Naturalisme* (1989); D. Baguley, *Naturalist Fiction: The Entropic Vision* (1990).

Naturisme, Le, see FAUVISM.

NAUDÉ, Gabriel (1600–53). Editor, antiquarian, scholar, and librarian, a member of the nascent European republic of letters and of the 'tétrade' of friends which included at various times *La Mothe le Vayer, *Gassendi, and *Patin. After studies at the University of Paris, Naudé went to Padua and came under the influence of Cremonini, who was widely suspected of atheism. While librarian to the président de Mesmes, he composed an *Avis pour dresser une bibliothèque* which appeared in 1627; but his first publication was a vigorous *Apologie pour les grands personnages faussement soupçonnés de magie* (1625), written in reply to a vituperative attack on suspected *libertins* by *Garasse in 1623. Naudé went to Italy with Cardinal di Bagno in the 1630s, where he acted as the correspondent of *Peiresc and sought the manuscripts of 16th-c. Italian philosophers such as Nifo and Cardano, some of which he later published. On his return to France he became the librarian of *Mazarin and built up his impressive collection only to see it dispersed during the *Fronde. Unlike Gassendi and Peiresc, he seems to have merited his subsequent reputation for discreet freethought, although only hearsay evidence of this survives. [IM]

Nausée, La. *Sartre's first novel, published 1939. It is sometimes criticized for being too philosophical, but it is rather an attempt to evoke in fictional form human experience as it is seen by *phenomenology and *Existentialism. The novel's hero, Antoine Roquentin, undergoes an existential crisis in the course of which he loses confidence in the old-established values and identities of ordinary social life. His relationship to himself, to other people, to physical objects, all come to appear problematic as he becomes aware of the absurdity and contingency of the world, its lack of pre-ordained meaning and purpose. The effect of this is experienced psychologically by Roquentin as anguish, and physiologically as nausea. Sartre may intend a certain irony when he leaves Roquentin unreconciled with existence, but finding a temporary respite in the 'imaginary' realm of art: listening to a jazz tune and contemplating writing a work of fiction himself. [CMH]

NAVARRE, Yves (1940–94). French novelist, playwright, poet, and essayist, noted for his contribution to debates on homosexual rights. His many works show a paradoxical, often provocative, combination of lyricism and violence, particularly in the portrayal of homosexual relationships (e.g. *Les Loukoums*, 1973). His novel *Le Jardin d'acclimatation* (1980) won the Prix Goncourt. In the 1980s his fiction reflected a growing concern with the writing process itself, from the transitional *Biographie* (1981) to *Romans, un roman* (1988). The AIDS crisis led him to re-evaluate the relation between sexuality and artistic creation in the moving novel *Ce sont amis que vent emporte* (1991). [CFR]

NAVILLE, Pierre (1904–93). French *Surrealist (1924–9) who played a vital role in the politicization of the movement. He was co-editor, with Benjamin *Péret, of the first numbers of the review *La Révolution surréaliste*, author of the automatic text 'Les Reines de la main gauche' and the pamphlet *La Révolution et les intellectuels* (1926). That period is recalled in *Le Temps du surréel* (1977). After his study of *Holbach (1943), his principal research was in the field of industrial sociology. His post-war works include *Théorie de l'orientation professionnelle* (1945), *La Vie de travail et ses problèmes* (1954), *La Classe ouvrière et le régime gaulliste* (1964), *Temps et technique* (1977), and *Le Nouveau Léviathan* (6 vols., 1957–81). [KRA]

NDAO, Cheikh Aliou (pseud. of Sidi Ahmet Alioune Ndao) (b. 1933). Senegalese novelist and dramatist. Having attended primary school in Senegal, he completed his secondary and university education in France. He has worked as an English teacher in France and Senegal and has held important posts in the Senegalese Ministry of Culture and at the Presidency. He has experimented in poetry, theatre, and the novel. Two collection of his poems have been published, *Kairée* (1964) and *Mogariennes* (1970), but it was his play, *L'Exil d'Alboury* (1967), prizewinner at the Pan-African Festival in Algiers (1969) which first attracted public attention. Other plays have followed: *La Décision* (1969), *Le Fils de l'Almamy* and *La Case de l'homme* (1973), *L'Île de Bahia* (1975), and *Du sang pour un trône* (1983). His novels, no less important than his plays, include *Buur Tilleen* (1972), *Excellence, vos épouses* (1983), and *Un bouquet d'épines pour elle* (1988). He has also written a collection of short stories, *Le Marabout de la sécheresse* (1979). Ndao's output has been continuous, and his creative inspiration is rich and varied, his relationship with traditional African culture always playing a major role. He has refused to choose between genres, wishing to be an all-round writer in the footsteps of other African writers whom he admires. He also writes original works in Wolof. [MKa]

N'DEBEKA, Maxime (b. 1944). Congolese poet and playwright. A former army officer, trained in Russia and China, N'Debeka was sentenced to death in 1972 for his role in an attempted coup. He was pardoned but spent 18 months in prison, during which he wrote the verse in *L'Oseille/Les Citrons* (1975). Other volumes include *Les Signes du silence* (1978) and *La Danse de N'Kumba ensorcelée* (1988). His plays include *Le Président* (1970) and *Équatorium* (1987). A volume of short stories, *Vécus au miroir*, came out in 1991. [VC]

NDIAYE, Marie (b. 1967). Franco-Senegalese writer, born in Pithiviers. Her first novel, *Quant au riche avenir* (1985), was followed by *Comédie classique* (1987), a novel composed in a single sentence. *La Femme changée en bûche* (1989) combines realism and fable in the tale of a woman who enlists the help of the devil in her vengeance on her husband. [NHi]

NECKER, Jacques (1732–1804). Genevan banker who became French finance minister in 1777, managing the economy with prudence and putting into practice some of *Turgot's ideas for reform. Resigning in 1781 because of court resistance to his plans (see his famous *Compte rendu* of that year), he published a *Traité de l'administration des finances de France* in

1784. In 1788 he came back to power on a wave of popularity, was dismissed just before the fall of the Bastille, and returned in triumph soon after. His lack of enthusiasm for major political change led to clashes with *Mirabeau, and he retired finally in 1790. [PF]

NECKER, Suzanne Curchod, Madame (1739–94). She received an excellent education in ancient and modern literature, then married Jacques *Necker. Their daughter became Germaine de *Staël. Perhaps the last *précieuse* [see PRECIOSITY], Necker ran a famous Paris *salon where men of letters and politicians met. She wrote prolifically, despite her husband's objections to literary women. He published five volumes of her collected works posthumously (1798–1802). [JDeJ]

NECKER DE SAUSSURE, Albertine (1766–1841). Cousin by marriage and friend of Germaine de *Staël, author of a *Notice sur le caractère et les écrits de Mme de Staël* (1820) and of a treatise on education and the position of women.

Nedjma. *Kateb Yacine's masterpiece, published in Paris in 1956, is the pre-eminent and most influential Maghrebian novel. It was the first Maghrebian work to take into account not only the unique realities of the North African colonial experience, but also the experimental tradition established by such writers as Joyce, Faulkner, and the French authors of the *Nouveau Roman. Most of the action of the novel takes place in eastern Algeria in the decade before the War of Independence. It describes the adventures of four young Algerian men—Rachid, Lakhdar, Mustapha, and Mourad—in a series of subplots and adventures, including imprisonment, murder, kif smoking, and voyages to the ancestral Nadhor and to Mecca, often with or in search of Nedjma, an ethereal object of desire and fantasy whose origins are ambiguous: she was conceived in a cave by an abducted French woman and one of the men who violated her, who include the main character Rachid's father and Si Mokhtar, an important character in the story.

The plot is so complex and rich that it defies brief summary. In any event, *Nedjma's* success lies in its powerful writing, its fragmented Postmodern structure which was new to Maghrebian discourse, and its several possible readings, authorizing, for example, interpretation of Nedjma (*nedjma* means 'star' in Arabic) as symbolic of the rising star of Algerian nationalism. [ES]

Nègres, Les. Play by *Genet, published 1958, first staged 1959. Writing to provide a script for black actors, Genet required that it be performed before a white audience. Some of the cast wear white masks and mimic traditional white figures of authority, while the rest actually apply black make-up and caricature the image of blacks prevalent among racist whites. Through provocation and outrage the black characters seek to go beyond racial stereotypes and scandalize whites out of their complacency—while diverting audience attention from the off-stage black militants organizing for concrete political action. Ultimately each side is seen to be playing roles determined by its view of how the other sees it. Self-consciously theatrical and spectacular, replacing traditional plot with orchestrated movement and mood, *Les Nègres* suggests that complex simulation and illusion lie at the heart of human reality. [DHW]

Négritude. Cultural movement born in a context of international ferment, marked by the rise of Communism, the mingling of peoples resulting from World War I, and the diffusion of the work of Delafosse, Delavignette, Hardy, and Monod on cultural relativism.

In Paris between 1930 and 1940 black intellectuals from Africa, America, and the Caribbean were meeting and debating together. Even before this, however, the Harlem Negro Renaissance of the 1920s, signalled by the work of W. E. B. Dubois and Marcus Garvey, had clearly posed the problem of the destiny of the black peoples, their consciousness and their solidarity, in other words, their identity. The presence in France of Jean Toomer, Countee Cullen, Claude McKay, and other writers from Harlem galvanized the black intellectuals, and in 1931–2 *La Revue du monde noir* published in French a number of texts of the Negro Renaissance.

In the *West Indies, most earlier writers, eager to promote their integration into metropolitan France, had favoured a literature of assimilation. The contact between African blacks and West Indians living in Paris led to a new awareness of the treatment accorded to black peoples. *Négritude* thus grew out of what *Fanon called 'l'expérience vécue du Noir'.

The theory of the movement appeared in periodicals such as *Les Continents*, *La Dépêche africaine*, *La Revue du monde noir*. The last-named, founded by Sajous and Paulette Nardal, was the first major meeting-place for black intellectuals, including *Price-Mars, Félix Ebony, *Maran, Étienne Léro, *Menil, *Césaire, *Senghor, and *Damas. One of their main concerns was to reassert the value of black cultures by setting the historical record straight. In spite of its commitment to truth, the *Revue* was a moderate publication; it appeared between November 1931 and April 1932.

On 1 June 1932, several former contributors to the *Revue*, declaring their allegiance to *Breton and *Surrealism, founded *Légitime défense*. This journal was strongly influenced by the West Indians, through the contributions of Léro, Menil, Jules-Marcel Monnerot, and Maurice-Sabas Quitmas. Claiming that the *Revue du monde noir* was a 'revue à l'eau de rose', in other words moderate and Catholic, they set out to 'develop an ideology of revolt'. The tone of the new journal irritated the

French authorities, who prevented more than one number appearing.

In 1935 a little journal, *L'*Étudiant noir*, was published containing the work of writers from both Africa (e.g. Senghor, *Socé Diop, Birago *Diop) and the West Indies (e.g. Césaire, Damas, Léonard Sainville). It was these publications that created the intellectual ferment which gave birth to *négritude*. The stated aim of the movement was to 'créer entre les Noirs du monde entier, sans distinction de nationalité, un lieu intellectuel et moral qui leur permette de mieux se connaître . . . et d'illustrer leur race'.

Négritude thus had both a cultural and a political dimension. If Césaire invented the term, it was Senghor, with his numerous writings, who appeared as the leading spirit and propagandist for the movement. For him, it represents 'le patrimoine culturel, les valeurs, et surtout l'esprit de la civilisation négro-africaine'.

Following in the wake of its American forerunner, the movement established itself as a place of rehabilitation for black culture. As a literary school, it produced such major works as Damas's *Pigments*, Césaire's *Cahier d'un retour au pays natal* and *Les Armes miraculeuses*, *Rabemananjara's *Rites millénaires*, or even *Rabéarivelo's *Traduit de la nuit* and *Vieilles chansons des pays d'Imérina*. Other writers such as *Camara Laye or *Sembène Ousmane also helped give body to the great 'cri nègre'.

But the concept of *négritude* is far from having won universal support among black intellectuals. By insisting on the cultural unity of the black world and the permanent qualities of the black soul, Senghor seems to have brushed to one side socio-historical considerations. For Fanon, a cultural renaissance was impossible in a context of oppression; it was essential above all to struggle against the domination of the black peoples. Césaire's *Discours sur le colonialisme* of 1955 is in the same vein.

Négritude was an essential turning-point in the awakening of political awareness in Africa and the West Indies. It occupies a vital place in the recovery of the historical initiative by dominated black peoples. But it has given rise to many different interpretations and controversies. Although Senghor continued to defend the original *négritude*, while modifying its content, many African intellectuals saw it as a dated movement, and in some cases an ideology of enslavement, e.g. Marcien Towa in *Léopold Sédar Senghor: négritude ou servitude* (1971). Others, including Stanislas Adotévi, author of *Négritude et négrologues* (1972), believe that the movement should confine itself to cultural questions, and that it has been misused for political purposes. (There is a clear allusion here to Senghor, who governed Senegal from 1960 to 1980 under the aegis of *négritude*.) The most extreme argue that, as the tiger does not go on about tigritude, the negro should not waste his time proclaiming his negritude, imprisoning himself in coterie politics. Such is the

position of Wole Soyinka and many English-speaking intellectuals, who prefer to speak simply of the African personality.

At all events, it seems that the debate on *négritude* is now closed. The movement has definitively entered the literary-historical Pantheon of the black peoples. [AK]

NELLIGAN, Émile (1879–1941). Canadian poet, described by Edmund Wilson as 'at once the *Rimbaud and the Gérard de *Nerval of French Canada'. His destiny was a tragic one. Born in Montreal, he grew up in the company of his mother and sisters, his father being often absent as postal inspector on the Gaspé peninsula. In 1897 he joined the École Littéraire de Montréal, a society of young writers intent on renewing French-Canadian literature. His father, disapproving of his poetic vocation, sent him off as a merchant seaman to Liverpool and attempted to get him employed as a clerk in Montreal. Then, in August 1899, Nelligan was admitted to a mental asylum, and spent the rest of his life in confinement, continuing to write spasmodically.

His œuvre consists of some 160 lyric poems, most of which first appeared in 1904 in a volume edited by his friend Louis Dantin, *Émile Nelligan et son œuvre*. The poetry eschews specific reference to Canada, and is heavily indebted to French and Belgian lyricism, combining the formal beauty of *Hérédia and the *Parnasse with the musicality and evocative imagery of *Verlaine, *Baudelaire, and the *Symbolists. Nelligan's verbal genius sometimes leads him into excessive artfulness, in the manner of the contemporary *Decadents, but many of his poems (e.g. the famous sonnet 'Le Vaisseau d'or') evoke in a haunting way a deep and sometimes tormented melancholy. Characteristically his lyrics conjure up a mood of seclusion and retreat, distaste and fear of the world, yearning for a lost ideal (often associated with childhood), and the fragile pleasures of art and beauty. All of this is familiar Romantic or Symbolist material, but is frequently made memorable by the striking interweaving of sound and image, as in the opening of 'Sérénade triste': 'Comme des larmes d'or qui de mon cœur s'égouttent, | Feuilles de mon bonheur, vous tombez toutes, toutes.' [PF]

Nemo, Le Capitaine. Hero of *Verne's *Vingt mille lieues sous les mers*, who reappears dramatically at the end of L'*Île mystérieuse*.

NEMOURS, Marie d'Orléans-Longueville, duchesse de (1625–1707), fought in the *Fronde alongside her stepmother, the duchesse de *Longueville and wrote public letters protesting against her father's imprisonment. Exiled to her estate, Coulommiers (1650), the immensely wealthy heiress married Henri II de Savoie only in 1657. Her *Mémoires* of the Fronde were published posthumously by *L'Héritier (1709). [JDeJ]

Neoclassicism

Neoclassicism. New and deliberate imitation of Greek and Roman subject-matter, ideas, and style which spread throughout mid-18th-c. Europe. It was stimulated by widespread interest and enthusiasm among the literati for the findings at archaeological excavations at Herculaneum and Pompeii and by the interpretative writings of J. J. Winckelmann, especially his *History of Ancient Art* (1764). Lessing's *Laocoon or Concerning the Limitations of Painting and Poetry* followed in 1766, demanding more restraint from the visual arts than from poetry. Joseph-Marie Vien (1716–1809) led the fashionable taste in France for subjects from the classics when he returned to Paris in 1750, full of ideas from Rome. He became arbiter of taste in France, counting *David among his famous pupils. The *Réflexions sur la sculpture* of *Falconet formed a similar bridge between the ideas of the *Rococo and Neoclassicism. La Live de Jully introduced Neoclassical decoration in his study in 1756, and Clerisseau, under the influence of Piranesi and Winckelmann, pioneered the new Roman style in architecture.

Winckelmann's favourite classical statue, the *Apollo Belvedere*, was looted from Italy by Napoleon and formed a touchstone for French Neoclassical taste. Training at the Academy resumed a more severe character and subjects for the Prix de Rome were taken from Stoic writers. A strong strand of realism, however, developed in portraiture and landscape subjects alongside this resumption of intellectual values. [See also CLASSICISM.]   [JPC]

Néologie, see MERCIER, L.-S.

Neoplatonism. The term properly describes the thought of Plotinus (3rd c. AD) and his early disciples Porphyry, Iamblichus, and Proclus, but loosely covers the influence of these writers, and any subsequent revival of Plato, more particularly in the 15th c. in Italy and the 16th c. in France. It is often difficult to separate the Plotinian tradition from a purer form of Platonism. In the Middle Ages Plato himself was not well known in the West, and scarcely at all in Greek. The *Timaeus* was known in Cicero's partial translation (and also in that of Chalcidius) and although the *Phaedo* and the *Meno* were translated into Latin in the 12th c. by Henry Aristippus their impact was slight. Knowledge of Plato came through the Latin writings of Cicero, Augustine, Macrobius, *Boethius, and Scotus Erigena, an Irishman living in Paris. In the 12th c. this Platonist tradition was further transmitted in Paris by Bonaventure, Duns Scotus, and other Franciscans, and by the school of Chartres, in contrast to the Aristotelian approach of the Dominicans. It must be stressed that it was not Platonism but Scholastic Aristotelianism which was the dominant philosophy in France at least until 1600 [see SCHOLASTICISM]. In literature there are some superficial parallels between Platonist thought and the idealized love of the *troubadours, as with the spiritual ideal of

Petrarch; the true revival of Plato does not, however, take place until the 15th c. The presence in Italy of the Byzantine scholars Chrysoloras, Bessarion, George of Trebizond, and Gemisthus Pletho generated interest in Greek language and literature; in about 1460 Cosimo de' Medici founded a Platonic Academy at Florence and it was frequented by poets and philosophers.

One man above all is responsible for the spread of Neoplatonism in the west, and especially in France, Marsilio Ficino (1433–99), a priest and humanist who edited and translated Plato, Plotinus, and other Neoplatonic and hermetic writings, and attempted a synthesis of Platonism and Christianity. His commentary on Plato's *Symposium* (published in Latin in 1484 and in Italian in 1544) is the direct source of many poems and treatises on love in Italian and French, among which are: the *Asolani* of Bembo (1505, French translation 1545), Mario Equicola's *Libro di natura d'amore* (written by 1496, published 1525), Castiglione's *Il Cortegiano* (1528, French translation 1537), Leone Ebreo's *Dialoghi d'amore* (written 1502, published 1535, two French translations, by Pontus de *Tyard and Denys Sauvage, 1551). It was thus from Italy that Neoplatonism came to France, through these treatises or directly from Ficino, with the support of Greek or Latin editions or French translations of Plato.

Among the first works to show signs of this influence were Symphorien *Champier's *Ianua logice et physice* (1498) and the fourth book of his *Nef des dames vertueuses* (1503), a partial commentary on the *Symposium* after Ficino. *Lefevre d'Étaples, though predominantly Aristotelian, was influenced by Plato, as were Bovelles, *Ramus, *Rabelais, and *Marguerite de Navarre in her mystical and spiritual works. *Héroët's *Androgyne* (1542) is another Ficinian translation and commentary on part of the *Symposium*, his *Parfaite Amie* shows the same inspiration. Other poets acquainted with the tradition are *Scève in his *Délie* (1544) and *Microcosme* (1562), *Du Guillet (*Rymes*, 1545), *Du Bellay (*L'Olive*, 1549, *Treize sonnets*, 1552), and especially Pontus de Tyard (*Erreurs amoureuses*, 1549, 1551, 1555). Mention should also be made of Charles Fontaine, Charles de *Sainte-Marthe, and Gilles Corrozet. In the second half of the century *Desportes's poems indicate a further revival.

The main impact of Platonism on French literature thus occurred in the 16th c. and concerned love-poetry. The philosophy of love was, however, grounded in epistemology (love as a kind of knowledge, or leading to self-knowledge), cosmology (love as producing the harmony of the world, man as a microcosm), and aesthetics or metaphysics (love as an ascent to the realm of ideas, the superiority of the ideal over the material world). French Renaissance writers, following Diotima's speech in the *Symposium*, described the poet-lover's ascent from the love of a beautiful woman (for the writer was usually a man and the Greek ideal of male homosexual love had been forgotten) to the contemplation and love of beauty itself and to an awareness of the union of beauty, truth, and goodness. The clearest expression of this comes in the closing sonnets of Du Bellay's *Olive* and in his *Treize sonnets de l'honnête amour*.

Yet in spite of this idealism, and whatever the theorists say, the poets often reject, almost simultaneously, the idealizing tendency with its implications of chastity and spirituality; Platonism, like *Petrarchism, has obvious limitations, and the sensual appreciation of beauty prevails in *Ronsard, *Baïf, and *Belleau. Aristophanes' humorous intervention in the *Symposium* also captured the Renaissance imagination: the myth of the Androgyne justified the search for one's original other half and symbolized (in Ficino, Héroët, and others) man's attempt to regain his lost innocence. Love is linked also to critical theory in the doctrine of divine madness, or enthusiasm, which came from the *Phaedrus* and the *Ion* through the intermediary of Ficino: the four furies (poetic, mystical, prophetic, and erotic) are all aspects of a divine force which inspire mankind and ultimately converge to lead it from disorder to the original unity it has lost and bring it to the generation of beauty. In France the leading exponents of this attitude were *Sebillet, Du Bellay, Tyard, and Ronsard. Platonism is also seen in the Socratic educational ideal in Rabelais and *Montaigne, as well as in political theory. Since the 16th c. Platonism has reappeared sporadically in different authors and different domains (e.g. the Romantic movement and early 20th-c. philosophy) but it is seen at its most dynamic in the humanist union of philosophy and literature.   [PS]

See R. V. Merrill and R. J. Clements, *Platonism in French Renaissance Poetry* (1957): A. H. T. Levi, 'The Neoplatonist Calculus', in Levi (ed.), *Humanism in France* (1970), and 'The Role of Neoplatonism in Ronsard's Poetic Imagination', in T. Cave (ed.), *Ronsard the Poet* (1973); F. Joukovsky, *Le Regard intérieur. Thèmes plotiniens chez quelques écrivains de la Renaissance* (1982).

NEOSTOICISM. This term covers a number of philosophical movements which draw on the ethics and psychology of the Stoics (although not their logic). Stoicism is known principally through the later accounts of other ancient philosophers: Cicero, Plutarch, Seneca, *Boethius, and most of all Epictetus, whose *Enchiridion* enjoyed an enormous vogue throughout Europe from the end of the 16th c. The revival of Stoicism has close connections with 15th-c. Florentine *Neoplatonism, especially in the writings of Ficino and Pico della Mirandola. Their exaltation of human moral autonomy and celebration of the figure of Socrates as an exemplar of pagan virtue were enormously influential in northern Europe. From the beginning of the 16th c. attempts were made by *Erasmus and others to reconcile Evangelical Christianity with optimistic Stoic

doctrines about man's capacity to control his will, to eradicate or harness his passions, and to regulate his own happiness.

This desired reconciliation is detectable in the works of *Rabelais, whose giant hero *Pantagruel embodies an ideal of Christian behaviour embodying piety, moral energy, and a belief both in the possibilities of 'right reason' and the perfectibility of man. Pantagruelism is described in the prologue of the *Quart Livre* as 'certaine gaieté d'esprit confite en mépris de choses fortuites'; the latter phrase alludes to the Stoic doctrine that man should strive to control only that which is in his power, namely his own desires. Reason is the sure guide to human moral choice and behaviour; in Rabelais's writings this is always allied to personal faith and to 'gaieté d'esprit' which is nurtured by human companionship. Stoic thought may also be detected at this time in the treatises setting out the ideal education for princes, among them those by *Budé and *Ronsard.

Another strand of Neostoicism stresses the consolation of philosophy and its strength as a bulwark for the individual against personal misfortune and a hostile social, physical, or intellectual environment. This grimmer version comes to prevail in the second half of the 16th c. It may be detected in the Latin letters of Michel de *l'Hôpital; it finds expression in the plays of *Garnier; *Du Bellay even describes his muse as a dispenser of Stoic fortitude and consolation. By the 1580s a number of prominent scholars and writers in Europe—Cardano (*De utilitate ex adversis capienda*, 1561), Justus Lipsius (*De constantia*, 1583), *Montaigne, *Du Vair—came to promote Neostoic ideas in the wake of the civil and religious unrest caused by the *Reformation. Their activity was complemented by new translations or adaptations of ancient Stoics such as Plutarch (translated by *Amyot in 1572), Epictetus (translated by *Du Vair in 1591), Seneca (translated by Goulart in 1595 and Pressac in 1598), and Boethius (translated by Malassis de Mente in 1597). Much of this material remained available throughout the 17th c.

Various versions of Neostoicism emerge by 1600: that of Justus Lipsius surprisingly accompanies an opportunistic and unprincipled view of politics, and a suggestion that those in public life can usefully abandon all notions of private integrity when acting politically. This contradicts the view expressed in the earlier part of the century that Stoic values need to be inculcated in princes. Montaigne echoes this latter judgement in the chapter of his *Essais* entitled 'De l'utile et de l'honnête', but stresses more the importance of abstaining from participation in political life. For him, Stoicism is seen as a means of anticipating and managing human suffering by the individual. At first he proposed that this could best be done by steeling oneself against future pain and evil and by suppressing one's passions, but in his later writing he comes to argue the benefits of a more relaxed attitude towards pain and pleasure. His initial identification of Stoic, acquired virtue with a moral élite gives way to an appreciation of the 'natural' virtue of peasants and the fortitude they display in the face of pain and death.

This populist tendency is found also in the writings of Du Vair, which are deeply influenced by Epictetus' *Enchiridion*; in his *De la constance et consolation ès calamités publiques* (published 1597) an attempt is made to ally Stoic doctrines to *Counter-Reformation piety, a tendency found also in Justus Lipsius's work. Neostoicism of this last kind was strongly encouraged in *Jesuit schools, and emerges as an important element in the writings of some of their most famous pupils. It may be detected in Guez de *Balzac's *Socrate chrétien* (1652); in Pierre *Corneille's early tragedies, which offer an optimistic vision of the moral autonomy of the high-born individual; and in *Descartes's ethics, which are strongly reminiscent of Neostoicism. But whereas Corneille portrays virile, self-assertive heroes possessing lucidity, integrity, and moral consistency, who overcome not only their own passions but also hostile political machinations by sheer strength of character (Rodrigue in *Le *Cid*, Auguste in *Cinna*, *Nicomède), Descartes's *Traité des passions* of 1649 is less élitist in tone and argues for the ability of all human beings to master their own emotions and to manage their lives felicitously.

These optimistic accounts of human powers were undermined by the growing prestige of scepticism on the one hand and Augustinianism on the other; although the conflict between Jesuits and *Jansenists did not bear on this issue only, the discussion of Stoic doctrines is a significant factor in the debates of the middle years of the 17th c. The subsequent decline of Neostoicism coincided with the rise of the absolutist state, whose repressive character was more in tune with the pessimistic Augustinian account of human mental impotence and corruption.   [IM]

See A. Levi, *French Moralists: The Theory of the Passions 1585–1649* (1964).

NERCIAT, André-Robert Andréa de (1739–1800). French soldier and traveller, author of poems, plays, and libertine novels which were consigned to the 'Enfer' of the *Bibliothèque Nationale until *Apollinaire resurrected them. They include *Le Diable au corps* (1786), *Les Aphrodites* (1793), and the rather more decorous *Félicia ou Mes fredaines* (1776), a lively first-person narrative whose cheerful eroticism contrasts with the darker works of *Laclos and *Sade.   [PF]

NERVAL, Gérard de (pseud. of Gérard Labrunie) 1808–55. Poet, traveller, story-writer. His father was a military surgeon who joined Napoleon's armies shortly after the poet's birth; his mother died in Silesia in 1810 and his father, permanently wounded, only returned to France in 1814. Relations between father and son were often somewhat strained. Nerval spent his childhood in the Valois region, of

which he always remained fond, then attended the Lycée Charlemagne, where he met his lifelong friend Théophile *Gautier. He began publishing in 1826, and his translation of the first part of Goethe's *Faust* appeared in 1827. Nerval also translated other texts from the German, and republished the poems of *Ronsard. A member of the *Petit Cénacle with Célestin Nanteuil, Pétrus *Borel, Alexandre *Dumas, and Gautier, he contributed regularly to various periodicals (travel literature, drama criticism, essays). In 1834 he inherited a considerable sum from his maternal grandfather which he quickly lost in an unfortunate publishing venture, and much of the rest of his life was spent in financial straits. In that same year he made his first voyage to Italy, and thereafter was an inveterate traveller, indeed at times a vagabond. Partly because of his love for the actress Jenny Colon, partly in order to achieve fame and money, he wrote a number of plays, often in collaboration, none of which was a great success. He also practised the fantastic tale and wrote a historical novel about the Revolution, *Le Marquis de Fayolle* (1849).

In 1841 he underwent his first crisis of madness, and thereafter until his death was hospitalized intermittently for varying periods of time. Diagnosed as 'theomanic' at the time, he seems to have suffered from manic depression and schizophrenia. In 1843 he took an extended trip to Cairo and Beirut which led to his *Voyage en Orient* (1851); this breaks with the traditions of travel literature in that much of the text is devoted to rewriting, in a quite personal way, a series of tales, including that of Solomon and the Queen of Sheba, where he expounds his theories about the artist and artistic creation. In 1850 he published *Faux saulniers*, a strangely complex work in both form and structure, playing with the Sterne–*Diderot tradition of the digressive and self-conscious novel and with the problems of realism and historical veracity. In 1852 *Les Illuminés, ou les Précurseurs du socialisme* brought together a series of portraits of representatives of the tradition of *Illuminism. *Nuits d'octobre* (1852) and *Promenades et souvenirs* (1854–6) belong to a different sort of travel literature, describing his peregrinations in and around Paris and in the Valois, but introducing anecdotes, reminiscences, and dreams. The *Petits Châteaux de Bohème* (1852) contain many of his poems framed with a commentary on life and literature. His most read work, *Sylvie* (1853), is a tale of his love for three women and their differences or resemblances, and of his return to the Valois, with reminiscences of his childhood. His intense and continuing interest in folk-songs and popular traditions, which he shared with George *Sand, is manifest in this work.

That year and the following, when he was suffering more and more from psychological instability, he was none the less extremely productive. He completed the writing of *Les Filles du feu et les Chimères*, containing *Sylvie* and also a number of other tales, each about a woman figure, and a series of sonnets rich in mythological allusions and often ambivalent in tone and complex in nature, of which the most haunting and commented on is 'El Desdichado'. He also wrote *Aurélia and Pandora, a tale of his loves in Vienna, perhaps the most extreme of his works in its structural innovations, as it moves between lucidity and the oneiric or unconscious world. Because of what his doctor considered a premature intervention by his friends, he left the asylum and was found dead by hanging. Though in all probability the death was a suicide, thanks to his doctor's pleas he was given a Christian burial at Notre-Dame.

Nerval was not considered a major writer until the 20th c., when *Barrès, then *Proust and the *Surrealists moved him into the literary canon; he has since been much commented on by various schools of criticism. For several reasons (the anonymous publication of some works, his tendency to publish texts in various forms and configurations), the task of editing Nerval is a complex one and readers are well advised to consult the new Pléiade edition (ed. Jean Guillaume and Claude Pichois).

Nerval was representative of *Romanticism in many ways—in his appreciation of the Renaissance, of the exotic and the fantastic, of the primitive and folklore, of irrationalism and the occultist tradition, of the oneiric—but often he both pursued these interests to the extreme and ironically questioned their validity. He had a rich sense of (as well as curiosity about) the numinous , but was also profoundly sceptical. Many of his (especially later) writings invite an autobiographical reading, but his quest for the self was clearly problematic and hence enriched by his investigations of reverie and dreams. Deeply indebted to a certain tradition of thought and of literature (from *Neoplatonism, Apuleius, and Virgil to *Restif de la Bretonne), his essential adventure was that of seeking a literary form adequate to the expression of his conceptions, whence his revolutionary contribution to such varied genres as travel literature, the sonnet, and the autobiographical novel. [FPB]

See L. Cellier, *Gérard de Nerval* (1963); M. Jeanneret, *La Lettre perdue* (1978); G. Malandain, *L'Incendie au théâtre* (1988).

NERVÈZE, Antoine de (c. 1575–c.1615). French author of numerous novels, love stories which were very successful in their day. He gave his name to the 'style Nervèze', an extravagantly affected brew of *pointes and other figures of speech, much mocked by subsequent generations.

Nesle, Tour de. This tower stood until 1663 on the left bank of the Seine, on the site now occupied by the *Institut de France. Its association with the lurid crimes of Marguerite de Bourgogne (c.1290–1315), who was reputed to have attracted her lovers there before having them thrown down into the Seine, made it popular with Romantic writers, including

Aloysius *Bertrand and *Dumas *père*. The latter's far-fetched historical drama, *La Tour de Nesle*, was performed in 1832.

NESSON, Pierre de (c.1383–before 1442). French author of several pious and patriotic poems, and notably of the penitential *Vigilles des Morts* (also known as *Les Neuf Leçons de Job*), a poem in *sixains* commenting on the Office of the Dead and lingering on the repellent and the macabre. [JHMT]

Neveu de Rameau, Le. Dialogue by *Diderot, begun c.1760. It was published in 1804 in Goethe's German translation; the first French publication was a retranslation. The original manuscript was discovered at the end of the 19th c. Today this short and vivid dialogue is widely regarded as Diderot's masterpiece. It was admired by Hegel, who gives it an important place in his *Phänomenologie des Geistes*, and its enigmatic quality has attracted many differing interpretations.

The two interlocutors ('Moi' and 'Lui') are based on real individuals, Diderot himself and the nephew of the composer *Rameau. They meet and talk in a Paris café on a great variety of subjects, including art, music, morality, and education. Against the *philosophe*'s conventional good conscience, the bohemian Rameau, whose gifts are for music, mime, and parasitism, sets a radically amoral view of human life. For him, virtue is a cant phrase, and society is ruled by the law of the jungle. With his histrionic gifts, racy language, and brutal cynicism, he seems to have the best of the dialogue, yet he too leads an unfulfilled life in the corrupt Paris of the day. Diderot does not conclude; the dialogue ends: 'Rira bien qui rira le dernier.' [PF]

Newspapers, see PRESS.

Nez qui voque, Le, see DUCHARME.

NGAL Mbwil a Mpaang (Georges) (b. 1946). Zaïrois novelist, critic, and academic. Ngal's training in philosophy and theology is revealed in the novel *Giambatista Viko ou le Viol du discours africain* (1975). He has also written a survey of francophone African literature and a study of Aimé *Césaire. He has taught in several European universities and has lived in Paris since 1980. [VC]

NGANDU NKASHAMA, Pius (b. 1946). A Zaïrois with degrees in philosophy and literature, Ngandu Nkashama wears the mantle of poet, novelist, playwright and critic. His six novels include *Le Fils de la tribu* (1983), *Étoiles écrasées* (1988), and two works published in 1991, *Des mangroves en terre haute* and *Un jour de grand soleil sur les montagnes de l'Éthiopie*. One of his plays, *Bonjour Monsieur le Ministre* (1983), a political satire, was signed Elimane Bokel. Two recent plays are *L'Empire des ombres vivants* (1991) and *May Britt de Santa Cruz* (1993). He has also published a survey of African literature, a critical anthology, and several critical works. [VC]

NIANE, Djibril Tamsir (b. 1932). A historian committed to decolonizing African history, Niane was born in Guinea but has taken Senegalese nationality. In his best-known literary work, *Soundjata ou l'Épopée mandingue* (1960), he recounts the story of the legendary founder of the Mali empire, as told to him by a traditional story-teller. Part of a wave of literature which sought to propose heroic models to the African people during the independence struggle, Niane's epic has been likened by Western critics to the works of Homer and *La Chanson de *Roland*. In *Sikasso ou la Dernière Citadelle* (1971), Niane deals with African resistance to the French, emphasizing how the French exploited divisions between African chiefs, and making a lucid appeal for African unity. Niane's interest in the past springs from his concern for the future of Africa. His collection of short stories, *Méry* (1975), is further evidence of his sober, objective, materialist analysis of African society and its relationship with the West. He consistently contests the West's claim to a monopoly of civilization, rationality, and science. What distinguishes him from the majority of writers of his generation is his ability to expose the underlying mechanisms of society. His materialist approach enables him to deal incisively with issues such as race with an unusual lack of emotionalism. His latest contribution to African artistic ventures is the translation into Bambara of the scenario of *Sembène's film, *Samory*.   [FNC]

NICOLAY, Nicolas de (1517–83). French traveller, soldier, artist, and royal cartographer; his topographies of the French provinces, commissioned by *Catherine de Médicis, were unpublished in his lifetime, but the lively account of his travels, *Navigations et pérégrinations orientales* (1567), was translated into five languages; Nicolay's illustrations of local costume are particularly fine.   [MJH]

NICOLE, Pierre (1625–95). French moralist and theologian. Having studied philosophy and theology, he became a part-time teacher in the 'Petites Écoles' of *Port-Royal. He wrote textbooks and collaborated with Antoine *Arnauld in writing the *Logique de Port-Royal* (1662). He contributed to the Mons New Testament [see BIBLE] and provided *Pascal with material for the *Lettres provinciales* (1656–7), which he also translated into Latin. Somewhat timorous as well as intelligent, he was less militant than Arnauld, with whom he drafted *La Perpétuité de la foi de l'église catholique touchant l'Eucharistie,* (1669–74). In *Les Imaginaires* (1664 onwards) he defended *Jansenism, although he did not share the Jansenist view of grace. He is also credited with the Jansenist distinction between the *question de droit* and the *question de fait*.

His opposition to mysticism in *Les Visionnaires* (1667) and *Traité de l'oraison* (1679), together with his refutation of *Quietism in 1695, indicate the increasing influence of Cartesianism on his thinking. From 1671 onwards he published the famous *Essais de morale*—moral and religious treatises, commentaries on the Bible, etc. Although briefly in exile with Arnauld and others, he characteristically made his peace with Church and State and was permitted to return to Paris in 1683.   [JC]

NICOLE BOZON, see ANGLO-NORMAN LITERATURE, 3b and 6c.

Nicomède. Tragedy by Pierre *Corneille, first performed 1651. The author proclaimed that his main intention was to depict the foreign policy of the Roman empire, but contemporaries saw in the play clear allusions to the *Fronde and the part played in it by *Condé. Nicomède, the disciple of Hannibal and son of Prusias, king of Bythinie, is threatened by the imperialist machinations of the Romans in league with his stepmother Arsinoë and his half-brother Attale. He and his betrothed, Laodice, queen of Armenia, defy their enemies with noble sarcasm; in the end, with the aid of popular support, Nicomède triumphs, and his 'générosité' wins over Prusias, Arsinoë, Attale, and even the Roman ambassador Flaminius. It is one of the best examples of the Cornelian tragedy founded on *admiration* rather than on pity and fear.   [PF]

NICOT, Jean, see DICTIONARIES, 2.

NIMIER, Roger (1925–61). The central figure of the right-wing *Hussards group of French writers, Nimier was important both as a novelist and as a literary journalist. His novels, *Les Épées* (1948), *Le Hussard bleu* (1950), and *Les Enfants tristes* (1951), cultivate a tone of harsh cynicism towards World War II and the post-war era which masks a poignant sense of emptiness. In his evocation of an impossible heroism, his work draws strongly upon the writers of the 1920s, particularly *Morand, and upon *Stendhal, for whose revival in the 1940s he was in large part responsible. As a journalist, he was a major contributor to *La Table Ronde*, *La Parisienne*, and *Arts*, and a distinguished editor of *Opéra* and *Le Nouveau Fémina*.   [NH]

NINON DE LENCLOS, see LENCLOS.

NISARD (Jean-Marie-Napoléon) Désiré (1806–88). French journalist, professor, and literary critic, a firm defender of 17th-c. classicism and adversary of the *Romantics. He produced a study of the *Bibliothèque Bleue.

NISSABOURY, Mostafa, see MOROCCO.

NIVELLE DE LA CHAUSSÉE, see LA CHAUSSÉE.

NIZAN, Paul (1905–40). From 1929 to 1939, Nizan worked hard as a Communist militant, journalist, and writer of fiction and polemical essays, to serve the joint but often warring causes of Communism and truthfulness. The son of a French railway engineer, he had performed brilliantly at the *École Normale Supérieure, where he formed a close friendship with *Sartre. He married in 1927, and in 1929 joined the Communist Party. Over the next 10 years, although entrusted with responsibilities in the cultural sphere (journalism, public lectures, a study-tour to the USSR, the organization of anti-fascist congresses), and although encouraged to stand in the 1932 elections, he suffered, like almost all intellectuals, from abiding mistrust by the Party hierarchy. Nevertheless, he silenced any doubts about his adherence until the Hitler–Stalin Pact of 1939, which he judged a betrayal of Communist efforts. He joined up, and was killed near Dunkirk in 1940.

His first published work, *Aden Arabie* (1931), is a caustic attack on imperialist capitalism, a violent, often pompous essay, in which he lacerates his own illusions as well as his enemies'. *Les Chiens de garde* (1932) are the intellectual cheer-leaders of the ruling establishment. This challenging essay asks the perennially awkward question: who does our thinking for us?

In *Antoine Bloyé* (1933) Nizan presents an upwardly mobile worker's fundamentally unlived life. Nizan's approach emphasizes personal responsibility as much as economic determinism. This novel's undeniable morbidity is rarely gratuitous, for it stems from an angry awareness of what people fail to do in order to counteract their imposed fates. The Marxist optic is a means of correcting lazy eyes.

In *Le Cheval de Troie* (1935) Nizan switches from the alienated individual to the militant group. He does not idealize them, for ideological dissension and private sexual woes complicate their solidarity. The time is that of the *Popular Front, with violent confrontations between a broad Left and fascistic street-gangs. The battles fought remain dubious, and any advance is only provisional.

His best novel, *La Conspiration* (1938), features a student group, still partly in hock and thrall to their bourgeois families and seeking different ways of escape from their *angst*. Nizan both analyses sympathetically and mocks their largely verbal activism and their ignorance of the real world. This novel benefits from an intelligent disgust with misapplied intellect, combined with a penetrating consciousness of multiple, competing conspiracies. The least anti-heroic of the group, Laforgue, survives a near-fatal illness to begin living again on more demandingly concrete terms. Of the traitor within the group, Pluvinage, Nizan writes with such understanding that, when he left the Party in 1939, he was accused by its hacks of having proved his own treachery in his fictional foray. It took the energetic championing of Sartre (notably in his preface to the 1960 edition of *Aden Arabie*) to restore him to proper recognition.

Irony was not Nizan's only mode. He wrote many passages of elegant, acerbic wit, of psychological finesse, of lyrical nature-descriptions, and of an anti-cerebral defence of the body's rights. As Sartre remarked, this revolutionary was singularly lacking in blindness. So much so that he presciently scooped Sartre in the area of problematic committed literature, and in scenes where characters subject each other to judgement via an unrelenting gaze (cf. the Sartrian *regard*). Nizan was as obsessed with the death-defying as he was with death itself.   [WDR]

See W. D. Redfern, *Paul Nizan* (1972).

NOAILLES, Anna de (1876–1933). French poet and novelist, showing a clear affiliation to the Romantic mode of personal lyricism, with an immediacy of emotional response and an energetic flow of imagery. A celebratory 'pantheistic' conflation of Nature, the universe, and God informs *Le Cœur innombrable* (1901), *Les Éblouissements* (1907), *Les Forces éternelles* (1920), and *Le Poème de l'amour* (1925). The novels chart strong emotional impulses towards religious purity or physical passion: *La Nouvelle Espérance* (1903), *Le Visage émerveillé* (1904). She also wrote evocative autobiographical and travel sketches: *De la rive d'Europe à la rive d'Asie* (1913), *Le Livre de ma vie* (1932).   [MMC]

Nobel Prize for Literature, see PRIZES.

Nobility. The nobility (*la noblesse*) was the second of the three orders, or estates, into which *ancien régime* French society was divided. In 1789 there were about 30,000 noble families—about 200,000 individuals, or fewer than 1 per cent of the population. Originally a military group, with its origins in the landowning élite of the Dark Ages and the ruling families of the era of *Charlemagne, by the 12th c. an aristocracy was identifiable as a warlike and governing class and an order in society [see FEUDALISM]. Gradually, the class of knightly retainers was admitted to the ranks of the nobility. At about the same time a clearly defined ethic emerged, based on prowess in battle, fidelity, honour, and virtue [see CHIVALRY]. Nobility had become transmissible through the male line, and the house or lineage was of vital concern to all members of the family.

From the 16th c. onwards, new elements were added to this definition of nobility. Noble culture became associated with courtly culture, as described in Castiglione's *The Book of the Courtier*, in which education, manners, and a whole concept of civility were important [see COURTOISIE]. The need to find a way of widening the ethic to incorporate as legitimate those ennobled by judicial administrative office or royal letters (as the financially hard-pressed monarchy sold titles to raise money) led to emphasis on the Renaissance concept of *vertu* as an essential trait. Above all, though, by the 17th and 18th c. nobility was a question of life-style. The gentleman should be able to live without doing demeaning manual labour or engaging in retail trade; he would be able to pursue a career at arms (but did not always do so), and would possess landed estates with lordships, and perhaps royal offices at court or

Noces

in the administration. By the late 18th c. more than half of the order could trace its noble ancestry back no further than the mid-17th c. It was thus neither a closed caste nor a class of conquerors going back to the Franks, as many in the late *ancien régime*, such as *Boulainviller and *Montesquieu, believed. Regardless of the type of nobility, whether *épée* (military) or *robe* (judicial), it was imperative to live nobly and to display the external signs of such an honourable rank in society. Here, two concepts are important: misalliance and *dérogéance*. The latter was the loss of noble status for engaging in any non-noble activity, and fear of it conditioned noble strategies. Misalliance was a term to describe marrying down, such as the joining by marriage of a noble and a rich bourgeois family.

Nobles enjoyed extensive rights and privileges. The most significant was exemption from personal *taxation, on the grounds that they paid their taxes in blood. Since the maintenance of status required independent means, nobility was ultimately defined as much by wealth as by ideology. Within the order, differences of wealth could be enormous. The provincial nobility was, in spite of complaints about its poverty, almost always the richest group in the area, even if a few of its members were relatively poor *hobereaux*. But provincial houses could rarely compete in terms of wealth with the grand houses drawing revenue from extensive properties in several provinces, court offices and pensions, governorships, and ecclesiastical sinecures. Most dukes were vastly wealthy, and by their presence at *court were well able to defend their family interests. By the 18th c. formerly bitter conflicts between robe and sword had lost their force; except at court the distinction was now usually one between careers. The several sons of an aristocratic household might go, one into the army, another to an office which the family might have held for generations, and a third into the Church.

The power structures and business of politics were profoundly aristocratic. The upper echelons of the judicial and financial administration as well as most of the ecclesiastical hierarchy and virtually all posts at court were the preserve of the nobility. The social prestige of the class combined with political and financial power to produce a vastly powerful and deeply entrenched élite. Not only was the political system dominated by nobles, but so too was the financial one, as surplus wealth was channelled into the profitable state finances. Nobility was abolished in June 1790, but was revived by *Napoleon, who also created new titles such as baron. Both before and after the Revolution usurpation of noble status was frequently attempted, often facilitatated by the popular misconception that a 'de' before the name was proof of nobility.   [PRC]

See J. Meyer, *La Noblesse bretonne* (1972); G. Chaussinand-Nogaret, *La Noblesse au XVIIIe siècle* (1976).

Noces, see JOUVE.

NODIER, Charles (1780–1844). French writer. His father was an active *Jacobin; he himself lived through the Revolution at Besançon and was deeply marked by the Terror. After various unsuccessful efforts at earning his living (as secretary, as government official in Illyria, where he encouraged the study of folk literature and tradition), in 1824 he became librarian of the *Bibliothèque de l'Arsenal in Paris, where he maintained an important literary salon [see ROMANTICISM, 2]. He was elected to the Académie Française in 1833.

A precursor and patron of the Romantic movement (its 'pilot' until *Hugo wrested leadership from him), Nodier dabbled in entomology, was an active and learned bibliophile, a philologist, and lexicographer. He stands out in his generation primarily, however, because of his fascination with folklore, the supernatural, the oneiric, madness, and the *vox populi*; these interests enriched many of his tales. He foreshadows both *Sand and *Nerval, but usually treats his themes in a somewhat playful manner. Yet his deep concern with violence, with incest and forbidden love, etc., have made him a happy hunting-ground for psychoanalytical criticism.

His major works include: his first novel, *Le Peintre de Salzbourg, journal des émotions d'un cœur souffrant* (1803), in the Werther mode; *Jean Sbogar* (1818), about a noble and unconventional Illyrian bandit; *Thérèse Aubert* (1819), a tragic tale of love with the Vendée revolts as background. But he is best known for his fantastic tales such as *Smarra, ou les Démons de la nuit* (1821), a nightmarish tale marked by reminiscences of the guillotine, combined with sadistic sexuality, vampirism, and echoes of Apuleius; it is typical of Nodier's frenetic mode. *Trilby, ou le Lutin d'Argail* (1822) is set in an ancient and fanciful Scotland where the troll Trilby brings fortune to a fisherman and his wife, and falls in love with the latter; the passion is reciprocated, but a local monk exorcizes the troll, and the wife dies. *La Fée aux miettes* (1832) is a framed first-person narrative of Michel, the carpenter, interned in a Scottish insane asylum, who recounts his love for a midget fairy who turns out to be also the Queen of Sheba. Michel undergoes a number of adversities and trials, some quite nightmarish, the last one being to quest for a singing mandrake root. He exemplifies the virtues of the innocent insane, and the tale's framework sharply questions condemnations of insanity and indeed the boundaries between sanity and madness. *Inès de las Sierras* (1837) is another fantastic tale, set in Spain during the Napoleonic era, where French soldiers spend Christmas Eve in a haunted castle and there encounter the beautiful and supposedly dead Inès. The second half of the tale provides a non-supernatural explanation, recounting in the Gothic-novel mode the tribulations and madness of Inès.

Many other tales reflect Nodier's concerns with the upheavals of history and with the *Illuminist tradition. His often witty and whimsical writing exemplifies the French form of Romantic irony.   [FPB]

See A. R. Oliver, *Charles Nodier, Pilot of Romanticism* (1964); H. Juin, *Charles Nodier* (1970).

Noël, see POPULAR SONG.

NOËL, Bernard (b. 1930). French poet, novelist, and essayist. His novel *Le Château de Cène* (1971) was prosecuted for 'outrage aux mœurs'. Influenced by writers such as *Bataille, *Blanchot, and *Artaud, he struggles in his dense poems (e.g. *Treizes cases du je*, 1975) to find a language adequate to the obscurity of bodily existence.   [PF]

NOËL, Marie (pseud. of Marie Rouget) (1883–1967). Widely recognized as one of the foremost Catholic poets of her time, Noël allies a profound religious sensibility with an intense feeling for the rustic beauty of her native Burgundy. Born at Auxerre, she lived there for the rest of her life publishing collections of poems at regular intervals (including *Les Chansons et les heures*, 1920; *Les Chants de la merci*, 1930; *Chants et psaumes d'automne*, 1947). The popular success she progressively built up was further enhanced by her charming volumes of *contes* (such as *La Rose rouge*, 1961). Classical in their versification, but generally song-like in register and rhythm, Noël's poems impress by their gentle solemnity and musicality. Her *Notes intimes* (1959) contain moving meditations on her spiritual life in its everyday context.   [MHTS]

Nœud de vipères, Le. Novel by François *Mauriac, published 1932. Written shortly after the resolution of Mauriac's extended religious crisis, the novel is one of the first to reconcile opposition to bourgeois hypocrisy with ultimate salvation. It takes the form of an extended letter written by an old lawyer, Louis, to his wife Isa, in which he details every example of their incompatibility and cries out his frustration. The death of his young daughter Marie has sealed this incompatibility and he is left an embittered old miser, plotting to avenge himself on the family he loathes by disinheriting them. This project changes course with the unexpected death of Isa, the intended victim of the text, which occasions both a new direction for the novel and a reconciliation between the newly converted Louis and his son and daughter, Hubert and Geneviève. His depth of spirituality, however, is only appreciated by his granddaughter Janine: in belief as in disbelief, in death as in life, Louis remains separate from and uncomprehended by the bourgeoisie, represented by his son and daughter. With his death, however, Louis achieves the salvation which *Thérèse Desqueyroux is denied.   [NH]

Noirisme. Term generally used to describe a racialist view of culture and politics among intellectuals in *Haiti. It became a fully fledged movement after the American occupation (1915–34) and under the influence of Jean *Price-Mars. In the 1930s it could be called the Haitian brand of *négritude*, with its emphasis on the African past, the Voodoo religion, and the need for authentic black leadership. It was promoted by the journal *Les *Griots*, organ of the ethnological movement started by Louis Diaquoi, Lorimer Denis, and François Duvalier. It became the ideological basis for the Duvalier regime in 1957.   [JMD]

NOKAN, Zegoua Gbessi (Charles) (b. 1936). Writer from Ivory Coast, teacher of sociology at the University of Abidjan. His published works often mix literary genres. A militant author, he portrays revolutionaries, e.g. the heroes of the plays *Le Soleil noir point* (1962) and *Les Malheurs de Tchako* (1968), and of the novel *Violent était le vent* (1966). *Cri* (1989) contains poetry and a previously published play.   [VC]

Noma Award (for Publishing in Africa). Established in 1979, the Noma Award is open to African writers and scholars whose work is published in Africa. The prize is given annually for an outstanding new book in any of three categories: scholarly or academic; books for children; literature and creative writing. Books are admissable in any of the languages of Africa, both indigenous and European. The Award's founder is the late Shoichi Noma, formerly president of Kodansha Ltd., the Japanese publishing giant.

The Award is now recognized as the most significant and influential book prize to honour indigenously published African authors—and it has drawn attention to the scope and vitality of African publishing throughout the continent, despite the considerable problems faced, and the most adverse conditions for book production. Writers and scholars from francophone Africa have won the prize on three occasions: the first recipient was Mariama *Ba for her novel *Une si longue lettre*. In 1985 the prize was awarded posthumously to the Cameroonian writer Bernard *Nanga for his *La Trahison de Marianne*. And in 1987 a pioneering scholarly study of urbanization and social change in pre- and postcolonial Ivory Coast, *Villes de Côte d'Ivoire, 1893–1940*, by Pierre Kipré was the winner of the award.   [HMZ]

Nominalists were those medieval philosophers who held that universal terms (e.g. the species 'Man' or the genus 'Animal') do not refer to anything in reality. By contrast, Realists believed that such terms refer either to an independently existing Idea (Platonic Realism); or to an essence—e.g. the form of man-ness which makes each man a man (roughly speaking, Aristotle's position); or to all the individuals of a sort taken as a collection. Nominalism appears to have been a medieval invention. *Abélard's teacher Roscelin is reputed to have been one of the earliest Nominalists, whilst Abélard himself developed a sophisticated version of the theory. The influence of Aristotle in the 13th c. ensured that almost all the thinkers of that time, such as Aquinas, Bonaventure, and Duns Scotus, adopted some form of (sophisticated) Realism. But in the early 14th c. Nominalism was revived by William of Occam and *Buridan. The terms *nominales* and *reales* were first used by writers of the later 12th c. to describe the philosophical factions of the time. By *nominales* they usually meant those who followed Abélard's logical teaching, both about universals and other subjects; all the other logical schools were called, collectively, *reales*.   [JAMM]

NORGE, Géo (pseud. of Georges Mogin) (1898–1990). Belgian poet, born in Brussels, a relatively popular poet who dares to rhyme. There is nothing ponderous or bombastic in Norge. He is a virtuoso, full of word-play, irony, and invention. He has a genuine lyric gift (in the English sense of the word), which provides great concreteness and density. He believes in communication, saying that poetry 'is a profession, a craft, not merely an inspiration'. His poems are published in *Œuvres poétiques* (1973).   [GDM]

NOSTREDAME, Michel de, usually known as Nostradamus (1503–66). Astrologer and prophet. He grew up and lived in Provence, where he was influenced by his doctor grandfather, a converted Jew. Having studied medicine in Montpellier, he practised in Agen until forced to leave in the face of the Inquisition. He dabbled in the occult, and from 1547 gave astrological consultations (annual *Prognostications* from 1555). He was called to Blois by *Catherine de Médicis and in legend became a 16th-c. Rasputin. He had a Paracelsian view of nature, but is best remembered for his prophetic quatrains, the *Centuries*, published in 1555 and augmented later (1558, 1566). It is claimed he prophesied Louis XVI's fate, the advent of Hitler, etc.   [KCC]

Notre-Dame de Paris—1482. Novel by Victor *Hugo set in 15th-c. Paris, begun in 1828 and completed after the fall of the Restoration monarchy in 1831. Parallels with Hugo's own time are evident.

The medieval stone cathedral is transformed into a historical novel with a Romantic cast of characters: Quasimodo, the monstrous bell-ringer capable of sublime love and self-sacrifice; Esméralda, the beautiful and innocent gypsy girl who becomes the focus of the Faustian priest Claude Frollo's lust; Pierre Gringoire [see GRINGORE], a writer of incoherent *mystery plays about Nobility, Clergy, Trade, and Labour, who fails to understand the significance of the events unfolding around him; the seething Paris underclass of the Cour des Miracles that lays siege to the cathedral in a scene reminiscent of the storming of the Bastille in 1789. Amongst the most original features of the work are Hugo's dramatic handling of crowd scenes, the imaginative use of historical documentation, and a depiction of the cathedral so erudite and familiar that it caused a revolution in architectural taste. The success of this darkly moving novel was immediate, establishing Hugo as the premier historical novelist of his time. *Lamartine called him 'the Shakespeare of prose fiction'.   [SN]

Notre jeunesse, see PÉGUY.

NOUGÉ, Paul (1895–1967). A founder member of the Belgian Communist Party, Nougé brought an austere and trenchant intellect to the service of *Surrealism, founding the review *Correspondance* in 1924 with Marcel *Lecomte and Camille Goëmans and masterminding a collective strategy for the Brussels group, whose diplomatic deflection of Parisian influences fostered a deceptive blend of seeming modesty and occasional abrupt assertiveness. A biochemist by training, Nougé wrote aphoristically, producing tracts, open letters, and theoretical essays, gathered in *Histoire de ne pas rire* (1956). His assiduous commentaries on the surreal canvases of his friend René *Magritte, printed as *Les Images défendues* in 1943, are as gnomic and provocative as the paintings.   [RC]

NOURISSIER, François (b. 1927). Author of many successful novels, columnist for Le *Figaro, member of the *Académie Goncourt. Rather like late *Montherlant, his novels, often openly autobiographical, give a sad picture of unheroic existence in modern France: see *Bleu comme la nuit* (1958), *Un petit bourgeois* (1963), and *Une histoire française* (1965). His exploration of 'la pauvreté du monde et des âmes' is continued in *La Crève* (1970) and the bestseller *Le Musée de l'homme* (1978).   [PF]

Nourritures terrestres, Les. Work by *Gide, published 1897. Its narrator addresses the reader directly as 'Nathanaël', recounting to this young man the essential features of Gide's own 'rebirth' and discovery of his sexuality during his travels in North Africa. A subtly structured collection of lyrical fragments, reminiscences, poems, travel notes, and aphorisms, the book exemplifies a doctrine of *disponibilité* and *ferveur*, challenging the reader to seek personal fulfilment without concern for tradition, convention, morality, or restrictive notions of religion. It came to command such a following after World War I that Gide wrote a preface stressing the work's self-critical dimension.   [DHW]

NOUVEAU, Germain (1851–1920). Increasingly appreciated for its freshness and musicality, Nouveau's poetry (*La Doctrine de l'amour*, 1904; *Valentines*, 1922) has slowly been salvaged from the wreckage of his chaotic and moving life. He was born in the village of Pourrières (Var), where he was also to die in abject poverty. A friend of *Rimbaud and *Verlaine, he studied (and later begged for alms) in Aix-en-Provence, and held various posts as journalist and teacher, but above all he wandered from place to place: London (with Rimbaud in 1874), Beirut, Aden, Santiago de Compostela, and elsewhere. Much of his writing belongs to a period following a mystical and nervous crisis which led him to be interned for some months, and precipitated his conversion to Christianity. From this point (1891) he led the life of a tramp and composed a substantial body of verse in which various forms of love—mystical, erotic, Franciscan—are blended in the modulations of an admirably pure lyric voice, first celebrated by the *Surrealists. [MHTS]

Nouveau Roman, Le. In the mid-1950s the name 'Nouveau Roman' was given to the work of a group of writers who saw themselves as challenging the traditional conception of the novel, particularly the conventions governing plot and characterization. Opinions differed somewhat as to who counted as a *nouveau romancier*, but the central figures—at first—were Alain *Robbe-Grillet, Nathalie *Sarraute, Michel *Butor, Claude *Simon, and Robert *Pinget (Marguerite *Duras was also often associated with them, but she was never interested in belonging to a group). All these novelists wanted to create a 'new realism' that would more adequately convey contemporary reality, but each of them interpreted the task in a different way. For Robbe-Grillet it meant asserting the separateness of external reality from man's anthropocentric projections; for Sarraute, the deconstruction of 'character' to reveal a hitherto unformulated level of psychological interaction; for Butor, an awareness of the historical and cultural basis of our vision of reality, and so on.

Despite these differences, however, they were further united by a common emphasis on the *seriousness* of fiction, considered as a means of enlightenment rather than mere entertainment. This was also *Sartre's view; but the *nouveaux romanciers* disagreed with his conception of writing as an act of *political* commitment. Several vehement exchanges between him and Robbe-Grillet, Sarraute, and Simon (Butor, on the other hand, remained close to Sartre) gave the Nouveau Roman additional publicity. Indeed, one of the group's main characteristics from the beginning was the importance they attached to the theory, as well as the practice, of fiction. Sarraute's L'Ère du soupçon (1956) and Robbe-Grillet's Pour un nouveau roman (1963) played as great a role in the novels themselves in establishing the identity of the Nouveau Roman. Their status as intellectual, avant-garde writers—associated with *Barthes, for instance, who wrote articles praising Robbe-Grillet and Butor—has persisted; as the initial controversial impact of their novels wore off, they have figured on many university syllabuses, and most of the authors have lectured extensively at universities throughout Europe and America.

To some extent, the collective existence of the group was a creation of the media. After an initially hostile response, they were promoted by L'*Express

and by the *Minuit publishing house, where Robbe-Grillet's position as editor ensured that he, Butor (until 1960), Simon, and Pinget were all 'Minuit writers'. Moreover, they began to be seen as the most significant writers of the period; 1957, which saw the publication of Robbe-Grillet's La *Jalousie, Butor's La *Modification, Simon's Le Vent, and the re-edition, by Minuit, of Sarraute's Tropismes, established a dominance which lasted for at least the next decade. In 1964, for instance, the three novelists selected by the European Community of Writers to represent France at a conference in Leningrad were Robbe-Grillet, Sarraute, and Butor (although illness prevented him from attending).

But their public success led to increasing tensions within the corporate identity of the Nouveau Roman, as the differences between individual members became more difficult to overlook. This process was greatly exacerbated by Jean *Ricardou who, along with Claude *Ollier, was a slightly later recruit to the group. Ricardou was on the editorial board of the journal *Tel Quel, whose promotion of *Structuralist-*Marxist literary theory both influenced and threatened the work of the Nouveau Roman. His attempt to define the collective project of the latter more rigorously than hitherto, and the dogmatic fervour with which he imposed his definition on the group, in fact precipitated its partial break-up. The argument centred on *realism, which Ricardou, following Tel Quel, saw as complicitous with bourgeois ideology. Therefore, he argued, the Nouveau Roman should not attempt to represent or express the real in any way at all; it was no longer a question of renewing realism but eliminating it altogether in favour of a subversive free play of language. Butor and Sarraute were unable to accept this. This conflict came to a head at a conference at *Cerisy which Ricardou organized in 1971: here he consolidated his dominance over the remaining *nouveaux romanciers*, going on to organize further conferences on Simon (1974) and Robbe-Grillet (1976). But while Robbe-Grillet's fiction had always had a provocative, playfully anti-realist dimension, Simon's acceptance of the new line necessitated a major reorientation in his work in the 1970s until, finally and dramatically, he rebelled against Ricardou with the publication of Les *Géorgiques in 1981. At a conference held in New York in 1982, Simon, Sarraute, Pinget, and Robbe-Grillet himself asserted their collective rejection of Ricardou, and the futility of any attempt to prescribe what their individual novels should be like.

There is thus a sense in which the *nouveaux romanciers* outlived the Nouveau Roman. They all continued to be productive throughout the 1980s, and much of their work in this period was characterized by a revalorization of real-life individual experience, e.g. the autobiographical texts of Sarraute, Robbe-Grillet, and Simon. But this was the only remaining common feature. The emphasis on clarifying and theorizing collective aims had entirely disappeared. Ricardou continued to develop his theories under the new title of 'textique'; Butor's work had for some time ceased to be fictional in any conventional sense; Robbe-Grillet was almost exclusively concerned with the textual and filmic representation of his sexual fantasies; and the others had remained remarkably faithful to their original individual concerns. They now looked back on the earlier phases of the Nouveau Roman with some scepticism and disillusionment.

But while it is true that the collective project eventually proved unrealizable, the contribution it made to the evolution of the novel is still extremely important. The significance of the Nouveau Roman is, in the first place, that of a group of writers theorizing their own fictional practice, engaging actively with wider contemporary intellectual movements (Marxism, Structuralism, *psychoanalysis), and in the process generating a debate which, if at times confused or acrimonious, was always lively, demystifying, and insightful. Equally, they have produced some of the major French novels of the 20th c. [See NOVEL IN FRANCE, 4.]　　　　　　　　　[CB]

See S. Heath; *The Nouveau Roman: A Study in the Practice of Writing* (1972); J. Ricardou and F. van Rossum-Guyon (eds.), *Le Nouveau Roman: hier, aujourd'hui*, 2 vols. (1972); A. Jefferson, *The Nouveau Roman and the Poetics of Fiction* (1980).

Nouveaux Philosophes, Les. In the late spring and summer of 1977 an eclectic group of young French philosophers took the media by storm. André *Glucksmann's *Les Maîtres penseurs* and Bernard-Henri *Lévy's *La Barbarie à visage humain* became overnight best-sellers. Within a few months, the 'new philosophers', who had been launched by *Les Nouvelles littéraires* in June 1976, became media celebrities in Europe and America (*Time* devoted a cover story to them). In addition to Lévy and Glucksmann, the group included Jean-Marie Benoist, Guy Lardreau, Christian Jambet, Jean-Paul Dollé, Michel Guérin, Philippe Némo, and Maurice *Clavel.

Critics accused these 'disc jockeys of ideas' of 'philosophical marketing'; *Deleuze denounced the whole phenomenon as 'a media racket mounted by the Right'. Coming from divergent political backgrounds, they nevertheless shared a common hostility towards *Marxism and the notions of progress, revolution, and the state. The success of the Nouveaux Philosophes is to be attributed less to the ideas they put forward, which date back to the 1950s, than to their timing. They appeared on the French political scene just before the parliamentary elections of March 1978, when a victory of the Left seemed imminent.　　　　　　　　　　[DM-S]

Nouvelle, see SHORT FICTION.

Nouvelle Critique, La, see CRITICISM, 4; LITERARY HISTORY, 2.

Nouvelle Droite, La. Name given to a group of right-wing French ideologists who had been in existence since the late 1960s, but attracted a good deal of media attention in 1979, at the same time as the *Nouveaux Philosophes, with whom they had much in common. They sought to forge a cultural renaissance, based on a rejection of the dominant Judaeo-Christian egalitarian tradition. The movement's claim to novelty resides in the absence from its ideology of the traditional right-wing themes of nation and Catholicism. Although it has eschewed involvement in vulgar party politics, the Nouvelle Droite is implicated in the activities of extreme-Right organizations, especially the Front National [see FASCISM]. The most prominent member of the group is Alain de *Benoist.　　　　　　　[GVR]

Nouvelle Héloïse, Julie ou la. Novel by Jean-Jacques *Rousseau, written at Montmorency and inspired by his love for Sophie d'*Houdetot. Published in 1761, it was an immediate best-seller (72 editions were published before 1800). It is written in letter form; many readers took the letters to be authentic, and Rousseau discusses this question teasingly in his second preface.

The scene is set on the shores of Lake Geneva. Julie, the loving daughter of the Baron d'Étange, falls in love with her tutor, the commoner Saint-Preux, but their wedding is prevented by her father's social prejudice. The Baron's violence causes her to miscarry. Exhorted by Julie's more playful cousin Claire and by his virtuous English friend Milord Edouard Bomston (whose own love story was omitted from the definitive version of the novel), Saint-Preux leaves for Paris. Remorseful at her mother's death, Julie agrees to sacrifice her love and marries her father's friend, the benevolent *philosophe Wolmar; she experiences a religious conversion during the ceremony. Her stricken lover now joins an expedition round the world; on his return, he finds Julie, Wolmar, and their children installed on an estate at Clarens, at the centre of a happily productive rural community. In spite of his amorous misgivings, he is admitted to the chosen company. Wolmar puts the former lovers to the test by leaving them alone; they triumph over temptation. But the idyll is fragile; Julie, who has written to Saint-Preux: 'le pays des chimères est en ce monde le seul digne d'être habité', dies willingly as a result of saving a child from drowning.

Rousseau thus combined his original story of passionate love and protest against the social order with an edifying tale of moral and social regeneration, even making the union of Julie and Wolmar an emblem of the reconciliation of religion and philosophy. Many letters express ideas dear to the author, such as Saint-Preux's report on the happy Swiss mountain-dwellers or his condemnation of the Paris opera. The *ménage à trois* embodies one of Jean-Jacques's dreams, and the patriarchal world of

Clarens is a vision of the happy state denied to him, an ideal blend of nature and culture. [PF]

Nouvelle Revue Française, La. The initials *NRF* on the cover of this famous French review have come to symbolize contemporary trends in literature, thought, and art. From its beginnings it has always been anxious to keep up the high standard of its contributions, maintaining its independence of any particular literary fashion, artistic school, or political slants, and jealously—though not always successfully—trying to guard its intellectual freedom. The *NRF* soon became a fundamental reference-point in the cultural scene, leading Otto Abetz, German ambassador in Paris, to state that: 'Il y a trois forces en France: le communisme, la grande banque, et la *NRF*.'

The journal began seriously in 1909. The driving force behind the venture was *Gide, who thought it was imperative that the new writing which was replacing *Symbolism should have a mouthpiece, after the closure of the review *L'Ermitage* in 1908. The founder members were *Schlumberger, *Copeau, Marcel Drouin, André Ruyters, *Ghéon, and Gide. They sought to encourage a new form of classical writing, sober, restrained, intelligent, rational, free from any constraints of ideology. The *NRF* encouraged new writers, and proved a magnet to those seeking acceptance into Parisian cultural life. It published extracts from new fiction, critical articles on art, music, ballet, and opera, and launched the careers of a whole host of writers, among whom were *Romains, *Giraudoux, *Duhamel, *Saint-John Perse, *Thibaudet, *Alain, and *Ponge—to name but a few from an endless list. It failed to recognize the genius of *Proust, however, and would have lost him but for *Rivière. One of its important features was the *Notes*, where well-known critics and thinkers kept readers up to date with all that was new and fashionable on the cultural scene.

The blackest and most controversial period in its existence was during the *Occupation, when the Germans wanted it to continue for propaganda purposes. Under the direction of *Drieu la Rochelle, it became an instrument for collaborationist writing from 1940 to 1943, thus compromising its cherished ideal of freedom from ideology. Its contributors during this period included *Giono, *Jouhandeau, Fabre-Luce, *Aymé, *Montherlant, Gide himself, and Ramon *Fernandez.

Having been associated with cultural collaboration, the famous review disappeared for a time, to rise again in 1953 with a new title, *La Nouvelle Nouvelle Revue Française*, once more directed by *Paulhan aided by Marcel *Arland. It has now reverted to its original title. It has tried to remain faithful to its original ideals. What has changed are the names of the contributors: *Le Clezio, *Lainé, *Tournier, *Sarraute . . . [ET]

Nouvelles de la République des Lettres, see BAYLE.

Nouvelles ecclésiastiques. This clandestine *Jansenist periodical, founded in 1723, survived many attempts to suppress it; it continued to appear until 1803.

Nouvelles françaises, Les, see SCARRON; SOREL, C.

Nouvelles Impressions d'Afrique, see ROUSSEL.

Nouvelle Vague. A term originally coined by Françoise *Giroud in *L'*Express* to describe the movement that from 1958-9—the years in which Chabrol, *Godard, *Resnais, and *Truffaut released their first feature films—revolutionized the French cinema. Inspired by the vitality of the Hollywood 'B' movie, the wider availability of equipment suitable for location filming, and the self-conscious iconoclasm of *Existentialism, the new directors showed a fierce determination to establish film as the cultural equal—if not the superior—of more 'respectable' art-forms such as the novel. Most of them had worked as film critics (generally for *Cahiers du cinéma*); all had spent much time in the Paris *Cinémathèque. Their trademarks included widespread use of the jump-cut (moving abruptly from the beginning of an action to the end), uncoupling of the image and the soundtrack (helped by almost universal location filming), and a rejection—often (as with Truffaut) contemptuous—of the older school of 'literary' cinema with its stress on décor and plot. Financial reasons determined all this as much as aesthetic ones: the Nouvelle Vague made low-budget filming outside the orbit of the big studios a reality for many.

Its major directors not listed separately were Claude Chabrol, influenced by Hitchcock and fond of lampooning the provincial bourgeoisie (*Le Beau Serge*, 1958; *Que la bête meure*, 1969; *Les Noces rouges*, 1973), and Jacques Rivette, whose convoluted stories-within-stories evoke the *Nouveau Roman or even *Perec (*Paris nous appartient*, 1961; *Céline et Julie vont en bateau*, 1974). Chris Marker, Jacques Demy, and Jacques Rozier are other important figures associated with the movement, though since it never issued a manifesto or formally constituted itself it is a matter of opinion who is or is not a 'Nouvelle Vague director'. By the same token, it is difficult to say when the Nouvelle Vague ceased to exist; *May 1968 and the Cinémathèque affair brought its main figures together in action, but their film-making practices had already begun to diverge widely. Its continuing influence is, however, shown by the fact that in 1990 Godard made a film—starring Alain Delon, an actor never associated with the movement—with the title *Nouvelle Vague*. [KAR]

See J. Monaco, *The New Wave* (1976).

Nouvel Observateur, Le. This weekly, sired out of *France Observateur* (1950), first appeared in November 1964. Jean Daniel, formerly of *L'*Express*, ran the journal as a left-of-centre news magazine, distinguished for its fine writing, from the 1960s to the 1990s. It played the Socrates of the Left: throughout the 1960s and 1970s it battled for the birth of a new Left, over and above the rivalries of existing parties and politicians. In 1981 Daniel hailed the accession of François *Mitterrand as president of the Republic. In its cultural pages, *Le Nouvel Observateur* has done much to stimulate and reflect cultural innovation in France. [MP]

NOVARINA, Valère (b. 1942). French playwright, whose prolific output is remarkable for its torrential verbal inventiveness, seeming to defy theatrical production—yet his plays have been acted with considerable success. *Théâtre* (1989) contains several early texts; see also *Le Discours aux animaux* (1987), *Je suis* (1991), and the manifestos gathered in *Le Théâtre des paroles* (1989). [PF]

Novel in France, The [for other francophone countries see relevant entries]

1. Romance and Novel before 1700

French has only one term, *roman*, for the English 'romance' and 'novel'. The French novel both continues the medieval *romance and defines itself against it. In the 16th c., romance is best represented by *Amadis de Gaule*, the butt of Cervantes's mockery in *Don Quixote*, the founding text of the modern novel. *Rabelais's unclassifiable work can be seen both as an 'anti-*roman*' in its parody of epic and romance, and (with Bakhtin) as a novel in its bringing together of the varied and conflicting voices of contemporary society.

Similarly, one important strand in the 17th-c. novel is the comic tradition, though this comes nowhere near the greatness of Cervantes or Rabelais. The best examples are Sorel's *Francion* and *Le Berger extravagant*, Scarron's *Roman comique*, and Furetière's *Roman bourgeois*; these novels, all written by men, mock the heroic or romantic pretensions of contemporary fiction, giving an often grotesque image of the reality of ordinary life.

The very existence of such novels, as of *Boileau's skittish *Dialogue des héros de roman*, shows the continuing popularity of romance, which had flourished from the end of the *Wars of Religion. In the 1620s Jean-Pierre *Camus began a series of spiritual romances in which tragic events are meant to give the lie to the illusions of profane fiction. Probably the most influential novel of the century, however, was d'Urfé's pastoral *L'*Astrée*; equally popular were the *romans héroïques* of *La Calprenède, *Gomberville, and Madeleine de *Scudéry. These immense narratives of love and adventure, set in idealized pastoral or classical worlds, often appealed (e.g. *Clélie*) by reason of their patient analysis of emotions and their transposition of *salon discussions.

The same concerns are visible in the shorter works set in the recent past which became popular around 1660. Called *nouvelles historiques* by their contemporaries [see SHORT FICTION], these are often misleadingly seen as the 'beginning of the French novel', in particular the one 17th-c. work of fiction to achieve classic status, Lafayette's *La *Princesse de Clèves*. This stands out by virtue of its clear-eyed concentration on the problems of love and marriage, but 'les désordres de l'amour' are also the central subject of the novellas of *Segrais (with the duchesse de *Montpensier) and *Villedieu, and of the intense *Lettres portugaises*.

2. Eighteenth Century

The novel, not being a genre vouched for by antiquity, was the object of suspicion and some contempt in the period of *classicism. It was a corrupting influence, concerned with love at the expense of more serious matters, and it was guilty of presenting fictions as historical truths. In 1670 *Huet had defended it as a poem in prose, but throughout the 18th c., as more and more novels were written [see BIBLIOTHÈQUE UNIVERSELLE DES ROMANS], novelists continued to worry about the authenticity of their work. It is revealing that the dominant forms were the *memoir-novel and the *epistolary novel, where fiction can be presented as a 'real-life' document (Rousseau deliberately entertained such confusion about his *La *Nouvelle Héloïse*).

There are separate entries for both the memoir-novel (illustrated above all by *Lesage, *Marivaux, *Prévost, *Crébillon *fils*, *Duclos, *Diderot, *Restif, and *Sade) and the epistolary novel (practised with varying degrees of success by *Montesquieu, *Graffigny, Rousseau, *Riccoboni, and *Laclos, among others). Third-person narratives were unusual at this time, and few if any display the narrative stance of a Fielding or of the major 19th-c. novelists. Diderot's *Jacques le fataliste*, largely in dialogue form, is a unique exploration of the possibilities of the novel.

Both social and psychological observation characterize the 18th-c. novel. Writers such as Lesage, Diderot, and Marivaux devote themselves to evoking ordinary contemporary life, the life of the city, the road, and the inn, of the different social classes, while the psychological concerns of Lafayette are taken further by Marivaux, Riccoboni, Crébillon, Laclos, and many others. In the last two writers, as in Duclos, Restif, and particularly Sade, there is a *libertin* element characteristic of this period [see also DULAURENS; FOUGERET DE MONBRON; LOUVET DE COUVRAY; EROTICISM AND PORNOGRAPHY]. Often, as with Diderot and Sade, the *libertin* strain is allied with the 'philosophical', and throughout the century writers use fiction for persuasive purposes, the most striking examples being Fénelon's modern didactic epic, *Télémaque*, Montesquieu's *Lettres persanes*, *Voltaire's stories, and *La Nouvelle Héloïse* (where a passionate romance grows into a novel of ideas).

3. Nineteenth Century

Sociological and technological changes brought a huge growth in the novel-reading public in this period. Appealing to a wide audience, writers such as *Pigault-Lebrun or *Ducray-Duminil launched what *Sainte-Beuve was to describe superciliously as 'la littérature industrielle' (*Stendhal, thinking of writers like Madame de *Genlis, wrote equally scornfully of the 'roman de femme de chambre'). New *periodicals such as *Girardin's La Presse allowed for the rise of the best-selling *romans-feuilletons of *Sue and others. Then bookseller-publishers (*Hetzel, *Hachette) improved the marketing of inexpensive novels, using such outlets as the new railway stations (whence the idea of the 'roman de gare'). Nor was there an unbridgeable gap between popular and literary novels; *Madame Bovary was first published serially, *Balzac, *Dumas père, *Zola, and *Verne profited from the new system to achieve earnings unthinkable for their 18th-c. predecessors. The 19th and 20th c. saw such a large and varied production of novels in France that it is only possible here to indicate some of the main writers, tendencies, and sub-genres.

The early years of the 19th c. saw several remarkable novels of individual experience, often written in the first person, usually about love (*Chateaubriand, *Constant, *Senancour, *Staël); this line was later developed by *Musset, Sainte-Beuve, and *Fromentin. The dominant type, however, was the novel where a number of powerful figures are seen in a broad social context; the writer's ambition was to be for modern society what Walter Scott was for the past, chronicling its conflicts, diversity, and evolution. This tradition is best represented in the first half of the century by Stendhal and, above all, Balzac, who was the first to conceive of a whole collection of novels forming a unified 'comédie humaine'. *Sand's stories of rural life are likewise contemporary chronicles, but her novels are generally more personal and more idealistic.

Something of the same realistic ambition is present in *Flaubert, though he repudiated the label of *Realism adopted by *Champfleury and *Duranty, and has been most influential as the precursor of the modern art novel, concerned above all with the language and the difficulties of representation. His disciple *Maupassant and other *Naturalists (the *Goncourt brothers, A. *Daudet, *Huysmans, and, by far the greatest, *Zola) concentrated on the depressing side of contemporary life, depicting victims rather than heroes. At the same time, following *Bernardin de Saint-Pierre and Chateaubriand, novelists (*Loti, Verne) were turning to more exotic scenes.

History was a prime source of colour and excitement. Many writers used the novel to explore the national past (*Vigny, *Mérimée, Balzac, Dumas, *Erckmann-Chatrian). *Hugo in particular spans French history from the Middle Ages (*Notre-Dame de Paris) to the early 19th c. (Les *Misérables, one of the greatest of French novels). The political commitment of much of Hugo's work is found in very different forms in the work of Sand, *Vallès, and *Darien.

4. Twentieth Century

In the 20th c. classification becomes very difficult, and the placing of writers in what follows could easily be challenged. Certain popular sub-genres are easily identified, including *detective fiction, whether in the French or American mode, the *roman noir, and *science fiction. The *roman d'aventure is a more composite category; in the novels of *Malraux or *Saint-Exupéry it becomes something more ambitious than a story of heroic action.

Historical fiction has been less important than in the 19th c., though one can cite the work of *France and *Yourcenar, among others. The chronicle of more or less contemporary life continues to attract writers and readers. A special development was the *roman-fleuve practised in the early 20th c. by *Martin du Gard, *Rolland, and *Duhamel. Other novels with a strong element of social or political observation include those of J. *Renard, *Aragon, *Dabit, *Nizan, *Guilloux, and *Curtis—and in a more fantastic vein the early work of *Céline, who in spite of political opprobrium has emerged as one of the most important novelists of the century. A particular place is occupied by the 'regional' novel; see e.g. the fiction of *Pergaud, *Aymé, *Pourrat, *Clancier, *Bosco, to whom one might add *Mauriac and *Giono, if the label did not seem too limiting for their work.

The figure who dominates the landscape of the 20th-c. novel is Proust, though his solitary eminence was not immediately apparent. Though *A la recherche du temps perdu found no direct imitators, it was to be crucially important for the *Nouveau Roman. At first, however, it was seen as belonging to the tradition of social observation and psychological analysis. A concentration on individual psychology is also evident in such different writers as *Bourget, *Colette, *Radiguet, Mauriac, *Green, and *Drieu la Rochelle. In some cases the exploration of inner worlds leads into a more fantastic, poetic world. Alain-Fournier's Le *Grand Meaulnes is an influential novel of this kind, as are the very dissimilar works of *Giraudoux, *Gracq, *Cocteau, *Breton, *Mandiargues, *Des Forets, and *Vian.

A feature of much 20th-c. fiction, including some of that already mentioned, is its philosophical or ideological nature. This is already evident in *Barrès and *Gide, both crucial figures for many writers in the first half of the century. From 1920 novelists including Malraux, Drieu, Mauriac, *Bernanos, Saint-Exupéry, *Sartre, *Beauvoir, and *Camus used the genre to raise metaphysical, moral, and political questions, and sometimes to suggest answers. Sartre and his allies proposed a politically committed novel [see ENGAGEMENT], usually on the side of the Left [see e.g. VAILLAND]; against this, writers such as the *Hussards group defended a 'non-aligned' (often right-wing) stance.

Novembre

Against both of these, the 1950s saw the rise of the apolitical Nouveau Roman. Rejecting a caricatural 'roman balzacien', the writers grouped under this label followed the self-reflexive, experimental line which springs from masters including Flaubert, Proust, *Roussel, Céline, Gide, and *Queneau. As important as the classic Nouveau Roman group (*Butor, *Robbe-Grillet, *Sarraute, C. *Simon, *Pinget) are such explorers of the possibilities and limits of the genre as *Beckett, *Blanchot, G. *Bataille, *Duras. A particularly striking phenomenon of the 1980s was the rise to prominence of Perec, whose La *Vie mode d'emploi is widely praised as one of the great novels of the century.

The Nouveau Roman was the last great movement to affect French fiction; with its critical approach to traditional story-telling, it seemed to some to portend the 'death of the novel'—a recurring phrase in recent decades. But the novel has not died; indeed, it continues to dominate the literary scene to excess, and captures almost all the important *prizes. In recent decades francophone novels from abroad have been at least as interesting as those produced in France. In France itself, the novelists who have attracted most critical attention since about 1960 include *Cixous, *Echenoz, *Ernaux, Hervé *Guibert, *Le Clézio, *Modiano, Christiane *Rochefort, *Tournier, and *Wittig. Such a list is bound to be invidious, but it suggests something of the continuing variety and vitality of the genre. [PF]

See H. Coulet, *Le Roman jusqu'à la Révolution*, 2 vols. (1967); M. Raimond, *Le Roman depuis la Révolution* (1967); M. Robert, *Roman des origines, origines du roman* (1972).

Novembre, see FLAUBERT.

Noyers de l'Altenburg, Les, see MALRAUX.

NUGUET, Émile (1864–1927). Poet whose finely crafted lyrics, collected in a series of slim volumes (*Éveils*, 1887; *Efflorescences*, 1895; *Le Pain des jours*, 1910; *Évaporations*, 1919), celebrate with an almost Gidean *ferveur* the joys and sorrows of an intensely private life, spent among the broad fields and simple people of his native Beauce. Appreciated in his day by *Valéry, but vilified by the *Surrealists, he is now remembered only by a small number of enthusiasts. [PF]

Nuits, Les, see MUSSET.

Nuits de Paris, Les, see RESTIF DE LA BRETONNE.

O

OBALDIA, René de (b. 1918). French writer, born in Hong Kong. Best known as a playwright, he has also written poems and novels. His plays resemble *Ionesco's in their verbal playfulness, though with narrower metaphysical horizons. They have an expansive comic force created by pursuing an absurd proposition to its logical limits. In *Genousie* (1960) it is the substitution of an imaginary language for French; in *Du vent dans les branches de sassafras* (1965), an accident-prone cowboy; in *Le Cosmonaute agricole* (1965), a spaceman falling to earth in a farming community. The latter is more typical of his later works, such as *Deux femmes pour un fantôme* (1971), where the fantasy is rooted more in satire of the modern world. [DWW]

Oberman (later *Obermann*) (1804). Epistolary novel by *Senancour, in which the deeply introspective hero, Oberman, having suffered disappointment in love, has retreated into the solitude of nature, where he writes of his spleen and despair. Its date of publication, together with its subject-matter and mood, inevitably place it alongside Constant's *Adolphe* and Chateaubriand's *René* as one of the key works exemplifying the *mal du siècle*. The influence of *Rousseau and *Bernardin de Saint-Pierre is evident. Despite its obvious affinities with other texts, *Oberman* remains one of the strangest and most individual works of French literature. Its intensity, austerity, and bleakness make it virtually inaccessible to most readers, but for those sensitive to Oberman's melancholy, lethargy, and nihilism, it retains a dark and insidious appeal. [BR]

OBEY, André (1892–1975). Dramatist, man of the theatre, and resident playwright of Michel Saint-Denis's Compagnie des Quinze (1930–4), for whom he wrote six plays. His ambition was to revive a form of poetic drama in which classical, biblical, and national myths could be reworked and made relevant for 20th-c. audiences by exploiting the company's disciplined ensemble playing and its use of stylized sets, rhythmic movement, mime, and choral speaking. *Noé* (1931) retains a certain folk vitality. Later plays likely to survive include *L'Homme de cendres* (1949), a version of the Don Juan legend, and *Lazare* (1951). [SBJ]

Occitan Language and Literature (Medieval). 'Occitan' is the name now most widely used to refer to the speech of an area comprising much of southern France and extending into northern Italy. It is famous for two main literary movements, widely separate in time: the court literature of *fin'amor created in the 12th and 13th c. by the *troubadours; and the 19th-c. revival pioneered by *Mistral.

Although now generally thought of as a variety of French, in the Middle Ages the *langue d'oc was considered a language in its own right, alongside the *langue d'oïl* (northern French) [see HISTORY OF THE FRENCH LANGUAGE]. The name Occitania was coined in the 13th c. following the Albigensian Crusade, a war waged under the banner of crusade but which resulted in the effective annexation of the south by the French Crown [see CATHARS]. Before then, the principal regions of the south (Poitou and Aquitaine, the county of Toulouse, and the county of Provence) enjoyed considerable political independence, and were more closely allied with Spanish courts or, following the marriage of *Eleanor of Aquitaine to Henry II Plantagenet, with those of the *Anglo-Norman empire than with those of northern France. Recent years have seen a growing desire among some Occitanians to return to the cultural and linguistic autonomy of the south which characterized the early Middle Ages.

Confusingly, Occitan is sometimes referred to by other names. Early scholars of the medieval language considered it to be the closest to Latin of the romance vernaculars, and baptized it *roman*. Under the influence of Mistral and his followers, the term *provençal* gained wide acceptance, and is still used by many scholars. A disadvantage of this term, however, is that it suggests identification with the county of Provence. In fact, the earliest troubadours came not from the east of the Occitan-speaking domain but from its extreme west: Poitou and Aquitaine. The literary movement spread eastwards gradually, with other early poets coming from the Limousin and the Auvergne. Their literary language and that of their successors, though not to be identified with any one local dialect, is closest to that of the Limousin.

Although the troubadours are the most famous poets composing in medieval Occitan, there are a few narrative works which pre-date the earliest-known troubadour, *Guilhem IX (1071–1126). A vernacular *Chanson de sainte Foy, concerning the patron saint of Agen martyred under Diocletian, survives from the 11th c., as does a fragment of an adaptation of *Boethius' Consolation of Philosophy. From the 12th c. we have two *chansons de geste, *Girart de Roussillon and *Daurel et Beton; and two other fragments, part of an *Alexander romance and a version of the Song of Antioch (Chanson d'Antioche) from the *crusade cycle. One of the finest literary productions of medieval Occitan is a 13th-c. *Flamenca, and there are a number of narrative works of this date, including more fragmentary *chansons de geste*, an Arthurian romance, *Jaufre, a *fabliau on the theme of adultery, a version of the *Cour d'amour, and the Vida sant Honorat. But it was *lyric poetry which established the reputation of Occitan as a literary language. From the late 12th c. onwards, Catalans (such as Guillem de Berguedà) and Italians (such as Sordello) writing in Occitan swell the ranks of the troubadours, and many poets from outside the Occitan-speaking region also try their hand at it.

From that period too, linguistic manuals were composed in order to assist novice poets to eliminate errors in their Occitan, so that they could then go on to produce their own compositions; the longest and most interesting of these is also the latest in date, the 14th-c. *Leys d'amors. Raimon Vidal, author of the earliest such manual, the Razos de Trobar, dated by its editor between 1190 and 1213, says that 'the French language is worth more, and is more suitable, for the composition of *romances and *pastourelles, but that of the Limousin is better for composing verses and *cansos and *sirventes'. In Raimon's account, this superiority seems to rely simply on authoritative precedent: the troubadours wrote a 'classical' poetry in Occitan, and this qualifies Occitan as the language of poetry. Nevertheless, medieval Occitan possesses linguistic features which certainly make it suited to lyric composition.

Troubadour poetry is formally very elaborate; although poets often use the same themes as one another, they rarely use the same metrical form as a predecessor. Formal intricacy and inventiveness, centring on rhyme, are the hallmarks of this tradition. Medieval Occitan has the advantage that both verbs and nouns possess a wide range of stressed suffixes. A poet could thus be assured of finding a large number and variety of rhymes relatively easily. For example, past participles offer a series in -a (amat, desirat, etc.); a series in -i (auzitz, chauzitz); and one in -u (volgut, mogut). Infinitives can provide masculine rhymes in -r, -er, or -ir. The existence of a case system for nouns provides derivational suffixes in -aire (nominative) in words such as amaire, 'lover', chantaire, 'singer', trobaire, 'poet'; or in -ador (oblique), such as amador, chantador, trobador; this last is still used today with the spelling troubadour. One of the commonest rhymes is furnished by a derivational suffix forming an abstract noun: amor, dolor, iror ('distress'), paor ('fear'), savor, etc. Unlike northern French at the same date, Occitan has four unstressed vowels which can appear in a final unstressed syllable (a, e, i, and o), and so add variety to feminine rhymes. In addition, the syntax of the language benefited from a relatively unfettered word order, which meant that it was just possible to compose stanzas with lines of six, five, four, three, two, and even, exceptionally, one syllable, without

forfeiting intelligibility. Finally, the vocabulary deployed in the songs had associations with religious and feudal usage (as illustrated, for example, by the Sainte Foy and the chansons de geste mentioned above). The word amor could designate love of God and/or the bond to one's overlord, as well as erotic attachment to the beloved. Similarly, fe could refer to religious faith, juridical commitment, or emotional loyalty. The key terms of lyric composition thus brought with them not only a sense of familiarity but also a weight of affective response.

The success of troubadour poetry not only inspired the composition of linguistic manuals. It gave rise to other more or less parasitic genres such as *ensenhamens, instructing *jongleurs, knights, or ladies on behaviour appropriate to their station; and to short prose works purporting to record the life of a troubadour (his *vida) or to explain the circumstances of composition of an individual song (razo). Although the content of these works is generally suspect from the point of view of the modern historian, they provide an interesting insight into the way 13th-c. readers interpreted troubadour poetry. Another literary by-product of the troubadours was the *Breviari d'amor by Matfre Ermengaud, a late 13th-c. encyclopaedic treatise studded with lyric quotations.

This tradition of reception and commentary outlived the productions on which it was based. At the start of the Albigensian Crusade (1209) vernacular court poetry was flourishing. It was recruiting new kinds of poets, notably women (the *trobairitz) and writers from the bourgeoisie or abroad. It was experimenting with new genres, such as the partimen or *jeu parti. And it was attracting new audiences: the very small number of courts which had patronized poets in the early 12th c. had grown continuously as the prestige of troubadour poetry increased. But the effect of the Crusade seems to have been to stifle these courts. Troubadours who lived through the Crusade complain of oppression by the northern French, and repression by the clergy—particularly the Inquisitors—who were perceived as their agents. A long and very fine chronicle in the manner of a chanson de geste, the *Canso de la crotzada, details the course of this war, highlighting, in its second part, the unjust sufferings of the supporters of the house of Toulouse. With its court infrastructure largely dismantled, Occitan literature became increasingly academic and nostalgic. The scholar-poets and commentators of the later 13th c. and beyond are, however, our great benefactors, since to their diligence we owe much of our knowledge of their more illustrious predecessors. [SK]

See J. Anglade, Histoire sommaire de la littérature méridionale au moyen age, des origines à la fin du XVe siècle (1921); R. Lafont and C. Anatole, Nouvelle Histoire de la littérature occitane (1970–1).

Occitan Literature (Post-Medieval). In the age of printing, literature in the six main dialects of the *langue d'oc* (Gascon, Languedocien, Provençal, Limousin, Auvergnat, and Provençal Alpin) is dominated by a few great authors, mainly poets. Yet hundreds of minor writers also made distinctive contributions. The reluctance or inability of many to publish in their lifetime complicates the pattern of recognition and influence.

In the 16th c., political, economic and social factors ensured that French continued to oust Occitan as an administrative and literary language [see HISTORY OF THE FRENCH LANGUAGE]. Despite evidence of continuing Occitan drama, apart from one journal, some arithmetical and religious works, and students' satires (*Cansons dau carrateyron*, composed in Aix, *c.*1530), little of significance was published until Pey de Garros's fine Gascon translations of the Psalms (1565) and his heroic and bucolic *Poesias gasconas* (1567), which standardized Gascon spelling. There followed a Provençal renaissance in Aix and Marseille, heralded by the fanciful *Vies des plus célèbres et anciens poètes provençaux* (1575) of Jean de Nostredame (brother of Michel de *Nostredame). This renaissance included poets less sober, more erotic and carnivalesque than Garros, such as Robèrt Ruffi, Miqueu Tronc, Pèire Paul and, above all, Loïs Bellaud de la Belaudiera (1543–88). Languedoc as yet produced little in Occitan save four volumes of crude though pedantic verse (1579–83) by the Protestant ex-soldier Auger Gaillard.

Between 1600 and 1660 gallicization continued despite some hostility to the crown after 1610 and intermittent opposition at the *Jeux Floraux in Toulouse. By virtue of its location, wealth, and compliance with royal authority, this city assumed a central role in the spreading Occitan renaissance. It attracted the Gascon poets Bertran Larade (b. 1581), a lawyer who won no prizes for his lively baroque love poetry, and Guilhem Ader (?1567–1638), a doctor who wrote verse homilies and a patriotic encomium of *Henri IV, *Lou Gentilome gascoun* (1610). Hailed as the foremost poet of Toulouse was Pèire Godolin (1580–1649), author of *Ramelet moundi* (1617), comprising festival poems and 16 burlesque prose prologues to ballets. In Montpellier his equivalent was Isaac Despuech (d. 1642), in Aix Glaudi Brueys (*fl.* 1628). In Agen Francés de Corteta (1586–1667) wrote a farce and two pastoral comedies, all unpublished and apparently unstaged in his lifetime. Aix and Béziers were important centres of theatrical activity.

The period 1660–1789, marked by Bourbon rule, harsh taxation, famine, and *Camisard revolt, produced a number of minor Occitan writers. A Toulousain school followed Godolin until 1694; in Provence, theatre flourished, as did *pastoral in Languedoc and Marseille. Joan de Cabanes (Aix, 1654–1717) wrote verse narratives, comedies, satires, and prose tales, still largely unpublished. Cibran Despourrins (Accous, 1698–1759) composed attractive songs in the Béarnais dialect, and priests throughout Occitania produced religious verse, especially carols. Two clerical authors stand out: in Languedoc, the impoverished anti-Voltairean humanist Joan-Batista Fabre (1727–83), whose voluminous writings include traditional yet original comedies, burlesques, and the classic of satirical prose *Istouera de Jan-l'an-pres*, all published posthumously; and in Rouergue Glaudi Peiròt (1709–95), read as far afield as Paris and Versailles, a lesser author of fashionably rural Rousseauesque descriptions fusing Virgilian echoes with agricultural practicality.

Despite Revolutionary hopes, the period 1789–1914 made Occitania subservient to the French nation. Yet the language continued to be widely spoken, and provincial intellectual life flourished, producing local learned societies (e.g. Béziers, Nîmes) and political clubs. After 1830, new *patois* writers emerged: revolutionary or conservative working-class authors who broke with the oral tradition, sympathizing intellectuals, and even resettled aristocrats. Against all odds, and unorganized, a second literary renaissance developed, notably in the Mediterranean coastal towns between Béziers and Marseille, but also in Bordeaux, Nice, the Toulouse region, and Béarn. Here the liberal intellectual Xavier Navarrot (1799–1862), bourgeois of Oloron and friend of *Béranger, wrote convivial and moving political songs (*Estreas bearnesas*, 1835). In the more central areas, *La Gazette du Bas-Languedoc* printed Roumanille's first critical essays [see below], while bourgeois authors like the Nîmes judge Louis *Aubanel, the Avignon academic Hyacinthe Morel and the Cévenol marquis de la Fare-Alais published Occitan works alongside working-class poets (e.g. the potter G.-A. Peiròtas of Clermont-l'Hérault) and realists such as the bitterly reactionary Victor Gelu (1806–85) of Marseille.

Meanwhile some writers worked in isolation. They included priests in Auvergne, the Gévaudan, and Limoges. 'Jasmin' (Jacques Boé, 1798–1864), the barber poet of Agen and author of *Las Papillotos* (1835), positively shunned disciples, even though his sentimental romances and, after 1830, political lyrics made him the most popular Occitan poet of his day, feted in Paris and honoured by the Pope for contributions to charity. In his preoccupation with enriching the language, his unqualified success since 'discovery' by *Nodier in 1832, and his very numerous poetry performances, he prefigures *Mistral.

Despite the increasingly rapid erosion of Occitan after 1852, an organized renaissance developed in Avignon from the meeting of Mistral and Joseph Roumanille (1818–91), the humorously moralizing writer of *Li Conte provençau* (1883), a sharp Catholic polemicist after 1848 and 1871, and father of the *Félibrige. Thanks to Mistral, this renaissance broadened after 1870 from a heterogeneous Avignon school (including Aubanel, Anselme Mathieu, and soon Alphonse Tavan, William Bonaparte-Wyse, Louis Roumieux, and Félix Gras) into a pan-Occitan organization with regional heads (*majoraux*), embracing writers as diverse as Paul *Arène, Valèri Bernard, Batisto Bonnet, Auguste Fourès, Albert Arnavielle, Arsène Vermenouze, Joseph Roux, Jean-Baptiste Chèze, Jean-François Bladé, Michel Camelat, and Philadelphe de Gerde.

Breadth inevitably brought conflict among local chauvinists, especially when spelling reforms were attempted. Enduring linguistic anarchy resulted, with friction between, on the one side, the Provençal modernists and continuers of the Félibrige, and on the other the members of the Escòla Occitana, who were based mainly in Upper Languedoc and admired the earlier local reformist poets Antonin Perbosc (1861–1944) and Prosper Estieu (1860–1939). Yet amid an increasing awareness of the minority status of Occitan after World War I, pan-Occitan federalism was revitalized by contact with Catalan nationalism in the 1920s and 1930s. It found expression in periodicals such as *Oc* (founded in Toulouse in 1923 by the Gascon Ismaël Girard) and *Occitània* (founded by the Marseille-born Charles Camproux), and in 1931 inspired the creation of the Societat d'Estudis Occitans.

However, the schismatic tendency reappeared during World War II when the Félibrige, now reactionary and responding to the Vichy government and Fascist sympathizers (notably *Maurras), was opposed by a variety of liberal and left-wing thinkers and writers, some of them Parisians seeking refuge in the 'free' zone and espousing the Occitan cause, others (e.g. Joë *Bousquet) being southerners by birth [see OCCUPATION AND RESISTANCE]. It was a coalition of French and Occitan writers (including Jean *Cassou, Tristan *Tzara, Ismaël Girard, Max Rouquette, René Nelli, and Pierre Rouquette) that secretly planned and, soon after the Liberation of France, launched the Institut d'Estudis Occitans, a major organization for the promotion of Occitan culture and research with branches throughout Occitania and in Paris.

Post-war writing has been dominated by IEO members, some of whom have transcended inter-dialectal rivalry and achieved international recognition (e.g. poets Max Rouquette, René Nelli, and Yves Rouquette, novelists Jean Boudou and Bernard Manciet, and polymath Robert Lafont). Notable among independents is the poet Max-Philippe Delavouët. Constant themes are alienation and self-awareness, cultural and linguistic *enracinement* and *déracinement*. Since May 1968, writers (including newcomers like Roland Pécout and Jean-Marie Pieyre) have endeavoured to break with tradition, truisms, and conformity, blending styles in a baroque mixture that reflects a shattered cultural identity. On a more popular level, traditional themes and contemporary political issues have been treated by Occitan singers, who have found sponsorship for their concerts and recordings (e.g. in Languedoc Claude Marti, Patric and Maria Roanet; in Limousin Jan dau Melhau; in Gascony Nadau; in

Provence Mont-Jòia). The future of Occitan literary activity depends largely on regional, central, and European Community funding and policy on minority language rights.   [PVD]

See R. Lafont and C. Anatole, *Nouvelle histoire de la littérature occitane* (1970–); P. Gardy and F. Pic (ed.), *Vingt ans de littérature d'expression occitane, 1968–1988* (1990).

Occupation and Resistance during World War II

1. History

In May 1940, after eight months of the *drôle de guerre*, Guderian's tanks crossed the Ardennes and the Meuse, and within four weeks the French armies had been defeated. In the débâcle, over eight million women, children, and old men were caught up in a nightmare *exode* towards the centre of France. There was no saving Battle of the Marne, no citizens' Valmy. Paris was declared an open city, and from Bordeaux Marshal *Pétain, aged 84, called for a cease-fire. In a sacrificial gesture he offered himself to France. It began a mythology of Pétain as the saviour of France, a conjuncture of the public's desperate need for reassurance and Pétain's own charismatic paternalism. The Armistice divided France into two major zones. In the *zone libre* at Vichy, Pétain was invested with full powers by the National Assembly, and created a new État Français, proclaiming the virtues of *Travail, Famille,* and *Patrie*. The regime launched a National Revolution based on the doctrinaire ideals of the nationalist Right, excluding Jews from civil rights, mobilizing youth, and abolishing trade unions. Vichy ruled across both zones, though subject to the German military authorities in the *zone occupée*, and the regime continued even after the Germans had occupied the whole country on 11 November 1942.

In Paris, French fascists and intellectual admirers of Nazism competed for German patronage and a dynamic role in the Nazi New Europe. Some 3,000 fought in German uniform on the Russian Front in the Légion des Volontaires Français (LVF), recruited by Jacques *Doriot, and in the south Joseph Darnand's Milice pursued Jews and Resisters with methods similar to the Gestapo. Pétain announced a policy of collaboration after his meeting and symbolic handshake with Hitler in October 1940, but what started essentially as coexistence became steadily more servile. Admiral Darlan almost took France to war on Germany's side over Syria, and in 1942–3 Pierre Laval justified the inhuman deportation of Jewish families from the Vichy zone as part of a shield policy to protect France from a possible *Gauleiter*. Vichy also collaborated, though more ambivalently, in the transfer of over 600,000 French workers to Germany under the Service du Travail Obligatoire (STO), and in 1944 the more extreme collaborators, Darnand, Déat, and the influential broadcaster Philippe *Henriot, were brought into the government. The last year of Vichy was fascist by any criterion.

From autumn 1941 Vichy was progressively rejected by the majority of the population. Pétainism survived longer. Resistance began with individual acts of defiance and freedom, notably General de *Gaulle's *appel* of 18 June 1940 from London, and grew into specialist escape and intelligence networks co-operating with the Free French or the British Special Operations Executive (SOE), and into multi-operational movements with their own clandestine press: *Combat, Libération, Défense de la France, Franc-Tireur, Cahiers du Témoignage Chrétien*, among many other titles, which marked the resilience of hundreds of small, disconnected groups in the first two years. The Communist-led movement Front National, with its activist groups Francs-Tireurs et Partisans (FTP) and party newspaper L'*Humanité*, was brought into closer rapport with the other movements by Jean Moulin, de Gaulle's special envoy, whose last achievement before his arrest, torture, and death was the Conseil National de la Résistance (CNR). The radical reforming Charter of the CNR indicated just how far the Resistance had become an alternative France, with its own publications, social services, urban *groupes francs*, and finally the *maquis*, formed in the hills and forests in 1943 and bringing together resisters on the run, anti-fascists from Spain and Central Europe, and *réfractaires* refusing STO. The *maquis* suffered tragic but heroic defeats in the mountains of Glières and Vercors, and elsewhere engaged in largely autonomous tactics of ambush and sabotage, backed by widespread community involvement throughout the countryside. The Germans, and the Milice, exacted ferocious reprisals on these communities, reaching the depths of horror with the shooting and burning of over 600 villagers at Oradour-sur-Glâne. It was June 1944, and the Germans were in full retreat. Between June and September they were driven out of France by the combined armies of the British, Americans, and Free French, and the actions of the Resistance coordinated in the Forces Françaises de l'Intérieur (FFI). The euphoria of the Liberation brought universal festivities and an extensive purge (*épuration*) of collaborators, and Vichy ministers were eventually brought back from Sigmaringen in Germany to stand trial. Due to the Free French and the internal Resistance, France emerged from the war acknowledged as one of the victorious powers.

2. Renewal and Conflict

In 1940 the first aspirations for revival seemed to share a similar vocabulary. Denis Saurat's *Regeneration* (1940) and Jean *Schlumberger's writings, both adopted by the Free French, called for cultural renewal in terms comparable to those employed at Vichy and by celebrants of the New Order, *Drieu la Rochelle, *Rebatet, and Jacques Chardonne. *Montherlant's *Solstice de Juin* (1940),

*Mounier's republication of *Esprit, *Claudel's ode to Pétain, and the article 'Retour à Molière' (1941) by Ramon *Fernandez were all statements of cultural reassertion and potential, despite, or even because of, the defeat. But the right to speak for France and for French literature was bitterly disputed. *Péguy's writings of patriotic defiance were appropriated both by nationalists at Vichy and by the first dissidents such as Edmond Michelet. Four years later Péguy's *Jeanne d'Arc* was mobilized for the *maquis*, with Jeanne's boast 'je serais chef de bande'. The historical *Jeanne was fêted first by Vichy, but increasingly by the Resistance. The myths of antiquity were diversely retold. Meanings became stipulative or covert. The authority of the word was fractured.

3. Collaborationism

Within the immediate German orbit, *Phönix oder Asche?* (Phoenix or Ashes?) was the title chosen by Bernhard Payr, head of the Nazi Literature Office, for his survey of the French literary scene in 1940–1. It was the prescriptive side of the 'Listes Otto' by which the Propaganda Abteilung banned 2,000 titles and 850 authors and translators, mostly for Jewish origins or left-wing affiliations. All the Paris publishers submitted. Payr found the language of *Céline and Rebatet crude and eccentric, but their ideas commendable. Céline's visceral *antisemitism was displayed in *Les Beaux Draps* (1941), and Rebatet's misanthropic nihilism indulged the taste for cultural masochism prevalent among the collaborationists: *Les Décombres* (1942) was the literary success of this viciously talented world. Drieu took over La *Nouvelle Revue Française* from *Paulhan, and made it into a fulcrum of the New Europe, visiting Weimar in 1941 with *Brasillach, Fernandez, Bonnard, Chardonne, and *Jouhandeau. The German exhibition 'Le Juif et la France' was reviewed in Jean Luchaire's *Les Nouveaux Temps* as 'un juste racisme', and the 'unmasking' of Jews in the theatre was personally undertaken by the envenomed critic Alain Laubreaux (alias Max Daxiat) in his column in *Le Cri du peuple* and *Je suis partout*.

4. Vichy

The approved press and literature of Vichy reflected less the German present than the glories of the French past, for which *Maurras developed his 'Uchronie', an ideal chronology to link Pétain with the *ancien régime* in a seamless continuum. His colleague Léon *Daudet was less dismissive of the recent past, and in an article on 'La Littérature de demain' (1940) gave Péguy, Claudel, *Proust, *Saint-Exupéry, and even *Gide as models. Early Vichy stressed the independence of the French literary tradition, but growing collaboration and the didactic role of Pétainism brought censorship and prescription, closing *Esprit* and dissolving the intellectual École des Cadres at *Uriage. Books were to have a nobility of moral purpose, and to celebrate familial and rural values. Maurras, Henri *Massis, and René Benjamin were Vichy's chroniclers and conscience, Henri *Pourrat and Jean de *la Varende its literary eminence, and Paul *Morand its public image as writer and diplomat. Pourrat's *Vent de Mars*, set in the countryside of the Auvergne, received the Prix Goncourt for 1941, bestowed with ceremony at Chamalières, in the heart of the region, and *Giono's *Regain* was recuperated by the regime. Outdoor life and sport became themes of revivalist fervour, and *Obey's drama spectacle *800 mètres* (1941), with music by Honegger, epitomized the 'joie de l'effort', according to Jean-Louis *Barrault, one of the main animators of the first performance at the Stade Roland Garros. The label 'Vichy' cannot be used indiscriminately to indicate all legalized publications and public performances in this period. Were it to be so, it would be attached to *Aragon's *Le Crève-cœur* (1941), Claude Vermorel's *Jeanne avec nous* (first performed 1942), *Sartre's *Les Mouches* (1943), all of which are held to have sustained ideas of resistance, and to *Valéry's *Mauvaises pensées et autres* (1942), which sought to establish the inviolability of French literature.

5. Publication and Ambiguity

Nevertheless, for certain writers any legalized publication of whatever kind did amount to compromise, not just with Vichy but with the Germans. It was argued that behind the censors lay the authority which executed the *savants* of the Musée de l'Homme in February 1942 and which perpetrated the savagery of the round-up of Jewish families at the Vélodrome d'Hiver in July 1942. The fact of publication was conditioned by these events: the only unequivocal defiance was to publish clandestinely as an act of resistance. Even silence could be misunderstood.

It is now more readily argued that ambiguity typifies much of the published work of the period, and there is a reluctance to assign all works to specific categories of thought and belief. Giono's writings, which appeared in *La Gerbe* and the *NRF*, *Anouilh's *Antigone* (1944), and Saint-Exupéry's *Pilote de guerre* (1942) all contain different kinds of ambiguity. The literary reviews *Confluences*, run by René Tavernier, and *Fontaine*, directed by Max-Pol *Fouchet in Algiers, were adept at defying the censor, and *Seghers published *Poésie* as an annual anthology, repeatedly successful in its evocation of dissidence. A greater pluralism in cultural practices under Vichy is now regularly affirmed.

6. Resistance

Publishing an underground newspaper was the most widespread collective act at the origins of Resistance. Words were action. It was the decision of Jacques Decour and Georges *Politzer to bring out a review, *La Pensée libre* (No. 1, February 1941), which inspired the first clandestine product of the Éditions de *Minuit—a run of 350 copies of *Le Silence de la mer* by *Vercors (Jean Bruller), originally intended for *La Pensée libre*. Decour's review was broken up by the Germans, and he himself arrested in January 1942 as he was preparing the first number of a larger project, *Les Lettres françaises*, finally launched in the following September.

The originators of Éditions de Minuit were Pierre de Lescure and Jacques Debû-Bridel, while the link between many literary resisters was made by Jean *Paulhan. At Minuit artisans and writers worked together as a collective; clandestine literature was process and not just product. For all its realism, Vercors's novel was more fable than document, one of the ways in which Resistance writers established a creative tension with the cause for which they were fighting. In the same way, *Triolet created in the Juliette of *Les Amants d'Avignon* (1943) an archetypal heroine, even if in fact many of the women who acted as liaison agents were not so very unlike her. The women facing torture and deportation in Claude *Aveline's intimate novel *Le Temps mort* (1944) lead lives which are both private and public, so that their struggles and the horrors they endure are seen in both personal and historic terms.

This fusion of private and public was taken to its highest literary level in poetry, which was as integral to the Resistance as counter-information and codes. Concise, using little ink or paper and easily memorized, much of the poetry of Aragon and *Éluard was functional in the same way as *Kessel and Marly's 'Chant des partisans', first printed in *Cahiers de Libération* in September 1943. Éluard's 'Liberté' was dropped in thousands from the air. But many poems went far further, consciously re-creating for the reader meanings that had been lost, recovering identity, giving new life: 'Il y a des mots qui font vivre | Et ce sont les mots innocents . . .' (Éluard, 'Gabriel Péri', 1944). This was the importance of Jean *Cassou's *33 Sonnets composés au secret* (1944) and of the anthology *L'Honneur des poètes* (1943), in which Éluard's carefully weighted poem 'Les Belles Balances de l'ennemi' first appeared, turning the German dominance round in the last line: 'Nous ferons justice du mal.' Emotive and active, Resistance poetry also re-mobilized history, legend, and locality—Paris above all, but the countryside too—breaking Vichy's monopoly of regionalism and fashioning a post-war generation of *Occitan poets.

7. Liberation and After

The significance of words under the Occupation and the fierce struggle for cultural legitimacy gave the purge of writers a central place in the retributive justice of the Liberation. Resistance intellectuals divided over the ethics and politics of the trials, *Camus, Debû-Bridel, and Claude Morgan arguing for the necessity of a purge, and *Mauriac and Paulhan warning against the use of scapegoats. Camus adjusted his position and signed the appeal for Brasillach, along with 58 others, and in August

1945 announced in *Combat* that the purges had failed and were now 'odious'.

The *épuration* at popular level was one of the elements which provoked a post-war genre of ambiguous and ironic writing about the Occupation, led by the semi-documentary *Mon village à l'heure allemande* (1945) by Jean-Louis *Bory and *Les Forêts de la nuit* (1947) by Jean-Louis *Curtis. It reached its satirical heights with *Aymé's *Uranus* (1948) and Jean *Dutourd's burlesque *Au bon beurre* (1952), and a point of bleak pessimism in *Nimier's *Les Épées* (1948). In contrast, *Chamson's *Le Puits des miracles* (1945) was a perpetuation of Resistance, and *Beauvoir's *Le Sang des autres* (1945) was received as a Resistance novel, despite her protestations. Six years later *Vailland's *Un jeune homme seul* (1951) marked the path of self-fulfilment through Resistance that the fourth volume of Sartre's *Chemins de la liberté* might well have taken. The allegory of Camus's *La *Peste* (1947) is for some debased, and for others heightened, by its symmetry with the Occupation, a literary debate which has its parallel among historians with the disagreements over the representative quality of the epic film documentary *Le Chagrin et la pitié* (1971) made by Marcel Ophuls. Equally contentious was the portrait of a peasant youth turned collaborator in Louis Malle and Patrick *Modiano's film *Lacombe Lucien* (1974).

The prevalence of myths, judgements, and deconstructions of the period in all branches of history, literature, and film during the 1970s and 1980s led Henry Rousso to discern a permanent *syndrome de Vichy*. Among specific treatments, the verve of local resistance has been captured by Jean-Pierre *Chabrol, the Cévenol novelist, in *Un homme de trop* (1958), and the experience of Jewish children has been evoked with humour and vitality in Joseph Joffo's *Un sac de billes* (1973), and with haunting poignancy by Louis Malle in *Au revoir les enfants* (1987), a film no less conclusive on the barbarity of the Holocaust than *Resnais's classic *Nuit et brouillard* (1956). Antisemitism is also at the heart of *Truffaut's film *Le Dernier Métro* (1980), one of the most convincing presentations of the personal ambiguities as well as the stark divisions of *les années noires*. [HRK]

See P. Seghers, *La Résistance et ses poètes* (1974); R. Kedward and R. Austin (eds.), *Vichy France and the Resistance* (1985); I. Higgins (ed.), *The Second World War in Literature* (1986); H. Rousso, *Le Syndrome de Vichy* (1987); J.-P. Rioux (ed.), *Politiques et pratiques culturelles dans la France de Vichy* (1988); M. Atack, *Literature and the Resistance* (1989).

Océantume, L', see DUCHARME.

Ode (from Greek *ōdē*, a poem to be sung, and thus a generic term for the lyric). In condemning the *ballade and other medieval *formes fixes* as 'épiceries', Du Bellay recommended in the *Défense*: 'Sing me

those odes, still unknown to the French muse, with a lute well tuned to the Greek and Roman lyre, and let no sound be without some mark of rare and ancient learning.' *Ronsard's five books of odes (1550–3) draw on the two large strains of odal inspiration: the Pindaric, with its mode of heroic celebration, its monumental triadic structures (strophe, antistrophe, epode), its cultivation of the sublime style, of mythological references, erudite allusion, apostrophes, invocations, and the impassioned public voice; and the Horatian (incorporating the Anacreontic), with its formal and thematic variety, epicurean leanings, quiet pleasure in the rural environment, and cultivation of the commonplace concerns of the private citizen, expressed with a mixture of affection and irony.

As the Pindaric ode developed in France, the ten-line isometric structure, the so-called *dizain isométrique classique* (ababccdeed, usually in octosyllables) favoured by *Malherbe became a privileged vehicle for exploring religious and philosophical topoi both in the 17th c. (e.g. *Racine, *Cantiques spirituels*) and in the 18th (e.g. Jean-Baptiste *Rousseau, *Odes*). One still finds this form occasionally in the odes of *Lamartine and *Hugo, but in very mixed company. The attractions of the *dizain* lie in its combination of all basic rhyme-schemes (*rimes croisées*, *rimes plates*, *rimes embrassées*); after the forward-moving developmental phase of the first four lines, the strophe reaches a fulcrum, or moment of suspension, at the couplet, before achieving the encompassing finality of the last four lines.

But alongside the Pindaric, the Horatian ode developed a multitude of shorter and often heterometric stanzas. Among these should be mentioned the 'shortened' form of the *dizain*, a *sixain* rhyming aabccb which often assumed the grander tones of the Pindaric (e.g. J.-B. Rousseau's 'Sur l'aveuglement des hommes du siècle'), but which equally addressed pastoral and amorous subjects (André *Chénier). The lighter ode reached its paroxysm with *Banville's *Odes funambulesques* (1857). Ironically this collection has among its pages, masquerading as odes, precisely those fixed forms (*rondeaux*, *triolets*, *villanelles*) decried by the Pléiade in favour of the ode. [See VERSIFICATION.] [CS]

Odéon, Théâtre de l'. Built for the *Comédie-Française on a new design with seats in the pit, this theatre opened in 1782 on a site close to the Palais du Luxembourg. It was twice destroyed by fire and rebuilt, emerging as an official theatre in the 19th c. In the 20th c. it was used by *Antoine and *Gémier, became a branch of the Comédie-Française in 1946, was the home of *Barrault's Théâtre de France from 1959, housed spectacular student meetings in *May 1968, and in 1971 became the Théâtre National de l'Odéon. [PF]

Odes et ballades, see HUGO.

Odette de Crécy

Odette de Crécy. Character in Proust's *A la recherche du temps perdu*. A *demi-mondaine*, she is loved by Swann in *Un amour de Swann* and figures as his wife in other volumes.

Œdipe. Tragedy by *Pierre Corneille, written for *Fouquet, first performed 1659. Introducing a love interest and playing down the horror, Corneille does his best to adapt the ancient legend to modern polite society. *Voltaire also wrote an *Œdipe* (1718).

Œuvre, L'. Novel by *Zola, published in 1886, the 14th in his *Rougon-Macquart* series. Set mainly in the artistic world of Paris in the 1860s, it is particularly significant as the most autobiographical work of the series, as an important *roman à clefs*, representing in fictional guise leading artistic figures of the day such as Cézanne, Monet, Manet, Pissarro, and Flaubert, and as a key text containing in the numerous discussions of art and literature by the characters many of Zola's essential ideas. The hero of the novel, Claude Lantier, son of Gervaise Macquart and Lantier from *L'*Assommoir*, is a tormented artist, torn between his vast ambitions as a painter and his love for his wife, Christine. Their child dies; Claude's work is received with hostile incomprehension and indifference; in a fit of desperation and self-doubt he hangs himself one night in front of the visionary painting of a naked woman that he has failed to complete. In this panorama of the life of the studios and salons of the turbulent period during which the *Impressionists were making their mark, Zola shows other artists to be more ready to compromise their ideals than Claude, including his closest friend, the novelist Pierre Sandoz, a thinly disguised self-portrait of a writer engaged upon the disciplined task of compiling a vast series of novels. Claude appears to be largely based on Zola's childhood friend *Cézanne, and the depiction of his failure is thought to have caused a rift between the two men.
[DB]

Œuvre, L'. Journal founded in 1904 by Gustave Téry as a monthly pamphlet (reminiscent of *Rochefort's *Lanterne* of 1868); it became a weekly in 1910 and a daily in 1915. Trenchant, left-of-centre, nonconformist, and opinionated, *L'Œuvre* married innovation in style and layout with editorial freedom that attracted journalists as different as Robert de Jouvenel (chief editor), *Séverine, and Henri Béraud. 'Idiots don't read L'Œuvre' was one promotional slogan of this daily, many of whose contributors, in the inter-war years, also wrote in Le *Canard enchaîné*. In the 1930s it reached a circulation of around 300,000. During the Occupation, under Marcel Déat's editorship, *L'Œuvre* was collaborationist.
[MP]

Œuvre, Théâtre de l', see LUGNÉ-POË.

Œuvre au noir, L', see YOURCENAR.

OFFENBACH, Jacques (1819–80), composer, see MEILHAC.

Ogier. *Chanson de geste* hero. Ogier the Dane is one of the 12 peers in *chansons de geste* associated with *Charlemagne; he has a major role, for example, in *Renaut de Montauban*, figuring as the cousin of the rebel baron Renaut. He is the chief protagonist of a long, early-13th-c. *chanson de geste* by Raimbaut de Paris, *La Chevallerie Ogier*. Here, in a plot closely modelled on *Renaut de Montauban*, Ogier's son is killed in a quarrel at Charlemagne's court by Charlemagne's own son, and when the king refuses to punish the killer, Ogier is driven into a career of exile and revolt. He and Charles are finally reconciled through the intermediacy of Turpin, when Ogier's help is needed to save France. The poem, which is manifestly a reworking of earlier material (a lost *Chanson d'Ogier de Danemarche?*), is somewhat uneven in quality but contains some magnificent scenes. Another surviving poem which takes Ogier as its hero is also a *remaniement*, by *Adenet le Roi; known as the *Enfances Ogier*, it retells in 10,000 lines the early part of Ogier's career. Ogier was one of the heroes who attracted the 14th-c. writer *Jean d'Outremeuse, who devoted to him a substantial part of his *Myreur des histors*, a text which recasts as prose 'history' the narratives of earlier *chansons de geste*. The epic hero Ogier is thought to be the legendary transformation of a historical figure, buried at Meaux and revered there as a saint.
[SK]

OGIER, François (1597–1670). Learned prior and friend of Guez de *Balzac. He was associated with the Illustres Bergers, a group of pastoral poets centred on Frénicle in the mid-1620s. He is best remembered, though, for his preface to *Schelandre's *tragicomedy *Tyr et Sidon* (1628), a spirited defence of current theatrical practice against the growing movement towards regularity in the construction of plays. He gives potent expression to a hedonist view of art—'la poésie ... n'est faite que pour le plaisir'— arguing that the more supple and irregular form of tragicomedy, which can accommodate complex plots and different registers, provides a varied, and consequently more *vraisemblable* and pleasurable, theatrical experience.
[GJM]

OLDENBOURG, Zoé (b. 1916). Russian *émigrée* whose first novels (*Argile*, 1946, and *La Pierre angulaire*, 1953) are set in the Middle Ages. Two autobiographical essays were followed by novels dealing with the Russian émigré community in the Paris of the inter-war years, in which love is a dominant theme. She is a member of the Prix Fémina jury.
[EAF]

OLIER, Jean-Jacques (1608–57), see DEVOTIONAL WRITING, 2.

Olive, L', see DU BELLAY.

OLIVÉTAN, Pierre Robert (*c*.1506–38). Compiler of the first French Protestant *Bible, published at Neuchâtel in 1535, with two prefaces by *Calvin; it owes much to the translations of *Lefèvre d'Étaples. Olivétan was probably instrumental in converting Calvin, his relative and school fellow, to the Reform. [MJH]

Olivier. One of the Twelve Peers of Charlemagne, friend of *Roland; he figures in the *Chanson de Roland* and *Girart de Vienne*.

OLIVIER, Juste, see SWISS LITERATURE IN FRENCH, 3.

OLIVIER DE LA MARCHE, see LA MARCHE.

OLLIER, Claude (b. 1922). French novelist, whose formal experimentation links him to the *Nouveau Roman. His fictional cycle *Le Jeu d'enfant* draws on his travels and includes texts mimicking and subverting a variety of traditional genres, e.g. *La Vie sur Epsilon* (1972), exploiting *science-fiction. His later writing—*Une histoire illisible* (1986), *Déconnection* (1988)—is more overtly autobiographical. [EAF]

O'NEDDY, Philothée (pseud. of Théophile Dondey) (1811–75). French poet and critic. His poems *Feu et flamme* (1833) are a good example of the writing of the *Frénétiques.

On ne badine pas avec l'amour. Play in three acts by *Musset, published 1834, first performed 1861. It is a comedy of love, full of playful writing, but it ends tragically. The heroine Camille refuses the love of Perdican who, to spite her, plans to marry a village girl, Rosette. This brings Camille to declare her love for Perdican; the scene is overheard by Rosette, who dies of grief, and the two lovers agree to part. [PF]

Opera. The French operatic tradition that dates from *Lully persists into the 20th c. It is characterized by the emphasis placed on ballet, the *merveilleux*, sensuous textures, and most importantly the subordination of the music to the text. A related feature is the use of a clear declamatory vocal style, in order that the text be understood [see also WORDS AND MUSIC]. An ironic fact about this French tradition is that, starting with Lully himself, through *Gluck, Cherubini, Spontini, Meyerbeer, and Stravinsky, so many of its principal protagonists have been foreigners.

Opera was slow to develop in 17th-c. France because of the firm entrenchment and success of both dramatic theatre and ballet. Lully's *tragédies en musique* of the 1670s successfully incorporated both these elements, by emphasizing the *tragédie* and featuring substantial ballets in all his works. From the 17th c., when Mazarin tried to convert the French to Italian opera, to Boïeldieu's chauvinistic clinging to *le genre national* (*opéra-comique*) in the early 19th c., the French resisted domination by Italian opera and maintained their distinctive national style. The respective values of Italian and French opera were one of the subjects of a continual stream of polemical literary debates that began in 1700 and were continued throughout the 18th c., more by men of letters than by composers [see GUERRE DES BOUFFONS]. The largely pro-Italian *philosophes* contributed numerous significant articles to the debate. Lully's operas remained in repertory well into the 18th c. and both *Rameau and Gluck continued in essence the tradition of giving central importance to the text. Gluck, with his emphasis on dramatic naturalness and simplicity, continued the aesthetics of the French tradition in both his operas and writings (see his preface to *Alceste* of 1769).

19th-c. Paris was very cosmopolitan. The Opéra was a fashionable place to visit and the majority of significant works performed there were not French. Although Italian opera had now fully infiltrated France, it was still performed in a separate theatre, the Théâtre Italian, where Rossini was for a time director, and drew a more aristocratic audience than the Opéra. *Stendhal was perhaps Italian opera's most passionate follower and wrote extensively on its attractions. The Opéra was also extremely popular with contemporary writers of the day and features frequently in works by both *littérateurs* and serious novelists: e.g. 'Gambera' (1837), a short story by *Balzac, has a lengthy discussion of Meyerbeer's opera *Robert le diable*. By mid-century Grand Opera, a form popularized by Meyerbeer, indulged spectacle to the point where it almost ran out of control; immense sums were spent on costumes and stage sets, while the standards of libretti deteriorated dramatically. The majority were written by Eugène *Scribe. For most of the 19th c. Paris was the musical capital of the world, and for a composer of any nationality the ultimate achievement was to have a work performed at the Paris Opéra. Verdi and Donizetti wrote works to French libretti, and even Wagner agreed to reorganize *Tannhäuser* for what turned out to be the débâcle of 1861.

Gluck's tradition, however, continued in *Berlioz's epic opera *Les Troyens* (partially staged 1863). The emphasis on spectacle is still a major feature (the opera incorporates ballets into the dramatic action) but the libretto, written by Berlioz himself, is once again of great importance. Berlioz did not agree, however, with Gluck's theory of the subordination of music to poetry, nor did he believe that Gluck had achieved it.

France's defeat in the *Franco-Prussian War was followed by a nationalistic upsurge and fostering of French music by composers such as *Saint-Saëns. However, the influence of Wagner's music and writings was also felt in France at this time, reaching a peak in the 1880s. Although Wagner influenced opera composition, he also had a remarkable effect on poets and writers, in particular *Baudelaire, *Villiers de l'Isle Adam, *Gautier and, slightly later, the *Symbolists *Verlaine and *Mallarmé.

In the late 19th to early 20th c. there were a large

number of French operas with libretti either specifically written by or based on works by important writers of the time. Often the collaboration between writer and composer was extremely close, as in the collaborations between *Massenet and Catulle *Mendès, *Bruneau and *Zola, *Debussy and *Maeterlinck, Honegger and *Claudel, *Poulenc and *Apollinaire, and *Milhaud and Claudel. The most important 20th-c. French opera is undoubtedly Debussy's *Pelléas et Mélisande (1902), based on a play of the same name by Maeterlinck. Debussy set Maeterlinck's play to music with very few alterations, and it could be argued that no other opera has managed so successfully to wed literature and music. His vocal line aims to capture the inflections and natural rhythms of the French language, and the musical techniques manage not only to capture the essence of the drama but also the Symbolist aesthetic underlying the play.

Works of mixed genres—theatre, opera, oratorio, ballet—became popular in the 20th c. One of the most important literary collaborators on works of mixed genre and on operas in the first half of the century is *Cocteau: Milhaud's opera *Le Pauvre Matelot* (1927) is a setting of a three-act Cocteau play; Stravinsky's opera-oratorio *Oedipus Rex* (1927) is a Latin translation of a text by Cocteau; Honneger's opera *Antigone* (1927) has a Cocteau text, as does Poulenc's opera *La Voix humaine* (1959). Poulenc's *Dialogues des carmélites* (1957), based on a libretto by *Bernanos, is another example of an opera in which minute attention is paid to the vocal line following the natural accentuation of the French language.

Henri Pousseur's opera *Votre Faust* (1969) questions the myth of Faust but also opera as a genre, and some of France's important contemporary composers have deliberately turned against opera for ideological reasons. Pierre *Boulez, for instance, although a famous conductor of opera, has never written one himself. On the other hand, Olivier Messiaen's three-act, five-hour-long *Saint François d'Assise* was performed at the Paris Opéra in 1983. The fact that Messiaen wrote the libretto, basing it on the saint's writings, is evidence of the continued importance of the text to French opera.   [KM]

See J.-M. Bailbé, *Le Roman et la musique sous la monarchie de juillet* (1969); D. Launay (ed.), *La Querelle des bouffons* (1973); J. F. Fulcher, *The Nation's Image: French Grand Opera* (1988).

Opéra, Théâtre de l'. When in 1673 *Lully obtained from *Louis XIV a monopoly for the performance of *opera, he established the Académie Royale de Musique in the theatre of the Palais-Royal. The Académie changed its title many times, and had to move repeatedly until it was finally installed under the official name of Académie Nationale de Musique in its pompous new building in the place de l'Opéra in 1875. A second national opera opened in the place de la Bastille in 1990.

Opéra-comique is defined as opera with spoken recitatives in contrast to opera with sung recitatives. It need not have comic subject-matter. Its 17th-c. origins were the *comédies-ballets with spoken dialogues alternating with song and dance, and the comedies performed at *théâtres de la *foire using popular *vaudeville tunes with new words. In 1716 a Théâtre de l'Opéra-Comique was established performing *comédies-vaudevilles. Charles-Simon *Favart was the most interesting writer of these and was in favour of introducing newly composed music. The visit of the Italian Opera Buffa troupe in 1752 and the *Guerre des Bouffons inspired a new type of national comic opera, soon known as *comédie mêlée d'ariettes*, where all the music was original and the libretti were at times sentimental and at times made use of social satire. The most important composers were Philidor and Monsigny, and later Grétry and Méhul. *Diderot in his *Entretiens sur le Fils naturel* (1757) outlined a *plan d'opéra-comique* which proved quite influential.

In 1762 the *Comédie-Italienne merged with the Théâtre de l'Opéra-Comique, and the resulting Opéra-Comique moved to the Salle Favart, which it still occupies. In the late 18th to early 19th c. the *opéra-comique* developed in two ways. The so-called 'Rescue' *opéra-comique* was in reality serious romantic opera often with a social and/or moral message in tune with the Revolutionary period. This was followed by another, lighter genre consisting of simple tuneful comedies and exemplified by the works of Francois-Adrien Boïeldieu (1775–1834) in the 1820s. Under the influence of Rossini a more worldly strain developed with the *opéras-comiques* of Auber and Hérold. *Bizet's *Carmen* (1875) is a later example of a serious work set in the traditional *opéra-comique* framework, but in general in the later 19th c. the more frivolous operetta took over [SEE MEILHAC AND HALÉVY].   [KM]

Opium et le bâton, L', see MAMMERI.

Opoponax, L', see WITTIG.

Orality.

1. Middle Ages

Few traces remain of a true medieval oral tradition. By definition, any medieval text that has survived to the present day did so by virtue of having been written down, and it is impossible to gauge precisely its resemblance to oral renditions. Certain early texts, however, such as the *Vie de saint Léger (10th c.) and the Oxford *Roland (c.1080; MS early 12th c.), do provide an indication of a *jongleur repertoire of *hagiographic and heroic tales. Such pieces no doubt flourished as an oral repertoire for quite some time both before and after they were written down. Songs and refrains of all kinds—such as *chansons de toile, *rondeaux, and the songs of the *troubadours and *trouvères—can also be viewed as representatives of an ongoing oral tradition. The enormous number of variants that characterizes the manuscript tradition of the earlier lyric in both *langue d'oc and langue d'oïl strongly suggests that the songs were transmitted at least in part by an oral performance tradition in which individual performers were free to add, subtract, or rearrange stanzas and to alter melodies or even to substitute entirely new ones [see WORDS AND MUSIC, 1].

The transition from an oral tradition to a written literature was long and gradual, extending throughout the later Middle Ages and beyond. One finds countless allusions in *romances and chronicles to the performance of songs and tales of various kinds. *Chansons de geste were performed by jongleurs, generally with accompaniment on the fiddle; *lais, by either professional performers or aristocrats, usually with harp though sometimes with other instrumentation. Most evidence suggests that chansons de toile, rondeaux, and other lyric forms could be sung either by minstrels or by the nobility themselves, sometimes as accompaniment for dance and frequently without instrumental accompaniment. Both men and women are described as performing songs and tales of all types. In *Jean Renart's Roman de la rose ou de Guillaume de Dole (early 13th c.), for example, a brother–sister pair performs some lines from a chanson de geste; both knights and ladies sing chansons de toile and rondeaux. *Romance tradition also contains numerous examples of men and women, both aristocrats and professional minstrels, who compose and perform lais with accompaniment on the harp.

Descriptions of performance found in chronicles and romances indicate a variety of performance contexts. Story-telling [see FOLK-TALE] was particularly associated with the humbler sectors of society, but not confined to them. Chansons de geste and lais could be performed in town squares or in court. Banquets always provided an occasion for musical performance and poetic declamation. Court performances often feature a close relationship between the musician and his or her audience. The performer may preface the piece with a narrative account of how or why it was written, the events that it refers to, how he or she came to learn it, and so on, and may answer questions from the audience. This dialogue often continues after the performance, and sometimes audience members want the performer to teach them the piece. While one must be cautious in using literary texts as evidence for social history, it is most likely that accounts of the general attitudes towards performance, the relations between performer and audience, and the overall role of the performer do reflect the then current practices. One can gather that songs and tales were performed in an intimate context that potentially included considerable narrative background and commentary from the performer and discussion of the piece by the members of the audience.

Such a performance tradition may well lie behind such written forms as the razos that appear in trou-badour chansonniers [see VIDA]. The prose commentaries in the manuscripts would take the place of the performer's commentary for someone encountering the songs in written rather than oral form. A related phenomenon is the romance with lyric insertions, which comes into being in the early 13th c., at about the same time as the compilation of the first surviving chansonniers. Such romances present the songs with a narrative context and re-create the performance situation. Conversely, the songs provide musical interludes to liven up an oral reading of the romance. And the descriptions of performance shed light on the highly visible narrator of medieval romance, who typically expresses opinions, makes sententious comments, and invites the audience to pass judgement on the events of the narrative.

The production of vernacular *manuscripts greatly increased in the 13th c., and at this time also one begins to find expressions of distrust with regard to the oral tradition. For example, the Pseudo-Turpin Chronicle—originally composed in Latin c.1145, and translated into French c.1200—presents itself as an eyewitness, written account of Roland's battle at Rencesvals, more reliable than the chansons de geste performed by the jongleurs who know it only from hearsay. Such comments by no means signal an end to itinerant performers and their repertoire, but they are representative of a gradual trend towards the establishment of French literature as a written tradition and the preservation of literary texts as the written work of a particular author.

Medieval orality is not limited to the performance of texts lacking a written tradition. Even such written forms as the romance or the chronicle were read aloud, as is clear from numerous allusions to the practice. In *Chrétien de Troyes's Chevalier au lyon (Yvain), for example, an aristocratic maiden reads a romance aloud to her parents. The practice of oral reading does not necessarily reflect illiteracy on the part of the audience. In the Espinette amoureuse, *Froissart portrays himself as encountering a young lady engaged in a private reading of a romance; he joins her and the two take turns reading aloud to one another. During the winter of 1388–9, Froissart entertained *Gaston Phébus with an oral reading of his newly completed romance Meliador, at the rate of seven pages a night; Froissart notes that Gaston frequently engaged him in discussions of the text. Even in the late 14th c., among people quite capable of reading to themselves, literature was commonly experienced through oral presentation in a social context.

When reading medieval texts, one must always bear in mind the importance of the performative tradition. These works were addressed to an audience that was accustomed to hearing texts sung or declaimed, and that might well receive even a prose text through oral reading. The stance adopted by the medieval narrator, the rhetorical techniques employed, the division of a long romance into self-contained episodes, the extremely popular practice

587

of inserting songs and refrains into romances—all this can be properly understood and appreciated only if we imagine the texts as destined for oral delivery. [SJH]

See P. Zumthor, *La Poésie et la voix dans la civilisation médiévale* (1984); C. Page, *The Owl and the Nightingale: Musical Life and Ideas in France 1100–1300* (1989).

2. Post-Medieval

The oral element has remained important in the French experience of literature in the post-medieval period. This is notably true for those genres which are, or seem to be, expressly designed for oral performance—theatre, *sermon, political *eloquence, and song [see POPULAR SONG; CHANSON FRANÇAISE]. Quite apart from these, however, there has continued to be a complex interplay between reading and hearing, writing and speaking.

Conversation has long been cultivated as an art in France, notably in the *salons of the 17th and 18th c. It was the central activity of polite society [see HONNÊTETÉ] and was often thought of as a French speciality. There were many books giving advice on the art, from the aristocratic work of a *Méré or a *La Rochefoucauld to the more basic politeness manuals of a *Courtin or a *Vaumorière. Volumes of model conversations were produced by writers such as *Bary or Madeleine de *Scudéry, and the latter's novels, following in the tradition established in *Marguerite de Navarre's *Heptaméron*, offer an image of how polite people should talk together.

The implications of this for literature were considerable. For many writers and readers speech had priority over writing; the latter was expected to comply with some of the norms of salon conversation: clarity, variety, wit, etc. The good writer had to be a person of good company. In his *Contre *Sainte-Beuve*, *Proust accused the great 19th-c. critic of adopting society values and subordinating the 'moi profond' of writing to the social self of conversation—the same could be said of most critics and readers of the *ancien régime*.

Many literary works were couched in forms compatible with the oral culture developed in the salons; this applies not only to the *dialogue, or *entretien*, which mimes polite conversation, but to such forms as the maxim (La Rochefoucauld), the portrait, the essay, and the many types of light verse which flourished at this time (*Voiture being their most famous exponent). The *ana* offered collections of the talk of celebrated writers. *Letter-writing, thought of as conversation at a distance, was part private activity, part public art.

It was common until the 19th c. for writers to read their works aloud in advance of publication. *Rousseau and *Chateaubriand gave lengthy readings from their autobiographies, but most of all this practice concerned the *conte*, which sought to maintain a link with the oral tradition [see SHORT FICTION]. *Voltaire read some of his tales to fashionable

audiences, and *Marmontel writes in his memoirs of the way he tested out his *Contes moraux* in the salons. More than a century later *Mérimée was reading his stories to the empress *Eugénie. At the same time, the *academies, more learned versions of the salons, provided the opportunity for the performance of *discours*, *éloges*, and the like, echoing the emphasis on the spoken word in French *education.

In the 20th c., while the influence of salons and academies has declined, the audio-visual media have confirmed that a literary work can exist as much for the ear as for the eye. What *Flaubert called 'l'épreuve du gueuloir' remains an important element in writing. And more importantly, the development of francophone literature overseas, particularly in *Africa and the *West Indies, has often been grafted on to older oral traditions. [PF]

See M. Fumaroli, *Le Genre des genres littéraires français: la conversation* (1992).

Oratorians (Congrégation de l'Oratoire). This religious order, springing from the *Counter-Reformation, was founded in 1570 in Italy by St Philip Neri to reinvigorate Catholic doctrine and to enhance the intellectual and moral qualities of the priesthood. Brought to France in 1611 by *Bérulle, the Order counted, by 1629, over 70 colleges, from Dieppe to Toulon, Nantes to Nancy. (Juilly, whose educational and pedagogical innovations would constantly inspire all sister establishments, was founded in 1638.) But such good fortune irritated powerful opponents (including the *Jesuits), who charged the Oratorians with disregarding their own regulations. Indeed, despite its clear commitment to education, the order had not been founded for that purpose but for the training of priests (in fact, the supreme goal of Condren, the second general of the order, would have been to obtain responsibility for the seminaries). Though rivalry in the field of education was to compromise the equanimity of the Oratorians, at least until the closing of the Jesuit colleges in 1762, a more serious cause of disturbance was *Jansenism: a small minority (starting with *Quesnel, Soanen, and Duguet) made the whole order suspect and long caused it much anxiety. By the time of its suppression (1792), the Oratorians had given to French religious and intellectual life *Mascaron, *Malebranche, *Massillon, *Thomassin, and *Lamy. [JR]

Oratory, see ELOQUENCE.

ORESME, Nicole (1320/5–1382). This outstandingly versatile *savant* belonged to the school of intellectuals gathered by Charles V. He wrote numerous treatises in Latin, on mathematics, astrology, theology, and the function of money, but he also wrote in French (apologizing for his 'rude manière de parler'), on economics and astrology, and most notably, between 1370 and 1377, at the commission of Charles, made the first translations into any vernacular of Aristotle's *Ethics, Politics, Economics,* and *Meteorologica,* with interpretative comments, designed explicitly to spread scientific knowledge not just to the specialist, but to the educated layman. [JHMT]

Orientales, Les, see HUGO.

Origines de la France contemporaine, Les. *Taine began this massive work in 1871 during the *Commune, and devoted his life to it. *Halévy called the title 'vaste, démesuré', and the project to understand the contemporary political and social reality of France through its origins in the *ancien régime* and the Revolution is grandiose. Taine invents a unique form, combining history which is social (ordinary people, the countryside, the provinces), constitutional (*Le Régime moderne*), and ideological (the *philosophes,* especially J.-J. *Rousseau) with sociology (*L'Église* and *L'École*) and psychology (the pathology of the *Jacobin), in a style which includes Stendhalien litotes (*L'Ancien Régime*) and a *Zola-like fascination with horror (*La Conquête jacobine*) while (remarkably for the time) giving full references to archive material. The work manifests Taine's unresolved conflicts: flux/system; *récit*/tableau; liberal-sceptical tolerance/anti-democratic traditionalism. But it has always been read tendentiously, arousing antagonism from all sides. The Left (and the University) vilified Taine for his anti-Revolutionary and anti-democratic position. The Right, while exploiting his work, never forgave him his account of the iniquities and absurdities of the *ancien régime*. The Church remembered his *anticlericalism. The Bonapartists were incensed at his treatment of their hero. The army thought him unpatriotic. . . . Such is the *grandeur et misère* of the intellectual.

Taine can be repetitive: see the abridged version (ed. F. Léger, 1974). [CHE]

Orléans. From the late 14th c. the younger brother of the French king bore the title of duc d'Orléans. Of those who did not become king, the most famous members of the house of Orléans were:

Charles d'Orléans, the poet;

Gaston d'Orléans(1608–60). Father of the duchesse de *Montpensier, he intrigued ceaselessly against *Richelieu and took part in the *Fronde;

Philippe d'Orléans (1674–1723), regent of France from 1715 to 1723 [see REGENCY; PALAIS-ROYAL];

Louis-Philippe-Joseph d'Orléans (1749–93), nicknamed 'Philippe-Égalité' because he threw in his lot with the *Revolution, hoping to become constitutional monarch. He was guillotined during the Terror; his son became King Louis-Philippe [see JULY MONARCHY].

ORMESSON, Jean d' (b. 1925). High-ranking French civil servant, editor of Le *Figaro, and novelist. He has published many successful books, including personal reflections (e.g. *Du côté de chez Jean,* 1959) and

several large-scale historical fictions, from *La Gloire de l'empire* (1971) to *L'Histoire du Juif errant* (1990).

Orphée, see COCTEAU.

Orphelin de la Chine, L' (1755). Tragedy by *Voltaire, in which Genghis Khan is shamed by virtuous examples into choosing the path of generosity and sparing the life of a child.

Orphism was the name used by *Apollinaire in 1913 of a group of painters (notably Robert *Delaunay but also *Léger, *Picabia, *Duchamp) whose assimilation of *Fauvist colour and *Cubist fragmentation of objects led them in the direction of non-figurative art. Delaunay, however, described his *Eiffel Tower* and *Windows* series (1909–12, 1912–13), *Ville de Paris* (1910–12), and *Disque* (the first French non-figurative painting, 1912) as *simultaneist* paintings, a word which also expressed the wider ambition to give formal structure to the representation of modern, urban civilization as the simultaneous presence of fragmented but interconnected experience. This, for Apollinaire, characterized all modern art and the term 'simultaneism' was applied to the work of *Cendrars, the *Unanimists, and Apollinaire himself. [JK]

ORVILLE, Xavier (b. 1932). Martinican novelist. His fiction uses whimsical fantasy, symbol, and parable to develop recurrent themes: the search for Caribbean identity and the plight of colonized peoples. Typical of his surrealistic narratives are *L'Homme aux sept noms et des poussières* (1981) and *Laissez brûler Laventurcia* (1989). [BJO]

Ossian in France, see BRITISH, IRISH, AND AMERICAN INFLUENCES.

OSTER-SOUSSENOV, Pierre (b. 1933). French poet, who places himself in the line of *Claudel and *Saint-John Perse, celebrating in eloquent and expansive verse the unity of creation. His collections, some of them with his notes on poetry, include *Le Champ de mai* (1955), *Solitude de la lumière* (1957), *Un nom toujours nouveau* (1960), *La Grande Année* (1964), *Les Dieux* (1970), *Requêtes* (1977, new version 1992). [PF]

Otage, L'. Written 1909–10, performed 1914, *L'Otage* is the first play in *Claudel's historical trilogy. Georges de Coûfontaine, a monarchist, has delivered Pope Pius VII from Napoleon and has brought him to his ancestral home, where his cousin Sygne helps to hide him. Turelure, a former peasant, now a Napoleonic prefect, threatens the pope's safety unless Sygne marries him. A priest, Badilon, reveals to Sygne, who loves Georges, her vocation to suffer to save the pope. At the Restoration Sygne, now Turelure's wife, dies saving Turelure's life from Georges. Turelure is made a count by the returning Louis XVIII.

The story of the family is continued in two further plays, *Le Pain dur* and *Le Père humilié*. [RMG]

Othon

Othon. Tragedy by Pierre *Corneille, first performed 1664, a complex play of matrimonial bargaining, in which Othon competes successfully with Pison for the Roman imperial throne.

OTON DE GRANDSON, see GRANDSON.

OUELLETTE, Fernand (b. 1930). Canadian poet, essayist, and novelist. Born in Montreal, he studied social sciences at the University of Montreal and worked for Radio-Canada. He was a founder member of the journal *Liberté*. He enjoyed early recognition, having 'Poésie à quatre voix' broadcast in France and a text on Varèse published in New York for the composer's 75th birthday concert. From 1967 on he won numerous prizes, but in 1970, because of the political climate, he refused the Governor-General's Award for his collected essays, *Les Actes retrouvés*.

Ouellette writes perceptively on his own poetry; his inspiration comes mainly from Europe, from Dante to Kierkegaard, Hölderlin to *Jouve, and his writing makes little reference to Quebec, though he is clearly a Quebec writer through his struggle with the dualism of flesh and spirit and owes a visible debt to *Grandbois. He wrote the best essay yet on the implications of bilingualism, declaring: 'Dès que j'ai essayé d'écrire, je me suis rendu compte que j'étais un *barbare*.' His poetry is powered by a thirst for the absolute and for light, invading his being and instigating literary creation; he returned to poetry, after two well-received novels, with *Les Heures* (1987). His work displays a great unity and consistency of inspiration.   [CRPM]

OUELLETTE-MICHALSKA, Madeleine (b. 1935). Canadian poet, novelist, and essayist. Her two volumes of essays, *L'Échappée des discours de l'œil* (1981) and *L'Amour de la carte postale* (1987), combine erudition and intellectual penetration in tracing the history of patriarchal attitudes and analysing various forms of cultural imperialism. Short stories and novels such as *La Femme de sable* (1979), *Le Plat de lentilles* (1979), and *La Fête du désir* (1989) marry political awareness with an elegant sensuality. *La Maison Trestler ou le 8e Jour d'Amérique* (1984), her most ambitious novel, is an evocation of an early period of colonization in which the narrator appears to exchange identities with her fictional heroine.   [SIL]

OULIPO (sometimes OuLiPo). Contraction of Ouvroir de Littérature Potentielle, a group of writers formed principally by Raymond *Queneau, François Le Lionnais, Jacques Bens, Jean Lescure, and Jean Queval and subsequently including Jacques *Roubaud, Georges *Perec, and Italo Calvino. Beginning as an offshoot of the Collège de *'Pataphysique, this group of writers concerned themselves above all with the principle of 'potential', seeing the creation of literature as arising most felicitously from the imposition of constraints of a rigid and sometimes mathematical nature. One of

their number offered the early definition of the group and its endeavours as: 'rats qui ont à construire le labyrinthe dont ils se proposent de sortir'— and indeed most of their works, whether original compositions or transformations of existing texts, have a labyrinthine quality as well as a strongly ludic dimension [see also ROUSSEL].

From initial meetings begun in November 1960, the group expanded its numbers—including corresponding members, sometimes writing in other languages—and its activities throughout the 1960s and 1970s. Two manifestos were published (*La Lipo* and *Le Second Manifeste*) by the mathematician François Le Lionnais, and a number of collective projects and publications were undertaken. The main body of the group's work—aside from the principal achievements of individuals—can be found in two publications: *La Littérature potentielle* (1973) and *Atlas de littérature potentielle* (1981), and perhaps the most inventive conjunction of the mathematical and the literary is to be found in Roubaud's ε (1967).

Citing the invention of the sonnet as an early example of 'littérature potentielle', since it combines great rigour with great freedom of invention, the group set out to propose as many new ways of creating literary works as possible. These 'lipos' (= littératures potentielles) were to operate in two fundamentally different ways: either as a set of constraints to be imposed on material of the author's own invention, whether in prose or in verse, or as a set of transformational rules applied to existing literary works. Thus Queneau, as an example of the latter, reduces *Mallarmé's celebrated sonnet: 'Coup d'aile ivre, | sous le givre, | aujourd'hui | pas fui' to a haiku-like form, while another celebrated method consists of replacing every word by that found seven places on in a nominated dictionary. Of the former type, perhaps Perec's adoption of the *lipogram—a form requiring the omission of one or more letters—has produced the best and best-known example in *La Disparition*—a novel written without the use of the letter *e*—and Queneau's *Cent mille milliards de poèmes* is evidence of the fruitfulness of the Oulipian approach to verse.   [IWR]

OUOLOGUEM, Yambo (b. 1940). Acclaimed as the author of one of the major African novels of the 20th c. and attacked as a plagiarist for that very novel, Ouologuem continues to attract critical attention. Born in Bandiagara, Mali, he completed his secondary education at the Lycée Henri IV in Paris, subsequently taking degrees in literature, philosophy, and English, and a doctorate in sociology. His novel *Le Devoir de violence* (1968), which won the Prix Renaudot, remains his only major work. He has also published a collection of essays, *Lettre à la France nègre* (1969), an erotic novel, *Les Mille et une Bibles du sexe* (published in 1969 under the pseudonym Utto Rudolf), and several short stories, articles, and poems.

Le Devoir de violence relates the history of a fictitious West African kingdom, Nakem, from 1202 to the mid-20th c., with the past related in a series of flashbacks inserted into the account of the adventures of Raymond Spartacus Kassoumi and his family. The novel was initially acclaimed for its complex time structure, its combination of various styles of writing, and its fast-moving portrayal of erotic and violent scenes. More importantly it attempted to explode the myth of colonialism as the major destructive element in African history, presenting ethnologists like Frobénius (through the character Shrobénius) as the dupes of wily African leaders rather than the preservers of oral tradition. However, critics soon began to notice similarities between parts of the novel and other works, notably André *Schwarz-Bart's *Le Dernier des justes* (1959) and Graham Greene's *It's a Battlefield* (1934). By 1972 the controversy was receiving attention in the *Times Literary Supplement*, the *Figaro littéraire*, and other newspapers. Ouologuem's defenders saw the work as imaginative borrowing from European literature rather than plagiarism, and his masterpiece retains a prominent place in the history of the African novel. [AMC]

OUVILLE, Antoine Le Métel, sieur d' (*c*.1590–*c*.1657), French dramatist and translator. His several adaptations of Spanish *comedias*, published between 1639 and 1646, were particularly successful, and set a trend in French comedy which continued for 20 years. He also published two volumes of comic *contes* and translations of Spanish *novelas*. [GJM]

Ouvriers-poètes. With the growth of the working-class movement and the development of working-class political consciousness in the *July Monarchy, there emerged the highly characteristic phenomenon of the artisan poet. *Baudelaire's interest in the poems of Pierre *Dupont, and particularly in 'Le Chant des ouvriers' (1846), is well known, but other worker-poets were 'discovered' and encouraged (e.g. Magu the weaver by George *Sand). Early 19th-c. *Saint-Simonians, *Fourierists, and *Cabétistes, along with 20th-c. socialists and communists, constantly sought out and published 'the voice of the people'. Olinde Rodrigues produced an early collection, *Poésies sociales des ouvriers* (1841). [BR]

Ovide moralisé, see CLASSICAL INFLUENCES, I.

OYONO, Ferdinand (b. 1929). Cameroonian writer. Like many francophone African writers, Oyono has managed to combine a highly successful literary career with activity in other spheres. During his twenties he produced in quick succession three novels which continue to enjoy wide readership and critical interest: *Une vie de boy* (1956), *Le Vieux Nègre et la médaille* (1956), *Chemin d'Europe* (1960). Then, following the independence of his country in 1960, Oyono turned his back on literature to devote himself to a career in diplomacy. In 1962 he was appointed ambassador to Liberia, and after postings to Brussels and Paris spent 10 years attached to the United Nations in New York. He was appointed director of UNICEF in 1977. He returned to Cameroon in 1985, where he became a government minister.

His novels are very representative of the period in which he wrote, since they largely focus on the injustices of the colonial system. What is fresh about his approach, however, is the reliance on comic effect to underline his message. The three novels all highlight the hypocrisy and the bad faith which characterize the behaviour of the whites and the relationships which they establish with the blacks. The promises implicit in the whole colonial enterprise, the so-called civilizing mission of the colonizers, and the religious evangelism which accompanied it are all exposed as mere sham. They are shown to be myths which colonizer and colonized alike may choose to believe, either through self-interest or stupidity. The chief source of the comedy lies in the constant juxtaposing of pious 'myth' and the harsh reality of colonial life. Hence, it serves Oyono's purposes to present naïve and rather credulous characters as his protagonists: Toundi in *Une vie de boy*, Meka in *Le Vieux Nègre et la médaille*, and Aki Barnabas in *Chemin d'Europe*. All, to a greater or lesser extent, take the whites at face value and experience a rude awakening.

Perhaps the explanation for Oyono's decision to embrace a career as a diplomat and politician rather than as a writer is simply that the granting of independence brought an end to the colonial system which his novels so thoroughly condemn. [MPC]

See R. Mercier and M. and S. Battestini, *Ferdinand Oyono, écrivain camerounais* (1964).

OYONO-MBIA, Guillaume (b. 1939). Cameroonian playwright. From a peasant family, he studied in England (Keele) and has been working for the Ministry of Culture and Information since 1972. He has exploited his knowledge of rural life in south Cameroon to excellent comic effect in a trilogy of plays with the common theme of marriage. His first comedy, *Trois prétendants un mari* (1964), was awarded the Ahmadou Ahidjo Literary Prize in 1970. The second, *Jusqu'à nouvel avis* (1970), was originally written in English and performed at the Edinburgh Festival, while the third, *Notre fille ne se mariera pas*, a radio play, won the Inter-African Theatre Competition organized by Radio France International in 1971. In addition, he has published three volumes of 'village chronicles', *Les Chroniques de Mvoutessi* (1972), also in comic vein, and a further comedy, *Le Train spécial de son Excellence* (1979). Oyono-Mbia claims that his aim is to entertain rather than teach, and his skilful use of a wide range of comic effects brings out all the ironic potential of the confrontation between traditional village ways and the westernized urban life-style. But his work is also an effective weapon against pomposity, pretentiousness, and the manipulation of others in either culture, and an invitation to youth and women to do battle for rights traditionally denied them. [FNC]

P

Page d'amour, Une. Novel by *Zola, published in 1878 and eighth in the *Rougon-Macquart* series. Written, purposely, in a decidedly minor key compared to the previous novel, L'*Assommoir, this work is the story of the adulterous affair of a widow, Hélène Grandjean, the daughter of Ursule Macquart. She falls in love with Dr Deberle, who has saved the life of her daughter Jeanne, a child of delicate health who has inherited many of the family weaknesses. When, jealous of her mother's affection for the doctor and struck down by an illness due in part to her mother's neglect, Jeanne dies of consumption, Hélène blames herself, gives up her lover, and marries an old family friend. The novel is a picture of bourgeois life, dealing with such themes as the education of young girls and the harmful influence of religion on women. It is Zola's attempt at the art of the psychological novel, of which critics had declared him incapable. But it is most often evoked for the impressionist, panoramic descriptions of Paris, in varying seasons and conditions of light, which close each of the five 'acts' of the drama of Hélène's episode of love. [DB]

Page disgrâcié, Le, see TRISTAN L'HERMITE.

PAGNOL, Marcel (1895–1974). Dramatist, film-maker, and novelist. Born in Aubagne (Bouches-du-Rhône), he achieved fame for his evocations of the Midi and the manners of its people. He studied English at the University of Aix-en-Provence, and founded the literary review *Fortunio,* which later became *Les Cahiers du sud.* After various teaching posts he was appointed to the Lycée Condorcet. He had already written plays and theatre criticism; in Paris he pursued his theatrical career with plays of sharp social observation, notably *Topaze* (1928). His Marseille trilogy, *Marius* (1929), *Fanny* (1931), and *César* (1936), demonstrated his mastery of characterization in tragicomic vein. In the 1930s, with the arrival of talking films, he came to regard the cinema as an even more effective medium than the theatre. After working on film versions of existing material, including open-air filming of *Giono's *Jofroi* (1933), and *Angèle* (1934) with Fernandel, he produced *Merlusse* (1935), his first original screenplay. Later successes included *Regain* (1937) and *La Femme du boulanger* (1938).

Pagnol's reputation as a dramatist and *cinéaste* was such that, after the war, which he had spent in Provence, he was elected to the Académie Française (1946), the first film-maker to be honoured in this way. However, with his light-hearted satire, use of regional vocabulary, and association with the new genre of the cinema, he was not always regarded as a 'serious' writer. Mindful of this, he published his *Notes sur le rire* (1947) and *La Critique des critiques* (1949), and translations into French of Shakespeare's *Hamlet* (1947) and *A Midsummer Night's Dream* (1970), and Virgil's *Bucolics* (1958). In addition to films, such as his adaptations from Alphonse *Daudet's *Lettres de mon moulin* (1953–4, 1967), he later turned to prose writing with his *Souvenirs d'enfance,* consisting of *La Gloire de mon père* and *Le Château de ma mère* (1957) and the posthumous *Le Temps des amours* (1977), and with his tragicomic celebration of the myth of water, *L'Eau des collines* (1963), a prose-fiction version of his over-long film *Manon des sources* (1952). This novel was, in turn, re-adapted for the screen by Claude Berri, as *Jean de Florette* and *Manon des sources* (1986), to wide popular acclaim. During his lifetime Pagnol's reputation waxed and waned; since his death the quality of his writing has been increasingly respected, and his reputation has benefited from the enhanced prestige of film as an art-form. [BCS]

See C. E. J. Caldicott, *Marcel Pagnol* (1977); G. Berni, *Merveilleux Pagnol* (1981).

Paix de l'Église, La, see JANSENISM.

Palace, Le, see SIMON, C.

Palais-Royal, Le. Palace and garden situated close to the *Louvre in Paris. Built for *Richelieu as the Palais Cardinal [see THEATRES AND AUDIENCES, I], it was given by him to the royal family. From the late 17th c. to the 19th c. it belonged to the *Orléans family, who rebuilt it completely. Under the *Regency the palace became the scene for *fêtes* and acquired a reputation as a centre of libertinism. In the 18th and 19th c. the gardens were developed as a place of public resort, with cafés and shops, and became a centre for gambling and prostitution (see Diderot's *Le *Neveu de Rameau*). During the Revolution it was a scene of political activity; it was here that Camille *Desmoulins called on the crowds to defend the Revolution and storm the Bastille. [PF]

PALATINE, Charlotte-Élisabeth de Bavière, princesse (1652–1722). Second wife of Louis XIV's brother, the duc d'Orléans, and mother of the Regent. Her letters (mostly translated from German) give an outspoken and entertaining outsider's view of the court and its denizens.

Palissot de Montenoy

PALISSOT DE MONTENOY, Charles (1730–1814). French playwright and satirist. His early tragedy *Zarès* (1751) received only three performances, but substantial success came with *Les Tuteurs* in 1754. 1755 saw the performance of his *Le Cercle, ou les Originaux*, which particularly pilloried *Rousseau. He again attacked the *philosophes*, especially *Diderot, in *Les Philosophes* (1760), which, thanks to his protectors, received 14 performances in its first run at the Comédie-Française, and followed this with another attack, the poem *La Dunciade*, in 1764. His animosity towards the *philosophes*, particularly Diderot, was motivated chiefly by what he saw as the sterility of philosophical language and the *philosophes'* uncritical admiration of each other's works. His *Petites lettres sur les grands philosophes* of 1757 include an intemperate attack on Diderot's *Le Fils naturel*. [JD]

PALISSY, Bernard (c.1510–1590). Scientific writer. Little is known of his early years. He travelled around France in the 1530s as a surveyor and observed natural phenomena. From 1539 in Saintes he helped found the Reform Church in the Saintonge and developed his art as a potter. In 1566 he moved to Paris and remained there until his death in the Bastille, except for a short period in the east after 1572. An autodidact, a committed Protestant, and a creator of fine pottery in the Italian style with original 'natural' designs, Palissy worked for Montmorency on the grotto at Écouen and for *Catherine de Médicis at the Tuileries. Influenced by Paracelsus, he described his scientific theories and his religious views first in the *Recette véritable* (1563), which reveals his belief in the absolute virtue of observation in matters scientific and his convinced Protestantism. His other major publication, the *Discours admirables* (1582), was based on his public lectures in Paris. Like the *Recette*, it is in dialogue form and explores numerous subjects (fountains, metals, salts, alchemy, etc.), and provides modern views on the use of fertilizers, origin of fossils, etc. Palissy was one of the first modern scientists and a proponent of the Protestant 'scientific ethic'. [KCC]

PALSGRAVE, John (c.1480–1554). English grammarian, tutor in French to Mary Tudor; his *Éclaircissement de la langue française* (1530) is the first comprehensive French *grammar and an invaluable source for the study of contemporary vocabulary, morphology, and syntax. [MJH]

Pamphlet Literature. A pamphlet is a short piece of writing, often of an apparently ephemeral nature (though some of the greatest examples have had a lasting literary impact). The most famous pamphlets have tended to be polemical, but pamphlets have also at times been used purely for the dissemination of information (taking the place, in early 17th-c. France, for example, of the modern newspaper),

and have served for the communication of reasoned political or religious ideas.

With the advent of printing, the possibility of conveying one's ideas to a very large audience by means of the printed word soon became clear to those with an axe to grind. In 16th-c. France the religious and political ferment that surrounded the *Wars of Religion produced a plethora of printed pamphlets. Though most were in prose, a number, by established 'literary' writers, were in verse. *Ronsard's various *Discours*, for example, are typical of similar writings by poets such as *Grévin and *La Taille. Later published in book form, they started as separate pamphlets addressed to royal personages, stating Ronsard's views on the contemporary situation of France. His *Réponse aux injures et calomnies de je ne sais quels prédicantereaux et ministreaux de Genève*, however, is an example of another contemporary trend: in the more violent mode of polemic, it employs the colourful and often vulgar imagery used by other contemporary polemicists. Probably the most famous, and the best-written, of the pamphlets of the Wars was the *Satire Ménippée* (1594), which attacked the Catholic *Ligue by producing a parody of the events and speeches at the opening of the *États Généraux of 1593.

The political upheavals of the first half of the 17th c. were an equally fertile ground for polemical pamphlets, culminating at the time of the *Fronde with the *mazarinades*, a series of attacks, from divers hands, upon Cardinal *Mazarin and others.

The greatest literary example of pamphleteering in France in the 17th c. is *Pascal's *Lettres provinciales* (1656–7), written in defence of *Arnauld against the *Jesuits. The subtlety and irony of these attacks, later collected in book form, are polemic at its highest. The main thrust of pamphlet literature, as the 17th c. progressed, was to lie in the area of literary debate. The various *querelles*, from those surrounding *Corneille's plays to the *Querelle des Anciens et des Modernes later in the century, gave rise to a vast amount of ephemeral literature. Religious argument, too, continued to flourish in pamphlet form, from the *Jansenist controversies of mid-century to the bitter debate on the *Quietist question in the 1690s. In the aftermath of the Fronde, however, and with the centralizing monarchy of Louis XIV's adulthood, the scope for political pamphleteering had become reduced.

This situation was to change in the 18th c. In the plethora of political and social pamphlet literature in that century, the contributions of *Voltaire stand out for their fire and mordant irony. Many political tracts by other hands, however, are equally distinguished. Outstanding examples are *Sieyès's four famous tracts produced in the run-up to the convocation of the États Généraux in 1789, and particularly the famous *Qu'est-ce que le Tiers État?*, in which his compressed, nervous, terse style conveys his ideas with the maximum of effect.

Most of the famous pamphlets of the 18th c. had

been, even when violent in tone, bound by the constraints of literary language. The later years of the century, however, saw the increasingly massive production of scurrilous *libelles*, generally directed against the alleged corruption and immorality of those in power, and this style of pamphleteering continued to flourish under the *Revolution. With the advent of the mass-publication daily *press in the 19th c., this popular violence and vulgarity found its place on a far broader platform, particularly in the polemics which surrounded the major political events of the century, from *Napoleon III's *coup d'état* in 1851 to the *Dreyfus Affair in 1897–9. Locutions from popular language, vicious invective based on physical traits, animal similarities, sexual innuendo, etc., dominate this polemic; and whole families of stock images create 'tribal languages' for the various political factions. Not since the 16th and early 17th c. had the language and tactics of the streets dominated in this way the printed writings of controversialists.

In one sense, the newspaper article had become the new form of the pamphlet. The daily outpourings of such masters of polemic as *Rochefort, *Veuillot, Gohier, *Tailhade, and Cassagnac hit the public in the same way that the pamphlets of the past had. Both the violent and the more moderate press could produce writings which, if ephemeral in intention, have at times lasted as works of art in their own right. Among the best-known articles from the Dreyfus Affair, for example, are *Maurras's 'Le Premier Sang' and *Zola's 'J'accuse', both of which have lasted to our own day as examples of the consummate use of the French language for a polemical purpose. True pamphlets, as opposed to articles, still abounded, however. Zola's *Lettre à la jeunesse* and *Lettre à la France* were both produced as *brochures*; and a large number of such *brochures* and broadsheets were issued by both sides in the Affair.

In the 20th c. the pamphlet tradition was to continue strongly, particularly among the journalists of the extreme Left and Right. Most such writers were equally famed for their pamphlets and their newspaper articles.

The *événements* of *May 1968 bore witness to the continuing power of the political pamphlet, as the collections of the ephemera of those months have shown. Pamphlet literature lies at the boundary between 'literature', as it used to be conceived, and popular culture. The fact that certain great writers have produced pamphlets of outstanding 'literary' value should not hide from us the fact that the vitality of the genre, particularly in the 16th and 17th c., and from the mid-19th c. onwards, has lain in its capacity to express mass emotions, often through 'unliterary' language and procedures. At its heights, it reaches capabilities of expression which are peculiar to itself, and which are now seen to be as worthy of consideration as the more conventional output of the traditional literary genres.

[RMG]

See C. Moreau, *Choix de mazarinades*, 2 vols. (1853); R. Darnton, *The Literary Underground of the Old Régime* (1982); R. M. Griffiths, *The Use of Abuse: The Polemics of the Dreyfus Affair and its Aftermath* (1992).

Panama, Affaire du. A financial scandal involving widespread official corruption which rocked France in the 1890s, following the failure of the company set up in 1881 to pierce a canal through the Isthmus of Panama.

PANARD, Charles-François (1694–1765). French author of light verse, *vaudevilles, epigrams, and numerous texts (comic operas, parodies, pantomime ballets, etc.) for the *théâtres de la *foire*. He wrote amusing *calligramme* poems in the shape of a bottle, a glass, etc.

PANCKOUCKE, Charles-Joseph (1736–98). Member of a famous family of bookseller-publishers, and friend of many writers. As well as being a proprietor of the *Mercure de France* and founder of the *Moniteur*, he was responsible for several major publishing ventures, in particular the 201-vol. reworking of the *Encyclopédie*, the *Encyclopédie méthodique* (1781–1832).

PANET, Léopold (1820–59). Half-caste Senegalese who, after accompanying French naval commissioner Raffenel up the River Senegal into the Sudanese hinterland (1847), in 1850 explored Western Sahara alone. His 'Relation d'un voyage du Sénégal à Soueira', in the *Revue coloniale* (1850), is the first published work in French by an African writer.

[DSB]

Pangloss. Irrepressible professor of 'métaphysico-théologo-cosmolo-nigologie', used by Voltaire to mock the philosophy of Optimism in *Candide*.

Pantagruel. Hero of Rabelais's *Pantagruel* and succeeding books. 'Penthagruel' was known in popular culture as a small devil who threw salt into the mouths of drunkards at night; he first appears in Rabelais as a mythical *giant* associated with drought and insatiable thirst. These associations are dropped in later books, where even Pantagruel's gigantic stature is only rarely evoked: he becomes primarily an embodiment of ideal wisdom in contrast to the foolish and self-preoccupied *Panurge. 'Pantagruélisme' is defined in the earlier books as a joyful, positive attitude of mind; later, it becomes 'a certain gaiety of spirit composed of a contempt for worldly things'. 'Pantagruélion' is the magic herb—a universal panacea having properties similar to hemp—which Pantagruel and his friends take with them on their voyage.

[TC]

Pantagruel and ***Gargantua*.** The works of *Rabelais begin, in their fictional order, with the story of the birth, education, and military prowess of the giant *Gargantua, and continue with the not-dissimilar story of his son *Pantagruel. However, *Pantagruel* (1532) was written first, and this causes some slight narrative inconsistencies: e.g. Frère Jean, a runaway monk introduced in *Gargantua* (1534/5), reappears in the later continuation of the Pantagruel story in the *Tiers Livre* (1546), the *Quart Livre* (1548/52), and the *Cinquième Livre* (1562/64) alongside Pantagruel's companion *Panurge. In these later books, in fact, Panurge takes centre stage. Unable to decide whether to get married, he first consults, with Pantagruel's assistance, a series of experts in domains ranging from divination and prophecy (the Sibyl of Panzoust, Raminagrobis), through sign-language (Nazdecabre), to theology (Hippothadée), medicine (Rondibilis), and law (Bridoye); when these fail to provide the answer he wants, he embarks on a voyage to seek the *dive bouteille* (divine bottle), which he finally reaches at the end of the (probably inauthentic) *Cinquième Livre*. Meanwhile, the voyage provides the pretext for a series of more or less discontinuous encounters with strange peoples and creatures: the inhabitants of Ennasin, whose couplings imitate proverbial sayings; the inhabitants of Ruach, who consume (and give off) nothing but wind; the Lenten monster Quaresmeprenant and his adversary Mardi Gras, supported by legions of Andouilles (Chitterlings); Gaster, personification of the stomach. Some of these—the Lenten figures and the egregious Papimanes (Pope-worshippers)—stage transparently satirical scenarios. Other instances (the 'frozen words' episode, the feast off the island of Chaneph) provide complex enactments of the perennial Rabelaisian theme of language.

As this summary suggests, narrative consistency is not Rabelais's main preoccupation. Even in the first two books, which follow a relatively clear and simple narrative line, there are many diversions and digressions, and the transition from one episode to the next is often abrupt. One of the most celebrated of all Rabelaisian inventions is itself a piece of digressive narrative: towards the end of *Pantagruel* the narrator Alcofrybas Nasier (an anagram of Rabelais's name) accidentally strays into Pantagruel's mouth, where he finds a whole new country, with mountains, towns, and an inhabitant who claims that *his* world, not the one 'outside', is the old world. Rabelais's comic imagination relies on this ability to surprise and disconcert the reader.

Rabelais is in any case not writing a modern novel. His work is in part a burlesque of medieval *epic and *romance, in part a French equivalent of the tall stories of the Greek writer Lucian, who was fashionable among humanists, and in part also an idiosyncratic development of the comic paradoxes of *Erasmus's celebrated *Praise of Folly*—Panurge's praise of debts and of the codpiece in the *Tiers Livre*, as well as the episode featuring the fool Triboullet, belong to this Renaissance tradition. Besides the shifts of tone and subject-matter from episode to episode, there is a marked difference between the

first two books and the later ones. *Pantagruel* and *Gargantua* were written at a time of relative optimism in the religious and political sphere, a time, too, when Rabelais's personal career was prospering. In both books, the giants are gigantic and exuberant; they are given the benefit of a super-humanist education; they dwarf their opponents (the imperialistic Picrochole in *Gargantua*, Loup-Garou in *Pantagruel*) and win their battles decisively. The spirit of Utopia is present, not least in the invention of the Abbaye de Thélème, an ideal anti-monastery where well-born, well-educated men and women live in harmonious freedom. But already, at the end of *Gargantua*, there are more sombre references to the possibility of persecution: it was precisely at this time (late 1534) that the French *Evangelicals provoked the *Sorbonne into a hard-line reaction against religious reform.

In the 12-year interval before the publication of the *Tiers Livre*, religious persecution had dramatically increased, Rabelais had lost two of his most powerful patrons (Guillaume du Bellay and Geoffroy d'Estissac, who both died in 1543), and the political climate had become sombre and tense. The Prologue of the *Tiers Livre* reflects this new atmosphere: Rabelais now projects himself as a writer on the margins, playing with his comic fictions while France prepares for war. All the learning of the experts whom Panurge consults cannot dispel his uncertainty; Pantagruel seems to have lost his gigantic physical stature and often remains aloof, while, in the *Quart Livre*, gigantic monsters like Quaresmeprenant manifest themselves as enemies whom even Pantagruel cannot defeat or tame. The more pessimistic mood is reflected, too, from early in the *Tiers Livre*, by borrowings from ancient Stoic philosophy [see NEOSTOICISM], tempered by expressions of Christian humility; while the vertiginous uncertainty that Panurge unleashes in the narrative is personified in Trouillogan, a caricature of the newly fashionable *Pyrrhonist philosophy.

The question of how to read this extraordinary comic fantasy has dominated critical studies on Rabelais: indeed, within the work itself both the reader and the characters are frequently confronted with enigmatic texts and other problems of interpretation. Some things are clear: Lucien Febvre, M. A. Screech, and others have shown conclusively that Rabelais was not, as his early 20th c. editor Abel Lefranc believed, an atheist; it is equally an error to regard him as a revolutionary 'voice of the people', although elements of popular culture play an important role in his work and the mood of the carnival is present in many episodes, especially in the earlier books (this interpretation is particularly associated with the Russian critic Mikhail Bakhtin). The emphasis on eating, drinking, and other bodily activities should be seen, not as some kind of out-dated schoolboy humour, but as a vigorous and far-reaching attempt to portray human nature as a whole: the way such matters are treated, in fact, changes considerably in the course of the work. Besides, if modern readers are offended by anything in Rabelais's works, it is likely to be not so much by what an earlier generation referred to as his 'coarseness', as by the moral attitude to women evinced by episodes such as the encounter between Panurge and the 'dame de Paris' in *Pantagruel*. Such problems are best dealt with by regarding the text as a powerful, moving, and often disturbing testimony to its times, all the more so because its vision embraces more than the formal expression of philosophical or religious ideas. Rabelais's deeply committed participation in the events and issues of his day [see the entry devoted to him] demands from the reader a serious effort of historical understanding, and repays this effort by embodying for us in its own idiosyncratic way the disconcertingly *different* world of the early 16th c. [TC]

See L. Febvre, *The Problem of Unbelief in the Sixteenth Century* (1942; trans. B. Gottlieb, 1982); E. Auerbach, *Mimesis* (1946; trans. W. Trask, 1953), ch. II; M. Bakhtin, *Rabelais and His World* (1965; trans. H. Iswolsky, 1968); M. A. Screech, *Rabelais* (1979); T. Cave, *The Cornucopian Text* (1979).

Panthéon, Le. Originally built to the grandiose neoclassical design of Soufflot as the Église Sainte-Geneviève, this Paris church was taken over almost immediately (1791) by the Assemblée Constituante as a national burial place for notable Frenchmen. It carries the inscription 'Aux grands hommes la Patrie reconnaissante'. *Mirabeau was the first person to be buried there; shortly afterwards the remains of *Voltaire and *Rousseau were transferred there.

Pantomime. Greek in origin, the term in its modern usage refers to a type of popular entertainment reflecting distinctive national traditions. In France the tradition centres on the originally noisy and exuberant dumb-show featuring the clown Pierrot, a character borrowed from the servant Pedrolino of the *commedia dell'arte*, but made more gauche, simple, and appealing in his French guise, dating from c.1665. Given a distinctive costume—loose white smock, long sleeves, ruff, broad-brimmed hat, and chalk-white face—he became a firm favourite of the public at the Paris fairs of the late 17th and 18th c. Over the years, while remaining recognizably the same, his dress was modified and his character underwent a number of changes. Most important were those introduced by the great mime Debureau (1796–1846), idol in the 1830s of the boisterous Théâtre des Funambules, who transformed Pierrot into a lovelorn and moonstruck figure of pathos, reducing the anarchical turbulence of the old-style scenarios. His successor Legrand continued this trend towards wistfulness and sentimentality. The popularity of pantomime at the Funambules declined in the 1850s and 1860s, but the genre experienced a short-lived revival in the more literary productions of the Cercle Funambulesque (1888). Its charm is preserved in *Carné's film *Les Enfants du paradis* (1945). The term 'pantomime' is also used by *Diderot and others to refer to the physical, gestural element which they wished to revive in the theatre. [SBJ]

Panurge. A character in Rabelais's *Pantagruel* and succeeding books. His name is derived from the Greek *panourgos* ('resourceful', 'cunning'), and he belongs to a large family of trickster-figures in world literature. He appears first as a polyglot adventurer whom Pantagruel befriends; in *Pantagruel*, although his exploits are often amoral, they are clearly meant in most cases to engage the complicity of the reader. In the *Tiers Livre* and *Quart Livre* he is increasingly presented as a victim of self-love ('philautie') and a coward (see the storm scene in the *Quart Livre*). Yet he remains energetic and resourceful, as in his virtuoso defence of debts and in the trick he plays on the merchant Dindenault. [TC]

Papiers collés, see PERROS.

PAPUS (pseud. of Gérard Encausse) (1865–1916). One of the leading figures in the resurgence of occultism during the late 19th c. with his *Traité élémentaire de science occulte* (1888), Papus contributed, through his contacts with the literary and artistic milieu, to the *Symbolist aspiration to reconcile scientific and mystical approaches to art. [JK]

Paquebot Tenacity, Le, see VILDRAC.

Parade, see FARCE, 2.

PARADIS, Suzanne (b. 1936). Canadian poet and novelist. She champions a poetry of intense personal feeling: *Les Enfants continuels* (1959), *Le Visage offensé* (1965), *Pour voir les plectrophanes naître* (1970), *Chevaux de verre* (1979). In her novels too she seeks an immediacy and richness of experience: *Miss Charlie* (1980). *Femme fictive et femme réelle* (1966) is a penetrating critical essay. [MMC]

Paradis artificiels, Les, see BAUDELAIRE.

Paradoxe sur le comédien, Le, see DIDEROT.

PARAIN, Brice (1897–1971). French philosopher of language. In his best-known work, *Recherches sur la nature et les fonctions du langage* (1942), Parain explored the limits and power of denomination and demonstration: language, he argued, is the source both of error and of creativity, and thus engages man's responsibility. Preoccupied with the truth-value of propositions, he reaffirmed the principle of non-contradiction and deplored the role of rhetoric in communication, education, and power-relations. He was convinced of the autonomy of language, which the written rather than the spoken word particularly confirms, and argued that its primary function is regulative and universalizing rather than representational or expressive. He evinced the

Parallèlle des anciens et des modernes

modern view that, situated within language, we are spoken by it, rather than speaking it; at the same time he more traditionally postulated the existence of God as guarantor of its integrity.   [REG]

Parallèle des anciens et des modernes, see PERRAULT, C.

Paravents, Les, see GENET.

Pardaillan. Hero of adventure stories by *Zévaco; an important figure for the young *Sartre (see *Les Mots*).

PARÉ, Ambroise (*c.*1510–1590). French doctor and medical writer. From Laval Paré moved to Paris where, without a formal humanist education, he won recognition for his skill as a surgeon, and served four kings. One of the founders of modern science, he based his method on observation and a strong belief in God. He is considered to be the father of military surgery—he advocated unguents rather than boiling oil to cure wounds and the use of the tourniquet after amputation. His work, written in accessible French, reveals the Renaissance mind which looks afresh at monsters and science. His *Œuvres complètes* were published in 1575.   [KCC]

Parents pauvres, Les. Original group title of two of the *Scènes de la vie parisienne* in Balzac's *Comédie humaine: La *Cousine Bette* and Le *Cousin Pons*.

Parfaite Amie, La, see HÉROËT.

Pari, Le, see PASCAL.

PÂRIS, François de (1690–1727). A severe, self-mortifying *Jansenist who deliberately remained at the humble level of deacon (hence known as 'le diacre Pâris'). He worked among the poor and spent periods in La Trappe [see RANCÉ] and among the Mont-Valérien hermits. Crowds flocked to his grave in the Saint-Médard cemetery in Paris where miraculous cures were claimed and increasing numbers of people indulged in manifestations of mass hysteria—convulsions, contorsions, prophesying, speaking in tongues ('les convulsionnaires'). The cemetery was officially closed in 1732, but these practices continued more furtively for a long time, doing harm to the reputation of Jansenism.   [JC]

PARIS, Gaston (1839–1903). French historian of medieval literature, professor at the *Collège de France. He wrote on many themes, including the *chansons de geste*, which he saw, in the Romantic tradition, as deriving from oral folk ballads.

Parisienne, La, see BECQUE.

Paris-Soir, see PRESS, 2.

PARIZEAU, Alice (1930–90/1). Born in Poland, active in the Resistance, and sent to a concentration camp, she studied in Paris before emigrating to Quebec in 1955. Set in Poland, France, and Quebec, her novels, of a traditional realist type, explore problems of identity, flight, and inheritance, from *Fuir* (1964) and *Les Lilas fleurissent à Varsovie* (1981) to *Nata et le professeur* (1988).   [EAF]

Parlements. In the *ancien régime*, final courts of appeal from lower courts, for this reason known as *cours souveraines*, with wide powers of jurisdiction. An offshoot from the *curia regis*, the first *parlement* took form in the mid-14th c. in Paris and had a jurisdiction over about three-fifths of the realm. It comprised three chambers: the *grand'chambre*, which received appeals from lower courts and judged cases from privileged officers and the peers in the first instance, and received *appels comme d'abus*; the *enquêtes*, which judged appeals on written evidence; and the *requêtes*, which received cases from those with letters of *committimus*. Before the temporary abolition of the Parlement de Paris in 1771, there were five *chambres des enquêtes* and two *chambres des requêtes*. A *chambre de la Tournelle* was created in 1515 to judge criminal cases. Each had a number of counsellors and presidents, and the Parlement was presided over by a *premier président*. Judicial offices were venal, conferring lifetime nobility, but the vast majority of the magistrates were already nobles of the robe or sword when recruited [see NOBILITY]. The *parquet* was the name given to the *gens du roi* who were the prosecuting attorneys: the *procureur général*, the three *avocats généraux*.

Provincial *parlements*, usually transformations of existing higher courts and possessing a corresponding structure, with fewer chambers, were established in Languedoc (1437), Dauphiné (1453), Bordeaux (1462), Burgundy (1477), Normandy (1499), Provence (1501), Brittany (1553), Béarn (1620), Metz (1633), Franche-Comté (1676), Flanders (1686), and Lorraine (1775) [see map on p. xxix]. Most cases were judged in the first instance in the 400 or so courts which existed in the local *bailliages* and *sénéchaussées*, minor cases in the numerous courts held by *prévôts*; about 70,000 seigneurial courts of very reduced competence still existed in 1789. *Bailliages* and *prévôtés* originated in the 13th c. and had administrative, judicial, and financial attributions.

The *parlements* were both judicial and administrative bodies with wide local responsibilities. With powers to preserve order, they had authority over highways, municipalities, charitable institutions, the grain trade, and many other areas of provincial life. They could issue administrative rulings (*arrêts*) which, if not contradicted by the royal council, eventually became part of the local legal corpus. Like all corporate bodies, they had their own traditions and a very strong sense of their own importance, even going so far as to regard themselves as the guardians of the legal forms of the monarchy (and claiming there were 'fundamental laws'); magistrates often compared themselves to Roman senators. To become law, edicts had to be registered before the courts, and this verification process was combined with their right of remonstrance against inconsistent or ill-conceived royal legal declarations to give them an ill-defined power of interference in the legislative process. Remonstrances could be ignored by the king's council and legislation registered in the *parlement* by *lettres de jussion* or in the presence of the king by a *lit de justice*. In 1648 the Parlement de Paris protested against the 'constitutional' changes wrought by *Mazarin's war policies, and this sparked off the *Fronde Parlementaire. *Louis XIV, while giving an impression of authoritarian dominance of the *parlements*, avoided conflict by being much more sensitive to their interests and jurisdiction. From the 1730s jurisdictional conflict, often over ecclesiastical issues (the bull *Unigenitus*) and *parlementaire* *Gallicanism, was exploited by *Jansenists in the *parlements* with radical constitutional ideas. The consequent running battle between the *parlements* and the council up to 1770 (which led to the abolition of the *parlements* from 1771 to 1774, by the coup *Maupeou of 1771), and from the mid-1780s, was one of many causes of the collapse of the monarchy in 1789. They were abolished along with the other courts in 1790.   [PRC]

Par les champs et par les grèves. Book of travel notes written jointly in 1847 by *Flaubert and *Du Camp, published posthumously.

Parnasse, Le. The Parnassian ideal was the dominant trend in French poetry during the Second Empire and early years of the Third Republic. Recognizing *Leconte de Lisle as their leader, a group of young poets, united in their ambition to free poetry from what they saw as outdated Romantic theories of inspiration in favour of a more disciplined, scientific approach to the content and forms of poetry, formed around Catulle *Mendès, initially in his short-lived *Revue fantaisiste* (1861) and subsequently in the three volumes of verse, *Le Parnasse contemporain* (1866, 1871, 1876). Considered for much of this century as a parenthesis between the major movements of *Romanticism and *Symbolism, it is now increasingly recognized as having played a pivotal role in the interaction between the two.

In theoretical terms at least, the Parnassians defended impersonality, impassivity, and formal perfection against Romanticism's lyrical expression of the self and commitment to the social value of art, as a result, on one level, of the failure of the 1848 Revolution and, on another, of their commitment to the scientific objectivity central to the Second Empire's positivist ideology [see COMTE]. Though they dismissed *Lamartine's 'poésie du cœur', *Hugo's descriptive poetry (*Les Orientales*, 1829) and the cosmic visions of *Les Contemplations* (1856) and *La Légende des siècles* (1859) were major influences. In his poems on the history of humanity in the *Poèmes antiques* and *Poèmes barbares*, Leconte

de Lisle created a personal vision of nature and human history, whose force derives largely from its engagement with Parnassian prosodic constraints. *Gautier's theory of 'l'*art pour l'art' became an increasingly powerful rallying-point, and his *Émaux et camées* (1852) extended the prosodic implications of the analogies with painting and sculpture which had already exercised the Romantic generation of the 1830s. His 1857 poem 'L'Art' became a Parnassian manifesto, and *Banville's *Petit traité de poésie française* (1872) codified this emphasis on the plastic qualities of verse and the essential structuring role of rhyme. Parnassian poetry failed when, in order to express its scientific or philosophical ambitions, it lapsed into precisely the 'didactisme rimé' to which it was in theory opposed, but its emphasis on poetry as an organized system of rhymes, stanzaic structures, and descriptive, picturesque effects defined the basis from which *Baudelaire, *Verlaine, *Mallarmé, and *Rimbaud would, in their different ways, 'creuser le vers'. In 1893 the success among the Symbolists of *Heredia's *Les Trophées*, in many respects an anthology of Parnassian themes and practices, testifies to their recognition of the importance of the Parnassian phase in 19th-c. French poetry.   [JK]

PARNY, Évariste-Désiré de Forges de (1753–1814). Poet. Born in the Île Bourbon (Reunion), he lived mainly in France, but drew inspiration from his native landscapes. He lost his fortune in the Revolution, obtained a post in the Ministry of Education, and was elected to the *Institut de France in 1803. His *Poésies érotiques* (1778–84) were compared by contemporaries to Tibullus for their sensual and emotional charm. The *Chansons madécasses* (1787), over-lush prose poems supposedly based on native songs, were set to music by *Ravel. Parny achieved notoriety with his anti-Christian burlesque epic *La Guerre des dieux* (1799). His elegiac and epicurean love poetry and his irreverent wit made him a favourite of Pushkin.   [PF]

Parody and Pastiche. Both of these forms involve the playful imitation of existing writings. Often parody is seen as more aggressively satirical, and pastiche as a literary exercise. *Genette proposes a clearer distinction, using parody to refer to texts in which an existing *text* is in some way rewritten or adapted for comic purposes, and pastiche for an imitation of an individual or generic *style*.

Understood in this way, the purest French example of parody is the *Chapelain décoiffé* by *Boileau, *Chapelle, and others, in which some scenes from *Le *Cid* are adapted to tell a grotesque story of the loss of a wig by their enemy *Chapelain. Similar transformations, though no longer for satirical purposes, are the rewritten proverb (e.g. *Prévert's 'Martyr, c'est pourrir un peu' for 'Partir, c'est mourir un peu') or the textual games played by *OULIPO. In their collection of pastiches, *A la*

Parole de femme

manière de . . ., *Reboux and Muller take maxims by
*La Rochefoucauld and invert them to produce
equally plausible sayings, e.g. 'Il y a de délicieux
mariages, mais il n'y en a point de bons' (this is both
parody and pastiche).

The second main type of parody is the rewriting
of an elevated text in a vulgar style. This was the
hallmark of the *burlesque which flourished in the
17th c.; in *Scarron's *Virgile travesti*, Dido, Aeneas,
and the narrator speak the language of plebeians.
Such burlesque parody was common in comedies
acted at the *théâtres de la *foire*, where the tragedies
of *Racine or *Corneille were transposed to low-life
settings. The same principle is at work in the
operettas co-authored by Offenbach, *Meilhac, and
Halévy (e.g. *La Belle Hélène*, 1864).

Pastiche, understood as the imitation of a style, is
a more ambitious affair. It can be distinguished from
*hoax in that it is meant to be appreciated as an imi-
tation, and from the continuation of an unfinished
work (e.g. *La *Vie de Marianne*) in that it gives pleasure by playing on the relation between two texts.
Sometimes the aim is to mock the original text by
exaggerating the tics of an author or the characteristic features of a genre; this is the case in the collections of Reboux and Muller mentioned above, or
(more subtly) in the mockery of *Marivaux's style in
L'Écumoire of *Crébillon *fils* (Marivaux himself
enjoyed such games, though he was more inclined
to burlesque parody). In 1978 M.-A. Burnier and
P. Rambaud, who had published *Parodies* the previous year, produced a whole book devoted to a
crude pastiche of Roland *Barthes's language, *Le
Roland Barthes sans peine*.

Often, however, pastiche is less aggressive, more
purely playful. Boileau's *Le Lutrin*, which he presents as a 'new kind of burlesque', is the classic
French example of the mock-heroic, in which the
author apparently enjoys manipulating the grand
manner he could never manage in earnest. In their
respective comedies *Le Menteur* and *Les Plaideurs*,
Corneille and Racine play with their own tragic
style—and indeed a good deal of classical comedy
relies on the humorous imitation of serious theatre.
Some three centuries later *Queneau, whose novels
are full of pastiche and mock solemnity, devoted his
remarkable *Exercices de style* (1947) to rewriting a
banal anecdote in 99 different and contrasting
modes (*noble, précieux, maladroit*, etc.).

Many other French writers have incorporated
pastiche into their writings, but the master of the
genre is *Proust. Imaginative imitations, based on
an intimate knowledge, and sometimes love, of the
originals, are to be found scattered through *A la
recherche du temps perdu*, but also in *Pastiches et
mélanges* (1919). The latter includes *L'Affaire Lemoine*,
where a contemporary news story is treated as if by
*Saint-Simon and a number of 19th-c. writers
(*Sainte-Beuve, *Renan, *Balzac, *Michelet,
*Chateaubriand, *Goncourt, *Flaubert, *Regnier).
The aim is sometimes satirical, more often apprecia-

tive; Proust's Flaubert, for instance, is a remarkable
example of sympathetic recreation.   [PF]

See G. Genette, *Palimpsestes* (1982).

Parole de femme, see LECLERC, A.

Paroles, see PRÉVERT.

Paroles d'un croyant, see LAMENNAIS.

Partage de Midi. In this play, written in 1905,
*Claudel explores the relationship between the
adulterous lovers Mesa and Ysé on two levels—the
real world (on a boat and in China) and the Platonic
eternity in which their union has been forged.
There is a tension between a Romantic, fatalistic
attitude to love and its effects, and Christian responsibility for evil; despite Claudel's later preface (to
the stage version of 1948), the tension is not
resolved even by the lovers' *Liebestod* in Act III. In
the *cadre* of a 'well-made play' on an adulterous
theme, Claudel succeeds in producing a drama of
cosmic dimensions.   [RMG]

Partie de chasse de Henri IV, La. Innovative historical play by *Collé.

Partimen, see JEU PARTI.

Parti pris (1963–8). A Canadian literary and political
journal which was the ideological forum for radical
québécois intellectuals during the Révolution
Tranquille period [see QUEBEC, 5]. Strongly influenced by the anti-colonialist writings of *Fanon and
others, the journal advocated separatism and socialism as the only cures for Quebec's alienated condition. Its call for the use of *joual in literature was
made on the grounds that a subjugated nation must
express itself in the impoverished language of its disinherited people. Despite the ambivalence of such a
view of language, the journal inspired a great deal of
vigorous and original writing in the vernacular
which undoubtedly helped modern Quebec literature to find its own distinctive voice. Many of the
texts it promoted appeared under its own imprint in
a fruitful publishing venture which outlived the
journal itself.   [SIL]

Parti pris des choses, Le, see PONGE.

Part maudite, La, see BATAILLE, G.

Partonopeu de Blois. This anonymous verse
romance of the late 12th c. recounts the fabulous
voyage of the French hero Partonopeu to the
Byzantine world of Chef d'Oire, where he meets the
powerful and learned princess Melior, empress of
Constantinople. The lady accords her favours on
condition that Partonopeu make love to her only in
the dark. At his mother's urging, Partonopeu shines
a lantern on his beloved; Melior loses her magical
powers and banishes the disconsolate Partonopeu.
He eventually wins back his lady in the course of a

three-day tournament where the two are reconciled. The lengthy romance (whose longest version comprises over 18,000 lines) is punctuated by amusing interventions of the poet, who compares his progress with his lady to that of Partonopeu and Melior. In the Epilogue, the poet says that he would continue his story if only his lady would wink. A continuation appended to some manuscripts experiments more boldly with poetic form as it tells the tale of the sultan Margaris, whom Melior refused. Enormously popular in the Middle Ages, *Partonopeu* was translated into German, Dutch, English, Italian, and other languages. [RLK]

PASCAL, Blaise (1623–62). One of the greatest advocates of Christian ideas, Pascal also displayed outstanding gifts as a mathematician, a scientist, a controversialist, and a literary stylist.

He was born in Clermont-en-Auvergne (now Clermont-Ferrand). His mother died when he was 3, and in 1631 his father, a member of the *noblesse de robe*, moved with his family to Paris and devoted himself increasingly to the education of Blaise and his two sisters, Gilberte and Jacqueline. Pascal eventually received a thorough grounding in Latin, mathematics, and science. He showed such intellectual precocity that in 1635 his father began taking him occasionally to the scientific academy recently founded by *Mersenne. Partly inspired by a member of the group, Pascal published an *Essai pour les coniques* (1640) at the age of 16. In this short paper, intended as part of a larger *Traité des coniques* which remained unfinished, he moved from Euclidean to projective geometry while deducing certain conic properties. Later mathematical activity included work on the theory of probability, especially in his letters of 1654 to Fermat on 'la règle des partis' and in his *Traité du triangle arithmétique* of the same year. A series of later works on the mathematics of chance and on the cycloid are important in themselves and for the extent to which they anticipated the integral calculus.

At the end of 1639 Pascal's father had been appointed tax commissioner for Normandy. The family joined him in Rouen early in 1640, and the next six or seven years were very important in Pascal's life. Before long he had invented an ingenious mechanical calculating machine ('la pascaline') to aid his father with his fiscal computations. A machine was constructed, with the help of a mechanic in Rouen, in 1644, and a series of improved models followed up to 1652. It was also around this period that Pascal carried out much of his most important experimental work on the nature of the vacuum and on atmospheric pressure. The lively practicality of his mind was shown much later, some 18 months before his death, when he devised a system of cheap public transport for Paris—the so-called 'carrosses à cinq sols'.

It was during the Rouen period that Pascal experienced what is sometimes called his 'first conversion'. In January 1646 two amateur bone-setters, the brothers Deschamps Deslandes and Deschamps de la Bouteillerie, were treating his father for a hip injury. They were keen religious proselytizers, and succeeded in converting all members of the family to *Jansenism. In the spring of 1647 Pascal became seriously ill (he suffered from very poor health for most of his life), and in the summer he and Jacqueline returned to Paris. They visited *Port-Royal quite frequently and Jacqueline became a nun there, despite her brother's opposition, in 1652. It was also in 1652 that Pascal was to witness some of the worst battles of the *Fronde; he later wrote that 'le plus grand des maux est les guerres civiles'. After his illness Pascal's doctors had recommended that he seek more recreation, and he went through a brief 'worldly' period. He became increasingly intimate with the duc de Roannez and his sister Charlotte, while also maintaining an acquaintanceship with such socialites as the chevalier de *Méré and the religious sceptic Damien Mitton. He is sometimes credited with a *Discours sur les passions de l'amour* said to have been written at this period. It seems unlikely that he was the author, however, or that it reflects a passionate relationship with Charlotte de Roannez (to whom he wrote letters of spiritual guidance in 1656).

The most decisive moment of Pascal's life came in 1654. On the night of 23 November he underwent an intense religious experience which brought him total conviction (of a kind inaccessible to the rational intellect alone) of God's reality and presence. Where the first conversion was essentially a matter of intellectual persuasion, this second experience brought a deep, inner transformation of a mystical kind. The 'Mémorial', a short ecstatic document in which he recorded his experience, was found, on his death, sewn into his doublet.

Meanwhile attacks on Jansenism increased, led by the *Jesuits, and Antoine *Arnauld's position in the Sorbonne became very insecure. A number of his Port-Royal friends turned to Pascal for support. He launched an immensely successful attack against the Jesuits in his 18 *Lettres provinciales* (January 1656–March 1657). This is one of the great polemical works of French literature, ranging in tone from ironical mockery to angry denunciation and using a number of very successful argumentational devices and tactics. Even *Voltaire, no friend of Pascal or of Jansenism, admired and praised Pascal's rhetorical skill. The first four letters cleverly and amusingly reduce the theological jargon about grace, as used by the enemies of Jansenism, to meaningless self-contradiction. Between the third and fourth letters Arnauld was condemned and dismissed from the Sorbonne, but Pascal's campaign continued. Partly using material supplied by *Nicole and Arnauld, he denounced Jesuit casuistry and moral laxity in letters 5 to 10. The remaining eight letters are chiefly designed to answer the counter-polemic which the first ten had provoked. The eleventh, for instance, contains a brilliant justification of the use of humour in defence of religion (the abbess of Port-Royal, Mère Angélique Arnauld, had been shocked by Pascal's tone). And the last two letters were a counter-attack against the king's confessor, the Jesuit père Annat. Official reaction to the *Provinciales* was severe. They were placed on the Index of forbidden books and burned by the Parlement of Aix. But they enjoyed great popular success and aroused much admiration, even among non-Jansenists.

In the *Écrits des curés de Paris* (1658), which Pascal wrote in collaboration with Arnauld and Nicole, a major topic in the *Lettres provinciales*—moral laxism—is the focus of an attack on Pirot's *Apologie pour les casuistes*. Pascal reopened the other main topic of the *Lettres*—the nature of grace—when he completed four important *Écrits sur la grâce* around the same period. It was probably in 1659, as he continued to suffer acute ill health, that he wrote his *Prière pour demander à Dieu le bon usage des maladies*. An important posthumously published document is the *Entretien avec M. de Saci*, which *Le Maître de Sacy's secretary, Nicolas Fontaine, appears to have recorded as it took place and in which Pascal analyses the strengths and inadequacies of Epictetus' stoicism and *Montaigne's scepticism.

There is no doubt that Pascal's greatest work remains the *Pensées*, which were posthumously published in 1670. This is a major exercise in Christian apologetics, even though it is mainly composed of notes and fragments jotted down in preparation for a systematic treatise which he did not live to complete. Since only a part of this material had been put into order by Pascal, there is much debate among editors concerning the intended design of his apologia. It is clear, however, that human nature is investigated in the *Pensées* at the psychological, social, metaphysical, and theological levels. In moral-psychological terms, Pascal finds in human beings a series of dramatic contradictions which, he argues, only the Christian doctrine of original sin can properly explain. At the social-political level, he points to the fragile nature of many social relationships and the unsatisfactoriness of the legal and political concepts of his day. Rather startlingly for the period, he holds social hierarchy to be based on arbitrariness rather than justice. As with his moral and social being, man's metaphysical nature is a source of dissatisfaction. He is a unique creature, but condemned to die in an infinite, impersonal universe. At all these levels, then, the picture of human beings is a dark and desperate one, but Pascal argues that when God is introduced at each level, the picture is transformed. The *Pensées*, therefore, use an analysis of the problem of human nature in order to interest the reader in the Christian solution. They seek to convince him or her further with evidence from the scriptures, miracles, Church history, etc. Above all, they insist that only faith which responds to God's grace, not purely intellectual enquiry, will explain human life properly and bring knowledge of God and true happiness.

Pascal remained conscious of the necessity—and difficulty—of interesting the *libertin* in these ideas. His famous *pari*, or wager, demonstrating that it is in our interest to bet on God's existence rather than against it, is usually seen not as a serious argument in itself but as an attempt to address the gambling *libertin* in language he will understand.   [JC]

See J. H. Broome, *Pascal* (1965); J. Mesnard, *Les Pensées de Pascal* (1976); R. Duchêne, *L'Imposture littéraire dans les Provinciales de Pascal* (1985).

Pasquier, Chronique des. Cycle of novels by *Duhamel.

PASQUIER, Étienne (1529–1615). French historian. As a lawyer and orator, Pasquier is best known for his famous attack against the *Jesuits, whom, as a good *Gallican, he detested. Many of his letters show a great deal of insight into the problems created by the *Wars of Religion (he was a typical member of the *Politique party); but he is best known today as the author of the *Recherches de la France*. Begun in the 1550s, the *Recherches* gradually expanded over the subsequent decades. Though not devoid of error, they are significant for the way in which Pasquier's social, political, historical, and linguistic curiosity enables him to build up a picture of France's medieval past, of which he is extremely proud.   [JJS]

Passager de l'Occident, Un, see FARÈS.

PASSERAT, Jean (1534–1602). Teacher at the Collège du Cardinal-Lemoine, then at the Collège de Boncourt, before replacing *Ramus at the Collège Royal. His posts as tutor and librarian for the family of Henri de Mesmes linked him with the nobility. His commentaries (in Latin) on Catullus, Tibullus, and Propertius (not published until 1608) highlight the link between academic scholarship and contemporary interest in poetry as exemplified by the *Pléiade. Passerat supplied some of the satirical verses for the *Satire Ménippée and wrote various pieces of patriotic and religious verse; but he is better known for a more light-hearted style, more reminiscent of Clément *Marot (*Recueil des œuvres poétiques*, 1606).   [JJS]

Passé simple, Le, see CHRAÏBI.

PASSEUR, Stève (pseud. of Étienne Morin) (1899–1966). French journalist, then playwright. He worked with many famous directors, including *Lugné-Poë (*L'Acheteuse*, 1930), *Jouvet (*Suzanne*, 1929; *Le Château de cartes*, 1937), and *Pitoeff (*Je vivrai un grand amour*, 1935). These and other plays express a generally cynical vision of love between dominating females and feeble males; his dialogue is tough and witty in an efficiently theatrical manner.   [PF]

Passion du Palatinus, La. The earliest surviving complete French *Passion play; it dates from the early 14th c. and dramatizes the events of Holy

Week, from Christ's entry to Jerusalem up to his appearances after the Resurrection. This fast-moving 2,000-line play is heavily dependent on the 13th-c. narrative *Passion des jongleurs*.   [GAR]

Passion Plays. *Mystery plays which dramatize the Crucifixion of Christ. The earliest examples concentrate simply on the events of Holy Week, from Christ's entry into Jerusalem up to the Resurrection, but the later plays include not only the whole life of Christ, but also some Old Testament episodes. Thus, in its fully developed form, the Passion play is a cyclical drama starting with the Creation of the Universe and ending with the Ascension. The earliest French Passion plays, dating from the 14th c., were relatively short: e.g. the *Passion du Palatinus* (2,000 lines) and the *Passion Sainte-Geneviève* (4,500 lines). The latest, from the mid-16th c., were long, e.g. the 1549 *Passion de Valenciennes* (40,000 lines).

The origins of the French Passion play are found, not in liturgical drama, but in the narrative *Passion des jongleurs*, a widely circulated compilation of a number of legends associated with the last week of Christ's life, based on apocryphal material as well as the Gospels. The *Passion du Palatinus* borrowed much of this, and was in turn copied in subsequent plays. The genre was particularly successful after the *Hundred Years War. Eustache Marcadé's *Passion d'Arras* (25,000 lines, *c*.1440) set the pattern for most of the major plays. He divided his text into four *journées*, devoted respectively to the Nativity and Childhood of Jesus, his Public Life, the Crucifixion, and the Resurrection. This action is framed by the allegorical *Procès de Paradis*, in which Miséricorde and Pitié plead with God the Father to save mankind. Marcadé's most famous successors were Arnoul *Gréban and Jehan *Michel. Few completely original Passion plays were composed after 1450; the dramatists (*fatistes*) normally adapted pre-existing texts, though these adaptations sometimes amounted to complete rewritings. It is thus possible to trace the genealogy of Passion plays. Although only one manuscript of most mystery plays was copied out, such copies circulated in a limited geographical area, and each province had its own Passion play tradition. Several versions of the *Passion d'Auvergne* were performed in Montferrand in 1452, 1477, and the early 16th c.; the *Passion du Palatinus* gave rise to several Burgundian plays, including the *Passion de Semur* (1488). The most influential tradition sprang from Gréban's play, itself modelled on Eustache Marcadé's.

A change in emphasis is noticeable as the plays grew longer. Whereas the 14th-c. texts are content to dramatize the story which is the basis of the Christian religion, the later plays seek to comment, interpret, sermonize, and moralize, as well as to provide entertainment, excitement, tension, and colour. The Passion plays had an educational function; they were books for the illiterate. Even so, like all mystery plays, they contained important realistic and comic elements.   [GAR]

See M. Accarie, *Le Théâtre sacré de la fin du moyen âge* (1979).

Passion Sainte-Geneviève, La. A 4,500-line one-day *Passion play preserved in the *Bibliothèque Sainte-Geneviève; it forms part of an anthology of six *mystery plays dating from the late 14th and early 15th c. Though it dramatizes virtually the same material as the *Passion du Palatinus*, it is independent of this and all other Passion plays.   [GAR]

Passions de l'âme, Les, see DESCARTES.

PASTEUR, Louis (1822–95). Founder of microbiology. After his training in chemistry and biology, Pasteur's early work on fermentation led him to discover the micro-organisms which cause it, and to propose methods of preservation, one of which was named pasteurization. He developed the theory of germs and the method of asepsis as well as vaccines for anthrax and rabies. His flair for striking demonstrations, sometimes exceeding his rigour, made him a household name, and he was elected to the Académie Française in 1881. He founded the Institut Pasteur in Paris, which has maintained France's reputation in microbiology, most recently distinguished by its work on AIDS.   [MHK]

Pastiche, see PARODY.

Pastoral [for pastoral in the Middle Ages see PASTORELA]. The modern pastoral tradition began to reach France in the 1540s through the diffusion of the major classical, Spanish, and Italian texts, and was most popular in the early decades of the 17th c. In prose fiction it was more through translation than imitation that the tradition was sustained during the 16th c. Sannazaro's *Arcadia* (trans. 1544), Longus' *Daphnis and Chloë* (trans. 1559), Gil Polo's *Diana enamorada* (trans. 1582), and above all Montemayor's *Diana* (trans. 1578) were widely read, but original French imitations were few, the most notable being *Belleforest's *La Pyrénée et pastorale amoureuse* (1571) and Nicolas de *Montreux's cumbersomely derivative *Les Bergeries de Juliette* (1585–98) in five volumes. It was only with d'Urfé's *L'*Astrée* (1607–27) that France produced its own masterpiece in the genre, a text which was to influence the taste, if not the fiction, of generations to come.

Manifestations of the tradition in the theatre were much more widespread and significant. The major Italian pastoral plays, Tasso's *Aminta* (trans. 1584) and Guarini's *Il pastor fido* (trans. 1595), together with episodes taken from the Spanish romances, inspired many dramatists in the early years of the 17th c.; such plays were uneven in style and quality, and often dominated by extensive lament or implausible plots. *Racan's *Bergeries* (performed *c*.1619) and *Mairet's *Sylvie* (performed 1626), more refined both in their language and in their analysis of love, saw the beginnings of more accomplished pastoral, and the publication of Mairet's *Silvanire* (1631), with its important preface, marked the association of the genre with the growing movement towards theatrical reform. Many plays adapted from or modelled on the Italian classics soon followed, often accompanied by theoretical prefaces: *Pichou's *Filis de Scire* (1630), *Gombauld's *Amaranthe* (1631), *Baro's *Clorise* (1630), d'*Alibray's *Aminte* (1632), and *Rayssiguier's *Aminte* (1632), among others. Such plays suggested principles of regularity in dramatic construction to be adopted subsequently in tragedy, but they served also to inspire a new kind of comedy which would ultimately supersede its model: the comedy of *Pierre Corneille, *Rotrou, and *Du Ryer, which transposed basic plots of love and its trials to more modern, urban settings. *Tristan's *Amarillis* (performed 1652), an adaptation of Rotrou's *Célimène*, represents a successful but brief reawakening of interest in pastoral, but *Molière's several experiments in the genre are more of an ironic, self-consciously stylized reminder of an outmoded tradition. More faithful to its spirit, albeit in modified form, are the works of *Marivaux.

Pastoral poetry took different forms in the course of the 16th and 17th c. *Scève's *Saulsaye, églogue de la vie solitaire* (1547) is personal and meditative in tone; *Belleau's *Bergerie* (1565) is largely inspired by Sannazaro; and *Ronsard's *Bergerie* (1565) is more overtly political. D'Urfé's derivative, but very popular, *Sireine* (1604) established a renewal of interest in the genre, and in the course of the 17th c. many poets found inspiration in the tradition. Basic commonplaces survive in the work of the Illustres Bergers, a group centred on Frénicle; Racan's 'Stances sur la retraite' (1618) embody and refashion classic Virgilian themes; and the work of *Théophile, Tristan, and *Saint-Amant offer different meditations on nature and happiness. *Sarasin's eclogues mark a rare survival of pastoral in the 1640s, largely dominated by witty salon poetry, but in the second half of the century poets often drew on the tradition in their search for a more direct expression of feelings. Some, like *Gilbert, *Segrais, or *Fontenelle, are pale and unimaginative, but other work is of more significance. *La Fontaine's *Adonis* (1658) is a richly sensuous idyll, and in the poetry of such women poets as *La Suze, *Villedieu, and particularly *Deshoulières, traditions of the bucolic are invested with individual sensitivity.

Traces of the pastoral are to be found in later times, although they tend to be isolated. Imprecise but recurrent echoes haunt the work of J.-J. *Rousseau, a self-confessed admirer of d'Urfé, and at the end of the century some familiar themes re-emerge, bathed in sentimentality. *Florian's *Estelle et Némorin* (1788), consciously retrospective, evokes the passing of a golden age, and in Bernardin de Saint-Pierre's *Paul et Virginie* (1788) the birth of love is explored, innocent and close to nature, yet tinged

with melancholy. The poetic idylls of George *Sand (*La *Mare au diable*, *La Petite Fadette*, *François le Champi*) represent a creative reworking of the tradition in the following century. [GJM]

See J. Marsan, *La Pastorale dramatique* (1905); C. Longeon (ed.), *Le Genre pastoral* (1980); A. Patterson, *Pastoral and Ideology* (1988).

Pastorela. Originally an Occitan lyric genre in which a knight and a shepherdess converse in rural surroundings. Sometimes he attempts to seduce her; sometimes she attempts seduction; alternatively, she offers him advice on how to treat courtly ladies; occasionally one of the protagonists moralizes about the state of the world. The *pastorela* may have had its origin in Latin pastoral poetry, but the vernacular tradition is nevertheless distinct. The earliest example, by *Marcabru, is arguably also the best: a witty shepherdess counters the advances of an oafish knight with skilful dialectical argument, fusing clerical learning with quaint peasant wisdom. Other well-known troubadours composed *pastorelas*, including *Giraut de Borneil and *Guiraut Riquier. A large number of northern French *pastourelles* survive. They are frequently more burlesque than Occitan *pastorelas*; some are overtly violent and culminate in the rape of the shepherdess. Both the Occitan and the northern traditions provide an interesting insight into the way clerical and courtly culture represented peasants. *Adam de la Halle's *Jeu de Robin et de Marion* owes a great deal to the *pastourelle* tradition. For texts, see W. D. Paden, *The Medieval Pastourelle*, 2 vols. (1989). [SG]

Pastourelle, see PASTORELA.

'Pataphysique, La. Name given to the 'science des solutions imaginaires' invented by Alfred *Jarry and set out most fully in his *Gestes et opinions du Docteur Faustroll* (1911). Standing in the same relation to metaphysics as the latter does to physics, it is the antithesis of positivist or rational science, addressing the universe as an accumulation of exceptions and accidents. It therefore enables no serious conclusions to be drawn, and can be seen as the basis of Absurdist aesthetics. The *Surrealists greatly admired *Faustroll* and 'pataphysics; in 1948 a 'Collège de 'Pataphysique' was established whose members included *Queneau, *Ionesco, *Prévert, and *Vian. [DHW]

Pathelin, La Farce de maistre Pierre. Probably the best and the best-known of all medieval *farces, though it is far from typical. Pathelin, a bogus lawyer in straitened circumstances, succeeds by flattery in getting a miserly draper to give him some cloth on credit. When the draper calls to collect his money he is told by Guillemette, Pathelin's wife, that her husband could not have bought cloth from him that morning since he is gravely ill; Pathelin, in order to convince the draper, has to feign illness and delirium, speaking in nine different languages. Later, Pathelin is asked by a shepherd who admits killing his master's sheep to defend him at his trial; Pathelin's advice is that he should say *bee* in answer to all questions. At the trial, the shepherd's accuser is none other than the draper; seeing Pathelin, he repeatedly confuses the two crimes of which he has been the victim. His confusion, and the shepherd's *bees*, cause the judge to absolve the shepherd. Pathelin, however, when asking the shepherd for payment, only gets *bee* in answer.

Though illustrating many of the features of the farce, *Pathelin* is untypical in its length (1,600 lines), its early date (*c.* 1460), its complexity (it could be broken down into three small farces), and in its learned aspects (monologues and literary allusions). The author remains unknown, but its subject-matter appears to link it with the *Basoches. Critics have also sought to provide localized interpretations; Paris and Angers have both been suggested.

[GAR]

PATIENT, Serge (b. 1934). Writer, educator, and politician from French Guiana. A collection of poems, *Guyane pour tout dire* (1980), contains a semi-autobiographical sequence of lyric and protest pieces, showing fidelity to French Guiana and an alert interest in its multilingual heritage. A historical nouvelle, *Le Nègre du gouverneur* (1972), is set in the time of Victor Hugues, governor of Guyane from 1800 to 1809. [BJ]

PATIN, Guy (1601–72). A Parisian physician and member of a number of academic societies, best known today for his letters on political, social, and intellectual issues of his day. He was dean of the Paris Faculty of Medicine for a short period (1650–2), and professor at the Collège Royal from 1654 to his death. His entertaining letters abound in gossip and trenchant comment on medical and political matters; they express a deep commitment to religious toleration and free scientific debate and enquiry. During the *Fronde he was an outspoken opponent of *Mazarin; his religious views are consistently *Gallican and anti-Jesuit; on medical issues, he was a conservative who opposed Harvey's theory of the circulation of the blood and was cautious about iatrochemical medicine. He was a clandestine book-dealer and did much to encourage the publication in France of foreign medical scholarship. [IM]

Patois and Dialect Writing (Post-medieval). The advent of French printing in 1470 confirmed the supremacy of Parisian French as a medium for cultural expression. Yet, very gradually, a reaction developed among educated, bilingual provincials in dialect-speaking *Switzerland, *Belgium, and non-*Occitan France, who saw the potential of their down-to-earth *patois* for offering an amusing or refreshing contrast to an increasingly refined standard language, especially to express satirical and conservative viewpoints. Ironically, to be printed,

dialectal literature has until recently had to rely on technology available only in towns responsible for disseminating Parisian French and threatening the survival of rural *patois*.

If one discounts the *noëls* [see POPULAR SONG] in Parisian French with a smattering of Angevin dialectalisms published in 1524 by 'maître Mitou' (alias abbé J. Daniel), the earliest non-Occitan literature to be printed in dialect is Franco-Provençal, the *Chanson de la complanta et desolasion dé paitré* (*c.*1535), a Protestant's nine-stanza mock-lamentation satirizing the Genevan clergy, followed by poems in Dauphinois (*c.* 1550–60) by the lawyer Laurent de Briançon, and songs and carols in Savoyard (Annecy, 1555) by the cleric Nicolas Martin of Saint-Jean-de-Maurienne. Publications in northern French dialects now began to appear, namely two satirical poems in Poitevin, the anonymous *Loittre de Tenot à Piarrot* (Paris, 1554) and the celebrated *Menelogue de Robin* by the lawyer Jean Boiceau de la Borderie (Poitiers, 1555), both reprinted with eight other, mostly rustic, poems in the popular dialectal collection *La Gente Poitevin'rie* (Poitiers, 1572, enlarged 1660). The end of the century saw the publication of the anonymous *Dialogue récréatif* (1599), humorously commenting in Norman on life after the Treaty of Vervins, and the mock-heroic *Histoire plaisante de la jalousie de Jennain sur la grossesse soudaine de Prigne sa femme* (Paris, 1598), written in Saint-Quentin Picard by a royal courtier, reprinted in 1640 with a parodic sermon in Picard prose, and given a sequel in 1648. Eventually publications in Lorrain and Walloon appeared with, in 1615, *La Grosse Enwaraye messine* (*La Grosse Amoureuse de Metz*), a verse monologue on rustic manners issued with a short *Fable récréative* parodying chivalric romances, and, at Liège, an anonymous ode to the theologian Mathieu Naveau (1620) and an anti-Protestant sonnet (1622) by the Capuchin Hubert Ora, whose invective anticipated by some 10 years the Walloon *pasquèyes* protesting against military abuses. Probably both ode and sonnet are facetiously intended. Among several works unpublished amid this first flowering are the jocular Burgundian dialogues, speeches, and *pastorales* (Paris, BN, ms. fr. 24039; *c.*1580) by the eminent citizens of Dijon who belonged to the exclusive Mère Folie society.

In the 17th and 18th c. production of non-Occitan dialectal literature was, on available evidence, sporadic. Prose continued to be a less-favoured medium than verse, which was generally narrative or moralizing. Theatre is thinly represented. Lyricism was confined to *noëls*, which between 1650 and 1750 achieved a climax of popularity, notably now in eastern France, and were sometimes dramatized as local, contemporary Nativity plays (especially in Walloon), even degenerating into satire. Printed *noëls* and orally transmitted popular songs tended to circulate outside their native region and be assimilated and adapted in other dialectal cultures.

Significant writers included: J. Drouhet in

Poitevin; D. Ferrand in Norman; Le Gras and F. Cottignies in Picard; L. de Ryckman and S. de Harlez in Walloon; A. Brondex in Lorrain; A. Piron and B. de La Monnoye in Burgundian; and M. Allard and B. Uchard in Franco-Provençal.

To judge by definitions in contemporary dictionaries, *patois* carried a social stigma. Yet a substantial proportion of the populace remained *patoisant*. In 1794 *Grégoire reported that, of an estimated French population of 25 million, only 3 million spoke 'pure' French. Whether or not this was true, the measures of the Revolutionary and 19th-c. French governments ensured the increasingly rapid decline of dialect, which caused concern among the new breed of philologists seeking to record it for posterity. Dialect also became a Romantic medium for expressing individuality and nostalgia for the past, particularly in personal lyric poetry. Rather as in the 16th c., a dialectal literary movement began in reaction to the general standardizing trend, originating in the Channel Islands and around Liège, then spreading to other regions in parallel with the closer-knit *Félibrige movement in Provence. It won support from the many popular regionalist societies, whose mouthpiece was the local or regional press. Thus eventually, between 1839 and 1914, a fair amount of dialectal prose was read in gazettes publishing anti-government satires, polemics, and open letters, and in non-polemical almanacs.

Significant writers included: E. Lacuve in Poitevin; J. H. Burgaud des Marets in Saintongeais; G. Métivier in Guernsey French; H. Carion, A. Desrousseaux, and J. Watteeuw in Picard; M. Renard in Walloon; D. Mory in Lorrain; H. Berthaut in Burgundian; and L. Bornet, J. Hornung, L. Favrat, and C. C. Denéréaz in Franco-Provençal.

This century the upheaval of two World Wars and the ever-increasing pressure of mass media have wrought an arguably terminal decline in dialectal literature. Yet productivity is higher than in pre-Revolutionary times, and desk-top publishing now allows writers to edit their own work with ease at home. New Channel Island, Picard, and Walloon titles appear regularly, as do re-editions and collected works. Modern authors treat broader themes, though humdrum or humorous realism still abounds. The work of scientifically transcribing oral material continues.

Significant writers include: A. J. Desnouettes in Norman; G. F. Le Feuvre in Jersey French; E. David in Picard and J. Mousseron, R. Ducorron, and P. André in the Rouchi sub-dialect; H. Simon and J. Calozet in Walloon; contributors to *Nate tére lôraine* and E. Mathis in Lorrain; contributors to *Le Bien public* and *Pays de Bourgogne* in Burgundian; and the prolific J. Surdez in Franco-Provençal. [See also HISTORY OF THE FRENCH LANGUAGE; LITERACY; OCCITAN LITERATURE (POST-MEDIEVAL)]   [PVD]

See M. Piron, 'Les Littératures dialectales du domaine d'oïl', in R. Queneau (ed.), *Histoire des littératures*, vol. 3 (1958); C. Guerlin de Guer and F. Lechanteur, *La Littérature patoisante* (1984).

Patriote français, Le. Political journal founded by *Brissot; it appeared from July 1789 to June 1793.

Patronage. Until the late 18th c., it was virtually impossible for French writers to live on their literary earnings. Even *Diderot, often regarded as one of the first professional writers, eked out his income from the *Encyclopédie* with gifts from Catherine the Great. Publishers paid badly, if at all. The theatre, where the richest pickings were to be had, rarely afforded a regular means of support. Many writers did not need payment for their work, having either unearned income or another profession; during the *ancien régime* such people tended to disdain publishers, literary earnings, and the 'hacks' who depended on them. But not all were so fortunate; for many, patronage (*le mécénat*) was an indispensable element of literary life.

Much of it came from rich and powerful individuals or families, in particular from the courts of monarchs, princes, and nobles, not only in France but abroad. In the High Middle Ages, for instance, *Eleanor of Aquitaine was a renowned protector of the arts, and in the 15th c. the *Burgundian court was an outstanding artistic centre. The French *Valois kings, particularly *François Ier, pursued a policy of cultural prestige which boded well for writers and artists, and in the following century *Louis XIV followed the same path. His protégé *Racine's career is a striking example of how royal patronage could enrich a writer. Even under Louis, however, there were many *mécènes apart from the king, notably such great princes as *Condé. The 17th and particularly the 18th c. saw the rise of financiers and tax-farmers such as *Helvétius, d'*Épinay, and La Popelinière as patrons of literature.

There was a tendency in the 17th and 18th c. for patronage to become more impersonal and official. Under *Colbert's direction, and with *Chapelain's guidance, pensions were distributed to many writers who were thought capable of enhancing the prestige of the monarchy. As the press developed, the government channelled pensions to writers through such journals as the *Mercure de France* or the *Journal des savants*, which had to make the payments from their profits. The payment of state pensions was notoriously irregular, depending on the royal finances, but it was more reliable than the one-off gifts in cash or in kind which from the earliest times had been the basic form of patronage. More reliable still were the innumerable sinecures or near-sinecures with which the crown and other patrons rewarded or encouraged devoted writers. The most important were church livings of various kinds; for many of these it was not necessary to have taken orders—the tonsure was enough. Some writers were active churchmen, but others contented themselves with receiving the salary; writers who were rewarded in this way ranged from *Machaut in the 14th c. to *Ronsard in the 16th, Racine in the 17th, and *Bernis (a particularly striking example) in the 18th.

In many cases, as well as receiving gifts or a salary, the writer was the 'domestique' (sometimes the secretary or librarian or bursar) of the patron, living in his or her house and eating at his or her table; *La Fontaine received help of this kind from Madame de *la Sablière. In such cases, writer and patron might live in close proximity, and relations between them could be close and friendly. Medieval manuscripts sometimes show the writer kneeling humbly and offering a work to a patron, but they also often speak of collaboration between the two, the writer giving shape to the patron's ideas [see AUTHORSHIP]. In the 17th c. *Segrais, secretary to the duchesse de *Montpensier, signed the *Nouvelles françaises* in which his patron had a large part. At the opposite extreme, Diderot's *Neveu de Rameau* presents an unforgettable, if biased, picture of the fawning yet insolent behaviour of writers at the table of a tax-farmer.

Many works were directly addressed from author to patron. *Marot, for instance, wrote a joking verse epistle to François Ier requesting money after being robbed. More normally, the work was preceded by a dedication in verse or prose; in the latter case it was often a separate dedicatory epistle. This can be regarded as a minor literary genre in its own right, an exercise in the rhetoric of praise. Many examples are fulsome to the point of absurdity, the most famous case being the eulogy of the financier Montoron at the head of Corneille's *Cinna*. Others made a point of praising more subtly and wittily, while yet others (e.g. *Scarron) made mock of the whole procedure. The dedicatory epistle appears to have lost favour in the 18th c., though it is interesting to note that Voltaire dedicated *Mahomet* to Pope Benedict XIV, who was certainly not his patron.

Private patronage declined in importance as the book-buying public grew in the 19th c. It did not by any means disappear, however, and wealthy individuals supported the work of many avant-garde writers and artists, including the *Surrealists. Much more important in recent times is public patronage, whether from industrial companies or from the state. During the Revolutionary period and the Second Empire, for instance, government had given financial encouragement to the arts, provided they supported the regime. The appointment of *Malraux as minister of culture in 1959 led to an unprecedented volume of state support for all the arts, including literature. This was carried a stage further, with a different political slant and a different definition of culture, by Jack Lang, minister of culture under François *Mitterrand. In 1992 Marc Fumaroli provoked vehement debates with his *L'État culturel*, a vitriolic attack on the effects of state patronage. [PF]

See J. Lough, *Writer and Public in France* (1978).

PATRU, Olivier (1604–81). Lexicographer and one of the most celebrated barristers of his day. His *Plaidoyers* (1670) are a collection of speeches reworked after delivery in the manner of Cicero. He had the reputation for purging forensic oratory of its technical jargon and learned references, making it once again a readable literary genre. He was elected to the *Académie Française as early as 1640 and inaugurated its still extant tradition of the *discours de réception*. His interest in language led him to contribute to the *dictionaries of Richelet (1680) and the Academy (1694). [PJB]

Paulette, La, see TAXATION.

Paul et Virginie. Novel by *Bernardin de Saint-Pierre, published in Volume 4 of his *Études de la nature* in 1788, and separately in the following year.

Paul and Virginie are brought up by their mothers on the tropical island of Mauritius as if they were brother and sister, even though their mothers are from opposite ends of the social scale. At puberty Virginie is sent to join her great-aunt in France and is educated there for some years. Nevertheless she rejects the idea of marrying anyone but Paul. On her return the ship carrying her is wrecked on the coast of Mauritius. A sailor offers to carry her to the shore if she takes off her clothes, but out of modesty she refuses, and is drowned. Paul and the other main characters on the island die of grief shortly afterwards, but the great-aunt lives on in Paris, tormented by remorse.

Despite its didacticism, its excessive sentimentality, and the oddity of its denouement, *Paul et Virginie* owes its continuing popularity with readers to its powerful orchestration of a number of deep mythical elements—the lost earthly paradise, the *Tristan legend and even, at a subconscious level, the taboo on incest. At the heart of this *pastorale* is a *Rousseauistic indictment of the corruption of modern Europe and an elegy for the lost Edenic childhood innocence of mankind. The descriptions of Mauritius are strikingly beautiful. [DW]

PAULHAN, Jean (1884–1968). French critic and essayist. Born into a Protestant family in Nîmes, Paulhan was brought up in a free-thinking atmosphere which was to mark his own attitudes and commitments throughout his life. He never shirked involvement, political or cultural, and the five volumes of his collected works, and volumes of letters, attest to the wide range of his writing, criticism, and friendships.

A teaching post in Madagascar in 1907 awakened his interest in its language and culture, resulting in *Les *Hain-teny merinas: poésies populaires malgaches recueillies et traduites par Jean Paulhan* (1913). The experiences of World War I started him on his long and varied career as a writer and critic interested in language, especially semantics—*Le Guerrier appliqué*

(1917) was a contender for the Prix Goncourt. His immediate literary success brought him into contact with *Gide and *Rivière, and was the beginning of a long association with the *Nouvelle Revue Française.

Paulhan had always been attracted to fringe, innovative groups, including Russian anarchists, so it is not surprising to see him involved with the *Dadaists and especially the Surrealists—*Breton, *Aragon, *Soupault, and *Éluard, a group alien to the tastes of the NRF. Paulhan was not fixed in his tastes, but was continually renewing himself, revising his positions and looking for fresh ideas; consequently, a public quarrel with Breton was inevitable.

After Rivière's death in 1925 Paulhan took over as chief editor of the NRF, bringing new vigour to literary criticism in the 1930s and 1940s, launching new publishing ventures, and encouraging fresh, unconventional writers—a brilliant group including *Artaud, *Caillois, Jean *Grenier, *Leiris, *Michaux, *Ponge, *Queneau, and *Supervielle, together with the well-established Rilke—writers who were to change the subject-range, form, and perceptions of literature. Paulhan contributed to the renewal with his own critical works, Les Fleurs de Tarbes (1941) and Clef de la poésie, Traité des figures ou la Rhétorique décryptée (1944), which treat what he called 'les incertitudes du langage'.

The *Occupation made his position within the NRF ambiguous; he left it, and threw himself into Resistance activity, founding, with Jacques Decour, the clandestine newspaper Les Lettres françaises. The post-war period was marked by a great interest in modern painting, especially *Cubism, and the painters *Braque and *Dubuffet. It was a period of feverish activity and output, including De la paille et du grain (1949) and Lettre au médecin (1959), but was soured by an embittered controversy with the Comité National des Écrivains, culminating in Lettre aux directeurs de la Résistance (1952). In 1953 he became editor of the renamed NRF, the NNRF, and his contribution to the cultural and literary life of France was recognized when he was elected to the Académie Française in 1963. [ET]

See R. Judrin, La Vocation transparente de Jean Paulhan (1984); A. d'Hôtel, Jean Paulhan (1987).

PAUVERT, Jean-Jacques (b. 1926). Independent French publisher, who was harassed by the law in the post-war period for his bold editorial policies. He specializes in 'les écrivains maudits', including *Breton, G.*Bataille, and *Roussel, and has published the complete works of *Sade.

Pauvre Christ de Bomba, Le, see BETI.

Pavia, Battle of, see FRANÇOIS Iᵉʳ.

Paysan de Paris, Le, see ARAGON.

Paysan parvenu, Le. Novel by *Marivaux, published in five parts, 1734–5. It was left unfinished,

though there was an anonymous sequel in three further parts. Where La *Vie de Marianne belongs to the moralizing and sentimental romance tradition, Le Paysan is a cynical comic novel of the way of the world, though both stories are full of subtle psychological observations. The tale is told in later life by the unashamed and good-humoured hero Jacob, who has risen from his peasant origins to a wealthy and respectable position as a tax-farmer thanks to his resourceful wit and his physical attractions. He profits amorally from the affections of a series of (usually older) women, some of them with reputations for piety; these adventures are recounted in a spirited style, with a sharp eye for the hypocrisy of the respectable. [PF]

Paysanne pervertie, La, see RESTIF DE LA BRETONNE.

Paysan perverti, Le, see RESTIF DE LA BRETONNE.

Paysans, Les. Unfinished novel by *Balzac, planned from 1838, published in part as a serial in 1844, completed by the author's widow and published posthumously in 1855. The most substantial of the Scènes de la vie de campagne in La *Comédie humaine, Les Paysans is an unremitting denunciation, in fictional mode, of the effects of representative government and early capitalist economics on the French countryside. The peasantry are characterized as brutish, promiscuous, and venal, manipulated by bloodsucking money-lenders and ruled by the malevolent passions of the lower bourgeoisie. Balzac's panorama of a demoralized peasantry on the brink of guerilla war (an early title for the work was Qui terre a, guerre a) is also a gallery of grotesques, and contains many scenes of a cruelly comic nature. Balzac himself believed that the solution to the moral and economic impoverishment of the countryside lay in a return to feudal rule; Marx, who paid great attention to Les Paysans, used Balzac's detailed analysis of rural usury as the basis for a different argument. Despite its unfinished and polemical nature, Les Paysans contains many portraits and group scenes of outstanding literary quality, which Zola attempted to emulate in La *Terre. [DMB]

Peasants. Agricultural workers, small landed proprietors, share-croppers, and smaller numbers of richer laboureurs formed the bulk (perhaps 80 per cent) of pre-industrial French society. Owning about one-third of the land, these peasants did all the agricultural work, and, until the *Revolution, even when they did own plots of land, a whole range of *feudal dues was attached to them, there being no outright ownership of the land in the modern sense. Tenure was by long- or short-term leases and by the widespread system of métayage (sharecropping), by which usually half of the fruits of the land went to the owner in return for the use of the land and the farm establishment.

Most peasants owned plots of land far too small to support a family; they therefore rented further plots and often plied some other trade, such as ditcher or wheelwright. They were poor, and only a few in any community were rich enough to own a plough team. In good years they survived by using the common lands, cultivating their yard for fruit and vegetables and keeping some poultry; in years when the harvest was poor and bread prices rose, many would be reduced to severe poverty and perhaps vagrancy. At such times they might resemble the 'animals' described by *La Bruyère and *Vauban during the terrible age of *Louis XIV. The happy, virtuous peasants portrayed by the brothers *Le Nain in the 17th c. and by *Greuze in the 18th would have been the untypical richer peasants: poverty was the norm, and life was lived in poor houses with floors of beaten mud, one large bed, and little furniture. Regional variations were great, however, and in many areas—such as in the south, where polyculture was usual—the standard of living might be higher and the diet better.

In this subsistence economy the basic productive unit was the household, in which women and children had roles to fulfil. Male and female spheres of activity were closely defined, as described in *Restif de la Bretonne's La Vie de mon père (1779). Rural life took place in the context of small communities of rarely more than two or three hundred inhabitants. In spite of divisions of wealth, the community had a real sense of solidarity. Everybody knew everyone else, they all went to the same parish church, harvested together, paid taxes as a community, and often had the same seigneur. Many peasants lived their whole life in a tiny locality in which culture was a matter of tradition, custom, religion, and superstition rather than of formal education. The books that were available to those who were truly literate were usually catechisms and chapbooks [see BIBLIOTHÈQUE BLEUE]. Another important aspect of life was festivity: after the harvest and at carnival time there were fêtes during which people escaped from the drudgery of life into an imaginary world of abundance and licence. Peasant revolts, or jacqueries, which were quite frequent in the 17th and 18th c. and continued into the mid-19th c., often included elements of the carnivalesque as a part of the protest.

*Education by both the Church and, later, the State gradually changed rural mentalities in the 17th and 18th c., as did increased commercialization and mobility. The overwhelming grievances of the peasantry in 1789 were poverty and the seigneurial regime. The Revolution enabled many peasants to emancipate themselves from the feudal dues and achieve their aspiration of sufficient landownership. However, overpopulation quickly led to poverty; if more peasants lived on the land in the 19th c. than ever before, they were not wealthy. Even so, it was not until after World War II that fewer than 50 per cent of the population lived in the countryside.

The peasantry has long been seen as the backbone of France and the repository of sound values.

*Romanticism and the enthusiasm for disappearing rural values led in the 19th c. to an idealization of rural life by many writers, at a time when the peasantry was in fact under great pressure. Education and the experience of World War I turned peasants with a localized outlook into Frenchmen with wider political views by the 1920s. The trend of rural depopulation has continued since the 1940s, as predominantly small farms have become increasingly unviable. Recent years have seen political activism from farmers hard-pressed by reductions in subsidies from the European Community.   [PRC]

See E. Le Roy Ladurie, The Peasants of Languedoc (tr. J. Day, 1974); G. Duby and E. Wallon (eds.), Histoire de la France rurale, 4 vols. (1975); E. Weber, Peasants into Frenchmen (1979).

'Peau d'âne'. Ancient folk-tale retold by *Perrault in elegant verse. The heroine, to escape her father's incestuous love, hides in an ass's skin; in this humble disguise, she wins the love of a prince.

Peau de Chagrin, La. Novel by *Balzac, written and published in 1831 and subsequently included in the *Comédie humaine as one of the Études philosophiques. The story is of the pact made by a penniless and talented young man, Raphaël de Valentin, with an aged antiquarian who warns him that 'vouloir nous brûle et pouvoir nous détruit, mais savoir laisse notre faible organisation dans un perpétuel état de calme'. The talisman Raphaël acquires is a piece of shagreen (wild-ass's skin) which accords its owner's every wish (even those that are not expressed), but it shrinks with every wish granted; when the skin has shrunk to nothing, the owner is dead. The novel thus moves logically from Raphaël's first lavish, witty dinner-party, through his unrequited love for Fedora, the woman with a heart of stone, to his last desperate attempts to wish for nothing at all. Written with great verve, full of topical jokes, La Peau de chagrin was Balzac's first public success; it also expresses the foundations of his approach to character and desire in a more accessible manner than the later *Louis Lambert, and is an essential introduction to the Comédie humaine as a whole.   [DMB]

Peau noire masques blancs, see FANON.

Pêcheur d'Islande, see LOTI.

PÊCHEUX, Michel (1938–83). French *Marxist philosopher. An early disciple of *Althusser, he wrote on the history of science and developed a critique of the implicit philosophical assumptions in linguistics. Pêcheux has been influential in the development of discourse analysis. See his Les Vérités de la Palice (1975).   [MHK]

PÉGUY, Charles (1873–1914). Socialist, and later Catholic, poet and polemicist, whose poetry and prose both make use, in different ways, of remarkable effects of powerful and repetitive rhetoric. In his gradual move towards Catholicism, and towards attitudes more usually associated with the Right of the period, some observers have seen a profound political reorientation; but there is a strong case for seeing these later attitudes as a logical and organic development of his fairly idiosyncratic socialism, which owed more to the French tradition than to international Marxism, containing strong elements of *Jacobin nationalism and working-class tradition-alism.

Born in Orléans of peasant stock, Péguy in 1894 entered the *École Normale Supérieure in Paris, where he came under the influence of *Herr and *Jaurès, and involved himself in socialist politics. In 1895 he returned to Orléans to start writing his first *Jeanne d'Arc* (published in 1897), a dramatic trilogy dedicated to all those who 'seront morts pour tâcher de porter remède au mal universel'.

In 1896 Péguy returned to the ENS and was soon writing for the *Revue socialiste*. The *Dreyfus Affair exploded in late 1897, and Péguy was among those young socialists who defied the conventional wisdom of *Guesde and his group (that socialists should stay out of the fight); a strong Dreyfusard, in 1899 he wrote a series of important articles for the *Revue blanche*. Appalled by official socialist attitudes, in January 1900 he started the journal *Les Cahiers de la quinzaine*, in which, over the next 14 years, a gifted band of collaborators including Daniel *Halévy, Israël Zangwill, Romain *Rolland, the Tharaud brothers, *Bernard-Lazare, and Georges *Sorel were to write. Péguy's own lengthy contributions count among the greatest examples of polemic in modern France. His disillusionment with those from the Dreyfus camp who now, after their victory, were substituting politics for the 'mystique' of the Dreyfus cause, culminated in his polemical masterpiece *Notre jeunesse* (1910). Meanwhile, in *Notre patrie* (1905), the divisions among Frenchmen were seen to fade into insignificance beside the reality of national fervour in the face of external threats. Other polemics were concerned with more intellectual problems: an attack on the 'scientific' historical method used by the Sorbonne; a defence of *Bergson's philosophy against his opponents; and a recurrent praise of the traditions of old France.

Around 1908 Péguy refound his faith as a Catholic Christian, and in 1910 published his *Mystère de la charité de Jeanne d'Arc*, a long poem in which, around the dialogues of the 1897 play, Jeanne, obsessed with the problems of suffering and damnation, meditates at length, the centre-piece being the vivid and moving description of Christ's Passion. This was followed by two further 'mysteries' in the same mode, *Le Porche du mystère de la deuxième vertu* (1911) and *Le Mystère des Saints-Innocents* (1912). Other powerful religious poems, such as the *Présentation de la Beauce à Notre-Dame de Chartres* (1913), culminated in the long meditation of *Ève* (1913), in which effects of almost monotonous repetition create a monumental and overwhelming effect.

In the years 1910–14 Péguy found himself perpetually at the centre of controversy, and reacted powerfully in a variety of articles. Catholic criticism of his *Jeanne d'Arc* led to a violent response in *Un nouveau théologien: M. Fernand Laudet* (1911); bitterness at the Sorbonne 'Cabale' led to vicious attacks on *Lavisse, *Lanson, etc. But above all, his hatred for Jaurès, once so greatly admired at the time of the Affair, but attacked in *Notre jeunesse* as having betrayed his former companions through his cynical misuse of Dreyfusist idealism for political ends, was now exacerbated by Jaurès's espousal of international pacifism; in *L'Argent* and *L'Argent suite* (1913) Péguy vilified Jaurès as a traitor, and an agent of 'Pangermanism'. Contemporary observers saw paranoia in Péguy's attitudes at this time. But, though there was much injustice involved, the prose articles of 1910–14 contain some of the most brilliant and effective polemics in the French language.

Within the first weeks of the war, on 5 September 1914, Péguy, a reservist, was killed fighting in the Battle of the Marne.　　　　　　　　　　[RMG]

See N. Jussem-Wilson, *Charles Péguy* (1965); E. Cahm, *Péguy et le nationalisme français* (1972).

PEIRE CARDENAL (c.1180–c.1278). Exceptionally prolific *troubadour, also noted for his longevity. His work consists mainly of *sirventes and devotional poetry, with just a few extant love poems. Peire's poems comment frequently on the aftermath of the Albigensian Crusade, and though clearly not a *Cathar, nor even a sympathizer, he is hostile to the French.　　　　　　　　　　[SG]

PEIRE D'ALVERNHE (*fl.* c.1146–c.1168). *Troubadour who composed *cansos, *sirventes, devotional poetry, and a satire about other troubadours, including *Peire Rogier, *Giraut de Bornelu, *Raimbaut d'Aurenga, and *Bernart de Ventadorn. Influenced by *Marcabru, Peire was an important figure in the evolution of the *trobar clus and the earliest troubadour mentioned in Dante's *De vulgari eloquentia*. The best edition of his work is that of A. del Monte (Turin, 1955).　　　　　　　　　　[SG]

PEIRE ROGIER (*fl.* third quarter of 12th c.). *Troubadour, and friend of *Raimbaut d'Aurenga, with whom he exchanged witty verses. The author of nine known poems, he was the earliest troubadour to address the majority of his poems to a female patron (Ermengarde of Narbonne) and pioneered the fashion for inner dialogue which was later exploited by the romance of *Flamenca*.　　[SK]

PEIRESC, Nicolas-Claude Fabri de (1580–1637). Priest, scholar, antiquarian, astronomer, and naturalist, well known for his extensive library and collection of curiosities. He corresponded indefatigably with the learned community throughout Europe and did much to stimulate the free communication of scientific and philosophical ideas. A native of

Provence, he kept in touch with others with Provençal connections: *Malherbe, *Gassendi, who was a very close friend, and *Du Vair, whom he accompanied to Paris as secretary between 1616 and 1623. His letters testify not only to his wide intellectual interests, but also to his deep faith and strong commitment to Catholicism. Although once grouped with the *libertins of his day, he is now considered as one of those thinkers in whom an interest in new scientific developments coincided with unshakeable orthodoxy. Gassendi wrote his biography, which appeared in Latin in 1641. [IM]

PEIRE VIDAL (*fl. c.*1183–1204). Said to be the son of a furrier from Toulouse, this author of nearly 50 songs is the jester among the *troubadours. Introducing a more familiar tone into courtly discourse, he gives fantasy its head, purporting at one moment to become wolf-like in his love for a lady Loba ('she-wolf'), at another to have been dismissed for timidly stealing a kiss and a piece of cord from his sleeping beloved; posing in turn as a swaggering knight, an emperor, and a landless outcast; criticizing those who fail to go on crusade and deciding not to give up home comforts to go himself. Peire Vidal travelled widely and his poetry, formally flawless, won patronage in Spain and Italy as well as in Toulouse. [SK]

PEIRÒT, Glaudi, see OCCITAN LITERATURE (POST-MEDIEVAL).

PÉLADAN, Joséphin (1859–1918). Self-publicist and self-proclaimed Grand Master and Sar of the Rosicrucian Order [see ROSE-CROIX], founder of the Salons de la Rose+Croix, Péladan was the author of *La Décadence latine* (1884–1907), a 14-novel epic and anthology of *Decadent themes in which he argued that the supremacy enjoyed by the Latin race since Christ was threatened by contemporary democracy, materialism, and philistinism and could only be saved by an élite order of Rosicrucian artists. His religion of Art, Beauty, and Tradition was a highly personal and authoritarian fusion of Catholicism, mystic ritual, Wagnerian legend, and the erotic charms of androgyny. [JK]

Pélagie-la-Charette, see MAILLET, ANTONINE.

PÉLÉGRI, Jean (b. 1920). Novelist born in Rovigo, a village not far from Algiers, into a family which had lived in Algeria for many generations. His father's farm and vineyards, and the people who worked there, play a major role in Pélégri's writing. He believed in the Algerian quest for independence, and the two people most dear to him after his family were Algerians: an old servant, Fatima, and a workman who became the model for his most memorable character, Slimane. After Algerian independence Pélégri, a *lycée* teacher, moved to Paris.
Pélégri's obsession with memories of his homeland and a sense of dispossession provide the impe-

tus of almost all his books. His major works are an autobiographical account of two generations of colonial wine-growers and Algerians, *Les Oliviers de la justice* (1959), made into a film by James Blue (in which Pélégri, also an actor, played the role of his own father); and his masterpiece, *Le Maboul* (1963; Prix Charles-Veillon 1964), in which the narrator, Slimane, reflects on the meaning of life, which he sees as somehow linked to a petrified snail in the middle of a stone. [ES]

Pèlerinage de Charlemagne, Le, see VOYAGE DE CHARLEMAGNE.

PELETIER DU MANS, Jacques (1517–82). French poet, critic, philosopher, and mathematician, who was equally at home with the *Pléiade and the poetic and humanist circles of Lyon. He published his verse translation of Horace's *Ars poetica* in 1541; his *Œuvres poétiques* of 1547 contain translations of Homer, Virgil, Horace, and Petrarch, his own lyrical poems, notably court poems of praise and hymns of the four seasons, and also the first published poems of *Du Bellay and *Ronsard. His *Amour des amours* (1554) combines abstract, ethereal love poetry, a Dantesque search for the absolute, and cosmic, scientific description. The *Art poétique* (1555), written in the revised spelling proposed in his *Dialogue* of 1549, is the most philosophical of the contemporary manifestos, insisting on poetry as a form of knowledge which gives access to universals, on its elevated élitist role, and the mutual interaction of nature and art. In spite of his acknowledging the value of the vernacular, as his poetry, translations, and mathematical works in French attest, he ended up writing principally in Latin and on mathematical subjects. His later poems include *La Savoie* (1572) and *Les Louanges* (1581). [PS]

Pelléas et Mélisande. *Symbolist drama by *Maeterlinck, first performed in 1893 and later made into an *opera by *Debussy (1902). Mélisande, a strange waif, is discovered weeping in the forest by Golaud, widower and son of King Arkel. Impulsively he marries her and brings her back to the royal castle, where she meets his stepbrother, Pelléas. While sitting with Pelléas beside a fountain, she drops and loses the wedding ring Golaud has given her, and this prepares us for their falling in love. The jealous Golaud surprises them in an embrace and kills Pelléas. Mélisande dies. [SBJ]

PELLERIN, Jean, see FANTAISISTES.

PELLETIER, Madeleine (1874–1939). French feminist and socialist writer. The rebellious autodidact child of barely literate *petits commerçants*, Pelletier was befriended by anarchists and succeeded against all odds in qualifying as a doctor, though her medical career was fraught with frustration. By turns anarchist, socialist, and freemason, but constantly feminist, she wrote a series of defiant and unorthodox books and pamphlets, from *Le Droit à l'avortement* (1911) to *La Rationalisation sexuelle* (1935), by way of *La Désagrégation de la famille* (n.d.). An isolated and courageous figure, who died tragically in an asylum after prosecution for inciting to abortion, she was largely forgotten until her rediscovery in the 1970s, when she was acknowledged as an intellectual precursor of Simone de *Beauvoir. [SR]

PELLISSON(-Fontanier), Paul (1624–93). French poet and man of letters. Brought up a Protestant, he was a lawyer in Castres, but then, disfigured by smallpox, came to Paris and devoted himself to literature. His most famous work is the *Histoire de l'Académie Française* (1653), an elegant piece of writing, later completed up to 1700 by abbé d'Olivet. He also wrote both religious and amorous verse (the latter frequently republished in a *Recueil de pièces galantes* with the poems of the comtesse de *La Suze). But his main role was that of literary linkman; possessing considerable charm and a catholic taste, he defended writing that was graceful, natural, and entertaining. He was a close friend of many writers, notably Madeleine de *Scudéry and *Sarasin (for whose works he wrote an important preface), and as a literary expert became *Fouquet's *homme de confiance*. On his master's downfall he remained courageously loyal, and was imprisoned in the Bastille for several years, amusing himself by taming a spider. In 1670 he converted to Catholicism, won the king's favour, and was appointed official historian. [PF]

Pensée libre, La. Clandestine journal first produced in February 1941 [see OCCUPATION AND RESISTANCE, 6].

Pensées, see PASCAL.

Pensée sauvage, La, see LÉVI-STRAUSS.

Pensées diverses sur la comète, see BAYLE.

Pensées philosophiques, see DIDEROT.

Pensées sur l'interprétation de la nature, see DIDEROT.

PÉPIN LE BREF, see CAROLINGIANS.

Perceforest, Le Roman de. First devised, probably in Hainaut, between 1314 and 1340, this vast prose romance was probably adapted in mid-15th-c. Burgundy. In one great pseudo-historical sweep, it links the cycles of *Alexander the Great and *Arthur. Inspired by the prowess of the former, Britain under Perceforest and his lineage becomes an oasis of civilization, prefiguring the Round Table, in which chivalric and spiritual values are increasingly established. Through a proliferation of quests and adventures, his tone varying from the farcical to the tragic, the anonymous writer follows a firm narrative thread culminating in the coming of

the *Grail and the birth of Merlin, and heralding the birth of Alexander's descendant, King Arthur.
[JHMT]

Perceval. Hero of *Chrétien de Troyes's *Le Conte du Graal* [see GRAIL ROMANCES].

PEREC, Georges (1936–82). Parisian novelist and writer 'in all the fields in which it is possible to write nowadays'; member of *OULIPO from 1967.

Born in Paris of Polish-Jewish parents, who died in 1940 (in the defence of France) and 1943 (at Auschwitz), respectively, Perec was hidden in a Catholic boarding-school at Villard-de-Lans (Isère) during the Nazi occupation of France and brought up in Paris after the Liberation by his paternal aunt Esther and her husband David Bienenfeld, a trader in fine pearls. Perec's early orphanage marked him deeply, and lies near the root of his highly defended but engagingly unpretentious literary personality.

He was educated in Paris and at Étampes, where Jean *Duvignaud encouraged him in his early decision to become a writer. Perec dropped out of a history degree at the Sorbonne and constructed his own 'university' through reading, through friendships (particularly with a group of Serbian thinkers), and through La Ligne Générale (1958–60), a cultural movement aiming to renew *Marxism from within, but which never published the review with which it planned to rival Les *Temps modernes. Perec did two years' military service in a parachute regiment (1958–9), then worked briefly in market research before spending a year at Sfax, in Tunisia. From 1961 until 1978 he was employed as a research librarian in a neurophysiological laboratory attached to the CNRS.

Many of Perec's early writings have yet to be published. Every one of his published works is an exercise in a different style. *Les Choses: une histoire des années soixante* (1965, Prix Renaudot) is an ironic portrait of a generation bewildered by the arrival of prosperity, written in a deceptively simple language intentionally echoing the style of Flaubert's' *L'*Éducation sentimentale*; it made Perec famous as a 'sociological' analyst of the generation of the 1960s.

His following works were not in the same vein and were less widely read until the 1980s. *Quel petit vélo à guidon chromé au fond de la cour?* (1966) is a mock-epic account of the 'finest hour' of La Ligne Générale. *Un homme qui dort* (1967) is a second-person narrative of adolescent depression in which the technique of collage is used almost invisibly (a film version was made by Perec and Bernard Queysanne in 1974), and *La Disparition* (1969) is a murder-mystery novel written under the constraint of a *lipogram on 'e'.

Perec became well known in Germany for a series of radio plays: *Die Maschine* (1968, with Eugen Helmle), *L'Augmentation* (1969), *Tagstimmen* (1971, with Eugen Helmle and Philippe Drogoz), etc. He also pursued 'alphabetic exercises' in the context of his membership of OULIPO (including a palindrome of over 1,200 words), which led him eventually to write heterogrammatic poetry (*Alphabets*, 1976).

Perec's incessant formal innovations accompany a lifelong concern with autobiography. *La Boutique obscure* (1973) is a record of his dreams; *Espèces d'espaces* (1974) is a personal reflection on his relationship to spatiality; *Je me souviens* (1978), a record of 'shared' memories. *W ou le Souvenir d'enfance* (1975, incorporating earlier texts) is Perec's most direct approach to self-description and self-analysis, but it is conducted by unusual means. The book consists of two apparently unrelated texts printed in alternating chapters in different typefaces, which converge on a common image at the end, that of the concentration camp. It has been compared to Stendhal's *Vie de Henry Brulard* and to *Sartre's Les Mots* for its renewal of the genre of autobiography. Its deceptive design is to make the reader share some of the inextinguishable anguish and guilt of a childhood survivor of the Shoah.

*La *Vie mode d'emploi* is indisputably Perec's masterpiece. Planned as early as 1969, presented as a project to OULIPO in 1972, described in *Espèces d'espaces* (1974), this copious 'encyclopaedia of fictions' was written after the death of *Queneau, to whose memory it is dedicated. It won the Prix Médicis in 1978 and, together with crossword puzzles for a weekly magazine, it gave Perec the means to leave his job at the CNRS. He continued to work on the history of his far-flung family, made a television film about Ellis Island, produced *Les Jeux de la comtesse Dolingen de Gratz*, a film directed by his companion Catherine Binet, and published *Un cabinet d'amateur* (1979), a novella about a forged painting representing many other paintings, each of which refers in some way to *La Vie mode d'emploi*.

After 1978 Perec also travelled more widely, notably to Australia, where he was writer-in-residence at the University of Queensland in September 1981. He fell ill towards the end of that year and died of lung cancer on 3 March 1982. He left an unfinished 'literary thriller', "*53 Jours*" (published 1989), and a huge gap in OULIPO, in French, and in world literature. [DMB]

See C. Burgelin, *Georges Perec* (1988); D. Bellos, *Georges Perec: A Life in Words* (1993).

Père de famille, Le, see DIDEROT.

Père Duchesne, Le, see HÉBERT, J.-R.

Père Goriot, Le. Novel by *Balzac (1834, published 1835). Planned as a short story about filial ingratitude for the *Revue de Paris, Le Père Goriot grew into one of the finest and most characteristic examples of Balzac's longer fictions. It was in the course of writing this novel that he hit upon the idea of reusing characters invented in earlier stories; he is said to have rushed round to his sister, Laure Surville, to

tell her that he was 'in the process of becoming a genius'. Eugène de Rastignac, the young man whose adventures and feelings are at the centre of Le Père Goriot, is an episodic character of La *Peau de chagrin* (1830), and most of the society figures whom he meets in this novel had appeared in earlier stories of Parisian life. After Le Père Goriot, Balzac systematically reused its characters in dozens of other stories and novels, notably in *Illusions perdues*, where the arch-criminal Vautrin crops up under another disguise.

In Le Père Goriot, set in 1820, Vautrin is a lodger at the Pension Vauquer, a sordid boarding-house in the Quartier Latin, alongside Rastignac, an ambitious but penniless student with distant relations in high society, and Jean-Joachim Goriot, a retired trader whose reduced circumstances derive from his generosity towards his two daughters, now married into the aristocracy (Anastasie) and the financial bourgeoisie (Delphine). Vautrin wishes to inveigle the student into a criminal plot, but is thwarted by two other lodgers, both police spies. Goriot declines into ever-deeper poverty and ill health. His deathbed delirium is a stylistic *tour de force* reminiscent of Dickens at his most sentimental. Balzac had Shakespeare in mind: one of his aims in the novel is to endow an 'ordinary' character with as much tragic grandeur as King Lear. Rastignac, with whom the narrator has a shifting, ironical, and sympathetic relationship, learns how the world works in the course of the novel: from Vautrin and from his first adventures in high society he learns the lessons of callousness, and from Goriot the almost equally horrifying lesson of self-sacrifice. Only Rastignac attends Goriot's funeral at Père Lachaise cemetery, where he sheds his last tear of youth and descends into the city to make his career, issuing his famous challenge: 'A nous deux maintenant!'

Like Stendhal's Le *Rouge et le noir, to which it is often compared, Le Père Goriot is a 'novel of education'; it is also a lament at the disappearance of older values, symbolized by Goriot, and a historically pertinent analysis of the circulation of money and of changes in the class structure of Restoration France. [DMB]

Père-Lachaise, cemetery, see LA CHAISE.

PÉRET, Benjamin (1899–1959). A steadfast member of the French *Surrealist group, which he helped to form, and a political militant who joined the Communist Party in 1927 and fought in the Spanish Civil War. He was an uncompromising believer in the revolutionary nature of poetry, but his collections of stories, e.g. *Main forte* (1946) and *Le Gigot, sa vie et son œuvre* (1957), as well as the poems of *Dormir, dormir dans les pierres* (1927), *Le Grand Jeu* (1928), *Je ne mange pas de ce pain-là* (1936), with their mixture of the marvellous, the humorous, the sacrilegious, and the scatological, reveal the subversive inventiveness of his language. [KRA]

PERGAUD, Louis (1882–1915). A novelist of rare humour, master of a classical style, yet a great innovator in the representation of colloquial and regional speech, Pergaud is notable as the painter of rural life in his native Doubs at the turn of the century. His fine sensitivity as interpreter of the animal world is seen in *De Goupil à Margot* (1910, Prix Goncourt) and *Le Roman de Miraut, chien de chasse* (1913). He was killed in the Great War. A renewal of interest in his works was stimulated by Yves Robert's film (1962) of *La Guerre des boutons* (1912), a joyous evocation of the intervillage rivalry of young adolescents in the mid-1890s.   [AHB]

Periodicals

1. Literary Journals [see also press]

The 17th c. saw the appearance in France of two types of literary periodical: the **Journal des savants* printed reviews of new books, while the **Mercure galant* was a **salon-related publication containing verse, literary discussions, and the like. While the *Mercure* continued as the *Mercure de France*, other reviewing journals appeared in the 18th c., often providing a forum for political or religious debate as well as literary arguments; major titles include the *Mémoires de *Trévoux*, Pierre Rousseau's *Journal encyclopédique* (an organ for **philosophe* thought), and the work of journalists such as **Desfontaines, **Raynal, **Grimm, **Linguet, and **Fréron, as well as of major writers such as **Marivaux or **Prévost.

The 19th c. was the golden age of the literary journal. Novels were often published in serial form, not only **romans-feuilletons*, but even **Madame Bovary*, which first appeared in the **Revue de Paris* (founded 1829). Other major periodicals of the century were the controversial *Le *Globe* (1824–32) founded by P.-F. Dubois [see ROMANTICISM], the **Revue des deux mondes* (founded 1829 and still appearing today), *La Presse* (founded by **Girardin in 1836), the **Revue blanche* (1889–1903), and for Belgium *La Jeune Belgique* (1881–97) and *La Wallonie* (1886–92). The *Revue blanche* was an organ of **Symbolism, a movement which expressed itself largely in a host of short-lived periodicals. **Surrealism was similarly to give birth to journals such as *Littérature* or *La Révolution surréaliste*.

Two of the most important journals in the early years of the 20th c. were the new **Mercure de France* (1890–1965) and the immensely influential **Nouvelle Revue Française*. *Europe* (founded 1923), which like the *NRF* continues to appear, contains a good deal of literary material. This was also the period of the short-lived but influential Swiss journal *Les Cahiers vaudois* (1914–19). World War II brought the appearance of many new publications, before and after the Liberation. **Combat* and *Les *Temps modernes* were mainly philosophical and political, whereas *Critique*, founded by Georges **Bataille in 1946, published, and continues to publish, searching discussions of new works. Other literary journals of the post-war decade include *Lettres nouvelles* (1953–7), **Tel Quel* and its continuation *L'Infini*, **Change*, and *Obliques* (founded 1972).

A particular development was the appearance of numerous poetry magazines, including the annual *Poésie* launched by **Seghers in 1940 and relaunched, after an interval, in 1984, *Action poétique* (1955–), *La Délirante* (1967–), **Bonnefoy's important *L'Éphémère* (1967–72), and *Po&sie* founded by **Deguy in 1977. Most of the titles mentioned above combine new writing with criticism; at the same time the general public is served by reviewing journals such as *Le Figaro littéraire* (1946–72, succeeded by the weekly supplement to *Le *Figaro*), *La Quinzaine littéraire*, *Le Magazine littéraire*, and the weekly supplement to *Le *Monde* (*Le Monde des livres*).

Literary journals have had an important cultural part to play in francophone countries outside France: in **Quebec **Liberté*, **Parti pris*, and *La *Relève*; in North Africa *Horizons maghrébins* (1984–); in the **West Indies **Tropiques* and *Les *Griots* [see also AFRICAN LITERARY JOURNALS and entries for specific areas].

2. Academic Journals

Of the current French academic periodicals with literary interests some have a theoretical or critical perspective, e.g. *Communications* (1962–), *Poétique* (1970–), and *Littérature* (1971–). Other, longer-established journals are more concerned with **literary history: *Revue d'histoire littéraire de la France* (1894–), *Revue des sciences humaines* (1927–), *Cahiers de l'Association Internationale des Études Françaises* (1951–). Journals specializing in particular periods include for medieval studies *Romania* (1872–) and *Revue de langues romanes* (1870–), and for later periods *Humanisme et renaissance* (1934– , later *Bibliothèque d'humanisme et renaissance*), *Dix-septième siècle* (1951–), the yearbook *Dix-huitième siècle* (1969–), and *Romantisme* (1971–). There are innumerable journals devoted to individual writers or literary groups.

Several well-established English-language periodicals are devoted primarily to French literature and culture: in Britain *French Studies* (1947–) and *Nottingham French Studies* (1962–); in America the *French Review* (1927–), *Yale French Studies* (1948–), and *L'Esprit créateur* (1961–); in Australia the *Australian Journal for French Studies* (1964–). More-recent arrivals, taking a new approach, include the theoretical journal *Paragraph* (1983–), the comparative *Franco-British Studies* (1986–), and the wide-ranging *French Cultural Studies* (1990–). *French Seventeenth-Century Studies* (1979–) and above all the voluminous *Studies on Voltaire and the Eighteenth Century* (1955–) are devoted to specific periods. And of course French literature occupies a considerable place in the numerous general journals such as the *Modern Language Review*, *Modern Language Notes*, and the *Proceedings of the Modern Languages Association of America*.   [PF]

Perlesvaus, see GRAIL ROMANCES.

Permission tacite, see CENSORSHIP.

PÉROL, Jean (b. 1932). Much living colour, sensory experience, and a strong rhythmic energy infuse the poetry of Pérol, who insists (*Morale provisoire*, 1978) on the relevance to the poet of lived experience: 'The real is not to be imitated . . . but dwelt in.' Nowhere in his work is this so vividly illustrated as in *Le Cœur véhément* (1968), product of his love-affair with, and some years of living in, Japan. In this collection Japanese and French imagery are fused together into a new harmony. See also *Ruptures* (1970), *Maintenant les soleils* (1972), *Histoire contemporaine* (1982). [GDM]

PERRAULT, Charles (1628–1703). Perrault is a household name today as the author of the **Histoires ou contes du temps passé* (usually known as the *Contes*), one of the most popular books in the language; he was known in his own time for writings of a quite different sort.

Born in Paris, the son of a lawyer, he was a twin, but his twin brother did not live—Soriano sees this as a significant factor in the composition of the *Contes*. Three of his surviving brothers also had successful careers: Nicolas (1611–61), a *Jansenist theologian; Claude (1613–88), a doctor, author, and designer of the new colonnade of the *Louvre; and Pierre (1608–80), one of *Colbert's right-hand men. Charles trained as a lawyer, and thanks to Pierre, entered the service of Colbert, subsequently becoming Contrôleur des Bâtiments. Protected by Colbert, he had a successful career, becoming a member, and in 1681 the director, of the Académie Française, and a member of the *Académie des Inscriptions. His wife, Marie Guichon, died in 1678 after only six years of marriage, leaving him four children. Dismissed from government service after Colbert's death in 1683, he devoted himself to his family; his Contes are a product of the education he gave to his youngest son, Pierre.

He started writing early, producing a satirical translation of *Aeneid VI* while still at school, and publishing in 1653 the *burlesque *Les Murs de Troie ou l'Origine du burlesque*, written in collaboration with his brothers. These playful early works betray a disrespect for the Ancients which was to blossom later in life. Subsequently, moving in fashionable circles, he wrote a number of lightweight pieces, including a 'Dialogue de l'Amour et de l'Amitié' (1657), which was presented to *Fouquet, and a *précieux* fantasy [see PRECIOSITY] in a mixture of prose and verse, 'Le Miroir, ou la Métamorphose d'Orante' (1661). Perrault's main concerns as a writer, however, were the celebration of the reign of *Louis XIV and the defence of contemporary artistic culture. Like many of his contemporaries, he wrote odes, speeches, and other texts in praise of the monarch and his artistic patronage. The newly created gardens of *Versailles provide the theme for 'Le Labyrinthe de Versailles'

(1675), in which Perrault invents ingenious amorous morals for the fountains (designed by *Le Brun) representing Aesop's fables.

The celebration of the regime, together with his burlesque and *précieux* inclinations, led Perrault to adopt an uncompromisingly modern position in the *Querelle des Anciens et des Modernes. In 1674 he defended Quinault's opera *Alceste* against the attacks of *Boileau and *Racine, claiming that it was superior to Euripides' tragedy. In 1686 he published a Christian epic, *Saint Paulin*, asserting, against the sarcasms of Boileau, that the modern Christian age, and in particular the glorious age of Louis XIV, should have its own Christian culture rather than seeking to emulate the Ancients. This position was proclaimed openly and provocatively in the poem 'Le Siècle de Louis le Grand', read at the Academy in January 1687. The poem began the most virulent phase of the Querelle, in which Perrault and Boileau did battle until being publicly reconciled in 1694.

Perrault's modernist position is spelled out in his *Parallèle des anciens et des modernes*, published in four volumes between 1688 and 1697. This is a dialogue, set in Versailles, in which the *ancien* position is defended by the not unreasonable president against a chevalier and Perrault's mouthpiece, the abbé. The discussion ranges over the arts and the sciences, eloquence, and poetry. Confident in the progress of humanity, Perrault dismisses the ancients as childish, irrational, immoral, or barbarous; in particular, in Book 3, he launches an assault on the puerility and vulgarity of Homer. The level of the discussion is not very high, and the praise of contemporary culture is not particularly convincing, but the work is vigorously written. The *Contes*, composed between 1691 and 1695, are associated with this defence and illustration of modern culture, but they quickly outgrew this polemic to become one of the classics of European literature. [PF]

See M. Soriano, *Les Contes de Perrault: culture savante et tradition populaire* (1968); J. Barchilon and P. Flinders, *Charles Perrault* (1981).

PERRAULT, Pierre (b. 1927). Montreal-born poet, film-maker, and broadcaster who attempts by the innovative use of lightweight equipment to capture the pioneer experience. Isolated communities, he claims, preserve in their poetic speech, traditional practices, and physical reflexes, an authentic record of the impact of North America. His essays, *De la parole aux actes* (1985), defend his cinematographic technique. His poetry, collected as *Chouennes* (1975) and *Gélivures* (1977), seeks to honour 'un pays fondé dans la rudesse des souches'. [CRPM]

PERREIN, Michèle (b. 1935). French novelist and essayist whose texts have a strong feminist and regional flavour. *La Sensitive* (1956) creates the prototype of her independent heroines who nevertheless seek dialogue with men, as in *Ave César* (1982). *Les Cotonniers de Bassalane* (1984, Prix Interallié) and

La Margagne (1989) place her heroines in her native Landes. [EAF]

PERROS, Georges (1923–78). French writer. After working in the theatre he retired to live in Brittany. He published poetry (*Poèmes bleus*, 1962), a modestly autobiographical poem in octosyllables entitled *Une vie ordinaire* (1967), the innovative private writing of his *Papiers collés* (3 vols., 1960–78), and (posthumously) the aphoristic *Lexique* (1981). *Papiers collés* contains both brief jottings and lengthy reflections on everyday life, together with many notes on art and literature, writers and artists. The writing is subtle and personal, throwing a flickering light on the situation of the modern writer. [PF]

PERROT, Michelle (b. 1928). French historian. Her intellectual itinerary (see M. Agulhon (ed.), *Ego Histoire*, 1986) reflects that of a generation of post-war academics. Starting from a position of left-wing Catholicism, she has recognized the successive influences of *Marxism, the *May 1968 movement, *Foucault, and *feminism on her historical writing. Her early work anatomized strike movements in 19th-c. France (*Les Ouvriers en grève*, 1974) and the nature of incarceration. In the 1980s, she became the best-known French representative of women's history, with a series of influential essays. She edited the 19th-c. volume of *Histoire de la vie privée* (1988), and was general editor and prime mover of the multi-volume *Histoire des femmes* (1990–2). While always maintaining a sense of the concreteness of lived experience, she has been a key influence over a younger generation of theorists of gender and history. [SR]

PERROT D'ABLANCOURT, Nicolas (1606–64). French translator, man of letters, and one of the early members of the Académie Française. Born a Huguenot, he converted to Catholicism at 20 but apostasized a few years later. He used much of his private income to travel in Holland and England and to study foreign and ancient languages; thereafter a need for financial independence played a role in his choice of profession. *Conrart encouraged him to translate some orations of Cicero, as a result of which he was elected to the Academy in 1637. There followed, first, a major version of Tacitus, then a spate of publications based on Greek and Spanish as well as Latin originals. So free were these translations that *Ménage coined the phrase 'les belles infidèles' to describe them; but, together with the work of Guez de *Balzac, they had a major impact on the formation of *classical taste in the mid-17th c. and contributed considerably to the evolution of French prose style. Another friend from the same circle, *Patru, wrote his biography. [PJB]

PERSE, Saint-John, see SAINT-JOHN PERSE.

Personalism (*Le Personnalisme*). A philosophy which takes the person as the fundamental reality and yardstick of value. In France it is most closely associated with Emmanuel *Mounier and the review *Esprit*. The concept of the 'person' has played an important, if intermittent, role in European philosophy since the medieval *scholastics, acquiring well-defined legal, moral, and psychological meanings. But 'Personalism' as a general tendency was a late 19th-c. development, with small Personalist movements developing in Britain, Germany, and America. Charles *Renouvier's book *Le Personnalisme* (1903) offered a Kantian neo-critical approach to ethics, though it was little followed in France. The emergence of a strong French Personalist movement in the early 1930s was an attempt to construct a viable social philosophy within the Catholic tradition. It was constructed under the aegis of Mounier and the group around *Esprit*, which included Jean *Lacroix and Paul-Louis Landsberg (d. 1944). Important contributions came from the *Ordre nouveau* groups, including Arnaud Dandieu (1897–1933), Robert Aron (1898–1975), and Denis de *Rougemont.

Elements of Personalism were drawn from *Bergson's vitalism; from *Maritain's neo-Kantian Thomism; from earlier socially oriented Catholic movements such as the *Sillon*, the *Semaines sociales*, and *Péguy's *Cahiers de la quinzaine*; and from Max Scheler's *phenomenology, which proposed an objective hierarchy of values, culminating in personhood.

The human person was conceived as a free centre of initiative, but distinguished from the abstract individual by its roots in natural, social, and spiritual dimensions. The person was characterized by his or her *incarnation*, combining both material and spiritual existence, *communication*, combining both autonomous and social existence, and *vocation*, combining both immanence and transcendence. The fulfilment of the person could only be envisaged in a dynamic balance between these dimensions, and depended on the natural, social, and spiritual processes of which the person was part.

Innovative work relating the person to the natural environment was produced by the Jesuit palaeontologist Pierre *Teilhard de Chardin. His major work, *Le Phénomène humain*, posthumously published in 1955, suggested that evolution was a process of *personnalisation*, with the whole of nature aspiring to the condition of a person, manifested now in conscious human existence, but eventually leading to a personal God at a future 'Omega point'.

Mounier focused on the person's insertion in the social world. He distinguished a number of levels of organization, culminating in an integrated community, where a person's potential could be most fully realized. He therefore criticized the 'désordre établi', pointing to the depersonalizing character of modern capitalist society, which stood in need of a Personalist and communitarian revolution. Mounier recognized that, while moral values should be proclaimed prophetically, they also needed to be put into practice in the real world, politically. He therefore argued the necessity of commitment, which would often involve difficult decisions.

Despite the opposition of more conservative supporters, Mounier developed a dialogue with Communists, especially those of humanist tendency, whom he saw as sharing key Personalist values. But generally, *Esprit* saw *Socialism or radical Christian Democracy as the closest political approximation of its ideals, and gave critical support to the *Popular Front. During the *Occupation Mounier attempted to influence the youth movements sponsored by the pro-Catholic Vichy government, though he and *Esprit* were eventually banned. With its Resistance credentials, *Esprit* became an influential journal in the post-war period, especially in Catholic circles. Personalist ideas were professed by several currents within the post-war French governments, and had some currency in philosophical and psychological circles. In addition to Mounier's own writings, they were expressed in the literary and cultural criticism of Claude-Edmonde Magny and Pierre-Aimé Touchard, and of Mounier's successors as director of *Esprit*, Albert *Béguin and Jean-Marie *Domenach.

Personalism was strongly articulated in the debates of the Second Vatican Council (1962–4), especially by Cardinal Jean Daniélou (1905–74), and the 'human person' largely supplanted the 'soul' as the focus of Catholic social thinking. These ideas also enjoyed a considerable following in Belgium, Switzerland, Germany, Italy, Poland, North and West Africa, South-East Asia, and Latin America.

[MHK]

See E. Mounier, *Le Personnalisme* (1949); M. Kelly, *Pioneer of the Catholic Revival* (1979).

Pertharite. Tragedy by Pierre *Corneille, first performed 1651. This play of dynastic and matrimonial intrigue, set in early medieval Lombardy, was a complete failure.

Pesanteur et la grâce, La, see WEIL.

Peste, La. Novel by Albert *Camus, published 1947. It was begun during the Nazi *Occupation of France, when Camus, cut off from his home and wife in Algeria, was undergoing medical treatment and working with the Resistance in the Lyon area. The book takes the form of a chronicle related (in third-person style) by Dr Rieux, who tells how the town of Oran is overcome by a plague epidemic. He traces the reactions of the townspeople from initial disbelief, through panic and hysteria, to a numbed acceptance of mass deaths, isolation from the outside world, and the imposition of restrictions such as curfews, quarantine regulations, rationing, and shortages. The literal narrative thus generates symbolic or allegorical parallels with occupied France or with life under any totalitarian regime. It also provides a metaphor for the universe of the absurd in which human aspirations are undermined by death or distorted into evil. The cast of characters develop a range of responses to the situation and enable Camus to adumbrate his philosophy of revolt while illustrating the shortcomings of religion, the dangers of nihilism, and the dilemma between the search for individual happiness and the need for collective solidarity.

[DHW]

PÉTAIN, Philippe (1856–1951). General Pétain made his name by his defence of Verdun in 1916; he was created a marshal in 1919. After the fall of France in 1940, aged 84, he headed the collaborationist Vichy regime till 1944 [see OCCUPATION AND RESISTANCE]. Condemned to death for treason, he was reprieved and imprisoned on the Île d'Yeu.

PETAU, Denis (1583–1652). French Jesuit theologian and scholar, editor of Greek texts and author of neo-Latin poems and plays.

Petit Cénacle, Le. A rebellious offshoot of the Hugo *cénacle; it flourished in the early years of the July Monarchy (1830–3). In the studio of the sculptor Jean Duseigneur there came together a group of fervent young writers and artists (including *Gautier, *Nerval, and *Borel) who dedicated themselves to the *vie d'artiste* and to the cult of Art in the new conditions of philistinism and utilitarianism.

[BR]

'Petit Chaperon rouge, Le'. One of Perrault's *Histoires ou contes du temps passé*, the familiar 'Little Red Riding Hood', without a happy ending.

Petit Chose, Le, see DAUDET, A.

PETIT DE JULLEVILLE, Louis (1841–1900), see HISTORIES OF FRENCH LITERATURE.

Petite Fadette, La, see SAND.

Petites Écoles, Les, see PORT-ROYAL.

Petit Jehan de Santré, Le, see LA SALE.

Petit Journal, Le. The first daily newspaper—popular in content, style, and price (1 *sou*)—to gain lasting success: its average circulation in the 1890s was 1 million. Launched in 1863 as a literary paper, *Le Petit Journal* long eschewed partisan politics and offered a mix of human-interest stories, *romans-feuilletons*, and garrulous editorials. The press magnate Moïse-Polydore Millaud organized its production, distribution, and promotion like that of a perishable product to be delivered fresh each morning throughout France. Serial novels were a key ingredient: *Ponson du Terrail, Émile Richebourg, *Gaboriau, *Verne, and Xavier de Montépin adorned its columns. By 1901 the paper was losing appeal: under its chief editor Ernest Judet it deserted political moderation for partisan polemics (anti-*Clemenceau, anti-*Dreyfusard), and began an inexorable decline.

[MP]

Petit Parisien, Le

Petit Parisien, Le. Founded in 1876, and managed by the Dupuy family from the 1880s, *Le Petit Parisien* replaced *Le *Petit Journal* as the top-selling daily in 1901. Generally moderate in tone in its coverage of politics, it concentrated on providing a satisfactory mix of **romans-feuilletons*, crime and human-interest stories, sports coverage, and distinguished reporting. Albert Londres (1884–1932)—after whom the annual prize for good reporting is named—exposed the conditions of prisons in Cayenne in its columns (1922). Exceeding 2.1 million, *Le Petit Parisien*'s circulation in 1917 was the highest ever attained by a French daily newspaper. It ceased publication in 1944. [MP]

'Petit Poucet, Le'. One of Perrault's **Histoires ou contes du temps passé*, not the British 'Tom Thumb' but a story of abandoned children defeating an ogre, comparable to the Grimm brothers' 'Hansel and Gretel'.

Petit Prince, Le. One of *Saint-Exupéry's best-known works, this children's fairy-tale, published in 1943, describes the meeting of the aviator-narrator with the diminutive ruler of the solar system's smallest planet. The Prince's journey through space, his encounter with varying forms of human vanity, his self-sacrifice, death, and rebirth, convey in fantastic form the author's predominant preoccupations with quest, innocence, and redemption. The author's illustrations are integral to the effect of the book. [NH]

Petits Enfants du siècle, Les, see ROCHEFORT, C.

Petrarchism. Term commonly applied both to the love poetry addressed to Laura by Petrarch (1304–74) and to the conventions which developed from the *Canzoniere*'s widespread influence on generations of 15th- and 16th-c. European lyric poets. Petrarch had assimilated elements from Christian Platonism and from classical and medieval amatory traditions (especially the ethos of *chivalry and **fin'amor*), and had expressed, with psychological realism and emotional conviction, the tensions between his spiritual idealism and the anguish of love. Numerous Italian imitators, and notably the 'precious' poets of the late 15th c. (the Quattrocentists Chariteo, Tebaldeo, Serafino), transmitted to future European love poets a common language and a mode of stylization, well suited to an aristocratic court audience, in which an over-refined, 'witty' manner and the mechanical reproduction of a cluster of thematic and formal features (especially antithesis) all too often replaced the psychological complexities of the love-experience.

Within the Petrarchist conventions the woman was idealized as a goddess and an icon of physical and spiritual perfection. Her beauty was described in stylized comparisons (flowers, precious jewels, and metals) and her virtues and accomplishments rendered by hyperbole. The overwhelming effect of this paragon on the lover is crystallized in the account of the first meeting (the *innamoramento*) with its associated religious and seasonal symbolism and its common core of conceits and images (Cupid's arrows, love as a paralysing poison, the poet as wounded or trapped animal). Based on service and fidelity, the poet's love is immutable. Because of the woman's coldness, however, it is also characterized by physical and mental suffering and by conflicting emotional states (hope/despair, love/hate, pleasure/pain); these often find expression in patterns of antithesis and oxymoron, in military metaphors, and in *concetti* (like that of the poet in a frail boat prey to storm and shipwreck). Although death is welcomed as a release from torment, the lover enjoys his anguish which, like a religious passion, purifies and perfects. The obsessive intensity of his love recalls his absent lady either in natural settings or in nocturnal visions, or it expresses itself in the wish to be transformed into an object in her presence. Nature reflects the lover's emotional state in a process of 'pathetic fallacy': it either comforts him in his solitude or isolates him even further by contrasting the extremity of his grief with the universal harmony of nature.

Mythological reference supports the themes of metamorphosis (Jupiter), suffering and bondage (Prometheus, Sisyphus), hubris and self-destruction (Acteon, Icarus). In addition to antithesis, oxymoron, metaphor, and hyperbole, the Petrarchist's preferred rhetorical figures include apostrophe, exclamation, periphrasis, adynaton, and anaphora, whilst concluding force is often provided by an epigrammatic or pithy final line. Within such a codified system the poetry should not be read as a reflection of lived experience or sincere feeling: in many cases the woman is a pretext, and ultimately what is of prime importance is a devotion to the beauty of poetry itself.

The history and nature of French *Renaissance Petrarchism are complex and are intertwined with developments in Italy in the 15th and 16th c. The first French imitators of the 1530s and early 1540s (*Marot, *Saint-Gelais, *Scève) were restrained in their Italian borrowings, and in the case of Marot in particular remained rooted in the native love tradition. Influenced less by Petrarch himself than by the Quattrocentist poets, on the whole these French poets preferred, as did their Italian models, the epigram (*strambotto*) to the sonnet—Scève's *Délie* (1544), for example, is a sequence of *dizains* which combines Petrarchist and *Neoplatonic features.

It was with the advent of the *Pléiade that Petrarch himself, Petrarchist conventions, and the sonnet form and cycle were fully and creatively acclimatized in France. *Tyard, *Du Bellay, *Baïf, and *Ronsard all published cycles of love poetry between 1549 and 1555 (exclusively or predominantly in sonnet form), in which the Petrarchist canon occupied a prominent place—sometimes fused with the mystical idealism of Neoplatonism—and in which the preferred models were Petrarch himself and the more 'classical' and restrained poets, Ariosto, Bembo, and Bembist disciples. Ronsard in particular demonstrates independence of his models, transcending and naturalizing inherited conventions by superlative craftsmanship and by the personal voice he gives to inner tensions between idealism and sensuality.

The final phase of French Renaissance Petrarchism again reflects developments in Italy, where, from about 1555, there had occurred a reaction against the restraint of Bembo and a return to the 'precious' manner of the Quattrocentists, especially as manifested in the recent poetry of the Neopolitans Costanzo, Tansillo, and Rota. Their influence was discernible in varying degrees in France in Les Soupirs of *Magny (1557), the sonnets of *Belleau's Bergerie (1565), the Sonnets pour Hélène of Ronsard (1578), and in the immensely popular love poetry of *Desportes.

In Renaissance France, as elsewhere in Europe, this widespread fashion for Petrarchism coexisted with an anti-Petrarchist tradition, which originated in Italy and which generally expressed itself in parodies of the artifices of the convention or in a rejection of some of its principal features. This counter-current, which never seriously called into question the legitimacy of the convention or diminished its validity as a means of serious poetic utterance, is found in France in Du Bellay's A une dame (1553; reproduced in variant form in 1558 as Contre les pétrarquistes) and in Ronsard's 'A son livre' (Nouvelle continuation des Amours, 1556).

If certain social factors help to explain the popularity of Petrarchism in Renaissance France—the increasing influence of Italians in French society and at the court of *Catherine de Médicis in particular, the improvement in the status of women at court and their role in the literary *salons of the day—it was similarly the external pressures of civil war and the developing religious imperatives of the century which ultimately caused poets to turn in their sonnet cycles to devotional expression of a more overtly Christian nature.   [MDQ]

See J. Vianey, Le Pétrarquisme en France au XVIe siècle (1909); H. Weber, La Création poétique au seizième siècle en France, 2 vols. (1956); L. Forster, The Icy Fire (1969).

Peuple, Le, see MICHELET.

PEYREFITTE, Roger (b. 1907). A French diplomat turned novelist whose reputation was established with Amitiés particulières (1944, Prix Renaudot), evoking male adolescent passions in the confines of a religious college. Later novels become increasingly provocative and amoral, satirizing a variety of milieux including the ambassadorial (in Les Ambassades, 1951) and the Jewish (Les Juifs, 1965).   [EAF]

Phalansteries (phalanstères), see FOURIER.

Pharaon, Le, see MEMMI.

Pharisienne, La. Novel by François *Mauriac, published 1941. It exploits one of his favourite themes, that of Christian bourgeois hypocrisy, through the description of the misery wrought by Brigitte Pian on her family and entourage. The novel is significant for its criticism of official sanctity at the time of the German Occupation and the Vichy regime and for its use of a deliberately non-directive and non-omniscient first-person narrator in the wake of *Sartre's criticism of Mauriac as a novelist.   [NH]

Phèdre. Tragedy by *Racine, generally regarded in the 20th c. as his masterpiece. First performed in 1677 as Phèdre et Hippolyte in competition with *Pradon's play of the same name, Phèdre is the last of Racine's secular tragedies. In the preface, in order to make his peace with the *Jansenists, he stresses its moral message, and *Arnauld declared that Phèdre was indeed a 'juste à qui la grâce a manqué'.

The story comes from the Hippolytus plays of Euripides and Seneca. Phèdre, wife of Thésée, king of Athens, is in love with her stepson Hippolyte, who in turn (against his father's orders) loves the princess Aricie. When Thésée is absent, presumed dead, Phèdre makes an involuntary confession of her love to Hippolyte, who is horrified. On Thésée's return, to protect Phèdre, her nurse Oenone accuses Hippolyte of attempted rape; Thésée curses his son, who is killed in a combat with a sea-monster (his death, dragged by horses, is described in the famous 'récit de Théramène'). Phèdre, racked by guilt and jealousy, confesses and poisons herself; Thésée is left with his world in ruins. The play is remarkable for the emotional power of the language and for the malevolent presence of the gods (Venus and Neptune), who destroy the admirable protagonists.   [PF]

Phenomenology. A method of philosophical enquiry developed by Edmund Husserl (1859–1938), modified by Martin Heidegger (1889–1976), and reinterpreted in France by, among others, *Marcel, *Ricœur and, notably, *Sartre and *Merleau-Ponty.

Phenomenology investigates the ground and constitution of meaning. It involves an intuitive and reflective scrutiny of the sense-giving acts of consciousness prior to their conceptual elaboration, and a description of phenomena in the various modes in which they are present to consciousness. The complementary relationship of consciousness and its objects implies that things are as they appear to us: being and appearing coincide. Phenomenology argues against the view that there are hidden 'things-in-themselves' which lie beyond phenomena; it attempts to transcend the opposition between the idealist reduction of the world to the knowledge we have of it and the realist postulate that the external world exists independently of the activity of the mind. The emphasis is upon the 'intentionality' of consciousness: i.e., the fact that consciousness is always consciousness *of* something, is directed towards its objects in acts not only of perception and cognition, identification and synthesis, but also of willing, desiring, imagining, etc. The goal of Husserl's investigation, to be sharply differentiated from that of traditional psychology, was to elucidate, through an 'eidetic reduction', the essential structures of our acts of consciousness. A necessary prior step was to eliminate, following the example of *Descartes, all presuppositions and prejudices, whether philosophical, scientific, or naïve, concerning the world and our knowledge of it. A more radical and controversial aspect of Husserl's method involved a reinterpretation of the *cogito* whereby belief in and judgements concerning the factual existence of phenomena are suspended, thus revealing, as the only certainty to survive this 'phenomenological reduction', the activity of the 'transcendental Ego' as the absolute source of knowledge.

This apparent return to idealism was called into question by Heidegger and by the phenomenologists of the French school. Heidegger reflected not upon 'pure' consciousness but upon man's 'being-in-the-world' and upon human existence in terms of its temporality and historicity; he described such categories of experience as anxiety and authenticity, and his ultimate aim, in an ambitious move towards ontology, was to elucidate the meaning of Being itself. Sartre argued against Husserl that the Ego is a secondary construct, an object *for* consciousness rather than a subject *within* consciousness (*La Transcendance de l'Ego*, 1936–7); for Merleau-Ponty the inherence in the world of the embodied subject is the primordial and irreducible experience (*Phénoménologie de la perception*, 1945).

However, the French existential phenomenologists drew selectively upon the theories of both Husserl and Heidegger [see EXISTENTIALISM]. In his early works Sartre explored the structures of emotion and imagination. For him our emotions are ways of 'intending' the world as hateful, hostile, or sympathetic: we unreflectively experience our emotions as though they were objective qualities of the world (*Esquisse d'une théorie des émotions*, 1939). The act of imagining, in that it exemplifies our freedom and our ability to envisage what is not the case, is the paradigm of consciousness in its powers of projection, negation, and sense-giving detachment from the real (*L'Imaginaire*, 1940). In *L'*Être et le néant* (1943) the translucent activity of consciousness or being-for-itself creates a meaningful world against the undifferentiated, opaque background of being-in-itself. Merleau-Ponty, while convinced that Husserl's 'reductions' fail to capture the richness of concrete phenomena, was impressed by the apparent primacy of the 'life-world' in his later thought. Implicitly critical of Sartre's dualistic ontology and of his apparent insistence on the translucency of consciousness, Merleau-Ponty argued that the body is the subject of pre-reflective intentionality, percep-

tion, and action. The body-subject and the world are complementary, the world offering a store of potential meanings which may be realized by the intentional acts of embodied consciousness.

Among those acts are those of the artist and the writer. Hence the close affinity between phenomenology and the 'worlds' revealed in art and literature, made visible in Sartre's creative writing, in Merleau-Ponty's reflections on painting, and in the literary criticism of, for instance, Georges *Poulet and Jean-Pierre *Richard. For them the latent patterns of meaning of those imaginary worlds lie beneath their superficial structure at a pre-conceptual level of sensation, image, and spatial and temporal configuration: it is the task of the critic to make those patterns manifest. [See also RICŒUR.]   [REG]

See H. Spiegelberg, *The Phenomenological Movement*, 3rd edn. (1982); M. Hammond, J. Howarth, and R. Keat, *Understanding Phenomenology* (1991).

Philinte. The 'raisonneur' and Alceste's friend in Molière's *Le *Misanthrope*; he also figures in a philosophical comedy by *Fabre d'Eglantine.

PHILIPE, Gérard (1922–59). French actor. The outstanding young male lead of his generation, he acted in the first productions of *Giraudoux's *Sodome et Gomorrhe* (1943) and *Camus's *Caligula* (1945). In the 1950s his warm and charismatic acting was a significant element in the popularity of the *Théâtre National Populaire, most memorably in *Le *Cid* and Musset's *Les *Caprices de Marianne*. His notable film successes included Claude Autant-Lara's *Le Diable au corps* and René Clair's *La Beauté du diable*.   [DWW]

PHILIPON, Charles (1800–62). Founder of *Le *Charivari.

PHILIPPE, Charles-Louis (1874–1909). Novelist. The son of a Bourbonnais clog-maker, Philippe wrote of the rural poor and the urban underprivileged. Having moved to Paris, he published *Quatre histoires de pauvre amour* (1897), *La Bonne Madeleine et la pauvre Marie* (1898), the poignant *La Mère et l'enfant* (1900/11), one of the important early statements about childhood in French fiction, *Bubu de Montparnasse* (1901), an acclaimed portrayal of the milieu of prostitution, *Le Père Perdrix* (1902), *Marie Donadieu* (1904), and *Croquignole* (1906). The unfinished versions of *Charles Blanchard*, a homage to his father, appeared in 1913. He was a democratizer of the French novel, and his understated style and blend of socio-psychological realism infused with a poetic understanding influenced the early *Nouvelle Revue Française* group.   [DAS]

PHILIPPE-AUGUSTE (Philippe II) (1165–1223) was king of France from 1180 to 1223. He made a vital contribution to the establishment of the French state and the expulsion of the English from France, and also to the development of Paris, where remains of his city wall (the *enceinte Philippe-Auguste*) can still be seen.

PHILIPPE DE BEAUMANOIR (*fl.* 13th c.). Philippe II de Rémi, referred to as Philippe de Beaumanoir after the death of his elder brother in 1280, was a lawyer whose *Coutumes de Beauvaisis* (1283) was a much used and frequently copied vernacular treatise on customary law. The two romances, *Jehan et Blonde* and *La Manekine* (*c.*1240–1270?), which appear under the name of Philippe de Rémi, are now assumed to be the work of the father of the lawyer, likewise called Philippe. He seems to have taken the title of lord of Beaumanoir sometime between 1249 and 1255, and he died in 1265. An adventure romance, *Jehan et Blonde* tells of Jean, a young squire from Dammartin who falls in love with Blonde, daughter of his lord the count of Oxford, and of the couple's adventures and eventual marriage in the face of adversity. It shows affinities with the *Anglo-Norman *Horn* and *Gui de Warewic*. *La Manekine*, which exploits folklore themes, is the story of a girl who escapes from her father's incestuous love at the cost of her hand, which, after many adventures including marriage to the king of Scotland and calumny, she succeeds in having restored.   [IS]

PHILIPPE DE CHAMPAGNE, see CHAMPAGNE.

PHILIPPE DE MÉZIÈRES (*c.*1327–1405). Soldier and diplomat, Philippe devoted his life to the furthering of the crusading movement, rallying support and founding an order of chivalry. Of his French and Latin works (primarily religious and moralistic), the most important is the *Songe du vieil pelerin* (1389). This vast dream allegory, descriptive and polemic, synthesizes world geography, comments on contemporary world politics, attacks Rome, and satirizes the decadent state of France; it also includes a *miroir des princes* for Charles VI, and finally a vision of the king's personal apotheosis, all couched in an almost inextricably complex web of personification and metaphor.   [JHMT]

PHILIPPE DE NOVARRE (*c.*1195–after 1264). He lived in Outremer (the Holy Land) from *c.*1218, and was author of a varied *œuvre*: feudal law (*Livre de forme de plait*), morality (*Des quatre tenz d'aage d'ome*), and especially his *Mémoires* (*c.*1252), now lost apart from two sections on contemporary political struggles; one of these interestingly uses figures from *Le *Roman de Renart*.   [JHMT]

PHILIPPE DE THAON, see ANGLO-NORMAN LITERATURE, 7.

PHILIPPE DE VITRY (1291–1361). A Champenois who was notary to Charles IV, and bishop of Meaux from 1351, renowned in his own day as a philosopher, mathematician, classical scholar, poet (Petrarch called him 'the only poet in France'), and musician. His few surviving works include motets in French and Latin, a bucolic ballade (*Le dit de Franc Gontier*, parodied by *Villon), and a longer allegorical poem in praise of crusading, *Le Chapel des trois fleurs de lis*. Today he is known principally as a great musical innovator, and the author of the *Ars nova*, one of the first textbooks of polyphony.   [NM]

'Philippe-Égalité', see ORLÉANS.

PHILIPPE LE BON; PHILIPPE LE HARDI, dukes of Burgundy, see BURGUNDIAN COURT LITERATURE.

PHILOMBE, René (pseud. of Philippe Louis Ombede) (b. 1930) Cameroonian writer of short stories (*Lettres de ma cambuse*, 1964), novels (*Sola ma chérie*, 1969; *Un sorcier blanc à Zangali*, 1969), plays (*Africapolis*, 1979), and several collections of poetry. His realism, concern for social justice, and broad humanism have helped to make his writings accessible to a wide audience in Cameroon.   [PGH]

Philosophe. Name given in the 18th c. to writers and thinkers sympathetic to *Enlightenment values. The word was used with both negative and positive connotations. In the *Encyclopédie*, the standard-bearer of the cause, the *philosophe* is glowingly defined in the article of that name as not only a scrupulous observer and rational thinker, but 'un honnête homme qui veut plaire et se rendre utile'.

In the second half of the century the *philosophes* came to be an influential party, who were able, under the leadership of d'*Alembert, to establish a powerful presence in the *Académie Française. Seen by their opponents as a sinister faction, they were the object of many attacks, including J.-N. Moreau's pamphlet against the *Cacouacs and *Palissot de Montenoy's satirical comedy *Les Philosophes*, in which *Diderot and other leading members of the party are lampooned. The word *philosophie* often has a cognate meaning in the 18th c.   [PF]

Philosophe sans le savoir, Le. *Drame by *Sedaine, in five acts and in verse, first performed at the Comédie-Française in 1765. It continued to be staged, usually in a censored version, into the 1880s. It is generally acknowledged to be the best example of the genre.

Vanderk, aristocrat turned merchant, shows his 'philosophic' qualities by coping simultaneously with his son's involvement in a duel and his daughter's marriage to a lawyer. Vanderk is an idealized character, and his role is developed at the expense of all the others. The plot offers suspense, but lacks verisimilitude. The setting is a good representation of upper-middle-class family life. Though the play is focused on the event of the duel, its main interest derives from its eulogy of the merchant figure, portrayed as the worthy cosmopolitan who contributes to the revitalization of the fatherland (in the aftermath of the Seven Years War). The play is a vindication of 'philosophic' virtues in action and a reply to *Palissot's *Les Philosophes*.   [JD]

Philosophes français du 18e siècle, Les

Philosophes français du 18e siècle, Les, see TAINE.

Philosophie zoologique, see LAMARCK.

Photography. France was the birthplace of photography, though England (with Fox Talbot) may claim a share in the invention. It was Nicéphore Niépce (1765–1833) who in the 1820s, cooperating with *Daguerre, developed the process from which modern photography derives.

In the 19th c. the new invention was used in France as elsewhere to record aspects of reality. It had its greatest success in portraiture [see NADAR], but also served to depict exotic places (*Du Camp left memorable images of the Egypt he visited with Flaubert) or to record social reality closer to home. Scientists used the camera to investigate movement—a development which contributed to the invention of the cinematograph in France [see CINEMA]. As photography became a profitable business, its status as an art was much disputed, but it found a major role in the reproduction of existing art works.

The first half of the 20th c. saw significant new developments. The creation of lightweight cameras made photography more accessible to all and allowed photographers to produce spontaneous-seeming images of everyday life. The fashion industry and *advertising both contributed to the development of the art. Photo-reportage developed rapidly, finding outlets in journals such as *Vu* (1928) and *Regards* (1931). Some of the most familiar images of French life were produced by photographers who came to prominence at this time, notably Eugène Atget (1857–1927), Jacques-Henri Lartigue (1894–1986), Henri Cartier-Bresson (b. 1908), and Robert Doisneau (1912–94). Gisèle Freund (b. 1912), an immigrant from Germany, followed Nadar's example in producing remarkable portraits of writers (Malraux, Beauvoir, Beckett, etc.).

At the same time, photography was welcomed and exploited by the literary avant-garde, particularly the *Surrealists. Their journals featured photography and photomontage, and *Breton combined photographers' iconic images and his own text in an arresting way in *Nadja*. The Surrealists appreciated (e.g. in the work of Atget) the raw 'document' quality of the photographic image, but equally its ability to reveal the strangeness of familiar reality—this was enhanced by deliberate distortion, collage, and similar techniques. Major talents associated with this movement were the American Man Ray (1890–1976), the Hungarian André Kertész (1894–1985), the German Germaine Krull (1897–1985), and the Transylvanian Brassaï (1899–1984), all of whom adopted Paris as their creative home. The continuing importance of photography in contemporary art can be seen, for example, in the work of Marcel *Duchamp and Yves Klein (1928–62).

Of the French writers who have meditated on the effects of photography, the most significant is Roland *Barthes. His critical essays, in *Mythologies* and elsewhere, express suspicion of the pseudo-real nature of the photographic image and its contribution to an illusory *imaginaire* [see SARTRE; LACAN], but he pays homage to its quasi-magical powers in his late essay, *La Chambre claire*. [PF]

Photo-roman or **Roman-photo.** In its popular form, its parentage is to be found in the *cinema (and particularly the *ciné-roman*, stills 'narrated' by extracts from the script) and the *bande dessinée*. The magazine serial *roman-photo* had its immediate origins in Italy, in 1947, and was transplanted into France in 1949 by the publishers Aldo and Cino Del Duca. Part of the *presse du cœur*, it subscribes to the conventions of romantic fiction (the *roman rose*), but allows excursions into the territory of the *roman policier* [see DETECTIVE FICTION].

The serious *photo-roman*, on the other hand, appeared only in the 1980s, as a development of the experimentalism of the *Nouveau Roman, intent on exploring the frictions between narrative and isolated image, the symbolic and the referential; this line of enquiry is represented by the work of H. *Guibert (*Suzanne et Louise*, 1980; *Le Seul Visage*, 1984), B. Peeters and M.-F. Plissart (*Fugues*, 1983; *Droits de regard*, 1985; *Le Mauvais Œil*, 1986) and, more recently, C. Bruel and X. Lambours (*La Mémoire des scorpions*, 1991). [CS]

Physiocrats. An influential group of 18th-c. economic theorists, usually known in their time (and sometimes derided) as *économistes*. They may be said to have founded scientific economics in France. Their leader was *Quesnay, whose disciples included *Dupont de Nemours, *La Rivière, and *Mirabeau *père*.

'Physiocratie' means the government of nature. In true *Enlightenment fashion, Quesnay believed in a God-given natural order; the philosopher's task is to develop this basic 'evidence' by scientific calculations leading to greater prosperity and happiness. Physiocracy's central tenet is that all wealth comes from the land; only agriculture provides a *produit net* (real return on investment) and this wealth, if allowed to circulate freely, generates the economic life of society. Corollaries include the sanctity of private property, protected by a benevolent monarchy, freedom of production and trade, and a single tax based on agricultural revenue. The more archaic aspects of this system, including its underestimation of industry and commerce, were rejected by *Turgot, who in his public role was briefly able to put Physiocracy into practice, modernizing agriculture, freeing it from old rules and customs, reforming taxation, and allowing free trade in grain. [PF]

Physiologies. Too often dismissed as shallow *petit-bourgeois* ephemera, the small books in the *Physiologie* genre, dedicated to recording the apparently trivial aspects of life in the *July Monarchy, are in fact a precious source for the study of the society, politics, and culture of this period. They remain a sprightly and witty testimony to the vitality of literary journalism in the Paris of the 1840s, and particularly of the *Charivari group of writers and illustrators. In the late 1820s and throughout the 1830s various works appeared entitled *Physiologie de . . .* , the most notable being *Brillat-Savarin's Physiologie du goût* (1826) and *Balzac's Physiologie du mariage* (1830). The grandiose, pseudo-scientific subtitles of these two works set the tone for the genre, which was to explode with 122 titles in the years 1840–2. Underlying all the *Physiologies* was the sense that modern city life had become both infinitely interesting and mysterious, as well as decidedly ridiculous and bathetic.   [BR]

PIAF, Édith (pseud. of Édith Gassion) (1915–63). French singer and occasionally songwriter ('La Vie en rose', 1947; 'Hymne à l'amour', 1949). A legendary figure of the *chanson française*, her importance lay in her ability to dramatize her songs in an intensely emotional and captivating way, investing even the most banal refrain with universal poetic appeal. After a wretched childhood she went from street-singer in the Pigalle quarter of Paris in 1935 to her first success at the ABC music-hall in 1937. Her international career in the 1950s was undermined by her tragic private life, alcoholism, and drug addiction, but she continued performing, despite her deteriorating health.   [PGH]

PIAGET, Jean (1896–1980). Swiss psychologist. A specialist in child psychology, Piaget elaborated a theory of progressive intellectual development through a number of stages, each of which incorporated and synthesized the previous one; these stages have been widely adopted in educational psychology and pedagogy. He developed a theory of cognitive psychology which characterized intelligence as the coordination of an organized intellectual system and the external world. His concern with epistemological categories of cognition, such as space, quantity, and causality, led him to a semiotic analysis of symbolic forms which he described as structuralist. He insisted, however, that structure must be integrated with notions of development, and, in contrast to more static theories, he argued for a genetic *Structuralism.   [MHK]

PIBRAC, Guy du Faur de (c.1529–1584). Born in Toulouse of a well-established family, Pibrac studied law in Toulouse and after several skirmishes with the authorities became established in Paris. As chancellor for Henri, duc d'Anjou, in Poland, he defended the kings's claim to the throne. His royal enthusiasm was already visible in his *Apologie de la Saint-Barthélemy* (1573). Later he was appointed chancellor to *Marguerite de Valois, but retired an embittered man. Praised for his 'docte parler', Pibrac was renowned for his oratory. His moral precepts or *Quatrains* (from 1574), long a standard school-text, are austere in format but embody a popular wisdom which is not superhuman in its demands.   [KCC]

PICABIA, Francis Martinez de (1879–1953). Although he can be described as a painter-poet and founder of reviews (*391, Cannibale*), he himself scorned such labels. Of Cuban extraction, he studied at the École Nationale des Beaux-Arts and exhibited at the Salon des Artistes Indépendants in 1903. The most fertile phase of his literary career coincided with his involvement in the *Dada movement, the ideal vehicle for his jovial, iconoclastic, and hedonistic nihilism, seen at its best in *Jésus-Christ Rastaquouère* (1920). Much of his writing is aphoristic, but some poems (e.g. *Pensées sans langage*, 1919) read like long, automatic monologues, and *Unique Eunuque* (1920) contains lines where the word-order seems random.   [KRA]

PICARD, Louis-Benoît, see COMEDY, 2; REVOLUTION, 2.

PICARD, Raymond, see BARTHES; LITERARY HISTORY, 2.

Picaresque Writing, see SPANISH INFLUENCES.

Picardy, see ARRAS; PATOIS AND DIALECT WRITING.

PICASSO, Pablo (1881–1973). During the first half of the 20th c. the Spanish-born Picasso was the dominant figure in Western art, which from 1907 he redirected with his *Les Demoiselles d'Avignon* and, alongside *Braque, his development of *Cubism. His friendship with Max *Jacob began the contacts with poets which from 1904 would make Picasso's Bateau-Lavoir studio in Montmartre 'le rendez-vous des poètes' (most notably *Apollinaire, *Salmon, *Jarry, *Reverdy), among whom the new art, as it evolved from the *Demoiselles* to the *papier collé* and collages (1912), encouraged parallel theories and practices of poetry in terms of an autonomous structure of interrelated fragments of image and sound. *Breton acknowledged Picasso's importance for *Surrealism, while the painter's friendship with poets (notably from the 1930s with *Éluard and *Char) produced numerous exchanges between the two arts. The painter's Surrealist play *Le Désir attrapé par la queue*, written in 1941, is still occasionally performed.   [JK]

PICCINI, Nicola (1728–1800), composer, see GLUCK.

PICHETTE, Henri (b. 1924). French poet and dramatist who achieved early fame with his allegorical *Les Épiphanies* (1947) in which a poet (first played by Gérard *Philipe) confronts a cynical devil and proclaims the rights of the imagination in a language of baroque extravagance. Other works include *Apoèmes* (1947) and the play *Nucléa* (1952).

PICHOT, Amédée (1795–1877). French translator of Byron and an important intermediary between French and British culture. He edited the influential *Revue britannique*.

PICHOU (*c*.1597–1631). French dramatist. He wrote four tragicomedies, including the successful *Folies de Cardenio* (1628), adapted from *Don Quixote*, and *La Filis de Scire* (1630), probably the first French adaptation of an Italian pastoral, and which earned the praise of *Richelieu. Isnard's preface to this play is an important early defence of regular theatre.

[GJM]

Picturesque. A term closely linking art and literature, 'picturesque' originally meant a natural landscape which looked as if *Claude might have painted it. Landscapes of magnificent ruined and overgrown Italian gardens, drawn by *Fragonard and Hubert *Robert in Rome, and fantastic conceptions of nature reclaiming man-made edifices published in Paris by the Italian Piranesi were taken up as leitmotifs of the resurgent power of nature during the *Romantic movement of the 19th c. William Gilpin claimed that picturesque views were rarely found in nature; Richard Payne Knight defined a set of principles for landscape gardening which united beauty and the picturesque in *The Landscape: A Didactic Poem*, dedicated to the picturesque theorist Sir Uvedale Price. Landscape gardeners of the 18th c. established principles of variety, irregularity, surprise, accident, and interest as new canons of beauty. In France, the marquis de *Girardin wrote an admired work, *De la composition des paysages, ou Des moyens d'embellir la nature*, and put it into practice on his estate at Ermenonville.

[JPC]

Pièce à machines, SEE MACHINE PLAY.

Pièce à thèse. A term first associated with the plays of *Augier and *Dumas *fils*. It refers to plays which focus on some moral, social, or political evil or abuse and in which complicated but schematic plots lead to a demonstration of the playwright's own convictions (the expression *roman à thèse* is used in a similar way). It has been inappropriately applied to the moral complexity of Ibsen's dramas.

[SBJ]

Piège sans fin, Un, see BHÊLY-QUÉNUM.

Pierre et Jean. Novel by *Maupassant, published 1888. Set in Le Havre, it relates the story of two brothers, Pierre, a doctor, and Jean, a lawyer, sons of a retired jeweller, Monsieur Roland. The novel presents a fine psychological study of Pierre's jealousy of his brother over the affections of Madame Rosémilly, and, in particular, over the fortune that Jean inherits from an old family friend, Léon Maréchal. As Pierre's suspicions about his mother's past infidelity with his brother's benefactor emerge, the novel deals with the familiar preoccupation of Maupassant with the problem of paternity. The hapless Pierre takes a post as a ship's doctor on a transatlantic liner. The novel is noteworthy for the skilful use of point of view.

An essay on the novel ('Le Roman'), which was published as a preface to *Pierre et Jean*, is an important statement of Maupassant's realist aesthetic and of his debt to *Flaubert, containing the famous remark that 'les Réalistes de talent devraient s'appeler des Illusionnistes'.

[DB]

PIERRE LE LOMBARD (Peter the Lombard), see SCHOLASTICISM, 2.

PIEYRE DE MANDIARGUES, André, see MANDIARGUES.

PIGALLE, Jean-Baptiste (1714–85). The greatest and most successful French sculptor of the 18th c. Employed by Madame de *Pompadour and the crown, Pigalle was one of the first to explore dramatic forms of naturalism in monumental commissions. His most famous works are the Tomb of the Maréchal de Saxe (1753–76), showing the young hero striding confidently to his death, and the shocking, life-size, gaunt nude of *Voltaire (1776).

[JPC]

PIGAULT-LEBRUN (pseud. of Charles-Antoine-Guillaume Pigault de l'Épinoy) (1753–1835). French playwright and novelist. The first of his many plays, *Charles et Caroline* (performed 1790, but written much earlier) is a melodrama based on his own turbulent life, during which his father had him declared legally dead. His vast output of novels (over 70 volumes), beginning with *L'Enfant du carnaval* (1792), have a satirical and libertine gaiety which won him great popularity. *Les Barons de Felsheim* (1798) paves the way for the action-packed romances of *Dumas *père*.

[PF]

Pigments, see DAMAS.

PIIS, Pierre-Antoine-Augustin de (1755–1832). A French Vicar of Bray, he served many regimes, while composing comic operas and light verse of all kinds, which he defended against fashionable melancholy in 'Aux détracteurs de la poésie badine'. His *L'Harmonie imitative de la langue française* (1785) is a lively verse treatise on poetic onomatopoeia, with detailed examples.

[PF]

PILES, Roger de (1635–1709). Well-travelled French diplomat and art historian who had a background of practical training. His writings, influenced by the poem *De arte graphica* by Charles-Alphonse du Fresnoy (1611–55), challenged accepted Academic principles such as the supremacy of historical subject-matter, the intellectual superiority of line over colour, and the importance of learnt rules over innate genius. His best-known work, *Cours de peinture par principes avec une balance des peintres* (1708), used a typically French analytical system of assessing the quality of paintings by allotting marks out of 20 to four 'essential parts': composition, drawing, colour, and expression. In this scale of values Rubens and Raphael emerged pre-eminent, with *Lebrun ahead of *Poussin, and Michelangelo well down in the charts.

[JPC]

PILHES, René-Victor (b. 1934). French novelist who abandoned a highly successful career in advertising to write baroque and playful texts. Some have a strong psychoanalytic flavour (*La Rhubarbe*, 1965; *Le Loum*, 1969); others carry a social message, notably *L'Imprécateur* (1974), a satirical attack on the power of multinational companies. *L'Hitlérien* (1988) parodies fascist discourse. He has won both the Prix Médicis and the Prix Femina. [EAF]

PINGAUD, Bernard (b. 1923). French novelist, noted literary critic (studies of *Camus, Madame de *Lafayette) and essayist, he co-founded the review *L'Arc* (1958) and collaborated on *Les *Temps modernes*. His novels reflect both an interest in problems of the emotional life and psychoanalysis (*L'Amour triste*, 1950, and *La Scène primitive*, 1965) and his political commitment (*Adieu Kafka*, 1989). [EAF]

PINGET, Robert (b. 1919). Novelist and playwright. Born in Geneva, he trained as a lawyer, settled in France in 1946, and has devoted himself to writing since 1951.

To win literary fame in modern France one must meet at least one of three criteria: be easily classifiable, engage in public polemic, or publish a *succès de scandale*. Pinger has met none of these, and the result is that, although often regarded as a principal exponent of the *Nouveau Roman, this major writer is far less well known than he ought to be, in spite of a dozen plays and a score of novels or other pieces of extended prose. From the start, with the short pieces that make up *Entre Fantoine et Agapa* (1951), and in novels like *Mahu ou le Matériau* (1952), *Le Renard et la boussole* (1953), and *Graal Flibuste* (1956), some of the constants of his work are apparent: the pull of place (idealized, intimately known, fantastic, ordinary); the preoccupation with insiders and outsiders; the awareness of the joys and risks of invention. Notable too is the exuberance of the writing. In this early phase, that is sometimes expressed in ways obvious enough: exotic scenes, extravagant utterances. But increasingly Pinget turns away from the extraordinary, to create instead a marvellous quotidian; to find in stones, not sermons only, but skulls, and splendours, and shames. The shift continues through *Baga* (1958), *Le Fiston* (1959), and *Clope au dossier* (1961), and the phase culminates in *L'Inquisitoire* (1962), in which, by way of the relentless interrogation of an uncomprehending *homme à tout faire*, the 'Pinget country', places and people, is assembled as a huge jigsaw might be.

The novels that follow take this as their ground, but to increasingly different effect. The natural idiom of small rural communities is gossip: endless speculation on whatever is new or unknown, producing stories as plausible as they are unverifiable. But such fabrication, Pinget sees, is exactly what novelists do; and, just as gossip may be malevolent as well as trivial, so narrating may be variously reli-

able. When, as in his own novels, it is wholly unreliable, exquisitely detailed evocations of scene and custom serve in fact to tantalize; for the intimate domestic patterns of *Quelqu'un* (1965) can convey cosiness, but also obsession. And in *Le Libera* (1968), *Passacaille* (1969), and *Fable* (1971), it is the space between these that Pinget explores. The tide of talk bears, alongside fragments of the reassuringly familiar, evidence of darker things: sexual and mystical violence. But the tension between the nice and the nasty is never resolved. For Pinget's supreme gift is his rendering of voice: 'seule capte mon intérêt la voix de celui qui parle', as he himself put it. The modulations of tone and style, invariably convincing, pull us this way and that, setting local pleasure against general bafflement. And it is more than a display of mimetic talent or a teasing of readers. If there is no solution to his riddles, it is because there is no solver, no voice that distances and situates all the other voices. This is further explored in *Cette voix* (1975), *L'Apocryphe* (1980), and *L'Ennemi* (1987), but its deeper implications appear in an unexpected corner of his work: the texts concerning 'Monsieur Songe', an elderly, self-important fusspot who appeared briefly in *Graal Flibuste*.

In 1982 Pinget revealed that for 20 years he had been writing Monsieur Songe stories as a relaxation from serious writing, and he has carried on: *Monsieur Songe* (1982), *Le Harnais* (1984), *La Charrue* (1985), and *Du nerf* (1990). And this unserious, and very funny, writing we must take very seriously indeed; for the risibly feeble Monsieur Songe has taken to writing—and become just as likely a model of 'the writer' as any the Romantics have bequeathed: pompous, opinionated, and beset intermittently by doubts. How then are we to tell novelists from gossips—or from the subjects of gossip; how to tell profound truth from impromptu invention, or avowable preferences from unconscious desires? For Pinget, we cannot. Writing, language itself, enacts the flow of experience; distinctions like true/false, serious/trivial, or even conscious/unconscious are simply our futile attempts to control it. His novels, at once effortlessly readable and endlessly enigmatic, celebrate the flow itself.

Given his preoccupation with voice, it is not surprising that Pinget has written also for the stage and for radio, with constant echoes from the prose works. These plays are often delightful, but seldom have the charge of the novels. But one early play, *La Manivelle* (1959), signposts an important connection: it was translated by Samuel *Beckett as *The Old Tune*, and reissued as a parallel text in 1960. Pinget's admiration for Beckett is apparent throughout his work. The other plays are: *Lettre morte* (1959); *Ici ou ailleurs*, *Architruc*, and *L'Hypothèse* (1961); *Autour de Mortin* (1965); *Identité* and *Abel et Bela* (1971); *Paralchimie* and *Nuit* (1973); and *Un testament bizarre* (1986). [GC]

See M. Praeger, *Les Romans de Robert Pinget: une écriture des possibles* (1987).

PIRON, Alexis (1689–1773). Comic playwright. A native of Dijon, Piron had confined his literary activities to satirical and erotic verse before going to Paris in 1718. Once there, he wrote some thirty *opéras-comiques* and compositions for the *théâtres de la *foire*. His outstanding early success was *Arlequin-Deucalion* (1722), a masterly satirical monologue in which the title-character, the only speaker, interacts with a variety of others whose mutism—enforced by the law which at the time forbade the *théâtres de la foire* to use dialogue—is itself turned to satirical ends. Among his seven plays performed at the Comédie-Française, his tragedies were failures, except for *Gustave Wasa* (1733), but his comedy *La Métromanie* (1738) was a resounding success. He was elected to the Académie Française in 1753. However, his licentious compositions, notably an early 'Ode à Priape', were shown to the king, who forbade him to take his seat, but granted him a pension.   [JD]

PITHOU, Pierre (1539–96). French jurist and humanist of essentially *Politique convictions, who contributed some of the harangues in the *Satire Ménippée*. Like many members of the same group (e.g. *Pasquier), he was also a *Gallican, arguing strongly that, papals bulls notwithstanding, French bishops had the right to lift *Henri IV's excommunication.   [JJS]

PITOËFF, Georges (1884–1939). Actor and theatre director who grew up and trained in Russia before moving to Geneva and thence to Paris, where he worked from 1919. In partnership with his wife Ludmilla, a gifted actress, he earned renown through his international repertoire and simple but striking set-design. He was a co-founder of the *Cartel.   [DHW]

PIVOT, Bernard, see APOSTROPHES; RADIO.

PIXERÉCOURT, Guilbert de (1773–1844). French playwright, known as 'le *Corneille des boulevards' on account of his sensational *melodramas of which the most famous were: *Victor ou l'Enfant de la forêt* (1798), *Coelina ou l'Enfant du mystère* (1801), *Le Chien de Montargis* (1814). The basic formula was stark: virtue rewarded and vice punished. A maltreated or despoiled hero/heroine is rescued from the clutches of a villain in a plot stuffed with suspense, coincidence, high emotion, and violent action. There are blood-curdling encounters located in sinister or spectacular settings (dungeons, ruins), miraculous escapes and sensational endings, all requiring elaborate stage machinery.   [SBJ]

PIZAN, Christine de, see CHRISTINE DE PIZAN.

Placards, Affaires des. On the night of 17–18 October 1534, posters with booklets attached, attacking the Mass in intemperate sacramentarian terms, appeared all over Paris and even in *François Ier's appartments at Amboise. They were the work of Antoine Marcourt, a follower of the Zurich Reformer Zwingli. The king, alarmed by this 'sedition', instigated repressive measures against religious extremists, which were intensified after a second outbreak of posters on 13–14 January 1535: all printing was banned, a list of proscribed 'Lutherans', including Clément *Marot, was published, and scores of suspects were burned; the king himself led a huge penitential procession through Paris. Repression ended in May, but left bitter memories amongst the Reformers.   [MJH]

Place Royale, La. Comedy by Pierre *Corneille, subtitled *L'Amoureux extravagant*. First performed in 1633–4, it shows the vain attempt of the young Alidor to keep his independence by refusing true love.

PLACOLY, Vincent (1946–92). Martinican novelist and dramatist. He was educated in Fort-de-France, and then at the Lycée Louis-le-Grand and the Sorbonne, where he was a member of the Jeunesses Communistes and president of the Association Générale des Étudiants Martiniquais. His first novel, *La Vie et la mort de Marcel Gonstran* (1971), is a searching study of the effects of colonialism on an individual, while his second, *L'Eau-de-mort guildive* (1973), ranges over the whole of contemporary Martinican society; both novels are written in a style that owes much to *Rimbaud, Faulkner, and the contemporary Latin American novel, and combine a recondite vocabulary with the patterns and rhythms of *Creole. A third novel, *Frères volcans* (1983), is written in a more documentary style and explores the emancipation of slaves in Martinique in 1848 from the point of view of a white slave-holder. Placoly's plays include *La Mort douloureuse et tragique d'André Aliker* (1969), *Dessalines, ou la Passion de l'indépendance* (1983), which was awarded the Premio Casa de las Americas by the Centre for Cultural Studies in Havana, and a reworking, in a French West Indian context, of the legend of Don Juan. Shortly before his death, Placoly was awarded the Prix Frantz Fanon for a collection of stories and essays entitled *Une journée torride* (1991). A founder-member of the far-left Groupe Révolution Socialiste in 1974, Placoly was an active supporter of independence for Martinique.   [RJC]

Plaideurs, Les (1668). Light comedy about the legal profession by *Racine, based on Aristophanes' *The Wasps*.

Plaie, La, see FALL, M.

Plaine, La, see MONTAGNARDS.

Plaisir du texte, Le, see BARTHES.

Plaisirs de l'Île Enchantée, Les. First and most famous of the multi-media *fêtes* put on at *Versailles in honour of *Louis XIV. Taking place in May 1664, it included contributions from *Lully and *Molière, and in particular, after several days of concerts, fireworks, feasts, horse-races, and the like, the only performance of the first version of *Tartuffe*.

Plaisirs et les jours, Les, see PROUST.

Planchon, Roger (b. 1931). French actor, playwright, and director, the leading exponent of 'théâtre populaire' in the 1960s and 1970s. After early experiments in directing avant-garde playwrights, he was greatly influenced by Brecht's theories of staging and developed a politically committed production style involving a blend of social realism and rich theatricality. He worked closely with *Adamov, but his most influential productions have been iconoclastic Marxist interpretations of classics by *Molière, Shakespeare, *Marivaux, and *Racine. In 1972 the title of *Théâtre National Populaire was transferred from Paris to his theatre in the working-class suburb of Villeurbanne, Lyon.   [DWW]

Planétarium, Le. Novel by *Sarraute, published 1959. This work represents an important advance towards Sarraute's goal of plunging the reader into a fluid mass of 'tropistic' movements. There are named individuals: Alain and his wife Gisèle, their relatives, a famous writer. But there is no consistent *narratorial* voice. The inter-subjective dramas centre on Alain's attempts to acquire his aunt's flat and to be accepted into the writer's circle, thus engaging the apparently antagonistic values of the wealthy bourgeoisie and the intelligentsia. But the opposition collapses to reveal the same insecurity, acquisitiveness, and inauthenticity on both sides: the stars that move around the 'planetarium' are artificial ones.   [CB]

Plassans. Town, based on Aix-en-Provence, which provides the setting for some of Zola's *Rougon-Macquart* novels.

Plat de porc aux bananes vertes, Un, see SCHWARZ-BART, S.

Pléiade, La. Name traditionally given to a constellation of seven poets active from 1549 to 1589 who, under the leadership of *Ronsard, endowed French poetry with a new dignity consistent with *humanist principles, The group, which initially called itself the 'Brigade', never had the tight organization of a 'school': even its membership fluctuated, for if the names of Ronsard, *Du Bellay, *Baïf, *Tyard, and *Jodelle remain constant, the two remaining places were occupied, according to texts of Ronsard, firstly by *Des Autels and *La Péruse (1553) and later by *Peletier and *Belleau (1555, 1556). *Binet, in his biography of Ronsard (1586), replaces Peletier by *Dorat, who, as principal of the Collège de Coqueret, was responsible from 1547 for the education of Ronsard, Baïf, and Du Bellay. The other Parisian college closely associated with the formation of the new poetic movement was Boncourt, where members and associates of the future Pléiade (Jodelle, Belleau, La Péruse, *Grévin) received their

education from *Muret and *Buchanan. Other figures, like Denisot, *Garnier, *Magny, and *Jamyn, gravitated round the nucleus of the group.

The ideals of the Pléiade, as expressed in the *Defense et illustration* (1549) and in subsequent poems and theoretical statements, focused on the renewal of a national poetic language, to be achieved by the creative imitation of Greco-Roman and Italian sources [see CLASSICAL INFLUENCES; ITALIAN INFLUENCES]. Importance was accorded to poetic technique and, especially, to inspiration, often described in *Neoplatonist terms as a 'divine madness'. Erudite, virtuous, and assured of immortality, the poet is considered as a prophet, an intermediary between the gods and man, an interpreter of divine secrets and the mysteries of the universe. Aware of the elevated status of poetry and of their mission, and conscious of their role as innovators, the new movement was at first unjustly dismissive of previous French poetry, relegating even its best exponents (including Clément *Marot) to an outworn medieval tradition and rejecting its genres in favour of the models and forms of classical antiquity (ode, epic, elegy, eclogue, epigram, satire, tragic and comic theatre) and Italy (*sonnet).

The legacy left by the Pléiade was considerable. They acclimatized in France many of the genres they inherited (including the sonnet), they imposed their presence in a wide diversity of fields—love poetry, religious, scientific, satirical, political, and official verse, tragedy, comedy, the pastoral, and the epic—and were equally innovative and influential in matters of metre, rhyme, and versification and in theories concerning the nature and function of poetry. [See also PETRARCHISM.]   [MDQ]

See H. Chamard, *Histoire de la Pléiade* (1939–40); G. Castor, *Pléiade Poetics* (1964); Y. Bellenger, *La Pléiade. La Poésie en France autour de Ronsard* (1988).

Pléiade, Bibliothèque de la. Collection of French and world literature, together with encyclopedic volumes, published by *Gallimard since 1931. These handsome and increasingly scholarly editions consecrate an author's status as a classic; one contemporary writer described publication here as the equivalent of a tombstone.

Pleurer-rire, Le, see LOPÈS.

PLEYNET, Marcelin (b. 1933). French poet and critic; assistant managing editor of *Tel Quel* (1963–82). Pleynet received the Prix Fénéon for his first book of poems, *Provisoires amants des nègres* (1962). Subsequent works include: *Paysages en deux* and *Les Lignes de la prose* (1963), *Comme* (1965), *Stanze* (1973), *Rime* (1981), *Fragments du chœur* (1984), *Plaisir à la tempête* (1987). He has also published a multivolume diary and a number of important critical works devoted to avant-garde art and literature: *Lautréamont* (1967), *Art et littérature* (1977), *Transculture* (1978), *Les États-Unis de la peinture* (1986),

Henri Matisse (1988), *Motherwell* (1988), *Les Modernes et la tradition* (1990). He contends that the poet, like the critic, cannot detach himself from social history, nor from the history of ideas. Historically situated in the wake of World War II, Pleynet's prolific work explores the question of modernity as a form of individual and transnational resistance to the various manifestations of fascism in our century.

[DM-S]

PLISNIER, Charles, see BELGIAN LITERATURE IN FRENCH.

PLIYA, Jean (b. 1931). Playwright from Dahomey (Benin). The first *agrégé* in geography of the present Benin Republic, Pliya has held a number of important government offices including that of vice-chancellor of the Université du Bénin.

His first play, *Kondo le requin* (1966), won the Grand Prix Littéraire d'Afrique Noire. Part of a wave of historical plays produced in francophone Africa in the first decade of Independence, it covers the resistance of the Dahomean king, Gbéhanzin, to the French in the late 19th c. His second play, *La Secrétaire particulière* (1970), is a comedy of manners satirizing the corruption of government officials in the independent regimes. He has also published two collections of short stories, *L'Arbre fétiche* (1971) and *Le Chimpanzé amoureux* (1977).

Much of Pliya's work is concerned with the values on which modern Africa should be built. The efforts of individuals play a major role in his vision of the future. His most recent work is *La Fille têtue* (1982), a collection of stories inspired by Fon oral literature.

[FNC]

Plouffe. Fictional family made popular by the works of the Canadian novelist Roger *Lemelin.

PLUCHE, Noël-Antoine, abbé (1686–1761). French priest and teacher, famous for his *Spectacle de la nature* (1732–50). This encyclopedic work in nine volumes gives a simple account of the natural world and the cosmos, the human body, and human society. It includes descriptions and plates of machines which prefigure those of the *Encyclopédie. Pluche uses the universe as proof of God's goodness, and takes side-swipes at the pretensions of *philosophes. The work is written in an engaging style and was a huge publishing success.

[PF]

Pluie et vent sur Télumée Miracle, see SCHWARZ-BART, S.

Plume, see MICHAUX.

Plupart du temps, see REVERDY.

POE, Edgar Allen (1809–49). Described by *Mallarmé as 'ce cas littéraire absolu', Poe occupies a more significant place in the history of French literature than in that of his native America. This French version of Poe, made available by

*Baudelaire's translations of and introductions to his work (1848–65), itself contained two distinct strands. On the one hand there was the poet of the macabre, whose *Extraordinary Tales* renewed French Gothic fiction through their exploration of psychological terror and portrayed a network of feelings on the edge of normal psychic life (loss of the mother, obsession with the body, permeable borders between living and dead) on which the *Decadents and *Surrealists would draw. On the other, there was the mathematician of poetic effects, whose *Philosophy of Composition*, with its theory of poetry as an autonomous and deliberate object of language and its attack on lyrical effusion, didacticism, and sentimentality, reinforced the French tradition of 'l'*art pour l'art' and profoundly influenced Mallarmé and *Valéry. The diversity of critical approaches which Poe's work has always stimulated in France has been very evident in modern literary theory in such work as *Bachelard's 1944 preface to Baudelaire's translation of *The Adventures of Gordon Pym* and the seminal debate initiated by *Lacan's Structuralist analysis of *The Purloined Letter* (1966) and *Derrida's Post-Structuralist response (1972).

[JK]

Poèmes à jouer, see TARDIEU.

Poèmes antiques et modernes, see VIGNY.

Poèmes antiques; Poèmes barbares, see LECONTE DE LISLE.

Poésie pure, La. Term promoted by abbé *Bremond in 1925 and associated with *Poe, *Baudelaire, *Mallarmé, and *Valéry and their individual attempts, as part of the wider literary movement of *Symbolism, to define and exemplify purity of formal expression in poetry. With its roots in 18th-c. aesthetics, followed by the 'l'*art pour l'art' ideals of *Gautier, 'la poésie pure' covers a complex range of associations ranging from Mallarmé's metaphysical attempts to purify a poetic 'self' (note also his own reference in 'Crise de vers' to a desire of his times to separate two functions of language, ordinary or 'essential'), to Valéry's affirmations of the indissolubility of form and meaning: poetry as a highly charged emotional state which is as different from non-poetic prose as dancing is from walking or musical sound from mere noise.

[CMC]

Poètes maudits, Les, see VERLAINE.

Poil de carotte, see RENARD, J.

POINCARÉ, Henri (1854–1912). French mathematician and an influential philosopher of science. Poincaré advanced the doctrine of conventionalism, arguing that the laws of mathematics and physics (e.g. those of Euclidean geometry or Newtonian mechanics) are neither true nor false, being freely created and adopted for their convenience, simplicity, and utility (*La Science et l'hypothèse*, 1903). A prolific innovator in numerous fields of pure and applied mathematics, he was convinced of the synthesizing and inventive power of intuition in mathematical induction. Although not in agreement with Einstein, he enunciated a theory of the relativity of time and space and, anticipating Heisenberg, of the interaction of the observer and the phenomenon observed.

His cousin Raymond was president of the Republic, 1913–20. [REG]

Pointe. A surprising, witty turn of phrase, comparable to the English 'conceit'. It often involves the ostentatious use of rhetorical figures, puns, antitheses, and startling or extended metaphors, a well-known example being Pyrrhus's line in *Andromaque* referring at once to the fires of love and the burning of Troy: 'Brûlé de plus de feux que je n'en allumai.' Belonging to a *baroque art of verbal creativity, the theory of which was written by the Italian Emanuele Tesauro and the Spaniard Baltasar Gracián, it came under fierce attack in mid-17th-c. France as childish and affected. Its most remarkable French exponent was *Cyrano de Bergerac in his letters and *Entretiens pointus*. [PF]

Poisons, Affaire des. Famous trial of 1677 in which a woman named La Voisin was charged with a plot to murder the king involving poison and sorcery; she was sentenced to be burnt alive. Many noblemen and courtiers (including *Racine) were named during the hearings, but nothing was proved against them.

Poissard. Term formerly used of the language spoken by vulgar and uneducated Parisians. A stylized form of *poissard* enjoyed a brief vogue in the mid-18th c., being used for comedies, parodies, dialogues, verse, and the libretti of *opéras-comiques*. The invention of the *genre poissard* is attributed to Jean-Joseph *Vadé, its best-known practitioner. [VGM]

POISSENOT, Bénigne (*c*.1558–*c*.1586). Author of a collection of anecdotes and *exempla*, *L'Été* (1583; see also YVER), in which the unusually realistic setting often breaks in on the discussions between three holidaying students at Narbonne. Poissenot's *Nouvelles histoires tragiques* (1586) continues the tradition of Bandello and *Belleforest. [MJH]

POISSON, Raymond (1630–90). Comic actor (under the name of Belleroche) at the *Hôtel de Bourgogne, where he created the role of Crispin. He also wrote comedies. Members of the same family wrote and acted in comedies in the 18th c.

Poissy, Colloque de, see COLLOQUE DE POISSY.

Polar. Familiar term for *roman* or [*film*] *policier*; see DETECTIVE FICTION.

Polexandre, see GOMBERVILLE.

Police. During the *ancien régime*, *police* was a nebulous concept that combined administrative and judicial powers, for to administer was to judge and judgement implied the power to carry out the decision. *Police* thus implied the responsibility for keeping good order within the jurisdiction of a court. *Parlements*, *prévôtés*, municipalities all had often conflicting local powers of police, over highways, the grain trade, charitable institutions, acts of disorder, etc.

The more modern sense of police also existed in the form of a number of royal officers given powers to preserve order and arrest criminals. In the early 16th c. the powers given to the Prévôt de Paris were systematized, and by 1535 there existed 32 commissioners, 3 lieutenants, 20 archers, and 10 sergeants. Similar organizations were supposed to exist in the provinces and major towns. Not until 1667 did an edict establish a lieutenant-general of police in Paris (La Reynie) with extensive powers, and similar offices were set up in the major towns. In Paris a vast number of spies and informers (*mouchards*) were in service, and the detailed knowledge of the population was the envy of other rulers. Nevertheless, the continued existence of privileged jurisdictions interfered with the pursuit of, for example, illegal publishers. In 1789 the civilian organization for the keeping of order was never in a position to quell revolutionary activity.

Order was kept, to the limited extent that it was, by the *maréchaussée*. This force of mounted archers had had responsibility for the pursuit of criminals (e.g. thieves, smugglers, seditious or sacrilegious persons, counterfeiters) since the time of *François Ier. From 1720 each *généralité* (administrative region) had a company of archers; 34 existed in 1789, totalling about 4,000 men. After 1791 the *maréchaussée* was converted into the *gendarmerie*. The Revolutionary legislation brought about a separation of justice and administration, but the French police is much more involved in aspects of the state administration than the British. In 1811 special commissioners were set up, suppressed during the *Restoration and re-established later. From 1829 uniformed police officers were employed; the force expanded and there were 3,000 *sergents de ville* in Paris in 1861; and growth continued such that in 1985 the Police Nationale numbered about 120,000 (all services) and the Gendarmerie Nationale a further 88,000, making France one of the most densely policed states in Europe. [PRC]

Policier, see DETECTIVE FICTION.

POLIGNAC, Jules-Auguste-Armand-Marie, comte de (1780–1847). As foreign minister and prime minister to *Charles X in 1829–30, he was held responsible for the repressive policies which caused the latter's downfall. He later published political writings, including *Études historiques, politiques et morales* (1845).

Politeness (*politesse*), see HONNÊTETÉ.

Politiques. Name given to (mainly Catholic) moderates who, in the *Wars of Religion, argued that it was better to seek a political solution to the troubles than to destroy the country by prolonging civil war. Such views were based less on the principle of religious toleration (which was, however, growing during this period) than on a pragmatic assumption that peace and order were preferable to civil strife. Given the generally fanatical religious climate, this meant that the Politiques were condemned as atheists by the extremists of both sides. Their view infringed the sacrosanct tradition that there should be 'une foi, une loi, un roi', and was accordingly hard to defend. Its apparent failure seemed to be confirmed by the dismissal of the moderate chancellor Michel de *l'Hôpital in 1568. It received support, however, in times of crisis, notably after the *St Bartholomew's Day Massacre, when many Catholics decided that attempts to exterminate the Protestants were both pointless and wrong, and after the death of Alençon in 1584. The latter left the Protestant Henri de Navarre (the future *Henri IV) as heir to the throne, and many Frenchmen, notably Montmorency-Damville (the quasi-autonomous ruler of Languedoc), decided that it was better to support the legitimate heir to the throne in the hope that he might be persuaded to abjure than to raise arms against him. Similar views were espoused by *Montaigne and by *Pasquier, as well as by the authors of the *Satire Ménippée.   [JJS]

Politique tirée de l'écriture sainte, see BOSSUET.

POLITZER, Georges (1903–42). Communist philosopher and psychologist. Hungarian-born, he joined the 'Philosophies' group in the 1920s, developing a *Marxist theory of psychology. A founder of the review La Pensée and prime mover of the intellectual Resistance, Politzer was shot by the Gestapo.
          [MHK]

Polyandre, see SOREL, C.

Polyeucte. Tragedy by Pierre *Corneille, first performed 1642–3. Polyeucte, an Armenian nobleman, is married to Pauline, daughter of Félix, the Roman governor of Armenia. She was previously in love with the Roman Sévère who, after being thought dead, arrives in Armenia as the favourite of the emperor Décie, the persecutor of the Christians. Polyeucte, converted to Christianity, seeks martyrdom by breaking the statues of Roman gods. Resisting the appeals of Pauline, whose love for her husband triumphs over her old passion, he persists in declaring his religion and is put to death by the time-serving and timorous Félix. But his death brings about the miraculous conversion of Pauline and Félix, and forces the respect of the sceptical Sévère.   [PF]

Polysynodie, see REGENCY; SAINT-PIERRE.

POMPADOUR, Antoinette Poisson, marquise de (1721–64). The most celebrated mistress of Louis XV came from a wealthy middle-class background. She exerted a very considerable political influence for 20 years, and was an enlightened patron of artists and writers, including many of the *philosophes.

Pompée, see MORT DE POMPÉE, LA.

POMPIDOU, Georges (1911–74). Prime minister under de *Gaulle, subsequently president of the Republic (1969–74). The strikingly functional arts centre which was built during the 1970s on the rue Beaubourg in central Paris was named the Centre Pompidou in his honour.

POMPIGNAN, Jean-Jacques Lefranc, marquis de (1709–84). Poet. Born in Montauban, he practised as a magistrate, then devoted himself to letters; he knew Hebrew and several other languages and possessed a remarkable library. His works include plays, odes, and lighter verse. He had an ear for the music of language; his *cantiques* and paraphrases of the psalms show eloquence and rhythmic originality. His reputation has suffered unduly because of his hostile relations with the *philosophes, whose views he attacked at his reception into the Académie Française in 1760. *Voltaire ridiculed him mercilessly.   [PF]

PONGE, Francis (1899–1988). Usually classified as a poet, to his own annoyance. Of Protestant origins, for a time a Communist (1937–47), Ponge lived a comparatively uneventful life, though periods of poverty show his absolute commitment to his literary ideal.

He compares his work to a scientific activity providing a form of knowledge (*Nioque*, 1983). The source and subject of his writing is the indescribability of the most commonplace objects. He spent his whole writing career struggling to describe such things as a pebble, a bar of soap, a snail, bread, water, moss. As he says (*Le Parti pris des choses*, 1942): 'Fix your attention on the first thing that catches your eye: you'll see at once that nobody has ever looked at it properly, and that the most elementary things remain to be said about it.' To see objects properly, we must break down the conventional linguistic categories which constrict our minds; we must free ourselves to see them anew. He tells us that his early writing faced a succession of problems: he found it impossible to express himself; he fell back on attempting to describe objects; he recognized the impossibility of describing objects; he resolved to publish descriptions or accounts of *failures to describe*. Consequently, works such as *Le Savon, La Fabrique du pré, La Rage de l'expression* contain repeated efforts to describe a wasp, mimosa, a pine-wood, etc. All these, though supposedly 'failures', are highly evocative of concrete reality and wonderfully enrich our perceptions. Other work is collected in *Le Grand Recueil* (1961) and *Tome premier* (1965).   [GDM]

PONSARD, François (1814–67). French dramatist. His output is forgotten, with the exception of *Lucrèce*, a classical tragedy which was staged with considerable success in 1843, soon after the failure of Hugo's Romantic drama *Les *Burgraves.*   [CC]

PONSON DU TERRAIL, Pierre-Alexis, vicomte de (1829–71). French author of an endless number of *romans-feuilletons*, rivalling *Féval in the Second Empire. His novels appeared in a vast range of newspapers and journals. His great celebrity rested principally on the huge popular success of the Rocambole series of novels, which were published from the late 1850s onwards; from the name of the central character is derived the adjective *rocambolesque*, meaning far-fetched or fantastic.   [BR]

Pontigny. This former Cistercian abbey in Burgundy, the property of Paul Desjardins (1859–1940), was the setting for the 'Décades de Pontigny', frequent gatherings of writers and intellectuals (including *Gide and *Paulhan) between 1905 and 1939. The tradition has been continued in such centres as *Cerisy.

Pont-Neuf, Le. Bridge over the Seine at the west end of the Île de la Cité in Paris. Built in 1578–1607, it became in the 17th and 18th c. a centre for popular entertainment, and in particular for *popular song.

PONTUS DE TYARD, see TYARD.

Popular Culture. In the second half of the 20th c. what is loosely called popular culture has been extensively studied and discussed in France. The term is perhaps too broad to be very useful, and it confuses two different types of cultural object, that produced by the 'people' (e.g. folk-tales, dances, certain types of popular song) and that produced for popular consumption (e.g. the chapbooks distributed by pedlars or the novels sold on station bookstalls). Because of its patronizing overtones, the very notion of popular culture is a political battleground; some of the positions adopted by writers such as *Barthes, *Baudrillard, *Bourdieu, or de *Certeau are outlined in Brian Rigby's *Popular Culture in Modern France* (1993).

In the present volume different aspects of what may be called popular culture and literature are discussed under the following heads: BANDE DESSINÉE; BIBLIOTHÈQUE BLEUE; BOOK TRADE; CHANSON FRANÇAISE; CINEMA; DETECTIVE FICTION; FOIRE, THÉÂTRES DE LA; FOLK-TALE; LIVRE DE POCHE; MAISONS DE LA CULTURE; MELODRAMA; MUSIC-HALL; PHOTO-ROMAN; POPULAR SONG; RADIO; ROMAN D'AVENTURE(S); ROMAN-FEUILLETON; ROMAN NOIR; SCIENCE FICTION; TELEVISION; VAUDEVILLE.   [PF]

Popular Front (Front Populaire). Name given both to the anti-fascist alliance of left-wing organizations and individuals in 1934–6 and to the resulting government, led by Léon *Blum in 1936–7. Historically it has been seen both as a high-point of left-wing achievement and as a glorious failure. Blum later said that the Popular Front was an 'instinctive defence reflex' against two dangers: the threat to the republic from the right-wing paramilitary *ligues, and the depression which hit the economy during the early 1930s. The alliance was inspired by the violent anti-parliamentarian demonstration on 6 February 1934 by several *ligues* in the wake of the *Stavisky affair. Police fired, killing demonstrators, and the new prime minister, Edouard Daladier, resigned. The prospect of fascism in France, with Hitler newly in power in Germany, stimulated a counter-protest and strike by left-wing groupings including the Socialists and the Communists. Once fratricidal enemies, the two parties embarked on a *rapprochement*, and the call for a Rassemblement Populaire (the name found interchangeably with Front Populaire at the time) resulted in a massive demonstration of unity on 14 July 1935, at which participants took an oath to defend democratic liberties and to call for bread, work, and peace.

'Populaire' means 'of the people', usually with an emphasis on the working class, but the Front aimed for a wider appeal. The moderate *Radical Party joined in 1935; and the French Communist Party surprised its allies by extending the hand of comradeship (*la main tendue*) to Catholics, farmers, and the *petite bourgeoisie* in the interests of the cause. Apart from the *ligues*, the Front's enemies were defined as the '200 familles', a reference to the governors of the Banque de France. A common programme was drafted for the election of April 1936, in which the Front Populaire parties won a majority of 376 to 222 seats and Blum formed a government. The victory had sparked off an unprecedented strike-wave in May–June, with factory occupations, and the cabinet's first task was to offer the workers a revolutionary package, the Accords Matignon, including paid holidays, a 40-hour week, and collective bargaining. In the popular imagination, the strikes and reforms, especially *les congés payés*, were the most lasting memory of the Front, explaining why it was both venerated by the Left and execrated by the Right.

Blum's government intended to innovate. It contained no Communists, who declined to join, but included three women junior ministers, at a time when Frenchwomen still could not vote, and a junior minister for leisure. In the short year of its existence it banned the *ligues* and passed further progressive legislation, including raising the school-leaving age to 14. But it was forced onto the defensive over the economy (flight of capital, devaluation, productivity problems) and the international situation (especially the Spanish Civil War, over which Blum stuck to a policy of non-intervention). Neither the Radicals nor the Communists maintained their support unwaveringly, and Blum resigned in June 1937 when the Senate refused to grant him special powers over finance.

The Popular Front was accompanied by a

Popular Song

number of sympathetic intellectual and cultural activities, including the founding of journals like *Vendredi*, the forming of the Intellectuals' Committee Against Fascism, and of Ciné-Liberté, the body behind the production of Jean *Renoir's *La Marseillaise*, a film which can be read as the French Revolution revisited through the Popular Front. It is associated in many minds with the outdoor movement, the vogue for youth hostels and youth organizations. The opposition it provoked, one component of which was antisemitism, was reflected in the conflict between Vichy and Resistance during the war [see OCCUPATION AND RESISTANCE]: *Pétain explicitly associated the Popular Front with the *esprit de jouissance* as opposed to the *esprit de sacrifice*, blaming it for the defeat of 1940, although modern historians acknowledge its role in belatedly boosting French arms production, and most of them view its social pro-worker measures as long overdue in 1936. It is evoked in many memoirs and novels, including *Queneau's *Le Dimanche de la vie*, and is frequently referred to as one of the *moments privilégiés* of the history of the Left: 'everyone was 20 years old in 1936' (J.-P. Le Chanois). [SR]

See B. Cacérès, *Allons au-devant de la vie* (1981); J. Kergoat, *La France du Front populaire* (1986); J. Jackson, *The Popular Front in France: Defending Democracy 1934–38* (1988).

Popular Song. For many centuries poetry and song were closely related in France [see LYRIC POETRY, 1; WORDS AND MUSIC]. From the 17th c., however, there has been a tendency to separate the literary from the oral or popular. While various types of 'chanson' have remained in the standard repertoire of lyric poets, song has therefore been given a minor place in literature. Nevertheless, there have at all times been those who have looked to the popular song tradition for a renewal of life and feeling, from Alceste in Molière's *Misanthrope* to *Nerval in his *Chansons et légendes du Valois*. The vogue of folklore was particularly strong in the *Romantic period. What is more, the song-writer *Béranger was acclaimed in his time (for instance by *Stendhal) as France's greatest poet, and since then many poets (e.g. *Hugo, *Aragon) have themselves written songs, appealing to a less narrow audience than the usual poetry-reading public. Song deserves to be considered an integral and important part of French literature.

Many of the best popular songs are anonymous, but no scholars would now subscribe to the German Romantic view of the folk-song issuing spontaneously from the unspoilt *Volk*, and radically different from the productions of courtly or urban civilization. The origins and trajectories of songs are complex, involving a to-and-fro between high and popular culture. From the earliest times one finds pastiches of popular song, from the 13th-c. *chansons de toile* to the 18th-c. *romances* of writers such as

*Moncrif and Arnaud *Berquin. A considerable part was played in the diffusion of such songs by the urban *chansonniers* (e.g. the singers on the *Pont-Neuf in Paris), by popular entertainments such as the *opéra-comique*, and by the *colporteurs* who carried broadsheets around the villages. Many of the most widely known songs have quite recent urban origins: 'Au clair de la lune' and 'Le bon roi Dagobert' both originate in Paris in the 1780s.

Even so, the folk-songs which were collected by the folklorists of the 19th c. were predominantly rural (as was the French population) and they were above all transmitted orally. Like *folk-tales, they were therefore liable to constant modification, so that, whatever their ultimate origin, they were the result of a kind of collective creation. There is no standard version of such songs. Similarly, the same song might be sung to different tunes, and above all the same tune could be endlessly reused for any number of songs; this is the basis of the *vaudeville.

Such folk-songs belong to different types. The *complaintes* are narrative songs with a strong element of dialogue, comparable to English or German ballads; the most famous is 'Le Roi Renaud', a tragic tale sung to a tune of apparently Gregorian origin. Some *complaintes* refer to historical events, e.g. the death of *Mandrin. *Noëls* are songs in honour of Christ's birth; like the Protestant versions of the psalms or the Catholic *cantiques*, these were written by the literate to encourage popular piety. Then there are drinking songs and love songs, including *chansons de mal-mariée*, songs of work, and all kinds of humorous songs. A particularly important place in the mental world of all French people is held by children's songs; with the exception of such things as counting rhymes (*comptines*), these were rarely meant for children from the outset; 'Il était un petit navire', for instance, was a sailor's song which was subsequently given a humourous form.

The songs of the peasants had long been appreciated and collected by connoisseurs, but the massive and systematic work of folklorists in this domain only began in the second half of the 19th c. This was partly due to Romantic ideology; it also had the effect of drawing attention away from the other main type of popular song, the generally urban song of political protest. This had flourished at all periods, particularly times of unrest such as the *Wars of Religion and the *Fronde [see MAZARINADES]. It included satirical attacks on powerful figures and songs deploring the hardships endured by the poor, including military service. The *Revolution saw a great wave of political songs of all tendencies. Some of these were genuinely popular creations; the '*Ça ira' and the '*Carmagnole', sung to dance tunes, were the work of unknown authors, and were subject to constant alterations and additions. Others, such as 'La Mort de Marat', 'Le Chant du départ', or the 'Hymne à l'Être Suprême', are songs written for propaganda purposes, then adopted by a popular audience. The 'Marseillaise' of *Rouget de l'Isle, endlessly imitated and adapted, is the most famous of these.

The political song throve in the 19th c., being used to express opposition to governments and marking the successive revolutionary movements of 1830, 1848, and 1871. The master of the genre was Béranger, followed by such figures as *Dupont, *Clément, and Charles Gille, and imitated by the Hugo of the Chansons des rues et des bois. Their songs were performed in cabarets such as Le *Caveau and the more working-class singing societies known as goguettes. The latter were shut down in 1852 but, later in the Second Empire and during the *Commune of 1871, song regained its political function. From about this period there is a growing tendency towards the commercialization of popular song in the *music-halls, cafés-concerts, and the like, but in the 20th c. song has continued to be used as propaganda by bodies such as the Communist Party and the Catholic Church. During World War II, 'Maréchal, nous voilà!' drummed up support for *Pétain, while the 'Chant des partisans' became the marching-song of the Resistance [see OCCUPATION AND RESISTANCE]. A more detailed view of popular song in the 20th c. is given under CHANSON FRANÇAISE. [PF]

See H. Davenson, Le Livre des chansons (1946); P. Barbier and F. Vernillat, Histoire de France par les chansons, 8 vols. (1956–61); D. Rieger (ed.), La Chanson française et son histoire (1988).

Population, see MARRIAGE.

Populism. A literary movement which sprang from debates on literature and the working class in France following World War I and whose principles were elaborated in greatest detail by André Thérive and Léon Lemonnier, particularly in 'Un manifeste littéraire: le roman populiste', which appeared in L'Œuvre on 27 August 1929. Derived from *Naturalism, the 'roman populiste' was to take as its subject-matter the lives of ordinary people and to reflect them as accurately as possible, without the construction of a political message. In this, the partisans of the 'roman populiste' such as *Dabit parted company both from Communist theorists and practitioners like *Barbusse and from exponents of a more politically active 'littérature prolétarienne', such as *Poulaille. [NH]

POQUELIN, see MOLIÈRE.

PORCHÈRES, Honoré Laugier de (1572–1653). French poet, editor of *Sponde, and Academician; highly regarded in his day, he came to be seen as a prime exponent of old-fashioned mannerism.

Pornography, see EROTICISM AND PORNOGRAPHY.

Porte étroite, La. Novel by *Gide (1909). Jérôme recounts his pious love for his cousin Alissa, who refused his wish to marry, encouraging him to renounce earthly passion in favour of religious fulfil-

ment, and herself dying in the attempt. Alissa's diary adds an ironic perspective to this modern rendering of courtly love mingled with suggestions of repressed sexuality. [DHW]

Porthos. One of the heroes of Dumas's Les *Trois Mousquetaires.

PORTO-RICHE, Georges de (1849–1930). One of the most successful playwrights in France at the turn of the century. A rich businessman and admirer of *Hugo, he won fame with Amoureuse (1891). This, like such later plays as Le Passé (1897) and Le Vieil Homme (1911), offers a cynical view of marriage and adultery expressed in rapid, glossy dialogue. [PF]

Portrait d'un inconnu. Novel by *Sarraute, published 1948 with an important preface by *Sartre. In an atmosphere of obsessive anxiety, an unnamed narrator explores the personalities of an elderly man and his daughter. He tries to imagine their relationship, probing the 'carapace' of clichés that categorize them—as old miser and neurotic spinster—to uncover the soft, sticky, fluid reality of their interaction. In his hesitant but tenacious struggle against socially defined normality and, simultaneously, classic fictional characterization, a visit to see the 'portrait' of the title frees him from his psychiatrist's reductive vision, but he is finally defeated by the overwhelmingly solid conventionality of the daughter's fiancé. [CB]

Port-Royal. The name refers to two convents closely identified with *Jansenism. Port-Royal des Champs, situated south-west of Paris, had been founded in 1204. When Jacqueline Arnauld (Mère Angélique) became abbess in 1602 (aged 11) the convent was in a state of moral disorder. After her conversion in 1608 she began the process of reform, enforcing poverty and strict enclosure. In 1626, because of the unhealthy nature of the site, the nuns moved to the Faubourg Saint-Jacques—Port-Royal de Paris, where *Saint-Cyran became a director of conscience in 1635. From 1637 the much admired 'Petites Écoles' for boys were set up at several sites by a group of mostly lay solitaires; *Racine was a pupil here. In 1646 shortage of space in Paris led to a renewal of conventual life in Port-Royal des Champs.

Around this time, however, *Jesuit animosity and controversy over the five allegedly heretical propositions of Jansenius's Augustinus brought nuns and solitaires considerable persecution. A first attempt to make the nuns sign a formulary condemning Jansenius was unsuccessful in 1655. With few exceptions they continued to resist, and in 1665 the recalcitrant nuns from Paris were herded into Port-Royal des Champs. In 1668 the Paris house ceased to be associated with Jansenism and Clement IX proclaimed a 'Peace of the Church' which Port-Royal enjoyed for ten years. In 1679 persecution was resumed, and in 1709 the remaining nuns were forcibly removed. Two years later Port-Royal des Champs was razed to the ground on the orders of Louis XIV. The unique history of this convent inspired *Sainte-Beuve's great five-volume work *Port-Royal* (1840–59). [JC]

Port-Royal. This 1954 *Montherlant play deals with the expulsion of the *Jansenist nuns from Port-Royal in 1664. Much in the public scenes is taken verbatim from contemporary documents. Against this background, which illustrates the fundamental conflict between rigorous purity and the world, Montherlant builds, in original scenes of dialogue, a brilliant psychological depiction of a spiritual crisis in which the leader, Sœur Angélique, moves from certainty to premonitions of doubt, and Sœur Françoise from doubt to serenity in the face of persecution. This sympathetic depiction, by an agnostic, of the workings of grace, appears more authentic than much Catholic literature. [RMG]

Positivism. 19th-c. philosophical system put forward by Auguste Comte; the word is also used in a more general sense [see COMTE].

POSTEL, Guillaume (?1510–81). Scholar and original thinker (*docte et fol*), born near Barenton. He studied oriental languages in Paris and was commissioned by *François Ier to buy manuscripts in the Near East. In 1538 he published *De originibus seu de hebraicae linguae et gentis antiquitate*, the first of a number of publications in French, Latin, and Hebrew on the affairs of the Middle East. Constantly attacked for his beliefs by both Catholics and Protestants, Postel led a chequered existence. In the early 1540s he formulated a theory he was to propound throughout his life, that of peace through a universal religion, *De orbis terrae concordia* (1543–4), drawing upon his knowledge of the Turks. He contemplated becoming a Jesuit, but a difference of views between him and Ignatius Loyola prevented him from doing so. He travelled around the Middle East, Italy, and Eastern Europe. In 1555 he was interrogated by the Inquisition; judged to be insane, he was imprisoned for four years in Rome. Although he was a staunch defender of the *Gallican Church against Rome, he was constantly criticized for the extreme and unorthodox nature of his views. An expert on languages, mathematics, and theology, Postel's work (much of which remains in manuscript) is exemplary of a society open to new ideas yet influenced by a 'medieval mentality', a mixture of rationalism and mysticism. [KCC]

Postmodernism. A movement in art and ideas which challenges the aspirations to unity, purpose, and order. Emerging first as a rejection of the classical aesthetic principles of modern architecture, Postmodernism is exemplified by the Pompidou Centre at Beaubourg in Paris, which displays all its components and starkly contrasts with its surroundings. Jean-François *Lyotard, in *La Condition post-moderne* (1979), generalized the idea into a diagnosis of the contemporary fragmentation of systems of knowledge. Postmodernism rapidly became a portmanteau term applied to a wide range of cultural phenomena, especially in art and cinema, but also extending to literature and philosophy. Throughout the 1980s it became a focus for debate in English-speaking intellectual circles, where it was seen, by supporters and opponents alike, as a reflection of and on the apparent success of free-market economics and culture, and the evident disarray of Marxist political and intellectual alternatives.

Like *Post-Structuralism, from which it is often difficult to distinguish it, Postmodernism is not a readily identifiable school of thought in France. It is most usually associated with Lyotard and *Baudrillard, but is often felt to include the later writings of *Derrida, *Deleuze, *Kristeva, and *Irigaray. A widely shared view was that there was a growing disintegration of the modern *grands récits*, the Hegelian, Marxist, or Freudian systems, each of which had sought to provide a coherent intellectual framework with which to understand and change the world. Their failure signalled the futility of *any* attempt to construct a Master Narrative, and could be construed as a liberation from the strait-jacket of totality and authority. The Postmodern posture was therefore to emphasize and enjoy difference(s) without seeking to bring them into unity; to disrupt fixed patterns or hierarchies which might exist or emerge; and to frustrate imperatives or directions which anyone might seek to impose on another. For this reason it is notably resistant to simple summary or definition.

Postmodernism shares many aspects of earlier cultural avant-garde movements, particularly *Surrealism, anarchism, and *Situationism, from which its members have drawn many techniques. A striking feature is the prevalence of pastiche in Postmodern works, drawing on elements from a variety of sources, which are then juxtaposed, often ironically. Beneix's film *Diva* (1981) exemplifies the approach, using elements of character, plot, setting, and composition from several cinematic genres. As with earlier modernism, these highly allusive works offer a special pleasure to the initiated. Critics of Postmodernism, such as Fredric Jameson and Jürgen Habermas, have suggested that it exacerbates the problems of personal and social disintegration, bewilderment, impotence, and despair which it attempts to portray. [MHK]

See T. Docherty (ed.), *Postmodernism: A Reader* (1993).

Post-Structuralism. A current of critical theory which both questions and continues the main preoccupations of *Structuralism. Post-Structuralism is more than usually resistant to precise definition, and its presumed representatives are frequently deemed to belong to Structuralism, *Postmodernism, deconstructionism, post-Freudianism, or *feminism. The main reason for this is that Post-Structuralism is primarily a term of convenience adopted by English-speaking critics, rather than a self-conscious movement in French thought.

In this sense, it refers to work which became influential in the mid-1970s, after the first wave of Structuralism had been assimilated into the avant-garde of 'Anglo-Saxon' literary, cultural, and social theory. Broadly speaking, the major figures are *Derrida, the later *Barthes, the later *Foucault, the later *Lacan, *Deleuze, Felix Guattari, the early *Lyotard, *Cixous, the later *Kristeva, and the early *Irigaray. Simply to enumerate them may be sufficient to suggest the impossibility of all but the most general characterization of what they were felt to share.

Of the many Structuralist preoccupations which these writers inherit and challenge, three may be singled out: language, theory, and the subject. The *Saussurean theory of language as a sign-system was one of the foundations of Structuralism. The passing of its heroic age was marked by Derrida's deconstruction of the philosophical presuppositions he detected. He criticized the metaphysics of presence which supported the primacy of speech over writing, and the bold assumption that difference could be bound in systems. The 'logocentrism' which he unravelled was rapidly seen to infect not only the theory of language, but also all the human sciences which had adopted the Saussurean model, and even, at the limit, the very enterprise of theory itself.

Feminist writers gave the knife a further twist by arguing that, historically, socially, and psychologically, logocentrism was a key part of the strategy for securing male phallic domination of female discourse and desire: an enterprise of 'phallogocentrism'. In the struggle for domination, human subjectivity was identified as a crucial site of contention. The Structuralist dismissal or dissolution of the subject (as an illusion, as a neurotic or an ideological construct), therefore, appeared as a problematic step, to be challenged either in order to empower real subjects or in order to restore some alternative locus for non-phallogocentric or power-free personal or social fulfilment.

Pitched necessarily in the critical or interrogative mode, the Post-Structuralist challenge was above all a moment of transition. Where it led, if indeed identity ('it') or direction ('led') may fairly be imputed to it, can only be determined in relation to particular practitioners and agendas which were deemed to compose it.   [MHK]

See R. Young, *Untying the Text: A Post-Structuralist Reader* (1981); K. Reader, *Intellectuals and the Left in France since 1968* (1987).

Pot-Bouille. Novel by *Zola, the 10th in the *Rougon Macquart* series, published in 1882. In this fierce satire of bourgeois manners, the ambitious ladies' man, Octave Mouret, exercises his seductive talents in a middle-class apartment-house in Paris, where he reveals the hypocrisy, egoism, and sordidness of the life of the inhabitants behind the respectable façade of the building.   [DB]

POTOCKI, Jean (1761–1815). Polish count and diplomat who committed suicide in protest against the failure of the post-Napoleonic settlement to restore Polish independence. He was the author of the *Manuscrit trouvé à Saragosse*, for long an obscure and legendary masterpiece. Legend claims that Chojecki destroyed the French manuscript after making his Polish translation (published 1847). René Radrizzani reconstructs the complete text in his Paris edition of 1989.

The novel is divided into 66 days and an epilogue, and consists of a labyrinth of stories—a formal *tour de force*, its elements are interlocked much more strongly than in a mere *roman à tiroirs*. The hero, Van Worden, undergoes a series of ordeals which make him doubt the evidence of his senses, and test his honour, courage, and resistance to superstition. These ordeals are (it transpires) arranged by a secret society which awaits the moment to propagate the true religion. The hero's successful initiation is rewarded by gold, honours, and two simultaneous wives. Potocki is sceptical of revealed religion, prudery, and superstition, and even the triumph of the benevolent secret religion is prevented. None the less, the irrational is given real power. The message is multi-faceted, like the form.   [GDM]

POTTIER, Eugène-Edme (1816–87). Working-class politician, member of the Paris *Commune, a 'Juvénal de faubourg', according to *Vallès. He wrote many political songs, including the words of 'L'Internationale', reflecting the spirit of resistance immediately after the crushing of the Commune in 1871. Set to music by Pierre Degeyter in 1888, it was adopted as the anthem of international socialism, and was until 1944 the national anthem of the Soviet Union.   [SR]

Poudrier, Séraphin. Famous miserly character invented by the Canadian writer Claude-Henri *Grignon.

POUGY, Liane de (pseud. of Marie Chassaigne, later Princess Ghika) (*c.*1870–1950). Novelist and famous courtesan of the *belle époque*. Her affair with Nathalie Clifford Barney is evoked in her novel *Idylle saphique* (1901), which is simultaneously a celebration and a guilty denial of lesbian desire. Other novels include *L'Insaisissable* (1898). Her diary, *Mes cahiers bleus*, was published in 1977. [See also EROTICISM AND PORNOGRAPHY.]   [JB]

Poujadism, see FASCISM.

POULAILLE, Henry (1896–1980). French novelist and advocate of proletarian culture, which he practised in his novels *Le Pain quotidien* (1931), *Les Damnés de la terre* (1935), *Pain de soldat* (1937), *Les Rescapés*

(1938), and promulgated in numerous critical articles on literature and on the cinema. His credo, not to be confused with the contemporary *populism of the inter-war years, favours the direct expression by workers of working-class consciousness. [DAS]

POULAIN DE LA BARRE, François (1647–1723). A disciple of Descartes who wrote three rationalist tracts between 1673 and 1675 which cogently argue the case for the equality of the sexes. After being ordained a Catholic priest in 1679, he was converted to Protestantism and fled to Geneva from Paris in 1688. His writings mark a departure from the old *Querelle des Femmes. [IM]

POULANTZAS, Nicos (1936–79). Marxist political theorist; husband of Annie *Leclerc. Born in Greece, he studied law before moving to Paris, where he joined the outlawed Greek Communist Party. Though initially attracted to *Sartre's existential *Marxism, he became a close associate of *Althusser, whose theoretical Marxism inspired a number of influential studies of social classes, political power, and the state. In his later work, his schematic *Structuralist analysis incorporated some of Gramsci's ideas on hegemony to address issues of specific political action. See his *Pouvoir politique et classes sociales* (1971). [MHK]

POULENC, Francis (1899–1963). French composer. An important member of the group known as 'Les *Six', Poulenc composed chamber, choral, and stage music, including ballets, incidental music for plays (by writers such as *Anouilh, *Salacrou, and *Cocteau), and film music. He possessed a unique lyrical gift and made great use of mimicry and parody in his music. Poulenc wrote a number of compositions based on works by *Éluard, *Apollinaire (for instance the *opéra bouffe Les Mamelles de Tirésias*, 1947), and Cocteau (most importantly the opera *La Voix humaine*, 1959). Much of his music can be placed in the 19th-c. salon tradition. [KM]

POULET, Georges (1902–92). Critic. A Belgian by birth, Poulet is associated with the *Geneva school of criticism. His work, usually in the form of short essays grouped round a central theme, is concerned less with the form and texture of individual texts than with the inner world of the subject, as seen in such fundamental concerns as the relation of the individual ego to time and space (*Études sur le temps humain*, 1949; *La Distance intérieure*, 1952; *Les Métamorphoses du cercle*, 1961). His *La Conscience critique* (1971) closes with the words: 'Toute critique est initialement et fondamentalement une critique de la conscience.' [PF]

POULIN, Jacques (b. 1937). Canadian novelist. He studied at Laval University, then worked as a translator. Like contemporary novelists *Beauchemin and *Caron, he eschews Montreal for a provincial setting. His half-dozen novels deftly mix fantasy with reality, fable with psychological realism. His protest against the 'adult' establishment is embodied in the lonely child of *Jimmy* (1969), the Amerindian in *Volkswagen Blues* (1984), the vulnerable, hunted writer in *Les Grandes Marées* (1978), the heart-transplantee of *Le Cœur de la baleine bleue* (1970). Poulin is an excellent story-teller. He gives his characters depth by showing them self-preoccupied in interesting ways and by skilful surprise effects. Salinger is an obvious influence and *Volkswagen Blues* an ingenious Quebec version of the North American Odyssey novel. A *Québécois* and an Indian girl cross the continent in search of a missing brother. The gathering of clues, the use of landmarks, the retracing of the history of a land, make for a fascinating narrative, part saga, part love-story, part lament for a lost past. [CRPM]

Pour et contre, Le, see PRÉVOST, A.-F.

POURRAT, Henri (1887–1959). Regional writer. Forced by tuberculosis to give up a career as an agronomist, he retired young to his native Auvergne, where he devoted his life to local history and the collection of folklore and legend. The four expansive volumes of his colourful 19th-c. chronicle, *Gaspard des Montagnes* (1922–31), were turned into a popular television series in the 1960s, but he also wrote many other novels, essays, biographies, and stories. The 13-volume *Trésor des contes* (1948–62), retelling local versions of French folk-tales, is perhaps his most important work. His 'novel' *Vent de mars* (in reality a nostalgic reflection on the essential French peasantry) won the Prix Goncourt in 1941 and was hailed as an expression of Vichy ruralist ideology, but later, during the German *Occupation, *Gaspard des Montagnes* inspired the local Resistance leader 'Colonel Gaspard'. [PF]

POURTALÈS, Guy de, see SWISS LITERATURE IN FRENCH, 4.

Pour un nouveau roman, see ROBBE-GRILLET.

Poussière sur la ville, see LANGEVIN.

POUSSIN, Nicolas (1594–1665). The most influential of all French artists. He met the Italian poet *Marini at the French court, and illustrated Ovid's *Metamorphoses* for him before moving to Rome. He became known as a reflective thinker, with high intellectual abilities and a wide range of literary knowledge. His friends were literati like Casiano dal Pozzo, librarian to the Barberini. Poussin contributed drawings of antique sculptures to his Museo Cartacheo. He painted elegiac scenes from Ovid, Virgil, and Tasso, and embodied the concept of 'ut pictura poesis' in the 1630s in Rome.

In addition to many subjects from the Old and New Testaments, he painted heroic and stoic themes, like those featured by *Corneille or derived from *Montaigne, for French intellectuals. He also executed important allegorical commissions for

Cardinal *Richelieu, exploring Tasso's theories of instructing by means of pleasing through veiled meanings. This idea was popular in both poetry and painting. Poussin visited France in 1640–1 at the behest of the king and painted the *Finding of Moses* for Jean Pointel. The second set of *Seven Sacraments* for Fréart de Chantelou focused attention on the notion of the modes in painting—an intellectual system paralleling that common in music. His superb late landscapes *The Seasons* reinterpret crucial episodes in the Old Testament, and his late scenes from Ovid's *Metamorphoses* introduce power and terror into the landscapist's repertoire. These sublime themes were taken up by Salvator Rosa and Poussin's brother-in-law Gaspard Poussin (Dughet). It was the reasoned commitment to clarity and appropriateness in Poussin's subject painting which influenced the next two centuries of Academic painting. [JPC]

POZZI, Catherine (1882–1934). French poet and diarist whose reputation will surely grow. Her formative influences were a reaction against religion and disunited parents. A marriage to the playwright Édouard *Bourdet in 1909 led to divorce. Their only son, Claude *Bourdet, became a noted left-wing journalist. In 1920 she began a stormy affair with Paul *Valéry, on whose intellectual plane she easily manœuvred and to whose *Cahiers* she made a considerable editorial contribution. Her short story 'Agnès' appeared in 1927. From 1926 to 1934 she wrote six remarkable poems, 'Vale', 'Ave', 'Nova', 'Scopolamine', 'Maya', and 'Nyx'. A philosophical essay, *Peau d'Âme*, appeared posthumously in 1935. Her important *Journal 1913–1934* was published in 1987. Striking a sharp and occasionally caustic note from highly strung syntax, she frankly records in it her often anguished struggle for female selfhood, spiritual authenticity, and intellectual communion in the glitzy world of Parisian *haute société* and within the framework of her disintegrating health. [DAS]

PRADES, Jean Martin, abbé de (1720–82). Contributor to the *Encyclopédie*. In 1752 he fled to Berlin when his theological thesis was condemned by the Sorbonne and the Parlement de Paris. The affair contributed to the suppression of volumes 1 and 2 of the *Encyclopédie* in 1752; *Diderot wrote a *Suite de l'Apologie de l'abbé de Prades* in his defence.

PRADON, Nicolas (1632–98). French playwright, much abused by posterity for daring to compete with *Racine, who savaged him in a series of epigrams. His *Phèdre et Hippolyte* (1677), backed against *Phèdre* by the influential clique of the duchesse de Bouillon, lacks any tragic force, but is not entirely without interest, showing a modern scepticism about the sublime and irrational elements of ancient culture. He left several other unmemorable tragedies (*Tamerlan*, 1676; *La Troade*, 1678; *Statira*, 1680; *Régulus*, 1689; *Scipion l'Africain*, 1697). [PF]

PRASSINOS, Gisèle (b. 1920). Poet and novelist, born in Constantinople. Her youthful collection of poems, *Sauterelle arthritique*, was published in 1935 and celebrated by the Surrealists. Later she wrote short prose texts and many novels. *Breton, who included her in his *Anthologie de l'humour noir*, wrote: 'C'est la *révolution permanente* en belles images coloriées à un sou . . . Tous les poètes en sont jaloux.' [PF]

Précellence de la langue française, De la, see ESTIENNE, H.

Précieuse, La, see PURE.

Précieuses ridicules, Les. One-act farce by *Molière, first performed 1659. Two spurned suitors, La Grange and Du Croisy, decide to take revenge on the affected Cathos and Magdelon whose ideas about courtship and society have been culled from the novels of Madeleine de *Scudéry. The suitors ask their valets, Mascarille and Jodelet, to dress up as members of the nobility and fashionable salongoers and to visit the gullible girls. The resultant conversation is the occasion for mordant satire of the current literary and social vogue for *preciosity, which earned Molière the hostility of at least one powerful Parisian clique. The farce was the first of Molière's great theatrical successes after his return to Paris in 1658. [IM]

Preciosity. Literary and linguistic movement generated in mid-17th-c. Parisian *salons. From 1653 to 1661 preciosity was a major force in the development of French culture. Subsequently it went into decline, although the preoccupations and the activities characteristic of preciosity remained vital throughout the history of the salon tradition.

Women had been gathering in the salons for nearly four decades before anyone spoke of preciosity. The new vocabulary was the creation of hostile outsiders: salon women do not seem to have spoken of themselves as *précieuses*. From its earliest appearances, *précieuse* has two clear connotations. First, these women were portrayed as modern-day Amazons, intent on creating a state within the state, 'the kingdom of the précieuses', as it was known. Secondly, it was implied that this separatist tendency resulted from a fear of sexuality. 'Jansenists of love', Ninon de *Lenclos called them, as if their behaviour imitated the moral severity of *Port-Royal's disciples. Others called them simply prudes.

The word 'précieuse' alone said this much. The fiction of preciosity, of what these prudes did in their separate world, was elaborated by a rash of contemporary satires, of which Molière's *Les *Précieuses ridicules* (1659) is the best-known. These often devastating parodies of the movement's manners and its goals, published when it was most celebrated, were so successful that they have almost entirely obscured preciosity's actual history. Preciosity is thus widely associated with linguistic

Préfet

excess. Its practitioners' efforts to do away with words they considered vulgar (they attempted to have 'poitrine' replaced with 'cœur', for example) and their abuse of affected expressions such as 'furieusement' and 'ravissant' are consistently documented. Preciosity provides a rare example of a literary movement whose accomplishments have always proved less interesting than its negative image: it is hard not to see this willingness to remember preciosity only as ridiculous as indicative of a long-standing prejudice against learned women, especially those who work together for common goals.

The *précieuses* were committed above all to literature. This distinguishes them from the first salon women, who were more concerned with creating a model of elegant conduct in the hope of refining the still-rustic French court. Preciosity is best known for its poetry. Numerous poets practised the light verse that, because it is almost exclusively occasional, does not hold up well outside the salon context. *Malherbe, *Voiture, *Racan, and *Mainard are the best known of a largely male group. Although their production received its share of criticism, these poets were never ridiculed and the masculine form *précieux* was almost never used. Malherbe's well-known reform of French prosody respects the key tenets of preciosity: the preference for the artificial and distrust of the authentic, the predilection for perfect technique and formal constraint.

During the reign of preciosity the salons also encouraged formal innovation, in particular through collective literary ventures. Through discussion and the circulation of manuscripts, new literary forms were invented. Three of these stand out—the portrait, the conversation, and the maxim. All share a collective origin—so much so that those who eventually signed individual works often admitted privately that they could not tell who had played the principal role in their composition—and all first appeared in collaborative volumes. The maxim won its place in literary history when *La Rochefoucauld gathered together collectively produced texts under his signature. However, the maxim's most decisive influence on the development of French literature may be due to its having been adopted, along with the portrait and the conversation, by the early French novelists, who made these forms the foundation of their attempt to increase the novel's psychological range. Preciosity's most important contribution to French literature is the new emphasis on interiority that it inspired. Because early novelists followed the example of *précieux* salons, in which the motivations for human conduct, especially amorous conduct, were endlessly debated, psychological realism became a major force in French literature during the second half of the 17th c.

Preciosity's influence on the development of the French language was also noteworthy. The invention of numerous expressions still widely used is but the most tangible evidence of the *précieuses*' passion for language—for correct usage, new metaphorical expressions, linguistic purity. *Vaugelas in his *Remarques sur la langue française*, declares that 'in cases of doubt about language, it is ordinarily best to consult women'. The language which he thus codified and made into the standard against which usage would be measured for generations was the French spoken and analysed in the *précieux* salons.

Despite this eventual recuperation of its linguistic values, the original movement can hardly be seen as a politically conservative force. The assemblies subsumed under the name 'preciosity' were feminist in the full sense of this modern term. They worked to change women's lives, to promote reforms, in particular in marital and family law, designed to give women greater control over their fates. The practical message of preciosity can best be appreciated in the conversations, maxims, and portraits of a vast (10,000-page) window onto women's concerns in that optimistic era, Madeleine de Scudéry's *Clélie, histoire romaine* (1654–60). Scudéry's characters often express radical beliefs. For example, her heroines argue that, until marriage is redefined so that the institution can no longer be used to enslave women, women should only enter into unofficial unions, sealed with private contracts under which they can guarantee their personal freedom and financial independence.

At the time such radical goals were Utopian. However, preciosity's constructive optimism inspired French women, in numbers unheard of before or since, to become writers. Some won greater independence in their private lives than they would have dared to do without the movement's encouragement. And, long after the multiform French literature of sociability lapsed into the cynicism that dominates its history, waves of new preciosity, each as feminist and as self-confident as the first, were launched from the salons and the writing of women such as *Lambert, *Riccoboni, and *Genlis. [See also WOMEN WRITERS.]   [JDeJ]

See R. Lathuillère, *La Préciosité* (1969); D. Backer, *Precious Women* (1974).

Préfet, see REGIONS AND DEPARTMENTS.

Pre-Romanticism. A seemingly self-evident literary-historical term, first introduced in 1912 by Fortunat Strowski in his *Tableau de la littérature française du 19e siècle*, and used to designate an ensemble of cultural phenomena which are said to prepare, in a timid or tentative way, the vigorous sensibility, the bold lyrical expansiveness of the Romantic movement proper. Rarely, however, has any critical term proved to be so singularly imprecise. Since critics can define *Pre*-Romanticism only by reference to what they understand *Romanticism itself to be, they have necessarily identified its presence in France at differing periods: 1760–89, 1780–1810, 1800–15, or any convenient permutation of those dates. In fact, when taken to seemingly logical (but surely eccentric) limits, such finalism in reverse can even assign to Pre-Romanticism three separate phases: 1715–60, 1760–70, 1770–89.

A much more serious matter for concern, however, is the fact that Pre-Romanticism is not a cultural reality with its own inner coherence. The truth is that it sprang from the politico-cultural affiliations of critics themselves. Succinctly put, the notion (fathered by *Brunetière's evolutionist method of literary history: *Natura non facet saltus*) grew out of the various attempts which were made, from *c.*1900 onwards, to counter robust nationalistic denigration of Romanticism as a vile aberration of the true French spirit which had been fostered by the English, the Germans, and above all by Jean-Jacques *Rousseau (another foreigner, who, moreover, had made the French Revolution possible). Liberal critics reacted by attempting to demonstrate that the Romantic explosion had, on the contrary, been heralded by various sensitive individuals during the 18th c. who were there to prove that the Romantics themselves, far from wrenching French literature from its natural paths, had actually given to established aspects of French sensitivity the means of expression which it had not previously possessed. Argument over the characteristics and the temporal limits of Pre-Romanticism has always been endemic. It is now the very notion itself, however, which is being questioned: specialists of the 18th c., with a sharper sense of intellectual or cultural history and its problems, see the salient features of 'Pre-Romanticism' as forming an inalienable part of the *Enlightenment itself.   [JR]

Présence africaine. Review founded in Paris by Alioune Diop in 1947. It rapidly became an important cultural weapon in the struggle for black freedom in both Africa and the Americas. As such, it was the successor to the *Revue du monde noir* and *Légitime défense*; but it went further than its predecessors in broadening the struggle, since its committee of patrons included not only blacks from Africa and elsewhere (e.g. *Senghor, Richard Wright) but also progressive Europeans (*Sartre, Théodore Monod, *Mounier).

Présence africaine was characterized by the openness of its approach and its determination to rise above ideological differences. It was the driving force behind two Congresses of Black Writers and Artists (Paris, 1956; Rome, 1959). From its early days it has been an influential force in black literature: it published Abdoulaye Sadji's *Nini* in its early issues (1947–8) and included Afro-American literature in its reviews.

Despite the political and linguistic Balkanization of Africa, *Présence africaine* continues to exert a unifying influence, notably by its inclusion of African literature in English. Fulfilling the ambition of Alioune Diop, it is an indispensable tool for any-body wishing to understand Africa in all its cultural, ethnic, and literary diversity.   [MK]

Presidents of the Republic [see also REPUBLICS]. There was no president of the First Republic. The Second Republic had one president, Louis-Napoléon Bonaparte (subsequently Emperor *Napoleon III), elected for a term of four years in 1848. Under the Third and Fourth Republics the president was elected for a term of seven years by both chambers voting together. Under the Fifth Republic a referendum organized by de *Gaulle in 1962 decided that the president, whose powers were much increased, should be elected for a term of seven years by direct universal suffrage.

Presidents of the Third, Fourth and Fifth Republics have been as follows:

Third Republic

1871–3 Adolphe *THIERS (1797–1877)
1873–9 Maréchal de MACMAHON (1808–93)
1879–87 Jules GRÉVY (1807–91)
1887–94 Marie-François-Sadi CARNOT (1837–94),
1894–5 Jean CASIMIR-PÉRIER (1847–1907)
1895–9 François-Félix FAURE (1841–99)
1899–1906 Émile LOUBET (1838–1920)
1906–13 Armand FALLIÈRES (1841–1931)
1913–20 Raymond POINCARÉ (1860–1934)
1920 Paul-Eugène-Louis DESCHANEL (1855–1922)
1920–4 Étienne-Alexandre MILLERAND (1859–1943)
1924–31 Gaston DOUMERGUE (1863–1937)
1931–2 Paul DOUMER (1857–1932)
1932–40 Albert LEBRUN (1871–1950)

Fourth Republic

1947–54 Vincent AURIOL (1884–1966)
1954–8 René COTY (1882–1962)

Fifth Republic

1958–69 Charles de *GAULLE (1890–1970)
1969–74 Georges *POMPIDOU (1911–74)
1974–81 Valéry GISCARD D'ESTAING (b. 1926)
1981– François *MITTERRAND (b. 1916)

Press [see also PERIODICALS]. French historians of the periodical press nowadays understand the term to include any printed publication appearing at regular intervals that claimed to report the news. The history of the press and of publishing in France is riven with polemics: for example, Strasbourg and Mainz continue to feud over their importance in the career of Gutenberg, the symbolical father-figure of European printing techniques. The successive phases in the history of the press are often portrayed as adjuncts to France's political history. Technology and finance, and the identification of different markets and networks of printed communication, receive, however, growing recognition as formative influences. Form, format, and frequency of publication influenced the style and content of what was published as much as the censor's pen and self-censorship.

Press

1. Beginnings to 1830

Some claim that the first publication printed regularly was *Cy est le Compost et Kalendrier des Bergiers*, published in Paris in 1491, shortly after the rector of the *Sorbonne invited German printers within the College precinct. *Almanacs and calendars formed the main body of regularly produced publications between the 1490s and the 1630s. To these may be added one-off publications—tracts, pamphlets, *libelles*, and *occasionnels*—some of which ran to the odd, irregular series. From the *occasionnels* arose the *canards*. Often adorned by lurid illustrations that would 'speak' to the illiterate—as did frescos and sculptures in churches throughout the land—the *canards* exploited the fantastic and supernatural in a colourful prose which, generations later, would be echoed by popular daily newspapers such as *Le *Petit Journal*. Pandering to the emotions, *canards* related apparently inexplicable and unclassifiable events (*faits divers*). They prefigured the use of the human-interest story and the *roman-feuilleton* by press magnates set on thrilling and entertaining a mass public.

The first lastingly successful weekly (*La Gazette*) was published in 1631; the first daily—containing the rudiments of today's general-interest newspaper—in 1777 (75 years later than in Britain). From 1631 to (at least) 1789 most periodical publications resembled the printed book, in presentation, layout, and typography. Many weekly or monthly journals were compilations whose issues were bound together at the end of the year—*La Gazette* and *Le *Journal des savants*, for instance. During the *Revolution there were probably more bi- and tri-weekly publications than dailies.

Speed in the collection of copy and in the printing and distribution of copies assumed growing urgency: the Revolution, during which journalists won the battle to report parliamentary proceedings, also saw concerted efforts to promote newspapers for informative, educational, and propaganda purposes among *les classes laborieuses*. Yet, for all the legend of journalistic terror symbolized by *Marat's *L'Ami du peuple*, a daily pamphlet of changing fortunes, the weekly *La Feuille villageoise* (founded in 1790) better illustrates the pace at which the broadening of the newspaper-reading public was proceeding: it had some 250,000 readers.

The cadence of the collation of news, comment, and opinion reflected an epistolary style of journalism for much of the 17th and 18th c. The quickening tempo of public life in pre-Revolutionary years was already reflected in the press, however: political news gradually assumed more importance than the arts, the sciences, or religious and philosophical debate. In the century spanning the period from the end of the *Fronde (1653) to the 1750s (when *Malesherbes was in name, as Directeur de la Librairie, chief censor), the reverse had been the case: *La Gazette* was alone authorized to publish official news.

La Gazette's founder, Théophraste *Renaudot, was the first of the many hybrid entrepreneurial and journalistic figures who fashioned the history of the French press. *La Gazette* itself was a government-inspired publication; finding himself obliged as a journalist to serve many masters, Renaudot commented, on launching his paper in 1631, that some wanted their news unadorned, while others demanded flowery language. He opted for sobriety, a choice some regretted. Writing to *Louvois in 1674, *Vauban stressed that nothing need prevent a journalist from exaggerating a good piece of news and minimizing the bad. Both in the *ancien régime* and after 1789 news-management skills were studied by journalists and their masters alike.

Calculations concerning the number of French-language periodicals (world-wide) suggest a steady but accelerating growth throughout the 18th c.: 40 in 1700; 76 in 1730; 137 in 1750; 188 in 1770; and 277 in 1780. Among the most influential of those not already mentioned were the *Mercure galant*, the *Mémoires de Trévoux*, *Fréron's *L'Année littéraire*, and *Linguet's *Annales politiques, civiles et littéraires*. The launch of the first daily, the *Journal de Paris*, in 1777, and the struggle for the freedom of the press (nurtured by *Diderot and other *philosophes*) indicated the growing political and social importance of the press.

Article 2 of the *Déclaration des droits de l'homme* affirmed, *inter alia*, the freedom of the press; it is probable that more periodicals and newspapers were founded in France in 1789 alone than in the previous century and a half. Some Revolutionary governments of the nascent republic none the less curbed press freedom. Skilled in news-management and attentive to the influence of the press over public opinion, *Napoleon suppressed many political newspapers: in 1811 only four Parisian dailies survived—*Le *Moniteur*, *La Gazette de France*, *Le Journal de l'Empire*, and *Le Journal de Paris*. Thereafter, their numbers, and circulation, slowly grew, some of the most important newcomers being *Le *Constitutionnel*, *Le *Globe*, *La *Revue de Paris*, and *La *Revue des deux mondes*. The struggle for the freedom of the press remained entwined with that for other democratic freedoms: the downfall of Charles X in 1830 was prompted, in part, by a revolution led by journalists. The freedom of the press from state control was finally—and, with brief exceptions, lastingly—established by the Third Republic, in the law of 29 July 1881.

2. 1830 to the Present

In 1830 *Thiers's *Le National*, which played a prominent role in 'the journalists' revolution', only had about 2,000 subscribers. In 1836 Émile de *Girardin and Armand Dutacq launched dailies (*La Presse* and *Le *Siècle*) with subscription rates and sale-prices significantly lower than those of the established titles. Circulations rose: within 18 months Girardin's *La Presse* had 20,000 subscribers. Improvements in printing technology contributed to the democratization of the press: the printer Hippolyte Marinoni developed the steam press and rotary-action presses for magnates of the popular press, such as Girardin and Moïse Millaud. In January 1870 Millaud's *Petit Journal* printed 495,000 copies of an issue reporting the execution of a murderer, whose crimes, arrest, and trial it had amply covered.

Dailies rarely ran to more than four pages before the turn of the century. On the other hand, it appears that by 1914 over 300 dailies were published in France (major titles included La *Croix, Le *Figaro, Le *Matin, L'*Œuvre, Le *Temps, L'*Écho de Paris). France had possibly the highest number of newspaper copies per capita in Europe— one copy for every four French people. Low sale-prices and bitter newspaper wars contributed to this. Decline set in with World War I, partly because newspaper collusion with government propaganda tarnished the reputation of a press already compromised by financial scandals. The only lastingly significant success of the inter-war years among Parisian dailies was Jean Prouvost's *Paris-Soir*, whose news-editorial formula reflected the impact of photo-journalism and the advent of the audio-visual age. (*Saint-Exupéry and *Simenon wrote for *Paris-Soir*.) Much of the finest literary and polemical journalism was more likely to appear in the vigorous weekly and monthly titles [see PERIODICALS] or else in the most partisan of the dailies— dailies whose ideological diversity ranged from L'*Action française to L'*Humanité. Long before 1939 the press feared the threat *radio posed as a news, entertainment, and advertising medium, and Parisian dailies lost readers in the provinces where regional dailies became further entrenched.

World War II and the *Occupation exacerbated these trends. Titles published in Paris and the northern zone were not distributed in the unoccupied zone and vice versa. Paper was rationed and pagination reduced. The propaganda of collaborationist, pro-German, pro-Vichy (and anti-Third-Republic, anti-Gaullist) publications encountered increasing disbelief, if not opprobrium. Local papers fared somewhat better: they published useful information (details of ration-cards, lists of prisoners, etc.). Resistance figures, some of whom founded underground newspapers, wanted, in 1944, to reform the press, root and branch.

Only 28 of the 206 dailies published in 1939 were allowed to resume publication in 1944: they included L'Humanité and Le Figaro (and, from February 1945, La Croix). The abundance of daily newspapers, and of newpaper copies, published in 1944–6 proved short-lived. The circulation of daily newspapers fell from 15 million in 1946 to 9.6 million in 1952; the number of Parisian dailies fell from 28 to 14 and of provincial dailies from 175 to 117 during the same period. Some of the new titles, like Le *Monde, survived and grew in prestige; more often, like Camus's *Combat, they experienced a slow decline after an initial success; very rarely, a title born of the Resistance died a slow death only to rise again— *Libération* expired in 1964, was resurrected in the wake of the *May 1968 events, and, having assumed many different guises, is the one signal success in the recent history of the daily press. In 1992 the French press boasted 86 daily newspapers, of which a handful were general-interest titles, published in Paris and commanding a national audience. In addition to the supplements or review sections of dailies, cultural and intellectual life was covered amply in the general and special-interest magazines and reviews [see EXPRESS; NOUVEL OBSERVATEUR; ELLE].

3. Political and Economic Control of the Press

Controls on publishing preceded the advent of the periodical press. In 1547 *Henri II sought to prevent the propagation of Protestant books. In the struggle for freedom of expression, Protestants were to the fore: Richelieu's protégé, Renaudot, was himself a Protestant convert, and the *gazettes* smuggled in from Holland, under Louis XIV and later, were an early form of subversive press. In the early 16th c. the authorities had begun the award of licenses, authorizing the holder to print an account of a recent event. From 1651 the licence system constituted, indeed, the main form of state control of the press. La Gazette was the sole newspaper authorized to publish official news (a task that Napoleon and Napoleon III assigned to Le Moniteur) and to act as the mouthpiece of French policy abroad (a role that many persisted, later, in ascribing to Le Temps and some, even today, to Le Monde). The state also sponsored and controlled the first scientific and cultural review: in 1663, the year when *Colbert founded the *Académie des Sciences, the licence awarded to publish the Journal des savants declared that sciences and the arts, no less than military prowess, illustrated the genius of the French nation.

Curbs on the press stimulated the pen while causing anguish to printers and publishers. This is one reason why press history is often indistinguishable from political history. Publications that discussed public affairs took greater or lesser account of what the authorities permitted, of rules and regulations, legislation, censorship, fiscal controls, etc. During the *Fronde as during the *Enlightenment, and whenever authority was sapped as France moved towards a *régime d'opinion*, skirmishing with the power of the day and testing the limits of what was tolerated proved an exercise that produced some of France's finest political journalism—*Voltaire and *Beaumarchais, but also *Prévost-Paradol and *Rochefort. An epigram speaks of 'le (bon) mot qui tue'; under Louis-Napoléon as under *le roi soleil*, controls on the political press led some of France's most skilful writers to deploy their irony, satire, and mastery of allusion in the literary press and *la presse légère*, from the *Mercure galant* to Le Figaro.

*Censorship was one of many tools used in attempts to contain the questioning of authority, be it temporal or spiritual. The comptroller of publishing had 82 censors at his disposal in 1751 and 121 in 1763. Pressure for freedom of the press formed part of the wider demand, in Enlightenment circles, for freedom of expression. In a period when literary criticism and cultural cosmopolitanism nourished intellectual debate, the advocates of press freedom found it might prove a double-edged sword. For example, *Fréron of L'Année littéraire was a master of irony who—according to Jules *Janin of Le *Journal des débats—founded criticism as a literary form. Voltaire feared the bite of his pen: although often a champion of press freedom, he pressed the comptroller of publishing, Malesherbes, to act against Fréron.

The Revolution swept away the crumbling edifice of press controls, although successive governments attempted to retain them. The July 1881 press law, as noted, still underpins press legislation today. Technology and newspaper finance—especially the latter—assumed increasing importance, in the 19th c., in French writing about the press.

There was considerable stability between the end of the 15th c. and the 1820s in printing technology—manually set type and manually operated press—but rapid change subsequently: in the 1980s electronic publishing transformed journalistic practice, as had the steam and rotary-presses, the electric telegraph, and the linotype in the 19th c. The transformation of the press into an industry was portrayed, and often pilloried, by *Balzac, *Maupassant, *Zola, *Barrès, and countless others. Balzac depicted some lasting traits of French journalism: although embittered by his own failures in journal publishing (La Revue parisienne, etc.), his critique of the press (*Illusions perdues; Monographie de la presse parisienne) was married to investigative skills—e.g. in his exposure of the role of the *Havas news agency. Girardin's La Presse in 1836 (which published Balzac's La Vieille Fille) and Millaud's Le Petit Journal in 1863 (publisher of *Ponson du Terrail and countless other highly paid *roman-feuilletonistes) signified the advent of the popular daily and the industrialization of the press. Substantial capital resources were needed; press groups emerged seeking, in today's parlance, a dominant market share (of *advertising, as well as sales, revenue). Girardin and Millaud followed in the steps trodden earlier by *Panckoucke, publisher in 1789 of La Gazette, Le Mercure, Le Moniteur, and other titles: newspaper publishers became press magnates, attentive to economies of scale and to maximizing advertising revenue (often of dubious provenance). Few holds were barred: duels—by the sword, as well as the pen—were frequent.

The relative lack of commercial-advertising revenue led many papers to depend over-much on financial (i.e. stock-market) advertising, especially during periods of intense speculation (see Zola, L'*Argent; Barrès, Les *Déracinés). During the 1920s, however, commercial advertisers increasingly invested in the press, and specialist or thematic advertising developed in dailies, magazines, and reviews, which accordingly grew in size. But the print media no longer enjoyed a monopoly: cinema, radio, and later television diverted creative talent and advertising revenue from the press.

None the less, economic censorship—symbolized by *Lammenais's 'silence aux pauvres'—never totally stifled nonconformist views, any more than did political controls. Literary journals like Le Magazine littéraire survived on a hand-to-mouth basis, and just as the anarchist Le Père Peinard mocked authority in the 1890s and Le *Canard enchaîné opposed brain-washing for most of the 20th c., so successive incarnations of Jean-Edern *Hallier's L'Idiot international played the king's fool from the late 1960s onwards [see also CHARLIE-HEBDO]. [MP]

See C. Bellanger et al., Histoire générale de la presse française, 5 vols. (1969–76); J. Sgard, Dictionnaire des journaux, 1600–1789, 2 vols. (1991).

Presse, La. Newspaper launched in 1836 by Émile de *Girardin [see PRESS, 2].

PRÉVERT, Jacques (1900–77). French poet. Set to music by Kosma, interpreted by Yves *Montand, learnt by heart in schools, dissected by academics, Prévert's poems have a uniquely important place in 20th-c. French culture. His is a poetry of the man in the street—essentially oral, often sentimental, disdainful of the high and mighty, respectful towards the underdog. Anarchic and playful, his spirit is pre-political, although the sketches he wrote during his participation in the agit-prop Groupe Octobre, some performed in factories in 1936, and his delightful script for *Renoir's film Le Crime de Monsieur Lange, are quintessential expressions of the *Popular Front ethos. A fringe member of the *Surrealist group from 1925, he soon joined the dissidents along with his friends from the 'Groupe de la rue du Château' (Tanguy, Marcel Duhamel, *Queneau).

Prévert began writing poems in the early 1930s. However, long before the publication of his first collection (Paroles, 1946) he had made his name as writer of film-scripts: Drôle de drame (1937), Quai des brumes (1938), Les Visiteurs du soir (1942), Les Enfants du Paradis (1945), all directed by Marcel *Carné and displaying a mixture of realism and poetry allied with a strong sense of character. The great success of Paroles after the war led Prévert to write more poetry (Spectacle, 1951; La Pluie et le beau temps, 1955) mostly of a similar kind, dominated by clever punning, a sense of the marvellous, and an unerring feel for the quality of everyday life. [MHTS]

PRÉVOST, Antoine-François, abbé (1697–1763). French novelist and translator. After 1728 he called himself Prévost d'Exiles.

Having done well as a pupil of the Jesuits, Prévost seemed destined to enter the priesthood. But he apparently interrupted his religious training and spent two periods in military service. He finally took his vows in 1721, as a Benedictine. In 1728 he obtained a transfer to a less strict branch of the order. However, he left his monastery before the transfer had been validated and so became a fugitive. The next six years were spent as an exile in England and Holland. This period includes his liaison with Lenki Eckhardt, whom some critics have assumed, mistakenly, to be the model for Manon Lescaut. Probably because of Lenki, Prévost got into financial difficulties, fled from Holland leaving debts unpaid, and falsified a bill of exchange in London. In 1734 he returned to France, having regularized his position, and two years later he became almoner to the prince de Conti. There was one more period of exile: in 1741 he was banished for involvement in a scandal-sheet about Paris and the court. From 1742 until his death he led a peaceful existence, mainly occupied with his writing.

His output was prolific and extremely varied. He wrote prefaces to, and/or edited, works by other writers. He edited a literary review, Le Pour et contre (1733–40), and wrote much of its contents. His translations of Latin and English works totalled 31 volumes, without counting the large amount of translation involved in his 15-volume compilation, Histoire générale des voyages (1746–59). Among the English novels he translated, his version of Richardson's Clarissa, which appeared as Lettres anglaises (1751), was probably the most influential. He also compiled a Manuel lexique (1750) of unusual French words. Then there are two romanced biographies: Histoire de Marguerite d'Anjou (1740) and Histoire de Guillaume le Conquérant (1742). However, the basis of his literary fame nowadays is his fiction, and in particular *Manon Lescaut.

Between 1728 and 1741 he published three long novels. The Mémoires et aventures d'un homme de qualité (1728–31) recounts first the sufferings of the narrator-hero, and then the adventures of the young nobleman whose mentor he becomes. (The seventh volume, the story of Manon, was soon published separately and was frequently reprinted.) Next came Le Philosophe anglais ou Histoire de monsieur Cleveland (1731–9). Cleveland is supposedly an illegitimate son of Oliver Cromwell; he pursues a long quest for, and eventually finds, emotional and spiritual contentment. Le Doyen de Killerine (1735–40) is set amid the Jacobite struggles, but the Dean is chiefly concerned with the entanglements of his sister and his two brothers. These three works won considerable popularity. They are all rich in action: the heroes make numerous journeys; coincidences and chance meeetings abound; there are cases of mistaken identity, etc. In the main they observe the bienséances, though there are suggestive episodes, as when Cleveland comes close to inadvertently committing incest. But adventure is not all: Prévost's narrators dwell at length on their feelings; they are all keenly aware of moral issues, and repeatedly seek to explain and justify their behaviour.

These traits reappear in the remaining novels, which are shorter. Here, although amour-passion is still powerful, it gives way to disillusionment. The narrator of Histoire d'une Grecque moderne (1740) sets free a slave-girl with whom he then falls in love, but he is left doubting her virtue. In the Mémoires pour servir à l'histoire de Malte (1741), the Commandeur is for a time swayed by love, but finally overcomes it. As for Les Campagnes philosophiques (1741), though the 'campaigns' are ostensibly military ones, the true interest lies in various amorous intrigues. Prévost frequently uses historical elements in his novels, but he refashions 'history' freely to suit the needs of his stories.

Both in his translations and in his original works Prévost has a fluent, attractive style. His writings contributed to several major trends of the period such as the rising vogue of *sensibilité, the development of the *memoir-novel, and the spread of anglomanie. The fact that his works are so clearly imbued with passing tendencies of his day may help to explain why, apart from Manon Lescaut, their appeal has faded.   [VGM]

See J. Sgard, Prévost romancier (1968).

PRÉVOST, Jean (1901–44). French novelist, critic, and essayist. Prévost was a complete modern humanist, celebrating powers of mind and body in his essays Plaisirs des sports (1926) and Essai sur l'introspection (1927), whilst empathizing with the lot of les petites gens in his novel Les Frères Bouquinquant (1930). His telling critical studies, La Création chez *Stendhal (1942) and *Baudelaire (1953), broke new methodological ground, and his earlier work on *Montaigne, on *Valéry, and on the French Epicureans is sound and shrewd. He was shot by the Germans in the maquis of the Vercors.   [DAS]

PRÉVOST-PARADOL, Lucien–Anatole (1829–70). Journalist (on the *Journal des débats) and professor, an important figure among the liberal opposition to the Second Empire. He committed suicide in 1870 on account of the *Franco-Prussian War while serving as French ambassador to the United States.

Prévôté, see PARLEMENTS.

PRICE-MARS, Jean (1876–1969). Intellectual, writer, and diplomat, considered *Haiti's foremost thinker of this century. His early work was directed at educational reform, but these interests were intensified by the nationalism provoked by the American Occupation (1915–34). In his most famous work, Ainsi parla l'oncle (1928), he attacked the Haitian élite for their 'bovarysme collectif' or for being too francophile. This work is a defence and illustration of Haitian popular culture, language, and religion. His work inspired *indigénisme, *noirisme, and novelists such as *Roumain and *Thoby-Marcelin. In the backlash against Duvalierism he has been criticized for facilitating the politics of racial mystification.
                                              [JMD]

Prière sur l'Acropole

'**Prière sur l'Acropole**', see RENAN.

Prince, Le, see BALZAC, J.-L.

Princesse de Babylone, La (1768). Oriental story by *Voltaire, something of a pot-pourri of his favourite themes.

Princesse de Clèves, La. Last work published by the comtesse de *Lafayette (1678), masterpiece of 17th-c. prose fiction. Some literary historians call it the first modern novel. Lafayette recreated the 16th-c. setting through painstaking historical documentation. Her major innovation is an unprecedented attention to psychology, an attention that provoked heated response from contemporary readers and that modern readers see as the mark of her literary modernity.

The heroine becomes the object of universal desire when she arrives at Henri II's court. Her mother, Madame de Chartres, marries her to the prince de Clèves, although she knows that her daughter does not love him. When the duc de Nemours continues his pursuit, the princess tells her husband of her attraction to another man, whom she refuses to name. To preserve her virtue, she asks to leave the court. Her husband's jealous obsession with her secret provokes his untimely death. The princess refuses to remarry and lives her last years alone.

17th-c. readers saw the novel as questioning the institution of marriage: were sincerity and marriage, even love and marriage, compatible? Readers today see the novel as documenting the difficulty, especially for a woman, of preserving individuality in a court obsessed with appearances and with conformity to received ideas of (female) conduct.   [JDeJ]

Princesse de Montpensier, La, see LAFAYETTE, COMTESSE DE.

Principes philosophiques, see DESCARTES.

Printing in France until 1600. [For book production before printing, see MANUSCRIPTS; for later periods and for such issues as state control and guild organization, see BOOK TRADE.] The printing-press came to France in 1470, over 20 years after Gutenberg's invention. The first press, set up in the *Sorbonne by Guillaume Fichet and Jean Heynlin, produced several classical texts, modern humanist works such as Valla's *Elegantiae* and Fichet's *Rhetoric*, and scholastic writers like Scotus, turning to religious and popular works after 1472. Other presses were soon established in Paris (around the rue Saint-Jacques), in 1473 in Lyon, and by 1500 in 40 other French towns. For the first century and more, traditional works, classical and medieval, were printed, almost half of these of religious interest. The dominant language was Latin [see LATINITY]; gradually the medieval Latin of the schools and ecclesiastical debate gave way to purer *humanist Latin, which became the language of serious inter-national discourse. Although the first book to be published in French, Bonhomme's *Croniques de France*, dates from 1476, and although publishers like Antoine Vérard, celebrated for his splendid Books of Hours, did bring out court poetry, *mystery plays, and chivalric *romances at the end of the 15 c., it is not until the middle of the 16th that printing can be said to have encouraged writing in the vernacular.

France soon began to surpass both Germany and Italy in the quality of its typography and book production [for the physical manufacture of books see BOOK TRADE]. The gothic type, based on medieval manuscripts, and used for religious, medical, and legal works, and also for vernacular writing until the 1520s, was replaced by a Roman type based on a humanist hand which became common after Galliot du Pré's *Roman de la Rose*, and his *Chartier and *Villon of around 1530. Then Claude Garamond invented a new Roman type which became the standard for several centuries, a non-Aldine italic type, and also the beautiful 'grecs du roi' after the handwriting of the Cretan scholar Angelo Vergetio. This attention to visual presentation is typical of the high standards of French publishers at the time. In Paris, Jean Petit, an academic publisher who produced over 100 editions, and his associate Josse Bade, the publisher of *Erasmus, together with Geoffroy *Tory (*Champ fleury*, 1529; royal printer from 1530) and Galliot du Pré, with his translations of the classics and editions of contemporary writers such as Clément *Marot, all helped to establish the tradition of fine printing and to favour the move to a more humanist and more imaginative production.

The following period, from about 1530 to 1560, was the high point of French publishing, when printing was at the service of both humanist scholarship and vernacular literature. The *Estienne dynasty (Henri I, Robert I, Henri II) was famous for scholarly editions of classical and biblical texts, and for works of lexicography; among other energetic publishers mention should be made of *Turnèbe, Wechel, Vascosan, and Morel, all closely associated with the *Pléiade. In Lyon, following the early success of Trechsel, and later of *Dolet, in the golden age of French printing we find Sébastien Gryphe, friend of Marot, *Scève, and *Rabelais, who produced dozens of high-quality small schoolbooks, usually in Latin, and Jean de Tournes, publisher of Scève, *Labé, and other Lyonnais vernacular writers, as well as of classical and technical works. A feature of de Tournes's books is the art typography and illustration, the work of Bernard Salomon, whose elegant woodcuts in the style of *Fontainebleau typify this period.

The second half of the century saw a decline in book-publishing in France, because of the disorders of the civil and religious wars and their disastrous economic effects. This is reflected in the poor quality of the paper, and in the inferior or worn type and woodcut blocks. France's leading role then passed to the Low Countries, first to Antwerp, where the

Frenchman Christophe Plantin and his son-in-law Moretus had their presses, and later to Amsterdam.

The history of printing is not only closely linked with the history of writing and of literature, but also reflects and affects broader social and cultural changes [see LITERACY]. Initially directed at a relatively well-off élite (with print-runs ranging from 200 to 1,000) it nevertheless encouraged people to learn to read and facilitated the diffusion of texts, since they could be reproduced more quickly and more cheaply than manuscripts. Eventually printing brought about the standardization of spelling, and also of grammar and syntax, imposing one acceptable form on regional linguistic variations. However, its position was ambivalent since it could be used both to preserve the old order (cultural, political, or religious) and to undermine it, accelerating the dissemination of new ideas and producing intellectual ferment, which in turn invited *censorship. Printing helped to communicate humanist ideas, for example, which undermined the previously prevailing order, but by the end of the century it was used by *Montaigne and Bacon for the sceptical rejection of classical authority. In a similar way, after the systematic publication of all the available scientific texts of antiquity, a new approach to scientific discovery, itself a by-product of the way knowledge was now classified and presented on the printed page, subverted received ideas and led to new discoveries. In religion printing was used by traditionalists to strengthen piety and maintain orthodoxy, and by *Evangelicals (*Lefèvre d'Étaples and Erasmus) and Reformers (*Luther and *Calvin) to promulgate their ideas and encourage a scholarly and critical reading of the Bible. As a result of all these tensions the practice of reading spread, the use of the vernacular increased, and imaginative literature prospered.   [PS]

See L. Febvre and H.-J. Martin, *L'Apparition du livre* (1958); A. Parent, *Les Métiers du livre à Paris au XVIe siècle* (1974); E. L. Eisenstein, *The Printing Press as an Agent of Change* (1979); H.-J. Martin *et al* (eds.), *Histoire de l'édition française*, vol. 1, *Le Livre conquérant* (1982).

Prise d'Orange, La. *Chanson de geste* of the Cycle de *Guillaume. Originally dating from the 1120s, the poem was much reworked; the extant version belongs to the 1190s. It tells of Guillaume's wooing and winning, with the often sarcastic support of his nephew Gui, of the Saracen princess Orable, who is baptized as Guibourc. The poem contains much parodic comedy in its exploitation of epic techniques (especially 'oral-formulaic' compositional devices), romance and lyric motifs (the 'Spring Opening' and *amour de loin*—'love from afar'), and the folk motif of the hero's visit to the Otherworld and his victory by cunning.   [PEB]

Prisonnière, La (1923). The fifth part of Proust's *A la recherche du temps perdu*.

Privilège, see BOOK TRADE, 2.

Prizes (*les prix littéraires*) play a large part (some would say too large) in modern French literary life. Their history goes back to the Middle Ages, when there were many literary competitions, usually for poetry, the most famous and long-lived being the *Jeux Floraux de Toulouse. From early on the *Académie Française offered prizes for poetry and eloquence, as did the provincial *academies. The 20th c. has seen a vast increase in their number; some are offered by public bodies, some by commercial organizations, others by private associations, and they cover writing of all kinds.

The 'big six', all given to novels, are the Goncourt (the most coveted prize, awarded by the *Académie Goncourt), the Fémina (with an all-woman jury), the Grand Prix du Roman of the Académie Française, the Renaudot, the Interallié, and the Médicis (particularly associated with 'modernity'). Considerable prestige is attached to the Prix des Libraires, and there are many other prizes offered for particular kinds of writing (poetry, *detective fiction, *bande dessinée, etc.). The top prizes may not guarantee lasting success, but provide a considerable commercial boost—the Goncourt often leads to sales in excess of 100,000. They are naturally subject to rumours of intrigue and fixing (and were vigorously attacked by *Gracq in *La Littérature à l'estomac*), but are rarely refused.

A considerable number of prizes are available for francophone writing outside France. These include the *Noma awards, the Grand Prix de la Francophonie of the Académie Française, and the *Grand Prix Littéraire d'Afrique Noire.

The Nobel Prize for literature has been awarded to the following French-speaking writers: *Sully-Prudhomme (1901), *Mistral (1904), *Maeterlinck (1911), Romain *Rolland (1915), Anatole *France (1921), *Bergson (1927), *Martin du Gard (1937), *Gide (1947), *Mauriac (1952), *Camus (1957), *Saint-John Perse (1960), *Sartre (1964, refused), *Beckett (1969), *Milosz (1980), *Simon (1985).   [PF]

Procès-verbal, Le, see LE CLÉZIO.

Profession de foi du vicaire savoyard. J.-J. Rousseau's extremely influential defence of natural religion and conscience, put in the mouth of a Savoy priest and included in Book 4 of *Émile*.

Projet de paix perpétuelle, see SAINT-PIERRE.

Projet pour une révolution à New York, see ROBBE-GRILLET.

Promenade du sceptique, La, see DIDEROT.

Promenades dans Rome, see STENDHAL.

Propos rustiques (1547). The best-known collection of tales by *Du Fail.

Prose Poem (*poème en prose*). A prose piece whose brevity produces the rhythmic poise and acoustic structuring, the expressive elisions and condensed imagery, normally associated with verse. Among the possible sources of the prose poem might be mentioned poetic prose from *Fénelon to *Chateaubriand, prose renderings of foreign lyrics, and biblical prose; as the site of contradictory forces, it relates to *Romanticism's *mélange des genres*.

Aloysius *Bertrand's pioneering *Gaspard de la nuit* (begun 1828, pub. 1842) oscillates between the meditative and the exhibitionist, while Maurice de *Guérin's 'Le Centaure' (1840) and 'La Bacchante' unite classical harmony and pagan convulsion. *Barbey d'Aurevilly calls his 'Niobé' 'cette rêverie qu'on croirait traduite d'un poète anglais', and the idea of the prose poem as the transposition of a verse original, in a lower key, is borne out by several of *Baudelaire's *Petits poèmes en prose* (*Le Spleen de Paris*) (1855–69). But Baudelaire is also in search of the genre appropriate to the impulsive, discontinuous experience of the urban *flâneur*. *Rimbaud's *Illuminations* (written 1872–6?) exploit prose's refusal of the preordained: nothing can be predicted, each new phrase reinvents reality for a reader made vulnerable by the lack of literary reference-points.

The prose poem's flexibility ensured its continuing vigour in the 20th c. With their desire to erase the boundaries between genres, between the literal and the figurative, chance and destiny, dream and reality, the *Surrealists were much attracted to the form. But it was also an indispensable vehicle for writers as different as *Reverdy, *Ponge, *Michaux, and *Char.   [CS]

PROSPER, Jean-Georges (b. 1933). Poet. Born on Mauritius, he left to attend the Sorbonne where he read for both a first degree and a doctorate. He became president of the Association des Écrivains de Langue Francaise and, from Paris, advised on French education on Mauritius. He is author of the seminal *Histoire de la littérature mauricienne de langue française* (1978) and the words of the Mauritian national anthem. Always offering a plurality of readings, Prosper's poems have become increasingly religious, as the title of his later collection, *Les Saignées du Saigneur* (1983), suggests.   [BEJ]

Protestantism. [For the pre-1600 period see REFORMATION; EVANGELICALS; WARS OF RELIGION.]

1. Before 1789

At the time of the *Edict of Nantes (1598) there were about 1,250,000 Protestants in France, almost all Calvinists, constituting about 6 per cent of the population. They were often called Huguenots (from the German *Eidgenossen*); their religion was officially referred to as the *religion prétendue réformée* (RPR). They were geographically concentrated in a long crescent stretching from La Rochelle to Valence, skirting the Massif Central. Some towns were almost exclusively Protestant, notably La Rochelle

and Montauban; others, like Nîmes and Montpellier, had strong Protestant majorities. Paris had about 15,000 Calvinists, about 5 per cent of the population.

The acquisition of most of Alsace (1648), the Pays de Montbéliard (1676), and Strasbourg (1681) brought to France a considerable population of Lutherans. Their theology was not radically different from that of the Calvinists (except perhaps in their belief in the Real Presence), but they had a different religious culture: in particular, they tolerated iconography, and they had a tradition of accepting princely authority. They were also largely German-speaking. They were not subject to the full rigours of the Edict of Fontainebleau (i.e. the Revocation of the Edict of Nantes), because Louis XIV could not risk such persecution in a newly acquired frontier region; they were, however, subject to severe persecution after 1685.

French Protestantism seems to have stood up fairly well to the often virulent persecution of the 17th c. However, the intensified persecution of the 1680s [see DRAGONNADES] and the Revocation of the Edict of Nantes in October 1685 forced many to leave the country [see REFUGE]. Most of the rest conformed outwardly, while in many areas keeping alive a family tradition of Bible-reading and prayer. In the early 18th c. millenarian Protestantism among the peasantry of the Cévennes broke out in the Guerre des *Camisards. Many Protestant notables found this kind of apocalyptic popular religion not to their taste, and welcomed the work of Antoine Court, who after 1713 began to preach a moderate religion more in keeping with Huguenot traditions. Protestant worship, however, was still illegal and had mostly to be conducted in *le Désert*, i.e. in secret meetings usually held in the open air. A number of pastors were executed for their religious activity. Despite continuing persecution, French Protestantism maintained itself and even flourished in the first half of the 18th c. From about 1750 state persecution began to decline, perhaps in the face of *Enlightenment principles of toleration and the increasing secularization of the concept of the state (a notable exception to this general trend is provided by the execution of Jean *Calas). In 1787 the Edict of Toleration gave Protestants the right to keep their own parish registers, which were to have legal validity (i.e. it accepted their right to a legal existence).

2. Since 1789

The Revolution of 1789 was generally welcomed by Protestants, partly because it rapidly turned against the Catholic Church, partly because the *Déclaration des droits de l'homme* (art. 10) decreed that 'no one ought to be harassed on account of his opinions, even religious, provided their manifestation does not disturb the public order established by law'. Protestants were, however, subject, along with Catholics, to the de-Christianization campaign of

1793–4. They welcomed the *Concordat of 1801, because it gave official state recognition to the Protestant religion and provided it with state financial support (until 1905). Since then, the only case of serious persecution of Protestants has been the White Terror in and around Nîmes in late 1815, which saw a wave of violence carried out by Catholics against Protestants, with a number of deaths; the motivation appears to have been partly religious and partly social (Catholic populace against Protestant élite). Protestants have remained largely sympathetic to the *republican tradition; they played an important part in the founding of the Third Republic in the 1870s, and a century later were prominent in the Socialist cabinets of the 1980s.

Until the 19th c. the pressure of persecution kept French Calvinism a reasonably united body. The first half of the 19th c., however, saw a split between liberals and partisans of the movement known as Le Réveil. The liberals adopted an increasingly rationalist and moralistic approach, and emphasized the human conscience as a source of moral and religious knowledge. Le Réveil, in the Romantic style, emphasized the intuitions of the heart as the way to know God; it was strongly Christocentric, and placed renewed emphasis on the Bible. By the mid-19th c. followers of Le Réveil constituted 40–45 per cent of the Calvinist faithful (rather less among Lutherans). The national synod of 1872 saw a formal split between 'evangelicals' (the inheritors of Le Réveil) and liberals, with the former constituting a two-thirds majority; in 1879 and 1882 they established separate national organizations (there were also some independent churches). The split was not fully resolved until 1938, when a reunified Église Réformée de France was set up (excluding a smallish minority of independents). The 19th c. also saw the establishment in France of a number of minority Protestant denominations, such as the Mennonites, Quakers, and Methodists.

3. Numbers and Distribution

Throughout this period the Protestant heartlands referred to in the first paragraph have remained largely unchanged. Estimates of the total Protestant population are riddled with difficulties, but the Table gives a recent estimate.

	All Protestants	% of population
1562	2,000,000	10.0
1598	1,250,000	6.0
1670	1,026,000	5.0
c.1760	659,000	3.0
c.1815	751,000	2.6
1866	802,339	2.1
c.1900	900,000	2.2
1950	754,000	1.8
1974	850–880,000	1.7
1980	850,000	1.6

The figures in the Table include the Lutherans (also a small number of minority groups). The Lutheran population is estimated at 70,000 in 1670, 59,000 in 1760. There were about 220,000 Lutherans in Alsace and the Pays de Montbéliard in the early 19th c. After the loss of Alsace-Lorraine in 1871 (regained in 1919) only 80,000 Lutherans remained (out of 280,000). In 1975 there were about 275,000.

Although never more than a small minority of the population, French Protestants have made a disproportionate impact on public life. They have been prominent among economic and (after the Revolution) political élites. The strength of Protestant élites should not, however, hide the fact that until very recently a large majority of Protestants were rural and poor. The economic decline of many Protestant rural heartlands has recently changed this picture somewhat. A 1980 survey suggested that Protestants were over-represented among cadres supérieurs et moyens and employés, under-represented among ouvriers and agriculteurs.   [RBG]

See J. Garrisson, L'Édit de Nantes et sa révocation: histoire d'une intolérance (1985); A. Encrevé, Les Protestants en France de 1800 à nos jours (1985); Dictionnaire du monde religieux dans la France contemporaine, vol. 5, Les Protestants, ed. A. Encrevé (1993).

PROU, Suzanne (b. 1920). Novelist who situates her fiction in her native Provence, an environment shown as propitious for tragedy. Early works of an often ferociously ironic tone (Méchamment les oiseaux, 1972) were followed by La Terrasse des Bernardini (1973, Prix Renaudot), revealing what lies behind the provincial facade. Le Dit de Marguerite (1986) recounts her mother's life.   [EAF]

PROUDHON, Pierre-Joseph (1809–65). French anarchist and socialist theorist. Born in Besançon, he grew up in poverty, but studied at the local collège thanks to a scholarship, and became a printer by trade. His prolific writings demonstrate his impressive but sprawling erudition and his affinity with Utopian socialists like *Fourier. His first major book, Qu'est-ce que la propriété? (1840), brought notoriety with its much-quoted answer that Property is Theft. In fact, he supported the personal ownership of wealth and attacked only the abuse of property to exploit the work of others. He attracted followers in working-class and revolutionary circles, first in Lyon and then in Paris. He was impressed by Russian and German political exiles, including Marx and Bakunin, from whom he adapted a version of Hegelian dialectics to argue, in his Système des contradictions économiques, ou Philosophie de la misère (1846), that both good and bad consequences flow from particular economic factors. He scandalized religious believers by his assertion that God is Evil, since He is responsible for the tyranny, poverty, and falsehood in the world, and argued that the self-emancipation of humanity from these evils could only be achieved through economic reform. Marx's polemical riposte, Misère de la philosophie (1847),

Proust

criticized Proudhon's truncated Hegelianism and economic Utopianism.

An active participant in the February Revolution of 1848, Proudhon argued the working-class cause in newspapers he edited and in the Assemblée Constituante, to which he was elected in June 1848 [see REPUBLICS, 2]. He championed radical property taxation and the establishment of a people's bank. Despite three years in prison for denouncing Louis-Napoléon's election as president, he continued to produce lengthy treatises, including *L'Idée générale de la révolution* (1851), which summarized his experience of revolution and his prescriptions for a society run on anarcho-syndicalist principles. His three-volume *De la justice dans la révolution et dans l'église* (1858) incurred prosecution on moral grounds, which he evaded by four years of exile in Belgium. Like his *La Guerre et la paix* (1861), which inspired Tolstoy's celebrated novel, it proposed a radical philosophy of justice and equality for all men, though it specifically excluded women and races which he considered to be inferior. *Du principe fédératif* (1863) set out a vision of Europe based on confederations of self-governing, non-national communities, and *De la capacité politique de la classe ouvrière* (1865) exhorted the working class to organize its own salvation outside the bourgeois state. His followers were active in founding the First International in 1864, and Proudhon's conceptions became a dominant current in the French labour and *socialist movements. [See also MARXISM IN FRANCE.]

[MHK]

See G. Woodcock, *Anarchism* (1962); P. Ansart, *Proudhon, textes et débats* (1984).

PROUST, Marcel (1871–1922). Regarded as the greatest 20th-c. French novelist, Proust owes his fame to one 3,000-page novel, **A la recherche du temps perdu*, which he began in his late thirties and on which he continued to work until his death.

He was born into an upper-middle-class Parisian family of strong scientific and artistic interests; these interests were to mark both the subject-matter of his writing and the metaphors through which he would convey his picture of the mind. His father was an eminent physician, conversant with French psychology of the day, and his mother—with whom he had the more intense relationship—was cultured and witty. The letters exchanged between mother and son show the ambivalent intimacy that may have set a pattern for his susceptible and often unhappy sexual relationships. These were homosexual; Proust was to be the first major European novelist to describe in detail the comic and tragic aspects of being a gay in a prejudiced society.

Proust's mother was Jewish; he and his younger brother were brought up as Catholics. He no doubt grew up with an awareness of the diversity of religious and cultural traditions; this awareness is part of what gives *A la recherche du temps perdu* its breadth. The adult Proust seems to have been an atheist or agnostic (albeit one with a keen sense of awe and mystery); certainly his mature work shows, in religious and other areas, a scepticism by turns quizzical or delighted or anguished. Such scepticism has been part of the French literary tradition for centuries, but Proust was to foreground it in a particularly modern mode.

He was educated at the Lycée Condorcet in Paris, then studied law and philosophy; he was a voracious reader, but his scholastic career was somewhat idiosyncratic, in part because of ill health (he was asthmatic from the age of 9). Of contemporary influences, he was perhaps most drawn to the philosophy of *Bergson (to whom he was related by marriage). But to speak of this influence only would be to make far too narrow an assessment of a catholic taste that had absorbed not only the finest writings of 19th-c. France and England but also the classics of world literature, music, and painting. Direct references in all of Proust's writing (whether letters, articles, or fiction) show his detailed knowledge of, for example, Greek myth, medieval epic, George Eliot, *Baudelaire; of plainsong and Bach; of the Italian Renaissance and Turner.

There has been a widely held picture of the young Proust as a dilettante—this in spite of a collection of short stories, 'portraits', and poems, brought out in his twenties (*Les Plaisirs et les jours*, 1896); the translation and annotation of some Ruskin in his thirties (*La Bible d'Amiens*, 1904; *Sésame et les lys*, 1906); the publication at various times of talented articles and pastiches [see PARODY AND PASTICHE]; and, starting 30 years after his death, successive discoveries by scholars of many unpublished sketches or drafts. Of these drafts, the most sustained and ambitious is an unfinished novel, *Jean Santeuil*, written mainly in Proust's mid-to-late twenties (published 1952). Perhaps the most influential posthumous publication has been that of a short extract from drafts for *A la recherche du temps perdu*, known as *Contre Sainte-Beuve* and written *c*.1909. This extract, in the form in which it was published in 1954, is part essay, part autobiography, part fiction. In it Proust suggests that the kind of literary criticism which seeks close connections between works of art and the artist's own life is at best naïve, at worst wilfully stupid; for (he argues) there is an absolute division between the self which socializes with others and the 'deeper' self which creates in solitude. The same idea is present in *A la recherche* (embodied most notably in the figure of the great composer Vinteuil, despised by his neighbours). But *Contre Sainte-Beuve* puts the case more forcefully and single-mindedly, and it was only after its publication that mainstream French literary criticism slowly started to move away from the biographical approach. *Contre Sainte-Beuve* probably prompted, or at least reinforced, important new critical and literary trends in the second half of the 20th c. [see CRITICISM, 4].

Proust was, then, a more committed writer than

his contemporaries and early commentators realized. Nevertheless, it is still true that, although clearly brilliant, he wrote nothing of real artistic importance until *A la recherche*. His previous writings show that he already had wit, all of his themes, many of his characters, and his gifts for metaphor, parody, and hyperbolic elaboration. But he was still groping towards a structure for these, and still often lacked complete stylistic control. It does seem that, round about 1908–9, he may have had a sudden inspiration comparable to that he gives to the narrator of *A la recherche*, even if it was only of how to use insights long held. Certainly, from about 1909–10 he devoted himself to a huge task of writing, revising, and expanding, using the ill health of these later years as a way of withdrawing from the fashionable social circles he had once courted. Surviving manuscripts, typescripts, and proofs of *A la recherche* show how meticulously and purposefully he shaped and reshaped successive drafts.

The first volume (*Du côté de chez Swann*) was published in 1913, and although well received did not become immediately famous. World War I then interrupted publication. During these four years Proust greatly developed the rest of his novel, partly under the influence of the war itself, partly under that of his most passionate and tragic love-affair, but mainly because he constantly saw newly fertile ways of turning the 1,500 pages he had already written into the still richer and more sophisticated 3,000 we now have. With the publication of the second volume (*A l'ombre des jeunes filles en fleurs*, 1919), and the award of the Prix Goncourt, his fame was assured, and by the time he died he was attracting an international readership which has continued to grow.

Although *A la recherche* occasionally teases the reader with the idea that it might be Proust's own autobiography, it is not: there are very many differences, small and large, between the life of Proust the man and that of the narrator of *A la recherche*. The work is a great one because it is an intellectually challenging and aesthetically exquisite fiction.

[AMF]

See *Correspondance de Marcel Proust*, ed. P. Kolb (1970–); R. Hayman, *Proust: A Biography* (1990).

Provençal, see OCCITAN LANGUAGE AND LITERATURE.

Proverbe dramatique. Short dramatic sketch composed to illustrate a proverb. The genre was popular as a form of private theatricals in the *salons of the 17th and 18th c. A vogue for it sprang up in the mid-18th c., disappearing with the advent of the Revolution. Its development owed most to *Carmontelle, whose preface to the 1773 edition of his *Proverbes dramatiques* claims for it the status of comedy. Revived in Restoration high society, notably by Théodore Leclercq (*Proverbes dramatiques*, 1820–30), the genre reached perfection with *Musset's witty and poetic plays, e.g. *On ne badine pas avec l'amour* (1834).   [SBJ]

Proverbs in Medieval Literature. Proverbial wisdom in Medieval French literature is usually coterminous with popular, peasant wisdom, and 'li vilains dit en reprovier' (so says the peasant in his proverb) is a widespread tag. Proverbs are, however, like their Latin equivalents the *sententiae*, impersonal public expressions of collective authority. They were much favoured by learned authors and formed part of literary rhetoric. *Chrétien de Troyes, for example, makes skilful use of them to modulate narrational voice, and as a literary device they remain a consistent feature of most genres, including, more predictably, homiletic texts. Their characteristically terse and bipolar nature makes proverbs favourite material for compilation, not only in Latin (Egbert of Liège and Serlo of Wilton), but in the French vernacular also, where numerous manuscripts of *Proverbes au vilain* and similar collections survive.   [IS]

Provinces, see REGIONS AND DÉPARTEMENTS.

Provinciales, see GIRAUDOUX. It is also the shortened version of the title of *Pascal's *Lettres provinciales*.

Pseudonyms can take several different forms. In the first place there is the use of initials or periphrases ('l'auteur de . . .') or labels ('un médecin'), all of which are close to *anonymity. Then the author's real name may be concealed in an anagram or near-anagram: Voltaire for Arouet, Alcofribas Nasier for François Rabelais. In these cases, Rabelais's anagram is simply a *nom de plume*, whereas Voltaire's replaced his real name not only on title-pages but in life, and is perhaps not a true pseudonym. Some of the best-known names in French literature are either pen-names or adopted names: they include Molière, Sand, Stendhal, Nerval, Lautréamont, France, Apollinaire, Alain, Céline, Éluard, Gracq, Vercors, Yourcenar, Duras, Beti. Sometimes a writer will adapt his original name (Alain-Fournier) or use the name of a relation or protector (Villon).

Different names may be used by the same person for different kinds of writing, e.g. Dard (San Antonio), Gary (Ajar), Vian (Sullivan)—the last two of these being close to *hoaxes. Or else a writer may use several different pseudonyms: Balzac, who had already added a 'de' to his original name, published under such names as Lord R'Hoone or Horace de Saint-Aubin; Stendhal (Henri Beyle) used all kinds of false names, though not usually on his title-pages; Voltaire (originally Arouet) used over 150 *noms de guerre* on his anti-establishment writings.

The motives for taking a new name are very various. They include prudence (Vercors), a challenge to the privileges of the opposite sex (Sand), and mystification (Gary). In the case of Alain and Céline, the pseudonym created the necessary space between writing and another profession. With Molière, Stendhal, and Apollinaire, the motivation is more problematic, though in all these cases there seems to have been the desire to take a different social or psychological identity from that associated with the original family name. The same may be true of Voltaire, although his later pen-names are a playful form of tactical disguise. [PF]

Pseudo-Turpin, see TURPIN.

PSICHARI, Ernest (1883–1914). Grandson of *Renan, author of militaristic and semi-mystical narratives. Reacting against the free-thinking environment in which he was brought up, he joined the army in 1903 and converted to Catholicism while serving in colonial Africa. In the travelogue *Terres de soleil et de sommeil* (1908) and the novel *L'Appel des armes* (1913) Africa is celebrated as a training-ground for French nationalism. Psichari's religious conversion inspired the journal *Les Voix qui crient dans le désert* (1920) and the novel *Le Voyage du centurion* (1916). He was killed in action on the Western Front. [AGH]

Psyché. 1. Tragédie-ballet devised by *Molière on the popular theme of Cupid and Psyche, performed with great success in the Salle des Machines of the Tuileries in 1671. Vigarani provided elaborate stage machinery, *Quinault wrote words to go with *Lully's music, while the play itself is the joint work of Molière and the ageing *Corneille, who wrote most of Acts 2–5, including some beautiful verse. 2. Philosophical epic by *Laprade.

Psychoanalysis in France. Freud's theory of unconscious mental functioning, and the therapeutic techniques that he developed on the basis of that theory, were slow to gain a following in France. For an extended period in 1885–6 Freud was an observer at *Charcot's neurological clinic at La Salpêtrière. He was greatly impressed by Charcot's intellectual authority, his diagnostic powers, and the entire attitude of detachment and precision-seeking that he brought to the study of mental disorders. For Charcot, mental disorders had physical causes, and it was the neurologist's responsibility to discover these, localize them in human bodies, and so organize his results that a comprehensive map of human suffering could eventually be drawn. In Charcot's hands, La Salpêtrière had become a vast museum of living human subjects, a classificatory system built in stone. Freud was to base his analysis of mental suffering not upon organic lesions, but upon the disruptions caused by infantile sexual traumas. But throughout the 1890s, when Freud's researches were gradually bringing him closer to that psychology of the unconscious which was to remain his principal scientific concern, Charcot continued to represent in Freud's mind an ideal of scientific rigour.

Freud's debt to Charcot, his admiration for French literature, and his fond memories of Paris did not however oblige the French to do anything in return. *Breton and the Surrealists were relatively isolated in their enthusiasm for his work. *Die Traumdeutung* (1900) did not appear in French until 1926 (as *La Science des rêves*, translated by I. Meyerson), and other major works followed haphazardly. The Société Psychanalytique de Paris was founded in 1926 by René Laforgue, Marie Bonaparte, Rodolphe Loewenstein, Édouard Pichon, and six others, and remained small until well after World War II. During the Occupation its activities were suppressed.

Three factors are especially important in explaining this slowness of response to psychoanalysis, both inside the medical profession and in French culture at large. First, psychiatry in France was ill prepared for the new doctrine. It had a strong tradition of research into the organic causes of mental illness, and possessed its own 'new' psychotherapist in the formidable person of Pierre Janet (1859–1947), a renegade pupil of Charcot's. Like Freud, he was seeking outside the physiological domain for modes of explanation which would give due weight to the emotional history of his patients and to their wishes for themselves. Although Janet took some account of sexuality, and made some play with the idea of the unconscious, he placed an emphasis in treatment on the role played by the patient's will and his or her power to make reasonable choices and pursue emotionally fulfilling activities. But there was enough general similarity between the range of problems tackled by the two thinkers to make them seem like competitors. And it clearly served the interests of aspiring junior members of the profession in France to acquiesce in the view that a world already containing a Janet could not possibly be in need of a Freud.

Secondly, in the absence of informed spokesmen and a full range of accurate translations, Freud's thought soon fell prey to scandalmongers and myth-making pamphleteers. He was regularly attacked as the purveyor of ideas which were newfangled and obscure, but which were all too clearly the products of a morbid and prurient interest in sex. For these writers, Freudianism was a moral disease rather than a therapeutic method.

Thirdly, intelligent critical voices were raised against Freud well before his ideas had received a full public hearing. Two of these voices are particularly impressive: those of Georges *Politzer in *Critique des fondements de la psychologie* (1928) and Sartre in *L'*Être et le néant* (1943). Although the two books are quite different in their aims and scope, both writers have the same general complaint to make against Freud: he seemed to promise, but failed to provide, a science of personality in which the deeds, motives, desires, intentions, and projects of the individual subject would retain their density and complexity; instead, he built a series of elaborate and conceptually insecure abstract models of the human mind. Politzer announced a 'concrete psychology' and Sartre an 'existential psychoanalysis', both of which were to do what Freud had failed to do.

From having been resistant to psychoanalysis earlier in the century, France became one of its principal intellectual centres from the early 1950s onwards. This change was brought about by a single original-minded and charismatic analytic practitioner: *Lacan. For many years the institutional history of Lacanian psychoanalysis was a troubled one, marked by a series of expulsions, secessions, and splits. But Lacan's reformulation of Freud's theory had two profound effects. On the one hand, it encouraged numerous French scholars to return to the Freudian texts, to elucidate them, and to carry on working in directions that Freud himself had only begun to explore. Sometime pupils of Lacan like André Green, Serge Leclaire, Jean Laplanche, and J.-B. Pontalis comprised an energetic second generation of French theorists, and Laplanche and Pontalis's *Vocabulaire de la psychanalyse* (1967) and the Laplanche essays collected as *Problématiques* (1981–) are among the outstanding psychoanalytic works produced anywhere since the death of Freud.

On the other hand, Lacan's teaching, especially in the two decades following the publication of his *Écrits* (1966), gave psychoanalytic concepts an extraordinary general currency in France. Together with Marxism, semiology, and deconstruction, psychoanalysis became one of the main component languages of an entire metropolitan culture. It was by way of a creative and committed reaction to psychoanalysis that such 'post-*Beauvoir' French feminists as *Irigaray, *Cixous, and *Kristeva achieved their distinctive political and theoretical voices.

Lacanian psychoanalysis now has the makings of an international movement comparable in scope to that of the largely Anglo-American International Psychoanalytical Association. Its peculiar osmotic relationship with literature, and the new glamour that it seems to many to confer upon literary interpretation, have caused it to displace orthodox Freudian approaches and the brilliant, eccentric 'psychocriticism' of Charles *Mauron in many of the humanities departments of Western universities.   [MB]

Psychocriticism, see MAURON.

Pucelle, La. Title of a notoriously bad epic about *Jeanne d'Arc by *Chapelain, and of a notorious mock-epic by *Voltaire.

PUJADE-RENAUD, Claude (b. 1932). French short-story writer, teacher of educational sciences. The short stories of *Un si joli petit livre* (1989) move between the savage irony of realism and the disquieting darkness of the worlds of Freud and Grimm. She shocks like *Tournier, and convinces like Angela Carter.   [GDM]

Pulchérie. *Comédie héroïque* by Pierre *Corneille, first performed 1672. The heroine, heiress to the Roman imperial throne, renounces her love for a humble soldier to ensure her 'gloire' by marrying (in name only) the old senator Martian.

PURE, Michel, abbé de (1620–80). Author of biographies, novels, and a translation of Quintilian. His 'novel', *La Précieuse ou le Mystère des ruelles* (1656–8), is a rich collection of anecdotes and dialogues, giving a sympathetic account of *preciosity and showing particular interest in the conversations of the *précieuses* and their radical ideas on marriage.   [PF]

PUVIS DE CHAVANNES, Pierre (1824–98). French painter who enjoyed an enormous reputation in artistic and literary circles in the final decade of the 19th c. Puvis specialized in large mural compositions of allegorical subjects. The decorative effects created by his pale colours, simplified drawing, and emphasis on the flat surface influenced *Seurat and *Gauguin in particular, and his timeless, universal themes (*Le Pauvre Pêcheur*, 1881) were greatly admired by the literary *Symbolists. In 1895 *Mallarmé made him the subject of his most optimistic homage poem.   [JK]

Puy or **Pui.** Name given to associations of medieval and Renaissance lyric poets, whose president was given the fictitious title 'prince' (hence the traditional address to a 'prince' in the *envoi* of ballades). They held periodic competitions where lyrics were performed and prizes awarded. The name perhaps derives from the *podium* which accommodated competitors and judges, or from Le Puy-en-Velay, where Occitan sources suggest these contests first flourished, briefly, in the late 12th c. Later fraternities centred mainly around northern and western French towns, notably *Arras (in the 13th c.) and Rouen (c.1486–1654).   [PVD]

Pyrame et Thisbé, see THÉOPHILE DE VIAU.

Pyrénées, Traité des. Signed in 1659, this treaty put an end to Franco-Spanish hostilities; it was sealed by the marriage between *Louis XIV and Marie-Thérèse, daughter of Philip IV of Spain.

Pyrrhonism. A version of scepticism, so called after Pyrrho of Elis (d. *c.*275 BC), but known in the Renaissance through the life of Pyrrho by Diogenes Laertius and the summary of his doctrines by Sextus Empiricus (*c.* AD 200). Pyrrhonian scepticism is usually distinguished from academic scepticism: the latter is identified with the claim that no knowledge is possible, whereas the former argues for suspension of judgement on all questions concerning knowledge. Pyrrhonism is associated with a technique of argumentation (the putting forward of propositions which contradict those of your adversary, followed by a refusal to come down on either side of the argument), and is sometimes confused with relativism; but whereas a relativist would argue that there can be no grounds for comparing the merits or truth values of competing systems of thought, the Pyrrhonist suspends judgement on such questions.

Pyrrhonism

Pyrrhonian scepticism as such became widely known through the publication in 1562 and 1569 of Latin translations of Sextus Empiricus' works. Already the ground had been prepared for acceptance of those ideas and philosophical practices by the anti-intellectual movements of the late Middle Ages (Thomas à Kempis, Nicholas of Cusa, Cornelius Agrippa) and by the various attacks on *scholastic Aristotelianism, notably that of *Ramus; the intellectual ferment provoked by the *Reformation with its implicit anti-dogmatism and anti-authoritarianism contributed also to the favourable reception of Pyrrhonism. Even before the publication of Sextus Empiricus, Guy de Bruès had written three, probably fictional, *Dialogues contre les nouveaux Académiciens* (1557), which pitted *Ronsard and Nicot, as representatives of traditional rationalism, against *Baïf and Aubert, who defend sceptical positions; but the full force of of Pyrrhonism is first represented in *Montaigne's *Essais*, and especially in his 'Apologie de Raymond Sebond'.

Montaigne had already had a medal struck which showed him to be aware of the distinction between anti-dogmatism, academic scepticism, and Pyrrhonism: it bore the device 'Que sçay-je?' When he came to write his defence of the 15th-c. Spanish theologian Sebond (Sabunde), whose *Theologia naturalis* he had translated in 1569 at his father's behest, he produced a comprehensive (but not systematic) account of Pyrrhonism, and showed how it could be employed in the service of Catholic apologetics. From a confusing welter of destructive argument, only Pyrrhonism, the philosophy of doubt, emerges unscathed; it is associated by Montaigne not only with intellectual humility but also with a marked tendency to conformism. In theology his exercise in Pyrrhonian philosophy results in the proposition of fideism (the doctrine of the separate truths of faith and reason), which is made consistent with the reassertion of the authority of the traditional Church. In ethics and politics it leads to both conformist and relativist views: conformist, because there can be no valid reason for changing from one's present mode of life; relativist, because there can be no way of establishing by reason which of a number of competing systems is to be preferred. Pyrrhonism constituted, furthermore, a powerful critique of humanism and its optimistic vision of human capacities; and it added weight to the anti-scholastic and anti-intellectual movements, which affected in turn the development of science and scientific method in the early 17th c.

Montaigne's arguments were repeated by *Charron, and were pressed into the service of the *Counter-Reformation by writers such as Jean-Pierre *Camus. They were violently opposed in turn by *Garasse and others, who perceived their potential for weakening the case for religion. This potential may be detected in the writings of *libertins* such as *La Mothe le Vayer and anti-Aristotelian philosophers such as *Gassendi. *Descartes recognized the need to answer Pyrrhonism (which to some degree is represented in the figure of the 'malin génie'), as did *Pascal. Their discussions of this philosophy definitively altered the terms in which the debate about hyperbolic doubt was conducted. [IM]

See R. Popkin, *The History of Scepticism from Erasmus to Descartes* (1960).

Q

Quadrilogue invectif, Le, see CHARTIER.

Quartier Latin, Le. The Latin quarter or university quarter of Paris, on the right bank of the Seine in the 5th and 6th *arrondissements* [see p. xxvi].

Quart Livre, Le, by *Rabelais, see PANTAGRUEL AND GARGANTUA.

Quasimodo. The hunchback of Notre-Dame, the bell-ringer in Hugo's *Notre-Dame de Paris*.

Quatre Évangiles, Les, see ZOLA.

Quatre Fils Aymon, Les, see RENAUT DE MONTAUBAN.

QUATREMÈRE DE QUINCY, Antoine-Chrysostome (1755–1849). Academically trained French sculptor, archaeologist, writer on architectural theory and the fine arts. He is a striking example of the persistence of classical precepts, which, despite tentative modifications, he largely reiterated in *Essai sur la nature, le but et les moyens de l'imitation dans les beaux-arts* (1823). [BR]

Quatrevingt-treize. Victor *Hugo's last novel, published after his return from exile in 1874, inspired in part by the violence of the *Commune. Set in the counter-revolutionary *Vendée, its title recalls the year that marked the beginning of the Terror with the decapitation of the king. Written ostensibly to justify revolutionary violence, the plot abounds in ironies produced by the conflicting political ideologies and personal loyalties in which the main characters are caught: the marquis de Lantenac, Royalist and intransigent leader of the 'whites', gives himself up to save some Vendean children from a burning tower; Gauvain, nephew of Lantenac, returns with the Republican army to liberate his homeland and is condemned to death by his spiritual father, Cimourdain, for showing mercy towards the heroic Lantenac; Cimourdain, ex-priest and doctrinaire ideologue of the extreme Left, commits suicide after commanding his beloved Gauvain's death. Vividly described scenes, such as that of the captured children playing while the tower burns, point up the absurdity of war. Hugo's troubled family history—his father, a soldier in the Republican army, met his mother, a Vendean, during the Terror—adds an important psychological dimension to the novel.
[SN]

Quebec. Of all the nations of the French diaspora, Quebec offers the most courageous example of cultural survival [see also ACADIA]. Quebec has a cultural vitality which belies its tiny population (7 million, over 80 per cent French-speaking) and its precarious situation. It is one of ten provinces in the Canadian Confederation, and in spite of strong centralizing pressures has achieved a considerable degree of autonomy. The tension created by dissatisfaction with lack of sovereignty has proved stimulating. However, too extreme a nationalist reading of Quebec culture should be avoided.

1. Beginnings

The myth of origins is a powerful one in Quebec [for the settlement of the province, see COLONIZATION, I]. The three log-books of Jacques Cartier have been described by more than one writer as Canada's Genesis. The 'relation de voyage' is a distinct genre in North American literature, a work of inauguration, founding the land, naming peoples, places, and things, and by the act of naming appropriating them, conveying something of the fear, surprise, and passion the new land inspires. The literary monument of New France is the series of *Relations des *Jésuites* published in Paris from 1632 to 1673, works of propaganda for the mission to Canada. They transcribe letters from widely scattered outposts, describing fearlessly the hardships and the joys, and the martyrdom of several of the missionaries.

The mystical writings of Marie de l'Incarnation [see DEVOTIONAL WRITING, 2], founder of Quebec's Ursuline Convent, earned her the title 'Thérèse du Canada' from *Bossuet. The independent mind and encyclopedic curiosity of *La Hontan make him one of the most caustic observers of life in New France, and the spirited letters of the devout Élisabeth Begon reveal that, despite the clergy, winter in Montreal was a lively time. *Molière and *Corneille were performed in Quebec in the 17th c., the Jesuits opened a seminary there in 1663, and the Recollets had theirs in Ville-Marie (Montreal). The Ursulines educated the young ladies. There were libraries, one of 2,000 volumes. The Indians were troublesome, fire and disease also threatened life, but there was little of the famine that was common in France. The poverty of the feudal superiors (the seigneurial system was founded in 1634) made for a reasonably egalitarian society.

2. 1763–1900

By the Treaty of Paris, which concluded the *Seven Years War, New France was ceded to Britain in 1763, and French ceased to be an official language of the colony until 1848. Excluded from public life, the previously urban *Canadiens* retreated into a folk society of subsistence farmers. This rural people found its voice in the years between the Conquest of 1763 and the rebellion of 1837–8, through journalism, education, and the political movement for responsible government, which led to armed insurrection. Michel Bibaud (1782–1837) edited five of the literary journals of the early 1800s and published the first literary work to appear in French in North America, *Épîtres, satires, chansons, épigrammes et autres pièces de vers* (1830). His most spirited writing comes in his satires inspired by *Boileau denouncing the ignorance, superstition, and lack of taste of his compatriots. But he salutes with hope and enthusiasm the founding of five new classical *collèges*. Georges Boucher de Boucherville, author of *Une de perdue, deux de trouvées* (1864–5), Joseph Doutre, future president of the Institut Canadien de Montréal, with a long historical novel, *Les Fiancés de 1812* (1844), his poet friend Joseph Lenoir, Eugène l'Écuyer, author of *La Fille du brigand* (1844), and the Cornelian tragedy, *Le Jeune Latour* (1844) by Antoine Gérin-Lajoie, all point to the quality of the education dispensed by the Jesuits.

These young men were attracted by the radical Louis-Joseph Papineau, inspirer of the insurrection for political reform of 1837, by *Lammenais and the Romantics, and by the courage of the Institut Canadien (1844), which repeatedly refused to ban books proscribed by the Church. The rebellion finds an echo in some of the writing of the time. The first Canadian novel in French, *L'Influence d'un livre* (1837) by the younger Philippe *Aubert de Gaspé, a haunting reflection of the rebellion, presents itself as the 'premier roman de mœurs canadien' but is, in reality, a *roman noir* in the manner of *Sue or *Nodier. His father and co-author, an impoverished *seigneur*, twice wrote his memoirs, the first time in the form of a novel, *Les Anciens Canadiens* (1863). The troubles produced a gripping novella, *Le Rebelle* (1841) by the French baron de Trobriand, and some moving letters from the chevalier de Lorimier, one of a dozen patriots executed, besides the many exiled.

The year 1839 saw the publication of the Durham Report, a disparaging account of the insurrection of 1837. The response to this was to be the monumental *Histoire du Canada* (1845–8) by Francois-Xavier *Garneau, a work of great erudition and literary merit which sets out to revive the spirits of the *Canadiens* by recounting the courage of their ancestors. The other outstanding publication from the same period is James Huston's *Répertoire national* (1848–50), collecting the best in Canadian writing from the previous fifty years. This includes the complete novel *La Terre paternelle* (1846) by Patrice Lacombe, the prototype of the 'roman de la fidélité' which dominated the form for 100 years (the tradition was continued in 1874 and 1876 in the two volumes of Antoine Gérin-Lajoie's influential *Jean Rivard*). In 1863, meanwhile, Joseph-Charles Taché published his collection of the legends, place-names,

folk-songs, and tales associated with fur trade and lumber-camp, *Forestiers et voyageurs*. In this way, with Garneau, Huston, the Aubert de Gaspés, Lacombe, and Taché, the foundations of a national literature were soundly laid in the space of 20 years.

The buoyant liberalism of the historian Garneau, though greatly admired, did not set the tone in the 19th c., the second half of which was marked by the ultra-conservative Catholic revival associated with Pius IX, and the Church's domination of Quebec society, often felt by writers as highly oppressive, was to last until 1960 (see below, Section 5). Abbé Henri-Raymond Casgrain saw to it that literature became the servant of this crusading ideology. Only the stylish Arthur Buies (1840–1901) saw the advantage of the railways, the great 19th-c. adventure, for economic growth and French influence.

Nothing so far had prepared for the genius of Émile *Nelligan. Interested only in French literature at school, he devoured the poetry printed in the Montreal journals *Le Samedi* and *Le Monde illustré*. He was greeted with rapturous acclaim when he read his poems, brilliant pastiches of *Baudelaire and *Verlaine, at public meetings of the École Littéraire de Montréal. Laure Conan (Félicité Angers) surprised readers too, with *Angéline de Montbrun* (1882), the first French-Canadian psychological novel to give any depth to characters and any subtlety to plot and situation.

3. 1900–1945

Quebec's literature is a colonial literature. It responds belatedly to changes in fashion in France. The influence of the *Realists and *Naturalists, for example, was slow to appear. Rodolphe Girard's *Marie Calumet* (1904) was condemned by the Church for its crude satire. Albert *Laberge, unwilling to risk his career as a journalist, circulated privately his bitter portrait of rural life, *La Scouine*. Louis Hémon's celebration of the pioneering life, *Maria Chapdelaine* (1914), outdid the *Québécois* at their own game. Claude-Henri *Grignon rewrote the rural myth, with a miser for the central character of *Un homme et son péché* (1933), and *Ringuet produced in *Trente arpents* (1938) the outstanding *québécois* rural novel, a portrait of decline inspired by *Maupassant. Germaine *Guèvremont renewed the genre completely, giving it a woman's angle from the interior of the farmhouse, injecting life into the static rural community through *Le Survenant* (1945), while creating an authentic Canadian prose style.

Un homme et son péché became a popular radio series. Robert Choquette wrote for radio his *Pension Leblanc* (1927), mirroring the impact of urban sophistication on the timeless countryside, and went on to a career in television. Both media were greeted avidly by the *Québécois*, starved of excitement. Literature, the minority pursuit of doctors, lawyers, journalists, and priests, a largely week-end occupation, became just one aspect of a multi-media culture.

If radio fed the popular imagination, the academic world did the same for the élite, pilloried by Jean-Charles *Harvey as the *Demi-civilisés* (1934), a novel banned by the Church for its depiction of free love. In the same period two clerics, Lionel *Groulx and Camille Roy (author of a *Manuel d'histoire de la littérature canadienne-francaise*, 1920), both helped create a sense of identity and self-sufficiency strong enough to take responsibility for its own destiny. Journalism and the *prose d'idées* is a major genre in French Canada, and Groulx's *Action francaise* (1921–8, later *Action nationale*), sounding readers' opinion through a score of social surveys, begins to confront the myth of French Canada with some solid social observation. Quebec culture was stimulated by the increasingly numerous 'retours d'Europe' and European visitors. The journal *La Relève* was given encouragement by *Mounier and inspired by the visit of *Maritain.

The most important genre in the first half of the 20th c. is poetry. Albert Lozeau, confined to bed with Pott's Disease, produced a number of books of intimist verse, beginning with *L'Âme solitaire* (1907). Many poets were, like him, solitary and hypersensitive. Guy Delahaye (Guillaume Lahaise), who spent a year at the Institut Pasteur in Paris, has a fine sense of the 'mensonge du cœur'. Jean-Aubert Loranger, who read 'retour d'Europe' and who had read the *NRF* of *Paulhan and *Éluard, found it hard to readjust: 'Ouvre cette porte où je pleure.'

Hector de *Saint-Denys Garneau, however, fled from the oppressive weight of France's high culture after only three weeks. He marks an important new departure for Quebec. Hitherto, writers had belonged exclusively to the educated and leisured middle-class. Theirs was the intellectual world of *Mauriac, *Gilson, and Maritain as purveyed second-hand by *Le Devoir* and the *Relations dominicaines*. Garneau was from the same milieu as these writers, and was conscious of his descent from the family of Francois-Xavier Garneau; he differed from them, however, in his intense commitment to the world of art and of the spirit.

François Hertel's *Leur Inquiétude* (1936), Rex Desmarchais's *La Chesnaie* (1942), and much later André Laurendeau's *Une vie d'enfer* (1965) catch the ideological turmoil and the spiritual malaise of this culture, out of step with its official image. Meanwhile the historical novel was glorifying the heroic age of Canada's pioneers (e.g. Léo-Paul *Desrosiers, *Nord–Sud*, 1931). For the critic Jacques Blais, however, the two outstanding works of the late 1930s are Saint-Denys Garneau's *Regards et jeux dans l'espace* and Félix-Antoine *Savard's prose epic *Menaud Maître-draveur*, both of 1937, the latter a parable pointing to the alarming influence of American capital and predatory life-style.

4. 1945–1960

Quebec was ripe for modernity when in 1948 *Borduas and his group published their Surrealist manifesto *Refus global*. It begins with a brief history of Quebec's spiritual deformity. The Church, says Borduas, maintained the French Canadians in a state of fear, in ignorance of international currents of thought, condemned to perpetual inferiority. There seemed no hope of escape from this spiritual blockade, but foreign wars and the salutary influence of certain 'poètes maudits' (*Lautréamont and *Rimbaud, no doubt, but also Nelligan and Garneau) brought the unhoped-for release. New publishing houses not tied to clerical censorship, the Éditions Erta (1949), the Éditions de l'Hexagone (1953), and journals such as *Cité libre* (1951) and *Liberté* (1959) and the intellectual journalism of André Laurendeau in *Le Devoir*, created a plurality of voices in opposition to the oppressive regime of premier Maurice Duplessis. A series of strikes in the 1950s and the lessons in democracy learnt by the trade-union movement gave depth to this opposition.

The post-war novel has a decidedly new look, not in its technique, which remains wedded to realism, but in its subject-matter, tone, and ambition. Gabrielle *Roy's *Bonheur d'occasion* (1945; Prix Fémina, 1947) and Roger *Lemelin's *Au pied de la pente douce* (1944) present powerful social frescos with the accent on the poverty and lack of social opportunity in the working-class suburbs of Montreal and Quebec. Jean-Jules Richard uses the war and the asbestos strike of 1949 (a turning-point in the history of Quebec) as the backdrop to his angry *Neuf jours de haine* (1948) and *Ville rouge* (1949). André *Langevin's tryptich, *Évadés de la nuit* (1951), *Poussière sur la ville* (1953), and *Le Temps des hommes* (1956), sounds the first stirrings of revolt. Alienation is the theme, too, of the prose writings of poet Anne *Hébert. 'J'étais un enfant dépossédé du monde', the first line of *Le Torrent* (1950), sets the tone of the 1950s.

5. The 'Révolution Tranquille'

Gaston *Miron and his friends founded Les Éditions de L'Hexagone in 1953 with an avowed policy of national action through publishing. He was one of the first to recognize the significance of *Refus global*. Miron believes that Quebec poetry has a hidden genealogy. He admires authentic Quebec poets such as Alfred Desrochers, author of *A l'ombre de l'Orford* (1930). His own gritty, awkward, heroic verse is the best writing Quebec has produced, slim though his production is. The generation of the Hexagone begins to offer signs of the camaraderie which characterizes the artistic exploration of the 1960s. Movements such as the group associated with *Parti pris, a left-wing journal and publishing house which issued Paul Chamberland's Ginsberg-like *L'Afficheur hurle* (1965), Jacques Renaud's fierce short stories in *Le Cassé* (1964), and Pierre Vallière's *Nègres blancs d'Amérique* (1968), are all symptoms of the transformation which followed the death of Maurice Duplessis in 1959.

Quebec

In the 'Révolution Tranquille', the Catholic Church rapidly lost its influence in politics, sold off its stake in education, and saw a rapid decline in vocations and in church-going. The contraceptive pill started a sexual revolution fuelled by American counter-culture. The Liberal governments (1960–6) created a Ministry of Education, a Ministry of Cultural Affairs, and a Société Générale de Financement to stimulate investment, reform the civil service, and nationalize Quebec's vast hydro-electric industry. This latter was carried through by René Lévesque, a popular television presenter, journalist, and trade-unionist, who became one of the most charismatic of Quebec's leaders in the 1960s and 1970s. The Federal Inquiry into Bilingualism and Biculturalism, dreamed up by André Laurendeau, became a national forum on the twin cultures of Canada, their coexistence, and the future of a distinct French identity. The democratization of education, the egalitarianism of hippy culture, and the quest for identity and authenticity which mark post-war *Existentialism led to experiments in *joual, literature written in the vernacular. More successful was the poetry of popular *hargne* in the writing of Gérald *Godin, *Les Cantouques* (1967): 'ouatche-toe stun crisse un tabarnaque' (i.e. 'watch out, he's a real so-and-so', the words 'crisse'and 'tabarnaque' being deformations of 'Christ' and 'tabernacle'). Like Miron, he showed that *joual* is a marvellous 'langue à sacres' (*sacrer* is *québécois* for 'to swear'). The political reforms introduced by the Liberals were rapidly overtaken on the Left by the student uprising of 1968 and the serious terrorism of the Front de Libération du Québec, culminating in the October crisis of 1970.

The most brilliant expression of the anger and turmoil of the 1960s comes in the fiction of Hubert *Aquin. The schizophrenia which drove him to suicide in 1975 does not mask the playfulness and the profound but oblique commentary on Quebec's situation offered by *Prochain épisode* (1965), *Trou de mémoire* (1968), and *L'Antiphonaire* (1969). If the Quebec writer was silenced by aphasia, the *chansonniers* (Félix Leclerc, Gilles *Vigneault, Pauline Julien, Monique Leyrac, Robert Charlebois, Diane Dufresne, Clémence Desrochers) were not only teaching Canada to sing its exuberance but were leading the international 'Francofête'.

Literature reflected the quest for independence. Michèle *Lalonde's 'Speak White' (1968) is a strident denunciation of the oppressive superiority of the language and culture of Shakespeare. Meanwhile, there were those whose commitment to art sat uneasily with any ideology. The *Liberté* group (led by the poet Jean-Guy Pilon) was suspicious of the parochial culture of French Canada and was always open to international influences through its 'rencontres d'écrivains'. The dominant theme of the 1960s is a disincarnated patriotism. The theme of the *pays* takes highly personal forms in the work of Roland *Giguère, poet of *L'Âge de la parole*, Yves

Préfontaine, creating a poetry of the Northlands, Paul-Marie *Lapointe, turning a Federal guide to the trees of Canada and Frère Marie-Victorin's *Flore laurentienne* (1935) into an ambitious celebration, Jacques *Godbout, film-maker and entrepreneur, publishing in Paris his sardonic fables *Salut Galarneau!* (1967), *D'Amour, P. Q.* (1972), and questioning the viability of Quebec culture in a monopolistic market.

There is something bleak and haunting about the Quebec psyche: witness first novels such as *La Fille laide* (Yves *Thériault, 1950), *La Belle Bête* (Marie-Claire *Blais, 1959), and *L'Avalée des avalés* (Réjean *Ducharme, 1966). The world of ugliness and Gothic horror is not rare. In a different dark vein, Gilbert *Laroque (*Après la boue*, 1972; *Serge d'entre les morts*, 1976) and Victor-Lévy *Beaulieu (*Jos Connaissant*, 1970) fictionalize brilliant, sordid fantasies, and Michel *Tremblay tenderly re-creates the grim family world of his plays in his novels of the 'Plateau Mont-Royal' chronicle. Claude *Jasmin vainly searches for a refuge from life in *La Corde au cou* (1960) and *Ethel et le terroriste* (1964). His *La Sablière* (1979) more serenely portrays the wonder of childhood, as do Antonine *Maillet, from *On a mangé la dune* (1962) to *L'Oursiade* (1990), and Jacques *Ferron in *l'Amélanchier* (1970), half-playful, half-polemical, quietly scornful of the 'mythe de la race'.

6. Since 1970

Two political events mark the 1970s and 1980s. In 1976 Quebec elected a Parti Québécois government which promptly acted to defend French language and education. The euphoria this generated released writers from the nagging feeling of being conscripts in a cultural battle, compelled to contribute their page to a corporate national text. The writer was now free to create, a freedom often strange and frightening. And then, in 1980, the 'yes' faction in a referendum on national sovereignty could only muster 40 per cent of the vote. This was not so much Quebec giving Canada a last chance, an offer Canada subsequently declined, as a failure of nerve by a nation asked to take the plunge. These events have produced a grave disarray, a cultural pluralism defying analysis.

The women's movement has burst upon the literary scene, triumphantly self-assured in an age of uncertainty. It has displayed great tenderness, wit, and sophistication in its handling of the many issues of feminism: the rewriting of sexist history, language, and mythology. Louky *Bersianik in *L'Euguélionne* (1976) has produced a women's bible; Madeleine *Gagnon has explored the psychology of the matriarchal heritage; Nicole *Brossard has renewed the language and the tools of fiction through her own writing and through the lead she has given in the journals *La Barre du jour* and *La Nouvelle BDJ*.

The feminist movement has also been strong in the theatre, where women's groups have participated enthusiastically in the innovatory forms of drama which have been one of the features of the 1980s and 1990s. This new theatre combines music, dance, mime, and movement to produce a dramatic form in which speech is only one of many expressive elements. Having no author in the conventional sense, and no published text, such productions are often the collective creation of the actors themselves. But they can often be attributed also to the individual talent of their artistic director, who has total control over all the elements of the work. Many of the outstanding dramatic events of recent times have been due to this new breed of theatrical personality working in concert with companies devoted to innovation. Such is the case of Gilles Maheu and Carbone 14 with *Le Rail* (1985) and *Le Dortoir* (1989); of J. P. Ronfard and NTE with *Vie et mort du roi boiteux* (1982); and Robert Lepage and Théâtre Répère with *La Trilogie du dragon* (1985), among many others. Lepage, indeed, has become a peripatetic international star, carrying his spectacular exercises in stagecraft into guest productions in London, Paris, New York, and elsewhere. This emphasis on ensemble production, however, does not spell the demise of the individual author. On the contrary, writers like Marie Laberge (*Aurélie, ma sœur*, 1988), René-Daniel Dubois (*Being at home with Claude*, 1985), Normand Chaurette (*Provincetown Playhouse, juillet 1919, j'avais 19 ans*, 1981), and Michel Marc Bouchard (*Les Feluettes*, 1989) constitute a new theatrical avant-garde worthy of their great predecessor Tremblay.

With such a surge of dramatic talent, and an equally strong profile in other areas such as ballet and modern dance, illustrated by companies like Là là là Human Steps and O Vertigo, Quebec has emerged as one of the leading nations in the performing arts. A significant achievement in cinema should not be forgotten either, although volume film-making in Quebec did not begin until the 1960s. Following the international successes in the 1970s of Claude Jutra (*Mon oncle Antoine*, 1971), Jean Beaudin (*J. A. Martin Photographe*, 1976), and Francis Manckiewicz (*Les Bons Débarras*, 1979), critical acclaim and commercial success have come more easily to increasing numbers of film-makers. Particularly notable are Denys Arcand (*Le Déclin de l'empire américain*, 1986; *Jésus de Montréal*, 1989), Léa Pool (*La Femme de l'hôtel*, 1984), and Jean-Claude Lauzon (*Un zoo la nuit*, 1987).

Altogether, despite the difficulties of Quebec's constitutional position within Canada and the deflating effect of the referendum result, literature and the arts have never been more flourishing than in the 1980s and 1990s. While this is essentially a spontaneous, self-generating phenomenon, it has been greatly boosted by generous government funding for every form of culture. Governments of all persuasions have seen the promotion of a strong *québécois* culture as fundamental for preserving Quebec's identity as a French-speaking nation in

North America. The results have certainly justified the investment.   [CRPM with SIL]

See L. Mailhot, *La Littérature québécoise*, 2nd edn. (1975); W. Toye (ed.), *The Oxford Companion to Canadian Literature* (1983); G. Vincenthier, *Histoire des idées au Québec* (1983); L. Gauvin and G. Miron, *Écrivains contemporains du Québec* (1989).

QUEFFÉLEC, Henri (1910–92). Novelist. His realistic fiction—*Tempête sur Douarnenez* (1951), *Un homme d'Ouessant* (1953), *Un royaume sous la mer* (1957)—celebrates his native Finistère, its wild sea-coast, its fishermen, and, as in *Un recteur de l'Île de Sein* (1944) which brought him fame, its fishers of men, for his maritime Celtic spirit is fused with Catholicism. A contributor to Mounier's *Esprit, he later concerned himself with environmental issues—*Quand la terre fait naufrage* (1965)—and published his autobiography, *Un Breton bien tranquille*, in 1978.   [DAS]

QUEFFÉLEC, Yann (b. 1949). Novelist and literary journalist, son of Henri. Among his novels are *Les Noces barbares* (1985, Prix Goncourt), a harrowing story of a child born after the multiple rape of his mother, *Le Maître des chimères* (1990), about the sordid inadequacies of an anti-hero, his self-deceit, self-destruction, and final salvation by an act of suicidal heroism, and *Prends garde au loup* (1992), which relates a child's desperate love for his cousin and his discovery of a hostile world. Queffelec's writing is always energetic and psychologically sharp.   [PS]

Que ma joie demeure, see GIONO.

QUENEAU, Raymond (1903–76). French poet, novelist, and essayist, and persistent rejector of the rigid separation of these categories. Queneau was early associated with *Breton and the *Surrealist group, collaborating in *La Révolution surréaliste* from 1924 onwards, but he broke definitively with them in 1929; his military service in the 3e Zouaves, which took him to Morocco (1925–7), together with his early years spent in Le Havre, probably had a more profound influence on him. Three early prose works, *Les Derniers Jours* (1936), *Odile* (1937), and *Les Enfants du limon* (1938), together with the verse novel *Chêne et chien* (1937), settle his accounts with childhood and psychoanalysis, thereafter leaving the writer free to invent and to innovate as few others have done.

It was above all in the field of language that Queneau found the challenge that inspired much of his work. By 1930 he was increasingly focusing on the problem of the nature of written French, which he saw as largely static in its vocabulary and syntax since the grammarians of the 17th c. had codified and policed the language of Renaissance France, and *Voltaire and his contemporaries had made of it the instrument of rational clarity. The literary instrument, however, bore little resemblance to the language spoken in everyday life; Queneau's military experience had driven that home to him, but it was his trip to Greece (where he spent July to September 1932 and composed the greater part of Le *Chiendent) which crystallized his views. He came to see the French language as threatened by the same radical schism which had split the literary and demotic forms of Greek—Le Voyage en Grèce (1973) gives details. His experiments with the transcription of the spoken tongue (what he was to call 'le néo-français') as a medium suitable for any form of literary expression make of him one of the most interesting stylists of the century, but his importance far exceeds that. If such experimentation led him early in the direction of a literature that is at the same time richly comic and a densely observed portrait of modern urban life, especially among the lower classes, it is also true to say of his works that they are able to combine a Joycean richness of texture with a whimsy worthy of Lewis Carroll; both Joyce and Carroll were important influences on his work.

Queneau's constantly experimental approach to literary form led him to found, with the mathematician François Le Lionnais, the Ouvroir de Littérature Potentielle (*OULIPO) in 1960. As with Exercices de style, which tells the same anecdote 99 different ways, ranging from 'latinate' to 'javanais' [see ARGOT], the task set themselves by Queneau and other OULIPO authors was to produce works obeying strict mathematical rules of composition. These are sometimes applied to the transformation of existing works, or simply words, sayings, etc. Perhaps the most remarkable of these is Queneau's own Cent mille milliards de poèmes, a collection of 10 sonnets composed on the same rhyme scheme and grammatical structure, originally published in a form allowing each line to be turned individually. It therefore becomes a machine capable of generating 10^{14} poems—substantially more than any single human lifetime could encompass.

Queneau's erudition, his pleasure in the arcane—he was editor of the Encyclopédie de la Pléiade [see ENCYCLOPEDIAS]—and his fascination with the banal make the characteristic tenor of all his work the always astonishing juxtaposition of high and low, of grand ideas and ordinary, even droll, words. In the same way, he refused to think of literary forms as rigid, while holding strictly to the notion that formal qualities are the essence of art, and typically professed his intention to 'faire du roman une sorte de poème.'

His best-known works in prose are Le Chiendent (1933), Pierrot mon ami (1942), Loin de Rueil (1944), Exercices de style (1947), *Zazie dans le métro (1959), and Les Fleurs bleues (1965); while his poems, from Les Ziaux (1943) to Fendre les flots (1969), have found, though rather more slowly, an appreciative audience, many of them, perhaps, beginning from Juliette *Greco's recording of his 'Si tu t'imagines', a demotic and barbed rendering of the carpe diem theme.   [IWR]

See J. Quéval, Raymond Queneau (1971); C. Shorley, Raymond Queneau (1985).

QUÉRARD, Joseph-Marie (1797–1865). French bibliographer; as well as the 10-volume La France littéraire (1827–39, supplements 1854, 1864), he published bibliographies of *hoaxes and anonymous writings (Les Supercheries dévoilées, 5 vols., 1845–56).

Querelle des Anciens et des Modernes, La. Rather than a pitched battle, this was a long series of skirmishes between two camps, from the mid-17th c. until about 1715. It was a far from straightforward affair, and some of the positions adopted seem paradoxical to modern readers. For the anciens, the classics of antiquity remained worthy of admiration and imitation; this did not imply slavish copying, but continuing an old tradition which had been revitalized at the *Renaissance. The modernes, even if they were not Cartesians, shared with *Descartes a sceptical attitude to tradition and favoured the creation of a distinctively modern French culture, whether in philosophy, literature, or the arts. In many cases they set modern Christianity against the errors of paganism. There was also a political aspect to the quarrel, though this was complex. Both sides expressed their devotion to the monarchy, but in general the anciens were closer to the official power of *Versailles, whereas their enemies were identified with the world of Paris, the précieux salons [see PRECIOSITY], and the *Mercure galant:

While the origins of the Querelle go back to *Richelieu's cultural policy, and indeed to the Renaissance, the first real hostilities date from the 1660s. They are mainly concerned with *epic poetry: *Marolles, Louis Le Laboureur (author of Charlemagne, 1664), and *Desmarets defended the modern Christian epic in which pagan mythological figures were replaced by angels and demons. At about the same time Le Laboureur and Desmarets both compared French with the ancient languages to the advantage of the former, and praised modern poetry above that of the ancients. The 1670s saw a vigorous polemic over the use of Latin or French for public inscriptions, *Charpentier defending the French cause. One of the centres of opposition to moderne views was the *Lamoignon academy, with figures including *Fleury, *Rapin, *Pellisson, *Bossuet, and above all *Boileau, who was to remain the chief champion of the anciens until the end of his life. His Art poétique (1674) and his translation of Longinus' treatise on the Sublime express the views of the Lamoignon circle, their advocacy of grand simplicity, and their hostility to modern frivolity—which they often associated with the women-dominated salons. In the mid-1670s Boileau, *Racine, and (somewhat ambiguously) *La Fontaine were grouped together as 'Messieurs du Sublime', supported by such powerful figures as *Condé, *La Rochefoucauld, and Madame de *Montespan. Subsequently *La Bruyère became an important supporter of the ancien cause.

The central episode in the quarrel was sparked off by *Perrault's reading of his moderne poem Le Siècle *de Louis XIV* at the *Académie Française in 1687. This aroused Boileau's indignation, and Perrault added fuel to the fire with his long and provocative *Parallèle des anciens et des modernes* (1688–97). Boileau replied in his *Réflexions critiques*, and eventually *Arnauld effected a somewhat fragile reconciliation between the two enemies. The quarrel mainly concerned literature; in his *Digression sur les anciens et les modernes* (1688) *Fontenelle widened the debate by arguing that, while human capacities remained the same through the ages, intellectual progress meant that in scientific matters the moderns inevitably surpassed the ancients.

A trivial postscript to this debate was provided by the 'querelle d'Homère', when Madame *Dacier took exception to *La Motte's adaptation of the *Iliad*. Montesquieu refers mockingly to this polemic in his *Lettres persanes* (letter 36). And indeed the whole of the Querelle may be viewed as an ephemeral squabble between literary factions. It is also, however, a symptom of much more important cultural change, the decline of classical learning [see LATINITY], the rise of modern philosophy and science, and the triumph of the spirit of criticism. In a sense, the *modernes* are the precursors of the *Enlightenment, and they may be seen to have won the battle in the long term. On the other hand, it was the *anciens* who imposed themselves as the great classic writers of 17th-c. France; it was they who most influenced the canon of French literature and succeeded in overshadowing the many achievements of their rivals. [PF]

See A. Adam, *Histoire de la littérature française du XVIIe siècle*, vols. 3 (1952) and 5 (1956); B. Magne, *Crise de la littérature sous Louis XIV: humanisme et nationalisme* (1976).

Querelle des Bouffons, La, see GUERRE DES BOUFFONS.

Querelle des Femmes, La. In its narrow sense, this term refers to a genre of writing in Latin and French in which the superiority of one or the other sex is proposed. The earliest examples are found *c.*1200, and the genre as such declined markedly after 1650. It attracted few prominent writers, and was largely governed by the rules of demonstrative rhetoric. In arguing the case for or against the superiority of women, writers may employ exclusively historical examples, as does Boccaccio's *De claris mulieribus* (composed 1360–74; translated several times into French), which is the prototype for many subsequent catalogues of famous women; or they may combine example with the rehearsal of theological, legal, and medical 'proofs' of excellence and with agreement from authority in the form of quotations from the ancients, the Bible, and the Church Fathers. The most accomplished and influential example of the latter type is Cornelius Agrippa's *De nobilitate et praecellentia foeminei sexus* (composed in 1509, published in 1529; translated into French in 1530).

From its beginnings, the Querelle is associated with clerical misogyny and misogamy, and many of its most notable contributions were written by clerics. It is also linked to female literary patronage and literary production, as in the cases of *Christine de Pizan, Boccaccio, Agrippa, *Marguerite de Navarre, Marie de *Romieu (1581), Marie de *Gournay, and Jacquette Guillaume (1668).

Throughout the 16th and early 17th c. there was a steady stream of contributions to the debate, the most notable being those produced by Gratien du Pont (1534), François de Billon (1553), Jean de Marconville (1564), and Alexis Trousset, alias Jacques Olivier, whose infamous but highly successful *Alphabet de l'imperfection et malice des femmes* (1617) reproduces in expanded form an alphabet of female vices composed by a 15th-c. Florentine archbishop. One of those to reply to Trousset was Marie de Gournay, whose *Égalité des hommes et des femmes* (1622) marks the shift of interest from rhetorical argument to the practical question of female education. This issue arises again in the exchange of letters between Rivet and Anna Maria van Schurman, published in Latin in 1638 and in French in 1646, and is central to the various feminist works of *Poulain de la Barre (1673–5), which are inspired by a Cartesian approach and mark the end of the Querelle des Femmes as such.

In the broader sense, the Querelle des Femmes encompasses all writing in which the relative merits of the sexes are discussed using arguments and material drawn from the more narrowly defined debate. Thus, the Querelle has been traced in the anti-feminist opinions expressed in *Jean de Meun's contribution to the *Roman de la Rose*, opposed by Martin *Lefranc's *Le Champion des dames* (1442); in the works of *Rabelais, notably in the academic debate about the nature of women and marriage which takes place in Chapters 29–36 of the *Tiers Livre*; in the *Heptaméron* of Marguerite de Navarre, especially in the discussion of Christian marriage; in the *Neoplatonist debate about the court lady between the poets Bertrand de *la Borderie, Charles Fontaine, and Antoine *Héroët (1541–2); in *Desportes's misogynist 'Stances du mariage' of 1571, which provoke a number of defences of women and marriage up to the end of the 16th c.; finally, in the opinions and arguments of some of *Molière's *barbons, notably Arnolphe in *L'*École des femmes* (1662). [See also FEMINISM; PRECIOSITY.] [IM]

See M. Angenot, *Les Champions des femmes* (1977); I. Maclean, *Woman Triumphant* (1977).

QUESNAY, François (1694–1774). French doctor and economist. Protected by Madame de *Pompadour and Louis XV, he was the leading spirit of the *Physiocrats, expounding the theories of the movement in the influential *Encyclopédie articles 'Grains', 'Fermiers', and 'Évidence', in his *Tableau économique* (1758), and in other writings published by *Dupont de Nemours in *Physiocratie* (1768). He is credited with the famous free-trade motto: 'Laissez faire, laissez passer.' [PF]

QUESNEL, Pasquier (1634–1719). French religious writer, originally an *Oratorian. His belief in Augustinian efficacious grace and his moral rigorism resulted in strong *Jansenist sympathies, which led to his banishment from Paris (1681) and his expulsion from the Oratoire (1684). Fearing persecution, he fled to Brussels, where he joined Antoine *Arnauld. On Arnauld's death (1694) he became leader of the Jansenist movement. He defended a scholarly approach to the Scriptures and held *Richerist views. His *Nouveau Testament en français avec des réflexions morales sur chaque verset* (1692) had been appearing in various forms since 1672. It became a central Jansenist text, and the papal bull *Unigenitus* (1713) condemned 101 sentences from it. [JC]

Qu'est-ce que la littérature? Immensely influential essay by *Sartre, first published in *Les *Temps modernes* in 1947 [see ENGAGEMENT].

Qu'est-ce que la propriété?, see PROUDHON.

Qu'est-ce que le Tiers État? Revolutionary pamphlet by *Siéyès.

Queste del Saint Graal, La, see GRAIL ROMANCES; LANCELOT ROMANCES.

Quietism. A tendency within mystical theology that commends the soul's self-abandoning acceptance of whatever God sends ('pure love'), and values silent contemplation above petitionary prayer. Discernible in the Renaissance Spanish mystics and elaborated by Miguel Molinos (1640–96), its promotion by Madame *Guyon led to a famous quarrel between *Fénelon, who defended her, and *Bossuet, who feared its potential for moral indifference and passive emotionalism. The effect of its condemnation by the papal brief *Cum alias* (1699) was to render all forms of mysticism suspect in the 18th-c. French Church; but German Pietism and British Methodism were to some extent its spiritual heirs. [PJB]

Quiet Revolution, The (La Révolution Tranquille), see QUEBEC, 5.

QUIGNARD, Pascal (b. 1948). French author of elaborate, often erudite texts, including novels such as *Carus* (1979) and critical essays on such topics as *Scève, *Deguy, and recondite areas of Latin literature (*Petits traités*, 1990).

QUINAULT, Philippe (1635–88). French dramatist. Although pilloried in *Boileau's *Satires*, he catered very successfully for the tastes of his society. The son of a Paris baker, he became, thanks to his plays, a member of the Académie Française (1670) and an *auditeur des comptes* (1671). *La Comédie sans comédie* (1654), a play-within-a-play, offers a show-case of different genres; between 1653 and 1671 the versatile Quinault wrote four comedies, seven tragicomedies, and five tragedies. Thereafter he devoted himself to writing libretti for *Lully's operas; in return for handsome payment, he produced one play a year, working closely with the composer and revising the text to meet his demands.

'Jusqu'à "je vous hais" tout s'y dit tendrement', wrote Boileau of Quinault's most successful tragedy, *Astrate* (1665). Love is indeed his great theme, but it is treated in several modes. *La Mère coquette* (1665), his best comedy, combines the usual matrimonial plot with satire against an ageing lady. His tragicomedies (e.g. *Stratonice*, 1660) reflect the idealized world of the *roman héroïque*, with complex plots and happy endings. Some of his tragedies also end well, with villains punished and virtuous couples rewarded, but *Astrate* and *Pausanias* (1666) both end in disaster for the lovers. Quinault's weak point is the monotony and prolixity of his verse. This no longer matters in the libretti; these texts, taken first from Greek mythology (e.g. *Alceste*, 1674; *Phaëton*, 1683) and then from the Middle Ages (e.g. *Roland*, 1683; *Armide*, 1686), combined admirably with the music, dance, and spectacle of the opera, offering Louis XIV's contemporaries the mixed pleasures of amorous fairy-tale and improving allegory. [PF]

Quincampoix, Rue. Street in Paris where John *Law established his ill-fated bank in 1716.

QUINET, Edgar (1803–75). French poet, historian, critic, and politician. Quinet's central interest lay in the meaning of history and the role which religion played in the unfolding of events. As a young man he was influenced by German philosophy and published a translation of Herder (1827–8). In 1833 he brought out an epic poem, *Ahasvérus*, in which the Wandering Jew symbolized mankind's anguished striving for the Absolute throughout history [see JUIF ERRANT]. In 1842 appeared *Le Génie des religions*, which argued that every society was the outgrowth of a religious idea. However, this did not make Quinet an ally of the Church; his view was that the religious principle realizing itself in history took the form of freedom and individuality.

He was appointed in 1842 to the *Collège de France; his lectures, together with those of his friend *Michelet, became political acts, the focus for opposition to the Catholic Church (*Les Jésuites*, 1843) and the spark for political discontent. He was elected to parliament during the Second Republic but fled into exile after the coup of 1851. Thereafter he produced works of the imagination (*Merlin l'enchanteur*, 1860), natural history (*La Création*, 1870), and a controversial critical reassessment of 1789 (*La Révolution*, 1865), on which his present reputation rests. [CC]

Quinze Joies de mariage, Les (late 14th/early 15th c.). This anonymous treatise—perhaps the work of a provincial cleric or lawyer—is structured around the devout *Quinze Joies de Nostre Dame*, and purports to warn the young man against the *nasse* (net) of marriage. He may experience a short-lived happiness, but soon his wife's demands will lead to financial difficulties and domestic strife, 'et finera miserablement ses jours'.

The work thus fits into a long tradition of medieval misogyny, but with a discretion and lightness of touch which attach it rather to the short story than to the dour diatribes of St Jerome or Eustache *Deschamps. Paradoxically, the writer's prime target is the sheer stupidity of the husband, his invincible gullibility and good nature. The *Joies* trace a 'typical' marriage via 'typical' husband and wife (the writer insists that both are representative)—courtship, the birth of the first child, the wife's inevitable infidelities, the husband's eventual abjection—to an extent which might suggest the history of a particular marriage. Each *joie* dramatizes a particular confrontation between husband and wife, couched in lively dialogue and set in a detailed *mise en scène* which relates the message to everyday preoccupations. Yet the writer accepts that he will be ignored—and indeed his epilogue invites the reader to see the *Quinze Joies* as merely ludic: he could write another treatise detailing the 'griefz et oppressions que les hommes font aux femmes'. [JHMT]

Qui se souvient de la mer, see DIB.

Quotations. This entry aims to dispel some uncertainties by identifying a few frequently encountered brief quotations from literary works. Drawn mostly from the classics of French literature, it inevitably has something of a '1066 and All That' feel about it. It does not include *obiter dicta* such as 'Qu'ils mangent de la brioche' (*Marie-Antoinette) or 'Messieurs les Anglais, tirez les premiers' [see FONTENOY]:

A la fin tu es las de ce monde ancien (Apollinaire, 'Zone')

Anne, ma sœur Anne, ne vois-tu rien venir? (Perrault, 'La Barbe Bleue')

A nous deux maintenant! (Balzac, *Le Père Goriot*)

Aujourd'hui maman est morte. Ou peut-être hier, je ne sais pas (Camus, *L'Étranger*)

Ce que l'on conçoit bien s'énonce clairement (Boileau, *Art poétique*)

C'est Vénus tout entière à sa proie attachée (Racine, *Phèdre*)

Chaque homme porte la forme entière de l'humaine condition (Montaigne, *Essais*, III, 2)

Comment peut-on être Persan? (Montesquieu, *Lettres persanes*)

Cueillez dès aujourd'hui les roses de la vie (Ronsard, *Sonnets pour Hélène*)

Dans ce pays-ci il est bon de tuer de temps en temps un amiral pour encourager les autres (Voltaire, *Candide*)

Dans un mois, dans un an, comment souffrirons-nous,
Seigneur, que tant de mers me séparent de vous?
(Racine, *Bérénice*)

Debout, les damnés de la terre! (Pottier, 'L'Internationale')

De la musique avant toute chose! (Verlaine, 'Art poétique')

Dieu! que le son du Cor est triste au fond des bois! (Vigny, 'Le Cor')

Donner un sens plus pur aux mots de la tribu (Mallarmé, 'Tombeau d'Edgar Poe')

Elle est retrouvée.
Quoi?—L'Éternité.
C'est la mer allée
Avec le soleil.
(Rimbaud, *Derniers vers*)

Emma retrouvait dans l'adultère toutes les platitudes du mariage (Flaubert, *Madame Bovary*)

Enfin Malherbe vint, et le premier en France,
Fit sentir dans les vers une juste cadence
(Boileau, *Art poétique*)

Et rose, elle a vécu ce que vivent les roses,
L'espace d'un matin
(Malherbe, 'Consolation à M. du Périer')

Et tout le reste est littérature (Verlaine, 'Art poétique')

Fais ce que voudras (Rabelais, *Gargantua*)

Familles! je vous hais! (Gide, *Les Nourritures terrestres*)

France, mère des arts, des armes, et des lois (Du Bellay, *Les Regrets*)

Frères humains, qui après nous vivez,
N'ayez les cœurs contre nous endurcis.
(Villon, 'Ballade des pendus')

Halt sunt li pui e li val tenebrus (*La Chanson de Roland*)

Heureux qui, comme Ulysse, a fait un beau voyage (Du Bellay, *Les Regrets*)

Hypocrite lecteur,—mon semblable,—mon frère! (Baudelaire, *Les Fleurs du mal*)

Il faut cultiver notre jardin (Voltaire, *Candide*)

Il faut imaginer Sisyphe heureux (Camus, *Le Mythe de Sisyphe*)

Quotations

Il pleure dans mon cœur
Comme il pleut sur la ville.
(Verlaine, *Romances sans paroles*)

J'accuse (Zola, title of article in *L'Aurore*)

J'aime la majesté des souffrances humaines (Vigny, 'La Maison du berger')

J'ai vu se préparer la fête de la Nuit à la fuite du jour.
Je proclame la Nuit plus véridique que le jour
(Senghor, *Éthiopiques*)

JE est un autre (Rimbaud, 'Lettre du voyant')

Je le ferais encor, si j'avais à le faire (Corneille, *Le Cid*)

Je pense, donc je suis (Descartes, *Discours de la méthode*)

Je suis comme je suis
Je suis faite comme ça.
(Prévert, *Paroles*)

Je suis le ténébreux,—le veuf,—l'inconsolé,
Le Prince d'Aquitaine à la tour aboli.
(Nerval, 'El Desdichado')

La beauté sera CONVULSIVE ou ne sera pas (Breton, *Nadja*)

La chair est triste, hélas! et j'ai lu tous les livres (Mallarmé, 'Brise marine')

L'amour-propre est le plus grand de tous les flatteurs (La Rochefoucauld, *Maximes*)

La politique au milieu des intérêts d'imagination, c'est un coup de pistolet au milieu d'un concert (Stendhal, *Le Rouge et le noir*)

La propriété . . . c'est le vol! (Proudhon, *Qu'est-ce que la propriété?*)

La raison du plus fort est toujours la meilleure (La Fontaine, 'Le Loup et l'agneau')

La terre est bleue comme une orange (Éluard, *L'Amour la poésie*)

Le bon sens est la chose du monde la mieux partagée (Descartes, *Discours de la méthode*)

Le cœur a ses raisons que la raison ne connaît point (Pascal, *Pensées*)

Le jour n'est pas plus pur que le fond de mon cœur (Racine, *Phèdre*)

Le nez de Cléopâtre, s'il eût été plus court, toute la face de la terre aurait changé (Pascal, *Pensées*)

L'enfer, c'est les autres (Sartre, *Huis clos*)

Les gueux se réconcilient à la gamelle (Diderot, *Le Neveu de Rameau*)

Le silence éternel de ces espaces infinis m'effraie (Pascal, *Pensées*)

Le temps s'en va, le temps s'en va, ma Dame,
Las! le temps non, mais nous nous en allons
(Ronsard, *Amours de Marie*)

Le vice et la vertu sont des produits comme le vitriol et le sucre (Taine, *Histoire de la littérature anglaise*)

L'homme est né libre, et partout il est dans les fers (Rousseau, *Du contrat social*)

L'homme est son propre Prométhée (Michelet, preface to *Histoire de France*)

L'hypocrisie est un hommage que le vice rend à la vertu (La Rochefoucauld, *Maximes*)

L'imaginaire est ce qui tend à devenir réel (Breton, *Le Revolver à cheveux blancs*)

Longtemps, je me suis couché de bonne heure. (Proust, *Du côté de chez Swann*)

Là, tout n'est qu'ordre et beauté,
Luxe, calme et volupté.
(Baudelaire, 'L'Invitation au voyage')

Ma bouche sera la bouche des malheurs qui n'ont point de bouche, ma voix, la liberté de celles qui s'affaissent au cachot du désespoir (Césaire, *Cahier d'un retour au pays natal*)

Mais où sont les neiges d'antan? (Villon, 'Ballade des dames du temps jadis')

Merdre! (Jarry, *Ubu roi*)

Mon ultime prière: Ô mon corps, fais de moi toujours un homme qui interroge! (Fanon, *Peau noire masques blancs*)

Nature est un doux guide, mais non pas plus doux que prudent et juste (Montaigne, *Essais*, III, 13)

Ni Dieu, ni César, ni tribun (Pottier, 'L'Internationale')

Nous autres, civilisations, nous savons maintenant que nous sommes mortelles (Valéry, *Variété*)

Nous avons changé tout cela (Molière, *Le Médecin malgré lui*)

On ne naît pas femme, on le devient (Beauvoir, *Le Deuxième Sexe*)

Ô temps, suspends ton vol! (Lamartine, 'Le Lac')

Paien unt tort e chrestïens unt dreit (*La Chanson de Roland*)

Plonger au fond du gouffre, Enfer ou Ciel, qu'importe?
Au fond de l'Inconnu pour trouver du *nouveau*!
(Baudelaire, 'Le Voyage')

Que diable allait-il faire dans cette galère? (Molière, *Les Fourberies de Scapin*)

Que sais-je? (Montaigne, *Essais*)

Que sont tous les nègres qu'on dit français? (Oyono, *Une vie de boy*)

> Que tu es sale Christ d'être avec les bourgeois
> Leur luxe est un veau d'or au cou de leurs
> bourgeoises.
> (Tchicaya U Tam'si, *Épitomé*)

Que vouliez-vous qu'il fît contre trois?—Qu'il mourût! (Corneille, *Horace*)

Qu'importe le flacon, pourvu qu'on ait l'ivresse? (Musset, *La Coupe et les lèvres*)

Revenons à ces moutons (*La Farce de Maître Pierre Pathelin*)

Rien n'est beau que le vrai. Le vrai seul est aimable. (Boileau, *Épître* ix)

Rire est le propre de l'homme (Rabelais, *Gargantua*)

Si Dieu n'existait pas, il faudrait l'inventer (Voltaire, *Épîtres*)

Sous le pont Mirabeau coule la Seine (Apollinaire, 'Le Pont Mirabeau')

T'as de beaux yeux, tu sais (Carné / Prévert, *Quai des brumes*)

Tel qu'en Lui-même enfin l'éternité le change (Mallarmé, 'Tombeau d'Edgar Poe')

Tire la chevillette, la bobinette cherra (Perrault, 'Le Petit Chaperon Rouge')

Toute ma vie, je me suis fait une certaine idée de la France (De Gaulle, *Mémoires de guerre*)

Tout est bien sortant des mains de l'Auteur des choses, tout dégénère entre les mains de l'homme (Rousseau, *Émile*)

Tout est dit, et l'on vient trop tard (La Bruyère, *Les Caractères*)

Tout est pour le mieux dans le meilleur des mondes possibles (Voltaire, *Candide*)

> Tout passe.—L'art robuste
> Seul a l'éternité
> (Gautier, *Émaux et camées*)

Tu causes, tu causes, c'est tout ce que tu sais faire (Queneau, *Zazie dans le métro*)

Un roman est un miroir qui se promène sur une grande route (Stendhal, *Le Rouge et le noir*)

Un seul être vous manque, et tout est dépeuplé (Lamartine, 'L'Isolement')

Vérité au-deçà des Pyrénées, erreur au-delà (Pascal, *Pensées*)

> Vous chantiez? J'en suis fort aise,
> Eh bien! dansez maintenant
> (La Fontaine, 'La Cigale et la fourmi')

Vous l'avez voulu, George Dandin, vous l'avez voulu (Molière, *George Dandin*)

Vous vous êtes donné la peine de naître, et rien de plus! (Beaumarchais, *Le Mariage de Figaro*)

Waterloo! Waterloo! Waterloo! morne plaine! (Hugo, 'L'Expiation').

R

RABBE, Alphonse (1786–1829/30). Often considered as exemplary of Romantic pessimism, Rabbe, young, handsome, and intelligent, was disfigured by syphilis and indulged excessively in opium. He wrote journalism and historical compilations of little value, and finally his *Album d'un pessimiste*, posthumously published (1835), in part an anthology of observations by Rabbe and others on the meaninglessness of life and the inevitability of death, together with extremely sardonic and bitter prose poems which inspired *Baudelaire. At times deeply moving, the volume is more than a literary curiosity. [FPB]

RABEARIVELO, Jean-Joseph (1901–37). One of the three major francophone writers of *Madagascar. Rabearivelo's poetry belongs to a very particular moment in the colonial history of the island. His work is, on the one hand, intensely focused on the self, displaying extraordinary inner coherence and self-referentiality, and on the other, symptomatic of a common experience of cultural and political conflict under a colonial power. A predictable progression is visible in texts that range from the early *La Coupe de cendres* (1924), *Sylves* (1927), and *Volumes* (1928), which follow regular verse forms and remain French poetry, to *Presque-songes* (1934) and *Traduit de la nuit* (1935), where both the formal and cryptic features of the traditional Malagasy *hain teny* are visible in a poetry more intimately bound up in a Malagasy landscape. The *Vieilles chansons des pays d'Imerina* (1939) are *hain teny*, transcribed and translated.

Rabearivelo's suicide ended a life dominated by illness, relative poverty, unsuccessful love-affairs, the death of a favourite daughter, an inability to find a place within colonial society, and a profound psychological difficulty in reconciling the French and Malagasy sides of himself. In the early poetry an obsession with death is consistent with the *Symbolist aesthetic. In the later work it has become part of a preoccupation with the Malagasy identity, and intimately associated with the idea of communication with ancestral voices. The sense of uncertain identity gradually becomes the poetic focus of Rabearivelo's work, paralleled by numerous antitheses (e.g. day and night) and moments of uncertainty and transition, such as twilight. [BEJ]

RABELAIS, François (d. 1553). French humanist, doctor, and author of comic fictions. Relatively little is known of his public life, virtually nothing of his

private life. The caricatural image of the author as a drunken buffoon was already beginning to be established at the time of his death; as an incarnation of the so-called 'esprit gaulois', it remains an important point of reference in the French cultural tradition. *Montaigne appreciated his works, and he was read throughout Europe in the 16th and 17th c.: Fischart's translation into German and the equally free rendering into English by *Urquhart and Le Motteux are major literary achievements in their own right. In France his reputation waned in the classical era, whose taste he offended, but it was revived in the 19th c. He was admired by both *Hugo and *Flaubert, while Gustave *Doré produced a famous set of illustrations for an edition of his works.

He may have been born in 1483, or possibly in 1494; his father was a lawyer from Chinon in the Loire valley. There is evidence that he himself studied law in his earlier years, but the first major recorded event in his life occurred in 1510–11, when he entered the order of the Observantine Franciscans at the monastery of Le Puy Saint-Martin in Fontenay-le-Comte, where he remained until 1524. In the later part of this period he corresponded with Guillaume *Budé; his first extant letter is dated March 1521. He had also been studying Greek: in 1523–4 he was apparently working on a translation of Lucian into Latin. Greek studies were at this time regarded as suspect because of their impact on biblical interpretation, and Rabelais was obliged to change orders, becoming a Benedictine at the less rigorous Saint-Pierre-de-Maillezais under the protection of Bishop Geoffroy d'Estissac.

By 1526 he appears to have abandoned holy orders. He may have studied medicine in Paris between 1526 and 1530, and it is probably at this time too that he became the father of two illegitimate children, legitimized by the pope some 10 years later. In 1530 he matriculated as a medical student at Montpellier; by 1531 he was lecturing there on Hippocrates and Galen, and in 1532 he published editions of various medical works. At the same time he had been writing his first comic work, *Pantagruel*, which was printed in Lyon that same year. In November he moved to Lyon as physician at the Hôtel-Dieu. A letter to *Erasmus, acknowledging his profound influence, dates from this time.

In 1534 Rabelais went to Rome for about three months with Bishop Jean du Bellay, uncle of the famous poet. His second comic book, *Gargantua*, dates from later in that year, or possibly early in 1535; during this period, he also produced a series of burlesque chapbooks under titles such as *Pantagruéline Prognostication*.

Rabelais returned to Rome with Du Bellay in 1535, abandoning his post at the Hôtel-Dieu, and obtained papal absolution for his 'apostasy' in leaving holy orders without permission. On his return, in 1536, he became a secular priest at Du Bellay's abbey at Saint-Maur-les-Fossés, which was itself secularized at this time. In 1537 he took up his medical studies again, first in Paris, then in Montpellier, obtaining his doctorate in medicine and lecturing on Hippocrates.

The next phase of Rabelais's career for which we have reliable evidence is the period 1540–2, which he spent in Turin and elsewhere in Piedmont assisting his patron Guillaume du Bellay, seigneur de Langey, who was the governor of Piedmont. The opening chapters of his *Tiers Livre* [for this and other books, see PANTAGRUEL AND GARGANTUA] are a distant echo of this experience; more centrally, the death of his beloved patron in 1543 is alluded to in some detail in the *Tiers Livre* and the *Quart Livre*.

At about this time, too, the *Sorbonne began to compile lists of censorable books, among which both *Pantagruel* and *Gargantua* were named. In 1545 *François Ier granted a royal privilege for Rabelais's *Tiers Livre*, which was dedicated to the king's sister *Marguerite de Navarre and was printed several times in 1546; despite this royal protection, it was placed on a new list of censorable books. Rabelais left Paris, first for Metz (1546), then for Rome (1547), where he remained until 1549. Meanwhile, a first, fragmentary version of the *Quart Livre* appeared (1548). After his return to France, Rabelais obtained the protection of Cardinal Odet de Châtillon, to whom an expanded *Quart Livre* was dedicated (1552). Not long after, the *Quart Livre* too was condemned.

In 1551 Rabelais had obtained two benefices, which had provided him with some hope of financial security; he resigned these in 1553, shortly before his death. A further fragment of comic fiction known as the *Île sonnante*, attributed to Rabelais, was published in 1562; this formed the first eight chapters of the *Cinquième Livre*, which appeared in 1564. The authenticity of these posthumous works is still disputed.

A reading of Rabelais's works according to this biography would draw attention to his familiarity both with the world of *humanism and with the movement of moderate religious reform in France [see EVANGELICALS] which was fostered by powerful families such as the Du Bellays; his knowledge of Greek, his admiration of Erasmus, his dedication of the *Tiers Livre* to Marguerite de Navarre, his vigorous satire of the Sorbonne, of monasticism, and of observances such as fasting and pilgrimages all point in this direction. He borrows from Sir Thomas More the notion of Utopia in order to sketch out a comic version of an ideal realm ruled by philosopher-giants; he stages in *Gargantua* a patriotic battle against a vicious invader (who might be identifiable

with the emperor Charles V); he satirizes the papacy from a nationalistic (though not a schismatic) standpoint in the Papimanes episode of the *Quart Livre*. In other words, Rabelais's work reads in that light like a serious satirical comment on crucial issues of its day.

However, it is important not to turn his scant biography into another kind of caricature, that of the pious scholar hiding his serious thoughts beneath a thin veneer of humour. The exuberant linguistic inventiveness of his writing, unparalleled in French literature, creates a self-contained imaginative world in which the real events and problems of the early 16th c. are transformed and transcended. It is that inventive power, above all, which has guaranteed the survival of Rabelais's works as comic masterpieces. [For further reading see under PANTAGRUEL AND GARGANTUA.]   [TC]

RABEMANANJARA, Jacques (b. 1913). One of the three best-known francophone writers of *Madagascar (with *Rabearivelo and *Ranaivo), Rabemananjara has written poetry, plays, and essays. Both his life and work have been dominated by politics. The earlier poetry, such as *Antsa* (1956; Malagasy for hymn or eulogy), *Lamba* (1948; Malagasy for the traditional strip of cloth worn as clothing), and *Antidote* (1961), was written during a period of considerable political instability and violence. The first two collections were published in the year of his release from prison and his move/exile to France. In 1958 he published *Nationalisme et problèmes malgaches*, and in 1960, the year the island gained independence, he returned, first as deputy, then minister, and finally vice-president of the Republic. Following President Tsiranana's fall in 1972 he has devoted most of his time to editorial work with the publishing house *Présence Africaine in Paris.

Antsa is a long, complex poem, dense with violent images of the primordial, sometimes reminiscent of *Césaire's early poetry. The poem culminates in the island's birth—and liberation. Origins, in this case the delivery of a fictional continent, is the focus of *Lamba*, another long poem. The importance of origins is combined with a desire for a return to a primordial innocence and coherence, symbolic of a pre-colonial time. The poems in the collection *Antidote* are militant, concerned with liberation often brought about through magic and ritual. These poems belong broadly within the protest tradition, but they are also difficult and complex texts.

Rabemananjara has also written three plays: *Les Dieux malgaches* (1942), *Les Boutriers de l'aurore* (1957), and *Les Agapes des dieux* (1962). The first two are historical dramas and all are, once again, dominated by a fascination with origins and man's primal relationship with his environment.   [BEJ]

Rabouilleuse, La. Novel by *Balzac, written and published in 1841–3, and one of the last of the *Scènes de la vie de province* in La *Comédie humaine*. Set partly in Paris, as the story of a mother's preference for her elder, swashbuckling, and more handsome son Philippe Bridau over his brother Joseph, a painter of genius, and partly at Issoudun, *La Rabouilleuse* owes its title to Flore Brazier, a peasant girl who is first seen muddying the water (*rabouiller*) of the local stream in search of crayfish. Flore becomes the servant-mistress of a slow-minded and repulsive *rentier*, Jean-Jacques Rouget, the uncle of the Bridau brothers and the inheritor of their grandfather's whole fortune. Through a plot of gripping complexity, the morally worthless Philippe captures both Flore and the inheritance, and Joseph, narrowly escaping death at the hands of a mob, retreats to Paris and to the service of art. *La Rabouilleuse* weaves together, in a rather loose narrative structure, many of Balzac's more personal themes: the injustice of families, the outrageous acquisitiveness of provincial life, the rights of genius, the manipulative power of women, and the corrupting impact on civilian life of the under-employed ex-soldiers of Napoleon's armies. [DMB]

RACAN, Honorat de Bueil, seigneur de (1589–1670). French poet. Having lost his father at an early age, he was taken into the care of the duc de Bellegarde. *Malherbe, on his arrival at the court in 1605, was assigned by the king to the Bellegarde household, and there he befriended the young man, whom he came to regard as his favourite pupil. The somewhat nonchalant Racan profited from Malherbe's discipline, though he disagreed with the master on some technical points and disliked excess of regulation. Nor did he share Malherbe's scorn of *Ronsard, and there is a strong vein of rustic realism in his work which recalls the 16th c. This gives authenticity to his well-known *stances*, 'A Tircis sur la retraite'; it blends well too with pastoral conventions in his play *Les Bergeries* (first performed as *Arthénice*, c.1619). In general his poetry is more relaxed, quieter than that of Malherbe, even in his odes, where the master's influence is at its strongest. In this respect he shows some affinity with *Tristan L'Hermite, and it is not surprising that *La Fontaine should have admired him. He left some interesting biographical notes on Malherbe. [AJS]

RACHEL (pseud. of Elisa Félix) (1820–58). Possibly France's greatest tragic actress. After inauspicious beginnings, she was taken up by Samson of the *Comédie-Française, himself a pupil of *Talma, and was soon responsible for reviving the glories of *Corneille and *Racine in performances of incandescent power, aided by superb diction and dignity of bearing. [SBJ]

RACHILDE (pseud. of Marguerite Eymery) (1860–1953). French writer who attained notoriety from the mid-1880s through a series of novels and plays (notably *Monsieur Vénus*, 1884; *La Marquise de Sade*, 1887; *Madame la Mort*, 1891) rich in *Decadent themes such as morbid and frenzied sexuality, Satanism, and artificiality. During the 1980s the *feminist movement led to a revival of interest in her work after a long period of neglect. Debate now centres on whether her portrayal of male–female power relationships should be considered pro- or anti-feminist, and whether stylistically her work can be said to have contributed to the development of a modernist aesthetic. [JK]

RACINE, Jean (1639–99). French tragic playwright. Early in his career he achieved a reputation which has never been eclipsed, even if he has not been as popular a writer as *Molière. Criticized in Stendhal's *Racine et Shakespeare* as a representative of stultifying *classicism, he has continued to be acted, read, praised, and interpreted. It is a time-honoured tradition to compare his plays with those of Pierre *Corneille—*La Bruyère said that Corneille depicts people as they should be, but that Racine depicts them as they are. In the 20th c. his works have often been a battleground for rival critical tendencies, the most famous episode being the dispute between *Barthes and the scholar Raymond Picard over the former's provocative *Sur Racine* [see LITERARY HISTORY, 2].

Racine was born in a middle-class family in La Ferté-Milon (Aisne). Orphaned while still a small child, he was brought up by his grandparents, then sent to the *Jansenist school at *Port-Royal des Champs. Although in 1666 he was to break with his mentors, writing a vitriolic attack on *Nicole, who had accused playwrights of being public poisoners, he was later reconciled with them. He completed his education in Paris, and left school with a knowledge of Greek literature that was unusual in his day. Having spent over a year in Uzès in the vain pursuit of an ecclesiastical living, he embarked in 1663 on a literary career in Paris. *La Fontaine was among his friends, soon to be joined by Molière and *Boileau. His first compositions, written to obtain a royal pension, were flattering odes on the marriage of *Louis XIV and the like. It was in the theatre, however, that he made his name.

He began in 1664 with *La Thébaïde* (*Les Frères ennemis*), a violent and somewhat bombastic play about the fatal rivalry of Oedipus' two sons. This was followed in 1665 by the very different *Alexandre le grand*. Heroic and optimistic rather than blackly tragic, this play gives a flattering image of Louis XIV under the guise of the conqueror of the world. It was put on, like *La Thébaïde*, by Molière's company, but after a few days Racine transferred it to the rival *Hôtel de Bourgogne, who performed all his subsequent secular tragedies. These now followed in a steady succession—*Andromaque* (1667), *Britannicus* (1669), *Bérénice* (1671), *Bajazet* (1672), *Mithridate* (1673), *Iphigénie* (1674), and *Phèdre* (1677). There is also a comedy, *Les Plaideurs* (1668), a satire on the legal profession which is remarkable for its linguistic virtuosity.

Racine's life during these years is little known. He lived a good deal with actors and actresses, and by some accounts led a fairly disreputable existence. At the same time he established himself socially and financially. He was elected to the Académie Française in 1672, *Colbert's protection brought him a lucrative sinecure, and he continued to receive a royal pension. His theatrical success involved him in quarrels and polemics, notably with the ageing Corneille and with the party of the *modernes* [see QUERELLE]. Against *Perrault and his allies he joined forces with Boileau in defence of antiquity (together they were known mockingly as 'Messieurs du Sublime').

In 1677 he and Boileau were made historiographers royal, a post that carried a handsome salary. In the same year he married, was reconciled with the Jansenists, and turned away from the theatre; it is unclear whether this 'retirement' was the result of an inner crisis or simply the next step in his career as a courtier. Certainly this career flourished, as he served the king with his pen. With Boileau he wrote a small amount of eloquent official history, he continued to attend the Academy and was made a member of the *Académie des Inscriptions, he wrote texts for court entertainments, and was admitted to the king's inner circle. In particular, in order to please Madame de *Maintenon, he wrote two biblical plays to be performed by the girls at the school of *Saint-Cyr, *Esther (1689) and *Athalie (1691). He was ennobled and made a *gentilhomme ordinaire de la chambre du roi* and *secrétaire ordinaire du roi*. Shortly before his death, however, he lost some of this favour because of his courageous defence of Port-Royal, whose history he wrote in the *Abrégé de l'histoire de Port-Royal* (composed 1698).

Racine wrote a few impressive religious poems, but his reputation rests essentially on his tragedies. These are more varied than is suggested by those who talk of 'Racinian tragedy' or the 'Racinian hero'. They are all very effective as theatre, this being due above all to their language and plot construction. The language has been described as simple (Racine uses a very small vocabulary), as elegant, and as poetic; it is all of these at times, but not to the exclusion of other qualities, for it is above all dramatic, giving memorable expression to the subtle and often extreme passions of the protagonists. The plots conform to the precepts of *classicism (unity of time, place, and action), but they stand out from those of contemporary dramatists by their tense concentration on a single knot of conflict, in which a small number of characters, often interrelated, pursue their goals of love and power. These protagonists—Greek, Roman, biblical, or Turkish—are all of exalted rank, but only rarely do they live up to the standard their position demands. They range from the feeble yet demonic Néron in *Britannicus* to the strong and saintly Esther, but most often they exemplify a human nature divided against itself, weak, impulsive, cruel, self-seeking,

yet aware of its degeneration from an unattainable ideal. Their existence is in striking contrast to the golden image of royalty which Racine had to paint as official historian; it seems like an illustration of *Pascal's vision of 'la misère de l'homme sans Dieu', and this has led many commentators to insist—perhaps excessively—on Racine's Jansenism.

Whether Jansenist-inspired or not, what distinguishes his writing in the end is the tragic vision of fate it conveys. There are optimistic elements in all his plays, but these are set against the usually stronger forces of destruction. Driven on by their futile hope as apparently free agents, yet condemned by their own nature or by some higher force to failure and ruin, these magnificent and lamentable men and women act out on their confined stage a splendid ceremonial of defeat. Racine often proclaimed his debt to the Greek tragedians; in France he is their only successor. [PF]

See O. de Mourgues, *Racine, or the Triumph of Relevance* (1967); R. C. Knight (ed.) *Racine: Modern Judgements* (1969); A. Niderst, *Les Tragédies de Racine, diversité et unité* (1975).

RACINE, Louis (1692–1763). Youngest son of Jean [see previous entry] and author of a large amount of religious poetry, frequently republished in the 18th c. *La Grâce* (1720) and *La Religion* (1742) are lengthy verse discourses in conventional alexandrine couplets, dealing in a *Pascalian way with faith and philosophy, man and God. Many of the *Odes saintes* (1730–43) are based on the Psalms; they use the rhetoric of the genre to express apparently sincere religious beliefs. He also published a prose translation of *Paradise Lost* (1755) and edifying *Mémoires sur la vie et les ouvrages de Jean Racine* (1747). [PF]

Racine et Shakespeare. Pamphlet published by *Stendhal in two instalments (1823, 1825). It starts as a manifesto in favour of national tragedy in prose, unhampered by the unities of time and place, and becomes an attempt to define *Romanticism. Stendhal ridicules both the *Académie Française's mediocre conservatism and the traditionalism of the liberal journalists. For him, Romanticism means writing for contemporary society. In their time Shakespeare and Racine were both Romantics. An imitation of Racine in 1823 is a dull anachronism, but it is just as wrong to imitate the admirable Shakespeare. What is needed is theatre capable of creating the maximum pleasure for the modern spectator. [PF]

Racines du ciel, Les, see GARY.

Radical Party. The Parti Radical was officially formed in 1901, by republicans of the moderate Left. Its heyday was the Third Republic, its constituency the provincial middle class, its philosophy that the best government was the least government, and its most passionately held belief *anticlericalism—many Radicals were also *freemasons. After the

*Dreyfus Affair and the separation of Church and State in 1905, under the Radical premier Émile Combes, the party's radicalism waned, since its targets (monarch, nobility, Church) posed little threat. The Radicals' links with economically backward elements of French society, as *Socialism and Communism appeared on its left, led to a more conservative identity: 'hearts on the left, wallets on the right.' Strategically dominant in parliamentary politics between the wars, it had a stranglehold on certain ministries, such as the Interior, and could block certain measures, such as women's suffrage. For all that, the party retained some elements of the republican ideal, formulated by its intellectual spokesman *Alain in 1925; it joined the *Popular Front in the 1930s; and it contained in its ranks major figures as diverse as *Clemenceau, *Herriot, Daladier, and *Mendès-France. It played little part in the Resistance, and after 1945 was never again a major force in political life, although it survived in parliamentary coalitions for some years, until terminal fragmentation set in under the Fifth Republic.   [SR]

RADIGUET, Raymond (1903–23). Radiguet is mostly known for his novel *Le Diable au corps*, a first-person narration which succeeds in combining an apparently classical style and technique with all the resources of modern ambiguity. After leaving school in 1918 Radiguet soon entered Parisian literary circles, becoming the inseparable companion of *Cocteau. After some poetry and articles, he started work in 1921, aged 18, on *Le Diable au corps*, which appeared in 1923. In December of that year Radiguet died of typhoid. A further novel, *Le Bal du comte d'Orgel*, was published posthumously in 1924, under Cocteau's care.   [RMG]

Radio. Coverage of the performing arts and of literature was a regular feature of news and feature programmes from the outset of sound broadcasting in France. In 1922–3 René Sudre, one of the founding fathers of the Syndicat National des Journalistes (1918), did much with André Delacour, on the *journal parlé* of the Tour Eiffel radio station, to define the parameters of coverage of the literary world. From the mid-1930s radio began to become a mass medium; there were both public and private stations, but only the former broadcast cultural programmes. Light entertainment dominated the more successful private stations.

During the *Occupation radio was the prime propaganda medium of Vichy France. Figures from the arts worked for, or were celebrated by, Vichy radio stations, whose star propagandist was Philippe *Henriot, the minister of information; his editorials, broadcast four times a day, were praised by the journalist Maurice Martin du Gard for their oratorical, polemical, and literary skills. The minor propagandist, Jean Herold-Pacquis, worked for the German-controlled *Radio-Paris* and became celebrated for his catch-phrase 'et l'Angleterre comme Carthage sera détruite'.

Periodically after 1945 the state reaffirmed its monopoly of broadcasting; only in 1981 were private radio stations again authorized to operate within France. Coverage of the arts and literature remained politically sensitive—especially before the development of television and of consumer society (and the reaction of *May 1968) in the 1960s. In 1948 the director of the books and drama department of RTF [see TELEVISION] lost his post after only 11 months: he had authorized a programme in which *Genet mentioned *Vian, and another in which *Sartre offended 'good taste'; the director, Fernand Pouey, was disavowed following his recording of a programme with *Artaud which his superiors refused to broadcast.

State radio thereafter gave ample coverage to more mainstream intellectual figures. From 1949 RTF broadcast lengthy interviews and discussions intended to promote understanding of authors such as *Gide, *Breton, *Carco, and *Mauriac. Thus, late in life, *Léautaud was 'discovered' by the listening public, following a series of interviews with Robert Mallet in 1950–1. While programmes devoted to more esoteric authors were occasionally broadcast on France-Culture, which catered for minority interests, the tradition of a mix of serious and lively coverage of the arts for a 'mass' or middle-brow public was maintained in cultural programmes on both radio and, later, television. Programmes of reviews and debates about books, theatre, and the cinema continued on public-service radio into the 1990s. *Le Masque et la plume*, for instance, began in 1954: it was the offspring of Michel Polac's *Pour l'amour du théâtre* and François-Régis Bastide's *Une idée pour une autre*. Authors such as *Camus and *Breton replied to critics (Robert Kanters, Claude *Mauriac, Morvan Lebesque, etc.) before a studio audience.

In the 1990s coverage of the arts, and of literature in particular, was no longer likely to occur in prime time, as had happened during the period when state broadcasters of RTF and ORTF (1964–74) were required to dispense culture to the nation. Coverage was increasingly personalized and geared to the brief attention-span of 'three-minute culture'. Television replaced radio as the main broadcasting medium covering the arts. However, on radio news bulletins, as on television newscasts, the literary world was occasionally featured. Media coverage of the arts reflected the high profile adopted by cultural policy-makers and *artistes*, notably when Jack Lang headed the Ministry of Culture (1981–6, 1988–93).   [MP]

Ragotin, see ROMAN COMIQUE.

RAIMBAUT D'AURENGA (*c.*1144–1173). As count of Orange, Raimbaut was a patron as well as a *troubadour, notably of *Giraut de Bornelh and *Peire

Rogier, though his relatively short life seems to have been plagued by financial crises. Metrically complex, his poetry is sophisticated and demanding; it is marked by an appealing sense of humour. Raimbaut frequently subverts the conventions of serious hermetic poetry with obscene metaphors, and in one poem undermines the tradition of the boasting poem by ironically vaunting his own castration. A key figure in the controversy over the *trobar clus*, Raimbaut probably also knew *Bernart de Ventadorn and may have exchanged lyrics with *Chrétien de Troyes. [SG]

RAIS, Gilles de, see GILLES DE RAIS.

RAKOTOSON, Michèle (b. 1948). Malagasy playwright and novelist. Several of her plays have won prizes and been staged but (except for *La Maison morte*, 1991) most are as yet unpublished. *Dadabé* (1984), a book of stories, whose title means 'grandfather', won the Grand Prix Littéraire du Madagascar in 1984. A novel, *Le Bain des reliques*, came out in 1988. She lives in Paris, where she works for Radio France. [VC]

Rambouillet, Hôtel de. *Hôtel particulier* (town house) constructed according to plans imagined by Catherine de Vivonne de Savelli, marquise de Rambouillet. It was famous for a design not previously used in French architecture, a suite of salons. The Hôtel de Rambouillet's salons culminated in the room famous as *la chambre bleue*. There, from about 1610 to her death in 1665, the marquise presided over the first French *salon. Especially in the 1620s–40s, her guests' judgements on matters literary and social were considered so authoritative that *Sévigné claimed that for a time 'the Hôtel de Rambouillet was the Louvre' (letter of 12 January 1680). [JDeJ]

RAMEAU, Jean-Philippe (1683–1764). French composer, performer, and author of one of the most influential treatises in music history, the *Traité de l'harmonie* (1722). Rameau's *tragédies lyriques* provided the basis for the major 18th-c. debates on music: Lullists against Ramists, French *opera against Italian, and finally *Gluckists against Piccinistes [see also GUERRE DES BOUFFONS]. In fact, his operas scarcely modified the model established by *Lully, but their intensity of expression and seeming succession of miniatures made them appear the quintessence of Frenchness to later composers. By the 1780s they began to slip out of the repertoire and Rameau was once again appreciated as a theorist rather than a composer. His nephew is the subject of one of *Diderot's most famous dialogues. [KM]

RAMSAY, Andrew Michael (1686–1743). French writer of Scottish birth, known as 'le chevalier Ramsay'. Converted to Catholicism by *Fénelon, he edited his master's works and wrote in his defence.

Les Voyages de Cyrus (1727), a philosophical novel in imitation of *Télémaque*, enjoyed great success. Ramsay was a Jacobite and an early *freemason.[PF]

RAMUS, Peter (Pierre de la Ramée) (1515–72). Educationalist and professor of philosophy and eloquence at the Collège Royal. He wrote, mainly in Latin, on a wide range of subjects: the arts of discourse (grammar, rhetoric, logic), mathematics, ethics, and theology. His first published works, *Dialecticae partitiones* and *Aristotelicae animadversiones* (1543), were tendentiously anti-Aristotelian; the *Dialectique* (1555) which grew out of them is the first substantial philosophical work in French and presents the theory of method which is central to his thought. Ramus believed that there was one single method for teaching any subject, based on Aristotle's laws of demonstration, and although the emphasis on deduction was later rejected by Bacon, Ramus's theories were influential for two centuries. His *rhetoric, published under the name of his collaborator Omer Talon (Talaeus) and also by his pupil Antoine Fouquelin (*La Rhétorique française*, 1555), is merely an adaptation of the classical theory of ornament; he had in fact removed the first two parts of classical rhetoric, invention and disposition, to logic and restricted rhetoric to *elocutio* (expression or style). His attempts at literary analysis are equally reductive. A convert to Protestantism from about 1560, he was brutally murdered in the *St Bartholomew's Day Massacre. Ramus is significant not as a philosopher but as an educational reformer and as a focus for debate about discourse and communication. [PS]

RAMUZ, Charles-Ferdinand (1878–1947). Swiss novelist and poet and acknowledged leader of the *renaissance vaudoise*, which first gave intellectual coherence to francophone literature in Suisse Romande [see SWISS LITERATURE IN FRENCH]. Born in Lausanne, he studied at Lausanne University before starting an uncompleted thesis on Maurice de *Guérin in Paris (1900–1). After a brief return to teach at Aubonne, he returned to Paris in 1902 to start a literary career, publishing his first poems on Swiss peasant life (*Le Petit Village*, 1903), tutoring in Weimar (1903–4), and contributing to a Suisse-Romande literary collection, *Les Pénates d'argile* (1904), which developed into *La Voile latine*, dedicated to creating a Suisse-Romande literature.

Living in Paris (1904–14) he published a first novel *Aline* (1905) and *Les Circonstances de la vie* (1907). After a first stay in the Valais (1907) he began his 'Valaisan' novels, notably *Le Village dans la montagne* (1908), *Jean-Luc persécuté* (1909), *La Séparation des races* (1923), *Farinet* (1932), *Derborence* (1934), and the semi-autobiographical novels *Aimé Pache, peintre vaudois* (1911) and *Vie de Samuel Belet* (1913), portraying the vocational dilemma of Swiss artists. He married a painter, Cécile Cellier, and visited *Cézanne in 1913. In 1914, with Budry and Ansermet, he launched *Cahiers vaudois* (1914–19), breaking away from Gonzague de Reynold and publishing a literary manifesto, 'Raison d'être', in the first issue, formulating the idea of *enracinement*.

He left Paris for Switzerland just before the outbreak of war. Meeting Stravinsky in 1915, he and Auberjonois collaborated with him to produce *Histoire du soldat* (1918). He moved to Lausanne in 1916, and finally to Pully (1930), publishing with Grasset from 1924, when French critics finally acknowledged his talent. He was awarded several prizes, including the Grand Prix Romand (1928).

Ramuz's works are remarkable for their lyricism, vernacular style, and powerful mythical, tragic, poetic vision of the mountain peasant, his rituals, stoicism, and resilience. His literary landscapes have a Cézanne-like painterly quality and symbolism. It is a work rooted in the landscape in which he was born. Like his hero Aimé Pache, 'il portait en lui sa race' and 'on ne saurait l'imaginer que Suisse' (Gide). [SSBT]

See G. Guisan, *C.-F. Ramuz* (1966); D. G. Bevan, *The Art and Poetry of Charles-Ferdinand Ramuz* (1977).

RANAIVO, Flavien (b. 1914). Malagasy poet. His father died two years after his birth. He began formal education only at the age of 8 and his schooling was entirely in Malagasy until he was 14. He became a teacher, and during World War II fought with the Free French. After the war he entered the Civil Service, occupying posts both in France and Madagascar. Since 1970 he has lived in France.

In many ways a continuation of *Rabearivelo's poetic project, Ranaivo's work is based on a synthesis of formal French and traditional Malagasy verse. His *œuvre* consists of just three small volumes: *L'Ombre et le vent* (1947), *Mes chansons de toujours* (1955), and *Le Retour au bercail* (1962). The boundaries of his poetic world are, however, more limited. Whereas his predecessor's preoccupation with origins and with the Malagasy landscape becomes part of a wider metaphorical exploration of Malagasy problems of identity, in Ranaivo's work the matrix of meaning functions locally within particular poems. [BEJ]

RANCÉ, Armand Jean le Bouthillier de (1626–1700). French monastic reformer. A godson of *Richelieu, when 12 years old he was already commendatory abbot of five religious houses, including the Cistercian abbey of La Trappe in Normandy. By the 1650s he was a wealthy, worldly cleric. Between 1657 and 1660, however, he underwent a profound religious conversion. He then disposed of many of his possessions, resigned his multiple benefices, and placed himself under the direction of *Arnauld d'Andilly. In 1663 he accepted a monastic vocation in the Cistercian order, underwent a year's strict novitiate, and became the regular, resident abbot of La Trappe, where he introduced austere reforms,

becoming widely influential as the leading figure among *Cistercians of the Strict Observance. Rancé believed that monastic life should be restricted to prayer and manual work. His *De la sainteté et des devoirs de la vie monastique* (1683) rejected learning and scholarship in the cloister, leading eventually to an extended but courteous debate with the Maurist *Mabillon. Major contributions to the argument include Mabillon's *Traité des études monastiques dans les cloîtres* (1691), Rancé's *Réponse au Traité des études monastiques* (1692), and Mabillon's *Réflexions sur la réponse de M. l'abbé de la Trappe* (1693). He was the subject of *Chateaubriand's swan-song, *La Vie de Rancé* (1844). [JC]

RANDAU, Robert (pseud. of Robert Arnaud) (1873–1950). French Algerian novelist. In works such as *Les Colons* (1907) and *Les Algérianistes* (1911) he presented European colonists as a vigorous antidote to the decadence of metropolitan France. He was seen by many in colonial *Algeria as the archetype of a literary school unique to North Africa. [AGH]

Raoul de Cambrai. One of the most violent and passionate of the Old French *chansons de geste*, this poem presents a sombre picture of social disintegration. Raoul's father dies while the hero is still an infant, and the king gives his fief to another of his barons. When Raoul comes of age, his obsessive desire to hold land plunges him into conflict with the king, his family, and his closest friend. It leads him even to commit acts of sacrilege, most notably the burning of an abbey church in which a convent of nuns, and all the inhabitants of their small town, have taken sanctuary. The horrific violence of this scene clearly impressed itself on medieval audiences, for there are many references to it in other texts. The abbess of the convent is the mother of Raoul's companion, Bernier, who has been obliged by his allegiance to Raoul to take up arms against his own relatives, for the king has unwisely decided to appease Raoul by giving him the lands which Bernier's father and uncles expect to inherit. After his mother's death, Bernier and Raoul quarrel, and Bernier joins forces with his family, eventually killing Raoul in the battle which ensues.

This narrative forms about one-third of the 8,500-line text which we now have, and probably results from the reworking of earlier material, now lost. Successive continuations were added in the late 12th and early 13th c., which follow the career of Bernier after Raoul's death and offer interesting reflections on the problems raised by the older poem. Although attempts are made to restore political order, the text closes with the murder of Bernier and the elimination of all the remaining male characters. Conflict and bloodshed are combined in this work with a growing conviction that the moral and political problems surrounding them are irresolvable. [SK]

RAOUL DE HOUDENC (*fl.* 1220–30). Writer of verse romances and didactic poems whose work displays range, rhetorical talent, and wit. Raoul's debt to *Chrétien de Troyes is apparent in *Meraugis de Portlesguez*, where the eponymous hero and his lady set off in quest of *Gauvain. In the course of their adventures the narrator ingeniously transforms and spoofs generic conventions, notably in a scene where Meraugis dresses as a woman to escape from an imperious lady. *La Vengeance Raguidel*, whose attribution to Raoul is contested, describes Gauvain's protracted and less-than-exemplary quest for an assassin; the hero's misadventures with two women are tinged with misogyny. In a more positive vein, the didactic *Roman des eles* allegorizes the obligations of knighthood as the feathers of the paired wings of largesse and courtesy. *Le Songe d'enfer*, probably Raoul's last work, is an allegorical dream poem of a voyage to hell that satirizes worldly vices. Raoul's authorship of *La Voie de paradis* is uncertain. [RLK]

RAPIN, Nicolas (1538–1608). French poet. Born in Fontenay-le-Comte, Rapin read law at Poitiers and had a successful—if contentious—career within legal administration, the magistrature, and local government. Equally critical of the extreme views of Reformists and the *Ligue, after Henri III's death (1589) Rapin's political allegiances lay with the moderate *Politiques and with the cause of Henri de Navarre (*Henri IV). Not only did he fight in Henri's army at Ivry—a victory he celebrated in anapaestic metre (1590)—but he collaborated in the composition of the *Satire Ménippée*, which prepared the king's entry into Paris (1594). Besides the pieces written for the *Satire Ménippée*, Rapin is best known today for his erotic contribution (written in 1579) to *La Puce de Madame *des Roches* (1583), for his classically measured verse (published in the posthumous *Œuvres complètes, latines et françaises*, 1610), and for the rustic evocation, modelled on Horace, of the *Plaisirs du gentilhomme champêtre* (1575, 1581, 1583). In addition, he published a slim volume of *Épitaphes* (1570) inspired, like so much of his poetry, by circumstance (the siege of Poitiers), a translation of the *XXVIIIe Chant du Roland furieux* of Ariosto (1572), and *Les Sept Psaumes pénitentiels* (1588). The natural simplicity of Rapin's poetry was much admired by Mathurin *Régnier. [MDQ]

RAPIN, René, père (1621–87). French Jesuit priest, poet, and critic. He taught at the Collège de Clermont and subsequently frequented the *Lamoignon circle, acquiring a considerable influence as an advocate of up-to-date classical theories. His *Réflexions sur la poétique* (1674–5) and *Réflexions sur l'éloquence* (1671) put forward theories akin to those of *Boileau, stressing the moral function and the truth-content of literature, and setting ancient grandeur against modern frivolity. These views are exemplified in a series of comparative studies: of Homer and Virgil (1669), of Demosthenes and Cicero (1670), of Thucydides and Livy (1681). He

also wrote against *Jansenism and was celebrated as the author of a number of Latin poems (in particular, the *Hortorum libri IV*, 1665), which are regarded as high points in modern *Latinity. [PF]

Rastignac, Eugène de. Character in Balzac's *Comédie humaine*; he appears first as a young man on the make in Le *Père Goriot, at the end of which he launches his famous challenge to Paris: 'A nous deux, maintenant!' Several other novels show his successful career.

RAVAISSON(-MOLLIEN), Félix (1813–1900). French spiritualist philosopher, professor, and administrator. A scholar of Aristotle, he made his reputation with *De l'habitude* (1838). He is also known for producing a widely disseminated *Rapport sur la philosophie en France au XIXe siècle* (1867).

RAVEL, Maurice (1875–1937). French composer, most renowned for his piano music and skill as an orchestrator. Although by nature a classicist, his music shows an intense pictorial imagination, and most of his compositions have pictorial and poetic titles. Ravel was a member of an artistic group called 'Les Apaches', and a fellow member of the group, Tristan *Klingsor, wrote the texts for his orchestral song-cycle *Schéhérazade* (1903). Ravel felt an affinity with *Symbolist poets and wrote a chamber music piece called *Trois poèmes de Stéphane Mallarmé* (1913). He also worked with *Colette on a *fantaisie lyrique*, *L'Enfant et les sortilèges* (1925). He wrote a small amount of music criticism. [KM]

Ravissement de Lol V. Stein, Le, see DURAS, M.

RAY, Jean (1887–1964). Enjoying a spurious reputation as sometime pirate and smuggler, the Belgian Ray reached a wide public with dozens of crimestories featuring the detective Harry Dickson, and a more serious output of weird tales, beginning with *Les Contes du whisky* (1925). Drawing on classic formulae of the *Fantastic, he elaborated an idiom of dark yet seductive fantasy in the novel *Malpertuis* (1943), with its Chinese-box narrative structure, and in collections of macabre spook-stories such as *Le Livre des fantômes* (1947). [RC]

RAYMOND, Marcel (1897–1981). Swiss critic, leading member of the *Geneva school with *Béguin and *Poulet. Influenced by *Rivière and *Du Bos, and by German philosophy, he practised a type of non-rationalistic criticism in which he sought to identify himself with the spirit or consciousness of a writer and to reproduce it in the quality of his own writing. He published studies of *Senancour, Rivière, *Valéry, and *Rousseau, and some remarkable works tracing the development of the poetic quest, notably *De Baudelaire au surréalisme* (1933) and *Baroque et renaissance poétique* (1955). [PF]

RAYNAL, Guillaume, abbé (1713–96). Educated by the Jesuits, he left the clergy to work as a journalist, being for a time editor of the *Mercure de France* and compiler of the *Nouvelles littéraires*. He frequented the salons of the *philosophes, several of whom he engaged as collaborators in his *Histoire des deux Indes (first edn. 1770), the massive work which brought him fame, persecution, and exile (Berlin, St Petersburg). Having been elected to the *États Généraux and acclaimed as a culture hero by the early revolutionaries, he disappointed and infuriated his admirers by an address to the Assemblée Constituante (31 May 1791) deploring the violence of current policies.   [PF]

RAYNOUARD, François-Juste-Marie (1761–1836). A member of the Académie Française (1807), he moved steadily away from playwriting towards the study of philology (he became a member of the Académie des Inscriptions in 1815). An early precursor of the *Félibriges, he composed—over a period of 20 years—numerous (if sometimes wrong-headed) studies on the 'langue romane' and *troubadour poetry.   [JR]

RAYSSIGUIER (d. 1660). French dramatist. He took a liberal attitude to the issue of regularity, and his six plays include an adaptation of Tasso's *Aminta* (published 1632), three tragicomedies taken from *L'*Astrée, and two others, *La Bourgeoise* (published 1633) and *Les Tuileries* (performed 1635), which contributed to the popularity of less romanesque, more modern and sophisticated love intrigues.   [GJM]

Razo, see VIDA.

Realism. [For the use of the term in medieval philosophy, see NOMINALISTS.] Originally a philosophical term opposed to idealism, realism gained currency as an aesthetic category when it appeared in art criticism in the mid-1840s. It is particularly associated with *Courbet, who called for the 'sincerity' and 'truth' of art in the context of a socialist politics, and declared in 1848 that he would paint only modern and popular subject-matter. *Un enterrement à Ornans* (1850) and *L'Atelier du peintre* (1855) were polemical paintings, and his 1855 exhibition of paintings refused by the official salons was entitled 'Le Réalisme'. *Champfleury, who wrote the exhibition catalogue, transposed Courbet's ideas to literature in *Le Réalisme*, a collection of essays serving as a manifesto. Louis *Duranty joined in with a journal, *Réalisme*, which ran to six issues in 1856 and 1857. His first attempt at a self-conscious Realist novel was *Le Malheur d'Henriette Gérard* (1860). Courbet, Champfleury, and Duranty are the three figures who espoused the term 'Realism' deliberately. Flaubert, whose *Madame Bovary was first published in 1856, despised the polemics as well as the implied aesthetics, and vigorously resisted the application of the term to his work.

The problem arises here of whether Realism is a literary movement, precisely located in history (coming after *Romanticism, preceding *Naturalism

and modernism, etc.), or whether it is simply an aesthetic label which escapes periodization and can be applied anachronistically. Even then, the value-judgements entailed in the term vary wildly and should doubtless be accounted for historically. Seen as a literary movement, Realism should probably be restricted to the period from the late 1840s to the mid-1860s. It implies a theory of subject-matter (that content should focus on ordinary, everyday lives, preferably lower-class) and a theory of documentation (i.e. a quasi-journalistic recourse to reliable sources).

However, 20th-c. critics tend to apply the term to a broader range of 19th-c. novelists, of whom the canonical examples tend to be *Stendhal, *Balzac, Flaubert, and *Zola. Erich Auerbach, who traces the history of mimesis in Western literature, attributes to 19th-c. France the key role in the rise of modern realism, stressing the complete break with classical prescriptions about appropriate styles and genres for the portrayal of everyday life. Realism chooses random people and events to illustrate general historical trends, and ordinary, low-class people earn the right to problematic and even tragic representation. The reality in which they are embedded is a strictly material one: it is political, social,. economic, and constantly evolving. George Lukács, who wanted to reroute the 20th-c. novel back to the path of 19th-c. Realism, similarly stresses the representation of 'total' human beings in 'total' surroundings that change in history. Lukács especially admired Balzac for linking his psychological and moral analyses to economic determinations and to political history; he felt he had achieved this through the construction of characters as artificial but historically accurate types. Though Lukács's belief that the ideal realist character will behave independently of its creator may seem misguided, his stress on typification nevertheless moves the debate into the question of the technical, aesthetic means by which realist writing might be achieved.

French Realism (and Balzac in particular) had a particularly bad press in the period of the *Nouveau Roman, when it was equated with a naïve belief in the transparency of language as the unproblematic vehicle of representations of the real world. The *Structuralist insistence on the non-referentiality of language fed into this view. However, *Barthes's famous reading of a Balzac story in *S/Z* (1970) lifted this block on serious work on realism. On the one hand his stress on the intertextuality of the codes of realist writing did indeed seem to dissolve the solid presence of 19th-c. France in the novels of the period. On the other hand, Barthes provided a thorough and insightful analysis of the conventions and devices whereby a realist text creates a representation of a recognizable reality. In a neat reversal of its original aesthetics, realism can be studied as a particular sort of discourse—one which achieves its effects by making plot details subservient to its own requirements.   [DK]

See G. Lukács, *Studies in European Realism* (trs. E. Bone, 1950); E. Auerbach, *Mimesis: The Representation of Reality in Western Literature* (trs. W. R. Trask, 1953); C. Prendergast, *The Order of Mimesis* (1986); L. Furst (ed.), *Realism* (1992).

Réalisme merveilleux, Le. An artistic movement begun in the 1920s by the *Surrealists, which later emerged in Latin America as the basis for an indigenous poetics. Made famous by the Cuban novelist Alejo Carpentier, 'marvellous realism' meant an assertion of a Caribbean and Latin American worldview which was different from Europe's. These ideas came to *Haiti by way of Carpentier's visit in 1943 and *Breton's visit in 1945. At the first Congress of Black Writers in 1956 the Haitian novelist *Alexis presented his 'Du réalisme merveilleux des Haïtiens'. It was an argument for seeing Haitian culture as creolized rather than neo-African, and for creating a new narrative method that would reflect the Haitian people's ability to combine the real and the fantastic in their imagination. [JMD]

RÉAUMUR, René-Antoine Ferchault de (1683–1757) French scientist whose many interests earned him the nickname of the Pliny of the 18th c. He is remembered for the thermometric scale that bears his name, and for his *magnum opus* of painstaking observation, *Mémoires pour servir à l'histoire naturelle des insectes* (6 vols., 1734–42).

REBATET, Lucien (1903–72). One of the most violent and outspoken *fascist intellectuals in France in the 1930s and the *Occupation. A journalist with both *L'*Action française* and *Je suis partout* in the 1930s, he broke with the former in 1940. He made his name in 1942 with the publication of *Les Décombres*, a violently antisemitic and anti-Republican account of the last years of the Third Republic which became a bestseller of the Occupation. He was condemned to death in 1946, but reprieved, and spent six years in prison, during which he wrote his only novel, *Les Deux Étendards* (1952). [NH]

REBOUX, Paul (1877–1963), and **MULLER,** Charles (1877–1914), composed three series of *A la manière de . . .* (1908, 1910, 1913); Reboux continued alone in 1925 and 1950. These pastiches are generally accurate and amusing; some, of authors now obscure, have lost their point, but others, aimed at classic targets, have worn better, e.g. 'Cleopastre', a fragment of *Racinian tragedy presented as if in a school edition, with notes; 'Un mot à la hâte', parodying *Proust. *Flaubert, *Gide, *Giono, *Mallarmé, *Verlaine, and *Zola, are also among those parodied, as are some foreign authors in translation. [SFN]

RÉCAMIER, Jeanne-Françoise, née Bernard (Juliette) (1777–1849). Born in Lyon, she married the rich and elderly banker Récamier. Of considerable beauty and charm but sexually seemingly chaste, she counted among her admirers and close, devoted friends many of the major literary figures of the age, including *Ballanche, a life-long companion, Germaine de *Staël (whose closest woman friend she was, sharing part of her exile), Benjamin *Constant, who fell passionately in love with her, and particularly *Chateaubriand, who visited her almost daily in his later years in her famed salon at L'Abbaye-aux-Bois, a fashionable convent-pension in the *Faubourg Saint-Germain. Her *Souvenirs et correspondance* were posthumously edited (1859) by her niece, Madame Lenormand. Both *David and Gérard did famous portraits of her. [FPB]

Recherche de l'absolu, La. One of the *Études philosophiques* in Balzac's *Comédie humaine*; the Flemish hero, Balthasar van Claës, ruins himself and his family in his search for the philosopher's stone.

Recherche de la vérité, La, see MALEBRANCHE.

Recherches de la France, see PASQUIER, E.

Récit de la mort, Le, see TATI-LOUTARD.

Récit de Théramène, Le. The dramatic account of Hippolyte's death at the end of Racine's *Phèdre*; it was often attacked as excessively long and ornate.

Récit du cirque de la vallée des morts, Le, see FANTOURÉ.

Récit secret, see DRIEU LA ROCHELLE.

RECLUS, Élisée (1830–1905). French geographer, remembered particularly for his monumental *Géographie universelle* (1875–94). A member of the Second International and an anarchist, he took an active part in resistance to the *coup d'état* of Louis-Napoléon in 1851 and in the *Commune of 1871, as did his elder brother Élie (1827–1904), a writer. Their younger brother Onésime (1837–1910) was a geographer and geologist specializing in Africa. [PF]

RECLUS DE MOLLIENS, LE (first third of 13th c.). Probably identifiable as a certain Barthélemy de Saint-Fuscien, and author of two verse treatises. Both the *Miserere* and the *Roman de Carité* are calls to penitence, the former reviewing the estates and listing the sins inspired by the senses, the latter lamenting the disappearance of charity. [JHMT]

RÉDA, Jacques (b. 1929). Since 1987 chief editor of the *Nouvelle Revue Française*, Réda is centrally a poet, though also a jazz critic (*Jazz Magazine*) with broad tastes and a meticulous ear. *L'Improviste* (1980) and *Jouer le jeu* (1985) contain essays (and the occasional poem) on jazz. The problem of metre in French has engaged him, and in his essays on poetry (*Celle qui vient à pas légers*, 1985) he has important things to say about the prosody of modern French, and draws a parallel between the proper writing of verse and the jazz musician's swing. The long title-poem in his second collection, *Récitatif* (1970), has

Redon

the freedom and compelling immediacy of an improvization. His first collection, *Amen* (1968), sets the tone for much of his work—elegiac, sensitive to hints of a secret reality behind the world's enigmatic surface. He is a dedicated *flâneur*, and his prose collections, such as *Les Ruines de Paris* (1977) and *L'Herbe des talus* (1984), illustrate the wonderful precision of his eye and ear. His later poetry (e.g. *Retour au calme*, 1989) shows an ever-increasing power to link concrete experience with metaphysical depth, and in recently published volumes, notably *Le Sens de la marche* (1990), he mingles prose and verse in an original synthesis.   [GDM]

REDON, Odilon (1840–1916). French artist, best known for the series of charcoals and lithographs (1879–88) whose fantastic subjects explore relationships between natural and human forms. His imaginative interpretation of the work of *Baudelaire, *Flaubert, and *Poe made Redon one of the heroes of the *Decadent movement following the description of his work in Huysmans's *À rebours (1884).
[JK]

REDONNET, Marie (b. 1948). French author of a striking trilogy: *Splendid Hôtel* (1986), *Forever Valley* (1987), and *Rose Mélie Rose* (1987). Each text elaborates a female strategy for survival in a strange and symbolic, *fin-du-monde* universe. Her plays include *Tir et Lir* (1988) and *Mobie-Diq* (1989); *Silsie* (1990) marks her return to the novel.   [EAF]

Réflexions critiques sur la poésie et la peinture, see DU BOS, J.-B.

Réflexions sur la formation et la distribution des richesses, see TURGOT.

Réflexions sur la violence, see SOREL, G.

Reformation, The (*La Réforme*). The course of the Reformation in France before the outbreak of the *Wars of Religion in 1562 was influenced, as was the Reformation movement generally, by social and political as well as theological issues. Many of the factors which contributed to the development of the *Renaissance also played a part in the religious revival: impatience with tradition, the growth of national and municipal feeling, the spread of *printing, and above all the new learning—the revival of Greek and Hebrew studies opened new areas to theological and philosophical enquiry. Among the Church's shortcomings identified by the proponents of reform were the ignorance, materialism, and undue privilege of the priesthood and monastic orders, the dullness and complexity of scholastic theology, and the tediousness and inaccessibility of Church ritual. Most conspicuous of all, according to *Luther, was the worldliness and ambition of the papacy.

The French Church had secured a measure of independence both from Rome and from the monarch under the Pragmatic Sanction of Bourges

(1438), which granted it special rights over taxation, the election of prelates, and the convocation of councils. The tradition of *Gallican independence was exploited by Louis XII when, during his struggle with Julius II, he convoked the particularist Council of Pisa (1512), and it was continued by *François Ier's *Concordat with Leo X (1516). Thus, the anti-papal storm which followed Luther's protest in 1517 was not entirely unwelcome in France. Moreover, in recent years many religious houses and educational establishments had been reformed, often under the aegis of the *Brethren of the Common Life, whose principles of personal piety and return to the pure sources of early Christianity were frequently contrasted by *humanist reformers with the noisy outward show of contemporary worship, and with the theologians' reliance on the accumulated commentaries of medieval *scholasticism. Finally, although the Concordat broke with tradition and concentrated ecclesiastical patronage in the hands of the monarch, on the whole François established an episcopate with reforming credentials.

The publication of *Erasmus's Greek New Testament in 1516, and Luther's denunciation of the trade in indulgences in the following year, are arguably the events which precipitated the Reformation. In France, Erasmus was already well known (though more as satirist and classical scholar than as theologian), and it did not take long for Luther's ideas to percolate. In 1521 the *Sorbonne followed the pope's excommunication of Luther with a vehement condemnation of his doctrine—which probably did much to disseminate his views. In the same year an influential group of *Evangelical reformers was gathered by Guillaume *Briçonnet in his diocese of Meaux. This included such diverse figures as *Lefèvre d'Étaples and Guillaume *Farel; in these confused early years of the intellectual ferment stirred up by Erasmus and Luther, unexpected alliances were not uncommon. Even the Sorbonne, so savagely represented by *Rabelais as monolithically obscurantist, had its share of moderate scholars not averse to reform, such as Briçonnet's teacher Josse Clichtove; moreover, it had inherited the tradition of Gallican independence and was by no means the puppet of Rome. However, the pugnacious Noël *Béda, syndic of the Faculty of Theology from 1520 to 1533, took the role of champion of orthodoxy, supported by the courts and in particular by the Parlement de Paris, and battle was joined.

Late in 1521 the Faculty condemned the works of Lefèvre, whose scriptural commentaries had anticipated Luther in some respects. In August 1523 occurred the first execution in Paris of a 'Lutheran heretic', Jean Vallière, an Augustinian from Normandy. Luther's translator Louis de *Berquin was arrested, his books burned, and his release secured only by François Ier's intervention. During the king's captivity after the Battle of Pavia (1525), the regent Louise de Savoie, alarmed by the Peasants' War in Germany and social unrest in France, permitted renewed repression of trouble-makers: Berquin was rearrested, and saved from the stake only by the king's return. At the same time pressure was put on the Meaux group, resulting in temporary exile for Lefèvre, whose translation of the New Testament was burned, and in retraction by Briçonnet. In February 1526 the Parlement forbade the preaching of 'Lutheran' doctrines and ordered the surrender of all French translations of scripture.

The king's return drove a wedge between the Sorbonne and the Parlement, which realized that it had been pushed too far by Béda's zeal. But François's need to restore national unity led him to sponsor a more modest episcopal and Gallican reform movement. Measures against extremism promulgated by the Council of Sens in 1528 led to condemnations and executions, culminating in the burning of the incorrigible Berquin in April 1529.

In the 1530s royal patronage frequently raised the hopes of the Evangelicals. The Sorbonne's influence was diminished in 1530 by the establishment of the independent royal professorships [see COLLÈGE DE FRANCE], by the Faculty's humiliation over its proposed censure of *Marguerite de Navarre's *Miroir de l'âme pécheresse*, and by Béda's banishment in 1533 for attacking the Evangelical preaching of Marguerite's protégé Roussel. On the other hand, bloody repression followed the two Affaires des *Placards (October 1534 and January 1535), whose apparent revelation of schismatic and seditious extremism led François to severe measures, including a short-lived ban on all printing. But in July 1535 his Edict of Coucy offered terms to all but the Zwinglians, whose doctrine the *placards* embodied. At the prompting of the liberal Cardinal Jean du Bellay, François invited Luther's colleague Melanchthon to Paris to debate the terms for religious peace. Melanchthon never appeared, but the cardinal's brother Guillaume, seigneur de Langey, attended a Diet of the German Lutheran princes in 1537, presenting a most conciliatory paper. Although clearly part of François's diplomatic offensive against Emperor Charles V, this event perhaps represents the high-water mark of Evangelical hopes in France, bolstered by the election of a reforming pope, Paul III, in 1534. But the suspicions of the princes and of Luther, and the shifting alliances between the great powers, frustrated the initiative; in 1538 François signed a truce with the emperor, who took upon himself much of the burden of conciliation. François then turned increasingly towards the enforcement of religious orthodoxy, defined for the French Church by the Sorbonne's 26 Articles of Faith, promulgated in 1543, and largely a reply to *Calvin's *Institution*. The ageing king was now particularly receptive to allegations of Reformist sedition, which may account for such dark deeds as the massacre of the Waldensians (*Vaudois) of Mérindol in 1545. But

in any case the opening in that year of the Council of Trent, the rise of the uncompromising Calvin, and the foundation of the *Jesuits, were clear indications that the era of potential conciliation was ending; the *Counter-Reformation was gathering pace.

*Henri II continued his father's policy of fostering Gallican interests whilst repressing potential sedition. Liberal churchmen such as cardinals Jean du Bellay and Odet de Châtillon enjoyed his confidence, and relations with the papacy became so strained (cf. Rabelais's *Quart Livre*) that in 1551 it seemed possible that France would seek an 'Anglican' solution to the question of reform (in the end, political necessity healed the breach). On the other hand, in 1547 Henri authorized the notorious *chambre ardente* as an inquisitorial adjunct to the Parlement and, though he was restrained from instituting a full-scale Inquisition on the Spanish model, the number of burnings increased steadily. Predictably, these deaths, chronicled in Jean Crespin's *Livre des martyrs*, failed to deter the Calvinists; numerous small congregations were founded, public services were held, and the first national assembly of the French Reformed Church met in 1559. The adherence of prominent aristocrats, including Gaspard de *Coligny and Louis de *Condé, emphasized the extent of Calvinist penetration; *L'Hôpital's policy of toleration, and the belated compromise attempted in 1561 at Poissy, where *Bèze led the Reformist delegation, did little to heal the divisions [see WARS OF RELIGION].

French Renaissance literature before 1562 was profoundly marked by the events and controversies of the Reformation. While producing nothing to match the sombre grandeur of *Ronsard's *Discours* or d'*Aubigné's *Tragiques*, inspired by the Wars of Religion, writers of the period could scarcely ignore debates which involved the very destiny of their souls—and those of their readers: justification by faith, predestination, the role of the Church and of Christ, the nature of the Eucharist. Theological debate is never far from the pages of those renowned entertainers Rabelais and *Marot, who both endured exile for their views, and a new, if somewhat eclectic, spirituality informs the poetry and drama of Marguerite de Navarre. Not least, the Reformation's challenge to established authority offered ideal conditions for the burgeoning of satire, exemplified by *Des Periers's *Cymbalum mundi* and the vernacular writings of *Dolet, Bèze, *Viret, and Calvin himself. [MJH]

See J. Delumeau, *Naissance et affirmation de la Réforme* (1973); R. M. Kingdon, *Church and Society in Renaissance Europe* (1985); M. Greengrass, *The French Reformation* (1987).

Réfractaires, Les. Members of the clergy who refused to accept the *Constitution Civile of 1790.

Refuge, Le. Term used to describe the Huguenot communities which fled from France, particularly after the Revocation of the *Edict of Nantes in 1685 (though there had been such exiles since the *Wars of Religion, and departures picked up again from the mid-1650s onwards). Estimates of the number who left in and after 1685 vary between 200,000 and 300,000. Most went to the Low Countries or England; by the late 17th c. there were between 50,000 and 80,000 Huguenots in England, constituting about 1 per cent of the English population. Most exiles were from the Huguenot élite; rural Huguenots, particularly in the Cévennes and the Languedoc in general, mostly stayed put. Many exiles were soldiers or sailors, and about 10,000 Huguenots fought in enemy ranks in the next war. It is often argued that the loss of the economic skills of the exiles, and also of much of their capital, had a serious retarding effect on French economic growth (though continuing warfare was probably a much more serious cause). Many Huguenot families remained abroad for generations. In the Low Countries in particular, pastors and spokesmen of the Refuge such as *Jurieu and *Bayle remained a constant centre of propaganda against French Catholicism and the French state.   [RBG]

Refus global, see BORDUAS.

Regard du roi, Le, see LAYE.

Regards sur le monde actuel, see VALÉRY.

Regency. The regencies in French history include that of Marie de Médicis during the minority of Louis XIII and that of *Anne d'Autriche during the minority of Louis XIV, but the term 'La Régence' is applied to that of Philippe, duc d'*Orléans, during the first eight years (1715–23) of the minority of Louis XV. With the support of the Parlement de Paris, the duke set aside *Louis XIV's will and assumed power, returning the ancient right of remonstrance to the Parlement and giving ministerial responsibility to a 'Polysynodie' of six councils composed largely of great nobles.

The Regency is usually seen as an explosion of freedom and frivolity after the austere devotion of Louis XIV's last years. In fact many of its dominant characteristics—politely dissolute manners, new fortunes, gambling, freedom of thought, and political enquiry—were already present in the preceding years in such milieux as the *Temple and the court of the duchesse du *Maine at Sceaux. But the influence of the Regent and the instability caused by *Law's economic experiments made such new tendencies more visible. In literary terms, the Regency sees the predominance of modernist tendencies in works such as Montesquieu's *Lettres persanes* and *Marivaux's comedies. It is a time of free enquiry, audacious satire, and a light, elegant style which can be seen as the literary equivalent of the *Rococo.
                                                  [PF]

Regions and *Départements* of France. The 'hexagone' of present-day France is the outcome of a long historical process, the creation of a nation by the gradual annexation of neighbouring territories. Over this long period, France has known a variety of internal administrative divisions.

1. The Creation of Modern France

The Frankish kingdom of the *Merovingians, and subsequently the empire of *Charlemagne, extended over most of present-day France (except for Brittany) and beyond. After the period of strife and anarchy following the death of Charlemagne, the territory controlled by the French king was much reduced. At the end of the 10th c. Hugues Capet ruled directly over a demesne corresponding roughly to the Île-de-France; he was, however, acknowledged as their feudal overlord by the rulers of many surrounding *duchés* and *comtés* [see MONARCHY; FEUDALISM]. By the end of the 12th c. virtually half of present-day France was part of the Angevin empire and subject to rule from England [see Map 1]; the reconquest of this territory began in earnest under *Philippe-Auguste, but it was only completed, after centuries of warfare, when Calais fell to the French in 1558.

Over the same centuries, by conquest, marriage, or treaty, the other lands which currently make up France were gradually added to the kingdom. The violence of the so-called Albigensian Crusade [see CATHARS] brought Languedoc under French rule; Dauphiné, *Brittany, and Provence were successively acquired; and after the feud of the *Armagnacs and Burgundians had torn France apart, the Burgundian lands finally became French at the end of the 15th c. By the end of the 16th c. the greater part of modern France was united under a single ruler.

The following three centuries saw the acquisition of the remaining major territories: Roussillon, Franche-Comté, and Alsace in the 17th c.; Lorraine and Corsica in the 18th; Nice and the northern part of the former Duchy of Savoy in the 19th. Alsace and Lorraine were lost to Germany in 1870–1918 and again in 1940–4. Until its independence in 1962, *Algeria was treated as part of metropolitan France, as were (and still are) certain French islands in the Caribbean and Indian Ocean [see DOM-TOM].

2. The Ancien Régime: Provinces and Généralités

In the 17th and 18th c. France was primarily divided into more than 30 major provinces or *gouvernements* [see Map 2]. These corresponded in part to the territories absorbed into France during the Middle Ages; they were controlled (in name at least) by provincial *gouverneurs*, high-ranking nobles whose role tended to become more honorific as a good deal of their power passed to the royal *intendants*. The latter presided over new administrative districts known as *généralités* (also sometimes called provinces, though they were not identical with the *gouvernements*).

There were many further divisions of *ancien régime* France, producing an administrative system of redoubtable complexity and inertia; local and provincial rights were jealously maintained. Judicially, the country was divided up between the 13 *parlements*, and there were innumerable sub-divisions: *prévôtés*, *baillages*, *sénéchaussées*, etc. [see PARLEMENTS]. In addition, there was a distinction between the *pays d'état* (provinces such as Brittany, Burgundy, Provence, and Languedoc which had been allowed to retain their *états*, regional assemblies) and the so-called *pays d'élection*; in the latter the *généralités* were divided up for fiscal purposes into *élections*, which originally corresponded to yet another type of division, ecclesiastical dioceses. *Taxation was very unevenly distributed, the *pays d'état* generally paying less than the *pays d'élection*.

3. Départements

Not surprisingly, the Revolutionary authorities set out to reorganize the rich chaos outlined above. They proceeded to a new carving-up of the country into *départements*, originally 83 in number. The frontiers of these tended to follow those of the old *gouvernements* where possible, but the names of the old provinces were eliminated (*départements* were named after geographical features such as rivers or mountains). Each *département* was of roughly equivalent size, the principle being that it was possible to ride a horse from any point in the *département* to its administrative centre (*chef-lieu*) in a day.

The *département* was in the charge of a *préfet* (now called *commissaire de la République*) appointed by the government, and the *corps préfectoral* became a powerful instrument for maintaining central control over the provinces. Each *département* was (and still is) divided into a number of *sous-préfectures* or *arrondissements* (the term also used for the districts of Paris). These in turn are divided into *cantons* and then into *communes*. The *commune*, the smallest administrative unit, is presided over by an elected mayor, who may be repeatedly re-elected and may thus come to exert great local power (it is possible, indeed common, for a mayor also to be a *député* in the Assemblée Nationale).

The administrative map established during the Revolution has lasted remarkably well. Among the subsequent changes one may mention the following: in the 1790s there were 15 annexed *départements* in Flanders in the East, while between 1870 and 1914 the departments of Alsace and Lorraine ceased to be part of France, with the exception of the small Territoire de Belfort; Algeria was divided into three *départements*, which were lost at Independence; several *départements* were renamed in the 1960s to avoid the supposedly humiliating connotations of certain adjectives (Seine Inférieure became Seine Maritime); at about the same time seven new *départements* took the place of the former Seine and Seine-et-Oise in the densely populated Paris area. There are currently (1993) 95 *départements* in metropolitan France plus four *départements d'outre-mer* [see DOM-TOM].

4. Regions

While the departmental system worked efficiently, it was less successful in attracting loyalty; many French people continued to feel that they belonged rather to the old provinces, such as Brittany, Picardy, or Provence. It was in relation to the provinces or smaller *terroirs* that a good deal of local culture defined itself throughout the 19th and 20th c. There was writing in the local languages or dialects [see PATOIS AND DIALECT WRITING], the collection of local folklore [see FOLK-TALE; POPULAR SONG], and particularly in the 20th c. the flourishing of the 'regional novel' (e.g. *Giono, *Pourrat, *Pergaud), written in French but distilling the character and manners of a given provincial area.

The persistence of regional loyalty was often accompanied by distrust of Paris, resentment at the discrimination against local language and culture, and hostility to the excessive, 'Jacobin' centralization of French political life. In the second half of the 20th c., building on previous endeavours, a number of important initiatives, including the establishment of *Maisons de la Culture and the *'décentralisation théâtrale', set out to redress the balance.

Regionalism and decentralization also became major political issues, constituting, for instance, a major plank in the programme of the new Parti Socialiste in the 1970s. Regional reform has been constantly on the agenda of successive governments during the Fourth and Fifth Republics. The 1950s saw the beginning of a new administrative division of France into regions. There are currently (1993) 22 metropolitan regions as follows: Alsace, Aquitaine, Auvergne, Basse-Normandie, Bourgogne, Bretagne, Centre, Champagne-Ardennes, Corse, Franche-Comté, Haute-Normandie, Île-de-France, Languedoc-Roussillon, Limousin, Lorraine, Midi-Pyrénées, Nord, Pays de la Loire, Picardie, Poitou-Charentes, Provence-Côte d'Azur, Rhône-Alpes. Some of the names are those of the old provinces, but the boundaries of regions and provinces rarely correspond.

The main task of the regions is to promote economic development. Under the presidency of François *Mitterrand steps were taken to promote greater regional autonomy; each region is administered both by a representative of central government (the *commissaire de la République*) and by a Conseil Régional (directly elected since 1986) and a Comité Économique et Social. However, the real autonomy of the regions and the nature of their relations both with central government and with the *départements* remain open questions.   [PF]

Règle du jeu, La, see LEIRIS; RENOIR, J.

Règles pour la direction de l'esprit, see DESCARTES.

REGNARD, Jean-François (1655–1709). French comic playwright; a widely travelled author, whose early experiences included eight months of slavery in

Algiers, fictionalized in *La Provençale* (1731). Regnard began his dramatic career in 1688, when his *Le Divorce* was performed at the *Comédie-Italienne. He wrote 11 comedies for the *Italiens*, including four in collaboration with *Dufresny. Their collaboration ended in 1696, when they quarrelled over the paternity of the outline of a play about a gambler. Regnard's *Le *Joueur*, written in five acts in verse (unusual at this time) was accepted and performed by the *Comédie-Française, but Dufresny's subsequent play, *Le Chevalier joueur*, met with little acclaim. Between 1696 and 1708, Regnard wrote eleven plays for the Comédie-Française.

Along with *Le Joueur* and *Les Folies amoureuses* (1704), his best-known play is *Le Légataire universel* (1708). Its form is classical, but like all his plays for the Comédie-Française, it bears the imprint of Regnard's career with the *Italiens*, such as the use of disguises, puns, *lazzi*, and scenes tangential to the plot. From his own day onwards, Regnard has been regarded as the best dramatist of his generation, but performances of his plays have dwindled since the mid-19th c. His verse has always been praised for its wit and musicality. But until the latter half of the 20th c. his work suffered from an inappropriate comparison with *Molière's, based on the misconception that his disinterested, schematic, and fantasized portrayal of human behaviour, his ludicrous, loosely structured, and often inconclusive plots, his caricatural characters, his 'borrowings' and quotations from classical playwrights, and his propensity for including burlesque and (sometimes scabrous) jokes at every opportunity denoted frivolity, cynicism, or an inability (or refusal) to take a moral stance. Recent criticism (e.g. Dorothy Medlin's *The Verbal Art of Jean-François Regnard*, 1966) has seen his achievement more positively. [JD]

RÉGNIER, François-Joseph (1807–85). Distinguished French actor whose long career at the *Comédie-Française (1831–71) was marked by almost unbroken success in the major comic roles of the classical repertory (*Molière, *Marivaux, *Beaumarchais). He was also esteemed for his performances in modern plays, e.g. *Scribe's *Bertrand et Raton* (1833). [SBJ]

RÉGNIER, Henri de (1864–1936). French poet who made an important contribution to the *Symbolist movement with *Poèmes anciens et romanesques* (1890) and *Tel qu'en songe* (1892), in which he combined *vers libre* and more traditional verse forms to express his sense of the mystery of experience. His later work, with its more descriptive clarity and regular rhythms, played its part in the neoclassical revival of the period, but he never renounced the Symbolist elements which corresponded to his delicate, nostalgic, and complex sensibility. In this way he helped to win a wider audience for Symbolist poetry, a fact borne out in 1911 when he became the first representative of the Symbolist movement to be elected to the Académie Française. [JK]

RÉGNIER, Mathurin (1573–1613). French poet and satirist, the nephew of *Desportes, whose benefice he inherited. Legend has exaggerated his reputation as a debauchee; he seems to have frequented learned circles more than the *cabaret*. He enjoyed the favour of *Henri IV and wrote a number of court poems, including verse for *royal entries. His work also includes both religious poetry and love poetry, but his reputation rests on a group of 17 satires, verse discourses addressed to friends and patrons. While some of these (e.g. Satire 13, a vivid portrait of the *entremetteuse* Macette) conform to the then current vogue for picturesque and grotesque sketches in the style of the Italian Berni [see SATIRE], his more constant aim was to raise satire to a proper dignity, following like the *Pléiade the model of the classics, notably Horace; to this end he uses alexandrines throughout. His poems contain much criticism of contemporary society, with the usual nostalgia for previous, more virtuous ages. He writes above all as a moralist, echoing *Montaigne's views on the variability of opinion and the weakness of the human will. His verse is full of life and variety and in Satire 9 he defends his freedom, together with the poetic ambitions of *Ronsard and the classics, against the modern purism of *Malherbe. [PF]

RÉGNIER-DESMARAIS, François-Séraphin (1632–1713). French poet and grammarian, active in the preparation of the first *dictionary of the Académie Française, and author of a *Traité de la grammaire française* (1705).

Regrets, Les, see DU BELLAY.

'Regrets de la Belle Heaulmière', see VILLON.

Reine d'Écosse, La. Tragedy by *Montchrestien, first published in 1601 as *L'Écossaise, ou le Désastre*; much revised, and republished as *La Reine d'Écosse* in 1604. The play falls into two parts; the first two acts show the reluctant Elizabeth Tudor being urged to sign the death-warrant of Marie Stuart; in the other three acts the Scottish queen is told of the death-sentence, she prepares to die, and her execution is reported. The abiding impression is of admiration and pity for Mary, but Elizabeth's dilemma is also made clear. There is some fine elegiac writing in choric poems, especially at the end of Act II. [GJ]

Reine morte, La. This 1942 *Montherlant play on the traditional theme of Inès de Castro is dominated by the figure of Ferrante, the king who kills his son's wife for the good of the kingdom. His actions show the irrationality and inconsistency of human behaviour, departing from the dramatic convention of coherence and unity of character. His reasons for killing Inès are never clear; he persuades himself of the reasons not to, before doing so. This is a typical Montherlant 'costume' play in its Iberian background and formal stylization, which clothe a realistic and 'unliterary' psychological examination of human behaviour. [RMG]

RÉJANE, Gabrielle (1857–1920). A leading French actress of the *belle époque*, she enjoyed great popularity, especially at the Vaudeville, in light comedies, like *Sardou's *Madame Sans-Gêne* (1893), in which she displayed exceptional charm, brio, and seductiveness, as she did in dramas of passion, such as *Porto-Riche's *Amoureuse* (1891). [SBJ]

Relations des Jésuites, see JESUITS; TRAVEL WRITING.

Relève, La (1934–41; *La Nouvelle Relève* 1941–8). Journal published by several educated young Montrealers (Claude Hurtubise, Robert Charbonneau, Jean Le Moyne). They rejected bourgeois philistinism and *terroirisme* for the *Personalism of Emmanuel *Mounier. Less committed than Mounier's *Esprit*, it became a mouthpiece for renewal through art and Catholic spirituality. *Saint-Denys Garneau contributed reviews, including 'Peintres français à la Galerie Scott', characteristic in its warm, idealistic aestheticism. [CRPM]

Religieuse, La. Novel by *Diderot. Written in 1760, it was published in the *Correspondance littéraire* in 1780, though a teasing set of letters (known as the 'Préface-annexe'), which describe the circumstances of composition, had been made public in 1770. It began life as a practical joke: in order to tempt the wealthy and humanitarian marquis de Croismare to return to Paris, Diderot, *Grimm, and others made up letters from a supposed nun, Suzanne Simonin, who had escaped from a convent and was seeking his protection. The novel that developed from this is presented as Suzanne's own story of her life.

For family reasons she is placed in a convent against her will, trapped into taking orders, and subjected to an improbable accumulation of sadistic persecutions. The story produces a powerful, melodramatic effect, like a Gothic horror novel. Diderot uses it to explore imaginatively the effects of claustration on a group of women—there is a remarkable sequence concerned with female homosexuality—and to expose the evils of forced vocations and the unnatural life of the convent. Whether it should be read as an attack on Christianity is doubtful.

A film by Jacques Rivette, based on Diderot's novel, was banned from the French screen in 1967. [PF]

Religious Writing, see DEVOTIONAL WRITING; SERMON.

Remarques sur la langue française, see VAUGELAS.

Remède de Fortune, Le, see MACHAUT.

RÉMOND DE SAINT-MARD, Toussaint (1682–1757). Epicurean French author of various short works, in particular *Réflexions sur la poésie en*

général (1733), stressing the appeal of poetry to the senses and the passions, and *Nouveaux dialogues des dieux* (1741, also published as *Éloge des plaisirs*), preceded by a 'Discours sur la nature du *dialogue', one of the few 18th-c. discussions of the genre. [PF]

Remonstrance, see PARLEMENTS.

RÉMUSAT, Charles, comte de (1797–1875). The son of Claire de *Rémusat, he had a political career as *député* and at times minister, but was primarily a historian of philosophy. His most famous work, *Abélard* (1845), is written in dramatic form and learnedly re-creates medieval philosophical debates. Much of his other work is on English philosophers: *Anselme de Cantorbéry* (1854), *Bacon* (1858), *Lord Herbert de Cherbury* (1874), and his *Histoire de la philosophie en Angleterre de Bacon jusqu'à Locke* (1875). [FPB]

RÉMUSAT, Claire-Élisabeth Gravier de Vergennes, comtesse de (1780–1824). Lady-in-waiting to the Empress Josephine and a woman of remarkable beauty and intelligence. Her major writings were published after her death. Her *Essai sur l'éducation des femmes* (1824) demanded a considerably richer intellectual development than *Rousseau proposed for women. Her *Mémoires* (1879–80) provide acute and valuable insights on the Napoleonic court. Her *Correspondance* (1881) with her son, Charles de *Rémusat, is enlightening about intellectual life during the period. [FPB]

Renaissance, The

1. The Idea of a Renaissance

The Renaissance was a movement in learned culture and the fine arts beginning in Italy in the 14th c.—Petrarch (1304–74) is often considered the first 'Renaissance man'—and spreading through most of Western Europe. By the late 16th c. it was beginning to give way to other movements [see BAROQUE; CLASSICISM] which may, however, also be seen as transformations of the Renaissance itself.

Writers of this period themselves spoke of a rebirth or renewal of culture (broadly, that of classical antiquity) after what they saw as the barbarism of the intervening centuries; *Rabelais and *Du Bellay provide famous versions of the theme. By the 18th c. historians had begun to characterize this cultural movement as a 'Renaissance of arts and letters'. However, the notion of the Renaissance as a self-contained period in the history of Western civilization is largely the invention of 19th-c. historians such as Burckhardt and *Michelet, who attributed to the period as a whole characteristics such as optimism, individualism, and an increasingly secular outlook. More recently, historians have shown that such generalizations are misleading, drawing attention to what 'Renaissance' writers and thinkers have in common with their 'medieval' predecessors, or to earlier 'Renaissances' such as that of the 12th c.

Renaissance

2. The Early Renaissance

In France, the sense of a cultural renewal begins to gather momentum in the last third of the 15th c. A *printing press was established in Paris in 1470, and *rhetoric and classical poetry were taught in extra-curricular hours at the University of Paris. *Lemaire de Belges, in his *Concorde des deux langages* of 1511, proposes a harmonious alliance of French and Italian culture, and the importance of Lyon as a cultural staging-post between France and Italy is already becoming clear as *Neoplatonist ideas emerge in the writings of Symphorien *Champier and others. During this period, too, the intermittent French military incursions into Italy certainly had some cultural consequences, although historians no longer attribute to this factor the importance it was once thought to have in the formation of the French Renaissance [see ITALIAN INFLUENCES].

The evolution of French culture at this time is in fact by no means wholly dependent on Italy. Northern European *humanism, ideally embodied in *Erasmus, provides a model for the reconciliation of ancient Greek and Roman wisdom with Christian faith. In 1517 *François Ier tried to persuade Erasmus to found a humanist college in Paris; this venture was unsuccessful, but in 1530 François established a group of *lecteurs royaux* in classical and biblical languages [see COLLÈGE DE FRANCE]. The leading French humanist of François Ier's reign was *Budé, who mastered Greek as well as Latin studies and corresponded extensively with Erasmus. It was at this time, too, that Rabelais acquired Greek: his knowledge of the ancient world is an essential element in his comic fiction.

The impact of Renaissance humanism on French vernacular writers had in fact been apparent from the 15th c. onwards: the *Rhétoriqueurs, often regarded by literary historians as backward-looking, were in part influenced by the humanist interest in rhetoric. In the second quarter of the 16th c. the *translation of Latin, Greek, and Italian texts into French was vigorously promoted by François Ier and his sister *Marguerite de Navarre, and French poets made increasing use of classical forms: Clément *Marot wrote eclogues, and *Scève, in his love-cycle *Délie*, adapted the Latin epigram form which was especially fashionable among poets of the 1540s. The influence of Petrarchan love-poetry on French poets is another central feature of this period [see PETRARCHISM]. *Délie* is the first Petrarchan love-sequence in French, although it was written in *dizains*, not sonnets; the *sonnet-form made its appearance in France at the end of the 1530s, but was not to be widely used until it was made fashionable by the *Pléiade.

Meanwhile, prose style was also evolving. Latin was still the primary focus of interest, as in the acrimonious debate over the value of Cicero as a model: Étienne *Dolet attacked Erasmus's flexible, eclectic approach in favour of a purist classical aesthetic, but it was Erasmus who was the more widely followed.

However, translation of Cicero and other prose-writers into the vernacular ensured that the issue was not limited to learned culture. Translation of biblical texts also raised the question of style; and French was by now being more and more widely used in the public arena—in law, for example, where the Edict of *Villers-Cotterêts (1539) specified the use of the French language in legal proceedings and court records. *Calvin's *Institutes of the Christian Religion*, of which the first version appeared in Latin in 1536, soon began to appear in French translation, thus becoming the first comprehensive work of theology in French. The medical writer Ambroise *Paré also chose French rather than Latin.

One of the most distinctive philosophical emphases of the European Renaissance was an interest in the dialogues of Plato as opposed to the more systematic, logic-based philosophy of Aristotle which had underpinned the thinking of the *scholastics. Originating in Florence in the late 15th c., the Neoplatonist movement soon began to find disciples in France. It was transmitted above all by the handbooks of courtly behaviour (Castiglione's *The Courtier* is the best-known example) which were fashionable in Italy and France in the first half of the 16th c. [see COURTOISIE]. These placed woman at the centre of courtly life and proposed a metaphysic and an ethic according to which human love was valued as the first phase of a spiritual ascent towards knowledge of the supreme good. Poets such as *Héroët exploited Neoplatonist arguments and images; Marguerite de Navarre, in her *Heptaméron*, drew rather more cautiously on such ideas in order to explore the problems and potentialities of human relationships. Counter-arguments were also vigorously defended, both by court poets and by some of the characters in the *Heptaméron* (itself, characteristically, a *dialogue). Yet Neoplatonism continued to be an important element in the 16th-c. imagination, at least at the higher social levels, and provided one of the means by which the status of women and their cultural activities could be enhanced. Marguerite de Navarre was only one of several prominent woman writers of the mid-16th c.: the poets Pernette *du Guillet and Louise *Labé, both from Lyon, rivalled the production of male contemporaries such as Scève.

The story of the French Renaissance in the reign of François Ier is closely bound up with religious developments. The Erasmian emphasis on understanding of the biblical texts as well as of the classics was taken up in France from the very beginning of the 16th c. by scholars such as *Lefèvre d'Étaples, and the opposition of the *Sorbonne to humanist learning was largely conditioned by the theological implications of new readings of scripture. The interweaving of these two currents—humanism and *Evangelism—is particularly well illustrated by the works of Rabelais, whereas in the circle of Marguerite de Navarre a more ambivalent attitude to the classics is apparent.

The most distinctive artistic achievement of the earlier 16th c. in France was the construction of a number of châteaux. The most ambitious of these was *Fontainebleau, but the châteaux of the Loire valley (Blois, Amboise, Chenonceaux, Chambord, and others) are equally celebrated and better preserved. Unlike the imposing fortified castles of the later Middle Ages, they were designed as elegant pleasure-palaces for the king himself and for members of the court, who enjoyed country pursuits such as hunting; at the same time they were manifestations of royal power and prosperity. Many of their architectural features—such as the staircases at Blois and Azay-le-Rideau—were borrowed from Italy, but these were blended with earlier native structures to form an independent and distinctive style. The châteaux were not only architectural achievements: they were decorated with paintings, sculptures, and tapestries which also exhibit the influence of Italian styles. France also has fine Renaissance churches: Saint-Étienne du Mont, in Paris, has an elegant François Ier interior within a late Gothic structure; particularly striking is the *jubé*, one of the very few choir screens to have survived in French churches.

3. High Renaissance and Late Renaissance

The accession of *Henri II (1547) and the death of Marguerite (1549) represent a major cultural watershed. The generation of the Evangelicals is all but over; so too is a period in which new literary forms, drafted in from classical antiquity and Italy, cohabited more or less comfortably with native French forms and genres inherited from the later Middle Ages. In the late 1540s a group of younger poets acquired from the humanist scholar Jean *Dorat at the Collège de Coqueret a thorough grounding in the poetry of Greece and Rome; in 1552 they joined forces with a similar group studying at the Collège de Boncourt, thus forming what came to be known as the Pléiade. Du Bellay's *Défense et illustration de la langue française* (1549) proclaimed a programme of systematic imitation of ancient and Italian poetry, famously rejecting as 'vieilles épiceries' virtually the entire native French tradition. The poetry of Du Bellay, *Ronsard, and others thus represents a 'High Renaissance' in French literature, naturalizing classical themes and myths and, in the process, forging some of the central tools of French poets for centuries to come (the sonnet, the *alexandrine). This is also the period when classicizing *tragedy begins to appear on the French scene with Jodelle's *Cléopâtre captive* (1552-3). These developments were vigorously opposed by Calvinist writers such as *Bèze, who saw them as a manifestation of paganism (although there is no reason to take this charge literally).

Neoplatonism continued to be an important element in the literature and thought of this period: the poets of the new generation exploited it in particular for a theory of divine inspiration that assigned dignity and seriousness to their writings. With the coming of the *Wars of Religion in the 1560s the mood changes, however, and writers turn to ancient philosophies designed to provide defences against adversity (*Neostoicism) or to give scope to metaphysical and epistemological uncertainty (*Pyrrhonism); elements of these modes of thought had been known and used by earlier generations, but they now begin to predominate. The *Essais* of Michel de *Montaigne exhibit both trends.

Montaigne, in fact, illustrates with great clarity the character of what may be called the 'Late Renaissance' in France. He too had received a humanist education: he was thoroughly familiar with classical Latin literature, quoting it on almost every page he wrote, and he read Greek works in translation (*Amyot's translation of the *Lives* and moral essays of Plutarch profoundly influenced the composition of the *Essais*). The transposition of this learning into a vernacular medium was also not in itself an innovation. Yet Montaigne takes one aspect of the humanist programme to unprecedented lengths. Both Erasmus and Du Bellay had stressed that the writer should make use of the whole range of classical materials, reworking them and 'digesting' them so that they re-emerged in a new and individual form: the first-person singular thus becomes a central organizing principle (Erasmus's letters and Du Bellay's *Regrets*, many of which are letter-poems, are key examples). In Montaigne's *Essais*, the perspective of the individual writer becomes so dominant that, especially in its later versions, the book becomes a 'self-portrait', anticipating a tradition of secular *autobiography which, four centuries later, we still recognize as distinctively modern. It is, no doubt, not an accident that painters cultivated the art of lifelike portraiture in this period: Jean *Clouet and his son François are the best-known French examples.

4. Later Developments and Historical Significance

Classical scholarship will continue to be a major aspect of European education and culture until the 20th c. [see LATINITY], but, in France at least, the culture of the court and of the higher levels of society increasingly moves, in the 17th c., towards the evolution of forms of expression which avoid the pedantic and the technical. Montaigne is a forerunner of this development; in poetry, a shift away from high-flown rhetoric and from the more arcane forms of classical allusion and mythology will eventually lead poets and theorists (*Malherbe, *Boileau) to reject out of hand the achievements of the Pléiade.

Understood in terms of a dialogue with classical antiquity, the French Renaissance may thus be charted both as a coherent phenomenon in its own right and as part of a wider cultural complex that includes the baroque and classicism. It should be stressed, however, that it is primarily a phenomenon of learning and of high culture, and that it cannot be safely extended to characterize the history of the period as a whole. Certainly, it is closely linked to—indeed enabled by—wider historical factors such as the economic expansion of the later 15th and the 16th c. and increased travel and trade (not least with the New World); writers like Montaigne help to foster greater cultural relativity and a more secular world-view. But it is now clear that Renaissance humanism was not primarily responsible for the rise in science and technology which was to play such a central role in the centuries that followed, and that pre-Renaissance modes of thought continued throughout the 16th c., not always in unenlightened ways. Renaissance humanists mounted a formidable and highly effective propaganda campaign which it is all too easy to accept as historical fact. Over-simplification may be avoided by treating the Renaissance as part of that broader historical phase now commonly referred to as the 'early modern period'. [TC]

See W. K. Ferguson, *The Renaissance in Historical Thought* (1948); F. Simone, *The French Renaissance* (1961; trans. H. G. Hall, 1969); P. Burke, *The Renaissance* (1964); A. J. Krailsheimer (ed.), *The Continental Renaissance* (1971).

RENAN, Ernest (1823–92). One of the leading French writers and thinkers of the 19th c. Born in Brittany, he studied for holy orders in Paris, leaving the seminary of Saint-Sulpice in 1845 as a result of the religious doubts his scientific enquiries had engendered, though he retained both a fascination for religion and a deep regret for his lost faith. He rapidly completed the *baccalauréat*, *licence*, and philosophy *agrégation*, in which he came first. After the February Revolution of 1848 he enthusiastically supported the liberal positions of *Lamartine, and drafted his first substantial work, *L'Avenir de la science* (published only in 1890), which sketched out his romantic vision of progress in nature and society, culminating in a synthesis of science and religion. His doctoral thesis on *Averroès et l'averroïsme* (1852) was much admired, and he published widely on philology and the history of religion, as well as contributing actively to the intellectual press.

Appointed to the chair of Hebrew at the *Collège de France in 1861, he was suspended after casting doubt on the divinity of Christ in his inaugural lecture. His controversial *Vie de Jésus* (1863), however, was an enormous popular success, and he followed it over the next 20 years with six further volumes, comprising his major *Histoire des origines du christianisme*, taking the account as far as Marcus Aurelius. His subsequent *Histoire du peuple d'Israël* (1887–93) was also acclaimed. Restored to his chair after the fall of the Second Empire, he wrote *La Réforme intellectuelle et morale* (1871) to advise on the stern measures he felt were required to restore authority, order, and progress. The Third Republic showed its appreciation in the official honours it showered on him, including election to the Académie Française in 1878. He continued to write trenchantly on matters of current political or philosophical interest, and several of his more important essays were collected as *Dialogues et fragments philosophiques* (1876). But his work was increasingly tinged with scepticism as to the value of his (or any) intellectual activity. He reviewed his personal and intellectual development in *Souvenirs d'enfance et de jeunesse* (1883), including the account of his loss of religious faith, entitled 'Prière sur l'Acropole', which has frequently figured in anthologies.

Renan's thought was compendious, eclectic, and flexible, rather than systematic. Outside his historical works he preferred to adopt the more open dialogue format, which enabled questions to be raised without necessarily reaching conclusions. This lent itself well to discussion of the major problem of how to reconcile the evident triumph of the natural sciences with the deep-seated desire for the consolations of religion. Trained as both a scholar and a priest, Renan felt the conflict personally and strove for a solution which would recognize the worth of both. He formulated a *loi des trois états*, drawing on both *Comte's Positivism and Hegel's dialectic, and suggesting that human development passed from an early spontaneous and intuitive syncretism, expressed as religion, to a later reflective and rational analysis, expressed as science, and finally to a synthesis of these in a higher unity, combining scientific knowledge with imaginative sympathy in an *esprit de finesse*. Ultimately, the progress of humanity would raise it to the perfection of God.

Renan rejected the supernatural as well as most forms of metaphysics, and championed the scientific method which he saw as encompassing and superseding philosophy. In particular, he regarded philology, his own speciality, as the science of humanity, since in studying the history of the human mind, philology revealed consciousness to be the product and goal of the history of the universe. This also confirmed for Renan that the final end of evolution is the realization of the Ideal, or God, who in an almost pantheistic sense can then be seen to be drawing the universe towards His own self-realization. It followed that men had a moral duty to promote the growth of consciousness, which was identified as a moral good. Renan recuperated many Christian practices in this light, as forerunners of the true religion of science. He also felt it important to offer the common people an accessible moral and religious framework which would guarantee social order.

Towards the end of his life, recognizing that his philological work was being superseded by others, and that his moral aspirations were unworkable, he adopted a more ludic and even cynical stance which stressed the value of sensual pleasures. Celebrated during his lifetime, Renan has been criticized for his ambiguity, self-indulgence, and conservatism, and his reputation has never regained its former peak, though many aspects of his work have informed later French thought. [MHK]

See D. G. Charlton, *Positivist Thought in France* (1959); K. Gore, *L'Idée de progrès dans la pensée de Renan* (1970).

RENARD, Jean-Claude (b. 1922). French poet. With *La Terre du sacre* (1965) Renard moved away from the fixed metres of his early years (e.g. *Juan*, 1945) to free-verse forms. A richly sensuous love of nature blends with awareness of a hidden supernatural reality in collections such as *La Braise et la rivière* (1969). The concision of the zen *koan* is achieved in *Toutes les îles sont secrètes* (1984). Renard rejects all dogmatic positions, and his prose texts (*Notes sur la poésie*, 1970; *Quand le poème devient prière*, 1987; and others) are essential reading. They explore with rigorous open-mindedness the problems of poetic creation and its relationship to mystical experience.
[GDM]

RENARD, Jules (1864–1910). Author of prose fiction and plays. Bred in the countryside of central France, he became a man of letters, frequenting literary, artistic, and theatrical circles and contributing to contemporary journals (*Le *Mercure de France, La *Revue blanche*). His one, indifferent book of poems, *Les Roses* (1886), was followed by the prose and plays on which his reputation as a minor classic rests. Drawing heavily on his observation of rural life in the provinces, he renders people with a wary, unsentimental, and tireless regard for truth, as in the character sketches of *Le Vigneron dans sa vigne* (1894) and his moving novel of an unhappy childhood, *Poil de carotte* (1894). He scrutinizes the world of nature—poppies, swallows, frogs—with a verbal precision and striking novelty of metaphor and simile that make us see them afresh. Such is the case with *Histoires naturelles* (1896), brilliantly illustrated by *Toulouse-Lautrec and *Bonnard and set to music by *Ravel. His plays punctiliously register human self-deception and pettiness and astringently expose them, as in *Le Plaisir de rompre* (1897), *Le Pain de ménage* (1898), *La Bigote* (1909). His *Journal* (posth., 1925–7) combines self-examination and a vivid picture of the *belle époque*.
[SBJ]

RENART, Jean, see JEAN RENART.

Renart, Le Roman de, see ROMAN DE RENART.

RENAUD (pseud. of Renaud Séchan) (b. 1952). Singer-songwriter. His songs, often using 'verlan', a kind of back-slang, are the contemporary equivalent of those of *Bruant, ironically celebrating the low-life of the Parisian suburbs, street gangs, petty criminals, drug addicts, etc. His anarchist political stance ('Hexagone', 1974) has been toned down by his support for *Mitterrand ('Tonton', 1991). His music mixes and parodies popular styles like the tango, the *valse musette*, rock and 'country and western' in much the same way as his lyrics lampoon aspects of contemporary French society.
[PGH]

RENAUD, Jacques (b. 1943). Canadian novelist who, in *Le Cassé* (1964), produced the first creative work in prose to use *joual extensively. It is a tale of a pointless, violent murder which graphically expresses the feelings of cultural and social alienation in French Canada that underlay the Révolution Tranquille [see QUEBEC, 5].
[SIL]

RENAUD, Madeleine (b. 1900). French actress, co-founder in 1946 with Jean-Louis *Barrault of the Compagnie Renaud-Barrault. After a brilliant début as a classical actress at the Comédie-Française before World War II, under Barrault's direction she became the leading interpreter of modern and avant-garde playwrights, from *Claudel in the 1940s, *Ionesco and *Beckett in the 1960s, to *Duras in the 1970s.
[DWW]

RENAUD, Pierre (1921–76). Mauritian writer. Renaud's *Les Balises de la nuit* (1974), for which he was awarded the Prix des Mascareignes, is a long poem which explores the Mauritian identity.
[BEJ]

RENAUDOT, Théophraste (1586–1653). A native of Loudun and friend of Scévole de *Sainte-Marthe. His exceptionally inventive mind and experiences as a doctor prompted him to set up *bureaux d'adresse et de rencontre* (job centres, later also free medical agencies) and the first *mont-de-piété*, or pawnshop, for the poor. The support these ventures elicited from Louis XIII, *Richelieu, and his **éminence grise* led in 1631 to his founding the weekly *Gazette*, the first French newspaper [see PRESS, 1].
[PJB]

Renaut de Montauban. A long and impressive *chanson de geste, also known by the title *Les Quatre Fils Aymon*. Its structure is biographical, following Renaut from a boyhood quarrel at *Charlemagne's court through many years of exile and warfare against the king to his final abandonment of the world; he works as a builder in the construction of Cologne Cathedral, and is killed by his fellow workers for undercutting accepted rates of pay, but his abnegation meets with divine favour, and he is finally revered as a saint.

Like *Raoul de Cambrai, *Renaut de Montauban* explores the breakdown of society and the collapse of authority within it; Charlemagne loses the support of the twelve peers, and his authority is symbolically dismantled by Renaut's extraordinary cousin, Maugis, a thief and magician who steals the royal insignia and even kidnaps the king himself. Another unexpected source of support to Renaut is his horse Bayart, who is more of a character than many of the humans in the text. He carries Renaut and his three brothers on his back, and actively participates in their struggles; Charlemagne vindictively tries to have him drowned, but the magnificent horse swims away to safety. The 12th c. French poem survives in a large number of manuscripts, and was recast in both verse and prose in the

14th and 15th c.; it was also adapted in medieval Dutch. [SK]

Rencesvals. Site of the famous battle against the Saracens [see ROLAND].

René. Short novel by *Chateaubriand, published first as part of *Le Génie du christianisme* in 1802, then separately in 1805. The somewhat autobiographical hero exemplifies the *vague des passions* or *mal du siècle*, he feels that the past is dead and in ruins and the future offers little hope. He leads an isolated life except for his sister Amélie who, however, enters a convent because of her incestuous passion for him. René, having discovered that passion, heads for the wilds of America and there tells his sad tale to Chactas, the hero of *Atala*. The settings—stormy sea-shore, wild nature, the Gothic chateau at Combourg—are in the Romantic melancholy mode. The text had an immense success, its hero's problems being seen as representative of the age. [FPB]

RENÉ D'ANJOU (1409–80). Count of Provence, claimant to several thrones, magnificent patron of the arts, 'le roi René''s own works are a *Traité de la forme et devis d'un tournoi* (c.1444), a handbook of tournament ritual, and two allegories: the *Mortifiement de vaine plaisance* (c.1453), and a lover's progress, *Le Livre du cuer d'amours espris* (c.1460). [JHMT]

RENOIR, Auguste (1841–1919). One of the founders and major figures of the *Impressionist movement, Renoir has become identified with its world of Parisian leisure (gardens, cafés, dances, boating-scenes) which he infused with a luminous sensuality derived from his apprenticeship as a painter on porcelain of 18th-c. rococo scenes. His later work is devoted primarily to the representation of the female nude, with which he is most associated. Among writers, support came from *Zola, *Huysmans, *Verhaeren, and above all *Mallarmé, one of his closest friends, whose portrait he painted in 1892. [JK]

RENOIR, Jean (1894–1979). French film director, son of the above; his *La Règle du jeu* (1939), consistently voted the greatest French film ever, is the summit of one of world cinema's richest bodies of work. Renoir began making films in the silent era, but came into his own only with sound. The 'realism' of such films as *La Chienne* (1931) or *Le Crime de M. Lange* (1936)—perhaps the key film of the *Popular Front years, about a workers' cooperative—might be compared with that of a *Balzac or a *Zola in the novel (Renoir indeed filmed La *Bête humaine in 1938). His most widely acclaimed works are *La Grande Illusion* (1937), set in a World War I prison-camp for officers, and *La Règle du jeu*, about an aris-tocratic house-party that is a microcosm of the corruptness and exhaustion of French society on the

eve of World War II. The latter film provoked riots at its first screenings and was banned successively by the French government and by Vichy [see OCCU-PATION AND RESISTANCE].

Renoir's subsequent work—in Hollywood during the war, largely in France afterwards—is not gener-ally thought to stand comparison with what had gone before. The fluidity of a visual style in which 'le détail non réaliste travaille à l'effet de réalité' (Larousse's *Dictionnaire du cinéma français*) made him for *Bazin and the *Cahiers critics the greatest of French film-makers, and the one most influential on post-war directors. [KAR]

RENOUVIER, Charles (1815–1903). French philoso-pher; best known for his development of 'neo-criticism', in which he questioned the Kantian doc-trine of the thing-in-itself, modified Kant's categories, and argued against his distinction between theoret-ical and practical reason (*Essais de critique générale*, 1854–64). For Renouvier personality was the highest and most concrete category, and freedom the most fundamental attribute of consciousness; knowledge and belief involve an act of will, which also affirms what we hold to be morally good. Respect for the individual person as a free moral agent led Renouvier to reject dogmatism in religion and authoritarian theories in politics (*La Science de la morale*, 1869), and to develop a concept of God as finite and limited. [REG]

Répertoire, see BUTOR.

Republicanism [see also REPUBLICS]. Support for the republic and republican values. In France, the word is often applied specifically to a set of values which crystallized under the Third Republic and can be seen as a particular interpretation of the French *Revolution.

Before 1789 the word 'republic' could be used to mean either *res publica*, the common weal, whatever the regime, or, by contrast, a specifically non-monarchical constitution. Thus *Rousseau could write that 'tout gouvernement légitime est républi-cain'; but *Montesquieu that 'le gouvernement républicain est celui ou le peuple en corps, ou seule-ment une partie du peuple, a la souveraine puis-sance'. The first sense carried over into the 19th c.: coins minted in 1805 carried the legend 'République française, Napoléon Empereur'. But the second sense prevailed, and is now linked to the founding event, the destitution of the monarchy on 10 August 1792, followed by the declaration of the republic on 22 September. A republican constitution, of which *Condorcet was a leading architect, was voted in 1793 (though never applied). During the 19th c. republicanism gradually acquired its identity as a philosophy looking back to the Revolution and opposed to the royal or imperial regimes of the day. *Michelet's lectures helped inspire the short-lived Second Republic and the republican opposition under the *Second Empire, a political training-ground for the leaders of the Third Republic.

The Third Republic commissioned the *Eiffel Tower to commemorate the centenary of 1789, and it is in the years before 1914, when a positive reading of the Revolution dominated, that historians see republicanism as taking root as a shared ideology among the regime's defenders. Its central principle was freedom from arbitrary or privileged rule, whether hereditary or feudal, whether based on wealth or on spiritual influence. The preferred regime was parliamentary and bicameral, with a government responsible to the assembly, a president with little power, and an independent judiciary. Political rights were identified as freedom of belief, speech, and the press, the right to a fair trial, equality before the law, and the right of the male citizen to choose representatives at fair and regular elections. Positivism, with its essentially progressive notion of political evolution and its faith in empirical science [see COMTE], was enlisted as the philosophy of the modern republic, and Comte, *Littré, *Lavisse, *Larousse, and *Alain were its organic intellectuals. A powerful set of symbols became attached to the Republic: its anthem 'La Marseillaise' [see ROUGET DE L'ISLE], its flag the tricolour, its motto Liberté, Égalité, Fraternité, and its personification *Marianne (la gueuse to her enemies), whose bust adorns many a town hall and who often bears a resemblance to *Delacroix's 'Liberty'.

Michel Winock has argued that the 'founding myth' of the republic was really the *Dreyfus Affair of the 1890s, the classic confrontation between raison d'état and the rights of the individual. As well as the issues of *antisemitism and the claim of the army to be above the law, the Affair raised the spectre of the overthrow of the republic as a regime, thus inspiring its supporters to rally to its defence. The tensions exposed by the Affair also identified the Catholic Church as the irreconcilable enemy of republican values—and it is no coincidence that Church and State were separated soon afterwards, in 1905.

*Education was the battleground of clerical and republican values. One of the Third Republic's most celebrated acts was the provision in the 1880s of 'l'école Jules *Ferry': free, compulsory, and secular primary education for all children. Its aim was to educate citizens and to counter the influence of the Church over the young. Instituteurs and institutrices, trained in state colleges where a secular philosophy dominated, became 'the hussars of the republic', dispatched into every village of France to bring enlightened rational values to its children and to do battle with the local curé. Although la querelle religieuse has abated, its memory remains green, and passions can be roused even in the late 20th c. over state policy towards Church schools. The more extreme feelings of the turn of the century are vividly—if not objectively—evoked in *Pagnol's portrait of his instituteur father in La Gloire de mon père (1957).

In the late 20th c. republicanism is still a meaningful term. Indeed, since the decline of *Marxism as an intellectual tradition there has been a revival in the rhetoric of the republic, though the historical references have changed. The golden legend of *Zola's 'J'accuse' and the école Jules Ferry is not forgotten, but is today fitted into a defence of human rights where the enemy is likely to be identified as the threat to individual freedom from authoritarian regimes or racial or religious intolerance in a multicultural society. In post-war years the Vichy regime [see OCCUPATION AND RESISTANCE] has been identified as the 'anti-republic', and the aspect of it most severely condemned is its antisemitism. It has been argued that the Fifth Republic—which was seen by some as running counter to the republican tradition and having certain affinities with *Bonapartism, namely a strong president and use of the referendum—has as a result successfully identified its own founding myth in the Resistance.

Republicanism has not always been viewed positively. The Third Republic version has sometimes been regarded as having stifled the development of liberal philosophy, while from a Marxist position, *Guesde suggested that its only merit was to render more visible the economic oppression of capitalism. And *feminists have pointed out that the universalism of the republican tradition broke down when it came to gender. It could be argued that the republic was constructed not so much without women as against them. Republican rhetoric speaks proudly of 'universal suffrage' being introduced as early as 1848, but republican politicians blocked women's suffrage until 1944, and French women did not acquire full civil rights on a par with men until the 1980s. An illustration of change within continuity, as well as uncertainty within the contemporary republican tradition, was provided by the 'affaire du foulard' of 1989. In the furore over Muslim schoolgirls who chose to cover their heads with scarves for religious reasons when attending class, both the religious neutrality of the state school and the rights of women were claimed as republican ideals.   [SR]

See E. Weber, Peasants into Frenchmen (1976); C. Nicolet, L'Idée républicaine en France (1982); P. Nora (ed.), Les Lieux de mémoire, i. La République (1984); S. Berstein and O. Rudelle (eds), Le Modèle républicain (1992); J. and M. Ozouf, La République des instituteurs (1992).

Republics

1. The First Republic [see REVOLUTION]

The Parisian insurrection of 10 August 1792 destroyed the Constitution of 1791, which had sought to establish a limited monarchy. The new parliament, the Convention, was elected by all French men over the age of 21 who had had a fixed domicile for one year and were not servants. On

21 September 1792 it abolished the monarchy and the following day proclaimed the Republic, with a constitution that had to be accepted by the will of the people. There were further constitutional changes, the biggest in practice being Bonaparte's seizure of power [see NAPOLEON, I]; the Republic came to an end in 1804 when he became emperor.

The First Republic was based on the rights of man [see DÉCLARATION DES DROITS DE L'HOMME] and the individual's right to vote, although these principles were rarely observed in the continuing crisis of the Revolution. Of a potential 7 million electors only some 700,000 voted in the election to the Convention, and some 1,800,000 approved the Constitution of 1793.

2. The Second Republic

This was proclaimed on 25 February 1848, as King Louis-Philippe fled the country [see JULY MONARCHY]; it lasted until Louis-Napoléon's *coup d'état* on 2 December 1851. Its most notable feature was the organization of elections to a constituent assembly on 23 April 1848 by universal manhood suffrage. Whereas under the July Monarchy only about a quarter of a million men had the right to vote, under this law nearly 10 million voted, making France the most democratic country in the world. However, public opinion showed itself to be hostile to the socialist and Utopian ideas of the leaders of the February Revolution; out of an Assembly of some 900 members, approximately 400 were monarchists and 400 moderate (as distinct from radical) republicans. When the government suspended the right to work and the *Ateliers Nationaux, the workers raised the red flag and set up barricades, but were crushed by military forces under Cavaignac in the savage street-fighting of the 'journées de juin' (23–6 June); this is described in Flaubert's L'*Éducation sentimentale.

The constitution that was subsequently elaborated provided for a president elected by manhood suffrage for a non-renewable period of four years; he could not command the army, dissolve parliament, veto legislation, or abrogate the constitution. On 10 December 1848 Louis-Napoléon was elected president by a large majority (*Lamartine only gained a few thousand votes).

The electoral law voted in February–March 1849 saw the first great electoral law organizing voting by manhood suffrage; most of it was adopted by the Third Republic in 1875. But the elections of May 1849 saw radical successes, and rumours of socialist plots provided a pretext for those who wished to remove the poorest from the electoral roll. The complications that ensued placed the prince-president in a strong position, and after his *coup d'état* there was little resistance. A plebiscite of 20 December 1851 approved the dissolution of the Assemblée and the extension of the prince-president's authority. A second plebiscite on 21–2 November 1852 approved the establishment of the hereditary empire [see SECOND EMPIRE].

3. The Third Republic

This had an inauspicious beginning. It was proclaimed by a small group of moderates on 4 September 1870, on the news of the French army's defeat [see FRANCO-PRUSSIAN WAR]. The elections of 8 February 1871 returned a majority of monarchists, and it was an anti-republican assembly which designated Adolphe *Thiers president of the republic on 31 August 1871. Only in January 1875 was the constitution finalized, and then only by a majority of one.

Nevertheless, the Third Republic was to last. It survived the conflict between a monarchist president, MacMahon, and a republican assembly (1877), the attempts of General *Boulanger to seize power (1877–9), many political crises, and the harrowing events of World War I. It became accepted that the president [see PRESIDENTS OF THE REPUBLIC] was a conciliator and a symbol of republican unity, while real power lay with the Assemblée Nationale. Because there were many parties, there was ministerial instability; the average length of a government was six to nine months, but changes were often slight and the centralized administrative system stayed in place.

The fundamental problems of the Third Republic concerned relations between the Catholic Church and the state [see ANTICLERICALISM], the acquisition of a colonial empire at a time when Germany seemed to represent the biggest danger to France [see COLONIZATION], and the existence of extreme political parties: the Communist Party [see SOCIALISM AND COMMUNISM] and various *fascist-type groups that flourished in the 1930s. It was a divided nation that was forced to meet the challenge of the 1939 war and the military defeat of 1940. Institutional weaknesses led to Marshal *Pétain being called on to form a government; the Senate and the Chambre des Députés met as a National Assembly at Vichy, suspended the constitution, and voted full powers to Pétain [see OCCUPATION AND RESISTANCE], thus effectively ending the Third Republic.

4. The Fourth Republic

This originated in a referendum called by General de *Gaulle in October 1945, in which 96 per cent of the voters (now including women) declared that the new assembly they were electing should be a constituent assembly. A further referendum which would have virtually abolished the president of republic and installed a single-chamber government was rejected in May 1946, and a new constitution, restoring the powers of the president in line with the practice of the Third Republic and instituting a second chamber (Conseil de la République), was approved by referendum in October 1946.

The central feature of this constitution was the importance of the Chambre des Députés and of the political parties represented there. Election was by proportional representation, and no party ever gained an overall majority. The country was therefore governed by coalitions, which became increasingly complex because of the existence of a strong Communist Party (which became isolated as the Cold War developed), the development of a new Social Catholic party (Mouvement Républicain Populaire), and the creation of a Gaullist party (Rassemblement du Peuple Français) in 1947. After the election of the Socialist Vincent Auriol as president in January 1947, the first official government of the Fourth Republic was headed by Paul Ramadier. There followed 20 further governments, ending with that of de Gaulle as prime minister before the inauguration of the Fifth Republic with his election as president in January 1959.

The crisis of the Fourth Republic arose from a revolt in Algiers on 13 May 1958 [see ALGERIAN WAR]. After 24 May, when parachutists from Algeria took over Corsica, there seemed a real danger of an invasion of the mainland and of civil war. On 27 May de Gaulle announced that he was forming a government; the National Assembly voted for the investiture of this government and gave it powers to prepare a new constitution, which was overwhelmingly approved by referendum on 28 September 1958.

5. The Fifth Republic

After the referendum of 28 September and the legislative elections of November, de Gaulle was elected president of the republic on 21 December by an electoral college of 80,000 voters. The new constitution was, according to de Gaulle, both presidential and parliamentary. The president, elected for seven years, is head of the executive, presides over the Conseil des Ministres, and assures the proper working of the institutions and the continuity and independence of the state. He appoints the prime minister and the ministers, the latter being proposed by the prime minister. Parliament is elected for a five-year period, but can be dissolved by the president (elections cannot be held twice within 12 months). The president can have recourse to a referendum, and by Article 16 of the Constitution can assume full powers in an emergency.

It had been widely forecast that this constitution was tailor-made for de Gaulle and would not last. But his presidency outlived the Algerian crisis, and he was defeated only in a referendum, seeking to change the powers of the Senate, in 1969. Although not obliged to do so, he resigned. His successors, Georges *Pompidou and Valéry Giscard d'Estaing, had been associated with Gaullism and had thereby accepted the constitution. François *Mitterrand, elected president in 1981, had been a consistent opponent of what he termed the 'coup d'état permanent'; however, as he put it, the institutions of the Fifth Republic had not been made with him in mind, but they suited him well.

The biggest change in the 1958 constitution came in 1962, when a referendum endorsed de Gaulle's proposal that the president be elected by direct universal suffrage. Three further details should be noted: Article 16 has been invoked only once, in April 1961; the referendum was used five times by de Gaulle, once by Pompidou, not at all by Giscard d'Estaing, and twice by Mitterrand; the Assemblée has been dissolved by presidential decision only four times, by de Gaulle in 1962 and 1968, and by Mitterrand in 1981 and 1988 (for the latter, each time after he had won presidental elections).

The relationship between president and prime minister is a problem in the Fifth Republic. It has been the practice of presidents to dismiss prime ministers when it suited them. But in 1986 Mitterrand was faced with a parliamentary majority hostile to him and was forced to undergo the experience of 'cohabitation' with a prime minister who was his rival, Jacques Chirac. Again in 1993, when the elections gave a massive majority to the former Opposition, he was obliged to appoint Édouard Balladur as his prime minister. In general it has been assumed that the president has a decisive role in foreign policy and defence matters.

In the political field, the Fifth Republic has been marked by *decolonization, the decline of the Communist Party, the rise of the extreme rightwing Front National, and France's full integration into the European Community. Socially and economically, it has seen a progressive modernization of France, and the decline of many traditional ways of life, such as agriculture and fishing. [DJ]

Resistance during World War II, see OCCUPATION AND RESISTANCE.

RESNAIS, Alain (b. 1922). French film-director. He began his career as a maker of documentaries, notably Nuit et Brouillard (1955) and Toute la mémoire du monde (1956); these films established the visual and narrative hallmarks of his work. Resnais's films (made in collaboration with writers such as *Duras, *Robbe-Grillet, *Semprun and *Cayrol) deal with the functioning of memory (Muriel, 1963) and the mind (Van Gogh, 1948; Hiroshima mon amour, 1959). Time is perceived as layered rather than chronological (La Vie est un roman, 1983). Past and present are alternately counterpointed and fused, generating a mood of uncertainty where time and space are ambiguous in construction and reconstruction (L'Année dernière à Marienbad, 1961). Visually this representation is achieved through a fast editing style (exceptions being Mon oncle d'Amérique, 1980 and Mélo, 1986), where past and present are sequenced in parallel and image, word, and music are counterpointed. [SH]

Restaurants, see CAFÉS AND RESTAURANTS.

RESTIF (or RÉTIF) DE LA BRETONNE, Nicolas-Edme (1734–1806). Author of novels, short stories, diary-documentaries, philosophical treatises and *Utopian legislative tracts, and a major 16-volume autobiography, *Monsieur Nicolas, ou le Cœur humain *dévoilé* (1794–7). Historiographer of the Parisian streets and their public during the Revolution (*Les Nuits de Paris, ou le Spectateur nocturne*, 1788–94) and obsessive chronicler of his own private sexual fantasies, Restif is a writer unique and innovatory in his perspectives and style. He cuts across all the categories of the classical canon and closes the gap between the psychological novel of the 18th c. and the social realism of the 19th.

The historian *Le Roy Ladurie has tellingly characterized Restif as the type of the many young men of well-to-do peasant families who came to Paris in the pre-Revolutionary period to seek their fortune (see *Monsieur Nicolas*, and the novels *Le Paysan perverti*, 1775, *La Paysanne pervertie*, 1784). Their experiences at the bottom of the urban pyramid (in Restif's case, as a printing-shop apprentice) stirred in them a revolutionary fervour that coexisted with a nostalgic longing for the security of the patriarchal hierarchy back home. This group, eager for reform but afraid of changes that might threaten their own precarious status, constitutes a major section of the new middle ground in which revolutionary politics, codified by Napoleon in 1804, eventually stabilized.

Much of Restif's writing focuses on the organization of sexuality and the family which he (like the Napoleonic Code) sees as fundamental to the proper organization of the state. The classification and regimentation of women in their social and sexual functions—daughter, spinster, wife, mother, whore—are the subject-matter of the observations and anecdotes and the vivid and vigorous dialogue in *Les Contemporaines* (1780–6), *Les Françaises* (1786), and *Le Palais-Royal* (1790). These put flesh on the bones of the legislative proposals in *Le Pornographe* (1769), which advocates state-run brothels to cement social stability, or in *Le Thesmographe* (1789), which sketches new laws on property, marriage, and divorce. Marriage as a bar to sexual freedom is the theme of the novels *La Femme infidèle* (1786), based on Restif's own unhappy marriage, and *Ingénue Saxancour* (written 1786, published 1789), a graphic fictionalization of his daughter's struggles to leave a violent and vicious husband. The latter is an interesting text to read in conjunction with the incest-fantasies of Restif's pornographic *L'Anti-Justine, ou les Délices de l'amour* (1798), which he presents as a more acceptable version of *Sade's text. [JB]

See M. Poster, *The Utopian Thought of Restif de la Bretonne* (1971).

Restoration, The. After *Napoleon's abdication (6 April 1814), the *Bourbon monarchy was restored to the throne in the person of Louis XVIII. This is usually called the first Restoration, since it was interrupted by Napoleon's escape from Elba and return to Paris (20 March 1815); the second Restoration began with his abdication (22 June 1815) and Louis's return to Paris. After Louis's death (16 September 1824), his brother *Charles X succeeded to the throne. The reign of the Bourbons ended with the Revolution of July 1830, provoked by the king's reactionary policies and disregard for representative government. Charles abdicated on 2 August 1830 [see JULY MONARCHY].

This period saw the introduction of parliamentary government on the constitutional basis of the Charter ('La Charte') proclaimed by the king on 4 June 1814. The right to vote was based on wealth, which was calculated by the amount of direct taxation paid; it has been calculated that one out of every 100 adult Frenchmen possessed this privilege. A chamber of peers was appointed by the monarch. In order to be eligible for election as a *député*, one had to be male, at least 40 years old, and paying a considerable sum in direct taxation. This meant that in some parts of provincial France only 10 men in a *département* might be eligible. The system was beset by fraud; one of the aims of the Liberal opposition was to make it more effectively parliamentary.

The Restoration was marked by a great intellectual, literary, and artistic activity [see ROMANTICISM]. According to one estimate, whilst in 1812 some 4,648 books were published within the extended frontiers of Imperial France, in 1825, within the restricted frontiers of Restoration France, some 7,542 were published. Among these publications, the increase in the number of historical works is significant (their number more than tripled), and historians such as *Barante, *Guizot, *Thiers, and *Thierry were among the most distinguished writers of the period.

But at first it was the scientists who most impressed observers from other countries. The mathematician Augustin Cauchy (1789–1857), the engineer Augustin Fresnel (1788–1827), the inventor of thermodynamics Sadi Carnot (1796–1832), were only a few of a famous group of scientists presided over by the Secrétaire Perpétuel of the *Académie des Sciences, *Cuvier. Many intellectual movements, such as socialism, economic liberalism, eclecticism, and positivism originated during the years of the Restoration. [DJ]

RETTÉ, Adolphe (1863–1930). An ardent supporter of the French *Symbolist movement, to which he contributed poetry (*Cloches en la nuit*, 1889), prose (*Thulé des brumes*, 1894), and literary and art criticism. He became an equally ardent leader of the anti-Symbolist reaction when, from late 1894, he denounced *Mallarmé and *Gauguin in the name of a return to traditional French values of clarity, lyricism, and love of nature. [JK]

RETZ, Jean-François-Paul de Gondi, cardinal de (1613–79). Ecclesiastic and would-be statesman whose career ended in spectacular disgrace and whose retirement was spent writing the most flamboyant of the many memoirs to have come down to us from the 17th c.

His family, of Florentine origin, had risen to prominence in France through *Catherine de Médicis; they had a virtual monopoly of the see of

Paris, upgraded in 1622 to an archbishopric. His father was a notably pious general of the galleys. After the death of an elder brother he was destined for the Church, though later describing himself as 'perhaps the least ecclesiastical soul there ever was'. Even in his brilliant career as a student he brushed with *Richelieu; after touring Italy he wrote the politically suspect *Conjuration de Fiesque* (not published until 1655). In 1643 he was appointed co-adjutor archbishop of Paris with the right of succession to his uncle. He zestfully built up influence as a preacher and reforming administrator, and when the civil unrest of the *Fronde broke out joined in the rebellion against *Mazarin.

The bulk of the *Mémoires* concerns the complex ebb and flow of hostilities, conspiracies, and negotiations that engulfed France from 1648 to 1652. At one point Mazarin offered Retz the bribe of a red hat, and he was finally made a cardinal in 1652. In the same year he was arrested and imprisoned in Vincennes. He attempted a come-back in 1654, when his uncle died and he had himself installed by proxy as archbishop; but after a few days was transferred as a prisoner to Nantes, where he made a daring escape and fled via Spain to Rome to seek papal protection. Not until 1662 did he formally resign the see and receive permission to return to France, where he was largely exiled to his estates. He remained, however, in contact with many of the leading personalities of Paris, and the anonymous lady to whom he addresses the *Mémoires* was almost certainly Madame de *Sévigné.

The *Mémoires* are less a confession than a theatrical reconstruction, in which the author plays tragic or comic, but always heroic, roles. The pithy phrase, vivid anecdote, and keenly perceptive character-portraits serve to narrate defeat so that it seems victory. They were published in 1717.   [PJB]

See A. Bertière, *Le Cardinal de Retz mémorialiste* (1977); D. A. Watts, *Cardinal de Retz: The Ambiguities of a Seventeenth-Century Mind* (1980).

Réunion, La (Reunion), see MAURITIUS AND REUNION.

Rêve, Le. Novel by *Zola, the 16th of the *Rougon-Macquart* series, published 1888. Combining the fairy-tale and the Naturalist novel, it is the story of the pious orphan Angélique, brought up by a childless couple, the Huberts, in the religious atmosphere of the cathedral city of Beaumont, who dies on the day of her marriage to the handsome Félicien on the steps of the cathedral after the wedding ceremony.   [DB]

Rêve de d'Alembert, Le. Name given to three dialogues composed by *Diderot in 1769; as well as being entertaining and poetic pieces of writing, they contain his boldest theorizing about human and animal life, seen in a materialist perspective. The interlocutors are Julie de *Lespinasse (who acts the part of the intelligent learner), d'*Alembert (whose

dream occupies a central position in the dialogues), and the doctor *Bordeu (who is more or less Diderot's mouthpiece).

The conversations concern the difference between living and non-living matter, and attempt in speculative fashion to account for the various phenomena of human thought and feeling. Numerous anecdotes from everyday life and from experimental work in biology and medicine are used to support the thesis that the origin of the most complex mental activities can be found in our material make-up (in particular, the brain and nervous system) without recourse to the idea of spirit or of God. These speculations lead to a number of conclusions which are destructive of conventional morality. The most powerful section of the dialogues is the dream sequence, which contains a vision of a universal flux of matter and adumbrates a theory of evolution.   [PF]

Réveil, Le, see PROTESTANTISM, 2.

Reverdie. In the Middle Ages, a spring song.

REVERDY, Pierre (1889–1960). A poet who strove to delete all textual vestige of his person, and who in 1926 abandoned the busy avant-garde scene of Paris to live in pious exile in a village in Normandy, Reverdy maintained over the years such consistency of tone and ascetic scruple as to achieve, in the end, an entirely compelling and individual voice. The early poems, reissued as *Plupart du temps* (1944), rely on the seemingly arbitrary strewing of fragmented and unaccentuated phrases upon the page to set hints of poetic meaning inching into consciousness. Nothing in Reverdy is emphatic, yet his laconic gatherings of lack-lustre observations, often of solitary figures in rooms with eventless prospects, enjoy a mysterious effect of magnification which draws the anecdotal shreds into an ephemeral yet magical coherence. Reverdy's later poetry is more confidently rhythmical, though the *vers libre* of collections like *Ferraille* (1937) sounds the same note of yearning and estrangement, at times opening onto existential panic. His collected essays on painting (*Note éternelle du présent*, 1973) evince an almost ethereal conception of aesthetics, while the theoretical notes gathered in *Le Gant de crin* (1927) and *Le Livre de mon bord* (1948) reflect a determined effort to define the very special way poets view reality.   [RC]

Rêveries du promeneur solitaire. Jean-Jacques *Rousseau's swan-song, left unfinished at his death, published with Part I of the *Confessions* in 1782. The final stage in his self-exploration, it is supposedly meant for himself rather than the reading public. Ten 'promenades' round Paris contain meditations on moral and religious questions, reflections on his behaviour and character, and, above all, memories. The highly constructed prose lovingly recreates moments of solitary ecstasy, above all in the fifth 'promenade', devoted to his brief stay on the Île de

689

Saint-Pierre, a key text in the development of *Romantic attitudes and sensibilities.   [PF]

Rêves portatifs, see BEMBA.

Reviews, see PERIODICALS.

Revocation of the Edict of Nantes, see EDICT OF NANTES.

Revolution. While the term 'La Révolution Française', or simply 'La Révolution' is reserved for the Revolution of 1789–99 (see below), the revolutionary movement produced three further major upheavals in 19th-c. France: the uprising of 27–9 July 1830 (*les trois glorieuses*) leading to the establishment of the *July Monarchy; the Revolution of 1848 [see REPUBLICS, 2]; and the *Commune de Paris of 1871. From the opposite end of the political spectrum, the Vichy government during World War II [see OCCUPATION AND RESISTANCE] claimed to be launching a 'Révolution Nationale'. [See also REPUBLICANISM.]

1. **The French Revolution: A Chronological Account**

(a) *1786–9.* By 1786 a long-standing, costly foreign policy had saddled France with a massive debt. Without radical reforms which would help to clear it, the country was clearly condemned to serious decline. Louis XVI, however, could no longer act without the goodwill of the privileged orders. Calonne, the controller-general, persuaded the king therefore to summon an Assembly of Notables who—he hoped—would approve his plans and initiate a movement of national consensus. They met (February 1787), but were not compliant. Calonne's successor, Brienne, dissolved the Assembly (May 1787) and embarked, 'unsanctioned', on a programme of sweeping reforms. So began a serious battle of wills. For amid mounting public antagonism, Versailles tried to outface the resistance which the *parlements* were demonstrating towards Brienne's initiatives. Having failed, Louis determined to destroy the *parlements.* Since, however, they were commonly seen as bastions against 'despotism', that hostile measure (the May Edicts of 1788) was greeted by a wave of rebellious disaffection and renewed calls for the convocation of the *États Généraux. Hoping to divide the opposition, Brienne conceded (8 August) that the Estates would meet (May 1789) in order to examine the nation's *cahiers de doléances.*

Though the situation had been momentarily defused, *Necker, Brienne's successor, was to experience far worse trouble: the state was now bankrupt, and the disastrous summer of 1788, followed by a catastrophic winter, brought severe economic problems. In parallel there came serious political problems; for, following the inflammatory decree of the Parlement de Paris that *Clergy, *Nobility, and *Tiers État should each have a similar number of deputies and should vote according to order, the Assembly of Notables was reconvened (November–

December) to advise on the composition and running of the Estates. Attention was consequently fixed on the question of privilege and on the proportion of representation to be accorded to the Tiers. The latter's favoured 'model', based on the newly revived Estates of Dauphiné (Vizille, 21 July 1788), required that the Tiers be double the size of other two orders, and that voting be, not by order, but by head. Louis received much reactionary advice on these matters, but did decide (27 December) to implement the first proposal. That still left one significant requirement unsatisfied.

(b) *1789–92.* Predictably the first issue to agitate the Estates when they met in Versailles (5 May 1789) was the vote by head. Clergy and Nobility (representing together perhaps half a million men) refused to meet other than separately. The Tiers, representing 25 million common people, and which had—in the frenetic electioneering of the previous six months—recognized itself as *the* significant political force, reacted in the spirit of *Siéyès's famous pamphlet of January 1789 (*Qu'est-ce que le Tiers État?*): it proclaimed itself the Assemblée Nationale (17 June), where voting would be by head. Responding immediately with an apparent *coup d'état*, Louis locked the deputies out of their respective meeting-places. Outraged, the Tiers—assembling in a nearby tennis-court—there swore the first, most famous, oath of the Revolution: the Serment du Jeu de Paume, i.e. not to separate until France had a Constitution and, with it, public regeneration.

On 9 July, underlining the primacy of the task, the Assemblée was to call itself the Assemblée Nationale Constituante. Such defiance, and accompanying public ferment, prompted Louis to order both the Clergy and the Nobility (some of whom had already taken the decision) to work with the Tiers (27 June). The coming days were nevertheless notable for widespread public disorder. Since January food-shortages and steep rises in the price of grain, flour, and bread had been raising the age-old spectre of the 'pacte de famine' and causing riots and peasant insurrections almost everywhere. At the same time, by ordering troop movements around Paris and Versailles, Louis was clearly attempting to intimidate the populace, causing further fear and disaffection. On 11 July there came another act of royal 'despotism': Louis dismissed Necker, the people's champion. In Paris the resultant anger was awesome. Rioting crowds destroyed the toll-gates; needing arms to counter an 'imminent' *coup de force*, they next invaded known or suspected arsenals. On the morning of 14 July the Invalides was forced, and cannon and muskets taken. Attention was then turned on that most formidable arsenal of all: the *Bastille.

Reports (and rumours) of events in Paris exacerbated unrest in the provinces, which rapidly spiralled down into psychosis (La Grande Peur, July–August). In many areas, known or imagined enemies of the popular cause were pre-emptively attacked, noble dwellings sacked, feudal records destroyed, barns raided, tithes reclaimed. From afar, the Assemblée magnified such events into a Dantesque vision. Believing that radical measures alone could calm such turmoil, the Assemblée—allowing civil disobedience to exert influence over the exercise of power—abandoned the whole *régime féodal* in the famous session of 4 August. Society had consequently to be 'recreated', starting with that new, now urgently required, Constitution. Most deputies agreed that it should be prefaced—as in the American States—by a Declaration of Rights. Rapidly promulgated (26 August), the *Déclaration des droits de l'homme et du citoyen* became the founding document of the Revolution. Debate, in which *Mirabeau played a dominating part, also intensified around the constitutional process to come. Should there be two chambers? Should the king—despite popular antipathy—have a power of veto? On 4 October Louis expressed reservations about the Declaration of Rights. His behaviour merely served to reinforce the people's belief that their destiny lay safely in their own hands alone. They had already organized politically [see JACOBINS; CORDELIERS; COMMUNE DE PARIS; etc]. They now acted again: on 5 October the march on Versailles culminated in the invasion of both the Assemblée and the Royal palace. On 6 October—under severe pressure—Louis agreed to reside in the capital. The Assemblée soon followed him. Both were henceforth under the eye of vigilant, suspicious Parisians who would not hesitate (1789–95) to 'interfere' in the conduct of national business.

Meanwhile the national debt, unchecked, had become massive. On 3 November the Assemblée—responding robustly—decided to nationalize and sell off Church lands [see ASSIGNATS]. (The Church was to be the greatest casualty of the Revolution, losing its power and its autonomy: dissolution of monasteries and convents, February 1790; Civil Constitution of the Clergy, July 1790, which required from clerics an oath of allegiance to the new order; etc.). However, despite this signal radicalization of the Revolution, the deputies still broadly enjoyed a national consensus: the Fête de la Fédération, the first great *fête révolutionnaire*, mounted throughout France (14 July 1790), proved the point.

Distressed by such increasing radicalism, and particularly by the activity of the Jacobins, Louis took flight to Varennes (20 June 1791), leaving behind a proclamation which denounced everything that had been accomplished since October 1789. He was arrested and brought back to Paris. His defection, like the Civil Constitution of the Clergy, further polarized opinion. But popular opposition and growing republicanism were dealt with energetically (e.g. the Massacre du Champ de Mars, 17 July 1791). The political battle was now moving into the final phase of polarization around limited versus democratic views of the Revolution. The former,

represented by the *Feuillants and such figures as *Barnave and *Lafayette, triumphed in the short term: the Constitution of 1791 trammelled the principles of liberty, equality, and revolutionary freedom (e.g. with limited franchise, restrictions on public and printed utterances, etc.). Louis signed that Constitution (14 September) and, its work complete, the Assemblée Constituante ended amid growing fears that the European monarchies were plotting to crush the Revolution.

The new Assemblée Législative (1 October 1791) was even more politicized than its predecessor. Notable for its bellicosity, it soon grew to believe that war could solve all current problems: it would divert fractious attention away from serious internal problems, regenerate the nation, and—neutralizing the league of foreign despots—consolidate the Revolution. Over the winter the mood of defiance grew. On 20 April 1792 the Assemblée declared war on Austria. Unfortunately, performance did not match mood. The army, weakened by emigration, disaffection, and sheer incompetence, met with defeats. The *Brissotin ministry was replaced (June) by a more royalist administration. Against a background of military reverses, of mounting suspicion (e.g. that Lafayette was preparing a *coup d'état*), and severe economic shortages, new popular leaders were beginning to emerge, mobilizing displays of popular strength.

The sense of impending disaster mounted. The *Patrie en danger* was proclaimed (11 July); sectional assemblies (Jacobins, etc.) went into permanent session (25 July). With the Brunswick Manifesto, the Austrian invasion, and the desertion of Lafayette, all 48 Paris sections—bar one—demanded the deposition of Louis. Initiative now slipped from the Assemblée to the new insurrectionary Commune which, invading the Tuileries (10 August), brought Louis's reign to an end. Over the next six weeks the Assemblée—in the paranoid atmosphere in which *Danton and *Marat reigned supreme—did the Commune's bidding. Serious reverses at Longwy and Verdun laid the road to Paris open to the Austrians. Panic swept the capital, leading to that most ferocious of pre-emptive strikes: the September Massacres of counter-revolutionary suspects held in various prisons. Amid violence and carnage, the Assemblée Législative bowed out—emasculated—to make way for the Convention Nationale, whose essential, and seemingly hopeless, task was to save the Revolution.

(c) 1792–4. The Convention, 'sujet de contemplation sombre, lugubre, effrayant, mais sublime' (Victor *Hugo), met on 20 September 1792 (the same day on which the invading Prussians were halted by the Revolutionary armies at the Battle of *Valmy). Its first act was to declare that Republic which radicals had increasingly been demanding. Abolishing the monarchy was easy. Knowing what to do with Louis was not, and his future was hotly debated, with *Girondins temporizing,

Revolution

*Montagnards arguing either for his trial or his immediate punishment (the popular insurrection of 10 August having been, said *Saint-Just, his trial already). Trial was the favoured solution and, after being portrayed variously and eloquently as a criminal or a victim of circumstance, Louis was condemned to death with no right of appeal to the nation (15 January 1793) and executed (21 January).

In the same spirit of defiance, the Convention took on even more enemies (including Britain) and embarked on protracted war. Initial failures (March–August 1793) were—after inspired reorganization of the army—spectacularly reversed: from the Battle of Hondschoote (8 September 1793) to Hohenlinden (3 December 1800), the armies of the Republic were almost invariably victorious. But it was war on two fronts. Nearer home, the Convention was embroiled with the *Vendée, Federalist revolts, counter-revolution, and treason. The Comité de Sûreté Générale alone (instituted 2 October 1792) was unequal to the gigantic task. To counteract these domestic dangers and to safeguard the Republic 'one and indivisible', the authorities created the Revolutionary Tribunal and *comités de surveillance* (March), the Comité de Salut Public (April), the *levée en masse* (May), a Revolutionary army to police the countryside (June), and finally—under pressure from the popular movement—government by Terror (September).

The stage is now occupied by the great Committee of Public Safety. From its inception it sought—as something akin to a war cabinet—to galvanize the nation's resolve; responding to numerous problems, it did indeed guide the Republic with increasing single-mindedness. Unfortunately its enormous task was not facilitated by its fellow Republicans. Inter-factional fighting now bedevilled the Convention: Montagnards fought Girondins (and eliminated them in the summer of 1793), while later the Montagnards themselves were to be overtaken on the far Left by the *Enragés, *Hébertistes, the Paris Commune, sundry populists, and the poorer sections of the capital. Nor was its task facilitated by the Convention's *représentants en mission*, who often defended the Republic with ferocious individual initiative: e.g. the purging of Lyon by *Collot d'Herbois; the punishment of Toulon by Barras; the repression of Bordeaux by *Tallien, of Nantes by Carrier; or the anarchic, often repulsive, 'dechristianization' practiced by *Fouché and Chaumette.

Such excesses—widely imitated—antagonized many ordinary supporters of the Republic (and indeed, *Robespierre came to view them as deliberate acts of political sabotage). Consequently the Comité took a firmer grip on affairs. Helped by the law of 4 December 1793 which gave extraordinary powers to the Comité de Salut Public, the latter could now restrain maverick behaviour on behalf of the Republic. Complaints about such abuse of power had, however, become the main thrust of the

campaign, animated by Danton and his allies, to abandon the Terror. Conversely, the Cordeliers and Hébert advocated continuing Terror and accelerated dechristianization, and called for an insurrectionary purge of the Convention. Thoroughly alarmed, the Comité struck. Within ten days the Hébertistes had been destroyed (24 March 1794), their ally—the Paris Revolutionary Army—dissolved (27 March), and the Commune purged (April–May).

Events now quickened, notably because Robespierre—a significant influence within the Comité—was becoming steadily obsessed with counter-revolutionary corruption and scheming. (His victims would include *Fabre d'Églantine, Danton, *Desmoulins, etc. and his weapons would include the infamous law of 22 Prairial [for Revolutionary dates see CALENDARS] which—simplifying the procedures of the Revolutionary Tribunal—meant that justice became expeditious and that the number of executions rose dramatically.) The Republic of Virtue was purging society of its contaminated elements, and was working hard for regeneration. But it was now Robespierre himself, with his moral fanaticism, who was being viewed as an increasingly dangerous individual. Since the autumn of 1792 he had been accused of aspiring to dictatorship. His peremptory denunciations of personal and public enemies now caused renewed suspicions of this possibility. Moreover, sheer dread gripped the Convention, where former over-zealous *représentants* felt distinctly vulnerable (e.g. Fouché, Tallien, etc.). The dénouement came on 26 July (8 Thermidor), when Robespierre delivered a rambling speech calling for the punishment of certain (unspecified) traitors in both the Convention and the two Comités. His clumsy declaration of war on his enemies—the meaning of which is still hotly debated—provoked the immediate counter-attack of 9 Thermidor. He was arrested and executed (along with *Couthon, Saint-Just, etc.) on the following day.

(*d*) *1794–9*. Within a month of the Thermidorian *coup d'état* the Convention had dismantled the central institutions of the Terror and Revolutionary Government. Reaction, much heartened, re-emerged in the form of right-wing and royalist journals, of the anti-Jacobin *Jeunesse dorée* and *Muscadins*, of revenge attacks on Jacobins and Jacobin clubs. Initially unmoved, the Convention chose to demonstrate continuing commitment to leftist republicanism. For example, it removed Mirabeau's remains from the Panthéon and replaced them with those of Marat, and refused to take action against the leading *terroristes* in the two Comités. But palinody soon proved more opportune: before long Carrier had been sacrificed and guillotined (16 December); the *maximum*—that ultimate bastion of Revolutionary government—abolished (24 December); laws against emigration relaxed (December–January); Marat's body removed from the Panthéon (8

February 1795); *Barère, Billaud, and Collot d'Herbois indicted (22 March).

Jacobin horror, even despair, at these happenings was exacerbated by runaway inflation and the sufferings caused by the severe winter. The result was the uprising of 12 Germinal (1 April), when the people invaded the Convention demanding bread and the Constitution of An II. Despite reprisals, the people repeated their insurrection on 1 Prairial (20 May). Revenge was swift. On 22 May the Saint-Antoine district of Paris received a savage punitive visit. This was followed in the coming weeks by generalized forms of repression. The popular movement in Paris, severely weakened by the Terror, was now all but destroyed. The events of December–May became the signal for anarchic (often royalist), vindictive acts of counter-terror (La Terreur Blanche) in the Lyonnais, the Rhône valley, and the South (May–June).

The main problem facing the Convention was, however, to devise a Constitution which would ensure stability, prevent any resurgence of radical republicanism and royalism, and respect the principles of 1789 (as opposed to those of 1793). That new Constitution of An III was approved on 22 August. The preceding six years having demonstrated the dangers of a single chamber, the legislature now became bicameral: the lower chamber (the Conseil des Cinq Cents) would initiate legislation, the upper (the Conseil des Anciens) would ratify or reject it. Executive power was now vested in five directors (the Directoire). The aim was general stability. Continuity was, moreover, guaranteed by decrees accompanying the Constitution which stipulated that two-thirds of the members of the founding Conseils should come from within the Convention: anger at this measure among royalists, and particularly radical republicans (who had also been disenfranchised), was extreme. On 5 October came the uprising of 13 Vendémiaire, when 25,000 insurgents converged on the Convention in what was to be Paris's last attempt to impose its will on the national representatives. The regular army, which was henceforth to become the supreme instrument of the Directoire at home and abroad, now saw action against Paris for the first time since April 1789. It took, however, much more determined effort from Bonaparte and his 6,000 troops than his legendary 'whiff of grapeshot' to carry the day.

The golden rule of the first directors (1 November) was to protect the Republic from political extremism. But their attention was equally focused on the dire economic situation which had followed the abandonment of the controlled economy. Speculation was rife, fortunes were being made and flaunted. This is the atmosphere in which *Babeuf eloquently expressed the grievances of the disinherited and the betrayed. But the glorious failure of his Conspiration des Égaux (April 1796), which had probably been manipulated by the Directoire, and the renewed anti-Jacobin repression

of the next 12 months, emboldened the royalists. In the partial elections of An V (April–May 1797) monarchists were heavily returned. Dismayed, the republican directors (*Barras, Reubell, and La Révellière-Lépeaux) forestalled any monarchist triumph: with Bonaparte's 'permission' they used the army for the *coup d'état* of 18 Fructidor (4 September). In the following Directorial Terror (lasting into 1798), the Conseils were purged and many 'leftist' measures implemented. Setting aside unwelcome results which it felt to be inimical to the implementation of its own policies was to become a Directorial imperative. It would do the same in the partial elections of April 1798. But in April 1799 the new Conseils proved less docile. Their own *coup d'état* of 30 Prairial (18 June) struck the directors themselves. Siéyès, one of the new directors, emerged with much-increased power. 1789 long forgotten, he now sought to strengthen the authority of the executive with military support. On 18 Brumaire (9 November 1799) Bonaparte ejected the Conseils and, with Ducos and Siéyès, assumed executive power. The Directoire was over and, with it, the Revolution. [See NAPOLEON.]

2. Literature in the Revolutionary Period

While the literature of the Revolutionary period is often dismissed, and certainly shows few innovations in the traditional genres, the demise of *censorship, the suppression of privileged corporations, and the gradual disappearance of the *salons brought about a transformation within the *République des lettres* which allowed this decade to demonstrate an effervescence of creativity (see Monglond's bibliography, *La France révolutionaire et impériale*) which stands comparison with that of 1670–80 or 1750–60.

Since the nation quickly became responsible for its own regeneration, areas of unprecedented innovation were political *eloquence and journalism. The years 1789–94 are remarkable for the rhetoric of the 'Left' in the unfolding political debates, which found few worthy opponents on the 'Right' (Cazalès, *Maury). The speeches of Mirabeau, of Barnave, *Vergniaud, and Brissot, of Danton, of Robespierre and Saint-Just—all ardent witnesses to both national and individual dramas—punctuated every important moment of the Revolution. Though they now sometimes appear pompous, theatrical, or abstract, they will always strike the 'listener' as being animated by a passionate conviction which epitomizes the growing turbulence of the period.

Political journalism, with its 1,500 separate publications in the same period, is equally ebullient [see also PRESS]. Transmission of facts (though not unknown, e.g. *La Gazette de France*, *Le *Moniteur*, etc.) was quickly outstripped by the formation of opinion, be it royalist or revolutionary. The journals of the former (e.g. *Les Actes des apôtres*, *Le Journal de la cour et de la ville*) are simplistic and politically

Revolution

shallow, whereas the latter, whether *L'Ami du peuple* (Marat), *Le Père Duchesne* (Hébert), or *Les Révolutions de France et de Brabant* (Desmoulins), are notable for their astuteness, their effulgent and sometimes frightening sincerity. After Thermidor the press becomes largely anti-Jacobin and often obliquely royalist, and will be severely reined in after Babeuf's Conspiration des Égaux. It was then left almost uniquely to the *Décade philosophique*, the political and literary organ of the Idéologues, to keep faith with republican and liberal opinion.

In turn the theatre, never a stranger to didacticism, readily became a vehicle for political education. The abundant repertoire of the period was, to begin with, decidedly 'national' (e.g. M.-J. *Chénier's Charles IX* and *Calas*), then republican, and the authorities used their not-inconsiderable powers to ensure that it remained so, although counter-revolutionary plays did occasionally command a hearing (e.g. *Laya). But not all is anchored in uplifting, didactic political themes. These years, preparing tastes to come, also see A.-V. Arnault, *Lemercier, G.-M. Legouvé, and *Raynouard, for example, turning for inspiration to exotic antiquity, Ossianism, or the Middle Ages; or, in a less elevated vein, the comic author Louis-Benoît Picard (1769–1828), keenly observing a society in flux (e.g. *Médiocre et rampant*, 1797). But this is perhaps the golden age of the *melodrama of *Pixerécourt and others which, like the *roman noir* or Gothic novel, was specifically designed for the people, and in which the values of society were reaffirmed.

Prose writers are just as prolific (e.g. *Loaisel de Tréogate, *Nerciat, *Pigault-Lebrun, Madame de *Genlis). Many of their texts, reflecting the social upheaval, are indeed so many historical documents. But the work of certain practitioners proved to have enduring value: in particular *Louvet de Couvray; *Bernardin de Saint-Pierre; *Restif de la Bretonne; and the marquis de *Sade, whose apocalyptic vision of the very real cruelty dormant in human nature was to be 'discovered' as a horrible reality by 20th-c. Europe. Other signs of things to come (more rapidly) and other conceptions of the novel are clearly there in *Senancour (*Aldomen*, 1795) or in Madame de *Staël's *Zulma* (1794), *Mirza, Adélaïde et Théodore*, and *Histoire de Pauline* (1795), which were prefaced by an *Essai sur les fictions* of which Goethe and Schiller took particular note.

Traditional poetry tends to be unremarkable, though innovation, particularly in subject-matter, is certainly to be seen (e.g. Ossianism, the Nordic world, the *genre troubadour*). But this is above all the time when André *Chénier created his own ardently personal and timeless poems (*Iambes*, 1794). Furthermore, as much real and vibrant poetry can be found in Revolutionary songs and hymns ('Le Chant du 14 juillet', 'La Marseillaise', 'Hymne à l'Être suprême', 'Le Chant du départ', etc.) as in *Volney's *Les Ruines* (1791).

Though contemporaries were assured that 'la Révolution n'a pas besoin de savants', the decade was singularly productive in scientists and mathematicians. *Lavoisier, *Laplace, and *Monge produced respectively three great works (*Traité de chimie*, 1789; *Exposition du système du monde*, 1796; *Traité de géométrie descriptive*, 1799), while the seminal work of *Cabanis (*Traité du physique et du moral de l'homme*, 1798–9) founded the study of psychophysiology, and that of Pinel (*Traité médico-philosophique sur l'aliénation mentale*, 1798) the study of psychopathology. And *Condorcet's *Esquisse d'un tableau des progrès de l'esprit humain* must surely be—given the circumstances of its production—one of the most moving expressions of confidence in human destiny ever penned.

Finally, one should not overlook the eminently personal reactions to the Revolution. They are particularly poignant among the *émigrés* (*Bonald, Xavier and Joseph de *Maistre, *Chateaubriand, *Sénac de Meilhan, *Rivarol, Madame de Genlis). Similarly, Madame *Roland and *Marmontel both wrote their *Mémoires* as their own direct response to the Revolution as a catastrophic transformation on both public and personal levels.

3. The Revolution and Posterity

The turbulent intensity of the Revolution (especially 1789–94), and the way in which it elicited the best and the worst from its actors, have inspired or terrified successive generations. From the very beginning it was clear that Europe was witnessing a mutation whose consequences were potentially cataclysmic. Given the mental equipment of the 18th c., almost all early commentators saw it as the result of human volition. Some invoked a type of providentialism, insisting that human pride and presumption were to blame (Burke). Others sought to shift responsibility wherever it could conveniently be placed. They blamed individuals—e.g. 'Philippe-Égalité' [see ORLÉANS]—or 'Pitt's gold', while equally popular culprits were Protestants or Jews, *freemasons or *philosophes. Joseph de *Maistre, on the other hand, claimed that the nation was being subjected to divine purification. The 'definitive' synthesis of such theories was given by the abbé Barruel in his *Mémoires pour servir à l'histoire du jacobinisme* (1797–9). Others were, however, sceptical. For example, J.-J. Mounier, replying to Barruel, in *De l'influence attribuée aux philosophes, francs-maçons et illuminés sur la Révolution de France* (1801), wrote: 'on a substitué à des causes très compliquées des causes simples, à la portée des esprits les plus paresseux et les plus superficiels.' But in turn, despite more evident intellectual distinction, writers such as Madame de Staël, *Thiers, *Michelet, *Quinet, and *Lamartine found it impossible to keep their own affiliations and preferences separate from their writings.

As Croce was to say: 'History is always contemporary History.' The events of 1830, 1848, and 1871 will all in turn, therefore, by a process which J. M.

Roberts has aptly termed 'mythological revivalism', generate either reverent evocation of the Great Revolution as a model to be imitated or expressions of distaste for an aberration to be condemned. That is why *Esquiros, for example, celebrating the Montagnards, could claim: 'Leur mémoire est comme une colonne de feu qui guide les générations errantes et indécises à la recherche d'une nouvelle terre promise.' That is precisely why *Toqueville and Marx (whose political opinions are amply betrayed in their own pronouncements on the Revolution) both believed that the men of 1848, haunted by the images and the rhetoric of 1789–94, were—by a process of mimesis—recreating the actions, the language, and the stances of their revolutionary grandfathers. But that belief was not confined to the Continent, nor to 1848 or the Commune. In 1837 Thomas Carlyle reacted in a similar way. Discerning a disturbing parallelism between contemporary events in Britain and the events of 1789–94, he produced his *French Revolution*, an apocalyptic vision in which unrelieved violence is the recurring theme. Some 20 years later Dickens's *Tale of Two Cities*, which remains fixed in the British consciousness, repeated the same lesson for the same reasons—with the result that these two works, themselves building on older, indelible memories of rabid anti-Revolutionary propaganda, have helped to create a popular (but widespread) view of the Revolution which is a caricature worthy of Cruikshank or Gillray, to which even the educated are still not immune.

Views of the Revolution among the French continued to be created in the ways exemplified by Madame de Staël, Thiers, Michelet, etc. down into the 20th c. However, with the Russian Revolution and the consequent reactivation of the very concept of revolution, there came both an internationalization and an intensification of the historiographical phenomenon itself. Three generations later there are consequently, across the world, numerous adherents of diverse 'tendencies'. At the risk of simplifying, we may define these as: counter-Revolutionary; Marxist-Leninist; libertarian Marxist; and liberal or neo-liberal 'revisionist'.

The simplest, the first, is prejudiced in favour of the *ancien régime* and proposes—as did *Taine, and diverse *Bonapartists or Legitimists—that the confrontation should have ended on 23 June 1789, the day when Louis XVI presented a 'perfectly satisfactory' blueprint for the future conduct of national affairs. This position is perhaps best exemplified by P. Gaxotte, whose *Révolution française* (1928)—written largely out of fear of the Bolshevik Revolution and organized subversion—is regularly reissued.

Marxist-Leninists (of whom the most eminent are G. *Lefebvre and A. Soboul) inherited much of the very orthodox and long-standing view which asserted that the bourgeoisie had seized power and used it to refashion society for its own ends. Intensifying that interpretation, the Revolution is now defined—by its economic content—as an inevitable conflict between the emerging forces of capitalist production and the declining feudalistic powers of the old social order. Russian historians and politicians, fixated by the 'inexorable' mechanism of the Great Predecessor, are particularly interesting: one result of their extreme tendency to draw inferences about the future direction of their own Revolution was the obsession of some (e.g. Trotsky) with the possibility of 'Thermidor', i.e. the brutal ending of a 'democratic' phase of the Revolution, or of 'Brumaire', i.e. the emergence of a soldier who would confiscate the state to his own advantage. They were not the first to appeal to historical analogies: Chateaubriand had already illustrated that approach in his *Essai sur les révolutions* (1797).

Libertarian Marxists owe less to Lenin than to Bakunin, Trotsky, and Rosa Luxemburg. They are intensely hostile to Marxist-Leninists, whom they revile as being tainted with an authoritarian Jacobinism which is deliberately unmindful of the popular democracy of An II. Such historians (e.g. Daniel Guérin, *La Lutte de classe dans la Première République*, 1944; *Bourgeois et Bras Nus*, 1973) believe that, in Year II, there came about a new type of class struggle which opposed the bourgeoisie to the urban workers, who constituted an embryonic proletarian revolution. One important result of this school has been the intensive examination of the popular strata of society in those pre-industrial times.

The 'revisionist' position seeks to demythify the Revolution by stripping away from it the accretions that are attributable to later visions. Essentially—without necessarily being 'right-wing'—it seeks to propose an alternative to the Marxist interpretation, either by placing the Revolution in a much wider temporal and spatial context (e.g. the Atlantic Revolution of R. R. Palmer or J. Godechot) or by attacking the basic concepts of Marxist historiography, which are claimed to be methodologically dubious. Classic statements of the latter position are those of Alfred Cobban (*The Social Interpretation of the French Revolution*, 1962) and François Furet (*Penser la Révolution française*, 1978); their influence was very noticeable in the many works produced in 1989 for the bicentenary of the Revolution (e.g. Simon Schama, *Citizens*). [JR]

Révolution du langage poétique, La, see KRISTEVA.

Révolution surréaliste, La, see SURREALISM.

Révolution Tranquille, La, see QUEBEC, 5.

Revue blanche, La. One of the most important of the many periodicals associated with *Symbolism and modern literary movements in late 19th-c. France. Founded in 1889, it merged with *La Revue* in 1903. It published writing by *Mallarmé, Henri de *Régnier, and others; *Debussy was its music critic, and the young Léon *Blum wrote theatrical and literary reviews.

Revue de Paris, La. A journal spanning—with many interruptions—140 years (1829-1970). It was founded in 1829 by Dr Véron (who later relaunched *Le *Constitutionnel*) and had many ties with *La *Revue des deux mondes*. In 1851 *Gautier, *Houssaye, and *Du Camp were among those who relaunched the journal; the Bonapartist authorities suppressed it in 1858. A more lasting revival occurred in 1894. Backed by the publisher Michel Lévy, the journal had as spiritual mentor the historian *Lavisse. It published pieces by *Barrès, *Renan, and the staunchly *Dreyfusard Anatole *France. This century, it was generally more literary in content than *La Revue des deux mondes*. [MP]

Revue des deux mondes, La. Founded in 1829 by Mauroy and Ségur-Dupeyron, this bimonthly review covered the arts and culture, politics, and economics. Early contributors included *Vigny, *Musset, *Balzac, and *Sand. Under the management of the Buloz family, the journal reflected the political liberalism and social conservatism of *July Monarchy Orléanism. It had close ties with the Rothschilds and *Le *Journal des débats*. Somewhat staid in literary tastes, *La Revue* was the most widely read of French reviews by the 1860s; in 1914 it still had 40,000 subscribers. It published pieces by *Leconte de Lisle and *Heredia, *Maupassant, *Loti, and Anatole *France. But, from the editorship of *Brunetière onwards (1893), it became something of an intellectual backwater. It supported Antoine Pinay and Edgar Faure under the Fourth Republic, and rallied to de *Gaulle under the Fifth. It was relaunched in 1982. [MP]

Revue du monde noir, La, see NÉGRITUDE.

Revue indigène, La, see THOBY-MARCELLIN.

Revue wagnérienne, La, see SYMBOLISM.

REYNOLD, Gonzague de, see SWISS LITERATURE IN FRENCH, 3.

REZVANI, Serge (b. 1928). Born in Teheran, but living in France since early childhood, Rezvani was a painter before turning to writing. His large output includes grotesque satires in the spirit of *May 1968, fables of life, love, and art (e.g. *La Loi humaine*, 1983), and autobiographical writings, from his first novel *Les Années-Lumière* (1967) to recent memoirs (e.g. *Variations sur les jours et les nuits*, 1985). These express the search for meaning by a writer who has difficulty feeling at home in French culture. [PF]

Rhetoric. Traditionally, rhetoric was defined as the art of persuasion, or the art of speaking well. For many centuries, it was a central element in the school curriculum and in literary culture in most of Europe, and notably in France, but suffered a loss of prestige in the 19th c. from which it has not fully recovered, though there have been many modern attempts to revive it.

The theoretical foundations of the discipline lie in the classics of Greece and Rome: Aristotle, Cicero, and Quintilian. In medieval France, though some of the key texts were lost, it flourished as a part of the *trivium* of language arts, even if it took third place to its sister arts, grammar and, above all, dialectic [see SCHOLASTICISM]. It was essentially concerned with the learning of Latin, and the study of Latin classics for stylistic purposes [see LATINITY], and it encompassed letter-writing and poetry (the 'art de seconde rhétorique'), as well as preaching and argumentation.

The *Renaissance saw the recovery of the great classical texts and a new stress on eloquence as a peak of human accomplishment. The *Jesuit colleges gave pride of place to rhetoric, and Cicero was the unsurpassed model. The complete discipline taught in the colleges of 16th–18th-c. France included the reading and analysis of classical texts, exercises of imitation (narration, fable, etc.), and carefully graded training in written and oral composition, culminating in the performance of full-scale orations. Dramatic productions were also used as an aid to public speaking. Attention was paid to all five parts of rhetoric: *inventio* (the discovery of the materials of persuasion), *dispositio* (the ordering of the material), *elocutio* (style, figures, etc.), memory, and *actio* (delivery and gesture). However, *Ramus transferred the first two to the domain of dialectic, which accentuated the tendency of rhetoric to concentrate on decorative language. As time went on, writing gained importance at the expense of speech.

In the 17th c. rhetoric was still Latin-based and was thus the province of the male students who attended Jesuit and other colleges. There was, however, a gradual increase in textbooks written in French (e.g. *Lamy, *De l'art de parler*, 1675) and in various reflections and essays by writers such as *Rapin and *Bouhours, aimed at a polite audience of both sexes. There were also works specifically concerned with the eloquence of the bar and the pulpit, the two careers most directly served by rhetoric. But at the same time rhetoric overlapped largely with poetics, so that many debates concerning literature, criticism, and taste found expression in rhetorical works. By the late 17th c. modern French writing was being studied in the rhetoric classes alongside the classics, and almost all French literature of the period bears the mark of rhetorical consciousness.

Ever since Plato, rhetoric had been subject to attack as an unscrupulous art, concerned less with truth than with persuasion or ostentation. Although St Augustine in his *De doctrina christiana* had recommended the adaptation of this pagan art for Christian purposes, puritanical believers remained suspicious of its powers. A greater threat came in the 18th c. from the new scientific philosophy. *Descartes had proclaimed (self-deludingly, of course) that no special art was needed to communicate thought, and *philosophes* such as d'*Alembert derided the traditional teaching of the colleges, suggesting that the stress on the 'places' (aids to the invention of subject-matter) and the figures led to empty declamation. A further threat to the subject emerged in the *Romantic period, when values of sincerity and individual self-expression challenged the idea of an art of writing or speaking that could be taught. Nevertheless, rhetoric retained its place in the lycées throughout the 19th c. By now it was concerned with French composition as much as with Latin and with writing as much as with speech. It remained a practical art, inculcating habits of expression which set the lycée pupils apart from the rest of the population. Only in 1902 was the classe de rhétorique renamed the classe de seconde. Triumphant positivism left little room in theory for the apparently empty ostentation of the orator. But it is easier to condemn rhetoric than to abandon it, and the values and habits of the rhetoric classes did not die because of a change of name.

The second half of the 20th c. has seen a powerful revival of interest in the old discipline, this being heralded by the subtle analyses of *Valéry and *Paulhan (Les Fleurs de Tarbes). The revival has taken several forms. There has been a new appreciation of the historical importance of rhetoric, illustrated above all by Marc Fumaroli's monumental study of Renaissance and classical rhetoric. At the same time, under the influence of *Structuralism, rhetoric has been seen as a precursor for the semiotic study of communication, as in the work of *Genette (who edited the forgotten work of *Fontanier) and the Rhétorique générale (1970) by a group of scholars headed by J. Dubois. More in keeping with the pragmatic nature of ancient rhetoric, Chaim Perelman and L. Olbrechts-Tyteca attempt in their La Nouvelle Rhétorique (1958) to formulate a modern rhetoric of persuasive argumentation. At the other end of the spectrum, writers associated with *Post-Structuralism stress the playful, subversive side of the subject. And finally, the 1980s saw the revived use of explicitly rhetorical models in composition classes in secondary schools to combat an apparent decline in pupil's communication skills. Rhetoric has not yet said its last word. [PF]

See P. France, Rhetoric and Truth in France, Descartes to Diderot (1972); M. Fumaroli, L'Age de l'éloquence (1980).

Rhétoriqueurs or **Grands Rhétoriqueurs.** Name generally given to a group of poets active from approximately 1450 to 1530, between *Villon and *Marot (principally *Chastellain, *Meschinot, *Molinet, Octovien de *Saint-Gelais, *Gringore, *Crétin, Jean *Lemaire de Belges, Jean *Marot, and Jean *Bouchet, who was still writing in 1550). Although they did not call themselves 'Rhétoriqueurs', they shared an intense preoccupation with *rhetoric—it was as 'l'art de seconde rhétorique' that late medieval tradition classified poetry.

They were mostly bourgeois, attached to royal or ducal households in France and Burgundy and paid to espouse the interests and celebrate the exploits of their patrons. They were specialists in chroniques and occasional verse or prose for propagandist purposes, hence the proliferation of pieces on births, marriages, and deaths, politics and wars (e.g. Jean Marot, Le Voyage de Venise).

Their shorter poems make extensive use of the *formes fixes: ballades, chants-royaux, rondeaux, virelais; longer pieces, such as déplorations or complaintes, often use mixed forms, combining Latin and French, prose and verse. The Rhétoriqueurs continue the traditions of the *Roman de la Rose, with an extensive use of allegory and abstraction and an overwhelming tendency to didacticism and moralizing. They have a certain, and in some cases (e.g. Lemaire de Belges, Octovien de Saint-Gelais) considerable, knowledge of the literature of antiquity, and an eagerness to display it, and this sometimes leads to an excessive use of Latinisms in pursuit of a high style. Their works show a concentration on purely formal devices, such as elaborate rhyme schemes (rimes léonines, couronnées, enchaînées, équivoquées), alliteration, puns, rebus, and other types of puzzles. All this is sometimes (inevitably) at the expense of clarity.

Their influence on Renaissance poetry, with all its formal experimentation, was considerable, though the *Pléiade poets denied this vigorously. *Rabelais too, with his love of puns and lists, can be seen as a direct heir of the Rhétoriqueur tradition. Late 19th-c and early 20th-c. criticism, with its emphasis on sincerity and spontaneity, tended to be contemptuous of the Rhétoriqueurs (see Henri Guy's L'École des Rhétoriqueurs, 1910). A major re-evaluation has been undertaken in recent years in the wake of *Zumthor's important book Le Masque et la lumière (1978). [CMSJ]

Rhin, Le. Descriptive work by *Hugo, mingling personal impressions of a visit to the Rhineland in 1839–40, legendary and historical material, and political reflections.

Rhinocéros, see IONESCO.

Rhyme. For a general view of rhyme and the different types of rhyme in French poetry, see VERSIFICATION, 3.

RIBEMONT-DESSAIGNES, Georges (1884–1974). One of 'les seuls vrais "dadas"', according to *Breton, he started composing poems after temporarily abandoning painting in 1913. His early plays, e.g. L'Empereur de Chine (1916), anticipate the Theatre of the *Absurd; his later ones are more fanciful. His novels and récits include L'Autruche aux yeux clos (1924), Ariane (1925), Le Bar du lendemain (1927), Céleste Ugolin (1928), which satirizes the *Surrealist movement, and Monsieur Jean ou l'Amour absolu (1934). As he grew older his poetry became more obviously lyrical: *Le Règne végétal* (1972) is probably his most important poetic text. His memoirs, *Déjà jadis* (1958), contain revealing insights into the *Dada and Surrealist movements. [KRA]

RIBOT, Théodule (1839–1916). Philosopher and pioneer of the modern psychological sciences in France. A professor at the Sorbonne and, from 1889, at the Collège de France, he wrote *Les Maladies de la mémoire* (1881) and studies on volition, personality, and attention. In these works he stressed the physiological basis of impaired mental functioning, but in his later writings gave increasing weight to emotional and affective factors. [MB]

RICARDOU, Jean (b. 1932). French novelist and theorist. Ricardou's first novels, *L'Observatoire de Cannes* (1961) and *La Prise de Constantinople* (1965), aligned him with the *Nouveau Roman, and for a while he was their leading theorist. He then invented the 'nouveau nouveau roman'—an even more radically and systematically anti-representational writing. His fictional texts are like difficult crossword puzzles; but he is most important for his substantial body of theoretical work. For Ricardou, the text subverts the ideological 'dogmas' of representation and expression through its self-referential structure and by maximizing the autonomous productivity of language through punning and anagrammatic wordplay. *Le Théâtre des métamorphoses* (1982) combines fiction and theory in a deliberately 'unclassifiable' text. [CB]

RICCOBONI, Marie-Jeanne Laboras de Mézières, Madame (1713–92). In 1734 Marie-Jeanne Laboras married Antoine-François Riccoboni and made her début as an actress in the *Comédie-Italienne, to which her husband belonged. She continued to perform until 1761, when her success as a writer allowed her to retire from the stage. In 1751 she wrote a *Suite* (published 1760) to La *Vie de Marianne*. Her first novel, *Lettres de mistriss Fanni Butlerd* (1757) was well received. Even more successful was *Lettres de milady Juliette Catesby* (1759), which was translated into five other languages. She wrote six more novels and four *nouvelles*. In 1762 she brought out a free translation of Fielding's *Amelia*, and later, with Thérèse Biancolelli, five English plays in translation (1768–9). By the time she corresponded with Laclos, criticizing *Les *Liaisons dangereuses*, she was therefore recognized as an author of some standing.

Her novels can be classed as *romans d'analyse*. Their heroines are portrayed, in most cases, as suffering through the attitudes and actions of men. She took great pains with her style, which was much admired by her contemporaries, including *Diderot. She usually avoids the hectic sensibility so common at the time; indeed, her letters show an independent mind, capable of irreverent and caustic comment. [VGM]

RICHARD, Jean-Pierre (b. 1922). Critic associated with the *Geneva school. His work, which is indebted to *Sartre and *Bachelard, seeks to describe the 'imaginary world' of writers, and in particular the way in which the imagination is shaped by physical sensation. *Littérature et sensation* (1954) contains richly detailed readings of novelists, especially *Flaubert and *Stendhal. Several works explore 19th- and 20th-c. poetry (*Poésie et profondeur*, 1955; *L'Univers imaginaire de *Mallarmé*, 1961; *Onze études sur la poésie moderne*, 1964), and subsequent studies concern *Chateaubriand, *Romanticism, and *Proust. [PF]

RICHELET, César-Pierre (1631–98), see DICTIONARIES, 2.

RICHELIEU, Armand du Plessis, cardinal de (1585–1642). The greatest French politician and statesman of his age, who was also an active and influential patron of the arts. He came to prominence at the *États Généraux of 1614, which he attended as bishop of Luçon (a see in the gift of his family, to which he had been appointed in 1607). After a period of time in the service of the Queen Mother, he became first minister of Louis XIII in 1628, and immediately made his mark by a successful campaign against the Protestants in France, who were forced to surrender important privileges after the siege of La Rochelle. He concentrated power in the royal government, and extended the frontiers of France by systematically opposing Spanish interests, a policy which led him into alliances with German Protestant states against the Catholic Empire.

His years in power were marked not only by ruthlessness and shrewd judgement at home and abroad, but also by an active, even interventionist, interest in the arts in general and literature in particular. He was instrumental in the foundation of the *Académie Française in 1634–5, and gave financial assistance and protection to many of its early members. His enthusiasm for the theatre was very great; not only did he build a theatre in his Paris residence, but he also formed a company of five authors (*Corneille, *Boisrobert, *Colletet, L'Estoille, and *Rotrou) who were brought together to write dramas under his direction and in collaboration with him. The resulting plays were not particularly well received. His relations with Corneille seem to have been strained: he it was who instructed the Academy to pass judgement on Le *Cid, whose celebration of Spanish chivalry and tacit acceptance of duelling among the nobility were uncongenial both to his foreign and his domestic policy. He left a *Testament politique*, and his ghost-written memoirs reproduce many of his confidential reports to Louis XIII. [IM]

RICHEPIN, Jean (1849–1926). French poet, novelist, dramatist. A bohemian vagabond who had spells as a sailor, boxer, and circus performer, he produced a volume of poems, *Les Chansons des gueux* (1876), which attracted sympathetic attention because of its picture of the miseries of vagrants and down-and-outs. Other verse followed (e.g. *Les Caresses*, 1877), but the transient fame he achieved in his day rested on his plays, usually in verse. Typical was *Le Chemineau* (1897), with its roving and roistering farmworker making amends to a servant-girl abandoned in pregnancy. He wrote *Nana-Sahib* (1883) for *Bernhardt. [SBJ]

RICHER, Edmond (1559–1631). French author of *De ecclesiastica et politica potestate* (1611), a short but influential brochure which summarizes his positive *Gallicanism. It also expresses his 'democratic' view of authority in the Church as something that is shared by all the members. This 'richérisme' strongly influenced 18th-c. *Jansenism. [JC]

RICŒUR, Paul (b. 1913). French philosopher and literary theorist. A major exponent of *phenomenology, Ricœur was particularly concerned with developing its implications for a theory and practice of interpretation. This hermeneutic approach, adopted in order to decipher such indirect expressions of lived experience as myths and symbols (*La Symbolique du mal*, 1960), led to a study of Freud's psychoanalytic discourse and of the dissimulating or distorting language of desire, and thence to an awareness of the inevitably conflictual but productive competition of interpretations in the absence of any absolute grounding for knowledge (*Freud et la philosophie*, 1965; *Le Conflit des interprétations*, 1969). Ricœur's appreciation of contemporary Anglo-American philosophy—rare among Continental thinkers—sharpened his well-informed critique of the *Structuralist model of language as a closed synchronic system. His rehabilitation of the communicative, referential, and semantic rather than semiotic functions of discourse informed his major study of metaphor as a source of new knowledge and meaning (*La Métaphore vive*, 1975), while his concern with the status of the written text and with the structures of temporality in human action, experience, and imagination inspired his monumental study of the function of narrative, and of the intersection of two modes of reference, in fictional and historical writing (*Temps et récit*, 1983–5). [REG]

RICTUS, Jehan (pseud. of Gabriel Randon de Saint-Amand) (1867–1933). French poet, novelist, and dramatist, remembered for the poetic texts, written in a kind of *argot and usually in octosyllables, which he performed in the *Chat Noir and other cabarets. His most famous collection, *Le Soliloque du pauvre* (1897), gives a voice to the miseries and emotions of the Parisian poor; it was admired by *Mallarmé. See also *Le Cœur populaire* (1914). [PF]

RIGAUD, Hyacinthe (1659–1743). Known for his formal Baroque portraits of *Louis XIV, Rigaud was also the first major portraitist in France to emulate the naturalism and psychological penetration of Rembrandt. His early paintings of other artists and his group of the printer Pierre-Frédéric Leonard and his family demonstrate this interest in realism. [JPC]

RIGAUT, Jacques-Georges (1898–1929). A founder-member of the Paris *Dada group, Rigaut was the specialist of verbal revolt, a master of elegant paradox and acid cynicism. His personal manifesto, 'Je serai sérieux comme le plaisir' (1920), was a characteristic provocation in its advocacy of despair and suicide; and his 'Pensées' comprise stunning aphorisms about the moral code of the nihilist and *dandy. Incapable of adjusting to *Surrealism, Rigaut left Paris for New York in 1924 and led a wastrel's life till he shot himself in 1929. His collected writings, nearly all posthumous, appeared as *Écrits* in 1970. [RC]

RIHOIT, Catherine (b. 1949). A university English specialist, Rihoit's novels range widely, from her own milieu, wittily described in *Le Bal des débutantes* (1978), to the Revolution in *La Nuit de Varennes* (1982); she ironically describes women and men in *Les Abîmes du cœur* (1980) and *Jeu de mémoire* (1988). [SFN]

RIMBAUD (Jean-Nicolas-)Arthur (1854–91). Few poets can have acquired so high a reputation as Arthur Rimbaud on the basis of so slender an *œuvre* and so brief a career. From the moment his legendary *Illuminations* saw print in 1886, the sheer inventiveness of his writings, seemingly indissociable from the eventfulness of his life, has been the subject of fervent and noisy debate, to the extent that the strict data of biography and literary production are now engulfed in innumerable theories and conflicting interpretations. Rimbaud remains the outstanding example in French literature of a meteoric talent giving rise to enduring controversy.

A crude summary of his life reduces it to two stretches of relatively steady existence on either side of the eruptive creative adventure at its centre. A model schoolboy, Rimbaud seemed content to please his mother by gaining annual prizes at his college in Charleville (in the Ardennes), until his early satirical verse began to voice his hatred of an environment he saw as totally debilitating, with abrasive attacks on the sanctity of bourgeois routine in 'A la musique', on Christianity in 'Les Premières Communions', and on orthodox notions of the beautiful in 'Vénus Anadyomène', a sonnet about a hag stepping from her bath-tub. Disruptions to local life due to the Prussian invasion of mid-1870 coincided with symptomatic episodes when the teenager repeatedly ran away from home; it is thought he may have witnessed the brief apogee of the Paris *Commune in the spring of 1871. The period of his late teens (c.1870–c.1874) saw the abrupt flowering of a unique talent as, like a gambler whose daring never fails, Rimbaud moved in the space of a few months from structured verse

699

through progressively more liberated verse (the poems known as 'Derniers vers') and on to the *prose poem, of which he would become one of the first masters. In September 1871, still not yet 17, he had tucked into his pocket an astonishing poem, 'Le Bateau ivre'—a maritime allegory of the visionary process—and taken leave of Charleville, journeying to Paris to take the literary establishment by storm. Almost at once he entered on a turbulent erotic relationship with *Verlaine, and travelled with him to London, the backdrop to several of the dream-like scenarios elaborated in *Illuminations*. After a violent break with Verlaine, Rimbaud spent some years drifting through casual jobs in northern and southern Europe, having by now effectively abandoned literature. By the end of the decade he had also abandoned Europe, pursuing a mercantile career in the obscure regions of Abyssinia, and only returning to his homeland because of illness. He died in Marseille in 1891, aged 37.

The terms of the Rimbaud legend were dictated by Verlaine, who first dubbed him a *poète maudit* and published *Illuminations* without their author's knowledge as the relics of a genius who had touched perfection and then moved on to the alternative ascesis of day-to-day existence. This narrative of striving and renunciation is consistent with the confessional themes of *Une saison en enfer*, completed in the summer of 1873, where the writer describes ecstatic visions which he later relinquishes because of the physical torment they entail. A plausible interpretation of the chapter 'L'Alchimie du verbe', when read in conjunction with two earlier texts which had excitedly announced the new visionary approach, the so-called 'Lettres du voyant' of May 1871, is that Rimbaud induced actual states of *voyance* by way of drugs and alcohol and then transliterated his experiences into an image-laden idiom embodying 'l'hallucination des mots'. The 40-odd prose pieces of the *Illuminations* cycle amount to a phantasmagorical documentation of the creative process, one which charts the itinerary of a consciousness visited by chimerical spectacles, by turns monstrous and ravishing and seemingly inseparable from the literary tropes wherein they find expression. Cryptic allusions to apocalyptic omens and ineffable harmonies, and the hint that 'illumination' is a transcendental (and thus extra-literary) event, have laid such texts open to religious readings which cast their author in the role of an unorthodox prophet. Other readings stress the virtuosity of a poetic discourse which marries baffling enigma to thrilling suggestion, and at a stroke transforms the reading experience from one of intellectual construal to one of emotional participation. 'J'ai seul la clef de cette parade sauvage', the poet warns us, although recent research indicates that many of his impenetrable formulations embody empirical references to contemporary society. Yet to acknowledge that Rimbaud's mature work echoes the lexical and cultural codes of his age is not necessarily to reduce all he wrote to mimetic explicitness and a univocal legibility. The irreducible strength of Rimbaud's 'alchemy of the word' remains its sheer rhetorical confidence, the inimitable assertiveness, the beguiling violence, of its imagery and tone. [RC]

See Y. Bonnefoy, *Rimbaud par lui-même* (1961); R. G. Cohn, *The Poetry of Rimbaud* (1973); A. Kittang, *Discours et jeu: essai d'analyse des textes d'Arthur Rimbaud* (1975); A. Borer (ed.), *L'Œuvre-Vie d'Arthur Rimbaud* (1991).

RINALDI, Angelo (b. 1940). French novelist, literary critic of *L'Express*. His novels are mainly set against a background of Corsican society and feature narrators who, in later life, attempt to understand the causes of their present materially successful but spiritually bleak existence. He is, in the fullest sense, a classical novelist, acutely aware of the presence of the ancient world in his landscape. His *La Maison des Atlantes* won the Prix Fémina in 1971. Subsequent novels include *La Dernière Fête de l'Empire* (1980) and *La Confession dans les collines* (1991) [IWR]

RINGUET (pseud. of Dr Philippe Panneton) (1895–1960). Canadian doctor, writer, and public figure who ended his career as Canadian ambassador to Portugal. The significance of his novel *Trente arpents* (1938) is broadly political as well as literary in that it decisively rejected the agrarian myth that had for so long sustained conservative ideologies in Quebec. Far from being an arcadian world of truth and beauty, the rural society of *Trente arpents* is seen to be retarded and decadent. Unlike similar attacks by writers such as Albert *Laberge, Ringuet's account has a sobriety which emphasizes the inevitability of social change without abandoning respect for the rural values that are condemned to extinction. Indeed, a marked nostalgia for the natural world, coupled with a distaste for the superficialities of modern urban life, permeate all his later works, *L'Héritage* (1946), *Fausse monnaie* (1947), and *Le Poids du jour* (1949). In these lesser pieces, however, Ringuet's conflicting attitudes are never as satisfactorily reconciled as in his masterwork. [SIL]

'Riquet à la houppe'. One of Perrault's *Histoires ou contes du temps passé*, the only one of Perrault's own invention. An ugly but witty boy loves a beautiful but stupid girl, and their good qualities are united in a happy end.

Rire, Le, see BERGSON.

Rivage des Syrtes, Le, see GRACQ.

RIVARD, Yvon (b. 1945). Canadian novelist. His novels, *Mort et naissance de Christophe Ulric* (1976), *L'Ombre et le double* (1979), and *Les Silences du corbeau* (1986), have a playful hermeticism and formal self-consciousness which are reminiscent of the French *Nouveau Roman, but their themes—imaginary voyages in search of self and country—are entirely typical of Quebec literature. [SIL]

RIVAROL, Antoine Rivaroli, self-styled comte de (1753–1801). Though intended for the Church, Rivarol chose instead to pursue a career in, or on the fringes of, the Parisian salons, where his verbal brilliance ('Il fut le dieu de la conversation', said *Chênedollé) and his genteel malice were to make him second only to *Chamfort as the scourge of the ailing *ancien régime*. Rivarol's life-style was, however, to hinder sustained literary production. Despite his admired translation of Dante's *Inferno* and despite finding fame with his prize-winning *Discours sur l'universalité de la langue française*, his penchant was for satire: in 1782 he produced an amusing parody of Delille's *Jardins* entitled *Le Chou et le navet*, and six years later taunted France's self-important literary mediocrities in his *Petit almanach de nos grands hommes* (1788).

The following year, though perfectly lucid about the deficiencies of the monarchy, and of Louis XVI in particular, he chose to defend the latter as the natural guarantor of the liberties of the nation and turned his talents as a satirist to political journalism. His articles for the *Journal politique et national* (July 1789–November 1790)—published collectively as a *Tableau historique et politique de l'Assemblée constituante* (1797)—prompted Edmund Burke to hail him as 'the Tacitus of the French Revolution'; those articles, taken in conjunction with his contributions to the *Actes des apôtres*, aroused the hatred of the Revolutionaries, and particularly those who had figured in his *Petit dictionnaire des grands hommes de la Révolution* (1790), whom he had branded as ambitious, small-minded upstarts. Prudence led him, on 10 June 1792, to emigrate to Brussels, then to London (1794), and finally to Hamburg (1795). There he undertook a philosophically orientated *Nouveau dictionnaire de la langue française*; all that exists of that work (which might well have been his best) is the *Prospectus* and the *Discours préliminaire*. Seven years after his death in Berlin, Fayolle and Chênedollé produced his *Œuvres complètes* in five volumes. [JR]

RIVETTE, Jacques, French film-maker, see NOUVELLE VAGUE.

RIVIÈRE, Jacques (1886–1925). When a bout of typhoid fever killed Rivière at the age of 38, the French literary scene lost one of its brightest young critics. His meeting with *Gide was decisive, professionally and formatively; launched into Parisian literary and artistic life, he became secretary of the *Nouvelle Revue Française* in 1911. Rivière was continually searching for the truth, torn between the acceptance of God and the quest for self-fulfilment and happiness. It was in 1906 that the young student from Bordeaux wrote to *Claudel for spiritual guidance, and there ensued a long and important correspondence. Another decisive meeting, resulting in a deep friendship and another important correspondence, was with *Alain-Fournier at the Lycée Lakanal. He wrote many articles on literature, music, and painting, collected as *Études* (1912) and *Nouvelles études* (posth., 1947). While a prisoner in Germany he wrote *L'Allemand, souvenirs et réflexions d'un prisonnier de guerre* (1919); *Aimée* (1922) a novel which was criticized for its apparently autobiographical exploration of *l'amour-passion*; and *A la trace de Dieu* (1925).

From 1919 to 1925 he was director of the *NRF*, and made it into the intellectual mouthpiece of France. He had an intuitive, penetrating grasp of the cultural trends of the time, encouraged new talent (e.g. *Proust), and opened up debates on the role of art versus intelligence, the intellectual in society, and the future of the novel. He helped to shape French literary tastes, always demanding a high standard of writing and intellectual honesty.

A number of his works were published posthumously by his wife, Isabelle Rivière. [ET]

RIVOYRE, Christine de (b. 1921), began as a journalist before writing a series of novels analysing contemporary relations between the sexes. In *Les Sultans* (1964), the tone is sardonic; in *Le Petit Matin* (1968), set in occupied France, passion turns to tragedy. *Reine-mère* (1985) offers a portrait of a woman whose strength lies in her passionate generosity. [EAF]

ROBBE-GRILLET, Alain (b. 1922). Breton-born novelist and film-maker. In the 1960s and 1970s, Robbe-Grillet was one of the most prominent and controversial of French avant-garde writers. He launched and publicized the *Nouveau Roman, through his novels and critical journalism and as editor at the *Minuit publishing house. His work is based on a rejection of realism—the traditional 19th-c. novel, and also *Sartre's politically committed realism. *Pour un nouveau roman* (1963) vigorously states Robbe-Grillet's position: the novelist must not accept any external constraints—whether literary conventions, political or moral concerns, or representational accuracy—but must let the text proceed freely, propelled only by its own formal logic. Humanist values must be replaced by a non-anthropocentric refusal of complicity between man and his environment.

His early novels—*Les Gommes* (1953), *Le Voyeur* (1955), *La *Jalousie* (1957), *Dans le labyrinthe* (1959)—introduced a striking new style: his flatly precise, largely visual descriptions, eliminating figurative language and 'human' significance, were labelled *chosiste*. But this apparently objective writing creates a strangely unstable fictional reality. Thus, from about 1960 critical interpretation of his fiction—reinforced by his screenplay for *Resnais's film *L'Année dernière à Marienbad* (1961), and then his own first film, *L'Immortelle* (1963)—swung round to the opposite pole: these were intensely *subjective* texts,

701

staging a world of dream, fantasy, and obsession. The contradiction between 'objectivist' and 'subjectivist' readings is sustained in *Instantanés* (1962), a collection of short texts characterized by a curious blurring of identity and difference. This is extended in *La Maison de rendez-vous* (1965), where the 'same' characters and events recur in different versions and on different levels of narrative. But this novel is also more explicitly ludic (as are his next two films, *Trans-Europ-Express*, 1966 and *L'Homme qui ment*, 1968)—playing games with our expectations of both narrative coherence and cultural meanings. A set of deliberately stereotyped fantasies and generic conventions—a Hong Kong brothel, drug-dealers, etc.—is combined to produce a logically impossible narrative sequence. The text is thus generated through an open-ended series of transformations of the relations between its elements. *Projet pour une révolution à New York* (1970) performs a similarly *Structuralist operation with an underground terrorist organization in New York. Robbe-Grillet argues that this effectively subverts the dominant ideology: the generative play exposes and defuses the cultural stereotypes. In subsequent novels and films, however, the insistent repetitiveness of sado-masochistic scenes has cast doubt upon Robbe-Grillet's supposedly critical position. *Topologie d'une cité fantôme* (1976) and *Souvenirs du triangle d'or* (1978) suggest a more ambivalent involvement in the fantasies staged by the text. (Also in 1978 *Le Régicide*, written in 1949, appeared for the first time.) The films of this period—*L'Éden et après* (1971), *Glissements progressifs du plaisir* (1974), *Le Jeu avec le feu* (1975), and the later *La Belle Captive* (1983)—are similarly provocative and troubling. *Djinn* (1981) returns to a more controlled playfulness, based on grammar: a systematic progression through increasingly complex syntactic forms, it also came out in America as a language textbook, with accompanying exercises.

In 1985 Robbe-Grillet published *Le Miroir qui revient*, the first volume of his autobiography. For an author who had so firmly denied any relevant connections between his life and his writing, this constitutes a major volte-face. Claiming that his earlier views have become a new orthodoxy to be overthrown, he now says that all his previous fiction was, despite appearances, essentially personal. *Le Miroir* mixes anecdote with literary criticism, Breton folklore, and the erotic desires and fears of his childhood. The second volume, *Angélique ou l'Enchantement* (1988), is more exclusively concerned with sexual fantasies staged in a fairy-tale landscape. The third volume, *Les Derniers Jours de Corinthe*, appeared in 1993.

Robbe-Grillet is a theorist and teacher as well as a producer of fiction and film. His work has been provocative, confrontational, and often opportunist, but has always posed radical questions about the relation between cultural stereotypes, fantasy, and anti-representational structure. [CB]

See O. Bernal: *Alain Robbe-Grillet: le roman de l'absence* (1964); *Obliques*, 16–17 (1978), special issue on Robbe-Grillet.

ROBERT, Hubert (1733–1808). French painter; a close friend of *Fragonard and abbé Saint-Non, with whom he travelled in Sicily and southern Italy. He developed a personal Romantic vision of a classical past, expressed in imaginative ruin-scapes, which influenced the picturesque landscapes of artists like Pillement. He was keeper of the king's pictures and curator of the Louvre. [JPC]

ROBERT, Marthe (b. 1914). French essayist. Her *L'Ancien et le nouveau* (1963) and *Roman des origines, origines du roman* (1972) are challenging discussions of the relation between modern literature and tradition. She has translated many German writers and written an important introduction to Freud, *La Révolution psychanalytique* (1964). [PF]

ROBERT DE BLOIS (*fl.* second third of 13th c.). Author of a range of narrative, lyric, religious, and didactic poetry which has survived in several manuscript compilations. Robert preached conservative courtly values with a measure of flair and wit. Among his best-known works, the *Enseignement des princes* is a didactic poem that instructs noblemen in their public life and describes the moral and religious duties of knights. By contrast, the *Chastoiement des dames* prescribes a domestic role for noblewomen and imparts rules of etiquette, dress, and table-manners; at times, the clerkly narrator adopts a bantering tone. *Floris et Lyriopé* is an extended Ovidian *exemplum recounting the exploits of Narcissus's parents: his father Floris seduces the innocent Lyriopé by cross-dressing as a woman. In one manuscript compilation these works are all contained within the nearly completed Arthurian romance *Beaudous*, in which the eponymous hero receives instructions from his mother before departing for Arthur's court, as does *Chrétien de Troyes's Perceval. [RLK]

ROBERT DE BORON. Late 12th-c. author of three *Grail romances, *Joseph d'Arimathie*, *Merlin*, and *Perceval*, the last two of which are preserved only in 13th-c. prose adaptations. He was the first to make an explicit link between the Grail and the events of the Crucifixion. [PEB]

Robert le Diable. Legendary folk-hero. His story, like that of his son Richard sans Peur, was endlessly reprinted and adapted in the *Bibliothèque Bleue. It first appears in a *dit of the 12th c., then in the *Chroniques de Normandie* and a *miracle play. Robert, supposed son of the duke of Normandy, is dedicated to the devil before his birth, leads a life of crime, but repents and redeems himself by fighting the Saracens. In some versions he marries the emperor's daughter, in others he becomes a saint. [PF]

ROBESPIERRE, Maximilien (1758–94). Radical Revolutionary leader who sat in the États Généraux, the Assemblée Constituante, and the Convention, but whose power base remained in the *Jacobin Club. He came centre-stage with his election to the Comité de Salut Public (July 1793), where he helped institute the Terror (September 1793–July 1794), helping—in the process—to save the Republic, but also engineering the downfall of the *Girondins, spearheading the liquidation of the *Hébertistes, and dispatching *Danton to the guillotine. The general fear in which he was increasingly held, both in the Comité and the Convention, led to the pre-emptive strike of 9 Thermidor and his execution.

Because of the often self-interested rhetoric of the Thermidorian reaction, Robespierre almost immediately became one of the most maligned and misunderstood of men. He was an idealist and a man of great, genuinely deserved, moral authority. But it is no less true that he was also a dogmatic, even academic, Revolutionary who seems to have worked from theoretical models and who—with his particularly exalted idea of humanity—had no sympathy whatsoever for opponents whom *ipso facto* he suspected of bad faith or furtive counter-revolutionary activity. Few politicians can, at their most influential, have so sadly and yet so genuinely misgauged the 'art of the possible'. His speeches and writings—like those of *Saint-Just—are fascinating examples of rhetorical skills and can conveniently be consulted in *Robespierre, textes choisis* (ed. J. Poperen, 1979) and *Robespierre: Écrits* (ed. C. Mazauric, 1989). [JR]

ROBINET, Jean-Baptiste (1733–1820). French scholar, author of philosophical and grammatical works. Having contributed to the supplement to the *Encyclopédie, he published an encyclopedic *Dictionnaire universel ou Bibliothèque de l'homme d'état et du citoyen* (30 vols., 1777–83).

ROBLÈS, Emmanuel (b. 1914). Born in Oran, of Spanish origin, Roblès left Algeria for France in 1958. A prolific novelist and playwright, and occasional poet, he is a great traveller, and his fiction and drama, while primarily Mediterranean in location, have been set as far afield as Japan and South America. Among his best-known works are the novels *Cela s'appelle l'aurore* (1952), *Saison violente* (1974), *Venise en hiver* (1981), and the play *Montserrat* (1948).

There is no metaphysical dimension to Roblès's fictional world; his heroes are unremarkable, frequently flawed men of modest circumstances who live under constant threat of death from accident, war, natural forces or disasters, or the enmity of brutal and unscrupulous aggressors. Typically, they are faced with the necessity of making a moral choice and, although tempted to adopt the easy solution, they choose to jeopardize their personal happiness, even their lives, to support a friend or cause or to protect the weak or under-privileged

against oppression through power, wealth, or authority. This rebellious, virile humanism finds satisfaction in making the right decision or achieving a challenging task, virtue in courage, loyalty and generosity of spirit, and tenderness and respite, occasionally, in the love of a woman. [RMJ]

Rocambole. The hero of adventure novels by *Ponson du Terrail.

ROCHE, Denis (b. 1937). French anti-poet associated with *Tel Quel*. His work might be described as late modernism's version of *poésie pure. Crying that poetry 'is inadmissible; besides, it doesn't exist', he advocates reducing it to a state where its pure conventionality is patent. Hence the arbitrary breaches and interruptions in subject, sentences, and grammar, less consequential than a game of consequences or the *Surrealist *cadavre exquis*. The occasional flicker of amusement or erotic interest might be felt while reading *Éros énergumène* (1968). Other works include *Le Mécrit* (1972), and he has translated Pound's *Pisan Cantos* and *ABC of Reading*. [GDM]

ROCHEFORT, Christiane (b. 1917). French feminist writer whose first novel, *Le Repos du guerrier* (1958), in which the heroine struggles with questions of sexuality and power within the couple, gained immediate success. Many of her subsequent texts have also proved best-sellers. *Les Petits Enfants du siècle* (1961) is narrated by a working-class girl living on a large housing-estate and offers a strong critique of French pro-natalist policies and the state's manipulation of consumer society. The heroine appears self-aware but eventually falls into the trap. In *Les Stances à Sophie* (1963) the working-class female narrator is again trapped when she marries into the wealthy bourgeoisie; this time, however, she becomes more radically alienated and, after the woman with whom she has an affair is killed, makes a new life for herself. In rather different vein to these realist texts *Une rose pour Morrison* (1966) and *Archaos ou le Jardin étincelant* (1972) adopt a fantasy mode to conduct their attack on the social control of sexuality. Desire and the impulse to break free of social models and constraints recur frequently in Rochefort's texts (*Printemps au parking*, 1969; *Encore heureux qu'on va vers l'été*, 1975). *La Porte du fond* (1988) deals with the painful subject of child sexual abuse. [EAF]

ROCHEFORT, Henri (Henri de Rochefort, marquis de Rochefort-Luçay) (1831–1913). One of the outstanding polemical journalists of his age, moving rapidly from the extreme Left to the extreme Right, Rochefort started as a critic of the Second Empire in his paper *La Lanterne*. A supporter of the *Commune in 1871, he was deported to New Caledonia, whence he escaped to Geneva. Returning to France under the 1880 amnesty, he founded *L'Intransigeant*. A fervent Boulangist, he went into exile in London from 1889 to 1895 after the collapse of the *Boulanger cause. In the *Dreyfus Affair Rochefort was one of the most powerful anti-Dreyfusard apologists. [RMG]

Rochefort, L'École de. Unlike the *Surrealist movement, whose influence it sought to supplant (preferring the examples of *Jacob, *Reverdy, or *Follain) the Rochefort school was not based on a common programme but brought together poets linked by strong ties of friendship and a shared desire to promote an accessible poetry of everyday lyricism. Although none of the prime movers was a poet of the first rank (*Cadou is probably the best known) the Rochefort spirit, distilled essentially in the numerous publications of series such as the 'Cahiers de l'École de Rochefort', was very pervasive in the 1940s and 1950s and for a time exerted a strong influence on such poets as *Frénaud, *Guillevic, and *Réda. Named after Rochefort-sur-Loire where it was founded in 1941, the school counted among its adherents Cadou, Marcel Béalu, *Fombeure, Jean Rousselot, and Luc Bérimont. [MHTS]

Rococo. The Rococo style is identified in France with the reign of Louis XV. In recent years it has come to be applied to literary style, but is commonly used of the visual arts. It derives from the term *rocaille*, or rockwork, and is principally a decorative style of shell-like forms, C curves, and asymmetrical scrolls. Variety and attractiveness are the hallmarks of Rococo sculpture, house painting, porcelain, and metalwork. An increase in the variety of subjects drawn from ordinary life and literature characterizes Rococo painting.

The popular grotesque engravings of Meissonnier (1695–1750), the delicate engravings of decorative landscapes by Lajoue (1686–1761), and the asymmetrical wall-panel drawings of Pineau (1684–1754) influenced interior decorations by painters like Oudry, *Watteau, Lancret, and *Boucher and, later, Oppenordt's schemes at Versailles. The Gros Pavillon (1752) at *Fontainebleau is covered with examples of the 'style pittoresque' [see PICTURESQUE].

Book illustrators used the same formulae, often binding vignette designs to the text with elaborate, curved frames. Hubert Gravelot (1699–1773), Boucher, and Moreau le Jeune were particularly inventive Rococo illustrators, and forged the closest link between literature and art. The many French authors illustrated by major Rococo engravers included J.-J. *Rousseau, *Corneille, *Montesquieu, *Marmontel, *La Fontaine, La Borde, and *Dorat. Painters as well as printmakers welcomed the rich range of new subjects provided by these texts. [JPC]

Rocroi, Battle of, see CONDÉ, PRINCE DE.

RODENBACH, Georges (1855–98). 'C'est très beau et très Poe, cela', said *Mallarmé of Le Règne du silence (1891), in whose poems Rodenbach expressed in melodious, intimist, and melancholy tones the mysterious analogies between poet and world which made him one of the leading figures of Belgian *Symbolism. In 1881 he co-founded La Jeune Belgique, in which he helped to open Belgian literature to the influences of the French *Decadents and Symbolists. He achieved greatest success with his novel Bruges-la-morte (1892), in which he brought together the theme of love for the deceased spouse with descriptions of the city's canals, rains, and mists and their links to the subconscious. *Bachelard described the novel as an illustration of the 'Ophelia complex', and this 'ophélisation d'une ville entière' made Bruges one of the privileged sites of fin-de-siècle sensibility. [JK]

RODIN, Auguste (1840–1917). Prolific French sculptor of major importance. In the manner of Michelangelo, he left some works 'unfinished', displaying created, smooth areas of form (the head in La Pensée) emerging from a block of uncut stone. Other signs of the creative imprint show in those of his cast bronzes which retain the marks of considerable working of the wax. The forms, always representational, are fluid, evoking, as in L'Age d'airain, nascent or surging movement of both body and spirit. Translating into the language of the visible their absorption in the writer's craft, and their vast designs, he produced remarkable portraits of Victor *Hugo (busts in bronze and marble, a marble monument) and the lionizing and indeed leonine *Balzac. [HEB]

Rodogune. Tragedy by Pierre *Corneille, first performed 1645, and remarkable for its powerful, if melodramatic, portrait of moral evil. The central character, Cléopâtre, queen of Syria, will sacrifice anything to retain power. Only she can decide between the rival claims of her twin sons, Antiochus and Séleucus, to inherit the throne; she promises her voice to whichever of the two will rid her of Rodogune, princess of Parthia, whose hand is destined to the new king. Both princes love Rodogune, but she confronts them with a terrible dilemma by promising love to whichever kills his mother. In desperation Cléopâtre kills Séleucus, the weaker of the twins, and prepares a poisoned cup for the wedding of Antiochus and Rodogune, but is forced into drinking it herself, and dies defiant. [PF]

Rodrigue. The young and glamorous hero of P. Corneille's Le *Cid.

ROHMER, Eric (b. 1920). French film-maker. Editor of *Cahiers du cinéma (1957–63), Rohmer turned to directing in the early 1960s. Seen by some as the consummate exponent of cinematic marivaudage, by others as the apotheosis of pretentious Gallicism, he deals with moral and ethical issues in a style whose dry humour and reliance on dialogue are unlike that of any other director. Ma nuit chez Maud (1969), one of his *Six contes moraux*, marked his first major success. The more recent series of *Comédies et proverbes* tackles problems of marriage, cohabitation, and solitude (*Le Beau Mariage*, 1982; *Les Nuits de la pleine lune*, 1984; *Le Rayon vert*, 1986), suggesting that the notoriously apolitical Rohmer may still be a major 'post-*soixante-huitard*' film-maker. [KAR]

Roi, Cycle du. Term used to refer to *chansons de geste* featuring *Charlemagne (e.g. the *Chanson de *Roland*) or, more rarely, some other *Merovingian or *Carolingian king, to distinguish them from the poems featuring William of Orange (Cycle de *Guillaume) and from the *geste* of *Doon de Mayence. The threefold classification derives from *Bertrand de Bar-sur-Aube's prologue to *Girart de Vienne*. [SK]

Roi des aulnes, Le. Set in the years 1938 to 1945, *Tournier's second novel (1970, Grand Prix de l'Académie Française) takes its title from Goethe's poem 'Der Erlkönig'. The protagonist, Abel Tiffauges, recounts his version of his life history with his left hand, the newly discovered power of which gives him a renewed perspective on his life. Proclaiming himself to be an ogre ('un monstre féerique émergeant de la nuit des temps'), Tiffauges sees himself as a reader of the signs that are everywhere to be found in the world and as sharing a particular complicity with history.

The first-person narration of the opening section is used to combine the fantastic with the historical, as the diary form charts the progress towards the outbreak of World War II, final proof for Tiffauges of the complicity of history with his own destiny. His discovery of his vocation to bear/carry children, filtered through his own *sinister* world-view, leads to his imprisonment (for child-molesting) and enforced recruitment into the army, where he eventually becomes a prisoner of the Germans. His entry into Germany appears to him as an entry into the promised land, and his activities as a prisoner take him progressively deeper into the lands and world of the Third Reich. He sees in Göring and in Hitler ogres whose conduct reflects his own in a negatively inverted way, while his activities as a trustee prisoner, turned recruiter for the Napola, are a reflection of his 'vocation phorique' towards children.

The final section of the novel reveals the extent to which all aspects of Tiffauges's life in Germany are themselves reflections of the horrors of Auschwitz, just as his proclaimed affection for the children he has snatched for the Napola leads directly to their deaths. The novel ends on his descent into the marshlands from which earlier the eponymous figure of a sacrificial victim had been disinterred.

The protagonist's propensity to identify himself with certain figures is never simply acceptable at face value, any more than is the morality of his world-view, but his insistence on the systematic

deciphering of the meaning of the world alerts the reader to other readings of the same phenomena and therefore to the systematic nature of our understanding of the world, history, etc. The real subject of the novel lies less in its fantastic depiction of events not normally considered suitable for any but the most documentary of treatments, than in its manner of transforming our awareness of the ways in which the self-in-the-world attempts to understand the world; here, in its drawing both on genetic theory and physiology as well as Freudian and post-Freudian psychology, lies its true originality. [IWR]

Roi miraculé, Le, see BETI.

Roi s'amuse, Le (1832). Poetic drama by *Hugo, the basis of Verdi's *Rigoletto*. François Ier's jester Triboulet, driven mad by the king's love for his daughter, plans to have him murdered, but finds instead that the body in the sack that he is about to throw into the Seine is that of his daughter.

Roi se meurt, Le, see IONESCO.

Rois fainéants, Les, see MEROVINGIANS.

ROLAND, Marie-Jeanne Phlipon, Madame (1754–93). Important French political figure, wife of Jean-Marie Roland, minister of the interior in the crucial Revolutionary year of 1792–3. The Rolands, having been passionately committed to the Revolution in its early stages, became its victims. On 2 June 1793, as members of the defeated *Girondin faction, Madame Roland was arrested and her husband fled into the country. When she was executed in November of that year, her husband committed suicide.

With the halo of a noble death, preceded by the words: 'O Liberté, que de crimes on commet en ton nom', she was regarded as a tragic heroine by Romantic historians such as Carlyle. In reality she was by no means a passive victim, and took an active part in political struggles, notably with *Danton, whom she detested. Her reputation now rests, however, on the remarkable *Mémoires* she wrote in prison (see the edition of P. de Roux, Mercure de France, 1986). First entitled *Appel à l'impartiale postérité*, these contain a far-from-impartial account of recent events, with some striking portraits of friends and enemies, but also her 'Mémoires particuliers', an autobiography inspired by her hero *Rousseau. Here she describes, in an appealing and apparently uninhibited way, her childhood and upbringing in the artistic bourgeoisie of Paris, attempting to create a unified image of a character remarkable both for sensibility and for energy. [PF]

Roland, La Chanson de. The most widely known of the hundred or so medieval French epics that have come down to us, and artistically the highest achievement of the genre, the *Chanson de Roland* is generally considered as synonymous with the version contained in the oldest extant manuscript (Oxford, Bodleian, Digby 23), an *Anglo-Norman copy made between 1130 and 1170. Acknowledged as 'pre-excellent' within the surviving tradition, it preserves a state of the legend of Rencesvals (Roncevaux) that goes back to at least the end of the 11th c. Its formal features are those of the earliest *chansons de geste, assonating decasyllables (3,998 in the case of the Oxford text) grouped in laisses of unequal length. A story of honour, treachery, and vengeance set in a zealous crusading atmosphere, it portrays conflicting feudal loyalties within an aristocratic warrior society.

The poem, which preserves distant echoes of *Charlemagne's defeat in the Pyrenees in 778 at the hands of the Basques/Gascons, tells of the end of the Frankish emperor's seven-year campaign against the Saracens of Spain. The Christians' unsuspecting acceptance of the pagans' deceitful offer of peace, opposed only by Charlemagne's nephew Roland, sets the tragedy in train. Ganelon, a spokesman for the appeasers, is nominated by Roland, his stepson, for the dangerous mission of negotiating with the Saracen king Marsile, and, insulted, he angrily swears vengeance. Ganelon conspires with the Saracens, who plan to ambush Charlemagne's army as it retreats over the pass of Rencesvals, and he arranges for Roland to command the rearguard. With the Franks hopelessly outnumbered, but before the attack, Olivier vainly urges his comrade-in-arms Roland to summon help. After heroic resistance by the Christians, Roland, the last survivor, dies from the exertion of blowing his oliphant to recall Charlemagne. God sends the Archangel Gabriel and St Michael to bear Roland's soul to heaven. The emperor arrives, pursues the Saracens, and takes vengeance. When pagan reinforcements arrive with the emir Baligant, East and West clash; Charlemagne emerges victorious from single combat. Back at Aix-la-Chapelle, Ganelon, accused of treason against the emperor's person, is tried; his case goes to judicial combat, and the guilty traitor is executed. Gabriel summons a weary Charlemagne to further wars against the pagans.

The Oxford text is characterized by a heavily oral-formulaic discourse and by an elaborate narrative structure which skilfully exploits parallelism and repetition. Stark bipolarities are everywhere in evidence. The narrative is unilinear, alternating between council scenes and highly stylized and formulaic descriptions of battles and single combats. An important role is allotted to dialogue. Action is at a premium, and motives are not articulated. Authorial intervention is rare. There is a pervasive rhetoric of hyperbole, but use of the supernatural is muted. Imagery is predominantly visual and gestural. The tone, which ranges from the noble, elevated, and pious to the crude, brutal, and genocidal, is militaristic and fiercely anti-Islamic.

There are two women in an otherwise exclusively male cast. Characters tend to be portrayed as figures and types and, therefore, to lack any sustained psychological elaboration. However, Roland, Ganelon, and to a lesser degree Charlemagne are given some personality traits. Olivier represents classical wisdom; Turpin is a populist embodiment of the Church militant. Roland, who exemplifies heroic extremism, nevertheless dies an exemplary Christian death. He is avenged by a rejuvenated Charlemagne who, roused from a singular passivity, singlehandedly triumphs over the forces of evil represented by Baligant. Vengeance is exacted from the Other, and Ganelon draws the wages of feudal sin. Modern criticism, after a long period of preoccupation with the Roland's literary (written versus oral) origins, belatedly turned to formalist and Structuralist analysis, though the old urge to offer moralizing readings of Roland's behaviour seems still to persist.

Curiously at variance with what we know to have been the Chanson de Roland's wide reception during the Middle Ages, it survives today in no more than seven manuscripts and two fragments. Only the 14th-c. Franco-Italian Venice 4 version is, like the Oxford text, in assonance, the others being rhymed redactions. There has been much critical debate on whether the Roland textual tradition is an exclusively written one, or whether, as the neo-traditionalists maintain, extant texts are but chance survivals from innumerable semi-improvised oral performances. Adherents of the former theory divide the manuscript stemma into two branches, the 'alpha' family comprising the Oxford version alone, and 'beta' family all other collateral texts. These, largely disregarded since *Bédier, are of course works in their own right. Amplification is the general tendency here, and the Châteauroux/Venice 7 version, for example, has over 8,000 lines. It enlarges at considerable length and with melodrama on the grief and death of Roland's fiancée Aude, whose appearance in the Oxford version had been fleeting and all but mute. It introduces a new character, Renier de Chartres, as well as a whole new episode into the narrative, the escape and dramatic recapture of Ganelon. This appears also in the Paris, Cambridge, and Lyon versions. Unlike all the others, which seem to move in varying degrees closer to the conventions of *romance, the Lyon text reduces the scope of the narrative, omitting both Ganelon's treason and the Baligant episode in order to highlight above all Roland's heroic role, though Aude is not forgotten here either.

Medieval translations and adaptations into Latin, Norse, German, Dutch, Welsh, and English are witnesses to the broad popularity enjoyed in the Middle Ages by what is now regarded as one of the masterpieces of world literature.   [IS]

See P. Le Gentil, La Chanson de Roland (1962); E. Vance, Reading the Song of Roland (1970).

Rolla, see MUSSET.

ROLLAND, Romain (Edme Paul-Émile) (1866–1944). French novelist, playwright, biographer, musicologist, and Nobel Prize winner (1915). As a student in Rome he was strongly influenced by the German socialist Malwida von Meysenbug. Her ideas, together with the teaching of Tolstoy, largely shaped his political, humanitarian, and internationalist ideas. These were tested by World War I, when his essay, *Au-dessus de la mêlée* (1915), with its appeal to the intellectuals of France and Germany to refuse war and strive for peace, made him many enemies. Later, he was to evolve towards a distinctly individual mixture of *Marxism and oriental mysticism.

In the first 45 years of the century Rolland published biographies of Beethoven (1903), Michelangelo (1908), Tolstoy (1911), Gandhi (1924), Ramakrishna (1929), Vivekananda (1930), and *Péguy (1944). His writings on music included a history of European opera before Lully and Scarlatti, and a six-volume study of Beethoven's work. His best-known plays were organized into two trilogies, *Le Théâtre de la Révolution* (1909) and *Les Tragédies de la foi* (1913), largely inspired by the 'popular theatre' ideas of Maurice Pottecher. His main novels are *Jean-Christophe* (1904–12), *Colas Breugnon* (1919), *Clérambault* (1920), and *L'Âme enchantée* (1922–33).

[JC]

ROLLIN, Charles (1661–1741). Professor at the University of Paris, known for his *Histoire ancienne* (1730–8), his *Histoire de Rome* (1738–48), and above all his *De la manière d'enseigner et d'étudier les belles-lettres*, better known as the *Traité des études*. First published in four volumes in 1726–32, this was allegedly based on Rollin's own practice. It remains faithful to humanist ideals of literary education in which emulation and performance play a central part, but is noteworthy for its advocacy of the study of French (volume 2 is a French rhetoric) and its humane attitude to the teacher–pupil relationship. Its moderate approach won it many followers and it was much translated. [PF]

ROLLINAT, Maurice (1846–1903), see BALLADE.

ROMAINS, Jules (pseud. of Louis Farigoule) (1885–1972). French novelist, dramatist, poet, and essayist, elected to the Académie Française in 1946. Early in his career he was associated with a short-lived artistic community, the Groupe de l'*Abbaye, which published his poems, *La Vie unanime*, in 1908. These poems, and much of his later verse and prose, were influenced by *Unanimist theories of social groups and collective psychology. Before the outbreak of war in 1914 he published more collections of poetry, a verse play, *L'Armée dans la ville* (1911), and two novels, *Mort de quelqu'un* (1911) and the farcical *Les Copains* (1913).

In 1919 Romains retired from teaching to become a full-time writer. He published more poetry, a film-script, *Donogoo Tonka* (1920), and another verse play, *Cromedeyre-le-vieil* (1920). The farcical comedies

Knock, ou le Triomphe de la médecine (1923), *M. Le Trouhadec saisi par la débauche* (1923), and *Le Mariage de M. Le Trouhadec* (1925) earned him much popularity. Interesting collections of essays include *Hommes, médecins, machines* (1959) and *Lettre ouverte contre une vaste conspiration* (1966)—with its strictures on modern cultural attitudes and standards. But his outstanding work remains his *roman-fleuve: Les *Hommes de bonne volonté* (1932–47). [JC]

Roman à thèse, see PIÈCE À THESE.

Roman bourgeois, Le (1666). Satirical novel by *Furetière, set among the bourgeoisie of the Place Maubert in Paris. It contains a number of different stories and digressions. The first part tells the mundane love story of Nicodème, a would-be fashionable lawyer, and Javotte, daughter of a *procureur;* the second is largely devoted to a satirical portrait of Charles *Sorel. The unlovely society depicted here is a mocking counterpart to the idealized world of the *roman héroïque, which *Boileau was attacking at the same time in his *Dialogue des héros de roman*. A myopic and slightly grotesque realism results; Furetière treats his subject with mocking condescension. [PF]

Romance (as a musical form), see WORDS AND MUSIC, 2.

Romance. Term used in English-language criticism of French literature for the *roman courtois*, or courtly romance, a narrative genre that flourished in the 12th and 13th c., first in verse and then in prose, and continued in various transformations throughout the Middle Ages. In Old French, *romanz* meant the vernacular, and the expression 'metre en roman' implied translation from Latin. As the first vernacular fictions treating the conflict between love and social obligations, these fictions are forerunners of the *roman*, the *novel.

1. Verse Romances

The first romances, the *romans d'antiquité*, dating from 1150–65, were translations or adaptations of Latin epics into octosyllabic couplets; the anonymous *Roman de Thèbes* and *Roman d'Enéas*, and Benoît de Sainte-Maure's *Roman de Troie* are remarkable for their amplification of description, their focus on individual characters, and particularly for the importance accorded to love and female characters. In addition, Latin accounts of the life of Alexander the Great inspired various *Alexander romances, of which the most notable was written in 12-syllable lines, later called *alexandrines. The *romans d'antiquité*, and other early works such as *Floire et Blancheflore*, *Marie de France's *Lais*, and Thomas's *Tristan*, evidence the public's taste for amorous conflicts, love casuistry, and description of social life and material surroundings.

Factors that fostered romance's development in *Anglo-Norman England and on the Continent

Romance

from 1160 to 1300 were the refinement and expansion of court life in a period of relative peace, the rise of the vernacular as a literary language, the emergence of a class of educated clerics, the presence of noblewomen as well as knights among the court audience, and the nobility's desire to define their social superiority. Early romances were written to be read orally before an assembled court audience; some are dedicated to a noble male or female patron. Beginning in the 13th c., works were increasingly written in prose or adapted from verse into prose. Romances were copied in manuscript compilations, sometimes grouped around a discernible theme or interest. Little is known about early romance authors, who were often anonymous; they were probably Church-educated male clerks who exercised a secular function at court.

Romance authors drew their material freely and inventively not only from Latin historiography, *hagiography, *rhetoric, sermons, and the Bible, but also from the *chansons de geste and from popular legends and folk-tales. Writers took pride in their ability to transform conventional materials in new ways. As contrasted with the epic, or chanson de geste, romance focused on the inner dilemma or quest of an individual knight, rather than on collective conflicts; it highlighted sentimental as well as chivalric education; its central conflict was often that of knightly duty versus private desire. Although women figured more prominently in romance than in epic, they were usually objects of the hero's quest rather than agents. None the less, many female characters display pragmatism, intelligence, and a capacity to manipulate situations through verbal wit or clever ruses.

If the epic narrator was often a spokesman for communally shared values, the verse romance narrator was an individual observer who commented on his craft and his subject-matter. Many romances are sophisticated literary artefacts that refer self-consciously to other works. Fantastic settings, marvellous objects and beasts, and supernatural events often spice these tales and heighten their mysterious charm. None the less, despite their idealized landscapes, romances, like the chansons de geste, invited their audience to reflect on serious social and moral problems.

In the last third of the 12th c. *Chrétien de Troyes wrote the first surviving full-length *Arthurian fiction, Erec et Enide, which was followed by four other romances. Chrétien inaugurated a vogue for Arthurian fiction that would expand throughout Europe during the Middle Ages and revive in the 19th c. [see MATIÈRE DE BRETAGNE]. His brilliant characterizations, harmonious structures, pointed irony, and rhetorical wit fostered his readers' reflection and inspired many imitators and continuators.

Verse romance after Chrétien was remarkably diverse. Non-Arthurian romances explored the themes of love and *chivalry in modes that ranged from the parodic, as in Hue de Rotelande's Ipomedon

(12th c.) [see ANGLO-NORMAN LITERATURE, 3a], to the lyrical, as in *Partonopeu de Blois (12th c.), or the marvellous, as in *Adenet le Roi's Cléomadès (13th c.). Arthurian romances were equally varied in stance. *Raoul de Houdenc's Meraugis de Portlesguez ingeniously replayed Chrétien's comic possibilities; Renaut de Beaujeu's Le *Bel Inconnu explored the quest for love and identity in a magical fairy world. A spate of narratives followed *Gauvain as hero. The intriguing *Roman de Silence described the adventures of a woman disguised as a knight. Four verse continuations of Chrétien's Conte du graal (Perceval) [see GRAIL ROMANCES] recounted the further adventures of Perceval and Gauvain. It is impossible to discern a single ideological bent in the rich variety of 13th-c. romances. Some were frankly misogynistic (*Raoul de Houdenc's La Vengeance Raguidel, Le Chevalier à l'Épée), others burlesqued courtly conventions (*Joufroi de Poitiers, the chantefable *Aucassin et Nicolette), while romances such as Durmart le Gallois attempted to preserve chivalric values.

Other 13th-c. romances have been dubbed 'romans réalistes' because of their contemporary geographical setting, historical figures, realistic descriptions, and absence of marvellous events; these include the romances of *Jean Renart, Jakemes's Le Roman du Castelain de Coucy et de la Dame de Fayel [see CHASTELAIN DE COUCI], and Gerbert de Montreuil's Le Roman de la Violette. Not infrequently, these romances analyse the plight of women as victims of the chivalric code of honour or, as in *Philippe de Beaumanoir's Manekine, as objects of incestuous desire; women in these stories excel as virtuous heroines or plucky survivors.

Another kind of roman written in octosyllabic couplets was the dream allegory, of which the most influential was the *Roman de la Rose, begun by Guillaume de Lorris in a lyrical mode and terminated in a tenor of scholastic debate by Jean de Meun [see also ROMAN DE LA POIRE]. Perhaps as a result of the Rose, an important 13th-c. stylistic development was the inclusion of lyric poems into the narrative frame, as in Jean Renart's Guillaume de Dole or Jakemes's Castelain de Coucy; in the latter, the romancer mirrors the stance of a lyric poet by addressing a beloved female reader.

2. Prose Romances

A major shift in the genre's evolution came in the 13th c. with the increasing use of prose for many works, as evidenced strikingly in the prose romances of the so-called Vulgate cycle (the *Lancelot and *Grail romances and the prose *Tristan). This monumental summa of Arthurian history combined Chrétien's Lancelot and Conte du Graal, and explored further the problems raised in them. It created an intricate interweaving of episodes that pursued a multiplicity of characters to their predestined fate; it deepened the conflict between earthly and spiritual values latent in

Chrétien; and it created a vast, totalizing cycle that merged Christian and Arthurian history. The Vulgate texts claimed to tell a more profound 'truth' than verse even as they displayed a heightened sense of their status as fiction. The 'je' of verse narration was replaced by 'li conte' as the storyteller; marvellous events were rationalized and Christianized; in works like the Queste del Saint Graal, a moralizing tone prevailed. The shift from verse to prose implied a shift from aural audience at a performance to private reading of a book; manuscripts were more lavishly illuminated for their owners.

Verse romances continued to be produced throughout the 13th c. and into the 14th; *Froissart's Meliador (1383–8) was the last Arthurian verse romance. But by the end of the 14th c. prose was the predominant form, as evidenced by the proliferation of new prose works and of mises en prose, which were adaptations of by-now archaic verse romances (Cligés, Erec, Tristan). The courts of *Burgundy and of Anjou were important centres of late-medieval romance production. In the wake of disastrous losses during the *Hundred Years War, chivalric exploits lost their transcendent ideological purpose. Critics speak of moral and aesthetic decline in some 14th- and early 15th-c. chivalric romances, where the episode or motif is presented as a pleasurable surface rather than as a meaningful element in a significant whole. Lengthy romances such as the prose *Perceforest concentrate more on the collective group of Arthurian knights than on a predestined individual. Lacking the critical angle of their predecessors, late romances tend to project an illusory image of an idealized past.

In the 15th c. a new mode of prose narrative emerged in the nouvelle, a brief tale with a contemporary setting and worldly ethic, whose humour was sometimes the vehicle for a more critical, even cynical vision, as in the earlier verse *fabliaux. The shift has been detected in the materialism and uncourtliness of Antoine de *la Sale's transitional Jehan de Saintré, which was ostensibly the story of a 'vaillant chevalier'. The taste for short comic tales was confirmed by the compilation of Les *Cent Nouvelles nouvelles for Philippe le Bon of Burgundy by an unknown redactor [see SHORT FICTION].

Old French romances transmitted their tales of love and chivalry throughout European national literatures by means of translations and adaptations; their new concern for subjectivity was a major step in the evolution of fiction. If the excesses of late chivalric romance [see AMADIS DE GAULE] were parodied by Cervantes and others, the aristocratic public's taste for lengthy pseudo-historical narratives of love and adventure continued in the 17th-c. *romans héroïques of *La Calprenède and Madeleine de *Scudéry. Arthurian themes revived in the 19th c., especially in England, and are still alive in literature and film (e.g., in France, *Bresson's Lancelot and *Rohmer's faithful adaptation of Chrétien's

Perceval). Any popular fiction relating adventures in a fantasy world or an idealized past might be considered a distant heir of romance; closer in spirit is Alain-Fournier's Le *Grand Meaulnes, which uses a dream-like setting to explore an adolescent sentimental crisis. But modern popular fantasies do not as a rule reflect the social concerns of their audience, as did so many of their medieval French counterparts. The critical social function of courtly romance ended with the waning of feudal society; what remains is the persistent desire to imagine another world. [RLK]

See J. Frappier and R. R. Grimm (eds.), Le Roman jusqu'à la fin du XIIIe siècle, in Grundriss der romanischen Literaturen des Mittelalters, ed. H. R. Jauss and E. Kohler, IV (1978); N. Lacy, D. Kelly, and K. Busby (eds.), The Legacy of Chrétien de Troyes (1987–8); D. Poirion (ed.), La Littérature française aux XIVe et XVe siècles, in Grundriss, VIII (1988).

Romancéro aux étoiles, see ALEXIS, J.-S.

Romances sans paroles (1874). Collection of lyric poems by *Verlaine, containing some of his most popular verse.

Roman comique, Le. Novel by *Scarron. Part 1 was published in 1651, Part 2 in 1657; a number of writers wrote sequels to the unfinished text. The title means not only 'comic novel', but 'novel about actors'. Drawing on his experience in Le Mans, Scarron paints the adventures, amorous and otherwise, of a company of travelling players and their dealings with their provincial patrons, in particular the diminutive lawyer Ragotin, who falls for one of the actresses and is remorselessly mocked and humiliated. Grotesque sits uneasily alongside romance in this rambling novel, which only appears to give a realistic view of provincial and theatrical life. It is remarkable above all for its playful style, the narrator's humorous presence in his story, and the parody of epic or romance, whereby Homeric battles are echoed in ridiculous night brawls in an inn. [PF]

Roman d'aventure(s)

1. Medieval

Term sometimes used to refer to medieval *romances such as Le Roman de la Violette or *Joufroi de Poitiers, which are characteristically 13th-c. or later, with a strong narrative line, relatively slight engagement with courtliness or *fin'amor, and little conspicuous use of magic or the marvellous. It distinguishes such works (though not with any rigour) from 'Arthurian' or 'courtly' romances, such as those of *Chrétien de Troyes.

2. Modern

The 18th-c. sources of this genre are twofold: the picaresque novel and *children's literature—*Perrault's Contes (1697) and Madame d'*Aulnoy's

Contes nouveaux (1698) released a current of fantasy and initiatory writing in which heroism, denied to the guileful *picaro*, was available to uncorrupted youth, facing the world alone. This latter trend was important for the 19th and 20th c. in two senses: many writers drew on the spirit of the fairy-tale (*Nodier, *Sand, *Daudet, *Alain-Fournier); and much 'adult' literature was adopted by, and increasingly geared to, a youthful readership. What had already happened to Swift and Defoe happened, in the course of the 19th c., to Walter Scott, Fenimore Cooper (see Gustave Aimard, *Les Trappeurs de l'Arkansas*, 1858; *La Loi de lynch*, 1859), *Hugo, *Dumas, and *Loti. Robinson Crusoe had his own particular progeny—Verne's *L'*Île mystérieuse* and *L'École des Robinsons* (1882); Louis Boussenard's *Les Robinsons de la Guyane* (1882); Tournier's *Vendredi, ou les Limbes du Pacifique* and its children's version, *Vendredi ou la Vie sauvage* (1971)—but the picaresque had bequeathed a whole legacy of travel adventures: *Verne's *Le Tour du monde en quatre-vingts jours* (1873); Boussenard's *Le Tour du monde d'un gamin de Paris* (1880); G. Bruno's *Le *Tour de la France par deux enfants*.

The 19th c. also saw the development of the third constitutive element of the genre, the *roman populaire*, or, in its earlier form, the *roman-feuilleton*. The launching of the cheap press by Émile de *Girardin in 1836 (*La Presse*) brought the novels of *Sue and Dumas to the public in gripping episodes; and later *Ponson du Terrail's *Rocambole* (1859), the work of *Gaboriau, and Xavier de Montépin's *La Porteuse de pain* (1884). As the century progressed, the inflated Romantic hero, the justice-seeker and self-redeemer of earlier *feuilletons*, was ousted from a sanctimonious world of pettier crimes and greater melodrama. Serials fell back on formula writing and a conformist ideology. But something of the original antisocial stance of the popular novel was recovered in Gaston *Leroux's *Chéri-Bibi* and Maurice *Leblanc's Arsène Lupin. The *roman d'aventures* had become enmeshed in the emergence of the *roman policier* [see DETECTIVE FICTION] and the *roman noir*. According to *Narcejac [see BOILEAU-NARCEJAC], the *roman policier* preserves the characters, the fundamental conflict between good and evil, and the *merveilleux* of the *roman d'aventures*. Whatever its modern generic affiliations, the *roman d'aventures* has survived in the *bande dessinée*, in children's heroes like *Tintin and *Astérix, and in the more adult, historical adventures of, e.g., François Bourgeon and Patrick Cothias.   [CS]

See J.-Y. Tadié, *Le Roman d'aventures* (1982).

Roman de Brut, Le, see WACE.

Roman de Fauvel, Le, see ROMAN DE LA ROSE.

Roman de la Poire, Le. Mid-13th-c. poem by Tibaut. Its use of first-person narrative and personifying allegory to describe the onset of love derives from the *Roman de la Rose*. The *Poire* incorporates a series of refrains whose initials form acrostics, and contains allusions to figures from medieval romance and classical mythology. The principal manuscript (BN fr. 2186), nearly contemporary with the poem, features an important series of full-page miniatures and historiated initials.   [SJH]

Roman de la Rose, Le (begun *c*.1225–40, completed *c*.1270–78). Poem in octosyllabic couplets, cast as an allegorical dream-vision, that describes a young man's initiation into love and his efforts to possess the rosebud of which he is enamoured. The first 4,058 lines were composed by *Guillaume de Lorris, of whom nothing further is known; the remainder—nearly 18,000 lines more—is the work of *Jean de Meun, a Parisian writer and intellectual. The *Rose* was the most widely read work of medieval French literature, surviving today in nearly 300 manuscripts dating from the late 13th to the early 16th c.; most are illustrated, many quite lavishly. Numerous printed editions date from the 15th and 16th c. Jean *Molinet produced a prose version with commentary, interpreting the *Rose* as spiritual allegory (1500); Clément *Marot adapted the poem into early modern French (1526). The *Rose* circulated outside France as well; it was read by such poets as Chaucer, Gower, Dante, and Petrarch. By the end of the 14th c. it had been translated into Italian, Dutch, and English.

Guillaume's poem, purportedly the story of the narrator's dream, is set in the allegorical Garden of Delight, where the dreamer meets the God of Love and his entourage, gazes into the fountain of Narcissus, and sees there a rosebud with which he falls in love. The God of Love delivers a sermon about behaviour in love, based largely on Ovid; Reason tries to dissuade the Lover; Ami offers courtship advice. The allegorical construct is such that there is no real figure for the lady, whose various attributes are represented by the Rose and by the figures that surround it. The two with whom the Lover interacts directly are male: Bel Acueil, a pleasant young boy who allows him to approach the Rose, and Danger, an obstreperous peasant who chases him away. Two other guardians of the Rose, Fear and Shame, are female. With the aid of Venus, the Lover manages to kiss the Rose; alerted by Male Bouche, Jealousy then constructs a fortified tower to protect it. The poem ends with the Lover's lament.

It is uncertain whether Guillaume intended to continue the poem beyond this point. The text remains true to the lyric model, whereby the Lover never achieves full consummation of his desires. None the less, an impulse to complete the narrative soon resulted in a brief anonymous continuation, pre-dating that of Jean de Meun, that allows the Lover to spend a night of bliss with the Rose. Jean's continuation, in turn, completely transformed the poem. It is constructed on a series of discourses by the major characters: Reason, Ami, Richesse, the

God of Love, Faux Samblant, the Old Woman who guards the Rose, Nature, and her priest Genius. In this way the framework of the poem is expanded to include rational, erotic, self-serving, procreational, and sacred forms of love. In a thinly disguised allegory of sexual intercourse, the Lover finally succeeds in penetrating to the inner sanctum where the Rose is enshrined; the poem ends with his awakening at daybreak.

The original *Rose* of Guillaume de Lorris introduced important innovations that profoundly influenced subsequent French literature. It is the first example in French of sustained first-person narrative and of narrative allegory. Jean's continuation, equally innovative, used Guillaume's allegorical framework as the vehicle for a literary review of encyclopedic proportions. Unlike Guillaume, whose romance remained within the closed world of the allegorical garden, Jean opened the poem up to the satire of contemporary society through such characters as the Jealous Husband, with his misogynistic attack on marriage; Faux Samblant, with his exposé of ecclesiastical corruption; and the Old Woman, who explains the sexual manipulation of men by women. Jean's expanded focus also allows for extended discussion of such diverse issues as language and signification; Fortune, destiny, and free will; government and justice; optics and meteorology; and the role of procreation in the cosmic order. He incorporated considerable material from the Latin tradition, especially Ovid, *Boethius, *Alan of Lille, and Guillaume de Saint-Amour. The result is a mixture that defies easy analysis—all the more so in that the material taken over from the Latin authors is subject to parodic distortion and seeming incongruities, such as Reason's defense of obscenity in a speech that otherwise maintains a lofty moral tone, and Genius's claim that heterosexual coupling is a means to eternal salvation.

As a result the *Rose* has been subject to divergent readings ever since it was written, and has inspired diverse literary responses. *Machaut, whose entire corpus is marked by the influence of the *Rose*, used it as the basis for an intellectualized vision of love which, though quite different from that portrayed in the *Rose*, owes much to Jean's blend of Ovidian eroticism and Boethian rationalism; a prime example is his *Remede de Fortune* (*c*.1341). Gervais du Bus drew on the *Rose* in the satirical *Roman de Fauvel* (1310–14); *Guillaume de Degulleville used it as a model for moral and spiritual allegory in *Le Pelerinage de vie humaine* (1330–1). A similar range of attitudes can be found in the variant versions of the text itself. It was subject to abridgements, both to produce a narrative more narrowly focused on the conquest of the Rose, and to delete bawdy passages in favour of the poem's moral and philosophical content. More often it was preserved intact and expanded through interpolations that contributed sometimes to its religious or didactic message, sometimes to its eroticism.

A debate about the *Rose*, initiated by *Christine de Pizan's *Epistre au Dieu d'Amours* (1399), unfolded during the opening years of the 15th c. [see QUERELLE DES FEMMES]. Christine attacked the *Rose* for defaming women, for justifying seduction and rape, and for bawdy language and a subversive use of authoritative material. *Gerson, chancellor of the University of Paris, joined her in attacking the poem as blasphemous and, in effect, pornographic. The *Rose* was defended by three royal secretaries, Jean de Montreuil and Gontier and Pierre Col, who argued that it was a satirical text intended to expose human follies. The documents of the Querelle, precious sources for the origins of French literary criticism, demonstrate the cultural importance of the *Rose* as a focal point for fundamental issues: language and authority, sexuality and gender, and the role of eros in the social, natural, and cosmic order.

[SJH]

See D. Poirion, *Le Roman de la Rose* (1973); P.-Y. Badel, *Le Roman de la Rose au XIVe siècle* (1980); D. Hult, *Self-fulfilling Prophecies* (1985).

Roman de la rose ou de Guillaume de Dole, Le, see JEAN RENART.

Roman d'Eneas, Le, see ROMANS D'ANTIQUITÉ.

Roman de Renart. The name given to a collection of 26 short texts or 'branches' recounting the outrageous behaviour of Renart, a fox, most frequently in his dealings with a wolf, Isengrin, in the context of a 'society' of animals presided over by a lion king. The existence of folk analogues for many of these narratives means that the Old French tales may have an oral prehistory which we cannot determine, but they began to circulate in something like their present form in the last quarter of the 12th c., and new branches were added until about 1250. The earliest branches (II and Va in the numbering established by E. Martin) are associated with the name of Pierre de Saint-Cloud, though it is now thought that he was not their sole author, rather a compiler and adaptor of existing stories. Virtually all the other branches are anonymous; all are composed in octosyllabic rhyming couplets. Most of the manuscripts preserving the *Renart* date from the mid-13th c. onwards and are cyclic, that is, they group together a substantial number of branches, marshalling them into a larger, though necessarily disjointed, narrative.

Often referred to as 'beast epic', the *Roman de Renart* recalls fables by its placing of animals in human narrative contexts, but its branches are considerably longer (between 400 and 1,000 lines long) and make no attempt to draw explicit morals (apart from the occasional warning not to be made a fool of). An animal world of large and small, powerful and weak, predator and victim, is thereby juxtaposed with elaborate social hierarchies, both secular (king, seneschal, constable, barons, lesser nobility, etc.) and religious (legate, archpriest, monks, and other clerics). The satirical potential of this juxtaposition clearly influenced later writers, who used the character of the fox in a number of poems, principally attacking the mendicant orders: *Renart le Nouvel, Le Couronnement Renart, Renart le Contrefait*, and the *Renart le Bestorné* by *Rutebeuf. The fox is even used by a 13th-c. historiographer: there is a *Renart* chapter in the *Récits d'un ménéstrel de Reims*. There are certainly some satirical elements in the earlier branches of the *Roman de Renart*, since most proposed datings for these are based on identification of topical allusions.

But the *Renart* is more comic than satirical. The protagonists have the elasticity of cartoon figures. Sometimes Renart has red fur and a tail, runs on all fours, lives in an earth, and relies on his teeth or speed, while at others he wears clothes, rides a horse, lives in a castle, and can talk his way out of any situation. Such protean bodies can be horribly mangled without its seeming to matter: Isengrin in particular loses his tail (branch III), and is flayed alive (branch X), yet bounces back in subsequent episodes as though nothing had happened. In this text the conditions of reality are suspended, and a space for play created. Indeed, the animal-characters are so unreal that they can be made to perform some very *risqué* routines indeed: one of the core episodes in the whole cycle is a rape, committed by the fox on Isengrin's wife (branch II), and the question of whether the act of intercourse took place and, if so, whether the she-wolf was consentient, recurs through subsequent branches. Another recurrent form of brinkmanship with respect to the proprieties is irreligion: Renart poses as a false monk (branch III), a false preacher (branch IV), a false pilgrim (branch I), and even eats his confessor (branch VII). The ideals of official culture, such as *fin'amor*, *chivalry, and *feudalism, which provide the doctrinal underpinning of its serious narrative genres (*chansons de geste* and *romances), are treated here as empty illusions.

The irreverence of the *Roman de Renart* anticipates that of the *fabliaux*. They, however, have chosen to use human protagonists. In using animals as vehicles of playfulness, the *Renart* responds to medieval debates about the nature of animals, and the nature of Nature, important themes of *scholasticism in the late 12th and 13th c., when the *Renart* texts we have today were put together. Some of the authors of the *Renart* were conversant with clerical culture; some of its branches are closely related to a Latin beast epic about monastic life, the *Ysengrimus*. The animals who commit the comic outrages of the *Renart* may offer its authors an alibi for their constant infringements of human social taboos: if animals are lower than human beings, they cannot be expected to live up to human standards. On the other hand, if humanity is part of Nature, then human pretentions to superiority are more precarious, and the comedy of the *Renart* is more disquieting.

The success of the fox did not prove to be dependent on a particular intellectual context. Like *Tristan, of whom he is a kind of burlesque double, Renart was an international success, and imitations or translations of the Old French *Roman de Renart* exist in Middle High German, Dutch, and Franco-Italian, as well as in Caxton's *Reynard the Fox*.   [SK]

See J. Flinn, *Le 'Roman de Renart' dans la littérature française et dans les littératures étrangères au moyen âge* (1963); J. R. Scheidegger, *Le 'Roman de Renart' ou le Texte de la dérision* (1989).

Roman de Rou, Le, see WACE.

Roman des deduis, Le, see GACE DE LA BUIGNE.

Roman de Silence, Le. Arthurian verse romance of the latter half of the 13th c., written by one Heldris de Cornuälle. This intriguing story recounts the adventures of Silence, whose parents raise her as a boy in order to circumvent an interdiction on female inheritance. The exemplary child excels in hunting and fighting as well as reading, writing, and singing; she becomes an outstanding knight in the French and English courts. Her adventures might seem to prove the equality of the sexes, but the narrator asserts woman's 'natural' role in several remarkable debates between the allegorical figures of Nature and Noreture (Nurture). Silence's true sexual identity is revealed inadvertently through the machinations of wicked Queen Eufeme, who tries to seduce the reluctant youth. To punish Silence for her refusal, Eufeme sends her off on the impossible task of catching Merlin, who can only be snared by a woman. The captured magician reveals Silence's secret as well as Eufeme's affair with a priest disguised as a nun. Eufeme is killed for her wanton sexuality, and Silence marries the king. The romance is fascinating not only for its inversion of gender roles, but also for its linguistic play and narratorial interventions. [RLK]

Roman de Thèbes, Le, see ROMANS D'ANTIQUITÉ.

Roman de Troie, Le, see BENOÎT DE SAINTE-MAURE.

Roman expérimental, Le. A collection of articles by *Zola, published 1880 and containing his essay on the 'experimental novel', his most forceful statement of his belief that the methods of the biological sciences should be applied to the field of literature. Zola's famous essay abounds in quotations and paraphrases from Claude *Bernard's *Introduction à la médecine expérimentale* (1865). Critics long ago dismissed Zola's arguments as untenable, but more recently the polemical and rhetorical force of this attempt to produce a theory of *Naturalism has come to be appreciated more.   [DB]

Roman-feuilleton. In statistical terms the *roman-feuilleton* was the dominant literary genre of the 19th c. The formula 'la suite au prochain numéro' had already been used in the *Revue de Paris* in 1829, but it was in 1836 that Émile de *Girardin first used serialized fiction in *La Presse* as the corner-stone of his marketing strategy. Girardin led the way, and Armand Dutacq was quick to follow in *Le *Siècle*, and all major Parisian dailies included serialized fiction after 1836.

Although dramatic for the period, the circulation figures now seem quite modest. In 1846 the three main Parisian dailies (*Le Siècle*, *Le *Constitutionnel*, and *La Presse*) had, respectively, 32,885, 24,771, and 22,170 subscribers. The total readership was, of course, much higher, given that the papers were read in family groups, clubs, and *cabinets de lecture*. Nevertheless, the increased audience for newspapers and for the emerging *roman-feuilleton* remained largely a middle-class one. Only later in the century did the *roman-feuilleton* find a significant lower-class readership. In these early years, the key novelists were *Balzac, *Sue, *Soulié, *Dumas *père*, and *Féval. Balzac never had the success of Sue or Dumas. Indeed, in 1844 publication of *Les *Paysans* was prematurely brought to a halt, and it was replaced by Dumas's *La Reine Margot*. It was Sue who first made a truly enormous impact with *Les *Mystères de Paris* (1842-3) and *Le Juif errant* (1844-5), which by itself increased subscriptions to *Le Constitutionnel* by 20,000.

The period 1842-8, generally seen as the high-point of the *roman-feuilleton*, was dominated by Dumas (*Les *Trois Mousquetaires*, 1844; *Le *Comte de Monte-Cristo*, 1844-6). But the formulas laid down by the pioneers were endlessly repeated and further elaborated throughout the century in the social, historical, sentimental, travel, and even space-fiction variants of the genre. Foreshadowing a long line of *detectives and future comic supermen, the early 19th-c. stories told of how Byronic hero figures penetrated the mysteries of the big city and braved the dangers of the criminal underworld in order to bring about justice and retribution on behalf of the repressed and the tyrannized. Sue's Rodolphe leads to *Ponson du Terrail's *Rocambole* series (1857-71), to *Gaboriau, to *Leblanc's Arsène Lupin, and to the *Fantômas* series, by which time the *cinema began to draw directly from the *roman-feuilleton*, heralding future television soaps. [See also PRESS.]   [BR]

See L. Queffélec, *Le Roman-feuilleton français au XIXe siècle* (1989).

Roman-fleuve. Term used to describe a series of novels following the fortunes of a character, a family, or a society. Inspired by *Balzac's *Comédie humaine* and *Zola's *Rougon-Macquart* novels, the form enjoyed great popularity at the beginning of the 20th c. in the hands of such writers as Romain Rolland (*Jean-Christophe*) and Jules Romains (*Les *Hommes de bonne volonté*). A similar structure informs the novel cycles of authors such as *Duhamel, *Aragon, and *Sartre.

Roman héroïque. Term used to refer to the multi-volume historical novel of love and adventure which was the dominant form of prose fiction in the 17th c. Its principal exponents were *Gomberville, *La Calprenède, and above all Madeleine de *Scudéry; *Artamène ou le Grand Cyrus* is perhaps the finest example of this once-popular genre.

Roman noir. Term used originally as the equivalent of the English 'Gothic novel', but more recently to cover the broad territory of the 'thriller'. Whatever the genre owes to *Gaboriau, Gaston *Leroux, and *Leblanc, its immediate sources are to be found in the 'hard-boiled' *detective fiction of 1920s and 1930s America (Hammett, Whitfield, Burnett) and the gangster movie. Serious writing in this genre has had some difficulty in maintaining itself against the mass-produced collections of 'brigadisme' published by Gérard de Villiers, Pierre Lucas, André Burnat, etc., and calling upon the services of writers such as Antoine Dominique, Michel Brice, and Jean-Pierre Bourre; these collections have added sadistic and pornographic resources to the *roman noir*'s already violent tendencies.

It is not difficult to agree with *Todorov that the *roman noir* differs fundamentally from the *roman policier*. In the *roman policier*, the crime (usually single) is committed before the narrative (or at its very beginning) by a criminal whom it is the detective's job to identify, in a single narrative; the detective works on his own and is impelled by the desire to defend the moral order. In the *roman noir*, multiple crimes are committed as an ongoing feature of multiple narratives, by criminals whose identity is known and whom it is the heroes' job to destroy (rather than apprehend); the heroes are usually part of an organization and are paid to defend a political order.   [CS]

Roman policier, see DETECTIVE FICTION.

Romans d'antiquité (or *romans antiques*). A group of verse romances dating from the mid-12th c., so-called in contradistinction to the *romans bretons* since they deal, at least loosely, with classical material, particularly that of 'Rome la grant'. Conventionally included under this heading, in probable order of composition, are the anonymous *Roman de Thèbes* and *Roman d'Eneas*, based respectively on Statius's *Thebaid* and on the *Aeneid*, and *Benoît de Sainte-Maure's *Roman de Troie*, elaborated on the primary sources of Dares Phrygius, *De excidio Troiae*, and Dictys Cretensis, *Ephemeridos Belli Troiani*. Often grouped with these full-length romances are the shorter anonymous poems *Piramus et Tisbé* and *Narcisus*, expanded from the stories in Ovid's *Metamorphoses*.

The treatment of the classical accounts is cavalier, and the source is taken as pretext for adaptation and elaboration after the fashion of contemporary taste. While there are, notably in the *Roman de Thèbes*, features reminiscent of the *chansons de geste* (lengthy and meticulous accounts of battles, discussions of strategy, and the use of epic formulae), authorial inventions tend to take one of two main forms. A considerable amount of space is devoted to description of the *merveilleux*, but the texts are less concerned with striking instances of the workings of magic and the supernatural—although the awesome portent may be retailed with relish—than with the wonders of the palpable world. They celebrate the marvels of nature and manufacture: amazing creatures of land and sea, artificial constructions of the architect, goldsmith, and weaver.

In the second place, the authors seize upon any textual opportunity afforded by their sources to construct a love-relationship between suitably qualified persons. The *Roman de Thèbes* invents love-episodes between Antigone and Parthenopeus and Ismene and Aton; the *Roman d'Eneas* follows the story of the passionate love of Dido and Aeneas with an extended love-idyll between Aeneas and Lavinia. Benoît de Sainte-Maure presents a spectrum of relationships: between Jason and Medea, Paris and Helen, Achilles and Polyxena, as well as the Troilus–Briseida story later taken up and developed by Boccaccio, Chaucer, and Shakespeare. The attitude to love expressed across these texts is remarkably coherent, and differs profoundly from *fin'amor*. Frequently the initiative is taken by the woman, whose sentiments are explored and expressed, on the whole, to the same degree and extent as those of the man; the relationship is endorsed by society and tends, ideally, to lead to marriage between two persons suited in respect of age, background, and inclination. The thoughts of the characters are conveyed in often lengthy monologues, which describe their amorous states in a style conventionally, but vaguely, referred to as 'Ovidian'. Recurring examples are descriptions of the ravages caused by love's arrow and its effect upon eyes and heart, and relations of the mysterious and contradictory symptoms of the 'sickness' of love.

Works of transition, brief flowering of a genre that did not survive, the *romans d'antiquité* had a decisive influence upon the future of the verse *romance as it was shaped by *Chrétien de Troyes.
[RMJ]

See R. M. Jones, *The Theme of Love in the 'Romans d'Antiquité'* (1972).

Romanticism (*Le Romantisme*)

1. General characteristics

Romanticism marked a profound shift in European culture, a crisis in belief and a change in sensibility. It was a complex phenomenon which contained diverse and sometimes contradictory elements, developing along different lines within individual national cultures. In France it affected politics, philosophy, literature, music, and the fine arts.

Romanticism was long presented first and foremost as a reaction against the rules imposed by a tired *classical aesthetic. It was held to be character-

ized by a vibrant assertion of the value of selfhood, individuality, and personal revolt. Although this view contains much that is true, it neglects the extent to which Romanticism was a much broader cultural phenomenon involving new evaluations of the relationship between self and society, new attitudes to nature and to history, and a new sense of the sacred. Moreover, one must bear in mind that in France, more than elsewhere, the development of Romanticism was intimately related to the experience of the *Revolution and its aftermath. Indeed, Romanticism was in large part a response to the general mood of post-Revolutionary instability.

In recent times entrenched and often highly polemical definitions of French Romanticism—which tended to focus on a narrow period such as 1820–43—have given way to a willingness to consider most literary work produced from the 1770s to at least 1850 as corresponding to the Romantic age (indeed, some critics go as far as to include *Symbolism and *Surrealism within an extended definition of Romanticism). Furthermore, the notion that there was a distinct early phase of Romanticism, called *Pre-Romanticism, which had earlier become a critical orthodoxy, has also now fallen from favour. The difficulty with considering almost a century of French culture as Romantic is obvious: can any term retain its usefulness if it is applied to such a diversity of cultural production? On the other hand, one advantage of adopting the extended time-scale and moving away from restricted definitions is that authors such as *Balzac and *Stendhal, who tended to be situated outside mainstream Romanticism, can now legitimately be placed at its centre.

2. Origins to 1830

The term 'Romantic' was popularized by Germaine de *Staël in *De l'Allemagne* (1810), where she advocated an openness towards foreign literatures and cultures, to values and qualities which had been excluded by classical taste. Romanticism marked a move away from 18th-c. sensationalist philosophy, which held that all knowledge came through the senses, in a new direction, one which valued inwardness and the truths of feeling. The scientific world-view was held to have sundered the individual from society, separated man from nature. Romanticism questioned the capacity of reason to arrive at the truth, valorizing instead mystery and fantasy, dream and reverie. Moreover, as the power of traditional Catholicism waned, the Romantics attributed to literature itself a revelatory function, casting themselves in the role of priests of the religion of art. In turning inwards and relying on the voice of conscience, Romanticism followed J.-J. *Rousseau; it also incorporated his identification of the natural as the locus of truth and authenticity. However, in the 19th c. political and social conditions had been transformed by the experience of the Revolution. At one level Romanticism's Prometheanism, its call for self-expression and emancipation, can be seen as an avatar of the revolutionary will to freedom. But at another level it represents a quest for new forms of knowledge and grounds of meaning, and also, paradoxically, for the restoration of a lost or imagined harmony. Indeed, Romanticism can be said to be characterized by a passionate desire for unity, a wish to transcend the contraries of mind and nature, subject and object, intellect and emotion.

In the early 1800s the quintessentially Romantic themes of spiritual longing, the inner void, solitude, restlessness, uncertainty, melancholia, the vanity of all things, and the obsession with love and death were embodied in Chateaubriand's highly influential *René*. The tale's protagonist became the archetypal victim of the *mal du siècle*. Was it only the intensity of suffering which gave purchase on life? *René* was included within Le Génie du christianisme (1802), Chateaubriand's apologia for the Christian religion, where the story functioned—somewhat ambiguously—as a cautionary tale. Le Génie du christianisme blended Rousseauism with Catholicism, and marked a sharp reaction against the liberalism and individualism of the *Enlightenment, which were held responsible for the social dislocation wrought by the Revolution. What mattered was the rebuilding of social cohesion, the reconstruction of the social bond.

Romanticism repudiated contractual theories and often ascribed primacy to society over the individual. This desire to re-forge the social bond often involved viewing society as an organism—this was the hallmark of anti-democratic conservative thought (e.g. J. de *Maistre, *Lamennais). Conservative Romantics revered the past as the repository of truth and value, rehabilitated the Gothic Middle Ages, and respected the ordering power of medieval Christianity. In the early years of the century their arguments were resisted by the *Idéologues, who defended the cause of moderate republicanism and individualism.

In the 1820s the Romantic school of poets came to prominence. *Vigny, *Hugo, and *Lamartine were young authors whose writing, with its personal, introspective, confessional tone, struck an immediate chord with readers [see also DESBORDES-VALMORE]. In political and religious terms the allegiance of these new writers lay with legitimist royalism and Catholicism. They met as a group, or *cénacle, in the salon of Charles *Nodier, and their views on literature were expressed in the pages of periodicals such as La Muse française (1823–4). However, the Romantic idea underwent significant modifications during the Restoration. In *Racine et Shakespeare (1823 and 1825) Stendhal related Romanticism to an artistic commitment to engage with contemporary reality, particularly in the theatre. In the mid-1820s a different, liberal Romanticism was formulated in the pages of Le *Globe, the organ of a rising generation of critics,

historians, and poets who were dissatisfied with the sceptical liberalism of the Idéologues. The later 1820s witnessed the coming together of Romanticism and liberalism.

In the Préface de *Cromwell Hugo formulated what amounted to a manifesto and a new aesthetic. He saw the task of art as grasping the complexity of reality in a totalizing vision, grounded his project in a philosophy of history, and formulated an aesthetic based upon oppositions and tensions which challenged the prescriptions and formal requirements of classicism. Romantic writers followed Hugo's example, holding that the old conventions were no longer adequate to express the conflicts of modernity. Artistic freedom involved technical innovation and questioning of the traditional genres. The battle of *Hernani (1830) is usually taken as a key date in the struggle to renew French drama by calling into question the rules of classical doctrine [for the drame romantique see DRAMA IN FRANCE SINCE 1789].

3. After 1830

The July Revolution of 1830 marked a watershed in the development of French Romanticism. After this date we find a growing concern for broader social themes and a sympathy for the plight of the masses suffering under the impact of industrialism [see JULY MONARCHY]. The artist was held to have social responsibilities. The poet, in particular, was cast in the role of interpreter of God's ways to man in what to many seemed to be a post-Christian world. In the wake of 1830 there was an explosion of new social religions in France [see SAINT-SIMON, MARQUIS DE; FOURIER]. There were also attempts to renew traditional religious forms: *Lamennais published his Paroles d'un croyant in 1834. Some authors, however, found the self-importance of the new believers difficult to accept. *Musset could not take seriously the new religions which proclaimed the goodness of the masses and relied upon a progressivist theory of history. *Gautier rejected the notion that art should serve political ends and advocated a different programme altogether, that of 'l'*art pour l'art'. Others, the *Frénétiques, developed a literature which focused on the violence, despair, and nihilism inherent in the critical dimension of Romanticism [see also BOUSINGOTS; JEUNES-FRANCE].

After 1830 the mal du siècle persisted, but its cause was no longer the loss of the ancien régime so much as the failure of France to regain her position in the vanguard of history, to extend the gains of the Revolutionary years. In the 1830s and 1840s *Quinet, Pierre *Leroux, and *Michelet proclaimed their faith in nationalism. Socialists, on the other hand, prized humanitarianism over nationalism; in their view social reorganization in the name of increased equality was of greater significance than political reform. In these years Romantic writing was drawn to the apocalyptic, to myths of rebirth and transformation. It created the intellectual climate which accompanied the Revolution of 1848 [see REPUBLICS,

2], with its exaggerated hopes of renewal and the inception of a new harmonious order. The disillusionment which followed the Second Republic's inability to incarnate the idealism of Romanticism in the world of fact produced an anti-Romantic backlash. Writers who none the less remained deeply Romantic in temperament (*Baudelaire, *Flaubert) questioned the metaphysical status of nature and history. Others reaffirmed, against the odds, the totalizing ambitions of Romanticism. After 1851 Michelet wrote expansive works of history and natural history and Hugo elaborated cosmic themes in his prophetic poetry.

4. Nature and History

French Romanticism's main centres of interest can be summed up by looking briefly at attitudes to nature and history. Romantic literature did more than use reference to nature as a way of evoking human feelings. Many authors believed that external nature was the embodiment of the divine and that the universe could be understood analogically as a network of secret relationships or correspondences. The artist obtained access to an invisible spiritual world (*Sand, *Les Sept Cordes de la 'lyre*, 1840); the imagination was viewed as a spiritual faculty, creative not imitative. Moreover, artistic knowledge of the sacred patterning of nature was linked to theories of the regeneration of society.

Equally central to Romanticism was a new relation to time. The God who was present in nature was also active in history, which became a ground of meaning, personal and collective. Romantic thinkers envisaged politics against the backdrop of world history. Poets and writers who were preoccupied with the fragmentation of the personality (e.g. *Nerval) turned to a poetics of memory as a way of beginning the reconstruction of selfhood. Romanticism believed that ideas moved history and that these ideas were embodied in peoples, collective subjects. Reviving the national past was a central part of creating a sense of belonging to community, and the recreation of the past was a central aspect of the novels of Hugo, *Vigny, and *Dumas.

Romantic writing surprises by its capacity to challenge our expectations. Personal lyricism combines with political commitment; the literature of exhaustion exudes energy and desire; the evocation of disintegration becomes a hymn to metamorphosis and transformation; the imagination which sets out to discover the divine presence uncovers unsettling truths about the unconscious and its workings; confidence in the goodness of nature and the purpose of history is undercut by parody or qualified by irony. The overarching Romantic desire to achieve synthesis and unity remained tempered by the critical inheritance of the 18th c.   [CC]

See H. Peyre, *Qu'est-ce que le romantisme?* (1971); M. Milner and C. Pichois, *Le Romantisme* (1973); P. Bénichou, *Le Temps des prophètes* (1977); D. G.

Charlton, *The French Romantics*, 2 vols. (1984); F. P. Bowman, *French Romanticism: Intertextual and Interdisciplinary Readings* (1990); C. Crossley, *French Historians and Romanticism* (1993).

Rome, Naples et Florence, see STENDHAL.

Rome, Prix de, see ACADÉMIE ROYALE DE PEINTURE ET DE SCULPTURE.

ROMIEU, Marie de (?1545–1590). Poet from Viviers in the Ardèche, whose *Premières œuvres* were published in 1581. Most of her work consisted of translations from Italian and neo-Latin poets, but she also composed a 'Bref discours de l'excellence de la femme' in reply to *Desportes's 'Stances du mariage' [see QUERELLE DES FEMMES]. This was reprinted several times after her death.   [IM]

Roncevaux. Site of the famous battle against the Saracens, now usually known to scholars as Rencesvals [see ROLAND].

Ronde, La, see HAITI, 2.

Rondeau, rondel. Fundamentally the *rondel* is a single-stanza lyric which opens and closes with a refrain whose first line(s) it repeats nearly half-way through. The form originated in songs accompanying a round dance perhaps associated with northern French May festivals—hence a chorus with somewhat constricting repetition. The AB | aA | ab | AB pattern of such *rondets de carole* (renamed *triolets* c.1488) enjoyed popularity from the 12th to 16th c. and in the late 18th and 19th c. The 14th-c. development of the ten-, eleven-, or thirteen-line *rondel tercet* (various patterns) and subsequent sixteen-line *rondel quatrain* (pattern generally: **ABBA | abAB | abba | AB**BA) led to the late 15th-c. rondeau, employed by *Marot, *Voiture, *Voltaire, and *Musset, which cut the refrain to the opening words, usually connected by sense to the previous line (pattern generally: Aabba | aab(A) | aabba(A)).   [PVD]

RONSARD, Pierre de (1524–85). Leader of the *Pléiade and the most diverse, accomplished, and influential poet of *Renaissance France. Victim of two centuries of unwarranted obscurity because of the classical reforms of *Malherbe and the strictures of *Boileau, Ronsard was 'rediscovered' by *Sainte-Beuve. Modern research has restored him to his rightful place in French poetry, emphasizing not only his superlative achievement as poet of love, wine, and nature, but also focusing attention increasingly on the qualities of his scientific, political, religious, and official poetry. In addition, a large corpus of Ronsard's work discusses the function and nature of poetry itself, either in theoretical treatises (*Art poétique*, 1565; prefaces to the *Odes*, 1550, and the *Franciade* of 1587) or in frequent poems about the activity of poetry.

His early childhood was mostly spent in his birthplace, the Château de la Possonnière near Vendôme. Destined for a military and diplomatic career, he became a page at court in 1536, first to the dauphin, then to Charles, duc d'Orléans, and finally to Charles's sister, Madeleine, whom he followed to Scotland upon her marriage to James V. After a second visit to Scotland (1539–40), Ronsard accompanied Lazare de *Baïf on a diplomatic mission to Alsace (1540): on his return a serious illness left him partially deaf and dashed hopes of a military career. Encouraged by *Peletier in his earliest poetic attempts, and educated under *Dorat at the Collège de Coqueret from about 1547, Ronsard collaborated in the writing of the *Défense et illustration (1549) and published his first collection, Les Quatre Premiers Livres des Odes (1550); a fifth book followed in 1552. Two sources predominate—Horace, whose 'naïve douceur' is exploited to excellent effect, and the Greek Pindar, whom Ronsard proudly introduces into French verse and whose sublime lyricism, triadic structure, and celebrational discourse Ronsard adapts to glorify patrons, important events and, most convincingly, poetry itself (Ode à Michel de l'Hôpital, 1552).

With the Odes of 1552 Ronsard published Les Amours, a cycle of 183 decasyllabic love sonnets, augmented for the second edition of 1553 by further poems (including the much-admired 'Mignonne, allons voir') and a commentary by *Muret. Accompanied in the 1552 edition by a supplement of musical settings and dedicated to Cassandre Salviati, this sequence is characterized by a tension between its idealized, *Petrarchan mode and a frustrated sensuality. A second cycle of love poetry followed in two collections (the Continuation and Nouvelle continuation des Amours of 1555 and 1556), composed essentially of chansons and alexandrine sonnets and addressed to an (as-yet) unidentified Marie. The Amours de Marie represented a temporary abandonment of Petrarchism for a more naturalistic conception of love and a simpler style, the 'beau style bas' which had already been heralded in the lighter poetry of Le Livret de folastries (1553), Le Bocage (1554), and Les Mélanges (1555).

In marked contrast, 1555–6 also saw the appearance of two books of Hymnes, poems conceived as miniature epics after classical models but more directly indebted to the Hymni of the neo-Latin poet Marullus. They are written mainly in alexandrine rhyming couplets as celebrations of powerful figures, natural phenomena, and abstract entities (Philosophy, Justice). The style is elevated and the content encyclopaedic, as befits a poet fulfilling his divine and social role as interpreter of the world's mysteries. The seasonal hymnes of the Recueil des nouvelles poésies (1563) centre on poetic and political concerns in allegorical form.

In 1560 Ronsard published the first collective edition of his work. He was nominated conseiller et aumônier du roi in 1558, and his poetry from the late 1550s to the mid-1560s became increasingly circum-

stantial, often reflecting the historical events of the period and the official interests of the monarchy and the Catholic Church. The outbreak of the *Wars of Religion in 1562 inspired the Institution pour l'adolescence du roi (1562), the Discours and the Continuation du Discours des misères de ce temps (1562), and the Remonstrance au peuple de France (1563); here Ronsard's private convictions and his public position coincide to produce powerful, emotional poetry which is theological, patriotic, and political in content. Attacked in Calvinist *pamphlets, Ronsard replied with his Réponse aux injures (1563), a sort of apologia pro vita sua. Two years later the Élégies, Mascarades et Bergerie appeared, a collection of official pieces written for the court entertainments of 1564 designed by *Catherine de Médicis to unite the Protestant and Catholic nobility behind *Charles IX.

From the mid-1560s much of Ronsard's energy was devoted to extensive revisions of his work in preparation for the six collective editions which appeared between 1567 and 1587. During a severe illness (1567–9), and more frequently after the failure of his epic La *Franciade (1572) and the death of Charles IX (1574), Ronsard spent lengthy periods away from court at the priories of Saint-Cosme and Croixval, which he had received in 1565–6 (tonsured in 1543, he could hold ecclesiastic benefices by way of patronage). Ronsard never enjoyed generous support from *Henri III, and the court increasingly showed a preference for *Desportes's poetry. It was, perhaps, partially to compete with Desportes and to respond to the Italianate fashion of the court that Ronsard included in his fifth collective edition (1578) a new cycle of Petrarchist verse—the Sonnets pour Hélène—dedicated to Hélène de Surgères, lady-in-waiting to Catherine de Médicis. New also to the 1578 edition, and completing the Marie cycle, was Sur la mort de Marie, a slim volume (including the memorable 'Comme on voit sur la branche . . .') written on behalf of Henri III to commemorate the death of Marie de Clèves in 1574. The illness which led to Ronsard's own death (27 December 1585) is graphically evoked in the Derniers vers (1586).

Ronsard's verse impresses by the breadth of its imaginative vision, by its copious diversity and energy, by the suggestiveness of his images, by the sensitive interplay between syntax, rhythm, and musicality, and by the consummate skill with which he surpasses and personalizes the models and conventions which have inspired him. He truly merits the title of 'Prince of Poets'. [MDQ]

See H. Weber, La Création poétique au XVIe siècle, 2 vols. (1956); T. Cave (ed.), Ronsard the Poet (1973); M. Quainton, Ronsard's Ordered Chaos (1980).

ROPS, Félicien (1833–98). 'En Belgique . . . pas d'artistes, excepté Rops', wrote *Baudelaire of the Belgian painter and engraver who is now chiefly remembered for his illustrations of texts by Baudelaire, *Mallarmé, *Barbey d'Aurevilly,

Roquentin

*Verlaine, and *Péladan. His work explores the sado-masochistic eroticism, satanism, and mysogony analysed at length by the *Goncourts and *Huysmans; this made Rops one of the leading artists of *fin-de-siècle* *Decadence.　　　[JK]

Roquentin, Antoine. The hero of Sartre's *La *Nausée.*

Rose-Croix, Frères de la. Name given in France to adherents of the so-called Society of Rosicrucians, a loose and secret grouping of thinkers and writers who, from the early 17th c., promoted various types of mystical enquiry. *Descartes was apparently attracted to their doctrines in his early years. In the 18th and 19th c. they tended to be associated with *freemasonry and with *Illuminist thinking, influencing *Balzac, and enjoying a new lease of life with the *Symbolists, especially *Péladan.　　　[PF]

ROSNY, J.-H. Pseudonym of the brothers Joseph Henri Boex (called J.-H. Rosny *aîné*) (1856–1940) and Séraphin Justin Boex (called J.-H. Rosny *jeune*) (1859–1948). The brothers began writing as confirmed *Naturalists, and even after their break with *Zola in 1887 ('Manifeste des Cinq'), social issues informed many of their novels (*Nell Horn de l'armée du Salut*, 1886; *Le Bilatéral*, 1887; *Le Termite*, 1890; *La Fauve*, 1899). When their collaboration ended in 1908, Rosny *jeune*'s work maintained this social preoccupation. But Rosny *aîné*, the more significant writer, had already established his originality in two often overlapping genres: *science fiction (*Les Xipéhuz*, 1887; *Le Cataclysme*, 1896; *La Force mystérieuse*, 1914) and the prehistoric novel (*Vamireh*, 1892; *Eyrimah*, 1895; *La Guerre du feu*, 1911). The brothers were founding members of the *Académie Goncourt, from 1896.　　　[CS]

ROSSINI, Gioacchino Antonio (1792–1868). Italian opera composer who lived and worked for many years in Paris, although his version of Beaumarchais's *Le *Barbier de Séville* was first performed in Rome in 1816. *Stendhal, who greatly admired him, wrote a *Vie de Rossini* (1823).

ROSTAND, Edmond (1868–1918). French playwright who marks the reaction against the seriousness and gloom of *Naturalist drama. At their best his plays have warmth, charm, wit, and poetic feeling, but they can be contrived and sentimental. *Les Romanesques* (1894), with its version of Romeo and Juliet, and *La Princesse lointaine* (1895), with its revival of the troubadours, are winsome but cloying. His great success is *Cyrano de Bergerac* (1897), a swashbuckling romantic drama, brilliantly ingenious in its versifying and still exciting and touching in performance. *Chantecler* (1910), an allegory using masks of birds and beasts, is an ambitious experiment.　　　[SBJ]

ROTROU, Jean (1609–50). French dramatist. A lawyer by training, he combined this profession with the theatre, and his legal duties may have cost him his life: he became a magistrate in his native town of Dreux in 1639 (having bought an office), and the account given of his death is that he refused to leave the town during a plague epidemic, perceiving it as his duty to stay, and died of the disease. For some years he was employed to write plays for the Comédiens du Roi at the *Hôtel de Bourgogne, but managed to free himself from this obligation in about 1634 (by which date he claimed to have written 30 plays), after which his output slowed down. He published 35 plays (17 tragicomedies, 12 comedies, 6 tragedies) and he may well have written 50 or more. He was one of *Richelieu's 'cinq auteurs' and a friend, as well as a rival, of Pierre *Corneille.

Rotrou drew some of his material from Seneca and the Greek dramatists, some from ancient historians, and much from Spanish sources (he was the first French dramatist to borrow from Spanish plays rather than novels or non-dramatic poetry). The plays most highly regarded by modern critics are three of the tragedies, *Le *Véritable saint Genest* (performed 1645), *Venceslas* (performed 1647), and *Cosroès* (performed c.1648). Many other plays are interesting, however, whether for their connections with other texts, or for their own merits, or both. *Antigone* (1637) and *Iphigénie en Aulide* (1640) treat Greek subjects later handled by *Racine in *La Thébaïde* (1664) and *Iphigénie* (1674), and *Molière borrowed from several of Rotrou's comedies. Like his contemporaries, Rotrou adapts and changes his material considerably, and this leads to some happy inventions, such as the spirited wife of Polynice in *Antigone*, who strikes up a friendship with Antigone when she meets her for the first time after Polynice's death.

The early play *La Bague de l'oubli* (performed 1629, published 1635), a comedy, was the first play taken from a Spanish dramatic source (Lope de Vega's *Sortija del olvido*). Unlike previous French comedies it has a courtly setting and several royal characters. The ring mentioned in the title is magical and induces amnesia in the wearer. It is used in a plot aimed at dethroning a king, a subject similar to those used in tragicomedy; but there are several comic characters, such as the king's jester and an inept general and admiral, and a certain amount of indelicate language, as well as the amusing surprises caused by the action of the ring, so that the tragic possibilities are muted by the comic tone.

Classed as a tragicomedy, *Laure persécutée* (1637) presents the triumph of young love over a tyrannical and thoroughly unscrupulous father who happens to be a king and therefore has more power than fathers in comedy. Although forced to recognize the beauty and virtue of Laure, whom his son loves, the king does not relent until she is improbably discovered to be of royal birth. Although Laure is threatened by the king first with death and then with rape, the perils seem fairly easily averted, and the tone is not unlike that of Shakespearean comedies such as *Much Ado About Nothing* (which the plot in part resembles, Laure being traduced just as Hero is).

Rotrou's theatre has been characterized as *baroque because of his fondness for devices such as disguise, real or feigned madness, illusory situations where a character is thought to be dead (or believes himself to be dead), ambiguity, or manipulations of dramatic illusion, as in *Le Véritable saint Genest*, through the play-within-a-play. It displays considerable freedom of technique, with violent action and spectacular effects on stage, numerous changes of place within a play, and expansiveness of time-scale. The language is often conspicuously rhetorical, in the sense both of stylized forms (stichomythia, monologues, passages of stanzaic verse) and of ornaments such as anaphora, apostrophe, and sententious utterances. The later plays still display this characteristic, while becoming more rigorous in form and showing more concern for *bienséance*, in keeping with current trends.   [GJ]

See J. Morel, *Jean Rotrou, dramaturge de l'ambiguïté* (1968).

Rotrouenge. A somewhat indistinct *trouvère* lyric form, perhaps best defined by its music. The name may derive from the *rote*, 'portable harp', serving as accompaniment. In strophic structure the *rotrouenge* eschews the two *pedes* plus *cauda* division of the *chanson*. Rather, it resembles the *ballette* despite its more elaborate verse-form and greater number of stanzas, which together permit a fuller development of content. This varies considerably. Musicologists identify 34 *rotrouenges* covering some ten thematic genres, notably *chansons courtoises* (9) and *pastourelles* (5). Although *troubadours adopted the *rotrouenge*, only five *retroensas* survive, including four late compositions.   [PVD]

ROUAULT, Georges (1871–1958). French painter and engraver; also a poet in *Paysages légendaires* (1929). His naturally calligraphic style developed into forceful outlining, partly indebted to an early training in stained-glass production. Large-format heads loomed into icons. He abhorred the wrongs of society, courtrooms, and war. Through his compassion for humanity (prostitutes, clowns, the accused) he revealed the soul while painting the body or the public costume. He respected *Baudelaire for recognizing the talent of *Daumier, whose penetrating observation and telling delineation Rouault echoed. For the dealer Ambroise Vollard he produced a series of nearly 60 huge etchings, *Miserere et Guerre*, and smaller etchings and wood-engravings illustrating Vollard's text *Les Réincarnations du Père Ubu*. *Rivière, *Apollinaire, and *Malraux reviewed his work.   [HEB]

ROUBAUD, Jacques (b. 1932). French mathematician, poet, novelist, a member of *OULIPO since 1966, author of authoritative studies of French verse and of the lyrics of the *troubadours, and disciple of

*Queneau. Roubaud's literary work is an exemplary demonstration of the creative potential of form and of the interpenetration of mathematics and literature. In ε (1967) he structured a poem-sequence according to the rules of the Japanese board-game go, which he helped introduce into France (*Petit Traité invitant à la découverte de l'art subtil du go*, 1969, in collaboration with Pierre Lusson and Georges *Perec). Together with Jean-Pierre *Faye, Roubaud launched the review *Change in 1970, to counter the influence of *Tel Quel. His best-known work of poetry, *Quelque chose noir* (1986), is a moving lamentation of the death of his second wife Alix Cléo Roubaud. Since then he has published a trilogy of comic novels (*La Belle Hortense, L'Enlèvement d'Hortense, L'Exil d'Hortense*) which take up themes and games from the works of Queneau; and a brilliant, difficult narrative account of a great work he can never write, entitled '*Le Grand Incendie de Londres*'. In this 'story with bifurcations and interpolations', Roubaud asserts that he now knows that he will never rival Sterne, Malory, Murasaki, Henry James, Szentkuthy, etc; readers may judge him less harshly, particularly after the appearance of the second 'branch' of his increasingly autobiographical 'project', *La Boucle* (1993).   [DMB]

ROUCH, Jean (b. 1917). French ethnographer and film-maker, whose thought was influenced by *Surrealism and *Leiris's *L'Afrique fantôme*. He made many short documentaries before emerging in 1958–62 as a pioneer of *cinéma-vérité*. His spontaneous, documentary-style films, notably *Moi un noir* (1958) and *Chronique d'un été* (1961, in collaboration with Edgar *Morin) pointed the way (for *Godard and others) to a new cinematic approach to social reality.   [PF]

ROUCHER, Jean-Antoine (1745–94). Poet from Montpellier, friend and admirer of J.-J. *Rousseau. He welcomed the Revolution, but was arrested in the Terror and went to the guillotine with André *Chénier. *Les Mois* (1779) is a descriptive poem in 12 cantos in the manner of Thomson's *Seasons*; often pompous or didactic in tone, it evokes the energy of the natural cycle.   [PF]

Rouge et le noir, Le. Novel by *Stendhal, published 1830, one of the summits of French fiction. Julien Sorel, a carpenter's son from the Franche-Comté, is a passionate devotee of *Napoleon. Devoured by ambition, he concludes that in the post-Napoleonic age, the Church is the only road to fortune. His ability to recite the Bible by heart allows him to start his climb to success by becoming tutor to the children of the local mayor, Monsieur de Rênal. In comic imitation of his hero, he imposes his will on his master and seduces the naïve and beautiful Madame de Rênal. His next step takes him to the seminary of Besançon, where his superiority riles his fellow students. He moves to Paris, as secretary to an *ultra nobleman, the marquis de la Môle, who sends him on political missions. His fire and intelligence allow him now to seduce the marquis's romantic, head-strong daughter, Mathilde; when the marquis learns that she is expecting his child, he is obliged to procure Julien an army commission under an aristocratic name. Then, at the height of his success, the hero is brought down by a letter of denunciation from Madame de Rênal to the marquis. He shoots her in a moment of alienation and gives himself up to justice. Although she is only wounded, his defiance of the jury as class enemies results in the death sentence. As he awaits his fate in the prison tower high above Besançon he is reunited in perfect love with Madame de Rênal, turning away from Mathilde and worldly ambition. She dies on the day of his execution; Mathilde, in imitation of a Renaissance ancestor, carries his severed head to burial.

The novel gives a remarkable satirical picture of different levels of French society. Stendhal was proud of his realism (in a famous aside he describes the novel as 'un miroir qui se promène sur une grande route')—which is shown also in the detailed exploration of the battle of love between Julien and Mathilde. But this witty, clear-eyed narrative, written in an admirably taut and rapid style, with many ironic comments from the narrator, also contains a romantic exaltation of energy and passion, and of love as the supreme value. Julien is no *Tartuffe; he is more a mixture of Napoleon and *Rousseau. The enigmatic title may be intended to represent the army and the Church; on a broader interpretation it sets generosity, energy, and life against boredom and oppression. [PF]

ROUGEMONT, Denis de (1906–85). Writer and cultural historian. Born in Neuchâtel, Switzerland, he dabbled in *Surrealism and occultism before rediscovering Protestant spirituality through Karl Barth. Moving to Paris, he participated in founding the *Personalist reviews *Esprit and Ordre nouveau, and wrote extensively on contemporary themes of personal dignity and political commitment. His exploration of modern concepts of love, L'Amour et l'occident (1938), remains a classic, examining historical, psychological, and ethical issues. He supported the Resistance from Switzerland, and on Swiss diplomatic service in the United States. Returning in 1947, de Rougemont founded the Centre for European Culture in Geneva, and campaigned energetically for European federalism, on which he wrote several influential essays. [MHK]

ROUGET DE LISLE, Claude-Joseph (1760–1836), wrote some forgotten verse and songs, but achieved immortality in 1792 when, as a French army officer, he wrote the words and music of the 'Chant de guerre pour l'armée du Rhin'. Renamed 'La Marseillaise' when sung by the Marseille fédérés, it was adopted as the national anthem and, with the exception of periods of reaction (e.g. under

Napoleon, during the Restoration), has kept its place ever since. [PF]

Rougon-Macquart, Les (1871–93). A series of 20 novels written by *Zola. As is indicated by the subtitle of the series, 'l'histoire naturelle et sociale d'une famille sous le Second Empire', the novels are related by their historical setting and by the novelist's ambition to study the effects of the transmission of hereditary traits down through different generations of the same family. Zola conceived the plan of the series in 1868, studied a number of works on physiology, and took detailed notes on La Physiologie des passions by Charles Letourneau and on the Traité de l'hérédité naturelle by Prosper Lucas, works which provided the novelist with a 'scientific' basis for the ten volumes that he originally intended to write. *Balzac was the literary model, though Zola was careful, in his preliminary notes, to define the differences between his future series and the Comédie humaine: 'My work will be less social than scientific.'

As he progressed through the series Zola kept a genealogical tree of his fictional family, which was first published in Une *page d'amour (1878), then, with numerous additions, in the last volume of the series, Le *Docteur Pascal (1893). It shows the Rougon-Macquart family divided into three main branches, all stemming from the common ancestor, the neurotic Adélaïde Fouque. Her son, Pierre Rougon, becomes the head of the legitimate branch of the family, whose members provide dramas of corruption and ambition in the higher reaches of Imperial society. Adélaïde's two illegitimate children by the drunken smuggler Macquart, Ursule and Antoine, have three children each. The Mourets become the source of the bourgeois dramas of neurotic characters; the Macquarts provide the more violent episodes of the series in novels of working-class or peasant life.

The first volume of the series, La Fortune des Rougon (1871), deals both with the origins of the *Second Empire, in a tale of political intrigue in a small Provençal town, Plassans, at the time of the coup d'état of December 1851, and with the origins of the family, as its various members are introduced. In the succeeding volumes the family is dispersed throughout French society, allowing Zola to vary considerably the milieux and topics with which they deal. La *Curée (1872) treats the financial speculation and corruption of the imperial regime and is followed by Le *Ventre de Paris (1873), set in the market district of Paris. La *Conquête de Plassans (1874), a story of the intrigues of a priest, returns to a provincial setting, as does La *Faute de l'abbé Mouret (1875). *Son Excellence Eugène Rougon (1876) follows the career of a ruthless member of the imperial government, whilst, by contrast, L'*Assommoir (1877), set in the slums of Paris, is the tragedy of a simple washerwoman. The domestic, low-key drama of Une page d'amour (1878) contrasts markedly with the scandalous *Nana (1880), the life and adventures of a courtesan. *Pot-Bouille* (1882), a savage satire of bourgeois life, has the same hero, Octave Mouret, as *Au Bonheur des Dames* (1883), which studies the new social phenomenon of the department store. *La *Joie de vivre* (1884) is set on the Normandy coast and deals with philosophical rather than social or political themes. Three 'Macquart' novels follow: *Germinal* (1885), a masterly work on industrialism and the class-struggle, which recounts the events of a strike in a mining community in the north of France; L'*Œuvre* (1886), which depicts the tragic failure of a painter, Claude Lantier, a 'roman à clefs' of considerable documentary and biographical interest on the artistic milieux of Paris; and La *Terre* (1887), Zola's controversial representation of peasant life. Le *Rêve* (1888) is the shortest and, seemingly, the most idealistic and innocent novel of the series, with its theme of religious mysticism, sandwiched between the brutalities of La *Terre* and La *Bête humaine* (1890), the novel of crime and violence in a railway setting. L'*Argent* (1891) brings the hero of La *Curée*, Saccard, back to centre stage for a further study of the world of finance. La *Débâcle* (1892) and Le Docteur Pascal (1893) close the series, the former concluding the social and political history of the Second Empire with an account of the fall of the regime in the *Franco-Prussian War and the *Commune, the latter rounding off the natural history of the family with a return to the problem of heredity, which, in point of fact, has played a lesser part in the series than Zola originally intended.

The *Rougon-Macquart* novels, as well as being studies of particular milieux or aspects of contemporary life, almost invariably contain, if not a love story, then a strong erotic element, which usually ends in misfortune. There is much political and social satire in the earlier volumes of the series and several of the novels typify the themes and techniques of literary *Naturalism, of which Zola was the leading representative. Despite the catastrophes and disasters that they continue to narrate, the later volumes of the series contain more optimistic strains of belief in the possible future regeneration of the family, the nation, and the world, anticipating the novelist's Utopian phase at the end of his career. Whilst recognizing the documentary value of Zola's panorama of society during the Second Empire, critics have especially emphasized the rich and complex fund of images, symbols, and myths contained in the series, which has come to be appreciated as the work of a visionary writer rather than the product of scientific analysis and realistic representation which the novelist claimed it to be.   [DB]

See H. Guillemin, *Présentation des Rougon-Macquart* (1964); M. Serres, *Feux et signaux de brume: Zola* (1975); A. Dezalay, *L'Opéra des Rougon-Macquart* (1983).

Rouletabille. Detective hero of novels by Gaston Leroux [see DETECTIVE FICTION; ROMAN D'AVENTURE(S)].

ROUMAIN, Jacques (1907–44). Poet, novelist, and essayist, regarded as one of *Haiti's greatest writers. He dominates Haitian literature in the 20th c. much as Aimé *Césaire does French Caribbean literature.

Born into Haiti's élite, he was educated in Switzerland and rose to prominence as an activist in the nationalist opposition to the American Occupation (1915–34). One of the founders of La *Revue indigène*, he epitomized his generation's desire to challenge the political and literary values of its forebears. He was as fierce in his determination to get rid of the Americans as he was to expose Haiti to the new writing of Latin America and the Harlem Renaissance. After founding the Haitian Communist Party in 1934 he was sent into exile, where he established links with international left-wing writers—Langston Hughes, Pablo Neruda, and Nicolas Guillen, among others. He returned to Haiti and in 1943 was made chargé d'affaires in Mexico, where he died one year later.

Given the turbulence of the years in which he lived and his irreverent, restless spirit, Roumain's political writings are as important as his literary output. He is the first in Haiti to use a Marxist methodology to examine folk culture, religion, and race. His approach was different from the essentialist doctrine of *noirisme*, which argued that race was the primordial factor in Haitian culture. His Marxist orientation was consistent in all his essays, whether on Haitian society (*L'Analyse schématique*, 1934), lynching in the United States (*Les Griefs de l'homme noir*, 1939), or voodoo (*Autour de la campagne anti-superstitieuse*, 1942).

Before the late 1930s his creative writing is surprisingly personal and melancholy. Despite his militancy during the American Occupation, his poems in La *Revue indigène* are private and meditative. His early prose works, *Les Fantoches* (1931) and *La Proie et l'ombre* (1930), are bleak satires of the Haitian élite. His depiction of the peasantry in *La Montagne ensorcelée* (1931) is no less depressing. He is best known for his later work, which is gloriously Utopian in intent. The poems of *Bois d'ébène* (1945) are epic and declamatory calls to universal revolt and human solidarity. His highly regarded novel *Gouverneurs de la rosée* (1944) has been translated into over a dozen languages and both filmed and produced as theatre. It is more than the usual Marxist *roman à thèse*. Set in a remote, drought-stricken village, it tells how the hero, Manuel, brings water to his sterile community. Into this work Roumain poured his knowledge of peasant society and his skills as a poet. His characters are not simply ideological abstractions, but invested with mythological power and a credibility that derives from his ethnological work. This novel and its author's politics were to leave an indelible mark on the writers of the following generation—especially *Depestre, *Brierre, and *Alexis.   [JMD]

See C. Fowler, *A Knot in the Thread: The Life and Work of Jacques Roumain* (1980); R. Dorsainville, *Jacques Roumain* (1981).

ROUMANILLE, Joseph, see FÉLIBRIGE; OCCITAN LIT-
ERATURE (POST-MEDIEVAL).

ROUMER, Émile, see HAITI, 2; INDIGÉNISME.

ROUPNEL, Gaston (1871–1946). Author of two successful novels, *Nono* (1910) and *Le Vieux Garain*
(1914), Roupnel became professor of Burgundian
history at Dijon in 1916 and in 1932 published his
seminal *Histoire de la campagne française*. Although
its underlying thesis that French open-field agrarian
structure dates to neolithic times was subsequently
challenged, the work's mystical timbre, empathy
with the peasant soul, and lyrical articulation of the
husbanded landscape make it memorable. A friend
of *Bachelard, Roupnel celebrated Burgundian folklore and wrote articles and stories collected in *Hé,
Vivant* (1927). [DAS]

ROUSSEAU, Henri, known as 'Le Douanier'
(1844–1910). Ambitious, self-taught French naïve
painter, who submitted work to the Salon des
Indépendants, and in whose honour *Picasso organ-
ised a banquet in the Bateau-Lavoir in 1908,
attended by artists and writers. Rousseau admired
past academic artists like Bouguereau, and took
direct inspiration from the Jardin des Plantes, but he
was adopted by the leaders of modern art, with
*Apollinaire often acting as publicist. Rousseau
measured Apollinaire for his portrait alongside
Marie Laurencin in *La Muse inspirant le poète*: the
resemblance is gauche yet unmistakable. Rousseau's
representations of exotic vegetation, his dream landscapes (admired by the *Surrealists), and his allegory
of war are compelling and atmospheric, with a curious formality and *gravitas*. [HEB]

ROUSSEAU, Jean-Baptiste (1671–1741). Poet. The
son of a well-to-do Paris shoemaker, he had a good
education and enjoyed social success, but was banished for allegedly publishing defamatory verse, and
lived the last 30 years of his life abroad. Known as 'le
grand Rousseau', he enjoyed great success in the
18th c. as a lyric poet, and had a high notion of
poetic genius. The bulk of his work consists of odes,
which show considerable variety of tone and subject-matter; a personal voice is sometimes heard
through the grand classical style. He wrote eloquent
paraphrases of the Psalms, but also *cantates* to be set
to music, and sharp epigrams. [PF]

ROUSSEAU, Jean-Jacques (1712–78). Swiss writer,
one of the most influential and controversial figures
ever to write in French. From the beginning his person and his books have attracted disciples and fierce
critics. His denunciation of contemporary society
and his evocations of lost innocence and alternative
worlds set off a wave of 'Rousseauism'. Readers—
from Madame *Roland to Tolstoy—sought to follow what they supposed to be his example, while on
the other hand he was reviled as a destroyer of traditional values. His influence marked the theory

and practice of education and politics, his novel *La
Nouvelle Héloïse was a model for life and literature,
and his *Confessions* inaugurated *autobiography as
a literary genre.

He was by birth a citizen of Geneva, a title he
proudly declared on his title-pages until 1763, when
his native city condemned two of his most important works. His father was a watchmaker. His
mother died shortly after his birth, and his father
left home when he was 10; he received little formal
education, being apprenticed at the age of 13, and
leaving Geneva in 1728 for a wandering life, which is
memorably described in the *Confessions*. Having
walked across the Alps to Turin (where he was temporarily converted to Catholicism), he was given
protection in Chambéry by Madame de Warens, an
agent of the king of Savoy; he lived in or near her
house for several years, and she was for him both
surrogate mother and lover. During this period he
educated himself by intensive private reading.
When an idyllic stay with Madame de Warens at
the country retreat of Les Charmettes had come to
an unhappy end as she took another lover, he
moved to Paris in 1742, hoping in vain to make a living by music—a permanent love of his life. He was
employed for a few months as secretary in the
French embassy in Venice, enjoyed the protection
of the rich Dupin family, and became friendly with
the *philosophes, including *Diderot, for whose
Encyclopédie he wrote articles on music and political economy. In 1745 he began a liaison with
Thérèse Levasseur which was to last for the rest of
his life and which he regularized by an unofficial
marriage in 1768. By his own account he deposited
their five children at a foundlings' home.

He had written nothing significant before 1749. In
that year, on the road to visit Diderot in prison at
Vincennes, he claims to have experienced a
moment of vision which changed his life. The first
fruit was his brief *Discours sur les sciences et les arts*,
which won the prize of the Académie de Dijon and
created a sensation on its publication in 1751. It is a
denunciation of intellectual and technical progress
as both cause and symptom of the moral decadence
of modern society. In the ensuing polemic,
Rousseau developed his theory into a speculative
account of human history as a decline from a hypothetical solitary state of nature through ever-
worsening states of society. Crucial turning-points
in this tragic fall are the institution of metallurgy
and agriculture, bringing in their wake private property, the division of labour, and the subsequent evolution of a political order in which the laws serve
the powerful. The resulting domination and inequality cannot be justified in nature and exacerbate
the *amour-propre* (vanity) which is a perversion of
natural *amour de soi* (the instinct of self-preservation). This is the theory eloquently expounded in
the *Discours sur l'origine et les fondements de l'inégalité
parmi les hommes* (1755), also submitted—unsuccessfully—for the Dijon prize.

His literary debut had brought him celebrity, and this was intensified in 1752 with the court production of his melodious pastoral opera, *Le Devin du village*. Conscious of the gap between his social success and his principles, Rousseau now attempted to break with polite society. Henceforth, although often patronized by the rich and powerful, he was to adopt the independent stance of the cynic Diogenes. Unwilling to make a living as an author, he set up as a music copyist. In 1756 he accepted the invitation of Madame d'*Épinay to live in the Hermitage, an isolated house on her country estate near Paris. This was to prove a disastrous move. His prickly resistance to her patronage, his unhappy love for her cousin Sophie d'*Houdetot, and the insensitivity of Madame d'Épinay and her lover *Grimm led Rousseau to break publicly with them, and with their friend Diderot, to whom he had been very close. He left the Hermitage and accepted hospitality nearby at Montmorency from one of his most influential patrons, the maréchal de *Luxembourg.

The years between 1756 and 1762 were Rousseau's most productive period. The three principal works were *Du *contrat social* (1762), **Émile* (1762), and *Julie ou la Nouvelle Héloïse* (1761). The first two were part of a philosophical programme, offering a positive remedy to the predicament outlined in the *Discours*. The third, an epistolary novel which became an immediate best-seller, came rather from its author's personal dreams and fantasies, though he attempted to make it too a part of his philosophical message. Three other significant works date from the same period, a group of four letters to *Malesherbes which are his first attempt at autobiography, the *Lettres morales* (1757) addressed to Sophie d'Houdetot as an attempt to salvage something from his amorous shipwreck, and the *Lettre à d'Alembert* (1758). The last of these was triggered by d'*Alembert's *Encyclopédie* article on Geneva, which called for the establishment of a theatre in Rousseau's native city. He replied with a long and very personal attack on the Paris theatre (including an unwittingly revealing critique of Molière's *Le *Misanthrope*), which is at the same time a defence of an idealized Swiss traditional culture.

When *Émile* and its author were condemned for religious unorthodoxy in 1762 by the Parlement de Paris, he felt obliged to flee to Switzerland, first to the Neuchâtel district, and then in 1765, after his house was stoned by his superstitious neighbours, to the Île de Saint-Pierre, on the Lac de Bienne. During these three years in Switzerland he crossed swords with critics of *Émile* and *Du contrat social*. The *Lettre à Christophe de Beaumont* (1763), a masterly piece of polemic, is directed against the archbishop of Paris, and the *Lettres écrites de la montagne* (1764) is a reply to Genevan critics, which allied Rousseau with the ordinary citizens of Geneva in their struggles against the political élite.

The last mentioned works contain an autobiographical element, which was to be amply developed in the *Confessions*. This work was begun in about 1764, and continued over the next six years, as Rousseau was driven from place to place. At the invitation of David Hume he went to England in 1765, but soon became involved in a violent public dispute with the Scot. Suffering increasingly—and not without cause—from feelings of persecution, he returned to France, taking refuge first in the Paris region, and then in the Dauphiné. In 1770, although still officially liable to arrest, he returned to Paris to confront his 'enemies' with public readings of the *Confessions*. Feeling that these had been unsuccessful, he continued his enterprise of self-justification in the extraordinary and obsessive *Dialogues*, also known as *Rousseau juge de Jean-Jacques*; in these 'Rousseau' and 'a Frenchman' try to arrive at a complete view of his life and works, which he insisted were indissoluble rather than contradictory. Then, in the last two years of his life, he composed his swan-song, the beautiful and self-absorbed *Rêveries du promeneur solitaire*. Just before his death he was offered his final refuge by the marquis de *Girardin at Ermenonville; here he was buried. Ermenonville quickly became a place of pilgrimage, and among the pilgrims was *Robespierre. Rousseau was to be one of the great heroes of the French revolutionaries, and in 1794 his remains were transferred to the *Panthéon.

Besides the works already mentioned, he published important books on a variety of subjects. These include the *Lettre sur la musique française* (1753), taking the Italian side in the *Guerre des Bouffons; the *Essai sur l'origine des langues* (composed about 1753), a work that has been much discussed in recent years, notably by *Derrida; the *Dictionnaire de musique* (1767); and various writings on botany. In two posthumously published political texts, the *Projet de constitution pour la Corse* (1765) and the *Considérations sur le gouvernement de Pologne* (1771), he attempted practical applications of the theories of *Du contrat social*. His correspondence runs to 50 volumes in the monumental edition by R. A. Leigh.

In the history of European ideas Rousseau occupies an ambiguous position. He was for many years a close friend of Diderot and an ally of the *philosophes*, and he participated in the *Enlightenment critique of existing institutions. But he broke violently with his former friends, for reasons that were both personal and philosophical. Against their belief in cultural progress, he proclaimed the superiority of simpler states of society. His treatment of institutional Christianity in the 'Profession de foi du vicaire savoyard' (*Émile*, Book 4) has much in common with *Voltaire's *deism ('Mock on, mock on, Voltaire, Rousseau!', wrote Blake), but he was hostile to the corrosive scepticism of his contemporaries and maintained an unorthodox loyalty to the Protestantism of his upbringing, exalting in particular the role of

723

Rousseau juge de Jean-Jacques

conscience in morality. In a long letter to Voltaire of 1756 he defended the consoling belief in providence against the latter's bitter poem on the Lisbon earthquake, and subsequently the two men were to become irreconcilable enemies.

It is possible, indeed, to detect many contradictions between the positions adopted in his various books. He had a gift for striking formulations (e.g. the opening of *Émile*: 'Tout est bien, sortant des mains de l'auteur des choses: tout dégénère entre les mains de l'homme'); this led him to adopt extreme positions which he subsequently qualified. Nevertheless, his writings express a coherent, if complex, view of life, a tragic view in which the fall from original nature into society plunges human beings into an alienated condition. Contrary to common belief, he saw no possibility of a 'return to nature', but the writings of his middle period show him attempting to overcome this alienation, imagining alternative forms of social organization. In spite of the uses made of *Du contrat social*, he was not a political revolutionary; his ideal was rather the small and harmonious social unit, based on the family—his view of woman's role being deeply traditional. In his own existence, however, because of his extreme susceptibility and the hostility of certain contemporaries, he found it difficult to maintain satisfactory social relationships. It was perhaps as a second-best that he sang the praises of solitude; even so, he made a deep impact on readers by the pictures he painted of individual happiness in natural settings, among the lakes and mountains of Switzerland.

Imagination played a key role in Rousseau's life, for better or worse. The dark side of imagination led him in his later years to invent a universal conspiracy against him, but it was also in imagination that he found a refuge from the pains of actual life. And although he often declared himself hostile to books and writing as a part of corrupt modern culture, it was in writing that he created for himself and his readers alternatives to the world as it is. His musical prose, though highly wrought and far from spontaneous, comes off the page with the warmth of personal conviction. This was mocked by his critics, who saw him as a hypocrite and a play-actor. To many, however, his voice conveyed a compelling vision of things as they are and things as they might be. [PF]

See G. May, *Rousseau par lui-même* (1961); J. Starobinski, *Jean-Jacques Rousseau: la transparence et l'obstacle*, 2nd edn. (1971): M. Launay, *Jean-Jacques Rousseau, écrivain politique* (1971); M. Cranston, *Jean-Jacques: The Early Life and Works of Jean-Jacques Rousseau* (1983) and *The Noble Savage: Jean-Jacques Rousseau, 1754–1762* (1991) (there will be a third and final volume of this biography).

Rousseau juge de Jean-Jacques. Three autobiographical and self-justifying dialogues written by J.-J. *Rousseau in 1775–6 (see above).

ROUSSEL, Gérard, see EVANGELICALS.

ROUSSEL, Raymond (1877–1933). An aura of the unreal and the artificial surrounds the reputation of this most curious of modernists, a French writer who from the outset cherished a self-image of incomparable genius when, at 19, he composed the verse novel *La Doublure* (1897) in a state of rapture. (The psychiatrist Pierre Janet, whom Roussel later consulted, was to write up his notes as the case-history of an ecstatic narcissist.) Roussel's world cruise of 1920–1; his meanderings across Europe in a luxury caravan, complete with bathroom and studio; his passion for chess, for expensive clothes, for pistols and barbiturates; his unexplained death in the Palermo hotel where Wagner had written *Parsifal*—such biographical details support the myth of the artist as *dandy, an exquisite solipsist all but refined out of existence.

Apart from the rare performances of such plays as *L'Étoile au front* (1924) and *La Poussière de soleils* (1926), which the Paris *Surrealists made a point of applauding in the face of general barracking, Roussel's work remained essentially unknown in his lifetime. He was in fact a most fastidious logophile, a man who would spend months making intricate verbal constructs in which an obsessional and highly rigorous method generates startling semantic variations. The posthumous *Comment j'ai écrit certains de mes livres* (1935) lifts the veil on some of his procedures, such as the punning mechanisms which underlie his early stories and the novel *Locus Solus* (1914), where elaborate descriptions of abstruse objects at the villa of an eccentric scientist-inventor appear to have been generated solely from the multiple suggestions of homonyms and echo phrases. Whereas the prose novel *Impressions d'Afrique* (1910) at least opens with a scene of shipwreck on the African coast, the 1,276 alexandrines of *Nouvelles impressions d'Afrique* (written between 1915 and 1928, and published in 1932) cultivate an unreal logocentricity that has strictly nothing to do with Africa: the book is essentially an exercise in hermeticism, the momentum of a given sentence being repeatedly forestalled by the insertion of parentheses, themselves in turn subverted by fresh parentheses, until the text at large becomes a maze of elaborate embeddings. Peppered with brilliant but arbitrary similes, and made even more mysterious by the 59 uncaptioned illustrations which Roussel commissioned from a commercial artist who never saw the text, *Nouvelles impressions* became an exemplary model for later experimentalists such as *Leiris and *Robbe-Grillet. [RC]

See J. Ferry, *Une étude sur Raymond Roussel* (1953); M. Foucault, *Raymond Roussel* (1963); R. Heppenstall, *Raymond Roussel: A Critical Guide* (1966).

ROUSSET, Jean (b. 1910). Swiss literary critic, one of the *Geneva school. He wrote an influential thematic study of *La Littérature de l'âge baroque en France* (1953), and in *Forme et signification* (1962) went some way towards reconciling thematic criticism with the *Structuralist approach which was soon to become dominant in France. [PF]

ROUSSIN, André (b. 1911), playwright, see COMEDY, 2.

Route des Flandres, La. Novel by Claude *Simon, published 1960, based on his wartime experiences. The central figure Georges remembers the defeat in 1940 of his cavalry regiment and his time in a German prisoner-of-war camp. His commanding officer, de Reixach, is accompanied by a former employee who may have had an affair with his wife Corinne. Georges sees de Reixach killed by a sniper, suspects him of deliberately exposing himself to death, and is haunted by the mystery of this possible suicide: was it motivated by the shame of military fiasco, or of his wife's adultery? In Georges's fantasies Corinne is the essentially desirable woman; after the war he sleeps with her, in an unsuccessful attempt both to resolve the enigma and to identify with de Reixach. Beyond its condemnation of war, the novel thus also explores issues of personal identity, sexual desire, and the limited knowledge we can have of events. Originally titled 'Description fragmentaire d'un désastre', it rejects linear narrative in favour of 'the purely sensory architecture of memory' (Simon), intertwining sequences forming series of loops around the moment of de Reixach's death, and alternating between first- and third-person narrative. It also hovers ambiguously between interior monologue and a spoken account given to fellow prisoner Blum and/or to Corinne. [CB]

ROUX, Jacques (1752–94), Revolutionary leader, see ENRAGÉS.

ROUX, Paul de (b. 1937). French poet, akin to *Réda in his imaginative use of near-traditional verse to evoke moments of day-to-day existence; see his *Poèmes des saisons* (1989).

Roxane is the name of the principal female figure in several French works, including Racine's *Bajazet*, Montesquieu's *Lettres persanes*, and *Rostand's *Cyrano de Bergerac*.

ROY, Claude (b. 1915). French poet and essayist. Drawn early into political commitment, he joined the PCF, but became disenchanted during the 1950s and moved to a nonconformist liberal humanism. His essays, travel writings, and theatre criticism show the same whimsical ebullience as his informative and revealing autobiographies, *Moi je* (1969), *Nous* (1972), and *Somme toute* (1976). [MHK]

ROY, Gabrielle (1909–83). Canadian novelist whose first work, *Bonheur d'occasion* (1945), is a classic of social realism and a landmark in Quebec literature. Breaking with the tradition of the rural novel, it depicted the poverty and social deprivation of the francophone working class of Montreal, at the time of World War II, with a pathos that is typical of her work and with a breadth of vision that she never again equalled. Apart from *Alexandre Chênevert* (1954), in which the theme of urban alienation is articulated through the figure of a lonely bank-clerk, and *La Montagne secrète* (1961), a somewhat laboured allegory of a painter in quest of his ideal, her subsequent works are slighter in scope and more personal in tone. Many of them are fictional sketches or semi-autobiographical short stories set in her native Manitoban prairies: *La Petite Poule d'eau* (1950), *Rue Deschambault* (1955), *La Route d'Altamont* (1966), *Un jardin au bout du monde* (1975), *Ces enfants de ma vie* (1977). Whether there or in other pastoral settings, like the Arctic north (*La Rivière sans repos*, 1970) or the Quebec countryside (*Cet été qui chantait*, 1972), they tend to concern sensitive characters in a quest for self-fulfilment and human understanding that is often ephemeral. The prevailing mood of her later work is one of compassion and sadness, quiet humour and precarious happiness—polarities that are reflected in the title of her posthumous autobiography, *La Détresse et l'enchantement* (1984). [SIL]

ROY, Jules (b. 1907). A French army officer, born in Algeria, whose novels and essays reflect his military experience. A critic of the *Algerian War, he wrote a series of novels entitled *Les Chevaux du soleil* (1968–72) set in French Algeria. *La Bataille de Dien Bien Phu* (1963) describes the crucial battle of the war in *Indo-China. *Mémoires barbares* (1989) recounts his life. [EAF]

Royal Entries. These ceremonial entries of the monarch into a city formed an increasingly important part of *court ritual at a time when the *monarchy was striving either to increase its power or to defend it. They enabled monarchs to reinforce their prestige whilst seeking to enhance their contacts with their people. As such, they were closely related both to the 'Royal Progress' (when the monarch toured his country) and to the court festival (where lavish display was seen both as a sign of prestige and as an opportunity for propaganda). The impact of a particularly impressive entry could be felt even by those who had not been present, since descriptions were often published. The organization of an entry was a collective affair, combining the visual arts, allegorical symbolism, music, ballets, *tableaux vivants*, and even plays. For this reason entries would often involve famous writers (like *Scève for the Royal Entry to Lyon in 1548), painters and humanists (like Antoine Caron and Jean *Dorat, who collaborated on the entry into Paris of the future *Henri III in 1573), and architects (Palladio, for instance, helped design the triumphal arch which greeted the same monarch on his arrival in Venice in 1574). [JJS]

ROYER-COLLARD, Pierre-Paul (1763–1845). French philosopher and politician. As a thinker, Royer-

Collard articulated the spiritualist critique of 18th-c. materialism. He argued in favour of the need to recognize an initial, organizing activity of consciousness. After 1811 he occupied the chair of the history of philosophy at the Sorbonne. Royer-Collard had welcomed the Revolution in its early, constitutionalist phase, but grew rapidly disenchanted and served the royalist cause. He is usually identified with the Doctrinaires, the group which included *Guizot and *Barante and which defended the constitutional monarchy against the attacks of the *ultras during the Restoration. [CC]

ROYÈRE, Jean (1871–1956). French poet. A devoted follower of *Mallarmé, from whom he derived his theory of a hermetic poetry based on the mystical power of sensations and to which he gave the name of 'Musicisme', Royère aimed to extend *Symbolism's exploration of the mystery of poetic language. His own poetry (notably Exil doré, 1898, and Eurythmies, 1904) tended to sacrifice ideas to verbal games, but the review La Phalange, which he founded in 1906 and edited until the outbreak of war in 1914, provided an important early link between Mallarméan poetics and definitions of *poésie pure. [JK]

Rubempré, Lucien de. One of the heroes of Balzac's *Illusions perdues.

RUBINSTEIN, Katia (b. 1944). Tunisian-Jewish writer born in Tunis but resident since 1959 in France, where she teaches philosophy. Her only work is Mémoire illettrée (1979), presented as the memories of 'une fillette d'Afrique du Nord à l'époque coloniale'. It is the only Maghrebian novel to date to be written in the usually unwritten languages actually spoken in these countries. The text is a tour-de-force which draws on the Francarabe, Italian, and Spanish-Hebrew of Tunis contrasted with the formality of written French. It needs to be read aloud, and remains an isolated experiment. [JKa]

Ruche, La, (1945–6). Weekly student newspaper founded in *Haiti by left-wing radicals—Jacques Stéphen *Alexis, René *Depestre, and Theodore Baker among others. It emerged in the intellectual effervescence of post-war Haiti and was shaped by the ideas of Jacques *Roumain, *Surrealism, and the reaction against fascism. It became the catalyst of the revolution which overthrew President Lescot in 1946. [JMD]

RUDEL, Jaufre, see JAUFRE RUDEL.

Ruelle, see SALONS.

Ruines, Les, see VOLNEY.

RULHIÈRE, Claude Carloman de (1734–91). French diplomat, historian, and poet. His agreeably satirical 'Discours sur les disputes' won high praise from

*Voltaire, but he is best known for his unfinished Histoire de l'anarchie de Pologne (published 1806) and his pro-tolerance Éclaircissements (1788) on the Revocation of the *Edict of Nantes. [PF]

Russia and France. From the beginning of the 18th c. French literature was a model for the new literature of Russia; the works of the classics of the age of Louis XIV were extensively translated and imitated. In the second half of the century the empress Catherine the Great, as part of her campaign to win a reputation for enlightenment, offered patronage to a number of French artists and writers. The sculptor *Falconet was invited to St Petersburg to create the famous 'Bronze Horseman' statue of Peter the Great, and among literary visitors were *Grimm and, above all, *Diderot, who spent several months in the Russian capital in the winter of 1773–4 as a sign of his gratitude for Catherine's money and protection. One result of this was that Diderot's library and a set of his manuscripts were sent to Russia after his death; the books were dispersed (unlike *Voltaire's library, which is still housed in St Petersburg), but the manuscripts were preserved.

Although the influence of German and English literature partly eclipsed French in the 19th c., French remained a normal language of communication for the upper classes. Much correspondence in French survives, as well as one major work of polemic, P. Y. Chaadayev's Lettres philosophiques (1829). Many Russian writers spent long periods in France; Turgenev, for instance, was a good friend of *Flaubert. At the same time, a few French writers, notably *Mérimée, *Custine, and *Dumas père, displayed an interest in Russia and Russian literature. When Turgenev tried to attract Flaubert to Pushkin, however, he met with the rejoinder: 'Il est plat, votre poète'; it was only with Tolstoy and subsequently Dostoevsky (much admired by *Gide among others) that Russian writers began to exert a serious influence on the French [see VOGÜÉ].

In the 20th c. the two-way traffic has continued in different ways. Russian Symbolism owed a debt to the poets and theorists of France, whereas after the Bolshevik Revolution Russia provided a pole of attraction for many radically inclined writers. *Aragon and Romain *Rolland, for instance, sang the praises of the new society. Gide's Retour de l'URSS is the most famous of a number of accounts of disillusionment with the failed Utopia. At the same time, many important Russian émigré writers, such as the poets Khodasevich and Tsvetaeva, settled in Paris, and the French capital has remained one of the principal centres of Russian culture abroad. [PF]

RUTEBEUF (fl. c.1249–c.1277). One of the most important French poets of the 13th c., Rutebeuf's real identity is unknown, the name being a pseudonym upon which he puns frequently. 56 texts survive in a large number of manuscripts, indicating considerable contemporary popularity. They range from short lyrics to narrative poems of several thousand lines. The style and content of many suggest that he was well-educated. Almost certainly a clerk, he was possibly also a semi-professional poet and in some way attached to the recently founded Paris University.

Rutebeuf is thought to have been from the Champagne region. His *Dit des Cordeliers* (1249) suggests he lived in Troyes for a time, but he probably moved to Paris shortly after 1250, and many of his poems can be linked to the dispute there between the secular teachers of the university and those from the Mendicant orders (who were mainly *Dominicans, though there were some *Franciscans). The Mendicants were disliked because chairs were reserved for them and because they taught for nothing. In 1252 the university tried to limit the number of chairs held by religious orders, and in 1253 all *maîtres* were obliged to take an oath to observe university statutes. The Mendicants refused and were consequently banned from teaching. From 1254 Guillaume de Saint-Amour, leader of the secular faction, headed a systematic attack on the Mendicants, but by 1256 it was clear that the university was not powerful enough to take on the orders, particularly once they had secured the support of the pope. Guillaume (d. 1272) was exiled. In poems like the *Discorde des Jacobins* (1255), *D'Hypocrisie* (1257), the *Dit de Guillaume de Saint-Amour* (1258), the *Complainte de Guillaume de Saint-Amour* (1258), *De Sainte Eglise* (1259), and *Les Ordres de Paris* (1260), Rutebeuf shows himself to be an ardent defender of the secular cause, an opponent of the Mendicant orders, and a passionate supporter of Guillaume. In the *Dit du mensonge* (1260), one of his finest and most amusing poems, he satirizes the Mendicants by constructing an elaborate ironic allegory in which Humility conquers the world.

Rutebeuf is best known to modern readers for the so-called 'poésies personnelles': *La Griesche d'hiver* (1260), *La Griesche d'été* (1260), *Le Mariage Rutebeuf* (1261), *La Complainte Rutebeuf* (1262), *La Repentance Rutebeuf* (1262), and *La Pauvreté Rutebeuf* (1277). In this sequence Rutebeuf constructs a fictional autobiography. He complains of his poverty and misfortune, which he attributes to gambling (*griesche* means dicing), drink, and an unfortunate marriage; finally he repents and turns to God. These poems are characterized by rampant punning and an often vulgar sense of humour. Some of the details he gives about his life are patently false and the entire tale of woe is probably fabricated, but he inaugurates a tradition of ostensibly autobiographical poetry about city life which culminates in the later Middle Ages with *Villon.

Rutebeuf's corpus is striking for its range. In addition to the university poems and the 'poésies personnelles', he wrote an important sequence about the Fourth Crusade, *fabliaux, a play (*Le Miracle de Théophile*, 1264), a poem related to the *Roman de Renart* (*Renart le Bestorné*), *hagiography, and comic narratives with moral denouements. If many of his poems indicate fervent religious commitment, there is no evidence of a progression in his work towards devotional poetry, as some critics have argued. He seems at home in a wide variety of genres, witness two texts which are almost contemporary: the wickedly irreverent *Le Dit de frère Denise* (1262), in which a young girl enters a male religious order in disguise with predictable, if hilarious, consequences, and the beautifully lyrical *La Vie de sainte Marie L'Egyptienne* (1263), a version of a well-known saint's life. Though diverse, the corpus derives a degree of unity from Rutebeuf's robust, often earthy sense of humour and from a sustained interest in linguistic play. [SG]

See N. F. Regalado, *Poetic Patterns in Rutebeuf* (1970); M. Zink, *La Subjectivité littéraire* (1985) and (ed.), *Rutebeuf: Œuvres complètes*, 2 vols. (1989–90).

Ruy Blas (1838). Verse drama, considered by many to be *Hugo's most successful play. Set in 17th-c. Spain ravaged by a dissolute nobility, it presents parallels with the Bourbon monarchies of 1789 and 1830. The hero, a commoner and a poet in love with the queen, temporarily becomes prime minister. His speech castigating the ministers reflects the values of true patriotism. Don César, a ruined noble turned street poet whose sudden appearance through a chimney constitutes a *coup de théâtre*, is a Falstaffian counter to Ruy Blas. The play has sumptuous, historically accurate decor, virtuoso use of Romantic verse style, and an important preface on the ideal audience. [SN]

S

SABATIER, Robert (b. 1923). French author of a nine-volume *Histoire de la poésie française* (1975–88). His novels, beginning with *Alain et le nègre* (1953), reinvent his childhood; from *Allumettes suédoises* (1969) onwards he recounts his real life in a series of best-selling autobiographies. *L'Oiseau de demain* (1981) collects together poems of cosmic and mythological inspiration. [EAF]

SABLÉ, Madeleine de Souvré, marquise de (1599–1678). Like many aristocrats of her generation, this lady-in-waiting of Marie de Médicis devoted considerable energy to political sedition before and during the *Fronde. She frequented the Hôtel de *Rambouillet and, after a legal separation freed her from an unhappy marriage, ran perhaps the most celebrated mid-century *salon. She was strongly influenced by *Jansenism and lived for years at *Port-Royal. Led by Sablé and *La Rochefoucauld, her circle invented a popular contemporary genre, the maxim. Members revised each other's maxims and published collectively. A volume of Sablé's maxims appeared posthumously (1678). [JDeJ]

SACHS, Maurice (pseud. of Jean-Maurice Etting Lausen) (1906–?1944). Essayist, memorialist, translator, and novelist. A wayward camp-follower of the glitterati of the inter-war years, Sachs captured the amoral tone and tempo of the Parisian jazz age in a number of spirited and stylish chronicles: *Au temps du Bœuf sur le Toit* (1939), *Le Sabbat* (1946), *Chronique joyeuse et scandaleuse* (1948), and a *roman à clefs, Alias* (1935). [DAS]

SACY, Le Maître de, see LE MAÎTRE DE SACY.

SACY, Sylvestre de (1758–1838). Noted French orientalist, professor at the École des Langues Orientales and at the *Collège de France.

SADE, Donatien-Alphonse-François, marquis de (1740–1814). For generations a forbidden author with a subversive attraction, the marquis de Sade has in recent decades acquired both literary and intellectual respectability and has become a classic. He is an essential point of reference for such 20th-c. writers as *Barthes, *Blanchot, and Georges *Bataille.

Of ancient Provençal nobility in straitened circumstances, he married into money (1763) to find financial freedom and spent the next 30 years struggling in the webs spun between family and state. Under the *ancien régime* he was pursued by *lettres de cachet* from his wife's family, who were horrified by his

scandalous conduct. He was arrested and imprisoned a number of times for assaults and attempted murders of prostitutes, and had been in prison for 12 years when the Revolution began. The decree of the Assemblée Constituante abolishing *lettres de cachet* (March 1790) led to his release in the following month. In June his wife took advantage of the new legislation to obtain a legal and financial separation.

His relations with the Revolution were no happier. He described himself in a letter to his agent, Gaufridy (December 1791), as neither aristocrat nor democrat, but possessed of a dislike of the *Jacobins. An 'Adresse au roi des Français' (June 1791) on the royal family's return from Varennes shows him in favour of a reformed monarchy. His anti-aristocratic drama *Le Comte Oxtiern, ou les Effets du libertinage*, which received two showings in October 1791, was a failed attempt to exploit revolutionary sentiment for dramatic success. The brochure 'Français, encore un effort si vous voulez etre républicains', included in *La Philosophie dans le boudoir* (1795), is a plea for licence for the passions, not political reform. But as a prudent man, Sade obtained from his section (Place Vendôme) in July 1790 his *carte de citoyen actif*, and performed the appropriate duties. Arrested on 8 December 1793 because his name appeared in error on a list with others denounced for conspiracy, he missed the guillotine by a bureaucratic accident and was released after the fall of *Robespierre in 1794. Sade and the new order were as ill-matched as Sade and the old. The publication of *Justine* in 1791 was met with cries of outrage, and Sade spent the rest of his career assiduously denying its authorship. He was nevertheless imprisoned in April 1801 (without trial, to avoid scandal) as part of the campaign for morality launched by Napoleon. He spent his last years confined to the mental asylum at Charenton, where he continued to write and organized plays performed by the inmates.

Sade was no politician. He remarks in *La Nouvelle Justine* (1800): 'Il n'y a vraiment aucun bon parti: celui de l'opinion générale est toujours le seul qu'il faut adopter.' The message of all his libertines is that, short of possessing absolute power, dissimulation is the sole key to freedom. Imagination, in his work, compensates for impotence. His writing reduces the whole universe to the manageable dimensions of the (imagined) human body, which becomes his theatre of power—or, more precisely, of desire for power denied.

A man of his time, he pushed to extremes the

ideas of the *philosophes, with the exception of their belief in historical progress and the perfectibility of human nature. He was a materialist and an atheist; the ideas presented in treatise form in his *Dialogue entre un prêtre et un mourant* (1782) reappear throughout his fictions. He took an equally keen interest in contemporary developments in imaginative fiction, acknowledging a special debt to Richardson and *Prévost for their treatment of the passions. His own well-argued study of the Gothic novel, *Idée sur les romans*, appeared as the introduction to his collection of short stories, *Les Crimes de l'amour* (1800). His extensive and varied œuvre experiments with the range of contemporary genres, including prose narrative (short stories, historical novels, *romans à tiroirs*) and drama, as well as pamphlets and philosophical treatises.

Sade began writing novels in the Bastille. From the beginning, he applied the whole Gothic apparatus—coincidence, melodrama, terror, sentimentality, and brutality—as well as a rationalist mind-set, which works in cold and effective contrast to the chaotic material it contains. From the start, too, the concept of story-telling is foregrounded. The procedures of art, the mechanisms of control, are crucial to Sade's eroticism: not blind instinct, but constructed desire.

Les 120 Journées de Sodome, written in the Bastille in 1784–5, was first published in 1904. The definitive text was produced in 1931–5 by Maurice Heine, whose work facilitated the passage of Sade's writing from the literary underground to open availability to creative writers (the *Surrealists, for example, were already provided with *Apollinaire's 1909 anthology of Sade) and scholars in psychology, literary history, and literary criticism. (The appearance in 1990 of the first volume of the Pléiade edition of Sade's complete works marks, as its editors say, the final admission of Sade into the university.) The *120 Journées*, which presents the most forbidden subjects in uncensored detail, has not lost its power to shock; it is like a parody of the operations of the well-run modern state: a careful categorization of crimes and perversions, carried out to a strict timetable and set of rules by a brilliantly caricatured group of contemporary authority figures—judges, financiers, churchmen. The institutions of the state thrive in the spaces of individual despotic desire: in the private depths of the family castle, the bodies of the family and the paid servants are the raw material on which tyranny practises.

Justine ou les Malheurs de la vertu (1791; an expanded version of a text of 1787) is a less hair-raising version of the same theme of the pleasure and power of evil. In this first-person narrative, which inevitably—perhaps in deliberate parody—invites comparison with Voltaire's *Candide, the naïve orphan, seeking only to live by an ethic of virtue and kindness, experiences a painful initiation into the logic of a Hobbesian universe. Subjected to a sequence of spectacular rapes and perverted cruelties at the hands of her fellow men and women,

Justine, unlike Candide, is denied the chance of a happy ending by a well-aimed, morally indifferent bolt of lightning. In contrast, Justine's sister Juliette, a paradigm of evil, thrives and prospers (*La Nouvelle Justine, ou les Malheurs de la vertu, suivie de l'Histoire de Juliette, sa sœur ou les Prospérités du vice*, 1797). Juliette, having served and survived her apprenticeship with the most wicked libertines in France, takes off on an early Cook's Tour, spreading death, disease, and immorality through all the antique sites and beauty spots of Western Europe, devastating the cultural inheritance.

Aline et Valcour, begun in the Bastille and finally published in 1795, had the merit, according to Sade, of predicting the Revolution, in the scattered references throughout the text to democratic principles and especially in its section on the Utopian kingdom of Zamé. In fact, the centre of the novel is the pleasure of incest: the baron de Blamont and his libertine friends engage in a complex seduction and exchange of daughters, closing the circle of desire.

[JB]

See S. de Beauvoir, 'Faut-il brûler Sade?' (originally, *Privilèges*, 1955); G. Lély, *Sade* (1967); J.-J. Pauvert, *Sade vivant* (1989).

SADJI, Abdoulaye (1910–61). Senegalese novelist. Though first published in the 1950s, Sadji's two novels were written earlier and form part of the first wave of 'ethnographic' novels encouraged by the French, who were anxious for 'horse's mouth' knowledge of their colony. Sadji's novels, like those of his fellow countryman *Socé Diop, provide a detailed account of Senegalese manners and attitudes in the 1930s. Though written mainly for European consumption, Sadji's work is popular with his own people. While in no way openly contesting the colonial enterprise, his novels, both of which have strong moral overtones, are a warning to young Africans against the superficial allure of Western culture. *Maimouna, la petite fille noire* (1953), which recounts the misadventures of a village girl in Dakar, is a pessimistic version of Socé's *Karim*, while *Nini, mûlatresse de Sénégal* (1954) is a condemnation of the Afro-European who despises her African cultural heritage. Sadji has also written *Tounka, une légende de la mer* (1952), an account of the early days of the Lebou tribe, in which traditional story-telling techniques are blended with Western narrative features to excellent effect. [FNC]

SADOUL, Georges (1904–67). French film-critic and historian of cinema. Moving with *Aragon from *Surrealism to communism, Sadoul virtually invented the scholarly study of cinema. Among his voluminous writings, the monumental *Histoire générale du cinéma* (1948–56) is still considered a classic. [MHK]

SAGAN, Françoise (pseud. of Françoise Quoirez) (b. 1935). French writer, who was first thrown into the

729

public eye at the age of 18 when she published her best-selling novel, *Bonjour tristesse* (1953). Studiedly subverting contemporary notions of morality, the novel describes adolescent sexuality in a casual yet poignant tone. The dominant mood of sadness and detachment is repeated in a series of more than a dozen best-selling romantic novels, such as *Dans un mois, dans un an* (1957) and *Aimez-vous Brahms?* (1959). Often the limitations of the social roles open to women are gently underlined: thus, Lucie of *La Chamade* (1965) is unable to engage in any meaningful life outside the cocoon which her wealthy lover provides. Sagan's combination of jet-setting lifestyle with vociferous support for left-wing causes has made her a media phenomenon. In 1984 she published an autobiographical text, *Avec mon meilleur souvenir*, in which she presents her writing as a revenge against life's constraints.   [EAF]

Sagesse, see VERLAINE.

Sagesse, De la, see CHARRON.

SAÏD, Amina (b. 1953). Tunisian poet, whose poetic language is at once erotic and esoteric. Her quest for an artistic identity, as expressed in her three volumes of poems, *Paysages, Nuit friable* (1980), *Sables funambules* (1988), and *Feux d'oiseaux* (1989), transcends national boundaries and embraces a wider humanity. Saïd received the Jean Malrieux Prize in 1989 for *Feux d'oiseaux*.   [HA-J]

SAINT-AMANT, Marc-Antoine de Gérard (or Girard), sieur de (1594–1661). Poet. The son of a Protestant merchant in Rouen, he was plain Antoine Girard at his baptism, but by 1629 had acquired this grander appellation. Though claiming small Latin and less Greek, he must have received a sound schooling, he knew Italian and Spanish, and was noted for his skill on the lute. Perhaps through his father's trading interests, he visited Senegal, the Canaries, and the Caribbean; but from about 1619 he was based in Paris. In the train of successive patrons, we find him in Belle-Île, in Rome, on active service with the Mediterranean fleet, in London twice, in Poland with the French-born queen, calling on Christina of Sweden on his way home. He converted to Catholicism c.1625, and was a founder member of the Académie Française.

The image of 'le bon gros Saint-Amant' as a sort of Falstaff among French poets, though largely promoted by himself, is misleading; nor, though a friend of *Théophile, should he be glibly classed as a *libertin*. His keen enjoyment of life is steadied by broad intellectual and artistic interests. Basically, his poetry is a lively response to the world he sees around him: it is a *peinture parlante* in many modes—pastoral, heroic, heroï-comic, *burlesque, satirical—precise and perceptive in its sense-notations, though often embellished with mythological fancy.

His *coup d'essai*, 'La Solitude', is already character-

istic—sketches loosely strung together according to his vagabond humour, his delight in every detail underlined by his exclamatory style. Nine of his poems bear the title 'Caprice'; more might well do so. Such 'licence', as he calls it, can lead to tonal discrepancies and blurred levels of significance; on the other hand, the poet is always at our elbow like a convivial guide. 'Le Melon' and similar poems are like 16th-century *blasons exploding with a new energy. Comic verve abounds too in his carousals and picaresque scenes, and in his satires (notably 'Rome ridicule' and 'L'Albion'). It is sustained with a sometimes virtuosic rhyming, and a zest for language that puts one in mind of *Rabelais.

Saint-Amant spent much effort in his later years on his *idylle héroïque*, *Moïse sauvé* (1653), but he does not achieve a happy balance there between action and description: the epic and pastoral components do not fit well together.   [AJS]

See J. Lagny, *Le Poète Saint-Amant* (1964); *Œuvres*, ed. J. Bailbé and J. Lagny, 5 vols. (1967–79).

SAINT-ANDRÉ, Guillaume de (*fl.* 1371–98), probably from Guérande, was a law student at Angers before entering the service of Duke Jean IV of Brittany, whose biography he sketched c.1385 in a verse life (4,305 lines), which is an important historical source. He also composed an allegorical *Jeu des échecs moralisés* (1,200 lines), associated with the biography in the only surviving complete manuscript, BN ms. fr. 5037; modern edition in *Romania*, 67 (1942–3).   [MJ]

St Bartholemew's Day Massacre (24 August 1572). The Protestants liked to believe that this crucial episode in the *Wars of Religion was the result of a prearranged plan. It is more likely, however, that it was the product of a panic decision taken after an unsuccessful attempt on the life of *Coligny. Fearing that they would be unmasked, *Catherine de Médicis and her younger son, the future *Henri III, persuaded *Charles IX (who had initially promised to punish the culprits) that his own life would be in danger if he failed to act against the admiral and his closest advisors. Once the killings started they prompted violence on an apparently unforeseen scale, as the Parisian mob took the opportunity to assassinate as many Protestants as possible (their numbers were swollen by those who had come to Paris to celebrate the wedding between the future *Henri IV and the king's sister). The number of casualties escalated still further when the massacre spread to the provinces. The massacre itself was an aberration from normal royal policy (which was by and large conciliatory). It produced, however, a marked change in Protestant resistance theory, which now became much more radical [see DU PLESSIS-MORNAY; GENTILLET; HOTMAN].   [JJS]

Saint-Cyr. Site of a convent school near Versailles, founded by Madame de *Maintenon in 1686 for young ladies from impoverished noble families. Racine's *Esther* and *Athalie* were written for performance by the pupils.

In 1808 the École Spéciale Militaire de Saint-Cyr, an officers' training college comparable to the British Sandhurst, was established in the former convent.

SAINT-CYRAN, Jean-Ambroise du Vergier de Hauranne, abbé de (1581–1643). A central figure in the renewal of early 17th-c. French Catholic piety. He took part in anti-Jesuit controversy and succeeded *Bérulle as leader of the *dévots* (1629). As a young man he became a close friend of Jansenius, sharing his Augustinian theology [see JANSENISM]. He imparted this doctrine to *Port-Royal on becoming spiritual director there in late 1635, exercising a powerful influence over Mère *Angélique, the nuns, and the *solitaires*. Imprisoned on *Richelieu's orders in 1638, he was released after the latter's death in 1642, but died the following year. [JC]

SAINT-DENYS GARNEAU, Hector de (1912–43). Canadian poet. Of aristocratic Quebec lineage, Saint-Denys Garneau was educated at a Catholic school in Montreal, but when in 1934 he learnt that a teenage illness had left a deep lesion in his heart he retreated from public life, eventually immuring himself in the ivy-clad family manor at Sainte-Catherine de Fossembault, a village on a tributary of the Saint-Lawrence. Grappling with private feelings of sinfulness, alienation, and doom, he inadvertently reflected in his poetry a more broadly felt unease and yearning for unity, and was posthumously hailed as a herald of the Quebec literary renaissance of the 1950s.

The one collection published in his lifetime, *Regards et jeux dans l'espace* (1937), deals with his rural childhood, nostalgically evoking a state of grace beyond recall. The poems of *Les Solitudes* came out posthumously (in *Poesies complètes*, 1949) and, along with his *Journal* (1954), portray an ascetic loner obsessed by thoughts of mortality and racked by an obscure psychic pain. The poet's spiritualized landscapes transpose suffering and intermittent ecstasy into images of overgrown pathways, distant birds in flight, or forest fires, or again a snowbound house with shuttered windows, a key symbol of confinement and flawed security. Saint-Denys Garneau drowned in a boating accident at the age of 31. [RC]

SAINTE-BEUVE, Charles-Augustin (1804–69). French poet, novelist, and critic. Even before the publication of *Contre Sainte-Beuve*, where *Proust used him as a straw man in order to define his own anti-intellectual conception of art, Sainte-Beuve had become the scapegoat for all the guilt of literary criticism, and he remains best remembered for his underestimation of *Balzac, *Stendhal, *Baudelaire, and *Flaubert, to whom he preferred *Béranger, Ernest *Feydeau, and many minor writers.

Notorious mostly as a critic—the 'prince of critics' and 'uncle Beuve', an academician in the July Monarchy and a senator of the Second Empire—he was also, and before this, a poet. *Vie, poésies et pensées de Joseph Delorme* (1829), where he poses as the anonymous editor of a dead poet, is marked by a rare realism, for instance in 'Les Rayons jaunes', and introduces day-to-day city life into lyric poetry. But Sainte-Beuve never attained the reputation of *Lamartine and *Hugo, whose glory would always stand in his way. He had come to Paris in 1818 and studied medicine, but quickly turned to literature. His early articles on Hugo and in defence of *Romanticism, in Le *Globe (1827), introduced him into the *Cénacle. He became a friend of Hugo while falling in love with the latter's wife, Adèle. His two other volumes of poetry, *Consolations* (1830) and *Pensées d'août* (1837), parallel the evolution of his feelings for Hugo, from ambivalence to hostility after their break in 1835. In 1834 he published his only novel, *Volupté*, a first-person narrative, where autobiographical elements abound.

Disappointed by the reception of his creative works, Sainte-Beuve later confined himself to criticism and created the 19th-c. genre through numerous articles in Le *Constitutionnel, Le *Moniteur, and Le *Temps, as well as lectures in Lausanne (1837–8), Liège (1848–9), and the *École Normale Supérieure (1858–61), all collected in volumes. His *Tableau historique et critique de la poésie française et du théâtre français au XVIe siècle* (1828) re-evaluates the *Pléiade and uses it to justify Romanticism; *Critiques et portraits littéraires* (1836–46, devoted to 17th-c. writers), *Portraits de femmes* (1844), and *Portraits contemporains* (1846) develop the biographical genre, explaining, through sympathy, the inspiration of literature by the life of authors. *Port-Royal* (1840–59), expanding on the lectures in Lausanne, and *Chateaubriand et son groupe littéraire sous l'Empire* (1861), based on the lectures in Liège, trace the broader picture of a period and milieu. In the almost 500 articles collected in *Causeries du lundi* (1851–2) and *Nouveaux lundis* (1863–70), Sainte-Beuve touched upon a great variety of literature, mostly French, but also classical and foreign. As distinct from the earlier 'portrait', the 'causerie' is more of an essay and leads to a judgement. Sainte-Beuve combines the criticism of a journalist and a professor; he still protests against theory and systems but, perhaps influenced by *Taine's determinism, he claims to create a 'histoire naturelle des esprits'.

Sceptical, disillusioned, politically ambiguous—students interrupted his lectures at the Collège de France in 1855 in protest against Napoleon III, but massively followed his funeral after he had become a liberal senator—Sainte-Beuve has succeeded in attracting widespread hostility, perhaps because he dared write on the literature of his own time, a risk that academic criticism was soon to avoid. His intimate notebooks, posthumously published in *Mes poisons* (1926) and *Le Cahier vert* (1974), should allow

Sainte Eulalie

us to reappraise a writer to whom history has been unfair. [AC]

See J. Cabanis, *Pour Sainte-Beuve* (1987); M. Proust, *Against Sainte-Beuve and Other Essays* (tr. J. Sturrock, 1988).

Sainte Eulalie, Séquence de. This 29-line poem, a hymn in praise of the saint composed *c.* AD 880–2, is one of only two extant French texts dating from the 9th c. Emanating from a monastic rather than the administrative milieu of the *Strasbourg Oaths, the *Saint Eulalie*, despite its brevity and latinisms, is apparently a more faithful record of Early Old French usage than the Oaths (e.g. in notating diphthongs), and displays greater syntactic variety. The text, surviving in a contemporary manuscript from Saint-Armand-les-Eaux near Valenciennes, displays certain northern and north-eastern phonological and morphological features, yet the language also suggests the early existence of a supra-regional awareness. [WA-B]

SAINTE-MARTHE, Charles de (1512–55) taught theology at Poitiers, and was imprisoned in Grenoble for Lutheranism. Subsequently he taught French, Latin, Greek, and Hebrew. He was protected by the duchesse d'Étampes and found favour at the court of *Marguerite de Navarre, for whom he compiled the *Tombeau de Marguerite de Valois reine de Navarre* (1551). In his *Poésie française* (1540) he is a disciple of *Marot in his choice of themes and genres, but distinguishes himself by his use of *Neoplatonic elements and his restrained, sober lyricism. [CMSJ]

SAINTE-MARTHE, Scévole de (1536–1623). French poet and humanist, nephew of the above. He bought various offices, including that of *trésorier-général* in Poitiers. His varied French poetry is akin to that of the *Pléiade in its imitation of the ancients and the Italians. He also wrote a good deal of Latin verse and oratorical *éloges* of the poets of his day (*Gallorum doctrina illustrium elogia*, 1598), later reworked by *Colletet in French. [PF]

SAINTE-MAURE, Benoît de, see BENOÎT DE SAINTE-MAURE.

SAINTE-PALAYE, La Curne de, see LA CURNE DE SAINTE-PALAYE.

Sainte-Pélagie. This former convent near the Jardin des Plantes served as a prison from the *Revolution to the end of the 19th c. Madame *Roland wrote her memoirs here, and in the 19th c. the prison housed many notable political prisoners, journalists, and men of letters.

SAINT-ÉVREMOND, Charles de Marguetel de Saint-Denis, sieur de (1613–1703). A man of the world who preferred conversation to books, he left a scattering of short pieces, much admired by contemporaries for their wit and natural style. Including essays and letters, together with some verse and

three comedies, they were mostly published as *Œuvres mêlées* (1705). Scholarly editions of the *Œuvres en prose* (4 vols., 1962–9) and the *Lettres* (2 vols., 1967–8) have been published by R. Ternois.

Only a few years younger than Pierre *Corneille, Saint-Évremond was born in Normandy and educated by the Jesuits. He served in *Condé's army, but inclined towards the court in the *Fronde. This did not prevent him from breaking with *Mazarin; when his satirical letter on the Paix des Pyrénées was discovered in 1661 he took refuge in England, where he moved in fashionable court circles for the rest of his life, with the exception of four years in Holland (1665–9). He placed great value on friendship and polite society; among his close friends were fellow nobles such as the maréchal de Créqui and witty, independent women such as Ninon de *Lenclos and the scandalous duchesse de Mazarin, niece of the cardinal, who joined him in his London exile in 1675. His letters to friends, often mixing prose and verse, are among his most attractive writings.

His poetry is pleasant, often personal in tone, but unremarkable. His comedies, *Les Académistes* (1643), *Sir Politick Would-Be* (1662), and *Les Opéra* (1675) are satirical squibs which remained unperformed in spite of their verve. The last mocks a woman obsessed by *Lully's art form, which is discussed in a more subtle way in his essay 'Sur les opéras'. A good deal of his prose is literary criticism; it is deliberately unpedantic, placing great stress on an unexamined notion of 'good taste', the prerogative of the few. Saint-Évremond knew the Latin classics well, but he belonged to the camp of the *modernes* [see QUERELLE]. He constantly praises the heroic drama of Corneille as against the love-centred tragedies of *Racine or the primitive productions of the ancient Greeks.

He wrote historical essays ('Réflexions sur les divers génies du peuple romain', 1662), but his most interesting pieces, such as 'Conversation du maréchal d'Hocquincourt avec le père Canaye' or 'A M. le maréchal de Créqui', concern morality and religion. He is an aristocratic disciple of *Montaigne, an Epicurean, and a *libertin*. For him, religion and philosophy are uncertain, tolerance is the only reasonable attitude, and sociability, politeness, and the pleasures of body and mind are better than stiff and strenuous virtue. [PF]

See A. M. Schmidt, *Saint-Évremond, ou l'Humaniste impur* (1932); H. T. Barnwell, *Les Idées morales et critiques de Saint-Évremond* (1957).

SAINT-EXUPÉRY, Antoine de (1900–44). One of the most important French metaphysical novelists of the inter-war years. An early aviation pioneer, a colleague of Jean Mermoz in the legendary Aéropostale, he uses his novels to raise flying and the figure of the pilot to a symbolic status by which they represent heroic transcendence of the human condition, in the same way that *Malraux is able to exploit adventure.

His first two novels, *Courrier-Sud* (1928) and **Vol de nuit* (1931), recount the heroic pioneering days of the establishment of the airmail link between Europe and South America. *Terre des hommes* (1939) uses a number of flying anecdotes, particularly one concerning a crash in the desert, to constitute a general reflection on the aviator as standard-bearer of humanism. *Pilote de guerre* (1942) is based upon his experience as a fighter pilot in the Battle of France. His posthumously published fictionalized essay *Citadelle* (1948) is an ambitious attempt to outline an entire social philosophy in which Christianity and humanism combine. In spite of a disturbing tendency, at its most marked in *Vol de nuit* and *Citadelle*, to emphasize the role of the leader and to concentrate upon the pilot as a figure apart from the rest of humanity, Saint-Exupéry was clearly aware of the ethical problems involved in a celebration of the hero, as is indicated in both *Terre des hommes* and the charming and deceptively simple children's story *Le *Petit Prince* (1943). [NH]

SAINT-GELAIS, Mellin de (*c.*1490–1558). The son of Octovien de *Saint-Gelais, he knew Greek, Latin, and Italian and was an accomplished musician. He held various posts at the courts of François Ier and Henri II (chaplain, librarian), but his principal function was that of court poet. He specialized in reading aloud or singing his own compositions—frivolous, witty pieces, satirical or amorous. He used a mixture of the old genres (rondeaux, ballades) and the new (*chansons*, *épigrammes*). Either he or *Marot was the first to write sonnets in French. His clash with the up-and-coming *Ronsard in the 1550s was symbolic of his decline in favour. [CMSJ]

SAINT-GELAIS, Octovien de (1468–1502). A *Rhétoriqueur who was born in Cognac into an illustrious family and became bishop of Angoulême. His most famous poem, the long, allegorical *Séjour d'honneur*, describes the poet's journey to the king's court. His translations of Ovid's *Heroides* and Virgil's *Aeneid*, despite their mediocrity, reveal him as a precursor of the Renaissance. [CMSJ]

***Saint Genest*, by *Rotrou, see VÉRITABLE SAINT GENEST, LE.**

***Saint Genet, comédien et martyr*, see GENET; SARTRE.**

Saint-Germain-des-Prés. Abbey on the left bank of the Seine in Paris, founded 588. In the 17th c. it became the chief house of the *Maurists. The cafés and night-clubs in this district were much frequented in the 1940s by artists and writers, and Saint-Germain-des-Prés became synonymous with the fashionable aspects of *Existentialism.

SAINT-JOHN PERSE (pseud. of Alexis Saint-Léger Léger) (1887–1975). A poet-diplomat, like *Claudel and Neruda, Perse achieved the highest distinction in both careers, becoming by 1940 Secrétaire Général at the Quai d'Orsay, and thus head of French diplomacy in a critical period, and receiving the Nobel Prize for literature in 1960. History had brought bitter reverses in both spheres, however. Perse vigorously opposed appeasement throughout the 1930s and was summarily dismissed by the prime minister Paul Reynaud just prior to France's defeat in 1940. The Vichy government subsequently stripped him of his nationality, and he went into exile in the United States, where he was to remain until 1957. In the turmoil a considerable body of poetic writing was lost (he had refrained from publication for career reasons since 1925).

Enforced retirement and the experience of exile were none the less to be beneficial to the writer. Exile had always been an essential pole of Perse's experience, sharpening his responses to that other vital pole: the intense jubilation provoked by the physical and human worlds in all their rich and interpenetrating diversity. Born in Guadeloupe, Perse enjoyed a paradisical childhood celebrated in 'Pour fêter une enfance' (written 1907, incorporated in *Éloges*, 1911), but was transplanted to France at the age of 12, an experience of loss and exile he transposed brilliantly in the 'Images à Crusoë' (written 1904, also in *Éloges*).

The publication of *Anabase* in 1924 under a newly minted pseudonym brought 'Saint-John Perse' considerable admiration, quickly extended to the English-speaking world by T. S. Eliot's translation. Written while he was at the embassy in Peking, the poem inaugurates Perse's grand manner: epic sweep, sustained but subtly modulated grandiloquence, endless curiosity about human institutions and artefacts throughout space and time, impatience with the mediocre compromises of bourgeois civilization, predilection for restless movement (in this case that of a nomadic society which forms and then disbands a fixed settlement). The formal constituents characteristic of Perse's work are also in place: successive cantos consisting of a number of *laisses* (verse paragraphs) grouping the rhythmical but metrically unconstrained *versets* which are the principal building-blocks of Perse's poetry.

The four poems of *Exil* (1944)—'Exil', 'Pluies', 'Neiges', and 'Poème à l'étrangère'—written during the war, show the full fruition of the *verset*. Infinitely flexible, and able to integrate metrical units such as the octosyllable and the *alexandrine, this unit can vary from a few syllables to a dozen or more lines. It provides the ideal medium for Perse's favourite devices, which include anaphora and enumeration, elaborate sound patterning and syntactic parallelism, recourse to rare and specialized words, and consistent play on etymology and the multiple associations of particular words and expressions.

Thematically, Perse's poetry tends to celebrate elemental realities: *Vents* (1946), *Amers* (1957), *Chronique* (1960). However, its form and rhetoric allow for easy movement between the personal and the cosmic. Seeking to embrace phenomena in both their particularity and their relation to a totality, Perse looks to such formal exemplars as the Pindaric ode and gives his poetry a ritualized and hieratic aspect. But at the same time his fervent admiration for the great variety of human aspirations and achievements, lauded by both *Breton and Auden, keeps his poetry in the concrete. In his speech at the Nobel banquet in 1960 Perse accepted on behalf of poetry itself, noting, 'par son adhésion totale à ce qui est, le poète tient pour nous liaison avec la permanence de l'être'. He continued to write poetry well into his eighties, and apart from a few essays (including an important tribute to Dante) devoted himself exclusively to this form.   [MHTS]

See R. Caillois, *Poétique de Saint-John Perse* (1954); R. Little, *Études sur Saint-John Perse* (1984).

SAINT-JUST, Louis de (1767–94). Austere young Conventionnel whose denunciations of Louis XVI, then of the *Girondins, the *Hébertistes, *Danton, and Camille *Desmoulins, were so effective that he became known as 'the Angel of death'. He was equally gifted in other domains, playing, for example, decisive roles in the drafting of the Constitution de l'An II and in the debates on economic and military affairs. As a member of the Comité de Salut Public (30 May 1793) he aligned himself with *Robespierre and Couthon, and played a leading part in the final internecine struggles that sent all three to the guillotine on 10 Thermidor [see REVOLUTION, 1C].   [JR]

SAINT-LAMBERT, Jean-François, marquis de (1716–1803). A French soldier and aristocrat, he was a friend of *Voltaire (in spite of his affair with Madame *du Châtelet) and of the *philosophes. He was elected to the Académie Française in 1770. His writings include poems and moralizing stories (e.g. 'Les Deux Amis', 1770); he achieved success with Les Saisons (1769), a descriptive poem modelled on Thomson's Seasons. This worthy but somewhat tedious effort, inspired in part by *Physiocrat ideas, offers absentee landowners an idealized image of country life, as well as castigating abuses such as the corvée.   [PF]

SAINT-LAURENT, Cecil, pseudonym used by Jacques *Laurent.

Saint-Lazare, Prison de. Formerly a leper-house, this was administered as a hospital from 1632 by the Lazarists of *Vincent de Paul. It became a place of detention for young men of good family, and during the Revolution a prison. André *Chénier and *Roucher went to their death from here.

Saint-Loup, Robert de. Character in Proust's *A la recherche du temps perdu*, a friend of the narrator, nephew of the duchesse de Guermantes, and eventually husband of Gilberte Swann.

SAINT-MARC GIRARDIN (pseud. of Marc Girardin) (1801–73). Politician, professor, and influ-

ential literary critic writing for the *Journal des débats and the *Revue des deux mondes. An adversary of the Romantics, he was elected to the Académie Française in 1844. His major work was his Cours de littérature dramatique (1843–68).   [CC]

SAINT-MARTIN, Louis-Claude de (1743–1803). The 'philosophe inconnu' was part of the French *Illuminist movement, but stands out in it because of the beauty of his prose and because he rejected such materialist trappings as *Mesmerism, proposing instead a purely spiritual doctrine, whence his other sobriquet, the 'Luther of occultism'. His aesthetic theories prefigure *Romanticism. The poet is a seer possessed of a symbolic vision; poetry is a matter of content, not form; the prophetic nature of literature requires the presence of both honey and gall, the ugly as well as the beautiful. The holy person is a 'man of desire', yearning for the good and the absolute, and charged by God with creating that good and absolute in the spiritual realm and also here below. Humanity in its history can go beyond Christ in restoring the harmony of all creation. Among his major works are L'Homme de désir (1790), Le Ministère de l'homme-esprit (1802), and his posthumously published Mon portrait historique et autobiographique. He was much admired by Germaine de *Staël, *Guttinguer, and *Sainte-Beuve.   [FPB]

Saint-Maur, Congrégation de, see MAURISTS.

Saint-Médard, see PÂRIS.

SAINT-PAVIN, Denis Sanguin de (c.1595/1600–1670). Friend of *Théophile and *libertin poet, agile author of sonnets and other light but daring verse. Although reputedly an atheist, he enjoyed an ecclesiastical benefice.

SAINT-PIERRE, Bernardin de, see BERNARDIN DE SAINT-PIERRE.

SAINT-PIERRE, Charles-Irénée Castel, abbé de (1658–1743). French political reformer. An indefatigable student of science, philosophy, and politics, he was close to the centre of power during the *Regency, but was expelled from the Académie Française because of his subversive ideas. His many projects, on subjects including taxation, education, and spelling reform, were described as the 'rêves d'un homme de bien' by Cardinal Dubois and condemned as impractically Utopian by J.-J. *Rousseau, who wrote analytic summaries of them. In fact they contain much that is far-sighted. The famous Projet de paix perpétuelle (1713–17) anticipates 20th-c. plans for a federal Europe, and his Discours sur la polysynodie (1718) condemns *Louis XIV's regime of 'vizirs' (i.e. powerful ministers) and argues for a monarchy guided by the collective wisdom of elected councils. He is credited with introducing the word bienfaisance into French.   [PF]

SAINT-POL-ROUX (pseud. of Paul Roux) (1861–1940). French *Symbolist poet, friend of *Mallarmé. Between 1893 and 1907 he published three volumes of prose poems, *Les Reposoirs de la procession*. His verse play *La Dame à la faulx* (1899) is the best expression of his conviction that 'le Drame est l'expression capitale de la Poésie'. Having moved to Brittany in 1898, he withdrew more and more from the world of letters. The *Surrealists, however, hailed him as 'le Maître de l'image' and 'le seul authentique précurseur du mouvement dit moderne'. He continued to write, but much of his life's work was destroyed when his manor-house at Camaret was pillaged in 1940. [KRA]

Saint-Preux. Hero of Rousseau's *La *Nouvelle Héloïse*.

SAINT-RÉAL, César Vichard, known as abbé de (1639–92). Historian, novelist, and diplomat who represented the court of Turin. In his native Savoy he met *Mazarin's niece, Hortense Mancini, and travelled to London with her entourage. In his historical writing, notably *De l'usage de l'histoire* (1671), Saint-Réal contended that history's goal was not to record facts but to understand the motivations of those who shaped history. He helped create the historical novel with *Don Carlos* (1672) and *La Conjuration des Espagnols contre la république de Venise en 1618* (1674), which imagine the human factors behind historical events. All his production was criticized as a novelization of history. [JDeJ]

Saints, Lives of the, see HAGIOGRAPHY.

Saint-Sacrement, Compagnie du. This secret society, which existed from the late 1620s until around 1665, developed in part from dissatisfaction with the apparently slow pace of moral and ecclesiastical reform at the period. It was founded by the duc de Ventadour as a joint venture in Christian discipleship by lay and ordained members of the Church seeking to strengthen piety and charity. Notable members included *Vincent de Paul, *Bossuet, and the prince de *Conti. By 1659 there were 58 groups spread throughout France and maintaining links with Paris. There was a strong emphasis on almsgiving, and determined opposition to duelling. Operations needed by the poor were paid for. Prison visiting, the reclaiming of prostitutes, support for missionary work at home and abroad, and the hounding of Protestants were also essential activities. The character of the company changed considerably with the death of the Paris superior, Gaston de Renty, in 1649, and the withdrawal of *Oratorian support. Sectarian fanatics and pious busybodies came increasingly to the fore, and this 'cabale des dévots' aroused much opposition in the 1650s and 1660s. The company was against the theatre and kept Molière's *Tartuffe* off the Paris stage for five years. [JC]

SAINT-SAËNS, Camille (1835–1921). French composer, performer, and writer. Essentially a classicist with fairly conservative tastes, in his lifetime Saint-Saëns was perceived as representing the French classical spirit and was popular both in France and internationally. In 1871 he formed the Société Nationale de Musique which, with the motto *ars gallica*, encouraged the performance of new music by French composers, in particular orchestral and chamber music. Saint-Saëns was a prolific composer and also a writer, not only on music (e.g. his autobiography, *École buissonnière: notes et souvenirs*, 1913) but also on philosophy, theatre, and painting. He also wrote poetry and plays. [KM]

SAINT-SIMON, Claude-Henri de Rouvroy, comte de (1760–1825). French social thinker. Of a collateral branch of the family of the 17th-c. duke [see below], Saint-Simon fought in the American War of Independence. He made money during the Revolution by speculation, but experienced real poverty during much of his later life. His *Lettres d'un habitant de Genève* (1802–3) contain in germ many of his later ideas, but between 1802 and 1814 his mental health was not of the best. Under the Restoration he published extensively, often in periodicals, and only in his last days produced his two major works, *Opinions littéraires, philosophiques et industrielles* and *Le Nouveau Christianisme* (both 1825). Augustin *Thierry and later Auguste *Comte served as his secretaries.

Saint-Simon turned the triad of human faculties described by the anatomist Bichat (thought, action, feeling) into a triple categorization of men: scientists, industrialists-workers, and artists-priests. If at first he gave pre-eminence to the scientists, later he proposed that it was the artists who created social unity and initiated progress; the scientists evaluated and criticized, the worker-industrialists executed. Rejecting both egotism and egalitarianism, he proposed rather that all should be able to express their aptitudes to the fullest, thus increasing productivity. Nature, rather than fellow man, was to become the object of aggression and conquest. He read history as an alternation between synthetic (or organic) and particular (or analytic) phases, and thought that his theories would lead mankind to a new organic age based on the full realization of the eternal Christian moral principle of fraternity, all the while emphasizing the importance of technical progress and of governmental encouragement of science and indistry.

His disciples were known as Saint-Simonians, the more extreme of whom pursued a picturesque evolution. Led by Prosper (Père) Enfantin, they demanded the emancipation of women and the rehabilitation of matter and of the flesh, creating a new religion including an androgynous definition of God and a quest for the female Messiah, and forming a Utopian community at Ménilmontant [see FEMINISM, 2]. In 1832 they were tried for immorality, and successfully turned the trial into a major public event. In later years various members of the group, including Michel Chevalier, exercised considerable influence, and *Napoleon III shared many of their convictions.   [FPB]

SAINT-SIMON, Louis de Rouvroy, duc de (1675–1755). Author of the celebrated *Mémoires*. His father was one of Louis XIII's favourites, and had been made a duke in 1635: the son was brought up to cherish the old king's memory, and reverence for the values of the early 17th c. afforded him a perspective from which to view critically the political and social developments of his own lifetime. The young duke was physically small (generally known as 'notre petit duc') and consumed with the importance of his rank. He served briefly in the army, but resigned because he found talent prized above seniority or birth. Thereafter he divided his time between his country estate at La Ferté and the court, where high rank entitled him to be constantly in attendance though he never secured the positions of importance he felt his due.

Saint-Simon was one of the group including *Fénelon, Beauvilliers, and the duc de Chevreuse, whose covert opposition to the regime of *Louis XIV's declining years focused on the duc de Bourgogne, and whose hopes for restoring order and prosperity in France were dashed by the young dauphin's death in 1712. Characteristically, Saint-Simon committed these *Projets de gouvernement du duc de Bourgogne* to paper only after this event, doubtless partly with the ambition of guiding policy under the now inevitable *Regency. Indeed, after Louis XIV's death in 1715 the regent was prepared to listen, and his dramatic overturning of the provision made for Louis's illegitimate offspring in his will is applauded in the *Mémoires*; but the only formal task entrusted to Saint-Simon was a mission to Spain in 1722 to bring back the princess engaged to the young Louis XV. She did not in fact become queen; but the event was profoundly to affect the future publication of the *Mémoires*, since all Saint-Simon's papers were at his death classified as state documents, and many of them remain to this day in the archives of the Quai d'Orsay.

They show him to have had an obsessive love of documentation, amassing legal and historical evidence bearing on the issues of the day while he waited in vain for political office in the years after the regent's death (1723). Ever since 1694 he had been recording what he had himself seen at court. Late in 1729 he was given a manuscript copy of the journals of court life which *Dangeau had dictated from 1684 till his death in 1720. He had them interleaved with blank pages which, over nine years, he annotated from his own range of sources. After this period of immense preparation, he composed the *Mémoires* in the decade 1740 to 1750. He lost his beloved wife in 1743, his elder son in 1749, his younger son and sole heir in 1754, and he himself died in 1755.

Far, then, from being a spontaneous report on events in the last years of Louis XIV and the first of Louis XV, the *Mémoires* are a retrospective analysis, contemporary with *Montesquieu's *Esprit des lois*, of what went wrong with France during those years. But Saint-Simon was not a *philosophe*. His perspective is partly religious, and an austerely Augustinian sense of the vanity of human endeavour informs his sombrest reflections. Like a baroque dramatist, he evokes the dream-world of *Versailles against an implicit background of unseen realities and divine judgements. His preface returns to the question on which, as a young man, he had sought counsel from no less stern a spiritual authority than *Rancé: may a Christian write the history of his own times without offending against charity? The answer, namely that it is permissible if undertaken for the greater good, serves also to explain the political perspective of the *Mémoires*. The evils he recounts are those of disorder. Usurpation of God-given authority by low-born adventurers has distorted the primitive ancient constitution of the realm. The venomous critiques of Madame de *Maintenon's malign influence, the ambitions of the duc du *Maine, the manœuvres of Cardinal Dubois, are ultimately accusations of illegitimacy. Those rightfully entrusted with the governance of France (dukes above all) have been dispossessed by a kind of diabolical subterfuge.

If this ideology militates against scientific historical accuracy, it imbues the *Mémoires* with powerfully dramatic energy. Saint-Simon has been aptly described as standing half-way between Dante and *Balzac. He shares with the novelist a gift for physical depiction by means of details that imply a moral judgement, and also an urgent, persuasive, at times breathless narrative. What may appear to a modern reader the *longueurs* of his accounts of ceremonies and genealogies are a vital element in creating an almost cosmic context of hierarchy within which disruptive forces are discerned at work. With him the genre of the character-portrait, refined over a century of *moraliste* writing, reaches its peak. The freshness of these descriptions springs from their combination of formality with the unexpected, the commonplace, even the vulgar. His writing ranges from the stately to the highly idiosyncratic, neologism jostling with archaism in his vocabulary, and the persuasive crescendo with the occasionally baffling ellipsis in his phrasing.

*Proust was one of his most fervent readers. It was, indeed, only at the turn of the 20th c. that the complete text of the *Mémoires* appeared, after more than a century of state sequestration and partial publication. He seems himself to have envisaged publication delayed until well after his death. [PJB]

See Y. Coirault, *L'Optique de Saint-Simon* (1965); D. van der Cruysse, *Le Portrait dans les 'Mémoires' de Saint-Simon* (1971) and *La Mort dans les 'Mémoires' de Saint-Simon* (1981).

SAINT-SORLIN, Desmarets de, see DESMARETS DE SAINT-SORLIN.

Saison au Congo, Une, see CÉSAIRE, A.

Saison dans la vie d'Emmanuel, Une, see BLAIS.

Saison en enfer, Une, see RIMBAUD.

Saisons, Les, see SAINT-LAMBERT.

SALACROU, Armand (1899–1989). Playwright whose intellectual energy and restless formal experiments make him an important, if uneven, figure in 20th-c. French drama. His plays are strongly auto-biographical, rooted in the intellectual and political tendencies of his time, and reflect the tension between private and collective, spiritual and material. From early failures to later successes, he subverts realism by recourse to fantasy, dream-projections, time-shifts, and parody. So *L'Inconnue d'Arras* (1935) and *Sens interdit* (1953) play with time; *Histoire de rire* (1939) up-ends the drama of adultery; *Dieu le savait* (1950) questions God, and *Boulevard Durand* (1961) the capitalist order. [SBJ]

Salammbô. Historical novel by *Flaubert, a considerable commercial success on its publication in 1862. Set after the first Punic War, it deals with the revolt against Carthage of its unpaid mercenary army. Mâtho, their strangely passive Libyan leader, falls under the spell of Salammbô, daughter of Hamilcar. The fortunes of Carthage are superstitiously allied with the theft and return of its talisman, the veil of the goddess Tanit. Stolen by Mâtho and his companion, it becomes increasingly associated with Salammbô herself, who is sent to Mâtho's tent to retrieve it in exchange for her virginity, and who eventually dies 'pour avoir touché au manteau de Tanit'. This oblique love-affair, interwoven with mythical and symbolic elements (especially connecting Salammbô and Mâtho to the moon and the sun), is equally interwoven with detailed accounts of the cruelty of both warring parties, from the sacrifice of children to Moloch, to lingering crucifixions, to the horrible torture of Mâtho on the final page. Flaubert, who massively researched his sources, engaged in a vigorous debate with *Sainte-Beuve and Froehner over the accuracy of his historical and archaeological details. He seems to have wallowed in the very unfamiliarity of an alien civilization, and to have worked at producing an aesthetic effect of strangeness and distance. [DK]

Salavin. Hero, or anti-hero, of a cycle of novels by *Duhamel.

SALES, François de, see FRANÇOIS DE SALES.

SALL, Amadou Lamine (b. 1951), works in the Senegalese Ministry of Culture and is a fervent admirer of *Senghor's work. His own poetry is characterized by striking imagery (e.g. the title of his second collection, *Comme un iceberg en flammes,* 1982) reflecting his rejection of the world created by his elders and his determination to build a new social order based on love. 'Pas une nation n'a pris comme idéologie l'amour', he notes in his first work, *Mante des aurores* (1979), in which he expresses confidence in the power of love and of the new generation of poets to rebuild Africa. [FNC]

SALL, Ibrahima (b. 1949). The early poetry of this young Senegalese writer is characterized by his sense of rootlessness in the alienating world created by the previous generation. *La Génération spontanée* (1975) is a cry against corruption and compromise by one who seeks to reject all ideologies. Sall's collection of short stories, *Crépuscules invraisemblables* (1977), in which his anger at his society is tempered by humour, are among the best produced in the genre in francophone Africa. His novel *Les Routiers de chimères* (1982), short-listed for the *Noma Award, poetic rather than realistic, is bitter with the dashed hopes of Africa's youth. His play *La République* (1985) condemns the thirst for power of both conservative and self-proclaimed 'popular' leaders. [FNC]

SALLENAVE, Danièle (b. 1940). French literary theoretician and novelist. Her early works, beginning with *Paysages de ruines avec personnages* (1975), are formal experiments; the narrative organization of *Le Voyage d'Amsterdam* (1977) resembles a musical score. *Villes et villes* (1991) explores Rome, Leningrad, and Calcutta. *Adieu* (1988) evokes a brief period a young man spends with his elderly uncle. [EAF]

SALMON, André (1881–1969). Poet, novelist, and art critic. A very Parisian figure, Salmon is best remembered as an impresario and chronicler of the arts who did much to promote the 'vie d'artiste' in *Montparnasse and the merits of artists such as *Picasso and Modigliani who were among his familiars (see his *Souvenirs sans fin,* 3 vols., 1955–61). An eclectic and enthusiastic critic, he launched the review *Le Festin d'Ésope* with *Apollinaire and *Jacob in 1903. His intensely lyrical poetry, always tinged with nostalgia but often humorous and linguistically playful, is at its best in *Créances* (1926), *Carreaux* (1928), and *Les Étoiles dans l'encrier* (1952). Of his novels, the best is probably *Le Manuscrit trouvé dans un chapeau* (1919). [MHTS]

Salons. [For artistic Salons see ART CRITICISM.] The literary salon was not invented in 17th-c. France. A tradition of such gatherings had existed in Renaissance France and Italy. However, in Paris between 1610 and 1650 this tradition was redefined. The new assemblies multiplied and became so influential that, until shortly after the Revolution, the salons rivalled the official literary society, the *Académie Française, for control over the Republic of Letters.

The first true salon was created at the Hôtel de *Rambouillet by the woman known as 'la divine Arthénice'. The marquise de Rambouillet received her guests lying in bed; she seated them in the *ruelle*, the space between the bed and the wall. This term came to designate any salon assembly. (Salons were also referred to by the day of the week on which they met; 'the Saturday', for example, meant the weekly meeting presided over by Madeleine de *Scudéry.) In the marquise's bedroom, the *chambre bleue*, a group whose membership remained remarkably stable over long periods of time met regularly to discuss matters of literary and social taste. The Hôtel de Rambouillet is often credited with having invented the obsession with social refinement that became associated with the French court only much later, under *Louis XIV. The original *ruelle* also gave birth to a literary style, *preciosity, and to a type of literary woman, the *précieuse*, the principal model for women writers of the *ancien régime*.

The *chambre bleue* defined the French salon tradition in two important ways. First, these assemblies were always presided over by women, providing a rare example of a literary sphere under female control. Secondly, they gave conversation extraordinary new prominence. Because of the salons, the French tradition, alone among national traditions, has treated conversation as a fine art. Conversely, the conversational style—the blend of wit, elegance, and oral brilliance first concocted in the salons—has often been considered the essence of the French style. Historians have stressed that the salons were intrinsic to the definition and diffusion of French culture during what is often considered its golden age. Some contend that, without them, the period 1650–1789 would never have witnessed such glory. However, the salons' relation to French culture was always double: they were also influential critics of the society they nurtured and perfected.

The first wave of salon activity was abruptly ended by the outbreak of the *Fronde. During the Fronde, many noted salon figures became politically prominent by leading the opposition to the monarchy. After the uprising had been crushed the salons reopened and entered their most brilliant period, the decade before the reign of *classicism, during which France seemed totally captivated by the style they were promoting. But appearances were deceiving, for the salons would never again be the same: political agitation had become part of their mission. Not all salons were overtly political; in some cases the political content of their agitation is easily overlooked. However, their apparently parochial concerns often produced more significant results than did the traditional forms of opposition to France's social structure under the absolute monarchy.

Influential contemporary thinkers, notably *Vauban, promoted, to little avail, the notion that French society should be revitalized by introducing the notion of a meritocracy. The salons made possible the only important modifications in this direction. From the beginning, salon debate took up what are thought of today as women's issues—from a woman's right to refuse marriage to her freedom

to limit the number of children she bore. In particular, salon women, although they were almost always aristocrats, nevertheless consistently maintained that merit rather than birth should determine the choice of a husband. When important numbers of them put this belief into practice, members of the bourgeoisie gained legitimate entry into the aristocracy and a new type of self-made noble was created. The salons were widely attacked for having thus undermined social purity.

After the Fronde the salon tradition continued uninterrupted until the Revolution. Throughout its existence it remained remarkably faithful to the blend of wit and subversion created by the early salon women. This continuity is logical: the salons that functioned until the end of the 17th c. were organized by women, notably *Sablé and *La Sablière, who had come of intellectual age in the original assemblies. By the time they disappeared, those who would define the 18th c. salon tradition, in particular *Lambert and *Tencin, had already begun to hold court—and *their* inheritors, such as *Du Deffand, were waiting in the wings.

Following the model of the 17th-c. Cartesian salons, certain 18th-c. assemblies were dominated by philosophical discussion; others were principally concerned with scientific debate, a phenomenon already present in some *ruelles*. However, in the age of Enlightenment all debate—whether political, philosophical, or scientific—became increasingly bold, as the *philosophes* who frequented salons, and in particular *Geoffrin's assembly, made their intellectual activity virtually synonymous with political ferment. The assemblies presided over by *Lespinasse and Suzanne *Necker Curchod are typical of the final incarnation of true French salons, in which the assemblies became centres of political unrest.

The salons declined in importance once the Revolution had eliminated the *ancien régime*, with which they had consistently entertained a relation simultaneously complicitous and subversive. Literary assemblies continued to function in the 19th and 20th c., but even their founders, Sophie *Gay for example, admitted that they never recreated the flavour of their pre-Revolutionary forerunners. In particular, women, even those who led salons, played secondary roles in post-Revolutionary assemblies: they no longer dictated the essence of French style.

Commentators have too often based their eulogies as well as their mockeries on the superficial aspects of salon activity such as linguistic affectation or fashion fads. However, unless we also remember how dramatically the salons brought about political, social, and literary change, we will never understand why powerful men found them threatening, or why powerful women first kept them going and then tried for generations to bring them back to life. [See FEMINISM; WOMEN WRITERS.]　　　[JDeJ]

See R. Picard, *Les Salons littéraires et la société*

française (1943); C. Lougee, *Le Paradis des Femmes: Women, Salons, and Social Stratification in 17th-Century France* (1976).

Salons, Les. Name given to the accounts by *Diderot of the biennial exhibitions of the *Académie Royale de Peinture et de Sculpture (there are also *Salons* by *Baudelaire and others). They are generally regarded as the beginning of art criticism in France. Diderot composed nine *Salons* between 1759 and 1781; writing for the subscribers to the *Correspondance littéraire*, he describes the works in detail, as well as discussing their value and his sometimes contradictory attitudes towards them.

His initial approach was literary, and he never ceased to value the 'sublime' theatrical element in a *Greuze or a *Vernet, particularly when it served an edifying purpose, but over the years, by frequenting artists, he acquired a genuine understanding of the painterly side of art. His artistic theory, which he spells out in the *Essais sur la peinture* (1766), is founded on the classical doctrine of the imitation of nature, which he interprets in a way hostile to academic art. He prizes the realism of *Chardin, but is also aware that 'le soleil du peintre n'est pas celui de l'univers'.

The *Salons*, in particular those of 1765 and 1767, are among Diderot's most attractive and personal works; he writes with great freedom, engaging the artists and his readers in imaginary dialogues, entering into the world of the paintings, and bringing out the unity of art and life. [For an account of the development of the Salons and the resulting critical writing see ART CRITICISM.]   [PF]

Salpêtrière, La. Impressive hospital in south-east Paris, built in the mid-17th c. on the site of a former saltpetre works. In the 18th c. it served as a place of confinement for vagrants, prostitutes, mad people, and others (described as 'le grand renfermement' in *Foucault's *Histoire de la folie*). One part of it, La Force, housed political prisoners during the *Revolution and was the scene of terrible massacres in September 1792.

Salut Galarneau!, see GODBOUT.

SAMAIN, Albert (1858–1900). The acclaim which greeted the publication in 1893 of *Au jardin de l'Infante* made Samain one of the most popular French poets of the late 19th c. Heavily influenced by *Baudelaire, *Verlaine, and *Poe, his lyrical poetry expresses in a minor key some of the essential elements of *fin-de-siècle* sensibility: the nostalgic melancholy and fleeting sensations characteristic of the *Decadence, but without its lurid eroticism; the musical and mystical tendencies of the *Symbolist aesthetic, but without its metaphysical ambition. Subsequent volumes (*Aux flancs de vase*, 1898, and *Contes*, 1902) reiterate the tone of delicate and refined langour related in no small measure to his permanently fragile health.   [JK]

SAM LONG, Jean-François (b. 1949). Writer from Reunion. A major promoter and editor of *réunionnais* writing, Sam Long has also produced a number of collections of poetry and prose writings of various lengths, including a novel, *Le Bassin du diable* (1977).   [BEJ]

SAN ANTONIO. Pen-name of Frédéric *Dard, and the name of the narrator-hero of his numerous novelettes.

SAND, George (1804–76). Pen-name of Aurore Dupin, baronne Dudevant, a prolific and important author. Her father, a military officer, died in 1808 and Aurore, the subject of some contention between mother and grandmother, was brought up in large part by the latter at Nohant, in Berry, where she spent much of her later life and about which she often wrote. For some years a boarder at an Augustinian convent, she was an unruly pupil, but also knew moments of intense mysticism. In 1822 she married Casimir Dudevant by whom she had her son Maurice; the marriage was not a happy one and led to a much-contested separation. She had a series of lovers, including Jules *Sandeau, *Musset, the leftist lawyer Michel de Bourges, and Chopin (for nine years). The relationships were often tumultuous and are reflected in both her writings and those of others, including her lovers. She was also a close friend of *Flaubert, who wrote 'Un cœur simple' in her honour.

Politically to the Left, especially in the late 1830s and 1840s, she was active in the Revolution of 1848, writing extensively on political matters, but after *Napoleon III's *coup d'état* of 1851 she largely withdrew from politics. Though she used a male pseudonym and often dressed as a man, she was in her way a feminist, sharply critical of the inequities of marriage as defined by the Napoleonic Code and of the inferior education and status given to women [see WOMEN WRITERS]. She refused, however, to stand for election to parliament in 1848 or to seek election to the Académie Française.

Her many works include novels, short stories, plays, travel literature, and autobiographical writings, as well as political literature and an extremely rich correspondence. She began by collaborating with others, notably Sandeau (it was at this time that she began to use her pseudonym). *Indiana* (1832), her first solo novel, a study of the fate of women in marriage, was an immediate success, as was *Valentine* (1832), which explores a problem she often treats, that of love or friendship among people of different classes. *Lélia* (1833), with a rather complicated and melodramatic plot, describes the *mal du siècle* as experienced by a heroine. Sand here broke with the tradition of the woman's novel as being primarily about love and joined Madame de *Staël in making it a vehicle for philosophical, religious, and political concerns. A second version (1839) ends more happily. *Jacques* (1834), an epistolary novel,

739

deals with the triangle of older husband–young wife–lover, and with suicide, and reflects her troubled relation with Musset. *Mauprat* (1837) recounts the transformation of the hero by his love for the heroine; it is the first of her novels to be situated in her native Berry.

Her writings of the following decade are much marked by her political preoccupations and by the influence of leftist intellectuals such as *Lamennais and Pierre *Leroux. *Spiridion* (1838–9) recounts a spiritual quest for a new religion and discusses the relation between religious and political progress. *Les Sept Cordes de la lyre* (1840), a closet drama in the mode of Goethe's *Faust*, adds to these problems various meditations on the nature of art, music, and inspiration, and on the role of woman in creating progress. *Le Compagnon du tour de France* (1840) presents these same preoccupations as experienced by the politically conscious workers of the period, and provides interesting insight into workers' organizations at the time. *Le Meunier d'Angibault* (1845), with a more plausible plot, depicts peasant life and ends with the proposed foundation of a Utopian community. Her most important novel of this period was *Consuelo*, with its sequel *La Comtesse de Rudolstadt*, partly inspired by the Hussite movement which she also analysed in two historical works, *Jean Zyska* and *Procope le Grand* (1842). All these works are deeply marked by her hopes for a spiritual and political renewal which would usher in the Joachimist third age; they are among the most important texts revealing the Romantic aspiration for Utopia. Later in life she would see in liberal Protestantism an acceptable form of that new religion; *Mademoiselle La Quintinie* (1863) examines this hope.

Already before the failure of the Revolution of 1848, however, she began producing those 'rustic novels' for which she was best known and appreciated by a broad public. *Jeanne* (1843) is a transposition of the story of *Jeanne d'Arc in the form of a saintly peasant girl coveted by various men, a highly successful combination of the rustic tradition and metaphysical and social concerns. *La *Mare au diable* (1846), *La Petite Fadette* (1848), dealing with superstition and love, *François le Champi* (1848), and *Les Maîtres sonneurs* (1853) continue in this vein; the last also provides meditations on the meaning of music and of initiation. As portraits of rustic life these novels often possess real anthropological value for the information they provide on folk tradition and folklore. But they are also governed by Sand's concerns with social equality and progress, with the love of justice and the constraining powers of convention, and with the relations between reason and sentiment.

Sand also wrote extensively for the theatre. If *Les Sept Cordes de la lyre* was not meant to be staged, *Cosima* was performed in 1840 and was followed by a number of other plays. Some of these are highly innovative in form. She also produced a considerable body of travel and autobiographical literature,

including the *Lettres d'un voyageur* (1837), mostly set in Italy but also describing her personal tribulations, and *Un hiver à Majorque* (1841). *Histoire de ma vie* (1854) is her lengthiest and most ambitious autobiographical work, including remarkable evocations of her childhood, her convent life, her early career as a writer, and reflections on the political events both of her past and of the time of writing. *Elle et lui* (1858) is a highly autobiographical novel about her relation with Musset. In her last years she wrote her *Contes d'une grand-mère* (1872–6), which rehearse in a more fantasized mode her lifelong preoccupation with forming character and meaningful relations despite the restrictions of social conformity and false beliefs.

Often disparaged by such contemporaries as *Baudelaire, Sand remains the major woman writer of French Romanticism and someone who renewed literature by her successful melding in innovative forms of the autobiographical, the amorous, and the pastoral tradition with political, moral, and philosophical concerns. Like *Hugo, she managed to write simultaneously for a wide public and for an intellectual élite, to combine visionary aspirations with a sharp sense of contemporary reality and its shortcomings, to blend realism and the poetic. [FPB]

See P. Salomon, *George Sand* (1984); D. Powell, *George Sand* (1990).

SANDEAU, Jules (1811–83). French novelist, who collaborated with *Sand (*Rose et Blanche*, 1831), with *Augier, and with *Houssaye (*Milla*, 1843, a study of the nefarious effects of reading novels). His own novels praise bourgeois values as opposed to the ravages of passion or indeed the pretensions of nobility. [FPB]

SANDRAS DE COURTILZ, see COURTILZ DE SANDRAS.

Sang des autres, Le, see BEAUVOIR.

SANGNIER, Marc (1873–1950). Generally recognized as the founder of Christian Democracy in France, Sangnier, from 1902 to 1910, presided over the *Sillon movement, which attracted numerous intellectuals. A newspaper and review editor, he was also a Catholic *député* from 1919 to 1924 and in the 1946 Assembly, and the founder, in 1929, of the French youth-hostel movement. [NH]

Sang noir, Le (1935). Novel by *Guilloux about one day in the life of a provincial town and of Cripure, an agonized *lycée* philosophy teacher. The brutal impact of 1917 carnage and mutinies interacts with his private neurosis. The title refers to the black bile of melancholy (ambiguous, for it also foments creativity), asphyxia, and the stain of Cripure's suicide. Though alert to the local *notables'* impostures, Cripure will not rebel. His febrile mental activity, betokened by his proliferating 'Chrestomathy of Despair', is spent more on self-laceration over his cautious compromises (weak-willed love, *petit-bour-geois* investments) than on social critique. Against the absurdity of existence, he chooses the absurdist and self-defeating strategy of accentuating its deri-siveness. Cripure has outsize feet and a rampant persecution-complex. His one clear action, the slap-ping of a noxious colleague for insulting common soldiers, is adventitious rather than truly willed. When the expected duel fails to materialize, Cripure shoots himself. This dubious hero, lucid but impo-tent, is surrounded by a rich cast of eccentric, obnoxious, or idealistic characters. *Le Sang noir* houses nightmare visions *à la* Poe. This highly the-atrical, baroque, and powerful text, drenched in lit-erary allusions (German and Russian, as well as French) is a distinguished pathfinder for Sartre's *La *Nausée.* [WDR]

Sans-culottes. Name given from 1791 or 1792 to the more committed partisans of the *Revolution, who wore trousers of coarse fabric rather than the aristo-cratic *culotte* (breeches). At first used mockingly, the name was adopted enthusiastically, the radical *sans-culotte* being contrasted with the conservative bour-geois. A *sans-culottide* was an extra day in the Revolutionary *calendar.

Sanseverina, La. Gina, the aunt of Fabrice del Dongo in *La *Chartreuse de Parme,* becomes duchesse de Sanseverina through a cynically arranged marriage. Passionate and energetic, she is one of Stendhal's greatest female characters.

Sans famille, see MALOT.

Sapho. Name under which Madeleine de *Scudéry was often known [see ARTAMÈNE].

SARASIN, Jean-François (1614–54). French salon poet whose multiple experiments with new or out-moded forms were an inadequate outlet for his undoubted talent. He is best remembered for his subtle 'Galanterie' to a lady nicknamed 'la souris', his ingenious gloss on *Benserade's 'Sonnet de Job', or the witty 'Pompe funèbre de *Voiture', whose original mixture of prose and verse was to be much imitated. And yet his output also contains odes writ-ten in the style of *Malherbe, eclogues with evoca-tive echoes of Virgil, and some serious works of historiography. His work was collected together and published posthumously by his friends *Pellisson and *Ménage. [GJM]

SARCEY, Francisque (1827–99). French journalist, lecturer, and influential drama critic of Le *Temps from 1867. His often witty writings display a scepti-cal, conservative view of literature.

SARDOU, Victorien (1831–1908). Highly successful French dramatist, a brilliant manipulator of empty but complicated plots and spectacular theatrical effects. Inheritor and perfecter of *Scribe's 'well-made play', he invented cardboard characters ide-ally suited to be animated by the personalities of stars like *Bernhardt. Several of his comedies of manners show charm and a light touch, but the melodramas and historical plays are merely sumptu-ously dressed machines for producing *coups de théâtre.* Such are *Fédora* and *Théodora* (1882 and 1884), both preposterous dramas involving royalty and their lovers; *Tosca* (1887), used by Puccini for his opera; and *Madame Sans-Gêne* (1893), featuring a laundress who marries a Napoleonic marshal. [SBJ]

Sarrasine. Short story by *Balzac, first published in November 1830, dealing with indeterminate sexual-ity in 18th-c. Rome and the origins of a wealthy Parisian household. The complexity of Balzac's nar-ration of a story touching on a theme considered improper in his time, the theme itself, and the description of a painting as part of the narrative, have made *Sarrasine* a much-studied text in the 20th c., notably in *Barthes's *S/Z* (1970). [DMB]

SARRAUTE, Nathalie (b. 1902). Russian-born French writer, author of eight novels, six plays, and an autobiography. Her reputation derives mainly from her being a founding member of the *Nouveau Roman group in the mid-1950s—although she started writing much earlier, and since the 1970s has pursued an increasingly independent, if still very consistent, course.

Her first publication, a collection of short texts, is entitled *Tropismes* (1939), and the 'tropism' has remained her central concern. The term, taken from biology, is adapted to denote a level of psycho-logical activity that Sarraute sees as fundamental to our subjective existence: the movements of attrac-tion and repulsion, attack and defence, approach and retreat that constitute our relations with others in a pre-verbal arena which normally escapes our full conscious attention. Individual differences between people cease to exist here; subjects merge in a generalized, amorphous psychical 'material', continuously engaged in tropistic interaction. This essentially non-verbal process is conveyed in the texts through a repertoire of distinctive imagery ranging from the nauseous (bursting abcesses, coil-ing tentacles, oozing fluids) to the paranoid (secret police, espionage, religious fanaticism). Speech, con-versely, is dominated by the cliché; conversation, in all Sarraute's fiction, is the inauthentic, conven-tional surface which, treacherously, both conceals and acts out the psychological warfare of the tro-pisms.

This vision of inter-subjective conflict is not dis-similar to *Sartre's; and he provided a laudatory preface for Sarraute's first novel, *Portrait d'un inconnu* (though later revising his opinion of her). *Portrait's* anxious excavation of the bland surfaces of social discourse is continued in *Martereau* (1953), where another first-person narrator explores, through a mixture of analysis and imaginary reconstruction, a nexus of relationships. He, however, is more substantially involved in it than was the narrator of *Portrait*; and this move away from a 'spectator' position reaches its logical conclusion in *Le *Planétarium* (1959) where there is no narrator at all. All Sarraute's subsequent novels are characterized by a disconcertingly mobile narrative point of view: the reader has to shift constantly and rapidly from one centre of consciousness to another. Also, the theme of literature itself, already introduced in *Le Planétarium*, becomes central to *Les Fruits d'or* (1963) which, satirically undermining the platitudes and the one-upmanship of literary critics, poses the whole question of aesthetic values. *Entre la vie et la mort* (1968) focuses on the creative process itself, as the writer struggles to find words that will sustain rather than destroy the 'living', nameless sensation or impulse that brings the text into being. *Vous les entendez?* marks another new development, in that the boundary between conversation and the 'sub-conversation' of the tropisms has been erased; it is now impossible to distinguish between real and imaginary, literal and figurative dialogues. The title itself, however, illustrates the permanence of another of Sarraute's techniques: a fragment of speech acts as a recurrent leitmotif and a focus of investigation for the whole text—as is also the case in *'disent les imbéciles'* (1976), in *L'Usage de la parole* (1980), where Sarraute reverts to the structure of her first book by producing a collection of short separate pieces, and in *Tu ne t'aimes pas* (1989).

Her dramatic writing has attracted less critical attention but is closely connected to the novels; the same anonymous psychological movements are conveyed here solely through the medium of a directly verbalized sub-conversation. She started writing plays—at first for the radio and then the theatre—in the 1960s, and published a collected edition of them in 1978: *Le Silence, Le Mensonge, Isma ou Ce qui s'appelle rien, C'est beau,* and *Elle est là*. These were followed by *Pour un oui ou pour un non* in 1982.

Equally, Sarraute has produced a considerable body of theoretical and critical writing. Early articles appeared in Sartre's journal *Les *Temps modernes*, but with the publication in 1956 of *L'Ère du soupçon*, seen with some justification as the first manifesto of the Nouveau Roman, her ideas reached a wider audience. She traces the evolution of the modern novel away from the traditional fictional character—a deceptively solid agglomerate of oversimplified emotions—towards a new psychological realism in which the reader is immersed in a swirling mass of indefinable tropistic interactions. (The Nouveau Roman as a whole, however, was less committed to the psychological.) Sarraute's most popular recent text is the autobiographical *Enfance* (1983), which consists of fragmentary memories of her childhood whose authenticity is constantly scrutinized by a sceptical *alter ego*. Here, as always, the struggle against the distorting power of clichés and the determination to express the true quality of individual experience are of paramount importance. [CB]

See A. S. Newman, *Une poésie du discours: essai sur les romans de Nathalie Sarraute* (1976); V. Minogue, *Nathalie Sarraute and the War of the Words* (1981).

SARRAZIN, Albertine (1937–67). Novelist. A foundling child, born in Algiers and adopted by French parents, she had a troubled early life which led her into teenage rebellion and delinquency, followed by a series of prison sentences, mostly for theft. Her talent for writing was already evident as a schoolgirl, and her diary as a young runaway was published without her knowledge in the magazine *Le Surréalisme* in 1954. She met Julien Sarrazin, whom she later married, in the circumstances related in *L'Astragale* (1965), her first and most successful autobiographical novel, which she described as a 'love poem' and which narrates her flight from prison with clarity and immediacy. Albertine Sarrazin spent a total of nine years in prison, with some gaps, followed by two years of literary celebrity before her early death, the result of an operation that went wrong. Her second novel, *La Cavale* (1965 but written earlier), is longer and more discursive than *L'Astragale*; it is a compelling and disturbing account of life in women's prisons and planned escapes. Her third novel, *La Traversière* (1966), is about *not* being in prison, a subject she found harder to handle. After her death several writings were published posthumously, including *Lettres à Julien* (1971) and *Journal de prison* (1972). Her voice is at once youthful and disillusioned, her extraordinary and isolated life history reflected in a poignant body of work oddly unrelated to the mainstream literature of the time, a marginal experience expressed in a mixture of vernacular and classical styles. [SR]

SARTRE, Jean-Paul (1905–80). Best known as a philosopher, Sartre was also a novelist, dramatist, critic, moralist, and biographer. He contributed to aesthetic theory, *psychoanalysis, politics, *phenomenology, and *Marxism. Within this immense diversity, a unity of purpose can none the less be detected: Sartre's central focus is the relationship between liberty and situation, his aim to reconcile a radical view of human freedom with a recognition of human limitations and facticity and the constraints of the world. The works which reveal the most concerted attempt to synthesize an *Existentialist conception of liberty with a Marxist theory of conditioning are the *Critique de la raison dialectique* (1960) and *L'Idiot de la famille* (1971–2), but the preoccupation is present in Sartre's writing from the outset.

He was born in Paris, where he spent most of his life apart from a few years in Meudon and La Rochelle as a child, and in Le Havre as a philosophy teacher in a *lycée* in the early 1930s. He attended the *École Normale Supérieure from 1924–9, where he failed the *agrégation* in 1928, and then took first place the following year; at this time he met his lifelong partner, Simone de *Beauvoir, and formed a close friendship with Paul *Nizan. In 1933 he went to Berlin to study phenomenology. The late 1930s constitutes the first phase of Sartre's philosophical career, in which a phenomenological and existential orientation is evident, but during which Sartre still defines himself in a fairly academic way in relation to the philosophers.

La Transcendance de l'Ego (1936) argues against Husserl that the self is not an inner core of character, source of our actions, feelings, and beliefs, but rather a synthesis or construct which we falsely imagine to be such a core. Similarly, the historical study *L'Imagination* (1936) and the later, more creative *L'Imaginaire* (1940) criticize previous theories of imagination on the grounds that they hold an erroneous view of the image as something immanent to consciousness. In Sartre's view, imagination is rather a relation, one of the modes in which consciousness relates to something outside itself. His *Esquisse d'une théorie des émotions* (1939) carries out an analogous demystification of the emotions, arguing that they are, on a deep level, chosen reactions to situations which are difficult to deal with rationally, quasi-'magical' retreats from problematic areas of experience, rather than themselves being the source of the feelings which accompany them. The phenomenological, existentialist novel *La *Nausée* (1939), which explores its hero's reactions to the realization of the contingency and absurdity of the world, is the chief literary work of this period, together with the remarkable collection of stories and novellas published in 1939 under the title *Le Mur*.

In 1939, Sartre was conscripted into the army in Nancy, where he kept the diary later published as *Carnets de la drôle de guerre* (1983), and was subsequently taken prisoner, escaping in 1941. Whilst a soldier and later a captive he worked on *L'Âge de raison*, the first volume of the unfinished trilogy set in wartime France, *Les *Chemins de la liberté*. He also composed and directed *Bariona*, a nativity play which, like the later and better-known *Les Mouches* (1943, a reworking of the Electra story), used a mythical drama to communicate a politics of resistance in a form sufficiently far from contemporary events to evade German censorship. He also spent some time during this period working on his best-known philosophical text *L'*Être et le néant* (1943), which explores the relationship of consciousness to the world and to other consciousnesses. But although Sartre takes over in it the Hegelian model of human relations as conflictual, rather than espousing the more positive Heideggerian notion of *Mitsein* (being-with-others), he does not explore the moral consequences of his position. He reserves these for a later work on ethics, never to be published in his lifetime.

L'Être et le néant is descriptive rather than committed: Sartre later declared that it was the experience of war that had led him to political commitment. Certainly, after his escape he took some part in the French Resistance [see OCCUPATION AND RESISTANCE], and in the post-war period he participated in founding the Rassemblement Démocratique Révolutionnaire, a radical left-wing alternative to the Communist Party. In 1945 he founded the journal *Les *Temps modernes* at the same time as publishing the play *Huis clos* (produced 1944, the famous portrayal of three characters fated to remain together for ever after death in a Second Empire salon, unable to escape from each other's gaze, source of the much misinterpreted slogan: 'L'Enfer, c'est les autres'). *Les Chemins de la liberté* (1945–9) and *L'Existentialisme est un humanisme* (1946, a public lecture in which Sartre attempted to draw more positive, quasi-Kantian ethical consequences from the basic tenets of Existentialism) also appeared in the years immediately following the war. The same fertile period saw the performance of the plays *Morts sans sépulture* (1946), *La Putain respectueuse* (1946), and *Les *Mains sales* (1947), and the publication of the screenplays *Les Jeux sont faits* (1947) and *L'Engrenage* (1948) and of the essays *Réflexions sur la question juive* (1947), *Qu'est-ce que la littérature?* (1947, see ENGAGEMENT), and *Baudelaire* (1947), together with the first of the mainly political essays published over a number of years in 10 volumes as *Situations* (1947–76).

In 1951 *Le *Diable et le Bon Dieu* and *Saint Genet, comédien et martyr* were published. Both are concerned to attack notions of moral absolutes in favour of a human, situational, relativist ethics; it was on these grounds that in the same year Sartre finally broke with his formerly close associate, Albert *Camus. *Saint Genet* gives a full-scale existential analysis of the novelist and poet Jean *Genet, in terms which relate his life as thief and homosexual to his internalization of the hostile judgements passed on him by others in his childhood and adolescence in a foster-home and later a reformatory. Sartre describes Genet as setting a trap for the bourgeois reader through the evocative and seductive lyricism of evil. Ultimately, however, he turns the tables on Genet by interpreting this trap in terms of its paradoxical moral utility to the reader, who is forced to imagine from the inside the life and experience of a social and moral outcast. Genet is reported to have been so traumatized by reading this lengthy psychoanalysis of his works that he abandoned writing for several years. For the rest of the 1950s Sartre's activities were primarily political, and in particular concerned with trying to ease relations between Western Europe and the USSR. This attempt came to an abrupt end in 1956 with the Soviet invasion of Hungary. Sartre then turned his attention to the question of French relations with Algeria, in particular the violation of human rights. This preoccupation was given dramatic form in *Les *Séquestrés d'Altona* (1959), which generalizes the ethical problems of torture by situating the action in post-war Germany, whilst calling the major protagonist Frantz.

In 1960 Sartre also published his second major philosophical work, the *Critique de la raison dialectique*, a 700-page attempt to reconcile Existentialism and Marxism. The radical philosophy of freedom was finally to earn its historical-materialist credentials through its insertion into an equally radical theory of social and historical conditioning. Sartre also attempted to save Marxism from what he saw as its current sclerosis by rejuvenating it, taking it back to the more complex and subtle of Marx's own ideas, and freeing it from the naïvely causal theories of determinism in which it had become entrenched. It is here that he proposes his theory of totalization as a necessary but impossible goal: the unrealizable dream of the *Critique* is to transcend inevitable human heterogeneity and found a total historical truth. It is symptomatic that the *practice* of such a totalizing project was destined to remain (in Volume II, posthumously published in 1985) in the form of unfinished notes.

Apart from the beautifully written, brief, allusive, and tantalizing autobiography of his early years, *Les Mots* (1966), the 1960s start and end with politics for Sartre. After the *Critique* came the publication of several volumes of essays in *Situations*, of primarily political rather than literary criticism. The decade ends with his support of the student movement in *May 1968, and with his taking over the editorship of the Maoist journal *La Cause du peuple*. But Sartre did not see his increased politicization as incompatible with very different kinds of writing, and he defended *L'Idiot de la famille* (1971–2), a mammoth 3,000-page biography of *Flaubert, as a politically committed text, despite its apparently aesthetic subject-matter, on the grounds that its dialectical methodology and epistemology were themselves revolutionary. In the 1970s Sartre's health deteriorated, his eyesight failed, and he turned to taped discussions as an alternative to writing, using his public prestige to intervene in a wide variety of political issues, particularly the Arab–Israeli question. He died on 15 April 1980 of oedema of the lungs, and was buried in Montparnasse cemetery attended by a huge funeral procession.

Sartre's influence on the social, moral, and political issues of his day was indisputable and was generally positive in its consequences, even if unpopular with the authorities of Church and State. His literary works are varied and innovative. Paradoxically, it is in the domain where his originality and creativity were greatest that his fortunes have been at their lowest ebb: that of philosophy. *Structuralism in the 1960s, deconstruction [see DERRIDA], and *Post-Structuralism in the 1970s and 1980s owed an immense debt to him as one of the first thinkers in France to draw the full consequences from the instability of meaning (in art as in philosophy), the human multiplicity of truths, and the important lessons to be learnt from a renewed Marxism. But in their desire to claim originality these currents of thought preferred parricide to acknowledgement of affinities or influences. A decade after Sartre's death the shadow began to lift, and his philosophical works are once more starting to be treated with the seriousness they deserve. [CMH]

See P. Caws, *Sartre* (1979); R. Aronson, *J.-P. Sartre: Philosophy in the World* (1980); R. Goldthorpe, *Sartre: Literature and Theory* (1984); C. Howells, *Sartre: The Necessity of Freedom* (1988).

SASSINE, Williams (b. 1944). Writer born in eastern Guinea of a Lebanese father and a Guinean mother. He had begun his studies at the Institut Polytechnique in Conakry when in 1963, at the age of 19, he was exiled by the brutal regime of Sékou Touré. He left Guinea for Paris, where he pursued studies in mathematics. In 1966 he became a teacher and has since worked in a number of African towns: Agboville, Abidjan, Monrovia, Freetown, Bamako, Niamey, and Libreville. He briefly returned to Guinea in 1985 after the death of Sékou Touré, but did not settle.

Sassine belongs to the generation of writers who sought, in the aftermath of colonial rule, to focus attention on an Africa left to its own devices. He thus aims to foreground African problems and African solutions, without necessarily referring to a white man's perspective. His first novel, *Saint-Monsieur Baly* (1973), is the tale of a retired schoolteacher who attempts to set up a school for pupils who have been rejected by the state system. As in the later novels, *Wirriyamu* (1976), which describes the destruction of an Angolan village by Portuguese troops, and *Le Jeune Homme de sable* (1979), where the narrative is filtered through the consciousness of a politically dissident adolescent, elements of a Utopian vision are presented in the context of an often nightmarishly hostile environment.

One of the recurring preoccupations of Sassine's work is the portrayal of alienated, marginalized members of communities and their efforts to achieve some form of integration. There is also a constant recourse to images of decay, putrefaction, and sickness which has clearly symbolic relevance. After writing a children's book, *L'Alphabête*, in 1982, he completed a fourth novel, *Le Zéhéros n'est pas n'importe qui* (1985), recounting the return of an exile to post-Touré Guinea in grotesquely comic, almost Ubuesque, terms.

In spite of the predominance of such apparently negative themes and images, there is an optimism and a faith in the future discernible in all of Sassine's work. He is never sectarian in his analyses of the social, political, and metaphysical struggles which his fictions present. Rather, he manages to combine lucidity and dispassionate rigour with an austerely poetic style. He is a man with few pretensions who studiously avoids being categorized as an intellectual. He prefers to refer to himself as a 'conteur' rather than an 'ecrivain'. [MPC]

Satire

SATIE, Erik (1866–1925). French composer, whose short, witty works experiment with dissonance and the mingling of styles in an innovatory way which influenced many composers, including Les *Six. *Cocteau, with whom he collaborated on the ballet *Parade* (1917), wrote a number of pieces about him.

Satire. A Protean term, satire can be understood as a particular genre with formal characteristics, or as an element or spirit that is present in works of many kinds.

In its restricted definition it means a discourse, usually in verse, mocking or condemning the follies of human beings and the abuses of society. It was present in the Middle Ages, in such forms as the *dit, but the term 'satire' was not then in use. Du Bellay in his *Défense et illustration called for satire on the classical model in place of the medieval *coq-à-l'âne. *Ronsard in his Discours provided a model of indignant verse in the Juvenalian mode, which is echoed in much of d'*Aubigné's Tragiques; similar denunciations of vice are found in the work of the Normandy satirists, *Auvray, *Angot de l'Éperonnière, *Sonnet de Courval, and *Du Lorens.

A more light-hearted vein can be traced from Ronsard's folastries and from the Italian Berni to poems of grotesque, often abusive description, where the interest is less in morality than in the pleasure of the game, e.g. the inventive, obscene verse of *Sigogne and *Motin. The serious and the playful coexist in the satires of *Régnier, who established the classic form, written in alexandrines, which *Boileau's much imitated Satires were to consecrate. Here the influence of Horace prevails over that of Juvenal. Boileau's prefaces and poems contain many defences of the genre, which was often condemned as low, particularly when, like Boileau, the satirist named names. In spite of such criticism (see *Voltaire's Mémoire sur la satire, 1739), satires full of abuse continued to be written throughout the 18th c., not least by Voltaire himself. *Gilbert's notorious Le Dix-Huitième Siècle was a model for polemic verse of all tendencies during the Revolutionary period, but the greatest satire of the time was the fierce and formally innovative Iambes of André *Chénier.

The same title, Iambes, was used in the next century by Auguste *Barbier, for his poems about the Revolution of 1830. In general, however, formal verse satire declined in importance in the 19th c. *Béranger's songs pick up a different tradition, that of the political *popular song, which had flourished in times of trouble such as the *Fronde and the Revolution. Hugo's Les *Châtiments are not, for the most part, satires as described above, but in every other sense are a summit in French satirical writing.

A different type of satire is derived from the Latin word satura, meaning a medley or hotchpotch. Such satires are characteristically in prose, or a mixture of prose and verse, and are often just as fiercely committed to political, social, moral, or religious denun-

ciation as Juvenalian verse satire. This vein is illustrated in the 16th c. by *Des Périers's Cymbalum Mundi, a set of Lucianesque dialogues, Henri *Estienne's Apologie pour Hérodote, and above all the *Satire Ménippée. Many other works, often in *dialogue form, could be seen as continuing this tradition, though not necessarily with the same vehemence. Several of Voltaire's miscellaneous writings are in fact Menippean satires, including dialogues such as 'Les ABC' and works usually included in his Contes, such as 'Pot-pourri' or 'Les Oreilles du comte de Chesterfield'. *Diderot actually entitled a brief piece of social observation 'Satire première', and gave Le *Neveu de Rameau the subtitle 'Satire seconde', thus associating it too with a classical form in which disorder reigned.

In its broader sense, which can extend to almost any form of mockery or criticism of people and society, satire is omnipresent in French writing. It is found in *pamphlets, in journalism, in songs, in novels and short stories, in poems and plays of many kinds, and is often virtually indistinguishable from *comedy. Critics have often associated it rather loosely with a bourgeois (as opposed to a courtly or heroic) way of thinking, but in reality it has not been the property of any social group.

In the Middle Ages the *fabliaux and *morality plays are full of laughter directed against human weaknesses and pretensions as well as against specific social groups, notably clerics. *Miroirs and similar didactic forms are largely satirical in content. Satire is central to the *Roman de Renart and the second part of the *Roman de la Rose, and it is an important element in the work of *Rutebeuf and in *Villon's Testament. In the Renaissance period *Rabelais's work could arguably be seen as the greatest of all Menippean satires, though very different from the Satire Ménippée itself. *Marot's poems contain much playful mockery, while *Du Bellay's Regrets are largely sustained by bitter mockery of the alien world of Rome. The social satire already present in medieval farce continues to figure in new types of comedy, and this satirical vein is exploited to the full by comic playwrights in the following two centuries, from *Desmarets de Saint-Sorlin (Les Visionnaires) to *Destouches (Le Glorieux). Recent criticism has tended to play down the satirical element in *Molière, focusing rather on the comedy of human inconsistencies and illusions, but there can be no denying the aggressive thrust of *Tartuffe or Les *Précieuses ridicules.

Otherwise, in the 17th and 18th c. satire thrives in the new genre of the novel, from the comic novels of *Scarron or *Furetière to the sharply observed scenes of *Marivaux or *Crébillon fils. Similar amused or censorious pictures are presented by La Fontaine in his *Fables (indirectly) and by *moralistes such as *La Bruyère. In the Enlightenment period there is a tendency for satire to become partisan again, as it had been in the Wars of Religion. Montesquieu, in the *Lettres persanes, and Voltaire,

745

in his philosophical tales and a great range of other work in prose and verse, pour scorn on established folly, while their enemies (*Palissot, *Fréron) respond in kind. Throughout all this period, and above all during the Revolution, there is a massive production of pamphlets, libels, and satirical songs.

In the novels and plays of the last two centuries the satirical representation of French society has been a constant element, as in the work of *Stendhal, *Flaubert, *Proust, or *Sartre, but it is rarely dominant—*Anatole France's *L'Île des pingouins* may be seen as an exception. The medley tradition of *satura* can be traced, for instance, in the novels of *Queneau or the later work of *Céline. But satire has found its purest expression in pamphlet literature and in the *press, from the writings of *Courier to the journalism of *Le* *Canard enchaîné, *Charlie-Hebdo, and the many other sharp-tongued periodicals of Right, Left, and centre. [PF]

See F. Fleuret, 'La Satire française au XVIe siècle' and 'La Satire française au XVIIe siècle', both in *De Ronsard à Baudelaire* (1935).

Satire Ménippée. The most famous of the satires created during the *Wars of Religion. It was given this name with reference to Menippus, the Syrian-Greek satirist of the 3rd c. BC, who wrote satires in this mixed form of verse and prose, but its first edition (1594) was entitled: *La Vertu du Catholicon d'Espagne*. In the *avant-propos*, two charlatans (one representing Spain and the other representing the Catholic *Ligue) attempt to sell a miraculous new drug—their version of the Catholic religion, which cures all evils and gives them power to do anything they wish. The choice of Spaniard and Ligueur is deliberate since the *Politique authors wish to attack the principal opponents of *Henri IV who, in a desperate attempt to prevent a Protestant from acceding to the throne, had convened the États Généraux of 1593 with the intention of electing a Catholic ruler. The authors of the *Satire Ménippée* (who include Nicolas *Rapin and Pierre *Pithou) appeal directly to moderate Catholics in search of stability and a return to traditional French values. They highlight the ridiculous and self-deflating speeches of the Ligueurs by contrasting them with a grave and impassioned speech by le sieur d'Aubray, who exploits the readers' war fatigue and sense of national pride. [JJS]

Saül le furieux, see LA TAILLE.

Saulsaye, La, see SCÈVE.

SAURIN, Bernard-Joseph (1706–81). French dramatist. Having begun as a lawyer, he was supported as a writer by a pension from *Helvétius and wrote plays in several genres. Fame came with *Spartacus* (1760), a heroic tragedy of political resistance in the style of P. *Corneille. *Beverlei* (1768), based on Moore's *Gamester* (which also inspired *Diderot), is a *drame in *vers libres*, a melodramatic concoction

culminating in a suicide which demonstrates the fatal effects of gambling. His comedies include *Les Mœurs du temps* (1760), a satire on snobbery, and *L'Anglomane* (1772), a skit on the vogue for things English, to which Saurin had himself contributed. [PF]

SAUSSURE, Ferdinand de (1857–1913). Linguist. Saussure spent all but 10 years of his life in Geneva, but his work has had more influence on French thought than that of any other Swiss national since *Rousseau. Similarly intriguing is the fact that he never published his major work: the *Cours de linguistique générale* (1916) was constructed posthumously from lecture plans and student notes of the period 1907–11. During his lifetime Saussure's publications were more language-specific: a dissertation on vowel systems in Indo-European languages in 1878, a doctoral thesis on Sanskrit, and studies of Lithuanian, medieval German legends, and anagrams in Latin poetry.

Saussure is generally considered to be the father of structural linguistics; he is also one of the forefathers of *Structuralism. He conceived of language as a system of signs, which could be analysed either in its specific empirical manifestations, i.e. as different *languages* which may be compared and contrasted, and whose historical evolution may be described; or, more abstractly, as part of a study of semiotics or semiology in which the main focus of interest is the nature of signification and of the sign itself. Saussure's analyses tend to be conducted in terms of a series of binary oppositions. The study of language may be diachronic (historical) or synchronic (structural). In his view, the state of a language at a particular point in time needs to be described before its evolution can be assessed. This gives the synchronic priority over the diachronic, but purely in the sense of the logical order of study. Secondly, language may be considered as *langue* or as *parole*, that is, either as the general set of semantic and syntactic rules of a particular language or as its individual utterances. Thirdly, Saussure describes the linguistic sign as comprising a *signifiant* (signifier) and a *signifié* (signified), that is, an aural or written form and the concept which it embodies. (Followers of Saussure have extended this bipartite structure to a tripartite one which also includes the object to which the sign refers, the referent.) The relationship between signifier and signified is arbitrary, and both depend on a vast network of differences. Furthermore, since language itself contributes to the understanding and division of the real, rather than being a mere nomenclature naming the already given, languages may not correspond readily to one another, and their 'arbitrary' divisions of the real may not be easily translatable. These theories of meaning have influenced not only linguistics but also literary theory [see BARTHES], anthropology [see LÉVI-STRAUSS], and psychoanalysis [see LACAN]. [CMH]

See J. Culler, *Saussure* (1976, rev. edn. 1988).

Sauvage, La, see ANOUILH.

SAVARD, Félix-Antoine (1896–1982). Canadian priest and writer whose *Menaud, maître-draveur* (1937), overtly inspired by Hémon's *Maria Chapdelaine*, is a major work of Quebec literary nationalism. It was Savard who, by making the venerable logger Menaud meditate on the dream voice which spoke to Maria Chapdelaine against the domination of French Canada by anglophones, gave Hémon's work the political resonance it now enjoys within the nationalist tradition. The lyrical qualities of Savard's style, his constant appeal to the beauties of nature, the simplicity of his peasant characters, and the artlessness of his narrative convincingly naturalized the political message as the expression of perennial human values. The same model was to be followed by many other writers, even as late in the century as Roch *Carrier.

None of Savard's other works achieve the mythic power of *Menaud*. The most considerable, *L'Abatis* (1943) and *Le Barachois* (1959), express his romantic naturalism in the form of short poetic and evocative prose pieces. The latter has the extra interest of offering documentary glimpses of the colonization movement of the 1930s—a Church-led project aimed at combating unemployment and preserving the traditional rural way of life of French Canada by opening up new farmlands in the inhospitable north of Quebec—in which Savard played a leading role as a socially committed priest. [SIL]

SAVARY, Jérôme (b. 1942). French actor, director, and script-writer. As founder of the Grand Magic Circus, which mounted a series of burlesques in the 1960s and 1970s, he created a highly popular brand of alternative theatre, part cabaret, part satirical revue. In the 1980s he applied his exuberant, festive style to classical and musical plays, most notably in a celebrated iconoclastic production of *Molière's Le Bourgeois gentilhomme*. [DWW]

SAVOIE, Jacques, see ACADIA.

SCALIGER, Jules-César (1484–1558), claimed to descend from the Della Scala of Verona. He was at various times a Franciscan monk and a soldier, but is best known for his violent attack on *Erasmus (*Oratio pro M. Tullio Cicerone*, 1531) and his *Poetices libri septem* (1561). The latter is a literary treatise based on Aristotle which had an enormous influence on 17th-c. French literary theory, especially in the field of drama, where his ideas on the importance of decorum, regularity, and control found an increasingly receptive audience [see CLASSICISM]. [JJS]

Scapin. One of the stock characters of the *commedia dell'arte*, usually a resourceful, amoral valet. His most famous French incarnation is in *Molière's *Les Fourberies de Scapin*, where he persuades old Géronte to hide in a sack and be beaten.

SCARAMOUCHE, Tiberio Fiorilli, known as (1608–94). A member of Torelli's Italian troupe, he settled in Paris from 1644 and became famous for his virtuosity as a mime. He was widely held to have influenced *Molière in the development of his expressive acting style during the years after 1658 when the Italians shared a theatre with Molière's troupe. The figure of Scaramouche was a stock character in the *commedia dell'arte*. [GJM]

SCARRON, Paul (1610–60). Poet, novelist, and comic playwright. Born in a Parisian legal family, he was destined for the Church. From 1629 he frequented literary circles in the capital, though from 1633 to 1640 he was based in Le Mans, where he was a canon of the cathedral. In 1638 he was struck down by a crippling disease, which paralysed him. He bore his suffering with courage and good humour, surrounded by friends (e.g. *Sarasin, *Ménage, *Pellisson) and cared for by his young wife, Françoise d'Aubigné, granddaughter of the poet, later to become famous as Madame de *Maintenon. He received a royal pension (humorously describing himself as 'le malade de la Reine'). A close friend of *Retz, he attacked *Mazarin during the *Fronde.

His writing career coincides with the time of his illness. In his poetry, much of it in the form of verse epistles, he projects an image of himself as a witty, but grotesquely misshapen figure. Laughter at his own expense alternates with good-humoured satire of the ridiculous world around him—though his *mazarinades* are bitterly scurrilous. His speciality is the *burlesque style; beginning with the *Recueil de quelques vers burlesques* (1643), and continuing with *Le Typhon ou la Gigantomachie* (1644) and his parody of the *Aeneid*, the *Virgile travesti* (1648–51), he poured out floods of sprightly octosyllabic verse in which poetry is brought down from Parnassus to the modern market-place. His language, full of dissonances and familiar or vulgar expressions, plays games at the expense of heroic, serious, or sentimental diction.

The same playful disrespect permeates his fiction and his comic drama, all of it freely imitated from Spanish models. His great success was the *Roman comique* (1651–7), but he also wrote five *Nouvelles tragi-comiques* (1655–60), largely satirical and sometimes realistic tales of love and deceit, set in Spain. 'La Précaution inutile' foreshadows Molière's *L'*École des femmes*. His comedies, following the Spanish model of love intrigues in five acts in verse, are remarkable for the fantastic exuberance of language of their central figures. In *Jodelet ou le Maître-Valet* (performed 1643) and *Les Trois Dorothées* (later *Jodelet soufleté*) (performed 1645) he uses the talents of the famous *farceur*; *L'Héritier ridicule* (performed 1649) centres on a valet dressed as a master, whereas *Don Japhet d'Arménie* (performed 1651–2) displays and cruelly mocks a Quixotesque fool. These comedies were very popular throughout the 17th c. and provided a model for later writers. [PF]

See E. Magne, *Scarron et son milieu* (1924).

Sceaux, Château de, see MAINE.

Scènes de la vie de Bohème, see MURGER.

*Scènes de la vie privée . . . de province . . . parisi-
enne . . . politique . . . militaire . . . de campagne.*
The six subdivisions of the *Études de mœurs* in
Balzac's *Comédie humaine.*

Scepticism. Important philosophical movement
which emerged in the 16th c. as a major opponent
of Aristotelianism and contributed significantly to
its demise and, indirectly, to the development of the
scientific revolution in the 17th c. It impinges on
French writing in its most influential form as
*Pyrrhonism.   [IM]

SCÈVE, Maurice (*c.*1500–1560). Lyonnais poet and
humanist, best known for his *Délie, objet de plus
haute vertu* (1544), the first French *canzoniere* of love
poems. It consists of 449 decasyllabic *dizains* and a
prefatory *huitain* and is illustrated by 50 emblematic
woodcuts, appearing regularly throughout the text;
they bear some relation to the neighbouring poems
and increase the aphoristic flavour of the writing.
Scève published his poem a few years before the
first work of the *Pléiade (who praised him, but
rather reluctantly); he was more firmly rooted in
the native French tradition, and closer to Clément
*Marot and the *Rhétoriqueurs than they were, but
he shares or anticipates many of their aims and preoccupations, such as the creative reading of classical
and Italian authors and the use of the vernacular in
the renewal of poetry. He stands outside his own
time and theirs, however, in the originality of his
linguistic and syntactic innovation, the concentration of his thought and its expression, and his ability
to unite abstract ideas and sensuous imagery.

Although Scève's poem starts with an *innamoramento* and proceeds through several absences and
partings to a final separation, and in spite of certain
anecdotal elements (such as boating in spring when
the shad are coming up the river) and some clear historical pointers, this is not the narrative of a love-
affair. Nor is the sequence significantly *Petrarchan.
Scève's first *dizain* does indeed contain a clear allusion to the first of Petrarch's sonnets, and his last
poem refers to the *Trionfi,* thus placing *Délie* firmly
in a Petrarchan frame, yet the final *dizain* emphasizes how far away from Petrarch he is since there is
no question of repudiating his love for Délie on religious or spiritual grounds. Délie may well be a pseudonym for Pernette *du Guillet with whom Scève
has long been associated, but the name has many
other resonances: it is just possible that its anagram
'L'idée' has links with the Platonic doctrine superficially present elsewhere in the poem; more certainly
the name is the focus of numerous allusions to classical literature (e.g. Tibullus' Delia) and to classical
mythology, especially in the person of Diana. The
geographical setting of Lyon provides a recurrent
symbol of the poet's love for Délie: the vigorous

Rhône and the slow-moving Saône, images of the
poet and his mistress, will sooner part, and the two
hills of Fourvière and Croix-Rousse come together,
than their love fail. The poet's physical jealousy is
powerfully and dramatically conveyed.

Scève was also the author of a translation of *La
Déplorable Fin de Flammette* (1535) by Juan de Flores
(who based himself on Boccaccio), and he composed
five *blasons (Sourcil, Larme, Front, Gorge, Soupir).
A more important work is his pastoral poem *La
Saulsaye, églogue de la vie solitaire* (1547); this is a
debate between two shepherds, Antire and Philerme,
on the subject of town and country and also the
court; Scève here shows the influence of Sannazaro
and *Marguerite de Navarre, but also much originality. Scève's versatility is evident in the work he did
for the *Royal Entry of *Henri II and *Catherine de
Médicis into Lyon in September 1548; he was the
overall artistic director of this enterprise, was responsible for the iconography and the written inscriptions, and was also the author of the printed account,
*La Magnificence de la superbe et triomphante entrée de la
noble et antique cité de Lyon* (1549). Finally, he published in 1562 another major work, *Microcosme.* This
is a long cosmic, scientific poem about the creation
of man, his fall, and his subsequent achievements, in
which Adam (man) is the little world reflecting the
whole universe. The book covers the period from
the creation to the death of Abel, but man's progress
up to the coming of Christ is foretold by means of a
dream of Adam's. Scève is writing at the end of a
long tradition of patristic and medieval thought, and
his work constitutes an encyclopedia in the manner
of Gregor Reisch's *Margarita philosophica,* stressing
the discovery and development of the arts and sciences, and man's dignity and freedom, yet stopping
short of the new Renaissance learning.   [PS]

See I. D. McFarlane (ed.), *The 'Délie' of Maurice
Scève* (1966); D. G. Coleman, *Maurice Scève, Poet of
Love* (1975); D. Fenoaltea, '*Si haulte architecture':
The Design of Scève's 'Délie'* (1982).

SCHEHADÉ, Georges (1910–89). A Lebanese member of the *Surrealist movement. Between 1938 and
1972 he published five wistful and whimsical volumes entitled *Poésies,* plus further collections of
poetry, *L'Écolier Sultan* (1950), *Si tu rencontres un
ramier* (1951), and *Le Nageur d'un seul amour* (1985).
He is better known as a dramatist whose plays
transpose to the stage the dreamy, playful qualities
of his poetry: see e.g. *Monsieur Bob'le* (written 1938,
performed 1951), *La Soirée des proverbes* (1954),
Histoire de Vasco (1956), and *L'Émigré de Brisbane*
(1965). He also wrote a *récit, Rodogune Sinne* (1947), a
so-called 'pantomime', *L'Habit fait le prince* (1973),
based on Gottfried Keller's 'Kleider machen Leute',
and, for Jacques Baratier, the scenario of the film
Goha.   [KRA]

SCHELANDRE, Jean de (*c.*1585–1635). French dramatist. His tragedy *Tyr et Sidon* appeared in 1608; it has

an involved, adventurous, and violent plot, but is in regular five-act form. There are choruses, as in earlier humanist tragedies, and incidents of violence are conveyed by *récits*, a practice common to earlier humanist and later classical tragedy. In 1628 it was republished as a *tragicomedy, not only with a happy ending but greatly expanded (to ten acts), including as on-stage action much of what had previously been communicated in *récits*. It was accompanied by a preface by François *Ogier arguing for the lifelike quality of tragicomedy's mixed tone.

[GJ]

SCHLUMBERGER, Jean (1877–1968). French novelist, important also for his part in founding the *Nouvelle Revue Française*. His novels explore family conflicts, moral choices, the individual's search for freedom: *L'Inquiète Paternité* (1911), *Un homme heureux* (1921), *Saint-Saturnin* (1931). He also wrote evocative memoirs (*Éveils*, 1950) and critical essays (*Plaisir à Corneille*, 1936; *Jalons*, 1944; *Madeleine et André Gide*, 1956). [MMC]

SCHNEIDER, Hortense (1833–1920). French singer and actress. After appearing in musical productions and acting in vaudeville, she was taken up by Offenbach at the Bouffes-Parisiens and soon became the unchallenged queen of operetta under the Second Empire, starring in *La Belle Hélène* (1864), *La Grande-Duchesse de Gerolstein* (1867), *La Périchole* (1868), etc. [SBJ]

SCHOELCHER, Victor, see SLAVERY.

Scholasticism. Although historians sometimes refer to 'scholastic philosophy', scholasticism is not a philosophical school or current of thought. Rather, it describes the *methods* of study characteristic of the medieval universities and also, in the view of some historians, the particular accommodation between Christian doctrine and rational investigation reached by scholars there.

1. Schools, Universities, and Scholasticism

Before about 1200 there were no universities in northern Europe. In the 8th, 9th, and 10th c. the leading centres of learning were the great monasteries. But by the late 11th c. it was in some of the schools attached to cathedrals, such as those at Chartres and Laon, that the most exciting intellectual developments were taking place. At this stage it was the fame of the individual teacher (usually a canon of the cathedral) which made a particular school popular. Over the next 50 years, however, Paris became pre-eminent as a centre of learning. In addition to the cathedral school of Notre-Dame, other schools opened there, so that by 1150 a whole variety of teachers—grammarians, logicians, and theologians—were competing for pupils.

The University of Paris the oldest and most important of the north European universities—was, in its origins, simply an association of the various masters teaching in Paris. Its earliest charter dates, conveniently, from exactly 1200. The masters formed a tightly organized guild, and the requirements for degrees (which books were to be studied and for how long) were formalized. Paris, like other medieval universities, was divided into faculties of arts and the smaller but 'higher' faculties of law, medicine, and theology, which students could not enter without having completed the arts course or its equivalent. Statutes also regulated many other aspects of university life, ranging from academic dress to the lavishness of graduation celebrations. But the written regulations are likely to give a misleading impression of universities as centralized institutions, offering a highly uniform education. In fact, the masters were all private, each with his own students, on whose fees he depended for his living. The various orders, especially the *Franciscans and the *Dominicans, had their own private houses of study within the university, catering for their own members, and from the 13th c. students increasingly resided and studied in semi-autonomous *colleges, the most famous of which was the *Sorbonne. Moreover, the majority of students did not complete even the whole arts course, whilst for most masters university teaching was a passing stage in their career. University statutes were, then, an attempt to impose some framework on institutions never far from chaos. Perhaps the same characteristic—an apparent rigidity of organization which disguises heterogeneous variety—is also found in the scholastic method, which dominated university studies.

2. The Scholastic Method

Each faculty in the medieval university had its own textbooks, and study was centred on them. In the arts faculties from the mid-13th c. onwards the near-complete corpus of Aristotle's works (in Latin translation) provided most of the set texts. In theology the set texts were the Bible and the *Sentences* of Peter the Lombard, a mid-12th-c. work which provided a convenient guide to the range of theological problems. In lectures, set texts received two different sorts of exposition. First, in an effort to explain exactly the meaning of each text, they were systematically divided and subdivided until the most basic units of argument were reached. Secondly, 'questions' (*quaestiones*) were posed about the topics raised by each portion of the text. Especially in commentaries on the *Sentences*, these questions—and the discussions raised in answering them—range far beyond any of the matters actually raised by Peter the Lombard and reflect rather the intellectual interests of the university theologians of the time.

In their polished, written version, scholastic *quaestiones* have a standard structure. A problem is put in the form of a question which can be answered 'yes' or 'no'. The writer then puts a series of arguments, from reason or authority, for the answer with which he disagrees. There follows a brief statement,

749

usually from an authoritative author, in favour of the opposing view, with which the author in fact agrees. Then comes the 'body' of the *quaestio*—the author's own arguments for the answer he favours (which sometimes involve modifying the terms of the original question). Finally, the arguments for the opposite answer set out at the beginning are answered in turn. Very often the rejection of these arguments, a large number of which are taken from the most authoritative Christian or classical authors, takes the form, not of a refutation, but of a demonstration that, though valid, they do not pertain to the matter at issue. The neatest example of the *quaestio* form is provided by Thomas Aquinas's famous *Summa theologiae*, written in the 1260s in an attempt (unsuccessful at the time) to provide a textbook to replace the Lombard's *Sentences*. In the 14th c., although the basic form of the *quaestio* was retained, there was a tendency for the 'body' section to grow into an independent essay, with its own divisions and subdivisions, and for the other parts to shrink into a mere formality.

In addition to lectures on set texts, the university year also included a number of disputations (*quaestiones disputatae*), either on a particular topic (such as the soul, evil, or truth) or else 'quodlibetal disputations', where any topic could be raised by a questioner. Although in their polished, written form disputations are hard to distinguish from *quaestio*-commentaries on texts, the organization of these disputations was complex, and they took place in two sessions, the first of which was probably far from orderly in its presentation of arguments and counter-arguments.

The way in which argument was conducted within the framework of a *quaestio* was deeply influenced by the intensive study of grammar and, especially, logic in the arts course. Not only did they often spell out arguments in explicitly syllogistic form, but also scholastic thinkers were skilled in the sophisticated analysis of logical form and of the different ways in which words could refer to their objects. In addition, the Aristotelian studies of the arts course were taken for granted among the theologians, and Aristotelian terms and ideas abound in their writings. It would be wrong, however, to imagine that scholastic thinkers were straightforward Aristotelians. In the arts faculties 'Aristotle's' views were, indeed, very often taken as a guide; but these were Aristotle's views as seen through a tradition of ancient and Arab commentaries, especially those of Avicenna (ibn Sina, 980–1037) and Averroes (ibn Rushd, 1126–98), and coloured by the inclusion of apocryphal works such as the *Liber de causis* (in fact a compilation based on the work of Proclus, a *Neoplatonist) within the Aristotelian canon. For the theologians, Aristotle's views were, at best, examples of what human reason unaided by revelation, could achieve; and from the late 13th c. onwards the theologians became increasingly bold in analysing the deficiencies of such a perspective,

even with regard to matters apparently within its scope.

3. Scholastic Thinkers

Understood as a method, scholasticism can only be said to have been established by the mid-13th c., when the universities of Paris and Oxford adopted an Aristotelian curriculum in the arts faculty. Already in the early 12th c., however, the pupils of Anselm of Laon and William of Champeaux, most notably Peter *Abélard, had begun to fashion the *quaestio* technique and to raise some of the theological problems which would preoccupy their successors. Theologians such as William of Auvergne, in the early 13th c., used a wide range of Aristotle's works, but they did not set out their work in the distinctively scholastic form. Thomas Aquinas (c.1225–1274), therefore, belonged to the first generation of properly scholastic thinkers. Although greatly respected, he did not enjoy in his own or the succeeding century the pre-eminence which he has been accorded by more recent historiography. The most influential figure of the next generation was Henry of Ghent (c.1217–1293). But it was Duns Scotus (c.1265–1308), a keen though admiring critic of Henry (and, less directly, of Aquinas), whose ideas became an inevitable point of reference for all his successors. The influence of William of Occam (c.1285–1347/9), once portrayed as the destroyer of the syntheses of Aquinas and Scotus, has been exaggerated. He is best seen as one of a set of brilliant Oxford scholars—among whom were Adam Wodeham and Walter Chatton—whose ideas influenced Parisian thought in the following decades. Although the great age of scholasticism had passed by about 1350, a number of outstanding scholastic thinkers worked in the late Middle Ages, such as John Wyclif (c.1330–1384) and Peter of Ailly (1350–1420/1). All these figures were theologians. But a few thinkers made their careers in the arts faculty. They include Siger of Brabant and Boethius of Dacia in the 1260s and 1270s, and John *Buridan in the 14th c.

4. The Idea of Scholasticism

Was scholasticism merely a set of methods, or did it also involve on a more abstract level a distinctive approach to intellectual life? Historians have been quick to point to the combination of faith and reason in the works of the scholastics. Scholastic thinkers, they say, neither relied uncritically on the authority of the ancients and Church Fathers, nor did they attempt to base their views on reason alone. Their independence from authorities marks them out from their early-medieval predecessors; their reliance on revelation distinguishes them from philosophers of the early-modern period and later.

Yet it is questionable whether such a characterization amounts to more than saying that the scholastic thinkers were, indeed, thinkers, and that most of them did their most important work as theologians. *No* thinker relies blindly on the authority of his predecessors, and scholastic writers differed from their early-medieval predecessors not by being independent from authorities, but in the methods by which they achieved this independence. Within the arts faculties scholars were not merely encouraged, but required to discuss only what reason could construct on the basis of self-evident premisses. In the theology faculties Christian doctrine provided the basic material for study, although this did not prevent theologians from spending much of their time analysing concepts, logical connections, and language. The relationship between what could be known without Christian revelation and what could not was a matter for constant sophisticated debate, in which no single solution became the accepted one. Scholasticism is, therefore, best regarded as a set of methods and, in a transferred sense, as the name for the large and various body of surviving logical, philosophical, scientific, legal, and theological texts which exemplify them. [JAMM]

See N. Kretzmann, A. Kenny, and J. Pinborg (eds.), *The Cambridge History of Later Medieval Philosophy* (1982); A. de Libera, *La Philosophie médiévale* (1989); J. Marenbon, *Later Medieval Philosophy (1150–1350): An Introduction*, 2nd edn. (1992).

SCHURÉ, Édouard (1841–1929). Schuré made two major contributions to the cultural and aesthetic context of French *Symbolism. The first was his publication in 1875 of *Le Drame musical*, which helped to establish the Wagner cult in France. The second was his publication in 1889 of *Les Grands Initiés*, a comparative study of the esoteric tradition whose aim was to reassert the spiritual unity of humanity. [JK]

SCHWARZ-BART, André (b. 1928). Novelist. His reputation rests largely on one remarkable novel, *Le Dernier des justes* (1959, Prix Goncourt). He was the son of a Polish immigrant family which perished in the Holocaust and a Resistance fighter; the book is a meditation on the Jewish people's destiny of suffering, depicted through successive generations of one family, from the death of the Jews in York in 1185 to the Auschwitz gas-chambers. The Talmudic legend of the 36 just men on whom the world's salvation depends forms the central myth and also points to the desperate conclusion: the modern world kills the last of the just.

Schwarz-Bart also collaborated with his wife Simone on *Un plat dé porc aux bananes vertes* [see below], and wrote *La Mulâtresse Solitude* (1972, see SLAVERY). [NW]

SCHWARZ-BART, Simone (b. 1938). Guadeloupean novelist, each of whose novels offers a different approach to the same central issue: the search for Caribbean cultural identity. While exploring the negative aspects of this quest—the inability to regain contact with ancestral, African roots, and the alienation of the West Indian in France—she also depicts the emotional strength of those who have a sure sense of their personal and racial identity. Non-militant in tone but positive in stance, her fiction is concerned less with revolt against white cultural domination than with the fostering of black cultural values.

Her first novel, *Un plat de porc aux bananes vertes* (1967), was written in collaboration with her husband, André [see above], and reflects a preoccupation common to both: the plight of minority groups within a hostile society. The novel's figure of alienation is an elderly, infirm Martinican woman living in an institution in France. Her vain search, in the wintry dark of Paris, for the warmth of a once-familiar Creole restaurant becomes the poignant symbol of her failure to achieve reintegration with her own cultural group.

Pluie et vent sur Télumée Miracle (1972), Schwarz-Bart's second work, is widely regarded as her masterpiece. The novel describes the humble, difficult, but ultimately serene lives of a peasant girl and her grandmother living in a remote, mountainous area of Guadeloupe in the early 20th c. Their unselfconscious sense of Caribbean identity depends both on their intimate contact with their own culture, and on their refusal to accept the moral judgements of colonialism regarding the black race. The narrative is deftly articulated in contrasting sequences of joy and disaster, generosity and betrayal, grief and an overriding faith in life.

Her third novel, *Ti Jean L'Horizon* (1979), borrows a hero from Caribbean folklore and places him in a timeless, epic dimension. Magic allows Ti Jean to realize the old slave dream of returning to Africa. But his spiritual odyssey turns into nightmare when his ancestors reject him because his line has been tainted by slavery. France, the object of his second pilgrimage, proves to be another false turning in the quest for cultural identity. Fleeing these bitter truths, Ti Jean pledges his loyalty to Guadeloupe—the branch once wrenched from the tree of Africa but now producing its own, unique, Caribbean fruit.

In recent years Simone Schwarz-Bart has turned from fiction to theatre. *Ton beau capitaine* (1987) explores the themes of betrayal and loss with a delicacy and poignancy characteristic of all her writing. [BNO]

SCHWOB, Marcel (1867–1905). French writer. Dismissed for much of this century as a period piece of the *Decadent and *Symbolist movements, as a polymath who had failed to give effective literary form to themes, images, and myths drawn from an exceptional range of intellectual interests (which included Greek, Latin, and Anglo-Saxon as well as medieval French literature, mystical and idealist philosophy, philology, and slang), Schwob and his work are currently the subject of renewed interest. In particular, *Le Roi au masque d'or* (1892) and *Vies imaginaires* (1896) are increasingly seen as engaging

Science Fiction

with themes (time, myth, sexuality) central to the modern sensibility. [JK]

Science Fiction. However long its ancestry—Jules *Verne, J.-H. *Rosny aîné, Gaston Leroux—science fiction only established itself in France in the early 1950s, with the launching of the collections 'Le Rayon fantastique' (1951) (Hachette-Gallimard), 'Anticipation' (1952) (Fleuve Noir), and 'La Présence du futur' (1954) (Denoël). Initially, these were largely vehicles for translations of Anglo-American texts. A consistent, if slender, French tradition already existed, one with a propensity for apocalyptic visions, e.g. J.-H. Rosny, *La Mort de la terre* (1912), Jacques Spitz, *L'Agonie du globe* (1925), René Barjavel, *Ravage* (1943), B. R. Bruss, *Et la planète sauta* (1946); but the new start made in the 1950s was faltering, not only because of suffocation by American material, but also because of critical resistance. It had to withstand charges of star-gazing, of simplistic psychology and philosophy, of escapism and hero-cults; it also had to overcome the discrediting of 19th-c. positivistic scientism by the nuclear present.

By 1968 French science fiction was in danger of atrophy; wedded to a pre-1960s American model, it was more concerned with the vague futurity of outer space than with the immediate future of our planet. 1968 saw the politicization of French science fiction with the publication of *nouvelles* by J.-P. *Andrevon, Daniel Walther, and Serge Nigon in *Fiction*. The need to imagine a specifically French future, given threats as diverse as the backlash from the Right, or chemical pollution, or overpopulation, was confronted by Robert *Merle in *Malevil* (1972), Michel Jeury in *Le Temps incertain* (1973), and Philippe *Curval in *Cette chère humanité* (1976). But the heroic-fantasy/space-opera dimension of science fiction has undergone no diminution, and it is in this form that it has flourished in the *bande dessinée*—Edgar Jacobs (Blake and Mortimer), Philippe Druillet (Lone Sloane), Guiraud (Arzach), J. Mézières et P. Christin (Valérian).

The generic status of science fiction remains problematic. It owes as much to the Gothic novel and the *roman d'épouvante* as it does to *Utopian writing and the exoticism of the *roman d'aventures*. But its concerns have remained consistent: cybernetics (androids, humanoids, mutants), nuclear and bacteriological apocalypse, parallel realities, the deconstruction of temporal, spatial, and psychological categories, parasitical aliens, a bureaucracy of machines. [CS]

See H. Baudin, *La Science-Fiction* (1971); J. Van Herp, *Panorama de la science-fiction: les thèmes, les genres, les écoles, les problèmes* (1973).

Science universelle, La, see SOREL, C.

Scorpion, Le, see MEMMI.

SCRIBE, Eugène (1791–1861). French dramatist. Father of the 'well-made play', he wrote some 300 plays, often with collaborators. His importance in theatre history lies in the way in which he transformed the mechanics of play-making by inventing plots which are complicated but neat and tight, connecting scenes and acts in a logical and coherent chain that leads to satisfying endings through a liberal use of surprise and suspense. Satirical comedies like *Bernard et Raton* (1833), historical plays like *Le Verre d'eau* (1840), and domestic dramas like *Une chaîne* (1841) owed their vast success to his plots. Masters like Ibsen learned from him. [SBJ]

SCUDÉRY, Georges de (1601–67). French military man of legendary vanity who, in about 1630, left the army for the theatre. He wrote numerous plays, 16 of which were staged between 1631 and 1644 alone, notably *La Comédie des comédiens* (1634) and *Arminius* (1643). Shortly after *Théophile de Viau's condemnation by the Church, Scudéry edited Théophile's *Œuvres* (1632) and in a preface courageously defended the poet against his enemies. On the other hand, he initiated the attack on Corneille's dramaturgy with *Observations sur le *Cid* (1637). In subsequent texts he defended the *Académie Française's position in the quarrel; he was later elected to its ranks. Many of his sister Madeleine's works, such as *Artamène, ou le Grand Cyrus*, were published under Georges's name; he may have collaborated to some extent in their production. He wrote an epic poem, *Alaric, ou Rome vaincue* (1654). After his marriage in 1654 he lived in Normandy. His widow was a favourite correspondent of *Bussy-Rabutin. [JDeJ]

SCUDÉRY, Madeleine de (1608–1701). The most prolific French novelist of her century, also the most successful—her novels sold so widely that they made her publisher wealthy. Orphaned at an early age, she received an unusually extensive education from an uncle. She began writing only in the early 1640s. Her most significant early work, *Les Femmes illustres* (1642), is a series of first-person accounts: famous women from antiquity (Sappho, Artemisia, and so forth) tell their own stories to refute the slanders of history.

Scudéry immediately began to experiment with the form that was the foundation of her success, the extended (up to 15,000 pages), serially published, historical prose fiction known today as the *roman héroïque*. Initially, in particular for *Ibrahim, ou l'Illustre Bassa* (1641–4), she collaborated with her brother Georges, who signed all her novels [see above]. However, Georges's role was far less important than some have claimed. His sister always used collaborators. It is likely that Georges's contribution was no more significant than those of *Huet, *Ménage, or *Pellisson, for decades Madeleine's intimate companion.

The 1650s marked the high point of Scudéry's career. She composed her most popular novels, ***Artamène, ou le Grand Cyrus* (1649–53) and **Clélie*, *histoire romaine* (1654–60). She founded her *salon, known as *le samedi*, which was among the century's most significant private cultural institutions. The two activities were intimately related. Elements later used in the novels, e.g. *Clélie's* famous *carte de *Tendre*, were originally created in her salon. In addition, Scudéry's first readers seem to have believed that the novels re-created salon society on a much broader scale; that, for example, characters were portraits of prominent individuals.

Scudéry later published other novels, novellas, and occasional poetry, but her audience was now less vast. She ended her career with four collections of 'conversations' (1680–92), dialogues on social ethics sometimes reprinted from her novels.

Scudéry's novels were translated into many languages. Prominent foreign intellectuals considered a visit to the novelist the highlight of their French sojourn. She won the first prize for eloquence awarded by the Académie Française (1671). Several academicians tried to have the ban against women lifted so that she could join their ranks. Her novels were widely read until the turn of the 19th c.— *Rousseau and *Chateaubriand count among her admirers.

Commentators have often presented Scudéry's work as an unambiguous eulogy of political absolutism and aristocratic privilege. They therefore eliminate the nuances in her political thinking—e.g. her eyewitness accounts of the *Fronde—that subtly predict the dangers of absolutism. The cautiously subversive Scudéry could find new readers today.   [JDeJ]

See R. Godenne, *Les Romans de Mademoiselle de Scudéry* (1983).

SCUTENAIRE, Louis, see BELGIAN LITERATURE IN FRENCH.

SEBBAR, Leïla (b. 1941). Novelist of Franco-Algerian descent. Her Algerian father and French mother were schoolteachers in colonial Algeria. Since the age of 17 she has lived in France, specializing in narratives dealing with the immigrant community, particularly the so-called *Beur generation. The condition of young women from immigrant families is highlighted in *Fatima ou les Algériennes au square* (1981), *Schérazade* (1982), *Les Carnets de Schérazade* (1985), and *Le Fou de Schérazade* (1991).   [AGH]

SEBILLET, Thomas (1512–89) published *L'Art poétique français* in 1548, one year before Du Bellay's *Défense et illustration*, apparently intending to forestall it. Sebillet's poetic manifesto combines a humanist conception of the poet's divine calling and inspiration with practical technical recommendations about verse-forms, rhythms, rhyme, and language. He belongs rather to Clément *Marot's generation and looks back to the late Middle Ages, but also relies on Horace, Cicero, and Quintilian. In 1549, adapting Greek metres to French, he published

a French translation of the *Iphigenia* of Euripides, an author made familiar by the Latin versions of *Erasmus and *Buchanan.   [PS]

Sebond, Apologie de Raymond, see MONTAIGNE.

SEBTI, Youssef (1943–93). Algerian writer and teacher of rural sociology. In 1981 he published a volume of poetry, *L'Enfer et la folie*, a log-book for 1962—including memories of the *Algerian War (*l'enfer*) and violent attacks on the new bureaucratic middle class (*la folie*). He also wrote a number of unpublished volumes of poetry and was a regular and outspoken contributor to the review *Révolution africaine* until his death by assassination.   [ET]

Second Empire. This lasted from Louis-Napoléon Bonaparte's assumption of imperial power in 1852 [see NAPOLEON III] until his defeat at Sedan in September 1870 [see FRANCO-PRUSSIAN WAR]. It was an authoritarian regime, though becoming more liberal in the 1860s. France was involved in several foreign wars (including the Crimean War) and in colonial expeditions [see COLONIZATION]. It was a period of considerable industrial growth, seeing notably the rapid expansion of the railway network. One of the Second Empire's most lasting legacies was the *haussmanisation* of Paris.

In his *Rougon-Macquart* series, Zola offers a vast tableau of Second-Empire France, stressing economic and social change, corruption, speculation, and the positivistic, materialist spirit of the age. [PF]

SEDAINE, Michel-Jean (1719–97). French librettist and dramatist. Sedaine was the son of a master mason whose financial ruin and early death obliged him to become a stonemason himself in order to support the family. Self-educated in his spare time, he was encouraged by his employer to develop his literary talents. His career as a librettist, during which he worked with Philidor, Monsigny, and Grétry, began in 1756 and produced, e.g., *Le Déserteur* (1769) and *Richard Cœur de Lion* (1784). He also wrote *Le *Philosophe sans le savoir* (1765), which was the most notable example of the *drame, and *La Gageure imprévue* (1768), a comedy reminiscent of the work of *Marivaux, both of which were well-received at the Comédie-Française.

Sedaine's importance lies in his contribution to the development of the *opéra-comique and the *drame*, which marks the decline of the traditional genres and style of production. Contemporaries admired him for his agreeable personality, intelligence, and sound judgement. He was a founder member of the Société des Auteurs Dramatiques in 1777. A modernist in drama, he was a friend of *Diderot and the *philosophes and shared the view that literature had an ethical responsibility for the propagation of social progress. He helped the painter *David at the beginning of his career but, though he supported the Revolution when it came, did not share David's Jacobinism. He was made secretary of the Académie d'Architecture in 1768 and elected to the Académie Française in 1786. [JD]

Sedan. Town near the Belgian frontier, scene of the French defeat in 1870 [see FRANCO-PRUSSIAN WAR] and of a German breakthrough in May 1940.

SEFRIOUI, Ahmed (b. 1915). Moroccan novelist. As chronicles of pre-independence Morocco, Sefrioui's books draw on the story-telling traditions of his native Fez. He showed himself aware of the danger of alienation through the use of French and of footnoting in works like *La Boîte à merveilles* (1954) and *Le Chapelet d'ambre* (1949), when he spoke of 'cette technique linguistique de depaysement'. Sefrioui's writing is indicative of the resilience of oral culture, which, like the old medina of Fez itself, remained beyond the reach of the French. This power may be due to his rooting himself in Sufi mysticism. He is a path-breaking author much imitated by Tahar *Ben Jelloun. [JKa]

SEGALEN, Victor (1878–1919). A naval doctor of Breton origin, Segalen drew the substance of his literary works from his journeys in exotic regions. He was, however, not interested in documentary realism and scorned the type of exoticism cultivated by *Loti: his enigmatic and idiosyncratic writings focus obsessively on the relationship between the imaginary and the real. If travel and writing were essentially paths towards self-discovery for him (he published little in his lifetime), none of his works is easily classified in terms of genre. *Les Immémoriaux* (1907), part-novel, part-documentary, is concerned with the extinction of tribal civilization in Tahiti. Long journeys and archaeological explorations undertaken in China provide the inspiration for the solemn, hieratic prose poems of *Stèles* (1912), Segalen's best-known work, as well as for his strange narrative *René Leys* (1921), in which the status of the narrator's account remains unclear to the end, and *Équipée* (1929), which recounts an imaginary expedition. Segalen's China, dominated by the figures of the Emperor, the Sage, and the Regent, is essentially symbolic and mythical, but the personal quest which underlies its creation is real and, despite Segalen's rather static style, often compelling. A friend of *Debussy, for whom he devised a libretto, *Orphée-Roi* (1921), Segalen also wrote interestingly about the visual arts. Characteristically, the works evoked to powerful effect in *Peintures* (1916) are largely imaginary. [MHTS]

SEGHERS, Pierre (1906–87). French poet, anthologist, and publisher. He first came to prominence in the context of Resistance poetry to which he made a massive contribution as writer and organizer [see OCCUPATION AND RESISTANCE]. *Poètes casqués* (1939–40) published soldiers' poetry. Thereafter, annual volumes (*Poésie 1940*, etc.), produced in the southern zone in collaboration with *Aragon, *Éluard, and others, gave poetry a cardinal role in the struggle against barbarism. The anthology *La Résistance et ses poètes* (1974) is an impressive monument to his achievements. After the war Seghers founded a publishing-house which is best known for the invaluable series 'Poètes d'Aujourd'hui' (over 100 titles), instrumental in bringing younger poets to public attention. In his own poetry (collected in *Le Temps des merveilles*, 1978) Seghers is always eloquent and accomplished, fusing public and private emotion in subtle but accessible language. [MHTS]

SEGRAIS, Jean Regnauld de (1624–1701). French man of letters who left the ecclesiastical life for poetry. He wrote verse and a tragedy and frequented the Hôtel de *Rambouillet. The most important stage of his career began in 1647 when he was introduced to the duchesse de *Montpensier. For over 20 years he served as her literary assistant. They collaborated on numerous publications, which Segrais signed, but whose principal author remains undecided. The *Nouvelles françaises* (1656–7) is known in particular for its important preface proclaiming the importance of plausibility for modern prose fiction. *La Galerie des peintures* (1659), which they co-edited, launched the mode of verbal portraits and self-portraits. He was elected to the Académie Française in 1662. After falling out with Montpensier, Segrais briefly played a similar role with Madame de *Lafayette. He collaborated on *Zayde*, which was published under his name; its preface, by his friend *Huet, is addressed to Segrais. He retired to Caen in 1676 and revived its Academy. [JDeJ]

SÉGUIER, Pierre (1588–1672). A lawyer of noble family, holder of many diplomatic and administrative positions. He became chancellor of France in 1635 and protector of the *Académie Française in 1643. A faithful servant of Louis XIV, he showed great zeal in prosecuting *Fouquet.

SÉGUR, Sophie Rostopchine, comtesse de (1799–1874). Writer of children's fiction. Despite charges of racism, feudalism, and indecency (dubious spanking scenes) levelled at her by modern critics, Madame de Ségur, born in St Petersburg, remains the *doyenne* of French childrens' writing which, a century and a half after *Perrault, she rescued from the wishy-washy clutches of Madame de *Genlis, *Berquin, and others. Written for middle- and upper-class readers, her stories are lively, realistic, and unprudish, with colourful use of dialogue. The books, including *Les Petites Filles modèles* (1857), *Les Malheurs de Sophie* (1864), *Le Général Dourakine* (1866), formed the backbone of Hachette's famous 'Bibliothèque Rose' and have delighted generations of French children. [DAS]

Seinte Resurreccion, La, see ANGLO-NORMAN LITERATURE, 5.

SELDEN, Camille, see TAINE.

Semaines, Les, see DU BARTAS.

Semaine sainte, La. Novel by *Aragon, published 1958. It deals with the Holy Week in 1815 when, following Napoleon's escape from Elba, Louis XVIII fled to Belgium in the company of the painter *Géricault. The novel explores, through Géricault's growing historical consciousness, the relationship between art and society. [NH]

Semaine sanglante, La, see COMMUNE DE PARIS (1871).

Sémantique structurale, see GREIMAS.

SEMBÈNE Ousmane (b. 1923) is famous as the pioneer of African cinema, but his contribution to literature is equally outstanding. His early novels, *Le Docker noir* (1956) and *Ô pays mon beau peuple* (1957), form part of the wave of anti-colonial literature of the 1950s, but it is with *Les Bouts de bois de Dieu* (1960) that he emerges as a major artist and thinker, a position which has been consolidated by his subsequent work.

Born in Senegal, Sembène's background distinguishes him from other writers of his generation, especially his famous compatriot *Senghor. Expelled from school at 14, Sembène worked as a builder before joining the army. World War II, he claims, was a major factor in his ideological education. During the 1950s he worked in France as a mechanic and later a docker, furthering his formal education in evening classes. He joined the Communist Party and was active in the trade-union movement, before returning to Africa in 1958.

Les Bouts de bois de Dieu is a fictional recreation of the 1947 railway workers' strike in the French Sudan. A beautifully constructed and deeply moving work, it belies the theory that aesthetic quality and ideological commitment are incompatible. One aspect of its originality lies in its introduction into the African novel of a collective, popular protagonist—the developing African proletariat—and of the idea of organized resistance. The novel reflects Sembène's belief that Africa will be liberated, not by the élite, but by the struggle of the working class. Women play a prominant role in the novel: for Sembène, sexual equality will be achieved through women's involvement in the class struggle rather than by separate feminist movements.

In *Les Bouts de bois de Dieu* Marxism equips Sembène to go beyond the false dichotomy of tradition and modernism in which many African intellectuals tend to flounder. His ideal, 'une Afrique indépendante et rénovée', involves a rejection of the Western capitalist development model, which perpetuates dependency, and also of the oppressive feudal, patriarchal, and gerontocratic residues of traditional society. The way forward embraces science and technology along with all aspects of popular traditional culture compatible with scientific socialism, such as self-reliance and the community spirit.

In 1963, after a short course on cinema in Moscow, Sembène made his first film. His involvement in cinema sprang from his concept of art as a means of raising the consciousness of the masses and his awareness of the limitations of literature in French for reaching an African public who do not know the language and cannot read. Sembène also participated in promoting literacy in the national languages, through the Wolof newspaper, *Kaddu*.

Unlike those writers who had illusions about Independence and consequently refrained from comment throughout the early 1960s, Sembène's critique of African leadership and their collusion with Western capitalism has been continuous. His only collection of short stories, *Voltaïques* (1962), was followed by *L'Harmattan* (1964), an incisive fictional recreation of the politics of the 1958 Referendum when, under Senghor, Senegal voted against a radical break with France. Two novellas, *Le Mandat* and *Véhi-Ciosane*, published in a single volume, won for Sembène his only literary prize, awarded by the 1966 Festival des Arts Nègres in Dakar. *Le Mandat* became a famous film, as did Sembène's next novel, *Xala* (1973), in which he reveals the link between cultural alienation and economic impotence. *Le Dernier de l'empire*, a *roman à clefs* which appeared in 1981, within months of Senghor's resignation as president of Senegal, is a hard-hitting review of Senegalese political history since Independence, and a critical meditation on democracy. Two more novellas, *Niiwam* and *Taaw*, drafted much earlier, appeared in a single volume in 1987.

Sembène has the great artist's ability to distill the essential structures and mechanisms of society into powerful, memorable images which become symbols of the times: the money-order, the (literally) impotent business man, the peasant forced by penury to convey his dead child's corpse to the cemetery in the bus. Consistently Afrocentric, his work in its entirety is an implicit condemnation of Senghor's *négritude* and the latter's promotion of *la *francophonie* and other aspects of French cultural hegemony. In Sembène's later work, he appears less optimistic about the revolutionary role of the proletariat, and seems to lean towards the military as the only viable symbol of African resistance and rehabilitation. [FNC]

See P. Vieyra, *Sembène Ousmane cinéaste* (1972); F. Pfaff, *The Cinema of Ousmane Sembène, a Pioneer of African Film* (1984).

Semiology, semiotics, see BARTHES; SAUSSURE.

SEMPRUN, Jorge (b. 1923). The son of a member of the Spanish Frente Popular government of 1932–8, Semprun was forced to take refuge in France when Franco overthrew it. As an active Communist he joined the Resistance but was captured and sent to Buchenwald. He survived and recorded his experiences in two novels, written in French, *Le Grand Voyage* (1963) and *Quel beau dimanche* (1981); the

Sénac

former in particular is remarkable for its conjunction of personal experience and narrative technique. Perhaps just as important are his two collaborations with Alain *Resnais, for whom he scripted *La Guerre est finie* (1965) and *Stavisky* (1974), since both films record, in different ways, a disaffection from the revolutionary struggle and the Marxist world-view. Equally interesting is his autobiographical work *L'Autobiographie de Féderico Sanchez* (1978), first published in Spanish. He returned to Spain to become minister of culture in the socialist government of Felipe Gonzalez.   [IWR]

SÉNAC, Jean (1926–73). Algerian poet who began, while very young, to frequent literary and artistic circles, and in 1948 met *Dib and *Camus, and later *Char, who were all to have a profound influence on him. Sénac's poems, published in reviews, were haunted by the human suffering around him, and filled with faith in a better future 'sous un soleil fraternel'. His first volume of poetry, *Poèmes* (1954), had an introduction by Char. When the *Algerian War broke out in the same year he became committed to the cause of his people and fought in the FLN; his poetry became the expression of the battle for independence: the colonialist enemy, the suffering of the country, and oppression. *Matinale de mon peuple* was published in 1961.

Sénac's non-war poetry is a search for his own truth, his own identity and origins, his father, his real name (*Avant-Corps, Diwân du Noûn*, 1968). He was concerned with the future of Algeria after independence, holding that no revolution is possible without love, and, for love to exist, the heart of man needs to change, 'Car il n'y a pas de Révolution sans Amour' (*Citoyens de beauté*, 1967). It was not only the political future of the country that concerned him; he did all he could to encourage its artistic talent. He worked for Algerian Radio, organized poetry recitals, and published, with an introduction written by himself, *Anthologie de la nouvelle poésie algérienne* (1971), introducing a number of young poets to a wider public. The sun, a recurrent theme in Sénac's writing, is the symbol of the fullness of fraternity—of harmony, of love, and of inspiration. He was disillusioned at times with the lack of progress after independence, and his support for cultures other than Arab, e.g. Berber and French, made his situation in Algiers rather difficult. He was murdered in mysterious circumstances in 1973.   [ET]

SÉNAC DE MEILHAN, Gabriel (1736–1803). A high-level French administrator who in later life wrote a variety of literary, political, and philosophical works, including *Considérations sur l'esprit et les mœurs de ce temps* (1787) and *Du gouvernement, des mœurs et des conditions en France avant la Révolution* (1795). He is now known, above all, for *L'Émigré* (1797), one of the only contemporary novels about the Revolution still available in bookshops. It deploys the rhetoric of sensibility to move the reader to sympathize with dispossessed aristocrats and to loathe the cruelty of the *Jacobins. He left France on the outbreak of Revolution and travelled in Russia, Germany, and Austria.   [BR]

SENANCOUR, Étienne Pivert de (1770–1846). Melancholic and pessimistic writer who subjected the self to intense and unremitting scrutiny in his novel *Oberman* (1804), a text which is inextricably associated with the *mal du siècle.

Senancour had an uneventful and highly reclusive life in Paris and in Switzerland. An unsuccessful marriage left him with a bitter and resigned outlook, but he found philosophical consolation in his disappointments and solitariness and nurtured them as the sources of his literary power. His bleak and comfortless philosophy of life, his misanthropy and misogyny, his failure to find adequate energy and reasons for action and belief—all appealed to those later writers who saw in him a fellow spirit (*Sainte-Beuve, Matthew Arnold). He was discovered by the Romantics in the early 1830s and became the focus of a small cult. Finely balanced between Enlightenment materialism and Romantic spirituality, he also wrote a series of dense and difficult philosophical and meditative texts: *Les Premiers Âges* (1792), *Sur les générations actuelles* (1793), *Rêveries sur la nature primitive de l'homme* (1798–1800), and *Libres. méditations d'un solitaire inconnu* (1819, and a later uncompleted version).   [BR]

Sénat, Le, see NATIONAL ASSEMBLIES.

SENAULT, Jean-François (c.1601–1672). Philosopher and preacher. The date of his birth at Antwerp is disputed. Under the influence of *Bérulle he first joined the *Oratorian congregation in 1618, and became its superior in 1662. His sermons and funeral orations were much imitated, and won him the favour of *Anne d'Autriche; *Voltaire commends him as an early restorer of the prestige of preaching in 17th-c. Paris. Senault is now best known for *De l'usage des passions* (1641), a two-part treatise which attempts to synthesize the Augustinian and *Neostoic moral traditions, and represents a current of thought which surfaces again in *Pascal and *La Rochefoucauld.   [PJB]

Sénéchaussée, see PARLEMENTS.

SENGHOR, Léopold Sédar (b. 1906). Joint founder with Aimé *Césaire, in Paris of the 1930s, of the black cultural movement of *négritude, Senghor is now widely regarded as the *doyen* of African francophone writing. He has vindicated the movement's objectives in both a literary and a political capacity. Not only a poet of world stature, he is also a critic, educational and social theorist, and a member of the Académie Française. In the practical world, following a distinguished academic and political career in France, he dominated the West African scene as a statesman for several

756

decades, being from 1960 to 1980 president of Senegal.

Senghor was born in the coastal town of Joal into a Christian merchant family of the Serer tribe; his writing in all fields draws strength from the cross-currents of his background and formative experiences. His position as a tribal and religious *minoritaire* enabled him to bypass internal rivalries as a leader in a Muslim state. The confluence in his education, first at mission schools, then at the Sorbonne, of his African heritage with orthodox French and classical culture, has nourished a body of poetry where sensual vibrancy and intensity combine distinctively with erudition, and the intricacies of traditional rhythm accommodate a polyvalent symbolism. Felt as the living core of his personality, *négritude* is also intellectually perceived as an anthropological and historical reality. His poetry, and no less his prose writings, offer a deliberately contrived *défense et illustration* of the vitality of African civilization and of its common ancestry with European counterparts; this was demonstrated in 1948 by his *Anthologie de la nouvelle poésie nègre et malgache de langue française*, with a preface entitled *Orphée noir (Black Orpheus)* by *Sartre. Senghor's eclecticism in the language and substance of his poetry, or in the content of his political doctrine, stems neither from convenience nor from accident. It springs rather from a coherent philosophical vision, formally underpinned by systematic scholarship, where cultural diversity is deemed capable of resolving itself through cross-fertilization in a *civilisation de l'universel*.

Senghor's poetry may be classed in the conventional categories of lyric, elegy, and eulogy. Simultaneously it records his own personal odyssey of exile, alienation, protest, and revolt through to healing and fulfilment, intimate joy, and public celebration. The poetry's meaning is invariably multilayered. Thus, its frank eroticism, exalting both human and natural fecundity, is generated by the dualism of woman and the continent of Africa. Jointly they constitute a territory of body and of soul where images and sensations, though concretely evoked, are endlessly interchangeable. For Senghor's intense sensuality, quintessentially African as it is, holds the key to his spirituality. At its deepest level his poetry is sacramental, not only inspired in its content and metre by traditional ritual, but in itself constituting, through the creative articulation of signs, an act of participation in the cycles and forces of nature. In such visionary aspirations Senghor displays affinities with *Claudel, while his conception of imagery as both analogical and associative recalls *Baudelaire, though the reality thus translated must be construed as vitalistic rather than ideal.

The poems comprise the following volumes: *Chants d'ombre* (1945); *Hosties noires* (1948); *Chants pour Naëtt* (1949); *Éthiopiques* (1956); *Nocturnes* (1961); *Lettres d'hivernage* (1973); together with *Élégies*

majeures (1979), composed in honour of friends and eminent contemporaries (e.g. Georges *Pompidou, Martin Luther King), and *Poèmes* (1984). Their subjects range from the black exile's search for identity and war's revelation of Europe's spiritual and moral bankruptcy, to the potency of Africa's landscape and the poignancy of separation from the beloved. Metrically, Senghor practises a form of free verse. He simulates the rhythmic effects of traditional music by incorporating the grammatical elisions and parallelisms characteristic of some African languages.

His prose writings, in a projected six volumes, bear the collective title *Liberté*. In contrast to the erudite hermeticism of his poetry, they display literary cosmopolitanism, pedagogic directness, and the shrewdness of a pragmatist. Almost always addressing cultural and political issues raised by *decolonization, Senghor explores the modalities of an African critical perspective. He shows particular skill in adapting such philosophical sources as Marx and, notably, *Teilhard de Chardin, to forge a flexible ideology and attainable programme for emergent African nations. [For critiques of Senghor's ideas and political practice, see for instance NÉGRITUDE; SEMBÈNE; SOW FALL.] [SMM]

See S. W. Bâ, *The Concept of Négritude in the Poetry of Léopold Sédar Senghor* (1973); M. M. Marquet, *Le Métissage dans la poésie de L. S. Senghor* (1983); R. Joanny, *Les Voies du lyrisme dans les 'Poèmes' de L. S. Senghor* (1986).

Sensibilité, La. A literary-cum-social phenomenon whose beginnings in France can be traced to the closing years of the 17th c., and whose apogee is the period between about 1760 and the Revolution. It consists of extreme emotional sensitivity, giving rise to lively manifestations of feeling. The emotions in question are usually the 'softer' ones: love, pity, sympathy, regret, grief, etc., and these are most frequently shown by violent gestures, tears, and broken speech (the last effect often indicated in print by a lavish use of exclamation marks and *points de suspension*). Hence the term *comédie larmoyante* for drama of this kind.

In plays and novels anyone who is truly *sensible* is generally taken to be made of finer stuff than the common herd and is therefore superior to colder, less demonstrative characters. (Des Grieux, in *Manon Lescaut*, asserts this explicitly.) *Sensibilité* is connected with kindness, so it acquired associations of virtue and goodness of heart, but in a secular rather than religious mode: the *acte de bienfaisance* replaces Christian charity. The 18th-c. *Tartuffe is, therefore, a *faux sensible* instead of a religious hypocrite; an example is Valmont's pretended act of kindness in Les *Liaisons dangereuses*.

Most *drames, like *Diderot's two works in this new genre, are rich in *sensibilité*. A high proportion of 18th-c. novels, especially those with edifying aims, also show *sensibilité* at work; the lovers in

Rousseau's *La *Nouvelle Héloïse*, for instance, are deeply *sensible*. The most prolific exponent of *sensibilité* was *Baculard d'Arnaud, immensely popular in his day but now forgotten. The phenomenon was not exclusively French: many English and German writers, for instance, displayed the same kind of sentimentality, with lush expressions of feeling. Certain authors, notably *Voltaire, mocked the cult of *sensibilité*; in fact a new term, *sensiblerie*, was coined to convey the notion of excessively emotional behaviour.

In real life some people, mainly those with the money and the leisure to demonstrate finer feelings, displayed the outward forms of *sensibilité*. At a deeper level it can be seen as one of the motives for a growing number of secular charitable works—homes for foundlings and orphans, hospitals for the poor, etc.—and for sympathy with the underprivileged, such as slaves. At this level *sensibilité* was part of a wider movement (which included rationalists, *philosophes*, and critics of *sensibilité*) that was attempting to awaken greater social awareness and to reduce the injustice and abuses of contemporary society. [VGM]

Sept Cordes de la lyre, Les, see SAND.

September Massacres, see REVOLUTION, 1b.

Séquestrés d'Altona, Les. Play by *Sartre, first performed 1959. It focuses on the fortunes of the Von Gerlach family in post-war Germany, but reflects Sartre's concern with issues raised by the *Algerian War. The younger son, Frantz, has incarcerated himself in his room since the war ended, unable to face the implications of the fact that he participated in torture, or of Germany's economic recovery. He seems half-mad, trapped in an incestuous relationship with his sister, Léni, and refusing to confront the truth about his own life or European history. It is Sartre's most pessimistic play. There appears no possibility of redemption or conversion. The forces of family and history conspire to reduce Frantz to impotence—he is victim and prisoner of both subjective and objective contradictions. Sartre's *rapprochement* with Marx and Freud here reveals the potential abyss of human alienation. The play seems to announce not now the death of God, but the death of *Existential man himself. Paradoxically, however, Frantz's suicide, his only way out of an intolerable situation, could be seen to bring him close to some kind of tragic authenticity. [CMH]

Séraphita. Novel by *Balzac, begun in 1834, published 1835 with *Les Proscrits* and *Louis Lambert* in *Le Livre mystique*. Set in an imaginary Nordic land, *Séraphita* presents an androgynous creature who 'has climbed rung by rung the mystic Ladder of Existence and is ready to be received into the company of the angelic hosts' (H. J. Hunt). One of Balzac's least successful novels, it preaches *Illuminist doctrines drawn from *Swedenborg and *Saint-Martin, and sits uneasily alongside the rest of *La Comédie humaine*, from which mysticism and religiosity are largely absent. [DMB]

SERGE, Victor (pseud. of Viktor Kibalchich) (1890–1947). Revolutionary politician. Of Russian origin, he was born in Brussels, was imprisoned as an anarchist in Paris, and took part in the Russian Revolution from 1919. His resistance to Stalinism led to exile in France and Mexico. His writings express his political convictions vigorously: *Mémoires d'un révolutionnaire* (1951) and five largely autobiographical novels, published as *Les Révolutionnaires* (1967). [PF]

SERHANE, Abdelhak (b. 1950). Moroccan Berber recorder of the bleakness of life in Azrou under French colonialism and after independence. In two outstanding novels, *Messaouda* (1983) and *Les Enfants des rues étroites* (1986), Serhane traces the brutal, illiterate reality of rural life while satirizing its transcription into an alien idiom via the Moroccan francophone novel developed for a foreign audience. A highly intelligent and principled writer, Serhane trained as a psychologist and obtained a teaching post at the University of Vemtra. [JKa]

Série Noire, La. Marcel Duhamel launched Gallimard's thriller collection in 1945, its punning title suggested by Jacques *Prévert. Translators, including Boris *Vian, adapted Chase, Cheyney, and Chandler for the post-war vogue of Americana, promising violence with style and humour, under intriguing titles and yellow-and-black covers. The first French author published, Serge Arcouët, pretended to be American ('Terry Stewart', *La Mort et l'ange*, 1948), as did *Amila; the first French signature was André Piljean, *Passons la monnaie* (1951). Thrillers, espionnage, and westerns are still imported, distinctly packaged as consumables: the thousandth title (American) appeared in 1966, the two-thousandth (French) in 1985. Aimed at a public taste formed by film, Série Noire action and atmosphere also inspired film-makers. Albert *Simonin and Auguste Le Breton (*Du rififi chez les hommes*, 1951) introduced authentic *argot, and, though still predominantly American, the series included, from the mid-1960s, more French authors: Francis Ryck, *Opération Millibar* (1966); Viard and Zacharias, a parodic *Hamlet* entitled *L'Embrumé* (1966). Diverse distinctive French notes are sounded: political in J.-P. *Manchette, *L'Affaire N'Gustro* (1971), reworking the Ben Barka case; grotesque in Pierre Siniac, *Luj Inferman' et la Cloducque* (1971); pastoral-comical in A.D.G., *Berry Story* (1973); amusingly inventive in Daniel Pennac, *Au bonheur des ogres* (1985), set in today's Paris. [See also DETECTIVE FICTION.] [SFN]

Serments de Strasbourg, Les, see STRASBOURG OATHS.

Sermon

1. The Sermon as a Literary Genre

Sermons form an important, at times even preponderant, element in French literary production, and preachers in French have greatly enriched the genre. Yet their contribution is largely inseparable from its international context. The Christian sermon has its origins in Scripture and was thoroughly elaborated by the early Church Fathers, often under the influence of secular Greek and Roman *rhetoric. These models have exercised a lasting influence, not least because preachers regularly aspire to prove their orthodoxy by appealing to antiquity, and are trained to do so. The result is that sermons of every period and in every tongue display more affinities than dissimilarities; it is hard to speak of an evolution or to identify elements specific to French-speaking countries. Manuals for preachers (abundant medieval Artes prædicandi and post-Renaissance Discours sur l'éloquence sacrée were written in France) adhere even more rigidly to the conventions of their genre.

None the less, it is because preachers partly aim to instruct their hearers by appealing to contemporary taste that they are of interest to social and literary as well as to religious historians. Though often a distorting mirror (for life is seen through the filter of biblical or classical analogies, and clerical preoccupations feature disproportionately), preaching before the advent of universal literacy and the mass media is a rich source of cultural information, with household names among its leading exponents. There is, however, in every age, a marked disjunction between what is heard in church and the texts that survive. Of the several categories of preaching, the bulk have gone unrecorded. In the French Catholic tradition this is above all the case of the weekly talk at Mass (homily or *prône*), though models for imitation have regularly appeared. From medieval times to the present day it is the series of addresses for Advent and Lent, saints' days, and major festivals which have been collected and preserved. From *Reformation days Protestant preaching has frequently been published in the form of commentaries on Scripture. Funeral orations, because they serve as obituaries, survive in greater number than, say, sermons for rural or colonial missions. This distinction to be drawn between the history of preaching and the history of the sermon is all the sharper because, until the advent of the tape-recorder, the written text is rarely a simple transcription of the oral address. It commonly has a different goal, as a formal essay or a thesaurus of ideas and authorities for others to plunder. Sometimes the text is based on the preacher's own jottings, sometimes on the notes of listeners or even professional secretaries: *Calvin employed a stenographer. Years may elapse between delivery and the appearance of a written, possibly unauthorized, version.

2. The Middle Ages

These distinctions are especially true of the Middle Ages. Preaching in Latin was restricted to the universities and clerical or monastic assemblies. But though elsewhere the vernacular was used, the written versions are almost invariably in Latin. The outstanding exception is *Gerson, nearly 60 of whose vernacular sermons survive. Sometimes the transcriptions are in a mixture of Latin and the vernacular, a practice running from the 10th c. (*Sermon sur Jonas*) to the late 15th c., and though the curious *'macaronic' sermons resulting from this process are amusingly parodied by *Rabelais, it would be wrong to suppose that they were delivered in this hybrid form.

The surviving earlier medieval sermons reflect the ebb and flow of influences in the Church—the *Cluniacs, the 12th-c. founding of the *Cistercians (important texts by *Bernard de Clairvaux) and the Victorines (Richard de St-Victor, d. 1173), the rise of the *Scholastics (with collections by *Abélard, *Alan of Lille, Maurice de Sully). This theological rather than pastoral emphasis continues with the emergence of the University of Paris and eventually flowers in the work of Gerson. As primarily academic sermons, their core is the fourfold interpretation of Scripture in its literal, moral, anagogical, and allegorical senses, though little space is given to purely historical aspects of exegesis.

In 1210 Innocent III granted the *Franciscans the right to preach, and they were followed by the *Dominicans or 'Order of Preachers'. The Mendicants provided training for preachers and unleashed a flood of manuals and encyclopaedias for this purpose throughout Europe. Their movement reaches its apogee in France with Olivier *Maillard and Michel *Menot. Late-medieval sermons conform to a set plan. The *prothema* is a miniature introductory sermon; then comes the *thema*, a scriptural text raising a point of theology or of canon law which is analysed into divisions and subdivisions, often with great subtlety and virtuosity. But these dry bones are animated by the use of *exempla* in the form of saints' lives, popular tales, and animal fables, and by dramatic techniques such as invented dialogue shot through with the language of the streets and taverns.

3. Reformation to the Present

With the Reformation, preaching in French achieves a fresh authority: the language of Calvin's sermons, widely diffused by the new printing-presses, allies the richly colloquial late-medieval inheritance with the prestige of the newly translated vernacular Scriptures. During the *Wars of Religion controversy between Catholics and Protestants frequently spilled over into politics: the *Ligue was notorious for rabble-rousing preachers such as Jean Boucher (1551-1646). By imposing discretion on both sides, *Henri IV is traditionally considered to have ushered in the golden age of the sermon.

759

Sermon joyeux

The Calvinist tradition was vigorously maintained in France by preachers such as Pierre du Moulin (1568–1658) and Moïse Amyraut (1596–1664) until the Revocation of the *Edict of Nantes (and continues in French-speaking Switzerland to our own day). In the Catholic world the Council of Trent had striven to revive the dignity of preaching, and the dissemination of its decrees in France, part of a wider renewal of spiritual fervour associated with *Bérulle and St *Vincent de Paul, coincided with a creative literary ferment. Already in the first half of the 17th c. published sermons by such as Jean-Pierre *Camus and Étienne Molinier (d. 1647) were in great demand. By the reign of Louis XIV pulpit oratory, shorn of vulgar *exempla* and imitations of popular speech, entered the mainstream of court life with *Bossuet, *Bourdaloue, *Fléchier, and *Massillon, whose works have remained classics. (Funeral orations for the illustrious dead were a particularly magnificent form of oratory.) *La Bruyère chides his contemporaries for allowing Christian discourse to become a spectacle; but grand eloquence in the pulpit, perhaps especially when the theatres were closed in Lent and Advent, answered a deeply felt need. He also mocks the rigidity of sermon structures, and it is true that at this point they (like drama) achieve a form which remains fixed for two centuries. The classical sermon begins with an ornate *avant-propos* leading up to a communally recited *Ave Maria*; the preacher then proposes a division of his scriptural text into three points, and considers each one in turn. The third point provides a synthesis and concludes with direct exhortation or with prayer. The structure is not dissimilar to the academic *dissertation française*.

Massillon was an *Oratorian, and members of his order, such as the Terrasson brothers (André, 1673–1723; Gaspard, 1680–1752), were the leading 18th-c. exponents of the full-dress sermon in its crystallized state. Though they incline to biblical metaphors, they remain in contact with contemporary ideas. The *Jesuits, notably Charles de Neuville (1693–1774), maintain Bourdaloue's use of the seductive character portrait. Increasingly they preach against the *philosophes*, with *Voltaire's enemy Le Chapelain (1710–79) becoming a pulpit satirist.

The dissolution of the Society of Jesus, the suppression of seminaries under the Revolution, and the general disorder of the French Church in its aftermath, led paradoxically to even greater reverence for the classics of the *grand siècle*. The 19th c. saw extensive reprinting of their works for use as models, culminating in J.-P. Migne's *Collection des orateurs sacrés*. But the same social conditions drove a wedge between the formal sermon and the re-evangelization of the countryside by the Mission de France or by rural apostles such as the Curé d'Ars, whose simple homilies over the period 1820 to 1850 display a return to everyday speech, anecdote, and relative formlessness. At this time, too, the Dominicans reappear as leading preachers, a posi-

tion they have maintained to our own day. *Lacordaire was the Order's most famous 19th-c. orator. His disciples and successors include Fathers Didon (1840–1900), Janvier (1860–1939), and Sertillanges (1863–1948). Their preaching on solemn occasions, not least during World War I, was diffused by the growing religious press. Between the wars the annual Lenten Conférences à Notre-Dame de Paris attracted huge audiences to hear the Oratorian Pierre Samson (1885–1955) and the Jesuit Henri Pinard de la Boullaye (1874–1958). Aided by the rise of broadcasting, these series maintain the tradition of the formal sermon as a special event.

[PJB]

See P. J. Bayley, *French Pulpit Oratory, 1598–1650* (1980); F. P. Bowman, *Le Discours sur l'éloquence sacrée à l'époque du romantisme* (1980); J.-P. Collinet and T. Goyet (eds.), *Bossuet: la prédication au XVIIe siècle* (1980); J. Longère, *La Prédication médiévale* (1983).

Sermon joyeux. A 15th- and 16th-c. theatrical genre, of which about 30 examples survive, in which an actor disguised as a preacher pronounces a short mock-sermon in a mixture of French and dog Latin. The themes vary from encomia on absurd objects (*Sermon de saint Hareng*) to risqué *exempla*. Structurally, they make use of the formal conventions of the sermon proper, proceeding from concocted texts in dog Latin or carefully chosen biblical texts, to a burlesque final lesson. Their deliberately irreverent choice of subject has links with the licence of carnival and the Feast of Fools. [JHMT]

SERREAU, Geneviève (1915–81). Co-founder of the Théâtre de Babylone, where her play *Les Peines de cœur d'une chatte anglaise* (1977) achieved great popularity, and author of an *Histoire du nouveau théâtre* (1966). She was married to Jean-Marie *Serreau. Her fiction, which tends to attack social and cultural stereotypes, includes *Un enfer très convenable* (1981), in which notions of paradise and hell are subtly explored. [EAF]

SERREAU, Jean-Marie (1915–73). Theatre director, husband of the above. A versatile and experimental explorer of dramatic forms, he is best remembered as one of the directors who helped to promote new playwrights of the 1950s, especially *Beckett, *Ionesco, *Adamov, and *Genet. [DWW]

SERRES, Michel (b. 1930). French philosopher and imaginative writer and member of the Académie Française who has moved from the rational analysis of his early work on Leibniz, mathematics, and information theory (see *Hermès*, I–V) to non-systematic creative thinking, grounded in sensual awareness of the world. Among his numerous works, *Le Parasite* (1980), *Genèse* (1982), *Rome: le livre des fondations* (1983), and *Détachement* (1983) deal centrally and peripherally with the origin of knowledge and the balance of power in relationships. *Les Cinq Sens*

(1985) is an extended literary meditation on intuition and practical sense-knowledge. *Statues* (1987) links aesthetics, religion, and philosophy. *Le Contrat naturel* (1990) proposes a new pact with nature to replace the social contract. Finally, *Le Tiers-Instruit* (1991) presents the motley result of all education, seeing knowledge as elliptical, a way from, not a way through (*exodus* not method).

Serres's work has become increasingly a kind of poetic philosophy, or a philosophical narration, mainly about knowledge and communication, rooted in lived experience, typically that of the seaman and the peasant; it constitutes an ecstatic personal quest for truth and an attempt to recover our primitive inheritance, too often obscured or atrophied by language, and his thought is shaped by his vibrant, exploratory, and culturally allusive writing.
[PS]

SERRES, Olivier de (1539–1619). French writer on rural economy. A Calvinist nobleman, he was a loyal servant of Henri IV, who greatly appreciated his *Théâtre d'agriculture et ménage des champs* (1600), and encouraged him to publish separately the section on silk, which led to the introduction of the silkworm into France.

Sertorius. Tragedy by Pierre *Corneille, first performed 1662. One of the best of his later plays, it tells of plots and counterplots in the unsuccessful struggle of the general Sertorius against the forces of the Roman senate led by Pompée. The high point is the debate between the two leaders in Act II.

Serventois, see SIRVENTES.

Servitude et grandeur militaire (1835). This volume by *Vigny contains three short stories which highlight the themes of duty, sacrifice, and service. Writing amidst what he calls 'le naufrage général des croyances', Vigny aspires to a new religion of conscience which he identifies with the idea of honour. The three stories are entitled *Laurette ou le Cachet rouge*, *La Veillée de Vincennes* and *La Vie et la mort du capitaine Renaud ou la Canne de jonc*. The first tale illustrates nicely the countervailing pressures of different loyalties. It recounts how, during the Directoire, the commander of a naval vessel grows to like and respect the prisoner whom he is transporting to Cayenne. However, at the equator the captain opens his sealed orders and discovers that he is required to execute the prisoner. The death sentence is duly carried out, but the captain subsequently leaves the navy and takes responsibility for the prisoner's wife, who has become insane. [CC]

Séthos, see TERRASSON.

Seuil, Éditions du. French publishing-house founded in 1937 by Jean Bardet and Paul Flamand. After World War II it published contemporary authors such as *Bernanos, *Emmanuel, Pierre-Henri Simon, *Teilhard de Chardin, and Graham Greene. Its collections include series of essays focusing on contemporary intellectual life, and it has a particularly noted role in the field of human sciences, especially linguistics and semiology, publishing *Barthes, *Greimas, *Kristeva, and *Todorov. It has also participated in avant-garde literary movements, notably that associated with *Sollers and *Tel Quel.
[EAF]

SEURAT, Georges (1859–91). French painter. Rejecting what he considered the intuitive, subjective treatment of colour in *Monet's work, Seurat sought to establish *Impressionism on a more scientific basis. His technique, which he called divisionism, was based on his study of *Delacroix, Chevreul's colour theories, and Charles *Henry's chromatic circle. Small dots of colour, instead of being mixed on the palette, were juxtaposed on the canvas and mingled in the eye of the spectator standing at the appropriate distance. *Fénéon defined the new style in *Les Impressionnistes en 1886* and *Kahn saw it as related to *Symbolist experimentation with *vers libre*. [JK]

SÈVE, Lucien (b. 1926). *Marxist philosopher. Born in Chambéry, he studied philosophy at the *École Normale Supérieure, passing the *agrégation* in 1949, and subsequently taught in several provincial *lycées*. He joined the PCF in 1950, was elected to its Central Committee in 1961, and subsequently directed its publishing house, Éditions Sociales. Sève's early writings were polemical assertions of Stalinist orthodoxy but, prompted by educational and psychological concerns, he developed an innovative theory of the social construction of personality. His philosophical synthesis, *Une introduction à la philosophie marxiste* (1980), drew strongly on Hegelian dialectics, and proved productive in debates on religion and the ethical implications of scientific advance, especially in biology. [MHK]

Seven Years War (1756–63). War between Prussia on the one hand and Austria, France, Russia, Sweden, and Saxony on the other; the battles between *Frederick the Great and the allies are described with ferocious irony in the early chapters of Voltaire's *Candide*. Britain joined Prussia, and the resulting naval warfare between France and Britain led to the French loss of Canada, described by Voltaire as 'quelques arpents de neige' [see QUEBEC]. [PF]

Sévérambes, Histoire des, see VEIRAS.

SÉVERINE. Pseudonym of Caroline Rémy, Madame Guebhard (1855–1929), a celebrated journalist of the Third Republic. A friend of *Vallès, she directed *Le Cri du peuple* from 1886 to 1888, then worked free-lance. She attacked *Rochefort and defended anarchist, Socialist, and Communist positions. See her *Pages rouges* (1893), *Notes d'une frondeuse* (1894), and *Pages mystiques* (1895). [PF]

SÉVIGNÉ, Marie de Rabutin-Chantal, marquise de (1626–96). No woman writer has exercised a greater influence over the history of French literature than the marquise de Sévigné. From the early 18th c., when the first overviews of the French tradition were composed, to the present day, Sévigné alone among women writers has found a place in every canon of French literature. She produced what is arguably the most celebrated correspondence of all time. The stability of her literary fortunes is founded on the enduring importance in the French tradition of *letter-writing, a genre seldom highly prized in other national literary canons.

Born into an old aristocratic family, Marie de Rabutin-Chantal lived her life at the centre of the privilege, power, and luxury that the contemporary nobility cultivated so successfully. Her family gave her an education more than respectable for a female child of her day. She received the name by which literary history remembers her from a brief early marriage (1644–51) to Henri, baron and marquis de Sévigné. When her husband was killed in a duel over another woman, he left a 25-year-old widow with two children, Françoise-Marguerite (the future comtesse de Grignan, who received the lion's share of her mother's correspondence) and Charles. Sévigné might well have fulfilled a literary stereotype of the classical age, the beautiful, young, well-born widow. She became instead the prototype of the woman intellectual of the *ancien régime*.

She first became known as an intellectual when she frequented the *salons, especially the Hôtel de *Rambouillet. There she met major literary figures, among others, the comtesse de *Lafayette, her cousin by marriage and lifelong dearest friend. For nearly half a century Sévigné entertained numerous correspondents with letters of very different sorts. Some are chronicles of the scandals and amusements of court life, close in content to such early public newspapers as Le *Mercure galant. Others are overtly political: witness her celebrated accounts of the trial of *Foucquet. Sévigné's unrelenting defence of Foucquet shows none of the prudent reserve demonstrated by the men of letters who had enjoyed his protection.

Her letters are often the only literary source of information on numerous controversial events, from famines to parliamentary revolts and their official suppression. In treating these topics, Sévigné departs from her habitual exuberance and expansiveness and adopts a severe, affectless tone. This stylistic austerity is not, however, a sign of personal indifference, but a prudent response to the ease with which Louis XIV's police violated correspondences. Very different in tone is the correspondence most appreciated by modern readers, Sévigné's letters to her daughter. This most intimate and sustained chronicle of a mother–daughter relationship ever recorded is alternately an outpouring of passion and a brilliant display of wit.

Sévigné's earliest extant letters date from 1646.

Her correspondence won instant acclaim; certain letters were widely circulated in her lifetime, although none appeared in print. A few were published in the year of her death. Others appeared, although often in censored or excerpted versions, in a steady stream of editions in the 18th and 19th c. Some 1,100 letters have now been recovered (see Sévigné, *Correspondance*, ed. Roger Duchêne, 3 vols., 1972), but we cannot know what part of Sévigné's total production they represent. This strange publication history made it easy for each age to construct its own Sévigné corpus, tailored to reflect the view of her letters it wanted to promote. Pedagogical editions have long used selected correspondence to portray the author as the model of *ancien régime* elegance, as a role-model for young women, and as a tender mother.

Sévigné can play all the roles we assign her because her correspondence has so many facets: it is the portrait of a protean woman; it is a window onto the most fascinating of French courts; it is a history of private life, with information on everything from birth-control to hair-dos; it is a manual of epistolary styles. Other famous correspondences give us the private life of noted writers; Sévigné's provides perhaps a unique example of epistolary artistry so memorable that its creator is known as a great author. [JDeJ]

See R. Duchêne, *Madame de Sévigné ou la Chance d'être une femme* (1982).

Sèvres, École Normale Supérieure de. *Grande école* founded in 1881 to train teachers for the new girls' *lycées* [see EDUCATION, 2b]; alumni are known as *sévriennes*. In the 1980s it was merged with the *École Normale Supérieure de la rue d'Ulm.

SEYSSEL, Claude de (*c*.1450–1520). Savoyard scholar, diplomat, and churchman, successively bishop of Marseille and archbishop of Turin. He collaborated with the Byzantine refugee Janus Lascaris on translations of ancient Greek historians, and distilled his political experience into *La Grant Monarchie de France* (1519), a cogent and influential analysis of contemporary institutions. [MJH]

Sganarelle. Comic character, originally played by *Molière, and figuring in many of his plays, including *Sganarelle, ou le Cocu imaginaire* (1660), of which he is the pusillanimous hero. In other plays he may be a peasant/doctor (Le *Médecin malgré lui*) or a valet (*Dom Juan*), but he is always ludicrous.

Shaba deux, see MUDIMBE.

Shakespeare in France. It was only in the early 18th c. that Shakespeare became known across the Channel, mainly through the writings of *Prévost and, in particular, Voltaire's *Lettres philosophiques*. Voltaire's praise of the English playwright was quite bold, and he drew inspiration from him for his own dramatic innovations (more spectacular stage action, local colour, etc.). However, his attitude was from the beginning divided (as was that of many English contemporaries), and in later years his hostility was expressed more openly. For all his genius, Shakespeare's irregular plays seemed monstrous by French standards—pearls in a dunghill. *Diderot described him grandly as a 'colosse gothique'.

The first translations were P.-A. de la Place's prose versions in his *Théâtre anglais* (1745–9). These were followed by the complete prose rendering of *Le Tourneur (1776–82). *Ducis, who knew no English, used both of these for his watered-down verse adaptations. But Shakespeare had little impact on French dramatic practice in the 18th c.

It was the *Romantic movement which established him in the French poetic Pantheon [see DRAMA IN FRANCE SINCE 1789, 1]. Of the *drames romantiques*, Musset's *Lorenzaccio* is probably the most Shakespearian—significantly, it was not meant for the stage. *Hugo's plays are quite un-Shakespearian, though later he wrote an essay on genius, *William Shakespeare* (1864), as a preface to the translation of the *Œuvres complètes* (1859–65) by his son François-Victor. This has remained the standard translation; it marks a great advance over its predecessors in its faithfulness to the original.

Since the mid-19th c. Shakespeare has had a secure place in French culture. There have been new translations of individual plays, notably by *Gide, *Supervielle, *Jouve, and in particular *Bonnefoy. Most important has been the revolution in Shakespeare performance, launched by *Lugné-Poë and *Copeau and continued by the *Cartel, *Vilar, *Barrault, and most of the major post-war directors, who have exploited to the full this opportunity for free and innovative staging.   [PF]

Short Fiction. Pieces of fiction shorter than the *novel have generally been known in France by two names: *conte* and *nouvelle*; these two forms can further be distinguished from such didactic short narratives as the *exemplum* and the fable. The term *conte* suggests the relation to the oral *conte populaire*, or *folk-tale, and it tends to mean a short story containing supernatural or otherwise improbable elements. *Nouvelle*, on the other hand, is frequently used for longer, more literary narratives of real, contemporary life. The distinction is often unclear, particularly in the 19th c. *Mérimée, in a single sentence, refers to his *La Vénus d'Ille* as both *conte* and *nouvelle*.

The medieval verse *fabliau* and *lai* may be seen as French ancestors of short prose fiction. The *nouvelle* first makes its appearance in the 15th c., notably in the successful Les *Cent Nouvelles nouvelles*, a collection of mainly bawdy stories modelled on Boccaccio's *Decameron*. Similar collections followed over the next 100 years, including the *Grand paragon des nouvelles nouvelles et délectables* (c.1535) of Nicolas de Troyes, the *Nouvelles récréations* of *Des Périers, the rustic tales of *Du Fail, and above all the

Heptaméron of Marguerite de Navarre, where traditional *fabliau* material sits alongside more serious stories, the whole sequence being enclosed, like the *Decameron*, by a frame of courtly conversation.

In the 17th c. the influence of *Spanish models became more important, in particular that of Cervantes. Spanish stories were translated, adapted, and imitated by writers such as *Scarron, *Sorel, and *Segrais, the last of whom offers a definition and defence of the genre in the *Nouvelles françaises* of 1658. At this time the *nouvelle* is seen as a short novel, coming as a welcome relief from the interminable *roman héroïque*; Madame de *Lafayette's *La *Princesse de Clèves*, now thought of as a key work in the history of the French novel, was known in its day as a *nouvelle historique*. The second half of the 17th c. saw a flowering of such medium-length 'historical' narratives, often extravagant stories of love and adventure, by authors such as *Saint-Réal, *Villedieu, *La Roche-Guilem, *Boursault, and *Le Noble. At the same time, in a different vein, *La Fontaine's *Contes* offer elegant verse treatments of the rather disreputable old repertory.

Contes en vers continued to be written throughout the following century; *Gresset's *Ver-vert* is a good example of this entertaining genre. More generally, the 18th c. was a golden age for the *conte*. The success of two of the great classics of the genre, Perrault's *Histoires ou contes* and Galland's Les *Mille et une Nuits*, launched a vogue for fairy-tales and then oriental tales (d'*Aulnoy, *Caylus, *Gueulette, *Le Prince de Beaumont, *Cazotte, etc.). These might explore psychological subtleties, but made little claim to verisimilitude. They were generally light-hearted, often parodic; a vein of 'libertine' story-telling was exploited by many writers, from *Crébillon *fils* (*Le Sopha*) to *Denon (*Point de lendemain*).

A notable 18th-c. development was the use of the non-realistic *conte* to explore philosophical questions. *Voltaire's *contes philosophiques*, the summit of his work, range from brief squibs such as the *Voyages de Scarmentado* to the full-scale narratives of *Zadig, *Candide, or *La Princesse de Babylone*, series of *contes* linked by a search for meaning and happiness. More realistic anecdotes illustrating moral questions abound in *Diderot's writings, mostly embedded in longer novels or dialogues. In a similar spirit, in the second half of the 18th c. *Marmontel's *Contes moraux* helped revive the fortunes of the *nouvelle*. The material is not always original, but such writers as *Loaisel de Tréogate, *Baculard d'Arnaud, *Sade, and (later) *Genlis often obtain new emotional effects in their very different stories.

The 19th c. saw the greatest flowering of short prose fiction in France. It has been argued, somewhat dramatically, that the modern short story was born in France in the 1830s, and *Baudelaire in his introduction to *Poe gave one of the best accounts of the appeal of the short *nouvelle*, the equivalent in prose of the brief and intensely experienced lyric poem. Innumerable stories were published in the many newly established periodicals and newspapers, in 'keepsakes' (anthologies of pieces in prose and verse), and in collective publications of which the most famous was the *Soirées de Médan*. Almost all the great novelists and poets of the *Romantic period (*Balzac, *Dumas, *Hugo, *Vigny, *Musset, *Gautier, *Stendhal, *Sand, etc.) wrote *contes* and *nouvelles*, as did the *Realists and *Naturalists (*Flaubert, *Gobineau, *Erckmann-Chatrian, *Zola) and writers of the *fin de siècle* (*Barbey d'Aurevilly, *Bloy, *France). Some important writers, moreover, made their name as authors of short stories (even if they themselves attached more significance to their longer works); these include *Nodier, Alphonse *Daudet, *Villiers de l'Isle-Adam, and above all Mérimée and *Maupassant.

It is a sign of the lack of prestige of the short story that the masterly work of both Mérimée and Maupassant has been less praised and studied than the novels of the period. Their stories range from the short novel (e.g. *Colomba) to the brief comic anecdote (e.g. Maupassant's 'Toine'). Maupassant is particularly remarkable for his attempt to maintain the oral character of the *conte* by way of frame stories, internal narrators, and the like—though his work remains poles apart from the folk-tale. Both writers make use of short fiction to explore exotic or unfamiliar cultures (in the case of Maupassant, the world of the Normandy peasants), and both, though in very different ways, exploit the *fantastic vein of horror and mystery so characteristic of their time.

Since Maupassant, the prestige of the *conte* or *nouvelle* has declined. Short stories continue to be written and read in quite large numbers, but they rarely win the prizes which dominate the French literary scene. No 20th-c. authors of short fiction have quite matched the achievement of their 19th-c. predecessors. Even so, the genre has been variously illustrated by (among many others) *Aymé's humorous tales, the stories of *Pergaud, *Morand, and *Dabit, the surreal fictions of *Supervielle and *Mandiargues, *Yourcenar's *Nouvelles orientales* (1938), *Gripari's merry children's stories, and the many collections of *Arland, one of the century's most dedicated short-story writers. The *conte philosophique* has been revived in a new form: *Sartre (*Le Mur*) and *Camus (*L'Exil et le royaume*) use thematically grouped collections to explore existential dilemmas, while *Tournier, in his *Le Coq de bruyère* (1978), offers iconoclastic reworkings of old myths and legends. Meanwhile, in francophone countries overseas many writers, from Birago *Diop in Senegal to *Carrier in Quebec, have drawn on local traditions of story-telling to renew the *conte*, bringing it closer to the oral tale from which it ultimately derives. [See also AFRICA (SOUTH OF THE SAHARA).]   [PF]

See M. Sachs (ed.), *The French Short Story in the Nineteenth Century* (1969); R. Godenne, *La Nouvelle*

française (1974); A. Martin (ed.), *Anthologie du conte en France, 1750–1799* (1981).

Sicilien, Le (1667). Comédie-ballet by *Molière in which a French lover (disguised as an artist) succeeds by stealth in stealing the bride-to-be of a jealous Sicilian.

Siècle, Le. Launched in July 1836 on the same day that *Girardin founded *La Presse*, *Le Siècle* was the archetypal left-of-centre opposition paper, cultivating Voltairean *anticlericalism. It was also a commercial success, under both its founder, Armand Dutacq, a lawyer's clerk and would-be press tycoon, and, later, the more prudent Léonor Havin. Dutacq succeeded—more than Girardin—in creating a low-priced daily, aimed at a popular readership, with the right blend of human-interest stories, *romans-feuilletons* (*Balzac, *Sue, etc.), and politics. During the Second Empire, at a time when the Republican press was proscribed, it did much to rally the disaffected among the lower middle classes.   [MP]

Siècle de Louis XIV, Le, see VOLTAIRE [for *Le Siècle de Louis le Grand* see PERRAULT].

Siège de Calais, Le. Patriotic play by de *Belloy, first performed with great success at the Comédie-Française in 1765. The plot is that Édouard (Edward III of England, pretender to the French throne), having defeated Philippe de Valois at Crécy, is besieging Calais. After prolonged resistance the town surrenders, and Édouard orders the death of six citizens in retribution. Many volunteer, including the mayor, and after various difficulties Édouard relents. The initial success of this five-act verse *drame* was due to its timely call to patriotism through the recall of exemplary figures from the past, following France's losses in the *Seven Years War. Its disparagement of cosmopolitanism (unintentional, according to de Belloy) earned it the contempt of the *philosophes.
                                              [JD]

Siege of Paris (1870–1), see FRANCO-PRUSSIAN WAR.

Siegfried et le Limousin, see GIRAUDOUX.

SIÉYÈS, Emmanuel-Joseph, abbé (1748–1836). French author of three pamphlets (the third was the famous *Qu'est-ce que le *Tiers État?*) which sufficed to have him elected by Paris to the États Généraux. As a politician in successive Revolutionary assemblies he was essentially a committee man of considerable (though momentarily declining) influence. He became more visible again after Thermidor and served in 1795 on the emasculated Comité de Salut Public. Elected to the Conseil des Cinq Cents, a member and then president of the Directoire, he was the drafter of the Constitution of Year VIII (as he had been, in 1789, of the *Déclaration des droits de l'homme*) and was one of the architects of the 18th Brumaire. Thereafter *Napoleon shunted him into honorific sidings.   [JR]

SIGNORET, Simone (pseud. of Simone Kaminker) (1921–85). French film actress, the most famous of whose many parts was probably in Becker's *Le Casque d'or*. Married for many years to Yves *Montand, she published a best-selling book of memoirs, *La Nostalgie n'est plus ce qu'elle était* (1976), and a novel, *Adieu Volodya* (1985).

SIGOGNE, Charles-Timoléon de Beauxoncles, seigneur de (*c.*1560–1611). Combatant in the *Wars of Religion and notable practitioner of the crudely vituperative and inventively picturesque form of *satire in vogue in the early 17th c. About 75 of his pieces figure in *recueils libres* (mixed collections) of the time.   [PF]

Silbermann, see LACRETELLE.

Si le grain ne meurt. Autobiography of André *Gide (1926). The work had been a long-term project, connected with Gide's determination from an early age to sound out and make manifest all aspects of his personality. In this respect it can be related to *Corydon,* Gide's justification of pederasty, published in 1924. It has been argued that *Si le grain ne meurt* was written mainly for the sake of its second part, which tells the story of Gide's journeys to North Africa in 1893–5, during which he underwent a serious illness, discovered a heightened sense of life on his recovery, and, encouraged by Oscar Wilde whom he met there, first gave expression to his homosexuality in encounters with Arab boys. But the volume concludes with his engagement to his cousin Madeleine: its full significance derives from his simultaneous attachment to the spiritual values he had known as a youth. The first part of the text seeks out the sources of his dual nature in a series of oppositions such as that between his father's family background in the Protestant Languedoc and his mother's partly Catholic antecedents in Normandy. At the same time it recounts his unsettled childhood and the development of his literary vocation.
                                          [DHW]

Silence de la mer, Le, see VERCORS.

Sillon, Le. Review founded in 1894 by Paul Renaudin, which, in 1902, under Marc *Sangnier, gave its name to the first French Christian Democrat movement; it attempted to unite students, workers, and the middle classes in progressive Catholic politics and had considerable attraction for Catholic intellectuals. Considered subversive, the movement and journal were dissolved in 1910 by order of Pius X.   [NH]

Si longue lettre, Une, see BA, M.

Silvanire, La, see MAIRET.

SILVIA (pseud. of Zanetta Benozzi). Leading actress in the *Comédie-Italienne after the company's return to Paris in 1716. *Marivaux admired her intensely and created many of his most memorable parts for her.

SIMENON, Georges (1903–89). Belgian-born novelist, one of the best-known and most prolific writers of the century. Born in Liège to a childhood of genteel poverty and promising studies cut short by his father's ill health, he was reporter and columnist on the *Gazette de Liège* before moving to Paris in 1922 to work as secretary to a novelist, and to an aristocrat. Over the next dozen years he wrote, under 20 or more pseudonyms, thousands of short stories and hundreds of popular novels. His independence thus assured, he began travelling the world, living in various places in France and the USA before settling in Switzerland at the end of the 1950s. His restless travelling is as legendary as his womanizing.

The 200-odd novels signed with his own name, from *Pietr-le-Letton* (1931), which introduced Commissaire Maigret, to the last, *Maigret et Monsieur Charles* (1972), use elements of his own experience: *Le Pendu de Saint Pholien* (1931) recounts an incident from his youth; the avid, ill-assured provincials of *Les Noces de Poitiers* (1946) and other titles are reflections of Simenon himself. He began his autobiography with *Je me souviens* (1945) and *Pedigree* (1948). His novels and stories, like his journalism, explore self-knowledge and dignity in perpetually renewed developments on the basic pattern of closed settings in which misplaced characters come to some realization.

In the 80 or so Maigret novels and stories the detective, by empathizing with victim and situation, achieves understanding of the killer's *vérité humaine.* After the first dozen Maigrets, Simenon began to publish novels without the character, though murder remained frequent: the first non-Maigret novel, *Le Passager du 'Polarlys'* (1932), is scarcely different; *Il pleut, bergère* (1941) contains a man-hunt, but turns on a child's realization of how trivialities can provoke adult quarrels. In *Maigret* (1934) the detective is retired until *Maigret revient* (1942), after which the number of Maigret titles rises gradually to about half of the six or so books published yearly.

Abandoning novels in 1972, Simenon returned to autobiography; the first of a score of volumes, *Un homme comme un autre* (1975), is significantly titled: Simenon's short novels take ordinary people in ordinary settings developed to the point at which they overturn into the exceptional.   [SFN]

See S. G. Eskin, *Simenon: A Critical Biography* (1987).

SIMON, Claude (b. 1913). The award of the Nobel Prize for literature in 1985 consolidated Simon's rather belatedly recognized position as one of France's major post-war novelists. Associated with the *Nouveau Roman group, he combines their commitment to formal innovation with a deep sense of human vulnerability and dispossession; his characters struggle to orientate themselves in a physical reality beyond their control. The world is constantly changing, and our perceptions of it, like our memories of the past, are always fragmentary and uncertain. Hence a mode of writing which refuses to impose order, aiming rather to reproduce the flux and simultaneity of perceptual experience. He has therefore been described as a *phenomenological writer; his novels were greatly admired by *Merleau-Ponty. More recent critics, however, have concentrated rather on the way in which the richness and energy of his language generates the texts through a play of imagery, alliteration, and punning.

Simon was born in Madagascar but brought up in south-west France. Soon after his birth his father was killed in World War I, and his mother died when he was 11. He originally wanted to be a painter, but decided he was not good enough; fascination with the visual arts, however, still pervades his writing (Femmes, 1966, for instance, was written to accompany a set of paintings by Joan Miró). In 1936 he fought briefly for the Republicans in the Spanish Civil War. In 1939 he was called up to serve in a cavalry regiment which, the following year, was annihilated by the Germans; he spent several months in a prisoner-of-war camp, then escaped and returned home. Here he finished his first novel, Le Tricheur, published 1945. This was followed by an autobiographical text, La Corde raide (1947), and two more novels, Gulliver (1952) and Le Sacre du printemps (1954). But it is Le Vent (1956) that is usually regarded as his first major novel; it marks his move to the more prestigious *Minuit publishing house, where he met *Robbe-Grillet, *Butor, and *Pinget. The influence of William Faulkner is strong here, as in all Simon's early writing, but Le Vent also inaugurates several typically Simonian themes and techniques: the absent, unknown, or rejected father; nature (here in the form of the wind) dominating and mocking human activity; and a narrative that is a hypothetical reconstruction of events on the basis of incomplete, disparate, and mainly second-hand accounts. The notion of man's subjection to the natural world is developed further in L'Herbe (1958): death is part of the natural cycle, and reality is always changing, as relentlessly but as imperceptibly as the grass grows. Simon's powers of visual description are much in evidence here.

Two years later he published La *Route des Flandres. Like this novel, Le Palace (1962) centres on memories of a wartime experience, but given a more overtly political perspective—the failure of the Republican cause in Spain in the 1930s. The novel expresses Simon's bitter disillusionment with the Marxist theory of revolution. The belief that men can make history is, he thinks, a dangerous illusion. In fact his scepticism extends beyond Marxism to all rationalist or idealist views of history, and informs almost all his writing. His solidarity with history's victims is all the stronger, and indeed he

has himself participated in political actions, notably the 'Manifeste des 121' in 1960 protesting against the conduct of the *Algerian War. *Histoire (1967) was followed by La Bataille de Pharsale in 1969. Both these novels contain a strong intertextual dimension; in La Bataille especially, fragments from *Proust and classical Greek and Latin writers come together to form a kind of textual collage.

This important novel also constitutes a turning-point in Simon's development; half-way through it, the characteristic long, sensuous, rambling sentences give way to a crisp impersonal style, while the 'phenomenological' concern with perception and memory is replaced by a formalist conception of the text as a construction of interrelated elements. This project is pursued further in Les Corps conducteurs (1971), Triptyque (1973), and Leçon de choses (1976); and the theoretical discussions that Simon begins to produce at this point, e.g. in the preface to Orion aveugle (1970) and the conference paper 'La Fiction mot à mot' (1971), stress this anti-realist focus on the text's 'shape' and internal 'logic of signifiers'. But the formalist texts nevertheless retain the elements of desire, fascination, and sense of loss that are more overtly, indeed overwhelmingly, present in novels such as Histoire and La Bataille de Pharsale. Les *Géorgiques, while integrating some of the formalist elements, returns to narrative and to the problems of subjectivity and history; and in Simon's subsequent texts—L'Invitation (1987) and L'Acacia (1989)—the autobiographical element which has all along been ambiguously present in his novels becomes dominant.

Simon has never whole-heartedly adopted the intellectual approach to the novel which characterized most of his fellow nouveaux romanciers; he has always seen himself as an artisan rather than a theorist, building up his texts bit by bit without any predetermined overall plan. Through this intuitive, exploratory, and workmanlike attitude towards writing, he illustrates *Lévi-Strauss's notion of bricolage: the reworking, by trial and error, of a set of elements into new patterns. Thus Simon's themes remain remarkably constant throughout his work. The power of his novels derives partly from this enduring quality, but equally from the inventiveness of the textual bricolage itself, and from the sheer intensity and concreteness of his vision of reality.

[CB]

See J. A. E. Loubère: The Novels of Claude Simon (1975); C. Britton (ed.), Modern Literatures in Perspective: Claude Simon (1993).

SIMON, Michel (1895–1975). Though Swiss by birth, the most anarchistic of French screen actors, whether disrupting an ordered bourgeois household (*Renoir's Boudu sauvé des eaux, 1932) or, paradoxically, preserving and restoring order on a canal barge (*Vigo's L'Atalante, 1934). For Renoir he was a memorable victim in La Chienne (1931), and his throaty voice and mobile, lined countenance were used by *Carné in *Drôle de drame* (1937) and *Quai des brumes* (1938). [KAR]

SIMON, Richard (1638–1712). French *Oratorian priest and Hebraic scholar, the foremost biblical critic of his time after *Spinoza. The first of his revolutionary accounts of the sacred texts was the *Histoire critique du Vieux Testament* (1678), which denied the Mosaic authorship of the Pentateuch. It was attacked by *Le Clerc among others. Analogous volumes followed on the New Testament (text, versions, and commentaries: 1689–93), then a translation (1702). The treatment of the Christian revelation by the same methods as secular writings shocked many, notably *Bossuet, who in a celebrated incident at Easter 1678 had Simon's work banned. [CJB]

SIMONIN, Albert (1905–80). French writer. His taxi-driver's experience of Paris characters and their *argot (*Voilà taxi*, 1935, with Jean Bazin) produced a number of novels, initially in the *Série Noire: *Touchez pas au grisbi* (1953), *Le Cave se rebiffe* (1954), and also a dictionary of argot, *Le Petit Simonin illustré* (1957). [SFN]

Simultaneism, see ORPHISM.

Sirventes. Important Occitan lyric genre which accounts for a large proportion of the surviving *troubadour lyric corpus. The word first appears c.1150 to denote poems with a political, satirical, or moralizing theme. Though *Marcabru never uses the word to designate his own compositions, he is clearly a key figure in the development of the genre. Whereas it appears to have been a point of honour for troubadours to find an original rhyme scheme for a *canso, sirventes frequently use the rhyme scheme and tune of other poems, often *cansos*.

Sirventes are often highly polemic and overtly slanderous. Many of the best-known troubadours composed *sirventes* as well as *cansos*, e.g. *Peire d'Alvernhe and *Giraut de Bornelh; some troubadours were obviously more at home in the genre than in any other, e.g. *Bertran de Born and *Peire Cardenal. Many *sirventes* seem impenetrable to the modern reader (particularly without a good critical edition) as they depend on precise topical allusions, but some of the finest troubadour songs are *sirventes* rather than *cansos*, and later medieval readers, such as Dante, for whom the topical allusions must also have been opaque, clearly appreciated *sirventes* as much as love poetry. Some *sirventes* by *trobairitz survive. [SG]

SISMONDI, Léonard Simonde de (1773–1842). Swiss economist, critic and historian, and member of the *Coppet Group. As a historian Sismondi is best remembered for his 16-volume *Histoire des républiques italiennes* (1807–18), which appealed to liberal sentiments. He also produced a massive *Histoire des Français* (1821–44). His historical work was writ-

ten in the 18th-c. tradition, and he was less than enthusiastic about the grand Romantic philosophies of history. In 1813 he published his influential *De la littérature du midi de l'Europe*. As an economic thinker his ideas underwent a significant evolution. He was initially strongly influenced by Adam Smith but later, in his *Nouveaux principes de l'économie politique* (1819), he mounted a critique of the notion of *laissez-faire*. [CC]

SISSOKO, Fily-Dabo (1900–64). Malian writer. A schoolteacher and later *chef de canton*, he made his first trip to France when he was elected Socialist *député* for the French Sudan to the French National Assembly in 1945. His main contributions to literature are a collection of Malinké proverbs translated into French, *Sagesse noire* (1953); a collection of brief portraits of local people, *Crayons et portraits* (1953), inspired by *La Bruyère; and his memoirs, *La Savane rouge* (1962), awarded a prize at the Black Arts Festival in 1965. Imprisoned and condemned to hard labour by the Malian president Modibo Keita, Sissoko died in jail in 1964. [FNC]

Situationism. One of the most important movements in the *May 1968 events. It aimed above all at destroying the 'société du spectacle', described by Guy Debord in his book of the same name (1967) as that in which 'tout ce qui était directement vécu s'est éloigné dans une représentation'. For Debord, political parties and the whole modern culture industry were inextricably wedded to the 'spectacle'; only the workers' council, supposedly unmediated by the pernicious illusions of ideology, could constitute the revolutionary class as a subject.

Closely connected with this were the notions of *dérive* and *détournement*, strategies for subverting the bourgeois concepts of artistic and political representation. May 1968's posters and wall-slogans, its stress on direct democracy, and its maximalist urge to transform everyday life all bore the imprint of Situationism, itself influenced by *Surrealism and Hegelian *Marxism.

That imprint first became manifest with the foundation of the Situationist International in 1957 to propagate political ideas and cultural practice, seen as indissociable. But by 1972 the Situationist International had dissolved itself, seeing the age of the artistic avant-garde as over. Situationism forms an important pre-text for *Lyotard and *Baudrillard, though its adherents would doubtless have considered them as much a part of the 'société du spectacle' as any other bourgeois representational mode. [KAR]

Six, Les. A group of composers, consisting of Louis Durey (1888–1979), Germaine Tailleferre (1892–1983), Georges Auric (1899–1983), Arthur Honegger (1892–1955), Darius *Milhaud, and Francis *Poulenc. For a brief period in the early 20th c. Les Six gave concerts together and jointly published a play-ballet, *Les Mariés de la tour Eiffel* (1921).

Slavery

Sponsored by the composer Erik *Satie, they were closely involved with *Cocteau, who did the text and choreography for Les Mariés and whose manifesto Le Coq et l'arlequin (1918) summed up many of the aims of their music, namely a search for simplicity and clarity and for inspiration from popular music. Today their music is known mainly through the works of Milhaud and Poulenc.   [KM]

Slavery (in the French *West Indies). Slaves of African origin were imported in small numbers into the islands of Martinique and Guadeloupe from the very beginning of their occupation by France in 1635, but slavery did not establish itself as the dominant mode of production in France's West Indian colonies until the last quarter of the 17th c. In Martinique blacks outnumbered whites by 15,000 to 6,500 in 1700; the slave population rose to 35,000 by 1719 and had doubled again by 1736. The slave population of Guadeloupe increased somewhat more slowly, but it was the colony of Saint-Domingue (modern *Haiti), acquired from Spain in 1697, that saw the largest number of slave imports from Africa. From around 2,000 in 1681, the colony's slave population rose to 117,000 in 1730 and to 480,000 in 1791, by which time there were 83,000 slaves in Martinique and 90,000 in Guadeloupe. With smaller numbers of slaves in lesser or newly acquired colonies such as French Guiana and Tobago, the total slave population of France's West Indian colonies stood at around 650,000 on the eve of the Revolution. Exports from slave colonies—principally sugar, but also cotton, coffee, and spices—amounted to 217.5 million livres (£9 million), compared with British West Indian exports of £5 million, produced by 480,000 slaves. The contribution of slavery and the slave trade (la traite) to the economy of the ancien régime was such that in 1763 France preferred to cede the bulk of its mainland colonies in the New World in order to retain the sugar colony of Martinique. The prosperity of Nantes, Le Havre, and Bordeaux was in large part dependent on la traite and West Indian trade.

Relations between masters and slaves were theoretically regulated by the Code Noir of 1685 which, amongst other measures, provided for the instruction of slaves in the Catholic faith, sought to limit sexual relations between whites and blacks, and specified punishments for a wide range of slave offences. The Code was, however, unable to prevent the growth of a large population of mixed race, many of whom were manumitted by their white fathers and/or owners, creating an intermediate group, the gens de couleur libres or affranchis, who, often slave-owners themselves, posed a growing threat to white social, economic, and finally political power. In addition, slavery was continually resisted by the slaves themselves, especially in Saint-Domingue, through a combination of flight (marronnage), sabotage, poisoning, and outright violence. The outbreak of revolution in France unleashed a complex series of events which, in Saint-Domingue, led to the slaves, under the leadership of Toussaint *Louverture, gaining freedom by their own efforts by the time the Convention formally abolished slavery on 16 Pluviôse An II (4 February 1794). In Guadeloupe the abolition decree was imposed and implemented by the remarkable Victor Hugues, but in Martinique slaveholders chose to surrender their island to Britain in order to preserve the institution on which their power and wealth depended.

Slavery was restored in the French colonies by Napoleonic decree in May 1802, provoking desperate but unsuccessful resistance in Guadeloupe led by Louis Delgrès and, in Saint-Domingue, full-scale guerrilla warfare against a French expeditionary force, which culminated in the colony's becoming independent as Haiti in 1804. France followed Britain in abolishing the slave trade in 1815, but the trade continued clandestinely until 1831 and, despite increasing competition from French-grown sugar-beet, slave-produced sugar from Martinique, Guadeloupe, and French Guiana continued to be profitable. There were major slave uprisings in Martinique in 1831 and 1834, and opposition to slavery in France was organized by the Société de Morale Chrétienne (founded 1821) and the Société Française pour l'Abolition de l'Esclavage (founded 1834). The diffusion of abolitionist ideas in the 1840s owed much to the propaganda efforts of Victor Schoelcher, author of L'Abolition de l'esclavage (1840) and Abolition immédiate de l'esclavage (1842), and abolition was one of the first measures decreed by the Second Republic when it came to power in 1848. Slavery was finally abolished by the Provisional Government on 27 April 1848, but before news of the decree reached the French West Indies the slaves of Martinique and Guadeloupe rose up against their masters and effectively liberated themselves. Slavery has been treated in a number of French and French West Indian novels, notably Le Quatrième Siècle (1965) by Édouard *Glissant and La Mulâtresse Solitude (1972) by André *Schwarz-Bart.

[RDEB]

See C. L. R. James, The Black Jacobins (1980); A. Gautier, Les Sœurs de Solitude (1985); R. Blackburn, The Overthrow of Colonial Slavery 1776–1848 (1988).

Smarra, see NODIER.

SOCÉ DIOP, Ousmane (1911–73). Senegalese novelist and poet, belonging to the generation of young black intellectuals who founded the négritude movement in Paris in the inter-war years. His pioneering first novel, Karim, roman sénégalais (1935) (awarded the Grand Prix Littéraire d'Afrique Occidentale, 1947), introduces into African fiction the theme of the African at the crossroads of two civilizations, attempting without success to preserve traditional values in a rapidly changing urban situation. The social scene is closely observed and the hero's dilemmas and vicissitudes described with a certain detachment leavened with humour. His second novel, *Mirages de Paris* (1937), is the progenitor of a long line of semi-autobiographical works dealing with the 'Negro in Paris' theme, including the emotional involvements of the *déraciné* hero with white women. Long passages of philosophical and moralizing discussion reduce the protagonists to marionnettes, acting out a *roman à thèse*. He published a collection of tales, heroic legends, and folk-fables, *Contes et légendes d'Afrique noire* (1938), drawn from his country's oral heritage. Like Birago *Diop, he claims to be the faithful scribe of the *griot*, singing the *chansons de geste* of Africa to the accompaniment of his guitar or khalam. His poems are entitled *Rythmes du khalam* (1948). In Dakar he founded the literary magazine *Bingo* as a vehicle for his compatriots' poems and short stories.   [DSB]

Socialism and Communism (in 20th-c. France). French Socialism as it emerged in the early 20th c. was heir to several traditions: the revolutionary tradition of 1789, 1793, and 1871; the Utopian socialism of *Fourier and *Saint-Simon; the syndicalism of the trade-union movement; the *ouvriérisme* of skilled workers inspired by *Proudhon; the gas-and-water socialism of the Possibilistes; and the class-based analysis of Marx and Engels, whose shorter texts were translated and popularized by the Guesdists [see MARXISM]. After the storms of the *Dreyfus Affair, it was chiefly through the efforts of *Jaurès that the various groupings formed the unified Socialist Party, the SFIO (Section Française de l'Internationale Socialiste) in 1905. Under Jaurès, the SFIO, with its daily paper L'*Humanité and a growing clientele in industrial areas, steadily increased its parliamentary numbers until the war. In 1914 the Socialist International failed to prevent the war, and Jaurès, ardent advocate of unity and internationalism, was assassinated in the last days of peace. The party, still in shock, joined the national government and the war effort.

The Bolshevik Revolution of 1917 faced all Socialists with the choice of supporting it or not. At the SFIO congress at Tours in December 1920 the French party split. The majority of delegates accepted Lenin's conditions for a new Communist Party (essentially iron discipline and suppression of dissidence) and formed the Parti Communiste Francais (PCF). The minority remained with Léon *Blum in the SFIO—although within a few years the position was reversed, as early turmoil within the PCF sent many members back to *la vieille maison*.

The infant Communist Party went through some lean years, isolated, engaged in bitter rivalry with its 'brother party', and riven by internal disputes. Losing ground electorally, it was nevertheless building a solid organization, rooted in the industrial towns and in the 'red belt' of suburbs round Paris. With *Thorez as leader, it came in from the cold to join the anti-fascist alliance of the *Popular Front, and in the 1936 elections won a record 70 seats. In the imagery of the day, 'the outstretched hand' had replaced 'the knife between the teeth'. After the Front's collapse the PCF campaigned for resistance to Hitler, but faced with the 1939 Nazi–Soviet pact the party, although shaken, accepted the new line and was outlawed in France as a result. Some individuals, such as *Nizan, left in protest, others lay low. But following Hitler's invasion of the USSR in 1941 the party wholeheartedly joined the Resistance, in which it became a major force [see OCCUPATION AND RESISTANCE]. Its organization lent itself to clandestinity and it could legitimately claim a roll-call of heroic wartime martyrs (the '75,000 fusillés').

At the Liberation, a revitalized PCF cooperated with other parties in the new Fourth Republic, to the extent of participating in de *Gaulle's and later governments. It was now at its peak in terms of members and voters, regularly receiving 25 per cent of the vote. The Cold War sent it into parliamentary opposition and Stalinist isolation after 1947, prompting Guy Mollet's jibe that the PCF was not on the left but 'in the east'. It retained electoral support, however, partly due to its championing of the working class and its opposition to the damaging colonial wars of the period. At this time many French intellectuals, teachers, and artists were members of the party (some of the best-known being *Aragon, *Althusser, and *Picasso), while others like *Sartre devoted much effort to defining their position in relation to it.

The Fifth Republic's new institutions damaged the PCF electorally after 1958, since the presidency was not attainable by a Communist and the two-ballot voting system reduced its numbers in parliament. Soviet repression in Eastern Europe had alienated sections of the membership, and the party was further damaged by the events of *May 1968 which showed that the younger generation rejected its monolithic structures, Stalinist identity, and defence of the USSR. Attempts to liberalize the party during the 'Eurocommunist' years of the late 1970s were half-hearted and failed to overcome the 'Solzhenitsyn factor', which led to a further exodus of members. Electoral alliance with the Socialist Party in these years (the Programme Commun) was to prove advantageous only to the Socialists. When the Socialist François *Mitterrand was elected president in 1981, the Communists were invited into government, but left again in 1984, by which time it was already clear that the party was in a state of historic decline and inner turmoil. By the 1990s, following the collapse of Communism in Eastern Europe, its vote had fallen to about 10 per cent, its membership was greatly reduced, and few intellectuals were to be found defending it.

The Socialist Party's fortunes followed a different curve, reaching an unexpected peak in the 1980s. The collapse of the Popular Front had brought

Socialisme ou barbarie

great disappointment, and during the war and Occupation the SFIO became fragmented. Many of its members were in the Resistance, but its hopes of a large post-war Socialist Party were dashed. Drawn into coalition governments after 1945, it had often reluctantly acquiesced in policies not to its taste. The most painful period for many was the Socialist-led Mollet government of 1956–7, which pursued an uneasy policy of continuing the *Algerian War. By the early 1960s the party seemed to many to be ageing, out of touch, and dominated by the old demons of *anticlericalism and windy Marxism. It had never had the same attraction for intellectuals as the PCF. However, a series of regrouping initiatives, given urgency by the events of May 1968, enabled the party to be rejuvenated, as the Parti Socialiste (PS) in 1969, largely thanks to Mitterrand, who aimed to win the presidency for the Left. The Programme Commun, while not without risks, brought Communist voters into electoral alliances, and the new PS, unlike the old, appealed to the 1968 generation, whose concerns included workers' control, the Third World, regionalism, *feminism, cultural renovation, and the environment, as well as social reform.

1981 saw the Left returned to power, with Mitterrand at the Élysée, and Socialist-dominated governments in 1981–6 and 1988–93. The Left had proved that it could rule within the framework of the Fifth Republic. But after a euphoric état de grâce, which saw a wave of judicial reforms, several nationalizations, and a deliberate attempt to expand the economy on Keynesian lines, the PS was forced to bow to the international recession and apply policies of economic rigour—for which the price was rising unemployment. It now seemed to be moving towards a new pragmatism, with an acceptance of modernization and the market. Reform was, however, pursued in other areas: decentralization, women's rights, and educational expansion, while in the cultural sphere many initiatives were taken under the energetic (though not universally appreciated) minister of culture, Jack Lang, with increased subsidies for the creative arts (cinema, theatre, music) and the endowment of sometimes controversial national monuments, such as the Bastille Opera. But; in the face of a dispiriting economic situation, support for the Socialists dwindled. By the 1993 elections the entire Left was in retreat and some disarray. Despite its high cultural profile, its organic intellectuals were not much in evidence. Its ideological commitment had been considerably modified over the decade, and the support it had hitherto received from academics, teachers, trade unionists, and the young had waned, in an age seen as less heroic than the confrontational 1930s or the immediate post-war period. [SR]

See J. Touchard, La Gauche en France depuis 1900 (1977); R. W. Johnson, The Long March of the French Left (1981); P. Hall et al., Developments in French Politics (1990).

Socialisme ou barbarie, see MARXISM.

Société des Anciens Textes, La, see MIDDLE AGES, 3.

Société des Gens de Lettres, La, see BOOK TRADE, 5.

Sociology. The study of human society (or societies) is as old as civilization, but the modern discipline of sociology is generally traced to French thinkers of the 18th and 19th c. From them arose three broad currents of sociological thought.

*Montesquieu's heroic attempt to codify the principles of different social formations was an application of the rationalist project of the *Enlightenment. His primary interest was in political structures and in their legal and philosophical underpinnings, an approach taken up by *Tocqueville in his influential studies of 18th-c. France and 19th-c. America. Together they dominate the current of liberal sociology, whose most recent exponents have included Élie *Halévy and Raymond *Aron.

Henri de *Saint-Simon was a fertile source of proposals on social organization and planning, particularly in respect of key social élites. Many of his ideas were systematized by *Comte, who attempted to extend the methods of the natural sciences to society, and coined the term 'sociology'. His positivist methodology and emphasis on empirical enquiry were developed by Frédéric Le Play (1806–82), especially in his study of the family, and by Émile *Durkheim, who dominated university sociology for 30 years before World War I. Durkheim's influential studies of suicide and of the division of labour drew on detailed statistical evidence. In them he emphasized the importance of social solidarities, and developed the concept of 'anomie' to describe the disastrous effects for individuals of their collapse. Durkheim's approach, developed by figures like Georges Gurvitch (1894–1965), still predominates in mainstream academic sociology.

The Utopian socialism of Saint-Simon and *Fourier was an early influence on Karl Marx (1818–83), whose ideas on society were championed in France at the turn of the century by Georges *Sorel, among others [see MARXISM]. It was chiefly after World War II, however, that Marxist ideas were widely adopted by French social thinkers, giving prominence to concepts of social class and addressing issues of change and conflict. Henri *Lefebvre entered sociology from a philosophical background during the 1950s and produced pioneering work on rural and urban sociology which emphasized the social production of space. Younger sociologists who followed his humanist Marxism included Edgar *Morin, with work on cognitive sociology, and Alain *Touraine, with analyses of post-industrial society and changing class structures. At the same time Lucien *Goldmann inaugurated the sociology of literature. A later generation, inspired by *Althusser and *Poulantzas, attacked their over-emphasis on empirical study and lack of a rigorous theoretical Marxist framework. In recent years the work of Pierre *Bourdieu on cultural and intellectual sociology has exercised a strong influence, developing concepts of the 'habitus' (a set of inherited and acquired dispositions), the 'field' within which people struggle to increase their economic or cultural capital, and the 'symbolic violence' which characterizes forms of domination within society.

By contrast with its Anglo-American counterpart, which has largely followed the positivist road, French sociology is distinguished by its focus on theoretical issues rather than empirical detail. Perhaps for this reason its international influence has been felt most strongly in cultural and political debate.   [MHK]

Socrate chrétien, Le, see BALZAC, J.-L.

Sodome et Gomorrhe (1921–2). The fourth part of Proust's *A la recherche du temps perdu.*

Soirées de Médan, Les. Collection of six stories, published in 1880 by members of the so-called 'groupe de Médan', supposedly the major representatives of literary *Naturalism. The volume consists of 'L'Attaque du moulin' by *Zola, 'Boule de suif' by *Maupassant, 'Sac au dos' by *Huysmans, 'La Saignée' by *Céard, 'L'Affaire du grand 7' by *Hennique, and 'Après la bataille' by *Alexis. The provocative preface and the publicity surrounding the appearance of this book created the myth which led critics to regard it as a kind of literary manifesto of the new school of Naturalist writers grouped around Zola and meeting frequently at his country-house in Médan. There is, however, more unity in the themes and techniques of this collection than there was amongst its authors. They all narrate, realistically and with mordant irony, incidents from the *Franco-Prussian War, and seek to expose the brutality, hypocrisy, and futility of war in general, in opposition to the militarist and revanchist spirit of the age.   [DB]

Soirées de Saint-Pétersbourg, Les, see MAISTRE, J. DE.

Soissons, Le Vase de. A famous incident in the life of the *Merovingian king Clovis involves the capital punishment (by the king's own hand) of a soldier who broke this precious vase. The question 'Qui a cassé le vase de Soissons?' (an equivalent of '1066 and all that') became the title of a nostalgic book by Gaston Bonheur (1963), a lovely evocation of primary-school French history.   [PF]

Soleils des indépendances, Les, see KOUROUMA.

SOLLERS, Philippe (pseud. of Philippe Joyaux) (b. 1936). Co-founder of *Tel Quel* and *L'Infini*, Sollers has been at the forefront of the Parisian literary scene ever since his fellow Bordelais Francois *Mauriac discovered him in 1957. That year the Prix Fénéon was awarded to Sollers's short novel *Le Défi.* A year later the novel *Une curieuse solitude* was acclaimed by *Aragon. Sollers never quite forgave the 'Vatican and Kremlin' for launching him. He subsequently repudiated these early texts, which he considered too 'traditional' and 'bourgeois'. In 1960 he co-founded *Tel Quel.* The following year he was awarded the Prix Médicis for his 'poem in novel form', *Le Parc.* In 1963 he published *Francis *Ponge* in the 'Poètes d'aujourd'hui collection' and a collection of essays, *L'Intermédiaire.* With *Drame* (1965) language became the sole subject of the novel.

In 1967 (the year of his marriage with Julia *Kristeva) Sollers's writing took on a political (Marxist) slant, which is evident in *Logiques* and *Nombres* (1968). *Entretiens avec Francis Ponge* was published in 1970. A supporter of the French Communist Party from 1967 to 1971, Sollers subsequently turned to Maoism. *Lois* (1972) and *Sur le matérialisme* (1974) are marked by the Chinese Cultural Revolution. In *H* (1973) Sollers freed the novel of all punctuation, thereby compelling the reader to explore the 'transfinite', 'poly-logical', and 'materialist' nature of language.

Sollers's shifting political views of the mid-1970s are evident in *Délivrance* (1977), a debate with Maurice Clavel aired on French radio. During this period he befriended the *Nouveaux Philosophes, repudiated Marxism, proclaimed the death of the avant-garde, and turned to America and the Bible. In 1981 he published *Paradis*, a novel greatly influenced by Dante, Joyce, and the Bible, and *Vision à New York* (an interview with David Hayman).

January 1983 marked a turning-point in his literary career. He left the Éditions du Seuil for Gallimard, where he published his first best-seller, *Femmes.* *Tel Quel'*s successor, *L'Infini*, was launched. Successive novels, such as *Portrait du joueur* (1984), *Le Cœur absolu* (1987), *Les Folies françaises* (1988), and *Le Lys d'or* (1989) are marked by a provocative, autobiographical tone (already apparent in *H*), and a return to southern, Catholic, Girondist, and libertine values. Other works of this period include: *Théorie des exceptions* (1986), *Paradis II* (1986), *Les Surprises de Fragonard* (1987), *Carnet de nuit* (1989), *La Fête à Venise* (1991), and *Le Secret* (1992).   [DM-S]

See S. Heath, *The Nouveau Roman* (1972); *Tel Quel,* 57 (1974), devoted to Sollers; R. Barthes, *Sollers écrivain* (1979).

SOMAIZE, Antoine Baudeau, sieur de (b. 1630). Obscure author of works devoted to *preciosity. He attacked *Molière, publishing a satirical comedy, *Les Véritables Précieuses* (1660), and two works entitled *Le Grand Dictionnaire des précieuses* (1660, 1661), containing lists of their new expressions, remarks on their customs, and anecdotal portraits, not entirely reliable, of several hundred women.   [PF]

Somme de poésie, Une

Somme de poésie, Une, see LA TOUR DU PIN.

Son Excellence Eugène Rougon. Novel by *Zola, the sixth in the *Rougon-Macquart* series, published 1876. It follows the vicissitudes of the political career of a Second Empire minister, Eugène Rougon, who falls victim to the intrigues of the seductive Clorinde Balbi; incarnating the unscrupulous opportunism of the regime, he returns to power with a brutal act of repression. [DB]

Song, see CHANSON FRANÇAISE; POPULAR SONG.

Songe de Vaux, Le, see LA FONTAINE.

Songe du vieil pelerin, see PHILIPPE DE MÉZIÈRES.

Sonnet (from Italian *sonetto*, a small sound or song). If Clément *Marot was the first French poet to publish one, in 1538, the honour of composing the first French sonnet usually goes to Mellin de *Saint-Gelais (1533/4). The sonnet structure favoured by both Mellin and Marot (abba | abba | ccd | eed), together with that introduced by *Peletier du Mans (abba | abba | ccd | eed), was popularized by *Ronsard (*Les Amours*, 1552–3) and *Du Bellay (*Les Regrets*, 1558); Ronsard follows in the *Petrarchizing footsteps of Du Bellay's *L'Olive* (1549), while *Les Regrets* show the sonnet's capabilities in elegy and satire. In the 17th c. the sonnet was as much an instrument of social exchange and partisanship as an aesthetic ideal (*Boileau: 'Un sonnet sans défaut vaut seul un long poème'): in 1638, for example, *Voiture's 'Sonnet d'Uranie' and *Benserade's 'Sonnet de Job' created the opposing *précieux* factions of the *uranistes* and the *jobelins*. After lying fallow in the 18th c., the sonnet gradually achieved lyric predominance in the latter half of the 19th c.; after *Sainte-Beuve's expressively tentative, but substantial output, and *Musset's 20-odd sonnets in lighter vein, *Gautier's sonnets of the 1830s and *Nerval's *Les Chimères* (1854) set the pattern for later *Parnassian and *Symbolist poets.

*Baudelaire outlines the thematic range of the sonnet in a letter to Armand Fraisse (18 February 1860): 'Tout va bien au sonnet, la bouffonnerie, la galanterie, la passion, la rêverie, la méditation philosophique.' If *Banville, *Corbière, and *Verlaine provide examples of 'bouffonnerie' and 'galanterie', then Baudelaire and *Mallarmé, and even *Heredia, explore the meditative, metaphysical potentialities of the sonnet, and put to advantage its apparent structural imbalance: 'le sonnet ressemble à une figure dont le buste serait trop long et les jambes seraient trop grêles et courtes' (Banville, *Petit Traité de poésie française*, 1872).

If abba | abba | ccd | ede is considered the 'regular' French form, then one may say that two self-enclosed, autonomous stanzaic structures, which confirm each other in their shared rhymes, give way to two stanzas which are interdependent and whose rhyme scheme is less predictable, with three rhymes in six lines rather than two in eight. This structural asymmetry creates highly unstable and mercurial relationships, not only between the tercets, but between the quatrains and tercets. As the four-square octave (the *status quo*) comes to an end, it moves into an accelerated, shifting, exploratory mode, seeking its destination in significance. Seen in this light, the sonnet is the ideal vehicle for Baudelairian 'surnaturalisme' or 'ironie', for Mallarmé's symbolic alchemy, and for Heredia's discovery of revealing intimacies at the heart of history. [See VERSIFICATION.] [CS]

SONNET DE COURVAL, Thomas (1577–1627). The 'Juvenal of Normandy', author of vehement political and social satires, notably the *Satires contre les abus et désordres de la France* (1622).

Sonnets pour Hélène, see RONSARD.

SONY LABOU TANSI (pseud. of Marcel Sony) (b. 1947). Congolese playwright and novelist. He is one of the most prolific and influential of the younger generation of francophone African writers, author of numerous plays performed since 1979 by his theatre company, the Rocado Zulu Théâtre of Brazzaville, Congo, and of a series of novels, the first and best-known being *La Vie et demie* (1979). His early plays, such as *Conscience de tracteur* (1973, published 1979), *Je soussigné cardiaque* (1976), *La Parenthèse de sang* (1978), published together in 1981, and *La Coutume d'être fou* (1980), were regularly awarded prizes in the annual drama competition organized by Radio France International; his early short stories were similarly acclaimed. *La Vie et demie*, hailed as a new departure in African fiction, marked the beginning of his career as a major novelist; it was followed in quick succession by *L'État honteux* (1981), *L'Anté-peuple* (written 1976, published 1983), *Les Sept Solitudes de Lorsa Lopez* (1985), and *Les Yeux du volcan* (1988). More recently Sony has concentrated on his theatrical writing, which has taken on an international dimension with regular presentations at the Festival des Francophonies at Limoges, tours and residencies in Paris and elsewhere, and collaborations with well-known French theatre directors, such as *La Rue des mouches* (1985, directed by Pierre Vial), *Antoine m'a vendu son destin* (1986, Daniel Mesguich), *Moi, veuve de l'empire* (1987, Michel Rostaing), and *Qui a mangé madame d'Avoine Bergotha?* (1989, Jean-Pierre Klein).

The themes of Sony's writings are the abuses of power in thinly disguised fictitious African states, such as 'la Katamalanasie' in *La Vie et demie*. The point of view may be that of the capricious and deluded dictator, such as Antoine in the play of that name, Walante in *Qui a mangé madame d'Avoine Bergotha?*, or the succession of 'providential guides' in *La Vie et demie*; or that of the unfortunate victims of their absurd and arbitrary decisions, such as the family of the resistance fighter Libertashio in *La Parenthèse de sang*. Women are often caught up in the cycle of brutality and cynicism, and reduced to exploiting their rampant sexuality as a weapon. This grim and often violent subject-matter is treated most often with black humour and the tone is usually one of grotesque farce, although some of the novels, such as L'Anté-peuple, adopt a more realistic mode.

What sustains these flights of fancy is the verve of Sony's language, which infuses into standard French—'une langue frigide'—a dose of 'tropicalités' based on the colourful street-language of the Congo. This produces a lyricism which constantly transgresses the boundaries of register to produce memorable formulations of the importance of self-expression as a therapeutic activity, exorcizing the horror of a nasty, brutish existence with a humorous vitality: 'On ne fait pas d'omelette sans casser les mots.' It is this bravura style which elevates Sony's writing above parody of the anarchic politics of African states to embrace a concern with human cruelty and suffering in general.   [PGH]

Sopha, Le, see CRÉBILLON, C.-P.-J. DE.

Sophonisbe. Title of several tragedies, including those by *Mairet (1634) and Pierre *Corneille (1663). They concern the death of the Carthaginian queen at the hands of the Romans.

Sorbonne, La. The history of the Sorbonne and that of the University of Paris are closely interwoven [see SCHOLASTICISM]. The college of the Sorbonne was founded in 1253 by Robert de Sorbon, chaplain and confessor to Louis IX, to provide free moral and theological education for poor students. Gradually the Sorbonne became identified in people's minds with the faculty of theology. Around the 13th c. the theological reputation of Paris was at its highest, with teachers like *Abélard, the Dominicans Albert the Great and Aquinas, and the Franciscans Bonaventure and Duns Scotus.

The next two centuries saw a period of decline, tempered, however, by the presence of figures like the mystical writer *Gerson (1363–1429), the reforms drawn up by Cardinal d'Estouteville in 1452, the founding of a chair of Greek in 1466 (though the Sorbonne was to become suspicious of Greek scholarship, in new translations of the *Bible), and the establishment of the first printing-press in France by two of its doctors. In the 16th c. the Sorbonne had to contend with both the spread of *humanism (symbolized by the Collège Royal, later *Collège de France) which was often at odds with its reactionary clerical culture, and the introduction of Lutheran and Calvinist ideas. The right of *censorship, by now invested in it and exercised in an ill-defined partnership with the king and the Parlement, affected not only theologians, but also philosophers like *Ramus (who published plans for reforming the university and weakening the power of the Sorbonne) and imaginative writers like *Marot and *Rabelais. The same repressive attitude is seen in its

rejection of both *Jansenists and *Jesuits in the 17th c. and of *philosophes in the 18th. Neither the faculty of theology, nor the Sorbonne as such, survived the suppression of the university at the Revolution.

The whole university was reorganized in the 1880s [see EDUCATION] and a new Sorbonne emerged. Unlike at Oxford and Cambridge, there are few physical remains of the medieval university colleges, and none of the Sorbonne: of *Richelieu's major rebuilding (1627–42) only Lemercier's chapel has survived. More recently, after the student riots of *May 1968, further reorganization has taken place, and there are now 13 different universities of Paris, three of which contain the old name: Panthéon-Sorbonne (Paris I), Sorbonne-Nouvelle (III) and Paris-Sorbonne (IV).   [PS]

SOREL, Charles (c.1599–1674). Novelist, critic, historiographer, one of the most versatile and innovative French writers of the century, yet one of the least well known. Of bourgeois origins, he published his first novel at the age of 22. His fiction, although at first reproducing many contemporary commonplaces (and excesses), showed increasing signs of originality. His Nouvelles françaises (1623) represent an unprecedented attempt to adapt Cervantes's popular Novelas ejemplares to a specifically French context, and from this same period dates the first version of his most successful and complex novel, *Francion. His Le Berger extravagant (1627–8), revised and republished as L'Anti-Roman (1633–4), reveals similar creative independence, as it moves beyond the parody of pastoral to incorporate a critical examination of the inadequacies of fiction itself. Notwithstanding this often unsparing analysis, Sorel made one final experiment with the genre in Polyandre (1648), his (unsuccessful) attempt to create a novel of everyday life, purged of the grotesque and burlesque, in which plot is subordinated to scenes of Parisian life and various satirical portraits.

In spite of these ambitious enterprises, Sorel continued to see fiction as a genre of little value, and sought recognition for his (often equally original) writing in other modes. A fertile historiographer— he bought the post of Historiographe du Roi from his uncle in 1635—he proposed a more sociological approach to historical enquiry in the 'Avertissement' to his Histoire de la monarchie française (1629–33). His massive La Science universelle (1634–41) is a courageous act of popularization which embraces not only developments in the physical sciences, but also political and moral questions. It is informed by a burning commitment to the progress of knowledge, and contains some bold, enlightened sympathy for scientific novateurs. From this time, too, dates the virtually unclassifiable La Maison de jeux (1642), a unique and fascinating blend of imaginative literature and social analysis which examines the creation of fiction(s) in the broader context of game.

Sorel was also a productive literary critic. His La

Bibliothèque française (1664), a critical bibliography of texts written in or translated into French, is a very early attempt at literary history with a clear sense of generic categories and developing traditions. His *De la connaissance des bons livres* (1671) contains searing attacks on contemporary fiction, but also offers sensitive comments on the criteria for literary judgement. Long ignored by scholars, the full range and originality of Sorel's *œuvre* is now beginning to attract attention. [GJM]

> See F. Sutcliffe, *Le Réalisme de Charles Sorel* (1965); G. Verdier, *Charles Sorel* (1984); R. Howells, *Carnival to Classicism* (1989).

SOREL, Georges (1847–1922). A powerful and original political thinker, unclassifiable as either 'Right' or 'Left', Sorel was, through his revolt against reason, to have a profound influence on 20th-c. ideologies. He started late; in 1892 he resigned from the civil service in order to study. He was a revolutionary syndicalist, and his *Réflexions sur la violence* (1908) depicted violence as alone being capable, through the use of 'myths' such as that of the general strike, of revitalizing decadent modern society. In the years before World War I Sorel moved nearer to the authoritarian Right. He has been seen as a precursor of *fascism. [RMG]

Sorel, Julien. The ambitious plebeian hero of Stendhal's *Le *Rouge et le noir*.

Sotie (or *sottie*). Short comic play of the 15th and 16th c.; about 60 have survived. It is clearly distinct from the *farce in several respects. Characters are often numerous and designated by a number rather than a name—Premier Sot, Second Sot . . . The place of the action is vague or symbolic, the language more stylized, and the tone cruelly sarcastic or fanciful; the *sotie* presents, not a slice of life leading to a clear denouement (as does the farce), but a series of verbal exchanges which constitute a vicious mockery of some social or political target. It is intellectual, conflictual drama which uses bitter laughter to provoke thought and political action. The Sot (Fool) is a public censor, who criticizes with impunity thanks to the excuse of his folly. Even when named, e.g. Teste-Verte, Sotte-Mine, Chascun, Chose Publique, the Sot is not individualized, but remains simply one of a number of points of view; the Sots are often controlled by a *meneur du jeu*, Mère Sotte. Traditionally, Sots wore a simple grey robe, and a hood with asses' ears—a sign of their folly, i.e. both of their exclusion from normal society and of their fools' superior wisdom. Although some later *soties* have a loose plot with chronological development, thus coming close to some *moralities, many are simple *parades* (as in the *Sotie des menus propos*, where three Sots exchange a series of disconnected satirical observations) or mock trials (e.g. the *Sotie des sots triumphants*, where Mère Sotte passes judgement on a series of complaints).

The origins of the *sotie* go back to the Fête des Fous and other ceremonies associated with Carnival, organized on the principle of the world turned upside-down. The juridical aspects of many *soties* suggest that their authors belonged to the *Basoches, and that they were aimed at an educated middle-class audience. [See also GRINGORE.]

In the 20th c. the label *sotie* was used by Gide for *Les *Caves du Vatican*. [GAR]

> See J.-Cl. Aubailly, *Le Monologue, le dialogue et la sottie* (1976).

SOUCHON, Alain (b. 1945). French singer-songwriter and film actor. Working with singer-musician Laurent Voulzy, Souchon benefited from a youthful admiration for Lennon and McCartney in creating his own ironic style of Gallic melancholy, childhood nostalgia, and existential anguish, expressed in schoolboy slang and integrated into a subtle, English-flavoured rock music. His popular successes of the late 1970s: 'Allo Maman bobo', 'Bidon', 'Y'a d'la Rumba dans l'air', 'Poulailler's Song', 'Papa Mambo' were not matched in the 1980s despite the sustained quality of his records and concerts (*On avance*, 1983). [PGH]

Souffles (1966–72). Major journal of *Maghrebian culture. Published in Rabat, Morocco, and edited by Abdellatif *Laâbi, *Souffles* drew to it all the most prominent francophone Moroccan writers and intellectuals of the post-Independence period: *Khatibi, *Ben Jelloun, *Chraïbi, Nissaboury. The journal provided a forum for the discussion of national culture and decolonization. Appearing quarterly over a six-year period, it reached out to the international stage in its alliance with the Vietnamese, Palestinian, and American anti-imperialist struggles. A major issue debated in its columns was the continued use of French and the avoidance of acculturation on the one hand, and the problem of Arab 'traditionalism' on the other. The recognition of Arabic as the national language led to the production of *Anfas* (eight issues only) as a parallel Arabic enterprise. *Souffles* was closed by order of the Moroccan government in 1972 and its editor Laâbi was arrested, tortured, and imprisoned along with other members of the Parti de la Libération et du Socialisme. [JKa]

SOULIÉ, Frédéric (1800–47). Prolific writer of *romans-feuilletons* whose novels appeared mainly in the *Journal des débats* from 1837 to 1845. His principal success was *Les Mémoires du diable* (1837–8). He wrote many novels on the history of the Languedoc and dramatized his own novels (*La Closerie des genêts*, 1846). [BR]

Soulier de Satin, Le. Written 1919–24, this play represents a new departure for *Claudel, who in it brilliantly uses many of the techniques of unreality both of the modern and of the Japanese theatre. Spread over four 'journées' like a medieval mystery play, the action celebrates the mission of the *Counter-Reformation. The whole world, and the battle for the faith and against heresy, is its theme. The action involves Spain, Africa, the Americas, Italy, Bohemia, the Far East. At the centre of it all lies the theme of the love of Rodrigue and Prouhèze; mystically, through vicarious suffering, the separation of the lovers counterbalances the sins of the world and creates the conditions for the triumph of Spain's mission. The bewildering confusion of scenes and events illustrates the apparent confusion of God's intentions; but just as the playwright's 'machinistes' such as 'L'Annoncier' partly explain what he intends, so the 'Ange Gardien' and the dying Jesuit who starts the play help to decipher the intentions of that other playwright, God. Originally considered unperformable, the play was successfully adapted for the stage by Claudel and *Barrault, and first performed in 1943; its subsequent stage success has outstripped all Claudel's other plays. [RMG]

SOUMET, Alexandre (1788–1845). French poet and dramatist of the Restoration and July Monarchy. He remains of interest on account of a late work, *La Divine Épopée* (1841), which occupies a significant place in the development of the Romantic *epic.

Soundjata, see NIANE.

SOUPAULT, Philippe (1897–1990). French poet and novelist, but also essayist, critic, anthologist, translator, journalist, and broadcaster. He was a *Dadaist and the co-author with *Breton of the first *Surrealist text, *Les Champs magnétiques* (1920). He published his first collection of poems, *Aquarium,* in 1917, followed by *Rose des vents* (1920), *Westwego* (1922), and *Georgia* (1926), all marked by a febrile modernism. Also in the 1920s he embarked on a succession of novels, including *Le Bon Apôtre* (1923), *Les Frères Durandeau* (1924), and *Les Dernières Nuits de Paris* (1928), where, as in many of his other writings, there is an almost obsessive oscillation between movement and immobility. During roughly the same period he produced a series of studies devoted to the Douanier *Rousseau, *Apollinaire, *Lautréamont, Blake, Lurçat, Uccello, Charlie Chaplin, and *Baudelaire.

After his expulsion from the Surrealist group in 1926 his wanderlust was partly satisfied by a new career as an international reporter, especially in the 1930s. In 1938 he was appointed director at Radio-Tunis and during the war he held a similar post with the Free French station in Algiers, where his contributions to the review *Fontaine* included the poem 'Ode à Londres bombardée'. After the war he combined his radio work with writing. [KRA]

Souper de Beaucaire, Le, see NAPOLEON,2 .

Sous le soleil de Satan, see BERNANOS.

Sous l'orage, see BADIAN.

Souvenirs d'égotisme. Autobiographical work by *Stendhal, dealing with the period 1822–30.

Souvenirs d'enfance et de jeunesse, see RENAN.

SOW FALL, Aminata (b. 1941). One of the earliest and best-known francophone African woman writers, author of four novels. Written from the point of view of the concerned citizen rather than the feminist, her work provides a running commentary on contemporary Senegalese social behaviour and attitudes.

Le Revenant (1976) is a critique of the new bourgeoisie, and their anxiety to impress others with their ill-won wealth. Her second novel, *La Grève des Bàttu* (1979), winner of the Grand Prix Littéraire d'Afrique Noire and short-listed for the Prix Goncourt, is her best-known and most impressive work to date. Set in the early 1970s, at a time when *Senghor's World-Bank inspired tourist campaign had resulted in a series of decrees and brutal police action against Dakar's beggars, this semi-fantasy about a retaliatory strike-action by the beggars is an indictment of Senghor's 'humanism' and at the same time a witty dig at the power-hungry politicians who surround him.

In Sow Fall's third novel, *L'Appel des arènes* (1982), which also featured on the Goncourt short-list and was awarded the Alioune Diop Prize, the theme of cultural alienation comes full circle. In contrast to the protagonists of her compatriots *Socé, *Sadji, and *Kane, who are psychologically destroyed by the superficial appeal of Western culture, Sow Fall's young hero, only child of highly westernized parents, is drawn back to his roots by the sound of the drums from the traditional wrestling arena. *L'Ex-Père de la nation* (1987), Sow Fall's latest novel, is a variant on the resignation-of-the-president theme instituted by *Sembène's *Le Dernier de l'empire* in 1981.

Sow Fall writes in a simple, accessible style: her aim, she says, is to provide people with a mirror to enable them to see and correct their shortcomings. A civil servant and educationist, she was a member of the Commission for Educational Reform responsible for the introduction of African literature into the French syllabus in Senegal. She has a good sense of the relationship between literature and 'market forces', and of the importance of promoting the literary product. She is head of the Centre d'Animation et d'Échanges Culturels in Dakar, and her publishing-house, Éditions Khoudia, was opened in 1990. [FNC]

Spanish Influences. Although Spanish writing has known periods of widespread popularity in France, its influence has not been as deep or formative as that of Italy in the 16th c. or of England in the 18th. It was from the Renaissance that Spanish writers became widely known. The work of Antonio de

775

Spanish Influences

Guevara was rapidly translated and particularly significant. His *Livre d'or de Marc-Aurèle* (trans. 1531) left its mark on moral and political thinking in the period; his *Mépris de la cour* (trans. 1542) inspired works by *Du Fail and *La Taille; and his *Épîtres dorées* (trans. 1556) were closely read by *Montaigne and *Brantôme, among others. The popularity of certain sentimental novels helped to create and sustain the idealized conception of love dominant in the century: *La Prison d'amour* of Diego de San Pedro (trans. 1526); and two novels of Juan de Flores, *Le Jugement d'amour* (trans. 1520) and *La Déplorable Fin de Flammette*, translated by *Scève in 1535. Similarly, the vogue for chivalric romance during this same period owed much to the many translations and adaptations of *Amadis de Gaule*.

The high point of Spanish popularity was the 17th c., when the major texts of the Golden Age were translated. However, the nature and degree of influence varies greatly. Least potent was poetry. The burlesque and satirical verses of Góngora were imitated by *Saint-Amant, *Voiture, and *Scarron, but the metaphorical, syntactical, and lexical complexities of *conceptismo* and *culteranismo* found little following. Some of the mystical writings of St John of the Cross or St Teresa of Avila were read and translated, but their influence on *devotional literature is slight.

It is in the fields of prose fiction and drama that Spanish writing was most prominent. Some texts were widely read, but their impact on French authors was uneven. The pastoral novels of Montemayor, Gil Polo, and Cervantes were very popular, provided plots for many plays, and helped diffuse the *Neoplatonic conceptions of love dominant in the first half of the century; but until the arrival of d'*Urfé few novelists moved beyond insipid imitation. The same is true of the *novela*. Cervantes's *Novelas ejemplares* (trans. 1615) were much appreciated, by *Sorel and Scarron among others, as were the many translations and adaptations of *novelas* by later writers. However, although regularly adapted for the stage, they inspired few original *nouvelles*; Sorel's *Nouvelles françaises* (1623) and *Segrais's collection of the same title (1656) are notable exceptions.

Other texts were more inspirational. Pérez de Hita's *Guerres civiles de Grenade* (trans. 1608) created a taste for exotic, sentimental Hispano-Moorish tales, seen in texts from *Gomberville's *Polexandre* to *Villedieu's *Galanteries grenadines* (1673). Similarly popular was Cervantes's *Don Quixote* (trans. 1614), which provided the plots of several comedies and became the model for comic novels from *Du Verdier's *Chevalier hypocondriaque* (1632) to *Subligny's *Fausse Clélie* (1670). Apart from Sorel's *Berger extravagant* (1627), though, such imitations lacked depth, reducing the hero's rootless idealism to mere vanity or madness.

The fictional tradition most creatively assimilated in French writing is perhaps the picaresque. The major texts were all known, from *Lazarillo de Tormes* to the novels of Alemán, Espinel, and Quevedo, and, though Lesage's *Gil Blas* is the first (and only) successful imitation of the form, several satirical or autobiographical novels of earlier years bear its traces: episodic form, attention to details of everyday life (where the presence of Rojas's *La Celestina* (trans. 1527), widely known but never imitated in France, is also evident), and the implied involvement of the reader in the first-person narrative: Sorel's *Francion*, *Théophile's *Fragments d'une histoire comique* (1623), and *Tristan's *Page disgracié* (1642) count among such texts.

In the theatre, dramatists from *Hardy to *Quinault found plots for tragedies and tragicomedies in both *novela* and *comedia*. Similarly, the mid-century saw a fashion for adaptations of Spanish comedies which blended romantic intrigue and burlesque; d'*Ouville, Scarron, Thomas *Corneille, and *Boisrobert published between them over 20 such plays. *Rotrou was probably the most prolific adaptor of Spanish texts, but the most successful was certainly Pierre *Corneille, whose *Le *Cid*, taken from the *Mocedades del Cid* of Guillén de Castro, and *Le *Menteur*, inspired by Alarcón's *La verdad sospechosa*, embody the qualities of creative understanding and theatrical imagination which so many other adaptations lacked.

In the 18th c. Spanish influence was more occasional. Much of Lesage's work is Hispanic in inspiration, from early adaptations of *comedias* to his very successful *Le *Diable boiteux*, based on a novel by Vélez de Guevara, and *Gil Blas*. At the end of the century, *Florian imitated Montemayor in his *Estelle et Némorin* (1788), and adapted the Hispano-Moorish tale in *Gonzalve de Cordoue* (1792). Elsewhere, though, Spain and Spanish writing is much less evident. *Voltaire expressed admiration for Gracián's *El criticón*, widely read at the beginning of the century, but its influence on his *contes philosophiques* is uncertain; *Beaumarchais wrote a *Mémoire sur l'Espagne* (1764), but the Spain of his comedies is little more than a convenient backdrop.

Spain re-emerged both as a theme and as a literary presence during the Romantic period, when there was a renewal of interest in the Golden Age. Quasi-authentic *couleur locale* informs the settings of several prose works, from *Nodier's *Inès de las sierras* (1837) to Mérimée's *Carmen*, and *Chateaubriand's *Aventures du dernier Abencérage* (1826) re-works the tradition of Hispano-Moorish tale. Abel Hugo's *Romances historiques* (1822) popularized the *romancero* (ballad), whose themes were taken up by *Vigny, *Heredia, and Victor *Hugo (*Orientales*, 1829), while more creative adaptation of Spanish forms was tried by *Gautier, and by Hugo in *La *Légende des siècles*. As for the theatre, countless Spanish literary echoes haunt *Mérimée's *Théâtre de Clara Gazul* (1825), and in Hugo's *Hernani* and *Ruy Blas* the spirit of the *romancero* is clear.

In this century Spain has been inspirational, if not

deeply influential. Spanish themes or settings pervade the theatre of *Claudel and *Montherlant, and the Civil War gave rise to works by *Malraux, *Sartre, *Éluard, and *Aragon. The Surrealist movement was clearly sensitive to the work of *Picasso and Dali, and the *Ficciones* (trans. 1951) of the Argentine writer Borges provided some stimulus to the development of the *Nouveau Roman. The impact of recent Latin American novels on modern French fiction remains to be determined. [GJM]

See G. Hainsworth, *Les Novelas ejemplares en France* (1933); P. van Tieghem, *Influences étrangères sur la littérature française* (1961); A. Cioranescu, *Le Masque et le visage* (1983).

Spanish Succession, War of the (1701–14). In this general European war, England, Holland, Austria, and their allies sought to curb the power of *Louis XIV, who, by placing his grandson on the Spanish throne threatened to upset the 'balance of power'. Its complicated and inconclusive course is notable for the campaigns of Marlborough, Prince Eugene of Austria, and the French generals Catinat and Villars.

Spectacle dans un fauteuil, Un, see MUSSET.

Spectacle de la nature, Le, see PLUCHE.

Spectateur français, Le, see MARIVAUX.

Speculum maius, see VINCENT DE BEAUVAIS.

SPINOZA, Baruch (1632–77). In France the great Judaeo-Cartesian philosopher was known largely from the article in *Bayle's *Dictionnaire* and an essay by *Boulainviller. For Cartesian rationalists like himself (e.g. *Fénelon), Spinoza's logic was irreligious and dangerous. Refuted both by less radical free-thinkers and Christian apologists, he was commonly seen by 18th-c. readers as a subversive critic of the Bible (in the *Tractatus theologico-philosophicus*) and a materialistic atheist denying free will (in the *Ethics*). *Condillac criticized him as a system-builder. *Voltaire in later works was comparatively impartial, but until the 19th c. few were sympathetic and knowledgeable except *Diderot. [CJB]

Spleen de Paris, Le (1869). Collection of prose poems by *Baudelaire, published posthumously, sometimes known as *Petits Poèmes en prose*.

'Spleen et idéal'. The first and most important section of Baudelaire's Les *Fleurs du mal*.

Splendeurs et misères des courtisanes. Novel-cycle by *Balzac, written in several distinct parts between 1838 and 1847 as a Parisian sequel to the unsuccessful adventures of the 'poet' Lucien de Rubempré (Lucien Chardon) in *Illusions perdues*. In this rambling, convoluted, fantastical thriller, Lucien is the catspaw of Balzac's maestro of the underworld, Jacques Collin, first introduced as Vautrin in Le *Père Goriot* and reappearing at the end of *Illusions perdues* as Carlos Herrera. Melodramatic by design, *Splendeurs et misères* purports to show the unity of Parisian society through the conspiracies which link high society, legitimate business, and crime, and it provides a model for much popular fiction and journalism of the 20th c. In the final episode Lucien commits suicide in prison, and his manipulator becomes chief of the Paris police. [DMB]

SPONDE, Jean de (1557–95). French *humanist and poet. Brought up as a Calvinist, he was given a humanist education and visited Basle, famous for its learning and its toleration. He was personally acquainted with Henri de Navarre (later *Henri IV) and held various public offices. When Henri IV was converted to Catholicism (1594) Sponde followed suit, and was violently attacked by leading Huguenots such as *Bèze and d'*Aubigné. He acquired a reputation as a humanist scholar, publishing Latin translations of Homer (1583) and Hesiod (1592) together with commentaries. His French works include a set of prose meditations on four psalms (1588), designed for the personal use of Henri de Navarre, but he is best known for his slender but striking collections of lyric verse: the *Amours*, published posthumously (c.1598), and the *Essai de poèmes chrétiens*, published with the psalm meditations. The Christian poems (twelve sonnets and a longer poem on death; a poem on the Eucharist) bear traces of Sponde's Calvinism; they also belong to a broader revival of devotional poetry in this period [see CHASSIGNET; LA CEPPÈDE; FAVRE]. Sponde's poetry was 'discovered' in 1930 by the critic Alan Boase, who judged it comparable with contemporary English metaphysical poetry. [TC]

STAAL, Marguerite-Jeanne Cordier de Launay, baronne de (c.1684–1750). Brilliantly educated, she frequented the most notable intellectuals of the day, and turned her first-hand knowledge of the *Regency—from its *fêtes* to its political conspiracies—into *Mémoires* (1755) too frank to be published during the lifetimes of all principal protagonists. She spent 40 years at the court at Sceaux in the service of the duchesse du *Maine, and wrote comedies staged at the court theatre and a celebrated correspondence. Late in her life the duc du Maine arranged a marriage with the baron de Staal to enhance her rank and privileges. [JDeJ]

STAËL, Anne-Louise-Germaine Necker, Madame de (1766–1817). Novelist, essayist, literary critic, and precursor of the modern comparative study of cultures.

Born the daughter of Jacques *Necker and Suzanne Curchod, Germaine Necker grew up in the world of her mother's literary salon. There she acquired a great facility and brilliance in conversation for which she was noted all her life, and a familiarity with the philosophical ideas of her time. In

1786 she entered into a loveless marriage with the Swedish ambassador to Paris, baron de Staël: of her three children by him only one survived to adult years, Auguste, who was to edit her Œuvres complètes in 1820. She held a salon at her home in the rue du Bac and in 1788 published privately Lettres sur les ouvrages et le caractère de J.-J. Rousseau, which aroused fierce controversy by its vigorous defence of La *Nouvelle Héloïse.

From 1790 she spent part of each year with her father at his chateau at *Coppet on the Lake of Geneva. During the Terror she made courageous efforts to rescue friends from the guillotine, and had a love-affair with a Swedish exile Count Ribbing in 1793. On 18 September 1794 she met Benjamin *Constant, who fell in love with her. Although it was some time before she returned his love, their intellectual and emotional intimacy was to be of central importance in their lives and also the source of great suffering. Both were fervent supporters of the moderate republican cause, and from 1795 onwards, in Paris and at Coppet, they worked together for political progress, founding the Club Constitutionnel in 1797. In the same year Germaine de Staël gave birth to a daughter, Albertine, possibly Constant's daughter. This was a period of prolific writing: De l'influence des passions (1796), Des circonstances actuelles qui peuvent terminer la Révolution (published only in 1988), and De la littérature considérée dans ses rapports avec les institutions sociales (1800). In 1800 she was officially separated from her husband, who died in 1802.

Her opposition to the tyranny of the military dictator Bonaparte became ever stronger, and in 1802, following the publication of her novel *Delphine, which incurred the First Consul's anger, she was banned from living in Paris. She visited Weimar with Constant, met Goethe, Schiller, and Wieland, and employed August Wilhelm von Schlegel as tutor to her children. Gradually the Groupe de Coppet formed around her: A. W. von Schlegel and his brother, *Bonstetten, *Sismondi, and the historian Prosper de *Barante, all with an interest in comparative cultural history. After touring Italy in 1805 she wrote her best-known novel, *Corinne ou l'Italie, completed in 1806 and published in 1807 as Constant was beginning *Adolphe, with which it has often been compared. In 1807 she set about the publication of her most celebrated work of non-fiction, De l'Allemagne, which was immediately seized by *Napoleon's minister of police, who ordered her into exile. In 1812, after the autobiographical Dix années d'exil (1811), she fled to London (via Vienna, Moscow, St Petersburg, and Stockholm), from where she continued her work in opposition to Napoleon. After his overthrow she spent much time at Coppet, meeting Lord Byron in the summer of 1816 and marrying her lover John Rocca secretly in October 1816. Her Considérations sur la Révolution française were published posthumously in 1818.

Germaine de Staël occupies a curious position in French literary history. Her style, sometimes diffuse and prolix, has often been criticized and compared unfavourably to Constant's, for example. Nevertheless, the originality of her perceptions is remarkable, and on many matters she was in advance of her time. Well travelled and open to new ideas, in De la littérature she surveys the literature of the past and of other cultures and points to the close relationship between literature and thought and the society in which they grow—a relatively original idea at the time [see LITERARY HISTORY]. France is caught between the old pagan world of Greece and Rome, with its stress on form and clarity, and the new imaginative world of the Germanic peoples of Christian northern Europe where 'romantic' literature, characterized by enthusiasm and feeling, has developed. In De l'Allemagne she introduces French readers to modern German writers such as Goethe and Schiller. The plot of Corinne, while similarly resting on an opposition between northern and southern Europe, may also reflect to some degree the novelist's sense of isolation as a woman and an artist in a male-dominated society. [DW]

See S. Balayé, Madame de Staël: lumières et liberté (1979); G. de Diesbach, Madame de Staël, 1983.

STAHL, P.-J., pseudonym of the publisher *Hetzel.

Stances à Sophie, Les, see ROCHEFORT, C.

STANISLAS I LESZCZYŃSKI (1677–1766). Nominal king of Poland from 1704 to 1766, Stanislas spent his last 30 years in exile in Lorraine. His brilliant court in Nancy and Lunéville welcomed artists and writers, and the king himself took part in the polemic over J.-J. *Rousseau's Discours sur les sciences et les arts.

STAROBINSKI, Jean (b. 1920). Critic. A Genevan, Starobinski trained as a psychiatrist. His most celebrated work, Jean-Jacques Rousseau, la transparence et l'obstacle (1957), offers a subtle and text-based view of the subject's inner world, close in some ways to the work of *Poulet and *Richard. Later writings, often long essays, explore many topics, from *Saussure's preoccupation with anagrams to melancholia in *Montaigne and *Baudelaire. Some of his best work is concerned with the 18th c.—*Diderot, *Rousseau, and the oratory and emblems of the *Revolution (L'Invention de la liberté, 1964). [PF]

STAVISKY, Alexandre (1886–1934). Shady financier, whose ruin and alleged suicide in 1933–4 led to an 'affaire' in which the government and important public figures were implicated. This provoked violent right-wing demonstrations [see CROIX-DE-FEU]. The legends surrounding the affair and its hero are treated in the film Stavisky (1974) by *Resnais and *Semprun.

STÉFAN, Jude (b. 1936). French poet, author of several collections, beginning with Cyprès (1967) and including *Suites slaves* (1983) and *A la Vieille Parque* (1989), remarkable for their organization of the verse line and the concentrated richness of their language. [PF]

Stèles, see SEGALEN.

Stello, see VIGNY.

STENDHAL (pseud. of Henri Beyle) (1783–1842). Though most widely known as the author of two great novels, *Le *Rouge et le noir* and *La *Chartreuse de Parme*, Stendhal wrote prolifically in many prose genres: travel literature, essays, journalism, art history, biography, and autobiography. All of these, together with his journals and correspondence, constitute a remarkable picture of Beyle the individual. The self is omnipresent in the writing, and it is this individual voice which most appeals to 'Stendhalians'; for Stendhal has been the object of a cult in the 20th c. He wrote for the 'Happy Few', and after a period of relative neglect posterity has justified his faith in a manner which he might have found embarrassing.

He grew up in Grenoble, a town he detested as a symbol of narrow French provincial life. The black picture painted in the autobiographical *Vie de Henry Brulard* of his childhood, stressing the early death of his mother, his antagonistic relations with his father, and his hate of priestly reaction, needs to be viewed with caution, but he was happy when his proficiency at mathematics took him to Paris in 1799 to study at the *École Polytechnique. As it turned out he worked in the War Ministry, and in May 1800 joined Napoleon's armies and crossed the Alps to Milan. Italy was henceforward to be for him the anti-France, a place of beauty, opera, passion, and happiness, and he lived much of his life there.

From 1802 to 1806 he lived in France, mainly Paris, receiving a pension from his father, reading intensively, and training to be a writer; his unfulfilled ambition was to be a comic playwright. His *Journal* of this period marks the beginning of the self-scrutiny (and self-creation) that was a dominant concern; he later applied to it the new word *égotisme*. From 1806 to 1814 he was much involved in political and military life in the service of the emperor, towards whom he developed ambivalent feelings which are reflected in many of his works (he wrote two lives of *Napoleon, 1817, 1836). His service took him all over Europe, culminating with the Moscow campaign, of which he was one of the few survivors.

On Napoleon's fall Stendhal went into exile in Milan, whence he was expelled as a revolutionary (*carbonaro*) by the Austrian government in 1821. Without being a plotter, he was hostile to the reactionary governments of post-1815 Europe; his works are full of political satire and liberal sentiments, yet as he himself admitted, he was for all his republicanism a natural aristocrat in his tastes, a believer in the value of superior beings, and in the beauty and passion which modern liberal democracy stifles.

Stendhal once composed his own epitaph beginning: 'Errico Beyle, Milanese: visse, scrisse, amò.' (Henri Beyle, Milanese: he lived, wrote, loved.) It was in Milan that he began to write for publication: derivative lives of Haydn, Mozart, and Metastasio; his *Histoire de la peinture en Italie* (1817); and the joyful travel notes, *Rome, Naples et Florence en 1817* (1817, enlarged edn. 1826), in which he begins to elaborate his Italian myth, with a great stress on opera. *Rome, Naples et Florence* marks the first appearance of the pseudonym Stendhal—perhaps to rival *Staël, perhaps for other reasons, but in any case deep psychological causes made Beyle a great user of masks and false names.

Love-affairs, successful or unsuccessful, were the second main business of his life (see the opening of *Vie de Henry Brulard*). Stendhalians have mapped his various liaisons in great detail. In Milan he had a stormy affair with Angela Pietragrua (1811–15), but was most marked by his unconsummated passion for Matilde Dembowski (Métilde), which is reflected in *De l'amour* (1822). Thereafter his most important loves were for the countess Clémentine Curial (1824–6) and for Giulia Rinieri (1830–3).

Between 1821 and 1830 he lived mainly in Paris, with visits to England, Italy, etc. At this time he acquired a reputation as a brilliant and ferocious conversationalist. Poorer than before, he wrote many important essays for the English press (*Chroniques pour l'Angleterre*). He took a keen interest in politics and literature, championing his own version of Romanticism in *Racine et Shakespeare* (1823–5). A second travel book, *Promenades dans Rome*, is more concerned with politics and society than *Rome, Naples et Florence*—this tendency was continued in the *Mémoires d'un touriste* (1838), a fictitious travel journal which is one of the first serious attempts at a description of France. The Parisian period also saw the beginnings of Stendhal's most famous body of work, his fiction, with *Armance (1827), *Vanina Vanini (written 1829), and his first masterpiece, *Le *Rouge et le noir* (1830).

After the July Days of 1830 he became French consul at the small port Civitavecchia in the Papal states, where he served until just before his death. It was a tedious posting, relieved only by trips to Rome and a long period of leave in Paris and France (1836–9). But this was his most productive period as a writer. In 1832 he wrote his first autobiographical work, *Souvenirs d'égotisme*, concerning his life in Paris in the 1820s. This was soon followed by the incomparable account of his childhood, *Vie de Henry Brulard*. And in the same period he worked on four major works of fiction, *Lucien Leuwen, *Chroniques italiennes, La *Chartreuse de Parme, and *Lamiel, on which he was working just before his death.

Stendhal originally wanted to be the *Molière of his time. The comic element is strong in his writings, which are full of critical, often biased, accounts of contemporary life. He had a low opinion of post-Revolutionary France, its hypocrisy, vanity, and

779

oppression. Always an enemy of power (he says he danced with joy on learning of the execution of Louis XVI), he wrote to celebrate liberty. However, although he remained faithful to a more or less radical political position, liberty for him was above all a matter for the individual spirit. In *Vie de Henry Brulard* he describes the liberating effect of reading Shakespeare, Ariosto, and Cervantes as a child; they represent art, beauty, and life. To them should be added *Rousseau; Stendhal's ironic realism, like his brilliant conversation, was often a mask for Romantic idealism. His ideal, which he tended to locate in other times and other places, was one of generosity of spirit; it involved the ability to feel and to act daringly, to pursue happiness without hypocrisy. Madame *Roland, who met death nobly, was an ideal female figure, and it is striking how often death, sacrifice, and suicide give the final nobility to his life-loving heroes and heroines.

At the same time, he knew how Romantic aspiration can become a pose. He ridicules the windy eloquence of a *Chateaubriand, and takes refuge either in humour and irony (loving the mixture of laughter and passion in Mozart's operas) or in a sharp, bare style, where no time is wasted on fine writing. To feel like Rousseau but write like *Montesquieu was his aim. It is in this mixture of the hard and the soft, the cynical and the tender, the ironic and the passionate that the particular charm of his writing lies. [PF]

See M. Bardèche, *Stendhal romancier* (1947); M. Tillett, *Stendhal: The Background to the Novels* (1971); S. Felman, *La 'Folie' dans l'œuvre romanesque de Stendhal* (1971); M. Crouzet, *Stendhal et l'italianité* (1982); R. Pearson, *Stendhal's Violin* (1988).

STEPHENSON, Élie (b. 1944). Economist and teacher who composes poetry, drama, and songs in French and in the *Creole of French Guiana. His plays place emphasis on self-reliance and solidarity (*Ô Mayouri!*, 1970), tackling issues such as migration (*Les Voyageurs*, 1977), and recreating local history (*Les Placers*, 1990). A tensely economical poetic line is as effective in traditional work-songs as in love lyrics. [BJ]

STERN, Daniel, pseudonym of the comtesse d'*Agoult.

Strasbourg Oaths (*Serments de Strasbourg*). Recorded by Nithard in a roughly contemporary Latin chronicle (MS late 10th c.), the Oaths were sworn in Strasbourg on 14 February 842, when two of *Charlemagne's grandsons, Charles the Bald and Louis the German, formed an alliance against their brother Lothair. The first oath of mutual support (*sacramentum firmitatis*) was sworn in French by Louis the German, and in German by the French-speaking Charles; each man's followers then swore a different oath (*sacramentum fidelitatis*) in their own language. The Oaths, despite their formulaic and conservative use of language, are of great signifi-cance to French philologists as the earliest extant document in the 'lingua romana' or vernacular of Gaul. [WA-B]

Structuralism. Movement of thought which exerted a great influence on French intellectual and literary life in the post-war period. It covers a wide range of disciplines, from *anthropology to *literary criticism, and a common definition is not easily found. Broadly, it seeks to define facts of human existence, from marriage customs to events in novels, in terms of organized structures of which they are parts. In studying cultural phenomena, it finds meaning not in single elements, but in their relationship (often one of binary opposition) to other elements within a given signifying system.

In the mid-1940s the anthropologist Claude *Lévi-Strauss used the term 'structuralist', inspired by contemporary *linguistics under the influence of Roman Jakobson, to characterize his method of analysis of social phenomena. 'Structuralism' thus became a label by which many intellectuals, or at least their commentators, were to denote until the mid-1970s an approach, a technique, or a fully fledged philosophy, depending on the degree of identification of the speaker. It can be said to have survived in the first two senses and to be embodied in permanent achievements in various disciplines, though conspicuously replaced on the fashionable and mythical plane by *Post-Structuralism and deconstruction [see DERRIDA]. But whereas Structuralism actively sought to supersede *Existentialism and *phenomenology, since it held that their reliance on consciousness and lived experience was what *Bachelard called an 'epistemological obstacle' to the scientific recognition of hidden structures, the relations between Structuralism and its successors is dialectical rather than purely antagonistic.

Nowhere is this more evident than in the work of *Barthes, who played a major part in the propagation of the Structuralist outlook, both because of a unique combination of gifts as a profound analyst and a popularizer of genius and because of the breadth of his interests. This was obvious early on in *Mythologies*, which laid the foundations of his enduring fame with the educated layman. In fact, the term he uses there to describe his account of society and its artefacts at one stroke, as communication ruled by sign systems, is 'semiology', a word we owe to the father of 'structuralist' linguistics, *Saussure. Lévi-Strauss's catholicism in applying his newly forged techniques not only to expected concerns such as kinship, totemism, or myths but also to modern practices in cookery, clothes, or town-planning is matched by Barthes's illuminating insights into contemporary behaviour and institutions. He bridges the heterogeneity of the media in order to reveal the coherence of the message conveyed through *advertising, scholarly or legal discourse, photographs, films, exhibitions, garments, or cars.

This universality of application is a typically Structuralist ambition. The description of 'the human mind', which is overtly Lévi-Strauss's long-term aim, is tacitly present in the work of all those who felt his influence. It allied his work with that of thinkers who had similarly broad ambitions, including Freud (via *Lacan), Marx (via *Althusser), *Sartre (via Barthes), ancient and modern theorists of *rhetoric (including *Genette and the Belgian 'Groupe μ'), and even contemporary physicists and biologists. While Michel *Foucault's work is not explicitly Structuralist, its regular inclusion under that label is fully justified by the contrast between its wide scope and its concentration on synchrony, where relations between historically contemporary elements are the sole source of intelligibility.

The regular coexistence of two features which are normally found at opposite ends of the cognitive spectrum, a concern for the multiplicity of phenomena and a stress on fundamentals, marks Structuralist authors as thinkers sensitive to the concrete charms of appearance despite their essential conviction that truth is found in immanence and not manifestation. It is, however, their assertion of the ultimate dominance of deep logico-semantic levels, whatever the variegated effects produced by 'transformations' of basic elements, which is the major cause of the keen objections levelled at Structuralism by those who—whether Existentialist, Christian, or *Marxist—sought to preserve an active belief in human agency in matters personal and historical. This outcry is understandable in view of the extreme and often blatantly provocative form in which the Structuralist rejection of the humanist basis of such philosophies was often expressed. Furthermore, the silence of most Structuralists during the events of *May 1968, together with the sometimes forbidding look of their books, readily led to accusations that their credo was the ideology of conservatism and technocracy. But the Structuralist way of exploring the depths automatically implies convincing descriptions of the surface, and this aspect, which makes up a large part of their appeal, also tempers the despondency naïve observers might feel on reading that they are not acting, speaking, or thinking but being 'acted', 'spoken', or 'thought out' by language and unconscious formations.

This dual focusing is reflected in the fact that many Structuralist authors are also good writers, and have taken a professional interest in the generation of literary effects. Barthes was again here first in the field, because he grasped a nettle which other Structuralists carefully avoided: the shortcomings of the Saussurean linguist's purely differential and binary definition of signs when one leaves the original source of Structuralism—phonology—to graduate to the complex realities of society and art, ruled by laws which, although shadowy, have more to do with more recent concerns of linguistics such as semantics and pragmatics.

Yet the binary principle, even taken only as one instance of the human mind's propensity to order and classify, was to prove heuristically fertile in literary and filmic analysis. Such analysis centred on journals such as *Communications* and *Poétique*; apart from Barthes, the most important figures included *Greimas, *Genette, *Metz, and *Todorov. Greimas also drew attention to other grammatical and semantic sources for the scientific grounding of modern poetics, especially the analysis of narrative, where he systematized two oppositions between surface and depth which had been described in various terminologies by theorists from different traditions without gaining, until then, the classic status they now have. One is the distinction between the 'story' as a catalogue of events and the various 'discourses' which, through different manipulations of these events, can foster wholly different effects, such as suspense. The other is the distinction between 'actors', or characters, the mimetic units which the naïve reader endows with a fictitious anthropomorphic identity, and 'actants', the logical forces whose constellation, deployed in time, generates the plot. The fact that characters have pertinence both on the syntactic plane of plot and the semiotic plane of general significance further highlights the similarity between a plot, a grammatical sentence, and even the semantic structure of a word (or 'sememe'), which has also been an extremely fertile notion, e.g. in the work of Umberto Eco.

As for the Structuralist obsession with epistemology, it foregrounds the human mind and its processes in a way which parallels the self-consciousness and formalism typical of modernist works. This made the study of the latter very rewarding for Structuralist analysis when it ventured beyond its prudent beginnings centred on folk-tales (following Vladimir Propp's pioneering work) or James Bond novels (e.g. in *Communications*, no. 8). This feature—which heralded the Post-Structuralist challenging of the 'human sciences', on the grounds that their reliance on natural languages destroys their claims to the metalanguage of science—eventually so reduced the distance between critic and writer that this traditional opposition all but disappeared, until the aspirations of authors such as Barthes or *Sollers rescued it.

Structuralism inherited from the *Nouveau Roman its insistence on the active reader or spectator. While this has become a tenet of recent critical orthodoxy, this invocation of the reader's activity is not only opportunistic; applied to art and to society as a whole, it is what will probably remain as the legacy of Structuralism, together with the memory of an exhilaratingly productive moment in intellectual history. The customary listing of Marx, Freud, and Nietzsche as the patron saints of the movement does not do justice to its extraordinarily populous and varied genealogy; yet the invocation of these 'masters of suspicion' is justified. For those who have learned from Structuralism to 'read' the entire human text, and nature itself, as something which

Style indirect libre

does not 'go without saying' but has instead to be decoded, the world will never be the same again.

[AL]

See J. Piaget, *Le Structuralisme* (1968); F. Wahl, *Qu'est-ce que le structuralisme?* (1968); O. Ducrot and T. Todorov, *Dictionnaire encyclopédique des sciences du langage* (1972); T. Hawkes, *Structuralism and Semiotics* (1977); A. Lavers, *Roland Barthes: Structuralism and After* (1982); J. Sturrock, *Structuralism* (1987).

Style indirect libre. Form of narration combining the features of reported and direct speech. Typically, the thoughts of a fictional character are expressed, but without any introductory formula ('She thought . . .') and in the imperfect tense. The narrator can thus move unobtrusively between objective and subjective narration, often suggesting an ironic view of the thoughts expressed. The form occurs in the 18th and early 19th c., but was used most powerfully by *Flaubert, and has become an essential feature of the modern novel. [PF]

SUARD, Jean-Baptiste-André (1732–1817). French journalist and translator. He edited the *Journal étranger* (1760–2) and the *Gazette littéraire d'Europe* (1764–6), and was on good terms with the *philosophes*, many of whom came to his wife's salon, but he eschewed their more radical ideas. In 1774 his worldly career was crowned by election to the Académie Française, and he became a censor (he did not approve of Le *Mariage de Figaro*). A prudent conformist, he was nevertheless harassed by both the Revolutionary and the Napoleonic regimes. His *Mélanges de littérature* were published in 1803–5. [PF]

SUARÈS, André (pseud. of Félix-André-Yves Scantrel) (1868–1948). French critic and poet who used other pseudonyms (André de Séipse, Caërdal, etc.). He devoted himself to the cult of greatness as manifested at the summits of artistic achievement. In a grandiloquent, lyrical style tuned to the void underlying all human experience, his numerous essays and portraits—*Tolstoï vivant* (1911), *Trois hommes: Pascal, Ibsen, Dostoïevski* (1913), *Le Voyage du condottiere* (1910–32)—sometimes illumine their subjects, although much of his own life was spent in shade, umbrage, and haughty isolation. [DAS]

SUBLIGNY, Adrien Perdou de (1639–96). French dramatist and novelist. His works include *La Folle Querelle* (1668), which combines both parody and more substantial criticism of *Andromaque*, and a *Dissertation sur la tragédie de Phèdre* (1677). His *La Fausse Clélie* (1670), written in the satirical tradition of Cervantes and *Sorel, has moments of insight into the dynamics of character which anticipate *Challe's *Illustres Françaises*. [GJM]

Sublime et le grotesque, Le. The idea of the sublime, which acquired wide currency in the 18th c.,

carried the sense of a powerful, awe-inspiring beauty. Victor *Hugo opened up a new direction in aesthetics by setting up creative tensions between the sublime and the grotesque. In the *Préface de *Cromwell*, he presented this opposition in terms of a dualism in which the grotesque contrasted with the sublime as body with soul, matter with spirit, and supported his argument with a historical overview dividing the development of civilization into three stages. Following *Chateaubriand, he made the dualism of body and soul constitutive of modern man. The modern spirit found expression in the drama, which encompassed the multiplicity and the complexity of the reality revealed by Christianity. Hence Hugo's conviction that modern art must include contrasting elements: 'c'est de la féconde union du type grotesque au type sublime que naît le génie moderne.' Henceforward art would include the ugly as well as the beautiful, the material as well as the spiritual, the comic as well as the tragic. Here was a manifesto for *Romantic art, a programme for aesthetic renewal. Art would no longer be bound by restrictive classical conventions, but would aspire to include the totality of experience. It would mirror the processes of life itself. [CC]

SUE, Eugène (1804–57). Celebrated French popular novelist. After a short spell as a naval surgeon in 1827, Sue took up the life of a literary dandy in Paris. His early works were sea novels (especially *Atar-Gull*, 1831). He was one of the first exponents of the *roman-feuilleton*, initially focusing on novels of fashionable life. It was when he turned his melodramatic and Romantic talents to low life that he achieved enormous success. Les *Mystères de Paris* ran from June 1842 to October 1843. It had France's roman-feuilleton readers on the edge of their seats. In this novel Sue set the pattern for modern mass fiction, with its super-heroes, its obsession with criminality, and its irresistible blend of the fantastic and the mysterious. His work became a precious commodity for newspapers eager to boost and retain their circulation figures. *Le Juif errant* (1844–5) and *Les Sept Péchés capitaux* (1847–8) followed the early successes. Sue became increasingly drawn to humanitarian and socialist causes. He was elected a *député* in 1850, but was forced into exile in 1851. His last big success was *Les Mystères du peuple* (1849–57). The Imperial Government promptly banned the publication of the complete work. [BR]

SUGER, Abbot, see LATINITY, 1.

Suivante, La. Comedy by Pierre *Corneille, first performed 1622–3. It contains a striking portrait of a heroine embittered by poverty.

SULIVAN, Jean, was the pseudonym adopted by abbé Joseph Lemarchand (1913–80) when he turned to literature as a means of expressing a vigorous Christian spirituality, while questioning received ideas and structures in the institutional Church. An essayist, poet, and novelist, he edited the Gallimard collection 'Voies ouvertes'.　　　　　　　　[BCS]

SULLIVAN, Vernon, see VIAN.

SULLY, Maximilien de Béthune, duc de (1559–1641). *Henri IV's great minister, whose financial and agrarian reforms largely repaired the damage done to the French economy by the *Wars of Religion, helping also to secure the position of the Bourbon dynasty. Discarded after Henri's death in 1610, Sully retired to his château, living in regal style and dictating his memoirs, the *Économies royales d'état, domestiques, politiques et militaires* (1638), a wide-ranging survey of his times but also an apologetic work, including the notorious account of Henri's (probably mythical) plan to create a United States of Europe, the so-called 'Grand Dessein'.　　　[MJH]

SULLY-PRUDHOMME (pseud. of René-François-Armand Prudhomme) (1839–1907). An engineer by training and the first recipient (in 1901) of the Nobel Prize for Literature, Sully-Prudhomme embodied most clearly the scientific and philosophical commitments of the *Parnassian movement in French poetry. He also shared its descriptive aesthetic and cult of formal perfection, which gradually displaced the intimate sentimentality and gentle melancholy of his early poetry (notably *Les Stances*, 1865). From his encounter with the writings of Lucretius, whom he translated (1869), and the impact of the military defeat of 1870 came *Les Destins* (1872); this inaugurated the scientific and philosophical poetry written in a literal and didactic epic form which had a wide appeal during the period 1875–1900, but ensured a rapid decline in his reputation thereafter.　　　[JK]

SUPERVIELLE, Jules (1884–1960). Poet. Born in Montevideo of Béarnese-Basque parents, he was taken at eight months to visit relatives in south-west France, where his parents died, perhaps of tainted water. He was brought up by his aunt, whom he thought to be his mother until the age of 9. After childhood he spent most of his life in France. After the collapse of the Supervielle Bank, he was made cultural attaché to the Uruguayan Embassy (1946).

Supervielle suffered from uncertainties of memory and an intermittent heartbeat; walking in the country he felt, ambiguously, that it penetrated him and that he was dispersed in it (see *Boire à la source*, 1933). By his own admission, he feared to confront the monsters of his imagination. It was not until *Débarcadères* (1922) that his true voice emerged. His best work is here and in *Gravitations* (1925), *Le Forçat innocent* (1930), and *Les Amis inconnus* (1934). His language is shy and tentative, but dense with personification, attributing unusual feeling to animals, plants, and objects. Thus, he has a 'theory of ghosts': the apparition of his dead mother is the product of his own longing for her; she feels emotions that reflect his own. He is perhaps the first poet to inhabit the world of the modern scientist,

where the furthest space, the furthest time connects, *now*, with *us*.

In his fiction he was an exponent of 'magical realism' *avant la lettre*. The Guanamiru of *L'Homme de la pampa* (1923), a novel whose brief length is burst apart by its immense inventiveness, is a magician who toys with volcanoes. The hero of *Le Voleur d'enfants* (1926) and *Le Survivant* (1928) suffers a miraculous demonstration of his own Freudian guilt. But it is hard to empathize with his characters. Is his touch too light, his caution too desperate? The title-story of the collection *L'Enfant de la haute mer* (1931) achieves genuine emotion—but we are dealing here again with the 'theory of ghosts'. His theatrical work is less satisfactory. The attempt to import magic into it leads to an easy shying-away from the problems of Shariar's cruelty in *Schéhérazade* (1949).

Supervielle's poetry is profoundly original—it is time it ceased being classified as 'minor'.　　[GDM]

See T. W. Greene, *Supervielle* (1958); J. A. Hiddleston, *L'Univers de Jules Supervielle* (1965).

Supplément au Voyage de Bougainville. Dialogue by *Diderot, begun *c.*1772, published posthumously in 1798. The work takes the form of a fictitious supplement to the recent account of a visit to Tahiti by *Bougainville. A series of conversations, anecdotes, and speeches sets the happy natural life of the islanders, and particularly their codes of sexual behaviour, against the absurd and harmful mores of modern Europe. Inspired by the Utopian notions of Dom *Deschamps, Diderot does not, however, take his dream entirely seriously; the concluding dialogue favours a provisional and critical acceptance of the *status quo*.　　　　　　　　[PF]

Suréna. Pierre *Corneille's last tragedy, first performed 1674. It is a movingly simple swan-song, in which two noble lovers, the Parthian general Suréna and Eurydice, accept death rather than giving in to the ambitious machinations of the king and his son.

SURIN, Jean-Joseph, see DEVOTIONAL WRITING, 2.

Surprise de l'amour, La. Attractive comedy by *Marivaux, first performed 1722. Lelio and the comtesse, professing to give up love, are gradually brought, in spite of themselves, to love one another. Its success was not matched by *La Seconde Surprise de l'amour* (1727).

Surrealism

1. Beginnings

Surrealism was a revolutionary movement that developed in Paris, partly in response to the carnage and futility of the *World War I. Calling for a revision of values, it was a reaction against positivism, realism, reason, logic, and the 19th-c. belief in progress. For two or three years its activity and personnel coincided with those of the Paris branch of

Surrealism

*Dada, but the publication of *Breton's *Manifeste du surréalisme* in 1924 finally established its supremacy, its greater creative potential.

Breton's examination of the nature of lyricism, begun during the war [see VACHÉ], and his interest in the ideas of Freud, sparked off by his medical studies, led to his discovery of automatic writing (*écriture automatique*) and to the first Surrealist text, *Les Champs magnétiques* (1920), written in conjunction with *Soupault. The exploration of the subconscious was also pursued through hypnotic sleep, the best exponent of which proved to be *Desnos, and the transcription of dreams. The fruits of these techniques, together with his reading of *Lautréamont and *Rimbaud and his conversations with *Reverdy, made Breton appreciate the crucial importance of the image; from then on, Surrealist works were to be dominated by the power of their images, both visual and verbal, especially those that juxtaposed, in a seemingly arbitrary manner, phenomena that would not normally be associated, e.g. the classic encounter of a sewing-machine and an umbrella on a dissecting table in Lautréamont's *Les Chants de Maldoror*. Consequently, both the imagination and inspiration were fully restored to favour.

In the 1924 *Manifeste* Breton provided a number of definitions, including the often-quoted: 'SURRÉAL-ISME, n.m. Automatisme psychique pur par lequel on se propose d'exprimer, soit verbalement, soit par écrit, soit de toute autre manière, le fonctionnement réel de la pensee, en l'absence de tout contrôle exercé par la raison, en dehors de toute préoccupation esthétique ou morale.' ('Pure psychical automatism, which has the aim of expressing, whether verbally, in writing, or in some other manner, the actual functioning of thought freed from any control of the reason and any aesthetic or moral preoccupation.') Breton conceived of the state of *surréalité* in terms of the fusion of dream and reality. Near the beginning of the *Second Manifeste du surréalisme* (1930) there is the expression of a belief in the existence of a point in the mind where pairs of opposites (e.g. life and death, the real and the imaginary, the past and the future) cease to be perceived as contradictory.

The movement's most important writers (Aragon, Artaud, Breton, Char, Crevel, Desnos, Éluard, Gracq, Péret, Soupault) are the subject of separate entries, but some of the key themes and concepts in their works should be mentioned: the quest, the city (especially Paris), the night, *le merveilleux*, surprise, coincidences (often seen in relation to *le hasard objectif*), chance encounters (not just with beautiful and intriguing women), the *femme-fée*, the *femme-enfant*, *la beauté convulsive*, *l'amour fou*, desire, and the championing of liberty in all walks of life.

2. Painting and Cinema

According to Breton, Surrealist painting came into being as a consequence of a growing awareness of *psychoanalytic theory and Gestalt psychology and of the perfecting of photographic and cinematographic techniques which invalidated the ambition of merely reproducing reality: the final objective was the synthesis of physical perception and mental representation. Throughout his life he sought out precursors for the movement, but at the end of World War I the paintings of Chirico, with their disturbing blend of the real and the unreal, not to mention their conflicting perspectives, seemed to offer the best way forward. Before long, however, Ernst, Masson, Miró, Tanguy, *Magritte, Man Ray, Dali, even *Picasso, in their different ways, were to produce works that were labelled 'Surrealist'.

Although a plastic equivalent of *écriture automatique* was quickly found in the form of automatic drawing, Surrealist art was marked by a multiplicity of approaches, styles, and techniques, including Ernst's *frottage* and collage, Magritte's veristic but enigmatic study of the relationship between the object and its representation, Dominguez's decalcomania, *Giacometti's elongated sculptures, and Dali's 'paranoiac-critical method'. For the public at large pictorial Surrealism was destined to be better known than its literary counterparts. This was doubtless due in part to the Surrealist exhibitions that were mounted periodically in such places as Copenhagen (1935), London (1936), Amsterdam (1938), as well as those in Paris in 1947 and 1965. Moreover, the Surrealists were able to open their own art gallery in Paris, A l'Étoile Scellée, in December 1952.

Within the context of the movement itself the true potential of the cinema has perhaps not been realized, despite the importance of Luis Buñuel, especially his early films made with Salvador Dali: *Un chien andalou* (1928), with its perennially shocking opening shot of the eye sliced by a razor, and *L'Âge d'or* (1929), a sacrilegious mix of quasi-scientific documentary, psychoanalytic symbolism, eye-catching visual imagery, and paean to both the marquis de Sade and *l'amour fou*. In the 1920s other members of the group published scenarios in their reviews, and indeed made films. In 1929 Man Ray created *Le Mystère du château de dés* with *Duchamp and *L'Étoile de mer*, based on a poem by Desnos, relying on improvisation to produce a kind of 'automatic cinema'. Other films of the same period that were regarded as 'Surrealist' included Germaine Dulac's dream-like *La Coquille et le clergyman*, with a script by *Artaud. Since then the label has tended to be used rather loosely with reference to film, but it is not completely inappropriate for works such as Borowczik's *Les Jeux des anges*. Some critics have even suggested that the basic rhetoric of cinema is Surrealist in essence.

3. Politics

If the Dadaists seemed to turn their backs on politics in the normal sense of the word, except for their basic anarchistic nihilism and their pursuit of scandal for scandal's sake, the Surrealists in the mid-1920s gradually sought a political role. In 1925 they began negotiations with the editors of *Clarté, a periodical close to the French Communist Party. Although plans to join forces on a new magazine to be called *La Guerre civile* came to nothing, the *Clartéistes* gave the Surrealists their first lessons in *Marxism and also their introduction to the Communists. Five of the Surrealists (Aragon, Breton, Éluard, Péret, and *Unik) officially joined the Party in 1927, but Breton was quickly disillusioned by the mundane tasks he was allotted: compiling statistics on steel production in Italy did not satisfy his revolutionary aspirations or correspond to the role he saw for himself within the Party. Such revelations are found in the *Second Manifeste*, which also includes the famous anarchistic pronouncement, 'l'acte surréaliste le plus simple consiste, revolvers aux poings, à descendre dans la rue et à tirer au hasard, tant qu'on peut, dans la foule'. Although Breton was infuriated by Michel Marty's claim 'si vous êtes marxiste, vous n'avez pas besoin d'être surréaliste', by 1932 Aragon was to opt definitively in favour of the Party. In 1935 the Franco-Soviet Pact and a clash between Breton and Ilya Ehrenburg led to the expulsion from the Party of its remaining Surrealist members, though Surrealists and Communists were united in their opposition to the fascist threat; Péret, for instance, went to Spain to fight in the Civil War. The possibilities of a new orientation, raised by Breton's visit to Trotsky in Mexico in 1938, were dashed by the latter's assassination two years later. After the war the Surrealists continued to take up political stances of an anti-colonial, anti-totalitarian nature, and in 1948 Breton was involved in Garry Davis's Citizens of the World movement.

4. Group Activities

The Surrealists constantly operated as a group centred on Breton. They disseminated tracts and pamphlets, devised and played various games (e.g. *le cadavre exquis*, something like the English game of 'consequences'), and published works written in collaboration, e.g. the very different texts from 1930, the poems of *Ralentir travaux* by Breton, Char, and Éluard, and *L'Immaculée Conception*, with its celebrated simulations of insanity by Breton and Éluard. For much of the the time the group had its own review, beginning with *Littérature*, launched by Aragon, Breton, and Soupault in 1919, and continuing in the 1920s and 1930s with *La Révolution surréaliste*, *Le Surréalisme au service de la révolution*, and in the post-war period with *Néon, Médium, Bief, Le Surréalisme, même* and *La Brèche*. In addition, *Minotaure* was dominated by the Surrealists. A feature of the reviews, apart from the publication of poems, accounts of dreams, automatic texts, photographs, and drawings, was the succession of investigations, with such questions as: 'Pourquoi écrivez-vous?'; 'Le suicide est-il une solution?';

'Quelle sorte d'espoir mettez-vous dans l'amour?'. This kind of enquiry was fostered by the opening of a Bureau de Recherches Surréalistes in 1925.

The dissolution of the group was threatened more than once. There were frequent expulsions, even at the beginning. The movement was rent asunder in 1929/30, but was saved by an influx of new blood, especially Buñuel, Char, and Dali, with their very distinctive contributions. During World War II its base shifted to New York, where Breton and others sought refuge, though in Paris the spirit of Surrealism was kept alive by a group called La Main à Plume. When Breton and Péret returned, there quickly gathered around them a new generation of writers and artists, including Sarane Alexandrian, Jean-Louis Bédouin, Jean-Pierre *Duprey, Gérard Legrand, and Jean Schuster. Breton's death in 1966 was to sound the death-knell, and the official Surrealist group agreed to disband three years later.   [KRA]

See F. Alquié (ed.), *Entretiens sur le surréalisme* (1968); P. Audoin, *Les Surréalistes* (1973); S. Alexandrian, *Le Surréalisme et le rêve* (1974).

Swann, Charles. A central figure in Proust's *A la recherche du temps perdu*, in which he acts as a kind of *alter ego* for the narrator, notably in his love for Odette de Crécy, recounted in *Un amour de Swann*. A member of fashionable society and connoisseur of the arts, he suffers as a Jew during the *Dreyfus Affair. Gilberte, the daughter of Swann and Odette, is the object of the narrator's youthful affections, but marries his friend Saint-Loup.

SWEDENBORG, Emmanuel (1678–1772). Swedish scientist, philosopher, and mystic whose works reached a wide audience across Europe despite their obscurity and difficulty. Before the Revolution his mystical doctrine appealed to those in France with interests in *Illuminism and esotericism. His work continued to attract attention in the 19th-c., when there were attempts to set up a Swedenborgian church. In the 1820s and 1830s his best-known devotees were Édouard Richer and abbé J.-G.-E. Œgger. Swedenborgianism was of interest to the *Romantics and to the *Symbolists on account of the importance it ascribed to emanation, regeneration, and analogical modes of explanation.   [CC]

Swiss Literature in French

1. General Characteristics

Francophone literatures can reveal both linguistic and cultural variation within a shared language, but they pass through distinct phases of growth. Early stages are usually spontaneous and undirected. Later developments will be more strongly marked culturally as writers assert their autonomy and collective self-consciousness. Later, writers will again de-emphasize their francophone role and establish themselves simply as writers in French. They will, however, benefit from an accepted cultural autonomy and momentum, a receptive local public, and receptive publishers. As a result, literatures such as that of Suisse Romande remain something of an abstraction, and many have doubted whether a French-Swiss literary culture exists as a reality. Some have seen Suisse Romande as 'un corps qui cherche une âme' (Amiel) or 'une province [de France] qui n'en est pas une' (Ramuz). Some suggest that it is itself a collection of distinctive regional literatures (Vaudois, Jurassien, etc.). Others say simply that: 'Il n'y a point de littérature romande, il n'y a que des écrivains romands' (P. André). Whatever the nomenclature adopted, Swiss literature in French has a distinctive history.

The Suisse Romande has a quarter of the Swiss population, but no natural ethnic or political identity. It embraces the French-speaking cantons of Geneva, Vaud, Neuchâtel, francophone Fribourg and Valais, and the isolated canton of Jura. Each mirrors the religious, ethnic, and cultural pluralism of Switzerland as a whole. Vaud joined the 1291 Confederation as recently as 1803; Geneva, Valais, and Neuchâtel in 1815; French-speaking Jura in 1979. The Swiss bourgeoisie was traditionally exposed to French, German, or Italian cultural imperialism, and Paris has long been the cultural catalyst of French-speaking intellectuals and artists. Many emigrated to France: *Rousseau, *Constant, de *Staël, Pourtalès, Borgeaud, Cingria, *Cendrars, Landry, etc. Rural communities, however, remained untouched by cosmopolitanism, and strongly cantonal or communal in culture. Any idea of a hermetic Suisse-Romande culture is to some extent a political or academic fabrication. Unlike other francophone countries, Suisse Romande generated no dialectal literature, though *patois* persisted in Valais, Gruyère, and elsewhere. When Charles-Ferdinand *Ramuz, the dominant figure of Suisse-Romande literature, set out to 'écrire une langue parlée: la langue parlée par ceux dont je suis né', he was in search of a distinctive voice, 'une inflexion'.

2. Beginnings to 1800

There was no major literature in French in Suisse Romande prior to the *Reformation though there were 13th-c. Jurassien *trouvère* poets: Simonin de Boncourt and Girard de Pleujose. There was also the 14th-c. Savoyard courtly poet Oton de *Grandson, known to *Froissart and Chaucer. With the coming of the Reformation in 1536, Geneva and its Académie (1559) became a cultural centre of European reformed religion. Much of the activity was that of immigrant writers: *Farel, *Calvin, *Bèze, and d'*Aubigné. The exception is the satirist Pierre *Viret, the first authentic Swiss-French writer, 'le sourire de la Réforme' and a native Vaudois. He was the creator of Tobie, an archetypal Vaudois *Panurge. His contemporary was François Bonivard (1493–1570, *Chroniques de Genève*, published 1831) the famous prisoner of Chillon.

There was then a fallow period until the second French Huguenot immigration after 1685, with Jean-Robert Chouet (1642–1731), Jean-Alphonse Turrettini (1671–1737), Jean Barbeyrac (1674–1744), and Firmin Abauzit (1679–1767). Their writing was dominated by science, liberal Protestant evangelical theology, and later pietism. Swiss *Enlightenment thinkers Jacob Vernet (1698–1789), Abraham Trembley (1710–84), and Charles Bonnet (1720–93) opposed *Voltaire's anticlericalism and secularism. Jean-Jacques Rousseau too championed his Genevese pastor friends against Voltaire, who was in exile near Geneva. In his *Confessions and *Rêveries, Rousseau, like Albrecht von Haller (1707–77, *Die Alpen*), first found literary inspiration in the Swiss landscape. His autobiographical writings foreshadow *Amiel, and there are clear areas in which Rousseau laid the foundations for later developments in Swiss-French writing.

3. Nineteenth Century

In the early 19th c. Germaine de Staël and Benjamin Constant abandoned their native cantons for Paris [see also COPPET]. Madame de Staël was above all cosmopolitan. Constant's work focused on the Paris scene, though his *Journal intime* set him in the autobiographical tradition. With the Napoleonic invasion of the cantons, a nationalist reaction against Paris brought closer ties with German Switzerland and a clearer Helvetic dimension.

In the later 19th c. liberal Protestant writing reawakened. Educational writing followed Rousseau and Pestalozzi (1746–1827) in developing the education of the whole man. The outstanding literary figure, however, was the Vaudois moralist and Christian thinker Alexandre Vinet (1797–1847). He left his mark on cultural, educational, and religious life, even on literature. This Christian tradition continued, remaining anti-dogmatic, devout, and evangelical. However, with its firm grip over academia, intellectuals, and scientists, it ossified easily into a middle-class morality which gave the cantons an ultra-puritanical image. Pourtalès would later highlight its hypocrisy, and Mercanton its repression of natural instinct. If we tend to associate the Suisse Romande with Protestant writing, Catholic writers were none the less active, predominantly in the Jura and Valais.

The move towards a French-language Helvetic literature (linked with Swiss-German *Helvetismus*) first emerged in the 18th c. with Philippe-Cyriaque (known as le doyen) Bridel (1757–1845, *Poésies helvétiennes* 1782). It developed briefly again in World War I under an academic historian Gonzague de Reynold (1880–1970). More significant was the mood set earlier by the Genevese Rodolphe Toepffer (1799–1846). He was a liberal Protestant thinker, novelist, satirist, caricaturist, and literary historian and a major transitional figure between Rousseau and Ramuz. Toepffer's appeal was limited outside Geneva, but he seriously influenced writers with his demonstration of vernacular art. Then came Juste

Olivier (1807–76) with his 'Un génie est caché dans tous ces lieux que j'aime' (later termed *génie du lieu*). These figures dominated the 1830–50 period and stirred a new consciousness of *terroir*. They were followed by Philippe Godet (1850–1922), who accused young Swiss intellects of creating 'un art d'importation et d'imitation, où il ne restera rien de romand', and pleaded for 'une patrie distincte de la France, mais liée à la France par la langue et la culture'. Others pursuing the vernacular in art included the Genevese painter Ferdinand Hodler (1853–1918), whose art anticipates Ramuz on canvas.

The most significant 19th-c. development was not in vernacular but in introspective writing. Henri-Frédéric Amiel wrote 174 *cahiers*, over 16,000 manuscript pages, in his private *Journal intime* (1839/47–81). Only a part of the journal was published, posthumously, revealing a lucid, contemplative, spiritually alive, and sexually repressed self-portrait. As a diarist of psychological and intellectual penetration, he established the contemplative self-portrait as a characteristic genre of Suisse-Romande literary expression.

4. Twentieth Century

The year 1904 is the watershed in Suisse-Romande writing, when a group of writers opened a fundamental debate on the character and function of a vernacular literature, first in *Pénates d'argile* and then in *La Voile latine* (1904–10). This first secession from French influence was led by Gonzague de Reynold and his associates, but it united writers in pursuit of an autonomous and autochthonous artistic culture. This first phase collapsed when literary Helvetism was abandoned by Ramuz and his Vaudois associates. They branded it as 'suissisme de château', 'enduit pastoral', and 'semis professoral', a product of academic intellectualism and patrician nostalgia. Reynold's formation of a group called the Nouvelle Société Helvétique in 1914 was an attempt to avoid the disintegration of the Confederation into linguistic areas. The Vaudois rejected it as 'voile latinerie' and launched a *renaissance vaudoise* through a journal that they provocatively named *Cahiers vaudois* (1913/14–19). This contained Ramuz's manifesto for a Swiss-French literature, 'Raison d'être', asserting the reality of the *pays* as the root of personal and ethnic identity. His *ars poetica* expanded Juste Olivier's *génie du lieu* into what we now term *enracinement*. He rejected *folklorisme*, *helvétisme*, political *engagement*, and the introspective tradition, coming closer to Toepffer and Hodler and closer still to *Cézanne, who clearly influenced him.

The *renaissance vaudoise* in its original form was led by the Helvetists Gonzague de Reynold, Robert de Traz (1884–1951), and Alexis François, but it had now narrowed to Ramuz, Edmond Gilliard (1875–1969), Paul Budry (1883–1949), and close associates. Ramuz in many ways parallels Gottfried Keller, his German-Swiss counterpart. Swiss-French literature became for him an autonomous area of

creative literary activity, sharing a common language with France but using Paris as a crucible rather than a mould. It created the voice of a region without relapsing into provincialism or regionalism. Ramuz and his followers claimed to have created an authentic, vernacular voice in art, the voice of *homo alpinus*.

If the period is inevitably dominated by Ramuz's charismatic figure, this has obscured the contribution of a major international talent: the Neuchâtelois Guy de Pourtalès (1881–1941). His *Marins d'eau douce* (1912), *Monclar* (1927), and *La Pêche miraculeuse* (1937) are marks of an extraordinary talent, deeply rooted in Neuchâtel, Geneva, and the Lac Léman. His genius is in many ways akin to Thomas Mann's. Other figures include the unclassifiable Charles-Albert Cingria (1883–1954), an anti-'Swiss', globe-trotting essayist of a Polish-Turkish family background; and the Neuchâtelois Blaise *Cendrars, travel-writer extraordinary, novelist, poet, and anti-poet.

The Vaudois *renaissance* cleared the way for autonomous and autochthonous creative activity in all the cantons, in the novel, in poetry, on stage and screen. Poets, many influenced by Rilke, are at least as significant as novelists in this development and they number major talents such as Edmond Gilliard (1875–1969), Pierre-Louis Matthey (1893–1970), Gustave Roud (1897–1976), and Edmond-Henri Crisinel (1897–1948), all in their twenties when *Cahiers vaudois* appeared. They were followed by others: Maurice Chappaz (b. 1916), Philippe *Jaccottet, Jacques Chessex (b. 1934), and Jurassiens such as Alexandre Voisard (b. 1930). Roud and Jaccottet above all have emerged as talents of international stature.

The Swiss identify their academic and critical tradition as a distinctive element. At the beginning of the century Ferdinand de *Saussure, lecturing in German, revolutionized the science of linguistics; his work had an incalculable effect on 20th-c. thought. A little later came a remarkable group of gifted literary critics, including Albert *Béguin, Charly Guyot (1898–1974), Marcel *Raymond, Jean *Starobinski, and Pierre-Olivier Walzer (b. 1915). To these we have to add the enabling activity of publisher-patrons, most recently Bertil Galland (b. 1931).

The modern Swiss-French novel, before and after World War II, is no longer marginalized by French or Swiss critics. It is the genre in which artistic activity is most evident to the Swiss themselves. Suisse Romande can boast an élite of men and women novelists outstanding by any standard. Ramuz himself, Pourtalès, Catherine Colomb (1893–1965: *Châteaux en enfance*, 1945; *Les Esprits de la terre* 1953), Alice Rivaz (b. 1901: *Jette ton pain*, 1978; *Ce n'est pas le mien*, 1980, Prix Ramuz), Jacques Mercanton (b. 1910: *Le Soleil ni la mort*, 1948; *La Sybille*, 1979), Corinna Bille (1912–79: *Théoda*, 1944; *La Demoiselle sauvage*, 1974; *Le Salon ovale*, 1976), Georges Borgeaud (b. 1914: *Le Préau*, 1952, Prix des Critiques; *Le Voyage à l' étranger*, 1974, Prix Renaudot), Jean-Pierre Monnier (b.1921: *La Clarté de la nuit*, 1956; *L'Arbre un jour*, 1971), and Jacques Chessex (b. 1934: *L'Ogre*, 1973, Prix Goncourt).

Other distinctive themes recur sufficiently in Suisse-Romande literature to warrant mention. There is the cross-fertilization of the arts, and the frequency with which writers invade the worlds of music and painting (Pourtalès, Ramuz, Landry). Many are both poets and novelists (Roud, Chessex, Chappaz), a factor profoundly affecting style and vision. There is an endemic globe-trotter syndrome (Cingria, Cendrars, Mercanton, Galland, Bille, Pourtalès) with its themes of departure, alienation, and return. The Protestant or Catholic conscience lives on, for moralist and *enfant terrible* (Chappaz, Chessex, Borgeaud, Monnier). There is the special optic of the diarist and autobiographer (Ramuz, Colomb, Borgeaud, Chessex, Zermatten), and the *mythos* of lake and mountain, mostly centred on the Valais (Ramuz, Chessex, Chappaz, Saussure, Zermatten). Polyglot writers are inevitably involved in translation (Jaccottet, Roud, Matthey).   [SSBT]

See C. Guyot (ed.), *Écrivains de Suisse française* (1961); A. Berchtold, *La Suisse Romande au cap du XXe siècle* (1966); M. Gsteiger, *La Nouvelle Littérature romande* (1978); J. L. Flood (ed.), *Modern Swiss Literature: Unity and Diversity* (1985).

SYAD, William J. F. (b. 1930). Somalian writer; he is a poet (*Khamsine*, 1959, partly written in English; *Cantiques*, 1976) and a novelist (*Naufragées du destin*, 1978).

SYGOGNE(S), see SIGOGNE.

Sylvie, see NERVAL.

Sylvie, La, see MAIRET.

Symbolism. Defined narrowly, Symbolism was the term adopted by Jean *Moréas in his manifesto article of 18 September 1886 to describe the rejection of the *Naturalist, *Parnassian, and *Decadent movements by young writers (notably Moréas, *Kahn, *Morice, *Ghil, *Dujardin, *Wyzewa, *Retté) grouped around *Mallarmé between 1885 and 1895. In broader terms it is used to refer to developments in French poetics between *Baudelaire and *Valéry which were then assimilated in different forms and to different degrees by the non-French literatures. Though too much effort has gone into the search for definitional purity (distinctions between precursors, true and peripheral Symbolists), it is around the poetical practice and critical ambition of Mallarmé that both narrow and broad definitions have crystallized.

In the course of the 1870s positivism [see COMTE] secured its position as the dominant intellectual system of the newly founded Third Republic, and the Naturalist novel and Parnassian poetry expressed its scientific, didactic ambition to describe external real-ity. For writers who saw themselves as alienated or marginalized by the republican ideology of progress, democracy, and economic liberalism, the renewal of the idealist tradition taking place during the same period (notably via translations of Schopenhauer and Hartmann) reactivated in new forms the legacy of *Romanticism's correspondences between the human and divine realms and the poet's responsibility for communication between the two. Though in the highly competitive Parisian avant-garde the polemic nature of literary manifestos encouraged simplification—Mallarmé never considered *Zola to be exclusively a Naturalist; aspects of the Parnassian ideal, such as impersonality, universality, and the cult of form were central to the Symbolist aesthetic; themes and language associated with Decadence remained deeply embedded in many Symbolist texts—Symbolism enabled idealist trends to achieve definition. It contained a programme, the search for the Absolute, and since this could not be expressed directly, it proposed formal strategies of indirect apprehension of the mysteries hidden behind appearances. In this sense Mallarmé's aesthetic of suggestion—'C'est le parfait usage de ce mystère qui constitue le symbole'—was flexible enough to embrace the group's diverse aspirations.

The catalyst was the founding in January 1885 by Dujardin and Wyzewa of *La Revue wagnérienne* (one of the many literary periodicals associated with Symbolism) and, in particular, Mallarmé's engagement there with Wagnerism later that year in his essay, 'Richard Wagner, rêverie d'un poëte français', and his sonnet in hommage to the musician. Such is the density of these texts that within the Symbolist group they obscured the distance which he placed there between himself and the Wagner cult, a distance central to the distinction between narrow and broad definitions mentioned initially. For Mallarmé, poetry had no need for Wagnerian myths and it was self-sufficient in music. His sonnet enacted this self-sufficiency. Unlike other Symbolists, he did not believe in the existence of a transcendent truth which it was poetry's task to manifest. For him, words in poetry were constellations; their modes of operation were poetry's subject and object. Mallarmé's radical experimentation with the nature and function of poetic language was French Symbolism's most important legacy to modernism, for it crystallized the loss of credibility of literature as representation of an extra-literary reality.

Wagnerism had several faces and offered a powerful, wide-ranging resource during the Symbolist period. Some used it mechanically as a source of alternative allegories. Others, such as Ghil with his briefly influential 'verbal instrumentism', sought in it the basis of a new theory of poetic expression. More significant was its contribution, affirmed by Dujardin, to two major developments of the Symbolist period, the *vers libre* in poetry and the *monologue intérieur* in fiction. Wagner's theory of the contiguity of the arts, which many believed to be the same as Baudelairean correspondences, led Wyzewa to attempt a definition of Wagnerian painting which was too general to be effective, but in *Aurier's hands the same theory encouraged powerful statements of the anti-naturalist trends in the painting of *Gauguin and *Van Gogh. In the theatre its emphasis on mysticism and ritual stimulated experimentation in all aspects of stage-craft and in the relationship between stage and public, as is seen in *Villiers de l'Isle-Adam's *Axël*, Maeterlinck's *Pelléas et Mélisande*, and Claudel's *Tête d'Or*.

In 1891 the Symbolist movement achieved its greatest influence within the avant-garde, but even as it did so the defection of Moréas to found his 'École Romane' was an early sign of a classical revival in which Symbolism would be attacked as a foreign tradition. Poets like *Verhaeren, *Vielé-Griffin, and Kahn returned to nature and/or the modern world in one form or another, themes around which new groupings such as the Naturists and *Unanimists reinforced the anti-Symbolist reaction. From the turn of the century it remained for others (notably Valéry, Claudel, and *Royère) to transmit the Mallarmean legacy to the modernist tradition.   [JK]

See A. Balakian, *The Symbolist Movement in the Literatures of European Languages* (1982); R. Furness, *Wagner and Literature* (1982).

Symphonie pastorale, La. Novel by *Gide (1919) in the form of a pastor's diary, recording his efforts to educate a blind girl he has rescued from destitution and introduced into his family. He progressively neglects his wife and children, distorting moral and religious precepts to justify a growing love he is unable fully to acknowledge.   [DHW]

Système de la nature, Le, see HOLBACH.

S/Z, see BARTHES.

T

TABARIN, Antoine Girard, known as (1584–1626), Parisian *farceur*. His performances on the Pont-Neuf with his brother, 'Mondor', drew large crowds and became a model of popular *farce in the early 1620s. Two volumes of *rencontres* and *questions tabariniques*, published 1622, suggest the rich, *Rabelaisian blend of the scatological, scholarly, and satirical which characterized his improvisations.   [GJM]

Tableau de Paris, Le, see MERCIER, L.-S.

Tableaux parisiens, see FLEURS DU MAL.

TABOUROT, Étienne (1549–90). A lawyer and a supporter of the *Ligue, he also wrote neo-Latin verse, a dictionary of French rhymes, and four medleys of comic writing, full of jokes, mock apophthegms, facetious and scurrilous tales, and word-play of all kinds: *Les Bigarrures* (1583); *Les Touches* (1585–8); *Les Apophtegmes du sieur Goulard* (1585), and *Les Écraignes dijonnaises* (1588).

TADJO, Véronique (b. ?1955). Poet and novelist from Ivory Coast, author of a prize-winning collection of poems, *Latérite* (1984), a novella, *A vol d'oiseau* (1986), and some collections of stories for children.   [PGH]

TAHUREAU, Jacques (1527–55). One of the more famous members of the group of humanist writers based in Poitiers (others were *Bouchet, *La Péruse). His collections of neo-Petrarchan poetry (*Premières poésies, Sonnets, odes et mignardises amoureuses de l'Admirée,* 1554) are now beginning to receive serious critical attention; but he is still best known for the posthumous *Dialogues* (1565), in which Démocritic (who shuns society) and Cosmophile (who is less critical) debate the follies of the world: love, the court, law, medicine, astrology—and, more dangerously, 'les forgerons de dieux'. Tahureau claims to exclude Christianity from his strictures; but his comments may be no more than a defensive measure (an absolute requirement at a period when atheism was punishable by death). The ambiguity shows how well he exploited the dialogue as a genre.   [IJS]

TAILHADE, Laurent (1854–1919). After *Parnassian beginnings in *Le Jardin des rêves* (1880), for which *Banville wrote the preface, Tailhade found his voice in the French tradition of satirical poetry to which he brought the anarchistic nihilism of the *fin-de-siècle* aesthete. A translator of Petronius and Plautus, his ferocious satires directed against individuals and against the values of the Third Republic led to duels (notably with *Barrès) and eventual imprisonment. *Mallarmé aptly called them 'des pièces d'artifice furieuses et magistralement réglées'. The *Poèmes aristophanesques* (1904), containing the collected satirical poems, illustrate his mastery of this form and the limitations of its rhetoric.   [JK]

Taille, La, see TAXATION.

TAILLEMONT, Claude de (*c.*1504–after 1588). A member of the Lyon group of writers, he is best known for the recently re-edited *Discours des Champs Faëz* (1553), in which Platonism combines with mediaeval chivalric romance and with discussions based on Boccaccio's *Decameron* to produce a defence of women which contributes to the *Querelle des Femmes. His collection of poems, *La Tricarite* (1556), is notable for its density (reminiscent of *Scève) and for its use of spelling designed to be closer to actual speech [see MEIGRET].   [IJS]

TAINE, Hippolyte-Adolphe (1828–93). French critic and historian. Taine is exemplary of the way in which a writer can dominate his era and yet be virtually unknown a century later. Lacking the armature of imagined form, ideas dissolve into the intellectual gene-pool. The irony is that Taine saw this with exceptional lucidity. In some ways he was the *Sartre of his time (Taine-and-*Renan/Sartre-and-*Camus); but where Sartre was able to produce works of the imagination as well as works of the intellect, the imaginative writer in Taine was repressed, finding an outlet only in occasional heightened language (the purple passages of Les *Origines de la France contemporaine,* 1875–93) and frequent similes (one of these—'Le vice et la vertu sont des produits comme le vitriol et le sucre'—is all that the average reader recalls of Taine's enormous output).

His year of crisis was 1862, and it is described in a rare diary entry reproduced in the *Vie et correspondance* (1902–7). At 34 this only son of a humble country lawyer from Vouziers in the Ardennes had become the leading critic of his generation. He had published articles on a wide range of subjects. Collected, recast, and prefaced, these became a series of influential books: *Les Philosophes français du XIXe siècle* (1857), an iconoclastic attack on the dominant *spiritualiste* philosophy (and on Victor *Cousin in particular); the *Essais de critique et d'histoire* (1858); the *Nouveaux essais de critique et d'histoire* (1865), in which he boldly championed *Balzac and *Stendhal; and the *Histoire de la littérature anglaise* (1864).

But he had unrealized ambitions as a philosopher and in 1862 he had recently discovered a vocation as a creative writer, beginning a novel, *Étienne Mayran* (published posthumously); at the same time he had a liaison with the novelist Camille Selden, a somewhat mysterious, romantic figure who had an association with Heine. His critical work had convinced him that greatness only comes from the imagination. But he chose reason rather than risk: he broke with Camille Selden and abandoned his novel. The shock of the *Commune may have been responsible for the anti-revolutionary emphasis of *Les Origines*, but the 'decision' to become a historian rather than a novelist is the resolution of the 1862 crisis.

The mythical opposition is a familiar, universal one—Sartre said he always felt inferior to writers like *Rimbaud because they, unlike him, 'ont su se perdre'. All his life Taine worked at this binary opposition: each individual he studied—Byron, *Shakespeare, *Michelet, *Guizot, Macaulay, *Racine, *Danton, *Napoleon—exemplified and extended it. The symbolic figure he called the 'Poet', the creator working with the imagination and (*avant la lettre*) the unconscious, achieves greatness, but it may be at the cost of his life or his sanity: and, for Taine, the same source that produces great works of the imagination produces the atrocities of the Terror. Better the safe world of the figure he calls the 'Orator', rational and controlled. This reflects Taine's historical moment—post-Romantic—but he knew well that posterity cherishes the poets and that orators get short shrift. He reflected on this—and implicitly on his own oblivion—in a series of poignant articles collected as *Derniers essais de critique et d'histoire* (1894).

Taine became the spokesman for the new positivist, determinist, *anticlerical, anti-Romantic philosophy which was to influence *Zola so much. Zola was, however (and for good reason), the only contemporary critic to see in him the repressed Romantic. Not until the publication of the correspondence and the early manuscript material was the Romantic metaphysician recognized. Pre-Freud and pre-Marx, Taine is still relevant as a psychologist (in *De l'intelligence*, 1870) and as a sociologist (in the *Origines*) because of the way he lived out the contradictions of the scientific method. His insistence on the need for empirical observation was in conflict with a heroic commitment to system. His explanatory concepts are often inadequate—as when he explains a writer by three forces, 'race', 'milieu', and 'moment', and by their 'contrariété' or 'concordance'. But his struggle to reconcile a rationalist, continental outlook with the empiricism characteristic of the English, objectivity with subjectivity, remains relevant a century after his death.

[CHE]

See C. Evans, *Taine: essai de biographie intérieure* (1975); F. Léger, *La Jeunesse d'Hippolyte Taine* (1980).

TALLEMANT DES RÉAUX, Gédéon (1619–92). French memorialist. He moved in *précieux* circles [see PRECIOSITY] and wrote some light verse, but his major work, the *Historiettes*, only began to be published in 1834. It is a collection of over 300 'brief lives', together with assorted salacious anecdotes. Most of his material dates from before 1660. Many famous names figure in Tallemant's gallery (*Richelieu, *Balzac, *Corneille, *La Fontaine, etc.); the stories he tells, in an entertaining and uninhibited style, are generally scandalous, but often borne out by other testimonies; they give a lively image of society life in the 17th c. [PF]

TALLEYRAND-PÉRIGORD, Charles-Maurice de (1754–1838). Aristocrat and diplomat. Because of lameness he entered the Church, and became bishop of Autun. He represented the clergy at the *États Généraux and was prominent in proposing nationalization of Church lands in the early years of the Revolution. After emigrating to England and America, he returned to France in 1796, becoming a permanent figure in political and diplomatic life. He was *Napoleon's chief adviser and was created prince de Bénévent; he negotiated the restoration of the Bourbons and represented France at the Congress of Vienna; he helped the duc d'Orléans to become King Louis-Philippe and was appointed French ambassador to London until 1834. On his deathbed he was reconciled to the Church, claiming that he was still bishop of Autun. His *Mémoires*, edited by the duc de Broglie (5 vols., 1891–2) may not have been written by him. [DJ]

TALLIEN, Jean-Lambert (1767–1835). Journalist and *Jacobin activist during the Revolution. He helped engineer *Robespierre's downfall, partly under the influence of his Spanish wife, Thérèse Cabarrus, who came to be known as Notre-Dame de Thermidor. The beautiful Madame Tallien later became the mistress of the banker Ouvrard and a leading figure in the salons of the Directoire. [PF]

TALMA, François-Joseph (1763–1826). Celebrated French tragic actor admired by Napoleon. On the stage of the Comédie-Française he played 247 parts in 195 plays old and new, including Racine's *Andromaque, *Voltaire's *Oedipe*, M.-J. *Chénier's *Charles IX* (1789), and Pierre-Antoine Lebrun's *Marie Stuart* (1820). He introduced important reforms in acting, staging, and costume. [SBJ]

TALON, Omer, see RAMUS.

TAMZA, Arriz (pseud. of Maya Boussselmania) (b. 1957). Algerian-born novelist, one of the most imaginative of *Beur writers. He was brought up from the age of 5 in Marseille, where his father was an immigrant worker. *Lune et Orian* (1987) and *Zaïd le mendiant* (1989) blend together mysticism and dreams against a backdrop of mythical Islamic lands. *Ombres* (1989) is a more autobiographical work. [AGH]

Tancrède

Tancrède (1760). Tragedy by *Voltaire, a romantic story of love and valour set in medieval Sicily.

TANSI, Sony Labou, see SONY LABOU TANSI.

Tant que la terre durera, see TROYAT.

TARDIEU, Jean (b. 1903). French writer. A sense of existential bewilderment, provoking both anxiety and a certain dark exhilaration, informs Tardieu's work in the two media he has worked in extensively: drama and poetry. In *Obscurité du jour* (1977) he traces the origin of a feeling of depersonalization and anonymity which he associates with the intermittent impression of being inhabited by a voice that is not his own. Accordingly, language and word-play, dialogue and monologue, doubles and figments feature consistently in his writing.

Tardieu's first published poems appeared in the *Nouvelle Revue Française* in 1927 (*Margeries*, 1986, reprints much early unpublished work), but the core of his poetry will be found in *Le Fleuve caché*, which groups collections published between 1938 and 1961. Often tinged with an ironic, burlesque, and sometimes black humour (also a feature of his plays), Tardieu's poetry is suffused by a feeling for the enigmatic dimension at the heart of experience which language, however widely its resources are exploited, tends to confirm rather than dispel. Later collections include the poetic prose of *La Part de l'ombre* (1972) and *L'Accent grave et l'accent aigu: poèmes 1976–1983* (1985), which deepen and ramify the same basic experiences and devices.

Tardieu contributed to many clandestine publications during the *Occupation, and after the war made his career in French radio. His output includes 'pièces radiophoniques', but his best-known plays, collected in *Théâtre de chambre* (1955) and *Poèmes à jouer* (1960), were written for the 'petites salles' of the Left Bank and have been widely performed and translated around the world. Generally very brief, a typical Tardieu play develops a single idea, situation, or convention: theatrical asides (*Oswald et Zénaide ou les Apartés*), the hollowness of social chat (*La Sonate et les trois messieurs*), the illusory nature and pitfalls of hope (*Qui est là?*), memory (*Une voix sans personne*), or self-knowledge (*Monsieur moi*). Many of these 'drames-éclair' use word-play, verbal rhythm, and linguistic distortion to great effect, and in some cases, notably in *Conversation-sinfonietta* (1966), Tardieu orchestrates his dialogue as in a musical composition. [MHTS]

See J. Onimus, *Jean Tardieu: un rire inquiet* (1985).

Tartarin de Tarascon. Hero of once-popular stories by Alphonse *Daudet. An ebullient and boastful Provençal, he survives astonishing adventures and mishaps as an amateur big-game hunter (*Tartarin de Tarascon*, 1872), a mountaineer (*Tartarin sur les Alpes*, 1885), and an explorer of the South Seas (*Port Tarascon*, 1890).

Tartuffe, Le. Five-act comedy by *Molière, first performed in a partial version in 1664. It was banned from public performance until 1669, because it dealt with the thorny issue of religious hypocrisy. It is subtitled *L'Imposteur.*

Orgon, a well-to-do Parisian, has become besotted with Tartuffe, whose hypocritical show of devoutness scandalizes the rest of Orgon's household and threatens the proposed marriage of his daughter Mariane to Valère. Tartuffe attempts to seduce Elmire, Orgon's wife; Damis, his son, witnesses this and denounces the hypocrite, only to find himself unjustly banished from the house. Orgon eventually himself witnesses another attempt at seduction, but is banished in turn, as it is revealed that the house now belongs by Orgon's deed of gift to Tartuffe. A *deus ex machina* in the guise of the king's legal representative restores order and arrests Tartuffe at the end of the play.

The name of the villain, derived from an Italian word meaning 'hypocrite', has passed into the French language. [IM]

TATI, Jacques (1907–82). Like Buster Keaton, at once a great comic actor and a great director. The benign, shambling hero of *Les Vacances de Monsieur Hulot* (1953) is perhaps the best-loved comic creation in French cinema, yet Tati came to regard Hulot as an incubus and to be more and more interested in increasingly elaborate burlesque choreography for the camera. *Playtime* (1967), a satire on the homogenizing effects of tourism, displays extraordinary richness and subtlety of visual detail. For many, however, the ingenuity of this and *Traffic* (1971) represents a loss compared to the warmth of *Jour de fête* (1948), *Hulot*, and *Mon oncle* (1958). [KAR]

TATI-LOUTARD, Jean-Baptiste (b. 1938). Congolese poet, novelist, and short-story writer, educated in Brazzaville and Bordeaux. He was very active in the educational sector until his administrative responsibilities drew him away from teaching and he became minister for culture, the arts, and sports.

He has published seven collections of poems, notably *Poèmes de la mer* (1968), *Les Racines congolaises* (1968), *L'Envers du soleil* (1970), and *La Tradition du songe* (1985), poems which explore the world that surrounds the poet and his relationship with it, along with the various constraints imposed by natural elements, portrayed symbolically through the seasons, the sun, moon, and sea, all in a kind of dream-like meditation. His short stories, *Chroniques congolaises* (1974) and *Nouvelles chroniques congolaises* (1980), give a lengthy and meticulous description of Congolese society. The latter was awarded the Prix des Lettres Africaines. In his first novel, *Le Récit de la mort* (1987), Tati-Loutard tries to rid himself of his lifelong obsession with death. Death is the central character, whether it be physical, intellectual, or political. The images and use of language remain highly poetic. He was awarded the Grand Prix

Littéraire d'Afrique Noire for this work, along with the Prix de la Culture pour la Paix.

[DRDT]

TAVERNIER, Jean-Baptiste (1605–89). French traveller. He made many trading voyages to the Orient, claiming in Les Six Voyages de Jean-Baptiste Tavernier to have travelled more than 60,000 leagues overland. His detailed and informative reports (particularly on Persia and India) contributed to a growing interest in the Orient and are among the main sources for Montesquieu's *Lettres persanes.

Taxation, Tax-Farmers (ancien régime). The *monarchy never found it easy to levy taxes during the ancien régime, since *feudal dues tended to be paid to the local seigneur before royal taxes, and the king was supposed to live off his own estates except in emergencies. There was no budget, and revenue was raised according to immediate need, with financiers and tax-farmers making advances to bridge the gap between collection and receipt.

The principal direct royal tax was the taille, levied either on individuals (taille personnelle) or on commoner lands (taille réelle) depending on the region, and reserved for the king by the ordinance of 1439; it was his chief source of strength. A host of indirect taxes existed, the most important of which was the gabelle, the monopoly on the sale of salt in many provinces, established in the 1330s; the gabelous (enforcement officers) were much hated, and smuggling was rife. Aides were taxes on the consumption of articles, often those considered luxuries but also including drinks, livestock, wood, and eventually almost anything. These went by various names, such as subvention (1656), gros, quatrième, cinq sols, and annuel (on the existence of distinct commercial premises). Their incidence and existence varied enormously according to province or town. Octrois were entry taxes levied on goods at customs barriers on entry to towns. Traites were taxes levied on goods on entry or exit from provinces or the kingdom.

Indirect taxes were usually collected by tax-farmers, who advanced the receipts to the royal treasury in return for the right to keep as profits the often substantial difference between the sums levied (minus costs) and the sum advanced. The Fermiers Généraux were a syndicate of 40 tax-farmers who had purchased the Royal General Farm, the combination from 1681 of the 'Cinq Grosses Fermes' of traites for 13 provinces and the aides, gabelles, and receipts from the royal domains. Nobles, clergy, and privileged urban bourgeois were usually exempt from many forms of taxation, but the paulette, a tax on offices from 1604, was a successful attempt to tax the normally exempt privileged venal office-holders in return for their right to pass on their offices to their heirs.

The 17th c. witnessed a massive increase in taxation from the 1630s until the end of the reign of *Louis XIV; in an attempt to tax the privileged orders, new wartime direct taxes were invented with the capitation of 1695 and the dixième of 1710. The vingtième appeared in 1749, and its attempt to tax even the privileged in peacetime created a crisis smaller in scale but similar in kind to the crisis over the reforms of 1787 [see REVOLUTION, 1a].

Throughout the ancien régime the monarchy's fiscal system was nearly inadequate and gave rise to several partial bankruptcies. This led to reliance for funds first, from the 16th c., on bankers, and second, in the 17th c., when royal needs outstripped the provision, on financiers or traitants. It was then that a system developed in which revenue was advanced by financiers, closely allied with courtly families, providing funds at high rates of interest. The huge fortunes made by some of these made them a target of bitter satire in the late 17th c. Corruption was endemic in the fiscal and financial system, to which the monarchy was tied, unable to reform itself for fear of antagonizing too many vested interests.

[PRC]

See F. Hinckner, Les Français devant l'impôt sous l'ancien régime (1971).

TCHICAYA U TAM'SI, Gérald-Félix (1931–88). One of the few authors writing in the Congo before Independence in 1960, he played a leading role in the development of Congolese literature and is now considered a major African poet.

Born in Mpili, the son of a politician, he was educated in Orléans and Paris, after which he abandoned study and took a series of unskilled jobs. However, his interest in writing brought him into contact with poets such as *Supervielle, and by 1955 he had written a novel, Les Cancrelats (not to appear until 1980), and published a collection of poems, Le Mauvais Sang. His literary output includes poetry, novels, and plays, and he won several literary prizes, including the Grand Prix de Poésie du Festival des Arts Nègres de Dakar for Épitomé in 1966 and the Italian Prix Simba in 1979. He worked briefly with ORTF before returning to his country in 1960 and becoming editor of Congo, the organ of Patrice Lumumba's Mouvement National Congolais. During this time he came into contact with the Congolese leader himself, an encounter which exerted considerable influence on his writing. Returning to France after Lumumba's death, he worked with UNESCO until 1986.

In Tchicaya's first collection, Le Mauvais Sang (1955), the influence of French poetry is clear, in standard forms such as six-syllable lines or alexandrines, and in stylistic devices suggesting the influence of *Verlaine, *Rimbaud, and *Mallarmé. However, Feu de brousse (1957) and A triche-cœur (1958) develop the specifically African themes of the earlier poems in a form and style which are recognizable as the poet's own. His poetry is characterized by an ironic attitude towards himself, an acute awareness of how colonialism has divorced the

Tchichellé Tchivela

African poet from his cultural heritage, and a syncretic combination of images from the natural world of West Africa and from Christianity, especially the Bible. In these and the following collections, *Épitomé* (1962) and *Le Ventre* (1964), the poet clearly distances himself from the writers of **négritude*, refusing to seek in a return to the African past a solution to the problems raised by his cultural identity.

In the 1970s Tchicaya turned his attention to the theatre with *Le Zulu*, first produced at Avignon in 1976. Critics drew parallels with Greek tragedy, Shakespeare, and *Corneille. The play relates the life of the pre-colonial African hero Shaka, developing the theme of the isolated leader already present in the poems. *Le Destin glorieux du Maréchal Nnikon Nniku prince qu'on sort* (1979) treats the same theme in a grotesque and farcical manner. In his novels the author concentrates on the life of ordinary Africans from the late 19th c. onwards. *Les Cancrelats* (1980), *Les Méduses ou les Orties de mer* (1982), and *Les Phalènes* (1984) form a trilogy, a saga of a family's history in Africa and Europe. Despite the importance of his contribution to the African novel and theatre, however, the style of all his works is essentially poetic, and it is ultimately as a poet that he is remembered.   [AMC]

TCHICHELLÉ TCHIVELA (pseud. of François Tchichellé) (b. 1940). Short-story writer from the Congo who trained originally as a doctor, only turning to writing at the age of 30. Tchivela is a nickname for 'thunder', which is the effect he wants his stories to have in the consciences of the leaders and population. He has published two collections, *Longue est la nuit* (1980) and *L'Exil ou la tombe* (1988).
                                                        [DRDT]

TEILHARD DE CHARDIN, Pierre (1881–1955). French Jesuit priest and palaeontologist, who worked mainly in China and sought to reconcile evidence about the origin of man with his Christian faith. Among his many books (unpublished in his lifetime to satisfy his superiors) is *Le Phénomène humain* (written 1938–40, published 1955), which explains the emergence of mind from matter by the increase in complexity and consciousness. For Teilhard, man can now control evolution as it moves towards Omega Point. Criticized by scientists for going beyond the evidence, and by the Church for underplaying sin and redemption, Teilhard remains an original, lucid, and persuasive writer, a scientist with the soul of a mystic.   [PS]

Télémaque. A pedagogical story which *Fénelon wrote *c.*1695 for the duc de Bourgogne and described as 'a fable narrated in the form of a heroic poem', though in prose. It is an imaginary continuation of Book IV of the *Odyssey*, where Telemachus learns that his father Ulysses is detained on Calypso's isle. He reappears only in Book XV; Fénelon supplies the missing adventures.

Accompanied by Mentor, Télémaque is shipwrecked on the isle, tells Calypso of his travels, and falls in love with the nymph Eucharis (Books 1–7). Mentor rescues him from this entanglement and they are carried to Salente, which Mentor reorganizes as an ideal city-state (Books 8–11), while Télémaque is sent on various missions, including a descent to Hades (Books 12–17), before they rejoin Ulysses at Ithaca.

When an unauthorized version circulated in 1699, the Salente episode was seized upon as a *roman à clefs* highly critical of *Louis XIV. It contributed both to Fénelon's disgrace and to his posthumous reputation as a precursor of the *Enlightenment. *Télémaque* was the book most frequently reprinted in the 18th c., and for two centuries the invariable prescribed text for students of French.   [PJB]

Television. Until 1982 television was a state monopoly in France. Before World War II the state had the monopoly of the Hertzian waves but was, by and large, non-interventionist. After the war the state inherited the organization put in place by the Germans during the Occupation. In 1945 the Radiodiffusion Télévision Française (RTF) was established as a public service attached to the government but placed under the tutelage of the Ministry of Information—and, after 1969, of the prime minister. Until deregulation in 1982 the RTF was—under various guises—the official voice of the state. In 1964, coinciding with the second channel, Antenne 2 (which was geared to broadcast in colour, introduced in France in 1970), the RTF was renamed the ORTF (Office de la Radio Télévision Française). In 1974 the ORTF was disbanded and broken up into seven different offices, a separate office for each radio and television branch (by 1973 the third channel, FR3, had been launched). This attempt at decentralizing did not, however, bring about a lessening of state intervention.

In 1982 the Socialist government voted a new audio-visual policy that would set in place a programme of deregulation, first, to stem state interventionist practices and, secondly, to expand the number of channels available. With regard to the first set of measures, all television channels were by 1990 governed by an independent authority, the Conseil Supérieur de l'Audiovisuel (CSA). The CSA was responsible for the appointment of the director of public-sector television and the allocation of its budgets, fixing of the licence fee, the content of broadcast advertisements (brand advertising was introduced in 1968), and for ensuring that the television channels' respective charters (*cahiers des charges*) were properly observed. On the more political front, the CSA ensured parity of exposure to all political parties.

With regard to the second measure, France had in 1990 seven terrestrial channels, three of which were state owned (A2, FR3, La Sept); three private (TF1, La5, M6), and Canal Plus, a pay-TV (also private).

Apart from Canal Plus (a movie and sports channel) and La Sept (the cultural channel), all the other channels were generalist ones (FR3 broadcast only a small percentage of regional programmes), which meant a predominant tendency towards a similarity in programming, especially in prime time.

On average, the French daily consumption of television amounts to three-and-a-half hours. TF1 is the favourite channel by far, and programme predilection is for game and variety shows, news at 8 p.m., American series, sports programmes, and films.

Deregulation, especially, brought in its wake a decline in programme quality. However, the beginnings of this decline reach back as far as the early 1970s when President *Pompidou forced the channels to be 'homologues mais compétitives'. Ever since, innovation has been on the wane and the science of programming on the ascendant. The golden age of television (1950–70) saw the first 'journal télévisé' in the world (1949); France was at the forefront of investigative journalism in the 1960s with its *Cinq colonnes à la Une*; literary adaptations abounded, and films were specially commissioned for television (the very first was *Bresson's Mouchette*, 1966, an adaptation of the *Bernanos novel). In 1970, and in the light of Pompidou's decree, everything changed. To secure a faithful audience the idea occurred to TF1 of presenting literary adaptations in serialized form; in 1970 a French version of the BBC's *Forsyte Saga* was broadcast in 15 episodes. The success with audience ratings was undeniable, and from this moment on most literary adaptations were programmed in this way—structurally resembling soap-opera. In the 1980s, given the increasing costs of making drama productions, the next stage was to transfer this successful formula to less expensive productions (single location, fixed sets, cameo performances by stars, etc). It was in this way that *Châteauvallon* (France's first soap) was conceived and, a bit later, the sitcom *Maguy*. The author too has had (and still has) a voice on TV, either through the dynamic but now defunct *Apostrophes* or the subsequent, more anodine *Ex Libris*. The tradition of satire is still alive, though on a lesser scale than in the heyday of Jean-Claude Averty's surreal satirical shows (*Les Raisins verts*, 1960s), in the form of *Le Bébête Show*.

The paradox for French television remains, therefore, that, although it is more depoliticized than ever before, nevertheless it has become an industry where capital rules, and in so doing has lost its public-service mission to inform, educate, and entertain. [SH]

Tel Quel. French avant-garde journal published by the Éditions du *Seuil (1960–82). For two decades *Tel Quel* succeeded in gathering under its aegis an impressive constellation of names that stand for what is most noteworthy and provocative in French intellectual thought and writing at this time, including *Barthes, Georges *Bataille, *Derrida, *Faye, *Foucault, *Guyotat, *Kristeva, *Ponge, *Ricardou, Denis *Roche, *Sollers, and *Todorov.

Tel Quel was launched in March 1960 by a group of writers in their mid-twenties: Philippe Sollers, Jean-Edern *Hallier, Jean-René *Huguenin, Renaud Matignon, Jacques Coudol, and Xavier de Boisrouvray. Within a few years no one remained from the original founding team except Sollers. He became the driving force behind the journal, along with Marcelin *Pleynet, who became assistant managing editor in 1963. *Tel Quel's* initial objective was to disengage literature from the reigning ideologies of the post-war years. It consequently supported the *Nouveau Roman, viewing it as a viable alternative to Sartrean *engagement.

From 1963 to 1966 *Tel Quel* explored the linguistic and philosophical implications of writing (*écriture*), and began to elaborate a critical theory which transcended generic and disciplinary boundaries. The literary models were Dante, *Sade, *Mallarmé, *Lautréamont, Joyce, *Artaud, Bataille, and Ponge; the theoretical references were the Russian Formalists, Derrida, and subsequently *Lacan and *Althusser. The importance of *psychoanalysis and *Marxism for *Tel Quel* is evident in the collective *Théorie d'ensemble* (1968), which contains a number of the most significant *Tel Quel* texts of this period.

In 1967 *Tel Quel* took on the avant-garde wager of revolutionizing literature and transforming society. It saw itself as the logical successor of *Surrealism, whose philosophical and political errors it set out to rectify. A fellow traveller of the French Communist Party from 1967 to 1971, the journal then became Maoist, devoting numerous articles to China until 1974. From the mid-1970s to the 1980s it relinquished Marxism, befriended the *Nouveaux Philosophes, turned to theology, and declared the avant-garde dead.

Despite an apparently erratic political trajectory, *Tel Quel* (subsequently *L'Infini* at Gallimard) nevertheless succeeded in preserving a certain aesthetic coherence. With its unconditional defence of literature from 1960 to 1982, it represents, in many respects, an attempt to resuscitate *La *Nouvelle Revue Française* in the wake of *Les *Temps modernes*. [DM-S]

Temple, Le. Complex of buildings east of central Paris originating with a 13th-c. tower, the headquarters of the Knights Templar, then of the Order of St John ('Knights of Malta'), joined by many younger sons of noble families. In the later 17th c., under Philippe de Vendôme as grand prior, the debauched suppers of the Temple were famous, and until the *Regency it was a centre of *libertinage and Epicurean poetry, from drinking songs to the works of *Chaulieu and *La Fare. The tower, used as a prison for Louis XVI and others, was demolished in 1811. [CJB]

Temple de Gnide, Le, see MONTESQUIEU.

Temps, Le

Temps, Le (1861–1942). An influential daily newspaper, *Le Temps* long bore the imprint of its founder, Auguste Nefftzer, a Protestant liberal from Alsace, and—later—that of his successor, the more worldly Adrien Hébrard. Nefftzer stressed objective newsreporting, extensive foreign coverage, and unwavering independence—as later did the paper's successor, Le *Monde*. Le Temps became the paper of the governing élite during the Third Republic, under the management of the Hébrard family. It combined insider knowledge with an austere tone and presentation. Its cultural pages, while less brilliant than those of Le *Figaro*, none the less carried pieces by writers such as Anatole *France and Francisque *Sarcey, drama critic from 1867 to 1899. Its circulation never exceeded 100,000.   [MP]

Temps modernes, Les. Monthly interdisciplinary journal founded by *Sartre, first published in 1945, with an editorial board which included *Beauvoir, *Leiris, *Merleau-Ponty, and Raymond *Aron. Its 'Présentation' by Sartre in the first issue situated it as part of an attempt to construct a left-wing post-war ethics and ideology compatible with *Marxism and conscious of its place in contemporary history. Its project was revolutionary in the sense of aiming to transform society in a radical fashion, and it welcomed young writers and thinkers who had not yet established their reputations, as well as fostering new movements and disciplines.

The review's primary interests were initially literature and politics, with a considerable place for the human sciences and the other arts, but politics took over increasingly from literature. It was the focus of several significant intellectual battles: between Sartre and Merleau-Ponty over philosophy and politics; around *psychoanalysis and anthropology with *Lévi-Strauss, Leiris, and Pontalis; and later about *Structuralism. The journal survived Sartre's death in 1980, though it has lost the place at the centre of controversy and contemporary intellectual debate which it held in the 1940s and 1950s.   [CMH]

Temps retrouvé, Le. The final part of Proust's *À la recherche du temps perdu*.

TENCIN, Claudine-Alexandrine Guérin, marquise de (1681–1749). For decades this sometime nun was notorious for her sexual indiscretions, often documented (d'*Alembert was the illegitimate son of her affair with a Chevalier Destouches) and more often wildly rumoured, and for the political intrigues plotted with her brother, Cardinal Tencin. After the *Regency, Tencin achieved respectability through the intellect for which she had long been celebrated. She founded a *salon in which former *Lambert regulars such as *Fontenelle mingled with *Montesquieu and *Marivaux (whose admission to the Académie Française she secured). She was also known as a novelist, especially for Le Comte de Comminge (1735) and Le Siège de Calais (1739).
                                                                        [JDeJ]

Tendre, La Carte de. Centrepiece of the first volume of Madeleine de *Scudéry's novel, *Clélie. The page unfolds to reveal the engraved map of a land called Tenderness. Scudéry's heroine presents the map as teaching the ways to win or lose a woman's heart. The *carte* inspired numerous authors to invent allegorical maps.   [JDeJ]

Tenso. Medieval Occitan lyric genre in which two voices engage in dialogue, usually in alternate stanzas; it was called *tenson* in northern French. The word *tenso* means 'dispute'. The authenticity of the dialogues in many *tensos* is a vexed issue: sometimes one of the voices is attributed to a known *troubadour, sometimes both, but some *tensos* are clearly fictional, e.g. there are *tensos* involving a poet and his horse or a poet and God. In the 13th c. there was a minor vogue for composing fictional dialogues with dead poets as a means of contrasting two positions, so even the use of the name of a known troubadour is no guarantee of authenticity.

Tensos cover a variety of topics, but the most common theme is love, and the genre offers an obvious forum for love casuistry. When the two voices of a *tenso* are attributed to known troubadours, the acrimony they may appear to show each other is obviously contrived, as such debates were not spontaneous, but composed collaboratively for performance. A number of *tensos* opposing male and female voices survive, some of which involved real *trobairitz; they may consequently represent female responses to the conventions of *fin'amor. See also the *jeu parti or partimen, a genre related to the *tenso*, in which two voices debate a specific question or problem set by the first speaker.   [SG]

Tentation de saint Antoine, La. A hybrid philosophical drama by *Flaubert, not meant for staging, part poem and part narrative. Flaubert was obsessed with this work, no doubt identifying with the 4th-c. hermit whose metaphysical temptations parade before the reader in a succession of visions. He produced three versions over 25 years (1849, 1856, and 1874), publishing only the final, shortened version. He had probably intended to publish the 1849 version, which he spent four days reading aloud to his friends *Du Camp and *Bouilhet. Supposedly, they advised him to throw such lyrical outpourings into the fire and to write a realist novel instead.   [DK]

TERRASSON, Jean, abbé (1670–1750). An early *freemason and member of the Académie Française and Académie des Inscriptions. He was a champion of the *modernes* (Dissertation sur l'Iliade d'Homère, 1715) [see QUERELLE], and wrote a long novel Séthos (1731), which is a combination of political instruction, a guide to Egyptian antiquity, and a novel of masonic initiation.   [PF]

Terre, La. Novel By *Zola, published 1887, the 15th work in his *Rougon-Macquart series. It is a novel of peasant life, set in a village in the Beauce, depicting the harsh labours of the peasants and their rapacious attachment to the earth. Jean Macquart, the son of Antoine Macquart, marries Françoise Fouan (*dite* Mouche) and finds himself embroiled in a terrible dispute over the property of old Fouan, which the old man had divided amongst his children. When both his wife and old Fouan are brutally killed by the former's sister, Lise, and the latter's son, Buteau, for possession of the family house, Jean leaves Rognes to join the army and figure in *La *Débâcle*. Lyrical descriptions of the countryside and of the eternal recurrence of the seasons contrast with the violent human actions in this reworking of the *King Lear* theme.

The novel provoked a hostile reaction, particularly, in *Le *Figaro* of 18 August 1887, from a group of self-proclaimed disciples of Zola, who denounced the excesses of the work in an article entitled '*La Terre*. A Emile Zola', which was immediately dubbed 'Le Manifeste des Cinq', a gesture that was taken to be the sign of a crisis in the movement of literary *Naturalism. [DB]

Terre des hommes, see SAINT-EXUPÉRY.

Terre et le sang, La, see FERAOUN.

Terror (*La Terreur*), see REVOLUTION, IC.

TESNIÈRE, Lucien, see LINGUISTICS.

Testament, Le, see VILLON.

Teste, see MONSIEUR TESTE.

Tête d'Or. Claudel's first play, written 1889 and published 1890. A sprawling *Symbolist drama with Shakespearean and Wagnerian overtones, it expresses much of the confusion he felt in this period, through imagery in which a Nietzschean desire for self-fulfilment is accompanied by a good deal of Christian symbolism. The power of Claudel's declamatory verse can already be felt.

The play is in three parts. In Part 1, Simon Agnel, who has broken loose from all family ties, is burying the woman who has been his companion. His freedom leaves him with a sense of a great destiny. In Part 2 an old emperor awaits the result of a battle, in which an unknown called Tête d'Or (Simon Agnel) is commanding his army. Tête d'Or returns triumphant, demands the throne, and kills the emperor. In Part 3 he has launched forth on a war of conquest, in the Caucasus, he is mortally wounded in battle. On to this simple base a bewildering range of symbolism, Christian and otherwise, is added, particularly in relation to the mystical figure of the princess, the emperor's daughter. In the second version of the play, published 1901, the Christian elements gain more prominence. [RMG]

THALY, Daniel, see WEST INDIES, 4.

Théâtre de chambre, see TARDIEU.

Théâtre de Clara Gazul, Le, see MÉRIMÉE.

Théâtre de la foire, see FOIRE, THÉÂTRES DE LA.

Théâtre du Soleil, Le, see MNOUCHKINE.

Théâtre Libre, Le, see ANTOINE.

Théâtre National Populaire, Le (TNP). State-subsidized company created in 1920 under the directorship of Firmin *Gémier. In the 1930s and 1940s it suffered from under-funding and lack of a clear artistic policy. In 1951 it was relaunched as the TNP with Jean *Vilar as its director [see AVIGNON, FESTIVAL OF]. Under Vilar in the 1950s it operated in the Palais de Chaillot with spectacular success as a 'service public', providing high-quality, inexpensive, and accessible productions of the classics for popular audiences. It went into decline again after 1968, and the title of TNP was transferred to Roger *Planchon's company in the Lyon suburb of Villeurbanne. Under Planchon and his co-directors Patrice *Chéreau and Georges Lavaudant, it was re-politicized and became a focus for innovative productions of the classics. [DWW]

Theatre of Cruelty, see ARTAUD.

Theatres and Audiences

1. 1500–1789

As in the Middle Ages [see MEDIEVAL DRAMA], dramatic events in the 16th c. usually took place in settings erected or adapted for the occasion, and this practice was to persist throughout the *ancien régime*, even after the establishment of regular theatres. Venues varied from royal courts at one extreme to city streets at the other. Renaissance drama was mainly performed in colleges and courts, palaces housed ballet and opera, streets were transformed for *royal entries or carnivals, while *farces amused crowds at the fairgrounds. The 18th c. saw an increased vogue for private theatricals (*théâtre de société*). Meanwhile, throughout the provinces, travelling players performed in private houses, inns, or tennis courts (*jeux de paume*); a vivid image of this type of theatre, well known to *Molière, is to be found in Scarron's *Roman comique*.

Gradually, however, proper theatres were set up, first in Paris and then, in the 18th c., in major provincial cities. The principal Parisian theatres in the early classical period are as follows:

(*a*) the *Hôtel de Bourgogne, the oldest theatre, where the Confrères de la Passion [see CONFRÉRIES] performed *mystery plays until the mid-16th c. At the beginning of the 17th c. a company called the Comédiens du Roi was set up there by Valleran le Comte; they performed plays by *Hardy alongside the much-loved farces of Turlupin, Gros-Guillaume, and *Gaultier-Garguille. Subsequently, with actors such as Floridor, *Montfleury, and La *Champmeslé, the Hôtel became the stronghold

797

Theatres and Audiences

of classical tragedy until 1680, when the theatre passed to the Italian players who were to become the *Comédie-Italienne.

(b) The Théâtre du Marais, set up by Le Noir and Montdory in 1629 and established in its permanent premises on the Right Bank in 1634, was associated above all with Pierre *Corneille. Its greatest period, when it rivalled the Hôtel, was between 1634 and 1646; thereafter it specialized increasingly in *machine plays.

(c) The theatre of the *Palais-Royal, originally *Richelieu's Palais-Cardinal, was built in 1641. It was the first example in France of the Italian style of theatre building. From 1661 to 1673 it was shared by Molière's company and the Italian actors, who had from 1658 to 1660 shared the Salle du Petit-Bourbon, previously a venue for *ballet de cour. In 1673 the Palais Royal became the home of the *Opéra.

After Molière's death in 1673 there were major reorganizations of the Paris theatre companies. Molière's company, now headed by *La Grange, fused with the Marais, and played at the Hôtel de Guénégaud, on the Left Bank, where they were joined in 1680 by the Hôtel de Bourgogne actors. The resultant company was to be known as the *Comédie-Française. A new theatre on the Left Bank was built for them in 1689, and they continued to play here until moving to the Salle des Machines of the Tuileries in 1770 and to the newly built Théâtre du Luxembourg (subsequently the *Odéon) in 1782.

Alongside the two official theatres, the Comédie-Française and the Opéra, other companies fought to establish themselves. The Comédie-Italienne, having been expelled from France in 1697 for insulting Madame de *Maintenon, returned in 1716 and enjoyed a period of great popularity, performing many of *Marivaux's comedies. In 1762 they formed the *Opéra-Comique in conjunction with players from the ever-popular théâtres de la *foire, who had survived their battle with the official theatres and developed a varied dramatic and musical repertoire. Finally, in the mid-18th c., a new generation of popular theatres came into existence on the boulevards surrounding Paris, the théâtres de *boulevard which were to flourish in the following century.

It is not easy to generalize about theatres, performances, and audiences at this period. The early theatres such as the Hôtel de Bourgogne and the Marais were long and narrow like the tennis courts that preceded them; only gradually did purpose-built theatres provide more suitable space for actors and spectators. The 17th c. saw the imposition of unitary sets at the expense of the old décor simultané (where different parts of the stage represented different places), and the increasing domination of the 'Italian' style in which proscenium arch and curtain separated stage from auditorium. Acting was highly stylized and (in tragedy) declamatory, but emotionally effective. While sets were relatively simple at the Hôtel, the general tendency was towards spectacular effects, with trompe l'œil decor and much stage machinery; this showy style reached its height—or nadir—at the Opéra.

As for audiences, private productions (e.g. at court) were obviously for an élite. Public theatres, having been rowdy, disreputable places in the reign of Henri IV, acquired a new respectability in Paris by 1640, and over the next 150 years occupied a central place in the rituals of polite sociability. Compared with the socially mixed medieval audiences, the public in the established theatres was limited—seat prices excluded the poor. Nevertheless, audiences were drawn from different ranks of society. John Lough has estimated that at the end of the 17th c. the Comédie-Française had between 10,000 and 17,000 regular patrons. Noblemen, bourgeois, servants, students, and writers stood together in the parterre (pit), women and respectable spectators sat in loges (boxes) at the sides and back of the auditorium, while men of fashion continued to make a nuisance of themselves by sitting on the stage itself until 1759 at the Comédie-Française. Audience behaviour became more polite with time, but could still be rowdy by modern standards. Since the auditorium could not be darkened during the candle-lit performances, the audience themselves were a part of the show.

Throughout the period the theatre was subject to official control. *Louis XIV, while protecting actors, imposed his will on the theatre, ordering the mergers of 1673 and 1680 and giving various forms of monopoly to the Opéra and the Comédie-Française. *Censorship was established in 1701. And the Church never became fully reconciled to the theatre, making its hostility felt in such episodes as the banning of *Tartuffe or *Bossuet's anti-theatrical outbursts. Louis XIV was godfather to Molière's child, but actors were refused burial in consecrated ground. [PF]

2. Post-1789

The Revolution of 1789 ushered in a period of chaotic competition in the theatre. The law of 13 January 1791 swept away the corporate monopolies and privileges of the *Comédie-Française and other official theatres, making it possible for any citizen to set up a public theatre and present plays of any kind. The result was a sharp increase in the number of theatres (over 20 in 1791 alone), most of them short-lived. A new kind of theatrical spectacle emerged with the *fêtes révolutionnaires of 1793–4 organized by the painter *David.

Stricter control returned with the Directoire and the Napoleonic regime which, in a series of decrees (1806–7), effectively restored the regulatory system of the ancien régime. No new theatre could be established in Paris without a licence; major provincial cities were restricted to two theatres and smaller towns to one. The approval of the préfet was required for running a theatre and that of the censor for staging a new play. The official Paris theatres were limited to four (Comédie-Française, Odéon, Opéra, Opéra-Comique), as were the 'secondary' theatres: Gaîté and Ambigu-Comique, given over to *melodrama, farce, and *pantomime; and Variétés and Vaudeville, devoted to parodies, musical sketches, and bawdy short plays.

Censorship and central control remained the rule under the Restoration and, in spite of attempts to introduce a more liberal system in the 1830s and 1840s, continued to apply during most of the Second Empire. By a decree of 6 January 1864, French theatres were in effect converted into commercial enterprises. They could open without prior approval and were not restricted in the sort of play they could offer, but were still subject to the laws of blasphemy and obscenity and required the prior assent of the censor. Censorship technically disappeared with an act of 1905, but the powers of the *préfets* remained unchanged in matters of public morals. Formal abolition of censorship had to wait until after World War II.

In the course of the 19th c. a democratization of theatre audiences occurred, aided by the expansion of state education and the growth of a mass press. A rising new commercial and manufacturing class, dating from the 1830s, looked to the stage to provide distraction from its humdrum life or a reflection of its concerns about money, property, and social mobility. From the Second Empire onwards the railways brought provincial visitors and foreign tourists to Paris, swelling the theatre public and the demand for spicy entertainment. Though *haussmannisation* forced the closure of some popular theatres (e.g. Funambules, 1862), it led to a boom in theatre building (e.g. Châtelet, 1862). Street entertainers were gradually squeezed out in favour of indoor theatrical performances, but the illegitimate stage flourished in the form of *cafés-concerts*, *music-halls, and cabarets (e.g. Le *Chat Noir, c.1880). Inevitably repertories and audience loyalties changed over the century, with many famous houses showing remarkable powers of survival. The old Gaîté moved from melodrama to operetta, the Porte-Saint-Martin from Romantic drama to spectacle, the Gymnase from *Scribe's 'well-made plays' to the serious drama of *Augier and *Dumas *fils*.

By the 1890s Parisian theatres attracted about half a million spectators weekly, and on the eve of World War I some 62 permanent theatres operated in the provinces, being especially vigorous in major cities (e.g. Bordeaux, Lyon, Marseille, Rouen) and garrison towns. Theatres, responding to a technical age, provided lavish sets and costumes, elaborate stage machinery, and opulent auditoriums. Sets became increasingly cluttered and there was a vogue for pictorialism and historical authenticity (e.g. *Sardou). Gas lighting (Opéra and Variétés, 1822), electric arc lamps (Opéra, c.1846), and carbon filament bulbs (Opéra, 1886) gradually displaced oil and paraffin lamps, producing a brilliantly lit space

which necessitated changes in acting and staging.

Actors themselves, while remaining stagey by 20th-c. standards, moved away from the declamation and formal gestures and poses of early 19th-c. theatre towards greater naturalness, intimacy, and flexibility of voice and movement. By the end of the century a cult of the star actor, fostered by foreign and provincial tours, had developed in both the commercial (or boulevard) theatres and the state-subsidized houses. Significantly, the decay of the Comédie-Française and Odéon into museums of dramatic art went hand in hand with the rise of star actors, from *Rachel and Delaunay in the 1850s to *Bartet and *Mounet-Sully in the 1890s.

Reaction against the sterility of the state theatres and a commercial stage dominated by stars, spectacle, and light entertainment was signalled by the revival of mime at the Cercle Funambulesque (1888), the vogue for puppets at Signoret's Petit Théâtre des Marionnettes (1888), and the emergence of three important avant-garde theatres: *Antoine's Théâtre Libre (1887–94), Paul *Fort's poetic Théâtre d'Art (1890–2), and *Lugné-Poë's Théâtre de l'Œuvre (1893–9). These initiated a revolution in acting, scenic design, and lighting, drawing on an adventurous foreign repertory (German, Russian, Scandinavian) and so highlighting the international character of the new 'art-theatre' movement.

Antoine and Lugné-Poë herald the era of the theatrical director, blazing the trail for the great reformers of the French stage between the wars: *Copeau at the Vieux-Colombier (1913–14, 1919–24), and the 'Cartel'—*Dullin at the Atelier (1922–40), *Jouvet at the Athénée (from 1934), *Baty at the Montparnasse (1930–47), *Pitoëff at the Mathurins (from 1934). Together these were responsible for the most innovative stage productions of the inter-war years, using a variety of means—bare stage, group movement, complex lighting plots, revival of the techniques of the circus and *commedia dell'arte—to create dynamic performances. Other valuable experimental groups of the period included *Artaud and his associates in the Théâtre de la Cruauté, Saint-Denis and the Compagnie des Quinze (1930–6), and the Laboratoire du Théâtre Art et Action (1917–39).

During World War II theatre in occupied France was controlled by the Germans through a front organization, the Comité d'Organisation des Entreprises de Spectacles. Paradoxically, theatre receipts soared in Paris and an impetus was given to small provincial touring companies, e.g. Le Rideau Gris (Lyon, 1941–2) and Jeune France (1940–2). This wartime revival offset the severe decline in the number of permanent theatre companies operating in the provinces after 1914, a decline countered by scattered enthusiasts, e.g. Pottecher's amateur Théâtre du Peuple de Bussang (from 1895), *Gémier's Théâtre National Ambulant (1911–12), and La Compagnie des Comédiens Routiers (1934–7). In the wartime activity of local companies and their predecessors lie the seeds of the movement for *décentralisation and the explosion of state-subsidized regional theatres (Centres Dramatiques Régionaux) that occurred after 1945, leading to some 55 established companies working outside Paris by 1980. Between the wars most new plays were produced in commercial or experimental theatres; by 1980 many were staged in Centres Dramatiques Régionaux. While the inter-war theatrical avant-garde tended to be literary and élitist, it became populist after 1945 (e.g. *Vilar's TNP, *Mnouchkine's Théâtre du Soleil), wedded to the idea of 'total performance', and open to foreign theorists and practitioners (e.g. Brecht, Grotowski, Peter *Brook). [SBJ]

See J. Lough, *Paris Theatre Audiences in the Seventeenth and Eighteenth Centuries* (1957); M. Carlson, *The French Stage in the Nineteenth Century* (1972); J. de Jomaron (ed.), *Le Théâtre en France*, 2 vols. (1988–9); D. Bradby, *Modern French Drama, 1940–1990* (1991).

Thébaïde, La, ou les Frères ennemis (1664). *Racine's first tragedy, presenting the bloody conflict of Oedipus' two sons, Eteocles and Polynices.

Thélème, L'Abbaye de. Ideal anti-monastery in *Rabelais's *Gargantua* [see PANTAGRUEL AND GARGANTUA]. Its one rule is: 'Fais ce que voudras.'

Théodore. Tragedy by Pierre *Corneille, first performed 1646. Set in Roman Antioch, it tells of the Christian princess Théodore, who is condemned to prostitution, but chooses martyrdom.

Théophilanthropie, La. A deistic religion which enjoyed a certain popularity during the Revolution from 1796 until the *Concordat of 1801. Using formerly Christian churches, it celebrated a religion based on belief in God, virtue, and immortality.

THÉOPHILE DE VIAU (1590–1626). French poet and dramatist. Born at Clairac, he studied at the Huguenot *académies* of Montauban and Saumur, and at Leiden. For two years he was playwright for a company of actors, but none of his early plays survives. In the service of the duc de Candale, he became prominent in the free-living, sometimes free-thinking, circles in and around the court, and in 1619 was exiled. His offence was probably involvement in political intriguing by his superiors, but the pretext alleged was impious and obscene poetry. He had to pay for his return to Paris by transferring his allegiance to the king's favourite, Luynes—a distressing reflection of which is his highly uncharacteristic sonnet celebrating the execution of Étienne *Durand. His reputation as a leading *libertin was, however, already established, and despite his conversion in 1622 he provided a conspicuous target for two unscrupulous Jesuits, Voisin and *Garasse. Tried in his absence, he was burned in effigy.

Arrested soon afterwards, he was held in harsh conditions for two years, but defended himself vigorously and received the mild sentence of banishment from Paris, not, in the event, enforced.

Much has been made of Théophile's debt to Italian naturalism, in particular that of *Vanini, with its denial of Providence, personal immortality, and other Christian doctrines; but the pervasive influence of *Montaigne should not be overlooked, especially in relation to Théophile's cult of individual freedom and truth to one's own nature.

These values are frequently affirmed in his poetry. He admires *Malherbe as well as *Ronsard, but will go his own 'modern', sensible way, heeding neither 'la sotte antiquité' nor over-scrupulous purists. The personal factor gives new life even to the eulogy of the great in *La Maison de Silvie* (1623–5), ten odes addressed to the duchesse de Montmorency, who with her husband had given sanctuary to the fugitive poet at Chantilly in 1622. Praising the duchess through the beauties of her park, he has scope for descriptions in the baroque mode which still retain something of the freshness of his early poems 'Le Matin' and 'La Solitude'. Whether in nature or in love, however, he finds no delight exempt from decay and death: his most original poems are low-key elegies in which he follows freely his fluctuating thought and feeling; and though in his tragedy *Pyrame et Thisbé* (published 1623) youthful passion burns as fiercely as in *Romeo and Juliet*, in the elegy 'Cloris, lorsque je songe, en te voyant si belle . . .' he finds himself concluding that the greatest of all pleasures lies in the creation of poetry. [AJS]

See A. Adam, *Théophile de Viau* (1935).

Théorèmes, Les, see LA CEPPÈDE.

THÉORET, France (b. 1942). Canadian writer who has published poetry, novels, drama, and essays. She began writing at the height of the feminist movement in Quebec in the mid-1970s; her collections of poetry, *Bloody Mary* (1970), *Une voix pour Odile* (1978), *Vertiges* (1979), and *Nécessairement putain* (1980), are all marked by a preoccupation with feminine identity, or rather non-identity. Language and writing are presented as highly problematic for the female subject; the identity of the poetic voice is fractured and unstable, difficult to identify with the author, despite an autobiographical element in her writing (the Odile, for example, of *Une voix pour Odile*, is her grandmother). However, the voice is always marked by a strong sense of rhythm and musicality. The 'Je' is again elided in the title of *Nous parlerons comme on écrit* (1982), described by its author as a novel and consisting of a series of experimental texts which play with the fluid movement of speech. *Entre raison et déraison* (1987) is a collection of essays pursuing the themes of language, poetry, women, and writing. [EAF]

Théorie d'ensemble, see TEL QUEL.

Théorie des lois civiles, see LINGUET.

THÉRÈSE DE LISIEUX, Saint, see DEVOTIONAL WRITING, 3.

Thérèse Desqueyroux. Novel by François *Mauriac, published 1927. Based on the Canaby trial in Bordeaux in 1905, the novel explores through an extended flashback the reasons which led the heroine to poison her husband Bernard. Set in the Landes, in an arid landscape of pine-trees and sand, the novel powerfully evokes the claustrophobia of one of Mauriac's nonconformists, which finally leads her to commit the crime. Benefiting from a *non-lieu* verdict, Thérèse is returned to her husband, who changes her metaphorical imprisonment into a literal one: she is confined to her room. The end of the novel sees her release in Paris, which, for all its excitement, is portrayed in the same arid imagery as the Landes. Thérèse's final attempt to explain her motives to Bernard ends in continuing and impenetrable incomprehension, maintaining both characters in their solitude. Mauriac's fascination with his heroine, whom he saw as an exceptional being struggling for salvation, prompted a further novel based on her, *La Fin de la nuit* (1935), and two short-stories, 'Thérèse chez le docteur' and 'Thérèse à l'hôtel', both published in *Plongées* (1938). [NH]

Thérèse Raquin. Novel by *Zola, published 1867, his most important work before the **Rougon-Macquart* series. Set in the claustrophobic atmosphere of a dingy haberdasher's shop in the passage du Pont-Neuf in Paris, this powerful novel tells how the heroine and her lover, Laurent, kill her husband, Camille, but are subsequently haunted by visions of the dead man and prevented from enjoying the fruits of their crime. They are progressively consumed by a crude form of remorse, under the accusing gaze of Camille's paralysed mother, until they are driven to suicide as the only relief from their torment. In a resounding preface to the second edition (1868), Zola claimed that his novel was a work of the new school of *Naturalism, a physiological analysis of the passions and temperaments of his bestial characters. In fact, much of this work, which shows the influence of *Balzac and *Taine, is taken up with physiological analysis, but there are also undeniable Gothic strains and melodramatic effects inherited from the popular novel. [DB]

THÉRIAULT, Yves (1915–83). Canadian novelist whose work, in quantity and diversity, is of monumental proportions. He is best known for his novels on the native peoples of Canada, depicting in epic terms their affinity with nature in the remote wildernesses of the north. Despite the grandeur of vision of the Inuit cycle—including *Agaguk* (1958), *Tayaout* (1969), *Agoak* (1975)—there is a questionable primitivism in its portrayal of the Inuit as noble savages ever inclined to lapse into violence and brutishness. In contrast, *Ashini* (1960) shows with great

sensitivity the destructive impact of Western civilization on traditional Amerindian culture, while *Aaron* (1954) shows the same process affecting the Jewish faith. In general, his work is more optimistic and sober when it deals with simple people in touch with nature, as in *Le Dernier Hâvre* (1970) and *Moi, Pierre Huneau* (1979), than when it depicts modern, materialistic society, where there is a heavy emphasis on the violence and depravity of alienated, rootless characters. His prodigious narrative skills are possibly seen at their best in two substantial collections of short stories, *La Femme Anna et autres contes* (1981) and *Valère et le grand canot* (1981). [SIL]

Thermidor. Name given to the coup of 9 Thermidor An II (27 July 1794) in which *Robespierre and his allies were overthrown [see REVOLUTION, IC].

Thésée. The last novel written by *Gide (1946). In it the mythological hero Theseus retells elements of his legendary life which serve as allegories for the moral issues Gide himself had confronted. Its final lines can be read as the author's own testament: 'Pour le bien de l'humanité future, j'ai fait mon œuvre. J'ai vécu.' [DHW]

THÉVENOT, Jean (1633–67). Traveller to the East. His accounts of Egypt, Arabia, Persia, and India were published together in five volumes of *Voyages* (1689). Clearly written, they provide a good deal of useful information, and show the detached, wide-ranging curiosity of one who travels for travelling's sake.

THEVET, André (1516–92). 'Cosmographe de quatre rois' (from *Henri II to *Henri III), this Franciscan friar from Angoulême cut a controversial figure: his *Cosmographie de Levant* (1554) is less an account of his pilgrimage to the Holy Land than a compilation from other works, while his supposedly first-hand tale of the French expedition to Brazil, *Les Singularités de la France antarctique* (1557), was challenged by the Calvinist Jean de *Léry. Thevet's most ambitious work was the *Cosmographie universelle* (1575), an immense patchwork of geography, history, and politics which drew accusations of vanity, gullibility, and plagiarism from Thevet's former collaborator *Belleforest. [MJH]

THIAM, Awa (b. c.1950). Born in Senegal, Thiam writes forcefully of the conditions of women today on the African continent. Her best-known book, *La Parole aux négresses* (1978), contains interviews and essays. It was followed in 1983 by another study of African women, *Continents noirs*. [VC]

THIBAUDET, Albert (1874–1936). French literary critic. By training a historian-geographer-philosopher, Thibaudet became the critical stalwart of the *Nouvelle Revue Française in the inter-war period. A trencherman for text, he pursued a method informed by *Bergsonian concepts of *élan* and *durée*, but personal and undogmatic, if somewhat prolix. He had a geographer's eye for the contours of a genre and a historian's for its evolution. From *La Poésie de Stéphane Mallarmé* (1912) to his seminal *Histoire de la littérature française de 1789 à nos jours* (1936), numerous volumes testify to his range— *Flaubert* (1922), *Paul Valéry* (1924), *Physiologie de la critique* (1930), *Stendhal* (1931). His *La République des professeurs* (1928) is a sociological study of French intellectuals. The foremost critic of his time, he still stimulates the mind. [DAS]

Thibault, Les. Roger *Martin du Gard's Tolstoyan fresco of bourgeois life, published between 1922 and 1940. In 1931, after the appearance of *Le Cahier gris* (1922), *Le Pénitencier* (1922), *La Belle Saison* (1923), *La Consultation* (1928), *La Sorellina* (1928), and *La Mort du père* (1929), the original epic scope of the *roman-fleuve* was drastically curtailed and the project completed in four further volumes, the three of *L'Été 1914* (1936) and *Épilogue* (1940).

The male-dominated story is told by an omniscient narrator, though with much use of dialogue, *style indirect libre*, a novel within a novel, letters, and towards the end a diary. The structure is based on a series of set episodes of varying duration and complexity. The novel follows the destinies of Antoine and Jacques Thibault, sons of an overbearing, intellectual, Catholic father. Both become materialist agnostics, Antoine a successful society doctor, Jacques a writer and socialist revolutionary. The Protestant de Fontanin family is a foil to the Thibaults. Daniel de Fontanin becomes a *Gidean sensualist and a painter; his sister Jenny and Jacques fall in love. His mother is perhaps the most admirable character portrayed, though the most striking female figure is the emancipated Rachel, Antoine's lover. The author is adept at working parallels and contrasts into his complex plot. Characters are not given as absolutes. The web of relationships is very convincingly handled, the psychology perceptive and discreet but rarely profound. Sexuality is treated with some frankness. Focus and tempo vary greatly. Sections of *La Mort du père* are sluggish, and parts of *L'Été 1914*, where analysis of the causes of the war predominates, tedious and artificial. The art of *Les Thibault* is one of tolerant humanist irony, indirect suggestion, and implicit meanings. Style is never allowed to obtrude. Time, death, love, loneliness, egoism, the alleviation of suffering through medicine and social justice are the main themes of this ambitious portrayal of the bourgeois human condition. [DAS]

THIBAUT DE BLAISON. *Trouvère* bearing the dynastic name of the lords of Blaison (Maine-et-Loire) and Mirebeau-en-Poitou (Vienne). A friend of *Thibaut de Champagne, he was probably the magnate attested from 1200 onwards who was seneschal of Poitou. His compositions include one *pastourelle* and six conventional *chansons courtoises*. A seventh

(in Franco-Occitan) and a *chanson de mal-mariée* are less reliably attributed in troubadour songbooks. [PVD]

THIBAUT DE CHAMPAGNE (1201–53). Like his ancestor *Guilhem IX, Count Thibaut IV of Champagne and Brie, king of Navarre (crowned 1234), is more remembered for his contribution to literature than for his chequered political career. The widespread diffusion of his 64 extant lyrics suggests he was as much admired as a *trouvère* as he was disliked as a ruler and fickle ally. His 36 *chansons courtoises*, three crusading songs, 12 *jeux partis*, five *débats*, two *pastourelles*, and six religious songs (five to the Virgin) show versatility, polished artifice, and preciosity rather than originality. [PVD]

THIERRY, Augustin (1795–1856). French historian who made an important contribution to the revival of historical studies under the Restoration. He wrote about ordinary people, made references to contemporary politics, and used anecdotes and legends to give colour and drama to his writing. His most famous and influential works were the *Histoire de la conquête de l'Angleterre par les Normands* (1825) and *Considérations sur l'histoire de France* (1840). He believed that every new epoch opened for history new points of view, and that the writing of history had constantly to be reviewed and revised.

His brother, Amédée Thierry, was also a historian. [DJ]

THIERS, Adolphe (1797–1877). French journalist, historian, and statesman. The only son of a modest Marseille family, educated at the *lycée* there and at the law faculty of Aix-en-Provence, he rapidly made a name for himself in Paris during the 1820s. As founder of the newspaper *Le National* he was an active promoter of the 1830 Revolution and was twice prime minister under the *July Monarchy. An opponent of *Napoleon III, he was prominent in negotiating for peace between France and Prussia in 1870–1, and became the dominant figure in the Third Republic and its first president. He was responsible for crushing the Paris *Commune of 1871.

His *Histoire de la révolution française* (1823–7) was one of the first to take account of basic economic factors. *Histoire du consulat et du l'empire* (1845–62) made great use of the oral evidence of many of the participants. [DJ]

THIRY, Marcel (1897–1977). Belgian poet and storyteller. Escaping from occupied Belgium in World War I, Thiry saw action with a Belgian corps in Galicia, was caught up in the Russian Revolution, and then contrived to return home to Liège via Siberia, North America, and France. His poetry, as in *Toi qui pâlis au nom de Vancouver* (1924), echoes the fitful nostalgia of a *Cendrars or an *Apollinaire, mingling exhilaration with a sense of disorientation, and developing an image of modernity both wistful and sceptical. Thiry's fantastic tales draw strength from an insistence upon plausible material fact (*Nouvelles du grand possible*, 1958); his science-fiction novel *Échec au temps* (1945) builds rigorously on the premiss that Napoleon won the Battle of Waterloo. [RC]

THOBY-MARCELIN, Philippe (1904–75). Haitian poet and novelist, and one of the founders of *La *Revue indigène* (1927–8), in which he published delicate mood poems inspired by peasant life. The same material is later apparent in his sometimes humorous fiction *Canapé vert* (1942), *La Bête de Musseau* (1946), *Le Crayon de dieu* (1952), and *Tous les hommes sont fous* (1970). [JMD]

THOMAS. 12th-c. Anglo-Norman poet, author of a *Tristan*.

THOMAS, Antoine-Léonard (1732–85). French writer, sometimes remembered for his philosophical ode 'Sur le temps' (which prefigures *Lamartine's 'Le Lac'), but principally for his grandiloquent *éloges* of great men (Marcus Aurelius, *Sully, *Descartes), which regularly won prizes from the Académie Française. His *Essai sur les éloges* (1773) gives his theory of the genre. [PF]

THOMAS, Henri (1912–93). French poet, novelist, and translator. Thomas's glassy, musical poetry, from *Travaux d'aveugle* (1941) to *A quoi tu penses* (1980), has been overshadowed by his translations of Shakespeare, Pushkin, and Jünger and by his successful novels: *John Perkins* (1960), *Le Promontoire* (1961). Muted personal variations on feelings of fragile mortality dominate his writing. [DAS]

THOMAS AQUINAS, see AQUINAS.

THOMASSIN, Louis de (1619–95). French *Oratorian theologian and teacher. His lengthy pedagogical treatises (e.g. *La Manière d'enseigner chrétiennement et solidement les lettres humaines*, 1681–2) belong in the tradition of Christian humanism.

THOREZ, Maurice (1900–64). Leader of the French Communist Party from 1934 until his death. He was held chiefly responsible for the party's unwavering loyalty to Moscow in the 1930s and 1940s, its *ouvriérisme* (illustrated by his own part-ghosted autobiography, *Fils du peuple*, 1936), and its Stalinist stance in the 1950s, when he encouraged the cult of his own personality and held at bay the changes of the Khrushchev years. [SR]

THOU, Jacques-Auguste de (1553–1617). Historian, and a typical representative of the French legal classes, who used his legal experience in the service of the restoration of the French monarchy (he helped to negotiate *Henri IV's entry into Paris in 1594 and to prepare the *Edict of Nantes). His fame rests on his enormous *Historia sui temporis*, much of which was translated into French in 1659 (a full

translation had to wait until 1734). The importance of the *Historia* lies in its impartiality and in de Thou's use of the extensive documentation available to him as a high-ranking Parisian magistrate. He also writes in a clear, readable way—hence *Bossuet's description of him as a 'grand auteur' and a 'fidèle historien'. [JJS]

Thriller, see DETECTIVE FICTION; ROMAN D'AVEN-TURE(S); ROMAN NOIR.

Tiers État, Le (or Le Tiers). The third of the three orders or estates that the society of the *ancien régime* was divided into, the first two being the *clergy and the *nobility. It therefore included all those excluded from the other orders, and had no real homogeneity, except that all could engage in trade without penalty and, as commoners, were theoretically subject to the *taille* [see TAXATION]. Consequently, the 'Third Estate' was of the most varied social composition: its members ranged from the wealthiest financial or judicial office-holder through all the fine gradations of urban ranks amongst tradesmen to the lowliest peasant. There was, in fact, an accepted (but sometimes contested) hierarchy reaffirmed by places in urban processions and forms of address. At the top were those who could 'live nobly' from their investments in land and office, followed by those living from intellectual labour, like lawyers and judicial office-holders, then merchants, master craftsmen, and tradesmen, down to those whose only means of income was unskilled manual labour.

In spite of the apparently strict hierarchy, society was complex, and in addition to regional variations in status there were the criteria of wealth and lifestyle, such that a non-noble tax-farmer might rank higher in the eyes of his contemporaries than many a provincial noble, while a wealthy merchant might receive more esteem than many a master craftsman. The order was riven with internal rivalries and suffered politically from the fact that its wealthiest members were generally attempting to flee it by purchasing titles of nobility. The upper echelons of the bourgeoisie acquired many privileges that gave them dignity, and already lived in a manner virtually indistinguishable from the nobles.

'Tiers État' was both the name for a collection of social groups and a term for its representation. The political representation of the Third Estate was limited to the infrequent meetings of the *États Généraux, to the periodic assemblies of provincial estates, and to membership of some town councils. Peasants never gained representation in person as members of the Tiers, although in 1789 they were allowed to vote in indirect elections and present *cahiers de doléances* along with the other groups. The elections to the Tiers at the États Généraux of 1789 resulted in the election of 448 judicial office-holders, lawyers, and notaries, and as few as 85 manufacturers, traders, and bankers from a total of

648. The representatives of the Tiers were thus overwhelmingly bourgeois.

The Tiers was the subject of a famous 1789 pamphlet by *Siéyès, which contains the questions and answers: 'Qu'est-ce que le Tiers État? Tout. Qu'a-t-il été jusqu'à présent dans l'ordre politique? Rien.'
[PRC]

Tiers Livre, Le, by *Rabelais, see PANTAGRUEL AND GARGANTUA.

Tiffauges, Abel. The hero of Tournier's Le *Roi des aulnes.

Ti Jean l'Horizon, see SCHWARZ-BART, S.

Timocrate (1656). Romantic tragedy by Thomas *Corneille, one of the great box-office successes of the 17th c.

Tintin. Cartoon character created by the Belgian artist Hergé (Georges Remi, 1907–83), whose mastery of the immediately legible image and of unflagging narrative made him the father of the modern *bande dessinée. Tintin first appeared in 'Tintin au pays des Soviets' (1929), in the pages of Le Petit Vingtième, the weekly children's supplement of Le Vingtième Siècle. Thereafter, in a succession of journals, appeared the further 22 albums which go to make up Les Aventures de Tintin. In the guise of a roving reporter, Tintin maintained many of his original boy-scout traits: celibacy, indefatigable adventurousness, clean-living candour, eternal youth, resourcefulness. Always accompanied by his uncannily human dog, Milou, Tintin gradually finds himself surrounded by entertaining auxiliaries: the pratfalling, word-playing pseudo-twins, the Dupond/t (Les Cigares du Pharaon, 1932–4); the miles gloriosus in maritime guise, Haddock (Le Crabe aux pinces d'or, 1940–1); the wilfully and serenely hard-of-hearing Professor Tournesol (Les Sept Boules de cristal, 1943–6); and the forbidding diva Bianca Castafiore (L'Affaire Tournesol 1954–6), conceited and egocentric. These characters tend to steal Tintin's thunder and deprive him of his heroic isolation, making him just one character among many in a male-orientated *roman d'aventures.
[CS]

TIRAQUEAU, André (c.1480–1558). The famous friend and protector of *Rabelais. Tiraqueau was a magistrate in the Parlement de Paris and wrote two influential treatises: the De legibus connubialibus (1513) and the De nobilitate (1549). Of these, the former is the best-remembered today, partly as a result of the debate which it prompted on the role and status of women, but mainly because of the way in which Rabelais exploited this debate in the Tiers Livre. [JJS]

TIROLIEN, Guy (1917–88). Guadeloupean poet and man of letters who spent most of his adult life in Africa, first as a colonial administrator and then as an official of the United Nations. His early poems, including the much-anthologized 'Prière d'un petit

enfant nègre', are collected in Balles d'or (1961). His other main work is a collection of poems and nouvelles entitled Feuilles vivantes au matin (1977); a series of interviews with Michel Tétu, De Marie-Galante à une poétique afro-antillaise (1990), was published after his death.
[RDEB]

Tite et Bérénice. Comédie héroïque by Pierre *Corneille, first performed 1670 in competition with Racine's *Bérénice. Corneille starts from the same story as Racine, the unwilling separation of two lovers, but makes of it a quite different play, introducing alongside Tite and Bérénice two new characters, Domitien and Domitie, and thereby weaving a complicated web of matrimonial intrigue where vanity seems more important than love. Corneille's play does not have Racine's tragic poetry, but with its false happy ending it offers a poignant image of noble reputation masking weakness and sterility.
[PF]

TITINGA, Frédéric Pacéré (b. 1943). Poet of Burkina Faso. Titinga, who places himself in the *griot tradition, is also a practising lawyer. He won the 1982 Grand Prix Littéraire d'Afrique Noire for two works: Poèmes pour l'Angola (1982) and La Poésie des griots (1982). Other volumes include Refrains sous le Sahel (1976), Quand s'envolent les grues couronnées (1976), and Du lait pour une tombe (1984). [VC]

TLILI, Mustapha (b. 1937). Tunisian novelist and diplomat. His largely autobiographical novels, La Rage aux tripes (1975), Le Bruit dort (1978), Gloire des sables (1982), and La Montagne du lion (1988), explore the traumas of the decolonized. Although Tlili is Tunisian, his protagonists are war-scarred Algerian intellectuals, caught in the bind between their past and their present. In many respects the novels read like detective stories; they are set in the milieu of international civil servants in the context of decolonization. (Tlili himself is a veteran international civil servant at the United Nations.)

His first three novels, although different in their style and techniques of writing, have a similar storyline: a Paris-bred Algerian journalist/intellectual moves in the diplomatic world of New York and is torn between political engagement and an artistic vocation. This traumatized character is restless and unsatisfied. His only anchorage is his writing, where all his tensions and obsessions are exhibited and exhausted. Tlili's recent novel, La Montagne du lion, is the most lyrical and accomplished of his work. It is an indictment of the regimes of Independence, symbolized by the recurrent image of the megalomaniac dictator, which have, in the name of progress, subverted the traditional order of things, 'l'ordre clair et délibéré des choses', in this desert community.
[HA-J]

TOCQUEVILLE, Alexis de (1805–59). Political thinker and politician; major French theorist of liberal democracy. Born into an aristocratic family connected with the Bourbon monarchy, he began a legal career in government service in 1827. In 1831–2 he spent a year in America helping to prepare a study of the penal system there, published in 1833. His two-volume *De la *démocratie en Amérique* (1835–40), based on this experience, was an immediate success and secured his reputation as a writer, as well as election to the Académie Française. Leaving government service, he entered politics, serving as an independent *député* for Valogne (Normandy) from 1839, and was briefly foreign minister in 1849. After Louis-Napoléon's *coup d'état*, which he opposed, he left politics to work on the history of the French Revolution, towards which he completed an influential introductory study, *L'Ancien Régime et la Révolution* (1856).

A conscientious but unimpressive politician, Tocqueville was a poor orator with a notoriously ponderous written style, and was uncomfortable with the single-mindedness and partisanship of his more successful fellow *députés*. He tried to reconcile the legitimist Right to democracy and the republican Left to law and order. Before the February Revolution of 1848 he warned that deteriorating social conditions and the disenfranchisement of the people could lead to revolution, but he supported the conservative factions of the Second Republic [see REPUBLICS, 2].

Tocqueville's dominant concern was liberty, conceived as the absence of restraint and coercion and the availability of choices. Liberty was a necessary precondition for moral actions and the ideal towards which society should aspire. He placed a high value also on equality, social and political, which he saw as the measure of progress towards a higher degree of civilization. He recognized that the liberty of some could conflict with that of others, and he also saw that liberty could potentially conflict with equality. His proposed solution was a democratic state, bound by the rule of law, in which power was distributed among a plurality of institutions and associations, linked in a framework of checks and balances. The guarantee of such a system was the widest possible involvement of citizens in making and carrying out decisions. Tocqueville considered that such a democracy was already well advanced in America, and would and should be introduced gradually in France. He feared, however, that its attempted introduction by revolutionary means would entail serious risks for freedom.

[MHK]

See J. Lively, *The Social and Political Thought of Alexis de Tocqueville* (1962); M. Hereth, *Alexis de Tocqueville* (1986).

TODOROV, Tzvetan (b. 1939). Literary theorist and essayist. Of Bulgarian origin, he introduced the Russian Formalists to France in the anthology *Théorie de la littérature* (1965). *Introduction à la littérature fantastique* (1970) and *Poétique de la prose* (1971) belong to *Structuralism in their systematic

approach to literary practice. His later writing is less scientific; it includes essays on *Rousseau (*Frêle Bonheur*, 1985) and politics (*Face à l'extrême*, 1991).

[PF]

TOEPFFER, Rodolphe, see SWISS LITERATURE IN FRENCH, 3.

Tombeau des rois, Le, see HÉBERT, A.

Topaze, see PAGNOL.

Torrent, Le, see HÉBERT, A.

TORTEL, Jean (1904–93). Materialist poet, born in Avignon and deeply attached to the Midi. He understands poetic writing as a place of passage where the ephemeral retinal images of nature, 'flat but sumptuously there', are 'transferred' into figures of their transformation. His precise, unadorned writing is artisanal, the 'gesture of someone who shapes wood, lifts a burden'. A regular contributor to the *Cahiers du Sud* from 1938 until 1966, his work includes an important body of criticism and over 20 books of poetry, including *Les Villes ouvertes* (1965), *Limites du regard* (1971), *Des corps attaqués* (1979), *Le Discours des yeux,* (1982), and *Les Saisons en cause* (1987). [SN]

TORY, Geoffroy (c.1480–after 1553). One of the first generation of *humanist teachers in Paris, Tory is best known as a printer and as the author of *Champ fleury* (1529). His defence of the French language ('il faut écrire en français comme Français nous sommes') puts him amongst the forerunners of the movement epitomized by Du Bellay's *Défense et illustration*; but his belief in the analogical relationship between the letters of the Roman alphabet and parts of the universe looks back towards the Middle Ages. [JJS]

TOULET, Jean-Paul (1867–1920). French poet. Though he was well-known during his lifetime as a writer of novels, short stories, and travelogues, it was his poetry published in reviews from 1910 and in volume form (*Contrerimes*) in 1921, which established Toulet's reputation among the *Fantaisistes. In these poems his virtuoso mastery of technique resulted occasionally in little more than gratuitous verbal games which have harmed his reputation as a poet, but in the best examples it served a wide range of feelings, sensations, and moods, from fantasy to self-mocking disillusion and gentle irony, which display a serious and profound analysis of the modern sensibility. [JK]

TOULOUSE-LAUTREC, Henri de (1864–1901). French painter and graphic artist whose name is synonymous with striking poster design. He admired and was influenced by Japanese prints. Lautrec allied a remarkable command of line (economic, nervous, expressive) to an exceptionally effective *mise en page*. As an observer and recorder

Touraine

of aspects of working-class women's life and work (washerwomen, prostitutes, dancers, singers) he ranks with *Daumier, *Guys, *Degas, and *Manet, like them inventive in viewpoint and skilful in capturing movement. Despite unrestrained subject-matter—brothel scenes, lesbian couples, and erotic drawings—he was neither voyeuristic nor censorious. Recent criticism has detached his shrewd professional drive from the trappings of legend around his Parisian life. [HEB]

TOURAINE, Alain (b. 1925). French sociologist. His distinctive contribution to sociological analysis lies in his emphasis upon the activity and evolution, whether spontaneous or organized, of social movements which expose, confront, and sometimes transform existing power-structures and institutions (*La Voix et le regard*, 1978). Stimulated by the eruption of student revolt within his own university department in *May 1968, he went on to study anti-nuclear protest, the movement for greater Occitan autonomy in France, and the rise of Solidarity in Poland, devising a method of 'sociological intervention' whereby the investigator would interact with militant groups within a given movement in order to promote a self-analytic awareness of its dynamics. [REG]

Tour de France, Le. Before being accepted as masters by many guilds of craftsmen, apprentices had to complete a 'tour de France' within the system of *compagnonnage* which developed from the 15th c. as an organization for solidarity among artisans (see Agricol Perdiguier, *Mémoires d'un compagnon*, 1853).

Today the Tour de France is above all an annual three-week cycle race, created in 1903. This high point of the French sporting calendar is analysed as a modern epic in *Barthes's *Mythologies*. [PF]

Tour de la France par deux enfants, Le. The 'best-loved schoolbook' of turn-of-century France. First published in 1877, shortly before compulsory primary schooling was introduced, it had sold 6 million copies by 1900 and was familiar to several generations of children until 1914 and after. The author, behind the pseudonym 'G. Bruno', was Madame Alfred Fouillée (born Augustine Tuillerie). The famous opening sentence: 'Par un épais brouillard du mois de septembre, deux enfants, deux frères, sortaient de la ville de Phalsbourg en Lorraine', introduces André and Julien, whose adventurous journey from their conquered province all over France takes a whole school year, and gives the young reader an illustrated tour of a still-rural but progressive country. More patriotic and geographical than historical or political, the content was sufficiently neutral over religion to be used in both Church and state schools, though the revised edition of 1906 caused controversy by removing even phrases like 'Mon Dieu'. Although it avoids explicit *republicanism, the book's message is clearly humanist in tone, praising justice, compassion, and

industry, while condemning tyranny, and it is identified as one of the 'Lieux de mémoire' of the Republic in the collection edited by P. Nora in 1985. [SR]

Tour de Nesle, La, see NESLE.

Tour du monde en quatre-vingts jours, Le, see VERNE.

Tour Eiffel, La, see EIFFEL.

Tournaments, which figure prominently in medieval French literature, evolved in the late 11th and early 12th c. to test the equestrian skills demanded of knights in battle. In the early days these *mêlées* were often unintentionally dangerous— Count Geoffrey of Brittany was killed in one in 1186. Consequently the Church banned all such meetings, and did not change its mind until 1316. But although the French monarchs were thereby deterred from participating, the ban was not otherwise effective in limiting the spread of what became a very popular sport. In the interests of safety the proceedings were sometimes pared down to 'hastiludes'—mounted combat using only spears—or even jousts (single combat), and the chief aim became to unhorse and ransom opponents. The popularity of such encounters derived from the opportunity they provided for knights to enrich themselves and to catch the eye of potential noble patrons. The most striking example of upward social mobility achieved largely through prowess in tournaments was the careeer of William Marshal, a knight in the service of the Angevin kings of England who ended his life as earl of Pembroke and regent for the young Henry III. His exploits were celebrated in the *Histoire de Guillaume le Mareschal* [see ANGLO-NORMAN LITERATURE, 4].

The 1170s marked a proliferation of tournaments under the patronage of Count Philip of Flanders, Henry the Liberal of Champagne, and Henry, heir to the Angevin king Henry II. They became a spectator sport with a particular appeal to the ladies of the courts, who encouraged the development of heraldic devices for ease of recognition. The increasing emphasis on the splendour of apparel and equipment led to escalating costs and prevented all but the richest of lords from staging these spectacles for the rest of the Middle Ages. But those who could afford to do so regarded it as a worthy demonstration of their high social status. Tournaments were held in special places appointed for the purpose, and in celebration of marriages, knighting ceremonies, or other important occasions. Frederick Barbarossa's plans for the Third Crusade were hatched at a tournament, as were those of the counts of Blois and Champagne for the Fourth Crusade. As late as 1559, Henri II died as a result of an accident sustained in a tournament. [JHD]

See R. Barber and J. Barker, *Tournaments* (1989).

TOURNIER, Michel (b. 1923). French novelist and short-story writer for both children and adults.

Tragedy

Tournier began his career as a writer relatively late in life after an initial failure to become a philosopher (he failed the *agrégation* and continued to bear a grudge against his examiners, since he considered himself to be 'le meilleur de ma génération'). After a period spent as a broadcaster with Europe No. 1, his first two novels—*Vendredi ou les Limbes du Pacifique* (1967) and Le *Roi des aulnes* (1970)—won immediate critical acclaim (the former being awarded the Grand Prix du Roman de l'Académie Française, while the latter carried off the Prix Goncourt). He has for some time been considered one of the major French novelists of the post-war period.

Born to parents who were both teachers of German, Tournier spent four years studying philosophy in Tübingen after the end of World War II, returning to Paris to receive the check in his career which ultimately turned him towards literature. He gives his own view of the importance of these matters in his intellectual autobiography Le Vent paraclet (1977). His works bear the clear stamp of his love of ideas and particularly of those forms of systematic thought embodied in the great Germanic tradition of metaphysics. Those French intellectuals who have most influenced his work are *Sartre (although Tournier's disillusionment with what followed L'*Être et le néant* was perhaps as important as the positive side), *Lacan, and *Lévi-Strauss. As a writer of fiction he must be seen, and presents himself, as being in sharp disaccord with the dominant forms of the novel in France during the 1950s, 1960s, and 1970s, so that here also he owes more to the German tradition of such as Thomas Mann and Hermann Broch.

While many aspects of Tournier's writing have proved provocative, e.g. his reading of Christianity in Gaspard, Melchior, Balthasar (1980), and while his massive novel Les Météores (1975) revelled in scandalous topics, perhaps the area in which he has gained the greatest notoriety is in the view of children, childhood, and adolescence that pervades his work both thematically and formally, since much of his more recent writing refuses to accept the lines traditionally drawn to separate the adult and the non-adult worlds. It is particularly, though not exclusively, in his work as a *conteur* that Tournier plays upon the multiplicity of readings that superficially simple forms evoke in multiple readers; his first volume of stories, Le Coq de bruyère (1978), with its rewriting and subversion of ancient stories, from Adam and Eve to *Perrault's 'Le Petit Poucet', provides ample evidence of these. His theory of the nature of the *conte*—to be found in a volume of reviews and essays, Le Vol du vampire (1981)—holds that the form, being half-way between the opaque realism of the *nouvelle* and the transparent moralizing of the fable, is especially suited to his conception of the function of the writer, namely to enrich but not to enlighten, to leave the reader in touch with 'des figures qu'il ne parvient pas à saisir tout à fait'. This form is, for Tournier, ideally suited to the meeting of myth with the familiar world. In one of his most recent works, La Goutte d'or (1985), the story of a North African boy who comes to France as an immigrant worker, this conjunction serves to explore both race-relations in the post-colonial world and the status of the self within the complex interplay of literature and social existence.

While much that Tournier has written is didactic in tone, the reader is well advised never to assume that an authoritative voice is speaking, and to accept that the view being proposed is capable of many inflections and, indeed, reversals, since it is inescapably part of a greater system and its significance will shift as one moves within that system. His works are saved from being dogmatic by their fruitful suspension between—as one critic has put it—'"sens" and "écriture", truth and dissemination, structure and freedom'. They are just as challengingly open to readers of different ages and races as the *conte* could be in the hands of Perrault.   [IWR]

See S. Koster, *Michel Tournier* (1986); A. Bouloumié, *Michel Tournier: le roman mythologique* (1988); C. Davis, *Michel Tournier: Philosophy and Fiction* (1988).

Tours, Congrès de, see SOCIALISM AND COMMUNISM.

TOUSSAINT, François-Vincent (1715–72). French *philosophe* now remembered only for Les Mœurs (1748), a work of social and moral criticism at first attributed to *Diderot and condemned to be burnt. He took refuge in the Low Countries and then Berlin, working as a journalist and publishing novels.

TOUSSAINT, Jean-Philippe (b. 1957). French novelist whose brief texts La Salle de bain (1985) and L'Appareil-Photo (1988) have an eerie oddness. He is much admired as belonging to a new generation of the *Nouveau Roman; the term 'minimalism' has been used of him. Toussaint's heroes are unnaturally passive (one of them rarely leaves his bathroom); his world and his characters are viewed from an inconsequential angle. There is minute attention to detail, but causality is puzzling and free will absent: things happen, rather than being made to happen. He charms with his gentle guileless humour.   [GDM]

TOUSSAINT LOUVERTURE, see LOUVERTURE.

Tragédie du Roi Christophe, La, see CÉSAIRE, A.

Tragedy flourished in France over a period of about 250 years, between 1550 and the Revolution, with a high point in the middle of the 17th c. It differs from other dramatic genres in having given rise to a great deal of theorizing, most of it related to Aristotle's *Poetics* as mediated through the scholars of the Renaissance [see CLASSICISM].

French tragedy is characterized not so much by the emotional effects (pity, terror, catharsis)

807

Tragedy

mentioned by Aristotle or the ideological schemes developed by modern criticism from Hegel onward, as by the notion of *grandeur*. It was, with epic, the most elevated literary genre. Until the 18th c. it presented only persons of high rank, usually given lustre by being drawn from the distant world of Greek, Roman, or biblical myth, legend, or history. It was almost always written in verse (for the most part, *alexandrines), at least until the 18th c., when *La Motte and others made unsuccessful attempts to launch prose tragedy [for the mould-breaking 'tragédie bourgeoise' of *Diderot see DRAME].

1. Before 1630

The early 16th-c. idea of tragedy was still close to that of Chaucer's 'Monk's Tale', insisting on the morality to be drawn from the fall of great men; it was only after 1570 that *La Taille and *Vauquelin de la Fresnaye outlined a theory of tragic drama inspired by Aristotle. Tragedy in French was preceded by the Latin works of *Buchanan at Bordeaux, and by Lazare de *Baïf's French translation of Sophocles' *Electra* (1537). The first original French tragedy was Bèze's *Abraham sacrifiant* (1550), but it was Jodelle's Senecan *Cléopâtre captive* (1552/3) which set the pattern for *humanist tragedy with its very simple plot, extremely long speeches interspersed with passages of rapid dialogue (stichomythia), moralizing choruses, and rhetorical elaboration. Similar plays were written over the next 50 years, sometimes with more elaborate plots and greater psychological interest, by *Grévin, La Taille, *Montchrestien, and above all *Garnier, whose plays possess considerable poetic power. His *Les *Juives* represents a high point in Renaissance tragedy.

This type of tragedy has in recent years been increasingly appreciated on its own terms rather than as a preparation for later achievements. It was a literary rather than a theatrical phenomenon, remaining virtually unperformed outside the *humanist colleges. On the other hand, in the later years of the 16th c. tragedies began to be performed in the provinces, and then at the *Hôtel de Bourgogne in Paris, which showed little attempt to conform to the new rules of tragedy. This 'tragédie irrégulière' is best exemplified in the many plays of *Hardy. Such action-packed, free tragedies, together with the popular new genre of *tragicomedy, came near to eclipsing regular tragedy altogether (significantly, in 1628 *Schelandre rewrote his tragedy *Tyr et Sidon* as a tragicomedy, and *Ogier defied learned criticism in his preface to this reworking).

2. 1630–1700

The 1630s saw a remarkable revival of tragedy. New works were produced during this decade by *Mairet, *Scudéry, *Rotrou, *Du Ryer, *La Calprenède, *Tristan, and above all Pierre *Corneille. All of these respected, though with some freedom, the rules for the genre which had been outlined by Renaissance theorists, but were now reiterated by Mairet in his preface to *Silvanire* and more dogmatically by *Chapelain. In the years that followed, writers such as *La Ménardière, *Sarasin ('Discours sur la tragédie', 1639), d'*Aubignac, and eventually *Boileau completed the theoretical code of French tragedy. The most famous rules concerned the unities of place, time, and action: a tragedy should take place in a single setting, within a period of time not exceeding 24 hours, and should confine itself to a single plot. There were other stipulations concerning language and form, e.g. that within each of the five acts all the scenes should be linked, and more general recommendations for the construction of well-made plays. But the cardinal precepts were those insisting on *vraisemblance* and *bienséance*. The former ensured that the actions of the stage characters would seem credible; this meant, above all, conforming to audience preconceptions—or prejudices—about human psychology and the limits of probability. *Bienséance* worked in a similar way: 'la bienséance interne' laid down that characters should act in accordance with their rank, situation, and nature (as understood by contemporary audiences); 'la bienséance externe', that they should observe a proper decorum. And finally, it was axiomatic to classical critics that tragedy should be morally improving.

It was these rules that were invoked by Chapelain in his critique of Corneille's *Le *Cid*. Corneille, the dominant figure in French tragedy before 1660, was often at odds with scholars and purists over the unities and other matters; in his three 1660 *Discours* (on dramatic poetry, tragedy, and the three unities) he asserted his independence, arguing in particular that truth, even when improbable, was as good a basis for tragedy as *vraisemblance*. He also claimed that 'admiration' was as valid a tragic emotion as the Aristotelian pity and terror. His own tragedies, particularly those written before 1651, often seem remote from modern ideas of tragedy, with their optimistic images of heroic self-creation—or alternatively their pictures of such self-proclaimed monsters as Cléopâtre in *Rodogune*. In his later tragedies, on the other hand, confusion and failure are more in evidence, and the tragic outcome of *Suréna* is as irrevocable as anything in *Racine.

It is, of course, the latter who is the great tragic playwright of the later 17th c., although one should also mention such figures as Thomas *Corneille and *Quinault; these both contributed to the revival of tragedy in 1656 after a brief eclipse, and managed at their best to produce moving and effective drama. In Racine's case, an apparently easy observation of classical precepts goes with a probing of the dark core of human nature that makes him, in plays such as *Andromaque*, *Britannicus*, and *Phèdre*, more obviously akin than Corneille to the great tragedians of Greece. Only in the early *Alexandre le Grand* and in the late and untypical religious tragedies, *Esther* and *Athalie*, do we find endings that could be called optimistic.

By the time of Racine tragicomedy had disappeared from the stage, and regular tragedy was in competition with the *machine plays and their successor, the increasingly popular *opera (often called *tragédie lyrique*), in which psychological drama is subordinate to spectacle, music, and dance. When Racine retired from the secular stage in 1677 there was no tragic author to fill the gap. *Pradon, who had challenged *Phèdre*, continued to write tragedies, as did, with varying degrees of contemporary success—but no posthumous recognition—*Campistron, *La Grange-Chancel, *Longepierre, and others.

3. After 1700

While Racine, and to a lesser extent Corneille, retained their classic status throughout most of the 18th c., they found few successors worthy of note. The tragedies of *La Motte, *Lemierre, and de *Belloy enjoyed success in their time. *Crébillon *père* won a great reputation with his horror-filled tragedies on the classical model, but his fame was soon eclipsed by that of *Voltaire, who set out to become Racine's heir, and was seen as such by contemporaries, if not by posterity. He too conformed to classical rules, making some innovations (e.g. use of spectacular effects and exotic settings) and seeking both to move audiences and to win them over to progressive causes (e.g. *Mahomet*). For all their skilful construction, his plays too have been consigned to literary history.

Tragedy was challenged in the mid-18th c. by the *drame*. Even if this new genre had no great successes at the time, the future belonged to it [see DRAMA IN FRANCE AFTER 1789]. Tragedies continued to be written, from M.-J. *Chénier's patriotic *Charles IX* (1789) to the work of *Raynouard, *Lemercier, and Casimir *Delavigne, and the briefly successful *Lucrèce* of *Ponsard (1843), but tragedy as a genre was dead. This did not mean, of course, the disappearance of the tragic element in literature, however the notoriously slippery word 'tragic' is defined. There is more that is truly tragic, as most people understand the word today, in the novels and plays of the 19th and 20th c. than in most plays called tragedies. To speak only of the theatre, one sees a powerful tragic element in certain Romantic dramas, notably Musset's *Lorenzaccio*, in Becque's Les *Corbeaux*, or in some of *Claudel's Symbolist works (e.g. *Partage de midi*). In more recent times, *Giraudoux and *Anouilh, among others, have reworked such tragic subjects as Electra and Antigone, though with a twist, while *Sartre and *Camus at times convey an apparently tragic vision of the world in their plays. And the playwrights associated with the Theatre of the *Absurd, above all *Beckett, offer haunting images (at once comic and tragic) of a humanity deprived of the old comforts of belief. [PF]

See J. Scherer, *La Dramaturgie classique* (1950); J. Truchet, *La Tragédie classique en France* (1973);

C. J. Gossip, *An Introduction to French Classical Tragedy* (1981); G. Jondorf, *French Renaissance Tragedy: The Dramatic Word* (1990).

Tragicomedy. The French genre of *tragi-comédie* was popular with audiences from the late 16th c. to the middle of the 17th c. It was generally a play of love and adventure, a theatrical equivalent of the *romance and the *roman héroïque*, with a complex plot, surprising effects, and a happy ending, but not necessarily any comic features. Though written in verse, it did not usually conform to the rules of classical *tragedy. The first important example is Garnier's *Bradamante* (1582); the scores of tragicomedies written in the following decades include *Schelandre's reworking of *Tyr et Sidon*, plays by *Hardy, *Scudéry, *Du Ryer, and *Rotrou, and above all Pierre *Corneille's Le *Cid. With slight modification, *Le Cid* was later renamed a tragedy, since tragicomedy had fallen from fashion.

After the decline of the genre, tragicomedy left its mark on serious theatre; it is, in fact, often difficult to distinguish it from various related forms carrying different labels. Corneille's *comédies héroïques* such as *Don Sanche d'Aragon* are tragicomedies in all but name, as are romantic 'tragedies' such as Thomas *Corneille's *Timocrate*. [PF]

Tragiques, Les. D'*Aubigné's poetic account of the *Wars of Religion and justification of the Protestant cause, published in 1616, though mostly written nearly 40 years earlier.

Misères, the first of the seven books, laments the wretched state to which religious and civil conflict has reduced France and appeals for divine vengeance against such unnatural forces. *Princes* constitutes an attack, fuelled by righteous anger, against the Valois court, the Catholic aristocrats, and political leaders in this 'siècle tortu', for their treachery and immorality. *La Chambre dorée*, a satire on the processes of justice, describes the *chambre ardente* of *Henri II as seen from heaven and contrasts Queen Elizabeth of England with *Catherine de Médicis, the French Jezebel. *Les Feux* is a gruesome account of the sufferings of Protestant martyrs, and *Les Fers* sees the history of the Huguenot cause as a conflict between God and Satan, presenting individual battles and massacres in a series of 'tableaux célestes'. *Vengeances* gives a selective history of the Church from primitive times, concluding that God will ensure that the elect are avenged. Finally, *Jugement* attacks Protestant renegades, and debates immortality and the resurrection of the dead, as well as the bliss of the elect as God ultimately triumphs over Satan.

In his preface d'Aubigné notes that the style rises from low (Book I) to elevated (Books VI and VII), claims that his overall aim is to move rather than teach his readers, and admits to his 'passion partisane'. It is this fanaticism which binds together the prophetic and apocalyptic biblical vision, the

Calvinist theology, the Senecan and Juvenalian disillusionment, the classical allegory, contemporary history, and the rich baroque rhetoric and poetry, into a cosmic, epic equation of the reformed church and the Chosen People. *Les Tragiques* was ideologically and aesthetically out of tune with the age in which it appeared, but, in spite of much monotony, its timeless qualities ensured its revival in the 19th c. and an increasing interest in it today.   [PS]

Trahison de Marianne, La, see NANGA.

Trahison des clercs, La, see BENDA.

Traitant, a tax farmer, see TAXATION.

Traité des études, see ROLLIN.

Traité des sensations (1749). *Condillac's key philosophical work; it contains the comparison of the human being to a statue successively endowed with the different senses.

Traité du choix et de la méthode des études, see FLEURY, C.

Traité du sublime, translated from Longinus, see BOILEAU-DESPRÉAUX.

Traité sur la tolérance, see VOLTAIRE.

Transcendance de l'Ego, La, see SARTRE.

Translation. Few writers who specialized in translation are still remembered, and the genre occupies only a small place in most histories of literature. Yet many major French writers have also translated, and translation is a vital element in the national literature. Together with various forms of imitation and adaptation, it has allowed the culture of other nations to shape French writing; the principal foreign influences are traced here in separate entries [see BRITISH, IRISH, AND AMERICAN INFLUENCES, etc.]. In addition, at certain periods, translation has been a workshop in which a national prose style has been developed.

1. Medieval and Renaissance

For most of the medieval period non-French writings, mainly in classical or contemporary Latin, were made French by a process which is best described as adaptation or transposition. The notion of *translatio studii* implies that the achievements of ancient or foreign culture can find their equivalent in modern times, as for instance in the *romans d'antiquité*. Until the 13th c. it was normal to translate even prose works into the verse of vernacular literature [see ANGLO-NORMAN LITERATURE, 6, 7]. The *Bible was rendered into both prose and verse, but prose translation began to come into its own in the 14th c., with such work as *Jean de Meun's version of *Boethius; it flourished in the following century at the court of *Burgundy. Almost always, medieval translation was done with a view to transmitting content rather than re-creating style, but the

*Rhétoriqueurs at the end of the 15th c. used their translations to create a more latinate French, and the *humanist scholars of the 16th c. were to follow their example.

The *Renaissance period saw a great increase in translating activity, still mainly from Latin, but sometimes from Greek, and the appearance of writers who were primarily translators. As in the Middle Ages, many writers were bilingual, and there was a good deal of self-translation: *Du Bellay published Latin and French versions of the same poems; *Dolet, author of *La Manière de bien traduire* (1540), translated his own neo-Latin poetry; and *Calvin reissued his *Institutio* in French. Some translations were meant to be useful to students (e.g. the work of *Aneau and *Cordier), others (e.g. the many produced by Michel de Tours) were strongly latinate, but the main thrust was towards a good vernacular French which would be a worthy equivalent of the original; Dolet advises his reader: 'Il ne faut pas s'asservir jusques à là que l'on rende mot pour mot.'

Of the classical authors translated at this time, alongside Cicero, Ovid was perhaps the most popular [see CLASSICAL INFLUENCES]. Most of the major Renaissance poets and prose writers did some translation (*Montaigne's rendering of Raymond Sebond led to one of his greatest essays). Blaise de *Vigenère's contribution, including his penitential Psalms, was important, but the most significant work in terms of both quality and long-term literary influence was *Amyot's Plutarch (Amyot also translated the very popular Greek novels of Heliodorus and Longus). At the same time the *Evangelical movement and the *Reformation produced many translations of sacred texts; the example of *Lefèvre d'Étaples's translation of the Bible was followed by many others. The Psalms in particular, translated by *Marot and *Bèze, became rallying cries for Protestants during the *Wars of Religion.

A noteworthy 16th-c. development was the growing number of translations from modern languages, in particular Italian and Spanish. In addition to translations of such major figures as Petrarch, Boccaccio, and Castiglione [see ITALIAN INFLUENCES] or Guevara [see SPANISH INFLUENCES], one can cite the influential rendering of Bandello's *Novelle* as *Histoires tragiques* by *Belleforest and *Boaistuau, Des Essarts's version of *Amadis de Gaule*, and the many *pastoral novels and plays of Italy and Spain. *Don Quixote*, like many Spanish classics of the Golden Age, was translated (by Oudin) in the early 17th c.

2. Seventeenth and Eighteenth Centuries

While learned men continued to be bilingual in the 17th c., literary culture was increasingly dominated by a courtly or urban audience whose knowledge of ancient languages could not be taken for granted [see HONNÊTETÉ]. They demanded works written in elegant, unpedantic French, and translations helped to satisfy this demand. Indeed, translation was an ideal means of forging a modern prose style. Such was the ambition of many writers associated with the *Académie Française. *Conrart in particular encouraged the work of translators, who included the grammarian *Vaugelas, author of a famous translation of Quintus Curtius, and above all the highly productive *Perrot d'Ablancourt. Perrot's versions of Cicero, Tacitus, Xenophon, Caesar, Lucian, Thucydides, and others were dubbed 'belles infidèles' by *Ménage because of their free approach to the original. Such freedom was the norm during the classical period; it was practised by both camps in the *Querelle des Anciens et des Modernes. At the beginning of the 18th c., however, the 'querelle d'Homère' brought *anciens* and *modernes* to blows about the respective merits of the faithful but prosaic Homer of Anne *Dacier and the 'improved' verse *Iliad* of *La Motte (who knew no Greek).

Apart from Perrot's work, the two most important literary translations of the 17th c. are probably *Boileau's *Traité du sublime*, based on Longinus, and *La Bruyère's version of Theophrastus, the starting-point for his own *Caractères*. More broadly significant were the versions of *Descartes's *Méditations* and *Principes*, and above all the translating work of *Port-Royal. The key figure here was *Lemaître de Sacy, who was not only largely responsible for the Port-Royal Bible, but also translated the *Imitation of Christ* and (for pedagogical purposes) Terence and Phaedrus. At the same time *Huet wrote a treatise on translation, *De optimo genere interpretandi* (1661).

18th-c. translators looked increasingly to sources other than Greek, Latin, Italian, and Spanish. At the very beginning of the century appeared one of the most influential translations in French literature, Galland's *Les *Mille et une Nuits*, translated from the Arabic; exotic in a different way were the translations of ancient Scandinavian poetry published in the 1750s by abbé Mallet. But the most striking development was the flood of works translated from the English. These included Pope, Richardson, 'Ossian', and *Shakespeare; some famous authors contributed, including *Voltaire and *Diderot, but the most important translators from English were *Prévost, whose vast output included a free version of *Clarissa*, and *Le Tourneur, responsible above all for Ossian and for a complete Shakespeare in prose.

One feature worth noting in 18th-c. literary translation was in fact the tendency to translate verse by prose. In many cases (e.g. Pope) competing verse and prose versions were available, or else, as in the case of Shakespeare, verse translations (*Ducis) were made on the basis of prose ones. This practice gave rise to an ongoing debate, in which Voltaire in particular fought on behalf of verse translation. In later centuries *Chateaubriand and *Gide were respectively to translate Miltonic and Shakespearian verse by prose, but generally speaking poetry has been rendered in verse (free or otherwise) in the last 200 years.

3. Nineteenth and Twentieth Centuries

Since 1800 ever broader areas of world literature have been brought into French culture by translation, so much so that by 1990 translation occupied a place almost equal to French and francophone literature in bookshops and literary journals. The most important new sources are *Germanic, *Russian, and American (both North and South). In the same period there has been a growth in the discussion of problems of translation, both by practitioners (e.g. *Larbaud, *Valéry) and by theorists (e.g. Georges Mounin's *Les Problèmes théoriques de la traduction*, 1963, and Henri *Meschonnic's *Pour la poétique II*, 1973). Generally, the tendency has been towards a greater respect for the specificity of the original, as implied by Romantic notions of cultural difference. Chateaubriand, in his prose *Paradise Lost* (1836), deliberately adopted an odd French style, close to Milton's own usage. Going even further, *Littré published in 1879 a translation of Dante's *Inferno* in Old French.

It is perhaps unjust that over this period, when so many excellent translations have been published, no translators have established a name for themselves comparable to that of Amyot (or of Scott-Moncrieff, the British translator of *Proust). Of writers specializing in translation, one might pick out Pierre Leyris for his versions of writers as different as Dickens, Hopkins, Eliot, and Shakespeare. The most celebrated modern translations, however, are famous largely because they are the work of authors known for their original writings: *Nerval's *Faust*; *Baudelaire's versions of *Poe; Proust's Ruskin; Larbaud's Butler, Joyce, and Coleridge; *Bonnefoy's Keats and Shakespeare; *Jaccottet's Hölderlin, Rilke, and Musil. [PF]

See R. Zuber, *Les 'Belles Infidèles', et la formation du goût classique* (1968); G. Steiner, *After Babel* (1975); V. Worth, *Practising Translation in Renaissance France* (1988).

Trappe, Abbaye de la, see RANCÉ.

TRAUNER, Alexandre (1906–93). A set-designer (of Hungarian origin) with probably the longest continuing career in French cinema—from assistant on Clair's *A nous la liberté* (1931) through to Besson's *Subway* (1985). His great achievement remains his sets for *Carné, responsible as much as the actors or *Prévert's scripts for the films' potent atmosphere.
[KAR]

Travailleurs de la mer, Les (1866). Novel by *Hugo. The narrative is introduced by a geographically precise account of 'the Channel Archipelago', inspired by the landscape of Hugo's exile. The plot, epic and mythic in its dimensions, centres on the struggle of a simple fisherman, Gilliatt, to rescue the newly invented engine of a steamship, wrecked on the rocks. Gilliatt's confrontation with the fury of the natural forces, most arrestingly described in his fight with a giant octopus, is symbolic of the triumph of the human spirit over the forces of darkness. [SN]

Travel Writing. Descriptions of journeys take many forms—diary, letter, retrospective narration—and the journeys themselves spring from many different impulses—business, pleasure, adventure, science, escape, self-discovery, etc. The first French travel writing was a by-product of the medieval pilgrimages and *Crusades. *Villehardouin and *Joinville give some account of the countries visited by the crusaders, as do some of the poems of the *Crusade Cycle and the unheroic epic *Voyage de Charlemagne*. There are also accounts by private travellers, e.g. the late-14th-c. *Voyage de Jherusalem* of Ogier d'Anglure, with its descriptions of pyramids, elephants, and giraffes (see *Jeux et sapience du moyen âge*, ed. A. Pauphilet, 1951). *Mandeville's *Voyages* (c.1356) are largely a work of compilation, but their mixture of curiosity and imaginary creation prefigures many later developments in travel writing.

Printed accounts of the great voyages of discovery launched the new genre on its popular course. Of the French writers of the 16th and 17th c., the most influential were those writing about the New World, including *Léry, *Thevet, and *Villegagnon for South America, and Jacques Cartier, Samuel de Champlain, and the *Jesuit authors of the famous *Relations* for Canada [see QUEBEC]. Jesuits also wrote accounts of their missions in other lands, including China and India; these are some of the most informative works of their kind. Other classic accounts of travels in Africa and Asia were written by *Belon du Mans, *Villamont, Ogier Ghiselin de Busbecq (*Turkish Letters*, written in Latin, 1555–62), *Bernier, *Chardin, *Tavernier, and *Thévenot. These travellers wrote with a view to publication; others, like *Montaigne and, in the 18th c., *Montesquieu, left travel diaries which were only published (posthumously) because of their authors' celebrity.

All these writers offered new information about the geography, fauna and flora, government, trade, customs, and culture of the countries they visited. Their writing was rarely subjective, more akin to science than to *autobiography. The same goes for their numerous successors in the 18th c., when the popularity of travel writing remained undiminished—being fed by *Prévost's 15-volume *Histoire générale des voyages* (1746–59). French travel writers of the period include *Labat, *Chastellux, *La Condamine, de *Brosses, *Bougainville, and *Bernardin de Saint-Pierre. An objective gaze did not, however, rule out a personal touch, as in the chattiness of de Brosses (admired by *Stendhal), the enthusiasm of Bougainville for Tahiti (an inspiration to *Diderot), and the romantic eloquence of Bernardin de Saint-Pierre.

Much travel writing was a vehicle for social, political, or philosophical comment; *La Hontan's accounts of his travels in North America are moulded by his subversive convictions. In the same way, inspired by real voyages, the many imaginary voyages of this period were full of criticism of the established order and dreams of *Utopia. Thomas

More's example was followed in their different ways by *Cyrano de Bergerac, *Veiras, *Foigny, *Tissot de Patot, and a century later by *Mercier and *Restif. The travel motif permeates much Enlightenment fiction, from Fénelon's *Télémaque* to Montesquieu's *Lettres persanes* and many of *Voltaire's *contes philosophiques*. 'Il est certain qu'il faut voyager', says *Candide during his improbable voyage of initiation into the ways of the world.

Travel writing underwent a sea-change with *Romanticism. While 19th-c. writers such as *Custine or *Gobineau continue to publish more or less accurate accounts of distant places, the emphasis is increasingly on the poetic sensibility of the observer, the ability to convey the essential quality of the alien place. Travel is also seen as a voyage of self-discovery, a way of reviving the exhausted energy of the tired European. Travel writing comes closer to autobiography. Two key figures here are Stendhal and *Chateaubriand. The former mixes compilation and first-hand observation in his Italian travel books, and breaks new ground with his description of the French provinces in the *Mémoires d'un touriste*, but always it is the author, with his opinions, aversions, and desires, who is at the centre of the picture. Chateaubriand's grandiose accounts of his American and oriental journeys are also pictures of the self, not without some fictional embellishment, and are recycled in his *Mémoires d'outre-tombe*. The early and mid-19th c. also saw the publication of distinctively personal travel books by *Nodier, *Gautier (*Voyage en Espagne*, 1843), *Hugo (*Le Rhin*, 1842), *Nerval (*Voyage en Orient*, 1851), and *Taine (*Voyage aux eaux des Pyrénées*, 1855).

The mid- to late 19th c. was the second great period of French *colonization. This is reflected in the travelogues of a *Fromentin (*Un été dans le Sahara*, 1857) or of a *Loti, and more indirectly in the imaginary voyages of Jules *Verne and the heroic adventures of *Malraux's novels. There is a strong globe-trotting element in much 20th-c. French literature, e.g. the fictions of *Larbaud, the poems of *Cendrars, and (in a blacker mode) Céline's *Voyage au bout de la nuit*, closely based on its author's travels. As for travel writing proper, two outstanding figures are the utterly different *Segalen and *Morand, but one should also mention *Gide's political journeys, *Michaux's inward-looking *Un barbare en Asie*, and *Leiris's *L'Afrique fantôme*. Many of these express a typically modern distrust of the confident travel narrative; writing at the end of Empire, *Lévi-Strauss too voices his dislike for the genre at the beginning of *Tristes tropiques*, which is in its way one of the great travel books of the 20th c.

Some prominent novelists of recent decades, including *Butor and *Le Clézio, have written extensively about foreign travel, and more generally the late 20th c. has seen a renewed interest in travel literature, witnessed in the republication of classics of the genre, the launching of the periodical *Gulliver*, and the essays collected in *Pour une littérature voyageuse* (1992). Among the writers associated with this movement are the Scottish-French poet Kenneth White (b. 1936); Michel Le Bris (b. 1944), author of *L'Homme aux semelles de vent* (1977); the Swiss writer Nicolas Bouvier (b. 1929), whose *L'Usage du monde* (1963, reissued 1985) is a landmark in the new travel writing; and Jacques *Lacarrière. Lacarrière's *Chemin faisant*, a journey through France, showed that travel writing need not be exotic. Even closer to home, François *Maspéro has described a journey through the depressed Parisian suburbs (*Les Passagers du Roissy-Express*), and Jacques *Réda writes evocatively in prose and verse of his wanderings through the heart of France.   [PF]

See G. Atkinson, *Les Relations de voyages au 17e siècle et l'évolution des idées* (1924); M. B. Campbell, *The Witness and the Other World: Exotic European Travel Writing, 400–1600* (1988); A. Borer et al., *Pour une littérature voyageuse* (1992).

Traversée, La, see MAMMERI.

TREMBLAY, Michel (b. 1942). Canadian dramatist and novelist whose work is the most significant achievement in modern Quebec theatre. His preeminence was established by his first play, *Les Belles-Sœurs* (1968), and reinforced by a long line of later works, including *A toi pour toujours, ta Marie-Lou* (1971), *Bonjour là, bonjour* (1974), and *Sainte Carmen de la Main* (1976).

While these plays express a mood of social frustration and alienation which had already been articulated by predecessors like *Dubé and *Gélinas, Tremblay's handling of such common themes is marked by powerful characterization and a refined sense of dramatic form. He sees his uncultured, mainly working-class, characters in part as social victims, deprived of opportunity and bemused into accepting their wretched lot by the mystifying power of the Catholic Church. But they can also be energetic, transcending their misfortunes through caustic lucidity and heroic action. Nowhere is this truer than in the sleazy underworld of male prostitutes and drag queens who are among his most colourful creations (*La Duchesse de Langeais*, 1969; *Hosanna*, 1973). Here sexual deviance is initially a mask for moral failure, but then becomes a courageous choice of personal identity. This boldness of vision is matched by formal inventiveness. The combination of vigorously demotic *joual with musical structures and chorus effects inspired by classical drama produces a theatre that is at once immediately popular and of great formal sophistication.

It is no doubt his sure sense of stagecraft that has enabled his work to evolve in pace with a changing social climate, while remaining remarkably close to its initial inspiration. Plays such as *Albertine en cinq temps* (1984), *Le Vrai Monde* (1987), and *La Maison suspendue* (1990) are in direct continuity with the early work, while being freer in tone and less sombre in mood. A more relaxed inspiration is also evident in the cycle of novels which represent his most substantial achievement outside the theatre. From *La Grosse Femme d'à côté est enceinte* (1978) to *Le Premier Quartier de la lune* (1989) these draw on the same Plateau Mont-Royal district of Montreal as his plays, and involve some of his stage characters, but they have in general a more easygoing realism, heightened by recurring moments of drama and fantasy. Although uneven in fictional power, they undoubtedly add to the weight and substance of his work, as do two very atmospheric volumes of memories of his childhood: *Les Vues animées* (1990) and *Douze coups de théâtre* (1992). Altogether he is the most considerable literary figure in contemporary Quebec and possibly in Canada as a whole.   [SIL]

TRENET, Charles (b. 1913). French singer-songwriter, also novelist and painter. The frenetically cheerful young man whom the critics called 'le fou chantant' when he took the ABC music-hall by storm in 1938 is also generally credited with the launching of the poetic current in the popular *chanson française* since the Liberation. His fantastical lyrics borrow elements from the playful side of *Surrealism and poets such as *Fort, *Cros, and *Jacob, set to racy, syncopated, jazz-inspired music ('Je chante', 1937). He can be subtly comic, or indulge in tongue-twisting word-play ('Débit de l'eau débit de lait', 1943); his nostalgic refrains ('La Mer', 1945) have the charm of *Verlaine allied with the catchiest of tunes ('Que reste-t-il de nos amours', 1943). With his 1988 concerts he celebrated 50 years of virtually uninterrupted popularity.[PGH]

Trente arpents, see RINGUET.

Trésorière, La, see GRÉVIN.

TRESSAN, Louis-Élisabeth de la Vergne, comte de (1705–83). French courtier and soldier, remembered for his pioneering collection of medieval *romances. He adapted many of the most famous stories (*Tristan, *Lancelot, etc.) for the *Bibliothèque universelle des romans*; these are patchworks of various versions, with Tressan's own comments.

Trévoux, Mémoires de (also known as the *Journal de Trévoux*). The first lastingly successful religious journal was founded in 1701 by the *Jesuits, partly to counter the *Journal des savants*. Generally published monthly, printed in eastern France but compiled in Paris, it reviewed new publications, concentrating on theological, philosophical, and historical works. Accountable to the father-general of the order, successive editors published articles combating Protestantism and the *Jansenists, and aspects of Cartesian, Newtonian, and *Enlightenment thinking. Attentive to issues concerning language and grammar, the journal also reflected the order's internationalism by its coverage of intellectual life

Tribulat Bonhomet

abroad. Its influence declined after the expulsion of the Jesuits. [MP]

Tribulat Bonhomet, see VILLIERS DE L'ISLE-ADAM.

Tribun du peuple, Le, see BABEUF.

Trilby, le lutin d'Argail, see NODIER.

Trimètre, L'Alexandrin, see VERSIFICATION, 2.

Triolet (verse form), see RONDEAU, RONDEL.

TRIOLET, Elsa (1896–1970). Of Russian origin (she was born Elsa Kagan and was the sister of Mayakovsky's lover Lili Brik), Triolet owes her reputation to her role in the Resistance: together with her partner Louis *Aragon, she was a founding member of the Comité National des Écrivains and worked on the clandestine *Les Lettres françaises*. Her fiction from the Occupation period constitutes her most powerful and accomplished work: two novels, *Mille regrets* (1942) and *Le Cheval blanc* (1943), and the collection of short stories which won the 1945 Prix Goncourt, *Le Premier Accroc coûte deux cents francs* (1945). Her post-war fiction was essentially Socialist Realist, but retained an element of fantasy and often returned to the preoccupation with the role of women in the Resistance. [NH]

Trissotin. Comic figure of a self-important writer in Molière's *Les *Femmes savantes*, reputedly modelled on *Cotin.

Tristan. Hero of one of the most influential legends in French literature, whose love for Iseut provided a model for adulterous love (both courtly and tragic) throughout the Middle Ages and down to the present day. Tristan's influence has been felt by lyric poets, romance writers, and novelists, as well as by non-literary artists. A comparison of the surviving 12th- and 13th-c. versions allows us to extrapolate the following underlying narrative scheme.

The nephew of King Mark of Cornwall, Tristan defends Mark's kingdom in judicial combat and kills the Irish champion, Morholt, who had come to claim a regular tribute of Cornish boys and girls. Later Tristan, who is Mark's heir, is instrumental in organizing his uncle's marriage with Iseut, princess of Ireland and Morholt's niece, but as a result of drinking a magic potion accidentally served by Iseut's maid Brangien, the nephew and the uncle's bride find themselves fatally committed to loving each other. There are several attempts by members of Mark's court to trap the pair and have them condemned; Mark's attitude is unstable, swinging from almost farcical jealousy (when he climbs a tree to spy on them) to a naïvely loving trust. The couple undergo a period of banishment together, and Iseut has to undergo trial by oath and ordeal; eventually Tristan is exiled to Brittany, where he marries a second Iseut but never consummates his marriage. Tristan dies of grief, succumbing to a poisoned

wound when, out of jealousy, his wife lies and tells him that Iseut la Blonde has refused to come to tend him. Iseut arrives to find Tristan dead, and herself dies of a broken heart. They are buried next to each other and a dog-rose and a vine grow from their graves, intertwining inseparably.

The origins of the legend seem to lie with the Picts of eastern Scotland. Tristan's name has been associated with Drust, a Pictish prince of the 8th c.; his home, Loonois, identified with Lothian; and the forest of Morrois, to which the lovers flee when condemned to death, with Moray. However, by the 12th c. the story is firmly located in Cornwall and Brittany, Tristan's own land being Léon (Finistère). The hero's name is now explained by his being an orphan, whose mother died giving birth to him. He is thus destined to sorrow ('tristesse').

Two full-length versions of his legend in verse survive from the 12th c., fragmentary texts by Béroul (4,400 continuous lines in one manuscript) and Thomas (3,080 lines in all, in seven fragmentary manuscripts, two of which were lost at the end of the 19th c.); a third by *Chrétien de Troyes (who refers to his version as being 'about King Mark and Iseut la Blonde') is lost. Béroul's version dates probably from the 1160s, though it has been placed in the 1190s, and is usually considered the 'non-courtly' version because of the comparative barbarity of some of the scenes, the bloodthirstiness exhibited by all characters in the pursuit of vengeance, and the survival of many folkore elements (Mark has horse's ears, Tristan is skilled in woodcraft, an important role is given to an astrologer-dwarf). Certainly Béroul was working in the oral tradition, as witness some of the inconsistencies of his text (the evil trinity of barons hounding the lovers is permanently reconstituted, even after one or other has been killed), but the scenes with King Arthur, the use of terms like *losengier* (tale-bearer), and the role of Brangien as go-between show that he was familiar with courtly literature. Also, although in Béroul the love potion acts as an instrument of external destiny robbing the lovers of any choice, he also uses it to conduct a debate on the role of intention in crime and sin, indicating that he was aware of contemporary learned controversy and probably working in courtly rather than popular circles.

The version by Thomas, dated to the 1170s, is normally described as the 'courtly' version, since the love between Tristan and Iseut is only partly determined by the potion, which is given a largely symbolic role in this text, thereby ensuring at least a measure of that free choice by the lovers which was considered vital to a genuinely 'courtly' relationship. Thomas also devotes much space to exploring the psychology of his characters through the kinds of interior debate favoured by the *romans d'antiquité* and Chrétien de Troyes. His version smooths out many of the violent edges of the Béroul version: the harsh life of outlaws led by the lovers in the forest of Morrois is replaced by an idyllic existence in a cave (an episode not extant in the surviving fragments); and later, in Brittany following his marriage, Tristan organizes a veritable chapel to his love in a grotto, complete with statues which he contemplates in a transport of adoration that gives concrete expression to the inherent fetishism of *fin'amor*. Tristan's marriage to a second Iseut, and his final death from a wound suffered serving the love of a second Tristan, permit the exploration of many facets of love, including the relationship between love, marriage, and jealousy and the place of adventure in love-service.

Tristan's periods of exile allowed many writers to invent episodes to fill this part of the biography. *Marie de France's *Chevrefoil* tells of a meeting in the forest as Iseut travels to court. The substance of the meeting is a brief interview, but the significance of the text lies in the characters carved on the hazel twig with which Tristan attracts Iseut's attention (a transposition into the 12th-c. French text of magic ogham or runic engravings), and in the symbol of the symbiotic existence of the honeysuckle and the hazel, which Tristan evokes.

Two writers of the early 13th c. composed versions of the *Folie Tristan*, in which Tristan, mad with love, disguises himself as a fool to return to court and exploits the privileges of his assumed role to recount in the presence of Mark significant episodes from his love for Iseut, who also hears them, the ultimate purpose being to gain a private meeting with his mistress. The texts, identified by the libraries which now house the manuscripts, are related, one to Béroul's version (*Folie de Berne*), one to Thomas's (*Folie d'Oxford*). Our knowledge of the fragmentary 12th-c. texts is completed by two translations into German (by Eilhard von Oberge and Gottfried von Strasburg) and by the Norse *Tristrams saga ok Isonde*. In the 13th c., under the influence of the prose *Lancelot*, the story of Tristan was developed in a vast prose romance (composed *c.*1230), in which the original tale is dwarfed by a long Arthurian elaboration. Far from fleeing to the Morrois, the lovers now remove themselves to Logres, where Tristan fights in a series of tournaments in which his chief opponent is a Saracen, Palamedés, also in love with Iseut, and his inseparable companion is Dinadan, a brave but cynical knight never slow to pour scorn on chivalric convention. Tristan also becomes a knight of the Round Table and participates in the Quest for the *Grail before leaving Logres to allow the inevitable denouement. [PEB]

See G. Schoepperle, *Tristan and Isold: A Study of the Sources of the Romance* (1913); P. Jonin, *Les Personnages féminins dans les romans français de Tristan au XIIe siècle* (1958); E. Baumgartner, *Le Tristan en prose: essai d'explication d'un roman du XIIIe siècle* (1975) and *Tristan et Yseut* (1987).

TRISTAN, Flora (1803–44). Early socialist and feminist writer, now celebrated for her passionate obser-

vation and denunciation of the social conditions of oppressed and marginal groups (*Promenades dans Londres*, 1840; *Le Tour de France*, published 1973), and for her struggle to achieve working-class solidarity (*L'Union ouvrière*, 1843) and to secure rights for women.

She was the daughter of a Spanish aristocrat, born in Peru, and grandmother of the painter *Gauguin. Brought up in Paris by a mother fallen on bad times, in 1821 Flora married the painter and lithographer André Chazul. His violence forced her to leave him. From 1825 to 1830 she served as companion to English ladies. In 1833 she left France for Peru, and this journey was later the subject of *Pérégrinations d'une paria* (1837). Back in France in 1834, she built up close links with the growing working-class movement and published her first political texts on women's questions. In 1838 her novel *Méphis* showed the female character Maréquita finding her emancipation through the proletarian artist Méphis.

[BR]

TRISTAN L'HERMITE (*c.*1601–1655). French poet and dramatist. François l'Hermite took this name because of a supposed family connection with Louis XI's counsellor so called; he is sometimes referred to as Monsieur (de) Tristan. Of noble birth, he was brought up in the royal household as page to Henri de Bourbon, until in 1616 he killed a stranger in a fit of temper and fled the country. In *Le Page disgrâcié* (1642–3) he gives a racy account of his adventures in England, Scotland, and Norway, with much picaresque embellishment. On his return he joined the household of Gaston d'*Orléans, with whom he remained, on and off, for some 20 years. He was elected to the Académie Française in 1649, with a deserved reputation both as poet and as dramatist.

At home in high society, he was in touch too with the freer spirits of the time such as *Théophile, and valued nothing more highly than the creative freedom of the artist. Much of his poetry, however, was written perforce for courtly circles—praise of the great, or elegant variations on the commonplaces of *galanterie* derived from the neo-*Petrarchans and *L'*Astrée*. He may have learned from *Malherbe his sure handling of odes, *stances*, and sonnets, but he replaces marmoreal grandeur with musical fluidity. He is fond of Ovid and the Italians, declaring Tasso superior to Virgil, and like *Marino, whom he often echoes, he lets *concetti* play freely over the surfaces of things; but he shares with Théophile a subtler sensitivity to nature, besides an ardent temperament, and the interfusion of these factors produces some highly attractive poetry, as in 'Le Promenoir des deux amants' (set to music by *Debussy). 'La Mer' is a remarkable exercise in baroque description. Other poems reveal an underlying moral seriousness and melancholy, and a Stoic dignity in the face of death.

In 1636, the same year as *Le *Cid*, Tristan achieved an outstanding success with his tragedy *La*

Tristes tropiques

Marianne. Among his other plays, *La Mort de Sénèque* (performed 1644) and the tragicomedy *La Folie du sage* (published 1645) are full of dramatic interest. Though with occasional lapses, he demonstrates the virtue of clear construction, vivid confrontations, and boldly conceived characters, in portraying which he shows sharp psychological insight. [AJS]

See N. M. Bernerdin, *Un précurseur de Racine: Tristan l'Hermite* (1895); A. Carriat, *Tristan ou l'Éloge d'un poète* (1955); D. Dalla Valle, *Il Teatro di Tristan l'Hermite* (1964).

Tristes tropiques, see LÉVI-STRAUSS.

Trobairitz. The Occitan term for a female *troubadour. For only two do we have more than one surviving piece: *Castelloza and the *Comtessa de Dia (both early 13th-c. composers of love songs). Single songs are attributed to Azalais de Porcairagues, Beatriz de Romans, Clara d'Anduza, and a fragmentary one (one stanza) to Tibors. There is one *sirventes*, a formal imitation (*contrafactum*) of a work by Guilhem de Figueira, attributed to a woman, Gormunda de Monpeslier. Several other *sirventes*, some of them fragmentary, appear to be by women, but are not ascribed to one by the manuscripts. A *salutz*, or letter of greeting, to a certain Clara is credited to Azalais d'Altier. It is difficult to say with certainty how many of the remaining poems containing stanzas in a first-person female voice were actually composed by women. There are several dialogue poems between two female voices; some exchanges of *coblas* [see CANSO] between a male and a female voice; some debate poems between a well-known male poet and a female voice; and a number of anonymous songs in a more popular style, allegedly sung by a woman, but whose authorship is simply unknown.

For only very few of the named women do we have any biographical information. The most famous is probably Maria de Ventadorn, participant in a *tenso with Gui d'Ussel, wife of Ebles V of Ventadorn and known elsewhere as a patron of troubadours. A few other *trobairitz*—the Comtessa de Dia, Garsenda de Proensa, and Lombarda—are named in charters. In most cases, the female name appearing in a manuscript is the sum total of our information. Arguments about attribution are not furthered by assertions from some quarters that certain stanzas ascribed to women are too proficient to be by anyone but men. With the limits of the corpus so uncertain, it is hard to characterize the poetry of the *trobairitz*. The love-songs veer between women's vindication of the right to sing their love and anxiety at being put in the wrong. In the dialogue genres, the women's stanzas often serve to undermine the 'courtly' posture of the male participant. The most interesting poem in some respects is *No.m puesc mudar no digua mon veiaire*, an attack on the misogyny of male poets such as *Marcabru. It is characteristic of the shadowy existence of the *trobairitz* that this *sirventes* is attributed to a man. Indeed, many of the songs ascribed to women are marginal to the manuscript tradition, being transmitted only by a single *chansonnier*. [SK]

See W. D. Paden (ed.), *The Voice of the Trobairitz: Perspectives on the Women Troubadours* (1989).

Trobar clus, Term used frequently by modern critics, but rarely by the *troubadours themselves, to designate a style of hermetic poetry thought to have been popular, though controversial, in mid-12th-c. Occitan courts. The *trobar clus*, literally 'closed poetry', is often opposed to the *trobar leu*, 'easy' or 'open' poetry, on the basis of a celebrated *tenso in which *Raimbaut d'Aurenga and *Giraut de Bornelh defend respectively the *clus* and *leu* styles. However, the piece is ironic in tone, offers no definitions, and is probably a joke at the expense of its audience. Though some troubadours and patrons enjoyed the hermetic style, it seems likely that courtly audiences demanded less exacting poetry. *Marcabru and *Peire d'Alvernhe are thought to have been influential in the evolution of the *trobar clus*, but neither uses the term; *Arnaut Daniel is considered a later practitioner. The *trobar clus* is difficult to define, as the term is never used by the troubadours with an exact technical sense. It is, however, possible to surmise that it is characterized by metrical complexity, difficult rhyme sounds, allusive metaphors, and opacity. The troubadours' thinking on style was clearly influenced by Latin rhetorical theory. [SG]

Trois contes. Collection of stories by *Flaubert, composed relatively quickly and published in 1877. Linked by the theme of sainthood, the stories are nevertheless very different in subject-matter, in historical and geographical setting, and above all in tone. The third, *Hérodias*, Flaubert's version of the beheading of John the Baptist at the behest of Salomé, follows the classical unities to trace events from one dawn to the next, largely from the viewpoint of Hérode-Antipas. The second, *La Légende de saint Julien l'Hospitalier*, recounts the life of the medieval saint. The willed naïvety of tone is emphasized by the famous closing reference to the narrator's supposed source (a stained-glass window in Rouen Cathedral), and serves to distance the sexuality and violence of the Oedipal story-line. The first, *Un cœur simple*, evokes the Normandy of Flaubert's own childhood, through the life of a simple and selfless servant who loses the objects of her devotion one after another (boyfriend, mistress's daughter, sailor nephew, mistress, parrot), and who ends her long life taking comfort in material remnants of her past. The most famous is her stuffed parrot, whom she confuses in a dying vision with the Holy Ghost. Flaubert claimed to have written this story to move his readers to tears, and purely to please his friend George *Sand who despaired of his cynicism. The stuffed parrot which he kept on his desk (to imbue his soul with the spirit of parrothood) has inclined many critics to an ironic reading. [DK]

Trois Glorieuses, Les. The three days of fighting (27–29 July 1830) which sealed the fate of the *Bourbon monarchy and ushered in the *July Monarchy.

Trois Mousquetaires, Les (1844). Novel by Alexandre *Dumas *père*. Serialized in *Le Siècle* from March to July 1844, *Les Trois Mousquetaires* was published in eight volumes later in the year. It is one of Dumas's truly great popular, pseudo-historical novels, whose appeal has never waned from its first appearance as a *roman-feuilleton* to the repeated revivals and adaptations in the press, cinema, and television. The names of D'Artagnan, Athos, Porthos, and Aramis have become an integral part of world mass culture, having been initially discovered by Dumas in *Courtil de Sandras's fictionalized *Mémoires de M. d'Artagnan* (1700).

Dumas wrote his novel in collaboration with Auguste *Maquet (who provided the historical notes and sketched out the chapters). Historical accuracy was not a priority for him. Once he had set the scene for four dashing musketeers to defend Louis XIII against the manœuvres of *Richelieu, Dumas was free to exploit all his talents for creating exciting and colourful narrative, held together by a sequence of duels, the ultimate of these being the conflict between D'Artagnan and the *femme fatale* Milady, agent of Richelieu. This sexual confrontation adds a deeper and darker dimension to the *Boy's Own* quality of the novel, which culminates in the thrilling Gothic finale of Milady's execution. [BR]

Trois Villes, Les, see ZOLA.

TRONCHIN, Jean-Robert (1702–88). Procureur Général of Geneva in 1762, responsible for the condemnation of *Rousseau's works. His anonymous *Lettres écrites de la campagne* (1763) provoked Rousseau's *Lettres écrites de la montagne*. Like his brother François and his cousin Théodore (1709–81), a famous physician, he was a close friend of *Voltaire.

Trophées, Les, see HEREDIA.

Tropiques (1941–5). Literary magazine founded by Aimé and Suzanne *Césaire and René *Ménil in Martinique under the Vichy regime (14 issues). Reassessing Caribbean reality (the African heritage of oral traditions, local natural history) in the light of *Surrealist poetics and the expanding horizons of *négritude*, the magazine had a revitalizing impact. [BJ]

Tropismes, see SARRAUTE.

TROTEREL, Pierre (b. *c.*1586). French dramatist. His varied output is one of the most theatrically

imaginative of the early 17th c., and includes *Les Corrivaux* (published 1612) and *Gillette* (performed 1619), comedies notable for their lively dialogue and satirical observation within the framework of farce, and *Sainte Agnès* (published 1615), one of the earliest religious tragedies to develop a dramatic conflict. [GJM]

Troubadours. Poets composing in medieval *Occitan and, more narrowly, composers of Occitan *lyric poetry, troubadours are the precursors of the northern French *trouvères. They were musicians and performers as well as poets. Troubadours came to be associated with all the major courts of Occitania, and were also in demand in the courts of Spain, Portugal, northern Italy, England, and northern France. Although less than half of their surviving compositions deal with love, it is to the troubadours that we owe the earliest literature of *fin'amor and the promotion of an ideal of *cortezia, or 'courtliness' [see COURTOISIE].

The earliest known troubadour, *Guilhem IX (1071–1126), established the importance of Poitou and Aquitaine as a centre of patronage, and the next generation of known troubadours (including *Marcabru, *Cercamon, *Jaufre Rudel) all had some degree of dependence on his successor, Guilhem X. The 'generation of 1170' (so called because in that year the troubadour *Peire d'Alvernhe composed a song, each of whose 12 stanzas sketches a satirical portrait of a fellow poet) numbers some of the most famous troubadours: *Bernart de Ventadorn, *Giraut de Bornelh, *Raimbaut d'Aurenga. In fact, the careers of several of these poets overlapped with that of Marcabru, at least; and in their works, which should often be read as interventions in a discussion rather than as isolated pieces, questions of love and poetic style are vigorously debated. The development of individual and even idiosyncratic views on these issues characterizes the next wave of major poets, all of whom have left substantial *œuvres*: *Gaucelm Faidit, *Arnaut Daniel, *Bertran de Born, *Peire Vidal, Raimon de Miraval. The Albigensian Crusade (1209–*c.*1229) [see CATHARS] prompted poetry of a different, more satirical or nostalgic cast, by such troubadours as *Peire Cardenal and Guilhem de Montanhagol. *Giraut Riquier (*c.*1230–1292) is usually thought of as 'the last of the troubadours'.

Although deriving from a wide range of social backgrounds, troubadours composed in the context of aristocratic courts, either because (like Guilhem IX, Jaufre Rudel, Raimbaut d'Aurenga, or Bertran de Born) they presided over one themselves or because they had court employment of some sort. We have the names of 460 persons held to have composed lyric poetry in Occitan, and, according to Istvan Frank's *Répertoire métrique* (1953–7), 2,542 works survive that can be attributed to some 350 troubadours, a few of whom were women poets (or *trobairitz). Individual poems of the troubadours are

Trouvères

identified by the number assigned to them in Pillet and Carsten's *Bibliographie der Trobadours* (1933). [See LYRIC POETRY, I.]

[SK]

See M. de Riquer, *Los Trovadores: historia literaria y textos*, 3 vols. (1975); L. T. Topsfield, *Troubadours and Love* (1975); L. M. Paterson, *Troubadours and Eloquence* (1975).

Trouvères. Medieval poets composing narrative and, especially, lyric verse in the *langue d'oïl* [see LANGUE D'OC] until the late 14th c. They were the northern French equivalents of the *troubadours, responsible *inter alia* for continuing the remarkable vogue of the love-lyric within and outside France both in the 13th c., when the *canso took second place to the *sirventes in the Midi, and in the 14th c., when the southern successors of the troubadours were less widely known or appreciated. Sociolinguistic factors played a part here, the growing status of the *langue d'oïl*, particularly as used by predominantly aristocratic poets, enhancing the appeal of poetry expressing *fin'amor*.

Generalizations about the *trouvères* require more than one caveat. Evidence about their lives is very often extremely thin. Unlike the troubadours, almost all lack the doubtful benefit of a medieval biography. At least eight late *trouvères* worked in southern courts. Also, the proportion of anonymous lyrics or lyrics of doubtful attribution is far higher for *trouvères* than for troubadours, impeding historical assessment from internal evidence. Nevertheless extant lyrics can be ascribed to 276 *trouvères*.

The earliest known *trouvère* may well be *Chrétien de Troyes, to whom song-books plausibly ascribe two lyrics. Though at least one anonymous lyric (c.1146) pre-dates his activity, *trouvères* seem to have started composition somewhat later than the troubadours, probably following contacts made in northern French courts after the marriages of *Eleanor of Aquitaine and her offspring. Picardy, Wallonia, Lorraine, and Champagne were prominent areas of *trouvère* activity.

Few *trouvères* were evidently low-born professionals seeking patronage from the nobility (exceptions are *Colin Muset, *Rutebeuf). One or two (*Adam de la Halle, Guillaume de *Machaut), while not necessarily seeking patronage, certainly found it. But most *trouvères* were aristocrats, knights or members of the gentry (e.g. *Blondel de Nesle, Le *Chastelain de Couci, *Conon de Béthune, *Gace Brulé, *Gautier de Dargies, *Thibaut de Blaison); four were monarchs (e.g. Richard Cœur-de-Lion, *Thibaut de Champagne); some were monks or churchmen (e.g. *Gautier de Coinci, *Hélinand, Le *Reclus de Molliens, *Richard de Fournival, Machaut); others represented the growing bourgeoisie (e.g. *Jehan Bretel, Adam de la Halle, *Baude Fastoul, Jean *Bodel), even if the last two suddenly became social outcasts. Two *chansons de femme* and three *jeux partis* are attributed to ladies.

Almost all these were amateur poets, but may nevertheless have performed their own compositions in courts or *puys. The time-honoured distinction between author and interpreter is as questionable for *trouvères* and *jongleurs as for troubadours and joglars. [See LYRIC POETRY, I.]

[PVD]

TROYAT, Henri (pseud. of Lev Tarassoff) (b. 1911). An immensely successful best-selling author, Troyat is one of the most accomplished practitioners of realist fiction in France in the 20th c. His reputation was initially established through a series of short psychological novels, of which *L'Araigne* (1938) won the Prix Goncourt. In the 1940s he embarked upon a series of extended *romans-fleuves, beginning with the *Tant que la terre durera* cycle (1947–50), based upon his own experience of Tsarist and revolutionary Russia, and at the same time established himself as a major biographer of Russian literary and political figures. Successful as this production is, it is in his collections of short stories, such as *Le Geste d'Ève* (1964), where fantasy coexists with realism, that Troyat shows himself at his most innovative. [NH]

TROYES, Nicolas de, story-teller, see SHORT FICTION.

TRUBLET, Nicolas-Charles-Joseph, abbé (1697–1770). Essayist. A Breton by origin, he attached himself in Paris to *La Motte and *Fénelon, sharing their critical attitude to verse. His attacks on La *Henriade earned him the dislike of Voltaire, who mocked him in *Le Pauvre Diable* ('il compilait, il compilait, il compilait'). His *Essais de morale et de littérature*, first published in 1735 and often reprinted in augmented editions, are a record of the typical views of polite society, and are valuable as such. In 1761, in spite of *philosophe opposition, he achieved his ambition, membership of the Académie Française. [PF]

TRUFFAUT, François (1932–84). French film-maker, one of the pillars of the *Nouvelle Vague. Beginning as a critic, he was a founder member of *Cahiers du cinéma* in 1951. His films can be grouped in three main categories: films about Antoine Doinel, fairly autobiographical in nature (e.g. *Les 400 Coups*, 1959; *Domicile conjugal*, 1970); the film noir series, frequently playful homages to Hitchcock (e.g. *Tirez sur le pianiste*, 1960; *Vivement dimanche*, 1983); films about love (e.g. *Jules et Jim*, 1961; *La Femme d'à côté*, 1981). All have in common the difficulty of human relationships; solitude is a hallmark of his narratives. His films are tightly structured, often in the form of diptychs, with the opening sequence foreshadowing the rest of the film. [SH]

Tueur sans gages, see IONESCO.

Tunisia. Like its Maghrebian and Sub-Saharan counterparts, Tunisian literature in French is the result of *colonization. Tunisia became an independent state in 1956. Most Tunisian writing is in Arabic but, although their overall literary production remains limited, francophone Tunisian writers of the post-Independence generation, unlike their fellow writers from *Algeria and *Morocco, have quickly and effectively transcended the problematics of *decolonization and national identity. In the last decade, in particular, Tunisian literature in French (published for the most part in France) has become a forum for cross-cultural experiments that are more in consonance with *Postmodern aesthetic conceptions and intellectual preoccupations than with the concerns of post-colonial politics.

The best exponent of this new versatility is Albert *Memmi, Tunisia's leading writer. In his earlier writings Memmi examines, in terms of *Sartrean dialectics, the colonial situation and its consequences (cultural alienation, loss of identity, bilingualism, mixed marriage), especially for the educated among the colonized. The theme of colonialism is extended in the essays of the 1960s to that of dominance and oppression; in his later symbolic novels and his only book of poems, *Le Mirliton du ciel* (1990), Memmi explores more universal questions.

Mustapha *Tlili has written fiction rooted in a multi-cultural and multiracial context. His novels explore the psychological and social after-effects of colonization on his expatriate characters and explore the dialectic of exile and creation. With his two novels, and his poem *Tombeau d'Ibn Arabi*, Abdelwahab *Meddeb has established a secure literary reputation as a writer in the Postmodernist manner. His writing is encyclopaedic in its scope and themes. He practises collage as an expression of his many sundered sensibilities and moods, and enters into dialogue with kindred spirits, ancient and modern, from East and West. Like Meddeb, Fawzi *Mellah uses intersubjectivity and intertextuality as dialogic practices in his novels.

Poetry, however, remains the dominant genre in contemporary Tunisian writing (there is little significant dramatic work). Hédi *Bouraoui, an academic by training, has tried his hand at every conceivable genre: fiction, poetry, criticism, and drama, often fusing them in a fascinating and original manner. The poetry of Mohamed *Aziza is a constant search for a truer and more authentic self. For Majid *El-Houssi poetic language is a tool with which he subverts and manipulates his cross-cultural reality. In the promising work of Tahar Bekri (b. 1951), *Poèmes bilingues* (1978), *Exils* (1979), *Le Laboureur du soleil*, *suivi de les Grappes de la nuit* (1983), *Les Lignes sont des arbres* (1984), and *Le Chant du roi errant* (1985), poetic exploration is concomitant with the quest for identity. While the poetry of Abdelaziz Kacem (b. 1933) is serene and urbane, dwelling on symbols and myths as in *Le Frontal, suivi de AL? Dresden, on efface ton nom* (1983), that of Salah Garmadi (1933–82) and Moncef Ghachem (b. 1946) is dominated by anger and denunciation and is anchored in everyday reality. They write in a populist vein, debunk bourgeois social values, and promote revolution and freedom.

For Amina *Saïd, the best known of a number of contemporary women writers, the feminine lyrical voice is not only a catharsis but the catalyst of social, moral, and cultural emancipation.   [HA-J]

Turcaret. Comedy by *Lesage, first performed at the Comédie-Française in 1709, in spite of the actors' reluctance to offend the targets of Lesage's satire. In this brilliant play, a cynical remake of Molière's *Bourgeois gentilhomme*, Turcaret, a rich and unscrupulous financier of low birth, with pretensions to elegant living, is duped by the Baronne, a flirtatious widow, and her double-dealing Chevalier, and is exposed to ridicule when the wife he had been keeping in the provinces comes to Paris to confront him. In the end Turcaret is ruined by the machinations of his valet Frontin, whose 'reign' is about to begin as the curtain falls.   [PF]

TURENNE, Henri de la Tour d'Auvergne, vicomte de (1611–75). Marshal of France and outstanding general who commanded the French forces in *Louis XIV's early campaigns; he was often compared to *Condé. His funeral oration by *Fléchier became an anthology piece, constantly cited by teachers of rhetoric. He is credited with the saying: 'Dieu est toujours pour les gros bataillons.'

TURGOT, Anne-Robert-Jacques (1727–81). French statesman and economist. Born into a magistrate's family, he showed remarkable gifts while still a student at the Sorbonne, producing an essay in philosophical history, the *Discours sur les progrès de l'esprit humain* (1750), which is regarded as one of the first clear statements of the new ideology of progress. He also wrote on philosophy, tolerance, and the origins of language (articles for the *Encyclopédie*), but his most important writings are on economics, in particular *Réflexions sur la formation et la distribution des richesses* (composed 1766) and *Lettres sur la liberté du commerce des grains* (1770). Close to the *Physiocrats, he advocated free trade and fair taxation in order to increase prosperity and relieve popular suffering.

Appointed *intendant of the backward Limousin region in 1761, he put his ideas into practice with great energy. In 1774, to the applause of his *philosophe friends, he became minister of finance and produced radical plans for introducing order and economy into the nation's affairs. In particular, he proposed spreading the tax burden equally over the whole population, including the nobility, and abolishing the *corvée* and the trade corporations. Faced by great resentment, and undermined by bad harvests and bread riots, he was forced to resign in 1776. It could be said, however, that his ideas triumphed in the long term, and he remains an exemplary figure of the *Enlightenment.   [PF]

TURLUPIN. One of the trio of *farceurs* at the *Hôtel de Bourgogne in the early 17th c. [see GAULTIER-GARGUILLE].

TURNÈBE, Adrien (1512–65). Reader in Greek at the Collège Royal from 1547, and royal printer of Greek (1552–6) (Aeschylus, Sophocles, the *Iliad*, philosophy). He was praised by *Ronsard and *Montaigne for his learning, judgement, and urbanity. His *Adversaria* (1564) contain textual and literary criticism; his *Opera omnia* (1600) include prefaces, speeches, and poems. [PS]

TURNÈBE, Odet de (1552–81). Humanist, lawyer, and dramatist, elder son of Adrien *Turnèbe, whose death in 1565 delayed until 1566 the first publication of work by his son. As well as his prose comedy *Les *Contents* (published 1584, written probably c.1580), he composed poetry, not only in French but also in Spanish and Italian. Little is known about his life other than that he studied law at Toulouse, spent some time at Poitiers in 1579, and was appointed Premier Président de la Cour des Monnaies shortly before his early death. [GJ]

TUROLDUS is named in the last line of the *Chanson de *Roland* ('Ci falt la geste que Turoldus declinet'), suggesting that he is the author, source, performer, or scribe of the poem. His identity remains enigmatic; a small figure apparently labelled Turold appears in one frame of the Bayeux Tapestry.

Turpin. *Charlemagne's archbishop in the *Chanson de *Roland* and other *chansons de geste, and alleged author of the *Chronicle of Pseudo-Turpin*. This immensely popular mid-12th-c. Latin prose text, purporting to give an eyewitness account of Charlemagne's Spanish campaigns, was subsequently translated and adapted into French prose in the early 13th c.

TYARD, Pontus de (1521–1605). Initially influenced by *Scève and later a member of the *Pléiade, Tyard was not only a poet, the translator of Leone Ebreo's *Dialoghi d'Amore* (1551), and a writer of philosophical treatises (often in dialogue form), but a man of science, a Christian Platonist, and a distinguished ecclesiastic (he was bishop of Chalon-sur-Saône from 1578 to 1589). His three books of *Erreurs amoureuses* (1549, 1551, 1555) employed the *Petrarchist canon together with a personal note of Platonic idealism, whilst his *Vers lyriques* (1552, 1555) revealed the developing influence of *Ronsard. The *Œuvres poétiques* (1573) collected together these previously published collections and added the *Recueil des nouvelles œuvres poétiques*, predominantly Petrarchist poems addressed to the maréchale de Retz, whose prestigious salon Tyard had frequented from about 1568.

Tyard's philosophical treatises (several of which are Platonic in inspiration) discuss poetry (*Solitaire premier*, 1552), music (*Solitaire second*, 1552), time (*Discours du temps, de l'an, et de ses parties*, 1556), the physical and spiritual universe (*L'Univers*, 1557), and astrology and divination (*Mantice*, 1558). These treatises, which received a collective edition in 1587 (*Discours philosophiques*), bear witness to an encyclopaedic mind and a robust prose style with a mastery of rhetoric. [MDQ]

Tyr et Sidon, see SCHELANDRE.

TYSSOT DE PATOT, Simon (1655–1738). Writer of the Huguenot diaspora, known for his *Voyages et aventures de Jaques Massé* (c. 1715, pre-dated '1710'). It is a clever pastiche of earlier imaginary-voyage books by *Veiras, *Foigny, etc. In dialogues alternating with tales of intrigue and romance, all kinds of heterodox ideas appear. Massé meets Australian deists, a stoical Chinese persecuted by the Inquisition in Portuguese Goa, and an aggressively atheist renegade Huguenot in Algiers, who tells a 'Fable des abeilles' (apparently unconnected with Bernard Mandeville's more famous *Fable of the Bees*). Tyssot's fable parodies Christian history, making out that biblical revelation is an imposture. [CJB]

TZARA, Tristan (1896–1963). Born Samuel Rosenstock, this Romanian poet took for his *nom de guerre* a name as staccato and aggressive as the nonsensical *'Dada'—the battle-cry of the cultural rebellion he helped launch in 1916 in the multilingual setting of Zurich. Tzara's iconoclastic *Manifeste Dada 1918*—written in French, as were all subsequent works—is a remarkable instance of utter nihilism propelled by a flood of positive verbal energy. In 1920 he moved to Paris to direct another Dada campaign until *Breton turned the group's attention towards *Surrealism.

Tzara settled permanently in France and later contributed to Surrealism with a book on dreams called *Grains et issues* (1935); in the post-war period he was to become a Communist and a stern critic of Surrealist idealism. While he refused to acknowledge any discontinuity in his poetic output, one may discern a shift from the asymmetrical verbal montages of the Dada period, which exploit incongruous newspaper headlines and printer's errors, to the smoother, even rhapsodic intonations of *L'Homme approximatif* (1931), where visionary prospects are imparted through glittering metaphors. A collector of African sculpture, Tzara also wrote knowledgeably on the visual arts. His *Œuvres complètes* (1975–91) comprise six volumes.

[RC]

U

Ubu Roi. Play by *Jarry, first performed as a puppet show for his school friends in Rennes in 1888, given its stage première by *Lugné-Poë in 1896. The opening word is 'Merdre'. Greedy, vulgar, cruel, cowardly, and vicious, Ubu murders the king of Poland, crowns himself, and embarks on a savagely farcical reign of terror and guzzling until overthrown in his turn. Crudely parodying the classical and naturalist tradition, the action evinces a juvenile delight in scatology, knockabout violence, and extravagant verbal invention. History subsequently revealed a sinisterly prophetic dimension to the play; the theatrical energies it unleashed shaped modern drama, notably the Theatre of the *Absurd. [DHW]

Ultra. Member of the ultra-royalist party after the *Restoration of 1815. Aspiring to a return to the *ancien régime*, the *ultras* defended the absolute monarchy and the power of the Church.

Ultramontanism. The term 'ultramontain' was applied to those French Catholics who looked to the authority of Rome (*ultra montes*—beyond the Alps), maintaining that the French Church was entirely subject to such authority. Ultramontanism was the antonym of *Gallicanism.

Ultramontane attitudes existed under the *ancien régime*, but as a minority opinion; it was the 19th c. that saw the triumph of Ultramontanism in France. This was partly because the fall of the last Bourbon in 1830 rendered the old royal Gallicanism largely irrelevant; partly because parish priests, subject to stronger episcopal tutelage than ever before, tended to look to Rome as a countervailing locus of power; and partly because the younger clergy increasingly saw in the papacy a source of spiritual inspiration. Such attitudes were inspired by the work of de *Maistre (especially in *Du pape*, 1819), and of *Lamennais (till his break with Rome in 1832–4). They triumphed with the declaration of papal infallibility at the First Vatican Council in 1870. Although Ultramontane doctrines were initially concerned with the primacy of papal authority in the French Church, they also came in the course of the 19th c. to be associated with illiberalism in politics and a certain anti-intellectualism in theology (e.g. the uncritical acceptance of the miraculous), of which Louis *Veuillot, editor of the Catholic newspaper *L'Univers*, was the champion. [RBG]

Unanimism. Described by its founder, Jules *Romains, as the expression of 'la vie unanime et collective', Unanimism (with which Pierre-Jean *Jouve and the *Abbaye poets were also associated) was an attempt, in the period preceding World War I, to express the individual's relationship to the collective nature of modern urban experience. Romains believed that every group of individuals, whatever their number or type of relationship, generated a collective 'soul' which shaped the feelings of each member. Its most important texts were Romains's first volume of poetry, *La Vie unanime*, whose themes and rhythms define an anti-*Symbolist, modern, urban, universal lyricism, and his monumental *Les *Hommes de bonne volonté*. [JK]

Unigenitus Dei Filius. The title of the papal bull which condemned the *Jansenist writings of *Quesnel in 1713, giving rise to fierce religious conflict.

UNIK, Pierre (1909–45). French poet, journalist, and script-writer. A *Surrealist between 1925 and 1932, he joined the Communist Party in 1927. He worked with Buñuel on three films, including *Terre sans pain*. In his lifetime he published one volume of poetry, *Le Théâtre des nuits blanches* (1931), but in 1972 another collection, *Chant d'exil*, and an unfinished novel, *Le Héros du vide*, appeared. [KRA]

Unities, The Three, see TRAGEDY, 2.

Univers, L', see VEUILLOT.

Universities, see EDUCATION; for the University of Paris in the Middle Ages see SCHOLASTICISM.

URFÉ, Honoré d' (1567–1625). Novelist, poet, and moralist. Born in Marseille into a family related on his mother's side to the ducal house of Savoy, he was to acquire a vast culture, embracing the classics, the writings of Ficino and Pico della Mirandola, and modern Italian and Spanish literature. He began to compose verse at the age of 16, but his first success was a pastoral poem, *Sireine*, completed in 1594 and published in 1604, clearly inspired by the ever-popular *Diana* of Montemayor. Like his two brothers he was a *ligueur* [see LIGUE], attached to the duc de Nemours and twice captured. In prison he composed the first volume of his *Épîtres morales* (1598), largely Stoic in inspiration. In 1600 he married Diane de Chateaumorand, whose marriage to his elder brother nearly 30 years before had been annulled, and lived from then until 1607 at Chateaumorand and Virieu. In 1608 he published the second volume of the *Épîtres*, whose bold blend of the Platonic and the Cabbalistic marked a significant change in

Uriage

philosophical outlook. He spent the rest of his life in the Forez or in Italy, principally concerned with the work which would bring him European acclaim: the pastoral novel *L'*Astrée*. [GJM]

Uriage. The École des Cadres, at Saint-Martin-d'Uriage in the Isère, was a controversial attempt in 1940–1 to establish a leadership training-school under the arm's-length sponsorship of the Vichy government. Trading on ideological resemblances with *Pétain's National Revolution, its director Pierre Dunoyer de Segonzac promoted a robust centre-left Catholic *Personalism with the support of *Mounier, *Lacroix, and others. Suspected of subversive intent, it was closed after a year. Many students, including *Domenach and *Beuve-Méry, joined the Resistance and later played influential roles in post-war life. [MHK]

URQUHART, Sir Thomas (*c*.1605–1660). Scottish baronet and eccentric, whose delicious translation of *Rabelais, whilst frequently unfaithful to the literal sense, captures fully the spirit of the original. Urquhart's translation of the first three books, published in part in 1653, was completed and published in 1694 by Pierre Le Motteux. [MJH]

Ursule Mirouet (1841). One of the *Scènes de la vie de province* in Balzac's *Comédie humaine*. The heroine, an orphan in Nemours, is cheated of an inheritance, but thanks to dreams is enabled to recover her fortune and marry the young Count Savinien.

Usage des passions, De l', see SENAULT.

Usbek. The older of the two Persian travellers in Montesquieu's *Lettres persanes*.

Utopia. The model for descriptions of the ideal state has always been Plato's *Republic*, but for the fictional version, the report of a far-off country, perfectly organized and happy, the pioneer was More (*Utopia*, 1516). He was inspired (like many imitators throughout Europe) by the first tales of exploration. In France (neglecting an isolated effort in 1616, the anonymous Huguenot *Royaume d'Antangil*), a tradition of Utopian fiction developed during the early *Enlightenment.

The pattern was fixed in the 1670s by the inventions of *Foigny and *Veiras, both set in the as-yet unexplored southern continent. *Tyssot de Patot's 'Austral Land' resembles Veiras's, as does the Saharan society found in the anonymous *Mémoires de Gaudence de Lucques* (1746). Other minor works (those by *Gilbert, *Lesconvel, and *Lassay deserve mention) vary the geography and other details, but not the assumption that reason can satisfy human nature by devising a prosperous society, carefully regulated, having social and sexual equality (within limits), and free from European miseries such as war.

More influential were works not strictly speaking Utopian, but containing Utopian episodes, above all Fénelon's *Télémaque*, imitated by his disciple *Ramsay (*Voyages de Cyrus*) and by *Terrasson (*Séthos*). Montesquieu's regenerated Troglodytes, in the *Lettres persanes*, and perhaps even the Eldoradans of *Candide*, are also Fénelonian. The critical potential of Utopia was also exploited: vigorously in *La Hontan's idealized, anti-European Native American society, more mildly in Marivaux's stage Utopia *L'*Île des esclaves*, and with humour, as regards religion and sex, in Diderot's Tahiti (*Supplément au Voyage de Bougainville*).

After 1750, as freedom of publication increased, political idealism was expressed more overtly, in treatises rather than fiction. *Morelly's Utopian epic, *La Basiliade*, was followed by his *Code de la nature*, legislating for a propertyless society. Both Rousseau's *Contrat social and (more justifiably) the domestic, rural society of Clarens in *La *Nouvelle Héloïse*, can be considered Utopian. *Mercier's *L'An 2440* broke new ground by putting an improved Paris into the future; it contains much direct criticism of the present, as does *Restif's *L'An 2000*. During the Revolution, the real re-creation of society swamped the Utopian variety. The next 50 years saw the expression of what Marx disdainfully called 'Utopian socialism' in *Saint-Simon and *Fourier; *Cabet expressed it traditionally, with sentimental trappings, in his *Voyage en Icarie*.

[CJB]

See R. Trousson, *Voyages aux pays de nulle part* (1975).

V

VACHÉ, Jacques-Pierre (1895–1919). Despite the slimness of his *œuvre*, Vaché enjoys a high reputation as the evangelist of French *Dada. It was in Nantes in 1916 that he met André *Breton and, startling him with his nonchalant cynicism, conveyed the essentials of those dissenting positions which the latter would impress upon Paris Dada and *Surrealism. A natural anarchist and dandy, Vaché cherished nothing but the task of mocking inherited cultural values. The *Lettres de guerre de Jacques Vaché* (1920) delineate a quirky, impulsive temperament prepared for anything—even, as Vaché proved in 1919, suicide. [RC]

VADÉ, Antoine, Catherine, Guillaume, and Jean-Joseph. The first three are imaginary characters, used as pseudonyms by *Voltaire. Catherine supposedly wrote the introduction to her 'cousin's' book, *Contes de Guillaume Vadé* (1764), which contains the 'Discours aux Welches' attributed to his 'brother' Antoine. Voltaire was alluding to the real author, Jean-Joseph Vadé (1719–57), best known for his works in *poissard*. [VGM]

VADEBONCŒUR, Pierre (b. 1920), *québécois* essayist, was legal adviser to the Confédération des Syndicats Nationaux (*En grève*, 1963). This 'lyrique aventuré dans l'action' (Maurice Blain) saluted the courage of *Borduas in *La Ligne du risque* (1963), the 'génie de la prime enfance' in *Un amour libre* (1970), the power of love and art to 'amener visiblement à portée l'ineffable de l'être' in *L'Absence* (1985), and the moral force of literature with *Les Deux Royaumes* (1978). [CRPM]

Vagabonde, La. Novel by *Colette, published 1910 under the name of Colette Willy, and her first major independant work. Strongly autobiographical, the novel recounts the music-hall career of the narrator, Renée, following the ending of her marriage to the painter Adolphe Taillandy, and the tension between her desire for Bohemian independance and the temptation of renewed comfort and respectability through marriage with the rich Maxime Dufferein-Chautel. The novel is remarkable for its evocative description of back-stage life in the music-hall of the *belle époque*, the *demi-monde* who frequent it, and the life of the artistes on tour through France, but its major importance lies in its clear assertion of the heroine's independance against the pressures towards orthodoxy: in spite of her love for Max and her emotional need for a permanent relationship, Renée discovers that her authenticity lies in the independance of the vagabond and not in the constraints of the wife. [NH]

VAILLAND, Roger (1907–65). French novelist and essayist. His main works of fiction, *Drôle de jeu* (1945), *Les Mauvais Coups* (1948), *Bon pied, bon œil* (1950), *Beau Masque* (1954), *325,000 francs* (1955), *La Loi* (1957, Prix Goncourt), *La Fête* (1960), *La Truite* (1960), demonstrate a tension between the individual will and *la chasse au bonheur* on the one hand, and a sense of Marxist-inspired social commitment on the other. Egalitarianism notwithstanding, quality of spirit alone allows his heroes survival and ultimate authorial approval. Vailland, an ex-Surrealist, a *résistant*, and a Communist until the invasion of Hungary, also wrote plays and probing essays—*Laclos par lui-même* (1953), *Éloge du cardinal de Bernis* (1956), *Le Regard froid* (1963). [DAS]

Valentine, see SAND.

VALÉRY, Paul (1871–1945). French poet, essayist, and thinker, Valéry is famous not only for literary works such as *La Soirée avec *Monsieur Teste* (1896) and major poems of the *Symbolist and post-Symbolist epoch, but also for the vast analytic enterprise of his *Cahiers*, the hundreds of notebooks written nearly every day at dawn for over 50 years, largely without thought of publication. Here, lyrical prose poems and snatches of self-analysis alternate with pages of more abstract or generalized reflection on the functioning of the human mind.

Valéry was born where he would most like to have been born, he tells us: the port of Sète on the French Mediterranean (his mother was Italian and his father Corsican), and indeed he describes in 'Inspirations meditérranéennes' (one of the many essays collected in *Variété*), how the three 'deities' of Sea, Sky, and Sun moulded his thought in its characteristic sense of universality. Valéry figures as a kind of intellectual Robinson Crusoe building a self-taught way of thinking tested constantly from his own experience and revived in its potentiality by primitive astonishment in the natural world.

Thwarted in his early desire to go to sea (insufficient mathematics to join the navy), he instead read law at the University of Montpellier, moving permanently to Paris in 1894. There, having worked for a short time in the War Office (1897–1900), he married Jeannie Gobillard, niece of the painter Berthe *Morisot, becoming in the same year (1900) the private secretary to Édouard Lebey at the Agence *Havas—an occupation which offered him the time and means to pursue his writing free of the need to make it a livelihood, right up to the death of his employer in 1922, the initial year of publication of his main collection of poems, *Charmes*. From then on his career developed with unusual rapidity, and he received a series of public honours: president of the PEN Club (1924), member of the Académie Française (1925), honorary degree from Oxford University (1931), administrator of the Mediterranean University Centre at Nice (1933), president of Intellectual Co-operation at the League of Nations (1936), professor of poetics at the *Collège de France (1937), where, holding a specially created chair, he lectured during the Occupation on the Jewish philosopher *Bergson (1941) and, not inappropriately, gave his last lecture, in December 1944, in commemoration of the 250th anniversary of the birth of *Voltaire. On his death in July 1945 a state funeral was held in Paris, and he was buried in Sète in the 'graveyard by the sea' which had inspired his most famous poem, 'Le Cimetière marin' (1920).

Valéry's earliest published verse appeared in the Symbolist review *La Conque* (1891), encouraged by his friendship with the young Symbolist poet and editor Pierre *Louÿs, who introduced him to *Gide (the beginning of a 50-year correspondance) and to *Mallarmé, whose poetry he at once admired and despaired of ever equalling. Together with *Poe's theory of poetic composition as an art of lucidly calculated linguistic effects, Mallarmé's poetry was to have a deeply formative role in allowing him to characterize and differentiate his own. In 1892, however, with the coming to a head of a severe crisis in values, Valéry rejected poetry and literature altogether as demanding a sacrifice of the intellect, devoting himself instead to the *Cahiers* (unlike Mallarmé, he was always to refuse poetry a place superior to other human languages like mathematics and science).

Centred on the famous 'nuit de Gênes'—the night of a violent thunderstorm when he felt himself divided between 'self' and 'self'—the crisis of 1892 provides an important signpost. Humiliated by the overwhelming power of 'irrational' ideas and images, Valéry began to concentrate not so much on the content of his thoughts and feelings as on the power of the conscious mind to observe them in action, in other words on secondary consciousness ('le Moi pur'): that profound note of existence which, once we have heard it, seems to dominate and shape a whole human life. It is from this period, in fact, that emerged both the mythical figure of Monsieur Teste and the essay *Introduction à la méthode de Léonard de Vinci* (1895), where the universal Renaissance genius is chosen to exemplify the 'central attitude from which both the undertakings of knowledge and the operations of art are equally possible'. Comparing the 'nuit de Gênes' to the mental crisis in which *Descartes is said to have formulated his 'cogito', Valéry saw himself in possession of an intellectual method based on observation

and understanding of the limits and possibilities of the mind experienced 'from within' as a unique source of self-reconstruction or improved mental yield.

Far from denying emotion, such an ideal was based precisely on the uncontrollable power of the sensibility, in turn a dynamic interaction of body, mind, and world. Indeed, it was his own unusually acute sensitivity which led Valéry to place such a high value on the experience of love—a potential masterpiece of co-ordinated intellectual and emotional energies which he explores symbolically in the figures of Faust and Lust in *Mon Faust* (modelled on the resources for dialogue in a single mind). Never mere rationalism, such a unity is none the less the fruit of self-awareness, 'rational' in its judgement and use of the human material from which, as in the act of poetic composition (the process of which, for Valéry, was always more important than the product), the human mind is able to construct itself anew.

Valéry's return to poetry in 1912 after what used to be called misleadingly the 'Great Silence' is similarly instructive from the point of view of the deep coherence of his work, and indeed of his own achievement of the 'central attitude' he attributes to Leonardo. Revising his old poems at the suggestion of *Gide and *Gallimard (the collection was published as *Album de vers anciens* in 1920), he intended to add a poem of some mere 30 lines as a kind of valediction to literature in general. Instead, he found himself composing what turned out to be the intensive four-year 'exercise' of 'La Jeune Parque', an immense dramatic monologue (published in 1917) of no less than 500 lines modelled on the contralto voice in a Gluck recitative, and in which, in a language as full of imagery and verbal music as possible, he attempts to convey the modulations of consciousness in a single night. This entails, if we turn to the ever-present symbolic level of the poem, the interaction of 'Être' and 'Connaître', the two great poles from which the human individual 'self' is ceaselessly recomposed (hence the characteristic Valéryan emblem of the 'ouroboros' or serpent biting its own tail). Here, as in the relatively more rapidly written poems of *Charmes* (1922; their title is derived from the Latin *carmina*, magic songs or hymns), Valéry paradoxically increases the power of the poem to resonate in the reader's sensibility by rejecting the Symbolist *vers libre* and maximizing the constraints of language: classical prosody in its richest, most varied forms (see for instance 'Fragments du Narcisse', 'Ébauche d'un serpent', and 'Le Cimetière marin'). The research of the *Cahiers* of the time into the conditions of the living/thinking human being, their sense of recurrent phases or cycles, in particular, provides a constant background to the poems, which are festivals of the intellect where abstract ideas are 'musicalized' in sensuous, universally dramatized form.

Valéry's subsequent literary works include: *L'Âme*

et la danse and Eupalinos ou l'Architecte in 1921 and 1923 (mock-Socratic dialogues extolling the dance as the epitome of pure, flame-like movement, or architecture and music as arts of pure form); Pièces sur l'art and Regards sur le monde actuel in 1931 (in the latter Valéry foresees many of the problems facing Europe because of its blind nationalism, and analyses the effect on that precious mental freedom he felt so essential to our humanity of the radical transformations brought about through technology); L'Idée fixe ou Deux hommes à la mer, a brilliant pirouette of ideas on mental obsession, also in dialogue form, in 1934; Degas Danse Dessin in 1938; collections of 'Voltairean' aphorisms such as Mélange, Tel quel, and Mauvaises pensées et autres in 1941, 1942, and 1943; Dialogue de l'arbre in 1943; the fifth and final volume of the essays of Variété together with Propos me concernant in 1944; and the unfinished play, Mon Faust, in 1946.

Famous in his lifetime for the eloquent lucidity of both his poetry and prose, Valéry is now receiving more and more attention as the innovatory thinker revealed in the Cahiers themselves (first published in facsimile version in 1957 and 1961 in 29 volumes of some 30,000 pages, and translated into many languages throughout the world). Here he can be found, in the field of mathematical thinking alone, anticipating by several decades the application of mathematical models to mental processes. Prefiguring Wittgenstein, Valéry also attacks traditional patterns of religious thought and philosophy for generating problems purely linguistic in origin, and, while pursuing a certain mystic resonance in human experience, orchestrates his crucial early insight into 'points of view' and our tendency to confuse mental imagery with the 'real'. Rivalling Freud in their distinctive approach to dreams, emotion, memory, and the unconscious, the Cahiers are emerging in turn as one of the most significant works of the 20th c., testimony to the limits and aspirations of a would-be universal human 'self'.

[CMC]

See P. O. Walzer, La Poésie de Valéry (1953); J. Hytier, La Poétique de Valéry (1953); Paul Valéry: Cahiers, ed. J. Robinson, vols. 1, 2 (1973–4); C. G. Whiting, Paul Valéry (1978); C. M. Crow, Paul Valéry and the Poetry of Voice (1982).

VALINCOUR, Jean-Henri du Trousset, sieur de (1653–1730). A friend of *Boileau and *Racine, he became historiographer to *Louis XIV. He is mainly remembered for his critical Lettre . . . sur le sujet de la *Princesse de Clèves (1678).

Valjean, Jean. A former convict, the central figure of Hugo's Les *Misérables.

VALLÈS, Jules (1832–85). The son of a provincial instituteur, Vallès is remembered above all as the author of a largely autobiographical trilogy of novels. Most of his working life he was a journalist, hack at first but graduating to editing his own papers (La Rue, Le Cri du peuple). His first published

work, L'Argent (1857), combined pointed satire and bandwaggoning in its heralding of 'industrial' literature based on the values of the Stock Exchange. Viscerally incapable of abstract theory, Vallès used his journalism to protest against censorship, social injustices, worship of the past, and the imitativeness inculcated in schoolchildren. He was jailed several times for attacking public authorities. A déclassé himself, he was most drawn to les réfractaires (showpeople, freaks, eccentric artists). His stamping-ground was la rue rather than the modish boulevard. Much of his dynamic journalism was collected in Les Réfractaires (1865) and La Rue (1866).

After the Paris *Commune he was sentenced to death and escaped to a nine-year exile in England. One product was La Rue à Londres (1883), which recorded his passionate nostalgia for Paris alongside his highly critical, impressionist sketch of England as a joyless, compartmentalized, and brutal society. The major outcome was the Jacques Vingtras trilogy: L'Enfant (1879), Le Bachelier (1881), and L'Insurgé (1886).

Long before *Sartre, he stressed the impossibility of uncommitted literature. L'Enfant starts on the domestic front, offering searing but frequently highly comic images of a battered—not loveless, but mis-loved—childhood. The style is sensationalist ('ocular greed, nasal libertinage'). Vallès energizes all he touches: a dumb aunt hypnotizes by her frenetic body-language. Mother and son wrestle for control of his will-power, but unwittingly her killjoy harshness teaches him the valuable art of survival.

Le Bachelier releases Jacques from the family prison into a hand-to-mouth existence in Paris. Hallucinatory hunger, wretched accommodation, and patched clothing periodically but not ultimately depress this only briefly employable in-between, who has paper qualifications but no real skills. His youthful idealism is repeatedly squelched by realistic workers and endangered by police surveillance. The climactic duel with his best friend is a shifting event of bravura, despair, and courage.

L'Insurgé finds Jacques first compromised in the teaching job he had sworn to avoid; later finding his feet clumsily in the press, and resisting the inane patriotism of 1870; and finally engaged up to the hilt in the Commune. There he upholds the freedom of the press for all persuasions, tries to abort lynchings, and writes honestly of atrocities and incendiarism. Despite the foreordained defeat, the Commune was for Vallès the joyous revenge, rendered with stoical gallows-humour, for a previously frustrated life. The trilogy lives intensely through its volatile narrative and its effervescent style. [WDR]

See W. Redfern, Feet First: Jules Vallès (1992).

Valmont, vicomte de. Leading character in Laclos's Les *Liaisons dangereuses.

Valmy. Famous battle in eastern France at which on 20 September 1792 the Revolutionary armies under Dumouriez and Kellermann turned back the advancing Prussians. Goethe saw it as a turning-point in world history.

Valois. Branch of the *Capetian family which reigned in France from 1328 until 1589. The direct line died out with Charles VIII, leaving the throne to Louis XII (Valois-Orléans) and then to the Valois-Angoulême (*François Iᵉʳ, *Henri II, François II, *Charles IX, *Henri III). The assassination of the last of these led to the accession of the *Bourbon dynasty.

VAN GENNEP, Arnold (1873–1959). Father of modern French folklore studies. Born in Germany in an *émigré* family, he came to live in France at the age of 6. His education and interests were unusually broad, and much of his life was devoted to private research outside the university system. His first works were devoted to anthropological questions (*Les Rites de passage*, 1909), but his most famous contribution was to French folklore, which he placed on a newly scientific footing (*Manuel du folklore français contemporain*, 1937–58).   [PF]

VAN GOGH, Vincent (1853–90). Dutch painter who worked mainly in France. The art of Van Gogh, with its intense colour and writhing forms, became, through its impact on the *Fauvists and German Expressionists, one of the major sources of 20th-c. painting, while his tragic biography is one of the most powerful examples of the myth of the artist as deranged and alienated visionary. *Aurier launched the legend in his definition of Van Gogh as a *Symbolist painter (1890), but its most important literary development is *Artaud's *Van Gogh et le suicidé de la société* (1947), which attempts to re-create in language what Artaud sees as the power of Van Gogh's painting to denounce institutions and restructure the world.   [JK]

Vanina Vanini. Short story by Stendhal, written in 1829, later included in the *Chroniques italiennes*. A story of passion, energy and politics, set in modern Rome, it prefigures many aspects of Stendhal's novels.

VANINI, Giulio Cesare (1585–1619). An Italian priest and doctor of laws who came to France in 1614 and was brutally executed at Toulouse in 1619 for having written two atheistic and impious tracts. The more notable of these was translated into French and published in 1616 with the title *Dialogues sur les secrets admirables de la nature, reine et déesse des mortels*. He was execrated by *Counter-Reformation theologians as an apostle of *libertin doctrines.   [IM]

VAN LERBERGHE, Charles (1861–1907). Belgian poet. A class-mate of *Maeterlinck in Ghent, Van Lerberghe wrote for *La Wallonie*, the focal review of Belgian *Symbolism. His first volume of poems, *Entrevisions* (1898), essays a tone of musical imprecision indebted to the Symbolist master *Mallarmé,

whom he visited in Paris in 1889. Of his poetic cycle *Chanson d'Ève* (1904), an evocation of Eve's awakening in the garden of Eden, Van Lerberghe told a friend that its true subject was 'le premier éveil, le premier murmure, le premier ravissement devant les choses'; and the tenuousness of his physical allusions reflects a Symbolist poetics whereby impulse melts into idea and sonority into suggestive silence. A discreet ardour colours his letters to Gabrielle Max, a young poet he met only twice (*Lettres à une jeune fille*, 1954). A year before he died he expressed a more robust sensuality in *Pan*, a play in which the young *Colette starred.   [RC]

VAN LOO. Important family of French painters. Jean-Baptiste (1684–1745) was admired by the English engraver Vertue. His brother, Carle (1705–65), was a lively and varied artist associated with Rococo ideas. Louis-Michel (1707–71), Jean's son, painted splendid official full-length portraits of Louis XV, admired for their convincing animation. In 1767 a portrait of *Diderot, richly clad, was exhibited in the Salon and wryly reviewed by the sitter.   [JPC]

VARDA, Agnès (b. 1928). Belgian-born French filmmaker. She studied at the École du Louvre and was a photographer before making her first film, *La Pointe courte*, in 1955. Her films often depend on an interplay of fiction and documentary. *Cléo de 5 à 7* (1962) uses 'real time' to show a singer waiting for two hours for the result of a cancer test. Subsequent films include the feminist *L'une chante, l'autre pas* (1977) and documentaries such as *Daguerréotypes* (1975), a fascinating picture of Varda's Paris street, the rue Daguerre. Her most remarkable achievement is *Sans toit ni loi* (1985), a half-documentary, *Citizen-Kane*-like exploration of the last, desperate months of a homeless young woman.   [PF]

Varennes, Flight to, see REVOLUTION, 1b.

Variété, see VALÉRY.

VATABLE, François (d. 1547). One of the first two professors of Hebrew at the Collège des Lecteurs Royaux [see COLLÈGE DE FRANCE]. Like many *humanists of the period, he combined a sincere interest in religion (see his translation of the *Biblia sacra hebraica*, 1539–43) and in the philosophers of antiquity, notably Aristotle (see e.g. his *Aristotelis de sensu et sensibili libri*, translation and commentary, 1546).   [JJS]

VATEL, François (d. 1671). *Maître d'hôtel* to *Fouquet and then *Condé. It was at the latter's palace at Chantilly that he committed suicide, when his honour was tarnished by the non-arrival of the fish course (*Sévigné tells the story).

VAUBAN, Sébastien Le Prestre, seigneur de (1633–1707). Genius of siegecraft and legendary military strategist who personally directed over 50 sieges and designed and built 333 fortified places, many of which still stand. His accomplishments are wide-ranging: he pioneered creative statistics, reorganized the army, and imagined the first modern draft system. Perhaps Vauban's greatest project, which establishes him as a founder of modern economics and a precursor of the *Enlightenment's socially concerned intellectuals, is La Dîme royale (1707). This far-reaching economic project proposed a total revision of the *taxation system and documented the economic misery of the lower classes. It was confiscated and destroyed on Louis XIV's decree.   [JDeJ]

Vaudeville. A term applied in the 15th c. to satirical couplets set to popular airs, and modified in the course of the 17th c. so as to denote satirical ballads, often of a political character. By the 18th c. it was used to refer to performances by the strolling players at the Paris fairs. Because of the monopoly of the *Comédie-Française over the classical repertory, plays staged by the théâtres de la *foire could only be given in dumb-show, using interpolated choruses based on popular tunes and often parodying the productions of the legitimate theatre. Ironically, this cheeky folk tradition survived and took off after the Napoleonic regime introduced (1806–7) dictatorial controls limiting the number of 'secondary' theatres in Paris to four: the Gaîté and Ambigu-Comique, restricted to *melodramas, *pantomimes, and *farces; and the Variétés and Vaudeville, limited to parodies, musical sketches, etc. Within this scheme, vaudeville blossomed into a form of short comedy of manners in prose, enlivened by farcical episodes, rhyming couplets, songs, and dance routines [see COMEDY, 2]. Zestful and naughty, it was also topical and irreverent, dominating the light stage for some 30 years after 1815. Offenbach was its natural heir [see MEILHAC and HALÉVY].   [SBJ]

Vaudois (or Waldensians). Heretical Christian sect which grew out of an anti-sacerdotal movement begun by Peter Waldo of Lyon in the 12th c. Practising apostolic poverty and moral austerity, they established a strong presence in rural regions, particularly the Alps, and like the *Cathars were much persecuted. In the 16th c. they began to make common cause with the *Reformation. In spite of a ferocious massacre in Provence in 1545 and another in 1655 (which provoked Milton's sonnet 'Avenge, O Lord, thy slaughtered saints'), they survived into the 20th c. on a small scale, mainly in Piedmont.   [PF]

VAUGELAS, Claude Favre de (1585–1650). Son of the famous jurisconsult, Antoine Favre, Vaugelas spent his early life in Savoy. On moving to Paris in 1607 he was employed in the households of, first, the duc de Nemours, then the king, and later Gaston d'*Orléans. As a member of the newly founded *Académie Française, Vaugelas presented it with his observations on French in 1637 and from 1639 worked on the compilation of its dictionary

until his death. He also frequented the *salons and cabinets, where linguistic problems were much discussed. Plagued by poverty at the end of his life, he led a miserable existence as the governor of Prince Thomas de Savoie-Carignan's sons.

Vaugelas is best known for his influential Remarques sur la langue française (1647), a collection of randomly ordered observations discussing aspects of good French usage, defined in élitist terms as that of the soundest part ('la plus saine partie') of the court and of contemporary authors. Good usage is subdivided into declared and doubtful usage, the latter furnishing the subject-matter of the observations, since his is not a systematic *grammar, but a discussion of areas of uncertainty on the part of the best speakers. Whilst in theory Vaugelas claims merely to record good usage, in practice he may resolve a doubt through recourse to etymology, regularity, euphony, or analogy, defined as a type of general usage applied to doubtful cases. Vaugelas also admits that reason plays a role in language behaviour, since, for example, most grammatical constructions are 'reasonable'; it must not, however, be allowed to regularize or question usage. Purity, clarity, an appropriateness of usage of word or phrase are deemed paramount. Syntactic ambiguity is abhorred, and neologism discouraged, since these might cause hesitation and therefore displeasure in listeners or readers. At a time of rapid social mobility, the Remarques—like a courtesy book—warned honnêtes gens seeking promotion at court against offending fellow courtiers through incorrect or awkward usage, and preached a sort of linguistic conformism [see HONNÊTETÉ]. As for the Nouvelles remarques, published in 1690 by Louis-Augustin Alemand, these are not fresh observations, but mainly those rejected in 1647.

For Vaugelas and his contemporaries, grammar and *translation went hand-in-hand. His translation from Spanish of Fonseca's Lenten Sermons (1615) is perhaps a juvenile exercise. More important is his translation of Quintus Curtius, on which he worked for some 30 years and which was published posthumously, edited first by *Conrart and *Chapelain (1653) and then by *Patru (1659). Considered a model of classical style, it was deemed worthy of annotation by the Academy in the early 1720s.   [WA-B]

See W. Ayres-Bennett, Vaugelas and the Development of the French Language (1987).

VAUMORIÈRE, Pierre d'Ortigue de (1610–93), frequented précieux circles [see PRECIOSITY] and the 'academy' of d'*Aubignac, completed *La Calprenède's Faramond, and published a number of works giving advice on writing and conversation, including collections of model letters and speeches and the relatively successful L'Art de plaire dans la conversation (1688).   [PF]

VAUQUELIN DE LA FRESNAYE, Jean (1535–1606). French poet. Having studied law at Poitiers, he eventually rose to high public office in Caen. He published an early collection of poetry (*Les Foresteries*, 1555), but is known principally for his *Art poétique* in verse, begun 1574 and published 1605 as the preface to his *Diverses poésies*. The *Art poétique* displays the influence of Aristotle's *Poetics* as well as of Horace's *Ars poetica*; it outlines the general principles of poetics and covers the major genres and forms, including tragedy, comedy, and epic. It reflects late-16th-c. practice without being especially innovative or controversial. [TC]

VAUQUELIN DES YVETAUX, Nicolas (1567–1649). Son of *Vauquelin de la Fresnaye, and a noted *libertin*. Having been tutor to the future Louis XIII, he lived a life of eccentric retirement, devoted to the epicurean pleasures celebrated in a famous sonnet beginning 'Avoir peu de parents, moins de train que de rente'. [PF]

VAUTHIER, Jean (1910–92). French playwright. Formerly a cartoonist with *Sud-Ouest*, he emerged in the wake of *Ionesco and others as the author of plays often classed with the Theatre of the *Absurd: *Capitaine Bada* (1952), *Le Personnage combattant* (1956), *Le Rêveur* (1961). Later works include *Le Sang* (1970), *Les Prodiges* (1970), and *Ton nom dans le feu des nuées*, *Elizabeth* (1976). More a poet than a natural playwright, he writes searing but unwieldy dramas showing characters undergoing a moment of truth about themselves. In spite of attracting many of the leading contemporary directors (notably Reybaz, *Barrault, *Vilar, Vitaly, Maréchal, Wilson, and *Mnouchkine), his plays have more often than not proved disappointing on stage. [DWW]

Vautrin. Master-criminal who appears under different names and disguises (his 'real' name being Jacques Collin) in several novels of Balzac's *Comédie humaine*, notably *Le *Père Goriot*, *Illusions perdues*, and *Splendeurs et misères des courtisanes*. Perhaps partly modelled on *Vidocq, he proclaims the power of the strong individual beyond good and evil.

VAUTRIN, Jean (pseud. of Jean Herman) (b. 1933). French film-maker (as Jean Herman), novelist (*Billy-Ze-Kick*, 1974; *Bloody-Mary*, 1979; *Canicule*, 1982; *La Vie ripolin*, 1986; and *Un grand pas vers le Bon Dieu*, 1989, Prix Goncourt), short-story writer (*Baby Boom*, 1985; *18 tentatives pour devenir un saint*, 1989; and *Courage, chacun*, 1992), and joint-author with Dan Franck of detective stories (*La Dame de Berlin*, 1987), featuring the adventures of Boro (Blèmia Borowicz). Vautrin gives a violent and sinisterly funny presentation of the quirks and obsessions of marginal people, universalizing them by the art of the *moraliste*; in his own words, he is linguistically versatile to the point of schizophrenia. [PS]

VAUVENARGUES. Luc de Clapiers, marquis de (1715–47), was a French career soldier who saw ser-

vice in the War of Austrian Succession. The disastrous siege of Prague and the retreat through Bohemia weakened his chronic poor health, leading him to make several unheeded requests for a career in diplomacy. *Voltaire, with whom he had been corresponding since April 1743, forced recognition of his merit. By then it was too late: Vauvenargues had contracted smallpox. Established in Paris in 1745, the *moraliste*, who was endowed with an acute sense of his own extraordinary but thwarted destiny, concentrated his long-standing, intense (even obsessive) meditation on the success which had been denied him in action, in ambition, and in glory. Feeling that his time was limited, he hastily produced his *Introduction à la connaissance de l'esprit humain suivie de réflexions et maximes* (1746), which reappeared in a 'definitive' posthumous edition in 1747.

This work, viewed globally, is a reaction against decades of Augustinian intellectual terrorism. For example, the deliberate denigration of the human condition, made with such apparent authority by *Pascal and *Bossuet, was anathema to him; their strident insistence that true happiness came only through faith was likewise intolerable. His own experience told him that there was no such thing as Original Sin, that life was good, that one must have confidence in it and in man. But the *Introduction*, viewed from one particular angle, hints strongly at a more pointed reaction than that; for Vauvenargues is offering to an élite, if not to all men, a viable alternative to what he felt was the stultifying pessimism (or, rather, the demoralizing reading all too readily made) of the *Maximes* of *La Rochefoucauld. Like the latter, Vauvenargues had known disappointed ambition and the incomprehension of a ruling circle which was insensitive to true merit. But animated by what he considered to be a more just, generous, and rounded vision of the human character, he chose to become a champion of heroic glory, a rehabilitator of the passions, a spokesman for man's true capacity for exploiting his own moral energy and his noble instincts.

Reading Vauvenargues—whom life treated so cruelly—reveals a man of great inner serenity and strength. Small wonder that his intimates (e.g. Voltaire, *Marmontel) gave him unreserved and tender admiration. Readers should be warned, however, that all editions (including the 'authoritative' one produced by D. L. Gilbert in 1857) fall well short of scholarly standards. [JR]

See G. Lanson, *Le Marquis de Vauvenargues* (1930); P. M. Fine, *Vauvenargues and La Rochefoucauld* (1974).

Vaux-le-Vicomte. Magnificent palace near Melun, built for *Fouquet in 1656–9. Incorporating the work of the architect Le Vau, the painter *Le Brun, and the landscape gardener Le Nôtre, it anticipated the splendours of *Versailles, and was the scene of lavish artistic festivals at which *Louis XIV was entertained before ordering Fouquet's arrest. *La

Fontaine, a frequent guest, sang its praises in his *Fragment du songe de Vaux.* [PF]

VEIRAS (or Vairasse, etc.), Denis (after 1622–c.1700). Writer of Huguenot extraction, who lived in England and France and published the *Histoire des Sévarambes* (5 vols., 1677–9; 1 vol. in English, 1675). It is the most important early *Utopian novel, integrating history and customs from ancient Greece and Persia, the Incas, the Old Testament, and *Louis XIV's France. The society organized in the Austral Land by Sevarias, an emigrant from Persia, has an elective ruler, governing both state and religion. The state owns all property, distributing to the citizens whatever they need. They are happy, industrious, but not perfect; illness and corruption occur (as some of the intercalated stories illustrate). All are equal, except for elected officials. The agrarian economy is prosperous, the public works impressive. The religion, lacking priests and doctrinally tolerant, combines theism and sun-worship. Life is elaborately regulated; numerous civil and religious rites mark stages of personal development. Boys and girls are educated together. Marriage is compulsory, military service also, for both sexes. Some of the book can be read as social criticism, but its publication was unhindered; it may have been meant to support indirectly the policies of *Colbert. [CJB]

Velche, see WELCHE.

Venceslas. Tragedy by *Rotrou, performed 1647, published 1648 (at first with the designation of tragicomedy, but republished as a tragedy later that year). It is loosely derived from a Spanish play (Francisco de Rojas Zorilla, *No hay ser padre siendo rey*, 1640). Venceslas, the ageing king of Poland, abdicates in favour of his dangerously wild son Ladislas in order to avoid having to uphold the death-sentence passed on Ladislas for murder. It was Rotrou's most successful play, enjoying frequent revivals (several by *Molière's company) and reprintings in the 17th c. [GJ]

Vendanges de Suresnes, Les, see DU RYER.

Vendée, Guerre de la. Cruel civil war fought in the west of France between 1793 and 1795, caused by the resentment that the traditional rural communities felt for the town-dwellers, whose encroaching *Revolution (with its ever more pronounced anti-monarchical, anti-religious policies) was becoming increasingly unacceptable. Disturbances had already occurred (October 1791, August 1792), but one piece of interference in local life finally proved intolerable: faced with the enforced military levy decreed by the Convention, the Vendée rose (10 March 1793). Despite initial successes (March–July), the insurgents were heavily defeated at Luçon (13 August). Thereafter the Republic took the initiative, implementing the scorched-earth policy agreed by the Convention. The 'war' ended with rebel defeats

at Le Mans and then at Savenay (23 December). The sporadic guerilla resistance of early 1794 was answered with vigorous counter-insurgency methods, especially through Turreau's 'infernal columns', and was then slowly contained (December 1794–November 1795).

Deaths through battle, disease, epidemics, starvation, and summary executions were numerous (probably in the region of 150,000). But current revisionists who speak of 'genocide' have merely rediscovered and tailored to their own needs the thesis first advanced by *Babeuf who, in *Le Système de dépopulation* (1794), accused *Robespierre of deliberately causing the extermination of 1 million people in the Vendée in the furtherance of his economic policies. [See also CHOUANNERIE.] [JR]

VENDÔME, Philippe de, see TEMPLE.

Vendredi ou les Limbes du Pacifique (1967, revised version 1972). First novel by *Tournier. This is a version of what he calls the myth of Robinson Crusoe, Friday, and the desert island, although, despite the promise of the title, Vendredi does not make his appearance until over half-way through, and it is he, not Robinson, who leaves the island for 'civilization'. This dense novel of ideas bears the marks of *Lévi-Strauss, Freud, *Lacan, and *Sartre, but above all engages the reader in a dialectical reading of myth and history. Tournier, the failed philosopher, admirably succeeds here as a creator of fiction. He produced a version for children, *Vendredi ou la Vie sauvage*, in 1971. [IWR]

Vengeance Radiguel, La, see RAOUL DE HOUDENC.

Vent, Le, see SIMON, C.

Ventre de Paris, Le. Novel by *Zola, the third in the *Rougon-Macquart* series, published 1873 and set in the market district of Paris, Les Halles. It is largely a political satire, a complement to La *Curée, dealing with the unprincipled support for the Empire from the materially contented lower bourgeoisie. Florent, a social idealist, returns to Paris after escaping from a penal colony in Cayenne, whence he had been deported after being wrongly arrested for resistance to the coup d'état of December 1851. He lodges with his half-brother Quenu, who now runs a prosperous delicatessen business with his wife Lisa, the daughter of Antoine Macquart. When Florent, dreaming of a just society, involves himself in a plot against the Empire, Lisa contributes to his arrest and subsequent deportation.

The novel presents an allegorical struggle between the 'Fat' (the comfortable, conservative, complacent, bourgeois supporters of the new regime) and the 'Thin' (the dissident political idealists like Florent, or artists like Claude Lantier, Lisa's nephew). It is Claude, the future hero of L'*Œuvre* (1886), who sums up the moral of the story in the final phrase: 'Quels gredins que les honnêtes gens!'

Besides its political theme, the novel is noteworthy for its impressive, *Hugolian evocation of Les Halles, and especially for its *nature morte* descriptions of market produce, notably the famous anthology piece, the 'symphony of cheeses'.   [DB]

Vénus d'Ille, La, see MÉRIMÉE.

Vénus physique, La, see MAUPERTUIS.

VERCINGÉTORIX. Gaulish chief of the first century BC, leader of resistance against Julius Caesar. He was victorious at Gergovia in the Auvergne but, having been defeated at Alesia in Burgundy, was taken in triumph to Rome and executed. Although defeated, he has acquired the aura of a French national hero [see also ASTÉRIX].

VERCORS (pseud. of Jean Bruller) (1902–91). Novelist and publisher. He began as an illustrator, then in World War II assumed his now-celebrated role as editor of the clandestine Éditions de *Minuit, linked to the London Cahiers du Silence. His influential novella *Le Silence de la mer* (1942) charts moral resistance through silence to the seductions of the cultured 'good' German, and embodies in a girl and an old man paradoxes of weakness and strength. *La Marche à l'étoile* (1943) describes the plight of patriotic French Jews betrayed by fellow countrymen. His later novels are analyses of collaboration and corruption, or humanist fables.   [MMC]

Vercors, Le. A high and inaccessible plateau between Grenoble and the Drome, the stronghold of an important *maquis* in World War II, and the scene of a tragic defeat for the Resistance [see OCCUPATION AND RESISTANCE].

Verdun. Town in the east of France, a place of great strategic importance over the centuries. It was the site of a legendary siege of World War I, in which the heroic and immensely costly French resistance was led by General *Pétain, the watchword being: 'Ils ne passeront pas.'

Verdurin, Monsieur and Madame. Bourgeois couple who figure prominently, together with their salon ('le petit clan') in Proust's *À la recherche du temps perdu*. Madame Verdurin eventually becomes the princesse de Guermantes.

VERGNIAUD, Pierre-Victurnien (1753–93). The most eloquent of the *Girondin orators during the *Revolution. Having practised as a lawyer in Bordeaux, he was elected to the Assemblée Législative in 1791 and played a leading role in the battles between Girondins and Montagnards in the Convention in April and May 1793. His magnificent, rather literary speeches, several of them directed against *Robespierre, were not enough to save his party from defeat, nor himself from execution. His *Éloge de Mirabeau* (1791) is an important text for the theory of revolutionary eloquence.   [PF]

VERHAEREN, Émile (1855–1916). One of the major figures of francophone Belgian literature and an important channel for Franco-Belgian literary relationships, particularly during the *Decadent and *Symbolist periods, Verhaeren began by publishing descriptive, *Parnassian poetry (*Les Flamandes*, 1883; *Les Moines*, 1886). This was followed by a period of intense anguish expressed in the sombre trilogy of *Les Soirs* (1887), *Les Débâcles* (1888), and *Les Flambeaux noirs* (1890), Verhaeren's first volume of *vers libre* poetry. Thereafter, a newly found affirmation of life and commitment to a socialist ethic led him to the highly personal adaptation of Symbolist mysticism found in the poetry of *Les Campagnes hallucinées* (1893), *Les Villes tentaculaires* (1895), and *Les Forces tumultueuses* (1902), for which he is best known. Here his regret at the demise of the countryside is countered by a Utopian vision of modern urban civilization, whose violent, creative energies are expressed in a lyricism of powerful images, varied rhythms, and fragmented structures of sounds. This has been related to Expressionism, notably that of Ensor, of whom Verhaeren wrote an important early study (1909). The themes and forms of this poetry made Verhaeren an important presence in the poetic trends which emerged from the Symbolist movement at the turn of the century while his poetry on Flemish landscapes (1904–11) made him his country's national poet.   [JK]

Véritable saint Genest, Le. Tragedy by *Rotrou, performed 1645, published 1647. At the court of the emperor Diocletian the actor-manager Genest is asked to stage a play on the conversion of St Adrian (martyred by Diocletian). Genest, playing Adrian, is himself converted during performance, so provoking his own martyrdom. The 'outer' play comments on the staging and rehearsing of the 'inner' play, and there is constant movement between different levels of 'reality', emphasized by the presence of the on-stage spectators of the 'inner' play. The play invites comparison with Pierre Corneille's martyr-plays *Polyeucte* and *Théodore* and with his *L'*Illusion comique*.   [GJ]

VERLAINE, Paul (1844–96), a poet of contrasts, moods, and musical lyricism, is generally considered to be one of the major French poets of the second half of the 19th c. With *Baudelaire, *Rimbaud, and *Mallarmé, he is sometimes seen as a precursor of the French Symbolist poets of the 1880s. If, however, the idea of French literary *Symbolism is viewed in the broader context of innovative and musical approaches to poetic creation—from Baudelaire to *Valéry—Verlaine may be regarded as a direct contributor to Symbolist poetics.

He was born in Metz, into a middle-class family, and died in penury in Paris, a generally respected literary figure but dependent on financial support from individuals and public authorities. He was educated at the Lycée Bonaparte (Condorcet) in Paris, and from 1862 studied at the Faculté de Droit. His academic progress was limited by his preference for café-life, literature, and drink; in 1864 his father withdrew him from the university and he was employed by an insurance company and then as a clerk at the Hôtel de Ville. He published poems in Le Parnasse contemporain (1866) [see PARNASSE]. An unstable, contradictory, often unpredictable character, he lived a life of extremes, by turns violent and loving, rebellious and orderly. He met Mathilde Mauté in 1867 and was married to her in 1870. He served in the Garde Nationale during the seige of Paris, 1870–1, and was associated with the *Commune.

In 1871 he invited Rimbaud to Paris, and thereafter began a series of often tempestuous escapades with him. His marriage, already unstable, broke up after the birth of their son, and was legally ended in 1874. In 1872–3 Verlaine and Rimbaud lived for a time in Brussels and then in London, where Verlaine—having been born in Metz, by now ceded to Germany—opted for French nationality. During this time Verlaine wrote the poems of Romances sans paroles. After their return to Brussels, Verlaine wounded Rimbaud with a revolver during a drunken quarrel in July 1873, and was sentenced to two years' imprisonment. During his imprisonment he wrote 'Art poétique', and following his separation from Mathilde he turned to the Catholic faith into which he had been born, a 'conversion' which was at the origin of poems in the collection Sagesse.

Following his release from prison, in January 1875, he eventually returned to England, where he held teaching posts in Stickney, Lincolnshire, and Bournemouth. He subsequently taught in various schools, including Notre-Dame in Rethel near Reims, where he befriended a pupil, Lucien Létinois, and at Lymington, Isle of Wight. He attempted farming, unsuccessfully. In 1885 he was fined and briefly imprisoned for attacking his widowed mother. In later years he suffered increasing ill health, including rheumatism, diabetes, and syphilis. However, he was becoming widely recognized as a poet of distinction, and in the late 1880s the poètes décadents [see DECADENCE] claimed him as a leader. He gave public lectures in several countries, and on the death of *Leconte de Lisle in 1894 he was elected 'Prince des Poètes'.

Verlaine's main poetical works were Poèmes saturniens (1866), Fêtes galantes (1869), La Bonne Chanson (1870, 1872), Romances sans paroles (1873–4), Sagesse (1880–1), Jadis et naguère (1885), Amour (1888), Parallèlement (1889), Bonheur (1891), Chansons pour elle (1891). His prose works include Les Poètes maudits (1884), short critical studies of several poets, including himself, under the anagram 'Pauvre Lelian'. His best work retains a wide appeal, for its musical qualities, its simplicity and directness of expression, its subtle, lyrical evocations of shades of feeling and desire. Verlaine was not a thinker, but a creator of moods, derived from his own sensations and shifting aspirations. A cautiously experimental prosodist, he rejected vers libre, preferring vers libéré, which he defined authoritatively in 'Art poétique'. This poem, published in Jadis et naguère, emphasizing musicality, fluidity, half-tones, variety of rhyme, and avoidance of grandiloquence, was an important contribution to the contemporary debate about the nature of poetry and to the development of French poetic technique since Romanticism. Verlaine's naïvety was far removed from artlessness, and his troubled life left a legacy of fine poetry.   [BCS]

See A. Adam. Verlaine (1953); V. P. Underwood, Verlaine et l'Angleterre (1956).

VERNE, Jules (1828–1905). French novelist. Long considered a minor author for young people, Verne is now accorded more critical attention; many French writers admit enthusiasm for him. While losing some of his status as a scientific seer, he has begun to shed the mantle of political prophet which almost replaced it. What remains are some 18 Voyages extraordinaires, the general title under which Verne's work appeared in volumes. Their freshness is sustained by narrative energy; their imaginative inventiveness, underpinned by scrupulous detail. They can be read naïvely, but there is also a vein of irony, even in the lists which appear to compel belief.

A studious pupil, though he apparently attempted to run away at the age of 11, Verne was expected to follow his father by studying law in Nantes. For sentimental reasons his studies continued in Paris; he obtained his licence in 1849, but was more interested in the theatre and had begun writing plays: thanks to *Dumas père, his comedy Les Pailles rompues was performed in 1850. In 1851 he became secretary of the new Théâtre Lyrique, and began publishing in the journal Le Musée des familles stories later reworked as Un drame au Mexique (1876) and Un drame dans les airs (in Le Docteur Ox, 1874).

Whilst still writing for the theatre with his musician friend Hignard, he became acquainted with scientists and explorers. Martin Paz appeared in the Musée in 1852, and Verne abandoned his studies, though his success in theatre was slight: on his marriage in 1857 he bought into a financial agency in Paris. In 1859 and 1861 he visited Scotland and Norway with Hignard, and in 1862 his friendship with *Nadar led him to write the story which, revised on the publisher *Hetzel's advice, was serialized in 1862 and published in volume form in 1863 as Cinq semaines en ballon. Success was immediate, and Hetzel retained Verne as a regular contributor to the Magasin d'éducation et de récréation. Verne later returned successfully to theatre with dramatizations of his novels.

The first works examine scientific preoccupations of the day. balloons (though, since they could not be steered, heavier-than-air flight later takes over in Robur le conquérant, 1886); the Earth inside and out in

Vernet

Voyage au centre de la terre (1864), and *De la terre à la lune* (1865); polar exploration in *Aventures du capitaine Hatteras* (1866). Verne, however, was not a scientist, and his wonderful machines generally extrapolate from what existed: a *Nautilus* had been tested in 1800; the *Great Eastern*, on which he travelled in 1867, described in *Une ville flottante* (1871), is enlarged to *L'Île à hélice* (1895). Electricity, which powers submarines in *Vingt mille lieues sous les mers* (1870) or *Mathias Sandorf* (1885), remains vague, although in *Le Château des Carpathes* (1892), a story of benighted love and electricity, Verne imagines a *téléphote* which would enable people to see each other at a distance. Travel and the exotic are themes as important as science in *Le Tour du monde en quatre-vingts jours* (1873), *Les Enfants du capitaine Grant* (1867), *Michel Strogoff* (1876), and others.

Education was his brief, and his books are geography lessons which do not escape the bias of their time. Verne shows oppressed peoples, but he is not so much anti-colonial—accepting French colonialism in *L'Invasion de la mer* (1905)—as anti-English (*P'tit Bonhomme*, 1892). Even when they are heroes, his Englishmen are figures of fun; his preferred anglophones are Scots or Americans, as in *L'*Île mystérieuse* (1874), though even Americans may be criticized for their arrogance, as in *Sens dessus dessous* (1889). Heroes may be challengers of society: Nemo, for example, or Robur, Thomas Roch in *Face au drapeau* (1895) or Kamyk Pacha in *Maître Antifer* (1894); but Robur is dangerous rather than admirable in *Maître du monde* (1904), and in *Les Naufragés du 'Jonathan'* (posthumous, 1909, published by his son Michel) events undermine Kaw-Djer's anarchism. Indeed, although Verne was a radical councillor in Amiens and a firm believer in scientific progress, his society is hierarchical: older men have authority rooted in knowledge, servants know their place, young men must learn and prove themselves; male friendship and rivalry are important, and, though women are not totally absent, his is a predominantly male universe, where man's search for knowledge is paramount.   [SFN]

See S. Vierne, *Jules Verne* (1986).

VERNET, Claude-Joseph (1714–89), came from a family of French artists. He first established his reputation in England, then exhibited at the Paris Salon from 1749 for 40 years. His lively, theatrical seascapes, in particular his late shipwreck scene from *Paul et Virginie*, were immensely popular; *Diderot greatly admired his painting. His son Carle (1758–1836) painted battle-scenes and portraits of Napoleon.   [JPC]

VÉRON, Louis-Désiré (1798–1867). French newspaper proprietor. A doctor by training, he founded the *Revue de Paris* and later bought and developed *Le *Constitutionnel*.

Versailles. A hunting-lodge and then a modest château in the reign of Louis XIII, Versailles became one of the main interests of the young *Louis XIV soon after he began to rule in 1661. The work was to last for 42 years and cost 82 million *livres*. The first stage was to enlarge Versailles in order to make an appropriate setting for court festivals, notably the *Plaisirs de l'Île Enchantée (1664). The gardens (designed by Le Nôtre), the fountains, and the statues were an essential part of the project. The next stage, the work of Le Vau, was to surround the original chateau with a U-shaped palace, the famous *enveloppe* (1668–74). What rendered this magnificent palace out of date almost as soon as it was finished was the king's decision to live there (together with his court and administration) on a more or less permanent basis. Jules Hardouin-Mansart, therefore, added two more floors to the palace, as well as designing the great Galerie des Glaces to accommodate *Lebrun's paintings of the king's most famous deeds. It was this third Versailles, inaugurated in 1682, which accommodated the king's everyday life, while *Marly (constructed from 1679 onwards) became his new palace of pleasure. Versailles, which was already becoming a tourist attraction, continued to house the royal administration and the court until the Revolution.   .   [UPB]

Vers et prose, see FORT.

Versification

1. Rhythm and Metre

In the standard view, the metrical foundation of regular French verse is syllabic, which is also to say isosyllabic: its lines are composed of a fixed and equal number of syllables. Although the principle of isosyllabism may imply that that syllables are quantitatively equal (isochronous), this is clearly not so, as experimental phonetics has demonstrated.

The ascendancy of the syllable as the unit of metric definition in French is a result of the gradual erosion of accent (stress): originally French accent was either oxytonic (falling on the last syllable of the word) or paroxytonic (falling on the penultimate syllable of the word, if the final syllable was an articulated *e* mute, or *e atone*). But as it weakened, accentuation shifted from word to word-group (syntactic segment), where, correspondingly, it fell on the final syllable of the group (if no *e atone* was involved).

French verse's system of accentuation, then, depends on the arrangement of word-groups within the line, which is itself constituted by a given number of syllables. The metrical rules for French verse are in fact minimal: the final syllable in the line must be accentuated, as must the final syllable of any unit (half-line) created by a caesura (see below); other accentuation is optional. Thus, the *alexandrine (12-syllable line), which has a fixed medial caesura, must have accents on its sixth and twelfth syllables. It usually has two further accents, one in each half-line (hemistich), but neither the occurrence nor the position of these 'secondary' accents is prescribed. The standard alexandrine might be presented thus:

$$\underline{-\ -\ \overset{(\prime)}{-}\ -\ \overset{\prime}{-}\ \|\ \ -\ -\ \overset{(\prime)}{-}\ -\ -\ \overset{\prime}{-}}$$

The octosyllable, on the other hand, which has no caesura—a caesura occurs only in lines of nine syllables or more—has just one obligatory accent, on the eighth syllable; but it usually has one other accent (sometimes two), which, again, may occur on any other syllable(s) in the line; thus:

$$\underline{-\ -\ \overset{(\prime)}{-}\ -\ \overset{(\prime)}{-}\ -\ \overset{\prime}{-}}$$

The rhythm of a French line is usually described in terms of the syllabic groups created by the accents:

J'étais séul | près des flóts ‖ par une núit | d'étóiles.

(3 + 3 + 4 + 2)

Pas un nuáge | aux ciéux, | sur les mérs | pas

de vóiles (4 + 2 + 3 + 3)
(*Hugo, 'Extase')

or

Allons, Julíe, il faut t'atténdre

(4 + 4)

A me vóir quelque jóur en céndre.

(3 + 3 + 2)
(*Musset, 'A Julie')

An important distinguishing feature of regular French verse has been the retention of the articulated *e atone*, long after its disappearance in the spoken language. In regular verse, an *e atone* within the line is counted as a syllable, and pronounced, when it is followed by a consonant or aspirate *h* (as in 'une' and 'quelque' above); it is elided before a vowel or mute *h* (as in 'nuage' and 'Julie' above). At the end of the line, it is treated as extra-metrical (not counted) and serves to define the rhyme as feminine (see below). When an articulated *e atone* occurs immediately after an accentuated vowel, as in *Baudelaire's lines:

Je t'adóre à l'égál ‖ de la vóûte noctúrne,

(3 + 3 + 3 + 3 + 3)

Ô váse de tristésse, ‖ ô gránde tacitúrne,

(2 + 4 + 2 + 4)

the consequences are twofold. First, the *e atone* is normally counted as part of the measure following that in which the accentuated syllable occurs—e.g. 'de la voû: | te nocturne'—creating a *coupe enjambante* (a word, 'voûte', straddles the *coupe*, or bar-line, of the measure): in other words, rhythmic measures are the syllabic spans between one accent and the next. Secondly, the *e atone* lengthens the accentuated vowel preceding it, and thus not only has a liaisory function between words, but also injects tonality or emotion (compassion, regret, irony, admiration) into the accentuated vowel. But there are occasions when, for syntactic or expressive reasons, the articulated e cannot be carried forward into the following measure. In *Racine's line, for example:

Mais párle: de son sórt ‖ qui t'a rendú l'arbítre?

(*Andromaque*, v. iii)

if we read 'Mais par: | le de son sort', we change the syntax of the line. We must instead read 'Mais parle: | de son sort', and notate the rhythm as 3' + 3 + 4 + 2, where the apostrophe on the first '3' indicates that the measure, unusually, ends with an *e atone*, called a *coupe lyrique*. In other instances, the *coupe lyrique*, because of its tendency to rupture the line, might be called upon to reinforce expressive effects. In *Leconte de Lisle's line from 'Midi':

Tout se tait. L'air flamboie ‖ et brûle sans haleine

a 3 + 3 + 3' + 3 reading might be preferred to a 3 + 3 + 4 + 2 one, simply to emphasize the literally breathtaking torridity, and to introduce the stillness which 'sans haleine' then confirms. Alternatively, one might feel that 3 + 3 + 4 + 2 does better justice to the sense of suffocating envelopment.

2. The Caesura

The nature of the caesura remains problematic. It is not a pause (interruption) properly speaking, though it may be accompanied by one; it is rather a point of linguistic and structural (semantic) insistence; it is best seen as a feature of the sixth syllable rather than as an event which takes place *after* the sixth syllable. In addition, the caesura is a syllabic checkpoint. If, as Cornulier's findings indicate (1982), the ear is incapable of reliable syllabic perception beyond a limit of eight syllables, then the caesura is a necessary safeguard of the line's syllabic presence and integrity.

The fixity of the caesura in the alexandrine came, in the 19th c., to represent all that was fossilized and mechanical in French verse. If, ironically, the decasyllable, whose caesura is not metrically fixed, saw its standard 4 ‖ 6 and 6 ‖ 4 divisions shift to a symmetrical 5 ‖ 5 in 19th-c. practice, the medial position of the alexandrine's caesura was felt to yoke the line to a rhetoric dominated not by organic variability but by repetitive binary relationships of antithesis, apposition, and equation. In order to oust declamation in favour of the speaking voice, the *Romantics sought to displace the caesura in two ways: first, by varying its location in the line, in the *alexandrin brisé*, and thus registering the fluctuations of dramatic speech; secondly, by effacing the caesura, in the *alexandrin trimètre*, where demands of syntactical cohesion override the demands of metrical separation and replace binary structure with a ternary one. Thus, a standard scansion of:

Il paraît donc assez simple et facile à croire

(Musset, 'Mardoche')

would interpose the caesura between an adverb ('assez') and the adjective ('simple') it governs. It would make better sense of the line's syntax to erase the caesura and read 'Il paraît donc | assez simple | et facile à croire' (4 + 3 + 5). But these 'innovations' need to be treated with circumspection.

The *alexandrin brisé*, as described by Ténint in 1844, is often only an alexandrine in which the natural hierarchy of accentual intensity has been changed, so that a secondary accent becomes primary, e.g.

> Plus d'unité. Les nœuds des États se défont.
> $(4 \parallel 2 + 3 + 3)$
> (Hugo, *Les Burgraves*, 2nd part, i)

But to read this line with a $4 \parallel 8$ division is to give undue weight to the major syntactic break and to define the caesura as a pause rather than as a metrico-structural articulation. The line reads perfectly well as $4 + 2 \parallel 3 + 3$, which has the added advantage, precisely, of undoing 'les nœuds ‖ des Etats'. Similarly, the *trimètre* often has more expressivity if read as a regular alexandrine with *enjambement at the caesura rather than as a *trimètre*: e.g.

> Cet homme fait le bon mauvais, le mauvais pire
> (Hugo, *Marion de Lorme*, iv. vi)

works better perhaps as $2 + 4 \parallel 2 + 4$ than as $4 + 4 + 4$, and

> Ne plus penser, ne plus aimer, ne plus haïr
> (*Gautier, 'Thébaïde')

better as $4 + 2 \parallel 2 + 4$ than as $4 + 4 + 4$. But there is no doubt that the alexandrine was becoming more fluid, more rhythmically ambiguous, and that it developed in the 19th c. towards the condition described by *Mallarmé: 'Les fidèles àl'alexandrin, notre hexamètre, desserrent intérieurement ce mécanisme rigide et puéril de sa mesure' ('Crise de vers').

3. Rhyme

It is often argued that rhyme was treated as indispensable to French verse, until the end of the 19th c., because it had a metrical or near-metrical function: the structural recurrence of rhyme is exploited to mark the end of the syllabic string; and the acoustic foregrounding that accompanies rhyme intensifies the line-terminal accent, reinforcing both the boundary and the intonational shape of the line. Some commentators are less convinced of rhyme's line-demarcative function than they are of its stanzaic function. Rhyme-schemes are rhythms of repeated sound, patterns of interval, sometimes complicated by syllabic variations in the line (heterosyllabic stanzas); the basic 'rhythms' are: enclosed rhyme, or *rimes embrassées* (abba); alternating rhyme, or *rimes croisées* (abab); and couplets, or *rimes plates* (aabbcc). Rhyme-schemes are also patterns of intonation: the last two lines of a stanza in *rimes croisées*, for example, tend to repeat the intonational configuration of the first two at a slightly lower pitch, while a stanza in *rimes embrassées* produces an intonational suspension in its third line, which the fourth resolves with a more definitive cadence.

The metrical importance of rhyme in French is complemented by its expressive flexibility: in contrast to English rhyme, French rhyme distinguishes between different degrees of rhyme (*pauvre*, *suffisante*, *riche*), and between masculine and femi-

nine rhymes, and their attendant 'tonalities'. In recent verse-analysis a classification of degrees of rhyme according to the number of phonemes involved, regardless of whether they precede or succeed the tonic vowel—thus, *rime pauvre* (one phoneme, the tonic vowel: beauté | aimé), *rime suffisante* (two phonemes: père | frère), *rime riche* (three or more phonemes: rêve | grève), *rime léonine* (two or more syllables: majestueuse | fastueuse)—has superseded the earlier distinction between rhymes that include the consonant preceding the tonic vowel (*consonne d'appui*) and those that do not; in the older system, a shared *consonne d'appui* was the mark of a *rime riche*. Rich rhyme was much canvassed by the Romantics, since it invests rhyme-words with more resonance, colour, and dramatic presence, guarantees the depth and authenticity of thought and feeling, and safeguards the rigour of the poetic vocation. Generally, however, poets tend to mix degrees of rhyme, both out of necessity and to vary rhyme's intrusiveness.

The rule that masculine and feminine rhyme-pairs should alternate became generalized in the latter half of the 16th c. and acquired sufficient obligatoriness to warrant its being treated as a metrical feature. Even though the *e atone*, which identifies feminine rhymes, has disappeared from pronunciation, commentators have been in the habit of distinguishing between the different expressive ranges of the masculine and the feminine: the masculine rhyme is abrupt, hard, dry; the feminine yielding, soft, evanescent. Even if one deplores this sexual (sexist) mythology, the fact remains that masculine syllables have a tendency to be open (consonant-vowel) and feminine ones to be closed (vowel-consonant), ending with a protractable consonant.

4. *Vers libéré* and *vers libre*

The erosion of the *loi de l'alternance des rimes* began in the 1860s, with the emergence of that looser form of regular verse known as *vers libéré*. Poets, among them *Verlaine, Mallarmé, *Rimbaud, *Corbière, and *Laforgue, exploited with more frequency those devices which undermine the equilibrium and integrity of the classical verse-line: *enjambement, the *trimètre*, the *coupe lyrique*, assonance in place of rhyme, and the *vers impair*, the line with an odd (as opposed to even) number of syllables, which sounds dangerously like a *vers faux*, a miscount, and thus helps to sap syllabic confidence. As a result, rhythms lost their firm contours and, consequently, their aptitude for controlled, oratorical utterance. Instead, they acquired a certain indeterminacy, an unpredictability, which favoured the intimate, the prosaic, the impromptu, the *fantaisiste*.

The final prosodic constraints, syllabism and rhyme (or assonance), were removed with the appearance of free verse (*le vers libre*) in 1886, in the pages of Gustave *Kahn's journal *La Vogue* (work by Rimbaud, Laforgue, Kahn himself, Paul *Adam, and

Jean *Moréas). The undoing of the syllabic system was facilitated by the increasingly ambiguous status of the *e atone*—should it be counted or not when unelided?—and by doubts about the syllabic value of contiguous vowels. Paradoxically, however, syllabic ambiguity produces rhythmic multiplicity; a single line of free verse is potentially several lines, each with its own inherited or invented associations. Furthermore, the dissolution of syllabism was accompanied by a corresponding renewal of interest in accent. Many analysts believed that the demands of accentual recurrence determined the relative length of measures and lineation, that rhythm was created by the distribution of accents rather than by numbers of syllables.

At the same time, accent was more flexibly perceived: aside from the *accent tonique*, the word-group accent which turns syntactic segments into rhythmic measures, theorists drew attention to sub-accents within the measure, and to accents which transcended the measure, the accents of speech act and sustaining tone. Rhythm was now intimately linked with accentual activity of an intense and varied kind, varied in both source and degree. Rhyme, too, contributed to this sensitization of verse texture: it ceased to be the servant of rhetoric and became the instrument of purely associative mechanisms; by varying the interval between rhymes, by introducing rhymelessness and repetition alongside rhyme, by increasing line-internal echoes, the poet was able to multiply the levels of consciousness at which the poem operated. By allowing the uncontrolled and the improvised to inhabit verse, the *vers-libristes* opened poetry to stream of consciousness. [See also PROSE POEM.]   [CS]

See J. Mazaleyrat, *Eléments de métrique française* (1974); C. Scott, *French Verse-Art: A Study* (1980); B. de Cornulier, *Théorie du vers* (1982).

Vers libre, Vers libéré, see VERSIFICATION, 4.

Vers libres classiques. As opposed to modern *vers libre* [see VERSIFICATION, 4], these are various fluid verse forms, mixing rhyme-schemes and lines of different lengths, used by many poets in the 17th and 18th c. The outstanding example is La Fontaine's *Fables*.

Ver-Vert, see GRESSET.

VEUILLOT, Louis-François (1813–83). Polemical journalist, director from 1842 of the very popular review *L'Univers*. The son of an illiterate cooper, converted to a fervent *Ultramontane Catholicism, a populist and a thorn in the flesh of the liberal bourgeoisie, he kept up a stream of virulent articles, pamphlets, and books (e.g. *Les Libres Penseurs*, 1848; *Les Odeurs de Paris*, 1867) against progressive ideas in politics and religion, against capitalists, Jews, and the free press. He also wrote poetry, novels, and literary criticism, and left an important and voluminous correspondence.   [PF]

VIAN, Boris (1920–59). French novelist, playwright, poet, jazz musician and critic, song-writer and singer ('Le Déserteur', 1954), frequenter of *Saint-Germain-des-Prés. He was an anti-*Existentialist, though closely linked with *Sartre and *Les *Temps modernes*, and a member of the Collège de *'Pataphysique from 1952. Vian wrote lively plays in a proto-*Absurdist vein, notably *Les Bâtisseurs d'empire* (1959), but his greatest literary achievement lies in his novels: *Vercoquin et le Plancton* (written 1943–4, published 1947), *L'Écume des jours* (1947), a sad, sentimental love-story with a disconcerting logic and beauty of its own (satirizing incidentally, and rather obviously, Jean-Sol Partre and his fans); *L'Automne à Pékin* (also 1947), which describes a journey to Exopotamia, and relates, more cynically, another story of impossible love; finally, *L'Herbe rouge* (1950), a personal view of childhood which reappears in *L'Arrache-cœur* (1953), a story of possessive maternal love. Vian was also the author of four novels published under the pen-name of Vernon Sullivan, including *J'irai cracher sur vos tombes* (1946), a pastiche, purporting to be a translation from the American, written in ten days and resulting in a conviction for pornography. Vian is irreverent, iconoclastic, provocative; he is also linguistically and lyrically inventive with a gift for satire, Surrealist fantasy, and a refined sense of logical absurdity.
                                         [PS]

VIAU, Théophile de, see THÉOPHILE DE VIAU.

Vicaire savoyard, Profession de foi du, see ÉMILE.

Vichy. This town in central France was the headquarters of the collaborationist government during the German *Occupation of France in World War II. The word is often used by itself to refer to the regime.

Victor, ou l'Enfant de la forêt, see PIXERÉCOURT.

Victor, ou les Enfants au pouvoir. *Surrealist farce by *Vitrac. The hero, Victor, a 9-year-old six-foot-tall prodigy, is shocked and demoralized by the ludicrous behaviour of the grown-ups. He denounces their stupidity, exposes his father's adultery, and dies on his birthday while his parents commit suicide. In this grotesque parody of the drawing-room play, death is represented by an elegant lady visitor who farts uncontrollably, much to everyone's consternation. The techniques and dialogue were later imitated by *Ionesco. *Anouilh mounted a notable production in 1962.   [DHW]

Vida. *Occitan for 'life', used of biographical narratives such as the *Vida sant Honorat*, and most frequently of the short prose biographies of the *troubadours, composed from the early 13th c. onwards. Sometimes only a few sentences long, *vidas* are fairly accurate when stating a poet's social rank and place of origin, but are considered generally untrustworthy as regards other circumstances

Vidal de la Blache

of his career, such as his amorous attachments. *Vidas* serve as prefaces to author sections in some troubadour *chansonnier* manuscripts. An analogous genre, the *razo*, is used to preface an individual song, 'explaining' the circumstances of its composition. Some *razos* are early instances of *novellas*. Both genres are chiefly interesting as early documents in the history of reception. [SK]

VIDAL DE LA BLACHE, Paul (1845–1918). French geographer. Seeking to integrate history and geography, he was especially concerned with the effects of human activity on the physical environment, and opposed the then prevailing conceptions of environmental determinism. From the 1880s to World War I he was professor at the Sorbonne, and the dominant force in French academic geography. Several of his works have remained classics, especially his posthumously published *Principes de la géographie humaine* (1926). [MHK]

VIDOCQ, François-Eugène (1775–1857). Criminal turned police chief, whose *Mémoires* (1828, probably ghosted) are said to have been an inspiration for the creation of Balzac's *Vautrin.

Vie, Une, see MAUPASSANT.

Vie de boy, Une, see OYONO.

Vie de Henry Brulard. Autobiographical work by *Stendhal, begun 1835, abandoned four months later. Disjointed and apparently spontaneous, it seeks to embody the workings and searchings of memory, its gaps and illuminations. Though there is constant reference to more recent times and to the moment of writing, it is above all concerned with its hero's sombre early years, his loss of his beloved mother, his antagonistic relations with father and aunt, his escape from detested Grenoble to Paris, and thence with Napoleon's armies to Italy and happiness. As an autobiography it was revolutionary; it is also one of the most quintessentially Stendhalian writings. [PF]

Vie de Jésus. Controversial study by *Renan, which enjoyed great success when published in 1863. Following a similar work of the same title by the German 'Young Hegelian' David Strauss, Renan approached the life of Jesus Christ respectfully, but in a historical rather than a theological perspective. Miracles and other supernatural manifestations were dismissed as incompatible with the laws of nature, and Jesus analysed as an extraordinary man but not a supernatural being. The success of Jesus's message was attributed to its expressing the best insights of the Jewish people and a powerful religious feeling which, in Renan's view, corresponds to the deep-seated aspirations of humanity to transcendence. [MHK]

Vie de Marianne, La. *Memoir-novel by Marivaux, published in instalments between 1731 and 1742. It is

unfinished, though there were some apocryphal endings, and Madame *Riccoboni wrote a continuation imitating the style of the original.

The heroine tells her tale from the vantage-point of advanced years and a secure social position, frequently digressing to reflect on the world in a manner typical of her creator. As a child she had been adopted by the sister of a priest after her parents had been killed by highwaymen. The novel tells how she makes her way in the world. She is at first protected by the hypocritical *dévot* Monsieur de Climal, who tries to seduce her, but she chances to meet Climal's nephew Valville, and they fall in love. She is then adopted by the benevolent Madame de Miran (modelled on Madame de *Lambert), who turns out to be Valville's mother. Family objections to an apparent misalliance are overcome, and all seems to be leading to a happy union when Valville switches his attentions to Marianne's friend Varthon. At this point the narrative breaks off, the last three of the eleven parts being taken up by the quite separate story of another orphan.

The novel is remarkable for the narrator's delicate analyses of thoughts and feelings. The tone is virtuous, and sometimes sentimental, but there are many touches of humour. Early readers were divided in their opinions, as with all of Marivaux's works, but almost all were shocked at the realistic picture of a slanging-match between a coachman and Marianne's landlady, Madame Dutour. [PF]

'Vie de Napoléon racontée dans une grange, La'. A famous episode in Balzac's Le *Médecin de campagne.

Vie de saint Alexis, La. In this biography of a 5th-c. saint, *hagiography gives French literature its first masterpiece. The version dating from c.1050, composed in epic decasyllabics grouped in regular five-line stanzas within a carefully controlled mathematical structure, tells of a patrician's son's renunciation of his bride and social position to live as a hermit, first in the Orient, then under the external staircase of his father's house in Rome. Formal laments over the lost son and husband and the final apotheosis of the saint give the poem a sparse grandeur, diluted in the *romance elaborations of the later versions. [PEB]

Vie de saint Léger, La. One of the earliest documents in French, the biography of St Léger, bishop of Autun, was composed in north-eastern France towards the end of the 10th c. The extant version, conserved at Clermont-Ferrand, was copied by a southern hand in the early 11th c. The text, translated from a Latin *Vita*, tells, in 240 octosyllabic couplets grouped in threes, of the saint's rise to influence under Clothair, his disgrace at the hands of Ebroin, *maire du palais under Chilperic II, and his murder (which occurred in 679/80). Only in the final scenes of martyrdom is the sober account of political intrigue replaced by miracle. [PEB]

Vie des insectes, La, see FABRE, J.-H.

Vie devant soi, La, see GARY.

Vie et demie, La, see SONY LABOU TANSI.

VIÉLÉ-GRIFFIN, Francis (1863–1937). Born in Virginia, Viélé-Griffin studied law in Paris before turning first to painting, then to literature. One of the major exponents of what he called the personal rhythm of *vers libre* (in *Joies,* 1889) and co-editor of the *Entretiens politiques et littéraires* (1890–2), sympathetic to the anarchist cause, he briefly achieved a dominant position within the *Symbolist movement with the publication of *La Chevauchée d'Yeldis* (1893) and *La Clarté de vie* (1897). His poetry, whether exploring mythological themes or evoking the landscapes of the Touraine where he spent much of his time, retained, unlike that of other Symbolists, a profound, simple, and optimistic faith in life.   [JK]

Vie mode d'emploi, La. Novel by *Perec, awarded the Prix Médicis in 1978. A brilliant reassertion of the author's control over the meaning of his text and over the reader's reconstruction of it, Perec's novel renews 19th-c. traditions of narrative copiousness and runs directly counter to the better-known trends of French fiction in the 1960s and 1970s. The vast cast of fictional and non-fictional characters pursue projects with a passion reminiscent of Balzac's *Comédie humaine,* in fields as diverse (and as contemporary) as academic careerism, anthropology, currency speculation, cycle-racing, *haute cuisine,* interior decoration, the theatre, the occult, transvestite cabaret, the history of the Spanish Church in the 17th c., painting, bibliography, and the making and solving of jigsaw puzzles. Few of these 'lives', some narrated at great length, others in a brief paragraph, meet success in the end: Perec's often comic 'manual' is full of the sadness of thwarted ambitions and of the frailty of human life itself.

Set in a Parisian apartment building towards eight in the evening on 23 June 1975, Perec's 'novel of infinite extensions' consists of 99 chapters describing what could be seen simultaneously in each of the rooms if the façade of the building had been removed. The central story of Percival Bartlebooth, an Anglo-American millionaire who spends 20 years of his life circumnavigating the globe and painting a seascape every fortnight, and the following 20 years reassembling the jigsaw puzzles made from those seascapes by the master-craftsman Gaspard Winckler, can be read as a metaphor for the novel itself and for Perec's conception of the work of art: for Bartlebooth's self-negating grand plan is brought to a premature end by blindness and death, and, ironically but foreseeably, leaves its trace in the world.

Perec's masterpiece was written on the basis of a set of formal constraints proposed by *OULIPO, notably the Knight's Tour Problem (for the order of the chapters) and the orthogonal Graeco-Latin bi-square of order 10 (for the chapter contents); it is also a compendium of unacknowledged (mis)quotations from a score of other authors. Not the least of the novel's achievements is to erase all trace of its scaffolding. In its place, Perec puts a mock-scholarly paraphernalia of indexes and alphabetical checklists which also function as extensions of the conventionally narrated fictions. *La Vie mode d'emploi* is labyrinthine by design, bewildering in its scope, an aggressive rejection of the solipsism and linguistic pessimism of Roland *Barthes and *Tel Quel and, in the words of Italo Calvino, 'the last great event in the history of the novel'.   [DMB]

VIEN, Joseph-Marie, see NEOCLASSICISM.

Vies des dames galantes; Vies des dames illustres; Vies des hommes illustres, see BRANTÔME.

Vieux Colombier, Théâtre du, see COPEAU.

Vieux Cordelier, Le, see DESMOULINS.

Vieux Nègre et la médaille, Le, see OYONO.

VIGÉNÈRE, Blaise de (1523–96). Appointed *secrétaire de la chambre* by *Henri III, Vigénère was involved in the Academie du Palais established by the king [see ACADÉMIE DE POÉSIE ET DE MUSIQUE]. His *Traité des chiffres ou Secrètes manières d'écrire* (1587) makes him (after *Postel) one of the best-known representatives of Renaissance cabbalistic science. His interest in alchemy and magic are apparent in the *Traité du feu et du sel* (1618) and the *Traité des comètes* (1578). Also worthy of note is his translation of the Penitential Psalms into 'prose mesurée', which attempts to retain the rhythmic qualities of the original.   [JJS]

VIGNEAULT, Gilles (b. 1928). Canadian poet and song-writer who has achieved a unique status in contemporary Quebec culture. One of his songs, 'Les Gens de mon pays' (1963), has become the unofficial national anthem of Quebec, while the refrain of 'Gens du pays' (1975) is the obligatory song at every birthday celebration. His success lies in his ability to combine modernity of outlook and style with a deep sense of traditional values. While the poems and songs collected in *Tenir paroles* (2 vols., 1983) display great verbal skill, they remain simple in form and have deep roots in the traditional language and culture of French Canada. Love of people and country, devotion to nature and the land, and continuity with the past despite the passage of time are his major themes. All of these concerns come together in the projection of his native village of Natashquan as the mythic heartland of his universe. For modern urban Quebec, the constant return to the village and the people which Vigneault expresses with both humour and tenderness is an important cultural value.   [SIL]

Vigny

VIGNY, Alfred de (1797–1863). Poet, dramatist, and novelist, a distinctive voice within the *Romantic movement in France. Vigny came from an aristocratic background with a tradition of service to the monarchy. As a young man during the *Restoration he served in the army but found military life unsatisfying and monotonous. He aspired to literary success, which came early with the publication of *Poèmes antiques et modernes* (1826), containing the often anthologized pieces 'Moïse' and 'Le Cor'. In the same year he brought out a historical novel *Cinq-Mars. He frequented leading Parisian salons, establishing a reputation as a major Romantic author, translated Shakespeare into French (1829), and turned his own hand to historical drama with *La Maréchale d'Ancre* (1831).

Vigny was always sensitive to the artist's position in society and aware of his difficult relation to political reality. Despite his loyalty to the Bourbons, he had little sympathy for the Restoration and in the wake of the 1830 Revolution he showed interest in the social movements which sought to regenerate society. An important poem of 1831, 'Paris', described the intellectual ferment which followed the 'trois glorieuses' [see JULY MONARCHY]. However, Vigny was disillusioned with political solutions and sceptical of authority. He was preoccupied by the tragic dimension of life and by the dilemma of the creative artist in modern society. In *Stello* (1832) he emphasized the need to separate art from political engagement; in *Chatterton* (1835), one of the classic works of Romantic drama, he developed at length his view of the poetic genius, victim of a materialistic society; and in *Servitude et grandeur militaires* (1835) he examined the military virtues of duty, honour, and service.

After 1835 Vigny published little. He tended to withdraw to his family château, Le Maine Giraud. However, a number of major poems appeared at intervals in the periodical press. These were included in his most important collection of verse, *Les Destinées*, published posthumously in 1864. This contained eleven philosophical poems, including 'La Maison du berger', 'Le Mont des Oliviers', 'La Mort du loup', and 'La Bouteille à la mer'. Vigny believed in the profound seriousness of poetry and in the responsibility of the artist to his age. His concern lay with how modern man, deprived of the traditional consolations of faith and faced with a seemingly meaningless universe, could construct an ethic for living. He emphasized the dignity of human suffering endured in silence, and advised abandoning as unproductive the struggle to answer unanswerable ultimate questions. In *Les Destinées* Vigny viewed poetry not as the outpouring of emotion but as the concentrated expression of thought. [CC]

See P.-G. Castex, *Vigny, l'homme et l'œuvre* (1952); P. Viallaneix, *Vigny par lui-même* (1964).

VIGO, Jean (1905–34). French film-maker. Vigo made only four films before his death from tuberculosis, yet these mark him as one of the greatest of directors. *Zéro de conduite* (1933) is about a revolt in a boys' boarding-school, with images of surrealistic violence (the attack on the headmaster and dignitaries at the end) and great tenderness (a slow-motion procession in the dormitory). *L'Atalante* (1934) tells of a young married couple's quarrel and reconciliation on board a barge, exploiting the oneiric qualities of water. [KAR]

VILAIRE, Etzer, see HAITI, 2.

VILAR, Jean (1912–71). French theatre-director and actor, a leading figure in *décentralisation* and *théâtre populaire*. After training under *Dullin and working in small independent arts theatres, he became frustrated with their narrow élitist horizons and devoted himself to 'people's theatre'. He created two hugely successful institutions, the Festival d'*Avignon and the TNP (the former *Théâtre National Populaire), which he took over in 1951. His production style was noted for its sparse, almost ascetic simplicity. His artistic policy, underpinned by his sense of theatre's social responsibility, was to bring theatre of the highest order, but especially the classical heritage, to the greatest possible number of people. [DWW]

VILDRAC, Charles (1882–1971). French poet and member of the Groupe de l'*Abbaye, he was established as a playwright by *Copeau's enduringly successful production of *Le Paquebot Tenacity* in 1920. In this play an emigrant worker is left to embark alone as his companion abandons him, taking the girl they have both fallen in love with. Though Vildrac wrote satire (*Le Jardinier de Samos*, 1932) and broad farce (*Trois mois de prison*, 1942), his forte remained intimate theatre, characterized by reticence and simplicity in melancholy scenes hinting at the unspoken feelings in relationships (*La Brouille*, 1930). Later works included art criticism, essays, and memoirs (*D'après l'écho*, 1949). [DHW]

VILLAMONT, Jacques de (c.1560–c.1625). His *Voyages*, the most popular French travel-book of its time, was reprinted 13 times between 1595 and 1609; ostensibly an account of Villamont's pilgrimage to the Holy Land, it owes much to its predecessors, particularly *Belon's *Observations*. Later editions contain a touching meditation on death, the final 'voyage'. [MJH]

Villanelle. A poem in fixed form, consisting of a number of tercets (usually five) and a concluding quatrain. It has only two rhymes, and the first and third lines of the poem are repeated in alternate tercets and at the end of the final quatrain. It established itself in the 16th c., being given its consecrated form by *Passerat, and was very popular with *Banville and the *Parnasse.

Ville, La, see CLAUDEL.

838

VILLEDIEU, Marie-Catherine Desjardins, known as Madame de (*c*.1640–1683). Prolific, best-selling novelist. Along with Madeleine de *Scudéry, she was the best-paid woman writer of the century; they were the only women authors to receive royal pensions. Her first publication is a striking self-portrait in the 1659 collection, *La Galerie des peintures*, edited by *Montpensier and *Segrais. Here Villedieu reveals a class-consciousness and political awareness almost unheard-of in her day. A similar willingness to expose aspects of life repressed by social norms is evident in much of her fiction, nowhere more so than in *Mémoires de la vie d'Henriette-Sylvie de Molière* (1672–4), an often racy and always lively picaresque novel that ranks among the 17th c.'s most unjustly neglected works. In these pseudo-memoirs Villedieu's flagrantly unconventional heroine presents herself as a sexual adventuress deliberately challenging a repressive social order.

In similar fashion, Villedieu herself seems to have lived perpetually at odds with the contemporary social order. Early literary historians, perhaps confusing the novelist with her heroine Henriette-Sylvie, described Villedieu as a woman of easy virtue whose conduct scandalized her contemporaries, and subsequent commentators have generally repeated this portrayal. However, as *Bayle first warned readers, this alleged biography cannot be documented. Surviving documents reveal simply an independent woman unbound by convention. As of 1655 Desjardins was living alone in Paris 'answering to no one'. The only recorded 'scandal' involves her open liaison with a soldier, Boisset de Villedieu, who broke off his formal promise of marriage. He even sold her letters to the publisher *Barbin, who published them, despite her protests, as *Lettres et billets galants* (1668). After Villedieu's death later that year she simply adopted his name as her official signature, apparently with some degree of consent from his family. She subsequently married Claude de Chaste and had a child by him.

Villedieu's collected works fill 12 volumes. *Molière staged successfully her tragedy *Manlius Torquatus* (1662) and her tragicomedy *Le Favori* (1665), which has been interpreted as a commentary on the *Fouquet affair. She wrote other plays, occasional poetry, and numerous works of prose fiction. She helped launch two major late-17th-c. sub-genres, the historical novel (especially with *Les *Désordres de l'amour*, her best-known work today) and the sentimental or 'gallant' novel (*Annales galantes*, 1670). In her vast production many works deserve reconsideration today.   [JDeJ]

See M. Cuénin, *Roman et société sous Louis XIV: Madame de Villedieu* (1979).

VILLEGAGNON, Nicolas Durand de (*c*.1510–1571). Knight of Malta who published accounts of his Mediterranean campaigns before attempting, at *Coligny's request, to found a French colony in the bay of Rio de Janeiro in Brazil (1555–8); the settlement's failure, largely due to religious disputes, was disparately chronicled by *Léry and *Thevet.
                    [MJH]

VILLEHARDOUIN, Geoffroi de (*c*.1150–*c*.1216). Chronicler. Born to a noble family in Champagne, he became a devoted servant of the counts of Champagne and their families, was made marshal in 1185, and in 1187 accompanied Count Henry II on the Third *Crusade, where he was captured at the siege of Acre. After his release from a Saracen gaol, and after Henry's coronation as king of Jerusalem, Geoffroi returned to Champagne in 1194 to assist the regent, Countess Marie, and then her son Thibaud III. He was present at the tournament in 1199 at which the Fourth Crusade was first mooted, and remained committed to it after the death of Thibaud in early 1201. With representatives from the counts of Flanders and Blois, he negotiated the treaty with the Venetians that arranged shipping for the expedition; and he was instrumental in securing Count Boniface of Montferrat as its leader in 1202. He then left France. After the conquest of Constantinople he helped to defend the newly acquired Latin empire.

Geoffroi's chief claim to fame was his *La Conquête de Constantinople*, written after 1207 in the Latin empire, but intended for circulation in France. This account of the Fourth Crusade and its aftermath, distinguished as the first major work in French prose, has excited controversy over the generations. According to Villehardouin, the expedition's diversion, first to capture Zara for the Venetians, and then to conquer Constantinople, arose from a series of accidents which were the workings of the divine will. Those who criticized the leaders and left the army were motivated by malice. The conquest of Constantinople was an achievement on so heroic a scale that all doubts as to its morality were proved unfounded. And the subsequent troubles that befell the crusaders, culminating in Boniface's death, were a deplorable witness to the West's failure to comprehend what had happened and to assist the warriors of God. This attitude has been variously interpreted as a military man's honest summary of events or as a subtle politician's half-truths. The echoes of epic formulae when Geoffroi describes his allies the Doge of Venice and Boniface of Montferrat add to the difficulty of determining his intentions. But despite its ambiguity, his work remains both an exciting venture in French prose and an invaluable source for the Fourth Crusade.
                    [JHD]

See J. Beer, *Villehardouin: Epic Historian* (1986).

VILLEMAIN, Abel-François (1790–1870). French historian, literary critic, and politician, author of often-reprinted literary histories such as the *Cours de littérature française* (1828–9). As a professor of French eloquence during the Restoration, he was held in high esteem by members of the younger generation who were eager for political change (e.g. *Michelet). In 1819 he published a study of Cromwell. Villemain played a significant political role during the *July Monarchy, twice holding the key post of minister of public instruction. He left the government in 1844 for reasons of ill health and abandoned politics altogether after 1848, devoting himself to his writing (including his *Souvenirs contemporains*) and to the Académie Française.   [CC]

Villers-Cotterêts, Edict of, see HISTORY OF THE FRENCH LANGUAGE, 3.

VILLIERS, Pierre, abbé de (1648–1728). Jesuit priest, then a Cluniac prior. He wrote critical essays (including a dialogue on the fairy-tale), poems, and devotional works.

VILLIERS DE L'ISLE-ADAM, Jean-Marie-Mathias-Philippe-Auguste, comte de (1838–89). Extolled by *Mallarmé as the exemplary *Symbolist who upheld visionary idealism in the face of the inadequacies and absurdities of material existence, Villiers de l'Isle-Adam was also an impoverished aristocrat scraping a living from his literary talents. While his tales owe much to *Poe, they fit squarely in the French tradition of the *Fantastic and offer variants on the ghost-story and the supernatural escapade, charged with an ornate spiritualism. First printed in reviews, then gathered in *Contes cruels* (1883) and *Nouveaux contes cruels* (1888), the stories address such uncanny happenings as a man approaching a beautiful deaf girl who intuits his every thought ('L'Inconnue'), or a dead woman being magically revived by her husband just so long as he can keep the thought of her demise out of his mind ('Véra'). Flimsy in outline, Villiers's fictions take on substance thanks to their provocative emphases, their often icy tone and occasional savage irony.

In the novel *Tribulat Bonhomet* (1887) he exploits his talent for sardonic mimicry, like a ventriloquist giving voice to the person he hates, by calling up that most odious of materialists, the bourgeois sceptic Dr Bonhomet, who embodies Villiers's polar opposite. This exercise in cultural black comedy is in stark contrast to the Wagnerian solemnity of *Axël* (1886), a play replete with occult allusion and seemingly designed less for the real theatre than for some disembodied mental stage: embracing the ineffably desirable Sara, Prince Axël proposes double suicide as the ultimate expression of contempt for banal existence. The novel *L'Ève future* (1886) breaks fresh ground as an experiment in science fiction, being the story of the inventor Thomas Edison and the lovely Hadaly, an android indistinguishable from a real woman. In such works Villiers seems able to launch Symbolist aspirations while escaping the dead hand of positivism and crude common sense: his deadpan ironies distance him and lend his tenuous transcendentalism a transparent protective shell that even the sceptical materialist might hesitate to try to crack.   [RC]

See A. W. Raitt, *Villiers de l'Isle-Adam et le mouvement symboliste* (1965); J.-H. Bornecque, *Villiers de l'Isle-Adam: créateur et visionnaire* (1974).

VILLON, François (*c.*1431–after 1463). Villon seems the most autobiographical of medieval French poets—tantalizingly so, because the little biographical information we have does not quite mesh with his confessional first-person narrator. Born, modestly, François de Montcorbier, he found a patron in his uncle Guillaume de Villon, a prosperous cleric under whose aegis he embarked on an academic career: *bachelier* in 1449, *licencié* and *maître-ès-arts* in 1452. This hopeful start was short-lived: in 1455, in a student riot, Villon mortally wounded a priest, and at Christmas 1456 he was one of a group which burgled the Collège de Navarre. He left Paris hastily, until *c.*1462; his whereabouts during this period are unknown, but he seems to have visited *Charles d'Orléans's court, where he composed two ballades (including 'Je meurs de soif auprès de la fontaine'), and was imprisoned by the bishop of Orléans at Meung. His return to Paris was marked promisingly by a pardon for the earlier burglary, but in November 1462 he was implicated in a serious riot and condemned to hang. On appeal, in January 1463, this was commuted to ten years' exile; we have no further concrete information.

Villon's *œuvre* consists partly of a miscellany of shorter poems. The *ballades en jargon*—six reliably attributed, five more doubtful—are linguistically rather than poetically interesting: they are undated and written in an underworld *argot which has now been patiently deciphered. The 16 *poésies diverses*—principally ballades—are a mixed bag: poems built on paradox ('Je congnois tout fors que moy mesmes') or on a virtuoso display of proverbs ('Tant grate chievre . . .'); occasional poetry juxtaposed with the remarkable 'Épitaphe Villon' ('Ballade des pendus'), a poignant plea for understanding on behalf of the hanged.

But it is on Villon's two major poems, the *Lais* (*Petit Testament*) and the *Grant Testament*, that his reputation is primarily based. The first was, he claims, written at Christmas 1456—ironically, because the flight from Paris after the burglary is attributed to a romantic exile from a lady 'felonne et dure'; a martyr to love, he shivers in a garret composing the 38 *huitains* of a last testament. After eight stanzas elaborating this persona, the poet adopts the traditional structure of the mock will: he leaves to his friends and acquaintances appropriate or paradoxical inn-signs or public objects or even—absurdly—his own dubious reputation, whereas his enemies receive bequests sometimes openly calumniatory, and sometimes interpretable as revenge through *double entendre* or antiphrasis.

The 320 lines of the *Lais* are a sketch for Villon's major work, the *Testament* (2,023 lines), written in 1461–2 (first published 1489). Another mock will, it adapts the outline of the authentic will, a prime innovation being the incorporation of a number of ballades and rondeaux, some perhaps drawn from his existing poetic stock, others probably written expressly. The *Testament* is bipartite. The first part (lines 1–792, sometimes called the *Regrets*) is based on a sustained fiction, that the *Testament* is dictated by a moribund Villon to his çlerk Firmin. The major theme is repentance subverted by irony: in a complex interweaving of biblical allusion and classical anecdote, orchestrating of others' voices and apparent self-revelation, Villon reflects on age, death, and dissolution. On the surface, Villon accumulates the poetic topoi of his time: contrast of youth and beauty 'with' age and ugliness in the 'Regrets de la Belle Heaulmière', *Ubi sunt* in the 'Ballade des dames du temps jadis'. But this surface reading ignores Villon's renewal of the commonplace—his linguistic inventiveness, carnavalesque humour, virtuoso use of rhetorical device, and, above all, his irony.

The remainder of the poem consists of burlesque bequests (many to the legatees of the *Lais*), designed to be read tangentially; understanding depends on word-play and paradox, antinomy and oxymoron. Some legacies are poetic: ballades ranging from the obscene to the courtly, from prayer ('Ballade pour prier Nostre Dame') to vituperation ('Ballade des langues envieuses'). Some lyrics pick up contemporary debate ('Contredits de Franc Gontier') or purport to dramatize Villon's own life ('Ballade de la Grosse Margot'). Villon's handling of metre and verse-structure is easy and elegant, sometimes sophisticated; his ambiguities, ambivalences, and paradoxes, his mix of sincerity and mask, make this the most elusive and the most fascinating of medieval poems, and Villon perhaps the most romantic of medieval poets. His startling life-story, and the biographical hints his work suggests, have given him a reputation as a *poète maudit* and have led to a posthumous and continuing notoriety, in novels, films, plays, and even opera, which obscures rather than illuminates Villon the poet.   [JHMT]

See P. Le Gentil, *Villon* (1967); J. Dufournet, *Recherches* and *Nouvelles recherches sur F. Villon* (1971, 1980); E. B. Vitz, *The Crossroads of Intentions* (1974).

VILMORIN, Louise de (1902–69). French poet and novelist. *Cocteau wrote of her in 1935: 'une sorte de prodige: une femme qui invente des choses illustres . . . neuves, fraîches, comiques, poétiques, féroces, légères jusqu'à l'incroyable'. Her fine-spun, disconcerting brief novels treat of love, death, and absence, and use fairy-tale elements, fantasy, ellipsis, lyricism: *Le Lit à colonnes* (1941), *Le Retour d'Érica* (1946), *Julietta* (1951), *Madame de* (1951, filmed by Max Ophüls 1952), *Histoire d'aimer* (1955), *Le Violon* (1960), *L'Heure Maliciôse* (1967). Her wistful distilled lyrics celebrate Nature, recall childhood and lost love, interrogate the future. The selected *Poèmes* were prefaced by her companion *Malraux (1970).   [MMC]

VINAVER, Michel (b. 1927). French novelist and playwright whose first play was directed by Roger *Planchon. His minimalist theatre dramatizes the effect on everyday life of wider political and even commercial issues: the Korean War in *Les Coréens* (1956), de *Gaulle's return to power in 1958 in *Iphigénie Hotel* (published 1963, performed 1977), and in *A la renverse* (1980) the collapse of the sun-cream industry.   [EAF]

Vincennes, Château de. Military fortress to the east of Paris, which served as a state prison under the *ancien régime. *Diderot was imprisoned here in 1749, and it was on his way to visit him on a hot summer's day that J.-J. *Rousseau experienced his decisive 'illumination'. It was here too that the duc d'*Enghien was shot.

VINCENT DE BEAUVAIS (1190–1264). *Dominican friar and tutor to the sons of the king of France, he wrote the most famous of all medieval encyclopedias, the *Speculum maius*, divided into the *Speculum naturale*, on the world of nature, the *Speculum doctrinale*, on the arts, sciences, and theology, and the *Speculum historicum*, a chronicle of history from creation up to 1254. Vincent works mainly by compiling excerpts from authoritative sources, but he also shows the influence of his great Dominican contemporaries Albert the Great and Thomas Aquinas, and of Islamic writers such as Avicenna and Averroes.   [JAMM]

VINCENT DE PAUL, Saint (1581–1660). Born the son of a ploughman in the then miserably poor region of the Landes, and a shepherd boy till the age of 15, he studied for the priesthood at Dax and Toulouse, was (according to some accounts) captured by Tunisian pirates, and in 1608 achieved his ambition of reaching Paris. There he was profoundly influenced by *Bérulle, became chaplain to the Gondi family, and met *François de Sales, Madame de Chantal, and *Saint-Cyran. He founded first the Congregation of the Mission, based on the priory of Saint-Lazare and hence called Lazarists, to evangelize the countryside and provide a retreat for ordinands, and later (with Louise de Marillac) the now world-wide order of the Daughters of Charity. He was a major force in the religious life of the mid-17th c., assisting Louis XIII on his deathbed and, in the subsequent Regency, sitting as a member of the Council of Conscience which dealt with Church preferment. The writings attributed to him are largely notes by disciples published posthumously. He was canonized in 1737.   [PJB]

VINET, Alexandre, see SWISS LITERATURE IN FRENCH, 3.

VINET, Élie (1509–87). Scholar, teacher, and historian of Bordeaux. Principal of the Collège de Guyenne for 25 years, he published works on mathematics, agriculture, and archaeology, the first

Vingt ans après

French translation of *Einhard's *Life of Charlemagne,* and numerous accounts of local antiquities. His pioneering editions of Roman historians and of Ausonius (1551) were much admired. [MJH]

Vingt ans après (1845). Historical novel by *Dumas père, continuing the adventures of *Les *Trois Mousquetaires.*

Vingt mille lieues sous les mers (1870). One of the most popular novels of Jules *Verne; it centres on the misanthropic Captain Nemo and his submarine, the *Nautilus.*

Vingtras, Jacques. Hero of the trilogy of novels by *Vallès; they are often known by his name.

Vinteuil. Composer in Proust's **A la recherche du temps perdu*; the *petite phrase* from one of his sonatas becomes the leitmotif of Swann's love.

Violence et le sacré, La, see GIRARD, R.

VIOLLET-LE-DUC, Eugène-Emmanuel (1814–79). French architect, restorer of medieval buildings, and prolific writer on architectural matters. At the age of 25 he was commissioned by *Mérimée to restore the abbey church of Vézelay, and it is through the lens of Viollet-le-Duc's inspired interventionism that this Romanesque masterpiece is still to be seen today. Later commissions included the Sainte-Chapelle, Notre-Dame de Paris, Saint-Denis, Amiens Cathedral, the ramparts of Carcassonne, and Saint-Sernin in Toulouse. As a writer on architecture he recommended a rational and functional approach that was curiously at odds both with his restorations and with the majority of his original buildings. [MB]

VION D'ALIBRAY, see ALIBRAY.

Vireli, Virelai. Like the *ballette* [see BALLADE], the mid-13th-c. *vireli* and later *virelai* were originally dance-song forms extending the *rondet de carole* [see RONDEAU] over several stanzas with intervening refrain, but lacking an internal refrain. *Vireli* was probably once an euphonic refrain based on *virer,* 'to gyrate', subsequently crossed with *lai,* 'lay'. The *virelai,* whose popularity rose from the early 14th c. but waned in the 15th, was a less fixed form than the rondeau or ballade. It had generally shorter, heterometric lines and could be one to seven or more stanzas long. Length of refrain and stanza was also variable. *Deschamps innovated by using two one-line refrains to end alternate stanzas. [PVD]

VIRET, Pierre (1511–71). Peripatetic Reformer, friend of *Calvin and often a moderating influence upon him. Viret was chief pastor of the congregation at Lausanne for 23 years and also conducted important ministries at Nîmes and Lyon; he spent his last years teaching in Béarn under the protection of Jeanne d'Albret. A prolific writer of satires and dialogues in

French, Viret used a simple, direct, and often sardonic style to persuade both his opponents, in apologetic works such as *L'Interim* (1565), and his co-religionists, in exhortations such as the *Remonstrances aux fidèles* (1547). His major theological work is the *Instruction chrétienne* (1564). [MJH]

Virgile, non, see WITTIG.

Virgile travesti, see SCARRON.

VIRILIO, Paul (b. 1932). French archaeologist, sociologist, and philosopher, who studies space and time in the electronic age: *Vitesse et politique* (1977), on accelerating speed and its effect on communication; *Esthétique de la disparition* (1980), on visual perception and the cinema; *L'Espace critique* (1984), on instantaneous telecommunication, real and deferred time, the audiovisual vehicle; *L'Inertie polaire* (1990), on relativity, space-speed, and luminocentrism. [PS]

VISÉ, Donneau de, see DONNEAU DE VISÉ.

Visionnaires, Les, see DESMARETS DE SAINT-SORLIN.

Visitandines, Les, see FRANÇOIS DE SALES.

VITEZ, Antoine (1930–90). French actor, director, and poet. His productions were remarkable for their virtuoso intelligence and inventive theatricality centred on the actor. His work on *Racine and *Molière set the dominant trend for Marxist-inspired interpretations of the classics in the 1970s and 1980s. As director of the Théâtre National de Chaillot (1981–8), then of the *Comédie-Française (1988–90), and charismatic teacher at the Conservatoire, he had an immense influence on the French stage of his time. [DWW]

VITRAC, Roger (1899–1952). French playwright. He was a pioneer of *Surrealism in the theatre and a collaborator with *Artaud, with whom he staged his own plays at the Théâtre Alfred Jarry after they were both excluded from the Surrealist group. Probably the most gifted dramatist to emerge from the movement, in *Les Mystères de l'amour* (1927) Vitrac attempted to reproduce on stage features of automatic writing and disordered fantasies intended to break down the barrier between the everyday and the unconscious. Amid violent and grotesque scenes unfolding in a set reminiscent of Surrealist paintings, striking poetic passages occur. **Victor ou les Enfants au pouvoir* (1928), his most successful work, adopts the form of a fantastical spoof on drawing-room comedy; while *Le Coup de Trafalgar* (1934), moving towards more conventional techniques in a depiction of Parisian society, exploits farcical humour to satirize the bourgeoisie. *Les Demoiselles du large* (1938) represents a novel departure in the direction of tragedy, though with *Le Loup-Garou* (1939), situated in a mental hospital, the crazy dialogue shows Vitrac reverting to an outlandish mocking comedy of a type which he continued to write, along with screenplays, until his death (*Le Sabre de mon père*, 1951). [DHW]

VITRY, Philippe de, see PHILIPPE DE VITRY.

VIVIEN, Renée, see GAY AND LESBIAN WRITING.

VLAMINCK, Maurice de (1876–1958). French *Fauvist painter who experimented as a novelist. In words and paint some unevenness of result can be ascribed to a volatile and anarchic temperament. He was influenced by *Van Gogh in his use of bold—even strident—colour, impasto, gestural brushwork, and rushing perspective. However, Vlaminck's work is less well resolved, particularly the post-Fauvist, more expressionist paintings. The recurrent motif o: an empty street or road in *perspective fuyante* has a haunting but slightly facile quality, and his calligraphic strokes are sometimes insufficiently founded. In *Portraits avant décès* (1943), which include Max *Jacob, *Jarry, Derain, Vollard, and *Picasso, his remarks on *Apollinaire typify his range: gossip, overstatement, occasional discernment. [HEB]

Vœux du paon, see ALEXANDER ROMANCES.

VOGÜÉ, Melchior, vicomte de (1850–1910), caught the interest of contemporary writers with the publication of *Le Roman russe* (1886), a study of Turgenev, Dostoevsky, and Tolstoy which contributed to the debate about literary theory in the *Naturalist and *Symbolist contexts. Its influence may be detected, for example, in the idealist theories of *Wyzewa and in the early works of *Gide. The same idealist temperament is also evident in de Vogüé's own novels, such as *Jean d'Agrève* (1897) and *Les Morts qui parlent* (1899). His contribution to literary history is acknowledged, though his works are now little read. [BCS]

Voie royale, La (1930). Novel by *Malraux set in French Indo-China, drawing partly on his own experience. Claude and Perken, prototypes of the adventurer hero, struggle against the jungle, hostile native tribes, and the French administration in a desperate effort to carry out their projects. Claude intends to remove valuable statues from a Khmer temple; Perken intends to master a native tribe. Both fail, but the status of adventure in the novel is metaphysical; convinced that 'la vie n'a aucun sens', the protagonists challenge death and destiny in their efforts to take the exercise of the will to extreme limits. [EAF]

VOILQUIN, Suzanne, née Monnier (1801–78). Early French feminist. Of working-class origin, she became a follower of the comte de *Saint-Simon, attracted by the teachings of Enfantin, but eventually disagreed with his theories about women and favoured a more autonomous women's movement, based on rejection of the patriarchal family. Her most active role was as the moving force behind the newpaper *Tribune des femmes* (1832–4), the last and most influential of a series of publications by the *saint-simoniennes*. She also joined the feminist team on Eugénie Niboyet's *Voix des femmes* in the heady days of 1848. Her personal life was eventful and often hard, and she died in poverty. [SR]

Voir dit, see MACHAUT.

VOITURE, Vincent (1597–1648). Born in Amiens the son of a wine merchant, he became a founder member of the Académie Française and the animating spirit in Madame de *Rambouillet's salon. As a poet, he perfected the art of witty, social verse, reviving outmoded forms and experimenting with new ones, combining flattery and impertinence, classical culture and frivolity in a manner reminiscent of *Marot. His charming 'Stance à la louange du soulier d'une dame' elegantly deflates the traditional celebration of a lady's beauty, and his 'Stances sur une dame dont la jupe fut retroussée' show his typically skilful blend of boldness and disarming *badinage*.

Similar sophistication characterizes his letters, first published after his death. They were to become extremely popular in the course of the century and an alternative model to the more self-conscious eloquence of Guez de *Balzac. Voiture's epistolary art is that of discreet control—of subject-matter, correspondent, and moment; in their multiple shadings of tone, they suggest his twin talents of judgement and linguistic flexibility. Around 1630 he wrote a *nouvelle mauresque*, the *Histoire d'Alcidalis et Zélide*, very popular in *galant* circles although never published in his life-time; its imaginative force reveals another side to a writer whose diverse skills are too easily dismissed as superficial. [GJM]

Voix du silence, Les, see MALRAUX.

Voix et le phénomène, La, see DERRIDA.

Vol de nuit. Novel by *Saint-Exupéry, published 1931. It recounts the attempt of the French pilots of the Aéropostale in the 1920s to win the mail contract from Europe to South America, which can only be achieved through dangerous night-flying over the Andes. The novel focuses upon a solitary pilot who is killed on a night mission, but is celebrated as guaranteeing the superiority of man, both through literal transcendance of the elements and through unique self-sacrifice, and upon the tragic status of Rivière, the airline manager, whose task it is to order his pilots to risk their lives. Criticized for its celebration of the leader, the novel is nevertheless a key heroic work of the inter-war years. [NH]

Voleur, Le (1897). Novel by *Darien. Its hero, Randal, is a bourgeois burglar, avenging crimes against his person (20 years of social programming in family, school, and barracks). Joining the criminal underworld, he finds to his disappointment that its denizens are no freer or lovelier than respectable citizens. Exotic henchmen and several violently intelligent women, exploiting sex as a variant subversion, act as sermonizing mentors for his unsentimental education. *Le Voleur* is a brilliant and paradoxical pastiche of the melodramatic serial novel. Darien does not definitively valorize crime, nor leave Randal uncontested: his virtues are mainly negatory, a mixture of intellectual vandal and dandy, fatalist and self-affirmer. He hungers for true individualism against the crushing evidence of an irremediably corrupt and enslaving world.

Le Voleur is a modernist text, greatly admired by *Jarry and *Breton, in that it offers a metaphor for literary production. By its very nature a theft, artistic creation is parasitic on real life; and the novelist can defraud his readers of complete information. This novel's inflationary rhetoric, a countermystification, attacks the lethal clichés of enemy discourse. Randal remains an enigmatic and blackly comic failure. If *Vautrin is the 'Napoleon of Crime', Randal is the *fin-de-siècle* Hamlet. The finale is not purgative but costive. [WDR]

Volkswagen Blues, see POULIN.

VOLLAND, Sophie, see DIDEROT.

VOLNEY, Constantin-François de Chassebœuf, comte de (1757–1820). Philosopher, historian, politician, travel writer, a central figure in the political and intellectual life of France during the Revolution and the Empire. He was a mainstay of the *Idéologues and, due to his early associations with major thinkers such as *Holbach, a direct link with the high period of the Enlightenment.

His most celebrated work was *Les Ruines, ou Méditations sur les révolutions des empires* (1791), said to have been the best-seller of the Revolutionary period. It offered a strange but characteristic blend of science, philosophy, and theology in its attack on religion and metaphysics, and in its championing of atheistic humanism as the foundation for future progress. It also had a vague atmosphere of pre-Romantic feeling, which continued to exert a fascination for Romantic writers in the early 19th c. More surprising was the long history of its political impact on republican thinking well beyond France. It was much translated, and was taken up and used by poets such as Shelley and by British radicals.

Volney's travel writing was also important for the development of the genre (*Voyage en Égypte et en Syrie*, 1787). Under Napoleon, along with other likeminded intellectuals, he tried in vain to maintain liberal and democratic principles. [BR]

VOLTAIRE (pseud. of François-Marie Arouet) (1694–1778). Held to be one of the three greatest French writers of the 18th c., Voltaire was perhaps its most representative, certainly its most prolific, and emphatically its most combative (he illustrated the virtues of *engagement long before *Sartre). Most of his life was spent in an increasingly vigorous battle against *l'infâme*, a concept generally taken to comprehend the evils resulting from religious bigotry and superstition but which is infinitely extensible and probably encompasses all that Voltaire abhorred in benighted human behaviour—particularly Establishment behaviour—and that served to thwart the realization of his resolutely modern vision of a secular, tolerant society.

1. The Tragic Poet

Born in Paris, the youngest child of a notary, a pupil of the Jesuits at Louis-le-Grand, Voltaire was precociously attracted towards poetry. Devoted as he would always be to the aesthetic prejudices of the *grand siècle*, with its strict code of values, he dreamed of success as his century's greatest tragic writer. To his contemporaries he became first and foremost precisely that: between *Œdipe* (1718) and *Irène* (1778) he composed—often to acclaim—28 tragedies on vastly differing subjects. Today the bulk of them are treated as so much literary history, despite the fact that Voltaire had a credible tragic dignity, a good sense of the dramatic possibilities of the stage, and above all ideas (in a period when the tragic theatre was remarkably stagnant) as to what constituted desirable innovations, e.g. an increase in action and spectacle (*Brutus, 1730; La Mort de César, 1731), or themes drawn from different times and places (*Zaïre, 1732; Adélaïde du Guesclin, 1734; Alzire, 1736; L'Orphelin de la Chine, 1755; Don Pèdre, 1761; etc.). His inability to equal *Corneille or *Racine is partly explicable by his lack of intense psychological insight and by his haste or impatience (although, paradoxically, he expended considerable energy on all his compositions), but it is mostly to be ascribed to his increasing desire to use the theatre—for long an 'école de mœurs'—as a vehicle also for *Enlightenment propaganda.

2. The *Philosophe*

Voltaire was always to look upon writing from the point of view of a *philosophe, even when it did express immutable aesthetic values. Later, magisterially dismissing *Rousseau, he was to say: 'Jean-Jacques n'écrit que pour écrire; moi j'écris pour agir.' Voltaire's 'action' can be detected as early as 1714 and is explicable by his growing dissatisfaction with the *status quo* (whether socio-political or religious), which had doubtless been fostered by his early frequentation of the Société du *Temple. Even so young, Voltaire was already notorious as a *frondeur* with an insolent tongue and a caustic pen. The latter earned him provincial exile (1716). It was, moreover, in the Bastille (1717–18) that he finished composing *Œdipe*, which brought him international attention, and began work on his epic poem *La Ligue*, published in 1723 (re-titled *La *Henriade* in 1728). Both these works—not to overlook his deistic *Le Pour et le contre* (1722)—betray, with their humanitarian and *anticlerical outbursts, a spirit of revolt, even a spirit in revolt. Friendship with Viscount

Bolingbroke (1722 onwards) ensured, moreover, Voltaire's interest in the complexities of the modern British state, ultimately setting the seal on his orientation as a *philosophe* ready to censure, systematically, whatever was contrary to liberty, tolerance, and common sense.

An opportunity to visit England came in 1726. Having, in his increasing self-regard, come to believe that a lionized poetic genius was second to none, Voltaire incautiously treated the chevalier de Rohan with 'disregard' (January 1726). Their altercation earned the poet (whose corporeal humiliation, administered by Rohan's lackeys, was largely treated by society with an indifference which Voltaire found incomprehensible and unjust) a further spell in the Bastille. Shortly afterwards he left for London, capital of that 'pays où on pense librement et noblement sans être retenu par aucune crainte servile'. He remained there for over two years, delving into all aspects of its dynamic 'republican' civilization, free to meditate on the iniquities he had seen (or experienced) at home. He returned to France (autumn 1728), rapidly completing *Brutus* (1730) and the *Histoire de Charles XII* (1731), which both amply betrayed the more dangerous potential of his preparatory work for the **Lettres philosophiques*. The latter, **Lanson's 'première bombe lancée contre l'Ancien Régime', immediately promoted the long-standing nuisance into a full-blown *persona non grata*.

Fleeing Paris to escape a **lettre de cachet*, Voltaire sought refuge at Cirey, home of his mistress, Madame **du Châtelet (Émilie). The stay there (1734–44) was a period of happiness and of intense activity. Increasingly addicted to the tragic theatre, Voltaire added *Alzire*, *Zulime*, **Mahomet*, and *Mérope* to his repertoire; but essentially he worked—often alongside Émilie—on science and mathematics, biblical exegesis, history, and philosophical matters, either laying in large stocks of ammunition for his later campaign against revealed religion or using the material to produce that important work of popularization, the *Éléments de la philosophie de Newton* (1736). Émilie approved of this initiative. But stung somewhat by her opinion that history was much less important than natural science, the author of *Charles XII* also commenced two influential works: the **Essai sur les mœurs* and *Le Siècle de Louis XIV*.

3. Historian and Courtier

Voltaire was henceforth to be constantly preoccupied by history, giving much thought to its practice and to its role in society. His works on **Louis XIV (1751), Peter the Great (1759–63), the philosophy of history (1765), the Parlement de Paris (1769), and Louis XV (1769) will all accentuate his determined break with the humanist and providentialist stances which he felt were characterized by credulity and prejudice, faulty emphasis and delusive rhetoric. Voltaire's own counterpoised, sceptical method (see *Essai sur les mœurs*) was to prove excellent. Not so

his practice. For, though endowed with all the qualities of the marvellously stylish narrator, he tended quite visibly to fall victim to his own scepticism. When, moreover, it came to describing great men and events, Voltaire the historian performed—on two counts—exactly like Voltaire the tragic writer. Lacking psychological finesse, he had not been born to work that 'résurrection intégrale' of the past which **Michelet, for example, so brilliantly illustrated. Secondly, being passionately engaged in the struggles of the century, he tended to reduce history to a utilitarian warning of what happens to humanity deprived of Enlightenment.

With the death of **Fleury (1743) official hostility to Voltaire slackened. Thanks to powerful advocates (Madame de **Pompadour, d'**Argenson, the duc de Richelieu), he regained a measure of favour and worked hard to redeem himself; momentarily he became a court poet, producing in particular *La Princesse de Navarre* (1744) and the eulogistic (officially printed) *Poème de Fontenoy* (1745). The rewards came despite Voltaire's numerous enemies, who were either hostile to his ideals or jealous of his success and the considerable fortune he had amassed over the previous decades by business deals: Louis XV appointed him historiographer of France (1745), a distinction which doubtless helped his election (after four unsuccessful attempts) to the Académie Française (1746). During this period (1744–50) Voltaire also produced **Zadig* and—jousting yet again with **Crébillon—three more tragedies: *Sémiramis* (1746), *Oreste*, and *Rome sauvée* (1749). 'Immortalized' and internationally famous, he now experienced relatively greater contentment. But the death of Émilie and diverse vexations and unpleasantness served to reactivate his restless, dissatisfied spirit. He decided to heed the siren-calls which **Frederick II of Prussia, in his admiration for the 'literary genius of the century' had for long been sending. So began the (ultimately disastrous) Berlin interlude (1750–3), during which Voltaire, laden with Frederick's honours, completed **Micromégas* and *Le Siècle de Louis XIV*, wrote the *Poème sur la loi naturelle*, continued work on the *Essai sur les mœurs*, and conceived the idea for what became the **Dictionnaire philosophique*. Unfortunately, however, the two men's initial euphoria soon turned to mutual disenchantment. The rupture came, inevitably, when Voltaire, espousing König's cause in his famous quarrel with **Maupertuis, demolished the latter (the president of Frederick's Academy of Science) with his bitterly satirical *Diatribe du docteur Akakia* (1753).

4. The Sage of Ferney

Now began the most sombre period in Voltaire's life (1753–7). Disgraced in Berlin, unwelcome in France, generally anathema to right-thinking societies, Voltaire wandered disconsolate, seeking a permanent home. He was now 60. Who and what was he? A celebrated poet and playwright, a controversial historian, a superb letter-writer, a skilful popularizer of scientific ideas, a brilliant nonconformist whose ideas and attitudes constantly irritated authority. This is the Voltaire, however, of whom *Valéry once said: 'S'il fût mort à 60 ans, il serait à peu près oublié aujourd'hui.' The assessment, if extreme, is understandable: the 'real' Voltaire, the Voltaire of legend and posterity, the Voltaire of *Candide, the Voltaire who campaigned against injustice, intolerance, and human imbecility, is the Sage of Ferney, the substantial estate just over the border from Geneva which Voltaire bought in 1758 and which he managed actively and profitably. Once there, secure from persecution, financially independent, conscious of his mission, he became less concerned with purely literary pursuits and more devoted to his and his disciples' accelerating crusade against all adversaries of the Enlightenment.

Since, by this time, Voltaire had for long been almost constantly absent from the intellectual milieux in Paris (with which, naturally, he remained in contact), and since, in parallel, he had become an international celebrity (whose letters were highly prized), we should perhaps mention here the outstanding importance of Voltaire's *Correspondence* (edited by Theodore Besterman). Contained in 45 stout volumes, it enshrines nearly 70 years of vital French history, and covers—with a superb mastery of all conceivable registers—all possible matters, whether social, political, philosophical, or cultural. Here we find, in contact with his 1,200 different correspondents of various nationalities, professions, opinions, and importance, a complex, ever-changing, multi-faceted Voltaire whose pen was superbly suited to all occasions. Lanson has suggested, with some justification, that it is the *Correspondence* which is his least-contested masterpiece.

This is also, unsurprisingly, the time when Voltaire's already numerous enemies multiplied alarmingly. However, his combination of wit, irony, Rabelaisian humour, and sheer vilification neutralized them all so effectively that their reputations were irreparably distorted (e.g. *Fréron, Lefranc de *Pompignan, *Chaumeix, La Beaumelle, Rousseau, Nonnotte, Coger, etc.). His concerns, as he crossed swords with them, were political, philosophical, and above all religious. His attacks on revealed religion multiplied substantially and alarmingly (*Extrait des sentiments de Jean Meslier*, 1762; *Dictionnaire philosophique*, 1764; *La Philosophie de l'histoire*, 1764; *Questions sur les miracles*, 1765; *Le Dîner du comte de Boulainvilliers*, 1767; etc.). In tandem, his more general *philosophe* concerns found expression in his mock-heroic epic about *Jeanne d'Arc, *La Pucelle* (1755–62), and in countless *romans* and *contes*, *facéties* and *dialogues*, which were even more accessible to that general public which avidly read his mordant, even scurrilous, productions. It is mainly these polemical pieces which—given their subject-matter—should have been perishable and yet which, paradoxically, proved to be eternal by their exuberance, their wonderful inventiveness. *Candide* had, for example, shown the propaganda value of the tale; now came *Jeannot et Colin* (1764), *L'*Ingénu* (1767), *L'Homme aux quarante écus* (1768), etc.

But that was not all. Having himself experienced the direst vexations, Voltaire was more than normally sensitive to injustice and persecution. He concerned himself, for example, with the problems of political emancipation in Geneva (1765–6). Other activities are, however, better known: brilliantly he fought for the rehabilitation of *Calas (1762–5) and Sirven (1765–71), victims of intolerance; or defended the memories of Lally (1766–78), *La Barre (1767–75), and Montbailli (1771–3), all unjustly (even callously) executed; or undertook the seemingly hopeless defence (1772–3) of Morangiés, stridently accused of fraud. His most significant contributions in this field—besides his abundant writings which stubbornly justified the above unfortunates—are the *Traité sur la tolérance* (1762), the *Commentaire sur le livre Des délits et des peines* (1766), and the *Prix de la justice et de l'humanité* (1778).

It is the humanitarian Voltaire who, in the last decade of his life, imposed himself on his public. For when, in February 1778, he returned triumphally to Paris after 28 years of officially willed absence, it was 'l'homme aux Calas' who received the delirious welcome. When, worn out, he died on 28 May 1778, he was for many the most honoured man in Europe, for many others the most hated in Christendom. Similar mutually exclusive interpretations are common currency today.

Few authors have demonstrated such complexity. A man of extremes who was both mercurial and Protean, Voltaire was that essential man of extremes: the dual personality whose life and activities constantly and kaleidoscopically covered the whole spectrum of human behaviour. Valéry nicely formulated the problem when he called him 'ce diable d'homme dont la mobilité, les ressources, les contradictions, font un personnage que la musique seule, la plus vive musique, pourrait suivre'. [JR]

See G. Lanson, *Voltaire* (1906); R. Naves, *Voltaire* (1942); J. Orieux, *Voltaire ou la Royauté de l'esprit* (1966); Th. Besterman, *Voltaire* (1976); R. Pomeau (ed.), *Voltaire en son temps* (1985–).

Volupté. Novel by *Sainte-Beuve, published 1834. Under a catchy title, this first-person narrative—comparable to Senancour's *Oberman and Musset's *Confession d'un enfant du siècle*—is the confession of Amaury, now a bishop, to a younger man, before a passage to America. Amaury tells of his adolescence in Brittany under the guidance of an uncle—a variant of Chateaubriand's *René—then of his painful state, torn between platonic infatuations and sensual desires. He meets Monsieur de Couaën, the leader of the royalists in the province, and becomes his close friend while falling in love with Madame de Couaën, who loves him but remains faithful. Amaury follows the couple in Paris where, unsatisfied by his pure love for the wife of his friend, he gives himself up to the sensuality of life in the city. Concluding that love does not bring happiness, Amaury becomes a priest. He will later return to the land of his childhood in time to confess Madame de Couaën and assist her in her death.

This 'analysis of an inclination, a passion, even a vice', as Sainte-Beuve calls it in the preface, is reminiscent of his own ambiguous relation with Victor and Adèle *Hugo. The preface also insists on the 'cathartic power' of literature to cure the evil it depicts, here the contradiction between desire and sublimation. A pessimistic work—Sainte-Beuve was then close to *Lamennais—which disconcerts by its cold, introspective distance and the omnipresence of the narrator's commentary, *Volupté* was a model for Balzac's *Le *Lys dans la vallée* and Flaubert's *L'*Éducation sentimentale*. [AC]

VOUET, Simon (1590–1649). The most influential artist working in France before *Lebrun. He was profoundly influenced by Venetian poetic colour and freedom of handling. He trained an entire generation of painters in large-scale, illusionistic, decorative allegories for mansions round Paris. [JPC]

Vous les entendez?, see SARRAUTE.

Voyage au bout de la nuit. Novel by *Céline, published 1932. An episodic novel in the picaresque tradition, it conveys a pessimistic vision of the world of the 20th c. by taking its hero, or anti-hero, Bardamu and his *alter ego* Robinson through World War I, the French African colonies, New York and Detroit, and the industrial suburbs of Paris. With some humour, but with increasing bleakness, the novel explores the constancy of the division between the 'maîtres' and the 'miteux' under capitalism, exemplified by the officers and the soldiers during the War, the colonists and the natives in Africa, and the rich and the poor in the New World, with the conclusion that the only firm value is to be found in survival and the rejection of pretension to any higher values.

Written in the first person, the novel adopts a relatively watered-down version of Céline's later exploitation of spoken French and *argot to convey both the alienation of the narrator Bardamu and his outrage at the social and economic barriers which imprison him. Seen as a major political novel in the 1930s, by Left and Right alike, *Voyage au bout de la nuit* is considerably more complex. Through the establishment of a hero and his shadow in Bardamu and Robinson, Céline not only acknowledges his debt to *Robinson Crusoe* and the tradition of adventure and survival literature, but also creates a psychological novel of the imagination in which the two characters are different reflections of the same personality. From this starting-point Céline creates his own 'voyage imaginaire', or 'Robinsonade', in which the characters, locations, and events of the novel are less the direct reflection of a social reality than elements of a feverishly imagined future

world. These are created, not just from the narrator's initial conversation with his fellow student Arthur Ganate, but also from a whole range of literary references, from *Proust and Conrad to *Montaigne and Macaulay. In this world, Bardamu is less the real actor than a ghost in a society in which he no longer belongs. [NH]

Voyage autour de ma chambre (1794). Once very popular work of Xavier de *Maistre, describing the feelings experienced in a period of temporary confinement.

Voyage dans la lune. Title sometimes given to Cyrano de Bergerac's *L'*Autre Monde*.

Voyage de Charlemagne, Le. Epic in form, comprising 870 assonating dodecasyllables in *laisses* [see CHANSON DE GESTE], and uniquely burlesque in tone, the *Voyage* (or *Pèlerinage*) *de Charlemagne* survives in a single Anglo-Norman copy and is thought to date probably from the second half of the 12th c. Its narrative point of departure is a challenge to *Charlemagne by his wife to prove himself the match of King Hugh of Constantinople. During the ensuing pilgrimage, the emperor and his Twelve Peers bemusedly witness the splendours of Jerusalem, where they re-enact the Last Supper, and of the East, where they are dazzled by automata. Nothing short of divine intervention enables them to accomplish a series of ludicrous *gabs*, or boasts, that place them in the most unheroic of postures. They return home triumphant and laden with relics. [IS]

Voyage de Monsieur Perrichon, Le, see LABICHE.

Voyage de saint Brendan, Le, see ANGLO-NORMAN LITERATURE, 6a.

Voyage du jeune Anacharsis en Grèce, see BARTHÉLEMY.

Voyage en Icarie, see CABET.

Voyage en Orient, see NERVAL.

Voyageurs de l'impériale, Les. Novel by *Aragon, published initially in 1942 and in its definitive version in 1948, and the final volume of the *Monde réel* trilogy, after Les *Cloches de Bâle* and Les *Beaux Quartiers*. The imaginary story of Aragon's maternal grandfather, it evokes the career of Pierre Mercadier, a history teacher, through the *belle époque* until his death at the beginning of World War I. [NH]

'Voyant, Lettres du', see RIMBAUD.

Voyeur, Le, see ROBBE-GRILLET.

Vraisemblance (verisimilitude), see TRAGEDY, 2.

VUILLARD, Édouard (1868–1940). A co-founder of the *Nabis in 1888, Vuillard painted décors for the Théâtre Libre and Théâtre de l'Œuvre. One of the artists grouped around the *Revue blanche*, he is best known for the interiors and garden scenes generally described as 'intimist', a misleading term which understates the firmness of their design, the strength of their colour harmonies, and his highly individual fusion of the natural forms derived from *Impressionism and the decorative patterning he saw in *Gauguin and Japanese art.   [JK]

Vulgate Cycle, see ROMANCE, 2.

W

W, ou le Souvenir d'enfance, see PEREC.

WACE (*fl.* 12th c.). Master Wace is best known for his *Roman de Brut* (1155), a highly popular adaptation of the *Historia regum britanniae* of *Geoffrey of Monmouth. A critical and scholarly poet, he was also a gifted stylist whose literary influence was considerable. His elaborately and rhetorically constructed descriptive passages are particularly characteristic. His amplification of the Arthurian part of his source (including his addition of the Round Table) makes him an important pioneer in the development and dissemination of the *matière de Bretagne*, and an inspirational precursor of the courtly *romance tradition which was to culminate in *Chrétien de Troyes. Wace's Norman chronicle, *Le Roman de Rou*, was begun in 1160, and interrupted and finally abandoned when he was replaced as Henry II's court chronicler by *Benoît de Sainte-Maure. Wace was also the author of two vernacular saints' lives (St Margaret and St Nicholas) and of *La Conception Nostre Dame*. Though his French is not strictly speaking Insular (he was born in Jersey and had also lived in Normandy), his works are *Anglo-Norman in all but name. His *Brut* was translated into Middle English by Laȝamon in the early 13th c.
[IS]

Wagner in France, see SYMBOLISM.

WAHL, Jean (1888–1974). French philosopher. A prolific historian of philosophy, and professor at the Sorbonne, he was one of the first to introduce Hegel to a wider French audience. His influential study *Le Malheur de la conscience dans la philosophie de Hegel* (1930) presented Hegel as a philosopher of conscience, while his major *Études kierkegaardiennes* (1938) developed the notion of a dialectic between Hegel's thought and that of the then little-known Danish philosopher. A supporter of *Personalism and Christian *Existentialism, he criticized the denial by *Sartre and *Camus of a religious dimension to transcendence, which he analysed at length in *L'Expérience métaphysique* (1965). [MHK]

Waldef, Le Roman de, see ANGLO-NORMAN LITERATURE, 3a.

Waldensians, see VAUDOIS.

Wallonie, La, see BELGIAN LITERATURE IN FRENCH.

WALTER DE BIBBESWORTH, see ANGLO-NORMAN LITERATURE, 7.

WARENS, Madame de, see ROUSSEAU, J.-J.

WARNER-VIEYRA, Myriam (b. 1939). A novelist born in Guadeloupe but settled in Senegal since 1961, Warner-Vieyra deals economically, in diary or flashback form, with the difficulty of being a Caribbean woman. Her pathetic heroines, trapped, uprooted, deranged, write out their traumas in *Le Quimboiseur l'avait dit* (1980) and *Juletane* (1982). [BJ]

Wars of Religion. France's recovery from the dismemberment threatened by the *Hundred Years War was relatively rapid. By the Renaissance, kings such as *François Ier and *Henri II ruled a stronger, much more centralized kingdom. The tensions created by the rivalry between the great houses of Montmorency and *Guise and by the deteriorating religious and economic climate were, however, by the premature death of Henri II in 1559. His successor, François II, was a minor and was quickly dominated by the duc de *Guise and the cardinal de *Lorraine, who were the uncles of his wife (*Marie Stuart). In the short term their power was contested not so much by the Montmorency family as by Louis de *Condé, brother of Antoine de Navarre, the ineffectual leader of the *Bourbon family and prince of the blood [see AMBOISE, CONJURATION DE]. Condé was able to use the cloak of the Protestant religion to mask his ambition, thereby setting the tone for a period of over 40 years of civil war, in which religious passions and factional disputes exacerbated French divisions to the point where the continued existence of the French monarchy was actually in doubt. The religious disputes between Protestants and Catholics were rendered much more serious by two factors. First, the conversion to Protestantism of many members of the *noblesse d'épée*, which provided the already highly organized Calvinist Church with a parallel military structure. Secondly, the clientage system, which enabled great lords—Catholic as well as Protestant—to enrol many nobles in their armies.

The French monarchy at first tried a policy of conciliation: through the Colloque de Poissy (1561), which failed to achieve the hoped-for religious compromises, and then through the Edict of January (1562), which granted a great deal of freedom to the Protestants. The Catholic backlash was immediate. The massacre of Protestant worshippers at Wassy by troops belonging to François de Guise (1562) unleashed a series of increasingly bloody civil wars. Despite several Catholic victories, the Protestants were granted very favourable peace terms in 1570 and appeared to be on the point of winning *Charles IX over to their cause when, in 1572, the inevitable Catholic reaction led to the *St Bartholomew's Day Massacre. This provoked a hardening of the Protestants' position, since it induced them openly to question the political authority of the French monarchy [see HOTMAN; GENTILLET].

The death of the duc d'Alençon in 1584, however, left the Protestant Henri de Navarre (the future *Henri IV) as heir presumptive to the throne. This immediately created a reversal in the relative positions of extremist Protestants and Catholics. The former suddenly became defenders of the royalist tradition, while the latter came to argue that, if the king jeopardized the fate of Catholicism, he could be deposed or even assassinated. *Henri III tried to overcome the problem by persuading Henri de Navarre to abjure the Protestant faith. The latter's refusal to comply gave the Catholic *Ligue the excuse it needed not only against the Protestant heir to the throne, but also against the Catholic king, who, it was felt, was not resolute enough in his defence of Catholicism. It is not clear whether Henri de Guise intended to depose Henri III; but his challenge to the royal authority eventually led to his assassination at the hands of the king's bodyguard in 1588. The reaction of the Ligue was predictably hostile, leading eventually to the assassination of Henri III in 1589. The Ligue declared the cardinal de Bourbon king in Henri de Navarre's place, but he was never king in more than name. The Ligue's position was weakened by its own increasingly revolutionary activities (especially in Paris), and by the fact that its various supporters had their own candidates for the French throne.

In the event, Henri de Navarre cut the ground from beneath their feet by removing the most serious obstacle to his own candidacy: his Protestantism. He converted to Catholicism (almost certainly as a result of political calculations) in 1593 and was finally absolved by the Pope in 1595. ('Paris vaut bien une messe' was a contemporary view of this conversion.) He still had to reconquer his kingdom and buy off his enemies. His conversion alienated many of his Protestant followers, but he was sufficiently loyal to them to enforce the *Edict of Nantes (1598), which granted them limited but none the less substantial concessions. In the meantime the experience of protracted civil war led many Frenchmen to believe that there was no alternative to a strong monarchy. In this way the Wars of Religion prepared, however paradoxically, the absolutism of *Louis XIV. The influence of the Religious Wars on literature is particularly evident in the *Tragiques of d'Aubigné, the polemical works of *Ronsard, and the Essais of *Montaigne. [See REFORMATION.]   [JJS]

See J. H. Salmon, Society in Crisis (1975).

Waterloo. The battle fought near Waterloo in Belgium on 18 June 1815 brought an end to *Napoleon's struggle to maintain power. When the allied army under Wellington was joined by the Prussian forces under Blücher, the French forces were routed, though the Imperial Guard resisted to the end. Famous, and very different, descriptions of the battle are to be found in Stendhal's La *Chartreuse de Parme (an innocent's eye-view), Hugo's 'L'Expiation' in Les *Châtiments, and his Les Misérables.

WATRIQUET DE COUVIN (14th c.). One of the few named authors of *fabliaux; a number of his moralistic dits also survive.

WATTEAU, Antoine (1684–1721). French painter. In 1702 Watteau was introduced to the theatre by Claude Gillot, illustrator of subjects from theatrical productions. He studied the poetic works of the great Venetians of the 16th and 17th c. in French collections and developed their ideas of the close association of the arts of music, dance, and painting. His subjects range from direct transcriptions of stage-sets like The Embarkation for Cythère (1712) and From Cythère (1717), derived from Les Trois Cousins by *Dancourt, to studies and portraits of named actors such as Philippe Poussin, or anonymous groups of actors in costume off-stage, relaxing, and of friends dressed up. Of great historical interest are paintings of events associated with the theatre like The Italian Comedians Leaving Paris [see COMÉDIE-ITALIENNE]. His two principal pupils, Jean-Baptiste Joseph Pater (1696–1736) and Nicolas Lancret (1690–1743), continued to paint fêtes galantes and personalities from the theatrical world.   [JPC]

WAUQUELIN, Jean (d. 1452) Originally from Picardy, a calligrapher, writer, and translator in the service of Philippe le Bon of Burgundy; now principally known as compiler of a magnificently illuminated life of Alexander the Great (1448), and histories of England (1444) and Hainaut (1447).
                                                          [JHMT]

Weights and Measures. In 1799 France became the first country in the world officially to adopt the metric system (metre, gramme, litre, hectare), although French people continued to use old weights and measures for many years after this. Under the ancien régime many different weights and measures were used in different parts of France, not always with the same meanings. Some of the most frequently encountered are as follows:

Pouce, approx. 1 inch, the twelfth part of a pied.
Pied, a little more than the English foot.
Aune, approx. 1.2 metres (sometimes much less).
Toise, six pieds.
Lieue (cf. English 'league'), approx. 4 kilometres.
Livre, approx. 1 pound (still used to mean half a kilogramme).

Quintal, 100 *livres*.

Boisseau, approx. 1 decalitre.

Pinte, a pint.

Setier, between 150 and 300 litres (grain); 8 pints (liquid).

Muid, approx. 268 litres (liquid); 1,872 litres (dry goods).

Arpent, a little more than one acre.

[Note: many of these terms were used with different meanings in Canada, where the *arpent* was also a measure of length, approx. 58 metres.]

WEIL, Simone (1909–43). French philosopher and mystic. One of the first female graduates of the *École Normale Supérieure, she taught philosophy in various provincial schools from 1931 to 1938. An active socialist, hostile to communism, which she equated with fascism, she gained first-hand experience of a worker's life on the Renault assembly line (1934–5); this, and her political conclusions, are related in *La Condition ouvrière* (published 1951). She sought to join the Republicans in the Spanish Civil War, but an accident forced her to return to France (1936). Following mystical experiences at Solesmes (1938), she converted to Christianity, but was never baptized, being hostile to dogma and institutional religion. Because of her Jewish origins she fled the Nazi advance and in 1942 went to the USA, then England, to offer her services to the Free French. She offered to serve in a front-line nursing detachment, but was refused (a motive of suicidal self-sacrifice was suspected). Pleading the reduced rations of occupied France, she did not eat properly and contracted tuberculosis. Her death is usually attributed to a combination of illness and self-neglect.

Weil's writing consists for the most part of articles written over some 15 years and collected into books after her death (her *Œuvres complètes* are being published by Gallimard). It would be misleading, therefore, to see her philosophy as all of a piece. Her political theory (e.g. *L'Enracinement*, 1949 and *Écrits de Londres*, 1957) is often in Utopian disharmony with its time. We need to have a sense of usefully belonging to our country ('enracinement'). We have not rights, but duties and needs. Democracy is needful, but political parties should be banned since they promote half-truths, injustice, and the collective passions on which oppression feeds. Politicians and judges should, at the end of their term of office, account for their actions before a tribunal; punishments would be 'severe'. Weil's belief that truth and justice are absolutes is perhaps disquieting, but she speaks out strongly for free speech.

Her mysticism (*La Pesanteur et la grâce*, 1947) is unusually tragic and world-rejecting. One should seek to achieve total detachment, and to kill the self. God is present in the world only in the form of absence. One must not suppose He is present in the world, for this would implicate Him in evil, and would excuse evil acts by His devotees. Atheism brings one closer to God than does faith without

experience of Him. The way to God is through suffering, which, freely accepted, destroys suffering.

Her style has a beautiful lapidary clarity, and the originality of her views inspires fresh thinking on any issue that she touches.   [GDM]

See R. Rees, *Simone Weil* (1966); F. d'Hauteville, *Tourment de Simone Weil* (1970); G. A. White, *Weil* (1981).

WEINGARTEN, Romain (b. 1926). French playwright. His plays are idiosyncratic but are broadly situated in the post-absurdist current of experimental verbal theatre. In inspiration perhaps closer to *Surrealism than to the *Absurd, they explore an immaterial world of feelings and fantasy, and have a strong poetic charge. His first play, *Akara*, set inside the brain of a woman and representing a nightmare, caused a sensation in 1948 when it won the Prix des Jeunes Compagnies. His greatest success, however, and the play for which he is chiefly remembered, is *L'Été* (1966). Viewing adult life through the eyes of two cats and two children, it has a whimsical charm which won many admirers.   [DWW]

Welche or **Velche.** Name given to the French by *Voltaire (e.g. the 'Discours aux Welches' published under the name of *Vadé). The word, derived from the German, is meant to suggest unenlightened ignorance.

WEREWERE LIKING (pseud. of Eddy Liking, née Njock) (b. 1950). Cameroonian painter, poet, novelist, playwright, theatre director, and ethnographic researcher; she has lived and worked in Abidjan, Ivory Coast, since 1979. Studying the theatricality of traditional ritual in her home Bassa region of Cameroon, in Mali, and in Ivory Coast led to experiments in *théâtre-rituel* with students on the campus of the University of Abidjan, in collaboration with Marie-José Hourantier, a French drama lecturer. After various essays, folk-tales, and dramatic texts, this association culminated in the joint publication of *Orphée Dafric* (1981), a poetic novel, with her collaborator's dramatic text *Orphée d'Afrique*. Her best-known work appeared in 1983: *Elle sera de jaspe et de corail*, a full-length lyrical dialogue in three voices on the theme of hope for a better Africa. A similar multi-vocal novel, *L'Amour-cent-vies*, appeared in 1988. In the mid-1980s she set up an independent theatre group called the Théâtre Ki-Yi at the villa of the same name, which serves as cultural centre, art college, and drama school for young Africans interested in exploring their traditional heritage. Her theatre group has been a regular visitor to the Festival des Francophonies in Limoges.   [PGH]

WERTH, Léon, see WORLD WAR I.

West Indies. Literary production in the French West Indies (here meaning the present *départements d'outre-mer* of Martinique (M), Guadeloupe (G), and French Guiana (Gu)), may be divided into a number of relatively distinct phases, each dominated by one segment of the ethnically and socially diverse population of the societies concerned. [For HAITI, see separate entry.]

1. 1635–1789

The earliest writing on the French West Indies—notably père du Tertre's *Histoire générale des Antilles habitées par les Français* (1667–71) and père *Labat's *Nouveaux voyages aux îles d'Amérique* (1722)—consisted essentially of narrative descriptions by visitors or semi-permanent residents of the islands' terrain, flora and fauna, their rapidly disappearing autochthonous Carib population, and their transformation, beginning with the settlement of the first French *colons* in 1635, into fully fledged plantation societies based on *slavery by the end of the 17th c. Before 1789 virtually no writing was produced either by the established local white population (here referred to as Creoles) or by the *gens de couleur libres* (free people of mixed European and African descent, also known as mulattos), who came to form a French-speaking intermediate stratum between the whites and the *Creole-speaking slave population. Only at the very end of this first period did a West-Indian-born writer, the white Guadeloupean Nicolas-Germain Léonard (1744–93), produce any substantial body of writing (*Idylles morales*, 1766 ; *La Nouvelle Clémentine*, 1744). He, significantly, spent almost all his life in France, returning to his native island for a three-year stay in 1784, on the basis of which he published what is, historically, the first work on the French West Indies by a French West Indian writer. Its title, *Lettre sur un voyage aux Antilles* (1787), indicates that the perspective adopted is still essentially that of a visitor from metropolitan France.

2. 1789–1848

A distinctive white Creole literature—distinctive in vision if not in style—first emerged in the aftermath of the Revolutionary and Napoleonic era. Although slavery (abolished in 1794 but reimposed in 1802) survived, this period gave the local whites a sharpened sense of what separated them from France; it inspired a series of novels and other works dedicated to the defence of slavery and the society that rested on it against mounting abolitionist pressure in France. Representative writers are the poet Poirié de Saint-Aurèle (G), author of *Les Veillées françaises* (1826), *Le Flibustier* (1827), and *Cyprès et palmistes* (1833), and the novelists Louis Maynard de Queilhe (M) (*Outre-mer*, 1835) and Jules Levilloux (M) (*Les Créoles, ou la Vie aux Antilles*, 1835). The latter, who may have been a mulatto, is perceptibly more liberal on the question of miscegenation than other writers of the period. Dominated by reactionary and openly racist white writing, the post-1815 period also witnessed the emergence, first expressed in the pamphlet *De la situation des hommes de couleur libres aux Antilles françaises* (1823), of a progressive mulatto voice committed to the acquisition of full French

citizenship for the *gens de couleur libres* (eventually secured in 1833) and, by extension, to the liberation of the black slave population (finally decreed in April 1848).

3. 1848–1900

After 1848, and still more after 1870, the political power of the white Creole élite was threatened by the mulatto middle classes who, identifying with republican France, demanded that the West Indian colonies be assimilated as *départements* into the *métropole*. Its economic strength also weakened. The white élite succumbed to virulent hatred of mulattos, blacks, and their republican allies in France, and in G. Souquet-Basiège's *Le Préjugé de race aux Antilles françaises* (M, 1883)—he meant the prejudice of non-whites against whites rather than the reverse—produced a minor classic of racist paranoia. The fears and resentments of the old élite are also amply represented in Rosemond de Beauvallon's novel *Hier! Aujourd'hui! Demain!, ou les Agonies créoles* (G, 1885) and, more light-heartedly, in the novels of René Bonneville (M) (*La Vierge cubaine* and *Le Triomphe d'Églantine*, both 1899). The outstanding literary work of the second half of the 19th c. is, however, *Atipa, roman guyanais*, published in 1885 under the pseudonym Alfred Parépou by an unknown (but evidently non-white) Guianese writer. Written in Creole, the expressive qualities of which it sets out systematically to defend and illustrate, it offers a vivid and mordant picture of colonial society in Guiana in the early years of the Third Republic.

4. 1900–1930

With this exception, the non-white population, be it rising mulatto or still-subordinate black, produced no significant literature until the early 1900s. When eventually it did so, it was largely in imitation of local white writers. They, in their turn, derived their styles and language, together with much of their vision, from alien models, either *Parnassian poetry (the leading practitioners of which, *Leconte de Lisle and *Heredia, were at least fellow Creoles) or the novels and travel writings of Lafcadio Hearn, whose *Two Years in the French West Indies* and *Youma* (both 1890) inspired much French West Indian writing between 1900 and 1930. The white Creole élite produced one minor poet of talent in Daniel Thaly (M), author of, amongst many other works, *Lucioles et cantharides* (1900) and *Le Jardin des tropiques* (1911), and one of genius in Alexis Léger (G), the future *Saint-John Perse, whose *Éloges et autres poèmes* both takes over and totally transfigures some of the leading preoccupations of white Creole writing of the late 19th and early 20th c. The modes of white Creole poetry were followed all too sedulously by mulatto poets such as Victor Duquesnay (M) (*Les Martiniquaises*, 1903) and Oruno Lara (G) (*Sous le ciel bleu de Guadeloupe*, 1912); these were the leading figures, along with Thaly, of the regionalist or, less kindly, 'doudouiste' school (after the stereotypical figure of *la doudou*, the smiling, sexually available mulatto woman who haunts their poems) that dominated French West Indian writing from 1900 to 1930, and for which the reviews *La Guadeloupe littéraire* (1907–9, edited by Lara) and *Lucioles* (M, 1926–7, edited by Auguste Joyau and Gilbert Gratiant) briefly provided a focus. If regionalist poetry disappoints through its sterile exoticism and superannuated forms and language, the pre-1930 novel [see also MARAN] is of greater interest. Novels such as Oruno Lara's *Questions de couleur* (1923) and Suzanne Lacascade's *Claire Solange âme africaine* (M, 1924) display an assertive racial self-consciousness that is commonly held to have been absent from non-white French West Indian writing before the mid-1930s.

5. 1930–1960

The view that an 'authentic' French West Indian literature (or, more broadly still, 'black' literature in French) 'began' with the publication of the manifesto **Légitime défense* (1932) and the single number of *L'*Étudiant noir* (March 1935) now seems a simplistic exaggeration. It cannot be doubted, however, that the intellectual ferment [discussed more fully in the entry NÉGRITUDE] born of the first sustained contacts in Paris in the 1930s between black African and black and mulatto West Indian students resulted in a literature that was fundamentally different in themes, tone, style, and above all quality from anything else that preceded it. With some exaggeration, *Pigments* (1937) by the Guianese poet Léon *Damas has been described as the first work by a French West Indian in which the writer actively advertises his non-whiteness. It is, more precisely, the first work in which a distinctive French West Indian *style* is brought to bear on themes distinctly and wholly French West Indian. In *Cahier d'un retour au pays natal*, Aimé *Césaire (M), deploying the full panoply of *négritude* themes with unequalled passion, intensity, and poetic inventiveness, created the first undoubted masterpiece of French West Indian writing, the catalytic effect of which continues to be felt to this day.

The new literature gathered momentum in Vichy-dominated Martinique between 1940 and 1943. The review **Tropiques*, edited by Césaire and with Suzanne Césaire and René *Ménil as leading contributors, brought together poetry, folk-tales, and anthropological and other texts which, for the first time, proclaimed the cultural and psychospiritual specificity of the French West Indies. Insisting on their fundamentally 'African' character, they called in question the assimilationist assumptions both of French colonialism and of the overwhelming majority of black and coloured French West Indians. Yet the transformation of Martinique, Guadeloupe, and Guiana into *départements* of France in 1946 initially had no stronger supporter than Césaire himself; for the next ten years he attempted to reconcile the anti-assimilationist dynamic inherent in his poetry (*Les Armes miraculeuses, Soleil cou*

coupé, Corps perdu) and in the ideology of *négritude* as a whole with the assimilationist political praxis imposed on him by his role as Communist *député* for the Fort-de-France constituency of Martinique.

Up to the mid-1950s the most characteristic French West Indian writing—notably the novels of the Martinicans Joseph *Zobel (*La Rue Case-Nègres*), Rafaël Tardon (*Starkenfirst*, 1947, and *La Caldeira*, 1948), and Léopold Sainville (*Dominique, nègre esclave*, 1951)—viewed French West Indian history as a continuous struggle against slavery, colonialism, and racism which, it was implied, departmentalization had brought to a successful conclusion. At the same time Frantz *Fanon (M) pointed, in *Peau noire masques blancs*, to the presence of unresolved sociopolitical and psychological conflicts beneath the 'mask' of constitutional integration into metropolitan France, and uncomfortably suggested that the assimilationist impulse, far from being a solution, might actually be the source of the multiple alienations of black and coloured French West Indians. A growing unease surfaces in the early poetry of Édouard *Glissant (M) and Guy *Tirolien (G) (*Balles d'or*, 1961), and in the poems, written in both French and Creole, of Sonny Rupaire (G), later collected in *Cette igname brisée qu'est ma terre natale* (1971). The publication of Césaire's *Lettre à Maurice Thorez* in 1956, his break with the PCF, and subsequent founding of the autonomist Parti Progressiste Martiniquais in 1958 may be said to mark the end of the post-1946 departmentalist 'honeymoon', in Martinique at least. Though the majority of French West Indians have continued, with varying degrees of enthusiasm, to support departmentalization, most French West Indian writing since 1960 has, with differing degrees of intensity and from a diversity of political and ideological viewpoints, called that status increasingly into question.

6. 1960–1990

Amidst the considerable bulk of writing produced in the French West Indies since 1960 a number of salient patterns can be discerned. In the first place, it is apparent that poetry has lost the central position it enjoyed during the 'heroic' period of the *négritude* movement between 1935 and 1960. Since *Ferrements* (1960), Césaire's poetic output has been slight and somewhat disappointing. While the work of Serge *Patient (Gu), Georges Desportes (M) (*Cette île qui est la nôtre*, 1973, and *Semailles de pollen*, 1985), Élie *Stephenson (Gu), Henri Corbin (G) (*Plongée au gré des deuils*, 1978; *La Lampe captive*, 1979; and *La Terre où j'ai mal*, 1982), and Ernest Pépin (M) (*Au verso du silence*, 1984) has many merits, it does not mark a major advance in terms of theme and language over the poetry of the 1940s and 1950s. More interesting are those poets such as Joby *Bernabé (M), Monchoachi (M) (*Dissidans*, 1976, and *Nostrom*, 1981), and Hector Poullet (G) (*Mi zanfan péyi la*, 1967, and *Pawòl an bouch*, 1982) who, following the notable example of Gilbert Gratiant (M) (*Fab' Compè Zicaque*,

1958), have used Creole as their principal medium of expression.

Drama, though restricted by the shortcomings of local performing facilities, has made a notable advance through the plays of Césaire, Daniel *Boukman (M), Maryse *Condé (G), Vincent *Placoly (M), and Ina *Césaire (M). Once again Creole has been used with great effect, by Georges Mauvois (M) in his pioneering play *Agénor Cacoul* (1966) and, more recently, by Sonny Rupaire (*Somanbile*, 1987), Joby *Bernabé, and Ina Césaire (*L'Enfant des passages*).

But it is undoubtedly the novel that has been the dominant genre in French West Indian writing since 1960. During the 1960s most fiction was broadly realist in character and, following the pattern of the 1950s, drew from an intense examination of the French West Indian past (notably slavery) an essentially optimistic vision of the future that is reflected in the titles of two of the best novels of the decade, Bertène *Juminer's *Au seuil d'un nouveau cri* (Gu, 1963) and Glissant's *Le Quatrième Siècle*, the 'prequel' to his equally forward-looking *La Lézarde* of 1958. A broadly optimistic view of the French West Indian past, present, and future is likewise to be found in the sequence of novels written jointly or severally by Simone *Schwarz-Bart (G) and her metropolitan French husband André [see also ETCHART].

From 1970 onwards, however, as the distinctive identity of the French West Indies appeared to many observers to be crumbling beneath the combined pressures of emigration, unemployment, and the replacement of the traditional economy and culture by goods, mentalities, and life-styles imported from the *métropole*, an insistently pessimistic note entered French West Indian fiction. This is reflected in the salience of the word 'mort' in the titles of many of the most characteristic novels of the decade: Placoly's *La Vie et la mort de Marcel Gonstran* and *L'Eau-de-mort guildive*, Glissant's *Malemort*, and *Mère la mort* and *La Meurtritude* by the then Martinique-based metropolitan novelist Jeanne *Hyvrard.

Novels of the 1980s have been ambivalent in tone and often experimental in form and language. The examination and reconstruction of the distant and recent past have been continued in Daniel *Maximin's *L'Isolé Soleil* (G), Glissant's *La Case du commandeur* and *Mahogany*, Placoly's *Frères volcans*, and Raphaël *Confiant's remarkable 're-creation' of Martinique under the Vichy régime, *Le Nègre et l'Amiral*. Other novelists of interest are Xavier *Orville (M), Max *Jeanne (G), and Ernest Moutoussamy (G), whose *Il pleure dans mon pays* (1980) and *Aurore* (1987) give voice for the first time to Guadeloupe's East Indian minority. A striking feature of French West Indian fiction since 1960 has been the large number of novels written by women, most of them, for reasons that remain obscure, Guadeloupean women: Schwarz-Bart, Michèle *Lacrosil, the prolific and highly popular Maryse *Condé, Jacqueline *Manicom, Myriam *Warner-Vieyra, Sylviane Telchid, Lucie Julia, Maryse Romanos, and Gisèle Pineau. To them may be added the Martinicans Suzanne Dracius-Pinalie (*L'Autre qui danse*, 1989) and Marie-Reine de Jaham, whose *La Grande Béké* (1989) provides a late-20th-c. example of white Creole writing.

Novels have been written entirely in Creole by Raphaël Confiant (*Bitako-a*; *Kod-yanm*; *Marisosé*), but the most important development stylistically and linguistically is the potent and subversive fusion of French and Creole that he and Patrick *Chamoiseau (M) (*Chronique des sept misères*; *Solibo magnifique*) have developed in their fiction. The link between fictional practice and broader ideological, cultural, and political issues is made evident in Glissant's massive *Le Discours antillais* (1981), in which the concept of *antillanité* is developed as a counter both to 'Eurocentric' assimilationism and 'Afrocentric' *négritude*. The concept, first developed in the short-lived *Acoma* (M, 1971–3) edited by Glissant, has received further elaboration in the review *Carbet* (M, founded 1983) and in the important manifesto *Éloge de la créolité* (1989) by Chamoiseau, Confiant, and the influential Creole linguist Jean Bernabé (M). Before 1970 there was, in a sense, no French West Indian *literature*, only books by French West Indians: the award of the Prix Goncourt to Chamoiseau's *Texaco* in 1992 marked the coming-of-age of an authentic French Caribbean style.   [RDEB]

See J. André, *Caraïbales: études sur la littérature antillaise* (1981); B. Ormerod, *An Introduction to the French Caribbean Novel* (1985); R. Toumson, *La Transgression des couleurs: littérature et langage des Antilles, 18e, 19e, 20e siècles* (1989); M. Rosello, *Littérature et identité créole aux Antilles* (1992).

WHITE, Kenneth, Scottish-French writer, see BRITISH, IRISH, AND AMERICAN INFLUENCES; TRAVEL WRITING.

WIESEL, Élie (b. 1928). Born in Hungary, he survived Auschwitz, Birkenau, and Buchenwald, studied in France, then became an American citizen. His work—novels, autobiography, plays, and essays, written in French—is a prolonged meditation on the Holocaust and the fate of the Jewish people over the centuries. His first book, the autobiographical *La Nuit* (1958), was followed by *L'Aube* (1960), set in post-war Palestine, and *Le Jour* (1961), a novel of memories of war. His numerous subsequent texts include *Le Mendiant de Jérusalem* (1968, Prix Médicis) and *Le Testament d'un poète juif assassiné* (1981). He won the Nobel Peace Prize in 1986.   [PF]

WILLIAM MARSHAL, see ANGLO-NORMAN LITERATURE, 4; TOURNAMENTS.

William Ponty, École. This *école normale* was founded in Gorée, Senegal, in 1913 to replace the earlier training college set up in Saint-Louis in 1903. In 1938 the school moved to Sébikhotane, 45 kilometres from Dakar, and later to Thiès (1938) and Kolda (1979). Ponty had three sections—Education, Administration, and Medicine. Students, drawn from all over French West Africa, were admitted after three years in a Senior Primary School on the basis on a competitive examination. The school turned out highly competent staff to assist the French in running the colonies. Many Ponty products took high office in their respective governments after Independence. The first African writers came from the school, which is best known as the cradle of modern African theatre: Ponty theatre owes its existence to the guidance and encouragement of the French. The achievements of the school stemmed from the fact that it represented the highest level of university education available in the colonial system, and was dedicated to turning out a new élite which would not be cut off from its African roots. [MKa]

WILLY, see COLETTE.

WITTIG, Monique (b. 1935). Committed *feminist and lesbian writer. Her first novel, *L'Opoponax* (1964), a formally innovatory text written from the perspective of a child, won the Prix Médicis. Later texts radically attack heterosexual assumptions and phallocentricity, creating in their place a women-centred mythology and culture. *Les Guérillères* (1969) presents a Utopian island community of female warriors whose power and aggressivity contradict the myth of female submissiveness. The women win their war at the end of the novel and generously offer men an opportunity to participate in a new society. *Le Corps lesbien* (1973) recites the female body, verbalizing its experiences often in violent terms. Wittig splits the female subject pronoun as 'J/e' to reflect women's alienation in language. *Brouillon pour un dictionnaire des amantes* (1976), written with Sande Zeig, also focuses on language, redefining words, often humorously, in a lesbian perspective. *Virgile, non* (1985), an exuberant parody of Dante's *Divine Comedy*, pursues the attempt to rewrite and reclaim culture for women. 'Wittig', the character who travels through Hell and Purgatory with her guide Manastabal, witnessing womens' torments, has to pass through many trials and review some key assumptions. She eventually discovers Paradise in the Angels' kitchen. [EAF]

Wolmar, Baron. Husband of Julie and representative of 'la philosophie' in Rousseau's La *Nouvelle Héloïse*.

Women Writers in France. All too often women's writing is described trans-historically, as though the conditions surrounding its production had been identical for all writers and at all periods. On the contrary, both the process by which a woman became a writer and the manner in which she practised her craft have varied widely from century to century and from one milieu to another.

Many kinds of factor determine the differences between the careers of any two women writers. We may take for example the cases of the comtesse de *Lafayette and George *Sand. The most evident discrepancies between their situations can be explained by social status or class. Because Lafayette was born into the highest rank of the nobility, she had the kind of access to the literary world otherwise inconceivable for women in her day. She had a reasonably extensive education (before the 20th c. a woman's education was almost never the equivalent of that received by a male contemporary). All her life she frequented the best-known figures on the intellectual scene, and was able to call on them for their collaboration—asking them, for example, to modify her style according to her specifications. Moreover, she enjoyed apparently complete financial and legal independence. She married early, but she and her husband soon appear to have worked out an amicable, unofficial separation.

George Sand's life for the most part stands in sharp contrast to this privileged existence. Though the woman born Aurore Dupin who became through marriage Baronne Dudevant was far from a social outsider, she was obliged to struggle to have a literary career. Her separation from her husband was hardly painless. When she arrived in Paris hoping to become a writer she was penniless. And, whereas before the end of her long career she frequented the major writers of her day, in the beginning she was an unknown, and subsequently the less important partner in her collaboration with Jules Sandeau. That she signed all her works as a man, with the pseudonym contrived for this early collaboration, says a great deal about women's writing in the 19th c.: a degree of male protection was often required before it could enter public circulation.

The comparison between Lafayette and Sand can be replicated, in earlier centuries, by that between *Marie de France and *Christine de Pizan. Nevertheless, it is true that until the end of the *ancien régime* the dominant figures in French writing are most often women of privilege. From Marie de France to the *trobairitz, to *Marguerite de Navarre in the 16th c., to Lafayette's contemporary the marquise de *Sévigné, and to such 18th-c. novelists as the marquise de *Tencin and the baronne de *Staël, women whose rank gave them access to the most influential contemporary circles were also those most easily able to find a place in the Republic of Letters. Indeed, after the events of 1789 had put an end to the foundation of the system of privilege, Germaine de Staël (who supported the Revolution) remarked that it was possible that women writers in France would never again have such an easy time.

Women did indeed have a harder time becoming writers after the *ancien régime*, and this fact undoubtedly goes a long way towards explaining why standard paradigms are inadequate to evaluate the

Women Writers

history of French women's writing. English-speaking critics often assume, in particular, that the example of women's writing in England is universally valid. According to this model, the history of women's writing is always that of steady progress from obscurity towards ever more public and equal status. The history of French women's writing, however, is more complicated: only in the second half of the 20th c. have women writers begun to recover the prominence they enjoyed during the last century of the *ancien régime*.

This renewed prominence can be explained by the fact that, in recent decades, women have finally obtained at least some form of access to all the institutions—from publishing-houses to literary academies—outside which it is impossible to have a literary career. In particular, in the second half of the 20th c., for the first time women find every aspect of the French educational system open to them. Not surprisingly, this new access has had rapid and impressive results: women are now publishing in France in record and ever-increasing numbers.

Our knowledge of the different periods in the tradition of French women's writing varies greatly. It is no surprise that we often know less about the earliest women writers. At a time when most literary composition was anonymous, the identity of many women writers was irretrievably lost and the sex of many authors is uncertain. For instance, the medieval *chanson de toile is generally considered a women's genre, but in the case of anonymous lyrics such as these it is not clear what this means. Are they actual examples of women's writing or early illustrations of the phenomenon Hélène *Cixous calls *écriture féminine, writing that so successfully simulates a female voice that it comes to be accepted as the authentic expression of a woman's point of view? (The case of the 17th-c. novel, *Lettres portugaises, is perhaps the definitive example of writing that is the perfect fulfilment of an epoch's vision of the way in which a woman should write.)

The cases in which we do have abundant information about early women writers—e.g. 16th-c. poets, notably those who worked in the circle of the dames *des Roches—indicate that we know most about pre-20th-c. women writers when they worked collectively in some way. This might mean that they wrote as part of an actual literary collective, a circle or a *salon whose members circulated works for mutual advice and approval. It might also mean a more informal type of collective project, instances in which women writers—e.g. Lafayette, Sévigné, and numerous lesser-known contemporaries—were conscious that they were not writing in isolation but as part of a tradition.

The surviving records of these collaborations—correspondences, journals, collective volumes—constitute the richest source of information about the changing practical conditions that facilitated or hindered the process by which women became writers. We can thus learn to understand better certain aspects of the business of literature—what a writer at a particular period was paid for a novel or how different writers dealt with readers' responses to their works. We learn about strategies women were forced to devise to deal with activities that would have been merely routine for their male counterparts—how they had recourse to intermediaries for their dealings with publishers, or what caused them to hide their identity behind male pseudonyms.

For obvious reasons, and as these records of female literary collaboration indicate, it was easier for women to become writers when they worked collaboratively. The period 1650–1780 was a golden age of French women's writing: women were not only publishing in significant numbers, but were widely viewed as innovators whose creations were changing the shape of literature. Most importantly, women such as *Scudéry, Lafayette, *Montpensier, and *Villedieu were seen as the principal creators of a new literary form, the novel of subjective experience [see NOVEL, 2]. The literary world at large recognized both this unprecedented female literary presence and the sense of belonging to a tradition that these women writers shared. At least a dozen volumes appeared entirely devoted to the history of women's writing in France, several of which review the origins of that history in the Middle Ages. The most comprehensive of these studies are the five-volume *Histoire littéraire des femmes françaises* attributed to Joseph de La Porte (1769) and Louise de Keralio Robert's 12-volume *Collection des meilleurs ouvrages français, composés par des femmes* (1786–8).

If this view of French literary history, which places the accomplishments of women writers on the same footing as those of their male counterparts, had continued to be diffused, women writers might have known a very different fate in modern times. However, beginning in the mid-18th c., but particularly in the early 19th c., the history of French literature was rewritten in volumes that mark the beginning of *literary history as we know it, volumes that imposed the vision of the *canon of French literature that is still dominant today. Women writers were virtually excluded from this new literary history: only a few exceptional literary women were granted canonic status; all memory of the *tradition* of French women's writing was erased.

In recent decades we have begun to recover a sense of the true history of women writers' participation in the French tradition. That process of recovery, however, is far from complete. Our knowledge of women writers' presence in many periods, of their contribution to most genres, remains fragmentary at best. Only with continuing archival research will we obtain a truly new vision of French literary history, one in which women writers through the ages take their place alongside their male counterparts. [See FEMINISM.]   [JDeJ]

856

[see also POPULAR SONG]

1. Medieval

Until the late 14th c. the performance of much medieval poetry (including narrative poetry) involved music. The exact proportion is difficult to gauge since the number of surviving melodies corresponds in varying degree with the number of literary texts: e.g. at least two-thirds of the *trouvère* repertory survives with melodies, compared with roughly one-tenth of the 2,600 *troubadour poems. Music survives for all the major *lyric genres (such as the chanson (*canso), *alba or aube, *pastourelle, *rondeau, *ballade, motet, and *lai) and, though the evidence is more sparse, for several narrative genres as well, such as *chansons de geste and saints' lives. One reason why music was not transmitted as widely as texts is because (as now) it required specialist skills both in copying and in reading the notation: we cannot assume, then, that in all cases where music does not survive, it was not intended. Much of it must have circulated only orally. On the other hand, the fact that several manuscript collections of songs contain only texts suggests that for certain patrons the words of the songs were of independent interest.

The relations between words and music vary noticeably from genre to genre. Troubadour poetry is marked by its metrical variety: the melodies have a similarly unfixed structure which creates its own pattern separate from the texts. Many troubadour songs fit the broad structural outline aab (the first section with its repeat—aa—is approximately the same length as b), to which both text and music conform. However, within this broad strophic framework poets employed enormous metrical ingenuity (in the entire corpus, some 1,200 metrical schemes are used only once). The melodies are also highly unpredictable: many involve a range of repetitive forms, whereas others are continuous or through-composed. More significantly, the variety of musical pattern often appears to have little connection with the rhyme-scheme and formal structure of the texts. Indeed, where several melodies exist for a single poem, their forms often differ, to the extent that one may have an aab structure and another be through-composed. This divergence has caused much controversy in attempts by modern scholars (in the absence of other evidence) to determine the musical rhythm of the songs from the poetry, since metrical irregularity in the texts makes it difficult to establish rhythmic regularity in the music.

Other lyric genres in the 12th and 13th c. have simpler, though still varied, musical structures. Trouvère poetry borrows much from the troubadours, but the general trend is towards lighter, less elaborate or intellectual melodies. Genres from Pierre Bec's 'popularisant' register [see LYRIC POETRY, 1a] (especially *refrain*, rondeau, *estampie*, *virelai*, *ballette*) are characterized by their association with dance, and hence by short, strongly rhythmic, tuneful melodies. Narrative song, such as the *pastourelle*, *aube*, or *reverdie*, represents a place where the otherwise highly divergent traditions of high courtly style and lower-style dance song meet: in musical terms, this results in short repetitive patterns, tonal stability, and balanced phrases. Some *pastourelles* have melodies that resemble the few that survive for the *chansons de geste*. These consist of two or possibly three phrases that would have been repeated for each laisse. The *lai*, by contrast, is constructed out of a principle of progressive repetition (related to the sequence), in which each versicle may have a different metrical pattern and a different melody, but may also recapitulate on earlier material. *Lai* melodies have highly distinctive, short, formulaic phrases, often repeated within versicles as well as across them.

Although it is usually assumed that in any of the above genres the words were composed first and then 'set' to a tune, there is evidence to show that the opposite was often the case. The best example is the widespread practice of *contrafactum* composition, where new words are given to an existing tune. The very existence of this practice indicates that there is no necessary expressive relation between the words and the music in medieval song, since the same melodies may be used for quite unrelated texts, and often texts in different languages. 13th-c. motets are a particularly interesting case in point, since two, three, or four voice-parts, all with different texts, are sung simultaneously, and because verbal and musical composition are mutually interdependent; for just as motet texts are composite arrangements of refrains and formulaic phrases from 'popular' love poetry, so the music is similarly generated by refrain melodies, to the extent that it is often difficult to perceive where the compositional division between text and melody lies.

In the early- to mid-14th c., when song form enters a more stable phase with the so-called *formes fixes* established by poet-composers such as Jehan de Lescurel and *Philippe de Vitry, words and music achieve a highly sophisticated relation in the output of Guillaume de *Machaut. Both a celebrated poet and the most important composer of the century, his work is highly innovative, often employing extreme formal constraints yet also full of experimentation with retrograde form, pitch levels, polyphonic balance, and complex rhythmic architecture. No subsequent French poet, however, manages to match Machaut's facility in the two arts which, after his death, begin to diverge. *Deschamps's *Art de Dictier* (1392) makes a distinction between 'musique naturelle' (poetry) and 'musique artificielle' (music), thus recognizing a technical gulf between them even as he insists that the conjunction between the two 'musiques' forms the most complete expression of the sweetness of sound. His argument does not so much represent a change in the way in which music and poetry were traditionally conceived, as an attempt to give poetry greater credence precisely by appealing to the notion that it is a form of music in its own right. From now on composers and poets tended to work separately, and much lyric poetry was not written to be sung. Text settings were common, however, and established 15th-c. composers, such as Guillaume Dufay and Gilles Binchois set numerous rondeaux, including texts by *Christine de Pizan, Alain *Chartier, and *Charles d'Orléans. But the popularity of the *formes fixes* waned towards the 16th c., and new genres such as the madrigal, lute song, and the four-voice 'Parisian chanson' (first printed 1528) attest to a move away from complex polyphonic structures to clearer, simpler settings, in which the often highly dissonant superimposition of voices and texts gives way to a desire to imitate or present a text more directly and freely. Such was the case for the poets of the *Pléiade, most of whose lyric poetry was written with a view to possible musical performance. Later in the 16th c. the *Académie de Poésie et de Musique was specifically created with the aim of making an alliance on fresh terms between poetry and music.   [ARTB]

See J. Stevens, *Words and Music in the Middle Ages* (1986).

2. After 1600 [see also OPERA; LULLY; CHANSON FRANÇAISE]
In the 17th c. music's role in text setting was to imitate the words and intensify the poetry; *Molière's music-master in *Le Bourgeois gentilhomme* comments on the absolute necessity of adapting the tune to the words. In the first few decades of the century *airs de cour* were extremely popular. Subsequently, Molière and *Quinault contributed texts, but most were either based on Italian *pastorals by Renaissance authors or modelled on Italian literature from an earlier period (*Desportes became the most important local writer of the texts). It was not uncommon for composers of *airs de cour* to ignore the natural rhythms of the text. The *airs de cour* became more expressive in the second half of the century and were called either plain *air* or *air sérieux* in contrast to other lighter and more popular song types of a pastoral or amorous nature.

By championing Italian music, the 18th-c. *Encyclopédistes* implied that music should be given a more important role in the collaboration between text and music. The secular *cantate française* of the early 18th c. is an example of Italian influence on French music at this time, even though the French respect for the text ensures that the attempt to unite two national styles still results in a distinctively French style. The initial literary format of the *cantate française* text was established by J.-B. *Rousseau.

The mid-18th c. saw the introduction of the romance, a simple, usually strophic song based on a sentimental text, often by *Florian. J.-J. *Rousseau's *Le Devin du village* (1752) contains one of the first

examples of the romance, which became common in the emerging genre of *opéra-comique*. During the Revolution and the Empire the romance was extremely popular. Texts were sometimes topical while others were written in imitation of medieval troubadour verse. In the first few decades of the 19th c. the pastoral element became less important, yet the sentimental still persisted into the 1830s, appealing to its bourgeois audience with titles such as 'La Mère du matelot' and 'La Bénédiction d'un père'. The best-known composers of romance in the early 19th c. were Boïeldieu, Loïsa Puget, Monpou, and Romagnesi. The majority of texts were unmemorable, although *Chateaubriand contributed some of merit.

Texts of literary value, however, were used by two romance composers, Louis Niedermeyer and Hippolyte Monpou. Niedermeyer's *Le Lac* (n.d.), set to *Lamartine's poem, was one of the most popular romances of the 19th c. Niedermeyer had some problems in wedding the text to the traditional strophic form of the romance, as did Monpou in setting the poetry of *Hugo and *Musset. Monpou was deliberately trying to break with tradition, yet he does not appear to have had the technical ability to carry through his ideas successfully.

The regeneration and transformation of the romance from a salon piece into a more serious art form, the *mélodie*, was stimulated by Romantic poetry and the introduction of the Schubertian *lied* into France. Translations of Schubert's *lieder* into French were called *mélodie* to distinguish them from romances, but the label *mélodie* was first used for a French composition by *Berlioz in his *Neuf mélodies* (1829), based on poems by Thomas Moore. Early in his career Berlioz wrote a number of songs (including the majority of the Moore *mélodies*) in the simple strophic settings of traditional romance. Yet he soon began to use a freer structure in which the musical phrasing was principally determined by the rhythms and phrasing of the text. *Les Nuits d'été* (1840–1), based on poems from *Gautier's *La Comédie de la mort*, is his most successful example of this freer setting.

The *mélodie* is distinguished first by the use of texts of high literary value; secondly, by the much freer musical setting forced upon composers by the freer style of versification of the poets; and thirdly, by the more important role given to expressive piano accompaniment with the aim, not of dominating the text, but of better expressing it. It took a while for the *mélodie* to divorce itself from its romance origins and for composers to adopt a freer rhythmic style that could be adapted to the texts.

The high point of *mélodie* composition is in the last quarter of the 19th c. and the early 20th c., with composers such as *Fauré, Henri-Eugène-Marie Duparc (1848–1933), and *Debussy, and the poets *Baudelaire, *Mallarmé, and *Verlaine. Verlaine was the catalyst for Fauré's most inspired settings, in particular *La Bonne Chanson* (1892). Fauré sought to bring out the general feeling of a poem, and despite the fact that he had no compunction in at times altering the order of lines in a poem, his *mélodies* follow the structure of the verse with an extraordinary sensitivity to poetic nuance. In his later songs his vocal style becomes more declamatory, although always marked by a restrained lyricism. Duparc often converted his text into prose and his musical structure was usually dictated by the words, with the piano part aiming at expressive evocation of the text. For Debussy the vocal line became intensified declamation. In his *Proses lyriques* (1892–3) and *Chansons de Bilitis* (1897–8) he set prose poetry by himself and Pierre *Louÿs. Debussy also based orchestral works on poetry. He insisted that his music for *Prélude à l'après-midi d'un faune* (1892–3), based on a Mallarmé poem, was decoration not narrative.

Literature continued to be important to French composers in the 20th c. *Poulenc wrote vocal works set to poetry by *Jammes, *Claudel, *Éluard, *Apollinaire, and *Cocteau. Henry Barraud has based compositions on works by Hugo, *Péguy, and *Rimbaud, and from 1955 until his death in 1973 Jean Barraqué based all his music on a French translation of *The Death of Virgil* by Broch. Messiaen wrote many works to his own texts. But perhaps the most significant use of poetry in 20th-c. France has been by Pierre *Boulez, particularly in his settings of *Char in *Le Marteau sans maître* (1952–4) and Mallarmé in *Pli selon pli* (1957–62). Boulez has stated that he does not aim to communicate the text in his music directly (you can go to the poem itself for that), but to offer some more fundamental understanding of the way in which the poem is structured and even created. In *Pli selon pli*, Mallarmé's poetic structure is mirrored in the formal structure of the music, but it could also be said that Boulez's musical techniques aim to encapsulate Mallarmé's views on language. [KM]

See F. Noske, *French Song from Berlioz to Duparc*, rev. edn. (1970); J. Anthony, *French Baroque Music*, rev. edn. (1978).

World War I (Literature of). In the Great War of 1914–18 the new technology of attack (high-velocity shells, machine-guns, tanks, aeroplanes) at first outstripped the defensive capacities of the combatant armies. The 'industrialized killing' which resulted called in question traditional attitudes to war and eventually made its conventional literary expression obsolete. The war cast a long shadow over subsequent writing: such movements as *Surrealism, for instance, may be seen as responses to the perceived collapse of European values.

In France the number of dead and wounded was proportionately higher than in any other country. A whole male generation was virtually wiped out: *Alain spoke of 'ce massacre mécanique', and Apollinaire, himself a victim of the war, wrote: 'J'ai pleuré ma génération sur son trépas sacré'.

Although bellicose patriotism was the dominant mood in France, especially in the first years of the war, this gave way to more complex and critical responses. Faced by new physical and moral dramas, very few writers could remain detached, many were directly involved, and a striking body of war literature was produced in France, as in Britain and Germany.

*Péguy, *Alain-Fournier, and *Psichari were among the writers killed in the opening weeks of the war. The first major novel to be published about the experience of war was *Gaspard* (1915) by René Benjamin (1885–1948). It was awarded the Prix Goncourt, but many later readers found Benjamin's attitude to physical suffering too light-hearted. Other early war novels included Jean des Vignes Rouges's *Bourru, soldat de Vauquois* (1916, supplemented in 1917 by the same author's *André Rieu, officier de France*), and above all *Barbusse's *Le Feu*. The latter was the first really graphic picture of the horrifying killing and maiming of trench warfare. It shared the Prix Goncourt with Adrien Bertrand's *L'Appel du sol* (1916); this was a more consciously patriotic work, but did not minimize the horror, while employing the language of high moral idealism. In 1916 also *Genevoix published his vivid novels about the soldier's experience, *Sous Verdun* and *Nuits de guerre*, which were published in 1950 together with *La Boue* (1921) and *Les Éparges* (1923) under the collective title *Ceux de 14*.

Other novelists who attracted considerable attention at the time were Henri Malherbe (*La Flamme au poing*, 1917) and G.-T. Franconi (*Un tel de l'armée française*, 1917). But apart from Barbusse and Genevoix, the best-known of the war novelists today are probably *Duhamel, whose collected sketches *Vie des martyrs, 1914–1916* (1917) and *Civilisation, 1914–1917* (1918, Prix Goncourt) are marked by a rather sentimental humanism; *Dorgelès, whose *Les Croix de bois* (1919) is one of the most balanced accounts of trench warfare; and Léon Werth, author of an excellent pacifist novel, *Clavel soldat* (1919). Among the most significant of the many war novels written after the end of hostilities one may cite *Montherlant's heroic *Le Songe* (1922), *Giono's eloquently pacifist *Le Grand Troupeau* (1931), *Drieu la Rochelle's bitter *La Comédie de Charleroi* (1934), and Jules *Romains's panoramic *Prélude à Verdun* (1937) and *Verdun* (1938). The first part of Céline's *Voyage au bout de la nuit* (1932) offers a nightmarish vision of the carnage.

France was notably less productive of good war poetry than Britain. There is much banal verse, and not a little patriotic bombast, in Henri de *Régnier's *1914–1916; poèmes* (1922), Maurice Rostand's *Le Vol de la Marseillaise* (1919), and *Claudel's *Poèmes de guerre 1914–1916* (1922). In *Verhaeren's *Les Ailes rouges de la guerre* (1917), by contrast, war is denounced. The experience of the trenches finds more adventurous literary expression in *Apollinaire's *Calligrammes* (1918), the finest French poetry of World War I. At times Apollinaire appears to delight in the beauty of war ('Ah Dieu! que la guerre est jolie'), but his poems also convey both the banality and the horror of military life.

Although the book trade and the press were subject to tighter controls during these years, the war inspired a great deal of journalism and argumentative prose. Three important works in particular display characteristically contrasting responses. *Barrès, the champion of right-wing nationalism before the war, wrote patriotic daily pieces in *L'Écho de Paris*, subsequently collected in the 14 volumes of *Chronique de la Grande Guerre* (1920–4). *Alain, in *Mars, ou la Guerre jugée* (1921), offered a rational analysis of war, its literary expression, and the moral harm it causes. Romain *Rolland, finally, working for the Red Cross in Geneva, called on the intellectuals of France and Germany to join in the rejection of war in *Au-dessus de la mêlée* (1915); denounced by patriots on both sides, he was awarded a Nobel Prize in 1916, the year when *Dada was launched in Zurich. [JC]

See N. Norton Cru, *Témoins: essai d'analyse et de critique des souvenirs de combattants édités en français de 1915 à 1928* (1929); L. Riegel, *Guerre et littérature: le bouleversement des consciences dans la littérature romanesque inspirée par la Grande Guerre* (1978); J. Cruickshank, *Variations on Catastrophe: Some French Responses to the Great War* (1982).

World War II, see OCCUPATION AND RESISTANCE.

WYZEWA, Téodor de (1863–1917). Polish in origin, and a leading spokesman of the *Symbolist movement, Wyzewa was responsible with *Dujardin for the creation in 1885 of *La Revue wagnérienne*, through which Wagner's work became one of the essential elements of Symbolism's aesthetic idealism. Of cosmopolitan literary tastes, his regular articles on foreign literature in the *Revue des deux mondes* had a significant impact on French awareness of European writing, notably the novels of Tolstoy. [JK]

X

Xala, see SEMBÈNE.

Y

Year, Beginning of the, see CALENDARS.

Yonville-l'Abbaye. The imaginary Normandy town in which Flaubert's **Madame Bovary* is set, a microcosm of provincial mediocrity.

YOUNG, Arthur (1741–1820). Suffolk agriculturalist, whose *Travels in France* (1792) record three lengthy journeys between 1787 and 1790. He gives a rich, often critical, picture of French economy and society, and particularly agriculture, at a particularly interesting historical moment. His work was translated with the approval of the Convention Nationale.

YOURCENAR, Marguerite (pseud. of Marguerite de Crayencour) (1903–87). Elected the first woman member of the Académie Française, she spoke in her official reception address of the women who should have taken their places there before her; her work, however, bears little overt trace of feminist concerns. Yourcenar is a poet (*Les Dieux ne sont pas morts,* 1922), a dramatist (*Électre ou la Chute des masques,* 1954; *Le Mystère d'Alceste,* 1963), a short-story writer (*La Mort conduit l'attelage,* 1934; *Comme l'eau qui coule,* 1982), an essayist (*Sous bénéfice d'inventaire,* 1962), a literary critic (studies of Virginia Woolf, Henry James, Thomas Mann, Mishima, and others), and an autobiographer (*Le Labyrinthe du monde: I. Souvenirs pieux,* 1974; *II. Archives du Nord,* 1977; *III. Quoi? l'Éternité,* 1988). Her reputation rests principally, however, on her historical novels, set in ancient Greece and Rome, the Renaissance period, and the early 20th c.

She was born in Belgium, the child of a wealthy couple. Her mother died shortly after the birth; she was brought up by her father and travelled the world with him at an early age. She began writing in the 1920s, producing most notably *Alexis ou le Traité du vain combat* (1929) and *Le Coup de grâce* (1939). *Alexis* takes the form of a long letter from the protagonist to his wife, confessing his problems in coming to terms with his homosexuality and raising more generally the difficulties of expressing in language deep desires and fears. *Le Coup de grâce,* set in the Baltic in 1919, also deals with a man of homosexual tendencies who eventually, in the circumstances of civil war, is obliged to execute a woman who loves him, but whom he is unable to love. Yourcenar's interest in male homosexuality marked her life as well as her work: in the 1930s she suffered a painful rejection by a homosexual friend, and in the last years of her life she was close to a young homosexual who died of AIDS. Most of her relationships, however, were with women.

The advent of World War II disrupted her writing; she went to the United States in 1939, largely as a result of her relationship with the American Grace Frick; after a period spent teaching she eventually began writing again in the late 1940s, took American citizenship (1947), and settled on the island of Mount Desert off the American east coast with Frick. She gained an international reputation with the publication of *Mémoires d'Hadrien,* in 1951. Based on meticulous research, the text is again a first-person narrative and builds up a historical and psychological portrait of Hadrian which includes the emperor's meditations on literature, philosophy, the running of the Roman Empire, and his love for a young Greek boy. In 1968 she was awarded the Prix Fémina for *L'Œuvre au noir*, a novel set in the Renaissance but whose hero, in his consistent challenging of the institutions and ideologies of his era, could be considered as a forerunner of the 1968 protestors. In Paris at the time of *May 1968, the unconventional Yourcenar and Frick, with their idiosyncratic dress, their vegetarianism, and their pacifist and ecological concerns, seemed curiously in tune with the times, despite their age.

In 1971 Yourcenar was elected to the Royal Belgian Academy, and the first of a number of French television crews made its way to Mount Desert. The increasingly serious illness of Frick kept Yourcenar at home throughout much of the 1970s; she completed two volumes of her autobiography which, rather than presenting her own life, investigate the history of her family. In 1979 she published *La Couronne et la lyre*, a thick volume of her translations (sometimes so free as to be adaptations) of ancient Greek poems; the same year Pivot interviewed her at home for a special number of *Apostrophes*. In December the death of Frick deprived Yourcenar of a devoted friendship which

had lasted for 40 years. In 1980 she was elected to the Académie Française, and in 1982 her works were collected and published in the Pléiade, a rare honour for a living writer. In her last years she travelled a good deal, wrote an essay on Mishima, and was writing the last volume of her autobiography, reaching up to her own birth, when she died. [EAF]

See J. Savigneau, *Marguerite Yourcenar* (1990).

Ysopet or **Isopet**. Name given in the Middle Ages to a collection of supposedly Aesopic fables [scc MARIE DE FRANCE].

Yvain, see CHRÉTIEN DE TROYES.

YVER, Jacques (1520–*c*.1571). French story-teller. The five tales of his very popular *Printemps* (1572) offer differing perspectives on love, in the style of Marguerite de Navarre's *Heptaméron*; set in a country-house during a lull in the *Wars of Religion, the narrative creates an interesting blend of realism, imagination, and erudition, despite Yver's mannered style.   [MJH]

Z

Zadig, ou la Destinée (1748). Philosophical tale by *Voltaire, originally published as *Memnon* (1747). Zadig, a virtuous young man, falls inexplicably from prosperity into deplorable misfortune and experiences many unpleasant mishaps before finally rising to a position more brilliant than the one from which he originally fell. By way of explanation, the angel Jesrad, disguised as a hermit, reveals to him that 'there is no evil which does not produce some benefit' and that 'there is no such thing as chance but that all is trial or punishment, recompense or prevision'. The object of the tale is to demonstrate that Providence leads us by paths that are understood only by Providence, but Zadig's response to the angel is: 'Mais . . .'.   [JR]

ZADI-ZAOUROU, Bernard (b. 1938). Ivoirian poet, playwright, and academic. Zadi-Zaourou, who teaches African written and oral poetry at the University of Abidjan, is also the founder-director of the theatre group the Compagnie du Didiga. His writing, including the volume of verse, *Fer de lance* (1975), and the play, *Les Sofas* (1975), shows the importance he places on African oral traditions.
                    [VC]

Zaïre (1732). The most frequently staged of all *Voltaire's tragedies. Zaïre, a Christian child taken captive by the Turks and raised in the harem, is about to make a marriage of mutual love with the sultan Orosmane. However, Lusignan, a French knight liberated by Orosmane, recognizes Zaïre and Nérestan (her former companion in captivity) as his lost son and daughter. Dismayed to learn that Zaïre is a Moslem, Lusignan persuades her to become a Christian. But, deliberately hiding this intention and the family relationship, Zaïre and Nérestan arouse the suspicions of Orosmane who, intercepting a letter arranging a secret meeting, murders Zaïre in blind jealousy. Enlightened by Nérestan, Orosmane kills himself.   [JR]

ZAMENGA, Batukezanga (b. 1933). One of Zaïre's most popular and widely read authors, Zamenga has been little read outside the country. A prolific prose writer, he has published almost a title a year since 1971. Uncomplicated in form, Zamenga's short novels (usually approximately 100 pages), explore contemporary social difficulties, in particular within the context of the family. Conflict between the generations and the breakdown in traditional marriage are recurrent subjects.   [BEJ]

Zayde. Second novel by the comtesse de *Lafayette. First published (1670), jointly with *Huet's eulogy of romance fiction, *Zayde* marks Lafayette's only attempt to revive Madeleine de *Scudéry's *roman héroïque*. The novel's setting in Moorish Spain permits exoticism and a tale of lovers from different cultures and religions. Because the Spanish prince Consalve does not speak the same language as Zayde, he can learn nothing about the mysterious beauty with whom he immediately falls in love. Lafayette constructs fascinating meditations on the perils of indirect communication and the effects of jealousy before she brings *Zayde* to a happy end in marriage, conversion, and national unity.   [JDeJ]

Zazie dans le métro (1959). The best-known of the novels of *Queneau, indeed, his only real commercial success. Ostensibly the story of a provincial child's weekend in Paris, where her greatest desire is to travel on the Métro—an ambition thwarted by a strike that is emblematic of the Paris of the day—Queneau's comic novel gave him a truly national (and international) reputation, but also led to his being popularly considered as primarily, even exclusively, a joker and player with words. Apart from employing what he had called 'le néo-français' to hilarious effect, this variation on Alice in Wonderland (Queneau's favourite work) uses a far-from-innocent protagonist to explore the theme of appearance and reality.   [IWR]

ZENOU, Gilles (1957–89). French-Moroccan author of three novels, *Mektoub* (1987), *Le Livre des cercles* (1988), and *La Désaffection* (1990); two short-story collections, *Les Nuits* (1989) and *Le Livre des dupes* (1989); and numerous philosophical essays. Zenou explores his identity as a Jew in relation to the themes of sexuality and writing, exile and death. His tragic death at the age of 31 reminds us, along with his brilliant work, that each one of us is but a 'temporary resident'.   [DM-S]

ZÉVACO, Michel (1860–1918). The last author to achieve fame as writer of *romans-feuilletons, Zévaco shared characteristics with his heroes. Seducer, soldier, libertarian, feminist, he published a volume of military sketches, *Le Boute-Charge* (1888), but earned notoriety, and went to prison, for his revolutionary socialist journalism in *La Tribune libre* and *L'Égalité*, where his first *feuilleton* was serialized in 1889. His reputation rests on the Pardaillan cycle, serialized from 1902 onwards, appearing in volumes from 1907: *Les Pardaillan*, *L'Épopée d'Amour*, followed by others, with titles and volumes varying in later editions. A hero of the 16th c., Pardaillan is in many aspects a 19th-c. libertarian. [SFN]

ZINSOU, Senouvo (previously Nestor Zinsou) (b. 1946). Togolese writer. Although he has published a number of short stories, his main activity is as a writer and director of plays. His *On joue la comédie* won the Grand Prix de l'ORTF in 1972, and in 1990 he was director of the Togolese National Theatre Company. [MPC]

ZOBEL, Joseph (b. 1915). Martinican novelist, best known for *La Rue Cases-Nègres* (1950), a semi-autobiographical account (subsequently filmed) of a black child growing up on a Martinican plantation in the first half of the 20th c. The physical and economic hardships suffered by the estate workers, including José's grandmother, recall the harsh conditions of the plantation system which, in former centuries, exploited the labour of their slave ancestors. However, the child's enthusiasm for the small pleasures of rural life provides a counterpoint to the theme of unremitting, ill-rewarded toil. As in many real West Indian households, the grandmother is the source of love, support, and ambition, motivating the boy towards the escape-route of scholarships and social mobility. *La Fête à Paris* (1953) follows José to France, the setting also of some of the short stories in *Le Soleil partagé* (1964). Zobel's fiction is, however, mainly devoted to the life of the working-class poor in Martinique; the note of compassionate social protest is already evident in the tales of *Laghia de la mort* (1946) and the peasant novel *Diab-là* (1946; written 1942). His more recent works include *Les Mains pleines d'oiseaux* (1978), *Quand la neige aura fondu* (1979), and *Mas Badara* (1983). [BNO]

ZOLA, Émile (1840–1902). A writer of enormous influence in France and abroad, once much scorned by the literary establishment, who has come to be recognized as a major literary figure of 19th-c. France. Primarily a novelist, he was the author of 31 novels, five collections of short stories, a number of plays and libretti, a large body of art, drama, and literary criticism, as well as numerous articles on political and social issues published in the French press at various stages of his career as a journalist. His most famous article was his open letter, in *L'Aurore* of 13 January 1898, to Félix Faure, president of the Republic, entitled (by the editor of the newspaper) 'J'accuse', his dramatic protest against the acquittal of Esterhazy in the *Dreyfus Affair.

Zola was born in Paris, but spent his childhood and youth (from 1843 to 1858) in Aix-en-Provence, where he formed a close friendship with *Cézanne. His father, a civil engineer of Italian stock, died in 1847, leaving his family in difficult financial circumstances. Zola moved to Paris with his mother in 1858 to complete his education, but failed the *baccalauréat* and was forced to seek, with little success, some suitable form of employment. He wrote

Romantic poetry and stories whilst frequenting artistic milieux in these years of financial straits, which were only eased when he obtained a modest position with the publisher *Hachette. He published a collection of tales, *Contes à Ninon*, in 1864 and his first novel, the autobiographical *La Confession de Claude*, the following year, then two serial novels for public consumption: *Le Vœu d'une morte* (1866) and *Les Mystères de Marseille* (1867). But his early works received little critical attention. He began to make his mark, however, as a journalist in the late 1860s, particularly with his *Salons*, his defence of *Manet, and his strong opposition to the Second Empire regime. Converted to realism in art and literature, much influenced by *Balzac and *Taine, Zola began promoting a scientific view of literature inspired by the aims and methods of physiology, which he termed *'Naturalism'. His fourth novel, *Thérèse Raquin* (1867), applied these ideas and attracted some critical attention. Having published another more realistic novel, *Madeleine Férat*, in 1868, he embarked before the fall of the Empire upon his vast *Rougon-Macquart series, which would be, as the subtitle defines it, the 'histoire naturelle et sociale d'une famille sous le Second Empire' and would take him until 1893 to complete. In 1870 he married Alexandrine Meley, who remained his lifelong companion.

During the years in which he wrote his 20-volume series [for titles see ROUGON-MACQUART], Zola virtually abandoned political journalism; after brushes with the authorities in the early years of the Third Republic, he mainly concentrated his efforts on his novels, but also—with limited success—made occasional incursions into the theatre, either by writing plays of his own, like *Les Héritiers Rabourdin* (1874) and *Le Bouton de rose* (1878), or by collaborating on adaptations from his novels. His first novel to achieve major success was *L'*Assommoir* (1877), a work that brought him not only fame and fortune but considerable hostile criticism. Partly in defence of his own works and of works by a growing number of younger writers attracted to his rising star, Zola also issued several volumes of critical and theoretical studies, previously published in the press, notably *Le *Roman expérimental* (1880), in which he put forward his theory of the 'experimental novel'—to little effect, since his influence was (and would always be) due immeasurably more to his fiction than to his theories. For a brief period he became the leader of a school of writers, frequently named 'le groupe de Médan' after the country house that Zola bought on the proceeds of *L'Assommoir*. The group produced the one-and-only collective Naturalist work, *Les *Soirées de Médan*. Though he was still under attack in France, particularly after the publication of *La *Terre* (1887), Zola's influence spread abroad and he gradually received due recognition for his talent, though he would never gain admission to the Académie Française.

Zola's novels after the *Rougon-Macquart* series,

inspired by his desire to respond to a different intellectual climate and to produce a better world for his two children by Jeanne Rozerot (his mistress since 1888), represent a considerable departure from his Naturalist principles and practices. His trilogy *Les Trois Villes*, consisting of *Lourdes* (1894), *Rome* (1896), and *Paris* (1898), deals with a priest, Pierre Froment, who abandons the Catholic faith to espouse a religion of humanity. Zola's final series, *Les Quatre Évangiles*, consists of largely Utopian works, *Fécondité* (1899), *Travail* (1901), and *Vérité* (published posthumously, 1903). Before he could begin the fourth, *Justice*, Zola died of carbon-monoxide poisoning from a blocked chimney in his Paris apartment. The verdict of accidental death has never entirely removed suspicion of foul play prompted by Zola's role in the Dreyfus case.

Despite the reductive formulas with which Zola's novels have usually been defined by critics and literary historians, and by the author himself in his own theoretical statements, his monumental work is, in fact, enormously varied; it is, furthermore, uncompromising in its representation of the harsh realities of life, abounding in vitality, rich in mythical and symbolic formulations, and inspired by Zola's attachment to humane values even in works in which he showed them threatened, undermined, or swept away from within by obscure, instinctive forces or from without by the impersonal forces of the modern world. [DB]

See A. Wilson, *Emile Zola: An Introductory Study of his Novels* (1952); F. W. J. Hemmings, *Émile Zola*, 2nd edn. (1966); P. Walker, *Zola* (1985).

Zulu, Le, see TCHICAYA U TAM'SI.

ZUMTHOR, Paul (b. 1915). Probably the most influential French medievalist of this century, and author of several novels. Zumthor's publications span more than 40 years, his most important book being his *Essai de poétique médiévale* (1972). Radically attacking traditional notions of 'genre', 'text', and 'authorship', he advances a complex theory of intertextuality (texts are linked by their common dependence on a particular poetic 'register' or *registre*) and textual instability (*mouvance*). His theoretical writings are grounded in a formidable command of literary history (his first major book was his *Histoire littéraire de la France médiévale VIe–XIVe siècles*, 1954); he is also a brilliant critic, writing particularly illuminatingly on texts in the lyric tradition from the *fatrasies* to the *Rhétoriqueurs. [SK]

ZUYLEN, Belle de, see CHARRIÈRE.